PHILIP'S

ROBERTSON

STRE

G000094538

London

First published 2000 by

Philip's, a division of
Octopus Publishing Group Ltd
2–4 Heron Quays
London E14 4JP

Second edition 2003
Third impression with revisions 2006
LONBC

ISBN-10   0-540-08465-4 paperback
ISBN-10   0-540-08464-6 spiral

ISBN-13   978-0-540-08465-4 paperback
ISBN-13   978-0-540-08464-7 spiral

© Philip's 2006

o|s Ordnance Survey®

This product includes mapping data licensed
from Ordnance Survey®, with the
permission of the Controller of Her Majesty's
Stationery Office.© Crown copyright 2006.
All rights reserved.
Licence number 100011710

This product contains driver restriction
information derived from Teleatlas
© TeleatlasDRI

Printed and bound in Spain
by Cayfosa-Quebecor.

Contents

II **Key to map pages**

IV Administrative and Postcode boundaries

VI **Route planning**

X **Key to map symbols**

1 **Street maps**

228 **Keys to enlarged map pages and symbols**

229 **Enlarged street maps**

271 **Index**

395 **List of numbered locations**

407 Hospitals

408 Shopping, theatres, cinemas

410 Central London buses

412 Local rail and London Underground

414 Places of interest

Digital Data

The exceptionally high-quality mapping found in this atlas is available as digital data in TIFF format, which is easily convertible to other bitmapped (raster) image formats.

The index is also available in digital form as a standard database table. It contains all the details found in the printed index together with the National Grid reference for the map square in which each entry is named.

For further information and to discuss your requirements, please contact
Philip's on 020 7644 6932 or james.mann@philips-maps.co.uk

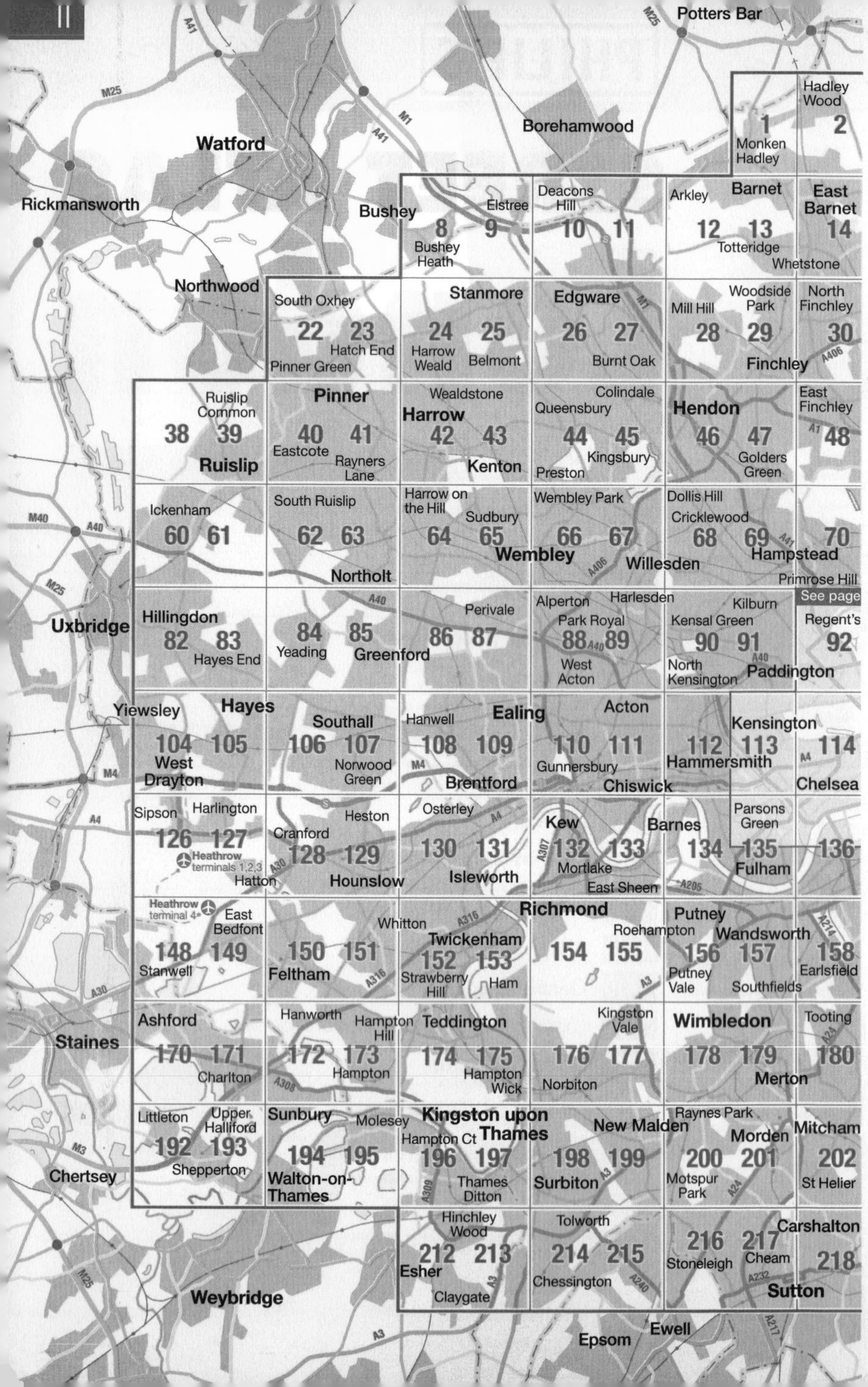

Potters Bar

M25

Hadley Wood

1 Monken Hadley | **2**

M25

Watford

A41 / A1 / M1

Borehamwood

Rickmansworth

Bushey
8 Bushey Heath | Elstree **9** | Deacons Hill **10** | **11** | Arkley **12** | **Barnet** **13** Totteridge | **East Barnet** **14**

Whetstone

Northwood

South Oxhey **22** | **23** Hatch End
Pinner Green | **Stanmore** **24** Harrow Weald | **25** Belmont | **Edgware** **26** | **27** Burnt Oak | Mill Hill **28** | Woodside Park **29** | North Finchley **30** Finchley

Pinner
Ruislip Common **38** | **39** | **40** Eastcote | **41** Rayners Lane
Ruislip | **Harrow** Wealdstone **42** | **43** **Kenton** | Colindale Queensbury **44** | **45** Kingsbury Preston | **Hendon** **46** | **47** Golders Green | East Finchley **48**

Ickenham **60** | **61** | South Ruislip **62** | **63** **Northolt** | Harrow on the Hill **64** | Sudbury **65** **Wembley** | Wembley Park **66** | **67** **Willesden** | Dollis Hill Cricklewood **68** | **69** | Hampstead **70** Primrose Hill

See page

Hillingdon **82** | **83** Hayes End | **84** Yeading | **85** **Greenford** | Perivale **86** | **87** | Alperton Harlesden Park Royal **88** | **89** West Acton | Kensal Green **90** | Kilburn **91** **Paddington** North Kensington | Regent's **92**

Uxbridge

Yiewsley | **Hayes** **104** | **105** West Drayton | Southall **106** | **107** Norwood Green | Hanwell **108** | **Ealing** **109** **Brentford** | Acton **110** | **111** Gunnersbury | Kensington **112** | **113** **Hammersmith** **Chiswick** | **114** **Chelsea**

Sipson | Harlington **126** | **127** Hatton | Cranford **128** | Heston **129** **Hounslow** | Osterley **130** | **131** **Isleworth** | **Kew** **132** | **133** Mortlake East Sheen | **Barnes** **134** | Parsons Green **135** | **136** **Fulham**

Heathrow terminals 1,2,3

A4

Heathrow terminal 4 | East Bedfont **148** | **149** Stanwell | Whitton **150** | **151** **Feltham** | **Twickenham** **152** | **153** Strawberry Hill | Ham **Richmond** **154** | **155** | **Putney** Roehampton **156** | **157** Putney Vale | **Wandsworth** Southfields | **158** Earlsfield

Staines

Ashford **170** | **171** Charlton | Hanworth **172** | Hampton Hill **173** Hampton | **Teddington** **174** | **175** Hampton Wick | Kingston Vale **176** | **177** Norbiton | **Wimbledon** **178** | **179** **Merton** | Tooting **180**

Littleton | Upper Halliford **192** | **193** Shepperton | **Sunbury** **194** | **195** Molesey | **Kingston upon** Hampton Ct **Thames** **196** | **197** Thames Ditton | New Malden **198** | **199** **Surbiton** | Raynes Park **200** Motspur Park | **Morden** **201** | Mitcham **202** St Helier

Chertsey

Weybridge

Hinchley Wood **212** | **213** **Esher** Claygate | Tolworth **214** | **215** Chessington | **216** Stoneleigh | **217** Cheam | **Carshalton** **218** **Sutton**

Ewell

Epsom

Key to map pages

Herne Hill **160** Tulse Hill — Atlas pages at 3½ inches to 1 mile

Parsons Green **125** — Central London atlas coverage at 7 inches to 1 mile (See page 228)

Scale
0 1 2 3 4 5 km
0 1 2 3 miles

3 Cockfosters	**4**	Clay Hill **5** Enfield Town	Forty Hill	Enfield Wash **6**	Enfield Lock **7** Brimsdown	Loughton

Enfield

Oakwood **15** Osidge | Winchmore Hill **16** | Bush Hill **17** Southgate | Ponders End **18** | **19** Lower Edmonton | **20** **21** Chingford | Buckhurst Hill

Friern Barnet **31** Muswell Hill | Edmonton **32** Wood Green | **33** Tottenham | **34** | **35** Higham Hill | Chingford Hatch **36** | **37** Woodford Green — **Woodford**

Hornsey **49** Highgate | **50** Finsbury Park | **51** | **Walthamstow** **52** Upper Clapton | **53** | Snaresbrook **54** | **55** **Wanstead** | Barkingside **56** | **57** Newbury Park | Little Heath **58** | **59** Goodmayes — **Romford**

Tufnell Park **71** Camden Town | **Stoke Newington** Highbury **72** Islington | **73** | Lower Clapton **74** Hackney | Lea Bridge **75** Hackney Wick | Leytonstone **Leyton** **76** Stratford | **77** Upton | **Ilford** **78** | **79** **Barking** | **80** | **81** **Dagenham** Becontree

228 for central London
Park **93** Marylebone | **Finsbury** **94** **95** **City of London** | Mayfair | Bethnal Green **96** **Stepney** | Bow **97** **Tower Hamlets** | **Newham** **98** | West Ham **99** Canning Town | East Ham **100** Beckton | **101** Creekmouth | Castle Green **102** | **103**

Mayfair **115** **Westminster** Lambeth | Southwark **116** **117** Walworth | Wapping **118** Bermondsey Rotherhithe | Canary Wharf **119** Isle of Dogs | Blackwall **120** **Greenwich** | Silvertown **121** | London City **122** **Woolwich** | **123** Plumstead | Thamesmead **124** Abbey Wood | **125** Belvedere

Battersea **137** Clapham | **Camberwell** **138** **Brixton** | **139** | Deptford **140** Nunhead | **141** New Cross | Charlton **142** Blackheath | **143** **Lewisham** | Shooters Hill **144** | **145** Falconwood | West Heath **146** Welling | **Erith** **147** **Bexley** — Erith / Crayford

159 Balham | Herne Hill **160** Tulse Hill | **161** Dulwich | Honor Oak **162** Forest Hill | Ladywell **163** Catford | Hither Green **164** | Lee **165** Grove Park | **Eltham** **166** | Avery Hill **167** New Eltham | Blackfen **168** | Old Bexley **169**

Streatham Furzedown **181** Norbury | **182** | **183** Upper Norwood | Crystal Palace **184** **Penge** | **185** **Beckenham** | Southend **186** Downham | **187** Plaistow **Bromley** | Elmstead **188** Bickley | **189** **Chislehurst** | Sidcup Foots Cray **190** St Paul's Cray | **191** — Swanley

203 Beddington Corner | Thornton Heath **204** | **205** Selhurst | Elmers End **206** Addiscombe | Eden Park **207** | Shortlands **208** | **209** Hayes | Petts Wood **210** Southborough | **211** Broom Hill

Beddington **219** **Wallington** | **Croydon** **220** | **221** | Shirley **222** | **223** Addington Selsdon | West Wickham **224** New Addington | **225** Keston | **Orpington** **226** Farnborough | **227**

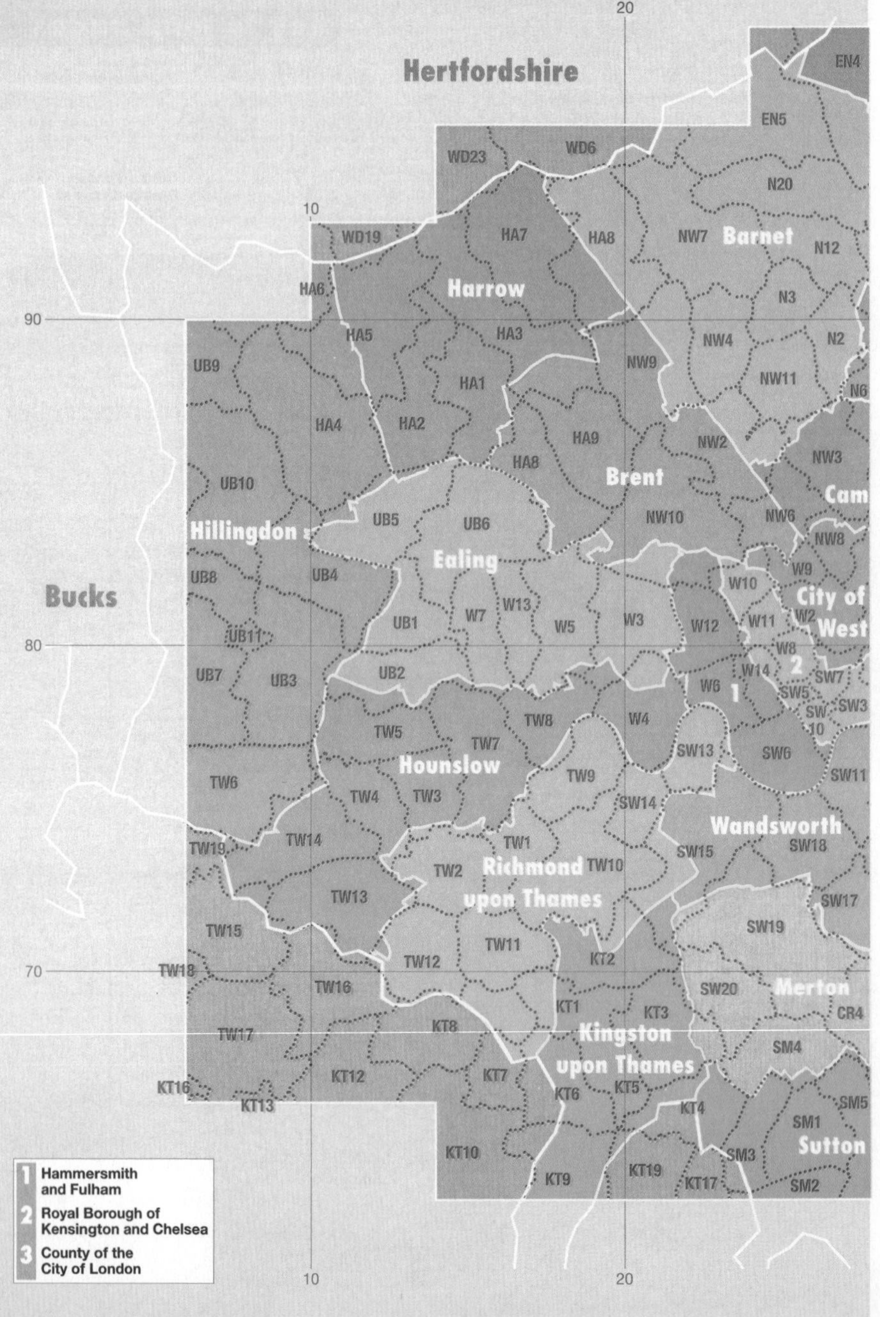

IV

Hertfordshire

Bucks

Barnet

Harrow

Hillingdon

Ealing

Brent

Hounslow

Richmond upon Thames

Kingston upon Thames

Wandsworth

Merton

Sutton

City of West

Cam

1 Hammersmith and Fulham
2 Royal Borough of Kensington and Chelsea
3 County of the City of London

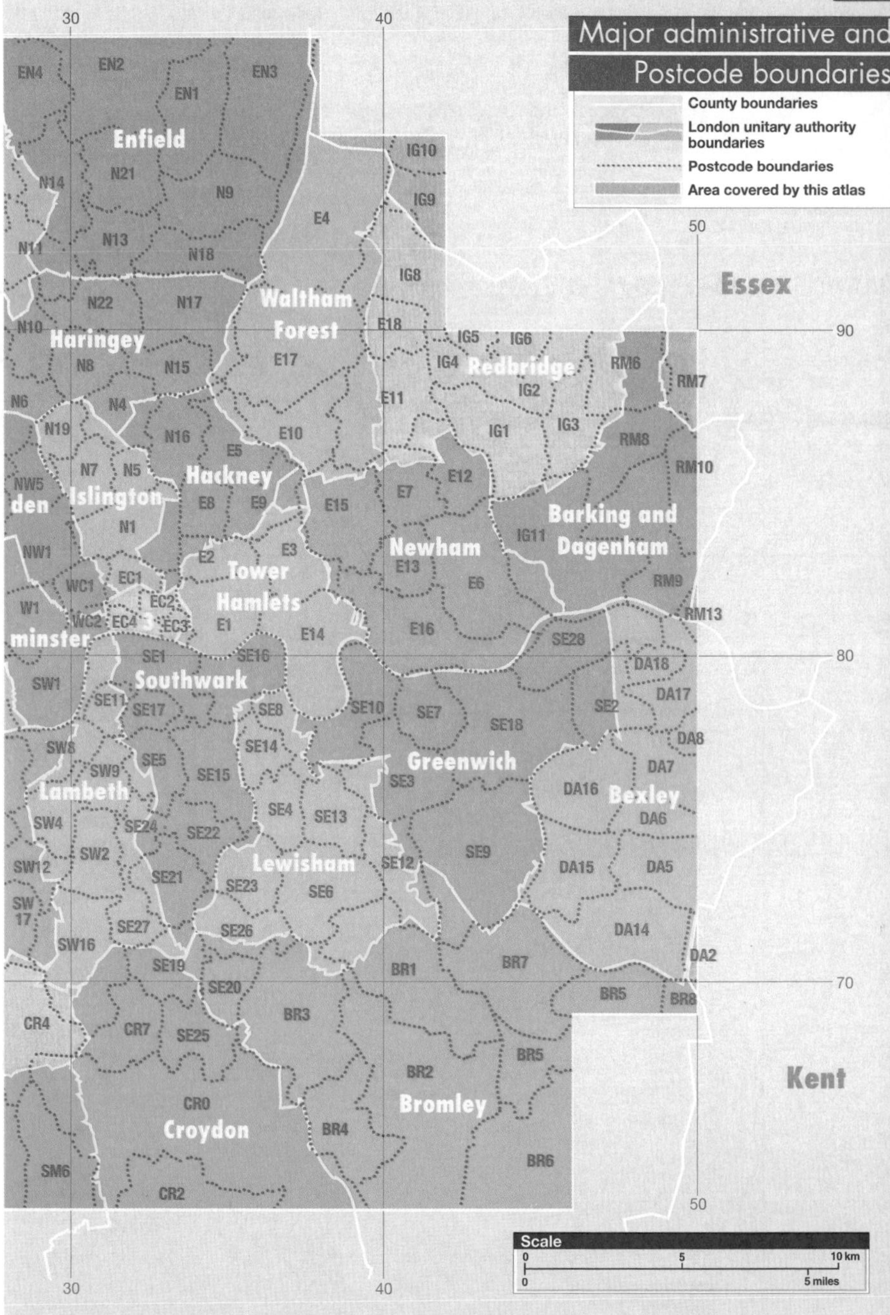

V

Major administrative and Postcode boundaries

County boundaries	
London unitary authority boundaries	
Postcode boundaries	
Area covered by this atlas	

Essex

Kent

Scale
0 — 5 — 10 km
0 — 5 miles

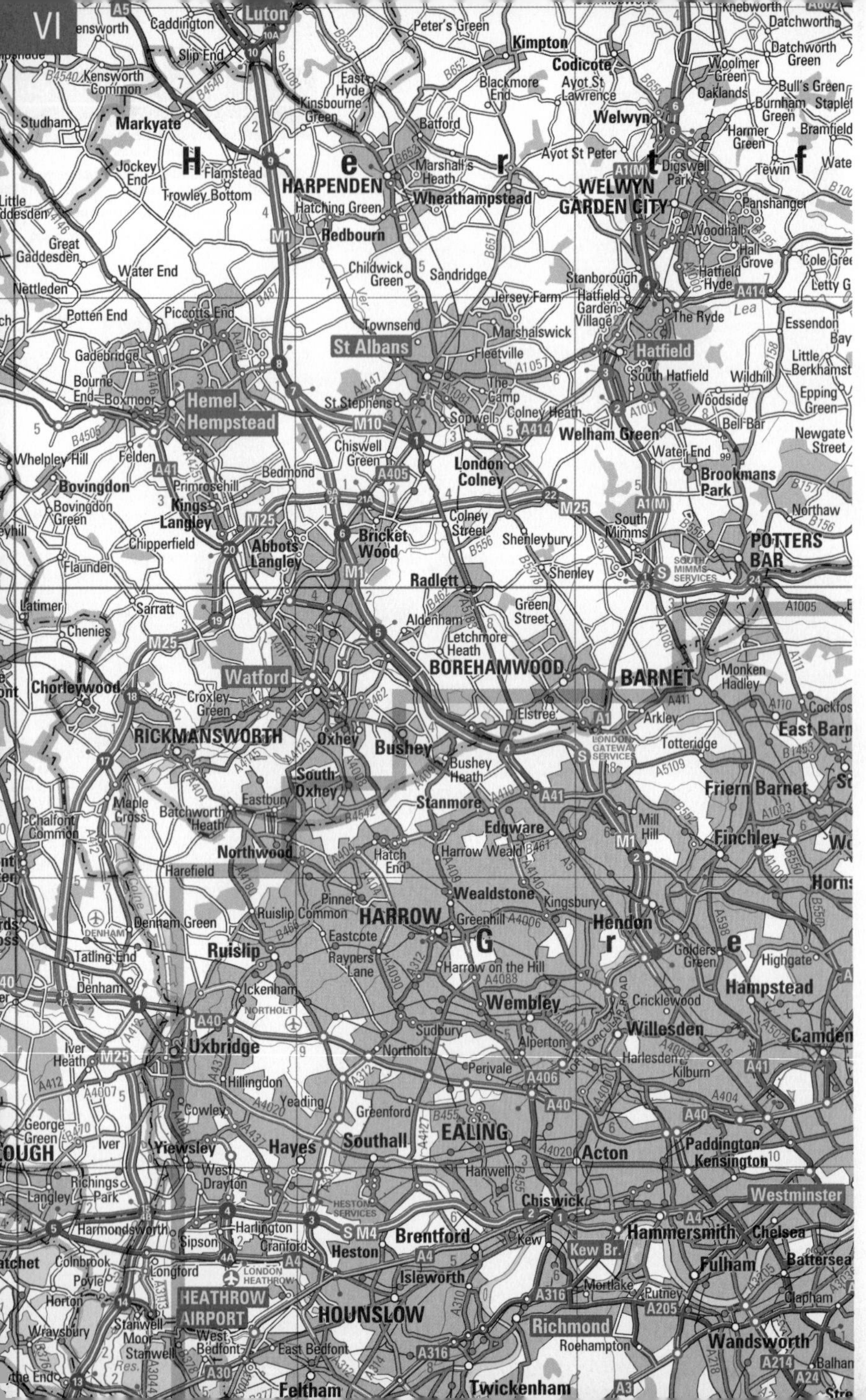

Luton
Caddington
Kensworth
Kensworth Common
Slip End
Studham
Markyate
Peter's Green
East Hyde
Kinsbourne Green
Kimpton
Codicote
Blackmore End
Ayot St Lawrence
Welwyn
Knebworth
Datchworth
Datchworth Green
Woolmer Green
Oaklands
Bull's Green
Burnham Green
Harmer Green
Bramfield
Tewin
Digswell Park
Ayot St Peter
Batford
Jockey End
Flamstead
Trowley Bottom
HARPENDEN
Marshall's Heath
Wheathampstead
WELWYN GARDEN CITY
Panshanger
Little Gaddesden
Hatching Green
Redbourn
Woodhall
Hall Grove
Cole Green
Great Gaddesden
Water End
Childwick Green
Sandridge
Stanborough
Hatfield Hyde
Letty Green
Nettleden
Jersey Farm
Hatfield Garden Village
The Ryde
Essendon
Potten End
Piccotts End
Townsend
Marshalswick
St Albans
Fleetville
Hatfield
Gadebridge
South Hatfield
Wildhill
Little Berkhamsted
Bourne End
Boxmoor
Hemel Hempstead
St Stephens
The Camp
Sopwell
Colney Heath
Woodside
Epping Green
Bell Bar
Welham Green
Newgate Street
Water End
Whelpley Hill
Felden
Chiswell Green
Bedmond
London Colney
Brookmans Park
Bovingdon
Bovingdon Green
Primrosehill
Kings Langley
Northaw
Colney Street
South Mimms
Chipperfield
Abbots Langley
Bricket Wood
Shenleybury
POTTERS BAR
Flaunden
Radlett
Shenley
SOUTH MIMMS SERVICES
Latimer
Sarratt
Green Street
Chenies
Aldenham
Letchmore Heath
BOREHAMWOOD
BARNET
Monken Hadley
Chorleywood
Watford
Croxley Green
Elstree
Arkley
Cockfosters
East Barnet
RICKMANSWORTH
Oxhey
Bushey
LONDON GATEWAY SERVICES
Totteridge
Bushey Heath
South Oxhey
Friern Barnet
Maple Cross
Batchworth Heath
Eastbury
Stanmore
Chalfont Common
Edgware
Mill Hill
Finchley
Northwood
Hatch End
Harrow Weald
Harefield
Pinner
Wealdstone
Kingsbury
Ruislip Common
HARROW
Greenhill
Hendon
Denham Green
DENHAM
Eastcote
Golders Green
Highgate
Tatling End
Ruislip
Rayners Lane
Harrow on the Hill
Hampstead
Denham
Ickenham
Wembley
Cricklewood
NORTHOLT
Willesden
Camden
Uxbridge
Sudbury
Alperton
Iver Heath
Northolt
Harlesden
Kilburn
Perivale
Hillingdon
Cowley
Yeading
Greenford
George Green
Iver
Yiewsley
Hayes
Southall
EALING
Acton
Paddington
Kensington
SLOUGH
West Drayton
Hanwell
Richings Park
Langley
Chiswick
Westminster
HESTON SERVICES
Harmondsworth
Harlington
Brentford
Hammersmith
Chelsea
Datchet
Colnbrook
Sipson
Cranford
Heston
Kew
Kew Br.
Fulham
Battersea
Poyle
Longford
LONDON HEATHROW
Isleworth
Mortlake
Putney
Clapham
Horton
HEATHROW AIRPORT
HOUNSLOW
Wraysbury
Stanwell Moor
Stanwell
West Bedfont
East Bedfont
Richmond
Roehampton
Wandsworth
Feltham
Twickenham
Balham
Lea
Ver
Colne
NORTH CIRCULAR ROAD
M1
M10
M25
M4
A1(M)
A41
A40
A4
A406
A414
A405
A1
A316
A205
A30
A3
A214
A24
A5109
A1005

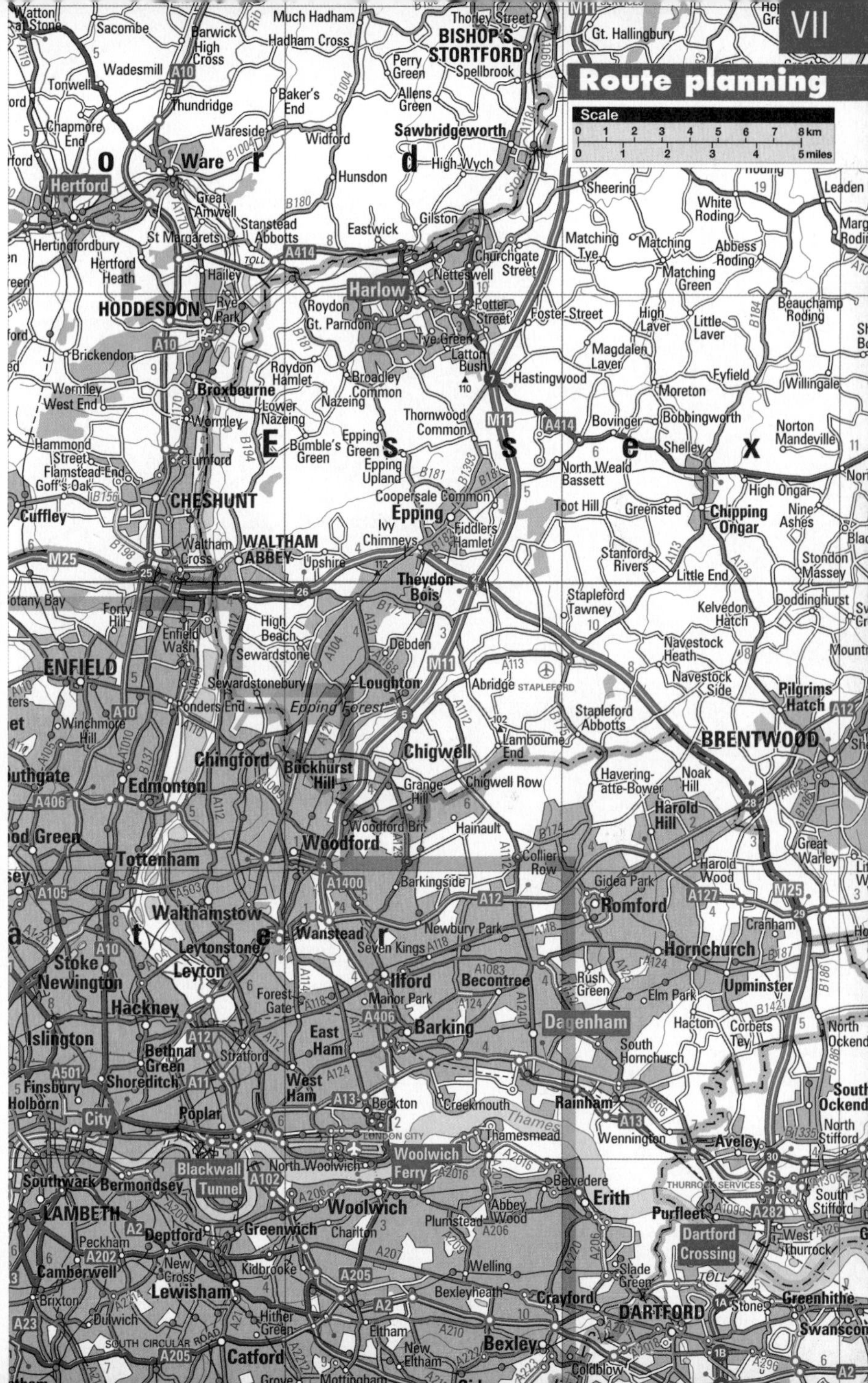

VII
Route planning
Scale
0 1 2 3 4 5 6 7 8 km
0 1 2 3 4 5 miles
Watton at Stone
Sacombe
Much Hadham
Barwick
High Cross
Hadham Cross
Thorley Street
BISHOP'S STORTFORD
Gt. Hallingbury
Perry Green
Spellbrook
Wadesmill
Tonwell
Thundridge
Baker's End
Allens Green
Chapmore End
Wareside
Widford
Sawbridgeworth
High Wych
Ware
Hertford
Hunsdon
Sheering
White Roding
Leaden
Great Amwell
Stanstead Abbotts
Eastwick
Gilston
St Margarets
Hertingfordbury
Hertford Heath
Hailey
Matching Tye
Matching
Abbess Roding
Churchgate Street
Netteswell
Matching Green
Harlow
HODDESDON
Rye Park
Roydon
Gt. Parndon
Potter Street
Foster Street
High Laver
Little Laver
Beauchamp Roding
Tye Green
Latton Bush
Magdalen Laver
Brickendon
Roydon Hamlet
Broadley Common
Hastingwood
Fyfield
Willingale
Wormley West End
Broxbourne
Lower Nazeing
Nazeing
Moreton
Wormley
Thornwood Common
Bovinger
Bobbingworth
Norton Mandeville
Hammond Street
Flamstead End
Goff's Oak
Turnford
Bumble's Green
Epping Green
Epping Upland
Shelley
North Weald Bassett
Coopersale Common
High Ongar
Cuffley
CHESHUNT
Epping
Toot Hill
Greensted
Chipping Ongar
Nine Ashes
Ivy Chimneys
Fiddlers Hamlet
Waltham Cross
WALTHAM ABBEY
Upshire
Stanford Rivers
Stondon Massey
Little End
Theydon Bois
Botany Bay
Forty Hill
Enfield Wash
High Beach
Stapleford Tawney
Kelvedon Hatch
Doddinghurst
Sewardstone
Debden
Navestock Heath
ENFIELD
Sewardstonebury
Loughton
Abridge
STAPLEFORD
Navestock Side
Pilgrims Hatch
Ponders End
Epping Forest
Stapleford Abbotts
Winchmore Hill
Lambourne End
BRENTWOOD
Chingford
Buckhurst Hill
Chigwell
Southgate
Edmonton
Grange Hill
Chigwell Row
Havering-atte-Bower
Noak Hill
Harold Hill
Woodford Bridge
Hainault
Wood Green
Tottenham
Woodford
Collier Row
Great Warley
Harold Wood
Barkingside
Gidea Park
Romford
Walthamstow
Wanstead
Newbury Park
Cranham
Seven Kings
Leytonstone
Hornchurch
Stoke Newington
Leyton
Ilford
Becontree
Rush Green
Upminster
Elm Park
Forest Gate
Manor Park
Hackney
East Ham
Barking
Dagenham
Hacton
Corbets Tey
North Ockendon
Islington
Bethnal Green
Stratford
South Hornchurch
Finsbury
Shoreditch
West Ham
Holborn
City
Poplar
Beckton
Creekmouth
Rainham
South Ockendon
Thames
Thamesmead
Wennington
Aveley
North Stifford
LONDON CITY
Woolwich Ferry
Blackwall Tunnel
North Woolwich
Southwark
Bermondsey
Belvedere
Erith
THURROCK SERVICES
South Stifford
LAMBETH
Woolwich
Abbey Wood
Purfleet
Greenwich
Charlton
Plumstead
Dartford Crossing
West Thurrock
Peckham
Deptford
New Cross
Camberwell
Kidbrooke
Welling
Slade Green
Lewisham
Bexleyheath
Crayford
TOLL
Brixton
Hither Green
DARTFORD
Stone
Greenhithe
Dulwich
Eltham
SOUTH CIRCULAR ROAD
New Eltham
Bexley
Swanscombe
Catford
Grove
Mottingham
Coldblow
Essex
Hertford
M25
M11
A10
A414
A406
A12
A13
A2

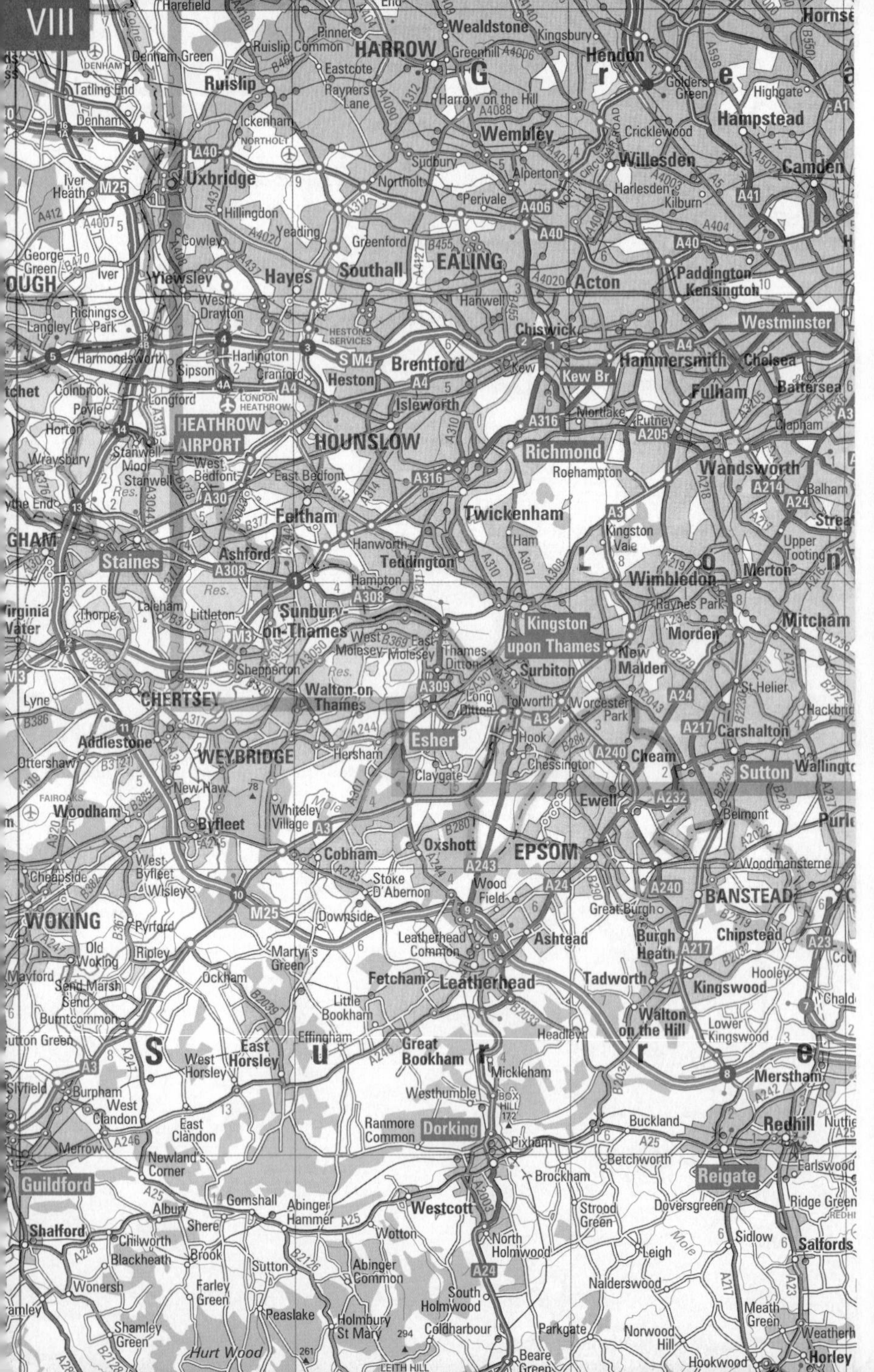

Harefield
Denham Green
DENHAM
Tatling End
Denham
Ruislip Common
Pinner
Wealdstone
Kingsbury
HARROW
Greenhill
Hendon
Horsey
Eastcote
Ruislip
Rayners Lane
Harrow on the Hill
Golders Green
Highgate
Hampstead
Ickenham
NORTHOLT
Wembley
Cricklewood
NORTH CIRCULAR ROAD
Iver Heath
Uxbridge
Sudbury
Alperton
Willesden
Camden
Northolt
Harlesden
Kilburn
Hillingdon
Perivale
Yeading
George Green
Cowley
Greenford
Iver
Yiewsley
Hayes
Southall
EALING
Acton
Paddington
Kensington
West Drayton
Hanwell
Richings Park
Langley
HESTON SERVICES
Chiswick
Westminster
Harmondsworth
Harlington
Hammersmith
Chelsea
Sipson
Cranford
Brentford
Kew
Kew Br.
Colnbrook
Heston
Fulham
Battersea
Poyle
Longford
LONDON HEATHROW
Isleworth
Mortlake
Putney
Horton
HEATHROW AIRPORT
HOUNSLOW
Clapham
Wraysbury
Stanwell Moor
Richmond
West Bedfont
Roehampton
Wandsworth
Stanwell
East Bedfont
Balham
Res.
Feltham
Twickenham
Kingston Vale
Upper Tooting
Hanworth
Ham
Ashford
Teddington
Staines
Wimbledon
Merton
Hampton
Res.
Laleham
Raynes Park
Thorpe
Littleton
Sunbury-on-Thames
Mitcham
Virginia Water
West Molesey
East Molesey
Kingston upon Thames
Morden
Thames Ditton
New Malden
Shepperton
Res.
Surbiton
St Helier
Lyne
CHERTSEY
Walton on Thames
Long Ditton
Tolworth
Worcester Park
Hackbridge
Esher
Carshalton
Addlestone
Hook
Ottershaw
WEYBRIDGE
Hersham
Chessington
Cheam
Sutton
Wallington
Claygate
FAIROAKS
New Haw
Ewell
Woodham
Whiteley Village
Belmont
Byfleet
Purley
Oxshott
EPSOM
Cobham
West Byfleet
Cheapside
Woodmansterne
Stoke D'Abernon
Wood Field
Wisley
BANSTEAD
WOKING
Downside
Great Burgh
Pyrford
Leatherhead Common
Ashtead
Burgh Heath
Chipstead
Old Woking
Ripley
Martyr's Green
Mayford
Send Marsh
Ockham
Fetcham
Leatherhead
Tadworth
Hooley
Kingswood
Send
Little Bookham
Chaldon
Burntcommon
Walton on the Hill
Sutton Green
Effingham
Headley
Lower Kingswood
West Horsley
East Horsley
Great Bookham
Mickleham
Merstham
Slyfield
Burpham
West Clandon
Westhumble
BOX HILL
East Clandon
Ranmore Common
Dorking
Buckland
Redhill
Nutfield
Merrow
Pixham
Betchworth
Earlswood
Newland's Corner
Brockham
Reigate
Guildford
Ridge Green
Gomshall
Abinger Hammer
Westcott
Strood Green
Doversgreen
Albury
Shere
Shalford
Chilworth
Wotton
North Holmwood
Sidlow
Salfords
Blackheath
Brook
Leigh
Sutton
Abinger Common
Wonersh
Farley Green
Nalderswood
South Holmwood
Meath Green
Peaslake
Holmbury St Mary
Coldharbour
Shamley Green
Parkgate
Norwood Hill
Hurt Wood
LEITH HILL
Beare Green
Hookwood
Horley
Mole
Colne
Res.
S
u
r
r
e
G
r
e
a
L
o
n
M25
M4
M3
A40
A4
A30
A308
A316
A205
A406
A41
A24
A214
A217
A232
A240
A243
A309
A3
A244
A307
A310
A25
A23
A312
A4020
A4088
A412
A4007
B470
B455
B2033
B2126

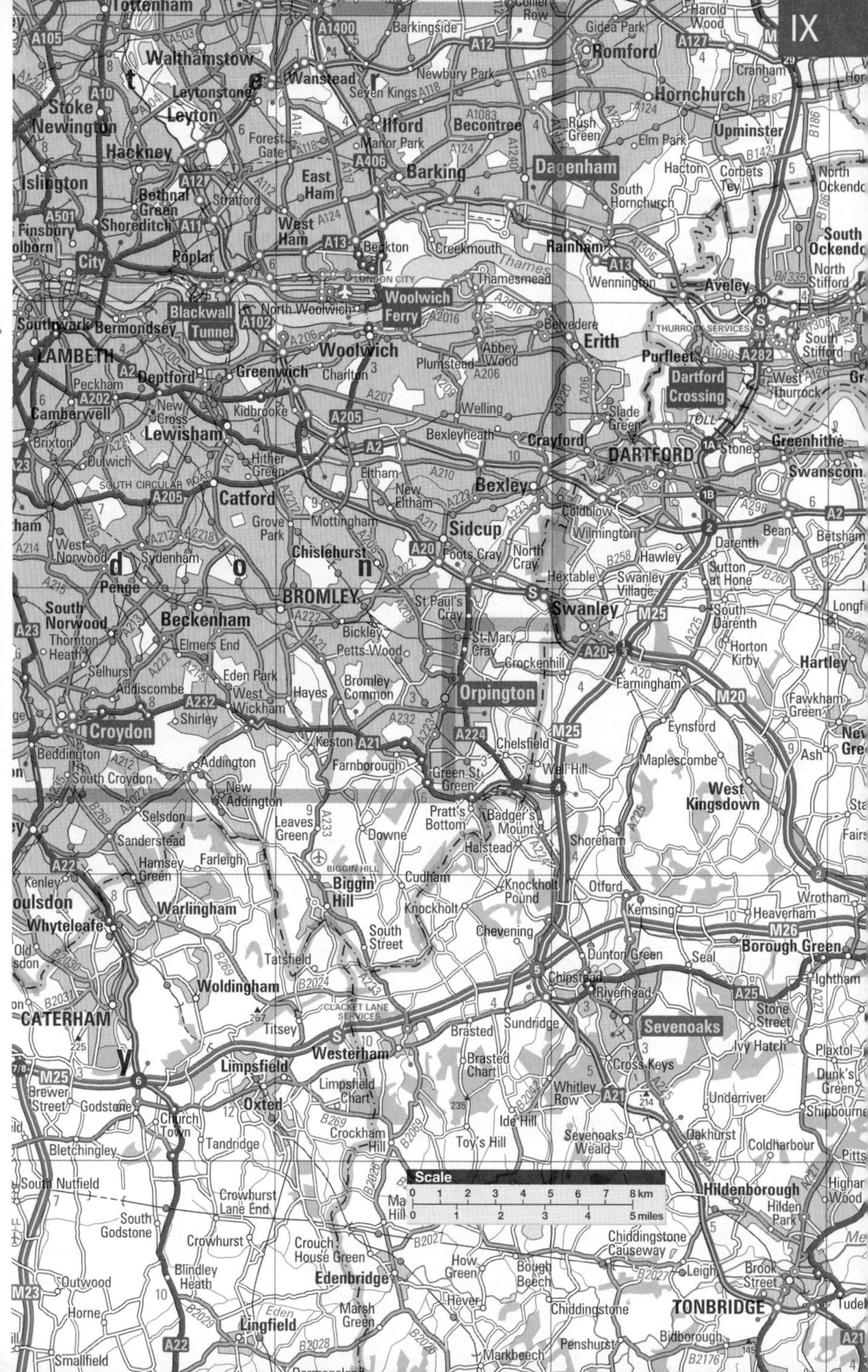
Tottenham
Collier Row
Harold Wood
Gidea Park
Barkingside
A1400
A12
Romford
A127
A105
A503
Walthamstow
Newbury Park
Cranham
Wanstead
Seven Kings
A118
Hornchurch
A10
Leytonstone
Stoke Newington
Leyton
Ilford
A1083
Becontree
Rush Green
Elm Park
Upminster
B186
Hackney
Forest Gate
Manor Park
A124
A1240
Dagenham
Hacton
Corbets Tey
B1421
North Ockendon
Islington
A406
Barking
East Ham
South Hornchurch
Bethnal Green
Stratford
A12
A112
A117
A501
Finsbury
Holborn
Shoreditch
A11
West Ham
A124
A13
Beckton
Creekmouth
Rainham
A1306
A13
South Ockendon
City
Poplar
LONDON CITY
Thames
Thamesmead
Wennington
Aveley
North Stifford
B1335
30
Blackwall Tunnel
North Woolwich
Woolwich Ferry
A2016
A102
A2041
Belvedere
Erith
THURROCK SERVICES
31
A1306
A1012
South Stifford
Southwark
Bermondsey
LAMBETH
A200
A206
Woolwich
Abbey Wood
Plumstead
A206
Purfleet
A1090
A282
A2
Deptford
Greenwich
Charlton
Dartford Crossing
West Thurrock
A126
Peckham
A202
Camberwell
New Cross
Kidbrooke
A207
A209
Welling
A220
A206
Slade Green
TOLL
Brixton
Lewisham
A205
A2
Bexleyheath
Crayford
DARTFORD
1A
Stone
Greenhithe
A23
Dulwich
A21
Hither Green
Eltham
A210
A207
A2018
Swanscombe
SOUTH CIRCULAR ROAD
A205
Catford
A2212
New Eltham
A222
Bexley
1B
A296
A2
A2199
A2218
A212
Grove Park
Mottingham
A211
Sidcup
A223
Coldblow
Wilmington
Bean
Betsham
A214
West Norwood
Sydenham
Chislehurst
A20
Foots Cray
North Cray
B258
Hawley
Darenth
Sutton at Hone
B260
B262
B255
A215
Penge
BROMLEY
A208
Hextable
Swanley Village
Swanley
M25
South Darenth
South Norwood
Thornton Heath
Beckenham
A213
A222
St Paul's Cray
St Mary Cray
Bickley
A21
Petts Wood
Elmers End
A222
Horton Kirby
Hartley
A20
Crockenhill
Farningham
Selhurst
Addiscombe
A214
Eden Park
West Wickham
Hayes
Bromley Common
Orpington
A232
M20
Fawkham Green
A232
Shirley
Croydon
A223
A224
Eynsford
Keston
A21
Chelsfield
M25
Beddington
A212
Addington
Farnborough
Well Hill
Maplescombe
Ash
A20
South Croydon
A2022
New Addington
Green St Green
West Kingsdown
A235
B269
Selsdon
Pratt's Bottom
Badger's Mount
A233
Leaves Green
Downe
Sanderstead
Halstead
A224
A225
Shoreham
Hamsey Green
Farleigh
BIGGIN HILL
A22
Kenley
Biggin Hill
Cudham
Knockholt Pound
Otford
Coulsdon
Knockholt
Kemsing
Wrotham
Heaverham
Warlingham
Whyteleafe
South Street
Chevening
M26
Borough Green
Old Coulsdon
B2030
B269
Tatsfield
Dunton Green
Seal
Woldingham
A233
B2024
Chipstead
Riverhead
A25
Ightham
A227
B2031
CLACKET LANE SERVICES
267
Titsey
Brasted
Sundridge
Sevenoaks
Stone Street
CATERHAM
225
Westerham
Ivy Hatch
Plaxtol
Limpsfield
Brasted Chart
Cross Keys
A225
Dunk's Green
M25
Brewer Street
Godstone
Church Town
Oxted
Limpsfield Chart
B2042
Whitley Row
A21
214
Underriver
Shipbourne
235
Bletchingley
Tandridge
B269
Crockham Hill
B2069
Toy's Hill
Ide Hill
Sevenoaks Weald
Oakhurst
B245
Coldharbour
South Nutfield
Crowhurst Lane End
B2026
Scale
0 1 2 3 4 5 6 7 8 km
0 1 2 3 4 5 miles
Hildenborough
A227
Hilden Park
South Godstone
Crowhurst
Crouch House Green
B2027
Chiddingstone Causeway
M23
Outwood
Blindley Heath
Edenbridge
How Green
Bough Beech
B2027
Leigh
Brook Street
Horne
Eden
Marsh Green
Hever
Chiddingstone
TONBRIDGE
A22
B2029
Lingfield
B2028
B2026
Penshurst
Bidborough
B2176
145
Smallfield
Markbeech
A21

Key to map symbols

Roads

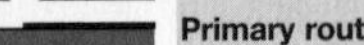

	Motorway with junction number (22a)
	Primary route – single, dual carriageway
	A road – single, dual carriageway
	B road – single, dual carriageway
	Through-route – single, dual carriageway
	Minor road – single, dual carriageway
	Road under construction
	Rural track, private road or narrow road in urban area
	Path, bridleway, byway open to all traffic, road used as public path
	Tunnel, covered road

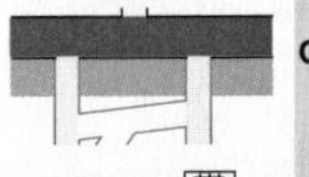

Congestion Charge Zone boundary
Roads within the zone are outlined in red

Gate or obstruction, car pound

 P **P&R** Parking, park and ride

 Crooked Billet Road junction name

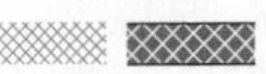

 Pedestrianised or restricted access area

Public transport

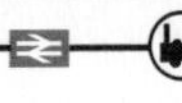

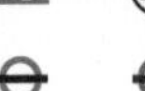

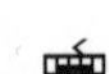

Railway station, private railway station

London Underground station, Docklands Light Railway station

Tramway or miniature railway with Tramlink station

Bus, coach station

Scale

3½ inches to 1 mile   1:18103

0   220yds   440yds   660yds   ½ mile

0   250m   500m   750m   1km

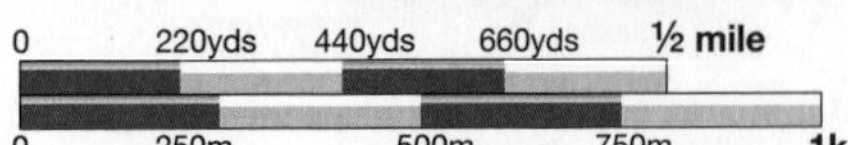

Emergency services

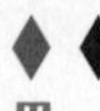

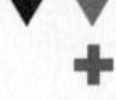

◆ ◆ ◆   Ambulance, police, fire station

H   ✚   Hospital, accident and emergency entrance

General features

⚒ 🗑	Market, public amenity site
🄸 PO	Information centre, post office
VILLA House	Roman, non-Roman antiquity
100 .304	House number, spot height – metres
✚	Christian place of worship
☾★ ☰	Mosque, synagogue
▫	Other place of worship

Houses, important buildings

Woods, parkland/common

123   Adjoining page number

Leisure facilities

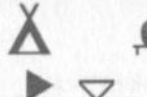

X ⛟   Camp site, caravan site

▶ ✗ ⚘   Golf course, picnic site, view point

Boundaries

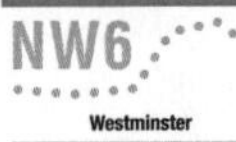

NW6 ⋯   Postcode boundaries

Westminster   County and unitary authority boundaries

Water features

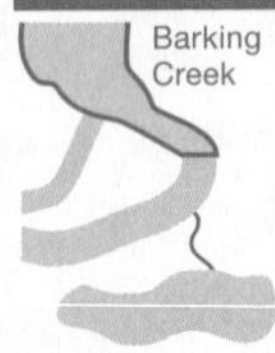

Barking Creek   Water name

Tidal water

River or canal – minor, major

Stream

Water

Abbreviations

Acad	Academy	Coll	College	Glf Crs	Golf Course	Ct	Law Court	
Allot Gdns	Allotments	Ct	Court	Drv Rng	Golf Driving Range	L Ctr	Leisure Centre	
Bndstd	Bandstand	Crem	Crematorium			LC	Level Crossing	
Btcl	Botanical	Crkt	Cricket	Gn	Green	Liby	Library	
Bwg Gn	Bowling	Ent	Enterprise	Gd	Ground	Mkt	Market	
Cemy	Cemetery	Ex H	Exhibition Hall	Hort	Horticultural	Meml	Memorial	
Ctr	Centre			Ind Est	Industrial Estate	Mon	Monument	
C Ctr	Civic Centre	Fball	Football			Mus	Museum	
CH	Club House	Gdns	Gardens	Inst	Institute	Nat Res	Nature Reserve	
Ctry Pk	Country Park	Glf C	Golf Course	Int	Interchange			

Obsy	Observatory	Sh Ctr	Shopping Centre
Pav	Pavilion	Sp	Sports
Pk	Park	Stad	Stadium
Pl Fld	Playing Field	Sw Pool	Swimming Pool
Pal	Royal Palace		
PH	Public House	Tenn Cts	Tennis
Recn Gd	Recreation Ground	TH	Town Hall
		Trad Est	Trading Estate
Resr	Reservoir		
Ret Pk	Retail Park	Univ	University
Sch	School	YH	Youth Hostel

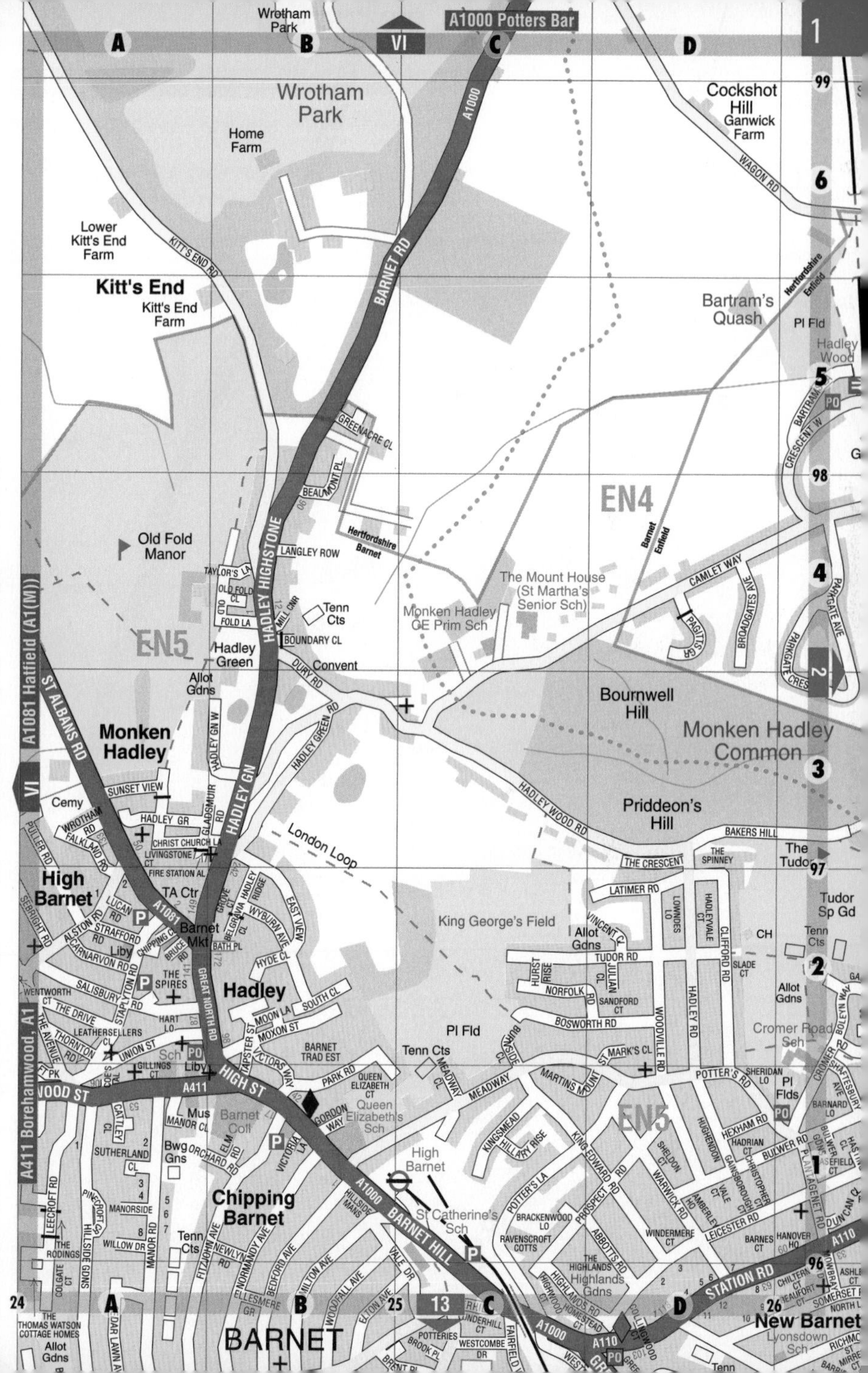
A1000 Potters Bar
VI
A
B
C
D
Wrotham Park
Home Farm
Lower Kitt's End Farm
Kitt's End
Kitt's End Farm
Cockshot Hill
Ganwick Farm
WAGON RD
KITT'S END RD
BARNET RD
A1000
Bartram's Quash
Hertfordshire Enfield
Pl Fld
Hadley Wood
GREENACRE CL
BEAUMONT PL
Hertfordshire Barnet
EN4
Barnet Enfield
Old Fold Manor
LANGLEY ROW
HADLEY HIGHSTONE
TAYLOR'S LA
OLD FOLD CL
FOLD LA
MILL CNR
BOUNDARY CL
Tenn Cts
The Mount House (St Martha's Senior Sch)
Monken Hadley CE Prim Sch
CAMLET WAY
BROADGATES AVE
PAGITTS GR
PARKGATE AVE
PARKGATE CRES
EN5
Hadley Green
Convent
DURY RD
Allot Gdns
Bournwell Hill
Monken Hadley Common
A1081 Hatfield (A1(M))
ST ALBANS RD
Monken Hadley
HADLEY GN W
HADLEY GREEN RD
HADLEY GN
HADLEY WOOD RD
Priddeon's Hill
BAKERS HILL
SUNSET VIEW
Cemy
WROTHAM RD
HADLEY GR
GLADSMUIR RD
FALKLAND RD
PULLER RD
CHRIST CHURCH LA
LIVINGSTONE CT
FIRE STATION AL
London Loop
THE CRESCENT
THE SPINNEY
The Tudor
High Barnet
TA Ctr
LATIMER RD
LOWNDES LO
HADLEYVALE CT
CLIFFORD RD
Tudor Sp Gd
SEBRIGHT RD
LUCAN RD
ALSTON RD
STRAFFORD RD
CARNARVON RD
A1081
Barnet Mkt
CHIPPING CL
BRUCE RD
GROVE CT
BELGRAVIA CL
HADLEY RIDGE
WYBURN AVE
EAST VIEW
King George's Field
VINCENT CL
Allot Gdns
CH
Tenn Cts
Liby
BATH PL
HYDE CL
TUDOR RD
HURST RISE
JULIAN CL
SLADE CT
WENTWORTH CT
SALISBURY RD
STAPLYTON RD
THE SPIRES
Hadley
SOUTH CL
NORFOLK RD
SANDFORD CT
HADLEY RD
Allot Gdns
THE DRIVE
HART LO
GREAT NORTH RD
MOON LA
MOXON ST
BOSWORTH RD
WOODVILLE RD
BOLEYN WAY
THE AVENUE
THORNTON RD
LEATHERSELLERS CL
UNION ST
Sch
PO
Pl Fld
Cromer Road Sch
BARNET TRAD EST
Tenn Cts
BURNSIDE CL
ST MARK'S CL
CROMER RD
SHAFTESBURY AVE
FT PK
GILLINGS CT
Liby
TAPSTER ST
VICTORS WAY
MEADWAY CL
MEADWAY
MARTINS MOUNT
POTTER'S RD
SHERIDAN LO
Pl Flds
WOOD ST
A411
HIGH ST
PARK RD
QUEEN ELIZABETH CT
Queen Elizabeth's Sch
BARNARD LO
CATTLEY CL
Mus
MANOR CL
Barnet Coll
GORDON WAY
KINGSMEAD
HILLARY RISE
KING EDWARD RD
EN5
HEXHAM RD
HADRIAN CT
BULWER RD
BULWER GDNS
HASTINGS
ASEFIELD CT
A411 Borehamwood, A1
SUTHERLAND CL
Bwg Gns
ORCHARD RD
ELM
VICTORIA LA
High Barnet
SHELDON CT
HUGHENDON
GAINSBOROUGH
CHRISTOPHER CT
PLANTAGENET RD
A1000
POTTER'S LA
PROSPECT RD
WARWICK RD
VALE CT
LEECROFT RD
PINECROFT CL
MANORSIDE
Chipping Barnet
HILLSIDE MANS
BARNET HILL
St Catherine's Sch
BRACKENWOOD LO
AMBERLEY HO
LEICESTER RD
DUNCAN CL
HILLSIDE GDNS
THE RODINGS
WILLOW DR
MANOR RD
Tenn Cts
FITZJOHN AVE
NEWLYN RD
NORMANDY AVE
BEDFORD AVE
MILTON AVE
VALE DR
RAVENSCROFT COTTS
ABBOTTS RD
WINDERMERE CT
BARNES CT
HANOVER HO
A110
COLGATE CT
WOODFALL AVE
ELTON AVE
THE HIGHLANDS
Highlands Gdns
HIGHLANDS RD
HIGHWOOD
HOMESTEAD CT
STATION RD
96
CHILTERN
BEAUFORT
ASHLEY
SOMERSET RD
NORTH LA
24
THE THOMAS WATSON COTTAGE HOMES
Allot Gdns
ELLESMERE GR
25
13
UNDERHILL CT
POTTERIES
BROOK PL
WESTCOMBE DR
FAIRFIELD
COLLINGWOOD CT
A110
26
New Barnet
Lyonsdown Sch
BARNET
99
6
5
98
4
2
3
97
2
1
BARTRAM
CRESCENT W

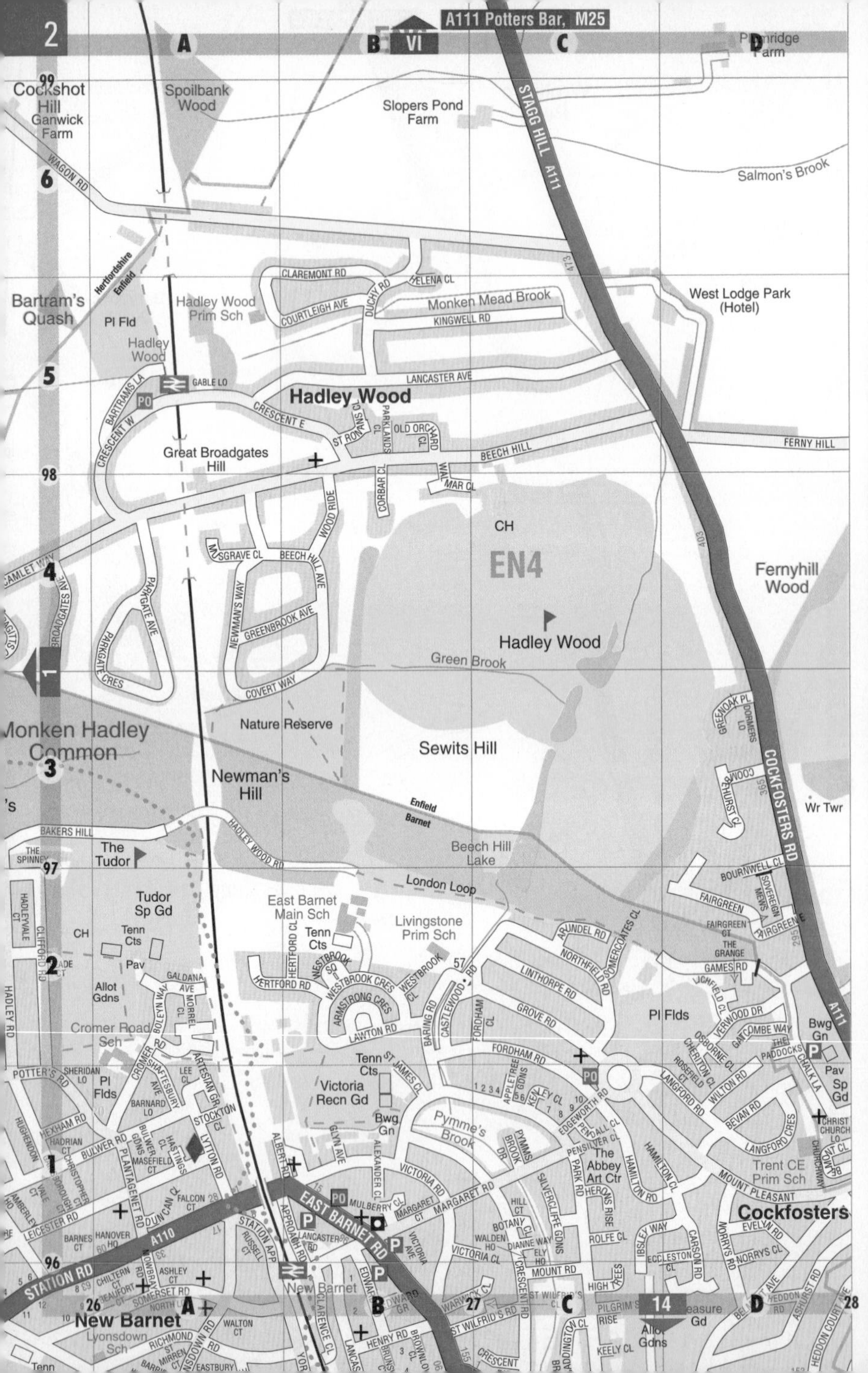
A111 Potters Bar, M25
VI
Cockshot Hill
Ganwick Farm
Spoilbank Wood
Slopers Pond Farm
Plumridge Farm
STAGG HILL
A111
Salmon's Brook
WAGON RD
Hertfordshire
Enfield
Bartram's Quash
Pl Fld
Hadley Wood Prim Sch
Hadley Wood
CLAREMONT RD
COURTLEIGH AVE
DUCHY RD
HELENA CL
Monken Mead Brook
KINGWELL RD
West Lodge Park (Hotel)
LANCASTER AVE
GABLE LO
Hadley Wood
BARTRAMS LA
PO
CRESCENT W
CRESCENT E
ST RONANS CL
PARKLANDS CL
OLD ORCHARD CL
BEECH HILL
FERNY HILL
Great Broadgates Hill
CORBAR CL
WALMAR CL
WOOD RIDE
CH
EN4
MUSGRAVE CL
BEECH HILL AVE
CAMLET WAY
BROADGATES AVE
PARKGATE AVE
NEWMAN'S WAY
GREENBROOK AVE
Fernyhill Wood
Hadley Wood
PARKGATE CRES
COVERT WAY
Green Brook
GREENOAK PL
DORMERS LO
Monken Hadley Common
Nature Reserve
Sewits Hill
COCKFOSTERS RD
Newman's Hill
Enfield
Barnet
Wr Twr
BAKERS HILL
HADLEY WOOD RD
THE SPINNEY
The Tudor
Beech Hill Lake
BOURNWELL CL
London Loop
SOVEREIGN MEWS
FAIRGREEN
FAIRGREEN CT
FAIRGREEN E
THE GRANGE
HADLEYVALE CT
CLIFFORD RD
Tudor Sp Gd
CH
Tenn Cts
East Barnet Main Sch
Tenn Cts
Livingstone Prim Sch
ARUNDEL RD
SOMERCOATES CL
NORTHFIELD RD
GAMES RD
LINTHORPE RD
Pav
GALDANA AVE
HERTFORD CL
WESTBROOK SQ
WESTBROOK CRES
WESTBROOK CL
CASTLEWOOD RD
HERTFORD RD
ARMSTRONG CRES
FORDHAM CL
GROVE RD
Pl Flds
LICHFIELD CL
VERWOOD DR
HADLEY RD
Allot Gdns
BOLEYN WAY
MORREL CL
LAWTON RD
BARING RD
GATCOMBE WAY
Bwg Gn
Cromer Road Sch
CROMER RD
ARTESIAN GR
FORDHAM RD
OSBORNE CL
CHERITON CL
THE PADDOCKS
CHALK LA
Pav
Sp Gd
POTTER'S RD
SHERIDAN LO
Pl Flds
SHAFTESBURY AVE
LEE CL
Tenn Cts
ST JAMES CL
Victoria Recn Gd
APPLETREE GDNS
KENLEY CL
EDGEWORTH RD
ROSEFIELD CL
LANGFORD RD
WILTON RD
BARNARD LO
STOCKTON CL
BEVAN RD
CHRIST CHURCH LO
HUGHENDON
HEXHAM RD
HADRIAN CT
BULWER RD
BULWER GDNS
HASTINGS
MASEFIELD CT
LYTTON RD
Bwg Gn
Pymme's Brook
PYMMS BROOK DR
PENDALL CL
PENSILVER CL
The Abbey Art Ctr
HAMILTON RD
HAMILTON CL
LANGFORD CRES
Trent CE Prim Sch
CHURCHWAY
BELMONT CL
CHRISTOPHER CT
BOROUGH CT
VALE CT
PLANTAGENET RD
DUNCAN CL
FALCON CT
ALBERT RD
GLYN AVE
ALEXANDER CL
VICTORIA RD
MARGARET RD
MULBERRY CL
MARGARET CT
SILVERCLIFFE GDNS
PARK RD
HERONS RISE
MOUNT PLEASANT
Cockfosters
AMBERLEY
LEICESTER RD
BARNES CT
HANOVER HO
A110
STATION APP
RUSSELL CT
APPROACH RD
EAST BARNET RD
LANCASTER RD
VICTORIA AVE
HILL CT
BOTANY CL
WALDEN HO
DIANNE WAY
ELY HO
VICTORIA CL
CRESCENT RD
IBSLEY WAY
CARSON RD
ROLFE CL
NORRYS RD
EVELYN RD
NORRYS CL
STATION RD
CHILTERN CT
BEAUFORT CT
MOWBRAY RD
ASHLEY CT
SOMERSET RD
New Barnet
EDWARD GR
MOUNT RD
ECCLESTON CL
HIGH TREES
BELMONT AVE
ASHURST RD
HEDDON RD
26
A
B
27
WARWICK CL
ST WILFRID'S CL
C
PILGRIM'S RISE
14
Pleasure Gd
D
28
New Barnet
NORTH LO
Lyonsdown Sch
RICHMOND RD
LANSDOWN RD
WALTON CT
CLARENCE CL
HENRY RD
BRUNSWICK
BROWNLOW
ST WILFRID'S RD
CRESCENT
ADDINGTON CL
Allot Gdns
KEELY CL
HEDDON COURT AVE
ST MIRREN CT
EASTBURY
Tenn
99
6
5
98
4
1
3
97
2
1
96

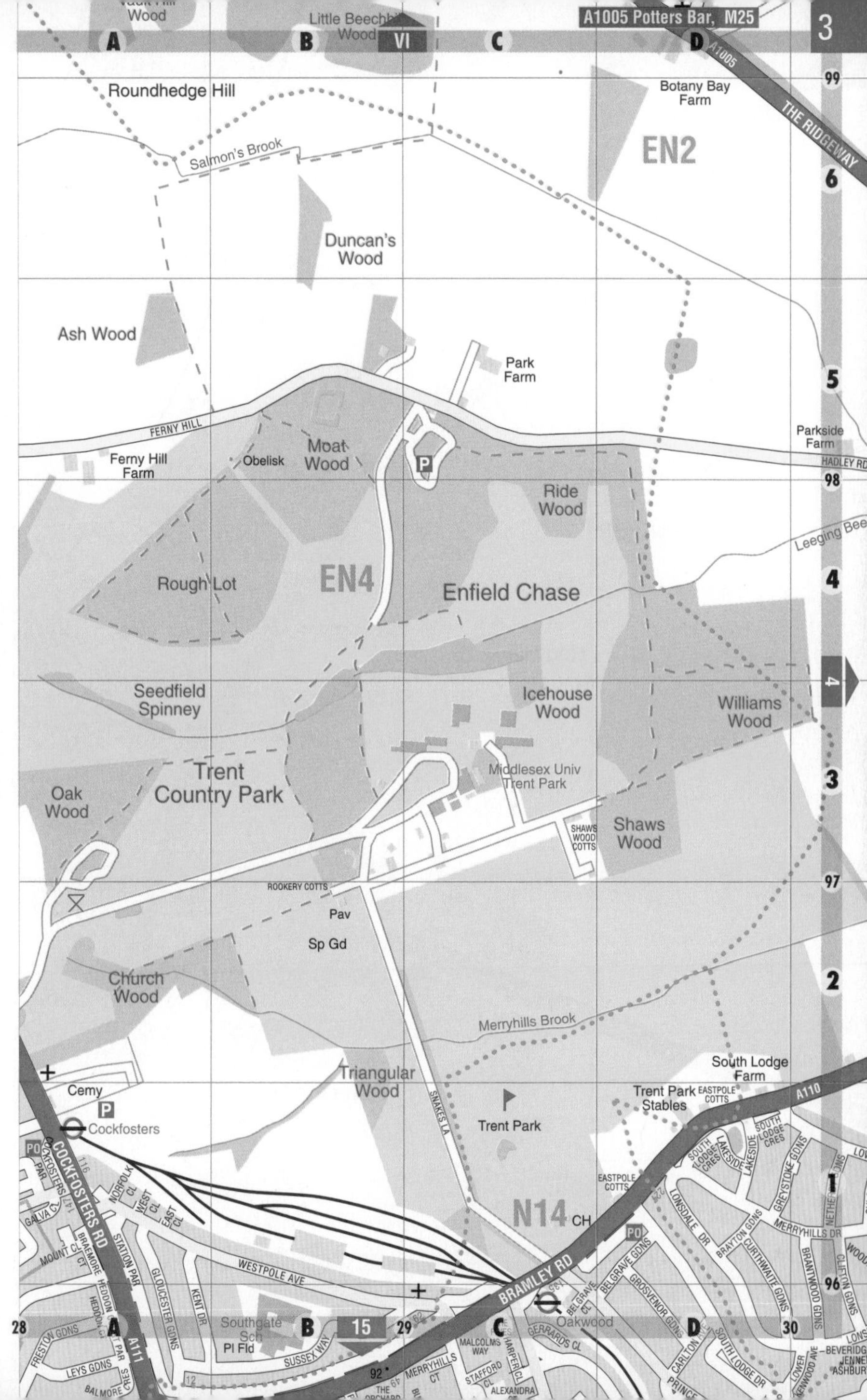
Little Beechhill Wood
VI
Roundhedge Hill
Botany Bay Farm
A1005
THE RIDGEWAY
EN2
Salmon's Brook
Duncan's Wood
Ash Wood
Park Farm
FERNY HILL
Ferny Hill Farm
Obelisk
Moat Wood
Parkside Farm
HADLEY RD
Ride Wood
Leeging Beech
EN4
Enfield Chase
Rough Lot
Seedfield Spinney
Icehouse Wood
Williams Wood
Trent Country Park
Middlesex Univ Trent Park
Oak Wood
Shaws Wood
SHAWS WOOD COTTS
ROOKERY COTTS
Pav
Sp Gd
Church Wood
Merryhills Brook
Triangular Wood
South Lodge Farm
Cemy
Cockfosters
SNAKES LA
Trent Park
Trent Park Stables
EASTPOLE COTTS
A110
COCKFOSTERS RD
N14
CH
BRAMLEY RD
WESTPOLE AVE
Oakwood
Southgate Sch
Pl Fld
15
SUSSEX WAY
A111
LAKESIDE
SOUTH LODGE CRES
GREYSTOKE GDNS
LONSDALE DR
BRAYTON GDNS
CURTHWAITE GDNS
MERRYHILLS DR
BRANTWOOD GDNS
CLIFTON GDNS
GROSVENOR GDNS
BELGRAVE GDNS
BELGRAVE CL
CARLTON AVE
SOUTH LODGE DR
GERRARDS CL
MALCOLMS WAY
STAFFORD CL
ALEXANDRA
HARPER CL
MERRYHILLS CT
THE ORCHARD
KENT DR
GLOUCESTER GDNS
STATION PAR
NORFOLK CL
WEST CL
EAST CL
MOUNT CL
BRAEMORE CT
HEDDON CT
GALVA CL
COCKFOSTERS PAR
FRESTON GDNS
LEYS GDNS
BALMORE CRES
BEVERIDGE
JENNER
ASHBURY
KENWOOD AVE
LOWER
PRINCE
NETHERLANDS
A B C D
99 98 97 96
6 5 4 3 2 1
28 29 30

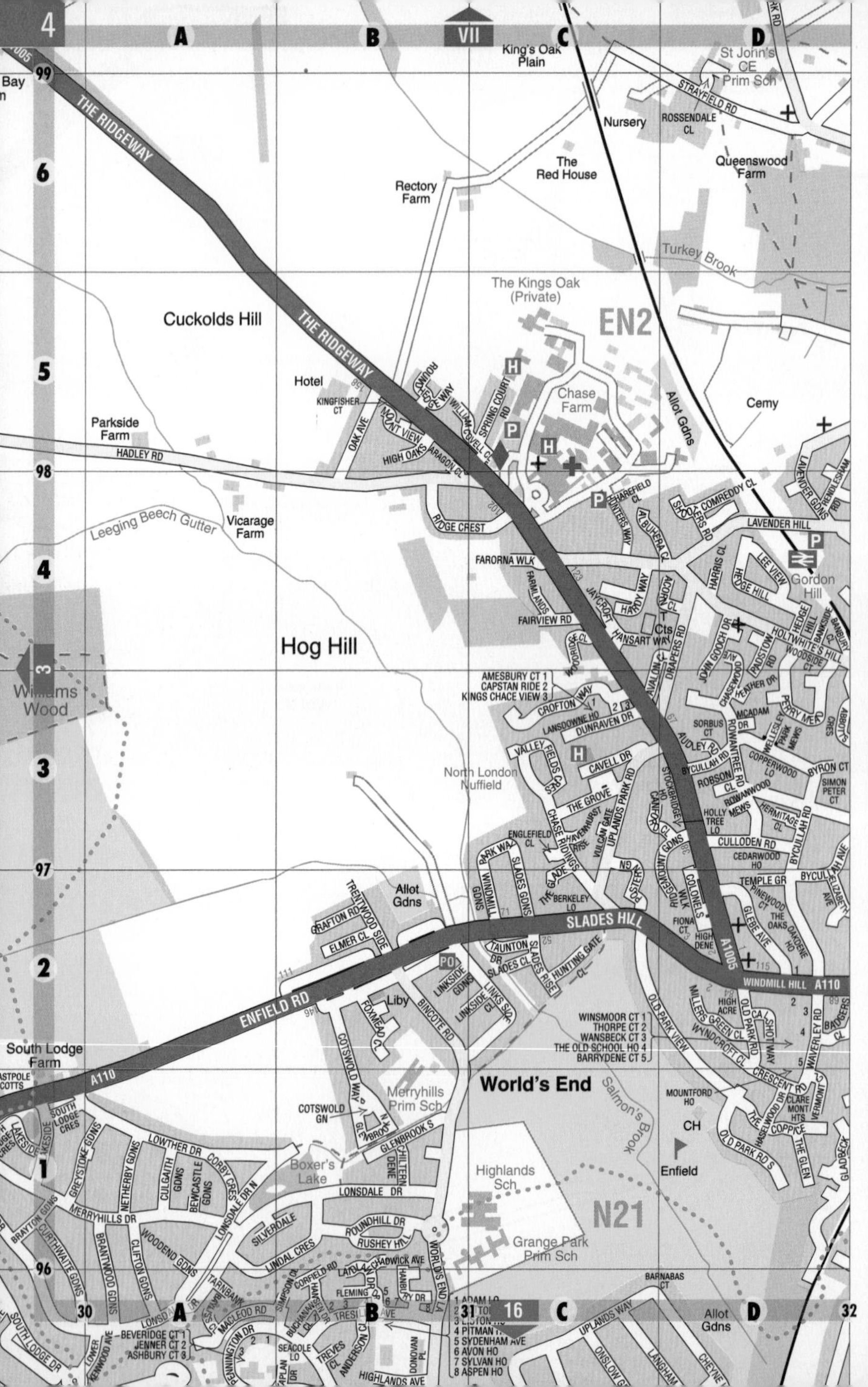

4
A
B
VII
C
D
King's Oak Plain
St John's CE Prim Sch
STRAYFIELD RD
Nursery
ROSSENDALE CL
The Red House
Queenswood Farm
Rectory Farm
THE RIDGEWAY
Turkey Brook
The Kings Oak (Private)
EN2
Cuckolds Hill
Hotel
KINGFISHER CT
OAK AVE
MOUNT VIEW
HIGH OAKS
ARAGON CL
ROUND HEDGE WAY
WILLIAM COVELL CL
SPRING COURT RD
Chase Farm
Allot Gdns
Cemy
Parkside Farm
HADLEY RD
RIDGE CREST
HAREFIELD CL
HUNTERS WAY
ALBUHERA CL
SHOOTERS RD
COMREDDY CL
LAVENDER HILL
LAVENDER GDNS
RENDLESHAM RD
Leeging Beech Gutter
Vicarage Farm
FARORNA WLK
FARMLANDS
JAYCROFT
HARDY WAY
ACORN CL
HARRIS CL
HEDGE HILL
LEE VIEW
Gordon Hill
FAIRVIEW RD
HANSART WAY
Cts
DRAPERS RD
JOHN GOOCH DR
PADSTOW RD
HOLTWHITE'S HILL
BANKSIDE
Hog Hill
Williams Wood
3
WOODGATE CL
AMESBURY CT 1
CAPSTAN RIDE 2
KINGS CHACE VIEW 3
CROFTON WAY
LANSDOWNE HO
DUNRAVEN DR
AVALON CL
CHASEWOOD AVE
FEATHER DR
WOODSIDE CT
PERRY MEAD
ABBOTS CRES
SORBUS CT
MCADAM DR
WELLESLEY PARK MEWS
AUDLEY RD
VALLEY FIELDS CRES
CAVELL DR
BYCULLAH RD
ROBSON CL
ROWANTREE RD
COPPERWOOD LO
BYRON CT
SIMON PETER CT
North London Nuffield
THE GROVE
UPLANDS PARK RD
STOCKBRIDGE HO
CANFORD CL
ROWANWOOD MEWS
HOLLY TREE LO
HERMITAGE CL
ENGLEFIELD CL
CHASE RIDINGS
HAVENHURST RISE
VULCAN GATE
PARK WAY
WINDMILL GDNS
SLADES GDNS
RIDGEMONT GDNS
CULLODEN RD
CEDARWOOD HO
BYCULLAH AVE
THE GLADE
POSTERN GN
COLONELS WLK
TEMPLE GR
PINEWOOD CT
THE OAKS
ELIZABETH AVE
TRENTWOOD SIDE
Allot Gdns
GRAFTON RD
ELMER CL
BERKELEY CL
SLADES HILL
FIONA CT
HIGH DENE
GLEBE AVE
OAKDENE HO
A1005
TAUNTON DR
SLADES CL
SLADES RISE
HUNTING GATE CL
WINDMILL HILL
A110
ENFIELD RD
PO
Liby
FOXMEAD CL
BINCOTE RD
LINKSIDE GDNS
LINKSIDE
LINKS SIDE CL
HIGH ACRE
MILLERS GREEN CL
OLD PARK RD
CALSHOT WAY
OLD PARK VIEW
WINSMOOR CT 1
THORPE CT 2
WANSBECK CT 3
THE OLD SCHOOL HO 4
BARRYDENE CT 5
WYNDCROFT CL
WAVERLEY RD
BADGERS CL
South Lodge Farm
EASTPOLE COTTS
COTSWOLD WAY
Merryhills Prim Sch
World's End
Salmon's Brook
MOUNTFORD HO
CRESCENT RD
CLAREMONT HTS
VERMONT CL
COTSWOLD GN
GLENBROOK N
GLENBROOK S
THE HASELWOOD DR
COPPICE
THE GLEN
CH
OLD PARK RD S
LAKESIDE
SOUTH LODGE CRES
GREYSTOKE GDNS
LOWTHER DR
CORBY CRES
NETHERBY GDNS
CULGAITH GDNS
BEWCASTLE GDNS
LONSDALE DR N
Boxer's Lake
CHILTERN DENE
Highlands Sch
Enfield
GLADBECK
LONSDALE DR
BRAYTON GDNS
MERRYHILLS DR
SILVERDALE
ROUNDHILL DR
CURTHWAITE GDNS
BRANTWOOD GDNS
CLIFTON GDNS
WOODEND GDNS
LONSDALE DR
RUSHEY HILL
N21
LINDAL CRES
Grange Park Prim Sch
CHADWICK AVE
WORLD'S END LA
SIMPSON CL
CORFIELD RD
LAIDLAW DR
HANBURY DR
FLEMING
TARNBANK
BARNABAS CT
30
A
B
31
16
C
D
32
MACLEOD RD
TRESILIAN AVE
BUCHANAN CL
HANSEN DR
1 ADAM HO
4 PITMAN HO
5 SYDENHAM AVE
6 AVON HO
7 SYLVAN HO
8 ASPEN HO
UPLANDS WAY
Allot Gdns
SOUTH LODGE DR
LOWER
KENWOOD AVE
BEVERIDGE CT 1
JENNER CT 2
ASHBURY CT 3
PENNINGTON DR
SEACOLE LO
TREVES CL
ANDERSON CL
DONOVAN PL
HIGHLANDS AVE
ONSLOW GDNS
LANGHAM
CHEYNE

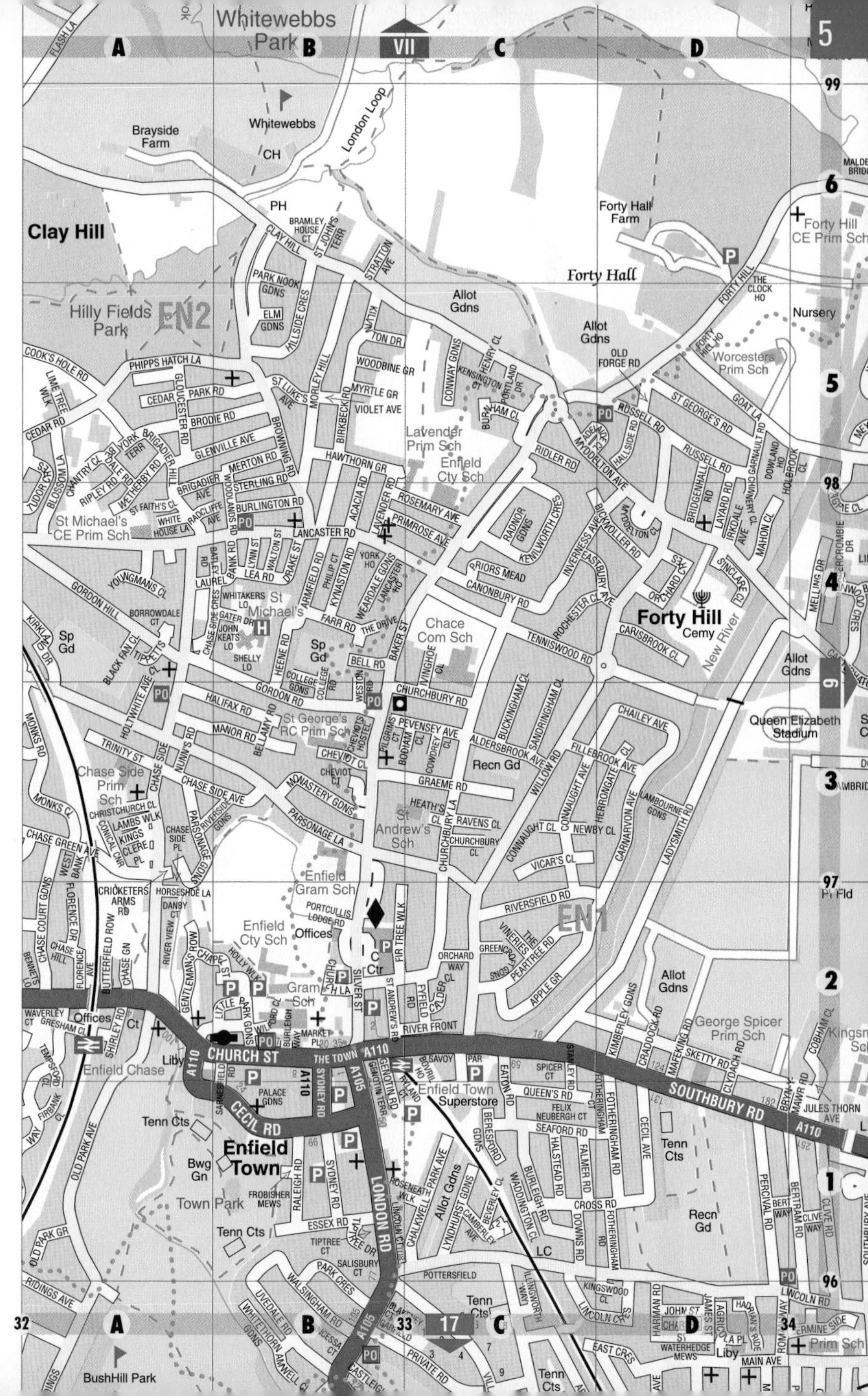
Whitewebbs Park
A
B
VII
C
D
99
Brayside Farm
Whitewebbs
CH
London Loop
PH
Clay Hill
Forty Hall Farm
Forty Hill CE Prim Sch
Forty Hall
Hilly Fields Park
EN2
Allot Gdns
Nursery
Worcesters Prim Sch
6
5
PHIPPS HATCH LA
COOK'S HOLE RD
CEDAR RD
CLAY HILL
BRAMLEY HOUSE CT
ST JOHN'S TERR
STRATTON AVE
PARK NOOK GDNS
ELM GDNS
HILLSIDE CRES
KILVINTON DR
WOODBINE GR
MYRTLE GR
VIOLET AVE
CONWAY GDNS
KENSINGTON CT
HENRY CL
PORTLAND DR
BURNHAM CL
OLD FORGE RD
RUSSELL RD
ST GEORGE'S RD
GOAT LA
FORTY HILL
THE CLOCK HO
PARK RD
GLOUCESTER RD
BRODIE RD
GLENVILLE AVE
ST LUKE'S AVE
MORLEY HILL
BIRKBECK RD
BROWNING RD
Lavender Prim Sch
Enfield Cty Sch
RIDLER RD
MYDDELTON AVE
HALLSIDE RD
BRIDGENHALL RD
LAYARD RD
IRKDALE AVE
GARNAULT RD
CHINNERY CL
DOWLAND HO
HOLBROOK CL
MAHON CL
98
HAWTHORN GR
ROSEMARY AVE
PRIMROSE AVE
LANCASTER RD
MERTON RD
STERLING RD
BURLINGTON RD
St Michael's CE Prim Sch
RADNOR GDNS
KENILWORTH CRES
BICKNOLLER RD
MYDDELTON CL
ORCHARD CL
SINCLARE CL
CANONBURY RD
PRIORS MEAD
INVERNESS AVE
EASTBURY AVE
ROCHESTER CL
Forty Hill Cemy
New River
CARISBROOK CL
TENNISWOOD RD
4
GORDON HILL
YOUNGMANS CL
BORROWDALE CT
WHITAKERS LO
St Michael's
GATER DR
JOHN KEATS LO
SHELLY LO
ARMFIELD RD
KYNASTON RD
WEARDALE GDNS
FARR RD
THE DRIVE
Sp Gd
Chace Com Sch
BELL RD
HEENE RD
BAKER ST
IVINGHOE CL
Allot Gdns
Queen Elizabeth Stadium
GORDON RD
CHURCHBURY RD
HALIFAX RD
St George's RC Prim Sch
BUCKINGHAM CL
SANDRINGHAM CL
CHAILEY AVE
MANOR RD
BELLAMY RD
PEVENSEY AVE
ALDERSBROOK AVE
WILLOW RD
FILLEBROOK AVE
CHEVIOT CL
Recn Gd
3
TRINITY ST
Chase Side Prim Sch
CHASE SIDE AVE
MONASTERY GDNS
GRAEME RD
HEATH'S CL
RAVENS CL
CONNAUGHT AVE
HERRONGATE CL
LAMBOURNE GDNS
LADYSMITH RD
MONKS RD
MONKS CL
PARSONAGE LA
St Andrew's Sch
CHURCHBURY LA
CONNAUGHT CL
NEWBY CL
CARNARVON AVE
CHASE GREEN AVE
VICAR'S CL
Enfield Gram Sch
97
Pl Fld
HORSESHOE LA
CRICKETERS ARMS RD
PORTCULLIS LODGE RD
FIR TREE WLK
RIVERSFIELD RD
EN1
THE VINERIES
PEARTREE RD
GREEN CROFT GDNS
Enfield Cty Sch
Offices
C Ctr
ORCHARD WAY
APPLE GR
Allot Gdns
2
KIMBERLEY GDNS
CRADDOCK RD
MAFEKING RD
George Spicer Prim Sch
COBHAM CL
Kingsmead Sch
CHURCH LA
SILVER ST
ST ANDREW'S RD
FYFIELD RD
CALDER CL
RIVER FRONT
MARKET PL
Offices
Enfield Chase
CHURCH ST
A110
THE TOWN
Liby
SAVOY
PAR
SPICER CT
STANLEY RD
SKETTY RD
CLYDACH RD
SOUTHBURY RD
BRYN-Y-MAWR RD
JULES THORN AVE
PALACE GDNS
CECIL RD
A105
GENOTIN RD
GENOTIN TERR
Enfield Town
Superstore
EATON RD
QUEEN'S RD
FELIX NEUBERGH CT
SEAFORD RD
FOTHERINGHAM CT
CECIL AVE
Tenn Cts
Tenn Cts
Bwg Gn
Town Park
FROBISHER MEWS
RALEIGH RD
SYDNEY RD
LONDON RD
ROSENEATH WLK
PARK AVE
Allot Gdns
BERESFORD GDNS
WADDINGTON CL
BURLEIGH RD
HALSTEAD RD
FALMER RD
CROSS RD
DOWNS RD
1
PERCIVAL RD
BERTRAM RD
CLIVE RD
Recn Gd
OLD PARK AVE
ESSEX RD
TIPTREE DR
CHALKWELL PARK AVE
LYNDHURST GDNS
CAMBERLEY AVE
LC
SALISBURY CT
PARK CRES
POTTERSFIELD
KINGSWOOD CL
LINCOLN CRES
LINCOLN RD
96
RIDINGS AVE
WALSINGHAM RD
UVEDALE RD
WHITETHORN GDNS
Tenn Cts
HARMAN RD
JOHN ST
JAMES ST
AGRICOLA PL
HADRIAN'S RIDE
ROMAN WAY
ERMINE SIDE
Prim Sch
32
33
17
34
Liby
EAST CRES
WATERHEDGE MEWS
MAIN AVE
PRIVATE RD
Bush Hill Park
Tenn Cts

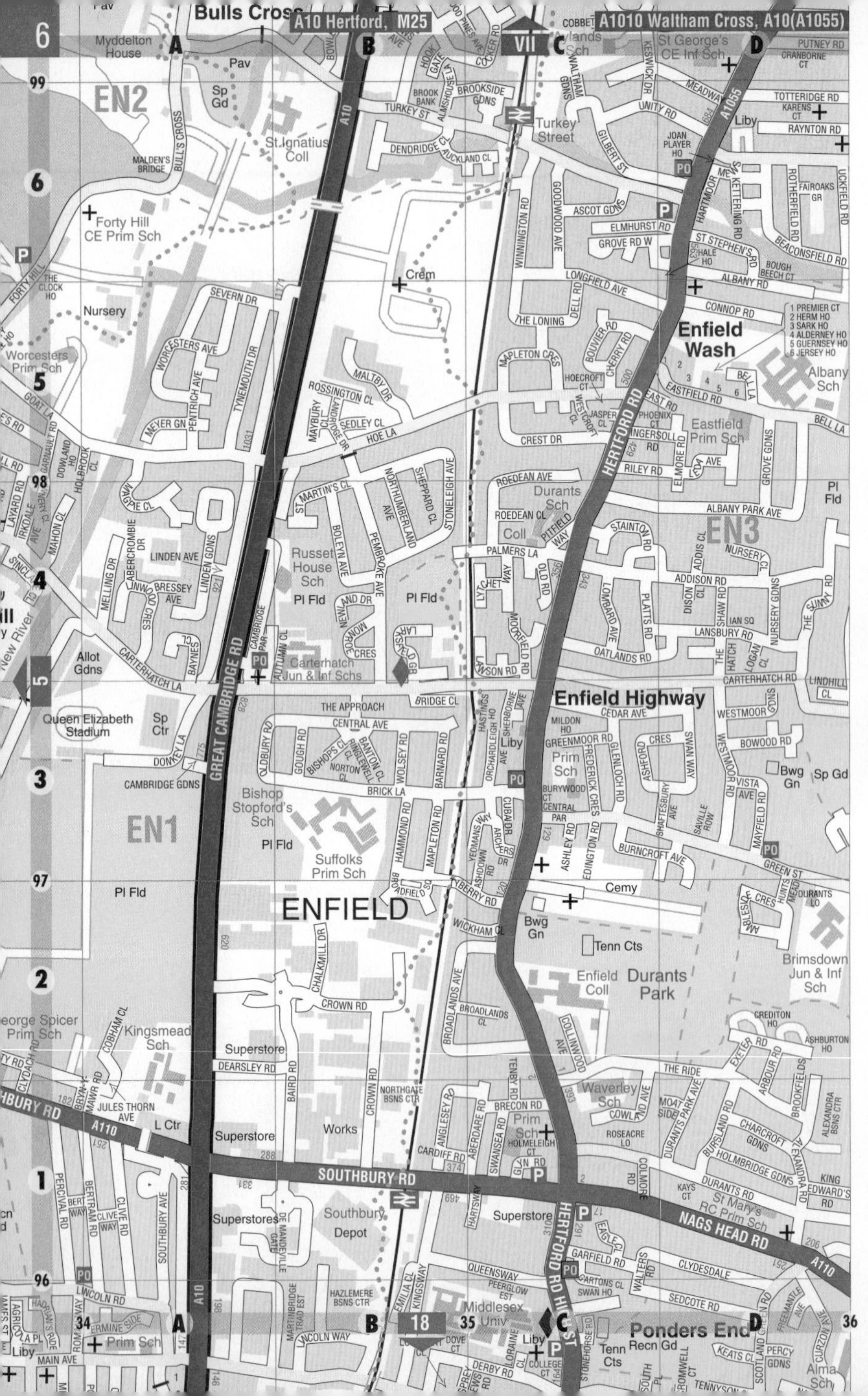

Bulls Cross
A10 Hertford, M25
A1010 Waltham Cross, A10(A1055)
VII
Myddelton House
EN2
EN3
EN1
Forty Hill CE Prim Sch
St.Ignatius Coll
Turkey Street
Crem
Enfield Wash
Albany Sch
Eastfield Prim Sch
Durants Sch
Russet House Sch
Carterhatch Jun & Inf Schs
Enfield Highway
Queen Elizabeth Stadium
Bishop Stopford's Sch
Suffolks Prim Sch
ENFIELD
Brimsdown Jun & Inf Sch
Enfield Coll
Durants Park
Kingsmead Sch
Waverley Sch
St Mary's RC Prim Sch
Southbury Depot
Middlesex Univ
Ponders End
GREAT CAMBRIDGE RD
HERTFORD RD
SOUTHBURY RD
NAGS HEAD RD
HOE LA
CARTERHATCH LA
BRICK LA
GREEN ST
5
18
34
35
36
96
97
98
99

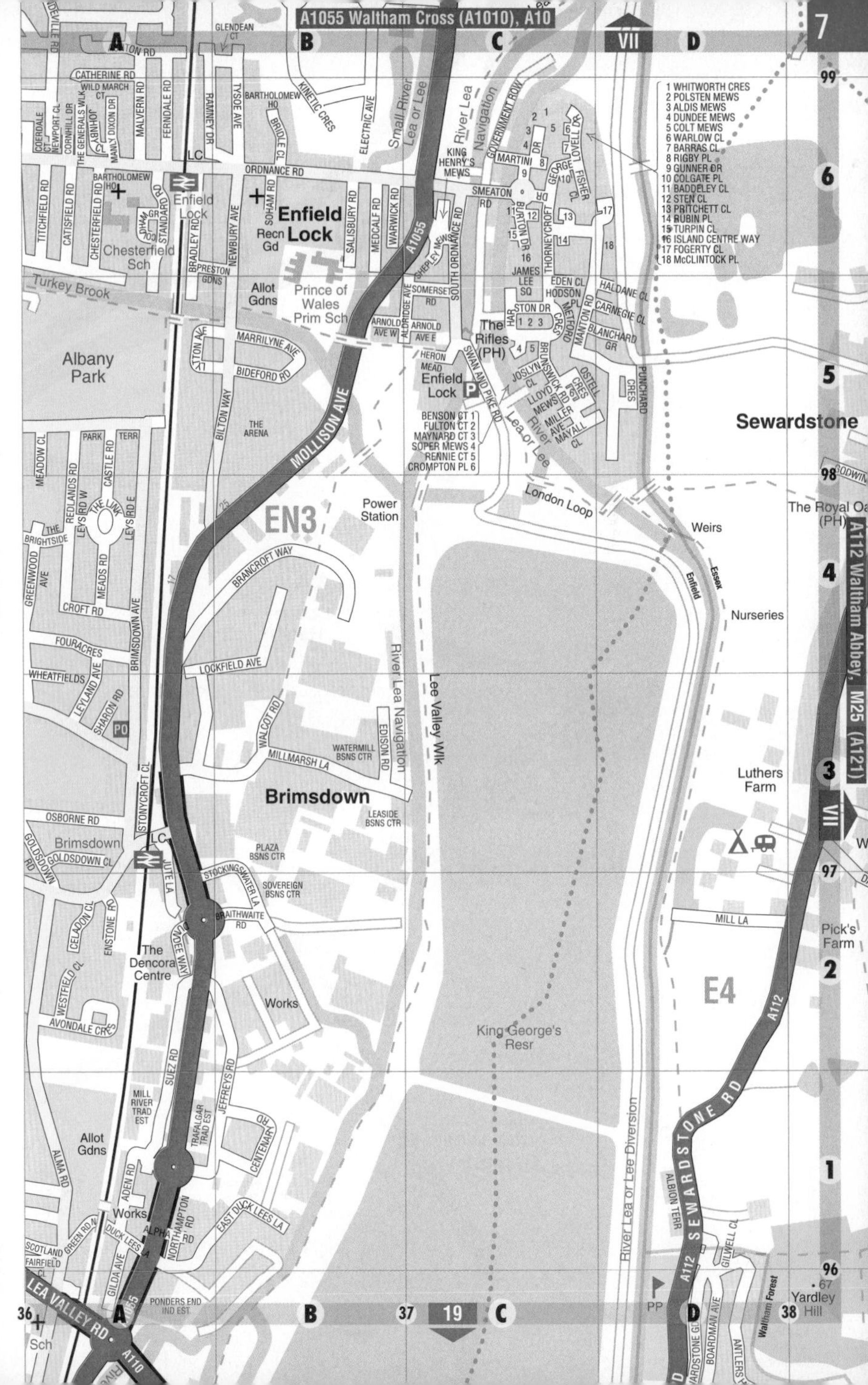
A1055 Waltham Cross (A1010), A10
VII
Enfield Lock
Recn Gd
Prince of Wales Prim Sch
Chesterfield Sch
Albany Park
Turkey Brook
Allot Gdns
THE ARENA
MOLLISON AVE
EN3
Power Station
The Rifles (PH)
London Loop
Weirs
Sewardstone
The Royal Oak (PH)
Nurseries
Luthers Farm
Pick's Farm
E4
King George's Resr
Lee Valley Wlk
River Lea Navigation
River Lea or Lee Diversion
Brimsdown
The Dencora Centre
Works
Mill River Trad Est
Trafalgar Trad Est
Ponders End Ind Est
LEA VALLEY RD
SEWARDSTONE RD
A112 Waltham Abbey, M25 (A121)
Yardley Hill
Waltham Forest
1 WHITWORTH CRES
2 POLSTEN MEWS
3 ALDIS MEWS
4 DUNDEE MEWS
5 COLT MEWS
6 WARLOW CL
7 BARRAS CL
8 RIGBY PL
9 GUNNER DR
10 COLGATE PL
11 BADDELEY CL
12 STEN CL
13 PRITCHETT CL
14 RUBIN PL
15 TURPIN CL
16 ISLAND CENTRE WAY
17 FOGERTY CL
18 McCLINTOCK PL
BENSON CT 1
FULTON CT 2
MAYNARD CT 3
SOPER MEWS 4
RENNIE CT 5
CROMPTON PL 6
19
36
37
38
99
98
97
96

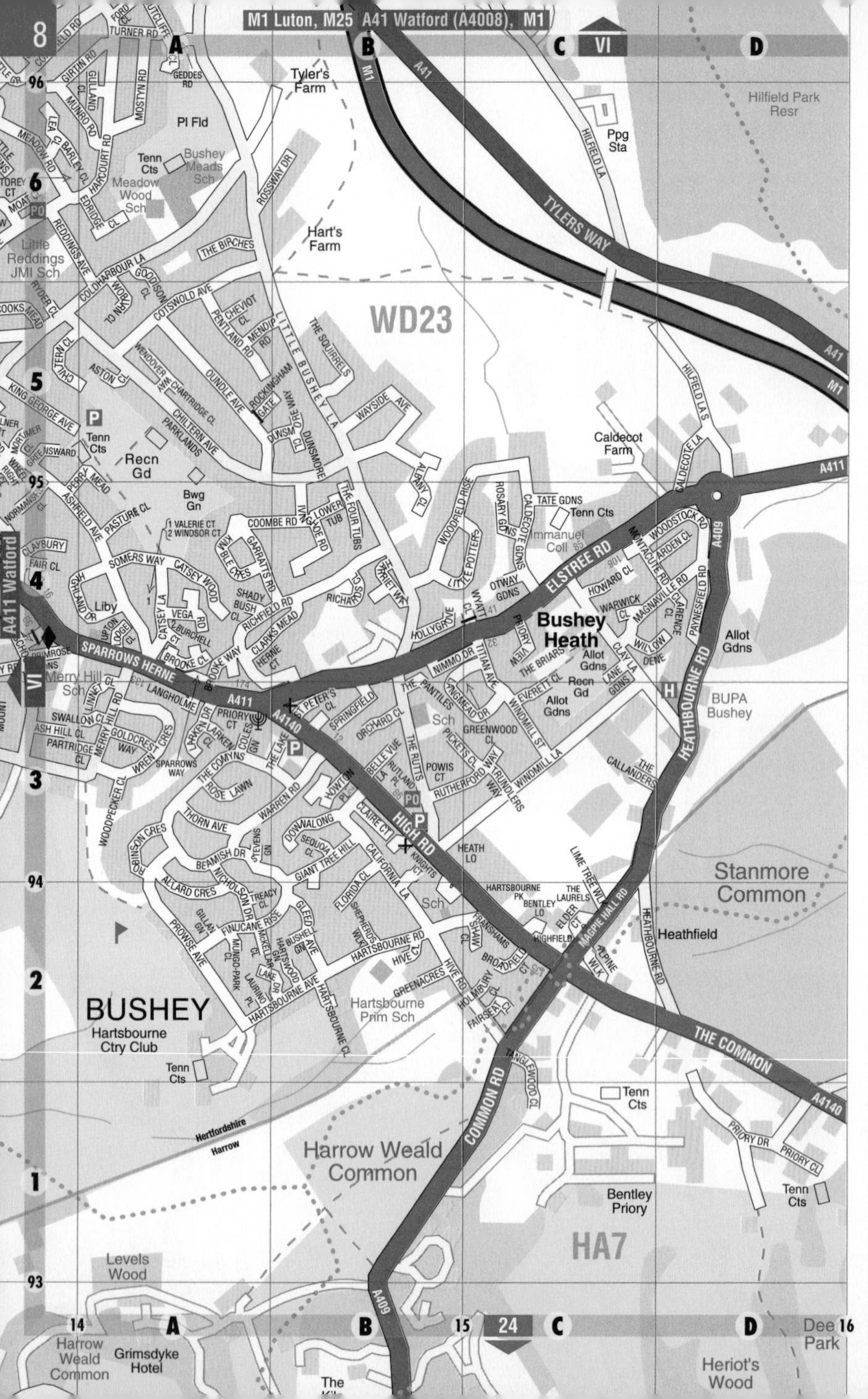
M1 Luton, M25 A41 Watford (A4008), M1
A
B
C
VI
D
96
6
5
95
4
3
94
2
1
93
Tyler's Farm
Pl Fld
Tenn Cts
Bushey Meads Sch
Meadow Wood Sch
PO
Little Reddings JMI Sch
Hart's Farm
Hilfield Park Resr
Ppg Sta
HILFIELD LA
TYLERS WAY
A41
M1
WD23
HILFIELD LAS
Caldecot Farm
CALDECOTE LA
A411
TURNER RD
GEDDES RD
GIRTIN RD
GULLAND CL
MUNRO RD
MOSTYN RD
MEADOW RD
LEA CL
BARLEY CL
HARCOURT RD
EDRIDGE CL
STOREY CT
MOAT CL
REDDINGS AVE
COLDHARBOUR LA
GOODISON CL
THE BIRCHES
ROSSWAY DR
RYDER CL
COOKS MEAD
COTSWOLD AVE
CHEVIOT CL
PENTLAND RD
MENDIP RD
LITTLE BUSHEY LA
THE SQUIRRELS
WENDOVER WAY
CHARTRIDGE CL
OUNDLE AVE
ROCKINGHAM GATE
MOORE WAY
CHILTERN CL
ASTON CL
KING GEORGE AVE
CHILTERN AVE
PARKLANDS
DUNSMORE
DUNSMORE CL
WAYSIDE AVE
ALBANY CL
Tenn Cts
Recn Gd
Bwg Gn
NORMANSHIRE DR
ASHFIELD AVE
PASTURE CL
PERRY MEAD
COOMBE RD
IVINGHOE RD
LOWER TUB
THE FOUR TUBS
WOODFIELD RISE
ROSARY GDNS
CALDECOTE GDNS
TATE GDNS
Tenn Cts
Immanuel Coll
ELSTREE RD
WOODSTOCK RD
MONTACUTE RD
ARDEN CL
HOWARD CL
WARWICK CL
MAGNAVILLE RD
CLARENCE CL
PAYNESFIELD RD
A409
Allot Gdns
1 VALERIE CT
2 WINDSOR CT
CLAYBURY
FAIR CL
SOMERS WAY
CATSEY WOOD
KIMBLE CRES
GARRATTS RD
HARRIET WAY
RICHARDS CL
LITTLE POTTERS
OTWAY GDNS
WYATT CL
Bushey Heath
A411 Watford
Liby
CATSEY LA
VEGA RD
SHADY BUSH CL
RICHFIELD RD
CLARKS MEAD
HERNE CT
HOLLYGROVE
PRIORY VIEW
THE BRIARS
Allot Gdns
CLAY LA
LANE GDNS
WILLOW DENE
H
HEATHBOURNE RD
BUPA Bushey
SPARROWS HERNE
Merry Hill Sch
BROOKE CL
BROOKE WAY
NIMMO DR
TITIAN AVE
Recn Gd
Allot Gdns
EVERETT CL
A411
ST PETER'S CL
SPRINGFIELD
ORCHARD CL
THE PANTILES
LONGMEAD DR
WINDMILL ST
LANGHOLME
PRIORY CT
COLES GN
A4140
Sch
GREENWOOD CL
THE CALLANDERS
SWALLOW CL
ASH HILL CL
PARTRIDGE CL
GOLDCREST WAY
WREN CRES
SPARROWS WAY
MERRY HILL RD
THE COMYNS
ROSE LAWN
THE LAKE
P
BELLE VUE LA
RUTLAND PL
THE RUTTS
POWIS CT
PICKETS CL
RUTHERFORD WAY
TRUNDLERS WAY
WINDMILL LA
HOWTON PL
PO
HIGH RD
WOODPECKER CL
THORN AVE
WARREN RD
DOWNALONG
CLAIRE CT
ROBINSON CRES
BEAMISH DR
STEVENS GN
SEQUOIA CL
GIANT TREE HILL
CALIFORNIA LA
KNIGHTS CT
HEATH LO
LIME TREE WLK
Stanmore Common
ALLARD CRES
NICHOLSON DR
TREACY CL
FLORIDA CL
Sch
HARTSBOURNE PK
THE LAURELS
BENTLEY LO
MAGPIE HALL RD
HEATHBOURNE RD
Heathfield
GILLAN GN
FINUCANE RISE
GLEED AVE
SHEPHERDS WLK
FRANSHAMS
ELDER CT
HIGHFIELD
ALPINE WLK
PROWSE AVE
MUNGO-PARK CL
McKELLAR CL
HARTSWOOD GN
BUSHELL GN
HARTSBOURNE RD
HIVE CL
SHAW CL
BROADFIELDS
HIVE RD
GREENACRES
LAURINO PL
LAKE DR
HARTSBOURNE AVE
HARTSBOURNE CL
HOLMBURY CT
FAIRSEAT CL
BUSHEY
Hartsbourne Ctry Club
Hartsbourne Prim Sch
THE COMMON
Tenn Cts
TANGLEWOOD CL
COMMON RD
Tenn Cts
A4140
Hertfordshire
Harrow
Harrow Weald Common
PRIORY DR
PRIORY CL
Bentley Priory
Tenn Cts
HA7
Levels Wood
A409
14
15
24
16
Harrow Weald Common
Grimsdyke Hotel
The
Dee Park
Heriot's Wood

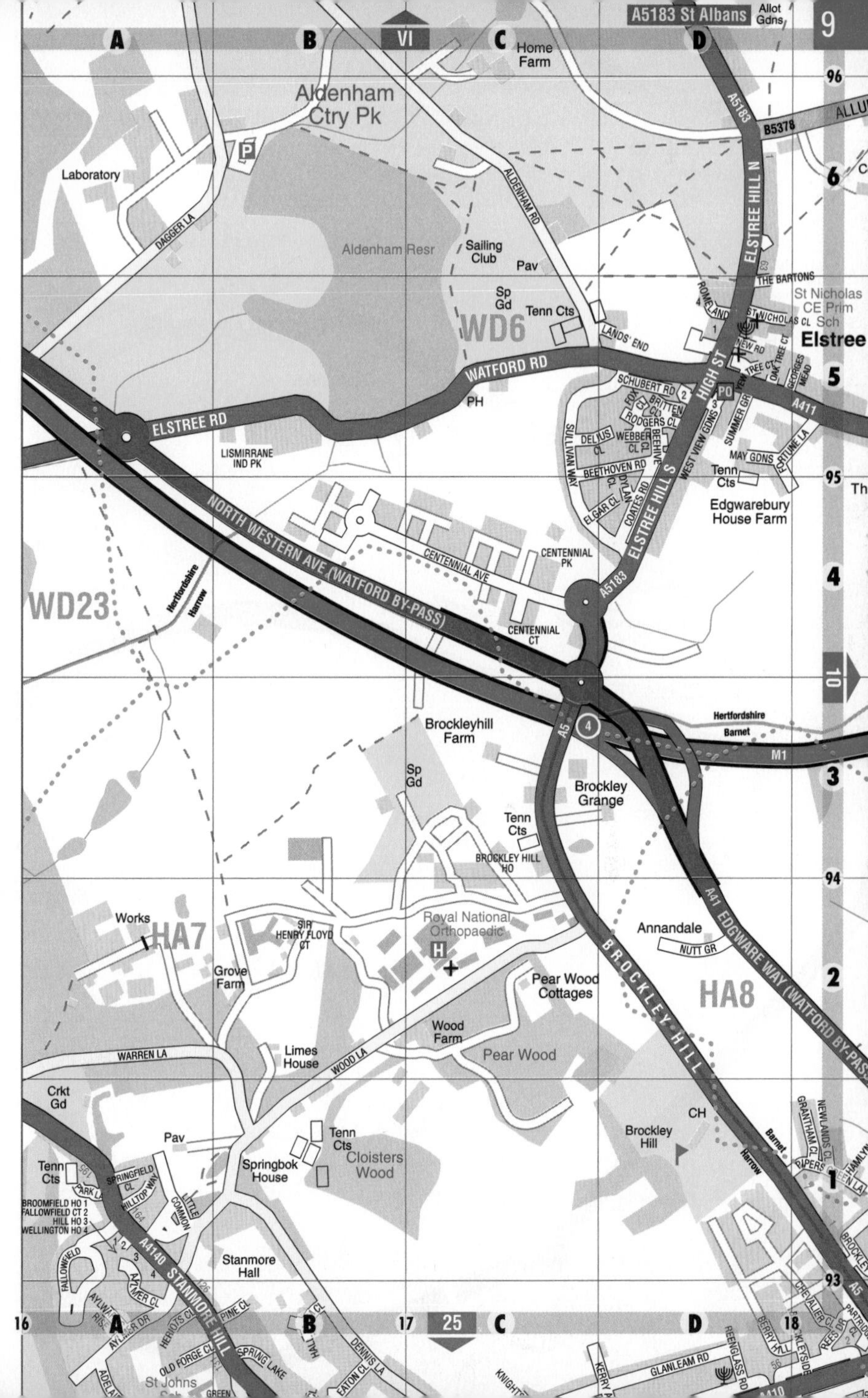
A5183 St Albans
Allot Gdns
VI
Home Farm
Aldenham Ctry Pk
Laboratory
DAGGER LA
ALDENHAM RD
Aldenham Resr
Sailing Club
Pav
Sp Gd
Tenn Cts
WD6
LANDS' END
WATFORD RD
ELSTREE RD
PH
LISMIRRANE IND PK
NORTH WESTERN AVE (WATFORD BY-PASS)
CENTENNIAL AVE
CENTENNIAL PK
CENTENNIAL CT
WD23
Hertfordshire
Harrow
A5183
ELSTREE HILL N
ELSTREE HILL S
B5378
THE BARTONS
ROME LAND
ST NICHOLAS CL
St Nicholas CE Prim Sch
Elstree
HIGH ST
NEW RD
YEW TREE CT
OAK TREE CT
GEORGES MEAD
SCHUBERT RD
FOX CL
BRITTEN CL
RODGERS CL
SULLIVAN WAY
DELIUS CL
WEBBER CL
BEEHIVE
BEETHOVEN RD
DYLAN CL
ELGAR CL
COATES RD
WEST VIEW GDNS
SUMMER GR
PO
A411
MAY GDNS
FORTUNE LA
Tenn Cts
Edgwarebury House Farm
10
Hertfordshire
Barnet
M1
A5
Brockleyhill Farm
Sp Gd
Brockley Grange
Tenn Cts
BROCKLEY HILL HO
Works
HA7
SIR HENRY FLOYD CT
Royal National Orthopaedic
Grove Farm
Annandale
NUTT GR
A41 EDGWARE WAY (WATFORD BY-PASS)
HA8
Pear Wood Cottages
BROCKLEY HILL
Wood Farm
Pear Wood
WARREN LA
Limes House
WOOD LA
Crkt Gd
Pav
Tenn Cts
Springbok House
Cloisters Wood
Brockley Hill
CH
Barnet
Harrow
GRANTHAM CL
NEWLANDS CL
PIPERS GREEN LA
Tenn Cts
SPRINGFIELD CL
PARK LA
HILLTOP WAY
LITTLE COMMON
BROOMFIELD HO 1
FALLOWFIELD CT 2
HILL HO 3
WELLINGTON HO 4
FALLOWFIELD
A4140 STANMORE HILL
AYLMER CL
Stanmore Hall
HERIOTS CL
PINE CL
OLD FORGE CL
SPRING LAKE
HALL CL
DENNIS LA
EATON CL
St Johns
KERRY
GLANLEAM RD
REENGLASS RD
BERRY HILL
CHEVALIER CL
A5
16
17
25
18
96
6
5
95
4
3
94
2
1
93

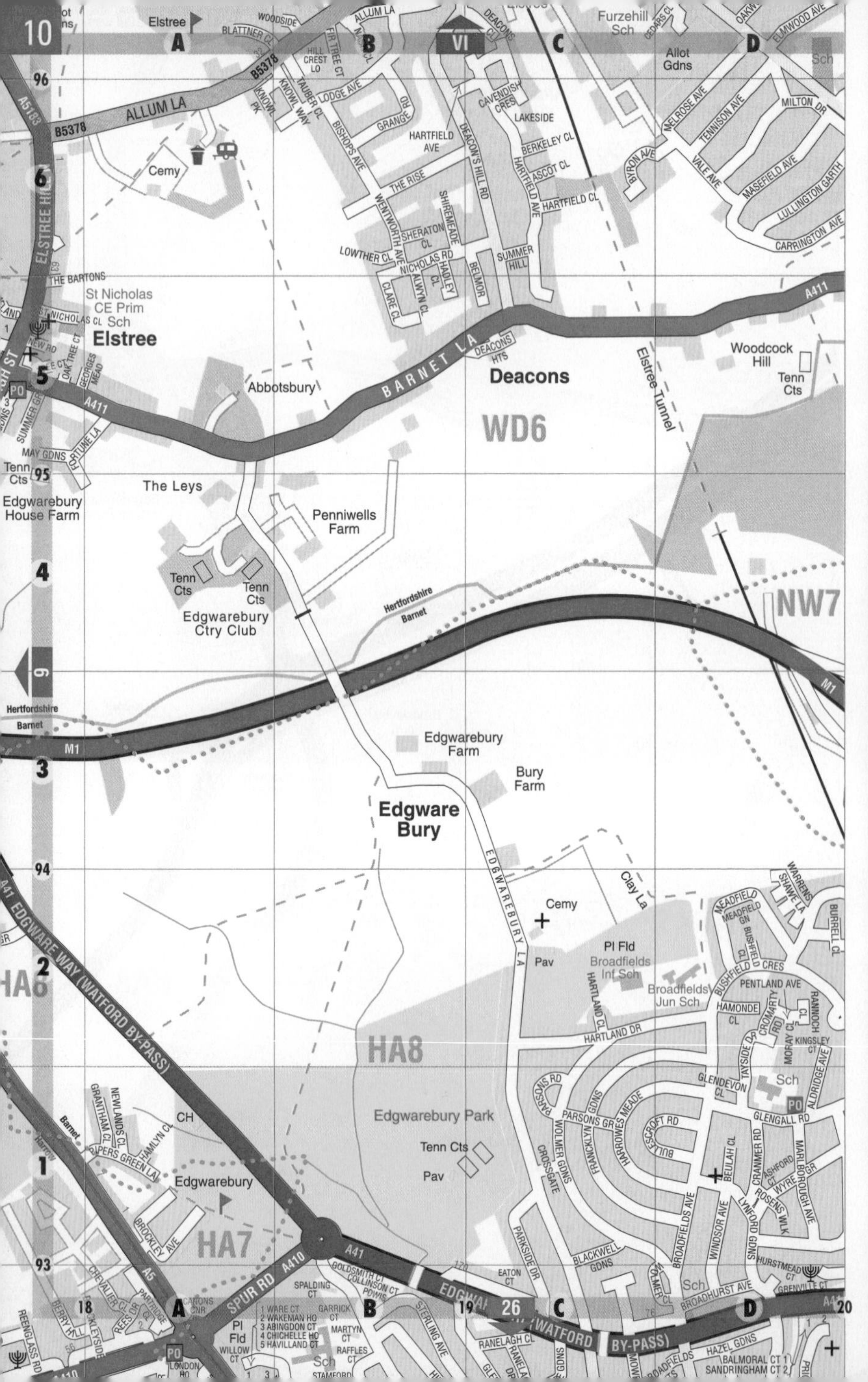
Elstree
Allum La
B5378
A5183
Elstree Hill
Cemy
Woodside
Blattner Cl
Fir Tree Ct
Hill Crest Lo
Tauber Cl
Knowl Way
Knowl Pk
Lodge Ave
Bishops Ave
Grange Rd
Hartfield Ave
The Rise
Wentworth Ave
Sheraton Cl
Shiremeade
Deacon's Hill Rd
Cavendish Cres
Lakeside
Berkeley Cl
Ascot Cl
Hartfield Cl
Lowther Cl
Nicholas Rd
Alwyn Cl
Hadley Cl
Clare Cl
Belmor
Summer Hill
Furzehill Sch
Allot Gdns
Cedars Cl
Melrose Ave
Tennison Ave
Milton Dr
Byron Ave
Vale Ave
Masefield Ave
Lullington Garth
Carrington Ave
Elmwood Ave
Sch
The Bartons
St Nicholas CE Prim Sch
St Nicholas Cl
Elstree
New Rd
Oak Tree Ct
Georges Mead
Barnet La
A411
Deacons Hts
Deacons
Elstree Tunnel
Woodcock Hill
Tenn Cts
Abbotsbury
WD6
PO
Summer Gr
Fortune La
May Gdns
Tenn Cts
Edgwarebury House Farm
The Leys
Penniwells Farm
Tenn Cts
Tenn Cts
Edgwarebury Ctry Club
Hertfordshire
Barnet
NW7
M1
Hertfordshire
Barnet
M1
Edgwarebury Farm
Bury Farm
Edgware Bury
Edgwarebury La
Clay La
Cemy
Pav
Pl Fld
Broadfields Inf Sch
Broadfields Jun Sch
Hartland Cl
Hartland Dr
Warrens Shawe La
Meadfield
Meadfield Gn
Bushfield Cl
Bushfield Cres
Burrell Cl
Pentland Ave
Hamonde Cl
Cromarty Rd
Rannoch Cl
Moray Cl
Kingsley Ct
Tayside Dr
Aldridge Ave
Glendevon Cl
Sch
PO
Glengall Rd
A41 Edgware Way (Watford By-Pass)
HA8
HA8
Edgwarebury Park
Tenn Cts
Pav
Parsons Rd
Parsons Gr
Harrowes Meade
Francklyn Gdns
Wolmer Gdns
Crossgate
Bullescroft Rd
Beulah Cl
Cranmer Rd
Ashford Cl
Wyre Gr
Marlborough Ave
Rosens Wlk
Lynford Gdns
Broadfields Ave
Windsor Ave
Parkside Dr
Blackwell Gdns
Wolmer Cl
Sch
Hurstmead Ct
Broadhurst Ave
Grenville Ct
Grantham Cl
Newlands Cl
Hamlyn Cl
Pipers Green La
CH
Barnet
Harrow
Edgwarebury
HA7
Brockley Ave
A5
Chevalier Cl
Rees Dr
Partridge Cl
Brockleyside
Berry Hill
Reenglass Rd
Canons Cnr
Spur Rd
A410
A41
Goldsmith Ct
Collinson Ct
Powis Ct
Spalding Ct
Garrick Ct
Martyn Ct
Raffles Ct
Sterling Ave
1 Ware Ct
2 Wakeman Ho
3 Abingdon Ct
4 Chichelle Ho
5 Havilland Ct
Pl Fld
Willow Ct
London Ho
Sch
Stamford
Eaton Ct
Ranelagh Cl
Edgware Way (Watford By-Pass)
Hazel Gdns
Balmoral Ct
Sandringham Ct
Broadfields
96
6
5
95
4
3
94
2
1
93
18
19
20
A
B
C
D
VI
9
26

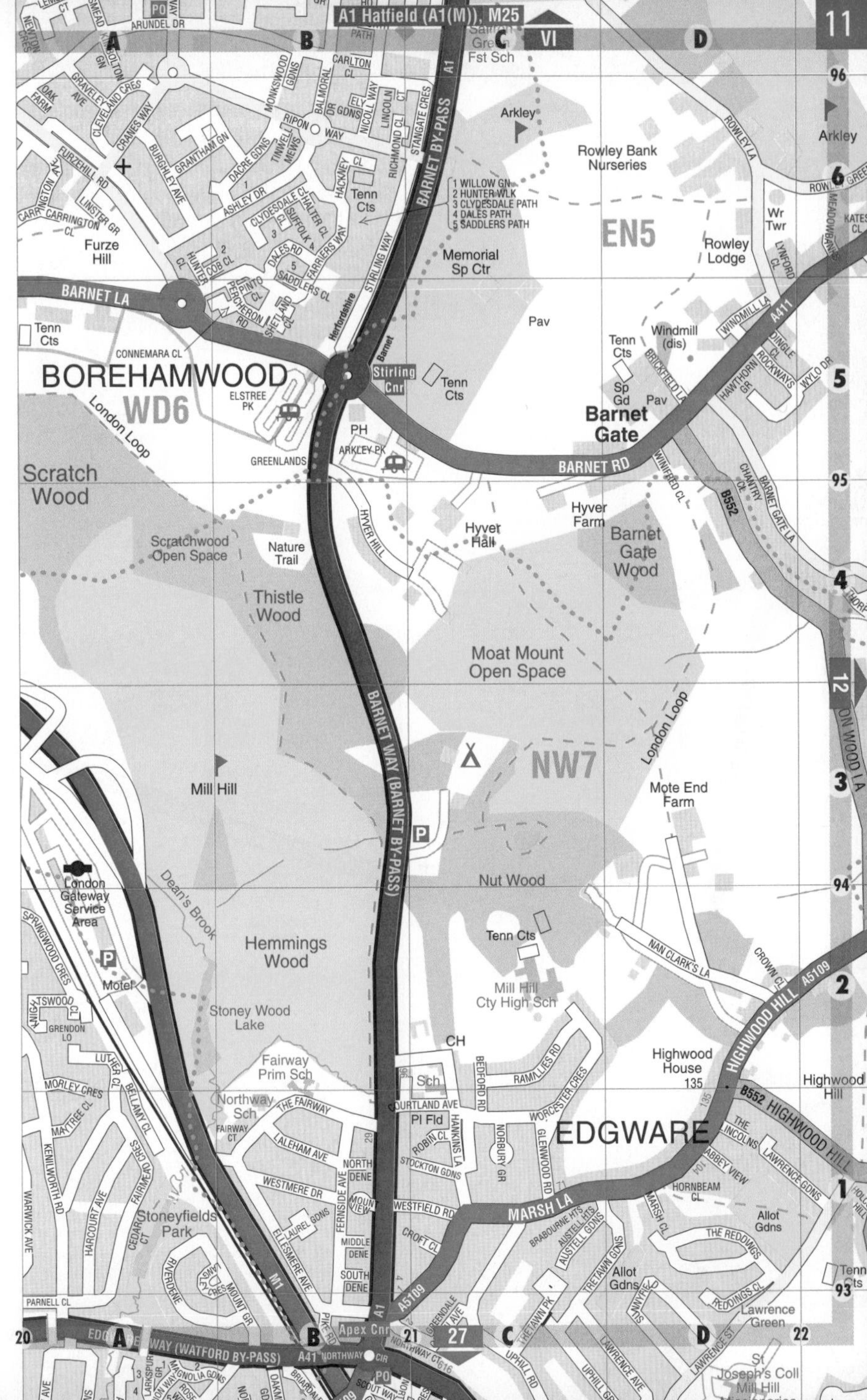
A1 Hatfield (A1(M)), M25
VI
Saffron Green Fst Sch
Arkley
Rowley Bank Nurseries
ROWLEY LA
ROWLEY GREEN RD
MEADOWBANKS
KATES CL
Wr Twr
Rowley Lodge
LYNFORD CL
EN5
Memorial Sp Ctr
1 WILLOW GN
2 HUNTER WLK
3 CLYDESDALE PATH
4 DALES PATH
5 SADDLERS PATH
ARUNDEL DR
KINGS MEAD
BOLTON GN
GRAVELEY AVE
OAK FARM
CLEVELAND CRES
CRANES WAY
MONKSWOOD GDNS
CARLTON CL
BALMORAL DR
ELY GDNS
NICOLL WAY
LINCOLN CT
STANGATE CRES
RIPON WAY
RICHMOND CL
TINWELL MEWS
GRANTHAM GN
DACRE GDNS
BURGHLEY AVE
HACKNEY CL
Tenn Cts
FURZEHILL RD
CARRINGTON AVE
CARRINGTON CL
LINSTER GR
ASHLEY DR
CLYDESDALE CL
HALTER CL
SUFFOLK CL
FARRIERS WAY
STIRLING WAY
BARNET BY-PASS
Furze Hill
HUNTER CL
COB CL
DALES RD
SADDLERS CL
PINTO CL
PERCHERON RD
SHETLAND CL
BARNET LA
Hertfordshire
Barnet
Stirling Cnr
CONNEMARA CL
BOREHAMWOOD
WD6
ELSTREE PK
London Loop
PH
ARKLEY PK
GREENLANDS
Pav
Windmill (dis)
Sp Gd
Barnet Gate
BARNET RD
BRICKFIELD LA
WINDMILL LA
A411
DINGLE CL
ROCKWAYS
HAWTHORN GR
WYLO DR
WINIFRED CL
CHANTRY CL
BARNET GATE LA
B552
Scratch Wood
Scratchwood Open Space
Nature Trail
HYVER HILL
Hyver Hall
Hyver Farm
Barnet Gate Wood
THORP CL
Thistle Wood
Moat Mount Open Space
12
BARNET WAY (BARNET BY-PASS)
NW7
Mill Hill
Mote End Farm
HOLLOW WOOD LA
Nut Wood
London Gateway Service Area
Dean's Brook
Hemmings Wood
Tenn Cts
NAN CLARK'S LA
CROWN CL
A5109
HIGHWOOD HILL
Mill Hill Cty High Sch
Motel
SPRINGWOOD CRES
KNIGHTSWOOD CL
GRENDON LO
Stoney Wood Lake
CH
Highwood House
Highwood Hill
LUTHER CL
BELLAMY CL
MORLEY CRES
MAYTREE CL
Fairway Prim Sch
Sch
RAMILLIES RD
BEDFORD RD
WORCESTER CRES
Northway Sch
THE FAIRWAY
COURTLAND AVE
Pl Fld
HANKINS LA
B552 HIGHWOOD HILL
FAIRWAY CT
ALEHAM AVE
ROBIN CL
NORBURY GR
GLENWOOD RD
EDGWARE
THE LINCOLNS
LAWRENCE GDNS
NORTH DENE
STOCKTON GDNS
ABBEY VIEW
HOLCOMBE HILL
KENILWORTH RD
FAIRMEAD CRES
HARCOURT AVE
WARWICK AVE
WESTMERE DR
FERNSIDE AVE
MOUNT VIEW
WESTFIELD RD
MARSH LA
HORNBEAM CL
Allot Gdns
Stoneyfields Park
CEDAR CT
LAUREL GDNS
ELLESMERE AVE
CROFT CL
BRABOURNE HTS
AUSTELL HTS
AUSTELL GDNS
MARSH CL
THE REDDINGS
MIDDLE DENE
SOUTH DENE
RIVERDENE
LANGLEY CRES
MOUNT GR
M1
A1
A5109
TRETAWN GDNS
Allot Gdns
SUNNYFIELD
REDDINGS CL
Tenn Cts
PARNELL CL
PIKE RD
Apex Cnr
GREENDALE
Lawrence Green
EDGWAREWAY (WATFORD BY-PASS)
A41
NORTHWAY CIR
NORTHWAY CT
27
TRETAWN PK
UPHILL RD
LAWRENCE AVE
LAWRENCE ST
St Joseph's Coll Mill Hill Missionaries
LARKSPUR GR
MAGNOLIA GDNS
ROSE
BRIARDALE
OAKMERE
SCOUT WAY
PO
A B C D
96 95 94 93
6 5 4 3 2 1
20 21 22

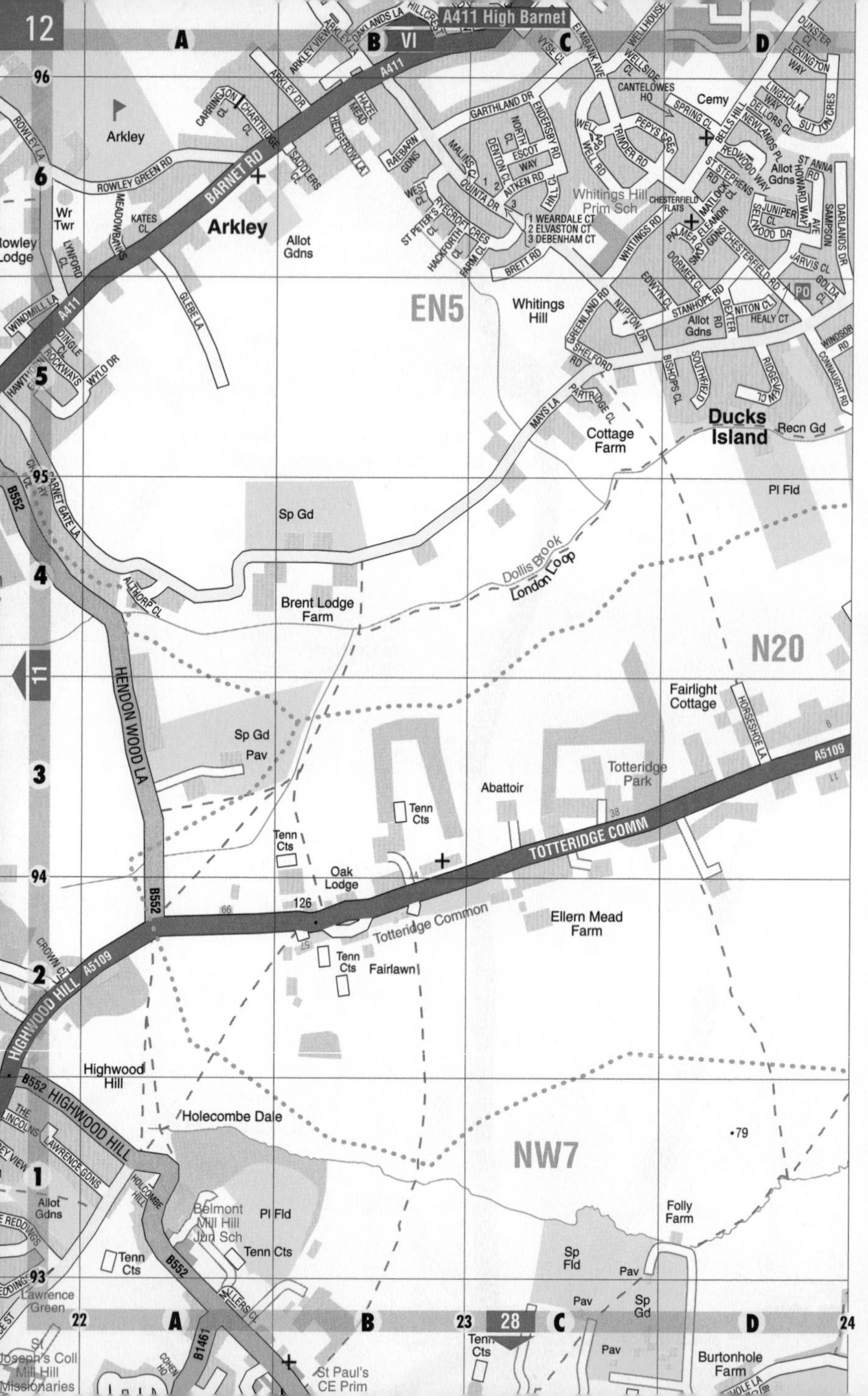
A411 High Barnet
VI
A
B
C
D
96
Arkley
Rowley Green Rd
Barnet Rd
A411
Arkley
Wr Twr
Rowley Lodge
Kates Cl
Allot Gdns
Glebe La
EN5
Whitings Hill
Whitings Hill Prim Sch
Cemy
Cantelowes Ho
Allot Gdns
1 Weardale Ct
2 Elvaston Ct
3 Debenham Ct
Ducks Island
Recn Gd
Cottage Farm
Mays La
Pl Fld
Sp Gd
Dollis Brook
London Loop
Brent Lodge Farm
N20
Fairlight Cottage
Horseshoe La
A5109
Totteridge Park
Abattoir
Tenn Cts
Totteridge Comm
Oak Lodge
126
Totteridge Common
Ellern Mead Farm
Fairlawn
Hendon Wood La
B552
Sp Gd
Pav
Highwood Hill
A5109
Highwood Hill
B552 Highwood Hill
Holecombe Dale
NW7
Allot Gdns
Belmont Mill Hill Jun Sch
Pl Fld
Tenn Cts
Folly Farm
Sp Fld
Pav
Sp Gd
Lawrence Green
Lawrence Gdns
St Joseph's Coll Mill Hill Missionaries
St Paul's CE Prim
Burtonhole Farm
B1461
22
23
24
28
11
6
5
4
3
2
1
95
94
93

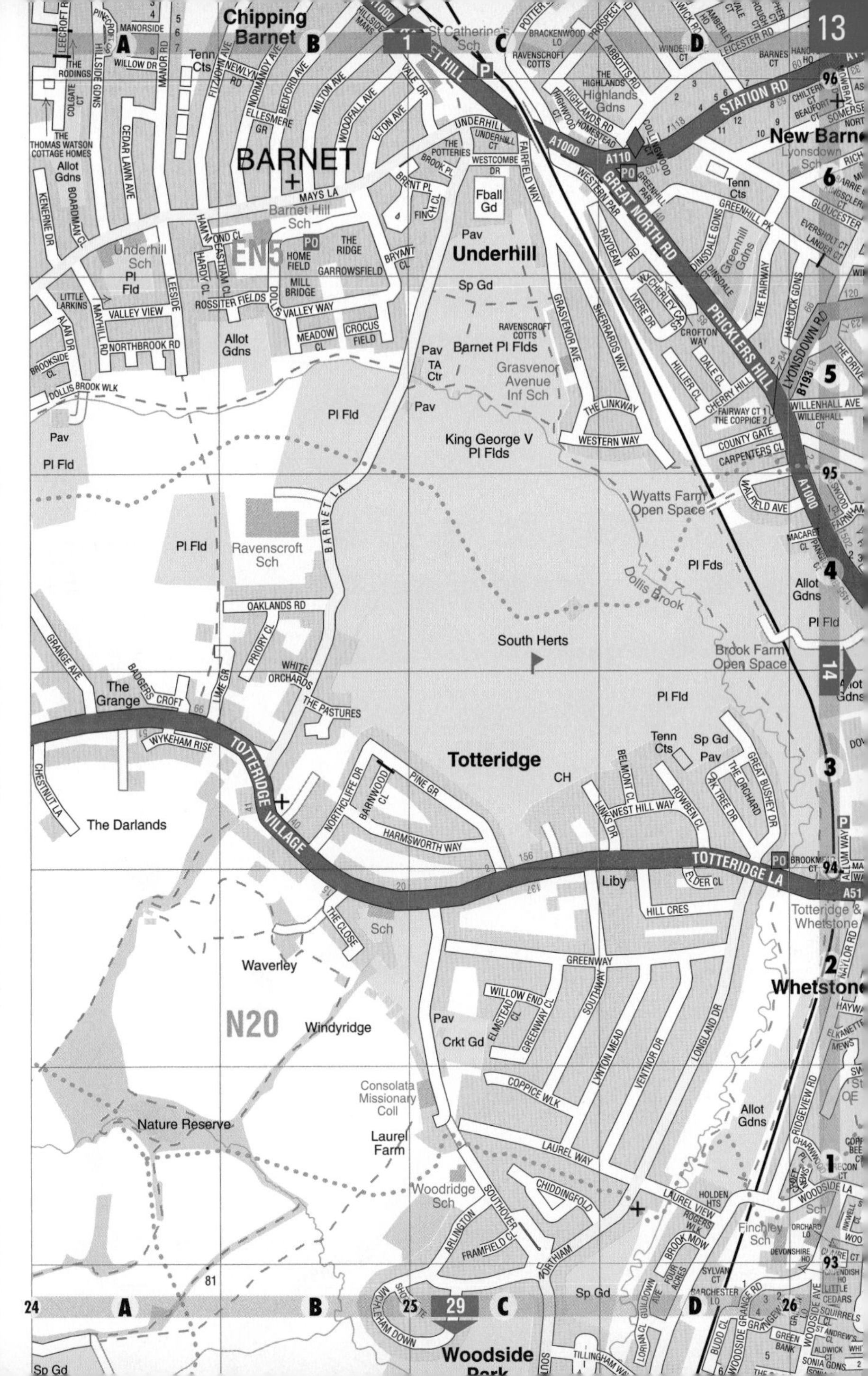

Chipping Barnet
BARNET
EN5
Underhill
New Barnet
Barnet Hill Sch
Underhill Sch
Ravenscroft Sch
Grasvenor Avenue Inf Sch
King George V Pl Flds
Barnet Pl Flds
Wyatts Farm Open Space
Brook Farm Open Space
Dollis Brook
South Herts
Totteridge
The Grange
The Darlands
Waverley
Windyridge
N20
Nature Reserve
Consolata Missionary Coll
Laurel Farm
Woodridge Sch
Whetstone
Totteridge & Whetstone
Woodside Park
GREAT NORTH RD
STATION RD
PRICKLERS HILL
TOTTERIDGE VILLAGE
TOTTERIDGE LA
BARNET LA
MAYS LA
UNDERHILL
WESTERN WAY
THE LINKWAY
SHERRARDS WAY
GRASVENOR AVE
LYONSDOWN RD
OAKLANDS RD
GRANGE AVE
WYKEHAM RISE
CHESTNUT LA
NORTHCLIFFE DR
HARMSWORTH WAY
PINE GR
BELMONT CL
WEST HILL WAY
ROWBEN CL
OAK TREE DR
THE ORCHARD
GREAT BUSHEY DR
GREENWAY
SOUTHWAY
LYNTON MEAD
VENTNOR DR
LONGLAND DR
COPPICE WLK
LAUREL WAY
LAUREL VIEW
CHIDDINGFOLD
SOUTHOVER
ARLINGTON
FRAMFIELD CL
NORTHIAM
RIDGEVIEW RD
WOODSIDE LA
DOLLIS BROOK WLK
NORTHBROOK RD
VALLEY VIEW
VALLEY WAY
ROSSITER FIELDS
MAYHILL RD
KENERNE DR
BOARDMAN CL
CEDAR LAWN AVE
HILLSIDE GDNS
MILTON AVE
BEDFORD AVE
NORMANDY AVE
FITZJOHN AVE
WOODFALL AVE
ELTON AVE
FAIRFIELD WAY
WESTCOMBE DR
A1000
A110
B193
A5109
1
29
14
A B C D
24 25 26

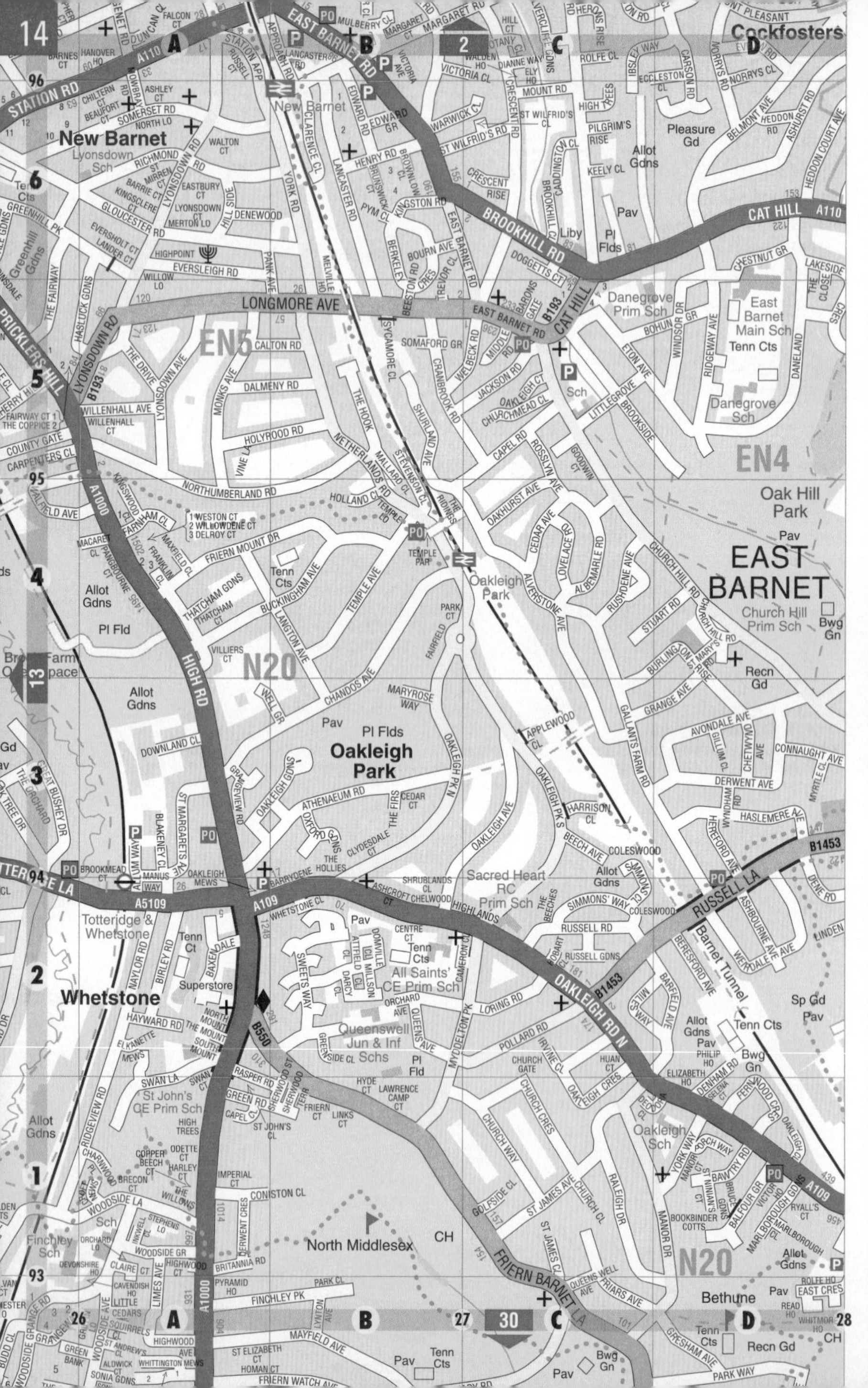

Cockfosters
New Barnet
Lyonsdown Sch
EN5
EN4
N20
EAST BARNET
Oakleigh Park
Whetstone
Totteridge & Whetstone
North Middlesex
Bethune
Oak Hill Park
STATION RD
EAST BARNET RD
BROOKHILL RD
CAT HILL
LONGMORE AVE
LYONSDOWN RD
PRICKLERS HILL
HIGH RD
A1000
A110
A109
A5109
B193
B1453
B550
RUSSELL LA
OAKLEIGH RD N
FRIERN BARNET LA
NORTHUMBERLAND RD
FRIERN MOUNT DR
CHANDOS AVE
OAKLEIGH PK N
OAKLEIGH PK S
CHURCH HILL RD
GALLANTS FARM RD
WOODSIDE LA
FINCHLEY PK
MAYFIELD AVE
Danegrove Prim Sch
Danegrove Sch
East Barnet Main Sch
Church Hill Prim Sch
Sacred Heart RC Prim Sch
All Saints' CE Prim Sch
Queenswell Jun & Inf Schs
St John's CE Prim Sch
Oakleigh Sch
Finchley Sch
Barnet Tunnel
Pleasure Gd
Allot Gdns
Tenn Cts
Pl Flds
Recn Gd
Superstore
2
13
30
A
B
C
D
1
2
3
4
5
6
93
94
95
96
26
27
28

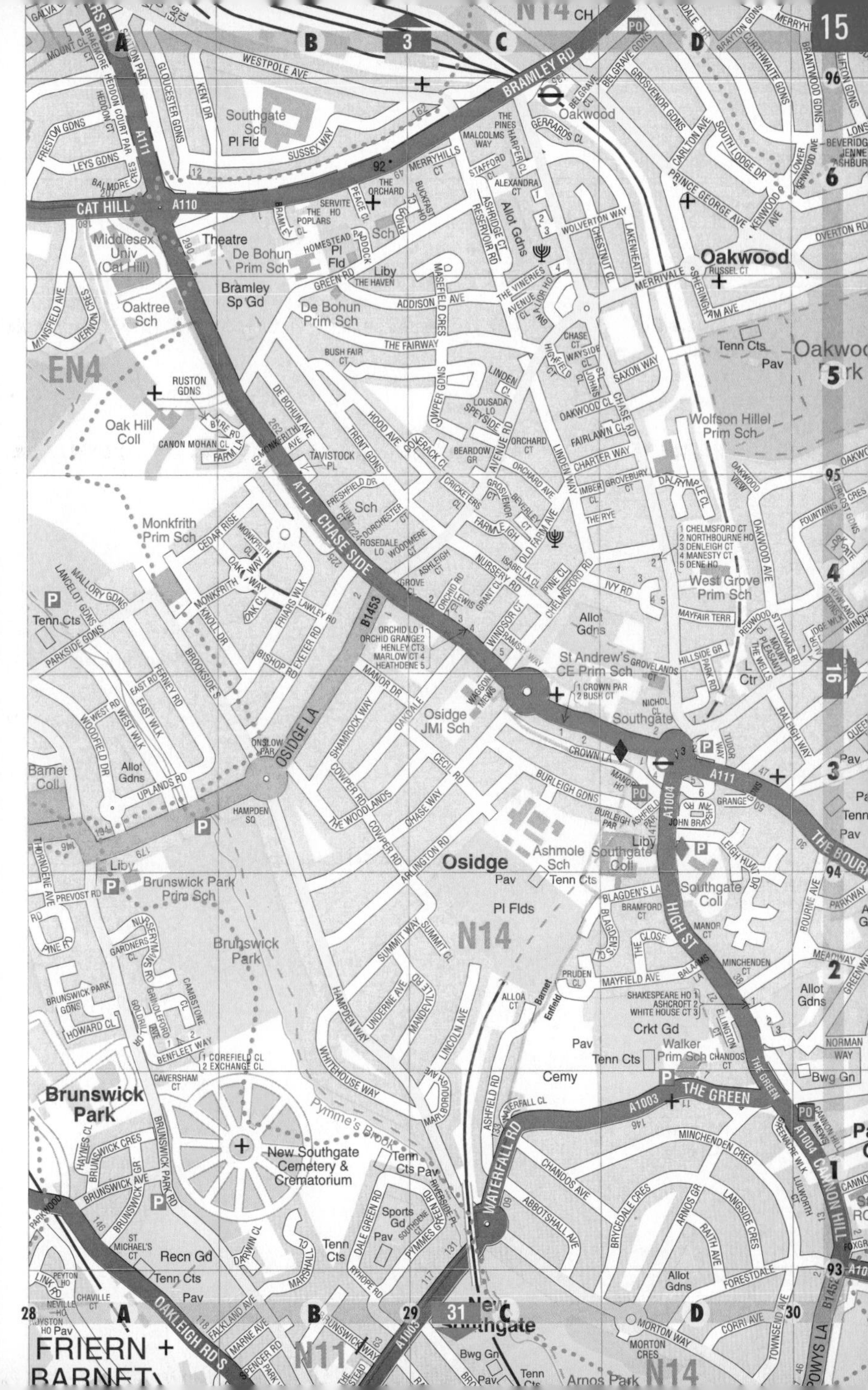

BRAMLEY RD
WESTPOLE AVE
Southgate Sch
Pl Fld
SUSSEX WAY
Oakwood
CAT HILL
A110
A111
Middlesex Univ (Cat Hill)
Theatre
De Bohun Prim Sch
Bramley Sp Gd
Oaktree Sch
EN4
Oak Hill Coll
Monkfrith Prim Sch
CHASE SIDE
OSIDGE LA
B1453
Osidge JMI Sch
Osidge
N14
Brunswick Park Prim Sch
Brunswick Park
New Southgate Cemetery & Crematorium
Pymme's Brook
WATERFALL RD
A1003
THE GREEN
HIGH ST
A1004
Southgate
Southgate Coll
Ashmole Sch
Walker Prim Sch
St Andrew's CE Prim Sch
West Grove Prim Sch
Wolfson Hillel Prim Sch
Oakwood Park
MERRIVALE
Cemy
Crkt Gd
Allot Gdns
Recn Gd
Sports Gd
OAKLEIGH RD S
FRIERN BARNET
N11
New Southgate
Arnos Park
CANNON HILL
THE BOURNE
POWYS LA

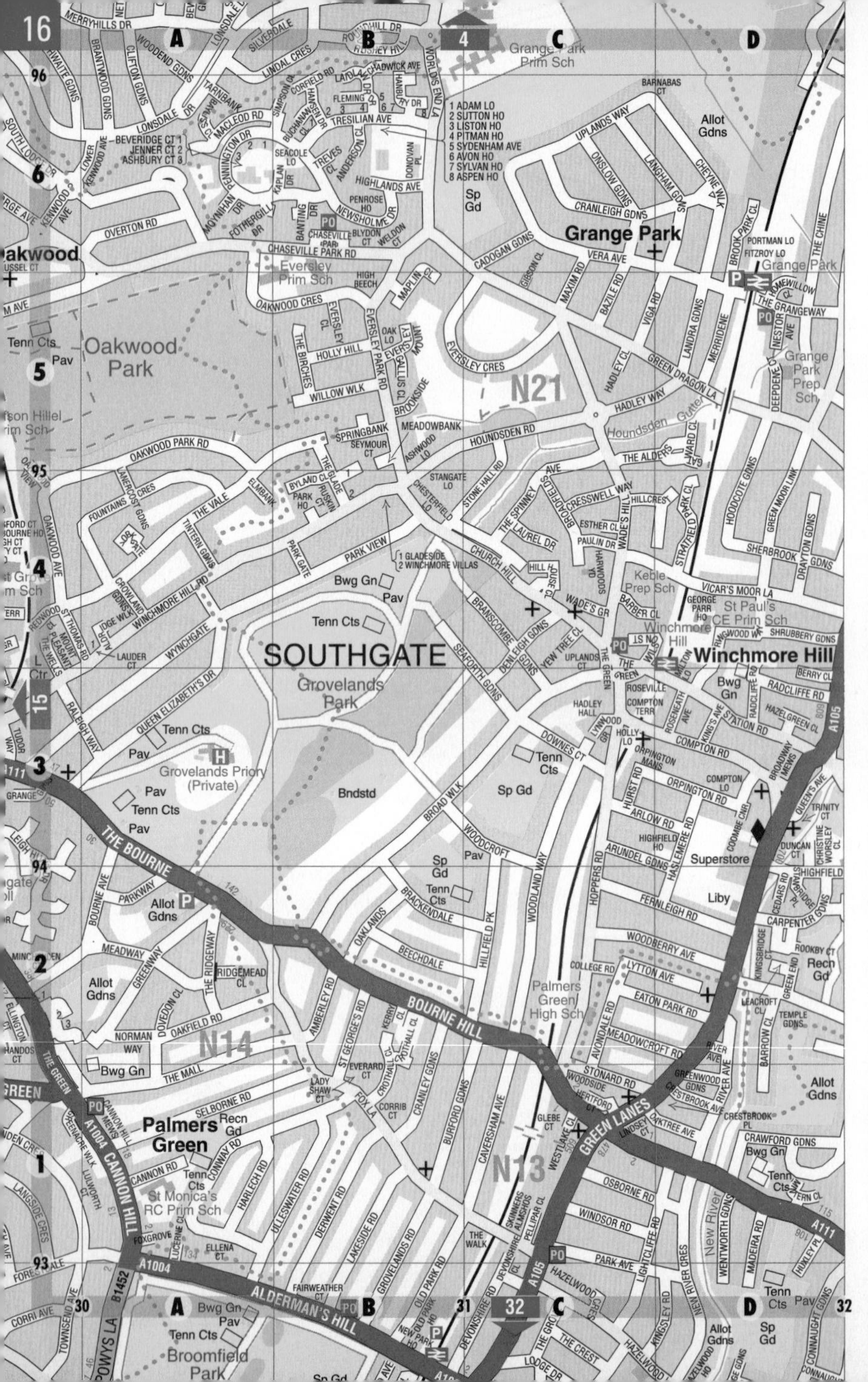

A
B
4
C
D
Grange Park Prim Sch
Grange Park
Oakwood
Oakwood Park
N21
SOUTHGATE
Grovelands Park
Grovelands Priory (Private)
Winchmore Hill
N14
Palmers Green
N13
Broomfield Park
St Paul's CE Prim Sch
Keble Prep Sch
Eversley Prim Sch
Grange Park Prep Sch
Palmers Green High Sch
St Monica's RC Prim Sch
THE BOURNE
BOURNE HILL
GREEN LANES
ALDERMAN'S HILL
CANNON HILL
CHASEVILLE PARK RD
HOUNDSDEN RD
CHURCH HILL
WINCHMORE HILL RD
GREEN DRAGON LA
1 ADAM LO
2 SUTTON HO
3 LISTON HO
4 PITMAN HO
5 SYDENHAM AVE
6 AVON HO
7 SYLVAN HO
8 ASPEN HO
1 GLADESIDE
2 WINCHMORE VILLAS
15
32

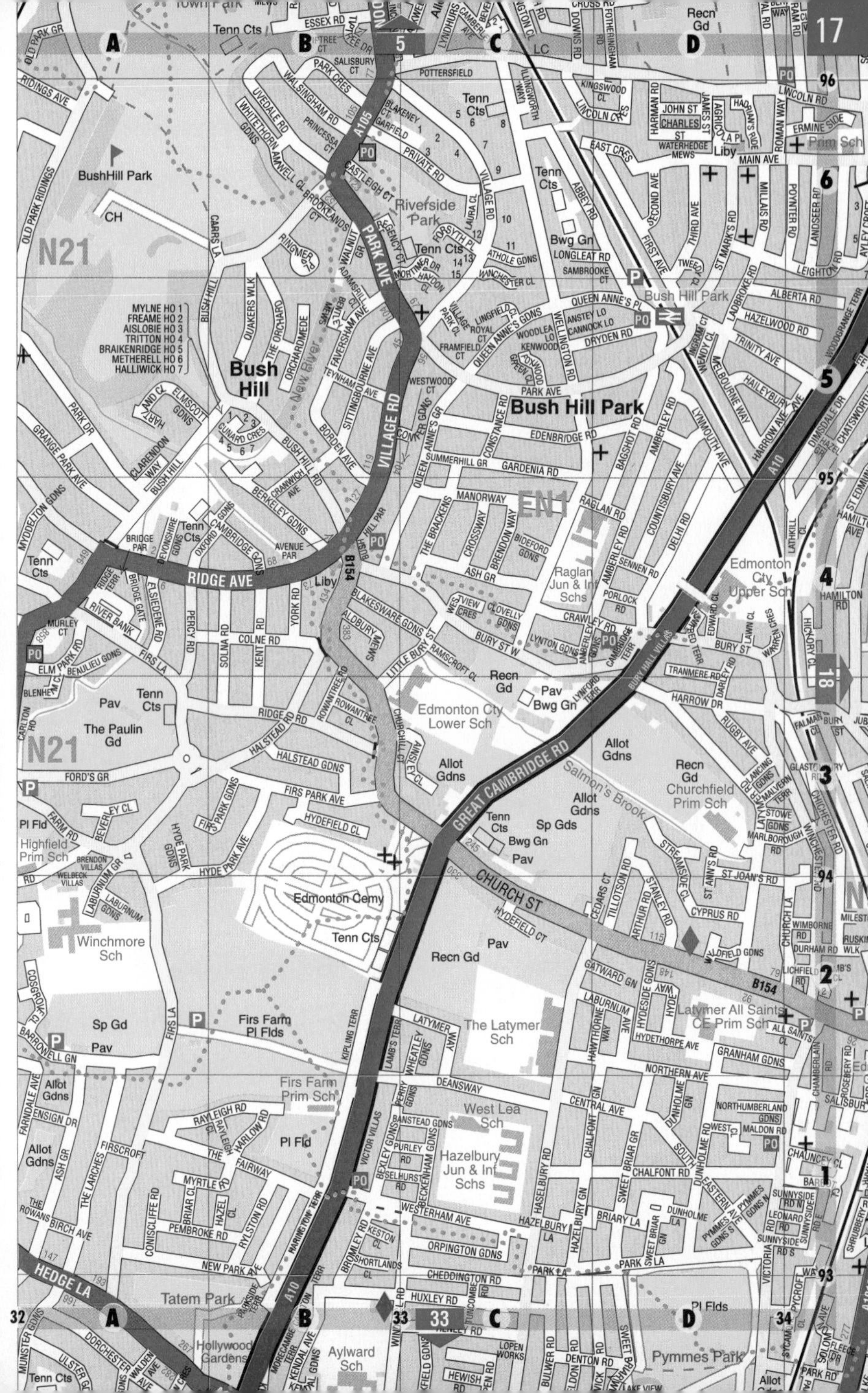
A
B
C
D
5
LC
Tenn Cts
ESSEX RD
SALISBURY CT
POTTERSFIELD
PARK CRES
WALSINGHAM RD
UVEDALE RD
PRINCESSA CT
WHITETHORN GDNS
A105
PO
BLAKENEY CT
GARFIELD
PRIVATE RD
VILLAGE RD
ILLINGWORTH WAY
KINGSWOOD CL
LINCOLN CRES
LINCOLN RD
HARMAN RD
JOHN ST
CHARLES ST
JAMES ST
AGRICOLA PL
HADRIAN'S RIDE
ROMAN WAY
ERMINE SIDE
Prim Sch
WATERHEDGE MEWS
Liby
MAIN AVE
EAST CRES
96
6
BushHill Park
CH
N21
CARRS LA
CASTLEIGH CT
BROOKLANDS CT
Riverside Park
REGENCY CT
PARK AVE
FORSYTH PL
Tenn Cts
Bwg Gn
LONGLEAT RD
SAMBROOKE CT
ABBEY RD
SECOND AVE
FIRST AVE
THIRD AVE
TWEED CT
ST MARK'S RD
MILLAIS RD
POYNTER RD
LANDSEER RD
AYLEY CROFT
LEIGHTON RD
ATHOLE GDNS
WINCHESTER CL
RINGMER PL
WALNUT GDNS
ADAMSHILL CL
HAYDON CL
MORTIMER DR
Bush Hill Park
QUEEN ANNE'S PL
ANSTEY LO
CANNOCK LO
DRYDEN RD
ALBERTA RD
LADBROKE RD
HAZELWOOD RD
TRINITY AVE
HAILEYBURY AVE
WOODGRANGE TERR
MYLNE HO 1
FREAME HO 2
AISLOBIE HO 3
TRITTON HO 4
BRAIKENRIDGE HO 5
METHERELL HO 6
HALLIWICK HO 7
BUSH HILL
QUAKERS WLK
THE ORCHARD
ORCHARDMEDE
Bush Hill
New River
FAVERSHAM AVE
TEYNHAM AVE
SITTINGBOURNE AVE
WESTWOOD CT
VILLAGE PARK CL
VILLAGE ROYAL CT
LINGFIELD CL
FRAMFIELD CT
QUEEN ANNE'S GDNS
WOODLEA LO
KENWOOD
WELLINGTON RD
PARK AVE
Bush Hill Park
INGRAM CT
WENDY CL
MELBOURNE AVE
MELBOURNE WAY
HARROW AVE
5
DIMSDALE DR
CHATSWORTH
ELMSCOTT GDNS
PARK DR
GRANGE PARK AVE
CLARENDON WAY
BUSH HILL
CUNARD CRES
BUSH HILL RD
BORDEN AVE
COWPER GDNS
QUEEN ANNE'S GR
CONSTANCE RD
EDENBRIDGE RD
SUMMERHILL GR
GARDENIA RD
BAGSHOT RD
AMBERLEY RD
LYNMOUTH AVE
COUNTISBURY AVE
A10
95
MYDDELTON GDNS
CRANWICH AVE
BERKELEY GDNS
MANORWAY
THE BRACKENS
CROSSWAY
BRENDON WAY
EN1
RAGLAN RD
DELHI RD
LATHKILL CL
HAMILTON AVE
Tenn Cts
BRIDGE PAR
DEVONSHIRE GDNS
OXFORD GDNS
CAMBRIDGE GDNS
AVENUE PAR
HILL PAR
BIDEFORD GDNS
ASH GR
Raglan Jun & Inf Schs
SENNEN RD
Edmonton Cty Upper Sch
4
HAMILTON RD
RIDGE AVE
B154
Liby
BRIDGE GATE
ELSIEDENE RD
PERCY RD
RIDGE TERR
RIVER BANK
MURLEY CT
YORK RD
BLAKESWARE GDNS
ALDBURY MEWS
LOVELLY GDNS
PORLOCK RD
CRAWLEY RD
EDWARD CL
LAWN CL
WARREN CRES
HICKORY CL
PO
ELM PARK RD
BEAULIEU GDNS
FIRS LA
SOLNA RD
KENT RD
COLNE RD
LITTLE BURY ST
RAMSCROFT CL
BURY ST W
LYNTON GDNS
CAMBRIDGE TERR
BURY HALL VILLAS
BURY ST
18
BLENHEIM CL
CARLTON RD
Pav
Tenn Cts
The Paulin Gd
N21
RIDGE RD
ROWANTREE RD
ROWANTREE CL
Recn Gd
Pav
Bwg Gn
LYNFORD TERR
TRANMERE RD
DARLEY RD
HARROW DR
Edmonton Cty Lower Sch
RUGBY AVE
HALSTEAD RD
HALSTEAD GDNS
CHURCHILL CT
AINSLEY CL
Allot Gdns
GREAT CAMBRIDGE RD
Allot Gdns
Recn Gd
Salmon's Brook
Churchfield Prim Sch
3
FORD'S GR
FIRS PARK AVE
FIRS PARK GDNS
HYDEFIELD CL
BEVERLEY CL
FARM RD
Pl Fld
Highfield Prim Sch
HYDE PARK GDNS
HYDE PARK AVE
Tenn Cts
Bwg Gn
Pav
Sp Gds
Allot Gdns
STREAMSIDE CL
ST ANN'S RD
ST JOAN'S RD
CHICHESTER RD
WINCHESTER RD
MARLBOROUGH RD
STOWE GDNS
BRENDON VILLAS
WELBECK VILLAS
LABURNUM GR
LABURNUM GDNS
Edmonton Cemy
CHURCH ST
HYDEFIELD CT
CEDARS CT
TILLOTSON RD
ARTHUR RD
STANLEY RD
CYPRUS RD
94
Winchmore Sch
Tenn Cts
Recn Gd
Pav
WILDFIELD GDNS
CHURCH LA
WIMBORNE RD
DURHAM RD
RUSKIN WLK
MILESTONE
COSGROVE CL
GATWARD GN
HYDESIDE GDNS
HYDE WAY
B154
LICHFIELD RD
2
Sp Gd
P
Firs Farm Pl Flds
KIPLING TERR
LATYMER WAY
The Latymer Sch
LABURNUM AVE
HAWTHORNE WAY
HYDETHORPE AVE
Latymer All Saints' CE Prim Sch
ALL SAINTS' CL
BARROWELL GN
Pav
Allot Gdns
FARNDALE AVE
ENSIGN DR
Firs Farm Prim Sch
LAMB'S TERR
WHEATLEY GDNS
PERRY GDNS
DEANSWAY
GRANHAM GDNS
NORTHERN AVE
CENTRAL AVE
CHAMBERLAIN
ROSEBERY RD
SALISBURY
NORTHUMBERLAND GDNS
MALDON RD
WEST CL
Allot Gdns
ASH GR
RAYLEIGH RD
RAYLEIGH CL
HARLOW RD
FIRSCROFT
Pl Fld
THE FAIRWAY
VICTOR VILLAS
BANSTEAD GDNS
PURLEY RD
BEXLEY GDNS
BECKENHAM GDNS
SELHURST RD
West Lea Sch
Hazelbury Jun & Inf Schs
HASELBURY RD
CHALFONT GN
SWEET BRIAR GR
DUNHOLME GN
DUNHOLME RD
SOUTH EASTERN AVE
CHALFONT RD
CHAUNCEY CL
1
THE LARCHES
THE ROWANS
BIRCH AVE
MYRTLE RD
BRIAR CL
HAZEL CL
CONISCLIFFE RD
RYLSTON RD
PEMBROKE RD
NEW PARK AVE
WESTERHAM AVE
KESTON CL
BROMLEY RD
ORPINGTON GDNS
HAZELBURY LA
BRIARY LA
DUNHOLME LA
PYMMES GDNS S
PYMMES GDNS N
SUNNYSIDE RD N
LEONARD RD
SUNNYSIDE RD S
VICTORIA RD
PARK LA
SHORTLANDS CL
CHEDDINGTON RD
HUXLEY RD
PYCROFT WAY
93
SHRUBBERY
HEDGE LA
Tatem Park
A10
32
A
B
33
33
C
D
34
Pl Flds
MUNSTER GDNS
DORCHESTER AVE
ULSTER GDNS
WALDEN AVE
Tenn Cts
Hollywood Gardens
MORECAMBE TERR
KENDAL AVE
Aylward Sch
HENLEY RD
LOPEN WORKS
HEWISH RD
BULWER RD
DENTON RD
Pymmes Park
SOLONA CL
FLEECE DR
PARK RD
Allot

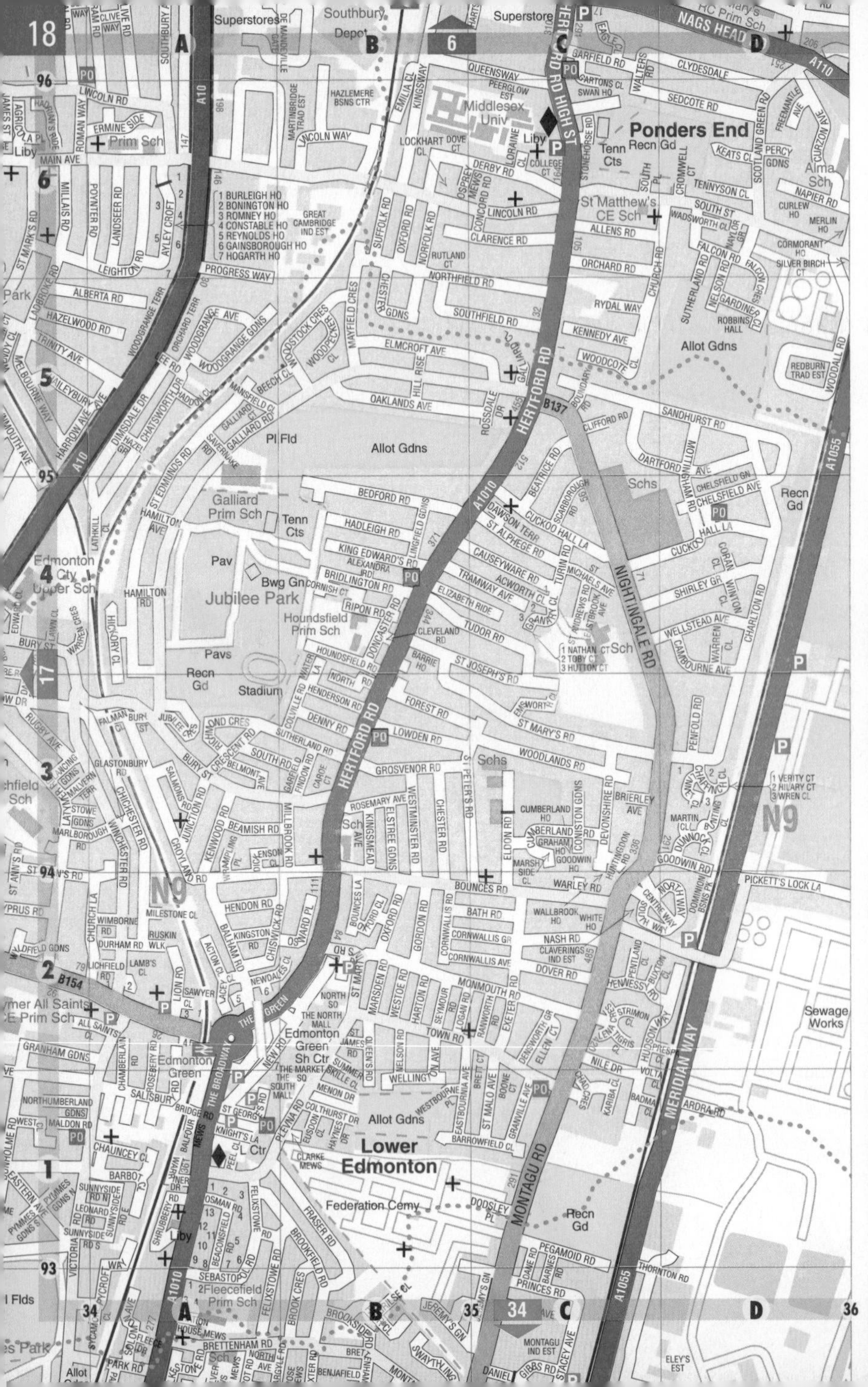

Ponders End
Lower Edmonton
Edmonton Green
Middlesex Univ
Jubilee Park
Southbury Depot
Superstores
Superstore
HAZLEMERE BSNS CTR
MARTINBRIDGE TRAD EST
GREAT CAMBRIDGE IND EST
1 BURLEIGH HO
2 BONINGTON HO
3 ROMNEY HO
4 CONSTABLE HO
5 REYNOLDS HO
6 GAINSBOROUGH HO
7 HOGARTH HO
Galliard Prim Sch
Houndsfield Prim Sch
Edmonton City Upper Sch
St Matthew's CE Sch
Alma Sch
Fleecefield Prim Sch
Pl Fld
Allot Gdns
Tenn Cts
Recn Gd
Stadium
Pav
Pavs
Bwg Gn
Schs
Sch
Liby
L Ctr
Federation Cemy
Sewage Works
Edmonton Green Sh Ctr
THE NORTH MALL
THE SOUTH MALL
THE MARKET SQ
NORTH SQ
REDBURN TRAD EST
CLAVERINGS IND EST
MONTAGU IND EST
DOMINION BSNS PK
ELEY'S EST
1 NATHAN CT
2 TOBY CT
3 HUTTON CT
1 VERITY CT
2 HILARY CT
3 WREN CL
HERTFORD RD
HERTFORD RD HIGH ST
NIGHTINGALE RD
MONTAGU RD
MERIDIAN WAY
THE BROADWAY
THE GREEN
NAGS HEAD RD
PICKETT'S LOCK LA
SOUTHBURY AVE
A10
A1010
A1055
A110
B137
B154
N9

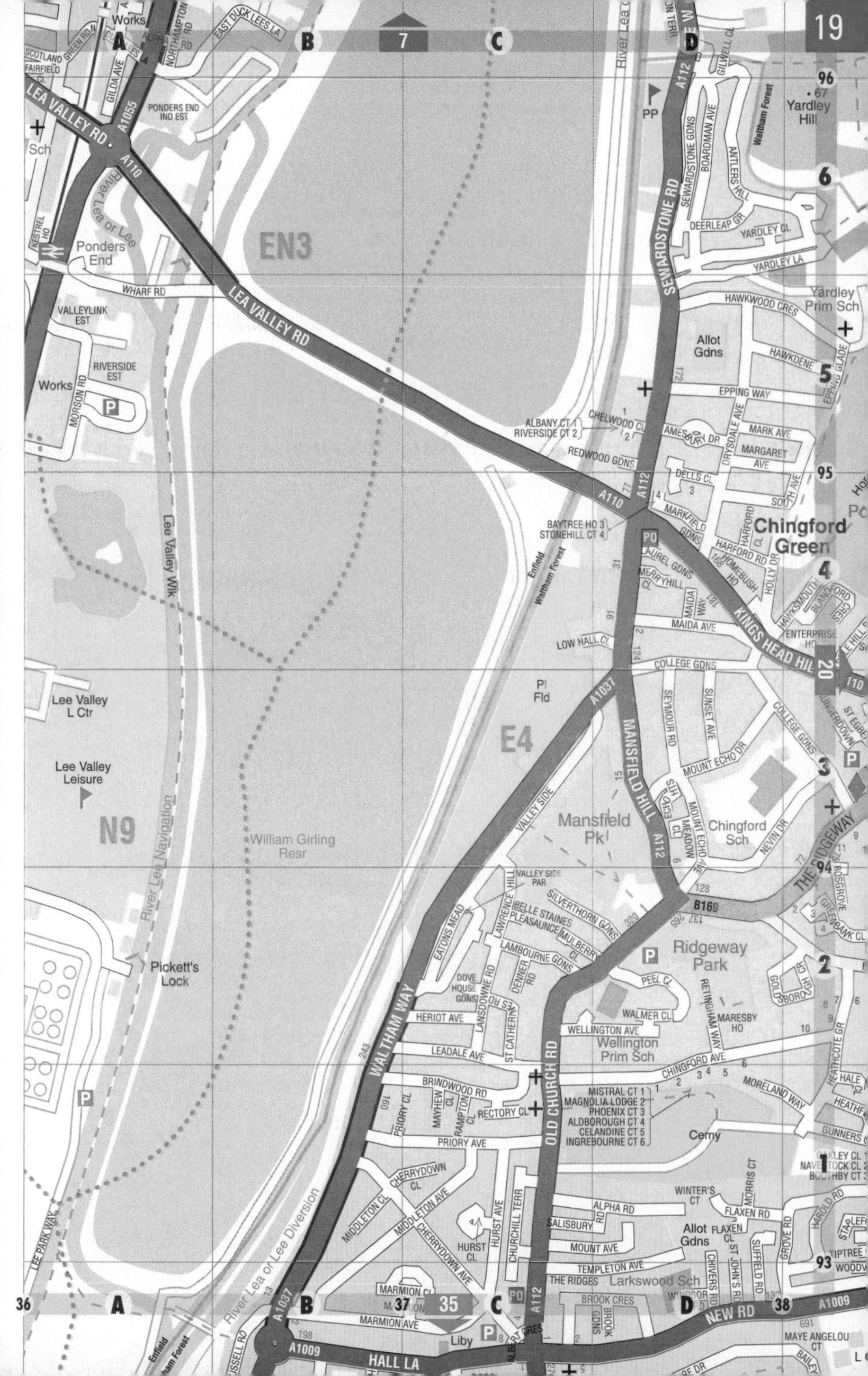
EN3
E4
N9
LEA VALLEY RD
Ponders End
PONDERS END IND EST
WHARF RD
VALLEYLINK EST
RIVERSIDE EST
Works
MORSON RD
Lee Valley Wlk
Lee Valley L Ctr
Lee Valley Leisure
River Lee Navigation
William Girling Resr
Pickett's Lock
LEE PARK WAY
River Lea or Lee Diversion
SEWARDSTONE RD
Yardley Hill
DEERLEAP GR
YARDLEY CL
YARDLEY LA
HAWKWOOD CRES
Yardley Prim Sch
Allot Gdns
HAWKDENE
EPPING WAY
EPPING GLADE
CHELWOOD CL
ALBANY CT 1
RIVERSIDE CT 2
REDWOOD GDNS
AMESBURY DR
DRYSDALE AVE
MARK AVE
MARGARET AVE
DELLS CL
SOUTH AVE
MARKFIELD GDNS
BAYTREE HO 3
STONEHILL CT 4
Chingford Green
LAUREL GDNS
HARFORD RD
HOMEBUSH HO
HOLLY DR
MERRYHILL CL
MAIDA WAY
MAIDA AVE
KINGS HEAD HILL
ENTERPRISE HO
LOW HALL CL
COLLEGE GDNS
Pl Fld
MANSFIELD HILL
SEYMOUR RD
SUNSET AVE
MOUNT ECHO DR
Mansfield Pk
Chingford Sch
NEVIN DR
THE RIDGEWAY
VALLEY SIDE
VALLEY SIDE PAR
SILVERTHORN GDNS
BELLE STAINES PLEASAUNCE
MULBERRY CL
LAMBOURNE GDNS
EATONS MEAD
DOVE HOUSE GDNS
DENNER RD
LANSDOWNE RD
Ridgeway Park
PEEL CL
RETINGHAM WAY
MARESBY HO
WALMER CL
WELLINGTON AVE
Wellington Prim Sch
HERIOT AVE
LEADALE AVE
WALTHAM WAY
CHINGFORD AVE
MORELAND WAY
BRINDWOOD RD
MISTRAL CT 1
MAGNOLIA LODGE 2
PHOENIX CT 3
ALDBOROUGH CT 4
CELANDINE CT 5
INGREBOURNE CT 6
PRIORY CL
MAYHEW CL
RAMPTON CL
RECTORY CL
OLD CHURCH RD
Cemy
PRIORY AVE
CHERRYDOWN CL
MIDDLETON CL
MIDDLETON AVE
CHERRYDOWN AVE
HURST AVE
HURST CL
CHURCHILL TERR
WINTER'S CT
MORRIS CT
FLAXEN RD
FLAXEN CL
ALPHA RD
SALISBURY RD
MOUNT AVE
TEMPLETON AVE
THE RIDGES
Larkswood Sch
BROOK CRES
BROOK GDNS
CHIVERS RD
ST JOHN'S RD
SUFFIELD RD
GROVE RD
HAROLD RD
MARMION CL
MARMION AVE
NEW RD
HALL LA
Liby
MAYE ANGELOU CT
GUNNERS
HEATHCOTE GR
ROSGROVE
GREENBANK CL
Enfield
Waltham Forest
A1055
A110
A112
A1037
A1009
B169

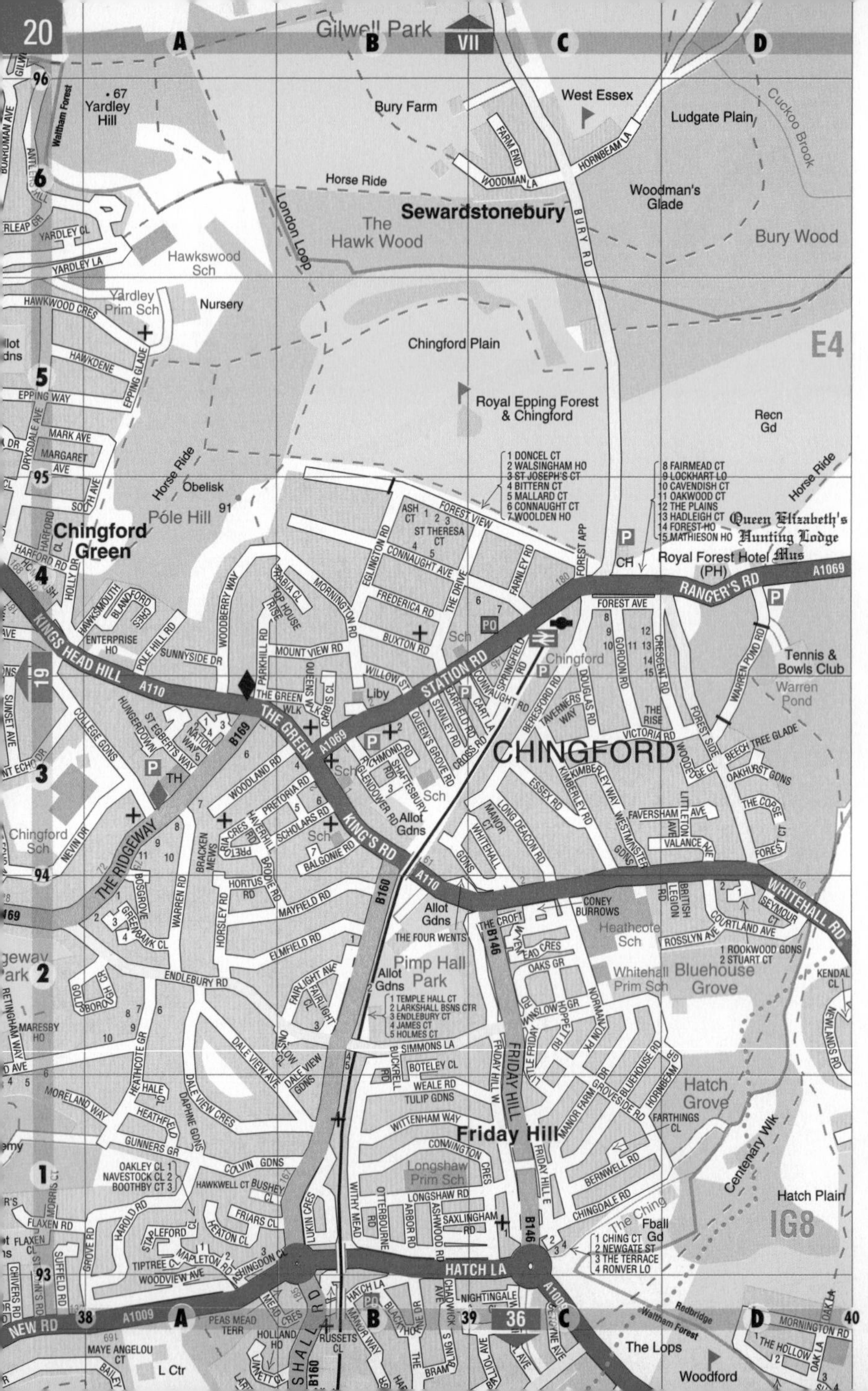

Gilwell Park
VII
A
B
C
D
Yardley Hill
Bury Farm
West Essex
Ludgate Plain
Cuckoo Brook
Horse Ride
Sewardstonebury
The Hawk Wood
Woodman's Glade
Bury Wood
London Loop
Hawkswood Sch
Yardley Prim Sch
Nursery
Chingford Plain
E4
Royal Epping Forest & Chingford
Recn Gd
Obelisk
Pole Hill
Chingford Green
Queen Elizabeth's Hunting Lodge
Royal Forest Hotel (PH)
Mus
RANGER'S RD
A1069
KINGS HEAD HILL
A110
STATION RD
THE GREEN
Chingford
Tennis & Bowls Club
Warren Pond
CHINGFORD
KING'S RD
THE RIDGEWAY
Chingford Sch
Allot Gdns
Heathcote Sch
Whitehall Prim Sch
Bluehouse Grove
WHITEHALL RD
Pimp Hall Park
Hatch Grove
Friday Hill
FRIDAY HILL
Longshaw Prim Sch
Centenary Wlk
Hatch Plain
IG8
The Ching
Fball Gd
HATCH LA
NEW RD
A1009
The Lops
Woodford
Waltham Forest
Redbridge
36
1 DONCEL CT
2 WALSINGHAM HO
3 ST JOSEPH'S CT
4 BITTERN CT
5 MALLARD CT
6 CONNAUGHT CT
7 WOOLDEN HO
8 FAIRMEAD CT
9 LOCKHART LO
10 CAVENDISH CT
11 OAKWOOD CT
12 THE PLAINS
13 HADLEIGH CT
14 FOREST HO
15 MATHIESON HO
1 ROOKWOOD GDNS
2 STUART CT
1 TEMPLE HALL CT
2 LARKSHALL BSNS CTR
3 ENDLEBURY CT
4 JAMES CT
5 HOLMES CT
1 CHING CT
2 NEWGATE ST
3 THE TERRACE
4 RONVER LO
OAKLEY CL 1
NAVESTOCK CL 2
BOOTHBY CT 3

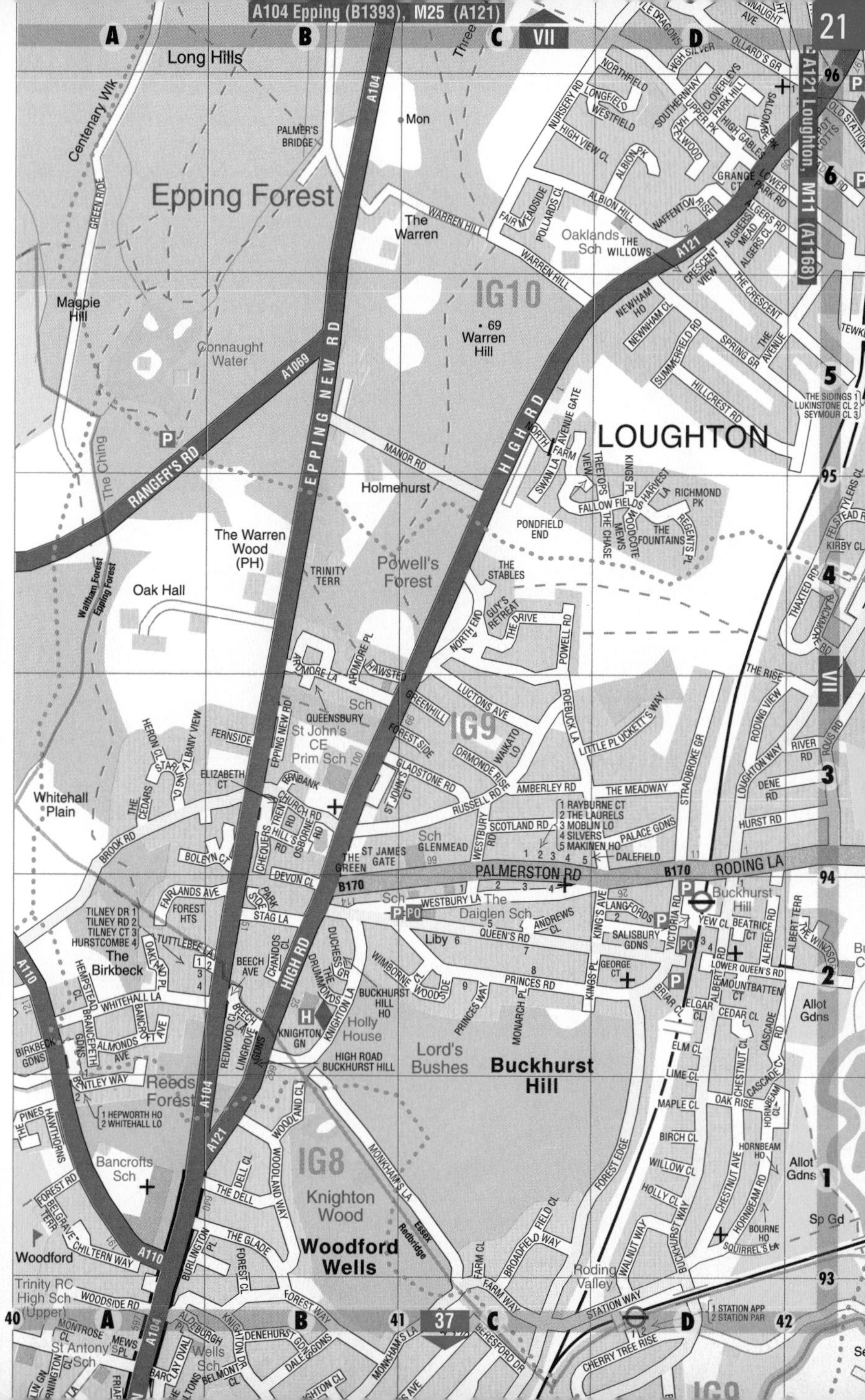
A104 Epping (B1393), M25 (A121)
VII
A121 Loughton, M11 (A1168)
Long Hills
Epping Forest
Centenary Wlk
Palmer's Bridge
Mon
The Warren
Warren Hill
IG10
69 Warren Hill
Magpie Hill
Connaught Water
Rangers Rd
Epping New Rd
High Rd
Manor Rd
Holmehurst
LOUGHTON
Oaklands Sch
The Warren Wood (PH)
Oak Hall
Powell's Forest
Trinity Terr
The Stables
Pondfield End
The Fountains
Richmond Pk
IG9
Queensbury
St John's CE Prim Sch
Whitehall Plain
The Ching
Palmerston Rd
Roding La
B170
Buckhurst Hill
The Birkbeck
Holly House
Lord's Bushes
Buckhurst Hill
Reeds Forest
Bancrofts Sch
IG8
Knighton Wood
Woodford Wells
Woodford
Trinity RC High Sch (Upper)
St Antony's Sch
Wells Sch
Roding Valley
Allot Gdns
Sp Gd
Essex
Redbridge
A104
A121
A110
A1069
1 Rayburne Ct
2 The Laurels
3 Moblin Lo
4 Silvers
5 Makinen Ho
Tilney Dr 1
Tilney Rd 2
Tilney Ct 3
Hurstcombe 4
1 Hepworth Ho
2 Whitehall Lo
The Sidings 1
Lukinstone Cl 2
Seymour Cl 3
1 Station App
2 Station Par
A
B
C
D
37
40
41
42
93
94
95
96
1
2
3
4
5
6

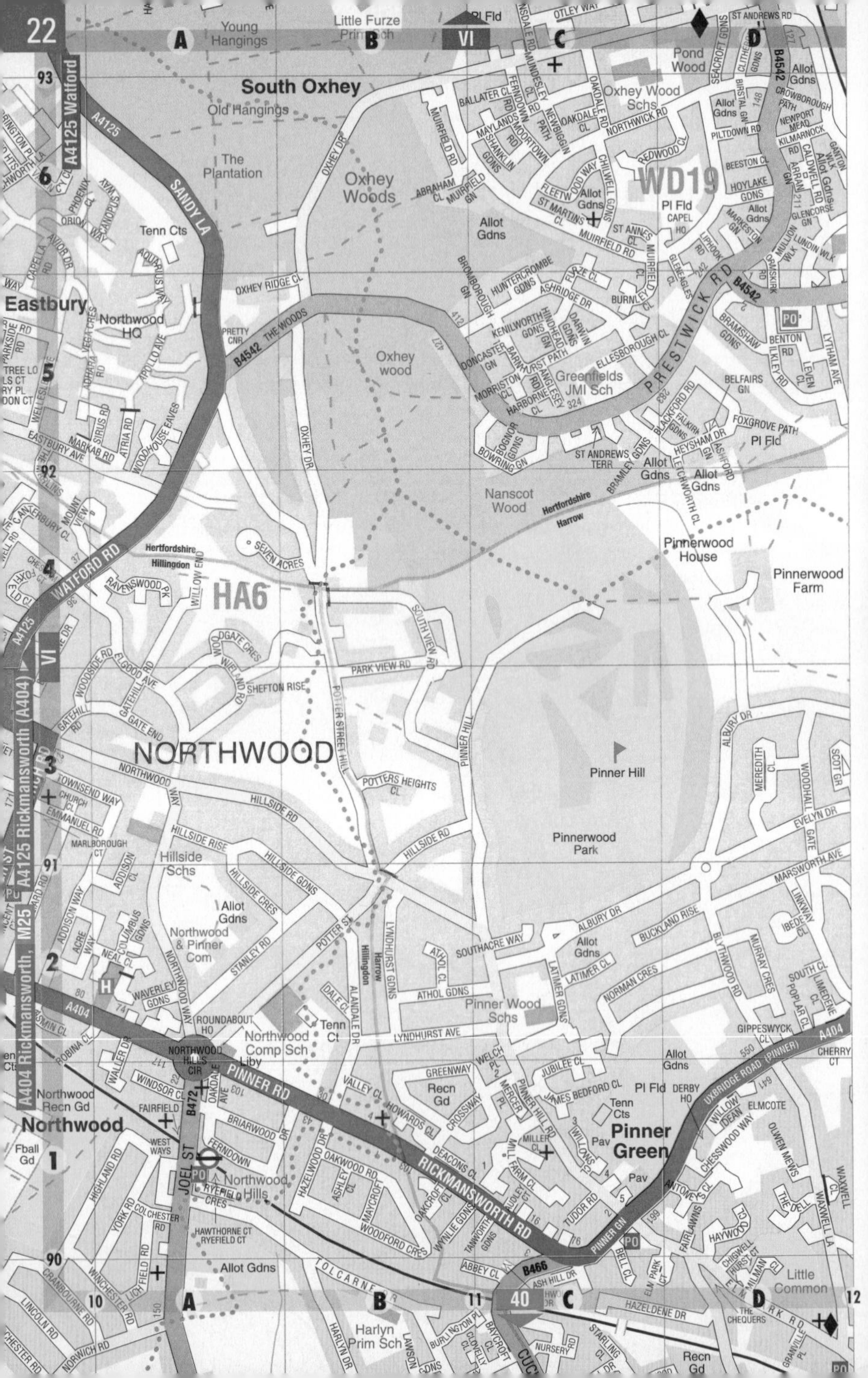

Young Hangings
Little Furze Prim Sch
South Oxhey
Old Hangings
The Plantation
Oxhey Woods
Oxhey wood
Pond Wood
Oxhey Wood Schs
WD19
Pl Fld
Allot Gdns
Greenfields JMI Sch
Nanscot Wood
Hertfordshire
Harrow
Pinnerwood House
Pinnerwood Farm
Pinner Hill
Pinnerwood Park
Eastbury
Northwood HQ
Tenn Cts
HA6
Hillingdon
NORTHWOOD
Hillside Schs
Northwood & Pinner Com
Northwood Comp Sch
Tenn Ct
Pinner Wood Schs
Recn Gd
Pinner Green
Northwood Recn Gd
Northwood
Northwood Hills
Fball Gd
Allot Gdns
Harlyn Prim Sch
Little Common
A4125 Watford
A4125
SANDY LA
WATFORD RD
B4542 THE WOODS
PRESTWICK RD
A404 Rickmansworth (A404)
A4125 Rickmansworth, M25
A404
PINNER RD
RICKMANSWORTH RD
UXBRIDGE ROAD (PINNER)
B472
B466
B4542
JOEL ST
OXHEY DR
OXHEY RIDGE CL
PRETTY CNR
MUIRFIELD RD
NORTHWICK RD
POTTER STREET HILL
PINNER HILL
SOUTH VIEW RD
PARK VIEW RD
SEVEN ACRES
WILLOW END
RAVENSWOOD PK
GATEHILL RD
ELGOOD AVE
SHEFTON RISE
HILLSIDE RD
HILLSIDE RISE
HILLSIDE GDNS
HILLSIDE CRES
STANLEY RD
POTTER ST
LYNDHURST GDNS
LYNDHURST AVE
ALANDALE DR
ATHOL GDNS
SOUTHACRE WAY
ALBURY DR
BUCKLAND RISE
MARSWORTH AVE
EVELYN DR
WOODHALL GATE
BLYTHWOOD RD
MURRAY CRES
NORMAN CRES
LATIMER CL
HAZELWOOD DR
OAKWOOD RD
WOODFORD CRES
TOLCARNE DR
HAZELDENE DR
PINNER GN
EASTBURY AVE
NORTHWOOD WAY
TOWNSEND WAY
EMMANUEL RD
ADDISON WAY
WAVERLEY GDNS
ROUNDABOUT HO
NORTHWOOD HILLS CIR
WINDSOR CL
BRIARWOOD DR
FERNDOWN
RYEFIELD CRES
HIGHLAND RD
YORK RD
COLCHESTER RD
WINCHESTER RD
LICHFIELD RD
CRANBOURNE RD
LINCOLN RD
NORWICH RD
HAWTHORNE CT
RYEFIELD CT
VI
40
A
B
C
D
93
92
91
90
6
5
4
3
2
1
10
11
12

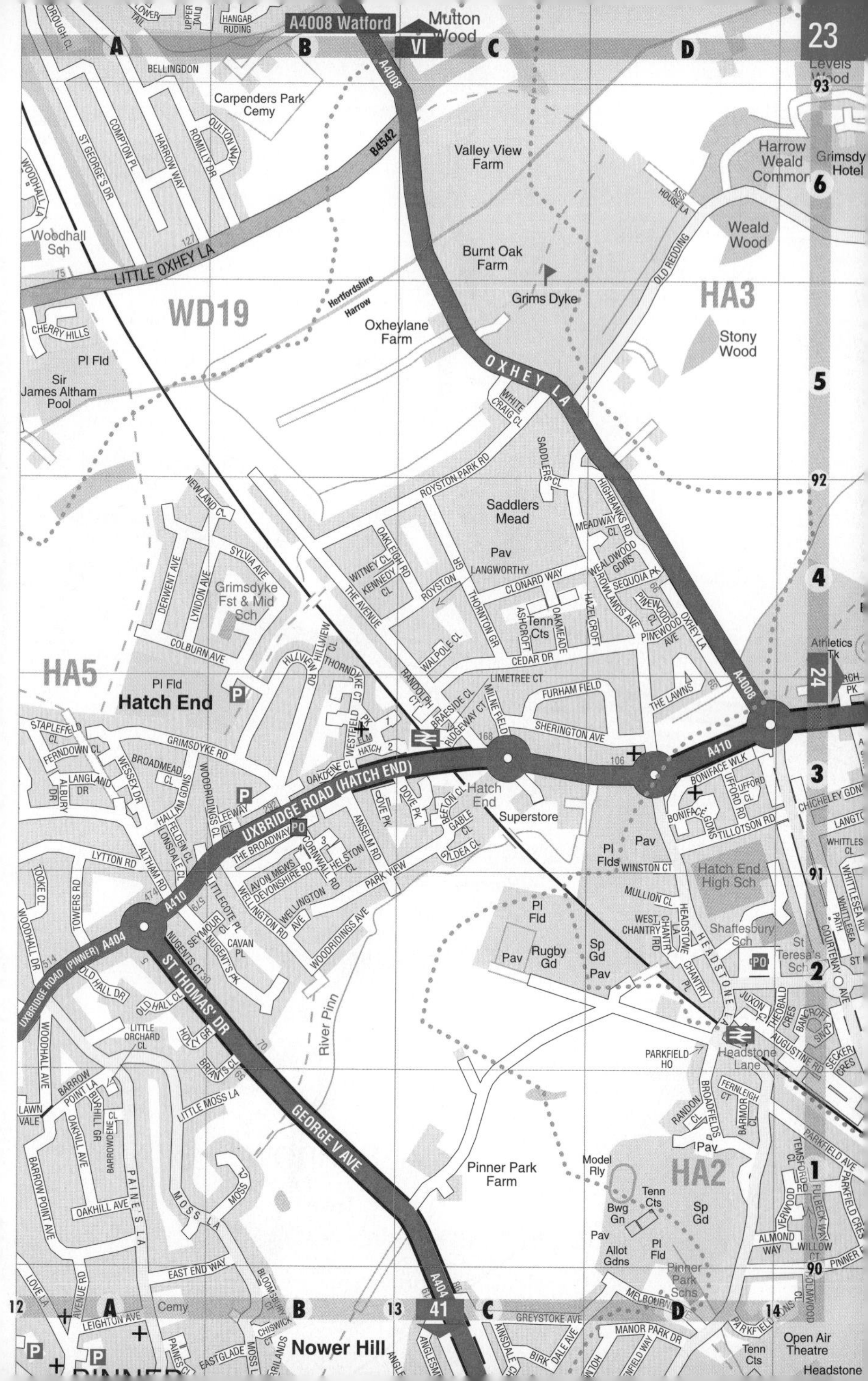
A4008 Watford
Mutton Wood
VI
A
B
C
D
Carpenders Park Cemy
Valley View Farm
Harrow Weald Common
Grimsdyke Hotel
Weald Wood
Burnt Oak Farm
Grims Dyke
HA3
WD19
Oxheylane Farm
Stony Wood
Woodhall Sch
LITTLE OXHEY LA
Sir James Altham Pool
Pl Fld
OXHEY LA
Saddlers Mead
Pav
Grimsdyke Fst & Mid Sch
Tenn Cts
HA5
Hatch End
UXBRIDGE ROAD (HATCH END)
Hatch End
Superstore
Athletics Tk
24
Hatch End High Sch
Shaftesbury Sch
St Teresa's Sch
Pl Flds
Rugby Gd
Sp Gd
River Pinn
Headstone Lane
ST THOMAS' DR
GEORGE V AVE
UXBRIDGE ROAD (PINNER)
Pinner Park Farm
HA2
Model Rly
Bwg Gn
Allot Gdns
Pinner Park Schs
Cemy
Nower Hill
41
Open Air Theatre
Headstone
6
5
4
3
2
1
93
92
91
90
12
13
14

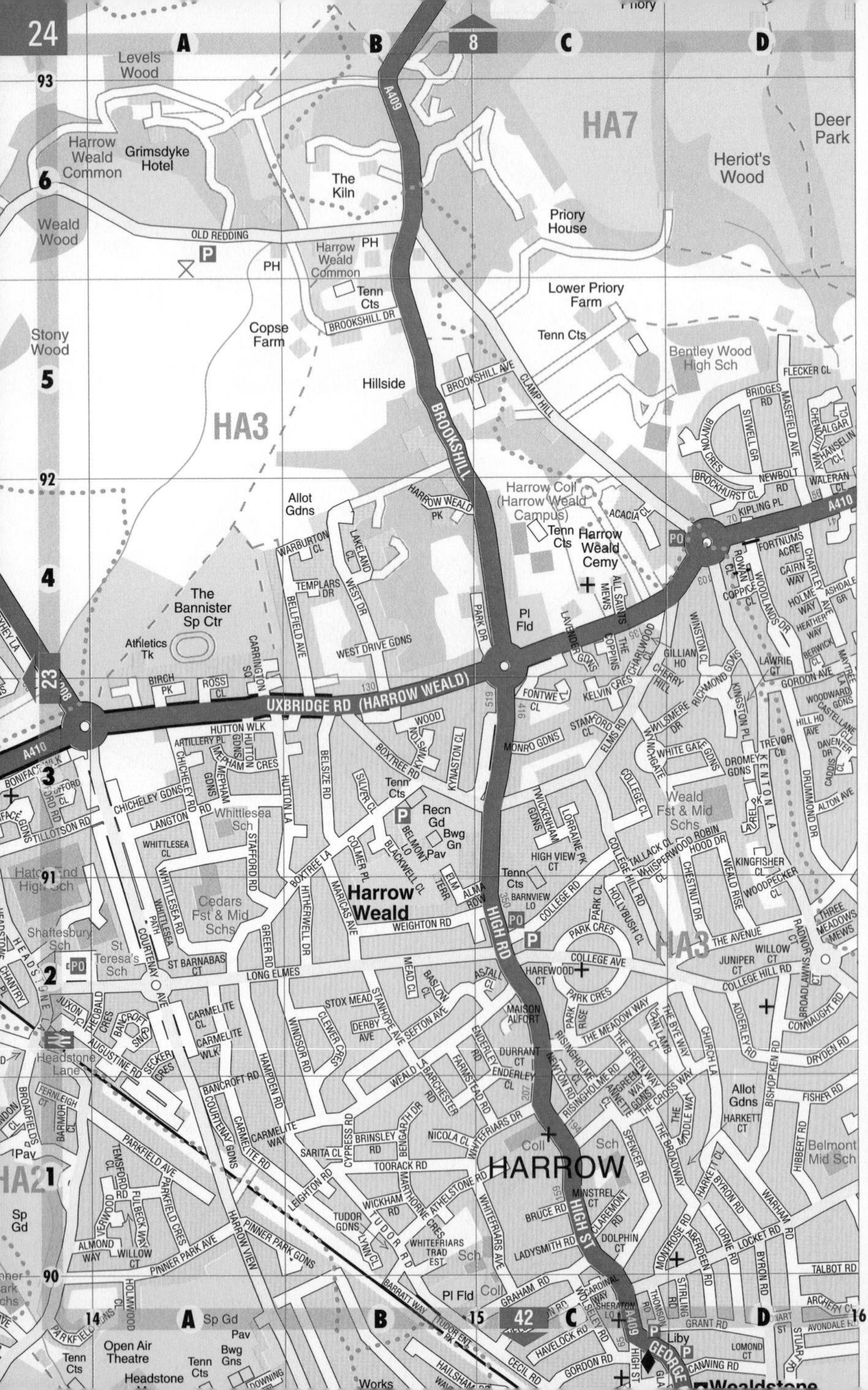
24
A
B
8
C
D
93
92
91
90
6
5
4
3
2
1
14
15
16
42
23
Levels Wood
Harrow Weald Common
Grimsdyke Hotel
Weald Wood
OLD REDDING
PH
Harrow Weald Common
The Kiln
Tenn Cts
BROOKSHILL DR
Copse Farm
Stony Wood
Hillside
HA3
HA7
Deer Park
Heriot's Wood
Priory House
Lower Priory Farm
Tenn Cts
Bentley Wood High Sch
BROOKSHILL AVE
CLAMP HILL
BROOKSHILL
A409
A410
FLECKER CL
BRIDGES RD
SITWELL GR
MASEFIELD AVE
BINYON CRES
CHENDUIT WAY
ALGAR CL
HANSELIN CL
BROCKHURST CL
NEWBOLT RD
WALERAN CL
KIPLING PL
Harrow Coll (Harrow Weald Campus)
ACACIA CL
Tenn Cts
Harrow Weald Cemy
Allot Gdns
HARROW WEALD PK
WARBURTON CL
LAKELAND CL
TEMPLARS DR
WEST DR
BELLFIELD AVE
WEST DRIVE GDNS
PARK DR
Pl Fld
LAVENDER GDNS
ALL SAINTS MEWS
COPPINS
THE
CHARLWOOD CL
FORTNUMS ACRE
ROWAN CL
COPPICE CL
CAIRN WAY
CHARTLEY AVE
WOODLANDS DR
HOLME WAY
ASHDALE GR
HEATHER WAY
BERWICK CL
WINSTON CL
GILLIAN HO
CHERRY HILL
RICHMOND GDNS
KINGSTON PL
LAWRIE CT
GORDON AVE
MAYTREE LA
WOODWARD GDNS
CASTELLANE CL
HILL HO AVE
DAVENTER DR
CADDIS CL
TREVOR CL
DROMEY GDNS
KENTON LA
DRUMMOND DR
ALTON AVE
LAUREL PK
KINGFISHER CL
WOODPECKER CL
The Bannister Sp Ctr
Athletics Tk
CARRINGTON SQ
BIRCH PK
ROSS CL
UXBRIDGE RD (HARROW WEALD)
FONTWELL CL
KELVIN CRES
STANFORD CL
ELMS RD
WILSMERE DR
WYNCHGATE
WHITE GATE GDNS
MONRO GDNS
WOOD
KYNASTON
KYNASTON CL
BOXTREE RD
HUTTON WLK
ARTILLERY PL
HUTTON GDNS
MEPHAM CRES
MEPHAM GDNS
CHICHELEY RD
CHICHELEY GDNS
HUTTON LA
BELSIZE RD
BONIFACE WLK
TUFFORD CL
BONIFACE GDNS
TILLOTSON RD
LANGTON RD
Whittlesea Sch
WHITTLESEA CL
STAFFORD RD
Tenn Cts
SILVER CL
Recn Gd
Bwg Gn
Pav
BELMONT LO
BLACKWELL CL
COLMER PL
BOXTREE LA
TWICKENHAM GDNS
LORRAINE PK
COLLEGE CL
Weald Fst & Mid Schs
HIGH VIEW CT
TALLACK CL
WHISPERWOOD CL
ROBIN HOOD DR
CHESTNUT DR
WEALD RISE
COLLEGE HILL RD
HOLLYBUSH CL
Hatch End High Sch
WHITTLESEA RD
WHITTLESEA PATH
Cedars Fst & Mid Schs
GREER RD
HITHERWELL DR
MARICAS AVE
Harrow Weald
ELM TERR
ALMA ROW
Tenn Cts
BARNVIEW LO
HIGH RD
COLLEGE RD
PARK CL
PARK CRES
THE AVENUE
HA3
JUNIPER CT
WILLOW CT
RADNOR CT
THREE MEADOWS MEWS
BROADLAWNS CT
Shaftesbury Sch
HEADSTONE LA
CHANTRY PL
St Teresa's Sch
COURTENAY AVE
ST BARNABAS CT
WEIGHTON RD
LONG ELMES
MEAD CL
BASLOW CL
ASTALL CL
HAREWOOD CT
COLLEGE AVE
COLLEGE HILL RD
ADDERLEY RD
CONNAUGHT RD
JUXON CL
THEOBALD CRES
BANCROFT GDNS
AUGUSTINE RD
CARMELITE CL
CARMELITE WLK
STOX MEAD
STANHOPE AVE
CLEWER CRES
DERBY AVE
SEFTON AVE
MAISON ALFORT
PARK RISE
THE MEADOW WAY
JOHN LAMB CT
THE BYE WAY
CHURCH LA
DRYDEN RD
Headstone Lane
SECKER CRES
BANCROFT RD
HAMPDEN RD
WINDSOR RD
WEALD LA
BARCHESTER
FARMSTEAD RD
ENDERLEY RD
DURRANT CT
ENDERLEY CL
RISINGHOLME CL
NEWTON RD
RISINGHOLME RD
GREEN WAY GDNS
THE GREEN WAY
ANNETTE CRES
THE CROSS WAY
THE MIDDLE WAY
BISHOP KEN RD
Allot Gdns
HARKETT CT
FISHER RD
FERNLEIGH CT
BROADFIELDS
BARMOR CL
COURTENAY GDNS
CARMELITE RD
CARMELITE WAY
CYPRESS RD
BENGARTH DR
NICOLA CL
WHITEFRIARS DR
Coll
Sch
HARROW
THE BROADWAY
SPENCER RD
HARKETT CL
BYRON RD
HIBBERT RD
Belmont Mid Sch
Pav
HA2
TEMSFORD CL
PARKFIELD AVE
FULBECK WAY
PARKFIELD CRES
VERWOOD RD
BRINSLEY RD
SARITA CL
TOORACK RD
LEIGHTON RD
MARTHORNE CRES
ATHELSTONE RD
WHITEFRIARS AVE
HIGH ST
MINSTREL CT
BRUCE RD
CLAREMONT RD
DOLPHIN CT
MONTROSE RD
ABERDEEN RD
LORNE RD
WARHAM RD
Sp Gd
ALMOND CL
WAY
WILLOW CT
PINNER PARK AVE
HARROW VIEW
PINNER PARK GDNS
WICKHAM RD
TUDOR RD
TUDOR GDNS
LYNN CL
WHITEFRIARS TRAD EST
Sch
LADYSMITH RD
LOCKET RD
TALBOT RD
HOLMWOOD CL
BARRATT WAY
Pl Fld
Coll
GRAHAM RD
CARDINAL WAY
WOLSELEY RD
SHERATON LO
THOMSON RD
STIRLING RD
ARCHERY CL
GRANT RD
AVONDALE RD
STUART RD
PARKFIELD GDNS
A
Sp Gd
Pav
Bwg Gns
B
TUDOR ENT PK
C
D
Open Air Theatre
Tenn Cts
Tenn Cts
Headstone
DOWNING
Works
HAILSHAM RD
CECIL RD
HAVELOCK RD
GORDON RD
GEORGE
Liby
LOMOND CT
CANNING RD
Wealdstone

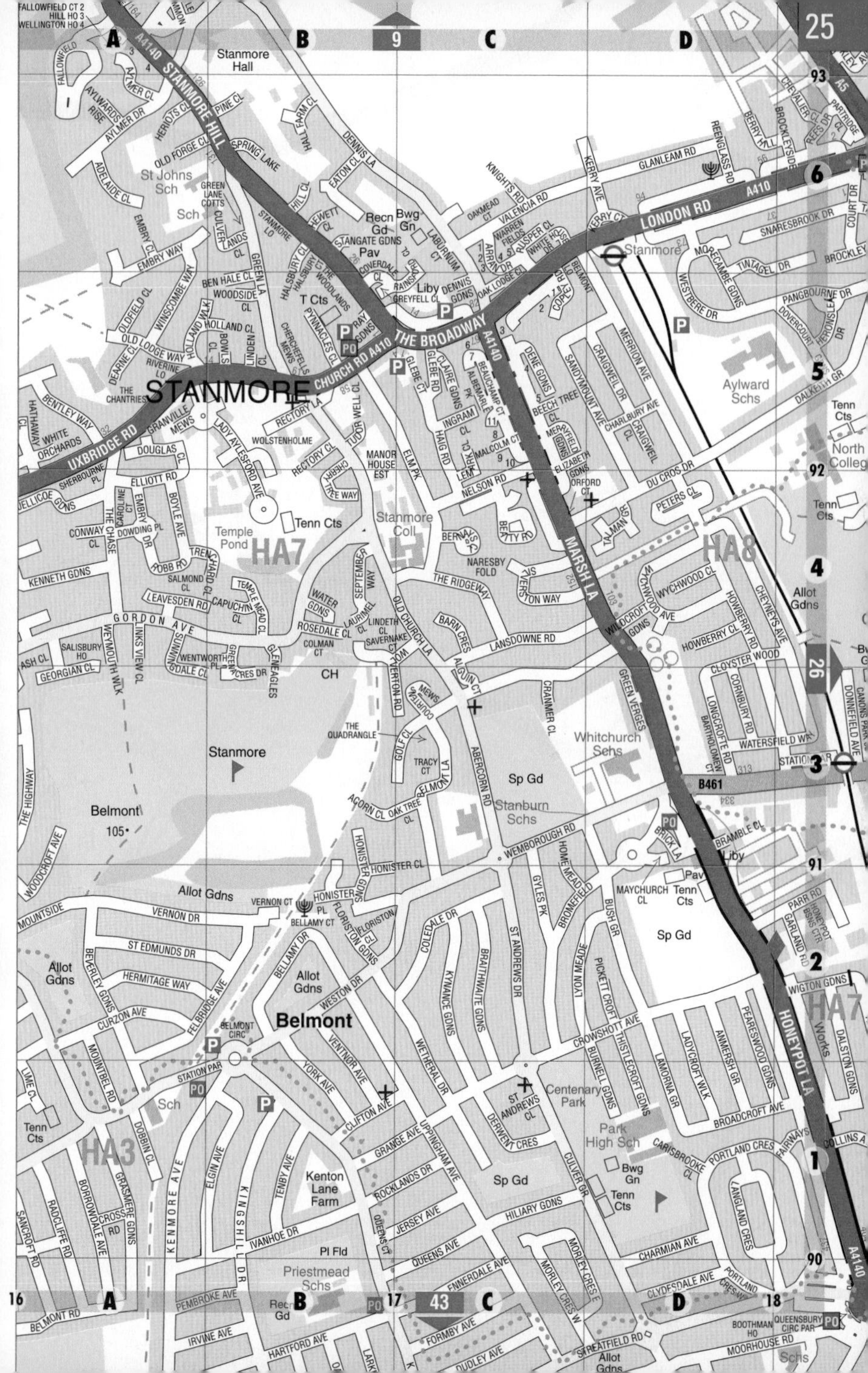
FALLOWFIELD CT 2
HILL HO 3
WELLINGTON HO 4
A
B
9
C
D
Stanmore Hall
STANMORE HILL
A4140
FALLOWFIELD
AYLMER CL
AYLWARDS RISE
AYLMER DR
HERIOTS CL
PINE CL
HALL FARM CL
DENNIS LA
SPRING LAKE
OLD FORGE CL
ADELAIDE CL
St Johns Sch
GREEN LANE COTTS
Sch
EMBRY CL
EMBRY WAY
CULVER LANDS
STANMORE LO
HILL CL
EATON CL
HEWETT CL
Recn Gd
Bwg Gn
STANGATE GDNS
Pav
LABURNUM CT
KNIGHTS RD
OAKMEAD CT
VALENCIA RD
WARREN FIELDS
RUSPER CL
ARRAN DR
WHITE HOUSE DR
KERRY AVE
KERRY CT
GLANLEAM RD
REENGLASS RD
BERRY HILL
CREVALIER CL
BROCKLEYSIDE
PARTRIDGE
REES DR
93
A5
6
A410
LONDON RD
SNARESBROOK DR
COURT DR
Stanmore
MORECAMBE GDNS
TINTAGEL DR
BROCKLEY
WESTBERE DR
PANGBOURNE DR
DOVERCOURT
HERONSLEA DR
BEN HALE CL
GREEN LA
HALSBURY CL
HALSBURY CT
THE WOODLANDS
COVERDALE
RAINSFORD
Liby
DENNIS GDNS
GREYFELL CL
OAK LODGE CL
BELMONT LO
COPLEY RD
WOODSIDE CL
T Cts
OLDFIELD CL
WINSCOMBE WAY
HOLLAND WLK
HOLLAND CL
PYNNACLES CL
RAY GDNS
CHERCHEFELLS MEWS
OLD LODGE WAY
DEARNE CL
BOWLS CL
LINDEN CL
RIVERINE LO
CHURCH RD A410
THE BROADWAY
GLEBE CT
GLEBE RD
CLAIRE GDNS
BEAUCHAMP CT
ALBEMARLE PK
DENE GDNS
SANDYMOUNT AVE
CRAIGWELL DR
MERRION AVE
5
Aylward Schs
DALKEITH GR
THE CHANTRIES
STANMORE
RECTORY LA
TUDOR WELL CL
INGRAM CL
HAIG RD
BEECH TREE CL
CHARLBURY AVE
CRAIGWELL CL
Tenn Cts
North Colleg
HATHAWAY CL
BENTLEY WAY
WHITE ORCHARDS
UXBRIDGE RD
GRANVILLE MEWS
LADY AYLESFORD AVE
WOLSTENHOLME
RECTORY CL
MANOR HOUSE EST
ELM PK
PARK CL
LEMON
MALCOLM CT
MERAYFIELD GDNS
ELIZABETH GDNS
DU CROS DR
92
SHERBOURNE PL
DOUGLAS CL
ELLIOTT RD
BOYLE AVE
JELLICOE GDNS
CAROLINE CT
EMBRY DR
DOWDING PL
CONWAY CL
THE CHASE
CHERRY TREE WAY
NELSON RD
ORFORD CT
PETERS CL
Temple Pond
HA7
Tenn Cts
Stanmore Coll
BERNAYS CL
BEATTY RD
TALMAN GR
HA8
ROBB RD
TRENCHARD CL
KENNETH GDNS
SALMOND CL
TEMPLE MEAD CL
CAPUCHIN CL
SEPTEMBER WAY
WATER GDNS
NARESBY FOLD
THE RIDGEWAY
VERSTON WAY
MARSH LA
WYCHWOOD CL
WYCHWOOD AVE
CHEYNEYS AVE
4
Allot Gdns
LEAVESDEN RD
GORDON AVE
ROSEDALE CL
LAURIMEL CL
LINDETH CL
SAVERNAKE CT
BARN CRES
LANSDOWNE RD
WILDCROFT GDNS
HOWBERRY RD
HOWBERRY CL
SALISBURY HO
ASH CL
GEORGIAN CL
WEYMOUTH WLK
LINKS VIEW CL
SUNNINGDALE CL
WENTWORTH PL
GREENACRES DR
GLENEAGLES
COLMAN CT
CH
OLD CHURCH LA
MOW
OVERTON RD
ALCUIN CT
CRANMER CL
GREEN VERGES
CLOYSTER WOOD
CORNBURY RD
LONGCROFTE RD
BARTHOLOMEW CT
26
DONNEFIELD AVE
CANONS PARK CL
COURTENAY MEWS
THE QUADRANGLE
GOLF CL
TRACY CT
BELMONT LA
ABERCORN RD
Whitchurch Schs
WATERSFIELD WAY
STATION PAR
3
Stanmore
Sp Gd
B461
THE HIGHWAY
Belmont
105
ACORN CL
OAK TREE CL
Stanburn Schs
WEMBOROUGH RD
HOME MEAD
BRICK LA
BRAMBLE CL
Liby
WOODCROFT AVE
HONISTER GDNS
HONISTER CL
GYLES PK
BROMEFIELD
Pav
MAYCHURCH CL
Tenn Cts
91
Allot Gdns
VERNON CT
HONISTER PL
BELLAMY CT
FLORISTON GDNS
FLORISTON CL
COLEDALE DR
ST ANDREWS DR
BUSH GR
PARR RD
GARLAND RD
HONEYPOT BSNS CTR
MOUNTSIDE
VERNON DR
ST EDMUNDS DR
HERMITAGE WAY
BEVERLEY GDNS
Allot Gdns
BELLAMY DR
Allot Gdns
KYNANCE GDNS
BRAITHWAITE GDNS
LYON MEADE
PICKETT CROFT
Sp Gd
2
WIGTON GDNS
HA7
Works
CURZON AVE
FELBRIDGE AVE
MOUNTBEL RD
BELMONT CIRC
Belmont
WESTON DR
VENTNOR AVE
WETHERAL DR
CROWSHOTT AVE
BURNELL GDNS
THISTLECROFT GDNS
LAMORNA GR
LADYCROFT WLK
AMMERSH GR
PEARESWOOD GDNS
HONEYPOT LA
DALSTON GDNS
LIME CL
STATION PAR
Sch
YORK AVE
CLIFTON AVE
ST ANDREWS CL
Centenary Park
Tenn Cts
DOBBIN CL
HA3
KENMORE AVE
ELGIN AVE
KINGSHILL DR
TENBY AVE
GRANGE AVE
UPPINGHAM AVE
DERWENT CRES
Park High Sch
CARISBROOKE CL
PORTLAND CRES
FAIRWAYS
BROADCROFT AVE
COLLINS AVE
1
SANCROFT RD
RADCLIFFE RD
BORROWDALE AVE
CROSS RD
GRASMERE GDNS
Kenton Lane Farm
ROCKLANDS DR
Sp Gd
CULVER GR
Bwg Gn
Tenn Cts
LANGLAND CRES
JERSEY AVE
HILIARY GDNS
QUEENS CT
IVANHOE DR
Pl Fld
QUEENS AVE
CHARMIAN AVE
MORLEY CRES
90
A4140
Priestmead Schs
ENNERDALE AVE
CLYDESDALE AVE
PORTLAND CRES
16
A
PEMBROKE AVE
B
Recn Gd
17
43
C
MORLEY CRES W
MORLEY CRES E
D
18
BELMONT RD
IRVINE AVE
HARTFORD AVE
FORMBY AVE
DUDLEY AVE
STREATFIELD RD
Allot Gdns
BOOTHMAN HO
QUEENSBURY CIRC PAR
MOORHOUSE RD
Schs

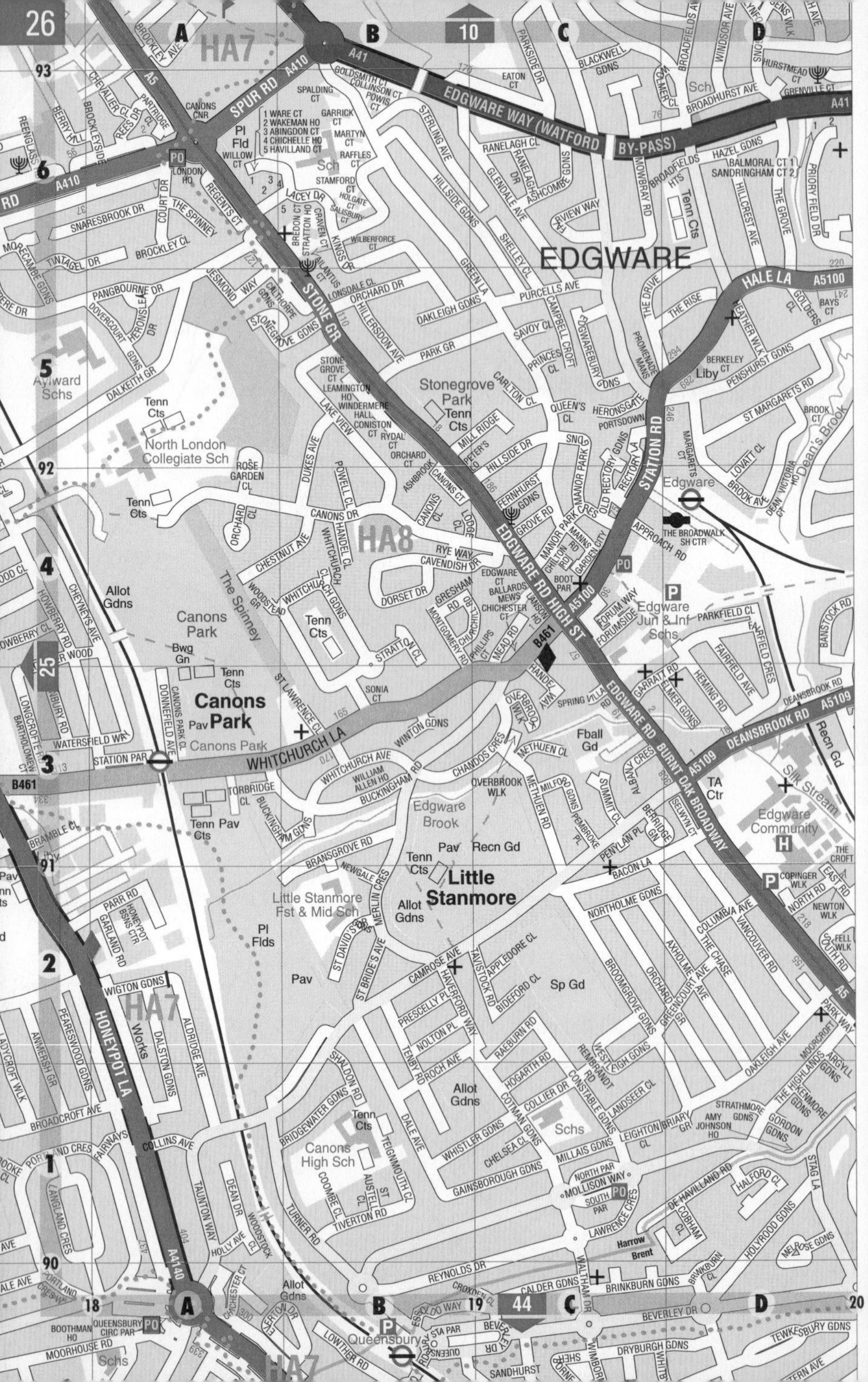

A
B
C
D
10
HA7
A5
A410
A41
SPUR RD
EDGWARE WAY (WATFORD BY-PASS)
EDGWARE
HALE LA
A5100
STONE GR
STATION RD
EDGWARE RD HIGH ST
EDGWARE RD BURNT OAK BROADWAY
DEANSBROOK RD
A5109
WHITCHURCH LA
B461
HA8
Stonegrove Park
North London Collegiate Sch
Aylward Schs
Canons Park
Canons Park
Little Stanmore
Little Stanmore Fst & Mid Sch
Edgware Brook
Edgware Jun & Inf Schs
Edgware Community
Edgware
THE BROADWALK SH CTR
HONEYPOT LA
A4140
Canons High Sch
Queensbury
Harrow
Brent
44
25
93
92
91
90
6
5
4
3
2
1
18
19
20

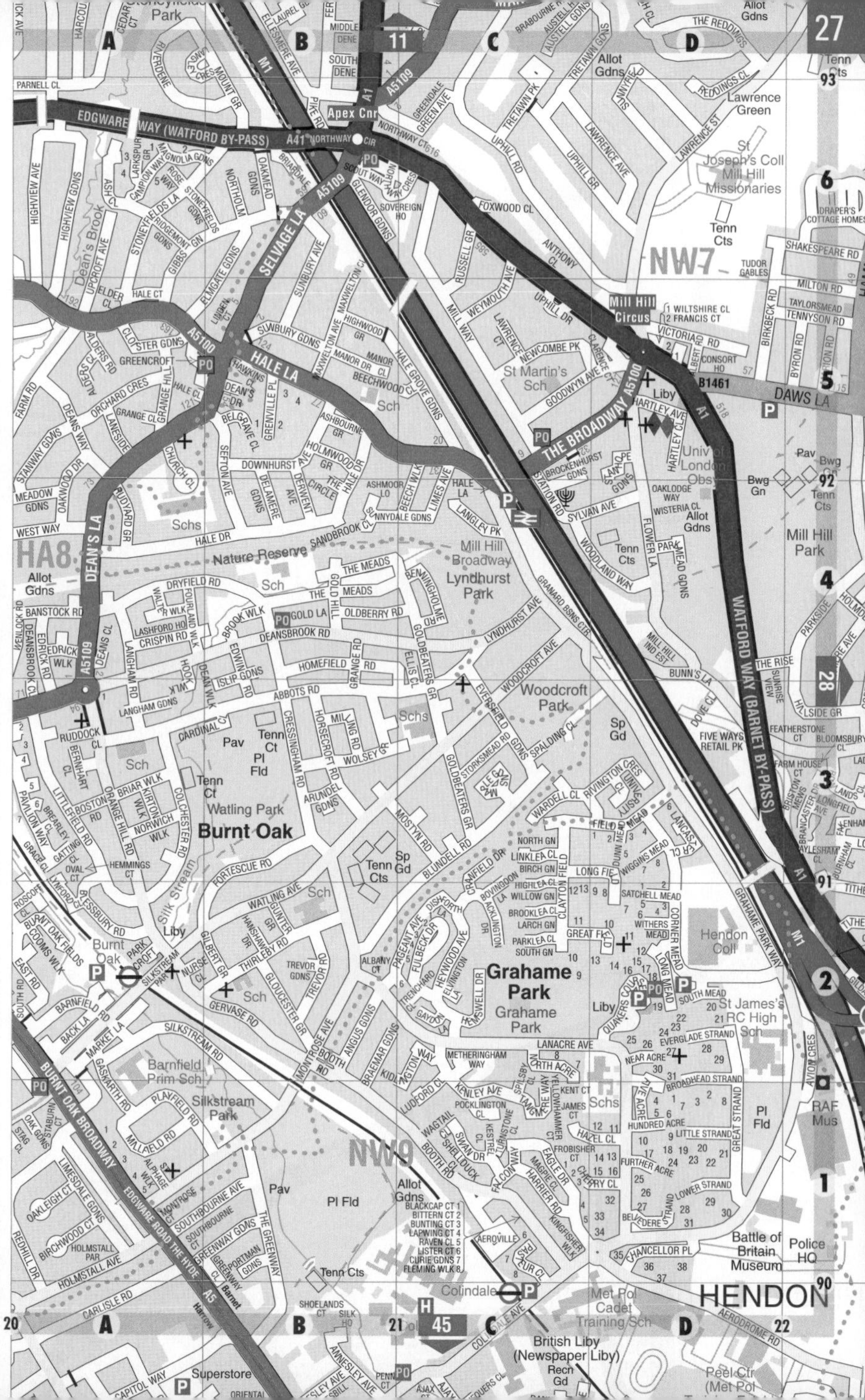

27
A
B
C
D
11
Apex Cnr
EDGWARE WAY (WATFORD BY-PASS)
A41
NORTHWAY CIR
M1
A1
A5109
A5100
A1
A5
Mill Hill Circus
1 WILTSHIRE CL
2 FRANCIS CT
NW7
HA8
NW9
HENDON
Burnt Oak
Grahame Park
Lawrence Green
St Joseph's Coll Mill Hill Missionaries
Allot Gdns
Tenn Cts
PARNELL CL
HIGHVIEW AVE
HIGHVIEW GDNS
Dean's Brook
UPCROFT AVE
STONEYFIELDS LA
SELVAGE LA
HALE LA
DEAN'S LA
HALE DR
SANDBROOK CL
Nature Reserve
Mill Hill Broadway
Lyndhurst Park
THE BROADWAY
DAWS LA
B1461
WATFORD WAY (BARNET BY-PASS)
Univ of London Obsy
Bwg Gn
Pav
Mill Hill Park
TUDOR GABLES
SHAKESPEARE RD
MILTON RD
TAYLORSMEAD
TENNYSON RD
BIRKBECK RD
BYRON RD
DRAPER'S COTTAGE HOMES
THE REDDINGS
REDDINGS CL
LAWRENCE ST
LAWRENCE AVE
UPHILL GR
UPHILL RD
TRETAWN GDNS
TRETAWN PK
FOXWOOD CL
ANTHONY CL
UPHILL DR
RUSSELL GR
WEYMOUTH AVE
MILL WAY
LAWRENCE CT
NEWCOMBE PK
St Martin's Sch
GOODWYN AVE
CLARENCE CT
VICTORIA RD
CONSORT HO
ALBERT RD
HARTLEY AVE
HARTLEY CL
BROCKENHURST GDNS
STATION RD
SYLVAN AVE
WOODLAND WAY
FLOWER LA
PARK MEAD GDNS
OAKLODGE WAY
WISTERIA CL
GRANARD BSNS CTR
MILL HILL IND EST
BUNN'S LA
DOVE CL
FIVE WAYS RETAIL PK
THE RISE
SUNRISE VIEW
HILLSIDE GR
FEATHERSTONE CT
BLOOMSBURY CL
FARM HOUSE CT
BRISTOW MEWS
BRANCASTER RD
LONGFIELD AVE
AYLESHAM
BURNHAM CL
PARKSIDE
HOLMDENE
28
Woodcroft Park
WOODCROFT AVE
LYNDHURST AVE
EVERSFIELD GDNS
SPALDING CL
STORKSMEAD RD
GOLDBEATERS GR
Sp Gd
RIVINGTON CRES
UNIVERSITY CL
WARDELL CL
FIELD MEAD
DUNN MEAD
LANCASTER CL
NORTH GN
LINKLEA CL
BIRCH GN
LONG FIELD
WIGGINS MEAD
HIGHLEA CL
WILLOW GN
SATCHELL MEAD
BROOKLEA CL
LARCH GN
WITHERS MEAD
PARKLEA CL
GREAT FIELD
SOUTH GN
CORNER MEAD
LONG MEAD
CLAYTON FIELD
Hendon Coll
GRAHAME PARK WAY
QUAKERS COURSE
SOUTH MEAD
St James's RC High Sch
LANACRE AVE
NORTH ACRE
NEAR ACRE
EVERGLADE STRAND
BROADHEAD STRAND
FIVE ACRE
HUNDRED ACRE
LITTLE STRAND
FURTHER ACRE
GREAT STRAND
LOWER STRAND
BELVEDERE STRAND
CHANCELLOR PL
Battle of Britain Museum
Police HQ
RAF Mus
AVION CRES
Pl Fld
AERODROME RD
Met Pol Cadet Training Sch
Colindale
COLINDALE AVE
British Liby (Newspaper Liby)
Rech Gd
Peel Ctr (Met Pol)
45
Superstore
CAPITOL WAY
ANNESLEY AVE
SHOELANDS CT
SILK HO
Tenn Cts
AEROVILLE
KINGFISHER WALK
HARRIER RD
MAGPIE CL
EAGLE DR
CHERRY CL
FROBISHER CT
HAZEL CL
JAMES CT
LOWTHER CL
FALCON WAY
TURNSTONE CL
KESTREL CL
SWAN DR
SHELDUCK CL
WAGTAIL CL
BOOTH RD
POCKLINGTON CL
KENLEY AVE
METHERINGHAM WAY
SPILSBY CL
TANGMERE WAY
KENT CT
LUDFORD CL
KIDDINGTON WAY
BLACKCAP CT 1
BITTERN CT 2
BUNTING CT 3
LAPWING CT 4
RAVEN CL 5
LISTER CT 6
CURIE GDNS 7
FLEMING WLK 8
Allot Gdns
Pl Fld
Pav
Silkstream Park
Barnfield Prim Sch
BURNT OAK BROADWAY
EDGWARE ROAD THE HYDE
THE GREENWAY
SOUTHBOURNE AVE
SOUTHBOURNE GDNS
GREENWAY GDNS
PORTMAN GDNS
CARLISLE RD
HOLMSTALL AVE
HOLMSTALL PAR
BIRCHWOOD CT
OAKLEIGH CT
LIMESDALE GDNS
REDHILL DR
STAG CL
MILLFIELD RD
PLAYFIELD RD
GASKARTH RD
SILKSTREAM RD
MARKET LA
BACK LA
BARNFIELD RD
GERVASE RD
THIRLEBY RD
GLOUCESTER GR
TREVOR RD
TREVOR GDNS
ALBANY CT
PAGEANT AVE
FULBECK DR
HEYWOOD AVE
HEMSWELL DR
CRANFIELD DR
BOVINGDON LA
ACKLINGTON DR
MONTROSE AVE
ANGUS GDNS
BRAEMAR GDNS
WATLING AVE
FORTESCUE RD
BLUNDELL RD
MOSTYN RD
Watling Park
Silk Stream
Liby
HAMPTON CL
BLESSBURY RD
EAST RD
SOUTH RD
COOMS WLK
BURNT OAK FIELDS
ROSCOFF CL
GRACE CL
PAVILION WAY
OVAL CT
GATTING CL
HEMMINGS CT
COLCHESTER RD
NORWICH WLK
KIRKTON WLK
BRIAR WLK
ORANGE HILL RD
BOSTON RD
LITTLEFIELD RD
BERNHART CL
RUDDOCK CL
CARDINAL CL
Watling Park
CRESSINGHAM RD
HORSECROFT RD
MILLING RD
WOLSEY GR
ARUNDEL GDNS
ABBOTS RD
LANGHAM GDNS
LANGHAM RD
ISLIP GDNS
HOMEFIELD RD
GRANGE RD
ELLIS CL
DEANSBROOK RD
CRISPIN RD
LASHFORD HO
WALTER WLK
FOULAND WLK
BROOK WLK
GOLD LA
OLDBERRY RD
GOLD HILL
THE MEADS
BENNINGHOLME RD
DRYFIELD RD
BANSTOCK RD
EDRICK WLK
DEANSBROOK CL
DEANS CL
WEST WAY
MEADOW GDNS
OAKWOOD DR
STANWAY GDNS
DEANS WAY
FARM RD
ALDERS RD
ORCHARD CRES
LANESIDE
GRANGE CL
CHURCH CL
RUDYARD GR
DOWNHURST AVE
SEFTON AVE
DELAMERE GDNS
DERWENT AVE
HOLMWOOD GR
THE CIRCLE
THE HALE DR
ASHBOURNE GR
ASHMOOR LO
BEECH WLK
LIMES AVE
HALE LA
LANGLEY PK
SUNNYDALE GDNS
HALE GROVE GDNS
BEECHWOOD CL
MANOR DR
MAXWELTON AVE
HIGHWOOD GR
SUNBURY GDNS
SUNBURY AVE
GLENDOR GDNS
SOVEREIGN HO
SCOUT WAY
BRIARDALE
OAKMEAD GDNS
NORTHOLM
STONEYFIELDS GDNS
RIDGEMONT GDNS
GIBBS GN
ELMGATE GDNS
LINDEN CT
HALE CT
ELDER CL
GREENCROFT
HAWKINS CL
DEAN'S DR
BELGRAVE CL
GRENVILLE PL
MAGNOLIA GDNS
CAMPION WAY
LARKSPUR GR
ROSE WAY
ASH CL
GREENDALE
GREEN AVE
PIKE RD
ELLESMERE AVE
LAUREL GDNS
MIDDLE DENE
SOUTH DENE
BRABOURNE HTS
AUSTELL GDNS
MOUNT GR
RIVERDENE
Stoneyfields Park
HARCOURT AVE
CEDAR CT
20
21
22
90
91
92
93
1
2
3
4
5
6

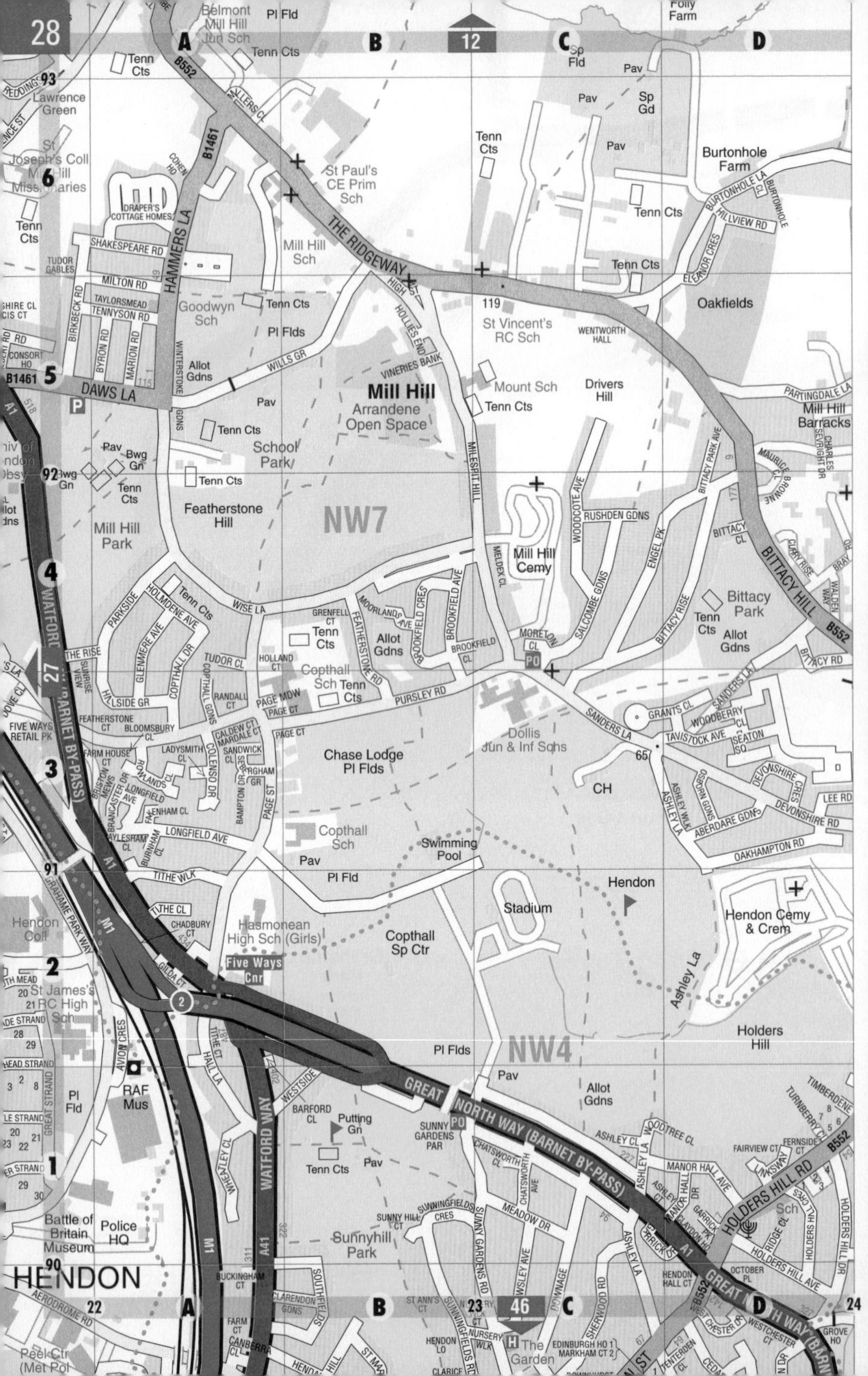
A
B
12
C
D
Belmont
Mill Hill
Jun Sch
Pl Fld
Folly
Farm
Tenn Cts
Sp Fld
Pav
Sp Gd
B552
93
Lawrence Green
St Joseph's Coll
Mill Hill Missionaries
6
Tenn Cts
B1461
St Paul's CE Prim Sch
Mill Hill Sch
THE RIDGEWAY
Burtonhole Farm
BURTONHOLE LA
HILLVIEW RD
DRAPER'S COTTAGE HOMES
HAMMERS LA
SHAKESPEARE RD
TUDOR GABLES
MILTON RD
TAYLORSMEAD
TENNYSON RD
BIRKBECK RD
BYRON RD
MARION RD
Goodwyn Sch
Pl Flds
HIGH ST
HOLLIES END
119
St Vincent's RC Sch
WENTWORTH HALL
ELEANOR CRES
Oakfields
5
B1461
DAWS LA
WILLS GR
Allot Gdns
VINERIES BANK
Mill Hill
Arrandene Open Space
Mount Sch
Drivers Hill
PARTINGDALE LA
Mill Hill Barracks
P
Pav
Bwg Gn
92
School Park
Featherstone Hill
NW7
MILESPIT HILL
WOODCOTE AVE
RUSHDEN GDNS
BITTACY PARK AVE
BITTACY CL
BITTACY HILL
Mill Hill Park
Mill Hill Cemy
MELDEX CL
ENGEL PK
SALCOMBE GDNS
BITTACY RISE
Bittacy Park
Allot Gdns
B552
4
WATFORD WAY (BARNET BY-PASS)
WISE LA
PARKSIDE
HOLMDENE AVE
GLENMERE AVE
COPTHALL DR
TUDOR CL
THE RISE
GRENFELL CT
MOORLAND AVE
FEATHERSTONE RD
BROOKFIELD CRES
BROOKFIELD AVE
BROOKFIELD CL
MORETON CL
PO
BITTACY RD
27
Copthall Sch
HOLLAND CT
PAGE MDW
PAGE CT
PURSLEY RD
SANDERS LA
GRANTS CL
WOODBERRY
TAVISTOCK AVE
SEATON SQ
FIVE WAYS RETAIL PK
FEATHERSTONE CT
BLOOMSBURY CL
Dollis Jun & Inf Schs
65
Chase Lodge Pl Flds
3
LADYSMITH CL
COLENSO DR
BAMPTON DR
PAGE ST
CH
DEVONSHIRE CRES
DEVONSHIRE RD
LEE RD
ASHLEY LA
ABERDARE GDNS
OAKHAMPTON RD
LONGFIELD AVE
Copthall Sch
Swimming Pool
Pav
91
A1
TITHE WLK
Pl Fld
Hendon
Stadium
Hendon Cemy & Crem
Hendon Coll
THE CL
CHADBURY CT
M1
GRAHAME PARK WAY
Hasmonean High Sch (Girls)
Copthall Sp Ctr
2
Five Ways Cnr
St James's RC High Sch
Ashley La
Holders Hill
AVION CRES
HALL LA
WATFORD WAY
NW4
Pl Flds
Pav
RAF Mus
GREAT NORTH WAY (BARNET BY-PASS)
Allot Gdns
Pl Fld
BARFORD CL
Putting Gn
SUNNY GARDENS PAR
WESTSIDE
1
Tenn Cts
WHEATLEY CL
CHATSWORTH AVE
MANOR HALL AVE
HOLDERS HILL RD
FAIRVIEW CT
TIMBERDENE
Battle of Britain Museum
Police HQ
Sunnyhill Park
MEADOW DR
SUNNY GARDENS RD
SHERWOOD RD
ASHLEY LA
A41
M1
Sch
HOLDERS HILL AVE
OCTOBER PL
HOLDERS HILL DR
90
HENDON
AERODROME RD
22
A
B
23
46
C
D
24
BUCKINGHAM CT
CLARENDON GDNS
SOUTHFIELDS
FARM CT
CANBERRA CL
NURSERY WLK
H
The Garden
EDINBURGH HO
MARKHAM CT
HENDON HALL CT
WESTCHESTER DR
GROVE HO
Peel Ctr (Met Pol

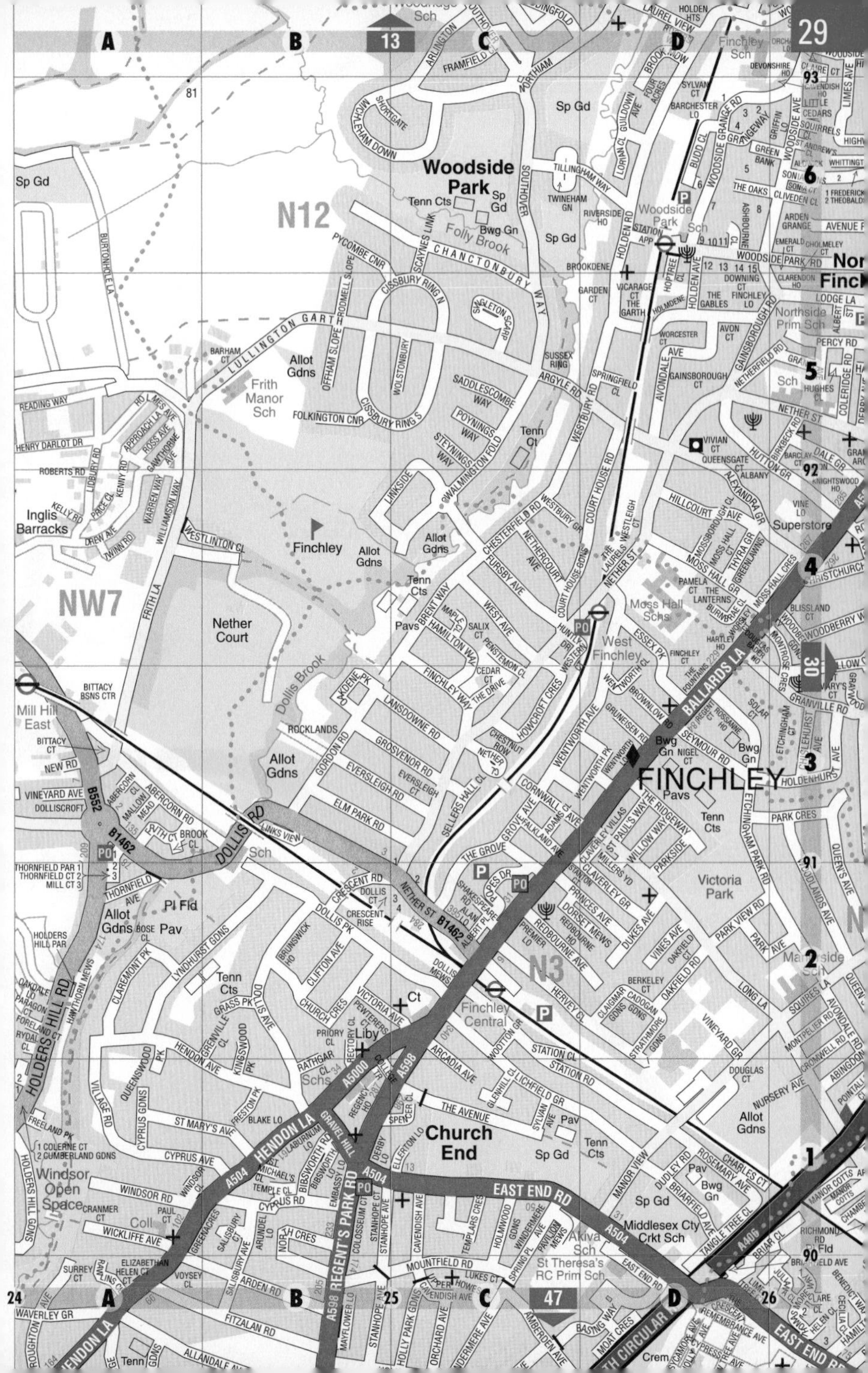
A
B
C
D
13
47
30
24
25
26
1
2
3
4
5
6
Woodside Park
N12
NW7
N3
FINCHLEY
Church End
Finchley
Nether Court
Frith Manor Sch
Inglis Barracks
Mill Hill East
West Finchley
Finchley Central
Woodside Park
Victoria Park
Windsor Open Space
Middlesex Cty Crkt Sch
St Theresa's RC Prim Sch
Akiva Sch
Moss Hall Schs
Northside Prim Sch
Folly Brook
Dollis Brook
BALLARDS LA
EAST END RD
REGENT'S PARK RD
HENDON LA
HOLDERS HILL RD
DOLLIS RD
NETHER ST
HOLDEN RD
CHANCTONBURY WAY
LULLINGTON GARTH
WOODSIDE PARK RD
ARGYLE RD
WESTBURY RD
COURT HOUSE RD
HENDON AVE
STATION RD
LONG LA
Superstore
Allot Gdns
Sp Gd
Tenn Cts

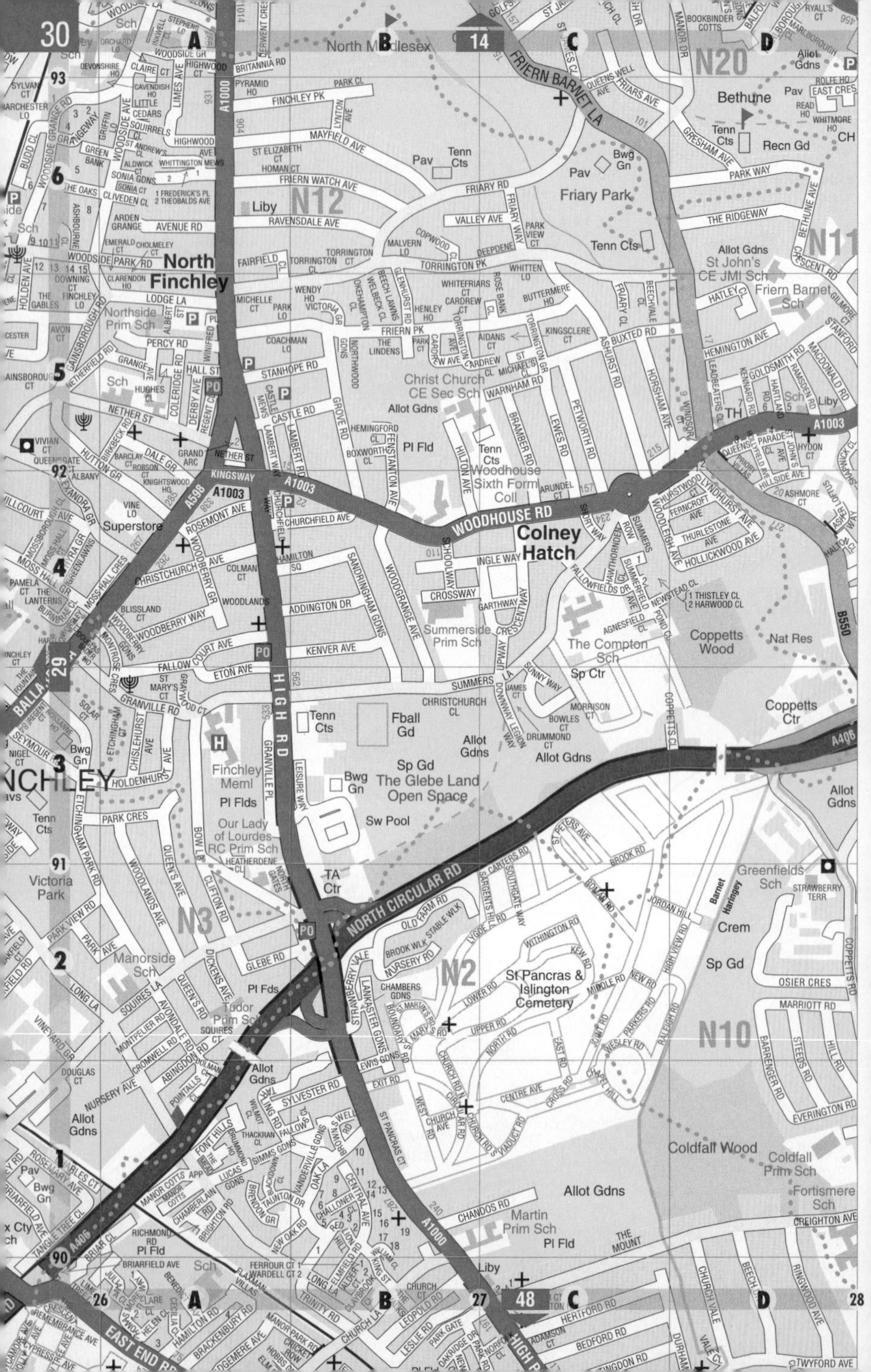
A
B
C
D
14
North Middlesex
N20
Bethune
Recn Gd
Friary Park
FRIERN BARNET LA
N12
Liby
North
Finchley
Northside
Prim Sch
Christ Church
CE Sec Sch
Allot Gdns
Pl Fld
Woodhouse
Sixth Form
Coll
WOODHOUSE RD
Colney
Hatch
Summerside
Prim Sch
The Compton
Sch
Coppetts
Wood
Nat Res
Coppetts
Ctr
St John's
CE JMI Sch
Friern Barnet
Sch
N11
Superstore
HIGH RD
Fball
Gd
Sp Gd
The Glebe Land
Open Space
Sw Pool
Finchley
Meml
Our Lady
of Lourdes
RC Prim Sch
TA
Ctr
NORTH CIRCULAR RD
N3
Victoria
Park
Manorside
Sch
Tudor
Prim Sch
N2
St Pancras &
Islington
Cemetery
Greenfields
Sch
Crem
N10
Coldfall Wood
Coldfall
Prim Sch
Fortismere
Sch
Martin
Prim Sch
ST PANCRAS CT
EAST END RD
KINGSWAY
A1000
A1003
A598
A406
B550
29
48
26
27
28
1
2
3
4
5
6
90
91
92
93

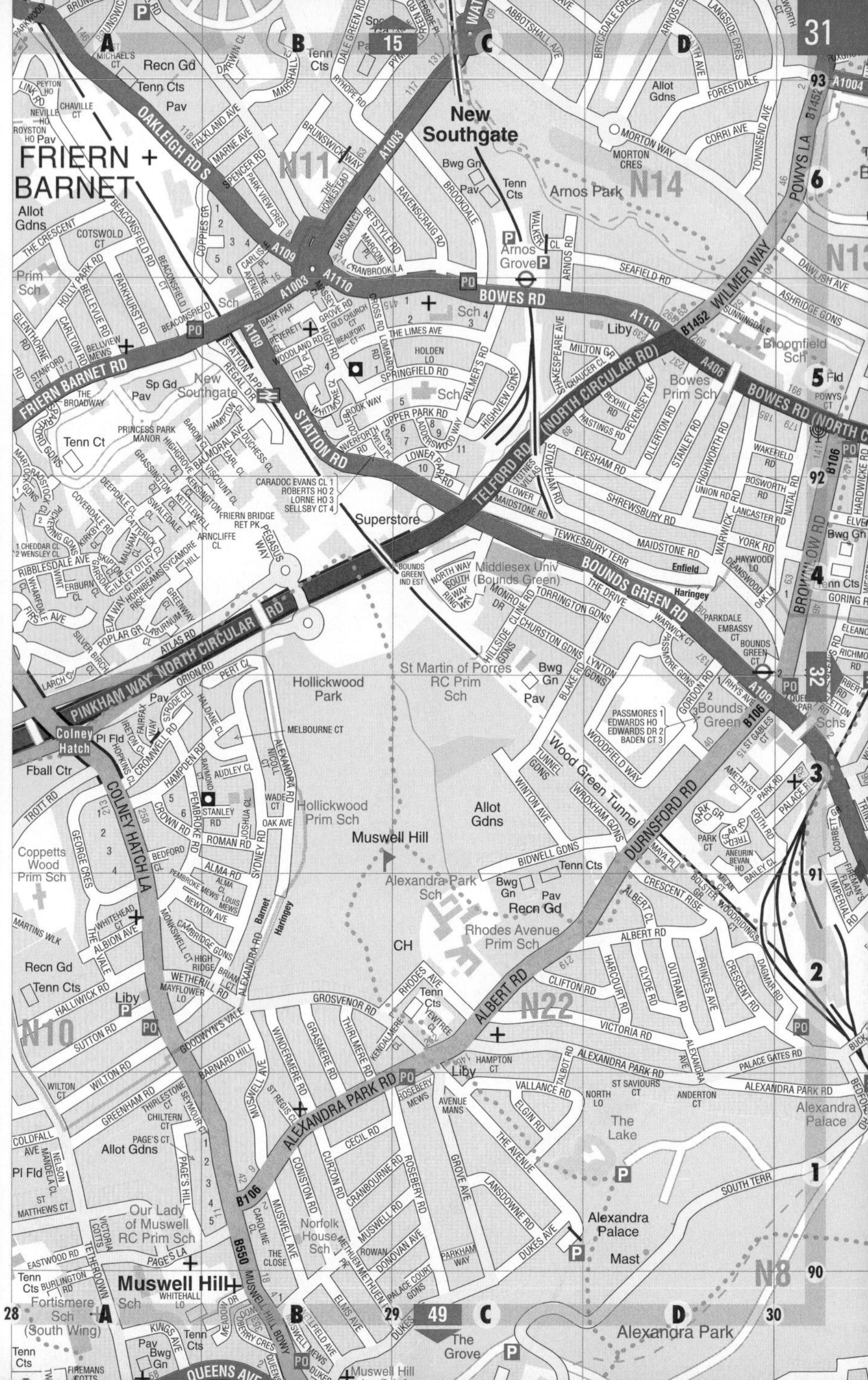

FRIERN BARNET
New Southgate
Arnos Park
N11
N14
N13
N22
N10
N8
Muswell Hill
Alexandra Palace
Alexandra Park
Hollickwood Park
Bounds Green
Colney Hatch
OAKLEIGH RD S
FRIERN BARNET RD
BOWES RD
STATION RD
TELFORD RD (NORTH CIRCULAR RD)
PINKHAM WAY NORTH CIRCULAR RD
BOUNDS GREEN RD
COLNEY HATCH LA
ALEXANDRA PARK RD
ALBERT RD
DURNSFORD RD
MUSWELL HILL BDWY
WILMER WAY
POWYS LA
BROWNLOW RD
Wood Green Tunnel
Middlesex Univ (Bounds Green)
St Martin of Porres RC Prim Sch
Hollickwood Prim Sch
Alexandra Park Sch
Rhodes Avenue Prim Sch
Coppetts Wood Prim Sch
Our Lady of Muswell RC Prim Sch
Norfolk House Sch
Fortismere Sch (South Wing)
Bowes Prim Sch
Bloomfield Sch
Superstore
The Lake
Mast
15
32
49
28
29
30

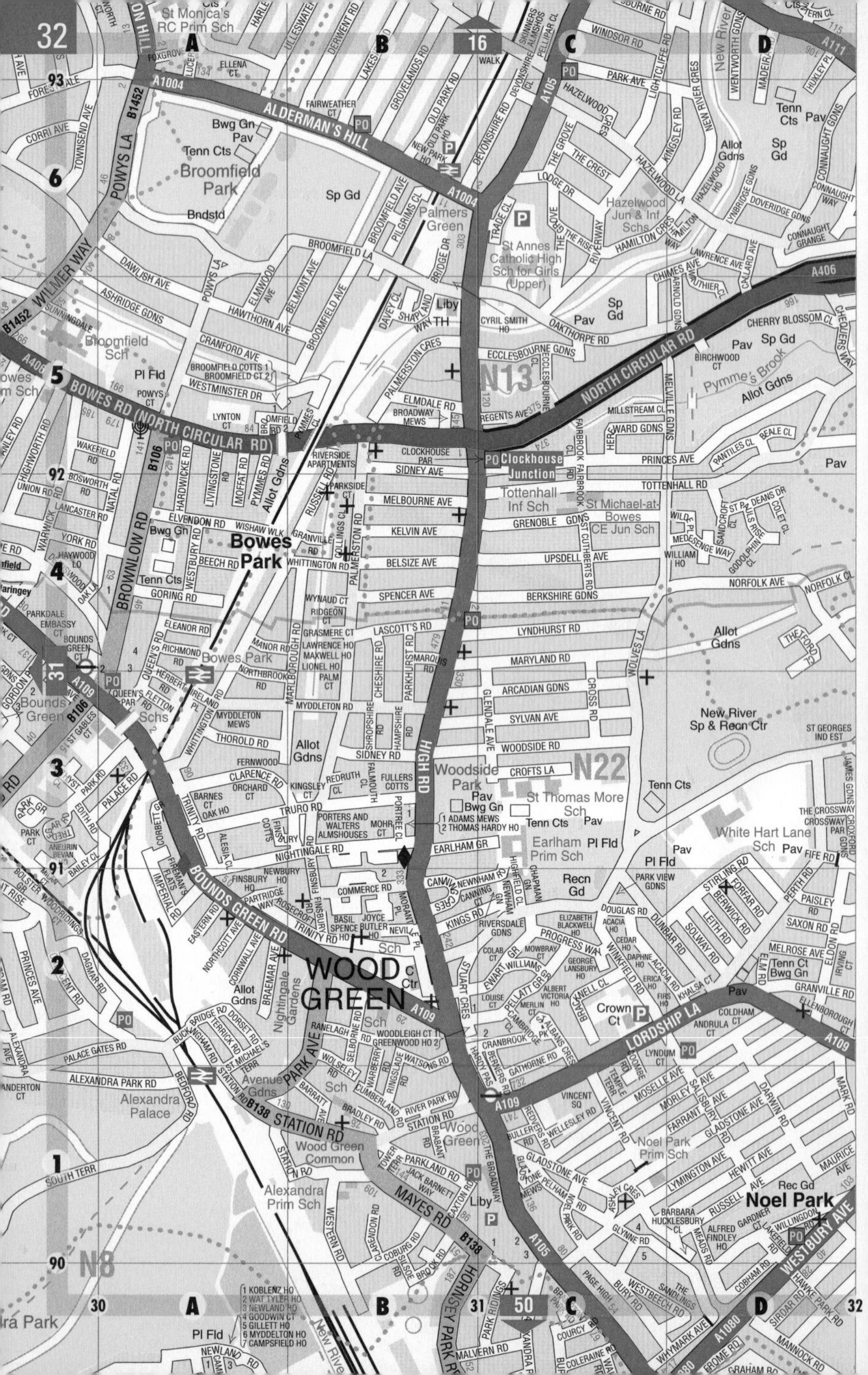
A
B
C
D
16
50
31
93
92
91
90
6
5
4
3
2
1
30
32
St Monica's RC Prim Sch
FOXGROVE
ELLENA CT
A1004
ALDERMAN'S HILL
FAIRWEATHER
PO
B1452
POWYS LA
CORRI AVE
TOWNSEND AVE
Bwg Gn Pav
Tenn Cts
Broomfield Park
Sp Gd
Bndstd
WILMER WAY
DAWLISH AVE
ASHRIDGE GDNS
SUNNINGDALE
Broomfield Sch
Pl Fld
A406
BOWES RD (NORTH CIRCULAR RD)
HAWTHORN AVE
CRANFORD AVE
BROOMFIELD COTTS 1
BROOMFIELD CT 2
WESTMINSTER DR
POWYS CT
LYNTON CT
ELMWOOD AVE
BELMONT AVE
BROOMFIELD AVE
BROOMFIELD LA
GROVELANDS RD
LAKESIDE
DERWENT RD
OLD PARK RD
NEW PARK HO
PILGRIMS CL
Palmers Green
BRIDGE DR
DEVONSHIRE RD
TRADE CL
St Annes Catholic High Sch for Girls (Upper)
WINDSOR RD
PARK AVE
HAZELWOOD CRES
LIGHTCLIFFE RD
KINGSLEY RD
NEW RIVER CRES
New River
WENTWORTH GDNS
MADEIRA
HUXLEY PL
A111
A105
THE GROVE
THE CREST
LODGE DR
RIVERWAY
THE RISE
HAZELWOOD LA
HAMILTON CRES
HAMILTON WAY
Hazelwood Jun & Inf Schs
Tenn Cts
Pav
Allot Gdns
Sp Gd
CONNAUGHT GDNS
LYNBRIDGE GDNS
DOVERIDGE GDNS
CONNAUGHT WAY
CONNAUGHT GRANGE
LAWRENCE AVE
CALLARD AVE
CHIMES AVE
ARNOLD GDNS
GAUTHIER CL
NORTH CIRCULAR RD
CHERRY BLOSSOM CL
CHEQUERS WAY
DAVEY CL
SHAPLAND WAY
Liby
TH
CYRIL SMITH HO
OAKTHORPE RD
Sp Gd
Pav
ECCLESBOURNE GDNS
ECCLESBOURNE CL
PALMERSTON CRES
N13
ELMDALE RD
BROADWAY MEWS
REGENTS AVE
BIRCHWOOD CT
Pymme's Brook
Allot Gdns
MILLSTREAM CL
MELVILLE GDNS
HEREWARD GDNS
FAIRBROOK CL
PANTILES CL
BEALE CL
PRINCES AVE
Pav
HIGHWORTH RD
WAKEFIELD RD
BOSWORTH RD
UNION RD
LANCASTER RD
NATAL RD
HARDWICKE RD
LIVINGSTONE RD
MOFFAT RD
PYMMES RD
Allot Gdns
PYMMES CL
RIVERSIDE APARTMENTS
CLOCKHOUSE PAR
Clockhouse Junction
SIDNEY AVE
PARKSIDE CT
RUSSELL RD
MELBOURNE AVE
Tottenhall Inf Sch
TOTTENHALL RD
St Michael-at-Bowes CE Jun Sch
GRENOBLE GDNS
ST CUTHBERTS RD
UPSDELL AVE
BERKSHIRE GDNS
NORFOLK AVE
NORFOLK CL
WILDE PL
MEDESENGE WAY
WILLIAM HO
SANDCROFT CL
DEANS DR
COLET CL
GODOLPHIN CL
ELVENDON RD
WISHAW WLK
WESTBURY RD
BEECH RD
Bwg Gn
Bowes Park
Tenn Cts
GORING RD
BROWNLOW RD
B106
WARWICK
YORK RD
HAYWOOD LO
OAK LA
GRANVILLE RD
COLLINGS CL
PALMERSTON RD
WHITTINGTON RD
KELVIN AVE
BELSIZE AVE
SPENCER AVE
WYNAUD CT
RIDGEON CT
GRASMERE CT
LAWRENCE HO
MAXWELL HO
LIONEL HO
PALM CT
LASCOTT'S RD
LYNDHURST RD
MARQUIS RD
MARYLAND RD
Allot Gdns
THE FORD CL
PARKDALE
EMBASSY CT
BOUNDS GREEN CT
ELEANOR RD
RICHMOND RD
QUEEN'S RD
HERBERT RD
IRELAND PL
MANOR RD
NORTHBROOK RD
Bowes Park
MARLBOROUGH RD
CHESHIRE RD
PARKHURST RD
ARCADIAN GDNS
CROSS RD
WOLVES LA
GLENDALE AVE
SYLVAN AVE
WOODSIDE RD
New River Sp & Recn Ctr
ST GEORGES IND EST
A109
Bounds Green
B106
ST GABLES CT
QUEEN'S PAR
FLETTON RD
Schs
MYDDLETON MEWS
THOROLD RD
WHITTINGTON RD
MYDDLETON RD
SHROPSHIRE RD
HAMPSHIRE RD
HIGH RD
SIDNEY RD
Allot Gdns
FERNWOOD
CLARENCE RD
ORCHARD CT
KINGSLEY CT
REDRUTH CL
FALMOUTH CL
FULLERS COTTS
Woodside Park
CROFTS LA
N22
Pav
Bwg Gn
St Thomas More Sch
Tenn Cts
Tenn Cts
PARK RD
PALACE RD
BARNES CT
OAK HO
TRINITY RD
TRURO RD
PORTERS AND WALTERS ALMSHOUSES
MOHR CT
PORTREE CL
1 ADAMS MEWS
2 THOMAS HARDY HO
Pav
THE CROSSWAY
CROSSWAY PAR
CROXFORD GDNS
White Hart Lane Sch
Pav
Pav
Pl Fld
FIFE RD
PARK CT
ANEURIN BEVAN CT
BAILEY CL
CORBETT GR
ALESIA CL
NIGHTINGALE RD
EARLHAM GR
Earlham Prim Sch
Pl Fld
HIGHFIELD CL
CHAPMAN GN
Recn Gd
PARK VIEW GDNS
STIRLING RD
FORFAR RD
PERTH RD
PAISLEY RD
SAXON RD
WOODRIDINGS CT
BOLSTER GR
FIREMAN'S FLATS
IMPERIAL RD
FINSBURY HO
NEWBURY HO
PARTRIDGE WAY
ROSECROFT
COMMERCE RD
CANNING CRES
NEWNHAM RD
CANNING CT
NEWNHAM
KINGS RD
BOUNDS GREEN RD
EASTERN RD
BASIL SPENCE HO
JOYCE BUTLER HO
NEVILLE PL
TRINITY RD
RIVERSDALE GDNS
ELIZABETH BLACKWELL HO
DOUGLAS RD
ACACIA HO
DUNBAR RD
BERWICK RD
LEITH RD
SOLWAY RD
PRINCES AVE
DAGMAR RD
NORTHCOTT AVE
CORNWALL AVE
BRAEMAR AVE
Sch
WOOD GREEN
C Ctr
STUART CRES
COLAB CT
EWART GR
MOWBRAY CT
WILLIAMS GR
PROGRESS WAY
GEORGE LANSBURY HO
CEDAR HO
DAPHNE HO
ERICA HO
FIRS HO
WINKFIELD RD
ACACIA RD
KHALSA CT
MELROSE AVE
ELM RD
Tenn Ct
Bwg Gn
ELDON RD
IRVING CT
GRANVILLE RD
Allot Gdns
Nightingale Gardens
LOUISE CT
PELLATT GR
ALBERT VICTORIA HO
MERLIN CT
BRACKNELL CL
Crown Ct
Pav
COLDHAM CT
ANDRULA CT
ELLENBOROUGH
LORDSHIP LA
ALEXANDRA
BUCKINGHAM RD
BRIDGE RD
DORSET RD
TERRICK RD
ST MICHAEL'S TERR
RANELAGH RD
SELBORNE RD
Sch
WOODLEIGH CT 1
GREENWOOD HO 2
CAMBRIDGE CT
ST ALBANS CRES
CRANBROOK
BERNERS RD
GATHORNE RD
LYNDUM CT
COOMBE RD
TEMPLE RD
PALACE GATES RD
PARK AVE
WOLSELEY RD
WARBERRY RD
RINGSLADE RD
WATSONS RD
HARDY PAS
MOSELLE AVE
MORLEY AVE
SALISBURY AVE
DARWIN RD
MARK RD
ALEXANDRA PARK RD
STATION RD
ANDERTON CT
Alexandra Palace
BEDFORD RD
Avenue Gdns
BARRATT AVE
CUMBERLAND RD
RIVER PARK RD
VINCENT SQ
VINCENT RD
WELLESLEY RD
FARRANT AVE
GLADSTONE AVE
B138
STATION RD
BRADLEY RD
STATION RD
BRABANT RD
Wood Green
Wood Green Common
REDVERS RD
BULLERS RD
Noel Park Prim Sch
SOUTH TERR
STATION CRES
TOWER TERR
PARKLAND RD
JACK BARNETT WAY
CAXTON RD
GLADSTONE AVE
GLADSTONE MEWS
PELHAM RD
NOEL PARK RD
ASHLEY CRES
LYMINGTON AVE
HEWITT AVE
MAURICE AVE
Rec Gd
Noel Park
Alexandra Prim Sch
WESTERN RD
MAYES RD
Liby
CLARENDON RD
COBURG RD
SILSOE RD
BROOK RD
HORNSEY PARK RD
THE BROADWAY
GLYNNE RD
BARBARA HUCKLESBURY CL
RUSSELL AVE
ALFRED FINDLEY HO
GARDNER CT
LAKEFIELD RD
WILLINGDON RD
WESTBURY AVE
N8
PAGE HIGH
WESTBEECH RD
THE SANDLINGS
MEADS RD
COBHAM RD
HAWKE PARK RD
SIRDAR RD
1 KOBLENZ HO
2 WAT TYLER HO
3 NEWLAND HO
4 GOODWIN CT
5 GILLETT HO
6 MYDDELTON HO
7 CAMPSFIELD HO
Pl Fld
NEWLAND RD
PARK RIDINGS
COURCY RD
COLERAINE RD
MALVERN RD
WHYMARK AVE
A1080
FROME RD
MANNOCK RD
GRAHAM RD

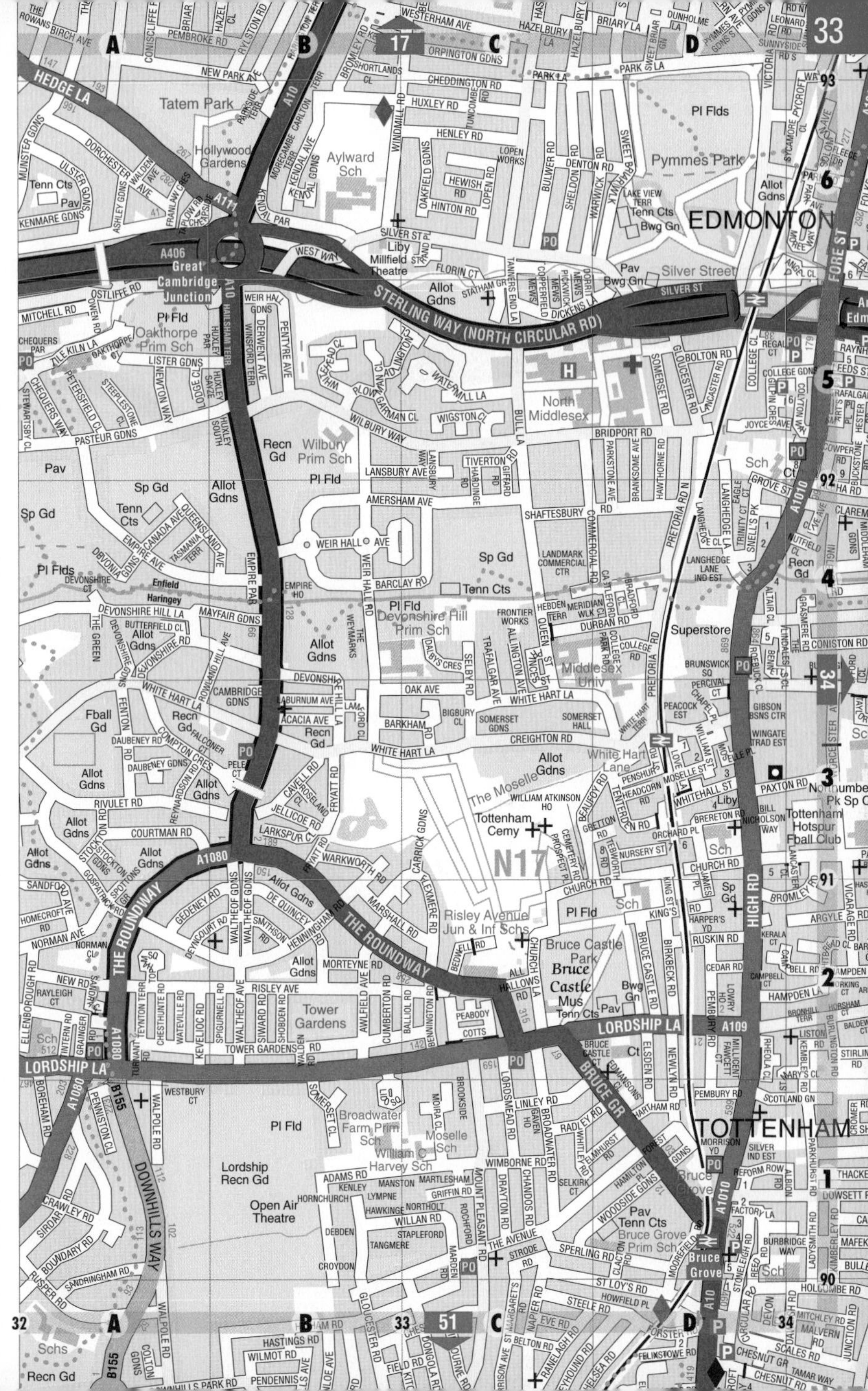

17
A
B
C
D
HEDGE LA
Tatem Park
Hollywood Gardens
Aylward Sch
Pymmes Park
Pl Flds
EDMONTON
Silver Street
A406
Great Cambridge Junction
STERLING WAY (NORTH CIRCULAR RD)
SILVER ST
Liby
Millfield Theatre
Allot Gdns
Oakthorpe Prim Sch
North Middlesex
Recn Gd
Wilbury Prim Sch
Pl Fld
Sp Gd
Tenn Cts
Pav
Enfield
Haringey
Devonshire Hill Prim Sch
Superstore
Middlesex Univ
White Hart Lane
The Moselle
Tottenham Cemy
N17
Tottenham Hotspur Fball Club
Northumberland Pk Sp C
Risley Avenue Jun & Inf Schs
Bruce Castle Park
Bruce Castle Mus
Tower Gardens
THE ROUNDWAY
A1080
A10
A1010
A109
HIGH RD
LORDSHIP LA
BRUCE GR
Broadwater Farm Prim Sch
Moselle Sch
William C Harvey Sch
Lordship Recn Gd
Open Air Theatre
TOTTENHAM
Bruce Grove
Bruce Grove Prim Sch
DOWNHILLS WAY
B155
34
51
32
33
6
5
4
3
2
1
93
92
91
90

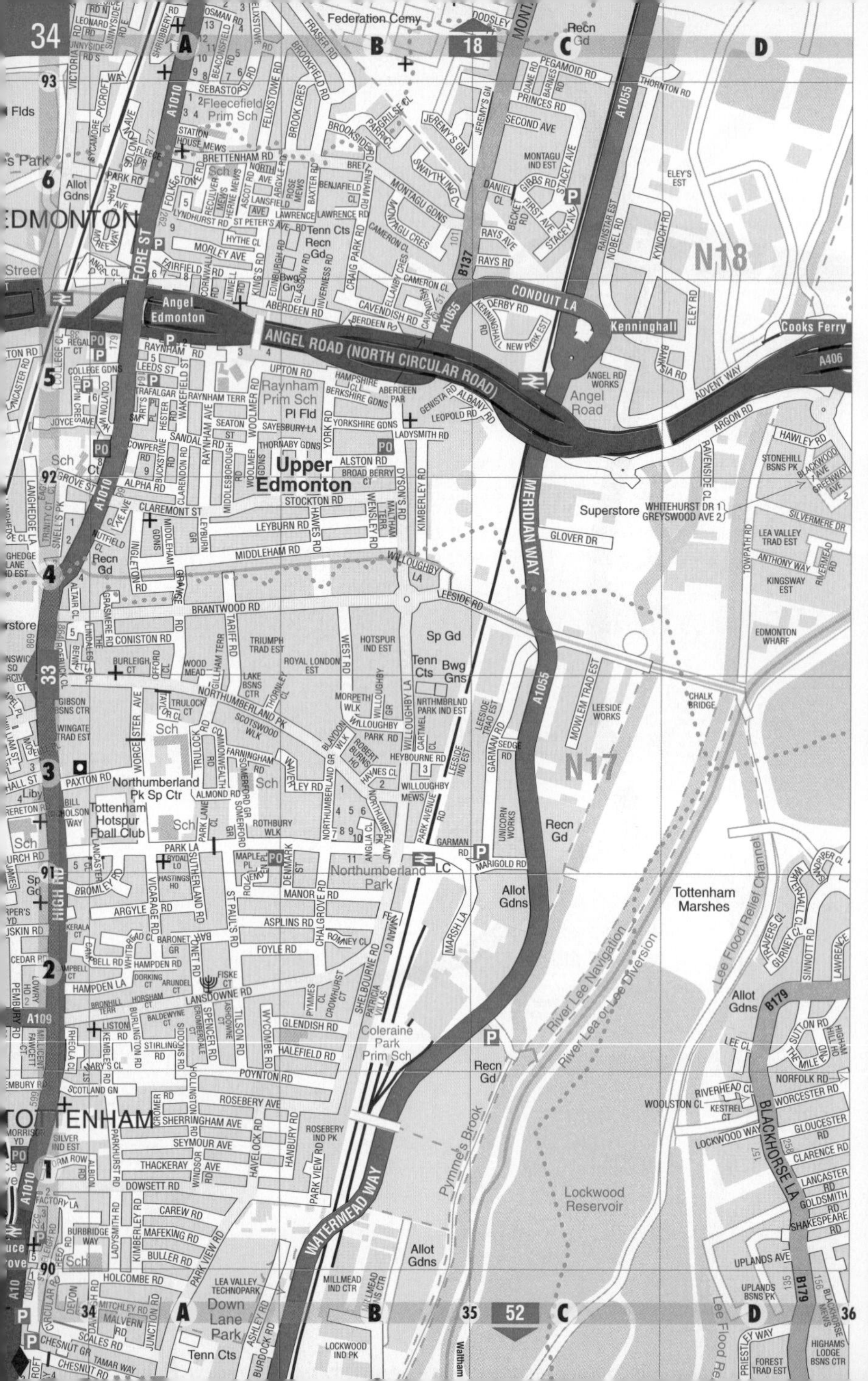

34
A
B
C
D
18
Federation Cemy
Recn Gd
EDMONTON
Fleecefield Prim Sch
Allot Gdns
Tenn Cts
Recn Gd
Bwg Gn
MONTAGU IND EST
ELEY'S EST
N18
CONDUIT LA
Kenninghall
Cooks Ferry
A406
Angel Edmonton
ANGEL ROAD (NORTH CIRCULAR ROAD)
Angel Road
ANGEL RD WORKS
ADVENT WAY
ARGON RD
Raynham Prim Sch
Pl Fld
Upper Edmonton
MERIDIAN WAY
A1055
A1010
FORE ST
B137
Superstore
STONEHILL BSNS PK
LEA VALLEY TRAD EST
KINGSWAY EST
EDMONTON WHARF
TRIUMPH TRAD EST
ROYAL LONDON EST
HOTSPUR IND EST
Sp Gd
Tenn Cts
Bwg Gns
NRTHMBRLND PARK IND EST
LEESIDE TRAD EST
LEESIDE IND EST
MOWLEM TRAD EST
LEESIDE WORKS
CHALK BRIDGE
N17
GIBSON BSNS CTR
WINGATE TRAD EST
Northumberland Pk Sp Ctr
Tottenham Hotspur Fball Club
Sch
Northumberland Park
UNICORN WORKS
Recn Gd
Allot Gdns
Tottenham Marshes
Lee Flood Relief Channel
River Lee Navigation
River Lea or Lee Diversion
Pymme's Brook
HIGH RD
Coleraine Park Prim Sch
ROSEBERY IND PK
TOTTENHAM
SILVER IND EST
Lockwood Reservoir
WATERMEAD WAY
BLACKHORSE LA
B179
UPLANDS BSNS PK
Allot Gdns
MILLMEAD IND CTR
LEA VALLEY TECHNOPARK
Down Lane Park
Tenn Cts
LOCKWOOD IND PK
FOREST TRAD EST
HIGHAMS LODGE BSNS CTR
Waltham
35
52
36

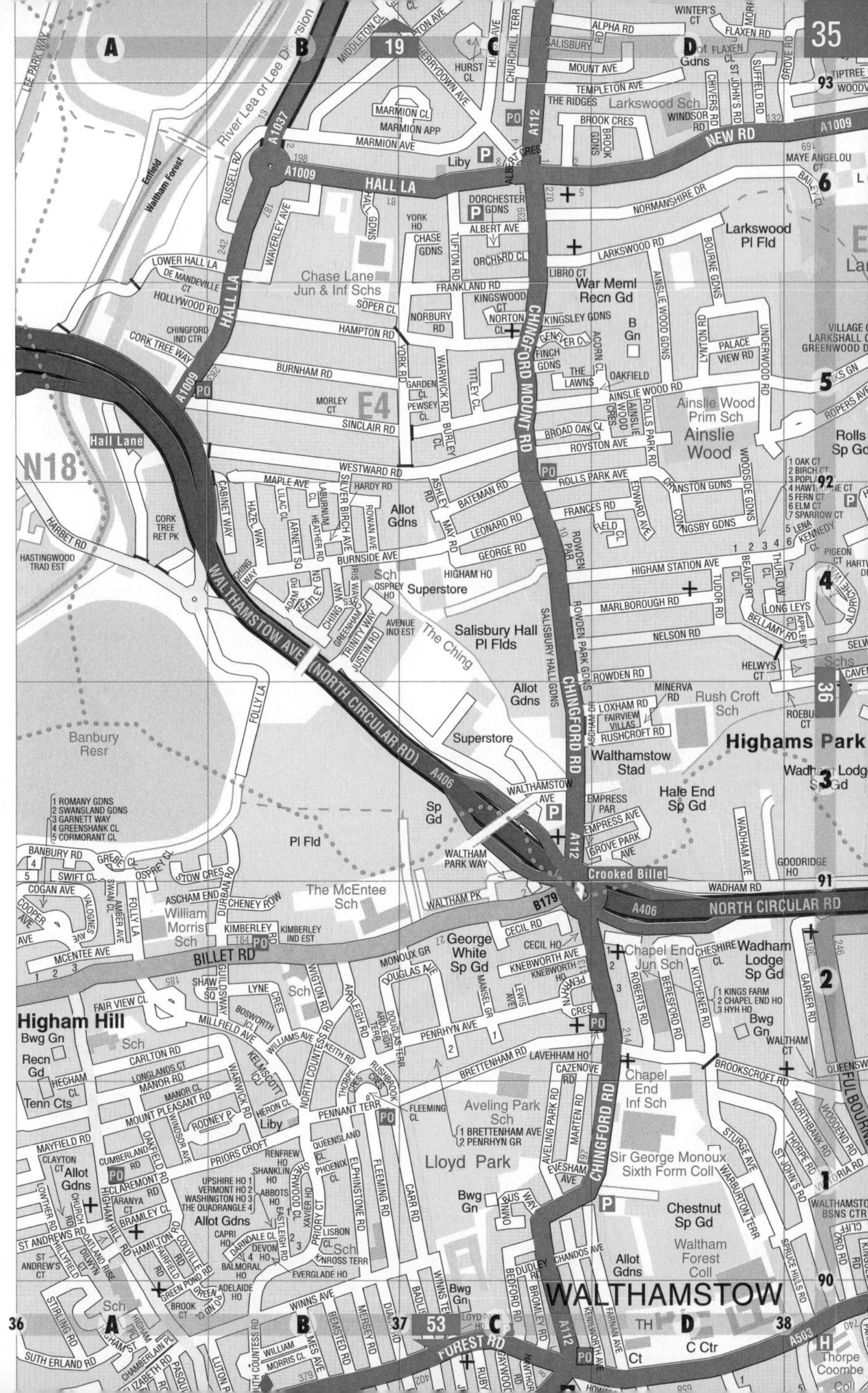

A
B
C
D
19
Enfield
Waltham Forest
River Lea or Lee Diversion
HALL LA
A1009
A1037
NEW RD
CHINGFORD MOUNT RD
CHINGFORD RD
A112
WALTHAMSTOW AVE (NORTH CIRCULAR RD)
A406
NORTH CIRCULAR RD
BILLET RD
B179
FOREST RD
E4
N18
Hall Lane
Chase Lane Jun & Inf Schs
Larkswood Sch
Larkswood Pl Fld
War Meml Recn Gd
Ainslie Wood Prim Sch
Ainslie Wood
Rolls Sp Gd
Allot Gdns
Superstore
Salisbury Hall Pl Flds
The Ching
Rush Croft Sch
Highams Park
Walthamstow Stad
Hale End Sp Gd
Wadham Lodge Sp Gd
Banbury Resr
Pl Fld
Sp Gd
Crooked Billet
The McEntee Sch
William Morris Sch
George White Sp Gd
Chapel End Jun Sch
Chapel End Inf Sch
Higham Hill
Bwg Gn
Recn Gd
Tenn Cts
Aveling Park Sch
Lloyd Park
Sir George Monoux Sixth Form Coll
Chestnut Sp Gd
Waltham Forest Coll
WALTHAMSTOW
Hastingwood Trad Est
Cork Tree Ret Pk
Chingford Ind Ctr
Kimberley Ind Est
Avenue Ind Est
Walthamstow Bsns Ctr
Thorpe Coombe
C Ctr
1 ROMANY GDNS
2 SWANSLAND GDNS
3 GARNETT WAY
4 GREENSHANK CL
5 CORMORANT CL
1 OAK CT
2 BIRCH CT
5 FERN CT
6 ELM CT
7 SPARROW CT
1 KINGS FARM
2 CHAPEL END HO
3 HYH HO
1 BRETTENHAM AVE
2 PENRHYN GR
UPSHIRE HO 1
VERMONT HO 2
WASHINGTON HO 3
THE QUADRANGLE 4
36
53
37
38
90
91
92
93

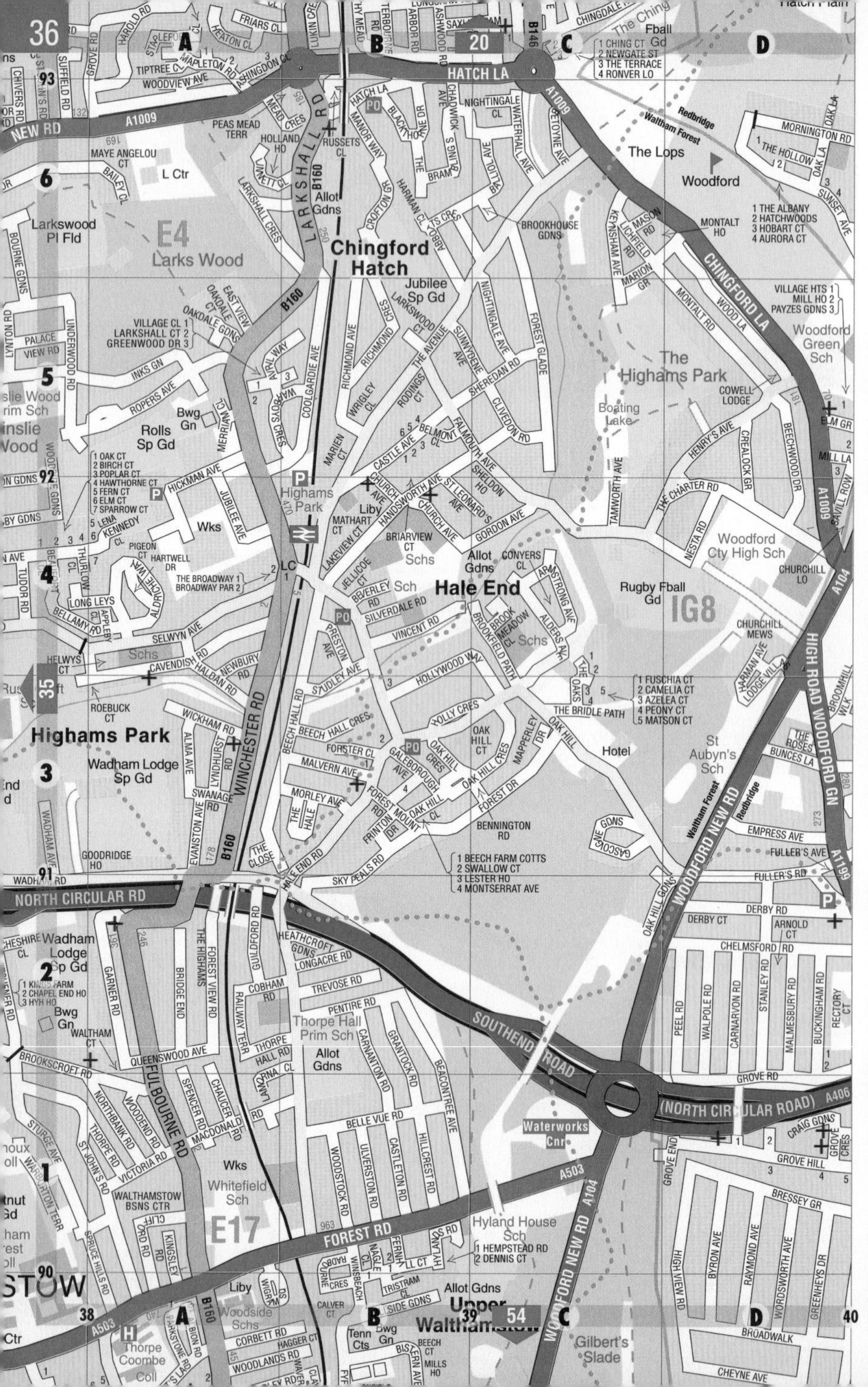
Chingford Hatch
Hale End
Highams Park
Larks Wood
Larkswood Pl Fld
The Highams Park
Boating Lake
The Lops
Woodford
Woodford Green Sch
Woodford Cty High Sch
Rugby Fball Gd
St Aubyn's Sch
Wadham Lodge Sp Gd
Rolls Sp Gd
Thorpe Hall Prim Sch
Whitefield Sch
Hyland House Sch
Waterworks Cnr
Upper Walthamstow
Gilbert's Slade
E4
IG8
E17
HATCH LA
NEW RD
LARKSHALL RD
WINCHESTER RD
NORTH CIRCULAR RD
SOUTHEND ROAD
(NORTH CIRCULAR ROAD)
FOREST RD
WOODFORD NEW RD
CHINGFORD LA
HIGH ROAD WOODFORD GN
FULBOURNE RD
Redbridge
Waltham Forest
1 CHING CT
2 NEWGATE ST
3 THE TERRACE
4 RONVER LO
1 THE ALBANY
2 HATCHWOODS
3 HOBART CT
4 AURORA CT
VILLAGE HTS 1
MILL HO 2
PAYZES GDNS 3
VILLAGE CL 1
LARKSHALL CT 2
GREENWOOD DR 3
1 OAK CT
2 BIRCH CT
3 POPLAR CT
4 HAWTHORNE CT
5 FERN CT
6 ELM CT
7 SPARROW CT
THE BROADWAY 1
BROADWAY PAR 2
1 FUSCHIA CT
2 CAMELIA CT
3 AZELEA CT
4 PEONY CT
5 MATSON CT
1 BEECH FARM COTTS
2 SWALLOW CT
3 LESTER HO
4 MONTSERRAT AVE
1 KINGS FARM
2 CHAPEL END HO
3 HYH HO
1 HEMPSTEAD RD
2 DENNIS CT
20
35
54
38
39
40

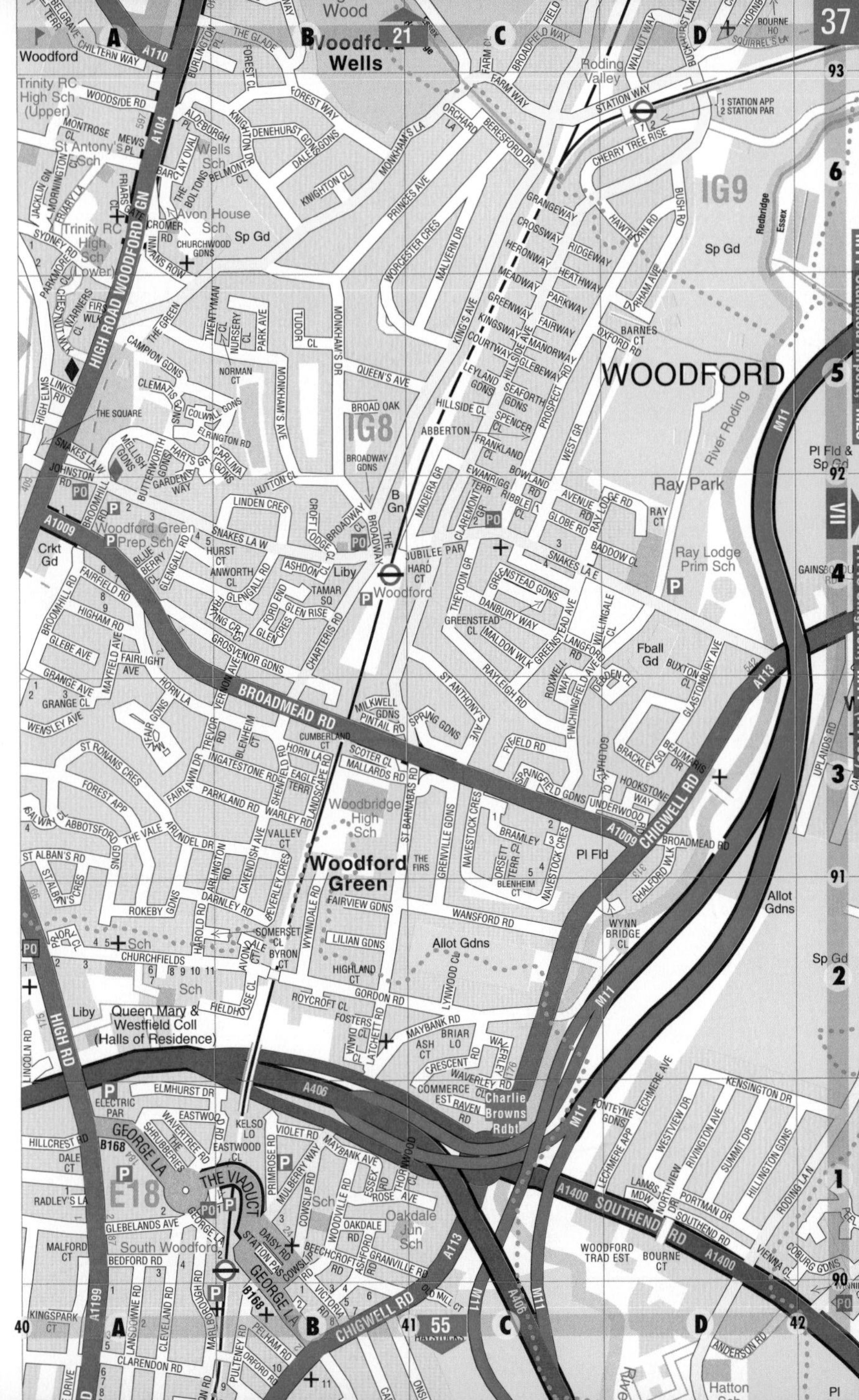

37
Woodford Wells
21
Woodford
Trinity RC High Sch (Upper)
St Antony's RC Sch
Trinity RC High Sch (Lower)
Wells Sch
Avon House Sch
Sp Gd
Roding Valley
STATION WAY
1 STATION APP
2 STATION PAR
IG9
IG8
E18
WOODFORD
M11 Stansted Airport, M25
A113 Chigwell, M11 (A1168)
River Roding
Ray Park
Pl Fld & Sp Gd
Ray Lodge Prim Sch
Fball Gd
HIGH ROAD WOODFORD GN
A104
A110
A1009
BROADMEAD RD
SNAKES LA W
SNAKES LA E
Woodford Green Prep Sch
Crkt Gd
Liby
Woodford
Woodbridge High Sch
Woodford Green
Pl Fld
Allot Gdns
Sp Gd
Queen Mary & Westfield Coll (Halls of Residence)
HIGH RD
A406
Charlie Browns Rdbt
A1400 SOUTHEND RD
CHIGWELL RD
A113
M11
South Woodford
GEORGE LA
THE VIADUCT
B168
Oakdale Jun Sch
WOODFORD TRAD EST
A1199
55
40
41
42
93
92
91
90
6
5
4
3
2
1
A
B
C
D
VII

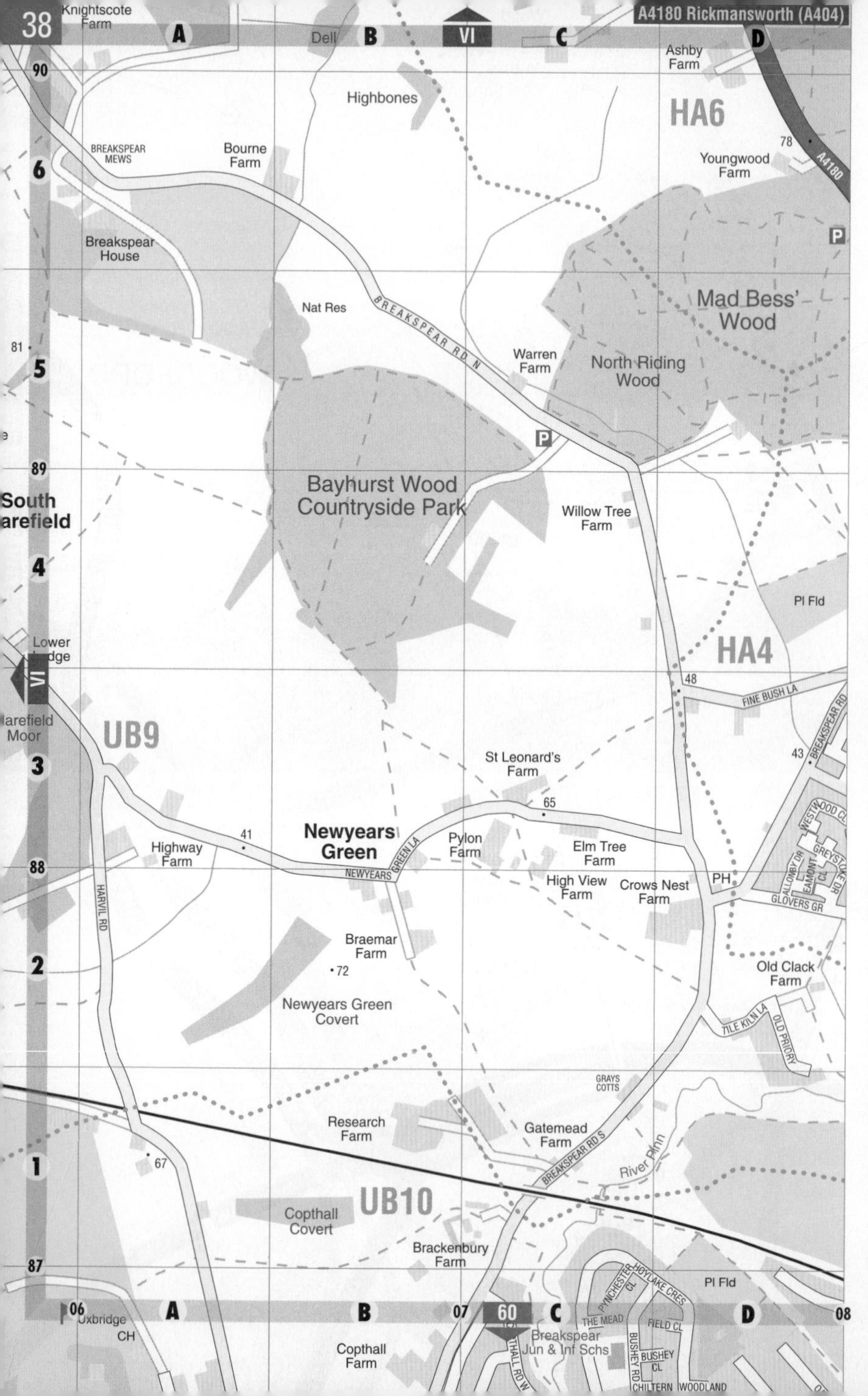
A4180 Rickmansworth (A404)
Knightscote Farm
Dell
Highbones
Ashby Farm
HA6
Youngwood Farm
A4180
BREAKSPEAR MEWS
Bourne Farm
Breakspear House
Mad Bess' Wood
Nat Res
BREAKSPEAR RD N
Warren Farm
North Riding Wood
Bayhurst Wood Countryside Park
South Harefield
Willow Tree Farm
Pl Fld
HA4
Lower Lodge
FINE BUSH LA
BREAKSPEAR RD
Harefield Moor
UB9
St Leonard's Farm
WESTWOOD CL
GREYSTOKE DR
ALLONBY DR
EAMONT CL
GLOVERS GR
Newyears Green
GREEN LA
NEWYEARS
Highway Farm
Pylon Farm
Elm Tree Farm
High View Farm
Crows Nest Farm
PH
HARVIL RD
Braemar Farm
Old Clack Farm
Newyears Green Covert
TILE KILN LA
OLD PRIORY
GRAYS COTTS
Research Farm
Gatemead Farm
BREAKSPEAR RD S
River Pinn
UB10
Copthall Covert
Brackenbury Farm
PYNCHESTER CL
HOYLAKE CRES
Pl Fld
Uxbridge CH
THE MEAD
FIELD CL
Breakspear Jun & Inf Schs
Copthall Farm
BUSHEY RD
BUSHEY CL
CHILTERN
WOODLAND
A B C D
06 07 08
90 89 88 87
6 5 4 3 2 1
VI
60

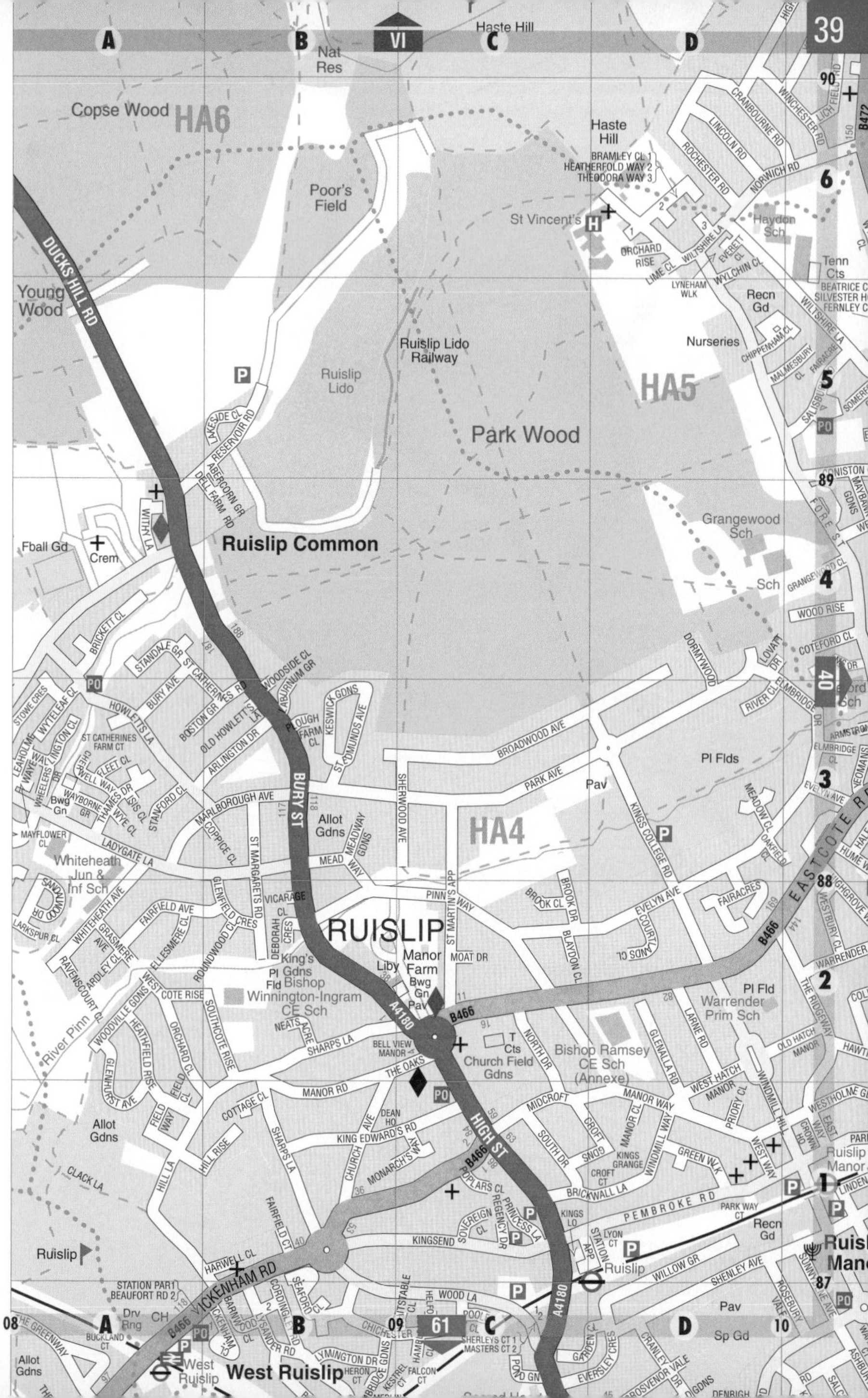
A
B
VI
C
D
Haste Hill
Nat Res
Copse Wood
HA6
Poor's Field
Haste Hill
BRAMLEY CL 1
HEATHERFOLD WAY 2
THEODORA WAY 3
St Vincent's
Haydon Sch
DUCKS HILL RD
Young Wood
Ruislip Lido Railway
Ruislip Lido
Nurseries
HA5
Park Wood
Tenn Cts
Recn Gd
Ruislip Common
Fball Gd
Crem
Grangewood Sch
Sch
BURY ST
HA4
RUISLIP
Allot Gdns
Pl Flds
Pav
Whiteheath Jun & Inf Sch
King's Gdns
Manor Farm
Liby
Bwg Gn
Pav
Pl Fld
Bishop Winnington-Ingram CE Sch
Warrender Prim Sch
Bishop Ramsey CE Sch (Annexe)
T Cts
Church Field Gdns
HIGH ST
A4180
B466
EASTCOTE RD
River Pinn
Allot Gdns
Ruislip
Ruislip Manor
Recn Gd
Pav
Sp Gd
West Ruislip
West Ruislip
Allot Gdns
61
40
08
09
10
87
88
89
90
1
2
3
4
5
6

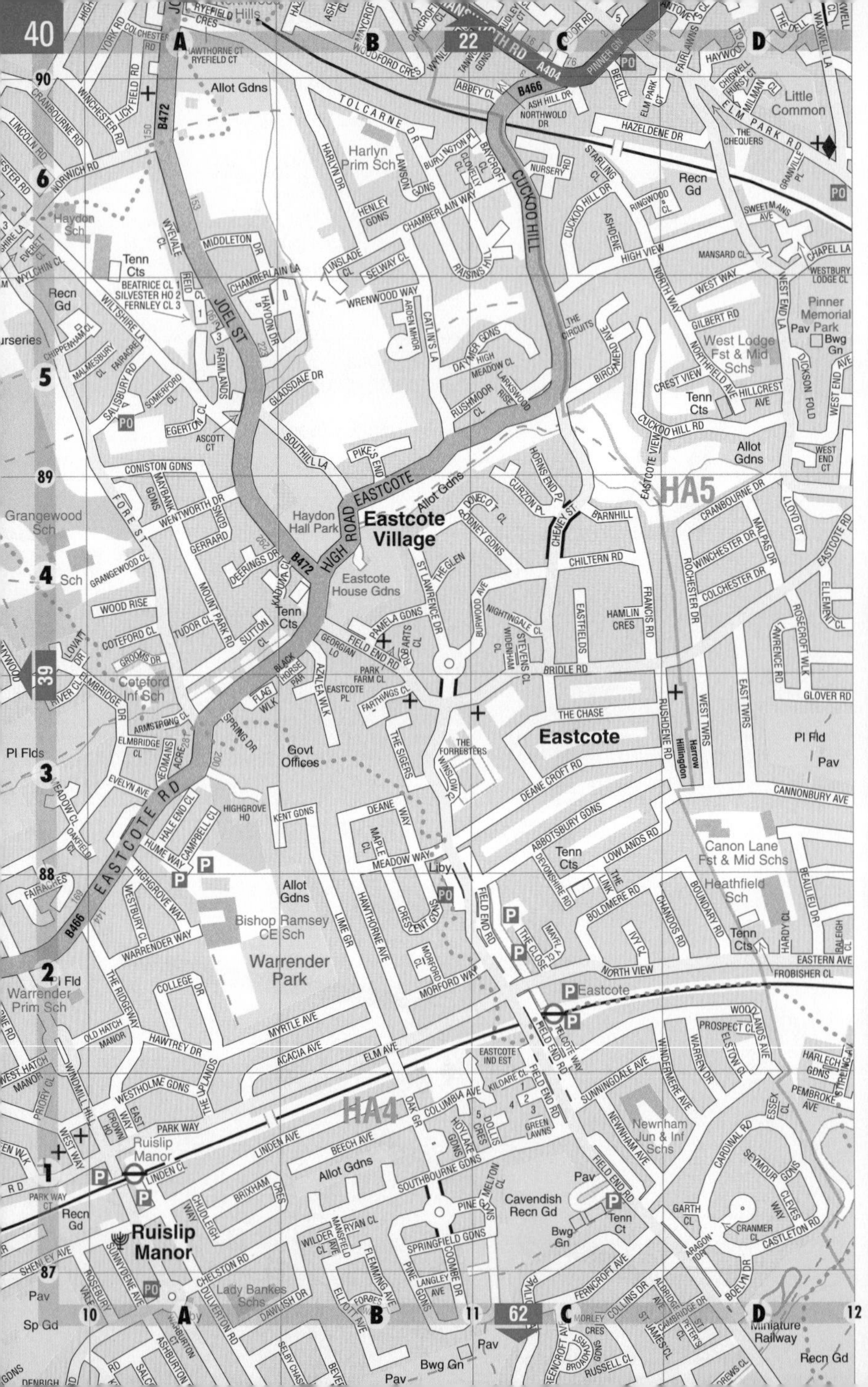

40
A
B
C
D
22
A404
B466
B472
90
6
5
89
4
3
88
2
1
87
39
10
11
12
62
Allot Gdns
Tolcarne Dr
Harlyn Prim Sch
Harlyn Dr
Henley Gdns
Lawson Gdns
Chamberlain Way
Burlington Pl
Baycroft Cl
Cuckoo Hill
Nursery Rd
Starling Cl
Recn Gd
Hazeldene Dr
Little Common
Elm Park Rd
Granville Pl
Ash Hill Dr
Northwold Dr
Abbey Cl
Pinner Gn
Bell Cl
Fairlawns Cl
Haywood Cl
Woodford Cres
Waxwell La
Tolcarne Dr
Norwich Rd
Cranbourne Rd
Lincoln Rd
Winchester Rd
Lichfield Rd
York Rd
Haydon Sch
Tenn Cts
Everett Cl
Wylchin Cl
Beatrice Cl 1
Silvester Ho 2
Fernley Cl 3
Wiltshire La
Wyevale Cl
Middleton Dr
Chamberlain La
Reid Cl
Joel St
Haydon Dr
Linslade Cl
Selway Cl
Wrenwood Way
Arden Mhor
Catlin's La
Raisins Hill
Daymer Gdns
High Meadow Cl
Larkswood Rise
Rushmoor Cl
The Circuits
Birchmead Ave
Cuckoo Hill Dr
Ashdene
Ringwood Cl
High View
North Way
West Way
Gilbert Rd
Mansard Cl
Sweetmans Ave
Chapel La
Westbury Lodge Cl
West End La
Pinner Memorial Park
Pav
Bwg Gn
West Lodge Fst & Mid Schs
Northfield Ave
Crest View
Hillcrest Ave
Dickson Fold
West End Ave
Cuckoo Hill Rd
Allot Gdns
West End Ct
Eastcote View
HA5
Cranbourne Dr
Lloyd Ct
Chippenham Cl
Malmesbury Cl
Fairacre
Salisbury Rd
Somerford Cl
Farmlands
Gladsdale Dr
Egerton Cl
Ascott Ct
Southill La
Pikes End
Eastcote High Road
Coniston Gdns
Maybank Gdns
Wentworth Dr
Gerrard Gdns
Grangewood Sch
Forest St
Haydon Hall Park
Eastcote Village
Dovecot Cl
Curzon Pl
Hornsend Pl
Cheney St
Barnhill
Rodney Gdns
St Lawrence Dr
The Glen
Chiltern Rd
Winchester Dr
Malpas Dr
Rochester Dr
Eastcote Rd
Colchester Dr
Sch
Grangewood Cl
Deerings Dr
Kaduna Cl
Eastcote House Gdns
Burwood Ave
Nightingale Cl
Eastfields
Hamlin Cres
Francis Rd
Ellement Cl
Wood Rise
Mount Park Rd
Tudor Cl
Sutton Cl
Pamela Gdns
Roberts Cl
Widenham Cl
Stevens Cl
Rosecroft Wlk
Lawrence Rd
Coteford Cl
Grooms Dr
Lovatt Dr
Georgian Lo
Field End Rd
Black Horse Par
Azalea Wlk
Park Farm Cl
Eastcote Pl
Farthings Cl
Bridle Rd
Rushdene Rd
West Twrs
East Twrs
Glover Rd
River Cl
Elmbridge Dr
Coteford Inf Sch
Flag Wlk
Armstrong Cl
Spring Dr
The Sigers
The Forresters
Winslow Cl
The Chase
Eastcote
Harrow
Hillingdon
Pl Fld
Pl Flds
Elmbridge Cl
Yeomans Acre
Govt Offices
Deane Croft Rd
Cannonbury Ave
Evelyn Ave
Meadow Cl
Oakfield
Eastcote Rd
Hale End Cl
Campbell Cl
Highgrove Ho
Kent Gdns
Deane Way
Maple Cl
Abbotsbury Gdns
Tenn Cts
Lowlands Rd
Canon Lane Fst & Mid Schs
Beaulieu Dr
Hume Way
Meadow Way
Liby
Devonshire Rd
The Link
Fairacres
Highgrove Way
Westbury Cl
Allot Gdns
Hawthorne Ave
Crescent Gdns
Boldmere Rd
Chandos Rd
Boundary Rd
Heathfield Sch
Hardy Cl
Raleigh Cl
Warrender Way
Bishop Ramsey CE Sch
Lime Gr
Morford Cl
The Close
Mayfly Cl
Ivy Cl
Tenn Cts
Eastern Ave
Warrender Park
Morford Way
North View
Frobisher Cl
Pl Fld
Warrender Prim Sch
College Dr
The Ridgeway
Eastcote
Woodlands Ave
Old Hatch Manor
Hawtrey Dr
Myrtle Ave
Prospect Cl
Elston Cl
Warren Dr
Harlech Gdns
Stirling Ave
Acacia Ave
Elm Ave
Eastcote Ind Est
Kildare Cl
Telcote Way
Sunningdale Ave
Windermere Ave
Pembroke Ave
West Hatch Manor
The Uplands
Westholme Gdns
Windmill Hill
Priory Cl
Crown Ho
East Way
Park Way
HA4
Oak Gr
Columbia Ave
Hoylake Gdns
Dollis Cres
Green Lawns
Newnham Ave
Newnham Jun & Inf Schs
Essex Cl
Cardinal Rd
Seymour Gdns
West Way
Ruislip Manor
Linden Ave
Beech Ave
Allot Gdns
Southbourne Gdns
Melton Cl
Pav
Field End Rd
Cleves Way
Linden Cl
Park Way Ct
Recn Gd
Brixham Cres
Chudleigh Way
Pine Gdns
Cavendish Recn Gd
Tenn Ct
Garth Cl
Cranmer Cl
Castleton Rd
Ruislip Manor
Wilder Cl
Ryan Cl
Mansfield Ave
Flemming Ave
Springfield Gdns
Coombe Dr
Bwg Gn
Aragon Dr
Shenley Ave
Rosebury Vale
Sunnydene Ave
Chelston Rd
Lady Bankes Schs
Langley Ave
Pine Gdns
Ferncroft Ave
Collins Dr
Albridge Ave
Boelyn Dr
Pav
Sp Gd
Dulverton Rd
Dawlish Dr
Elliott Ave
Forbes Way
St James Cl
Cambridge Dr
St Peter's
Morley Cres
Miniature Railway
Recn Gd
Ashburton Rd
Selby Chase
Bwg Gn
Pav
Greencroft Ave
Broadhurst Gdns
Russell Cl
Denbigh

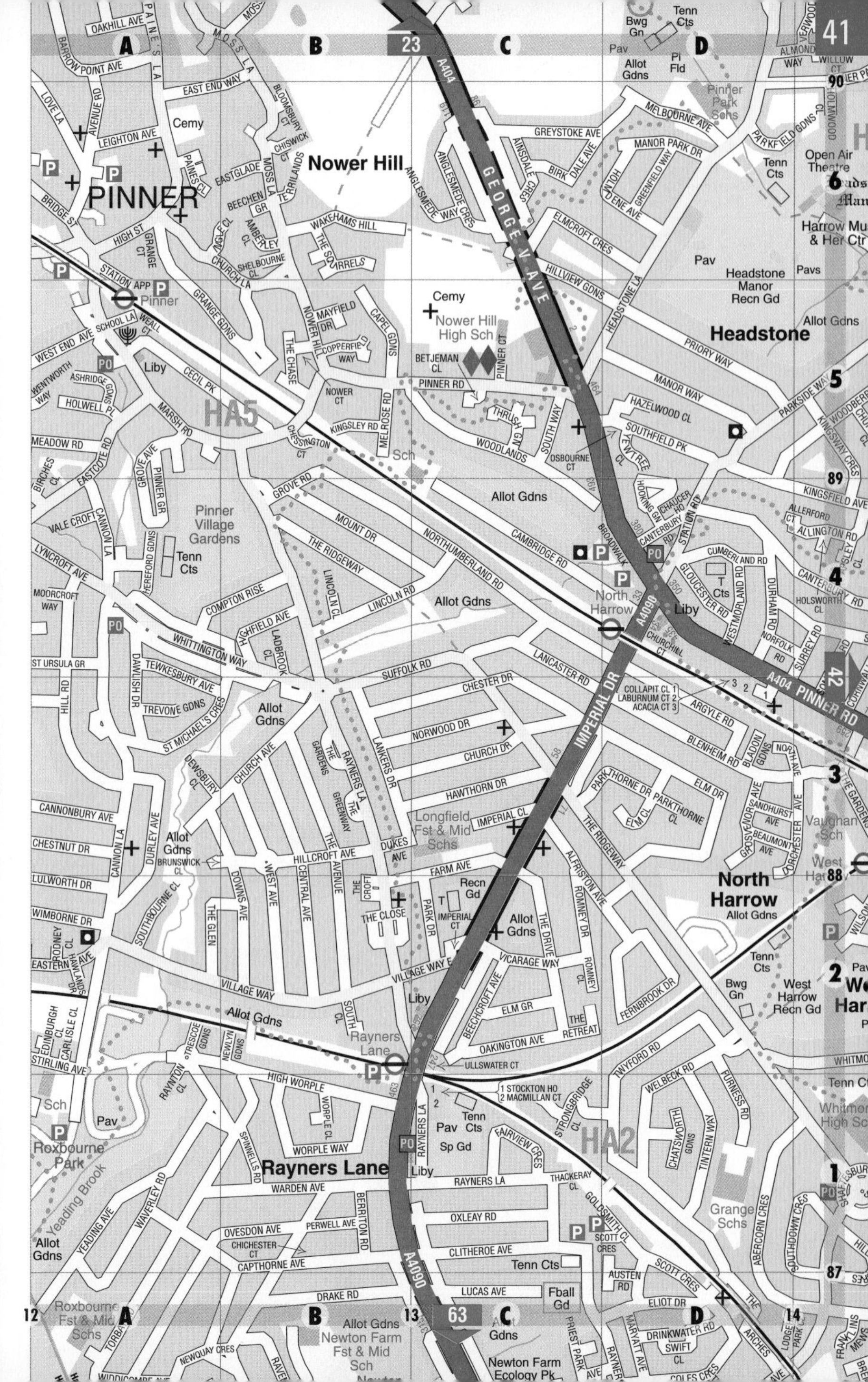
A
B
C
D
23
63
42
A404
A4090
PINNER
Nower Hill
Headstone
North Harrow
Rayners Lane
HA5
HA2
OAKHILL AVE
PAINES LA
MOSS LA
BARROW POINT AVE
EAST END WAY
LOVE LA
AVENUE RD
BLOOMSBURY CT
LEIGHTON AVE
Cemy
CHISWICK CT
PAINES CL
EASTGLADE
TERRILANDS
BRIDGE ST
BEECHEN GR
AMBER CL
ANGLESMEDE CRES
ANGLESMEDE WAY
GEORGE V AVE
GREYSTOKE AVE
AINSDALE CRES
BIRKDALE AVE
MELBOURNE AVE
MANOR PARK DR
HOLMDENE AVE
GREENFIELD WAY
Pinner Park Schs
Tenn Cts
Bwg Gn
Pav
Allot Gdns
Pl Fld
PARKFIELD GDNS
Open Air Theatre
Harrow Mus & Her Ctr
HIGH ST
GRANGE CT
CHURCH LA
WAKEHAMS HILL
THE SQUIRRELS
SHELBOURNE CL
ELMCROFT CRES
HILLVIEW GDNS
HEADSTONE LA
Headstone Manor Recn Gd
Pavs
STATION APP
Pinner
SCHOOL LA
WEALL CT
GRANGE GDNS
MAYFIELD DR
CAPEL GDNS
Nower Hill High Sch
PINNER CT
COPPERFIELD WAY
NOWER HILL
THE CHASE
BETJEMAN CL
PINNER RD
PRIORY WAY
MANOR WAY
WEST END AVE
WENTWORTH WAY
ASHRIDGE GDNS
HOLWELL PL
Liby
CECIL PK
MARSH RD
NOWER CT
KINGSLEY RD
MELROSE RD
THRUSH GN
SOUTH WAY
WOODLANDS
HAZELWOOD CL
SOUTHFIELD PK
YEW TREE CL
OSBOURNE CT
PARKSIDE WAY
KINGSWAY CRES
WOODBERRY
MEADOW RD
EASTCOTE RD
CHESSINGTON CT
Sch
GROVE AVE
PINNER GR
BIRCHES CL
GROVE RD
Allot Gdns
HOOKING GN
CHAUCER HO
CANTERBURY RD
STATION RD
KINGSFIELD AVE
ALLERFORD CT
ALLINGTON RD
Pinner Village Gardens
VALE CROFT
CANNON LA
MOUNT DR
THE RIDGEWAY
NORTHUMBERLAND RD
CAMBRIDGE RD
BROADWALK
CUMBERLAND RD
GLOUCESTER RD
WESTMORLAND RD
DURHAM RD
CANTERBURY RD
HEREFORD GDNS
LYNCROFT AVE
LINCOLN CL
LINCOLN RD
MOORCROFT WAY
COMPTON RISE
North Harrow
HOLSWORTH CL
NORFOLK RD
SURREY RD
HIGHFIELD AVE
LADBROOK CL
CHURCHILL CT
WHITTINGTON WAY
ST URSULA GR
DAWLISH DR
TEWKESBURY AVE
SUFFOLK RD
LANCASTER RD
IMPERIAL DR
PINNER RD
COLLAPIT CL 1
LABURNUM CT 2
ACACIA CT 3
ARGYLE RD
CHESTER DR
HILL RD
TREVONE GDNS
ST MICHAEL'S CRES
NORWOOD DR
BLENHEIM RD
BLADON GDNS
NORTH AVE
DEWSBURY CL
CHURCH AVE
THE GARDENS
RAYNERS LA
LANKERS DR
CHURCH DR
PARKTHORNE DR
PARKTHORNE CL
ELM CL
ELM DR
HAWTHORN DR
THE GREENWAY
CANNONBURY AVE
DURLEY AVE
Longfield Fst & Mid Schs
IMPERIAL CL
SANDHURST AVE
GROSVENOR AVE
BEAUMONT AVE
DORCHESTER AVE
Vaughan Sch
CHESTNUT DR
BRUNSWICK CL
HILLCROFT AVE
THE AVENUE
DUKES AVE
ALFRISTON AVE
ROMNEY DR
LULWORTH DR
WEST AVE
DOWNS AVE
CENTRAL AVE
FARM AVE
THE CROFT
Recn Gd
West Harrow
WIMBORNE DR
SOUTHBOURNE CL
THE GLEN
THE CLOSE
PARK DR
IMPERIAL CT
THE DRIVE
RODNEY CL
HAWLANDS DR
EASTERN AVE
VILLAGE WAY
VILLAGE WAY E
VICARAGE WAY
ROMNEY CL
FERNBROOK DR
Bwg Gn
West Harrow Recn Gd
BEECHCROFT AVE
ELM GR
THE RETREAT
SOUTH CL
EDINBURGH CL
CARLISLE CL
STIRLING AVE
TRESCOE GDNS
NEWLYN GDNS
OAKINGTON AVE
ULLSWATER CT
TWYFORD RD
WHITMORE
Rayners Lane
RAYNTON CL
HIGH WORPLE
WORPLE CL
1 STOCKTON HO
2 MACMILLAN CT
STRONGBRIDGE CL
WELBECK RD
FURNESS RD
Whitmore High Sch
Sch
Pav
Roxbourne Park
SPINNELLS RD
WORPLE WAY
RAYNERS LA
Sp Gd
FAIRVIEW CRES
CHATSWORTH GDNS
TINTERN WAY
Yeading Brook
WAVERLEY RD
WARDEN AVE
RAYNERS LA
THACKERAY CL
SHAFTESBURY
YEADING AVE
BERRITON RD
OXLEAY RD
GOLDSMITH CL
Grange Schs
ABERCORN CRES
SOUTHDOWN CRES
OVESDON AVE
PERWELL AVE
CHICHESTER CT
SCOTT CRES
CLITHEROE AVE
CAPTHORNE AVE
Tenn Cts
AUSTEN RD
SCOTT CRES
DRAKE RD
LUCAS AVE
Fball Gd
ELIOT DR
THE ARCHES
Roxbourne Fst & Mid Schs
TORBAY
Allot Gdns
Newton Farm Fst & Mid Sch
PRIEST PARK
MARYATT AVE
DRINKWATER RD
SWIFT CL
LODGE PARK
FRANKLINS MEWS
NEWQUAY CRES
Newton Farm Ecology Pk
COLES CRES
12
13
14
90
89
88
87
1
2
3
4
5
6

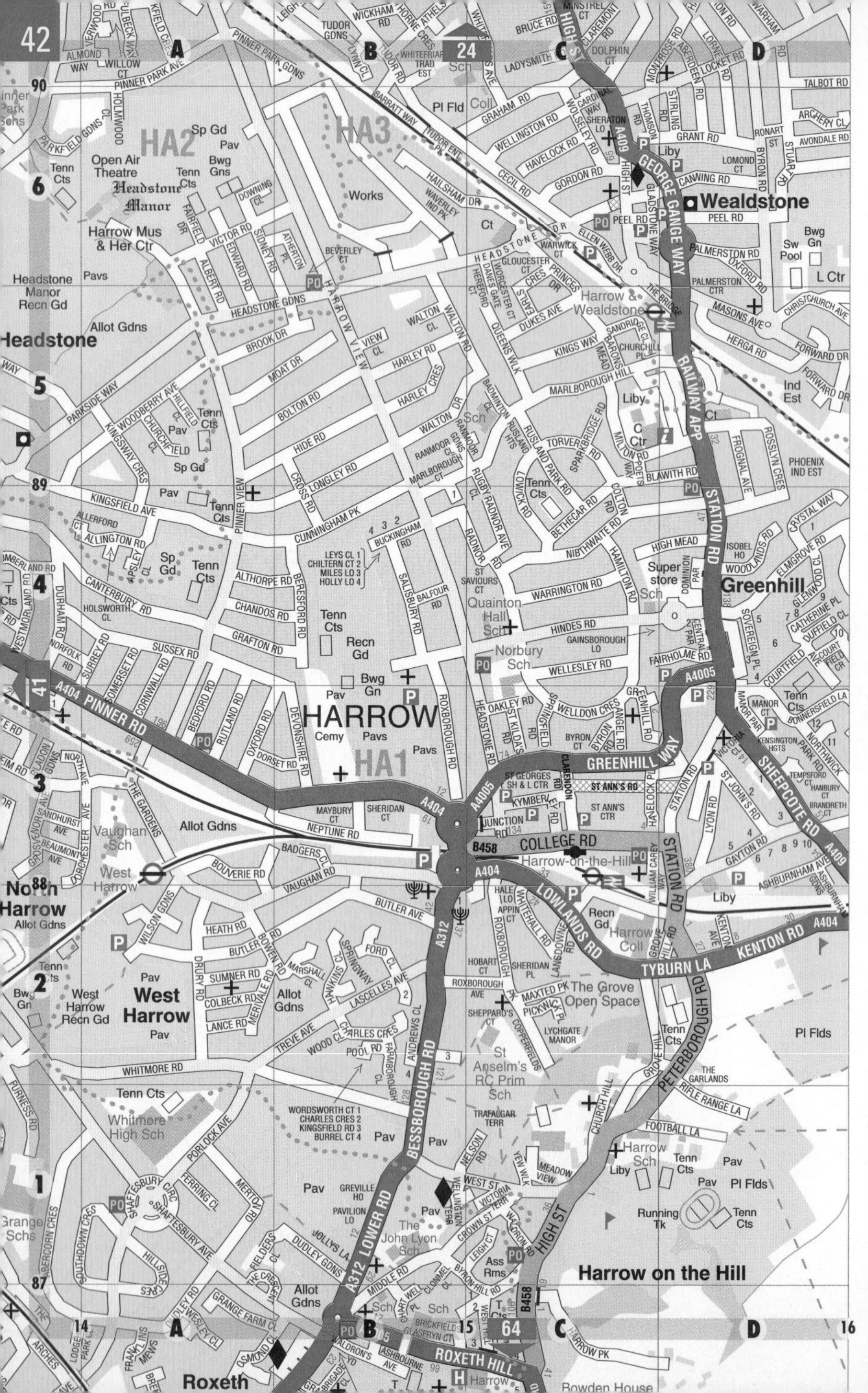

24
41
64
A
B
C
D
14
15
16
90
89
88
87
6
5
4
3
2
1
HA1
HA2
HA3
HARROW
Wealdstone
Headstone
Greenhill
West Harrow
North Harrow
Harrow on the Hill
Roxeth
Headstone Manor
Harrow Mus & Her Ctr
Open Air Theatre
Headstone Manor Recn Gd
Harrow & Wealdstone
Harrow-on-the-Hill
West Harrow
Harrow Coll
The Grove Open Space
Whitmore High Sch
The John Lyon Sch
Harrow Sch
St Anselm's RC Prim Sch
Quainton Hall Sch
Norbury Sch
Vaughan Sch
Phoenix Ind Est
Running Tk
A404 PINNER RD
A404
A4005
A409
A312 LOWER RD
B458
GEORGE GANGE WAY
RAILWAY APP
STATION RD
GREENHILL WAY
KENTON RD
TYBURN LA
LOWLANDS RD
COLLEGE RD
HIGH ST
BESSBOROUGH RD
PETERBOROUGH RD
SHEEPCOTE RD
ROXETH HILL

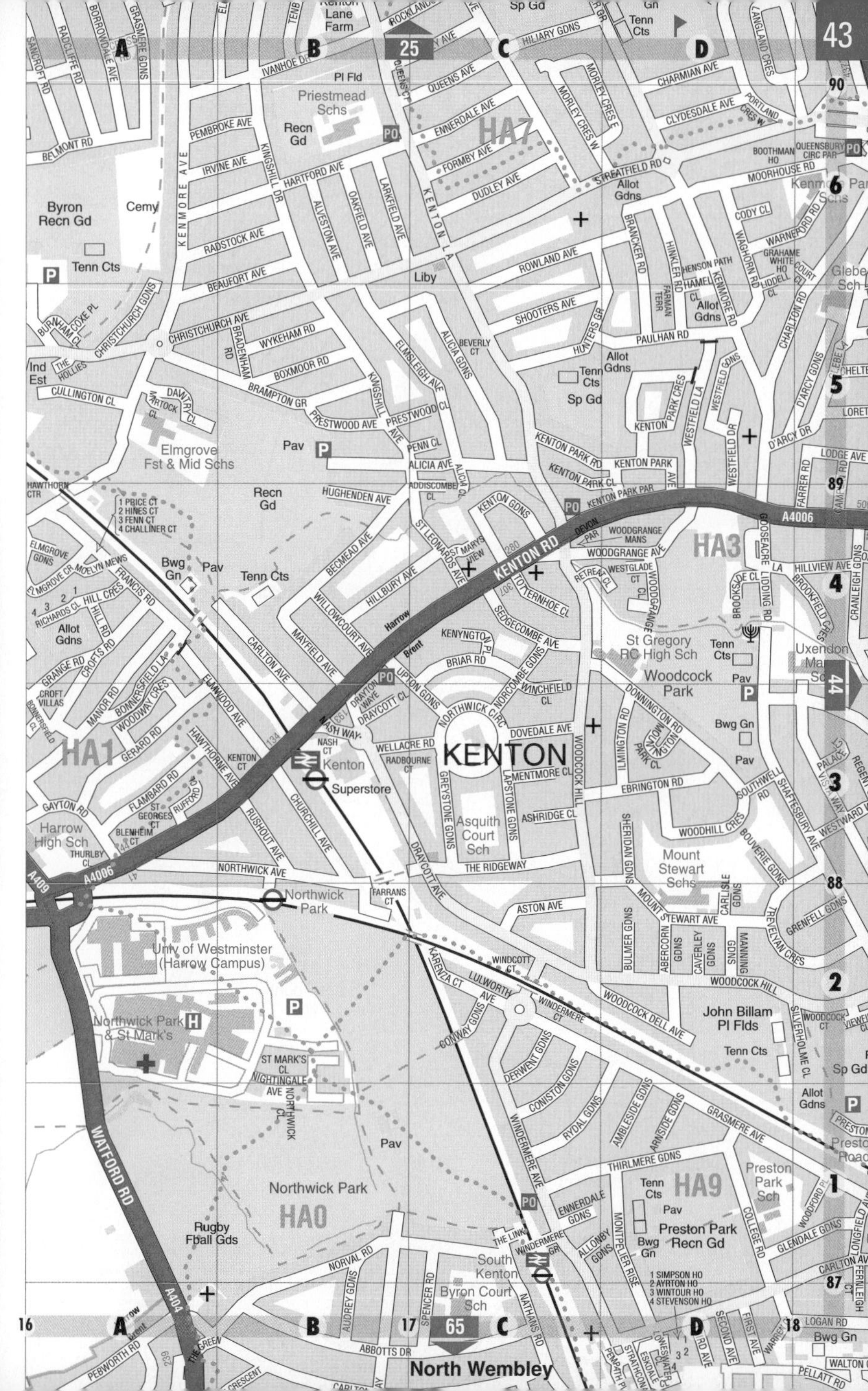
A
B
25
C
D
Kenton Lane Farm
Sp Gd
Tenn Cts
Priestmead Schs
Recn Gd
Pl Fld
HA7
Byron Recn Gd
Cemy
Tenn Cts
Liby
Allot Gdns
Kenmore Park Schs
Glebe Sch
Ind Est
Elmgrove Fst & Mid Schs
Recn Gd
Pav
Bwg Gn
Tenn Cts
Allot Gdns
Sp Gd
KENTON RD
A4006
HA3
St Gregory RC High Sch
Woodcock Park
Uxendon Manor Sch
HA1
KENTON
Kenton
Superstore
Asquith Court Sch
Mount Stewart Schs
Harrow High Sch
Northwick Park
Univ of Westminster (Harrow Campus)
Northwick Park & St Mark's
John Billam Pl Flds
Preston Road
Preston Park Sch
Preston Park Recn Gd
Northwick Park
HA0
HA9
Rugby Fball Gds
South Kenton
Byron Court Sch
WATFORD RD
A404
North Wembley
65
16
17
18
1
2
3
4
5
6
44
87
88
89
90

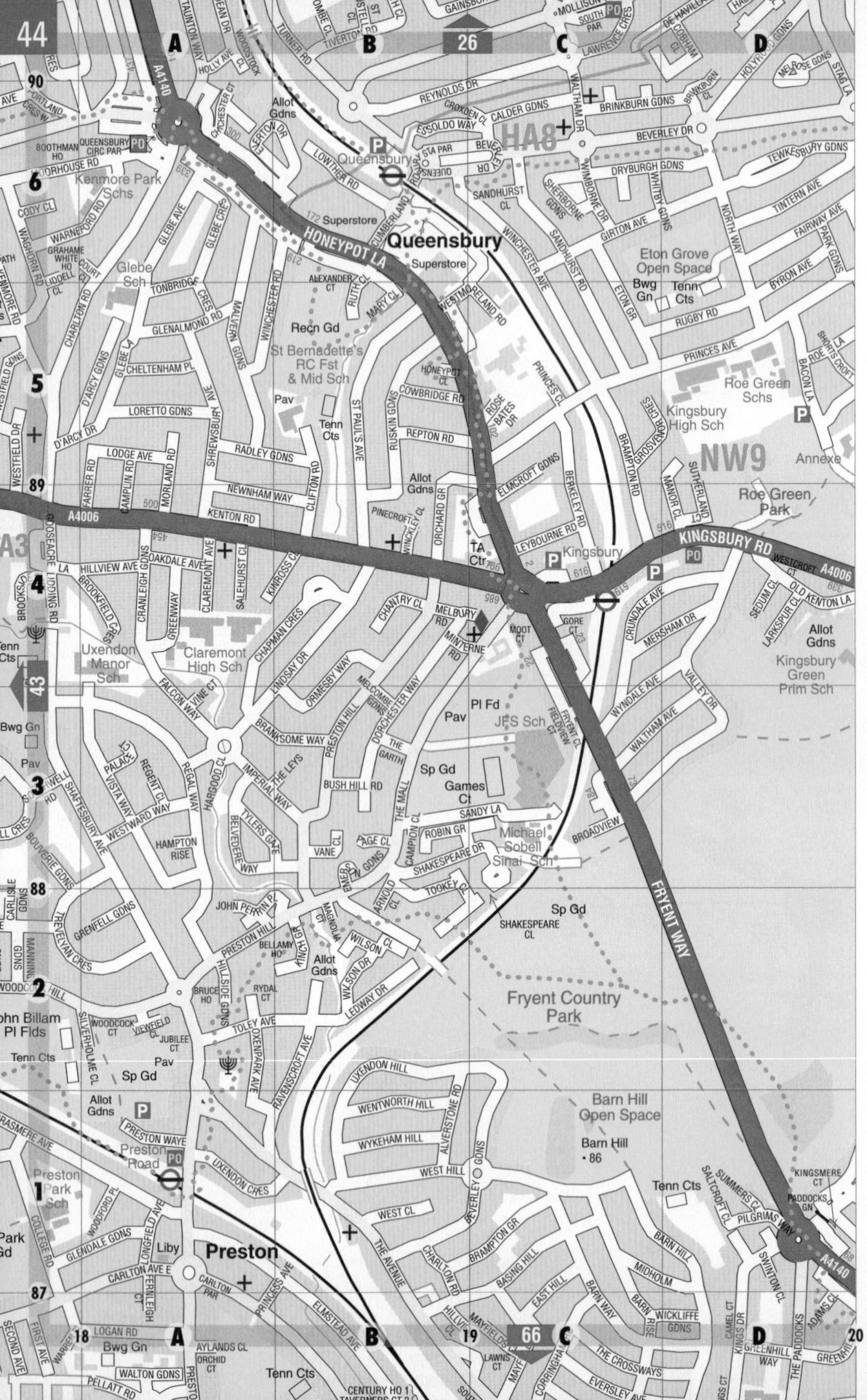
A
B
C
D
26
43
66
90
89
88
87
18
19
20
6
5
4
3
2
1
A4140
A4006
A3
HA8
NW9
Queensbury
Kingsbury
Preston
Preston Road
HONEYPOT LA
KINGSBURY RD
FRYENT WAY
Fryent Country Park
Barn Hill Open Space
Barn Hill
• 86
Eton Grove Open Space
Roe Green Park
Roe Green Schs
Kingsbury High Sch
Kingsbury Green Prim Sch
Annexe
Claremont High Sch
Uxendon Manor Sch
Glebe Sch
Kenmore Park Schs
St Bernadette's RC Fst & Mid Sch
JFS Sch
Michael Sobell Sinai Sch
Preston Park Sch
John Billam Pl Flds
Recn Gd
Allot Gdns
Superstore
Tenn Cts
Bwg Gn
Pav
Pl Fd
Sp Gd
Games Ct
TA Ctr
Liby
QUEENSBURY CIRC PAR
BOOTHMAN HO
MOORHOUSE RD
CODY CL
WARNEFORD RD
WAGHORN RD
GRAHAME WHITE HO
LIDDELL CL
COURT
KENMORE RD
PORTLAND CRES W
TAUNTON WAY
HOLLY AVE
WOODSTOCK CL
CHICHESTER CT
TURNER RD
TIVERTON RD
GAINSBOROUGH
MOLLISON
SOUTH PAR
LAWRENCE CRES
DE HAVILLAND
COBHAM CL
HOLYROOD GDNS
MELROSE GDNS
STAG LA
REYNOLDS DR
CROXDEN CL
CALDER GDNS
ESSOLDO WAY
BRINKBURN GDNS
BRINKBURN CL
BEVERLEY DR
TEWKESBURY GDNS
WALTHAM DR
STA PAR
QUEENS
DRYBURGH GDNS
SHERBORNE GDNS
WIMBORNE DR
WHITBY GDNS
NORTH WAY
TINTERN AVE
FAIRWAY AVE
PARK GDNS
BYRON AVE
GIRTON AVE
SANDHURST CL
SANDHURST RD
WINCHESTER AVE
LOWTHER RD
CUMBERLAND RD
ETON GR
RUGBY RD
PRINCES AVE
SHORTS CROFT
ROE LA
BACON LA
PRINCES CL
GLEBE AVE
GLEBE CRES
GLEBE LA
TONBRIDGE CRES
GLENALMOND RD
MALVERN GDNS
WINCHESTER RD
ALEXANDER CT
RUTH CL
MARY CL
WESTMORELAND RD
CHARLTON RD
D'ARCY GDNS
CHELTENHAM PL
LORETTO GDNS
SHREWSBURY AVE
D'ARCY DR
WESTFIELD GDNS
WESTFIELD DR
LODGE AVE
CAMPLIN RD
MORLAND RD
FARRER RD
RADLEY GDNS
NEWNHAM WAY
KENTON RD
CLIFTON RD
ST PAUL'S AVE
RUSKIN GDNS
COWBRIDGE RD
HONEYPOT CL
REPTON RD
ROSE BATES DR
ELMCROFT GDNS
BERKELEY RD
BRAMPTON RD
GROSVENOR CRES
MANOR CL
SUTHERLAND CT
ORCHARD GR
PINECROFT
WINCKLEY CL
LEYBOURNE RD
GOOSEACRE LA
HILLVIEW AVE
OAKDALE AVE
CLAREMONT AVE
SALEHURST CL
KINROSS CL
CRANLEIGH GDNS
GREENWAY
BROOKFIELD CRES
BROOKSIDE
LIDDING RD
WESTCROFT CT
SEDUM CL
OLD KENTON LA
LARKSPUR CL
CHANTRY CL
MELBURY RD
MINTERNE RD
MOOT CT
GORE CT
CRUNDALE AVE
MERSHAM DR
WYNDALE AVE
VALLEY DR
WALTHAM AVE
FRYENT CL
FIELDVIEW CT
CHAPMAN CRES
LINDSAY DR
ORMESBY WAY
MELCOMBE GDNS
DORCHESTER WAY
PRESTON HILL
FALCON WAY
VINE CT
BRANKSOME WAY
THE GARTH
THE LEYS
IMPERIAL WAY
HARGOOD CL
REGAL WAY
BUSH HILL RD
THE MALL
SANDY LA
ROBIN GR
CAMPION CL
SHAKESPEARE DR
SHAKESPEARE CL
TOOKEY CL
BROADVIEW
PALACE CT
VISTA WAY
REGENT CL
WESTWARD WAY
SHAFTESBURY AVE
HAMPTON RISE
TYLERS GATE
BELVEDERE WAY
VANE CL
EMBERTON GDNS
ARNOLD CL
MAGNOLIA CT
WILSON CL
WILSON DR
BOUVERIE GDNS
CARLISLE GDNS
TREVELYAN CRES
GRENFELL GDNS
JOHN PERRIN PL
BELLAMY HO
KINCH GR
LEDWAY DR
MANNING GDNS
WOODCOCK HILL
HILLSIDE GDNS
BRUCE HO
RYDAL CT
TOLEY AVE
OXENPARK AVE
RAVENSCROFT AVE
SILVERHOLME CL
WOODCOCK CT
VIEWFIELD CL
JUBILEE CT
GRASMERE AVE
PRESTON WAYE
UXENDON CRES
UXENDON HILL
WENTWORTH HILL
WYKEHAM HILL
ALVERSTONE RD
WEST HILL
WEST CL
BEVERLEY GDNS
KINGSMERE CT
PADDOCKS GN
SUMMERS CL
SALTCROFT CL
PILGRIMS WAY
SWINTON CL
WOODFORD PL
COLLEGE RD
GLENDALE GDNS
LONGFIELD AVE
FERNLEIGH CT
CARLTON AVE E
CARLTON PAR
PRINCESS AVE
ELMSTEAD AVE
THE AVENUE
CHARLTON RD
BRAMPTON GR
BASING HILL
EAST HILL
BARN WAY
BARN HILL
MIDHOLM
BARN RISE
WICKLIFFE GDNS
HILLVIEW CL
MAYFIELDS
CAMEL CT
KINGS DR
THE PADDOCKS
ADAMS CL
GREENHILL WAY
LOGAN RD
AYLANDS CL
ORCHID CT
WALTON GDNS
PELLATT RD
SECOND AVE
FIRST AVE
WARREN
LAWNS CT
CORRINGHAM
THE CROSSWAYS
EVERSLEY AVE
CENTURY HO
TAVERNERS CT

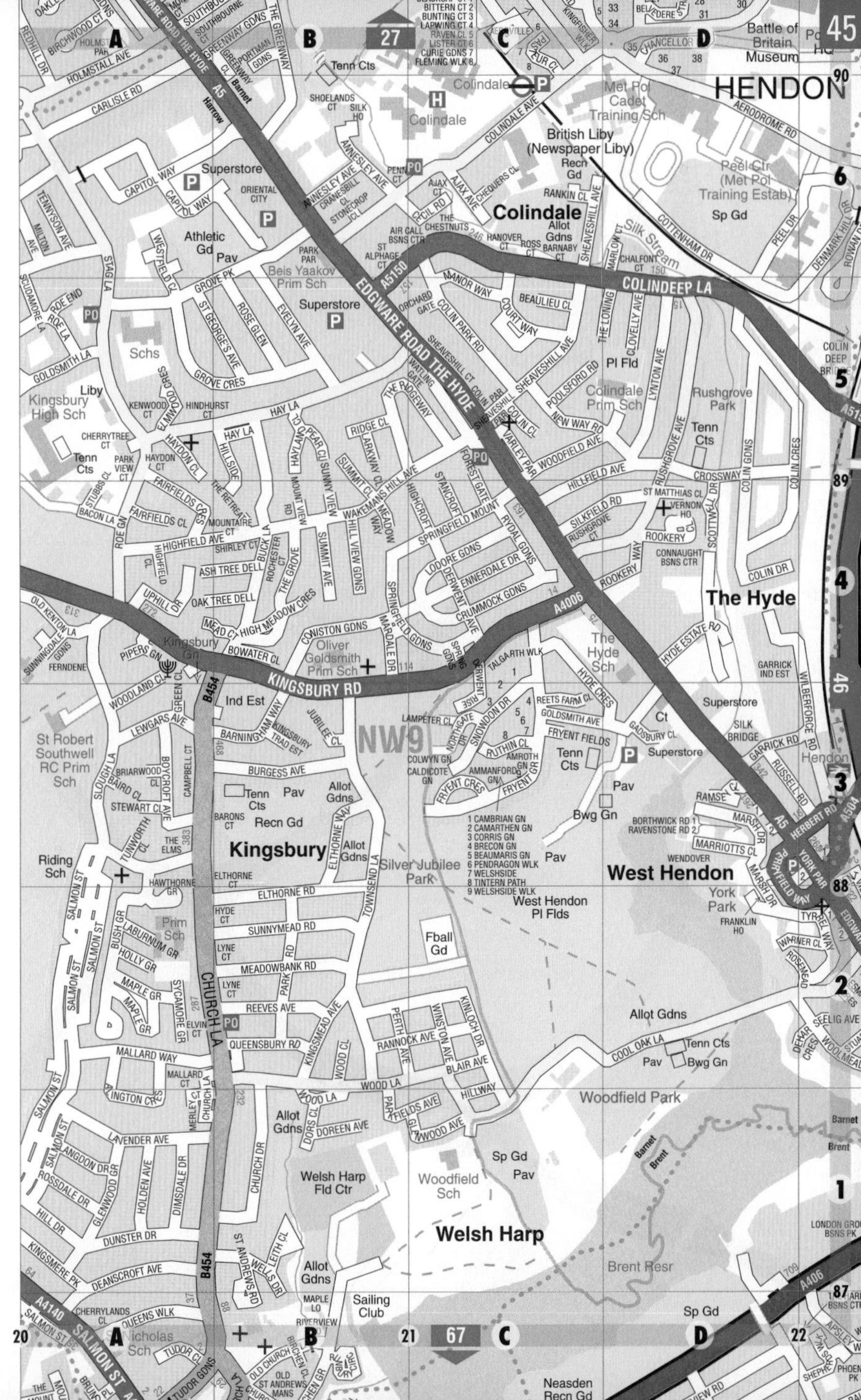

HENDON
Colindale
The Hyde
Kingsbury
West Hendon
Welsh Harp
NW9
EDGWARE ROAD THE HYDE
COLINDEEP LA
KINGSBURY RD
CHURCH LA
Battle of Britain Museum
British Liby (Newspaper Liby)
Met Pol Cadet Training Sch
Peel Ctr (Met Pol Training Estab)
Colindale Prim Sch
Rushgrove Park
The Hyde Sch
Oliver Goldsmith Prim Sch
Kingsbury High Sch
St Robert Southwell RC Prim Sch
Silver Jubilee Park
West Hendon Pl Flds
York Park
Woodfield Park
Woodfield Sch
Welsh Harp Fld Ctr
Sailing Club
Brent Resr
Neasden Recn Gd
Beis Yaakov Prim Sch
Garrick Ind Est
1 CAMBRIAN GN
2 CAMARTHEN GN
3 CORRIS GN
4 BRECON GN
5 BEAUMARIS GN
6 PENDRAGON WLK
7 WELSHSIDE
8 TINTERN PATH
9 WELSHSIDE WLK
BLACKCAP CT 1
BITTERN CT 2
BUNTING CT 3
LAPWING CT 4
RAVEN CL 5
LISTER CT 6
CURIE GDNS 7
FLEMING WLK 8
BORTHWICK RD 1
RAVENSTONE RD 2

27
46
67

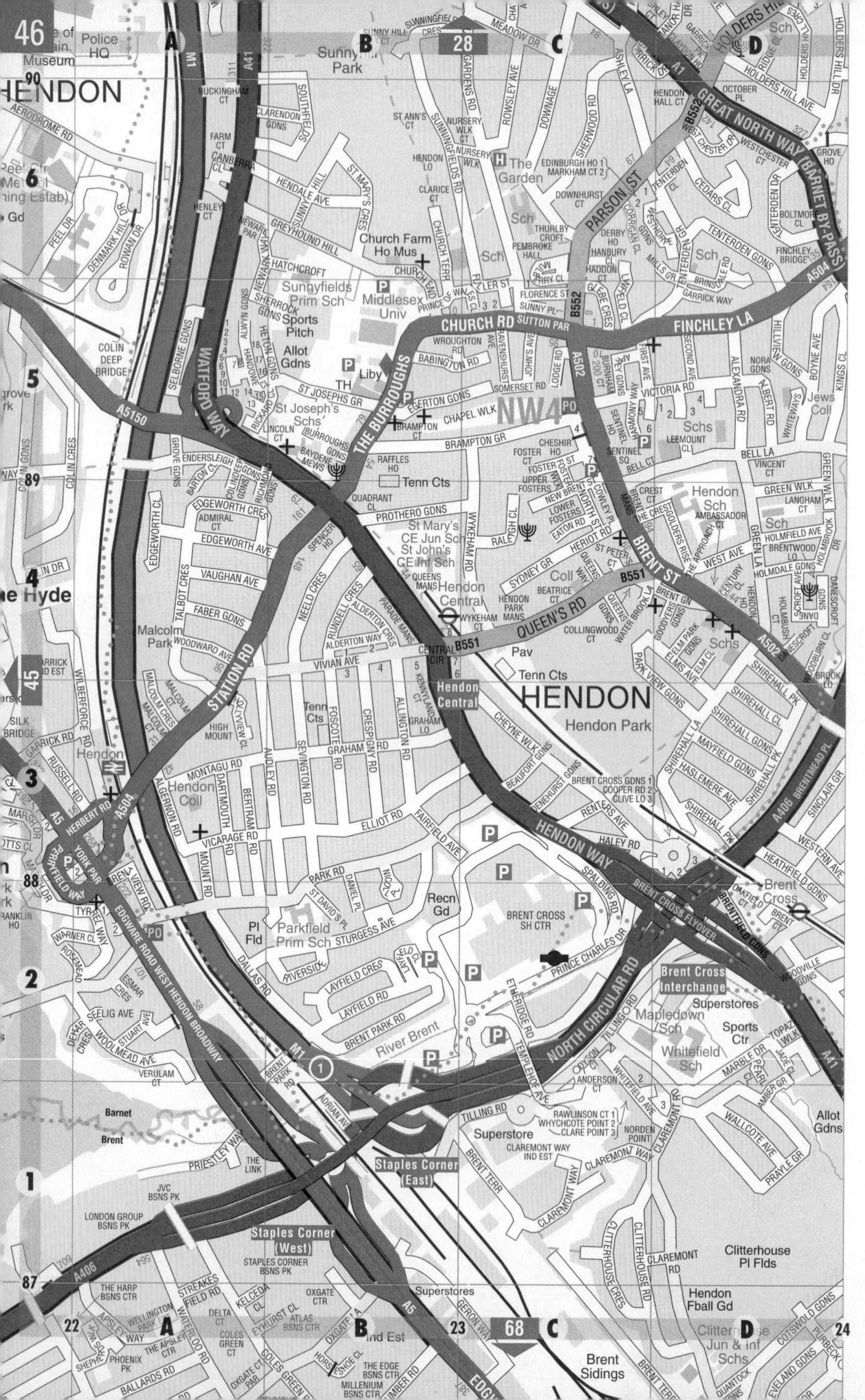
HENDON
Police HQ
Sunny Hill Park
28
A
B
C
D
Church Farm Ho Mus
Middlesex Univ
Sunnyfields Prim Sch
Sports Pitch
Allot Gdns
Liby
TH
St Joseph's Schs'
NW4
The Garden
Hendon Sch
Jews Coll
Hendon Central
Hendon Park
Tenn Cts
Pav
Malcolm Park
Hendon Coll
Parkfield Prim Sch
Recn Gd
BRENT CROSS SH CTR
Brent Cross Interchange
Brent Cross
Mapledown Sch
Whitefield Sch
Superstores
Sports Ctr
Staples Corner (East)
Staples Corner (West)
Clitterhouse Pl Flds
Hendon Fball Gd
Clitterhouse Jun & Inf Schs
Brent Sidings
River Brent
Barnet
Brent
45
68
WATFORD WAY
STATION RD
THE BURROUGHS
CHURCH RD
FINCHLEY LA
BRENT ST
QUEEN'S RD
HENDON WAY
NORTH CIRCULAR RD
GREAT NORTH WAY (BARNET BY-PASS)
EDGWARE ROAD WEST HENDON BROADWAY
BRENT CROSS FLYOVER
PARSON ST
A41
M1
A5
A406
A504
A502
A5150
B551
B552
A1
22
23
24
87
88
89
90
1
2
3
4
5
6

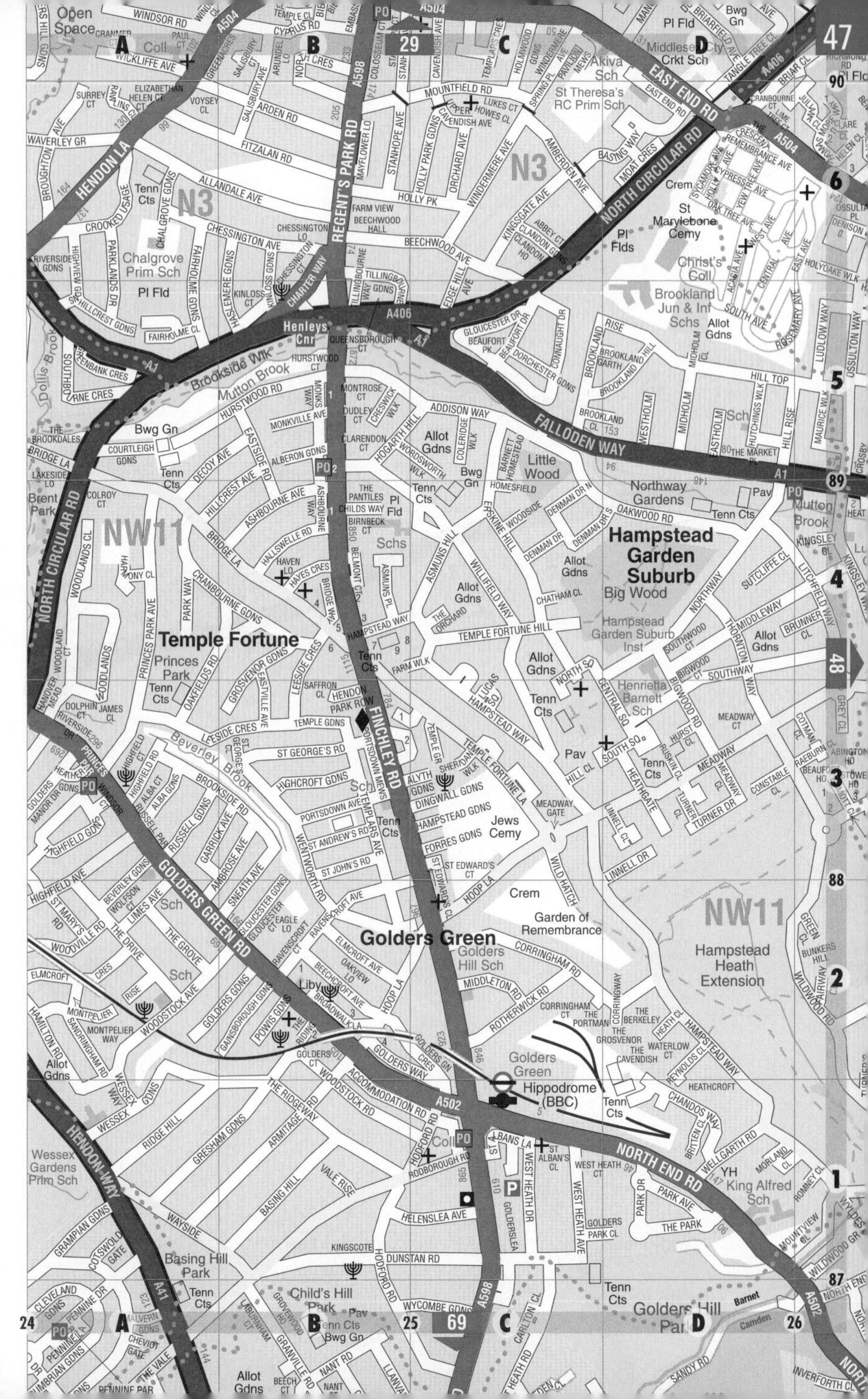

47
A
B
C
D
29
6
5
4
3
2
1
90
89
88
87
48
24
25
69
26
A504
A406
A598
A1
A502
A41
N3
NW11
Open Space
WINDSOR RD
CYPRUS RD
WICKLIFFE AVE
GREENACRES
SALISBURY CT
ARUNDEL LO
NORTH CRES
REGENT'S PARK RD
COLOSSEUM CT
STANHOPE AVE
CAVENDISH AVE
TEMPLARS CRES
HOLMWOOD GDNS
WINDERMERE AVE
PAVILION MEWS
Akiva Sch
Pl Fld
Middlesex Cty Crkt Sch
BRIARFIELD AVE
Bwg Gn
TANGLE TREE CL
EAST END RD
St Theresa's RC Prim Sch
MOUNTFIELD RD
LUKES CT
HOWES CL
SPRING PL
SURREY CT
ELIZABETHAN CT
HELEN CT
VOYSEY CL
ARDEN RD
FITZALAN RD
WAVERLEY GR
HENDON LA
BROUGHTON AVE
ALLANDALE AVE
Tenn Cts
CROOKED USAGE
PARKLANDS DR
CHALGROVE GDNS
CHESSINGTON AVE
CHESSINGTON LO
Chalgrove Prim Sch
Pl Fld
FAIRHOLME GDNS
HASLEMERE GDNS
KINLOSS CT
KINLOSS GDNS
CHARTER WAY
RIVERSIDE GDNS
HIGHVIEW GDNS
HILLCREST GDNS
FAIRHOLME CL
FARM VIEW
BEECHWOOD HALL
MAYFLOWER LO
HOLLY PARK GDNS
ORCHARD AVE
HOLLY PK
BEECHWOOD AVE
WINDERMERE AVE
KINGSGATE AVE
AMBERDEN AVE
BASING WAY
MOAT CRES
NORTH CIRCULAR RD
ABBEY CT
CLANDON GDNS
CLANDON HO
Pl Flds
EDGE HILL AVE
TILLINGBOURNE WAY
TILLINGBOURNE GDNS
Crem
St Marylebone Cemy
Christ's Coll
Brookland Jun & Inf Schs
Allot Gdns
SYCAMORE AVE
HOLLY AVE
CYPRESS AVE
YEW TREE AVE
OAK TREE AVE
THE CRESCENT
REMEMBRANCE AVE
ACACIA AVE
CENTRAL AVE
EAST AVE
WEST AVE
SOUTH AVE
ROSEMARY AVE
HOLYOAKE WLK
LUDLOW WAY
OSSULTON WAY
DENISON CL
BRIAR CL
CRANBOURNE CT
Henleys Cnr
QUEENSBOROUGH CT
HURSTWOOD CT
GLOUCESTER DR
BEAUFORT DR
BEAUFORT PK
DORCHESTER GDNS
CONNAUGHT DR
BROOKLAND RISE
BROOKLAND HILL
BROOKLAND GARTH
BROOKLAND CL
MIDHOLM CL
MIDHOLM
WESTHOLM
EASTHOLM
HILL TOP
HUTCHINGS WLK
HILL RISE
MAURICE WLK
THE MARKET PL
Sch
Brookside Wlk
Mutton Brook
Dollis Brook
GREENBANK CRES
SOUTHBOURNE CRES
HURSTWOOD RD
MONKS WAY
MONTROSE CT
DUDLEY CT
CRESWICK WLK
MONKVILLE AVE
CLARENDON CT
ADDISON WAY
HOGARTH HILL
WORDSWORTH WLK
COLERIDGE WLK
BARNETT HOMESTEAD
Little Wood
FALLODEN WAY
THE BROOKDALES
BRIDGE LA
Bwg Gn
COURTLEIGH GDNS
LAKESIDE LO
Brent Park
COLROY CT
DECOY AVE
EASTSIDE RD
ALBERON GDNS
HILLCREST AVE
ASHBOURNE AVE
ASHBOURNE WAY
THE PANTILES
CHILDS WAY
BIRNBECK CT
HOMESFIELD
DENMAN DR N
DENMAN DR S
DENMAN DR
Northway Gardens
OAKWOOD RD
Pav
Mutton Brook
NORTH CIRCULAR RD
WOODLANDS CL
HARMONY CL
CRANBOURNE GDNS
PARK WAY
HALLSWELLE RD
HAVEN LO
HAYES CRES
BRIDGE WAY
BELMONT CT
Schs
ASMUNS PL
ASMUNS HILL
ERSKINE HILL
WOODSIDE
WILLIFIELD WAY
THE ORCHARD
Hampstead Garden Suburb
Big Wood
CHATHAM CL
Hampstead Garden Suburb Inst
NORTHWAY
SUTCLIFFE CL
LITCHFIELD WAY
KINGSLEY CL
KINGSLEY WAY
MIDDLEWAY
BRUNNER CL
SOUTHWOOD CT
THORNTON WAY
Temple Fortune
PRINCES PARK AVE
Princes Park
WOODLAND CT
HANOVER MEAD
OAKFIELDS RD
GROSVENOR GDNS
EASTVILLE AVE
LEESIDE CRES
HAMPSTEAD WAY
TEMPLE FORTUNE HILL
FARM WLK
LUCAS SQ
NORTH SQ
CENTRAL SQ
Henrietta Barnett Sch
BIGWOOD CT
BIGWOOD RD
SOUTHWAY
MEADWAY CT
GREY CL
COTMAN CL
ABINGTON HO
RAEBURN CL
STOWE HO
BEAUFORT HO
DOLPHIN CT
JAMES CL
SAFFRON CL
HENDON PARK ROW
TEMPLE GDNS
FINCHLEY RD
PORTSDOWN MEWS
TEMPLE GR
SHERIDAN WLK
TEMPLE FORTUNE LA
SOUTH SQ
RUSKIN CL
HURST CL
HEATHGATE
MEADWAY
CONSTABLE CL
RIVERSIDE DR
PRINCES PAR
HIGHFIELD CT
HIGHFIELD RD
Beverley Brook
ST GEORGE'S CT
ST GEORGE'S RD
HIGHCROFT GDNS
ALYTH GDNS
DINGWALL GDNS
HAMPSTEAD GDNS
Jews Cemy
Sch
MEADWAY GATE
HILL CL
LINNELL CL
TURNER CL
TURNER DR
GOLDERS MANOR DR
HEATHER GDNS
WINDSOR CT
ALBA CT
ALBA GDNS
BROOKSIDE RD
RUSSELL PAR
RUSSELL GDNS
GARRICK AVE
AMBROSE AVE
PORTSDOWN AVE
TEMPLARS AVE
ST ANDREW'S RD
FORRES GDNS
WILD HATCH
LINNELL DR
HIGHFIELD GDNS
GOLDERS GREEN RD
ST JOHN'S RD
ST EDWARD'S CT
ST EDWARDS CL
HOOP LA
Crem
Garden of Remembrance
NW11
HIGHFIELD AVE
ST MARY'S RD
BEVERLEY GDNS
WOLFSON CT
LIMES AVE
SNEATH AVE
GLOUCESTER GDNS
WENTWORTH RD
RAVENSCROFT AVE
Golders Green
Golders Hill Sch
CORRINGHAM RD
Hampstead Heath Extension
GREEN CL
BUNKERS HILL
WILDWOOD RD
FAIRWAY
WOODVILLE RD
THE DRIVE
THE GROVE
EAGLE LO
RAVENSCROFT CT
ELMCROFT AVE
OAKVIEW LO
BEECHCROFT CT
ELMCROFT CRES
Sch
RISE
WOODSTOCK AVE
GOLDERS GDNS
GAINSBOROUGH GDNS
POWIS GDNS
Liby
BROADWALK LA
THE RIDING
HOOP LA
MIDDLETON RD
ROTHERWICK RD
CORRINGHAM CT
CORRINGWAY
THE PORTMAN
THE BERKELEY
THE GROSVENOR
THE CAVENDISH
HEATH CL
WATERLOW CT
HAMPSTEAD WAY
MONTPELIER RD
MONTPELIER WAY
HAMILTON RD
SANDRINGHAM RD
Allot Gdns
GOLDERS CT
GOLDERS WAY
GOLDERS GN CRES
Golders Green
Hippodrome (BBC)
Tenn Cts
REYNOLDS CL
HEATHCROFT
CHANDOS WAY
WESSEX WAY
WESSEX GDNS
THE RIDGEWAY
WOODSTOCK RD
ACCOMMODATION RD
RIDGE HILL
GRESHAM GDNS
ARMITAGE RD
HODFORD RD
Coll
ST ALBANS LA
ST ALBAN'S CL
WEST HEATH DR
WEST HEATH CT
BRITTEN CL
WELLGARTH RD
NORTH END RD
MORLAND CL
ROMNEY CL
YH
King Alfred Sch
Wessex Gardens Prim Sch
HENDON WAY
BASING HILL
VALE RISE
RODBOROUGH RD
GOLDERSLEA
WEST HEATH AVE
PARK DR
PARK AVE
GOLDERS PARK CL
THE PARK
MOUNTVIEW CL
WYLDES CL
WILDWOOD GR
WAYSIDE
HELENSLEA AVE
GRAMPIAN GDNS
COTSWOLD GATE
KINGSCOTE
DUNSTAN RD
Basing Hill Park
Child's Hill Park
Pav
Tenn Cts
Bwg Gn
WYCOMBE GDNS
Golders Hill Park
Barnet
Camden
CLEVELAND GDNS
PENNINE DR
MALVERN GDNS
CHEVIOT GATE
CUMBRIAN GDNS
PENNINE LA
THE VALE
LABURNUM CT
GROVEWOOD HO
GRANVILLE RD
NANT RD
BEECH CT
Allot Gdns
PENNINE PAR
CARLTON CL
SANDY RD
INVERFORTH CL
NORTH END

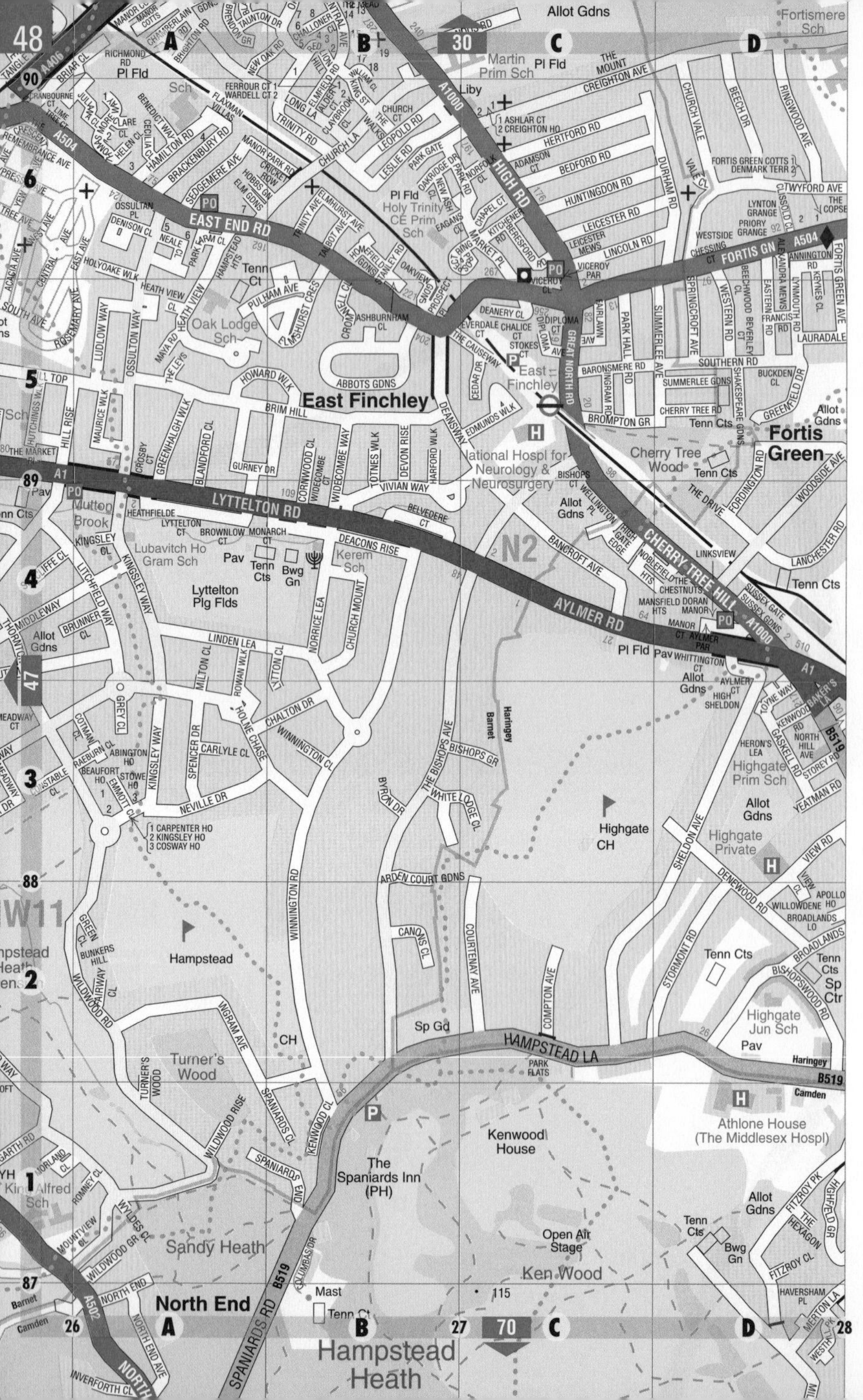

48
East Finchley
Fortis Green
N2
East End Rd
High Rd
Great North Rd
Lyttelton Rd
Aylmer Rd
Cherry Tree Hill
Fortis Gn
Hampstead La
Spaniards Rd
Winnington Rd
The Bishops Ave
Kingsley Way
Sheldon Ave
Holy Trinity CE Prim Sch
Oak Lodge Sch
Martin Prim Sch
National Hospl for Neurology & Neurosurgery
Cherry Tree Wood
Lyttelton Plg Flds
Lubavitch Ho Gram Sch
Kerem Sch
Highgate CH
Highgate Prim Sch
Highgate Private
Highgate Jun Sch
Hampstead
Turner's Wood
Sandy Heath
Kenwood House
Ken Wood
Open Air Stage
The Spaniards Inn (PH)
Athlone House (The Middlesex Hospl)
North End
Hampstead Heath
Mutton Brook
Fortismere Sch
Allot Gdns
A B C D
30
70
47
26 27 28
87 88 89 90
1 2 3 4 5 6

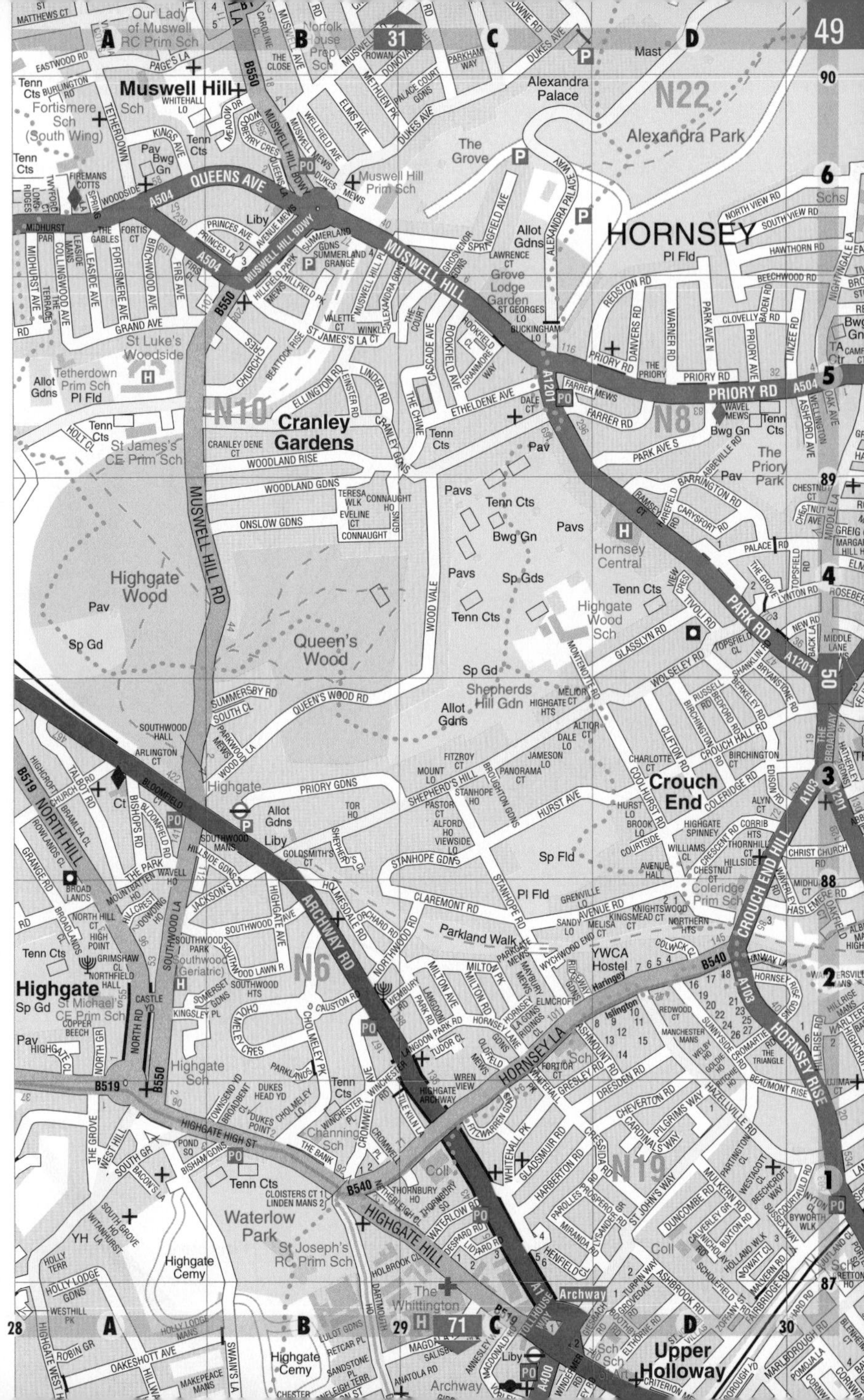
49
A
B
C
D
31
90
Muswell Hill
Alexandra Palace
N22
Alexandra Park
The Grove
Mast
HORNSEY
QUEENS AVE
A504
MUSWELL HILL
MUSWELL HILL BDWY
MUSWELL HILL RD
B550
PRIORY RD
A1201
PARK RD
N10
N8
N6
N19
Cranley Gardens
Highgate Wood
Queen's Wood
Hornsey Central
Highgate Wood Sch
Shepherds Hill Gdn
Crouch End
CROUCH END HILL
HORNSEY RISE
A103
The Priory Park
Highgate
NORTH HILL
B519
ARCHWAY RD
HIGHGATE HIGH ST
HIGHGATE HILL
HORNSEY LA
Parkland Walk
YWCA Hostel
Waterlow Park
Highgate Cemy
The Whittington
Channing Sch
Archway
Upper Holloway
A400
A1
B540
St Luke's Woodside
Tetherdown Prim Sch
St James's CE Prim Sch
St Michael's CE Prim Sch
St Joseph's RC Prim Sch
Coleridge Prim Sch
Muswell Hill Prim Sch
Our Lady of Muswell RC Prim Sch
Fortismere Sch (South Wing)
6
5
89
4
50
3
88
2
1
87
28
29
71
30

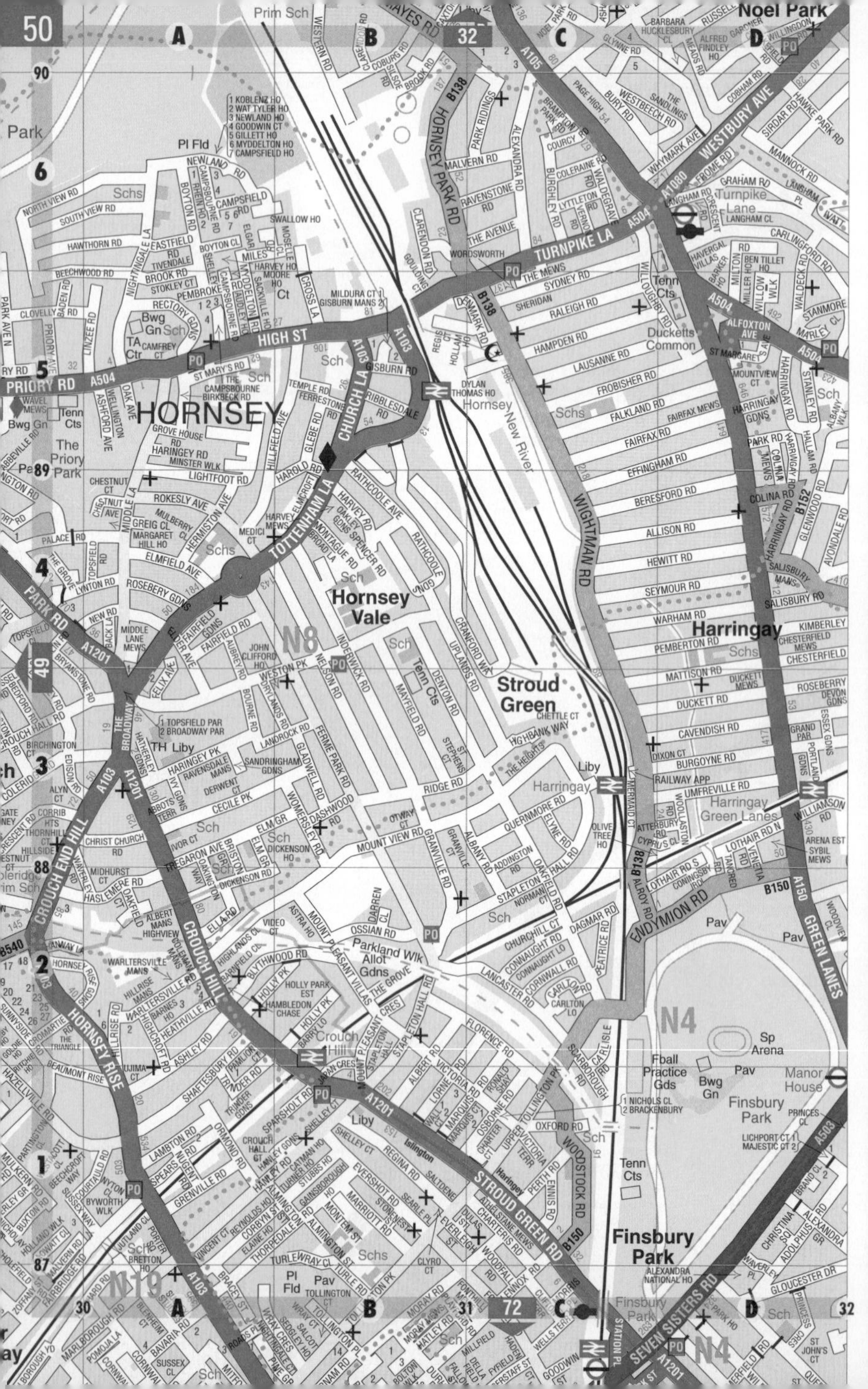
A
B
C
D
32
90
6
5
89
4
3
88
2
1
87
30
31
72
49
Noel Park
Park
Pl Fld
1 KOBLENZ HO
2 WAT TYLER HO
3 NEWLAND HO
4 GOODWIN CT
5 GILLETT HO
6 MYDDELTON HO
7 CAMPSFIELD HO
HORNSEY
HIGH ST
PRIORY RD
A504
The Priory Park
Bwg Gn
Tenn Cts
Schs
Sch
TOTTENHAM LA
CHURCH LA
A103
A1201
A105
B138
HORNSEY PARK RD
TURNPIKE LA
Turnpike Lane
WESTBURY AVE
A1080
WIGHTMAN RD
Ducketts Common
Hornsey
New River
Hornsey Vale
N8
Stroud Green
Harringay
Harringay Green Lanes
GREEN LANES
A150
B150
ENDYMION RD
N4
Sp Arena
Fball Practice Gds
Finsbury Park
Manor House
SEVEN SISTERS RD
STROUD GREEN RD
CROUCH HILL
Crouch Hill
CROUCH END HILL
HORNSEY RISE
Parkland Wlk
Allot Gdns
N19
PARK RD
THE BROADWAY
TH Liby
Liby
Islington
Haringey
B540
A503
WOODSTOCK RD
STATION PL
Finsbury Park

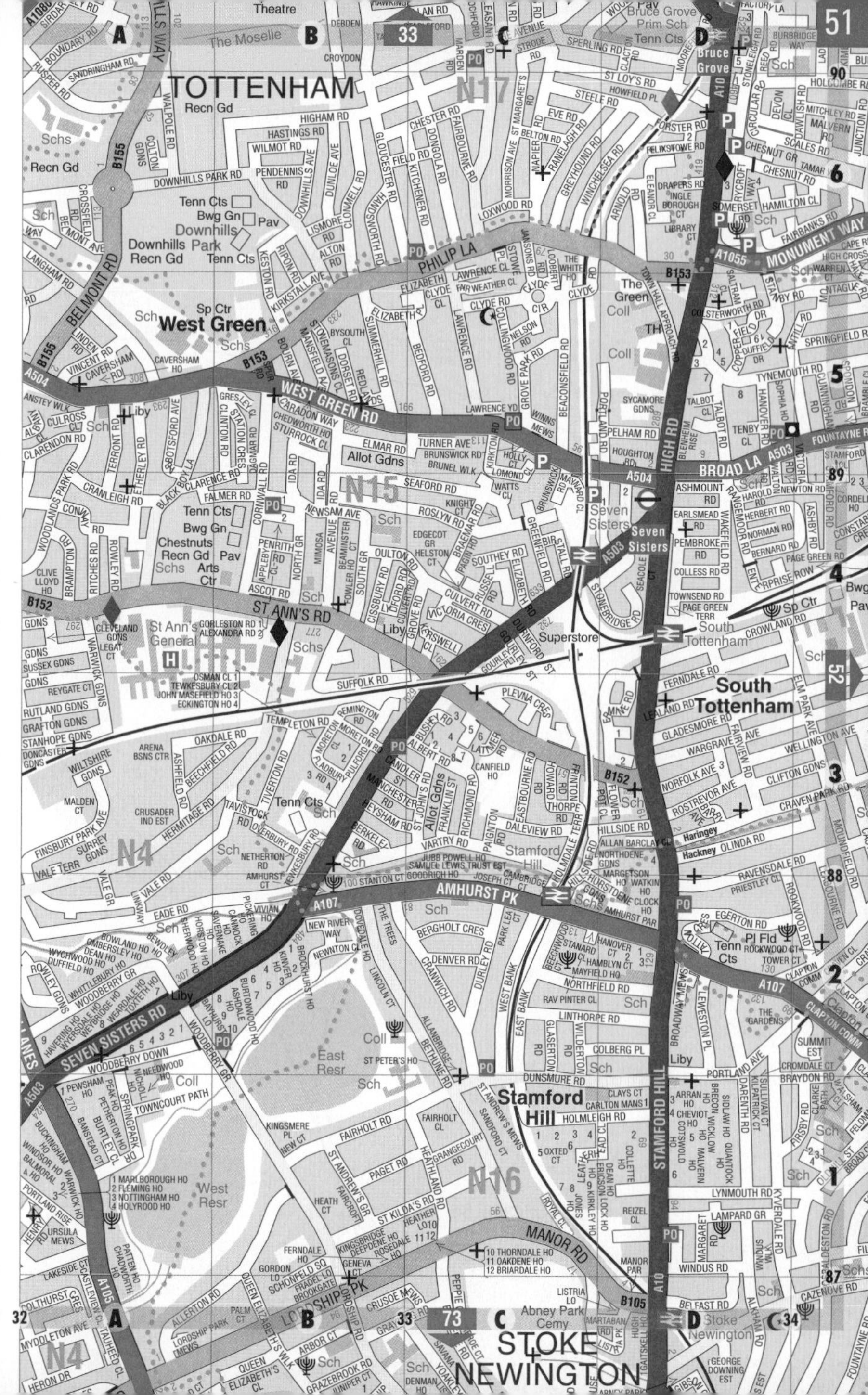
TOTTENHAM
West Green
South Tottenham
Stamford Hill
STOKE NEWINGTON
N17
N15
N4
N16
33
52
73
32
34
A
B
C
D
1
2
3
4
5
6
Bruce Grove
Seven Sisters
South Tottenham
Stamford Hill
Downhills Park
Downhills Recn Gd
Chestnuts Recn Gd
St Ann's General
East Resr
West Resr
Abney Park Cemy
Superstore
PHILIP LA
WEST GREEN RD
ST ANN'S RD
SEVEN SISTERS RD
AMHURST PK
BROAD LA
HIGH RD
STAMFORD HILL
MANOR RD
MONUMENT WAY
BELMONT RD
LORDSHIP PK
A10
A107
A503
A504
A105
A1055
B152
B153
B155
B105

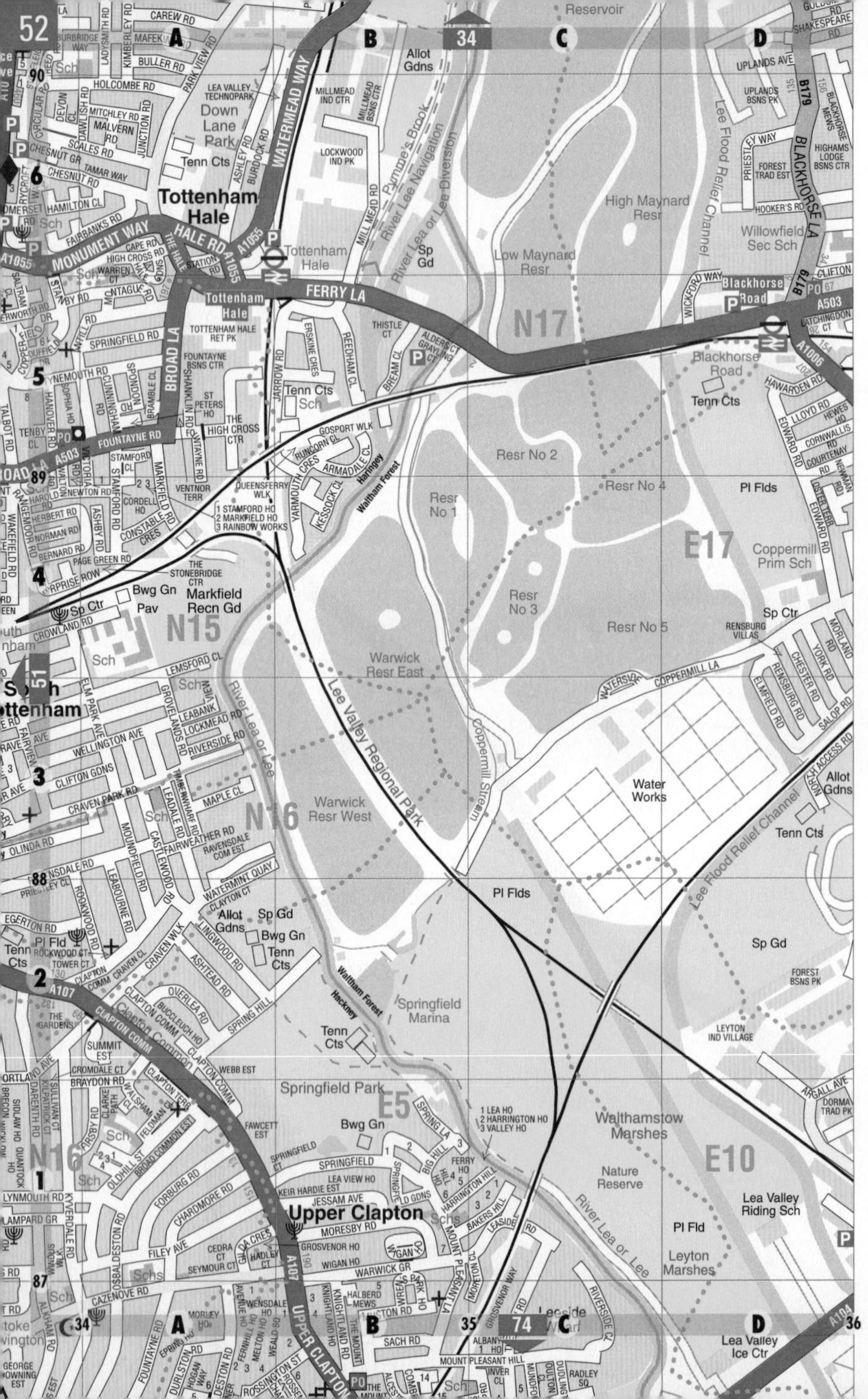

A
B
34
C
D
Reservoir
Allot Gdns
CAREW RD
MAFEKING
BULLER RD
HOLCOMBE RD
MITCHLEY RD
MALVERN RD
SCALES RD
CHESNUT GR
CHESNUT RD
TAMAR WAY
HAMILTON CL
FAIRBANKS RD
MONUMENT WAY
HALE RD
WATERMEAD WAY
LEA VALLEY TECHNOPARK
Down Lane Park
Tenn Cts
Tottenham Hale
MILLMEAD IND CTR
LOCKWOOD IND PK
MILL MEAD RD
Pymme's Brook
River Lee Navigation
River Lea or Lee Diversion
Sp Gd
High Maynard Resr
Low Maynard Resr
Lee Flood Relief Channel
UPLANDS AVE
UPLANDS BSNS PK
PRIESTLEY WAY
FOREST TRAD EST
HOOKER'S RD
HIGHAMS LODGE BSNS CTR
BLACKHORSE LA
B179
Willowfield Sec Sch
WICKFORD WAY
Blackhorse Road
FERRY LA
A1055
A503
A1006
N17
Tottenham Hale
TOTTENHAM HALE RET PK
FOUNTAYNE BSNS CTR
SPRINGFIELD RD
BROAD LA
FOUNTAYNE RD
ST PETERS HO
THE HIGH CROSS CTR
JARROW RD
ERSKINE CRES
REEDHAM CL
THISTLE CT
BREAM CL
ALDERS CT
GRAYLING CT
HAWARDEN RD
LLOYD RD
EDWARD RD
CORNWALLIS
COURTENAY
Resr No 2
Resr No 4
Resr No 1
Resr No 3
Resr No 5
Pl Flds
E17
Coppermill Prim Sch
Sp Ctr
RENSBURG VILLAS
COPPERMILL LA
WATERSIDE
MORLAND RD
YORK RD
CHESTER RD
ELMFIELD RD
SALOP RD
GOSPORT WLK
RUNCORN CL
ARMADALE CL
YARMOUTH CRES
KESSOCK CL
QUEENSFERRY WLK
1 STAMFORD HO
2 MARKFIELD HO
3 RAINBOW WORKS
Haringey
Waltham Forest
THE STONEBRIDGE CTR
Markfield Recn Gd
Bwg Gn
Pav
N15
CROWLAND RD
Sch
51
South Tottenham
LEMSFORD CL
ELM PARK AVE
GROVELANDS RD
LEABANK
LOCKMEAD RD
RIVERSIDE RD
WELLINGTON AVE
CLIFTON GDNS
CRAVEN PARK RD
MAPLE CL
River Lea or Lee
Warwick Resr East
Warwick Resr West
Lee Valley Regional Park
Coppermill Stream
Water Works
N16
FAIRWEATHER RD
RAVENSDALE COM EST
WATERMINT QUAY
CLAYTON CT
Allot Gdns
Sp Gd
Bwg Gn
Tenn Cts
Pl Flds
NORTH ACCESS RD
Allot Gdns
Tenn Cts
Sp Gd
FOREST BSNS PK
LEYTON IND VILLAGE
ARGALL AVE
DORMA TRAD PK
A107
CLAPTON COMM
Clapton Common
SUMMIT EST
WEBB EST
Springfield Marina
Tenn Cts
Springfield Park
E5
Walthamstow Marshes
Nature Reserve
E10
Lea Valley Riding Sch
Pl Fld
Leyton Marshes
River Lea or Lee
1 LEA HO
2 HARRINGTON HO
3 VALLEY HO
FAWCETT EST
SPRINGFIELD
KEIR HARDIE EST
JESSAM AVE
Upper Clapton
MORESBY RD
GROSVENOR HO
WIGAN HO
WARWICK GR
MOUNT PLEASANT LA
HARRINGTON HILL
BAKERS HILL
LEASIDE RD
GROSVENOR WAY
RIVERSIDE CL
Leaside Wharf
74
35
36
A104
Lea Valley Ice Ctr
UPPER CLAPTON
CAZENOVE RD
FOUNTAYNE RD
DURLSTON RD
MOUNT PLEASANT HILL
RADLEY SQ
GEORGE DOWNING EST
N16
LYNMOUTH RD
KYVERDALE RD
ALKHAM RD
6
5
4
3
2
1
90
89
88
87

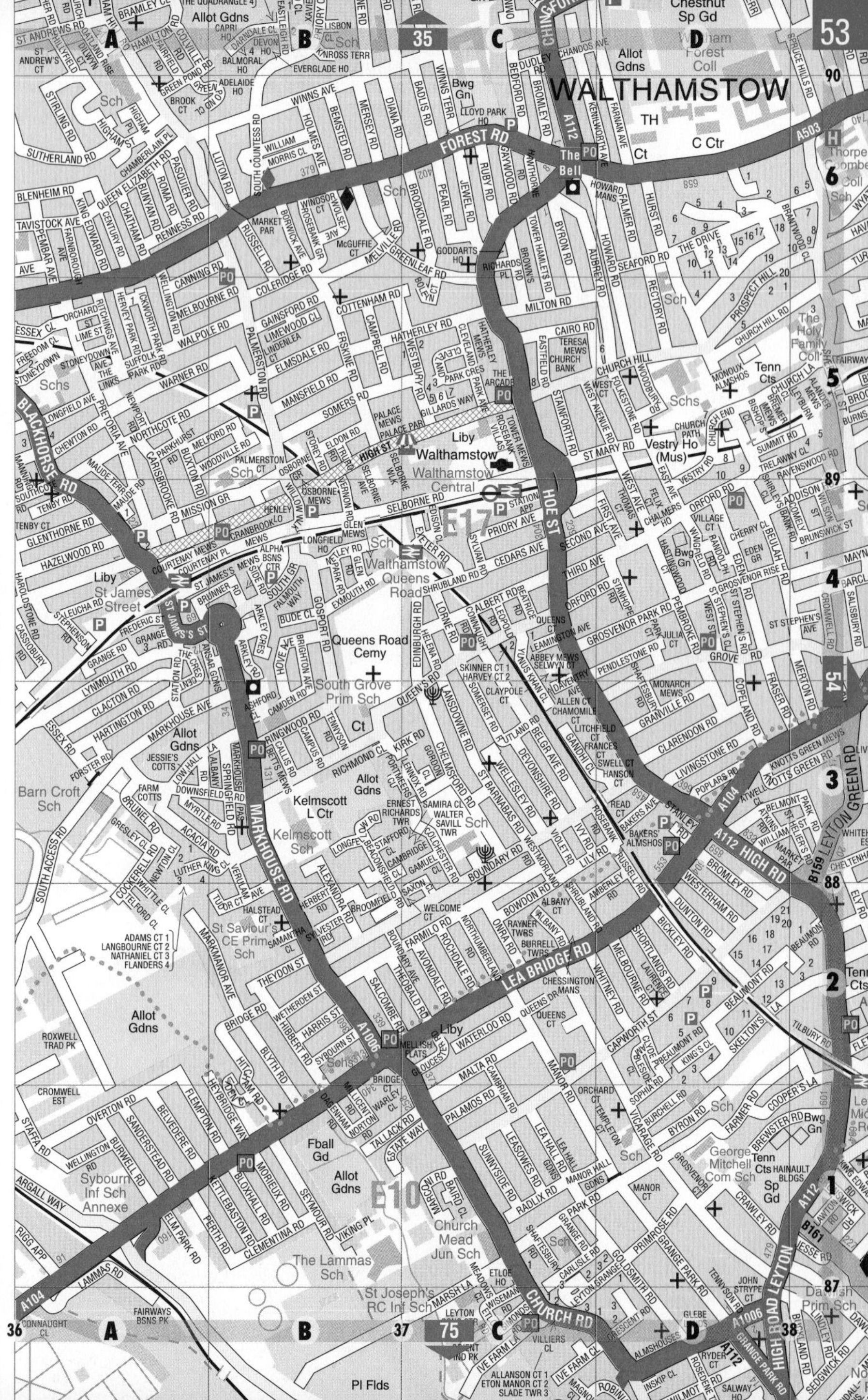

53
35
A
B
C
D
WALTHAMSTOW
E17
E10
Chestnut Sp Gd
Waltham Forest Coll
Allot Gdns
TH
C Ctr
Ct
The Bell
FOREST RD
A503
A112
Thorpe Coombe Coll
90
6
5
89
4
3
88
2
1
87
54
75
36
37
38
WINNS AVE
HOLMES AVE
BEMSTED RD
MERSEY RD
DIANA RD
BADLIS RD
WINNS TERR
BEDFORD RD
BROMLEY RD
CHANDOS AVE
KENILWORTH AVE
FARNAN AVE
HURST RD
HOWARD RD
FALMER RD
AUBREY RD
BYRON RD
TOWER HAMLETS RD
BROWNING
RICHARDS PL
MILTON RD
SEAFORD RD
RECTORY RD
PROSPECT HILL
THE DRIVE
BRAINTWOOD CL
CHURCH HILL RD
CHURCH HILL
The Holy Family Coll
CHURCH LA
CHURCH END
CHURCH PATH
Vestry Ho (Mus)
VESTRY RD
ST MARY RD
SUMMIT RD
TRELAWNY CL
RAVENSWOOD RD
ADDISON
ORFORD RD
HOE ST
Walthamstow Central
Liby
Walthamstow
HIGH ST
SELBORNE RD
PRIORY AVE
CEDARS AVE
SECOND AVE
THIRD AVE
FIRST AVE
GROSVENOR PARK RD
PEMBROKE RD
ST STEPHEN'S RD
GROSVENOR RISE RD
BEULAH RD
COMELY BANK RD
BRUNSWICK ST
WILSON
ST STEPHEN'S AVE
CROMWELL RD
SALISBURY RD
MERTON RD
FRASER RD
COPELAND RD
GRANVILLE RD
CLARENDON RD
LIVINGSTONE RD
POPLARS RD
A104
A112 HIGH RD
B159 LEYTON GREEN RD
KNOTTS GREEN MEWS
KNOTTS GREEN RD
WESTERHAM RD
BROMLEY RD
DUNTON RD
BICKLEY RD
SHORTLANDS RD
MELBOURNE RD
WHITNEY RD
BEAUMONT RD
Tenn Cts
Queens Road Cemy
Walthamstow Queens Road
South Grove Prim Sch
Kelmscott L Ctr
Kelmscott Sch
MARKHOUSE RD
MARKHOUSE AVE
LEA BRIDGE RD
A1006
Liby
St James Street
ST JAMES'S ST
BLACKHORSE RD
Barn Croft Sch
SOUTH ACCESS RD
Allot Gdns
ROXWELL TRAD PK
CROMWELL EST
Sybourn Inf Sch Annexe
ARGALL WAY
RIGG APP
LAMMAS RD
FAIRWAYS BSNS PK
CONNAUGHT CL
A104
Fball Gd
Church Mead Jun Sch
The Lammas Sch
St Joseph's RC Inf Sch
MARSH LA
CHURCH RD
VILLIERS CL
IVE FARM LA
Pl Flds
ALLANSON CT 1
ETON MANOR CT 2
SLADE TWR 3
ADAMS CT 1
LANGBOURNE CT 2
NATHANIEL CT 3
FLANDERS 4
St Saviour's CE Prim Sch
George Mitchell Com Sch
Sp Gd
HIGH ROAD LEYTON
B161
Dawlish Prim Sch
GRANGE PARK RD
PRIMROSE RD
VICARAGE RD
MANOR RD
CAPWORTH ST
SKELTON'S LA
TILBURY RD
COOPER'S LA
CRAWLEY RD
FARMER RD
BREWSTER RD
HAINAULT BLDGS
ALMSHOUSES
GLEBE
CHANGE PARK RD
SUTHERLAND RD
BLENHEIM RD
TAVISTOCK AVE
STIRLING RD
ST ANDREWS RD
HIGHAM ST
CHATHAM RD
ROMA RD
RENNESS RD
RUSSELL RD
COLERIDGE RD
COTTENHAM RD
HATHERLEY RD
CAMPBELL RD
WESTBURY RD
ERSKINE RD
ELMSDALE RD
MANSFIELD RD
SOMERS RD
WARNER RD
WALPOLE RD
MELBOURNE RD
CANNING RD
NORTHCOTE RD
PRETORIA AVE
CHEWTON RD
GLENTHORNE RD
HAZELWOOD RD
TENBY RD
MISSION GR
CARISBROOKE RD
BUXTON RD
LYNMOUTH RD
CLACTON RD
HARTINGTON RD
ESSEX RD
MARKHOUSE AVE
GOSPORT RD
EXMOUTH RD
EDINBURGH RD
LORNE RD
SHRUBLAND RD
ALBERT RD
CHELMSFORD RD
LANSDOWNE RD
RICHMOND RD
SOMERSET RD
WELLESLEY RD
DEVONSHIRE RD
BELGRAVE RD
ST BARNABAS RD
BOUNDARY RD
WESTMORLAND RD
VIOLET RD
IVY RD
LILY RD
RUSSELL RD
ROSEBANK
GANDHI CL
YUNUS KHAN CL
FARMILO RD
ROCHDALE RD
AVONDALE RD
NORTHUMBERLAND RD
ONRA RD
BOWDON RD
SALCOMBE RD
THEOBALD RD
HIBBERT RD
HARRIS ST
BLYTH RD
BRIDGE RD
WATERLOO RD
MALTA RD
PALAMOS RD
SUNNYSIDE RD
LEASOWES RD
LEA HALL RD
RADLIX RD
PARK RD
OVERTON RD
SANDERSTEAD RD
BELVEDERE RD
FLEMPTON RD
BURWELL RD
WELLINGTON RD
KETTLEBASTON RD
BLOXHALL RD
MORIEUX RD
CLEMENTINA RD
SEYMOUR RD
VIKING PL
PERTH RD
ELM PARK RD
THEYDON ST
WETHERDEN ST

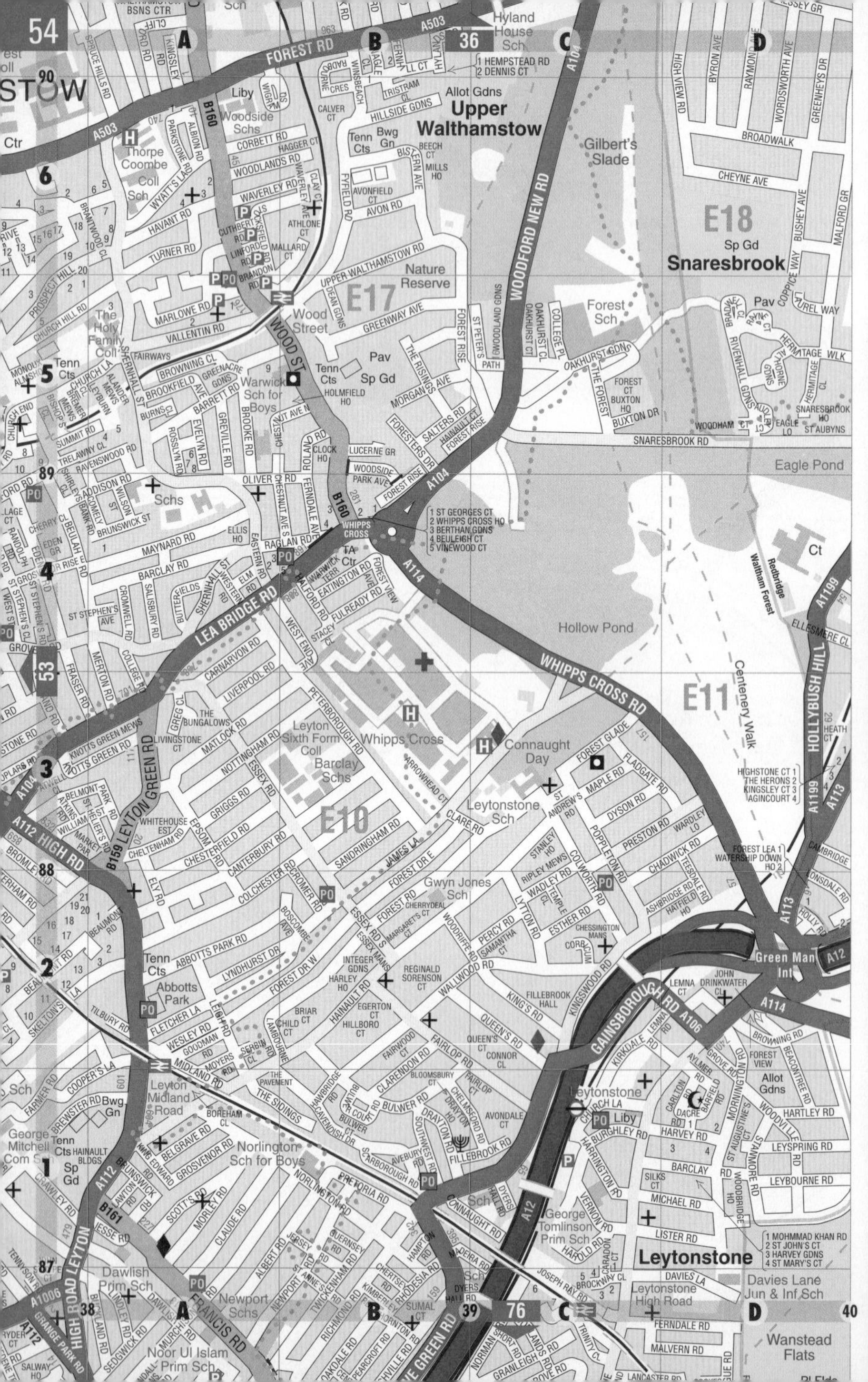

A
B
C
D
36
Hyland House Sch
FOREST RD
A503
1 HEMPSTEAD RD
2 DENNIS CT
Allot Gdns
Upper Walthamstow
STOW
Liby
Woodside Schs
Thorpe Coombe
Coll Sch
Gilbert's Slade
WOODFORD NEW RD
A104
E18
Sp Gd
Snaresbrook
BROADWALK
CHEYNE AVE
HIGH VIEW RD
BYRON AVE
RAYMOND AVE
WORDSWORTH AVE
GREENHEYS DR
BUSHEY AVE
MALFORD GR
COPPICE WAY
LAUREL WAY
Pav
HERMITAGE WLK
Forest Sch
OAKHURST GDNS
SNARESBROOK RD
SNARESBROOK HO
ST AUBYNS
Eagle Pond
Nature Reserve
E17
Wood Street
WOOD ST
GREENWAY AVE
UPPER WALTHAMSTOW RD
Tenn Cts
Bwg Gn
Sp Gd
Warwick Sch for Boys
THE RISINGS
MORGANS AVE
FORESTERS DR
SALTERS RD
FOREST RISE
ST PETER'S PATH
WOODLAND GDNS
OAKHURST CL
COLLEGE PL
THE FOREST
BUXTON DR
WOODHAM CT
The Holy Family Coll
CHURCH HILL RD
PROSPECT HILL
TURNER RD
HAVANT RD
MARLOWE RD
VALLENTIN RD
FAIRWAYS
BROWNING CL
SHERNHALL ST
ADDISON RD
OLIVER RD
Schs
MAYNARD RD
BARCLAY RD
ST STEPHEN'S AVE
RAGLAN RD
WHIPPS CROSS
B160
1 ST GEORGES CT
2 WHIPPS CROSS HO
3 BERTHAN GDNS
4 BEULEIGH CT
5 VINEWOOD CT
TA Ctr
A114
Ct
Redbridge
Waltham Forest
A1199
ELLESMERE CL
Hollow Pond
LEA BRIDGE RD
WHIPPS CROSS RD
E11
Centenary Walk
HOLLYBUSH HILL
HIGHSTONE CT 1
THE HERONS 2
KINGSLEY CT 3
AGINCOURT 4
A113
53
CARNARVON RD
LIVERPOOL RD
PETERBOROUGH RD
Leyton Sixth Form Coll
Barclay Schs
Whipps Cross
Connaught Day
FOREST GLADE
MAPLE RD
FLADGATE RD
DYSON RD
PRESTON RD
THE BUNGALOWS
KNOTTS GREEN MEWS
KNOTTS GREEN RD
LEYTON GREEN RD
MATLOCK RD
NOTTINGHAM RD
ESSEX RD
E10
Leytonstone Sch
CLARE RD
A112
HIGH RD
B159
CHELTENHAM RD
GRIGGS RD
CHESTERFIELD RD
CANTERBURY RD
COLCHESTER RD
SANDRINGHAM RD
JAMES LA
FOREST DR E
Gwyn Jones Sch
POPPLETON RD
CHADWICK RD
COLWORTH RD
FOREST LEA 1
WATERSHIP DOWN HO 2
CAMBRIDGE
88
ELY RD
Tenn Cts
ABBOTTS PARK RD
LYNDHURST DR
FOREST DR W
Abbotts Park
FLETCHER LA
WESLEY RD
KINGSWOOD RD
FILLEBROOK HALL
KING'S RD
QUEEN'S RD
GAINSBOROUGH RD
A106
Green Man Int
A12
A114
LEMNA CT
JOHN DRINKWATER CL
BROWNING RD
Leyton Midland Road
MIDLAND RD
TILBURY RD
COOPER'S LA
THE SIDINGS
CLARENDON RD
FAIRLOP RD
BULWER RD
DRAYTON RD
AVONDALE CT
Leytonstone
CHURCH LA
Liby
HARVEY RD
BARCLAY RD
Allot Gdns
HARTLEY RD
LEYSPRING RD
LEYBOURNE RD
George Mitchell Com Sch
Sp Gd
Norlington Sch for Boys
GROSVENOR RD
BELGRAVE RD
NORLINGTON RD
PRETORIA RD
FILLEBROOK RD
CONNAUGHT RD
George Tomlinson Prim Sch
MICHAEL RD
LISTER RD
1 MOHMMAD KHAN RD
2 ST JOHN'S CT
3 HARVEY GDNS
4 ST MARY'S CT
Leytonstone
87
HIGH ROAD LEYTON
Dawlish Prim Sch
FRANCIS RD
Newport Schs
DAVIES LA
Davies Lane Jun & Inf Sch
Leytonstone High Road
38
39
76
40
FERNDALE RD
MALVERN RD
Wanstead Flats
Noor Ul Islam Prim Sch
GRANGE PARK RD
A1006
SEDGWICK RD
LEYTONSTONE RD

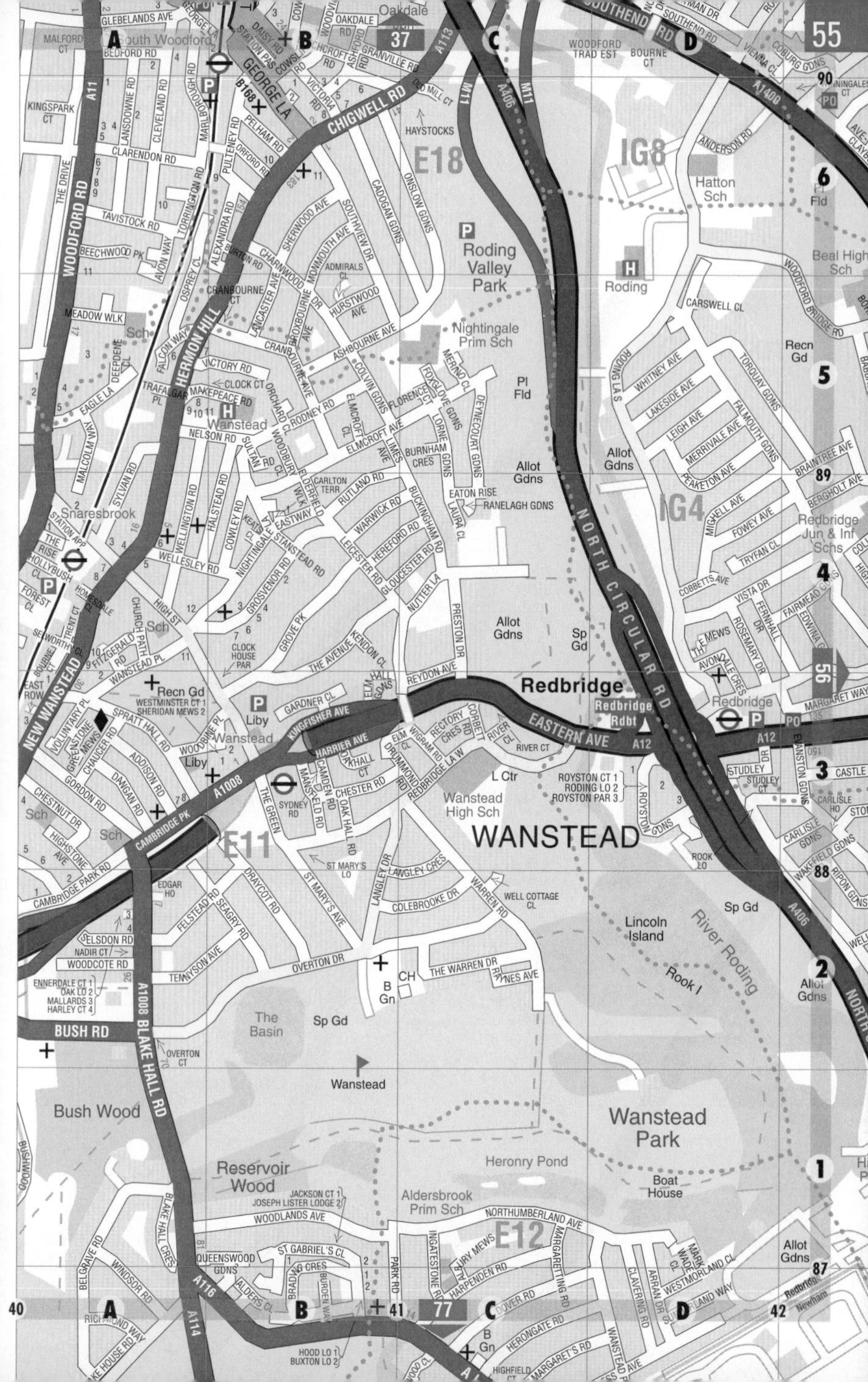

South Woodford
Oakdale
37
A
B
C
D
GLEBELANDS AVE
MALFORD CT
BEDFORD RD
KINGSPARK CT
LANSDOWNE RD
CLEVELAND RD
MARLBOROUGH RD
GEORGE LA
B168
DAISY RD
STATION PAS
COWSLIP RD
OAKDALE RD
ASHFORD RD
GRANVILLE RD
VICTORIA RD
CHIGWELL RD
A113
OLD MILL CT
HAYSTOCKS
E18
CLARENDON RD
PELHAM RD
ORFORD RD
PULTENEY RD
THE DRIVE
WOODFORD RD
A11
TAVISTOCK RD
TORRINGTON RD
BEECHWOOD PK
AVON WAY
ALEXANDRA RD
BURTON RD
OSPREY CL
CRANBOURNE CT
HERMON HILL
MEADOW WLK
Sch
DEEPDENE CL
FALCON WAY
VICTORY RD
CLOCK CT
TRAFALGAR PL
MAKEPEACE RD
EAGLE LA
MALCOLM WAY
Wanstead
NELSON RD
SYLVAN RD
Snaresbrook
STATION APP
THE RISE
HOLLYBUSH CL
FOREST CL
HOMESDALE CL
TRENT CT
SELWORTHY CL
BOURNE CT
EAST ROW
NEW WANSTEAD
CHURCH PATH
HIGH ST
FITZGERALD RD
WANSTEAD PL
OVERTON CT
WELLINGTON RD
HALSTEAD RD
COWLEY RD
WELLESLEY RD
NIGHTINGALE LA
KEATS CL
GROSVENOR RD
SULTAN RD
WOODBURY CL
ORCHARD CL
CARLTON TERR
ELDERFIELD WLK
EASTWAY
STANSTEAD RD
CHARNWOOD DR
LANCASTER AVE
BROXBOURNE AVE
SHERWOOD AVE
MONMOUTH AVE
SOUTHVIEW DR
ADMIRALS CL
HURSTWOOD AVE
CADOGAN GDNS
ONSLOW GDNS
CRANBOURNE AVE
ASHBOURNE AVE
COLVIN GDNS
ELMCROFT CL
ELMCROFT AVE
RODNEY RD
FLORENCE CT
FOXGLOVE GDNS
MERINO CL
LORNE GDNS
DEYNECOURT GDNS
BURNHAM CRES
IMES AVE
RUTLAND RD
WARWICK RD
HEREFORD RD
BUCKINGHAM RD
LEICESTER RD
GLOUCESTER RD
NUTTER LA
PRESTON DR
EATON RISE
RANELAGH GDNS
LAURA CL
Roding Valley Park
Nightingale Prim Sch
Pl Fld
Allot Gdns
GROVE PK
THE AVENUE
KENDON CL
CLOCK HOUSE PAR
Recn Gd
WESTMINSTER CT 1
SHERIDAN MEWS 2
VOLUNTARY PL
GREENSTONE MEWS
SPRATT HALL RD
CHAUCER RD
ADDISON RD
DANGAN RD
GORDON RD
CHESTNUT DR
HIGHSTONE AVE
WOODBINE PL
Liby
GARDNER CL
ELM HALL GDNS
KINGFISHER AVE
HARRIER AVE
REYDON AVE
Redbridge
Redbridge Rdbt
EASTERN AVE
A12
A1008
CAMBRIDGE PK
CAMBRIDGE PARK RD
E11
THE GREEN
SYDNEY RD
CAMDEN RD
MANSFIELD RD
OAKHALL CT
CHESTER RD
OAK HALL RD
DRUMMOND RD
ELM CL
WIGRAM RD
RECTORY CRES
CORBETT RD
REDBRIDGE LA W
RIVER CL
RIVER CT
L Ctr
Wanstead High Sch
WANSTEAD
ROYSTON CT 1
RODING LO 2
ROYSTON PAR 3
ROYSTON GDNS
ROOK LO
EDGAR HO
FELSTEAD RD
SEAGRY RD
DRAYCOT RD
ST MARY'S AVE
ST MARY'S LO
LANGLEY DR
LANGLEY CRES
COLEBROOKE DR
WARREN RD
WELL COTTAGE CL
SELSDON RD
NADIR CT
WOODCOTE RD
ENNERDALE CT 1
OAK LO 2
MALLARDS 3
HARLEY CT 4
TENNYSON AVE
OVERTON DR
THE WARREN DR
RAYNES AVE
B Gn
CH
BUSH RD
A1008 BLAKE HALL RD
OVERTON CT
The Basin
Sp Gd
Lincoln Island
River Roding
Rook I
Bush Wood
Reservoir Wood
Heronry Pond
Wanstead Park
Boat House
Aldersbrook Prim Sch
JACKSON CT 1
JOSEPH LISTER LODGE 2
WOODLANDS AVE
NORTHUMBERLAND AVE
E12
MARGARETTING RD
QUEENSWOOD GDNS
ST GABRIEL'S CL
BRADING CRES
BURDEN WAY
ALDERS CL
PARK RD
INGATESTONE RD
ALBURY MEWS
HARPENDEN RD
CLAVERING RD
ARRAN DR
MARK CL
WADE CL
WESTMORLAND CL
SUNDERLAND WAY
DOVER RD
HERONGATE RD
ST MARGARET'S RD
WANSTEAD PARK AVE
HIGHFIELD CT
HOOD LO 1
BUXTON LO 2
BLAKE HALL CRES
BELGRAVE RD
WINDSOR RD
RICHMOND WAY
A116
A114
BUSHWOOD
40
41
77
42
Redbridge
Newham
SOUTHEND RD
WOODFORD TRAD EST
BOURNE CT
VIENNA CL
COBURG GDNS
A1400
90
PO
A406
M11
IG8
ANDERSON RD
Hatton Sch
6
Pl Fld
Beal High Sch
H
Roding
WOODFORD BRIDGE RD
CARSWELL CL
Recn Gd
5
RODING LA S
WHITNEY AVE
LAKESIDE AVE
TORQUAY GDNS
LEIGH AVE
MERRIVALE AVE
FALMOUTH GDNS
PEAKETON AVE
BRAINTREE AVE
89
BERGHOLT AVE
IG4
MICHELL AVE
FOWEY AVE
TRYFAN CL
Redbridge Jun & Inf Schs
4
COBBETTS AVE
VISTA DR
FERNHALL DR
FAIRMEAD GDNS
EDWINA GDNS
THE MEWS
ROSEMARY DR
AVONDALE CRES
NORTH CIRCULAR RD
56
MARGARET WAY
STUDLEY DR
STUDLEY CT
EVANSTON GDNS
3
CASTLE
CARLISLE HO
CARLISLE GDNS
WAKEFIELD GDNS
RIPON GDNS
88
2
Allot Gdns
1
87

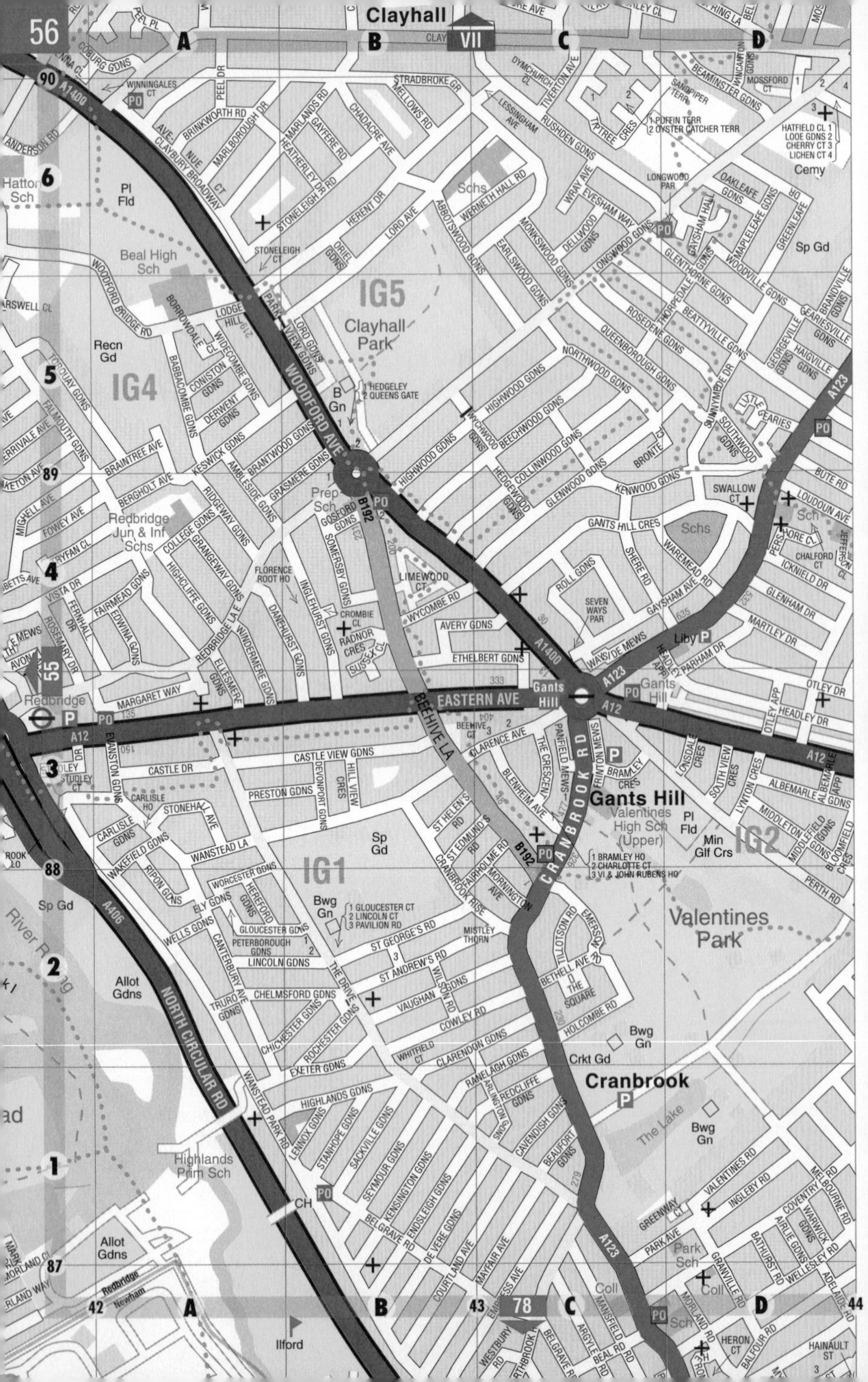
Clayhall
VII
A
B
C
D
6
5
4
3
2
1
90
89
88
87
42
43
44
55
78
IG5
IG4
IG1
IG2
Clayhall Park
Beal High Sch
Hatton Sch
Pl Fld
Recn Gd
Redbridge Jun & Inf Schs
Redbridge
Gants Hill
Valentines High Sch (Upper)
Valentines Park
Min Glf Crs
Cranbrook
The Lake
Crkt Gd
Bwg Gn
Sp Gd
Allot Gdns
Highlands Prim Sch
River Roding
Cemy
Schs
Sch
Prep Sch
Liby
Park Sch
Coll
Ilford
WOODFORD AVE
EASTERN AVE
CRANBROOK RD
NORTH CIRCULAR RD
BEEHIVE LA
A1400
A12
A123
A406
B192
WOODFORD BRIDGE RD
CLAYBURY BROADWAY
LORD AVE
STRADBROKE GR
RUSHDEN GDNS
TIVERTON AVE
BEAMINSTER GDNS
LONGWOOD GDNS
NORTHWOOD GDNS
QUEENBOROUGH GDNS
HIGHWOOD GDNS
BEECHWOOD GDNS
COLLINWOOD GDNS
GLENWOOD GDNS
KENWOOD GDNS
GANTS HILL CRES
GAYSHAM AVE
WOODVILLE GDNS
GLENTHORNE GDNS
BEATTYVILLE GDNS
SUNNYMEDE DR
SOUTHWOOD GDNS
ROSEDENE GDNS
BRAINTREE AVE
BERGHOLT AVE
KESWICK GDNS
GRASMERE GDNS
AMBLESIDE GDNS
RIDGEWAY GDNS
REDBRIDGE LA E
MARGARET WAY
CASTLE DR
CASTLE VIEW GDNS
PRESTON GDNS
WANSTEAD LA
ST GEORGE'S RD
ST ANDREW'S RD
LINCOLN GDNS
CHELMSFORD GDNS
COWLEY RD
CLARENDON GDNS
RANELAGH GDNS
HIGHLANDS GDNS
EXETER GDNS
BELGRAVE RD
COURTLAND AVE
MAYFAIR AVE
VALENTINES RD
INGLEBY RD
COVENTRY RD
MELBOURNE RD
PARK AVE
GRANVILLE RD
WELLESLEY RD
HOLCOMBE RD
BETHELL AVE
THE SQUARE
PERTH RD
ALBEMARLE GDNS
OTLEY DR
HEADLEY DR
PARHAM DR
MARTLEY DR
GLENHAM DR
ICKNIELD DR
LOUDOUN AVE
BUTE RD
1 HEDGELEY
2 QUEENS GATE
1 PUFFIN TERR
2 OYSTER CATCHER TERR
HATFIELD CL 1
LOOE GDNS 2
CHERRY CT 3
LICHEN CT 4
1 BRAMLEY HO
2 CHARLOTTE CT
3 VI & JOHN RUBENS HO
1 GLOUCESTER CT
2 LINCOLN CT
3 PAVILION RD

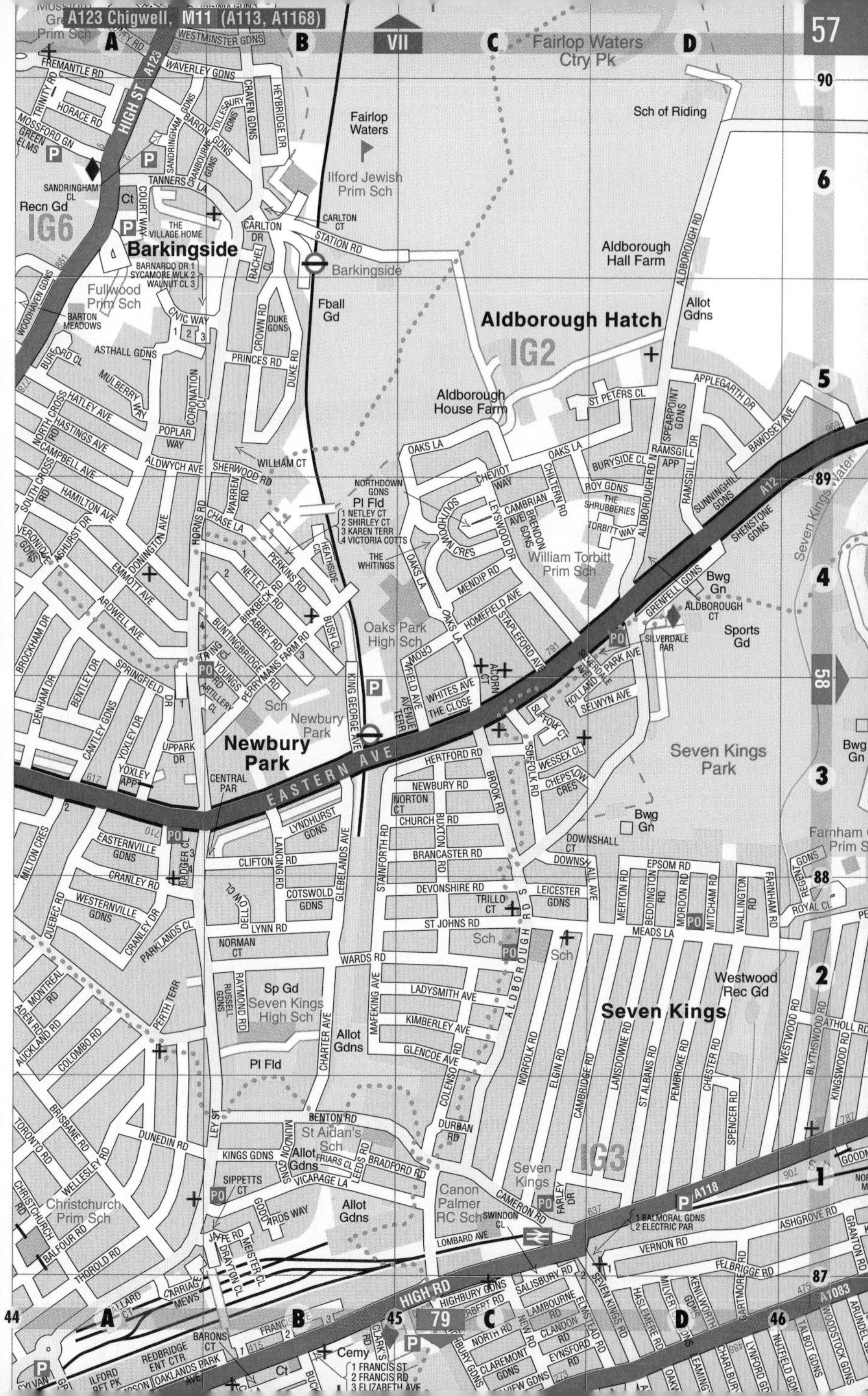
A123 Chigwell, M11 (A113, A1168)
Fairlop Waters Ctry Pk
Fairlop Waters
Ilford Jewish Prim Sch
Barkingside
Fullwood Prim Sch
Fball Gd
Sch of Riding
Aldborough Hall Farm
Aldborough Hatch
IG2
Aldborough House Farm
IG6
Recn Gd
Allot Gdns
William Torbitt Prim Sch
Oaks Park High Sch
Sports Gd
Newbury Park
Seven Kings Park
EASTERN AVE
Sp Gd
Seven Kings High Sch
Seven Kings
Westwood Rec Gd
Pl Fld
St Aidan's Sch
Christchurch Prim Sch
Canon Palmer RC Sch
IG3
Farnham Prim Sch
HIGH RD
Cemy
A12
A118
A1083
79
58
VII

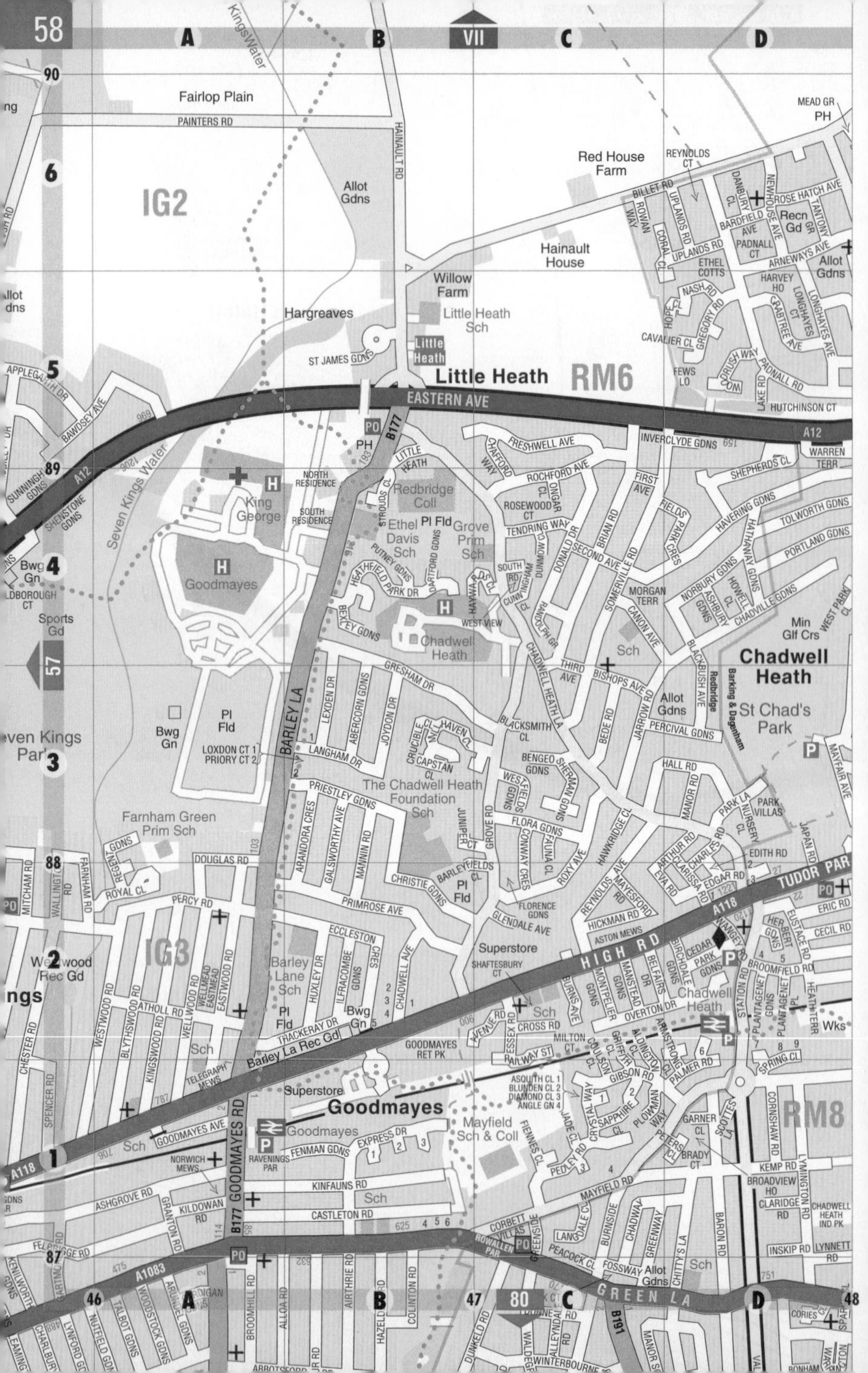

A
B
VII
C
D
Fairlop Plain
PAINTERS RD
HAINAULT RD
IG2
Allot Gdns
Red House Farm
REYNOLDS CT
BILLET RD
ROWAN WAY
CORAL CL
UPLANDS RD
DANBURY CL
NEWHOUSE AVE
ROSE HATCH AVE
BARDFIELD AVE
Recn Gd
TANTONY GR
PADNALL CT
ARNEWAYS AVE
MEAD GR
PH
Hainault House
Willow Farm
Little Heath Sch
ETHEL COTTS
NASH RD
HOPE CL
GREGORY RD
HARVEY HO
LONGHAYES CT
CRABTREE AVE
LONGHAYES AVE
CAVALIER CL
FEWS LO
DRUSH WAY
PADNALL RD
LAKE RD
HUTCHINSON CT
Hargreaves
ST JAMES GDNS
Little Heath
Little Heath
RM6
EASTERN AVE
A12
B177
PO
APPLEGARTH DR
BAWDSEY AVE
SUNNINGHILL GDNS
SHENSTONE GDNS
Seven Kings Water
NORTH RESIDENCE
SOUTH RESIDENCE
King George
Goodmayes
LITTLE HEATH
STROUDS CL
Redbridge Coll
Ethel Davis Sch
Pl Fld
Grove Prim Sch
CHAFFORD WAY
FRESHWELL AVE
ROCHFORD AVE
ONGAR CL
ROSEWOOD CT
TENDRING WAY
INVERCLYDE GDNS
FIRST AVE
SHEPHERDS CL
WARREN TERR
HAVERING GDNS
TOLWORTH GDNS
PORTLAND GDNS
FIELDS PARK CRES
HATHAWAY GDNS
DONALD DR
BRIAN RD
DUNMOW CL
SECOND AVE
SOMERVILLE RD
MORGAN TERR
NORBURY GDNS
ASHBURY GDNS
HOWELL CL
CHADVILLE GDNS
WEST PARK CL
Min Glf Crs
Chadwell Heath
St Chad's Park
Redbridge
Barking & Dagenham
MAYFAIR AVE
PUTNEY GDNS
DARTFORD GDNS
HEATHFIELD PARK DR
HAYWARDS CL
SOUTH RD
CUNNINGHAM CL
RANDOLPH GR
WEST VIEW
Chadwell Heath
BEXLEY GDNS
Sports Gd
Bwg Gn
ALDBOROUGH CT
57
Seven Kings Park
GRESHAM DR
LEXDEN DR
ABERCORN GDNS
JOYDON DR
CRUCIBLE CL
ANVIL WAY
HAVEN CL
CAPSTAN CL
LANGHAM DR
BARLEY LA
Pl Fld
Bwg Gn
LOXDON CT
PRIORY CT
THIRD AVE
BISHOPS AVE
CANON AVE
Sch
BLACKBUSH AVE
Allot Gdns
JARROW RD
BEDE RD
CHADWELL HEATH LA
BLACKSMITH CL
PERCIVAL GDNS
BENGEO GDNS
SHERMAN GDNS
WESTFIELDS GDNS
HALL RD
MANOR RD
PARK LA
NURSERY CL
PARK VILLAS
JAPAN RD
The Chadwell Heath Foundation Sch
PRIESTLEY GDNS
ARANDORA CRES
GALSWORTHY AVE
MANNIN RD
JUNIPER CT
GROVE RD
FLORA GDNS
CONWAY CRES
FAUNA CL
ROXY AVE
HAWKRIDGE CL
ARTHUR RD
CHARLES RD
CLARISSA RD
EVA RD
EDITH RD
EDGAR RD
TUDOR PAR
Farnham Green Prim Sch
REGENT GDNS
DOUGLAS RD
MITCHAM RD
WALLINGTON RD
FARNHAM RD
ROYAL CL
CHRISTIE GDNS
BARLEYFIELDS CL
Pl Fld
FLORENCE GDNS
REYNOLDS AVE
MAYESFORD RD
HICKMAN RD
ASTON MEWS
PO
ERIC RD
PERCY RD
PRIMROSE AVE
GLENDALE AVE
A118
CEDAR PARK GDNS
WANGEY RD
HERBERT GDNS
EUSTACE RD
CECIL RD
IG3
ECCLESTON CRES
Barley Lane Sch
ILFRACOMBE GDNS
HUXLEY DR
CHADWELL AVE
Superstore
SHAFTESBURY CT
HIGH RD
BURNS AVE
MONTPELIER GDNS
MANSTEAD GDNS
BELFAIRS DR
BIRCHDALE GDNS
BROOMFIELD RD
Westwood Rec Gd
WESTWOOD RD
BLYTHSWOOD RD
ATHOLL RD
WELLWOOD RD
WELLMEAD
EASTMEAD
EASTWOOD RD
Pl Fld
Bwg Gn
OVERTON DR
Chadwell Heath
STATION RD
PLANTAGENET GDNS
PLANTAGENET PL
HEATH TERR
Wks
Kings
CHESTER RD
KINGSWOOD RD
Sch
THACKERAY DR
Barley La Rec Gd
AVENUE RD
ESSEX RD
Sch
CROSS RD
MILTON CT
ARMSTRONG CL
ALDINGTON CL
GOODMAYES RET PK
RAILWAY ST
COULSON CL
GRIFFITH CL
PALMER RD
SPRING CL
TELEGRAPH MEWS
Superstore
Goodmayes
ASQUITH CL 1
BLUNDEN CL 2
DIAMOND CL 3
ANGLE GN 4
GIBSON RD
CRYSTAL WAY
SAPPHIRE CL
PLOWMAN WAY
JADE CL
SPENCER RD
Sch
GOODMAYES AVE
GOODMAYES RD
Goodmayes
EXPRESS DR
FENMAN GDNS
Mayfield Sch & Coll
FIENNES CL
PEDLEY RD
PETERS CL
GARNER CL
BRADY CT
SCOTTES LA
CORNSHAW RD
RM8
A118
NORWICH MEWS
RAVENINGS PAR
KINFAUNS RD
Sch
KEMP RD
LYMINGTON RD
BROADVIEW HO
CLARIDGE RD
CHADWELL HEATH IND PK
ASHGROVE RD
GRANTON RD
KILDOWAN RD
CASTLETON RD
MAYFIELD RD
BURNSIDE
CHADWAY
GREENWAY
CHITTY'S LA
BARON RD
LANGDALE CL
CORBETT VILLAS
GREENSIDE
ROWALLEN PAR
PO
PEACOCK CL
FOSSWAY
Allot Gdns
Sch
INSKIP RD
LYNNETT RD
FELBRIDGE RD
GARTMORE RD
KENILWORTH GDNS
A1083
PO
46
A
B
47
80
C
D
48
GREEN LA
B191
CHARLBURY
LYNFORD GDNS
NUTFIELD GDNS
TALBOT GDNS
WOODSTOCK GDNS
ARUNDEL GDNS
BROOMHILL RD
ALLOA RD
AIRTHRIE RD
COLINTON RD
DUNKELD RD
ALLEYNDALE RD
WALDEGRAVE
WINTERBOURNE
MANOR
CORIES CL
SPARSHOLT
BONHAM
ABBOTSFORD
90
6
5
89
4
3
88
2
1
87

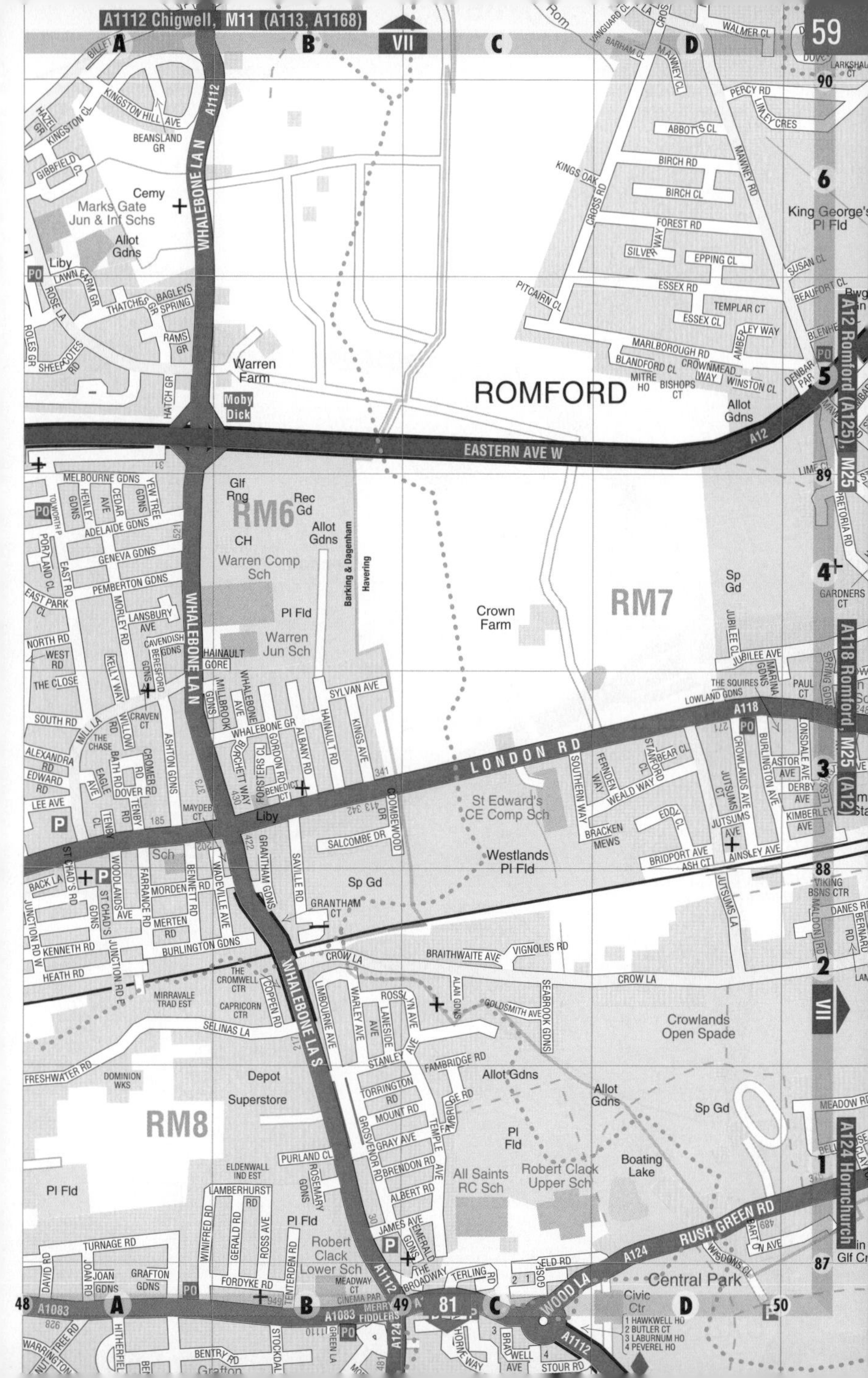

A1112 Chigwell, M11 (A113, A1168)
VII
ROMFORD
RM6
RM7
RM8
WHALEBONE LA N
WHALEBONE LA S
EASTERN AVE W
LONDON RD
RUSH GREEN RD
CROW LA
WOOD LA
A12 Romford (A125), M25
A118 Romford, M25 (A12)
A124 Hornchurch
Marks Gate Jun & Inf Schs
Warren Farm
Moby Dick
Warren Comp Sch
Warren Jun Sch
Crown Farm
St Edward's CE Comp Sch
Westlands Pl Fld
Crowlands Open Space
Robert Clack Upper Sch
Robert Clack Lower Sch
All Saints RC Sch
Boating Lake
Central Park
Civic Ctr
King George's Pl Fld
Barking & Dagenham
Havering
Dominion Wks
Depot
Superstore
Eldenwall Ind Est
Mirravale Trad Est
Capricorn Ctr
The Cromwell Ctr
Viking Bsns Ctr
1 HAWKWELL HO
2 BUTLER CT
3 LABURNUM HO
4 PEVEREL HO
81

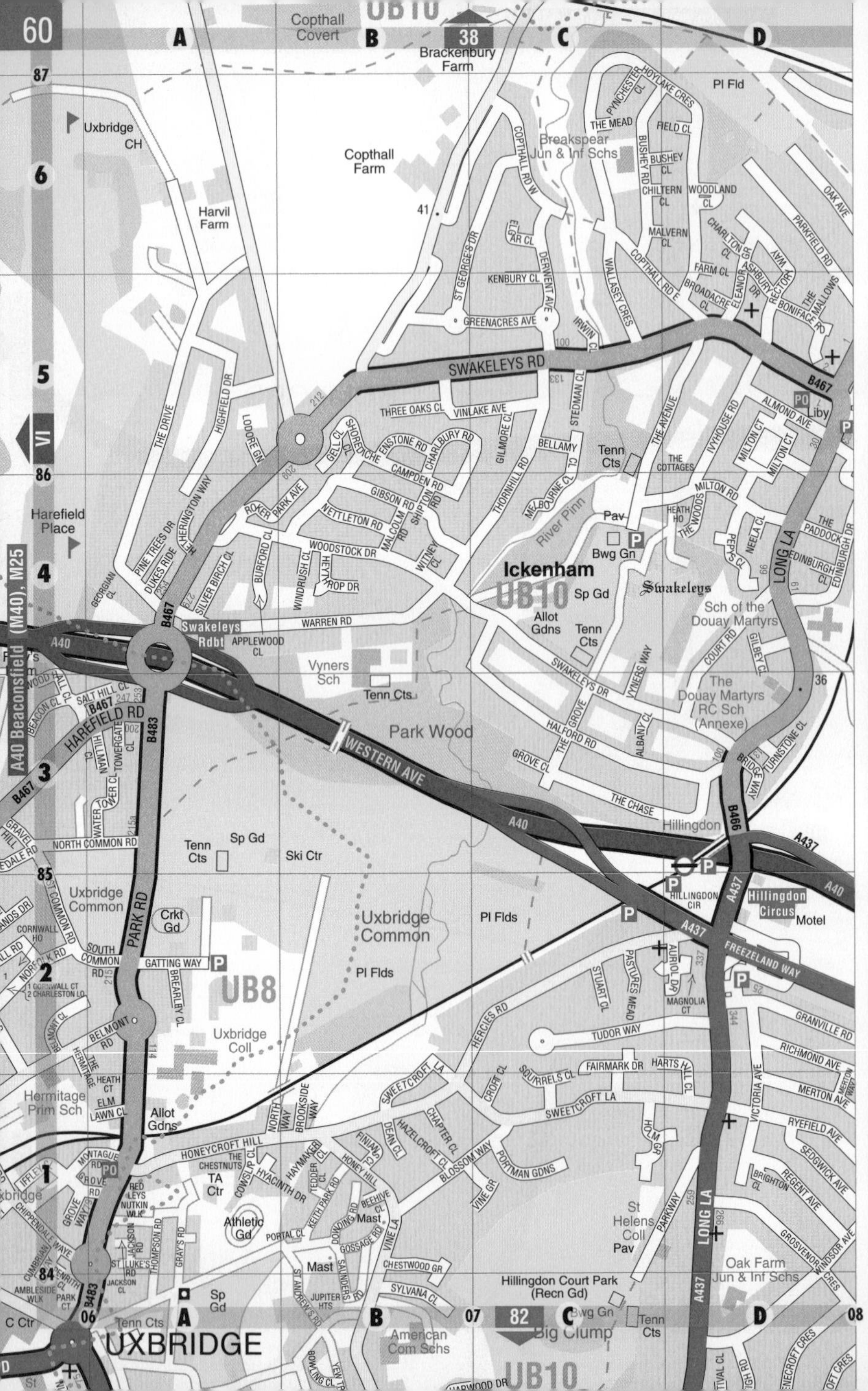

Copthall Covert
Brackenbury Farm
38
Uxbridge CH
Copthall Farm
Harvil Farm
Breakspear Jun & Inf Schs
Pl Fld
SWAKELEYS RD
B467
Harefield Place
Ickenham
UB10
Swakeleys
Sch of the Douay Martyrs
The Douay Martyrs RC Sch (Annexe)
Swakeleys Rdbt
Vyners Sch
Tenn Cts
Park Wood
WESTERN AVE
A40
A40 Beaconsfield (M40), M25
HAREFIELD RD
B483
PARK RD
Hillingdon
Hillingdon Circus Motel
A437
FREEZELAND WAY
LONG LA
B466
Uxbridge Common
Ski Ctr
Pl Flds
UB8
Uxbridge Coll
Hermitage Prim Sch
Allot Gdns
TA Ctr
Athletic Gd
Mast
St Helens Coll
Hillingdon Court Park (Recn Gd)
Oak Farm Jun & Inf Schs
UXBRIDGE
American Com Schs
Big Clump
82
06
07
08

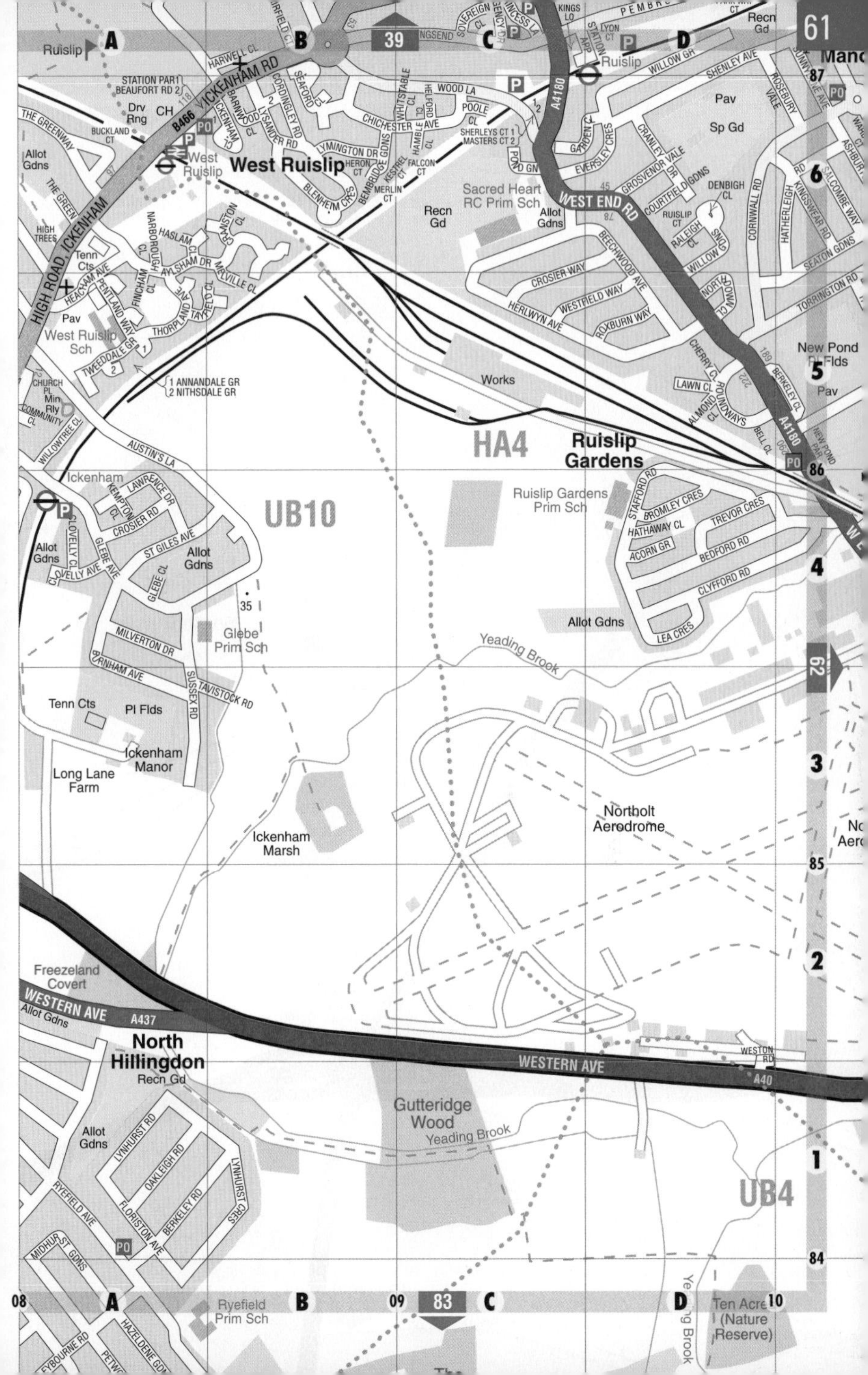

Ruislip
West Ruislip
HA4
UB10
Ruislip Gardens
Works
Sacred Heart RC Prim Sch
Recn Gd
Allot Gdns
Ruislip Gardens Prim Sch
Glebe Prim Sch
Ickenham
Ickenham Manor
Long Lane Farm
Ickenham Marsh
Northolt Aerodrome
Yeading Brook
Freezeland Covert
WESTERN AVE
A437
A40
A4180
B466
North Hillingdon
Gutteridge Wood
Ryefield Prim Sch
Ten Acre (Nature Reserve)
UB4
New Pond Pl Flds
West Ruislip Sch
HIGH ROAD, ICKENHAM
WEST END RD
Pav
Sp Gd
Tenn Cts
Pl Flds
Allot Gdns

39
62
83

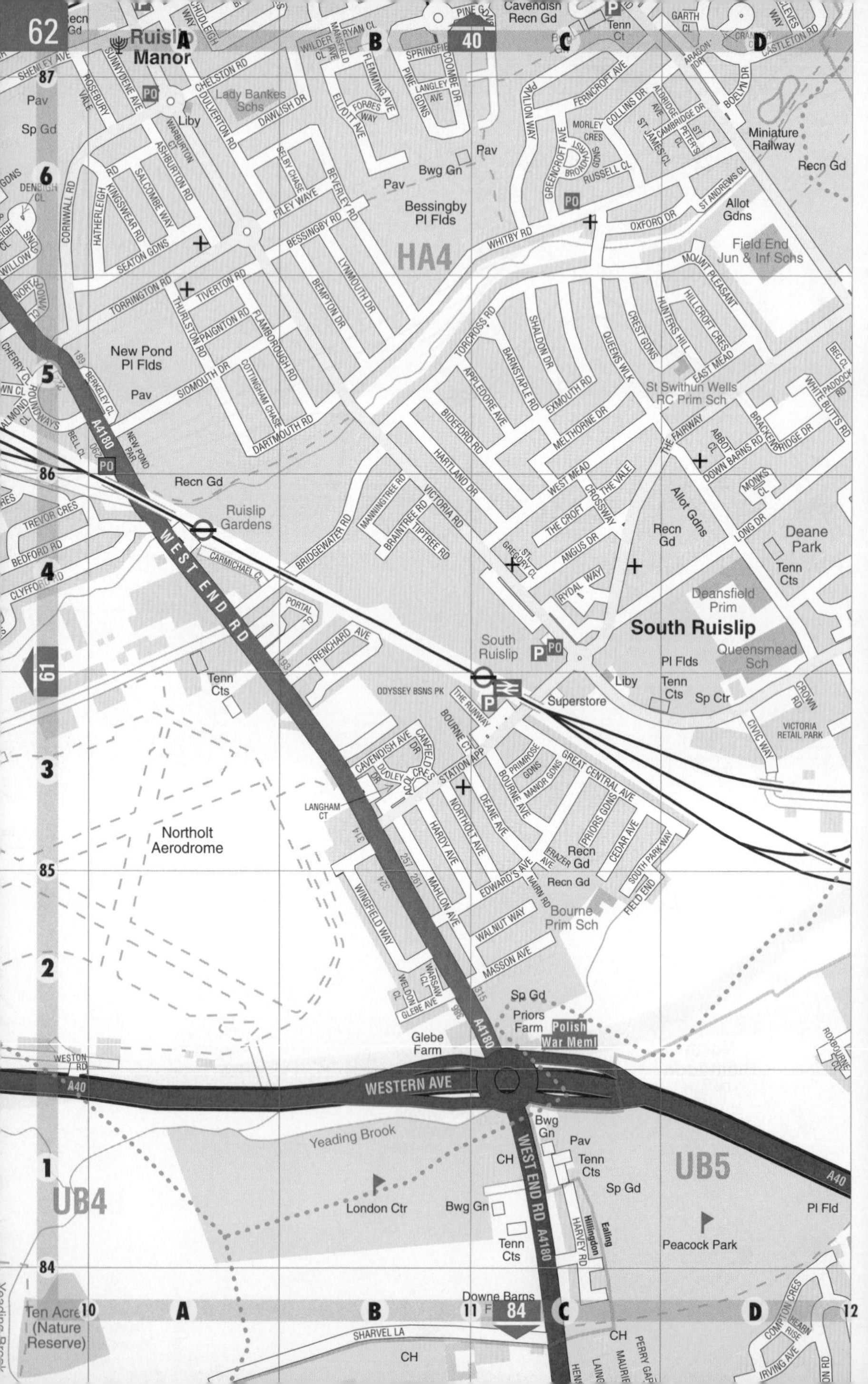
62
Ruislip Manor
A
B
C
D
40
87
86
85
84
6
5
4
3
2
1
61
10
11
12
84
HA4
UB4
UB5
Lady Bankes Schs
Liby
PO
Pav
Sp Gd
Recn Gd
Cavendish Recn Gd
Tenn Ct
Bwg Gn
Bessingby Pl Flds
Miniature Railway
Allot Gdns
Field End Jun & Inf Schs
New Pond Pl Flds
St Swithun Wells RC Prim Sch
Ruislip Gardens
Deane Park
Tenn Cts
Deansfield Prim
South Ruislip
Queensmead Sch
Pl Flds
Sp Ctr
Superstore
ODYSSEY BSNS PK
VICTORIA RETAIL PARK
Northolt Aerodrome
Bourne Prim Sch
Priors Farm
Polish War Meml
Glebe Farm
Yeading Brook
London Ctr
CH
Peacock Park
Pl Fld
Ten Acre (Nature Reserve)
Downe Barns F
Hillingdon
Ealing
WEST END RD
A4180
WESTERN AVE
A40
SHEMLEY AVE
SUNNYDENE AVE
ROSEBURY VALE
CHELSTON RD
DULVERTON RD
DAWLISH DR
WARBURTON CT
ASHBURTON RD
SALCOMBE WAY
KINGSWEAR RD
HATHERLEIGH RD
CORNWALL RD
SEATON GDNS
TORRINGTON RD
TIVERTON RD
THURLSTON RD
PAIGNTON RD
FLAMBOROUGH RD
COTTINGHAM CHASE
DARTMOUTH RD
SIDMOUTH DR
SELBY CHASE
FILEY WAYE
BESSINGBY RD
BEVERLEY RD
LYNMOUTH DR
BEMPTON DR
FLEMMING AVE
ELLIOTT AVE
FORBES WAY
PINE GDNS
LANGLEY AVE
COOMBE DR
WILDER CL
RYAN CL
MANSFIELD
PAVILION WAY
FERNCROFT AVE
COLLINS DR
GREENCROFT AVE
MORLEY CRES
BROADHURST GDNS
RUSSELL CL
ALDRIDGE AVE
CAMBRIDGE DR
ST JAMES CL
ST PETER'S CL
ST ANDREWS CL
GARTH CL
CASTLETON RD
BOELYN DR
ARAGON DR
WHITBY RD
OXFORD DR
MOUNT PLEASANT
HILLCROFT CRES
HUNTERS HILL
CREST GDNS
QUEENS WLK
SHALDON DR
TORCROSS RD
BARNSTAPLE RD
EXMOUTH RD
APPLEDORE AVE
BIDEFORD RD
HARTLAND DR
MELTHORNE DR
EAST MEAD
WEST MEAD
THE FAIRWAY
ABBOT CL
DOWN BARNS RD
BRACKENBRIDGE DR
WHITE BUTTS RD
PADDOCK RD
BEC CL
MONKS CL
LONG DR
THE VALE
CROSSWAY
THE CROFT
ANGUS DR
ST GREGORY CL
RYDAL WAY
MANNINGTREE RD
VICTORIA RD
BRAINTREE RD
TIPTREE RD
BRIDGEWATER RD
BERKELEY CL
ROUNDWAYS
BELL CL
NEW POND PAR
TREVOR CRES
BEDFORD RD
CLYFFORD RD
CARMICHAEL CL
PORTAL CL
TRENCHARD AVE
THE RUNWAY
BOURNE CT
CAVENDISH AVE
CANFIELD DR
DUDLEY DR
ACOL CRES
STATION APP
LANGHAM CT
PRIMROSE GDNS
MANOR GDNS
BOURNE AVE
GREAT CENTRAL AVE
PRIORS GDNS
CEDAR AVE
SOUTH PARK WAY
DEANE AVE
NORTHOLT AVE
HARDY AVE
MAHLON AVE
FRAZER AVE
EDWARD'S AVE
NAIRN RD
FIELD END
WINGFIELD WAY
WALNUT WAY
MASSON AVE
WARSAW CL
WELDON CL
GLEBE AVE
CROWN RD
CIVIC WAY
ROXBOURNE CL
WESTON RD
HARVEY RD
SHARVEL LA
COMPTON CRES
HEARN RISE
IRVING AVE
PERRY GARTH

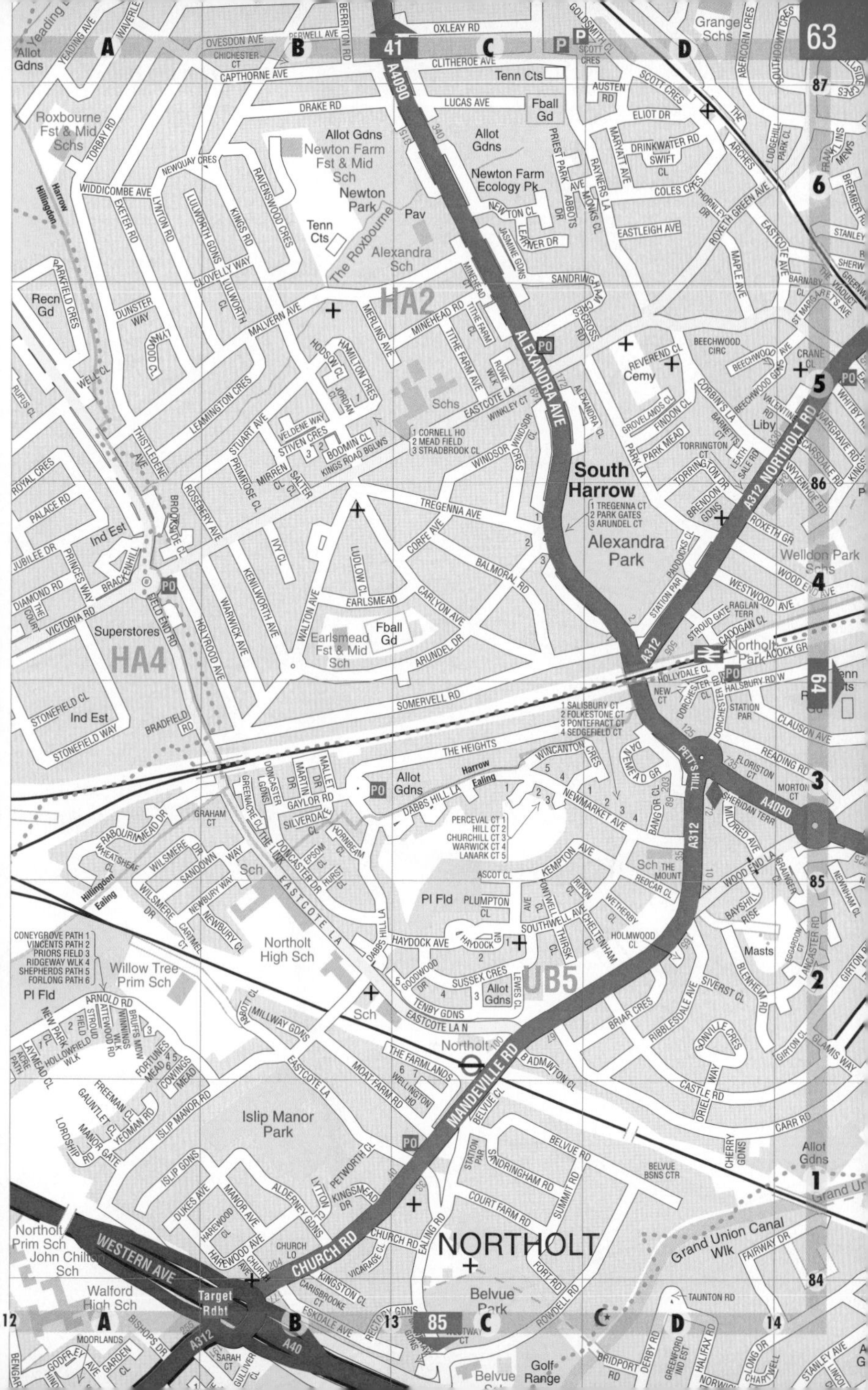

63
A
B
C
D
41
A4090
Allot Gdns
Yeading
YEADING AVE
WAVERLEY
OVESDON AVE
CHICHESTER CT
PERWELL AVE
BERRITON RD
OXLEAY RD
GOLDSMITH CL
SCOTT CRES
Grange Schs
ABERCORN CRES
SOUTHDOWN CRES
87
CAPTHORNE AVE
CLITHEROE AVE
Tenn Cts
AUSTEN RD
SCOTT CRES
DRAKE RD
LUCAS AVE
Fball Gd
ELIOT DR
Roxbourne Fst & Mid Schs
TORBAY RD
Allot Gdns
Newton Farm Fst & Mid Sch
Allot Gdns
PRIEST PARK AVE
MARYATT AVE
DRINKWATER RD
SWIFT CL
THE ARCHES
LODGEHILL PARK CL
FRANKLINS MEWS
Harrow
Hillingdon
NEWQUAY CRES
Newton Park
Newton Farm Ecology Pk
RAYNERS LA
COLES CRES
6
WIDDICOMBE AVE
EXETER RD
LYNTON RD
LULWORTH GDNS
KINGS RD
RAVENSWOOD CRES
Tenn Cts
The Roxbourne
Pav
NEWTON CL
ABBOTS DR
MONKS CL
THORNLEY DR
ROXETH GREEN AVE
EASTCOTE AVE
BREMBER RD
STANLEY
LEARNER DR
EASTLEIGH AVE
Alexandra Sch
JASMINE GDNS
MAPLE AVE
SHERW
CLOVELLY WAY
LULWORTH CL
SANDRINGHAM CRES
THE VIADUCT
BARNABY CL
ST MARGARET'S AVE
PARKFIELD CRES
Recn Gd
DUNSTER WAY
MALVERN AVE
HA2
MERLINS AVE
MINEHEAD RD
MINEHEAD CT
TITHE FARM CL
TITHE FARM AVE
CROSS RD
LYNWOOD CL
HODSON CL
HAMILTON CRES
ALEXANDRA AVE
PO
REVEREND CL
Cemy
BEECHWOOD CIRC
BEECHWOOD AVE
BEECHWOOD GDNS
CRANE CL
5
WHITBY
WELL CL
RUFUS CL
LEAMINGTON CRES
JORDAN CL
ROWE WLK
EASTCOTE LA
Schs
WINKLEY CT
ALEXANDRA CL
GROVELANDS CL
FINDON CL
CORBIN'S LA
BARNETTS CT
VALENTINE RD
Liby
NORTHOLT RD
A312
WARGRAVE RD
VELDENE WAY
STIVEN CRES
BODMIN CL
KINGS ROAD BGLWS
1 CORNELL HO
2 MEAD FIELD
3 STRADBROOK CL
WINDSOR CRES
WINDSOR CL
PARK MEAD
TORRINGTON CT
LEATH
SALE RD
CARSDALE RD
THISTLEDENE AVE
STUART AVE
PRIMROSE CL
MIRREN CL
SALTER CL
South Harrow
PARK LA
TORRINGTON DR
WYVENHOE RD
86
ROYAL CRES
ROSEBERY AVE
BROOKSIDE CL
TREGENNA AVE
1 TREGENNA CT
2 PARK GATES
3 ARUNDEL CT
BRENDON GDNS
ROXETH GR
PALACE RD
Ind Est
IVY CL
CORFE AVE
LUDLOW CL
Alexandra Park
PADDOCKS CL
Welldon Park Schs
JUBILEE DR
PRINCES WAY
BRACKENHILL
BALMORAL RD
WOOD END AVE
4
DIAMOND RD
THE COURT
VICTORIA RD
FIELD END RD
KENILWORTH AVE
WARWICK AVE
HOLYROOD AVE
WALTON AVE
EARLSMEAD
CARLYON AVE
STATION PAR
WESTWOOD AVE
RAGLAN TERR
STROUD GATE
CADOGAN CL
Superstores
Earlsmead Fst & Mid Sch
Fball Gd
ARUNDEL DR
A312
Northolt Park
ACOCK GR
HA4
HOLLYDALE CL
DORCHESTER RD
HALSBURY RD W
64
NEW CT
DORCHESTER CL
STATION PAR
STONEFIELD CL
Ind Est
SOMERVELL RD
1 SALISBURY CT
2 FOLKESTONE CT
3 PONTEFRACT CT
4 SEDGEFIELD CT
CLAUSON AVE
STONEFIELD WAY
BRADFIELD RD
THE HEIGHTS
WINCANTON CRES
DANEMEAD GR
PETT'S HILL
FLORISTON CT
READING RD
DONCASTER LGDNS
MALLET DR
MARTIN DR
Allot Gdns
Harrow
Ealing
MORTON CT
3
GREENACRE CL
GAYLOR RD
PO
DABBS HILL LA
NEWMARKET AVE
BANGOR CL
SHERIDAN TERR
A4090
GRAHAM CT
SILVERDALE CL
HORNBEAM
PERCEVAL CT 1
HILL CT 2
CHURCHILL CT 3
WARWICK CT 4
LANARK CT 5
MILLFORD AVE
RABOURNMEAD DR
WHEATSHEAF CL
WILSMERE DR
SANDOWN WAY
THE LINK
EPSOM CL
KEMPTON AVE
Sch
THE MOUNT
A312
WOOD END LA
GRAINGER CL
85
NEWNHAM CL
Hillingdon
Ealing
NEWBURY WAY
DONCASTER DR
HURST CL
ASCOT CL
RIPON CL
REDCAR CL
BAYSHILL RISE
WILSMERE DR
NEWBURY CL
EASTCOTE LA
Pl Fld
PLUMPTON CL
FONTWELL CL
WETHERBY CL
SOUTHWELL AVE
CHELTENHAM CL
THIRSK CL
HOLMWOOD CL
CARTMEL CT
Sch
CONEYGROVE PATH 1
VINCENTS PATH 2
PRIORS FIELD 3
RIDGEWAY WLK 4
SHEPHERDS PATH 5
FORLONG PATH 6
Northolt High Sch
Willow Tree Prim Sch
DABBS HILL LA
HAYDOCK AVE
HAYDOCK GN
Masts
EGGARDON CT
LANCASTER RD
GIRTON RD
Pl Fld
GOODWOOD DR
SUSSEX CRES
Allot Gdns
LEWES CL
UB5
SIVERST CL
BLENHEIM RD
2
ARNOLD RD
ATTEWOOD RD
WINNINGS WLK
BRUFFS MDW
NEW PARK CL
STROUD FIELD
HOLLOWFIELD WLK
ABBOTT CL
TENBY GDNS
Sch
EASTCOTE LA N
BRIAR CRES
RIBBLESDALE AVE
CONVILLE CRES
GIRTON CL
GLAMIS WAY
LAYMEAD CL
ACRE PATH
FORTUNES MEAD
COWINGS MEAD
MILLWAY GDNS
THE FARMLANDS
Northolt
BADMINTON CL
WELLINGTON HO
MOAT FARM RD
MANDEVILLE RD
ORIEL WAY
CASTLE RD
GAUNTLET CL
FREEMAN CL
YEOMAN RD
ISLIP MANOR RD
EASTCOTE LA
Islip Manor Park
BELVUE CL
NORTHOLT RD
CARR RD
LORDSHIP RD
MANOR GATE
PO
PETWORTH CL
STATION PAR
BELVUE RD
BELVUE BSNS CTR
CHERRY GDNS
Allot Gdns
ISLIP GDNS
SANDRINGHAM RD
1
Grand Union
DUKES AVE
MANOR AVE
ALDERNEY GDNS
LYTTON CL
KINGSMEAD DR
COURT FARM RD
SUMMIT RD
HAREWOOD CL
Northolt Prim Sch
John Chilton Sch
WESTERN AVE
HAREWOOD AVE
CHURCH LO
CHURCH RD
EALING RD
NORTHOLT
Grand Union Canal Wlk
FAIRWAY DR
VICARAGE CL
FORT RD
84
Walford High Sch
Target Rdbt
KINGSTON CL
CARISBROOKE CT
Belvue Park
ROWDELL RD
TAUNTON RD
12
A
B
13
85
C
D
14
ESKDALE AVE
RECTORY GDNS
BISHOPS DR
MOORLANDS
A312
A40
GODFREY AVE
GARDEN CL
SARAH CT
GULIVER CL
Belvue
Golf Range
BRIDPORT RD
DERBY RD
GREENFORD IND EST
HALIFAX RD
NORWICH
LONG DR
CHARTWELL
STANLEY AVE
LINCOLN
BENGARTH

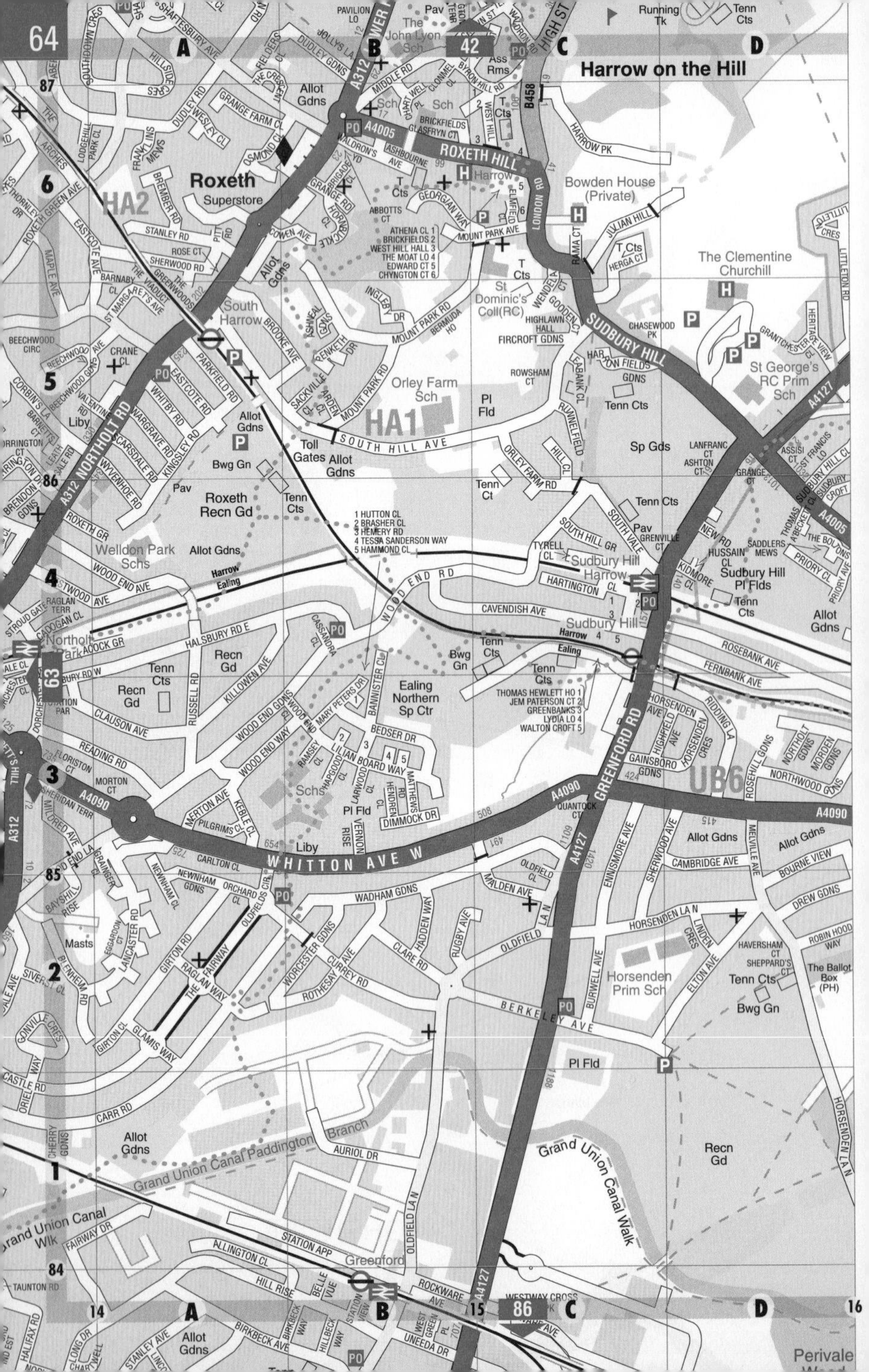

Harrow on the Hill
Roxeth
Superstore
HA2
HA1
UB6
South Harrow
Sudbury Hill
Sudbury Hill Harrow
Northolt Park
Greenford
Perivale
The John Lyon Sch
Ass Rms
Running Tk
Tenn Cts
Bowden House (Private)
The Clementine Churchill
St George's RC Prim Sch
St Dominic's Coll(RC)
Orley Farm Sch
Pl Fld
Sp Gds
Sudbury Hill Pl Flds
Allot Gdns
Roxeth Recn Gd
Welldon Park Schs
Toll Gates
Bwg Gn
Pav
Liby
Recn Gd
Ealing Northern Sp Ctr
Schs
Masts
Horsenden Prim Sch
The Ballot Box (PH)
Grand Union Canal Paddington Branch
Grand Union Canal Walk
Grand Union Canal Wlk
Harrow
Ealing
ROXETH HILL
SUDBURY HILL
NORTHOLT RD
GREENFORD RD
LONDON RD
HIGH ST
WHITTON AVE W
SOUTH HILL AVE
WOOD END RD
BERKELEY AVE
OLDFIELD LA N
HORSENDEN LA N
A312
A4005
A4127
A4090
B458
1 HUTTON CL
2 BRASHER CL
3 HEMERY RD
4 TESSA SANDERSON WAY
5 HAMMOND CL
ATHENA CL 1
BRICKFIELDS 2
WEST HILL HALL 3
THE MOAT LO 4
EDWARD CT 5
CHYNGTON CT 6
THOMAS HEWLETT HO 1
JEM PATERSON CT 2
GREENBANKS 3
LYDIA LO 4
WALTON CROFT 5
42
63
86
A
B
C
D
14
15
16
87
86
85
84
1
2
3
4
5
6

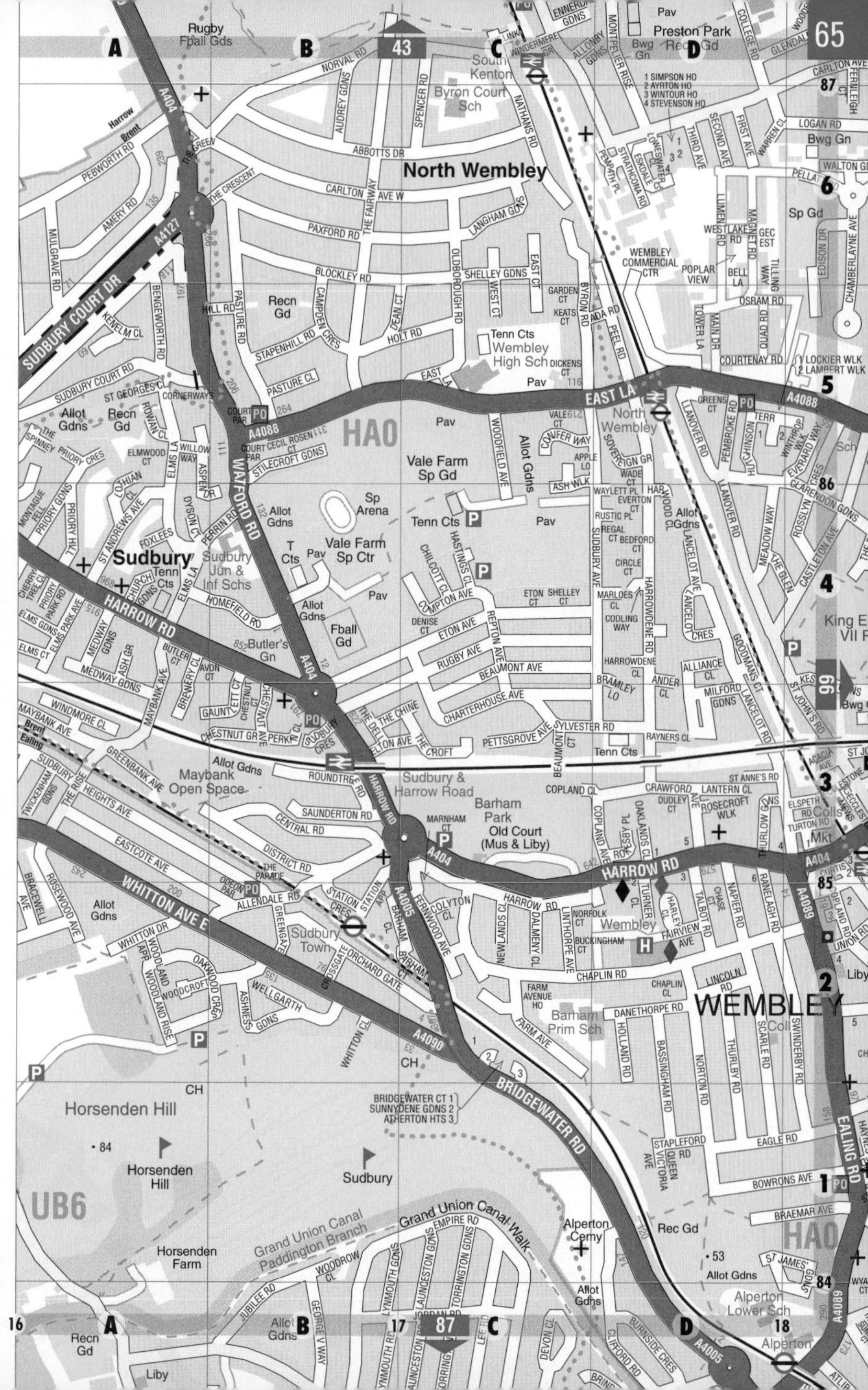

A
B
C
D
43
87
16
17
18
North Wembley
Sudbury
WEMBLEY
HA0
UB6
Horsenden Hill
Sudbury & Harrow Road
Sudbury Town
Vale Farm Sp Gd
Vale Farm Sp Ctr
Barham Park
Maybank Open Space
Wembley High Sch
Byron Court Sch
Wembley Commercial Ctr
Grand Union Canal Paddington Branch
Grand Union Canal Walk
Alperton Cemy
Alperton Lower Sch
Barham Prim Sch
Horsenden Farm
HARROW RD
WATFORD RD
EAST LA
EALING RD
BRIDGEWATER RD
WHITTON AVE E
SUDBURY COURT DR
A404
A4088
A4005
A4090
A4089
A4127

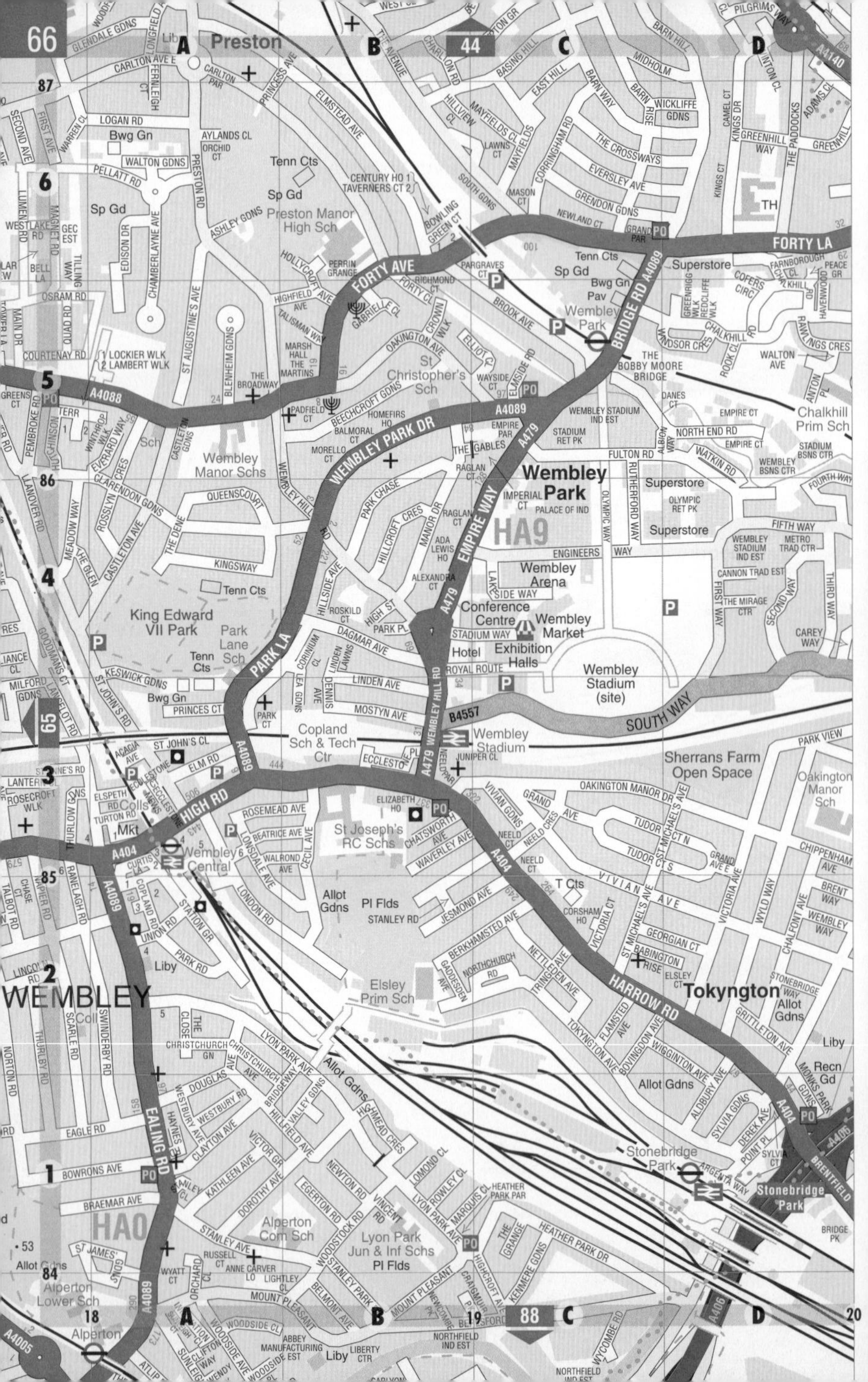

Preston
44
A
B
C
D
87
6
5
86
4
3
85
2
1
84
18
19
20
88
65
GLENDALE GDNS
CARLTON AVE E
CARLTON PAR
LONGFIELD
FERNLEIGH CT
PRINCESS AVE
THE AVENUE
CHARLTON RD
BASING HILL
BARN HILL
MIDHOLM
PILGRIMS WAY
A4140
LINTON CL
ELMSTEAD AVE
HILLVIEW CL
MAYFIELDS CL
EAST HILL
BARN WAY
BARN RISE
WICKLIFFE GDNS
KINGS DR
CAMEL CT
THE PADDOCKS
ADAMS CL
GREENHILL WAY
GREENHILL
LOGAN RD
Bwg Gn
AYLANDS CL
ORCHID CT
Tenn Cts
LAWNS CT
MAYFIELDS
CORRINGHAM RD
THE CROSSWAYS
EVERSLEY AVE
KINGS CT
SECOND AVE
FIRST AVE
WARREN CL
WALTON GDNS
PELLATT RD
PRESTON RD
CENTURY HO 1
TAVERNERS CT 2
SOUTH GDNS
MASON CT
GRENDON GDNS
TH
Sp Gd
Sp Gd
LUMEN RD
MAGNET RD
WESTLAKE RD
GEC EST
EDISON DR
CHAMBERLAYNE AVE
ASHLEY GDNS
Preston Manor High Sch
BOWLING GREEN CT
NEWLAND CT
GRAND PAR
PO
FORTY LA
BELL LA
TILLING WAY
HOLLYCROFT AVE
PERRIN GRANGE
FORTY AVE
PARGRAVES CT
Tenn Cts
Sp Gd
Bwg Gn
Pav
Superstore
FARNBOROUGH CL
PEACE GR
OSRAM RD
ST AUGUSTINE'S AVE
HIGHFIELD AVE
RICHMOND CT
FORTY CL
BROOK AVE
BRIDGE RD
A4089
GREENRIGG WLK
REDCLIFFE WLK
COFERS CIRC
CHALKHILL RD
HAVENWOOD
MAIN DR
QUAD RD
BLENHEIM GDNS
TALISMAN WAY
GABRIELLE CL
CROWN WLK
Wembley Park
WINDSOR CRES
CHALKHILL
RAWLINGS CRES
COURTENAY RD
1 LOCKIER WLK
2 LAMBERT WLK
MARSH HALL
THE MARTINS
OAKINGTON AVE
ELLIOT CL
ELMSIDE RD
THE BOBBY MOORE BRIDGE
ROOK CL
WALTON AVE
THE BROADWAY
St Christopher's Sch
WAYSIDE CT
ANTON PL
GREENS CT
PEMBROKE RD
A4088
PADFIELD CT
BEECHCROFT GDNS
HOMEFIRS HO
A4089
DANES CT
EMPIRE CT
Chalkhill Prim Sch
HUTCHINSON TERR
WINTHROP WLK
EVERARD WAY
CASTLETON GDNS
BALMORAL CT
WEMBLEY PARK DR
EMPIRE PAR
WEMBLEY STADIUM IND EST
STADIUM RET PK
ALBION WAY
NORTH END RD
Sch
Wembley Manor Schs
MORELLO CT
THE GABLES
A479
FULTON RD
RUTHERFORD WAY
WATKIN RD
STADIUM BSNS CTR
WEMBLEY BSNS CTR
LLANOVER RD
CLARENDON GDNS
ROSSLYN CRES
WEMBLEY HILL RD
RAGLAN CT
Wembley Park
FOURTH WAY
QUEENSCOURT
PARK CHASE
IMPERIAL CT
PALACE OF IND
Superstore
OLYMPIC RET PK
MEADOW WAY
THE GLEN
CASTLETON AVE
THE DENE
HILLCROFT CRES
MANOR DR
RAGLAN CT
EMPIRE WAY
HA9
OLYMPIC WAY
Superstore
FIFTH WAY
ADA LEWIS HO
ENGINEERS WAY
WEMBLEY STADIUM IND EST
METRO TRAD CTR
KINGSWAY
HILLSIDE AVE
ALEXANDRA CT
Wembley Arena
CANNON TRAD EST
SECOND WAY
THIRD WAY
FIRST WAY
Tenn Cts
ROSKILD CT
HIGH ST
LAKESIDE WAY
THE MIRAGE CTR
King Edward VII Park
Park Lane Sch
PARK PL
Conference Centre
Wembley Market
P
GOODMANS CT
DAGMAR AVE
STADIUM WAY
CAREY WAY
Tenn Cts
PARK LA
CORINIUM CL
LINDEN LAWNS
Hotel
Exhibition Halls
Wembley Stadium (site)
ALLIANCE CL
MILFORD GDNS
LANCELOT RD
KESWICK GDNS
LEA GDNS
DENNIS AVE
LINDEN AVE
ROYAL ROUTE
ST JOHN'S RD
Bwg Gn
PRINCES CT
PARK CT
MOSTYN AVE
B4557
SOUTH WAY
Copland Sch & Tech Ctr
Wembley Stadium
ST JOHN'S CL
ACACIA AVE
PARK VIEW
ST ANNE'S RD
LANTERN CL
ROSECROFT WLK
ECCLESTONE MEWS
ELM RD
A4089
ECCLESTON PL
JUNIPER CL
NEELD PAR
Sherrans Farm Open Space
Oakington Manor Sch
HIGH RD
OAKINGTON MANOR DR
GRAND AVE
THURLOW GDNS
ELSPETH RD
TURTON RD
Colls
ROSEMEAD AVE
ELIZABETH HO
VIVIAN GDNS
TUDOR CT N
ST MICHAEL'S AVE
Mkt
BEATRICE AVE
St Joseph's RC Schs
CHATSWORTH AVE
NEELD CT
NEELD CRES
GRAND AVE E
CHIPPENHAM AVE
A404
Wembley Central
WALROND AVE
CECIL AVE
WAVERLEY AVE
TUDOR CT S
BRENT WAY
CHASE CT
NAPIER RD
RANELAGH RD
CURTIS LA
LONSDALE AVE
LONDON RD
A404
NEELD CT
VIVIAN AVE
VICTORIA AVE
WYLD WAY
TALBOT RD
COPLAND RD
Allot Gdns
Pl Flds
T Cts
WEMBLEY WAY
STATION GR
STANLEY RD
JESMOND AVE
CORSHAM HO
VICTORIA CT
CHALFONT AVE
UNION RD
BERKHAMSTED AVE
GEORGIAN CT
PARK RD
NORTHCHURCH RD
NETTLEDEN AVE
BABINGTON RISE
ELSLEY CT
LINCOLN RD
Liby
GADDESDEN AVE
TRINGDEN AVE
STONEBRIDGE WAY
WEMBLEY
Elsley Prim Sch
HARROW RD
Tokyngton
Allot Gdns
Coll
SCARLE RD
SWINDERBY RD
THE CLOSE
FLAMSTED AVE
GRITTLETON AVE
THURLBY RD
CHRISTCHURCH GN
CHRISTCHURCH AVE
LYON PARK AVE
TOKYNGTON AVE
BOVINGDON AVE
WIGGINTON AVE
Liby
NORTON RD
DOUGLAS AVE
BRIDGEWAY
VALLEY GDNS
Allot Gdns
Recn Gd
WESTBURY AVE
WESTBURY RD
HILLFIELD AVE
HIGHMEAD CRES
ALDBURY AVE
MONKS PARK GDNS
EAGLE RD
HAYNES CL
CLAYTON AVE
VICTOR GR
SYLVIA GDNS
DEREK AVE
A404
A406
BOWRONS AVE
PO
EALING RD
KATHLEEN AVE
NEWTON RD
LOMOND CL
Stonebridge Park
POINT PL
SYLVIA CT
ARGENTA WAY
BRENTFIELD
STANLEY CL
DOROTHY AVE
EGERTON RD
VINCENT RD
LYON ROWLEY CL
HEATHER PARK PAR
Stonebridge Park
BRAEMAR AVE
HA0
WOODSTOCK RD
MARQUIS CL
THE GRANGE
HEATHER PARK DR
ST JAMES' GDNS
Alperton Com Sch
Lyon Park Jun & Inf Schs
LYON PARK AVE
KENMERE GDNS
BRIDGE PK
Allot Gdns
RUSSELL CT
ANNE CARVER LO
STANLEY AVE
STANLEY PARK
BELMONT AVE
Pl Flds
HIGHCROFT AVE
Alperton Lower Sch
WYATT CT
ORCHARD CL
LIGHTLEY CL
MOUNT PLEASANT
NEWCOMBE PK
CRAIGMUIR PK
A4089
BERESFORD
A406
A4005
Alperton
WOODSIDE CL
ABBEY MANUFACTURING EST
LIBERTY CTR
Liby
NORTHFIELD IND EST
WYCOMBE RD
WOODSIDE AVE
CLIFTON WAY
ATLIP

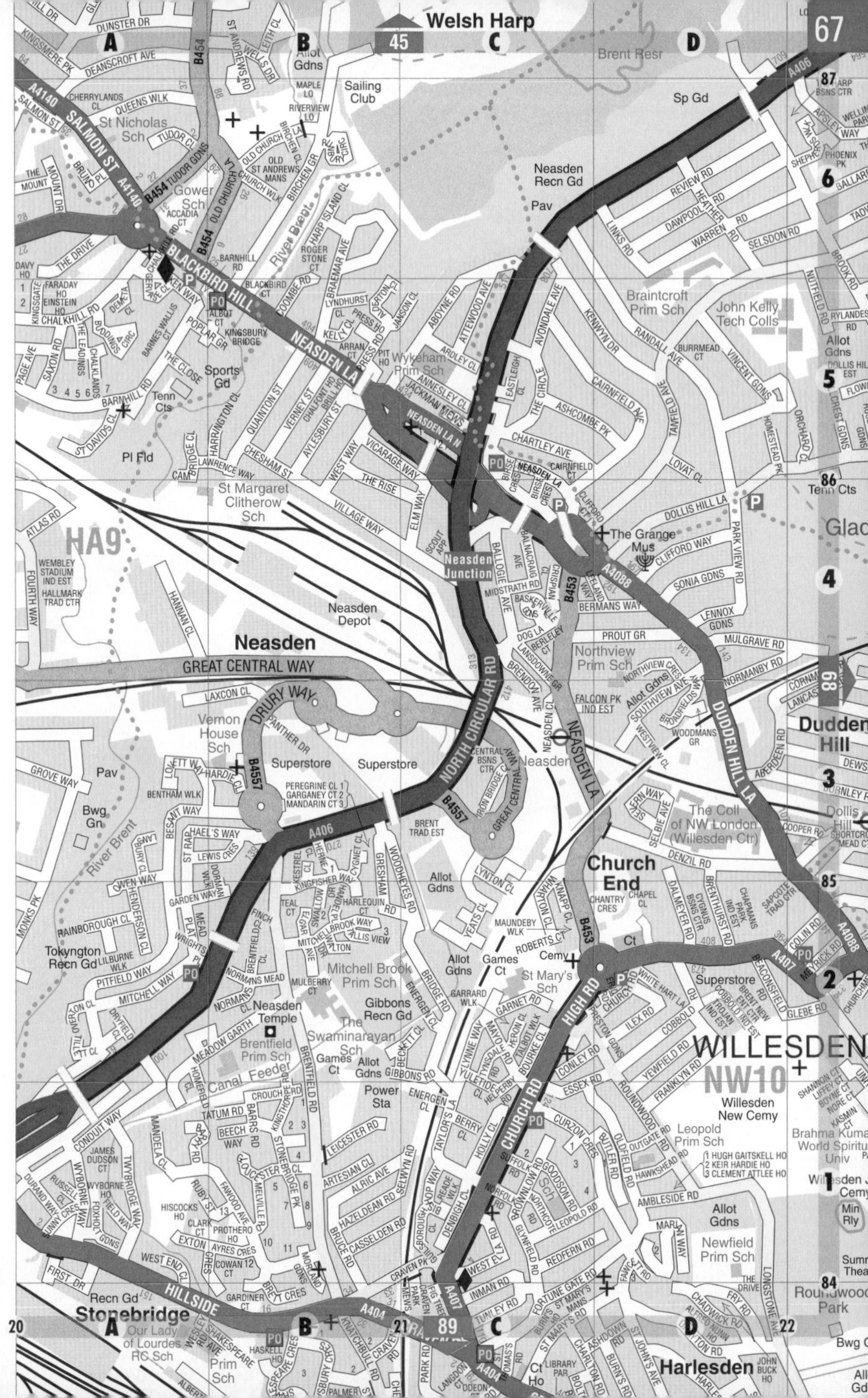

Welsh Harp
45
A
B
C
D
Brent Resr
Sailing Club
Sp Gd
Neasden Recn Gd
Pav
St Nicholas Sch
Gower Sch
BLACKBIRD HILL
NEASDEN LA
SALMON ST
A4140
B454
A406
Braintcroft Prim Sch
John Kelly Tech Colls
Allot Gdns
Sports Gd
Tenn Cts
Pl Fld
Wykeham Prim Sch
St Margaret Clitherow Sch
HA9
Neasden Depot
Neasden
Neasden Junction
The Grange Mus
A4088
B453
GREAT CENTRAL WAY
DRURY WAY
NORTH CIRCULAR RD
Northview Prim Sch
DUDDEN HILL LA
Dudden Hill
Vernon House Sch
Superstore
Superstore
B4557
Pav
Bwg Gn
River Brent
BRENT TRAD EST
The Coll of NW London (Willesden Ctr)
Church End
Allot Gdns
Tokyngton Recn Gd
Mitchell Brook Prim Sch
Gibbons Recn Gd
St Mary's Sch
Neasden Temple
Brentfield Prim Sch
The Swaminarayan Sch
Canal Feeder
Power Sta
HIGH RD
CHURCH RD
Superstore
WILLESDEN
NW10
Willesden New Cemy
Leopold Prim Sch
Brahma Kuma World Spiritu Univ
Allot Gdns
Newfield Prim Sch
Roundwood Park
HILLSIDE
A404
A407
Stonebridge
Our Lady of Lourdes RC Sch
Prim Sch
Harlesden
89
20
21
22
87
86
85
84
6
5
4
3
2
1
68

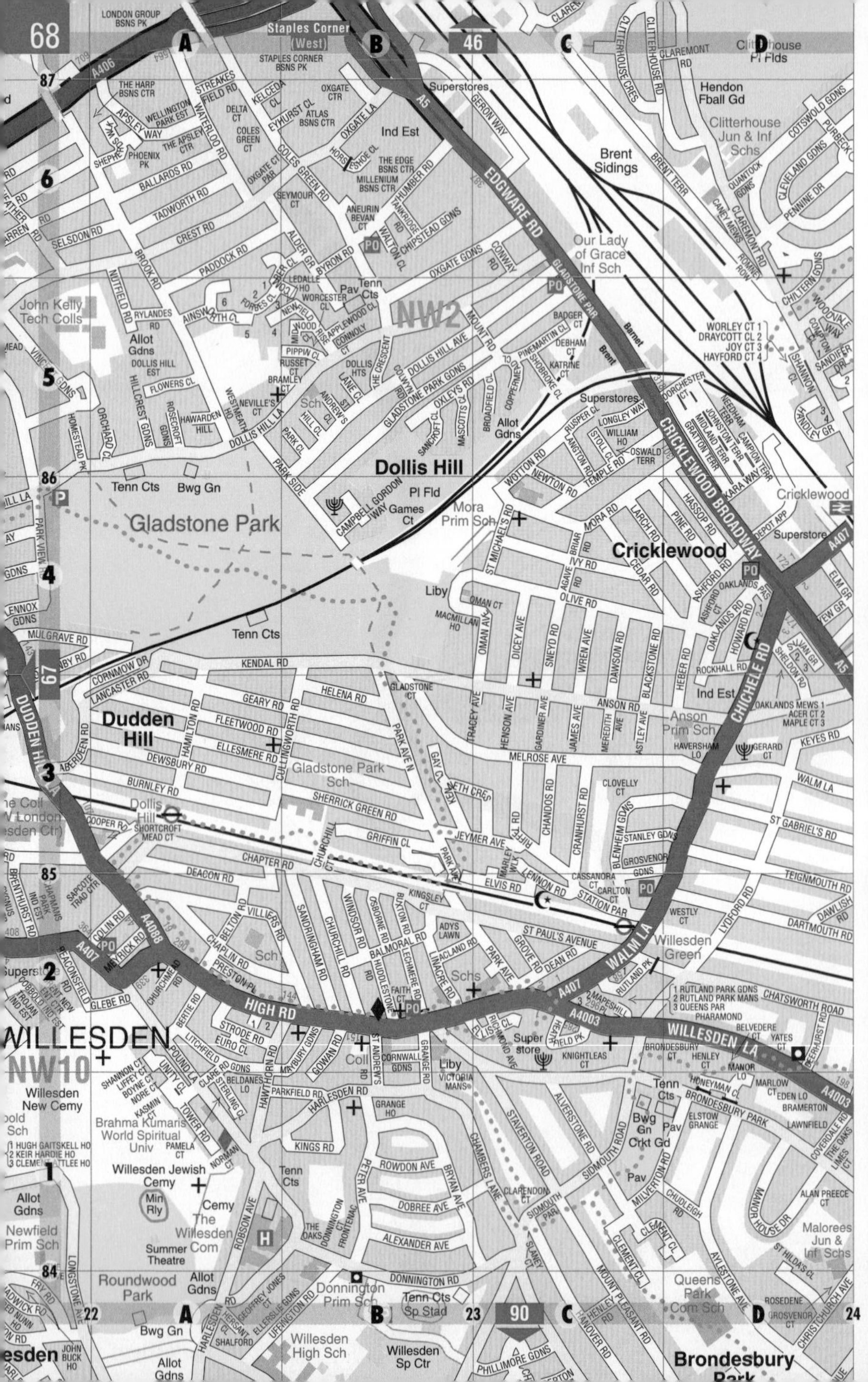

68
A
B
C
D
46
Staples Corner (West)
LONDON GROUP BSNS PK
STAPLES CORNER BSNS PK
A406
87
THE HARP BSNS CTR
WELLINGTON PARK EST
APSLEY WAY
THE APSLEY CTR
PHOENIX PK
STREAKES FIELD RD
WATERLOO RD
DELTA CT
COLES GREEN CT
KELCEDA CL
EYHURST CL
ATLAS BSNS CTR
OXGATE CTR
OXGATE LA
OXGATE CT PAR
COLES GREEN RD
Ind Est
HORSESHOE CL
THE EDGE BSNS CTR
MILLENIUM BSNS CTR
HUMBER RD
TANKRIDGE RD
CHIPSTEAD GDNS
WALTON CL
ANEURIN BEVAN CT
SEYMOUR CT
Superstores
GERON WAY
A5
EDGWARE RD
GLADSTONE PAR
CLITTERHOUSE CRES
CLITTERHOUSE RD
CLAREMONT RD
Clitterhouse Pl Flds
Hendon Fball Gd
Clitterhouse Jun & Inf Schs
COTSWOLD GDNS
PURBECK DR
CLEVELAND GDNS
PENNINE DR
QUANTOCK GDNS
Brent Sidings
BRENT TERR
CANEY MEWS
CLAREMONT RD
ROMNEY ROW
CHILTERN GDNS
WOODVALE WAY
COMPTON CL
SANDIFER DR
SHANNON CL
HANDLEY GR
WORLEY CT 1
DRAYCOTT CL 2
JOY CT 3
HAYFORD CT 4
Our Lady of Grace Inf Sch
6
BALLARDS RD
TADWORTH RD
CREST RD
SELSDON RD
PADDOCK RD
BROOK RD
NUTFIELD RD
ALDER GR
BYRON RD
LEDALLE HO
WORCESTER CL
FORBES CL
NEWFIELD RISE
Pav
Tenn Cts
OXGATE GDNS
CONWAY RD
APPLEWOOD CL
CONNOLY CT
NW2
MOUNT RD
BADGER CT
DEBHAM CT
KATRINE CT
PINEMARTIN CL
SHOBROKE CL
COPPERMEAD CL
Barnet
Brent
John Kelly Tech Colls
RYLANDES RD
AINSWORTH CL
Allot Gdns
DOLLIS HILL EST
PIPPIN CL
RUSSET CT
DOLLIS HTS
THE CRESCENT
COLWYN RD
DOLLIS HILL AVE
GLADSTONE PARK GDNS
OXLEYS RD
BROADFIELD CL
MASCOTTS CL
SANCROFT CL
5
VINCENT GDNS
HOMESTEAD PK
ORCHARD CL
HILLCREST GDNS
FLOWERS CL
ROSECROFT GDNS
HAWARDEN HILL
WESTMEATH HO
NEVILLE'S CT
BRAMLEY CT
Sch
HILL CL
ST ANDREW'S CL
LANE CL
DOLLIS HILL LA
PARK CL
PARK SIDE
Allot Gdns
Superstores
DORCHESTER CT
RUSPER CL
LONGLEY WAY
WILLIAM HO
LANGTON RD
STOLL CL
OSWALD TERR
TEMPLE RD
WOTTON RD
NEWTON RD
CRICKLEWOOD BROADWAY
NEEDHAM TERR
JOHNSTON TERR
MIDLAND TERR
GRATTON TERR
CAMPION TERR
KARA WAY
Cricklewood
86
Tenn Cts
Bwg Gn
Dollis Hill
Pl Fld
CAMPBELL GORDON WAY
Games Ct
Mora Prim Sch
Gladstone Park
PARK VIEW RD
ST MICHAEL'S RD
MORA RD
BRIAR RD
LARCH RD
HASSOP RD
PINE RD
DEPOT APP
Superstore
A407
Cricklewood
IVY RD
AGAVE RD
CEDAR RD
ASHFORD RD
OAKLANDS PAS
ELM GR
VIEW GR
4
LENNOX GDNS
Liby
OMAN CT
MACMILLAN HO
OMAN AVE
DICEY AVE
OLIVE RD
SNEYD RD
WREN AVE
DAWSON RD
BLACKSTONE RD
HEBER RD
ASHFORD CT
OAKLANDS RD
HOWARD RD
CHICHELE RD
SHELDON RD
VAN GR
MULGRAVE RD
Tenn Cts
67
KENDAL RD
CORNMOW DR
LANCASTER RD
GEARY RD
HELENA RD
GLADSTONE CT
ROCKHALL RD
Ind Est
TRACEY AVE
HENSON AVE
GARDINER AVE
JAMES AVE
MEREDITH AVE
ASTLEY AVE
ANSON RD
Anson Prim Sch
OAKLANDS MEWS 1
ACER CT 2
MAPLE CT 3
DUDDEN HILL LA
Dudden Hill
ABERDEEN RD
HAMILTON RD
FLEETWOOD RD
ELLESMERE RD
CULLINGWORTH RD
DEWSBURY RD
PARK AVE N
Gladstone Park Sch
MELROSE AVE
HAVERSHAM LO
GERARD CT
KEYES RD
3
BURNLEY RD
GAY CL
NETH CRES
WALM LA
SHERRICK GREEN RD
CHANDOS RD
CRANHURST RD
RIFFEL RD
CLOVELLY CT
Dollis Hill
COOPER RD
SHORTCROFT MEAD CT
GRIFFIN CL
JEYMER AVE
BLENHEIM GDNS
STANLEY GDNS
GROSVENOR GDNS
ST GABRIEL'S RD
CHAPTER RD
CHURCHILL CT
MARLEY WLK
LENNON RD
ELVIS RD
85
BRENTHURST RD
CHAPMANS PARK IND EST
SAPCOTE TRAD CTR
DEACON RD
KINGSLEY CT
CASSANORA CT
CARLTON CT
STATION PAR
TEIGNMOUTH RD
LYDFORD RD
DAWLISH RD
DARTMOUTH RD
A4088
COLIN RD
MEYRICK RD
BELTON RD
VILLIERS RD
SANDRINGHAM RD
CHURCHILL RD
WINDSOR RD
OSBORNE RD
BUXTON RD
ADYS LAWN
ACLAND RD
BALMORAL RD
LECHMERE RD
LINACRE RD
ST PAUL'S AVENUE
GROVE RD
DEAN RD
PARK AVE
WESTLY CT
Willesden Green
2
Superstore
BEACONSFIELD RD
TROJAN IND EST
COBBOLD IND EST
CHAPLIN RD
PRESTON RD
Sch
CHURCHMEAD RD
HUDDLESTONE RD
FAITH CT
Schs
A407
RUTLAND PK
1 RUTLAND PARK GDNS
2 RUTLAND PARK MANS
3 QUEENS PAR
PHARAMOND
CHATSWORTH ROAD
GLEBE RD
HIGH RD
PRESTON PL
BERTIE RD
STRODE RD
EURO CL
A4003
MAPESHILL PL
HEATHFIELD PK
RICHMOND AVE
ELLIS CL
Super store
KNIGHTLEAS CT
WILLESDEN LA
BELVEDERE CT
YATES CT
DEERHURST RD
WILLESDEN
NW10
LITCHFIELD GDNS
POUND LA
UNITY CL
CLARE RD
STERLING CL
BELDANES LO
HAWTHORN RD
MAYBURY GDNS
GOWAN RD
Coll
ST ANDREW'S RD
CORNWALL GDNS
GRANGE RD
Liby
VICTORIA MANS
BRONDESBURY CT
HENLEY CT
MANOR LO
HONEYMAN CL
MARLOW CT
EDEN LO
BRAMERTON
BRONDESBURY PARK
LAWNFIELD
Willesden New Cemy
SHANNON CT
LIFFEY CT
BOYNE CT
NORE CT
KASMIN CT
TOWER RD
PARKFIELD RD
HARLESDEN RD
GRANGE HO
STAVERTON ROAD
ALVERSTONE RD
SIDMOUTH ROAD
Tenn Cts
Bwg Gn
Crkt Gd
Pav
ELSTOW GRANGE
COVERDALE RD
THE OAKS
LIMES CT
Brahma Kumaris World Spiritual Univ
PAMELA CT
NORMAN CT
1 HUGH GAITSKELL HO
2 KEIR HARDIE HO
3 CLEMENT ATTLEE HO
KINGS RD
1
ROWDON AVE
BRYAN AVE
Willesden Jewish Cemy
Tenn Cts
Cemy
Min Rly
The Willesden Com
Summer Theatre
ROBSON AVE
H
PETER AVE
DOBREE AVE
THE OAKS
DONNINGTON CT
FRONTENAC
ALEXANDER AVE
CHAMBERS LANE
CLARENDON CT
SIDMOUTH PAR
SLANEY PL
CLEMENT CL
MILVERTON RD
CHUDLEIGH RD
Pav
MANOR HOUSE DR
ALAN PREECE CT
Malorees Jun & Inf Schs
Allot Gdns
Newfield Prim Sch
LONGSTONE AVE
84
FRY RD
Roundwood Park
Allot Gdns
GEOFFREY JONES CT
DONNINGTON RD
Donnington Prim Sch
Tenn Cts
Sp Stad
CLEMENT CL
MOUNT PLEASANT RD
AYLESTONE AVE
Queens Park Com Sch
ST HILDA'S CL
ROSEDENE
GROSVENOR CT
CHRISTCHURCH AVE
22
23
90
24
Bwg Gn
HARLESDEN RD
HERSANT CL
ELLERSLIE GDNS
UFFINGTON RD
SHALFORD
Willesden High Sch
Willesden Sp Ctr
PHILLIMORE GDNS
HENLEY RD
HANOVER RD
Brondesbury Park
JOHN BUCK HO
Allot Gdns

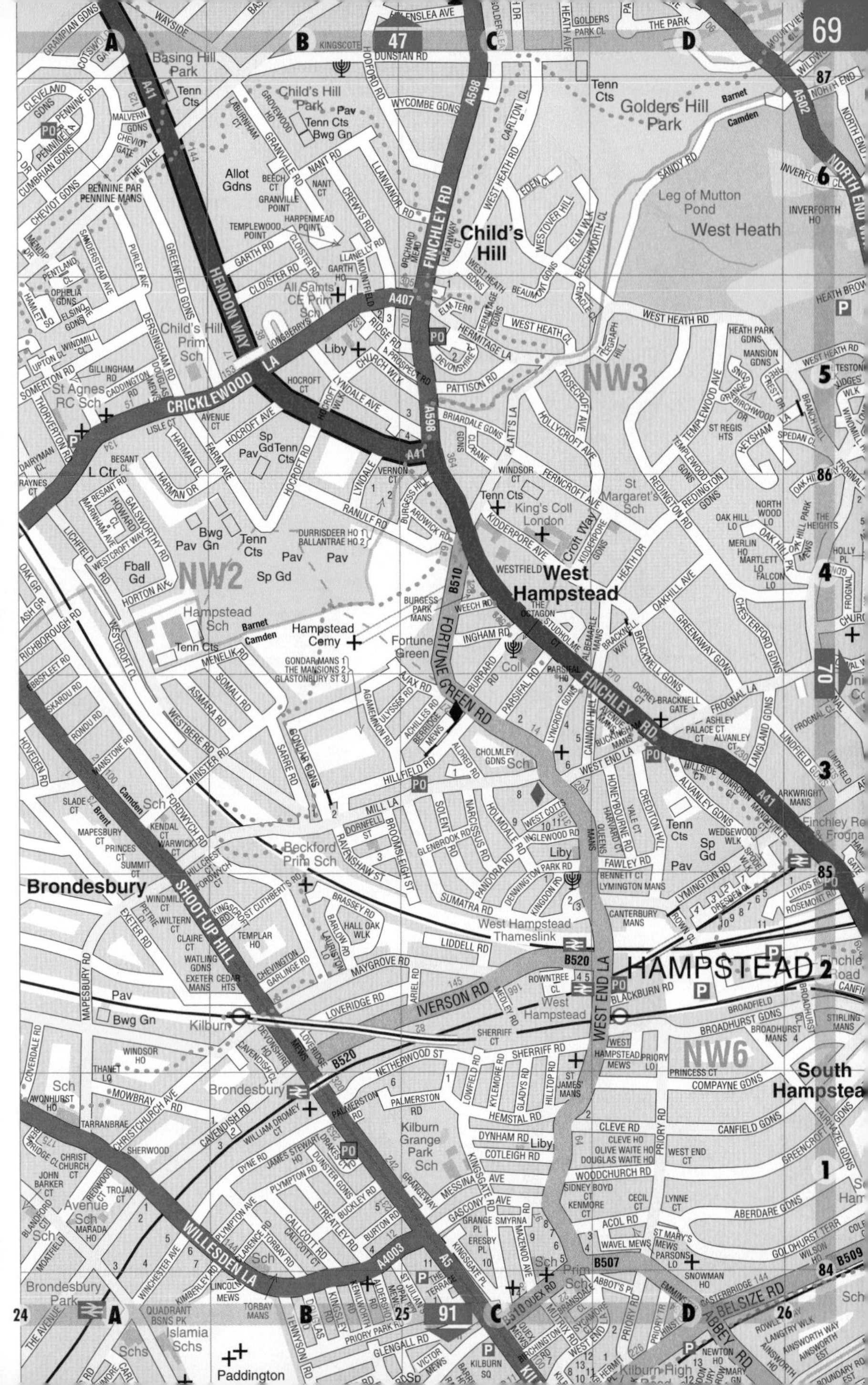

A
B
C
D
47
KINGSCOTE
DUNSTAN RD
HELENSLEA AVE
GOLDERS PARK CL
THE PARK
HEATH AVE
WAYSIDE
GRAMPIAN GDNS
COTSWOLD
Basing Hill Park
Tenn Cts
Child's Hill Park
Pav
Tenn Cts
Bwg Gn
HODFORD RD
WYCOMBE GDNS
A598
CARLTON CL
Golders Hill Park
Barnet
Camden
A502
NORTH END
NORTH END RD
87
MOUNTVIEW CL
WILDWOOD
A41
CLEVELAND GDNS
PENNINE DR
MALVERN GDNS
CHEVIOT GATE
THE VALE
CUMBRIAN GDNS
CHEVIOT GDNS
PENNINE PAR
PENNINE MANS
Allot Gdns
GROVEWOOD HO
LABURNHAM CT
GRANVILLE RD
NANT RD
NANT CT
BEECH CT
GRANVILLE POINT
LLANVANOR RD
CREWYS RD
HARPENMEAD POINT
TEMPLEWOOD POINT
GARTH RD
CLOISTER RD
FINCHLEY RD
WEST HEATH RD
EDEN CL
WESTOVER HILL
ELM WLK
BEECHWORTH CL
SANDY RD
Leg of Mutton Pond
West Heath
INVERFORTH CL
INVERFORTH HO
6
Child's Hill
HENDON WAY
All Saints' CE Prim Sch
A407
LLANELLY RD
MOUNTFIELD
GARTH HO
ORCHARD MEAD
HEATHWAY CT
BEAUMONT GDNS
WEST HEATH GDNS
ELM TERR
HERMITAGE GDNS
HERMITAGE LA
WEST HEATH CL
WEST HEATH RD
HEATH BROW
PURLEY AVE
GREENFIELD GDNS
SANDERSTEAD AVE
PENTLAND CL
OPHELIA GDNS
ELSINORE GDNS
HAMLET SQ
MENDIP
Child's Hill Prim Sch
DERSINGHAM RD
LONGBERRYS
RIDGE RD
Liby
PO
PROSPECT RD
DEVONSHIRE
CHURCH WLK
PATTISON RD
TELEGRAPH HILL
NW3
HEATH PARK GDNS
MANSION GDNS
TEMPLEWOOD AVE
WEST HEATH RD
TESTON
JUDGES' WLK
5
UPTON CL
WINDMILL CT
SOMERTON RD
GILLINGHAM RD
CADDINGTON RD
St Agnes RC Sch
THORVERTON RD
CRICKLEWOOD LA
HOCROFT CT
HOCROFT WLK
LYNDALE AVE
A598
BRIARDALE GDNS
PLATT'S LA
ROSECROFT AVE
HOLLYCROFT AVE
GRANGE GDNS
BIRCHWOOD DR
ST REGIS HTS
HEYSHAM LA
SPEDAN CL
BRANCH HILL
WINDMILL HILL
DAIRYMAN CL
AVENUE CT
LISLE CT
HARMAN CL
FARM AVE
HOCROFT AVE
Sp Gd
Tenn Cts
Pav
HOCROFT RD
A41
VERNON CT
LYNDALE
CLORANE GDNS
WINDSOR CT
FERNCROFT AVE
St Margaret's Sch
REDINGTON RD
REDINGTON GDNS
TEMPLEWOOD GDNS
OAK HILL WAY
FROGNAL
86
BESANT CL
L Ctr
RAYNES CT
HARMAN DR
BESANT RD
HOWARD CL
MARNHAM AVE
GALSWORTHY RD
WESTCROFT WAY
RANULF RD
BURGESS HILL
ARDWICK RD
DURRISDEER HO
BALLANTRAE HO
Tenn Cts
King's Coll London
KIDDERPORE AVE
Croft Way
KIDDERPORE GDNS
NORTH WOOD LO
OAK HILL PARK
OAK HILL LO
MERLIN HO
MARTLETT LO
FALCON LO
OAK HILL PK MEWS
THE HEIGHTS
HOLLY PL
LICHFIELD RD
Fball Gd
Bwg Gn
Pav
Tenn Cts
Pav
Pav
Sp Gd
NW2
HORTON AVE
B510
WESTFIELD
West Hampstead
HEATH DR
OAKHILL AVE
4
OAK GR
ASH GR
RICHBOROUGH RD
WESTCROFT CL
Hampstead Sch
Barnet
Camden
Tenn Cts
MENELIK RD
Hampstead Cemy
BURGESS PARK MANS
WEECH RD
FORTUNE GREEN RD
Fortune Green
INGHAM RD
THE OCTAGON
STUDHOLME CT
ALBEMARLE MANS
BRACKNELL WAY
BRACKNELL GDNS
GREENAWAY GDNS
CHESTERFORD GDNS
70
EBBSFLEET RD
SKARDU RD
SOMALI RD
ASMARA RD
GONDAR MANS
THE MANSIONS
GLASTONBURY ST
AJAX RD
ULYSSES RD
AGAMEMNON RD
ACHILLES RD
BERRIDGE MEWS
BURRARD RD
Coll
PARSIFAL RD
PARSIFAL HO
FINCHLEY RD
OSPREY CT
BRACKNELL GATE
FROGNAL LA
LANGLAND GDNS
LINDFIELD GDNS
FROGNAL CT
RONDU RD
HOVEDEN RD
MANSTONE RD
WESTBERE RD
MINSTER RD
SARRE RD
GONDAR GDNS
ALDRED RD
HILLFIELD RD
CHOLMLEY GDNS
Sch
LYNCROFT GDNS
CANNON HILL
AVENUE MANS
BUCKINGHAM MANS
WEST END LA
PO
ASHLEY PALACE CT
ALVANLEY CT
HILLSIDE CT
DUNROBIN CT
A41
ARKWRIGHT MANS
3
SLADE CT
Camden
Brent
FORDWYCH RD
Sch
KENDAL CT
WARWICK CT
MAPESBURY CT
PRINCES CT
SUMMIT CT
MILL LA
DORNFELL ST
BROOMSLEIGH ST
RAVENSHAW ST
SOLENT RD
NARCISSUS RD
HOLMDALE RD
GLENBROOK RD
WEST COTTS
INGLEWOOD RD
HONEYBOURNE RD
HARVARD CT
QUEENS MANS
YALE CT
CREDITON HILL
ALVANLEY GDNS
MANDEVILLE
Tenn Cts
Sp Gd
Pav
WEDGEWOOD WLK
Finchley Rd & Frognal
Beckford Prim Sch
Brondesbury
HILLCREST CT
FORDWYCH CT
ST CUTHBERT'S RD
PANDORA RD
DENNINGTON PARK RD
KINGDON RD
Liby
FAWLEY RD
BENNETT CT
LYMINGTON MANS
LYMINGTON RD
SPODE WLK
DRESDEN CL
LITHOS RD
ROSEMONT RD
85
WINDMILL CT
PETRIE CL
WILTERN CT
KINGSCROFT
EXETER RD
CLAIRE CT
SHOOT-UP HILL
BRASSEY RD
BARLOW RD
HALL OAK WLK
LAURISTON LO
TEMPLAR HO
SUMATRA RD
West Hampstead Thameslink
CANTERBURY MANS
ROWN CL
MAPESBURY RD
WATLING GDNS
EXETER MANS
CEDAR HTS
CHEVINGTON
GARLINGE RD
MAYGROVE RD
LIDDELL RD
B520
WEST END LA
ROWNTREE CL
HAMPSTEAD
Finchley Road
2
CANFIELD
Pav
Bwg Gn
Kilburn
LOVERIDGE RD
ARIEL RD
IVERSON RD
MEDLEY RD
West Hampstead
BLACKBURN RD
BROADFIELD
BROADHURST GDNS
BROADHURST MANS
BROADHURST CL
STIRLING MANS
COVERDALE RD
WINDSOR HO
THANET LO
DEVONSHIRE MEWS
CAVENDISH CL
LOVERIDGE MEWS
B520
NETHERWOOD ST
SHERRIFF CT
SHERRIFF RD
LOWFIELD RD
KYLEMORE RD
GLADYS RD
HILLTOP RD
ST JAMES' MANS
WEST HAMPSTEAD MEWS
PRIORY LO
NW6
PRINCESS CT
COMPAYNE GDNS
South Hampstead
Sch
AVONHURST HO
MOWBRAY RD
Brondesbury
TARRANBRAE
CHRISTCHURCH AVE
CAVENDISH RD
WILLIAM DROMEY CT
PALMERSTON RD
Kilburn Grange Park Sch
HEMSTAL RD
CLEVE RD
CLEVE HO
OLIVE WAITE HO
DOUGLAS WAITE HO
PRIORY RD
WEST END CT
CANFIELD GDNS
GREENCROFT GDNS
FAIRHAZEL GDNS
1
SHERWOOD
CHRIST CHURCH CT
JOHN BARKER CT
REDWOOD CT
TROJAN CT
DYNE RD
JAMES STEWART HO
DRAKES CTYD
DUNSTER GDNS
PLYMPTON RD
DYNHAM RD
Liby
COTLEIGH RD
MESSINA AVE
KINGSGATE RD
WOODCHURCH RD
SIDNEY BOYD CT
KENMORE CT
CECIL CT
LYNNE CT
ABERDARE GDNS
Avenue Sch
Sch
MARADA HO
BLANDFORD CL
MOATFIELD
WINCHESTER AVE
WILLESDEN LA
PLYMPTON AVE
CLARENCE RD
TORBAY RD
CALLCOTT RD
CALLCOTT CT
STREATLEY RD
BUCKLEY RD
BURTON RD
GRANGEWAY
GASCONY AVE
GRANGE CT
SMYRNA
ERESBY PL
MAZENOD AVE
ACOL RD
WAVEL MEWS
ST MARY'S MEWS
PARSONS LO
SNOWMAN HO
GOLDHURST TERR
WILSON HO
B509
84
Brondesbury Park
KIMBERLEY RD
LINCOLN MEWS
A4003
ALDERSHOT RD
KENILWORTH RD
ST JULIAN'S
THE TERRACE
KINGSGATE PL
A5
Sch
Prim Sch
QUEX RD
ABBOT'S PL
B507
GASTERBRIDGE
BELSIZE RD
ABBEY RD
EMMINS
Sch
24
THE AVENUE
QUADRANT BSNS PK
TORBAY MANS
B
KINGSLEY RD
25
91
C
B510
QUEX MEWS
MUTRIX RD
SYCAMORE CT
BRANSDALE CL
WEST END LA
PRIORY RD
D
26
ROWLEY WAY
LANGTRY WLK
AINSWORTH WAY
AINSWORTH EST
Islamia Schs
Schs
Paddington
TENNYSON RD
DOUGLAS RD
PRIORY PARK RD
GLENGALL RD
VICTOR MEWS
KILBURN SQ
BIRCHINGTON RD
NEWTON HO
Kilburn High Rd

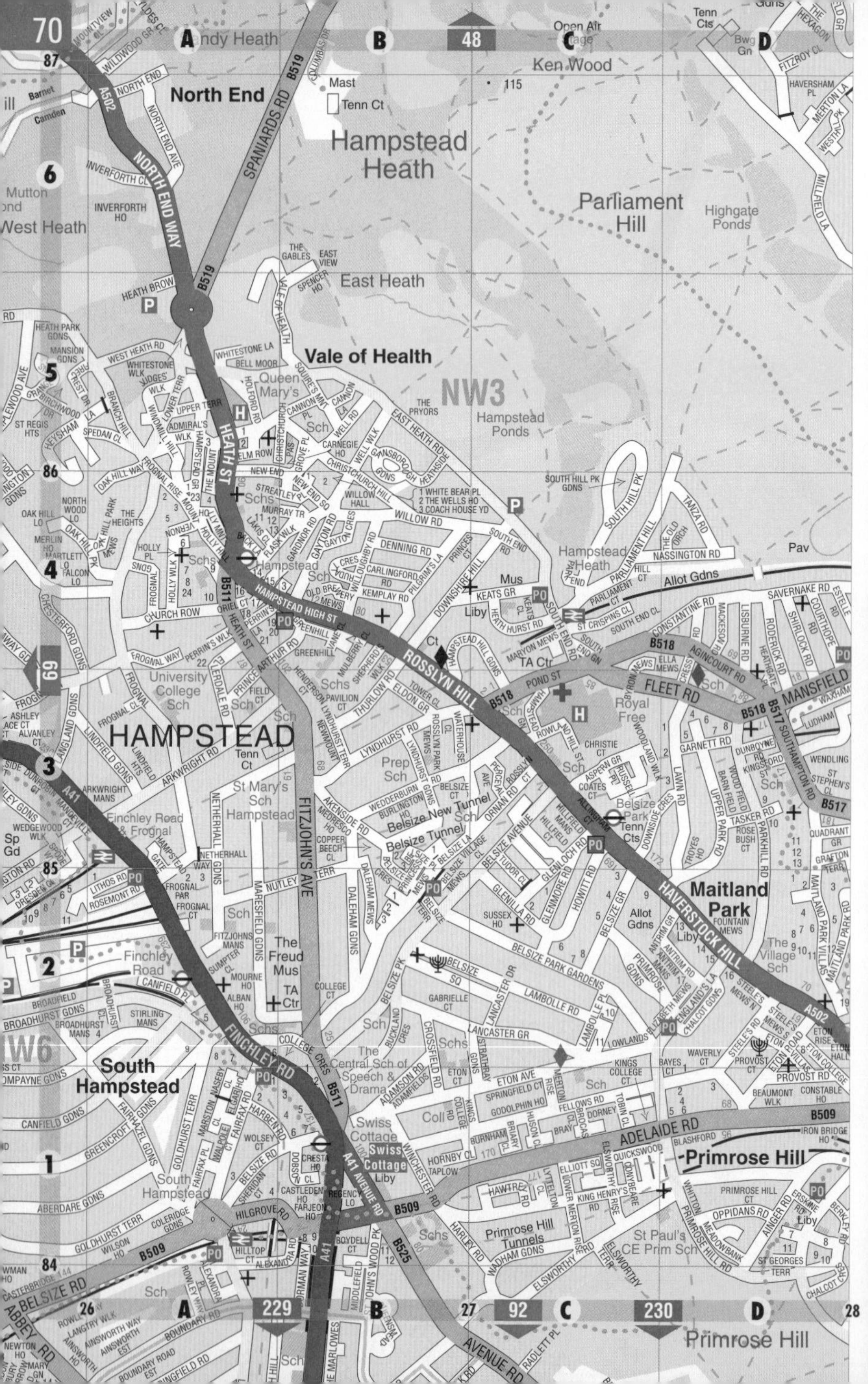
48
North End
Hampstead Heath
Ken Wood
Parliament Hill
Highgate Ponds
West Heath
East Heath
Vale of Health
NW3
Hampstead Ponds
HAMPSTEAD
Royal Free
Maitland Park
South Hampstead
Swiss Cottage
Primrose Hill
Finchley Road & Frognal
Finchley Road
The Freud Mus
Belsize Tunnel
Belsize New Tunnel
Primrose Hill Tunnels
The Central Sch of Speech & Drama
St Paul's CE Prim Sch
University College Sch
St Mary's Sch Hampstead
NORTH END WAY
SPANIARDS RD
HEATH ST
HAMPSTEAD HIGH ST
ROSSLYN HILL
HAVERSTOCK HILL
FITZJOHN'S AVE
FINCHLEY RD
ADELAIDE RD
BELSIZE RD
AVENUE RD
FLEET RD
POND ST
SOUTH END RD
EAST HEATH RD
WILLOW RD
BELSIZE PARK GARDENS
ETON AVE
LANCASTER GR
ARKWRIGHT RD
FROGNAL
CANFIELD GDNS
69
229
92
230

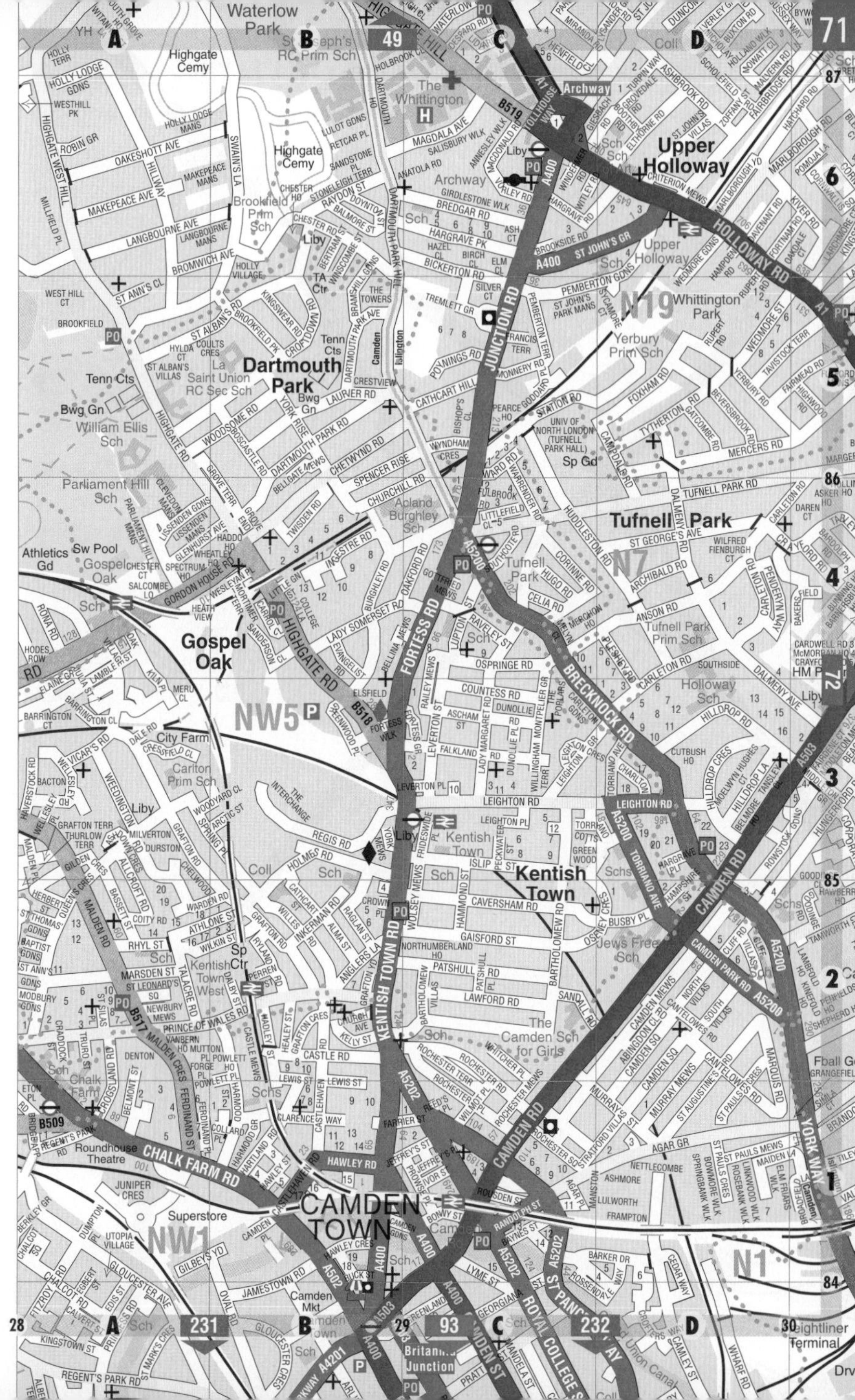

A
B
C
D
49
Waterlow Park
Highgate Cemy
The Whittington
Archway
Upper Holloway
Dartmouth Park
N19
Whittington Park
Tufnell Park
N7
Gospel Oak
NW5
Kentish Town
City Farm
The Camden Sch for Girls
Roundhouse Theatre
CAMDEN TOWN
NW1
N1
Camden Mkt
Britannia Junction
Superstore
HIGHGATE RD
FORTESS RD
JUNCTION RD
KENTISH TOWN RD
CAMDEN RD
BRECKNOCK RD
HOLLOWAY RD
CHALK FARM RD
YORK WAY
TUFNELL PARK RD
DARTMOUTH PARK HILL
LEIGHTON RD
MALDEN RD
ROYAL COLLEGE ST
ST PANCRAS WAY
231
93
232
28
29
30
87
86
85
84
6
5
4
3
2
1
72

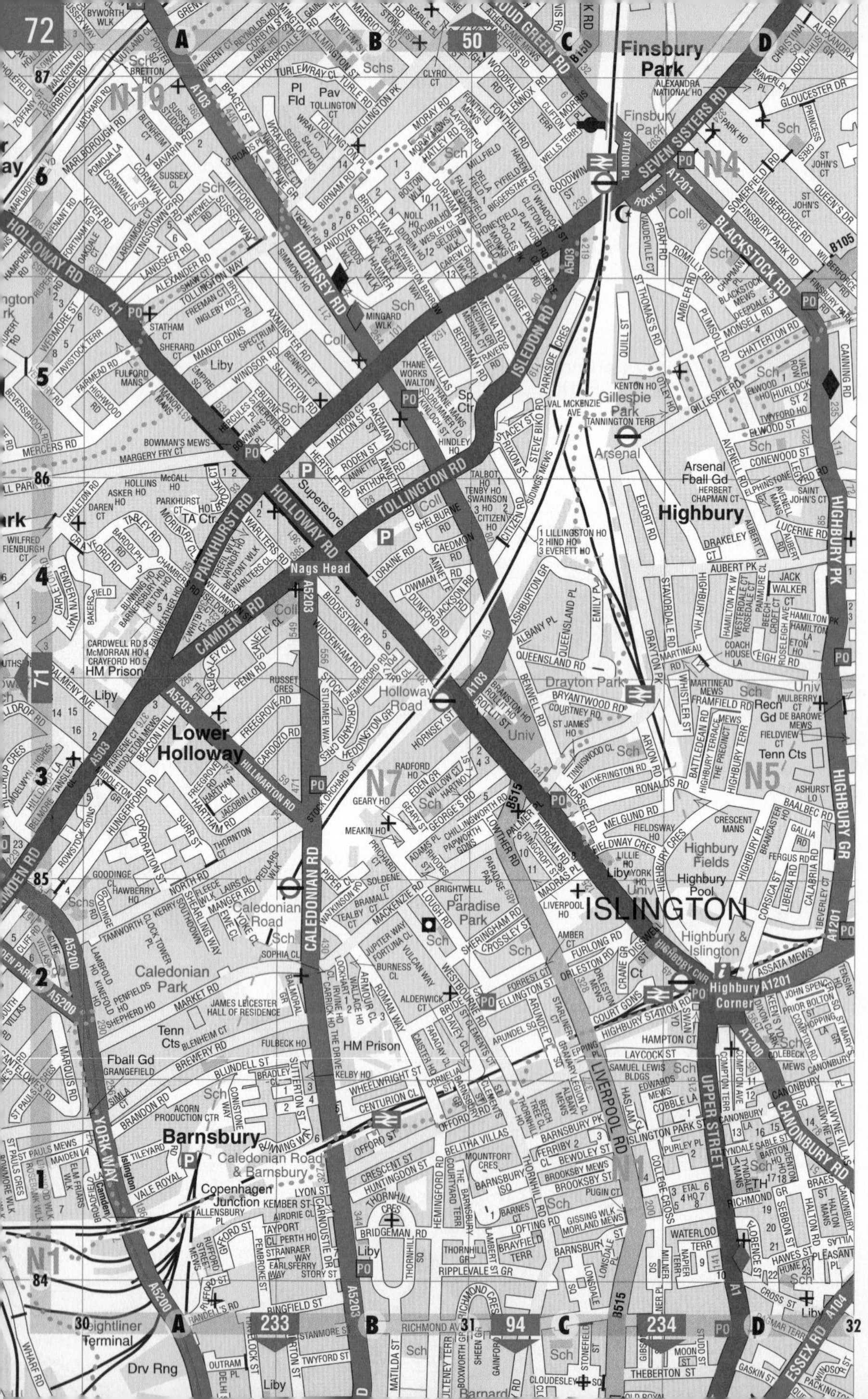

Finsbury Park
N19
N4
N7
N5
N1
Highbury
ISLINGTON
Lower Holloway
Barnsbury
Caledonian Park
Paradise Park
Highbury Fields
Nags Head
Holloway Road
Caledonian Road
Arsenal
Drayton Park
Highbury & Islington
Highbury Corner
Caledonian Road & Barnsbury
Copenhagen Junction
Gillespie Park
Arsenal Fball Gd
HM Prison
HOLLOWAY RD
SEVEN SISTERS RD
CALEDONIAN RD
CAMDEN RD
HORNSEY RD
TOLLINGTON RD
PARKHURST RD
ISLEDON RD
BLACKSTOCK RD
HIGHBURY PK
HIGHBURY GR
LIVERPOOL RD
UPPER STREET
CANONBURY RD
YORK WAY
ESSEX RD
50
71
94
233
234

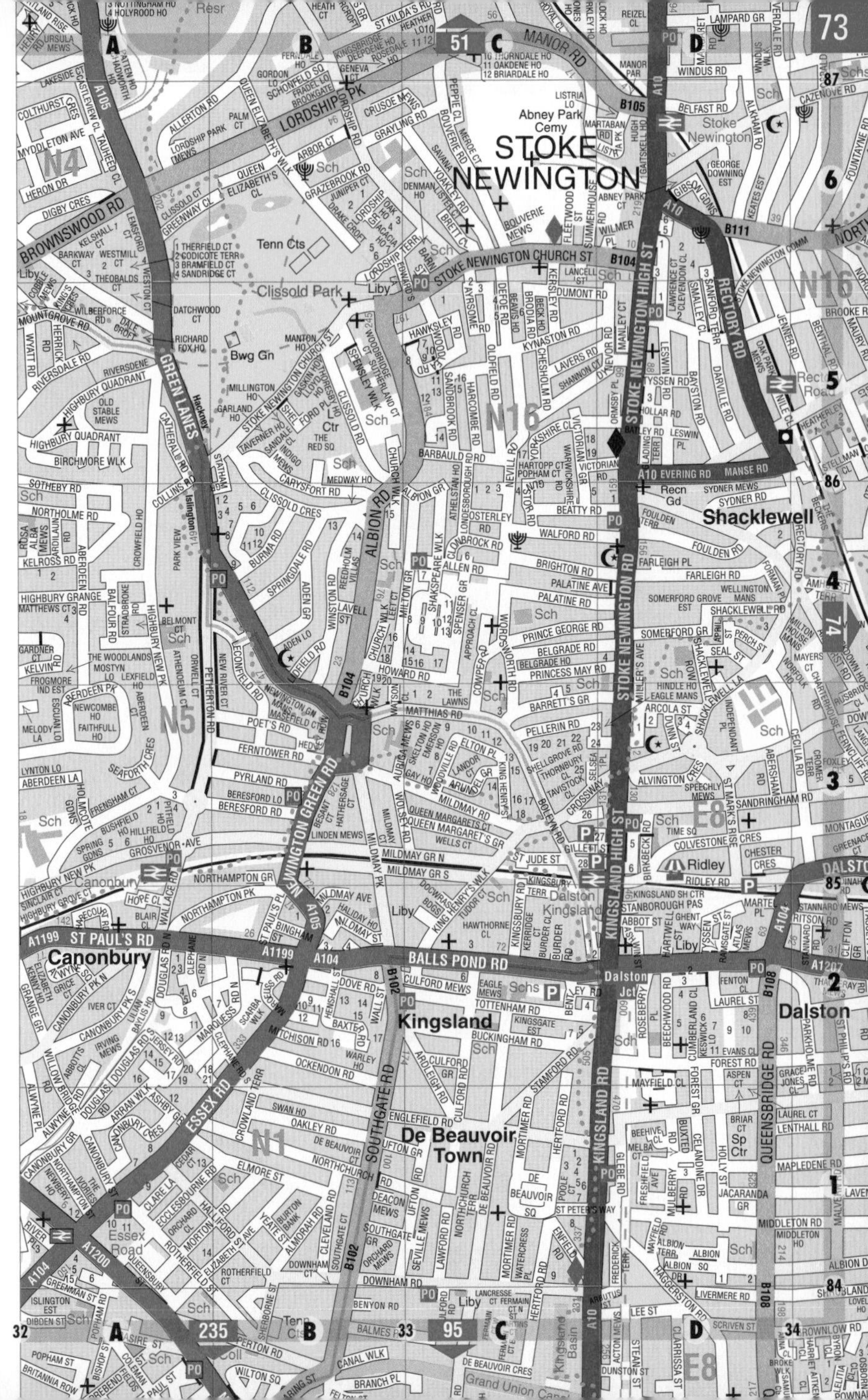
51
STOKE NEWINGTON
Abney Park Cemy
Stoke Newington
MANOR RD
LORDSHIP PK
BROWNSWOOD RD
GREEN LANES
Clissold Park
STOKE NEWINGTON CHURCH ST
STOKE NEWINGTON HIGH ST
RECTORY RD
Rectory Road
EVERING RD
Shacklewell
ALBION RD
KINGSLAND HIGH ST
NEWINGTON GREEN RD
Canonbury
ST PAUL'S RD
BALLS POND RD
Dalston Kingsland
Dalston Jct
Dalston
Kingsland
De Beauvoir Town
ESSEX RD
Essex Road
SOUTHGATE RD
KINGSLAND RD
QUEENSBRIDGE RD
Ridley
Grand Union Canal
Kingsland Basin
N4
N16
N5
N1
E8
74
235
95
32
33
34
84
85
86
87

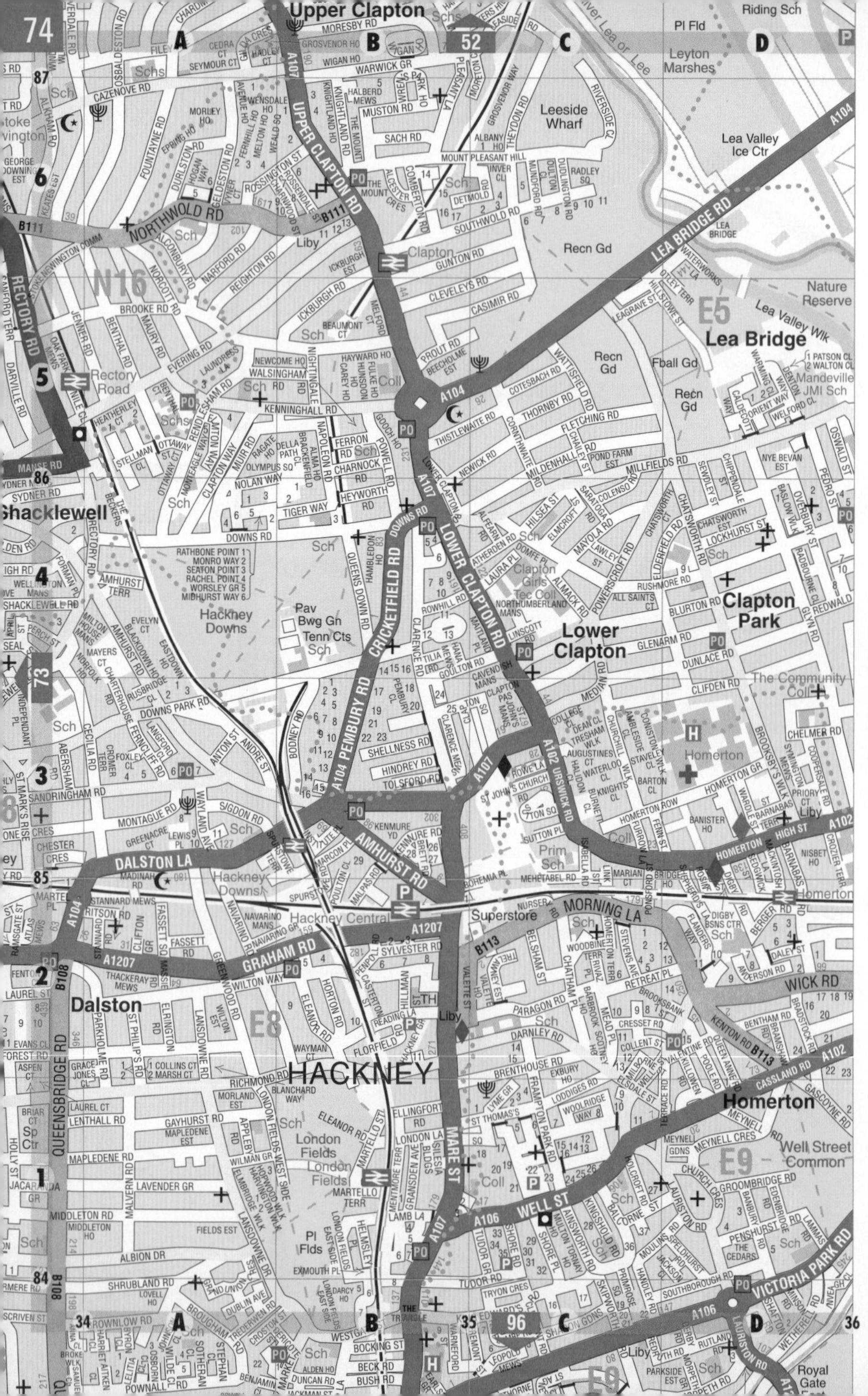
Upper Clapton
52
Riding Sch
Pl Fld
Leyton Marshes
River Lea or Lee
Leeside Wharf
Lea Valley Ice Ctr
A104
LEA BRIDGE RD
LEA BRIDGE
Nature Reserve
Lea Valley Wlk
E5
Lea Bridge
Mandeville JMI Sch
Recn Gd
Fball Gd
N16
RECTORY RD
Rectory Road
NORTHWOLD RD
B111
UPPER CLAPTON RD
A107
Clapton
CAZENOVE RD
MOUNT PLEASANT HILL
SOUTHWOLD RD
GUNTON RD
CLEVELEYS RD
CASIMIR RD
KENNINGHALL RD
MANSE RD
Shacklewell
DOWNS RD
Hackney Downs
CRICKETFIELD RD
LOWER CLAPTON RD
Clapton Girls Tec Coll
Lower Clapton
Clapton Park
MILLFIELDS RD
CHATSWORTH RD
GLENARM RD
The Community Coll
Homerton
HOMERTON HIGH ST
A102
HOMERTON GR
PEMBURY RD
A104
AMHURST RD
DALSTON LA
Hackney Downs
Hackney Central
GRAHAM RD
A1207
MORNING LA
B113
WICK RD
Superstore
Dalston
E8
HACKNEY
London Fields
MARE ST
WELL ST
A106
Homerton
CASSLAND RD
Well Street Common
E9
VICTORIA PARK RD
QUEENSBRIDGE RD
B108
Sp Ctr
Royal Gate
96
73
A B C D
34 35 36

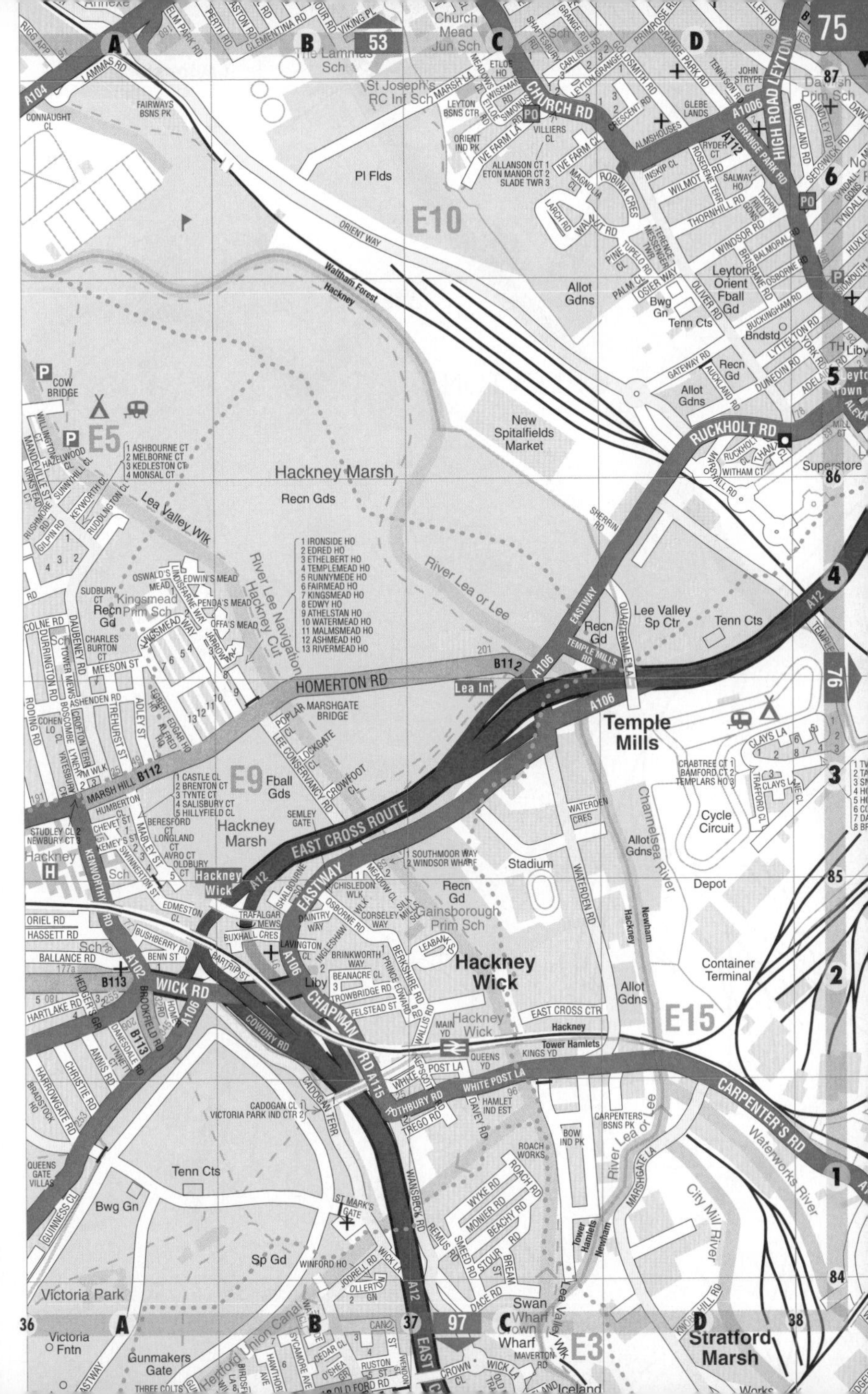

A
B
C
D
53
Church Mead Jun Sch
The Lammas Sch
St Joseph's RC Inf Sch
LAMMAS RD
A104
RIGG APP
ELM PARK RD
PERTH RD
CLEMENTINA RD
VIKING PL
FAIRWAYS BSNS PK
CONNAUGHT CL
MARSH LA
LEYTON BSNS CTR
ORIENT IND PK
IVE FARM LA
VILLIERS CL
ALLANSON CT 1
ETON MANOR CT 2
SLADE TWR 3
CHURCH RD
PO
GOLDSMITH RD
PRIMROSE RD
GRANGE PARK RD
GLEBE LANDS
ALMSHOUSES
CRESCENT RD
JOHN STRYPE CT
A1006
A112
HIGH ROAD LEYTON
GRANGE PARK RD
BUCKLAND RD
SEDGWICK RD
87
6
Pl Flds
E10
ORIENT WAY
Waltham Forest
Hackney
ROBINIA CRES
MAGNOLIA
LARCH RD
WALNUT RD
INSKIP CL
WILMOT RD
ROSEDENE TERR
RYDER CT
SALWAY HO
THORNHILL RD
WINDSOR RD
BALMORAL RD
OSBORNE RD
BRISBANE RD
TERENCE MESSENGER TWR
PINE CL
TUPELO RD
PALM CL
OSIER WAY
Bwg Gn
Tenn Cts
Allot Gdns
Leyton Orient Fball Gd
OLIVER RD
BUCKINGHAM RD
Bndstd
LYTTELTON RD
YORK RD
DUNEDIN RD
ADELAIDE RD
GATEWAY RD
AUCKLAND RD
Recn Gd
Allot Gdns
TH
Liby
5
RUCKHOLT RD
RUCKHOLT CL
WITHAM CT
MARSHALL RD
Superstore
86
New Spitalfields Market
COW BRIDGE
E5
1 ASHBOURNE CT
2 MELBORNE CT
3 KEDLESTON CT
4 MONSAL CT
Hackney Marsh
Recn Gds
Lea Valley Wlk
WILLINGTON RD
MANDEVILLE ST
HAZELWOOD CL
SUNNYHILL CL
KIRKSTEAD CT
RUSHMORE RD
KEYWORTH CL
RUDDINGTON CL
GILPIN RD
SHERRIN RD
River Lea or Lee
River Lee Navigation
Hackney Cut
1 IRONSIDE HO
2 EDRED HO
3 ETHELBERT HO
4 TEMPLEMEAD HO
5 RUNNYMEDE HO
6 FAIRMEAD HO
7 KINGSMEAD HO
8 EDWY HO
9 ATHELSTAN HO
10 WATERMEAD HO
11 MALMSMEAD HO
12 ASHMEAD HO
13 RIVERMEAD HO
OSWALD'S MEAD
EDWIN'S MEAD
LINDISFARNE WAY
PENDA'S MEAD
OFFA'S MEAD
JARROW WAY
KINGSMEAD WAY
SUDBURY CT
Kingsmead Prim Sch
Recn Gd
CHARLES BURTON CT
COLNE RD
DURRINGTON RD
DAUBENEY RD
TOWER MEWS
MEESON ST
EASTWAY
A106
QUARTERMILE LA
TEMPLE MILLS RD
Recn Gd
Lee Valley Sp Ctr
Tenn Cts
4
A12
201
B112
HOMERTON RD
Lea Int
POPLAR CL
MARSHGATE BRIDGE
LEE CONSERVANCY RD
LOCKGATE CL
CROWFOOT CL
ASHENDEN RD
TREHURST ST
ADLEY ST
EGBERT HO
EDGAR HO
ALFRED HO
COHEN LO
BOSCOMBE CL
CROFTON TERR
RODING RD
LYNEHAM WLK
YATESBURY CT
MARSH HILL
B112
1 CASTLE CL
2 BRENTON CT
3 TYNTE CT
4 SALISBURY CT
5 HILLYFIELD CL
E9
Fball Gds
SEMLEY GATE
EAST CROSS ROUTE
Temple Mills
76
CLAYS LA
CRABTREE CT 1
BAMFORD CT 2
TEMPLARS HO 3
TRAFFORD CL
CLAYS LANE CL
3
Cycle Circuit
WATERDEN CRES
Channelsea River
Allot Gdns
Stadium
Depot
85
HUMBERTON CL
CHEVET ST
KEMEY'S ST
MABLEY ST
BERESFORD CT
LONGLAND CT
AVRO CT
OLDBURY CT
SWINNERTON ST
STUDLEY CL 2
NEWBURY CT 3
Hackney
H
KENWORTHY RD
Hackney Marsh
Hackney Wick
Sch
EDMESTON CL
1 SOUTHMOOR WAY
2 WINDSOR WHARF
SHALBOURNE SQ
CHISLEDON WLK
MEADOW CL
OSBORNE RD
DAINTRY WAY
CORSELEY WAY
SILK MILLS SQ
Recn Gd
Gainsborough Prim Sch
WATERDEN RD
Hackney
Newham
ORIEL RD
HASSETT RD
BALLANCE RD
TRAFALGAR MEWS
BUXHALL CRES
BUSHBERRY RD
BENN ST
BARTRIP ST
LAVINGTON CL
INGLESHAW WAY
BRINKWORTH WAY
BEANACRE CL
TROWBRIDGE RD
FELSTEAD ST
BERKSHIRE RD
PRINCE EDWARD RD
LEABANK SQ
Hackney Wick
Container Terminal
2
B113
A102
WICK RD
A106
HARTLAKE RD
HEDGER'S GR
BROOKFIELD RD
HOMER RD
DANESDALE RD
LYNNETT RD
B113
Liby
CHAPMAN RD
EASTWAY
WALLIS RD
EAST CROSS CTR
Hackney Wick
MAIN YD
Hackney
Tower Hamlets
KINGS YD
QUEENS YD
Allot Gdns
E15
COWDRY RD
CADOGAN TERR
A115
WHITE POST LA
WHITE POST LA
HEPSCOTT RD
ROTHBURY RD
TREGO RD
DAVEY RD
HAMLET IND EST
CARPENTER'S RD
HARROWGATE RD
CHRISTIE RD
ANNIS RD
BRADSTOCK RD
CADOGAN CL 1
VICTORIA PARK IND CTR 2
ROACH WORKS
CARPENTERS BSNS PK
BOW IND PK
River Lea or Lee
MARSHGATE LA
Waterworks River
City Mill River
1
QUEENS GATE VILLAS
GUINNESS CL
Tenn Cts
Bwg Gn
ST MARK'S GATE
WANSBECK RD
WYKE RD
MONIER RD
ROACH RD
BEACHY RD
REMUS RD
SMEED RD
STOUR RD
BREAM ST
DACE RD
Sp Gd
WINFORD HO
JODRELL RD
WICK LA
OLLERTON GN
A12
Swan Wharf
Lea Valley Wlk
Tower Hamlets
Newham
KNOBS HILL RD
84
Victoria Park
36
A
B
37
97
C
D
38
Victoria Fntn
Gunmakers Gate
Hertford Union Canal
SYCAMORE AVE
CEDAR CL
O'SHEA GR
RUSTON ST
CANAL ST
WENDON ST
OLD FORD RD
HAWTHORN AVE
Crown Wharf
CROWN CL
WICK LA
MAVERTON RD
E3
Stratford Marsh
EAST
EASTWAY
THREE COLTS
Iceland
Works

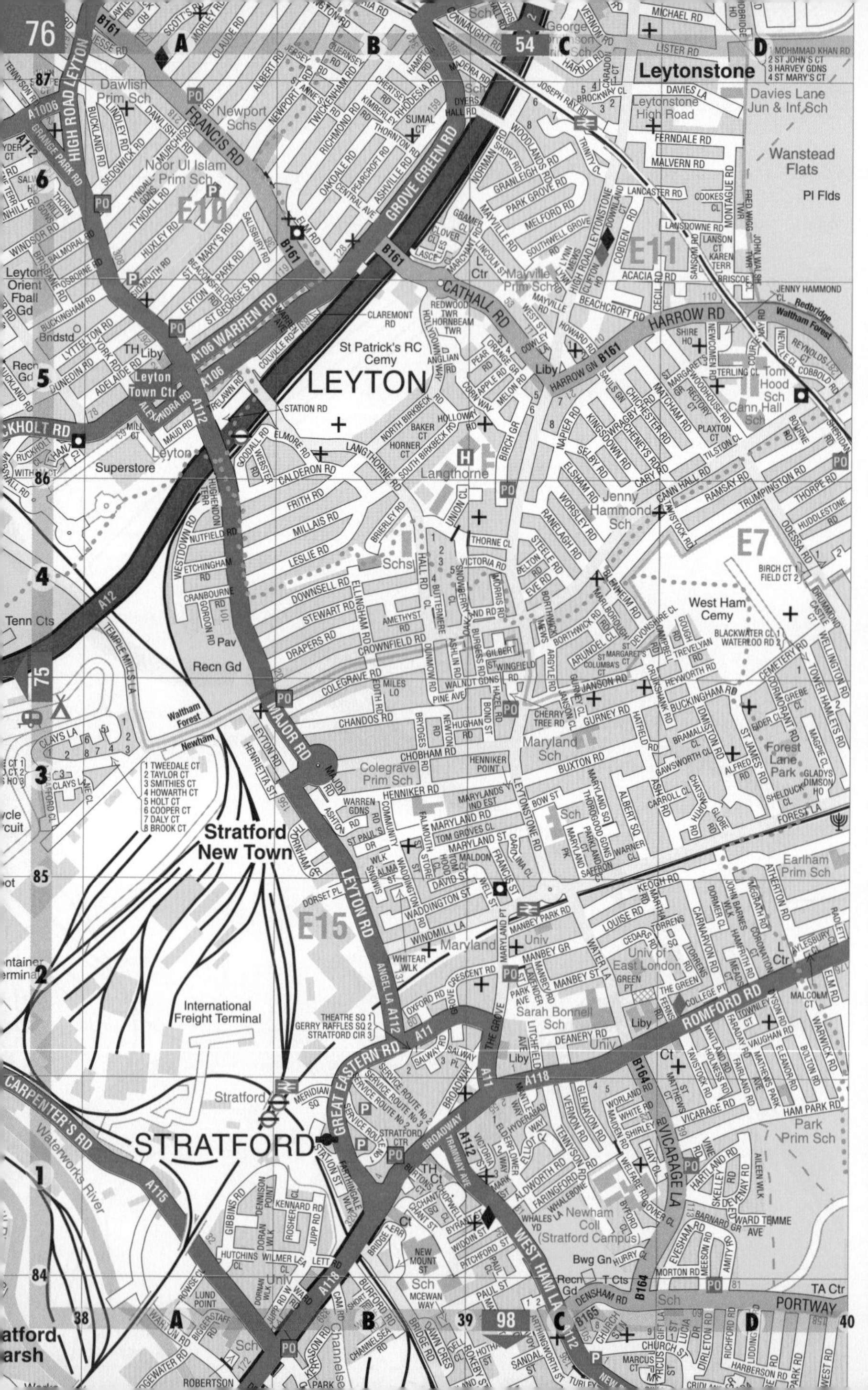

76
A
B
C
D
54
98
75
87
86
85
84
38
39
40
6
5
4
3
2
1
Leytonstone
LEYTON
STRATFORD
Stratford New Town
E10
E11
E15
E7
HIGH ROAD LEYTON
FRANCIS RD
GROVE GREEN RD
CATHALL RD
HARROW RD
A106 WARREN RD
LEYTON RD
MAJOR RD
ANGEL LA
GREAT EASTERN RD
ROMFORD RD
WEST HAM LA
VICARAGE LA
CARPENTER'S RD
PORTWAY
BROADWAY
THE GROVE
CANN HALL RD
HIGH ROAD LEYTONSTONE
TEMPLE MILLS LA
LEYTONSTONE RD
St Patrick's RC Cemy
West Ham Cemy
Wanstead Flats
Davies Lane Jun & Inf Sch
Leyton Orient Fball Gd
Noor Ul Islam Prim Sch
Newport Schs
Dawlish Prim Sch
Mayville Prim Sch
Jenny Hammond Sch
Tom Hood Sch
Colegrave Prim Sch
Maryland Sch
Forest Lane Park
Earlham Prim Sch
Univ of East London
Sarah Bonnell Sch
Newham Coll (Stratford Campus)
Park Prim Sch
International Freight Terminal
Langthorne
Superstore
Leyton Town Ctr
Recn Gd
Waterworks River
Stratford
Maryland
1 TWEEDALE CT
2 TAYLOR CT
3 SMITHIES CT
4 HOWARTH CT
5 HOLT CT
6 COOPER CT
7 DALY CT
8 BROOK CT
1 MOHMMAD KHAN RD
2 ST JOHN'S CT
3 HARVEY GDNS
4 ST MARY'S CT
THEATRE SQ 1
GERRY RAFFLES SQ 2
STRATFORD CIR 3

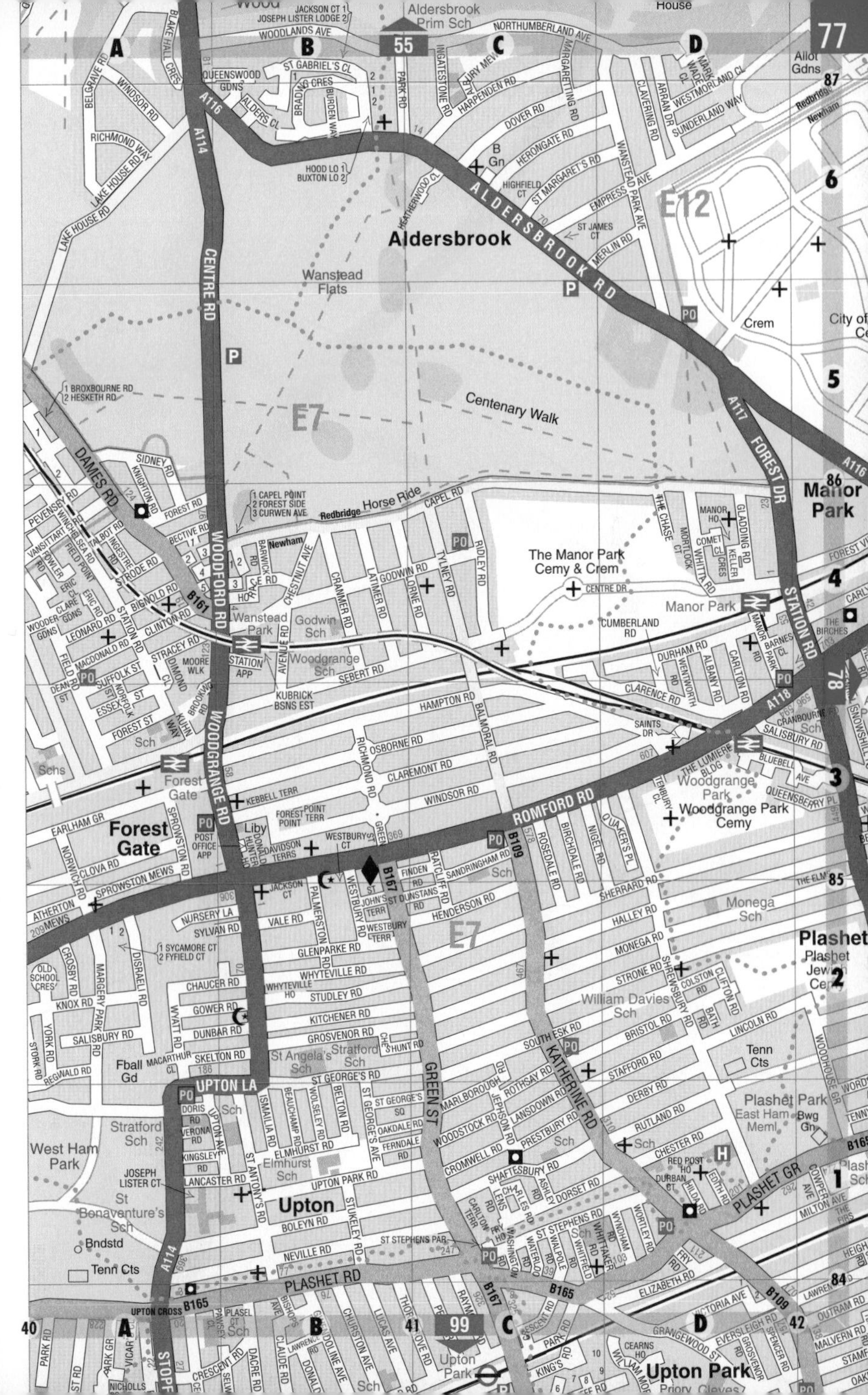

77
55
78
99
A
B
C
D
1
2
3
4
5
6
40
41
42
84
85
86
87
Aldersbrook
Aldersbrook Prim Sch
JACKSON CT 1
JOSEPH LISTER LODGE 2
WOODLANDS AVE
NORTHUMBERLAND AVE
BLAKE HALL CRES
QUEENSWOOD GDNS
ST GABRIEL'S CL
BRADWELL CRES
BURDEN WAY
ALDERS CL
PARK RD
INGATESTONE RD
HARPENDEN RD
MARGARETTING RD
CLAVERING RD
ARRAN DR
MARK WADE CL
WESTMORLAND CL
SUNDERLAND WAY
Allot Gdns
Redbridge
Newham
BELGRAVE RD
WINDSOR RD
RICHMOND WAY
LAKE HOUSE RD
A116
A114
HOOD LO 1
BUXTON LO 2
DOVER RD
HERONGATE RD
B Gn
HEATHERWOOD CL
ALDERSBROOK RD
HIGHFIELD CT
ST MARGARET'S RD
EMPRESS AVE
WANSTEAD PARK AVE
ST JAMES CT
MERLIN RD
E12
Wanstead Flats
CENTRE RD
P
PO
Crem
City of
1 BROXBOURNE RD
2 HESKETH RD
E7
Centenary Walk
A117
FOREST DR
DAMES RD
SIDNEY RD
KNIGHTON RD
1 CAPEL POINT
2 FOREST SIDE
3 CURWEN AVE
Redbridge Horse Ride
CAPEL RD
Manor Park
FOREST RD
PEVENSEY RD
VANSITTART RD
WINCHELSEA RD
TALBOT RD
INGESTRE RD
BECTIVE RD
STRODE RD
FOWLER RD
FIELD POINT
BARWICK RD
CHESTNUT AVE
CRANMER RD
LATIMER RD
GODWIN RD
LORNE RD
TYLNEY RD
RIDLEY RD
The Manor Park Cemy & Crem
CENTRE DR
THE CHASE
MORTLOCK CT
WHITTA RD
MANOR HO
COMET CL
KELLER CRES
GLADDING RD
STATION RD
WOODFORD RD
B161
HORACE RD
BIGNOLD RD
CLINTON RD
ERIC RD
CLARE GDNS
LEONARD RD
WOODER GDNS
MACDONALD RD
STRACEY RD
Wanstead Park
Godwin Sch
Woodgrange Sch
AVENUE RD
SEBERT RD
STATION APP
KUBRICK BSNS EST
DIMOND CL
MOORE WLK
SUFFOLK ST
NORFOLK ST
ESSEX ST
DEAN ST
FIELD RD
FOREST ST
Sch
KUHN WAY
BROOKING RD
CUMBERLAND RD
DURHAM RD
WENTWORTH RD
ALBANY RD
CARLTON RD
MANOR PARK RD
BARNES CL
CLARENCE RD
THE BIRCHES
A118
CRANBOURNE RD
SALISBURY RD
HAMPTON RD
BALMORAL RD
OSBORNE RD
RICHMOND RD
CLAREMONT RD
WINDSOR RD
SAINTS DR
THE LUMIERE BLDG
Woodgrange Park
BLUEBELL AVE
QUEENSBERRY PL
Woodgrange Park Cemy
Schs
Forest Gate
WOODGRANGE RD
KEBBELL TERR
FOREST POINT
POINT TERR
ROMFORD RD
TENBURY CL
QUAKERS PL
NIGEL RD
BIRCHDALE RD
ROSEDALE RD
B109
EARLHAM GR
SPROWSTON RD
POST OFFICE APP
Liby
DONALD RD
HUNTER RD
DAVIDSON TERRS
WESTBURY CT
GREEN ST
SANDRINGHAM RD
NORWICH RD
CLOVA RD
SPROWSTON MEWS
ATHERTON MEWS
JACKSON CT
PALMERSTON RD
WESTBURY RD
ST JOHN'S TERR
ST DUNSTANS RD
FINDEN RD
RATCLIFF RD
B167
HENDERSON RD
SHERRARD RD
THE ELMS
Monega Sch
HALLEY RD
MONEGA RD
Plashet
Plashet Jewish Cem
NURSERY LA
VALE RD
SYLVAN RD
WESTBURY TERR
1 SYCAMORE CT
2 FYFIELD CT
GLENPARKE RD
WHYTEVILLE RD
WHYTEVILLE HO
STUDLEY RD
OLD SCHOOL CRES
CROSBY RD
MARGERY PARK RD
DISRAELI RD
CHAUCER RD
GOWER RD
WYATT RD
DUNBAR RD
KNOX RD
YORK RD
SALISBURY RD
STORK RD
REGINALD RD
KITCHENER RD
GROSVENOR RD
CHESHUNT RD
STRONE RD
SHREWSBURY RD
COLSTON RD
CLIFTON RD
BATH RD
William Davies Sch
LINCOLN RD
BRISTOL RD
SOUTH ESK RD
KATHERINE RD
Tenn Cts
WOODHOUSE GR
Fball Gd
MACARTHUR CL
SKELTON RD
St Angela's Sch
Stratford Sch
UPTON LA
ST GEORGE'S RD
ISMAILIA RD
BEAUCHAMP RD
WOLSELEY RD
BELTON RD
ST GEORGE'S AVE
ST GEORGE'S SQ
OAKDALE RD
FERNDALE RD
MARLBOROUGH RD
ROTHSAY RD
JEPHSON RD
LANSDOWN RD
STAFFORD RD
DERBY RD
Plashet Park
East Ham Meml
Bwg Gn
DORIS RD
VERONA RD
UPTON AVE
KINGSLEY RD
LANCASTER RD
ST ANTONY'S RD
ELMHURST RD
Elmhurst Sch
UPTON PARK RD
WOODSTOCK RD
PRESTBURY RD
CROMWELL RD
SHAFTESBURY RD
RUTLAND RD
CHESTER RD
RED POST HO
DURBAN CT
EDITH RD
HILDA RD
H
PLASHET GR
B165
COWPER AVE
MILTON AVE
THE FIRS
West Ham Park
JOSEPH LISTER CT
St Bonaventure's Sch
Bndstd
Tenn Cts
Upton
BOLEYN RD
NEVILLE RD
STUKELEY RD
ST STEPHENS PAR
CARLTON TERR
CHARLES RD
ASHLEY RD
DORSET RD
ST STEPHENS RD
WASHINGTON RD
WATERLOO RD
WALPOLE RD
WHITFIELD RD
WHITTAKER RD
WYNDHAM RD
WORTLEY RD
FRY RD
ELIZABETH RD
PLASHET RD
A114
UPTON CROSS
PLASEL CT
VICTORIA AVE
GRANGEWOOD ST
EVERSLEIGH RD
GROSVENOR RD
SPENCER RD
LAWRENCE RD
OUTRAM RD
MALVERN RD
PARK RD
PARK GR
ST RD
VICAR
NICHOLLS
PAMSEY CT
CRESCENT RD
DACRE RD
CLAUDE RD
BISHOPS AVE
DONALD
MADELINE AVE
CHURSTON AVE
LUCAS AVE
THORNGROVE RD
Upton Park
KING'S RD
CRESCENT RD
CEARNS HO
WILLIAM MORRIS
Upton Park
Priory
Cleves

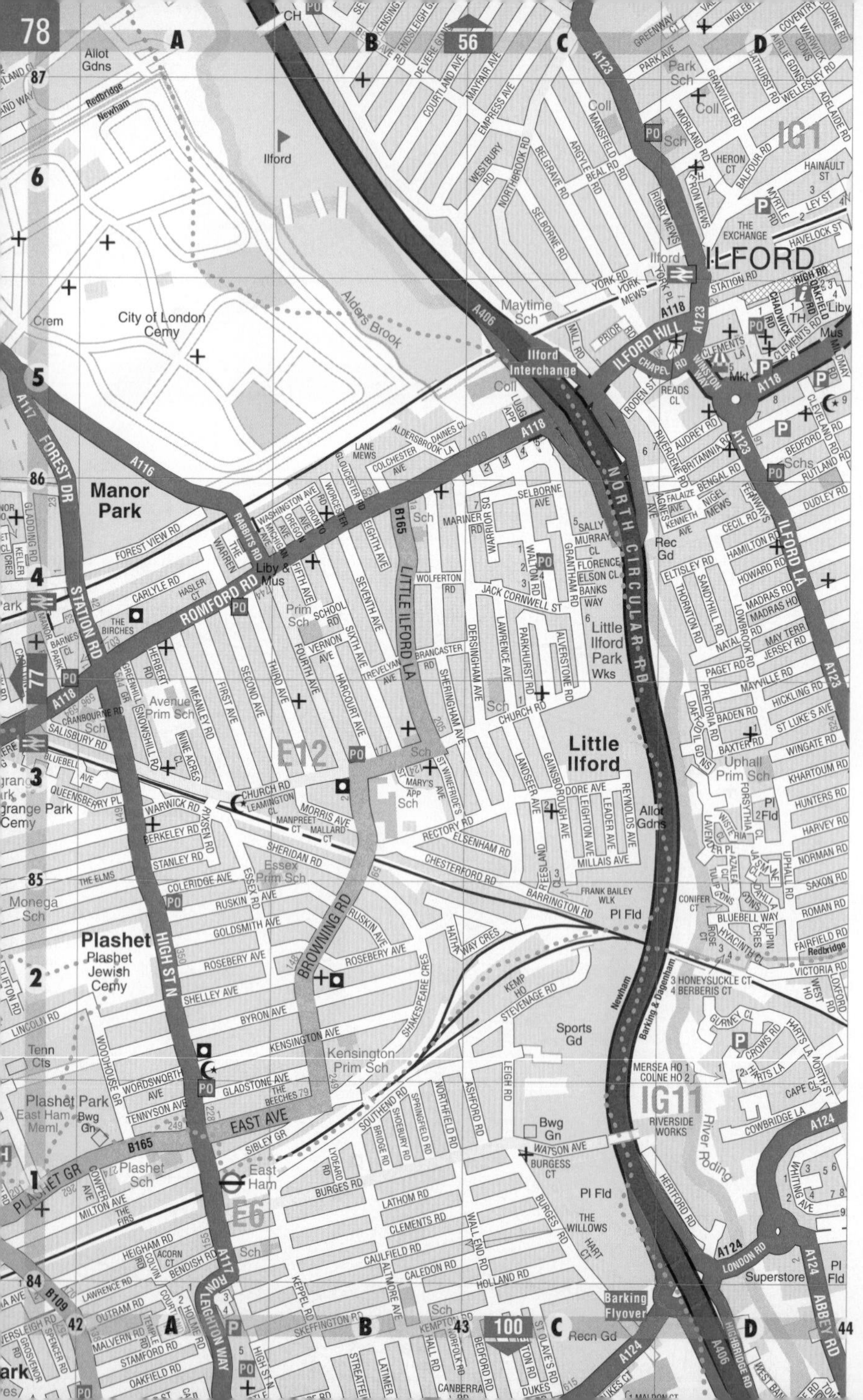

A
B
C
D
56
Allot Gdns
Redbridge
Newham
Ilford
City of London Cemy
Crem
Alders Brook
Park Sch
Coll
IG1
ILFORD
THE EXCHANGE
HAVELOCK ST
HAINAULT ST
LEY ST
BALFOUR RD
HERON CT
MORLAND RD
GRANVILLE RD
BATHURST RD
WELLESLEY RD
ADELAIDE RD
PARK AVE
GREENWAY
A123
MANSFIELD RD
ARGYLE RD
BEAL RD
BELGRAVE RD
NORTHBROOK RD
WESTBURY RD
SELBORNE RD
EMPRESS AVE
MAYFAIR AVE
COURTLAND AVE
DE VERE GDNS
ENDSLEIGH GDNS
RIGBY MEWS
YORK RD
YORK MEWS
YORK PL
STATION RD
HIGH RD
CHADWICK RD
CLEMENTS RD
Liby
Mus
TH
Maytime Sch
MILL RD
PRIOR RD
A406
A118
ILFORD HILL
CHAPEL RD
RODEN ST
READS CL
WINSTON WAY
CLEMENTS LA
Mkt
Ilford Interchange
Coll
LUGG APP
A116
A117
Manor Park
FOREST DR
FOREST VIEW RD
RABBITS RD
THE WARREN
WASHINGTON AVE
MICHIGAN AVE
OREGON AVE
TORONTO AVE
WORCESTER RD
GLOUCESTER RD
COLCHESTER AVE
LANE MEWS
ALDERSBROOK LA
DAINES CL
EIGHTH AVE
SEVENTH AVE
SIXTH AVE
FIFTH AVE
FOURTH AVE
THIRD AVE
SECOND AVE
FIRST AVE
MEANLEY RD
NINE ACRES CL
ROMFORD RD
Liby & Mus
STATION RD
CARLYLE RD
HASLER CT
THE BIRCHES
BARNES CL
MANOR PARK
GLADDING RD
KELLER CRES
Park
77
CRANBOURNE RD
SALISBURY RD
HERBERT RD
GREENHILL GR
SNOWSHILL RD
Avenue Prim Sch
Prim Sch
SCHOOL RD
VERNON AVE
HARCOURT AVE
TREVELYAN AVE
B165
LITTLE ILFORD LA
Sch
MARINER RD
WARRIOR SQ
SELBORNE AVE
SALLY MURRAY CL
FLORENCE ELSON CL
BANKS WAY
GRANTHAM RD
WALTON RD
WOLFERTON RD
JACK CORNWELL ST
BRANCASTER RD
SHERINGHAM AVE
DERSINGHAM AVE
LAWRENCE AVE
PARKHURST RD
ALVERSTONE RD
Little Ilford Park Wks
CHURCH RD
NORTH CIRCULAR RD
E12
Little Ilford
ST MARY'S APP
ST WINEFRIDE'S AVE
Sch
LANDSEER AVE
GAINSBOROUGH AVE
DORE AVE
LEIGHTON AVE
LEADER AVE
REYNOLDS AVE
MILLAIS AVE
Allot Gdns
RECTORY RD
ELSENHAM RD
CHESTERFORD RD
REESLAND CL
FRANK BAILEY WLK
BARRINGTON RD
Pl Fld
BLUEBELL AVE
QUEENSBERRY PL
Cemy
CHURCH RD
LEAMINGTON CL
MORRIS AVE
MANPREET CT
MALLARD CT
WARWICK RD
BERKELEY RD
PIXSEN RD
STANLEY RD
SHERIDAN RD
Essex Prim Sch
ESSEX RD
THE ELMS
COLERIDGE AVE
Monega Sch
RUSKIN AVE
GOLDSMITH AVE
Plashet
Plashet Jewish Cemy
HIGH ST N
BROWNING RD
ROSEBERY AVE
SHELLEY AVE
BYRON AVE
KENSINGTON AVE
Kensington Prim Sch
SHAKESPEARE CRES
HATHAWAY CRES
KEMP HO
STEVENAGE RD
Sports Gd
LINCOLN RD
CLIFTON RD
Tenn Cts
WOODHOUSE GR
WORDSWORTH AVE
TENNYSON AVE
GLADSTONE AVE
THE BEECHES
EAST AVE
Plashet Park
East Ham Meml
Bwg Gn
Plashet Sch
PLASHET GR
COWPER AVE
MILTON AVE
THE FIRS
SIBLEY GR
East Ham
E6
SOUTHEND RD
BRIDGE RD
SHOEBURY RD
SPRINGFIELD RD
NORTHFIELD RD
ASHFORD RD
LEIGH RD
LYDEARD RD
BURGES RD
LATHOM RD
CLEMENTS RD
CAULFIELD RD
CALEDON RD
HOLLAND RD
WALL END RD
Bwg Gn
WATSON AVE
BURGESS CT
BURGES RD
Pl Fld
THE WILLOWS
HART CT
IG11
RIVERSIDE WORKS
River Roding
HEIGHAM RD
ACORN CT
COLVIN RD
BENDISH RD
LAWRENCE RD
OUTRAM RD
MALVERN RD
STAMFORD RD
OAKFIELD RD
TEMPLE RD
HOLME RD
COURTENAY
LEIGHTON WAY
B109
84
42
43
44
100
KEPPEL RD
ALTMORE AVE
SKEFFINGTON RD
KEMPTON RD
HALL RD
NORFOLK RD
BEDFORD RD
ST OLAVE'S RD
Recn Gd
Barking Flyover
A124
HIGHBRIDGE RD
ABBEY RD
Superstore
LONDON RD
HERTFORD RD
COWBRIDGE LA
CAPE CL
HARTS LA
CROWS RD
GURNEY CL
MERSEA HO
COLNE HO
NORTH ST
WHITING AVE
Pl Fld
Barking & Dagenham
Newham
HONEYSUCKLE CT
BERBERIS CT
HYACINTH CL
ROSE CT
LUPIN CRES
BLUEBELL WAY
CONIFER CT
TULIP GDNS
DAHLIA GDNS
AZALEA CL
JASMINE CL
LAVENDER PL
WISTERIA CL
FORSYTHIA CL
Uphall Prim Sch
Pl Fld
UPHALL RD
LOXFORD
VICTORIA RD
FAIRFIELD RD
ROMAN RD
SAXON RD
NORMAN RD
HARVEY RD
HUNTERS RD
KHARTOUM RD
WINGATE RD
ST LUKE'S AVE
HICKLING RD
MAYVILLE RD
JERSEY RD
MAY TERR
MADRAS RD
HOWARD RD
HAMILTON RD
CECIL RD
DUDLEY RD
RUTLAND RD
BEDFORD RD
CLEVELAND RD
MILDMAY RD
ILFORD LA
Schs
BAXTER RD
BADEN RD
PAGET RD
PRETORIA RD
DAFFODIL GDNS
NATAL RD
LOWBROOK RD
SANDYHILL RD
THORNTON RD
ELTISLEY RD
Rec Gd
KENNETH AVE
AGNES AVE
FALAIZE AVE
NIGEL MEWS
BENGAL RD
BRITANNIA RD
AUDREY RD
RIVERDENE RD
FERNWAYS

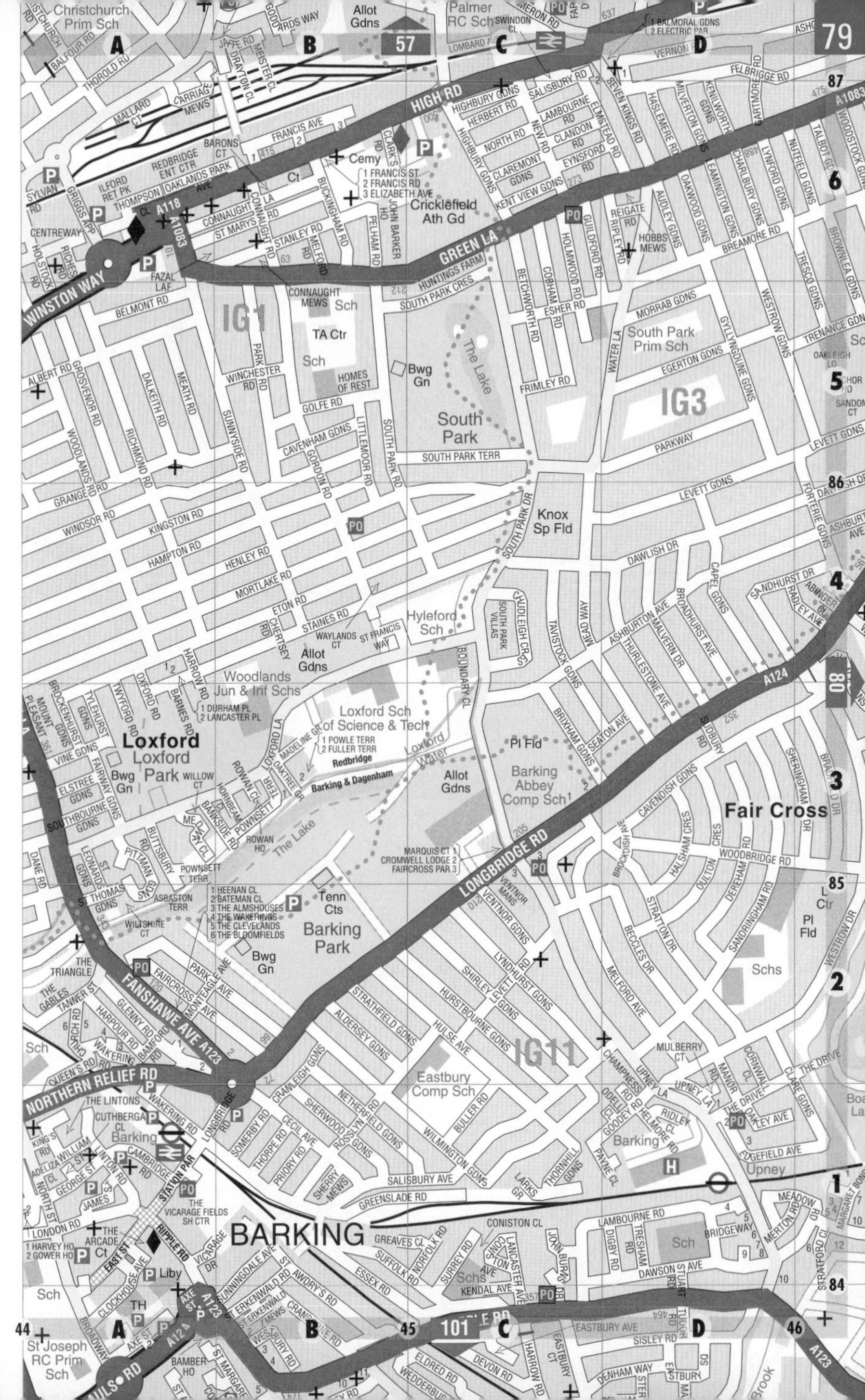

79
A
B
C
D
57
101
80
87
86
85
84
6
5
4
3
2
1
44
45
46
Christchurch Prim Sch
Allot Gdns
Palmer RC Sch
1 BALMORAL GDNS
2 ELECTRIC PAR
HIGH RD
GREEN LA
WINSTON WAY
A118
A1083
A124
A123
A12
IG1
IG3
IG11
Cemy
1 FRANCIS ST
2 FRANCIS RD
3 ELIZABETH AVE
Cricklefield Ath Gd
REDBRIDGE ENT CTR
ILFORD RET PK
CENTREWAY
CONNAUGHT MEWS
TA Ctr
Sch
HOMES OF REST
Bwg Gn
The Lake
South Park
SOUTH PARK TERR
SOUTH PARK CRES
SOUTH PARK DR
SOUTH PARK RD
HUNTINGS FARM
South Park Prim Sch
Knox Sp Fld
Hyleford Sch
WAYLANDS CT
ST FRANCIS WAY
Allot Gdns
Woodlands Jun & Inf Schs
1 DURHAM PL
2 LANCASTER PL
Loxford Sch of Science & Tech
1 POWLE TERR
2 FULLER TERR
Redbridge
Barking & Dagenham
Loxford Water
Loxford
Loxford Park
Pl Fld
Barking Abbey Comp Sch
MARQUIS CT 1
CROMWELL LODGE 2
FAIRCROSS PAR 3
LONGBRIDGE RD
Fair Cross
1 HEENAN CL
2 BATEMAN CL
3 THE ALMSHOUSES
4 THE WAKERINGS
5 THE CLEVELANDS
6 THE BLOOMFIELDS
Tenn Cts
Barking Park
FANSHAWE AVE
NORTHERN RELIEF RD
THE LINTONS
Barking
Eastbury Comp Sch
THE VICARAGE FIELDS SH CTR
BARKING
THE ARCADE
1 HARVEY HO
2 GOWER HO
Liby
TH
St Joseph RC Prim Sch
Upney
MULBERRY CT
THE DRIVE
Boat Lake
Schs
L Ctr
Pl Fld
Sch
EASTBURY AVE
SALISBURY AVE
GREENSLADE RD
LAMBOURNE RD
DAWSON AVE
KENDAL AVE
CONISTON CL
BRIDGEWAY

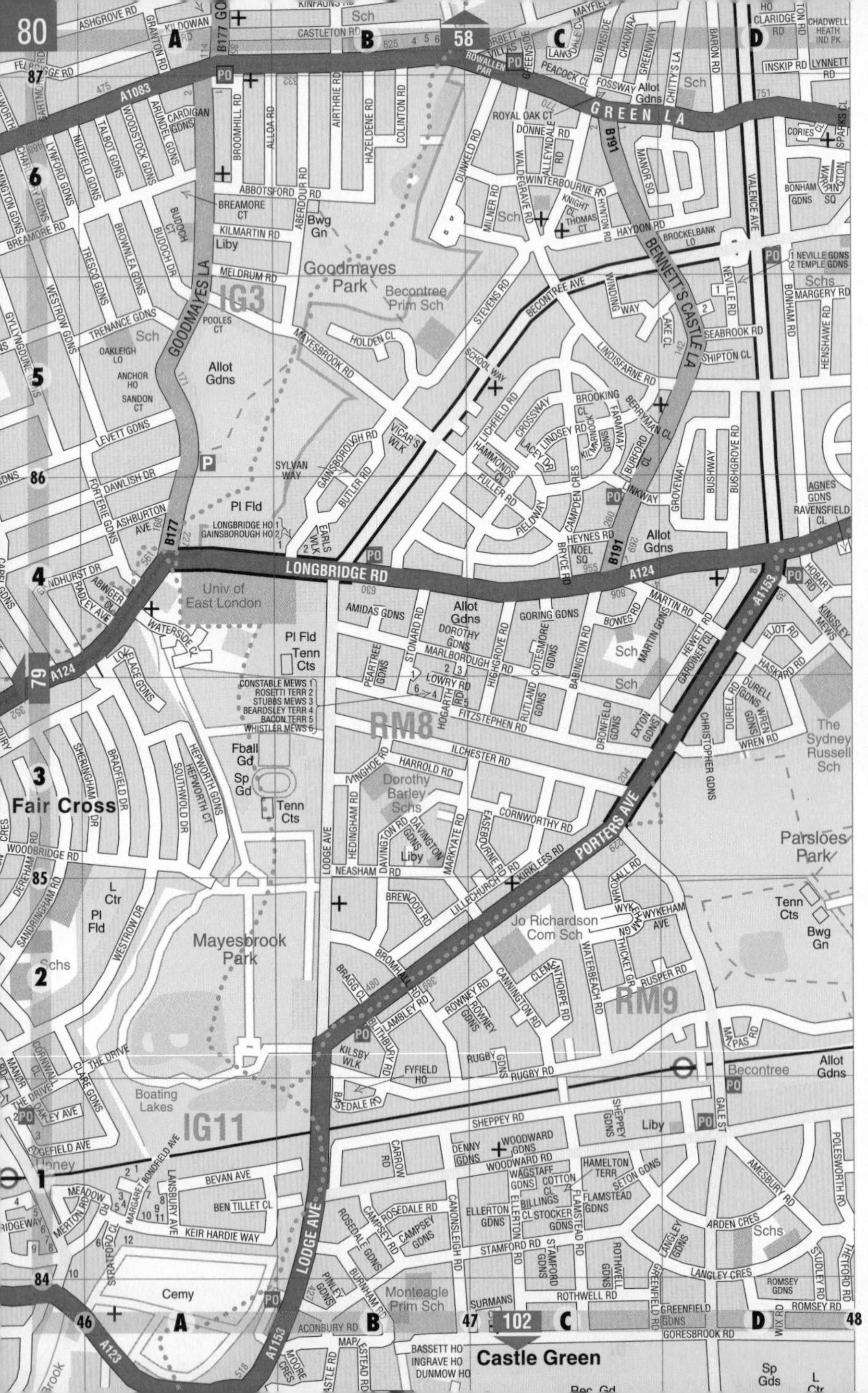
58
A
B
C
D
IG3
Goodmayes Park
Becontree Prim Sch
Allot Gdns
GOODMAYES LA
GREEN LA
A1083
B177
B191
BENNETT'S CASTLE LA
BECONTREE AVE
LONGBRIDGE RD
A124
Univ of East London
RM8
Dorothy Barley Schs
Fair Cross
Mayesbrook Park
Boating Lakes
IG11
PORTERS AVE
A1153
LODGE AVE
Jo Richardson Com Sch
RM9
Parsloes Park
The Sydney Russell Sch
Becontree
Monteagle Prim Sch
Cemy
A123
Castle Green
102
79
87
86
85
84
46
47
48
6
5
4
3
2
1

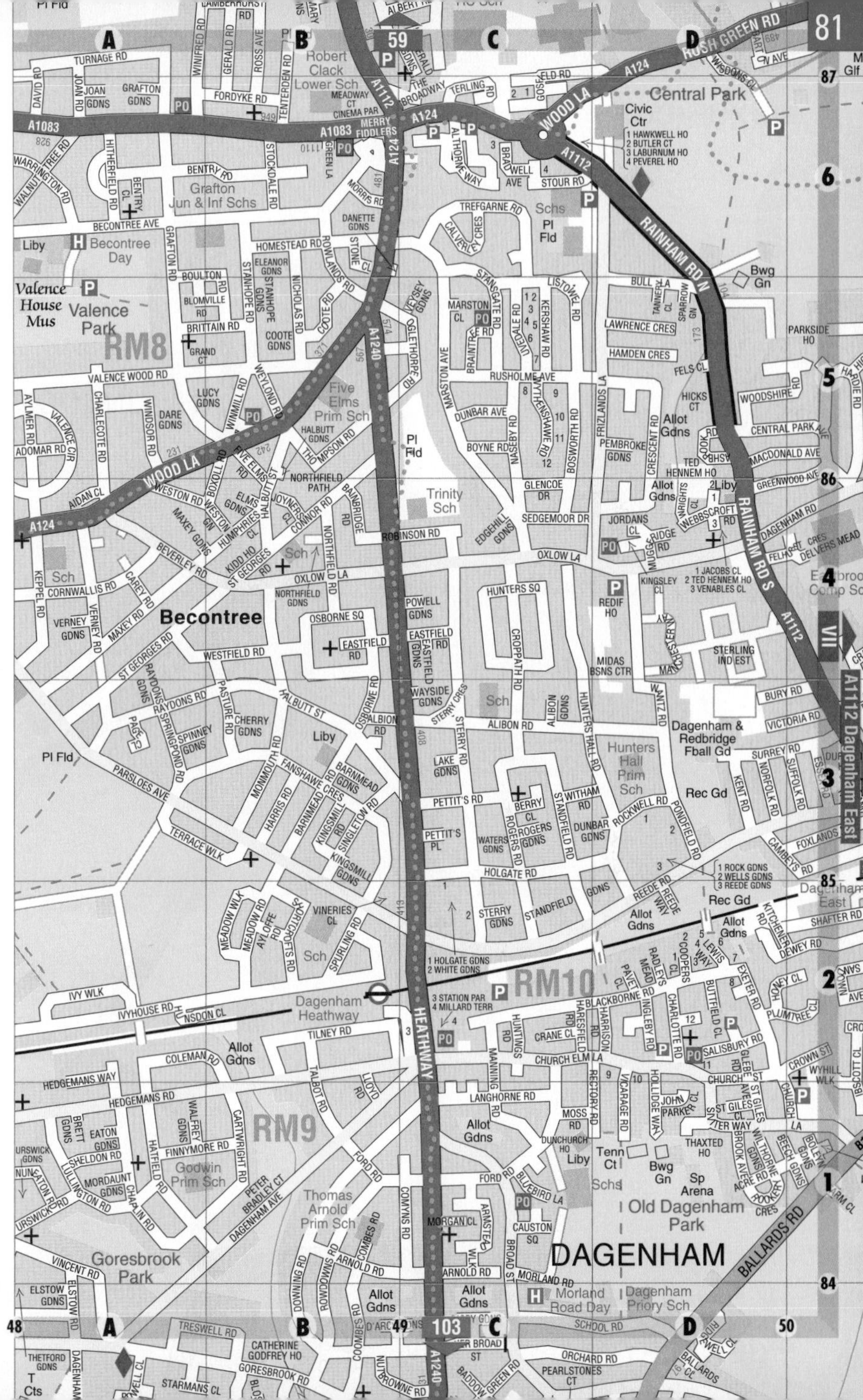
A
B
C
D
59
103
87
6
5
86
4
3
85
2
1
84
48
49
50
RUSH GREEN RD
TURNAGE RD
Robert Clack Lower Sch
Central Park
Civic Ctr
1 HAWKWELL HO
2 BUTLER CT
3 LABURNUM HO
4 PEVEREL HO
WOOD LA
A124
A1112
A1083
MERRY FIDDLERS
THE BROADWAY
FORDYKE RD
JOAN GDNS
GRAFTON GDNS
DAVID RD
WINIFRED RD
GERALD RD
ROSS AVE
TENTERDEN RD
MEADWAY CT
CINEMA PAR
TERLING RD
ALTHORNE WAY
BRAD WELL AVE
STOUR RD
WARRINGTON RD
WALNUT TREE RD
HITHERFIELD RD
BENTRY CL
BENTRY RD
Grafton Jun & Inf Schs
STOCKDALE RD
GREEN LA
MORRIS RD
BECONTREE AVE
Liby
Becontree Day
Valence House Mus
Valence Park
RM8
GRAFTON RD
HOMESTEAD RD
DANETTE GDNS
ROWLANDS RD
STONE CL
TREFGARNE RD
CALVERLEY CRES
Schs
Pl Fld
RAINHAM RD N
Bwg Gn
BOULTON RD
BLOMVILLE RD
BRITTAIN RD
GRAND CT
STANHOPE RD
ELEANOR GDNS
STANHOPE GDNS
NICHOLAS RD
COTE RD
COOTE GDNS
VEYSEY GDNS
OGLETHORPE RD
A1240
MARSTON CL
STANSGATE RD
LISTOWEL RD
BULL LA
TANNERY CL
SPARROW GN
LAWRENCE CRES
HAMDEN CRES
PARKSIDE HO
FELS CL
VALENCE WOOD RD
LUCY GDNS
WEYLOND RD
MARSTON AVE
BRAINTREE RD
UVEDALE RD
KERSHAW RD
RUSHOLME AVE
FRIZLANDS LA
HICKS CT
WOODSHIRE RD
CENTRAL PARK AVE
AYLMER RD
VALENCE CIR
CHARLECOTE RD
WINDSOR RD
DARE GDNS
WINMILL RD
Five Elms Prim Sch
HALBUTT GDNS
THOMPSON RD
DUNBAR AVE
BOYNE RD
NASEBY RD
WYTHENSHAWE RD
BOSWORTH RD
PEMBROKE GDNS
CRESCENT RD
Allot Gdns
TED HENNEM HO
MACDONALD AVE
ADOMAR RD
FIVE ELMS
NORTHFIELD PATH
GLENCOE DR
Trinity Sch
GREENWOOD AVE
AIDAN CL
WESTON RD
BOXOLL RD
ELMS GDNS
HALBUTT ST
JOYNERS CL
CONNOR RD
BAINBRIDGE
SEDGEMOOR DR
JORDANS CL
WRIGHTS CL
WEBBSCROFT RD
DAGENHAM RD
MAXEY GDNS
WESTON GN
HUMPHRIES CL
EDGEHILL GDNS
ROBINSON RD
RIDGE RD
DELVERS MEAD
FELHURST CRES
BEVERLEY RD
KIDD HO
ST GEORGES RD
Sch
OXLOW LA
NORTHFIELD RD
HUNTERS SQ
KINGSLEY CL
1 JACOBS CL
2 TED HENNEM HO
3 VENABLES CL
Eastbrook Comp Sch
KEPPEL RD
CORNWALLIS RD
CAREY RD
NORTHFIELD GDNS
POWELL GDNS
REDIF HO
RAINHAM RD S
VERNEY GDNS
VERNEY RD
MAXEY RD
Becontree
OSBORNE SQ
EASTFIELD RD
EASTFIELD GDNS
CROPPATH RD
VII
WESTFIELD RD
MIDAS BSNS CTR
STERLING IND EST
ST GEORGES RD
RAYDONS GDNS
RAYDONS RD
PASTURE RD
HALBUTT ST
OSBORNE RD
WAYSIDE GDNS
STERRY CRES
ALBION GDNS
HUNTERS HALL RD
WANTZ RD
BURY RD
A1112 Dagenham East
CHERRY GDNS
SPINNEY GDNS
SPRINGPOND RD
PAGE CL
ALBION RD
ALIBON RD
Dagenham & Redbridge Fball Gd
VICTORIA RD
Pl Fld
PARSLOES AVE
MONMOUTH RD
FANSHAWE CRES
BARNMEAD GDNS
LAKE GDNS
STERRY RD
Hunters Hall Prim Sch
SURREY RD
KENT RD
NORFOLK RD
SUFFOLK RD
HARRIS RD
BARNMEAD RD
KINGSMILL RD
SINGLETON RD
PETTIT'S RD
BERRY CL
WITHAM RD
ROCKWELL RD
Rec Gd
PONDFIELD RD
TERRACE WLK
PETTIT'S PL
WATERS GDNS
ROGERS RD
ROGERS GDNS
STANDFIELD RD
DUNBAR GDNS
FOXLANDS RD
CAMBEYS RD
KINGSMILL GDNS
HOLGATE RD
1 ROCK GDNS
2 WELLS GDNS
3 REEDE GDNS
REEDE RD
REEDE WAY
Dagenham East
MEADOW WLK
MEADOW RD
AYLOFFE RD
SHORTCROFTS RD
VINERIES CL
SPURLING RD
STERRY GDNS
STANDFIELD
KITCHENER RD
SHAFTER RD
DEWEY RD
LEWIS WAY
COOPERS
RADLEYS MEAD
1 HOLGATE GDNS
2 WHITE GDNS
RM10
PAVET CL
EXETER RD
HONEY CL
IVY WLK
IVYHOUSE RD
HUNSDON CL
Dagenham Heathway
3 STATION PAR
4 MILLARD TERR
HEATHWAY
BLACKBORNE RD
HARESFIELD RD
HARRISON RD
INGLEBY RD
CHARLOTTE RD
BUTTFIELD CL
PLUMTREE CL
TILNEY RD
HUNTINGS RD
CRANE CL
SALISBURY RD
COLEMAN RD
MANNING RD
CHURCH ELM LA
CROWN ST
HEDGEMANS WAY
TALBOT RD
LLOYD RD
RECTORY RD
VICARAGE RD
HOLLIDGE WAY
CHURCH ST
GLEBE AVE
ST GILES CL
WYHILL WLK
HEDGEMANS RD
WALFREY GDNS
CARTWRIGHT RD
LANGHORNE RD
MOSS RD
JOHN PARKER CL
ST GILES
SAVILE WAY
BRETT GDNS
EATON GDNS
RM9
DUNCHURCH HO
THAXTED HO
BROOK AVE
WILTHORNE GDNS
BEECH GDNS
BOLEYN GDNS
URSWICK GDNS
SHELDON RD
FINNYMORE RD
HATFIELD RD
Godwin Prim Sch
FORD RD
Allot Gdns
Tenn Ct
Bwg Gn
Sp Arena
ACRE RD
ROOKERY CRES
NUNEATON RD
MORDAUNT GDNS
LULLINGTON RD
CHAPLIN RD
PETER BRADLEY CT
DAGENHAM AVE
Thomas Arnold Prim Sch
COMBES RD
COMYNS RD
FORD RD
BLUEBIRD LA
Liby
Schs
Old Dagenham Park
URSWICK RD
MORGAN CL
ARMSTEAD WLK
CAUSTON SQ
DAGENHAM
BALLARDS RD
Goresbrook Park
VINCENT RD
ARNOLD RD
ROWDOWNS RD
DOWNING RD
BROAD ST
MORLAND RD
ELSTOW GDNS
ELSTOW RD
Morland Road Day
Dagenham Priory Sch
D'ARCY GDNS
SCHOOL RD
TRESWELL RD
CATHERINE GODFREY HO
COOMBES RD
ORCHARD RD
THETFORD GDNS
T Cts
STARMANS CL
GORESBROOK RD
NUTBROWNE RD
BADDOW GREEN RD
PEARLSTONES CT
BALLARDS CL
JEWELL CL
DAGENHAM RD

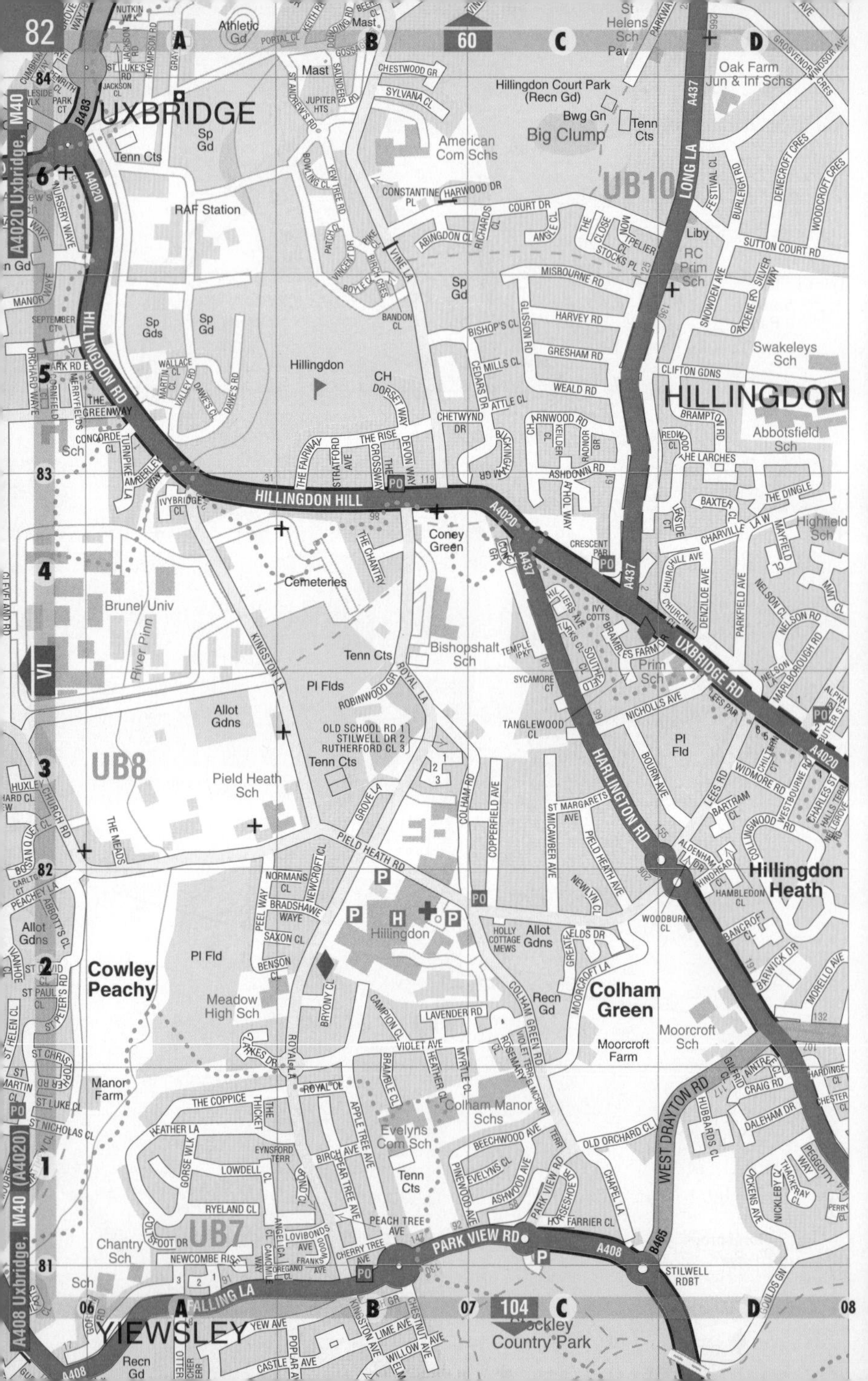
A
B
60
C
D
UXBRIDGE
Athletic Gd
Mast
St Helens Sch Pav
Oak Farm Jun & Inf Schs
Hillingdon Court Park (Recn Gd)
Bwg Gn
Tenn Cts
Big Clump
American Com Schs
Sp Gd
Tenn Cts
RAF Station
UB10
LONG LA
A437
A4020
B483
HILLINGDON RD
HILLINGDON HILL
Hillingdon
CH
Sp Gds
Sp Gd
Liby
RC Prim Sch
Swakeleys Sch
HILLINGDON
Abbotsfield Sch
Highfield Sch
Coney Green
Cemeteries
Brunel Univ
River Pinn
Tenn Cts
Bishopshalt Sch
Pl Flds
Allot Gdns
UB8
Pield Heath Sch
Tenn Cts
Prim Sch
Pl Fld
UXBRIDGE RD
HARLINGTON RD
Hillingdon Heath
Hillingdon
Cowley Peachy
Pl Fld
Meadow High Sch
Allot Gdns
Recn Gd
Colham Green
Moorcroft Sch
Moorcroft Farm
Manor Farm
Colham Manor Schs
Evelyns Com Sch
Tenn Cts
WEST DRAYTON RD
UB7
Chantry Sch
Sch
PARK VIEW RD
A408
B465
STILWELL RDBT
FALLING LA
YIEWSLEY
Recn Gd
104
Stockley Country Park
06
07
08
1
2
3
4
5
6
81
82
83
84
A4020 Uxbridge, M40
A408 Uxbridge, M40 (A4020)
VI
PO
P
H

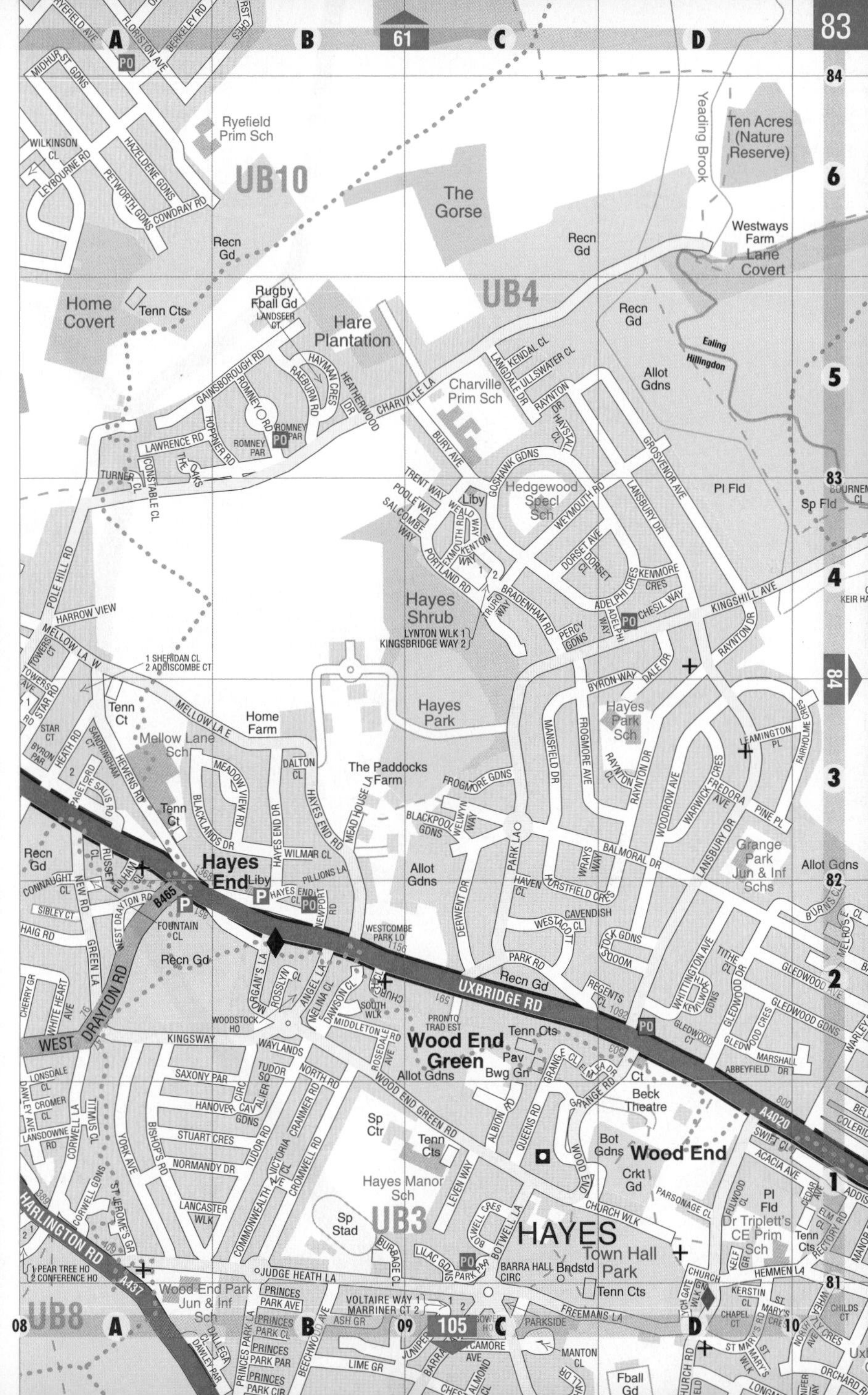
A
B
61
C
D
Ryefield Prim Sch
UB10
The Gorse
Ten Acres (Nature Reserve)
Yeading Brook
Westways Farm Lane Covert
Recn Gd
Home Covert
Tenn Cts
Rugby Fball Gd
Hare Plantation
UB4
Allot Gdns
Ealing
Hillingdon
Charville Prim Sch
Hedgewood Specl Sch
Liby
Pl Fld
Sp Fld
Hayes Shrub
LYNTON WLK 1
KINGSBRIDGE WAY 2
1 SHERIDAN CL
2 ADDISCOMBE CT
Home Farm
Hayes Park
Hayes Park Sch
Mellow Lane Sch
The Paddocks Farm
Tenn Ct
Grange Park Jun & Inf Schs
Hayes End
UXBRIDGE RD
Wood End Green
Pav
Bwg Gn
Beck Theatre
Sp Ctr
Bot Gdns
Wood End
Crkt Gd
Hayes Manor Sch
UB3
Sp Stad
HAYES
Town Hall Park
Dr Triplett's CE Prim Sch
Bndstd
Wood End Park Jun & Inf Sch
UB8
VOLTAIRE WAY 1
MARRINER CT 2
1 PEAR TREE HO
2 CONFERENCE HO
105
Fball Gd
08
09
10
84
6
5
83
4
3
82
2
1
81

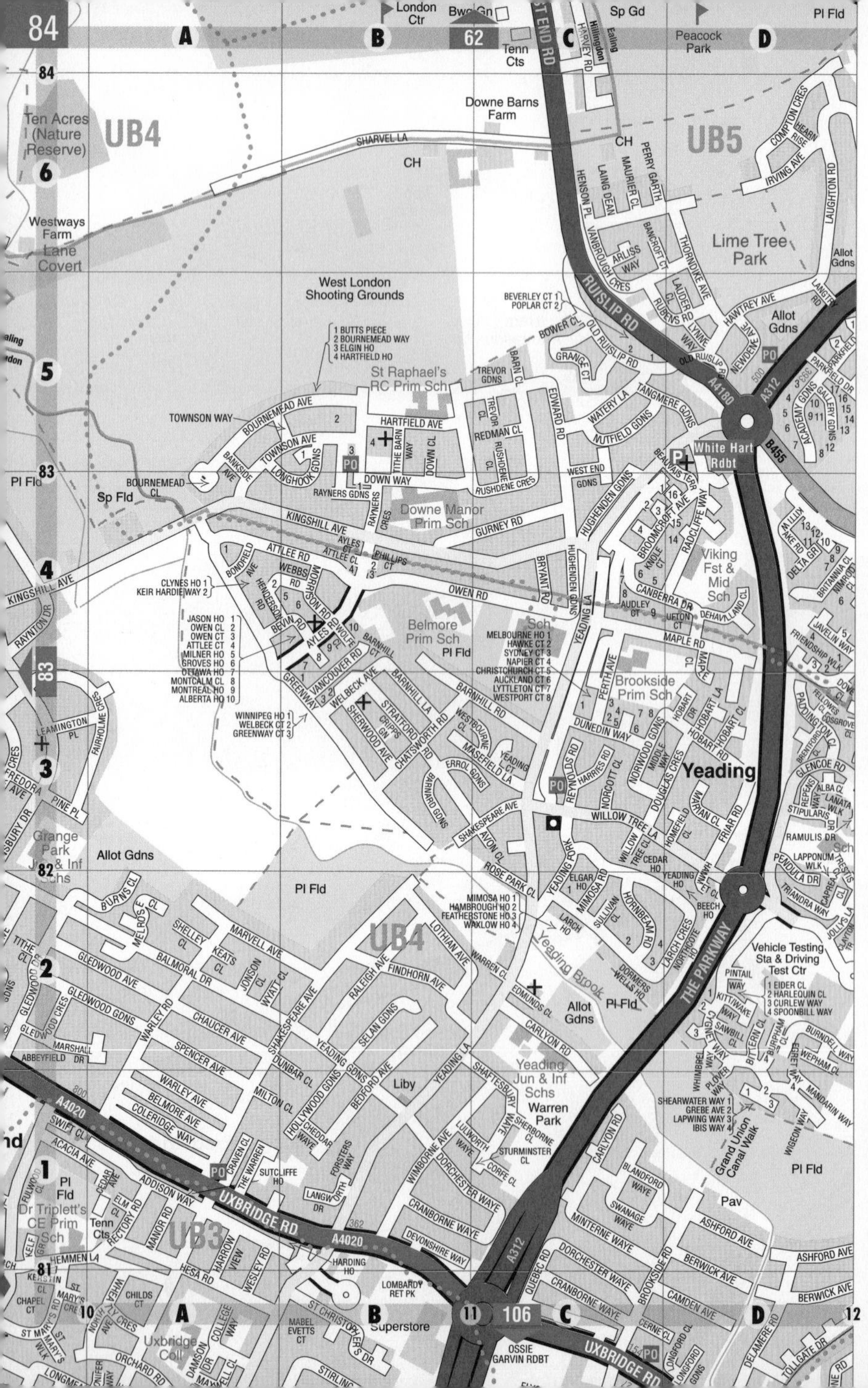

A
B
C
D
62
London Ctr
Bwg Gn
Tenn Cts
Sp Gd
Pl Fld
Peacock Park
WEST END RD
HARVEY RD
Hillingdon
Ealing
Ten Acres (Nature Reserve)
UB4
Downe Barns Farm
SHARVEL LA
CH
UB5
COMPTON CRES
HEARN RISE
IRVING AVE
LAUGHTON RD
HENSON PL
LAING DEAN
MAURIER CL
PERRY GARTH
Westways Farm
Lane Covert
VANBROUGH CRES
ARLISS WAY
BANCROFT CT
THORNDIKE AVE
Lime Tree Park
Allot Gdns
West London Shooting Grounds
BEVERLEY CT 1
POPLAR CT 2
RUISLIP RD
LAUDER CL
RUBENS RD
LYNNE WAY
HAWTREY AVE
LANGTRY RD
BOWER CL
OLD RUISLIP RD
GRANGE CT
NEWDENE AVE
A4180
A312
PO
1 BUTTS PIECE
2 BOURNEMEAD WAY
3 ELGIN HO
4 HARTFIELD HO
St Raphael's RC Prim Sch
TREVOR GDNS
BARN CL
TREVOR CL
EDWARD RD
WATERY LA
TANGMERE GDNS
NUTFIELD GDNS
White Hart Rdbt
B455
PARKFIELD DR
ACADEMY GDNS
GALLERY GDNS
TOWNSON WAY
BOURNEMEAD AVE
HARTFIELD AVE
TOWNSON AVE
TITHE BARN WAY
DOWN CL
REDMAN CL
RUSHDENE CL
RUSHDENE CRES
BEAUVAIS TERR
BANKSIDE AVE
LONGHOOK GDNS
BOURNEMEAD CL
DOWN WAY
RAYNERS GDNS
WEST END GDNS
HUGHENDEN GDNS
BROOMCROFT AVE
RADCLIFFE WAY
Pl Fld
Sp Fld
KINGSHILL AVE
RAYNERS CRES
Downe Manor Prim Sch
GURNEY RD
AYLES CT
ATTLEE CL
PHILLIPS CT
ATTLEE RD
BONDFIELD AVE
WEBBS RD
MORRISON RD
BRYANT RD
KNOLE CT
Viking Fst & Mid Sch
KITTIWAKE RD
DELTA GR
BRITANNIA CL
WINROOD
CLYNES HO 1
KEIR HARDIE WAY 2
HENDERSON RD
OWEN RD
YEADING LA
CANBERRA DR
AUDLEY CT
UFTON CT
DEHAVILLAND CL
RAYNTON DR
JASON HO 1
OWEN CL 2
OWEN CT 3
ATTLEE CT 4
MILNER HO 5
GROVES HO 6
OTTAWA HO 7
MONTCALM CL 8
MONTREAL HO 9
ALBERTA HO 10
BEVIN RD
AYLES RD
WOLFE CL
BARNHILL CT
Belmore Prim Sch
Sch
MELBOURNE HO 1
HAWKE CT 2
SYDNEY CT 3
NAPIER CT 4
CHRISTCHURCH CT 5
AUCKLAND CT 6
LYTTLETON CT 7
WESTPORT CT 8
MAPLE RD
MAPLE CL
JAVELIN WAY
FRIENDSHIP WLK
VANCOUVER RD
GREENWAY
WELBECK AVE
BARNHILL LA
BARNHILL RD
PERTH AVE
Brookside Prim Sch
HOBART DR
HOBART LA
HOBART CL
HOBART RD
PADDINGTON CL
WINNIPEG HO 1
WELBECK CT 2
GREENWAY CT 3
STRATFORD RD
CRIPPS GN
SHERWOOD AVE
CHATSWORTH RD
WESTBOURNE AVE
MASEFIELD LA
YEADING CT
DUNEDIN WAY
NORWOOD GDNS
MIDDLE WAY
DOUGLAS CRES
LEAMINGTON PL
FAIRHOLME CRES
Yeading
GLENCOE RD
ERROL GDNS
BARNARD GDNS
REYNOLDS RD
HARRIES RD
NORCOTT CL
ALBA CL
LANATA WLK
STIPULARIS DR
PINE PL
FREDORA AVE
SHAKESPEARE AVE
AVON CL
WILLOW TREE LA
HOMEFIELD CL
MARLIAN CL
FRIAR RD
RAMULIS DR
Grange Park Jun & Inf Schs
Allot Gdns
ROSE PARK CL
YEADING FORK
WILLOW TREE CL
CEDAR HO
YEADING HO
LAPPONUM WLK
PENDULA DR
TRIANDRA WAY
BURNS CL
MELROSE CL
MIMOSA HO 1
HAMBROUGH HO 2
FEATHERSTONE HO 3
WAXLOW HO 4
ELGAR HO
MIMOSA RD
SULLIVAN CL
HORNBEAM RD
BEECH HO
SHELLEY CL
MARVELL AVE
KEATS CL
LARCH HO
LARCH CRES
NORTHCOTE HO
THE PARKWAY
Vehicle Testing Sta & Driving Test Ctr
TITHE CL
GLEDWOOD AVE
BALMORAL DR
JONSON CL
WYATT CL
LOTHIAN AVE
FINDHORN AVE
RALEIGH AVE
WARREN CL
Yeading Brook
DORMERS WELLS HO
PINTAIL WAY
KITTIWAKE WAY
1 EIDER CL
2 HARLEQUIN CL
3 CURLEW WAY
4 SPOONBILL WAY
GLEDWOOD CRES
GLEDWOOD GDNS
WARLEY RD
CHAUCER AVE
SELAN GDNS
EDMUNDS CL
Allot Gdns
Pl Fld
CARLYON RD
CYGNET WAY
SAWBILL CL
BITTERN CL
BURPHAM CL
EGRET WAY
BURNDELL WAY
WEPHAM CL
MARSHALL DR
ABBEYFIELD DR
SPENCER AVE
DUNBAR CL
YEADING GDNS
BEDFORD AVE
YEADING LA
SHAFTESBURY WAYE
Yeading Jun & Inf Schs
WHIMBREL WAY
PLOVER WAY
MANDARIN WAY
WARLEY AVE
MILTON CL
HOLLYWOOD GDNS
Liby
Warren Park
SHEARWATER WAY 1
GREBE AVE 2
LAPWING WAY 3
IBIS WAY 4
A4020
BELMORE AVE
COLERIDGE WAY
CHEDDAR WAYE
SHERBORNE CL
STURMINSTER CL
LULWORTH WAYE
Grand Union Canal Walk
WIGEON WAY
SWIFT CL
ACACIA AVE
CRAVEN CL
THE WARREN
SUTCLIFFE HO
FORSTERS WAY
WIMBORNE AVE
DORCHESTER AVE
CORFE CL
CARLYON RD
BLANDFORD WAYE
Pl Fld
FULWOOD CL
CEDAR AVE
Pl Fld
ELM CL
ADDISON WAY
LANGWORTH DR
CRANBORNE WAYE
DORCHESTER WAYE
SWANAGE WAYE
Pav
Dr Triplett's CE Prim Sch
Tenn Cts
RECTORY RD
MANOR RD
UXBRIDGE RD
UB3
HARROW VIEW
WESLEY RD
DEVONSHIRE WAY
A312
MINTERNE WAYE
ASHFORD AVE
ASHFORD AVE
KELF GR
HEMMEN LA
HARDING HO
QUEBEC RD
DORCHESTER WAYE
BROOKSIDE RD
BERWICK AVE
KERSTIN CL
HESA RD
LOMBARDY RET PK
CRANBORNE WAYE
CAMDEN AVE
BERWICK AVE
CHAPEL CT
ST MARY'S RD
ST MARY'S CRES
CHILDS CT
10
A
B
11
106
C
D
12
WHEATLEY CRES
ST CHRISTOPHER'S DR
MABEL EVETTS CT
Superstore
CERNE CL
DELAMERE RD
ST MARY'S WLK
Uxbridge Coll
COLLEGE WAY
DAMSON DR
MAXWELL CL
ORCHARD RD
STIRLING
OSSIE GARVIN RDBT
UXBRIDGE RD
LONGFORD CL
LONGFORD GDNS
TOLLGATE DR

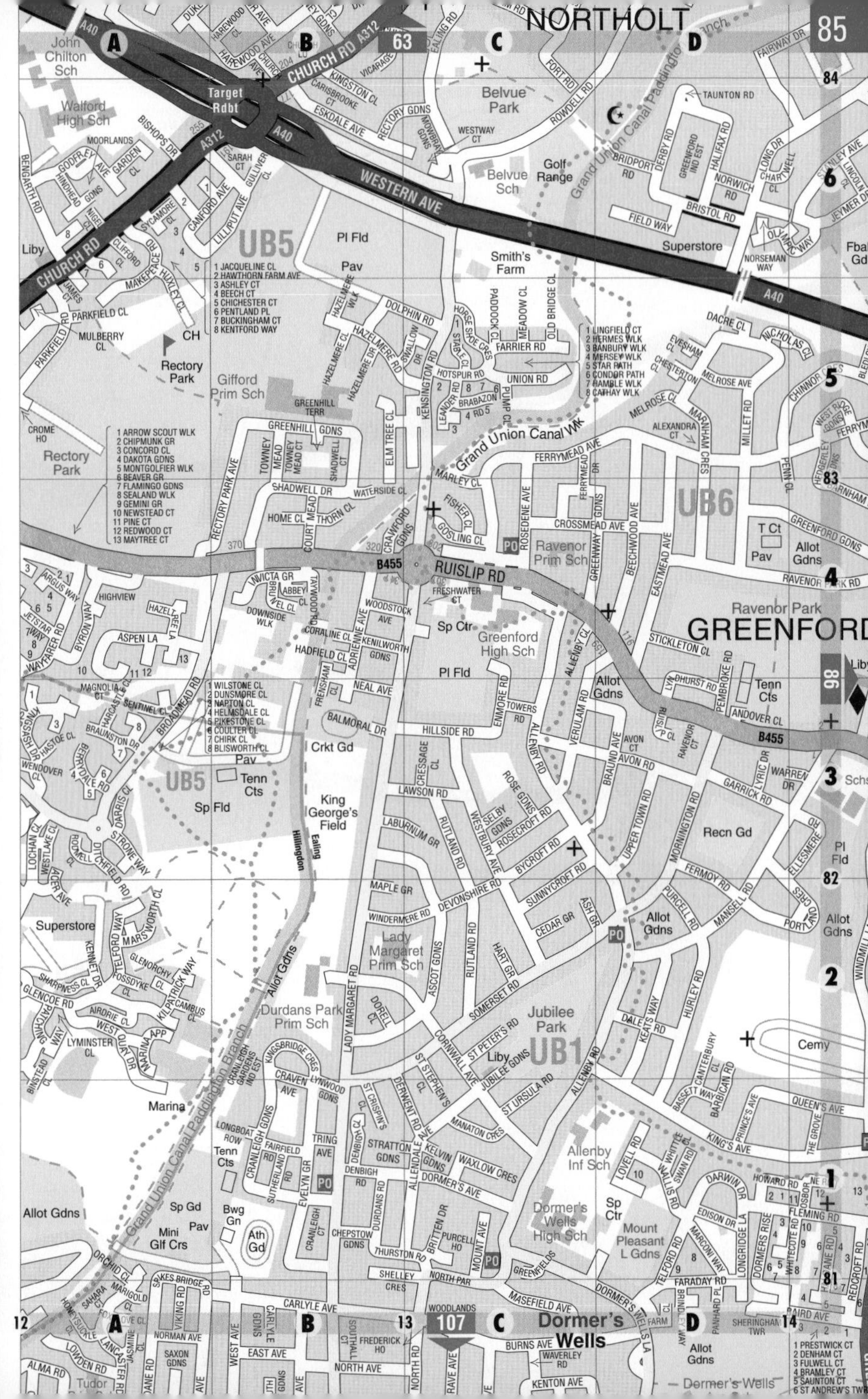

NORTHOLT
GREENFORD
Dormer's Wells
UB5
UB6
UB1
WESTERN AVE
CHURCH RD
RUISLIP RD
Target Rdbt
Grand Union Canal Paddington Branch
Grand Union Canal Wk
Belvue Park
Belvue Sch
Golf Range
Smith's Farm
Rectory Park
Gifford Prim Sch
Ravenor Prim Sch
Ravenor Park
Greenford High Sch
King George's Field
Lady Margaret Prim Sch
Durdans Park Prim Sch
Jubilee Park
Allenby Inf Sch
Dormer's Wells High Sch
Mount Pleasant L Gdns
Walford High Sch
John Chilton Sch
Superstore
Marina
Cemy
1 JACQUELINE CL
2 HAWTHORN FARM AVE
3 ASHLEY CT
4 BEECH CT
5 CHICHESTER CT
6 PENTLAND PL
7 BUCKINGHAM CT
8 KENTFORD WAY
1 LINGFIELD CT
2 HERMES WLK
3 BANBURY WLK
4 MERSEY WLK
5 STAR PATH
6 CONDOR PATH
7 RAMBLE WLK
8 CATHAY WLK
1 ARROW SCOUT WLK
2 CHIPMUNK GR
3 CONCORD CL
4 DAKOTA GDNS
5 MONTGOLFIER WLK
6 BEAVER GR
7 FLAMINGO GDNS
8 SEALAND WLK
9 GEMINI GR
10 NEWSTEAD CT
11 PINE CT
12 REDWOOD CT
13 MAYTREE CT
1 WILSTONE CL
2 DUNSMORE CL
3 NAPTON CL
4 HELMSDALE CL
5 PIKESTONE CL
6 COULTER CL
7 CHIRK CL
8 BLISWORTH CL
1 PRESTWICK CT
2 DENHAM CT
3 FULWELL CT
4 BRAMLEY CT
5 SAUNTON CT
6 ST ANDREW'S TWR
63
107
98

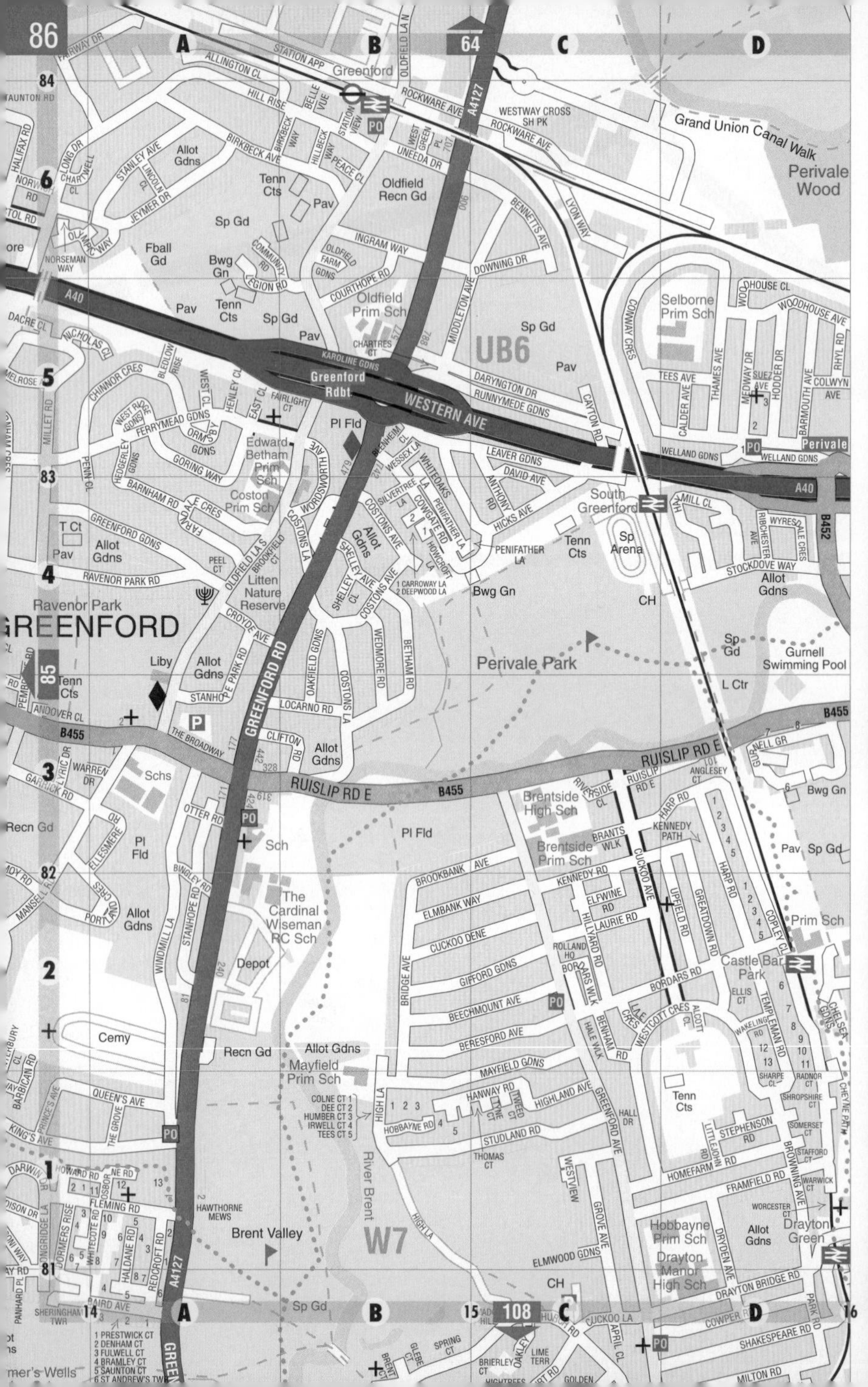
86
A
B
C
D
64
108
84
85
6
5
4
3
2
1
83
82
81
14
15
16
Greenford
STATION APP
ALLINGTON CL
HILL RISE
BELLE VUE
OLDFIELD LA N
ROCKWARE AVE
WESTWAY CROSS SH PK
Grand Union Canal Walk
Perivale Wood
A4127
BIRKBECK AVE
STANLEY AVE
JEYMER DR
LONG DR
CHARTWELL CL
HALIFAX RD
NORWICH RD
UNEEDA DR
PEACE CL
Oldfield Recn Gd
INGRAM WAY
BENNETTS AVE
LYON WAY
DOWNING DR
COURTHOPE RD
Oldfield Prim Sch
MIDDLETON AVE
CONWAY CRES
Selborne Prim Sch
WOODHOUSE AVE
Allot Gdns
Tenn Cts
Pav
Sp Gd
Fball Gd
Bwg Gn
COMMUNITY RD
LEGION RD
NORSEMAN WAY
OLYMPIC WAY
A40
DACRE CL
NICHOLAS CL
MELROSE
CHINNOR CRES
BLEDLOW RISE
WEST CL
HENLEY CL
EAST CL
FAIRLIGHT CT
KAROLINE GDNS
CHARTRES CT
Greenford Rdbt
WESTERN AVE
UB6
DARYNGTON DR
RUNNYMEDE GDNS
CAYTON RD
TEES AVE
CALDER AVE
THAMES AVE
MEDWAY DR
HODDER DR
BARMOUTH AVE
COLWYN AVE
RHYL RD
WELLAND GDNS
Perivale
MILLET RD
PENN CL
FERRYMEAD GDNS
HEDGERLEY GDNS
GORING WAY
BARNHAM RD
FARNDALE CRES
GREENFORD GDNS
Edward Betham Prim Sch
Coston Prim Sch
Pl Fld
WORDSWORTH AVE
COSTONS LA
BLENHEIM CL
WESSEX LA
WHITEOAKS
SILVERTREE LA
COWGATE RD
PENIFATHER LA
LEAVER GDNS
DAVID AVE
ANTHONY RD
HICKS AVE
South Greenford
Sp Arena
HAMILL CL
WYRESDALE CRES
RIBCHESTER AVE
STOCKDOVE WAY
B452
T Ct
RAVENOR PARK RD
PEEL CT
OLDFIELD LA S
BROOKFIELD CT
Litten Nature Reserve
SHELLEY AVE
SHELLEY CL
COSTONS AVE
HOWCROFT LA
1 CARROWAY LA
2 DEEPWOOD LA
Bwg Gn
CH
Ravenor Park
GREENFORD
CROYDE AVE
Liby
PE PARK RD
STANHOPE
GREENFORD RD
OAKFIELD GDNS
WEDMORE RD
BETHAM RD
Perivale Park
Gurnell Swimming Pool
L Ctr
ANDOVER CL
B455
THE BROADWAY
LOCARNO RD
CLIFTON RD
RUISLIP RD E
GURNELL GR
ANGLESEY CT
LYRIC DR
WARREN DR
GARRICK RD
Schs
OTTER RD
PO
Sch
Recn Gd
ELLESMERE RD
Brentside High Sch
RIVERSIDE CL
HARP RD
KENNEDY PATH
BRANTS WLK
Brentside Prim Sch
BROOKBANK AVE
KENNEDY RD
ELFWINE RD
LAURIE RD
CUCKOO AVE
UPFIELD RD
GREATDOWN RD
COPLEY CL
Prim Sch
MANSELL RD
PORTLAND CRES
BINGLEY RD
STANHOPE RD
The Cardinal Wiseman RC Sch
WINDMILL LA
ELMBANK WAY
CUCKOO DENE
GIFFORD GDNS
BEECHMOUNT AVE
BERESFORD AVE
MAYFIELD GDNS
HILLYARD RD
ROLLAND HO
BORDARS WLK
BORDARS RD
Castle Bar Park
ELLIS CT
TEMPLEMAN RD
Depot
BRIDGE AVE
Cemy
WESTCOTT CRES
ALCOTT CL
HALE WALK
BENHAM RD
WAKELING RD
SHARPE CL
RADNOR CT
CHELSEA GDNS
Mayfield Prim Sch
HANWAY RD
HIGHLAND AVE
SHROPSHIRE CT
CHEYNE PATH
BARBICAN RD
PRINCE'S AVE
QUEEN'S AVE
THE GROVE
KING'S AVE
COLNE CT 1
DEE CT 2
HUMBER CT 3
IRWELL CT 4
TEES CT 5
HIGH LA
HOBBAYNE RD
STUDLAND RD
THOMAS CT
HALL DR
GREENFORD AVE
STEPHENSON RD
LITTLEJOHN RD
SOMERSET CT
STAFFORD CT
HOMEFARM RD
FRAMFIELD RD
BROWNING AVE
WARWICK CT
WORCESTER CT
Drayton Green
DARWIN DR
HOWARD RD
FLEMING RD
HAWTHORNE MEWS
River Brent
WESTVIEW
GROVE AVE
Hobbayne Prim Sch
DRYDEN AVE
Drayton Manor High Sch
Brent Valley
W7
ELMWOOD GDNS
DRAYTON BRIDGE RD
WHITECOTE RD
HALDANE RD
REDCROFT RD
JORMERS RISE
LONGRIDGE LA
BAIRD AVE
SHERINGHAM TWR
PANHARD PL
Sp Gd
CUCKOO LA
APRIL CL
COWPER RD
PARK RD
SHAKESPEARE RD
MILTON RD
1 PRESTWICK CT
2 DENHAM CT
3 FULWELL CT
4 BRAMLEY CT
5 SAUNTON CT
6 ST ANDREW'S TWR
BRENT CT
GLEBE CT
SPRING CT
BRIERLEY CT
OAKLEY
LIME TERR
GOLDEN

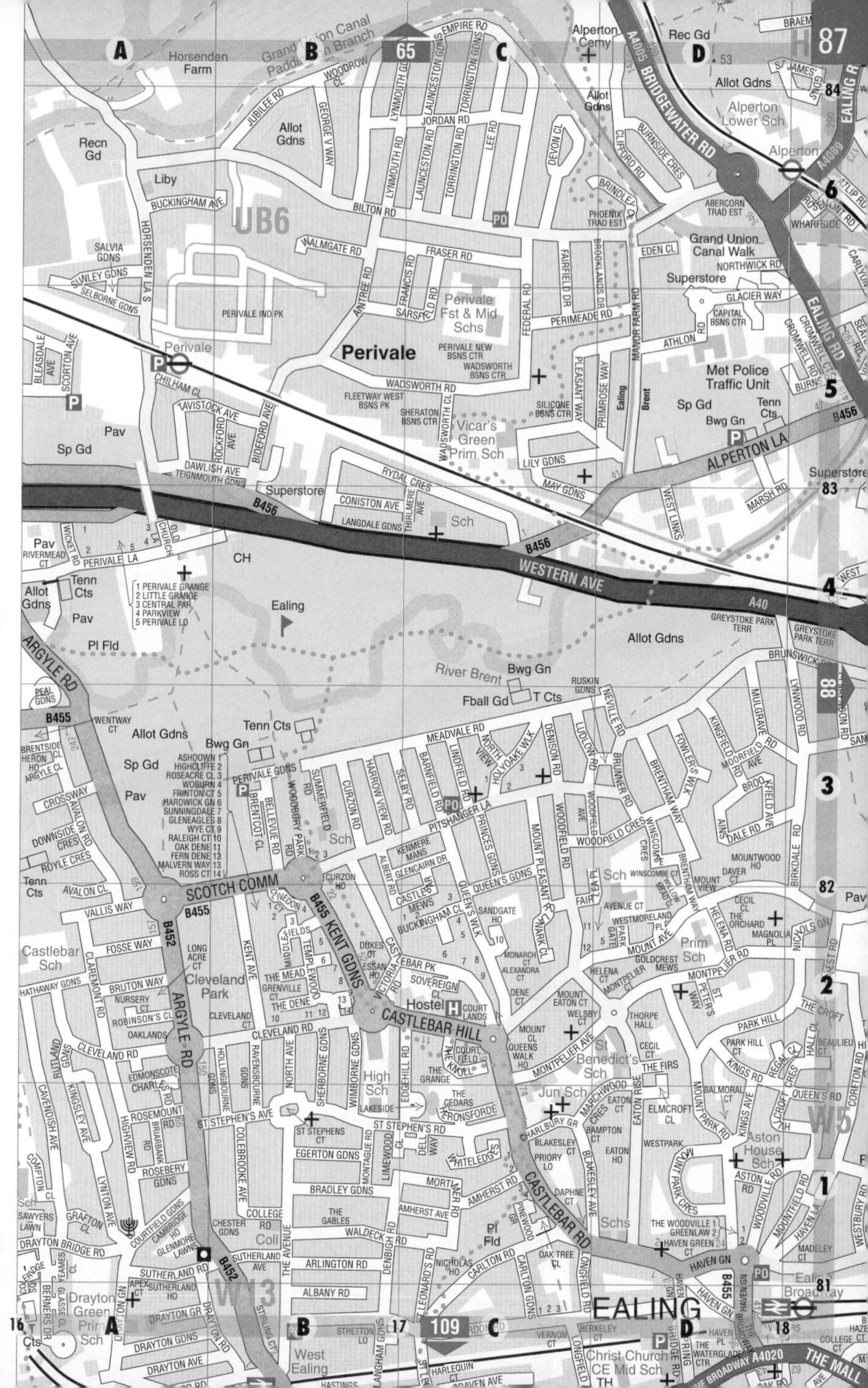

87
65
109
88
A
B
C
D
1
2
3
4
5
6
16
17
18
81
82
83
84
Horsenden Farm
Grand Union Canal Paddington Branch
EMPIRE RD
WOODROW CL
JUBILEE RD
GEORGE V WAY
LYNMOUTH GDNS
LAUNCESTON GDNS
TORRINGTON GDNS
JORDAN RD
LYNMOUTH RD
LAUNCESTON RD
TORRINGTON RD
LEE RD
DEVON CL
Alperton Cemy
Allot Gdns
Rec Gd
BRAEMAR
A4005 BRIDGEWATER RD
ST JAMES' GDNS
Alperton Lower Sch
Alperton
EALING RD
A4089
CLIFFORD RD
BURNSIDE CRES
BRINDLEY CL
PHOENIX TRAD EST
ABERCORN TRAD EST
ATLIP RD
ROSEMONT RD
WHARFSIDE
Recn Gd
Liby
BUCKINGHAM AVE
HORSENDEN LA S
UB6
BILTON RD
PO
WALMGATE RD
FRASER RD
SALVIA GDNS
SUNLEY GDNS
SELBORNE GDNS
PERIVALE IND PK
ANTREE RD
FRANCIS RD
SARSFIELD RD
Perivale Fst & Mid Schs
FEDERAL RD
FAIRFIELD DR
BROOKLANDS DR
MANOR FARM RD
EDEN CL
Grand Union Canal Walk
NORTHWICK RD
Superstore
GLACIER WAY
CAPITAL BSNS CTR
PERIMEADE RD
ATHLON RD
CROMWELL RD
CARLYON RD
BLEASDALE AVE
SCORTON AVE
Perivale
Perivale
PERIVALE NEW BSNS CTR
WADSWORTH BSNS CTR
Met Police Traffic Unit
BURNS RD
CHILHAM CL
WADSWORTH RD
PLEASANT WAY
PRIMROSE WAY
Ealing
Brent
FLEETWAY WEST BSNS PK
SHERATON BSNS CTR
WADSWORTH CL
SILICONE BSNS CTR
Sp Gd
Tenn Cts
Bwg Gn
B456
TAVISTOCK AVE
ROCKFORD AVE
BIDEFORD AVE
Pav
Sp Gd
Vicar's Green Prim Sch
LILY GDNS
MAY GDNS
ALPERTON LA
Superstore
DAWLISH AVE
TEIGNMOUTH GDNS
RYDAL CRES
CONISTON AVE
THIRLMERE AVE
LANGDALE GDNS
Sch
WEST LINKS
MARSH RD
Superstore
OLD CHURCH LA
Pav
RIVERMEAD CT
WICKET RD
PERIVALE LA
CH
WESTERN AVE
A40
Allot Gdns
Tenn Cts
1 PERIVALE GRANGE
2 LITTLE GRANGE
3 CENTRAL PAR
4 PARKVIEW
5 PERIVALE LO
Ealing
Pav
Allot Gdns
GREYSTOKE PARK TERR
ARGYLE RD
Pl Fld
River Brent
Bwg Gn
BRUNSWICK RD
RUSKIN GDNS
PEAL GDNS
Fball Gd
T Cts
B455
WENTWAY CT
Allot Gdns
Tenn Cts
MEADVALE RD
NEVILLE RD
LYNWOOD RD
BRENTSIDE
HERON HO
ARGYLE CL
Bwg Gn
ASHDOWN 1
HIGHCLIFFE 2
ROSEACRE CL 3
WOBURN 4
FRINTON CT 5
HARDWICK GN 6
SUNNINGDALE 7
GLENEAGLES 8
WYE CT 9
RALEIGH CT 10
OAK DENE 11
FERN DENE 12
MALVERN WAY 13
ROSS CT 14
Sp Gd
Pav
PERIVALE GDNS
NORTH VIEW
HOLYOAKE WLK
DENISON RD
LUDLOW RD
BRUNNER RD
BRENTHAM WAY
FOWLER'S WLK
KINGFIELD RD
MULGRAVE RD
MOORFIELD RD
MOORFIELD AVE
BROOKFIELD AVE
AINSDALE RD
CROSSWAY
AVALON RD
DOWNSIDE CRES
ROYLE CRES
BRENTCOT CL
BELLEVUE RD
WOODBURY PARK RD
SUMMERFIELD RD
CURZON RD
HARROW VIEW RD
SELBY RD
BARNFIELD RD
LINDFIELD RD
PITSHANGER LA
PRINCES GDNS
MOUNT PLEASANT RD
WOODFIELD RD
WOODFIELD AVE
WOODFIELD CRES
WINSCOMBE CRES
Sch
MOUNTWOOD HO
DAVER CT
BIRKDALE RD
Tenn Cts
AVALON CL
VALLIS WAY
SCOTCH COMM
B455
CURZON HO
KENMERE MANS
ALBERT RD
GLENCAIRN DR
CASTLEBAR MEWS
QUEEN'S GDNS
QUEEN'S WLK
SANDGATE HO
MONARCH CT
ALEXANDRA CT
Sch
WINSCOMBE CT
MOUNT VIEW
AVENUE CT
WESTMORELAND PL
PARK GATE
MOUNT AVE
CECIL CT
THE ORCHARD
MAGNOLIA PL
NICHOLS GN
Pav
Castlebar Sch
FOSSE WAY
CLAREMONT RD
B452
LONG ACRE CT
KENT AVE
MIDDLEFIELDS
TEMPLEWOOD
B455 KENT GDNS
DUKES CT
ESSAN HO
VICTORIA RD
CASTLEBAR PK
SOVEREIGN CL
BUCKINGHAM CL
DENE CT
MARK CL
HELENA CT
MONTPELIER CT
GOLDCREST MEWS
Prim Sch
MONTPELIER RD
HELENA RD
ST PETER'S WAY
WEST RD
HATHAWAY GDNS
BRUTON WAY
NURSERY CT
ROBINSON'S CL
OAKLANDS
Cleveland Park
ARGYLE RD
THE MEAD
GRENVILLE CT
THE DENE
CLEVELAND CT
Hostel
COURTLANDS
CASTLEBAR HILL
MOUNT EATON CT
WELSBY CT
MOUNT CL
QUEENS WALK HO
THORPE HALL
PARK HILL
THE CROFT
PARK HILL CT
REGAL CL
HALL CL
BEAULIEU CT
CORFTON RD
RUTLAND GDNS
CLEVELAND RD
CLEVELAND RD
NORTH AVE
SHERBORNE GDNS
WIMBORNE GDNS
EDGEHILL RD
COURTFIELD
THE KNOLL
THE GRANGE
MONTPELIER AVE
St Benedict's Sch
CECIL CT
THE FIRS
KINGS RD
KINGS AVE
BALMORAL CT
QUEEN'S RD
CAVENDISH AVE
KINGSLEY AVE
EDMONSCOTE
CHARLES HO
HOLLINGBOURNE GDNS
RAVENSBOURNE GDNS
High Sch
LAKESIDE
THE CEDARS
HERONSFORDE
Jun Sch
MARCHWOOD CRES
EATON CT
EATON RISE
ELMCROFT CL
MOUNT PARK RD
W5
HIGHVIEW RD
ROSEMOUNT RD
BRIARBANK RD
ST STEPHEN'S AVE
COLEBROOKE AVE
ST STEPHENS CT
ST STEPHEN'S RD
LIMEWOOD CL
DELL WAY
WHITELEDGES
CHARLBURY GR
BAMPTON CT
BLAKESLEY CT
EATON HO
WESTPARK
Aston House Sch
ROSEBERY GDNS
EGERTON GDNS
MONTAGUE RD
MORTIMER RD
PRIORY LO
CASTLEBAR RD
BLAKESLEY AVE
ASTON RD
WOODVILLE RD
MOUNTFIELD RD
HAVEN LA
WESTBURY RD
COMPTON CL
LYNTON AVE
BRADLEY GDNS
AMHERST RD
DAPHNE CT
MOUNT PARK CRES
Sch
SAWYERS LAWN
GRAFTON CL
COURTFIELD GDNS
CAMBRIDGE RD
GLENMORE LAWNS
CHESTER GDNS
COLLEGE RD
THE GABLES
AMHERST AVE
Pl Fld
PINEWOOD GR
Schs
THE WOODVILLE 1
GREENLAW 2
HAVEN GREEN CT
MADELEY CT
DRAYTON BRIDGE RD
Coll
WALDECK RD
NICHOLAS HO
CARLTON RD
OAK TREE CL
LONGFIELD RD
HAVEN GN
COLERIDGE
BERNERS DR
YEAMES CL
GLASSE CL
SUTHERLAND RD
APEX CT
SUTHERLAND HO
B452
SUTHERLAND AVE
THE AVENUE
ARLINGTON RD
DENBIGH RD
CARLTON GDNS
B455
HAVEN GN CT
Ealing Broadway
Drayton Green Prim Sch
DRAYTON GR
DRAYTON RD
W13
ALBANY RD
ST LEONARD'S RD
EALING
Cts
DRAYTON GDNS
STIRLING CT
STRETTON LO
LANGHAM GDNS
VERNON CT
BERKELEY CT
BRIDGE RD
SPRING
HAVEN PL
THE WATERGLADE CTR
THE BROADWAY A4020
THE MALL
HAZEL CT
COLLEGE CT
DRAYTON AVE
West Ealing
HARLEQUIN CT
RAVEN AVE
HASTINGS
Christ Church CE Mid Sch

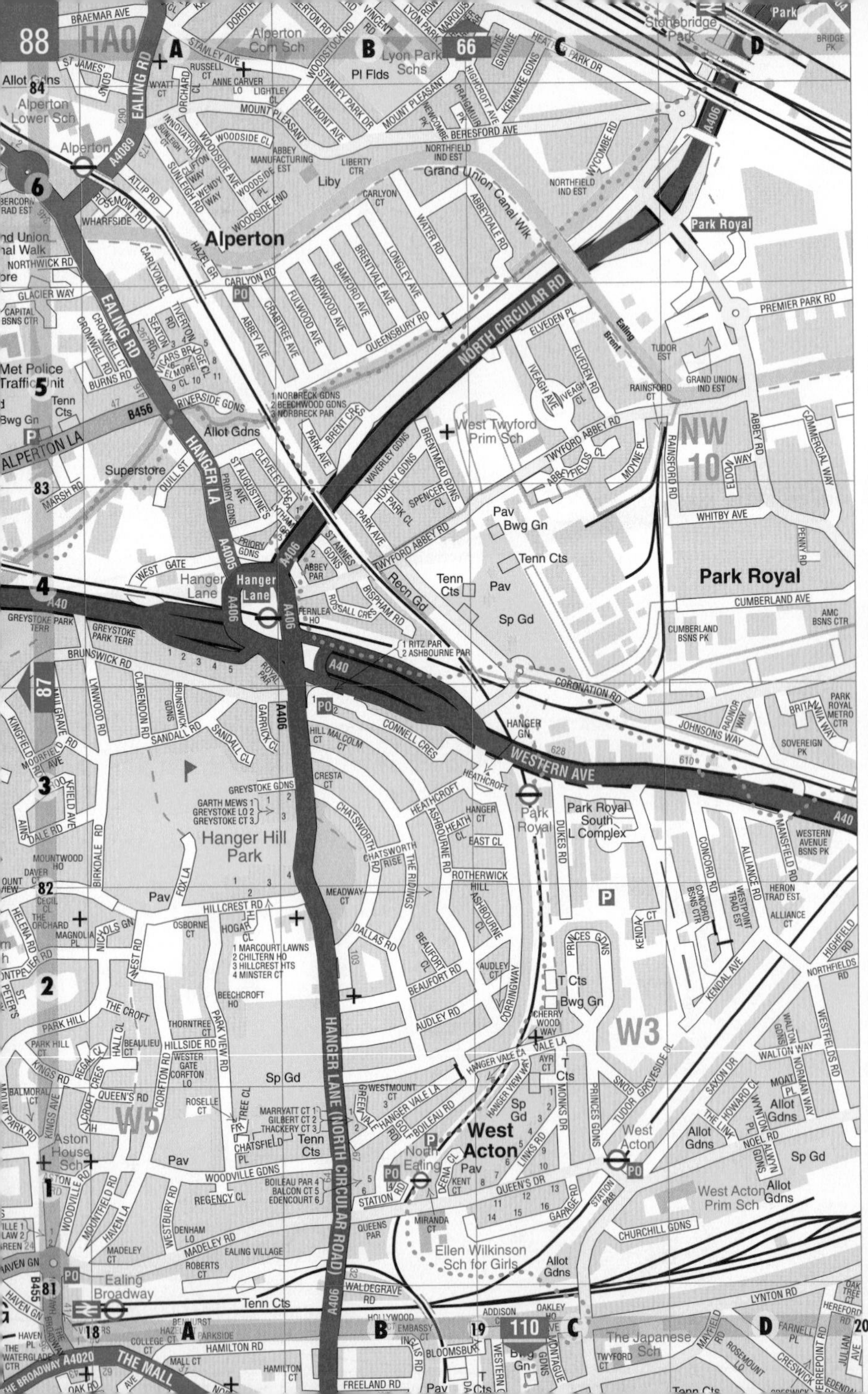
HA0
A
B
C
D
66
Park
Stonebridge Park
BRIDGE PK
BRAEMAR AVE
STANLEY AVE
Alperton Com Sch
Lyon Park Schs
Pl Flds
WOODSTOCK RD
VINCENT
LYON PARK
MARQUIS
THE GRANGE
HEATHER PARK DR
ST JAMES' GDNS
Allot Gdns
84
Alperton Lower Sch
EALING RD
A4089
RUSSELL CT
ANNE CARVER LO
WYATT CT
ORCHARD CL
LIGHTLEY CL
MOUNT PLEASANT
STANLEY PARK DR
BELMONT AVE
NEWCOMBE PK
CRAIGMUIR PK
HIGHCROFT AVE
KENMERE GDNS
BERESFORD AVE
Alperton
6
INNOVATION CL
SUNLEIGH CT
CLIFTON WAY
WENDY WAY
WOODSIDE CL
WOODSIDE AVE
WOODSIDE PL
WOODSIDE END
SUNLEIGH RD
ABBEY MANUFACTURING EST
LIBERTY CTR
Liby
NORTHFIELD IND EST
Grand Union Canal Wlk
WYCOMBE RD
A406
ATLIP RD
ROSEMONT RD
WHARFSIDE
ABERCORN TRAD EST
Grand Union Canal Walk
NORTHWICK RD
GLACIER WAY
CAPITAL BSNS CTR
Alperton
CARLYON CT
WATER RD
ABBEYDALE RD
Park Royal
HAZEL GR
CARLYON CL
CARLYON RD
PO
ABBEY AVE
CRABTREE AVE
FULWOOD AVE
NORWOOD AVE
BAMFORD AVE
BRENTVALE AVE
LONGLEY AVE
QUEENSBURY RD
NORTH CIRCULAR RD
ELVEDEN PL
ELVEDEN RD
Ealing
Brent
TUDOR EST
PREMIER PARK RD
GRAND UNION IND EST
CROMWELL RD
CROMWELL CT
SEATON RD
TIVERTON RD
VICARS BRIDGE CL
ELMORE CL
BURNS RD
Met Police Traffic Unit
5
Tenn Cts
Bwg Gn
P
ALPERTON LA
B456
RIVERSIDE GDNS
1 NORBRECK GDNS
2 BEECHWOOD GDNS
3 NORBRECK PAR
BRENT CRES
PARK AVE
IVEAGH AVE
IVEAGH CL
RAINSFORD CT
RAINSFORD RD
NW 10
ABBEY RD
COMMERCIAL WAY
West Twyford Prim Sch
TWYFORD ABBEY RD
ABBEYFIELDS CL
MOYNE PL
EDGOW WAY
Allot Gdns
HANGER LA
Superstore
QUILL ST
ST AUGUSTINES AVE
PRIORY GDNS
CLEVELEY CRES
WAVERLEY GDNS
BRENTMEAD GDNS
HUXLEY GDNS
SPENCER CL
PARK CL
83
MARSH RD
WHITBY AVE
Pav
Bwg Gn
PENNY RD
A4005
PRIORY GDNS
ST ANNES GDNS
ABBEY PAR
Tenn Cts
Tenn Cts
Pav
Park Royal
WEST GATE
Hanger Lane
4
A40
Recn Gd
Sp Gd
CUMBERLAND AVE
AMC BSNS CTR
CUMBERLAND BSNS PK
GREYSTOKE PARK TERR
FERNLEA HO
ROSSALL CRES
BISPHAM RD
1 RITZ PAR
2 ASHBOURNE PAR
BRUNSWICK RD
ROYAL PAR
CORONATION RD
87
LYNWOOD RD
CLARENDON RD
BRUNSWICK GDNS
SANDALL RD
SANDALL CL
GARRICK CL
PO
HILL CT
MALCOLM CT
CONNELL CRES
HANGER GN
JOHNSONS WAY
RADNOR WAY
BRITANNIA WAY
PARK ROYAL METRO CTR
SOVEREIGN PK
KINGFIELD RD
MILGRAVE RD
MOORFIELD RD
3
KFIELD AVE
DALE RD
CRESTA CT
WESTERN AVE
628
610
HEATHCROFT
GREYSTOKE GDNS
GARTH MEWS 1
GREYSTOKE LO 2
GREYSTOKE CT 3
CHATSWORTH RD
HANGER CT
HEATH CL
EAST CL
Park Royal
Park Royal South L Complex
DUKES RD
CONCORD RD
ALLIANCE RD
MANSFIELD RD
WESTERN AVENUE BSNS PK
Hanger Hill Park
BIRKDALE RD
MOUNTWOOD HO
DAVER CT
82
CHATSWORTH RISE
THE RIDINGS
ASHBOURNE RD
ROTHERWICK HILL
ASHBOURNE CL
CONCORD BSNS CTR
WESTPOINT TRAD EST
HERON TRAD EST
ALLIANCE CT
P
CECIL CL
THE ORCHARD
MAGNOLIA PL
HELENA RD
NICHOLS GN
Pav
FOX LA
HILLCREST RD
OSBORNE CT
HOGARTH CL
MEADWAY CT
DALLAS RD
KENDAL CT
PRINCES GDNS
HIGHFIELD RD
NORTHFIELDS RD
1 MARCOURT LAWNS
2 CHILTERN HO
3 HILLCREST HTS
4 MINSTER CT
BEAUFORT CL
BEAUFORT RD
AUDLEY CT
CORRINGWAY
T Cts
Bwg Gn
KENDAL AVE
2
ST PETERS
WEST RD
BEECHCROFT HO
103
AUDLEY RD
CHERRY WOOD WAY
W3
WALTON GDNS
WESTFIELDS RD
PARK HILL
THE CROFT
THORNTREE CT
PARK VIEW RD
HILLSIDE RD
WESTERGATE
CORFTON LO
HANGER VALE LA
VALE LA
AYR CT
T Cts
TUDOR GDNS
GROVESIDE CL
SAXON DR
WALTON WAY
NORMAN WAY
MOAT PL
REGAL CL
BEAULIEU CT
KINGS RD
CROFT CRES
HALL CL
CORFTON RD
Sp Gd
WESTMOUNT CT
GREEN VALE
HANGER VIEW WAY
Sp Gd
HOWARD CL
WYNTON PL
Allot Gdns
BALMORAL CT
QUEEN'S RD
ROSELLE CT
FIR TREE CL
MARRYATT CT 1
GILBERT CT 2
THACKERY CT 3
BOILEAU RD
GOLF CL
P
West Acton
MONKS DR
PRINCES GDNS
THE LINK
ALWYN GDNS
NOEL RD
Allot Gdns
KINGS AVE
W5
Tenn Cts
LINKS RD
West Acton
PO
Sp Gd
Aston House Sch
CHATSFIELD PL
Pav
North Ealing
OKENA CL
Pav
KENT CT
1
WOODVILLE RD
MOUNTFIELD RD
HAVEN LA
WESTBURY RD
WOODVILLE GDNS
REGENCY CL
BOILEAU PAR 4
BALCON CT 5
EDENCOURT 6
PO
STATION RD
MIRANDA CT
QUEEN'S DR
GARAGE RD
STATION PAR
West Acton Prim Sch
Allot Gdns
DENHAM LO
MADELEY RD
MADELEY CT
QUEENS PAR
CHURCHILL GDNS
HAVEN GN
PO
81
Ealing Broadway
B455
ROBERTS CT
EALING VILLAGE
Ellen Wilkinson Sch for Girls
Allot Gdns
HANGER LANE (NORTH CIRCULAR ROAD)
A406
WALDEGRAVE RD
Tenn Cts
HOLLYWOOD CT
EMBASSY CT
ADDISON
OAKLEY
LYNTON RD
OAK TREE CT
HEREFORD
18
HAVEN PL
HAZELHURST
PARKSIDE
A
B
19
110
C
D
20
FARNELL PL
MAYFIELD RD
ROSEMOUNT LO
The Japanese Sch
TWYFORD CT
CRESWICK
JULIAN
HAMILTON RD
COLLEGE CT
MALL CT
INGLIS RD
BLOOMSBURY
WESTERN
Bwg Gn
MONTAGUE GDNS
THE WATERGLADE CTR
THE BROADWAY
A4020
THE MALL
HAMILTON CT
FREELAND RD
OAK RD
Pav
T Cts
Tenn Cts

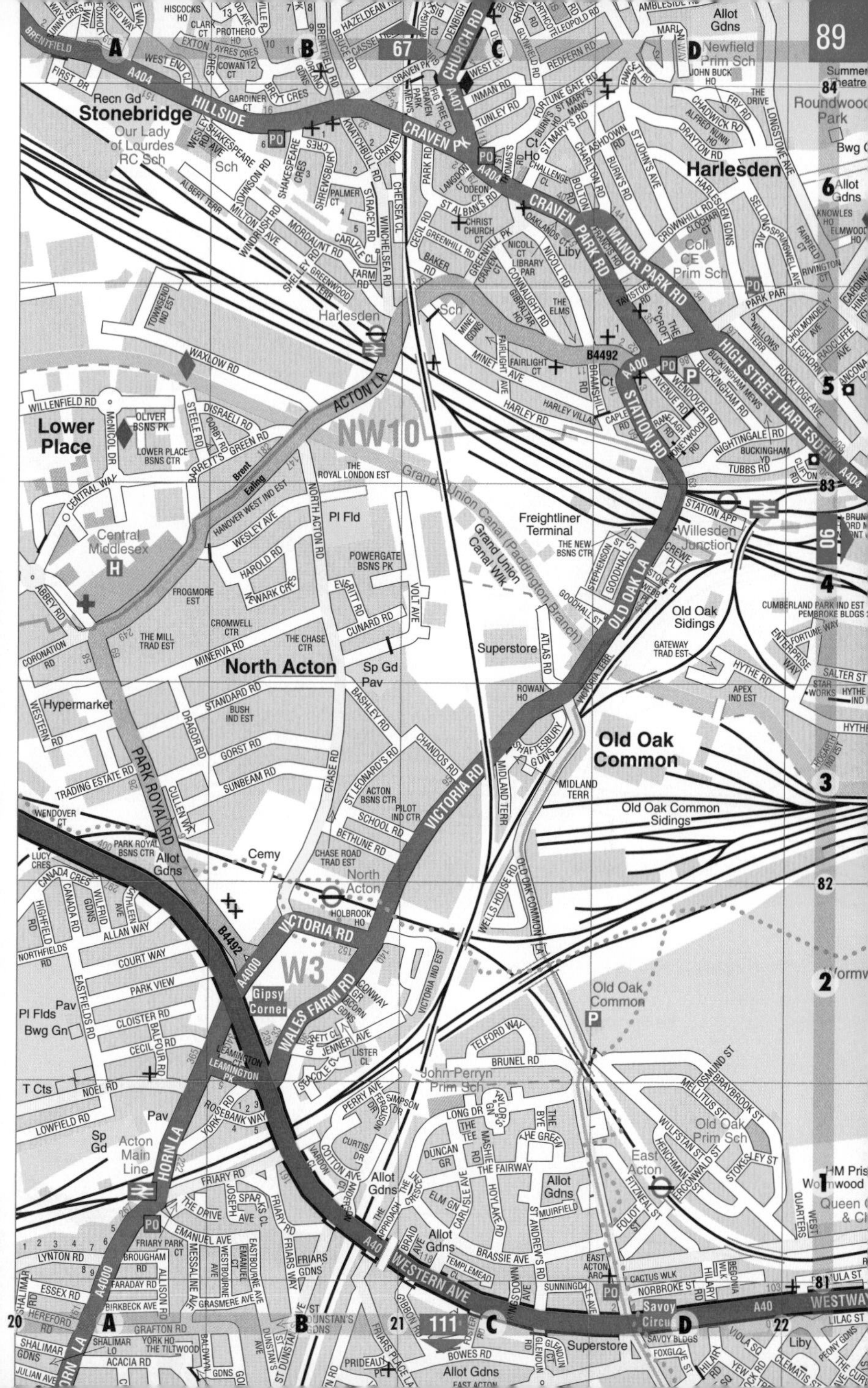

Stonebridge
Harlesden
Lower Place
NW10
North Acton
Old Oak Common
W3
Central Middlesex
Freightliner Terminal
Willesden Junction
Old Oak Sidings
Old Oak Common Sidings
Grand Union Canal (Paddington Branch)
HILLSIDE
CRAVEN PK
CRAVEN PARK RD
MANOR PARK RD
HIGH STREET HARLESDEN
STATION RD
OLD OAK LA
ACTON LA
PARK ROYAL RD
VICTORIA RD
WALES FARM RD
WESTERN AVE
HORN LA
CHURCH RD
Gipsy Corner
Acton Main Line
East Acton
North Acton
Harlesden
Savoy Circus

67
90
111

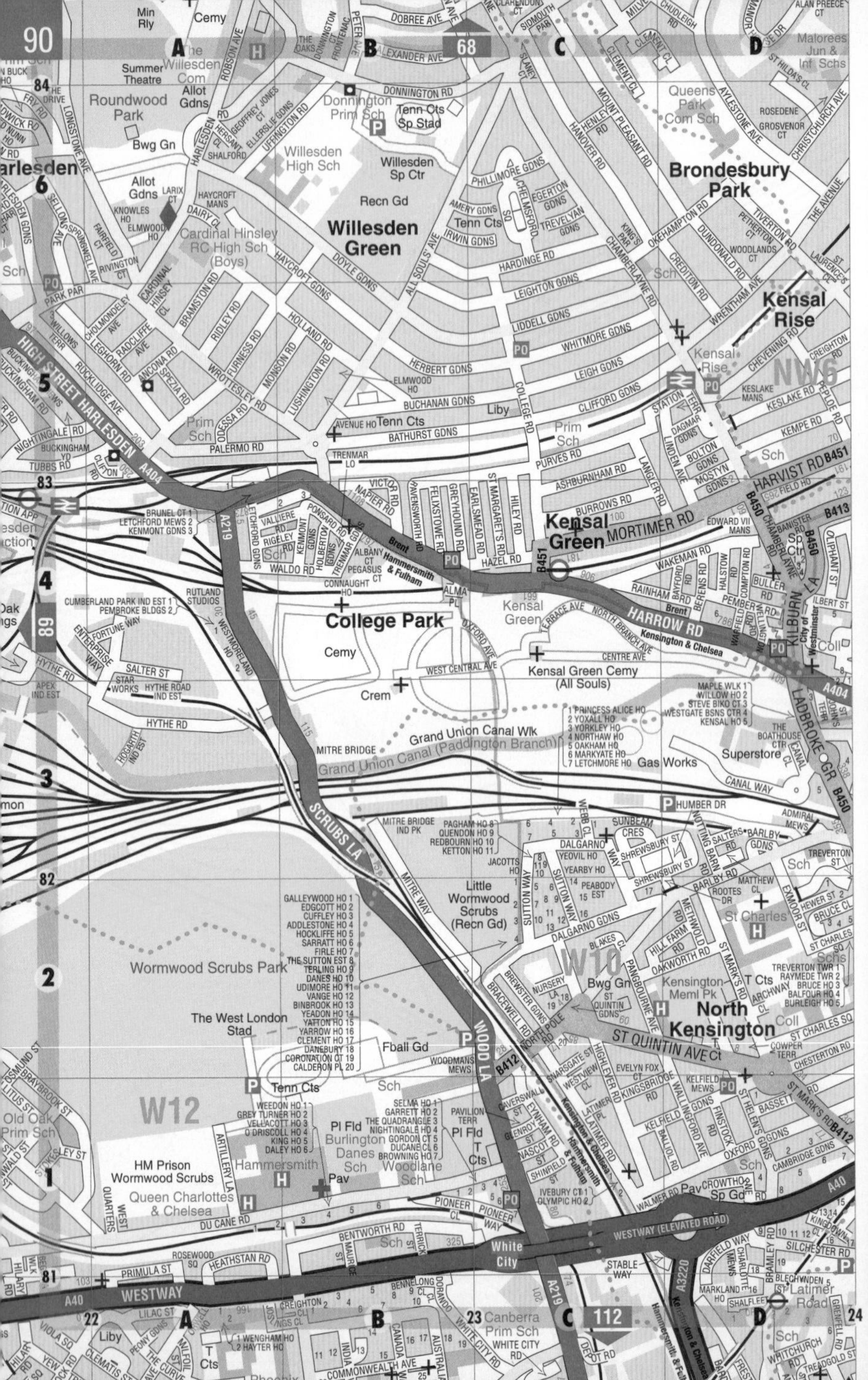

90
A
B
C
D
68
Willesden Green
Harlesden
Brondesbury Park
Kensal Rise
NW6
Kensal Green
College Park
Cemy
Crem
Kensal Green Cemy (All Souls)
Grand Union Canal Wlk
Grand Union Canal (Paddington Branch)
Gas Works
Superstore
Wormwood Scrubs Park
Little Wormwood Scrubs (Recn Gd)
The West London Stad
Fball Gd
W10
W12
North Kensington
HM Prison Wormwood Scrubs
Hammersmith
Queen Charlottes & Chelsea
White City
Roundwood Park
Willesden High Sch
Willesden Sp Ctr
Recn Gd
Cardinal Hinsley RC High Sch (Boys)
Queens Park Com Sch
Donnington Prim Sch
HIGH STREET HARLESDEN
HARROW RD
SCRUBS LA
WOOD LA
WESTWAY
WESTWAY (ELEVATED ROAD)
LADBROKE GR
ST QUINTIN AVE
DU CANE RD
MORTIMER RD
HARVIST RD
CHAMBERLAYNE RD
KILBURN LA
A404
A219
A40
A3220
B450
B451
B412
B413
Old Oak Prim Sch
Kensington Meml Pk
Burlington Danes Sch
Woodlane Sch
St Charles
Canberra Prim Sch
Latimer Road
112
22
23
24
81
82
83
84
1
2
3
4
5
6

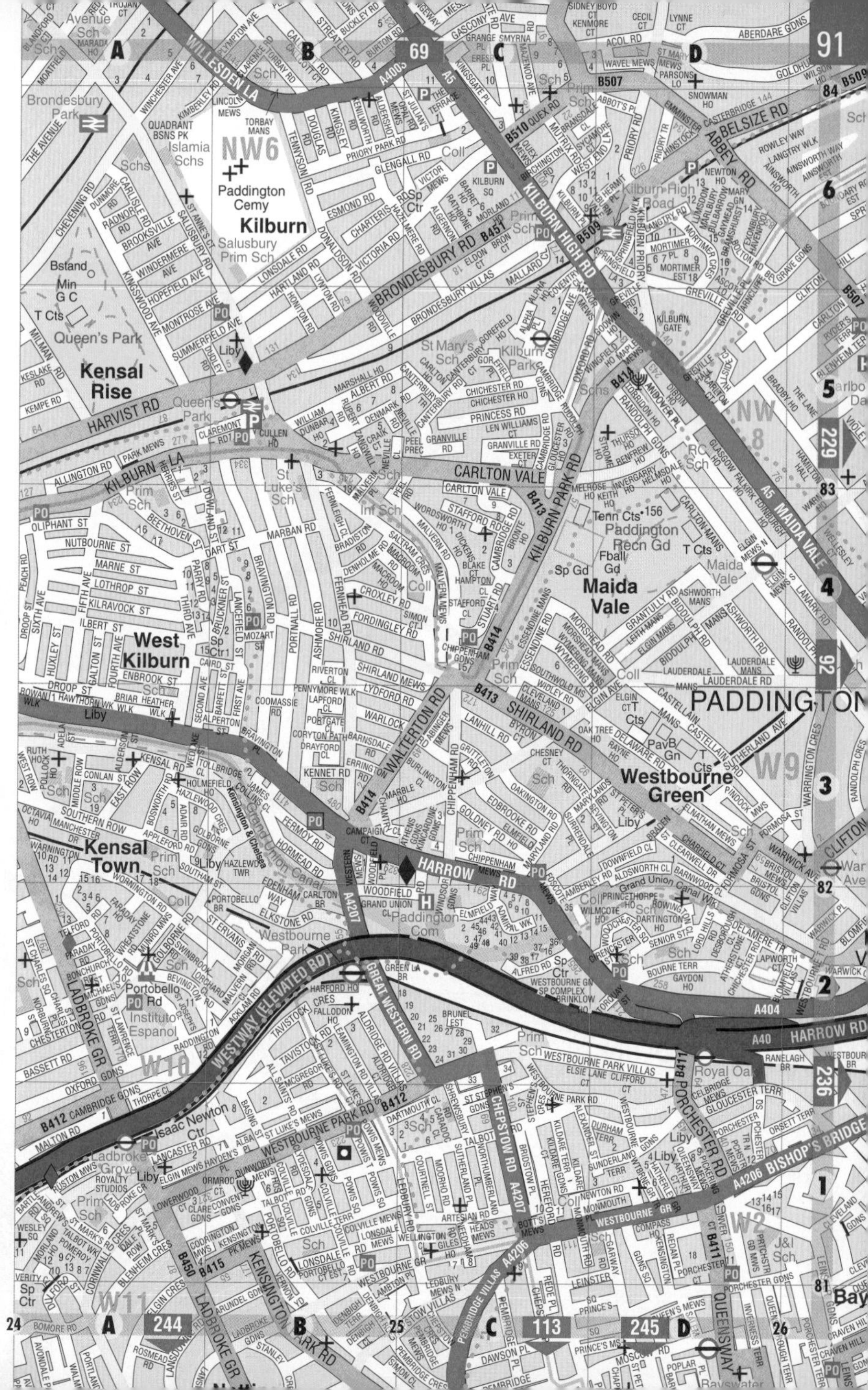
91
A
B
C
D
69
NW6
Kilburn
Paddington Cemy
Kensal Rise
Queen's Park
West Kilburn
Kensal Town
Maida Vale
PADDINGTON
Westbourne Green
W9
W10
W11
W2
NW8
Brondesbury Park
WILLESDEN LA
BRONDESBURY RD
KILBURN HIGH RD
KILBURN LA
HARVIST RD
CARLTON VALE
KILBURN PARK RD
MAIDA VALE
SHIRLAND RD
HARROW RD
WALTERTON RD
WESTWAY (ELEVATED RD)
GREAT WESTERN RD
LADBROKE GR
WESTBOURNE PARK RD
WESTBOURNE GR
PORCHESTER RD
CHEPSTOW RD
BISHOP'S BRIDGE RD
ABBEY RD
BELSIZE RD
Grand Union Canal
Paddington Recn Gd
Royal Oak
Westbourne Park
Ladbroke Grove
Portobello Rd
6
5
4
3
2
1
229
92
236
24
244
25
113
245
26

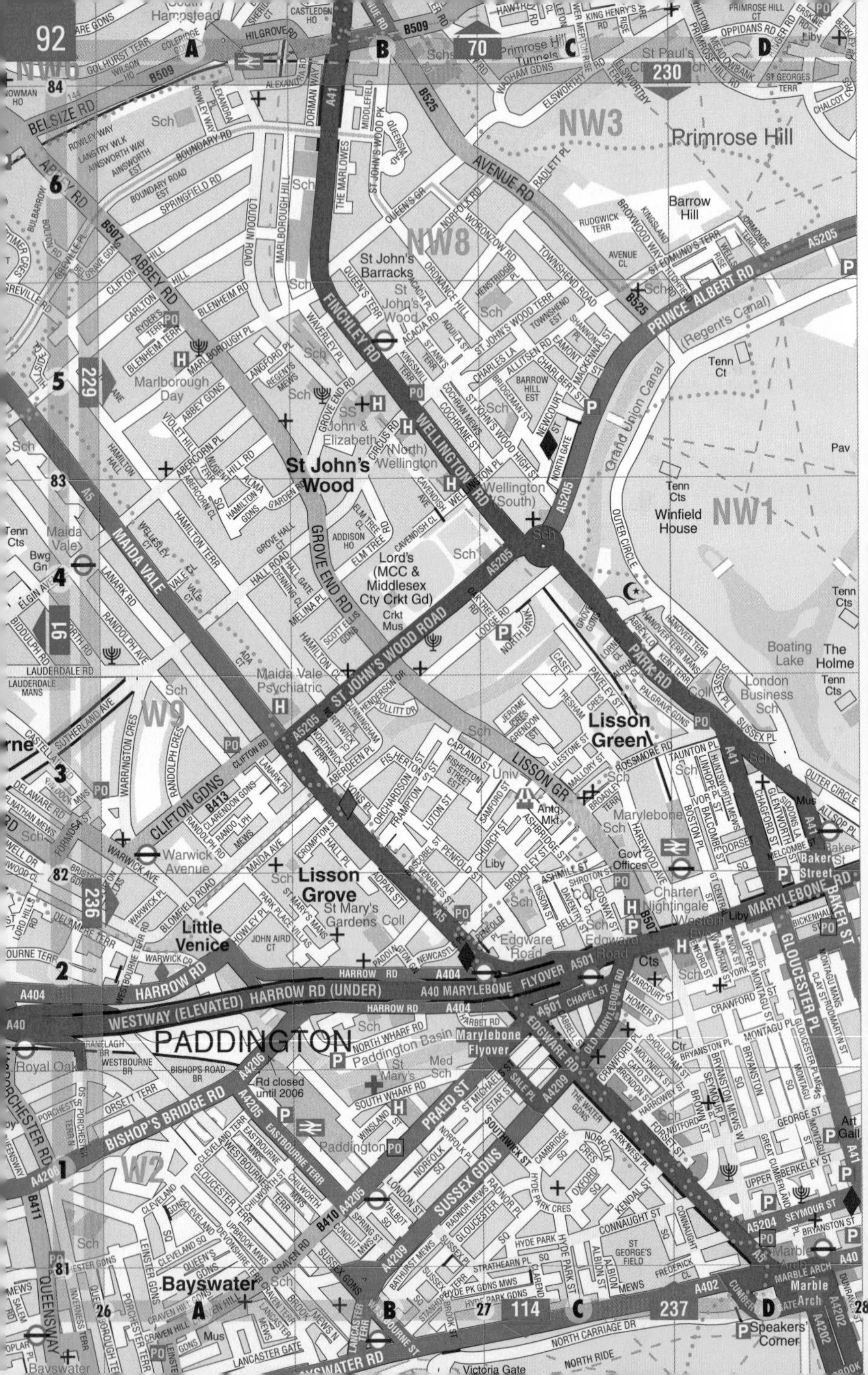

A
B
C
D
70
230
NW6
NW3
NW8
NW1
W9
W2
Primrose Hill
Barrow Hill
St John's Wood
St John's Barracks
Lord's (MCC & Middlesex Cty Crkt Gd)
Crkt Mus
Maida Vale
Lisson Green
Lisson Grove
Little Venice
Warwick Avenue
PADDINGTON
Paddington Basin
Paddington
Bayswater
Royal Oak
Marylebone
Marylebone Flyover
Edgware Road
Marble Arch
Speakers' Corner
Winfield House
Boating Lake
The Holme
London Business Sch
Grand Union Canal
(Regent's Canal)
FINCHLEY RD
WELLINGTON RD
PRINCE ALBERT RD
AVENUE RD
ABBEY RD
MAIDA VALE
GROVE END RD
ST JOHN'S WOOD ROAD
LISSON GR
PARK RD
OUTER CIRCLE
HARROW RD
WESTWAY (ELEVATED) HARROW RD (UNDER)
A40 MARYLEBONE FLYOVER
MARYLEBONE RD
GLOUCESTER PL
BAKER ST
EDGWARE RD
PRAED ST
SUSSEX GDNS
BISHOP'S BRIDGE RD
CLIFTON GDNS
QUEENSWAY
BAYSWATER RD
NORTH CARRIAGE DR
NORTH RIDE
Victoria Gate
6
5
4
3
2
1
26
27
28
81
82
83
84
91
114
229
236
237

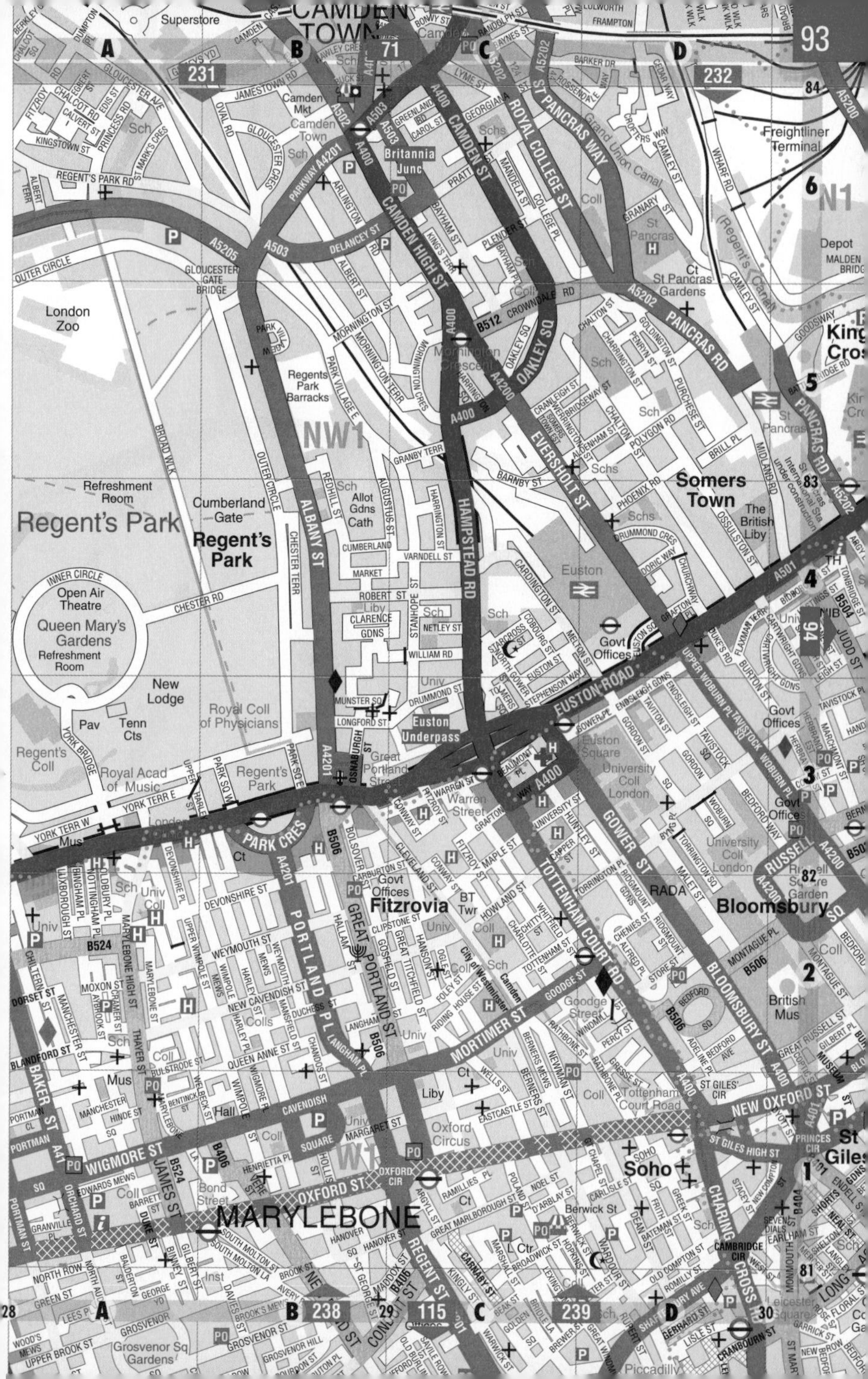

CAMDEN TOWN
Camden Mkt
Camden Town
Britannia Junc
Superstore
Freightliner Terminal
N1
Depot
Grand Union Canal
(Regent's Canal)
St Pancras Gardens
St Pancras
Kings Cross
London Zoo
Regents Park Barracks
NW1
Regent's Park
Cumberland Gate
Refreshment Room
Open Air Theatre
Queen Mary's Gardens
Inner Circle
Outer Circle
New Lodge
Royal Coll of Physicians
Regent's Coll
Royal Acad of Music
Pav
Tenn Cts
Euston
Euston Underpass
Somers Town
The British Liby
Govt Offices
Euston Square
University Coll London
Great Portland Street
Warren Street
Fitzrovia
BT Twr
City of Westminster
Camden
Goodge Street
RADA
Bloomsbury
Russell Square Garden
British Mus
Tottenham Court Road
Oxford Circus
Bond Street
MARYLEBONE
Soho
Berwick St
St Giles
Grosvenor Sq Gardens
Piccadilly
Leicester Square
ALBANY ST
HAMPSTEAD RD
CAMDEN HIGH ST
CAMDEN ST
ROYAL COLLEGE ST
ST PANCRAS WAY
PANCRAS RD
EUSTON ROAD
EVERSHOLT ST
GOWER ST
TOTTENHAM COURT RD
BLOOMSBURY ST
PORTLAND PL
GREAT PORTLAND ST
MORTIMER ST
OXFORD ST
NEW OXFORD ST
WIGMORE ST
BAKER ST
REGENT ST
CHARING CROSS
PARK CRES
PARKWAY
DELANCEY ST
MORNINGTON CRES
OAKLEY SQ
CROWNDALE RD
A
B
C
D
1
2
3
4
5
6
231
232
71
94
238
115
239
28
29
30
81
82
83
84

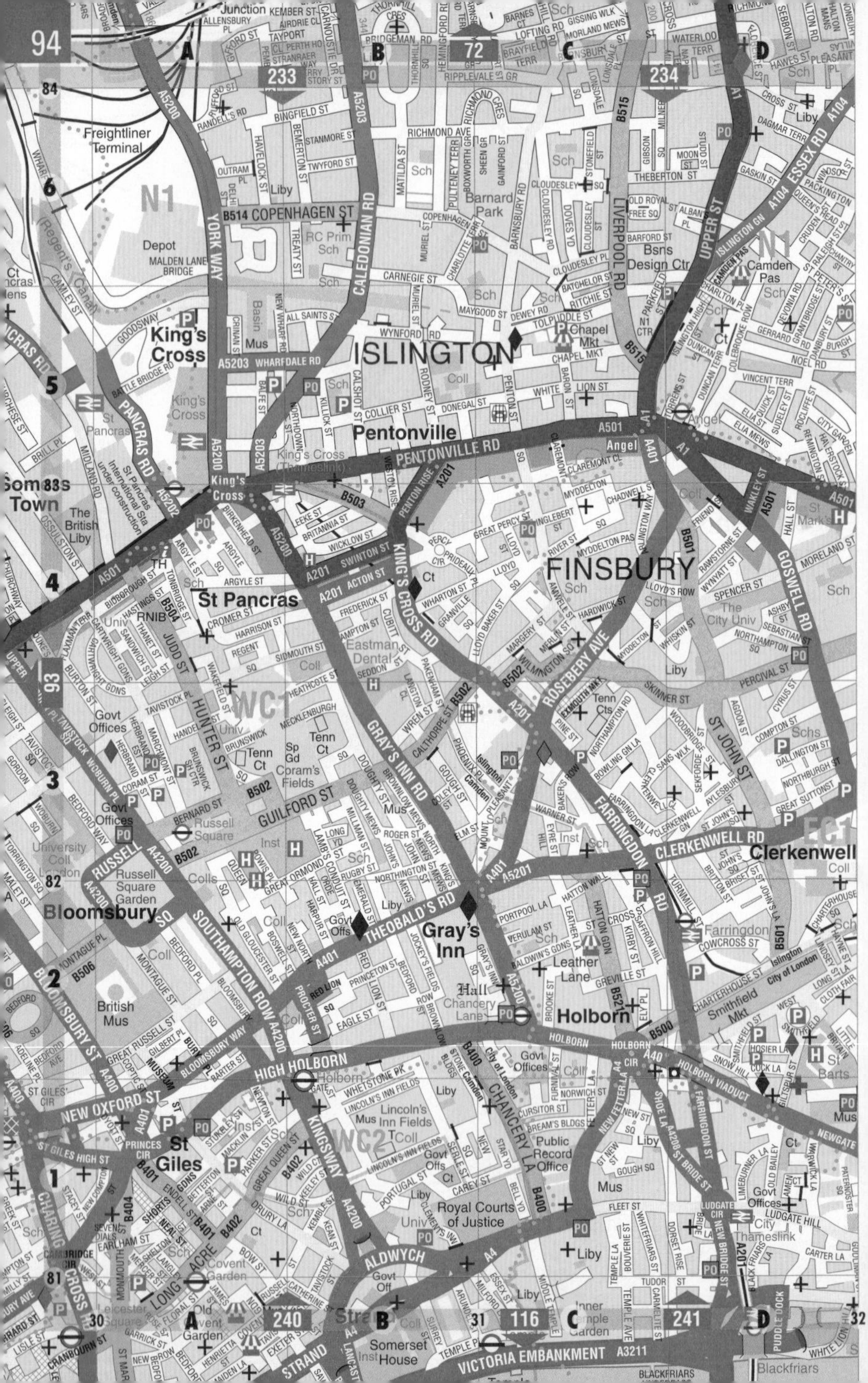
72
233
234
Freightliner
Terminal
N1
Depot
MALDEN LANE
BRIDGE
YORK WAY
CALEDONIAN RD
B514 COPENHAGEN ST
RC Prim
Sch
Barnard
Park
LIVERPOOL RD
UPPER ST
ESSEX RD
ISLINGTON GN
Bsns
Design Ctr
Camden
Pas
King's
Cross
ISLINGTON
Chapel
Mkt
Pentonville
PENTONVILLE RD
Angel
St
Pancras
PANCRAS RD
St Pancras
International Sta
under construction
Somers
Town
The
British
Liby
King's Cross
(Thameslink)
FINSBURY
The
City Univ
GOSWELL RD
St Pancras
KING'S CROSS RD
ROSEBERY AVE
WC1
Eastman
Dental
Govt
Offices
Tenn
Ct
Sp
Gd
Coram's
Fields
GUILFORD ST
GRAY'S INN RD
FARRINGDON RD
CLERKENWELL RD
Clerkenwell
EC1
Russell
Square
University
Coll
London
Russell
Square
Garden
Bloomsbury
THEOBALD'S RD
Gray's
Inn
Leather
Lane
Holborn
Farringdon
Smithfield
Mkt
British
Mus
SOUTHAMPTON ROW
HIGH HOLBORN
HOLBORN VIADUCT
NEW OXFORD ST
Lincoln's
Inn Fields
WC2
KINGSWAY
CHANCERY LA
Public
Record
Office
St
Giles
CHARING CROSS RD
LONG ACRE
Covent
Garden
Royal Courts
of Justice
ALDWYCH
FLEET ST
LUDGATE HILL
City
Thameslink
Strand
Somerset
House
Inner
Temple
Garden
VICTORIA EMBANKMENT
STRAND
Blackfriars
240
116
241
A
B
C
D
1
2
3
4
5
6

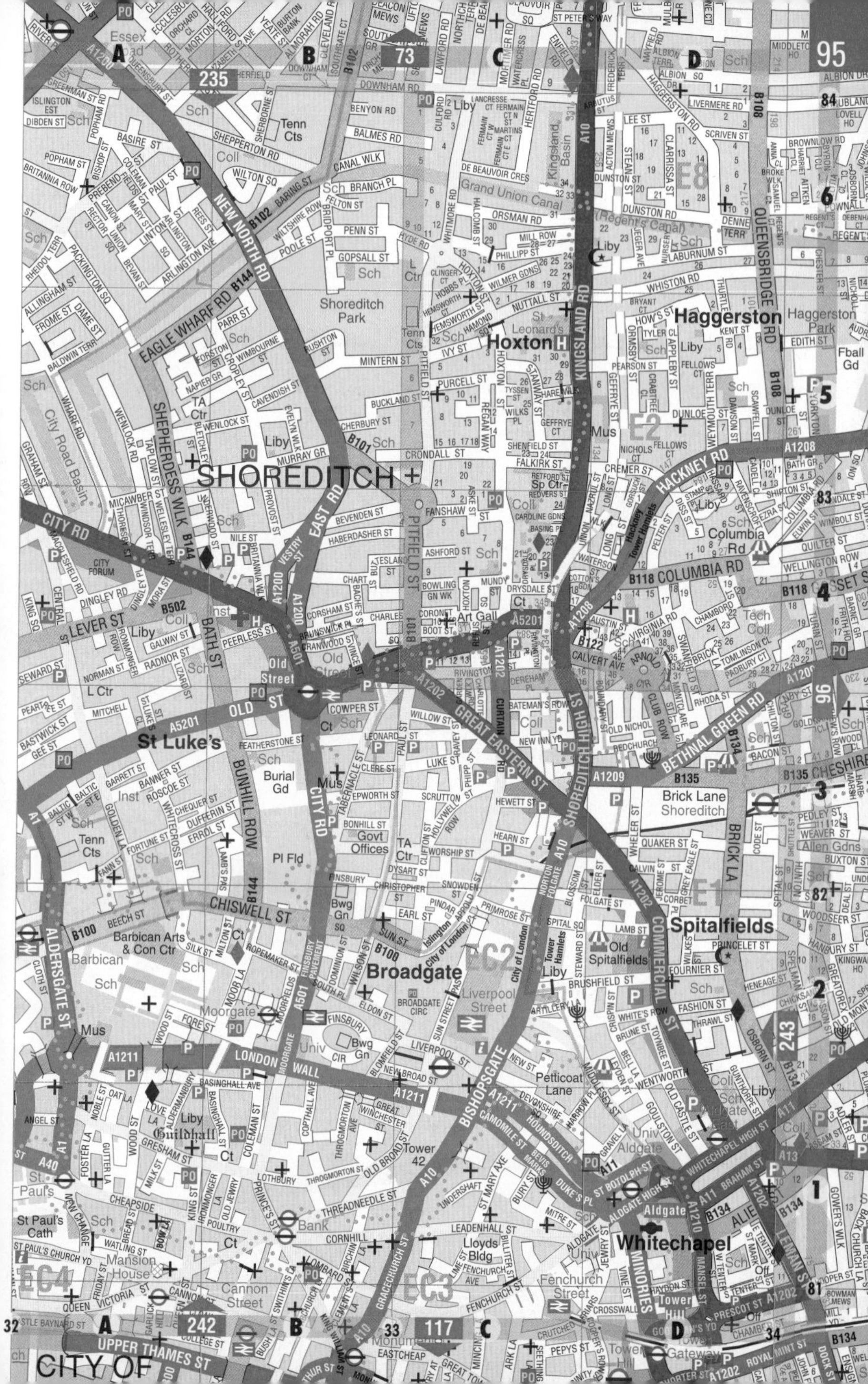

95
SHOREDITCH
Hoxton
Haggerston
Haggerston Park
St Luke's
Spitalfields
Broadgate
Whitechapel
Aldgate
Barbican
Barbican Arts & Con Ctr
Shoreditch Park
City Road Basin
Kingsland Basin
Grand Union Canal
(Regent's Canal)
Brick Lane Shoreditch
Old Spitalfields
Liverpool Street
Moorgate
Old Street
Bank
Mansion House
Cannon Street
St Paul's
St Paul's Cath
Guildhall
Tower 42
Lloyds Bldg
Fenchurch Street
Tower Hill
Tower Gateway
Petticoat Lane
Columbia Rd
CITY OF
E8
E2
E1
EC2
EC3
EC4
A
B
C
D
1
2
3
4
5
6
73
235
242
117
243
96
32
33
34
81
82
83
84
NEW NORTH RD
KINGSLAND RD
CITY RD
EAST RD
OLD ST
GREAT EASTERN ST
SHOREDITCH HIGH ST
HACKNEY RD
BETHNAL GREEN RD
COLUMBIA RD
COMMERCIAL ST
BISHOPSGATE
LONDON WALL
CHISWELL ST
ALDERSGATE ST
BUNHILL ROW
SHEPHERDESS WLK
QUEENSBRIDGE RD
BRICK LA
WHITECHAPEL HIGH ST
UPPER THAMES ST
GRACECHURCH ST
CHEAPSIDE
QUEEN VICTORIA ST
MINORIES
LEMAN ST
PITFIELD ST
EAGLE WHARF RD

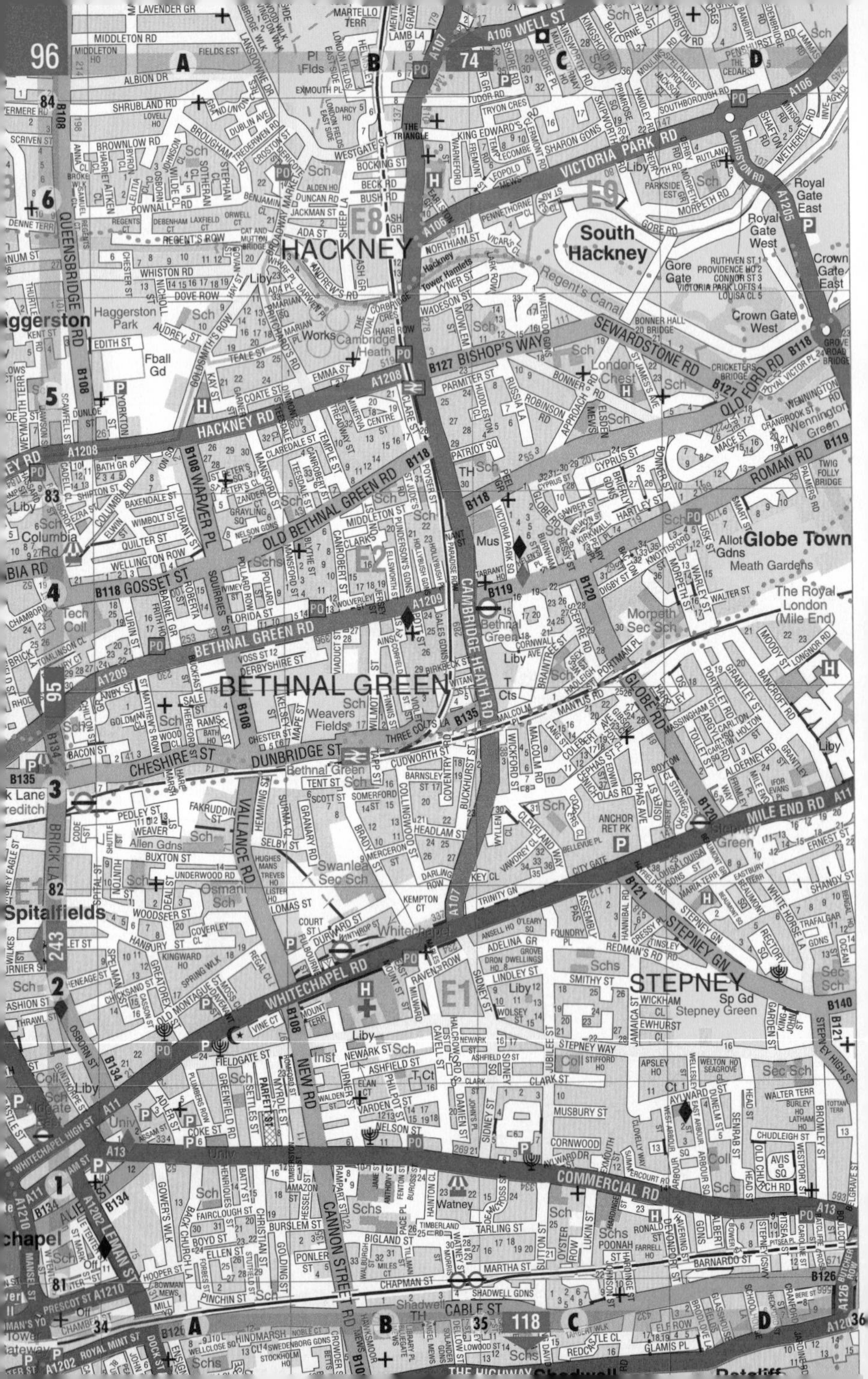

96
A
B
C
D
74
HACKNEY
E8
South Hackney
E9
Haggerston
Haggerston Park
BETHNAL GREEN
E2
Globe Town
STEPNEY
E1
Spitalfields
QUEENSBRIDGE RD
HACKNEY RD
OLD BETHNAL GREEN RD
BETHNAL GREEN RD
CAMBRIDGE HEATH RD
VICTORIA PARK RD
BISHOP'S WAY
SEWARDSTONE RD
OLD FORD RD
ROMAN RD
MILE END RD
WHITECHAPEL RD
COMMERCIAL RD
CANNON STREET RD
NEW RD
VALLANCE RD
BRICK LA
CHESHIRE ST
DUNBRIDGE ST
GOSSET ST
WARNER PL
GLOBE RD
STEPNEY GN
STEPNEY WAY
CABLE ST
LEMAN ST
Regent's Canal
Cambridge Heath
Bethnal Green
Whitechapel
Stepney Green
Shadwell
Weavers Fields
Swanlea Sec Sch
Meath Gardens
Morpeth Sec Sch
The Royal London (Mile End)
Royal Gate East
Royal Gate West
Gore Gate
Crown Gate East
Crown Gate West
Sp Gd Stepney Green
Allen Gdns
Osmani Sch
Watney
Columbia Rd
Tech Coll
Anchor Ret Pk
95
243
118
6
5
4
3
2
1
84
83
82
81
34
35
36

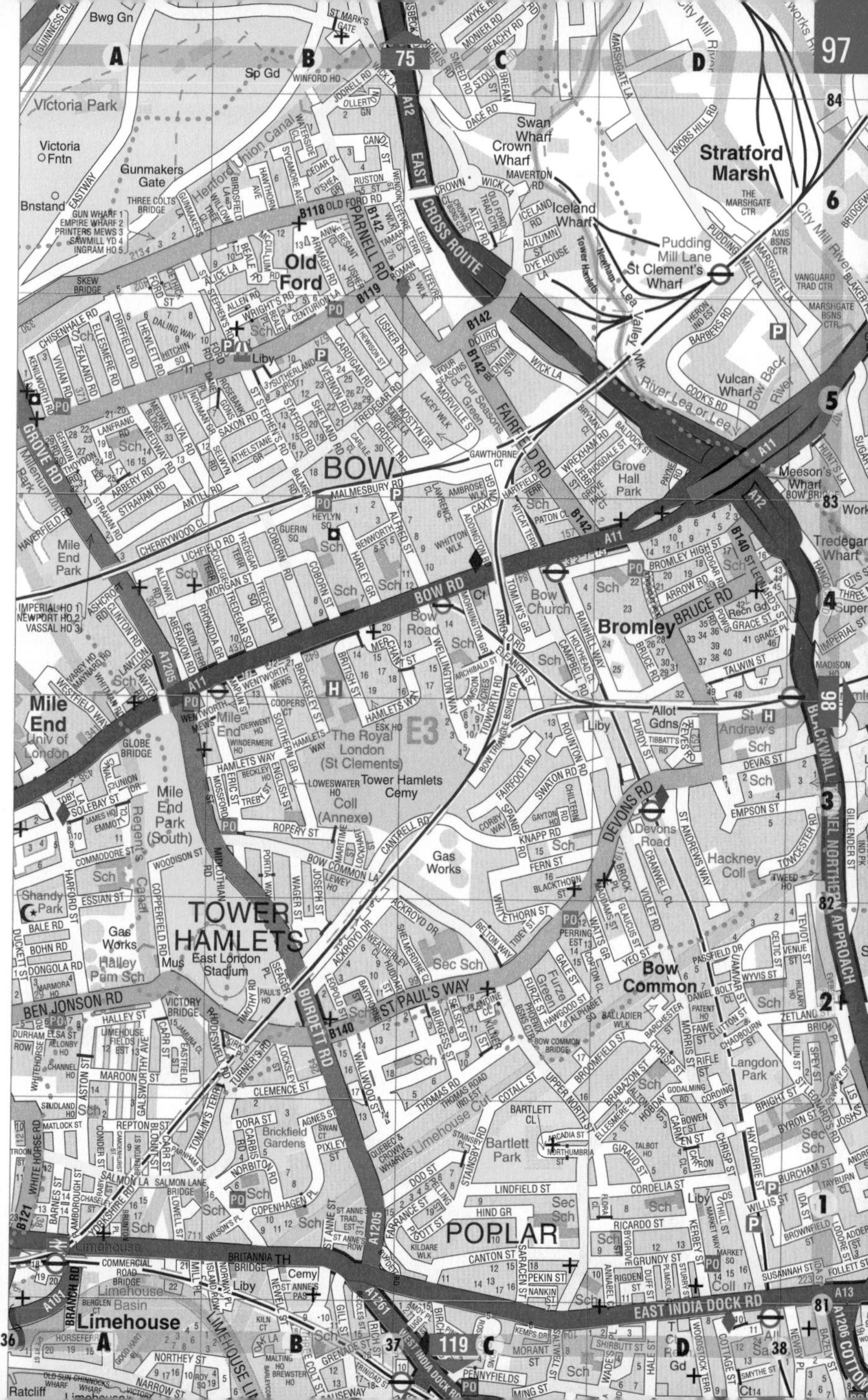

A
B
C
D
75
Victoria Park
Victoria Fntn
Gunmakers Gate
Bnstand
EASTWAY
Hertford Union Canal
Sp Gd
Bwg Gn
OLD FORD RD
B118
B119
Old Ford
PARNELL RD
B142
EAST CROSS ROUTE
A12
WICK LA
Swan Wharf
Crown Wharf
Iceland Wharf
Pudding Mill Lane
St Clement's Wharf
Stratford Marsh
THE MARSHGATE CTR
City Mill River
MARSHGATE LA
KNOBS HILL RD
Tower Hamlets
Newham
Lea Valley Wlk
River Lea or Lee
Bow Back River
Vulcan Wharf
COOK'S RD
BARBERS RD
HERON IND EST
AXIS BSNS CTR
VANGUARD TRAD CTR
MARSHGATE BSNS CTR
84
6
5
4
3
2
1
83
82
81
98
FAIRFIELD RD
Four Seasons Green
BOW
GROVE RD
Mile End Park
MALMESBURY RD
A11
BOW RD
Bow Road
Bow Church
Bromley
BROMLEY HIGH ST
BRUCE RD
B140
ST LEONARDS ST
Grove Hall Park
Meeson's Wharf
BOW BRIDGE
Tredegar Wharf
A1205
Mile End
Univ of London
GLOBE BRIDGE
Mile End Park (South)
Regent's Canal
E3
The Royal London (St Clements)
Tower Hamlets Cemy
Coll (Annexe)
Allot Gdns
St Andrew's
DEVONS RD
Devons Road
Gas Works
Hackney Coll
BLACKWALL TUNNEL NORTHERN APPROACH
TOWER HAMLETS
BURDETT RD
ST PAUL'S WAY
BOW COMMON LA
Bow Common
East London Stadium
Halley Prim Sch
BEN JONSON RD
Shandy Park
Furze Green
Langdon Park
Sec Sch
Limehouse Cut
Brickfield Gardens
Bartlett Park
POPLAR
CORDELIA ST
LINDFIELD ST
A1205
EAST INDIA DOCK RD
A13
A1206
COTTON
WEST INDIA DOCK RD
A1261
BRITANNIA BRIDGE
COMMERCIAL ROAD BRIDGE
Limehouse Basin
Limehouse
LIMEHOUSE LINK
BRANCH RD
A101
B121
WHITE HORSE RD
NARROW ST
Ratcliff
36
37
38
119

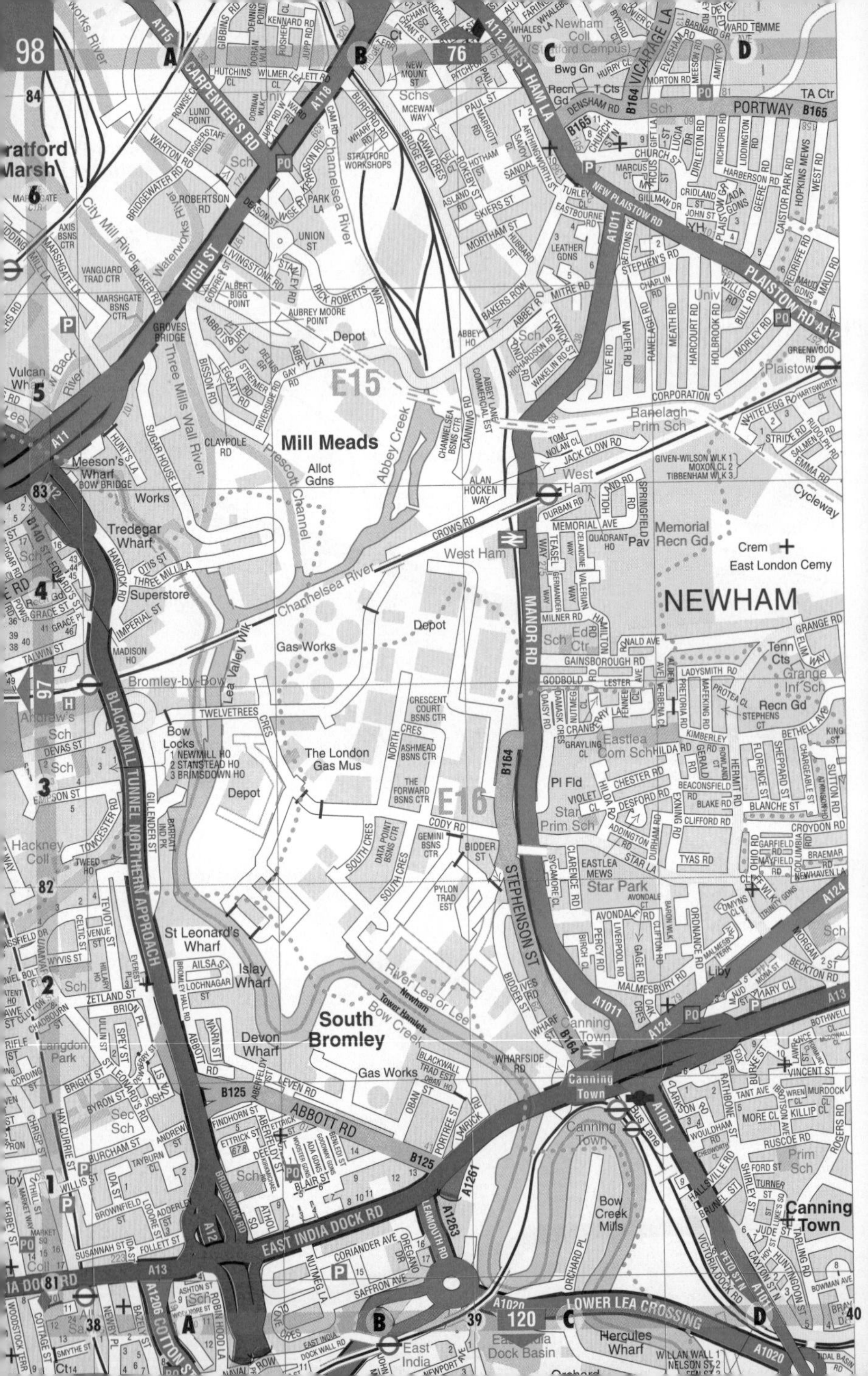

98
76
A
B
C
D
Stratford Marsh
Newham Coll (Stratford Campus)
CARPENTER'S RD
A112 WEST HAM LA
VICARAGE LA
PORTWAY B165
HIGH ST
NEW PLAISTOW RD
PLAISTOW RD A112
Plaistow
City Mill River
Waterworks River
Channelsea River
Three Mills Wall River
Prescott Channel
Abbey Creek
Mill Meads
E15
Depot
Allot Gdns
Ranelagh Prim Sch
CORPORATION ST
West Ham
Memorial Recn Gd
Crem
East London Cemy
Cycleway
NEWHAM
MANOR RD
Tredegar Wharf
Superstore
Gas Works
Lea Valley Wlk
Bromley-by-Bow
BLACKWALL TUNNEL NORTHERN APPROACH
TWELVETREES CRES
Bow Locks
The London Gas Mus
E16
Eastlea Com Sch
Star Prim Sch
Star Park
STEPHENSON ST
St Leonard's Wharf
Islay Wharf
River Lea or Lee
Bow Creek
South Bromley
Devon Wharf
ABBOTT RD
EAST INDIA DOCK RD
Canning Town
Bow Creek Mills
LOWER LEA CROSSING
Hercules Wharf
East India Dock Basin
East India
120
39
40
97
84
83
82
81
38

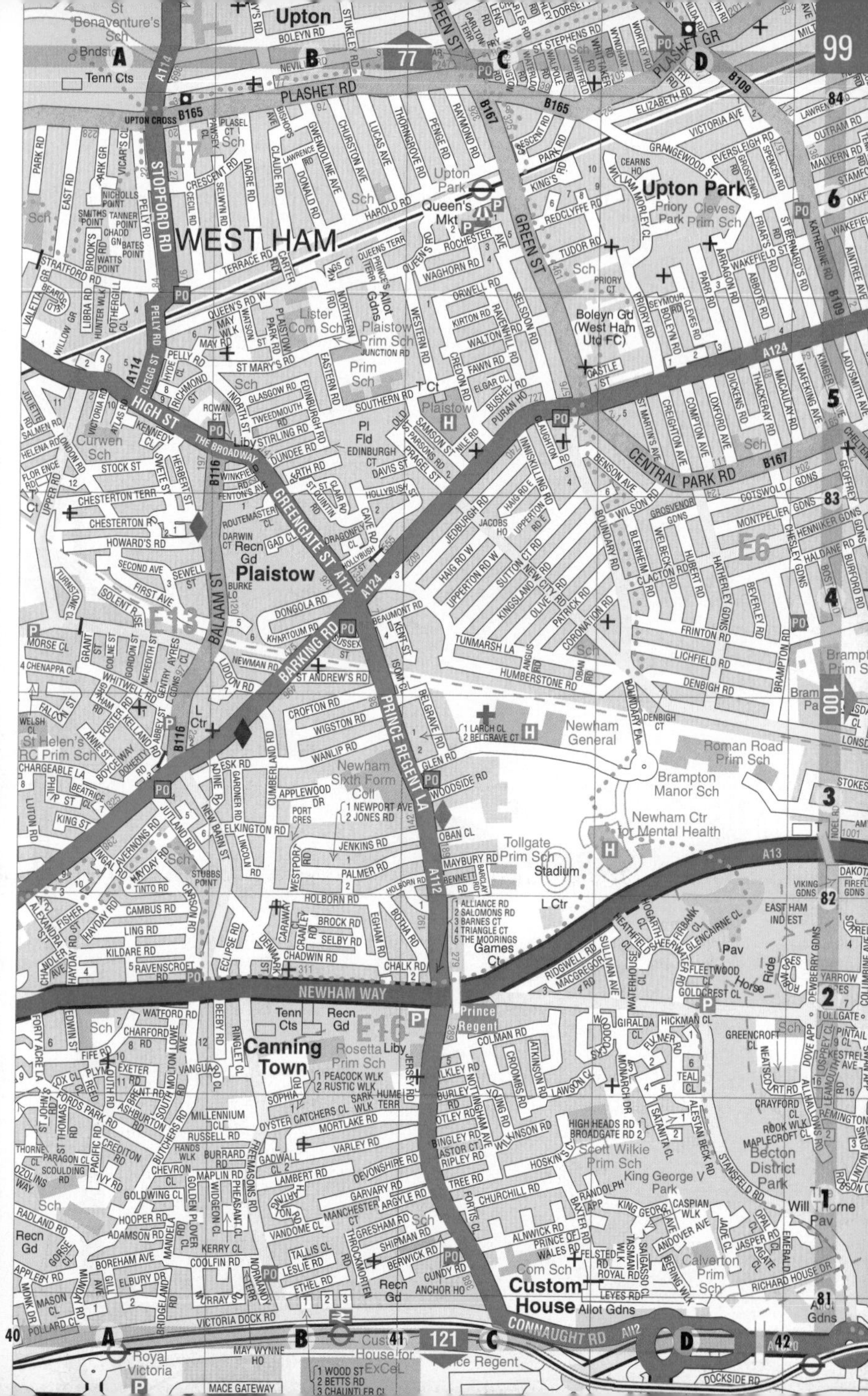
99
Upton
Upton Park
WEST HAM
Plaistow
Canning Town
Custom House
E7
E13
E6
E16
STOPFORD RD
PLASHET RD
PLASHET GR
BOLEYN RD
GREEN ST
HIGH ST
THE BROADWAY
GREENGATE ST
BARKING RD
PRINCE REGENT LA
BALAAM ST
CENTRAL PARK RD
NEWHAM WAY
CONNAUGHT RD
VICTORIA DOCK RD
UPTON CROSS
Upton Park
Queen's Mkt
Boleyn Gd (West Ham Utd FC)
Priory Park
Cleves Prim Sch
Lister Com Sch
Plaistow Prim Sch
Newham General
Roman Road Prim Sch
Brampton Manor Sch
Newham Ctr for Mental Health
Tollgate Prim Sch
Stadium
Newham Sixth Form Coll
Rosetta Prim Sch
Scott Wilkie Prim Sch
King George V Park
Becton District Park
Calverton Prim Sch
St Helen's RC Prim Sch
Curwen Sch
St Bonaventure's Sch
Prince Regent
Custom House for ExCeL
Royal Victoria
Games Ct
Allot Gdns
Recn Gd
Tenn Cts
A114
A124
A112
A13
B165
B167
B109
B116
77
100
121
40
41
42
81
82
83
84

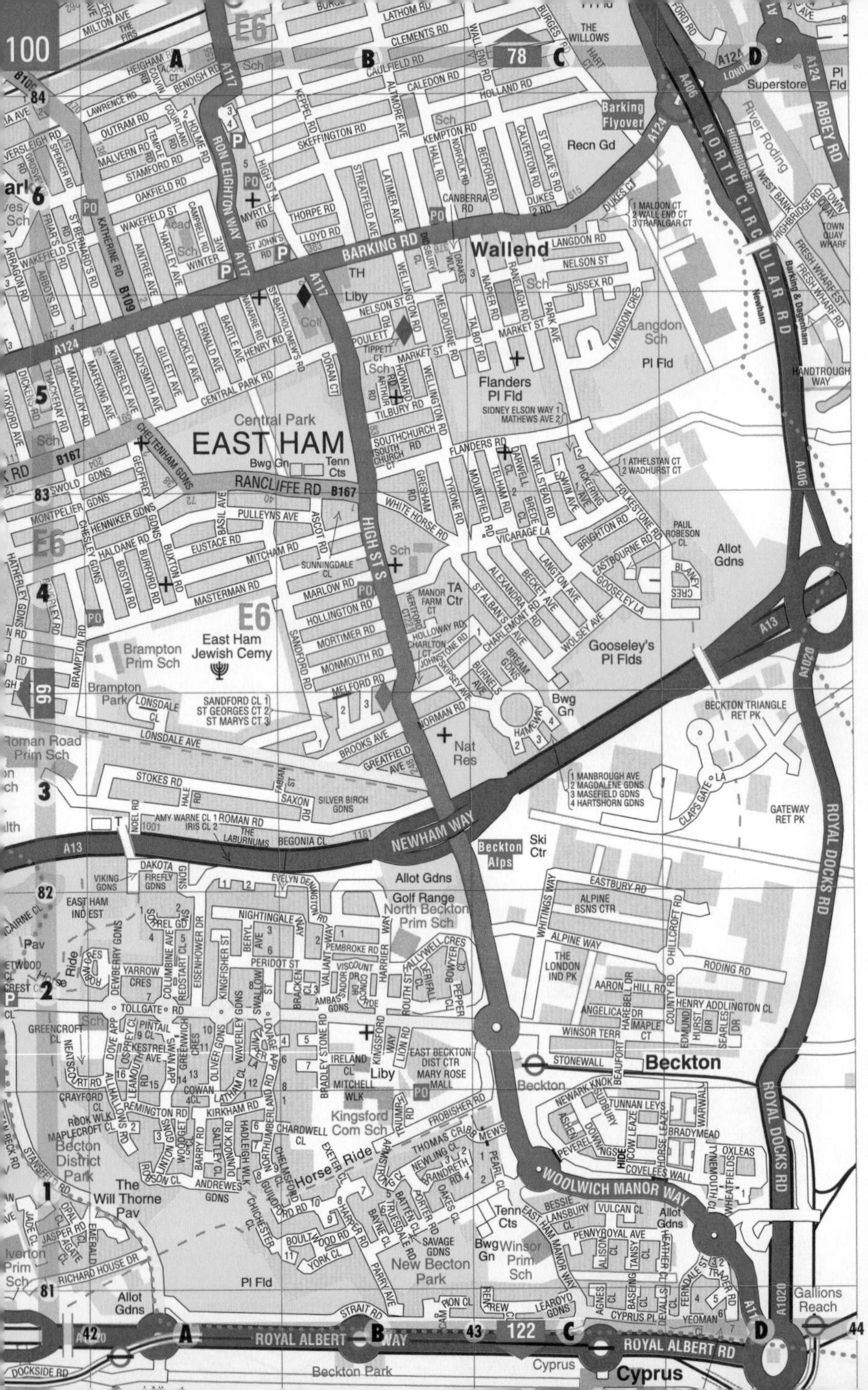

100
A
B
C
D
E6
78
EAST HAM
Central Park
Wallend
Beckton
Cyprus
Flanders Pl Fld
Langdon Sch
Pl Fld
Recn Gd
Barking Flyover
Superstore
River Roding
Allot Gdns
Gooseley's Pl Flds
Bwg Gn
Nat Res
TA Ctr
Manor Farm Ct
Beckton Triangle Ret Pk
Gateway Ret Pk
Beckton Alps
Ski Ctr
Golf Range
North Beckton Prim Sch
Alpine Bsns Ctr
The London Ind Pk
East Beckton Dist Ctr
Mary Rose Mall
Kingsford Com Sch
New Becton Park
Winsor Prim Sch
Tenn Cts
Beckton Park
Beckton District Park
The Will Thorne Pav
East Ham Ind Est
East Ham Jewish Cemy
Brampton Prim Sch
Brampton Park
Roman Road Prim Sch
Gallions Reach
Barking Rd
Ron Leighton Way
High St N
High St S
North Circular Rd
Royal Docks Rd
Newham Way
Woolwich Manor Way
Royal Albert Way
Royal Albert Rd
Abbey Rd
Katherine Rd
Rancliffe Rd
Central Park Rd
Lonsdale Ave
Stokes Rd
Roman Rd
Tollgate Rd
Horse Ride
Eastbury Rd
Alpine Way
Roding Rd
Winsor Terr
Stonewall
Dockside Rd
Richard House Dr
East Ham Manor Way
Barking & Dagenham
Newham
A124
A117
A406
A13
A1020
B167
B109
82
83
84
81
42
43
44
99
122
1
2
3
4
5
6

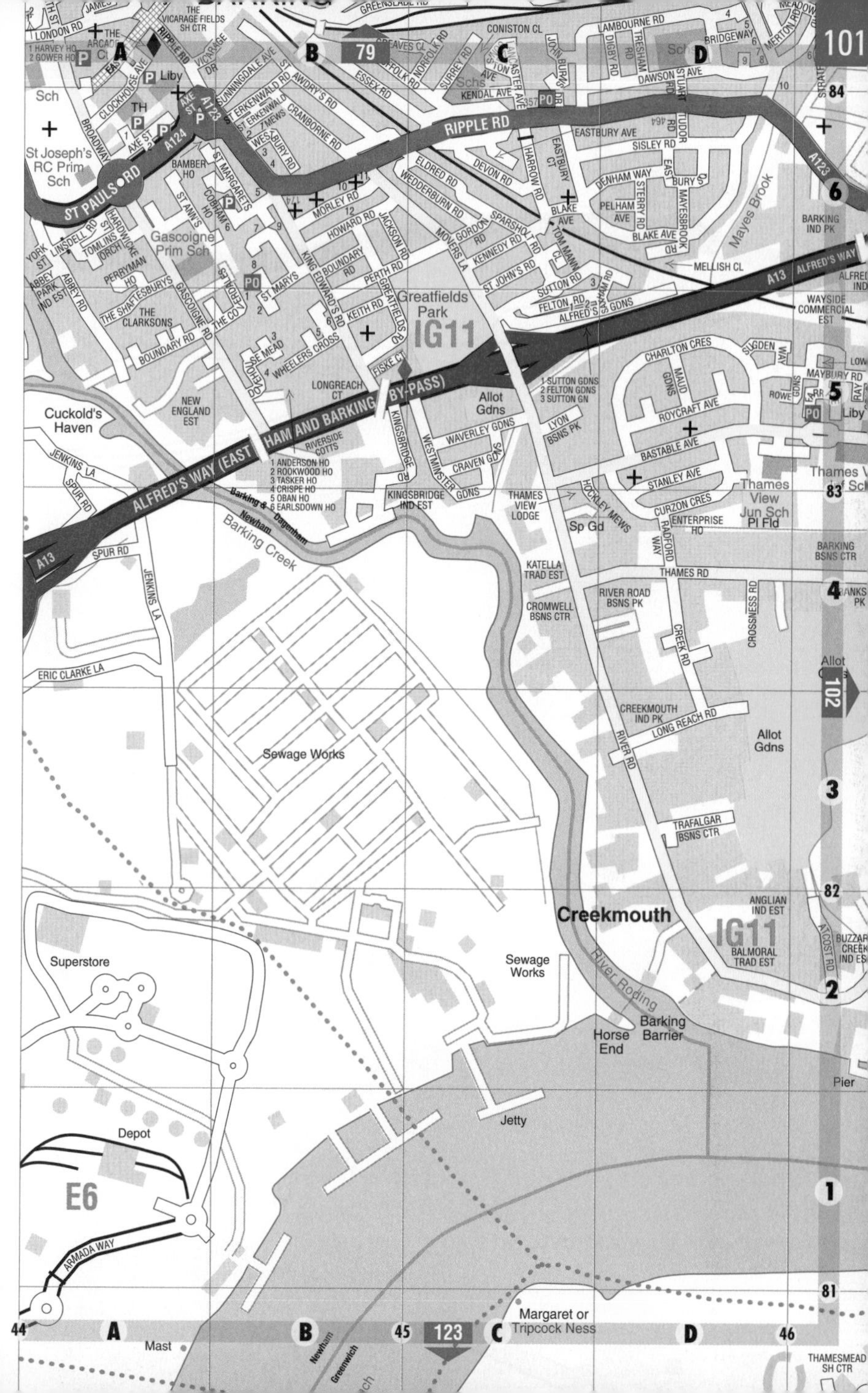

RIPPLE RD
ST PAULS RD
St Joseph's RC Prim Sch
Gascoigne Prim Sch
Greatfields Park
IG11
ALFRED'S WAY (EAST HAM AND BARKING BY-PASS)
Cuckold's Haven
Barking Creek
Sewage Works
Creekmouth
River Roding
Barking Barrier
Horse End
Jetty
Superstore
Depot
E6
ARMADA WAY
Margaret or Tripcock Ness
Mast
Thames View Jun Sch
THAMES RD
RIVER RD
LONG REACH RD
Allot Gdns
Mayes Brook
BARKING IND PK
THAMESMEAD SH CTR

79
102
123

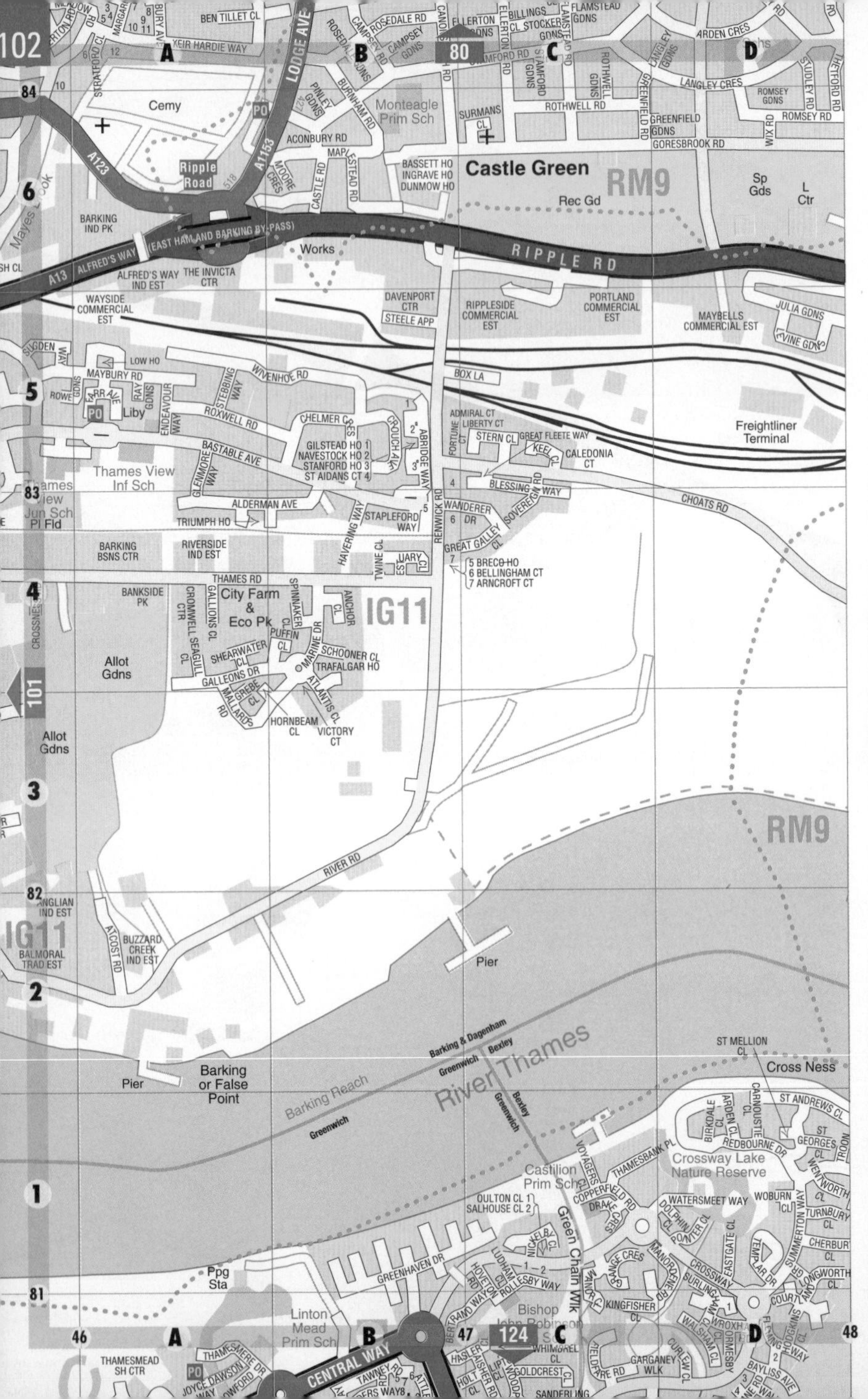
Cemy
Ripple Road
Monteagle Prim Sch
Castle Green
RM9
Rec Gd
Sp Gds
L Ctr
RIPPLE RD
ALFRED'S WAY
(EAST HAM AND BARKING BY-PASS)
Works
BARKING IND PK
ALFRED'S WAY IND EST
THE INVICTA CTR
WAYSIDE COMMERCIAL EST
DAVENPORT CTR
STEELE APP
RIPPLESIDE COMMERCIAL EST
PORTLAND COMMERCIAL EST
MAYBELLS COMMERCIAL EST
Freightliner Terminal
Thames View Inf Sch
BARKING BSNS CTR
RIVERSIDE IND EST
BANKSIDE PK
City Farm & Eco Pk
IG11
Allot Gdns
RIVER RD
ANGLIAN IND EST
BUZZARD CREEK IND EST
BALMORAL TRAD EST
Pier
Barking or False Point
Barking Reach
River Thames
Cross Ness
Crossway Lake Nature Reserve
Castilion Prim Sch
Ppg Sta
Linton Mead Prim Sch
Bishop John Robinson Sch
THAMESMEAD SH CTR
CENTRAL WAY
Green Chain Wlk
CHOATS RD
RENWICK RD
THAMES RD
80
101
124
46
47
48
84
83
82
81

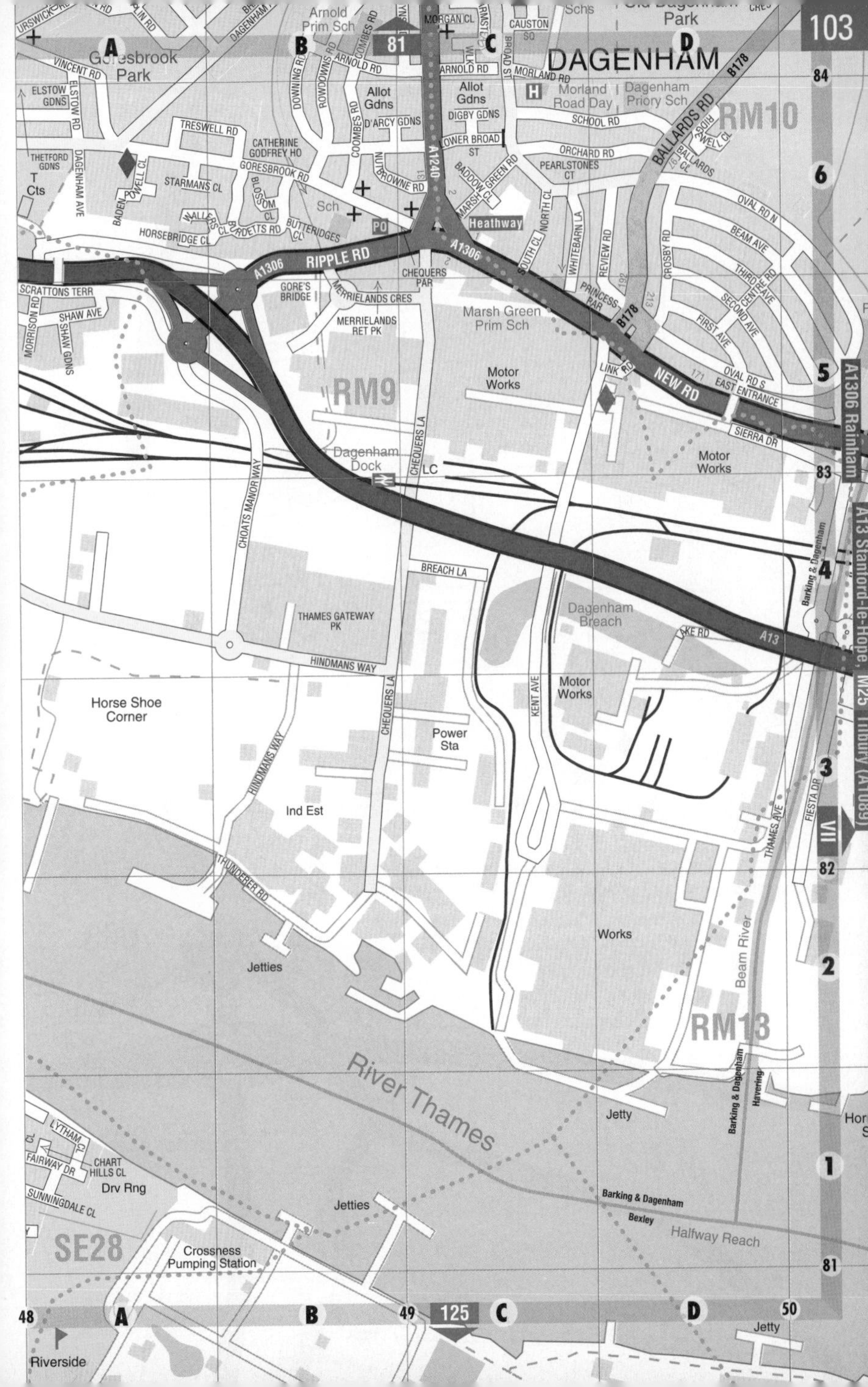
A
B
C
D
81
DAGENHAM
Goresbrook Park
Arnold Prim Sch
ARNOLD RD
MORGAN CL
CAUSTON SQ
ARNOLD RD
MORLAND RD
BROAD ST
Park
B178
84
VINCENT RD
ELSTOW GDNS
ELSTOW RD
DOWNING RD
ROWDOWNS RD
Allot Gdns
COOMBES RD
Allot Gdns
Morland Road Day
Dagenham Priory Sch
RM10
TRESWELL RD
D'ARCY GDNS
DIGBY GDNS
SCHOOL RD
BALLARDS RD
CATHERINE GODFREY HO
LOWER BROAD ST
A1240
ORCHARD RD
THETFORD GDNS
DAGENHAM AVE
GORESBROOK RD
NUTBROWNE RD
BADDOW CL
MARSH GREEN RD
PEARLSTONES CT
BALLARDS CL
6
T Cts
STARMANS CL
BADEN POWELL CL
BLOSSOM CL
Sch
NORTH CL
WHITEBARN LA
REVIEW RD
CROSBY RD
OVAL RD N
WALLERS CL
BURDETTS RD
BUTTERIDGES CL
PO
Heathway
BEAM AVE
HORSEBRIDGE CL
RIPPLE RD
A1306
A1306
SOUTH CL
THIRD AVE
CENTRE RD
CHEQUERS PAR
SCRATTONS TERR
GORE'S BRIDGE
MERRIELANDS CRES
PRINCESS PAR
SECOND AVE
MORRISON RD
SHAW AVE
SHAW GDNS
MERRIELANDS RET PK
Marsh Green Prim Sch
B178
FIRST AVE
5
A1306 Rainham
RM9
Motor Works
LINK RD
NEW RD
OVAL RD S
EAST ENTRANCE
SIERRA DR
Dagenham Dock
LC
Motor Works
83
CHOATS MANOR WAY
A13 Stanford-le-Hope, M25 Tilbury (A1089)
BREACH LA
4
Barking & Dagenham
Dagenham Breach
THAMES GATEWAY PK
A13
HINDMANS WAY
KENT AVE
Motor Works
Horse Shoe Corner
CHEQUERS LA
Power Sta
HINDMANS WAY
3
Ind Est
THAMES AVE
FIESTA DR
VII
82
THUNDERER RD
Works
Jetties
Beam River
2
RM13
River Thames
Barking & Dagenham
Havering
Jetty
LYTHAM CL
CHART HILLS CL
FAIRWAY DR
Drv Rng
1
SUNNINGDALE CL
Jetties
Barking & Dagenham
Bexley
Halfway Reach
SE28
Crossness Pumping Station
81
48
A
B
49
125
C
D
50
Jetty
Riverside

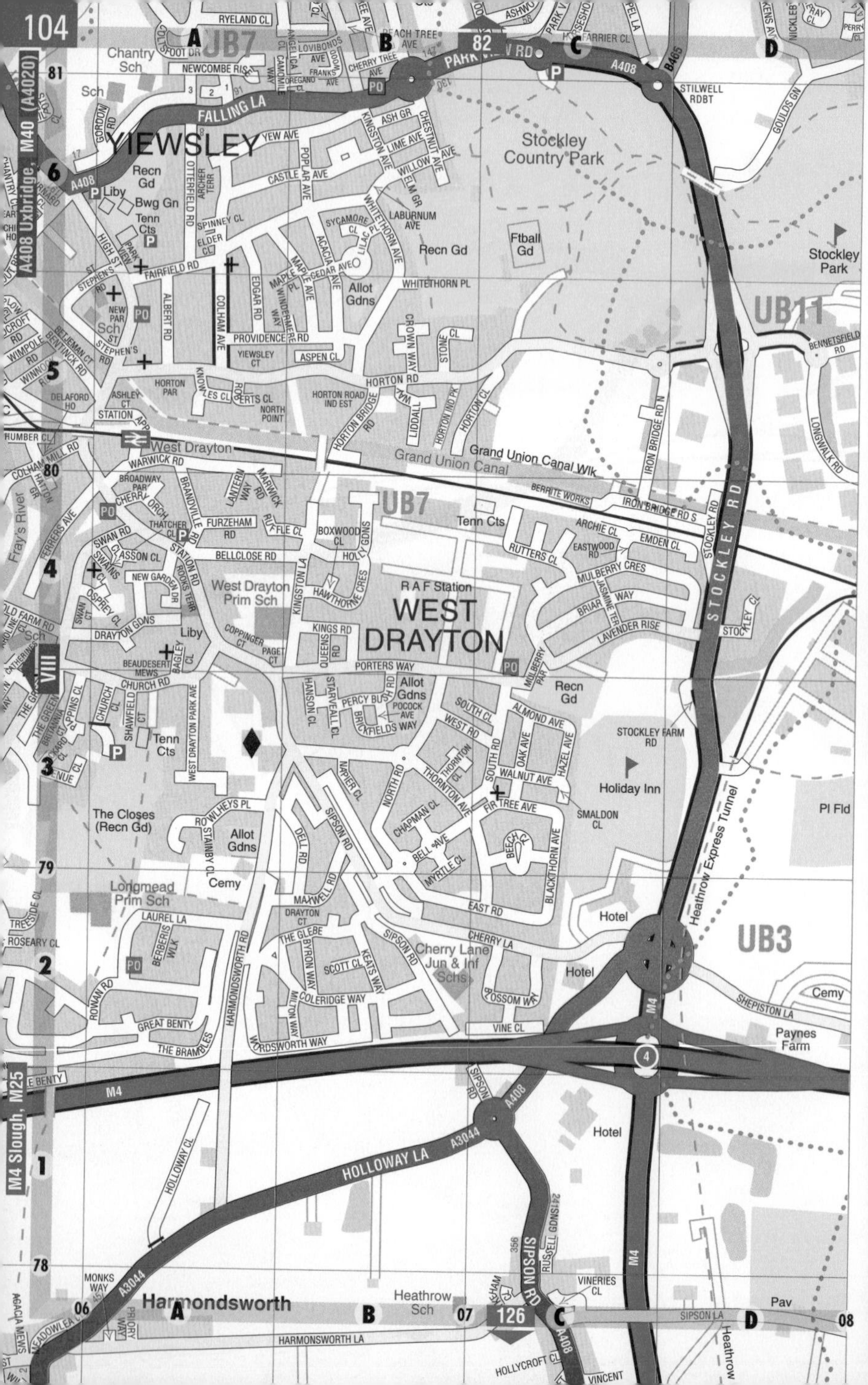

YIEWSLEY
WEST DRAYTON
Harmondsworth
Stockley Country Park
Stockley Park
UB7
UB11
UB3
M4 Slough, M25
A408 Uxbridge, M40 (A4020)
82
126
VIII
Chantry Sch
FALLING LA
PARK VIEW RD
STILWELL RDBT
HORTON RD
HORTON ROAD IND EST
West Drayton
Grand Union Canal
Grand Union Canal Wlk
R A F Station
West Drayton Prim Sch
STOCKLEY RD
STOCKLEY FARM RD
Holiday Inn
Heathrow Express Tunnel
The Closes (Recn Gd)
Longmead Prim Sch
Cherry Lane Jun & Inf Schs
HOLLOWAY LA
SIPSON RD
SIPSON LA
HARMONDSWORTH LA
SHEPISTON LA
Paynes Farm
Heathrow Sch
Heathrow
Hotel
Pl Fld
Cemy
Allot Gdns
Recn Gd
Tenn Cts
Ftball Gd
06
07
08

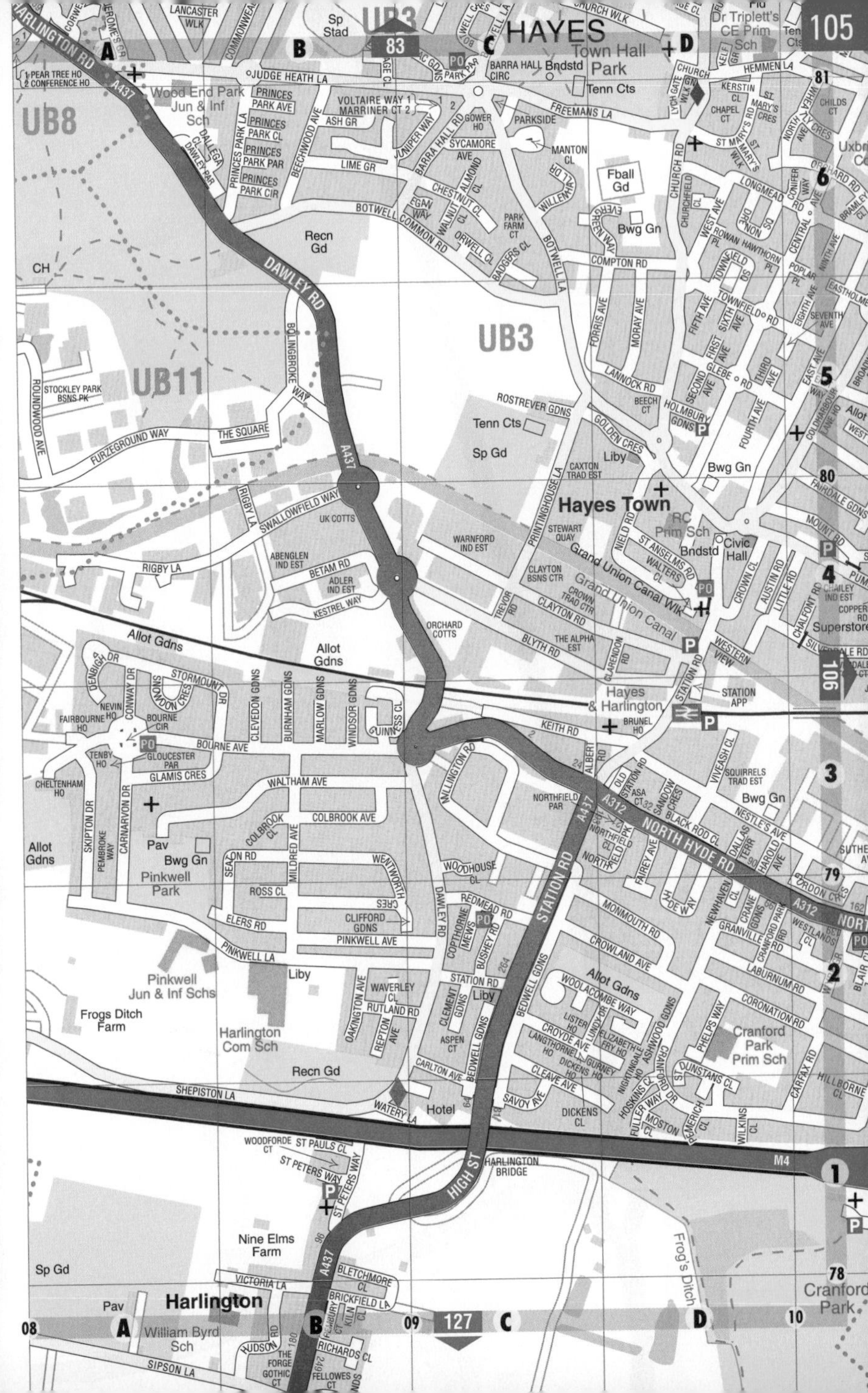
HAYES
UB3
UB8
UB11
Hayes Town
Harlington
Hayes & Harlington
Grand Union Canal
DAWLEY RD
STATION RD
NORTH HYDE RD
HIGH ST
M4
Cranford Park
Town Hall Park
Pinkwell Park
Stockley Park Bsns Pk
Harlington Com Sch
Pinkwell Jun & Inf Schs
Wood End Park Jun & Inf Sch
Dr Triplett's CE Prim Sch
Cranford Park Prim Sch
William Byrd Sch
Frogs Ditch Farm
Nine Elms Farm

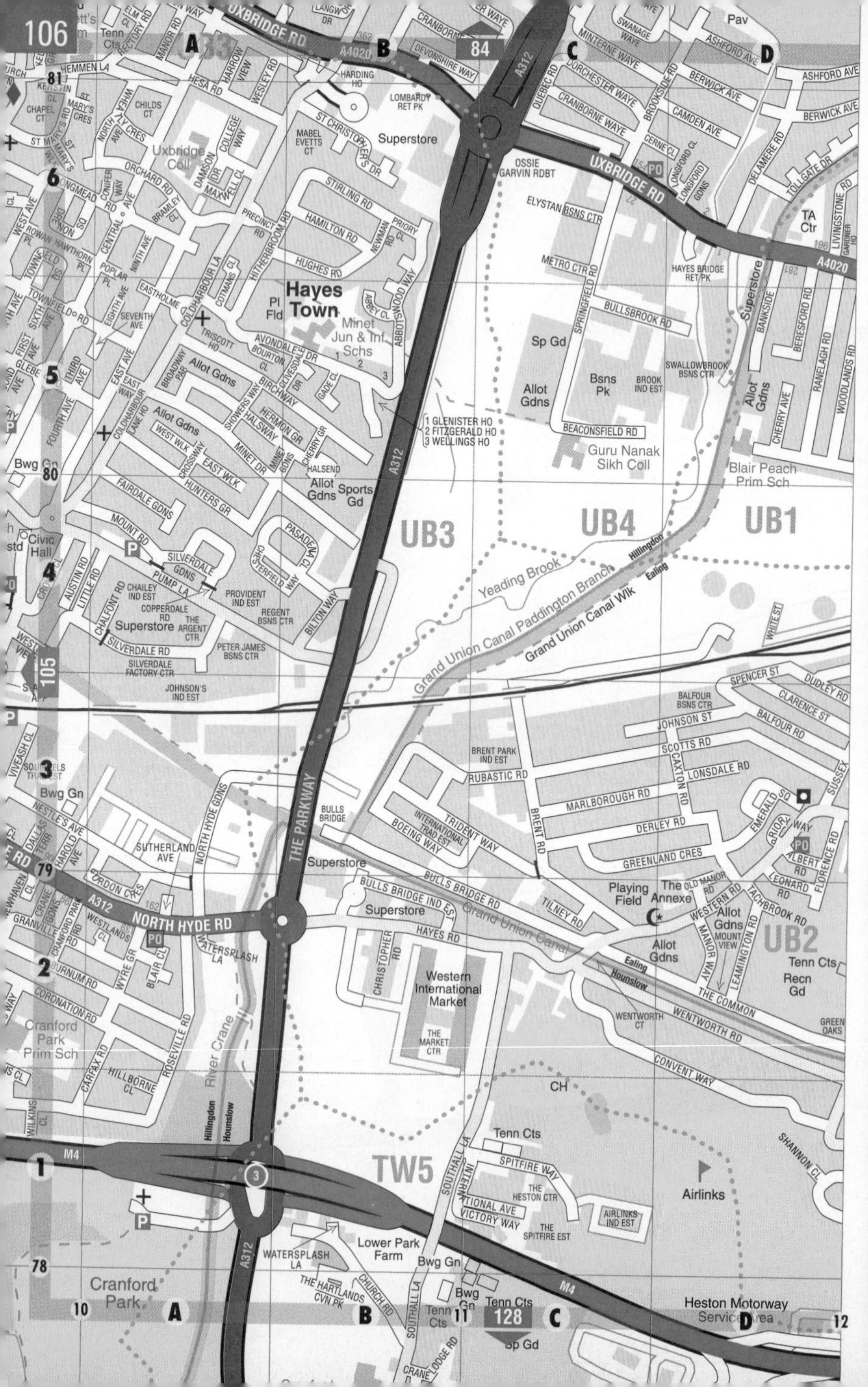

UXBRIDGE RD
A4020
84
A312
Hayes Town
Superstore
LOMBARDY RET PK
OSSIE GARVIN RDBT
ELYSTAN BSNS CTR
METRO CTR
HAYES BRIDGE RET PK
BULLSBROOK RD
SPRINGFIELD RD
Sp Gd
Allot Gdns
Bsns Pk
BROOK IND EST
SWALLOWBROOK BSNS CTR
BEACONSFIELD RD
Guru Nanak Sikh Coll
Blair Peach Prim Sch
Uxbridge Coll
Minet Jun & Inf Schs
1 GLENISTER HO
2 FITZGERALD HO
3 WELLINGS HO
UB3
UB4
UB1
UB2
TW5
Yeading Brook
Grand Union Canal Paddington Branch
Grand Union Canal Wlk
Civic Hall
Superstore
SILVERDALE RD
PROVIDENT IND EST
REGENT BSNS CTR
PETER JAMES BSNS CTR
SILVERDALE FACTORY CTR
JOHNSON'S IND EST
105
THE PARKWAY
BULLS BRIDGE
BULLS BRIDGE IND EST
Western International Market
THE MARKET CTR
HAYES RD
NORTH HYDE RD
BRENT PARK IND EST
INTERNATIONAL TRAD EST
BALFOUR BSNS CTR
Playing Field
The Annexe
Grand Union Canal
THE COMMON
WENTWORTH RD
CONVENT WAY
Tenn Cts
Recn Gd
Cranford Park Prim Sch
River Crane
M4
TW5
THE HESTON CTR
AIRLINKS IND EST
THE SPITFIRE EST
Airlinks
Lower Park Farm
THE HARTLANDS CVN PK
Cranford Park
Heston Motorway Service Area
128
Sp Gd
A
B
C
D
1
2
3
4
5
6
10
11
12

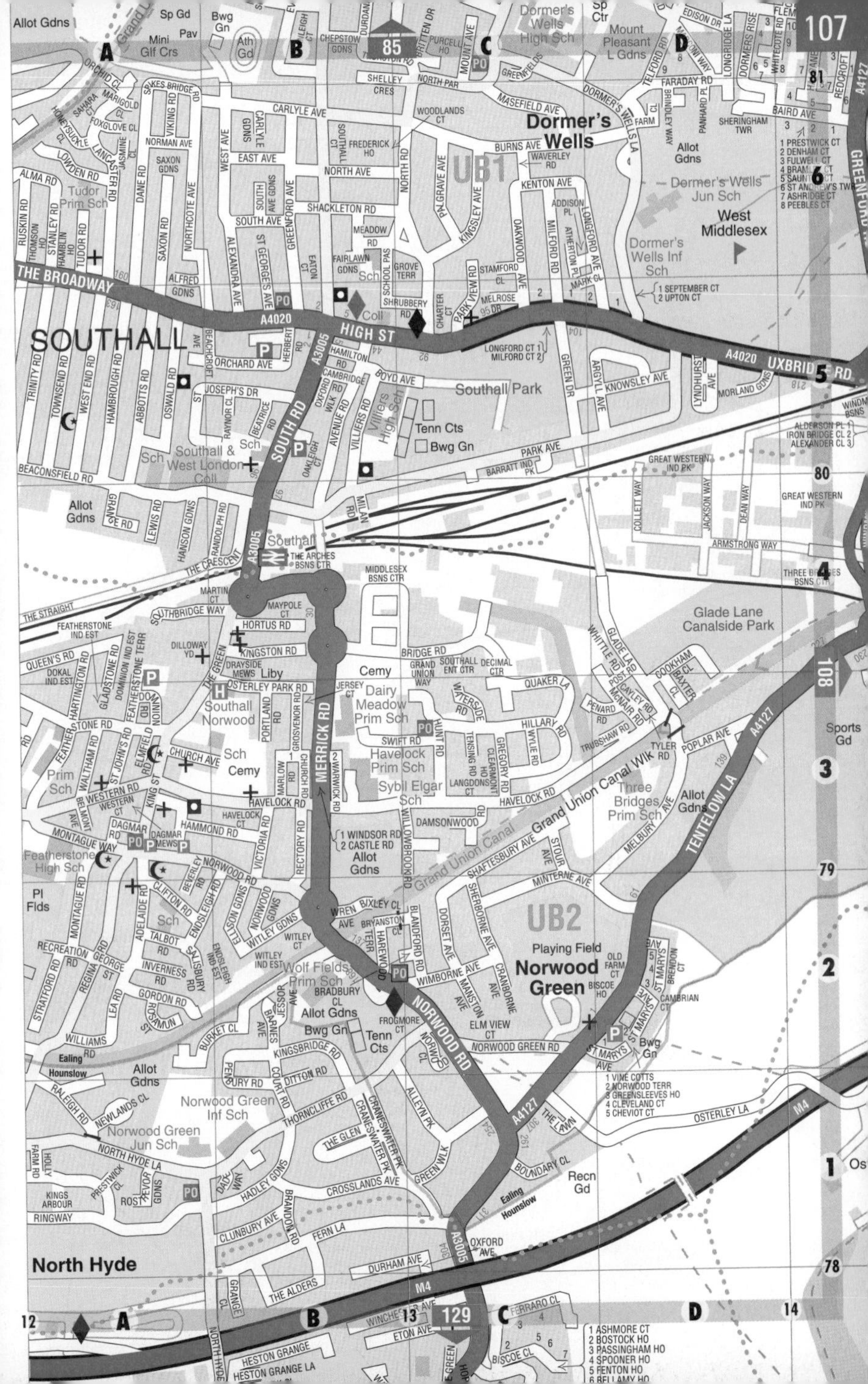
85
A
B
C
D
Dormer's Wells
UB1
SOUTHALL
THE BROADWAY
A4020
HIGH ST
UXBRIDGE RD
SOUTH RD
A3005
MERRICK RD
NORWOOD RD
A4127
TENTELOW LA
GREENFORD RD
Southall Park
Southall
Glade Lane Canalside Park
Grand Union Canal
Grand Union Canal Wlk
UB2
Norwood Green
Playing Field
North Hyde
M4
129
108
Tudor Prim Sch
Dormer's Wells High Sch
Dormer's Wells Jun Sch
Dormer's Wells Inf Sch
West Middlesex
Villiers High Sch
Southall & West London Coll
Dairy Meadow Prim Sch
Havelock Prim Sch
Sybil Elgar Sch
Three Bridges Prim Sch
Featherstone High Sch
Wolf Fields Prim Sch
Norwood Green Inf Sch
Norwood Green Jun Sch
Southall Norwood
Mount Pleasant L Gdns
Allot Gdns
Cemy
Liby
Tenn Cts
Bwg Gn
Recn Gd
Sports Gd
Pl Flds
Ealing
Hounslow
1 PRESTWICK CT
2 DENHAM CT
3 FULWELL CT
4 BRAMLEY CT
5 SAUNTON CT
6 ST ANDREW'S TWR
7 ASHRIDGE CT
8 PEEBLES CT
1 SEPTEMBER CT
2 UPTON CT
LONGFORD CT 1
MILFORD CT 2
ALDERSON PL 1
IRON BRIDGE CL 2
ALEXANDER CL 3
1 WINDSOR RD
2 CASTLE RD
1 VINE COTTS
2 NORWOOD TERR
3 GREENSLEEVES HO
4 CLEVELAND CT
5 CHEVIOT CT
1 ASHMORE CT
2 BOSTOCK HO
3 PASSINGHAM HO
4 SPOONER HO
5 FENTON HO
6 BELLAMY HO
1
2
3
4
5
6
12
13
14
78
79
80
81

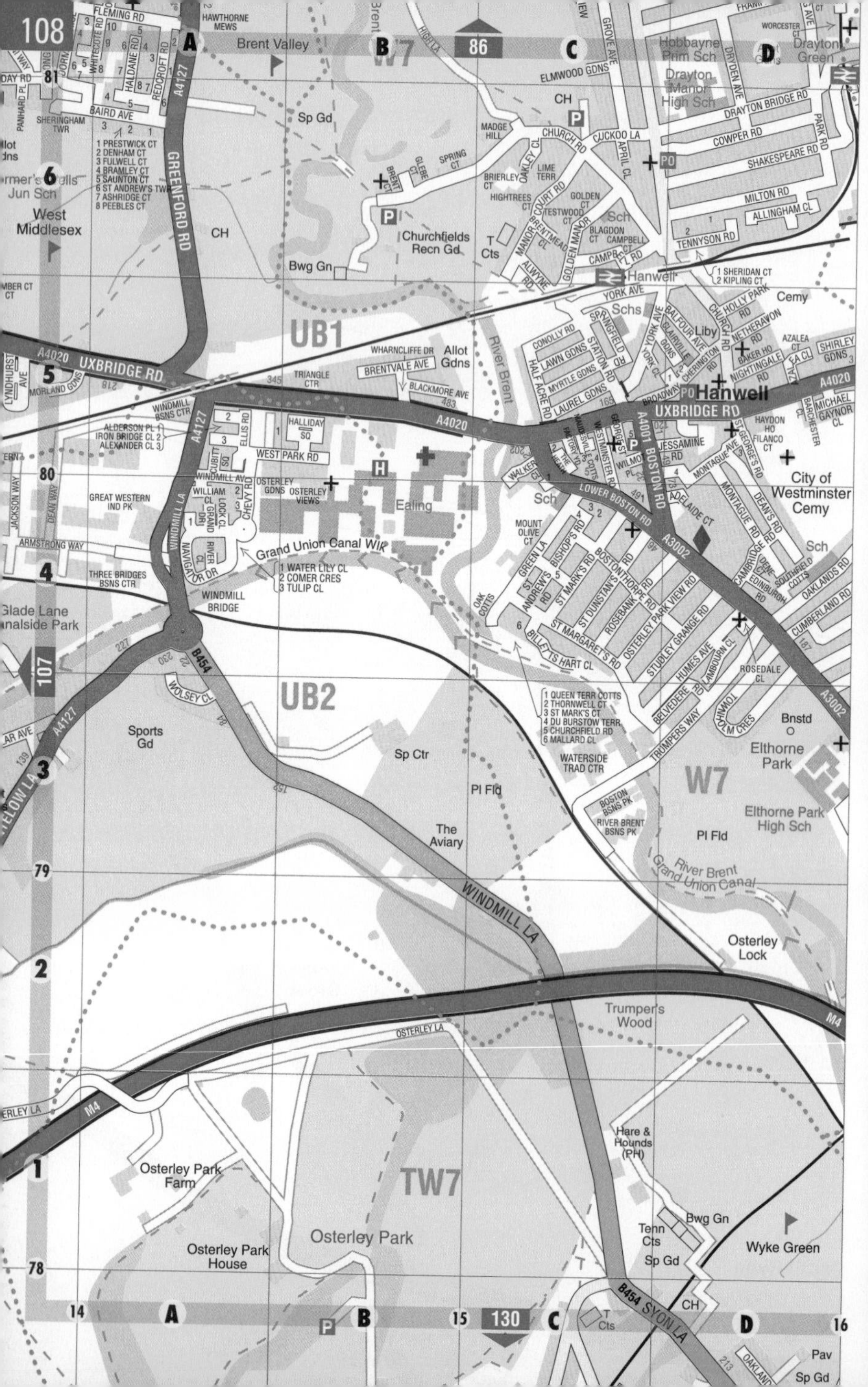
108
A
B
C
D
86
Brent Valley
W7
HAWTHORNE MEWS
FLEMING RD
WHITECOTE RD
HALDANE RD
REDCROFT RD
BAIRD AVE
PANHARD PL
SHERINGHAM TWR
81
1 PRESTWICK CT
2 DENHAM CT
3 FULWELL CT
4 BRAMLEY CT
5 SAUNTON CT
6 ST ANDREW'S TWR
7 ASHRIDGE CT
8 PEEBLES CT
6
West Middlesex
CH
GREENFORD RD
A4127
Sp Gd
HIGH LA
ELMWOOD GDNS
GROVE AVE
Hobbayne Prim Sch
Drayton Manor High Sch
DRYDEN AVE
WORCESTER CT
Drayton Green
DRAYTON BRIDGE RD
COWPER RD
SHAKESPEARE RD
PARK RD
MILTON RD
ALLINGHAM CL
TENNYSON RD
1 SHERIDAN CT
2 KIPLING CT
MADGE HILL
CHURCH RD
CUCKOO LA
APRIL CL
PO
SPRING CT
GLEBE CT
BRENT CT
BRIERLEY CT
OAKLEY CL
LIME TERR
HIGHTREES CT
COURT RD
GOLDEN CT
TESTWOOD CT
BRENTMEAD CL
MANOR CT
GOLDEN MANOR
BLAGDON CT
CAMPBELL CT
CAMPBELL RD
ALWYNE RD
Churchfields Recn Gd
T Cts
Bwg Gn
Sch
Hanwell
YORK AVE
Schs
HOLLY PARK RD
Cemy
NETHERAVON RD
AZALEA CT
SHIRLEY GDNS
BAKER HO
NIGHTINGALE RD
SEA CL
UB1
A4020
UXBRIDGE RD
LYNDHURST AVE
5
MORLAND GDNS
218
345
TRIANGLE CTR
WHARNCLIFFE DR
BRENTVALE AVE
BLACKMORE AVE
483
Allot Gdns
River Brent
CONOLLY RD
SPRINGFIELD RD
HALF ACRE RD
LAWN GDNS
STATION RD
MYRTLE GDNS
LAUREL GDNS
YORK CL
BALFOUR AVE
CLAIRVILLE GDNS
CHERINGTON RD
Liby
BROADWAY
Hanwell
MICHAEL GAYNOR CL
BARCHESTER ST
HAYDON HO
FILANCO CT
WINDMILL BSNS CTR
ALDERSON PL
IRON BRIDGE CL
ALEXANDER CL
ELLIS RD
HALLIDAY SQ
WEST PARK RD
H
Ealing
WINDMILL AV
OSTERLEY GDNS
OSTERLEY VIEWS
WILLIAM CL
LOCK CL
CHEVY RD
GRAND DR
CUBITT SQ
WINDMILL LA
GREAT WESTERN IND PK
JACKSON WAY
DEAN WAY
80
ARMSTRONG WAY
RIVER CL
NAVIGATOR DR
Grand Union Canal Wlk
1 WATER LILY CL
2 COMER CRES
3 TULIP CL
THREE BRIDGES BSNS CTR
WINDMILL BRIDGE
4
Glade Lane Canalside Park
WALKER CL
GEORGE ST
WESTMINSTER RD
WILMOT PL
JESSAMINE RD
A4001 BOSTON RD
LOWER BOSTON RD
ADELAIDE CT
MONTAGUE AVE
ST GEORGE'S RD
City of Westminster Cemy
MONTAGUE RD
DEAN'S RD
Sch
MOUNT OLIVE CT
BISHOP'S RD
GREEN LA
ST ANDREW'S RD
ST MARK'S RD
BOSTON RD
ST DUNSTAN'S RD
HANTHORPE RD
ROSEBANK RD
OSTERLEY PARK VIEW RD
STUDLEY GRANGE RD
A3002
CAMBRIDGE RD
DENE CT
EDINBURGH RD
SOUTHFIELD COTTS
OAKLANDS RD
CUMBERLAND RD
OAK COTTS
ST MARGARET'S RD
BILLETS HART CL
HUMES AVE
LAMBOURN CL
ROSEDALE CL
187
107
227
250
B454
WOLSEY CL
UB2
1 QUEEN TERR COTTS
2 THORNWELL CT
3 ST MARK'S CT
4 DU BURSTOW TERR
5 CHURCHFIELD RD
6 MALLARD CL
BELVEDERE RD
TRUMPERS WAY
HOLM CRES
Bnstd
Elthorne Park
Sports Gd
Sp Ctr
WATERSIDE TRAD CTR
W7
3
139
Pl Fld
BOSTON BSNS PK
RIVER BRENT BSNS PK
Elthorne Park High Sch
Pl Fld
The Aviary
152
79
WINDMILL LA
River Brent
Grand Union Canal
Osterley Lock
2
M4
Trumper's Wood
OSTERLEY LA
Hare & Hounds (PH)
1
Osterley Park Farm
TW7
Bwg Gn
Tenn Cts
Sp Gd
Wyke Green
Osterley Park
Osterley Park House
78
B454 SYON LA
CH
14
15
130
16
T Cts
213
OAKLAND
Pav
Sp Gd

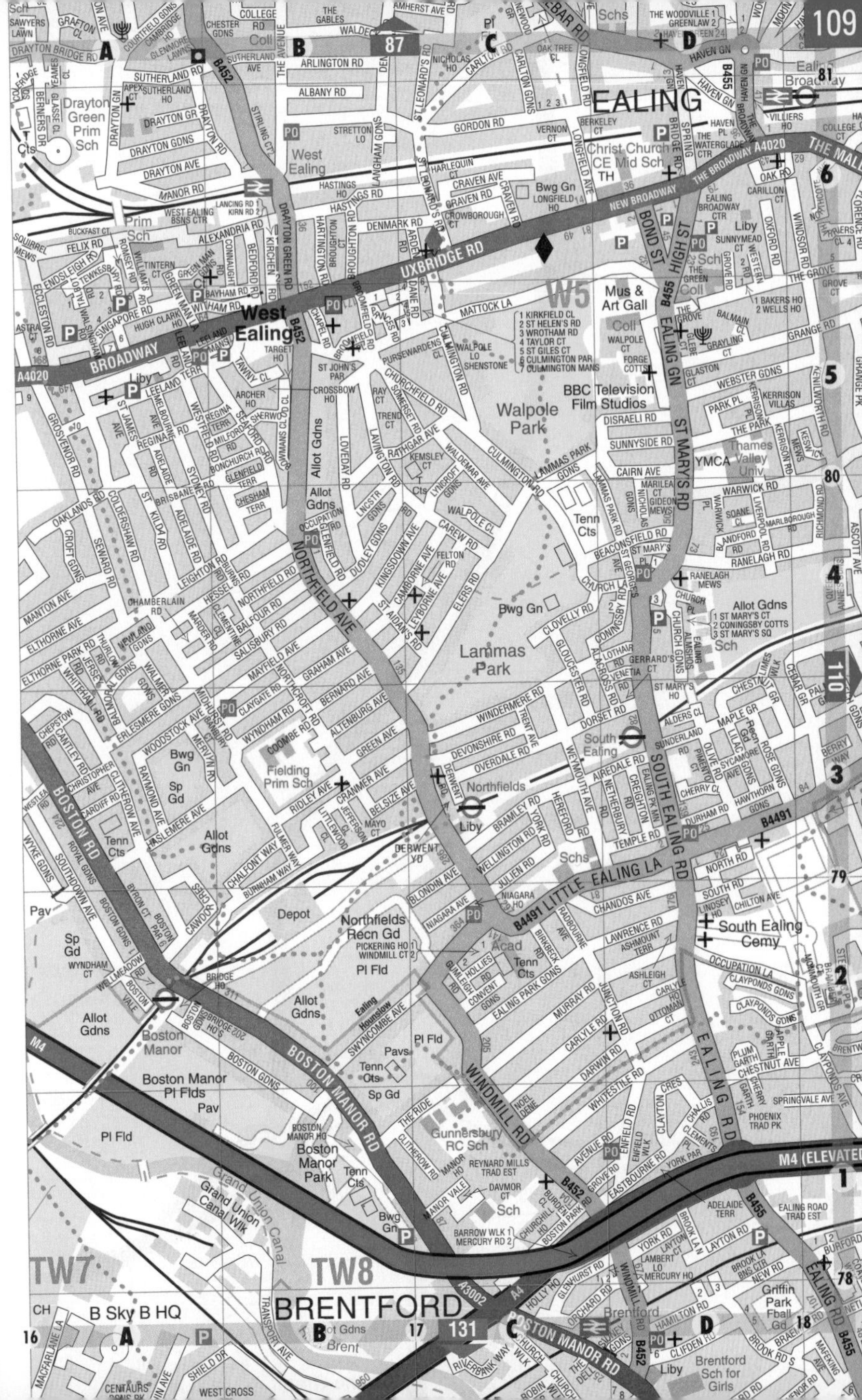

EALING
West Ealing
BRENTFORD
W5
TW7
TW8
UXBRIDGE RD
BROADWAY
A4020
NEW BROADWAY
THE BROADWAY A4020
THE MALL
B452
B455
B4491
A3002
A4
M4
M4 (ELEVATED)
NORTHFIELD AVE
DRAYTON GREEN RD
BOSTON RD
BOSTON MANOR RD
WINDMILL RD
SOUTH EALING RD
ST MARYS RD
EALING RD
LITTLE EALING LA
HIGH ST
BOND ST
EALING GN
Walpole Park
Lammas Park
BBC Television Film Studios
Mus & Art Gall
Christ Church CE Mid Sch
Thames Valley Univ
YMCA
Drayton Green Prim Sch
Fielding Prim Sch
Gunnersbury RC Sch
Brentford Sch for Girls
Northfields Recn Gd
Boston Manor Pl Flds
Boston Manor Park
South Ealing Cemy
Griffin Park Fball Gd
B Sky B HQ
Grand Union Canal
Grand Union Canal Wlk
Depot
Derwent Yd
Northfields
South Ealing
Boston Manor
Brentford
Phoenix Trad Pk
Ealing Road Trad Est
Reynard Mills Trad Est
Ealing Hounslow
87
131
110
A
B
C
D
1
2
3
4
5
6
16
17
18
78
79
80
81

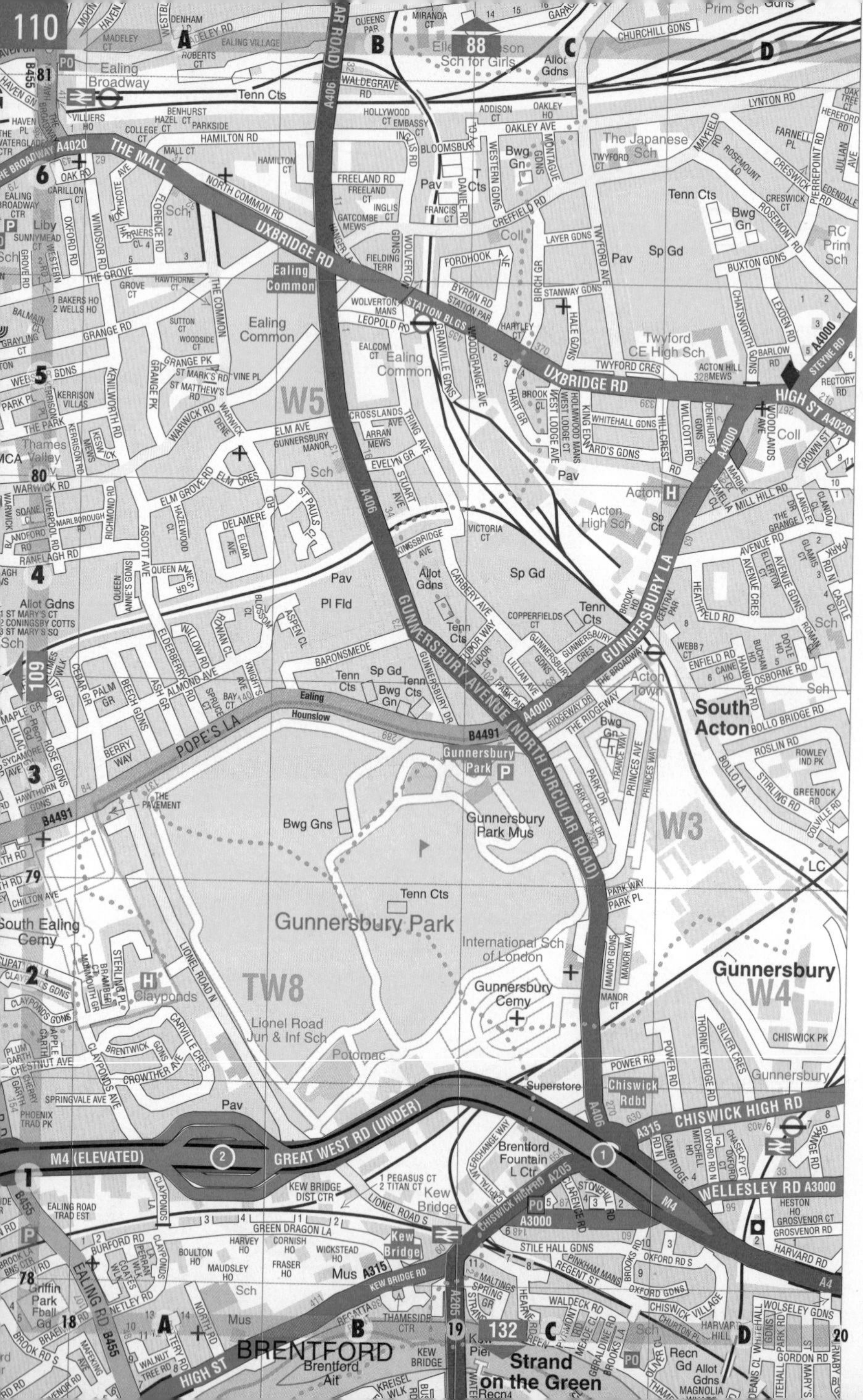

88
109
132
Ealing Broadway
Ealing Common
W5
W3
W4
TW8
Gunnersbury Park
Gunnersbury Park Mus
Gunnersbury Cemy
International Sch of London
South Acton
Acton Town
Acton High Sch
Twyford CE High Sch
The Japanese Sch
Gunnersbury
Chiswick Rdbt
Brentford Fountain L Ctr
Kew Bridge
BRENTFORD
Brentford Ait
Strand on the Green
South Ealing Cemy
Claypond
Lionel Road Jun & Inf Sch
Griffin Park Fball Gd
Thames Valley Univ
UXBRIDGE RD
THE MALL
GUNNERSBURY AVENUE (NORTH CIRCULAR ROAD)
GUNNERSBURY LA
POPE'S LA
GREAT WEST RD (UNDER)
M4 (ELEVATED)
CHISWICK HIGH RD
WELLESLEY RD A3000
KEW BRIDGE RD
EALING RD
HIGH ST
HIGH ST A4020
A406
A4000
A4020
B4491
A315
A205
B455

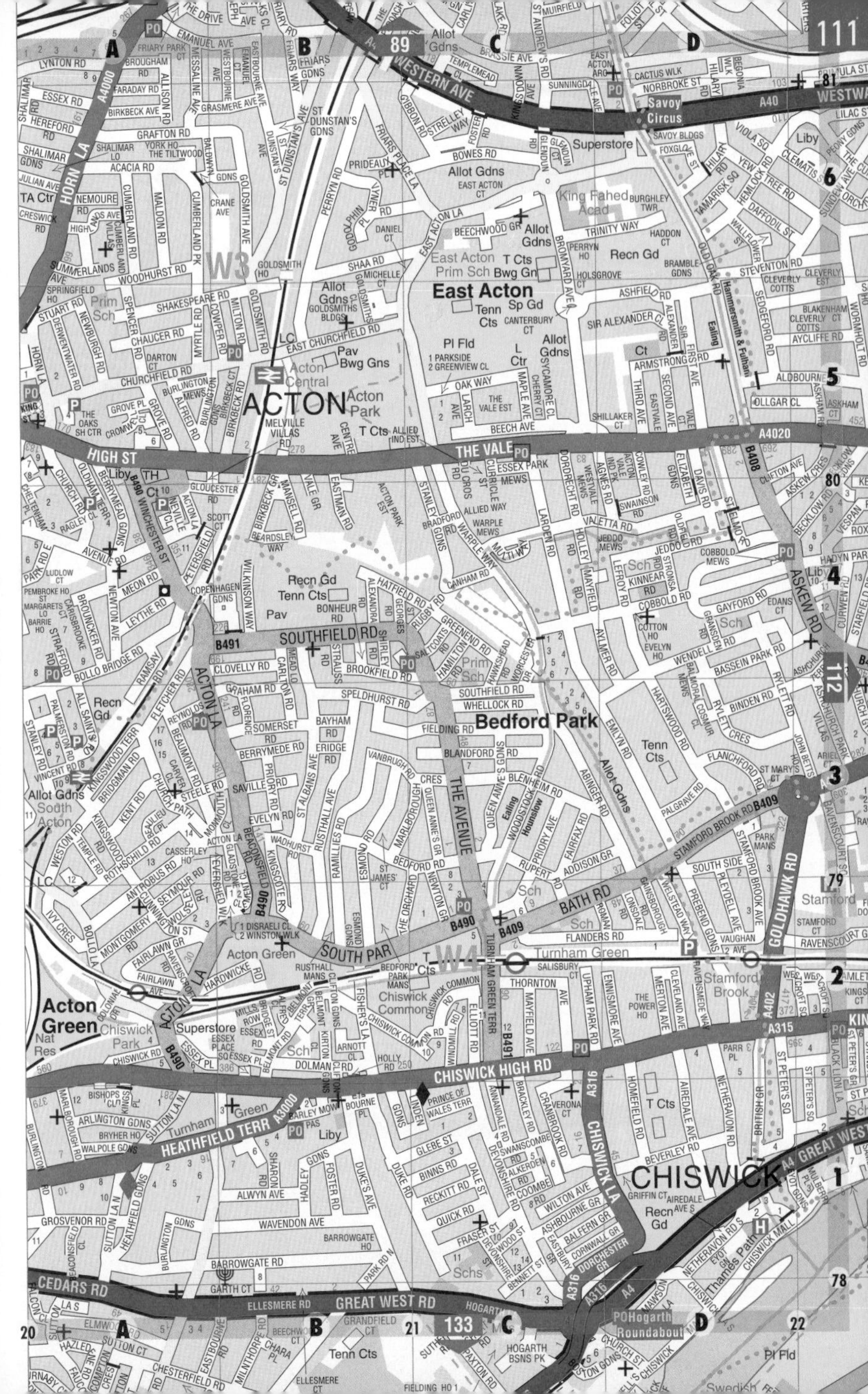

A
B
C
D
89
WESTERN AVE
A40
WESTWAY
Savoy Circus
HORN LA
A4000
EMANUEL AVE
FRIARY PARK CT
LYNTON RD
BROUGHAM RD
FARADAY RD
ESSEX RD
HEREFORD RD
BIRKBECK AVE
GRASMERE AVE
GRAFTON RD
SHALIMAR GDNS
ACACIA RD
JULIAN AVE
TA Ctr
NEMOURE RD
CRESWICK RD
CUMBERLAND PK
MALDON RD
CRANE AVE
GOLDSMITH AVE
W3
SUMMERLANDS AVE
SPRINGFIELD HO
WOODHURST RD
SHAKESPEARE RD
STUART RD
DERWENTWATER RD
NEWBURGH RD
SPENCER RD
CHAUCER RD
MYRTLE RD
COWPER RD
MILTON RD
GOLDSMITH RD
Prim Sch
DARTON CT
CHURCHFIELD RD
BURLINGTON MEWS
ALFRED RD
BIRKBECK RD
GROVE PL
GROVE RD
THE OAKS SH CTR
KING ST
ACTON
Acton Central
Acton Park
LC
EAST CHURCHFIELD RD
Pav
Bwg Gns
FRIARS WAY
FRIARS GDNS
ST DUNSTAN'S AVE
ST DUNSTAN'S GDNS
PERRYN RD
Allot Gdns
GIBBON RD
STRELLEY WAY
FOSTER RD
TEMPLEMEAD CL
BRASSIE AVE
KINGS DOWN AVE
ST ANDREW'S RD
EAST ACTON ARC
CACTUS WLK
NORBROKE ST
HILARY RD
BEGONIA WLK
PRIMULA ST
SUNNINGDALE AVE
GLENDUN RD
GLENDUN CT
Superstore
SAVOY BLDGS
FOXGLOVE ST
VIOLA SQ
Liby
LILAC ST
PEONY GDNS
CLEMATIS ST
SUNDEW AVE
BOWES RD
PRIDEAUX PL
FRIARS PLACE LA
EAST ACTON CT
King Fahed Acad
BURGHLEY TWR
TRINITY WAY
HADDON CT
Recn Gd
BRAMBLE GDNS
TAMARISK SQ
YEW TREE RD
HEMLOCK RD
DAFFODIL ST
WALLFLOWER ST
STEVENTON RD
CLEVERLY EST
CLEVERLY COTTS
EAST ACTON LA
BEECHWOOD GR
DANIEL CT
East Acton Prim Sch
T Cts
Bwg Gn
SHAA RD
MICHELLE CT
GOLDSMITHS BLDGS
East Acton
Tenn Cts
Sp Gd
CANTERBURY CT
BROMYARD AVE
PERRYN HO
HOLSGROVE CT
ASHFIELD RD
SIR ALEXANDER CL
ALEXANDER RD
OLD OAK RD
Hammersmith & Fulham
Ealing
SEDGEFORD RD
BLAKENHAM CT
CLEVERLY COTTS
AYCLIFFE RD
WORMHOLT RD
Pl Fld
1 PARKSIDE
2 GREENVIEW CL
L Ctr
Allot Gdns
SYCAMORE CL
OAK WAY
LARCH AVE
MAPLE AVE
CHERRY CL
THE VALE EST
Ct
ARMSTRONG RD
THIRD AVE
SECOND AVE
FIRST AVE
EASTVALE
VALE CT
SHILLAKER CT
ALDBOURNE RD
OLLGAR CL
ASKHAM RD
ASKHAM CT
BEECH AVE
MELVILLE VILLAS RD
CENTRE AVE
T Cts
ALLIED IND EST
THE VALE
A4020
B408
HIGH ST
Liby
TH
Ct
B490
WINCHESTER ST
GLOUCESTER RD
BIRKBECK GR
MANSELL RD
VALE GR
EASTMAN RD
ACTON PARK EST
DU CROS RD
CURRICLE ST
ESSEX PARK MEWS
ALLIED WAY
WARPLE MEWS
DORDRECHT RD
WESTVALE MEWS
AGNES RD
ACTON VALE IND PK
COWLEY RD
SWAINSON RD
ELIZABETH GDNS
DAVIS RD
ST ELMO RD
CLIFTON AVE
ASKEW CRES
BECKLOW RD
VESPAN RD
ROXWELL RD
80
CHURCH RD
OLDHAM TER
BERRYMEAD GDNS
CHELTENHAM PL
RAGLEY CL
NEVILLE CL
ACTON LA
SCOTT CT
PETERSFIELD RD
BEARDSLEY WAY
STANLEY GDNS
BRADFORD RD
WARPLE WAY
VALETTA RD
MUTI WAY
LARDEN RD
HOLLEY RD
JEDDO MEWS
JEDDO RD
COBBOLD MEWS
HADYN PARK RD
AVENUE RD
PARK RD E
LUDLOW CT
MEON RD
NEWTON AVE
PEMBROKE HO
ST MARGARETS LO
BARRIE HO
BROUCKER RD
CARISBROOKE
STRAFFORD RD
LEYTHE RD
COPENHAGEN GDNS
WILKINSON WAY
Recn Gd
Tenn Cts
Pav
BONHEUR RD
HATFIELD RD
ALEXANDRA RD
GEORGES RD
RUGBY RD
CANHAM RD
MAYFIELD RD
LEFROY RD
STRONSA RD
KINNEAR RD
COBBOLD RD
GAYFORD RD
EDANS CT
ASKEW RD
CURWEN RD
STARFIELD RD
4
BOLLO BRIDGE RD
RAMSAY RD
B491
SOUTHFIELD RD
STRAUSS RD
SHIRLEY RD
GREENEND RD
SALTCOATS RD
HAWKSHEAD RD
WORCESTER RD
AYLMER RD
COTTON HO
EVELYN HO
GRANSDEN RD
WENDELL RD
BASSEIN PARK RD
ASHCHURCH TER
112
CLOVELLY RD
CARLTON RD
MEAD RD
BROOKFIELD RD
HAMILTON RD
Prim Sch
SOUTHFIELD RD
WHELLOCK RD
HARTSWOOD RD
BALMORAL MEWS
COSMUR CL
RYLETT RD
BINDEN RD
ASHCHURCH PARK VILLAS
Recn Gd
ALL SAINTS RD
PALMERSTON RD
STANLEY RD
ACTON LA
GRAHAM RD
FLORENCE RD
SPELDHURST RD
FIELDING RD
Bedford Park
EMLYN RD
RYLETT CRES
SOMERSET RD
BAYHAM RD
ERIDGE RD
BLANDFORD RD
Tenn Cts
JOHN BETTS HO
KINGSWOOD TERR
BRIDGMAN RD
REYNOLDS RD
BEAUMONT RD
BERRYMEDE RD
PRIORY RD
VANBRUGH RD
QUEEN ANNE'S GDNS
ABINGER RD
FLANCHFORD RD
ST MARY'S CT
ARIEL CT
3
VINCENT RD
CARVER CL
STEELE RD
SAVILLE RD
ST ALBANS AVE
RUSTHALL AVE
CRES
THE AVENUE
BLENHEIM RD
Ealing
Hounslow
WOODSTOCK RD
PRIORY AVE
FAIRFAX RD
Allot Gdns
PALGRAVE RD
STAMFORD BROOK RD
B409
RAVENSCOURT SQ
Allot Gdns
South Acton
WESTON RD
KENT RD
CHURCH PATH
MONMOUTH CL
BEACONSFIELD RD
EVELYN RD
RAMILLIES RD
QUEEN ANNE'S GR
MARLBOROUGH CRES
KINGSWOOD RD
ROTHSCHILD RD
TEMPLE RD
ACTON LA HO
CASSERLEY HO
GLADSTONE RD
EVERSHED WLK
WADHURST RD
ESMOND RD
BEDFORD RD
ADDISON GR
RUPERT RD
SOUTH SIDE
PLEYDELL AVE
PARK MANS
GOLDHAWK RD
79
Stamford
LC
ANTROBUS RD
SEYMOUR RD
KINGSCOTE RD
ST JAMES' CT
THE ORCHARD
NEWTON GR
BATH RD
Sch
ROMAN RD
LONSDALE RD
GAINSBOROUGH RD
WELSTEAD WAY
PREBEND GDNS
STAMFORD BROOK AVE
IVY CRES
BOLLO LA
MONTGOMERY RD
CUNNINGTON ST
WOLSEY RD
1 DISRAELI CL
2 WINSTON WLK
ESMOND GDNS
B490
B409
FLANDERS RD
VAUGHAN AVE
STAMFORD CT
RAVENSCOURT GDNS
FAIRLAWN GR
RAVENSCOURT RD
Acton Green
SOUTH PAR
W4
TURNHAM GREEN TERR
Turnham Green
SALISBURY CT
2
FAIRLAWN AVE
HARDWICKE RD
RUSTHALL MANS
BEDFORD PARK MANS
T Cts
THORNTON AVE
UPHAM PARK RD
ENNISMORE AVE
MERTON AVE
CLEVELAND AVE
RAVENSMEDE WAY
Stamford Brook
WEST CROFT SQ
HAMLET GDNS
KINGS CT
Acton Green
Nat Res
COLONIAL DR
ACTON LA
Chiswick Park
Superstore
MILLS ROW
BRIDGE ST
ESSEX PL
BELMONT TERR
CLIFTON GDNS
FISHER'S LA
CHISWICK COMMON RD
Chiswick Common
WINDMILL RD
ELLIOTT RD
MAYFIELD AVE
THE POWER HO
A402
A315
KING ST
CHISWICK RD
ESSEX PLACE SQ
BELMONT RD
KIRTON GDNS
ARNOTT CL
HOLLY RD
PARR PL
ST PETER'S SQ
BLACK LION LA
B491
A316
CHISWICK HIGH RD
DOLMAN RD
MARLBOROUGH RD
BISHOPS CL
KINGS PL
ARLINGTON GDNS
BRYHER HO
WALPOLE GDNS
SUTTON LA N
Green
Turnham
HEATHFIELD TERR
A3000
PAS
Liby
BARLEY MOW PAS
BOURNE PL
LINDEN GDNS
PRINCE OF WALES TERR
ANNANDALE RD
BRACKLEY RD
CRANBROOK RD
VERONA CT
CHISWICK LA
HOMEFIELD RD
AIREDALE AVE
NETHERAVON RD
BRITISH GR
T Cts
Sch
BURLINGTON LA
HEATHFIELD GDNS
SHARON RD
HADLEY GDNS
FOSTER RD
DUKE'S AVE
DUKE RD
GLEBE ST
BINNS RD
RECKITT RD
DALE ST
DEVONSHIRE RD
SWANSCOMBE RD
ALKERDEN RD
COOMBE RD
BEVERLEY RD
CHISWICK
A4
GREAT WEST RD
1
ALWYN AVE
WILTON AVE
GRIFFIN CT
AIREDALE AVE S
Recn Gd
GROSVENOR RD
WAVENDON AVE
QUICK RD
ASHBOURNE GR
BALFERN GR
NETHERAVON RD S
CHISWICK MALL
Thames Path
BARROWGATE HO
FRASER ST
CORNWALL GR
DORCHESTER GR
BARROWGATE RD
PARK RD N
Schs
BENNETT ST
78
CEDARS RD
GARTH CT
GREAT WEST RD
ELLESMERE RD
HOGARTH
Hogarth Roundabout
MAWSON LA
20
A
B
133
C
D
22
21
ELMWOOD RD
SUTTON CT
HAZLEDENE RD
GRANDFIELD CT
BEECHWOOD CT
CHARA PL
Tenn Cts
HOGARTH BSNS PK
CHURCH ST
Pl Fld
COMPTON CRES
CHESTERFIELD RD
EASTBOURNE RD
MILNTHORPE RD
ELLESMERE CT
PAXTON RD
FIELDING HO

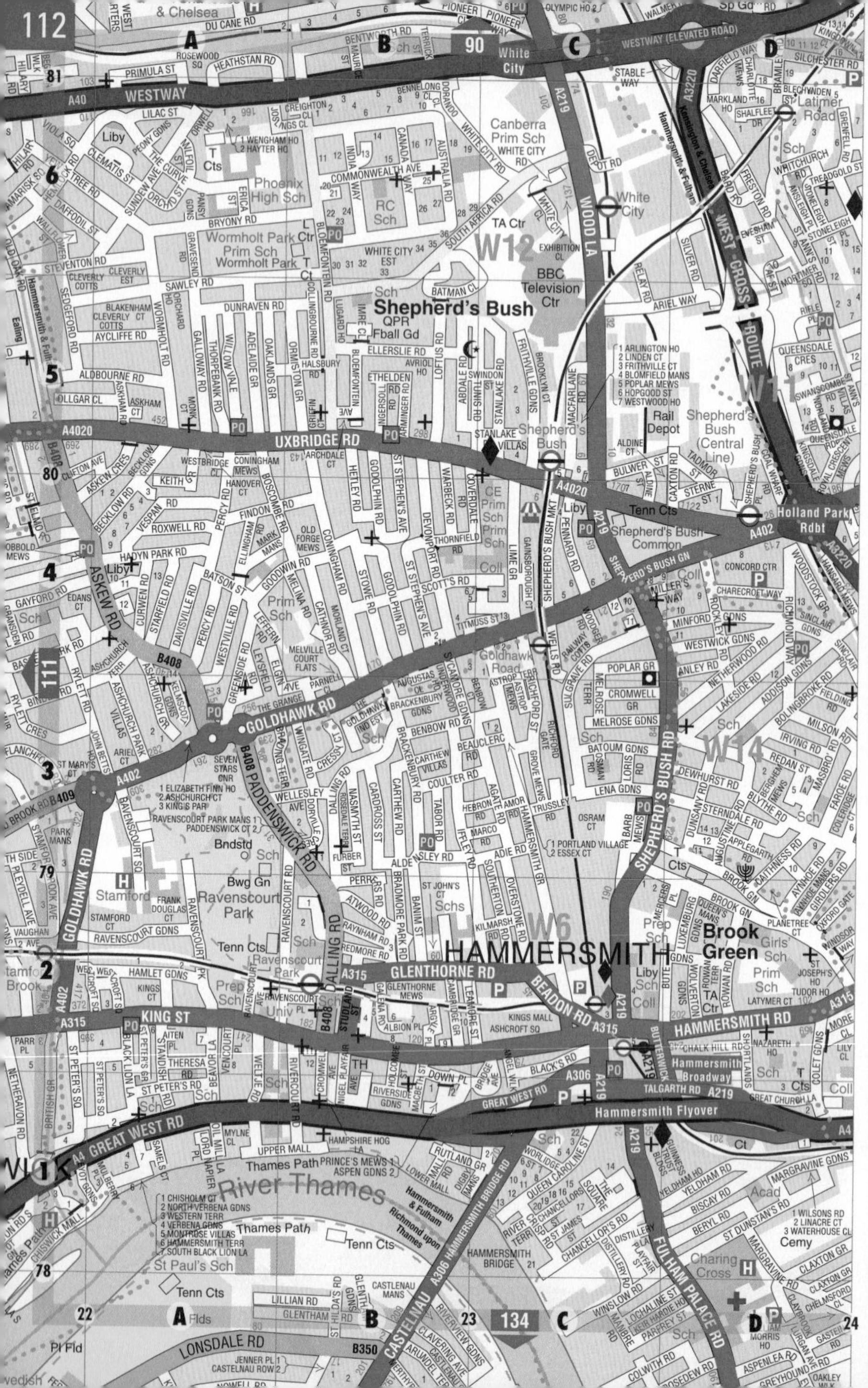
A
B
C
D
90
White City
WESTWAY
WESTWAY (ELEVATED ROAD)
A40
DU CANE RD
Canberra Prim Sch
Phoenix High Sch
Wormholt Park Prim Sch
Wormholt Park
RC Sch
W12
BBC Television Ctr
Shepherd's Bush
QPR Fball Gd
WOOD LA
WEST CROSS ROUTE
Latimer Road
W11
Shepherd's Bush (Central Line)
Holland Park Rdbt
UXBRIDGE RD
A4020
Shepherd's Bush Common
SHEPHERD'S BUSH GN
ASKEW RD
GOLDHAWK RD
Goldhawk Road
SHEPHERD'S BUSH RD
W14
Brook Green
PADDENSWICK RD
Ravenscourt Park
Stamford Brook
Ravenscourt Park
HAMMERSMITH
W6
GLENTHORNE RD
BEADON RD
KING ST
HAMMERSMITH RD
Hammersmith Broadway
Hammersmith Flyover
GREAT WEST RD
A4
River Thames
Thames Path
St Paul's Sch
HAMMERSMITH BRIDGE
CASTELNAU
FULHAM PALACE RD
Charing Cross
LONSDALE RD
134
6
5
4
3
2
1
111
22
23
24

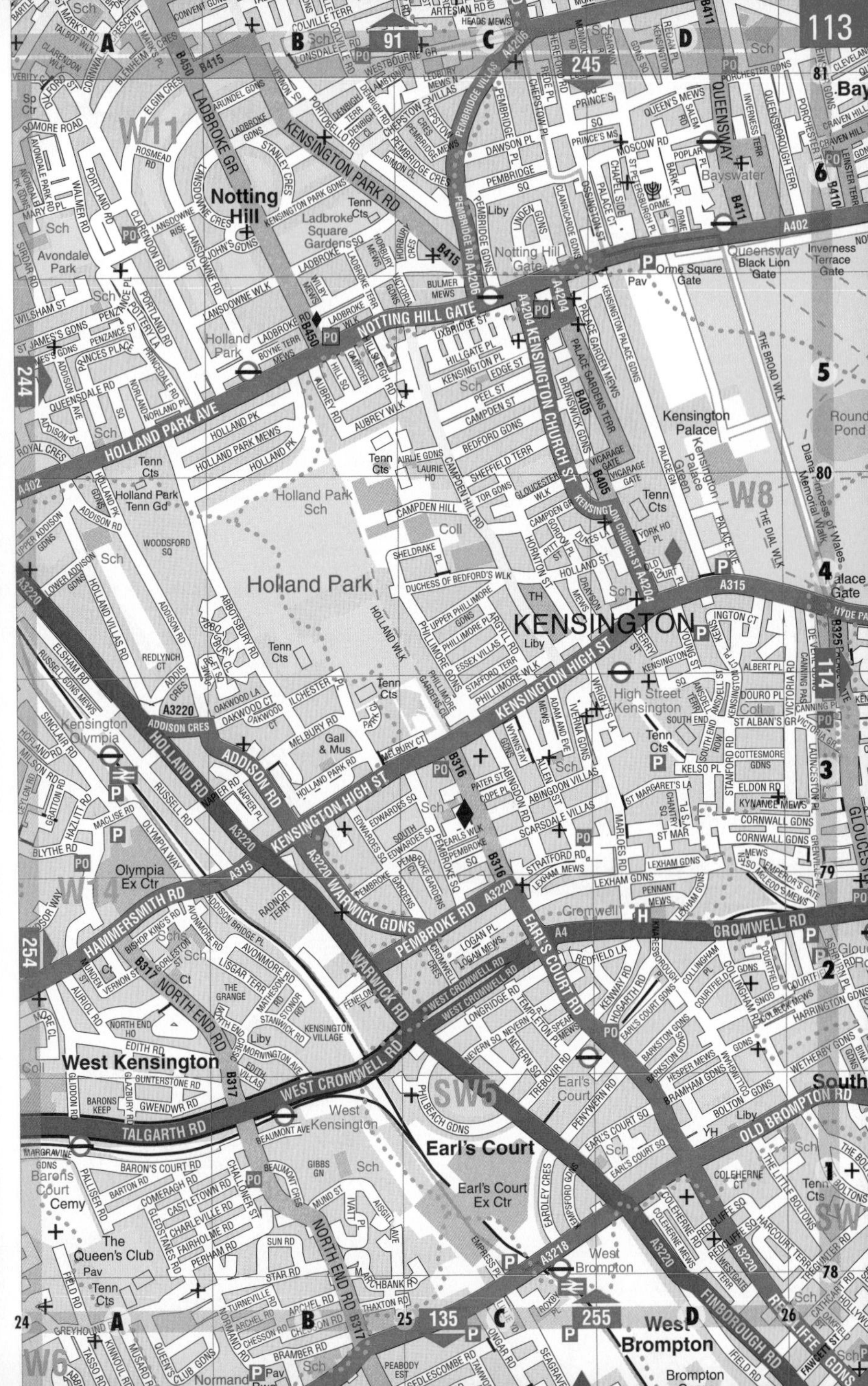
Notting Hill
W11
Holland Park
KENSINGTON
Kensington Palace
Round Pond
W8
W14
Olympia Ex Ctr
Kensington Olympia
West Kensington
SW5
Earl's Court
Earl's Court Ex Ctr
West Brompton
The Queen's Club
Barons Court Cemy
Bayswater
Queensway
High Street Kensington
NOTTING HILL GATE
HOLLAND PARK AVE
KENSINGTON HIGH ST
KENSINGTON CHURCH ST
HOLLAND RD
CROMWELL RD
WEST CROMWELL RD
TALGARTH RD
NORTH END RD
EARL'S COURT RD
WARWICK RD
LADBROKE GR
KENSINGTON PARK RD
HAMMERSMITH RD
OLD BROMPTON RD
FINBOROUGH RD
91
245
244
254
114
135
255
W6
24
25
26

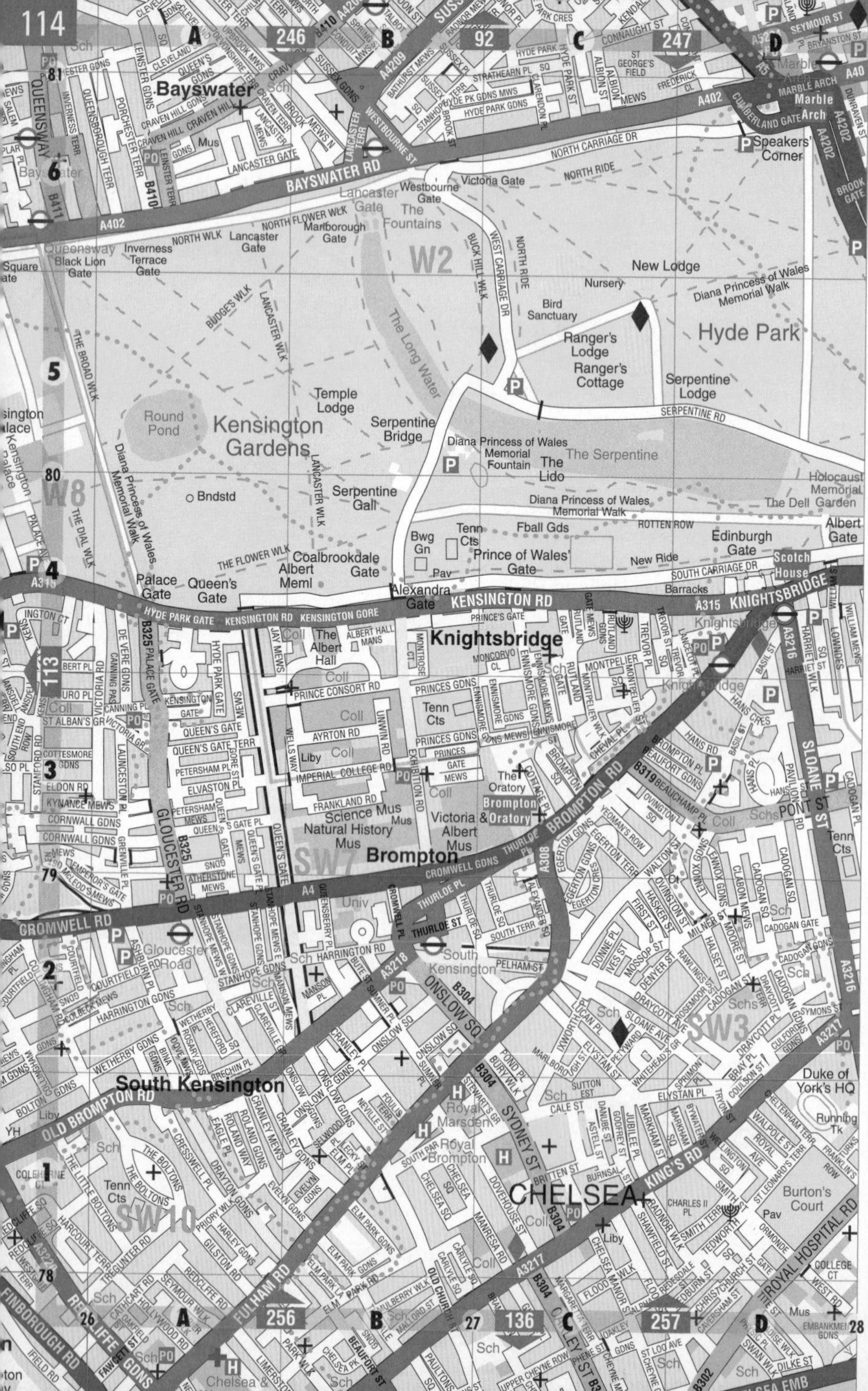

246
92
247
A
B
C
D
Bayswater
Queensway
Leinster Gdns
Queensborough Terr
Porchester Terr
Craven Hill Gdns
Craven Hill
Lancaster Gate
Westbourne St
Sussex Gdns
Bathurst Mews
Hyde Park Gdns
Hyde Park St
Connaught St
Seymour St
Bryanston St
Marble Arch
Cumberland Gate
Speakers' Corner
Bayswater Rd
A402
North Carriage Dr
North Ride
Victoria Gate
Westbourne Gate
Lancaster Gate
The Fountains
Marlborough Gate
North Flower Wlk
North Wlk
Inverness Terrace Gate
Black Lion Gate
W2
Buck Hill Wlk
West Carriage Dr
New Lodge
Nursery
Diana Princess of Wales Memorial Walk
Bird Sanctuary
Ranger's Lodge
Ranger's Cottage
Hyde Park
Serpentine Lodge
Serpentine Rd
The Long Water
Budge's Wlk
Lancaster Wlk
The Broad Wlk
Round Pond
Kensington Gardens
Temple Lodge
Serpentine Bridge
Diana Princess of Wales Memorial Fountain
The Lido
The Serpentine
Holocaust Memorial
The Dell
Garden
Serpentine Gall
Bndstd
W8
The Dial Wlk
Bwg Gn
Tenn Cts
Fball Gds
Rotten Row
Edinburgh Gate
Albert Gate
Prince of Wales' Gate
New Ride
South Carriage Dr
Scotch House
Barracks
The Flower Wlk
Coalbrookdale Gate
Albert Meml
Palace Gate
Queen's Gate
Alexandra Gate
Kensington Rd
Knightsbridge
A315
Hyde Park Gate
Kensington Gore
Prince's Gate
The Albert Hall
Knightsbridge
Prince Consort Rd
Princes Gdns
Ennismore Gdns
Rutland Gate
Montpelier Sq
Trevor Sq
Hans Cres
Sloane St
Brompton Rd
Imperial College Rd
Exhibition Rd
Science Mus
Natural History Mus
Victoria & Albert Mus
Brompton Oratory
The Oratory
Brompton
SW7
Beauchamp Pl
Pont St
Cadogan Pl
Gloucester Rd
B325
Cromwell Rd
Cromwell Gdns
Thurloe Pl
A4
Queen's Gate
Elvaston Pl
Launceston Pl
Victoria Gr
Cornwall Gdns
Kynance Mews
Eldon Rd
Stanhope Gdns
Thurloe St
Thurloe Sq
South Kensington
Pelham St
Harrington Rd
Onslow Sq
B304
A3218
Walton St
Egerton Gdns
Draycott Pl
Cadogan Sq
Cadogan Gate
SW3
Sloane Ave
Elystan Pl
A3216
A3217
Duke of York's HQ
Running Tk
South Kensington
Old Brompton Rd
The Boltons
Tenn Cts
SW10
Drayton Gdns
Royal Marsden
Royal Brompton
Sydney St
Fulham Rd
Chelsea
King's Rd
Burton's Court
Royal Hospital Rd
Coll
Liby
Finborough Rd
Redcliffe Gdns
Fawcett St
Beaufort St
Old Church St
Oakley St
Flood St
Chelsea Manor St
Tedworth Sq
Christchurch St
256
136
257
26
27
28
78
79
80
81
113
1
2
3
4
5
6

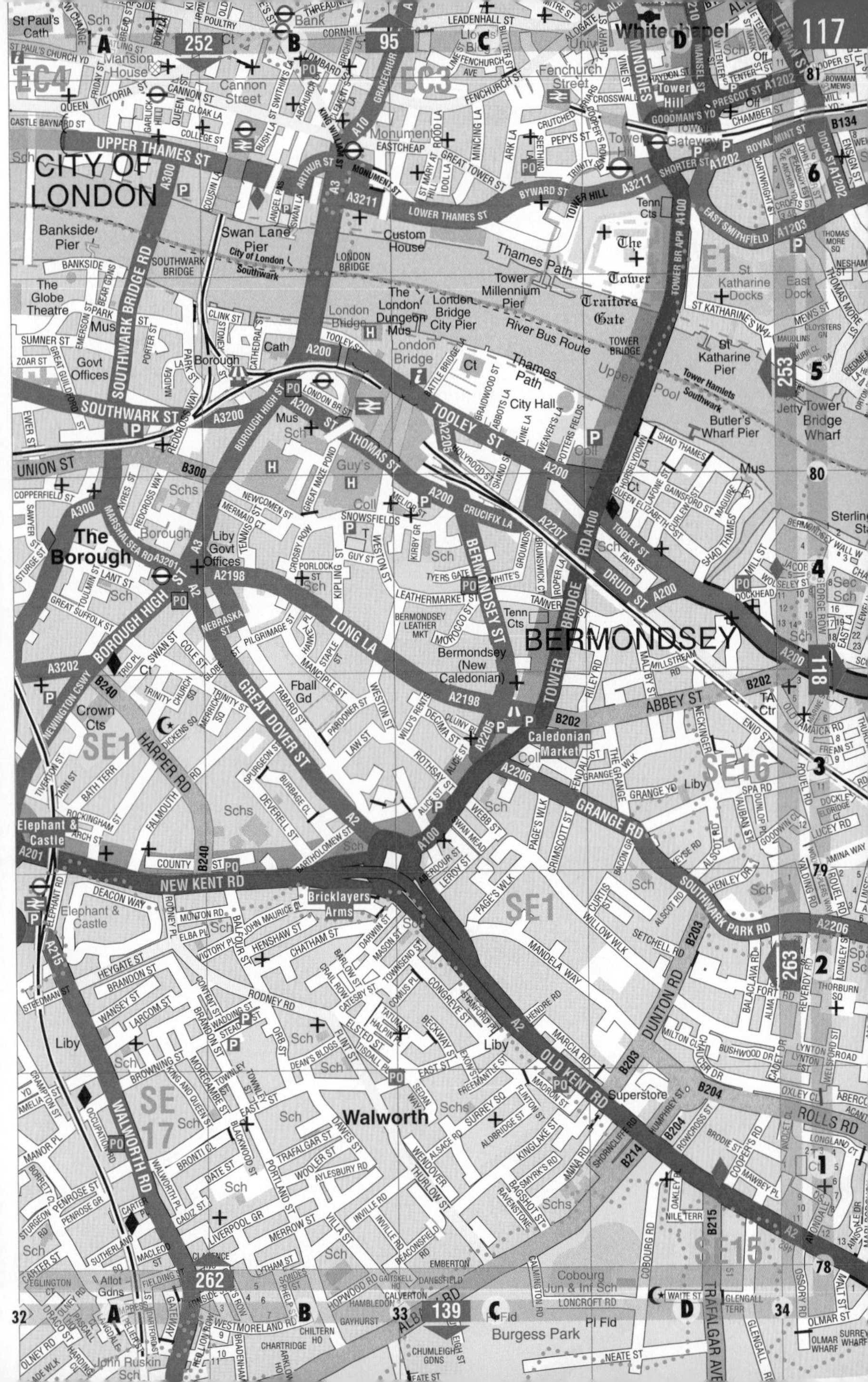

A
B
C
D
252
95
EC4
EC3
E1
SE1
SE16
SE17
SE15
St Paul's Cath
Mansion House
Cannon Street
Bank
Monument
Fenchurch Street
Whitechapel
Tower Hill
Tower Gateway
CITY OF LONDON
UPPER THAMES ST
LOWER THAMES ST
Bankside Pier
Swan Lane Pier
City of London
Southwark
Custom House
LONDON BRIDGE
Thames Path
The Tower
Traitors Gate
Tower Millennium Pier
The Globe Theatre
The London Dungeon Mus
London Bridge City Pier
River Bus Route
TOWER BRIDGE
St Katharine Docks
East Dock
St Katharine Pier
253
Tower Hamlets
Southwark
Upper Pool
City Hall
Butler's Wharf Pier
Jetty
Tower Bridge Wharf
London Bridge
Borough
Govt Offices
SOUTHWARK BRIDGE RD
SOUTHWARK ST
UNION ST
TOOLEY ST
THOMAS ST
Guy's
CRUCIFIX LA
The Borough
BOROUGH HIGH ST
Liby Govt Offices
LONG LA
BERMONDSEY ST
TOWER BRIDGE RD
BERMONDSEY
Bermondsey (New Caledonian)
Caledonian Market
ABBEY ST
DRUID ST
118
Crown Cts
HARPER RD
GREAT DOVER ST
GRANGE RD
SOUTHWARK PARK RD
Elephant & Castle
NEW KENT RD
Bricklayers Arms
OLD KENT RD
263
Walworth
WALWORTH RD
Superstore
DUNTON RD
ROLLS RD
262
Cobourg Jun & Inf Sch
Burgess Park
Pl Fld
139
ALBANY RD
TRAFALGAR AVE
John Ruskin Sch
Allot Gdns
32
33
34
1
2
3
4
5
6
78
79
80
81

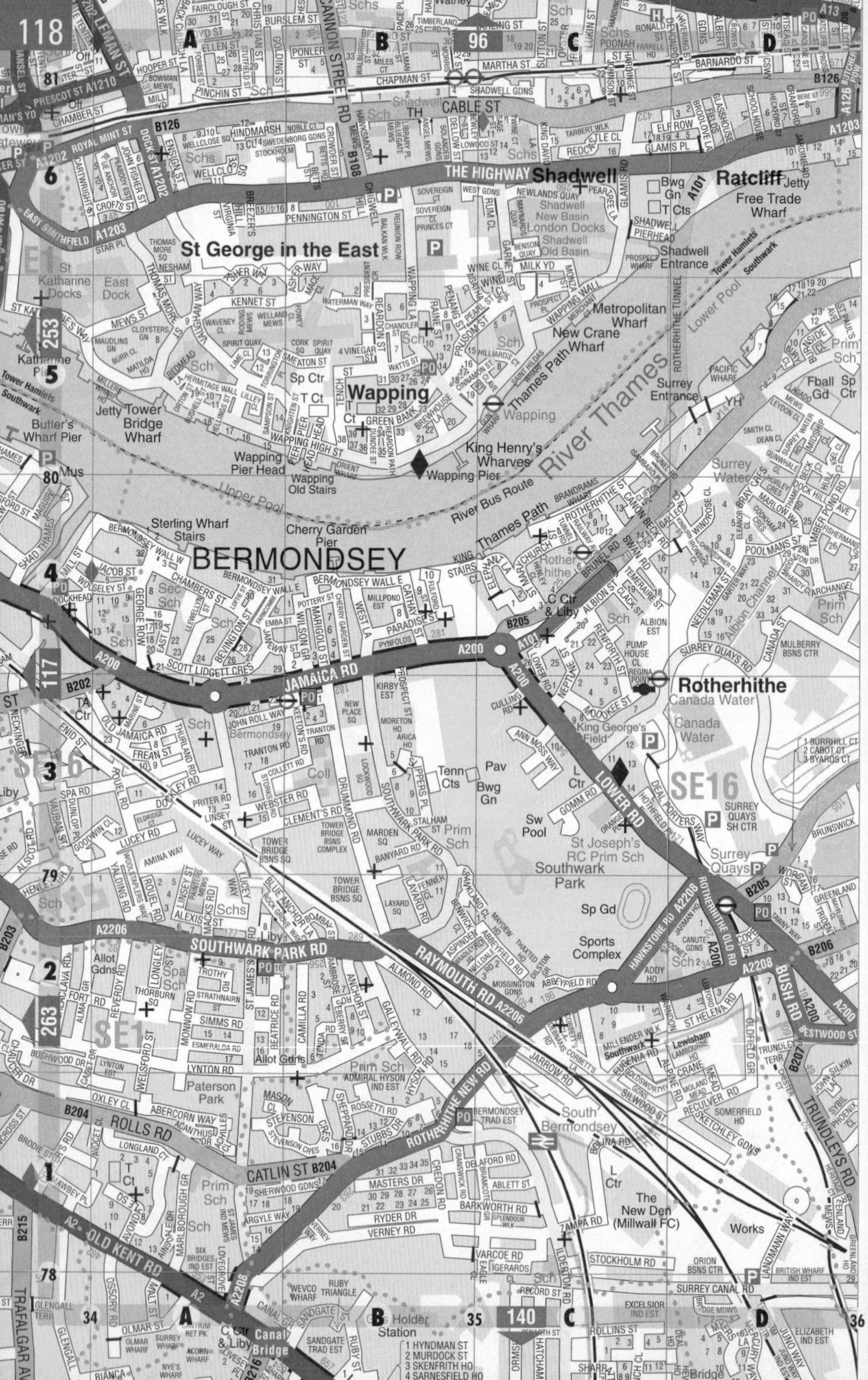
A
B
C
D
96
LEMAN ST
FAIRCLOUGH ST
CHRISTIAN ST
BURSLEM ST
CANNON STREET RD
BACK CHURCH LA
GOLDING ST
PONLER ST
HOOPER ST
PINCHIN ST
PRESCOT ST A1210
CHAMBER ST
CHAPMAN ST
MARTHA ST
SHADWELL GDNS
CABLE ST
Shadwell
BARNARDO ST
ROYAL MINT ST
DOCK ST A1202
HINDMARSH
SWEDENBORG GDNS
STOCKHOLM HO
WELLCLOSE SQ
CROWDER ST
HAWKSMOOR MEWS
B108
THE HIGHWAY
Shadwell
Ratcliff
GLAMIS PL
GLAMIS RD
CARTWRIGHT ST
JOHN FISHER ST
CROFTS ST
EAST SMITHFIELD A1203
PENNINGTON ST
SOVEREIGN CT
NEWLANDS QUAY
Shadwell New Basin
London Docks
Shadwell Old Basin
Shadwell Pierhead
Shadwell Entrance
Free Trade Wharf
ROTHERHITHE TUNNEL
St George in the East
E1
St Katharine Docks
East Dock
THOMAS MORE ST
VAUGHAN WAY
KENNET ST
ASHER WAY
WAPPING LA
WINE CL
MILK YD
WAPPING WALL
Metropolitan Wharf
New Crane Wharf
Lower Pool
Tower Hamlets
Southwark
253
MEWS ST
WAVENEY CL
CLOYSTERS GN
SPIRIT QUAY
WATERMAN WAY
CHANDLER ST
PRUSOM ST
CINNAMON ST
HILLIARDS CT
Katharine Pier
5
HERMITAGE WALL
TORRINGTON PL
Sp Ctr
T Ct
Wapping
Thames Path
Wapping
River Thames
Surrey Entrance
PACIFIC WHARF
Fball Gd
Prim Sch
Jetty
Tower Bridge Wharf
Butler's Wharf Pier
WAPPING HIGH ST
GREEN BANK
BREWHOUSE LA
King Henry's Wharves
Wapping Pier
Wapping Pier Head
Wapping Old Stairs
Upper Pool
80
Mus
SHAD THAMES
River Bus Route
Sterling Wharf Stairs
Cherry Garden Pier
BERMONDSEY
Thames Path
ROTHERHITHE ST
BRUNEL RD
SURREY WATER RD
Surrey Water
POOLMANS ST
TIMBER POND RD
4
MILL ST
JACOB ST
WOLSELEY ST
DOCKHEAD
BERMONDSEY WALL W
BERMONDSEY WALL E
CHAMBERS ST
GEORGE ROW
BEVINGTON ST
WILSON GR
MARIGOLD ST
CHERRY GARDEN ST
WEST LA
PARADISE ST
CATHAY ST
FULFORD ST
KING STAIRS CL
ST MARYCHURCH ST
Rotherhithe
C Ctr & Liby
ALBION ST
CLACK ST
TEMERAIRE ST
NEEDLEMAN ST
Albion Channel
CANADA ST
ARCHANGEL ST
MULBERRY BSNS CTR
SCOTT LIDGETT CRES
JAMAICA RD
A200
B205
A101
LOWER RD
NEPTUNE ST
RENFORTH ST
PUMP HOUSE CL
SURREY QUAYS RD
117
B202
TA Ctr
OLD JAMAICA RD
JOHN ROLL WAY
Bermondsey
KEETON'S RD
KIRBY EST
PROSPECT ST
NEW PLACE SQ
MORETON HO
CULLING RD
MOODKEE ST
Rotherhithe
Canada Water
Canada Water
King George's Field
3
SE16
NECKINGER
ENID ST
THURLAND RD
FREAN ST
TRANTON RD
COLLETT RD
Coll
LOCKWOOD SQ
SLIPPERS PL
Tenn Cts
Pav
Bwg Gn
ANN MOSS WAY
L Ctr
SE16
1 BURRHILL CT
2 CABOT CT
3 BYARDS CT
Liby
SPA RD
DUNLOP PL
ROUEL RD
DOCKLEY RD
PRITER RD
WEBSTER RD
CLEMENT'S RD
DRUMMOND RD
SOUTHWARK PARK RD
Prim Sch
Sw Pool
GOMM RD
St Joseph's RC Prim Sch
Southwark Park
DEAL PORTERS WAY
SURREY QUAYS SH CTR
BRUNSWICK
VAUBAN ST
LUCEY RD
LUCEY WAY
AMINA WAY
TOWER BRIDGE BSNS SQ
TOWER BRIDGE BSNS COMPLEX
MARDEN SQ
BANYARD RD
Surrey Quays
79
HENLEY DR
Sch
ALEXIS ST
Schs
BLUE ANCHOR LA
LAYARD SQ
LAYARD RD
Sp Gd
ROTHERHITHE OLD RD
HAWKSTONE RD
A2208
B205
GREENLAND
B203
A2206
SOUTHWARK PARK RD
Liby
RAYMOUTH RD A2206
Sports Complex
B206
2
Allot Gdns
TROTHY RD
STRATHNAIRN ST
SIMMS RD
ST JAMES'S RD
BEATRICE RD
CAMILLA RD
ANCHOR ST
GALLEYWALL RD
ALMOND RD
ABBEYFIELD RD
MOSSINGTON GDNS
ADDY HO
ST HELENA RD
OLDFIELD GR
BUSH RD
A200
263
SE1
MONNOW RD
ESMERALDA RD
LYNTON RD
Allot Gdns
Prim Sch
ADMIRAL HYSON IND EST
HYSON RD
JARROW RD
CORBETT'S LA
MILLENDER WLK
Southwark
Lewisham
EUGENIA RD
CRANE
MEAD
SILWOOD ST
RECULVER RD
SOMERFIELD HO
TRUNDLEYS TERR
BESTWOOD ST
B207
CHAUCER DR
BUSHWOOD DR
Paterson Park
OXLEY CL
ABERCORN WAY
ROLLS RD
B204
MASON CL
STEVENSON CRES
ROSSETTI RD
SHEPPARD DR
STUBBS DR
ROTHERHITHE NEW RD
BERMONDSEY TRAD EST
South Bermondsey
BOLINA RD
KETCHLEY GDNS
TRUNDLEYS RD
JOHN SILKIN LA
1
LONGLAND CT
T Ct
CATLIN ST B204
Prim Sch
SHERWOOD GDNS
MASTERS DR
CREDON RD
DELAFORD RD
ABLETT ST
BARKWORTH RD
RYDER DR
VERNEY RD
Sch
L Ctr
The New Den (Millwall FC)
Works
LANDMANN WAY
ZAMPA RD
B215
OLD KENT RD
A2
MARLBOROUGH GR
SIX BRIDGES IND EST
VARCOE RD
IGERARDS
STOCKHOLM RD
ORION BSNS CTR
BRITISH WHARF IND EST
78
TRAFALGAR AV
GLENGALL TERR
34
A
WEVCO WHARF
RUBY TRIANGLE
B
Gas Holder Station
35
140
C
RECORD ST
ILDERTON RD
SURREY CANAL RD
EXCELSIOR IND EST
D
36
ELIZABETH IND EST
OLMAR ST
OLMAR WHARF
SURREY WHARF
ACORN WHARF
C Ctr & Liby
Canal Bridge
SANDGATE ST
SANDGATE TRAD EST
RUBY ST
1 HYNDMAN ST
2 MURDOCK ST
3 SKENFRITH HO
4 SARNESFIELD HO
ROLLINS ST
ORMSIDE ST
HATCHAM
JUNO WAY
BIANCA
GLENGALL

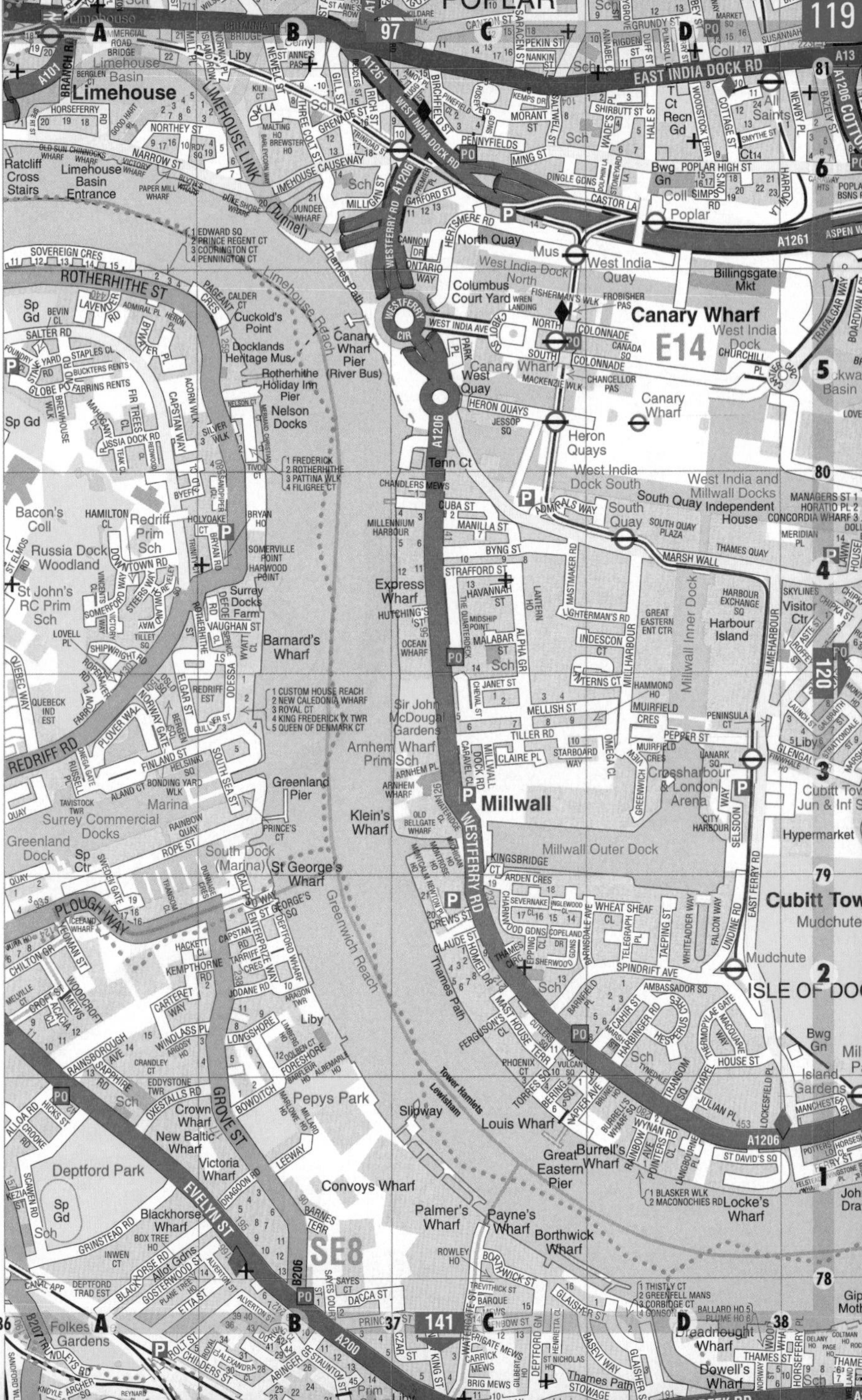

POPLAR
97
Limehouse
Limehouse Basin
BRANCH RD
A101
COMMERCIAL RD
BRIDGE
BRITANNIA BRIDGE
NEWELL ST
ST ANNE'S PAS
HORSEFERRY RD
NORTHEY ST
NARROW ST
LIMEHOUSE LINK
LIMEHOUSE CAUSEWAY
Ratcliff Cross Stairs
Limehouse Basin Entrance
PAPER MILL WHARF
DUKE SHORE WHARF
DUNDEE WHARF
MILLIGAN ST
GRENADE ST
THREE COLT ST
RICH ST
GILL ST
A1261
WEST INDIA DOCK RD
BIRCHFIELD ST
PENNYFIELDS
MING ST
MORANT ST
SALTWELL ST
CANTON ST
PEKIN ST
NANKIN ST
SARACEN ST
GRUNDY ST
RIGDEN ST
EAST INDIA DOCK RD
A13
A1206
SHIRBUTT ST
WADE'S PL
HALE ST
Ct Recn Gd
WOODSTOCK TERR
COTTAGE ST
All Saints
NEWBY PL
BAZELY ST
POPLAR HIGH ST
Bwg Gn
Coll
SIMPS RD
HARROW LA
Poplar
CASTOR LA
DINGLE GDNS
GARFORD ST
WESTFERRY RD
HERTSMERE RD
North Quay
Mus
West India Dock North
West India Quay
Billingsgate Mkt
A1261
ASPEN WAY
CANNON DR
ONTARIO WAY
Columbus Court Yard
WREN LANDING
FISHERMAN'S WLK
FROBISHER PAS
Canary Wharf
E14
West India Dock
WESTFERRY CIR
WEST INDIA AVE
CABOT SQ
NORTH COLONNADE
SOUTH COLONNADE
CANADA SQ
CHURCHILL PL
CARTIER CIRC
TRAFALGAR WAY
BOARDWALK PL
MACKENZIE WLK
CHANCELLOR PAS
West Quay
HERON QUAYS
JESSOP SQ
Heron Quays
1 EDWARD SQ
2 PRINCE REGENT CT
3 CODRINGTON CT
4 PENNINGTON CT
SOVEREIGN CRES
ROTHERHITHE ST
PAGEANT CRES
CALDER CT
Cuckold's Point
Docklands Heritage Mus
Limehouse Reach
Thames Path
Canary Wharf Pier (River Bus)
Rotherhithe Holiday Inn Pier
Nelson Docks
Sp Gd
SALTER RD
STAPLES CL
BUCKTERS RENTS
FARRINS RENTS
GLOBE POND
FIR TREES CL
CAPSTAN WAY
ACORN WLK
SILVER WLK
ISSIA DOCK RD
Sp Gd
1 FREDERICK
2 ROTHERHITHE
3 PATTINA WLK
4 FILIGREE CT
Tenn Ct
CHANDLERS MEWS
CUBA ST
MANILLA ST
MILLENNIUM HARBOUR
BYNG ST
STRAFFORD ST
West India Dock South
West India and Millwall Docks
South Quay
Independent House
ADMIRALS WAY
SOUTH QUAY PLAZA
MARSH WALL
THAMES QUAY
MANAGERS ST
HORATIO PL
CONCORDIA WHARF
MERIDIAN PL
80
Bacon's Coll
HAMILTON CL
Redriff Prim Sch
HOLYOAKE CT
BRYAN RD
Russia Dock Woodland
DOWNTOWN RD
St John's RC Prim Sch
SOMERVILLE POINT
HARWOOD POINT
Surrey Docks Farm
DEFOE CL
VAUGHAN ST
Barnard's Wharf
Express Wharf
HUTCHING'S ST
HAVANNAH ST
LANTERN HO
MASTMAKER RD
Millwall Inner Dock
HARBOUR EXCHANGE SQ
Harbour Island
LIMEHARBOUR
Visitor Ctr
SKYLINES
LIGHTERMAN'S RD
GREAT EASTERN ENT CTR
MILLHARBOUR
INDESCON CT
OCEAN WHARF
MALABAR ST
ALPHA GR
Sch
LOVELL PL
SHIPWRIGHT RD
QUEBEC WAY
QUEBECK IND EST
REDRIFF RD
PLOVER WAY
NORWAY GATE
ELGAR ST
ODESSA ST
REDRIFF EST
1 CUSTOM HOUSE REACH
2 NEW CALEDONIA WHARF
3 ROYAL CT
4 KING FREDERICK IX TWR
5 QUEEN OF DENMARK CT
JANET ST
CHEVAL ST
LANTERNS CT
HAMMOND HO
MUIRFIELD CRES
PENINSULA CT
120
Sir John McDougal Gardens
Arnhem Wharf Prim Sch
MELLISH ST
TILLER RD
CLAIRE PL
STARBOARD WAY
OMEGA CL
PEPPER ST
Crossharbour & London Arena
LANARK SQ
Liby
3
Cubitt Town Jun & Inf Sch
FINLAND ST
HELSINKI SQ
SOUTH SEA ST
BONDING YARD WLK
Greenland Pier
Marina
Surrey Commercial Docks
RAINBOW QUAY
Greenland Dock
Sp Ctr
ROPE ST
South Dock (Marina)
St George's Wharf
Klein's Wharf
Millwall
WESTFERRY RD
Millwall Outer Dock
SELSDON WAY
CITY HARBOUR
Hypermarket
KINGSBRIDGE CT
ARDEN CRES
79
Cubitt Town
Mudchute
EAST FERRY RD
PLOUGH WAY
SWEDEN GATE
CALYPSO WAY
ST GEORGE'S SQ
DEPTFORD WHARF
Greenwich Reach
WHEAT SHEAF CL
TELEGRAPH PL
TAEPING ST
WHITEADDER WAY
FALCON WAY
UNDINE RD
CREWS ST
CLAUDE ST
HOMER DR
THAMES CIRC
SPINDRIFT AVE
AMBASSADOR SQ
Mudchute
2
ISLE OF DOGS
CHILTON GR
KEMPTHORNE RD
CARTERET WAY
JODANE RD
Liby
WINDLASS PL
LONGSHORE
FORESHORE
Thames Path
FERGUSON'S CL
MAST HOUSE TERR
Sch
CAHIR ST
HARBINGER RD
THERMOPYLAE GATE
MACQUARIE WAY
HOUSE ST
Bwg Gn
RAINSBOROUGH AVE
SAPPHIRE RD
CRANDLEY CT
EDDYSTONE TWR
OXESTALLS RD
GROVE ST
BOWDITCH
Pepys Park
Tower Hamlets
Lewisham
Slipway
Louis Wharf
PHOENIX CT
TORRES SQ
NAPIER AVE
JULIAN PL
LOCKESFIELD PL
Island Gardens
MANCHESTER GR
A1206
Crown Wharf
New Baltic Wharf
Victoria Wharf
DRAGOON RD
LEEWAY
Deptford Park
Sp Gd
Sch
Convoys Wharf
Great Eastern Pier
Burrell's Wharf
WYNAN RD
ST DAVID'S SQ
1 BLASKER WLK
2 MACONOCHIES RD
Locke's Wharf
1
EVELYN ST
BARNES TERR
Blackhorse Wharf
GRINSTEAD RD
BOX TREE HO
INWEN CT
Allot Gdns
SE8
Palmer's Wharf
Payne's Wharf
Borthwick Wharf
ROWLEY HO
BORTHWICK ST
78
B206
DEPTFORD TRAD EST
CANAL APP
BLACKHORSE RD
GOSTERWOOD ST
ETTA ST
ALVERTON ST
SAYES COURT
DACCA ST
TREVITHICK ST
BARQUE MEWS
GLAISHER ST
1 THISTLY CT
2 GREENFELL MANS
3 CORBIDGE CT
4 GONSON ST
BALLARD HO
PLUME HO
36
A
Folkestone Gardens
B
A200
37
141
C
CZAR ST
KING ST
WATERGATE ST
FRIGATE MEWS
CARRICK MEWS
BRIG MEWS
DEPTFORD GN
BASEVI WAY
Thames Path
STOWAGE
D
Dreadnought Wharf
38
THAMES ST
Dowell's Wharf
HORSEFERRY PL
ROLT ST
CHILDERS ST
ABINGER GR
STAUNTON ST

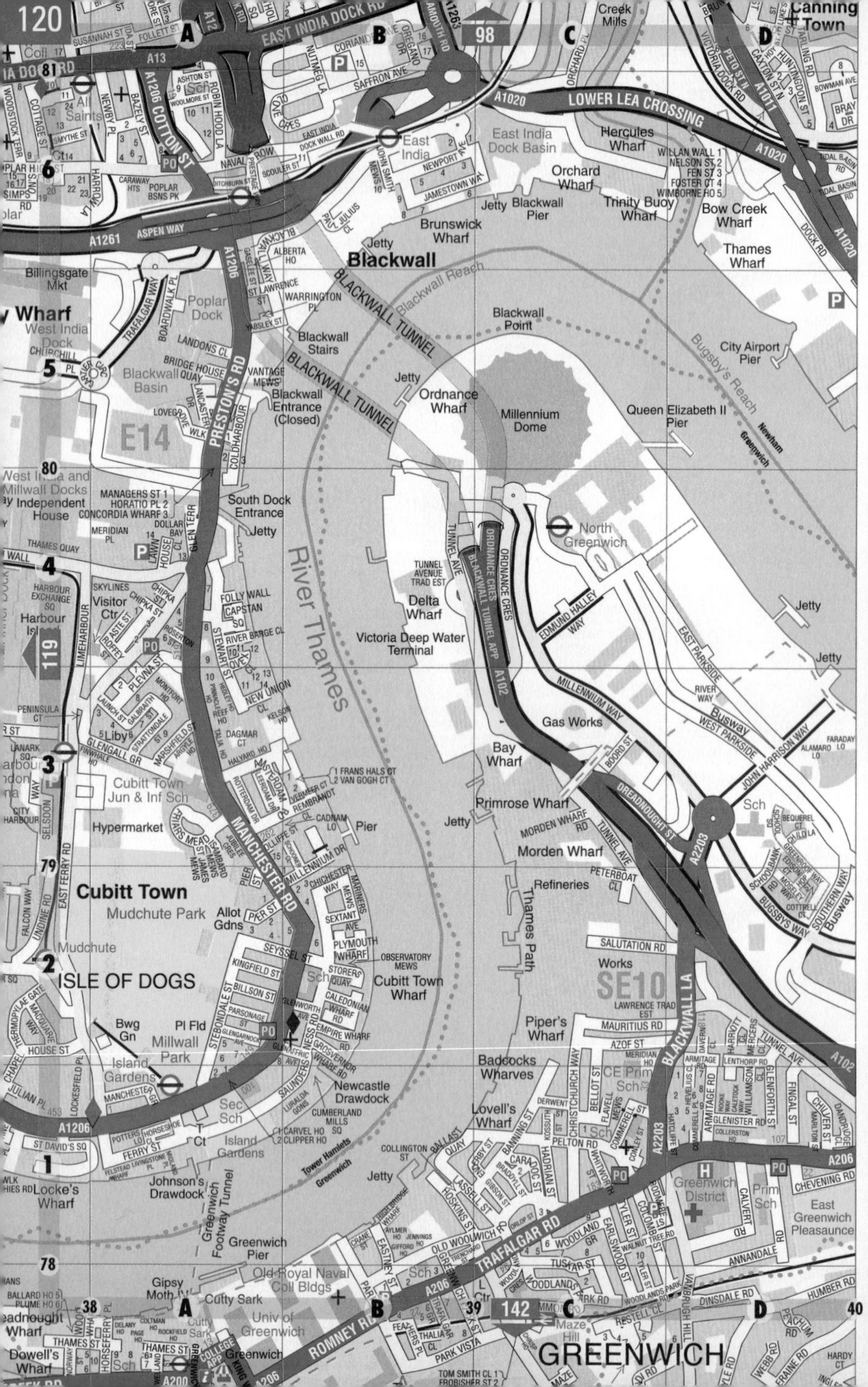

98
Canning Town
East India Dock Rd
Lower Lea Crossing
East India
East India Dock Basin
Hercules Wharf
Orchard Wharf
Trinity Buoy Wharf
Bow Creek Wharf
Thames Wharf
Blackwall Pier
Brunswick Wharf
Blackwall
Blackwall Tunnel
Blackwall Reach
Blackwall Point
Blackwall Stairs
Billingsgate Mkt
Poplar Dock
West India Dock
Blackwall Basin
Blackwall Entrance (Closed)
E14
Ordnance Wharf
Millennium Dome
City Airport Pier
Bugsby's Reach
Queen Elizabeth II Pier
Newham
Greenwich
North Greenwich
West India and Millwall Docks
Independent House
South Dock Entrance
Preston's Rd
River Thames
Tunnel Avenue Trad Est
Delta Wharf
Victoria Deep Water Terminal
Harbour Exchange Sq
Visitor Ctr
119
Gas Works
Bay Wharf
Primrose Wharf
Morden Wharf
Refineries
Thames Path
Cubitt Town Jun & Inf Sch
Hypermarket
Manchester Rd
Cubitt Town
Mudchute Park
Mudchute
Isle of Dogs
Cubitt Town Wharf
SE10
Blackwall La
Piper's Wharf
Badcocks Wharves
Lovell's Wharf
Millwall Park
Island Gardens
Newcastle Drawdock
Johnson's Drawdock
Greenwich Footway Tunnel
Greenwich Pier
Locke's Wharf
Tower Hamlets
Old Royal Naval Coll Bldgs
Gipsy Moth IV
Cutty Sark
Univ of Greenwich
Trafalgar Rd
Greenwich District
East Greenwich Pleasaunce
142
Maze Hill
GREENWICH
Romney Rd
Dreadnought Wharf
Dowell's Wharf
A B C D
1 2 3 4 5 6
38 39 40
78 79 80 81

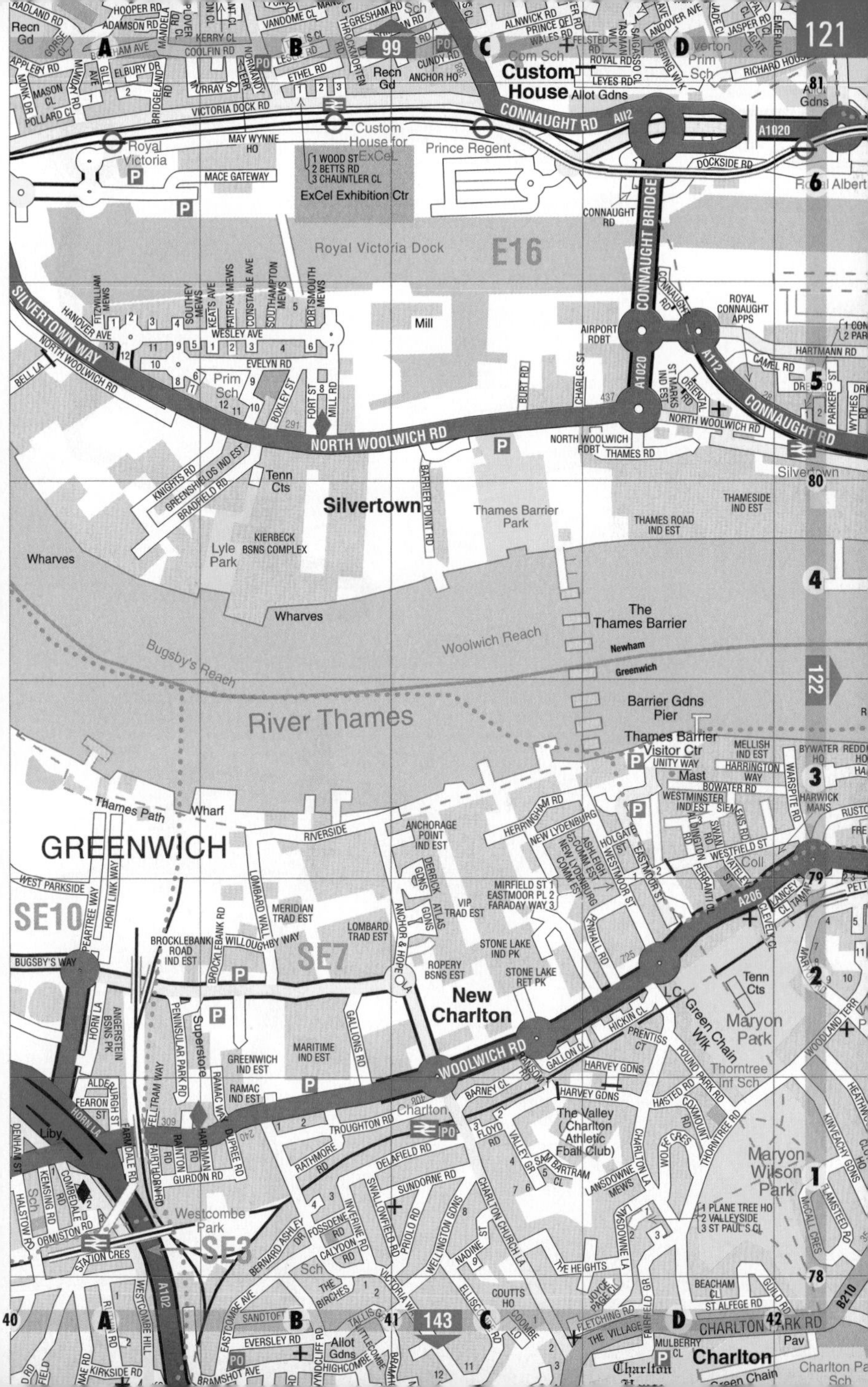
99
Custom House
Royal Victoria
Custom House for ExCeL
Prince Regent
ExCel Exhibition Ctr
Royal Victoria Dock
E16
CONNAUGHT RD
CONNAUGHT BRIDGE
SILVERTOWN WAY
NORTH WOOLWICH RD
Silvertown
Thames Barrier Park
Lyle Park
Wharves
The Thames Barrier
Woolwich Reach
Bugsby's Reach
River Thames
Barrier Gdns Pier
Thames Barrier Visitor Ctr
122
GREENWICH
SE10
SE7
New Charlton
WOOLWICH RD
The Valley (Charlton Athletic Fball Club)
Maryon Park
Maryon Wilson Park
Westcombe Park
SE3
Charlton
143
CHARLTON PARK RD

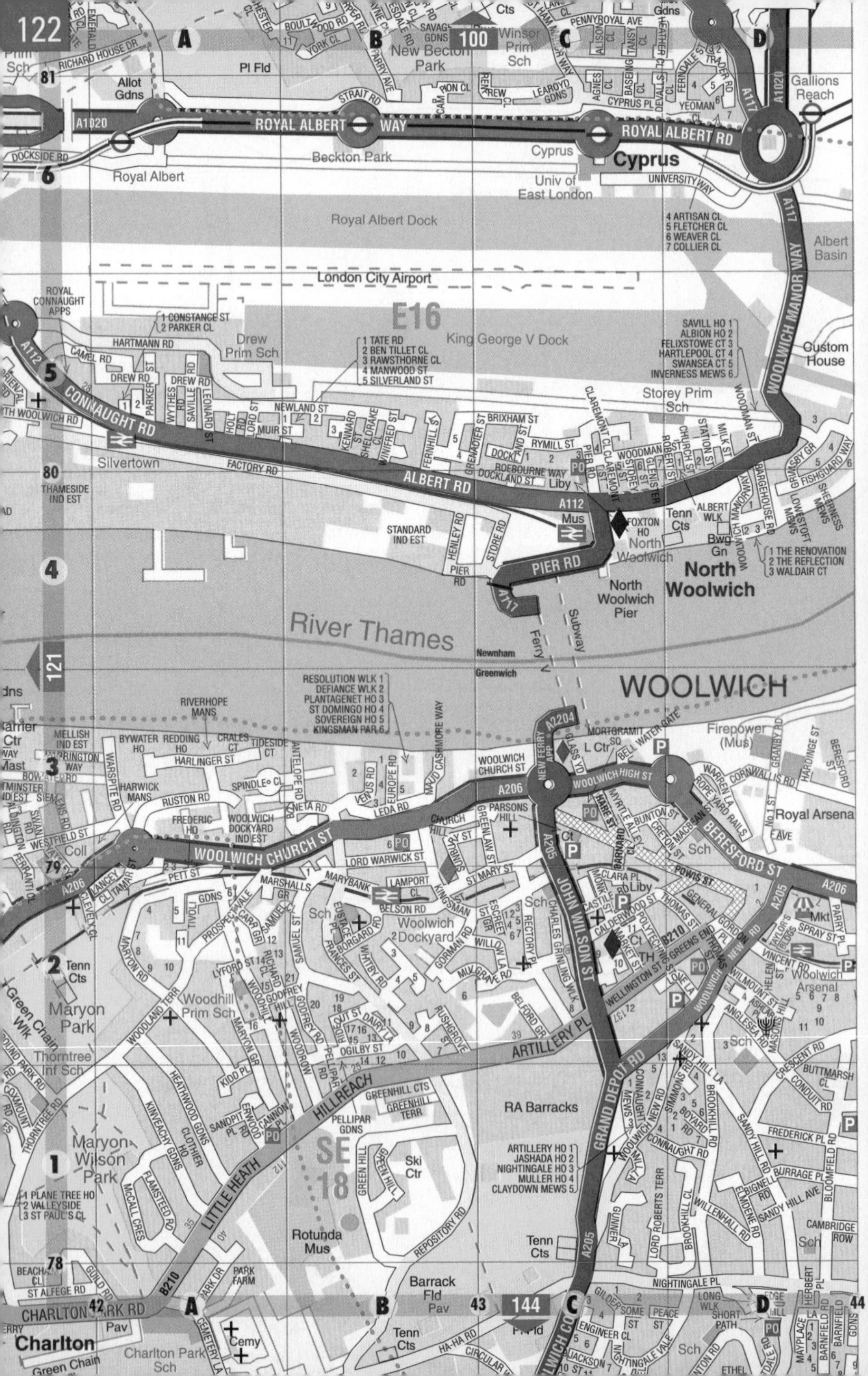

A
B
C
D
100
New Beckton Park
Winsor Prim Sch
Pl Fld
Allot Gdns
81
A1020
ROYAL ALBERT WAY
ROYAL ALBERT RD
STRAIT RD
DOCKSIDE RD
6
Royal Albert
Beckton Park
Cyprus
Univ of East London
UNIVERSITY WAY
Gallions Reach
A117
Royal Albert Dock
4 ARTISAN CL
5 FLETCHER CL
6 WEAVER CL
7 COLLIER CL
Albert Basin
London City Airport
E16
King George V Dock
ROYAL CONNAUGHT APPS
1 CONSTANCE ST
2 PARKER CL
HARTMANN RD
Drew Prim Sch
1 TATE RD
2 BEN TILLET CL
3 RAWSTHORNE CL
4 MANWOOD ST
5 SILVERLAND ST
SAVILL HO 1
ALBION HO 2
FELIXSTOWE CT 3
HARTLEPOOL CT 4
SWANSEA CT 5
INVERNESS MEWS 6
WOOLWICH MANOR WAY
Custom House
A112
5
CONNAUGHT RD
Silvertown
FACTORY RD
ALBERT RD
Storey Prim Sch
80
THAMESIDE IND EST
STANDARD IND EST
Mus
FOXTON HO
North Woolwich
Tenn Cts
ALBERT WLK
Bwg Gn
1 THE RENOVATION
2 THE REFLECTION
3 WALDAIR CT
4
PIER RD
North Woolwich Pier
River Thames
Subway
Ferry
Newnham
Greenwich
121
WOOLWICH
RESOLUTION WLK 1
DEFIANCE WLK 2
PLANTAGENET HO 3
ST DOMINGO HO 4
SOVEREIGN HO 5
KINGSMAN PAR 6
RIVERHOPE MANS
A2204
Firepower (Mus)
3
A206
WOOLWICH CHURCH ST
WOOLWICH HIGH ST
BERESFORD ST
Royal Arsenal
79
Coll
Woolwich Dockyard
JOHN WILSON ST
A205
B210
Mkt
Woolwich Arsenal
2
Tenn Cts
Maryon Park
Green Chain Wlk
Woodhill Prim Sch
Thorntree Inf Sch
ARTILLERY PL
HILLREACH
GRAND DEPOT RD
RA Barracks
ARTILLERY HO 1
JASHADA HO 2
NIGHTINGALE HO 3
MULLER HO 4
CLAYDOWN MEWS 5
1
Maryon Wilson Park
1 PLANE TREE HO
2 VALLEYSIDE
3 ST PAUL'S CL
LITTLE HEATH
SE 18
Ski Ctr
Rotunda Mus
Tenn Cts
78
CHARLTON PARK RD
42
Barrack Fld
43
144
44
Charlton
Charlton Park Sch
Cemy
Tenn Cts

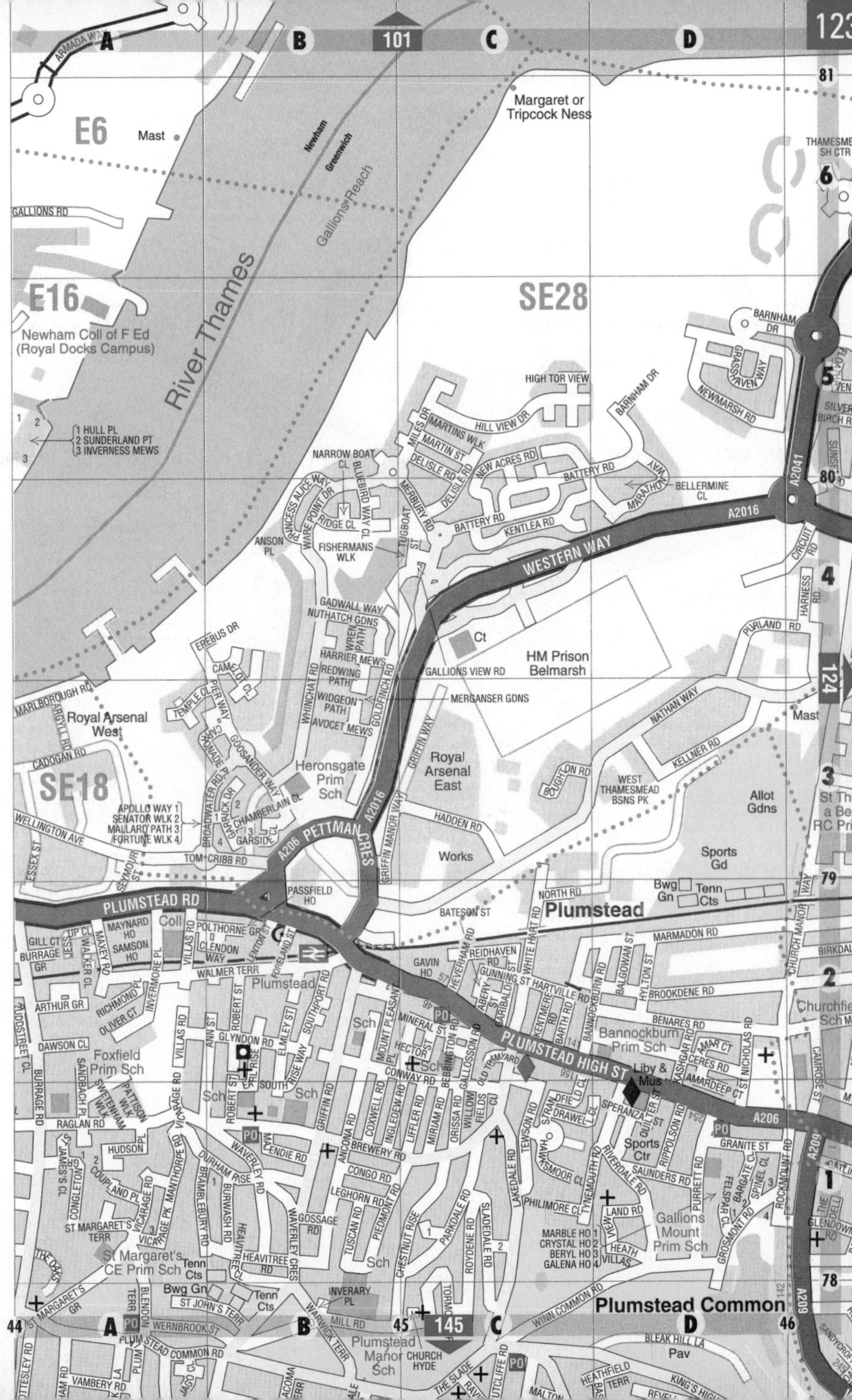

A
B
101
C
D
81
80
79
78
44
45
145
46
124
E6
E16
SE28
SE18
Mast
Margaret or
Tripcock Ness
Newham
Greenwich
Gallions Reach
River Thames
GALLIONS RD
ARMADA WAY
Newham Coll of F Ed
(Royal Docks Campus)
1 HULL PL
2 SUNDERLAND PT
3 INVERNESS MEWS
THAMESMEAD
SH CTR
BARNHAM DR
GRASSHAVEN WAY
NEWMARSH RD
HIGH TOR VIEW
HILL VIEW DR
BARNHAM DR
MILES DR
MARTINS WLK
MARTIN ST
DELISLE RD
NEW ACRES RD
BATTERY RD
MARATHON WAY
BELLERMINE CL
KENTLEA RD
NARROW BOAT CL
BLUEBIRD WAY
PRINCESS ALICE WAY
WARE POINT DR
RIDGE CL
MERBURY RD
TUGBOAT ST
ANSON PL
FISHERMANS WLK
WESTERN WAY
A2016
A2041
CIRCUIT RD
HARNESS RD
PURLAND RD
GADWALL WAY
NUTHATCH GDNS
WREN PATH
HARRIER MEWS
REDWING PATH
WIDGEON PATH
AVOCET MEWS
GOLDFINCH RD
WHINCHAT RD
MERGANSER GDNS
Ct
HM Prison
Belmarsh
GALLIONS VIEW RD
EREBUS DR
CAMELOT CL
TEMPLE CL
PIER WAY
CARRONADE PL
GOOSANDER WAY
Royal Arsenal
West
MARLBOROUGH RD
ARGYLL RD
CADOGAN RD
Heronsgate
Prim
Sch
GRIFFIN WAY
Royal
Arsenal
East
NATHAN WAY
KELLNER RD
BOUGHTON RD
WEST
THAMESMEAD
BSNS PK
Mast
Allot
Gdns
St Thomas
a Becket
RC Prim
APOLLO WAY 1
SENATOR WLK 2
MALLARD PATH 3
FORTUNE WLK 4
BROADWATER RD
GARRICK DR
CHAMBERLAIN CL
GARSIDE CL
WELLINGTON AVE
A206
PETTMAN CRES
GRIFFIN MANOR WAY
HADDEN RD
Works
Sports
Gd
ESSEX ST
SEYMOUR ST
TOM CRIBB RD
PLUMSTEAD RD
PASSFIELD HO
NORTH RD
Bwg
Gn
Tenn
Cts
Plumstead
BATESON ST
CHURCH MANOR WAY
MARMADON RD
BIRKDALE RD
GILL CT
JESSUP CL
MAXEY RD
MAYNARD HO
SAMSON HO
Coll
POLTHORNE GR
CLENDON WAY
LENTON ST
FORELAND ST
BURRAGE GR
WALKER CL
INVERMORE PL
VILLAS RD
WALMER TERR
Plumstead
GAVIN HO
HEVERHAM RD
REIDHAVEN RD
GUNNING ST
HARTVILLE RD
WHITE HART RD
BALGOWAN ST
HYLTON ST
BROOKDENE RD
ARTHUR GR
RICHMOND PL
OLIVER CT
ROBERT ST
SOUTHPORT RD
Sch
MOUNT PLEASANT
PO
MINERAL ST
PLUMSTEAD HIGH ST
BENARES RD
Churchfield
Sch
DAWSON CL
GLYNDON RD
ANN ST
ELMLEY ST
HECTOR ST
Bannockburn
Prim Sch
BANNOCKBURN RD
KENTMERE RD
BARTH RD
ABERY ST
GARIBALDI ST
CAMROSE ST
MYRA ST
Foxfield
Prim Sch
SANDBACH PL
SWETENHAM WLK
PATTISON WLK
EARL RISE
SOUTH RISE WAY
CONWAY RD
BEBBINGTON RD
GALLOSSON RD
OLD TRAMYARD
Liby &
Mus
KASHGAR RD
CERES RD
AMARDEEP CT
ST NICHOLAS RD
BURRAGE RD
RAGLAN RD
VICARAGE RD
Sch
GRIFFIN RD
ANCONA RD
COXWELL RD
INGLEDEW RD
LIFFLER RD
MIRIAM RD
ORISSA RD
WILLOW FIELDS CL
TEWSON RD
STRANDFIELD CL
DRAWELL CL
SPERANZA ST
QUILTER ST
RIPPOLSON RD
A206
ST JAMES'S CL
HUDSON
CONGLETON GR
COUPLAND PL
MANTHORPE RD
DURHAM RISE
WAVERLEY RD
MAXENDIE RD
BREWERY RD
CONGO RD
HAWKSMOOR CL
Sports
Ctr
RIVERDALE RD
GRANITE ST
A209
BRAMBLEBURY RD
BURWASH RD
LEGHORN RD
PIEDMONT RD
TUSCAN RD
GOSSAGE RD
LAKEDALE RD
SLADEDALE RD
PARKDALE RD
PHILIMORE CL
TYNEMOUTH RD
SAUNDERS RD
PURRETT RD
FELSPAR CL
BARGATE CL
SPINEL CL
ROCKMOUNT RD
GLENDOWN RD
THE DELL
ST MARGARET'S TERR
VICARAGE PK
HEAVITREE CL
HEAVITREE RD
WAVERLEY CRES
CHESTNUT RISE
ROYDENE RD
MARBLE HO 1
CRYSTAL HO 2
BERYL HO 3
GALENA HO 4
LAND RD
VIEW
HEATH VILLAS
Gallions
Mount
Prim Sch
GROSMONT RD
St Margaret's
CE Prim Sch
Tenn
Cts
Bwg Gn
ST JOHN'S TERR
Tenn
Cts
INVERARY PL
Sch
THE OAKS
ST MARGARET'S GR
TERR
BLENDON
WERNBROOK ST
MILL RD
WARWICK TERR
WINN COMMON RD
Plumstead Common
PLUMSTEAD COMMON RD
Plumstead
Manor
Sch
CHURCH
HYDE
BLEAK HILL LA
Pav
SANDYCROFT
VAMBERY RD
JAGO CL
THE SLADE
SUTCLIFFE RD
HEATHFIELD TERR
KING'S HIGHWAY

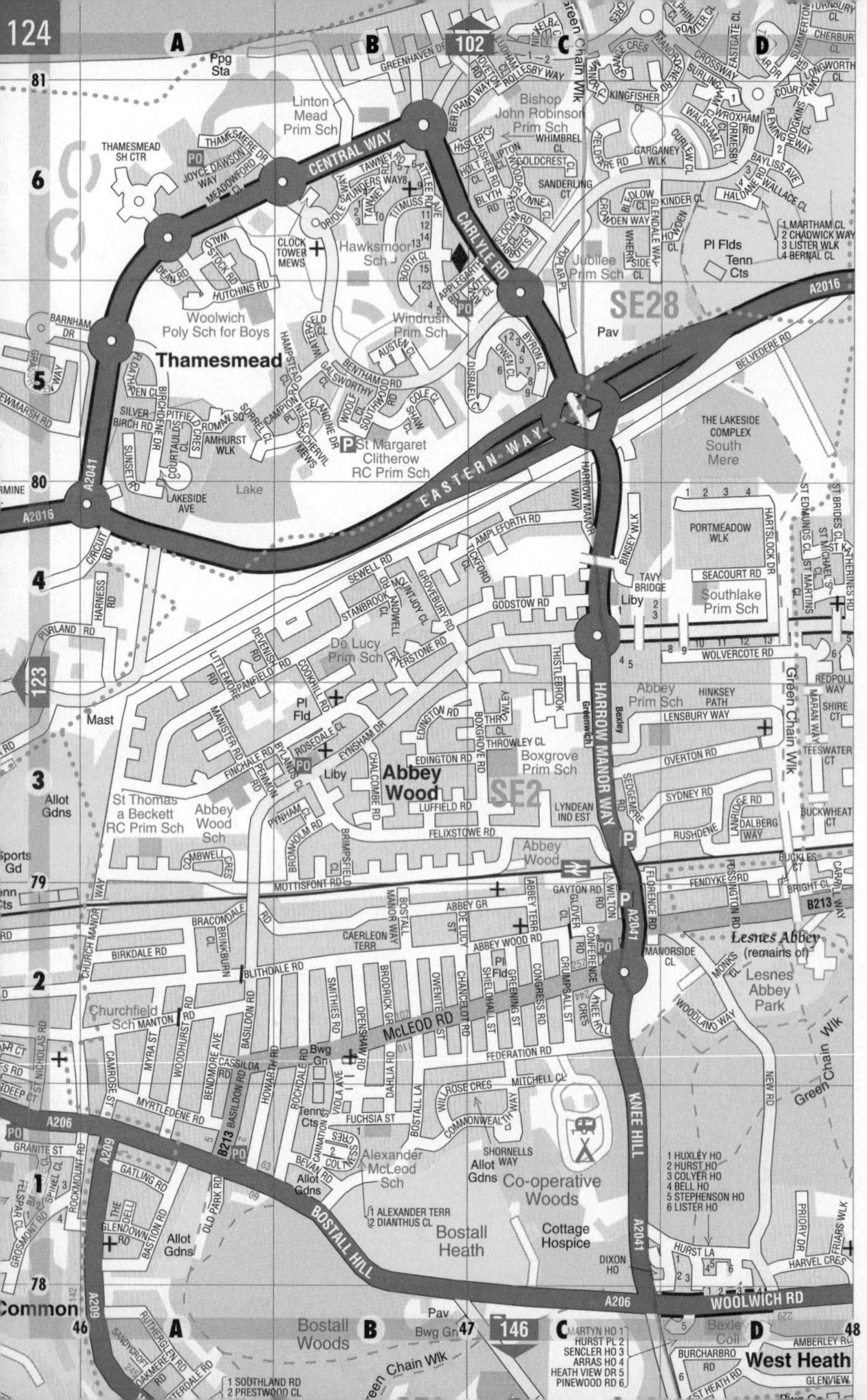
A
B
C
D
102
Ppg Sta
Linton Mead Prim Sch
Bishop John Robinson Prim Sch
THAMESMEAD SH CTR
CENTRAL WAY
CARLYLE RD
Green Chain Wlk
GREENHAVEN DR
ROLLESBY WAY
KINGFISHER CL
CROSSWAY
EASTGATE CL
CHERBURY CL
LONGWORTH CL
WHIMBREL CL
GOLDCREST CL
SANDERLING CT
GARGANEY WLK
CURLEW CL
WROXHAM RD
ORMESBY
WALSHAM CL
BAYLISS AVE
WALLACE CL
HALDANE RD
1 MARTHAM CL
2 CHADWICK WAY
3 LISTER WLK
4 BERNAL CL
Pl Flds
Tenn Cts
JOYCE DAWSON WAY
MEADOWFORD CL
THAMESMERE DR
CLOCK TOWER MEWS
Hawksmoor Sch
TITMUSS AVE
ATTLEE RD
BOOTH CL
APPLEGARTH RD
Jubilee Prim Sch
POPLAR PL
SE28
A2016
DEAN RD
HUTCHINS RD
Woolwich Poly Sch for Boys
BARNHAM DR
Thamesmead
Windrush Prim Sch
AUSTEN CL
BENTHAM RD
GALSWORTHY CL
BYRON CL
OWEN CL
DISRAELI CL
BELVEDERE RD
Pav
THE LAKESIDE COMPLEX
South Mere
EASTERN WAY
SILVER BIRCH RD
BIRCHDENE DR
PITFIELD CRES
ROMAN SQ
SORREL CL
AMHURST WLK
SUNSET RD
LAKESIDE AVE
Lake
St Margaret Clitherow RC Prim Sch
A2041
80
HARROW MANOR WAY
BINSEY WLK
PORTMEADOW WLK
HARTSLOCK DR
SEACOURT RD
Southlake Prim Sch
TAVY BRIDGE
Liby
AMPLEFORTH RD
SEWELL RD
GODSTOW RD
STANBROOK RD
MOUNTJOY CL
GROVEBURY RD
CIRCUIT
HARNESS RD
PURLAND RD
123
De Lucy Prim Sch
PEVERSTONE RD
WOLVERCOTE RD
LITTLEMORE RD
PANFIELD RD
DEVENISH RD
COOKHILL RD
THISTLEBROOK
Abbey Prim Sch
HINKSEY PATH
LENSBURY WAY
Green Chain Wlk
REDPOLL WAY
MARAN WAY
SHIRE CT
TEESWATER CT
Mast
Pl Fld
MANISTER RD
ROSEDALE CL
EYNSHAM DR
EDINGTON RD
BOXGROVE RD
THROWLEY CL
Boxgrove Prim Sch
OVERTON RD
FINCHALE RD
BYLANDS CL
PENMON RD
Abbey Wood
SE2
SEDGEMERE RD
SYDNEY RD
BUCKWHEAT CT
LANRIDGE RD
DALBERG WAY
RUSHDENE
Allot Gdns
St Thomas a Beckett RC Prim Sch
Abbey Wood Sch
PYNHAM CL
BROMHOLM RD
CHALCOMBE RD
LUFFIELD RD
LYNDEAN IND EST
FELIXSTOWE RD
Sports Gd
COMBWELL CRES
BRIMPSFIELD CL
BUCKLES CT
79
MOTTISFONT RD
GAYTON RD
HAMILTON RD
FLORENCE RD
FENDYKE RD
POSSINGTON RD
BRIGHT CL
CARRILL WAY
B213
BRACONDALE RD
CHURCH MANOR WAY
ABBEY GR
ABBEY TERR
CAERLEON TERR
ABBEY WOOD RD
GLOVER CL
CONFERENCE RD
MANORSIDE CL
Lesnes Abbey (remains of)
Lesnes Abbey Park
BIRKDALE RD
BRINKBURN CL
BLITHDALE RD
McLEOD RD
CRUMPSALL ST
CONGRESS RD
GREENING ST
SHIELDHALL ST
CHANCELOT RD
OWENITE ST
BRODRICK GR
SMITHIES RD
OPENSHAW RD
WOODLAND WAY
Churchfield Sch
MANTON RD
MYRA ST
WOODHURST RD
BENDMORE AVE
BASILDON RD
HOWARTH RD
ROCHDALE RD
DAHLIA RD
BOSTALL LA
FEDERATION RD
ST NICHOLAS RD
CAMROSE ST
CASSILDA RD
Bwg Gn
VIOLA AVE
MITCHELL CL
WILLROSE CRES
COMMONWEALTH WAY
KNEE HILL
NEW RD
Green Chain Wlk
MYRTLEDENE RD
A206
A209
FUCHSIA ST
Tenn Cts
CARNATION ST
GRANITE ST
GATLING RD
ROCKMOUNT RD
SPINEL CL
FELSPAR CL
GROSMONT RD
Alexander McLeod Sch
BEVAN RD
Allot Gdns
SHORNELLS WAY
Co-operative Woods
OLD PARK RD
BOSTALL HILL
1 HUXLEY HO
2 HURST HO
3 COLYER HO
4 BELL HO
5 STEPHENSON HO
6 LISTER HO
THE DELL
GLENDOWN RD
BASTION RD
Allot Gdns
1 ALEXANDER TERR
2 DIANTHUS CL
Bostall Heath
Cottage Hospice
PRIORY DR
FRIARS WLK
HURST LA
DIXON HO
HARVEL CRES
78
Common
WOOLWICH RD
46
Bostall Woods
Pav
Bwg Gn
47
146
MARTYN HO 1
HURST PL 2
SENCLER HO 3
ARRAS HO 4
HEATH VIEW DR 5
PINEWOOD RD 6
Bexley Coll
48
AMBERLEY RD
BURCHARBRO RD
West Heath
GLENVIEW
SANDYCROFT
OAKMERE RD
RUTHERGLEN RD
1 SOUTHLAND RD
2 PRESTWOOD CL
Green Chain Wlk

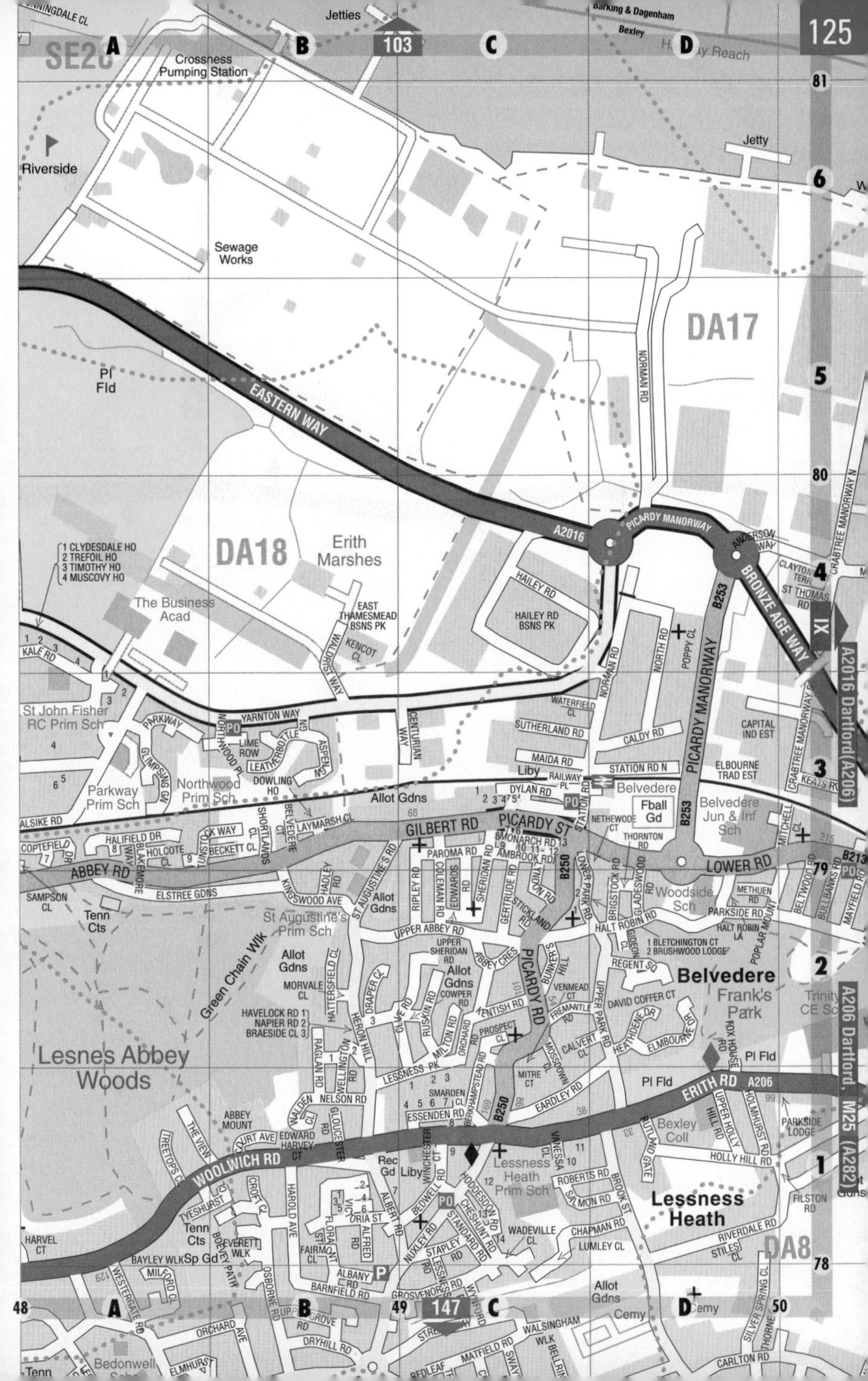

Jetties
103
Barking & Dagenham
Bexley
Crossness Pumping Station
Riverside
Sewage Works
Jetty
DA17
Pl Fld
EASTERN WAY
NORMAN RD
A2016
PICARDY MANOREWAY
ANDERSON WAY
BRONZE AGE WAY
DA18
Erith Marshes
1 CLYDESDALE HO
2 TREFOIL HO
3 TIMOTHY HO
4 MUSCOVY HO
The Business Acad
EAST THAMESMEAD BSNS PK
KENCOT CL
WALDRIST WAY
HAILEY RD
HAILEY RD BSNS PK
NORTH RD
POPPY CL
PICARDY MANORWAY
B253
CRABTREE MANORWAY N
CLAYTON TERR
ST THOMAS RD
A2016 Dartford (A206)
KALE RD
St John Fisher RC Prim Sch
YARNTON WAY
PARKWAY
NORTHWOOD PL
LIME ROW
LEATHERBOTTLE GN
ASPEN GN
CENTURIAN WAY
WATERFIELD CL
SUTHERLAND RD
MAIDA RD
CALDY RD
STATION RD N
CAPITAL IND EST
ELBOURNE TRAD EST
CRABTREE MANORWAY S
KEATS RD
GLIMPSING GN
Parkway Prim Sch
Northwood Prim Sch
DOWLING HO
Liby
RAILWAY PL
DYLAN RD
Belvedere
Fball Gd
Belvedere Jun & Inf Sch
ALSIKE RD
Allot Gdns
SHORTLANDS
BELVEDERE CT
LAYMARSH CL
GILBERT RD
PICARDY ST
STATION RD
NETHEWODE CT
THORNTON RD
MITCHELL CL
COPTEFIELD DR
HALIFIELD DR
TUNSTOCK WAY
HOLCOTE CL
BECKETT CL
MONARCH RD
AMBROOK RD
PAROMA RD
LOWER RD
B213
ABBEY RD
BLAKEMORE WAY
ELSTREE GDNS
KINGSWOOD AVE
HADLEY RD
ST AUGUSTINE'S RD
COLEMAN RD
EDWARDS RD
SHERIDAN RD
GERTRUDE RD
NUXLEY RD
B250
LOWER PARK RD
BRIGSTOCK RD
GLADESWOOD RD
Woodside Sch
METHUEN RD
BELTWOOD RD
BULLBANKS RD
MAYFIELD RD
SAMPSON CL
Tenn Cts
Allot Gdns
RIPLEY RD
STICKLAND RD
HALT ROBIN RD
PARKSIDE RD
HALT ROBIN LA
POPLAR MOUNT
St Augustine's Prim Sch
UPPER ABBEY RD
GIDEON RD
1 BLETCHINGTON CT
2 BRUSHWOOD LODGE
Green Chain Wlk
Allot Gdns
HATTERSFIELD CL
UPPER SHERIDAN RD
ABBEY CRES
PICARDY RD
BUNKER'S HILL
REGENT SQ
Belvedere
Frank's Park
Trinity CE Sch
A206 Dartford, M25 (A282)
MORVALE CL
DRAPER CL
Allot Gdns
COWPER RD
VENMEAD CT
FREMANTLE RD
DAVID COFFER CT
HAVELOCK RD 1
NAPIER RD 2
BRAESIDE CL 3
OLIVE RD
RUSKIN RD
KENTISH RD
HEATHDENE DR
ELMBOURNE DR
HERON HILL
MILTON RD
PROSPECT CL
UPPER PARK RD
CALVERT CL
FOX HOUSE RD
Lesnes Abbey Woods
RAGLAN RD
WELLINGTON RD
LESSNESS PK
ORCHARD RD
MOSSDOWN CL
Pl Fld
Pl Fld
MITRE CT
ERITH RD
A206
SMARDEN CL
BERKHAMPSTEAD RD
EARDLEY RD
UPPER HOLLY HILL RD
HOLMHURST RD
WALDEN CL
NELSON RD
ESSENDEN RD
PARKSIDE LODGE
ABBEY MOUNT
COURT AVE
EDWARD HARVEY CT
GLOUCESTER RD
VANESSA WAY
RUTLAND GATE
Bexley Coll
TREETOPS CL
THE VIEW
WOOLWICH RD
Rec Gd
Liby
WINCHESTER CT
Lessness Heath Prim Sch
HOLLY HILL RD
HARVEL CT
TYESHURST
CROFT CL
HAROLD AVE
VICTORIA ST
FLORA ST
ALBERT RD
ALFRED RD
BEDWELL RD
HODDESDON RD
CHESHUNT RD
ROBERTS RD
SALMON RD
BROOK ST
Lessness Heath
FILSTON RD
Tenn Cts
EVERETT WLK
BOEVEY PATH
FAIRMONT CL
STANDARD RD
STAPLEY RD
WADEVILLE CL
CHAPMAN RD
LUMLEY CL
RIVERDALE RD
STILES CL
DA8
BAYLEY WLK
Sp Gd
WESTERGATE RD
MILFORD CL
OSBORNE RD
ALBANY RD
BARNFIELD RD
LESSNESS RD
Allot Gdns
GROSVENOR RD
WYNFORD
147
Cemy
Cemy
UPPER GROVE RD
ORCHARD AVE
DRYHILL RD
WALSINGHAM WLK
SILVER SPRING CL
THORNE
Bedonwell Sch
ELMHURST
MATFIELD RD
BELLRING
CARLTON RD
A B C D
81 6 5 80 4 3 79 2 1 78
48 49 50

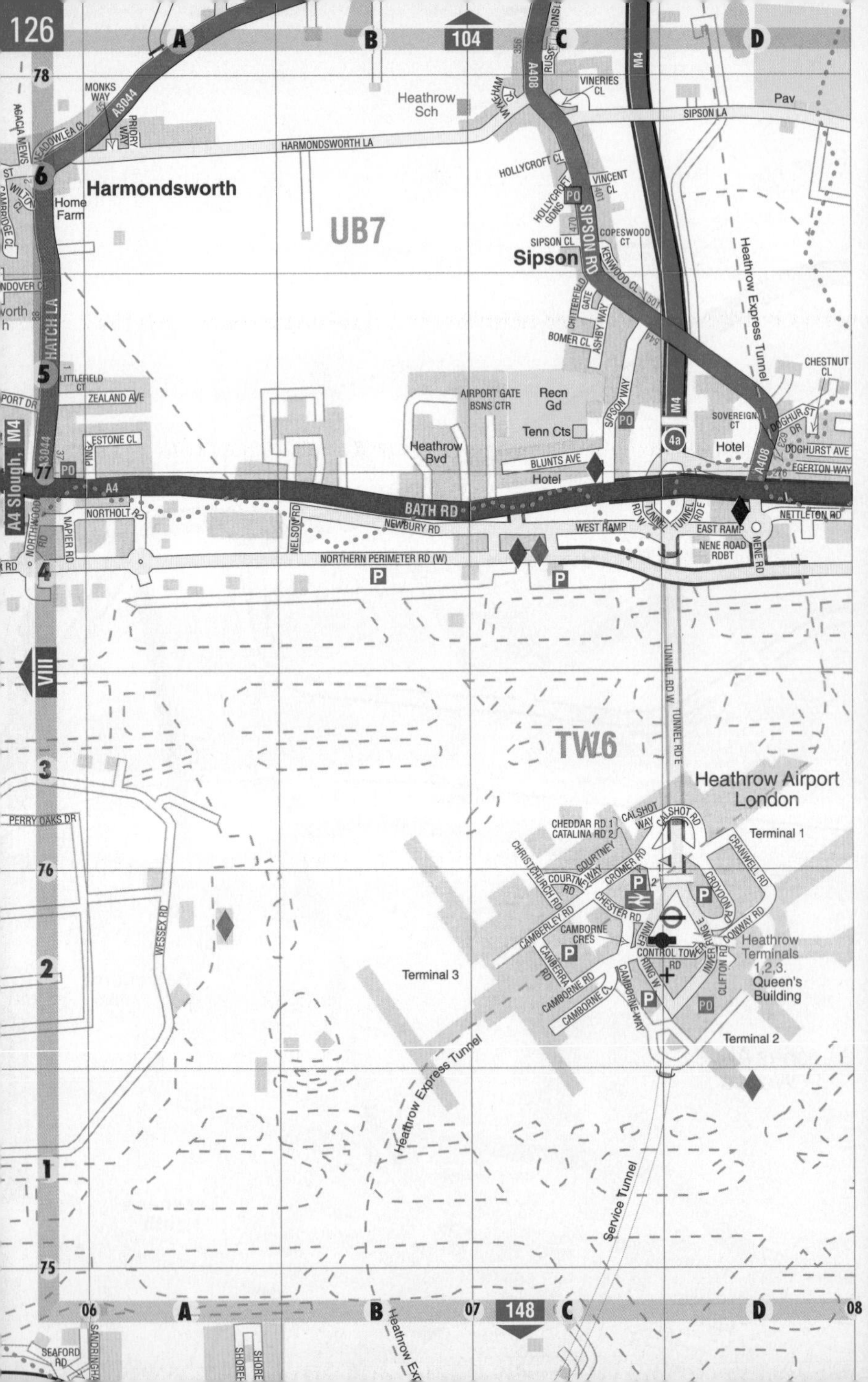

Harmondsworth
UB7
Sipson
TW6
Heathrow Airport London
Heathrow Sch
Home Farm
HARMONDSWORTH LA
SIPSON LA
SIPSON RD
HATCH LA
BATH RD
NORTHERN PERIMETER RD (W)
NEWBURY RD
NORTHOLT RD
NAPIER RD
NELSON RD
ZEALAND AVE
LITTLEFIELD CT
ESTONE CL
MONKS WAY
PRIORY WAY
MEADOWLEA CL
ACACIA MEWS
WILTON CL
CAMBRIDGE CL
VINERIES CL
WYKEHAM CL
HOLLYCROFT CL
HOLLYCROFT GDNS
VINCENT CL
COPESWOOD CT
KENWOOD CL
CHITTERFIELD GATE
ASHBY WAY
BOMER CL
SIPSON WAY
AIRPORT GATE BSNS CTR
Recn Gd
Tenn Cts
BLUNTS AVE
Heathrow Bvd
Hotel
WEST RAMP
EAST RAMP
TUNNEL RD W
TUNNEL RD E
NENE ROAD RDBT
NENE RD
NETTLETON RD
SOVEREIGN CT
CHESTNUT CL
DOGHURST DR
DOGHURST AVE
EGERTON WAY
Heathrow Express Tunnel
Service Tunnel
PERRY OAKS DR
WESSEX RD
Terminal 1
Terminal 2
Terminal 3
Heathrow Terminals 1,2,3. Queen's Building
CHEDDAR RD 1
CATALINA RD 2
CALSHOT WAY
CALSHOT RD
CHRISTCHURCH RD
COURTNEY RD
CROMER RD
CHESTER RD
CAMBERLEY RD
CAMBORNE CRES
CANBERRA RD
CAMBORNE RD
CAMBORNE CL
CAMBORNE WAY
INNER RING W
INNER RING E
CONTROL TOWER RD
CLIFTON RD
CROYDON RD
CRANWELL RD
CONWAY RD
A4 Slough, M4
A3044
A408
M4
4a
Pav
SEAFORD RD
SANDRINGHAM
SHORE
104
148
VIII

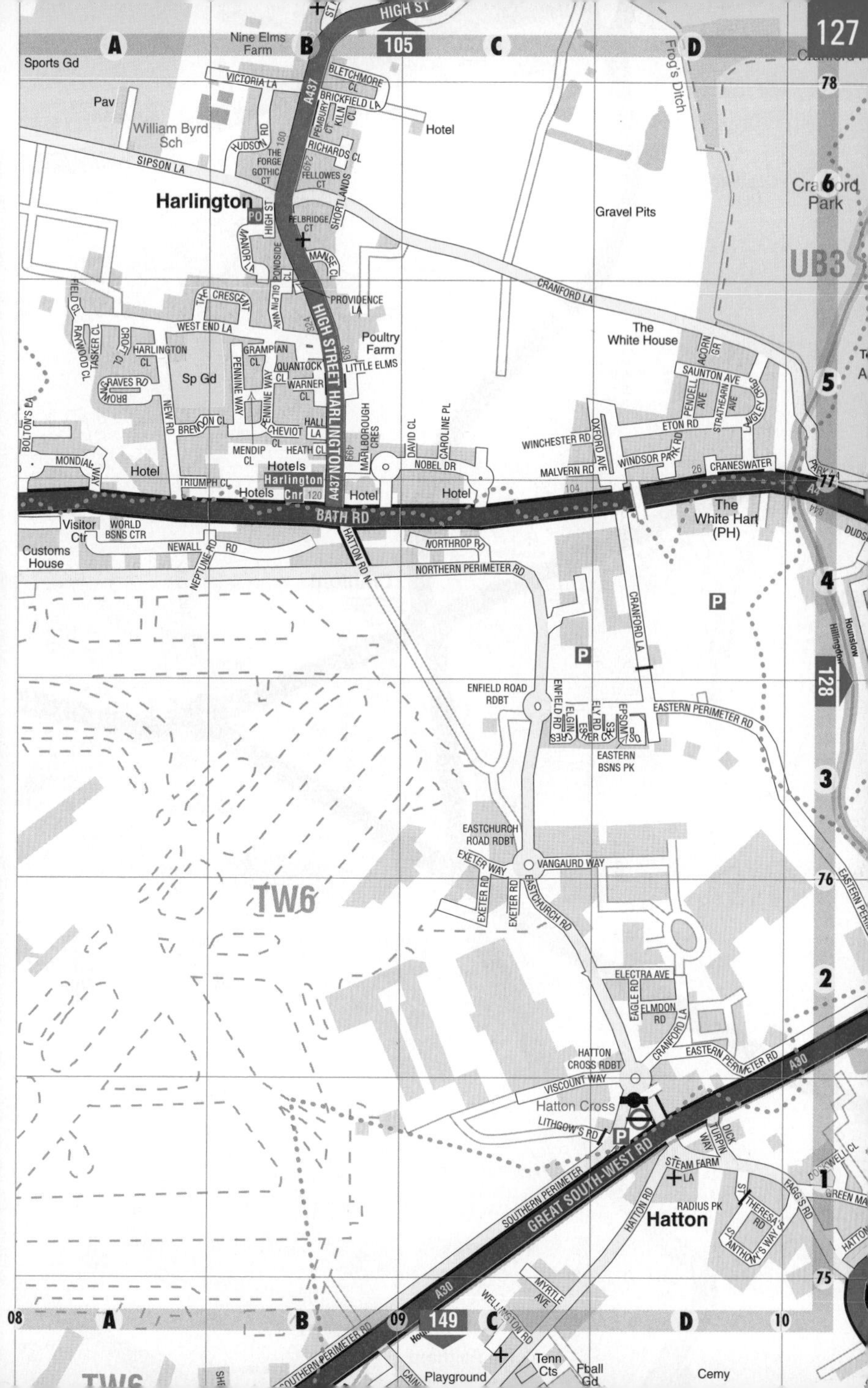

HIGH ST
105
Nine Elms Farm
Sports Gd
Pav
William Byrd Sch
VICTORIA LA
BLETCHMORE CL
BRICKFIELD LA
PEMBURY CT
KILN CL
Hotel
Frog's Ditch
HUDSON RD
THE FORGE
GOTHIC CT
RICHARDS CL
FELLOWES CT
SHORTLANDS
SIPSON LA
Harlington
PO
HIGH ST
FELBRIDGE CT
MANOR LA
PONDSIDE CL
MANSE CL
Gravel Pits
Cranford Park
UB3
CRANFORD LA
FIELD CL
THE CRESCENT
GILPIN WAY
PROVIDENCE LA
HIGH STREET HARLINGTON
A437
Poultry Farm
LITTLE ELMS
WEST END LA
RAYWOOD CL
TASKER CL
CROFT CL
HARLINGTON CL
GRAMPIAN CL
QUANTOCK CL
WARNER CL
Sp Gd
PENNINE WAY
RAVES RD
NEW RD
BRENDON CL
CHEVIOT CL
HALL LA
HEATH CL
MENDIP CL
MARLBOROUGH CRES
DAVID CL
CAROLINE PL
NOBEL DR
The White House
ACORN GR
SAUNTON AVE
PENDELL AVE
STRATHEARN AVE
LANGLEY CRES
ETON RD
WINCHESTER RD
OXFORD AVE
WINDSOR PARK RD
MALVERN RD
CRANESWATER
PARK LA
BOLTON'S LA
MONDIAL WAY
Hotel
Hotels
Harlington Cnr
TRIUMPH CL
Hotels
Hotel
Hotel
BATH RD
A4
The White Hart (PH)
Visitor Ctr
WORLD BSNS CTR
Customs House
NEWALL RD
NEPTUNE RD
HATTON RD N
NORTHROP RD
NORTHERN PERIMETER RD
CRANFORD LA
P
P
Hounslow
Hillingdon
128
ENFIELD ROAD RDBT
ENFIELD RD
ELGIN CRES
ELY RD
ESHER CRES
EPSOM SQ
EASTERN PERIMETER RD
EASTERN BSNS PK
EASTCHURCH ROAD RDBT
EXETER WAY
VANGAURD WAY
EXETER RD
EXETER RD
EASTCHURCH RD
TW6
ELECTRA AVE
EAGLE RD
ELMDON RD
CRANFORD LA
HATTON CROSS RDBT
EASTERN PERIMETER RD
A30
VISCOUNT WAY
Hatton Cross
LITHGOW'S RD
P
DICK TURPIN WAY
STEAM FARM LA
SOUTHERN PERIMETER RD
GREAT SOUTH-WEST RD
HATTON RD
RADIUS PK
Hatton
ST THERESA'S RD
ST ANTHONY'S WAY
FAGG'S RD
DOCKWELL CL
GREEN MAN
MYRTLE AVE
WELLINGTON RD
SOUTHERN PERIMETER RD
149
Playground
Tenn Cts
Fball Gd
Cemy
A
B
C
D
78
6
5
77
4
3
76
2
1
75
08
09
10

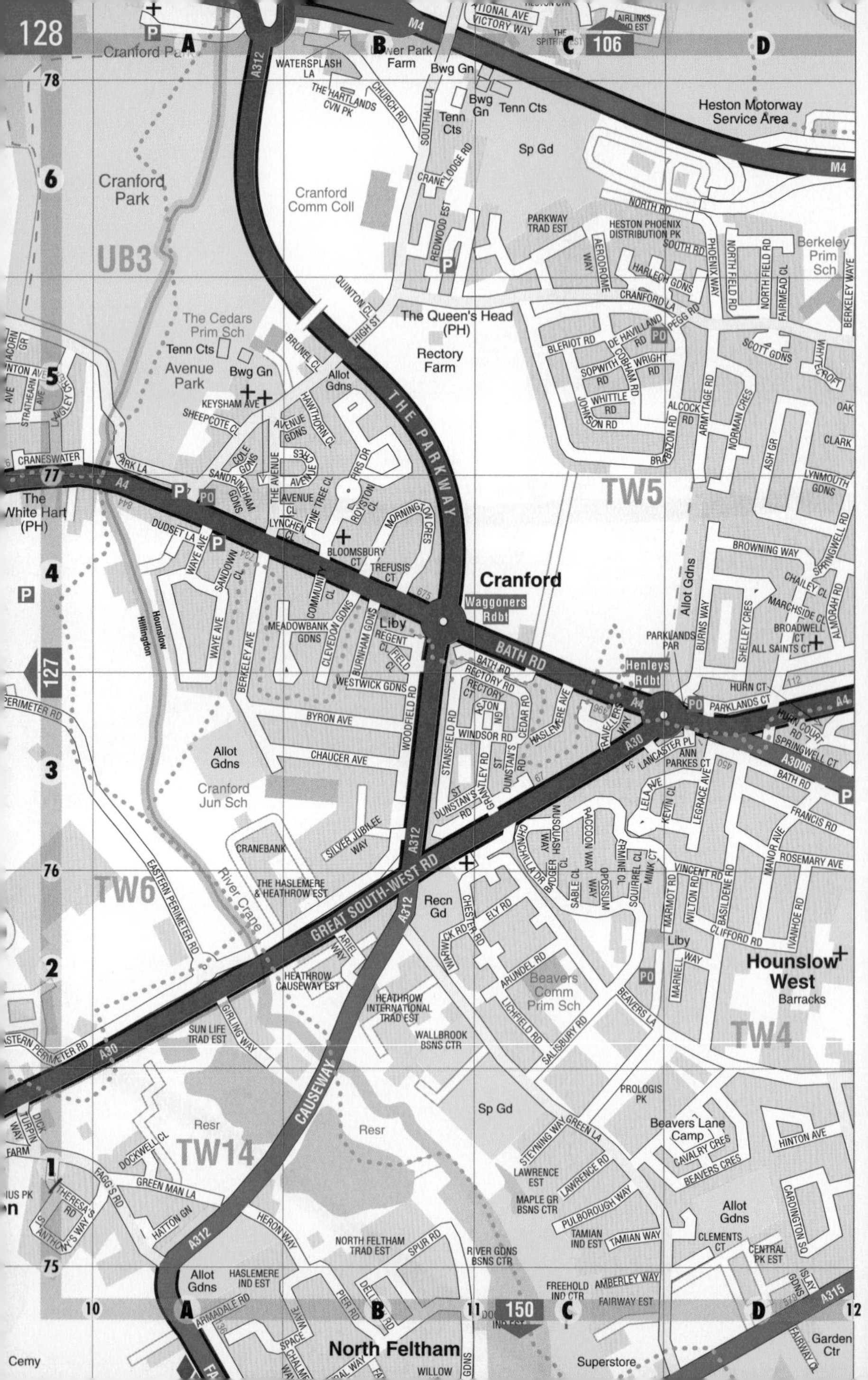

A
B
C
D
106
Cranford Park
Lower Park Farm
Watersplash La
The Hartlands Cvn Pk
Church Rd
Southall La
Bwg Gn
Tenn Cts
Heston Motorway Service Area
M4
A312
Cranford Park
UB3
Cranford Comm Coll
Crane Lodge Rd
Sp Gd
Redwood Est
North Rd
Parkway Trad Est
Heston Phoenix Distribution Pk
South Rd
Aerodrome Way
Phoenix Way
North Field Rd
Fairmead Cl
Berkeley Prim Sch
Berkeley Waye
Harlech Gdns
Cranford La
Pegg Rd
Quinton Cl
High St
The Queen's Head (PH)
Rectory Farm
The Cedars Prim Sch
Tenn Cts
Avenue Park
Bwg Gn
Brunel Cl
Allot Gdns
Keysham Ave
Sheepcote Cl
Hawthorn Cl
Avenue Gdns
The Parkway
Bleriot Rd
De Havilland Rd
Sopwith Rd
Cobham Rd
Wright Rd
Whittle Rd
Johnson Rd
Alcock Rd
Armytage Rd
Norman Cres
Brabazon Rd
Scott Gdns
Whytecroft
Ash Gr
Clark
Lynmouth Gdns
Craneswater
Park La
Cole Gdns
Sandringham Gdns
The Avenue
Avenue Cres
Avenue Cl
Firs Dr
Pine Tree Cl
Royston Cl
Lynchen Cl
Morningtons Cres
Bloomsbury Ct
Trefusis Ct
TW5
The White Hart (PH)
A4
Dudset La
Waye Ave
Sandown Cl
Cranford
Waggoners Rdbt
Browning Way
Springwell Rd
Chailey Cl
Marchside Cl
Almorah Rd
Broadwell Ct
All Saints Ct
Allot Gdns
Burns Way
Shelley Cres
Parklands Par
Community Cl
Meadowbank Gdns
Clevedon Gdns
Burnham Gdns
Liby
Regent Cl
Field Cl
Bath Rd
Rectory Rd
Rectory Ct
Acton Gn
Cedar Rd
Haslemere Ave
Travellers Way
Henleys Rdbt
Hurn Ct
Parklands Ct
Hurn Court Rd
Springwell Ct
A3006
127
Hounslow
Hillingdon
Perimeter Rd
Berkeley Ave
Westwick Gdns
Woodfield Rd
Byron Ave
Chaucer Ave
Windsor Rd
Stansfield Rd
Grantley Rd
St Dunstan's Rd
Lancaster Pl
Ann Parkes Ct
Lela Ave
Kevin Cl
Legrace Ave
Bath Rd
Francis Rd
A30
Allot Gdns
Cranford Jun Sch
Cranebank
Silver Jubilee Way
Musquash Way
Raccoon Way
Chinchilla Dr
Badger Cl
Sable Cl
Ermine Cl
Opossum Way
Squirrel Cl
Mink Ct
Manor Ave
Rosemary Ave
TW6
Eastern Perimeter Rd
River Crane
The Haslemere & Heathrow Est
Great South-West Rd
Recn Gd
Chester Rd
Ely Rd
Warwick Rd
Marmot Rd
Wilton Rd
Vincent Rd
Basildene Rd
Clifford Rd
Ivanhoe Rd
Liby
Marnell Way
Hounslow West
Barracks
Ariel Way
Heathrow Causeway Est
Heathrow International Trad Est
Arundel Rd
Beavers Comm Prim Sch
Lichfield Rd
Beavers La
Salisbury Rd
TW4
Sun Life Trad Est
Girling Way
Wallbrook Bsns Ctr
Eastern Perimeter Rd
Prologis Pk
Causeway
Resr
Sp Gd
Steyning Way
Green La
Beavers Lane Camp
Cavalry Cres
Beavers Cres
Hinton Ave
Dick Turpin Way
Dockwell Cl
TW14
Lawrence Est
Lawrence Rd
Maple Gr Bsns Ctr
Pulborough Way
Allot Gdns
Cardington Sq
Theresa Rd
Fagg's Rd
Green Man La
Hatton Gn
St Anthony's Way
Heron Way
North Feltham Trad Est
Spur Rd
River Gdns Bsns Ctr
Tamian Ind Est
Tamian Way
Clements Ct
Central Pk Est
Allot Gdns
Haslemere Ind Est
Dell Rd
Pier Rd
Freehold Ind Ctr
Amberley Way
Fairway Est
Islay Gdns
A315
10
11
150
12
Armadale Rd
Space Waye
North Feltham
Cemy
Willow
Superstore
Garden Ctr
Fairway Cl
78
6
5
77
4
3
76
2
1
75

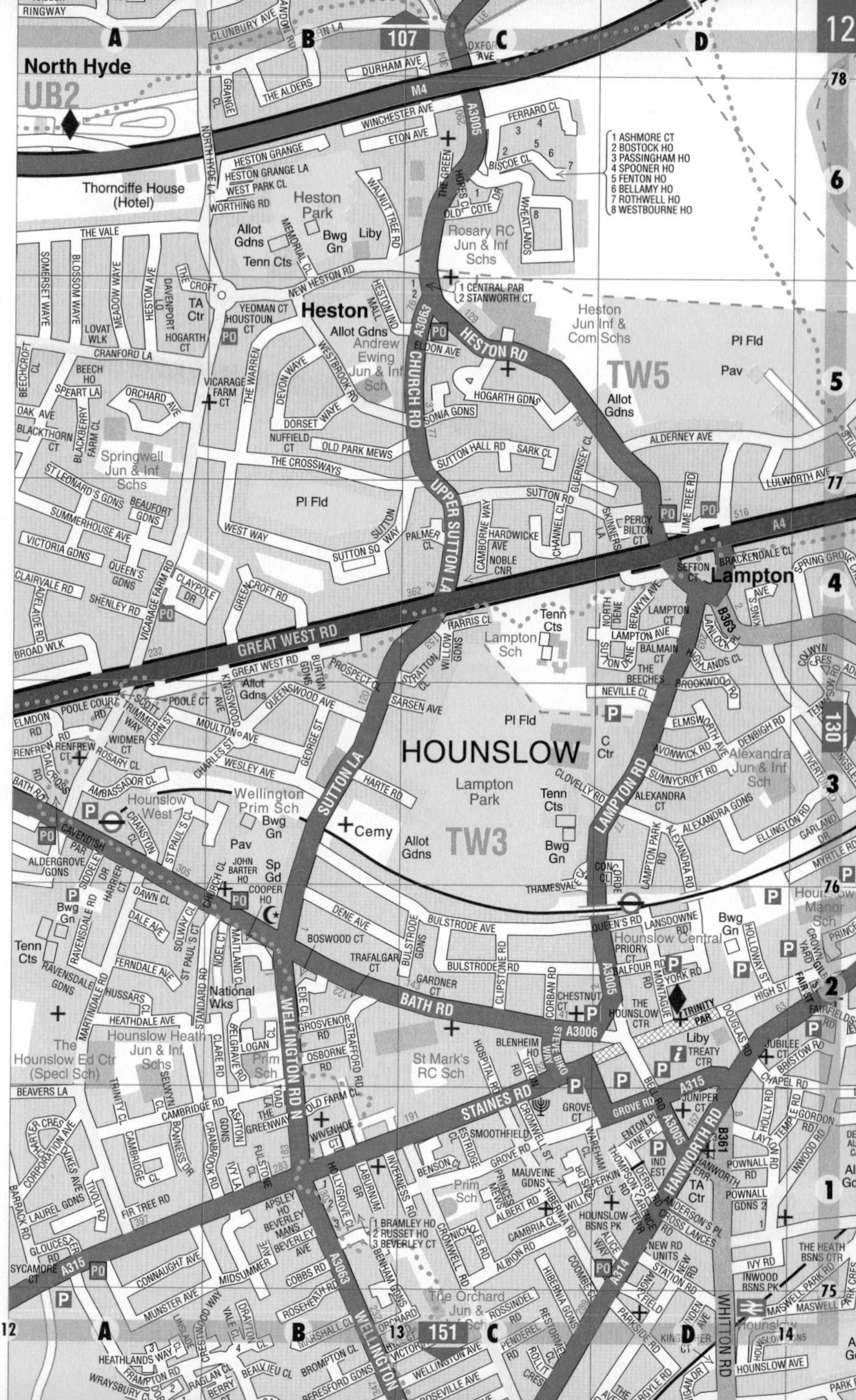
North Hyde
UB2
Thorncliffe House (Hotel)
Heston Park
Heston
TW5
Lampton
HOUNSLOW
Lampton Park
TW3
Hounslow West
Hounslow Central
GREAT WEST RD
BATH RD
STAINES RD
HESTON RD
CHURCH RD
UPPER SUTTON LA
SUTTON LA
LAMPTON RD
WELLINGTON RD N
HANWORTH RD
WHITTON RD
M4
A4
A3005
A3063
A315
A3006
A314
B363
B361
1 ASHMORE CT
2 BOSTOCK HO
3 PASSINGHAM HO
4 SPOONER HO
5 FENTON HO
6 BELLAMY HO
7 ROTHWELL HO
8 WESTBOURNE HO
1 CENTRAL PAR
2 STANWORTH CT
1 BRAMLEY HO
2 RUSSET HO
3 BEVERLEY CT
107
130
151

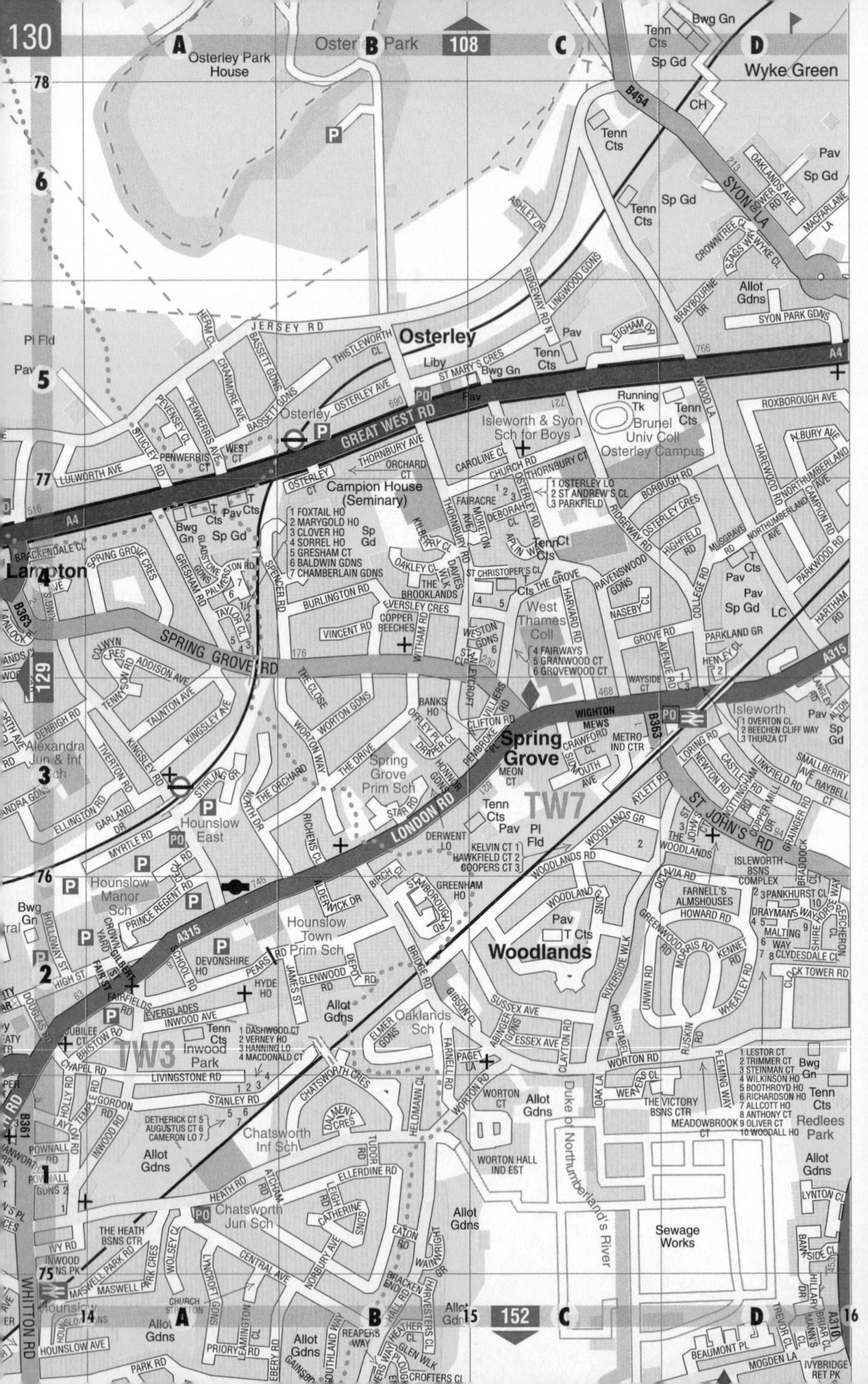

A
B
C
D
Osterley Park
108
Osterley Park House
Tenn Cts
Bwg Gn
Sp Gd
Wyke Green
78
B454
CH
P
Tenn Cts
6
Pav
Sp Gd
OAKLANDS AVE
GOWER RD
SYON LA
ASHLEY DR
Tenn Cts
Sp Gd
MACFARLANE LA
CROWNTREE CL
STAGS WAY
WYKE CL
RIDGEWAY RD N
LINGWOOD GDNS
BRAYBOURNE DR
Allot Gdns
SYON PARK GDNS
JERSEY RD
HERM CL
BASSETT GDNS
THISTLEWORTH CL
Osterley
LEIGHAM DR
Pav
Pl Fld
Tenn Cts
Liby
ST MARY'S CRES
Bwg Gn
A4
Pav
5
CRANMORE AVE
OSTERLEY AVE
PO
Pav
PEVENSEY CL
PENWERRIS AVE
BASSETT GDNS
Osterley
P
GREAT WEST RD
Running Tk
Tenn Cts
ROXBOROUGH AVE
Isleworth & Syon Sch for Boys
Brunel Univ Coll Osterley Campus
STUCLEY RD
PENWERRIS CT
WEST CT
THORNBURY AVE
ORCHARD CT
CAROLINE CL
CHURCH RD
THORNBURY CT
ALBURY AVE
HAREWOOD RD
NORTHUMBERLAND AVE
77
LULWORTH AVE
OSTERLEY CT
Campion House (Seminary)
1 OSTERLEY LO
2 ST ANDREW'S CL
3 PARKFIELD
BOROUGH RD
CAMPION RD
T Cts
Pav
T Cts
FAIRACRE
DEBORAH CL
OSTERLEY RD
OSTERLEY CRES
A4
Bwg Gn
Sp Gd
1 FOXTAIL HO
2 MARYGOLD HO
3 CLOVER HO
4 SORREL HO
5 GRESHAM CT
6 BALDWIN GDNS
7 CHAMBERLAIN GDNS
Sp Gd
THORNBURY RD
MORETON AVE
KILBERRY CL
Tenn Ct
Cts
RIDGEWAY RD
HIGHFIELD RD
MUSGRAVE RD
NORTHUMBERLAND AVE
PARKWOOD RD
BRACKENDALE CL
SPRING GROVE CRES
GRESHAM RD
GLADSTONE GDNS
PALMERSTON RD
SPENCER RD
OAKLEY CL
DAVIES WLK
ST CHRISTOPHER'S CL
THE GROVE
RAVENSWOOD GDNS
T Cts
Pav
Lampton
4
THE BROOKLANDS
Cts
HARVARD RD
NASEBY CL
COLLEGE RD
Pav
Sp Gd
LC
HARTHAM RD
B363
BURLINGTON RD
EVERSLEY CRES
West Thames Coll
TAYLOR CL
COPPER BEECHES
WITHAM RD
VINCENT RD
WESTON GDNS
GROVE RD
PARKLAND GR
SPRING GROVE RD
COLWYN CRES
ADDISON AVE
176
STANLEY CL
230
4 FAIRWAYS
5 GRANWOOD CT
6 GROVEWOOD CT
AVENUE RD
HENLEY CL
A315
129
TENNYSON RD
THE CLOSE
STANLEYCROFT
WAYSIDE CT
468
TAUNTON AVE
KINGSLEY AVE
WORTON GDNS
BANKS HO
VILLIERS RD
WIGHTON MEWS
PO
Isleworth
1 OVERTON CL
2 BEECHEN CLIFF WAY
3 THURZA CT
Pav
Sp Gd
DENBIGH RD
TIVERTON RD
KINGSLEY RD
OFFLEY PL
DRAPER CL
CLIFTON RD
PEMBROKE PL
Spring Grove
CRAWFORD CL
B363
METRO IND CTR
LORING RD
NEWTON RD
CASTLE RD
LINKFIELD RD
SMALLBERRY AVE
RAYBELL CT
Alexandra Jun & Inf Sch
3
STIRLING GR
WORTON WAY
THE DRIVE
Spring Grove Prim Sch
HONNOR GDNS
MEON CT
SIDMOUTH AVE
AYLETT RD
NOTTINGHAM RD
COPPER MILL DR
ELLINGTON RD
GARLAND DR
P
NORTH DR
THE ORCHARD
STAR RD
LONDON RD
Tenn Cts
Pav
TW7
Pl Fld
ST JOHN'S RD
ST JOHN'S CT
GRAINGER RD
Hounslow East
RICHENS CL
DERWENT LO
KELVIN CT 1
HAWKFIELD CT 2
COOPERS CT 3
WOODLANDS GR
THE WOODLANDS
94
BRADDOCK CL
MYRTLE RD
PO
P
WOODLANDS RD
ISLEWORTH BSNS COMPLEX
76
P
Hounslow Manor Sch
CECIL RD
PRINCE REGENT RD
P
746
ALDERWICK DR
BIRCH CL
STANBOROUGH RD
GREENHAM HO
WOODLAND GDNS
OCTAVIA RD
FARNELL'S ALMSHOUSES
HOWARD RD
2 3 PANKHURST CL
DRAYMANS WAY
4 5
MALTING WAY
SHIRE HORSE WAY
PERCHERON CL
Bwg Gn
HOLLOWAY ST
CROWN YARD
GILBERT ST
P
A315
Hounslow Town Prim Sch
Pav
T Cts
Woodlands
GREENWOOD RD
MORRIS RD
KENNET RD
6 7 8 CLYDESDALE CL
CLOCK TOWER RD
2
HIGH ST
FAIR ST
P
SCHOOL RD
DEVONSHIRE HO
PEARS RD
JAMES ST
HYDE HO
GLENWOOD RD
DEPOT RD
BRIDGE RD
GIBSON CL
SUSSEX AVE
RIVERSIDE WLK
UNWIN RD
WHEATLEY RD
63
DOUGLAS RD
FAIRFIELDS
EVERGLADES
INWOOD AVE
Allot Gdns
Oaklands Sch
ELMER GDNS
ABINGER GDNS
ESSEX AVE
CHRISTABEL CL
CLAYTON RD
RUSKIN RD
JUBILEE CT
BRISTOW RD
P
Tenn Cts
1 DASHWOOD CT
2 VERNEY HO
3 HANNING LO
4 MACDONALD CT
TW3
Inwood Park
FARNELL RD
PAGET LA
WORTON RD
WEAVERS CL
FLEMING WAY
1 LESTOR CT
2 TRIMMER CT
3 STEINMAN CT
4 WILKINSON HO
5 BOOTHROYD HO
6 RICHARDSON HO
7 ALLCOTT HO
8 ANTHONY CT
9 OLIVER CT
10 WOODALL HO
Bwg Gn
Tenn Cts
CHAPEL RD
LIVINGSTONE RD
STANLEY RD
CHATSWORTH CRES
HELDMANN CL
WORTON CT
Allot Gdns
Duke of Northumberland's River
OAK LA
THE VICTORY BSNS CTR
MEADOWBROOK CT
Redlees Park
HOLLY RD
TEMPLE RD
GORDON RD
LAYTON RD
INWOOD RD
DETHERICK CT 5
AUGUSTUS CT 6
CAMERON LO 7
DALMENY CRES
B361
POWNALL RD
POWNALL GDNS
Chatsworth Inf Sch
TUDOR RD
WORTON HALL IND EST
Allot Gdns
1
Allot Gdns
ELLERDINE RD
ATCHAM RD
LEIGH RD
HEATH RD
CATHERINE GDNS
LYNTON CL
PO
Chatsworth Jun Sch
THE HEATH BSNS CTR
EATON RD
Allot Gdns
Sewage Works
IVY RD
MASWELL PARK RD
MASWELL PARK CRES
WOLSEY CL
LYNCROFT GDNS
CENTRAL AVE
NORBURY AVE
WAINWRIGHT GR
BANKSIDE CL
INWOOD BSNS PK
75
Hounslow
CHURCH STATION
LEAMINGTON CL
BRACKEN END
HALL RD
HARVESTERS CL
HILLARY DR
WHITTON RD
14
A
B
Allot Gdns
15
152
C
D
TREVOR CL
MANN'S CL
BRIAR CL
A310
16
HOUNSLOW AVE
Allot Gdns
PRIORY RD
EBERY RD
Allot Gdns
SOUTHLAND WAY
REAPERS WAY
HEATHER CL
GLEN WLK
BEAUMONT PL
PARK RD
CROFTERS CL
MOGDEN LA
IVYBRIDGE RET PK

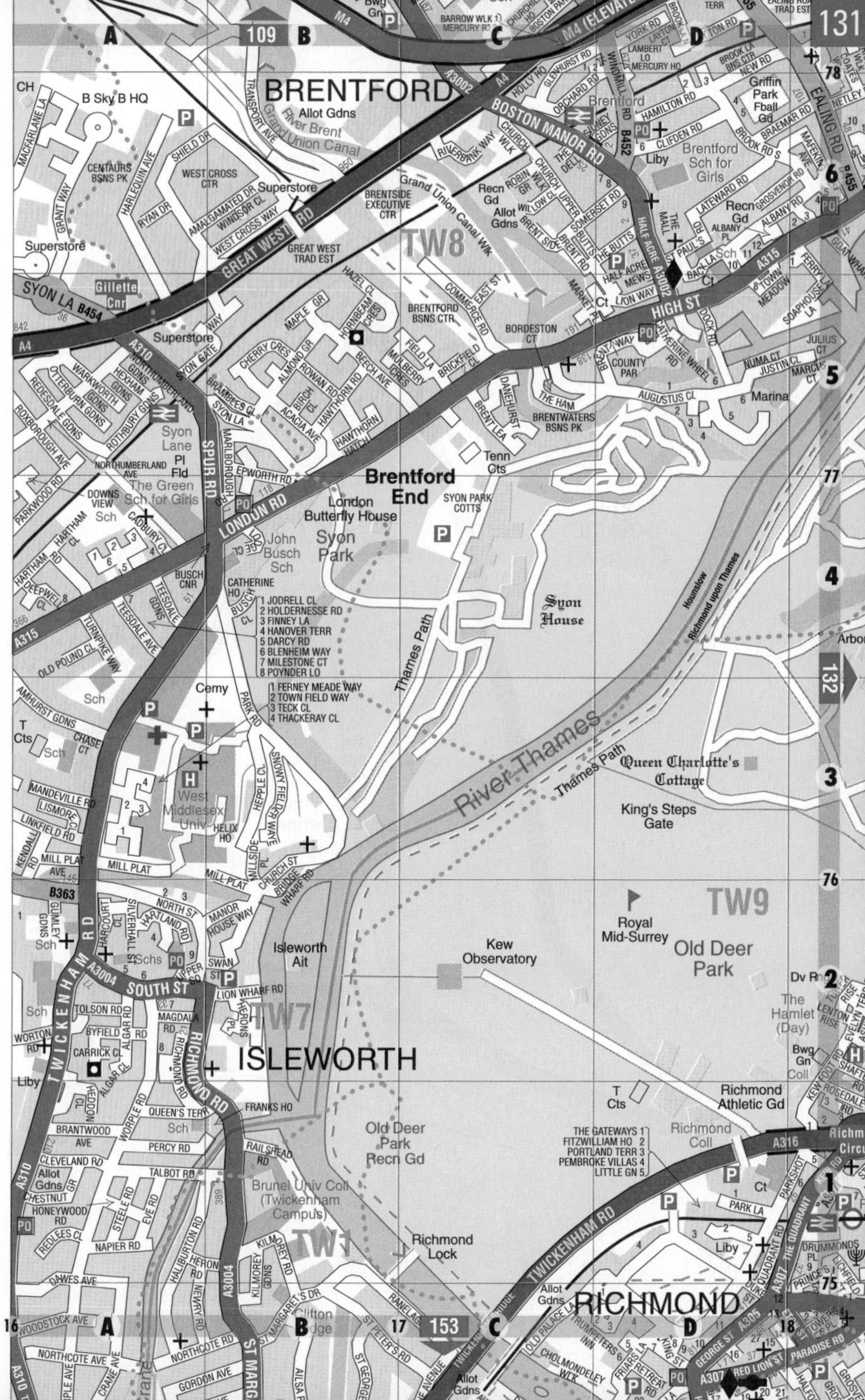

109
153
132
A
B
C
D
BRENTFORD
Brentford End
ISLEWORTH
RICHMOND
TW8
TW7
TW9
TW1
M4
A4
A315
A310
A3002
A3004
A316
A307
B452
B454
B363
B455
GREAT WEST RD
BOSTON MANOR RD
HIGH ST
LONDON RD
SPUR RD
SYON LA
TWICKENHAM RD
RICHMOND RD
SOUTH ST
HALF ACRE
EALING RD
River Thames
River Brent
Grand Union Canal
Grand Union Canal Wlk
Thames Path
Syon Park
Syon House
London Butterfly House
Syon Lane
Brentford
B Sky B HQ
Centaurs Bsns Pk
West Cross Ctr
Great West Trad Est
Brentside Executive Ctr
Brentford Bsns Ctr
Brentwaters Bsns Pk
Gillette Cnr
Superstore
Griffin Park Fball Gd
Brentford Sch for Girls
The Green Sch for Girls
John Busch Sch
West Middlesex Univ
Isleworth Ait
Kew Observatory
Royal Mid-Surrey
Old Deer Park
Old Deer Park Recn Gd
Queen Charlotte's Cottage
King's Steps Gate
Richmond Lock
Richmond Athletic Gd
Richmond Coll
Brunel Univ Coll (Twickenham Campus)
Marina
Hounslow
Richmond upon Thames
1 JODRELL CL
2 HOLDERNESSE RD
3 FINNEY LA
4 HANOVER TERR
5 DARCY RD
6 BLENHEIM WAY
7 MILESTONE CT
8 POYNDER LO
1 FERNEY MEADE WAY
2 TOWN FIELD WAY
3 TECK CL
4 THACKERAY CL
THE GATEWAYS 1
FITZWILLIAM HO 2
PORTLAND TERR 3
PEMBROKE VILLAS 4
LITTLE GN 5

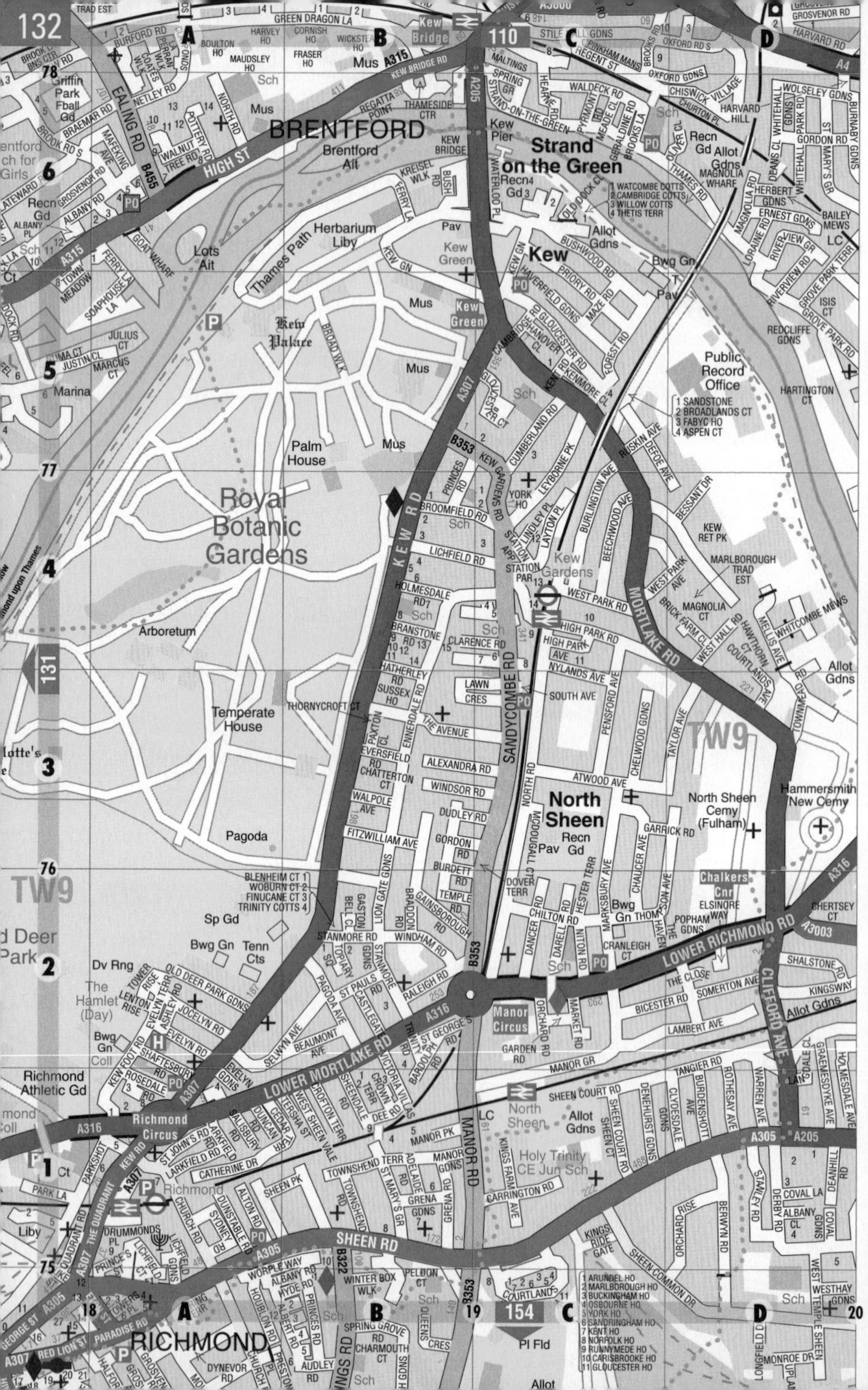

132
A
B
C
D
110
Kew Bridge
BRENTFORD
Brentford Ait
Strand on the Green
Griffin Park Fball Gd
EALING RD
HIGH ST
KEW BRIDGE RD
Lots Ait
Herbarium Liby
Thames Path
Kew Green
Kew Pier
Kew
Kew Palace
BROAD WLK
Palm House
Royal Botanic Gardens
Arboretum
Temperate House
Pagoda
KEW RD
Kew Gardens
SANDYCOMBE RD
MORTLAKE RD
Public Record Office
KEW RET PK
MARLBOROUGH TRAD EST
TW9
North Sheen
North Sheen Cemy (Fulham)
Hammersmith New Cemy
Chalkers Cnr
LOWER RICHMOND RD
CLIFFORD AVE
LOWER MORTLAKE RD
Manor Circus
MANOR RD
North Sheen
Holy Trinity CE Jun Sch
SHEEN RD
Richmond Circus
Richmond Athletic Gd
Old Deer Park
Dv Rng
The Hamlet (Day)
Sp Gd
Bwg Gn
Tenn Cts
RICHMOND
Richmond
PARADISE RD
RED LION ST
GEORGE ST
154
Pl Fld
131
1
2
3
4
5
6
75
76
77
78
18
19
20
1 ARUNDEL HO
2 MARLBOROUGH HO
3 BUCKINGHAM HO
4 OSBOURNE HO
5 YORK HO
6 SANDRINGHAM HO
7 KENT HO
8 NORFOLK HO
9 RUNNYMEDE HO
10 CARISBROOKE HO
11 GLOUCESTER HO
1 SANDSTONE
2 BROADLANDS CT
3 FABYC HO
4 ASPEN CT
1 WATCOMBE COTTS
2 CAMBRIDGE COTTS
3 WILLOW COTTS
4 THETIS TERR
BLENHEIM CT 1
WOBURN CT 2
FINUCANE CT 3
TRINITY COTTS 4

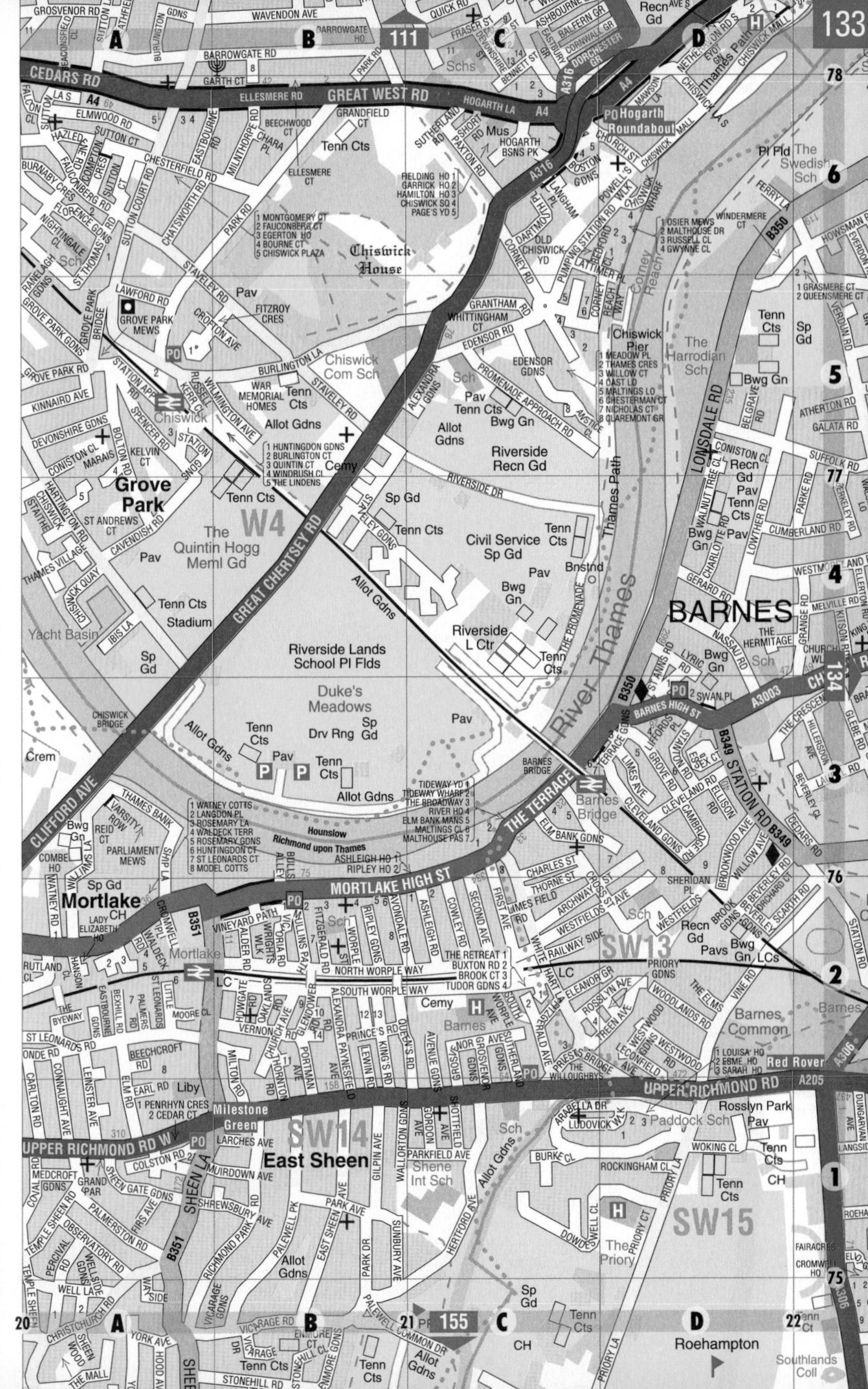

A
B
C
D
111
78
6
5
77
4
3
76
2
1
75
20
21
155
22
134
CEDARS RD
GREAT WEST RD
A4
HOGARTH LA
A316
DORCHESTER GR
Hogarth Roundabout
GROSVENOR RD
WAVENDON AVE
BARROWGATE RD
GARTH CT
ELLESMERE RD
ELMWOOD RD
SUTTON CT
CHESTERFIELD RD
SUTTON COURT RD
CHATSWORTH RD
EASTBOURNE RD
MILNTHORPE RD
PARK RD
GRANDFIELD CT
Tenn Cts
Mus
HOGARTH BSNS PK
1 FIELDING HO
2 GARRICK HO
3 HAMILTON HO
4 CHISWICK SQ
5 PAGE'S YD
1 MONTGOMERY CT
2 FAUCONBERG CT
3 EGERTON HO
4 BOURNE CT
5 CHISWICK PLAZA
Chiswick House
STAVELEY RD
LAWFORD RD
GROVE PARK MEWS
FITZROY CRES
CROFTON AVE
GRANTHAM RD
WHITTINGHAM CT
EDENSOR RD
EDENSOR GDNS
CHURCH ST
CHISWICK MALL
POWELL'S WLK
OLD CHISWICK YD
CORNEY RD
PUMPING STATION RD
CORNEY REACH WAY
Corney Reach
Chiswick Pier
1 MEADOW PL
2 THAMES CRES
3 WILLOW CT
4 OAST LO
5 MALTINGS LO
6 CHESTERMAN CT
7 NICHOLAS CT
8 CLAREMONT CT
1 OSIER MEWS
2 MALTHOUSE DR
3 RUSSELL CL
4 GWYNNE CL
WINDERMERE CT
Pl Fld
The Swedish Sch
FERRY LA
B350
The Harrodian Sch
LONSDALE RD
1 GRASMERE CT
2 QUEENSMERE CT
Tenn Cts
Sp Gd
Bwg Gn
BURLINGTON LA
Chiswick Com Sch
Chiswick
GROVE PARK RD
KINNAIRD AVE
DEVONSHIRE GDNS
WAR MEMORIAL HOMES
Allot Gdns
PROMENADE APPROACH RD
Riverside Recn Gd
RIVERSIDE DR
1 HUNTINGDON GDNS
2 BURLINGTON CT
3 QUINTIN CT
4 WINDRUSH CL
5 THE LINDENS
Cemy
Grove Park
W4
The Quintin Hogg Meml Gd
GREAT CHERTSEY RD
Civil Service Sp Gd
Thames Path
Bnstnd
Stadium
Yacht Basin
Riverside Lands School Pl Flds
Riverside L Ctr
River Thames
THE PROMENADE
BARNES
THE HERMITAGE
Duke's Meadows
Drv Rng
CHISWICK BRIDGE
Crem
CLIFFORD AVE
BARNES HIGH ST
A3003
B349
STATION RD
BARNES BRIDGE
THE TERRACE
Barnes Bridge
1 WATNEY COTTS
2 LANGDON PL
3 ROSEMARY LA
4 WALDECK TERR
5 ROSEMARY GDNS
6 HUNTINGDON CT
7 ST LEONARDS CT
8 MODEL COTTS
1 TIDEWAY YD
2 TIDEWAY WHARF
3 THE BROADWAY
4 RIVER HO
5 ELM BANK MANS
6 MALTINGS CL
7 MALTHOUSE PAS
Hounslow
Richmond upon Thames
1 ASHLEIGH HO
2 RIPLEY HO
MORTLAKE HIGH ST
Mortlake
B351
SW13
1 THE RETREAT
2 BUXTON RD
3 BROOK CT
4 TUDOR GDNS
NORTH WORPLE WAY
SOUTH WORPLE WAY
Barnes Common
1 LOUISA HO
2 ESME HO
3 SARAH HO
Red Rover
A306
A205
UPPER RICHMOND RD
UPPER RICHMOND RD W
Milestone Green
1 PENRHYN CRES
2 CEDAR CT
Liby
SW14
East Sheen
Paddock Sch
Rosslyn Park
SW15
The Priory
Shene Int Sch
SHEEN LA
PALEWELL COMMON DR
Roehampton
Southlands Coll

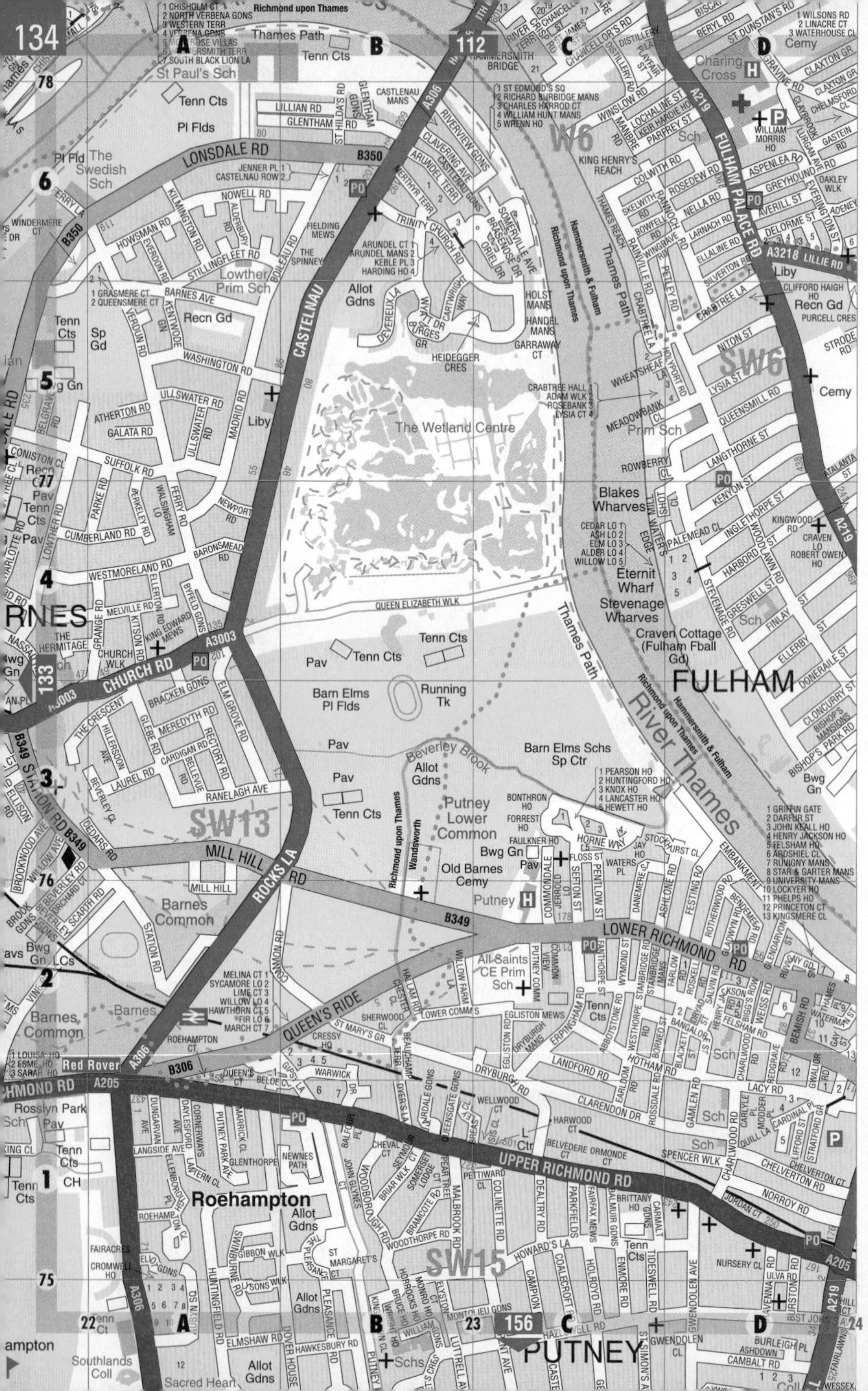
A
B
C
D
112
133
156
1 CHISHOLM CT
2 NORTH VERBENA GDNS
3 WESTERN TERR
4 VERBENA GDNS
6 HAMMERSMITH TERR
7 SOUTH BLACK LION LA
Richmond upon Thames
Thames Path
Tenn Cts
St Paul's Sch
HAMMERSMITH BRIDGE
Pl Flds
LILLIAN RD
GLENTHAM RD
CASTELNAU MANS
RIVERVIEW GDNS
CLAVERING AVE
ARUNDEL TERR
CASTELNAU GDNS
LONSDALE RD
B350
Pl Fld
The Swedish Sch
JENNER PL
CASTELNAU ROW
NOWELL RD
KILMINGTON RD
HOWSMAN RD
EVERDON RD
ALDERBURY RD
STILLINGFLEET RD
BOILEAU RD
FIELDING MEWS
THE SPINNEY
MERTHYR TERR
TRINITY CHURCH RD
ARUNDEL CT
ARUNDEL MANS
KEBLE PL
HARDING HO
SOMERVILLE AVE
BRASENOSE DR
ORIEL DR
WINDERMERE CT
B350
Lowther Prim Sch
1 GRASMERE CT
2 QUEENSMERE CT
BARNES AVE
VERDUN RD
KENTWOOD GN
Recn Gd
Allot Gdns
DEVEREUX LA
WYATT DR
BURGES GR
CARTWRIGHT WAY
HEIDEGGER CRES
HOLST MANS
HANDEL MANS
GARRAWAY CT
Tenn Cts
Sp Gd
WASHINGTON RD
CASTELNAU
Bwg Gn
ULLSWATER RD
ATHERTON RD
GALATA RD
MADRID RD
Liby
The Wetland Centre
CRABTREE HALL
ADAM WLK
ROSEBANK
LYSIA CT
CONISTON CL
Recn Gd
Pav
Tenn Cts
SUFFOLK RD
PARKE RD
BERKELEY RD
WALSINGHAM LO
FERRY RD
NEWPORT RD
CUMBERLAND RD
BARONSMEAD RD
LOWTHER RD
WESTMORELAND RD
ELLERTON RD
BYFIELD GDNS
MELVILLE RD
GRANGE RD
KITSON RD
KING EDWARD MEWS
QUEEN ELIZABETH WLK
RNES
THE HERMITAGE
CHURCH WLK
CHURCH RD
A3003
Bwg Gn
THE CRESCENT
HILLERSDON AVE
BRACKEN GDNS
MEREDYTH RD
GLEBE RD
CARDIGAN RD
RECTORY RD
ELM GROVE RD
BELLEVUE RD
LAUREL RD
RANELAGH AVE
BEVERLEY CL
Pav
Tenn Cts
Barn Elms Pl Flds
Running Tk
Beverley Brook
Allot Gdns
B349
STATION RD
CEDARS RD
SW13
MILL HILL RD
MILL HILL
ROCKS LA
BROOKWOOD AVE
WILLOW AVE
BEVERLEY RD
ORCHARD CT
SCARTH RD
Barnes Common
STATION RD
Bwg Gn
LCs
Barnes
COMMON RD
Richmond upon Thames
Wandsworth
Putney Lower Common
Old Barnes Cemy
Putney
MELINA CT
SYCAMORE LO
LIME CT
WILLOW LO
HAWTHORN CT
FIR LO
MARCH CT
ROEHAMPTON CT
QUEEN'S RIDE
CRESSY HO
ST MARY'S GR
SHERWOOD CL
HALLAM RD
CHESTER CL
WILLOW FARM LA
LOWER COMMON
All Saints CE Prim Sch
PUTNEY COMM
COMMON VIEW
1 LOUISA HO
2 ESME HO
3 SARAH HO
Red Rover
A306
B306
RICHMOND RD
A205
QUEEN'S CT
BELOE CL
WARWICK DR
GIPSY LA
BEAUCHAMP TERR
DYER'S LA
Rosslyn Park
Sch
Pav
Tenn Cts
CH
DUNGARVAN AVE
DAYLESFORD AVE
CORNERWAYS
PUTNEY PARK AVE
MARRICK CL
LANGSIDE AVE
ELLENBOROUGH PL
LANTERN CL
GLENTHORPE
NEWNES PATH
Roehampton
Allot Gdns
CHEVAL CT
SEYMOUR CT
BRIAR WLK
SOMERSET LODGE
PEAR TREE CL
MALBROOK RD
PETTIWARD CL
COLINETTE RD
DEALTRY RD
PARKFIELDS
FAIRFAX MEWS
BRITTANY HO
BALMUIR GDNS
CARMALT GDNS
UPPER RICHMOND RD
JOHN GLYNES
WOODBOROUGH RD
BRAMCOTE RD
WOODTHORPE RD
ROEHAMPTON CL
FAIRACRES
CROMWELL HO
SWINBURNE RD
GIBBON WLK
SONS WLK
HUNTINGFIELD RD
ST MARGARET'S CT
PLEASANCE RD
HORROCKS HO
MONRO HO
BRUCE HO
ELYSTON
SW15
HOWARD'S LA
CAMPION
COALECROFT RD
HOLROYD RD
ENMORE RD
TIDESWELL RD
GWENDOLEN AVE
Tenn Cts
NURSERY CL
AVENNA RD
ULVA RD
BURSTON RD
A219
A205
MONTOLIEU GDNS
HAZLEWELL RD
Allot Gdns
ELMSHAW RD
DOVER HOUSE
HAWKESBURY RD
Schs
LUTTRELL AV
PUTNEY
GWENDOLEN CL
BURLEIGH PL
ASHDOWN
CAMBALT RD
Southlands Coll
Sacred Heart
Allot Gdns
22
23
24
75
76
77
78
1
2
3
4
5
6
RIVER TERR
CRISP RD
CHANCELLOR'S RD
DISTILLERY RD
PLAYFAIR ST
ST JAMES
Charing Cross
1 ST EDMUND'S SQ
2 RICHARD BURBIDGE MANS
3 CHARLES HARROD CT
4 WILLIAM HUNT MANS
5 WRENN HO
W6
WINSLOW RD
LOCHALINE ST
KEIR HARDIE HO
PARFREY ST
MANBRE RD
Sch
KING HENRY'S REACH
BISCAY RD
BERYL RD
ST DUNSTAN'S RD
1 WILSONS RD
2 LINACRE CT
3 WATERHOUSE CL
Cemy
CLAXTON GR
GRAVINE RD
FULHAM PALACE RD
A219
WILLIAM MORRIS HO
CLAYBROOK RD
LURGAN AVE
CHELMSFORD CL
GASTEIN RD
COLWITH RD
ROSEDEW RD
ASPENLEA RD
GREYHOUND RD
OAKLEY WLK
SKELWITH RD
RANNOCH RD
NELLA RD
AVERILL ST
EVERINGTON ST
BOWFELL RD
WINGRAVE RD
LARNACH RD
DELORME ST
ELLALINE RD
SILVERTON RD
A3218
LILLIE RD
Liby
Hammersmith & Fulham
Richmond upon Thames
Thames Path
THAMES REACH
RAINVILLE RD
PELLEY RD
CRABTREE LA
CLIFFORD HAIGH HO
Recn Gd
PURCELL CRES
NITON ST
STRODE RD
SW6
WHEATSHEAF LA
HOLYPORT RD
LYSIA ST
QUEENSMILL RD
Cemy
MEADOWBANK CL
Prim Sch
LANGTHORNE ST
ROWBERRY CL
KENYON ST
ATALANTA ST
Blakes Wharves
CEDAR LO
ASH LO
ALDER LO
WILLOW LO
TOM WATERS EDGE
PALEMEAD CL
INGLETHORPE ST
WOODLAWN RD
KINGWOOD RD
CRAVEN LO
ROBERT OWEN HO
HARBORD ST
STEVENAGE RD
Eternit Wharf
Stevenage Wharves
GRESWELL ST
FINLAY ST
Sch
Craven Cottage (Fulham Fball Gd)
ELLERBY ST
DONERAILE ST
FULHAM
CLONCURRY ST
BISHOP'S MANSIONS
BISHOP'S PARK RD
River Thames
Barn Elms Schs Sp Ctr
1 PEARSON HO
2 HUNTINGFORD HO
3 KNOX HO
4 LANCASTER HO
5 HEWETT HO
BONTHRON HO
FORREST HO
FAULKNER HO
HORNE WAY
Bwg Gn
Pav
JAY HO
WATERS PL
STOCKHURST CL
EMBANKMENT
Bwg Gn
1 GRIFFIN GATE
2 DARFUR ST
3 JOHN KEALL HO
4 HENRY JACKSON HO
5 FELSHAM HO
6 ARDSHIEL CL
7 RUVIGNY MANS
8 STAR & GARTER MANS
9 UNIVERSITY MANS
10 LOCKYER HO
11 PHELPS HO
12 PRINCETON CT
13 KINGSMERE CL
FLOSS ST
SEFTON ST
PENTLOW ST
DANEMERE ST
ASHLONE RD
FESTING RD
ROTHERWOOD RD
BENDEMEER RD
COMMONDALE
JERROLD LO
LOWER RICHMOND RD
FANTHORPE ST
WYMOND ST
STANBRIDGE RD
FARLOW RD
ROSKELL RD
SALVIN RD
GLADWYN RD
GLENDARVON ST
RUVIGNY GDNS
EGLISTON MEWS
ERPINGHAM RD
ABBOTSTONE RD
WESTHORPE RD
BORNEO ST
BANGALORE ST
HENRY JACKSON RD
BIGGS ROW
WEISS RD
BEMISH RD
THAMES PL
FELSHAM RD
EGLISTON RD
DRYBURGH MANS
Tenn Cts
LANDFORD RD
HOTHAM RD
BLACKETT ST
CHARLWOOD RD
REDGRAVE RD
GWALIOR RD
DRYBURGH RD
WELLWOOD CT
EARLDOM
ROSSDALE RD
GAMLEN RD
CLARENDON DR
LACY RD
CARLYLE PL
CARDINAL PL
QUILL LA
STRATFORD GR
LIFFORD ST
HARWOOD CT
L Ctr
BELVEDERE CT
ORMONDE CT
Sch
SPENCER WLK
CHARLWOOD RD
CHELVERTON RD
CHELVERTON CT
NORROY RD
JORDAN CT

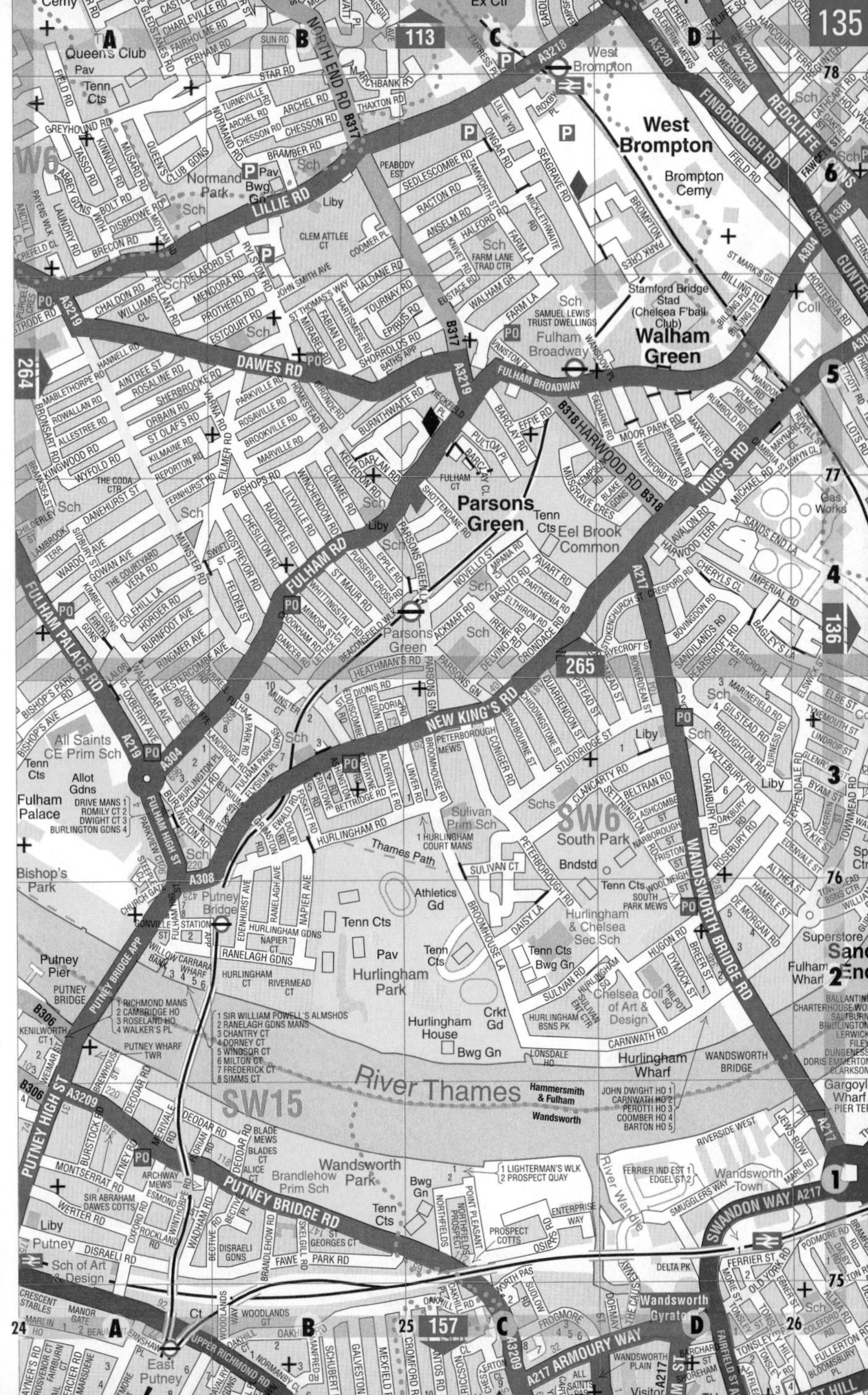

113
A
B
C
D
78
Queen's Club
Pav
Tenn Cts
West Brompton
West Brompton
Brompton Cemy
W6
Normand Park
Lillie Rd
North End Rd
B317
A3218
A3220
Finborough Rd
Redcliffe Gdns
Greyhound Rd
Kinnoul Rd
Musard Rd
Queen's Club Gdns
Normand Rd
Archel Rd
Chesson Rd
Turneville Rd
Star Rd
Sun Rd
Thaxton Rd
Bramber Rd
Peabody Est
Sedlescombe Rd
Racton Rd
Anselm Rd
Halford Rd
Farm La
Seagrave Rd
Ongar Rd
Tamworth St
Micklethwaite Rd
Roxby Pl
Lillie Yd
Ifield Rd
Brompton Park Cres
Clem Attlee Ct
Coomer Pl
Farm Lane Trad Ctr
Walham Gr
Eustace Rd
Haldane Rd
Tournay Rd
Epirus Rd
Shorrolds Rd
Baths App
Stamford Bridge Stad (Chelsea F'ball Club)
Samuel Lewis Trust Dwellings
Fulham Broadway
Walham Green
Billing Rd
St Mark's Gr
Coll
Hortensia Rd
Gunter Gr
6
5
264
A3219
Chaldon Rd
Williams Cl
Delaford St
Mendora Rd
Prothero Rd
Estcourt Rd
Rylston Rd
John Smith Ave
St Thomas's Way
Hartismere Rd
Fabian Rd
Mirabel Rd
Dawes Rd
Fulham Broadway
Hannell Rd
Aintree St
Rosaline Rd
Sherbrooke Rd
Orbain Rd
St Olaf's Rd
Kilmaine Rd
Reporton Rd
Mablethorpe Rd
Rowallan Rd
Allestree Rd
Kingwood Rd
Wyfold Rd
Bronsart Rd
Varna Rd
Parkville Rd
Rosaville Rd
Brookville Rd
Marville Rd
Homestead Rd
Burnthwaite Rd
Heckfield Pl
Barclay Rd
Effie Rd
Pulton Pl
B318
Harwood Rd
Gedarne Rd
Moor Park Rd
Waterford Rd
Britannia Rd
Maxwell Rd
Rumbold Rd
Holmead Rd
King's Rd
Michael Rd
Maynard Cl
Lots Rd
77
Gas Works
Parsons Green
Tenn Cts
Eel Brook Common
Kempson Rd
Musgrave Cres
Blake Gdns
The Coda Ctr
Danehurst St
Fernhurst Rd
Filmer Rd
Bishops Rd
Chesilton Rd
Radipole Rd
Lilyville Rd
Winchendon Rd
Clonmel Rd
Kelvedon Rd
Darlan Rd
Fulham Ct
Shottendane Rd
Lambrook Terr
Sidbury St
Gowan Ave
Wardo Ave
The Courtyard
Vera Rd
Colehill La
Horder Rd
Burnfoot Ave
Ringmer Ave
Munster Rd
Felden St
Rostrevor Rd
Fulham Rd
Epple Rd
Pursers Cross Rd
St Maur Rd
Whittingstall Rd
Mimosa St
Bookham Rd
Dancer Rd
Novello St
Mpana Rd
Favart Rd
Basuto Rd
Parthenia Rd
Elthiron Rd
Irene Rd
Ackmar Rd
Delvino Rd
Crondace Rd
Beaconsfield Wlk
Avalon Rd
Harwood Terr
Sands End La
Cheryls Cl
Imperial Rd
Cresford Rd
Stokenchurch St
Bovingdon Rd
Sandilands Rd
Pearscroft Rd
Bagley's La
Ryecroft St
A217
136
4
Fulham Palace Rd
Heathman's Rd
Parsons Gn
265
Bishop's Park Rd
Bishop's Ave
Hestercombe Ave
Waldemar Ave
Oxberry Ave
Dornoliffe Rd
Fulham Park Gdns
Dionis Rd
Eddiscombe Rd
Doria Rd
Gliddon Rd
New King's Rd
Bradbourne St
Chiddingstone St
Quarrendon St
Studdridge St
Peterborough Mews
Coniger Rd
Broomhouse Rd
Linver Rd
Alderville Rd
Ashington Rd
Bettridge Rd
Hurlingham Rd
All Saints CE Prim Sch
Allot Gdns
Fulham Palace
Drive Mans 1
Romily Ct 2
Dwight Ct 3
Burlington Gdns 4
A219
A304
Fulham High St
Burlington Rd
Rigault Rd
Elysium Pl
Landridge Rd
Ewald Rd
Dolby Rd
Foskett Rd
Grimston Rd
Sulivan Prim Sch
1 Hurlingham Court Mans
Thames Path
Schs
SW6
South Park
Bndstd
Clancarty Rd
Beltran Rd
Settrington Rd
Ashcombe St
Narborough St
Friston St
Sch
Liby
Marinefield Rd
Gilstead Rd
Broughton Rd
Furness Rd
Hazlebury Rd
Cranbury Rd
Oakbury Rd
Rosebury Rd
Stephendale Rd
Byam St
Townmead Rd
Elbe St
Tynemouth St
Linorop St
Glenrosa St
3
Sp Ctr
76
Bishop's Park
Putney Bridge
A308
Church Gate
Conville
Station App
Edenhurst Ave
Ranelagh Ave
Napier Ave
Hurlingham Gdns
Napier Ct
Ranelagh Gdns
Hurlingham Ct
Rivermead Ct
Athletics Gd
Tenn Cts
Pav
Hurlingham Park
Hurlingham House
Bwg Gn
Crkt Gd
Sulivan Ct
Broomhouse La
Daisy La
Peterborough Rd
Hurlingham & Chelsea Sec Sch
Tenn Cts
Bwg Gn
Sulivan Rd
Chelsea Coll of Art & Design
Hurlingham Bsns Pk
Carnwath Rd
Hugon Rd
Dymock St
Breer St
Philpot Sq
South Park Mews
Wandsworth Bridge Rd
De Morgan Rd
Hamble St
Althea St
Superstore
Sands End
Fulham Wharf
2
Putney Pier
Putney Bridge
Putney Bridge App
Willow Bank
Carrara Wharf
1 Richmond Mans
2 Cambridge Ho
3 Roseland Ho
4 Walker's Pl
1 Sir William Powell's Almshos
2 Ranelagh Gdns Mans
3 Chantry Ct
4 Dorney Ct
5 Windsor Ct
6 Milton Ct
7 Frederick Ct
8 Simms Ct
Putney Wharf Twr
Hurlingham Wharf
Wandsworth Bridge
Lonsdale Ho
River Thames
Hammersmith & Fulham
Wandsworth
John Dwight Ho 1
Carnwath Ho 2
Perotti Ho 3
Coomber Ho 4
Barton Ho 5
Ballantine St
Charterhouse Works
Saltburn Ho
Bridlington Ho
Lerwick Ho
Filey Ho
Dungeness Ho
Doris Emmerton Ct
Clarkson Ho
Gargoyle Wharf
Pier Terr
SW15
B306
Kenilworth Ct
Weimar St
Brewhouse La
Deodar Rd
Putney High St
A3209
Burstock Rd
Blade Mews
Blades Ct
Alice Ct
Merivale Rd
Florian Rd
Montserrat Rd
Atney Rd
Archway Mews
Esmond Rd
Sir Abraham Dawes Cotts
Werter Rd
Oxford Rd
Rockland Rd
Winthorpe Rd
Wadham Rd
Bective Rd
Bective Pl
Disraeli Gdns
Disraeli Rd
Putney Bridge Rd
Brandlehow Prim Sch
Wandsworth Park
Brandlehow Rd
Skelgill Rd
St Georges Ct
Fawe Park Rd
Bwg Gn
Tenn Cts
Northfields
Northfields Prospect
Point Pleasant
1 Lighterman's Wlk
2 Prospect Quay
Prospect Cotts
Osiers Rd
Enterprise Way
River Wandle
Riverside West
Ferrier Ind Est 1
Edgel St 2
Smugglers Way
Wandsworth Town
Jews Row
Marl Rd
Swandon Way
1
Delta Pk
Ferrier St
Old York Rd
Morie St
Ebner St
Tonsley Hill
Tonsley St
Alma Rd
Podmore Rd
Dalby Rd
Coleford Rd
Fullerton Rd
Bloomsbury Pl
75
Liby
Putney
Sch of Art & Design
Crescent Stables
Manor Gate
Ct
Woodlands Way
Woodlands Gt
Oakhill Rd
Frogmore
Sudlow Rd
Dormay St
The Causeway
Wandsworth Gyratory
A217 Armoury Way
Wandsworth Plain
All Saints Pl
Barchard St
Shoreham Cl
Fairfield St
Upper Richmond Rd
East Putney
Mercier Rd
Galveston Rd
Mexfield Rd
Cromford Rd
Schubert Rd
Manfred Rd
Normanby Cl
24
25
157
26

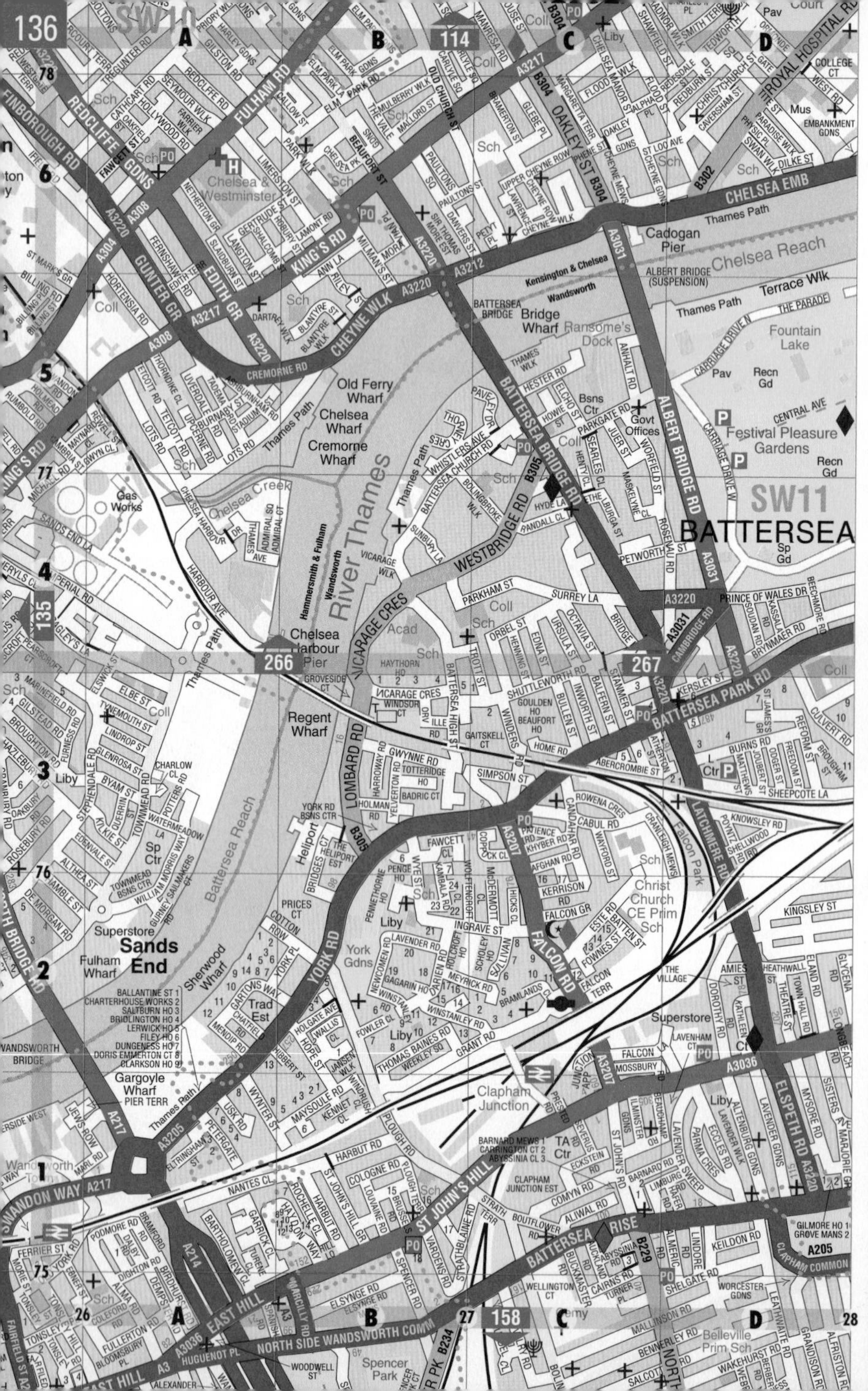

SW10
A
B
114
C
D
78
6
5
77
4
135
3
76
2
1
75
26
27
28
266
267
158
FINBOROUGH RD
REDCLIFFE GDNS
FULHAM RD
GUNTER GR
EDITH GR
KING'S RD
CHEYNE WLK
CREMORNE RD
BEAUFORT ST
OLD CHURCH ST
OAKLEY ST
ROYAL HOSPITAL RD
CHELSEA EMB
Chelsea & Westminster
Cadogan Pier
Chelsea Reach
ALBERT BRIDGE (SUSPENSION)
Kensington & Chelsea
Wandsworth
BATTERSEA BRIDGE
Bridge Wharf
Ransome's Dock
Thames Path
Terrace Wlk
THE PARADE
CARRIAGE DRIVE N
Fountain Lake
Festival Pleasure Gardens
CENTRAL AVE
SW11
BATTERSEA
Old Ferry Wharf
Chelsea Wharf
Cremorne Wharf
River Thames
Hammersmith & Fulham
Gas Works
Chelsea Creek
CHELSEA HARBOUR DR
HARBOUR AVE
Chelsea Harbour Pier
BATTERSEA BRIDGE RD
ALBERT BRIDGE RD
WESTBRIDGE RD
VICARAGE CRES
PRINCE OF WALES DR
BATTERSEA PARK RD
SURREY LA
PARKHAM ST
Regent Wharf
LOMBARD RD
BATTERSEA HIGH ST
Heliport
YORK RD
FALCON RD
LATCHMERE RD
Falcon Park
Christ Church CE Prim Sch
THE VILLAGE
Superstore
Sands End
Fulham Wharf
Sherwood Wharf
Battersea Reach
Trad Est
WANDSWORTH BRIDGE
Gargoyle Wharf
PIER TERR
Clapham Junction
ST JOHN'S HILL
BATTERSEA RISE
ELSPETH RD
LAVENDER SWEEP
CLAPHAM COMMON
SWANDON WAY
Wandsworth Town
EAST HILL
NORTH SIDE WANDSWORTH COMM
Spencer Park
Belleville Prim Sch
A3220
A3217
A308
A304
A3212
A3031
B304
B302
B305
A3207
A3036
A3205
A217
A214
A3
B229
B234
A205

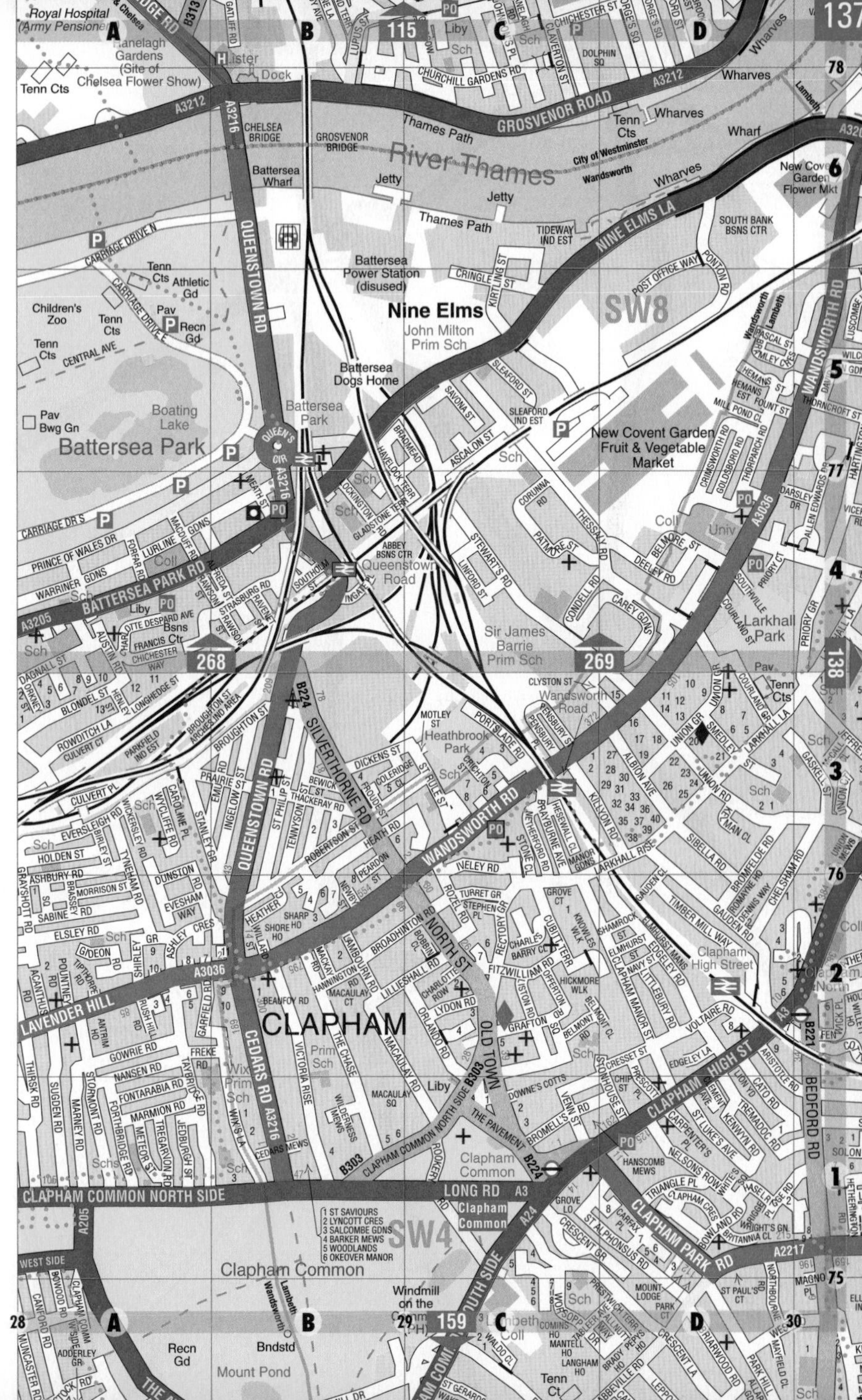
River Thames
Battersea Park
Nine Elms
SW8
SW4
CLAPHAM
Clapham Common
Battersea Power Station (disused)
Battersea Dogs Home
New Covent Garden Fruit & Vegetable Market
New Covent Garden Flower Mkt
Queenstown Road
Wandsworth Road
Clapham High Street
Clapham North
Larkhall Park
Heathbrook Park
QUEENSTOWN RD
GROSVENOR ROAD
NINE ELMS LA
WANDSWORTH RD
BATTERSEA PARK RD
LAVENDER HILL
CEDARS RD
CLAPHAM COMMON NORTH SIDE
LONG RD
CLAPHAM HIGH ST
CLAPHAM PARK RD
BEDFORD RD
SILVERTHORNE RD
NORTH ST
OLD TOWN
115
268
269
138
159
1 ST SAVIOURS
2 LYNCOTT CRES
3 SALCOMBE GDNS
4 BARKER MEWS
5 WOODLANDS
6 OKEOVER MANOR
A
B
C
D
28
29
30
1
2
3
4
5
6

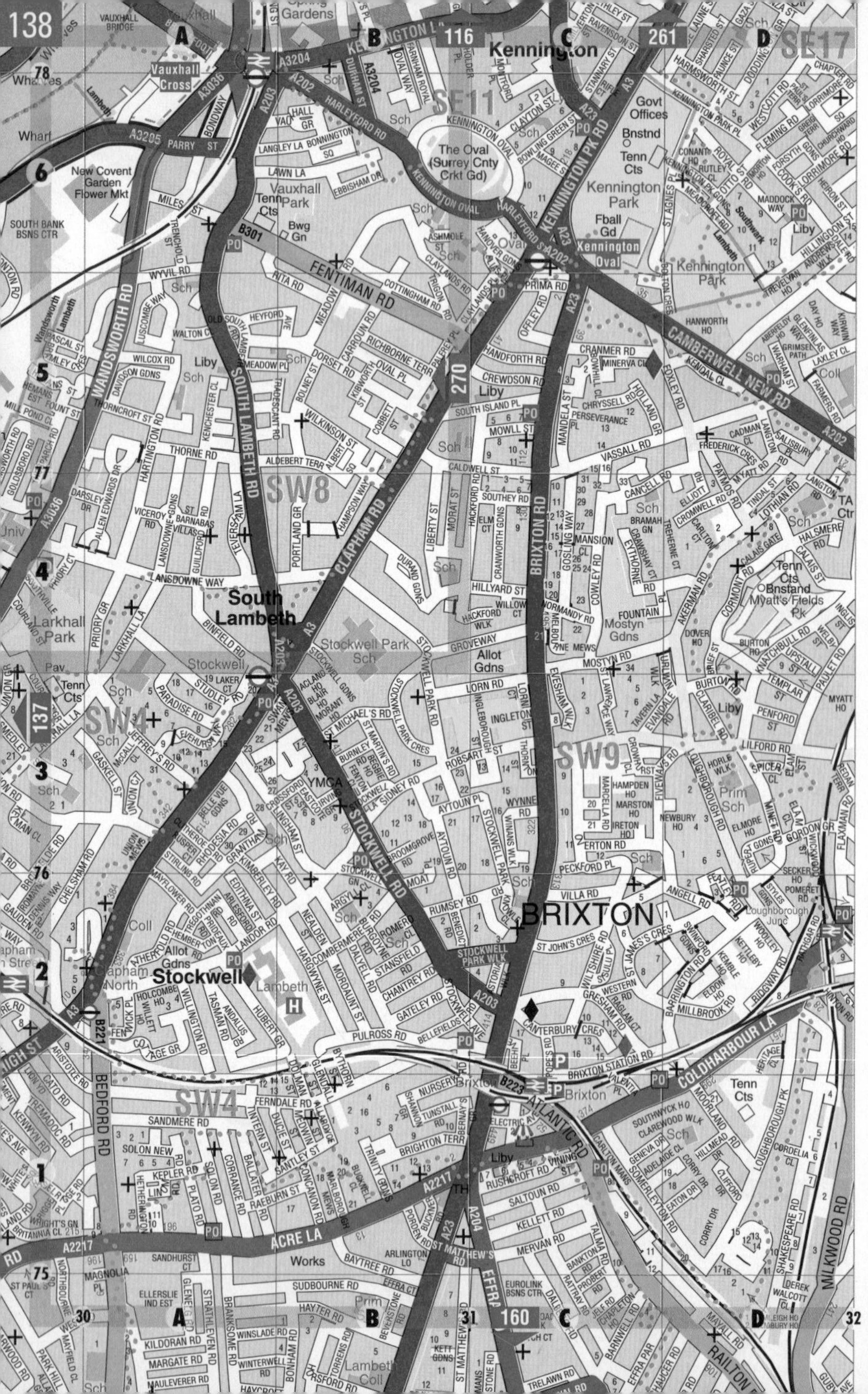
Kennington
SE11
The Oval (Surrey Cnty Crkt Gd)
Kennington Park
Kennington Oval
SE17
Vauxhall Cross
Vauxhall Park
New Covent Garden Flower Mkt
SW8
South Lambeth
Stockwell
SW4
SW9
BRIXTON
Clapham North
Myatt's Fields Pk
Loughborough Junc
WANDSWORTH RD
SOUTH LAMBETH RD
CLAPHAM RD
KENNINGTON PK RD
BRIXTON RD
CAMBERWELL NEW RD
STOCKWELL RD
COLDHARBOUR LA
ACRE LA
ATLANTIC RD
BEDFORD RD
MILKWOOD RD
FENTIMAN RD
HARLEYFORD RD
LANSDOWNE WAY
116
261
270
137
160
A
B
C
D
1
2
3
4
5
6
30
31
32
75
76
77
78

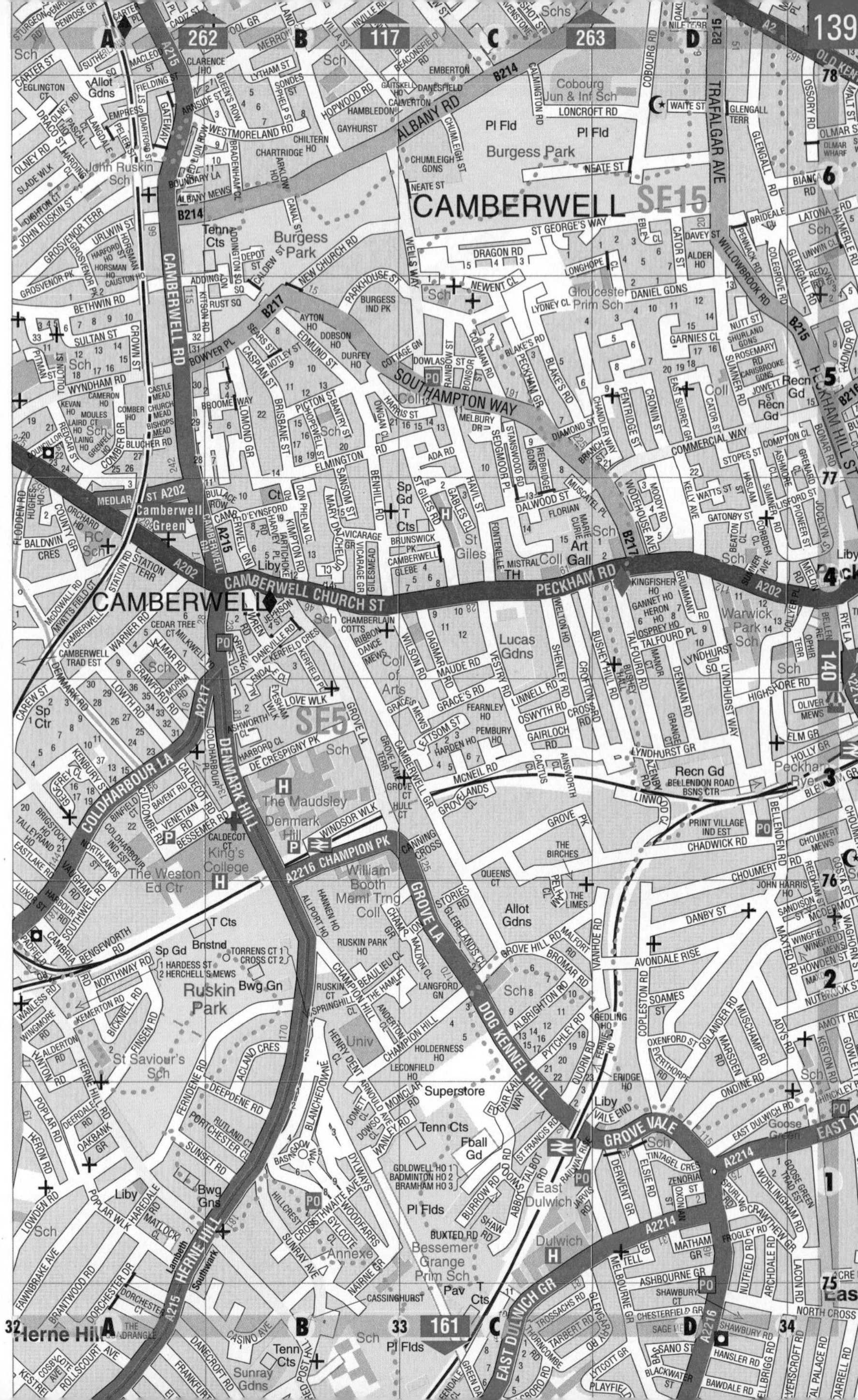

262
117
263
A
B
C
D
CAMBERWELL
SE15
SE5
Burgess Park
Cobourg Jun & Inf Sch
Pl Fld
ALBANY RD
B214
TRAFALGAR AVE
OLD KENT RD
A2
CAMBERWELL RD
A215
John Ruskin Sch
Tenn Cts
NEW CHURCH RD
B217
SOUTHAMPTON WAY
Gloucester Prim Sch
COMMERCIAL WAY
PECKHAM HILL ST
B215
B216
Recn Gd
Camberwell Green
A202
CAMBERWELL CHURCH ST
PECKHAM RD
CAMBERWELL
Liby
Art Gall
Coll
St Giles
Lucas Gdns
Warwick Park Sch
Coll of Arts
140
COLDHARBOUR LA
A2217
DENMARK HILL
The Maudsley
Denmark Hill
King's College
The Weston Ed Ctr
A2216 CHAMPION PK
William Booth Meml Trng Coll
GROVE LA
DOG KENNEL HILL
Allot Gdns
Peckham Rye
CHOUMERT RD
Ruskin Park
Bwg Gn
Sp Gd
Bnstnd
St Saviour's Sch
Univ
Superstore
Tenn Cts
Fball Gd
Pl Flds
East Dulwich
GROVE VALE
A2214
Goose Green
EAST DULWICH RD
Dulwich
Bessemer Grange Prim Sch
Annexe
HERNE HILL
Lambeth
Southwark
EAST DULWICH GR
Herne Hill
Sunray Gdns
161
32
33
34
78
77
76
75
6
5
4
3
2
1
East

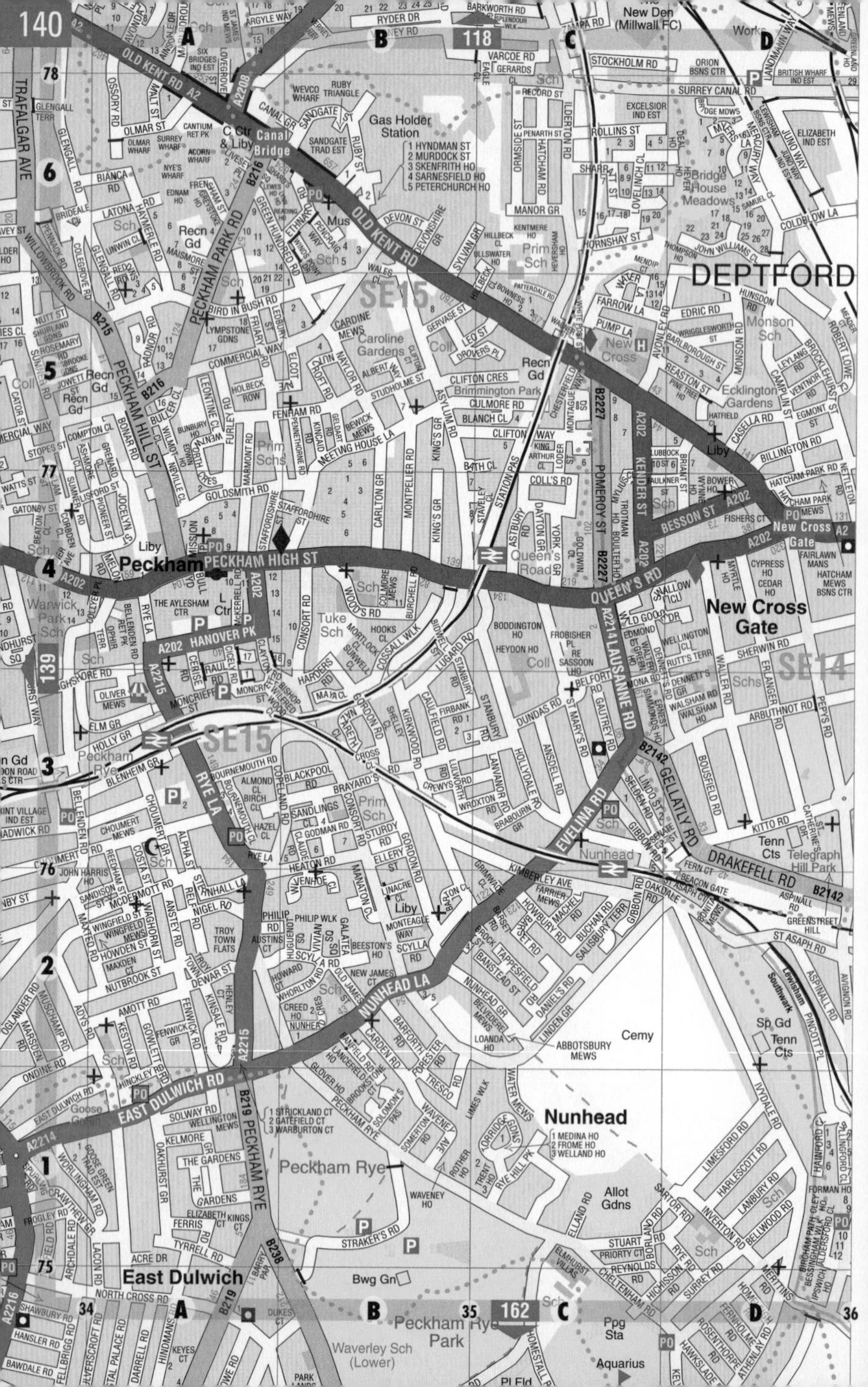

A
B
C
D
118
New Den
(Millwall FC)
Works
OLD KENT RD A2
A2208
Canal Bridge
C Ctr & Liby
Gas Holder Station
1 HYNDMAN ST
2 MURDOCK ST
3 SKENFRITH HO
4 SARNESFIELD HO
5 PETERCHURCH HO
OLD KENT RD
DEPTFORD
SE15
SE14
TRAFALGAR AVE
PECKHAM PARK RD
PECKHAM HILL ST
B215
B216
Recn Gd
Caroline Gardens
Brimmington Park
Peckham
PECKHAM HIGH ST
A202
QUEEN'S RD
New Cross
New Cross Gate
Ecklington Gardens
Bridge House Meadows
Queen's Road
B2227
POMEROY ST
KENDER ST
BESSON ST
A2214 LAUSANNE RD
B2142
GELLATLY RD
DRAKEFELL RD
Telegraph Hill Park
Tenn Cts
HANOVER PK
A2215
RYE LA
Peckham Rye
EVELINA RD
Nunhead
KIMBERLEY AVE
NUNHEAD LA
Cemy
ABBOTSBURY MEWS
EAST DULWICH RD
A2214
B219 PECKHAM RYE
1 STRICKLAND CT
2 GATEFIELD CT
3 WARBURTON CT
Peckham Rye
1 MEDINA HO
2 FROME HO
3 WELLAND HO
Allot Gdns
East Dulwich
NORTH CROSS RD
B238
Bwg Gn
Peckham Rye Park
Waverley Sch (Lower)
162
Ppg Sta
Aquarius
Sp Gd
Lewisham
Southwark
34
35
36
78
77
76
75
6
5
4
3
2
1
139

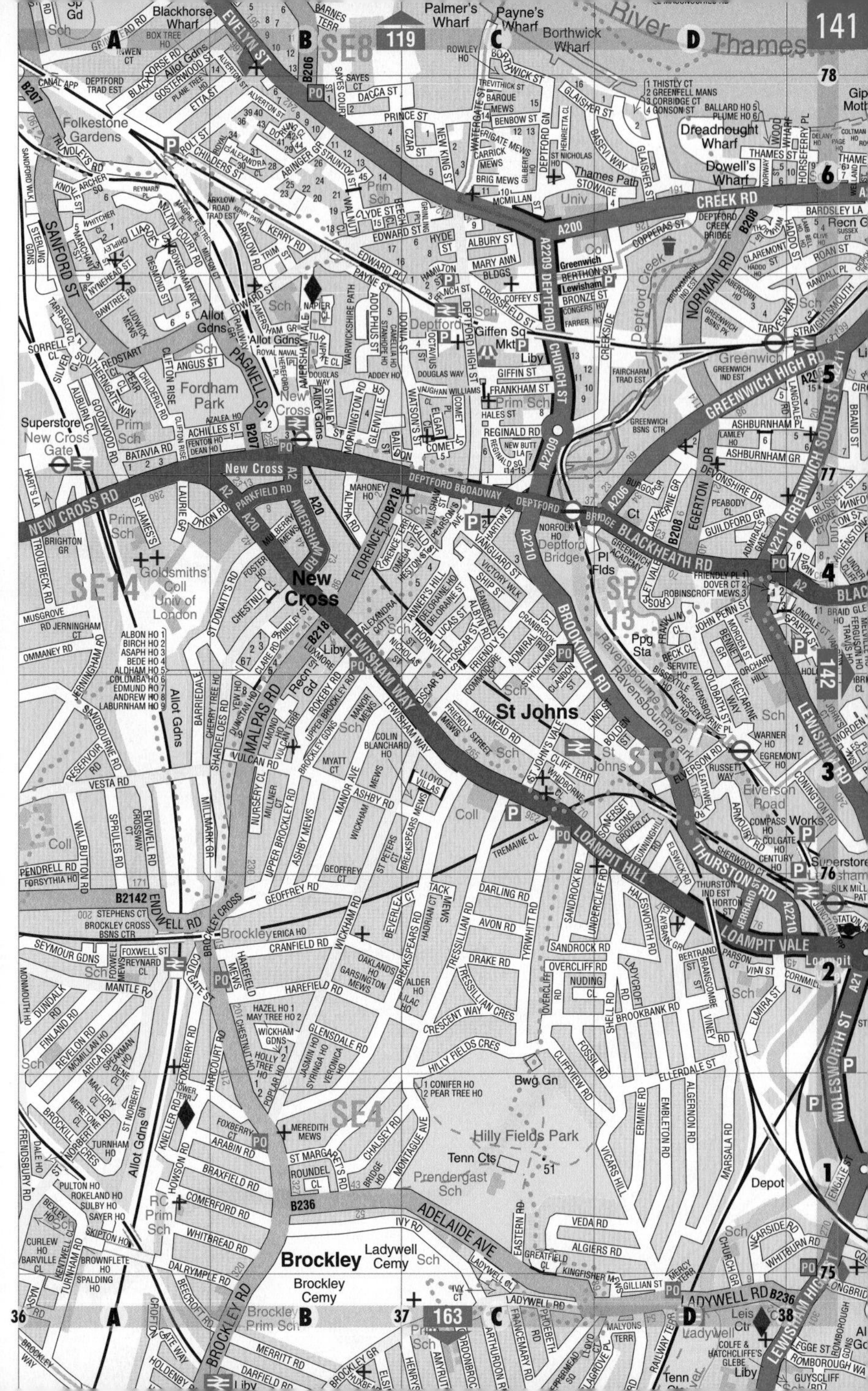
River Thames
Palmer's Wharf
Payne's Wharf
Borthwick Wharf
Blackhorse Wharf
Dreadnought Wharf
Dowell's Wharf
119
SE8
A
B
C
D
EVELYN ST
B206
B207
B208
A200
A2209
DEPTFORD CHURCH ST
CREEK RD
Folkestone Gardens
SANFORD ST
Thames Path
STOWAGE
Univ
Coll
Greenwich
Lewisham
Deptford Creek
NORMAN RD
Greenwich
GREENWICH HIGH RD
GREENWICH SOUTH ST
A2211
Deptford
Giffen Sq Mkt
Liby
DEPTFORD HIGH ST
PAGNELL ST
Fordham Park
New Cross
Superstore
New Cross Gate
NEW CROSS RD
New Cross
DEPTFORD BROADWAY
DEPTFORD BRIDGE
Deptford Bridge
BLACKHEATH RD
A2
A20
A206
A2210
AMERSHAM RD
FLORENCE RD
B218
LEWISHAM WAY
SE14
Goldsmiths' Coll Univ of London
SE13
Ravensbourne River
Ravensbourne Park
BROOKMILL RD
St Johns
St Johns
SE8
Elverson Road
142
LEWISHAM RD
MALPAS RD
Allot Gdns
Recn Gd
LOAMPIT HILL
LOAMPIT VALE
THURSTON RD
Superstore
B2142
ENDWELL RD
BROCKLEY CROSS
Brockley
SE4
Hilly Fields Park
Bwg Gn
Tenn Cts
Prendergast Sch
B236
ADELAIDE AVE
Brockley
Ladywell Cemy
Brockley Cemy
Brockley Prim Sch
LADYWELL RD
Ladywell
Leis Ctr
MOLESWORTH ST
LEWISHAM HIGH ST
Depot
Liby
BROCKLEY RD
36
37
163
38
1
2
3
4
5
6
75
76
77
78

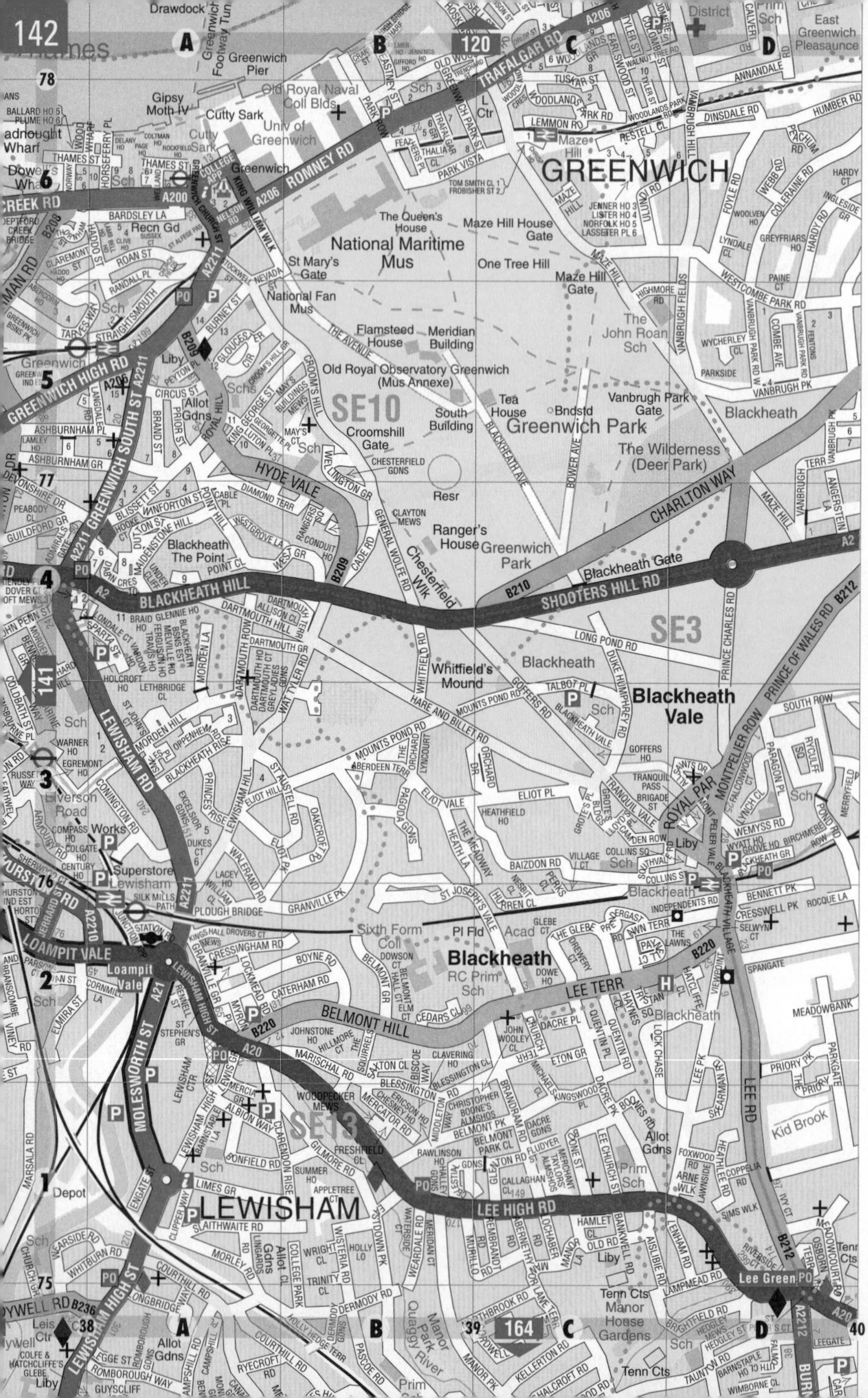

GREENWICH
SE10
Greenwich Park
National Maritime Mus
The Queen's House
Old Royal Naval Coll Blds
Univ of Greenwich
Cutty Sark
Gipsy Moth IV
Greenwich Pier
Greenwich Footway Tun
Drawdock
Old Royal Observatory Greenwich (Mus Annexe)
Flamsteed House
Meridian Building
South Building
Tea House
Bndstd
One Tree Hill
Maze Hill House Gate
Maze Hill Gate
St Mary's Gate
National Fan Mus
Croomshill Gate
Vanbrugh Park Gate
The Wilderness (Deer Park)
Ranger's House
Resr
Blackheath Gate
The John Roan Sch
East Greenwich Pleasaunce
Blackheath
SE3
Blackheath Vale
Whitfield's Mound
Blackheath The Point
Blackheath RC Prim Sch
Sixth Form Coll
Pl Fld
Acad
SE13
LEWISHAM
Loampit Vale
Lewisham Ctr
Superstore Lewisham
Elverson Road
Works
Depot
Lee Green
Manor House Gardens
Quaggy River
Manor Park
Kid Brook
Allot Gdns
Tenn Cts
Leis Ctr
Colfe & Hatchcliffe's Glebe
TRAFALGAR RD
ROMNEY RD
KING WILLIAM WLK
GREENWICH CHURCH ST
CREEK RD
GREENWICH HIGH RD
GREENWICH SOUTH ST
ROYAL HILL
CROOM'S HILL
THE AVENUE
BLACKHEATH AVE
MAZE HILL
VANBRUGH HILL
VANBRUGH PK
WESTCOMBE PARK RD
CHARLTON WAY
SHOOTERS HILL RD
BLACKHEATH HILL
HYDE VALE
GENERAL WOLFE RD
Chesterfield Wlk
DARTMOUTH HILL
DARTMOUTH ROW
LEWISHAM RD
LEWISHAM HILL
PRINCES RISE
LONG POND RD
PRINCE CHARLES RD
PRINCE OF WALES RD
MONTPELIER ROW
ROYAL PAR
TRANQUIL VALE
HARE AND BILLET RD
MOUNTS POND RD
ELIOT PL
ELIOT VALE
LEE TERR
BELMONT HILL
LEWISHAM HIGH ST
MOLESWORTH ST
LOAMPIT VALE
LEE HIGH RD
LEE RD
BLACKHEATH VILLAGE
BURNT ASH
120
141
164
A B C D
1 2 3 4 5 6
38 39 40
75 76 77 78

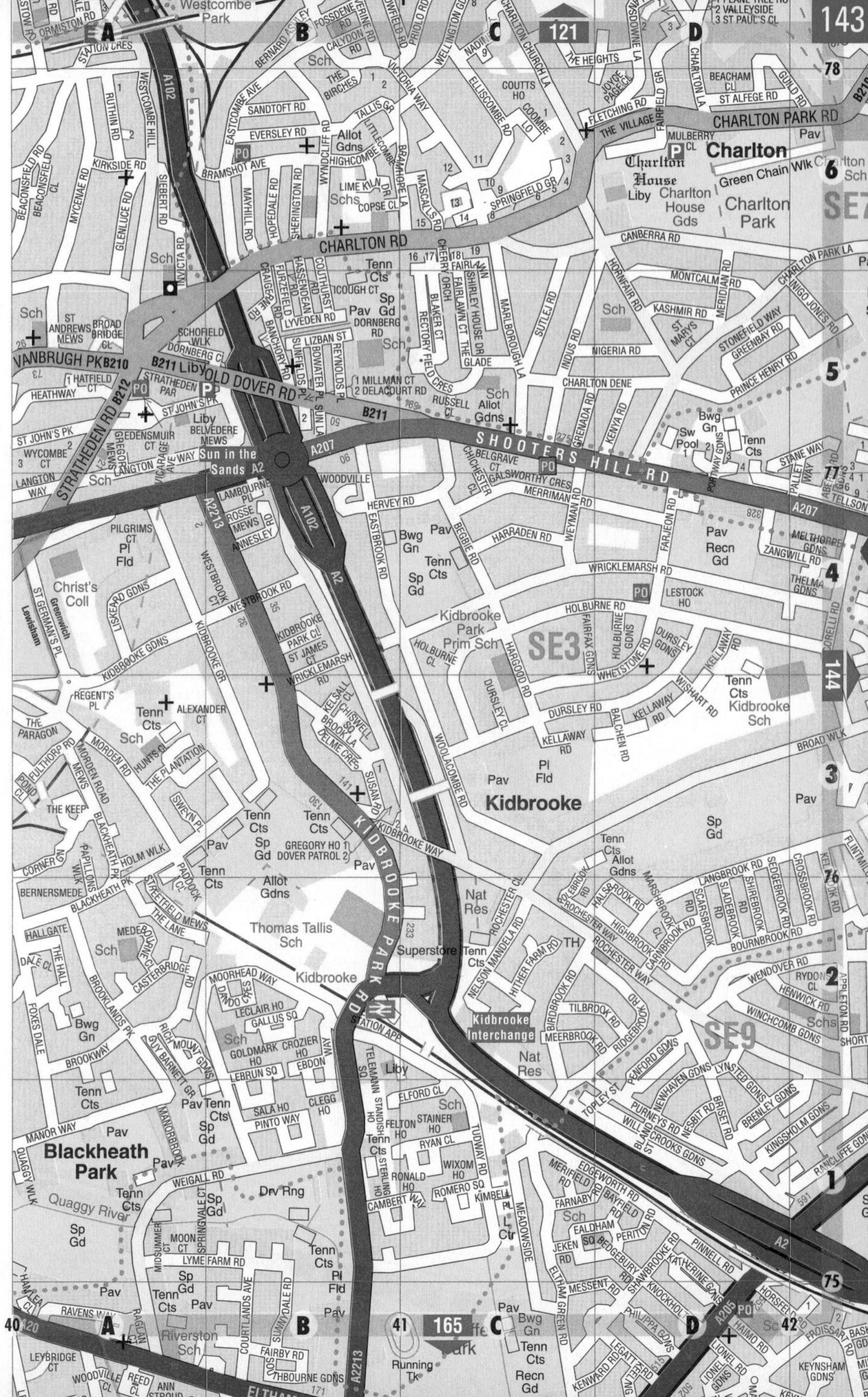

Westcombe Park
ORMISTON RD
STATION CRES
A102
BERNARD ASHLEY DR
FOSSDENE RD
CALYDON RD
VICTORIA WAY
PRIOLO RD
WELLINGTON GDNS
NADINE
CHARLTON CHURCH LA
121
1 PLANE TREE HO
2 VALLEYSIDE
3 ST PAUL'S CL
THE HEIGHTS
JOYCE PAGE CL
CHARLTON LA
BEACHAM CL
ST ALFEGE RD
GUILD RD
78
B210
CHARLTON PARK RD
COUTTS HO
COOMBE LO
ELLISCOMBE RD
THE BIRCHES
EASTCOMBE AVE
SANDTOFT RD
TALLIS GR
EVERSLEY RD
Allot Gdns
WYNDCLIFF RD
HIGHCOMBE
LITTLECOMBE
BRAMHOPE LA
RUTHIN RD
WESTCOMBE HILL
BEACONSFIELD RD
BEACONSFIELD CL
KIRKSIDE RD
MYCENAE RD
GLENLUCE RD
SIEBERT RD
BRAMSHOT AVE
MAYHILL RD
HOPEDALE RD
SHERINGTON RD
LIME KILN DR
COPSE CL
MASCALLS RD
SPRINGFIELD GR
FLETCHING RD
THE VILLAGE
FAIRFIELD GR
MULBERRY CL
Charlton
Charlton House
Liby
Charlton House Gds
Charlton Park
Green Chain Wlk
Pav
SE7
INVICTA RD
CHARLTON RD
CANBERRA RD
CHARLTON PARK LA
HORNFAIR RD
MONTCALM RD
MERIDIAN RD
KASHMIR RD
INIGO JONES RD
ST MARYS CT
STONEFIELD WAY
GREENBAY RD
PRINCE HENRY RD
NIGERIA RD
CHARLTON DENE
SUTLEJ RD
INDUS RD
MARLBOROUGH LA
CRAIGERNE RD
FURZEFIELD RD
HASSENDEAN RD
COUTHURST RD
ICOUGH CT
LYVEDEN RD
Tenn Cts
Sp Gd
DORNBERG RD
CHERRY ORCH
FAIRLAWN
SHIRLEY HOUSE DR
BLAKER CT
RECTORY FIELD CRES
THE GLADE
ST ANDREWS MEWS
BROAD BRIDGE CL
SCHOFIELD WLK
DORNBERG CL
VANBRUGH PK
B210
B211
B212
Liby
OLD DOVER RD
LIZBAN ST
SUNFIELDS PL
BOWATER PL
REYNOLDS PL
BANCHORY RD
1 MILLMAN CT
2 DELACOURT RD
RUSSELL CL
Allot Gdns
HATFIELD CT
HEATHWAY
STRATHEDEN PAR
STRATHEDEN RD
ST JOHN'S PK
GEDENSMUIR CT
GREGOR MEWS
BELVEDERE MEWS
WYCOMBE CT
LANGTON WAY
VICARAGE AVE
Sun in the Sands
A2
A207
SHOOTERS HILL RD
BELGRAVE CT
GALSWORTHY CRES
CHICHESTER CL
GRENADA RD
KENYA RD
Bwg Gn
Sw Pool
PORTWAY GDNS
STANE WAY
PALLET WAY
TELLSON AVE
MERRIMAN RD
WEYMAN RD
FARJEON RD
WOODVILLE
HERVEY RD
LAMBOURNE PL
ROSSE MEWS
ANNESLEY RD
A2213
A102
EASTBROOK RD
BEGBIE RD
HARRADEN RD
WRICKLEMARSH RD
Recn Gd
MELTHORPE GDNS
ZANGWILL RD
THELMA GDNS
LESTOCK HO
PILGRIMS CT
Pl Fld
Christ's Coll
Lewisham
Greenwich
ST GERMAN'S PL
LISKEARD GDNS
WESTBROOK CT
WESTBROOK RD
KIDBROOKE PARK CL
ST JAMES CT
KIDBROOKE GDNS
KIDBROOKE GR
Kidbrooke Park Prim Sch
HOLBURNE CL
HOLBURNE RD
SE3
HARGOOD RD
FAIRFAX GDNS
HOLBURNE GDNS
WHETSTONE RD
DURSLEY GDNS
KELLAWAY RD
CORELLI RD
144
Kidbrooke Sch
REGENT'S PL
ALEXANDER CT
THE PARAGON
FULTHORP RD
MORDEN RD
MORDEN ROAD MEWS
HUNTS CL
THE PLANTATION
SWEYN PL
POND CL
THE KEEP
KELSALL CL
CHISWELL SQ
BROOK LA
DELME CRES
SUSSAN RD
DURSLEY CL
DURSLEY RD
WISHART RD
BALCHEN RD
KELLAWAY RD
WOOLACOMBE RD
BROAD WLK
Kidbrooke
KIDBROOKE WAY
KIDBROOKE PARK RD
GREGORY HO 1
DOVER PATROL 2
BLACKHEATH PK
HOLM WLK
CORNER GN
PAPILLONS WLK
BERNERSMEDE
PADDOCK CL
Nat Res
ROCHESTER CL
ROCHESTER WAY
Thomas Tallis Sch
STREETFIELD MEWS
THE LANE
HALLGATE
THE HALL
DALE CL
MEDEBOURNE CL
CASTERBRIDGE RD
BROOKLANDS PK
FOXES DALE
Superstore
NELSON MANDELA RD
HITHER FARM RD
TH
HALSBROOK RD
HIGHBROOK RD
MARSHBROOK CL
CARNBROOK RD
SCARSBROOK RD
SLADEBROOK RD
SHIREBROOK RD
LANGBROOK RD
SEDGEBROOK RD
CROSSBROOK RD
BOURNBROOK RD
KELLYBROOK RD
FLINTMILL CRES
76
WENDOVER RD
RYDON CL
HENWICK RD
APPLETON RD
WINCHCOMB GDNS
Schs
SHORTWAY
SE9
MOORHEAD WAY
DANDO CRES
LECLAIR HO
GALLUS SQ
GOLDMARK HO
CROZIER HO
LEBRUN SQ
EBDON WAY
STATION APP
Kidbrooke Interchange
TILBROOK RD
BIRDBROOK RD
MEERBROOK RD
RIDGEBROOK RD
PENFORD GDNS
NEWHAVEN GDNS
LYNSTED GDNS
BRENLEY GDNS
TOPLEY ST
PURNEYS RD
NESBIT RD
BRISET RD
KINGSHOLM GDNS
RANCLIFFE GDNS
WILLIAM BLAND ST
CROOKS GDNS
RICH MOUNT GDNS
GUY BARNETT GR
MANORBROOK
BROOKWAY
TELEMANN SQ
STANDISH HO
Liby
ELFORD CL
SALA HO
PINTO WAY
CLEGG HO
STAINER HO
FELTON HO
RYAN CL
TUDWAY RD
WIXOM HO
ROMERO SQ
KIMBELL PL
MANOR WAY
Blackheath Park
QUAGGY WLK
WEIGALL RD
Drv Rng
STERLING HO
RONALD HO
CAMBERT WAY
L Ctr
MEADOWSIDE
EDGEWORTH RD
MERIFIELD RD
BAYFIELD RD
FARNABY RD
EALDHAM SQ
PERITON RD
Quaggy River
SPRINGVALE CT
MIDSUMMER CT
MOON CT
LYME FARM RD
COURTLANDS AVE
SUNNYDALE RD
JEKEN RD
BEDGEBURY RD
SHAWBROOKE RD
KATHERINE GDNS
KNOCKHOLT RD
PINNELL RD
MESSENT RD
ELTHAM GREEN RD
PHILIPPA GDNS
A205
A2
75
HORSFELD RD
HAIMO RD
FROISSART RD
BASKERVILLE GDNS
HAMLEA CL
RAVENS WAY
RAGLAN
Riverston Sch
FAIRBY RD
SOUTHBOURNE GDNS
41
165
Running Tk
Recn Gd
KENWARD RD
LEGATT RD
LIONEL RD
LIONEL GDNS
KEYNSHAM GDNS
LEYBRIDGE CT
WOODVILLE CL
REED CL
ANN STROUD
ELTHAM RD
40
42
A
B
C
D
1
2
3
4
5
6

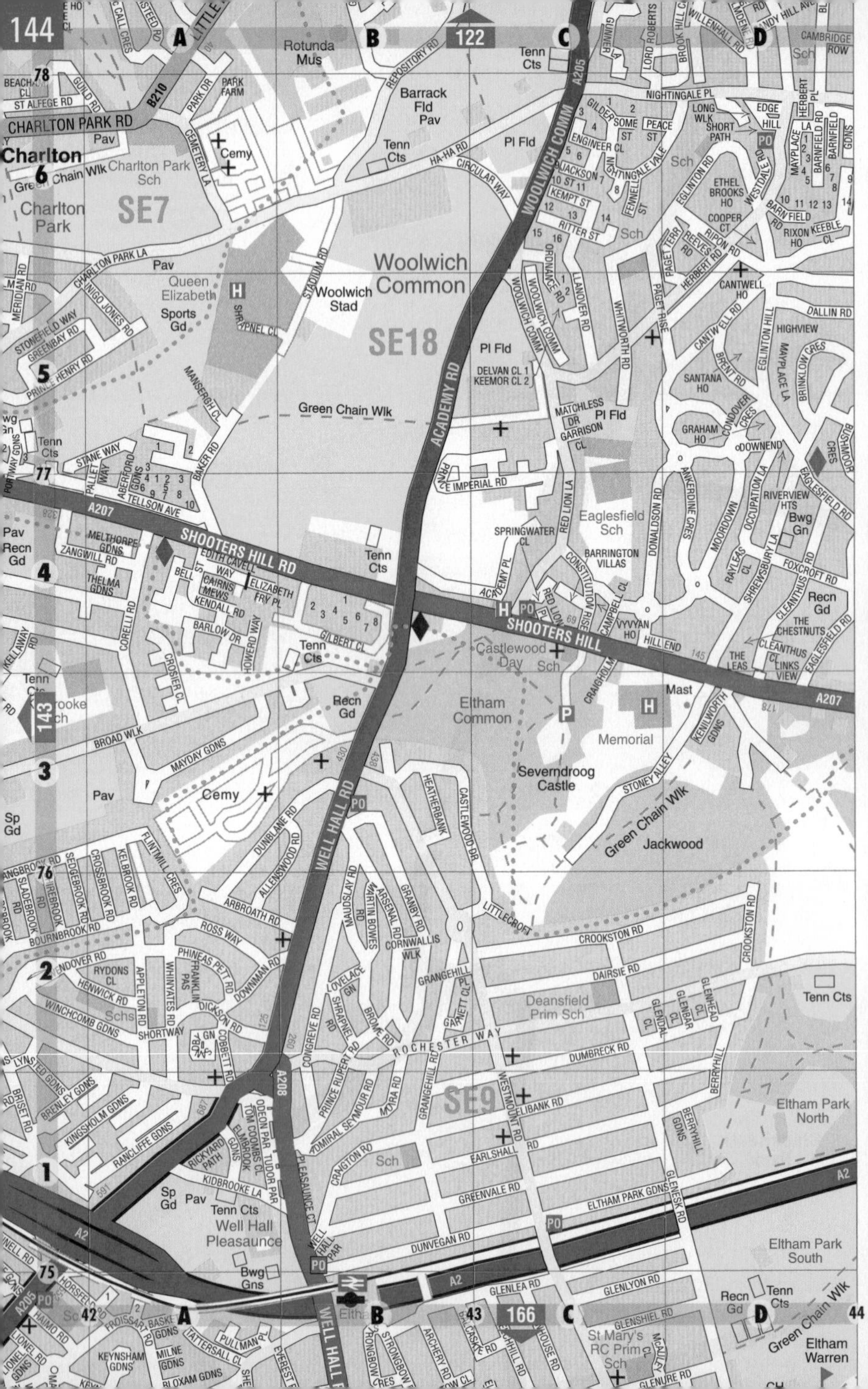
144
A
B
122
C
D
Rotunda Mus
Barrack Fld Pav
Tenn Cts
Charlton
Charlton Park Sch
Charlton Park
SE7
Cemy
Pl Fld
Woolwich Common
Woolwich Stad
Queen Elizabeth
Sports Gd
SE18
Green Chain Wlk
CHARLTON PARK RD
ST ALFEGE RD
CHARLTON PARK LA
CEMETERY LA
PARK DR
PARK FARM
HA-HA RD
CIRCULAR WAY
REPOSITORY RD
WOOLWICH COMM
A205
NIGHTINGALE PL
NIGHTINGALE VALE
GILDERSOME ST
PEACE ST
ENGINEER CL
JACKSON ST
KEMPT ST
RITTER ST
FENNELL ST
EGLINTON RD
ETHEL BROOKS HO
COOPER CT
RIPON RD
HERBERT RD
PAGET TERR
PAGET RISE
CANTWELL HO
CANTWELL RD
EGLINTON HILL
DALLIN RD
HIGHVIEW
MAYPLACE LA
BRINKLOW CRES
SANTANA HO
BRENT RD
GRAHAM HO
CONDOVER CRES
DOWNEND
WHITWORTH RD
LLANOVER RD
ORDNANCE RD
STADIUM RD
SHRAPNEL CL
MANSERGH CL
BAKER RD
ACADEMY RD
DELVAN CL
KEEMOR CL
MATCHLESS DR
GARRISON CL
PRINCE IMPERIAL RD
RED LION LA
Eaglesfield Sch
DONALDSON RD
ANKERDINE CRES
MOORDOWN
OCCUPATION LA
RIVERVIEW HTS
Bwg Gn
EAGLESFIELD RD
SHREWSBURY LA
RAYLEAS CL
FOXCROFT RD
CLEANTHUS RD
Recn Gd
THE CHESTNUTS
CLEANTHUS CL
LINKS VIEW
THE LEAS
SPRINGWATER CL
BARRINGTON VILLAS
CONSTITUTION RISE
CAMPBELL CL
VYVYAN HO
HILL END
SHOOTERS HILL
SHOOTERS HILL RD
A207
Castlewood Day Sch
CRAIGHOLM
Mast
Eltham Common
Memorial
Severndroog Castle
KENILWORTH GDNS
STONEY ALLEY
Jackwood
STONEFIELD WAY
GREENBAY RD
PRINCE HENRY RD
INIGO JONES RD
MERIDIAN RD
STANE WAY
PALLET WAY
ABERFORD GDNS
TELLSON AVE
MELTHORPE GDNS
ZANGWILL RD
THELMA GDNS
EDITH CAVELL WAY
ELIZABETH FRY PL
CAIRNS MEWS
KENDALL RD
BARLOW DR
HOWERD WAY
GILBERT CL
CORELLI RD
CROSIER CL
BROAD WLK
MAYDAY GDNS
Pav
Recn Gd
Sp Gd
WELL HALL RD
HEATHERBANK
CASTLEWOOD DR
DUNBLANE RD
ALLENSWOOD RD
ARBROATH RD
ROSS WAY
PHINEAS PETT RD
FRANKLIN PAS
WHINYATES RD
DOWNMAN RD
APPLETON RD
RYDONS CL
HENWICK RD
WINCHCOMB GDNS
SHORTWAY
DICKSON RD
COBBETT RD
FLINTMILL CRES
KELBROOK RD
CROSSBROOK RD
SEDGEBROOK RD
FIREBROOK RD
SLADEBROOK RD
BOURNBROOK RD
ENDOVER RD
MAUDSLAY RD
MARTIN BOWES RD
ARSENAL RD
GRANBY RD
CORNWALLIS WLK
LITTLECROFT
CROOKSTON RD
DAIRSIE RD
GRANGEHILL PL
GARNETT CL
LOVELACE GN
SHRAPNEL RD
BROME RD
Deansfield Prim Sch
GLENDAL CL
GLENBAR CL
GLENHEAD CL
Tenn Cts
ROCHESTER WAY
DUMBRECK RD
BERRYHILL
CONGREVE RD
PRINCE RUPERT RD
ADMIRAL SEYMOUR RD
MOIRA RD
GRANGEHILL RD
SE9
WESTMOUNT RD
ELIBANK RD
BERRYHILL GDNS
Eltham Park North
A208
LYNSTED GDNS
BRISET RD
BRENLEY GDNS
KINGSHOLM GDNS
RANCLIFFE GDNS
ODEON PAR
TOM COOMBS CL
TUDOR PAR
ELMBROOK GDNS
RICKYARD PATH
KIDBROOKE LA
PLEASAUNCE CT
CRAIGTON RD
Sch
EARLSHALL RD
GLENESK RD
GREENVALE RD
ELTHAM PARK GDNS
DUNVEGAN RD
A2
Well Hall Pleasaunce
Bwg Gns
WELL HALL PAR
PO
Eltham Park South
GLENLEA RD
GLENLYON RD
GLENSHIEL RD
St Mary's RC Prim Sch
GLENURE RD
Recn Gd
Tenn Cts
Eltham Warren
HORSFELD RD
HAIMO RD
FROISSART RD
BASKET GDNS
TATTERSALL CL
PULLMAN PL
MILNE GDNS
KEYNSHAM GDNS
BLOXAM GDNS
LIONEL RD
EVEREST RD
STRONGBOW RD
ARCHERY RD
WELL HALL RD
166
42
43
44
1
2
3
4
5
6
75
76
77
78
143

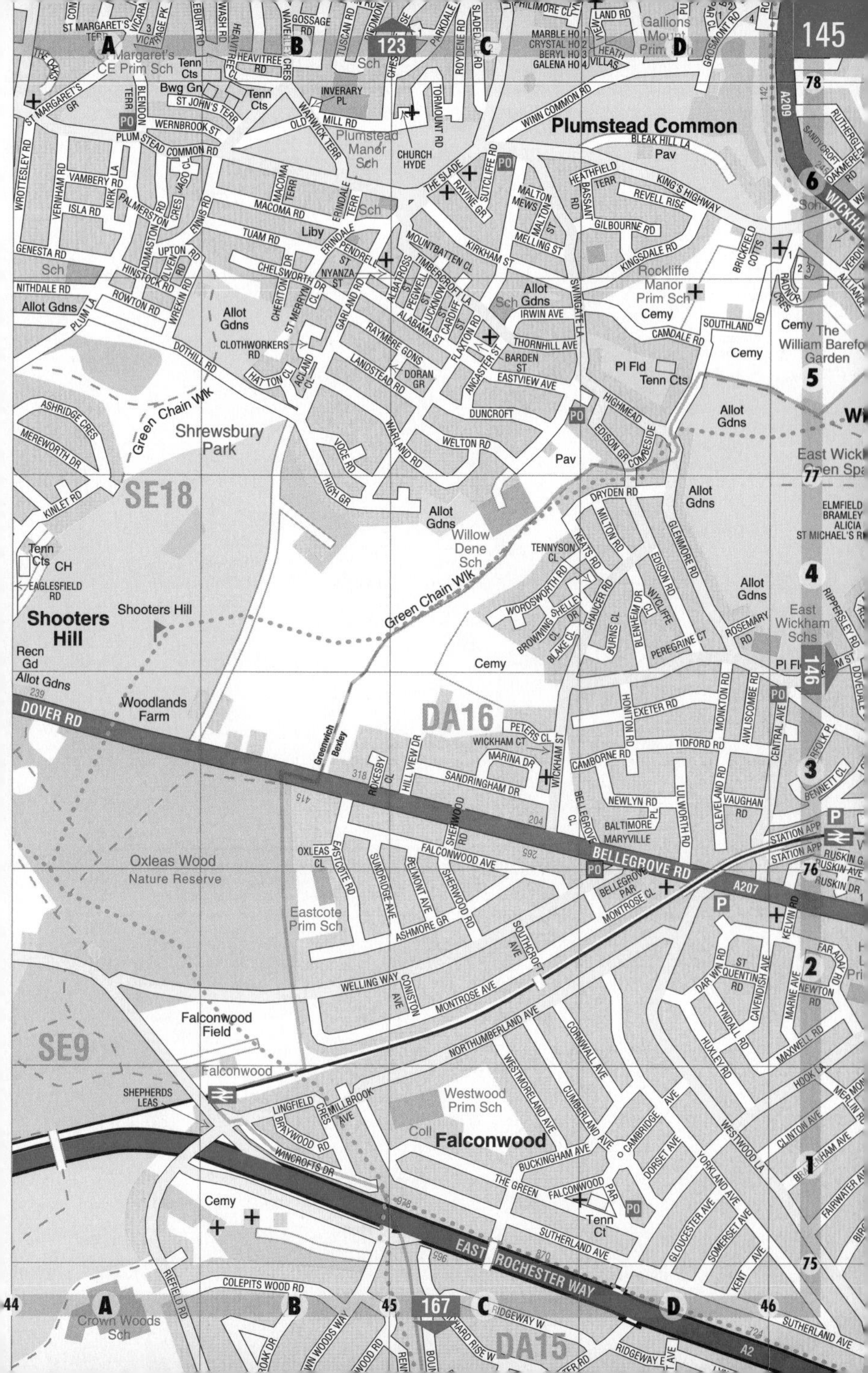

145
123
A
B
C
D
St Margaret's CE Prim Sch
Plumstead Common
Plumstead Manor Sch
Gallions Mount Prim Sch
WINN COMMON RD
KING'S HIGHWAY
BLEAK HILL LA
PLUMSTEAD COMMON RD
WERNBROOK ST
ST JOHN'S TERR
HEAVITREE RD
MILL RD
OLD MILL RD
WARWICK TERR
INVERARY PL
CHURCH HYDE
TORMOUNT RD
ROYDENE RD
SLADEDALE RD
THE SLADE
RAVINE GR
SUTCLIFFE RD
MALTON MEWS
MALTON ST
MELLING ST
KIRKHAM ST
HEATHFIELD TERR
BASSANT RD
REVELL RISE
GILBOURNE RD
KINGSDALE RD
BRICKFIELD COTTS
Rockliffe Manor Prim Sch
SWINGATE LA
IRWIN AVE
THORNHILL AVE
EASTVIEW AVE
BARDEN ST
ANCASTER ST
FLAXTON RD
CAMDALE RD
SOUTHLAND RD
Cemy
The William Barefoot Garden
Pl Fld
Tenn Cts
HIGHMEAD
EDISON GR
COMBESIDE
Allot Gdns
East Wickham Open Space
WICKHAM
A209
MACOMA RD
MACOMA TERR
TUAM RD
Liby
ERINDALE
ERINDALE TERR
PENDRELL ST
NYANZA ST
CHELSWORTH DR
CHERITON DR
ST MERRYN CL
GARLAND RD
ALBATROSS ST
PEGWELL ST
LUCKNOW ST
CARDIFF ST
ALABAMA ST
TIMBERCROFT LA
MOUNTBATTEN CL
RAYMERE GDNS
LANDSTEAD RD
DORAN GR
CLOTHWORKERS RD
HATTON CL
ACLAND CL
DUNCROFT
WELTON RD
WARLAND RD
VOCE RD
HIGH GR
Pav
WROTTESLEY RD
VERNHAM RD
VAMBERY RD
ISLA RD
KIRK LA
PALMERSTON CRES
ADMASTON RD
JAGO CL
ENNIS RD
UPTON RD
OLVEN RD
HINSTOCK RD
WREKIN RD
GENESTA RD
NITHDALE RD
ROWTON RD
PLUM LA
DOTHILL RD
Green Chain Wlk
Shrewsbury Park
ASHRIDGE CRES
MEREWORTH DR
KINLET RD
SE18
EAGLESFIELD RD
Shooters Hill
Recn Gd
Woodlands Farm
DOVER RD
Willow Dene Sch
DRYDEN RD
MILTON RD
KEATS RD
TENNYSON CL
WORDSWORTH RD
SHELLEY DR
BROWNING CL
BLAKE CL
CHAUCER RD
BURNS CL
BLENHEIM DR
WYCLIFFE CL
EDISON RD
GLENMORE RD
PEREGRINE CT
ROSEMARY RD
East Wickham Schs
RIPPERSLEY RD
146
DA16
Greenwich
Bexley
PETERS CL
WICKHAM CT
MARINA DR
WICKHAM ST
SANDRINGHAM DR
ROKESBY CL
HILL VIEW DR
HONITON RD
EXETER RD
TIDFORD RD
CAMBORNE RD
MONKTON RD
AWLISCOMBE RD
CENTRAL AVE
NEWLYN RD
LULWORTH RD
CLEVELAND RD
VAUGHAN RD
BALTIMORE PL
MARYVILLE
BELLEGROVE CL
BELLEGROVE RD
BELLEGROVE PAR
MONTROSE CL
A207
STATION APP
RUSKIN GR
RUSKIN AVE
RUSKIN DR
BENNETT CL
Oxleas Wood Nature Reserve
OXLEAS CL
EASTCOTE RD
Eastcote Prim Sch
SUNDRIDGE AVE
BELMONT AVE
SHERWOOD RD
FALCONWOOD AVE
ASHMORE GR
SOUTHCROFT AVE
WELLING WAY
CONISTON AVE
MONTROSE AVE
KELVIN RD
DARWIN RD
ST QUENTIN RD
CAVENDISH AVE
TYNDALL RD
MARINE AVE
FARADAY RD
NEWTON RD
MAXWELL RD
HUXLEY RD
HOOK LA
Falconwood Field
SE9
Falconwood
SHEPHERDS LEAS
NORTHUMBERLAND AVE
WESTMORELAND AVE
CORNWALL AVE
CUMBERLAND AVE
Westwood Prim Sch
Coll
LINGFIELD CRES
MILLBROOK AVE
BRAYWOOD RD
WINCROFTS DR
BUCKINGHAM AVE
THE GREEN
FALCONWOOD PAR
CAMBRIDGE AVE
DORSET AVE
YORKLAND AVE
WESTWOOD LA
CLINTON AVE
BRANKSHAM AVE
FAIRWATER AVE
Tenn Ct
SUTHERLAND AVE
GLOUCESTER AVE
SOMERSET AVE
KENT AVE
EAST ROCHESTER WAY
RIEFIELD RD
COLEPITS WOOD RD
Crown Woods Sch
167
RIDGEWAY W
DA15
A2
44
45
46
75
76
77
78

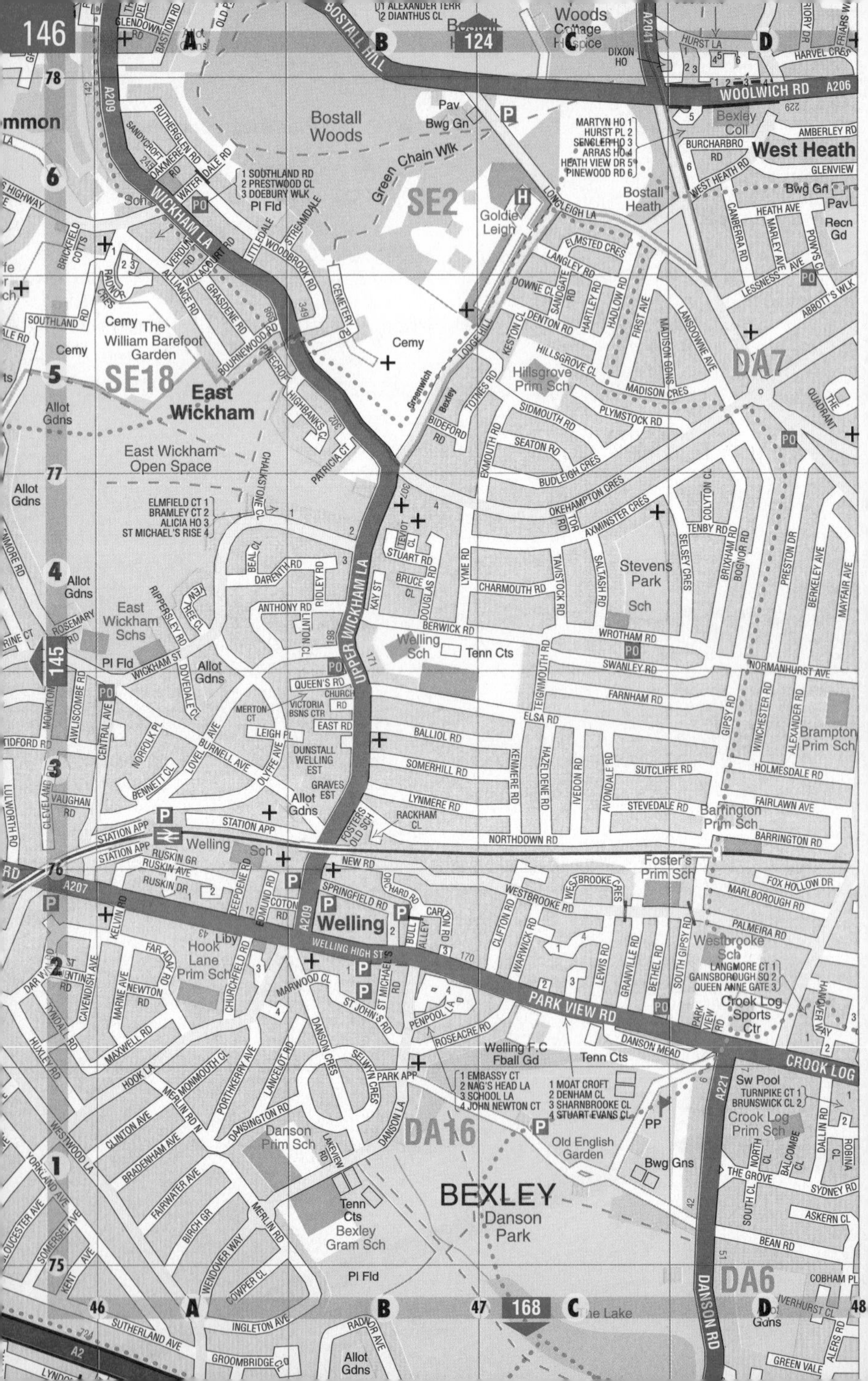

Bostall Woods
SE2
West Heath
Bostall Heath
Goldie Leigh
East Wickham
SE18
East Wickham Open Space
DA7
Stevens Park
Welling
DA16
BEXLEY
Danson Park
DA6
Bexley Gram Sch
Hook Lane Prim Sch
Danson Prim Sch
Hillsgrove Prim Sch
Welling Sch
Foster's Prim Sch
Barrington Prim Sch
Brampton Prim Sch
Westbrooke Sch
Crook Log Sports Ctr
Crook Log Prim Sch
Welling F.C Fball Gd
Old English Garden
The William Barefoot Garden
East Wickham Schs
Woods Cottage Hospice
Bexley Coll
WICKHAM LA
UPPER WICKHAM LA
WELLING HIGH ST
PARK VIEW RD
CROOK LOG
DANSON RD
WOOLWICH RD
BOSTALL HILL
LODGE HILL
LONGLEIGH LA
Green Chain Wlk
124
145
168

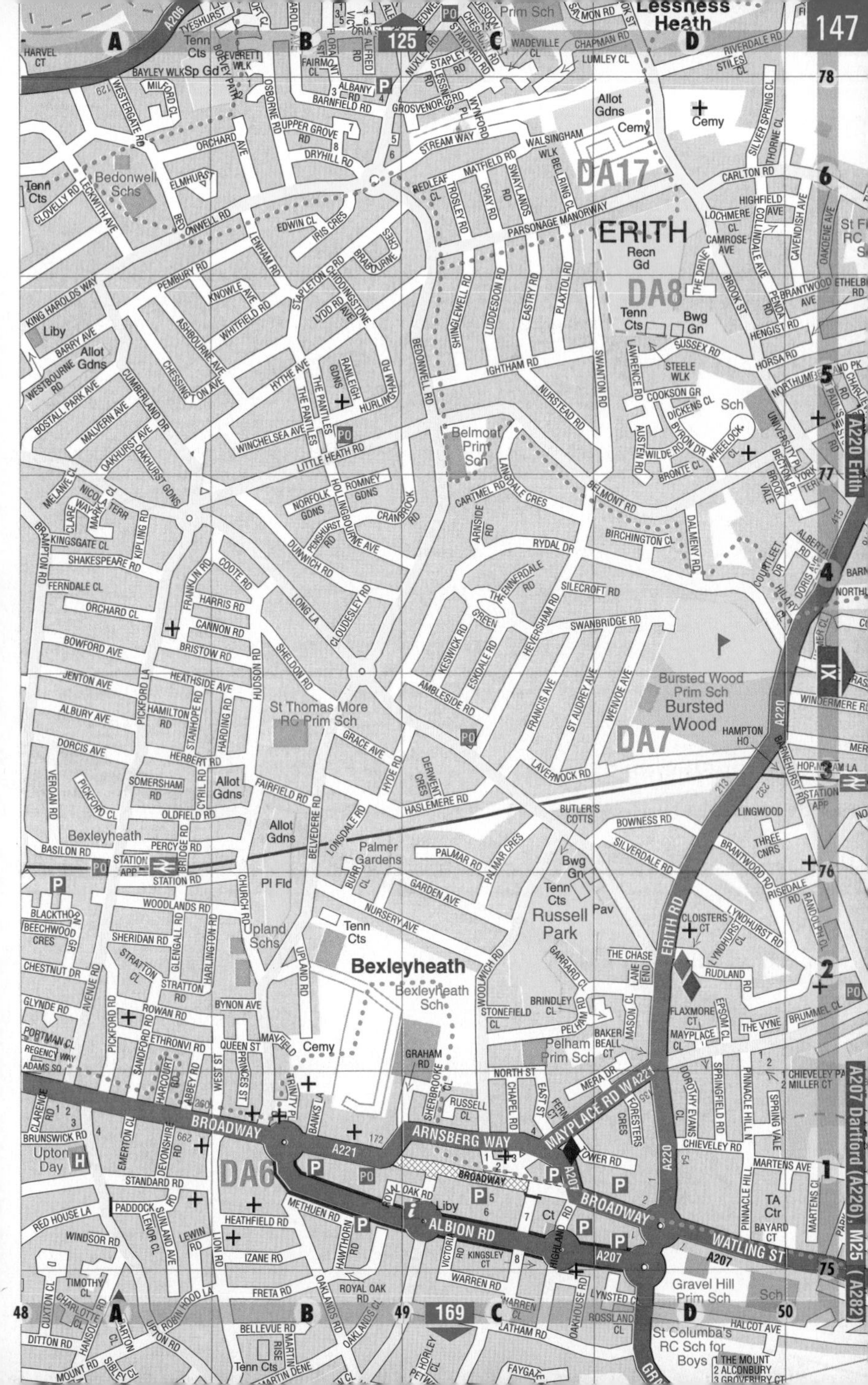

Lessness Heath
A
B
C
D
125
78
6
5
77
4
3
76
2
1
75
48
49
50
169
A206
TYESHURST CL
Tenn Cts
Sp Gd
HARVEL CT
BAYLEY WLK
EVERETT WLK
BEDDEVEY PATH
MILFORD CL
WESTERGATE RD
OSBORNE RD
FAIRMONT CL
FLORA ST
ALFRED RD
ALBANY RD
BARNFIELD RD
UPPER GROVE RD
DRYHILL RD
NUXLEY RD
STAPLEY RD
LESSNESS RD
STANDARD RD
CHESHUNT RD
WADEVILLE CL
CHAPMAN RD
LUMLEY CL
RIVERDALE RD
STILES CL
Prim Sch
SALMON RD
GROSVENOR RD
WYNFORD PL
STREAM WAY
WALSINGHAM WLK
Allot Gdns
Cemy
SILVER SPRING CL
THORNE CL
CARLTON RD
DA17
ORCHARD AVE
ELMHURST
Bedonwell Schs
Tenn Cts
CLOVELLY RD
LECKWITH AVE
BEDONWELL RD
REDLEAF CL
TROSLEY RD
MATFIELD RD
CRAY RD
SWAYLANDS RD
BELLRING CL
PARSONAGE MANORWAY
ERITH
Recn Gd
HIGHFIELD AVE
LOCHMERE CL
CAMROSE AVE
COLLINDALE AVE
CAVENDISH AVE
OAKDENE AVE
EDWIN CL
IRIS CRES
BRADBOURNE CRES
LENHAM RD
PEMBURY RD
KNOWLE AVE
WHITFIELD RD
ASHBOURNE AVE
CHESSINGTON AVE
STAPLETON RD
CHIDDINGSTONE AVE
LYDD RD
SHINGLEWELL RD
LUDDESDON RD
EASTRY RD
PLAXTOL RD
DA8
THE DRIVE
BROOK ST
PENDA RD
BRANTWOOD AVE
ETHELBERT RD
HENGIST RD
KING HAROLDS WAY
Liby
BARRY AVE
Allot Gdns
WESTBOURNE RD
BOSTALL PARK AVE
CUMBERLAND DR
MALVERN AVE
OAKHURST AVE
OAKHURST GDNS
HYTHE AVE
THE PANTILES
RANLEIGH GDNS
HURLINGHAM RD
BEDONWELL RD
IGHTHAM RD
SWANTON RD
NURSTEAD RD
Tenn Cts
Bwg Gn
SUSSEX RD
LAWRENCE RD
STEELE WLK
COOKSON GR
DICKENS CL
Sch
HORSA RD
NORTHUMBERLAND PK
WINCHELSEA AVE
LITTLE HEATH RD
Belmont Prim Sch
AUSTEN RD
WILDE RD
BYRON DR
BRONTE CL
WHEELOCK CL
UNIVERSITY PL
BECTON PL
BROOK VALE
YORK TERR
A220 Erith
MELANIE CL
NICOLA TERR
CLARE WAY
MARK CL
HOLLINGBOURNE AVE
ROMNEY GDNS
NORFOLK GDNS
CRANBROOK RD
CARTMEL RD
LANGDALE CRES
BELMONT RD
KINGSGATE CL
BRAMPTON RD
SHAKESPEARE RD
KIPLING RD
PENSHURST RD
DUNWICH RD
ARNSIDE RD
RYDAL DR
BIRCHINGTON CL
DALMENY RD
ALBERTA RD
COURTLEET DR
DORIS AVE
HILARY CL
FERNDALE CL
ORCHARD CL
FRANKLIN RD
COOTE RD
HARRIS RD
CANNON RD
LONG LA
CLOUDESLEY RD
THE ENNERDALE RD
GREEN
SILECROFT RD
HEVERSHAM RD
SWANBRIDGE RD
BOWFORD AVE
BRISTOW RD
SHELDON RD
KESWICK RD
ESKDALE RD
JENTON AVE
HEATHSIDE AVE
PICKFORD LA
HUDSON RD
ALBURY AVE
HAMILTON RD
STANHOPE RD
HARDING RD
St Thomas More RC Prim Sch
AMBLESIDE RD
FRANCIS AVE
ST AUDREY AVE
WENVOE AVE
Bursted Wood Prim Sch
Bursted Wood
HAMPTON HO
A220
WINDERMERE RD
DA7
DORCIS AVE
HERBERT RD
GRACE AVE
PO
LAVERNOCK RD
BARNEHURST RD
HOPINGHAM LA
STATION APP
VEROAN RD
PICKFORD CL
SOMERSHAM RD
CYRIL RD
Allot Gdns
FAIRFIELD RD
HYDE RD
DERWENT CRES
HASLEMERE RD
BUTLER'S COTTS
BOWNESS RD
LINGWOOD
OLDFIELD RD
Bexleyheath
BASILON RD
PERCY RD
BRIDGE RD
Allot Gdns
BELVEDERE RD
LONSDALE RD
Palmer Gardens
PALMAR RD
PALMAR CRES
SILVERDALE RD
THREE CNRS
BRANTWOOD RD
STATION APP
STATION RD
Pl Fld
BURR CL
GARDEN AVE
Bwg Gn
Tenn Cts
Russell Park
Pav
RISEDALE RD
RANDOLPH CL
BLACKTHORN GR
BEECHWOOD CRES
WOODLANDS RD
CHURCH RD
NURSERY AVE
CLOISTERS CT
LYNDHURST CL
LYNDHURST RD
SHERIDAN RD
GLENGALL RD
HARLINGTON RD
Upland Schs
Tenn Cts
ERITH RD
THE CHASE
LANE END
CHESTNUT DR
STRATTON CL
STRATTON RD
Bexleyheath
GARRARD CL
RUDLAND RD
GLYNDE RD
AVENUE RD
BYNON AVE
UPLAND RD
Bexleyheath Sch
WOOLWICH RD
BRINDLEY CL
STONEFIELD CL
PELHAM RD
MASON CL
FLAXMORE CT
MAYPLACE CL
EPSOM CL
THE VYNE
BRUMMEL CL
PORTMAN CL
REGENCY WAY
PICKFORD RD
SANDFORD RD
ROWAN RD
ETHRONVI RD
QUEEN ST
MAYFIELD RD
Cemy
GRAHAM RD
BAKER BEALL CT
Pelham Prim Sch
ADAMS SQ
HARCOURT RD
ABBEY RD
WEST ST
PRINCES ST
TRINITY PL
BANKS LA
NORTH ST
CHAPEL RD
EAST ST
FERN CT
MERA DR
MAYPLACE RD W
FORESTERS CRES
DOROTHY EVANS CL
SPRINGFIELD RD
PINNACLE HILL N
SPRING VALE
1 CHIEVELEY PA
2 MILLER CT
A207 Dartford (A226), M25 (A282)
CLARENCE RD
BROADWAY
A221
ARNSBERG WAY
SHERBROOKE CL
RUSSELL CL
MAYPLACE RD W
A221
BRUNSWICK RD
EMERTON CL
DEVONSHIRE RD
TOWER RD
CHIEVELEY RD
Upton Day
DA6
BROADWAY
MARTENS AVE
STANDARD RD
ROYAL OAK RD
Liby
A207
PINNACLE HILL
TA Ctr
MARTENS CL
PADDOCK CL
LENOR CL
SUNLAND AVE
HEATHFIELD RD
METHUEN RD
ALBION RD
BROADWAY
BAYARD CT
RED HOUSE LA
WINDSOR RD
LEWIN RD
LION RD
IZANE RD
HAWTHORN RD
VICTORIA RD
KINGSLEY CT
HIGHLAND RD
A207
WATLING ST
A207
WARREN RD
TIMOTHY CL
ROBIN HOOD LA
FRETA RD
ROYAL OAK RD
OAKLANDS RD
OAKHOUSE RD
LYNSTED CL
Gravel Hill Prim Sch
Sch
CUXTON CL
CHARLOTTE CL
WARREN CL
ROSSLAND CL
HALCOT AVE
UPTON RD
BELLEVUE RD
RISE
MARTIN DENE
LATHAM RD
St Columba's RC Sch for Boys
DITTON RD
HANSOL RD
CARTON CL
OAKLANDS CL
HORLEY CL
Tenn Cts
MOUNT RD
SIBLEY CL
FAYGATE
1 THE MOUNT
2 ALCONBURY
3 GROVEBURY CL

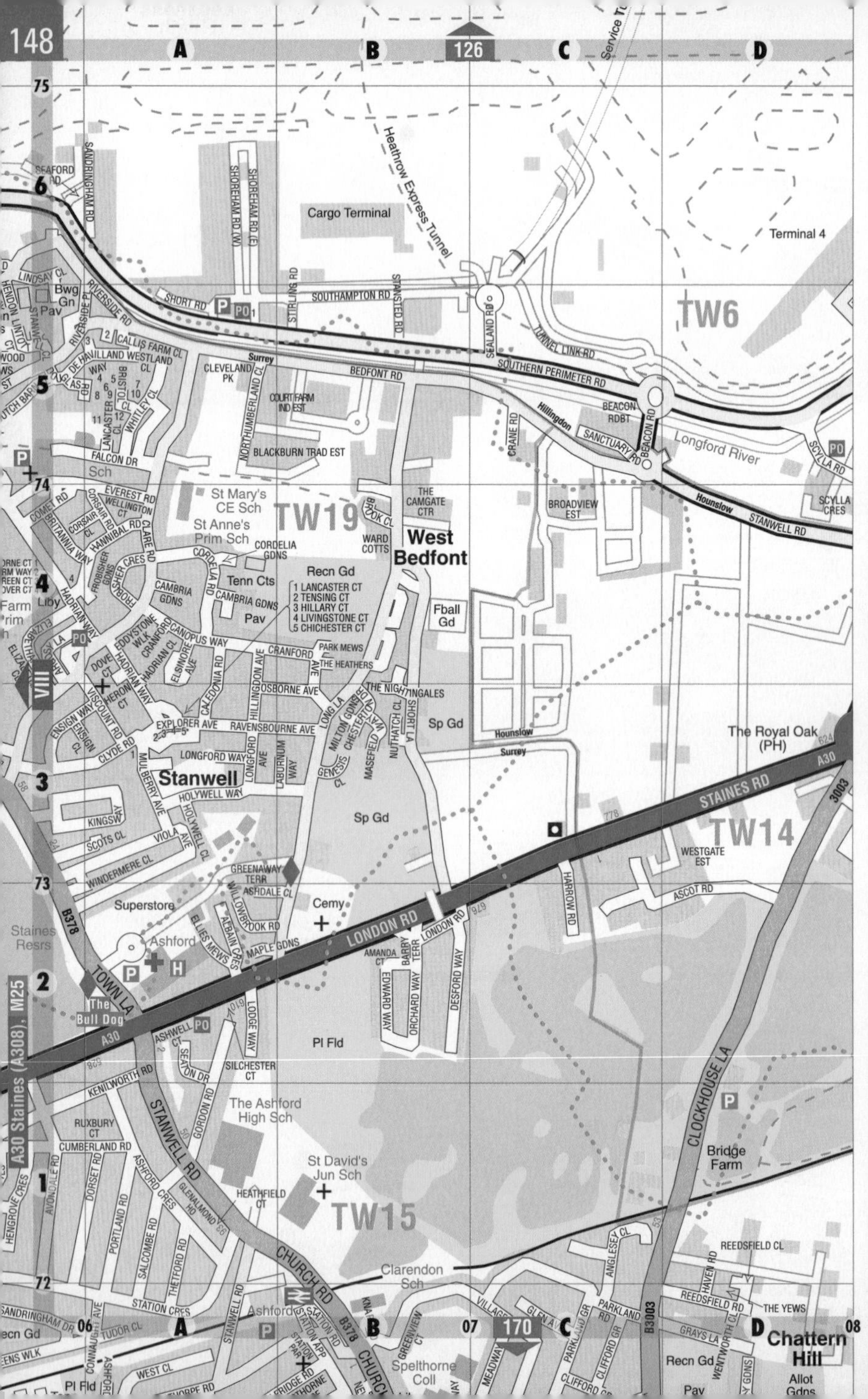

A
B
126
C
D
Cargo Terminal
Heathrow Express Tunnel
Terminal 4
TW6
SHOREHAM RD (E)
SHOREHAM RD (W)
SANDRINGHAM RD
SEAFORD RD
SHORT RD
SOUTHAMPTON RD
STIRLING RD
STANSTED RD
SEALAND RD
TUNNEL LINK RD
SOUTHERN PERIMETER RD
BEDFONT RD
RIVERSIDE RD
CALLIS FARM CL
DE HAVILLAND WESTLAND CL
CLEVELAND PK
NORTHUMBERLAND CL
COURT FARM IND EST
BLACKBURN TRAD EST
BEACON RDBT
BEACON RD
CRANE RD
SANCTUARY RD
Longford River
SCYLLA RD
SCYLLA CRES
STANWELL RD
BROADVIEW EST
THE CAMGATE CTR
BROOK CL
WARD COTTS
West Bedfont
St Mary's CE Sch
St Anne's Prim Sch
TW19
FALCON DR
EVEREST RD
WELLINGTON CT
CORSAIR RD
COMET RD
BRITANNIA WAY
HANNIBAL RD
CLARE RD
CORDELIA GDNS
CORDELIA RD
Recn Gd
Tenn Cts
CAMBRIA GDNS
1 LANCASTER CT
2 TENSING CT
3 HILLARY CT
4 LIVINGSTONE CT
5 CHICHESTER CT
Pav
Fball Gd
Liby
HADRIAN WAY
FROBISHER GDNS
CANOPUS WAY
CRANFORD AVE
PARK MEWS
THE HEATHERS
EDDYSTONE WLK
HADRIAN CL
ELSINORE AVE
CALEDONIA RD
HILLINGDON AVE
OSBORNE AVE
THE NIGHTINGALES
DOVE CT
HERON CT
VISCOUNT RD
ENSIGN WAY
EXPLORER AVE
RAVENSBOURNE AVE
LONG LA
MILTON GDNS
CHESTERTON
NUTHATCH CL
SHORT LA
Sp Gd
CLYDE RD
LONGFORD WAY
LONGFORD AVE
LABURNUM WAY
GENESIS CL
MASEFIELD
Stanwell
HOLYWELL WAY
MULBERRY AVE
KINGSWAY
SCOTS CL
VIOLA AVE
HOLYWELL CL
WINDERMERE CL
The Royal Oak (PH)
STAINES RD
A30
TW14
WESTGATE EST
ASCOT RD
HARROW RD
GREENAWAY TERR
ASHDALE CL
WILLOWBROOK RD
ALBAIN CRES
ELLIES MEWS
MAPLE GDNS
Cemy
LONDON RD
Superstore
Staines Resrs
Ashford
B378
TOWN LA
The Bull Dog
AMANDA CT
BARRY TERR
EDWARD WAY
ORCHARD WAY
DESFORD WAY
ASHWELL CT
SEATON DR
LODGE WAY
SILCHESTER CT
Pl Fld
A30 Staines (A308), M25
KENILWORTH RD
RUXBURY CT
CUMBERLAND RD
STANWELL RD
GORDON RD
The Ashford High Sch
CLOCKHOUSE LA
Bridge Farm
St David's Jun Sch
TW15
HEATHFIELD CT
GLENALMOND HO
AVONDALE RD
DORSET RD
PORTLAND RD
SALCOMBE RD
THETFORD RD
ASHFORD CRES
HENGROVE CRES
CHURCH RD
Clarendon Sch
ANGLESEY CL
REEDSFIELD CL
HAVEN RD
REEDSFIELD RD
THE YEWS
STATION CRES
STANWELL RD
STATION RD
STATION APP
PARKLAND RD
PARKLAND GR
CLIFFORD GR
B3003
GRAYS LA
WENTWORTH CL
Chattern Hill
Recn Gd
Allot Gdns
Spelthorne Coll
GREENVIEW CT
MEADWAY
GLEN AV
VILLAGE
SANDRINGHAM DR
TUDOR CL
CONNAUGHT AVE
WEST CL
Pl Fld
06
07
08
170
75
74
73
72
6
5
4
3
2
1
VIII

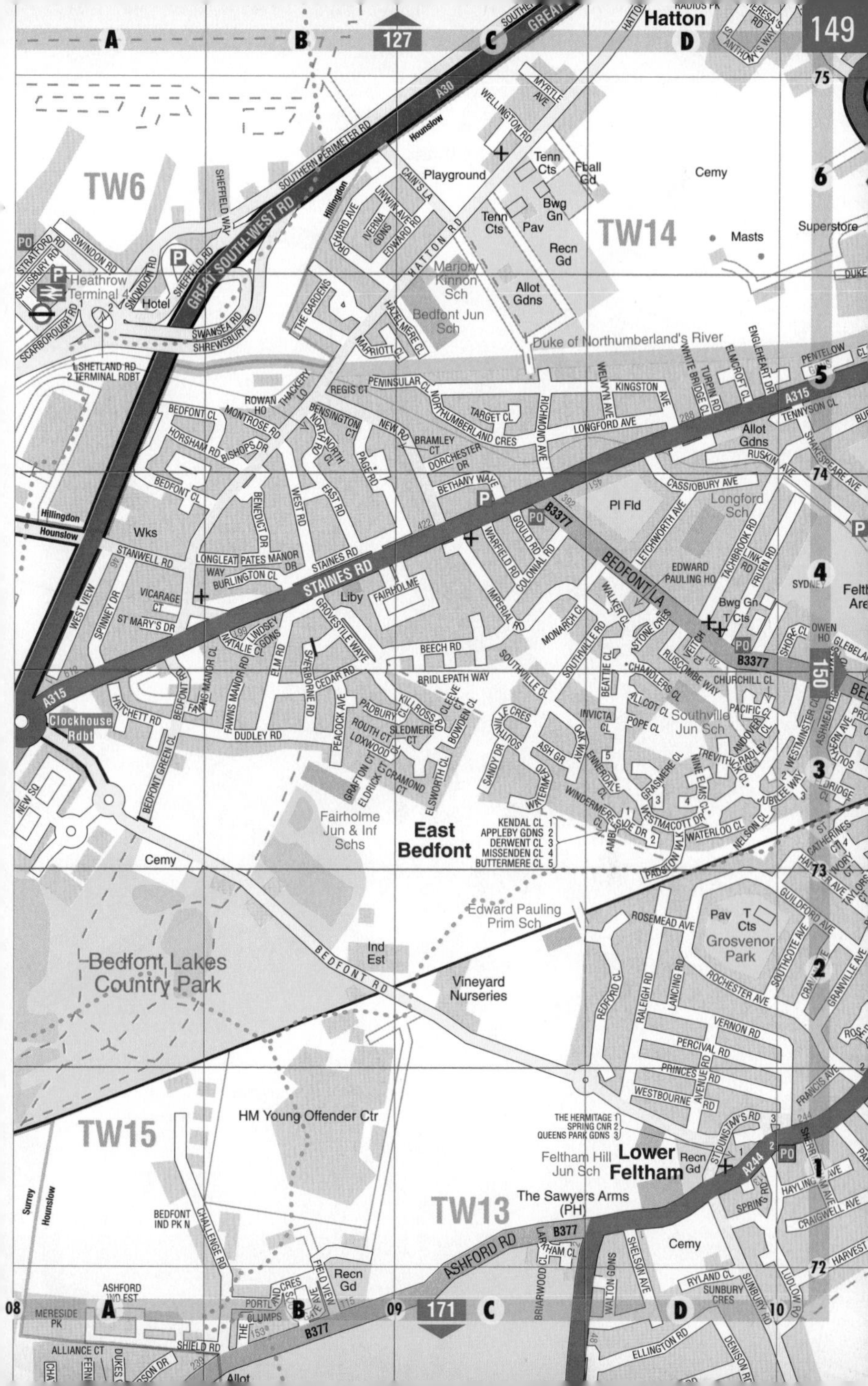

A
B
127
C
D
Hatton
TW6
TW14
TW15
TW13
SOUTHERN PERIMETER RD
A30
GREAT SOUTH-WEST RD
Hounslow
Hillingdon
SHEFFIELD WAY
SHEFFIELD RD
SWINDON RD
STRATFORD RD
SALISBURY RD
Heathrow Terminal 4
SNOWDON RD
Hotel
SCARBOROUGH RD
SWANSEA RD
SHREWSBURY RD
1 SHETLAND RD
2 TERMINAL RDBT
MYRTLE AVE
WELLINGTON RD
Playground
Tenn Cts
Fball Gd
Cemy
Bwg Gn
Pav
Recn Gd
Masts
Superstore
CAIN'S LA
UNWIN AVE
IVERNA GDNS
EDWARD RD
ORCHARD AVE
HATTON RD
Marjory Kinnon Sch
Allot Gdns
Bedfont Jun Sch
THE GARDENS
HAZELMERE CL
MARRIOTT CL
Duke of Northumberland's River
WHITE BRIDGE CL
TURPIN RD
ELMCROFT CL
ENGLEHEART DR
PENTELOW GDNS
PENINSULAR CL
REGIS CT
KINGSTON AVE
WELWYN AVE
NORTHUMBERLAND CRES
TARGET CL
RICHMOND AVE
LONGFORD AVE
A315
TENNYSON CL
ROWAN HO
THACKERY LO
BEDFONT CL
MONTROSE RD
BENSINGTON CT
NORTH RD
NORTH CL
NEW RD
BRAMLEY CT
DORCHESTER DR
HORSHAM RD
BISHOPS DR
PAGE RD
BETHANY WAYE
Allot Gdns
RUSKIN AVE
SHAKESPEARE AVE
CASSIOBURY AVE
Pl Fld
Longford Sch
Hillingdon
Hounslow
Wks
BENEDICT DR
WEST RD
EAST RD
B3377
GOULD RD
WARFIELD RD
COLONIAL RD
LETCHWORTH AVE
TACHBROOK RD
LINK RD
FRUEN RD
STANWELL RD
LONGLEAT WAY
PATES MANOR DR
BURLINGTON CL
STAINES RD
EDWARD PAULING HO
BEDFONT LA
SYDNEY
Felth Are
VICARAGE CT
WEST VIEW
SPINNEY DR
ST MARY'S DR
Liby
FAIRHOLME
IMPERIAL RD
WALKER CL
Bwg Gn
T Cts
OWEN HO
GLEBELA
SHORE CL
GROVESTILE WAYE
MONARCH CL
STONE CRES
VEITCH CL
LINDSEY GDNS
NATALIE CL
ELM RD
BEECH RD
SOUTHVILLE RD
RUSCOMBE WAY
B3377
150
SHERBORNE RD
BRIDLEPATH WAY
SOUTHVILLE CL
BEATTIE CL
CHANDLERS CL
CHURCHILL CL
FAWNS MANOR CL
FAWNS MANOR RD
CEDAR RD
PADBURY CL
KILLROSS RD
CLEEVE CT
BOWDEN CL
ALLCOT CL
Southville Jun Sch
PACIFIC CL
HATCHETT RD
Clockhouse Rdbt
PEACOCK AVE
ROUTH CT
SLEDMERE CT
INVICTA CL
POPE CL
ANDOVER CL
WESTMINSTER CL
DUDLEY RD
LOXWOOD CL
SOUTHVILLE CRES
OAK WAY
ASH GR
GRASMERE CL
TREVITHICK CL
RADLEY CL
NINE ELMS CL
JUBILEE WAY
ELDRIDGE CL
NEW SQ
BEDFONT GREEN CL
GRAFTON CT
ELDRICK CT
CRAMOND CT
ELSWORTH CL
SANDY DR
WATERMERE AVE
ENNERDALE CL
WINDERMERE SIDE DR
WESTMACOTT DR
WATERLOO CL
NELSON CL
Fairholme Jun & Inf Schs
East Bedfont
KENDAL CL 1
APPLEBY GDNS 2
DERWENT CL 3
MISSENDEN CL 4
BUTTERMERE CL 5
AMBLESIDE CL
PADSTOW WLK
ST CATHERINES CL
73
Cemy
Edward Pauling Prim Sch
ROSEMEAD AVE
Pav
T Cts
Grosvenor Park
GUILDFORD AVE
SOUTHCOTE AVE
GRANVILLE AVE
Ind Est
Bedfont Lakes Country Park
BEDFONT RD
Vineyard Nurseries
REDFORD CL
RALEIGH RD
LANCING RD
ROCHESTER AVE
VERNON RD
PERCIVAL RD
PRINCES RD
AVENUE RD
WESTBOURNE RD
FRANCIS AVE
HM Young Offender Ctr
THE HERMITAGE 1
SPRING CNR 2
QUEENS PARK GDNS 3
ST DUNSTAN'S RD
A244
Feltham Hill Jun Sch
Lower Feltham
Recn Gd
The Sawyers Arms (PH)
HAYLING AVE
CRAIGWELL AVE
Surrey
Hounslow
BEDFONT IND PK N
CHALLENGE RD
B377
LARKHAM CL
ASHFORD RD
SHELSON AVE
Cemy
HARVEST
72
ASHFORD IND EST
Recn Gd
FIELD VIEW
PORTLAND CRES
BRIARWOOD CL
WALTON GDNS
RYLAND CL
SUNBURY CRES
SUNBURY RD
LUDLOW RD
08
MERESIDE PK
A
THE CLUMPS
B
09
171
C
D
10
SHIELD RD
ALLIANCE CT
DUKES
ELLINGTON RD
DENISON RD
Allot
75
6
5
74
4
3
2
1

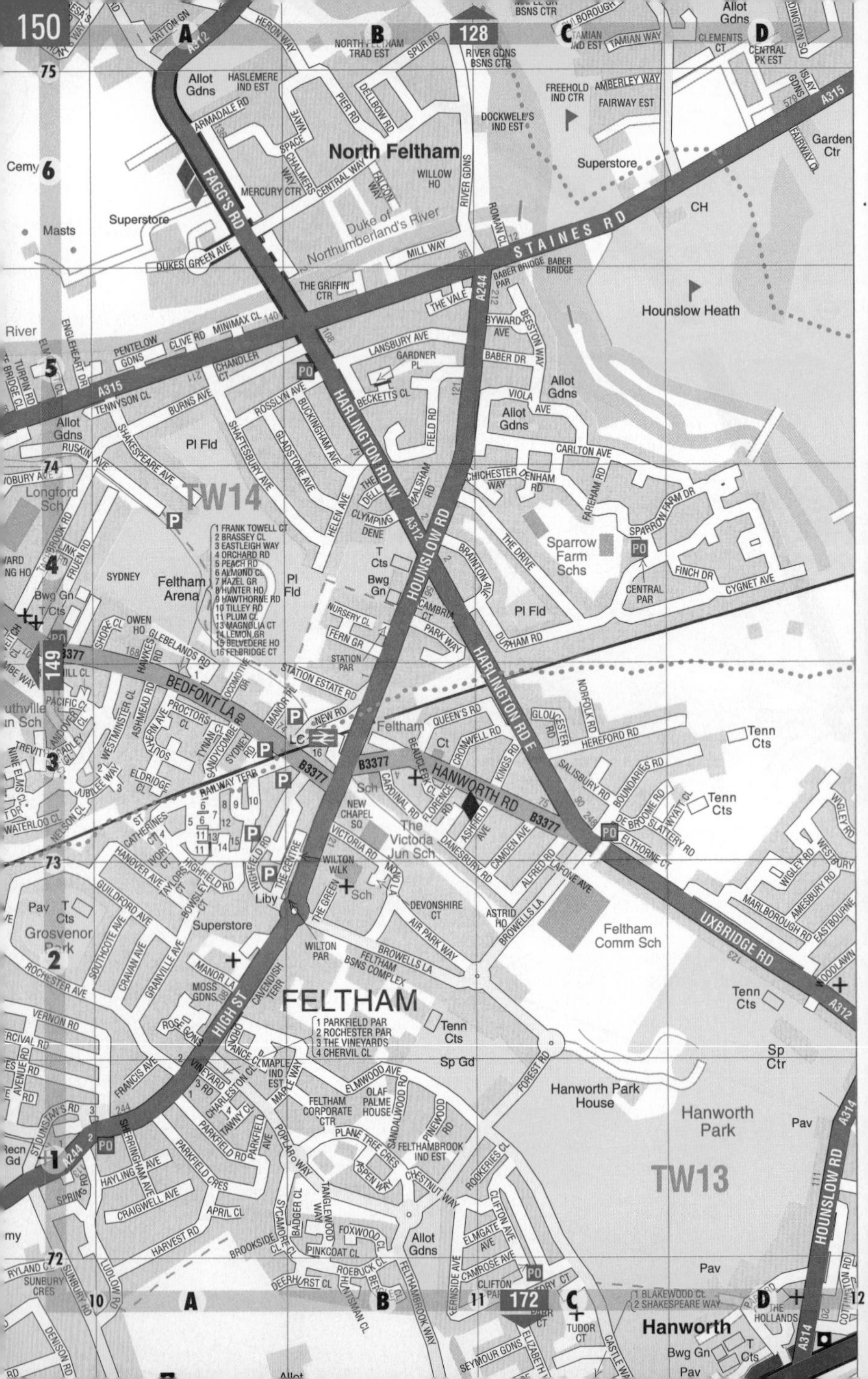

128
North Feltham
FELTHAM
Feltham
Hanworth
Hounslow Heath
Hanworth Park
TW14
TW13
STAINES RD
HARLINGTON RD W
HARLINGTON RD E
HOUNSLOW RD
HANWORTH RD
BEDFONT LA
UXBRIDGE RD
HIGH ST
FAGG'S RD
Feltham Arena
Sparrow Farm Schs
Feltham Comm Sch
Hanworth Park House
149
172

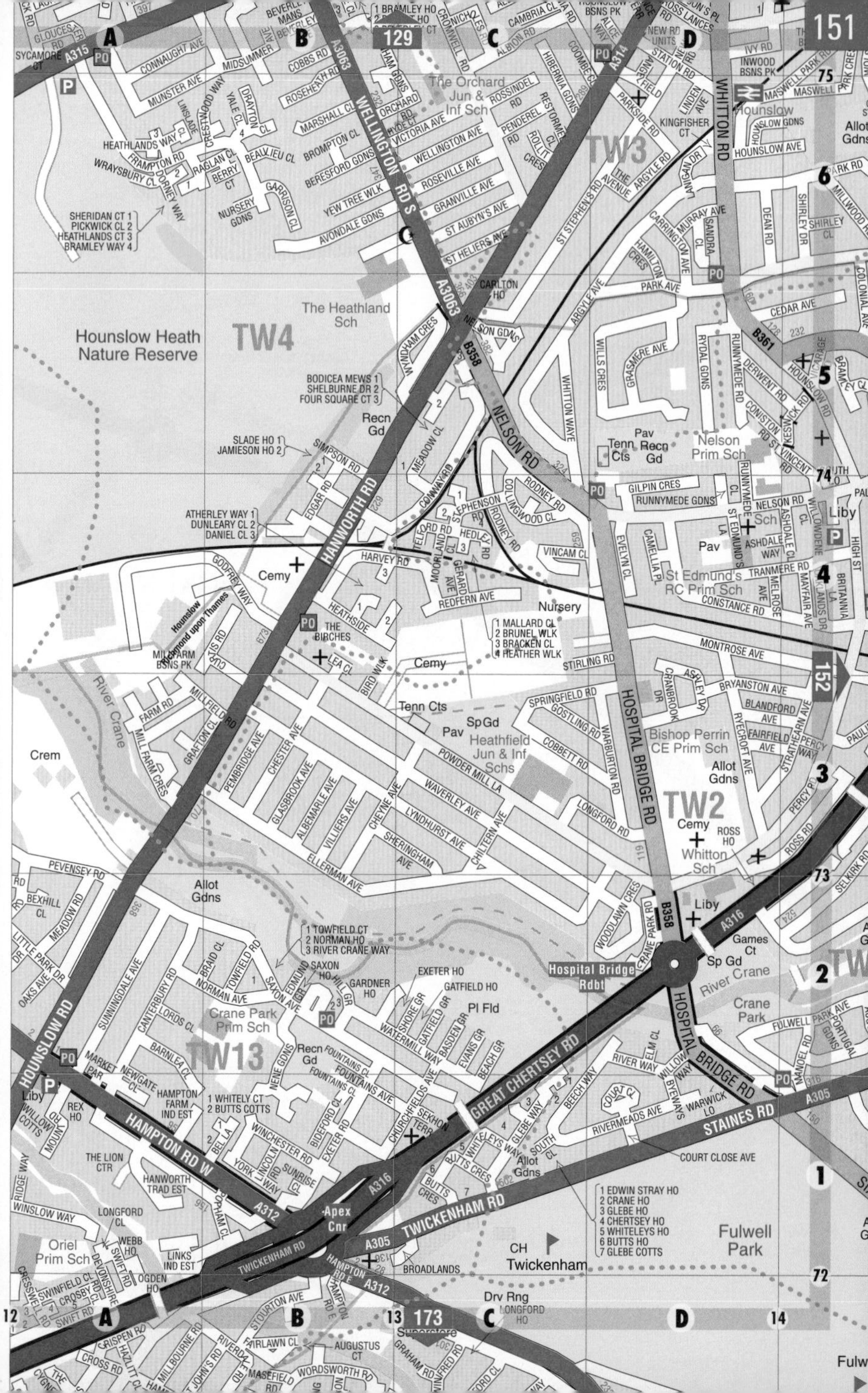
A
B
C
D
129
A315
A3063
A314
WELLINGTON RD S
TW3
TW4
Hounslow Heath Nature Reserve
The Heathland Sch
The Orchard Jun & Inf Sch
Hounslow
WHITTON RD
B358
NELSON RD
HANWORTH RD
B361
HOSPITAL BRIDGE RD
TW2
TW13
Hospital Bridge Rdbt
GREAT CHERTSEY RD
A316
STAINES RD
A305
TWICKENHAM RD
HAMPTON RD W
A312
Apex Cnr
HOUNSLOW RD
River Crane
Crane Park
Fulwell Park
CH Twickenham
Heathfield Jun & Inf Schs
Bishop Perrin CE Prim Sch
St Edmund's RC Prim Sch
Nelson Prim Sch
Crane Park Prim Sch
Oriel Prim Sch
Whitton Sch
Crem
Cemy
SHERIDAN CT 1
PICKWICK CL 2
HEATHLANDS CT 3
BRAMLEY WAY 4
BODICEA MEWS 1
SHELBURNE DR 2
FOUR SQUARE CT 3
SLADE HO 1
JAMIESON HO 2
ATHERLEY WAY 1
DUNLEARY CL 2
DANIEL CL 3
1 MALLARD CL
2 BRUNEL WLK
3 BRACKEN CL
4 HEATHER WLK
1 TOWFIELD CT
2 NORMAN HO
3 RIVER CRANE WAY
1 WHITELY CT
2 BUTTS COTTS
1 EDWIN STRAY HO
2 CRANE HO
3 GLEBE HO
4 CHERTSEY HO
5 WHITELEYS HO
6 BUTTS HO
7 GLEBE COTTS
152
173
12
13
14
75
74
73
72
6
5
4
3
2
1

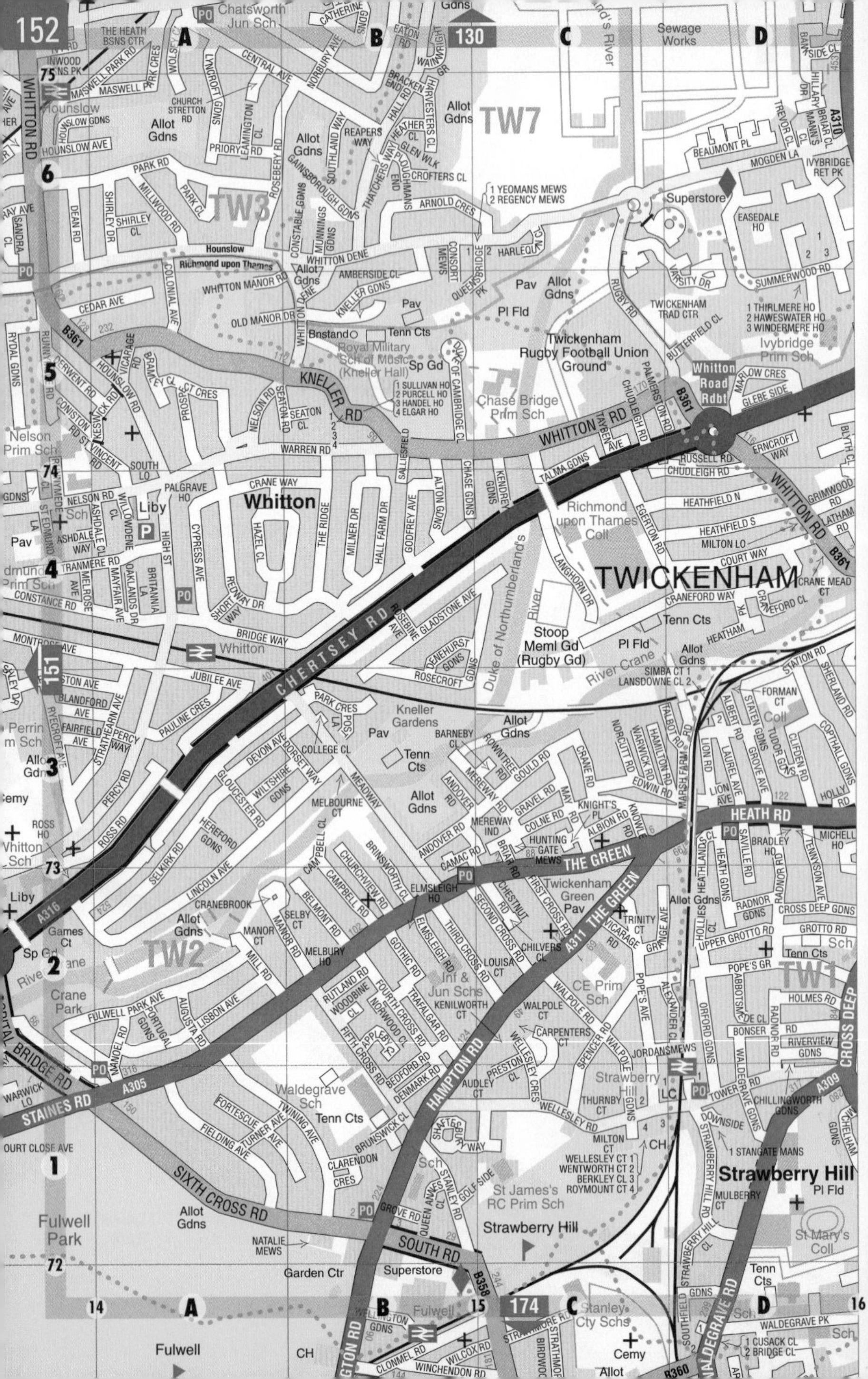
130
A
B
C
D
Chatsworth Jun Sch
THE HEATH BSNS CTR
INWOOD BSNS PK
75
WHITTON RD
Hounslow
MASWELL PARK RD
MASWELL PK
PARK CRES
WOLSEY
LYNCROFT GDNS
CENTRAL AVE
CHURCH STRETTON RD
NORBURY AVE
CATHERINE GDNS
EATON RD
WAINWRIGHT GR
BRACKEN END
HARVESTERS CL
HALL RD
Sewage Works
BANKSIDE CL
HILLARY DR
MANN'S CL
BRIAR CL
TREVOR CL
A310
HOUNSLOW GDNS
HOUNSLOW AVE
Allot Gdns
LEAMINGTON CL
PRIORY RD
ROSEBERY RD
SOUTHLAND WAY
REAPERS WAY
HEATHER CL
GLEN WLK
TW7
BEAUMONT PL
MOGDEN LA
IVYBRIDGE RET PK
6
PARK RD
MILLWOOD RD
GAINSBOROUGH GDNS
THATCHERS WAY
PLOUGHMANS END
CROFTERS CL
1 YEOMANS MEWS
2 REGENCY MEWS
Superstore
TW3
SHIRLEY DR
SHIRLEY CL
DEAN RD
PARK CL
CONSTABLE GDNS
MUNNINGS GDNS
ARNOLD CRES
EASEDALE HO
SANDRA CL
Hounslow
Richmond upon Thames
WHITTON DENE
CONSORT MEWS
QUEENSBRIDGE PK
HARLEQUIN CL
PO
COLONIAL AVE
WHITTON MANOR RD
AMBERSIDE CL
KNELLER GDNS
Pav
Allot Gdns
VARSITY DR
RUGBY RD
SUMMERWOOD RD
TWICKENHAM TRAD CTR
1 THIRLMERE HO
2 HAWESWATER HO
3 WINDERMERE HO
CEDAR AVE
OLD MANOR DR
Pl Fld
B361
Bnstand
Tenn Cts
Royal Military Sch of Music (Kneller Hall)
Sp Gd
DUKE OF CAMBRIDGE CL
Twickenham Rugby Football Union Ground
BUTTERFIELD CL
Ivybridge Prim Sch
RYDAL GDNS
RUNNYMEDE RD
DERWENT RD
5
HOUNSLOW RD
VICARAGE
BRAMLEY CL
PROSPECT CRES
KNELLER RD
Whitton Road Rdbt
MARLOW CRES
GLEBE SIDE
1 SULLIVAN HO
2 PURCELL HO
3 HANDEL HO
4 ELGAR HO
Chase Bridge Prim Sch
PALMERSTON RD
CHUDLEIGH RD
CONISTON
KESWICK RD
NELSON RD
SEATON RD
SEATON CL
SALLIESFIELD
WHITTON RD
TAYBEN AVE
ERNCROFT WAY
BLYTH CL
Nelson Prim Sch
ST VINCENT RD
SOUTH LO
WARREN RD
RUSSELL RD
CHUDLEIGH RD
74
PALGRAVE HO
CRANE WAY
CHASE GDNS
KENDREY GDNS
TALMA GDNS
Whitton
ALTON GDNS
Richmond upon Thames Coll
HEATHFIELD N
WHITTON RD
GRIMWOOD RD
RUNNYMEDE CL
NELSON RD
ASHDALE CL
WILLOWDENE CL
Liby
HIGH ST
HAZEL CL
THE RIDGE
MILNER DR
HALL FARM DR
GODFREY AVE
HEATHFIELD S
LATHAM CL
ST EDMUNDS LA
ASHDALE WAY
CYPRESS AVE
EGERTON RD
MILTON LO
Pav
4
TRANMERE RD
OAKLANDS DR
BRITANNIA LA
COURT WAY
B361
Edmund's Prim Sch
MELROSE AVE
MAYFAIR AVE
REDWAY DR
SHORT WAY
ROSEBINE AVE
GLADSTONE AVE
Duke of Northumberland's River
LANGHORN DR
TWICKENHAM
CRANEFORD WAY
CRANE MEAD CT
CRANEFORD CL
CONSTANCE RD
Tenn Cts
MONTROSE AVE
BRIDGE WAY
Whitton
CHERTSEY RD
DENEHURST GDNS
Stoop Meml Gd (Rugby Gd)
Pl Fld
HEATHAM PK
Allot Gdns
STATION RD
151
BLANDFORD AVE
ROSECROFT GDNS
River Crane
SIMBA CT 1
LANSDOWNE CL 2
FORMAN CT
SHERLAND RD
JUBILEE AVE
FAIRFIELD AVE
STRATHEARN AVE
PERCY WAY
PAULINE CRES
PARK CRES
POST LA
Kneller Gardens
Allot Gdns
BARNEBY CL
ROWNTREE RD
NORCUTT RD
WARWICK RD
HAMILTON RD
TALBOT RD
ALBERT RD
STATEN GDNS
TUDOR GDNS
COPTHALL GDNS
Coll
Perrin Sch
RYECROFT AVE
DEVON AVE
DORSET WAY
COLLEGE CL
Pav
Tenn Cts
MEREWAY RD
GOULD RD
CRANE RD
EDWIN RD
LION RD
LAUREL AVE
GROVE AVE
CLIFDEN RD
3
PERCY RD
GLOUCESTER RD
WILTSHIRE GDNS
MEADWAY
ANDOVER RD
Allot Gdns
GRAVEL RD
MAY RD
KNIGHT'S PL
KNOWLE RD
LION AVE
HOLLY RD
MELBOURNE CT
COLNE RD
ALBION RD
HEATH RD
MARSH FARM RD
Cemy
ROSS HO
ROSS RD
HEREFORD GDNS
CAMPBELL CL
BRINSWORTH CL
ANDOVER RD
MEREWAY IND
HUNTING GATE MEWS
HEATHLANDS CL
SAVILLE RD
BRADLEY HO
RADNOR RD
TENNYSON AVE
MICHELL HO
Whitton Sch
73
SELKIRK RD
CHURCHVIEW RD
GAMAC RD
BRIAR RD
THE GREEN
LINCOLN AVE
CAMPBELL RD
ELMSLEIGH HO
FIRST CROSS RD
Twickenham Green Pav
Allot Gdns
HEATH GDNS
RADNOR GDNS
CROSS DEEP GDNS
Liby
A316
CRANEBROOK
BELMONT RD
SELBY CT
SECOND CROSS RD
CHESTNUT RD
TRINITY CT
GRANGE AVE
HOLLIES CL
UPPER GROTTO RD
GROTTO RD
Games Ct
Allot Gdns
MANOR CT
MANOR RD
ELMSLEIGH RD
THIRD CROSS RD
A311 THE GREEN
VICARAGE RD
Sch
Sp Gd
TW2
MELBURY HO
GOTHIC RD
LOUISA CT
CHILVERS CL
POPE'S GR
Tenn Cts
2
River Crane
MILL RD
RUTLAND RD
Inf & Jun Schs
CE Prim Sch
ABBOTSMEDE CL
TW1
Crane Park
WOODBINE CL
FOURTH CROSS RD
TRAFALGAR RD
KENILWORTH CT
WALPOLE RD
POPE'S AVE
ALEXANDER CL
ORFORD GDNS
HOLMES RD
FULWELL PARK AVE
AUGUSTA RD
LISBON AVE
NORWOOD CL
WALPOLE CT
BONSER RD
CROSS DEEP
PORTUGAL GDNS
APPLEBY CL
FIFTH CROSS RD
CARPENTERS CT
WELLESLEY CRES
SPENCER RD
WALPOLE GDNS
JORDANS MEWS
RADNOR RD
RIVERVIEW GDNS
BRIDGE RD
MANOEL RD
BEDFORD RD
HAMPTON RD
PRESTON CL
Strawberry Hill
WALDEGRAVE GDNS
TOWER RD
DENMARK RD
AUDLEY CT
THURNBY CT
LC
CHILLINGWORTH GDNS
A309
WARWICK LO
STAINES RD
A305
FORTESCUE AVE
TWINING AVE
Waldegrave Sch
Tenn Cts
WELLESLEY RD
DOWNSIDE
CHELHAM WAY
TURNER AVE
FIELDING AVE
BRUNSWICK CL
SHAFTESBURY WAY
MILTON CT
CH
1 STANGATE MANS
COURT CLOSE AVE
1
CLARENDON CRES
Sch
GOLFSIDE
WELLESLEY CT 1
WENTWORTH CT 2
BERKLEY CL 3
ROYMOUNT CT 4
Strawberry Hill
STRAWBERRY HILL RD
Sixth Cross Rd
St James's RC Prim Sch
MULBERRY CT
Pl Fld
Fulwell Park
Allot Gdns
GROVE RD
QUEEN ANNES CL
STANLEY RD
Strawberry Hill
STRAWBERRY HILL CL
St Mary's Coll
NATALIE MEWS
SOUTH RD
72
Garden Ctr
Superstore
B358
WALDEGRAVE RD
Tenn Cts
14
A
B
Fulwell
15
174
C
Stanley Cty Schs
SOUTHFIELD GDNS
D
16
Sch
WELLINGTON GDNS
STRATHMORE RD
WALDEGRAVE PK
Fulwell
CH
CLONMEL RD
WILCOX RD
BIRDWOOD
Cemy
1 CUSACK CL
2 BRIDGE CL
WINCHENDON RD
Allot
B360

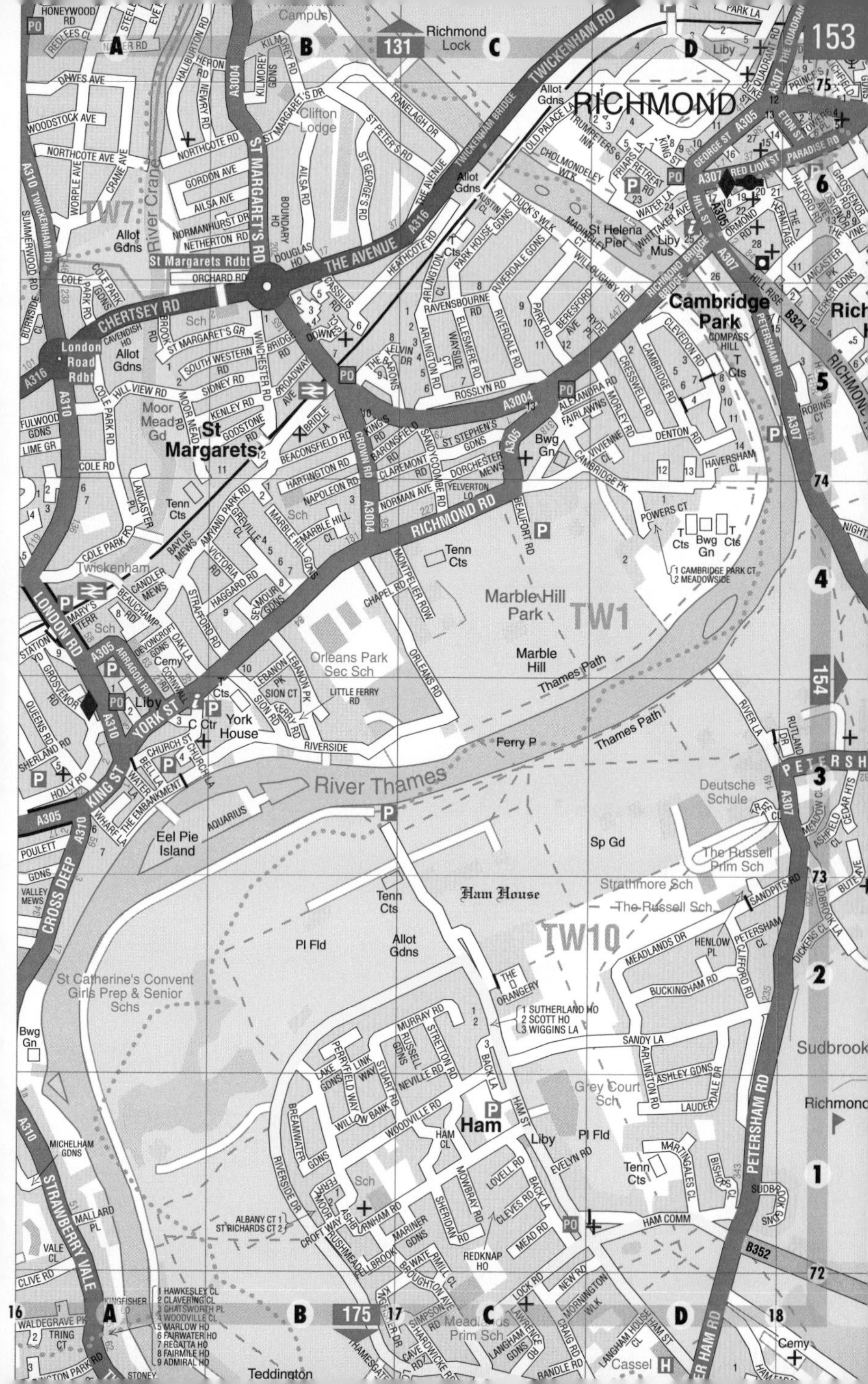

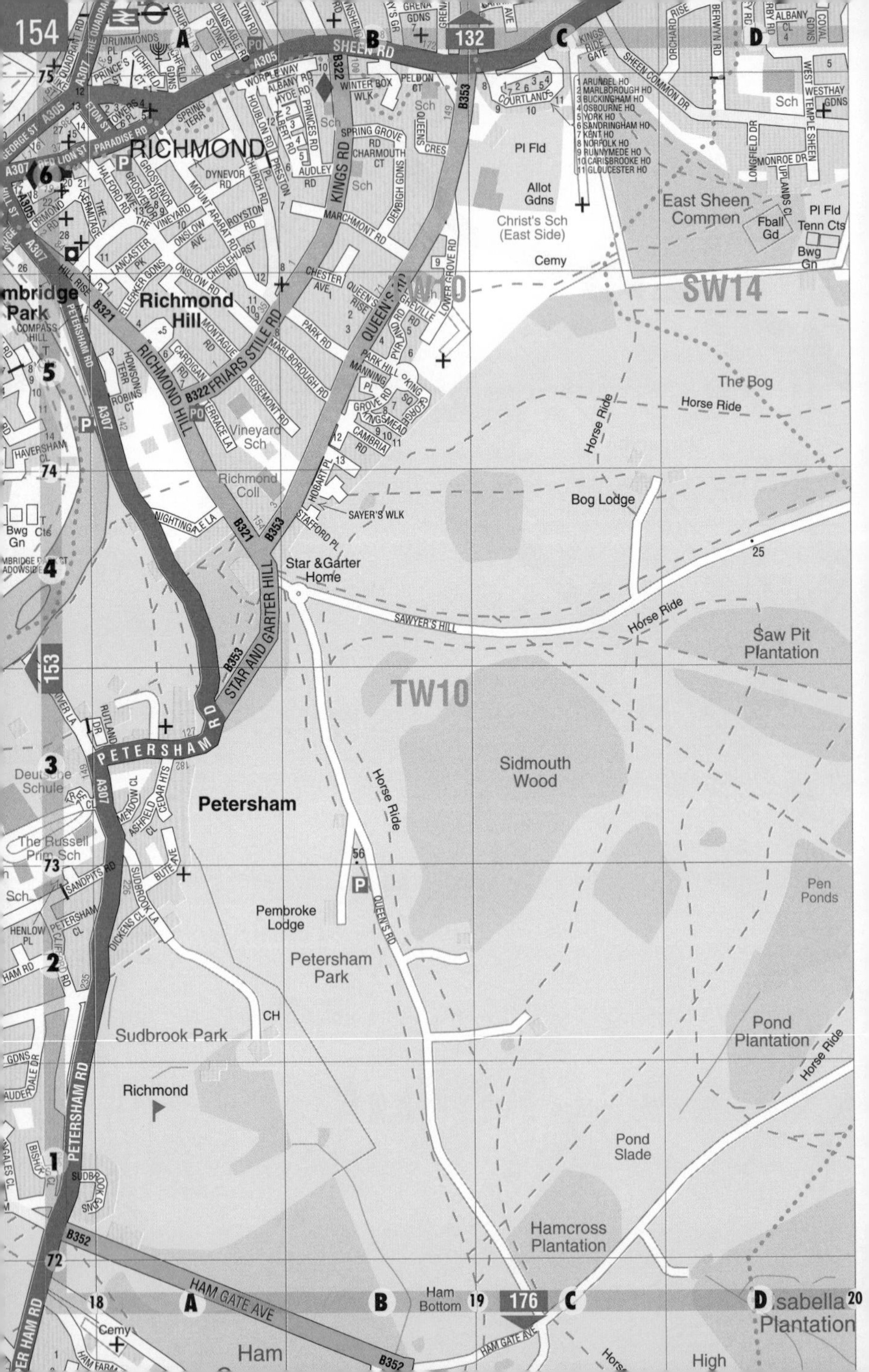

RICHMOND
Richmond Hill
Petersham
East Sheen Common
SW14
TW10
The Bog
Bog Lodge
Star &Garter Home
Saw Pit Plantation
Sidmouth Wood
Pembroke Lodge
Petersham Park
Sudbrook Park
Richmond
Pen Ponds
Pond Plantation
Pond Slade
Hamcross Plantation
Ham Bottom
Isabella Plantation
Ham
High
Horse Ride
SHEEN RD
KINGS RD
QUEEN'S RD
RICHMOND HILL
FRIARS STILE RD
STAR AND GARTER HILL
PETERSHAM RD
SAWYER'S HILL
HAM GATE AVE
Vineyard Sch
Richmond Coll
Christ's Sch (East Side)
Cemy
Allot Gdns
Pl Fld
Fball Gd
Tenn Cts
Bwg Gn
Deutsche Schule
The Russell Prim Sch
1 ARUNDEL HO
2 MARLBOROUGH HO
3 BUCKINGHAM HO
4 OSBOURNE HO
5 YORK HO
6 SANDRINGHAM HO
7 KENT HO
8 NORFOLK HO
9 RUNNYMEDE HO
10 CARISBROOKE HO
11 GLOUCESTER HO
132
153
176
A
B
C
D
1
2
3
4
5
6
18
19
20

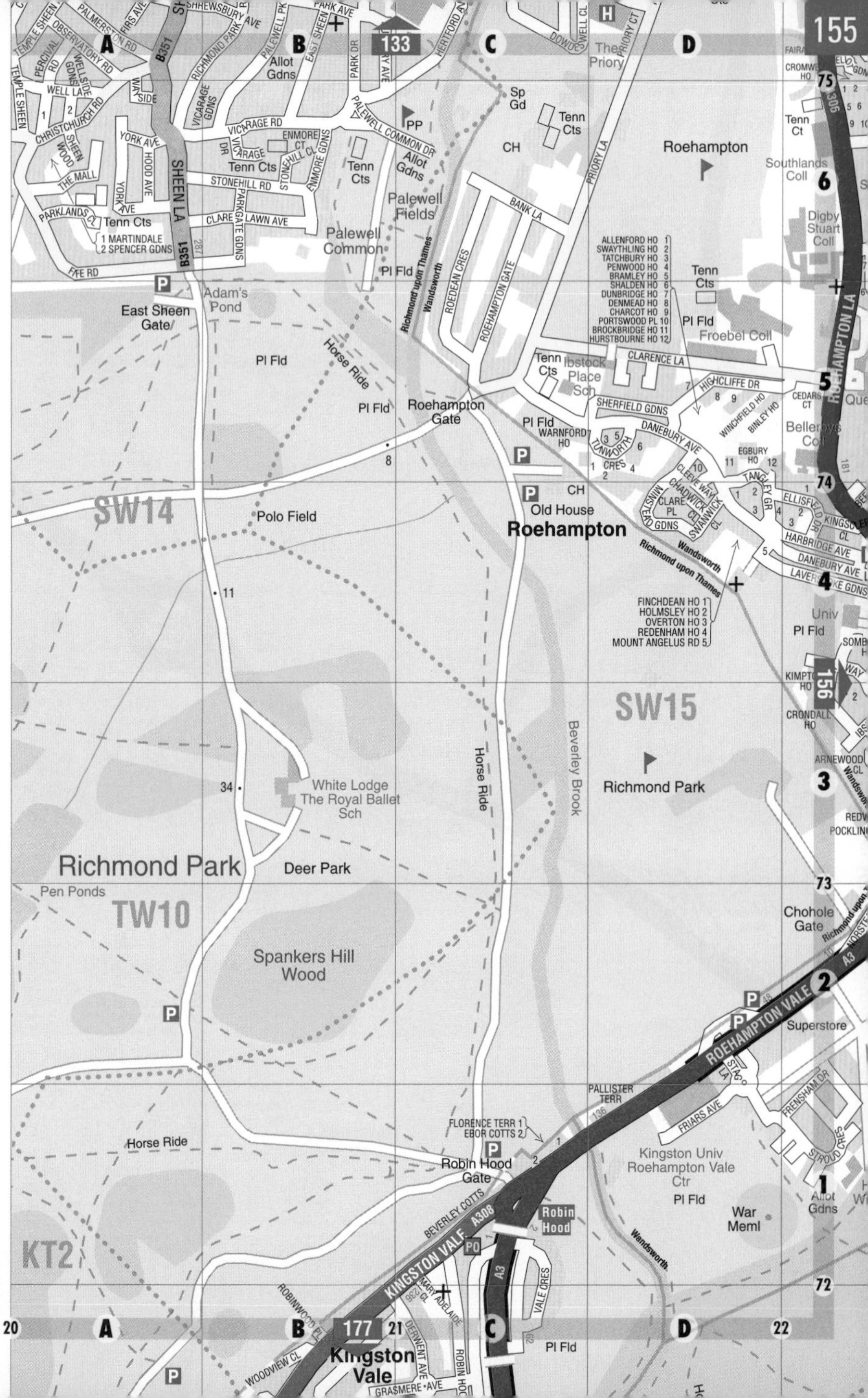
A
B
C
D
133
The Priory
Allot Gdns
Sp Gd
Tenn Cts
CH
Roehampton
Tenn Ct
Southlands Coll
6
Digby Stuart Coll
PP
Allot Gdns
Tenn Cts
Palewell Fields
Palewell Common
Pl Fld
Tenn Cts
1 MARTINDALE
2 SPENCER GDNS
SHEEN LA
B351
East Sheen Gate
Adam's Pond
Pl Fld
Horse Ride
Pl Fld
Roehampton Gate
Richmond upon Thames
Wandsworth
ALLENFORD HO 1
SWAYTHLING HO 2
TATCHBURY HO 3
PENWOOD HO 4
BRAMLEY HO 5
SHALDEN HO 6
DUNBRIDGE HO 7
DENMEAD HO 8
CHARCOT HO 9
PORTSWOOD PL 10
BROCKBRIDGE HO 11
HURSTBOURNE HO 12
Tenn Cts
Pl Fld
Froebel Coll
Tenn Cts
Ibstock Place Sch
5
ROEHAMPTON LA
Pl Fld
WARNFORD HO
Bellerbys Coll
74
CH
Old House
Roehampton
SW14
Polo Field
FINCHDEAN HO 1
HOLMSLEY HO 2
OVERTON HO 3
REDENHAM HO 4
MOUNT ANGELUS RD 5
4
Univ
Pl Fld
156
SW15
Beverley Brook
Richmond Park
3
White Lodge
The Royal Ballet Sch
Horse Ride
Richmond Park
Deer Park
Pen Ponds
TW10
73
Chohole Gate
Spankers Hill Wood
2
ROEHAMPTON VALE
Superstore
PALLISTER TERR
FLORENCE TERR 1
EBOR COTTS 2
Horse Ride
Robin Hood Gate
Kingston Univ Roehampton Vale Ctr
Pl Fld
War Meml
1
Allot Gdns
Robin Hood
KINGSTON VALE
A308
A3
KT2
72
20
A
B
177
21
C
D
22
Pl Fld
Kingston Vale

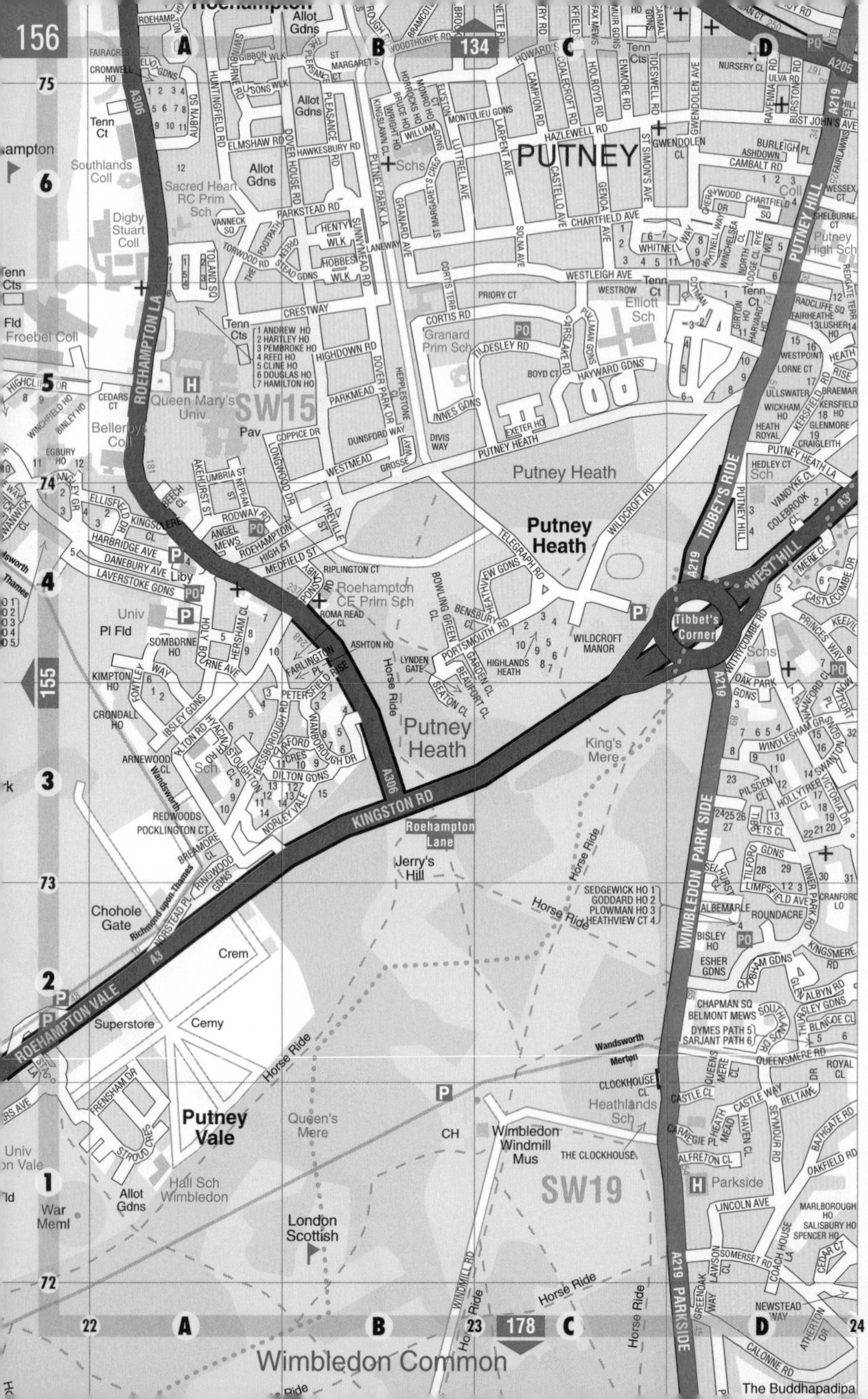

Roehampton
PUTNEY
SW15
SW19
Putney Heath
Putney Vale
Wimbledon Common
Tibbet's Corner
Jerry's Hill
King's Mere
Queen's Mere
Wimbledon Windmill Mus
London Scottish
Queen Mary's Univ
Southlands Coll
Digby Stuart Coll
Froebel Coll
Bellerbys Coll
Sacred Heart RC Prim Sch
Roehampton CE Prim Sch
Granard Prim Sch
Elliott Sch
Putney High Sch
Heathlands Sch
Hall Sch Wimbledon
Parkside
Chohole Gate
Crem
Cemy
Superstore
War Meml
Roehampton Lane
ROEHAMPTON LA
ROEHAMPTON VALE
KINGSTON RD
PUTNEY HEATH
PUTNEY HILL
TIBBET'S RIDE
WEST HILL
WIMBLEDON PARK SIDE
PARKSIDE
WINDMILL RD
TELEGRAPH RD
WILDCROFT RD
PORTSMOUTH RD
ROEHAMPTON HIGH ST
MEDFIELD ST
DANEBURY AVE
LAVERSTOKE GDNS
HARBRIDGE AVE
HOLYBOURNE AVE
PUTNEY PARK LA
DOVER HOUSE RD
DOVER PARK DR
GRANARD AVE
CHARTFIELD AVE
WESTLEIGH AVE
HAZLEWELL RD
ST SIMON'S AVE
GWENDOLEN AVE
CORTIS RD
TILDESLEY RD
HAYWARD GDNS
INNES GDNS
WESTMEAD
CRESTWAY
HIGHDOWN RD
PARKMEAD
DUNSFORD WAY
PUTNEY HEATH LA
WINDLESHAM GRO
INNER PARK RD
QUEENSMERE RD
LINCOLN AVE
SOMERSET RD
CALONNE RD
A3
A205
A219
A306
Horse Ride
Wandsworth
Merton
Richmond upon Thames
134
155
178
A B C D
22 23 24
72 73 74 75
1 2 3 4 5 6
The Buddhapadipa

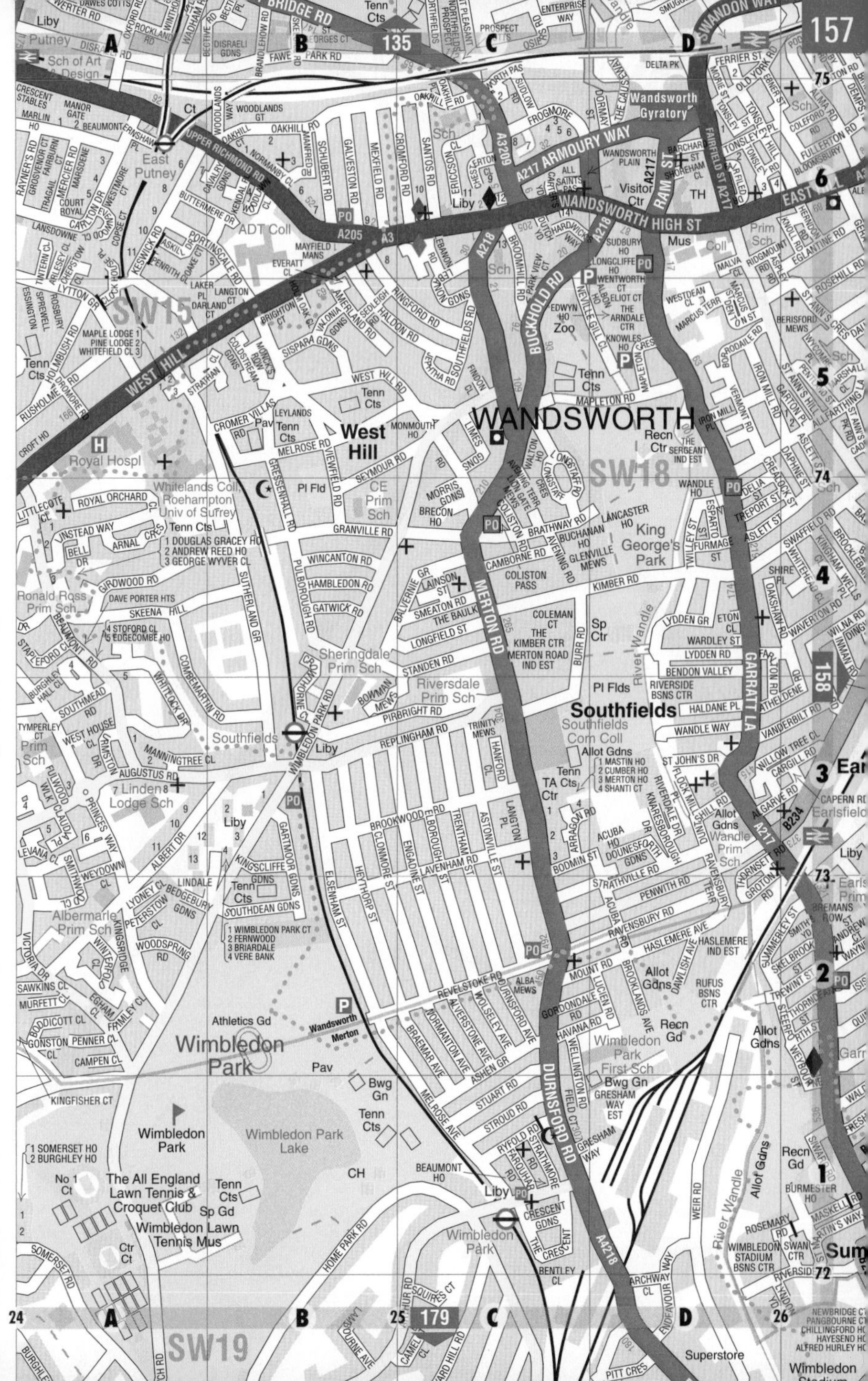
A
B
C
D
135
75
6
5
74
4
3
73
2
1
72
158
179
24
25
26
WANDSWORTH
West Hill
Southfields
Wimbledon Park
East Putney
SW15
SW18
SW19
Putney
Sch of Art & Design
Wandsworth Gyratory
A217 ARMOURY WAY
WANDSWORTH HIGH ST
WANDSWORTH PLAIN
Visitor Ctr
Mus
TH
ALL SAINTS PAS
RAM ST
FAIRFIELD ST A217
EAST HILL
UPPER RICHMOND RD
A205
A3
A3209
A218
WEST HILL
BUCKHOLD RD
MERTON RD
GARRATT LA
DURNSFORD RD
A4218
WIMBLEDON PARK RD
ADT Coll
Royal Hospl
Whitelands Coll, Roehampton Univ of Surrey
Ronald Ross Prim Sch
Sheringdale Prim Sch
Riversdale Prim Sch
Southfields Com Coll
Linden Lodge Sch
Albermarle Prim Sch
Wandle Prim Sch
Wimbledon Park First Sch
King George's Park
River Wandle
Athletics Gd
Wimbledon Park Lake
The All England Lawn Tennis & Croquet Club
Wimbledon Lawn Tennis Mus
No 1 Ct
Ctr Ct
Wandsworth
Merton
Zoo
Recn Ctr
THE SERGEANT IND EST
THE KIMBER CTR
MERTON ROAD IND EST
Sp Ctr
Pl Flds
RIVERSIDE BSNS CTR
HASLEMERE IND EST
RUFUS BSNS CTR
GRESHAM WAY EST
WIMBLEDON STADIUM BSNS CTR
Allot Gdns
Recn Gd
Tenn Cts
Liby
PO
Superstore
Earlsfield
Wimbledon Stadium

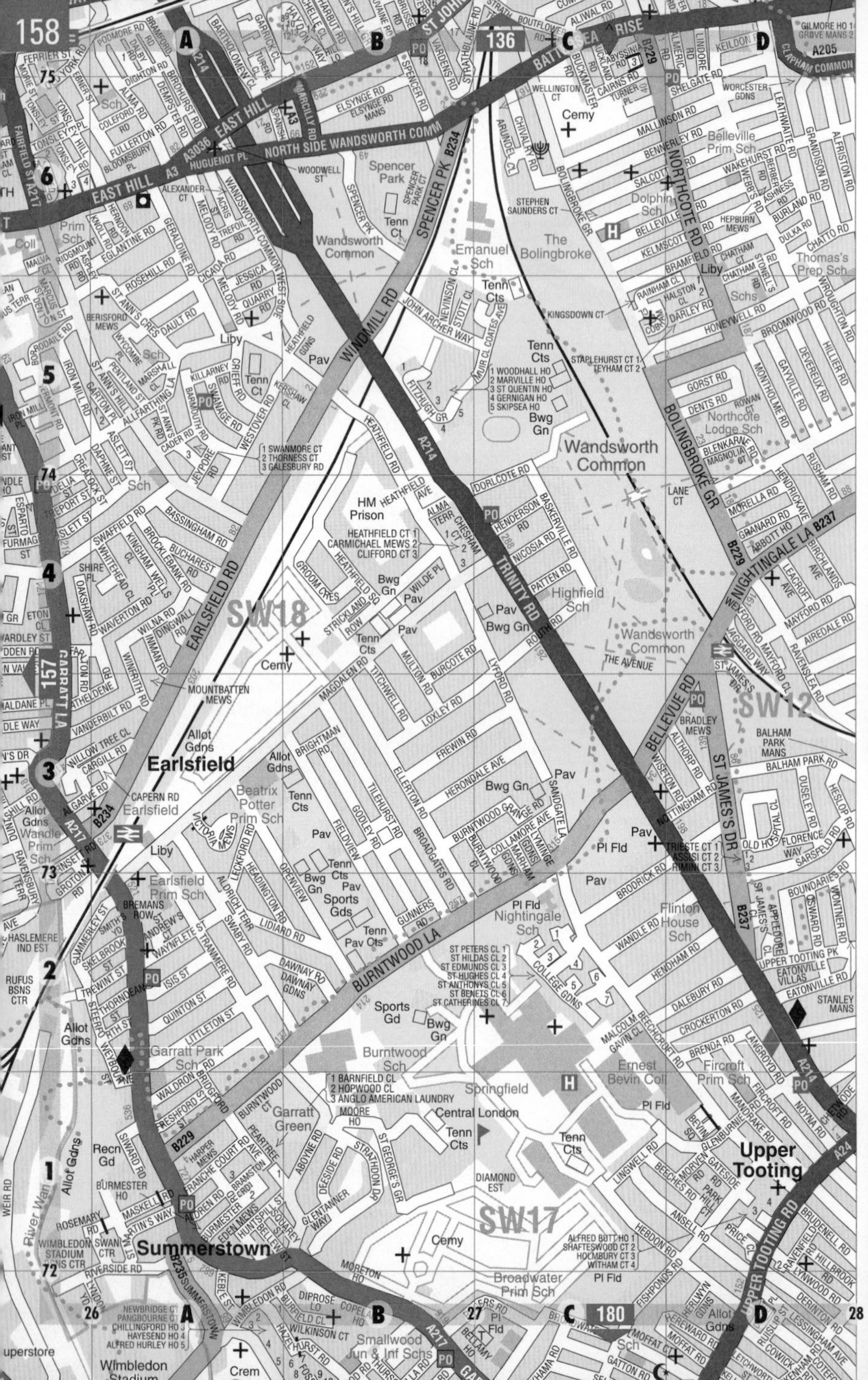
136
157
180
A
B
C
D
75
6
5
74
4
3
2
1
73
72
26
27
28
SW18
SW12
SW17
Earlsfield
Summerstown
Upper Tooting
Wandsworth Common
The Bolingbroke
Spencer Park
Emanuel Sch
HM Prison
Highfield Sch
Beatrix Potter Prim Sch
Earlsfield Prim Sch
Garratt Park Sch
Burntwood Sch
Springfield
Central London
Ernest Bevin Coll
Fircroft Prim Sch
Flinton House Sch
Nightingale Sch
Northcote Lodge Sch
Belleville Prim Sch
Dolphin Sch
Thomas's Prep Sch
Broadwater Prim Sch
Smallwood Jun & Inf Schs
Garratt Green
Wimbledon Stadium
Wandle Prim Sch
Cemy
Crem
Allot Gdns
Recn Gd
Sports Gds
Sports Gd
Tenn Cts
Bwg Gn
Pav
Pl Fld
Liby
Sch
EAST HILL
NORTH SIDE WANDSWORTH COMM
WANDSWORTH COMMON WEST SIDE
SPENCER PK
WINDMILL RD
EARLSFIELD RD
TRINITY RD
GARRATT LA
BURNTWOOD LA
NIGHTINGALE LA
BELLEVUE RD
ST JAMES'S DR
BOLINGBROKE GR
NORTHCOTE RD
BATTERSEA RISE
UPPER TOOTING RD
CLAPHAM COMMON
A3
A214
A3036
A217
A205
A24
B229
B234
B235
B237
THE AVENUE
FAIRFIELD ST
RIVER WANDLE

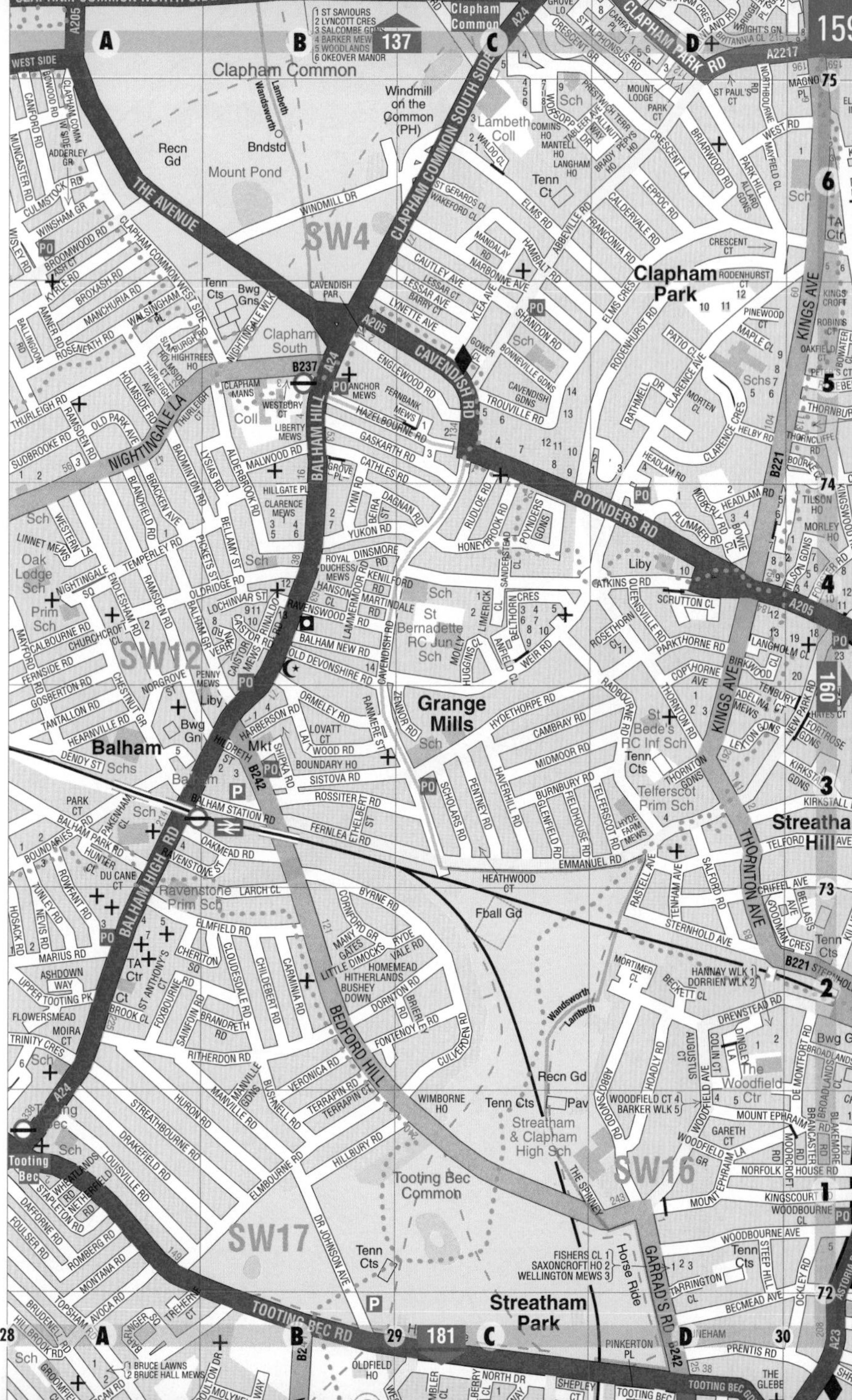
Clapham Common
Clapham Park
Balham
Grange Mills
Streatham Hill
Streatham Park
Tooting Bec Common
SW4
SW12
SW16
SW17
137
160
181
1 ST SAVIOURS
2 LYNCOTT CRES
3 SALCOMBE GDNS
4 BARKER MEWS
5 WOODLANDS
6 OKEOVER MANOR
THE AVENUE
CLAPHAM COMMON SOUTH SIDE
BALHAM HILL
BALHAM HIGH RD
CAVENDISH RD
POYNDERS RD
KINGS AVE
THORNTON AVE
BEDFORD HILL
NIGHTINGALE LA
TOOTING BEC RD
CLAPHAM PARK RD
Windmill on the Common (PH)
Mount Pond
Recn Gd
Bndstd
Lambeth Coll
Clapham South
Tooting Bec
Streatham & Clapham High Sch
St Bernadette RC Jun Sch
St Bede's RC Inf Sch
Telferscot Prim Sch
Ravenstone Prim Sch
Oak Lodge Sch
HANNAY WLK 1
DORRIEN WLK 2
FISHERS CL 1
SAXONCROFT HO 2
WELLINGTON MEWS 3
1 BRUCE LAWNS
2 BRUCE HALL MEWS
WOODFIELD CT 4
BARKER WLK 5

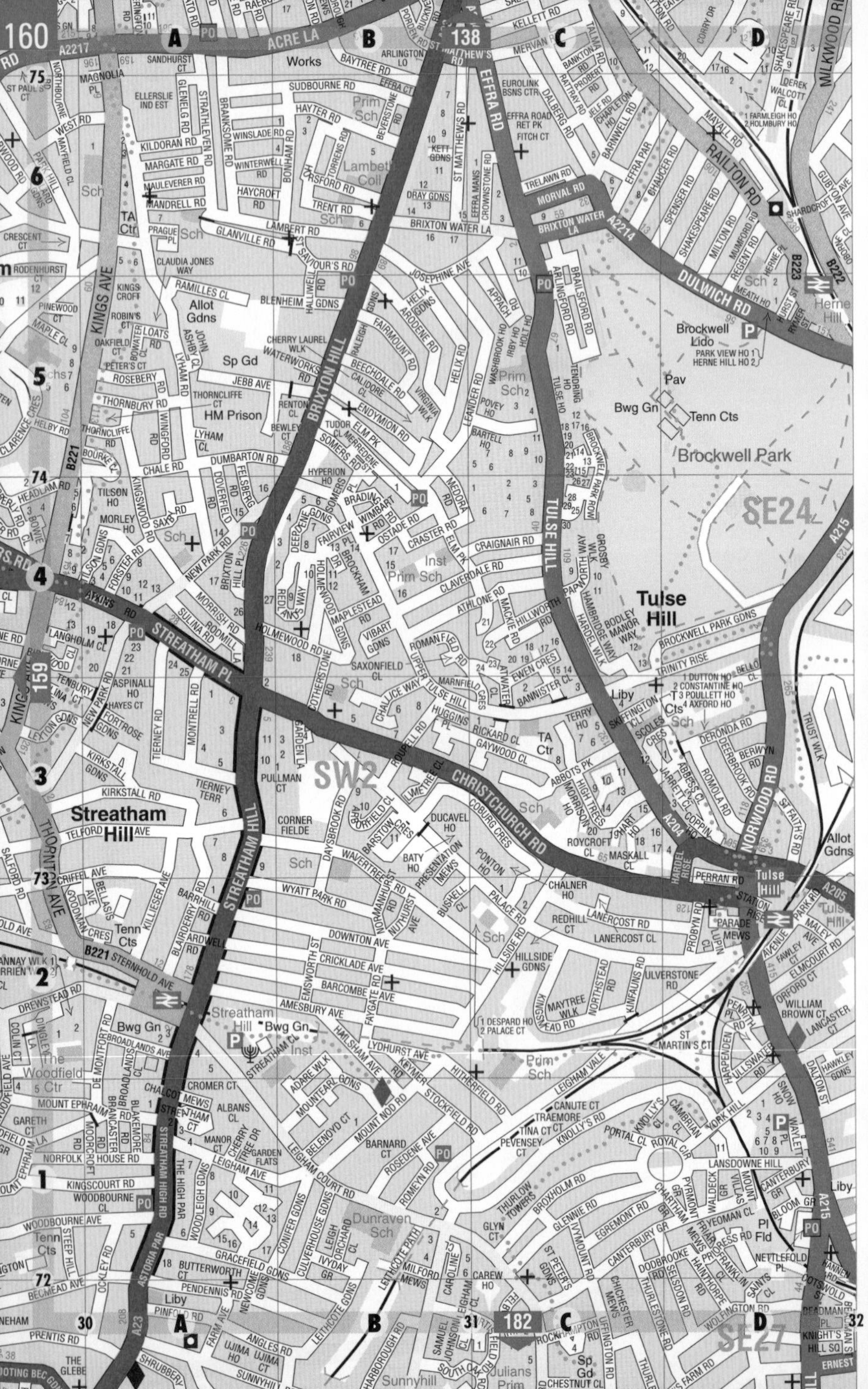
160
138
159
182
A
B
C
D
A
B
C
D
6
5
4
3
2
1
75
74
73
72
30
31
32
ACRE LA
A2217
SANDHURST CT
MAGNOLIA PL
NORTHBOURNE RD
ST PAUL'S CT
Works
BAYTREE RD
ARLINGTON LO
ST MATTHEW'S RD
KELLETT RD
MERVAN RD
TALMA RD
BANKTON RD
RATTRAY RD
PROBERT RD
CORRY DR
SHAKESPEARE RD
MILKWOOD RD
DEREK WALCOTT CL
1 FARMLEIGH HO
2 HOLMBURY HO
SUDBOURNE RD
EFFRA CT
EFFRA RD
EUROLINK BSNS CTR
EFFRA ROAD RET PK
FITCH CT
DALBERG RD
JELF RD
CHAPLETON HO
BARNWELL RD
EFFRA PAR
CHAUCER RD
SPENSER RD
SHAKESPEARE RD
MILTON RD
MUMFORD RD
REGENT RD
HERNE PL
ELLERSLIE IND EST
GLENELG RD
STRATHLEVEN RD
BRANKSOME RD
HAYTER RD
Prim Sch
BEVERSTONE RD
WINSLADE RD
WINTERWELL RD
KILDORAN RD
MARGATE RD
MAULEVERER RD
MANDRELL RD
HAYCROFT RD
BONHAM RD
TORRENS RD
Lambeth Coll
KETT GDNS
ST MATTHEWS RD
DRAY GDNS
TRENT RD
EFFRA MANS
CROWNSTONE RD
TRELAWN RD
MORVAL RD
RAILTON RD
SHARDCROFT AVE
GUBYON AVE
BRIXTON WATER LA
A2214
DULWICH RD
B223
B222
Herne Hill
MEATH HO
HURST ST
RYMER ST
Brockwell Lido
PARK VIEW HO 1
HERNE HILL HO 2
Pav
Bwg Gn
Tenn Cts
Brockwell Park
SE24
A215
Sch
TA Ctr
PRAGUE PL
GLANVILLE RD
LAMBERT RD
ST SAVIOUR'S RD
JOSEPHINE AVE
APPACH RD
ARLINGFORD RD
BRAILSFORD RD
CLAUDIA JONES WAY
RAMILLES CL
BLENHEIM GDNS
HALLIWELL RD
HELIX GDNS
ARODENE RD
FAIRMOUNT RD
CRESCENT CT
RODENHURST CT
KINGS AVE
KINGS CROFT
ROBIN'S CT
PINEWOOD CT
MAPLE CL
Allot Gdns
LOATS RD
OAKFIELD CT
BOWATER CT
JOHN ASHBY CL
LYHAM RD
PETER'S CT
ROSEBERY RD
Sp Gd
JEBB AVE
THORNBURY RD
THORNCLIFFE CT
HM Prison
CHERRY LAUREL WLK
WATERWORKS RD
RALEIGH GDNS
BEECHDALE RD
CALIDORE CL
VIRGINIA WLK
HELIX RD
LEANDER RD
WASHBROOK HO
IRBY HO
HOLT HO
TENDRING HO
TULSE HO
POVEY HO
BARTELL HO
BROCKWELL PARK ROW
RENTON CL
BEWLEY CT
ENDYMION RD
TUDOR CL
MERREDENE ST
ELM PK
SOMERS RD
HYPERION HO
BRIXTON HILL
CLARENCE CRES
HELBY RD
THORNCLIFFE RD
LYHAM CL
DUMBARTON RD
BOURKE CL
CHALE RD
B221
HEADLAM RD
TILSON HO
MORLEY HO
KINGSWOOD RD
DOVERFIELD RD
FELSBERG RD
SAXBY RD
MEDORA RD
BRADING RD
WIMBART RD
OSTADE RD
CRASTER RD
DEEPDENE GDNS
FAIRVIEW PL
CRAIGNAIR RD
TULSE HILL
CROSBY WLK
NEW PARK RD
BRIXTON HILL PL
Inst
Prim Sch
CLAVERDALE RD
PAPWORTH WAY
HAMBRIDGE WAY
TILSON GDNS
FORSTER RD
HOLMEWOOD RD
BROCKHAM DR
REDLANDS WAY
ATHLONE RD
MACKIE RD
HILLWORTH RD
Tulse Hill
HARDEL WLK
BODLEY MANOR WAY
BROCKWELL PARK GDNS
STREATHAM PL
ATKINS RD
MORRISH RD
RODMILL LA
SULINA RD
HOLMEWOOD GDNS
MAPLESTEAD RD
VIBART GDNS
ROMAN RISE
ROMANFIELD RD
EWEN CRES
LANGHOLM CL
ASPINALL HO
HAYES CT
TENBURY CT
NEW PARK RD
FORTROSE GDNS
LEXTON GDNS
SAXONFIELD CL
UPPER TULSE HILL
MARNFIELD CRES
ATWATER CL
BANNISTER CL
Liby
TRINITY RISE
1 DUTTON HO
2 CONSTANTINE HO
3 POULLETT HO
4 AXFORD HO
BELLO CL
SKIFFINGTON CL
Cts
CHALLICE WAY
HUGGINS PL
RICKARD CL
TERRY HO
SCOLES CRES
DERONDA RD
DEERBROOK RD
BERWYN RD
TRUST WLK
TIERNEY RD
MONTRELL RD
ROUPELL RD
GAYWOOD CL
ABBOTS PK
KIRKSTALL GDNS
KIRKSTALL RD
TIERNEY TERR
GARDEN LA
PULLMAN CT
SW2
LIMETREE CL
CHRISTCHURCH RD
COBURG CRES
MORRISON HO
HIGH TREES
HART HO
JARRETT CL
ABBESS CL
ROMOLA RD
NORWOOD RD
ST FAITH'S RD
Streatham Hill
THORNTON AVE
TELFORD AVE
CORNER FIELDE
ARBORFIELD CL
BARSTOW CRES
DAYSBROOK RD
DUCAVEL HO
BATY HO
PRESENTATION MEWS
PONTON HO
ROYCROFT CL
MASKALL CL
COPPIN
A204
HARDEL RISE
PERRAN RD
Allot Gdns
SALFORD RD
CRIFFEL AVE
BELLASIS AVE
KILLIESER AVE
BARRHILL RD
STREATHAM HILL
WAVERTREE RD
WYATT PARK RD
NORMANHURST RD
NUTHURST AVE
BUSHELL CL
PALACE RD
CHALNER HO
STATION RISE
PARK RD
A205
Tulse Hill
GOODMAN CRES
Tenn Cts
BLAIRDERRY RD
ARDWELL RD
DOWNTON AVE
HILLSIDE RD
REDHILL CT
LANERCOST RD
LANERCOST CL
PROBYN RD
LUPIN CL
PARADE MEWS
AVENUE PK RD
MALEY AVE
FAWLEY CT
ELMCOURT RD
B221
STERNHOLD AVE
DREWSTEAD RD
CRICKLADE AVE
BARCOMBE AVE
EMSWORTH ST
FAYGATE RD
HILLSIDE GDNS
NORTHSTEAD RD
KINFAUNS RD
ULVERSTONE RD
ORFORD CT
WILLIAM BROWN CT
LANCASTER AVE
AMESBURY AVE
MAYTREE WLK
KINGSMEAD RD
1 DESPARD HO
2 PALACE CT
ST MARTIN'S CT
PENRITH PL
HARPENDEN RD
ULLSWATER RD
HAWKLEY GDNS
DALTON ST
COLIN CT
DINGLEY LA
The Woodfield Ctr
DE MONTFORT RD
BROADLANDS AVE
BROADLANDS
Bwg Gn
STREATHAM CL
LYDHURST AVE
HALLSHAM AVE
KEYMER RD
HITHERFIELD RD
LEIGHAM VALE
Prim Sch
SNOW HO
WAYLETT PL
CROMER CT
ADARE WLK
MOUNTEARL GDNS
CHALCOT MEWS
ALBANS CL
STOCKFIELD RD
CANUTE CT
TRAEMORE CT
TINA CT
KNOLLY'S RD
PORTAL CL
KNOLLY'S CL
CAMBRIAN CL
YORK HILL
MOUNT EPHRAIM RD
BRANCASTER RD
BLAKEMORE RD
STREATHAM CT
MOUNT NOD RD
BELENOYD CT
LEIGHAM COURT RD
BARNARD CT
ROSEDENE AVE
PEVENSEY CT
ROYAL CIR
LANSDOWNE HILL
CANTERBURY GR
GARETH CT
MOORCROFT RD
MANOR CT
CHERRY TREE DR
GARDEN FLATS
NORFOLK HOUSE RD
KINGSCOURT RD
WOODBOURNE CL
STREATHAM HIGH RD
THE HIGH PAR
WOODLEIGH GDNS
LEIGHAM AVE
THURLOW TOWERS
BROXHOLM RD
GLENNIE RD
PYRMONT GR
WALDECK GR
MOUNT VILLAS
BLOOM GR
Liby
A215
WOODBOURNE AVE
Tenn Cts
STEEP HILL
OCKLEY RD
CONIFER GDNS
CULVERHOUSE GDNS
LEIGH ORCHARD CL
Dunraven Sch
ROMEYN RD
GLYN CT
EGREMONT RD
IVYMOUNT RD
CHARTHAM GR
FRIAR MEWS
YEOMAN CL
PRIORESS RD
FRANKLIN CL
Pl Fld
NETTLEFOLD PL
BECMEAD AVE
ASTORIA PAR
BUTTERWORTH CT
GRACEFIELD GDNS
IVYDAY GR
LEITHCOTE PATH
MILFORD MEWS
CAROLINE CL
CAREW HO
ST PETER'S GDNS
CHICHESTER MEWS
DODBROOKE RD
SELSDON RD
HAINTHORPE RD
SAINTS CL
COTSWOLD ST
PENDENNIS RD
NEWCOME GDNS
Liby
PINFOLD RD
LEITHCOTE GDNS
WOLFINGTON RD
DEADMAN
KNIGHT'S HILL SQ
ERNEST
SE27
PRENTIS RD
A23
FARM AVE
ANGLES RD
UJIMA HO
UJIMA CT
HARBOROUGH RD
SAMUEL JOHNSON CL
SOUTH OAK RD
Sunnyhill
Julians Prim
ROCKHAMPTON CL
UFFINGTON RD
THURLESTONE RD
Sp Gd
CHESTNUT CL
THE GLEBE
SHRUBBERY
SUNNYHILL
TOOTING BEC GDNS

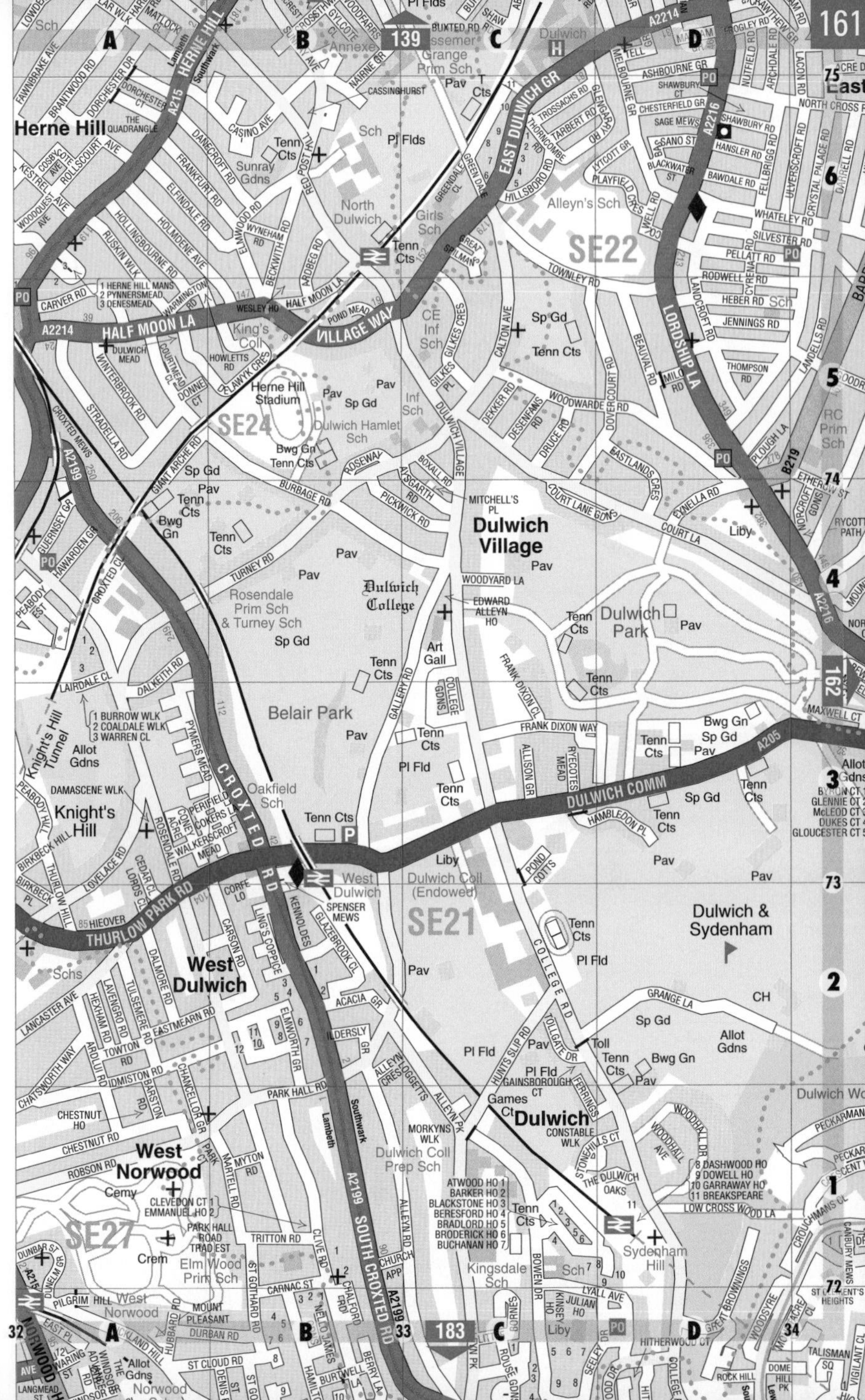

A
B
C
D
139
183
162
Herne Hill
HERNE HILL
A215
Lambeth
Southwark
FAWNBRAKE AVE
BRANTWOOD RD
DORCHESTER DR
DORCHESTER CT
THE QUADRANGLE
CASINO AVE
DANECROFT RD
FRANKFURT RD
ELFINDALE RD
HOLMDENE AVE
HOLLINGBOURNE RD
RUSKIN WLK
ROLLSCOURT AVE
KESTREL AVE
WOODQUEST AVE
CARVER RD
1 HERNE HILL MANS
2 PYNNERSMEAD
3 DENESMEAD
WARMINGTON
A2214
HALF MOON LA
WESLEY HO
DULWICH MEAD
WINTERBROOK RD
COURTMEAD CL
HOWLETTS RD
ELAWYK CRES
DONNE CT
STRADELLA RD
CROXTED MEWS
A2199
GUERNSEY GR
HAWARDEN GR
CROXTED CL
PEABODY EST
LAIRDALE CL
1 BURROW WLK
2 COALDALE WLK
3 WARREN CL
Knight's Hill Tunnel
Allot Gdns
DAMASCENE WLK
Knight's Hill
PEABODY HILL
BIRKBECK HILL
THURLOW HILL
LOVELACE RD
BIRKBECK PL
CEDAR CL
LORDS CL
HIEOVER
THURLOW PARK RD
Schs
LANCASTER AVE
HEXHAM RD
LAVENGRO RD
TULSEMERE RD
DALMORE RD
EASTMEARN RD
TOWTON RD
ARDLUI RD
CHATSWORTH WAY
IDMISTON RD
BARSTON RD
CHANCELLOR GR
CHESTNUT HO
CHESTNUT RD
ROBSON RD
West Norwood
Cemy
Crem
SE27
CLEVEDON CT 1
EMMANUEL HO 2
PARK HALL ROAD TRAD EST
Elm Wood Prim Sch
DUNBAR ST
DUNELM GR
PILGRIM HILL
West Norwood
MOUNT PLEASANT
DURBAN RD
EAST PL
WARING ST
NORWOOD H
WINDSOR
ST CLOUD RD
Allot Gdns
Norwood
LANGMEAD ST
HUBBARD RD
ST GOTHARD RD
DENIS
ST
SG
32
33
34
Sunray Gdns
Tenn Cts
Sch
Pl Flds
North Dulwich
ELMWOOD RD
WYNEHAM RD
BECKWITH RD
ARDBEG RD
RED POST HILL
NAIRNE GR
CASSINGHURST
GYLCOTE CL
WOODFARRS
BUXTED RD
Bessemer Grange Prim Sch
Annexe
Pav
Dulwich
Girls Sch
HALF MOON LA
POND MEAD
VILLAGE WAY
King's Coll
CE Inf Sch
Herne Hill Stadium
SE24
Dulwich Hamlet Sch
Sp Gd
Bwg Gn
ROSEWAY
GIANT ARCHE RD
BURBAGE RD
TURNEY RD
Rosendale Prim Sch & Turney Sch
Dulwich College
Belair Park
DALKEITH RD
PYMERS MEAD
CROXTED RD
PERIFIELD
CONEY ACRE
COKERS LA
WALKERSCROFT MEAD
ROSENDALE RD
Oakfield Sch
P
West Dulwich
SPENSER MEWS
KENNOLDES
GLAZEBROOK CL
LING'S COPPICE
CARSON RD
CORFE LO
West Dulwich
ACACIA GR
ELMWORTH GR
ILDERSLY GR
PARK HALL RD
MYTON RD
MARTELL RD
TRITTON RD
CLIVE RD
CHALFORD RD
CARNAC ST
NELLO JAMES
HAMILTON
BURTWELL LA
BERRY LA
SOUTH CROXTED RD
CHURCH APP
ALLEYN RD
Dulwich Coll Prep Sch
ALLEYN CRES
LOGGETTS
ALLEYN PK
MORKYNS WLK
ATWOOD HO 1
BARKER HO 2
BLACKSTONE HO 3
BERESFORD HO 4
BRADLORD HO 5
BRODERICK HO 6
BUCHANAN HO 7
Kingsdale Sch
BOWEN DR
ROUSE GDNS
BORNES
Liby
KINSEY HO
JULIAN HO
SEELEY DR
LYALL AVE
Gallery Rd
ART Gall
COLLEGE GDNS
EDWARD ALLEYN HO
WOODYARD LA
Dulwich Village
MITCHELL'S PL
PICKWICK RD
AYSGARTH RD
BOXALL RD
DULWICH VILLAGE
GILKES PL
GILKES CRES
Inf Sch
CALTON AVE
DEKKER RD
DESENFANS RD
DRUCE RD
WOODWARDE RD
DOVERCOURT RD
EASTLANDS CRES
COURT LANE GDNS
COURT LA
EYNELLA RD
Liby
Dulwich Park
FRANK DIXON CL
FRANK DIXON WAY
ALLISON GR
RYECOTES MEAD
DULWICH COMM
A205
HAMBLEDON PL
POND COTTS
Dulwich Coll (Endowed)
SE21
COLLEGE RD
Pl Fld
Games Ct
HUNTS SLIP RD
TOLLGATE DR
Toll
GAINSBOROUGH CT
FERRINGS
Dulwich
CONSTABLE WLK
STONEHILLS CT
THE DULWICH OAKS
Sydenham Hill
WOODHALL AVE
WOODHALL DR
8 DASHWOOD HO
9 DOWELL HO
10 GARRAWAY HO
11 BREAKSPEARE
LOW CROSS WOOD LA
HITHERWOOD CT
GREAT BROWNINGS
WOODSYRE
COLLEGE
Dulwich & Sydenham
GRANGE LA
CH
Allot Gdns
Dulwich Wood
PECKARMANS
CRESCENT WOOD
CROUCHMANS CL
CANBURY MEWS
ST CLEMENT'S HEIGHTS
TALISMAN SQ
DOME HILL PK
ROCK HILL
VIGILANT CL
GREENDALE CL
GREEN DALE
EAST DULWICH GR
TROSSACHS RD
TARBERT RD
GLENGARRY RD
THORNCOMBE
HILLSBORO RD
LYCOTT GR
PLAYFIELD CRES
Alleyn's Sch
SE22
TOWNLEY RD
BEAUVAL RD
MILO RD
LORDSHIP LA
A2216
MELBOURNE GR
ASHBOURNE GR
SHAWBURY CT
CHESTERFIELD GR
SAGE MEWS
SHAWBURY RD
SANO ST
HANSLER RD
BLACKWATER ST
BAWDALE RD
CO WELL RD
LANDCROFT RD
CYRENA RD
PELLATT RD
SILVESTER RD
WHATELEY RD
RODWELL RD
HEBER RD
JENNINGS RD
THOMPSON RD
LANDELLS RD
PLOUGH LA
B219
ETHEROW ST
NORCROFT GDNS
RYCOTT PATH
CROGLEY RD
CRAWTHEW GR
NUTFIELD RD
ARCHDALE RD
LACON RD
NORTH CROSS RD
ULVERSCROFT RD
CRYSTAL PALACE RD
FELLBRIGG RD
DARRELL RD
East
RC Prim Sch
BARRY
MOUNT
MAXWELL CT
Allot Gdns
BYRON CT 1
GLENNIE CT 2
McLEOD CT 3
DUKES CT 4
GLOUCESTER CT 5
75
74
73
72
6
5
4
3
2
1

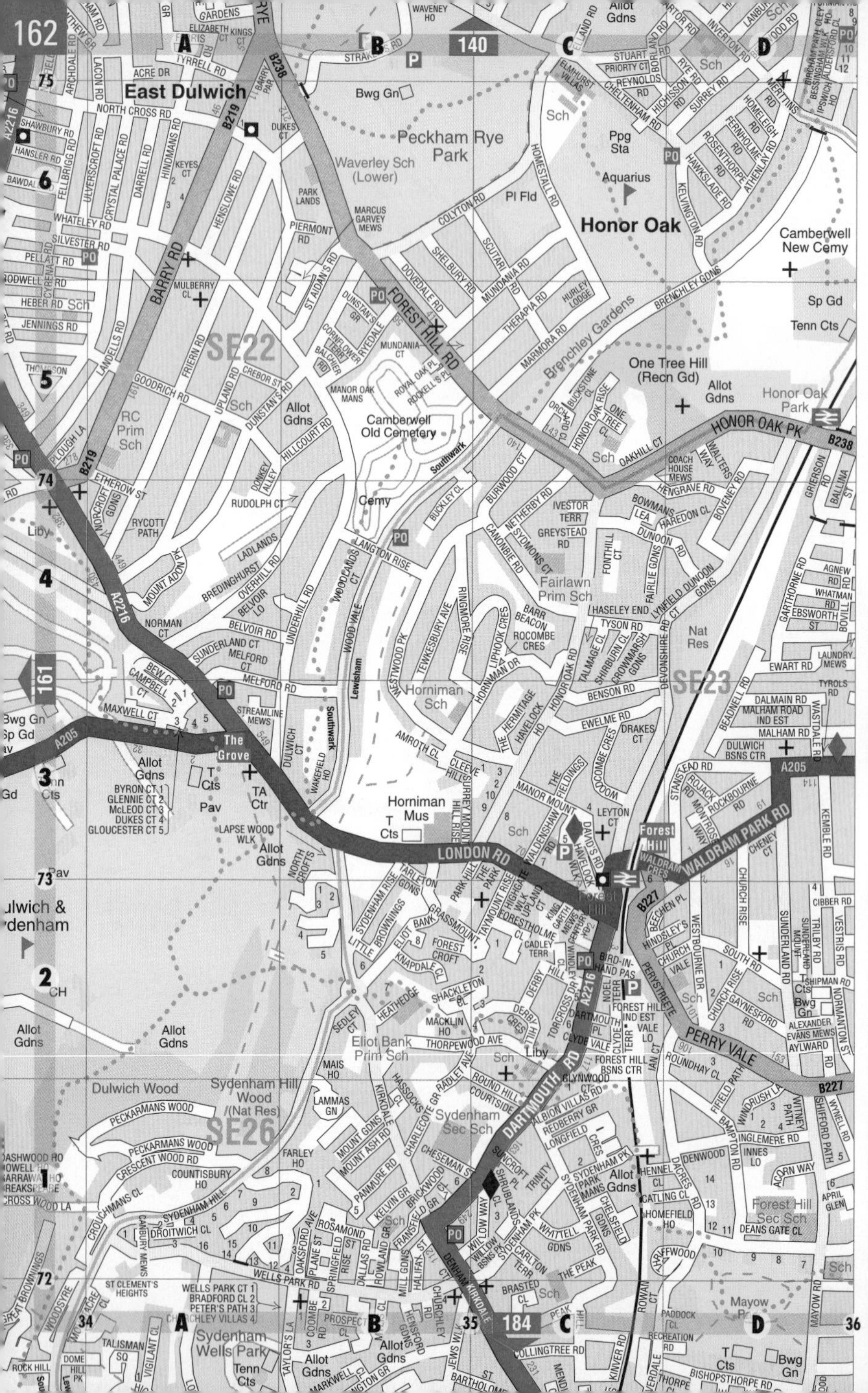
East Dulwich
Peckham Rye Park
Honor Oak
Camberwell New Cemy
SE22
One Tree Hill (Recn Gd)
Camberwell Old Cemetery
Brenchley Gardens
Honor Oak Park
Fairlawn Prim Sch
Horniman Sch
Horniman Mus
SE23
Forest Hill
LONDON RD
WALDRAM PARK RD
PERRY VALE
DARTMOUTH RD
Eliot Bank Prim Sch
Dulwich Wood
Sydenham Hill Wood (Nat Res)
SE26
Sydenham Sec Sch
Forest Hill Sec Sch
Sydenham Wells Park
Dulwich & Sydenham
FOREST HILL RD
BARRY RD
HONOR OAK PK
WOOD VALE
SYDENHAM HILL
The Grove
Waverley Sch (Lower)
Mayow Pk
140
161
184
34
35
36
A
B
C
D
1
2
3
4
5
6
72
73
74
75

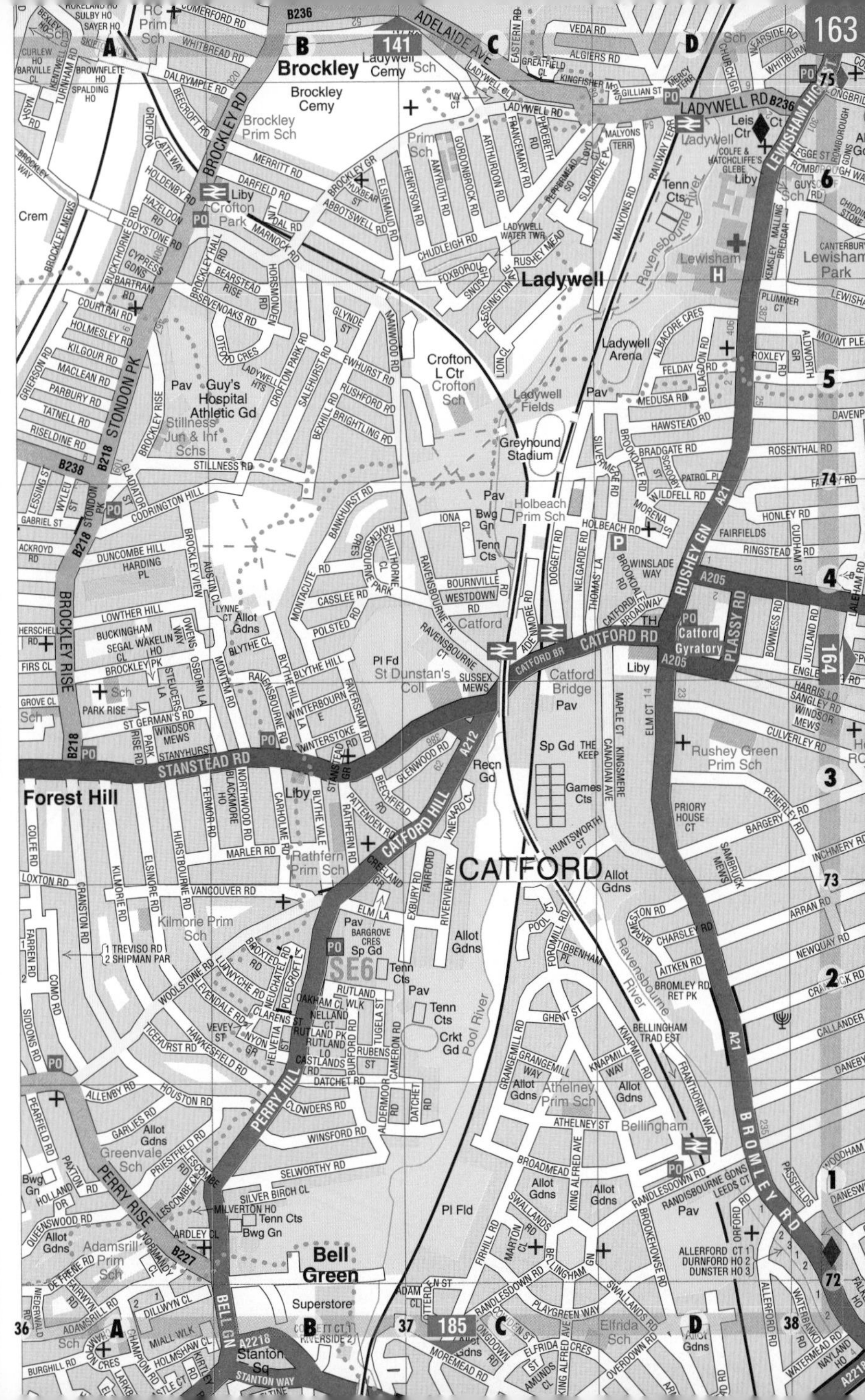
A
B
C
D
141
Brockley
Ladywell Cemy
Brockley Cemy
Brockley Prim Sch
ADELAIDE AVE
B236
VEDA RD
ALGIERS RD
LADYWELL RD
Ladywell
Crem
BROCKLEY RD
Liby
Crofton Park
PO
MERRITT RD
DARFIELD RD
ABBOTSWELL RD
MARNOCK RD
HENRYSON RD
AMYRUTH RD
GORDONBROCK RD
ARTHURDON RD
FRANCEMARY RD
PHOEBETH RD
SLAGROVE PL
MALYONS RD
RAILWAY TERR
Tenn Cts
Ravensbourne River
Lewisham
LEWISHAM HIGH ST
Lewisham Park
CHUDLEIGH RD
Ladywell
LADYWELL WATER TWR
6
HOLDENBY RD
HAZELDON RD
EDDYSTONE RD
BUCKTHORNE RD
CYPRESS GDNS
BARTRAM RD
COURTRAI RD
HOLMESLEY RD
KILGOUR RD
MACLEAN RD
PARBURY RD
TATNELL RD
RISELDINE RD
STONDON PK
BEARSTEAD RISE
SEVENOAKS RD
OTFORD CRES
HORSMONDEN RD
CROFTON PARK RD
SALEHURST RD
GLYNDE ST
EWHURST RD
RUSHFORD RD
BRIGHTLING RD
BEXHILL RD
MANWOOD RD
Crofton L Ctr
Crofton Sch
Ladywell Arena
Ladywell Fields
ALBACORE CRES
FELDAY RD
MEDUSA RD
HAWSTEAD RD
BRADGATE RD
ROSENTHAL RD
ROXLEY RD
5
Pav
Guy's Hospital Athletic Gd
Stillness Jun & Inf Schs
STILLNESS RD
Greyhound Stadium
B238
B218
CODRINGTON HILL
GABRIEL ST
ACKROYD RD
DUNCOMBE HILL
HARDING PL
BROCKLEY RISE
BROCKLEY VIEW
AUSTIN CL
BANKHURST RD
MONTACUTE RD
CASSLEE RD
POLSTED RD
IONA CL
Holbeach Prim Sch
HOLBEACH RD
BOURNVILLE RD
WESTDOWN RD
RAVENSBOURNE PARK
RAVENSBOURNE PK
DOGGETT RD
NELGARDE RD
THOMAS LA
BROOKDALE RD
WINSLADE WAY
CATFORD BROADWAY
RUSHEY GN
A21
FAIRFIELDS
RINGSTEAD RD
HONLEY RD
CUDHAM ST
4
A205
PLASSY RD
Catford Gyratory
BOWNESS RD
JUTLAND RD
164
LOWTHER HILL
BUCKINGHAM
SEGAL WAKELIN HO
BROCKLEY PK
FIRS CL
HERSCHELL RD
GROVE CL
PARK RISE
ST GERMAN'S RD
WINDSOR MEWS
STANYHURST
Allot Gdns
BLYTHE CL
BLYTHE HILL
Pl Fd
St Dunstan's Coll
SUSSEX MEWS
Catford
CATFORD BR
CATFORD RD
Catford Bridge
Liby
ADENMORE RD
ELM CT
MAPLE CT
KINGSMERE
CANADIAN AVE
Sp Gd
THE KEEP
Games Cts
STANSTEAD RD
Forest Hill
BLACKMORE HO
FERMOR RD
NORTHWOOD RD
HURSTBOURNE RD
CARHOLME RD
BLYTHE VALE
STANSTEAD GR
GLENWOOD RD
A212
CATFORD HILL
Recn Gd
Rushey Green Prim Sch
CULVERLEY RD
3
PRIORY HOUSE CT
BARGERY RD
PENERLEY RD
INCHMERY RD
COLFE RD
LOXTON RD
CRANSTON RD
KILMORIE RD
ELSINORE RD
MARLER RD
VANCOUVER RD
Rathfern Prim Sch
RATHFERN RD
CATFORD
Allot Gdns
73
Kilmorie Prim Sch
1 TREVISO RD
2 SHIPMAN PAR
FARREN RD
COMO RD
SIDDONS RD
WOOLSTONE RD
ELM LA
Pav
BARGROVE CRES
Sp Gd
SE6
Tenn Cts
Pav
Crkt Gd
Pool River
FORDMILL RD
TIBBENHAM PL
Ravensbourne River
ARRAN RD
NEWQUAY RD
CHARSLEY RD
AITKEN RD
BROMLEY RD RET PK
2
CALLANDER RD
GHENT ST
BELLINGHAM TRAD EST
HOUSTON RD
ALLENBY RD
PEARFIELD RD
GARLIES RD
Greenvale Sch
PERRY HILL
PERRY RISE
CLOWDERS RD
WINSFORD RD
SELWORTHY RD
SILVER BIRCH CL
MILVERTON HO
Tenn Cts
Bwg Gn
Pl Fld
Athelney Prim Sch
ATHELNEY ST
Bellingham
BROADMEAD
KING ALFRED AVE
Allot Gdns
RANDLESDOWN RD
RANDISBOURNE GDNS
Pav
BROMLEY RD
1
Bwg Gn
HOLLAND DR
QUEENSWOOD RD
Allot Gdns
Adamsrill Prim Sch
ARDLEY CL
B227
Bell Green
Superstore
BELLINGHAM GN
SWALLANDS RD
PLAYGREEN WAY
ALLERFORD CT 1
DURNFORD HO 2
DUNSTER HO 3
72
36
37
185
38
ADAMSRILL RD
DILLWYN CL
MIALL WLK
HOLMSHAW CL
BELL GN
A2218
Stanton Sq
STANTON WAY
Elfrida Sch
ELFRIDA CRES
OVERDOWN RD
MOREMEAD RD
WATERMEAD RD
NAYLAND HO

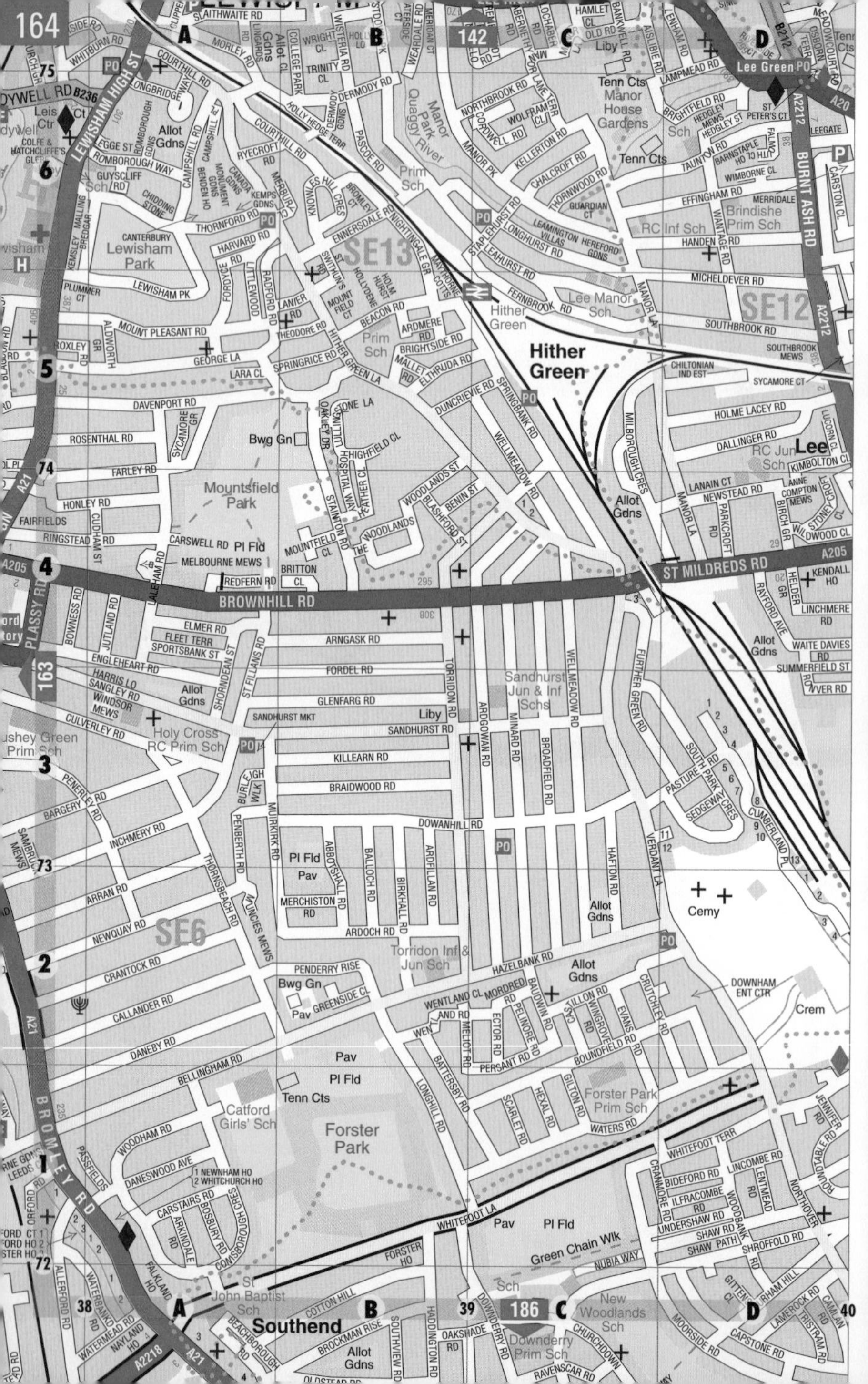
A
B
C
D
142
SLAITHWAITE RD
MORLEY RD
WHITBURN RD
COURTHILL RD
LONGBRIDGE WAY
LADYWELL RD B236
Leis Ctr
COLFE & HATCHCLIFFE'S GLEBE
LEWISHAM HIGH ST
LEGGE ST
ROMBOROUGH WAY
GUYSCLIFF RD
CAMPSHILL RD
Allot Gdns
WRIGHT CL
TRINITY CL
COLLEGE PARK
WISTERIA RD
DERMODY RD
HOLLY HEDGE TERR
RYECROFT RD
MERBURY CL
PASCOE RD
Manor Park
Quaggy River
Prim Sch
NORTHBROOK RD
CORDWELL RD
WOLFRAM CL
KELLERTON RD
CHALCROFT RD
THORNWOOD RD
MANOR PK
Tenn Cts
Manor House Gardens
Liby
Lee Green
A20
A2212
B212
ST PETER'S CT
LEEGATE
TAUNTON RD
BARNSTAPLE HO
WIMBORNE CL
EFFINGHAM RD
MERRIDALE
Brindishe Prim Sch
RC Inf Sch
HANDEN RD
MICHELDEVER RD
SOUTHBROOK RD
SE12
BURNT ASH RD
CARSTON CL
KEMPS GDNS
THORNFORD RD
CANTERBURY
Lewisham Park
HARVARD RD
ENNERSDALE RD
NIGHTINGALE GR
SE13
STAPLEHURST RD
LEAHURST RD
LONGHURST RD
LEAMINGTON VILLAS
HEREFORD GDNS
GUARDIAN CT
LEWISHAM PK
PLUMMER CT
FORDYCE RD
LITTLEWOOD
RADFORD RD
LANIER RD
THEODORE RD
HOLLYDENE
MOUNT FIELD CT
BEACON RD
ARDMERE RD
BRIGHTSIDE RD
Hither Green
FERNBROOK RD
Lee Manor Sch
MANOR LA
MOUNT PLEASANT RD
ALDWORTH GR
ROXLEY RD
GEORGE LA
LARA CL
SPRINGRICE RD
HITHER GREEN LA
MALLET RD
ELTHRUDA RD
CHILTONIAN IND EST
SOUTHBROOK MEWS
SYCAMORE CT
DAVENPORT RD
SYCAMORE GR
ROSENTHAL RD
FARLEY RD
HONLEY RD
FAIRFIELDS
RINGSTEAD RD
CUDHAM ST
Bwg Gn
Mountsfield Park
OAKLEY DR
HIGHFIELD CL
HOSPITAL WAY
DUNCRIEVIE RD
SPRINGBANK RD
WELLMEADOW RD
WOODLANDS ST
BENIN ST
BLASHFORD ST
THE WOODLANDS
MOUNTFIELD CL
STAINTON RD
MILBOROUGH CRES
HOLME LACEY RD
DALLINGER RD
Lee
RC Jun Sch
KIMBOLTON CL
LANAIN CT
NEWSTEAD RD
ANNE COMPTON MEWS
PARKCROFT RD
BIRCH GR
WILDWOOD CL
CARSWELL RD
Pl Fld
MELBOURNE MEWS
LALEHAM RD
REDFERN RD
BRITTON CL
A205
ST MILDREDS RD
KENDALL HO
BROWNHILL RD
PLASSY RD
BOWNESS RD
JUTLAND RD
ELMER RD
FLEET TERR
SPORTSBANK ST
ENGLEHEART RD
ARNGASK RD
FORDEL RD
GLENFARG RD
SANDHURST MKT
SANDHURST RD
TORRIDON RD
Sandhurst Jun & Inf Schs
FURTHER GREEN RD
RAYFORD AVE
HELDER GR
LINCHMERE RD
WAITE DAVIES RD
SUMMERFIELD ST
163
HARRIS LO
SANGLEY RD
WINDSOR MEWS
CULVERLEY RD
SHORNDEAN ST
ST FILLANS RD
Holy Cross RC Prim Sch
Rushey Green Prim Sch
KILLEARN RD
BRAIDWOOD RD
ARDGOWAN RD
MINARD RD
BROADFIELD RD
SOUTH PARK CRES
PASTURE RD
SEDGEWAY
CUMBERLAND PL
PENERLEY RD
BARGERY RD
INCHMERY RD
BURLEIGH WLK
PENBERTH RD
MUIRKIRK RD
DOWANHILL RD
HAFTON RD
VERDANT LA
SAMBRUCK MEWS
ARRAN RD
ABBOTSHALL RD
BALLOCH RD
BIRKHALL RD
ARDFILLAN RD
Pav
MERCHISTON RD
Cemy
NEWQUAY RD
SE6
THORNSBEACH RD
MUNCIES MEWS
ARDOCH RD
Torridon Inf & Jun Sch
CRANTOCK RD
PENDERRY RISE
HAZELBANK RD
DOWNHAM ENT CTR
GREENSIDE CL
WENTLAND CL
MORDRED RD
BAUDWIN RD
CASTILLON RD
WINGROVE RD
EVANS RD
CRUTCHLEY RD
Crem
CALLANDER RD
DANEBY RD
BELLINGHAM RD
MELFORT RD
ECTOR RD
PELINORE RD
PERSANT RD
BOUNDFIELD RD
BATTERSBY RD
LONGHILL RD
Catford Girls' Sch
Tenn Cts
Forster Park
SCARLET RD
HEXAL RD
GILTON RD
Forster Park Prim Sch
WATERS RD
JENNIFER RD
ROUNDTABLE RD
WOODHAM RD
DANESWOOD AVE
1 NEWNHAM HO
2 WHITCHURCH HO
PASSFIELDS
BROMLEY RD
A21
CARSTAIRS RD
BOSBURY RD
ARKINDALE RD
CONSBOROUGH CRES
WHITEFOOT TERR
CRANMORE RD
BIDEFORD RD
ILFRACOMBE RD
LINCOMBE RD
LENTMEAD RD
WOODBANK RD
NORTHOVER
UNDERSHAW RD
SHAW RD
SHAW PATH
SHROFFOLD RD
WHITEFOOT LA
Green Chain Wlk
NUBIA WAY
FORSTER HO
FALKLAND HO
St John Baptist Sch
ALLERFORD RD
WATERBANK RD
WATERMEAD RD
NAYLAND HO
COTTON HILL
Southend
BROCKMAN RISE
SOUTHVIEW RD
HADDINGTON RD
OAKSHADE RD
DOWNDERRY RD
186
Downderry Prim Sch
New Woodlands Sch
CHURCHDOWN
RAVENSCAR RD
GITTENS CL
MOORSIDE RD
CAPSTONE RD
LAMEROCK RD
TRISTRAM RD
CAMLAN RD
BEACHBOROUGH
A2218
38
39
40
72
73
74
75
1
2
3
4
5
6

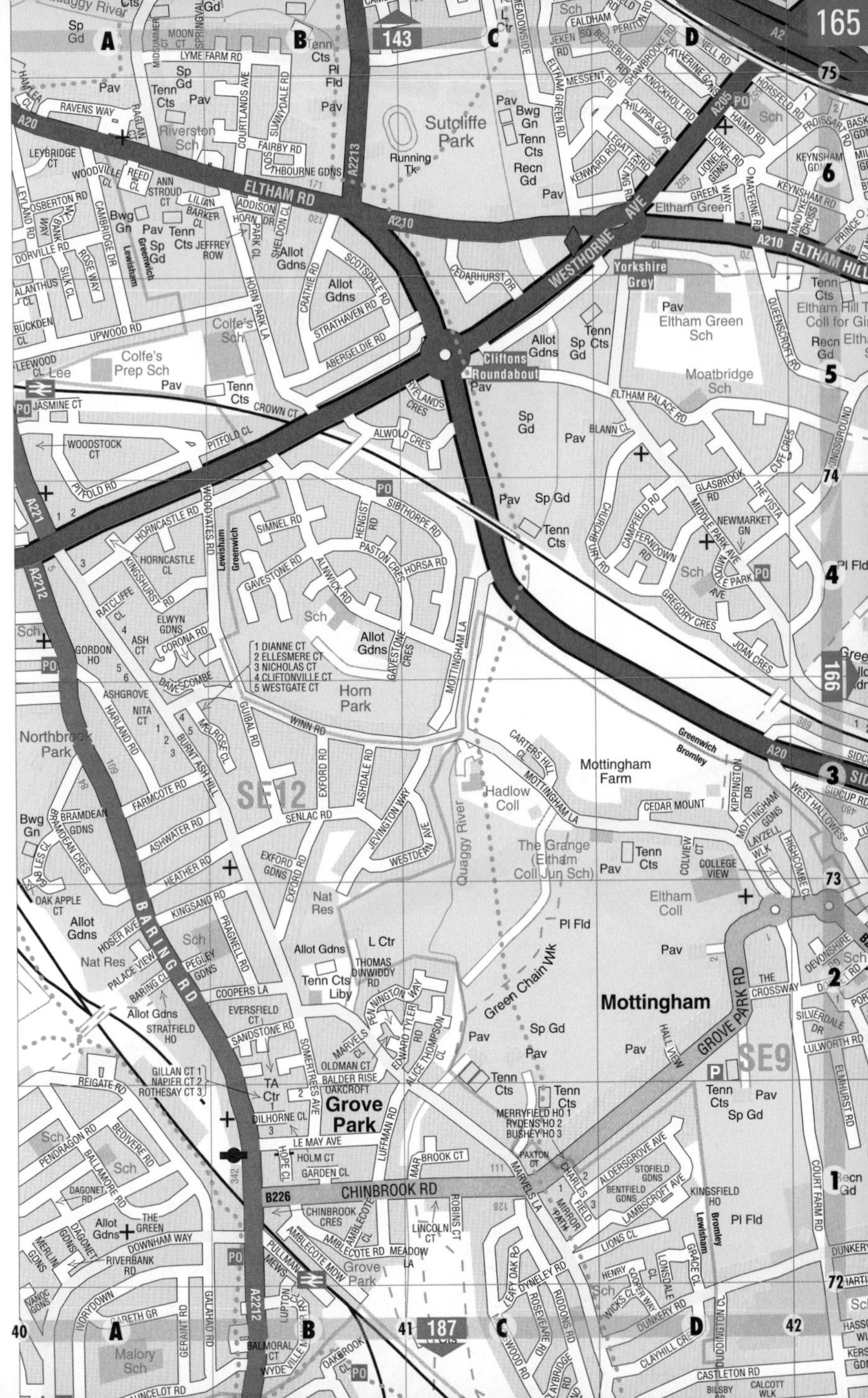
143
A2
75
Sutcliffe Park
Running Tk
A2213
ELTHAM RD
A210
A20
A205
WESTHORNE AVE
ELTHAM HILL
Eltham Green
Yorkshire Grey
Eltham Green Sch
Eltham Hill Tech Coll for Girls
Moatbridge Sch
Cliftons Roundabout
Colfe's Sch
Colfe's Prep Sch
Riverston Sch
Lee
LYME FARM RD
RAVENS WAY
COURTLANDS AVE
SUNNYDALE RD
FAIRBY RD
SOUTHBOURNE GDNS
LEYBRIDGE CT
WOODVILLE CL
REED CL
ANN STROUD CT
LILIAN BARKER CL
ADDISON DR
HORN PARK CL
HORN PARK LA
JEFFREY ROW
SHELDON CL
OSBERTON RD
CAMBRIDGE DR
DORVILLE RD
ROSE WAY
SILK CL
ALANTHUS CL
BUCKDEN CL
UPWOOD RD
LEEWOOD CL
JASMINE CT
CROWN CT
PITFOLD CL
PITFOLD RD
WOODSTOCK CT
CRATHIE RD
SCOTSDALE RD
STRATHAVEN RD
ABERGELDIE RD
RYELANDS CRES
ALWOLD CRES
CEDARHURST DR
ELTHAM GREEN RD
MESSENT RD
SHAWBROOKE RD
KNOCKHOLT RD
PHILIPPA GDNS
KENWARD RD
LEGATT RD
KEELING RD
HAIMO RD
LIONEL RD
LIONEL GDNS
GREEN WAY
OMAYERNE RD
HORSFELD RD
FROISSART RD
KEYNSHAM GDNS
KEYNSHAM RD
VANDYKE CROSS
PRINCE JOHN RD
QUEENSCROFT RD
ELTHAM PALACE RD
BLANN CL
KINGSGROUND
CUFF CRES
THE VISTA
GLASBROOK RD
CHURCHBURY RD
CAMPFIELD RD
FERNDOWN
MIDDLE PARK AVE
NEWMARKET GN
GREGORY CRES
JOAN CRES
HORNCASTLE RD
HORNCASTLE CL
KINGSHURST RD
WOODYATES RD
SIMNEL RD
SIBTHORPE RD
HENGIST RD
PASTON CRES
HORSA RD
GAVESTONE RD
ALNWICK RD
GAVESTONE CRES
MOTTINGHAM LA
RATCLIFFE CL
ELWYN GDNS
CORONA RD
ASH CT
GORDON HO
DANSCOMBE
ASHGROVE
NITA CT
HARLAND RD
MELROSE CL
BURNT ASH HILL
GUIBAL RD
1 DIANNE CT
2 ELLESMERE CT
3 NICHOLAS CT
4 CLIFTONVILLE CT
5 WESTGATE CT
Horn Park
WINN RD
EXFORD RD
ASHDALE RD
JEVINGTON WAY
WESTDEAN AVE
SENLAC RD
EXFORD GDNS
SE12
Northbrook Park
FARMCOTE RD
BRAMDEAN GDNS
BRAMDEAN CRES
ASHWATER RD
HEATHER RD
OAK APPLE CT
KINGSAND RD
PRAGNELL RD
HOSER AVE
BARING RD
PALACE VIEW
BARING CL
PEGLEY GDNS
COOPERS LA
EVERSFIELD CT
SANDSTONE RD
STRATFIELD HO
GILLAN CT 1
NAPIER CT 2
ROTHESAY CT 3
REIGATE RD
Quaggy River
Nat Res
THOMAS DINWIDDY RD
PENNINGTON WAY
EDWARD TYLER RD
ALICE THOMPSON CL
MARVELS CL
OLDMAN CT
BALDER RISE
OAKCROFT
SOMERTREES AVE
DILHORNE CL
Grove Park
LE MAY AVE
HOPE CL
HOLM CT
GARDEN CL
LUFFMAN RD
MARBROOK CT
CHINBROOK RD
B226
CHINBROOK CRES
AMBLECOTE CL
AMBLECOTE RD
AMBLECOTE MDW
MEADOW LA
LINCOLN CT
ROBINS CT
PULLMAN MEWS
LUPTON CL
Hadlow Coll
Mottingham Farm
CARTERS HILL CL
MOTTINGHAM LA
CEDAR MOUNT
KIPPINGTON DR
MOTTINGHAM GDNS
LAYZELL WLK
FISHCOMBE CL
The Grange (Eltham Coll Jun Sch)
COLVIEW CT
COLLEGE VIEW
Eltham Coll
Green Chain Wlk
Mottingham
THE CROSSWAY
GROVE PARK RD
HALL VIEW
SE9
DEVONSHIRE RD
SILVERDALE DR
LULWORTH RD
ELMHURST RD
COURT FARM RD
MERRYFIELD HO 1
RYDENS HO 2
BUSHEY HO 3
PAXTON CT
CHARLES FIELD
MIRROR PATH
MARVELS LA
ALDERSGROVE AVE
STOFIELD GDNS
BENTFIELD GDNS
LAMBSCROFT AVE
KINGSFIELD HO
LIONS CL
HENRY COOPER WAY
WICKS CL
LONSDALE
GRACE CL
DUNKERY RD
DUDDINGTON CL
CLAYHILL CRES
CASTLETON RD
BILSBY GR
CALCOTT WLK
LEAFY OAK RD
DYNELEY RD
ROSEVEARE RD
RIDDONS RD
PENDRAGON RD
BEDIVERE RD
BALLAMORE RD
DAGONET RD
DAGONET GDNS
THE GREEN
DOWNHAM WAY
MERLIN GDNS
RIVERBANK RD
VANOC GDNS
IVORYDOWN
GARETH GR
GERAINT RD
GALAHAD RD
Malory Sch
LANCELOT RD
BALMORAL CT
WYDEVILLE MANOR RD
OAKBROOK CL
A2212
A221
Lewisham
Greenwich
Bromley
166
187
SIDCUP RD
WEST HALLOWES
A
B
C
D
1
2
3
4
5
6
40
41
42
72
73
74

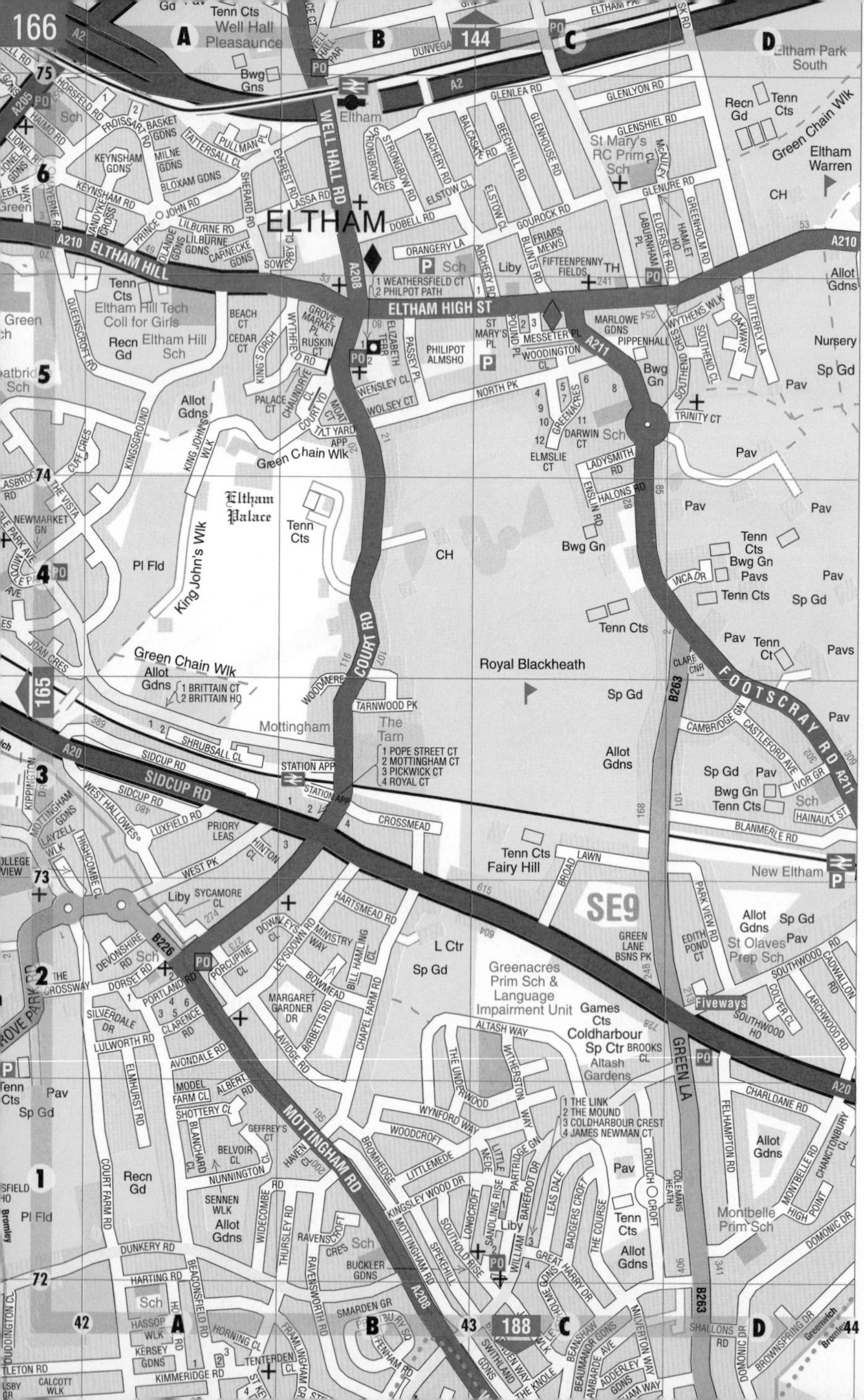
ELTHAM
Well Hall Pleasaunce
Eltham Park South
Eltham Warren
ELTHAM HILL
ELTHAM HIGH ST
WELL HALL RD
Eltham Hill Tech Coll for Girls
Eltham Hill Sch
Eltham Palace
King John's Wlk
Green Chain Wlk
COURT RD
Royal Blackheath
FOOTSCRAY RD
SIDCUP RD
Mottingham
The Tarn
Fairy Hill
New Eltham
SE9
Greenacres Prim Sch & Language Impairment Unit
Coldharbour Sp Ctr
Altash Gardens
GREEN LA
MOTTINGHAM RD
St Olaves Prep Sch
Montbelle Prim Sch
St Mary's RC Prim Sch
Fiveways
144
165
188
A2
A20
A210
A208
A211
B263
B226

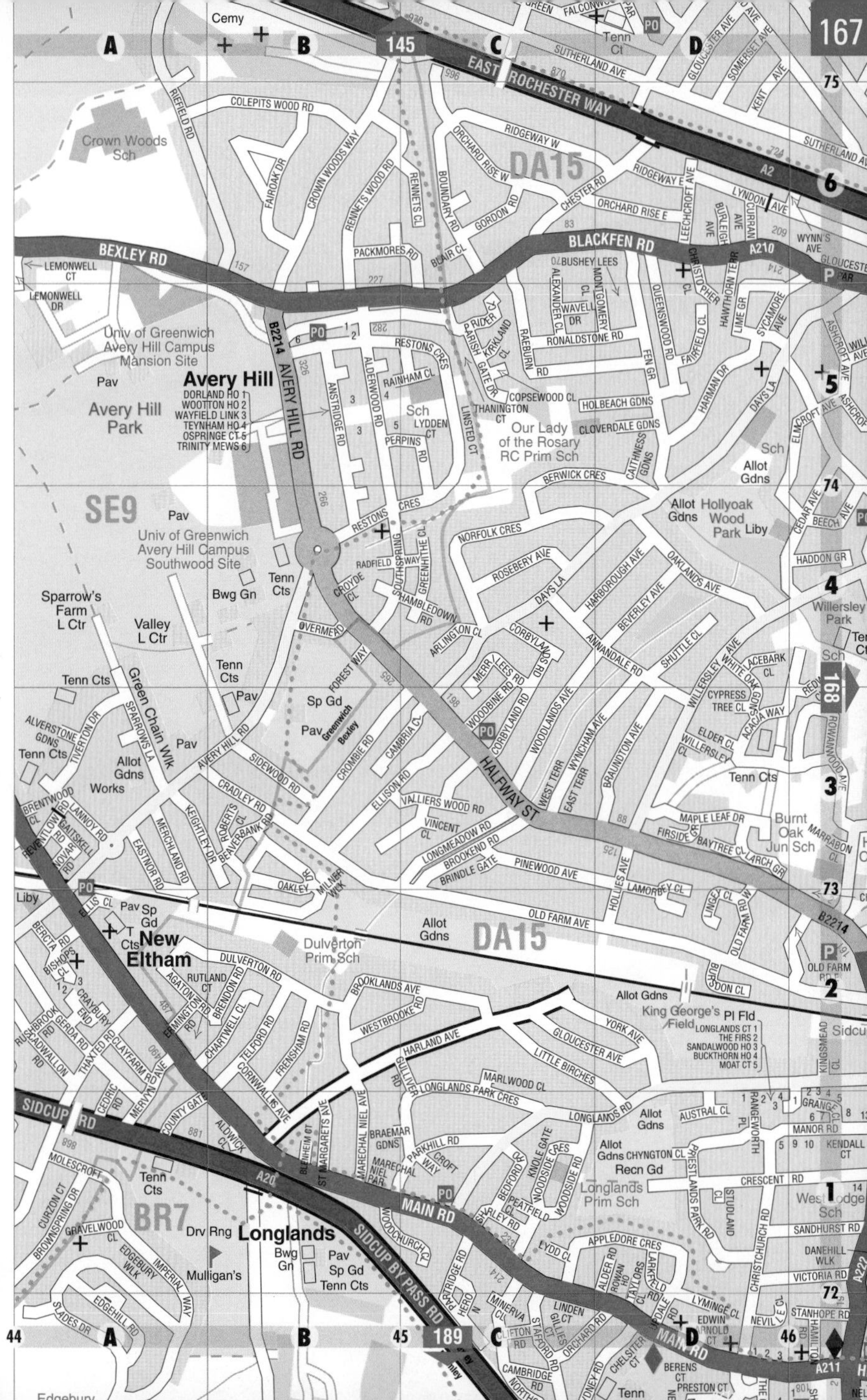

Cemy
145
EAST ROCHESTER WAY
SUTHERLAND AVE
GLOUCESTER AVE
SOMERSET AVE
KENT AVE
Tenn Ct
COLEPITS WOOD RD
RIEFIELD RD
Crown Woods Sch
FAIROAK DR
CROWN WOODS WAY
RENNETS WOOD RD
RENNETS CL
BOUNDARY RD
ORCHARD RISE W
RIDGEWAY W
DA15
GORDON RD
CHESTER RD
RIDGEWAY E
LEECHCROFT AVE
ORCHARD RISE E
BURLEIGH AVE
CURRAN AVE
LYNDON AVE
A2
WYNN'S AVE
BEXLEY RD
LEMONWELL CT
LEMONWELL DR
PACKMORES RD
BLAIR CL
BLACKFEN RD
A210
GLOUCESTER PAR
BUSHEY LEES
ALEXANDER CL
MONTGOMERY CL
WAVELL DR
QUEENSWOOD RD
CHRISTOPHER CL
HAWTHORN TERR
LIME GR
SYCAMORE AVE
ASHCROFT AVE
B2214
AVERY HILL RD
RESTONS CRES
RIDER
PARISH GATE DR
KIRKLAND CL
RAEBURN RD
RONALDSTONE RD
FEN GR
FAIRFIELD CL
HARMAN DR
DAYS LA
Univ of Greenwich Avery Hill Campus Mansion Site
Pav
Avery Hill
DORLAND HO 1
WOOTTON HO 2
WAYFIELD LINK 3
TEYNHAM HO 4
OSPRINGE CT 5
TRINITY MEWS 6
Avery Hill Park
ANSTRIDGE RD
ALDERWOOD RD
RAINHAM CL
Sch
LYDDEN CT
PERPINS RD
LINSTED CT
THANINGTON CT
COPSEWOOD CL
HOLBEACH GDNS
CLOVERDALE GDNS
CAITHNESS GDNS
Our Lady of the Rosary RC Prim Sch
ELMCROFT AVE
Allot Gdns
SE9
Univ of Greenwich Avery Hill Campus Southwood Site
BERWICK CRES
Hollyoak Wood Park
Liby
CEDAR AVE
BEECH AVE
HADDON GR
NORFOLK CRES
ROSEBERY AVE
HARBOROUGH AVE
OAKLANDS AVE
Willersley Park
Sparrow's Farm L Ctr
Valley L Ctr
Bwg Gn
Tenn Cts
CROYDE CL
RADFIELD WAY
SOUTHSPRING
GREENHITHE CL
HAMBLEDOWN RD
ARLINGTON CL
CORBYLANDS RD
BEVERLEY AVE
ANNANDALE RD
SHUTTLE CL
WILLERSLEY AVE
WHITE OAK GDNS
LACEBARK CL
OVERMEAD
FOREST WAY
Sp Gd
Green Chain Wlk
SPARROWS LA
ALVERSTONE GDNS
TIVERTON DR
168
CYPRESS TREE CL
ACACIA WAY
ROWANWOOD AVE
MERRILEES RD
WOODBINE RD
CORBYLAND RD
WOODLANDS AVE
WYNCHAM AVE
BRAUNDTON AVE
ELDER CL
WILLERSLEY CL
Greenwich Bexley
CROMBIE RD
CAMBRIA CL
ELLISON RD
AVERY HILL RD
SIDEWOOD RD
HALFWAY ST
WEST TERR
EAST TERR
Works
BRENTWOOD
LANNOY RD
REVENTLOW RD
GAITSKELL RD
NOVAR RD
CRADLEY RD
ROBERTS CL
BEAVERBANK RD
KEIGHTLEY DR
MERCHLAND RD
EASTNOR RD
VALLIERS WOOD RD
VINCENT CL
LONGMEADOW RD
BROOKEND RD
BRINDLE GATE
PINEWOOD AVE
MAPLE LEAF DR
FIRSIDE GR
BAYTREE CL
LARCH GR
Burnt Oak Jun Sch
MARRABON CL
Liby
ELLIS CL
OAKLEY DR
MILNER WLK
LAMORBEY CL
HOLLIES AVE
LINGEY CL
OLD FARM RD W
OLD FARM AVE
B2214
OLD FARM RD E
New Eltham
BERCTA RD
BISHOPS CL
CRAYBURY END
Dulverton Prim Sch
DULVERTON RD
RUTLAND CT
AGATON RD
BRENDON RD
ERMINGTON RD
CHARTWELL CL
BROOKLANDS AVE
WESTBROOKE RD
BURSDON CL
King George's Field
Pl Fld
LONGLANDS CT 1
THE FIRS 2
SANDALWOOD HO 3
BUCKTHORN HO 4
MOAT CT 5
YORK AVE
GLOUCESTER AVE
LITTLE BIRCHES
KINGSMEAD
Sidcup
RUSHBROOK RD
GERDA RD
CADWALLON RD
THAXTED RD
CLAYFARM RD
MERVYN AVE
TELFORD RD
FRENSHAM RD
CORNWALLIS AVE
HARLAND AVE
GULLIVER RD
MARLWOOD CL
LONGLANDS PARK CRES
LONGLANDS RD
AUSTRAL CL
RANGEWORTH PL
GRANGE CL
MANOR RD
KENDALL CT
SIDCUP RD
CEDRIC RD
COUNTY GATE
ALDWICK CL
BLENHEIM CT
ST MARGARETS AVE
MARECHAL NIEL AVE
BRAEMAR GDNS
MARECHAL NIEL PAR
PARKHILL RD
CROFT WAY
KNOLE GATE
WOODSIDE CRES
WOODSIDE RD
CHYNGTON CL
Recn Gd
PRIESTLANDS PARK RD
STUDLAND CL
CRESCENT RD
West Lodge Sch
MOLESCROFT
Tenn Cts
A20
MAIN RD
Longlands Prim Sch
BEDFORD RD
PEATFIELD CL
CHRISTCHURCH RD
SANDHURST RD
BR7
CURZON CT
BROWNSPRING DR
GRAVELWOOD CL
EDGEBURY WLK
IMPERIAL WAY
Drv Rng
Longlands
Mulligan's
Bwg Gn
Pav
Sp Gd
Tenn Cts
SIDCUP BY PASS RD
WOODCHURCH CL
PARTRIDGE RD
MINERVA CL
LYDD CL
APPLEDORE CRES
ALDER RD
ROWAN HO
TAYLORS CL
LARKFIELD
LYMINGE CL
DANEHILL WLK
VICTORIA RD
NEVILLE CL
STANHOPE RD
HAMILTON RD
A222
EDGEHILL RD
SLADES DR
LINDEN CT
GILLIES CT
ORCHARD RD
CLIFTON RD
STAFFORD RD
CAMBRIDGE RD
NORTHCOTE RD
CHELSITER CT
UPDALE RD
EDWIN ARNOLD CT
BERENS CT
PRESTON CT
A211
Tenn
Edgebury
44
45
46
189
75
74
73
72

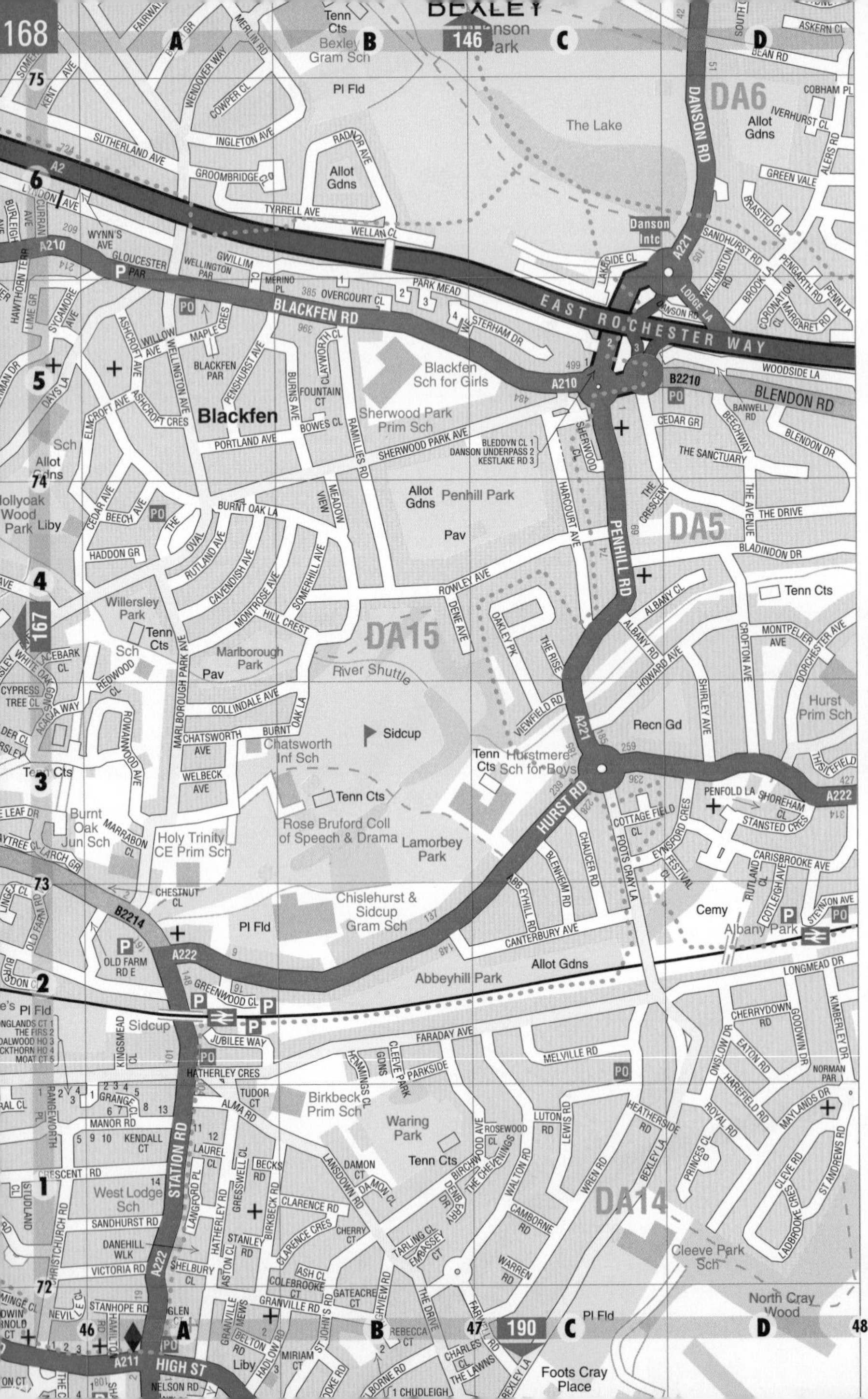
BEXLEY
146
Danson Park
Bexley Gram Sch
Pl Fld
The Lake
DA6
DANSON RD
Allot Gdns
Blackfen
Blackfen Sch for Girls
Sherwood Park Prim Sch
EAST ROCHESTER WAY
BLACKFEN RD
BLENDON RD
Danson Intc
Penhill Park
DA5
DA15
PENHILL RD
River Shuttle
Sidcup
Marlborough Park
Willersley Park
Chatsworth Inf Sch
Hurstmere Sch for Boys
Rose Bruford Coll of Speech & Drama
Lamorbey Park
Holy Trinity CE Prim Sch
Burnt Oak Jun Sch
Chislehurst & Sidcup Gram Sch
HURST RD
Recn Gd
Hurst Prim Sch
Cemy
Albany Park
Abbeyhill Park
Birkbeck Prim Sch
Waring Park
West Lodge Sch
STATION RD
DA14
Cleeve Park Sch
North Cray Wood
HIGH ST
Foots Cray Place
167
190
48

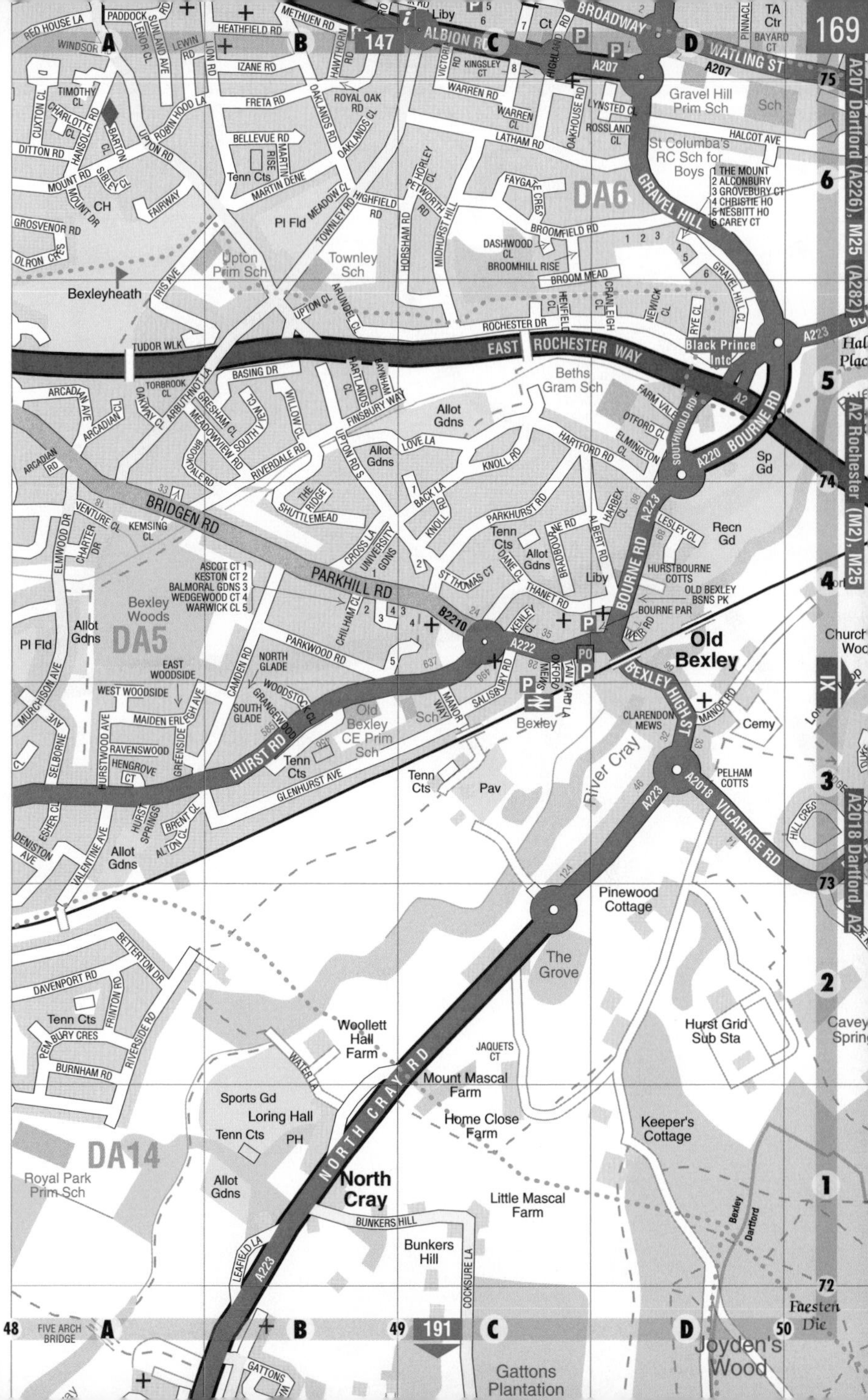

147
ALBION RD
BROADWAY
WATLING ST
A207
A207 Dartford (A226), M25 (A282)
RED HOUSE LA
PADDOCK
LENOR CL
SUNLAND AVE
HEATHFIELD RD
METHUEN RD
WINDSOR
LEWIN RD
LION RD
IZANE RD
HAWTHORN
Liby
KINGSLEY CT
WARREN RD
HIGHLAND RD
TIMOTHY CL
CHARLOTTE CL
CUXTON CL
HANSOL RD
BARTON CL
ROBIN HOOD LA
FRETA RD
ROYAL OAK RD
OAKLANDS RD
OAKLANDS CL
WARREN CL
OAKHOUSE RD
LYNSTED CL
ROSSLAND CL
Gravel Hill Prim Sch
Sch
HALCOT AVE
St Columba's RC Sch for Boys
1 THE MOUNT
2 ALCONBURY
3 GROVEBURY CT
4 CHRISTIE HO
5 NESBITT HO
6 CAREY CT
DITTON RD
MOUNT RD
SIBLEY CL
UPTON RD
BELLEVUE RD
MARTIN RISE
Tenn Cts
MARTIN DENE
LATHAM RD
DA6
GRAVEL HILL
FAYGATE CRES
CH
FAIRWAY
MOUNT DR
MEADOW CL
HIGHFIELD RD
PETWORTH CL
HORLEY CL
GROSVENOR RD
Pl Fld
TOWNLEY RD
HORSHAM RD
MIDHURST HILL
BROOMFIELD RD
OLRON CRES
Upton Prim Sch
Townley Sch
DASHWOOD CL
BROOMHILL RISE
BROOM MEAD
GRAVEL HILL CL
Bexleyheath
IRIS AVE
ARUNDEL CL
UPTON CL
HENFIELD CL
CRANLEIGH CL
NEWICK CL
RYE CL
ROCHESTER DR
TUDOR WLK
EAST ROCHESTER WAY
Black Prince Intc
A223
Hal Plac
BASING DR
BAYNHAM CL
HARTLANDS CL
FINSBURY WAY
Beths Gram Sch
FARM VALE
TORBROOK CL
ARCADIAN AVE
OAKWAY CL
ARBUTHNOT LA
GRESHAM CL
MEADOWVIEW RD
SOUTH VIEW CL
WILLOW CL
Allot Gdns
OTFORD CL
ELMINGTON CL
SOUTHWOLD RD
A2
BOURNE RD
A2 Rochester (M2), M25
ARCADIAN CL
ARCADIAN RD
BROOKDALE RD
RIVERDALE RD
UPTON RD S
LOVE LA
KNOLL RD
HARTFORD RD
A220
Sp Gd
BRIDGEN RD
THE RIDGE
SHUTTLEMEAD
BACK LA
PARKHURST RD
VENTURE CL
KEMSING CL
CHARTER DR
ELMWOOD DR
CROSS LA
UNIVERSITY GDNS
ST THOMAS CT
BRADBOURNE RD
ALBERT RD
HARBEX CL
LESLEY CL
Recn Gd
DANE CL
HURSTBOURNE COTTS
ASCOT CT 1
KESTON CT 2
BALMORAL GDNS 3
WEDGEWOOD CT 4
WARWICK CL 5
PARKHILL RD
THANET RD
OLD BEXLEY BSNS PK
BOURNE PAR
Bexley Woods
Allot Gdns
DA5
Pl Fld
CHILHAM CL
B2210
KENLEY CL
A222
WEIR RD
Old Bexley
Church Woo
PARKWOOD RD
NORTH GLADE
EAST WOODSIDE
WEST WOODSIDE
MAIDEN ERLEGH AVE
RAVENSWOOD
HENGROVE CT
CAMDEN RD
WOODSTOCK CT
GRANGEWOOD
SOUTH GLADE
SALISBURY RD
OXFORD MEWS
TANYARD LA
PO
BEXLEY HIGH ST
MANOR RD
MANOR WAY
Sch
Bexley
Old Bexley CE Prim Sch
CLARENDON MEWS
Cemy
MURCHISON AVE
SELBORNE AVE
HURSTWOOD AVE
GREENSIDE
HURST RD
Tenn Cts
GLENHURST AVE
Tenn Cts
Pav
River Cray
PELHAM COTTS
A2018
VICARAGE RD
HILL CRES
A2018 Dartford, A2
ESHER CL
DENISTON AVE
HURST SPRINGS
BRENT CL
ALTON CL
VALENTINE AVE
Allot Gdns
Pinewood Cottage
The Grove
BETTERTON DR
DAVENPORT RD
FRINTON RD
RIVERSIDE RD
Tenn Cts
PEMBURY CRES
BURNHAM RD
Woollett Hall Farm
WATER LA
JAQUETS CT
Mount Mascal Farm
Hurst Grid Sub Sta
Cavey Sprin
NORTH CRAY RD
Sports Gd
Loring Hall
Tenn Cts
PH
Home Close Farm
Keeper's Cottage
DA14
Royal Park Prim Sch
Allot Gdns
North Cray
Little Mascal Farm
BUNKERS HILL
Bunkers Hill
LEAFIELD LA
COCKSURE LA
Bexley
Dartford
Faesten Dic
FIVE ARCH BRIDGE
191
Joyden's Wood
GATTONS
Gattons Plantation
A
B
C
D
48
49
50
75
6
5
74
4
3
73
2
1
72
IX

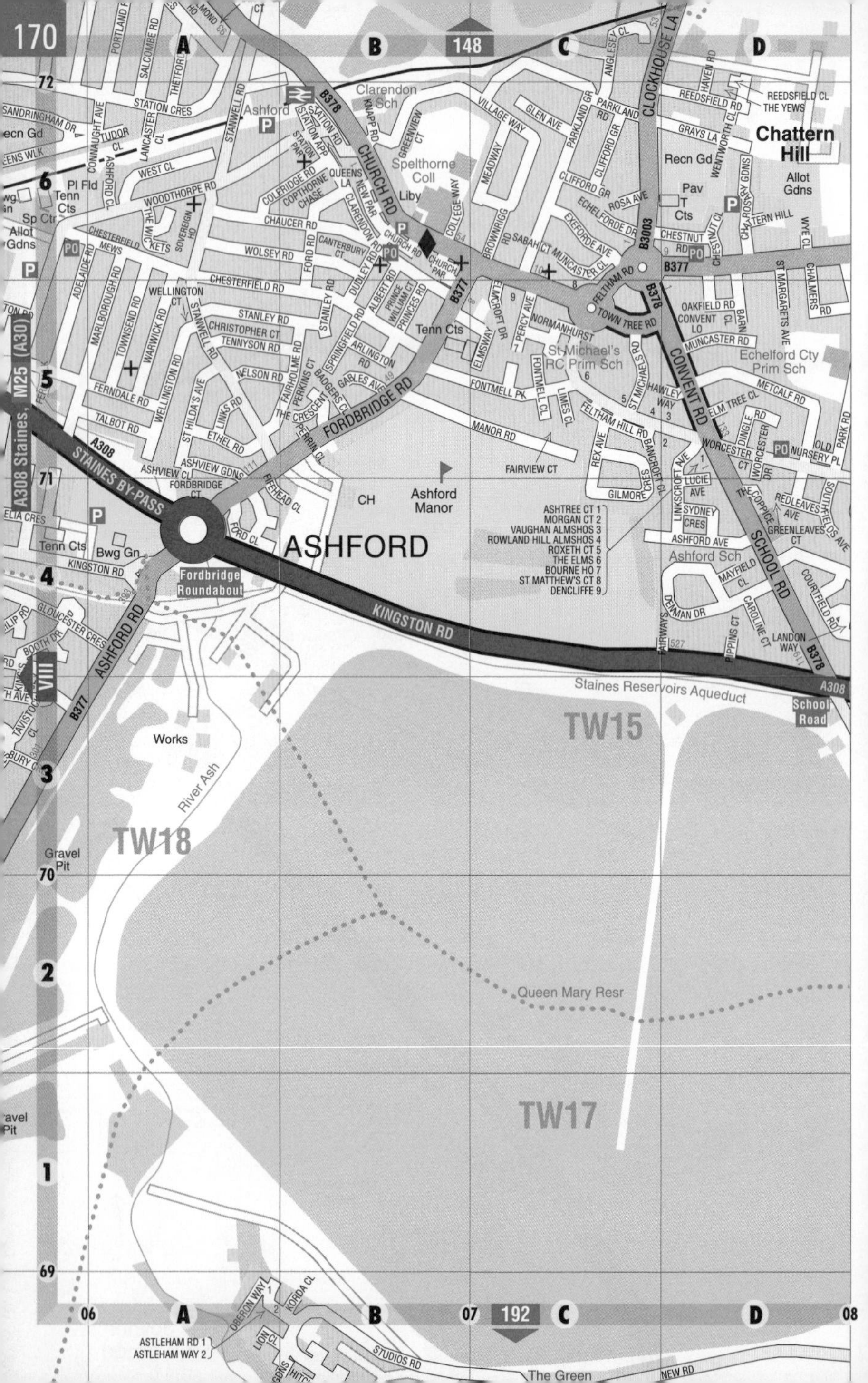

148
192
ASHFORD
Chattern Hill
TW15
TW18
TW17
Ashford Manor
Fordbridge Roundabout
School Road
Staines Reservoirs Aqueduct
Queen Mary Resr
River Ash
Spelthorne Coll
Clarendon Sch
St Michael's RC Prim Sch
Echelford Cty Prim Sch
Ashford Sch
KINGSTON RD
STAINES BY-PASS
CHURCH RD
FORDBRIDGE RD
CONVENT RD
SCHOOL RD
CLOCKHOUSE LA
ASHFORD RD
A308 Staines, M25 (A30)
ASHTREE CT 1
MORGAN CT 2
VAUGHAN ALMSHOS 3
ROWLAND HILL ALMSHOS 4
ROXETH CT 5
THE ELMS 6
BOURNE HO 7
ST MATTHEW'S CT 8
DENCLIFFE 9
ASTLEHAM RD 1
ASTLEHAM WAY 2
Works
Gravel Pit
The Green

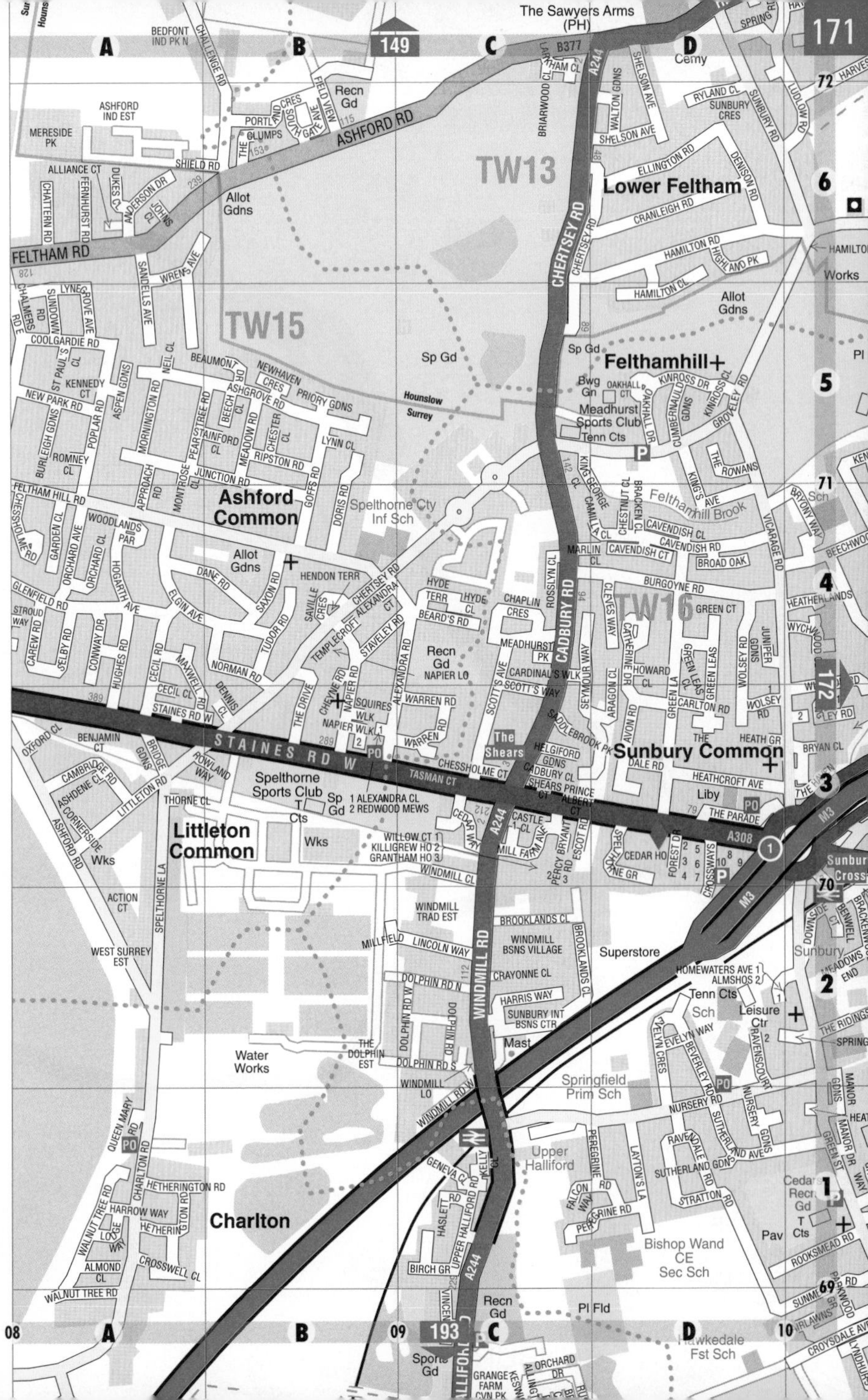
The Sawyers Arms (PH)
Lower Feltham
Felthamhill
Ashford Common
Sunbury Common
Littleton Common
Charlton
Upper Halliford
TW13
TW15
TW16
ASHFORD RD
FELTHAM RD
CHERTSEY RD
CADBURY RD
STAINES RD W
WINDMILL RD
Spelthorne Sports Club
Spelthorne Cty Inf Sch
Springfield Prim Sch
Bishop Wand CE Sec Sch
Hawkedale Fst Sch
Water Works
Superstore
Windmill Trad Est
Windmill Bsns Village
Sunbury Int Bsns Ctr
Meadhurst Sports Club
Feltham hill Brook
Hounslow
Surrey
149
172
193

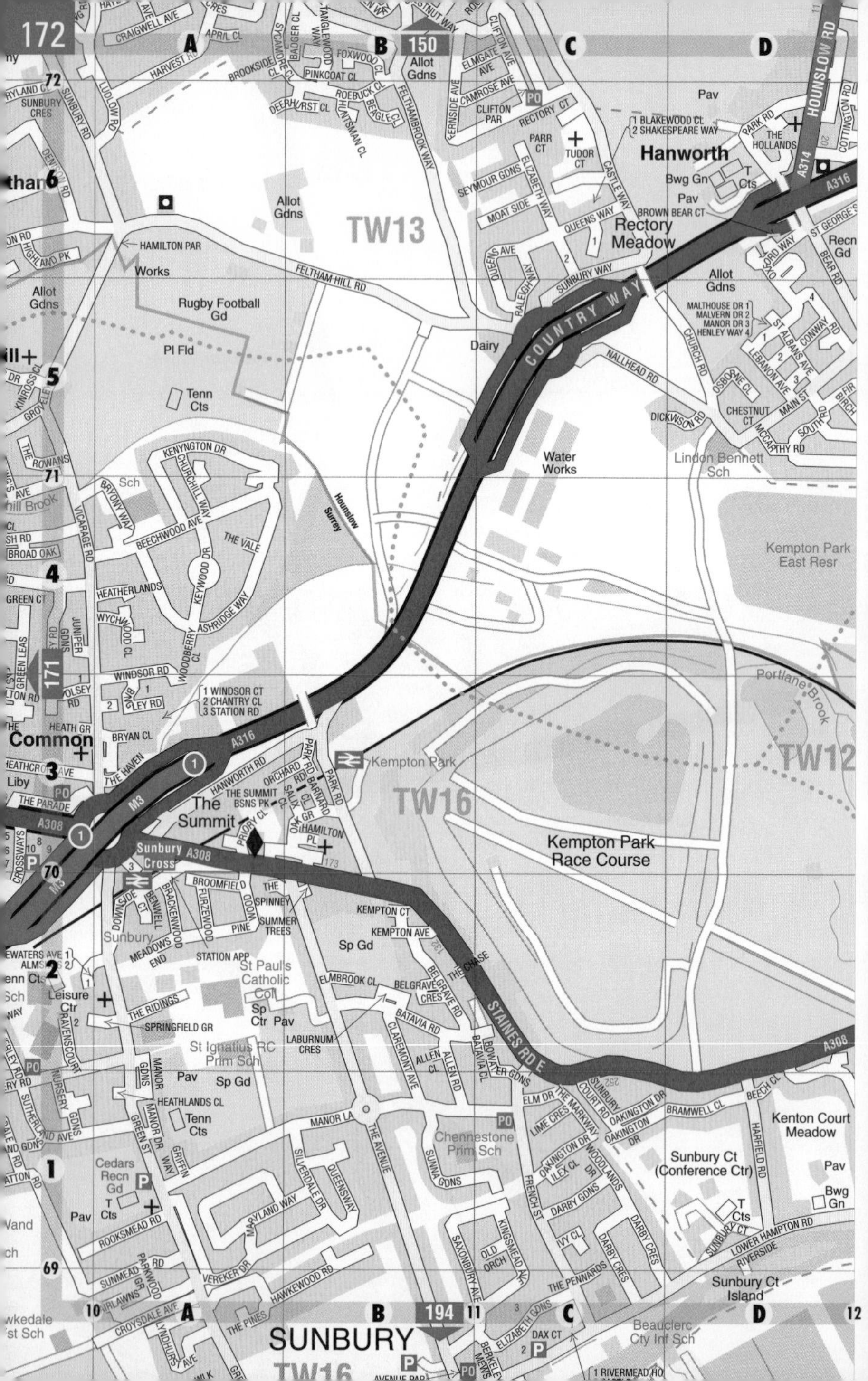

172
A
B
C
D
150
171
194
173
Hanworth
TW13
TW16
TW12
Common
The Summit
SUNBURY
Rectory Meadow
Kempton Park
Kempton Park Race Course
Kempton Park East Resr
Water Works
Portlane Brook
Hounslow
Surrey
COUNTRY WAY
HOUNSLOW RD
A314
A316
A308
M3
STAINES RD E
THE CHASE
Sunbury Cross
Sunbury
Allot Gdns
Rugby Football Gd
Pl Fld
Tenn Cts
Works
Dairy
Sch
Lindon Bennett Sch
St Paul's Catholic Coll
St Ignatius RC Prim Sch
Chennestone Prim Sch
Sunbury Ct (Conference Ctr)
Kenton Court Meadow
Sunbury Ct Island
Beauclerc Cty Inf Sch
Leisure Ctr
Cedars Recn Gd
Sp Gd
Sp Ctr
Pav
Bwg Gn
T Cts
Recn Gd
Liby
PO
P
CRAIGWELL AVE
APRIL CL
HARVEST RD
LUDLOW RD
SUNBURY RD
SUNBURY CRES
BROOKSIDE CL
SYCAMORE CL
BADGER CL
TANGLEWOOD WAY
FOXWOOD CL
PINKCOAT CL
ROEBUCK CL
HUNTSMAN CL
BEAGLE CL
DEERHURST CL
FELTHAMBROOK WAY
ELMGATE AVE
CAMROSE AVE
CLIFTON AVE
CLIFTON PAR
FERNSIDE AVE
RECTORY CT
PARR CT
TUDOR CT
1 BLAKEWOOD CL
2 SHAKESPEARE WAY
PARK RD
THE HOLLANDS
COTTINGTON RD
SEYMOUR GDNS
ELIZABETH WAY
CASTLE WAY
MOAT SIDE
QUEENS WAY
BROWN BEAR CT
QUEENS AVE
RALEIGH WAY
SUNBURY WAY
ST GEORGE'S
OXFORD WAY
BEAR RD
HAMILTON PAR
FELTHAM HILL RD
HIGHLAND PK
DENISON RD
MALTHOUSE DR 1
MALVERN DR 2
MANOR DR 3
HENLEY WAY 4
ST ALBANS AVE
CONWAY RD
CHURCH RD
NALLHEAD RD
LEBANON AVE
OSBORNE CL
CHESTNUT CT
MAIN ST
SOUTH RD
BIRCH
DICKWISON RD
MCCARTHY RD
KINROSS CL
GROVELEY
THE ROWANS
KENYNGTON DR
CHURCHILL WAY
BRYONY WAY
BEECHWOOD AVE
THE VALE
KEYWOOD DR
VICARAGE RD
BROAD OAK
HEATHERLANDS
WYCHWOOD CL
ASHRIDGE WAY
WOODBERRY CL
JUNIPER GDNS
GREEN CT
GREEN LEAS
WINDSOR RD
BINGLEY RD
1 WINDSOR CT
2 CHANTRY CL
3 STATION RD
HEATH GR
BRYAN CL
THE HAVEN
HEATHCROFT AVE
THE PARADE
CROSSWAYS
HANWORTH RD
ORCHARD RD
PARK RD
BARNARD CL
SALIX CL
THE SUMMIT BSNS PK
PRIORY CL
OAK GR
HAMILTON PL
DOWNSIDE
BENWELL CT
BRACKENWOOD
FURZEWOOD
BROOMFIELD
THE SPINNEY
SUMMER TREES
PINE WOOD
MEADOWS END
STATION APP
KEMPTON CT
KEMPTON AVE
BELGRAVE CRES
ELMBROOK CL
BATAVIA RD
LABURNUM CRES
THE RIDINGS
SPRINGFIELD GR
RAVENSCOURT
MANOR GDNS
MANOR DR
HEATHLANDS CL
GREEN ST
GRIFFIN WAY
NURSERY GDNS
SUTHERLAND AVE
CLAREMONT AVE
ALLEN CL
ALLEN RD
BATAVIA CL
BOWATER GDNS
ELM DR
LIME CRES
THE MARKWAY
COURT RD
SUNBURY
OAKINGTON DR
BRAMWELL CL
BEECH CL
HARFIELD RD
MANOR LA
THE AVENUE
SILVERDALE DR
QUEENSWAY
SUNNA GDNS
ILEX CL
WOODLANDS DR
FRENCH ST
DARBY GDNS
DARBY CRES
IVY CL
MARYLAND WAY
SAXONBURY AVE
KINGSMEAD AV
OLD ORCH
THE PENNARDS
SUNBURY CT
LOWER HAMPTON RD
RIVERSIDE
ROOKSMEAD RD
SUNMEAD RD
PARKWOOD GR
FIRLAWNS
VEREKER DR
HAWKEWOOD RD
CROYSDALE AVE
THE PINES
LYNDHURST AVE
ELIZABETH GDNS
DAX CT
BERKELEY MEWS
AVENUE PAR
1 RIVERMEAD HO
72
71
70
69
6
5
4
3
2
1
10
11
12

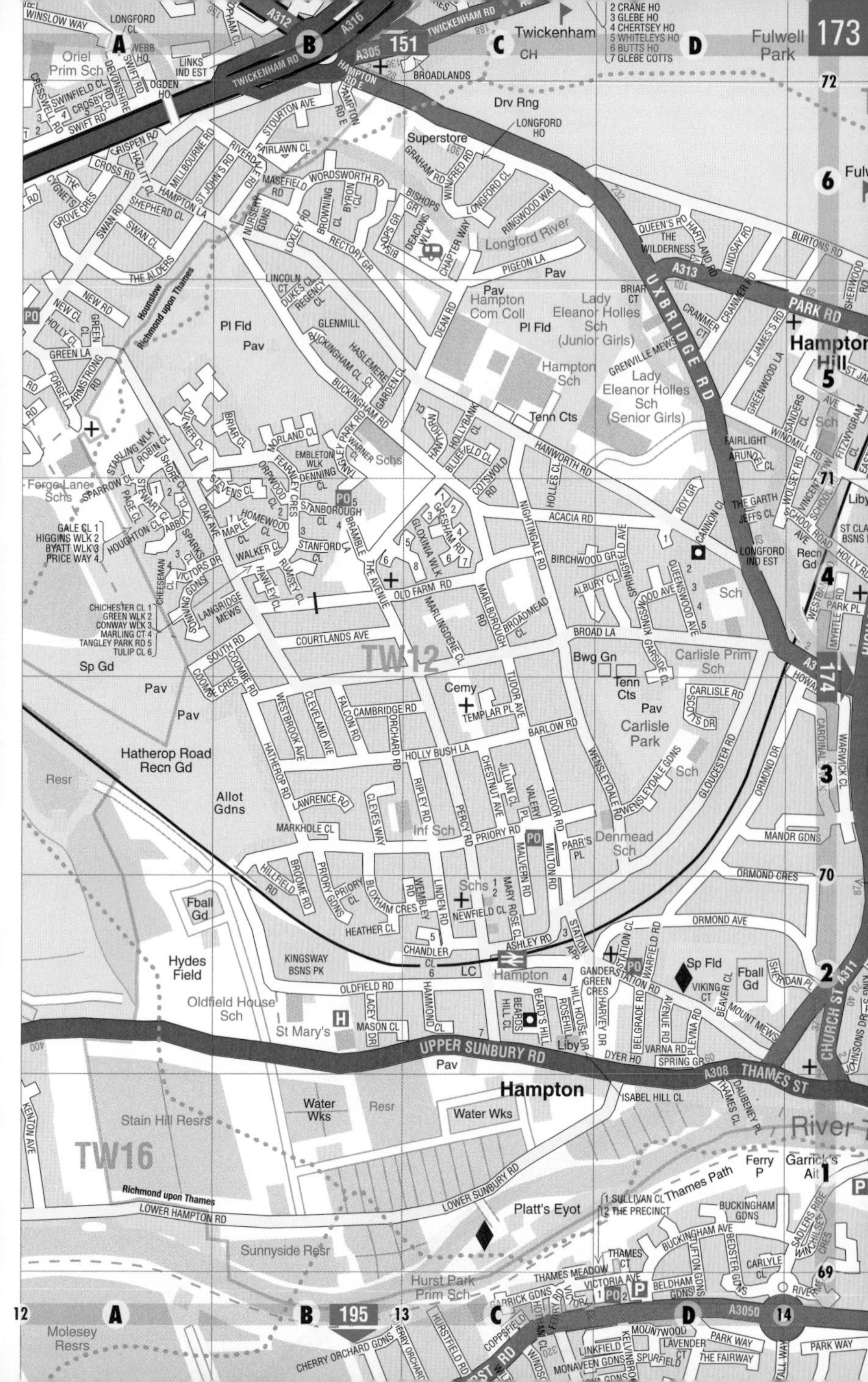

Twickenham
Fulwell Park
Hampton Hill
Hampton
TW12
TW16
Hampton Com Coll
Lady Eleanor Holles Sch (Junior Girls)
Lady Eleanor Holles Sch (Senior Girls)
Hampton Sch
Carlisle Park
Hatherop Road Recn Gd
Hydes Field
Stain Hill Resrs
Sunnyside Resr
Molesey Resrs
Platt's Eyot
Garrick's Ait
UXBRIDGE RD
UPPER SUNBURY RD
THAMES ST
LOWER SUNBURY RD
LOWER HAMPTON RD
HANWORTH RD
TWICKENHAM RD

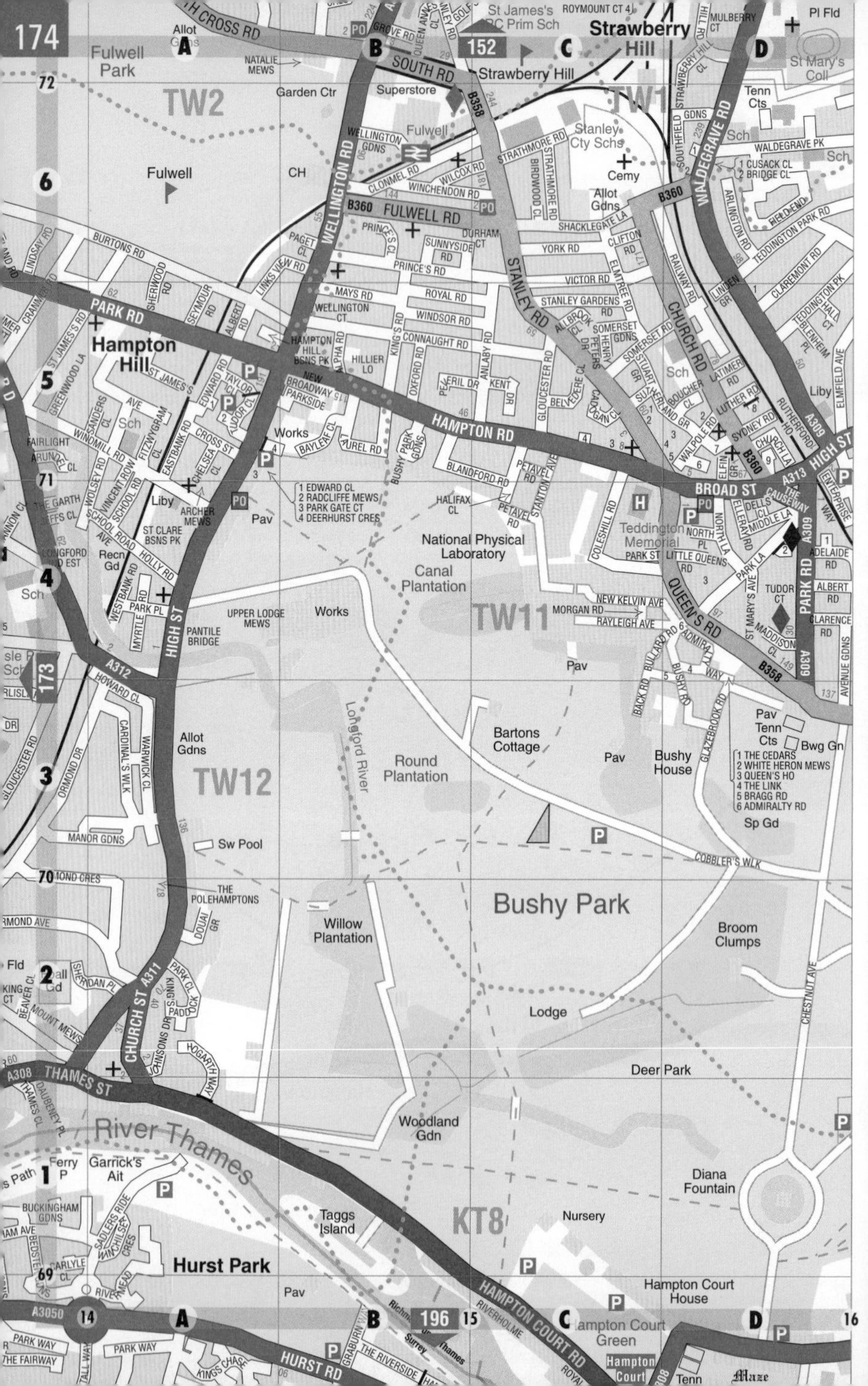
Fulwell Park
TW2
Fulwell
CH
Hampton Hill
Garden Ctr
Superstore
St James's RC Prim Sch
Strawberry Hill
152
TW1
Stanley Cty Schs
Cemy
Allot Gdns
WELLINGTON RD
FULWELL RD
SOUTH RD
STANLEY RD
WALDEGRAVE RD
PARK RD
HAMPTON RD
BROAD ST
HIGH ST
CHURCH RD
Teddington Memorial
National Physical Laboratory
Canal Plantation
TW11
Works
UPPER LODGE MEWS
PANTILE BRIDGE
QUEEN'S RD
1 EDWARD CL
2 RADCLIFFE MEWS
3 PARK GATE CT
4 DEERHURST CRES
1 THE CEDARS
2 WHITE HERON MEWS
3 QUEEN'S HO
4 THE LINK
5 BRAGG RD
6 ADMIRALTY RD
173
TW12
Allot Gdns
Round Plantation
Longford River
Bartons Cottage
Bushy House
Sw Pool
THE POLEHAMPTONS
Bushy Park
Willow Plantation
Broom Clumps
Lodge
Deer Park
CHURCH ST
THAMES ST
River Thames
Woodland Gdn
Diana Fountain
Garrick's Ait
Taggs Island
KT8
Nursery
Hurst Park
Hampton Court House
Hampton Court Green
HAMPTON COURT RD
HURST RD
196
Maze

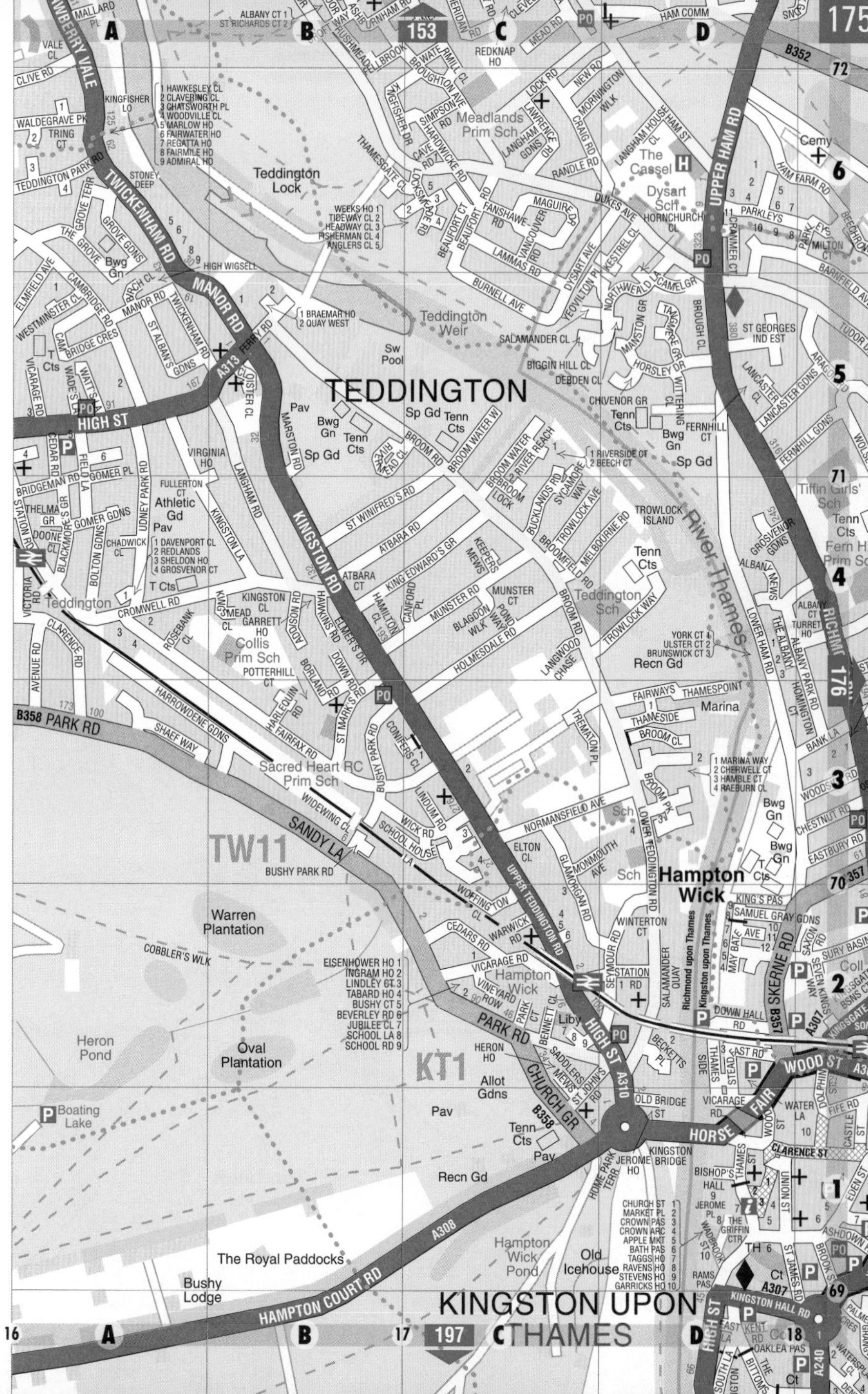

TEDDINGTON
KINGSTON UPON THAMES
Hampton Wick
TW11
KT1
153
197
176
Teddington Lock
Teddington Weir
River Thames
Trowlock Island
Meadlands Prim Sch
The Cassel
Dysart Sch
St Georges Ind Est
Tiffin Girls' Sch
Fern Hill Prim Sch
Teddington Sch
Collis Prim Sch
Sacred Heart RC Prim Sch
Athletic Gd
Warren Plantation
Oval Plantation
Heron Pond
Boating Lake
The Royal Paddocks
Bushy Lodge
Hampton Wick Pond
Old Icehouse
Allot Gdns
Recn Gd
Marina
Cemy
KINGSTON RD
TWICKENHAM RD
MANOR RD
HIGH ST
UPPER HAM RD
UPPER TEDDINGTON RD
HAMPTON COURT RD
PARK RD
SANDY LA
CHURCH GR
KINGSTON BRIDGE
HORSE FAIR
WOOD ST
BROOM RD
BROOM WATER W
CROMWELL RD
STATION RD
RICHMOND RD
SKERNE RD
KINGSTON HALL RD
LOWER HAM RD
LOWER TEDDINGTON RD
NORMANSFIELD AVE
Teddington

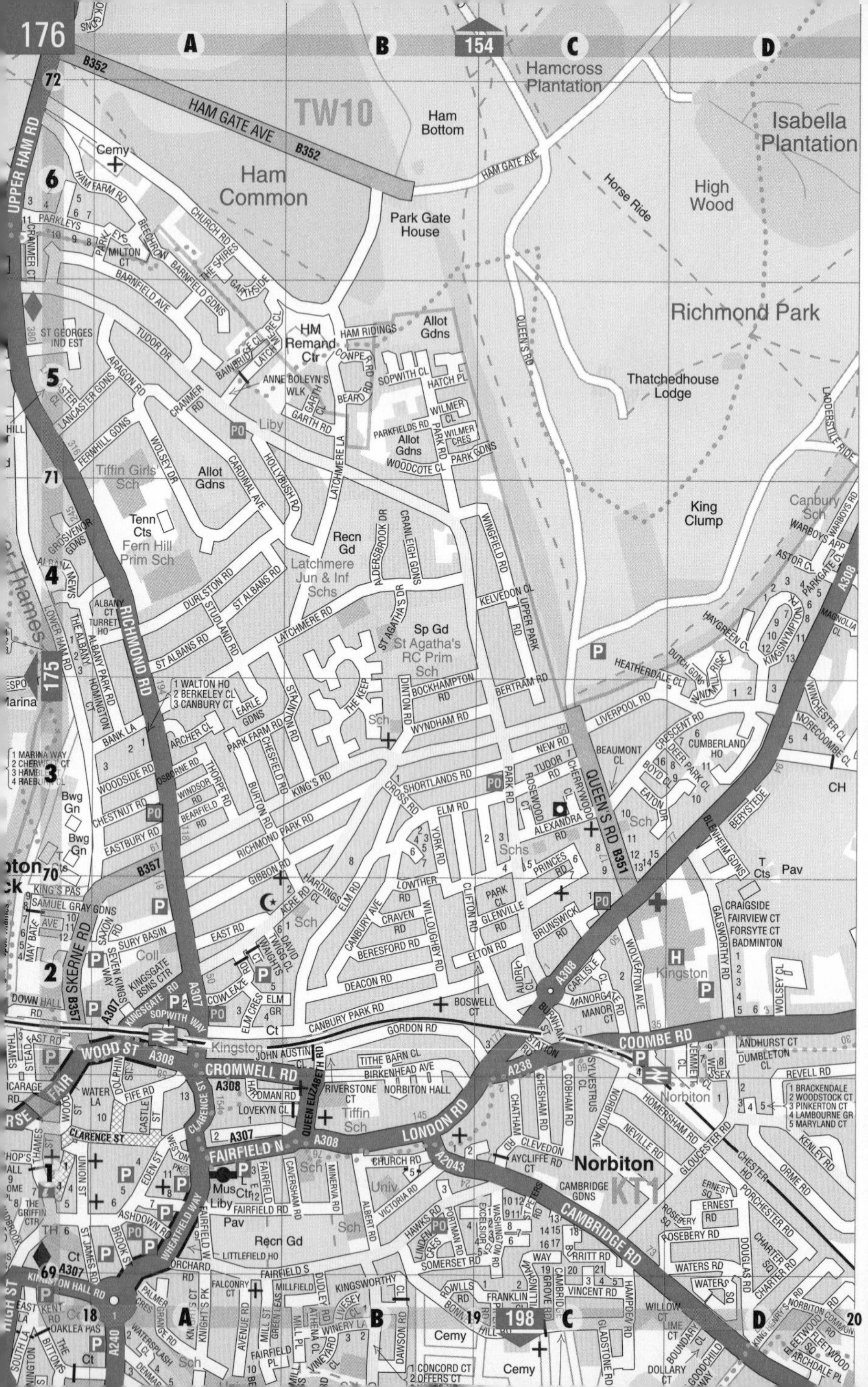
A
B
154
C
D
Hamcross Plantation
TW10
Ham Bottom
Isabella Plantation
HAM GATE AVE
B352
Ham Common
High Wood
Horse Ride
Park Gate House
Richmond Park
Thatchedhouse Lodge
HM Remand Ctr
Allot Gdns
UPPER HAM RD
RICHMOND RD
King Clump
Canbury Sch
Recn Gd
Latchmere Jun & Inf Schs
Sp Gd
St Agatha's RC Prim Sch
Tiffin Girls' Sch
Fern Hill Prim Sch
QUEEN'S RD
175
Kingston
COOMBE RD
Norbiton
WOOD ST
CROMWELL RD
LONDON RD
FAIRFIELD N
CAMBRIDGE RD
Norbiton
KT1
Recn Gd
Mus Ctr Liby
Tiffin Sch
Univ
Cemy
198
19
20
18
69
70
71
72
A
B
C
D
1
2
3
4
5
6

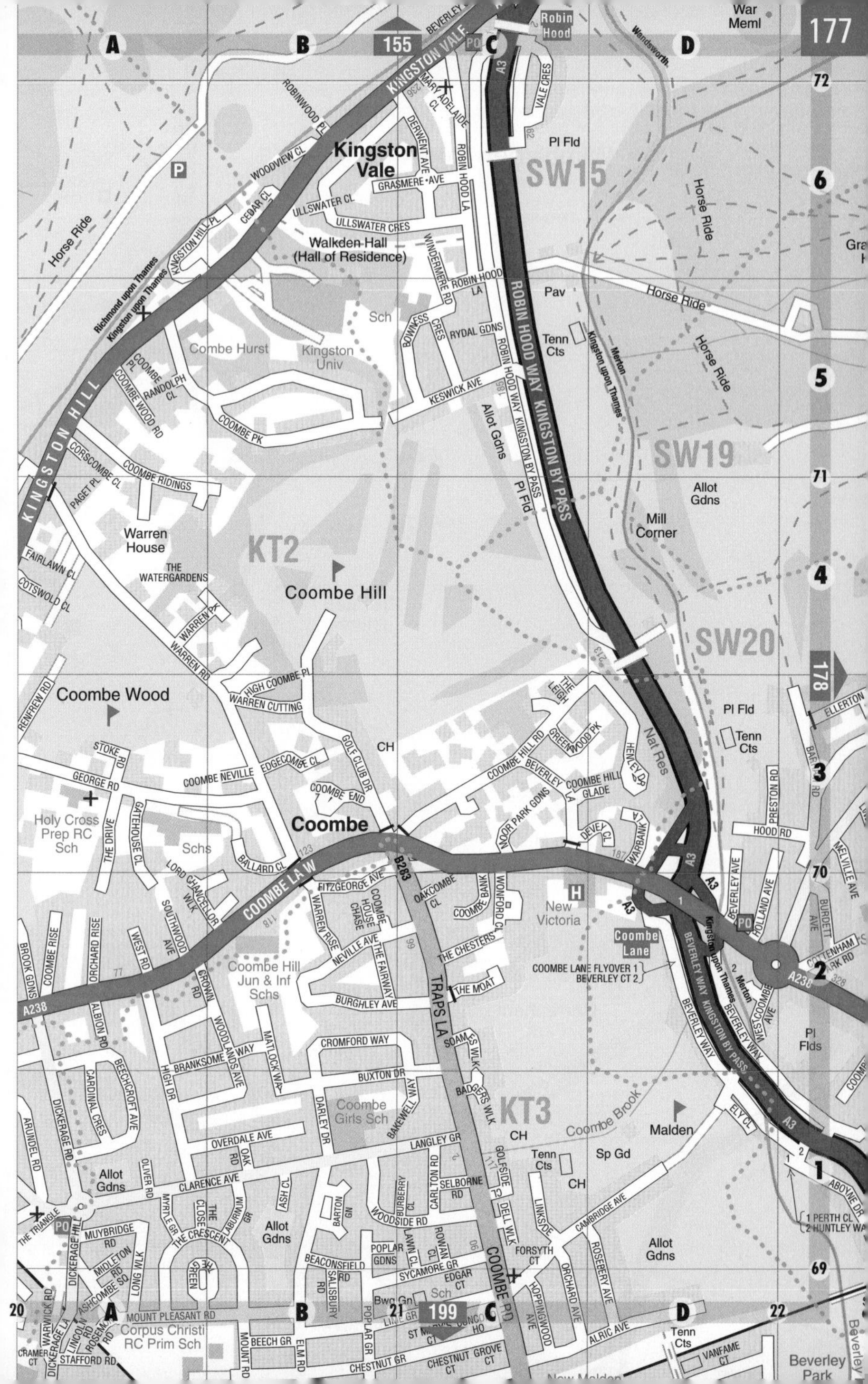

155
199
178
Kingston Vale
Walkden Hall
(Hall of Residence)
Combe Hurst
Kingston Univ
Warren House
Coombe Hill
Coombe Wood
Holy Cross Prep RC Sch
Coombe
Coombe Hill Jun & Inf Schs
Coombe Girls Sch
New Victoria
Mill Corner
Malden
Corpus Christi RC Prim Sch
SW15
SW19
SW20
KT2
KT3
KINGSTON VALE
KINGSTON HILL
ROBIN HOOD WAY
KINGSTON BY PASS
COOMBE LANE
TRAPS LA
COOMBE RD
BEVERLEY WAY
A3
A238
B283
Horse Ride
Robin Hood
War Meml
Coombe Lane
COOMBE LANE FLYOVER 1
BEVERLEY CT 2
1 PERTH CL
2 HUNTLEY WAY
Beverley Park

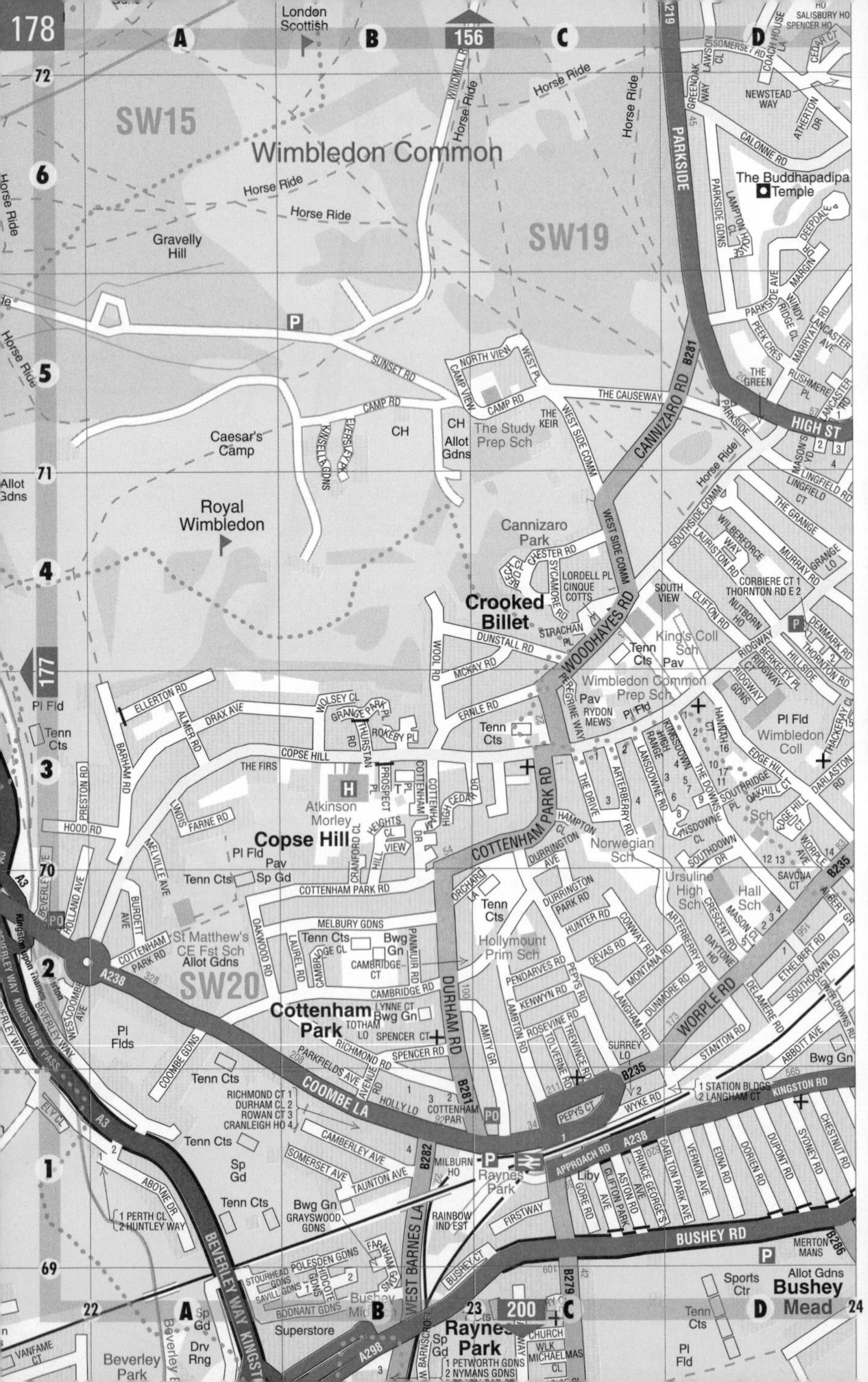
A
B
C
D
156
London Scottish
72
SW15
Wimbledon Common
Horse Ride
Windmill Rd
6
Gravelly Hill
SW19
PARKSIDE
A219
B281
Somerset Rd
Lawson Cl
Coach House La
Salisbury Ho
Spencer Ho
Cedar Ct
Greenoak Way
Newstead Way
Atherton Dr
Calonne Rd
The Buddhapadipa Temple
Parkside Gdns
Lampton Ho Cl
Deepdale
Margin Dr
Parkside Ave
Windy Ridge Cl
Peek Cres
Marryat Rd
Lancaster Ave
The Green
Rushmere Pl
Lancaster Rd
High St
5
Sunset Rd
North View
Camp View
West Pl
Camp Rd
The Causeway
Cannizaro Rd
The Keir
West Side Comm
Caesar's Camp
Kinsella Gdns
Eversley Pk
CH
The Study Prep Sch
Allot Gdns
Parkside
Mason's Yd
Lingfield Rd
Lingfield Ct
71
Royal Wimbledon
Cannizaro Park
Chester Rd
Beech Cl
Sycamore Rd
Lordell Pl
Cinque Cotts
Southside Comm
Wilberforce Way
Lauriston Rd
The Grange
Murray Rd
Grange Lo
Corbiere Ct 1
Thornton Rd E 2
4
Crooked Billet
Woodhayes Rd
South View
Clifton Rd
Nutborn Ho
Denmark Rd
Strachan Pl
Dunstall Rd
Wool Rd
McKay Rd
King's Coll Sch
Tenn Cts
Pav
Ridgway
Berkeley Pl
Ridgway Gdns
Hillside
Thornton Rd
177
Pl Fld
Ellerton Rd
Almer Rd
Drax Ave
Wolsey Cl
Grange Park Pl
Ernle Rd
Peregrine Way
Wimbledon Common Prep Sch
Rydon Mews
Kingsdown High Range
Hamilton Ct
Wimbledon Coll
Thackeray Cl
3
Barham Rd
Thurstan Rd
Rokeby Pl
Copse Hill
The Firs
Preston Rd
Prospect Pl
Cottenham Dr
Cottenham Pl
High Cedar Dr
Cottenham Park Rd
The Drive
Arterberry Rd
Lansdowne Rd
The Downs
Southridge Pl
Oakhill Ct
Edge Hill
Edge Hill Ct
Darlaston Rd
Hood Rd
Lindis
Farne Rd
Melville Ave
Atkinson Morley
Heights Cl
Hill View
Hampton Cl
Durrington Ave
Norwegian Sch
Lansdowne Cl
Southdown Dr
Worple Ave
Savona Ct
B235
70
A3
Beverley Ave
Holland Ave
Cranford Cl
Pl Fld
Pav
Tenn Cts
Sp Gd
Cottenham Park Rd
Orchard La
Durrington Park Rd
Ursuline High Sch
Hall Sch
Mason Cl
Albert Gr
PO
Burdett Ave
St Matthew's CE Fst Sch
Melbury Gdns
Oakwood Rd
Tenn Cts
Bwg Gn
Hunter Rd
Crescent Rd
2
Kingston upon Thames
Cottenham Park Rd
Allot Gdns
Laurel Rd
Cambridge Cl
Cambridge Ct
Panmuir Rd
Hollymount Prim Sch
Devas Rd
Conway Rd
Daytone Ho
Ethelbert Rd
Pl Fld
A238
SW20
West Coombe Ave
Cambridge Rd
Durham Rd
Pendarves Rd
Montana Rd
Arterberry Rd
Southdown Rd
Beverley Way
Kingston By Pass
Cottenham Park
Lynne Ct
Bwg Gn
Totham Lo
Spencer Ct
Kenwyn Rd
Pepys Rd
Dunmore Rd
Langham Rd
Worple Rd
Delamere Rd
Lower Downs Rd
Pl Flds
Richmond Rd
Parkfields Ave
Avenue Rd
Spencer Rd
Amity Gr
Lambton Rd
Rosevine Rd
Tolverne Rd
Trewince Rd
Surrey Lo
Stanton Rd
Abbott Ave
Bwg Gn
Coombe Gdns
Tenn Cts
Coombe La
Holly Lo
Cottenham Par
Richmond Ct 1
Durham Cl 2
Rowan Ct 3
Cranleigh Ho 4
B235
Pepys Ct
Wyke Rd
1 Station Bldgs
2 Langham Ct
Kingston Rd
Ely Cl
Camberley Ave
Somerset Ave
Taunton Ave
Tenn Cts
Sp Gd
1
Aboyne Dr
1 Perth Cl
2 Huntley Way
B282
Milburn Ho
Raynes Park
Approach Rd
A238
Liby
Gore Rd
Clifton Park Ave
Aston Rd
Prince George's Ave
Carlton Park Ave
Vernon Ave
Edna Rd
Dorien Rd
Dupont Rd
Sydney Rd
Chestnut Rd
Tenn Cts
Bwg Gn
Grayswood Gdns
Farnham Gdns
Rainbow Ind Est
Firstway
Bushey Rd
Merton Mans
B286
69
Beverley Way
Stourhead Gdns
Savill Gdns
Polesden Gdns
Hidcote Gdns
Bodnant Gdns
West Barnes La
Bushey Ct
B279
Sports Ctr
Allot Gdns
Bushey Mead
22
23
200
24
Sp Gd
Superstore
Drv Rng
Beverley Park
Vanfame Ct
A298
Raynes Park
Church Wlk
Michaelmas Cl
1 Petworth Gdns
2 Nymans Gdns
Tenn Cts
Pl Fld

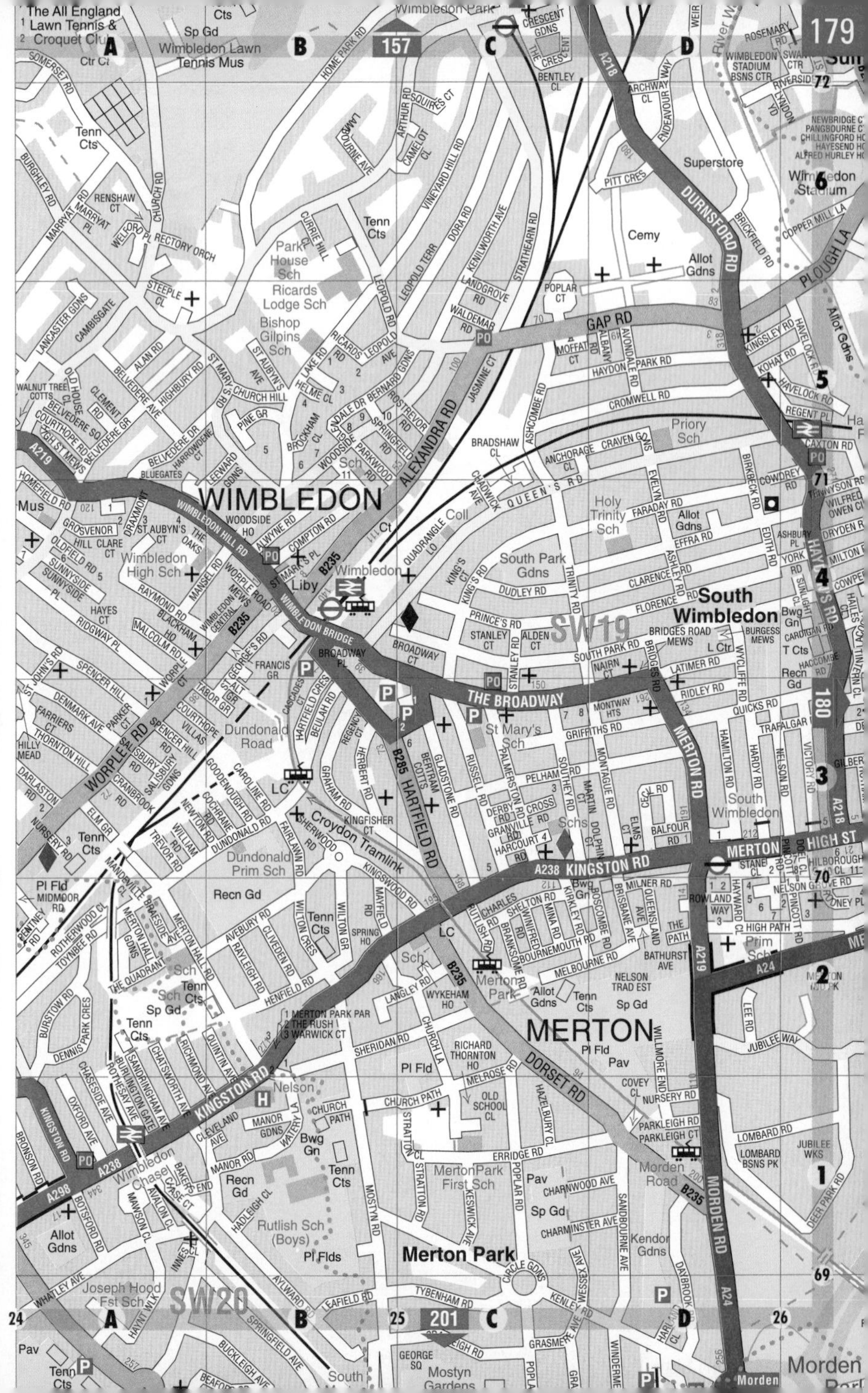

179
157
201
180
A
B
C
D
1
2
3
4
5
6
24
25
26
69
70
71
72
The All England Lawn Tennis & Croquet Club
Wimbledon Lawn Tennis Mus
Wimbledon Park
Sp Gd
Tenn Cts
WIMBLEDON
South Wimbledon
SW19
SW20
MERTON
Merton Park
Morden
Wimbledon Stadium
Wimbledon Chase
Wimbledon
Dundonald Road
Merton Park
Morden Road
Croydon Tramlink
Park House Sch
Ricards Lodge Sch
Bishop Gilpins Sch
Wimbledon High Sch
Holy Trinity Sch
Priory Sch
St Mary's Sch
Dundonald Prim Sch
Rutlish Sch (Boys)
Merton Park First Sch
Joseph Hood Fst Sch
Superstore
Cemy
Allot Gdns
Recn Gd
Pl Fld
Pl Flds
Bwg Gn
South Park Gdns
Nelson
Nelson Trad Est
Kendor Gdns
Jubilee Wks
Lombard Bsns Pk
Wimbledon Stadium Bsns Ctr
Liby
Coll
Mus
Sch
Schs
Pav
LC
L Ctr
Prim Sch
Gdns
T Cts
Ct
WIMBLEDON HILL RD
WORPLE RD
ALEXANDRA RD
WIMBLEDON BRIDGE
THE BROADWAY
HARTFIELD RD
KINGSTON RD
MERTON RD
MERTON HIGH ST
MORDEN RD
DURNSFORD RD
HAYDONS RD
PLOUGH LA
GAP RD
QUEEN'S RD
DORSET RD
CHURCH RD
HOME PARK RD
VINEYARD HILL RD
STRATHEARN RD
ARTHUR RD
SOUTH PARK RD
KINGSWOOD RD
CHURCH LA
ERRIDGE RD
MOSTYN RD
POPLAR RD
SANDBOURNE AVE
KENLEY RD
TYBENHAM RD
AYLWARD RD
WHATLEY AVE
OXFORD AVE
BOTSFORD RD
ST GEORGE'S RD
DUNDONALD RD
MERTON HALL RD
AVEBURY RD
RAYLEIGH RD
CLIVEDEN RD
HENFIELD RD
SHERIDAN RD
RIDGWAY PL
SPENCER HILL
DENMARK AVE
THORNTON HILL
DARLASTON RD
COTTENHAM PARK RD
RIDLEY RD
LATIMER RD
QUICKS RD
TRAFALGAR RD
HIGH PATH
BATHURST AVE
JUBILEE WAY
LOMBARD RD
DEER PARK RD
LEE RD
MILNER RD
MELBOURNE RD
BOURNEMOUTH RD
CHARNWOOD AVE
CHARMINSTER AVE
PARKLEIGH RD
NURSERY RD
HAZELBURY CL
MELROSE RD
CHURCH PATH
STRATTON RD
MANOR RD
CLEVELAND AVE
WATERY LA
BURSTOW RD
DENNIS PARK CRES
CHASESIDE AVE
ROTHESAY AVE
SANDRINGHAM AVE
CHATSWORTH AVE
RICHMOND AVE
QUINTIN AVE
KINGFISHER CT
GRAHAM RD
HERBERT RD
GLADSTONE RD
RUSSELL RD
PALMERSTON RD
SOUTHEY RD
MONTAGUE RD
PELHAM RD
GRIFFITHS RD
PRINCE'S RD
DUDLEY RD
FLORENCE RD
CLARENCE RD
EFFRA RD
FARADAY RD
TRINITY RD
EVELYN RD
BIRKBECK RD
CROMWELL RD
HAYDON PARK RD
KINGSLEY RD
HAVELOCK RD
REGENT PL
CAXTON RD
COWDREY RD
TENNYSON RD
DRYDEN RD
MILTON RD
ASHBURY PL
YORK RD
HAMILTON RD
HARDY RD
NELSON RD
VICTORY RD
BRIDGES RD
WYCLIFFE RD
BRICKFIELD RD
COPPER MILL LA
ARCHWAY CL
ENDEAVOUR WAY
PITT CRES
LEOPOLD RD
LEOPOLD AVE
KENILWORTH AVE
DORA RD
LANDGROVE RD
WALDEMAR RD
RICARDS RD
LAKE RD
ST MARY'S RD
CHURCH HILL
HIGHBURY RD
ALAN RD
BELVEDERE AVE
BELVEDERE DR
CAMBISGATE
LANCASTER GDNS
RECTORY ORCH
MARRYAT RD
BURGHLEY RD
SOMERSET RD
HOMEFIELD RD
OLDFIELD RD
SUNNYSIDE
HAYES CT
RAYMOND RD
MALCOLM RD
BLACKHAM HO
A218
A219
A238
A24
A298
B235
B285

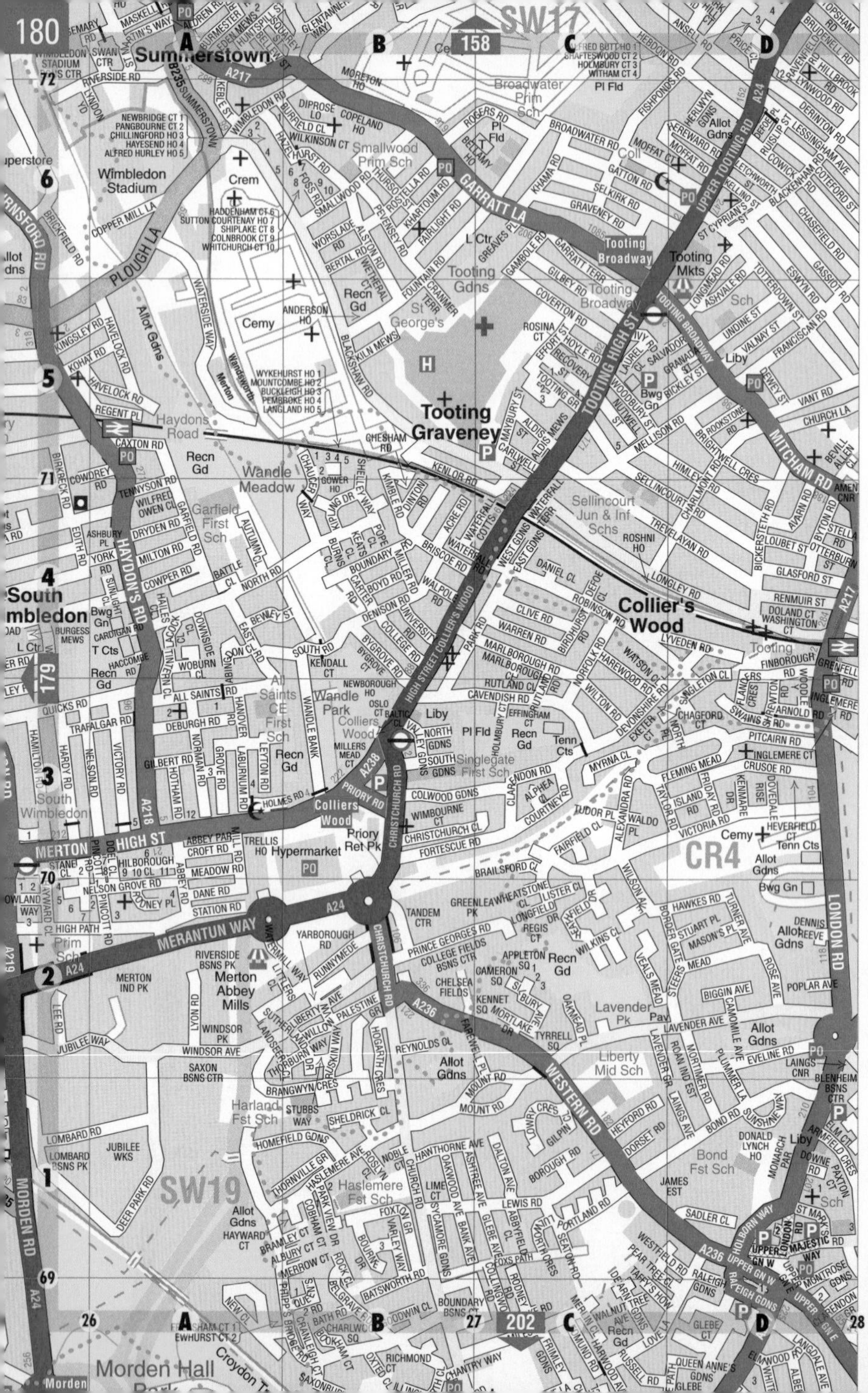
SW17
158
A
B
C
D
Summerstown
Wimbledon Stadium
Crem
Cemy
Smallwood Prim Sch
Broadwater Prim Sch
Pl Fld
GARRATT LA
Tooting Broadway
Tooting Mkts
UPPER TOOTING RD
TOOTING HIGH ST
TOOTING BROADWAY
MITCHAM RD
Tooting Gdns
St George's
Tooting Graveney
Haydons Road
Wandle Meadow
Garfield First Sch
Sellincourt Jun & Inf Schs
Collier's Wood
Tooting
South Wimbledon
HAYDON'S RD
HIGH STREET COLLIER'S WOOD
All Saints CE First Sch
Wandle Park
Colliers Wood
Singlegate First Sch
Priory Ret Pk
Hypermarket
MERTON HIGH ST
MERANTUN WAY
CHRISTCHURCH RD
CR4
Merton Abbey Mills
Merton Ind Pk
Lavender Pk
Liberty Mid Sch
WESTERN RD
LONDON RD
Harland Fst Sch
Haslemere Fst Sch
Bond Fst Sch
SW19
MORDEN RD
Morden Hall
202
26
27
28
69
70
71
72
1
2
3
4
5
6
179

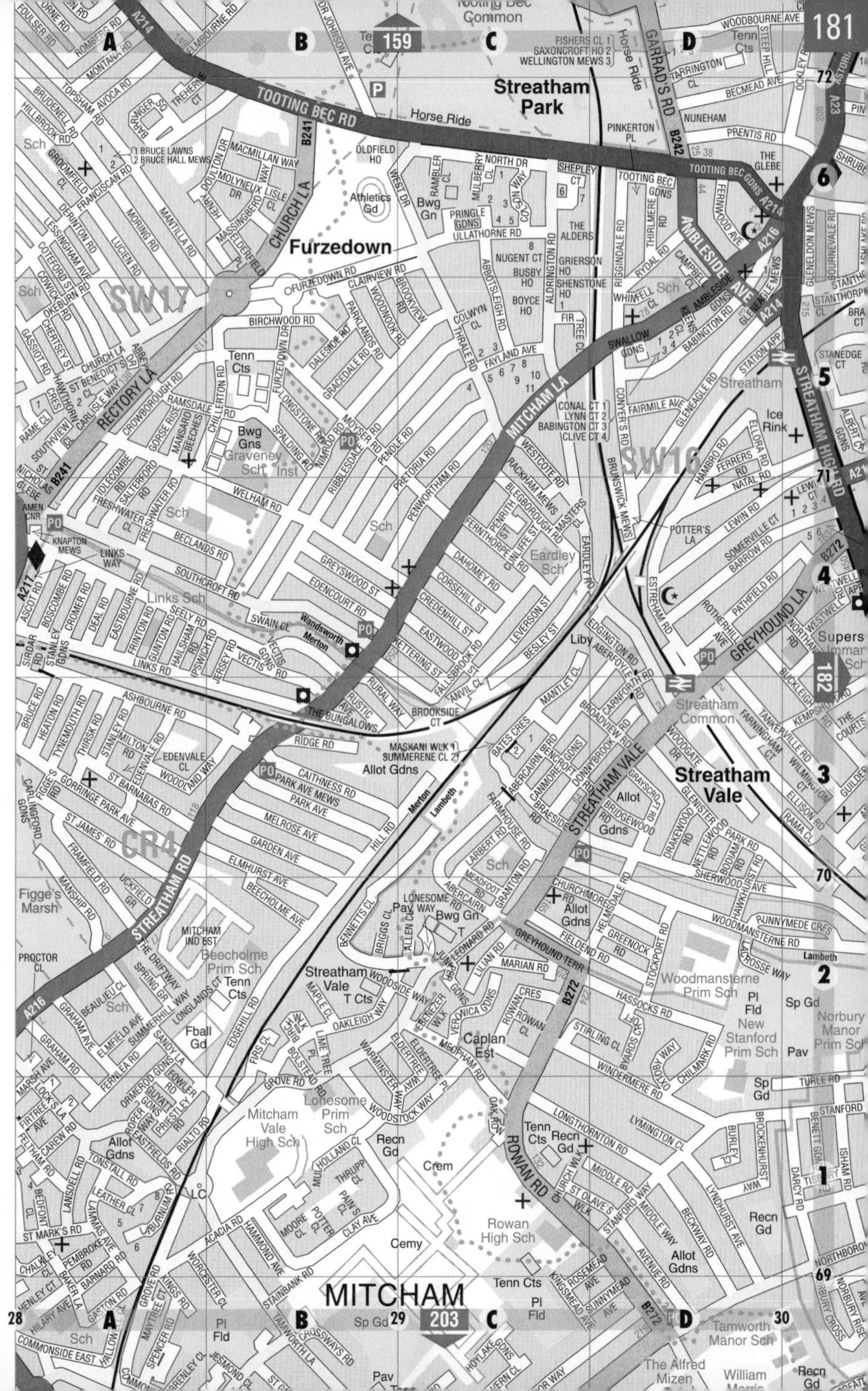
181
159
203
182
Streatham Park
Furzedown
Streatham
Streatham Vale
MITCHAM
SW17
SW16
CR4
Tooting Bec Common
TOOTING BEC RD
TOOTING BEC GDNS
MITCHAM LA
STREATHAM RD
STREATHAM VALE
STREATHAM HIGH RD
GREYHOUND LA
AMBLESIDE AVE
RECTORY LA
CHURCH LA
ROWAN RD
GARRAD'S RD
Horse Ride
Athletics Gd
Graveney Sch
Eardley Sch
Links Sch
Streatham Common
Figge's Marsh
Beecholme Prim Sch
Mitcham Vale High Sch
Lonesome Prim Sch
Woodmansterne Prim Sch
New Stanford Prim Sch
Norbury Manor Prim Sch
Rowan High Sch
Tamworth Manor Sch
Caplan Est
Mitcham Ind Est
Allot Gdns
Crem
Cemy
Recn Gd
Ice Rink
Liby
Wandsworth
Merton
Lambeth
A B C D
28 29 30
69 70 71 72
1 2 3 4 5 6

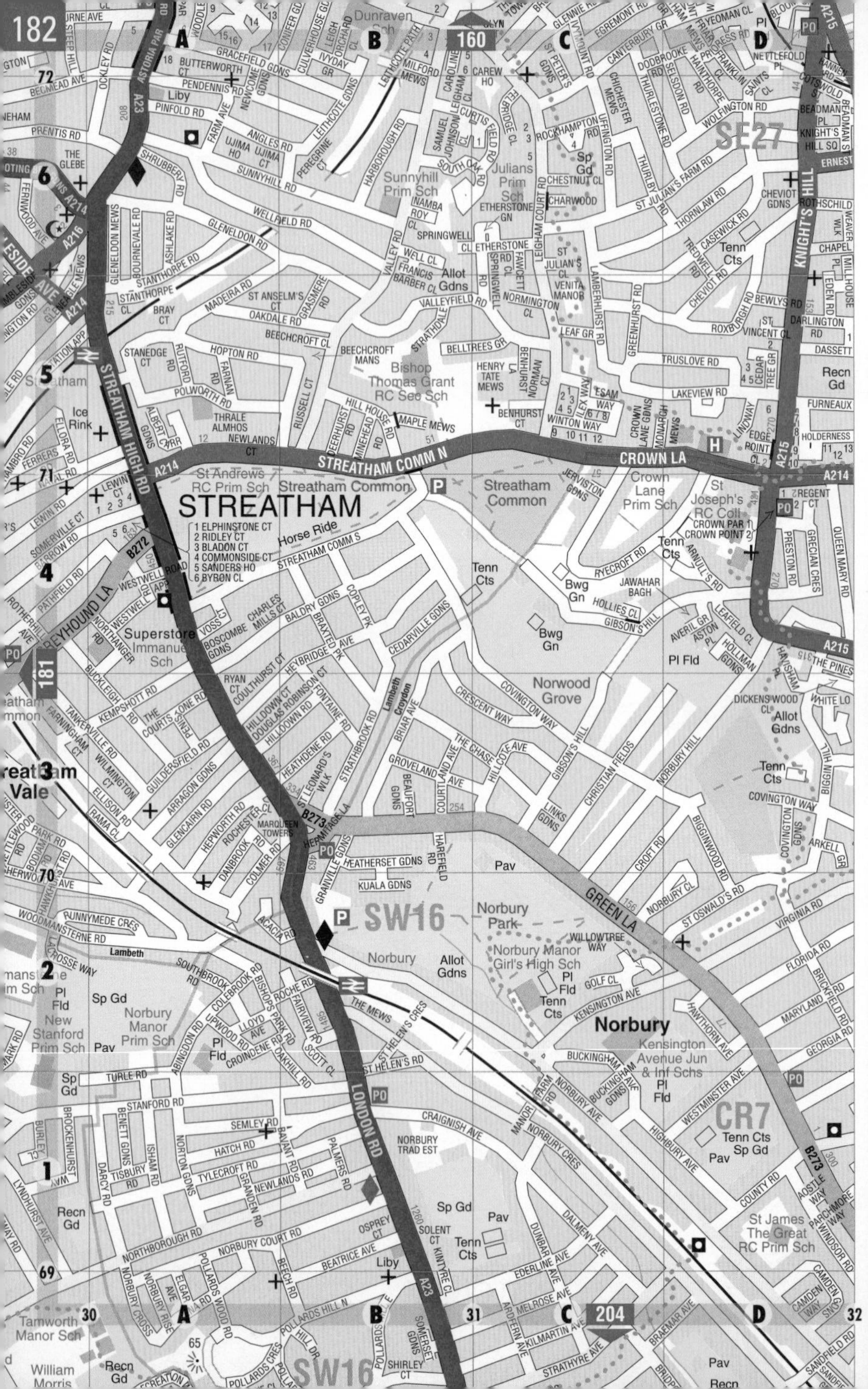
160
181
204
A
B
C
D
6
5
4
3
2
1
72
71
70
69
30
31
32
SE27
SW16
CR7
STREATHAM
Norbury
Streatham Common
Streatham Vale
Norwood Grove
Norbury Park
STREATHAM HIGH RD
STREATHAM COMM N
STREATHAM COMM S
CROWN LA
GREEN LA
LONDON RD
KNIGHT'S HILL
A23
A214
A215
A216
B272
B273
GREYHOUND LA
ASTORIA PAR
BUTTERWORTH CT
PENDENNIS RD
PINFOLD RD
PRENTIS RD
BECMEAD AVE
OCKLEY RD
GRACEFIELD GDNS
NEWCOMBE GDNS
FARM AVE
ANGLES RD
UJIMA HO
UJIMA CT
SHRUBBERY RD
SUNNYHILL RD
WELLFIELD RD
GLENELDON RD
GLENELDON MEWS
BOURNEVALE RD
ASHLAKE RD
STANTHORPE RD
STANTHORPE CL
BRAY CT
MADEIRA RD
ST ANSELM'S CT
GRASMERE RD
OAKDALE RD
BEECHCROFT CL
BEECHCROFT MANS
HOPTON RD
STANEDGE CT
RUTFORD RD
FARNAN RD
POLWORTH RD
RUSSELL CT
THRALE ALMHOS
NEWLANDS CT
ALBERT CARR GDNS
LEITHCOTE GDNS
LEITHCOTE PATH
MILFORD MEWS
PEREGRINE CT
HARBOROUGH RD
CULVERHOUSE GDNS
CONIFER GDNS
LEIGH ORCHARD CL
IVYDAY GR
Dunraven Sch
Sunnyhill Prim Sch
NAMBA ROY CL
VALLEY RD
WELL CL
FRANCIS BARBER CL
SPRINGWELL CL
Allot Gdns
VALLEYFIELD RD
STRATHDALE
Bishop Thomas Grant RC Sec Sch
BELLTREES GR
HENRY TATE MEWS
BENHURST LA
BENHURST CT
NORMAN CT
DEERHURST RD
MINEHEAD RD
HILL HOUSE RD
MAPLE MEWS
CAROLINE CT
JOHNSON CL
SAMUEL JOHNSON CL
CURTIS FIELD RD
SOUTH OAK RD
CAREW HO
Julians Prim Sch
ETHERSTONE GN
ETHERSTONE RD
FAWCETT CL
SPRINGWELL RD
NORMINGTON CL
LEIGHAM COURT RD
ST JULIAN'S CL
VENITA MANOR
ROCKHAMPTON RD
CHESTNUT CL
CHARWOOD
Sp Gd
ST PETER'S GDNS
IVYMOUNT RD
GLENNIE RD
EGREMONT RD
CHICHESTER MEWS
UFFINGTON RD
CANTERBURY GR
DODBROOKE RD
SELSDON RD
THURLESTONE RD
HAINTHORPE RD
FRANKLIN CL
PRIORESS RD
YEOMAN CL
NETTLEFOLD PL
WOLFINGTON RD
SAINTS CL
THURLBY RD
ST JULIAN'S FARM RD
THORNLAW RD
LAMBERHURST RD
GREENHURST RD
LEAF GR
ILEX WAY
ESAM WAY
WINTON WAY
TRUSLOVE RD
LAKEVIEW RD
CROWN LANE GDNS
MONARCH MEWS
CASEWICK RD
TREDWELL RD
CHEVIOT RD
CHEVIOT GDNS
ROXBURGH RD
BEWLYS RD
ST VINCENT CL
CEDAR TREE GR
LINDWAY
EDGE POINT CL
Tenn Cts
BEADMAN ST
BEADMAN PL
KNIGHT'S HILL SQ
ERNEST
ROTHSCHILD
CHAPEL
MILLHOUSE
EDEN RD
DARLINGTON RD
DASSETT
Recn Gd
FURNEAUX
HOLDERNESS
A214
REGENT CT
St Joseph's RC Coll
CROWN PAR
CROWN POINT
Crown Lane Prim Sch
JERVISTON GDNS
St Andrews RC Prim Sch
Horse Ride
1 ELPHINSTONE CT
2 RIDLEY CT
3 BLADON CT
4 COMMONSIDE CT
5 SANDERS HO
6 BYRON CL
Ice Rink
LEWIN RD
LEWIN CT
SOMERVILLE CT
BARROW RD
PATHFIELD RD
ELLORA RD
FERRERS RD
WESTWELL RD
WESTWELL ROAD APP
NORTHANGER RD
Superstore
Immanuel Sch
VOSS CT
BOSCOMBE GDNS
CHARLES MILLS CT
BALDRY GDNS
COPLEY PK
BRAXTED PK
CEDARVILLE GDNS
HEYBRIDGE AVE
RYAN CT
COULTHURST CT
BUCKLEIGH RD
KEMPSHOTT RD
THE COURTS
PENISTONE RD
TANKERVILLE RD
FARNINGHAM CT
WILMINGTON CT
GUILDERSFIELD RD
ARRAGON GDNS
HILLDOWN CT
DOUGLAS ROBINSON CT
HILLDOWN RD
FONTAINE RD
HEATHDENE RD
ST LEONARD'S WLK
STRATHBROOK RD
BRIAR AVE
Lambeth
Croydon
RYECROFT RD
Bwg Gn
JAWAHAR BAGH
HOLLIES CL
GIBSON'S HILL
AVERIL GR
ASTON PL
LEAFIELD CL
HOLLMAN GDNS
ARNULL'S RD
PRESTON RD
GRECIAN CRES
QUEEN MARY RD
Pl Fld
HAVISHAM
THE PINES
DICKENS WOOD CL
WHITE LO
BIGGIN HILL
COVINGTON WAY
COVINGTON GDNS
ARKELL GR
CRESCENT WAY
THE CHASE
HILLCOTE AVE
GROVELAND AVE
BEAUFORT GDNS
COURTLAND AVE
LINKS GDNS
CHRISTIAN FIELDS
NORBURY HILL
BIGGINWOOD RD
CROFT RD
NORBURY CL
ST OSWALD'S RD
VIRGINIA RD
ELLISON RD
RAMA CL
GLENCAIRN RD
HEPWORTH RD
ROCHESTER CL
MARQUEEN TOWERS
DANBROOK RD
COLMER RD
HERMITAGE LA
GRANVILLE GDNS
HEATHERSET GDNS
KUALA GDNS
HAREFIELD RD
Pav
PARK RD
BODIAM RD
SHERWOOD AVE
HAWKHURST RD
WOODMANSTERNE RD
RUNNYMEDE CRES
ACACIA RD
LACROSSE WAY
SOUTHBROOK RD
Norbury Manor Girl's High Sch
WILLOWTREE WAY
GOLF CL
KENSINGTON AVE
Kensington Avenue Jun & Inf Schs
Pl Fld
Sp Gd
New Stanford Prim Sch
Norbury Manor Prim Sch
COLEBROOK RD
BISHOPS PARK RD
ROCHE RD
FAIRVIEW RD
UPWOOD RD
LLOYD AVE
ABINGDON RD
CROINDENE RD
OAKHILL RD
SCOTT CL
THE MEWS
ST HELEN'S CRES
ST HELEN'S RD
HAWTHORN AVE
FLORIDA RD
BRICKFIELD RD
MARYLAND RD
GEORGIA RD
BUCKINGHAM AVE
BUCKINGHAM GDNS
NORBURY AVE
FARM RD
MANOR RD
WESTMINSTER AVE
TURLE RD
STANFORD RD
BENETT GDNS
ISHAM RD
NORTON GDNS
SEMLEY RD
BAVANT RD
PALMERS RD
CRAIGNISH AVE
NORBURY TRAD EST
NORBURY CRES
HIGHBURY AVE
HATCH RD
TYLECROFT RD
GRANDEN RD
NEWLANDS RD
TISBURY RD
DARCY RD
BROCKENHURST AVE
BURLEY CL
LYNDHURST AVE
NORTHBOROUGH RD
NORBURY COURT RD
OSPREY CT
SOLENT CT
KINTYRE CL
Tenn Cts
BEATRICE AVE
Liby
BEECH RD
ELGAR AVE
NORBURY RISE
NORBURY CROSS
POLLARDS WOOD RD
POLLARDS HILL N
POLLARDS CRES
HILL DR
SOMERSET GDNS
SHIRLEY CT
ARDERN AVE
MELROSE AVE
EDERLINE AVE
DUNBAR AVE
DALMENY AVE
KILMARTIN AVE
STRATHYRE AVE
BRAEMAR AVE
COUNTY RD
AOSTLE WAY
PARCHMORE WAY
WINDSOR RD
St James The Great RC Prim Sch
CAMDEN GDNS
CAMDEN WAY
SANDFIELD RD
Tamworth Manor Sch
William Morris
Recn Gd
PO
P
H

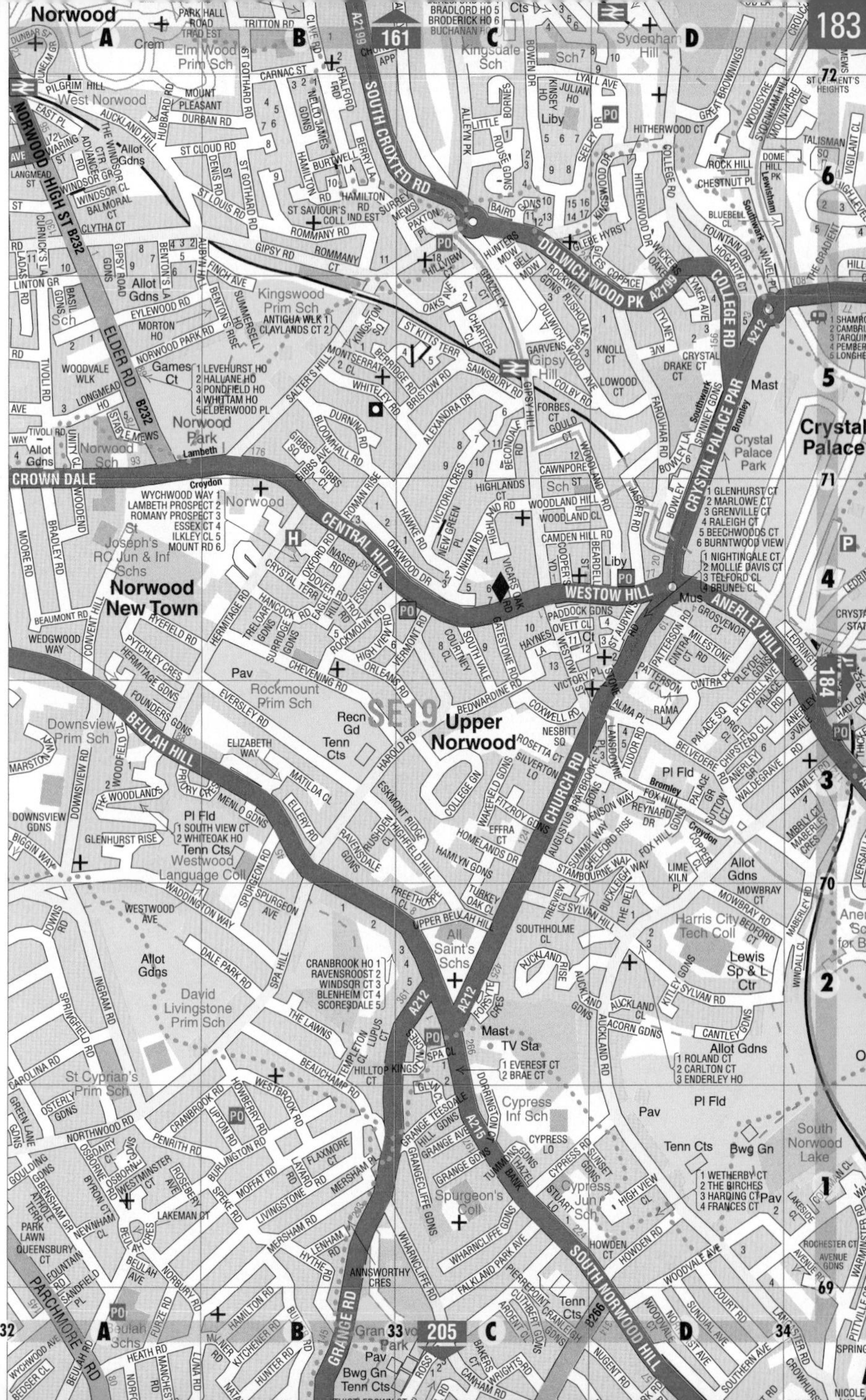

Norwood
Norwood New Town
Upper Norwood
Crystal Palace
SE19
West Norwood
Sydenham Hill
Gipsy Hill
South Norwood Lake
CROWN DALE
CENTRAL HILL
WESTOW HILL
BEULAH HILL
CHURCH RD
CRYSTAL PALACE PAR
ANERLEY HILL
SOUTH CROXTED RD
DULWICH WOOD PK
COLLEGE RD
NORWOOD HIGH ST B232
ELDER RD
GIPSY RD
SOUTH NORWOOD HILL
GRANGE RD
PARCHMORE RD
161
184
205

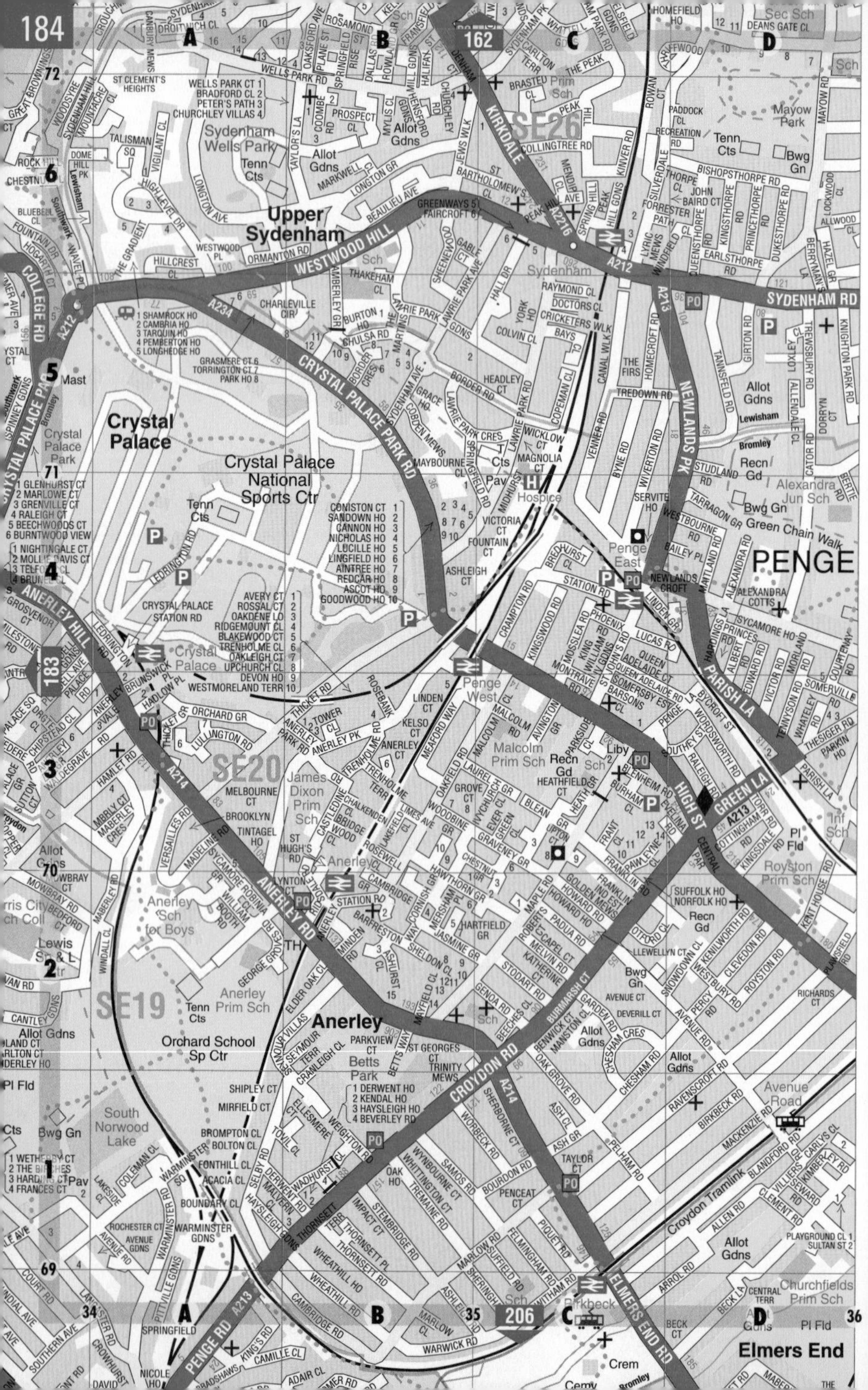

162
183
206
SE26
SE20
SE19
Upper Sydenham
Sydenham Wells Park
Sydenham
Crystal Palace
Crystal Palace Park
Crystal Palace National Sports Ctr
Penge
Penge East
Penge West
Anerley
Elmers End
Birkbeck
Mayow Park
Betts Park
South Norwood Lake
Croydon Tramlink
Avenue Road
James Dixon Prim Sch
Malcolm Prim Sch
Anerley Sch for Boys
Anerley Prim Sch
Orchard School Sp Ctr
Alexandra Jun Sch
Royston Prim Sch
Churchfields Prim Sch
Green Chain Walk
Hospice
Westwood Hill
Sydenham Rd
Kirkdale
Crystal Palace Park Rd
Crystal Palace Parade
College Rd
Anerley Hill
Anerley Rd
Croydon Rd
Penge Rd
Elmers End Rd
Newlands Pk
Parish La
High St
Green La
Lewisham
Bromley
Southwark
Croydon
A212
A213
A214
A234
A2216
34
35
36
69
70
71
72

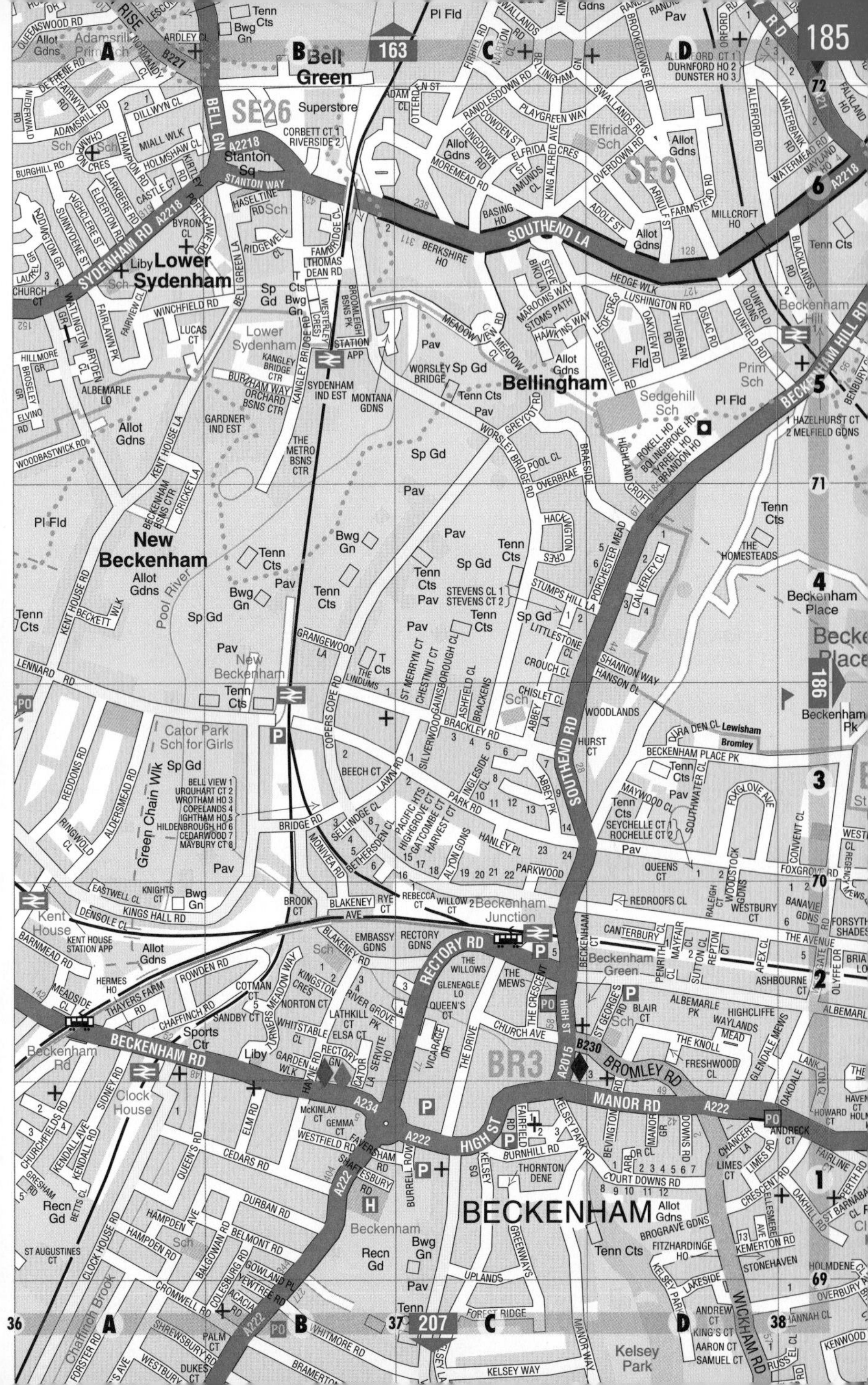
163
Bell Green
SE26
Superstore
Stanton Sq
STANTON WAY
SYDENHAM RD
A2218
BELL GN
Lower Sydenham
SOUTHEND LA
SE6
Elfrida Sch
Bellingham
Sedgehill Sch
BECKENHAM HILL RD
Beckenham Hill
Lower Sydenham
Sydenham Ind Est
New Beckenham
Pool River
Beckenham Place
Beckenham Pk
186
Lewisham
Bromley
SOUTHEND RD
Cator Park Sch for Girls
Green Chain Wlk
Kent House
Beckenham Junction
RECTORY RD
Beckenham Green
BR3
BECKENHAM RD
Clock House
Beckenham Rd
B230
BROMLEY RD
MANOR RD
A222
A234
A2015
HIGH ST
BECKENHAM
Beckenham
Recn Gd
Tenn Cts
Kelsey Park
WICKHAM RD
KELSEY WAY
Chaffinch Brook
207
36
37
38
A
B
C
D
1
2
3
4
5
6
69
70
71
72

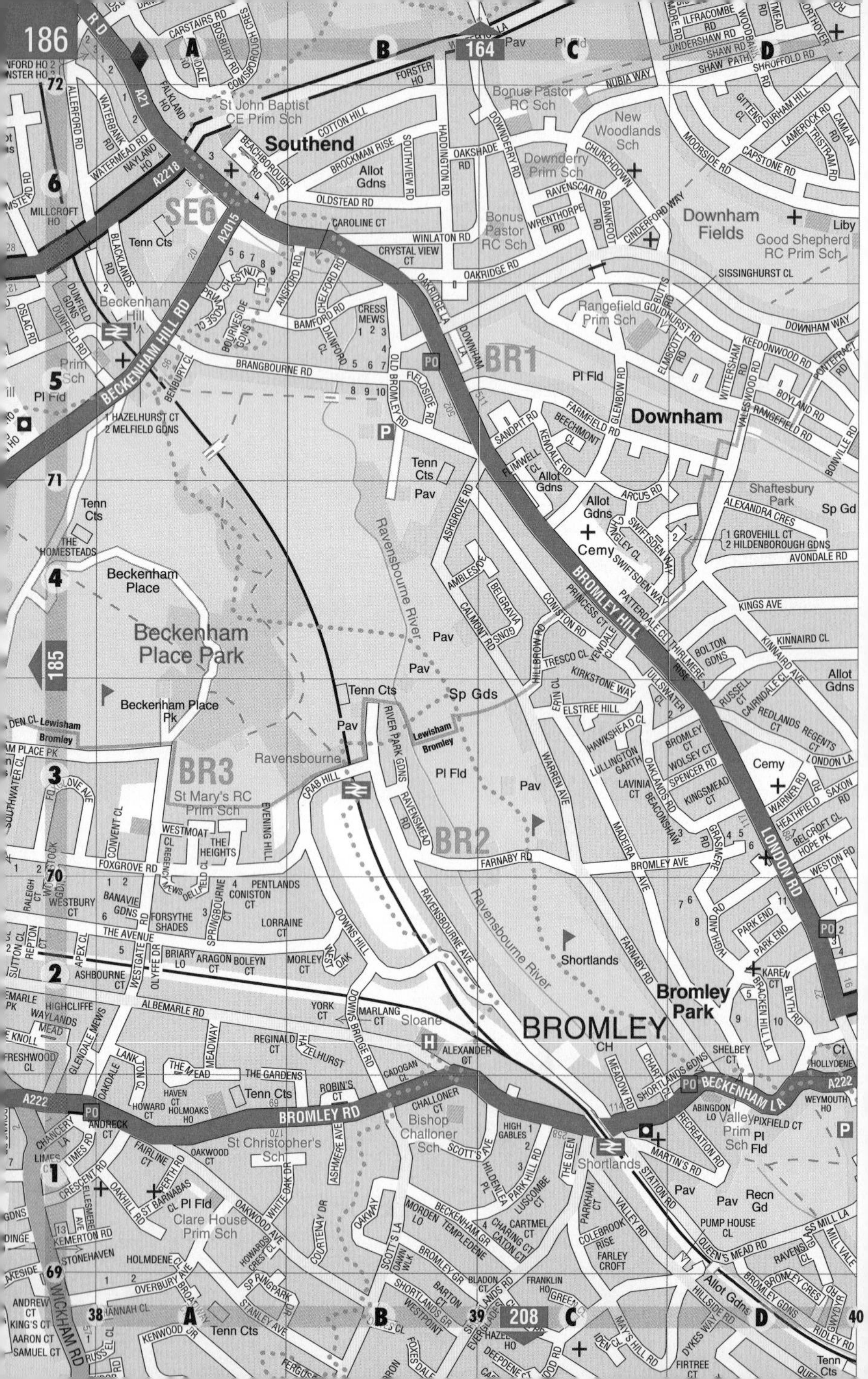
A
B
164
C
D
Southend
SE6
Downham Fields
Downham
BR1
Beckenham Place Park
Beckenham Place
Ravensbourne River
BR3
BR2
BROMLEY
Bromley Park
Shortlands
185
BROMLEY HILL
LONDON RD
BECKENHAM HILL RD
BROMLEY RD
BECKENHAM LA
WICKHAM RD
St John Baptist CE Prim Sch
Bonus Pastor RC Sch
New Woodlands Sch
Downderry Prim Sch
Good Shepherd RC Prim Sch
Rangefield Prim Sch
St Mary's RC Prim Sch
Bishop Challoner Sch
St Christopher's Sch
Clare House Prim Sch
Valley Prim Sch
Beckenham Hill
Ravensbourne
Sloane
Shaftesbury Park
208
6
5
4
3
2
1
72
71
70
69
38
39
40

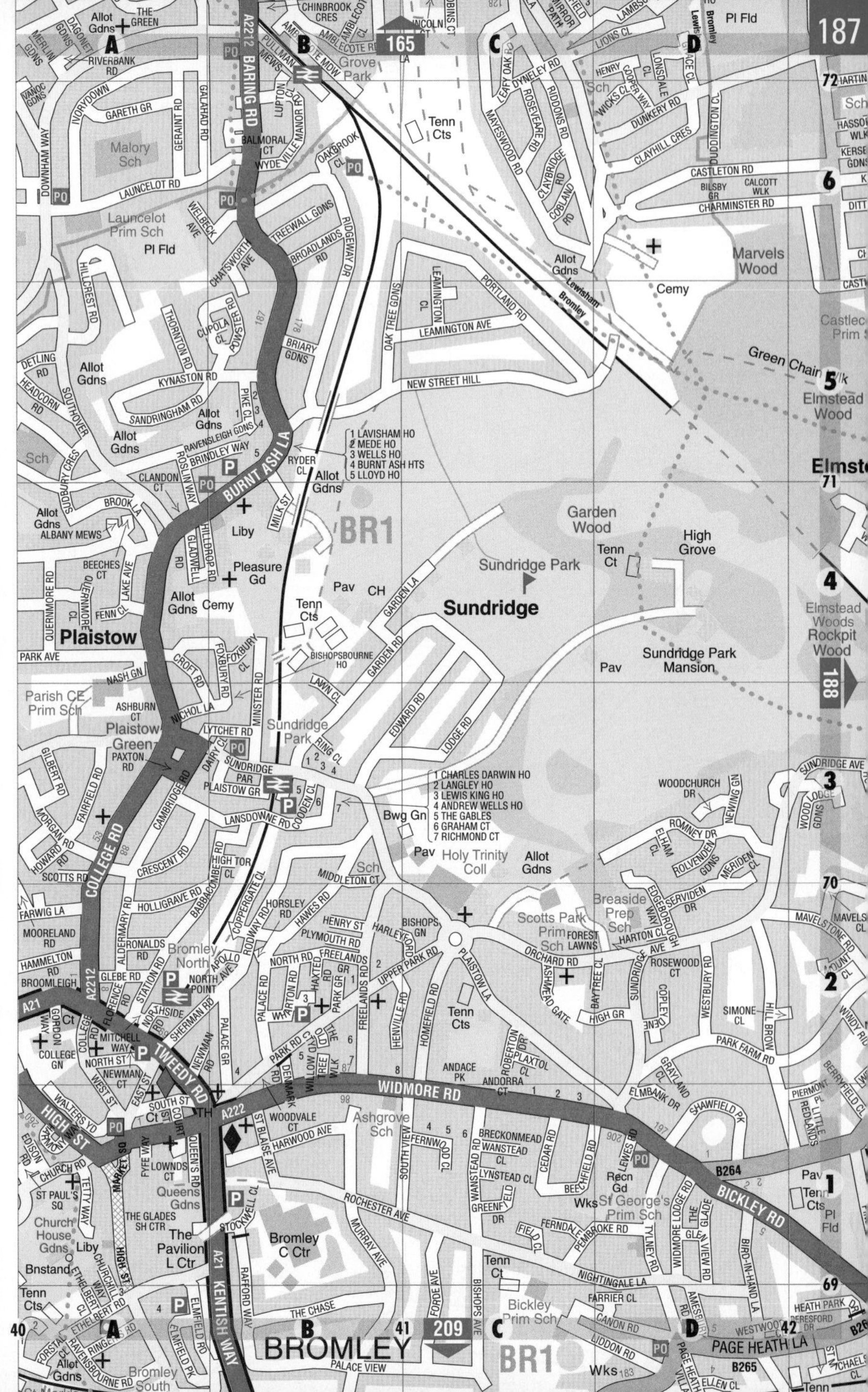
Plaistow
Sundridge
Sundridge Park
BR1
BROMLEY
Bromley North
Plaistow Green
Sundridge Park Mansion
Garden Wood
High Grove
Marvels Wood
Elmstead Wood
Elmstead Woods Rockpit Wood
Holy Trinity Coll
Bromley C Ctr
The Pavilion L Ctr
Queens Gdns
Church House Gdns
Launcelot Prim Sch
Malory Sch
Parish CE Prim Sch
Scotts Park Prim Sch
Breaside Prep Sch
Ashgrove Sch
Bickley Prim Sch
St George's Prim Sch
Grove Park
Bromley South
BARING RD
BURNT ASH LA
COLLEGE RD
TWEEDY RD
KENTISH WAY
HIGH ST
WIDMORE RD
BICKLEY RD
PAGE HEATH LA
PLAISTOW LA
NEW STREET HILL
LEAMINGTON AVE
PORTLAND RD
GARDEN RD
EDWARD RD
LODGE RD
SUNDRIDGE AVE
PARK FARM RD
NIGHTINGALE LA
ROCHESTER AVE
UPPER PARK RD
LANSDOWNE RD
CASTLETON RD
CHARMINSTER RD
CLAYHILL CRES
LAUNCELOT RD
1 LAVISHAM HO
2 MEDE HO
3 WELLS HO
4 BURNT ASH HTS
5 LLOYD HO
1 CHARLES DARWIN HO
2 LANGLEY HO
3 LEWIS KING HO
4 ANDREW WELLS HO
5 THE GABLES
6 GRAHAM CT
7 RICHMOND CT
165
188
209

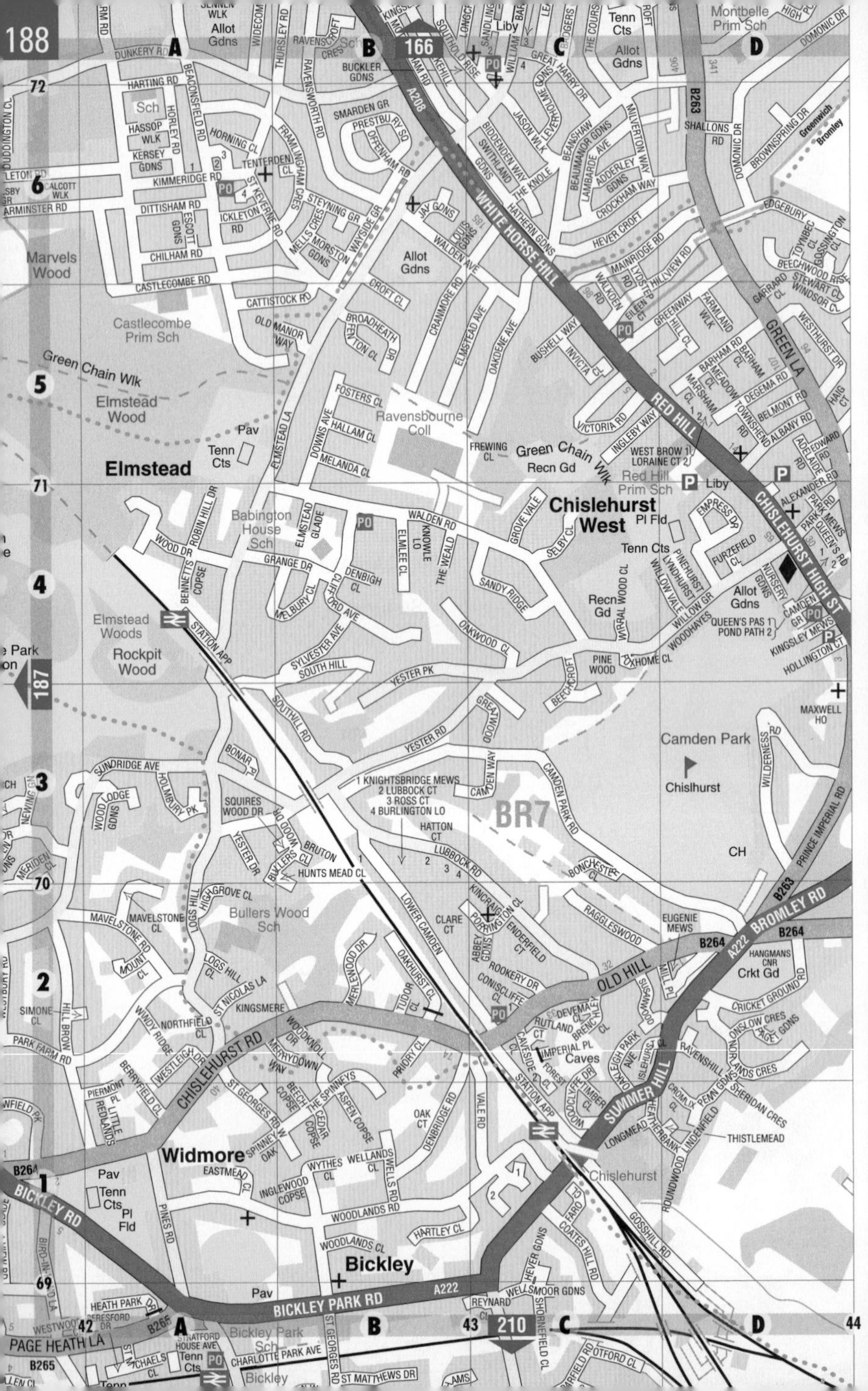

166
210
187
Elmstead
Chislehurst West
Widmore
Bickley
Elmstead Woods
Rockpit Wood
Marvels Wood
Elmstead Wood
Castlecombe Prim Sch
Green Chain Wlk
Ravensbourne Coll
Babington House Sch
Bullers Wood Sch
Camden Park
Chislhurst
Red Hill Prim Sch
Bickley Park Sch
Chislehurst
Caves
BR7
WHITE HORSE HILL
RED HILL
CHISLEHURST HIGH ST
GREEN LA
CHISLEHURST RD
BICKLEY PARK RD
BICKLEY RD
SUMMER HILL
OLD HILL
BROMLEY RD
PRINCE IMPERIAL RD
YESTER RD
YESTER PK
WALDEN RD
CAMDEN PARK RD
LOWER CAMDEN
ELMSTEAD LA
PAGE HEATH LA

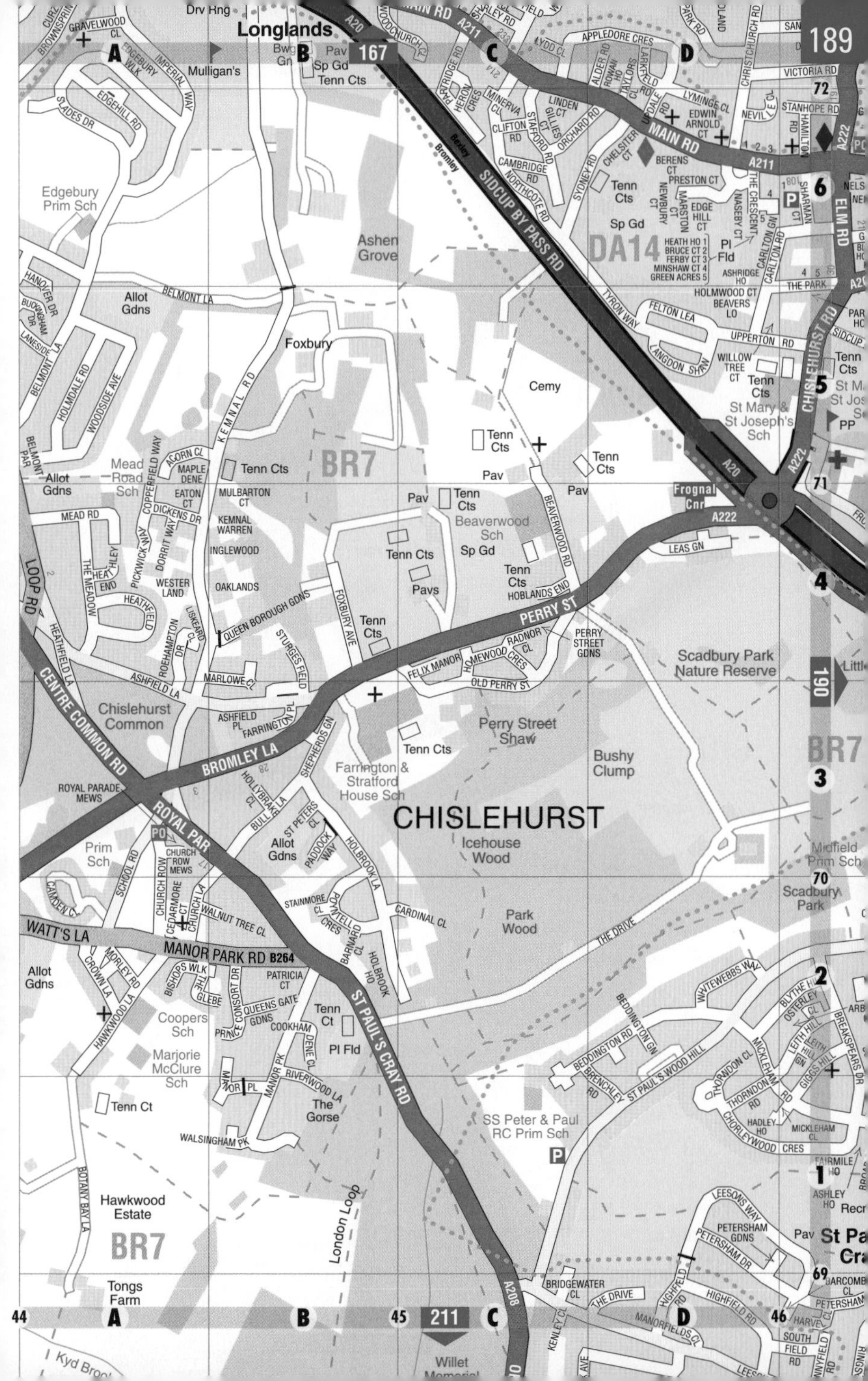
Longlands
Mulligan's
Edgebury Prim Sch
Ashen Grove
BR7
DA14
Foxbury
Allot Gdns
Cemy
Mead Road Sch
Beaverwood Sch
Frognal Cnr
Scadbury Park Nature Reserve
Chislehurst Common
Perry Street Shaw
Bushy Clump
Farrington & Stratford House Sch
CHISLEHURST
Icehouse Wood
Park Wood
Midfield Prim Sch
Scadbury Park
Coopers Sch
Marjorie McClure Sch
The Gorse
SS Peter & Paul RC Prim Sch
Hawkwood Estate
Tongs Farm
London Loop
St Mary & St Joseph's Sch
SIDCUP BY PASS RD
PERRY ST
BROMLEY LA
CENTRE COMMON RD
ROYAL PAR
MANOR PARK RD B264
WATT'S LA
ST PAUL'S CRAY RD
KEMNAL RD
MAIN RD
CHISLEHURST RD
ELM RD
BELMONT LA
LOOP RD
THE DRIVE
ST PAUL'S WOOD HILL
Willet Memorial
Kyd Brook
167
190
211
44
45
46
69
70
71
72

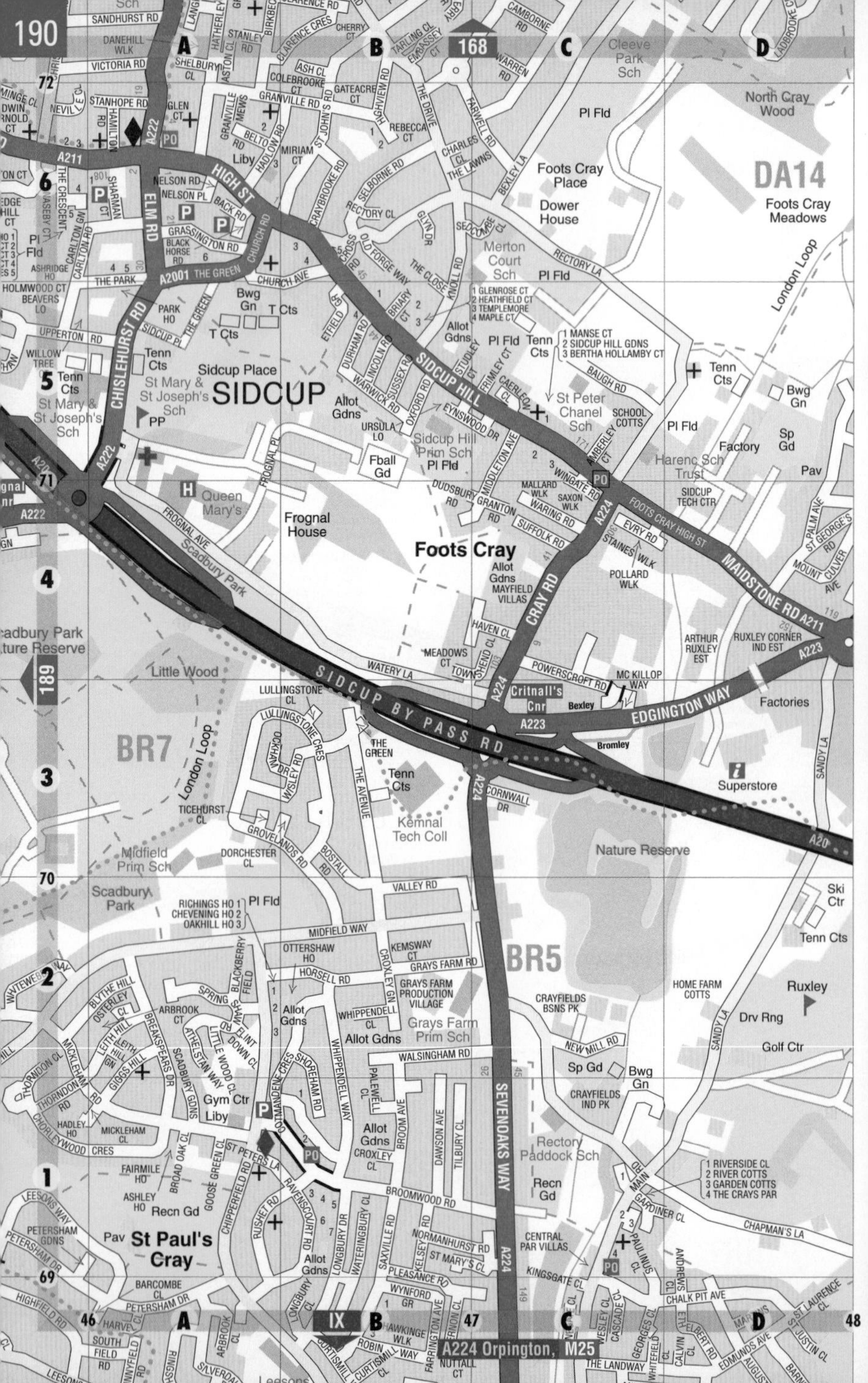

A
B
C
D
168
189
IX
46
47
48
72
71
70
69
6
5
4
3
2
1
SIDCUP
Foots Cray
St Paul's Cray
DA14
BR7
BR5
SANDHURST RD
DANEHILL WLK
VICTORIA RD
STANHOPE RD
NEVILLE CL
HAMILTON RD
A222
A211
HIGH ST
ELM RD
NELSON RD
NELSON PL
BACK RD
GRASSINGTON RD
BLACK HORSE RD
CHURCH RD
A2001 THE GREEN
CHURCH AVE
THE PARK
THE CRESCENT
CARLTON GN
CARLTON RD
SHARMAN CT
NASEBY CT
ASHRIDGE HO
HOLMWOOD CT
BEAVERS LO
UPPERTON RD
WILLOW TREE CT
CHISLEHURST RD
SIDCUP PL
PARK HO
THE GREEN
Tenn Cts
T Cts
Bwg Gn
Sidcup Place
St Mary & St Joseph's Sch
PP
Queen Mary's
Frognal House
FROGNAL PL
FROGNAL AVE
Scadbury Park
Scadbury Park Nature Reserve
Little Wood
London Loop
A20
A222
LANGDON
HATHERLEY
STANLEY RD
ASTON CL
SHELBURY CL
CLARENCE CRES
CLARENCE RD
BIRKBECK
GLEN CT
GRANVILLE MEWS
BELTON RD
HADLOW RD
Liby
PO
COLEBROOKE CT
ASH CL
GRANVILLE RD
MIRIAM CT
ST JOHN'S RD
CRAYBROOKE RD
GATEACRE CT
HIGHVIEW RD
CHERRY CT
TARLING CL
EMBASSY CT
THE DRIVE
REBECCA CT
CHARLES CL
THE LAWNS
SELBORNE RD
RECTORY CL
GLYN DR
OLD FORGE WAY
THE CLOSE
KNOLL RD
SEDCOMBE CL
CROSS RD
BRIARY CT
ETFIELD
DURHAM RD
LINCOLN RD
SUSSEX RD
WARWICK RD
OXFORD RD
SIDCUP HILL
EYNSWOOD DR
URSULA LO
Allot Gdns
Sidcup Hill Prim Sch
Pl Fld
Fball Gd
STUDLEY CT
FRIMLEY CT
CAERLEON CL
MIDDLETON AVE
DUDSBURY RD
GRANTON RD
CAMBORNE RD
WARREN RD
FARWELL RD
BEXLEY LA
Cleeve Park Sch
Foots Cray Place
Dower House
Merton Court Sch
RECTORY LA
1 GLENROSE CT
2 HEATHFIELD CT
3 TEMPLEMORE
4 MAPLE CT
1 MANSE CT
2 SIDCUP HILL GDNS
3 BERTHA HOLLAMBY CT
BAUGH RD
St Peter Chanel Sch
SCHOOL COTTS
AMBERLEY CT
WINGATE RD
MALLARD WLK
SAXON WLK
WARING RD
SUFFOLK RD
EVRY RD
STAINES WLK
POLLARD WLK
A224
CRAY RD
FOOTS CRAY HIGH ST
MAIDSTONE RD A211
North Cray Wood
Foots Cray Meadows
LADBROOKE CRES
Factory
Harenc Sch Trust
SIDCUP TECH CTR
Sp Gd
Pav
ST PALM AVE
ST GEORGE'S RD
MOUNT CULVER AVE
ARTHUR RUXLEY EST
RUXLEY CORNER IND EST
A223
Factories
EDGINGTON WAY
MC KILLOP WAY
POWERSCROFT RD
Critnall's Cnr
Bexley
Bromley
Allot Gdns
MAYFIELD VILLAS
HAVEN CL
MEADOWS CT
TOWNSHEND CL
WATERY LA
SIDCUP BY PASS RD
LULLINGSTONE CL
LULLINGSTONE CRES
OCKHAM DR
WISLEY RD
THE GREEN
THE AVENUE
Kemnal Tech Coll
CORNWALL DR
TICEHURST CL
GROVELANDS RD
BOSTALL RD
DORCHESTER CL
Midfield Prim Sch
Superstore
Nature Reserve
SANDY LA
Ski Ctr
Tenn Cts
Ruxley
Drv Rng
Golf Ctr
HOME FARM COTTS
VALLEY RD
RICHINGS HO 1
CHEVENING HO 2
OAKHILL HO 3
MIDFIELD WAY
OTTERSHAW HO
KEMSWAY CT
GRAYS FARM RD
HORSELL RD
CROXLEY GN
GRAYS FARM PRODUCTION VILLAGE
WHIPPENDELL CL
Grays Farm Prim Sch
WHIPPENDELL WAY
SEVENOAKS WAY
CRAYFIELDS BSNS PK
NEW MILL RD
Sp Gd
Bwg Gn
CRAYFIELDS IND PK
WALSINGHAM RD
PALEWELL CL
BROOM AVE
DAWSON AVE
TILBURY CL
BLYTHE HILL
OSTERLEY CL
SPRING SHAW RD
BLACKBERRY FIELD
ARBROOK CT
ATHELSTAN WAY
FLINT DOWN CL
LITTLE WOOD CL
BREAKSPEARS DR
SCADBURY GDNS
LEITH HILL
LEITH HILL GN
GIGGS HILL
MICKLEHAM CL
MICKLEHAM RD
THORNDON CL
THORNDON RD
HADLEY HO
CHORLEYWOOD CRES
Gym Ctr
Liby
COTMANDENE CRES
SHOREHAM RD
ST PETERS LA
BROAD OAK CL
GOOSE GREEN CL
CHIPPERFIELD RD
RUSHET RD
RAVENSCOURT RD
FAIRMILE HO
ASHLEY HO
Recn Gd
CROXLEY CL
BROOMWOOD RD
LONGBURY DR
WATERINGBURY CL
SAXVILLE RD
KELSEY RD
NORMANHURST RD
ST MARY'S CL
PLEASANCE RD
WYNFORD GR
HAWKINGE WLK
FARRINGTON AVE
ROBIN WAY
CURTISMILL CL
CURTISMILL WAY
NUTTALL CT
LONGBURY CL
Rectory Paddock Sch
Recn Gd
CENTRAL PAR VILLAS
KINGSGATE CL
MAIN RD
GARDINER CL
PAULINUS CL
1 RIVERSIDE CL
2 RIVER COTTS
3 GARDEN COTTS
4 THE CRAYS PAR
CHAPMAN'S LA
ANDREWS CL
CHALK PIT AVE
ELBERT RD
CALVIN CL
WHITEFIELD CL
GEORGES CL
CASCADE CL
WESLEY CL
EDMUNDS AVE
ST LAURENCE CL
ST JUSTIN CL
THE LANDWAY
LEESONS WAY
PETERSHAM GDNS
PETERSHAM DR
BARCOMBE CL
HIGHFIELD RD
SOUTH FIELD RD
ARBROOK CL
Leesons
A224 Orpington, M25

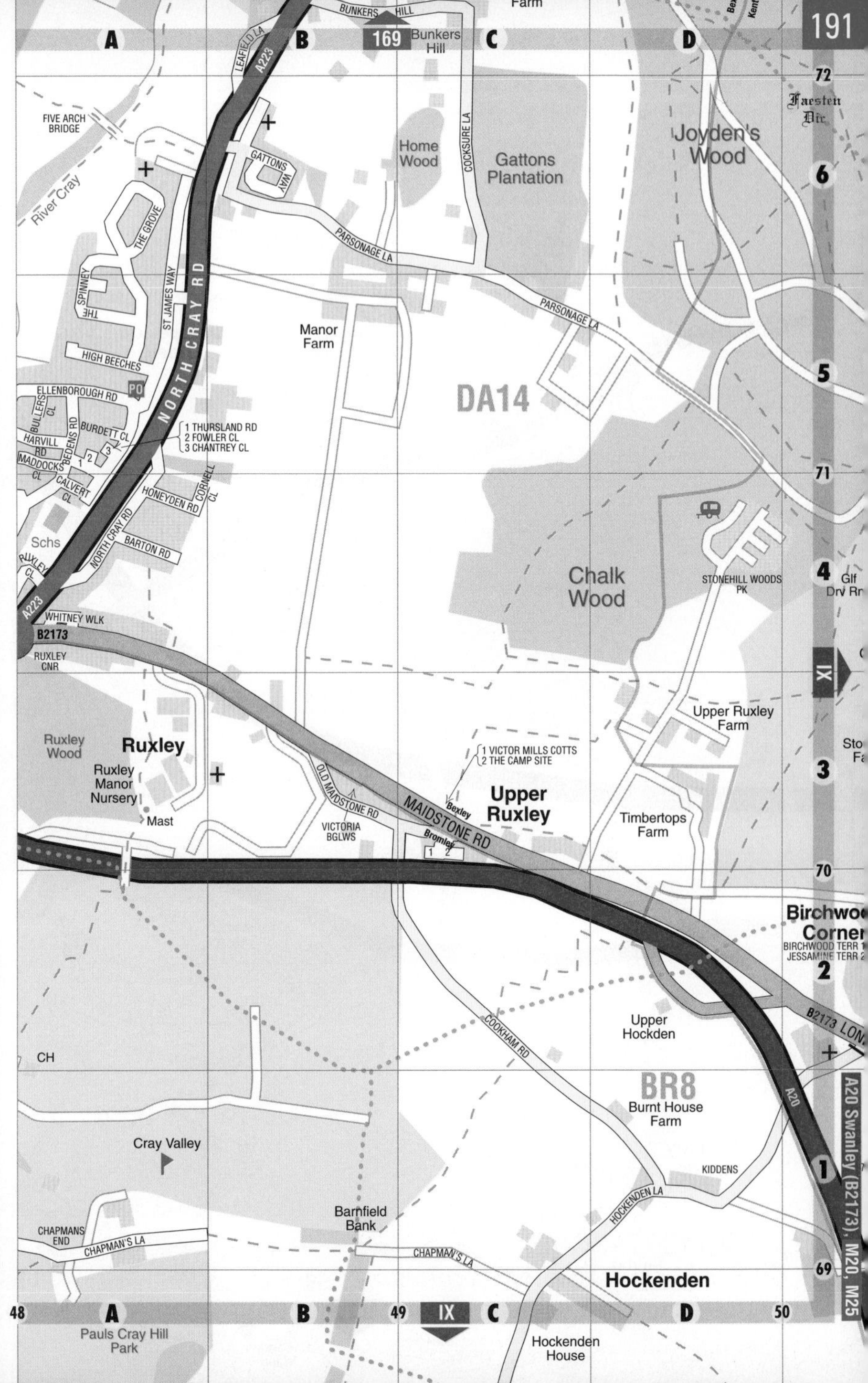

A
B
169
Bunkers Hill
C
D
BUNKERS HILL
LEAFIELD LA
A223
FIVE ARCH BRIDGE
River Cray
GATTONS WAY
Home Wood
COCKSURE LA
Gattons Plantation
Joyden's Wood
Faesten Dic
THE GROVE
PARSONAGE LA
THE SPINNEY
ST JAMES WAY
NORTH CRAY RD
Manor Farm
HIGH BEECHES
DA14
ELLENBOROUGH RD
PO
BULLERS CL
BEDENS RD
BURDETT CL
HARVILL RD
MADDOCKS CL
CALVERT CL
1 THURSLAND RD
2 FOWLER CL
3 CHANTREY CL
HONEYDEN RD
CORNELL CL
Schs
NORTH CRAY RD
BARTON RD
RUXLEY CL
Chalk Wood
STONEHILL WOODS PK
Glf Drv Rn
WHITNEY WLK
B2173
RUXLEY CNR
IX
Upper Ruxley Farm
Ruxley Wood
Ruxley
Ruxley Manor Nursery
Mast
1 VICTOR MILLS COTTS
2 THE CAMP SITE
Upper Ruxley
OLD MAIDSTONE RD
VICTORIA BGLWS
MAIDSTONE RD
Bexley
Bromley
Timbertops Farm
Birchwood Corner
BIRCHWOOD TERR 1
JESSAMINE TERR 2
CH
COOKHAM RD
Upper Hockden
B2173 LON
BR8
Burnt House Farm
A20
A20 Swanley (B2173), M20, M25
Cray Valley
KIDDENS
HOCKENDEN LA
Barnfield Bank
CHAPMANS END
CHAPMAN'S LA
Hockenden
48
49
50
Pauls Cray Hill Park
Hockenden House
72
6
5
71
4
3
70
2
1
69

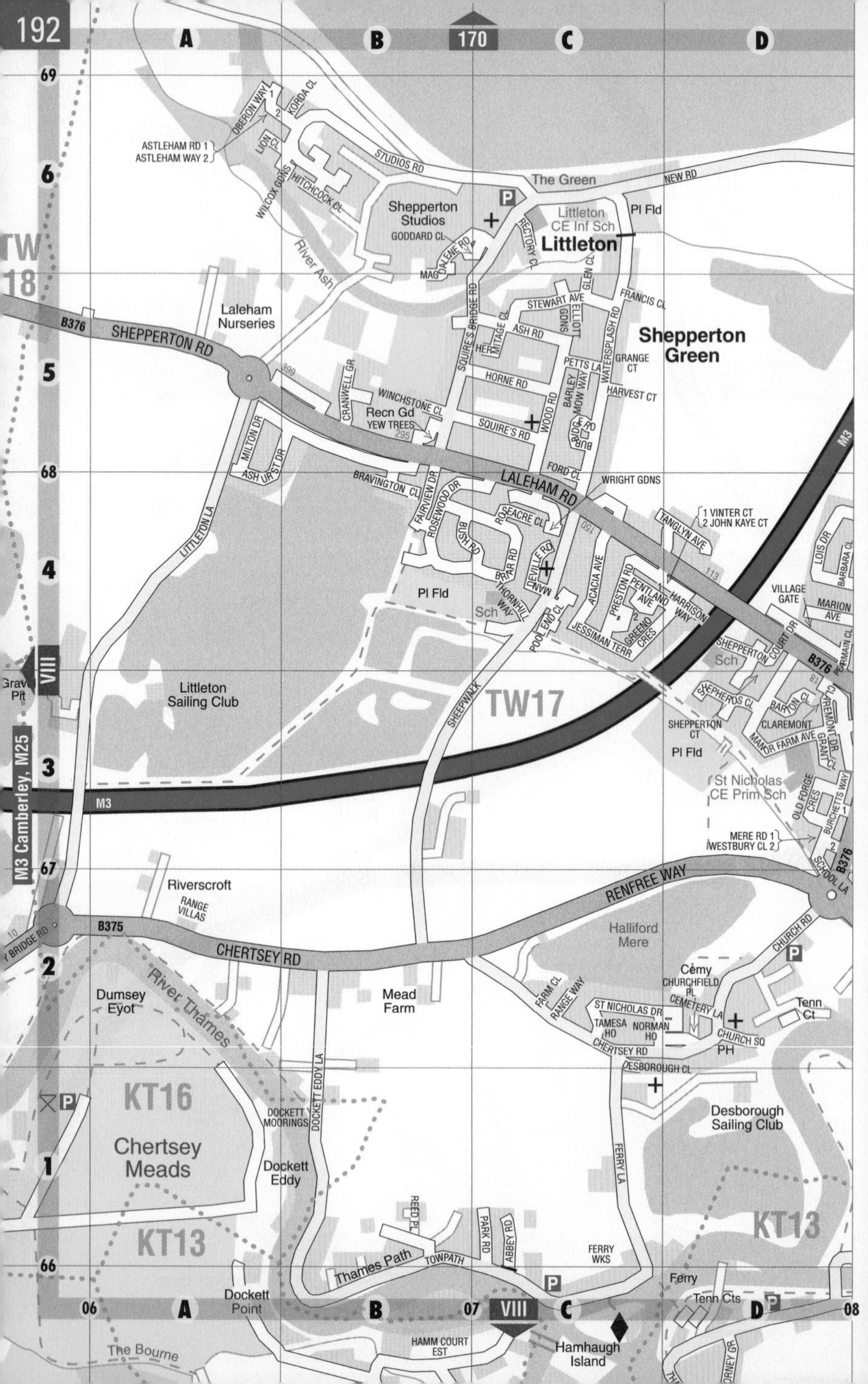

170
A
B
C
D
69
68
67
66
6
5
4
3
2
1
06
07
08
TW 18
ASTLEHAM RD 1
ASTLEHAM WAY 2
OBERON WAY
KORDA CL
LION CL
STUDIOS RD
WILCOX GDNS
HITCHCOCK CL
The Green
NEW RD
Shepperton Studios
GODDARD CL
DALENE RD
MAG
RECTORY CL
Littleton CE Inf Sch
Littleton
Pl Fld
River Ash
GLEN CL
FRANCIS CL
STEWART AVE
ELLIOTT GDNS
WATERSPLASH RD
Laleham Nurseries
B376
SHEPPERTON RD
SQUIRE'S BRIDGE RD
MITAGE CL
HERI
ASH RD
Shepperton Green
PETTS LA
BARLEY MOW WAY
GRANGE CT
HORNE RD
HARVEST CT
CRANWELL GR
WINCHSTONE CL
Recn Gd
YEW TREES
SQUIRE'S RD
WOOD RD
BURGE RD
MILTON DR
ASHURST DR
FORD CL
BRAVINGTON CL
FAIRVIEW DR
ROSEWOOD DR
LALEHAM RD
WRIGHT GDNS
ROSEACRE CL
1 VINTER CT
2 JOHN KAYE CT
TANGLYN AVE
LITTLETON LA
BUSH RD
BRIAR RD
DEVILLE RD
MAN
ACACIA AVE
PRESTON RD
PENTLAND AVE
HARRISON WAY
M3
LOIS DR
BARBARA CL
VILLAGE GATE
MARION AVE
Pl Fld
THORNHILL WAY
Sch
POOL END CL
JESSIMAN TERR
GREENO CRES
SHEPPERTON COURT DR
PERMAIN CL
VIII
Gravel Pit
Littleton Sailing Club
TW17
SHEPWALK
Sch
SHEPHERDS CL
BARTON CL
CLAREMONT
CLAREMONT DR
MANOR FARM AVE
GRANT CL
SHEPPERTON CT
Pl Fld
M3 Camberley, M25
M3
St Nicholas CE Prim Sch
OLD FORGE CRES
BURCHETTS WAY
MERE RD 1
WESTBURY CL 2
SCHOOL LA
Riverscroft
RANGE VILLAS
RENFREE WAY
BRIDGE RD
B375
CHERTSEY RD
Halliford Mere
CHURCH RD
Dumsey Eyot
River Thames
Mead Farm
FARM CL
RANGE WAY
Cemy
CHURCHFIELD PL
CEMETERY LA
Tenn Ct
ST NICHOLAS DR
TAMESA HO
NORMAN HO
CHERTSEY RD
CHURCH SQ
PH
DESBOROUGH CL
KT16
DOCKETT MOORINGS
DOCKETT EDDY LA
Desborough Sailing Club
Chertsey Meads
Dockett Eddy
FERRY LA
KT13
REED PL
PARK RD
ABBEY RD
KT13
FERRY WKS
Thames Path
TOWPATH
Ferry
Dockett Point
Tenn Cts
VIII
HAMM COURT EST
Hamhaugh Island
The Bourne
CORNEY GR

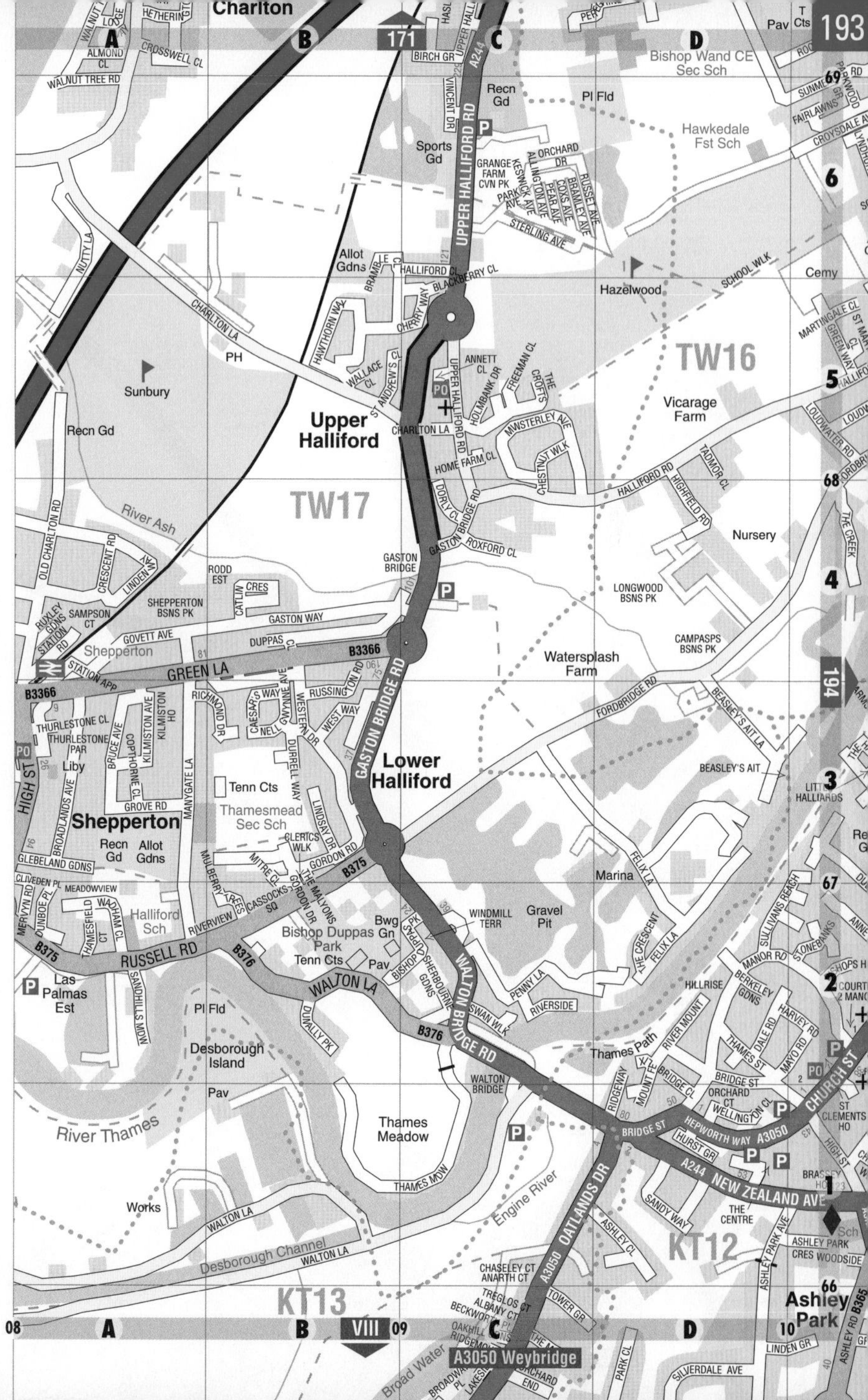

Charlton
171
A
B
C
D
Bishop Wand CE Sec Sch
Recn Gd
Pl Fld
Sports Gd
Hawkedale Fst Sch
UPPER HALLIFORD RD
A244
Allot Gdns
Hazelwood
Cemy
SCHOOL WLK
TW16
CHARLTON LA
PH
Sunbury
Recn Gd
Upper Halliford
TW17
Vicarage Farm
HALLIFORD RD
River Ash
Nursery
GASTON BRIDGE
GASTON BRIDGE RD
LONGWOOD BSNS PK
CAMPASPS BSNS PK
SHEPPERTON BSNS PK
GASTON WAY
GREEN LA
B3366
Shepperton
Watersplash Farm
FORDBRIDGE RD
194
Lower Halliford
Tenn Cts
Thamesmead Sec Sch
Shepperton
Recn Gd
Allot Gdns
Liby
HIGH ST
Marina
Gravel Pit
BEASLEY'S AIT
B375
RUSSELL RD
Halliford Sch
Bishop Duppas Park
Bwg Gn
Tenn Cts
Pav
WALTON LA
B376
WALTON BRIDGE RD
Las Palmas Est
Pl Fld
Desborough Island
Pav
Thames Path
WALTON BRIDGE
River Thames
Thames Meadow
BRIDGE ST
HEPWORTH WAY
A3050
NEW ZEALAND AVE
CHURCH ST
Works
Engine River
OATLANDS DR
Desborough Channel
KT12
KT13
Ashley Park
VIII
A3050 Weybridge
Broad Water
08
09
10
66
67
68
69
1
2
3
4
5
6

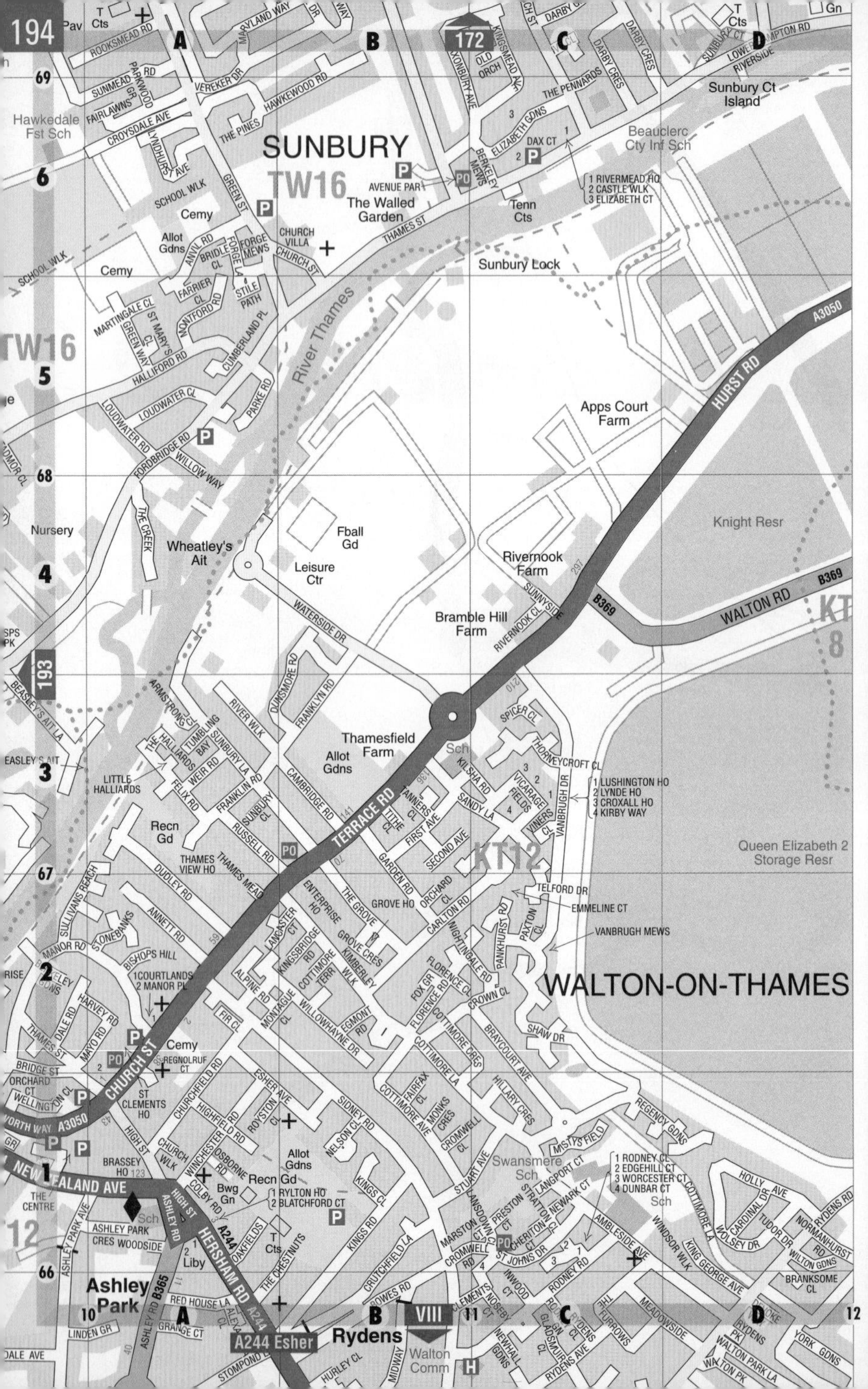
SUNBURY
TW16
The Walled Garden
Sunbury Lock
River Thames
Sunbury Ct Island
Beauclerc Cty Inf Sch
Hawkedale Fst Sch
Apps Court Farm
Knight Resr
Fball Gd
Leisure Ctr
Wheatley's Ait
Nursery
Rivernook Farm
Bramble Hill Farm
Thamesfield Farm
Allot Gdns
Recn Gd
KT12
Queen Elizabeth 2 Storage Resr
WALTON-ON-THAMES
Swansmere Sch
Ashley Park
Rydens
Walton Comm
HURST RD
TERRACE RD
WALTON RD
CHURCH ST
NEW ZEALAND AVE
HERSHAM RD
A244 Esher
172
193
VIII
1 RIVERMEAD HO
2 CASTLE WLK
3 ELIZABETH CT
1 LUSHINGTON HO
2 LYNDE HO
3 CROXALL HO
4 KIRBY WAY
1 RODNEY CL
2 EDGEHILL CT
3 WORCESTER CT
4 DUNBAR CT
1 RYLTON HO
2 BLATCHFORD CT
1 COURTLANDS
2 MANOR PL

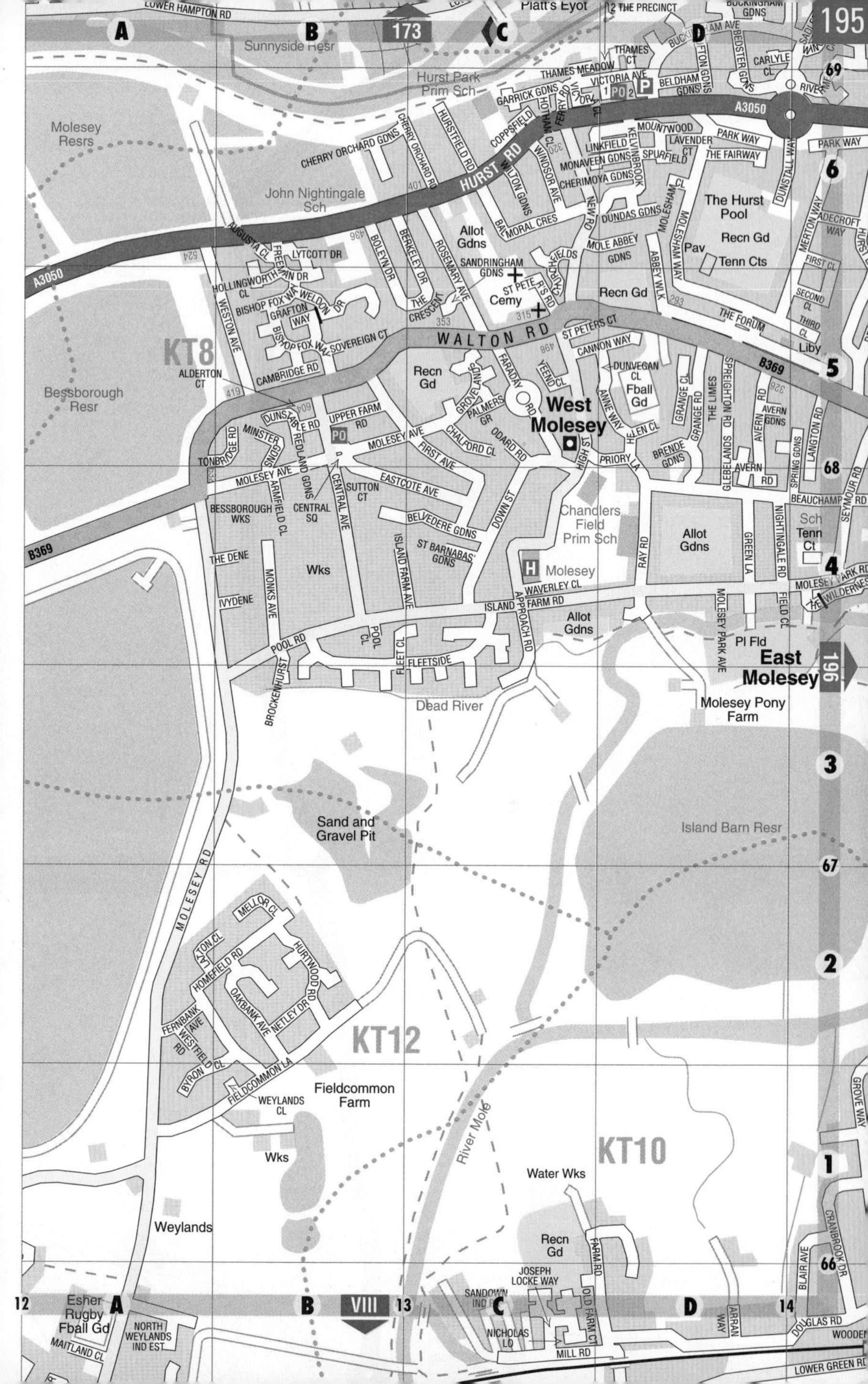

A
B
C
D
173
196
VIII
12
13
14
69
6
5
68
4
3
67
2
1
66
KT8
KT12
KT10
West Molesey
East Molesey
Platt's Eyot
Sunnyside Resr
Hurst Park Prim Sch
Molesey Resrs
John Nightingale Sch
Bessborough Resr
The Hurst Pool
Recn Gd
Pav
Tenn Cts
Allot Gdns
Cemy
Fball Gd
Chandlers Field Prim Sch
Molesey
Wks
Dead River
Molesey Pony Farm
Pl Fld
Sand and Gravel Pit
Island Barn Resr
Fieldcommon Farm
Weylands
Water Wks
River Mole
Esher Rugby Fball Gd
Liby
Sch
Tenn Ct
A3050
B369
HURST RD
WALTON RD
MOLESEY RD
LOWER HAMPTON RD
2 THE PRECINCT
THAMES MEADOW
VICTORIA AVE
BELDHAM GDNS
BUCKINGHAM AVE
CARLYLE CL
PARK WAY
THE FAIRWAY
DUNSTALL WAY
ISLAND FARM RD
MOLESEY AVE
HIGH ST
PRIORY LA
FIELDCOMMON LA
MILL RD
LOWER GREEN RD

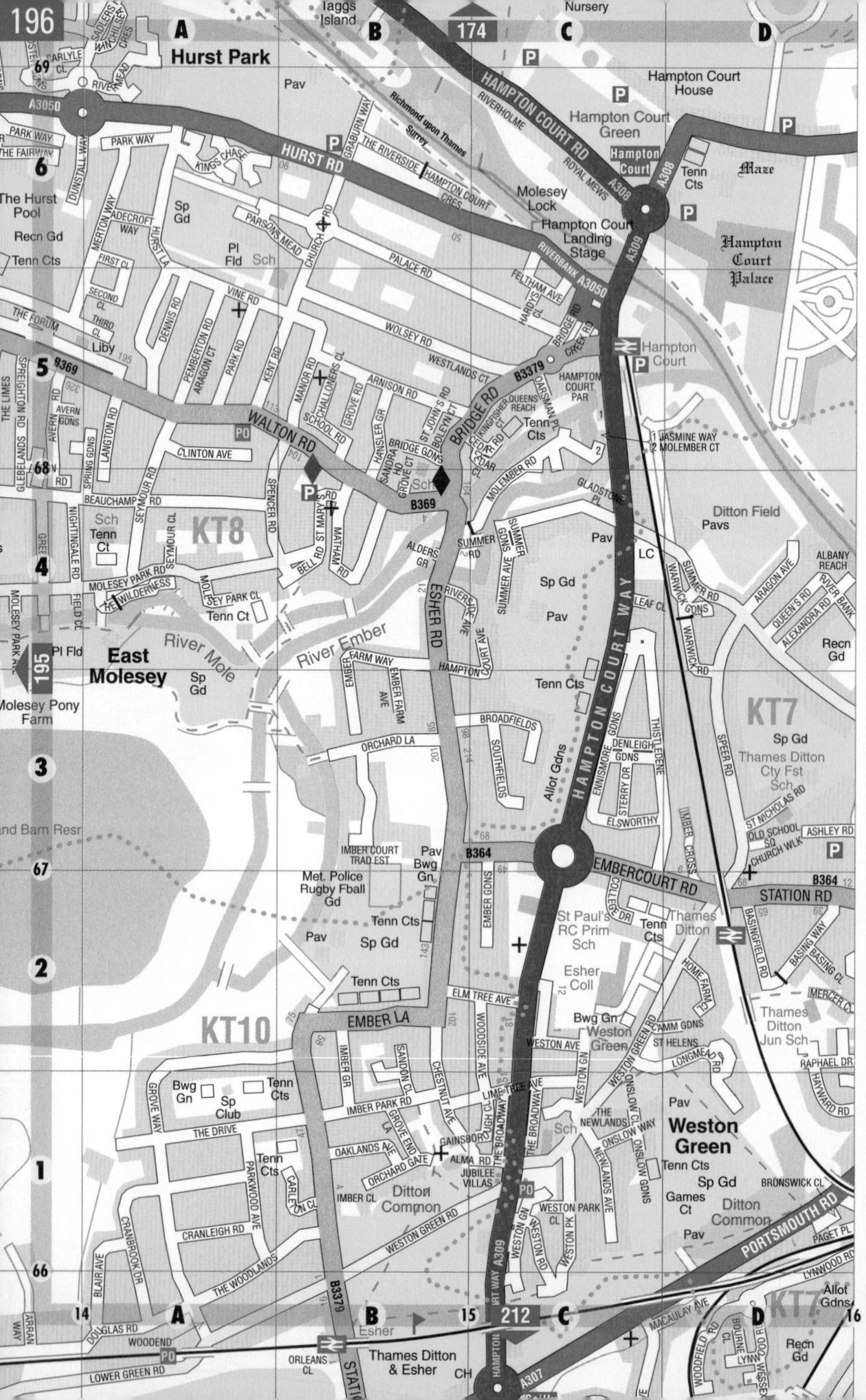
Hurst Park
Hampton Court House
Hampton Court Green
Hampton Court
Molesey Lock
Hampton Court Landing Stage
Hampton Court Palace
Maze
HAMPTON COURT RD
HURST RD
PALACE RD
WOLSEY RD
WALTON RD
BRIDGE RD
ESHER RD
HAMPTON COURT WAY
EMBERCOURT RD
STATION RD
PORTSMOUTH RD
EMBER LA
East Molesey
River Mole
River Ember
KT8
KT7
KT10
Ditton Field
Thames Ditton
Weston Green
Ditton Common
The Hurst Pool
Molesey Pony Farm
Met. Police Rugby Fball Gd
Imber Court Trad Est
Esher Coll
St Paul's RC Prim Sch
Thames Ditton Cty Fst Sch
Thames Ditton Jun Sch
Thames Ditton & Esher
Esher
174
195
212

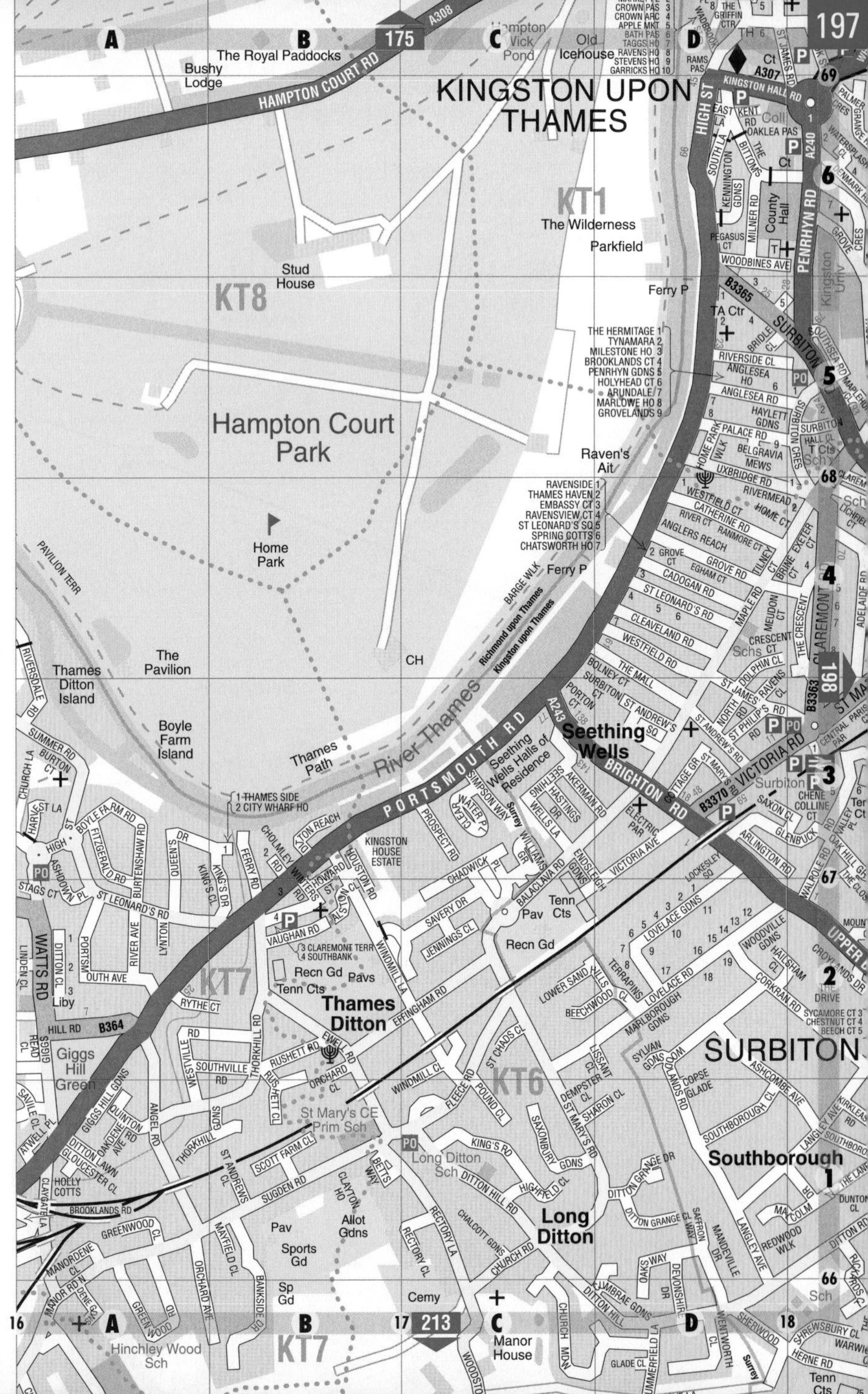

A
B
175
C
D
A308
Hampton Wick Pond
Old Icehouse
The Royal Paddocks
Bushy Lodge
HAMPTON COURT RD
KINGSTON UPON THAMES
CROWN PAS 3
CROWN ARC 4
APPLE MKT 5
BATH PAS 6
TAGGS HO 7
RAVENS HO 8
STEVENS HO 9
GARRICKS HO 10
THE GRIFFIN CTR
RAMS PAS
A307
KINGSTON HALL RD
HIGH ST
EAST LA
KENT RD
OAKLEA PAS
SOUTH LA
KENNINGTON GDNS
THE BITTONS
MILNER RD
County Hall
PENRHYN RD
A240
PEGASUS CT
WOODBINES AVE
Kingston Univ
KT1
The Wilderness
Parkfield
Stud House
KT8
Ferry P
B3365
SURBITON RD
TA Ctr
THE HERMITAGE 1
TYNAMARA 2
MILESTONE HO 3
BROOKLANDS CT 4
PENRHYN GDNS 5
HOLYHEAD CT 6
ARUNDALE 7
MARLOWE HO 8
GROVELANDS 9
RIVERSIDE CL
ANGLESEA HO
ANGLESEA RD
HAYLETT GDNS
SURBITON CRES
PALACE RD
BELGRAVIA MEWS
HOME PARK WLK
UXBRIDGE RD
RIVERMEAD
Hampton Court Park
Raven's Ait
RAVENSIDE 1
THAMES HAVEN 2
EMBASSY CT 3
RAVENSVIEW CT 4
ST LEONARD'S SQ 5
SPRING COTTS 6
CHATSWORTH HO 7
WESTFIELD CT
CATHERINE RD
RIVER CT
RANMORE CT
HOME CT
ANGLERS REACH
GROVE CT
EGHAM CT
GROVE RD
TILNEY CT
BRINE CT
EXETER CT
Home Park
PAVILION TERR
Ferry P
BARGE WLK
Richmond upon Thames
Kingston upon Thames
CADOGAN RD
ST LEONARD'S RD
CLEAVELAND RD
WESTFIELD RD
MAPLE RD
MEUDON CT
THE CRESCENT
CRESCENT CT
CLAREMONT RD
ADELAIDE RD
Schs
DOLPHIN CL
198
B3363
The Pavilion
CH
RIVERSDALE RD
Thames Ditton Island
Boyle Farm Island
River Thames
PORTSMOUTH RD
A243
BOLNEY CT
THE MALL
SURBITON CT
PORTON CT
ST ANDREW'S SQ
NORTH RD
ST JAMES' RD
RAVENS CT
ST PHILIP'S RD
Seething Wells
Seething Wells Halls of Residence
Thames Path
SUMMER RD
BURTON CT
CHURCH LA
HARVEST LA
1 THAMES SIDE
2 CITY WHARF HO
SIMPSON WAY
CLEAR WATER PL
SEETHING WELLS LA
HASTINGS DR
AKERMAN RD
BRIGHTON RD
ELECTRIC PAR
COTTAGE GR
ST MARY'S RD
B3370
VICTORIA RD
Surbiton
CHENE COLLINE CT
SAXON CL
GLENBUCK RD
ARLINGTON RD
VALLEY PL
OAK HILL
WALPOLE RD
THE CLOSE
BOYLE FARM RD
FITZGERALD RD
BURTENSHAW RD
QUEEN'S DR
KING'S DR
KING'S CL
FERRY RD
CHOLMLEY RD
DITTON REACH
KINGSTON HOUSE ESTATE
PROSPECT RD
WILLIAMS GR
ENDSLEIGH GDNS
VICTORIA AVE
LOCKESLEY SQ
ASHDOWN PL
STAGS CT
ST LEONARD'S RD
WINTERS RD
HOWARD ST
HOUSTON RD
ALSTON CL
CHADWICK PL
BALACLAVA RD
SAVERY DR
JENNINGS CL
Pav
Tenn Cts
Recn Gd
LOVELACE GDNS
UPPER
VAUGHAN RD
3 CLAREMONT TERR
4 SOUTHBANK
WINDMILL LA
WOODVILLE GDNS
HAILSHAM CL
CROYLANDS DR
WATTS RD
LINDEN CL
DITTON CL
PORTSMOUTH AVE
RIVER AVE
LYNTON RD
KT7
RYTHE CT
Recn Gd
Pavs
Tenn Cts
Thames Ditton
EFFINGHAM RD
LOWER SAND HILLS
TERRAPINS
BEECHWOOD CL
LOVELACE RD
MARLBOROUGH GDNS
CORKRAN RD
THE DRIVE
SYCAMORE CT 3
CHESTNUT CT 4
BEECH CT 5
Liby
HILL RD
B364
READ CL
Giggs Hill Green
WESTVILLE RD
SOUTHVILLE RD
THORKHILL RD
RUSHETT RD
EWELL RD
ORCHARD CL
RUSHETT CL
WINDMILL CL
FLEECE RD
POUND CL
ST CHADS CL
KT6
LISSANT CL
DEMPSTER CL
SHARON CL
SYLVAN GDNS
BLOOMFIELD RD
COPSE GLADE
ASHCOMBE AVE
SURBITON
SAVILE CL
ATWELL PL
GIGGS HILL GDNS
QUINTON RD
OAKDENE AVE
ANGEL RD
THORKHILL GDNS
St Mary's CE Prim Sch
SAXONBURY GDNS
ST MARY'S RD
SOUTHBOROUGH CL
LANGLEY AVE
KIRKLEAS RD
Southborough
DITTON LAWN
GLOUCESTER CL
ST ANDREWS CL
SCOTT FARM CL
BETTS WAY
Long Ditton Sch
KING'S RD
DITTON HILL RD
HIGHFIELD CL
DITTON GRANGE DR
DITTON GRANGE CL
SAFFRON WAY
MANDEVILLE DR
MALCOLM DR
DUNTON CL
REDWOOD WLK
DITTON RD
HOLLY COTTS
CLAYGATE LA
BROOKLANDS RD
SUGDEN RD
CLAYTON HO
Allot Gdns
RECTORY LA
CHALCOTT GDNS
CHURCH RD
Long Ditton
GREENWOOD CL
MANORDENE CL
MAYFIELD CL
ORCHARD AVE
BANKSIDE DR
Pav
Sports Gd
RECTORY CL
OAKS WAY
DEVONSHIRE DR
UMBRAE GDNS
DITTON HILL
Sp Gd
Cemy
RICKARDS CL
Sch
MANOR RD N
DENE GDNS
GREENWOOD RD
CHURCH MDW
SUMMERFIELD LA
WENTWORTH CL
SHERWOOD
SHREWSBURY CL
WARWICK
HERNE RD
Tenn Cts
16
A
B
17
213
C
D
18
Hinchley Wood Sch
KT7
Manor House
GLADE CL
WOODSTOCK
Surrey

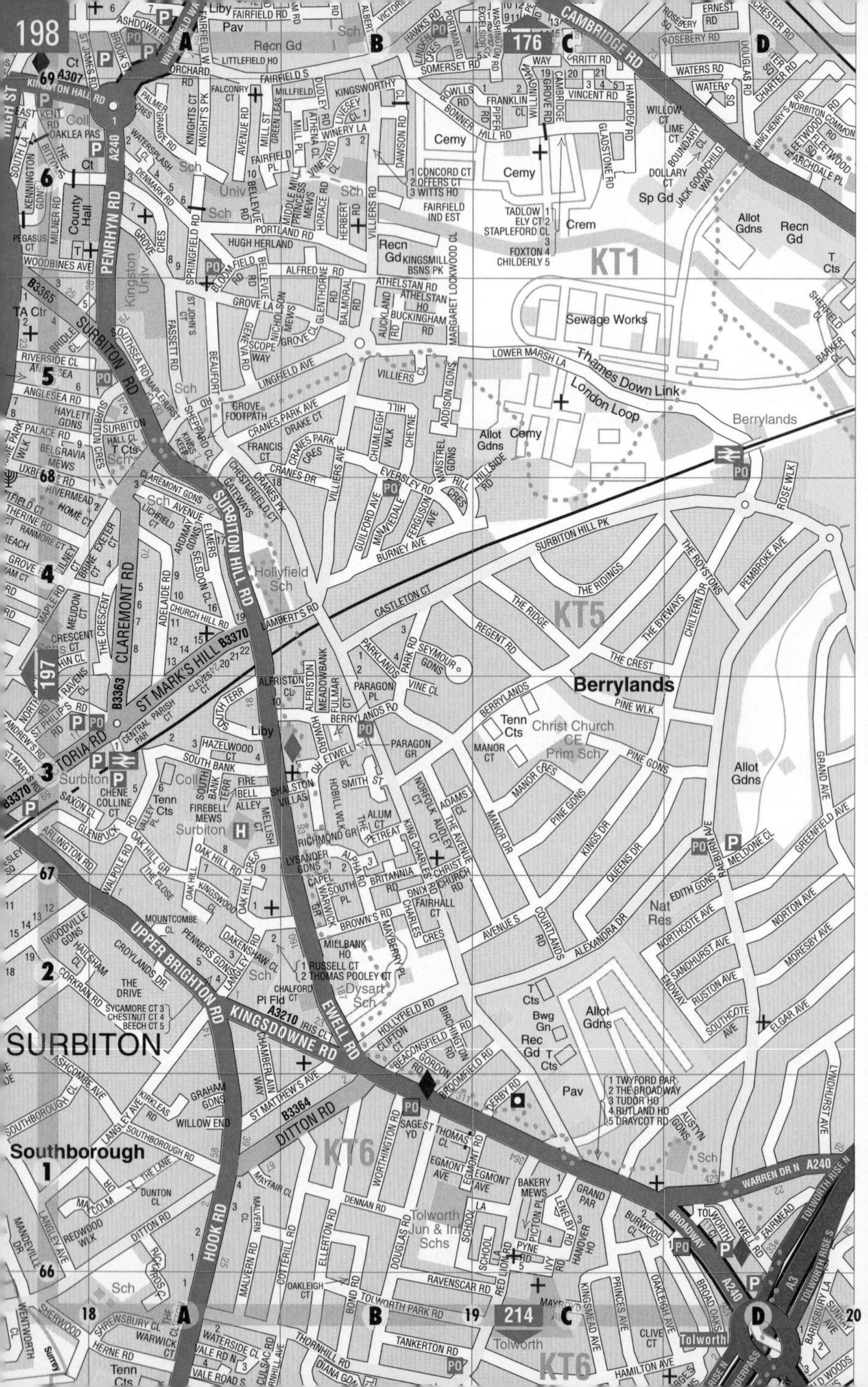

A
B
C
D
176
214
197
KT1
KT5
KT6
SURBITON
Southborough
Berrylands
Surbiton
Tolworth
CAMBRIDGE RD
KINGSTON HALL RD
A307
A240
PENRHYN RD
SURBITON RD
B3365
SURBITON HILL RD
ST MARK'S HILL
B3370
B3363
CLAREMONT RD
VICTORIA RD
UPPER BRIGHTON RD
KINGSDOWNE RD
A3210
EWELL RD
HOOK RD
DITTON RD
B3364
BROADWAY
WARREN DR N
TOLWORTH RISE N
TOLWORTH RISE S
A3
FAIRFIELD RD
Recn Gd
LITTLEFIELD HO
ORCHARD RD
FAIRFIELD S
KINGSWORTHY CL
SOMERSET RD
ROWLLS RD
FRANKLIN CL
VINCENT RD
WATERS RD
ROSEBERY RD
ERNEST RD
BONNER HILL RD
GLADSTONE RD
GROVE RD
Cemy
Crem
CONCORD CT
OFFERS CT
WITTS HO
FAIRFIELD IND EST
TADLOW
ELY CT
STAPLEFORD CL
FOXTON
CHILDERLY
Sp Gd
DOLLARY CT
JACK GOODCHILD WAY
BOUNDARY CL
WILLOW CT
LIME CT
Allot Gdns
County Hall
Kingston Univ
Univ
Sch
Coll
KENNINGTON GDNS
MILNER RD
PEGASUS CT
WOODBINES AVE
TA Ctr
RIVERSIDE CL
ANGLESEA RD
HAYLETT GDNS
PALACE RD
BELGRAVIA MEWS
RIVERMEAD
HOME CT
RANMORE CT
PORTLAND RD
HUGH HERLAND
ALFRED RD
ATHELSTAN RD
BUCKINGHAM RD
KINGSMILL BSNS PK
MARGARET LOCKWOOD CL
GROVE LA
LINGFIELD AVE
LOWER MARSH LA
Thames Down Link
London Loop
Sewage Works
Berrylands
VILLIERS CL
VILLIERS AVE
ADDISON GDNS
CHEYNE HILL
CRANES PARK AVE
CRANES PARK CRES
CRANES DR
CRANES PK
DRAKE CT
FRANCIS CT
GROVE FOOTPATH
EVERSLEY RD
GUILFORD AVE
MINNIEDALE
FERGUSON AVE
BURNEY AVE
HILLSIDE RD
ROSE WLK
SURBITON HILL PK
THE RIDINGS
THE ROYSTONS
PEMBROKE AVE
THE RIDGE
REGENT RD
CASTLETON CT
THE BYEWAYS
CHILTERN DR
THE CREST
SEYMOUR GDNS
PARKLANDS
PARK RD
VINE CL
PARAGON PL
PARAGON GR
BERRYLANDS RD
PINE WLK
PINE GDNS
Christ Church CE Prim Sch
Tenn Cts
MANOR CT
MANOR CRES
MANOR DR
KINGS DR
QUEENS DR
ALEXANDRA DR
COURTLANDS RD
AVENUE S
RAEBURN AVE
MELDONE CL
EDITH GDNS
GREENFIELD AVE
GRAND AVE
NORTON AVE
MORESBY AVE
NORTHCOTE AVE
SANDHURST AVE
RUSTON AVE
SOUTHCOTE AVE
ELGAR AVE
ENDWAY
Nat Res
LYNDHURST AVE
Hollyfield Sch
LAMBERT'S RD
CHURCH HILL RD
ADELAIDE RD
ELMERS
SELSDON CL
ARDMAY GDNS
LICHFIELD CT
CLAREMONT GDNS
AVENUE ELMERS
GATEWAYS
CHESTERFIELD CT
MEADOWBANK
ALFRISTON CL
FULMAR CT
HOWARD RD
ETWELL PL
SMITH ST
HOBILL WLK
NORFOLK CT
AUDLEY CT
ADAMS CL
THE AVENUE
KING CHARLES RD
CHRIST CHURCH RD
FAIRHALL CT
RICHMOND GR
THE RETREAT
ALPHA RD
BRITANNIA RD
LYSANDER GDNS
CAPEL
WARWICK GR
BROWN'S RD
MAYBERRY PL
MILLBANK HO
RUSSELL CT
THOMAS POOLEY CT
CHALFORD CT
Dysart Sch
HOLLYFIELD RD
CLIFTON RD
BEACONSFIELD RD
GORDON RD
BIRCHINGTON RD
BLOOMFIELD RD
DERBY RD
Pav
Rec Gd
Bwg Gn
TWYFORD PAR
THE BROADWAY
TUDOR HO
RUTLAND HO
DRAYCOT RD
AUSTYN GDNS
Liby
SOUTH TERR
HAZELWOOD CT
SOUTH BANK
SOUTH BANK TERR
FIREBELL MEWS
FIRE BELL ALLEY
MELLISH
SHALSTON VILLAS
Surbiton H
CHENE COLLINE CT
SAXON CL
GLENBUCK RD
VALLEY PL
OAK HILL GR
OAK HILL RD
OAK HILL CRES
THE CLOSE
KINGSWOOD CL
MOUNTCOMBE CL
PENNERS GDNS
OAKENSHAW CL
LANGLEY RD
ARLINGTON RD
WALPOLE RD
CROYLANDS DR
HAILSHAM CL
WOODVILLE GDNS
CORKRAN RD
THE DRIVE
SYCAMORE CT
CHESTNUT CT
BEECH CT
Pl Fld
CHAMBERLAIN WAY
ST MATTHEW'S AVE
GRAHAM GDNS
WILLOW END
KIRKLEAS RD
SOUTHBOROUGH RD
SOUTHBOROUGH CL
ASHCOMBE AVE
LANGLEY AVE
THE LANE
DUNTON CL
MALCOLM DR
REDWOOD WLK
MANDEVILLE DR
RUCKROSS CL
SHERWOOD
SHREWSBURY CL
WENTWORTH
HERNE RD
WARWICK CT
WATERSIDE CL
VALE RD N
VALE ROAD S
MAYFAIR CL
MALVERN CL
MALVERN RD
COTTERILL RD
ELLERTON RD
OAKLEIGH CT
BOND RD
TOLWORTH PARK RD
DOUGLAS RD
DENNAN RD
WORTHINGTON RD
SAGE ST YD
THOMAS CL
EGMONT AVE
EGMONT RD
SCHOOL LA
Tolworth Jun & Inf Schs
BAKERY MEWS
PICTON PL
RED LION RD
PYNE RD
IVY RD
LENELBY RD
HANOVER HO
GRAND PAR
BURWOOD CL
RAVENSCAR RD
TANKERTON RD
THORNHILL RD
DIANA GDNS
KINGSMEAD AVE
PRINCES AVE
OAKLEIGH AVE
CLIVE CT
HAMILTON AVE
BROAD OAKS
FAIRMEAD
EWELL RD
BARNSBURY LA
SUNRAY AVE
Surrey

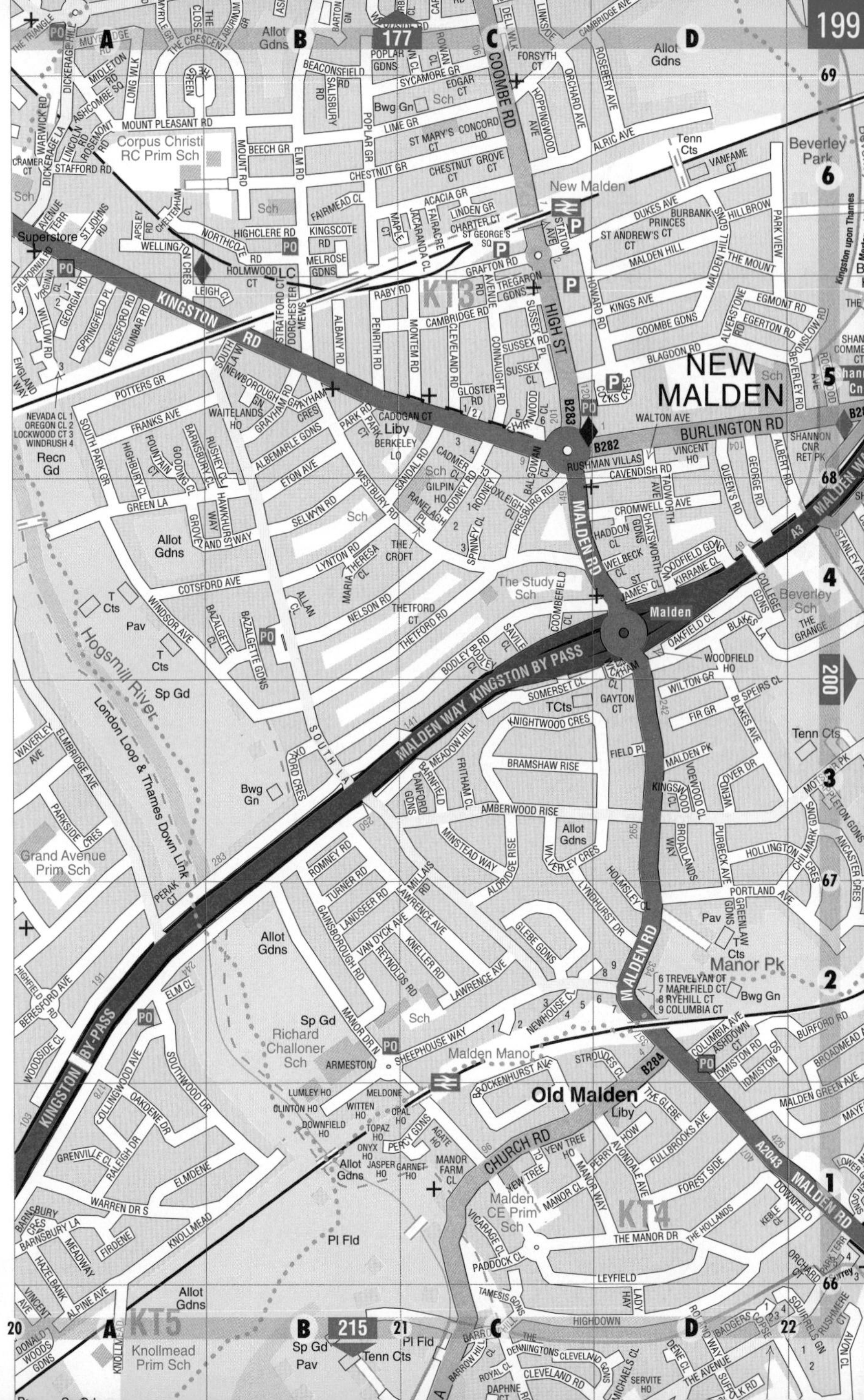
177
A
B
C
D
Allot Gdns
69
6
5
68
4
200
3
67
2
1
66
20
21
22
215
KT3
KT4
KT5
NEW MALDEN
Old Malden
New Malden
Malden Manor
Malden
KINGSTON RD
KINGSTON BY PASS
MALDEN WAY
KINGSTON BY-PASS
COOMBE RD
HIGH ST
MALDEN RD
BURLINGTON RD
CHURCH RD
B283
B282
B284
A3
A2043
Hogsmill River
London Loop & Thames Down Link
Beverley Park
Beverley Brook
Kingston upon Thames
Merton
Corpus Christi RC Prim Sch
Grand Avenue Prim Sch
Richard Challoner Sch
Malden CE Prim Sch
Knollmead Prim Sch
Beverley Sch
The Study Sch
Superstore
Liby
Recn Gd
Sp Gd
Pav
Pl Fld
Bwg Gn
Tenn Cts
T Cts
TCts
Manor Pk
Shannon Cnr Ret Pk
MOUNT PLEASANT RD
STAFFORD RD
CHESTNUT GR
BEECH GR
ELM RD
MOUNT RD
POPLAR GR
LIME GR
SYCAMORE GR
BEACONSFIELD RD
SALISBURY RD
ROWAN CL
EDGAR CT
FORSYTH CT
ORCHARD AVE
ROSEBERY AVE
CAMBRIDGE AVE
ALRIC AVE
HOPPINGWOOD AVE
VANFAME CT
DUKES AVE
PRINCES
BURBANK
HILLBROW
PARK VIEW
ST ANDREW'S CT
MALDEN HILL
MALDEN HILL GDNS
THE MOUNT
STATION AVE
HOWARD RD
KINGS AVE
COOMBE GDNS
EGMONT RD
EGERTON RD
ALVERSTONE RD
BLAGDON RD
BEVERLEY RD
DUNSLOW RD
GRAFTON RD
TREGARON GDNS
CAMBRIDGE RD
CLEVELAND RD
CONNAUGHT RD
SUSSEX RD
SUSSEX CL
GLOSTER RD
MONTEM RD
PENRITH RD
ALBANY RD
RABY RD
KINGSCOTE RD
MELROSE GDNS
FAIRMEAD CL
ACACIA GR
LINDEN GR
CHARTER CT
ST GEORGE'S SQ
HIGHCLERE RD
NORTHCOTE RD
WELLINGTON CRES
HOLMWOOD CT
LEIGH CL
STRATFORD CT
DORCHESTER MEWS
CALIFORNIA RD
VIRGINIA CL
GEORGIA RD
SPRINGFIELD PL
BERESFORD RD
DUNBAR RD
WILLOW RD
ENGLAND WAY
NEVADA CL 1
OREGON CL 2
LOCKWOOD CT 3
WINDRUSH 4
POTTERS GR
FRANKS AVE
SOUTH PARK GR
HIGHBURY CL
BARNSBURY CL
RUSHEY CL
HAWKHURST WAY
GROVELAND WAY
GREEN LA
SELWYN RD
ETON AVE
ALBEMARLE GDNS
WAITELANDS HO
GRAYHAM CRES
NEWBOROUGH GN
CADOGAN CT
BERKELEY LO
WESTBURY RD
SANDAL RD
CADMER CL
GILPIN HO
RODNEY RD
RANELAGH PL
SPINNEY CL
OXLEIGH CL
PRESBURG RD
BALGOWAN CL
THE CROFT
LYNTON RD
MARIA THERESA CL
COTSFORD AVE
ALLAN CL
NELSON RD
THETFORD RD
THETFORD CT
WINDSOR AVE
BAZALGETTE CL
BAZALGETTE GDNS
RUSHMAN VILLAS
CAVENDISH RD
VINCENT HO
WALTON AVE
CROMWELL AVE
TADWORTH AVE
HADDON CL
CHATSWORTH GDNS
WELBECK CL
ST JAMES' CL
WOODFIELD GDNS
KIRRANE CL
QUEEN'S RD
GEORGE RD
ALBERT RD
COLLEGE GDNS
STANLEY AVE
COOMBEFIELD CL
SAVILE CL
BODLEY RD
BODLEY CL
OAKFIELD CL
BLAKES LA
THE GRANGE
WOODFIELD HO
WILTON GR
SPEIRS CL
FIR GR
BLAKES AVE
SOMERSET CL
GAYTON CT
KNIGHTWOOD CRES
BRAMSHAW RISE
FIELD PL
MALDEN PK
VOEWOOD CL
KINGSWOOD CL
OVER DR
AMBERWOOD RISE
FRITHAM CL
MEADOW HILL
BARNFIELD
CANFORD GDNS
OXFORD CRES
SOUTH LA
MINSTEAD WAY
ALDRIDGE RISE
WAVERLEY CRES
BROADLANDS WAY
PURBECK AVE
HOLLINGTON CRES
CHILMARK GDNS
ANCASTER CRES
PORTLAND AVE
GREENLAW GDNS
HOLMSLEY CL
LYNDHURST DR
GLEBE GDNS
ROMNEY RD
TURNER RD
GAINSBOROUGH RD
LANDSEER RD
LAWRENCE RD
MILLAIS
VAN DYCK AVE
LAWRENCE AVE
REYNOLDS RD
KNELLER RD
MANOR DR N
SHEEPHOUSE WAY
NEWHOUSE CL
6 TREVELYAN CT
7 MARLFIELD CT
8 RYEHILL CT
9 COLUMBIA CT
COLUMBIA AVE
ASHDOWN CT
IDMISTON RD
BURFORD RD
BROADMEAD AVE
MALDEN GREEN AVE
STROUDES CL
BROCKENHURST AVE
THE GLEBE
FULLBROOKS AVE
AVONDALE AVE
MANOR WAY
YEW TREE HO
NEW TREE
MANOR CL
FOREST SIDE
KEBLE CL
DOWNFIELD
THE HOLLANDS
THE MANOR DR
VICARAGE CL
PADDOCK CL
LEYFIELD
LADY HAY
TAMESIS GDNS
HIGHDOWN
ROUND WAY
BADGERS COPSE
SQUIRRELS GN
RUSHMERE CT
ORCHARD CT
PARK TERR
ARMESTON
LUMLEY HO
MELDONE
CLINTON HO
WITTEN HO
OPAL HO
DOWNFIELD HO
TOPAZ HO
ONYX HO
JASPER HO
GARNET HO
AGATE HO
PERCY GDNS
MANOR FARM CL
WAVERLEY AVE
ELMBRIDGE AVE
PARKSIDE CRES
PERAK CT
HIGHFIELD RD
BERESFORD AVE
WOODSIDE CL
ELM CL
COLLINGWOOD AVE
SOUTHWOOD DR
OAKDENE DR
GRENVILLE CL
RALEIGH DR
ELMDENE
WARREN DR S
KNOLLMEAD
BARNSBURY CRES
BARNSBURY LA
MEADWAY
FIRDENE
HAZELBANK
VINCENT AVE
ALPINE AVE
DONALD WOODS GDNS
BARROW HILL CL
ROYAL CL
DAPHNE CT
DENNINGTONS
CLEVELAND RD
CLEVELAND GDNS
MICHAELS CL
SERVITE HO
DENE CL
THE AVENUE
SUFFOLK RD
AVON CL
DICKERAGE HILL
DICKERAGE LA
WARWICK RD
MIDDLETON RD
ASHCOMBE SQ
LONG WLK
LINCOLN RD
ROSEMONT RD
CRAMER CT
THE CRESCENT
THE GREEN
THE CLOSE
MYRTLE GR
LABURNUM
ST JOHNS RD
AVENUE TERR
APSLEY RD
CHELTENHAM

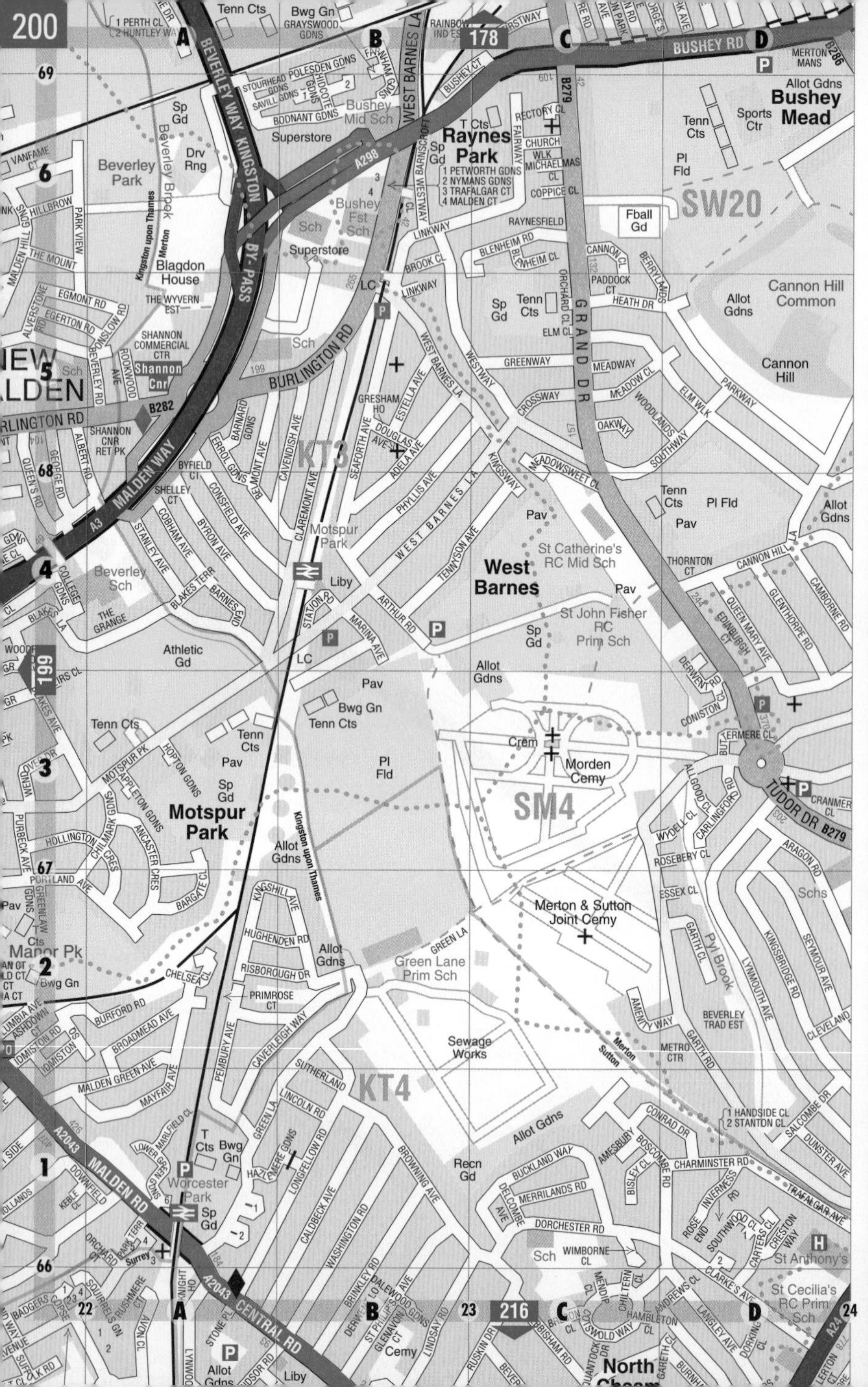

178
199
216
Raynes Park
West Barnes
Motspur Park
Bushey Mead
Cannon Hill Common
Cannon Hill
New Malden
SW20
KT3
SM4
KT4
Beverley Way Kingston By-Pass
Bushey Rd
West Barnes La
Burlington Rd
Grand Dr
Malden Way
Malden Rd
Central Rd
Tudor Dr
Morden Cemy
Merton & Sutton Joint Cemy
St Catherine's RC Mid Sch
St John Fisher RC Prim Sch
Green Lane Prim Sch
Sewage Works
Blagdon House
Beverley Park
Beverley Sch
Bushey Mid Sch
Bushey Fst Sch
Shannon Cnr
Worcester Park
St Anthony's
St Cecilia's RC Prim Sch
North Cheam
Beverley Trad Est
Metro Ctr
Kingston upon Thames
Merton
Sutton
Surrey

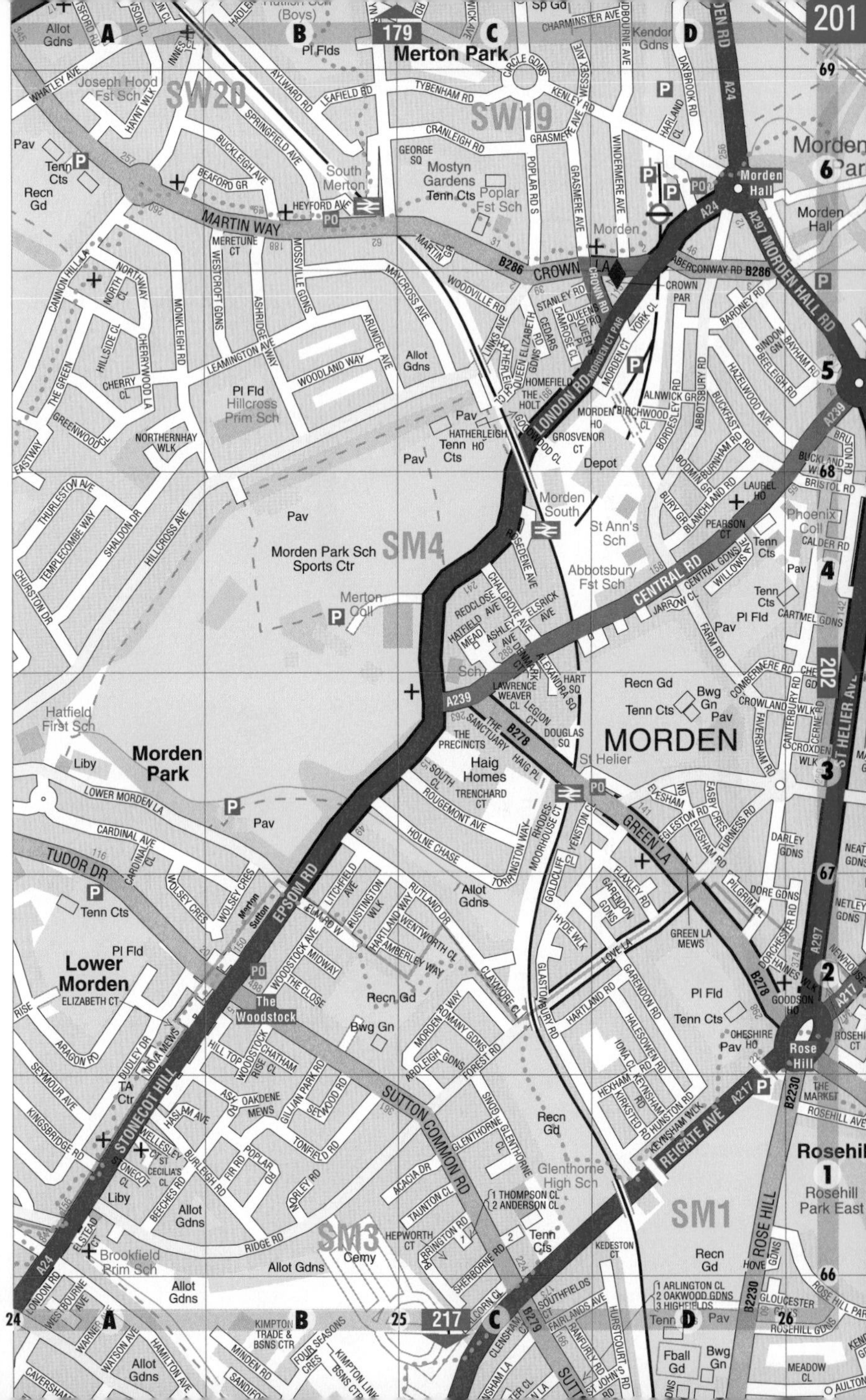
A
B
C
D
179
Merton Park
Allot Gdns
Pl Flds
Charminster Ave
Kendor Gdns
Whatley Ave
Joseph Hood Fst Sch
SW20
Aylward Rd
Leafield Rd
Tybenham Rd
Circle Gdns
Kenley Rd
SW19
Haynt Wlk
Springfield Ave
Buckleigh Ave
Beaford Gr
Cranleigh Rd
George Sq
Mostyn Gardens
Tenn Cts
Poplar Fst Sch
Grasmere Ave
Windermere Ave
Daybrook Rd
Harland Cl
Morden Rd
A24
Morden Hall
Morden Park
Pav
Tenn Cts
Recn Gd
South Merton
Heyford Ave
PO
Martin Way
Meretune Ct
Morden
Martin Gr
Crown La
B286
Abberconway Rd
Crown Par
Morden Hall Rd
A297
Cannon Hill La
Northway
North Cl
Westcroft Gdns
Monkleigh Rd
Ashridge Way
Mossville Gdns
Maycross Ave
Woodville Rd
Stanley Rd
Cedars
Camrose Cl
Queens Rd
Crown Rd
Morden Ct Par
Morden Ct
York Cl
Bardney Rd
Bindon Gn
Beeleigh Rd
Bayham Rd
Hillside Cl
Cherrywood La
Cherry Cl
The Green
Leamington Ave
Woodland Way
Arundel Ave
Allot Gdns
Links Ave
Hatherleigh Cl
Queen Elizabeth Gdns
Homefield
The Holt
London Rd
Alnwick Gr
Abbotsbury Rd
Buckfast Rd
Hazelwood Ave
Greenwood Cl
Pl Fld
Hillcross Prim Sch
Northernhay Wlk
Hatherleigh Ho
Goodwood Cl
Morden Ho
Birchwood Cl
Grosvenor Ct
Bordesley Rd
Bodmin Gr
Burnham Rd
Buckland Wlk
Bruton Rd
Bristol Rd
Eastway
Thurleston Ave
Templecombe Way
Shaldon Dr
Hillcross Ave
Depot
Morden South
Bury Gr
Blanchland Rd
Laurel Ho
Pearson Ct
Phoenix Coll
Calder Rd
Churston Dr
Morden Park Sch Sports Ctr
SM4
Rosedene Ave
St Ann's Sch
Abbotsbury Fst Sch
Central Rd
Central Gdns
Willows Ave
Merton Coll
Redclose Ave
Chalgrove Ave
Elsrick Ave
Hatfield Mead
Ashley Ave
Denmark Ct
Alexandra Sq
Jarrow Cl
Farm Rd
Cartmel Gdns
202
Sch
Hart Sq
Recn Gd
Bwg Gn
Combermere Rd
Crowland Wlk
Faversham Rd
Canterbury Rd
Cerne Rd
A239
Lawrence Weaver Cl
Legion Ct
Douglas Sq
MORDEN
St Helier
St Helier Ave
Croxden Wlk
Hatfield First Sch
Liby
Morden Park
The Sanctuary
The Precincts
B278
Haig Pl
Haig Homes
South Cl
Rougemont Ave
Trenchard Ct
Evesham Gn
Easby Cres
Furness Rd
Lower Morden La
Cardinal Ave
Cardinal Cl
Tudor Dr
Holne Chase
Torrington Way
Rhodes-Moorhouse Ct
Yenston Cl
Green La
Egleston Rd
Evesham Rd
Darley Gdns
Neath Gdns
Wolsey Cres
Merton
Sutton
Epsom Rd
Litchfield Ave
Rustington Wlk
Rutland Dr
Allot Gdns
Goldcliff Cl
Flaxley Rd
Garendon Gdns
Pilgrim Cl
Dore Gdns
Netley Gdns
Elm Rd W
Hartland Way
Wentworth Cl
Amberley Way
Hyde Wlk
Love La
Green La Mews
Dorchester Rd
Haines Wlk
Goodson Ho
Newhouse
A217
Pl Fld
Lower Morden
Elizabeth Ct
Woodstock Ave
Midway
The Close
The Woodstock
Recn Gd
Claymore Cl
Glastonbury Rd
Hartland Rd
Garendon Rd
Halesowen Rd
Pl Fld
Tenn Cts
Cheshire Ho
Rose Hill
Rosehill Ct
Rise
Aragon Rd
Dudley Dr
Nova Mews
Hill Top
Woodstock Rise
Chatham Cl
Gillian Park Rd
Selwood Rd
Bwg Gn
Morden Way
Romany Gdns
Ardleigh Gdns
Forest Rd
Iona Cl
Keynsham Rd
Hexham Rd
Kirksted Rd
Hunston Rd
Keynsham Wlk
Reigate Ave
The Market
Rosehill Ave
Seymour Ave
TA Ctr
Stonecot Hill
Haslam Ave
Oakdene Mews
Fir Rd
Poplar Rd
Tonfield Rd
Sutton Common Rd
Glenthorne Cl
Glenthorne Gdns
Recn Gd
Kingsbridge Rd
Wellesley Cres
Stonecot Cl
St Cecilia's Cl
Burleigh Rd
Beeches Rd
Morley Rd
Acacia Dr
Taunton Cl
Glenthorne High Sch
Rosehill
Rosehill Park East
1 Thompson Cl
2 Anderson Cl
Liby
Allot Gdns
Ridge Rd
SM3
Hepworth Ct
Barrington Rd
Sherborne Rd
Tenn Cts
SM1
Kedeston Ct
Recn Gd
Rose Hill
Hove Gdns
B2230
Elstead Ct
Brookfield Prim Sch
Cemy
Allot Gdns
Allot Gdns
1 Arlington Cl
2 Oakwood Gdns
3 Highfields
Southfields
Fairlands Ave
Hurstcourt Rd
Gloucester Gdns
Rose Hill Par
Rosehill Gdns
24
A
Westbourne Ave
London Rd
Warner Ave
Watson Ave
Hamilton Ave
Allot Gdns
B
Kimpton Trade & Bsns Ctr
Minden Rd
Four Seasons Cres
Kimpton Link Bsns Ctr
25
217
C
Alcorn Cl
Clensham Ct
Clensham La
B279
Ranfurly Rd
St John's Rd
D
Tenn Cts
Pav
26
Fball Gd
Bwg Gn
Meadow Cl
Aultone
66
67
68
69
1
2
3
4
5
6

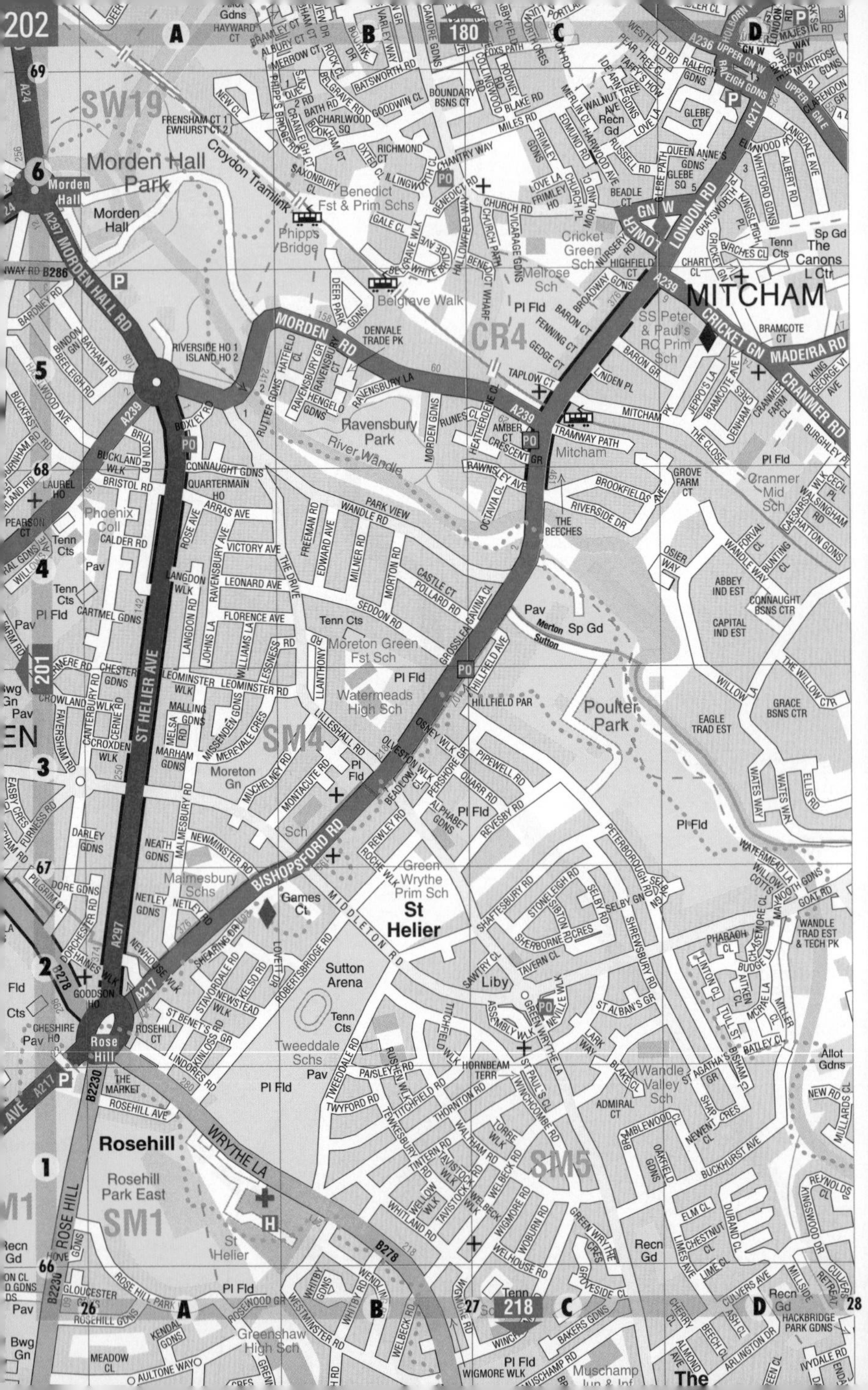
A
B
C
D
180
SW19
Morden Hall Park
Morden Hall
Croydon Tramlink
Benedict Fst & Prim Schs
Phipps Bridge
Belgrave Walk
MORDEN HALL RD
MORDEN RD
DENVALE TRADE PK
Ravensbury Park
River Wandle
CR4
MITCHAM
SS Peter & Paul's RC Prim Sch
Cricket Green Sch
Melrose Sch
The Canons L Ctr
LONDON RD
CRICKET GN
MADEIRA RD
CRANMER RD
Mitcham
Cranmer Mid Sch
Phoenix Coll
ST HELIER AVE
Moreton Green Fst Sch
Watermeads High Sch
Poulter Park
ABBEY IND EST
CONNAUGHT BSNS CTR
CAPITAL IND EST
GRACE BSNS CTR
EAGLE TRAD EST
SM4
Moreton Gn
Malmesbury Schs
BISHOPSFORD RD
Green Wrythe Prim Sch
St Helier
Sutton Arena
Tweeddale Schs
Wandle Valley Sch
WANDLE TRAD EST & TECH PK
Rose Hill
Rosehill
Rosehill Park East
SM1
SM5
WRYTHE LA
St Helier
Greenshaw High Sch
201
218
1
2
3
4
5
6
26
27
28
66
67
68
69

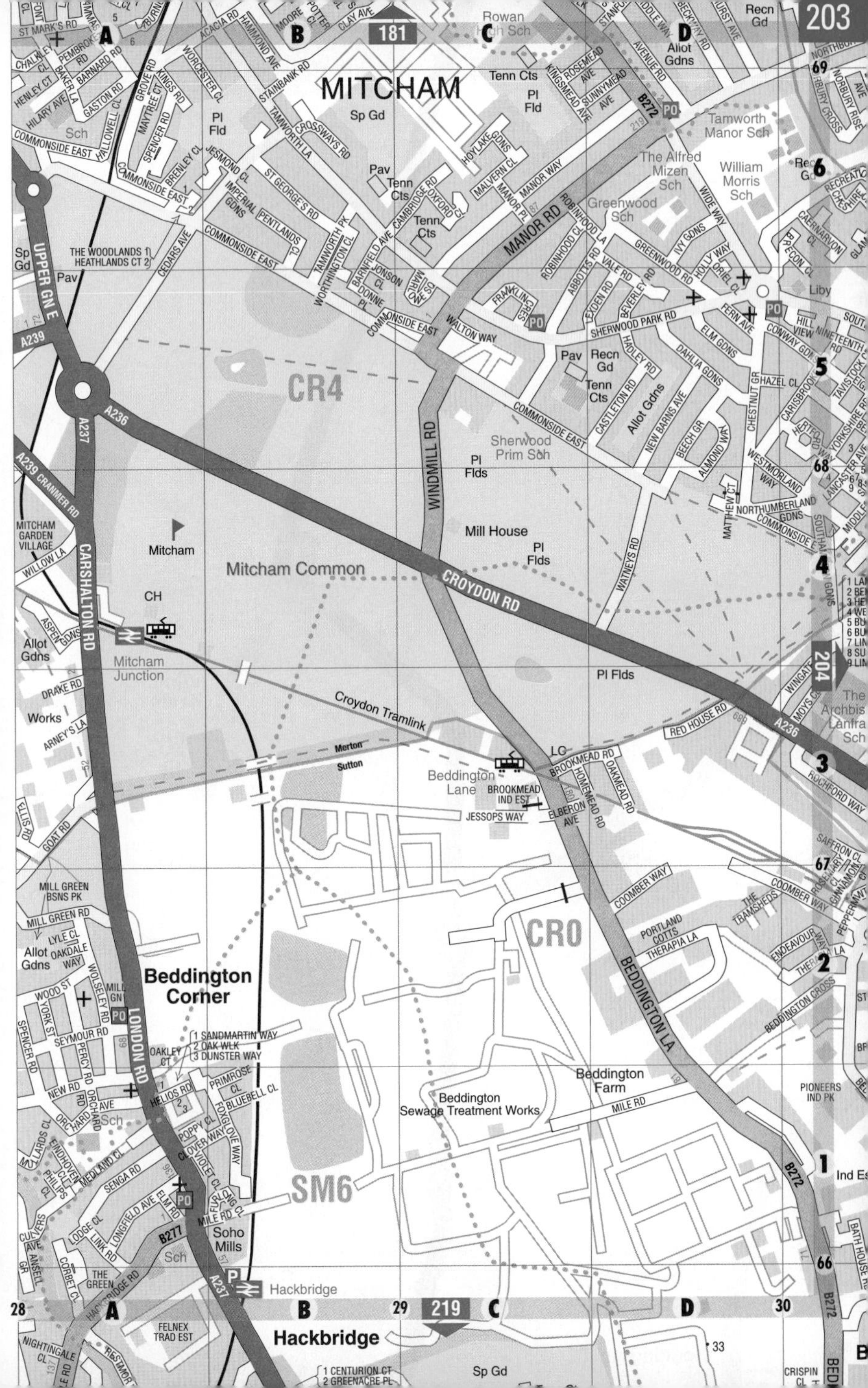
MITCHAM
CR4
CR0
SM6
Mitcham Common
Beddington Corner
Hackbridge
Beddington Sewage Treatment Works
Beddington Farm
Mitcham Junction
Croydon Tramlink
Beddington Lane
Mill House
Sherwood Prim Sch
Tamworth Manor Sch
The Alfred Mizen Sch
William Morris Sch
Greenwood Sch
Rowan High Sch
CROYDON RD
WINDMILL RD
CARSHALTON RD
LONDON RD
BEDDINGTON LA
MANOR RD
COMMONSIDE EAST
UPPER GN E
A236
A237
A239
B272
B277
181
204
219
A
B
C
D
1
2
3
4
5
6
28
29
30
66
67
68
69

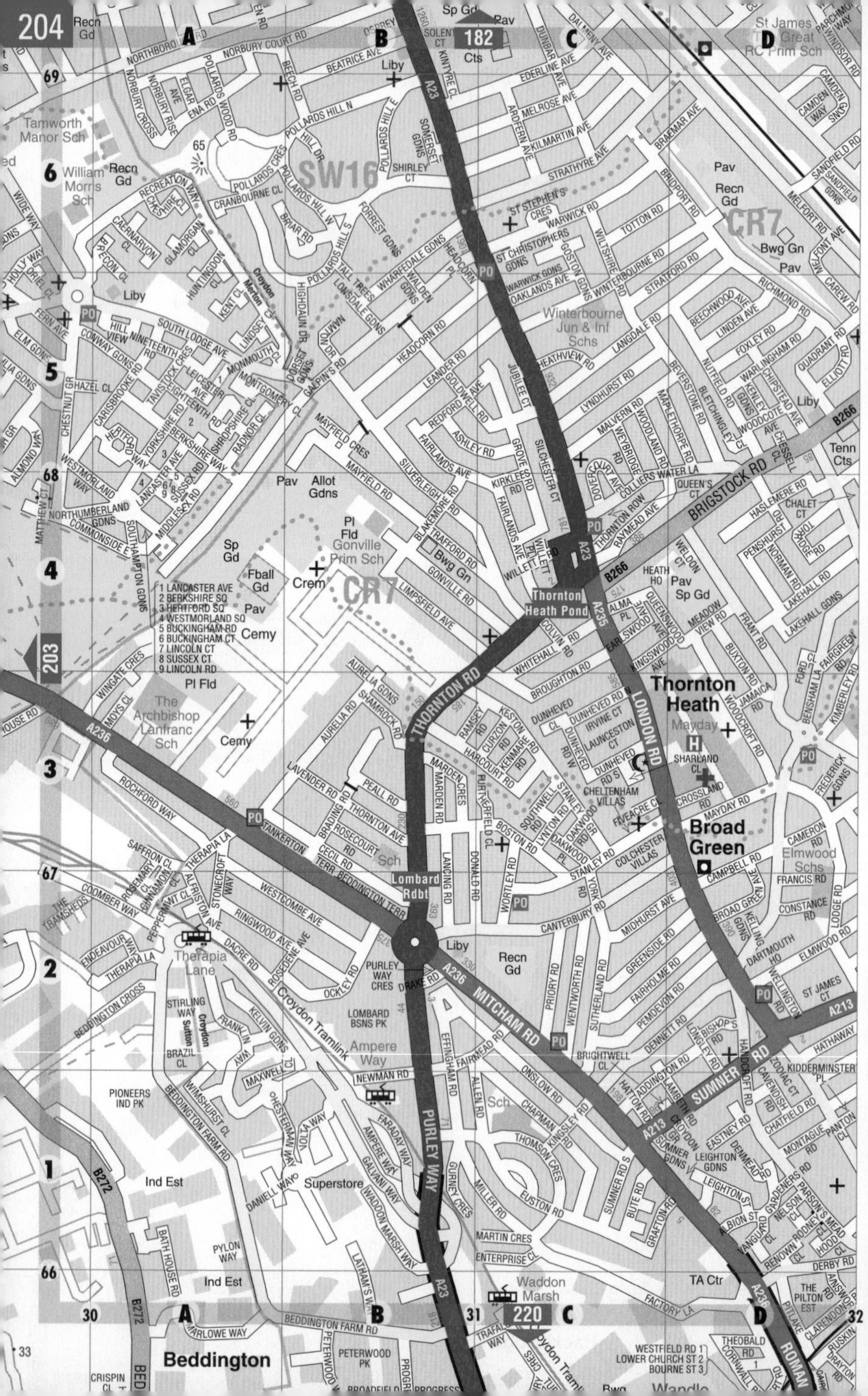
A
B
C
D
182
Recn Gd
NORTHBOROUGH RD
NORBURY COURT RD
BEATRICE AVE
Liby
Sp Gd
Pav
Cts
SOLENT CT
KINTYRE CL
DALMENY AVE
DUNBAR AVE
St James The Great RC Prim Sch
PARCHMORE WAY
WINDSOR RD
69
NORBURY CROSS
NORBURY RISE
ELGAR AVE
ENA RD
POLLARDS WOOD RD
BEECH RD
POLLARDS HILL N
POLLARDS HILL E
SOMERSET GDNS
EDERLINE AVE
MELROSE AVE
ARDFERN AVE
KILMARTIN AVE
BRAEMAR AVE
CAMDEN RD
CAMDEN WAY
Tamworth Manor Sch
65
SW16
SHIRLEY CT
STRATHYRE AVE
BRIDPORT RD
SANDFIELD RD
6
William Morris Sch
Recn Gd
RECREATION WAY
CHESHIRE CL
CRANBOURNE CL
POLLARDS CRES
POLLARDS HILL W
HILL DR
Pav
Recn Gd
CR7
MELFORT RD
WIDE WAY
CAERNARVON CL
GLAMORGAN CL
BRIAR RD
FORREST GDNS
POLLARDS HILLS
ST STEPHEN'S CRES
WARWICK RD
TOTTON RD
Bwg Gn
Pav
MELFONT AVE
CAREW RD
HOLLY WAY
ORIEL CL
BRECON CL
HUNTINGDON CL
Croydon
Merton
KENT CL
Liby
HIGHDAUN DR
TALL TREES
WHARFEDALE GDNS
LONSDALE GDNS
WALDEN GDNS
HEADCORN PL
PO
ST CHRISTOPHERS GDNS
WARWICK GDNS
OAKLANDS AVE
GOSTON GDNS
WILTSHIRE RD
WINTERBOURNE RD
STRATFORD RD
RICHMOND RD
BEECHWOOD AVE
LINDEN AVE
FERN AVE
ELM GDNS
CONWAY GDNS
HILL VIEW
NINETEENTH RD
SOUTH LODGE AVE
LINDSEY CL
DORSET GDNS
NAMTON DR
HEADCORN RD
Winterbourne Jun & Inf Schs
LANGDALE RD
FOXLEY RD
WARLINGHAM RD
QUADRANT RD
ELLIOTT RD
5
HAZEL CL
CHESTNUT GR
CARISBROOKE RD
TAVISTOCK CRES
LEICESTER AVE
EIGHTEENTH RD
MONMOUTH CL
MONTGOMERY CL
GALPIN'S RD
LEANDER RD
GOLDWELL RD
REDFORD AVE
HEATHVIEW RD
JUBILEE CT
LYNDHURST RD
BEVERSTONE RD
NUTFIELD RD
BLETCHINGLEY CL
KENLEY GDNS
CHIPSTEAD AVE
WOODCOTE AVE
Liby
B266
ALMOND WAY
HERTFORD WAY
YORKSHIRE RD
BERKSHIRE WAY
SHROPSHIRE CL
RADNOR CL
MAYFIELD CRES
FAIRLANDS AVE
ASHLEY RD
GROVE RD
SILCHESTER CT
MALVERN RD
WEYBRIDGE RD
WOODLAND RD
MAPLETHORPE RD
CHESSELL CL
Tenn Cts
68
WESTMORLAND WAY
LANCASTER AVE
SUSSEX RD
MIDDLESEX RD
Pav
Allot Gdns
MAYFIELD RD
SILVERLEIGH RD
KIRKLEES RD
DOVERCOURT AVE
COLLIERS WATER LA
QUEEN'S CT
BRIGSTOCK RD
HASLEMERE RD
CHALET CT
MATTHEW CT
NORTHUMBERLAND GDNS
COMMONSIDE E
SOUTHAMPTON GDNS
Pl Fld
Gonville Prim Sch
BLAKEMORE RD
TRAFFORD RD
FAIRLANDS AVE
WILLETT PL
WILLETT RD
THORNTON ROW
RAYMEAD AVE
WELDON CT
PENSHURST RD
NORMAN RD
TORRIDGE RD
4
Sp Gd
Fball Gd
Crem
Bwg Gn
GONVILLE RD
CR7
B266
HEATH HO
Pav
Sp Gd
LAKEHALL RD
1 LANCASTER AVE
2 BERKSHIRE SQ
3 HERTFORD SQ
4 WESTMORLAND SQ
5 BUCKINGHAM RD
6 BUCKINGHAM CT
7 LINCOLN CT
8 SUSSEX CT
9 LINCOLN RD
Pav
Cemy
LIMPSFIELD AVE
Thornton Heath Pond
A235
ALMA PL
QUEENSWOOD AVE
MEADOW VIEW RD
FRANT RD
LAKEHALL GDNS
203
COLVIN RD
WHITEHALL RD
EARLSWOOD AVE
KINGSWOOD AVE
BUXTON RD
FORD CL
BENSHAM LA
FAIRGREEN RD
WINGATE CRES
Pl Fld
AURELIA GDNS
SHAMROCK RD
THORNTON RD
BROUGHTON RD
LONDON RD
Thornton Heath
JAMAICA RD
WOODCROFT RD
KIMBERLEY RD
HOUSE RD
MOYS CL
The Archbishop Lanfranc Sch
Cemy
AURELIA RD
RAMSEY RD
CURZON RD
KESTON RD
KENMARE RD
HARCOURT RD
DUNHEVED CL
DUNHEVED RD N
IRVINE CT
LAUNCESTON CT
DUNHEVED RD W
DUNHEVED RD S
Mayday
H
SHARLAND CL
CROSSLAND RD
PO
FREDERICK GDNS
A236
3
ROCHFORD WAY
LAVENDER RD
PEALL RD
MARDEN CRES
MARDEN RD
FURTHERFIELD CL
SOUTHWELL RD
STANLEY RD
LYNTON RD
OAKWOOD RD
CHELTENHAM VILLAS
FIVEACRE CL
MAYDAY RD
THORNTON AVE
PO
TANKERTON TERR
BRADING RD
ROSECOURT RD
Sch
BOSTON RD
OAKWOOD PL
COLCHESTER VILLAS
STANLEY RD
Broad Green
CAMERON RD
Elmwood Schs
SAFFRON CL
THERAPIA LA
ROSEMARY CL
CINNAMON CL
ALFRISTON AVE
STONECROFT WAY
CECIL RD
BEDDINGTON TERR
Lombard Rdbt
LANCING RD
DONALD RD
WORTLEY RD
YORK RD
CAMPBELL RD
BROAD GREEN AVE
FRANCIS RD
67
THE TRANSHEDS
COOMBER WAY
PEPPERMINT CL
WESTCOMBE AVE
RINGWOOD AVE
PO
CANTERBURY RD
MIDHURST AVE
KELLING GDNS
CONSTANCE RD
LODGE RD
ENDEAVOUR WAY
THERAPIA LA
Therapia Lane
DACRE RD
ROSEDENE AVE
OCKLEY RD
PURLEY WAY CRES
DRAKE RD
Liby
A236
Recn Gd
PRIORY RD
WENTWORTH RD
SUTHERLAND RD
GREENSIDE RD
FAIRHOLME RD
DARTMOUTH HO
ELMWOOD RD
2
BEDDINGTON CROSS
STIRLING WAY
Sutton
Croydon
FRANKLIN WAY
KELVIN GDNS
Croydon Tramlink
LOMBARD BSNS PK
MITCHAM RD
PEMDEVON RD
WELLINGTON
ST JAMES CT
PO
A213
BRAZIL CL
Ampere Way
MAXWELL CL
NEWMAN RD
EFFINGHAM RD
FAIRMEAD RD
ALLEN RD
ONSLOW RD
PO
BRIGHTWELL CL
DENNETT RD
LONGLEY RD
BISHOP'S RD
HANDCROFT RD
HATHAWAY
KIDDERMINSTER PL
PIONEERS IND PK
WIMSHURST CL
BEDDINGTON FARM RD
CHESTERMAN WAY
VIOLA AVE
FARADAY WAY
PURLEY WAY
Sch
CHAPMAN RD
KINGSLEY RD
HATTON RD
ADDINGTON RD
LAMBETH RD
SUMNER RD
ZODIAC CT
CAVENDISH RD
CHATFIELD RD
1
B272
Ind Est
DANIELL WAY
Superstore
AMPERE WAY
GALVANI WAY
WADDON MARSH WAY
GURNEY CRES
MILLER RD
THOMSON CRES
EUSTON RD
SUMNER RD S
BUTE RD
GRAFTON RD
A213
CROYDON
SUMNER GDNS
LEIGHTON GDNS
EASTNEY RD
DENMEAD RD
LEIGHTON ST
MONTAGUE RD
PANTON CL
GARDENERS RD
PARSON'S MEAD
NELSON CL
ALBION ST
VANGUARD CL
RODNEY CL
HOOD CL
RENOWN CL
66
BATH HOUSE RD
PYLON WAY
Ind Est
LATHAM'S WAY
MARTIN CRES
ENTERPRISE CL
Waddon Marsh
TA Ctr
FACTORY LA
DERBY RD
THE PILTON EST
PITLAKE
ANSWORTH
CLARENDON RD
30
A
B
31
220
C
D
32
MARLOWE WAY
BEDDINGTON FARM RD
PETERWOOD WAY
TRAFALGAR WAY
Croydon Tramlink
THEOBALD RD
CORNWALL RD
RUSKIN
DRAYTON RD
ROMAN WAY
33
Beddington
PETERWOOD PK
WESTFIELD RD 1
LOWER CHURCH ST 2
BOURNE ST 3
CRISPIN CL
BROADFIELD
PROGRESS
Wandle

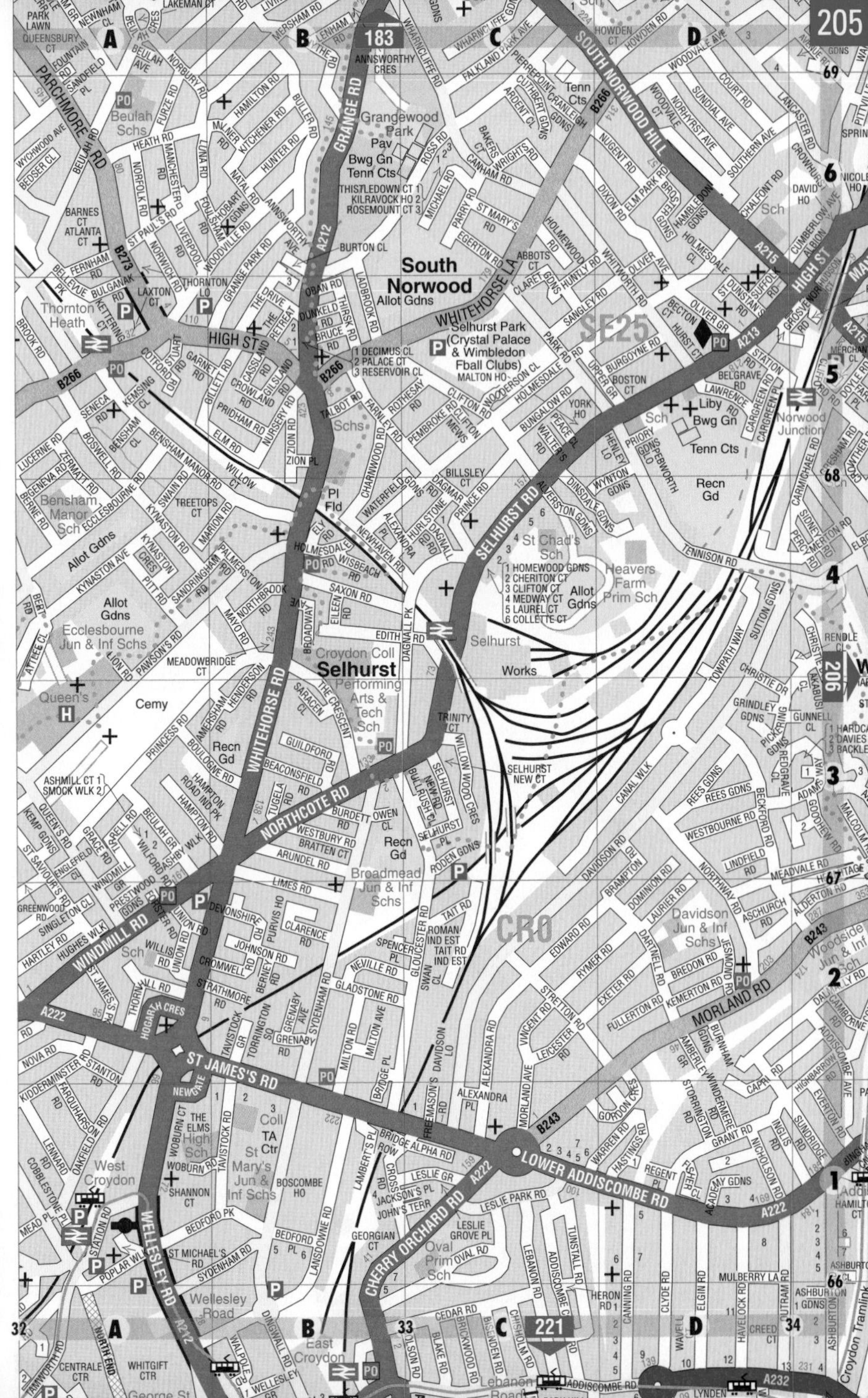
South Norwood
Selhurst
Thornton Heath
Norwood Junction
West Croydon
East Croydon
SE25
CR0
Grangewood Park
Selhurst Park (Crystal Palace & Wimbledon Fball Clubs)
Croydon Coll Selhurst Performing Arts & Tech Sch
Heavers Farm Prim Sch
Davidson Jun & Inf Schs
Broadmead Jun & Inf Schs
Ecclesbourne Jun & Inf Schs
Bensham Manor Sch
Oval Prim Sch
St Mary's Jun & Inf Schs
Wellesley Road
Croydon Tramlink
SOUTH NORWOOD HILL
WHITEHORSE RD
WHITEHORSE LA
SELHURST RD
GRANGE RD
NORTHCOTE RD
WINDMILL RD
ST JAMES'S RD
LOWER ADDISCOMBE RD
MORLAND RD
CHERRY ORCHARD RD
WELLESLEY RD
PARCHMORE RD
HIGH ST
TENNISON RD
183
221
206

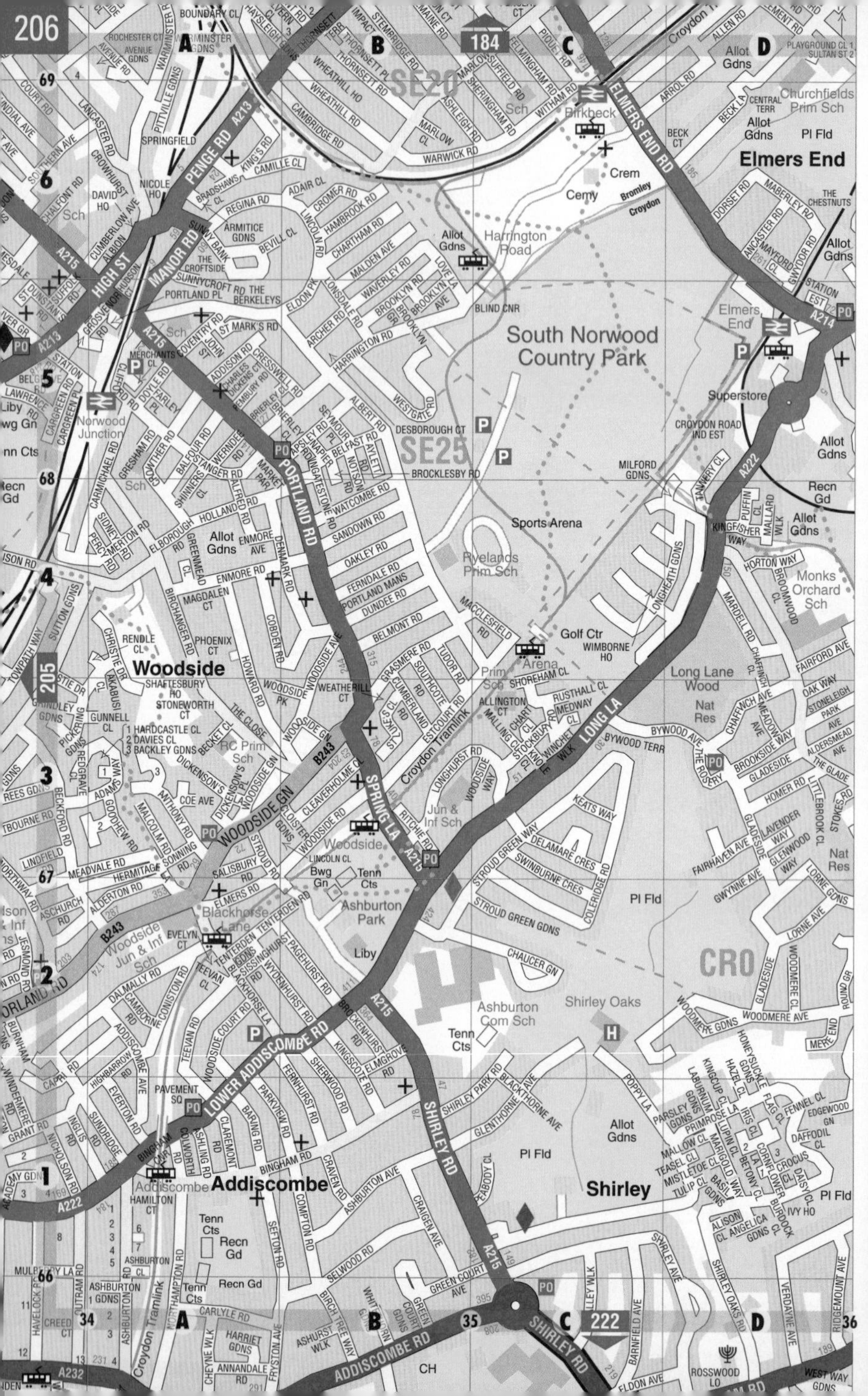
184
222
205
SE20
SE25
CR0
Elmers End
South Norwood Country Park
Woodside
Addiscombe
Shirley
Birkbeck
Norwood Junction
Harrington Road
Elmers End
Arena
Woodside
Blackhorse Lane
Addiscombe
Crem
Cemy
Sports Arena
Golf Ctr
Long Lane Wood
Nat Res
Ashburton Park
Ashburton Com Sch
Shirley Oaks
Ryelands Prim Sch
Churchfields Prim Sch
Monks Orchard Sch
Superstore
Croydon Road Ind Est
Croydon Tramlink
PENGE RD
HIGH ST
MANOR RD
PORTLAND RD
SPRING LA
SHIRLEY RD
LONG LA
ELMERS END RD
LOWER ADDISCOMBE RD
ADDISCOMBE RD
WOODSIDE GN
STROUD GREEN WAY
WOODMERE AVE
A213
A215
A214
A222
A232
B243
Allot Gdns
Pl Fld
Recn Gd
Tenn Cts
Liby

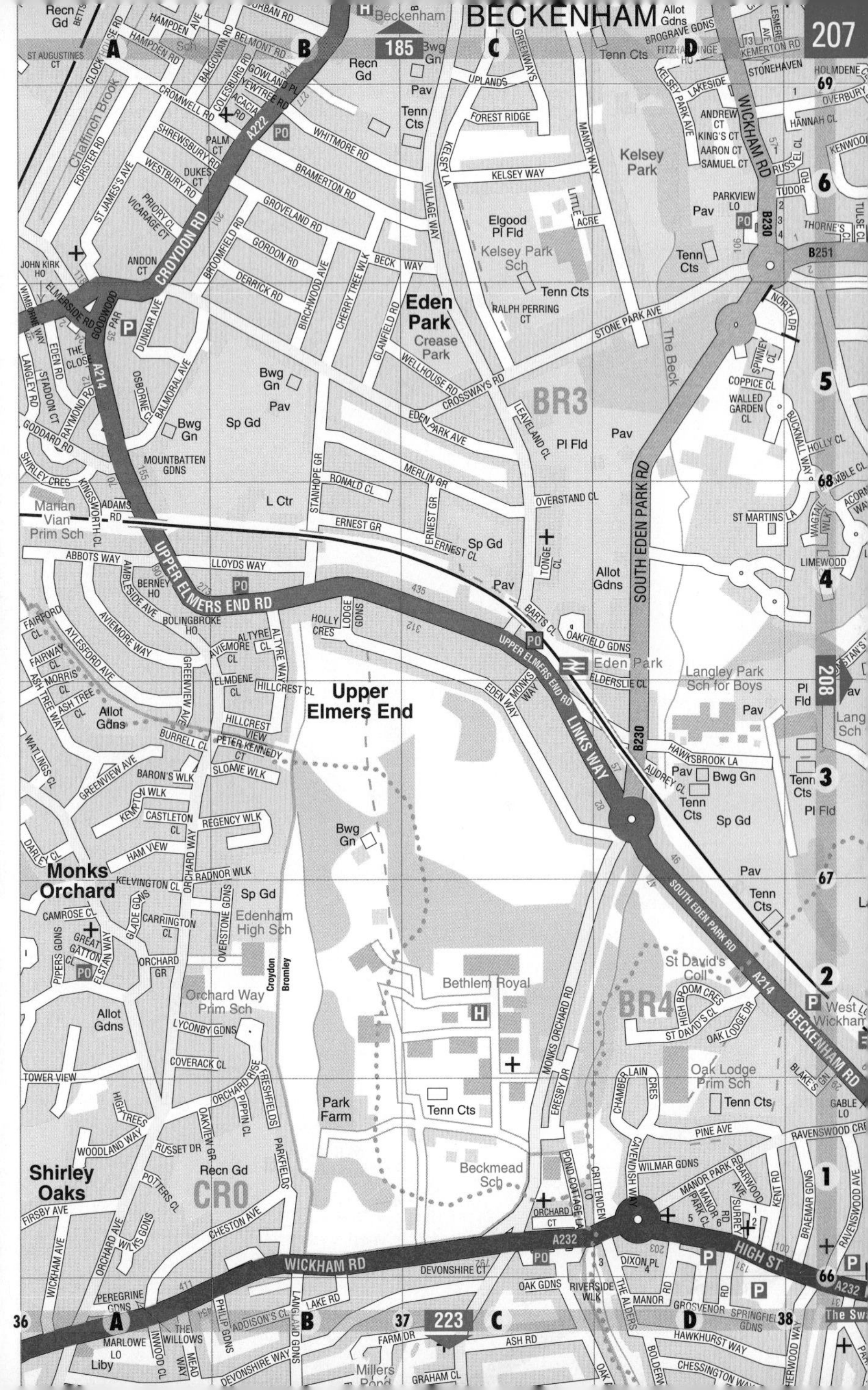

207
BECKENHAM
185
223
208
A
B
C
D
1
2
3
4
5
6
36
37
38
66
67
68
69
Beckenham
Recn Gd
Allot Gdns
Tenn Cts
Bwg Gn
Pav
HAMPDEN AVE
HAMPDEN RD
BELMONT RD
CLOCK HOUSE RD
ST AUGUSTINES CT
BALGOWAN RD
COLESBURG RD
GOWLAND PL
YEWTREE RD
ACACIA RD
CROMWELL RD
A222
Chaffinch Brook
FORSTER RD
SHREWSBURY RD
PALM CT
WHITMORE RD
BRAMERTON RD
WESTBURY RD
DUKES CT
ST JAMES'S AVE
PRIORY CL
VICARAGE CT
CROYDON RD
GROVELAND RD
GORDON RD
BROOMFIELD RD
DERRICK RD
BIRCHWOOD AVE
CHERRY TREE WLK
BECK WAY
GLANFIELD RD
VILLAGE WAY
KELSEY LA
UPLANDS
FOREST RIDGE
GREENWAYS
MANOR WAY
KELSEY WAY
Kelsey Park
LITTLE ACRE
Elgood Pl Fld
Kelsey Park Sch
RALPH PERRING CT
STONE PARK AVE
Eden Park
Crease Park
WELLHOUSE RD
CROSSWAYS RD
BR3
EDEN PARK AVE
LEAVELAND CL
Pl Fld
The Beck
SOUTH EDEN PARK RD
BROGRAVE GDNS
FITZHARDINGE HO
KEMERTON RD
STONEHAVEN
LAKESIDE
KELSEY PARK AVE
ANDREW CT
KING'S CT
AARON CT
SAMUEL CT
WICKHAM RD
RUSSELL CL
TUDOR RD
PARKVIEW LO
B230
B251
THORNE'S CL
TULSE CL
HOLMDENE CT
OVERBURY
HANNAH CL
KENWOOD
NORTH DR
SPINNEY CL
COPPICE CL
WALLED GARDEN CL
BUCKNALL WAY
HOLLY CL
WAGTAIL WLK
ST MARTINS LA
LIMEWOOD
JOHN KIRK HO
ANDON CT
ELMERSIDE RD
WIMBORNE WAY
GOODWOOD
EDEN RD
THE CLOSE
LANGLEY RD
STADDON CL
RAYMOND RD
GODDARD RD
SHIRLEY CRES
DUNBAR AVE
OSBORNE CL
BALMORAL AVE
A214
Sp Gd
MOUNTBATTEN GDNS
KINGSWORTH CL
ADAMS RD
Marian Vian Prim Sch
L Ctr
STANHOPE GR
RONALD CL
MERLIN GR
ERNEST GR
ERNEST CL
OVERSTAND CL
TONGE CL
Allot Gdns
ABBOTS WAY
LLOYDS WAY
AMBLESIDE AVE
BERNEY HO
UPPER ELMERS END RD
BARTS CL
OAKFIELD GDNS
Eden Park
ELDERSLIE CL
BOLINGBROKE HO
FAIRFORD CL
AYLESFORD AVE
AVIEMORE WAY
FAIRWAY CL
MORRIS CL
ASH TREE WAY
ASH TREE CL
AVIEMORE CL
ALTYRE CL
ALTYRE WAY
GREENVIEW AVE
HOLLY CRES
LODGE GDNS
ELMDENE CL
HILLCREST CL
HILLCREST VIEW
PETER KENNEDY CT
Upper Elmers End
EDEN WAY
MONKS WAY
LINKS WAY
Langley Park Sch for Boys
HAWKSBROOK LA
AUDREY CL
BURRELL CL
BARON'S WLK
SLOANE WLK
KEMPTON WLK
CASTLETON CL
REGENCY WLK
WATLINGS CL
DARLEY CL
HAM VIEW
ORCHARD WAY
RADNOR WLK
Monks Orchard
KELVINGTON CL
OVERSTONE GDNS
Edenham High Sch
CAMROSE CL
GLADE GDNS
CARRINGTON CL
GREAT GATTON CL
ELSTAN WAY
PIPERS GDNS
ORCHARD GR
Croydon
Bromley
Orchard Way Prim Sch
LYCONBY GDNS
COVERACK CL
TOWER VIEW
HIGH TREES
ORCHARD RISE
PIPPIN CL
FRESHFIELDS
OAKVIEW GR
WOODLAND WAY
RUSSET DR
Shirley Oaks
POTTERS CL
CR0
FIRSBY AVE
ORCHARD AVE
WILKS GDNS
CHESTON AVE
PARKFIELDS
WICKHAM AVE
Park Farm
Bethlem Royal
Beckmead Sch
MONKS ORCHARD RD
ERESBY DR
POND COTTAGE LA
CRITTENDEN LO
ORCHARD CT
St David's Coll
BR4
HIGH BROOM CRES
ST DAVID'S CL
OAK LODGE DR
Oak Lodge Prim Sch
CHAMBERLAIN CRES
BLAKE'S GN
BECKENHAM RD
West Wickham
GABLE LO
PINE AVE
RAVENSWOOD CRES
CAVENDISH WAY
WILMAR GDNS
MANOR PARK RD
MANOR PARK CL
BARWOOD AVE
SURREY RD
KENT RD
BRAEMAR GDNS
RAVENSWOOD AVE
A232
HIGH ST
WICKHAM RD
DEVONSHIRE CT
DIXON PL
OAK GDNS
RIVERSIDE WLK
THE ALDERS
MANOR RD
GROSVENOR RD
SPRINGFIELD GDNS
PEREGRINE GDNS
LAKE RD
ADDISON'S CL
PHILIP GDNS
THE WILLOWS
MARLOWE LO
Liby
INWOOD CL
MEAD WAY
LANGLAND GDNS
DEVONSHIRE WAY
FARM DR
ASH RD
Millers Pond
GRAHAM CL
HAWKHURST WAY
CHESSINGTON WAY
BOLDERWOOD WAY
HERWOOD WAY
The Swan

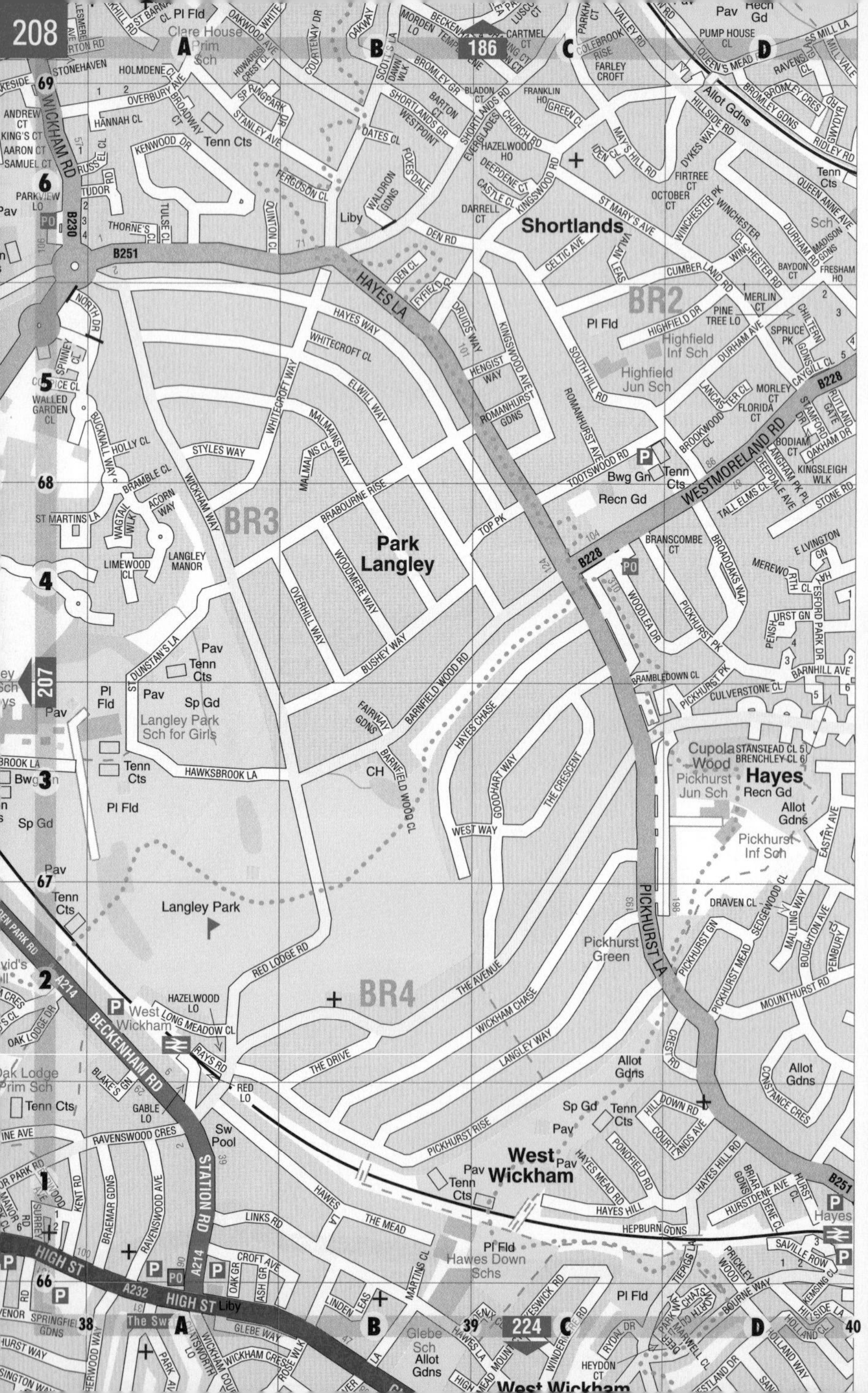
A
B
C
D
186
207
224
38
39
40
69
6
5
68
4
3
67
2
1
66
Shortlands
BR2
BR3
Park Langley
BR4
Hayes
West Wickham
Langley Park
Pickhurst Green
Cupola Wood
Clare House Prim Sch
Highfield Inf Sch
Highfield Jun Sch
Langley Park Sch for Girls
Pickhurst Jun Sch
Pickhurst Inf Sch
Oak Lodge Prim Sch
Hawes Down Schs
Glebe Sch
Langley Manor
WICKHAM RD
B230
B251
B228
A214
A232
HAYES LA
WESTMORELAND RD
PICKHURST LA
BECKENHAM RD
STATION RD
HIGH ST
SHORTLANDS RD
ST MARY'S AVE
CUMBERLAND RD
HIGHFIELD DR
DURHAM AVE
SOUTH HILL RD
ROMANHURST AVE
TOOTSWOOD RD
BRABOURNE RISE
STYLES WAY
WICKHAM WAY
WHITECROFT WAY
HAYES WAY
WHITECROFT CL
ELWILL WAY
MALMAINS WAY
MALMAINS CL
WOODMERE WAY
OVERHILL WAY
BUSHEY WAY
BARNFIELD WOOD RD
BARNFIELD WOOD CL
FAIRWAY GDNS
HAYES CHASE
GOODHART WAY
THE CRESCENT
WEST WAY
THE AVENUE
WICKHAM CHASE
LANGLEY WAY
THE DRIVE
PICKHURST RISE
RED LODGE RD
HAWKSBROOK LA
ST DUNSTAN'S LA
LONG MEADOW CL
RAYS RD
HAYES MEAD RD
HAYES HILL
PONDFIELD RD
HAYES HILL RD
HILLDOWN RD
COURTLANDS AVE
CREST RD
CONSTANCE CRES
MOUNTHURST RD
PICKHURST MEAD
PICKHURST GN
SEDGEWOOD CL
MALLING WAY
BOUGHTON AVE
PEMBURY CL
DRAVEN CL
EASTRY AVE
HURSTDENE AVE
HEPBURN GDNS
SAVILLE ROW
BOURNE WAY
PRICKLEY WOOD
TIEPIGS LA
HOLLAND WAY
HILLSIDE LA
KEMSING CL
LINKS RD
THE MEAD
HAWES LA
MARTINS CL
LINDEN LEAS
GLEBE WAY
WICKHAM CRES
ROSE WALK
CROFT AVE
OAK GR
ASH GR
RAVENSWOOD CRES
RAVENSWOOD AVE
BRAEMAR GDNS
KENT RD
SURREY RD
BLAKE'S GN
GABLE LO
OAK LODGE DR
HAZELWOOD LO
RED LO
WOODLEA DR
PICKHURST PK
BRAMBLEDOWN CL
CULVERSTONE CL
BROADOAKS WAY
BRANSCOMBE CT
BARNHILL AVE
MEREWORTH CL
TALL ELMS CL
DEEPDALE AVE
LANGHAM PK PL
STONE RD
KINGSLEIGH WLK
OAKHAM DR
STAMFORD DR
RUTLAND GATE
BODIAM CT
FLORIDA CT
MORLEY CT
LANCASTER CL
BROOKWOOD CL
SPRUCE PK
CHILTERN GDNS
CAYGILL CL
MERLIN CT
PINE TREE LO
KINGSWOOD AVE
ROMANHURST GDNS
HENGIST WAY
DRUIDS WAY
FYFIELD CL
DEN CL
DEN RD
CELTIC AVE
VALAN LEAS
DARRELL CT
CASTLE CL
DEEPDENE CT
KINGSWOOD RD
HAZELWOOD HO
CHURCH RD
EVERGLADES
WALDRON GDNS
FERGUSON CL
OATES CL
FOXES DALE
WESTPOINT
SHORTLANDS GR
BROMLEY GR
BARTON CT
STANLEY AVE
SPRINGPARK DR
BROADWAY
OVERBURY AVE
HOLMDENE CL
HANNAH CL
KENWOOD DR
TULSE CL
QUINTON CL
THORNE'S CL
TUDOR RD
RUSSELL CL
STONEHAVEN
NORTH DR
SPINNEY CL
COPPICE CL
WALLED GARDEN CL
BUCKNALL WAY
HOLLY CL
BRAMBLE CL
ACORN WAY
WAGTAIL WLK
ST MARTINS LA
LIMEWOOD CL
QUEEN ANNE AVE
DURHAM RD
MADISON GDNS
BAYDON CT
FRESHAM HO
WINCHESTER PK
WINCHESTER RD
OCTOBER CT
FIRTREE CT
DYKES WAY
HILLSIDE RD
MAY'S HILL RD
IDEN CL
GREEN CL
FRANKLIN HO
FARLEY CROFT
COLEBROOK RISE
PUMP HOUSE CL
QUEEN'S MEAD RD
BROMLEY CRES
BROMLEY GDNS
RAVENS CL
RIDLEY RD
MILL VALE
Allot Gdns
Tenn Cts
Pl Fld
Sp Gd
Pav
Recn Gd
Bwg Gn
Sw Pool
Liby
CH
West Wickham
Hayes

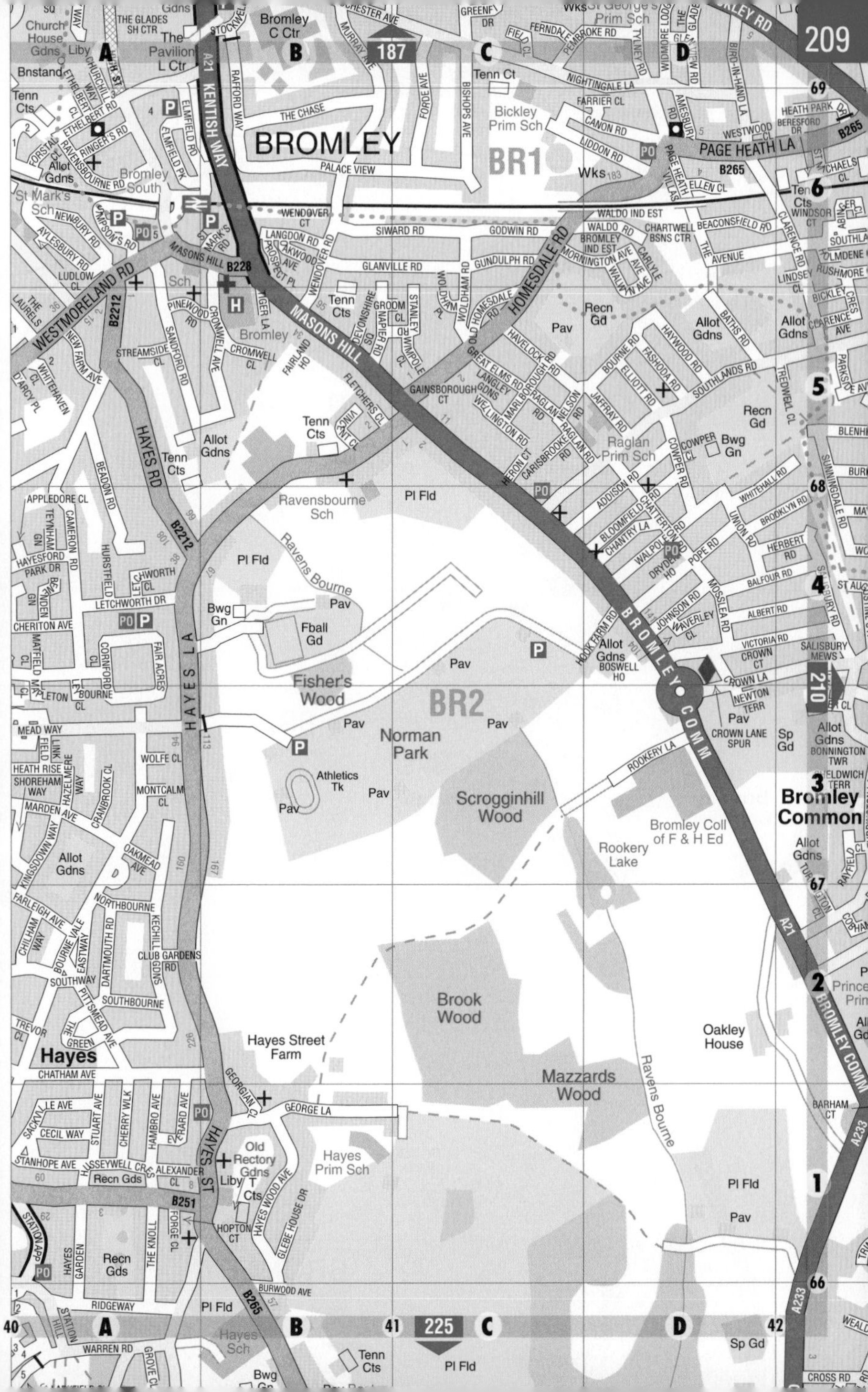
187
A
B
C
D
BROMLEY
BR1
BR2
Bromley South
Bromley C Ctr
The Pavilion L Ctr
Church House Gdns
Liby
Bnstand
Tenn Cts
Allot Gdns
St Mark's Sch
KENTISH WAY
A21
STOCKWELL
RAFFORD WAY
THE CHASE
MURRAY AVE
FORDE AVE
BISHOPS AVE
PALACE VIEW
Bickley Prim Sch
Tenn Ct
NIGHTINGALE LA
FARRIER CL
CANON RD
LIDDON RD
Wks
PAGE HEATH LA
PAGE HEATH VILLAS
ELLEN CL
WESTWOOD CL
B265
HEATH PARK DR
BERESFORD DR
69
6
WENDOVER CT
SIWARD RD
GODWIN RD
WALDO IND EST
WALDO RD
BROMLEY IND EST
CHARTWELL BSNS CTR
BEACONSFIELD RD
THE AVENUE
MORNINGTON AVE
CARLYLE AVE
WALWYN AVE
LANGDON RD
OAKWOOD AVE
PROSPECT PL
WENDOVER RD
GLANVILLE RD
GUNDULPH RD
HOMESDALE RD
WOLDHAM RD
WOLDHAM PL
OLD HOMESDALE RD
MASONS HILL
B228
WESTMORELAND RD
B2212
NEWBURY RD
AYLESBURY RD
LUDLOW CL
THE LAURELS
SIMPSON'S RD
ST MARK'S RD
Sch
H
Bromley
PINEWOOD RD
CROMWELL AVE
CROMWELL CL
TIGER LA
SANDFORD RD
STREAMSIDE CL
NEW FARM AVE
WHITEHAVEN CL
D'ARCY PL
DEVONSHIRE SQ
NAPIER RD
GROOM CL
STANLEY RD
WYMPOLE CL
FAIRLAND HO
FLETCHERS CL
VINCENT CL
GAINSBOROUGH CT
Tenn Cts
GREAT ELMS RD
LANGLEY GDNS
WELLINGTON RD
MARLBOROUGH RD
RAGLAN RD
NELSON RD
HAVELOCK RD
BOURNE RD
ELLIOTT RD
FASHODA RD
HAYWOOD RD
JAFFRAY RD
BATHS RD
SOUTHLANDS RD
TREDWELL CL
Recn Gd
Pav
Allot Gdns
5
Raglan Prim Sch
COWPER CL
COWPER RD
Bwg Gn
HERON CT
CARISBROOKE RD
ADDISON RD
BLOOMFIELD RD
CHANTRY LA
CHATTERTON RD
WALPOLE RD
DRYDEN HO
POPE RD
UNION RD
WHITEHALL RD
BROOKLYN RD
HERBERT RD
BALFOUR RD
ALBERT RD
VICTORIA RD
JOHNSON RD
WAVERLEY CL
MOSSLEA RD
HOOK FARM RD
BOSWELL HO
CROWN CT
CROWN LA
NEWTON TERR
CROWN LANE SPUR
SALISBURY MEWS
SALISBURY RD
SUNNINGDALE RD
68
4
210
HAYES RD
HAYES LA
BEADON RD
APPLEDORE CL
TEYNHAM GN
CAMERON RD
HAYESFORD PARK DR
HURSTFIELD
LETCHWORTH CL
LETCHWORTH DR
CHERITON AVE
MATFIELD CL
CORNFORD CL
FAIR ACRES
LE BOURNE CL
MEAD WAY
LINK FIELD
WOLFE CL
MONTCALM CL
HEATH RISE
SHOREHAM WAY
HAZELMERE WAY
CRAINBROOK CL
MARDEN AVE
Ravensbourne Sch
Ravens Bourne
Pl Fld
Bwg Gn
Fball Gd
Fisher's Wood
Norman Park
Athletics Tk
Scrogginhill Wood
ROOKERY LA
Bromley Coll of F & H Ed
Rookery Lake
BROMLEY COMM
Sp Gd
Bromley Common
BONNINGTON TWR
ELDWICH TERR
3
67
2
Prince Prim
KINGSDOWN WAY
OAKMEAD AVE
NORTHBOURNE
KECHILL GDNS
FARLEIGH AVE
CHILHAM WAY
BOURNE VALE
EASTWAY
DARTMOUTH RD
CLUB GARDENS RD
SOUTHWAY
PITTSMEAD AVE
SOUTHBOURNE
TREVOR CL
THE GREEN
Hayes
Brook Wood
Oakley House
Hayes Street Farm
Mazzards Wood
BARHAM CT
A233
CHATHAM AVE
SACKVILLE AVE
STUART AVE
CHERRY WLK
HAMBRO AVE
EVERARD AVE
CECIL WAY
STANHOPE AVE
HUSSEYWELL CRES
ALEXANDER CL
Recn Gds
GEORGIAN CL
GEORGE LA
HAYES ST
Old Rectory Gdns
Hayes Prim Sch
Liby
T Cts
HAYES WOOD AVE
GLEBE HOUSE DR
HOPTON CT
FORGE CL
B251
STATION APP
HAYES GARDEN
THE KNOLL
Recn Gds
BURWOOD AVE
RIDGEWAY
Pl Fld
B265
Pav
1
66
40
STATION HILL
WARREN RD
GROVE CL
Hayes Sch
Bwg Gn
41
225
42
Tenn Cts
Sp Gd
CROSS RD
WEALD

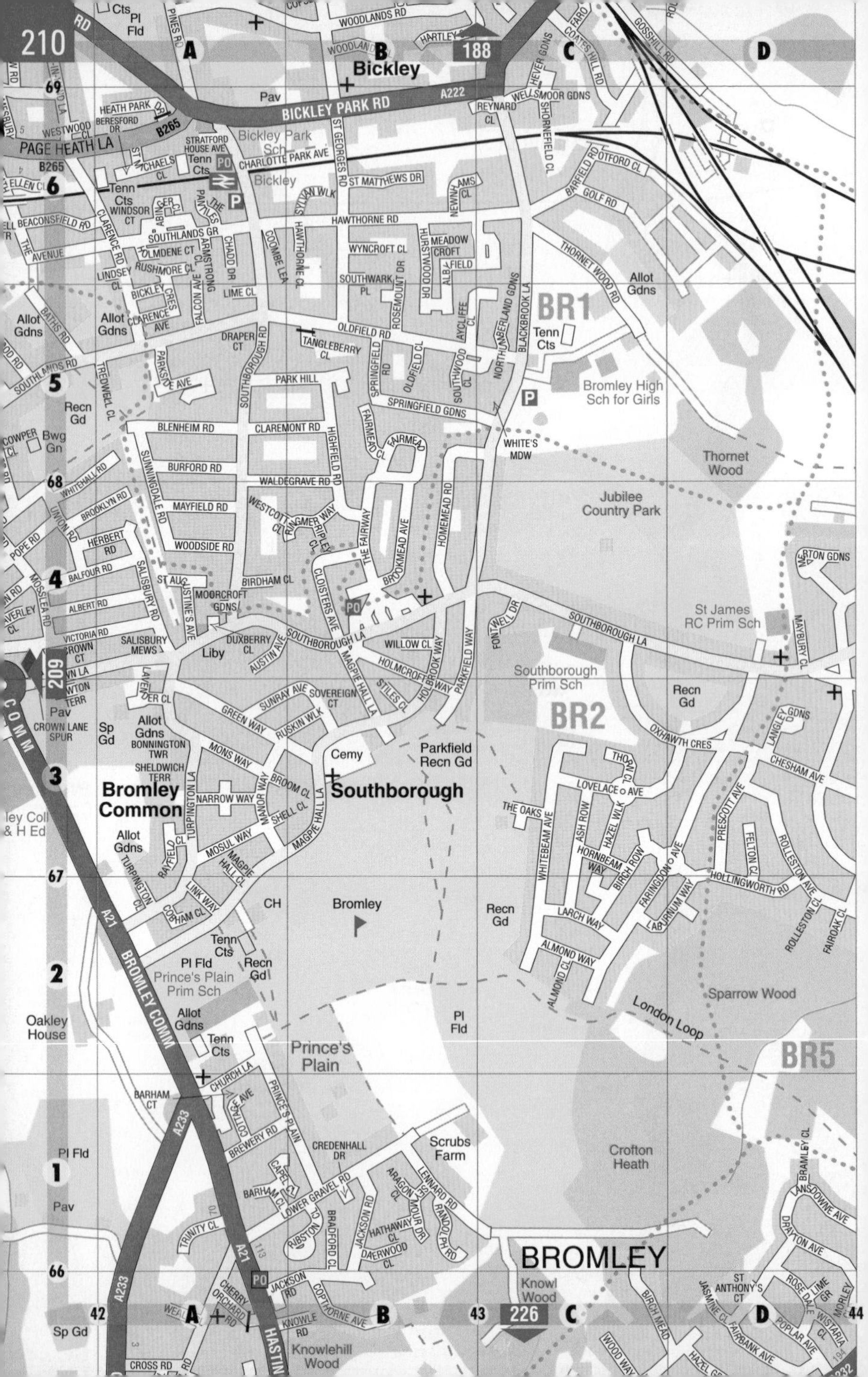
Bickley
BICKLEY PARK RD
A222
188
PAGE HEATH LA
B265
Bickley Park Sch
Bickley
CHARLOTTE PARK AVE
ST GEORGES RD
ST MATTHEWS DR
HAWTHORNE RD
BR1
Allot Gdns
Tenn Cts
Bromley High Sch for Girls
OLDFIELD RD
SOUTHBOROUGH RD
BLENHEIM RD
CLAREMONT RD
BURFORD RD
WALDEGRAVE RD
MAYFIELD RD
WOODSIDE RD
SPRINGFIELD GDNS
WHITE'S MDW
Thornet Wood
Jubilee Country Park
St James RC Prim Sch
SOUTHBOROUGH LA
Southborough Prim Sch
BR2
Recn Gd
OXHAWTH CRES
Liby
Cemy
Parkfield Recn Gd
Southborough
Bromley Common
209
COMM
Allot Gdns
Sp Gd
LOVELACE AVE
WHITEBEAM AVE
HOLLINGWORTH RD
CH
Bromley
Recn Gd
LARCH WAY
ALMOND WAY
A21
BROMLEY COMM
Tenn Cts
Pl Fld
Prince's Plain Prim Sch
Oakley House
Sparrow Wood
London Loop
BR5
Prince's Plain
Pl Fld
CHURCH LA
BARHAM CT
A233
BREWERY RD
CREDENHALL DR
Scrubs Farm
Crofton Heath
LOWER GRAVEL RD
LENNARD RD
BROMLEY
Knowl Wood
JACKSON RD
COPTHORNE AVE
KNOWLE RD
Knowlehill Wood
CROSS RD
HASTIN
A B C D
1 2 3 4 5 6
66 67 68 69
42 43 44
226

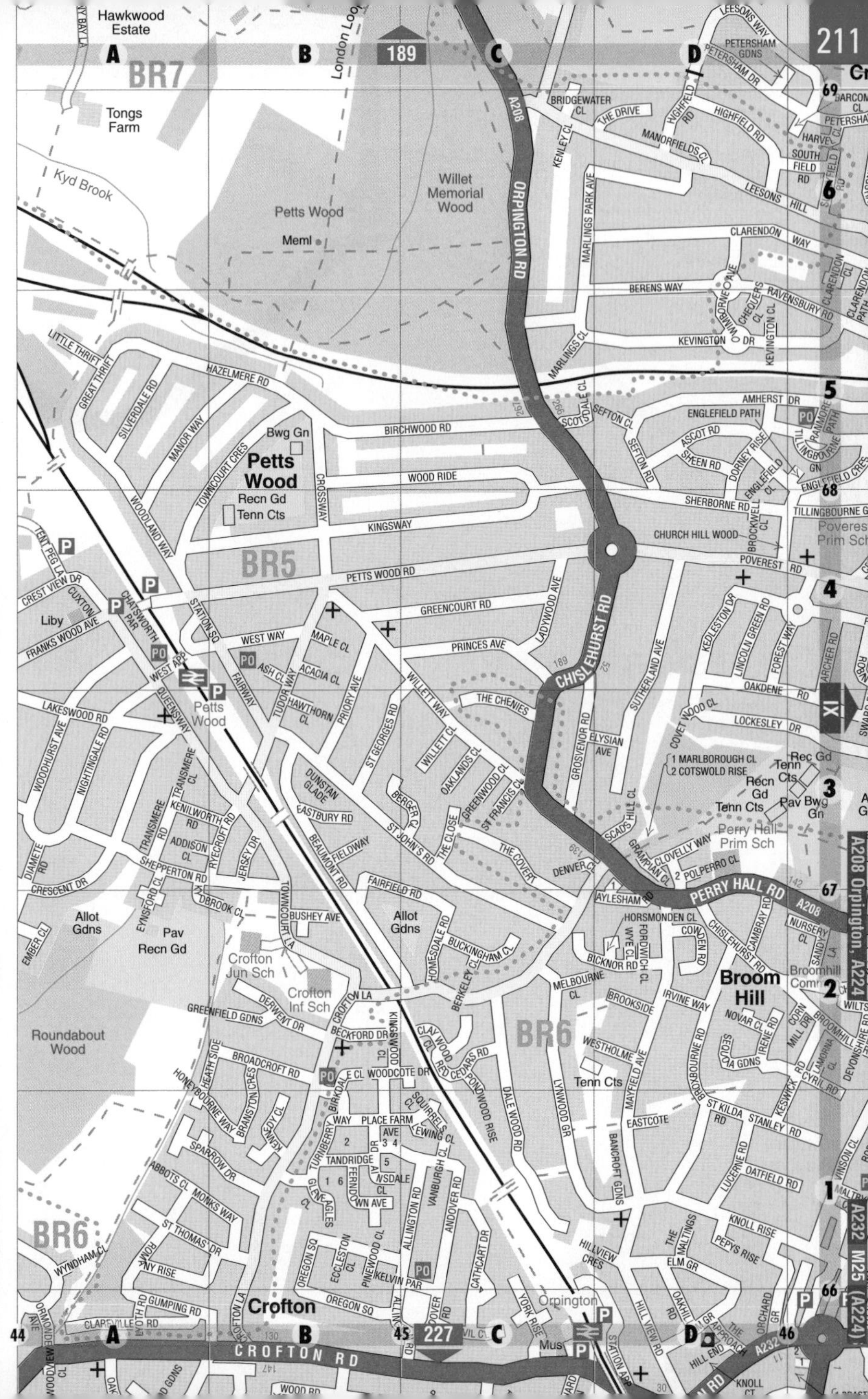

211
Hawkwood Estate
A
B
189
C
D
BR7
London Loop
Tongs Farm
Kyd Brook
Petts Wood
Meml
Willet Memorial Wood
A208
ORPINGTON RD
BRIDGEWATER CL
THE DRIVE
KENLEY CL
LEESONS WAY
PETERSHAM GDNS
PETERSHAM DR
HIGHFIELD RD
MANORFIELDS CL
LEESONS HILL
SOUTHFIELD RD
HARVEL
MARLINGS PARK AVE
CLARENDON WAY
BERENS WAY
WIMBORNE AVE
CHEQUERS CL
RAVENSBURY RD
KEVINGTON CL
KEVINGTON DR
MARLINGS CL
CLARENDON PATH
69
6
5
68
4
3
67
2
1
66
LITTLE THRIFT
GREAT THRIFT
SILVERDALE RD
HAZELMERE RD
MANOR WAY
Bwg Gn
Petts Wood
Recn Gd
Tenn Cts
TOWNCOURT CRES
BIRCHWOOD RD
WOOD RIDE
CROSSWAY
KINGSWAY
WOODLAND WAY
SCOTSDALE CL
SEFTON CL
SEFTON RD
AMHERST DR
ENGLEFIELD PATH
ASCOT RD
SHEEN RD
DORNEY RISE
ENGLEFIELD CL
ENGLEFIELD CRES
TILLINGBOURNE GN
RANMORE PATH
SHERBORNE RD
TILLINGBOURNE GN
CHURCH HILL WOOD
BROCKWELL CL
Poverest Prim Sch
POVEREST RD
BR5
PETTS WOOD RD
TENT PEG LA
CREST VIEW DR
CUXTON
CHATSWORTH PAR
Liby
FRANKS WOOD AVE
STATION SQ
GREENCOURT RD
LADYWOOD AVE
CHISLEHURST RD
WEST WAY
MAPLE CL
PRINCES AVE
KEDLESTON DR
LINCOLN GREEN RD
FOREST WAY
ARCHER RD
WEST APP
ASH CL
ACACIA CL
TUDOR WAY
FAIRWAY
QUEENSWAY
Petts Wood
LAKESWOOD RD
HAWTHORN CL
PRIORY AVE
ST GEORGES RD
WILLETT WAY
THE CHENIES
SUTHERLAND AVE
OAKDENE RD
COVET WOOD CL
LOCKESLEY DR
WOODHURST AVE
NIGHTINGALE RD
TRANSMERE CL
KENILWORTH RD
TRANSMERE RD
ADDISON CL
RYECROFT RD
JERSEY DR
DUNSTAN GLADE
EASTBURY RD
WILLETT CL
OAKLANDS CL
BERGER CL
GREENWOOD CL
ST FRANCIS CL
GROSVENOR RD
ELYSIAN AVE
1 MARLBOROUGH CL
2 COTSWOLD RISE
Rec Gd
Tenn Cts
Recn Gd
Tenn Cts
Pav
Bwg Gn
Perry Hall Prim Sch
DIAMETER RD
SHEPPERTON RD
CRESCENT DR
EYNSFORD CL
KYDBROOK CL
TOWNCOURT LA
BEAUMONT RD
FIELDWAY
ST JOHN'S RD
THE CLOSE
THE COVERT
SCADS HILL CL
GRAMPIAN CL
CLOVELLY WAY
POLPERRO CL
DENVER CL
AYLESHAM RD
PERRY HALL RD
A208
Allot Gdns
EMBER CL
Pav
Recn Gd
BUSHEY AVE
FAIRFIELD RD
Allot Gdns
HOMESDALE RD
BUCKINGHAM CL
HORSMONDEN CL
WYE CL
FORDWICH CL
COWDEN RD
CAMBRAY RD
CHISLEHURST RD
NURSERY CL
SANDY LA
Crofton Jun Sch
Crofton Inf Sch
BERKELEY CL
BICKNOR RD
MELBOURNE CL
Broom Hill
Broomhill Comm
CROFTON LA
GREENFIELD GDNS
DERWENT DR
BROOKSIDE
IRVINE WAY
Roundabout Wood
BECKFORD DR
KINGSWOOD CL
CLAYWOOD CL
RED CEDARS RD
BR6
WESTHOLME
NOVAR CL
IRENE RD
CORN MILL DR
BROOMHILL RD
HEATH SIDE
BROADCROFT RD
WOODCOTE DR
PONDWOOD RISE
DALE WOOD RD
LYNWOOD GR
MAYFIELD AVE
BROXBOURNE RD
LAMORNA CL
CYRIL RD
DEVONSHIRE RD
HONEYBOURNE WAY
BRANSTON CRES
KENNEDY CL
BIRKDALE CL
Tenn Cts
KESWICK RD
SQUIRRELS CL
TURNBERRY WAY
PLACE FARM AVE
EWING CL
EASTCOTE
ST KILDA RD
STANLEY RD
SPARROW DR
TANDRIDGE DR
FERNDOWN AVE
NSDALE CL
VANBURGH CL
ANDOVER RD
BANCROFT GDNS
LUCERNE RD
OATFIELD RD
VINSON CL
ABBOTS CL
MONKS WAY
GLENEAGLES CL
BR6
ST THOMAS' DR
WYNDHAM CL
OREGON SQ
ECCLESTON CL
PINEWOOD CL
ALLINGTON RD
CATHCART DR
HILLVIEW CRES
THE MALTINGS
KNOLL RISE
PEPYS RISE
ELM GR
KELVIN PAR
OAKHILL RD
ORCHARD GR
GUMPING RD
OREGON SQ
Crofton
YORK RISE
Orpington
HILL VIEW RD
ORMONDE AVE
CLAREVILLE RD
44
130
45
227
46
CROFTON RD
STATION APP
Mus
HILL END
APPROACH
KNOLL
WOOD RD
A232
A208 Orpington, A224
A232 M25 (A224)
IX

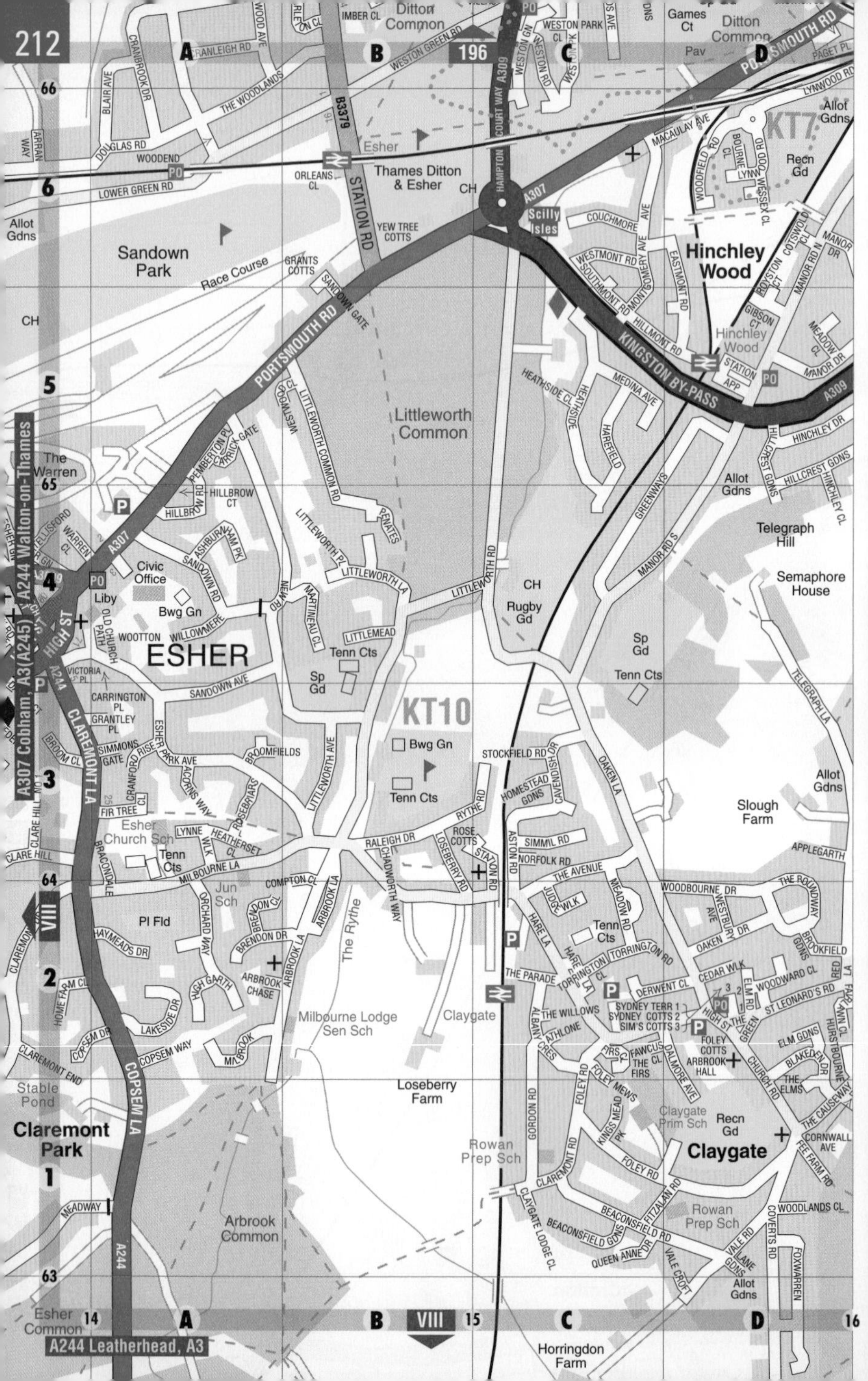

196
A
B
C
D
66
6
5
65
4
3
64
2
1
63
14
15
16
VIII
Ditton Common
Games Ct
Pav
PORTSMOUTH RD
KT7
Allot Gdns
Recn Gd
Esher
Thames Ditton & Esher
Sandown Park
Race Course
Scilly Isles
Hinchley Wood
KINGSTON BY-PASS
A309
A307
B3379
STATION RD
HAMPTON COURT WAY
Littleworth Common
The Warren
A307 Cobham, A3(A245) A244 Walton-on-Thames
Civic Office
Liby
Bwg Gn
ESHER
HIGH ST
CLAREMONT LA
Telegraph Hill
Semaphore House
CH
Rugby Gd
Sp Gd
Tenn Cts
KT10
Slough Farm
Esher Church Sch
Jun Sch
Pl Fld
The Rythe
Milbourne Lodge Sen Sch
Claygate
Loseberry Farm
Rowan Prep Sch
Claygate Prim Sch
Stable Pond
Claremont Park
COPSEM LA
Arbrook Common
Esher Common
Horringdon Farm
A244 Leatherhead, A3

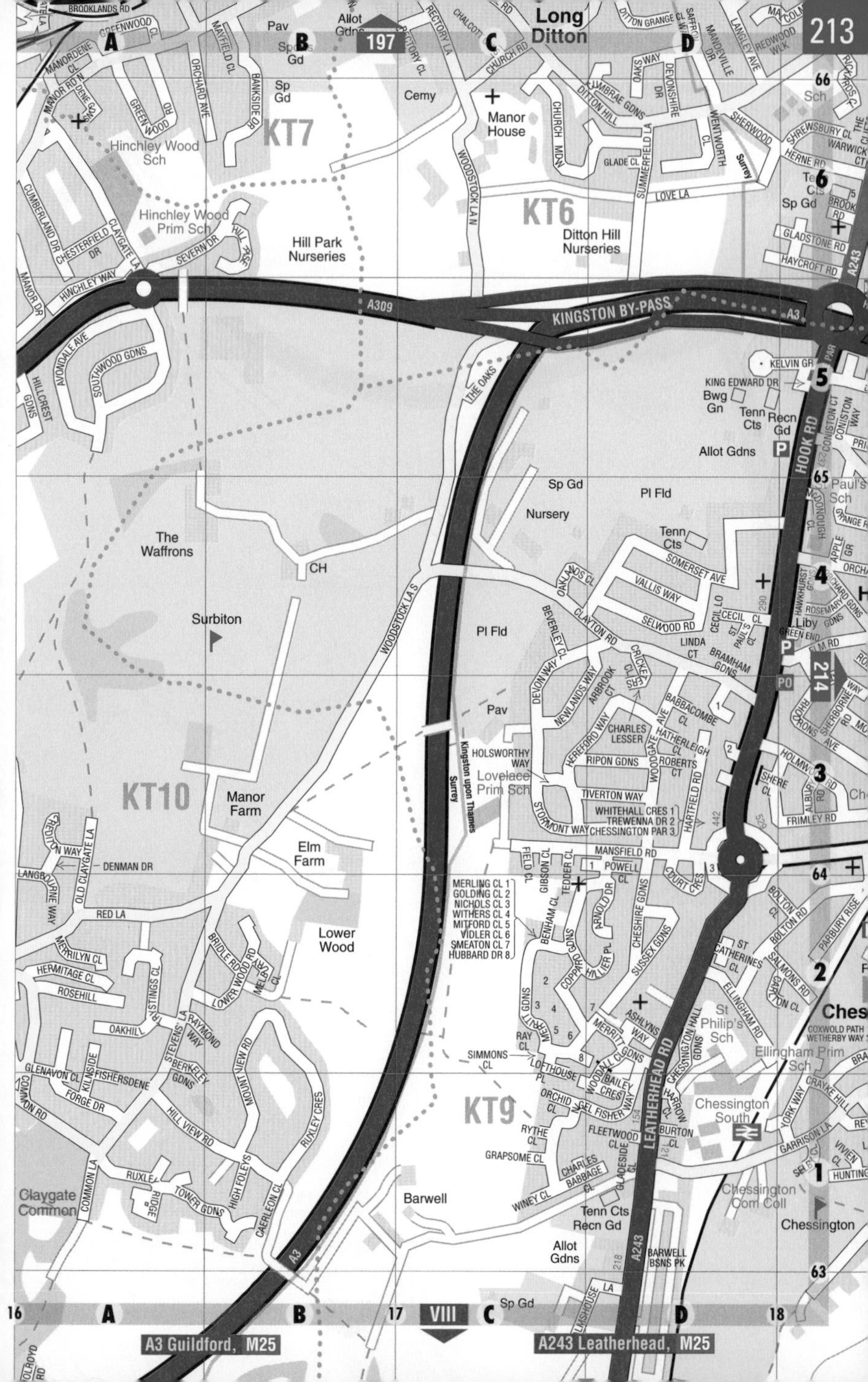
Long Ditton
KT7
KT6
KT10
KT9
Hinchley Wood Sch
Hinchley Wood Prim Sch
Hill Park Nurseries
Manor House
Ditton Hill Nurseries
KINGSTON BY-PASS
A309
A3
A243
HOOK RD
LEATHERHEAD RD
WOODSTOCK LA S
The Waffrons
Surbiton
Manor Farm
Elm Farm
Lower Wood
Barwell
Claygate Common
Lovelace Prim Sch
St Philip's Sch
Ellingham Prim Sch
Chessington South
Chessington Com Coll
Chessington
St Paul's Sch
BARWELL BSNS PK
A3 Guildford, M25
A243 Leatherhead, M25

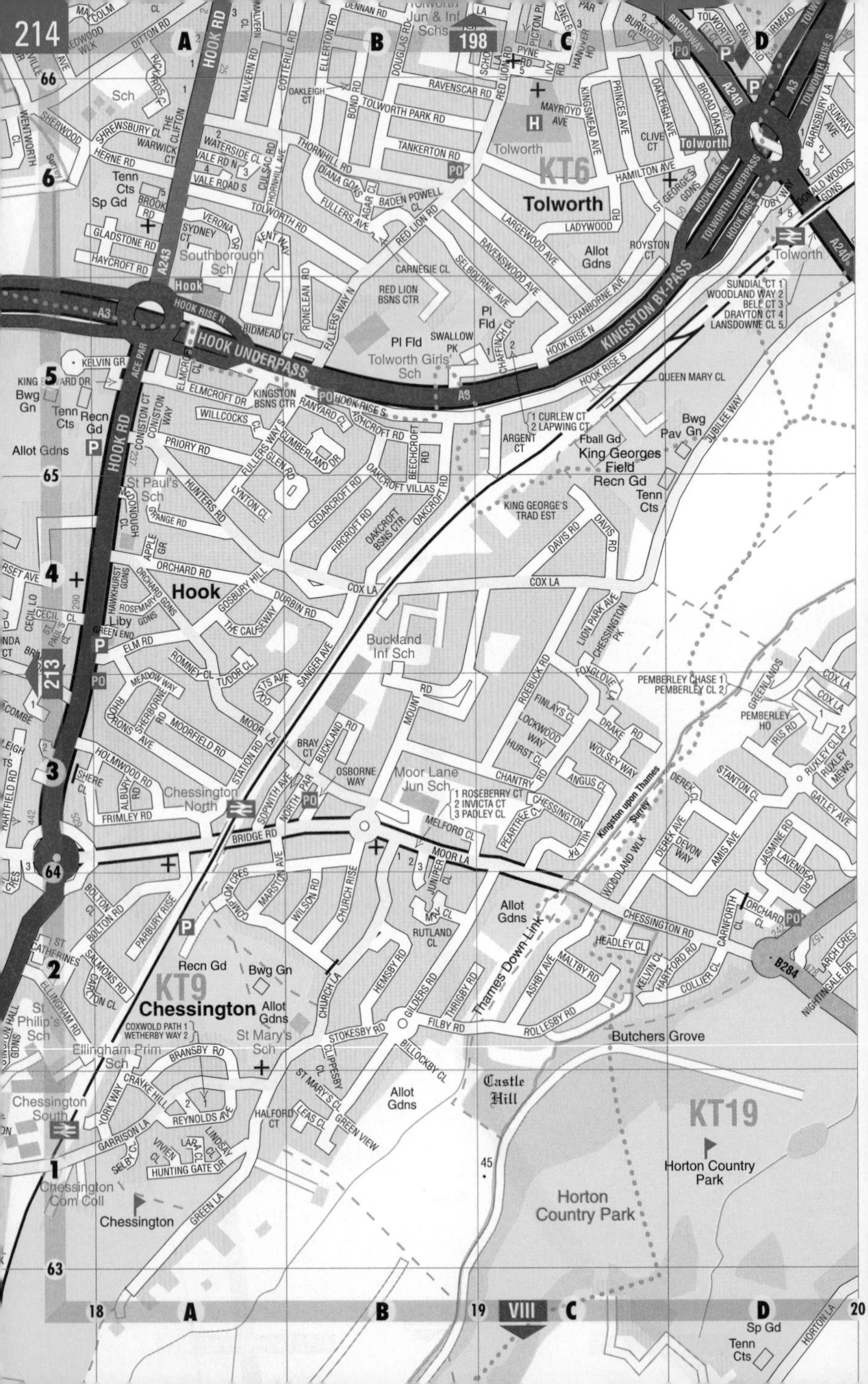
A
B
C
D
198
213
VIII
18
19
20
66
65
64
63
6
5
4
3
2
1
KT6
KT9
KT19
Tolworth
Hook
Chessington
HOOK RD
A243
A3
A240
B284
HOOK UNDERPASS
KINGSTON BY-PASS
TOLWORTH UNDERPASS
HOOK RISE N
HOOK RISE S
TOLWORTH RISE S
BROADWAY
Tolworth Jun & Inf Schs
DITTON RD
MALVERN RD
COTTERILL RD
ELLERTON RD
DOUGLAS RD
RAVENSCAR RD
OAKLEIGH CT
BOND RD
TOLWORTH PARK RD
TANKERTON RD
THORNHILL RD
DIANA GDNS
AGAR CL
BADEN POWELL CL
FULLERS AVE
TOLWORTH RD
RED LION RD
MAYROYD AVE
KINGSMEAD AVE
PRINCES AVE
OAKLEIGH AVE
BROAD OAKS
CLIVE CT
HAMILTON AVE
ST GEORGE'S GDNS
LARGEWOOD AVE
LADYWOOD RD
RAVENSWOOD AVE
SELBOURNE AVE
CRANBORNE AVE
ROYSTON CT
Allot Gdns
BARNSBURY LA
SUNRAY AVE
DONALD WOODS GDNS
TOBY WAY
SUNDIAL CT 1
WOODLAND WAY 2
BELL CT 3
DRAYTON CT 4
LANSDOWNE CL 5
SHREWSBURY CL
WARWICK CT
THE CLIFTON
WATERSIDE CL
VALE RD N
VALE ROAD S
CULSAC RD
HERNE RD
Tenn Cts
Sp Gd
BROOK RD
VERONA DR
SYDNEY CT
KENT WAY
GLADSTONE RD
HAYCROFT RD
Southborough Sch
CARNEGIE CL
RED LION BSNS CTR
RONELEAN RD
FULLERS WAY N
Pl Fld
SWALLOW PK
CHAFFINCH CL
Tolworth Girls' Sch
BIDMEAD CT
KELVIN GR
KING EDWARD DR
Bwg Gn
Recn Gd
ACE PAR
ELMCROFT DR
KINGSTON BSNS CTR
RANYARD CL
ASHCROFT RD
WILLCOCKS CL
CONISTON CT
CONISTON WAY
PRIORY RD
FULLERS WAY S
CUMBERLAND DR
GLEN RD
BEECHCROFT RD
OAKCROFT RD
OAKCROFT VILLAS
CEDARCROFT RD
FIRCROFT RD
OAKCROFT BSNS CTR
1 CURLEW CT
2 LAPWING CT
ARGENT CT
QUEEN MARY CL
Fball Gd
King Georges Field
Pav
JUBILEE WAY
KING GEORGE'S TRAD EST
DAVIS RD
St Paul's Sch
HUNTERS RD
LYNTON CL
GRANGE RD
APPLE GR
ORCHARD RD
HAWKHURST GDNS
ORCHARD GDNS
ROSEMARY GDNS
GOSBURY HILL
DURBIN RD
THE CAUSEWAY
COX LA
LION PARK AVE
CHESSINGTON PK
Liby
GREEN END
ELM RD
CECIL CL
Buckland Inf Sch
ROMNEY CL
TUDOR CL
COUTTS AVE
SANGER AVE
MOUNT RD
ROEBUCK RD
FOXGLOVE LA
FINLAYS CL
LOCKWOOD WAY
HURST CL
DRAKE RD
WOLSEY WAY
PEMBERLEY CHASE 1
PEMBERLEY CL 2
PEMBERLEY HO
GREENLANDS
IRIS RD
RUXLEY CL
RUXLEY MEWS
GATLEY AVE
STANTON CL
DEREK CL
MEADOW WAY
SHERBORNE RD
RONS AVE
MOORFIELD RD
MOOR LA
STATION RD
BRAY CT
BUCKLAND RD
OSBORNE WAY
Moor Lane Jun Sch
1 ROSEBERRY CT
2 INVICTA CT
3 PADLEY CL
CHANTRY RD
ANGUS CL
CHESSINGTON HILL PK
PEARTREE CL
Kingston upon Thames
Surrey
WOODLAND WLK
DEREK AVE
DEVON WAY
AMIS AVE
JASMINE RD
LAVENDER RD
HOLMWOOD RD
SHERE CL
ALBURY RD
FRIMLEY RD
Chessington North
SOPWITH AVE
NORTH PAR
BRIDGE RD
MELFORD CL
MOOR LA
JUNIPER CL
HARTFIELD RD
COMPTON CRES
MARSTON AVE
WILSON RD
CHURCH RISE
MAY CL
RUTLAND CL
CHESSINGTON RD
HEADLEY CL
CARNFORTH CL
ORCHARD CL
LARCH CRES
NIGHTINGALE DR
BOLTON CL
BOLTON RD
PARBURY RISE
ST CATHERINES
SALMONS RD
CARLTON CL
ELLINGHAM RD
Recn Gd
Bwg Gn
HEMSBY RD
GILDERS RD
THRIGBY RD
Thames Down Link
ASHBY AVE
MALTBY RD
KELVIN CL
HARTFORD RD
COLLIER CL
St Philip's Sch
COXWOLD PATH 1
WETHERBY WAY 2
St Mary's Sch
CHURCH LA
STOKESBY RD
FILBY RD
ROLLESBY RD
Butchers Grove
Ellingham Prim Sch
BRANSBY RD
CLIPPESBY CL
BILLOCKBY CL
Castle Hill
YORK WAY
CRAYKE HILL
REYNOLDS AVE
LINDSAY CL
HALFORD CT
LEAS CL
ST MARY'S CL
GREEN VIEW
Chessington South
GARRISON LA
SELBY CL
VIVIEN CL
LARA CL
HUNTING GATE DR
Chessington Com Coll
Chessington
GREEN LA
45
Horton Country Park
HORTON LA

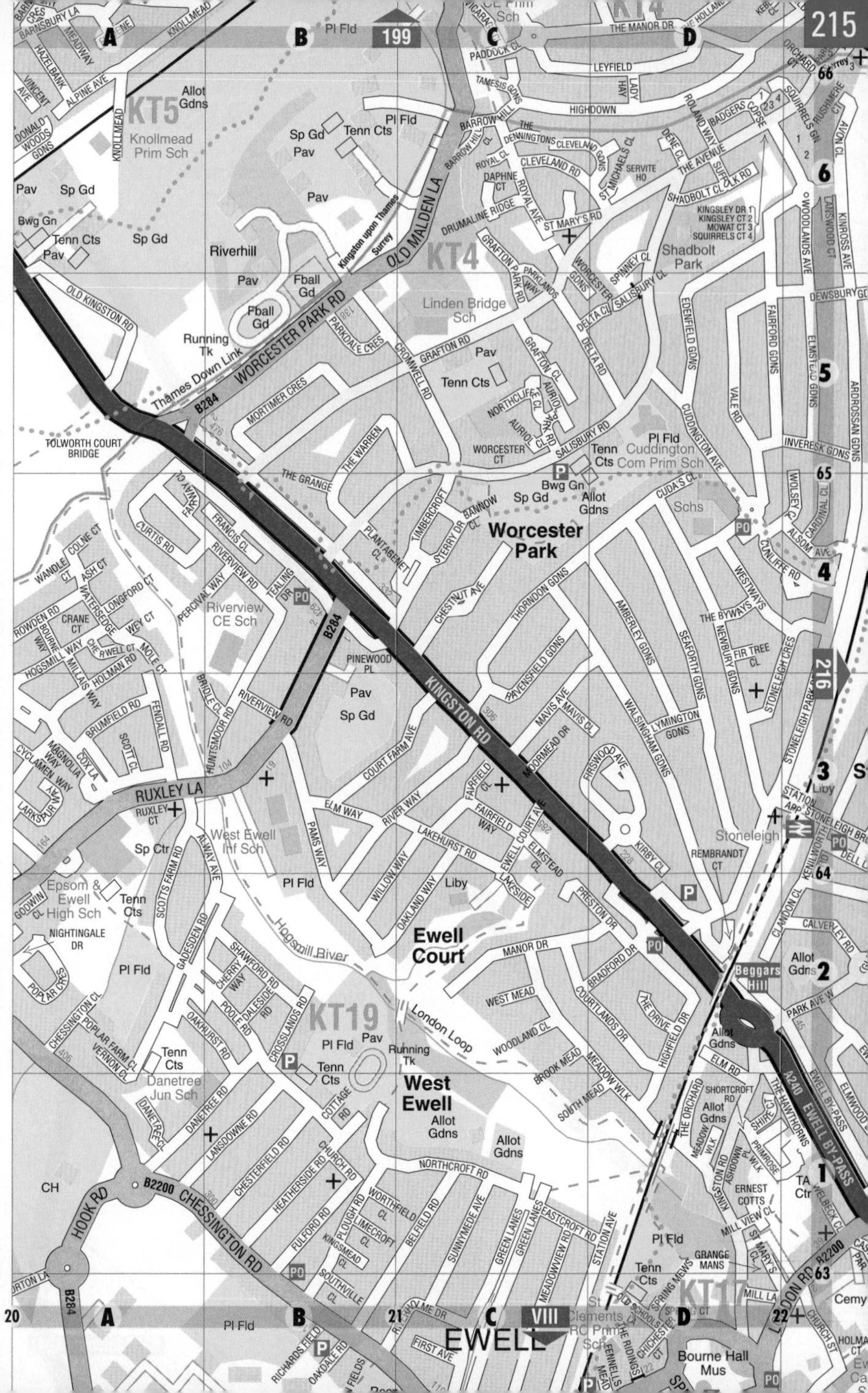

199
216
VIII
Worcester Park
Ewell Court
West Ewell
EWELL
Stoneleigh
KT5
KT4
KT19
KT17
KINGSTON RD
WORCESTER PARK RD
OLD MALDEN LA
RUXLEY LA
CHESSINGTON RD
HOOK RD
EWELL BY-PASS
LONDON RD
Knollmead Prim Sch
Riverhill
Linden Bridge Sch
Cuddington Com Prim Sch
Shadbolt Park
Riverview CE Sch
West Ewell Inf Sch
Epsom & Ewell High Sch
Danetree Jun Sch
Hogsmill River
London Loop
Beggars Hill
Bourne Hall Mus
TOLWORTH COURT BRIDGE
Thames Down Link

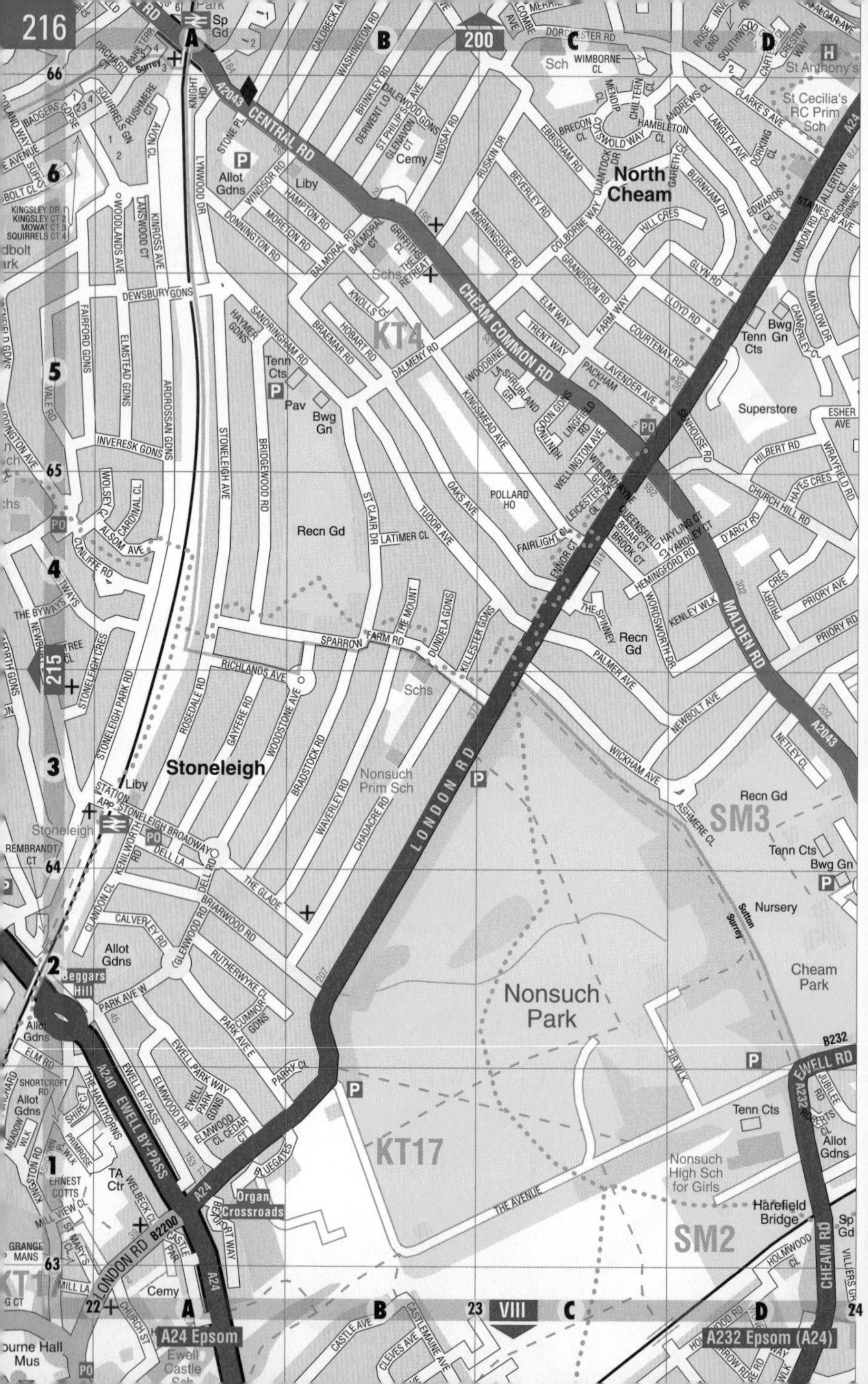

North Cheam
Stoneleigh
Nonsuch Park
Cheam Park
KT4
KT17
SM3
SM2
CENTRAL RD
CHEAM COMMON RD
LONDON RD
MALDEN RD
EWELL BY-PASS
EWELL RD
CHEAM RD
STONELEIGH BROADWAY
THE AVENUE
Beggars Hill
Organ Crossroads
Nonsuch Prim Sch
Nonsuch High Sch for Girls
Harefield Bridge
St Anthony's
St Cecilia's RC Prim Sch
Superstore
Recn Gd
Tenn Cts
Bwg Gn
Allot Gdns
Cemy
Nursery
200
215
VIII
A24 Epsom
A232 Epsom (A24)

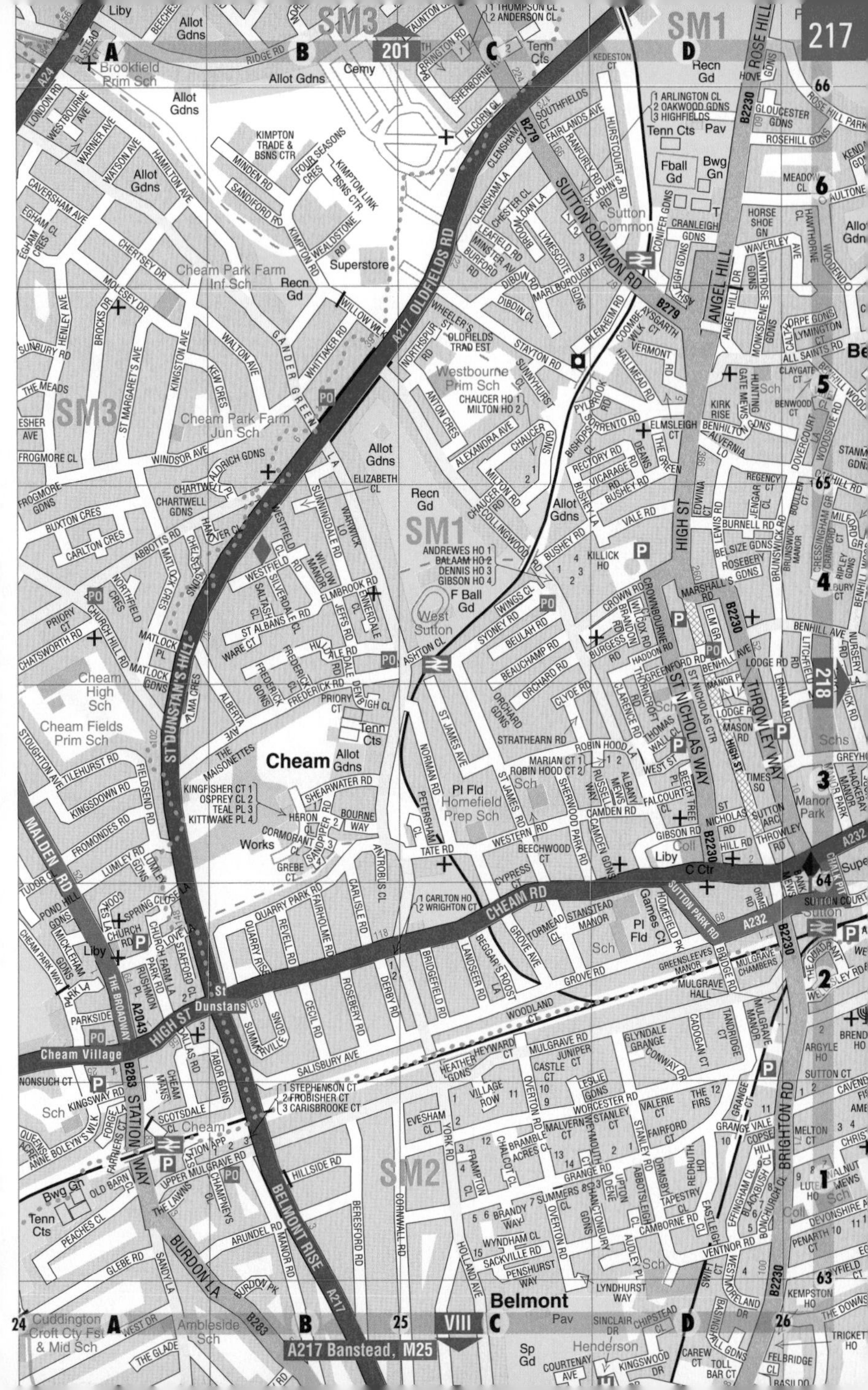

SM3
201
SM1
A
B
C
D
Liby
Allot Gdns
Brookfield Prim Sch
Cemy
Tenn Cts
Recn Gd
1 THOMPSON CL
2 ANDERSON CL
RIDGE RD
BARRINGTON RD
SHERBORNE RD
KEDESTON CT
ROSE HILL
HOVE GDNS
66
GLOUCESTER GDNS
ROSEHILL PARK
ROSEHILL GDNS
1 ARLINGTON CL
2 OAKWOOD GDNS
3 HIGHFIELDS
Pav
Fball Gd
Bwg Gn
A24
LONDON RD
WESTBOURNE AVE
WARNER AVE
WATSON AVE
HAMILTON AVE
KIMPTON TRADE & BSNS CTR
FOUR SEASONS CRES
KIMPTON LINK BSNS CTR
MINDEN RD
SANDIFORD RD
KIMPTON RD
WEALDSTONE RD
Superstore
ALCORN CL
SOUTHFIELDS CT
FAIRLANDS AVE
HURSTCOURT RD
RANFURLY RD
ST JOHN'S RD
CLENSHAM CT
CLENSHAM LA
B279
SUTTON COMMON RD
Sutton Common
CONIFER GDNS
CRANLEIGH GDNS
B2230
ANGEL HILL
HORSE SHOE GN
MEADOW CL
6
AULTONE
Allot Gdns
CAVERSHAM AVE
EGHAM CL
EGHAM CRES
CHERTSEY DR
Cheam Park Farm Inf Sch
MOLESEY DR
HENLEY AVE
BROCKS DR
CHESTER CL
BROOK LEAFIELD RD
MINSTER AV
BURFORD RD
LYMESCOTE GDNS
MARLBOROUGH RD
DIBDIN RD
DIBDIN CL
WAVERLEY AVE
MONTROSE GDNS
HAWTHORNE CL
WOODEND
MONKSDENE GDNS
ANGEL HILL DR
ASH LEIGH GDNS
COOMBE WLK
AYSGARTH CT
BLENHEIM RD
VERMONT RD
HALLMEAD RD
WILLOW WLK
WHITTAKER RD
GANDER GREEN LA
A217
OLDFIELDS RD
WHEELER'S LA
OLDFIELDS TRAD EST
NORTHSPUR RD
STAYTON RD
SUNNYHURST CL
Westbourne Prim Sch
CHAUCER HO 1
MILTON HO 2
ANTON CRES
SUNBURY RD
THE MEADS
SM3
ST MARGARET'S AVE
KINGSTON AVE
KEW CRES
WALTON AVE
Cheam Park Farm Jun Sch
PO
ESHER AVE
FROGMORE CL
WINDSOR AVE
ALDRICH GDNS
CHARTWELL PL
CHARTWELL GDNS
FROGMORE GDNS
ALEXANDRA AVE
CHAUCER GDNS
MILTON RD
CHAUCER RD
COLLINGWOOD RD
PYLBROOK RD
BISHOPS CL
SORRENTO RD
ELMSLEIGH CT
RECTORY RD
VICARAGE RD
BUSHEY LA
BUSHEY RD
DEANS RD
THE GREEN
HIGH ST
EDWINA CT
LEWIS RD
JENGAR CL
BURNELL RD
BELSIZE GDNS
ROSEBERY GDNS
BRUNSWICK RD
BRUNSWICK MANOR
BOULLEN CT
CRESSINGHAM GR
MILFORD GR
CRANFORD CL
RIPLEY GDNS
4
Be
ALL SAINTS RD
CLAYGATE CT
LYMINGTON CL
HUNTING GATE MEWS
KIRK RISE
BENHILTON GDNS
ALVERNIA LO
REGENCY CT
DOVERCOURT LA
WOODSIDE RD
BENWOOD CT
5
65
Sch
BUXTON CRES
CARLTON CRES
ABBOTTS RD
HANOVER CL
CHELSEA GDNS
MATLOCK CRES
NORTHFIELD CRES
ELIZABETH CL
SUNNINGDALE RD
WARWICK LO
WESTFIELD CL
WESTFIELD RD
WILLOW MANOR
SILVERDALE CL
SALTASH CL
Recn Gd
SM1
ANDREWES HO 1
BALAAM HO 2
DENNIS HO 3
GIBSON HO 4
Allot Gdns
KILLICK HO
P
PO
CHURCH HILL RD
PRIORY CT
CHATSWORTH RD
MATLOCK PL
MATLOCK GDNS
ALMA CRES
ST ALBANS RD
ELMBROOK RD
JEFFS RD
ENNERDALE CL
WARE CT
HILLDALE RD
FREDERICK RD
FREDERICK GDNS
FREDERICK CL
DENBIGH CL
PRIORY CT
F Ball Gd
West Sutton
ASHTON CL
WINGS CL
SYDNEY RD
BEULAH RD
BEAUCHAMP RD
ORCHARD RD
ORCHARD GDNS
CROWN RD
BURGESS RD
CROWNBOURNE CT
WILCOX RD
BRANDON RD
HADDON RD
GREENFORD RD
THORNCROFT RD
CLARENCE RD
CLYDE RD
ST NICHOLAS WAY
ST NICHOLAS CTR
ELM GR
MARSHALL'S RD
B2230
BENHILL AVE
MANOR PL
LODGE PL
THROWLEY WAY
LODGE RD
LENHAM RD
LITCHFIELD RD
NURSERY RD
BENHILL AVE
218
Cheam High Sch
Cheam Fields Prim Sch
STOUGHTON AVE
TILEHURST RD
KINGSDOWN RD
FIELDSEND RD
ST DUNSTAN'S HILL
ALBERTA AVE
THE MAISONETTES
Cheam
Allot Gdns
Tenn Cts
NORMAN RD
ST JAMES AVE
STRATHEARN RD
THOMAS WALL CL
ROBIN HOOD LA
MARIAN CT 1
ROBIN HOOD CT 2
WEST ST
BEECH TREE PL
TIMES SQ
MASON RD
Schs
3
Manor Park
THACKERAY MANOR
GREYHOUND
KINGFISHER CT 1
OSPREY CL 2
TEAL PL 3
KITTIWAKE PL 4
SHEARWATER RD
HERON CT
BOURNE WAY
SANDPIPER RD
CORMORANT CL
GREBE CT
Works
ANTROBUS CL
PETERSHAM CL
Pl Fld
Homefield Prep Sch
ST JAMES RD
SHERWOOD PARK RD
RUSSELL WAY
ALBANY MEWS
CAMDEN RD
CAMDEN GDNS
FALCOURT CL
ST NICHOLAS RD
SUTTON ARC
THROWLEY RD
GIBSON RD
HILL RD
Liby
Coll
C Ctr
A232
CHALK PIT
Supe
64
BANK MEWS
MALDEN RD
FROMONDES RD
LUMLEY RD
LUMLEY GDNS
TUDOR CL
POND HILL GDNS
TATE RD
WESTERN RD
BEECHWOOD CT
CYPRESS CT
CHEAM RD
1 CARLTON HO
2 WRIGHTON CT
QUARRY PARK RD
QUARRY RISE
REVELL RD
FAIRHOLME RD
CARLISLE RD
TORMEAD CL
STANSTEAD MANOR
GROVE AVE
BEGGAR'S ROOST LA
Sch
Games Ct
Pl Fld
HOMEFIELD PK
SUTTON PARK RD
ORME RD
SUTTON COURT
Sutton
THE QUADRANT
WESTMORLAND
SPRING CLOSE LA
COOK LA
CHURCH RD
STAFFORD RD
LOVE LA
CHURCH FARM LA
PARK RD
MICKLEHAM GDNS
CHEAM PARK WAY
Liby
PARK LA
RUSHMON PL
THE BROADWAY
A2043
ST Dunstans
PARKSIDE
BRIDGEFIELD RD
LANDSEER RD
DERBY RD
ROSEBERY RD
CECIL RD
SUMMERVILLE GDNS
GROVE RD
GREENSLEEVES MANOR
BRIDGE RD
MULGRAVE CHAMBERS
MULGRAVE HALL
2
WOODLAND CT
MULGRAVE MANOR
Cheam Village
HIGH ST
B283
TABOR GDNS
HEYWARD CT
MULGRAVE RD
JUNIPER CT
GLYNDALE GRANGE
CADOGAN CT
TANDRIDGE CT
CONWAY DR
SALISBURY AVE
HEATHER GDNS
CASTLE CT
LESLIE GDNS
BRENDON HO
ARGYLE HO
SUTTON CT
NONSUCH CT
KINGSWAY RD
CHEAM MANS
1 STEPHENSON CT
2 FROBISHER CT
3 CARISBROOKE CT
VILLAGE ROW
OVERTON RD
WORCESTER RD
STANLEY CT
VALERIE CT
THE FIRS
GRANGE CT
Sch
FORGE LA
STATION WAY
SCOTSDALE CL
Cheam
QUEENS ACRES
ANNE BOLEYN'S WLK
FARRIERS CT
STATION APP
UPPER MULGRAVE RD
EVESHAM CL
YORK RD
MALVERN CT
WEYMOUTH CT
STANLEY RD
FAIRFORD CT
GRANGE VALE
COPSE HILL
MELTON CT
CHRIST
1
Bwg Gn
OLD BARN CL
HILLSIDE RD
SM2
CHAMPNEYS CL
THE LAWNS
BRAMBLE ACRES CL
CHALCOT CL
FRAMPTON CL
GRANGE RD
SUMMERS CL
UPTON DENE
ABBOTSLEIGH RD
ORMSBY
REDRUTH HO
TAPESTRY CL
EFFINGHAM CL
BLACKBUSH CL
BONCHURCH CL
BRIGHTON RD
LUTEA HO
WALNUT MEWS
Sch
Tenn Cts
PEACHES CL
ARUNDEL RD
MANOR RD
BERESFORD RD
CORNWALL RD
BRANDY WAY
CHANCTONBURY GDNS
CAMBORNE RD
EASTLEIGH CL
VENTNOR RD
DEVONSHIRE AVE
PENARTH CT
Coll
GLEBE RD
SANDY LA
BURDON LA
BURDON PK
BELMONT RISE
WYNDHAM CL
SACKVILLE RD
PENSHURST WAY
HOLLAND AVE
AUDLEY PL
LYNDHURST WAY
SWIFT CT
WESTMORELAND DR
KEMPSTON HO
63
THE DOWNS
24
Cuddington Croft Cty Fst & Mid Sch
WEST DR
Ambleside Sch
B283
25
VIII
Belmont
Pav
SINCLAIR DR
CHIPSTEAD CL
26
BASINGHALL GDNS
TRICKETT HO
A217 Banstead, M25
THE GLADE
Sp Gd
Henderson
COURTENAY AVE
KINGSWOOD DR
CAREW CT
TOLL BAR CT
FELBRIDGE CL

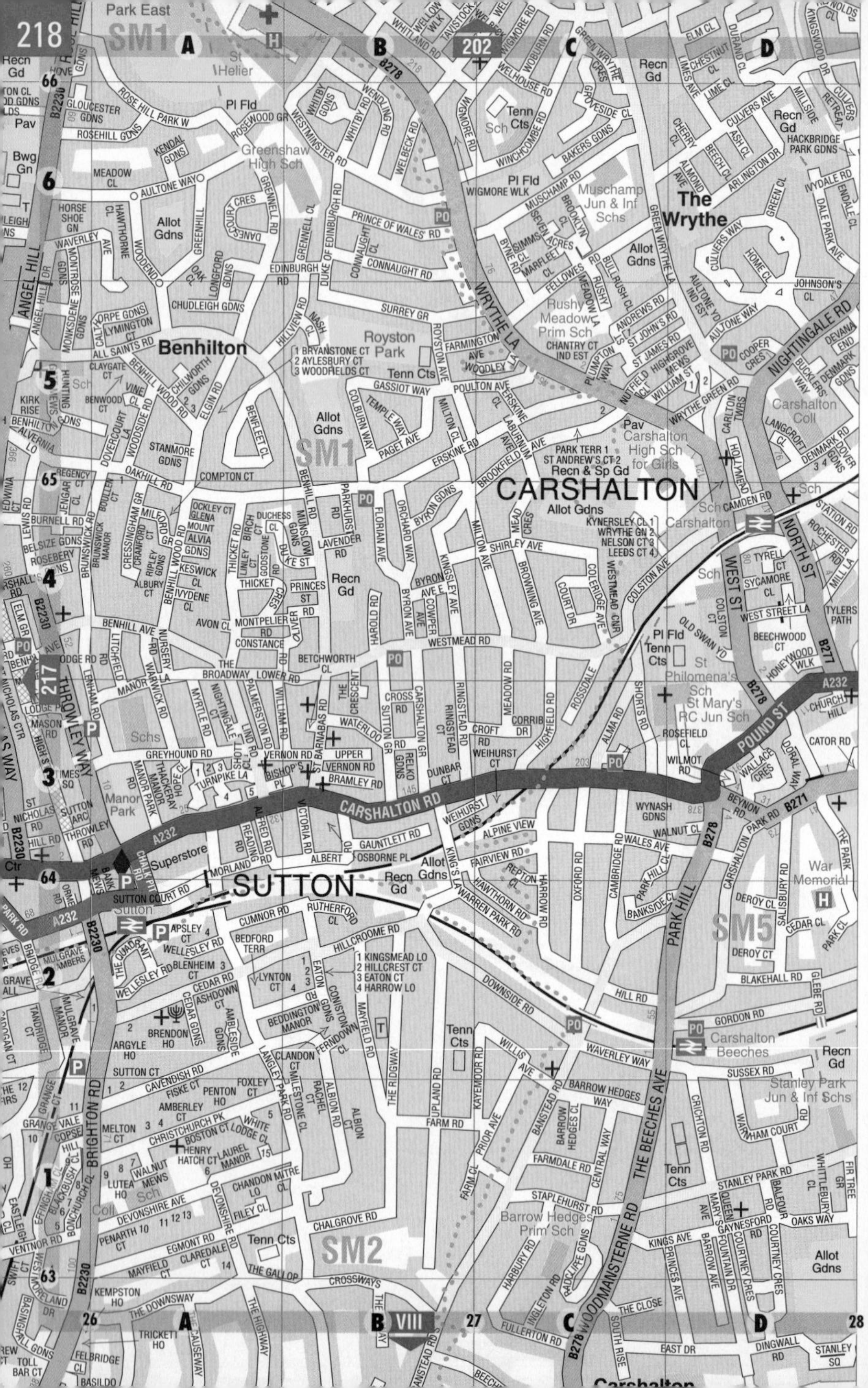

A
B
C
D
202
217
VIII
SM1
SM2
SM5
Park East
St Helier
Recn Gd
Pl Fld
Greenshaw High Sch
Allot Gdns
Benhilton
Royston Park
Tenn Cts
Muschamp Jun & Inf Schs
The Wrythe
Rushy Meadow Prim Sch
Carshalton Coll
Carshalton High Sch for Girls
CARSHALTON
Recn & Sp Gd
Carshalton
St Philomena's Sch
St Mary's RC Jun Sch
Manor Park
Schs
Superstore
SUTTON
Sutton
War Memorial
Carshalton Beeches
Stanley Park Jun & Inf Schs
Barrow Hedges Prim Sch
ROSE HILL PARK W
ROSEHILL GDNS
GLOUCESTER GDNS
MEADOW CL
AULTONE WAY
KENDAL GDNS
ROSEWOOD GR
WHITLAND RD
WESTMINSTER RD
WHITBY RD
WENDLING RD
WELBECK RD
WIGMORE RD
WIGMORE WLK
WOBURN RD
WELHOUSE RD
WINCHCOMBE RD
BAKERS GDNS
GROVESIDE CL
GREEN WRYTHE CRES
GREEN WRYTHE LA
MUSCHAMP RD
PRINCE OF WALES' RD
CONNAUGHT RD
EDINBURGH RD
DUKE OF EDINBURGH RD
SURREY GR
WRYTHE LA
ANGEL HILL
HORSE SHOE GN
HAWTHORNE AVE
WAVERLEY AVE
MONTROSE GDNS
CHUDLEIGH GDNS
LYMINGTON CT
ALL SAINTS RD
BENHILL WOOD RD
CLAYGATE CT
BENWOOD CT
VINE CL
KIRK RISE
BENHILTON GDNS
DOVERCOURT LA
WOODSIDE RD
STANMORE GDNS
OAKHILL RD
COMPTON CT
ELGIN RD
HILLVIEW RD
NASH CL
1 BRYANSTONE CT
2 AYLESBURY CT
3 WOODFIELDS CT
GASSIOT WAY
COLBURN WAY
TEMPLE WAY
PAGET AVE
ROYSTON AVE
FARMINGTON AVE
WOODLEY CL
POULTON AVE
MILTON CL
ERSKINE RD
ERSKINE CL
LABURNUM AVE
BROOKFIELD AVE
PARK TERR 1
ST ANDREW'S CT 2
PLUMPTON WAY
ANDREWS RD
ST JOHN'S RD
ST JAMES RD
NUTFIELD CL
HIGHGROVE MEWS
WILLIAM ST
WRYTHE GREEN RD
CARLTON TWRS
COOPER CRES
NIGHTINGALE RD
BUCKLERS' WAY
DENMARK GDNS
LANGCROFT CL
DENMARK RD
DOVER
CULVERS AVE
CULVERS WAY
HOME CL
AULTONE YD IND EST
JOHNSON'S CL
ARLINGTON DR
HACKBRIDGE PARK GDNS
IVYDALE RD
DALE PARK AVE
KINGSWOOD DR
MILLSIDE
CULVERS RETREAT
ELM CL
CHESTNUT CL
LIMES AVE
LIME CL
CHERRY CL
ASH CL
BEECH CL
ALMOND AVE
DURAND CL
CAMDEN RD
NORTH ST
STATION RD
ROCHESTER RD
TYRELL CT
SYCAMORE CL
WEST STREET LA
MILL LA
TYLERS PATH
BEECHWOOD CT
HONEYWOOD WLK
WEST ST
B277
B278
B271
B2230
A232
POUND ST
CHURCH HILL
CATOR RD
WALLACE CRES
DORAL WAY
BEYNON RD
CARSHALTON PARK RD
THE PARK
SALISBURY RD
DEROY CL
CEDAR CL
PARK CL
BLAKEHALL RD
GLEBE RD
GORDON RD
HILL RD
KYNERSLEY CL 1
WRYTHE GN 2
NELSON CT 3
LEEDS CT 4
COLSTON AVE
OLD SWAN YD
COLSTON CT
ROSEFIELD CL
WILMOT RD
WYNASH GDNS
WALNUT CL
WALES AVE
PARK HILL
PARK HILL CL
BANKSIDE CL
CAMBRIDGE RD
OXFORD RD
HARROW RD
REPTON CL
FAIRVIEW RD
ALPINE VIEW
HAWTHORN RD
WARREN PARK RD
KING'S LA
WEIHURST GDNS
WEIHURST CT
CROFT RD
CORRIB DR
HIGHFIELD RD
ROSSDALE
ALMA RD
SHORTS RD
WESTMEAD RD
WESTMEAD CNR
COLERIDGE AVE
COURT DR
BROWNING AVE
MEAD CRES
SHIRLEY AVE
MILTON AVE
KINGSLEY AVE
BYRON GDNS
BYRON AVE
BYRON AVE E
COWPER AVE
ORCHARD WAY
FLORIAN AVE
HAROLD RD
PARKHURST RD
LAVENDER RD
MUNSLOW GDNS
DUKE ST
DUCHESS CL
GOODSTONE
BIRCH CT
LINLEY CT
THICKET RD
THICKET CRES
PRINCES ST
OLIVER RD
MONTPELIER RD
CONSTANCE RD
BETCHWORTH CL
BENHILL RD
BENHILL AVE
AVON CL
NURSERY RD
LITCHFIELD RD
THE BROADWAY
LOWER RD
MANOR LA
WARWICK RD
MYRTLE RD
NIGHTINGALE CT
PALMERSTON RD
WILLIAM RD
ST BARNABAS RD
THE CRESCENT
WATERLOO RD
SUTTON GR
CROSS RD
CARSHALTON GR
RELKO GDNS
RINGSTEAD RD
RINGSTEAD CT
MEADOW RD
DUNBAR CT
CARSHALTON RD
VERNON RD
UPPER VERNON RD
BRAMLEY RD
BISHOP'S PL
TURNPIKE LA
GREYHOUND RD
LIND RD
THACKERAY MANOR
HOPE CL
ALFRED RD
READING RD
VICTORIA RD
GAUNTLETT RD
OSBORNE PL
ALBERT RD
MORLAND RD
CHALK PIT RD
BANK MEWS
SUTTON COURT RD
CUMNOR RD
RUTHERFORD CL
HILLCROOME RD
BEDFORD TERR
APSLEY CT
WELLESLEY RD
BLENHEIM CT
CEDAR RD
ASHDOWN CT
CEDAR GDNS
AMBLESIDE GDNS
BRENDON HO
ARGYLE HO
SUTTON CT
CAVENDISH RD
FISKE CT
PENTON HO
FOXLEY CT
AMBERLEY CT
CHRISTCHURCH PK
BOSTON CT
WHITE LODGE CL
HENRY HATCH CT
LAUREL MANOR
WALNUT MEWS
LUTEA HO
CHANDON LO
MITRE CL
DEVONSHIRE AVE
DEVONSHIRE RD
FILEY CL
PENARTH CT
EGMONT RD
MAYFIELD CT
CLAREDALE CT
THE GALLOP
KEMPSTON HO
THE DOWNSWAY
TRICKETT HO
CAUSEWAY
THE HIGHWAY
FELBRIDGE CL
BASILDON
1 KINGSMEAD LO
2 HILLCREST CT
3 EATON CT
4 HARROW LO
LYNTON CT
EATON RD
CONISTON GDNS
BEDDINGTON MANOR
FERNDOWN
CLANDON CT
MILESTONE CL
RACHEL CT
ALBION RD
ALBION CT
LANGLEY PARK RD
MAYFIELD RD
THE RIDGWAY
UPLAND RD
KAYEMOOR RD
FARM RD
FARM CL
PRIOR AVE
WILLIS AVE
DOWNSIDE RD
WAVERLEY WAY
BARROW HEDGES WAY
BARROW HEDGES CL
BANSTEAD RD
CENTRAL WAY
FARMDALE RD
STAPLEHURST RD
CHALGROVE RD
CROSSWAYS
HARBURY RD
RADCLIFFE GDNS
INGLETON RD
FULLERTON RD
WOODMANSTERNE RD
THE BEECHES AVE
SOUTH RISE
THE CLOSE
EAST DR
DINGWALL RD
STANLEY SQ
KINGS AVE
PRINCES AVE
BARROW AVE
FOUNTAIN DR
QUEEN MARY'S AVE
GAYNESFORD RD
COURTNEY RD
COURTNEY CRES
BALFOUR RD
STANLEY PARK RD
OAKS WAY
WHITTLEBURY CL
FIR TREE GR
WARNHAM COURT RD
CRICHTON RD
SUSSEX RD
BRIGHTON RD
THROWLEY WAY
THROWLEY RD
HIGH ST
TIMES SQ
SUTTON ARC
ST NICHOLAS RD
HILL RD
MULGRAVE RD
MULGRAVE MANOR
THE QUADRANT
TANDRIDGE CT
GRANGE VALE
COPSE HILL
BLACKBUSH CL
BONCHURCH CL
EFFINGHAM CT
EASTLEIGH CL
VENTNOR RD
WESTMORELAND DR
BASINGHALL GDNS
BELSIZE GDNS
ROSEBERY GDNS
ELM GR
BURNELL RD
LEWIS RD
JENGAR CL
REGENCY CT
BOULLEN CT
BRUNSWICK RD
BRUNSWICK MANOR
CRESSINGHAM GR
MILFORD GR
CRANFORD CL
RIPLEY GDNS
ALBURY CT
KESWICK CL
IVYDENE CL
ALVIA GDNS
GLENA MOUNT
OCKLEY CT
MASON RD
LODGE PL
LENHAM RD
26
27
28
63
64
65
66

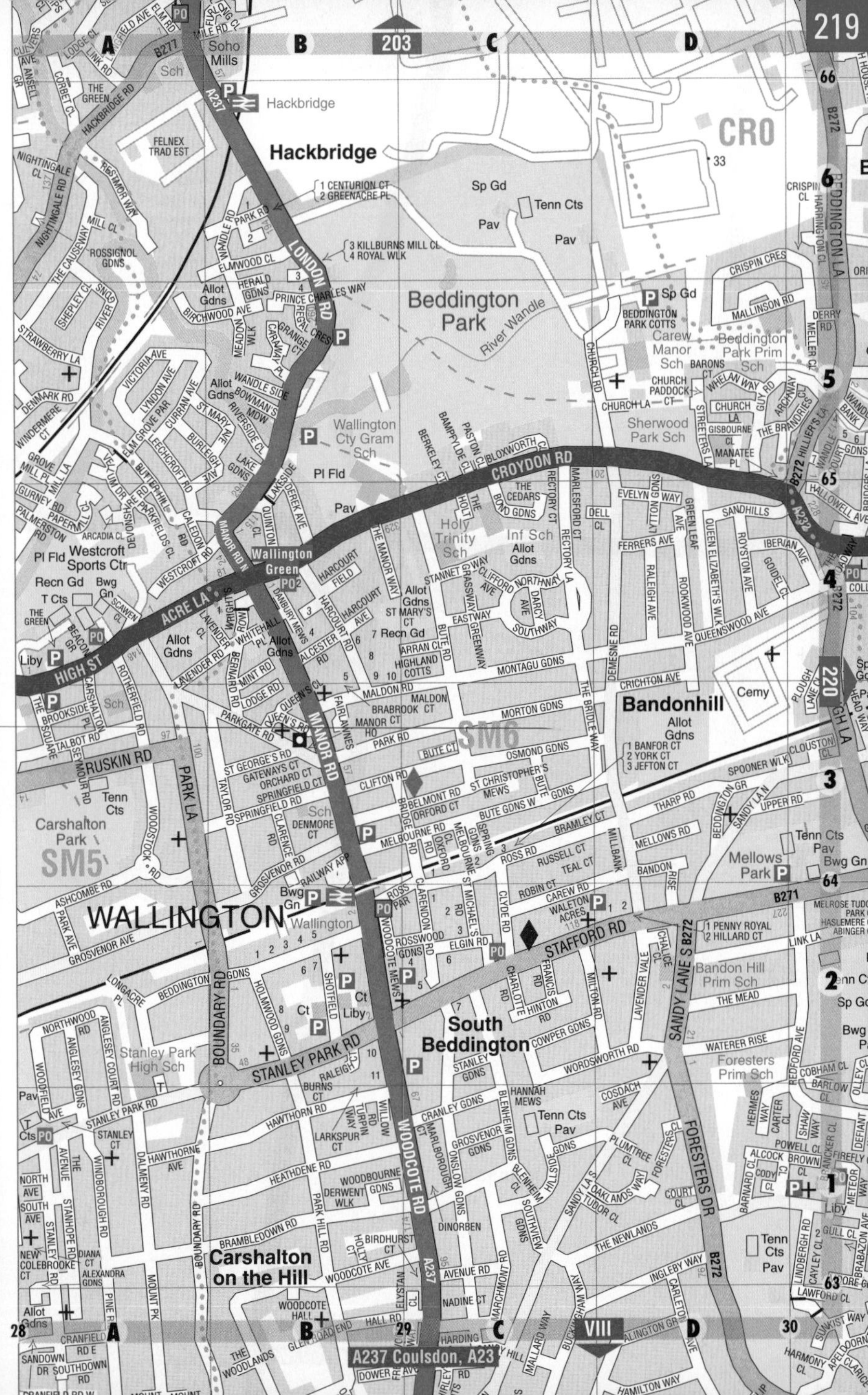

A
B
C
D
203
Soho Mills
Hackbridge
FELNEX TRAD EST
CRO
33
Sp Gd
Tenn Cts
Pav
1 CENTURION CT
2 GREENACRE PL
3 KILLBURNS MILL CL
4 ROYAL WLK
LONDON RD
A237
B277
HACKBRIDGE RD
NIGHTINGALE RD
NIGHTINGALE CL
RESTMOR WAY
THE CAUSEWAY
ROSSIGNOL GDNS
SHEPLEY CL
RIVER GDNS
STRAWBERRY LA
DENMARK RD
WINDERMERE CT
GROVE MILL PL
GURNEY RD
PAPERMILL CL
PALMERSTON RD
ARCADIA CL
Westcroft Sports Ctr
Pl Fld
Recn Gd
Bwg Gn
T Cts
THE GREEN
BEACON GR
Liby
HIGH ST
ACRE LA
WESTCROFT RD
CALEDON RD
Wallington Green
MANOR RD N
ELMWOOD CL
HERALD GDNS
PRINCE CHARLES WAY
BIRCHWOOD AVE
MEADOW WLK
REGAL CRES
GRANGE CT
CARAWAY PL
Allot Gdns
VICTORIA AVE
LYNDON AVE
CURRAN AVE
ST MARY AVE
BURLEIGH AVE
LEECHCROFT RD
ELM GROVE PAR
WANDLE SIDE
BOWMAN'S MDW
RIVERSIDE CL
LAKE GDNS
LAKESIDE
DEREK AVE
QUINTON CL
Beddington Park
River Wandle
Wallington Cty Gram Sch
Pl Fld
Pav
BEDDINGTON PARK COTTS
Carew Manor Sch
Beddington Park Prim Sch
BARONS CT
WHELAN WAY
CHURCH PADDOCK CT
CHURCH LA
CHURCH RD
Sherwood Park Sch
STREETERS LA
GISBOURNE CL
MANATEE PL
GUY RD
ARCHWAY
THE BRANDRIES
HILLIER'S LA
B272
BEDDINGTON LA
CRISPIN CL
HARRINGTON CL
CRISPIN CRES
MALLINSON RD
DERRY RD
MELLER CL
CROYDON RD
BLOXWORTH CL
PASTON CL
BAMPFYLDE CL
BERKELEY CT
THE HOLT
THE CEDARS
BOND GDNS
RECTORY CT
RECTORY LA
MARLESFORD CT
DELL CL
EVELYN WAY
LYTTON GDNS
GREEN LEAF AVE
SANDHILLS
FERRERS AVE
QUEEN ELIZABETH'S WLK
ROYSTON AVE
IBERIAN AVE
GOIDEL CL
A232
HALLOWELL AVE
Holy Trinity Sch
Inf Sch
Allot Gdns
THE MANOR WAY
HARCOURT FIELD
HARCOURT AVE
HARCOURT RD
STANNET WAY
GRASSWAY
CLIFFORD AVE
NORTHWAY
DARCY AVE
SOUTHWAY
EASTWAY
GREENWAY
RALEIGH AVE
ROOKWOOD AVE
QUEENSWOOD AVE
ST MARY'S CT
Recn Gd
ARRAN CL
HIGHLAND COTTS
BUTE RD
MONTAGU GDNS
CRICHTON AVE
DEMESNE RD
THE BRIDLE WAY
Cemy
PLOUGH LANE CL
220
Bandonhill
Allot Gdns
1 BANFOR CT
2 YORK CT
3 JEFTON CT
SM6
LAVENDER CL
LAVENDER RD
WHITEHALL PL
BERNARD RD
MINT RD
LODGE RD
DANBURY MEWS
ALCESTER RD
MALDON RD
MALDON CT
BRABROOK CT
QUEEN'S CL
QUEEN'S RD
FAIRLAWNES
MANOR CT
MANOR HO
PARKGATE RD
PARK RD
MORTON GDNS
MANOR RD
ROTHERFIELD RD
CARSHALTON PL
BROOKSIDE
THE SQUARE
TALBOT RD
SEYMOUR RD
RUSKIN RD
PARK LA
Tenn Cts
Carshalton Park
SM5
WOODSTOCK RD
ST GEORGE'S RD
GATEWAYS CT
ORCHARD CT
SPRINGFIELD CT
SPRINGFIELD RD
TAYLOR RD
CLARENCE RD
DENMORE CT
GROSVENOR RD
RAILWAY APP
BUTE CT
OSMOND GDNS
CLIFTON RD
BELMONT RD
ST CHRISTOPHER'S MEWS
BUTE GDNS
BUTE GDNS W
ORFORD CT
MELBOURNE RD
SPRING GDNS
BRIDGE RD
OXFORD RD
ROSS RD
RUSSELL CT
TEAL CT
BRAMLEY CT
MILLBANK
MELLOWS RD
BANDON RISE
THARP RD
SPOONER WLK
CLOUSTON CL
BEDDINGTON GR
SANDY LA N
UPPER RD
Tenn Cts
Pav
Mellows Park
Bwg Gn
ASHCOMBE RD
PARK AVE
GROSVENOR AVE
WALLINGTON
Wallington
Bwg Gn
ROSS PAR
CLARENDON RD
ST MICHAEL'S RD
CLYDE RD
ROBIN CT
CAREW RD
WALETON ACRES
STAFFORD RD
CHALICE CL
SANDY LANE S
B271
1 PENNY ROYAL
2 HILLARD CT
LINK LA
MELROSE
HASLEMERE CL
ABINGER CL
WOODCOTE MEWS
ROSSWOOD GDNS
ELGIN RD
LONGACRE PL
BEDDINGTON GDNS
BOUNDARY RD
HOLMWOOD GDNS
SHOTFIELD
Ct
Liby
CHARLOTTE RD
FRANCIS RD
HINTON RD
MILTON RD
LAVENDER VALE
Bandon Hill Prim Sch
THE MEAD
South Beddington
COWPER GDNS
WORDSWORTH RD
WATERER RISE
REDFORD AVE
Foresters Prim Sch
COBHAM CL
BARLOW CL
NORTHWOOD RD
ANGLESEY COURT RD
ANGLESEY GDNS
WOODFIELD AVE
Stanley Park High Sch
STANLEY PARK RD
RALEIGH CT
BURNS CT
STANLEY GDNS
HANNAH MEWS
COSDACH AVE
Tenn Cts
Pav
HERMES WAY
CARTER CL
SHAW WAY
POWELL CL
ALCOCK CL
BROWN CL
CODY CL
BARNARD CL
METEOR WAY
FIREFLY CL
DEFIANT WAY
Pav
T Cts
STANLEY CT
HAWTHORNE AVE
DALMENY RD
HAWTHORN RD
TURPIN WAY
LARKSPUR CT
WILLOW RD
WOODCOTE RD
CRANLEY GDNS
MARLBOROUGH CT
GROSVENOR GDNS
BLENHEIM GDNS
PLUMTREE CL
FORESTERS CL
FORESTERS DR
NORTH AVE
SOUTH AVE
THE AVENUE
STANHOPE RD
WINDBOROUGH RD
HEATHDENE RD
WOODBOURNE GDNS
DERWENT WLK
PARK HILL RD
ONSLOW GDNS
HILLSIDE GDNS
SANDY LA S
OAKLANDS WAY
TUDOR CL
COURT CL
Liby
GULL CL
LINDBERGH RD
CAYLEY CL
BRABAZON AVE
STANLEY RD
NEW COLEBROOKE CT
DIANA CT
ALEXANDRA GDNS
BRAMBLEDOWN RD
BIRDHURST CT
HOLLY CT
DINORBEN
SOUTHVIEW GDNS
THE NEWLANDS
Tenn Cts
Pav
Carshalton on the Hill
WOODCOTE AVE
AVENUE RD
MARCHMONT RD
INGLEBY WAY
CARLETON AVE
LAWFORD CL
SUNKIST WAY
MOUNT PK
PINE RD
Allot Gdns
WOODCOTE HALL
NADINE CT
HALL RD
ELYSTAN CL
HARDING
VIII
MALLARD WAY
BUCKINGHAM WAY
28
29
30
CRANFIELD RD E
SANDOWN DR
SOUTHDOWN RD
GLENROAD END
THE WOODLANDS
A237 Coulsdon, A23
DOWER AVE
HAMILTON WAY
HARMONY CL
APELDOORN
1
2
3
4
5
6
63
64
65
66

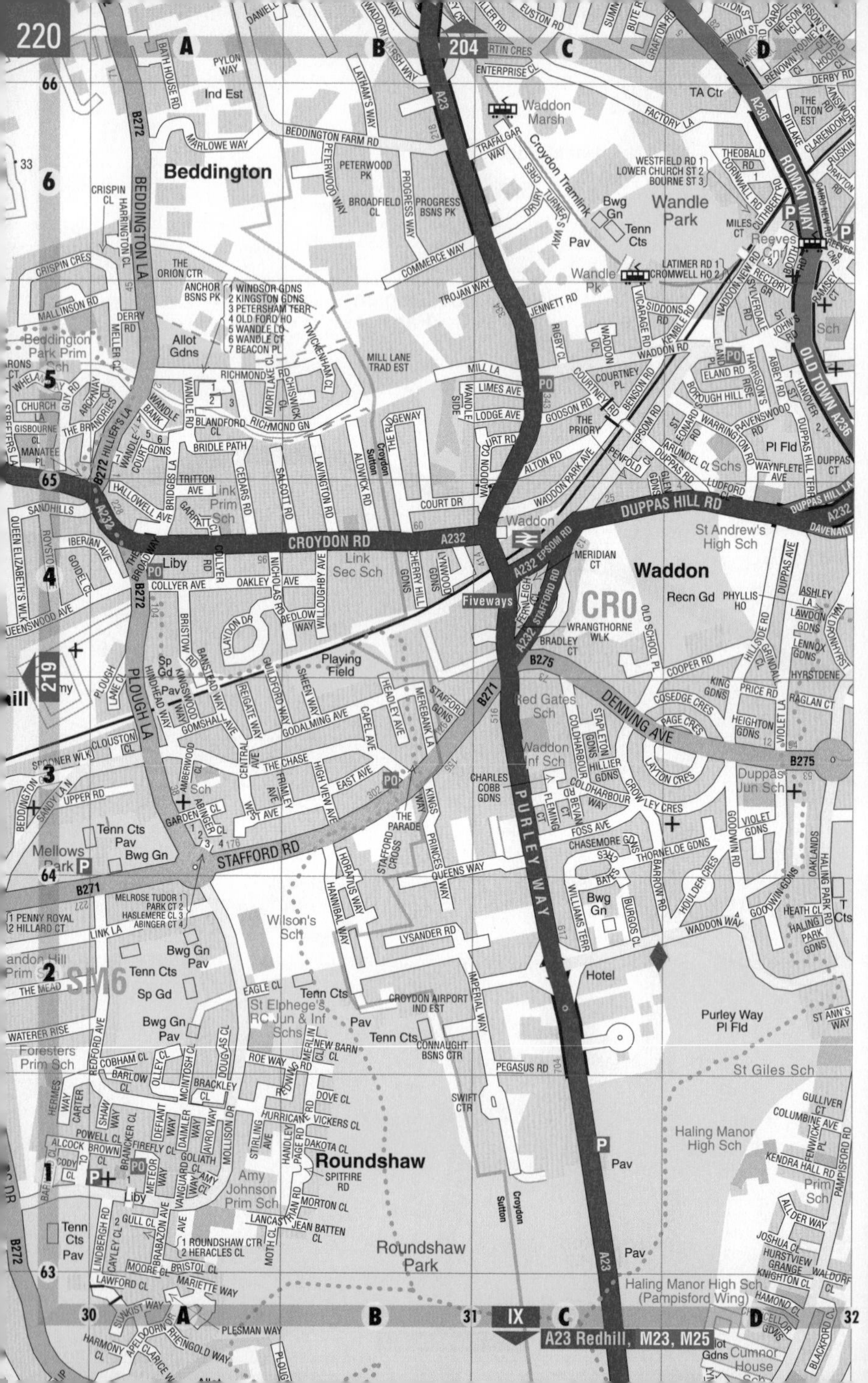

Beddington
Waddon
Roundshaw
Wandle Park
CR0
SM6
Waddon Marsh
Croydon Tramlink
Wandle Pk
Reeves Cnr
Fiveways
Waddon
Ind Est
Link Prim Sch
Link Sec Sch
Playing Field
Red Gates Sch
Waddon Inf Sch
Duppas Jun Sch
St Andrew's High Sch
Wilson's Sch
St Elphege's RC Jun & Inf Schs
Amy Johnson Prim Sch
Roundshaw Park
Purley Way Pl Fld
St Giles Sch
Haling Manor High Sch
Haling Manor High Sch (Pampisford Wing)
Mellows Park
Foresters Prim Sch
Beddington Park Prim Sch
CROYDON RD
DUPPAS HILL RD
PURLEY WAY
DENNING AVE
STAFFORD RD
PLOUGH LA
BEDDINGTON LA
OLD TOWN A236
ROWAN WAY
A23 Redhill, M23, M25
204
219
IX

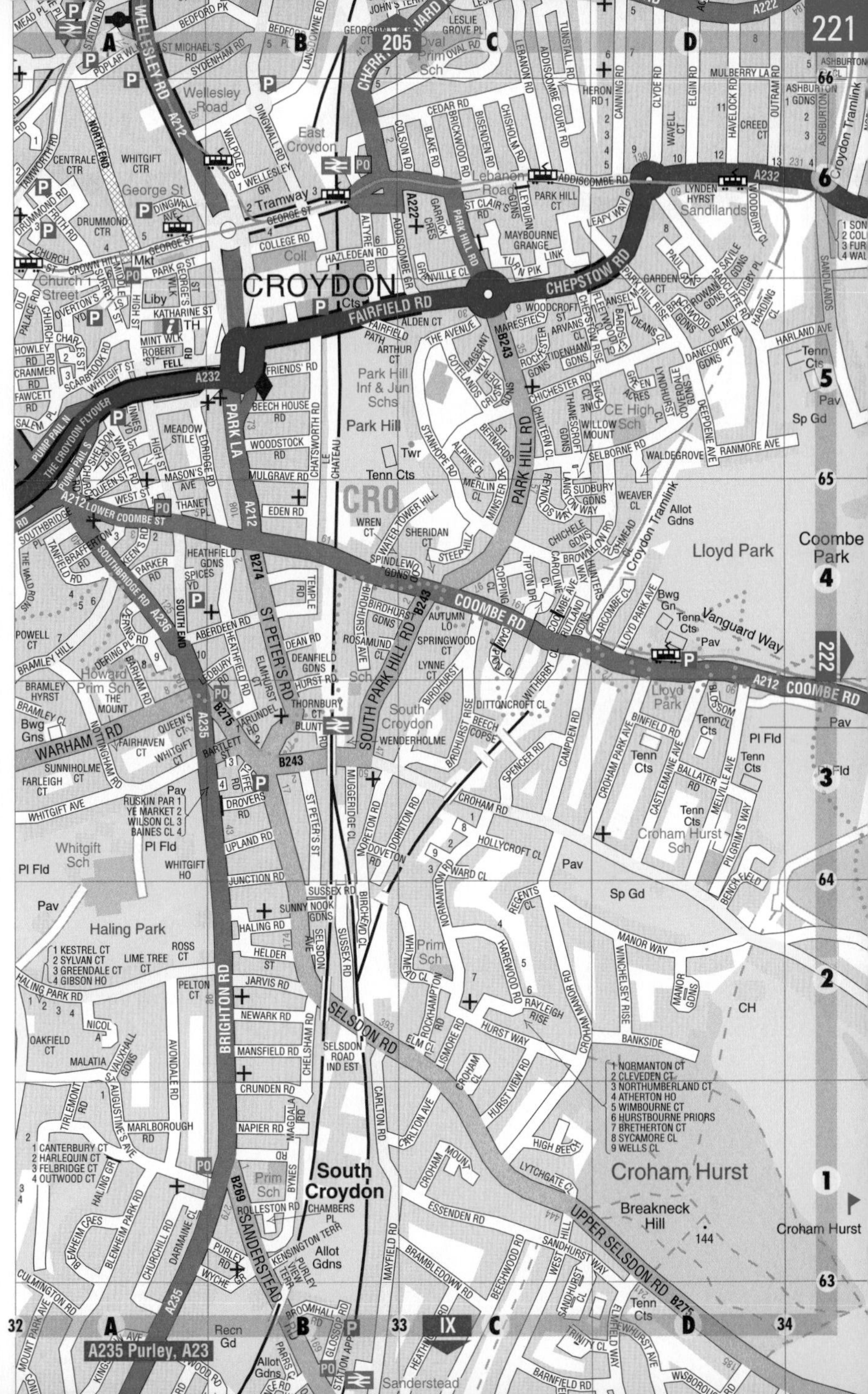
CROYDON
South Croydon
Croham Hurst
Lloyd Park
Coombe Park
Park Hill
Haling Park
Breakneck Hill
Sandilands
Sanderstead
East Croydon
George St
Wellesley Road
Lebanon Road
Church Street
WELLESLEY RD
FAIRFIELD RD
CHEPSTOW RD
ADDISCOMBE RD
PARK HILL RD
PARK LA
COOMBE RD
LOWER COOMBE ST
ST PETER'S RD
SOUTH PARK HILL RD
BRIGHTON RD
SELSDON RD
UPPER SELSDON RD
SANDERSTEAD RD
WARHAM RD
CROHAM RD
CHERRY ORCHARD RD
THE CROYDON FLYOVER
Croydon Tramlink
Vanguard Way
CENTRALE CTR
WHITGIFT CTR
DRUMMOND CTR
Park Hill Inf & Jun Schs
CE High Sch
Croham Hurst Sch
Whitgift Sch
Howard Prim Sch
Oval Prim Sch
SELSDON ROAD IND EST
1 KESTREL CT
2 SYLVAN CT
3 GREENDALE CT
4 GIBSON HO
1 CANTERBURY CT
2 HARLEQUIN CT
3 FELBRIDGE CT
4 OUTWOOD CT
RUSKIN PAR 1
YE MARKET 2
WILSON CL 3
BAINES CL 4
1 NORMANTON CT
2 CLEVEDEN CT
3 NORTHUMBERLAND CT
4 ATHERTON HO
5 WIMBOURNE CT
6 HURSTBOURNE PRIORS
7 BRETHERTON CT
8 SYCAMORE CL
9 WELLS CL
205
222
IX
A235 Purley, A23
A B C D
32 33 34
63 64 65 66
1 2 3 4 5 6

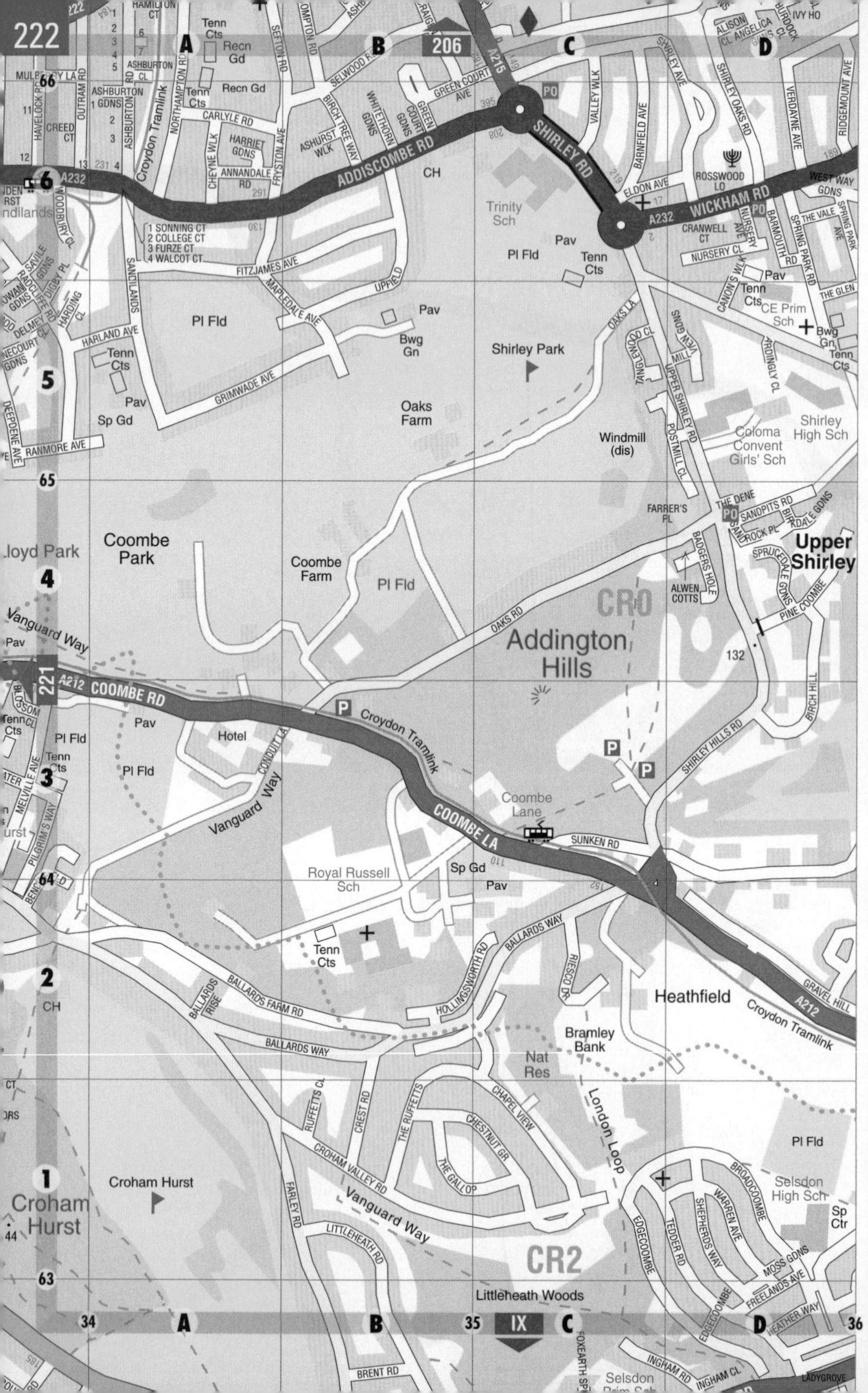

206
A
B
C
D
Tenn Cts
Recn Gd
Recn Gd
HAMILTON CT
ASHBURTON CL
ASHBURTON GDNS
MULBERRY LA RD
HAVELOCK RD
OUTRAM RD
CREED CT
ASHBURTON RD
Croydon Tramlink
NORTHAMPTON RD
CARLYLE RD
CHEYNE WLK
HARRIET GDNS
ANNANDALE RD
FRYSTON AVE
SEFTON RD
SELWOOD RD
BIRCH TREE WAY
ASHURST WLK
WHITETHORN GDNS
GREEN COURT GDNS
GREEN COURT AVE
A215
SHIRLEY RD
ADDISCOMBE RD
A232
CH
PO
Trinity Sch
VALLEY WLK
BARNFIELD AVE
SHIRLEY AVE
SHIRLEY OAKS RD
VERDAYNE AVE
RIDGEMOUNT AVE
ALISON CL
ANGELICA GDNS
BURDOCK CL
IVY HO
ELDON AVE
ROSSWOOD LO
WICKHAM RD
WEST WAY GDNS
CRANWELL CT
NURSERY AVE
NURSERY CL
BARMOUTH RD
SPRING PARK RD
THE VALE
SPRING PARK AVE
1 SONNING CT
2 COLLEGE CT
3 FURZE CT
4 WALCOT CT
FITZJAMES AVE
MAPLEDALE AVE
UPFIELD
SANDILANDS
WOODBURY CL
SAVILE GDNS
RADCLIFFE RD
DIGBY PL
DELMEY CL
HARDING CL
HARLAND AVE
DEEPDENE AVE
RANMORE AVE
Pl Fld
Pav
Tenn Cts
Bwg Gn
Sp Gd
GRIMWADE AVE
Shirley Park
Oaks Farm
OAKS LA
TANGLEWOOD CL
MILL VIEW GDNS
UPPER SHIRLEY RD
POSTMILL CL
Windmill (dis)
Coloma Convent Girls' Sch
Shirley High Sch
CANON'S WLK
CE Prim Sch
THE GLEN
ARDINGLY CL
FARRER'S PL
THE DENE
SANDPITS RD
ROCK PL
BIRDALE GDNS
BADGERS HOLE
ALWEN COTTS
Upper Shirley
SPRUCEDALE GDNS
PINE COOMBE
BIRCH HILL
Coombe Park
Lloyd Park
Coombe Farm
Pl Fld
CR0
OAKS RD
Addington Hills
132
Vanguard Way
A212 COOMBE RD
221
BLOSSOM CL
Pav
Pl Fld
Hotel
P
Croydon Tramlink
CONDUIT LA
MELVILLE AVE
PILGRIM'S WAY
SHIRLEY HILLS RD
Coombe Lane
COOMBE LA
SUNKEN RD
Royal Russell Sch
Sp Gd
Pav
BENCHFIELD
Tenn Cts
BALLARDS WAY
HOLLINGSWORTH RD
RIESCO DR
Heathfield
GRAVEL HILL
A212
BALLARDS RISE
BALLARDS FARM RD
BALLARDS WAY
CH
Bramley Bank
Nat Res
London Loop
RUFFETTS CL
CREST RD
THE RUFFETTS
CHESTNUT GR
CHAPEL VIEW
THE GALLOP
CROHAM VALLEY RD
Croham Hurst
Vanguard Way
FARLEY RD
LITTLEHEATH RD
CR2
Littleheath Woods
EDGECOOMBE
TEDDER RD
SHEPHERDS WAY
WARREN AVE
BROADCOOMBE
Pl Fld
Selsdon High Sch
Sp Ctr
MOSS GDNS
FREELANDS AVE
HEATHER WAY
INGHAM RD
INGHAM CL
BRENT RD
FOXEARTH SP
Selsdon Prim Sch
LADYGROVE
IX
34
35
36
66
65
64
63
6
5
4
3
2
1

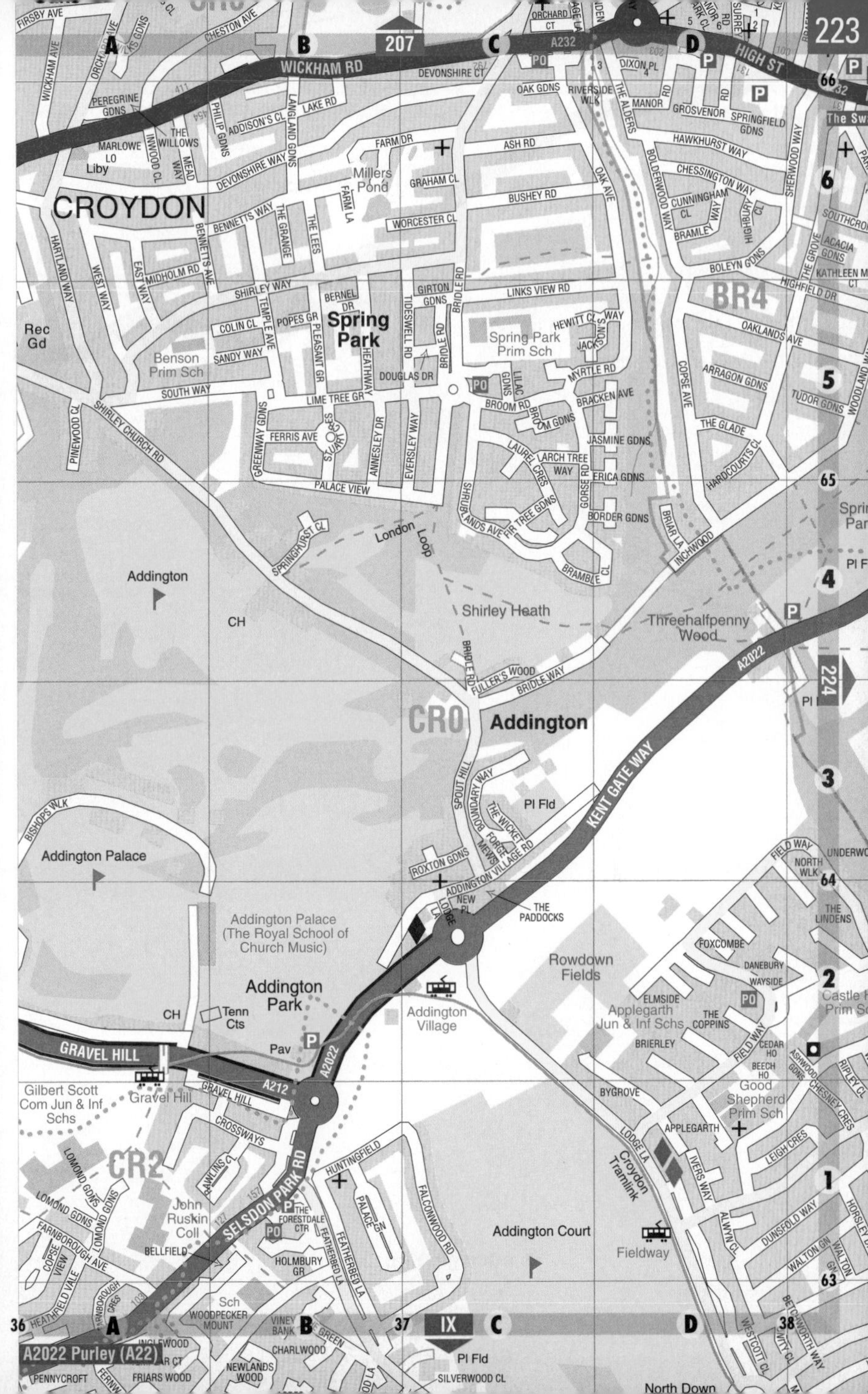

CROYDON
Spring Park
BR4
CR0
Addington
CR2
Shirley Heath
Threehalfpenny Wood
Addington Palace
Addington Palace (The Royal School of Church Music)
Addington Park
Addington Village
Rowdown Fields
Applegarth Jun & Inf Schs
Good Shepherd Prim Sch
Addington Court
Fieldway
Croydon Tramlink
Gilbert Scott Com Jun & Inf Schs
Gravel Hill
John Ruskin Coll
Benson Prim Sch
Spring Park Prim Sch
Millers Pond
London Loop
WICKHAM RD
HIGH ST
A232
A2022
A212
KENT GATE WAY
GRAVEL HILL
SELSDON PARK RD
SHIRLEY CHURCH RD
ADDINGTON VILLAGE RD
A2022 Purley (A22)
207
224
IX
A
B
C
D
36
37
38
63
64
65
66
1
2
3
4
5
6

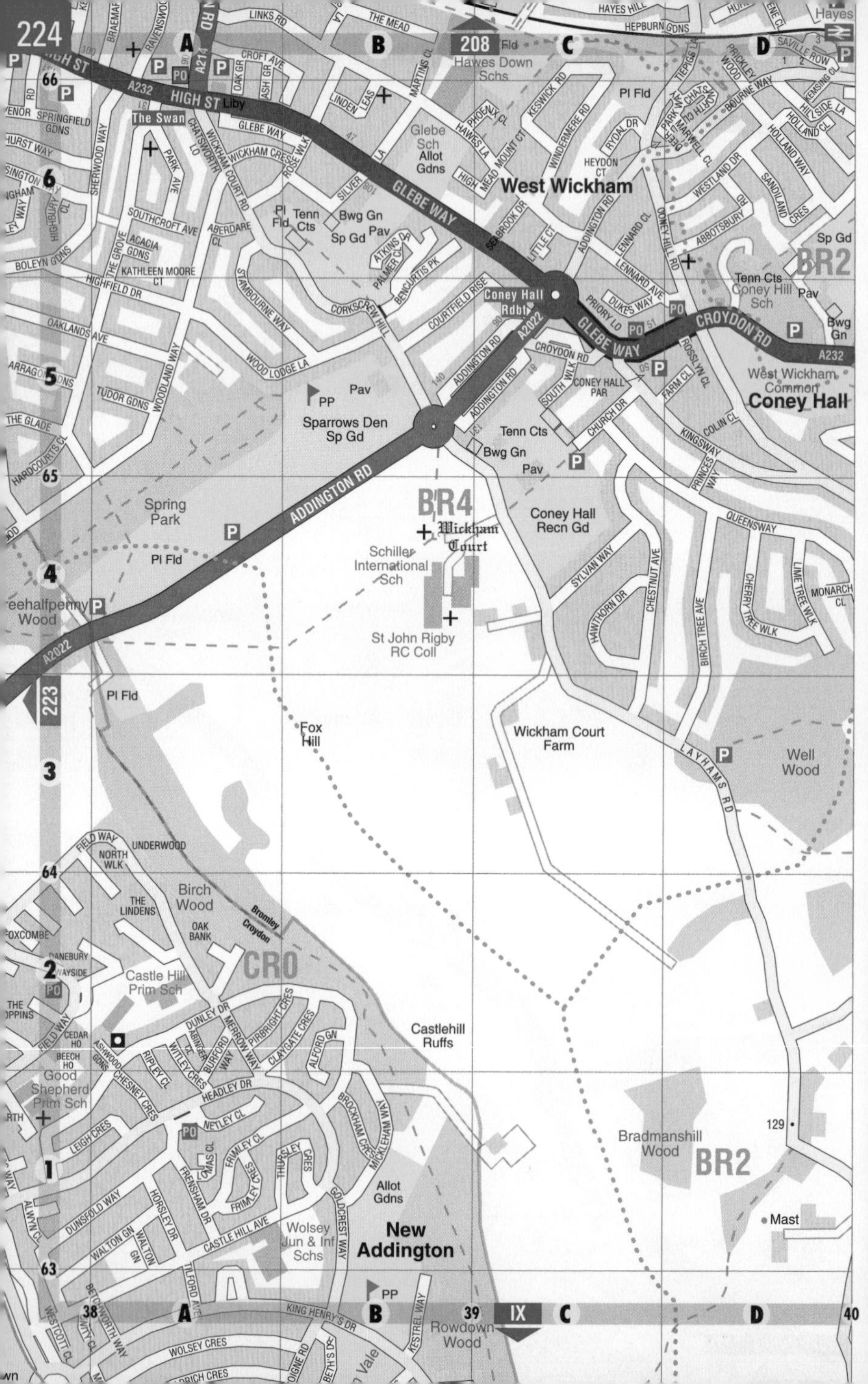

224
208
223
IX
A
B
C
D
6
5
4
3
2
1
66
65
64
63
38
39
40
West Wickham
Coney Hall
New Addington
BR4
BR2
CR0
HIGH ST
GLEBE WAY
CROYDON RD
ADDINGTON RD
LAYHAMS RD
A232
A214
A2022
Coney Hall Rdbt
The Swan
Liby
Hayes
Hawes Down Schs
Glebe Sch
Allot Gdns
Sparrows Den Sp Gd
Spring Park
Pl Fld
Wickham Court
Schiller International Sch
St John Rigby RC Coll
Coney Hall Recn Gd
Wickham Court Farm
Well Wood
West Wickham Common
Coney Hill Sch
Fox Hill
Birch Wood
Castle Hill Prim Sch
Castlehill Ruffs
Good Shepherd Prim Sch
Bradmanshill Wood
Wolsey Jun & Inf Schs
Rowdown Wood
Threehalfpenny Wood
Mast
Bromley
Croydon

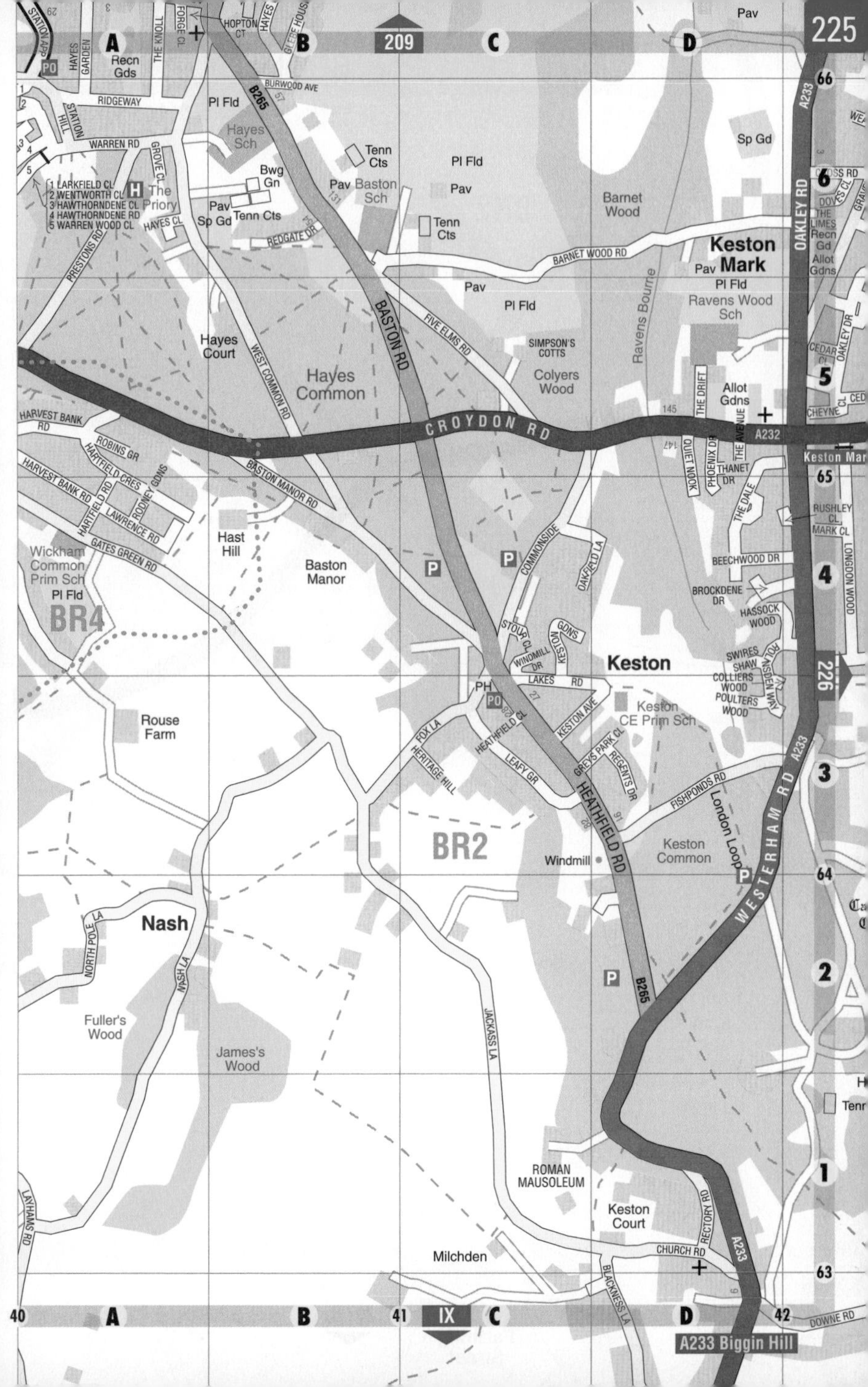
209
A
B
C
D
Recn Gds
Pl Fld
Hayes Sch
The Priory
Tenn Cts
Bwg Gn
Pav
Sp Gd
Baston Sch
Barnet Wood
Keston Mark
Ravens Wood Sch
Hayes Court
Hayes Common
Colyers Wood
SIMPSON'S COTTS
Allot Gdns
CROYDON RD
BASTON RD
WEST COMMON RD
FIVE ELMS RD
BARNET WOOD RD
OAKLEY RD
A232
A233
B265
Wickham Common Prim Sch
BR4
Hast Hill
Baston Manor
Keston
Keston CE Prim Sch
Rouse Farm
BR2
HEATHFIELD RD
WESTERHAM RD
Keston Common
London Loop
Windmill
Nash
Fuller's Wood
James's Wood
JACKASS LA
NASH LA
NORTH POLE LA
ROMAN MAUSOLEUM
Keston Court
Milchden
CHURCH RD
RECTORY RD
BLACKNESS LA
LAYHAMS RD
DOWNE RD
A233 Biggin Hill
IX
226
1 LARKFIELD CL
2 WENTWORTH CL
3 HAWTHORNDENE CL
4 HAWTHORNDENE RD
5 WARREN WOOD CL

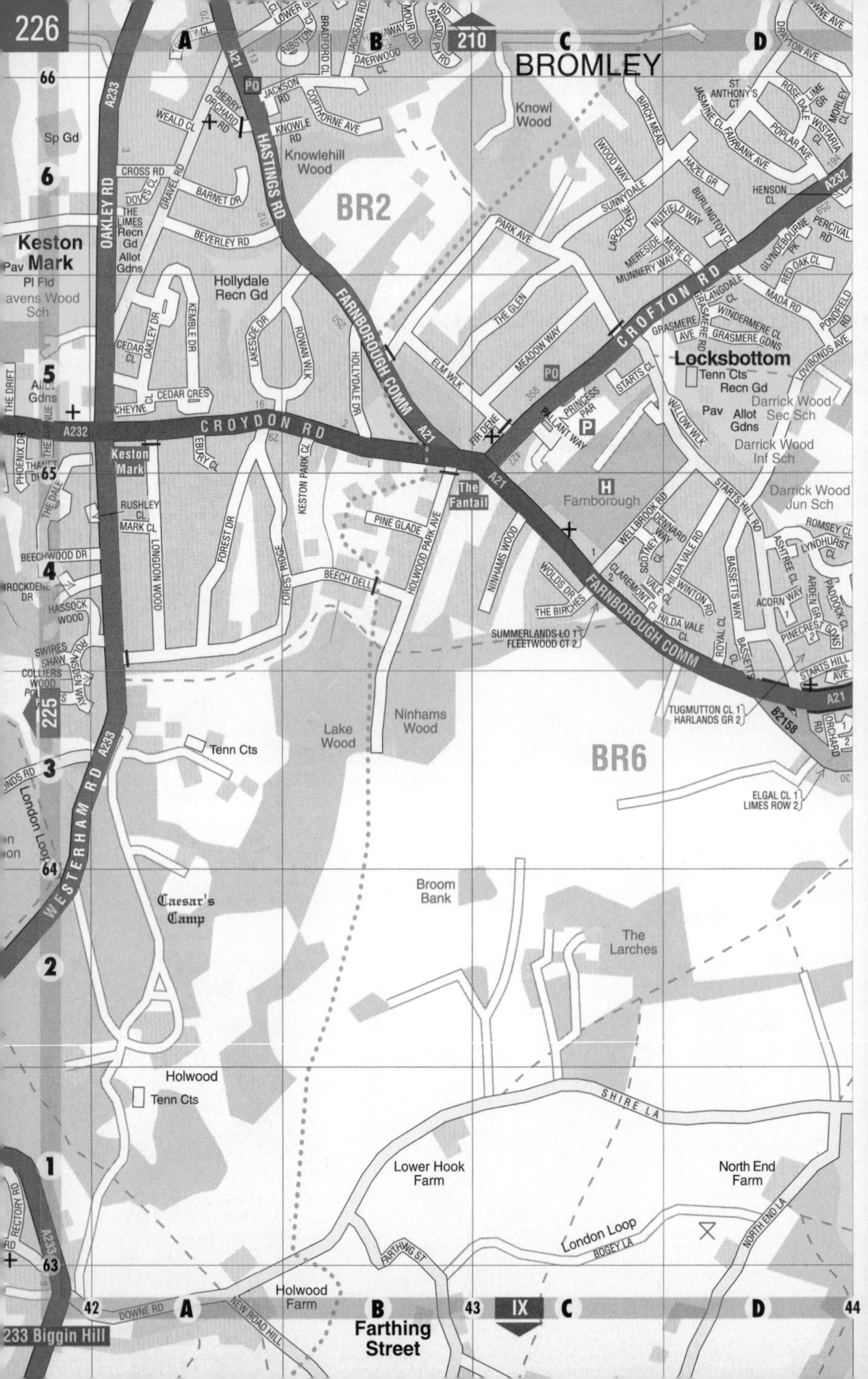
210
A
B
C
D
BROMLEY
Knowl Wood
Knowlehill Wood
BR2
Keston Mark
Hollydale Recn Gd
Locksbottom
Tenn Cts
Recn Gd
Darrick Wood Sec Sch
Darrick Wood Inf Sch
Darrick Wood Jun Sch
Farnborough
The Fantail
CROYDON RD
FARNBOROUGH COMM
HASTINGS RD
OAKLEY RD
CROFTON RD
WESTERHAM RD
Lake Wood
Ninhams Wood
BR6
Caesar's Camp
Broom Bank
The Larches
Holwood
Lower Hook Farm
North End Farm
London Loop
SHIRE LA
BOGEY LA
FARTHING ST
NEW ROAD HILL
DOWNE RD
NORTH END LA
Holwood Farm
Farthing Street
IX
233 Biggin Hill
225
42
43
44
66
65
64
63
1
2
3
4
5
6

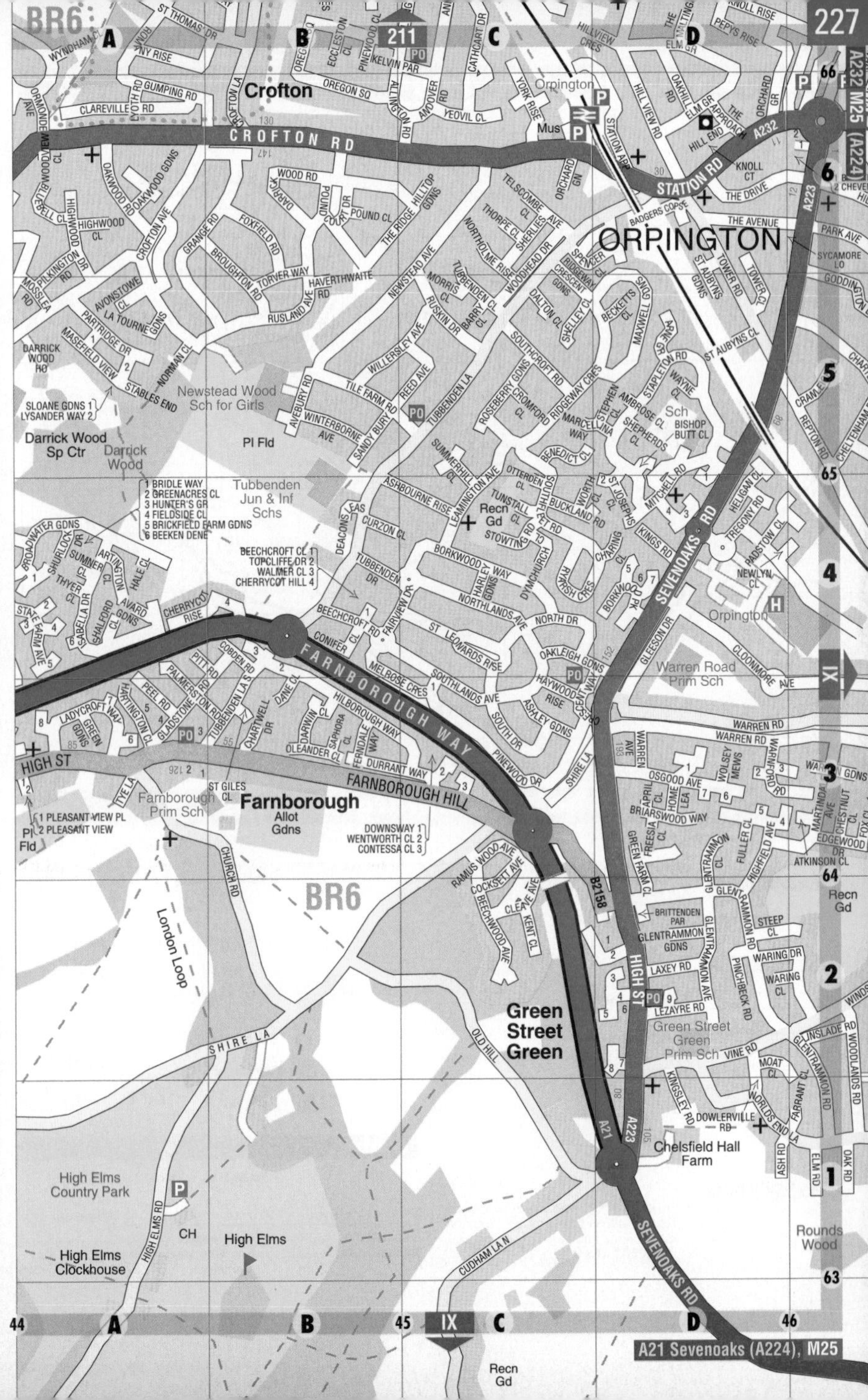
BR6
211
Crofton
CROFTON RD
Orpington
ORPINGTON
STATION RD
Newstead Wood Sch for Girls
Darrick Wood Sp Ctr
Darrick Wood
Tubbenden Jun & Inf Schs
Pl Fld
Recn Gd
FARNBOROUGH WAY
HIGH ST
FARNBOROUGH HILL
Farnborough
Farnborough Prim Sch
Allot Gdns
Warren Road Prim Sch
SEVENOAKS RD
Green Street Green
Green Street Green Prim Sch
Chelsfield Hall Farm
High Elms Country Park
High Elms Clockhouse
High Elms
London Loop
SHIRE LA
Rounds Wood
A232 M25 (A224)
A21 Sevenoaks (A224), M25
IX

Key to enlarged map pages

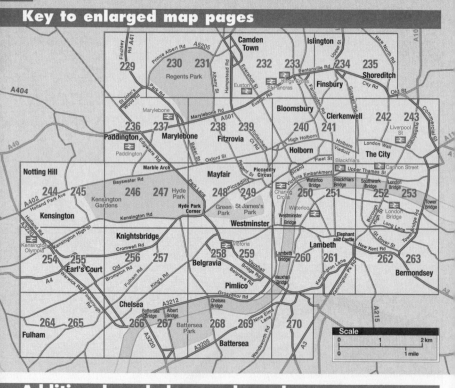

Finchley Rd A41 · Prince Albert Rd A5205

Camden Town

Islington · Upper St · New North Rd · A10

229 · **230** · **231** · **232** · **233** · **234** · **235**

Regents Park · Hampstead Rd · Eversholt St · Euston Rd · Rentonville Rd · King's Cross St Pancras · Farringdon Rd · Gray's Inn Rd · City Rd · Old St

A404 · St John's Wood Rd · Park Rd · Albany St · Euston Rd

Finsbury · **Shoreditch**

Marylebone · Marylebone Rd A501 · Euston Rd

Bloomsbury · **Clerkenwell**

A40 · **Paddington** · **236** · **237** · **238** · **239** · **240** · **241** · **242** · **243**

Edgware Rd · **Marylebone** · **Fitzrovia** · Trottenham Ct Rd · High Holborn · Holborn Viaduct · Liverpool St · Commercial St

Paddington · Baker St · Oxford St

Holborn · **The City**

Fleet St · Blackfriars · Upper Thames St · Cannon Street

Notting Hill · Marble Arch · **Mayfair** · Park Lane · **Piccadilly Circus** · Strand · Victoria Embankment · Blackfriars Bridge · Southwark Bridge · London Bridge

244 · **245** · **246** · **247** · **248** · **249** · **250** · **251** · **252** · **253**

A402 · Holland Park Ave · Bayswater Rd · Hyde Park · Charing Cross · Waterloo Bridge · Borough · Tower Bridge

Kensington Gardens · Hyde Park Corner · Green Park · St James's Park · Waterloo · London Bridge · Long Lane · Tower Bridge Rd

Kensington · Kensington Rd · **Westminster** · Westminster Bridge · Gt Dover St

Kensington Olympia · **Knightsbridge** · Cromwell Rd · Victoria · **Lambeth** · Elephant and Castle · New Kent Rd

254 · **255** · **256** · **257** · **258** · **259** · **260** · **261** · **262** · **263**

Earl's Court · Old Brompton Rd · Fulham Rd · **Belgravia** · Vauxhall Bridge Rd · Lambeth Bridge · Kennington Lane · **Bermondsey**

A4 · Warwick Rd · Finborough Rd · King's Rd · **Pimlico** · Belgrave Rd · Grosvenor Rd · Vauxhall Bridge · Kennington Pk Rd

A3212 · Battersea Bridge · Albert Bridge · Chelsea Bridge · Nine Elms Lane · A3 · A215

Chelsea · **264** · **265** · **266** · **267** · Battersea Park · **268** · **269** · **270**

Fulham · A3220 · A3205 · **Battersea** · Wandsworth Rd

Scale

0 — 1 — 2 km

0 — 1 mile

Additional symbols on enlarged maps

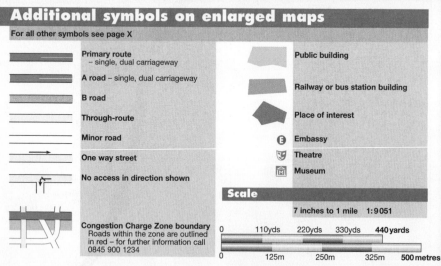

For all other symbols see page X

Primary route
– single, dual carriageway

A road – single, dual carriageway

B road

Through-route

Minor road

One way street

No access in direction shown

Congestion Charge Zone boundary
Roads within the zone are outlined
in red – for further information call
0845 900 1234

Public building

Railway or bus station building

Place of interest

Ⓔ Embassy

♟ Theatre

▥ Museum

Scale

7 inches to 1 mile   1:9051

0 — 110yds — 220yds — 330yds — **440 yards**

0 — 125m — 250m — 325m — **500 metres**

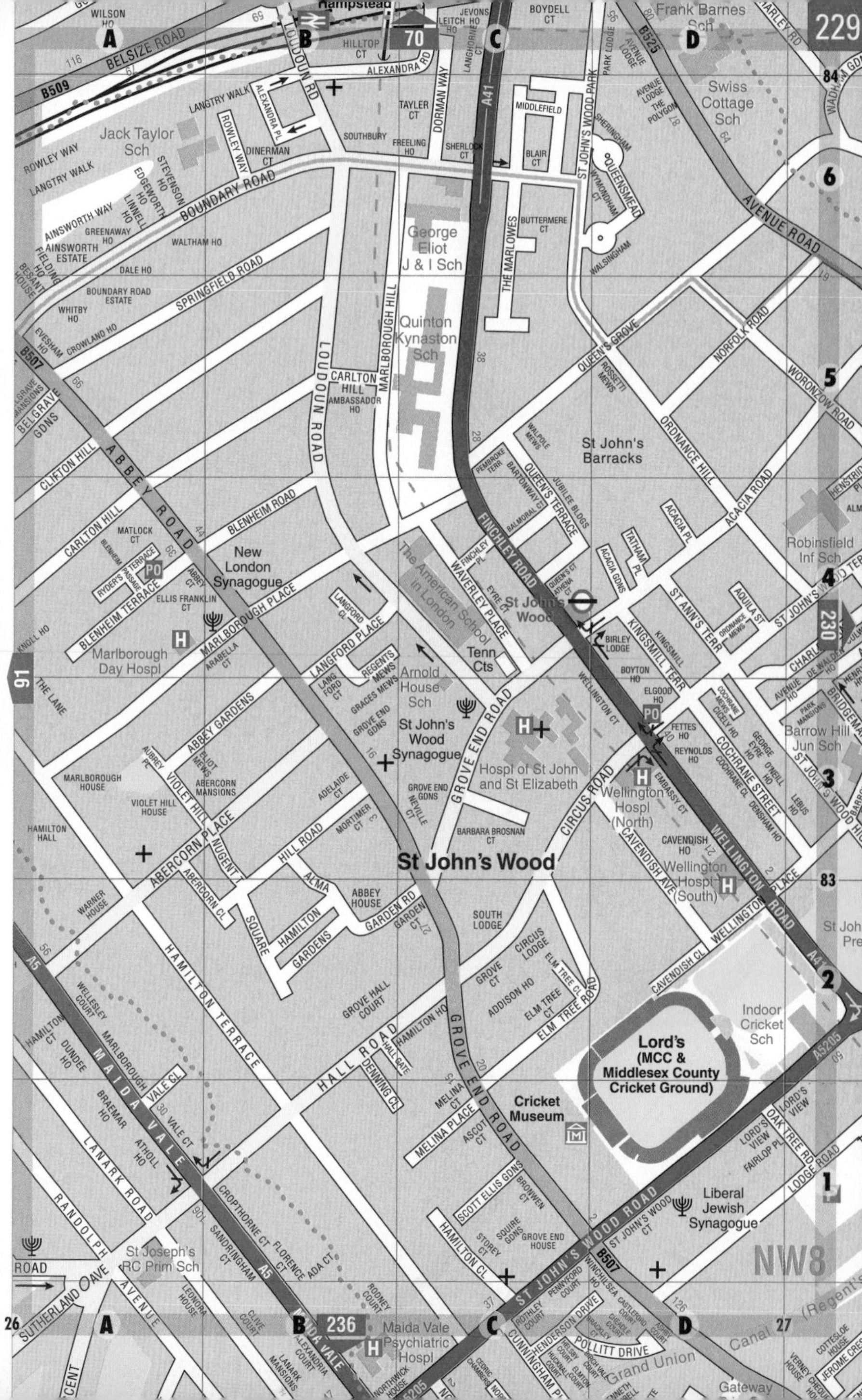

St John's Wood
NW8
Lord's (MCC & Middlesex County Cricket Ground)
Cricket Museum
Indoor Cricket Sch
Liberal Jewish Synagogue
St John's Barracks
St John's Wood
The American School in London
Hospl of St John and St Elizabeth
Wellington Hospl (North)
Wellington Hospl (South)
George Eliot J & I Sch
Quinton Kynaston Sch
Swiss Cottage Sch
Frank Barnes Sch
Jack Taylor Sch
New London Synagogue
Marlborough Day Hospl
Arnold House Sch
St John's Wood Synagogue
Robinsfield Inf Sch
Barrow Hill Jun Sch
St Joseph's RC Prim Sch
Maida Vale Psychiatric Hospl
Grand Union Canal (Regent's
ABBEY ROAD
FINCHLEY ROAD
WELLINGTON ROAD
GROVE END ROAD
ST JOHN'S WOOD ROAD
MAIDA VALE
BOUNDARY ROAD
BELSIZE ROAD
LOUDOUN ROAD
MARLBOROUGH HILL
QUEEN'S GROVE
AVENUE ROAD
ACACIA ROAD
ORDNANCE HILL
NORFOLK ROAD
WORONZOW ROAD
CIRCUS ROAD
HALL ROAD
HAMILTON TERRACE
ABERCORN PLACE
MARLBOROUGH PLACE
BLENHEIM ROAD
CARLTON HILL
CLIFTON HILL
SPRINGFIELD ROAD
LANARK ROAD
RANDOLPH AVENUE
SUTHERLAND AVE
ELM TREE ROAD
LODGE ROAD
CAVENDISH AVE
COCHRANE STREET
KINGSMILL TERR
ST ANN'S TERR
WAVERLEY PLACE
LANGFORD PLACE
HILL ROAD
GARDEN RD
HAMILTON GARDENS
VIOLET HILL
ABBEY GARDENS
HENDERSON DRIVE
POLLITT DRIVE
CUNNINGHAM PL
A41
A5
B507
B509
B525
A5205
70
230
236
91
A
B
C
D
1
2
3
4
5
6
83
84
26
27

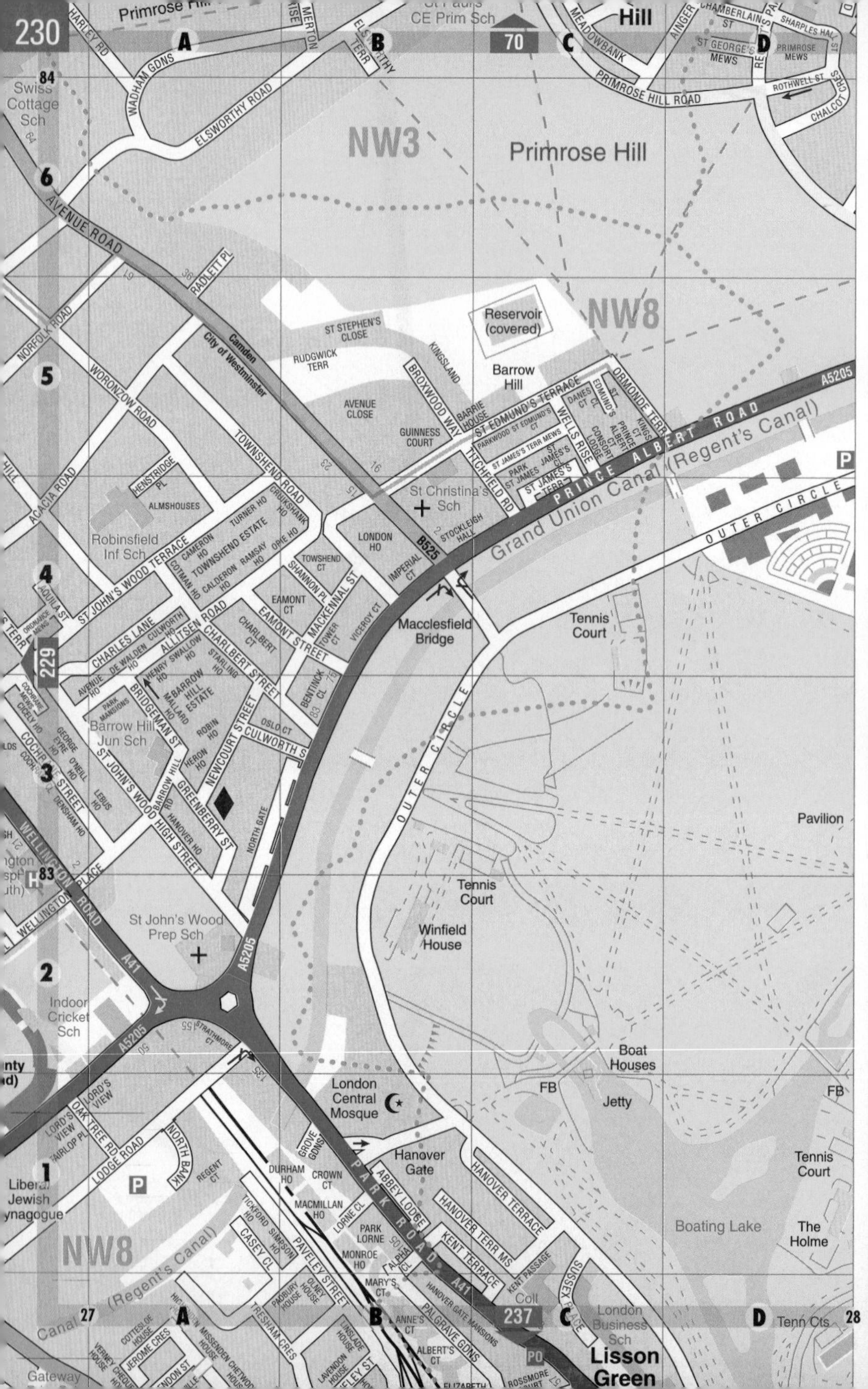

A
B
70
C
D
Primrose Hill
St Pauls CE Prim Sch
Hill
Swiss Cottage Sch
NW3
Primrose Hill
NW8
Reservoir (covered)
Barrow Hill
AVENUE ROAD
ELSWORTHY ROAD
WADHAM GDNS
PRIMROSE HILL ROAD
PRINCE ALBERT ROAD
Grand Union Canal (Regent's Canal)
OUTER CIRCLE
St Christina's Sch
Robinsfield Inf Sch
ALMSHOUSES
Macclesfield Bridge
Tennis Court
Barrow Hill Jun Sch
Pavilion
Winfield House
St John's Wood Prep Sch
Indoor Cricket Sch
Boat Houses
FB
Jetty
London Central Mosque
Hanover Gate
Tennis Court
Boating Lake
The Holme
Liberal Jewish Synagogue
NW8
PARK ROAD
WELLINGTON ROAD
ST JOHN'S WOOD HIGH STREET
ST JOHN'S WOOD TERRACE
London Business Sch
Lisson Green
Tenn Cts
229
237
84
83
27
28
6
5
4
3
2
1

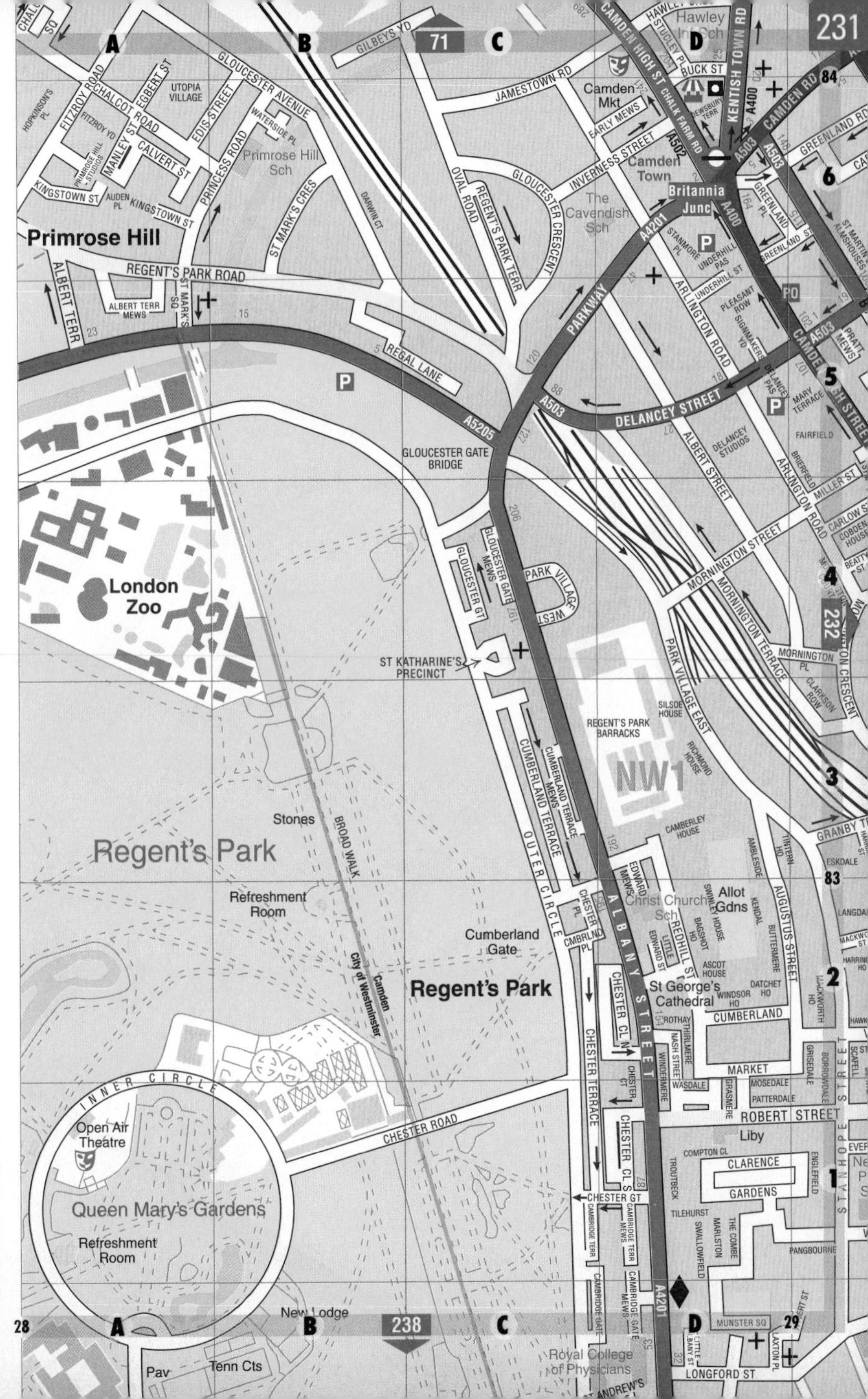

A
B
C
D
71
Primrose Hill
Utopia Village
Fitzroy Road
Chalcot Road
Egbert St
Gloucester Avenue
Edis Street
Princess Road
Calvert St
Kingstown St
Regent's Park Road
Albert Terr
Primrose Hill Sch
St Mark's Cres
Jamestown Rd
Oval Road
Regent's Park Terr
Gloucester Crescent
Inverness Street
Camden High St
Chalk Farm Rd
Kentish Town Rd
Camden Rd
Camden Mkt
Camden Town
Britannia Junc
The Cavendish Sch
Parkway
Arlington Road
Delancey Street
Albert Street
Regal Lane
A5205
A503
A4201
A400
A502
London Zoo
Gloucester Gate Bridge
Park Village West
St Katharine's Precinct
Mornington Street
Mornington Terrace
Park Village East
Regent's Park Barracks
NW1
Cumberland Terrace
Outer Circle
Albany Street
Stones
Broad Walk
Regent's Park
Refreshment Room
Cumberland Gate
Camden
City of Westminster
Chester Terrace
Christ Church Sch
Allot Gdns
Augustus Street
St George's Cathedral
Cumberland Market
Robert Street
Stanhope Street
Liby
Clarence Gardens
Chester Gt
Chester Road
Inner Circle
Open Air Theatre
Queen Mary's Gardens
New Lodge
Pav
Tenn Cts
Royal College of Physicians
Longford St
Munster Sq
Granby Ter
Greenland Rd
Mornington Crescent
232
238
28
29
1
2
3
4
5
6
83
84

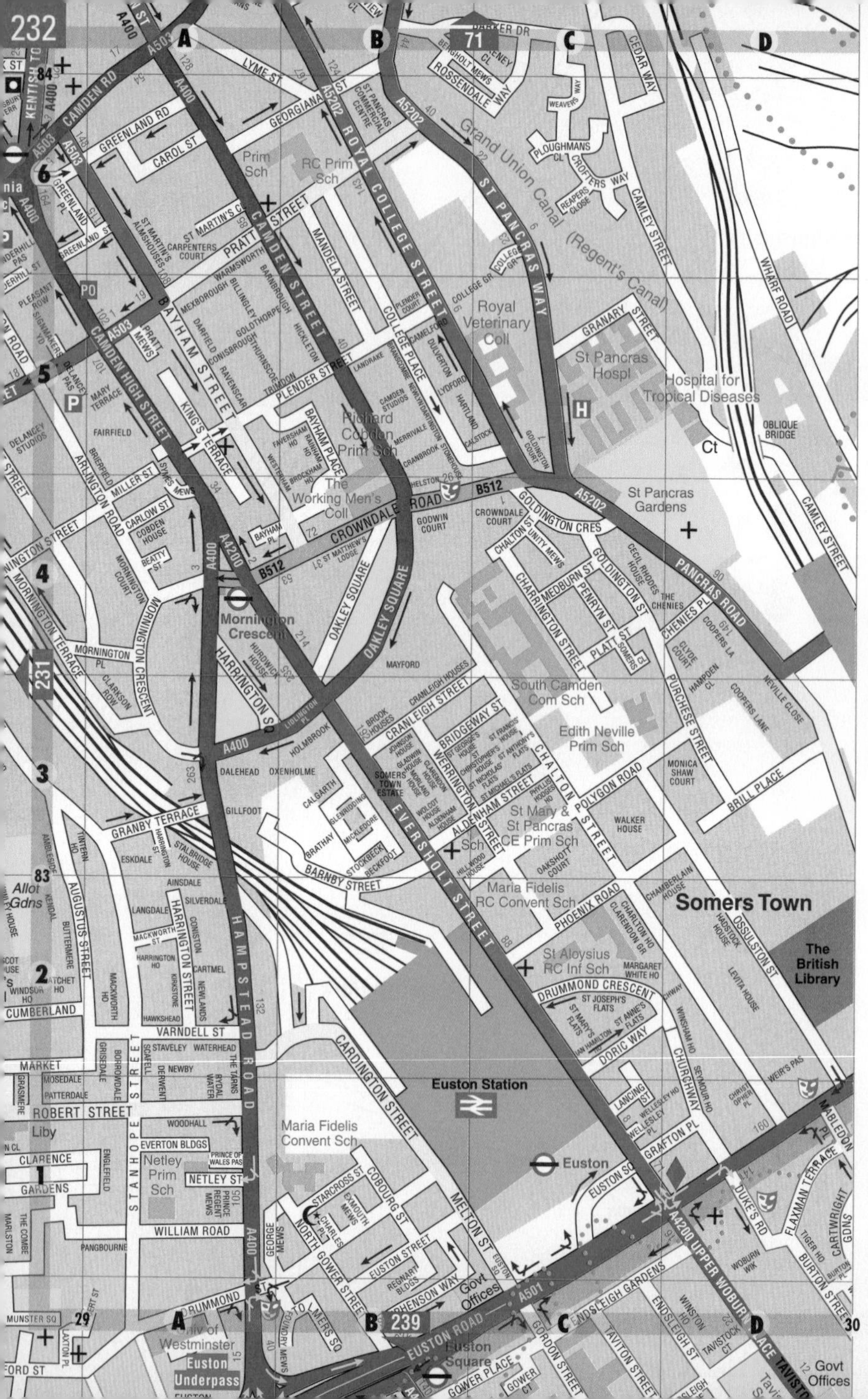

A
B
C
D
71
231
239
30
29
84
83
1
2
3
4
5
6
CAMDEN RD
KENTISH TOWN RD
LYME ST
GEORGIANA ST
GREENLAND RD
CAROL ST
GREENLAND PL
GREENLAND ST
ST MARTIN'S ALMSHOUSES
ST MARTIN'S CL
CARPENTERS COURT
PRATT STREET
PRATT MEWS
CAMDEN STREET
CAMDEN HIGH STREET
BAYHAM STREET
BAYHAM PLACE
BAYHAM PL
KING'S TERRACE
MANDELA STREET
ROYAL COLLEGE STREET
COLLEGE PLACE
COLLEGE GR
ST PANCRAS WAY
ST PANCRAS COMMERCIAL CENTRE
Prim Sch
RC Prim Sch
Grand Union Canal (Regent's Canal)
ROSSENDALE WAY
BERGHOLT MEWS
PARKER DR
CEDAR WAY
WEAVERS WAY
PLOUGHMANS CL
CROFTERS WAY
REAPERS CLOSE
CAMLEY STREET
WHARF ROAD
GRANARY STREET
Royal Veterinary Coll
St Pancras Hospl
Hospital for Tropical Diseases
OBLIQUE BRIDGE
Ct
PLENDER STREET
PLENDER COURT
MEXBOROUGH
BILLINGLEY
WARMSWORTH
BARNBROUGH
GOLDTHORPE
DARFIELD
CONISBROUGH
THURNSCOE
RAVENSCAR
TRIMDON
HICKLETON
LANDRAKE
BRANSCOMBE
NEWLYN
DARTINGTON
CAMELFORD
DULVERTON
LYDFORD
HARTLAND
CALSTOCK
CAMDEN STUDIOS
MERRIVALE
CRANBROOK
STONEHOUSE
HELSTON
Richard Cobden Prim Sch
FAVERSHAM HO
RAINHAM HO
WESTERHAM
BROCKHAM HO
The Working Men's Coll
CROWNDALE ROAD
B512
A5202
A5202
A502
A503
A400
A4200
A501
PO
P
H
DELANCEY PAS
DELANCEY STUDIOS
MARY TERRACE
FAIRFIELD
ARLINGTON ROAD
BRIERFIELD
MILLER ST
SYMES MEWS
CARLOW ST
COBDEN HOUSE
BEATTY ST
MORNINGTON STREET
MORNINGTON COURT
MORNINGTON CRESCENT
MORNINGTON TERRACE
MORNINGTON PL
CLARKSON ROW
Mornington Crescent
HURDWICK HOUSE
HARRINGTON SQ
LIDLINGTON PL
ST MATTHEW'S LODGE
OAKLEY SQUARE
GODWIN COURT
CROWNDALE COURT
GOLDINGTON COURT
GOLDINGTON CRES
GOLDINGTON ST
CHALTON ST
UNITY MEWS
CHARRINGTON STREET
MEDBURN ST
PENRYN ST
PLATT ST
SOMERS CL
CECIL RHODES HOUSE
THE CHENIES
CHENIES PL
COOPERS LA
CLYDE COURT
HAMPDEN CL
St Pancras Gardens
PANCRAS ROAD
NEVILLE CLOSE
COOPERS LANE
MAYFORD
South Camden Com Sch
Edith Neville Prim Sch
PURCHESE STREET
MONICA SHAW COURT
BRILL PLACE
POLYGON ROAD
WALKER HOUSE
CRANLEIGH HOUSES
CRANLEIGH STREET
BROOK HOUSES
BRIDGEWAY ST
JOHNSON HOUSE
GLADWIN HOUSE
CLARENDON HOUSE
NORLAND HOUSE
WERRINGTON STREET
ST GEORGE'S HOUSE
ST CHRISTOPHER'S HOUSE
ST FRANCIS' HOUSE
ST ANTHONY'S FLATS
ST NICHOLAS' FLATS
ST MICHAEL'S FLATS
PHYLLIS HODGES HO
CHALTON STREET
ALDENHAM STREET
WOLCOT HOUSE
ALDENHAM HOUSE
St Mary & St Pancras CE Prim Sch
Sch
HILLWOOD HOUSE
OAKSHOTT COURT
SOMERS TOWN ESTATE
HOLMBROOK
DALEHEAD
OXENHOLME
CALGARTH
GLENRIDDING
MICKLEDORE
BRATHAY
STOCKBECK
BECKFOOT
BARNBY STREET
EVERSHOLT STREET
Maria Fidelis RC Convent Sch
PHOENIX ROAD
CHARLTON HO
CLARENDON GR
CHAMBERLAIN HOUSE
Somers Town
HADSTOCK HOUSE
OSSULSTON ST
LEVITA HOUSE
The British Library
St Aloysius RC Inf Sch
MARGARET WHITE HO
DRUMMOND CRESCENT
ST JOSEPH'S FLATS
ST MARY'S FLATS
ST ANNE'S FLATS
DORIC WAY
CHURCHWAY
WINSHAM HO
SEYMOUR HO
LANCING ST
WELLESLEY HO
WELLESLEY PL
GRAFTON PL
CHRISTOPHER PL
WEIR'S PAS
MABLEDON PL
DUKE'S RD
FLAXMAN TERRACE
CARTWRIGHT GDNS
TIGER HO
BURTON ST
BURTON STREET
WOBURN WLK
UPPER WOBURN PLACE
TAVISTOCK CT
TAVISTOCK
Govt Offices
GILLFOOT
GRANBY TERRACE
HARRINGTON ST
STALBRIDGE HOUSE
ESKDALE
AINSDALE
SILVERDALE
LANGDALE
MACKWORTH ST
HARRINGTON HO
HARRINGTON STREET
CONISTON
CARTMEL
KIRKSTONE
NEWLANDS
HAWKSHEAD
TINTERN HO
AMBLESIDE
KENDAL
BUTTERMERE
AUGUSTUS STREET
Allot Gdns
HATCHET HO
WINDSOR HO
MACKWORTH HO
CUMBERLAND
MARKET
VARNDELL ST
STAVELEY
WATERHEAD
SCAFELL
DERWENT
NEWBY
RYDAL WATER
THE TARNS
MOSEDALE
PATTERDALE
GRISEDALE
BORROWDALE
GRASMERE
ROBERT STREET
STANHOPE STREET
HAMPSTEAD ROAD
Liby
WOODHALL
EVERTON BLDGS
PRINCE OF WALES PAS
Netley Prim Sch
NETLEY ST
PRINCE REGENT MEWS
CLARENCE GARDENS
ENGLEFIELD
MARLSTON
THE COMBE
WILLIAM ROAD
PANGBOURNE
DRUMMOND ST
MUNSTER SQ
LAXTON PL
FORD ST
Univ of Westminster
Euston Underpass
FOUNDRY MEWS
TOLMERS SQ
CARDINGTON STREET
Maria Fidelis Convent Sch
Euston Station
STARCROSS ST
EXMOUTH MEWS
COBOURG ST
CHARLES PL
NORTH GOWER STREET
GEORGE MEWS
EUSTON STREET
REGNART BLDGS
STEPHENSON WAY
MELTON ST
EUSTON SQ
Euston
EUSTON ROAD
Euston Square
GOWER PLACE
GOWER CT
GORDON STREET
ENDSLEIGH GARDENS
ENDSLEIGH ST
TAVITON STREET
WINSTON HO

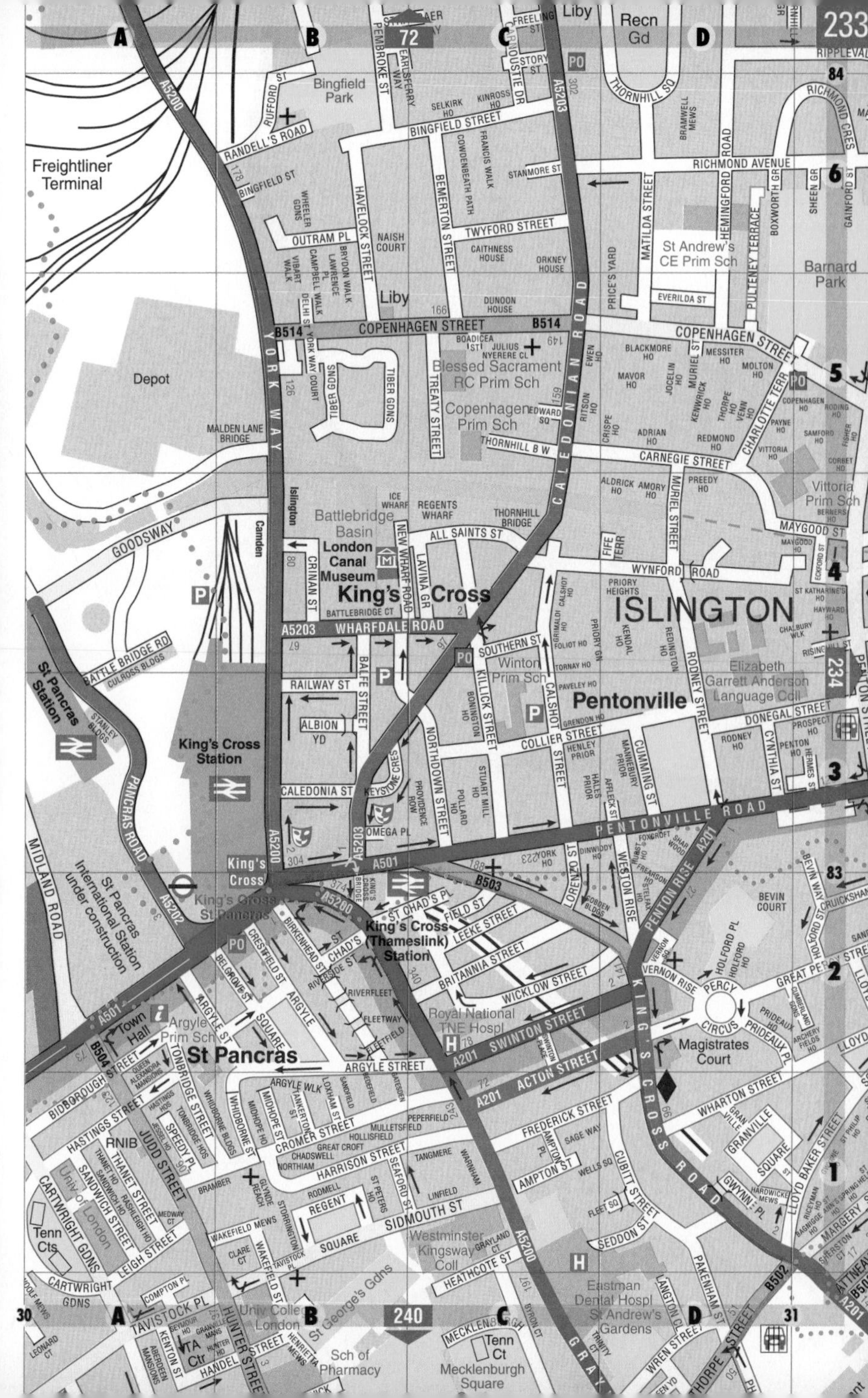
A
B
C
D
72
Liby
Recn
Gd
RIPPLEVALE
84
Freightliner
Terminal
Bingfield
Park
RUFFORD ST
RANDELL'S ROAD
BINGFIELD ST
PEMBROKE ST
EARLSFERRY WAY
FREELING ST
CARNOUSTIE DR
STORY ST
SELKIRK HO
KINROSS HO
BINGFIELD STREET
COWDENBEATH PATH
FRANCIS WALK
STANMORE ST
THORNHILL SQ
BRAMWELL MEWS
RICHMOND CRES
RICHMOND AVENUE
HEMINGFORD ROAD
BOXWORTH GR
SHEEN GR
GAINFORD ST
6
WHEELER GDNS
OUTRAM PL
HAVELOCK STREET
NAISH COURT
BEMERTON STREET
TWYFORD STREET
CAITHNESS HOUSE
ORKNEY HOUSE
DUNOON HOUSE
PRICE'S YARD
MATILDA STREET
PULTENEY TERRACE
St Andrew's
CE Prim Sch
EVERILDA ST
Barnard
Park
VIBART WALK
CAMPBELL WALK
LAWRENCE PL
BRYDON WALK
DELHI ST
COPENHAGEN STREET
B514
BOADICEA ST
JULIUS NYERERE CL
YORK WAY
YORK WAY COURT
TIBER GDNS
TREATY STREET
Blessed Sacrament
RC Prim Sch
Copenhagen
Prim Sch
EDWARD SQ
CALEDONIAN ROAD
RITSON HO
EWEN HO
CRISPE HO
BLACKMORE HO
MAVOR HO
ADRIAN HO
JOCELIN HO
MURIEL ST
KENWRICK HO
THORPE HO
VENN HO
MESSITER HO
MOLTON HO
REDMOND HO
CHARLOTTE TERR
COPENHAGEN HO
RODING HO
PAYNE HO
SAMFORD HO
FISHER HO
VITTORIA HO
CORBET HO
5
Depot
MALDEN LANE BRIDGE
THORNHILL B W
CARNEGIE STREET
ALDRICK HO
AMORY HO
PREEDY HO
MURIEL STREET
Vittoria
Prim Sch
BERNERS HO
Islington
Camden
ICE WHARF
REGENTS WHARF
THORNHILL BRIDGE
Battlebridge
Basin
ALL SAINTS ST
FIFE TERR
MAYGOOD ST
MAYGOOD HO
GOODSWAY
London
Canal
Museum
CRINAN ST
NEW WHARF ROAD
LAVINA GR
King's Cross
WYNFORD ROAD
PRIORY HEIGHTS
ECKFORD ST
4
ISLINGTON
ST KATHARINE'S HO
HAYWARD HO
BATTLEBRIDGE CT
A5203
WHARFDALE ROAD
SOUTHERN ST
CALSHOT HO
GRIMALDI HO
FOLIOT HO
PRIORY GN
KENDAL HO
REDINGTON HO
CHALBURY WLK
RISINGHILL ST
BATTLE BRIDGE RD
CULROSS BLDGS
St Pancras
Station
STANLEY BLDGS
PO
Winton
Prim Sch
KILLICK STREET
TORNAY HO
PAVELEY HO
RAILWAY ST
BALFE STREET
Elizabeth
Garrett Anderson
Language Coll
234
PENTON ST
King's Cross
Station
ALBION YD
BONINGTON HO
CALSHOT STREET
Pentonville
RODNEY STREET
DONEGAL STREET
GRENDON HO
COLLIER STREET
HENLEY PRIOR
MANNEBURY PRIOR
CUMMING ST
RODNEY HO
CYNTHIA ST
PROSPECT HO
PENTON HO
HERMES ST
3
NORTHDOWN STREET
KEYSTONE CRES
CALEDONIA ST
PROVIDENCE ROW
STUART MILL HO
POLLARD HO
HALES PRIOR
AFFLECK ST
PANCRAS ROAD
OMEGA PL
PENTONVILLE ROAD
A5200
A501
YORK HO
DINWIDDY HO
FOXCROFT HO
SHARWOOD
MIDLAND ROAD
King's Cross
King's Cross
St Pancras
A5202
St Pancras
International Station
under construction
B503
LORENZO ST
WESTON RISE
FREARSON HO
COBDEN BLDGS
PENTON RISE
A201
BEVIN WAY
83
CRUICKSHANK
BEVIN COURT
KING'S CROSS BRIDGE
ST CHAD'S PL
FIELD ST
LEEKE STREET
King's Cross
(Thameslink)
Station
BIRKENHEAD ST
ST CHAD'S ST
CRESTFIELD ST
BELGROVE ST
RIVERSIDE ST
RIVERFLEET
BRITANNIA STREET
WICKLOW STREET
VERNON SQ
VERNON RISE
HOLFORD PL
HOLFORD HO
HOLFORD ST
PERCY CIRCUS
GREAT PERCY STREET
CUMBERLAND GDNS
SANDS
2
LLOYD
ARGYLE SQUARE
ARGYLE ST
ARGYLE
FLEETWAY
FLEETFIELD
Royal National
TNE Hospl
SWINTON STREET
SWINTON PLACE
KING'S CROSS ROAD
PRIDEAUX PL
ARCHERY FIELDS HO
Town
Hall
Argyle
Prim Sch
St Pancras
B504
QUEEN ALEXANDRA MANSIONS
TONBRIDGE STREET
ARGYLE STREET
ACTON STREET
Magistrates
Court
LLOYD
BIDBOROUGH STREET
HASTINGS HO
TONBRIDGE HOS
WHIDBORNE BLDGS
WHIDBORNE ST
ARGYLE WLK
MIDHOPE ST
MIDHOPE HO
TANKERTON ST
LOXHAM ST
SANDFIELD
REDEFIELD
GATESDEN
WHARTON STREET
HASTINGS STREET
JESSEL HO
SPEEDY PL
CROMER STREET
PEPPERFIELD
MULLETSFIELD
HOLLISFIELD
FREDERICK STREET
AMPTON PL
SAGE WAY
GRANVILLE SQUARE
GRANVILLE
LLOYD BAKER STREET
ST PHILIP
RNIB
THANET HO
SANDWICH HO
GREAT CROFT
CHADSWELL
NORTHIAM
HARRISON STREET
TANGMERE
WARNHAM
WELLS SQ
1
JUDD STREET
THANET STREET
SANDWICH STREET
RASHLEIGH HO
CARTWRIGHT GDNS
Univ of London
BRAMBER
GLYNDE REACH
RODMELL
ST PETERS HO
SEAFORD ST
LINFIELD
AMPTON ST
CUBITT STREET
GWYNNE PL
HARDWICKE MEWS
RICEYMAN
BAGNIGGE HO
ANN'S
SPRING HO
MARGERY ST
Tenn
Cts
MEDWAY CT
LEIGH STREET
STORRINGTON
REGENT SQUARE
SIDMOUTH ST
FLEET SQ
GRAYLAND CT
Westminster
Kingsway
Coll
SEDDON ST
SHERSTON CT
WAKEFIELD MEWS
CLARE CT
WAKEFIELD ST
TAVISTOCK PL
HEATHCOTE ST
Eastman
Dental Hospl
PAKENHAM ST
B502
ATTNEAVE
CARTWRIGHT GDNS
COMPTON PL
LANGTON CL
St Andrew's
Gardens
A201
B502
30
TAVISTOCK PL
SEYMOUR HO
GRANVILLE MANS
HUNTER HO
Univ Coll
London
St George's Gdns
240
MECKLENBURGH
BYRON CT
GRAY
TRINITY CT
31
LEONARD CT
KENTON ST
ABERDEEN MANSIONS
TA
Ctr
HUNTER STREET
HANDEL STREET
HENRIETTA MEWS
Sch of
Pharmacy
Tenn
Ct
Mecklenburgh
Square
WREN STREET
THORPE STREET

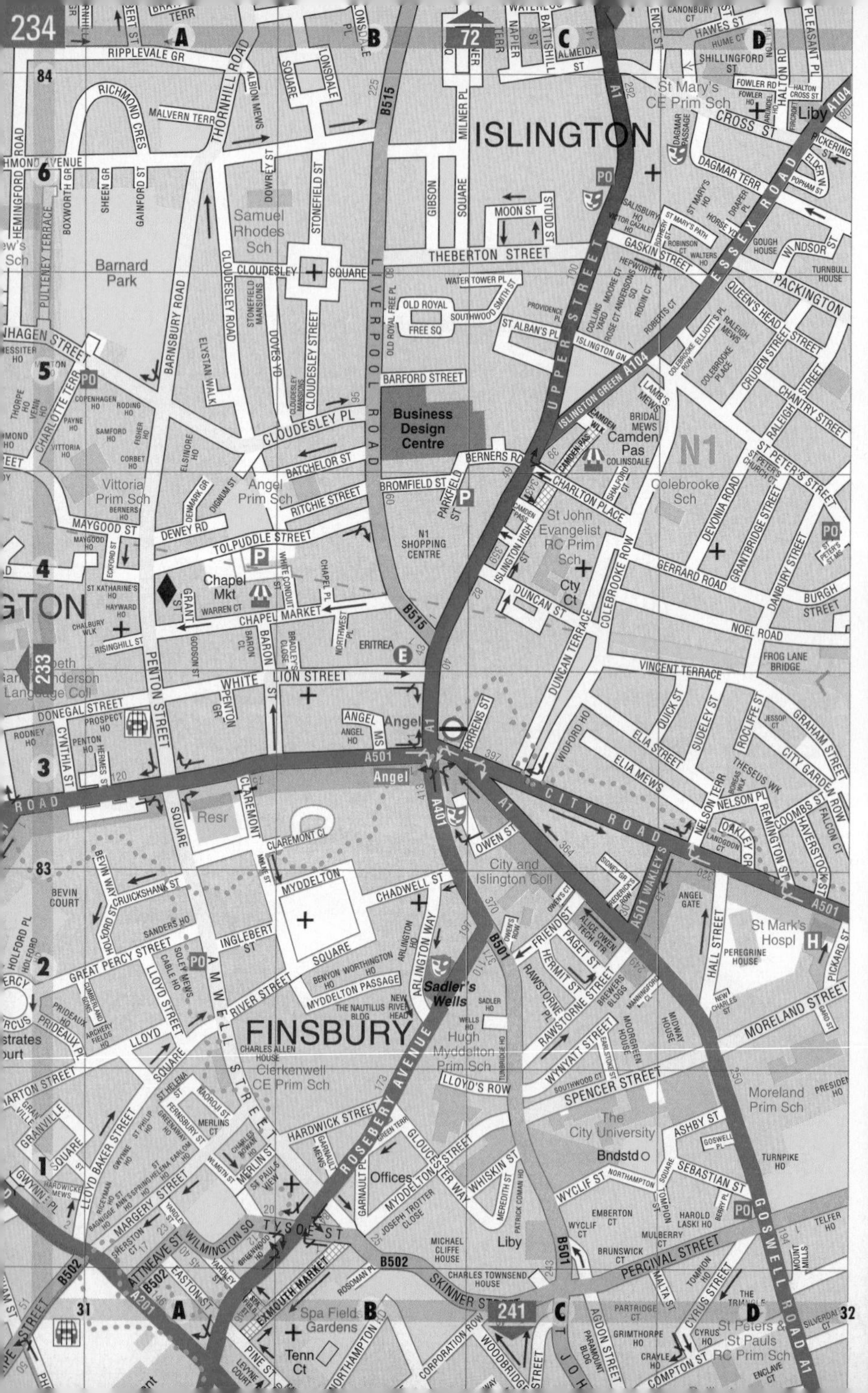
A
B
C
D
72
ISLINGTON
FINSBURY
N1
6
5
4
3
2
1
84
83
31
32
233
241
RIPPLEVALE GR
RICHMOND CRES
MALVERN TERR
THORNHILL ROAD
ALBION MEWS
LONSDALE SQUARE
MILNER PL
GIBSON SQUARE
ALMEIDA ST
SHILLINGFORD ST
HAWES ST
CANONBURY CT
PLEASANT PL
HALTON RD
St Mary's CE Prim Sch
CROSS ST
Liby
DAGMAR PASSAGE
DAGMAR TERR
ESSEX ROAD
A104
A1
B515
PO
MOON ST
STUDD ST
THEBERTON STREET
GASKIN STREET
WINDSOR ST
GOUGH HOUSE
TURNBULL HOUSE
PACKINGTON
QUEEN'S HEAD STREET
CRUDEN STREET
RALEIGH STREET
CHANTRY STREET
ST PETER'S STREET
Samuel Rhodes Sch
Barnard Park
BARNSBURY ROAD
CLOUDESLEY ROAD
CLOUDESLEY SQUARE
CLOUDESLEY STREET
STONEFIELD ST
DOWREY ST
SHEEN GR
GAINFORD ST
BOXWORTH GR
HEMINGFORD ROAD
PULTENEY TERRACE
RICHMOND AVENUE
LIVERPOOL ROAD
OLD ROYAL FREE SQ
WATER TOWER PL
SOUTHWOOD SMITH ST
ST ALBAN'S PL
UPPER STREET
ISLINGTON GREEN
BARFORD STREET
Business Design Centre
ELYSTAN WALK
DOVES YD
COPENHAGEN STREET
CHARLOTTE TERR
CLOUDESLEY PL
BATCHELOR ST
RITCHIE STREET
BERNERS RD
BROMFIELD ST
PARKFIELD ST
CAMDEN PAS
Camden Pas
CHARLTON PLACE
Colebrooke Sch
DEVONIA ROAD
GRANTBRIDGE STREET
DANBURY STREET
Vittoria Prim Sch
Angel Prim Sch
MAYGOOD ST
DEWEY RD
TOLPUDDLE STREET
Chapel Mkt
N1 SHOPPING CENTRE
St John Evangelist RC Prim Sch
ISLINGTON HIGH ST
COLEBROOKE ROW
GERRARD ROAD
BURGH STREET
DUNCAN ST
Cty Ct
CHAPEL MARKET
WHITE CONDUIT ST
PENTON STREET
RISINGHILL ST
NOEL ROAD
DUNCAN TERRACE
VINCENT TERRACE
FROG LANE BRIDGE
WHITE LION STREET
DONEGAL STREET
ANGEL MS
Angel
TORRENS ST
ELIA STREET
ELIA MEWS
QUICK ST
SUDELEY ST
ROCLIFFE ST
GRAHAM STREET
CITY GARDEN ROW
A501
CITY ROAD
A401
CLAREMONT SQUARE
Resr
NELSON TERR
NELSON PL
OAKLEY CR
REMINGTON ST
HAVERSTOCK ST
COOMBS ST
FALCON CT
OWEN ST
City and Islington Coll
MYDDELTON SQUARE
CHADWELL ST
BEVIN COURT
BEVIN WAY
CRUICKSHANK ST
INGLEBERT ST
GREAT PERCY STREET
AMWELL STREET
LLOYD STREET
ARLINGTON WAY
Sadler's Wells
RIVER STREET
MYDDELTON PASSAGE
ROSEBERY AVENUE
B501
RAWSTORNE STREET
WYNYATT STREET
ANGEL GATE
HALL STREET
St Mark's Hospl
PEREGRINE HOUSE
MORELAND STREET
PICKARD ST
Hugh Myddelton Prim Sch
LLOYD'S ROW
SPENCER STREET
The City University
Moreland Prim Sch
Clerkenwell CE Prim Sch
LLOYD BAKER STREET
GRANVILLE SQUARE
MARGERY STREET
HARDWICK STREET
GLOUCESTER WAY
Offices
WHISKIN ST
ASHBY ST
SEBASTIAN ST
Bndstd
WYCLIF ST
NORTHAMPTON SQUARE
TURNPIKE HO
GOSWELL ROAD
WILMINGTON SQ
TYSOE ST
EXMOUTH MARKET
B502
SKINNER STREET
PERCIVAL STREET
Liby
CYRUS STREET
A201
Spa Fields Gardens
Tenn Ct
NORTHAMPTON RD
CORPORATION ROW
AGDON STREET
COMPTON ST
St Peters & St Pauls RC Prim Sch
PINE ST

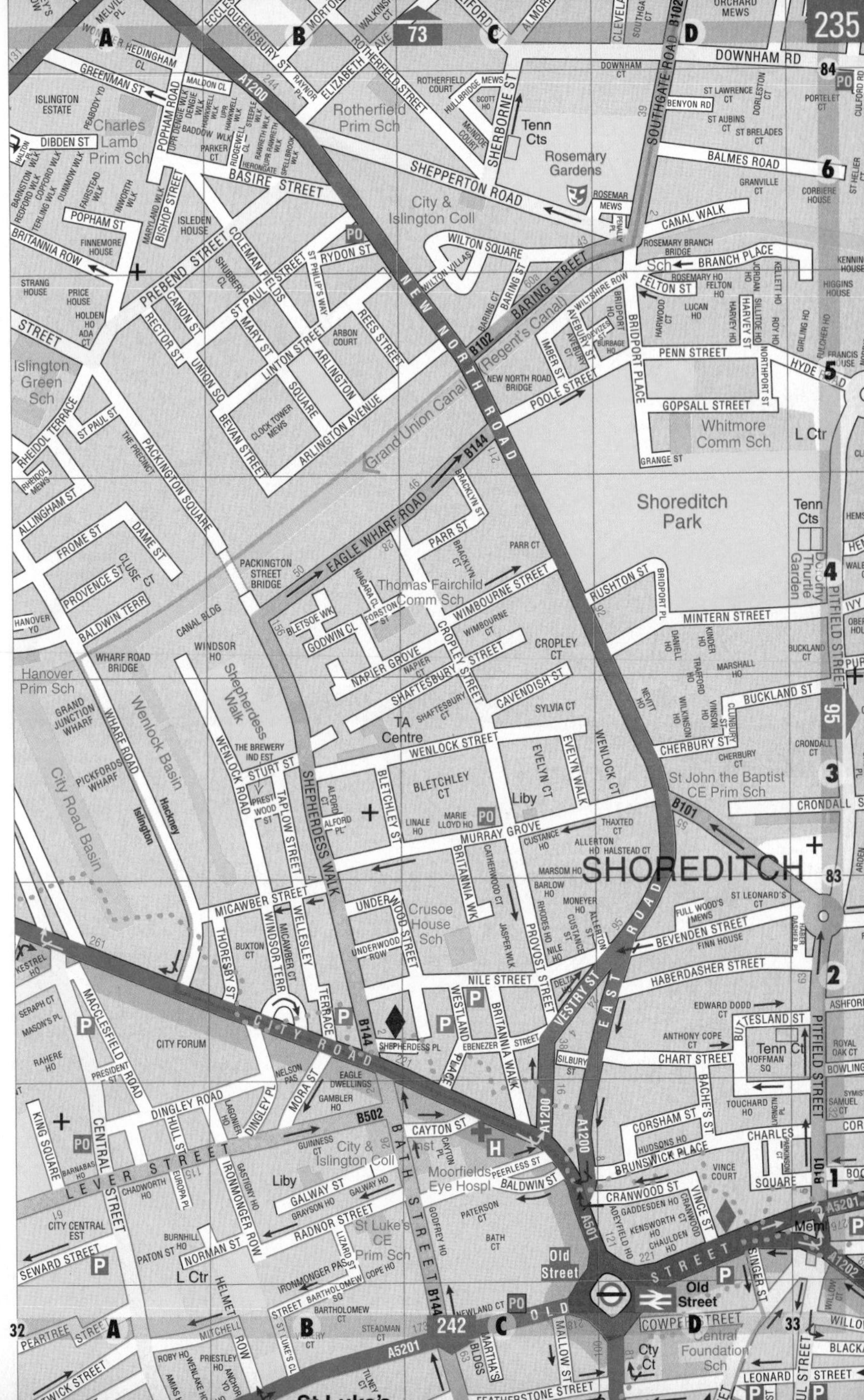

A
B
C
D
73
QUEENSBURY ST
ROTHERFIELD STREET
ELIZABETH AVE
SOUTHGATE ROAD
B102
DOWNHAM RD
DOWNHAM CT
ORCHARD MEWS
84
HEDINGHAM CL
GREENMAN ST
ISLINGTON ESTATE
PEABODY YD
POPHAM ROAD
MALDON CL
DIBDEN ST
Charles Lamb Prim Sch
BADDOW WLK
PARKER CT
HERONGATE
SPELLBROOK WLK
BASIRE STREET
BISHOP STREET
MARYLAND WLK
POPHAM ST
FINNEMORE HOUSE
BRITANNIA ROW
STRANG HOUSE
PRICE HOUSE
HOLDEN HO
ADA CT
STREET
Islington Green Sch
A1200
Rotherfield Prim Sch
ROTHERFIELD COURT
HULLBRIDGE MEWS
SCOTT HO
McINDOE COURT
SHERBORNE ST
Tenn Cts
Rosemary Gardens
SHEPPERTON ROAD
BENYON RD
ST LAWRENCE CT
DORLESTON CT
PORTELET CT
CULFORD RD
ST AUBINS CT
ST BRELADES CT
BALMES ROAD
6
GRANVILLE CT
CORBIERE HOUSE
ST HELIER CT
ROSEMAR MEWS
PENALLY PL
CANAL WALK
City & Islington Coll
ISLEDEN HOUSE
PREBEND STREET
COLEMAN FIELDS
SHUBBERY CL
CANON ST
RECTOR ST
UNION SQ
ST PAUL STREET
RYDON ST
ST PHILIP'S WAY
MARY ST
LINTON STREET
ARBON COURT
REES STREET
ARLINGTON SQUARE
ARLINGTON AVENUE
CLOCK TOWER MEWS
BEVAN STREET
WILTON SQUARE
WILTON VILLAS
BARING ST
BARING CT
BARING STREET
ROSEMARY BRANCH BRIDGE
BRANCH PLACE
Sch
ROSEMARY HO
FELTON HO
FELTON ST
WILTSHIRE ROW
BRIDPORT HO
HARWOOD CT
LUCAN HO
JORDAN HO
SILLITOE HO
HARVEY ST
HARVEY HO
KELLETT HO
ROY HO
GIRLING HO
FULCHER HO
KENNING HOUSE
HIGGINS HOUSE
FRANCIS HOUSE
NORRIS HO
AVEBURY ST
DEVIZES ST
BURBAGE HO
IMBER ST
BRIDPORT PLACE
PENN STREET
NORTHPORT ST
HYDE ROAD
5
Regent's Canal
NEW NORTH ROAD
NEW NORTH ROAD BRIDGE
POOLE STREET
GOPSALL STREET
Whitmore Comm Sch
L Ctr
GRANGE ST
Grand Union Canal
B144
RHEIDOL TERRACE
RHEIDOL MEWS
ST PAUL ST
THE PRECINCT
PACKINGTON SQUARE
ALLINGHAM ST
FROME ST
DAME ST
CLUSE CT
PROVENCE ST
BALDWIN TERR
HANOVER YD
EAGLE WHARF ROAD
BRACKLYN ST
BRACKLYN CT
PARR ST
PARR CT
Shoreditch Park
Tenn Cts
Dorothy Thurtle Garden
4
PITFIELD STREET
PACKINGTON STREET BRIDGE
NIAGARA CL
Thomas Fairchild Comm Sch
WIMBOURNE STREET
WIMBOURNE CT
RUSHTON ST
BRIDPORT PL
MINTERN STREET
DANIELL HO
KINDER HO
TRAFFORD HO
MARSHALL HO
BUCKLAND CT
CANAL BLDG
WINDSOR HO
BLETSOE WK
GODWIN CL
FORSTON ST
NAPIER GROVE
NAPIER CT
CROPLEY STREET
CROPLEY CT
SHAFTESBURY ST
SHAFTESBURY CT
CAVENDISH ST
SYLVIA CT
NEVITT HO
WILKINSON HO
VINSON HO
CLUNBURY ST
BUCKLAND ST
95
WHARF ROAD BRIDGE
Hanover Prim Sch
GRAND JUNCTION WHARF
WHARF ROAD
Wenlock Basin
Shepherdess Walk
WENLOCK ROAD
THE BREWERY IND EST
STURT ST
PREST WOOD ST
TAPLOW STREET
SHEPHERDESS WALK
TA Centre
WENLOCK STREET
EVELYN CT
EVELYN WALK
WENLOCK CT
CHERBURY ST
CHERBURY CT
CRONDALL CT
3
St John the Baptist CE Prim Sch
CRONDALL ST
PICKFORDS WHARF
City Road Basin
Islington
Hackney
ALFORD CT
ALFORD PL
BLETCHLEY ST
BLETCHLEY CT
LINALE HO
MARIE LLOYD HO
Liby
MURRAY GROVE
THAXTED CT
ALLERTON CT
HALSTEAD CT
B101
CUSTANCE HO
BRITANNIA WK
CATHERWOOD CT
MARSOM HO
SHOREDITCH
83
BARLOW HO
RHODES HO
MONEYER HO
ST LEONARD'S CT
FULL WOOD'S MEWS
MICAWBER STREET
UNDERWOOD STREET
Crusoe House Sch
JASPER WLK
PROVOST STREET
NILE HO
ALLERTON ST
EAST ROAD
BEVENDEN STREET
FINN HOUSE
HABERDASHER PL
THORESBY ST
BUXTON CT
WINDSOR TERR
MICAWBER CT
WELLESLEY TERRACE
UNDERWOOD ROW
NILE STREET
DELTA ST
VESTRY ST
HABERDASHER STREET
2
KESTREL HO
SERAPH CT
MASON'S PL
MACCLESFIELD ROAD
RAHERE HO
CITY ROAD
B144
SHEPHERDESS PL
WESTLAND PLACE
BRITANNIA WALK
EBENEZER STREET
SILBURY ST
EDWARD DODD CT
ASHFORD
BUTTESLAND ST
ANTHONY COPE CT
Tenn Ct
HOFFMAN SQ
ROYAL OAK CT
CHART STREET
BOWLING
CITY FORUM
PRESIDENT ST
NELSON PAS
MORA ST
EAGLE DWELLINGS
GAMBLER HO
A1200
BACHE'S ST
TOUCHARD HO
SYMISTER
SAMUEL CT
KING SQUARE
CENTRAL STREET
DINGLEY ROAD
HULL ST
LAGONIER HO
DINGLEY PL
B502
BATH STREET
CAYTON ST
CAYTON PL
Inst
H
CORSHAM ST
HUDSONS HO
CHARLES SQUARE
BRUNSWICK PLACE
VINCE COURT
B101
1
BARNABAS HO
LEVER STREET
CHADWORTH HO
EUROPA PL
IRONMONGER ROW
GASTIGNY HO
GUINNESS CT
City & Islington Coll
Liby
GALWAY ST
GALWAY HO
GRAYSON HO
Moorfields Eye Hospl
PEERLESS ST
BALDWIN ST
CRANWOOD ST
GADDESDEN HO
ADEYFIELD HO
KENSWORTH CT
CHAULDEN HO
CRANWOOD ST
VINCE ST
A5201
CITY CENTRAL EST
SEWARD STREET
BURNHILL HO
PATON ST
NORMAN ST
L Ctr
RADNOR STREET
St Luke's CE Prim Sch
LIZARD ST
GODFREY HO
PATERSON CT
BATH CT
A501
Old Street
STREET
Meml
A1202
SINGER ST
IRONMONGER PAS
COPE HO
BARTHOLOMEW SQ
BARTHOLOMEW CT
NEWLAND CT
Old Street
CITY
A5201
32
PEARTREE STREET
MITCHELL ST
HELMET ROW
ST LUKE'S CL
STEADMAN CT
242
MARTHA'S BLDGS
MALLOW ST
OLD STREET
COWPER STREET
Central Foundation Sch
Cty Ct
33
WILLOW
BLACKA
LEONARD STREET
ROBY HO
PRIESTLEY HO
ANCHOR YD
WENLAKE HO
AMIAS HO
TILNEY CT
FEATHERSTONE STREET
St Luke's

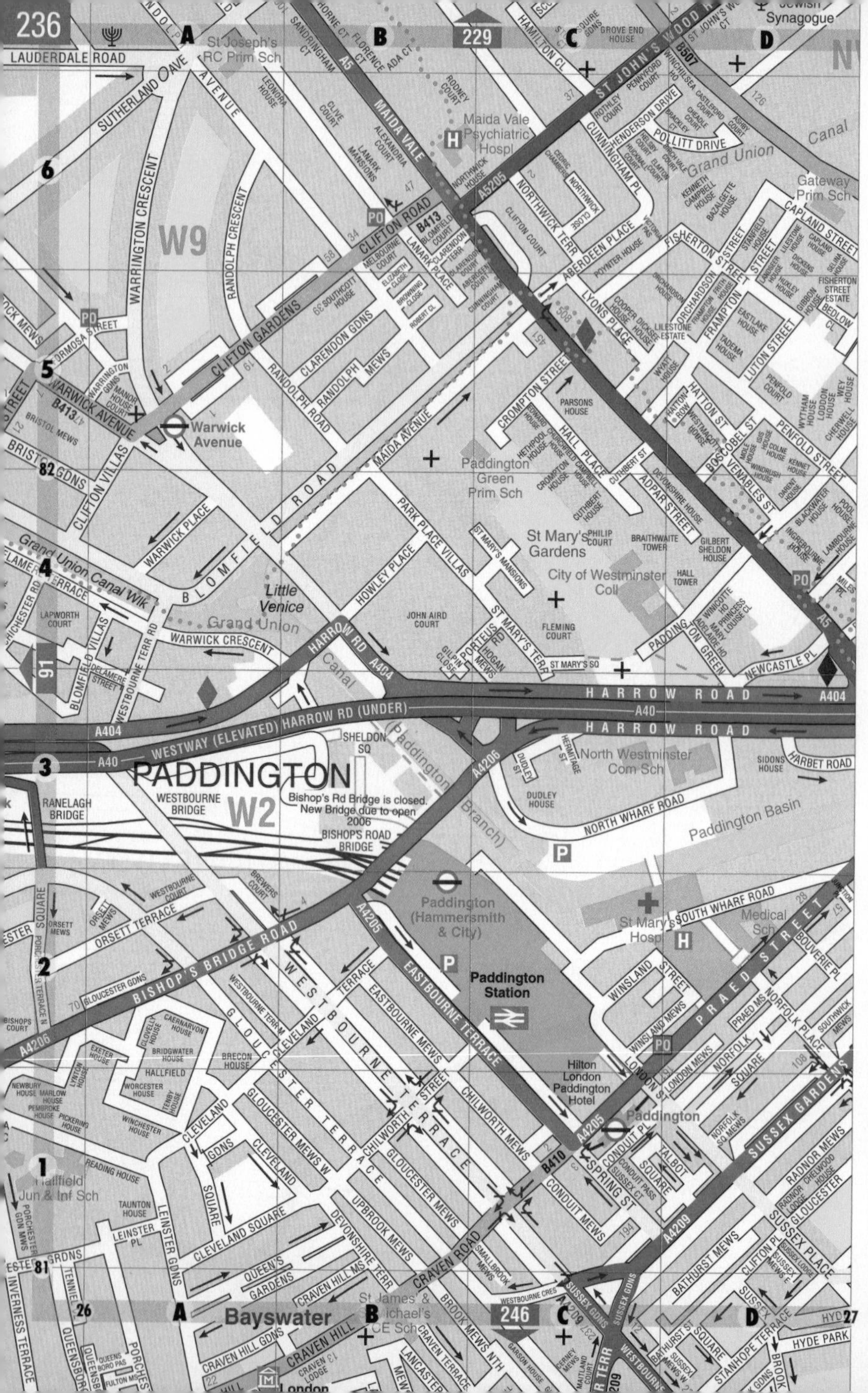
229
246
A
B
C
D
6
5
4
3
2
1
W9
W2
PADDINGTON
Bayswater
LAUDERDALE ROAD
SUTHERLAND AVENUE
WARRINGTON CRESCENT
RANDOLPH CRESCENT
CLIFTON ROAD
CLIFTON GARDENS
MAIDA VALE
ST JOHN'S WOOD ROAD
Maida Vale Psychiatric Hospl
St Joseph's RC Prim Sch
Jewish Synagogue
Grand Union Canal
Gateway Prim Sch
Warwick Avenue
WARWICK AVENUE
CLIFTON VILLAS
WARWICK PLACE
BLOMFIELD ROAD
MAIDA AVENUE
Little Venice
Grand Union Canal Wlk
WARWICK CRESCENT
HARROW RD
HARROW ROAD
WESTWAY (ELEVATED) HARROW RD (UNDER)
Paddington Green Prim Sch
St Mary's Gardens
City of Westminster Coll
North Westminster Com Sch
NORTH WHARF ROAD
Paddington Basin
Bishop's Rd Bridge is closed. New Bridge due to open 2006
BISHOPS ROAD BRIDGE
BISHOP'S BRIDGE ROAD
WESTBOURNE BRIDGE
RANELAGH BRIDGE
Paddington (Hammersmith & City)
Paddington Station
EASTBOURNE TERRACE
St Mary's Hosp
SOUTH WHARF ROAD
PRAED STREET
Hilton London Paddington Hotel
Paddington
SUSSEX GARDENS
WESTBOURNE TERRACE
GLOUCESTER TERRACE
CLEVELAND SQUARE
CRAVEN ROAD
CRAVEN HILL
Hallfield Jun & Inf Sch
St James' & St Michael's CE Sch
HYDE PARK
INVERNESS TERRACE
QUEENSBOROUGH TERRACE
PORCHESTER SQUARE
ORSETT TERRACE
LEINSTER GDNS
QUEEN'S GARDENS
DEVONSHIRE TERR
LONDON ST
NORFOLK SQUARE
SUSSEX PLACE
STANHOPE TERRACE
BATHURST MEWS
SPRING ST
CONDUIT MEWS

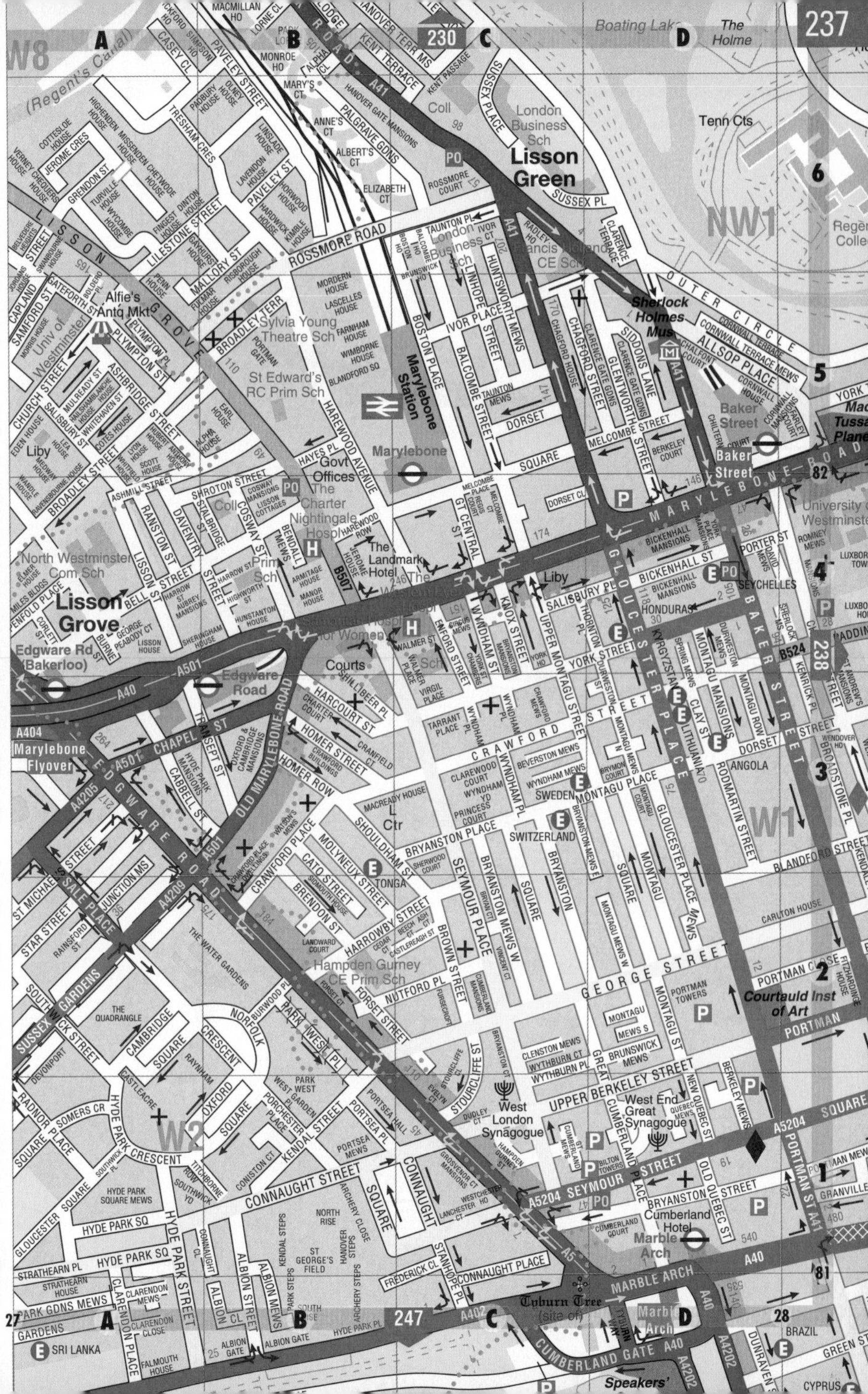
Lisson Green
Lisson Grove
Marylebone Station
Marylebone
Baker Street
Edgware Road
Edgware Rd (Bakerloo)
Marylebone Flyover
Marble Arch
Sherlock Holmes Mus
Alfie's Antq Mkt
Univ of Westminster
London Business Sch
Francis Holland CE Sch
Sylvia Young Theatre Sch
St Edward's RC Prim Sch
North Westminster Com Sch
The Landmark Hotel
The Western Eye Hosp
Samaritan Hosp for Women
Courts
Govt Offices
Hampden Gurney CE Prim Sch
West London Synagogue
West End Great Synagogue
Cumberland Hotel
Courtauld Inst of Art
Tyburn Tree (site of)
Speakers'
Tenn Cts
Regent's College
Madame Tussauds Planetarium
University of Westminster
Boating Lake
The Holme
(Regent's Canal)
NW1
W1
W2
W8
ROSSMORE ROAD
MARYLEBONE ROAD
EDGWARE ROAD
OLD MARYLEBONE ROAD
GLOUCESTER PLACE
BAKER STREET
CRAWFORD STREET
GEORGE STREET
SEYMOUR STREET
CONNAUGHT STREET
UPPER BERKELEY STREET
DORSET SQUARE
BRYANSTON SQUARE
MONTAGU SQUARE
PORTMAN SQUARE
OUTER CIRCLE
CUMBERLAND GATE
MARBLE ARCH
230
238
247

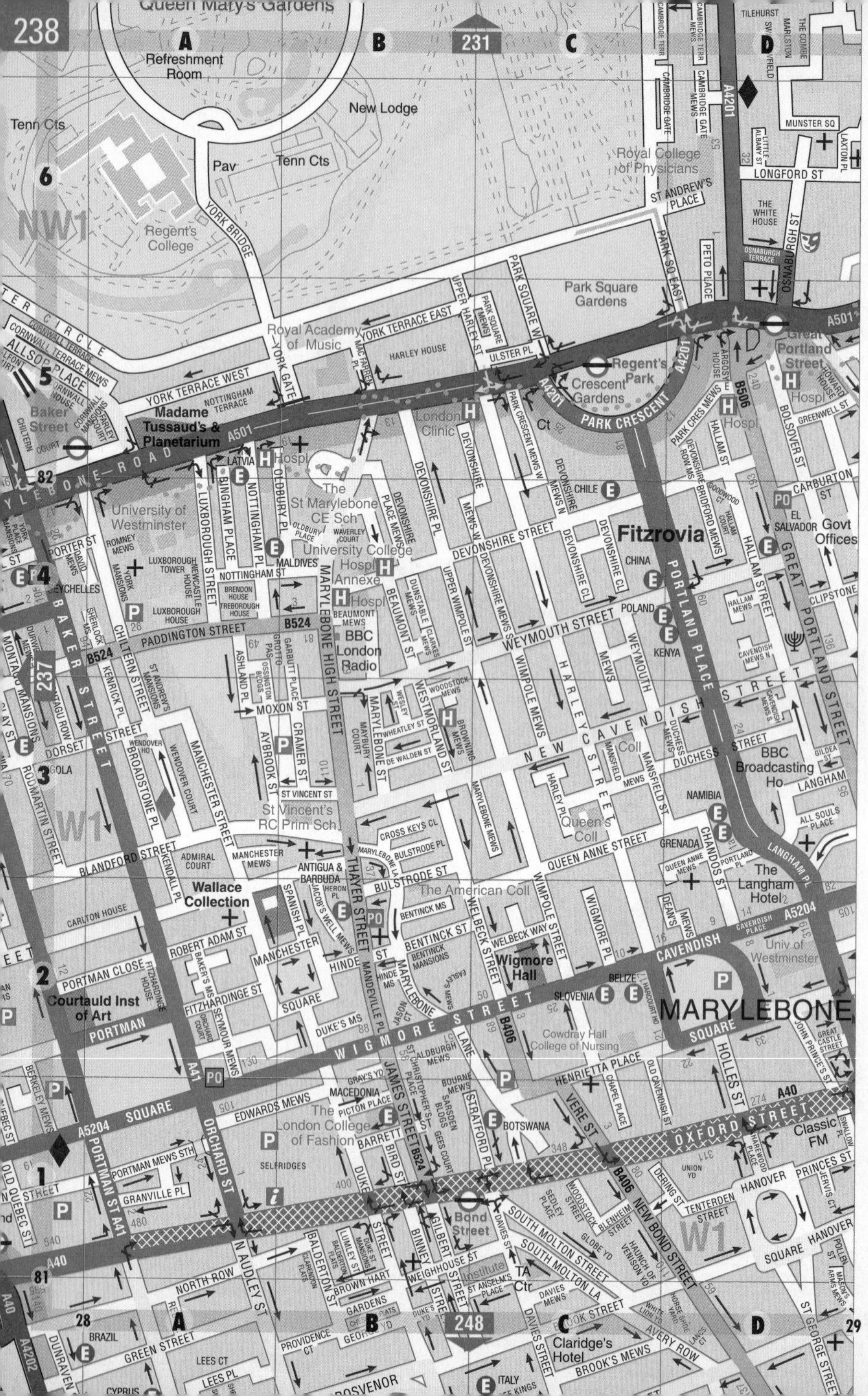

Queen Mary's Gardens
Refreshment Room
New Lodge
Tenn Cts
Pav
NW1
Regent's College
York Bridge
Royal College of Physicians
St Andrew's Place
Park Square Gardens
Royal Academy of Music
York Terrace East
York Terrace West
Nottingham Terrace
York Gate
Harley House
Ulster Pl
Park Square West
Park Square East
Peto Place
Osnaburgh St
Osnaburgh Terrace
The White House
Longford St
Munster Sq
Great Portland Street
Regent's Park
Crescent Gardens
Park Crescent
Madame Tussaud's & Planetarium
Baker Street
Marylebone Road
London Clinic
Hospl
University of Westminster
The St Marylebone CE Sch
University College Hospl Annexe
Devonshire Street
Devonshire Place
Upper Wimpole St
Weymouth Street
Fitzrovia
Portland Place
Carburton St
Govt Offices
El Salvador
China
Poland
Kenya
Chile
Latvia
Maldives
Seychelles
Luxborough Street
Nottingham Pl
Nottingham St
Bingham Place
Oldbury Pl
Paddington Street
B524
Marylebone High Street
Beaumont St
BBC London Radio
Moxon St
Cramer St
Aybrook St
Chiltern Street
Baker Street
Dorset Street
Manchester Street
Blandford Street
Wallace Collection
New Cavendish Street
Harley Street
Wimpole Mews
Wimpole Street
Queen Anne Street
Queen's Coll
Mansfield St
Duchess Street
BBC Broadcasting Ho
Langham
All Souls Place
The Langham Hotel
Namibia
Grenada
Chandos St
The American Coll
Bulstrode St
Thayer Street
Welbeck Street
Wigmore Hall
Wigmore Street
Cavendish Square
Univ of Westminster
MARYLEBONE
Belize
Slovenia
Cowdray Hall College of Nursing
Henrietta Place
Holles St
Courtauld Inst of Art
Portman Square
Portman Close
Orchard St
Edwards Mews
Macedonia
The London College of Fashion
Selfridges
James Street
Oxford Street
Stratford Pl
Botswana
Vere St
New Bond Street
Classic FM
Hanover Square
Princes St
Tenterden Street
South Molton Street
Bond Street
Davies St
North Row
N Audley St
Balderton St
Brown Hart Gardens
Weighhouse St
Gilbert Street
Brook Street
Claridge's Hotel
Brook's Mews
Avery Row
St George Street
Green Street
Brazil
Italy
Lees Pl
Dunraven
W1
A40
A41
A501
A5204
A4201
B406
A B C D
1 2 3 4 5 6
231
237
248
28
29
81
82

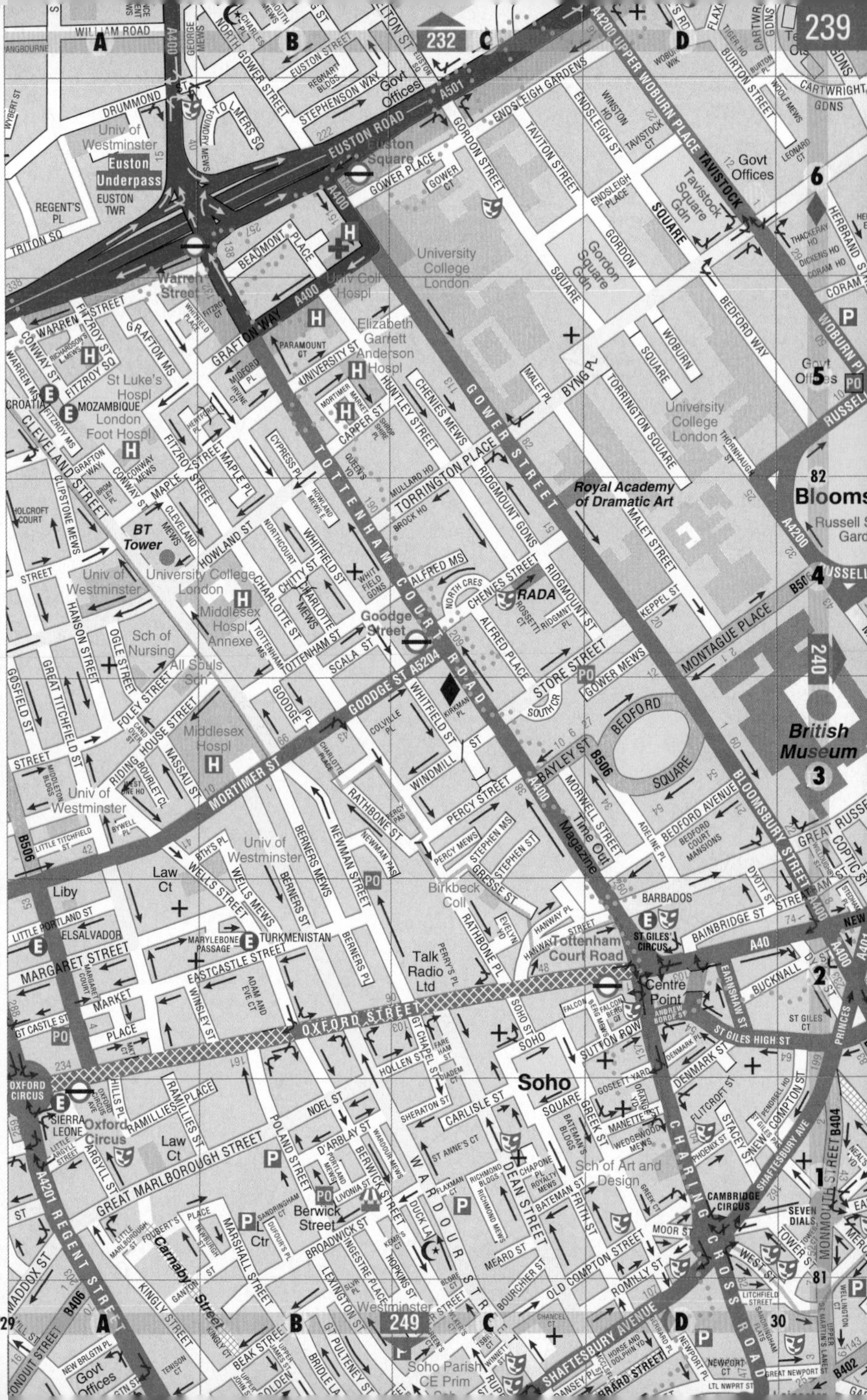

232
WILLIAM ROAD
A
B
C
D
A400
GOWER STREET
EUSTON STREET
STEPHENSON WAY
Govt Offices
DRUMMOND ST
EUSTON ROAD
A501
Euston Square
Univ of Westminster
Euston Underpass
EUSTON TWR
REGENT'S PL
TRITON SQ
GOWER PLACE
GOWER CT
BEAUMONT PLACE
Warren Street
GRAFTON WAY
Univ Coll Hospl
University College London
Elizabeth Garrett Anderson Hospl
ENDSLEIGH GARDENS
ENDSLEIGH ST
ENDSLEIGH PLACE
TAVITON STREET
GORDON STREET
WINSTON HO
TAVISTOCK CT
A4200 UPPER WOBURN PLACE
TAVISTOCK SQUARE
Tavistock Square Gdn
Govt Offices
BURTON STREET
CARTWRIGHT GDNS
LEONARD CT
THACKERAY HO
DICKENS HO
CORAM HO
HERBRAND STREET
CORAM
GORDON SQUARE
Gordon Square Gdn
BEDFORD WAY
WOBURN SQUARE
TORRINGTON SQUARE
WOBURN PL
Govt Offices
6
5
RUSSELL
MALET PL
BYNG PL
University College London
THORNHAUGH ST
Royal Academy of Dramatic Art
MALET STREET
82
Blooms
Russell S Garde
A4200
WARREN STREET
FITZROY STREET
FITZROY SQ
CONWAY ST
WARREN MS
GRAFTON MS
St Luke's Hospl
MOZAMBIQUE
CROATIA
London Foot Hospl
CLEVELAND STREET
CLIPSTONE MEWS
HOLCROFT COURT
MAPLE STREET
MAPLE PL
CONWAY MEWS
CLEVELAND MEWS
BT Tower
HOWLAND ST
UNIVERSITY ST
PARAMOUNT CT
MIDFORD PL
HUNTLEY STREET
CHENIES MEWS
CAPPER ST
MORTIMER MARKET
CYPRESS PL
QUEEN'S YD
MULLARD HO
TORRINGTON PLACE
BROCK HO
TOTTENHAM COURT ROAD
GOWER STREET
RIDGMOUNT GDNS
RIDGMOUNT ST
CHENIES STREET
NORTH CRES
ALFRED MS
ALFRED PLACE
RADA
KEPPEL ST
MONTAGUE PLACE
B506
4
240
British Museum
3
WHITFIELD ST
CHARLOTTE ST
CHARLOTTE MEWS
CHITTY ST
NORTHCOURT
WHITFIELD GDNS
Goodge Street
TOTTENHAM ST
SCALA ST
University College London
Univ of Westminster
STREET
HANSON STREET
OGLE STREET
Middlesex Hospl Annexe
Sch of Nursing
All Souls Sch
GOSFIELD ST
GREAT TITCHFIELD STREET
FOLEY STREET
RIDING HOUSE STREET
NASSAU ST
Middlesex Hospl
GOODGE PL
GOODGE ST A5204
KIRKMAN PL
STORE STREET
SOUTH CR
GOWER MEWS
BEDFORD SQUARE
BAYLEY ST
B506
MORWELL STREET
BEDFORD AVENUE
BEDFORD COURT MANSIONS
ADELINE PL
BLOOMSBURY STREET
GREAT RUSSELL
COPTIC ST
MORTIMER ST
BOURLET CL
Univ of Westminster
LITTLE TITCHFIELD ST
COLVILLE PL
CHARLOTTE PLACE
RATHBONE ST
PERCY PAS
WINDMILL ST
PERCY STREET
PERCY MEWS
STEPHEN MS
STEPHEN ST
GRESSE ST
Time Out Magazine
NEWMAN STREET
NEWMAN PAS
BERNERS MEWS
BERNERS ST
WELLS STREET
WELLS MEWS
Univ of Westminster
Law Ct
Liby
LITTLE PORTLAND ST
ELSALVADOR
MARYLEBONE PASSAGE
TURKMENISTAN
EASTCASTLE STREET
MARGARET STREET
MARKET PLACE
WINSLEY ST
ADAM AND EVE CT
Birkbeck Coll
RATHBONE PL
HANWAY PL
HANWAY STREET
Tottenham Court Road
Talk Radio Ltd
PERRY'S PL
BARBADOS
ST GILES' CIRCUS
BAINBRIDGE ST
DYOTT ST
STREATHAM
A40
NEW
EARNSHAW ST
BUCKNALL
2
Centre Point
ST GILES HIGH ST
ST GILES CT
PRINCES
OXFORD STREET
GT CASTLE ST
OXFORD CIRCUS
SIERRA LEONE
Oxford Circus
RAMILLIES PLACE
RAMILLIES ST
Law Ct
GREAT MARLBOROUGH STREET
ARGYLL ST
POLAND STREET
NOEL ST
D'ARBLAY ST
BERWICK STREET
WARDOUR MEWS
HOLLEN ST
GT CHAPEL ST
SHERATON ST
CARLISLE ST
ST ANNE'S CT
SOHO ST
SOHO SQUARE
Soho
SUTTON ROW
GOSLETT YARD
MANETTE ST
GREEK ST
BATEMAN'S BLDGS
DENMARK ST
FLITCROFT ST
STACEY ST
NEW COMPTON ST
SHAFTESBURY AVE
MONMOUTH STREET B404
1
Sch of Art and Design
DEAN STREET
CHAPONE PL
ROYALTY MEWS
RICHMOND BLDGS
RICHMOND MEWS
FLAXMAN CT
WARDOUR STREET
DUCK LA
BATEMAN ST
FRITH ST
CAMBRIDGE CIRCUS
SEVEN DIALS
CHARING CROSS ROAD
A4201 REGENT STREET
GREAT MARLBOROUGH STREET
LITTLE MARLBOROUGH ST
FOUBERT'S PLACE
MARSHALL STREET
Carnaby Street
Berwick Street
BROADWICK ST
LIVONIA ST
INGESTRE PLACE
HOPKINS ST
LEXINGTON STREET
MEARD ST
BOURCHIER ST
OLD COMPTON STREET
ROMILLY ST
MOOR ST
WEST ST
TOWER ST
LITCHFIELD STREET
MADDOX ST
B406
KINGLY STREET
GANTON ST
Westminster
249
A
B
C
D
29
30
81
SHAFTESBURY AVENUE
BEAK STREET
GT PULTENEY ST
BRIDLE LA
Soho Parish CE Prim
NEW BRLGTN PL
Govt Offices
TENISON CT
NEWPORT CT
GREAT NEWPORT ST
B402

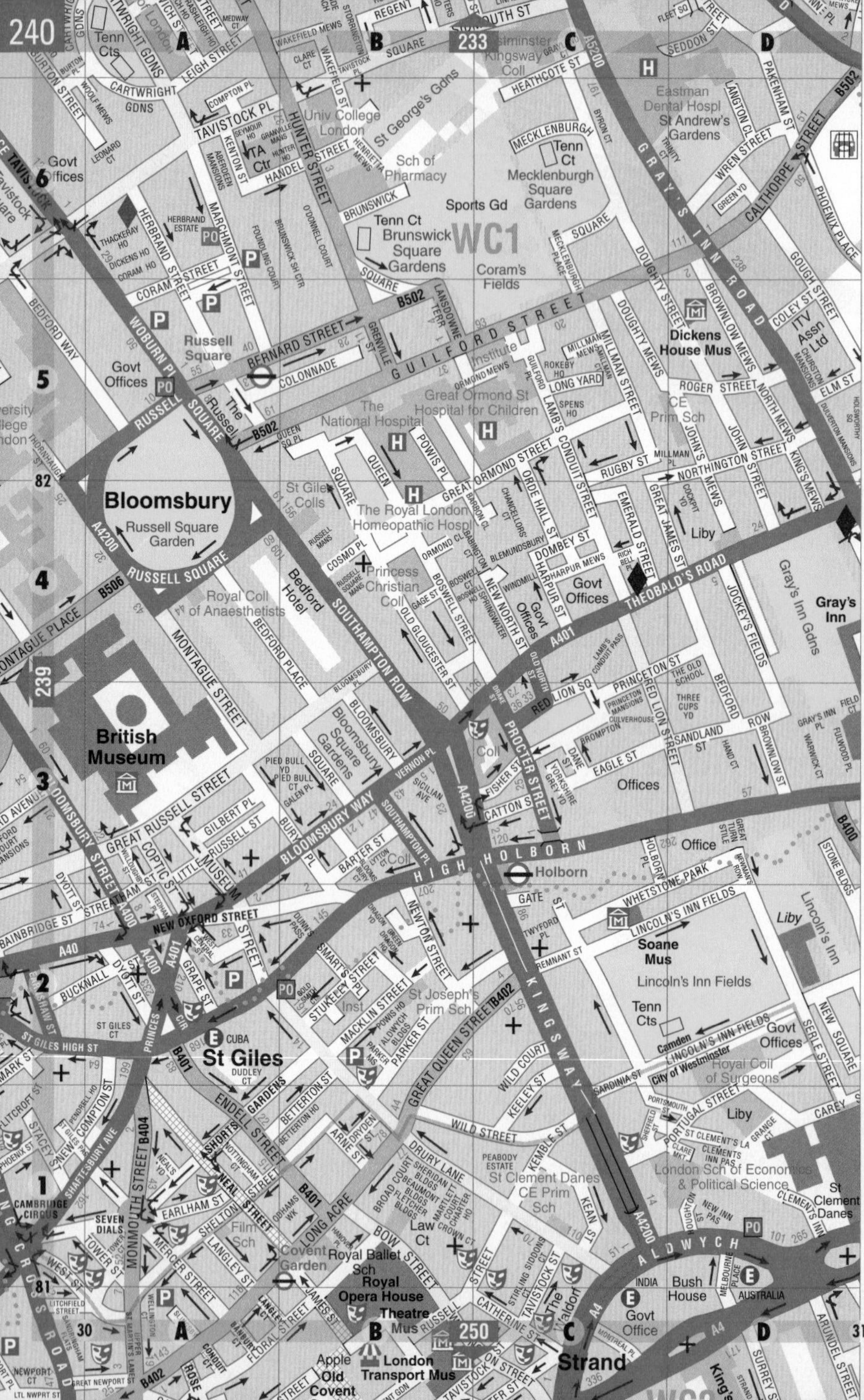
A
B
C
D
233
Tenn Cts
Cartwright Gdns
Leigh Street
Tavistock Pl
Compton Pl
Woolf Mews
Leonard Ct
Burton Pl
Wakefield Mews
Regent Square
Clare Ct
Hunter Street
Univ College London
St George's Gdns
Sch of Pharmacy
Handel Street
Brunswick
Westminster Kingsway Coll
Heathcote St
Mecklenburgh
Tenn Ct
Mecklenburgh Square Gardens
Sports Gd
Byron Ct
Gray's Inn Road
Eastman Dental Hospl
St Andrew's Gardens
Langton Cl
Wren Street
Pakenham St
Calthorpe Street
Phoenix Place
Green Yd
Seddon St
Fleet Sq
B502
6
Govt Offices
Tavistock Square
Thackeray Ho
Dickens Ho
Coram Ho
Herbrand Estate
Herbrand Street
Marchmont Street
Foundling Court
Brunswick Sh Ctr
O'Donnell Court
Kenton St
Aberdeen Mansions
TA Ctr
Tenn Ct
Brunswick Square Gardens
WC1
Coram's Fields
Mecklenburgh Square
Mecklenburgh Place
Doughty Street
Doughty Mews
Brownlow Mews
Gough Street
Coley St
ITV Assn Ltd
Coram Street
Woburn Pl
Bedford Way
Russell Square
Govt Offices
Bernard Street
Colonnade
Grenville St
Lansdowne Terr
Guilford Street
Institute
Ormond Mews
Guilford Pl
Rokeby Ho
Long Yard
Millman Mews
Millman Street
Spens Ho
Dickens House Mus
Roger Street
Elm St
CE Prim Sch
John's Mews
John Street
North Mews
King's Mews
5
University College London
The Russell
Queen Sq Pl
The National Hospital
Great Ormond St Hospital for Children
Powis Pl
Queen Square
Great Ormond Street
Orde Hall St
Lamb's Conduit Street
Rugby St
Millman Pl
Northington Street
Cockpit Yd
Great James St
Emerald Street
Liby
Thornhaugh St
82
Bloomsbury
Russell Square Garden
A4200
St Giles Colls
The Royal London Homeopathic Hospl
Russell Mans
Cosmo Pl
Barbon Cl
Chancellors Ct
Ormond Cl
Blemundsbury
Dombey St
Harpur Mews
Rich Bell Pl
Theobald's Road
Gray's Inn Gdns
Gray's Inn
4
Montague Place
B506
Russell Square
Royal Coll of Anaesthetists
Bedford Hotel
Southampton Row
Princess Christian Coll
Old Gloucester St
Gage St
Boswell Street
Boswell Ct
Windmill
New North St
Harpur St
Govt Offices
Jockey's Fields
239
Bedford Place
Montague Street
Bloomsbury Pl
A401
Old North St
Lamb's Conduit Pass
Red Lion Sq
Princeton St
Princeton Mansions
The Old School
Three Cups Yd
Red Lion Street
Bedford Row
Gray's Inn Pl
Warwick Ct
Field Ct
Fulwood Pl
British Museum
Bloomsbury Square Gardens
Bloomsbury Square
Pied Bull Yd
Pied Bull Ct
Galen Pl
Vernon Pl
Sicilian Ave
Coll
Procter Street
Fisher St
Catton St
Drake St
Culverhouse
Brompton
Dane St
Yorkshire Grey Yd
Eagle St
Sandland St
Hand Ct
Brownlow St
Offices
3
Bedford Avenue
Bloomsbury Street
Great Russell Street
Gilbert Pl
Russell St
Coptic St
Little Museum
Bury Pl
Bloomsbury Way
Southampton Pl
Barter St
Lytton Ct
High Holborn
Holborn
Great Turnstile
Office
Holborn Pl
B400
Stone Bldgs
Dyott St
Streatham
Bainbridge St
New Oxford Street
A40
A400
A401
West Central
Dunn's Pass
Dragon Yd
Newton Street
Gate St
Twyford Pl
Remnant St
Whetstone Park
Newman's Row
Lincoln's Inn Fields
Soane Mus
Lincoln's Inn Fields
Liby
Lincoln's Inn
2
Bucknall St
Dyott St
Grape St
Smart's Pl
Stukeley Street
St Joseph's Prim Sch
Inst
Macklin Street
Powis Ho
Aldwych Bldgs
Parker St
Parker Ms
Great Queen Street
B402
Kingsway
Tenn Cts
Camden
City of Westminster
Govt Offices
Royal Coll of Surgeons
New Square
Serle Street
St Giles High St
St Giles Ct
Shaftesbury Avenue
Princes Cir
Cuba
St Giles
Dudley Ct
B401
Endell Street
Betterton St
Betterton Ho
Wild Court
Keeley St
Sardinia St
Portsmouth St
Portugal Street
Sheffield St
Liby
Carey
Flitcroft St
Stacey St
New Compton St
Phoenix St
Shaftesbury Ave
Monmouth Street
B404
Neal's Yd
Shorts Gardens
Nottingham Ho
Neal Street
Arne St
Dryden St
Wild Street
Drury Lane
Peabody Estate
St Clement Danes CE Prim Sch
Kemble St
St Clement's La
Clare Mkt
Clements Inn Pas
Grange Ct
London Sch of Economics & Political Science
St Clement Danes
1
Cambridge Circus
Seven Dials
Earlham St
Tower St
Mercer Street
Shelton St
Langley St
Film Sch
Obhams Wk
Long Acre
Broad Court
Sheridan Bldgs
Beaumont Bldgs
Fletcher Bldgs
Martlett Ct
Courtier Ho
Charter Ho
Law Ct
Crown Ct
Kean St
Houghton St
New Inn Pas
Clements Inn
A4200
Aldwych
Charing Cross Road
West St
Litchfield Street
81
Covent Garden
Royal Ballet Sch
Royal Opera House
Theatre Mus
Bow Street
Hanover Pl
Catherine St
Stirling Siddons Ct
Tavistock St
The Waldorf
India
Bush House
Melbourne Place
Australia
Govt Office
Arundel Street
Wellington Ct
Upper St Martin's Lane
Banbury Ct
Floral Street
Langley Ct
James St
Russell
Conduit Ct
Rose
B402
250
Apple
Old Covent
London Transport Mus
Strand
Montreal Pl
A4
King's
Surrey St
Strand
Newport Pl
Newport Ct
Great Newport St
Ltl Nwprt St
30
31

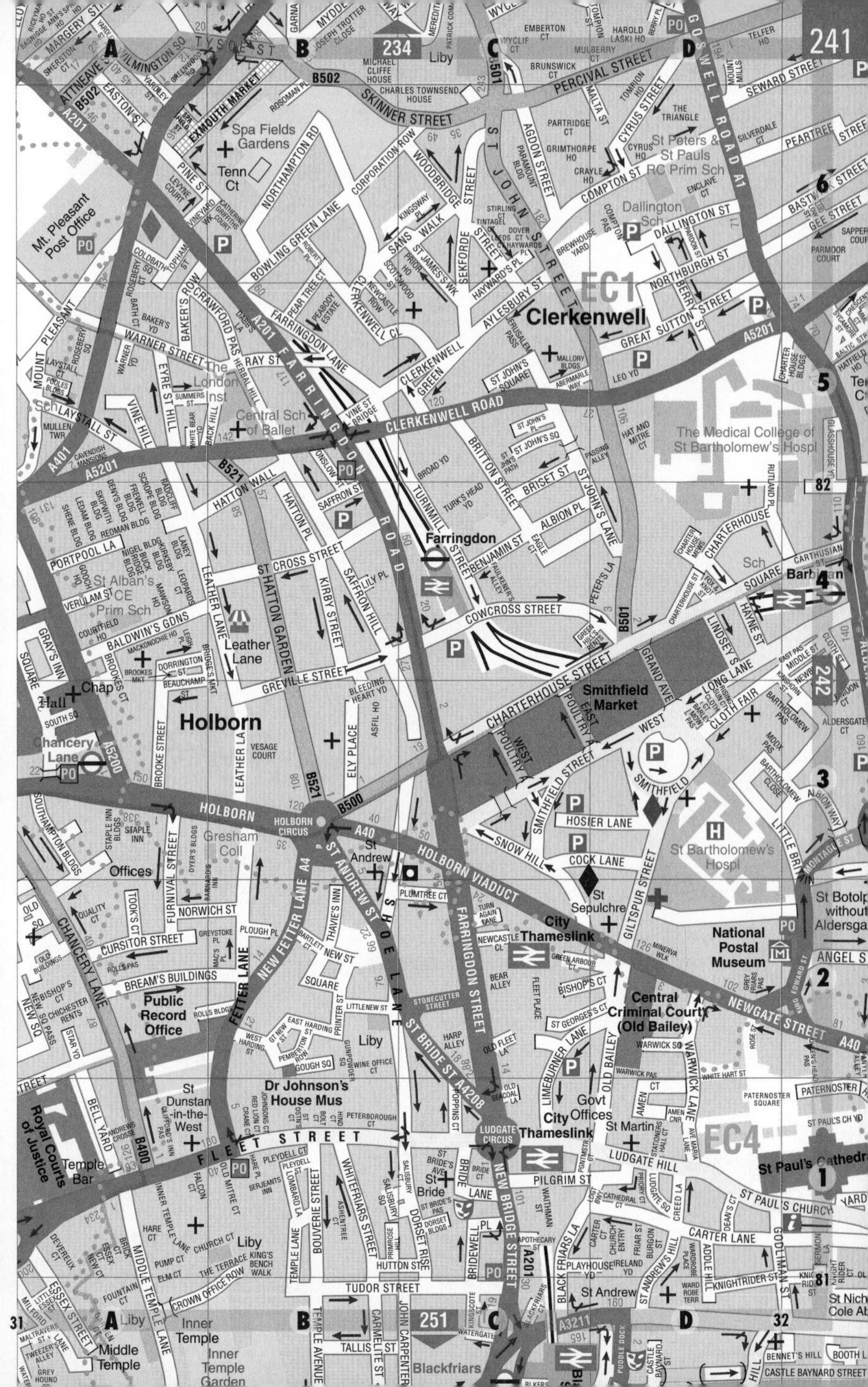
234
Liby
EMBERTON CT
HAROLD LASKI HO
MULBERRY CT
TELFER HO
MARGERY STREET
WILMINGTON SQ
TYSOE ST
JOSEPH TROTTER CLOSE
MICHAEL CLIFFE HOUSE
CHARLES TOWNSEND HOUSE
B502
SKINNER STREET
BRUNSWICK CT
PERCIVAL STREET
GOSWELL ROAD A1
SEWARD STREET
ATTNEAVE ST
EASTON ST
EXMOUTH MARKET
Spa Fields Gardens
ROSOMAN PL
NORTHAMPTON RD
CORPORATION ROW
WOODBRIDGE STREET
ST JOHN STREET
AGDON STREET
PARTRIDGE CT
GRIMTHORPE HO
CYRUS STREET
THE TRIANGLE
St Peters & St Pauls RC Prim Sch
PEARTREE STREET
A201
PINE ST
Tenn Ct
Mt. Pleasant Post Office
PO
P
COMPTON ST
BASTWICK STREET
GEE STREET
DALLINGTON ST
Dallington Sch
BOWLING GREEN LANE
SANS WALK
ST JAMES'S WK
SEKFORDE STREET
HAYWARD'S PL
BREWHOUSE YARD
NORTHBURGH ST
PARMOOR COURT
SAPPERTON COURT
EC1
Clerkenwell
AYLESBURY ST
BERRY ST
GREAT SUTTON ST
A5201
MOUNT PLEASANT
BAKER'S ROW
CRAWFORD PAS
WARNER STREET
RAY ST
FARRINGDON LANE
FARRINGDON ROAD
CLERKENWELL CL
CLERKENWELL GREEN
ST JOHN'S SQUARE
LEO YD
The London Inst
Central Sch of Ballet
LAYSTALL ST
VINE HILL
EYRE ST HILL
CLERKENWELL ROAD
The Medical College of St Bartholomew's Hospl
A401
A5201
B521
HATTON WALL
TURNMILL STREET
BRITTON STREET
BRISET ST
ST JOHN'S LANE
ALBION PL
HAT AND MITRE CT
RUTLAND PL
82
CHARTERHOUSE
Farringdon
PORTPOOL LA
St Alban's CE Prim Sch
LEATHER LANE
HATTON GARDEN
ST CROSS STREET
KIRBY STREET
SAFFRON HILL
BENJAMIN ST
COWCROSS STREET
PETER'S LA
B501
CHARTERHOUSE SQUARE
Barbican
4
5
6
GRAY'S INN SQUARE
BALDWIN'S GDNS
Leather Lane
GREVILLE STREET
CHARTERHOUSE STREET
Smithfield Market
GRAND AVE
LINDSEY ST
LONG LANE
CLOTH FAIR
242
ALDERSGATE
Chap
Hall
Holborn
Chancery Lane
A5200
BROOKE STREET
VESAGE COURT
ELY PLACE
WEST POULTRY AVE
EAST POULTRY AVE
WEST SMITHFIELD
SMITHFIELD STREET
HOSIER LANE
COCK LANE
St Bartholomew's Hospl
LITTLE BRITAIN
MONTAGUE ST
3
HOLBORN
HOLBORN CIRCUS
B521
B500
A40
A4
Gresham Coll
St Andrew
HOLBORN VIADUCT
SNOW HILL
GILTSPUR STREET
St Sepulchre
St Botolph without Aldersgate
Offices
FURNIVAL STREET
NORWICH ST
NEW FETTER LANE
ST ANDREW ST
SHOE LANE
FARRINGDON STREET
City Thameslink
National Postal Museum
ANGEL ST
2
CHANCERY LANE
CURSITOR STREET
FETTER LANE
NEW ST SQUARE
BREAM'S BUILDINGS
Public Record Office
STONECUTTER STREET
FLEET PLACE
BISHOP'S CT
Central Criminal Court (Old Bailey)
NEWGATE STREET
Liby
ST BRIDE ST A4208
OLD BAILEY
LIMEBURNER LANE
WARWICK SQ
WARWICK LANE
PATERNOSTER SQUARE
PATERNOSTER ROW
Dr Johnson's House Mus
St Dunstan-in-the-West
Royal Courts of Justice
BELL YARD
LUDGATE CIRCUS
Govt Offices
St Martin
EC4
FLEET STREET
B400
Temple Bar
NEW BRIDGE STREET
LUDGATE HILL
St Paul's Cathedral
1
PILGRIM ST
St Bride
ST PAUL'S CHURCH YARD
CARTER LANE
WHITEFRIARS STREET
BOUVERIE STREET
DORSET RISE
BRIDEWELL PL
A201
BLACK FRIARS LA
PLAYHOUSE YD
IRELAND YD
ST ANDREW'S HILL
GODLIMAN ST
KNIGHTRIDER ST
81
MIDDLE TEMPLE LANE
INNER TEMPLE LANE
CHURCH CT
Liby
KING'S BENCH WALK
CROWN OFFICE ROW
TEMPLE LANE
HUTTON ST
TUDOR STREET
St Andrew
A3211
ESSEX STREET
A
B
C
D
Liby
Inner Temple
Middle Temple
Inner Temple Garden
TEMPLE AVENUE
CARMELITE ST
TALLIS ST
JOHN CARPENTER ST
251
Blackfriars
31
32
BENNET'S HILL
CASTLE BAYNARD STREET
St Nicholas Cole Abbey

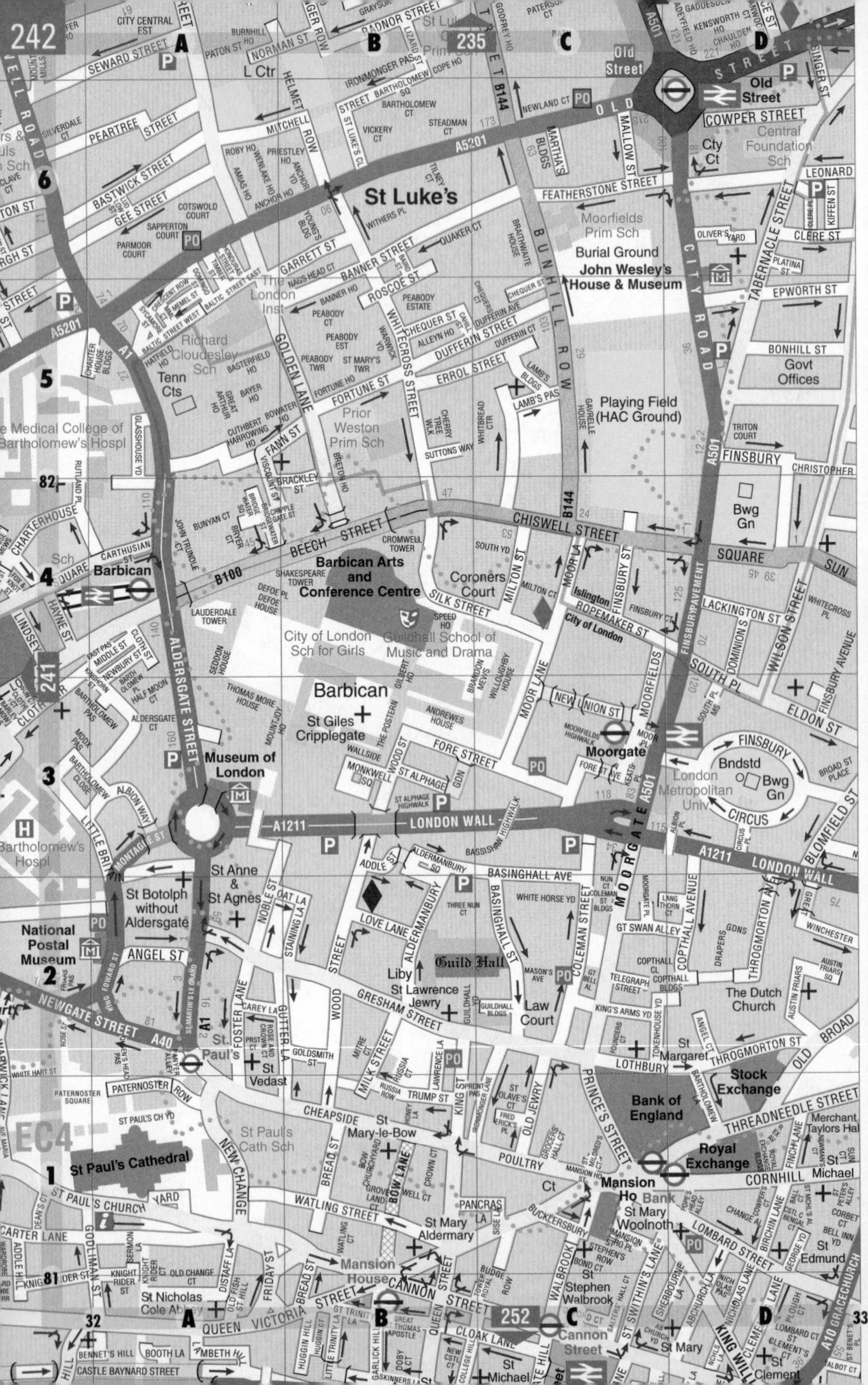

235
A
B
C
D
Old Street
St Luke's
Moorfields Prim Sch
Burial Ground
John Wesley's House & Museum
Central Foundation Sch
Govt Offices
Playing Field (HAC Ground)
Prior Weston Prim Sch
Richard Cloudesley Sch
Tenn Cts
Medical College of Bartholomew's Hospl
Barbican
Barbican Arts and Conference Centre
Coroners Court
City of London Sch for Girls
Guildhall School of Music and Drama
St Giles Cripplegate
Museum of London
Moorgate
London Metropolitan Univ
Bndstd
Bwg Gn
St Bartholomew's Hospl
St Anne & St Agnes
St Botolph without Aldersgate
National Postal Museum
Guild Hall
Liby
St Lawrence Jewry
Law Court
The Dutch Church
St Margaret
Stock Exchange
Bank of England
Royal Exchange
Mansion Ho
Bank
St Mary Woolnoth
St Paul's
St Vedast
St Pauls Cath Sch
St Paul's Cathedral
EC4
St Mary-le-Bow
St Mary Aldermary
Mansion House
St Stephen Walbrook
St Nicholas Cole Abbey
St Michael
St Edmund
St Clement
Cannon Street
252
241
1
2
3
4
5
6
32
33
81
82
OLD STREET
CITY ROAD
ALDERSGATE STREET
LONDON WALL
BEECH STREET
CHISWELL STREET
MOORGATE
CHEAPSIDE
QUEEN VICTORIA STREET
CANNON STREET
NEWGATE STREET
THREADNEEDLE STREET

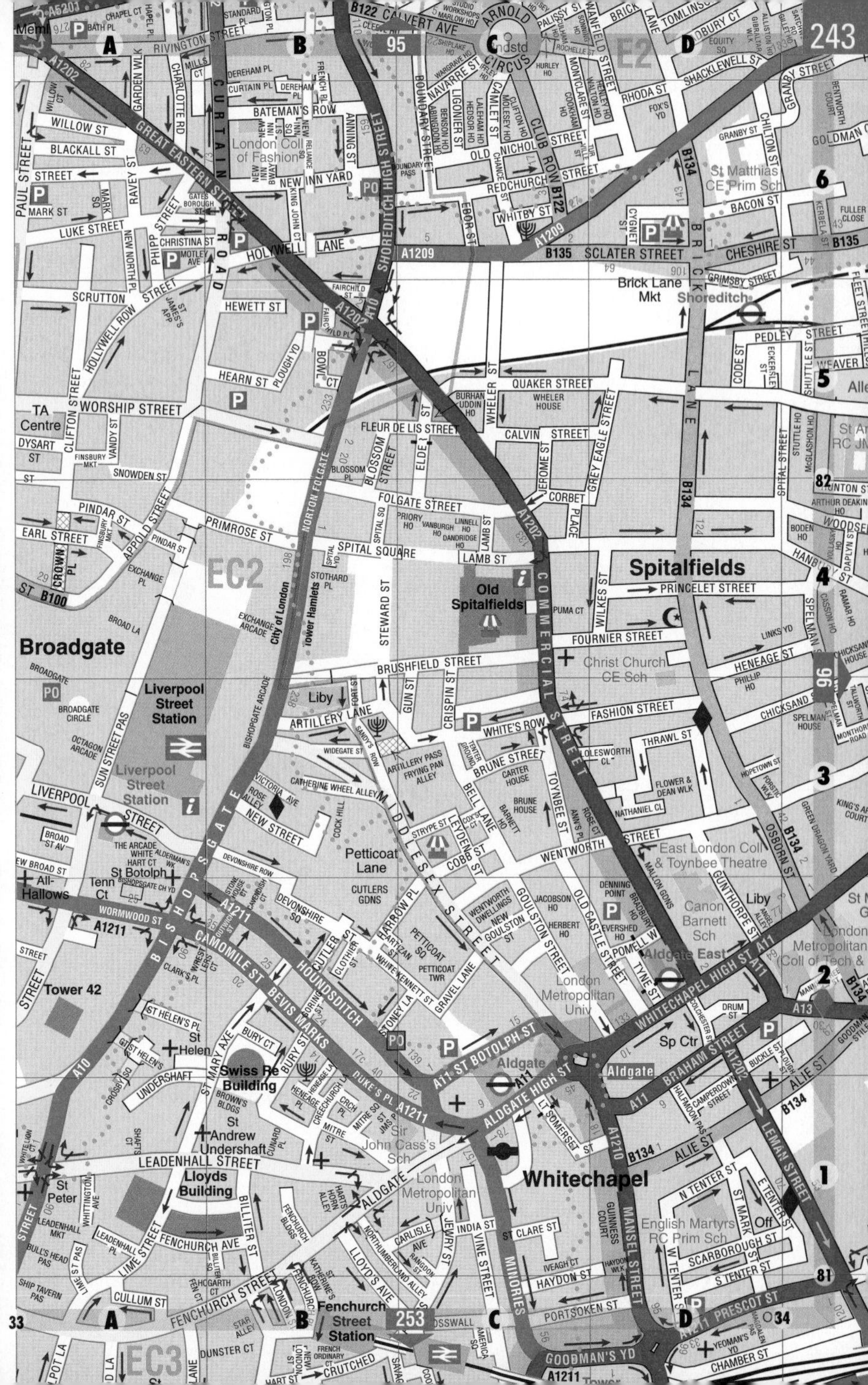
Broadgate
Liverpool Street Station
Spitalfields
Old Spitalfields
Petticoat Lane
Whitechapel
Aldgate
Aldgate East
Shoreditch
Brick Lane Mkt
Fenchurch Street Station
Tower 42
Swiss Re Building
Lloyds Building
London Coll of Fashion
Christ Church CE Sch
East London Coll & Toynbee Theatre
London Metropolitan Univ
English Martyrs RC Prim Sch
St Matthias CE Prim Sch
EC2
EC3
E2
COMMERCIAL STREET
BISHOPSGATE
SHOREDITCH HIGH STREET
GREAT EASTERN STREET
WHITECHAPEL HIGH ST
LEMAN STREET
BRICK LANE
MIDDLESEX STREET
HOUNDSDITCH
LEADENHALL STREET
FENCHURCH STREET
MINORIES
MANSEL STREET
ALDGATE HIGH ST
95
96
253
33
34

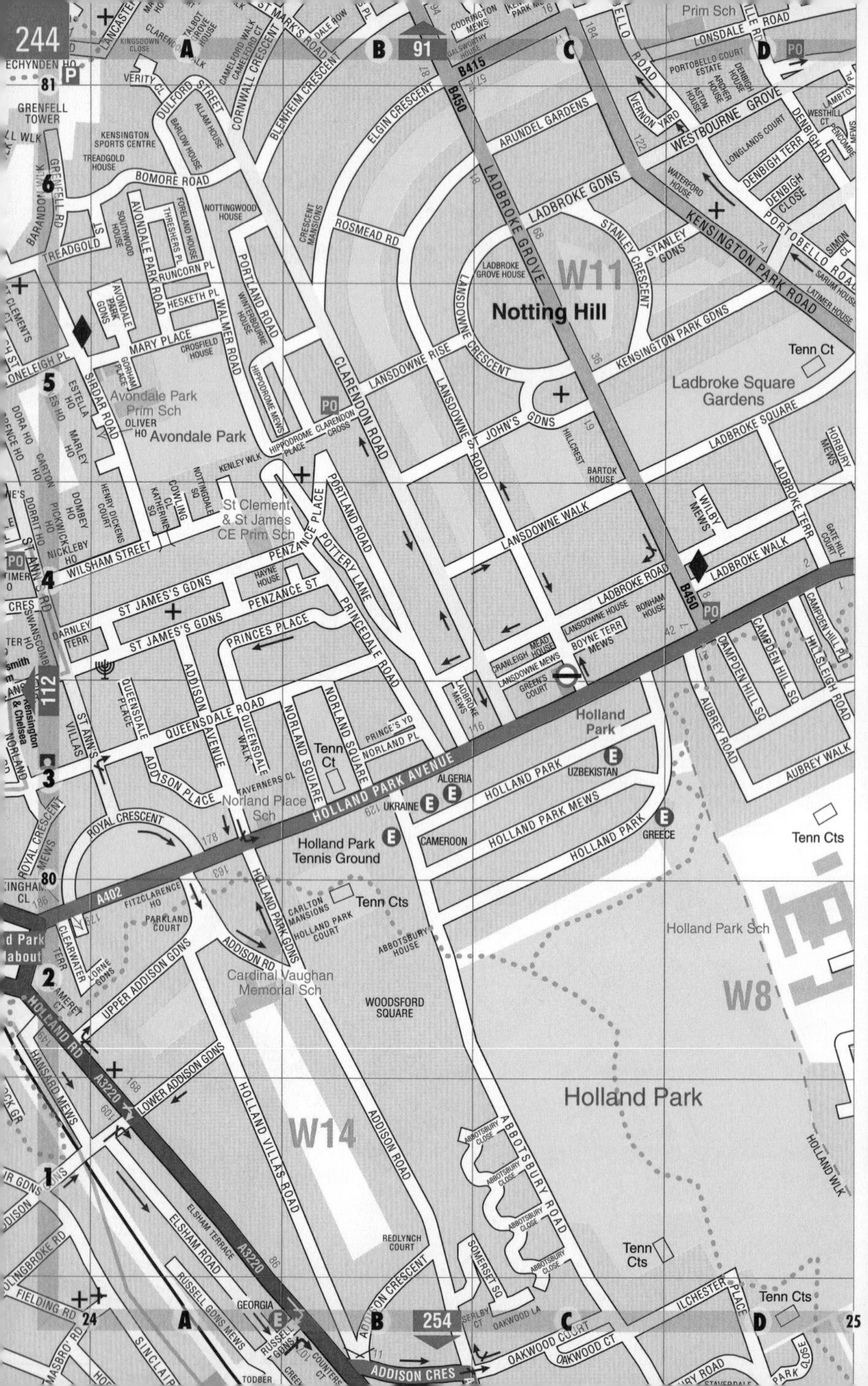
91
A
B
C
D
W11
Notting Hill
Ladbroke Square Gardens
Avondale Park
Avondale Park Prim Sch
St Clement & St James CE Prim Sch
Holland Park
Holland Park Tennis Ground
Norland Place Sch
Cardinal Vaughan Memorial Sch
Holland Park Sch
W8
W14
Holland Park
112
Kensington & Chelsea
Grenfell Tower
Kensington Sports Centre
Ladbroke Grove
Ladbroke Gdns
Lansdowne Crescent
Lansdowne Rise
Lansdowne Road
Lansdowne Walk
Ladbroke Road
Ladbroke Square
Ladbroke Terr
Ladbroke Walk
Kensington Park Road
Kensington Park Gdns
Stanley Crescent
Stanley Gdns
Westbourne Grove
Portobello Road
Ledbury Road
Denbigh Terr
Denbigh Rd
Denbigh Close
Elgin Crescent
Arundel Gardens
Blenheim Crescent
Cornwall Crescent
Clarendon Road
Clarendon Cross
Portland Road
Walmer Road
Mary Place
Bomore Road
Treadgold St
Sirdar Road
Wilsham Street
St James's Gdns
Penzance Place
Penzance St
Pottery Lane
Princedale Road
Princes Place
Queensdale Road
Addison Avenue
Addison Place
Norland Square
Royal Crescent
St Ann's Villas
Holland Park Avenue
Holland Park Mews
Holland Park Gdns
Aubrey Road
Aubrey Walk
Campden Hill Sq
Hillsleigh Road
Upper Addison Gdns
Lower Addison Gdns
Addison Rd
Addison Road
Holland Villas Road
Holland Rd
Elsham Road
Russell Gdns Mews
Abbotsbury Road
Abbotsbury Close
Ilchester Place
Oakwood Court
Oakwood La
Somerset Sq
Addison Crescent
Addison Cres
Holland Walk
Woodsford Square
A402
A3220
B450
B415
Tenn Ct
Tenn Cts
Algeria
Ukraine
Uzbekistan
Greece
Cameroon
Georgia
254
24
25

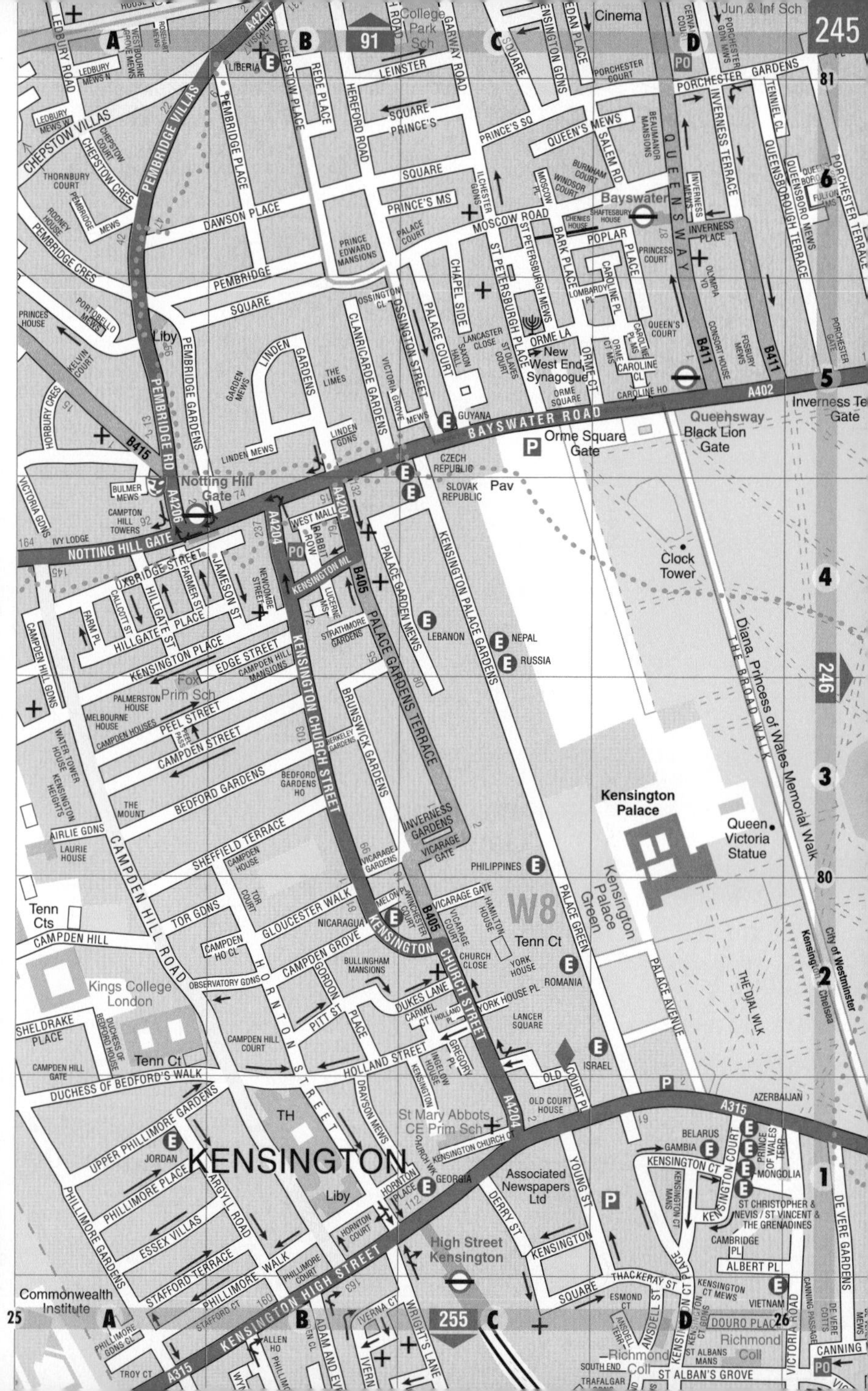

KENSINGTON
W8
Notting Hill Gate
Bayswater
Queensway
High Street Kensington
Kensington Palace
Kensington Palace Green
Kings College London
Commonwealth Institute
Associated Newspapers Ltd
St Mary Abbots CE Prim Sch
Fox Prim Sch
Clock Tower
Queen Victoria Statue
Diana, Princess of Wales Memorial Walk
THE BROAD WALK
THE DIAL WALK
BAYSWATER ROAD
NOTTING HILL GATE
KENSINGTON HIGH STREET
KENSINGTON CHURCH STREET
KENSINGTON PALACE GARDENS
PALACE GREEN
PALACE AVENUE
CAMPDEN HILL ROAD
PEMBRIDGE VILLAS
PEMBRIDGE RD
QUEENSWAY
New West End Synagogue
Orme Square Gate
Black Lion Gate
Inverness Terrace Gate
City of Westminster
Kensington Chelsea
91
246
255

A
B
C
D
236
TAUNTON HOUSE
LEINSTER PL
CLEVELAND SQUARE
DEVONSHIRE TERR
QUEEN'S GARDENS
CRAVEN HILL MS
CRAVEN RD
SMALLBROOK MEWS
WESTBOURNE CRES
SUSSEX GDNS
BATHURST MEWS
CLIFTON PL
SUSSEX PLACE
SUSSEX LODGE
SUSSEX MEWS E
SUSSEX SQUARE
HYDE PARK
TENNIEL CL
INVERNESS TERRACE
QUEENSBOROUGH TERRACE
QUEENSBORO MEWS
QUEENS BORO PAS
FULTON MS
PORCHESTER TERRACE
LEINSTER GARDENS
Bayswater
CRAVEN HILL GDNS
CRAVEN HILL
CRAVEN LODGE
St James's & St Michael's CE Prim Sch
London Toy & Model Museum
BROOK MEWS NTH
CRAVEN TERRACE
LANCASTER MEWS
GARSON HO
GILRAY HO
CERNEY MEWS
MAITLAND COURT
A4209
LANCASTER TERR
WESTBOURNE STREET
BATHURST ST
SUSSEX MEWS W
STANHOPE TERRACE
HYDE PARK GDNS
BROOK ST
Royal Lancaster Hotel
LEINSTER TERR
LEINSTER MEWS
GDNS
SPIRE HOUSE
LANCASTER GATE
COSTA RICA
CARROLL HOUSE
ELMS MEWS
LANCASTER COURT
BARRIE HOUSE
HYDE PARK TOWERS
B410
PORCHESTER GATE
OLYMPIA
CONSORT HOUSE
FOSBURY MEWS
B411
A402
BAYSWATER ROAD
A402
Victoria Gate
Westbourne Gate
Lancaster Gate
Marlborough Gate
NORTH FLOWER WALK
Lancaster Gate
St Agnes' Well
The Fountains
Bayard's Watering Place (site of)
W2
Inverness Terrace Gate
NORTH WALK
Black Lion Gate
BUCK HILL WALK
Speke's Monument
Peter Pan Statue
BUDGE'S WALK
LANCASTER WALK
The Long Water
Diana, Princess of Wales Memorial Walk
245
THE BROAD WALK
Statue
Temple Lodge
Serpentine Bridge
Round Pond
Kensington Gardens
Queen Victoria Statue
Diana, Princess of Wales Memorial Fountain
Serpentine Gallery
Bandstand
LANCASTER WALK
Kensington & Chelsea
City of Westminster
DIAL WALK
Tenn Cts
Bwg Gn
Pav
THE FLOWER WALK
Albert Memorial
Coalbrookdale Gate
AZERBAIJAN
A315
Palace Gate
Alexandra Gate
Queen's Gate
PRINCES GATE
LARUS
PRINCE OF WALES TERR
KENSINGTON COURT
MONGOLIA
HYDE PARK GATE
KENSINGTON ROAD
KENSINGTON GORE
Royal College of Art
ALBERT HALL MANSIONS
AFGHANISTAN
TUNISIA
ETHIOPIA
IRAN
UNITED ARAB EMIRATES
ST CHRISTOPHER & NEVIS / ST VINCENT & THE GRENADINES
B325
THORNEY COURT
BROADWALK HOUSE
FIJI
NETHERLANDS
ZAMBIA
RESTON PLACE
JAY MEWS
Royal Albert Hall
Royal Geographical Society
PRINCES GATE COURT
MONTROSE CT
CAMBRIDGE PL
ALBERT PL
DE VERE GARDENS
HYDE PARK GATE MEWS
CHANCELLOR HOUSE
ESTONIA
QUEEN'S GATE MEWS
ALBERT COURT
JAMAICA
KENSINGTON CT MEWS
VIETNAM
CANNING PASSAGE
DE VERE COTTS
PALACE GATE
Royal College of Science
BREMNER RD
PRINCE CONSORT ROAD
PRINCES GARDENS
Tenn Cts
DOURO PLACE
BULGARIA
256
Richmond Coll
VICTORIA ROAD
KENSINGTON GATE
CANNING PLACE
Royal College of Music
CALLENDAR RD
SW7
ALBANS MANS
QUEEN'S GATE MEWS
6
5
4
3
80
2
1
26
27

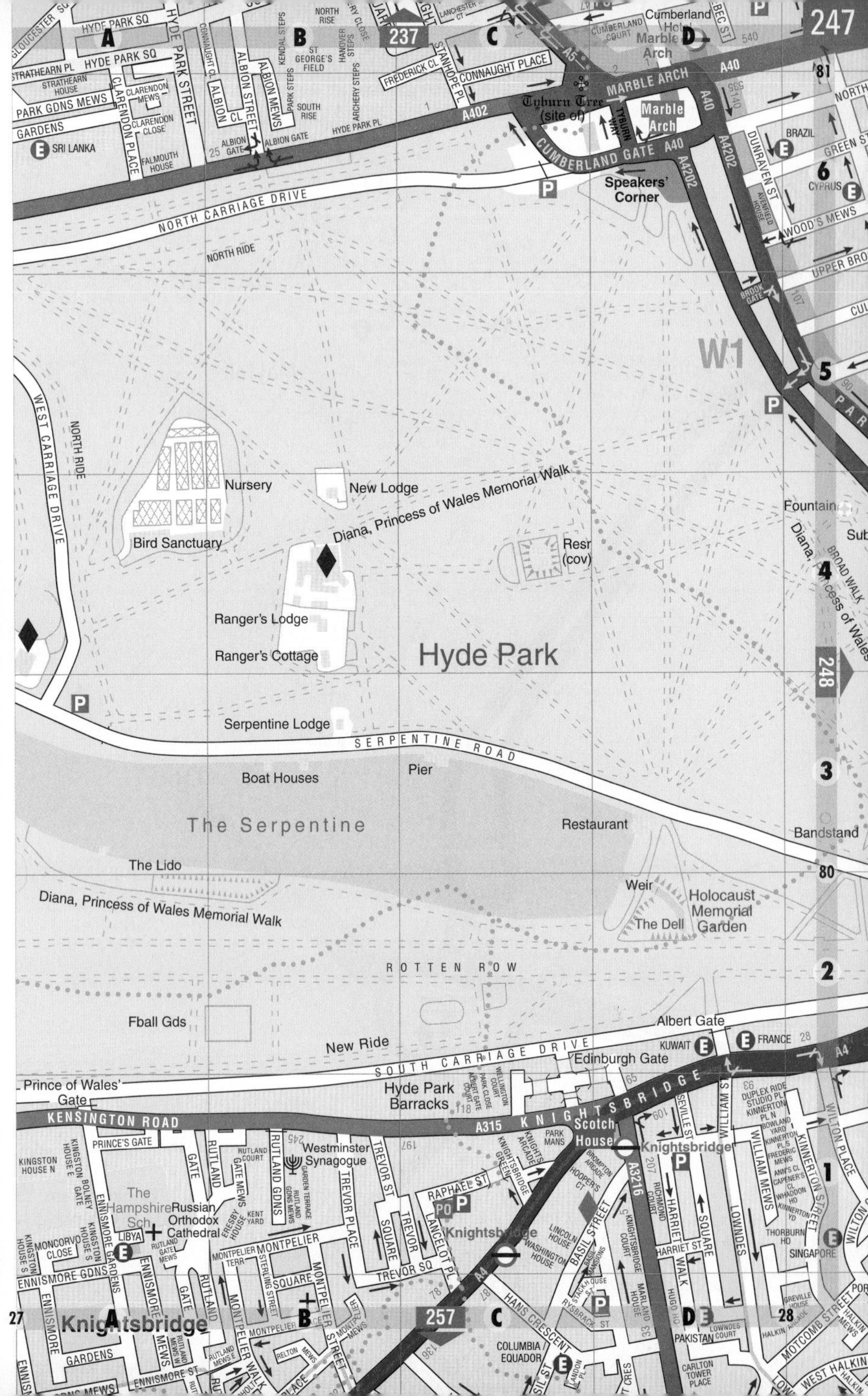

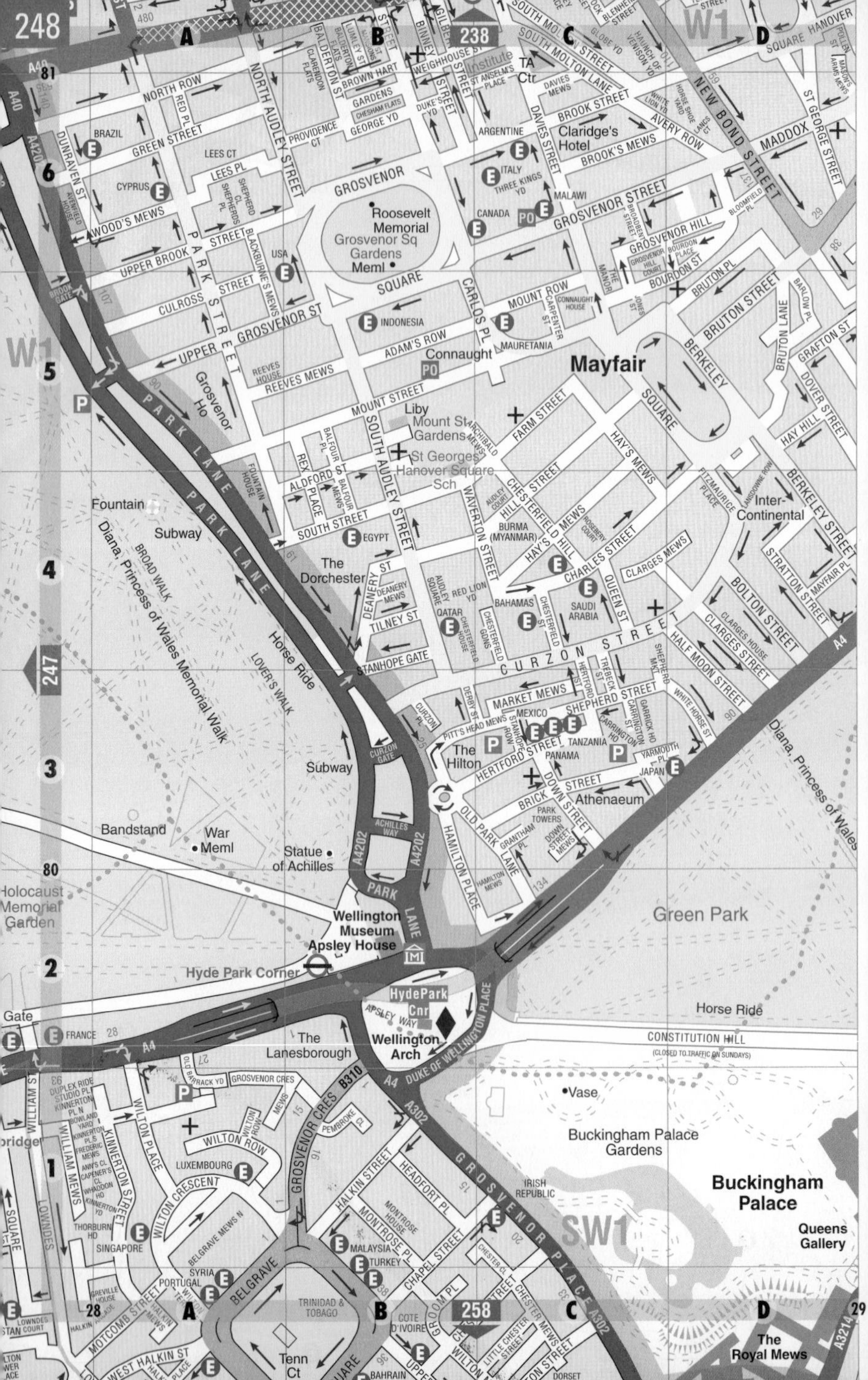

238
247
258
Mayfair
Claridge's Hotel
Roosevelt Memorial
Grosvenor Sq Gardens Meml
Connaught
Liby
Mount St Gardens
St Georges Hanover Square Sch
The Dorchester
Inter-Continental
The Hilton
Athenaeum
Fountain
Subway
Diana, Princess of Wales Memorial Walk
Horse Ride
Bandstand
War Meml
Statue of Achilles
Holocaust Memorial Garden
Wellington Museum
Apsley House
Hyde Park Corner
HydePark Cnr
Wellington Arch
The Lanesborough
Green Park
Constitution Hill
(CLOSED TO TRAFFIC ON SUNDAYS)
Vase
Buckingham Palace Gardens
Buckingham Palace
Queens Gallery
The Royal Mews
PARK LANE
GROSVENOR PLACE
CURZON STREET
BERKELEY SQUARE
NEW BOND STREET
GROSVENOR SQUARE
NORTH AUDLEY STREET
SOUTH AUDLEY STREET
PARK STREET
UPPER GROSVENOR ST
UPPER BROOK STREET
GREEN STREET
NORTH ROW
BROOK STREET
GROSVENOR STREET
MOUNT STREET
SOUTH STREET
HALF MOON STREET
PICCADILLY
HAMILTON PLACE
OLD PARK LANE
BELGRAVE SQUARE
WILTON CRESCENT
KINNERTON STREET
MOTCOMB STREET
W1
SW1

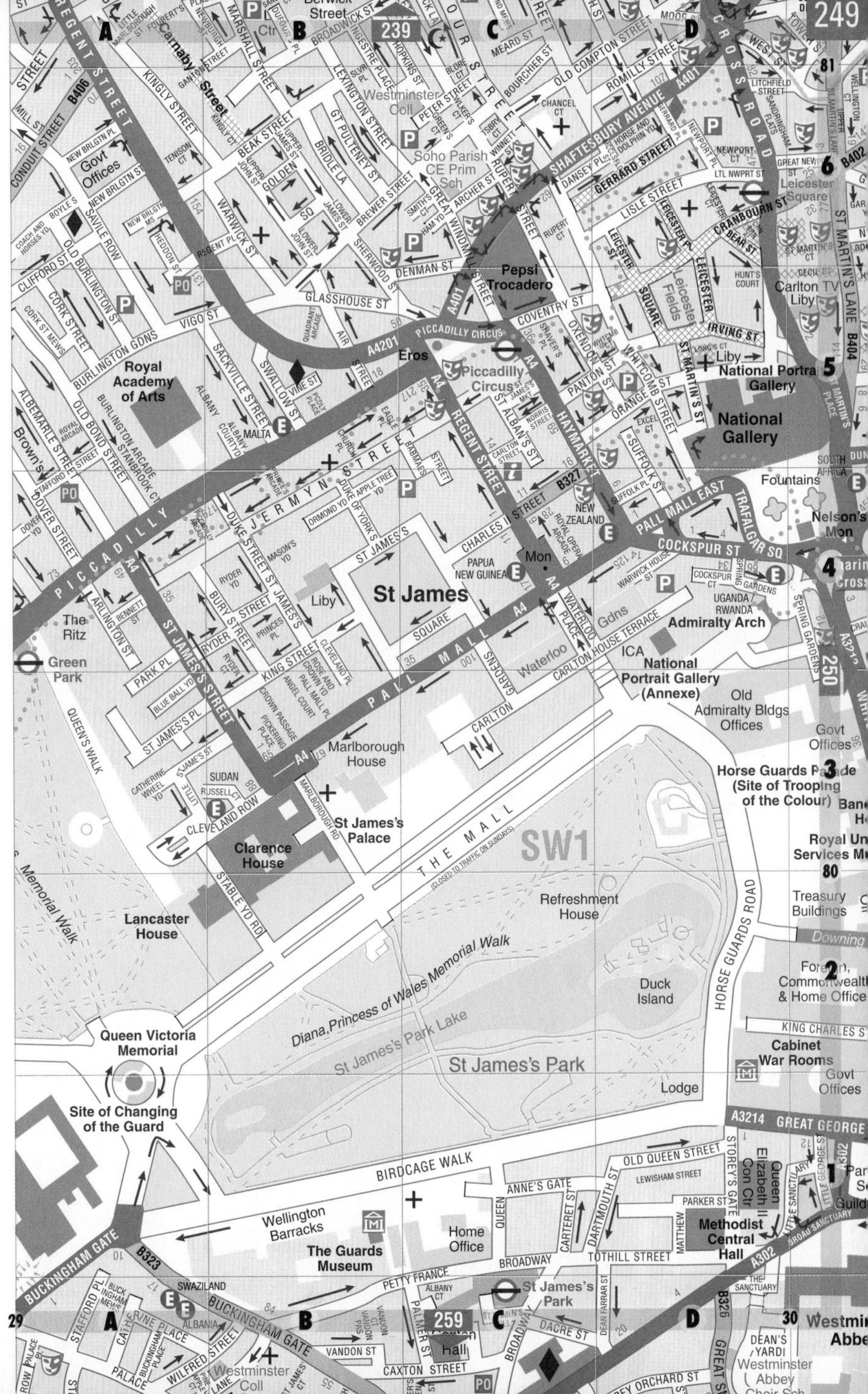

Regent Street
Carnaby Street
Kingly Street
Marshall Street
Broadwick St
Berwick Street
Westminster Coll
Soho Parish CE Prim Sch
Old Compton Street
Shaftesbury Avenue
Charing Cross Road
Gerrard Street
Lisle Street
Cranbourn St
Leicester Square
Leicester Fields
St Martin's Lane
Carlton TV Liby
Irving St
National Portrait Gallery
National Gallery
Pepsi Trocadero
Coventry St
Piccadilly Circus
Eros
Haymarket
Jermyn Street
Piccadilly
Royal Academy of Arts
Savile Row
Old Bond Street
Albemarle Street
Govt Offices
Conduit Street
Golden Sq
Brewer Street
Glasshouse St
Vigo St
Sackville Street
Burlington Gdns
Burlington Arcade
Duke Street St James's
St James
St James's Square
Liby
Charles II Street
Pall Mall
Pall Mall East
Cockspur St
Trafalgar Sq
Fountains
Nelson's Mon
South Africa
Admiralty Arch
Uganda / Rwanda
Papua New Guinea
New Zealand
Waterloo Place
Waterloo Gdns
Carlton House Terrace
ICA
National Portrait Gallery (Annexe)
Old Admiralty Bldgs Offices
Horse Guards Parade (Site of Trooping of the Colour)
Royal United Services M
Treasury Buildings
Downing
Foreign, Commonwealth & Home Office
King Charles St
Cabinet War Rooms
Govt Offices
Great George
The Ritz
Green Park
Queen's Walk
St James's Street
King Street
Marlborough House
St James's Palace
Clarence House
Lancaster House
Cleveland Row
Stable Yd Rd
Marlborough Rd
The Mall
(Closed to traffic on Sundays)
SW1
Memorial Walk
Diana, Princess of Wales Memorial Walk
St James's Park Lake
St James's Park
Refreshment House
Duck Island
Horse Guards Road
Lodge
Queen Victoria Memorial
Site of Changing of the Guard
Birdcage Walk
Wellington Barracks
The Guards Museum
Home Office
Old Queen Street
Lewisham Street
Queen Anne's Gate
Dartmouth St
Storey's Gate
Queen Elizabeth II Con Ctr
Methodist Central Hall
Parker St
Tothill Street
Broadway
Petty France
St James's Park
Buckingham Gate
Swaziland
Albania
Caxton Street
Caxton Hall
Vandon St
Dacre St
Great Smith St
Dean's Yard
Westminster Abbey Choir Sch
Westminster Abbey
Little Sanctuary
Broad Sanctuary
The Sanctuary
Westminster Coll
Wilfred Street
Catherine Place
Stafford Pl
Buckingham Place
Palace St
Old Orchard St
239
250
259
A
B
C
D
1
2
3
4
5
6
29
30
80
81

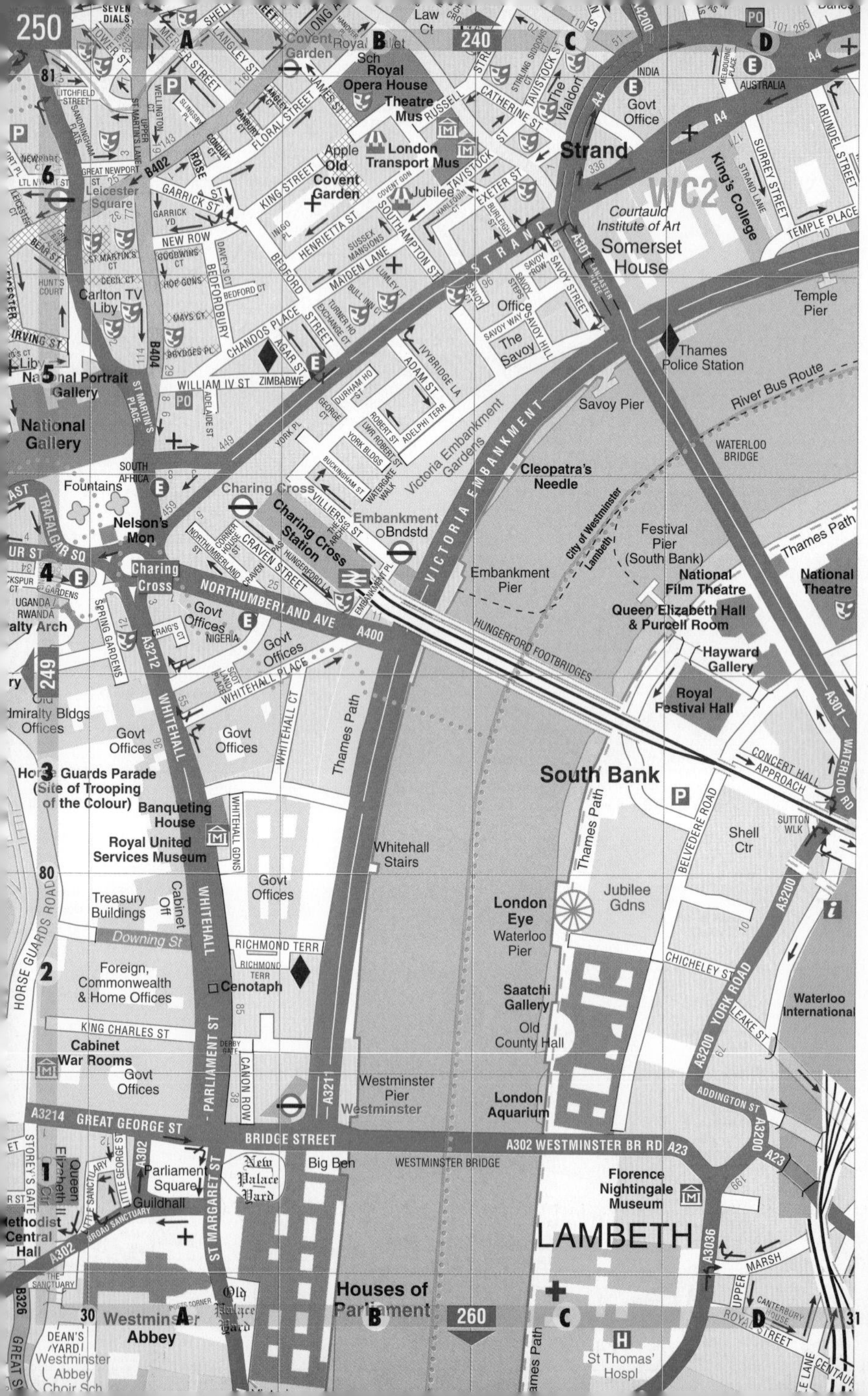

Covent Garden
Royal Ballet Sch
Royal Opera House
Theatre Mus
London Transport Mus
Apple
Old Covent Garden
Jubilee
Strand
WC2
King's College
Courtauld Institute of Art
Somerset House
Govt Office
INDIA
AUSTRALIA
Temple Pier
TEMPLE PLACE
ARUNDEL STREET
SURREY STREET
STRAND LANE
Leicester Square
Carlton TV
Liby
National Portrait Gallery
National Gallery
Charing Cross
Charing Cross Station
Embankment
Bndstd
Victoria Embankment Gardens
VICTORIA EMBANKMENT
Savoy Pier
Cleopatra's Needle
Thames Police Station
River Bus Route
WATERLOO BRIDGE
Festival Pier (South Bank)
National Film Theatre
National Theatre
Queen Elizabeth Hall & Purcell Room
Hayward Gallery
Royal Festival Hall
Embankment Pier
HUNGERFORD FOOTBRIDGES
City of Westminster
Lambeth
Thames Path
South Bank
CONCERT HALL APPROACH
BELVEDERE ROAD
Shell Ctr
SUTTON WLK
WATERLOO RD
Jubilee Gdns
London Eye
Waterloo Pier
Saatchi Gallery
Old County Hall
London Aquarium
CHICHELEY ST
YORK ROAD
LEAKE ST
Waterloo International
ADDINGTON ST
Florence Nightingale Museum
LAMBETH
MARSH
UPPER
CANTERBURY HOUSE
ROYAL STREET
St Thomas' Hospl
Fountains
Nelson's Mon
TRAFALGAR SQ
NORTHUMBERLAND AVE
CRAVEN STREET
Govt Offices
NIGERIA
WHITEHALL PLACE
WHITEHALL CT
WHITEHALL
Horse Guards Parade (Site of Trooping of the Colour)
Banqueting House
Royal United Services Museum
Treasury Buildings
Cabinet Off
Downing St
RICHMOND TERR
Foreign, Commonwealth & Home Offices
Cenotaph
KING CHARLES ST
Cabinet War Rooms
HORSE GUARDS ROAD
PARLIAMENT ST
CANON ROW
Westminster Pier
Westminster
GREAT GEORGE ST
BRIDGE STREET
A302 WESTMINSTER BR RD
WESTMINSTER BRIDGE
Big Ben
New Palace Yard
Parliament Square
Guildhall
BROAD SANCTUARY
Methodist Central Hall
ST MARGARET ST
Old Palace Yard
Houses of Parliament
Westminster Abbey
DEAN'S YARD
Westminster Abbey Choir Sch
240
249
260

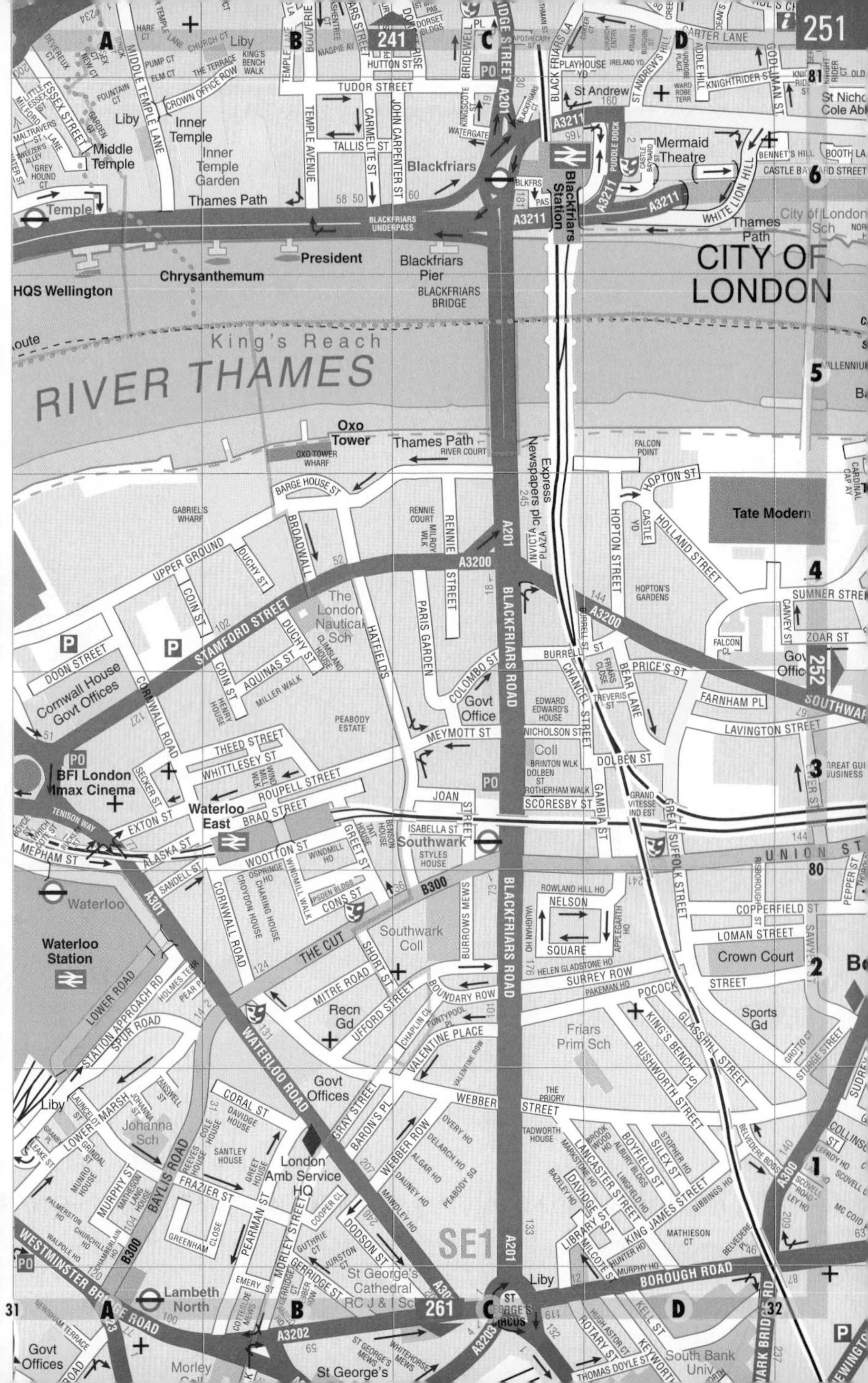
241
A
B
C
D
Temple
Inner Temple
Inner Temple Garden
Middle Temple
Thames Path
Blackfriars
Blackfriars Station
Mermaid Theatre
St Andrew
BLACKFRIARS UNDERPASS
President
Chrysanthemum
HQS Wellington
Blackfriars Pier
BLACKFRIARS BRIDGE
CITY OF LONDON
City of London Sch
King's Reach
RIVER THAMES
Oxo Tower
OXO TOWER WHARF
Thames Path
RIVER COURT
FALCON POINT
Express Newspapers plc
Tate Modern
GABRIEL'S WHARF
UPPER GROUND
STAMFORD STREET
The London Nautical Sch
BLACKFRIARS ROAD
HOPTON STREET
HOLLAND STREET
HOPTON'S GARDENS
SUMNER STREET
ZOAR ST
252
SOUTHWARK
Cornwall House Govt Offices
CORNWALL ROAD
PEABODY ESTATE
Govt Office
Coll
BFI London Imax Cinema
Waterloo East
Southwark
UNION ST
Waterloo
Waterloo Station
THE CUT
Southwark Coll
NELSON SQUARE
Crown Court
Sports Gd
Recn Gd
Friars Prim Sch
WATERLOO ROAD
LOWER MARSH
BAYLIS ROAD
Johanna Sch
Govt Offices
London Amb Service HQ
WEBBER STREET
SE1
St George's Cathedral RC J & I Sc
BOROUGH ROAD
Lambeth North
WESTMINSTER BRIDGE ROAD
ST GEORGE'S CIRCUS
261
Govt Offices
South Bank Univ
Liby
PO
1
2
3
4
5
6
31
32
80
81

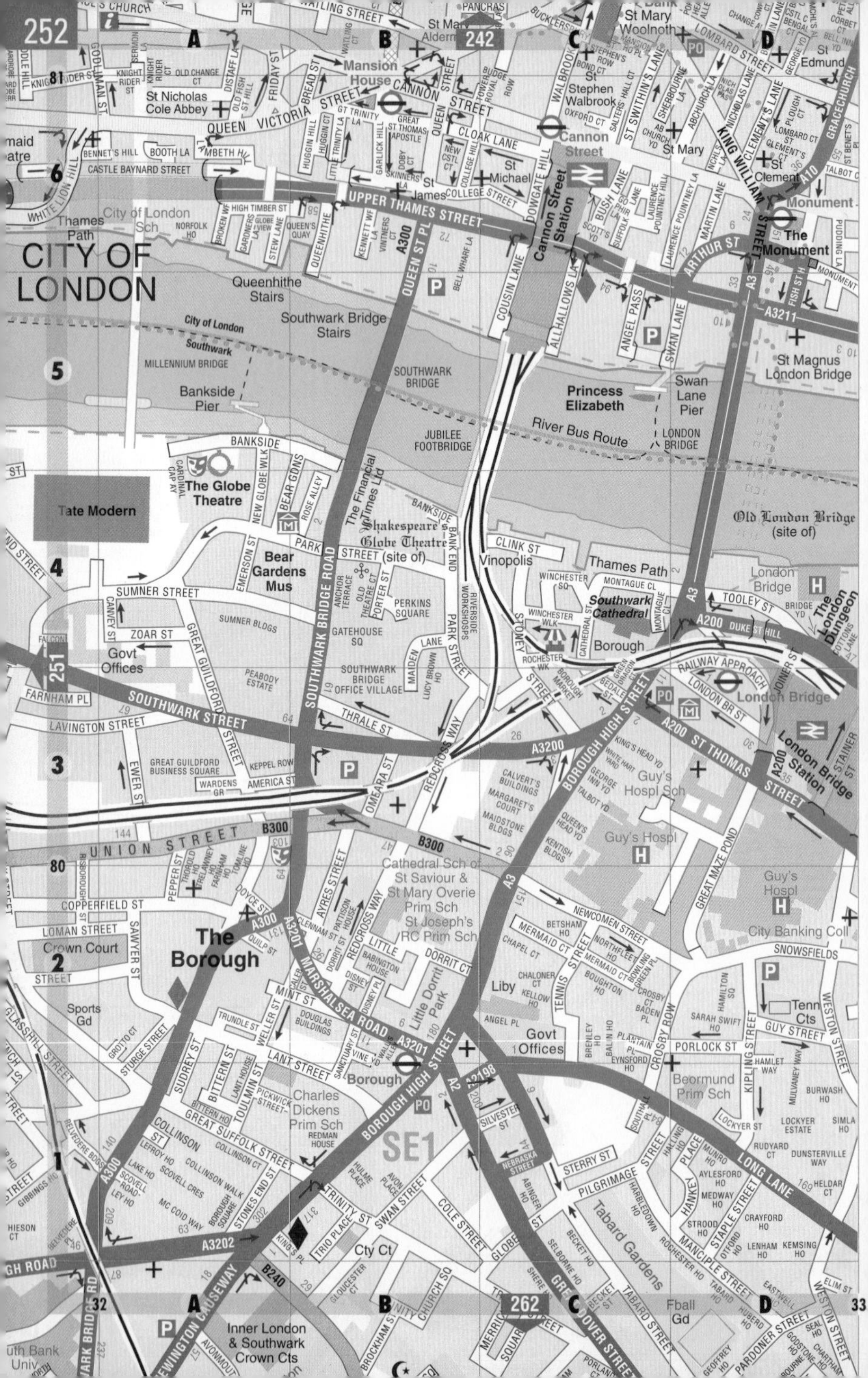

A
B
C
D
242
81
6
5
4
3
80
2
1
32
33
262
251
St Mary Woolnoth
St Mary Aldermary
Mansion House
CANNON STREET
QUEEN VICTORIA STREET
St Nicholas Cole Abbey
St Stephen Walbrook
Cannon Street
Cannon Street Station
St Mary
St Edmund
St Clement
Monument
The Monument
St Michael
St James
UPPER THAMES STREET
QUEEN ST PL
A300
CITY OF LONDON
Thames Path
City of London Sch
Queenhithe Stairs
Southwark Bridge Stairs
City of London
Southwark
MILLENNIUM BRIDGE
Bankside Pier
SOUTHWARK BRIDGE
JUBILEE FOOTBRIDGE
Princess Elizabeth
River Bus Route
Swan Lane Pier
LONDON BRIDGE
St Magnus London Bridge
A3211
A3
A10
LOMBARD STREET
GRACECHURCH
KING WILLIAM STREET
ARTHUR ST
BANKSIDE
The Globe Theatre
Tate Modern
Shakespeare's Globe Theatre (site of)
Old London Bridge (site of)
The Financial Times Ltd
Vinopolis
CLINK ST
Thames Path
London Bridge
Southwark Cathedral
Borough
The London Dungeon
TOOLEY ST
A200
DUKE ST HILL
RAILWAY APPROACH
London Bridge
London Bridge Station
Bear Gardens Mus
PARK STREET
SUMNER STREET
SOUTHWARK BRIDGE ROAD
SOUTHWARK STREET
Govt Offices
A3200
BOROUGH HIGH STREET
ST THOMAS STREET
Guy's Hospl Sch
Guy's Hospl
City Banking Coll
UNION STREET
B300
Cathedral Sch of St Saviour & St Mary Overie Prim Sch
St Joseph's RC Prim Sch
NEWCOMEN STREET
SNOWSFIELDS
The Borough
Crown Court
Sports Gd
MARSHALSEA ROAD
A3201
Little Dorrit Park
Liby
Govt Offices
Tenn Cts
GUY STREET
Beormund Prim Sch
Borough
Charles Dickens Prim Sch
SE1
GREAT SUFFOLK STREET
LONG LANE
A3202
A2
A2198
Tabard Gardens
City Ct
Inner London & Southwark Crown Cts
Fball Gd
GREAT DOVER STREET
NEWINGTON CAUSEWAY
B240

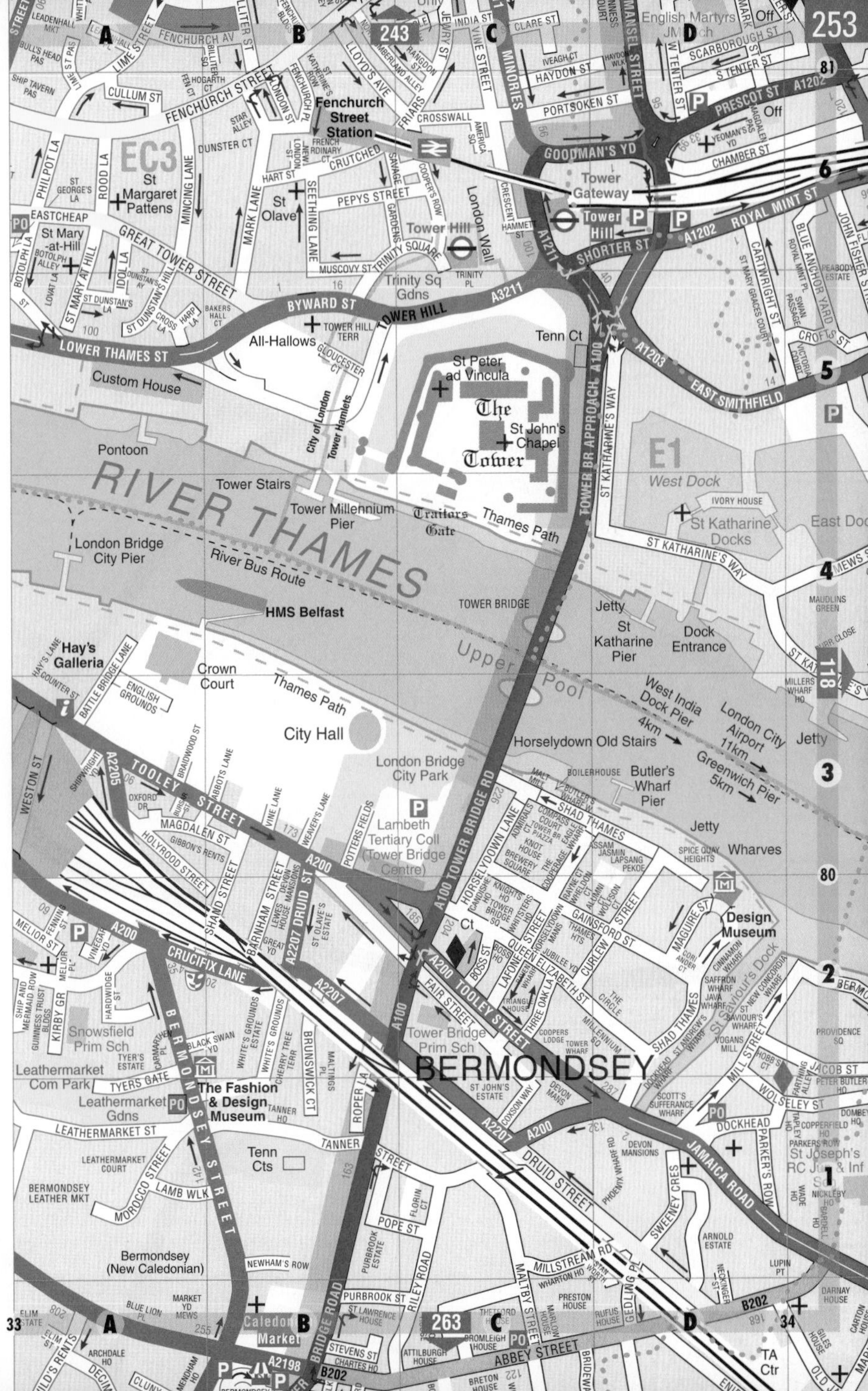

A
B
C
D
243
EC3
Fenchurch Street Station
St Margaret Pattens
St Olave
St Mary -at-Hill
Tower Hill
Tower Gateway
London Wall
Trinity Sq Gdns
BYWARD ST
TOWER HILL
LOWER THAMES ST
All-Hallows
Custom House
Tenn Ct
St Peter ad Vincula
The Tower
St John's Chapel
Traitors Gate
Pontoon
RIVER THAMES
Tower Stairs
Tower Millennium Pier
Thames Path
London Bridge City Pier
River Bus Route
HMS Belfast
TOWER BRIDGE
E1
West Dock
St Katharine Docks
East Dock
Jetty
St Katharine Pier
Dock Entrance
Upper Pool
Hay's Galleria
Crown Court
City Hall
West India Dock Pier 4km
London City Airport 11km
Greenwich Pier 5km
Horselydown Old Stairs
London Bridge City Park
Butler's Wharf Pier
Lambeth Tertiary Coll (Tower Bridge Centre)
Design Museum
Wharves
TOOLEY STREET
BERMONDSEY
Tower Bridge Prim Sch
Snowsfield Prim Sch
Leathermarket Com Park
Leathermarket Gdns
The Fashion & Design Museum
Tenn Cts
BERMONDSEY STREET
Bermondsey (New Caledonian)
Caledonian Market
St Joseph's RC Jun & Inf Sch
JAMAICA ROAD
DRUID STREET
ABBEY STREET
TA Ctr
263
118
6
5
4
3
2
1
33
34

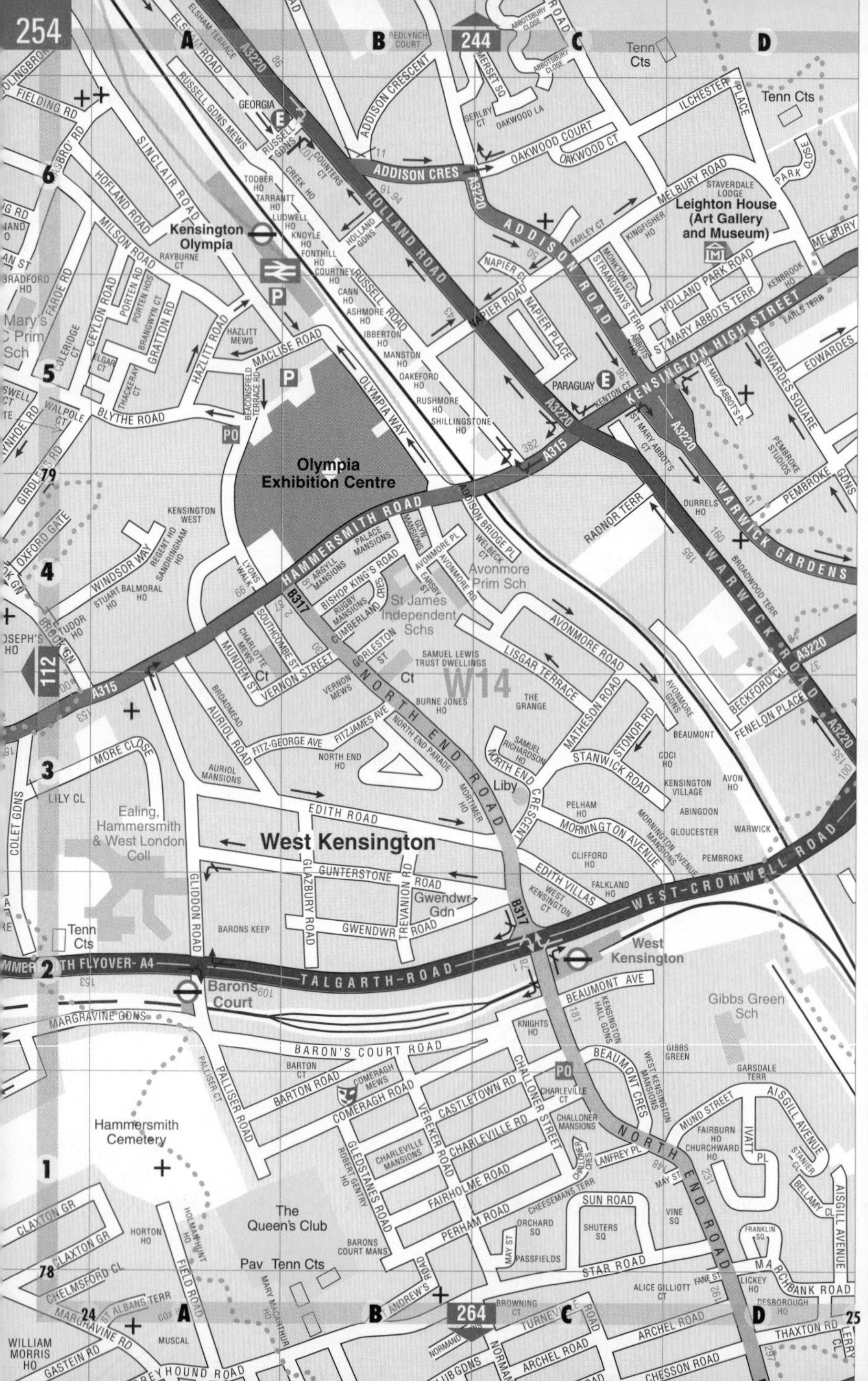

Kensington Olympia
Olympia Exhibition Centre
Leighton House (Art Gallery and Museum)
West Kensington
W14
Avonmore Prim Sch
St James Independent Schs
Ealing, Hammersmith & West London Coll
Hammersmith Cemetery
The Queen's Club
Barons Court
West Kensington
Gibbs Green Sch
HAMMERSMITH ROAD
HOLLAND ROAD
ADDISON ROAD
KENSINGTON HIGH STREET
WARWICK ROAD
WARWICK GARDENS
NORTH END ROAD
WEST CROMWELL ROAD
TALGARTH ROAD
HAMMERSMITH FLYOVER A4
EDITH ROAD
BLYTHE ROAD
AVONMORE ROAD
BARON'S COURT ROAD
PALLISER ROAD
GLIDDON ROAD

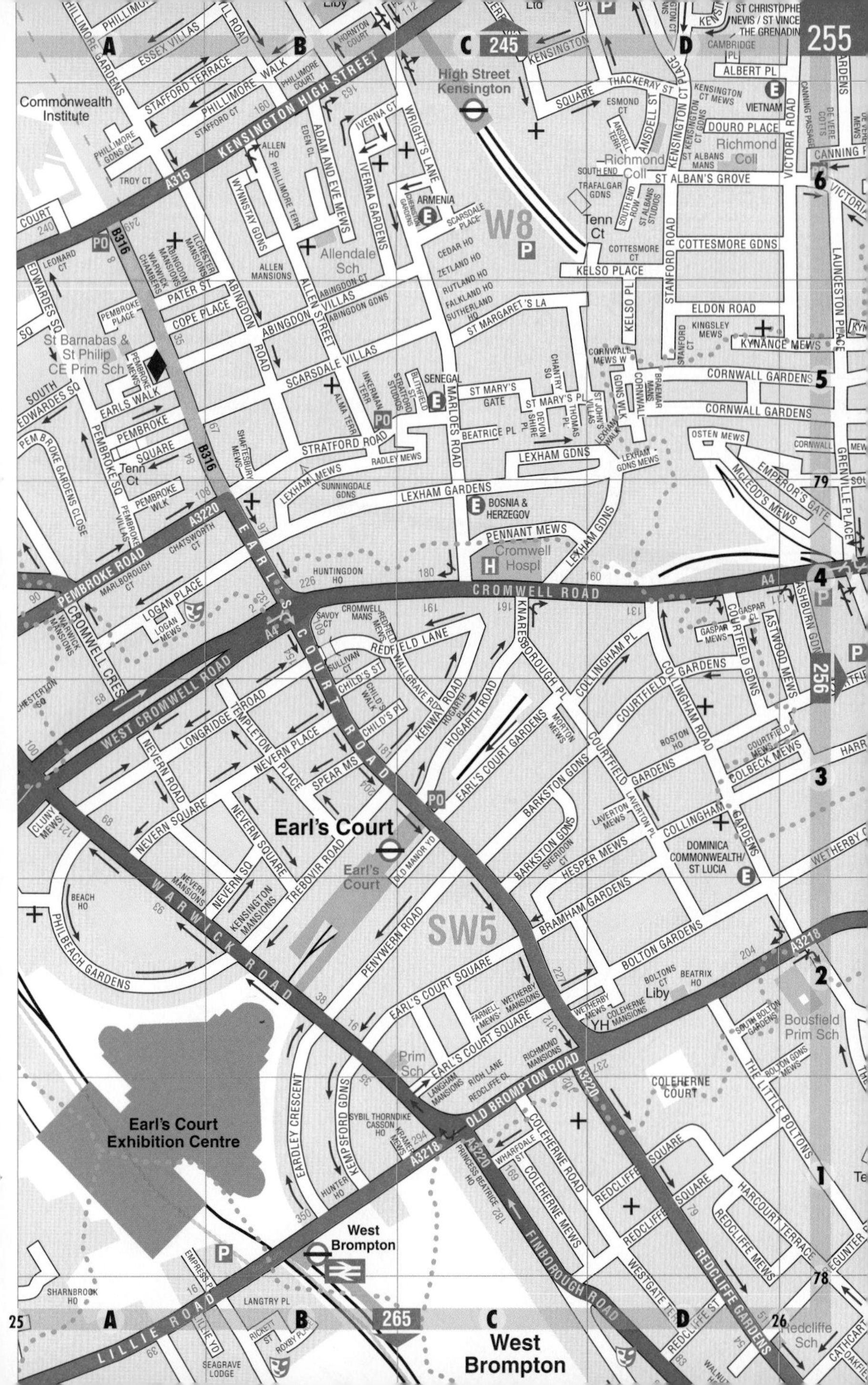
A
B
C
D
245
High Street
Kensington
Commonwealth
Institute
ESSEX VILLAS
STAFFORD TERRACE
PHILLIMORE WALK
PHILLIMORE GARDENS
PHILLIMORE GDNS CL
STAFFORD CT
KENSINGTON HIGH STREET
A315
TROY CT
HORNTON COURT
PHILLIMORE COURT
ADAM AND EVE MEWS
EDEN CL
IVERNA CT
IVERNA GARDENS
WRIGHT'S LANE
ALLEN HO
PHILLIMORE TERR
WYNNSTAY GDNS
ARMENIA
SCARSDALE PLACE
W8
Allendale
Sch
CEDAR HO
ZETLAND HO
RUTLAND HO
FALKLAND HO
SUTHERLAND HO
ST MARGARET'S LA
KENSINGTON SQUARE
THACKERAY ST
ESMOND CT
ANSDELL ST
ANSDELL TERR
KENSINGTON CT PLACE
KENSINGTON CT MEWS
ST ALBANS MANS
VIETNAM
ALBERT PL
CAMBRIDGE PL
DOURO PLACE
Richmond
Coll
ST ALBAN'S GROVE
SOUTH END
TRAFALGAR GDNS
SOUTH END ROW
ST ALBANS STUDIOS
Tenn
Ct
COTTESMORE CT
COTTESMORE GDNS
KELSO PLACE
KELSO PL
STANFORD ROAD
ELDON ROAD
KINGSLEY MEWS
STANFORD CT
KYNANCE MEWS
VICTORIA ROAD
CANNING PASSAGE
DE VERE COTTS
LAUNCESTON PLACE
6
5
CORNWALL GARDENS
CORNWALL MEWS W
BRAEMAR MANS
GDNS WLK
CORNWALL
ST JOHN'S VILLAS
LEXHAM WALK
COURT
240
PO
B316
EDWARDES SQ
LEONARD CT
ALLEN MANSIONS
ABINGDON MANSIONS
WARWICK CHAMBERS
ILCHESTER MANSIONS
PATER ST
ABINGDON ROAD
ABINGDON VILLAS
ABINGDON GDNS
ABINGDON CT
ALLEN STREET
PEMBROKE PLACE
COPE PLACE
St Barnabas &
St Philip
CE Prim Sch
SCARSDALE VILLAS
SOUTH EDWARDES SQ
PEMBROKE MEWS
EARLS WALK
PEMBROKE SQUARE
PEMBROKE SQ
PEMBROKE GARDENS CLOSE
PEMBROKE WLK
PEMBROKE VILLAS
SHAFTESBURY MEWS
ALMA TERR
INKERMAN TERR
STRATFORD STUDIOS
BLITHFIELD ST
SENEGAL
MARLOES ROAD
ST MARY'S GATE
CHANTRY SQ
ST MARY'S PL
DEVONSHIRE PL
THOMAS PL
BEATRICE PL
STRATFORD ROAD
RADLEY MEWS
LEXHAM MEWS
SUNNINGDALE GDNS
LEXHAM GDNS
LEXHAM GARDENS
LEXHAM GDNS MEWS
BOSNIA &
HERZEGOV
PENNANT MEWS
Cromwell
Hospl
OSTEN MEWS
EMPEROR'S GATE
McLEOD'S MEWS
GRENVILLE PLACE
79
A3220
CHATSWORTH CT
PEMBROKE ROAD
MARLBOROUGH CT
LOGAN PLACE
LOGAN MEWS
EARL'S COURT ROAD
HUNTINGDON HO
CROMWELL ROAD
A4
4
ASHBURN GDNS
GASPAR CL
GASPAR MEWS
COURTFIELD GDNS
ASTWOOD MEWS
256
WARWICK MANSIONS
CROMWELL CRES
SAVOY CT
CROMWELL MANS
REDFIELD MEWS
REDFIELD LANE
KNARESBOROUGH PL
COLLINGHAM PL
COURTFIELD GARDENS
COLLINGHAM ROAD
WEST CROMWELL ROAD
CHESTERTON SQ
LONGRIDGE ROAD
TEMPLETON PLACE
SULLIVAN CT
CHILD'S ST
CHILD'S WALK
CHILD'S PL
WALLGRAVE RD
KENWAY ROAD
HOGARTH PL
HOGARTH ROAD
EARL'S COURT GARDENS
MORTON MEWS
BOSTON HO
COURTFIELD MEWS
COLBECK MEWS
3
NEVERN ROAD
NEVERN PLACE
SPEAR MS
NEVERN SQUARE
BARKSTON GDNS
LAVERTON MEWS
LAVERTON PL
COLLINGHAM GARDENS
CLUNY MEWS
Earl's Court
NEVERN SQ
TREBOVIR ROAD
OLD MANOR YD
SHERIDON CT
HESPER MEWS
DOMINICA
COMMONWEALTH/
ST LUCIA
WETHERBY G
BEACH HO
NEVERN MANSIONS
WARWICK ROAD
KENSINGTON MANSIONS
PENYWERN ROAD
SW5
BRAMHAM GARDENS
BOLTON GARDENS
A3218
PHILBEACH GARDENS
EARL'S COURT SQUARE
FARNELL MEWS
WETHERBY MANSIONS
BOLTONS CT
BEATRIX HO
Liby
2
WETHERBY MEWS
YH
COLEHERNE MANSIONS
SOUTH BOLTON GARDENS
Bousfield
Prim Sch
Prim
Sch
RICHMOND MANSIONS
LANGHAM MANSIONS
RICH LANE
REDCLIFFE CL
OLD BROMPTON ROAD
COLEHERNE COURT
BOLTON GDNS MEWS
THE LITTLE BOLTONS
Earl's Court
Exhibition Centre
EARDLEY CRESCENT
KEMPSFORD GDNS
SYBIL THORNDIKE CASSON HO
KRAMER MEWS
WHARFDALE ST
COLEHERNE ROAD
COLEHERNE MEWS
REDCLIFFE SQUARE
HARCOURT TERRACE
1
HUNTER HO
PRINCESS BEATRICE HO
FINBOROUGH ROAD
REDCLIFFE MEWS
REDCLIFFE GARDENS
West
Brompton
EMPRESS PL
WESTGATE TER
78
SHARNBROOK HO
LANGTRY PL
LILLIE ROAD
LILLIE YD
RICKETT ST
ROXBY PL
265
REDCLIFFE ST
Redcliffe
Sch
SEAGRAVE LODGE
West
Brompton
25
26

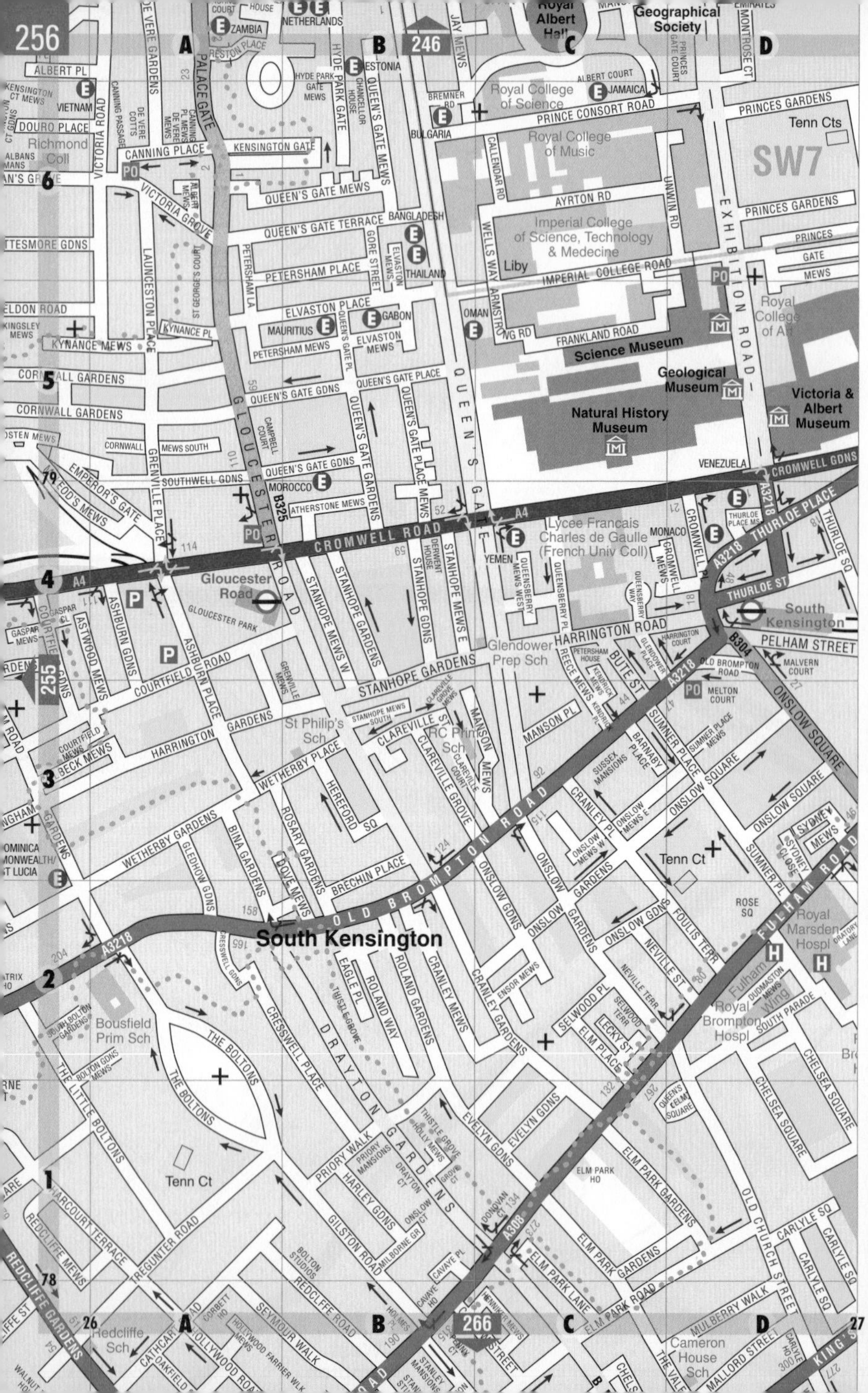
A
B
C
D
246
266
255
6
5
4
3
2
1
79
78
26
27
Royal Albert Hall
Geographical Society
ZAMBIA
NETHERLANDS
ESTONIA
RESTON PLACE
DE VERE GARDENS
PALACE GATE
HYDE PARK GATE
QUEEN'S GATE MEWS
JAY MEWS
BREMNER RD
BULGARIA
ALBERT COURT
JAMAICA
PRINCES GATE COURT
MONTROSE CT
Royal College of Science
PRINCE CONSORT ROAD
PRINCES GARDENS
Tenn Cts
SW7
ALBERT PL
KENSINGTON CT MEWS
VIETNAM
DOURO PLACE
VICTORIA ROAD
CANNING PASSAGE
DE VERE COTTS
Richmond Coll
CANNING PLACE
KENSINGTON GATE
Royal College of Music
CALLENDAR RD
AYRTON RD
UNWIN RD
EXHIBITION ROAD
VICTORIA GROVE
QUEEN'S GATE MEWS
QUEEN'S GATE TERRACE
BANGLADESH
Imperial College of Science, Technology & Medecine
Liby
IMPERIAL COLLEGE ROAD
PRINCES GATE MEWS
LAUNCESTON PLACE
ST GEORGE'S COURT
PETERSHAM LA
PETERSHAM PLACE
GORE STREET
ELVASTON MEWS
THAILAND
ELDON ROAD
KINGSLEY MEWS
KYNANCE PL
KYNANCE MEWS
ELVASTON PLACE
MAURITIUS
GABON
QUEEN'S GATE PL
PETERSHAM MEWS
ELVASTON MEWS
OMAN
WELLS WAY
ARMSTRONG RD
FRANKLAND ROAD
Science Museum
Royal College of Art
CORNWALL GARDENS
QUEEN'S GATE GDNS
QUEEN'S GATE PLACE
QUEEN'S GATE
Geological Museum
Natural History Museum
Victoria & Albert Museum
GLOUCESTER ROAD
CAMPBELL COURT
QUEEN'S GATE PLACE MEWS
QUEEN'S GATE GARDENS
CORNWALL
MEWS SOUTH
EMPEROR'S GATE
GRENVILLE PLACE
SOUTHWELL GDNS
QUEEN'S GATE GDNS
MOROCCO
ATHERSTONE MEWS
VENEZUELA
CROMWELL GDNS
B325
CROMWELL ROAD
A4
Lycee Francais Charles de Gaulle (French Univ Coll)
MONACO
CROMWELL PL
THURLOE PLACE MS
THURLOE PLACE
A3218
THURLOE SQ
THURLOE ST
YEMEN
QUEENSBERRY MEWS WEST
QUEENSBERRY PL
QUEENSBERRY WAY
CROMWELL MEWS
Gloucester Road
GLOUCESTER PARK
ASHBURN GDNS
ASTWOOD MEWS
GASPAR MEWS
GASPAR CL
COURTFIELD GARDENS
STANHOPE MEWS W
STANHOPE GARDENS
DERWENT HOUSE
STANHOPE GDNS
STANHOPE MEWS E
South Kensington
PELHAM STREET
HARRINGTON ROAD
Glendower Prep Sch
PETERSHAM HOUSE
HARRINGTON COURT
GLENDOWER PLACE
B304
MALVERN COURT
OLD BROMPTON ROAD
COURTFIELD ROAD
ASHBURN PLACE
GRENVILLE MEWS
STANHOPE GARDENS
REECE MEWS
KENDRICK MEWS
BUTE ST
MELTON COURT
ONSLOW SQUARE
St Philip's Sch
STANHOPE MEWS SOUTH
CLAREVILLE GROVE MEWS
RC Prim Sch
MANSON MEWS
MANSON PL
SUMNER PLACE
SUMNER PLACE MEWS
HARRINGTON GARDENS
COURTFIELD MEWS
BECK MEWS
WETHERBY PLACE
CLAREVILLE ST
CLAREVILLE COURT
CLAREVILLE GROVE
SUSSEX MANSIONS
BARNABY PLACE
HEREFORD SQ
ROSARY GARDENS
CRANLEY PL
ONSLOW MEWS E
ONSLOW MEWS W
ONSLOW SQUARE
SYDNEY MEWS
SYDNEY CLOSE
WETHERBY GARDENS
GLEDHOW GDNS
BINA GARDENS
DOVE MEWS
BRECHIN PLACE
OLD BROMPTON ROAD
ONSLOW GDNS
ONSLOW GARDENS
Tenn Ct
SUMNER PL
FULHAM ROAD
DOMINICA
COMMONWEALTH/ ST LUCIA
ROSE SQ
Royal Marsden Hospl
ORATORY LANE
South Kensington
A3218
CRESSWELL GDNS
EAGLE PL
THISTLE GROVE
ROLAND WAY
ROLAND GARDENS
CRANLEY MEWS
ENSOR MEWS
CRANLEY GARDENS
ONSLOW GDNS
NEVILLE ST
NEVILLE TERR
FOULIS TERR
Fulham Wing
DUDMASTON MEWS
Royal Brompton Hospl
SOUTH PARADE
SOUTH BOLTON GARDENS
Bousfield Prim Sch
BOLTON GDNS MEWS
THE BOLTONS
CRESSWELL PLACE
DRAYTON GARDENS
SELWOOD PL
SELWOOD TERR
LECKY ST
ELM PLACE
QUEEN'S ELM SQUARE
CHELSEA SQUARE
THE LITTLE BOLTONS
Tenn Ct
PRIORY WALK
PRIORY MANSIONS
HOLLY MEWS
THISTLE GROVE
DRAYTON CT
GROVE CT
EVELYN GDNS
EVELYN GARDENS
ELM PARK HO
ELM PARK GARDENS
OLD CHURCH STREET
HARCOURT TERRACE
REDCLIFFE MEWS
TREGUNTER ROAD
HARLEY GDNS
GILSTON ROAD
MILBORNE GR
ONSLOW CT
DONOVAN CT
A308
ELM PARK LANE
CARLYLE SQ
BOLTON STUDIOS
REDCLIFFE ROAD
CAVAYE PL
CAVAYE HO
ELM PARK ROAD
MULBERRY WALK
REDCLIFFE GARDENS
CORBETT HO
HOLLYWOOD ROAD
SEYMOUR WALK
HOLLYWOOD FARRIER WLK
HOLMES PL
HENNIKER MEWS
Redcliffe Sch
CATHCART ROAD
OAKFIELD
STANLEY MANSIONS
PENNY CT
Cameron House Sch
MALLORD STREET
CARLYLE HO
KING'S ROAD
WALNUT HO
REDCLIFFE ST

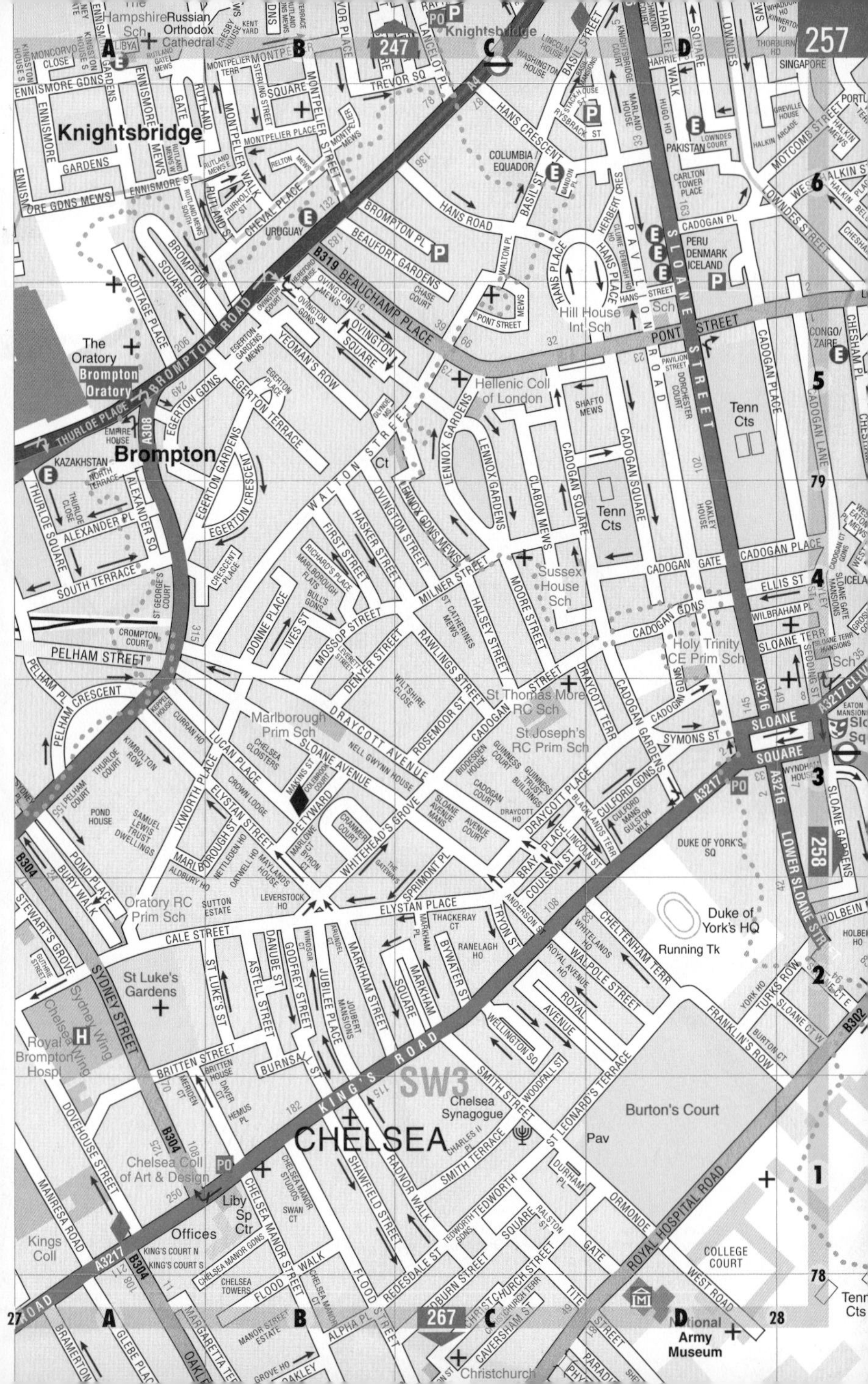
A
B
C
D
247
Knightsbridge
Russian Orthodox Cathedral
Hampshire Sch
LIBYA
MONCORVO CLOSE
ENNISMORE GDNS
ENNISMORE GARDENS
ENNISMORE MEWS
ENNISMORE ST
ENNISMORE GDNS MEWS
RUTLAND GATE
MONTPELIER SQUARE
MONTPELIER STREET
MONTPELIER PLACE
MONTPELIER WALK
MONTPELIER MEWS
MONTPELIER TERR
STERLING STREET
TREVOR SQ
TREVOR PLACE
LANCELOT PL
RELTON MEWS
FAIRHOLT ST
CHEVAL PLACE
RUTLAND ST
RUTLAND MEWS SOUTH
URUGUAY
HANS CRESCENT
HANS ROAD
HANS PLACE
HANS STREET
BASIL ST
BASIL STREET
LINCOLN HOUSE
WASHINGTON HOUSE
KNIGHTSBRIDGE COURT
MARLAND HOUSE
RYSBRACK ST
COLUMBIA / EQUADOR
HERBERT CRES
PAVILION ROAD
HARRIET WALK
HUGO HO
LOWNDES SQUARE
LOWNDES STREET
LOWNDES COURT
PAKISTAN
SINGAPORE
THORBURN HO
HALKIN ARCADE
GREVILLE HOUSE
MOTCOMB STREET
HALKIN MEWS
WEST HALKIN ST
CARLTON TOWER PLACE
CADOGAN PL
PERU
DENMARK
ICELAND
SLOANE STREET
BROMPTON SQUARE
BROMPTON PL
BEAUFORT GARDENS
CHASE COURT
B319 BEAUCHAMP PLACE
OVINGTON MEWS
OVINGTON GDNS
OVINGTON SQUARE
OVINGTON STREET
WALTON PL
WALTON STREET
PONT STREET
PONT STREET MEWS
Hill House Int Sch
COTTAGE PLACE
The Oratory
Brompton Oratory
BROMPTON ROAD
THURLOE PLACE
A308
EGERTON GDNS
EGERTON GARDENS
EGERTON GARDENS MEWS
EGERTON TERRACE
EGERTON CRESCENT
EGERTON PLACE
YEOMAN'S ROW
Hellenic Coll of London
LENNOX GARDENS
LENNOX GDNS MEWS
SHAFTO MEWS
CADOGAN SQUARE
CLABON MEWS
Tenn Cts
CADOGAN PLACE
CADOGAN LANE
CHESHAM PL
CONGO/ ZAIRE
PAVILION STREET
DORCHESTER COURT
OAKLEY HOUSE
EMPIRE HOUSE
Brompton
KAZAKHSTAN
NORTH TERRACE
THURLOE SQUARE
THURLOE CLOSE
ALEXANDER PL
ALEXANDER SQ
SOUTH TERRACE
CRESCENT PLACE
ST GEORGE'S COURT
CROMPTON COURT
PELHAM STREET
PELHAM PL
PELHAM CRESCENT
FIRST STREET
HASKER STREET
RICHARD'S PLACE
MARLBOROUGH FLATS
BULL'S GDNS
DONNE PLACE
IVES ST
MOSSOP STREET
LEVERETT STREET
DENYER STREET
MILNER STREET
ST CATHERINES MEWS
HALSEY STREET
MOORE STREET
RAWLINGS STREET
Sussex House Sch
CADOGAN GATE
CADOGAN GDNS
CADOGAN GARDENS
ELLIS ST
WILBRAHAM PL
SLOANE TERR
Holy Trinity CE Prim Sch
SEDDING ST
A3217
A3216
SLOANE SQUARE
SLOANE GARDENS
LOWER SLOANE STREET
WYNDHAM HOUSE
258
WILTSHIRE CLOSE
ROSEMOOR ST
CADOGAN STREET
St Thomas More RC Sch
St Joseph's RC Prim Sch
DRAYCOTT TERR
DRAYCOTT AVENUE
DRAYCOTT PLACE
SYMONS ST
CULFORD GDNS
BLACKLANDS TERR
GULSTON WALK
Marlborough Prim Sch
CHELSEA CLOISTERS
SLOANE AVENUE
NELL GWYNN HOUSE
MAKINS ST
COLEBROOK COURT
PETYWARD
CRAMMER COURT
WHITEHEAD'S GROVE
BIDDESDEN HOUSE
GUINNESS COURT
GUINNESS TRUST BUILDINGS
CADOGAN COURT
SLOANE AVENUE MANS
AVENUE COURT
BRAY PLACE
LINCOLN ST
COULSON ST
DUKE OF YORK'S SQ
Duke of York's HQ
Running Tk
KEPPEL HOUSE
CURRAN HO
KIMBOLTON ROW
THURLOE COURT
LUCAN PLACE
IXWORTH PLACE
CROWN LODGE
ELYSTAN STREET
ELYSTAN PLACE
MARLBOROUGH ST
PELHAM COURT
POND HOUSE
SAMUEL LEWIS TRUST DWELLINGS
POND PLACE
BURY WALK
Oratory RC Prim Sch
SUTTON ESTATE
LEVERSTOCK HO
SPRIMONT PL
MARKHAM ST
MARKHAM SQUARE
MARKHAM STREET
THACKERAY CT
RANELAGH HO
TRYON ST
BYWATER ST
ANDERSON ST
WHITELANDS HO
CHELTENHAM TERR
WALPOLE STREET
ROYAL AVENUE
FRANKLIN'S ROW
TURKS ROW
HOLBEIN PL
B304
CALE STREET
ST LUKE'S ST
DANUBE ST
ASTELL STREET
GODFREY STREET
JUBILEE PLACE
JOUBERT MANSIONS
STEWART'S GROVE
SYDNEY STREET
St Luke's Gardens
Royal Brompton Hospl
Sydney Wing
Chelsea Wing
BRITTEN STREET
BURNSALL ST
KING'S ROAD
SW3
WELLINGTON SQ
SMITH STREET
WOODFALL ST
ST LEONARD'S TERRACE
Burton's Court
Chelsea Synagogue
CHELSEA
SMITH TERRACE
DOVEHOUSE STREET
Chelsea Coll of Art & Design
MANRESA ROAD
Kings Coll
Liby
Sp Ctr
Offices
CHELSEA MANOR STREET
CHELSEA MANOR GDNS
SWAN CT
SHAWFIELD STREET
RADNOR WALK
TEDWORTH SQUARE
Pav
DURHAM PL
ORMONDE GATE
ROYAL HOSPITAL ROAD
COLLEGE COURT
WEST ROAD
KING'S COURT N
KING'S COURT S
CHELSEA TOWERS
FLOOD WALK
FLOOD STREET
REDESDALE ST
CHRISTCHURCH STREET
CAVERSHAM ST
TITE STREET
MANOR STREET ESTATE
ALPHA PL
267
National Army Museum
Christchurch
GLEBE PLACE
MARGARETTA TERR
BRAMERTON
OAKLEY
1
2
3
4
5
6
27
28
78
79

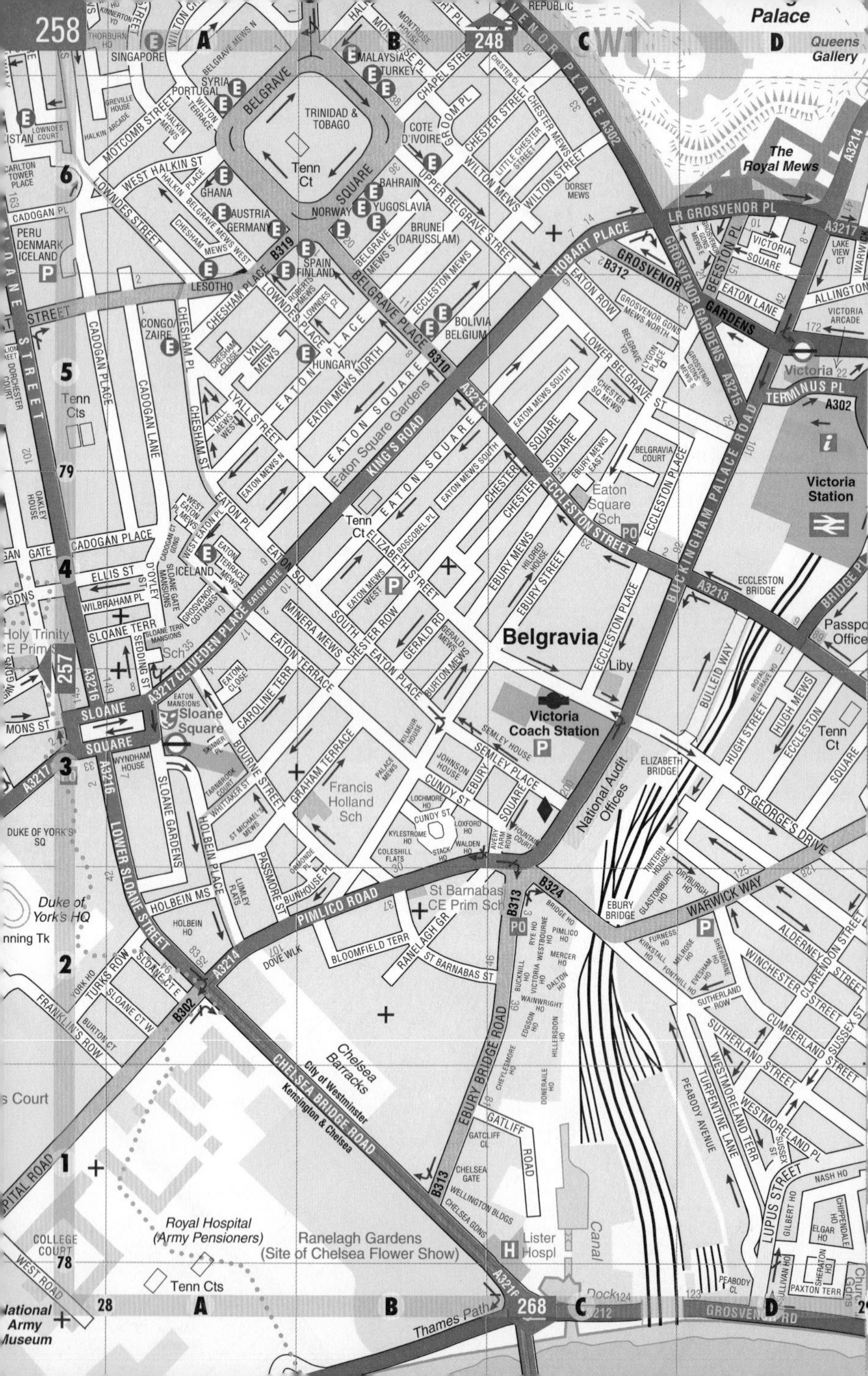

258
248
268
257
A
B
C
D
SW1
Palace
Queens Gallery
The Royal Mews
Belgravia
Victoria Station
Victoria Coach Station
Belgrave Square
Eaton Square
Eaton Square Gardens
King's Road
Sloane Square
Sloane Street
Lower Sloane Street
Buckingham Palace Road
Grosvenor Gardens
Hobart Place
Eccleston Street
Ebury Bridge Road
Chelsea Bridge Road
Pimlico Road
Warwick Way
St George's Drive
Chelsea Barracks
City of Westminster
Kensington & Chelsea
Royal Hospital (Army Pensioners)
Ranelagh Gardens (Site of Chelsea Flower Show)
Duke of York's HQ
Francis Holland Sch
Lister Hospl
National Audit Offices
Thames Path
Grosvenor Rd
National Army Museum

A
B
C
D
249
Wellington Barracks
The Guards Museum
Methodist Central Hall
Westminster Abbey
BUCKINGHAM GATE
PETTY FRANCE
BROADWAY
TOTHILL STREET
St James's Park
DACRE ST
SWAZILAND
ALBANIA
STAFFORD PL
CATHERINE PLACE
PALACE
WILFRED STREET
VANDON ST
CAXTON STREET
Caxton Hall
Westminster Coll
SW1
Westminster City Sch
Westminster City Hall
SPENSER ST
KOREA
New Scotland Yard
ABBEY ORCHARD ST
ABBEY ORCHARD ST ESTATE
GREAT SMITH STREET
Westminster Abbey Choir Sch
DEAN'S YARD
THE SANCTUARY
OLD PYE STREET
St Matthews Sch Westminster
Govt Offices
STAG PLACE
GLEN HO
BRESSENDEN PLACE
VICTORIA STREET
Strutton Ground
STRUTTON GD
Govt Offs
HOWICK PLACE
GREAT PETER STREET
GREAT COLLEGE ST
TUFTON STREET
Westminster Cathedral
WESTMINSTER
GREYCOAT PL
HORSEFERRY ROAD ESTATE
CHADWICK ST
Channel 4 TV Corp
Govt Offices
MONCK STREET
The Grey Coat Hosp CE Sch
RHS (Lawrence Hall & Conf Ctr)
TA Ctr
MEDWAY ST
ROMNEY ST
HORSEFERRY ROAD
ASHLEY PL
CARLISLE PLACE
St Vincent De Paul RC Prim Sch
AMBROSDEN AVENUE
THIRLEBY ROAD
GREENCOAT ROW
ROCHESTER ROW
ROCHESTER ST
Westminster Cath Choir Sch
Westminster Coll
Coroner's Court
St John's Gdns
MARSHAM STREET
KING'S SCHOLAR'S PASSAGE
MORPETH TERR
FRANCIS STREET
STILLINGTON ST
GREENCOAT PLACE
VINCENT SQUARE
RHS (Lindley Hall)
MAUNSEL ST
RUTHERFORD ST
PAGE STREET
WILTON ROAD
GILLINGHAM STREET
WILLOW PLACE
Tenn Cts
Pl Fld
Pav
VINCENT STREET
Offices
260
Civil Service Coll
GUILDHOUSE ST
LONGMOORE ST
VAUXHALL BRIDGE ROAD
The Gordon Hospl
Tenn Ct
HIDE PLACE
TA Ctr
REGENCY STREET
Millbank Prim Sch
ERASMUS STREET
HERRICK STREET
JOHN ISLIP STREET
Tate Britain
WARWICK WAY
B324
BELGRAVE ROAD
CHURTON ST
TACHBROOK STREET
Offices
The Grey Coat Hospl St Michaels (Sch)
DOUGLAS STREET
CHAPTER ST
ATTERBURY ST
WARWICK SQUARE
Tenn Ct
CHARLWOOD PL
CURETON ST
Royal Army Medical Coll
Fairley House Sch
CAUSTON STREET
PONSONBY PLACE
PONSONBY TER
ST GEORGE'S DRIVE
GLOUCESTER STREET
DENBIGH STREET
DENBIGH PLACE
CHARLWOOD STREET
MORETON PLACE
MORETON STREET
RAMPAYNE STREET
Pimlico
Liby
BESSBOROUGH ST
BESSBOROUGH GDNS
A3213
A202
A3212
Thames Path
CAMBRIDGE ST
WINCHESTER STREET
Pimlico
LUPUS STREET
Westminster Cath RC Prim Sch
BESSBOROUGH PLACE
Pimlico Sch
ST GEORGE'S SQUARE
St George's Square Gdns
AYLESFORD STREET
CROWN REACH
Churchill Gardens Prim Sch
CHICHESTER STREET
CLAVERTON STREET
DOLPHIN SQUARE
ST GEORGE'S SQUARE MEWS
Wharves
St Gabriel's CE Prim Sch
CHURCHILL GARDENS ROAD
Wharves
City of Westminster
Wandsworth
Lambeth
29
A
B
269
C
D
30
TELFORD TERRACE
CHURCHILL GARDENS
GROSVENOR ROAD
Tenn Ct
Thames Path
Westminster Boating Base
Wharves
1
2
3
4
5
6
78
79

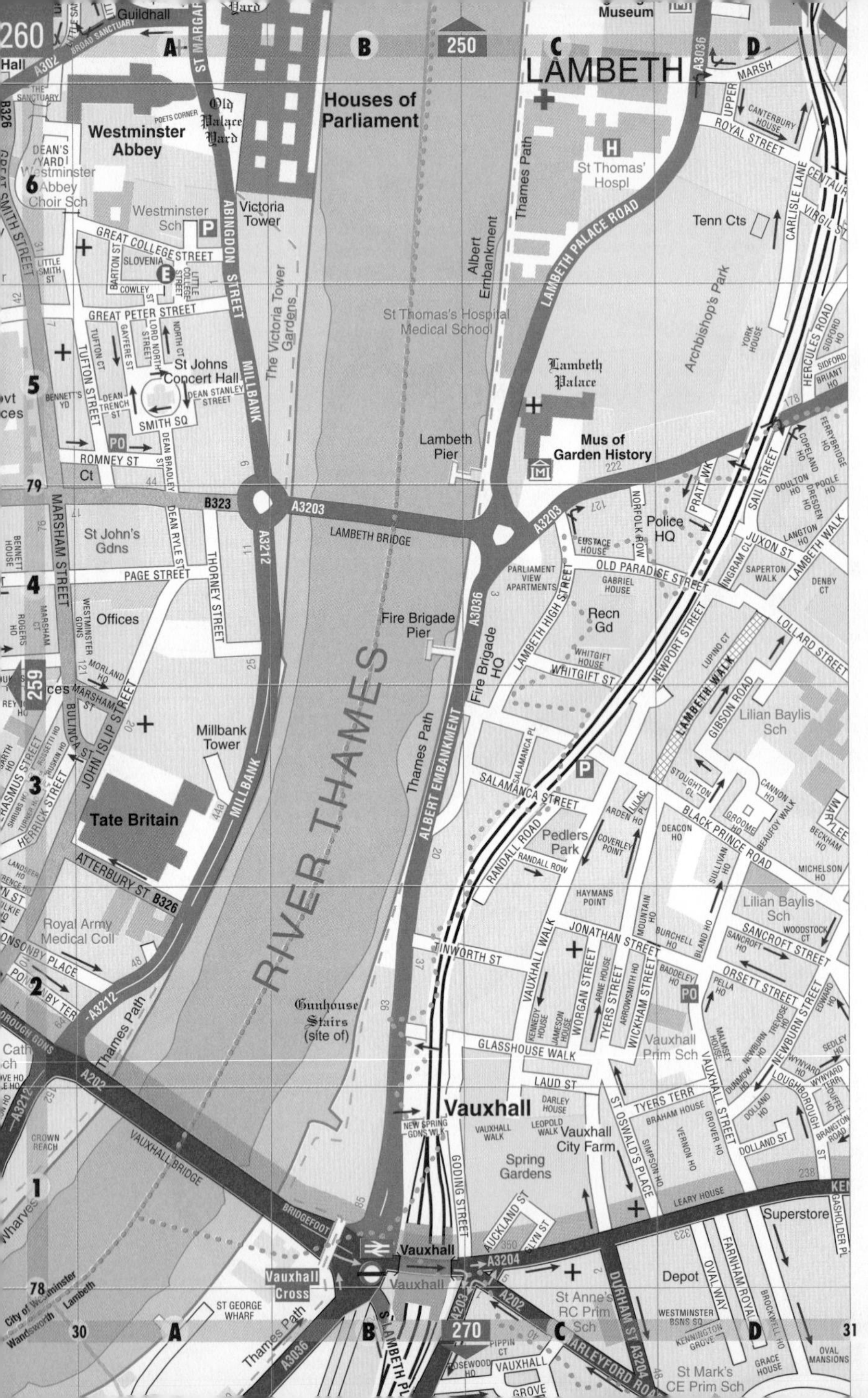

260
250
259
270
LAMBETH
Houses of Parliament
Westminster Abbey
Westminster Abbey Choir Sch
Westminster Sch
Victoria Tower
The Victoria Tower Gardens
St Thomas' Hospl
St Thomas's Hospital Medical School
Lambeth Palace
Mus of Garden History
Archbishop's Park
Lambeth Pier
St Johns Concert Hall
SMITH SQ
St John's Gdns
Offices
Millbank Tower
Tate Britain
Royal Army Medical Coll
RIVER THAMES
Fire Brigade Pier
Fire Brigade HQ
Police HQ
Recn Gd
Pedlers Park
Lilian Baylis Sch
Vauxhall Prim Sch
Vauxhall
Vauxhall City Farm
Spring Gardens
Gunhouse Stairs (site of)
Superstore
Depot
St Anne's RC Prim Sch
St Mark's CE Prim Sch
Vauxhall Cross
Thames Path
MILLBANK
ABINGDON STREET
LAMBETH BRIDGE
LAMBETH PALACE ROAD
ALBERT EMBANKMENT
VAUXHALL BRIDGE
GREAT PETER STREET
GREAT COLLEGE STREET
MARSHAM STREET
PAGE STREET
THORNEY STREET
JOHN ISLIP STREET
ATTERBURY ST
OLD PARADISE STREET
LAMBETH HIGH STREET
BLACK PRINCE ROAD
SALAMANCA STREET
JONATHAN STREET
VAUXHALL WALK
VAUXHALL STREET
GLASSHOUSE WALK
TINWORTH ST
GODING STREET
KENNINGTON LANE
DURHAM ST
HARLEYFORD ROAD
ROYAL STREET
CARLISLE LANE
HERCULES ROAD
LAMBETH WALK
LOLLARD STREET
SANCROFT STREET
ORSETT STREET
NEWPORT STREET
A3036
A3203
A3212
A202
A3204
B323
B326
A302

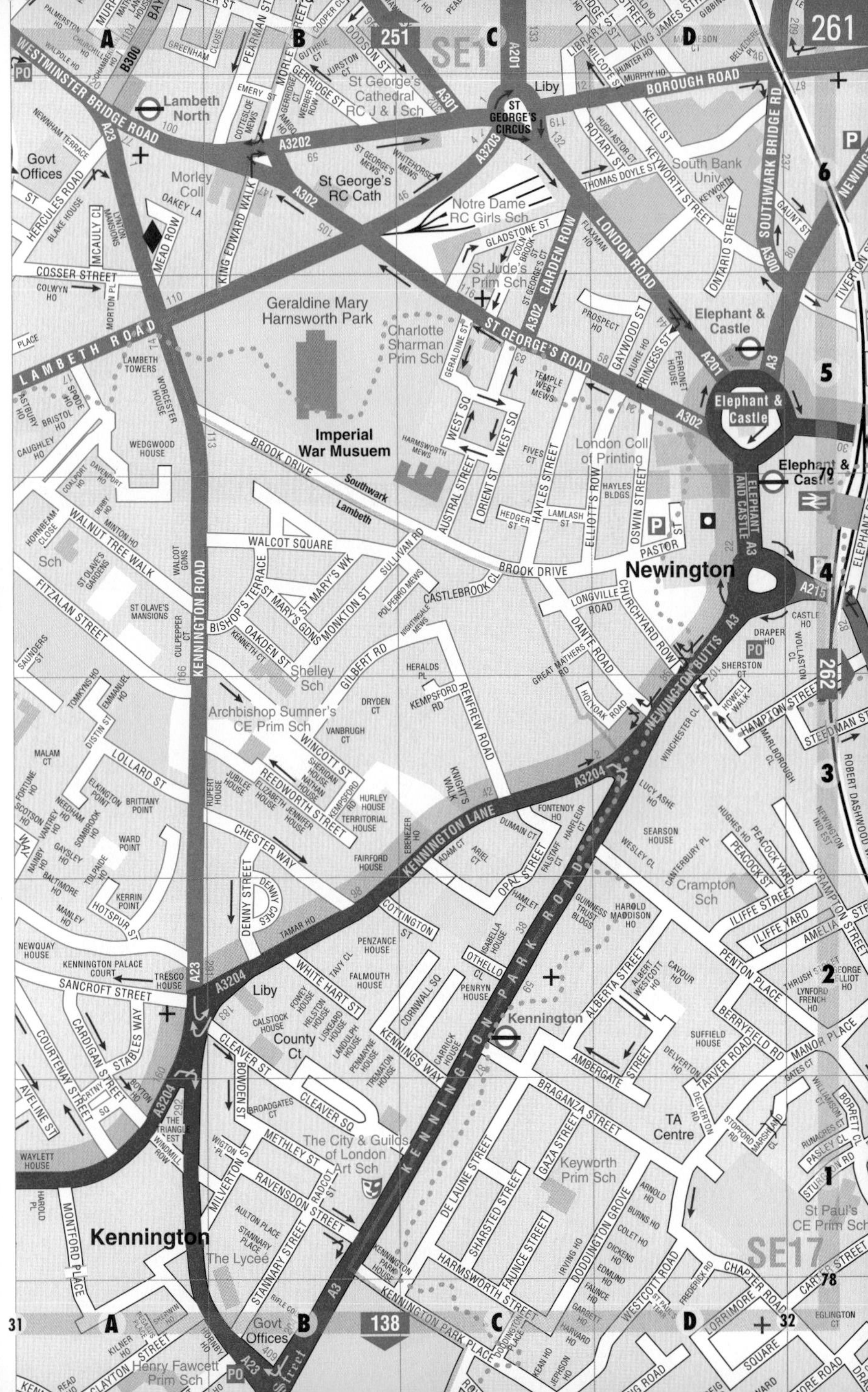
A
B
C
D
251
SE1
WESTMINSTER BRIDGE ROAD
Lambeth North
Govt Offices
HERCULES ROAD
Morley Coll
OAKEY LA
MEAD ROW
KING EDWARD WALK
COSSER STREET
A3202
A302
A3203
A301
A201
ST GEORGE'S CIRCUS
St George's Cathedral RC J & I Sch
St George's RC Cath
Notre Dame RC Girls Sch
Liby
BOROUGH ROAD
LONDON ROAD
GARDEN ROW
South Bank Univ
SOUTHWARK BRIDGE RD
KEYWORTH STREET
ONTARIO STREET
LAMBETH ROAD
Geraldine Mary Harnsworth Park
Charlotte Sharman Prim Sch
St Jude's Prim Sch
ST GEORGE'S ROAD
Elephant & Castle
Imperial War Musuem
WEST SQ
London Coll of Printing
BROOK DRIVE
Southwark
Lambeth
WALCOT SQUARE
KENNINGTON ROAD
WALNUT TREE WALK
FITZALAN STREET
Newington
ELEPHANT AND CASTLE A3
A215
NEWINGTON BUTTS
Shelley Sch
Archbishop Sumner's CE Prim Sch
GILBERT RD
RENFREW ROAD
DANTE ROAD
KENNINGTON LANE
A3204
REEDWORTH STREET
CHESTER WAY
LOLLARD ST
HAMPTON STREET
ROBERT DASHWOOD WAY
262
Crampton Sch
CRAMPTON STREET
PENTON PLACE
MANOR PLACE
KENNINGTON PARK ROAD
Kennington
SANCROFT STREET
A23
Liby
County Ct
CLEAVER SQ
BRAGANZA STREET
TA Centre
The City & Guilds of London Art Sch
Keyworth Prim Sch
DODDINGTON GROVE
WESTCOTT ROAD
HARMSWORTH STREET
St Paul's CE Prim Sch
SE17
CHAPTER ROAD
Kennington
The Lyceé
KENNINGTON PARK PLACE
Govt Offices
Henry Fawcett Prim Sch
CLAYTON STREET
1
2
3
4
5
6
31
32
78
79
138

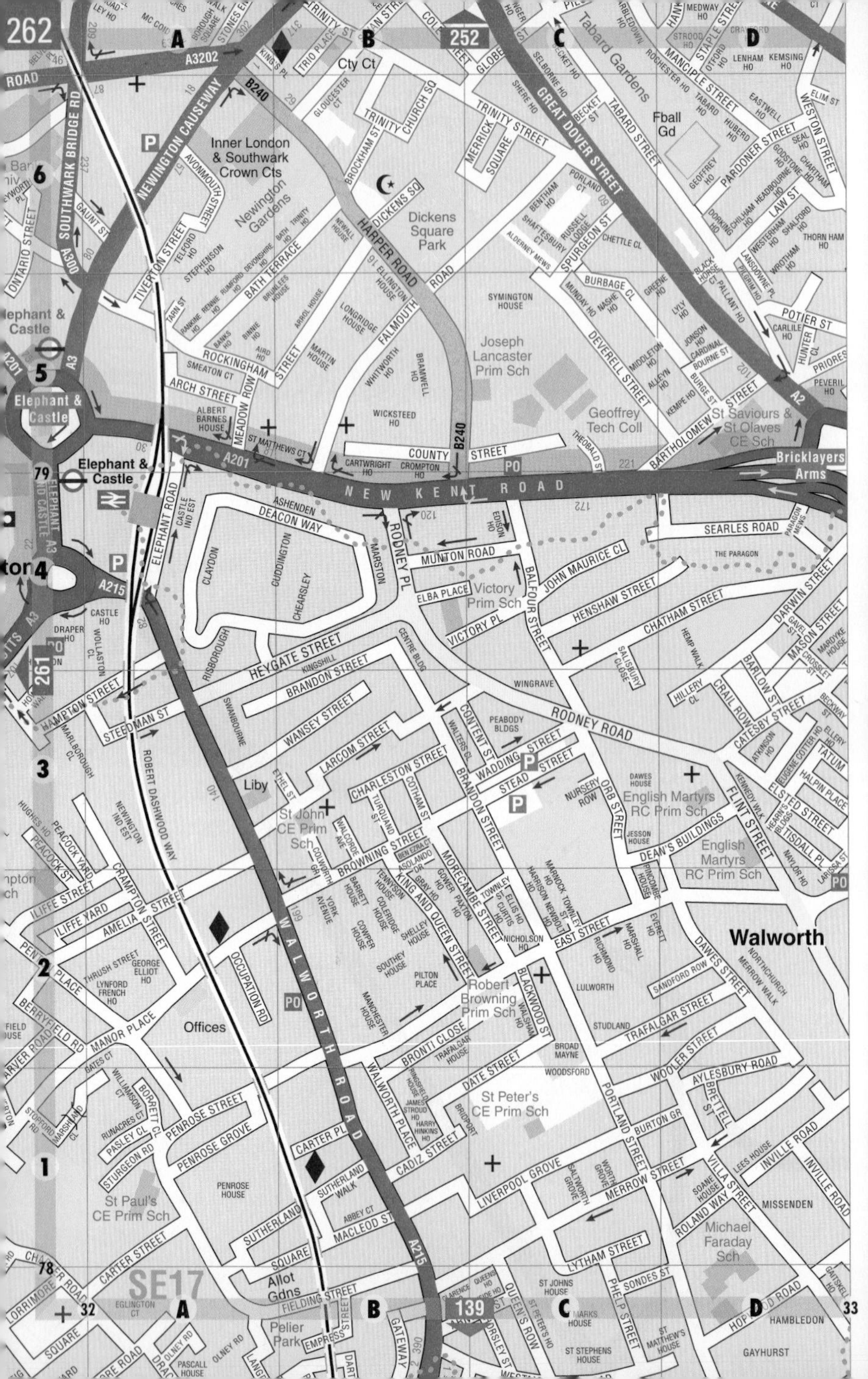

262
A
B
C
D
252
A3202
B240
Cty Ct
Trinity St
Trio Place
King's Pl
Globe St
Tabard Gardens
Medway Ho
Staple Street
Crawford
Lenham Ho
Kemsing Ho
Manciple Street
Rochester Ho
Tabard Ho
Huberd Ho
Eastwell Ho
Weston Street
Elim St
Pardoner Street
Seal Ho
Godstone Ho
Chartham
Headbourne
Chilham
Geoffrey Ho
Dorking Ho
Law St
Westerham Ho
Shalford Ho
Thorn Ham Ho
Wrotham Ho
Lansdowne Pl
Pilgrim Ho
Fball Gd
Road
Southwark Bridge Rd
A300
Gaunt St
Ontario Street
Newington Causeway
Inner London & Southwark Crown Cts
Avonmouth Street
Newington Gardens
Gloucester Ct
Trinity Church Sq
Brockham St
Dickens Sq
Dickens Square Park
Harper Road
Merrick Square
Trinity Street
Great Dover Street
Becket St
Tabard Street
Selborne Ho
Shere Ho
Bentham Ho
Porland Ct
Shaftesbury Ct
Russell Lodge
Spurgeon St
Alderney Mews
Chettle Cl
Burbage Cl
Greene Ho
Munday Ho
Nashe Ho
Lyly Ho
Black Horse Ct
Pallant Ho
Potier St
Carlile Ho
Hunter Cl
Priores
Peveril Ho
Tiverton Street
Telford Ho
Stephenson Ho
Bath Terrace
Rockingham Street
Smeaton Ct
Arch Street
Meadow Row
Albert Barnes House
Longridge House
Ellington House
Falmouth Road
Symington House
Martin House
Whitworth Ho
Bramwell Ho
Wicksteed Ho
Joseph Lancaster Prim Sch
Deverell Street
Middleton Ho
Alleyn Ho
Jonson Ho
Cardinal Bourne St
Burge St
Kempe Ho
Bartholomew Street
Geoffrey Tech Coll
Theobald St
St Saviours & St Olaves CE Sch
A2
6
5
4
3
2
1
Elephant & Castle
A201
St Matthews Ct
County Street
Cartwright Ho
Crompton Ho
PO
Bricklayers Arms
New Kent Road
79
Elephant and Castle A3
Elephant Road
Castle Ind Est
Ashenden
Deacon Way
Claydon
Cuddington
Chearsley
Marston
Rodney Pl
Munton Road
Edison Ho
Searles Road
Paragon Mews
The Paragon
A215
Castle Ho
Draper Ho
Wollaston Cl
261
John Maurice Cl
Elba Place
Victory Prim Sch
Victory Pl
Balfour Street
Henshaw Street
Chatham Street
Darwin Street
Risborough
Heygate Street
Kingshill
Brandon Street
Centre Bldg
Salisbury Close
Hemp Walk
Mason Street
Gavel St
Mardyke House
Crosslet St
Barlow St
Hampton Street
Steedman St
Swanbourne
Wansey Street
Wingrave
Hillery Cl
Crail Row
Catesby Street
Beckway St
Ellery
Rodney Road
Content St
Walters Cl
Peabody Bldgs
Wadding Street
Atkinson Ho
Eugene Cotter Ho
Tatum
Marlborough Cl
Robert Dashwood Way
Larcom Street
Stead Street
Dawes House
Halpin Place
Ethel St
Liby
Charleston Street
Cotham St
Nursery Row
Orb Street
English Martyrs RC Prim Sch
Kennedy Walk
Flint Street
Elsted Street
Hearn's Bldgs
St John CE Prim Sch
Walcorde Ave
Turquand St
Jesson House
Dean's Buildings
Tisdall Pl
Naylor Ho
Larissa St
Hughes Ho
Peacock Yard
Peacock St
Newington Ind Est
Browning Street
Ben Ezra Ct
Asolando Dr
Marnock Ho
Harrison Ho
Newbolt Ho
Townley St
Pincombe House
Crampton Street
Iliffe Street
Iliffe Yard
Amelia Street
Colworth Gr
York Avenue
Barrett House
Tennyson House
Coleridge House
Gray Ho
Gower Ho
Paxton Ho
Morecambe Street
King and Queen Street
Townley Ho
St Curtis Ho
Ellis Ho
Everett Ho
Walworth
Cowper House
Shelley House
Nicholson Ho
East Street
Marshall Ho
Richmond Ho
Dawes Street
Northchurch
Merrow Walk
Penton Place
Thrush Street
George Elliot Ho
Lynford French Ho
Occupation Rd
Walworth Road
Southey House
Pilton Place
Manchester House
Robert Browning Prim Sch
Blackwood St
Walsham Ho
Lulworth
Sandford Row
Berryfield Rd
Manor Place
Offices
Bronti Close
Trafalgar House
Studland
Trafalgar Street
Carver Road
Bates Ct
Williamson Ct
Borrett Cl
Ringsfield House
James Stroud Ho
Harry Hinkins Ho
Date Street
Broad Mayne
Woodsford
Wooler Street
Aylesbury Road
Brettell St
St Peter's CE Prim Sch
Portland Street
Burton Gr
Stopford Rd
Marshland Cl
Runacres Ct
Pasley Cl
Sturgeon Rd
Penrose Street
Penrose Grove
Bridport
Carter Pl
Cadiz Street
Walworth Place
Liverpool Grove
Saltworth Grove
Worth Grove
Merrow Street
Soane House
Lees House
Inville Road
Villa Street
Roland Way
Missenden
Penrose House
St Paul's CE Prim Sch
Sutherland Walk
Abbey Ct
Macleod St
Sutherland Square
Lytham Street
Michael Faraday Sch
Carter Street
Chapter Road
78
Lorrimore
Allot Gdns
Fielding Street
Clarence
Queens Ho
St Johns House
Sondes St
Phelp Street
Hopwood Road
Gaitskell Ho
SE17
32
Eglington Ct
Empress Street
139
Queen's Row
St Peter's Ho
Marks House
33
Hambledon
Pelier Park
Olney Rd
Pascall House
Gateway
St Stephens House
St Matthew's House
Gayhurst
Square

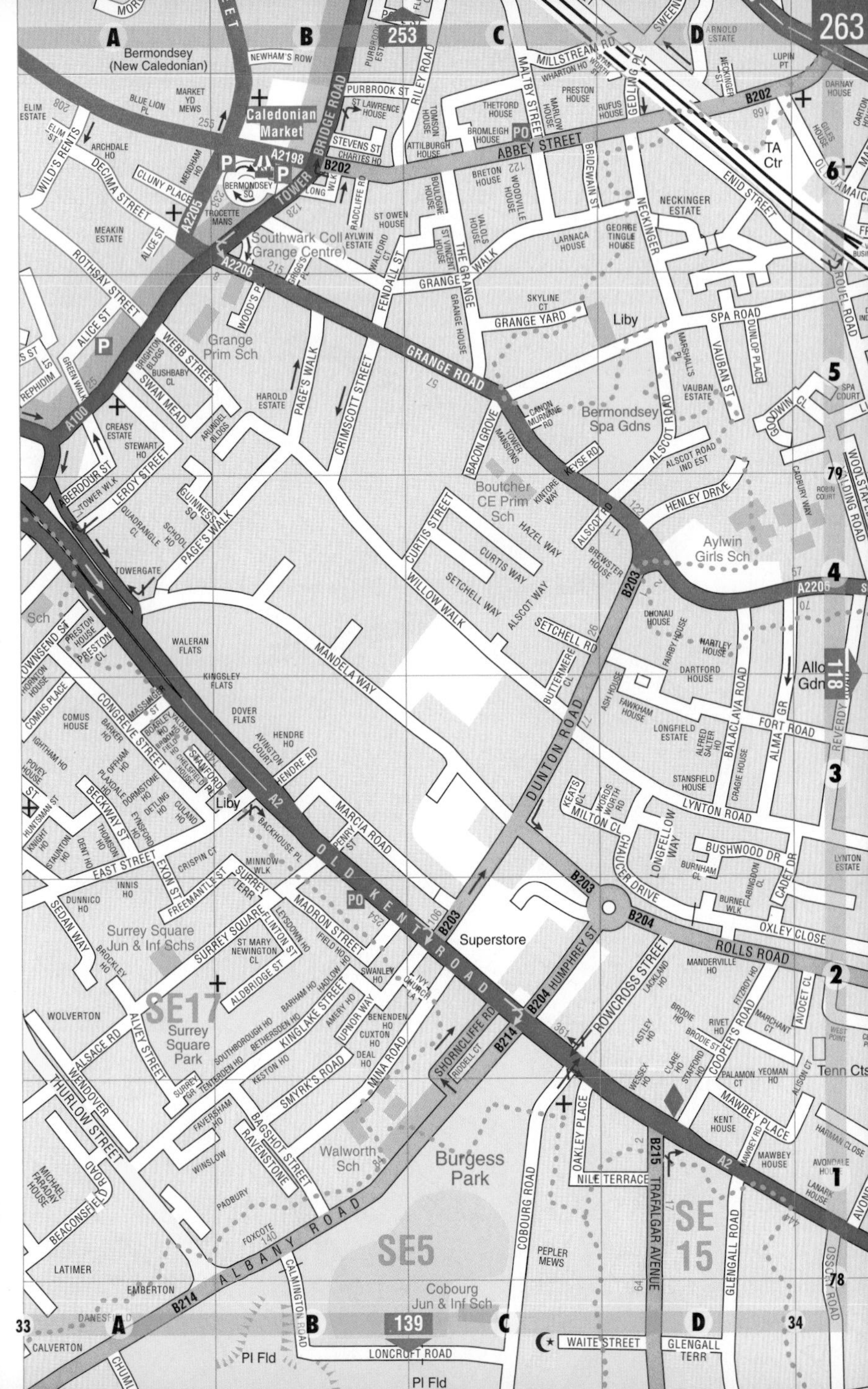

253
Bermondsey (New Caledonian)
Caledonian Market
ABBEY STREET
TOWER BRIDGE ROAD
GRANGE ROAD
GRANGE WALK
SPA ROAD
Bermondsey Spa Gdns
Grange Prim Sch
Boutcher CE Prim Sch
Aylwin Girls Sch
Southwark Coll (Grange Centre)
MANDELA WAY
WILLOW WALK
DUNTON ROAD
OLD KENT ROAD
ROLLS ROAD
LYNTON ROAD
Superstore
Surrey Square Jun & Inf Schs
Surrey Square Park
SE17
Walworth Sch
Burgess Park
SE5
SE 15
Cobourg Jun & Inf Sch
ALBANY ROAD
TRAFALGAR AVENUE
COBOURG ROAD
GLENGALL ROAD
WAITE STREET
LONCROFT ROAD
Tenn Cts
Allo Gdn
118
139

A
B
C
D
254
The Queen's Club
Pav Tenn Cts
HORTON HO
CLAXTON GR
CHELMSFORD CL
78
ST ALBANS TERR
MARGRAVINE RD
COX HO
MUSCAL
WILLIAM MORRIS HO
GASTEIN RD
6
GREYHOUND ROAD
SPENCER MEWS
TASSO ROAD
KINNOUL ROAD
MUSARD ROAD
MARY MACARTHUR HO
FIELD ROAD
BARONS COURT MANS
ST ANDREW'S ROAD
ORCHARD SQ
MAY ST
PASSFIELDS
SHUTERS SQ
VINE SQ
STAR ROAD
ALICE GILLIOTT CT
FANE ST
LICKEY HO
MARCHBANK ROAD
DESBOROUGH HO
THAXTON RD
BROWNING CT
TURNEVILLE ROAD
NORMAND MEWS
ARCHEL ROAD
QUEEN'S CLUB GDNS
NORMAND ROAD
CHESSON ROAD
B317
A3218
BRAMBER ROAD
Normand Park Prim Sch
BEAUFORT MEWS
GEORGE'S SQUARE
PEABODY ESTATE
W6
Tenn Cts
QUEEN'S CLUB GARDENS
P
Pav
MULGRAVE RD
CHESTNUT CT
CHESTNUT ALLEY
CHUTER EDE HO
OAKLEY WLK
CRAMMOND CL
ABBEY GARDENS
TASSO YD
Normand Park
Bwg Gn
Liby
ADENEY CL
WENTWORTH CT
HOBBITT ROAD
DISBROWE ROAD
St Augustine's RC Prim Sch
LILLIE ROAD
JIM GRIFFITHS HO
STAFFORD CRIPPS HO
5
PAYENS WLK
LAMPETER SQ
LAUNDRY RD
MOYLAN ROAD
LITTLE ROAD MANS
TOM WILLIAMS HO
HUGH GAITSKELL CL
ELLEN WILKINSON HO
MANNY HINWELL HO
MARGARET HERBISON HO
COOMER MEWS
ANCILL CL
BRECON ROAD
LINTAINE CL
TILTON ST
HERBERT MORRISON HO
CLEM ATTLEE CT
HAROLD WILSON HO
COOMER PL
CROWTHER CL
CREFELD CL
CAROLINE WLK
BAYONNE RD
A3218
Sir John Lillie Prim Sch
DELAFORD STREET
RYLSTON ROAD
P
MARGARET INGRAM CL
LEN FREEMAN PL
DOUGLAS JOHNSTONE HO
JOHN WHEATLEY HO
JOHN STRACHEY HO
FRANK BESWICK HO
FRANK SOSKICE HO
KENNETH YOUNGER HO
BUCKLER'S ALLEY
HALDANE ROAD
PURCELL CRES
TWYNHOLM MANS
PO
A3219
CHALDON ROAD
WILLIAMS CL
PELLANT ROAD
MENDORA ROAD
JOHN SMITH AVE
GEORGE LINDGREN HO
EDITH SUMMERSKILL HO
NYE BEVAN HO
ST THOMAS'S WAY
TOURNAY ROAD
Recn Ground
STRODE ROAD
HARTOPP POINT
CHASEMORE HO
PROTHERO ROAD
ROCQUE HO
CLYDE FLATS
MATON HO
ESTCOURT ROAD
MIRABEL ROAD
FABIAN ROAD
HARTISMERE ROAD
EPIRUS ROAD
4
DONNELLY CT
LANNOY POINT
BEDFORD PAS
ROYAL PAR
St Thomas of Canterbury RC Prim Sch
Fulham Cross Sec Sch
HANNELL ROAD
DAWES ROAD
PO
SHORROLDS ROAD
PALACE MEWS
BATHS APP
134
AINTREE STREET
ROSALINE ROAD
ROSALINE TERR
SHERBROOKE TERR
SHERBROOKE ROAD
LETTERSTONE RD
SALISBURY MEWS
PARKVILLE ROAD
HOMESTEAD ROAD
GOATER'S ALLEY
GIRONDE ROAD
MABLETHORPE ROAD
MUNSTER ROAD
Cemetery
ROWALLAN ROAD
VARNA ROAD
ORBAIN ROAD
ROSAVILLE ROAD
BURNTHWAITE ROAD
3
BRONSART ROAD
ALLESTREE ROAD
ST OLAF'S ROAD
BROOKVILLE ROAD
WHEATSHEAF TERR
THE QUADRANGLE
KILMAINE ROAD
ST PETER'S TERR
FILMER ROAD
MARVILLE ROAD
LANCASTER CT
KINGWOOD ROAD
WYFOLD ROAD
REPORTON RD
BLOOM PARK RD
DARLAN ROAD
ATALANTA ST
BRANKSEA ST
77
KELVEDON RD
ARUNDEL MANSIONS
MARRAYAT SQ
THE CODA CTR
FERNHURST RD
BISHOPS RD
CLONMEL RD
WINCHENDON RD
Henry Compton Sec Sch
DANEHURST ST
MUNSTER RESIDENCES
FLORENCE MANS
HAZELWOOD MANSIONS
LILYVILLE RD
Kensington Prep Sch
Liby
2
CHILDERLEY ST
CONNAUGHT MANS
ROSTREVOR MANS
PENHURST MANS
AVONDALE MANS
DEEPDENE MANS
CHESILTON RD
RADIPOLE RD
A304
A219
St John's CE Prim Sch
FILMER HO
FILMER ROAD STUDIOS
QUENTINGTON MANSIONS
Al-Muntada Islamic Sch
SIDBURY ST
LAMBROOK TERR
WARDO AVE
GOWAN AVE
SW6
SWIFT ST
ROSTREVOR RD
FULHAM RD
PURSERS CROSS RD
EPPLE RD
FINLAY ST
FULHAM
THE COURTYARD
VERA RD
FELDEN ST
ST MAUR RD
ELLERBY ST
FULHAM PALACE RD
KIMBELL GDNS
PARK MANSIONS
COLEHILL LA
PO
MIMOSA ST
WHITTINGSTALL MANSIONS
WHITTINGSTALL RD
BEACONSFIELD WLK
1
EDGARLEY TERR
FIRTH GDNS
HORDER RD
BURNFOOT AVE
MUNSTER RD
CROOKHAM RD
DONERAILE ST
ELY COURT FLATS
DANCER RD
LETTICE ST
WOODLAWN RD
RINGMER AVE
WALDEMAR AVENUE MANSIONS
HESTERCOMBE AVE
HEATHMAN'S RD
CLONCURRY ST
COLEHILL GDNS
DURRELL RD
CLARIDGE CT
WILLIAM BANFIELD HO
Tenn Cts
LALOR ST
WILSTON CT
ARTHUR HENDERSON HOUSE
ST DIONIS RD
BISHOP'S PARK RD
BISHOP'S MANSION
24
WALDEMAR AVE
DORNCLIFFE RD
135
MUNSTER CT
PLATO PL
MUSTOW PL
EDDISCOMBE RD
GUION RD
DORIA RD
25
BISHOP'S AVE
Pav
OXBERRY AVE
FULHAM PARK RD
ETHEL RANKIN CT

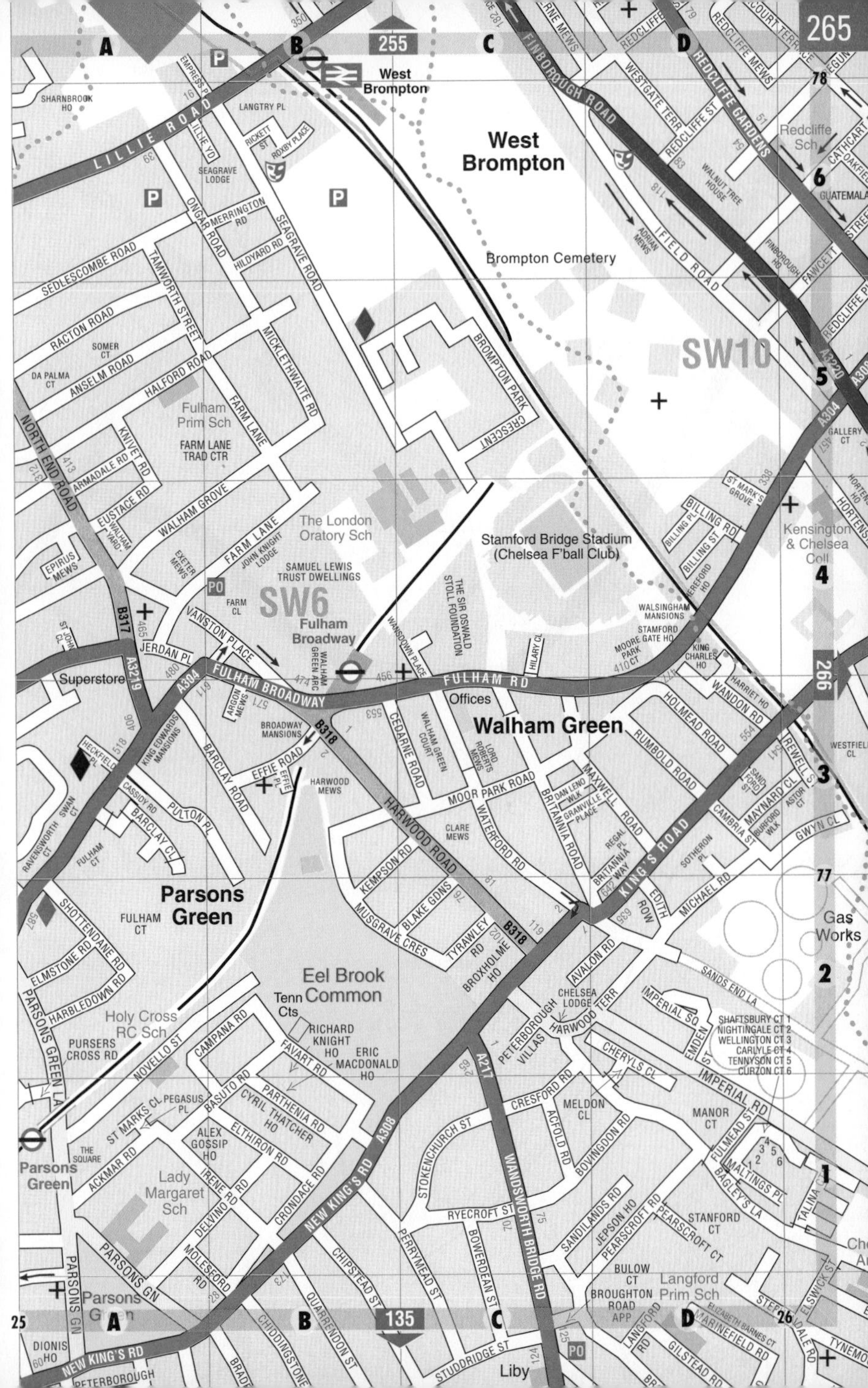
West Brompton
Brompton Cemetery
SW10
SW6
Stamford Bridge Stadium (Chelsea F'ball Club)
The London Oratory Sch
Fulham Prim Sch
Fulham Broadway
Walham Green
Parsons Green
Eel Brook Common
Holy Cross RC Sch
Lady Margaret Sch
Langford Prim Sch
Kensington & Chelsea Coll
Redcliffe Sch
Gas Works
Superstore
Offices
LILLIE ROAD
FULHAM RD
FULHAM BROADWAY
KING'S ROAD
NEW KING'S RD
NORTH END ROAD
HARWOOD ROAD
WANDSWORTH BRIDGE RD
FINBOROUGH ROAD
REDCLIFFE GARDENS
SEAGRAVE ROAD
IFIELD ROAD
IMPERIAL RD
SANDS END LA
SHAFTSBURY CT 1
NIGHTINGALE CT 2
WELLINGTON CT 3
CARLYLE CT 4
TENNYSON CT 5
CURZON CT 6

255
266
135

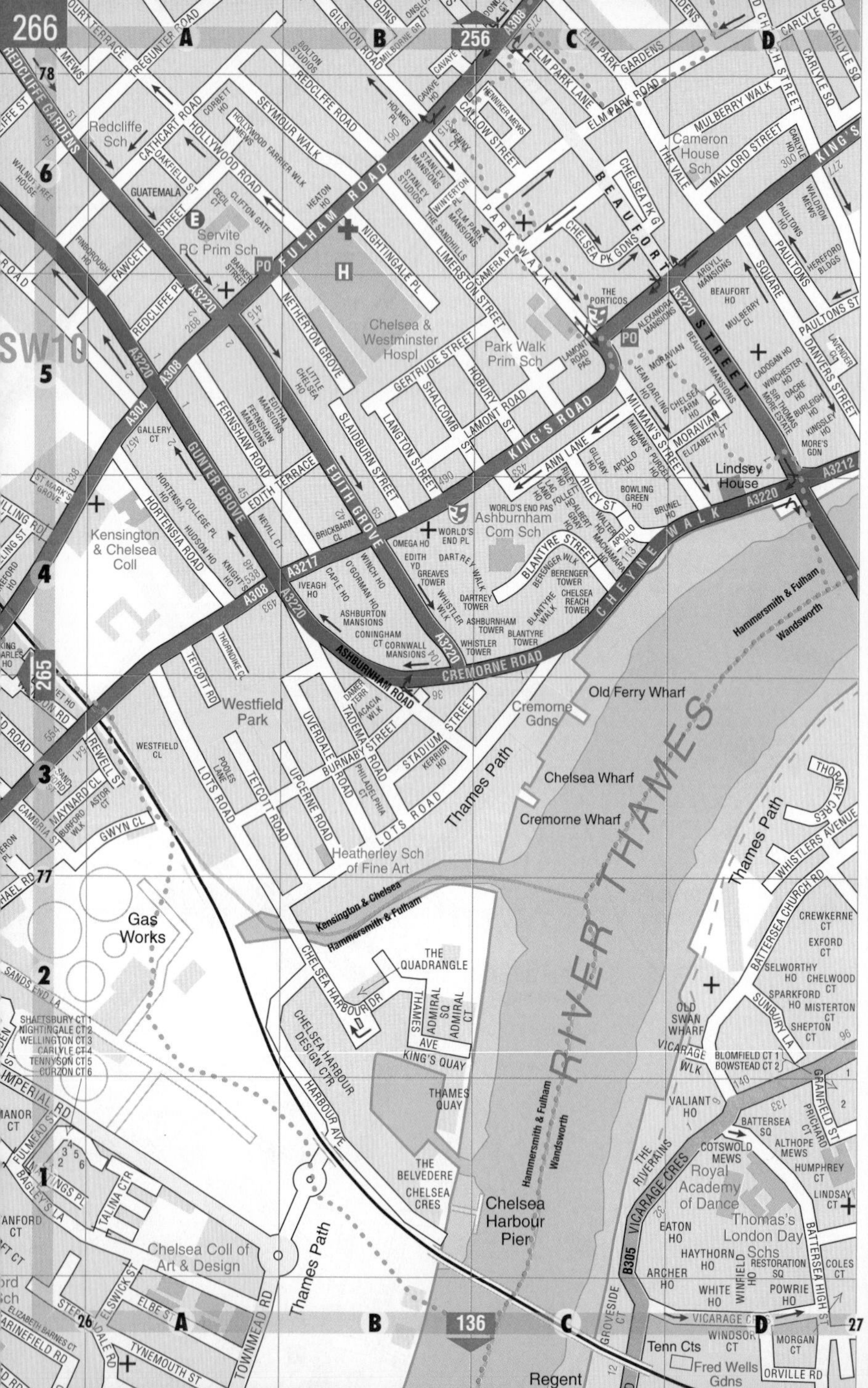

A
B
C
D
256
136
265
SW10
1
2
3
4
5
6
REDCLIFFE GARDENS
TREGUNTER ROAD
GILSTON ROAD
REDCLIFFE ROAD
BOLTON STUDIOS
SEYMOUR WALK
HOLLYWOOD ROAD
CATHCART ROAD
OAKFIELD ST
CLIFTON GATE
CECIL CT
GUATEMALA
Redcliffe Sch
Servite RC Prim Sch
FAWCETT STREET
FINBOROUGH HO
REDCLIFFE PL
BARKER STREET
FULHAM ROAD
NIGHTINGALE PL
NETHERTON GROVE
Chelsea & Westminster Hospl
HOLMES PL
CAVAYE PL
ELM PARK LANE
ELM PARK GARDENS
ELM PARK ROAD
CALLOW STREET
HENNIKER MEWS
STANLEY MANSIONS
STANLEY STUDIOS
WINTERTON PL
THE SANDHILLS
LIMERSTON STREET
CAMERA PL
PARK WALK
BEAUFORT STREET
CHELSEA PK GDNS
CHELSEA PK G
MULBERRY WALK
MALLORD STREET
THE VALE
Cameron House Sch
CARLYLE SQ
CHURCH STREET
KING'S ROAD
PAULTONS SQUARE
PAULTONS ST
DANVERS STREET
HEREFORD BLDGS
WALDRON MEWS
ARGYLL MANSIONS
BEAUFORT HO
MULBERRY CL
BEAUFORT MANSIONS
THE PORTICOS
ALEXANDRA MANSIONS
LAMONT ROAD PAS
Park Walk Prim Sch
GERTRUDE STREET
HOBURY ST
SHALCOMB ST
LAMONT ROAD
LANGTON STREET
SLAIDBURN STREET
EDITH GROVE
EDITH TERRACE
FERNSHAW ROAD
GUNTER GROVE
GALLERY CT
HORTENSIA ROAD
COLLEGE PL
HUDSON HO
Kensington & Chelsea Coll
ST MARK'S GROVE
MILMAN'S STREET
ANN LANE
MORAVIAN CL
MORAVIAN PL
CHELSEA FARM HO
ELIZABETH CT
JEAN DARLING HO
Lindsey House
CHEYNE WALK
RILEY ST
GILLRAY HO
APOLLO HO
BOWLING GREEN HO
BRUNEL HO
Ashburnham Com Sch
WORLD'S END PAS
WORLD'S END PL
BLANTYRE STREET
BERENGER WLK
BERENGER TOWER
CHELSEA REACH TOWER
BLANTYRE TOWER
DARTREY WALK
DARTREY TOWER
WHISTLER WLK
WHISTLER TOWER
ASHBURNHAM TOWER
GREAVES TOWER
EDITH YD
OMEGA HO
WINCH HO
O'GORMAN HO
CAPLE HO
IVEAGH HO
ASHBURTON MANSIONS
CONINGHAM CT
CORNWALL MANSIONS
ASHBURNHAM ROAD
CREMORNE ROAD
THORNDIKE CL
TETCOTT RD
Westfield Park
WESTFIELD CL
LOTS ROAD
POOLES LANE
TETCOTT ROAD
UPCERNE ROAD
UVERDALE ROAD
BURNABY STREET
TADEMA ROAD
DAMER TERR
ACACIA WLK
PHILADELPHIA CT
STADIUM STREET
KERRIER HO
Cremorne Gdns
Old Ferry Wharf
Chelsea Wharf
Cremorne Wharf
Thames Path
RIVER THAMES
Heatherley Sch of Fine Art
Kensington & Chelsea
Hammersmith & Fulham
Wandsworth
Gas Works
REWELL ST
MAYNARD CL
ASTOR CT
BURFORD WLK
GWYN CL
CAMBRIA ST
SANDS END LA
SHAFTSBURY CT 1
NIGHTINGALE CT 2
WELLINGTON CT 3
CARLYLE CT 4
TENNYSON CT 5
CURZON CT 6
IMPERIAL RD
FULMEAD ST
BAGLEY'S LA
TALINA CTR
ELSWICK ST
ELBE ST
STEPHENDALE RD
TYNEMOUTH ST
TOWNMEAD RD
Chelsea Coll of Art & Design
CHELSEA HARBOUR DR
CHELSEA HARBOUR DESIGN CTR
HARBOUR AVE
THE QUADRANGLE
THAMES AVE
ADMIRAL SQ
ADMIRAL CT
KING'S QUAY
THAMES QUAY
THE BELVEDERE
CHELSEA CRES
Chelsea Harbour Pier
THORNEY CRES
WHISTLERS AVENUE
BATTERSEA CHURCH RD
CREWKERNE CT
EXFORD CT
SELWORTHY HO
CHELWOOD CT
SPARKFORD HO
MISTERTON CT
SHEPTON CT
SUNBURY LA
OLD SWAN WHARF
VICARAGE WLK
BLOMFIELD CT 1
BOWSTEAD CT 2
VALIANT HO
GRANFIELD ST
PRICHARD CT
BATTERSEA SQ
ALTHOPE MEWS
HUMPHREY CT
LINDSAY CT
COTSWOLD MEWS
Royal Academy of Dance
Thomas's London Day Schs
THE RIVERAINS
VICARAGE CRES
EATON HO
HAYTHORN HO
WINFIELD HO
RESTORATION SQ
COLES CT
ARCHER HO
WHITE HO
POWRIE HO
BATTERSEA HIGH ST
GROVESIDE CT
WINDSOR CT
MORGAN CT
Tenn Cts
Fred Wells Gdns
ORVILLE RD
Regent
A308
A3220
A3217
A304
A3212
B305

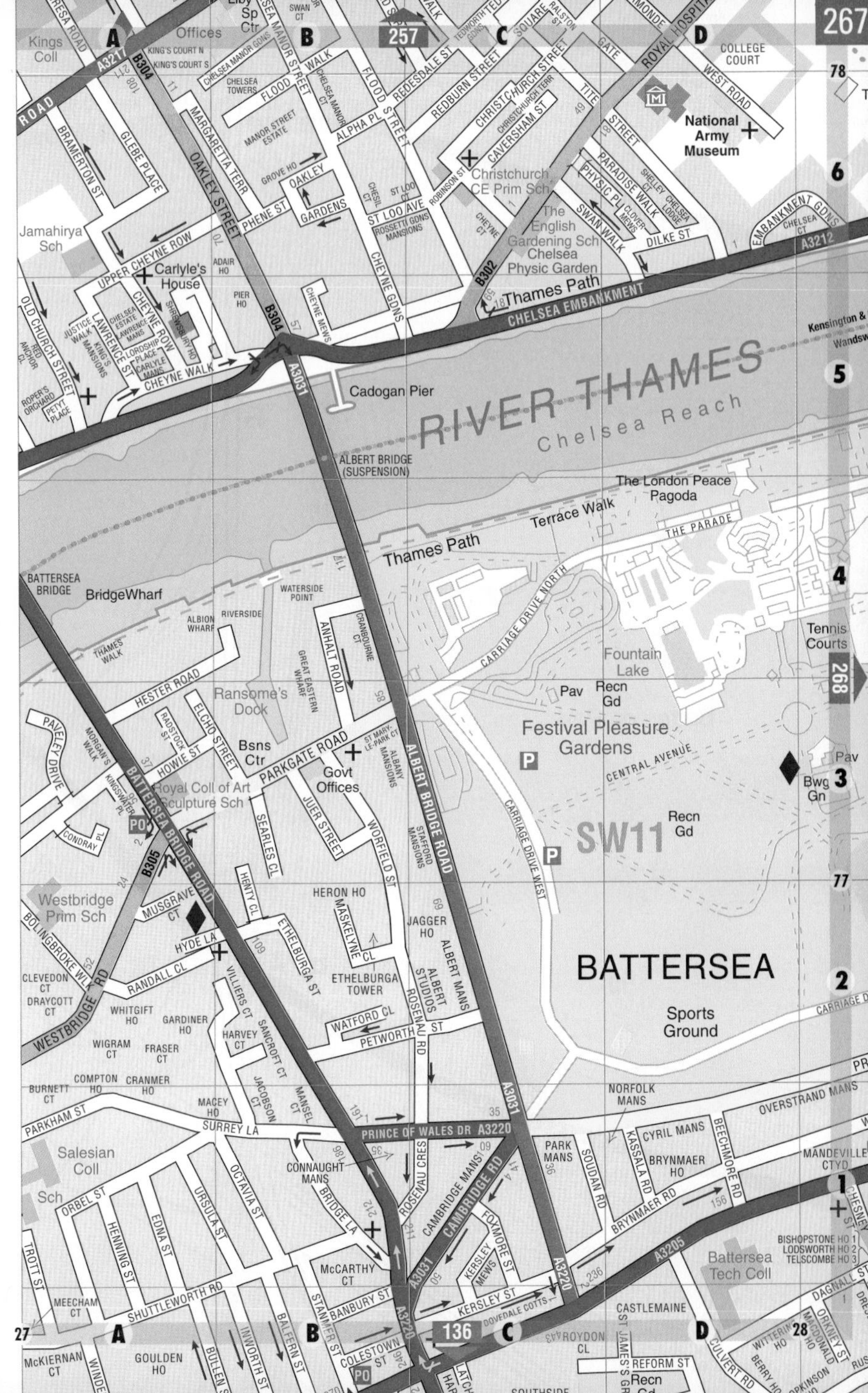

RIVER THAMES
Chelsea Reach
BATTERSEA
SW11
Festival Pleasure Gardens
National Army Museum
Chelsea Physic Garden
Carlyle's House
Cadogan Pier
ALBERT BRIDGE (SUSPENSION)
The London Peace Pagoda
Thames Path
Terrace Walk
BridgeWharf
Ransome's Dock
Fountain Lake
Sports Ground
CHELSEA EMBANKMENT
ALBERT BRIDGE ROAD
BATTERSEA BRIDGE ROAD
OAKLEY STREET
CHEYNE WALK
PRINCE OF WALES DR A3220
PARKGATE ROAD
Battersea Tech Coll
Salesian Coll
Westbridge Prim Sch
Royal Coll of Art Sculpture Sch
Kensington & C
Wandsw
257
268
136

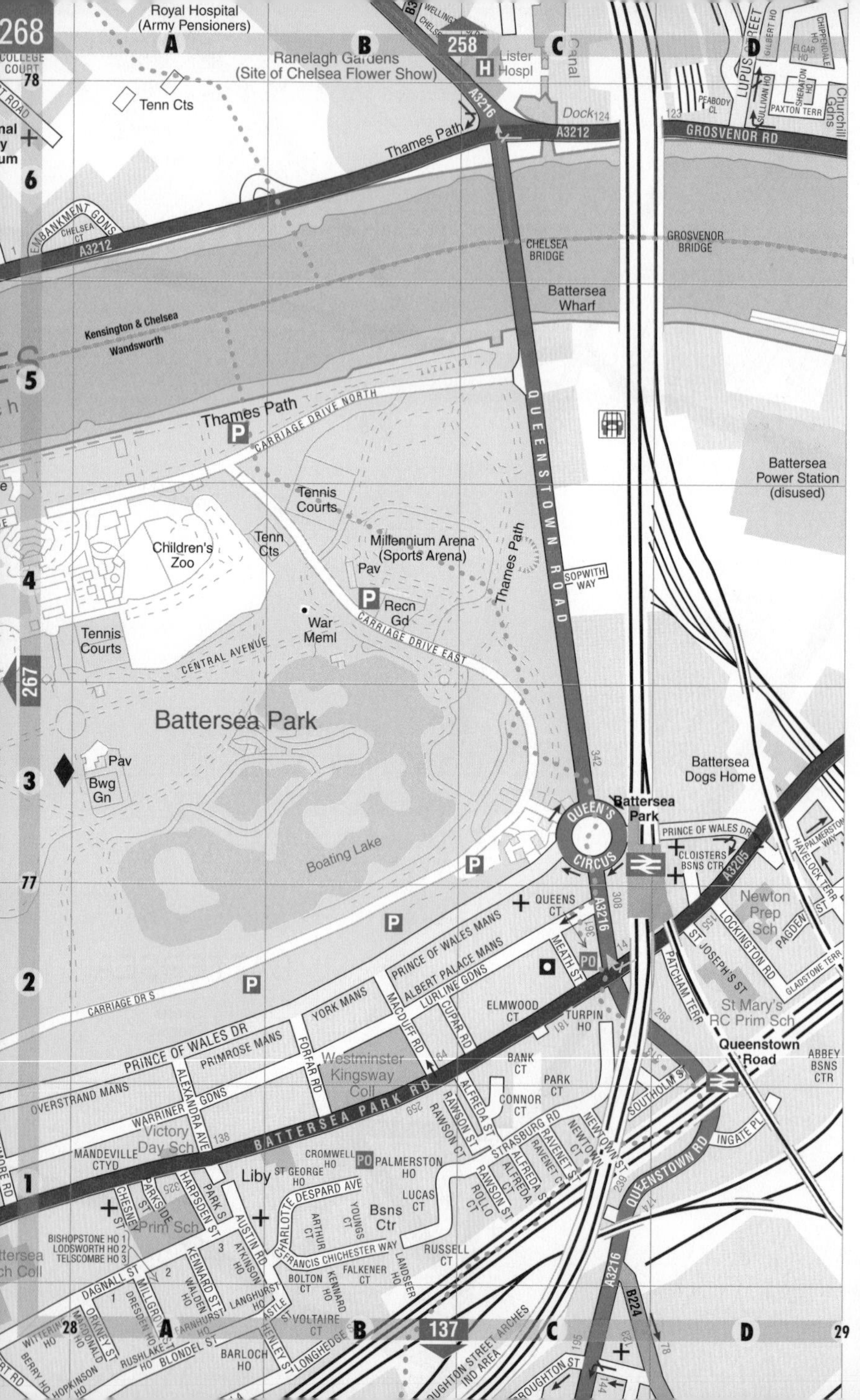
Royal Hospital (Army Pensioners)
Ranelagh Gardens (Site of Chelsea Flower Show)
Lister Hospl
Canal
Dock
Tenn Cts
Thames Path
A3216
A3212
GROSVENOR RD
LUPUS STREET
PEABODY CL
PAXTON TERR
Churchill Gdns
EMBANKMENT GDNS
CHELSEA CT
CHELSEA BRIDGE
GROSVENOR BRIDGE
Battersea Wharf
Kensington & Chelsea
Wandsworth
Thames Path
CARRIAGE DRIVE NORTH
QUEENSTOWN ROAD
Battersea Power Station (disused)
Tennis Courts
Children's Zoo
Tenn Cts
Millennium Arena (Sports Arena)
Pav
Recn Gd
SOPWITH WAY
War Meml
CARRIAGE DRIVE EAST
CENTRAL AVENUE
Tennis Courts
Battersea Park
Pav
Bwg Gn
Boating Lake
Battersea Dogs Home
Battersea Park
QUEEN'S CIRCUS
PRINCE OF WALES DR
CLOISTERS BSNS CTR
A3205
QUEENS CT
Newton Prep Sch
LOCKINGTON RD
PAGDEN ST
HAVELOCK TERR
ST JOSEPH'S ST
PATCHAM TERR
GLADSTONE TERR
St Mary's RC Prim Sch
PRINCE OF WALES MANS
ALBERT PALACE MANS
LURLINE GDNS
MEATH ST
ELMWOOD CT
TURPIN HO
CARRIAGE DR S
YORK MANS
MACDUFF RD
CUPAR RD
PRINCE OF WALES DR
PRIMROSE MANS
FORFAR RD
Westminster Kingsway Coll
BATTERSEA PARK RD
BANK CT
PARK CT
Queenstown Road
ABBEY BSNS CTR
OVERSTRAND MANS
ALEXANDRA AVE
WARRINER GDNS
Victory Day Sch
ALFREDA ST
RAWSON ST
CONNOR CT
SOUTHOLM ST
STRASBURG RD
RAVENET ST
NEWTOWN ST
INGATE PL
QUEENSTOWN RD
MANDEVILLE CTYD
Liby
CROMWELL HO
PALMERSTON HO
ST GEORGE HO
CHARLOTTE DESPARD AVE
LUCAS CT
ROLLO CT
Bsns Ctr
CHESNEY ST
PARKSIDE ST
HARPSDEN ST
PARK S
Prim Sch
AUSTIN RD
ARTHUR CT
YOUNGS CT
FRANCIS CHICHESTER WAY
RUSSELL CT
BISHOPSTONE HO 1
LODSWORTH HO 2
TELSCOMBE HO 3
KENNARD ST
ATKINSON HO
WALDEN HO
DAGNALL ST
MILLGROVE
DRESDEN HO
LANGHURST HO
BOLTON CT
FALKENER CT
LANDSEER HO
B224
ORKNEY ST
MACDONALD HO
FARNHURST HO
ASTLE ST
HENLEY ST
VOLTAIRE CT
WITTERING HO
BERRY HO
HOPKINSON HO
RUSHLAKE HO
BLONDEL ST
BARLOCH HO
LONGHEDGE ST
BROUGHTON STREET ARCHES IND AREA
BROUGHTON ST
258
267
137
A B C D
28 29
1 2 3 4 5 6
77 78

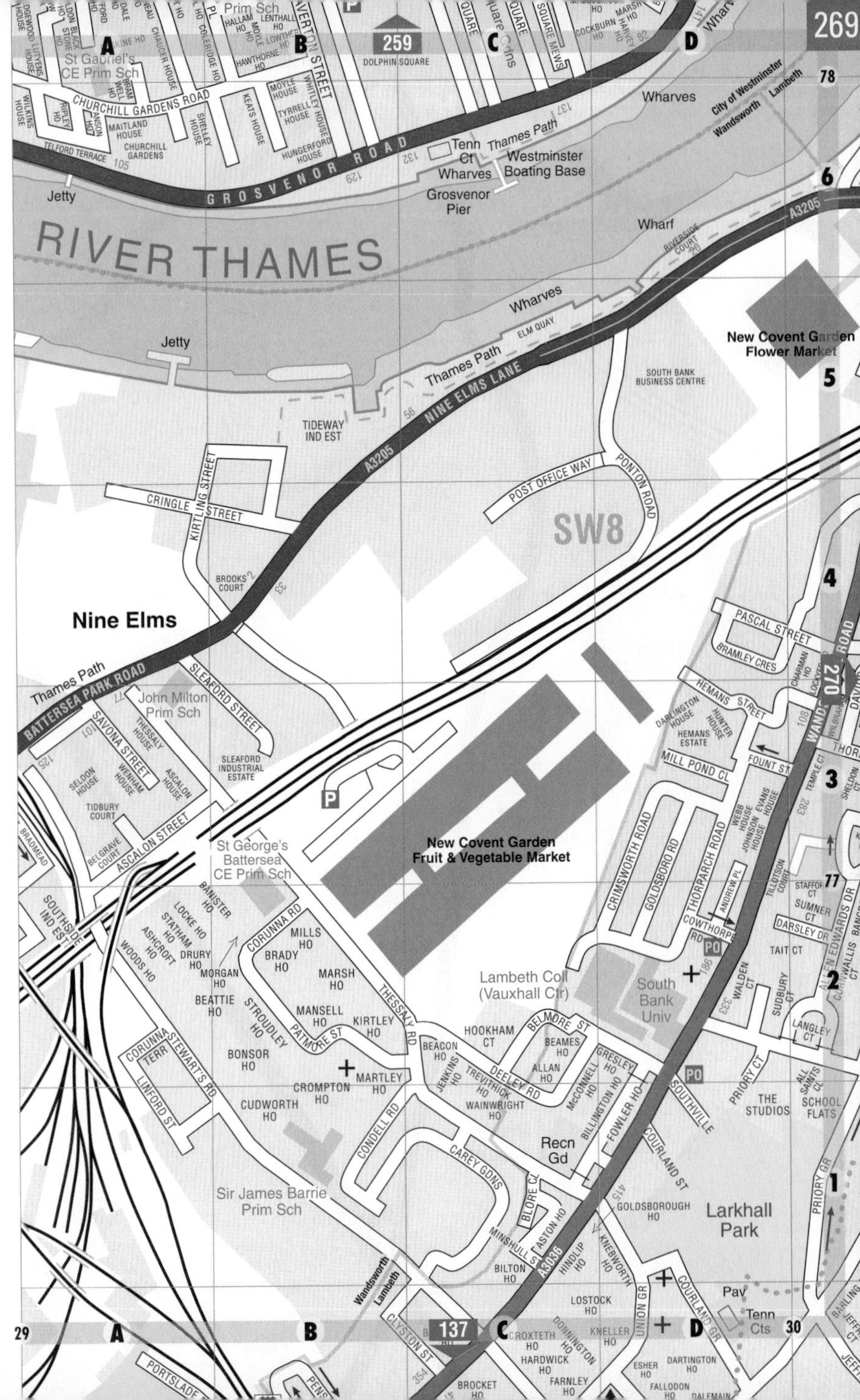

259
DOLPHIN SQUARE
St Gabriel's CE Prim Sch
CHURCHILL GARDENS ROAD
CHURCHILL GARDENS
TELFORD TERRACE
GROSVENOR ROAD
Tenn Ct
Thames Path
Westminster Boating Base
Wharves
Grosvenor Pier
Jetty
RIVER THAMES
Wharf
City of Westminster
Lambeth
Wandsworth
RIVERSIDE COURT
A3205
Wharves
ELM QUAY
New Covent Garden Flower Market
Jetty
Thames Path
NINE ELMS LANE
SOUTH BANK BUSINESS CENTRE
TIDEWAY IND EST
CRINGLE STREET
KIRTLING STREET
POST OFFICE WAY
PONTON ROAD
SW8
BROOKS COURT
Nine Elms
PASCAL STREET
BRAMLEY CRES
HEMANS STREET
HEMANS ESTATE
Thames Path
BATTERSEA PARK ROAD
John Milton Prim Sch
SLEAFORD STREET
SAVONA STREET
SLEAFORD INDUSTRIAL ESTATE
MILL POND CL
FOUNT ST
270
ASCALON STREET
TIDBURY COURT
BELGRAVE COURT
St George's Battersea CE Prim Sch
New Covent Garden Fruit & Vegetable Market
CRIMSWORTH ROAD
GOLDSBORO RD
THORPARCH ROAD
ANDREW PL
COWTHORPE RD
SOUTHSIDE IND EST
CORUNNA RD
Lambeth Coll (Vauxhall Ctr)
South Bank Univ
THESSALY RD
PATMORE ST
BELMORE ST
DEELEY RD
CORUNNA TERR
STEWART'S RD
LINFORD ST
SOUTHVILLE
COURLAND ST
THE STUDIOS
SCHOOL FLATS
Recn Gd
CONDELL RD
CAREY GDNS
Sir James Barrie Prim Sch
Larkhall Park
A3036
Wandsworth
Lambeth
COURLAND GR
UNION GR
Tenn Cts
Pav
CLYSTON ST
137
PORTSLADE
A
B
C
D
1
2
3
4
5
6
29
30
77
78

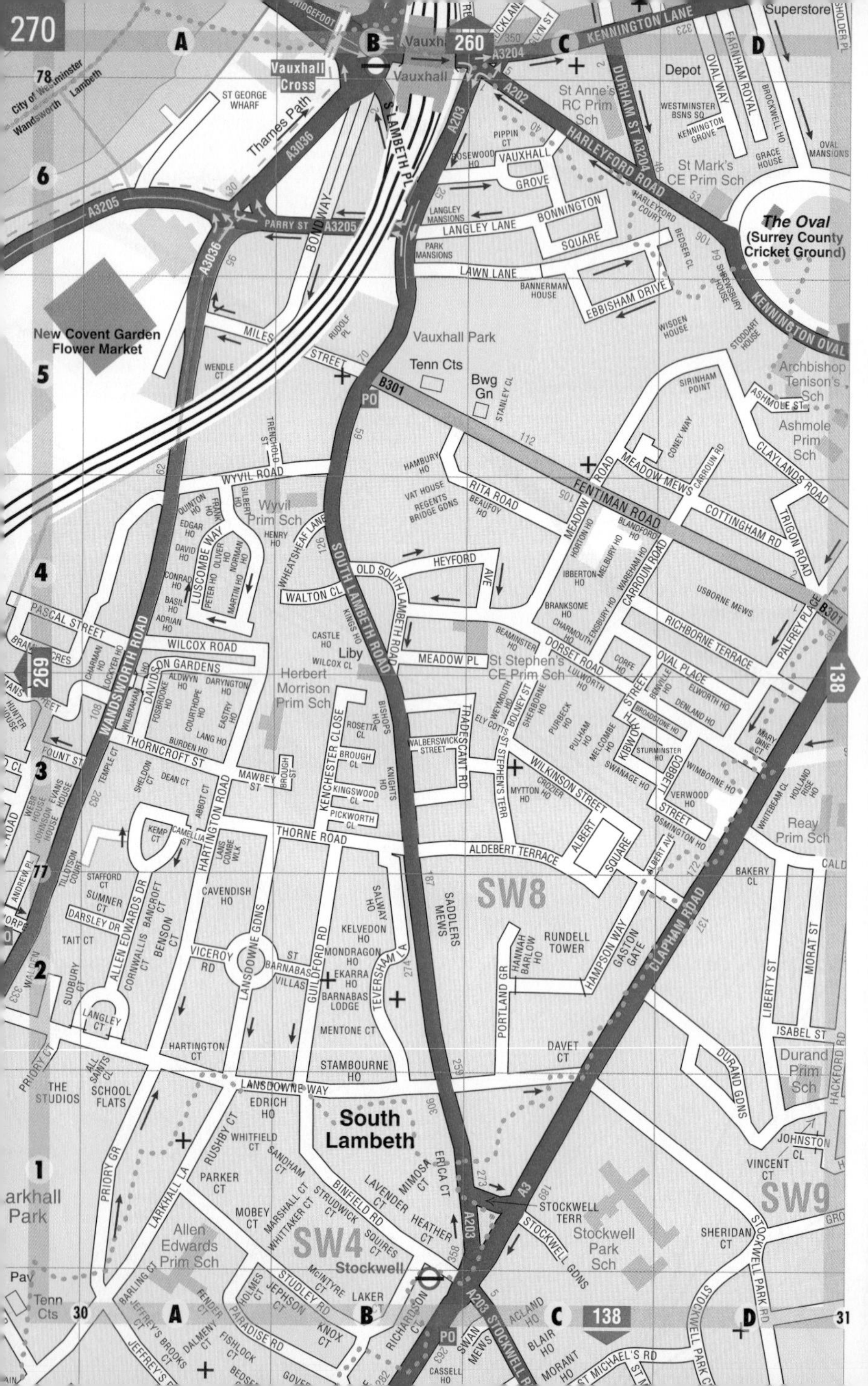
Vauxhall Cross
Vauxhall
Thames Path
ST GEORGE WHARF
City of Westminster
Wandsworth
Lambeth
KENNINGTON LANE
DURHAM ST
HARLEYFORD ROAD
The Oval (Surrey County Cricket Ground)
KENNINGTON OVAL
St Anne's RC Prim Sch
St Mark's CE Prim Sch
Depot
Superstore
OVAL WAY
FARNHAM ROYAL
BROCKWELL HO
WESTMINSTER BSNS SQ
KENNINGTON GROVE
GRACE HOUSE
OVAL MANSIONS
VAUXHALL GROVE
BONNINGTON SQUARE
LANGLEY LANE
LANGLEY MANSIONS
PARK MANSIONS
LAWN LANE
BANNERMAN HOUSE
EBBISHAM DRIVE
HARLEYFORD COURT
BEDSER CL
SHREWSBURY HOUSE
WISDEN HOUSE
STODDART HOUSE
PIPPIN CT
ROSEWOOD HO
S LAMBETH PL
PARRY ST
BONDWAY
MILES ST
WENDLE CT
RUDOLF PL
New Covent Garden Flower Market
Vauxhall Park
Tenn Cts
Bwg Gn
STANLEY CL
Archbishop Tenison's Sch
Ashmole Prim Sch
ASHMOLE ST
CLAYLANDS ROAD
SIRINHAM POINT
CONEY WAY
MEADOW ROAD
MEADOW MEWS
CARROUN RD
FENTIMAN ROAD
COTTINGHAM RD
TRIGON ROAD
USBORNE MEWS
RICHBORNE TERRACE
PALFREY PLACE
OVAL PLACE
RITA ROAD
HAMBURY HO
VAT HOUSE
REGENTS BRIDGE GDNS
BEAUFOY HO
TRENCHOLD ST
WYVIL ROAD
Wyvil Prim Sch
HENRY HO
WHEATSHEAF LANE
SOUTH LAMBETH ROAD
HEYFORD AVE
OLD SOUTH LAMBETH ROAD
WALTON CL
KINGS HO
CASTLE HO
WILCOX CL
Liby
MEADOW PL
St Stephen's CE Prim Sch
BEAMINSTER HO
DORSET ROAD
BRANKSOME HO
CHARMOUTH HO
IBBERTON HO
HORTON HO
MELBURY HO
BLANDFORD HO
WAREHAM HO
ENSBURY HO
CORFE HO
LULWORTH HO
QUINTON HO
FRANK HO
GILBERT HO
EDGAR HO
DAVID HO
LUSCOMBE WAY
CONRAD HO
BASIL HO
ADRIAN HO
PETER HO
OLIVER HO
NORMAN HO
MARTIN HO
PASCAL STREET
WILCOX ROAD
WANDSWORTH ROAD
DAVIDSON GARDENS
ALDWYN HO
DARYNGTON HO
FOSBROOKE HO
COURTHOPE HO
EASTRY HO
LANG HO
BURDEN HO
WILBRAHAM HO
CHARMAN HO
LOCKYER HO
THORNCROFT ST
FOUNT ST
TEMPLE CT
SHELDON CT
DEAN CT
ABBOT CT
HARTINGTON ROAD
MAWBEY ST
BROUGH ST
Herbert Morrison Prim Sch
KENCHESTER CLOSE
ROSETTA CL
BROUGH CL
KINGSWOOD CL
PICKWORTH CL
BISHOPS HO
KNIGHTS HO
WALBERSWICK STREET
TRADESCANT RD
ELY COTTS
WEYMOUTH HO
BOLNEY ST
ST STEPHEN'S TERR
SHERBORNE HO
PURBECK HO
PULHAM HO
MELCOMBE HO
KIBWORTH STREET
BROADSTONE HO
STURMINSTER HO
SWANAGE HO
COBBETT STREET
BENVILLE HO
ELWORTH HO
DENLAND HO
WIMBORNE HO
VERWOOD HO
OSMINGTON HO
MARY DINE CT
WILKINSON STREET
CROZIER HO
MYTTON HO
ALBERT SQUARE
ALBERT AVE
WHITEBEAM CL
HOLLAND RISE HO
Reay Prim Sch
BAKERY CL
WEBB HOUSE
EVANS HOUSE
JOHNSON HOUSE
KEMP CT
CAMELLIA ST
THORNE ROAD
ALDEBERT TERRACE
LANSCOMBE WLK
TILLOTSON COURT
ANDREW PL
STAFFORD CT
SUMNER CT
DARSLEY DR
TAIT CT
ALLEN EDWARDS DR
BANCROFT CT
CORNWALLIS CT
BENSON CT
CAVENDISH HO
VICEROY RD
LANSDOWNE GDNS
ST BARNABAS VILLAS
GUILDFORD RD
SALWAY HO
KELVEDON HO
MONDRAGON HO
EKARRA HO
BARNABAS LODGE
TEVERSHAM LA
MENTONE CT
STAMBOURNE HO
SADDLERS MEWS
SW8
HANNAH BARLOW HO
RUNDELL TOWER
PORTLAND GR
HAMPSON WAY
GASTON GATE
CLAPHAM ROAD
LIBERTY ST
MORAT ST
ISABEL ST
DURAND GDNS
Durand Prim Sch
HACKFORD RD
WALDEN
SUDBURY CT
LANGLEY CT
HARTINGTON CT
DAVET CT
PRIORY CT
THE STUDIOS
ALL SAINTS CL
SCHOOL FLATS
LANSDOWNE WAY
EDRICH HO
South Lambeth
RUSHBY CT
WHITFIELD CT
SANDHAM CT
PARKER CT
BINFIELD RD
LAVENDER CT
MIMOSA CT
ERICA CT
JOHNSTON CL
VINCENT CT
SW9
Larkhall Park
PRIORY GR
LARKHALL LA
MOBEY CT
MARSHALL CT
WHITTAKER CT
STRUDWICK CT
SQUIRES CT
HEATHER CT
STOCKWELL TERR
STOCKWELL GDNS
Stockwell Park Sch
SHERIDAN CT
STOCKWELL PARK RD
Allen Edwards Prim Sch
SW4
Stockwell
McINTYRE CT
LAKER CT
Pav
Tenn Cts
BARLING CT
JEFFREY'S CT
FENDER CT
HOLMES CT
JEPHSON CT
STUDLEY RD
KNOX CT
RICHARDSON CT
PARADISE RD
DALMENY CT
FISHLOCK CT
BROOKS CT
STOCKWELL RD
ACLAND HO
BLAIR HO
MORANT HO
ST MICHAEL'S RD
SWAN MEWS
CASSELL HO
STOCKWELL PARK CRES
A3205
A3036
A3204
A202
A203
A3
B301
260
269
138
PO
A
B
C
D
1
2
3
4
5
6
30
31
77
78

Index

Church Rd **6** Beckenham BR2..........**53** C6 **228** C6

Place name
May be abbreviated on the map

Location number
Present when a number indicates the place's position in a crowded area of mapping

Locality, town or village
Shown when more than one place (outside London postal districts) has the same name

Postcode district
District for the indexed place

Standard scale reference
Page number and grid reference for the standard mapping

Enlarged scale reference
Page number and grid reference for the central London enlarged mapping, underlined in red

Public and commercial buildings are highlighted in magenta
Places of interest are highlighted in blue with a star★

Index of localities, towns and villages

A

Abbey Wood 124 B3
Acton 111 B5
Acton Green 111 A2
Addington 223 C3
Addiscombe 206 A1
Aldborough Hatch ...57 C5
Aldersbrook 77 C6
Alperton 88 A6
Anerley 184 B2
Arkley 12 A6
Ashford 170 B4
Ashford Common ..171 B4
Avery Hill 167 B5

B

Balham 159 A3
Bandonhill 219 D3
Barbican 95 A2
Barking 79 B1
Barkingside 57 A6
Barnes 133 D4
Barnet 13 B6
Barnet Gate 11 D5
Barnsbury 72 A1
Battersea 136 D4
Bayswater 114 A6
Beckenham 185 C1
Beckton 100 D2
Becontree 81 A4
Beddington 220 A6
Beddington Corner .203 A2
Bedford Park 111 C3
Belgravia 115 B2
Bell Green 163 B1
Bellingham 185 C5
Belmont 25 B2
Belsize Park 70 C3
Belvedere 125 D2
Benhilton 218 A5
Bermondsey 118 A4
Berrylands 198 C3
Bethnal Green 96 B4
Bexley 146 B1
Bexleyheath 147 B2
Bickley 188 B1
Blackfen 168 A5
Blackheath 142 C2
Blackheath Park ...143 A1
Blackheath Vale ...142 D3
Blackwall 120 B6
Bloomsbury 93 D2
Borehamwood 11 C5
Borough The 117 A4
Bow 97 B5
Bow Common 97 D2
Bowes Park 32 A4
Brent Cross 46 D2
Brentford 131 B6
Brentford End 131 C4
Brimsdown 7 B3
Brixton 138 C2
Broad Green 204 D3
Broadgate 95 C2
Brockley 141 B1
Bromley 186 C2
Bromley (Tower Hamlets) ...97 D4
Bromley Common ..210 A3
Bromley Park 186 D2
Brompton 114 B3
Brondesbury 69 A2
Brondesbury Park ...90 D6
Brook Green 112 D2
Broom Hill 211 D2
Brunswick Park 15 A1
Buckhurst Hill 21 C2
Burnt Oak 27 B3
Bush Hill Park 17 C5
Bushey 8 A2
Bushey Heath 8 C4
Bushey Mead 200 D6

C

Camberwell 139 A4
Camden Town 71 B1
Canary Wharf 119 D5
Canning Town 99 B1
Canonbury 73 A2
Canons Park 26 A3
Carshalton 218 C4
Carshalton Beeches 218 D1
Carshalton on the Hill 219 B1
Castle Green 102 C6
Catford 163 C3
Chadwell Heath 58 D4
Charlton (Greenwich) 143 D6
Charlton (Surrey) ..171 B1
Chattern Hill 170 D6
Cheam 217 B3
Chelsea 114 C1
Chertsey Meads ...192 A1
Chessington 214 A2
Child's Hill 69 C6
Chingford 20 C3
Chingford Green 20 A4
Chingford Hatch 36 B6
Chipping Barnet 1 B1
Chislehurst 189 C3
Chislehurst West ..188 C4
Chiswick 111 D1
Church End (Barnet) 29 C1
Church End (Brent) .67 D2
City of London 117 A6
Clapham 137 B2
Clapham Common .137 B1
Clapham Junction .136 C1
Clapham Park 159 D6
Clapton Park 74 D4
Clay Hill 5 A6
Claygate 212 D1
Clayhall 56 B6
Clerkenwell 94 D3
Cockfosters 2 D1
Colham Green 82 C2
Colindale 45 C6
College Park 90 B4
Collier's Wood 180 C4
Colney Hatch 30 C4
Coney Hall 224 D5
Coombe 177 B3
Copse Hill 178 B3
Cottenham Park ...178 B2
Covent Garden 116 A6
Cowley Peachy 82 A2
Cranbrook 56 C1
Cranford 128 C4
Cranley Gardens 49 B5
Creekmouth 101 D2
Cricklewood 68 D4
Crofton 227 B6
Crooked Billet 178 C4
Crouch End 49 D3
Croydon 221 B5
Crystal Palace 184 A5
Cubitt Town 120 A2
Custom House 121 C6
Cyprus 122 C6

D

Dagenham 81 D1
Dalston 74 A2
Dartmouth Park 71 B5
De Beauvoir Town ...73 C1
Deacons Hill 10 C5
Deptford 140 D6
Dollis Hill 68 B5
Dormer's Wells 107 C6
Downham 186 C5
Ducks Island 12 D5
Dudden Hill 68 A3
Dulwich 161 C1
Dulwich Village 161 C4

E

Ealing 109 D6
Earl's Court 113 C1
Earlsfield 158 A3
East Acton 111 C5
East Barnet 14 D4
East Bedfont 149 C3
East Dulwich 162 A6
East Finchley 48 B5
East Ham 100 A5
East Molesey 196 A4
East Sheen 133 B1
East Wickham 146 A5
Eastbury 22 A5
Eastcote 40 C3
Eastcote Village 40 B4
Eden Park 207 C5
Edgware 26 C6
Edgware Bury 10 B3
Edmonton 33 D6
Elmers End 206 D6
Elmstead 188 A5
Elstree 10 A5
Eltham 166 B6
Enfield 6 B2
Enfield Highway 6 C3
Enfield Lock 7 B6
Enfield Town 5 B1
Enfield Wash 6 D5
Erith 147 D6
Esher 212 A4
Euston 93 C4
Ewell 215 C1

F

Fair Cross 79 D3
Falconwood 145 C1
Farnborough 227 B3
Farthing Street 226 B1
Feltham 150 A3
Felthamhill 171 D5
Finchley 29 D3
Finsbury 94 C4
Finsbury Park 50 D1
Fitzrovia 93 C1
Foots Cray 190 B4
Forest Gate 77 A3
Forest Hill 163 A3
Fortis Green 48 D5
Forty Hill 5 D4
Friday Hill 20 C1
Friern Barnet 31 A6
Fulham 134 D4
Furzedown 181 B6

G

Gants Hill 56 C3
Globe Town 96 D4
Golders Green 47 B4
Goodmayes 58 B1
Gospel Oak 70 D2
Grahame Park 27 C2
Grange Park 16 C6
Green Street Green 227 C2
Greenford 86 A4
Greenhill 42 D4
Greenwich 142 C6
Grove Park (Hounslow) 133 A4
Grove Park (Lewisham) 165 B1
Gunnersbury 110 D2

H

Hackbridge 219 B6
Hackney 74 B2
Hackney Wick 75 C2
Hadley 1 B2
Hadley Wood 2 B5
Haggerston 95 D5
Hale End 36 C4
Ham 153 C1
Hammersmith 112 C2
Hampstead 70 A3
Hampstead Garden Suburb 47 D4
Hampton 173 C1
Hampton Court 196 C5
Hampton Hill 174 A5
Hampton Wick 175 D3
Hanwell 108 D5
Hanworth 172 D6
Harlesden 89 D6
Harlington 127 A6
Harmondsworth 126 A6
Harringay 50 D4
Harrow 42 B3
Harrow on the Hill ..42 C1
Harrow Weald 24 B2
Hatch End 23 A3
Hatton 127 D1
Hayes (Bromley) ...209 A2
Hayes (Hillingdon) 83 C1
Hayes End 83 B3
Hayes Town 106 B5
Headstone 41 D5
Hendon 46 C3
Herne Hill 161 A6
Heston 129 B5
High Barnet 1 A2
Higham Hill 35 A2
Highams Park 36 A3
Highbury 72 D4
Highgate 49 A2
Hillingdon 82 D5
Hillingdon Heath 82 D2
Hinchley Wood 212 D6
Hither Green 164 C5
Holborn 94 C2
Homerton 74 D1
Honor Oak 162 C6
Hook 214 A4
Hornsey 50 A5
Hornsey Vale 50 B4
Hounslow 129 C3
Hounslow West 128 D2
Hoxton 95 C5
Hurst Park 174 A1
Hyde Park 114 D5
Hyde The 45 D4

I

Ickenham 60 C4
Ilford 78 D6
Isle of Dogs 120 A2
Isleworth 131 B2
Islington 72 D2

K

Kennington 116 C1
Kensal Green 90 C4
Kensal Rise 91 A5
Kensal Town 91 A3
Kensington 113 C4
Kentish Town 71 C3
Kenton 43 C3
Keston 225 D4
Keston Mark 225 D6
Kew 132 C6
Kidbrooke 143 C3
Kilburn 91 B6
King's Cross 94 A5
Kingsbury 45 B3
Kingsland 73 C2
Kingston Upon Thames 197 C6
Kingston Vale 177 B6
Kitts End 1 A5
Knightsbridge 114 C4

L

Ladywell 163 C6
Lambeth 116 B4
Lampton 129 D4
Lea Bridge 74 D5
Lee 74 D5
Lessness Heath 125 D1
Lewisham 142 A1
Leyton 76 B5
Leytonstone 54 D1
Limehouse 119 A6
Lisson Green 92 C3
Lisson Grove 92 B2
Little Heath 58 B5
Little Ilford 78 C3
Little Stanmore 26 B2
Littleton 192 C6
Littleton Common ..171 B3
Locksbottom 226 D5
London City Airport 122 B5
Long Ditton 197 C1
Longlands 167 B1
Loughton 21 D5
Lower Clapton 74 C4
Lower Edmonton 18 B1
Lower Feltham 149 D1
Lower Green 195 D1
Lower Halliford 193 C3
Lower Holloway 72 A3
Lower Morden 201 A2
Lower Place 89 A5
Lower Sydenham ..185 A6
Loxford 79 A3

M

Maida Vale 91 D4
Maitland Park 71 A2

Manor Park 78 A4
Marylebone 93 B1
Mayfair 115 B6
Merton 179 C2
Merton Park 179 C1
Mile End 97 A3
Mill Hill 28 B5
Mill Meads 98 B5
Millwall 119 C3
Mitcham 202 D5
Monken Hadley 1 A3
Monks Orchard 207 A3
Morden 201 D3
Morden Park 201 A3
Mortlake 133 A2
Motspur Park 200 A3
Mottingham 165 D2
Muswell Hill 49 A6

N

Nash 225 A2
Neasden 67 B4
New Addington 224 B1
New Barnet 14 A6
New Beckenham 185 A4
New Charlton 121 C2
New Cross 141 B4
New Cross Gate 140 D4
New Eltham 167 A2
New Malden 199 D5
New Southgate 31 C6
Newbury Park 57 B3
Newham 98 D4
Newington 116 D2
Newyears Green 38 B3
Nine Elms 137 C5
Noel Park 32 D1
Norbiton 176 C1
Norbury 182 C2
North Acton 89 B4
North Cheam 216 C6
North Cray 169 B1
North End 70 A6
North Feltham 150 B6
North Finchley 30 A6
North Harrow 41 D2
North Hillingdon 61 A2
North Hyde 107 A1
North Kensington 90 D2
North Sheen 132 C3
North Wembley 65 C6
North Woolwich 122 D4
Northolt 63 C1
Northwood 22 A3
Northwood Hills 22 A1
Norwood Green 107 C2
Norwood New Town 183 A4
Notting Hill 113 B6
Nower Hill 41 B6
Nunhead 140 C1

O

Oakleigh Park 14 B3
Oakwood 15 D6
Old Bexley 169 D4
Old Ford 97 B6
Old Malden 199 C1
Old Oak Common 89 D3
Orpington 227 D6
Osidge 15 C3
Osterley 130 B5

P

Paddington 92 A2
Palmers Green 16 A1
Park Langley 208 B4
Park Royal 88 D4
Parsons Green 135 C4
Peckham 140 A4
Penge 184 D4
Pentonville 94 B5
Perivale 87 B5
Petersham 153 D3
Petts Wood 211 B5
Pimlico 115 C1
Pinner 41 A6
Pinner Green 22 C1
Pinnerwood Park 22 C3
Plaistow (Bromley) 187 A4
Plaistow (Newham) 99 B4
Plashet 78 A2
Plumstead 123 C2
Plumstead Common 145 D6
Ponders End 18 D6
Poplar 97 C1
Preston 44 A1
Primrose Hill 70 D1
Putney 156 C6
Putney Heath 156 C6
Putney Vale 156 A1

Q

Queensbury 44 B6

R

Ratcliff 118 D6
Rayners Lane 41 B1
Raynes Park 200 C6
Redbridge 55 D3
Regent's Park 93 B4
Richmond 154 A6
Richmond Hill 154 A5
Richmond Park 155 A3
Roehampton 155 C4
Romford 59 C5
Rosehill 202 A1
Rotherhithe 118 D3
Roundshaw 220 B1
Roxeth 64 A6
Ruislip 39 B2
Ruislip Common 39 B4
Ruislip Gardens 61 D5
Ruislip Manor 40 A1
Ruxley 191 A3

S

Sands End 136 A2
Seething Wells 197 D3
Selhurst 205 B4
Selsdon 223 A1
Seven Kings 57 D2
Sewardstonebury 20 C6
Shacklewell 73 D4
Shadwell 118 C6
Shepherd's Bush 112 B5
Shepperton 193 A3
Shepperton Green 192 D5
Shirley 206 C1
Shooters Hill 145 A4
Shoreditch 95 B5
Shortlands 208 C6
Sidcup 190 A5
Silvertown 121 C4
Sipson 126 C6
Snaresbrook 54 D6
Soho 93 D1
Somers Town 93 D4
South Acton 110 D3
South Bank 116 B4
South Beddington 219 C2
South Bromley 98 B2
South Croydon 221 B1
South Hackney 96 C6
South Hampstead 70 A1
South Harrow 63 D5
South Kensington 114 A1
South Lambeth 138 A4
South Norwood 205 C6
South Oxhey 22 B6
South Ruislip 62 D4
South Tottenham 51 D4
South Wimbledon 179 D4
Southall 107 A5
Southborough (Bromley) 210 B3
Southborough (Kingston Upon Thames) 197 D1
Southend 186 B6
Southfields 157 C3
Southgate 16 B4
Southwark 117 B5
Spitalfields 95 D2
Spring Grove 130 C3
Spring Park 223 B5
St George in the East 118 A6
St Giles 94 A1
St Helier 202 B2
St James 115 C5
St John's 141 C3
St John's Wood 92 B5
St Luke's 95 A3
St Margarets 153 A5
St Pancras 94 A4
St Paul's Cray 190 A1
Stamford Hill 51 C1
Stanmore 25 B2
Stanwell 148 A3
Stepney 96 D2
Stockwell 138 A2
Stoke Newington 73 C6
Stonebridge 89 A6
Stoneleigh 216 A3
Strand 116 B6
Strand on the Green 132 C6
Stratford 76 A1
Stratford Marsh 97 D6
Stratford New Town 76 A3
Strawberry Hill 152 D1
Streatham 182 A4
Streatham Hill 160 A3
Streatham Park 181 C6
Streatham Vale 181 D3
Stroud Green 50 C3
Sudbury 65 A4
Summerstown 158 A1
Sunbury 194 B6
Sunbury Common 171 D3
Sundridge 187 C4
Surbiton 198 A2
Sutton 218 A1
Syon Park 131 B4

T

Teddington 175 C5
Temple Mills 75 D3
Thames Ditton 197 B2
Thamesmead 124 A5
Thornton Heath 204 D3
Tokyngton 66 D2
Tolworth 214 C6
Tooting 180 D4
Tooting Graveney 180 B5
Tottenham 33 D1
Tottenham Hale 52 A6
Totteridge 13 C3
Tower Hamlets 97 B2
Tufnell Park 71 D4
Tulse Hill 160 D4
Twickenham 152 D4

U

Underhill 13 C6
Upper Clapton 52 B1
Upper Edmonton 34 B5
Upper Elmers End 207 B4
Upper Halliford 193 B5
Upper Holloway 71 D6
Upper Norwood 183 C3
Upper Ruxley 191 C3
Upper Shirley 222 D4
Upper Sydenham 184 A6
Upper Tooting 158 D1
Upper Walthamstow 54 C6
Upton 77 B1
Upton Park 99 D6
Uxbridge 82 A6

V

Vale of Health 70 B5
Vauxhall 116 A1

W

Waddon 220 D4
Walham Green 135 D5
Wallend 100 C6
Wallington 219 A2
Walthamstow 53 D6
Walton-on-Thames 194 C2
Walworth 117 B1
Wandsworth 157 C5
Wanstead 55 C3
Wapping 118 B5
Waterloo 116 C4
Wealdstone 42 D6
Welling 146 B2
Welsh Harp 45 C1
Wembley 66 A2
Wembley Park 66 C5
West Acton 88 C1
West Barnes 200 C4
West Bedfont 148 C4
West Brompton 135 D6
West Drayton 104 B4
West Dulwich 161 A2
West Ealing 109 B5
West Ewell 215 C1
West Green 51 A5
West Ham 99 B6
West Hampstead 69 C4
West Harrow 42 A2
West Heath 146 D6
West Hendon 45 D3
West Hill 157 B5
West Kensington 113 A2
West Kilburn 91 A4
West Molesey 195 C5
West Norwood 161 A1
West Ruislip 61 B6
West Wickham 224 C6
Westbourne Green 91 D3
Westminster 115 C4
Weston Green 196 D1
Whetstone 14 A2
Whitechapel 95 D1
Whitton 152 A4
Widmore 188 A1
Willesden 68 A4
Willesden Green 90 B6
Wimbledon 179 B4
Wimbledon Park 157 B2
Winchmore Hill 16 D4
Wood End 83 D1
Wood End Green 83 C2
Wood Green 32 B2
Woodford 37 D5
Woodford Green 37 B3
Woodford Wells 21 B1
Woodlands 130 C2
Woodside 206 A4
Woodside Park 29 C6
Woolwich 122 D3
Worcester Park 215 C4
World's End 4 C1
Wrythe The 218 D6

Y

Yeading 84 D3
Yiewsley 104 A6

Abbreviations used in the index

Abbreviation	Meaning
Acad	Academy
App	Approach
Arc	Arcade
Art Gall	Art Gallery
Ave	Avenue
Bglws	Bungalows
Bldgs	Buildings
Bsns Ctr	Business Centre
Bsns Pk	Business Park
Bvd	Boulevard
Cath	Cathedral, Catholic
CE	Church of England
Cemy	Cemetery
Cir	Circus
Circ	Circle
Cl	Close
Cnr	Corner
Coll	College
Com	Community
Comm	Common
Comp	Comprehensive
Con Ctr	Conference Centre
Cotts	Cottages
Cres	Crescent
Cswy	Causeway
Ct	Court
Ctr	Centre
Crkt	Cricket
Ctry Pk	Country Park
Cty	County
Ctyd	Courtyard
Dr	Drive
Ent Ctr	Enterprise Centre
Ent Pk	Enterprise Park
Est	Estate
Ex Ctr	Exhibition Centre
Ex Hall	Exhibition Hall
Fst	First
Gdn	Garden
Gdns	Gardens
Gn	Green
Gr	Grove
Gram	Grammar
Her Ctr	Heritage Centre
Ho	House
Hospl	Hospital
Hts	Heights
Ind Est	Industrial Estate
Inf	Infant
Inst	Institute
Int	International
Intc	Interchange
Jun	Junior
Junc	Junction
La	Lane
L Ctr	Leisure Centre
Liby	Library
Mans	Mansions
Mdw/s	Meadow/s
Meml	Memorial
Mid	Middle
Mix	Mixed
Mkt	Market
Mon	Monument
Mus	Museum
Obsy	Observatory
Orch	Orchard
Par	Parade
Pas	Passage
Pav	Pavilion
Pk	Park
Pl	Place
Prec	Precinct
Prep	Preparatory
Prim	Primary
Prom	Promenade
RC	Roman Catholic
Rd	Road
Rdbt	Roundabout
Ret Pk	Retail Park
Sch	School
Sec	Secondary
Sh Ctr	Shopping Centre
Sp	Sports
Specl	Special
Sports Ctr	Sports Centre
Sq	Square
St	Street, Saint
Sta	Station
Stad	Stadium
Tech	Technical/Technology
Terr	Terrace
Trad Est	Trading Estate
Twr/s	Tower/s
Univ	University
Wlk	Walk
Yd	Yard

A

Aaron Ct BR3 207 D6
Aaron Hill Rd E6 100 C2
Abady Ho SW1 259 D4
Abberley Mews 9
SW8 137 B2
Abberton IG8 37 C5
Abbess Cl 11 E6 100 A2
Streatham SW2 160 D3
Abbeville Mews 3
SW4 137 D1
Abbeville Rd N8 49 D5
SW4 159 C6
Abbey Ave HA0 88 A5
Abbey Bsns Ctr
SW8 137 B4 268 D2
Abbey Cl Hayes UB3 106 B5
Northolt UB5 85 B4
Pinner HA5 40 C6
Abbey Cres DA17 125 C2
Abbey Ct N3 47 C6
NW8 229 A4
SE17 262 B1
6 W12 111 C3
Abbeydale Ct 6 UB1 85 D1
Abbeydale Rd HA0 88 C6
Abbey Dr SW17 181 A5
Abbeyfield UB4 83 D2
Abbeyfield Rd SE16 118 C2
Abbeyfields Cl NW10 88 C5
Abbey Gdns
NW8 92 A5 229 B3
9 SE16 118 A2
W6 135 A6 264 A5
Chislehurst BR7 188 C2
Abbey Gr SE2 124 B2
Abbeyhill Rd DA15 168 C2
Abbey Ho E15 98 C5
NW8 229 B2
Abbey Ind Est CR4 202 D4
Abbey La E15 98 B5
Beckenham BR3 185 C3
Abbey Lane Commercial Est
E15 98 C5
Abbey Lo NW8 230 B1
1 Ealing W5 109 C6
Abbey Manufacturing Est
HA0 88 B6
Abbey Mews E17 53 C4
Abbey Mount DA17 125 B1
Abbey Orchard St
SW1 115 D3 259 D6
Abbey Orchard Street Est
SW1 259 D6
Abbey Par Ealing NW10 88 B4
Merton SW19 180 A3
Abbey Park Ind Est
IG11 101 A6
Abbey Pk BR3 185 C3
Abbey Prim Sch SE2 124 C3
Abbey Rd E15 98 C5
NW8 92 A5 229 A4
Barking IG11 100 D6
Bexley DA6,DA7 147 A1
Croydon CR0 220 D5
Enfield EN1 17 C6
Erith DA17 125 A3
Ilford IG2 57 B4
Lower Halliford TW17 192 C1
Merton SW19 180 A2
Wembley NW10 88 D5
Abbey St E13 99 A3
SE1 117 D3 263 C6
Abbey Terr SE2 124 C2
Abbey Tutorial Coll W2 91 C1
Abbey View NW7 11 D1
Abbey Wlk KT8 195 D5
Abbey Wood Rd SE2 124 C2
Abbey Wood Sch SE2 124 A3
Abbey Wood Sta SE2 124 C3
Abbot Cl HA4 62 D5
Abbot Ct SW8 270 A3
Abbot Ho 13 E14 119 D6
Abbotsbury Cl E15 98 A5
W14 113 B4 244 C1
Abbotsbury Fst Sch
SM4 201 D4
Abbotsbury Gdns HA5 40 C3
Abbotsbury Ho W14 244 B2
Abbotsbury Mews
SE15 140 C2
Abbotsbury Rd
W14 113 B4 244 C1
Coney Hall BR2,BR4 224 D6
Morden SM4 201 D5
Abbots Cl BR5 211 A1
Abbots Ct SE25 205 C6
Abbots Dr HA2 63 C6
Abbotsfield Sch UB10 82 D5
Abbotsford Ave N15 51 A5
Abbotsford Gdns IG8 37 A3
Abbotsford Rd IG3 80 B6
Abbots Gdns N2 48 B5
Abbots Gn CR0,CR2 222 D2
Abbotshade Rd 15
SE16 118 D5
Abbotshall Ave N14 15 C1
Abbotshall Rd SE6 164 B2
Abbots Ho E17 35 B1
SW1 259 C1
W14 254 C5
Abbots La SE1 117 C5 253 B3
Abbotsleigh Cl SM2 217 D1
Abbotsleigh Rd SW16 181 C5
Abbotsmede Cl TW1 152 D2
Abbots Pk SW2 160 C3
Abbot's Pl NW6 91 D6
Abbots Rd E6 99 D6
HA8 27 B3
Abbot St E8 73 D2
Abbots Terr N8 50 A3
Abbotstone Ho 4 E5 74 A6
Abbotstone Rd SW15 134 C2
Abbots Way BR3 207 A4
Abbotswell Rd SE4 163 B6
Abbotswood Cl 7
DA17 125 A3
Abbotswood Gdns IG5 56 B6
Abbotswood Rd SE22 139 C1
Streatham SW16 159 D1
Abbotswood Way UB3 106 B5
Abbott Ave SW20 178 D2
Abbott Cl
Hampton TW12 173 A4
Northolt UB5 63 B2
Abbott Ho SW12 158 D4
Abbott Rd E14 98 B1
Abbotts Cl N1 73 A2
Romford RM7 59 D6
Woolwich SE28 124 C6
Abbotts Cres
Chingford E4 36 B6
Enfield EN2 4 D3
Abbotts Ct HA2 64 B6
Abbotts Dr HA0 65 B6
Abbotts Park Rd E10 54 A2
Abbotts Rd Barnet EN5 1 D1
Cheam SM3 217 A4
Mitcham CR4 203 C5
Southall UB1 107 A5
Abbott's Wlk DA7 146 D5
Abbyfield Cl CR4 180 C1
Abchurch La
EC2,EC4 117 B6 252 D6
Abchurch Yd EC4 252 C6
Abdale Rd W12 112 B5
Abel Ho 7 SE11 138 C6
Abenglen Ind Est UB3 105 B4
Aberavon Rd E3 97 A4
Abercairn Rd SW16 181 C3
Aberconway Rd SM4 201 D5
Abercorn Cl NW7 29 A3
NW8 92 A4 229 A2
Abercorn Cres HA2 41 D1
Abercorn Gdns
Harrow HA3 43 D2
Ilford RM6 58 B3
Abercorn Gr HA4 39 B5
Abercorn Ho SE10 141 D5
Abercorn Mans NW8 229 B3
Abercorn Mews 10
TW10 132 B1
Abercorn Pl
NW8 92 A5 229 A3
Abercorn Rd NW7 29 A3
Stanmore HA7 25 C3
Abercorn Trad Est HA0 87 D6
Abercorn Way SE1 118 A1
Abercrombie Dr EN1 6 A4
Abercrombie Ho 1
W12 112 B6
Abercrombie St SW11 136 C3
Aberdale Ct 22 SE16 118 D4
Aberdare Cl BR4 224 A6
Aberdare Gdns NW6 69 D1
NW7 28 D3
Aberdare Rd EN3 6 C1
Aberdeen Ct N5 73 A3
W2 236 C5
Aberdeen La N5 73 A3
Aberdeen Mans WC1 240 A6
Aberdeen Par N18 34 B5
Aberdeen Pk N5 73 A3
Aberdeen Pl
NW8 92 B3 236 C6
Aberdeen Rd N5 73 A4
NW10 67 D3
Croydon CR0 221 B4
Edmonton N18 34 B5
Harrow HA3 24 D1
Aberdeen Terr SE3 142 B3
Aberdour Rd IG3 80 B6
Aberdour St
SE1 117 C3 263 A4
Aberfeldy Ho SE5 138 D5
Aberfeldy St E14 98 A1
Aberford Gdns SE18 144 A4
Aberfoyle Rd SW16 181 D4
Abergeldie Rd SE12 165 B5
Abernethy Rd SE13 142 C1
Abersham Rd E8 73 D3
Abery St SE18 123 C2
Abingdon W14 254 D3
Abingdon Cl NW1 71 D2
SE1 263 D2
Hillingdon UB10 82 B6
Abingdon Cl *continued*
Wimbledon SW19 180 A4
Abingdon Ct W8 255 B5
Edgware HA8 26 A6
Abingdon Gdns W8 255 B5
Abingdon Ho E2 243 C6
Abingdon Lo BR2 186 D1
Abingdon Mans W8 255 A6
Abingdon Rd N3 30 A1
W8 113 C3 255 B5
Thornton Heath SW16 182 A2
Abingdon St
SW1 116 A3 260 A6
Abingdon Villas
W8 113 C3 255 B5
Abinger Cl BR1 210 A6
Barking IG11 80 A4
New Addington CR0 224 A2
Wallington SM6 220 A3
Abinger Ct
3 Ealing W5 109 C6
Wallington SM6 220 A3
Abinger Gdns TW7 130 C2
Abinger Gr SE8 141 B6
Abinger Ho SE1 252 C1
2 Kingston KT2 176 D3
Abinger Mews W9 91 C3
Abinger Rd W4 111 C3
Abington Ho NW11 48 A3
Ablett St SE16 118 C1
Abney Gdns 5 N16 73 D6
Abney Park Cemetery★
N16 73 C6
Abney Park Ct N16 73 D6
Aborfield 6 NW5 71 C3
Aboyne Dr SW20 178 A1
Aboyne Rd NW10 67 C5
Wandsworth SW17 158 B1
Abraham Cl WD19 22 B6
Abridge Way IG11 102 B5
Abyssinia Cl SW11 136 C1
Abyssinia Rd SW11 136 C1
Acacia Ave N2 47 D6
Brentford TW8 131 B5
Hayes UB3 83 D1
Littleton TW17 192 C4
Ruislip HA4 40 B2
Tottenham N17 33 B3
Wembley HA9 66 A3
Yiewsley UB7 104 B6
Acacia Bsns Ctr 1 E11 76 C5
Acacia Cl BR5 211 B4
SE8 119 A2
Penge SE20 184 A1
Stanmore HA7 24 C4
Acacia Ct Harrow HA1 41 D3
5 West Norwood
SW16 182 C5
Acacia Dr SM3 201 C1
Acacia Gdns NW8 229 D4
West Wickham BR4 224 A6
Acacia Gr Dulwich SE21 161 B2
Kingston KT3 199 C6
Acacia Ho N16 73 B6
1 New Malden KT3 199 C5
Wood Green N22 32 C2
Acacia Pl NW8 92 B5 229 D4
Acacia Rd E11 76 C6
E17 53 A3
NW8 92 B5 229 D4
W3 111 A6
Beckenham BR3 207 B6
Enfield EN2 5 B4
Hampton TW12 173 C4
Mitcham CR4 181 B1
Thornton Heath SW16 182 A2
Wood Green N22 32 C2
Acacias Lo EN4 14 B6
Acacias The EN4 14 B6
Acacia Way DA15 167 D3
Acacia Wlk SW10 266 B3
Academy Ct 13 E2 96 C4
Academy Gdns
Croydon CR0 205 D1
Northolt UB5 84 D5
Academy Pl SE18 144 C4
Academy Rd SE18 144 B5
Academy The 2 N19 49 C1
Acanthus Dr SE1 118 A1
Acanthus Rd SW11 137 A2
Accadia Ct NW9 67 A6
Accommodation Rd
NW11 47 B1
Ace Par KT9 214 A5
Acer Ave UB4 85 A2
Acer Ct NW2 68 D4
Acfold Rd SW6 265 C1
Achilles Cl SE1 118 A1
Achilles Ho 16 E2 96 B5
Achilles Rd NW6 69 C3
Achilles St SE14 141 A5
Achilles Way W1 248 B3
Acklam Rd W10 91 B2
Acklington Dr NW9 27 C2
Ackmar Rd
SW6 135 C4 265 A1
Ackroyd Dr E3 97 C2
Ackroyd Rd SE23 163 A4
Acland Burghley Sch
NW5 71 B4
Acland Cl SE18 145 B5
Acland Cres SE5 139 B2
Acland Ho SW9 138 B3
Acock Gr UB5 64 A4
Acol Cres HA4 62 B3
Acol Ct 3 NW6 69 C1
Acol Rd NW6 69 D1
Aconbury Rd RM9 102 B6
Acorn Cl Chingford E4 35 D5
Chislehurst BR7 189 A5
Enfield EN2 4 D4
1 Hampton TW12 173 D4
Stanmore HA7 25 B3
Acorn Ct E6 78 A1
Ilford IG2 57 C4
Acorn Gdns W3 89 B2
South Norwood SE19 183 D2
Acorn Gr
Harlington UB3 127 D5
Ruislip HA4 61 D4
Acorn Par 7 SE15 140 B5
Acorn Production Ctr
N7 72 A1
Acorns The 21 SW19 156 D3
Acorns Way KT10 212 A3
Acorn Way
Beckenham BR3 208 A4
Forest Hill SE23 162 D1
Orpington BR6 226 D4
Acorn Wharf SE1 140 A6
Acorn Wlk SE16 119 A5
Acre Dr SE22 140 A1
Acrefield Ho 4 NW4 46 D5
Acre La SW2 138 B1
Wallington SM5 219 A4
Acre Path UB5 63 A2
Acre Rd Dagenham RM10 81 D1
Kingston KT2 176 B2
Mitcham SW19 180 B4
Acre Way HA6 22 A2
Acris St SW18 158 A6
Action Ct TW15 171 A2
Acton Bsns Ctr NW10 89 B3
Acton Central Ind Est 4
W3 110 D5
Acton Central Sta W3 111 B5
Acton Cl N9 18 A2
Acton High Sch W3 110 C4
Acton Hill Mews W3 110 D5
Acton Ho 16 E8 95 D6
5 W3 89 A1
Acton Hospl W3 110 C4
Acton La Acton NW10 89 B5
Acton W3 111 A4
Acton W4 111 A2
Acton Main Line Sta
W3 89 A1
Acton Mews E8 95 D6
Acton Park Est W3 111 B4
Acton St WC1 94 B4 233 C1
Acton Town Sta W3 110 C4
Acton Vale Ind Pk W3 111 D5
Acuba Ho SW18 157 D3
Acuba Rd SW18 157 D2
Acworth Cl N9 18 C4
Acworth Ho 1 SE18 144 D6
Ada Ct N1 235 A5
W9 92 A4 229 B1
Ada Gdns E15 98 D6
South Bromley E14 98 B1
Ada Ho 23 E2 96 A6
Adair Cl SE25 206 B6
Adair Ho SW3 267 B6
Adair Rd W10 91 A3
Adair Twr 7 W10 91 A3
Ada Kennedy Ct 6
SE10 142 A5
Ada Lewis Ho HA9 66 B4
Adam Cl SE6 185 C6
Adam Ct SE11 261 C3
Adam & Eve Ct W1 239 B2
Adam & Eve Mews
W8 113 C3 255 B6
Adamfields NW3 70 B1
Adam Lo N21 16 B6
Adam Rd E4 35 B4
Adams Cl N3 29 C3
NW9 66 D6
Surbiton KT5 198 B3
Adams Ct E17 53 A3
Adams Gardens Est 5
SE16 118 C4
Adams Ho
3 South Bromley E14 98 B1
3 Streatham SW16 181 C5
Adams Mews N22 32 B3
Adamson Ct N2 48 C6
Adamson Rd E16 99 A1
NW3 70 B1
Adams Pl N7 72 B3
Adams Rd
Beckenham BR3 207 A4
Tottenham N17 33 B1
Adamsrill Cl EN1 17 B5
Adamsrill Prim Sch
SE26 163 A1
Adamsrill Rd SE26 185 A6
Adam's Row
W1 115 A6 248 B5
Adams Sq DA6 147 A2
Adam St WC2 116 A6 250 B5
Adams Way CR0 206 A3
Adams Wlk 11 KT1 176 A1
Adam Wlk SW6 134 C5
Ada Pl E2 96 A6
Ada Rd SE5 139 C5
Wembley HA0,HA9 65 D5
Adare Wlk SW16,SW2 160 B2
Ada St E8 96 B6
Adcot Wlk 6 BR6 227 D4
Adderley Gdns SE9 188 C6
Adderley Gr SW11 159 A6
Adderley Rd HA3 24 D2
Adderley St E14 98 A1
Addey Ho SE8 141 B5
Addey & Stanhope Sch
SE14 141 C4
Addington Ct 7 SW14 133 B2
Addington Dr N12 30 B4
Addington Gr SE26 185 A6
Addington Ho 13 SW9 138 B3
Addington Palace (The
Royal Sch of Church
Music) CR9 223 B2
Addington Rd E16 98 C3
E3 97 C4
N4 50 C3
Thornton Heath CR0 204 C1
West Wickham BR4 224 C6
West Wickham BR4,CR0 224 B4
Addington Sq SE5 139 B5
Addington St
SE1 116 B4 250 D1
Addington Village Rd
CR0 223 C3
Addington Village Sta
CR0 223 C2
Addis Cl EN3 6 D4
Addiscombe Ave CR0 206 A2
Addiscombe Cl HA3 43 C4
Addiscombe Court Rd
CR0 221 C6
Addiscombe Ct UB10 83 A3
Addiscombe Rd CR0 222 B6
Addiscombe Sta CR0 206 A1
Addison Ave
W11 113 A5 244 A3
Hounslow TW3 130 A4
Southgate N14 15 C5
Addison Bridge Pl
W14 113 B2 254 C4
Addison Cl
Northwood HA6 22 A2
Orpington BR5 211 A3
Addison Cres
W14 113 A3 254 B6
Addison Ct W5 110 C6
Addison Dr SE12 165 B6
Addison Gdns W14 112 D3
Kingston KT5 198 B5
Addison Gr W4 111 C3
Addison Ho
NW8 92 B4 229 C2
Addison Park Mans 12
W14 112 D4
Addison Pl
W11 113 A5 244 A3
Southall UB1 107 C6
Addison Prim Sch
W14 112 D3
Addison Rd BR2 209 D4
E17 54 A4
W14 113 B3 254 C6
Croydon SE25 206 A5
Enfield EN3 6 D4
Teddington TW11 175 B4
Wanstead E11 55 A3
Addison's Cl CR0 223 B6
Addison Way NW11 47 C5
Hayes UB3 84 A1
Northwood HA6 22 A2
Addle Hill EC4 241 D1
Addle St EC2 242 B3
Addlestone Ho W10 90 C2
Addy Ho SE16 118 C2
Adecroft Way KT8 196 A6
Adela Ave KT3 200 B5
Adela Ho 9 W6 112 C1
Adelaide Ave SE4 141 C1
Adelaide Cl SW9 138 C1
Enfield EN1 5 C5
Stanmore HA7 25 A6
Adelaide Ct NW8 229 B3
W7 108 D4
15 Beckenham BR3 185 C3
Adelaide Gdns RM6 59 A4
Adelaide Gr W12 112 A5
Adelaide Ho E17 53 B6
Adelaide Rd E10 76 A5
NW3 70 C1
2 SW18 157 C6
Ashford TW15 170 A6
Chislehurst BR7 188 D5
Ealing W13 109 A4
Heston TW5 129 A4
Ilford IG1 78 D6
Adelaide Rd *continued*
Kingston KT6 198 A4
Richmond TW9 132 B1
Southall UB2 107 A2
Teddington TW11 174 D4
Adelaide St WC2 250 A5
Adelaide Terr TW8 109 D1
Adela St W10 91 A3
Adelina Gr E1 96 C2
Adelina Mews SW12 159 D3
Adeline Pl WC1 93 D2 239 D3
Adeliza Cl IG11 79 A1
Adelphi Cres UB4 83 D4
Adelphi Ct 20 SE16 118 D4
Adelphi Terr WC2 250 B5
Adelphi Way UB4 83 D4
Adeney Cl W6 134 D6
Aden Gr N16 73 B4
Aden Ho 12 E1 96 D2
Aden Lo N16 73 B4
Adenmore Rd SE6 163 C4
Aden Rd Enfield EN3 7 A1
Ilford IG1 57 A2
Adeyfield Ho EC1 235 D1
Adhara Rd HA6 22 A5
Adie Rd W6 112 C3
Adine Rd E13 99 B3
Adisham Ho 4 E5 74 B3
Adler Ind Est UB3 105 B4
Adler St E1 96 A1
Adley St E5 75 A3
Adlington Cl N18 33 C5
Admaston Rd SE18 145 A6
Admiral Ct NW4 46 A4
SW10 136 A4 266 B2
W1 238 A3
Barking IG11 102 C5
Carshalton SM5 202 C1
Admiral Ho TW11 175 A6
Admiral Hyson Ind Est
SE16 118 B1
Admiral Mews W10 90 D3
Admiral Pl SE16 119 A5
Admirals Cl E18 55 B5
Admirals Ct 3 E6 100 D1
SE1 253 C3
32 Putney SW19 156 D3
Admiral Seymour Rd
SE9 144 B1
Admirals Gate SE10 141 D4
Admiral Sq
SW10 136 A4 266 B2
Admiral St SE8 141 C4
Admirals Way E14 119 C4
Admiral's Wlk NW3 70 A5
Admiralty Arch★
SW1 249 D4
Admiralty Cl 1 SE8 141 C4
Admiralty Rd TW11 174 D4
Admiralty Way TW11 174 D4
Admiral Wlk W9 91 C2
Adolf St SE6 185 D6
Adolphus Rd N4 50 D1
Adolphus St SE8 141 B5
Adomar Rd RM8 81 A5
Adpar St W2 92 B2 236 C4
Adrian Ave NW2 46 B1
Adrian Bolt Ho 2 E2 96 B4
Adrian Ho N1 233 D5
SW8 270 A4
Adrian Mews SW10 265 D6
Adriatic Bldg 18 E14
Adriatic Ho 18 E1 96 D3
Adrienne Ave UB1 85 B4
Adron Ho 9 SE16 118 C2
Adstock Ho 5 N1 72 D1
ADT Coll SW15 157 B6
Advance Rd SE27 183 A6
Adventurers Ct 4 E14 120 B6
Advent Way N18 34 D5
Adys Lawn NW2 68 B2
Adys Rd SE15 139 D2
Aerodrome Rd NW4,
NW9 45 D6
Aerodrome Way TW5 128 C6
Aeroville NW9 27 C1
Affleck St N1 233 D3
Afghan Rd SW11 136 C3
Agamemnon Rd NW6 69 B3
Agar Cl KT6 214 B6
Agar Gr NW1 71 D1
Agar Ho 6 KT1 198 A6
Agar Pl NW1 71 C1
Agar St WC2 250 B5
Agate Cl E16 99 D1
Agate Ho
New Malden KT4 199 C1
12 Penge SE26 184 B5
Agate Rd W6 112 C3
Agatha Cl E1 118 C5
Agaton Rd BR7,SE9 167 A2
Agave Rd NW2 68 C4
Agdon St EC1 94 D3 241 C6
Agincourt E11 54 D3
Agincourt Rd NW3 70 D4
Agnes Ave IG1 78 D4

Agnes Cl E6 122 C6
Agnes Ct 11 SW18 136 B1
Agnesfield Cl N12 30 C4
Agnes Gdns RM8 80 D4
Agnes Ho 13 W11 112 D6
Agnes Rd W3 111 D4
Agnes St E14 97 B1
Agnew Rd SE23 162 D4
Agricola Pl EN1 17 D6
Aidan Cl RM8 81 A4
Aidans Ct N12 30 C5
Aigburth Mans 5 SW9 138 C5
Ailantus Ct HA8 26 B5
Aileen Wlk E15 76 D1
Ailsa Ave TW1 153 B6
Ailsa Rd TW1 153 B6
Ailsa St E14 98 A2
Ainger Rd NW3 70 D1
Ainsdale NW1 232 A2
Ainsdale Cl BR6 211 B1
Ainsdale Cres HA5 41 C6
Ainsdale Dr SE1 118 A1
Ainsdale Rd W5 87 D3
Ainsley Ave RM7 59 D3
Ainsley Cl N9 17 C3
Ainsley St E2 96 B4
Ainsley Wood Prim Sch E4 35 D5
Ainslie Ct 2 HA0 88 A5
Ainslie Wood Cres E4 35 D5
Ainslie Wood Gdns E4 35 D5
Ainslie Wood Rd E4 35 D5
Ainsty St 14 SE16 118 C4
Ainsworth Cl NW2 68 A5
SE5 139 C3
Ainsworth Est NW8 92 A6 229 A6
Ainsworth Ho NW8 91 D6
Ainsworth Rd E9 74 C1
Croydon CR0 220 D6
Ainsworth Way NW8 92 A6 229 A6
Aintree Ave E6 100 A6
Aintree Cl UB8 82 D2
Aintree Ho SE26 184 B4
Aintree Rd UB6 87 B5
Aintree St SW6 135 A5 264 B4
Airborne Ho 10 SM6 219 B4
Air Call Bsns Ctr NW9 45 C6
Aird Ho SE1 262 A5
Airdrie Cl N1 72 B1
Hayes UB4 85 A2
Airedale Ave W4 111 D1
Airedale Ave S W4 111 D1
Airedale Rd W5 109 D3
Balham SW12 158 D4
Airlie Gdns W8 113 C5 245 A3
Ilford IG1 56 D1
Airlinks Ind Est TW5 106 C1
Air Park Way TW13 150 B2
Airport Gate Bsns Ctr UB7 126 B5
Airport Rdbt E16 121 D5
Air St W1 249 B5
Airthrie Rd IG3 80 B6
Aisgill Ave SW5 113 B1 254 D1
Aisher Rd SE28 124 C6
Aislibie Rd SE12 142 C1
Aislobie Ho N21 17 B5
Aiten Pl W6 112 A2
Aithan Ho 9 E14 97 B1
Aitken Cl E8 96 A6
Carshalton CR4 202 D2
Aitken Rd Barnet EN5 12 C6
Catford SE6 163 D2
Ajax Ave NW9 45 C6
Ajax Ho 15 E2 96 B5
Ajax Rd NW6 69 C3
Akabusi Cl SE25 206 A3
Akbar Ho 7 E14 119 D2
Akehurst St SW15 156 A4
Akenside Ct 3 NW3 70 B3
Akenside Rd NW3 70 B3
Akerman Rd SW9 138 D4
Kingston KT6 197 C3
Akintaro Ho 7 SE8 141 B6
Akiva Sch N3 29 D1
Alabama St SE18 145 C5
Alacross Rd W5 109 D4
Alamaro Lo SE10 120 D3
Alandale Dr HA5 22 B2
Aland Ct SE16 119 A3
Alander Mews E17 54 A5
Alan Dr EN5 13 A5
Alan Gdns RM7 59 C2
Alan Hocken Way E15 98 C5
Alan Lo N3 29 C2
Alan Preece Ct NW6 68 D1
Alan Rd SW19 179 A5
Alanthus Cl SE12 165 A5
Alaska St SE1 251 A3
Alba Cl UB4 84 D3
Albacore Cres SE13 163 D5
Alba Gdns NW11 47 A3
Albain Cres TW15 148 A2
Alba Mews SW18, SW19 157 C2
Alban Ho NW3 70 A2
Albans Cl SW16 160 A1
Albany N12 29 D4
W1 249 A5
Albany Cl N15 50 D5
Bushey WD23 8 B5
Ickenham UB10 60 C3
Mortlake SW14 132 D1
Sidcup DA5 168 D4
Albany Coll The NW4 46 C4
Albany Cres
Claygate KT10 212 C2
Edgware HA8 26 C3
Albany Ct E10 53 C2
HA8 27 B2
NW10 90 B4
SW1 259 C6
Kingston KT2 176 A4
Richmond TW10 153 B1
Chingford E4 19 D5
Albany Ctyd W1 249 B5
Albany Ho E5 74 C6
6 Brentford TW8 132 A6
Albany Mans SW11 267 B3
Albany Mews BR1 187 A4
N1 72 C1
SE5 139 A6
Kingston KT2 175 D4
Sutton SM1 217 D3
Albany Par 4 TW8 132 A6
Albany Park Ave EN3 6 D4
Albany Park Rd KT2 176 A4
Albany Park Sta DA14 168 D2
Albany Pas 12 TW10 154 A6
Albany Pl N7 72 C4
Brentford TW8 131 D6
Albany Rd E10 53 C2
E12 77 D4
E17 53 A3
N18 34 C5
N4 50 C3
SE5 139 C6
Brentford TW8 131 D6
Chislehurst BR7 188 D5
Dagenham RM6 59 B3
Ealing W13 109 B6
Enfield EN3 6 D5
Erith DA17 147 B6
New Malden KT3 199 B5
Richmond TW10 154 A6
Sidcup DA5 168 C4
Wimbledon SW19 179 D5
Albany Reach KT7 196 D4
Albany Sch EN3 6 D5
Albany St NW1 93 B4 231 D2
Albany Terr 6 TW10 154 B6
Albany The
Kingston KT2 175 D4
Woodford IG8 36 D6
Albany View IG9 21 A3
Albany Wlk N15 50 D5
Alba Pl W11 91 B1
Albatross 31 NW9 27 D1
Albatross St SE18 145 C5
Albemarle SW19 156 D2
Albemarle App IG2 56 D3
Albemarle Ave TW2 151 B3
Albemarle Gdns
Ilford IG2 56 D3
New Malden KT3 199 B5
Albemarle Ho SE8 119 B2
Albemarle Lo SE26 185 A5
Albemarle Mans NW3 69 D4
Albemarle Pk
Beckenham BR3 185 D2
Stanmore HA7 25 C5
Albemarle Prim Sch SW19 157 A2
Albemarle Rd
Beckenham BR2,BR3 186 A2
East Barnet EN4 14 C4
Albemarle St W1 115 C6 249 A5
Albemarle Way EC1 241 C5
Albermarle Ho 3 SW9 138 C2
Alberon Gdns NW11 47 B5
Alberta Ave SM1 217 B3
Alberta Ct 1 TW10 154 B6
Alberta Ho E14 120 A5
Hayes UB4 84 B4
Alberta Rd Bexley DA7 147 D4
Enfield EN1 18 A5
Alberta St SE17 116 D1 261 D2
Albert Ave SW8 270 C3
Chingford E4 35 C6
Albert Barnes Ho SE1 262 A5
Albert Bigg Point E15 98 A6
Albert Bridge Rd SW11 136 D5 267 C3
Albert Carr Gdns SW16 182 A5
Albert Cl 11 E9 96 B6
Albert Cl *continued*
N22 31 D2
Albert Cotts 2 E1 96 A2
Albert Cres E4 35 C6
Albert Ct SW7 246 C1
9 Putney SW19 157 A3
Albert Dr SW19 157 A3
Albert Emb SE1 116 A2 260 B3
Albert Gate Ct SW1 247 C1
Albert Gdns E1 96 D1
Albert Gr SW20 178 D2
Albert Gray Ho SW10 266 C4
Albert Hall Mans SW7 114 B4 246 C1
Albert Ho 5 E18 55 B6
Albert Mans N8 50 A2
SW11 267 C2
Albert Memorial* SW7 114 B4 246 C1
Albert Mews W8 256 A6
Albert Palace Mans SW11 268 B2
Albert Pl N3 29 C2
W8 113 D4 245 D1
Albert Rd BR2 209 D4
E10 54 A1
E17 53 C4
N15 51 C3
N4 50 B2
NW4 46 D5
NW6 91 B5
NW7 27 D5
Ashford TW15 170 B5
Buckhurst Hill IG9 21 D2
Chislehurst SE9 166 A1
Croydon SE25 206 B5
Dagenham RM8 59 C1
Ealing W5 87 B3
East Barnet EN4 2 A1
Erith DA17 125 B1
Hampton TW12 174 A5
Harrow HA2 42 A6
Hayes UB3 105 C3
Hounslow TW3 129 C1
Ilford IG1 79 A5
Kingston KT1 176 B1
Mitcham CR4 202 D6
Newham E16 122 B4
New Malden KT3 199 D5
Penge SE20 184 D4
Richmond TW10 154 B6
Sidcup DA5 169 D4
Southall UB2 106 D3
Sutton SM1 218 B3
Teddington TW11 174 D4
Twickenham TW1 152 D3
4 Wanstead E18 55 B6
Wood Green N22 31 C2
Yiewsley UB7 104 A5
Albert's Ct NW1 237 B6
Albert Sq E15 76 C3
SW8 138 B5 270 C3
Albert St N12 30 A5
NW1 93 B6 231 D5
Albert Starr Ho 7 SE8 118 D2
Albert Studios SW11 267 C2
Albert Terr NW10 89 A6
NW1 93 A6 231 A5
Buckhurst Hill IG9 21 D2
Albert Terr Mews NW1 231 A5
Albert Victoria Ho N22 32 C2
Albert Way SE15 140 B5
Albert Westcott Ho SE17 261 D2
Albert Whicher Ho 3 E17 54 A5
Albert Wlk E16 122 D4
Albion Ave N10 31 A2
SW8 137 D3
Albion Cl W2 247 B6
Albion Ct 2 SE7 122 A2
7 W6 112 B2
Sutton SM2 218 B1
Albion Dr E8 74 A1
Albion Est SE16 118 C4
Albion Gate W2 247 B6
Albion Gdns 1 W6 112 B2
Albion Gr N16 73 C4
Albion Hill IG10 21 D6
Albion Ho E16 122 D5
Albion Mews N1 234 A6
W2 114 C6 247 B6
6 W6 112 B2
Albion Pk IG10 21 D6
Albion Pl EC1 241 C4
EC2 242 D3
W6 112 B2
South Norwood SE25 206 A6
Albion Prim Sch SE16 118 C4
Albion Rd E17 54 A6
N16 73 B4
Bexley DA6 147 C1
Dagenham RM10 81 B3
Hayes UB3 83 C1
Hounslow TW3 129 C1
Kingston KT2 177 A2
Albion Rd *continued*
Sutton SM2 218 B1
Tottenham N17 34 A1
Twickenham TW2 152 C3
Albion Sq E8 73 D1
Albion St SE16 118 C4
W2 114 C6 247 B6
Thornton Heath CR0 204 D1
Albion Terr E8 73 D1
Sewardstone E4 7 D1
Albion Villas Rd SE23, SE26 162 C1
Albion Way EC1 242 A3
SE13 142 A1
Wembley HA9 66 C5
Albion Wharf SW11 267 A4
Albion Yd N1 233 B3
Albon Ho SE14 141 B4
Wandsworth SW18 157 D5
Albrighton Rd SE5, SE22 139 C2
Albuhera Cl EN2 4 C4
Albury Ave DA7 147 A3
Hounslow TW7 130 D5
Albury Bldgs SE1 251 D1
Albury Cl TW12 173 D4
Albury Ct
4 Croydon CR0 221 A4
Mitcham CR4 180 B1
6 Northolt UB5 84 C4
Sutton SM1 218 A4
Albury Dr HA5 22 D3
Albury Lo 7 SW2 160 B4
Albury Mews E12 77 C6
Albury Rd KT9 214 A3
Albury St SE8 141 C6
Albyfield BR1 210 B6
Albyn Rd SE8 141 C4
Alcester Cres E5 74 B6
Alcester Ct 4 SM6 219 B4
Alcester Rd SM6 219 B4
Alcock Cl SM6 219 D1
Alcock Rd TW5 128 D5
Alconbury DA6 169 D6
Alconbury Rd E5 74 A6
Alcorn Cl SM3 217 C6
Alcott Cl W7 86 D2
Aldborough Ct
Chingford E4 19 D1
Ilford IG2 57 D4
Aldborough Rd IG2 57 D6
Aldborough Rd N IG2 57 D4
Aldborough Rd S IG3 57 C2
Aldbourne Rd W12 112 A5
Aldbridge St SE17 117 C1 263 B2
Aldburgh Mews W1 238 B2
Aldbury Ave HA9 66 D1
Aldbury Ho SW3 257 A3
Aldbury Mews N9 17 B4
Aldebert Terr SW8 138 B5 270 C3
Aldeburgh Cl 16 E5 74 B6
Aldeburgh Pl IG8 37 A6
Aldeburgh St SE10 121 A1
Alden Ave E15 98 D4
Alden Ct
South Croydon CR0 221 C5
Wimbledon SW19 179 C4
Aldenham Ctry Pk WD6 9 B6
Aldenham Dr UB8 82 D3
Aldenham Ho NW1 232 B3
Aldenham Rd WD6 9 C6
Aldenham St NW1 93 D5 232 C3
Alden Ho E8 96 B6
Aldensley Rd W6 112 B3
Alderbrook Prim Sch SW12 159 B4
Alderbrook Rd SW12 159 B5
Alderbury Rd SW13 134 A6
Alder Ct N2 48 B6
3 West Norwood SW16 182 C5
Alder Gr NW2 68 B6
Aldergrove Gdns TW4 129 A3
Aldergrove Ho 3 E5 74 A6
Alder Ho 1 NW3 70 D2
SE15 139 D6
SE4 141 C2
Alderley Ho 36 SW8 137 D3
Alder Lo SW6 134 D4
Alderman Ave IG11 102 A4
Aldermanbury EC2 95 A1 242 B2
Aldermanbury Sq EC2 242 B3
Alderman Judge Mall 6 KT1 176 A1
Alderman's Hill N13 32 B6
Alderman's Wlk EC2 243 A3
Aldermary Rd BR1 187 A2
Aldermead 2 TW3 129 D1
Alder Mews 9 N19 71 C6
Aldermoor Rd SE6 163 B1
Alderney Ave TW5 129 D5
Alderney Gdns UB5 63 B1
Alderney Ho 16 N1 73 A2
Enfield EN3 6 D5
Alderney Mews SE1 262 C6
Alderney Rd E1 96 D3
Alderney St SW1 115 B1 258 D2
Alder Rd DA14 167 D1
Mortlake SW14 133 B2
Alders Ave IG8 36 C4
Aldersbrook Ave EN1 5 C3
Aldersbrook Dr KT2 176 B4
Aldersbrook House Coll of Railway Tech E12 78 C5
Aldersbrook La E12 78 B5
Aldersbrook Prim Sch E12 77 C6
Aldersbrook Rd E11,E12 77 C6
Alders Cl HA8 27 A5
W5 109 D3
Wanstead E11 77 B6
Alders Ct N17 52 B5
Aldersey Gdns IG11 79 B2
Aldersford Cl SE4 140 D1
Aldersgate Ct EC1 242 A3
Aldersgate St EC1 95 A2 242 A3
Alders Gr KT8 196 B4
Aldersgrove Ave SE9, SE12 165 D1
Aldershot Rd NW6 91 B6
Aldersmead Ave CR0 206 D3
Aldersmead Rd BR3 185 A3
Alderson Pl UB2 108 A5
Alderson St W10 91 A3
Alders Rd HA8 27 A5
Alders The
Feltham TW13 173 A6
Heston TW5 129 B6
Southgate N21 16 C5
Streatham SW16 181 C6
West Wickham BR4 223 D6
Alderton 9 KT2 176 D2
Alderton Cl NW10 67 B5
Alderton Cres NW4 46 B4
Alderton Ct KT8 195 B5
Alderton Rd SE24 139 A2
Croydon CR0 206 A2
Alderton Way NW4 46 B4
Alderville Rd SW6 135 B3
Alderwick Ct N7 72 B2
Alderwick Dr TW3 130 B2
Alderwood Prim Sch SE9 167 C5
Alderwood Rd SE9 167 B5
Aldford St W1 115 A5 248 B4
Aldgate EC3 95 C1 243 B1
Aldgate East Sta E1 95 D1 243 D2
Aldgate High St EC3 95 D1 243 C1
Aldgate Sta EC3 95 D1 243 C1
Aldham Hall 1 E11 55 A3
Aldham Ho SE4 141 B4
Aldine Ct W12 112 C5
Aldine St W12 112 C4
Aldington Cl RM8 58 C1
Aldington Ct 1 E8 74 A1
Aldington Rd SE18 121 D3
Aldis Mews
Holdbrook EN3 7 C6
Upper Tooting SW17 180 C5
Aldis St SW17 180 C5
Aldred Rd NW6 69 C3
Aldren Rd SW17 158 A1
Aldriche Way E4 36 A4
Aldrich Gdns SM3 217 B5
Aldrich Terr SW18 158 A2
Aldrick Ho N1 233 D4
Aldridge Ave
Edgware HA8 10 D1
Holdbrook EN3 7 C5
Ruislip HA4 62 D6
Stanmore HA7 26 A2
Aldridge Ct W11 91 B2
Aldridge Rd Villas W11 91 B2
Aldridge Rise KT3 199 C3
Aldridge Wlk N14 16 A4
Aldrington Rd SW16 181 C6
Aldsworth Cl W9 91 D3
Aldwick Cl BR7 167 B1
Aldwick Ct N12 30 A6
Aldwick Rd CR0 220 B4
Aldworth Gr SE13 164 A5
Aldworth Rd E15 76 C1
Aldwych WC2 94 B1 240 D1
Aldwych Ave IG6 57 A5
Aldwych Bldgs WC2 240 B2
Aldwyn Ho SW8 270 A3
Alers Rd DA6 168 D6
Alesia Cl N22 32 A3
Alestan Beck Rd E16 99 D1
Alexander Ave NW10 68 B1
Alexander Cl Barnet EN4 2 B1
Hayes BR2 209 A1
Sidcup DA15 167 C5
Southall UB2 108 A5
Twickenham TW2 152 D2
Alexander Ct SW18 158 A6
Beckenham BR3 186 B2
Greenwich SE3 143 B3
Stanmore HA7 44 B6
14 Surbiton KT6 197 D2
Alexander Evans Mews SE23 162 D2
Alexander Ho 9 E14 119 C3
Alexander McLeod Jun Sch SE2 124 B1
Alexander McLeod Prim Sch SE2 124 B1
Alexander Mews 2 W2 91 D1
Alexander Pl SW7 257 A4
Alexander Rd N19 72 A6
Bexley DA16 146 D3
Chislehurst BR7 188 D5
Alexander Sq SW3 114 C2 257 A4
Alexander St W2 91 C1
Alexander Terr SE2 124 B1
Alexandra Ave N22 31 D2
SW11 268 A1
Harrow HA2 63 C5
Southall UB1 107 B6
Sutton SM1 217 C5
Alexandra Bsns Ctr EN3 6 D1
Alexandra Cl SE8 141 B6
Ashford TW15 171 B3
Harrow HA2 63 D5
Alexandra Cotts SE14 141 B4
Penge SE20 184 D4
Alexandra Cres BR1 186 D4
Alexandra Ct 4 N16 73 D4
5 W12 112 A4
W9 236 B6
Ashford TW15 171 B4
Ealing W5 87 C2
Greenford UB6 85 D5
Hounslow TW3 129 D3
Southgate N14 15 C6
Wembley HA9 66 B4
Alexandra Dr
Surbiton KT5 198 C2
West Norwood SE19 183 C5
Alexandra Gdns N10 49 B5
Chiswick W4 133 C5
Hounslow TW3 129 D3
Wallington SM5 219 A1
Alexandra Gr N12 29 D4
N4 50 D1
Alexandra Ho 13 W6 112 C1
Alexandra Inf Sch
Kingston KT2 176 C3
Penge BR3 184 D3
Alexandra Jun & Inf Sch TW3 129 D3
Alexandra Jun Sch SE26 184 D4
Alexandra Mans
6 NW6 69 C3
SW3 266 C5
Alexandra Mews N2 48 D6
Alexandra National Ho N4 72 D6
Alexandra Palace* N22 31 D1
Alexandra Palace Sta N22 32 A1
Alexandra Palace Way N10 49 C6
Alexandra Park Rd N10, N22 31 D2
Alexandra Park Sch N22 31 C2
Alexandra Pl NW8 92 A6 229 B6
Croydon CR0 205 C1
South Norwood SE25 205 B4
Alexandra Prim Sch N22 32 B1
Alexandra Rd E10 76 A5
E17 53 B2
N10 31 B3
N15 51 B4
N8,N22 50 C6
NW4 46 D5
NW8 70 B1
W4 111 B4
Ashford TW15 171 C4
10 Brentford TW8 131 D6
Croydon CR0 205 C2
Dagenham RM6 59 A3
Edmonton N9 18 B4
Enfield EN3 6 D1
Hounslow TW3 129 D3
Kingston KT2 176 C3
Mitcham SW19 180 C3
Mortlake SW14 133 B2
Penge SE26 184 D4
Richmond TW9 132 B3
Thames Ditton KT7 196 D4
Twickenham TW1 153 C5
Wallend E6 100 C4
Wanstead E18 55 B6
Wimbledon SW19 179 C5
Alexandra Sch HA2 63 C6
Alexandra Sq SM4 201 C4
Alexandra St E16 99 A2
5 SE14 141 A5
Alexandra Wlk 8 SE19 183 C5
Alexandria Rd W13 109 B6

Alex Gossip Ho SW6 265 A1
Alexis St SE16 118 A2
Alfearn Rd E5 74 C4
Alford Ct N1 235 B3
5 Belmont SM2 217 D1
Alford Gn CR0 224 B2
Alford Ho N6 49 C3
6 SE18 144 D6
Alford Pl N1 235 B3
Alfoxton Ave N8,N15 50 D5
Alfreda Ct SW11 268 C1
Alfreda St
SW11 137 B4 268 C1
Alfred Butt Ho SW17 158 D1
Alfred Cl W4 111 B2
Alfred Findley Ho N22 32 D1
Alfred Gdns UB1 107 A6
Alfred Ho E9 75 A3
Alfred Hurley Ho
SW17 180 A6
Alfred Mews W1,WC1 239 C4
Alfred Mizen Prim Sch The
CR4 203 D6
Alfred Nunn Ho NW10 89 D6
Alfred Pl WC1 93 D2 239 C4
Alfred Prior Ho 6 E12 78 C4
Alfred Rd E15 76 D3
W2 91 C2
W3 111 A5
Buckhurst Hill IG9 21 D2
Croydon SE25 206 A4
Erith DA17 125 B1
Feltham TW13 150 C2
Kingston KT1 198 B6
Sutton SM1 218 A3
Alfred Salter Ho SE1 263 D3
Alfred Salter Prim Sch
SE16 118 D4
Alfred's Gdns IG11 101 C5
Alfred St E3 97 B4
Alfred's Way (East Ham & Barking By-Pass)
IG11 101 B5
Alfred's Way Ind Est
IG11 102 A6
Alfred Villas 9 E17 54 A5
Alfreton Cl SW19 156 D1
Alfriston KT5 198 B3
Alfriston Ave
Harrow HA2 41 C2
Thornton Heath CR0 204 A2
Alfriston Cl KT5 198 B3
Alfriston Rd SW11 158 D6
Algar Cl Isleworth TW7 131 A2
Stanmore HA7 24 D5
Algar Ho SE1 251 C1
Algar Rd TW7 131 A2
Algarve Rd SW18 157 D3
Algernon Rd NW4 46 A3
NW6 91 C6
SE13 141 D1
Algers Cl IG10 21 D6
Algers Rd IG10 21 D6
Alghers Mead IG10 21 D6
Algiers Rd SE13 141 C1
Alguin Ct HA7 25 C3
Alibon Gdns RM10 81 C3
Alibon Rd RM10 81 C3
Alice Ct SW15 135 B1
Alice Gilliott Ct W14 264 D6
Alice La E3 97 B6
Alice Mews 8 TW11 174 D5
Alice Owen Tech Ctr
EC1 234 C2
Alice Shepherd Ho 7
E14 120 A4
Alice St SE1 117 C3 263 A5
Alice Thompson Cl
SE12 165 C2
Alice Walker Cl 8
SE24 138 D1
Alice Way TW3 129 D1
Alicia Ave HA3 43 C5
Alicia Cl HA3 43 C5
Alicia Gdns HA3 43 C5
Alicia Ho DA16 146 B4
Alie St E1 95 D1 243 D1
Alington Cres NW9 45 A1
Alison Cl E6 100 C1
Croydon CR0 206 D1
Alison Ct 1 SE1 118 A1
Aliwal Rd SW11 136 C1
Alkerden Rd W4 111 C1
Alkham Rd N16 73 D6
Allam Ho W11 244 A6
Allan Barclay Cl N15 51 D3
Allanbridge N16 51 C2
Allan Cl KT3 199 B4
Allandale Ave N3 47 B6
Allan Ho SW8 269 C2
Allanson Ct E10 75 C6
Allan Way W3 89 A2
Allard Cres WD23 8 A2
Allard Gdns SW4 159 D6
Allardyce St SW4,SW9 138 B1
Allbrook Cl TW11 174 C5
Allbrook Ho 4 SW15 156 A4
Allcot Cl TW14 149 D3
Allcott Ho TW7 130 D2
Allcroft Rd NW5 71 A2
Allder Way CR2 220 D1
Allenby Cl UB6 85 C4
Allenby Inf Sch UB1 85 D1
Allenby Rd
Forest Hill SE23 163 A1
Southall UB1 85 C3
Allen Cl Streatham CR4 181 C2
Sunbury TW16 172 B2
Allen Ct E17 53 C3
Allendale Ave UB1 85 C1
Allendale Cl SE5 139 B4
Forest Hill SE26 184 D5
Allendale Rd UB6 65 B2
Allendale Sch
W8 113 C3 255 B6
Allen Edwards Dr
SW8 138 A4 270 A2
Allen Edwards Prim Sch
SW4 138 A4 270 A1
Allenford Ho 1 SW15 155 D5
All England Lawn Tennis & Croquet Club The
SW19 157 A1
Allen Ho W8 255 B6
Allen Mans W8 255 B6
Allen Rd E3 97 B5
N16 73 C4
Penge BR3 184 D1
Sunbury TW16 172 B1
Thornton Heath CR0 204 C1
Allensbury Pl NW1 72 A1
7 NW1 71 D1
Allens Rd EN3 18 C6
Allen St W8 113 C3 255 B5
Allenswood 12 SW19 157 A3
Allenswood Rd SE9 144 B3
Allerdale Ho 7 N4 51 B2
Allerford Ct
Catford SE6 163 D1
Harrow HA2 42 A4
Allerford Rd SE6 185 D6
Allerton Ct 5 NW4 28 D1
North Cheam SM3 216 D6
Allerton Ho N1 235 D3
4 Merton SW19 180 A3
Allerton Rd N16 73 A6
Allerton St N1 235 D2
Allerton Wlk 11 N7 72 B6
Allestree Rd
SW6 135 A5 264 A3
Alleyn Cres SE21 161 B2
Alleyndale Rd RM8 80 C6
Alleyn Ho EC1 242 B5
SE1 262 C5
Alleyn Pk Dulwich SE21 161 C1
Southall UB2 107 C1
Alleyn Rd SE21 161 C1
Alleyn's Sch SE22 161 C6
Allfarthing La SW18 158 A5
Allfarthing Prim Sch
SW18 158 A5
Allgood Cl SM4 200 D3
Allgood St 10 E2 95 D5
Allhallows La EC4 252 C5
Allhallows Rd E6 100 A1
All Hallows Rd N17 33 C2
Alliance Cl HA0 65 D4
Alliance Ct Acton W3 88 D2
Ashford TW15 171 A6
Alliance Rd Acton W3 88 D3
Newham E16 99 C2
Woolwich SE18 146 A5
Allied Ind Est W3 111 C5
Allied Way W3 111 C4
Allingham Cl W7 108 D6
Allingham Ct NW3 70 C3
Allingham St
N1 95 A5 235 A4
Allington Ave
Tottenham N17 33 C4
Upper Halliford TW17 193 C6
Allington Cl
Greenford UB6 64 A1
3 Wimbledon SW19 178 D5
Allington Ct 6 SW8 137 C3
Croydon CR0 206 C3
Allington Rd NW4 46 B3
W10 91 A5
Harrow HA2 42 A4
Orpington BR6 211 C1
Allington St SW1 258 D5
Allison Cl SE10 142 A4
Allison Gr SE21 161 C3
Allison Rd N8 50 D4
W3 111 A6
Alliston Ho 27 E2 95 D4
Allitsen Rd
NW8 92 C5 230 A4
Allnutt Way SW4 159 D6
Alloa Ct N14 15 C2
Alloa Rd SE8 119 A1
Ilford IG3 80 A6
Allom Ct 11 SW4 138 A3
Allonby Dr HA4 38 D2
Allonby Gdns HA9 43 C1
Allonby Ho E14 97 A2
Alloway Rd E3 97 A4
Allport Ho SE5 139 B2
Allport Mews 33 E1 96 C3
All Saints' Benhilton CE Prim Sch SM1 217 D5
All Saints CE First Sch
SW19 180 A3
All Saint's CE Jun Sch SE19
All Saints' CE Prim Sch
N20 14 B2
NW2 69 B5
SE3 142 C3
All Saints CE Prim Sch
SW15 134 C2
All Saints' CE Prim Sch
SM5 219 A3
All Saints' Cl N9 18 A2
All Saints Ct 9 E1 118 C6
E5 74 C4
Heston TW5 128 D4
All Saints Dr SE3 142 D3
All Saint's Inf Sch SE19
All Saints Mews HA3 24 C4
All Saints Pas SW18 157 C6
All Saints RC Sch RM8 59 C1
All Saints Rd W11 91 B1
All Saints' Rd W3 111 A3
All Saints Rd
Merton SW19 180 A3
Sutton SM1 218 A5
All Saints St N1 94 B5 233 C4
All Saints Sta E14 119 D6
All Saints Twr 18 E10 53 D2
Allsop Pl NW1 92 D3 237 D5
All Souls' Ave NW10 90 B6
All Souls CE Prim Sch
W1 93 C2 239 A4
All Souls Pl W1 238 D3
Allum La WD6 10 A6
Allum Way N20 14 A3
Allwood Cl SE26 184 D6
Alma Ave E4 36 A3
Alma Birk Ho 1 NW6 69 B1
Almack Rd E5 74 C4
Alma Cl N10 31 B2
Alma Cres SM1 217 A3
Alma Gr SE1 117 D2 263 D3
Alma Ho E5 74 B5
7 Brentford TW8 132 A6
2 Edmonton N9 34 A6
Alma Pl NW10 90 B4
Penge SE19 183 D3
Thornton Heath CR7 204 C4
Alma Prim Sch SE16 118 A2
Enfield EN3 18 D6
Alma Rd N10 31 B3
SW18 158 A6
Carshalton SM5 218 C3
Enfield EN3 7 A1
Sidcup DA14 168 A1
Southall UB1 107 A6
Thames Ditton KT10,KT7 196 C1
Alma Row HA3 24 B2
Alma Sq NW8 92 A4 229 B2
Alma St E15 76 B2
NW5 71 B2
Alma Terr W8 255 B5
Wandsworth SW18 158 B4
Almeida St 10 N1 72 D1
Almeric Rd SW11 136 D1
Almer Rd SW20 178 A3
Almington St N4 50 B1
Almond Ave W5 110 A3
Carshalton SM5 218 D6
Uxbridge UB10 60 D5
West Drayton UB7 104 C3
Almond Cl BR2 210 C2
SE15 140 A3
Charlton TW17 171 A1
Hayes UB3 105 C6
Ruislip HA4 61 D5
Feltham TW14 150 A3
Almond Gr TW8 131 B5
Almond Ho SE4 141 B3
Almond Rd SE16 118 B2
Tottenham N17 34 A3
Almonds Ave IG9 21 A2
Almond Way BR2 210 C2
Harrow HA2 24 A1
Mitcham CR4 203 D5
Almorah Rd N1 73 B1
Heston TW5 128 D4
Almshouse La EN1 6 B6
Almshouses E10 75 D6
Sunbury TW16 171 D2
Almshouses The IG11 79 A2
Al-Muntada Islamic Sch
SW6 135 B4 264 D2
Alnmouth Ct 10 UB1 86 A1
Alnwick 8 N17 34 B3
Alnwick Gr SM4 201 D5
Alnwick Rd
Eltham SE12 165 B4
Newham E16 99 C1
Alonso Ct 4 DA17 125 C1
Alperton Com Lower Sch
HA0 87 D6
Alperton Com Sch HA0 66 B1
Alperton La UB6 87 D5
Alperton St W10 91 B3
Alperton Sta HA0 88 A6
Alphabet Gdns SM5 202 B3
Alphabet Sq E3 97 C2
Alpha Bsns Ctr E17 53 B4
Alpha Cl NW8 92 C4 230 B1
Alpha Ct 6 NW5 71 B2
Alpha Est The UB3 105 C4
Alpha Gr E14 119 C4
Alpha Ho NW6 91 C5
NW8 237 B5
19 SW4 138 B1
Alpha Pl NW6 91 C5
SW3 136 C6 267 B6
Alpha Rd SE14 141 B4
Chingford E4 19 D1
Croydon CR0 205 C1
Edmonton N18 34 A4
Enfield EN3 7 A1
Hillingdon UB10 82 D3
Surbiton KT5 198 B3
Teddington TW12 174 B5
Alpha St SE15 140 A3
Alphea Cl SW19 180 C3
Alpine Ave KT5 215 A6
Alpine Bsns Ctr E6 100 C2
Alpine Cl CR0 221 C5
Alpine Copse 2 BR1 188 C1
Alpine Gr 36 E9 74 C1
Alpine Rd SE16 118 D1
Walton-on-T KT12 194 A2
Alpine View SM1 218 C3
Alpine Way E6 100 C2
Alpine Wlk HA7 8 C2
Alric Ave NW10 67 B1
Kingston KT3 199 D6
Alroy Rd N4 50 C2
Alsace Rd
SE17 117 C1 263 A2
Al Sadiq & Al Zahra Schs
NW6 91 A6
Alscot Rd SE1 117 D3 263 D5
Alscot Road Ind Est
SE1 263 D5
Alscot Way SE1 263 C4
Alsike Rd DA18 125 A3
Alsom Ave KT19,KT4 216 A4
Alston Cl KT7 197 B2
Alston Ct EN5 1 A2
Alston Rd Barnet EN5 1 A2
Edmonton N18 34 B5
Upper Tooting SW17 180 B6
Altair Cl N17 33 D4
Altash Way SE9 166 C2
Altenburg Ave W13 109 B3
Altenburg Gdns SW11 136 D1
Alt Gr SW19 179 A3
Altham Rd HA5 23 A3
Althea St SW6 135 D2
Althope Mews SW11 266 D1
Althorne Gdns E18 54 D5
Althorne Way RM10 81 C6
Althorp Cl EN5 12 A4
Althorpe Rd HA1 42 A4
Althorp Rd SW17 158 D3
Altior Ct N6 49 C3
Altmore Ave E6 100 B6
Altmore Inf Sch E6 100 B6
Alton Ave HA7 24 D3
Alton Cl DA5 169 A3
Isleworth TW7 130 D3
Alton Ct 18 BR3 185 C3
Alton Gdns
Beckenham BR3 185 C3
Twickenham TW2 152 B4
Alton Ho 3 E3 97 D4
Alton Rd N17 51 B6
Croydon CR0 220 C5
Richmond TW10,TW9 132 A1
Roehampton SW15 156 A3
Alton St E14 97 D2
Altyre Cl BR3 207 B4
Altyre Rd CR0 221 B6
Altyre Way BR3 207 B4
Alum Ct KT5 198 B3
Alumni Ct SE1 253 D2
Alvanley Ct NW3 69 D3
Alvanley Gdns NW6 69 D3
Alvanley Ho 14 SW9 138 C4
Alverstone Ave
East Barnet EN4 14 C4
Wimbledon SW18,SW19 157 C2
Alverstone Gdns SE9 167 A3
Alverstone Ho 11
SE11 138 C6
Alverstone Rd NW2 68 C1
Little Ilford E12 78 C4
New Malden KT3 199 D5
Wembley HA9 44 B1
Alverston Gdns SE25 205 C4
Alverton St SE8 141 B6
Alveston Ave HA3 43 B6
Alvey St SE17 263 A2
Alvia Gdns SM1 218 A4
Alvington Cres E8 73 D3
Alway Ave KT19 215 B3
Alwen Cotts CR0
Alwold Cres SE12 165 C5
Alwyn Ave W4 111 B1
Alwyn Cl
Borehamwood WD6 10 B5
Alwyn Cl *continued*
New Addington CR0 223 D1
Alwyne La N1 72 D1
Alwyne Pl N1 73 A1
Alwyne Rd N1 73 A1
Ealing W7 108 C6
Wimbledon SW19 179 B4
Alwyne Sq N1 73 A2
Alwyne Villas N1 72 D1
Alwyn Gdns NW9 46 A5
Acton W3 88 D1
Alyn Ct N8 49 D3
Alyth Gdns NW11 47 C3
Alzette Ho 11 E2 96 D5
Amalgamated Dr TW8 131 B6
Amanda Ct TW15 148 B2
Amar Ct SE18 123 D2
Amardeep Ct SE18 123 D1
Amazon St E1 96 B1
Ambassador Cl TW3 129 A3
Ambassador Ct NW4 46 D4
9 NW6 69 C3
Ambassador Gdns E6 100 B2
Ambassador Ho NW8 229 B5
Ambassador Sq E14 119 D2
Amber Ave E17 35 A2
Amber Ct N7 72 C2
NW9 45 C6
Mitcham CR4 202 C5
Amberden Ave N3 47 C6
Ambergate St
SE17 116 D1 261 D2
Amber Gr NW2 46 D1
Amberley Cl
2 Orpington BR6 227 D3
Pinner HA5 41 B6
Amberley Ct 2 SW9 138 D2
Sidcup DA14 190 C5
Sutton SM2 218 A1
Amberley Gdns
Enfield EN1 17 C4
Worcester Park KT19 215 D4
Amberley Gr
Croydon CR0 205 D2
Penge SE26 184 B5
Amberley Ho EN5 1 D1
Amberley Rd E10 53 D2
SE2 146 D6
W9 91 C2
Buckhurst Hill IG9 21 C3
Enfield EN1 17 D5
Palmers Green N13 16 B2
Amberley Way
Heston TW4 150 C6
Morden SM4 201 B2
Romford RM7 59 D5
Uxbridge UB10 82 A5
Amberside Cl TW2 152 B5
Amber Wharf 29 E2 95 D6
Amberwood Cl SM6 220 A3
Amberwood Rise KT3 199 C3
Amblecote Cl SE12 165 B1
Amblecote Mdw SE12 165 B1
Amblecote Rd SE12 165 B1
Ambler Prim Sch N4 72 D6
Ambler Rd N4 72 D5
Ambleside NW1 231 D3
Catford BR1 186 B4
13 Putney SW19 157 A3
Ambleside Ave
Beckenham BR3 207 A4
Streatham SW16 181 D6
Walton-on-T KT12 194 C1
Ambleside Cl E10 53 D2
E9 74 C3
Ambleside Cres EN3 6 D2
Ambleside Dr TW14 149 D3
Ambleside Gdns
Redbridge IG4 56 A4
Streatham SW16 181 D5
Sutton SM2 218 A2
Wembley HA9 43 D1
Ambleside Jun Sch
KT12 194 C1
Ambleside Point 1
SE15 140 C5
Ambleside Rd DA7 147 C3
NW10 67 D1
Ambrook Rd DA17 125 C3
Ambrosden Ave
SW1 115 C3 259 B5
Ambrose Ave NW11 47 B3
Ambrose Cl 6 E6 100 B2
Orpington BR6 227 D5
Ambrose Ho 9 E14 97 C2
Ambrose Mews 2
SW11 136 D3
Ambrose St SE16 118 B2
Ambrose Wlk E3 97 C5
AMC Bsns Ctr NW10 88 D4
Amelia Cl W3 110 D4
Amelia Ho 5 W6 112 C1
Amelia St
SE17 117 A1 262 A2
Amen Cnr EC4 241 D1
Streatham SW17 181 A4
Amen Ct EC4 94 D1 241 D1
Amenity Way SM4 200 C2
American Coll The
W1 93 A1 238 B2
American Com Schs
UB10 82 B6
American Sch in London
The NW8 92 B5 229 C4
America Sq EC3 253 C6
America St SE1 252 A3
Amerland Rd SW18 157 B5
Amersham Ave N18 33 B4
Amersham Gr SE14 141 B5
Amersham Rd SE14 141 B4
Thornton Heath CR0 205 B3
Amersham Vale SE14,
SE8 141 B5
Amery Gdns NW10 90 B6
Amery Ho SE17 263 B2
Amery Rd HA1 65 A6
Amesbury Ave SW2 160 B2
Amesbury Cl KT4 200 C1
Amesbury Ct EN2 4 C3
Amesbury Dr E4 19 D5
Amesbury Rd BR1 209 D6
Dagenham RM9 80 D1
Feltham TW13 150 D2
Amesbury Twr 4
SW8 137 C3
Ames Cotts 14 E3 97 A2
Ames Ho 10 E2 96 D5
Amethyst Cl N11 31 D3
Amethyst Rd E15 76 B4
Amherst Ave W13 87 C1
Amherst Dr BR5 211 D5
Amherst Gdns 2 W13 87 C1
Amherst Prim Sch E8 74 A3
Amherst Rd W13 87 C1
Amhurst Ct N4 51 B2
Amhurst Gdns TW7 131 A3
Amhurst Par N16 51 D2
Amhurst Pk N4,N16 51 C2
Amhurst Rd E8,N16 74 A4
Amhurst Terr E8 74 A4
Amhurst Wlk SE28 124 A5
Amias Ho EC1 242 A6
Amidas Gdns RM8 80 B4
Amiel St 17 E1 96 C3
Amies St SW11 136 D2
Amigo Ho SE1 261 B6
Amina Way SE16 118 A3
Amis Ave KT19 214 D3
Amity Gr SW20 178 C2
Amity Rd E15 76 D1
Ammanford Gn NW9 45 C3
Amner Rd SW11 159 A5
Amor Rd W6 112 C3
Amory Ho N1 233 D4
Amott Rd SE15 140 A2
Amoy Pl E14 119 C6
Ampleforth Rd SE2 124 C4
Ampton Pl WC1 233 C1
Ampton St WC1 94 B4 233 C1
Amroth Cl SE23 162 B3
Amroth Gn NW9 45 C3
Amstel Ct 11 SE15 139 D5
Amsterdam Rd E14 120 A3
Amundsen Ho 5 NW10 67 B1
Amwell Cl EN2 17 B6
Amwell St EC1 94 C4 234 A2
Amyand Cotts 12 TW1 153 B5
Amyand Park Gdns 2
TW1 153 B4
Amyand Park Rd TW1 153 B4
Amy Cl SM6 220 A1
Amy Johnson Ho HA8 26 D1
Amy Johnson Prim Sch
SM6 220 A1
Amyruth Rd SE4 163 C6
Amy Warne Cl E6 100 A3
Anarth Ct KT13 193 C1
Anatola Rd N19 71 C6
Ancaster Cres KT3 200 A3
Ancaster Rd BR3 206 D6
Ancaster St SE18 145 C5
Anchorage Cl SW19 179 C5
Anchorage Point E14 119 C4
Anchorage Point Ind Est
SE7 121 C3
Anchor Bsns Pk CR0,
SM6 220 A5
Anchor Cl IG11 102 B4
Anchor Ct 5 EN1 17 C6
Anchor Ho EC1 242 A6
Ilford IG3 80 A5
Newham E16 99 C1
Anchor & Hope La
SE7 121 C2
Anchor Mews SW12 159 B5
Anchor Ret Pk E1 96 C3
Anchor St SE16 118 B2
Anchor Terr SE1 252 B4
Anchor Yd EC1 242 B6
Ancill Cl W6 135 A6 264 A5
Ancona Rd NW10 90 A5
SE18 123 B1
Andace Pk BR1 187 C2
Andalus Rd SW9 138 A2

Andaman Ho 3 E1 ... 97 A2
Ander Cl HA0 ... 65 D4
Anderson Cl W3 ... 89 B1
Morden SM3 ... 201 C1
Southgate N21 ... 16 B6
Anderson Ct NW2 ... 46 C2
Anderson Dr TW15 ... 171 A6
Anderson Ho 10 E14 ... 120 A6
Barking IG11 ... 101 B5
Upper Tooting SW17 ... 180 B5
Anderson Rd E9 ... 74 D2
Redbridge IG8 ... 55 D6
Anderson's Pl TW3 ... 129 D1
Andersons Sq N1 ... 234 C5
Anderson St SW3 ... 257 C2
Anderson Way
Erith DA17 ... 125 D4
Erith DA17 ... 125 D4
Anderton Cl SE5 ... 139 B2
Anderton Ct N22 ... 31 D1
Andhurst Ct KT2 ... 176 D2
Andon Ct BR3 ... 207 A6
Andorra Ct BR1 ... 187 C2
Andover Ave E16 ... 99 D1
Andover Cl
East Bedfont TW14 ... 149 D3
Greenford UB6 ... 85 D3
Andover Ho 5 N7 ... 72 B6
Andover Pl NW6 ... 91 D5
Andover Rd N7 ... 72 B6
Orpington BR6 ... 211 C1
Twickenham TW2 ... 152 B3
Andoversford Ct 7
SE15 ... 139 C6
Andreck Ct BR3 ... 186 A1
Andre St E8 ... 74 A3
Andrew Borde St
WC2 ... 239 D2
Andrew Ct
Beckenham BR3 ... 207 D6
Forest Hill SE23 ... 162 D2
Andrewes Gdns E6 ... 100 A1
Andrewes Ho EC2 ... 242 B3
Sutton SM1 ... 217 C4
Andrew Ewing Jun & Inf
Sch TW5 ... 129 B4
Andrew Ho SE4 ... 141 B3
Putney SW15 ... 156 A6
Andrew Marvell Ho 12
N16 ... 73 C4
Andrew Pl SW8 ... 269 D2
Andrew Reed Ho
SW18 ... 157 A4
Andrews Cl BR5 ... 190 D1
Buckhurst Hill IG9 ... 21 C2
Harrow HA1 ... 42 B2
North Cheam KT4 ... 216 D6
Andrews Crosse WC2 ... 241 A1
Andrews Ct 2 W7 ... 108 C5
Andrew's Rd E8 ... 96 B6
Andrew St E14 ... 98 A1
Andrews Wlk SE17 ... 138 D6
Andrew Wells Ho BR1 187 B3
Andringham Lo 4
BR1 ... 187 B2
Andrula Ct N22 ... 32 D2
Andwell Cl SE2 ... 124 B4
Anerley Ct SE20 ... 184 B3
Anerley Gr SE19 ... 183 D3
Anerley Hill SE19 ... 183 D4
Anerley Park Rd SE20 . 184 B3
Anerley Pk SE20 ... 184 B3
Anerley Prim Sch
SE20 ... 184 A2
Anerley Rd SE20 ... 184 B2
Anerley Sch for Boys
SE20 ... 184 A2
Anerley Sta SE20 ... 184 B2
Anerley Station Rd
SE20 ... 184 B2
Anerley Vale SE19 ... 184 A3
Aneurin Bevan Ct NW2 . 68 B6
Aneurin Bevan Ho N11 31 D3
Anfield Cl SW12 ... 159 C4
Angel EC1 ... 94 C5 234 B3
Angela Ct 2 SE23 ... 162 C3
Angela Davis Ind Est 21
SW9 ... 138 D1
Angel Alley E1 ... 243 D2
Angel Cl N18 ... 34 A6
Angel Corner Par 6
N18 ... 34 A6
Angel Ct EC2 ... 242 D2
SW1 ... 249 B3
Angel Edmonton N18 .. 34 A5
Angelfield TW3 ... 151 D6
Angel Gate EC1 ... 234 D2
Angel Hill SM1 ... 217 D5
Angel Hill Dr SM1 ... 217 D5
Angel Ho N1 ... 234 B3
Angelica Cl UB7 ... 82 B1
Angelica Dr E6 ... 100 C2
Angelica Gdns CR0 ... 206 D1
Angelina Ho 2 SE15 ... 140 A4
Angel La E15 ... 76 B2
Hayes UB3 ... 83 B2
Angell Park Gdns 5
SW9 ... 138 C2
Angell Rd SW9 ... 138 D2
Angel Mews N1 ... 234 B3
Putney SW15 ... 156 A4
Stepney E1 ... 118 B6
Angel Pas EC4 117 B6 252 C5
Angel Pl SE1 ... 252 C2
1 Edmonton N18 ... 34 A5
Angel Prim Sch
N1 ... 94 C5 234 B4
Angel Rd Harrow HA1 ... 42 C3
Thames Ditton KT7 ... 197 A1
Angel Rd (North Circular
Rd) N18 ... 34 B5
Angel Rd Works N18 ... 34 C5
Angel Road Sta N18 ... 34 C5
Angel St EC1 ... 95 A1 242 A2
Angel Sta EC1 .. 94 C5 234 B3
Angel Wlk W6 ... 112 C2
Angerstein Bsns Pk
SE10 ... 121 A2
Angerstein La SE3 ... 142 D4
Anglebury 5 W2 ... 91 C1
Angle Cl UB10 ... 82 C6
Angle Gn RM8 ... 58 C1
Anglers Cl TW10 ... 175 C6
Anglers La NW5 ... 71 B2
Anglers Reach KT6 ... 197 D4
Anglesea Ave 4 SE18 122 D2
Anglesea Ho KT1 ... 197 D5
Anglesea Rd SE18 ... 122 D2
Kingston KT1 ... 197 D5
Anglesey Cl TW15 ... 148 C1
Anglesey Court Rd
SM5 ... 219 A2
Anglesey Ct W7 ... 86 D3
Anglesey Gdns SM5 .. 219 A2
Anglesey Ho 9 E14 ... 97 C1
Anglesey Rd Enfield EN3 .. 6 B1
South Oxhey WD19 ... 22 C5
Anglesmede Cres HA5 . 41 C6
Anglesmede Way HA5 . 41 C6
Angles Rd SW16 ... 182 A6
Anglia Cl N17 ... 34 B3
Anglia Ho 15 E14 ... 97 A1
Anglian Ind Est IG11 . 101 D2
Anglian Rd E11 ... 76 B5
Anglo American Laundry
SW17 ... 158 A1
Anglo Rd 24 E3 ... 97 B5
Angrave Ct 4 E8 ... 95 D6
Angrave Pas 5 E8 ... 95 D6
Angus Cl KT9 ... 214 C3
Angus Dr HA4 ... 62 C4
Angus Gdns NW9 ... 27 B2
Angus Ho 12 SW12 ... 159 D4
Angus Rd E13 ... 99 C4
Angus St SE14 ... 141 A5
Anhalt Rd
SW11 ... 136 C5 267 B4
Ankerdine Cres SE18 . 144 D4
Anlaby Rd TW11 ... 174 C5
Anley Rd W14 ... 112 D4
Anmersh Gr HA7 ... 25 D2
Annabel Cl E14 ... 97 D1
Anna Cl E8 ... 95 D6
Annandale Gr UB10 ... 61 A5
Annandale Prim Sch
SE10 ... 120 D1
Annandale Rd DA15 ... 167 D4
SE10 ... 120 D1
W4 ... 111 C1
Croydon CR0 ... 222 A6
Anna Neagle Cl 2 E7 .. 77 A4
Anne Boleyn's Wlk
Belmont SM3 ... 217 A1
Kingston KT2 ... 176 A5
Anne Carver Lo HA0 ... 66 A1
Anne Compton Mews
SE12 ... 164 D4
Anne Goodman Ho 3
E1 ... 96 C1
Anne Kerr Ct 18 SW15 156 D5
Anne's Ct NW8 ... 237 B6
Annesley Ave NW9 ... 45 B6
Annesley Cl NW10 ... 67 C5
Annesley Dr CR0 ... 223 B5
Annesley Ho 15 SW9 .. 138 C5
31 SW9 ... 138 C4
Annesley Rd SE3 ... 143 B4
Annesley Wlk N19 ... 71 C6
Anne St E13 ... 99 A3
Annett Cl TW17 ... 193 C5
Annette Cl HA3 ... 24 C1
Annette Cres 9 N1 ... 73 A1
Annette Ct N7 ... 72 B5
Annette Rd N7 ... 72 B4
Annett Rd KT12 ... 194 A2
Anne Way KT8 ... 195 D5
Annie Besant Cl E3 ... 97 B6
Annie Taylor Ho 1 E12 78 C4
Anning St E2 ... 243 B6
Annington Rd N2 ... 48 D6
Annis Rd E9 ... 75 A2
Ann La SW10 .. 136 B6 266 C5
Ann Moss Way SE16 ... 118 C3
Ann Parkes Ct TW5 ... 128 D3
Ann's Cl SW1 ... 248 A1
Ann's Pl E1 ... 243 C3
Ann St SE18 ... 123 B2
Ann Stroud Ct SE12 ... 165 A6
Annsworthy Ave CR7 .. 205 B6
Annsworthy Cres CR7 . 183 B1
Annunciation RC Inf Sch
The HA8 ... 27 B2
Annunciation RC Jun Sch
The HA8 ... 27 B4
Ansar Gdns E17 ... 53 B4
Ansdell Rd SE15 ... 140 C3
Ansdell St W8 113 D3 255 D6
Ansdell Terr
W8 ... 113 D3 255 D6
Ansell Gr SM5 ... 203 A1
Ansell Ho E1 ... 96 C2
Ansell Rd SW17 ... 158 D1
Anselm Cl CR0 ... 221 D5
Anselm Rd
SW6 ... 135 C6 265 A5
Pinner HA5 ... 23 B3
Ansford Rd BR1,SE6 ... 186 B6
Ansleigh Pl W11 ... 112 D6
Anslie Wlk 8 SW12 ... 159 B4
Anson 30 NW9 ... 27 D1
Anson Ho 6 E1 ... 97 A3
SW1 ... 269 A6
Anson Pl SE28 ...
Anson Prim Sch NW2 .. 68 D3
Anson Rd N7 ... 71 D4
NW2 ... 68 C3
Anstey Ct 6 W3 ... 110 D4
Anstey Ho 8 E9 ... 96 C6
Anstey Lo EN1 ... 17 C5
Anstey Rd SE15 ... 140 A2
Anstey Wlk N15 ... 51 A5
Anstice Cl W4 ... 133 C5
Anstridge Rd SE9 ... 167 B5
Antelope Rd SE18 ... 122 B3
Antenor Ho 11 E2 ... 96 B5
Anthony Cl NW7 ... 27 C6
Anthony Cope Ct N1 .. 235 D2
Anthony Ct TW7 ... 130 D2
Anthony Ho NW8 ... 237 A5
Anthony Rd DA16 ... 146 A4
Croydon SE25 ... 206 A3
Greenford UB6 ... 86 C4
Anthony St E1 ... 96 B1
Antigua Wlk SE19 ... 183 B5
Antilles Bay 7 E14 ... 120 A4
Antill Rd E3 ... 97 A4
N15 ... 52 A5
Antill Terr 5 E1 ... 96 D1
Antlers Hill E4 ... 19 D6
Anton Cres SM1 ... 217 C5
Antoneys Cl HA5 ... 22 D1
Anton Pl HA9 ... 66 D5
Anton St E8 ... 74 A3
Antony Ho 4 SE14 ... 140 D5
2 SE16 ... 118 C2
Antrim Gr NW3 ... 70 D2
Antrim Ho SW11 ... 137 A2
Antrim Mans NW3 ... 70 D2
Antrim Rd NW3 ... 70 D2
Antrobus Cl SM1 ... 217 B3
Antrobus Rd W4 ... 111 A3
Anvil Cl SW16 ... 181 C3
Anvil Ho 10 N9 ... 18 A1
Anvil Rd TW16 ... 194 A6
Anworth Cl IG8 ... 37 B4
Apex Cl BR3 ... 185 D2
Apex Cnr NW7 ... 27 B6
Twickenham TW13 ... 151 B1
Apex Ct W13 ... 87 A1
Apex Ind Est NW10 ... 89 D3
Aphrodite Ct 2 E14 ... 119 C2
Aplin Way TW7 ... 130 C4
Apollo Ave BR1 ... 187 B2
Moor Park HA6 ... 22 A5
Apollo Bldg 20 E14 ... 119 C2
Apollo Ho 31 E2 ... 96 B5
N6 ... 48 D2
SW10 ... 266 C5
Apollo Ind Bsns Ctr 29
SE8 ... 140 D6
Apollo Pl E11 ... 76 C5
SW10 ... 266 C4
Apollo Studios 18 NW5 71 D3
Apollo Way SE18 ... 123 B3
Apostle Way CR7 ... 182 D1
Apothecary St EC4 ... 241 C1
Appach Rd SW2 ... 160 C5
Appin Ct HA1 ... 42 C2
Appleby Cl N15 ... 51 B4
Chingford E4 ... 36 A4
Twickenham TW2 ... 152 B2
Appleby Gdns TW14 ... 149 D3
Appleby Rd E16 ... 99 A1
E8 ... 74 A1
Appleby St E2 ... 95 D5
Appledore Ave HA4 ... 62 C5
Appledore Cl BR2 ... 209 A4
Edgware HA8 ... 26 C2
Upper Tooting SW12,
SW17 ... 158 D2
Appledore Cres DA14,
DA15 ... 167 D1
Appleford 8 NW5 ... 71 C3
Appleford Ho 6 W10 ... 91 A3
Appleford Rd W10 ... 91 A3
Applegarth
Claygate KT10 ... 212 D3
New Addington CR0 ... 223 D1
Apple Garth TW8 ... 109 D2
Applegarth Dr IG2 ... 57 D5
Applegarth Ho SE1 ... 251 D2
8 SE15 ... 140 A5
Applegarth Inf Sch
CR0 ... 223 D2
Applegarth Jun Sch
CR0 ... 223 D2
Applegarth Rd W14 ... 112 D3
Woolwich SE28 ... 124 C6
Apple Gr
Chessington KT9 ... 214 A4
Enfield EN1 ... 5 C2
Apple Lo HA0 ... 65 C5
Apple Mkt★ WC2 ... 250 B6
Kingston KT1 ... 175 D1
Apple Rd E11 ... 76 C5
Appleshaw Ho 4 SE5 139 C2
Appleton Gdns KT3 ... 200 A3
Appleton Rd SE9 ... 144 A2
Appleton Sq CR4 ... 180 C2
Apple Tree Ave UB7 ... 82 B1
Appletree Cl 5 SE20 ... 184 B2
Appletree Ct SE13 ... 142 B1
Appletree Gdns EN4 ... 2 C1
Apple Tree Yd SW1 ... 249 B4
Applewood Cl N20 ... 14 C3
NW2 ... 68 B5
Ickenham UB10 ... 60 A4
Applewood Dr E13 ... 99 B3
Appold St EC2 .. 95 C2 243 A4
Appollo Ct 7 SW9 ... 138 C4
Apprentice Way 6 E5 . 74 B4
Approach Cl N16 ... 73 C4
Approach La NW7 ... 29 A5
Approach Rd E2 ... 96 C5
Ashford TW15 ... 171 A4
East Molesey KT8 ... 195 C4
Edgware HA8 ... 26 C4
Merton SW20 ... 178 C1
New Barnet EN4,EN5 ... 2 B1
Approach The BR6 ... 227 D6
NW4 ... 46 D4
W3 ... 89 B1
Enfield EN1 ... 6 B3
Aprey Gdns NW4 ... 46 C5
April Cl Ealing W7 ... 108 C6
Feltham TW13 ... 150 A1
Orpington BR6 ... 227 D3
April Ct 20 E2 ... 96 A5
April Glen SE23 ... 162 D1
April St E8 ... 73 D4
Apsley Cl HA2 ... 42 A4
Apsley Ct SM2 ... 218 A2
Apsley Ctr The NW2 ... 68 A6
Apsley Ho E1 ... 96 C2
Hounslow TW4 ... 129 B1
Apsley Rd
Croydon SE25 ... 206 B5
Kingston KT3 ... 199 A6
Apsley Way NW2 ... 68 A6
W1 ... 248 B2
Aquarius TW1 ... 153 B3
Aquarius Way HA6 ... 22 A6
Aquila St NW8 . 92 B5 229 D4
Aquinas St
SE1 ... 116 C5 251 B3
Arabella Ct NW8 ... 229 B4
Arabella Dr SW15 ... 133 C1
Arabia Cl E4 ... 20 B4
Arabian Ho 3 E1 ... 97 A3
Arabin Rd SE4 ... 141 B1
Aragon Ave KT7 ... 196 D4
Aragon Cl BR2 ... 210 B1
Ashford TW16 ... 171 D3
Enfield EN2 ... 4 B5
Aragon Ct
Beckenham BR3 ... 186 A2
East Molesey KT8 ... 196 A5
Aragon Dr HA4 ... 40 D1
Aragon Rd
Kingston KT2 ... 176 A5
West Barnes SM4 ... 200 D3
West Barnes SM4 ... 201 A2
Aragon Twr SE8 ... 119 B2
Arakan Ho 4 N16 ... 73 B4
Aral Ho 14 E1 ... 96 D3
Arandora Cres RM6 ... 58 B2
Aranya Ct E17 ... 35 A1
Arapiles Ho 6 E14 ... 98 B1
Arbery Rd E3 ... 97 A5
Arbon Ct N1 ... 235 B5
Arbor Cl BR3 ... 185 D1
Arbor Ct N16 ... 73 B6
Arborfield Ho 6 E14 119 C6
Arbor Rd E4 ... 20 B1
Arbourfield Cl SW2 ... 160 B3
Arbour Ho 3 E1 ... 96 D1
Arbour Rd EN3 ... 6 D2
Arbour Sq E1 ... 96 D1
Arbroath Rd SE9 ... 144 A2
Arbrook Chase KT10 .. 212 A2
Arbrook Ct BR5 ... 190 A2
Chessington KT9 ... 213 D3
Arbrook Hall KT10 ... 212 D2
Arbrook La KT10 ... 212 B2
Arbury Terr 3 SE26 ... 162 B1
Arbuthnot La DA5 ... 169 A5
Arbuthnot Rd SE14 ... 140 D3
Arbutus St E8 ... 95 D6
Arcade Ho 7 NW11 ... 47 B4
Arcade The E17 ... 53 C5
EC2 ... 243 A3
1 N7 ... 72 A4
2 SE9 ... 166 C5
Barking IG11 ... 79 A1
Arcadia Ave N3 ... 29 C2
Arcadia Cl SM5 ... 219 A4
Arcadian Ave DA5 ... 169 A5
Arcadian Cl DA5 ... 169 A5
Arcadian Gdns N22 ... 32 C3
Arcadian Rd DA5 ... 169 A5
Arcadia St E14 ... 97 C1
Archangel St SE16 ... 118 D4
Archbishop Lanfranc Sch
The CR0 ... 204 A3
Archbishop Michael
Ramsey Tech Coll
SE5 ... 138 D5
Archbishop's Pl 1
SW2 ... 160 B4
Archbishop Sumner's CE
Prim Sch
SE11 ... 116 C2 261 B3
Archbishop Tenison's CE
High Sch CR0 ... 221 D5
Archbishop Tenison's Sch
SE11 ... 138 B6 270 D5
Archdale Ct W12 ... 112 B5
Archdale Ho SE1 ... 263 A6
Archdale Pl KT3 ... 198 D6
Archdale Rd SE22 ... 139 D1
Archdeacon Cambridge's
CE Prim Sch TW2 ... 152 C2
Archel Rd W14 135 B6 264 C6
Archer Cl KT2 ... 176 A3
Archer Ho 25 N1 ... 95 C6
1 SW11 ... 136 B3
W11 ... 244 D6
Ealing W13 ... 109 B5
Archer Mews TW12 ... 174 A4
Archer Rd SE25 ... 206 B5
Archers Dr EN3 ... 6 C3
Archers Lo 14 SE16 ... 118 A1
Archer Sq SE14 ... 141 A6
Archer St W1 ... 249 C6
Archer Terr UB7 ... 104 A6
Archery Cl W2 ... 237 B1
Harrow HA3 ... 42 D6
Archery Fields Ho
WC1 ... 234 A2
Archery Rd SE9 ... 166 B6
Archery Steps W2 ... 247 B6
Arches Bsns Ctr The
UB2 ... 107 B4
Arches The WC2 ... 250 B4
Harrow HA2 ... 63 D6
Archibald Mews W1 ... 248 C5
Archibald Rd N7 ... 71 D4
Archibald St E3 ... 97 C4
Archie Cl UB7 ... 104 C4
Arch St SE1 ... 117 A3 262 A5
Archway N19 ... 71 C6
Archway Bsns Ctr 5
N19 ... 71 D5
Archway Cl W10 ... 90 D2
Wallington SM6 ... 220 A5
Wimbledon SW19 ... 179 D6
Archway Hts 5 N19 ... 49 C1
Archway Mews SW15 .. 135 A1
Archway Rd N6 ... 49 B2
Archway St SW13,
SW14 ... 133 C2
Archway Sta N19 ... 71 C6
Arcola St E8 ... 73 D3
Arctic St NW5 ... 71 B3
Arcus Rd BR1 ... 186 C4
Ardbeg Rd SE24 ... 161 B6
Arden 17 SW19 ... 156 D3
Arden Cl Bushey WD23 ... 8 D4
Erith SE28 ... 102 D1
Harrow HA1 ... 64 B5
Arden Court Gdns N2 .. 48 B3
Arden Cres E14 ... 119 C2
Dagenham RM9 ... 80 D1
Arden Gr BR6 ... 226 D4
Arden Grange N12 ... 30 A6
Arden Ho 21 N1 ... 95 C5
SE11 ... 260 C3
29 SW9 ... 138 A3
Arden Mhor HA5 ... 40 B5
Arden Rd N3 ... 47 B6
Ealing W13 ... 109 C6
Ardent Cl SE25 ... 205 C6
Ardent Ho 28 E3 ... 97 A5
Ardfern Ave SW16 ... 204 C6
Ardfillan Rd SE6 ... 164 B2
Ardgowan Rd SE6 ... 164 C3
Ardilaun Rd N5 ... 73 A4
Ardingly Cl CR0 ... 222 D5
Ardleigh Gdns SM3 ... 201 C2
Ardleigh Rd E17 ... 35 B2
N1 ... 73 C2
Ardleigh Terr E17 ... 35 B2
Ardley Cl NW10 ... 67 C5
Forest Hill SE6 ... 163 A1
Ruislip HA4 ... 39 A2
Ardlui Rd SE27 ... 161 A2
Ardmay Gdns KT6 ... 198 A4
Ardmere Rd SE13 ... 164 B5
Ardmore La IG9 ... 21 B4
Ardmore Pl IG9 ... 21 B4
Ardoch Rd SE6 ... 164 B2
Ardra Rd N9 ... 18 D1
Ardrossan Gdns KT4 .. 216 A5
Ardshiel Cl SW15 ... 134 D2
Ardwell Ave IG6 ... 57 A4
Ardwell Rd SW2 ... 160 A2
Ardwick Rd NW2 ... 69 C4
Arena Bsns Ctr N4 ... 51 A3
Arena Est N4 ... 50 D3
Arena Sta SE25 ... 206 C4
Arena The EN3 ... 7 B5
Ares Ct 8 E14 ... 119 C2
Arethusa Ho 8 E14 .. 119 D2
Argall Ave E10 ... 52 D1
Argall Ho 3 DA18 ... 125 A3
Argall Way E10 ... 53 A1
Argenta Way NW10 ... 66 D1
Argent Ct KT6 ... 214 C5
Argent Ctr The UB3 .. 106 A4
Argon Mews SW6 ... 265 B3
Argon Rd N18 ... 34 D5
Argos Ct 5 SW9 ... 138 C4
Argos Ho 8 E2 ... 96 B5
Argosy Ho SE8 ... 119 A2
W1 ... 238 D5
Argus Way UB5 ... 85 A4
Argyle Cl W13 ... 87 A3
Argyle Ho E14 ... 120 A3
Sutton SM2 ... 218 A2
Argyle Pl W6 ... 112 B2
Argyle Prim Sch WC1 . 233 A2
Argyle Rd E1 ... 96 D3
E15 ... 76 C4
N12 ... 29 C5
Ealing W13 ... 87 A2
Edmonton N18 ... 34 A6
Harrow HA2 ... 41 D3
Hounslow TW3 ... 151 D6
Ilford IG1 ... 78 C6
Newham E16 ... 99 B1
Tottenham N17 ... 34 A2
Argyle Sq WC1 . 94 A4 233 B2
Argyle St WC1 .. 94 A4 233 B2
Argyle Way SE16 ... 118 A1
Argyle Wlk WC1 ... 233 B1
Argyll Ave UB1 ... 107 D5
Argyll Cl SW9 ... 138 B2
Argyll Ct 15 SW2 ... 160 A4
Argyll Gdns HA8 ... 26 D2
Argyll Mans SW3 ... 266 D6
W14 ... 254 B4
Argyll Rd SE18 ... 123 A3
W8 ... 113 C4 245 B1
Argyll St W1 ... 93 C1 239 A1
Arica Ho SE16 ... 118 B3
Arica Rd SE4 ... 141 A2
Ariel Ct SE11 ... 261 C3
W12 ... 112 A3
5 Belvedere DA17 ... 125 C1
Ariel Rd NW6 ... 69 C2
Ariel Way W12 ... 112 C5
Hounslow TW4 ... 128 B2
Aristotle Rd SW4 ... 137 D2
Arkansas Ho 21 N19 ... 49 D2
Arkell Gr SW16 ... 182 D3
Arkindale Rd SE6 ... 164 A1
Arkley Cres E17 ... 53 B4
Arkley Dr EN5 ... 12 B6
Arkley Pk EN5 ... 11 B5
Arkley Rd E17 ... 53 B4
Arklow Ho SE17 ... 139 B6
Arklow Mews 4 KT6 . 214 A6
Arklow Rd SE14 ... 141 B6
Arklow Road Trad Est
SE14 ... 141 B6
Arkwright Ho 23 SW2 . 160 A4
Arkwright Mans NW3 ... 70 A3
Arkwright Rd NW3 ... 70 A3
Arlesey Cl SW15 ... 157 A6
Arlesford Rd SW9 ... 138 A2
Arless Ho 8 HA1 ... 42 D4
Arlingford Rd SW2 ... 160 C5
Arlington N12 ... 13 C1
Arlington Ave
N1 ... 95 A6 235 B5
Arlington Cl DA15 ... 167 C4
Sutton SM1 ... 217 C6
Twickenham TW1 ... 153 C5
Arlington Ct N6 ... 49 A3
4 Twickenham TW1 ... 153 C5
Arlington Dr
Carshalton SM5 ... 218 D6
Ruislip HA4 ... 39 B3
Arlington Gdns W4 ... 111 A1
Ilford IG1 ... 56 C1
Arlington Ho EC1 ... 234 B2
3 SE8 ... 141 B6
W12 ... 112 B5
Arlington Lo SW2 ... 138 B1
Arlington Park Mans 1
W4 ... 111 A1

Arlington Pl 7 SE10 142 A5
Arlington Rd N14 15 C3
NW1 93 B6 231 D5
Ashford TW15 170 B5
Ealing W13 87 B1
Richmond TW10 153 D2
Surbiton KT6 197 D3
Teddington TW11 174 D6
Twickenham TW1 153 C5
Woodford IG8 37 B3
Arlington Sq N1 95 A6 235 B5
Arlington St
SW1 115 C5 249 A4
Arlington Way
EC1 94 C4 234 B2
Arliss Way UB5 84 C6
Arlow Rd N21 16 C3
Armada Ct 11 SE8 141 C6
Armadale Cl N17 52 B5
Armadale Rd SW6 265 A5
Feltham TW14 150 A6
Armada St 10 SE8 141 C6
Armada Way E6 101 A1
Armagh Rd E3 97 B6
Armeston KT3 199 B2
Armfield Cl KT8 195 B4
Armfield Cotts 3
SW19 180 D1
Armfield Cres CR4 180 D1
Armfield Rd EN2 5 B4
Arminger Rd W12 112 B5
Armitage Ho
NW1 92 C2 237 B4
Armitage Rd NW11 47 B1
SE10 120 D1
Armitice Gdns SE25 206 A6
Armour Cl N7 72 B2
Armoury Rd SE8 141 D3
Armoury Way SW18 157 C6
Armsby Ho 15 E1 96 C2
Armstead Wlk RM10 81 C1
Armstrong Ave IG8 36 C4
Armstrong Cl BR1 210 A6
Dagenham RM8 58 D2
Newham E6 100 B1
Pinner HA5 40 A3
Walton-on-T KT12 194 A3
Armstrong Cres EN4 2 B2
Armstrong Ho 8
SW15 156 D5
Armstrong Rd SW7 256 C5
W3 111 D5
Feltham TW13 173 A5
Armstrong Way UB2 107 D4
Armytage Rd TW5 128 D5
Arnal Cres SW18 157 A4
Arncliffe NW6 91 D6
Arncliffe Cl N11 31 A4
Arncroft Ct IG11 102 B4
Arne Gr BR6 227 D5
Arne Ho SE11 260 C2
Arne St WC2 94 A1 240 B1
Arnett Sq E4 35 B4
Arneways Ave RM6 58 D6
Arneway St SW1 259 D5
Arne Wlk SE3 142 D1
Arnewood Cl SW15 156 A3
Arney's La CR4 203 A3
Arngask Rd SE6 164 B4
Arnhem Pl E14 119 C3
Arnhem Way 3 SE22 161 C6
Arnhem Wharf E14 119 C3
Arnhem Wharf Prim Sch
E14 119 C3
Arnison Rd KT8 196 B5
Arnold Ave E EN3 7 C5
Arnold Ave W EN3 7 B5
Arnold Cir E2 95 D4
Arnold Cl HA3 44 B2
Arnold Cres TW7 152 B6
Arnold Ct E18 36 D2
Arnold Dr KT9 213 D2
Arnold Est SE1 253 D1
Arnold Gdns N13 32 D5
Arnold Ho 9 N16 73 C5
SE17 261 D1
Arnold House Sch
NW8 92 B5 229 C3
Arnold Rd E3 97 C4
N15 51 D6
Dagenham RM10 81 C1
Mitcham SW17 180 D3
Northolt UB5 63 A2
Arnos Gr N14 15 D1
Arnos Grove Ct 4 N11 31 C5
Arnos Grove Sta N11 31 C6
Arnos Rd N11 31 C6
Arnot Ho 27 SE5 139 A5
Arnott Cl SE28 124 C5
W4 111 B2
Arnould Ave SE5 139 B1
Arnsberg Way DA7 147 C1
Arnside Gdns HA9 43 D1
Arnside Ho 2 SE17 139 B6
Arnside Rd DA7 147 C4
Arnside St SE17 139 A6
Arnulf St SE6 185 D6
Arnull's Rd SW16 182 D4
Arodene Rd SW2 160 B5
Arosa Rd 4 TW1 153 D5
Arragon Gdns
Streatham SW16 182 A3
West Wickham BR4 223 D5
Arragon Rd E6 99 D6
Wandsworth SW18 157 C3
Arran Cl SM6 219 C4
Arran Ct NW10 67 B5
32 NW9 27 D1
Arrandene Ho 3 BR5 190 B1
Arran Dr Stanmore HA7 25 C6
Wanstead E12 77 D6
Arran Ho N16 51 D1
Arran Mews W5 110 B5
Arran Rd SE6 164 A2
Arran Wlk N1 73 A1
Arras Ave SM4 202 A4
Arras Ho SE2 146 D6
Arrol Ho SE1 262 B5
Arrol Rd BR3 206 D6
Arrowe Ct 7 E5 74 B4
Arrowhead Ct E11 54 B3
Arrow Ho 24 N1 95 C6
Arrow Rd E3 97 D4
Arrow Scout Wlk UB5 85 A4
Arrowsmith Ho SE11 260 C2
Arsenal Rd SE9 144 B2
Arsenal Sta N5 72 C5
Artemis Ct 6 E14 119 C2
Arterberry Rd SW20,
SW19 178 D2
Artesian Cl NW10 67 B1
Artesian Gr EN5 2 A1
Artesian Rd W2 91 C1
Arthingworth St E15 98 C6
Arthur Ct SW11 268 B1
10 W10 90 D1
W2 91 D1
South Croydon CR0 221 B5
Arthur Deakin Ho 1
E1 96 A2
Arthurdon Rd SE4 163 C6
Arthur Gr SE18 123 A2
Arthur Henderson Ho
9 N19 49 D2
9 Fulham SW6 135 B3
Arthur Newton Ho 20
SW11 136 B2
Arthur Rd E6 100 B5
N7 72 B4
Dagenham RM6 58 D3
Edmonton N9 17 D2
6 Kingston KT2 176 C3
West Barnes KT3 200 B4
Wimbledon SW19 179 C6
Arthur Ruxley Est
DA14 190 D4
Arthur St EC4 117 B6 252 D6
Arthur Wade Ho 7 E2 95 D4
Arthur Walls Ho 3 E12 78 C5
Artichoke Hill 8 E1 118 B6
Artichoke Mews 5
SE5 139 B4
Artichoke Pl SE5 139 B4
Artillery Cl IG2 57 A3
Artillery Ho SE18 122 C1
Artillery La E1 95 C2 243 B3
W12 90 A1
Artillery Pass E1 243 B3
Artillery Pl SE18 122 C2
Harrow HA3 24 A3
Artillery Row SW1 259 C5
Artington Cl BR6 227 A4
Artisan Cl E16 122 D6
Artizan St E1 243 B2
Arton Wilson Ho 12
SW15 156 A6
Arts Educational Sch The
W4 111 C2
Arundale KT1 197 D5
Arundel Ave SM4 201 B5
Arundel Bldgs SE1 263 B5
Arundel Cl E15 76 C4
SW11 158 C6
Croydon CR0 220 D5
Hampton TW12 173 D5
Sidcup DA5 169 B5
Arundel Ct 2 DA6 147 A1
N12 30 C4
SW3 257 B2
Barnes SW13 134 B6
4 Beckenham BR2 186 C1
Harrow HA2 63 C4
Putney SW15 156 D6
Tottenham N17 34 A2
Arundel Dr Harrow HA2 63 C4
Woodford IG8 37 A3
Arundel Gdns HA8 27 B3
W11 113 B6 244 C6
Ilford IG3 80 A6
Southgate N21 16 C3
Arundel Gr N16 73 C3
Arundel Ho N1 94 D6 234 D6
3 W3 110 D4
Croydon CR0 221 B3
Arundel Lo N3 29 B1
Arundel Mans SW6 264 D2
Barnes SW13 134 B6
Arundel Pl N1,N7 72 C2
Arundel Rd
Belmont SM2 217 B1
Cockfosters EN4 2 C2
Hounslow TW4 128 C2
Kingston KT1 177 A1
Thornton Heath CR0 205 B3
Arundel Sq N7 72 C2
Arundel St
WC2 116 B6 250 D6
Arundel Terr SW13 134 B6
Arun Ho 5 KT2 175 D2
Arvon Rd N5 72 C3
Asa Ct UB3 105 D3
Asaph Ho SE14 141 B4
Asbaston Terr IG11 79 A2
Ascalon Ct 16 SW2 160 B4
Ascalon Ho SW8 269 A3
Ascalon St
SW8 137 C5 269 A3
Ascham Dr E4 35 C3
Ascham End E17 35 A2
Ascham St NW5 71 C3
Aschurch Rd CR0 205 D2
Ascot Cl
Borehamwood WD6 10 C6
Northolt UB5 63 C3
Ascot Ct DA5 169 B4
NW8 229 C1
8 SW4 138 A1
Ascot Gdns Enfield EN3 6 C6
Southall UB1 85 C2
Ascot Ho NW1 231 D2
6 W4 111 A1
1 W9 91 C2
Penge SE26 184 B4
Ascot Lo NW6 91 D5
Ascot Par 9 SW4 138 A1
Ascot Rd E6 100 B4
N15 51 B4
East Bedfont TW14 148 D2
Edmonton N18 34 A6
Orpington BR5 211 D5
Streatham SW17 181 A4
Ascott Ave W5 110 A4
Ascott Ct HA5 40 A5
Asfil Ho EC1 241 B3
Ashbourne Ave DA7 147 A5
N20 14 D2
NW11 47 B4
Harrow HA2 64 B6
Wanstead E18 55 B5
Ashbourne Cl N12 29 D6
Ealing W5 88 C2
Ashbourne Ct E5 75 A4
11 N12 29 D6
Beckenham BR3 186 A2
Ashbourne Gr NW7 27 B5
SE22 139 D1
W4 111 C1
Ashbourne Par
2 NW11 47 B5
Ealing W5 88 B3
Ashbourne Rd
Ealing W5 88 B3
Mitcham CR4 181 A3
Ashbourne Rise BR6 227 C4
Ashbourne Terr 1
SW19 179 C3
Ashbourne Way NW11 47 B4
Ashbridge Rd E11 54 D2
Ashbridge St
NW8 92 C3 237 A5
Ashbrook HA8 26 B4
Ashbrook Rd N19 71 D6
Dagenham RM10 81 D5
Ashburn Ct BR1 187 A3
Ashburn Gdns SW7 256 A4
Ashburnham Ave HA1 42 D3
Ashburnham Cl N2 48 B5
Ashburnham Com Sch
SW10 266 C4
Ashburnham Gdns HA1 42 D3
Ashburnham Gr SE10 141 D5
Ashburnham Pk KT10 212 A4
Ashburnham Pl SE10 141 D5
Ashburnham Rd NW10 90 C5
SW10 136 A5 266 B3
Richmond TW10 153 B1
Ashburnham Retreat 6
SE10 141 D5
Ashburnham Twr
SW10 266 C4
Ashburn Pl
SW7 114 A2 256 A3
Ashburton Ave
Croydon CR0 206 B1
Ilford IG3 79 D4
Ashburton Cl CR0 206 A1
Ashburton Com Sch
CR9 206 B2
Ashburton Gdns CR0 222 A6
Ashburton Gr N7 72 C4
Ashburton Ho EN3 6 D2
Ashburton Jun & Inf Sch
CR0 206 B3
Ashburton Mans
SW10 266 B4
Ashburton Rd E16 99 A1
Croydon CR0 222 A6
Ashburton Rd *continued*
Ruislip HA4 62 A6
Ashburton Terr 2 E13 99 A5
Ashbury Ct N21 16 A6
Ashbury Dr UB10 60 D5
Ashbury Gdns RM6 58 D4
Ashby Ave KT19,KT9 214 C2
Ashby Ct NW8 236 D6
Ashby Gr N1 73 A1
Ashby Grange 7 SM6 219 C2
Ashby Ho 8 N1 73 A1
6 SW9 138 D3
Ashby Mews SE4 141 B3
Ashby Rd N15 52 A4
SE4 141 B3
Ashby St EC1 94 D4 234 D1
Ashby Way UB7 126 C5
Ashby Wlk CR0 205 A3
Ashchurch Ct W12 112 A3
Ashchurch Gr W12 112 A3
Ashchurch Park Villas
W12 112 A3
Ashchurch Terr W12 112 A3
Ash Cl BR5 211 B4
HA8 27 A6
Carshalton SM5 218 D6
Kingston KT3 177 B1
Penge SE20 184 C1
Sidcup DA14 168 B1
Stanmore HA7 25 A4
Ashcombe Ave KT6 197 D2
Ashcombe Ct 4 SW15 157 A6
Ashcombe Gdns HA8 26 C6
Ashcombe Ho 39 E3 97 D4
Ashcombe Pk NW2 67 C5
Ashcombe Rd
Wallington SM5 219 A2
Wimbledon SW19 179 C5
Ashcombe Sq KT3 199 A6
Ashcombe St SW6 135 D3
Ashcroft N14 15 D2
Pinner HA5 23 C4
Ashcroft Ave DA15 168 A5
Ashcroft Cres DA15 168 A5
Ashcroft Ct N20 14 B2
5 SE9 166 C5
Ashcroft Ho SW8 269 A2
Ashcroft Rd E3 97 A4
Chessington KT9 214 B5
Ashcroft Sq W6 112 C2
Ash Ct N19 71 C6
SE12 165 A4
SW11 159 A6
W1 237 C2
Chingford E4 20 B4
Romford RM7 59 D3
West Ewell KT19 215 A4
2 West Norwood
SW16 182 C5
Woodford E18 37 C2
Ashdale Cl
Stanwell TW19 148 A2
Twickenham TW2 152 A4
Ashdale Gr HA7 24 D4
Ashdale Ho N4 51 B2
Ashdale Rd SE12 165 B3
Ashdale Way TW2 151 D4
Ashdene 6 SE15 140 B5
Pinner HA5 40 C6
Ashdene Cl TW15 171 A3
Ashdon Cl IG8 37 B4
Ashdown Ealing W13 87 B2
Putney SW15 156 D6
Ashdown Cl 13 BR3 185 D1
Ashdown Cres NW5 71 A3
Ashdown Ct
New Malden KT4 199 D2
Sutton SM2 218 A2
Ashdowne Ct N17 34 A2
Ashdown Ho 7 E5 74 A6
Ashdown Pl
Ewell KT17 215 D1
Thames Ditton KT7 197 A2
Ashdown Rd NW10 89 D6
Enfield EN3 6 C3
Hillingdon UB10 82 C5
Kingston KT1 176 A1
Ashdown Way SW17 159 A2
Ashdown Wlk 15 E14 119 C2
Ashe Ho 8 TW1 153 D5
Ashen E6 100 C1
Ashenden SE17 262 B4
Ashenden Rd E5 75 A3
Ashen Gr SW19 157 C2
Ashentree Ct EC4 241 B1
Asher Loftus Way N11 30 D4
Asher Way E1 118 A6
Ashfield Ave
Bushey WD23 8 A4
Feltham TW13 150 B3
Ashfield Cl
Beckenham BR3 185 C3
Richmond TW10 154 A3
Ashfield Ho 5 N5 73 A3
Ashfield La BR7 189 A3
Ashfield Par N14 15 D3
Ashfield Pl BR7 189 B3
Ashfield Rd N14 15 C1
N4 51 A3
Ashfield Rd *continued*
W3 111 D5
Ashfield St E1 96 C2
Ashford Ave N8 50 A5
Ashford TW15 170 D4
Hayes UB4 84 D1
Ashford CE Prim Sch
TW15 170 D4
Ashford Cl E17 53 B3
Ashford TW15 170 A6
Ashford Cres
Ashford TW15 148 A1
Enfield EN3 6 C3
Ashford Ct NW2 68 D4
Edgware HA8 10 D1
Ashford Gn WD19 22 D5
Ashford High Sch The
TW15 148 A1
Ashford Ho 11 SE8 141 B6
14 SW9 138 D1
Ashford Hospl TW15 148 A2
Ashford Ind Est TW15 171 A6
Ashford Rd NW2 68 D4
Feltham TW13,TW15 171 B6
Littleton TW15,TW17 171 A3
Staines TW18 170 A4
Wallend E6 78 C1
Woodford E18 37 B1
Ashford St N1 95 C4
Ash Gr E8 96 B6
NW2 69 A4
W5 110 A3
East Bedfont TW14 149 C3
Edmonton N13 17 A1
Enfield EN1 17 C4
Hayes UB3 105 B6
Heston TW5 128 D5
Penge SE20 184 C1
Southall UB1 85 C2
Wembley HA0 65 A4
West Wickham BR4 208 A1
Yiewsley UB7 104 B6
Ashgrove SE12 165 A3
Ashgrove Ct 2 W9 91 C2
Ashgrove Ho SW1 259 D2
Ashgrove Rd
Ashford TW15 171 B5
Catford BR1 186 B4
Ilford IG3 58 A1
Ashgrove Sch BR1 187 B1
Ash Hill Dr HA5 40 C6
Ash Ho 3 E14 120 A4
SE1 263 D3
Ashingdon Cl E4 20 A1
Ashington 1 NW5 71 B2
Ashington Ho 16 E1 96 B3
Ashington Rd SW6 135 B3
Ashlake Rd SW16 182 A6
Ashland Pl W1 238 A4
Ashlar Ct N2 48 C6
Ashlar Pl SE18 122 D2
Ashleigh Commercial Est
SE7 121 D3
Ashleigh Ct N14 15 C4
W5 109 D2
Penge SE26 184 B4
Ashleigh Gdns SM1 217 D6
Ashleigh Ho SW14 133 C2
Ashleigh Point 8
SE26 162 D1
Ashleigh Rd
Mortlake SW14 133 C2
Penge SE20 206 B6
Ashley Ave SM4 201 C4
Ashley CE Prim Sch
KT12 194 A1
Ashley Cl NW4 28 C1
Oatlands Park KT12,
KT13 193 D1
Pinner HA5 22 B1
Ashley Cres SW11 137 A2
Wood Green N22 32 C1
Ashley Ct 19 N16 73 C3
NW3 69 D3
NW4 28 C1
New Barnet EN5 14 A6
Northolt UB5 85 A6
Yiewsley UB7 104 A5
Ashley Dr
Borehamwood WD6 11 B6
Hounslow TW7 130 C6
Twickenham TW2 151 D3
Ashley Gdns
Edmonton N13 33 A6
Orpington BR6 227 C3
Richmond TW10 153 D2
Wembley HA9 66 A6
Ashley Ho BR5 190 A1
Ashley La NW4 28 C1
NW7 28 D3
Croydon CR0 220 D4
Ashley Park Ave KT12 193 D1
Ashley Park Cres
KT12 194 A1
Ashley Pl SW1 115 C3 259 A5
Ashley Rd E7 77 C1
N17 52 A6
N19 50 A2
Chingford E4 35 C4
Ashley Rd *continued*
Enfield EN3 6 C3
Hampton TW12 173 C2
Richmond TW9 132 A2
Thames Ditton KT7 196 D3
Thornton Heath CR7 204 B5
Walton-on-T KT12 194 A1
Wimbledon SW19 179 D4
Ashley Wlk NW7 28 D3
Ashling Rd CR0 206 A1
Ashlin Rd E15 76 B4
Ash Lo
2 Ashford TW16 171 D3
Fulham SW6 134 D4
Ashlone Rd SW15 134 D2
Ashlyns Way KT9 213 D2
Ashmead 4 N14 15 C6
Ashmead Bsns Ctr E16 98 B3
Ashmead Gate BR1 187 C2
Ashmead Ho E9 75 A3
Ashmead Prim Sch
SE8 141 C3
Ashmead Rd SE8 141 C3
East Bedfont TW14 150 A3
Ashmere Ave BR3 186 B1
Ashmere Cl SM3 216 D3
Ashmere Gr 11 SW2,
SW4 138 A1
Ashmere Ho 10 SW2 138 A1
Ashmill Ct CR0 205 A3
Ashmill St NW8 92 C2 237 A4
Ashmole Prim Sch
SW8 138 B6 270 D5
Ashmole Sch N14 15 C3
Ashmole St SW8 270 D5
Ashmoor Lo NW7 27 B4
Ashmore NW1 71 D1
Ashmore Cl SE15 139 D5
Ashmore Ct N11 30 D4
Heston TW5 129 C6
Ashmore Gr DA16 145 C2
Ashmore Ho W14 254 B5
Ashmore Rd W9 91 B4
Ashmount Prim Sch N6 49 C2
Ashmount Rd N15 51 D4
N19 49 D2
Ashmount Terr W5 109 D2
Ashneal Gdns HA1 64 B5
Ashness Gdns UB6 65 B2
Ashness Rd SW11 158 D6
Ashpark Ho 4 E14 97 B1
Ash Rd E15 76 D3
Cheam SM3 201 B1
Croydon CR0 223 C6
Littleton TW17 192 C5
Orpington BR6 227 D1
Ashridge Cl HA3 43 C3
Ashridge Cres SE18 145 A5
Ashridge Ct
Southall UB1 108 A6
Southgate N14 15 C6
Ashridge Dr WD19 22 C5
Ashridge Gdns
Bowes Park N13 32 A5
Pinner HA5 41 A5
Ashridge Ho DA14 189 D6
Ashridge Way
Ashford TW16 172 A4
Merton SM4 201 B5
Ash Row BR2 210 C3
Ashtead Ct 15 SW19 156 D3
Ashtead Rd E5 52 A2
Ashton Cl SM1 217 C4
Ashton Ct
1 Beckenham BR3 185 B2
Harrow HA1 64 D5
Ashton Gdns
Dagenham RM6 59 A3
Hounslow TW4 129 B1
Ashton Ho 13 SW9 138 C5
Roehampton SW15 156 B4
Ashton Rd E15 76 B3
Ashton St E14 120 A6
Ashtree Ave CR4 180 B1
Ashtree Cl BR6 226 D4
Ash Tree Cl
Croydon CR0 207 A3
1 Surbiton KT6 198 A1
Ashtree Ct TW15 170 D5
Ash Tree Dell NW9 45 B4
Ash Tree Way CR0 207 A3
Ashurst Cl SE20 184 B2
Ashurst Dr
Ilford IG2,IG6 57 A4
Littleton TW17 192 A4
Ashurst Lo N5 72 D3
Ashurst Rd N12 30 C5
Cockfosters EN4 14 D6
Ashurst Wlk CR0 222 B6
Ashvale Rd SW17 180 D5
Ashview Cl TW15 170 A5
Ashview Gdns TW15 170 A5
Ashville Rd E11 76 B6
Ashwater Rd SE12 165 A3
Ashway Ctr 5 KT2 176 A2
Ashwell Cl 8 E6 100 A1

Ayrton Rd
SW7 114 B3 256 C6
Aysgarth Ct SM1 217 D5
Aysgarth Rd SE21 161 C4
Ayston Ho 19 SE8 118 D2
Ayton Ho SE5 139 B5
Aytoun Ct 17 SW9 138 B3
Aytoun Pl SW9 138 B3
Aytoun Rd SW9 138 B3
Azalea Cl Ealing W7 108 D5
Ilford IG1 78 D3
Azalea Ct W7 108 D5
Azalea Ho SE14 141 B5
Azalea Wlk HA5 40 B3
Azelea Ct IG8 36 C3
Azenby Rd SE15 139 D3
Azof St SE10 120 C2
Azov Ho 9 E1 97 A3

B

Baalbec Rd N5 72 D3
Babbacombe Cl KT9 213 D3
Babbacombe Gdns IG4 56 A5
Babbacombe Rd BR1 187 A2
Baber Bridge Par
TW14 150 C5
Baber Dr TW14 150 C5
Babington Ct WC1 240 B4
Streatham SW16 181 D5
Babington Ho SE1 252 B2
Babington House Sch
BR7 188 B4
Babington Rd NW4 46 B5
Dagenham RM8 80 C4
Streatham SW16 181 D5
Babington Rise HA9 66 C2
Babmaes St SW1 249 C5
Bacchus Wlk 12 N1 95 C5
Bache's St N1 95 B4 235 D1
Back Church La E1 96 A1
Back Hill EC1 241 B5
Backhouse Pl SE1 263 B3
Back La HA8 27 A2
N8 50 A4
NW3 70 A4
Brentford TW8 131 D6
Dagenham RM6 59 A2
Richmond TW10 153 C2
Sidcup DA5 169 C4
Backley Gdns SE25 206 A3
Back Rd Sidcup DA14 190 A6
Teddington TW11 174 C3
Bacon Gr SE1 117 D3 263 C5
Bacon La NW9 44 D5
Edgware HA8 26 C2
Bacon's Coll SE16 119 A4
Bacon's La N6 49 A1
Bacon St E2 95 D3 243 D6
Bacon Terr RM8 80 B3
Bacton NW5 71 A3
Bacton St E2 96 C4
Baddeley Cl EN3 7 C6
Baddeley Ho SE11 260 D2
Baddow Cl
Dagenham RM10 103 C6
Woodford IG8 37 D4
Baddow Wlk N1 235 A6
Baden Ct N11 31 D3
Baden Pl SE1 252 C2
Baden Powell Cl
Dagenham RM9 103 A6
Surbiton KT6 214 B6
Baden Powell Ho 11
DA17 125 C3
Baden Powell Sch E5 74 B5
Baden Rd N8 49 D5
Ilford IG1 78 D3
Badger Cl
Feltham TW13 150 B1
Hounslow TW4 128 C2
Ilford IG2 57 A2
Badger Ct NW2 68 C5
Badgers Cl
Ashford TW15 170 B5
Enfield EN2 4 D2
Harrow HA1 42 B3
Hayes UB3 105 C6
Badgers Copse BR6 227 D6
Worcester Park KT4 215 D6
Badgers Croft SE9 166 C1
Barnet N20 13 A3
Badgers Hole CR0
Badgers Wlk KT3 177 C1
Badlis Rd E17 53 C6
Badma Cl N9 18 C1
Badminton KT2 176 D2
Badminton Cl
Harrow HA1 42 C5
Northolt UB5 63 C2
Badminton Ct 9 N4 51 A2
Badminton Ho SE22 139 C1
Badminton Mews 10
E16 121 A5
Badminton Rd SW12 159 A5
Badric Ct SW11 136 B3
Badsworth Rd 3 SE5 139 A4
Bagley Cl UB7 104 A4
Bagley's La
SW6 135 D4 265 D1
Bagleys Spring RM6 59 A5
Bagnigge Ho WC1 234 A1
Bagshot Ho NW1 231 D2
Bagshot Rd EN1 17 D5
Bagshot St
SE17 117 C1 263 B1
Baildon 28 E2 96 C5
Baildon St SE8 141 B5
Bailey Cl N11 31 D3
Chingford E4 36 A6
Bailey Cres KT9 213 D1
Bailey Ct 9 W12 112 A4
4 Chingford E4 36 B5
Bailey Ho 11 SE26 184 B5
Bailey Mews W4 132 D6
Bailey Pl SE26 184 D4
Bainbridge cl KT2 176 A5
Bainbridge Rd RM9 81 B4
Bainbridge St WC1 239 D2
Baines Cl CR2 221 B3
Bain Ho 23 SW9 138 A3
Baird Ave UB1 108 A6
Baird Cl E10 53 C1
NW9 45 A3
Baird Gdns SE19 183 C6
Baird Ho 29 W12 112 B6
12 Belvedere DA17 125 C3
Baird Rd EN1 6 B1
Baird St EC1 242 B6
Baizdon Rd SE3 142 C3
Baker Beall Ct DA7 147 D2
Baker Ct E11 76 B5
Baker Ho 12 E3 97 D4
Ealing W7 108 D5
Baker La CR4 203 A6
Baker Rd NW10 89 C6
SE18 144 A4
Bakers' Almshouses
E10 53 D3
Bakers Ave E17 53 D3
Bakers Ct SE25 205 C6
Bakers End SW20 179 A1
Bakers Field N7 72 A4
Bakers Gdns SM5 218 C6
Bakers Hall Ct EC3 253 B5
Bakers Hill E5 52 C1
Barnet EN5 1 D3
Bakers Ho W5 109 D5
Baker's La N6 48 D3
Bakers Mews 9 BR6 227 D2
Baker's Mews W1 238 A2
Bakers Rents 13 E2 95 D4
Bakers Row E15 98 C5
Baker's Row
EC1 94 C3 241 A5
Baker St W1 92 D2 237 D4
Enfield EN1 5 B4
Baker Street
W1 92 D2 237 D4
Baker Street Sta
NW1 92 D3 237 D5
Baker's Yd EC1 241 A5
Bakery Cl SW9 270 D3
Bakery Mews KT6 198 C1
Bakewell Way KT3 177 C1
Balaam Ho SM1 217 C4
Balaams La N14 15 D2
Balaam St E13 99 B4
Balaclava Rd
SE1 117 D2 263 D3
Kingston KT6 197 C2
Balcaskie Rd SE9 166 B6
Balchen Rd SE3 143 D3
Balchier Rd SE22 162 B5
Balcombe Cl DA6 146 D1
Balcombe Ho NW1 237 C6
3 Streatham SW2 160 B3
Balcombe St
NW1 92 D3 237 C5
Balcon Ct W5 88 B1
Balcorne St E9 74 C1
Balder Rise SE12 165 B2
Balderton Flats W1 238 B1
Balderton St
W1 93 A1 238 B1
Baldewyne Ct N17 34 A2
Baldock Ho 32 SE5 139 A3
Baldock St E3 97 D5
Baldrey Ho 1 SE10 120 D1
Baldry Gdns SW16 182 B4
Baldwin Cres SE5 139 A4
Baldwin Gdns TW3 130 A4
Baldwin Ho 15 SW2 160 C3
Baldwin's Gdns
EC1 94 C2 241 A4
Baldwin St EC1 235 C1
Baldwin Terr
N1 95 A5 235 A4
Baldwyn Gdns W3 111 B6
Bale Rd E1 97 A2
Bales Coll W10 90 D4
Balfern Gr W4 111 C1
Balfern St SW11 136 C3
Balfe St N1 94 A5 233 B3
Balfour Ave W7 108 D5
Balfour Bsns Ctr UB2 106 D3
Balfour Gr N20 14 D1
Balfour Ho W10 90 D2
Balfour Mews W1 248 B4
Edmonton N9 18 A1
Balfour Pl W1 248 B5
Putney SW15 134 B1
Balfour Rd BR2 209 D4
N5 73 A4
W13 109 B4
W3 89 A2
Croydon SE25 206 A5
Harrow HA1 42 B4
Hounslow TW3 129 D2
Ilford IG1 57 A1
Merton SW19 179 D3
Southall UB2 106 D3
Wallington SM5 218 D1
Balfour St
SE17 117 B2 262 C4
Balfron Twr 2 E14 98 A1
Balgonie Rd E4 20 B3
Balgowan Cl KT3 199 C5
Balgowan Prim Sch
BR3 185 A1
Balgowan Rd BR3 185 B1
Balgowan St SE18 123 D2
Balham Gr SW12 159 A4
Balham High Rd
SW12,SW17 159 A3
Balham Hill SW12 159 B5
Balham New Rd SW12 159 B4
Balham Park Mans
SW12 158 D3
Balham Park Rd SW12,
SW17 159 A3
Balham Rd N9 18 A2
Balham Sta SW12 159 B3
Balham Station Rd
SW12 159 B3
Balin Ho SE1 252 C2
Balkan Wlk E1 118 B6
Balladier Wlk E14 97 D2
Ballamore Rd BR1 165 A1
Ballance Rd E9 75 A2
Ballantine St SW18 136 A1
Ballantrae Ho NW2 69 B4
Ballard Cl KT2 177 B3
Ballard Ho SE10 141 D6
Ballards Cl RM10 103 D6
Ballards Farm Rd CR0,
CR2 222 A2
Ballards La N3 29 D3
Ballards Mews HA8 26 C4
Ballards Rd NW2 68 A6
Dagenham RM10 103 D6
Ballards Rise CR2 222 A2
Ballards Way CR0,CR2 222 B2
Ballast Quay SE10 120 B1
Ballater Cl WD19 22 C6
Ballater Rd SW2,SW4 138 A1
South Croydon CR2 221 D3
Ball Ct EC3 242 D1
Ballina St SE23 162 D4
Ballin Ct 9 E14 120 A4
Ballingdon Rd SW11 159 A5
Ballinger Point 18 E3 97 D4
Balliol Ave E4 36 C6
Balliol Ho 11 SW15 156 D5
Balliol Rd DA16 146 B3
W10 90 D1
Tottenham N17 33 C2
Balloch Rd SE6 164 B2
Ballogie Ave NW10 67 C4
Ballow Cl 23 SE5 139 C5
Ball's Pond Pl 3 N1 73 B2
Ball's Pond Rd N1 73 C2
Balmain Cl W5 109 D5
Balmain Ct TW3 129 D4
Balman Ho 3 SE16 118 D2
Balmer Rd E3 97 B5
Balmes Rd N1 95 B6 235 D6
Balmoral Ave N11 31 B5
Beckenham BR3 207 A5
Balmoral Cl 1 SW15 156 D5
Balmoral Cres KT8 195 C6
Balmoral Ct NW8 229 C4
SE12 187 B6
21 SE16 118 D5
11 Belmont SM2 217 C1
Ealing W5 87 D1
Edgware HA8 26 D6
North Cheam KT4 216 B6
Wembley HA9 66 B5
West Norwood SE27 183 A6
Balmoral Dr
Borehamwood WD6 11 B6
Hayes UB4 83 D3
Southall UB1 85 B3
Balmoral Gdns DA5 169 B4
W13 109 A3
Ilford IG3 57 D1
Balmoral Gr N7 72 B2
Balmoral Ho E17 35 B1
N4 51 A1
W14 254 A4
Balmoral Mews W12 111 D3
Balmoral Rd E10 75 D6
E7 77 C3
NW2 68 B2
Harrow HA2 63 C4
Balmoral Rd *continued*
Kingston KT1 198 B5
North Cheam KT4 216 B6
Balmoral Trad Est
IG11 101 D2
Balmore Cres EN4 15 A6
Balmore St N19 71 B6
Balmuir Gdns SW15 134 C1
Balnacraig Ave NW10 67 C4
Balniel Gate SW1 259 D2
Balsam Ho 8 E14 119 D6
Baltic Cl SW19 180 B3
Baltic Ho 7 SE5 139 A3
Baltic St E EC1 95 A3 242 A5
Baltic St W EC1 95 A3 242 A5
Baltimore Ho SE11 261 A2
Baltimore Pl DA16 145 D3
Balvaird Pl SW1 259 D1
Balvernie Gr SW18 157 C4
Bamber Ho 5 IG11 101 A6
Bamborough Gdns 12
W12 112 C4
Bamburgh 9 N17 34 B3
Bamford Ave HA0 88 B5
Bamford Ct E15 75 D3
Bamford Rd
Barking IG11 79 A2
Catford BR1 186 B5
Bampfylde Cl SM6 219 C5
Bampton Ct W5 87 D1
Bampton Dr NW7 28 A3
Bampton Rd SE23 162 D1
Banavie Gdns BR3 186 A2
Banbury Cl EN2 4 D4
Banbury Ct W13 109 A3
WC2 250 A6
8 Belmont SM2 217 C1
Banbury Ho 5 E9 74 D1
Banbury Rd E17 35 A3
E9 74 D1
Banbury St 3 SW11 136 C3
Banbury Wlk UB5 85 C5
Banchory Rd SE3 143 B5
Bancroft Ave N2 48 C4
Woodford IG9 21 A2
Bancroft Cl
Ashford TW15 170 C5
Hillingdon UB8 82 D2
Bancroft Ct SW8 270 A2
Northolt UB5 84 C6
Bancroft Gdns BR6 211 D1
Harrow HA3 24 A2
Bancroft Ho 10 E1 96 C3
Bancroft Rd E1 96 D3
Harrow HA3 24 A1
Bancrofts Sch IG8 21 A1
Bandon Cl UB10 82 B5
Bandon Hill Prim Sch
SM6 219 D2
Bandon Rise SM6 219 D3
Banff Ho 1 NW3 70 C2
Banfield Rd SE15 140 B2
Banfor Ct SM6 219 C3
Bangabandhu Prim Sch
E2 96 C4
Bangalore St SW15 134 D2
Bangor Cl UB5 63 D3
Banim St W6 112 B2
Banister Ho E9 74 D3
SW8 269 B2
15 W10 91 A4
Banister Rd W10 90 D4
Bank Ave CR4 180 B1
Bank Ct SW11 268 C2
Bank End SE1 252 B4
Bankfoot Rd BR1 186 C6
Bankhurst Rd SE6 163 B4
Bank La Kingston KT2 176 A3
Roehampton SW15 155 C6
Bank Mews SM1 218 A2
Bank of England★
EC2 242 C1
Bank Par N11 31 B5
Banks Ho SE1 262 A5
Isleworth TW7 130 C3
Banksia Rd N18 34 D5
Bankside SE1 117 A6 252 A5
SE1 252 B4
Enfield EN2 4 D5
Southall UB1 106 D5
South Croydon CR2 221 D2
Bankside Ave UB5 84 A5
Bankside Cl
Carshalton SM5 218 C2
Isleworth TW7 130 D1
Bankside Dr KT7 213 B6
Bankside Pier
SE1 117 A6 252 A5
Bankside Pk IG11 102 A4
Bankside Rd IG1 79 B3
Bankside Way 6 SE19 183 C4
Banks La DA6 147 B1
Bank Sta EC3 95 B1 242 D1
Banks Way E12 78 C4
Bank The N6 49 B1
Bankton Rd SW2 138 C1
Bankwell Rd SE13 142 C1
Banner Ho EC1 242 B5
Bannerman Ho SW8 270 C5
Banner St EC1 95 A3 242 B6
Banning Ho 4 SW19 156 D3
Banning St SE10 120 C1
Bannister Cl
Greenford UB6 64 B3
Streatham SW2 160 C3
Bannister Ho 28 SE14 140 D6
Bannister Sports Ctr The
HA3 24 A4
Bannockburn Prim Sch
SE18 123 D2
Bannockburn Rd SE18 123 D2
Bannow Cl KT19 215 C4
Banqueting House★
SW1 250 A3
Banstead Ct N4 51 A1
Banstead Gdns N9 17 C1
Banstead Rd SM2,SM5 218 C1
Banstead St SE15 140 C2
Banstead Way SM6 220 A3
Banstock Rd HA8 26 D4
Banting Dr N21 16 B6
Banting Ho 6 NW2 68 A5
Bantock Ho 14 W10 91 A4
Banton Cl EN1 6 B3
Bantry Ho 13 E1 96 D3
Bantry St SE5 139 B5
Banwell Rd DA5 168 D5
Banyan Ho 8 NW3 69 D2
Banyard Rd SE16 118 B3
Baptist Gdns NW5 71 A2
Barandon Wlk 6 W11 112 D6
Barbanel Ho 19 E1 96 C3
Barbara Brosnan Ct
NW8 229 C3
Barbara Cl TW17 192 D4
Barbara Hucklesbury Cl
N22 32 D1
Barbara Martin Ho 1
N11 31 C5
Barbara Ward Ct 3
E11 76 C6
Barbauld Rd N16 73 C5
Barber Beaumont Ho 21
E1 96 D4
Barber Cl N21 16 C4
Barbers Alley 1 E13 99 B4
Barbers Rd E15 97 D5
Barbican★ EC2 95 A2 242 B3
Barbican Arts & Con Ctr★
EC2 95 A2 242 B4
Barbican Rd UB1 85 D1
Barbican Sta
EC1 95 A2 242 A4
Barb Mews W6 112 C3
Barbon Cl WC1 240 C4
Barbot Cl N9 18 A1
Barbrook Ho E9 74 C2
Barchard St SW18 157 D6
Barchester Cl W7 108 D5
Barchester Lo N12 29 D6
Barchester Rd HA3 24 B1
Barchester St E14 97 D2
Barclay Cl
SW6 135 C5 265 A3
Barclay Ct N12 30 A5
Barclay Ho 21 E9 74 C1
Barclay Jun & Inf Schs
E10 54 B3
Barclay Oval IG8 37 A6
Barclay Rd E11 54 D1
E13 99 C3
E17 54 A5
SW6 135 C5 265 B3
Edmonton N18 33 B4
South Croydon CR0 221 B5
Barcombe Ave SW2 160 B2
Bardell Ho 14 SE1 118 A4
Barden St SE18 145 C5
Bardfield Ave RM6 58 D6
Bardney Rd SM4 201 D5
Bardolph Rd N7 72 A4
Richmond TW9 132 B2
Bard Rd W10 112 D6
Bardsey Pl 35 E1 96 C3
Bardsey Wlk 2 N1 73 A2
Bardsley Cl CR0 221 D5
Bardsley Ho 5 SE10 142 A6
Bardsley La SE10 142 A6
Barents Ho 10 E1 96 D3
Barfett St W10 91 B3
Barfield Ave N20 14 D2
Barfield Rd BR1,BR7 210 C6
E11 54 D1
Barfleur Ho SE8 119 B2
Barford Cl NW4 28 A2
Barford Ho 19 E3 97 B5
Barford St N1 94 C6 234 B5
Barforth Rd SE15 140 B2
Barfreston Way SE20 184 B2
Bargate Cl SE18 123 D1
New Malden KT3 200 A2
Bargehouse Rd E16 122 D4
Barge House St SE1 251 B4
Bargery Rd SE6 163 D3
Barge Wlk KT1,KT6,KT7 197 C3
Bargrove Cl 8 SE20 184 A3
Bargrove Cres SE6 163 B2
Barham Cl
Chislehurst BR7 188 D5
Keston Mark BR2 210 A1
Wembley HA0 65 C2
Barham Ct N12 29 B5
8 Croydon CR2 221 A4
Keston Mark BR2 210 A1
Wembley HA0 65 C2
Barham Ho SE17 263 B2
Barham Prim Sch HA0 65 C2
Barham Rd
Chislehurst BR7 188 D5
Croydon CR2 221 A3
Wimbledon SW20 178 A3
Baring Cl SE12 165 A2
Baring Ct N1 235 C5
Baring Ho 11 E14 97 C1
Baring Prim Sch SE12 165 A4
Baring Rd SE12 165 A2
Barnet EN4 2 B2
Croydon CR0 206 A1
Baring St N1 95 B6 235 C5
Barker Cl KT3 198 D5
Barker Dr NW1 71 D1
Barker Ho N15 50 D5
SE17 263 A3
Dulwich SE21 161 C1
Barker Mews SW4 137 B1
Barker St SW10 266 A6
Barker Wlk SW16 159 D1
Barkham Rd N17 33 C3
Barking Abbey Comp Sch
IG11 79 D2
Barking Abbey Comp Sch
(Lower Sch) IG11 79 C3
Barking Bsns Ctr IG11 102 A4
Barking Flyover IG11 78 D1
Barking Hospl IG11 79 D1
Barking Ind Pk IG11 102 A6
Barking Rd E13 99 B4
E6 100 B6
Barkingside Sta IG6 57 B6
Barking Sta IG11 79 A1
Bark Pl W2 113 D6 245 C6
Barkston Gdns
SW5 113 D2 255 C3
Barkway Ct N4 73 A6
Barkwith Ho 27 SE14 140 D6
Barkworth Rd SE16 118 C1
Barlborough St SE14 140 D5
Barlby Gdns W10 90 D3
Barlby Prim Sch W10 90 D3
Barlby Rd W10 90 D2
Barley Cl WD23 8 A6
Barleycorn Way E14 119 B6
Barleyfields Cl RM6 58 C2
Barley La IG3 58 B3
Barley Lane Prim Sch
RM6 58 B2
Barley Mow Pas EC1 241 D3
W4 111 B1
Barley Mow Way
TW17 192 C5
Barling 6 NW1 71 B1
Barling Ct 1 SW4 138 A3
Barlings Ho 2 SE4 140 D1
Barloch Ho 13 SW11 137 A3
Barlow Cl SM6 220 A1
Barlow Dr SE18 144 A4
Barlow Ho N1 235 C2
14 SE16 118 B2
W11 244 A6
Barlow Pl W1 248 D5
Barlow Rd NW6 69 B2
Acton W3 110 D5
Hampton TW12 173 C3
Barlow St
SE17 117 B2 262 D3
Barmeston Rd SE6 163 D2
Barmor Cl HA2 23 D1
Barmouth Ave UB6 86 D5
Barmouth Ho 6 N7 72 B6
Barmouth Rd SW18 158 A5
Croydon CR0 222 D6
Barnabas Ct N21 16 D6
Barnabas Ho EC1 235 A1
Barnabas Lo SW8 270 B2
Barnabas Rd E9 74 D3
Barnaby Cl HA2 64 A6
Barnaby Ct NW9 45 C6
Barnaby Pl SW7 256 C3
Barnard Cl
Chislehurst BR7 189 B2
Sunbury TW16 172 B3
Wallington SM6 219 D1
Woolwich SE18 122 C3
Barnard Ct SW16 160 B1
Barnard Gdns
Hayes UB4 84 B3
West Barnes KT3 200 A5
Barnard Gr E15 76 D1
Barnard Hill N10 31 B2
Barnard Ho 17 E2 96 B4
Barnard Lo 10 W9 91 C2
New Barnet EN5 2 A1
Barnard Mews SW11 136 C1

Barnardo Dr IG6 57 A5
Barnardo Gdns 1 E1 118 D6
Barnardo St E1 96 D1
Barnard Rd SW11 136 C1
Enfield EN1 6 B3
Mitcham CR4 181 A1
Barnard's Inn EC4 241 B2
Barnbrough NW1 232 A5
Barnby Sq 1 E15 98 C6
Barnby St 2 E15 98 C6
NW1 93 C4 232 B2
Barn Cl 19 NW5 71 D3
Ashford TW15 170 D5
Northolt UB5 84 C5
Barn Cres HA7 25 C4
Barn Croft Sch E17 53 A3
Barneby Cl TW2 152 C3
Barnehurst Rd DA7 147 D3
Barnersbury Ho N7 72 A4
Barnes Ave
Barnes SW13 134 A5
Southall UB2 107 B2
Barnes Bridge Sta
SW13 133 C3
Barnes Cl E12 77 D4
Barnes Common★
SW13 134 A2
Barnes Ct N1 72 C1
Barnet EN5 1 D1
Newham E16 99 C2
South Norwood CR7 205 A6
Woodford IG8 37 D5
Wood Green N22 32 A3
Barnes End KT3 200 A4
Barnes High St SW13 133 D3
Barnes Ho 14 E2 96 C5
N19 50 A2
26 SE14 140 D6
8 Barking IG11 101 B6
Barnes Hospl SW14 133 C2
Barnes Rd N18 34 C6
Ilford IG1 79 A3
Barnes St E14 97 A1
Barnes Sta SW13 134 A2
Barnes Terr SE8 119 B1
Barnes Wallis Ct HA9 67 A5
Barnet Coll EN4 15 A3
Barnet Coll of F Ed EN5 1 B1
Barnet Dr BR2 226 A6
Barnet Gate La EN5 11 D4
Barnet Gr E2 96 A4
Barnet Hill EN5 1 C1
Barnet Hill JMI Prim Sch
EN5 13 B6
Barnet Ho 36 SE5 139 A3
Barnet La
Barnet EN5,N20 13 B4
Borehamwood WD6 10 B5
Barnet Mus★ EN5 1 A1
Barnet Rd Barnet EN5 1 B5
Edgware EN5 11 C5
Barnett Ho E1 243 C3
Barnett Homestead
NW11 47 C5
Barnet Trad Est EN5 1 B2
Barnetts Ct HA2 63 D5
Barnett St 8 E1 96 B1
Barnet Way (Barnet
By-Pass) EN5,NW7,
WD6 11 B3
Barnet Wood Rd BR2 225 C6
Barney Cl SE7 121 C1
Barn Field NW3 70 D3
Barnfield KT3 199 C3
Barnfield Ave
Croydon CR0 222 C6
Kingston KT2 176 A5
Mitcham CR4 203 B6
Barnfield Cl N4 50 A2
Wandsworth SW17 158 A1
Barnfield Gdns SE18 144 D6
Kingston KT2 176 A5
Barnfield Pl E14 119 C2
Barnfield Prim Sch
HA8 27 A2
Barnfield Rd HA8 27 A2
SE18 144 D6
Ealing W5 87 C3
Erith DA17 147 B6
Barnfield Wood Cl
BR3 208 B3
Barnfield Wood Rd
BR3 208 B3
Barnham Dr SE28 123 D5
Barnham Rd UB6 86 A4
Barnham St SE1 253 B2
Barnhill HA5 40 C4
Barn Hill HA9 44 D1
Barnhill Ave BR2 208 D4
Barnhill Com High Sch
UB4 84 C4
Barnhill Ct UB4 84 B4
Barnhill La UB4 84 B3
Barnhill Rd Hayes UB4 84 C3
Wembley HA9 67 A5
Barnhurst Path WD19 22 C5
Barningham Way NW9 45 B3
Barnlea Cl TW13 151 A2
Barnmead Gdns RM9 81 B3
Barnmead Rd
Dagenham RM9 81 B3
Penge BR3 185 A2
Barn Rise HA9 66 C6
Barnsbury Cl KT3 199 A5
Barnsbury Cres KT5 199 A1
Barnsbury Gr N7 72 B1
Barnsbury Ho 12 SW4 159 D5
Barnsbury La KT5 199 A1
Barnsbury Pk N1 72 C1
Barnsbury Rd
N1 94 C6 234 A5
Barnsbury Sq N1 72 C1
Barnsbury St N1 72 C1
Barnsbury Terr N1 72 B1
Barnscroft SW20 200 B6
Barnsdale Ave E14 119 C2
Barnsdale Rd W9 91 B3
Barnsley St E1 96 B3
Barn St N16 73 C6
Barnstaple Ho SE12 164 D6
Barnstaple La SE13 142 A1
Barnstaple Rd HA4 62 C5
Barnston Wlk N1 235 A6
Barnview Lo HA3 24 C2
Barn Way HA9 66 C6
Barnwell Ho 1 SE5 139 C4
Barnwell Rd SW2 160 C6
Barnwood Cl W9 91 D3
Barnet N20 13 B3
Ruislip HA4 61 B6
Baron Cl N1 234 A4
N11 31 B5
Baron Ct CR4 202 C5
Baroness Rd 5 E2 95 D4
Baronet Gr N17 34 A2
Baronet Rd N17 34 A2
Baron Gdns IG6 57 A6
Baron Gr CR4 202 C5
Baron Rd RM8 58 D1
Barons Court Mans
W14 254 B1
Baron's Court Rd
W14 113 A1 254 B2
Barons Court Sta
W14 113 A1 254 A2
Barons Ct NW9 45 B3
Ilford IG1 79 B6
Wallington SM6 219 D5
Baronsfield Rd TW1 153 B5
Barons Gate 18 W4 111 A3
East Barnet EN4 14 C5
Barons Keep
W14 113 A1 254 A2
Barons Lo 8 E14 120 A2
Barons Mead HA1 42 C5
Baronsmead Rd SW13 134 A4
Baronsmede W5 110 B4
Baronsmere Ct 7 EN5 1 A1
Baronsmere Rd N2 48 C5
Baron's Pl SE1 116 C4 251 B1
Baron St N1 94 C5 234 A4
Barons The TW1 153 B5
Baron's Wlk CR0 207 A3
Baron Wlk E16 98 D2
Barque Mews SE8 141 C6
Barrack Rd TW4 129 A1
Barra Hall Cir UB3 83 C1
Barra Hall Rd UB3 105 C6
Barras Cl EN3 7 C6
Barratt Ave N22 32 B1
Barratt Ho 15 N1 72 D1
Barratt Ind Pk E3 98 A3
Southall UB1 107 C5
Barratt Way HA3 42 B6
Barr Beacon SE23 162 C4
Barrenger Rd N10 30 D1
Barret Ho NW6 91 C6
Barrett Rd E17 54 A5
Barrett's Gr N16 73 C3
Barrett's Green Rd
NW10 89 B5
Barrett St W1 93 A1 238 B1
Barrhill Rd SW2 160 A2
Barrie Ct EN5 14 A6
Barriedale SE14 141 A3
Barrie Ho 8 N16 73 C5
NW8 230 B5
W2 246 B5
Acton W3 111 A4
Edmonton N9 18 B4
Barrier Gdns Pier E16 121 D3
Barringer Sq SW17 181 A6
Barrington Cl NW5 71 A3
Barrington Ct 4 N10 31 B1
NW5 71 A3
31 SW9 138 A3
Barrington Prim Sch
DA16 146 D3
Barrington Rd N8 49 D4
SW9 138 D2
Bexley DA16 146 D3
Cheam SM3 201 C1
Little Ilford E12 78 C2
Barrington Villas
SE18 144 C4
Barrington Wlk 9
SE19 183 C4
Barrow Ave SM5 218 D1
Barrow Cl N21 16 D2
Barrow Ct 6 SE6 164 D3
Barrowdene Cl HA5 23 A1
Barrowell Gn N21 17 A2
Barrowfield Cl N9 18 C1
Barrowgate Ho W4 111 B1
Barrowgate Rd W4 111 B1
Barrow Hedges Cl
SM5 218 C1
Barrow Hedges Prim Sch
SM5 218 C1
Barrow Hedges Way
SM5 218 C1
Barrow Hill KT4 215 C6
Barrow Hill Cl KT4 215 C6
Barrow Hill Est
NW8 92 C5 230 A3
Barrow Hill Jun Sch
NW8 92 C5 230 A3
Barrow Hill Rd NW8 230 A3
Barrow Point Ave HA5 23 A1
Barrow Point La HA5 23 A1
Barrow Rd
Croydon CR0 220 C3
Streatham SW16 181 D4
Barrow Wlk TW8 109 C1
Barrs Rd NW10 67 B1
Barry Ave DA7 147 A5
N15 51 D3
Barry Cl BR6 227 C5
Barry Ct SW4 159 C5
Barrydene N20 14 B2
Barrydene Ct EN2 4 D2
Barry Ho 4 SE16 118 B1
Barry Lo N4 50 B2
Barry Par SE22 140 A1
Barry Rd E6 100 A1
NW10 67 A1
SE22 162 A6
Barry Terr TW15 148 B2
Barset Rd SE15 140 C2
Barsons Cl SE20 184 C3
Barston Rd SE27 161 A1
Barstow Cres SW2 160 B3
Bartell Ho SW2 160 C5
Barter St WC1 94 A2 240 B3
Bartholomew Cl EC1 242 A3
SW18 136 A1
Bartholomew Ct EC1 242 B6
Edgware HA8 25 D3
5 Poplar E14 120 B6
Bartholomew Ho
23 SE5 139 A3
Enfield EN3 7 A6
Enfield EN3 7 B6
Bartholomew La EC2 242 D1
Bartholomew Pas EC1 241 D3
Bartholomew Pl EC1 242 A3
Bartholomew Rd NW5 71 C2
Bartholomew Sq 18 E1 96 B3
Bartholomew St
SE1 117 B3 262 D5
Bartholomew Villas
NW5 71 C2
Barth Rd SE18 123 C2
Bartle Ave E6 100 A5
Bartle Rd W11 91 A1
Bartlett Cl E14 97 C1
Bartlett Ct EC4 241 B2
Bartletts Ho 10 RM10 81 D2
Bartlett St CR2 221 B3
Bartok Ho W11 244 C5
Bartolomew Sq EC1 242 B6
Barton Ave RM7 59 D1
Barton Cl E9 74 C3
NW4 46 A5
SE15 140 B2
Bexley DA6 169 A6
2 Newham E6 100 B1
Shepperton TW17 192 D3
Barton Ct 10 SW4 138 A3
W14 254 B2
Beckenham BR2 208 B6
Barton Gn KT3 177 B1
Barton Ho 8 E3 97 D4
N1 72 D1
SW6 135 D2
Barton Mdws IG6 57 A5
Barton Rd
W14 113 A1 254 B1
Sidcup DA14 191 A4
Barton St SW1 260 A6
Bartons The WD6 9 D5
Bartonway NW8 229 C4
Bartram Cl UB8 82 D3
Bartram Rd SE4 163 A5
Bartrams La EN4 2 A5
Bartrip St E9 75 B2
Barts Cl BR3 207 C4
Barville Cl SE4 141 A1
Barwell Ho 6 E2 96 A3
Barwick Dr UB8 82 D2
Barwick Ho 7 W3 111 A4
Barwick Rd E7 77 B4
Barwood Ave BR4 207 D1
Bascome St 13 SW2 160 C5
Basden Gr TW13 151 C2
Basedale Rd RM9 80 B1
Baseing Cl E6 122 C6
Basevi Way SE8 141 D6
Bashley Rd NW10 89 B3
Basil Ave E6 100 A4
Basildene Rd TW4,
TW5 128 D2
Basildon Rd SE2 124 A1
Basil Gdns
Croydon CR0 206 D1
West Norwood SE27 183 A5
Basil Ho 14 E1 96 A1
SW8 270 A4
Basil Mans SW1 247 C1
Basilon Rd DA7 147 A3
Basil Spence Ho N22 32 B2
Basil St SW1 114 D3 247 C1
SW1,SW3 114 D3 257 C6
Basin App 22 E14 97 A1
Basing Cl KT7 196 D2
Basing Ct 12 SE15 139 D4
Basingdon Way SE5 139 B1
Basing Dr DA5 169 B5
Basingfield Rd KT7 196 D2
Basinghall Ave
EC2 95 B1 242 C2
Basinghall St
EC2 95 B1 242 C2
Basing Hill NW11 47 B1
Wembley HA9 44 C1
Basing Ho
7 Barking IG11 101 B6
Catford SE6 185 C6
Basing House Yd 23 E2 95 C4
Basing Pl E2 95 C4
Basing St W11 91 B1
Basing Way N3 47 D6
Thames Ditton KT7 196 D2
Basire St N1 95 A6 235 B6
Baskerville Gdns NW10 67 C4
Baskerville Rd SW18 158 C4
Basket Gdns SE9 166 A6
Baslow Cl HA3 24 B2
Baslow Wlk E5 74 D4
Basnett Rd 8 SW11 137 A2
Basque Ct 21 SE16 118 D4
Bassano St SE22 161 D6
Bassant Rd SE18 145 D6
Bassein Park Rd W12 111 D4
Bassett Gdns TW7 130 A5
Bassett Ho RM9 102 B6
Bassett Rd W10 90 D1
Bassetts Cl BR6 226 D4
Bassett St NW5 71 A2
Bassetts Way BR6 226 D4
Bassett Way UB1 85 D1
Bassingbourn Ho 3
N1 72 D1
Bassingham Rd
Wandsworth SW18 158 A4
Wembley HA0 65 D2
Bassishaw Highwalk
EC2 242 C3
Basswood Cl SE15 140 B2
Basstable Ave IG11 102 A5
Basterfield Ho EC1 242 A5
Bastion Rd SE18,SE2 124 A1
Baston Manor Rd BR2,
BR4 225 B4
Baston Rd BR2 225 B5
Baston Sch BR2 225 B6
Bastwick St EC1 95 A3 242 A6
Basuto Rd
SW6 135 C4 265 B1
Batavia Cl TW16 172 C2
Batavia Ho 1 SE14 141 A5
Batavia Mews 3 SE14 141 A5
Batavia Rd SE14 141 A5
Sunbury TW16 172 B2
Batchelor St N1 94 C6 234 B5
Bateman Cl IG11 79 A2
Bateman Ho 8 SE17 138 D6
Bateman Rd E4 35 C4
Bateman's Bldgs W1 239 C1
Bateman's Row
EC2 95 C3 243 B6
Bateman St W1 93 D1 239 C1
Bates Cres
Croydon CR0 220 C3
Streatham SW16 181 C3
Bateson St SE18 123 C2
Bates Point E13 99 A6
Bate St 10 E14 119 B6
Bath Cl SE15 140 B5
Bath Ct EC1 235 C1
EC1 241 A5
3 Forest Hill SE26 162 A1
Bathgate Ho 8 SW9 138 D4
Bathgate Rd SW19 156 D1
Bath Gr E2 96 A5
Bath Ho E2 96 A3
SE1 262 B6
Bath House Rd CR0 204 A1
Bath Pas KT1 175 D1
Bath Pl 11 EC2 95 C4
14 W6 112 C1
Barnet EN5 1 B2
Bath Rd E7 77 D2
Bath Rd *continued*
N9 18 C2
W4 111 C2
Cranford TW3,TW4,TW5 128 C4
Dagenham RM6 59 A3
Harlington TW6,UB7,
TW5 127 B4
Harmondsworth TW6,
UB7 126 B4
Baths App
SW6 135 B5 264 D4
Baths Rd BR1,BR2 209 D5
Bath St EC1 95 B4 235 C1
Bath Terr SE1 117 A3 262 A6
Bathurst Ave SW19 179 D2
Bathurst Gdns NW10 90 B5
Bathurst Ho 2 W12 112 B6
Bathurst Mews
W2 114 B6 246 D6
Bathurst Rd IG1 56 D1
Bathurst St W2 246 D6
Bathway 17 SE18 122 C2
Batley Cl CR4 202 D2
Batley Pl 3 N16 73 D5
Batley Rd N16 73 D5
Enfield EN2 5 B4
Batman Cl W12 112 B5
Batoum Gdns W6 112 C3
Batson Ho 21 E1 96 A1
Batson St W12 112 A4
Batsworth Rd CR4 202 B6
Battenberg Wlk 10
SE19 183 C5
Batten Cl E6 100 B1
Batten Ho 8 E17 53 D6
7 SW4 159 C6
13 W10 91 A4
Batten St SW11 136 C2
Battersby Rd SE6 164 B1
Battersea Bridge Rd
SW11 136 C5 267 A3
Battersea Church Rd
SW11 136 B4 266 D2
Battersea Dogs Home
SW8 137 B5 268 D3
Battersea Park★
SW11 137 A5 268 A3
Battersea Park Rd
SW11,SW8 267 D1
Battersea Park Sta
SW8 137 B5 268 C3
Battersea Power
Station(dis)★
SW8 137 B6 268 D6
Battersea Rise SW11 136 C1
Battersea Sq SW11 266 D1
Battersea Tech Coll
SW11 136 D4 267 D1
Battery Rd SE28 123 C4
Battishill St 9 N1 72 D1
Battlebridge Ct NW1 233 B4
Battle Bridge Ctr
NW1 233 A4
Battle Bridge La
SE1 117 C5 253 A3
Battle Bridge Rd
NW1 94 A5 233 A4
Battle Cl SW19 180 A4
Battledean Rd N5 72 D3
Battle Ho 8 SE15 140 A6
Battle of Britain Mus★
NW9 27 D1
Batty St E1 96 A1
Baty Ho SW2 160 B3
Baudwin Rd SE6 164 C2
Baugh Rd DA14 190 C5
Baulk The SW18 157 C4
Bavant Rd SW16 182 B1
Bavaria Rd N19 72 A6
Bavent Rd SE5 139 A3
Bawdale Rd SE22 161 D6
Bawdsey Ave IG2 57 D5
Bawtree Rd SE14 141 A5
Bawtry Rd N20 14 D1
Baxendale N20 14 A2
Baxendale St E2 96 A4
Baxter Cl
Hillingdon UB10 82 D4
Southall UB2 107 D3
Baxter Ho 11 E3 97 D4
Baxter Rd N1 73 B2
Edmonton N18 34 B6
Ilford IG1 78 D3
Newham E16 99 C1
Bayard Ct DA7 147 D1
Baycliffe Ho 8 E9 74 D2
Baycroft Cl HA5 40 C6
Bay Ct 7 E1 96 D3
W5 110 A3
Baydene Mews NW4 46 B5
Baydon Ct BR2 208 D6
Bayer Ho EC1 242 A5
Bayes Ct NW3 70 D1
Bayeux Ho 10 SE7 143 C6
Bayfield Ho 3 SE4 140 D1
Bayfield Rd SE9 143 D1
Bayford Rd NW10 90 D4
Bayford St 5 E8 74 B1
Bayford St Ind Ctr 4
E8 74 B1
Bayham Pl NW1 93 C6 232 B5
Bayham Rd W4 111 B3
Ealing W13 109 B5
Morden SM4 202 A5
Bayham St NW1 93 C6 232 A5
Bayhurst Lo N4 51 A2
Bayhurst Wood Countryside
Park UB9 38 B4
Bayleaf Cl TW12 174 B5
Bayley St WC1 239 C3
Bayley Wlk SE2 125 A1
Baylis Mews TW1 153 A4
Baylis Rd SE1 116 C4 251 A1
Bayliss Ave SE28 124 D6
Bayliss Cl N21 16 A6
Bayne Cl E6 100 B1
Baynes Cl EN1 6 A4
Baynes Mews 2 NW3 70 B2
Baynes St NW1 71 C1
Baynham Cl DA5 169 B5
Bayon Ho 27 N19 49 D2
Bayonne Rd W6 264 A5
Bays Cl SE26 184 C5
Bays Ct HA8 26 D5
Bayshill Rise UB5 63 D2
Bayston Rd N16 73 D5
Bayswater Rd
W2 114 B6 246 C5
Bayswater Sta
W2 113 D6 245 D6
Baythorne St 5 E3 97 B2
Bayton Ct 2 E8 74 A1
Baytree Cl DA15 167 D3
Bromley BR1 187 D2
Baytree Ho E4 19 D4
Baytree Rd SW2 138 B1
Bazalgette Cl KT3 199 B4
Bazalgette Gdns KT3 199 B4
Bazalgette Ho NW8 236 D6
Bazeley Ho SE1 251 C1
Bazely St E14 120 A6
Bazile Rd N21 16 C5
BBC Television Ctr
W12 112 C5
Beacham Cl SE7 143 D6
Beachborough Rd
BR1 186 A6
Beachcroft Ave UB1 107 B5
Beachcroft Rd E11 76 C5
Beach Ct SE9 166 A5
Beach Gr TW13 151 C2
Beach Ho SW5 255 A2
Beachy Rd E3 75 C1
Beaconfield Terrace Rd
W14 254 A5
Beacon Gate SE14 140 D2
Beacon Gr SM5 219 A4
Beacon Hill N7 72 A3
Beacon Ho 19 SE5 139 C5
SW8 269 C2
10 Penge SE26 184 B5
Beacon House Sch
W5 110 B5
Beacon Pl CR0 220 A5
Beacon Rd SE13 164 B5
Harlington TW19,TW6 148 C5
Beacon Rdbt TW6 148 C5
Beacons Cl 10 E6 100 A2
Beaconsfield Cl N11 31 A5
SE3 143 A6
W4 111 A1
Beaconsfield Ct N11 31 A5
Beaconsfield Gdns
KT10 212 C1
Beaconsfield Par 1
SE9 188 A6
Beaconsfield Prim Sch
UB2 107 A5
Beaconsfield Rd BR1 209 D6
E10 76 A5
E16 98 D3
E17 53 B3
N11 31 A6
N15 51 C5
NW10 67 D2
SE17 117 C1 263 A1
SE9 188 A6
W4 111 B3
W5 109 D4
Claygate KT10 212 C1
Edmonton N9 18 A1
Enfield EN3 6 D6
Greenwich SE3 143 A5
Hayes UB4 106 C5
Kingston KT3 177 B1
Southall UB1 107 A5
Surbiton KT5 198 B2
Thornton Heath CR0 205 B3
Twickenham TW1 153 B5
Beaconsfield Wlk
SW6 135 B4 264 D1
Beaconshaw BR1 186 C3
Beacontree Ave E17 36 B1
Beacontree Rd E11 54 D2
Beadle Ct CR4 202 C6
Beadlow Cl SM4 202 B3
Beadman Pl SE27 182 D6

Beadman St SE27 182 D6
Beadnell Rd SE23 162 D3
Beadon Rd BR2 209 A4
W6 112 C2
Beaford Gr SW20 201 B6
Beagle Cl TW13 172 B6
Beak St W1 115 C6 249 B6
Beal Cl DA16 146 A4
Beale Cl N13 32 D5
Beale Ho 7 SW9 138 B3
Beale Pl E3 97 B5
Beale Rd E3 97 B6
Beal High Sch IG5 56 A5
Beal Rd IG1 78 C6
Beam Ave RM10 103 D6
Beames Ho SW8 269 C2
Beaminster Ct N15 51 B4
Beaminster Gdns IG6 56 D6
Beaminster Ho SW8 270 C4
Beamish Dr WD23 8 A3
Beamish Ho 5 SE16 118 C2
Beamish Rd N9 18 A3
Beanacre Cl E9 75 B2
Bean Rd DA6 146 D1
Beanshaw SE9 188 C6
Beansland Gr RM6 59 A6
Bear Alley EC4 241 C2
Bear Cl RM7 59 D3
Bear Croft Ho 6 SW6 135 B3
Beardell St SE19 183 D4
Beardow Gr N14 15 C5
Beard Rd TW10 176 B5
Beardsfield E13 99 A5
Beard's Hill TW12 173 C2
Beards Hill Cl TW12 173 C2
Beardsley Terr RM8 80 B3
Beardsley Way W3 111 B4
Beard's Rd TW15,TW16 171 C4
Bearfield Rd KT2 176 A3
Bear Gardens Mus★
SE1 117 A5 252 A4
Bear Gdns SE1 117 A5 252 A4
Bear La SE1 116 D5 251 D3
Bear Rd TW13 172 D6
Bear St WC2 249 D6
Bearstead Rise SE4 163 B6
Bearsted Terr 2 BR3 185 C2
Beasley's Ait TW17 193 D3
Beasley's Ait La TW16,
TW17 193 D3
Beaton Cl SE15 139 D4
Beatrice Ave
Thornton Heath SW16 182 B1
Wembley HA9 66 A3
Beatrice Cl E13 99 A3
Pinner HA5 40 A5
Beatrice Ct NW4 46 C4
Buckhurst Hill IG9 21 D2
Beatrice Ho 1 SW2 160 B6
4 W6 112 C1
Beatrice Pl W8 255 C5
Beatrice Rd E17 53 C4
N4 50 C2
N9 18 C4
SE1 118 A2
2 Richmond TW10 154 B6
Southall UB1 107 B5
Beatrice Tate Sch E2 96 B4
Beatrice Webb Ho 3
E3 97 A5
Beatrix Ho SW5 255 D2
Beatrix Potter Prim Sch
SW18 158 A3
Beattie Cl TW14 149 D3
Beattie Ho SW8 269 B2
Beattock Rise N10 49 B5
Beatty Rd N16 73 C4
Stanmore HA7 25 C4
Beatty St NW1 232 A4
Beattyville Gdns IG6 56 D5
Beauchamp Cl 16 W4 111 A3
Beauchamp Ct HA7 25 C5
Beauchamp Pl
SW3 114 C3 257 B5
Beauchamp Rd E7 77 B1
SW11 136 D1
East Molesey KT8 196 A4
South Norwood SE19 183 B2
Sutton SM1 217 C4
Twickenham TW1 153 A4
Beauchamp St EC1 241 A3
Beauchamp Terr
SW15 134 B2
Beauclerc Cty Inf Sch
TW16 194 C6
Beauclerc Rd W6 112 B3
Beauclere Ho 1 SM2 218 A1
Beauclerk Cl TW13 150 B3
Beauclerk Ho 10
SW16 160 A1
Beaudesert Mews
UB7 104 A4
Beaufort E6 100 C2
Beaufort Ave HA3 43 B6
Beaufort Cl Chingford E4 35 D4
Ealing W5 88 B2
Putney SW19 156 B4
Beaufort Ct N11 31 B5
New Barnet EN5 14 A6
Beaufort Ct *continued*
Richmond TW10 175 C6
Beaufort Dr NW11 47 C5
Beaufort Gdns NW4 46 C3
SW3 114 C3 257 B6
Heston TW5 129 A4
Ilford IG1 56 C1
South Norwood SW16 182 B3
Beaufort Ho 7 N15 51 D5
NW11 48 A3
SW1 259 C1
SW11 136 C3
SW3 266 D5
1 Wimbledon SW20 178 D2
Beaufort Mans SW3 266 D5
Beaufort Mews SW6 264 D6
Beaufort Pk NW11 47 C5
Beaufort Rd Ealing W5 88 B2
Kingston KT1,KT5,KT6 198 A5
Richmond TW10 175 C6
Ruislip HA4 61 B6
Twickenham TW1 153 C4
Beaufort St
SW3 136 B6 266 C6
Beaufort Way KT17 216 A1
Beaufoy Ho SW8 270 C4
3 West Norwood SE27 160 D1
Beaufoy Rd 11 SW8 137 B2
Tottenham N17 33 C3
Beaufoy Wlk
SE11 116 B2 260 D3
Beaulieu Ave 1 E16 121 B5
Forest Hill SE26 184 B6
Beaulieu Cl NW9 45 C5
SE5 139 B2
Hounslow TW4 151 B6
Mitcham CR4 181 A2
13 Twickenham TW1 153 D5
Beaulieu Ct W5 88 A2
Beaulieu Dr HA5 40 D2
Beaulieu Gdns N21 17 A4
Beaulieu Ho NW4 28 D1
Beaulieu Pl W4 111 A3
Beaumanor Gdns SE9 188 C6
Beaumanor Mans W2 245 D6
Beaumaris 4 N11 32 A4
Beaumaris Dr IG8 37 D3
Beaumaris Gn NW9 45 C3
Beaumaris Twr 2 W3 110 D4
Beaumont W14 254 D3
Putney SW15 157 A6
Beaumont Ave
W14 113 B1 254 C2
Harrow HA2 41 D3
Richmond TW9 132 B2
Wembley HA0 65 C4
Beaumont Bldgs WC2 240 B1
Beaumont Cl KT2 176 C3
Beaumont Cres
W14 113 B1 254 C1
Beaumont Ct E5 74 B5
16 NW9 27 D1
10 W4 111 A1
6 Mitcham CR4 181 A1
Wembley HA0 65 C3
16 Wimbledon SW19 178 D3
Beaumont Dr TW15 171 B5
Beaumont Gdns NW3 69 C5
Beaumont Gr E1 96 D3
Beaumont Ho 11 E10 53 D2
1 Streatham SW2 160 A3
Wimbledon SW19 157 C1
Beaumont Pl
NW1,WC1,W1 93 C3 239 B6
Barnet EN5 1 B4
Isleworth TW7 152 D6
Beaumont Rd E10 53 D2
E13 99 B4
W4 111 A3
Orpington BR5,BR6 211 B3
Putney SW15,SW19 157 A4
South Norwood SE19 183 A4
Beaumont Rise N19 49 D1
Beaumont Sch The E10 53 D1
Beaumont Sq E1 96 D2
Beaumont St W1 238 B4
Beaumont Terr 1
SE13 164 C4
Beaumont Wlk NW3 70 D1
Beauvais Terr UB5 84 D4
Beauvale 6 NW1 71 A1
Beauval Rd SE22 161 D5
Beaverbank Rd DA15,
SE9 167 B3
Beaver Cl
Hampton TW12 173 D2
9 Penge SE20 184 A3
Beaver Gr UB5 85 A4
Beavers Comm Prim Sch
TW4 128 C2
Beavers Cres TW4 128 D1
Beavers La TW4 128 C2
Beavers Lo DA14 189 D5
Beaverwood Rd BR7 189 C4
Beaverwood Sch for Girls
BR7 189 C4
Beavis Ho N16 73 C5
Beavor La W6 112 A1
Bebbington Rd SE18 123 C2
Beblets Cl 4 BR6 227 D3
Bec Cl HA4 62 D5
Beccles Dr IG11 79 D2
Beccles St E14 119 B6
Bechervaise Ct 2 E10 53 D1
Beck Cl SE13 141 D4
Beck Ct BR3 206 D6
Beckenham Bsns Ctr
BR3 185 A4
Beckenham Ct BR3 185 C2
Beckenham Gdns N9 17 C1
Beckenham Gr BR2 186 B1
Beckenham Hill Rd
BR3,SE6 186 A5
Beckenham Hill Sta
SE6 186 A5
Beckenham Hospl
BR3 185 B1
Beckenham Junction Sta
BR3 185 C2
Beckenham La BR1,
BR2 186 D1
Beckenham Place Pk
BR3 185 D3
Beckenham Rd
Penge BR3 185 A2
West Wickham BR3,BR4 208 A2
Beckenham Rd Sta
BR3 185 A2
Beckers The N16 74 A4
Becket Ave E6 100 C4
Becket Cl Croydon SE25 206 A3
2 Merton SW19 179 D2
Becket Fold HA1 42 D4
Becket Ho SE1 252 C1
Becket Rd N18 34 C6
Becket St SE1 262 C6
Beckett Cl DA17 125 B3
NW10 67 C2
Streatham SW16 159 D2
Beckett Ho 12 E1 96 C2
28 SW9 138 A3
Becketts Cl
Feltham TW14 150 B5
Orpington BR6 227 D5
Becketts Pl KT1 175 D2
Beckett Wlk BR3 185 A4
Beckfoot NW1 232 B3
Beckford Cl W14 254 D3
Beckford Dr BR5,BR6 211 B2
Beckford Ho 18 N16 73 C3
Beckford Prim Sch
NW6 69 B3
Beckford Rd CR0 205 D3
Beckham Ho SE11 260 D3
Beck Ho N16 73 C5
4 Edmonton N18 34 A5
Beckington 18 NW5 71 A2
Beck La BR3 206 D6
Beckley Ho E3 97 B3
Becklow Mews 7
W12 112 A4
Becklow Rd W12 112 A4
Beckmead Sch BR3 207 C1
Beck Rd E8 96 B6
Beck River Pk 3 BR3 185 C2
Becks Rd DA14 168 A1
Beckton Alps E6 100 C3
Beckton Alps Ski Ctr
E6 100 C3
Beckton Park Sta E16 122 B6
Beckton Rd E16 98 D2
Beckton Sta E6 100 C2
Beckton Triangle Ret Pk
E6 100 D3
Beck Way BR3 207 B6
Beckway Rd SW16 181 D1
Beckway St
SE17 117 C2 263 A3
Beckwith Ho 22 E2 96 B5
Beckwith Rd SE24 161 B6
Beclands Rd SW17 181 A4
Becmead Ave
Harrow HA3 43 B4
Streatham SW16 181 D6
Becondale Rd SE19 183 C5
Becontree Ave RM8 80 C5
Becontree Day RM8 81 A6
Becontree Prim Sch
RM8 80 B5
Becontree Sta RM9 80 D2
Bective Pl SW15 135 B1
Bective Rd E7 77 A4
Putney SW15 135 B1
Becton Pl
Erith DA7,DA8 147 D5
Erith DA8 147 D5
Bedale Rd EN2 5 A5
Bedale St SE1 252 C3
Beddington Cross
CR0 204 A2
Beddington Farm Rd
CR0 204 A1
Beddington Gdns SM5,
SM6 219 A2
Beddington Gn BR5 189 D2
Beddington Gr SM6 219 D3
Beddington Inf Sch
SM6 219 C4
Beddington La
Wallington CR0 220 A6
Wallington CR0 203 D2
Beddington Lane Sta
CR0 203 C3
Beddington Manor
SM2 218 B2
Beddington Park Cotts
SM6 219 D5
Beddington Park Prim Sch
CR0 219 D5
Beddington Rd BR5 189 D2
Ilford IG3 57 D2
Beddington Terr CR0 204 B2
Bede Cl HA5 22 D2
Bedefield WC1 233 B1
Bede Ho SE14 141 B4
5 Putney SW15 156 D5
Bedelsford Sch KT1 198 A6
Bedens Rd DA14 191 A5
Bede Rd RM6 58 C3
Bedfont Cl
East Bedfont TW14 149 A5
Mitcham CR4 181 A1
Bedfont Green Cl
TW14 149 A3
Bedfont Ind Pk N
TW15 149 A1
Bedfont Jun Sch
TW14 149 C5
Bedfont La TW14,
TW13 149 D4
Bedfont Lakes Ctry Pk
TW14 149 A2
Bedfont Rd
East Bedfont TW13,
TW14 149 B2
Stanwell TW19 148 B5
Bedford Ave
WC1 93 D2 239 D3
Barnet EN5 13 B6
Hayes UB4 84 B1
Bedfordbury
WC2 116 A6 250 A5
Bedford Cl N10 31 A3
Chiswick W4 133 D6
Bedford Cnr 3 W4 111 C2
Bedford Court Mans
WC1 239 D3
Bedford Ct WC2 250 A5
6 Richmond TW9 132 B1
South Norwood SE19 183 D2
Wembley HA0 65 D4
Bedford Gardens Ho
W8 245 B3
Bedford Gdns
W8 113 C5 245 B3
Bedford Hill SW12 159 B2
Bedford Ho 7 SW4 138 A1
2 W4 111 C2
Bedford Park Cnr 5
W4 111 C2
Bedford Park Mans
W4 111 B2
Bedford Pas SW6 264 B4
Bedford Pk CR0 205 A1
Bedford Pl WC1 94 A2 240 A4
Croydon CR0 205 B1
Bedford Rd E17 53 C6
N15 51 C5
N2 48 C6
N8 49 D3
NW7 11 C1
SW2,SW4 138 A1
W4 111 C3
Barking E6 100 C6
Ealing W13 109 B6
Edmonton N9 18 B4
Harrow HA1 42 A3
Ilford IG1 78 D5
North Cheam KT4 216 C6
Ruislip HA4 61 D4
Sidcup DA15 167 C1
Twickenham TW2 152 B1
Woodford E18 37 A1
Wood Green N22 32 A1
Bedford Row
WC1 94 B2 240 D3
Bedford Sq
WC1 93 D2 239 D3
Bedford St
WC2 116 A6 250 B5
Bedford Terr SM2 218 A2
Bedford Way
WC1 93 D3 239 D5
Bedgebury Gdns
SW19 157 A2
Bedgebury Rd SE9 143 D1
Bedivere Rd BR1 165 A1
Bedlow Cl NW8 236 D4
Bedlow Way CR0 220 B4
Bedonwell Inf Sch
SE2 147 A6
Bedonwell Jun Sch
DA17 147 A6
Bedonwell Rd
Bexley DA7,DA17 147 A6
Erith DA7 147 C5
Bedser Cl SE11 270 D6
Bedser Cl *continued*
South Norwood CR7 205 A6
Bedser Ct 7 SW4 138 A3
Bedser Dr UB6 64 B3
Bedster Gdns KT8 195 D6
Bedwardine Rd SE19 183 C3
Bedwell Ct 4 RM6 58 D2
Bedwell Gdns UB3 105 C2
Bedwell Ho 19 SW9 138 C3
Bedwell Rd
Belvedere DA17 125 C1
Tottenham N17 33 C2
Beeby Rd E16 99 B2
Beech Ave N20 14 C3
W3 111 C5
Brentford TW8 131 B5
Chigwell IG9 21 B2
Ruislip HA4 40 B1
Sidcup DA15 168 A4
Beech Cl SE8 141 B6
Ashford TW15 171 B5
Carshalton SM5 218 D6
Enfield N9 18 B5
Putney SW15 156 A4
Sunbury TW16 172 D1
West Drayton UB7 104 C3
Wimbledon SW19 178 C4
Beech Copse BR1 188 B1
South Croydon CR2 221 C3
Beechcroft BR7 188 C3
3 Kingston KT2 176 D2
Beechcroft Ave NW11 47 B2
Harrow HA2 41 C2
Kingston KT1,KT3 177 A1
Beechcroft Cl BR6 227 B4
Heston TW5 129 A5
Streatham SW16 182 B5
Beechcroft Ct 6 N12 29 D6
3 NW11 47 B2
Beech Croft Ct N5 72 D4
Beechcroft Gdns HA9 66 B5
Beechcroft Ho W5 88 A2
Beechcroft Lo 6 SM2 218 A1
Beechcroft Mans
SW16 182 B5
Beechcroft Rd BR6 227 B4
Chessington KT9 214 B5
Mortlake SW14 133 A2
Upper Tooting SW17 158 C2
Woodford E18 37 B1
Beechcroft Way N19 49 D1
Beech Ct E17 54 B6
NW2 69 B6
W1 237 C2
43 W2 91 C2
Beckenham BR3 185 B3
3 Buckhurst Hill IG9 21 D2
Hayes UB3 105 D5
6 Ilford E12 78 C5
Northolt UB5 85 A6
Surbiton KT6 198 A2
Teddington TW11 175 C4
4 West Norwood
SW16 182 C5
Beechdale N21 16 B2
Beechdale Rd SW2 160 B5
Beech Dell BR2,BR6 226 B4
Beechdene 4 SE15 140 B4
Beech Dr N2 48 D6
Beechen Cliff Way
TW7 130 D3
Beechen Gr HA5 41 B6
Beechen Pl SE23 162 C2
Beeches Ave The SM5 218 C1
Beeches Cl SE20 184 C2
Beeches Ct BR1 187 A4
Beeches Rd
Cheam SM3 201 A1
Upper Tooting SW17 158 D1
Beeches The E12 78 B1
1 N19 50 A1
N20 14 C2
Hounslow TW3 129 D4
Mitcham CR4 202 C4
Beechey Ho 30 E1 118 B5
Beech Farm Cotts IG8 36 B3
Beechfield Cotts 3
BR1 187 C1
Beechfield Ct 7 CR2 221 A4
Beechfield Rd BR1 187 C1
N4 51 A3
Forest Hill SE6 163 B3
Beech Gdns W5 110 A3
Dagenham RM10 81 D1
Beech Gr Kingston KT3 199 B6
Mitcham CR4 203 D5
Beech Hall Cres E4 36 B3
Beech Hall Rd E4 36 B3
Beech Hill EN4 2 C5
Beech Hill Ave EN4 2 B4
Beechhill Rd SE9 166 C6
Beech Ho 7 DA15 168 A1
5 N16 73 B6
6 NW3 70 D2
16 SE16 118 C4
Hayes UB4 84 D2
Heston TW5 129 A5
New Addington CR0 223 D2
Beech House Rd CR0 221 B5
Beech La IG9 21 B2
Beech Lawns N12 30 B5
Beechmont Cl BR1 186 C5
Beechmore Gdns SM3 216 D6
Beechmore Rd
SW11 136 D4 267 D1
Beechmount Ave W7 86 C2
Beecholme 18 N12 29 D6
Beecholme Ave CR4 181 B2
Beecholme Est E5 74 B5
Beecholme Prim Sch
CR4 181 B2
Beech Rd
Bowes Park N11 32 A4
East Bedfont TW14 149 C4
Thornton Heath SW16 204 B6
Beechrow KT2 176 A6
Beech St EC2 95 A2 242 B4
Beech Tree Cl N1 72 C1
Stanmore HA7 25 C5
Beech Tree Glade E4 20 D3
Beech Tree Pl SM1 217 D3
Beechvale Cl N12 30 C5
Beechway DA5 168 D5
Beech Way NW10 67 B1
Twickenham TW2 151 C1
Beech Wlk NW7 27 C4
Beechwood Ave N3 47 C6
Ashford TW16 172 A4
Greenford UB6 85 D4
Harrow HA2 63 D5
Hayes UB3 105 B6
Hillingdon UB8 82 C1
Orpington BR6 227 C2
Richmond TW9 132 C4
Ruislip HA4 61 D6
Thornton Heath CR7 204 D5
Beechwood Circ HA2 63 D5
Beechwood Cl N2 48 D5
NW7 27 C5
Surbiton KT6 197 D2
Beechwood Cres DA7 147 A2
Beechwood Ct N16 51 C2
Carshalton SM5 218 D4
Chiswick W4 133 B6
Sutton SM1 217 C3
Beechwood Dr
Keston BR2 225 D4
Woodford IG8 36 D5
Beechwood Gdns
Ealing NW10 88 B4
Harrow HA2 63 D5
Ilford IG5 56 C5
Beechwood Gr W3 111 C6
Beechwood Hall N3 47 B6
Beechwood Ho 22 E2 96 A5
Beechwood Mews 2
N9 18 A2
Beechwood Pk E18 55 A6
Beechwood Rd E8 73 D2
N8 50 A5
South Croydon CR2 221 C1
Beechwood Rise BR7 188 D6
Beechwoods Ct SE19 183 D5
Beechworth Cl NW3 69 C6
Beecroft Rd SE4 163 A6
Beehive Cl E8 73 D1
Elstree WD6 9 D5
Hillingdon UB10 60 B1
Beehive Ct IG1 56 B3
Beehive La IG1 56 B3
Beehive Pl SW9 138 C2
Beehive Prep Sch IG4 56 B4
Beeken Dene BR6 227 A4
Beeleigh Rd SM4 201 D5
Beeston Cl 5 E8 74 A3
South Oxhey WD19 22 D6
Beeston Pl SW1 258 D6
Beeston Rd EN4 14 B5
Beeston's Ho SE15 140 B2
Beeston Way TW14 150 C5
Beethoven Rd WD6 9 D5
Beethoven St W10 91 A4
Beeton Cl HA5 23 C3
Begbie Ho SW9 138 B3
Begbie Rd SE3 143 C4
Beggars Hill KT17 215 D2
Beggar's Roost La
SM1,SM2 217 C2
Begonia Cl E6 100 B3
Begonia Pl 1 TW12 173 C4
Begonia Wlk W12 89 D1
Beira St SW12 159 B4
Beis Rachel D'Satmar Girls
Sch N16 51 C2
Beis Yaakov Prim Sch
NW9 45 B6
Bekesbourne St 19 E14 97 A1
Belcroft Cl BR1 186 D3
Beldanes Lo NW10 68 A1
Beldham Gdns KT8 195 D6
Belenoyd Ct SW16 160 B1
Belfairs Dr RM6 58 C2
Belfairs Gn WD19 22 D5
Belfast Rd N16 73 D6
Croydon SE25 206 B5

Belfield Rd KT19 ....215 C1
Belfont Wlk N7 ....72 A4
Belford Gr SE18 ....122 C2
Belford Ho 7 E8 ....95 D6
Belfort Rd SE15 ....140 C3
Belfry Cl 33 SE16 ....118 B1
Belgrade Ho N16 ....73 C4
Belgrade Rd N16 ....73 C4
Hampton TW12 ....173 D2
Belgrave Cl NW7 ....27 B5
1 Acton W3 ....111 A4
Southgate N14 ....15 C6
Belgrave Cres TW16 ..172 B2
Belgrave Ct E13 ....99 C3
SE3 ....143 C5
SW8 ....269 A3
8 W4 ....111 A1
Belgrave Gdns NW8 ..91 D6
Southgate N14 ....3 D1
1 Stanmore HA7 ....25 C5
Belgrave Mans NW8 ..229 A5
Belgrave Mews N
SW1 ....248 A1
Belgrave Mews S
SW1 ....115 A3 258 B6
Belgrave Mews W
SW1 ....258 A6
Belgrave Pl
SW1 ....115 A3 258 B5
Belgrave Rd E10 ....54 A1
E13 ....99 C3
E17 ....53 C3
SW1 ....115 C2 259 A3
Barnes SW13 ....133 D5
Hounslow TW4 ....129 B2
Mitcham CR4 ....202 B6
Redbridge IG1 ....56 B1
South Norwood SE25 ..205 D5
Sunbury TW16 ....172 B2
Wanstead E11 ....55 A1
Belgrave Sq
SW1 ....115 A3 258 A6
Belgrave St E1 ....96 D1
Belgrave Terr IG8 ....21 A1
Belgrave Wlk CR4 ....202 B6
Belgrave Wlk Sta CR4 202 B5
Belgrave Yd SW1 ....258 C5
Belgravia Cl EN5 ....1 B2
Belgravia Ct SW1 ....258 C5
Belgravia Gdns BR1 ..186 C4
Belgravia Ho 11 SW4 .159 D5
Teddington TW11 ....175 C3
Belgravia Mews KT1 .197 D5
Belgrove St WC1 ....233 B2
Belham Wlk 18 SE5 ..139 B4
Belinda Rd 8 SW9 ..138 D2
Belitha Villas N1 ....72 C1
Bel La TW13 ....151 B1
Bellamy Cl 7 E14 ....119 C4
HA8 ....11 A1
SW5 ....254 D1
Uxbridge UB10 ....60 C5
Bellamy Ct HA7 ....25 B2
Bellamy Dr HA7 ....25 B2
Bellamy Ho Harrow HA3 44 A2
Heston TW5 ....129 C6
Upper Tooting SW17 ..180 B6
Bellamy Rd Chingford E4 35 D4
Enfield EN2 ....5 B3
Bellamy's Ct 16 SE16 .118 D5
Bellamy St SW12 ....159 B4
Bellasis Ave SW2 ....160 A2
Bell Ave UB7 ....104 B3
Bell Cl Pinner HA5 ....40 C6
Ruislip HA4 ....61 D5
Bellclose Rd UB7 ....104 A4
Bell Ct NW4 ....46 C5
Tolworth KT5 ....214 D6
Bell Dr SW18 ....157 A4
Bellefields Rd SW9 ..138 B2
Bellegrove Cl DA16 ..145 D3
Bellegrove Par DA16 .145 D2
Bellegrove Rd DA16 ..145 D3
Bellenden Rd SE15 ..139 D3
Bellenden Rd Ret Pk
SE15 ....140 A4
Bellenden Sch SE15 ..140 A3
Bellendon Road Bsns Ctr
SE15 ....139 D3
Bellerbys Coll SW15 .156 A5
Bellermine Cl SE28 ..123 D4
Belle Staines Pleasaunce
E4 ....19 C2
Belleville Prim Sch
SW11 ....158 D6
Belleville Rd SW11 ..158 D6
Belle Vue UB6 ....86 B6
Belle Vue Gdns SW9 ..138 A3
Belle Vue La WD23 ....8 B3
Bellevue Pk CR7 ....205 A5
Bellevue Pl E1 ....96 C3
Bellevue Rd DA6 ....169 B6
N11 ....31 A5
Barnes SW13 ....134 A3
Ealing W13 ....87 B3
Kingston KT1 ....198 A6
Bellevue Rd *continued*
Upper Tooting SW17 ...158 D3
Belle Vue Rd E17 ....36 B1
Bellew St SW17 ....158 A1
Bellfield CR0 ....223 B1
Bellfield Ave HA3 ....24 B4
Bellflower Cl 2 E6 ...100 A2
Bellgate Mews NW5 ...71 B5
Bell Gn SE26 ....185 B6
Bell Green La SE26 ..185 B6
Bellhill 6 CR0 ....221 A6
Bell Ho SE10 ....142 A6
SE2 ....124 D1
6 Dagenham RM10 ....81 D2
15 Streatham SW2 ....160 C4
Bellina Mews NW5 ....71 C4
Bell Ind Est 2 W4 ....111 A2
Bellingham 10 N17 ....34 B3
Bellingham Ct IG11 ..102 B4
Bellingham Gn SE6 ...163 C1
Bellingham Rd SE6 ...164 A1
Bellingham Sta SE6 ..163 D1
Bellingham Trad Est
SE6 ....163 D2
Bell Inn Yd EC3 ....242 D1
Bell La E1 ....95 D2 243 C3
E16 ....121 A5
NW4 ....46 D5
Enfield EN3 ....6 D5
Twickenham TW1 ....153 A3
Wembley HA9 ....65 D6
Bell Lane Prim Sch
NW4 ....46 D5
Bellmaker Ct 19 E3 ....97 C2
Bell Mdw SE19 ....183 C6
Bell Moor NW3 ....70 A5
Bellmore Ct 5 CR0 ..205 D1
Bello Cl SE24,SW2 ...160 D3
Bellot Gdns 1 SE10 ..120 C1
Bellot St SE10 ....120 C1
Bell Rd
East Molesey KT8 ....196 B4
Enfield EN1 ....5 B4
Hounslow TW3 ....129 D1
Bellring Cl DA17 ....147 C6
Bells Hill EN5 ....12 D6
Bell St NW1 ....92 C2 237 A4
SE18 ....144 A4
Bell The E17 ....53 C6
Belltrees Gr 1 SW16 .182 C5
Bell View BR3 ....185 B3
Bell View Manor HA4 ..39 C2
Bellview Mews N11 ....31 A5
Bell Water Gate SE18 .122 C3
Bell Wharf La EC4 ...252 B6
Bellwood Rd SE15 ...140 D1
Bell Yd WC2 ....94 C1 241 A1
Belmont Ave DA16 ...145 C2
N17 ....51 A6
Bowes Park N13 ....32 B5
Cockfosters EN4 ....14 D6
Edmonton N9 ....18 A3
Southall UB2 ....107 A3
Wembley HA0 ....88 B6
West Barnes KT3 ....200 A5
Belmont Circ HA3 ....25 B2
Belmont Cl N20 ....13 D3
SW4 ....137 C2
Chingford E4 ....36 B5
Cockfosters EN4 ....2 D1
Uxbridge UB8 ....60 A2
Woodford IG8 ....37 B6
Belmont Ct 6 N16 ....51 C1
N5 ....73 A4
NW11 ....47 B4
Belmont Gr SE13 ....142 B2
W4 ....111 B2
Belmont Hall Ct SE13 .142 B2
Belmont Hill SE13 ...142 B2
Belmont Jun & Inf Schs
N22 ....51 A6
Belmont La
Chislehurst BR7 ....189 A5
Stanmore HA7 ....25 C3
Belmont Lo Harrow HA3 24 B3
Stanmore HA7 ....25 C6
Belmont Mews SW19 .156 D2
Belmont Mid Sch HA3 .24 D1
Belmont Mill Hill Jun Sch
NW7 ....12 A1
Belmont Par 2 NW11 ..47 B4
Chislehurst BR7 ....189 A5
Belmont Park Cl SE13 142 C1
Belmont Park Rd E10 ..53 D3
Belmont Pk SE13 ....142 C1
Belmont Prim Sch W4 111 B2
Erith DA7 ....147 C5
Belmont Rd N15,N17 ..51 A5
SW4 ....137 C2
W4 ....111 B2
Beckenham BR3 ....185 B1
Chislehurst BR7 ....188 D5
Croydon SE25 ....206 B4
Erith DA8 ....147 D4
Harrow HA3 ....43 A6
Ilford IG1 ....79 A5
Twickenham TW2 ....152 B2
Uxbridge UB8 ....60 A2
Wallington SM6 ....219 C3
Belmont Rise SM1,SM2 217 B1
Belmont St NW1 ....71 A1
Belmont Terr W4 ....111 B2
Belmor WD6 ....10 C5
Belmore Ave UB4 ....84 A1
Belmore Ho N7 ....71 D3
Belmore Prim Sch UB4 84 B4
Belmore St
SW8 ....137 D4 269 C2
Beloe Cl SW15 ....134 A1
Belsham St E9 ....74 C2
Belsize Ave NW3 ....70 C3
W13 ....109 B3
Bowes Park N13 ....32 B4
Belsize Court Garages 1
NW3 ....70 B3
Belsize Cres NW3 ....70 B2
Belsize Ct NW3 ....70 B3
Belsize Gdns SM1 ....217 D4
Belsize Gr NW3 ....70 C2
Belsize La NW3 ....70 B3
Belsize Mews NW3 ....70 B2
Belsize Park Gdns NW3 70 C2
Belsize Park Mews 1
NW3 ....70 B2
Belsize Park Sta NW3 ..70 C3
Belsize Pk NW3 ....70 B2
Belsize Pl NW3 ....70 B3
Belsize Rd NW6 ....91 D6
NW8 ....229 A6
Harrow HA3 ....24 B3
Belsize Sq NW3 ....70 B2
Belsize Terr NW3 ....70 B2
Belson Rd SE18 ....122 B2
Beltane Dr SW19 ....156 D1
Belthorn Cres SW12 ..159 C4
Belton Rd E11 ....76 C4
E7 ....77 B1
N17 ....51 C6
NW2 ....68 A2
Sidcup DA14 ....190 A6
Belton Way E3 ....97 C2
Beltran Rd SW6 ....135 D3
Belvedere Ave SW19 ..179 A5
Belvedere Bldgs SE1 .251 D1
Belvedere Cl TW11 ...174 C5
Belvedere Ct DA17 ...125 B3
N2 ....48 B4
NW2 ....68 D2
7 SW4 ....159 D5
8 Kingston KT2 ....176 C3
Putney SW15 ....134 C1
Belvedere Dr SW19 ..179 A5
Belvedere Gdns KT8 ..195 C4
Belvedere Gr SW19 ..179 A5
Belvedere Heights
NW8 ....237 A6
Belvedere Ho TW14 ..150 A3
Belvedere Jun & Inf Sch
DA17 ....125 D3
Belvedere Mews SE15 140 C2
SE3 ....143 B5
Belvedere Pl SE1 ....251 D1
18 SW2 ....138 B1
Belvedere Rd
SE1 ....116 B4 250 D3
W7 ....108 D3
Bexley DA7 ....147 B3
Erith SE28 ....124 D5
Penge SE19 ....183 D3
Walthamstow E10 ....53 A1
Belvedere Sq SW19 ..179 A5
Belvedere Sta DA17 ..125 D3
Belvedere Strand NW9 .27 D1
Belvedere The SW10 ..266 B1
Belvedere Way HA3 ....44 A3
Belvoir Cl SE9 ....166 A1
Belvoir Lo SE22 ....162 A4
Belvoir Rd SE22 ....162 A4
Belvue Bsns Ctr UB5 ..63 D1
Belvue Cl UB5 ....63 C1
Belvue Rd UB5 ....63 C1
Belvue Sch UB5 ....85 C6
Bembridge Cl NW6 ....69 A1
Bembridge Gdns HA4 ..61 B6
Bembridge Ho 8 SE8 119 B2
Wandsworth SW18 ....157 D5
Bemersyde Point 6
E13 ....99 B4
Bemerton St N1 94 B6 233 C6
Bemish Rd SW15 ....134 D2
Bempton Dr HA4 ....62 B5
Bemsted Rd E17 ....53 B6
Benabo Ct 6 E8 ....74 A3
Benares Rd SE18,SE2 ..123 D2
Benbow Ct W6 ....112 B3
Benbow Ho 12 SE8 ....141 C6
Benbow Rd W6 ....112 B3
Benbow St SE8 ....141 C6
Benbury Cl BR1 ....186 A5
Bence Ho 13 SE8 ....119 A2
Bench Field CR2 ....221 D3
Bencroft Rd SW16 ....181 C3
Bencurtis Pk BR4 ....224 B6
Bendall Mews NW1 ....237 B4
Bendemeer Rd SW15 ..134 D2
Benden Ho SE13 ....164 A6
Bendish Rd E6 ....78 A1
Bendmore Ave SE2 ...124 A2
Bendon Valley SW18 ..157 D4
Benedict Cl BR6 ....227 C5
9 Erith DA17 ....125 A3
Benedict Ct RM9 ....59 B3
Benedict Dr TW14 ...149 B4
Benedict Fst Sch CR4 .202 B6
Benedict Prim Sch
CR4 ....202 B6
Benedict Rd SW9 ....138 B2
Mitcham CR4 ....202 B6
Benedict Way N2 ....48 A6
Benedict Wharf CR4 ..202 C6
Benenden Gn BR2 ....209 A4
Benenden Ho SE17 ...263 B2
Benett Gdns SW16 ...182 A1
Ben Ezra Ct SE17 ....262 B3
Benfleet Cl SM1 ....218 A5
Benfleet Ct 6 E8 ....95 D6
Benfleet Way N11 ....15 A2
Bengal Ct EC3 ....242 D1
Bengal Ho E1 ....96 D2
Bengal Rd IG1 ....78 D5
Bengarth Dr HA3 ....24 B1
Bengarth Rd UB5 ....85 A6
Bengeo Gdns RM6 ....58 C3
Bengeworth Rd SE5 ..139 A2
Harrow HA1 ....65 A5
Ben Hale Cl HA7 ....25 B5
Benham Cl 1 SW11 ..136 B2
Chessington KT9 ....213 C2
Benham Gdns TW3,
TW4 ....151 B6
Benham Rd W7 ....86 C2
Benham's Pl 8 NW3 ..70 A4
Benhill Ave SM1 ....218 A4
Benhill Rd SE5 ....139 B4
Sutton SM1 ....218 B4
Benhill Wood Rd SM1 218 A4
Benhilton Gdns SM1 .217 D5
Benhurst Ct Ealing W5 .110 A6
12 Penge SE20 ....184 B2
West Norwood SW16 ..182 C5
Benhurst La SW16 ...182 C5
Benin St SE13 ....164 B4
Benjafield Cl N18 ....34 B6
Benjamin Cl E8 ....96 A6
Benjamin Ct
4 Ealing W7 ....108 C5
4 Erith DA17 ....147 B6
Littleton TW15 ....171 A3
Benjamin St EC1 ....241 C4
Ben Jonson Ct 30 N1 ..95 C5
Ben Jonson Prim Sch
E1 ....97 A3
Ben Jonson Rd E1 ....97 A2
Benledi St E14 ....98 B1
Bennelong Cl W12 ....90 B1
Bennerley Rd SW11 ..158 D6
Bennetsfield Rd UB11 104 D5
Bennet's Hill EC4 ....251 D6
Bennets Lo EN2 ....5 A2
Bennett Cl DA16 ....146 A3
Teddington KT1 ....175 C2
Bennett Ct N7 ....72 B5
NW6 ....69 D2
7 W3 ....110 D4
Bennett Gr SE13 ....141 D4
Bennett Ho SW1 ....259 D4
2 Streatham SW4 ....159 D4
Bennett Pk SE3 ....142 D2
Bennett Rd E13 ....99 C3
Dagenham RM6 ....59 A2
Bennetts Ave
Croydon CR0 ....223 A6
Greenford UB6 ....86 C6
Bennett's Castle La
RM8 ....80 D5
Bennetts Cl
Mitcham CR4,SW16 ....181 B2
Tottenham N17 ....33 D4
Bennetts Copse BR7 ..188 A4
Bennett St SW1 ....249 A4
W4 ....111 C1
Bennetts Way CR0 ....223 B6
Bennett's Yd SW1 ....259 D5
Benn Ho 7 SE7 ....121 C1
Benningholme Rd HA8 .27 C4
Bennington Rd
Chingford IG8 ....36 C3
Tottenham N17 ....33 C2
Benn St E9 ....75 A2
Benns Wlk 8 TW9 ....132 A1
Bensbury Cl SW15 ...156 C4
Bensham Cl CR7 ....205 A5
Bensham Gr CR7 ....183 A1
Bensham La CR0,CR7 ..204 D3
Bensham Manor Rd
CR7 ....205 A5
Bensham Manor Sch
CR7 ....205 A4
Bensington Ct TW14 ..149 B5
Bensley Cl 7 N11 ....30 D5
Ben Smith Way 21
SE16 ....118 A3
Benson Ave E13,E6 ....99 D5
Benson Cl Hillingdon UB8 82 A2
Hounslow TW3 ....129 C1
Benson Ct 1 N19 ....71 C4
SW8 ....270 A2
Benson Ct *continued*
Holdbrook EN3 ....7 C5
Benson Ho E2 ....243 C6
SE1 ....251 B3
Benson Prim Sch CR0 223 A5
Benson Quay E1 ....118 C6
Benson Rd
Croydon CR0 ....220 C5
Forest Hill SE23 ....162 C3
Bentall Sh Ctr The 10
KT2 ....176 A1
Bentfield Gdns SE9 ..165 D1
Benthal Ct N16 ....74 A5
Benthal Prim Sch N16 .74 A5
Benthal Rd N16 ....74 A5
Bentham Ct 10 N1 ....73 A1
Bentham Ho SE1 ....262 C6
Bentham Rd E9 ....74 D2
Woolwich SE28 ....124 B5
Bentham Wlk NW10 ...67 A3
Ben Tillet Cl
Barking IG11 ....80 A1
Newham E16 ....122 B5
Ben Tillet Ho N15 ....50 D6
Bentinck Cl NW8 ....230 B3
Bentinck Ho 4 W12 ..112 B6
Bentinck Mans W1 ...238 B2
Bentinck Mews W1 ...238 B2
Bentinck Rd UB7 ....104 A5
Bentinck St W1 93 A1 238 B2
Bentley Cl SW19 ....157 C1
Bentley Dr IG2 ....57 A3
Bentley Ho 4 SE5 ...139 C4
6 Bow E3 ....97 C3
Bentley Lo WD23 ....8 C2
Bentley Mews EN1 ....17 B5
Bentley Rd N1 ....73 C2
Bentley Way
Stanmore HA7 ....25 A5
Woodford IG8 ....21 A1
Bentley Wood High Sch
HA7 ....24 D5
Benton Rd Ilford IG1,IG2 57 B1
South Oxhey WD19 ....22 D5
Benton's La SE27 ....183 A6
Benton's Rise SE27 ..183 B5
Bentry Cl RM8 ....81 A6
Bentry Rd RM8 ....81 B6
Bentworth Ct 1 E2 ...96 A3
Bentworth Prim Sch
W12 ....90 B1
Bentworth Rd W12 ....90 B1
Benville Ho SW8 ....270 D3
Benwell Ct TW16 ....172 A2
Benwell Rd N7 ....72 C3
Benwick Cl SE16 ....118 B2
Benwick Ct SE20 ....184 C2
Benwood Ct SM1 ....218 A5
Benworth St E3 ....97 B4
Benyon Ho EC1 ....234 B2
Benyon Rd N1 ....95 B6 235 D6
Beormund Prim Sch
SE1 ....117 B4 252 D1
Bequerel Ct SE10 ....120 D3
Berberis Ct IG1 ....78 D2
Berberis Ho 15 E3 ....97 C2
Berberis Wlk UB7 ....104 A2
Berber Pl 15 E14 ....119 C6
Berber Rd SW11 ....158 D6
Berberry Cl HA8 ....27 A6
Bercta Rd SE9 ....167 A2
Berebinder Ho 17 E3 ...97 B5
Berenger Twr SW10 ...266 C4
Berenger Wlk SW10 ..266 C4
Berens Ct DA14 ....189 D6
Berens Rd NW10 ....90 D4
Berens Way BR5,BR7 ..211 D6
Beresford Ave N20 ....14 D2
Ealing W7 ....86 C2
Tolworth KT5 ....199 A2
Twickenham TW1 ....153 C5
Wembley HA0 ....88 C6
Beresford Ct E9 ....75 A3
11 Twickenham TW1 ....153 C5
Beresford Dr BR1 ....210 A6
Woodford IG8 ....37 C6
Beresford Gdns
Dagenham RM6 ....59 A4
Enfield EN1 ....5 C1
Hounslow TW4 ....151 B6
Beresford Ho 14 SW4 .138 A1
Dulwich SE21 ....161 C1
Beresford Lo N4 ....73 B3
Beresford Rd N2 ....48 C6
N5 ....73 B3
N8 ....50 D4
Belmont SM2 ....217 B1
Chingford, Chingford Green
E4 ....20 C3
Chingford, Highams Park
E17 ....35 D2
Harrow HA1 ....42 B4
Kingston KT2 ....176 B2
New Malden KT3 ....199 A5
Southall UB1 ....106 D5
Beresford Sq 1 SE18 .122 D2
Beresford St SE18 ....122 D3
Beresford Terr 3 N5 ..73 A3
Bere St E1 ....118 D6
Berestede Rd 4 W6 ..111 D1
Bergen Ho 1 SE5 ....139 A3
Bergen Sq SE16 ....119 A3
Berger Cl BR5 ....211 C3
Berger Prim Sch E9 ...74 D2
Berger Rd E9 ....74 D2
Berghem Mews W14 .112 D3
Bergholt Ave IG4 ....56 A4
Bergholt Cres N16 ....51 C2
Bergholt Mews 4 NW1 71 D1
Berglen Ct E14 ....
Bering Sq E14 ....119 C1
Bering Wlk E16 ....99 D1
Berisford Mews SW18 158 A5
Berkeley Ave DA16 ...146 D4
Cranford TW4 ....128 A3
Northolt UB6 ....64 C2
Berkeley Cl
Borehamwood WD6 ....10 C6
Kingston KT2 ....176 A3
Orpington BR5,BR6 ....211 C2
Ruislip HA4 ....62 A5
Berkeley Cres EN4 ....14 B6
Berkeley Ct N3 ....29 D2
NW1 ....237 D5
1 NW11 ....47 B2
Ealing W5 ....109 C6
Edgware HA8 ....26 D5
18 Streatham SW2 ....160 C3
Wallington SM6 ....219 C4
Berkeley Dr KT8 ....195 C6
Berkeley Gdns W8 ....245 B3
Claygate KT10 ....213 A2
Southgate N21 ....17 B4
Walton-on-T KT12 ....193 D2
Berkeley Ho 17 E3 ....97 C4
8 SE8 ....119 B1
11 Brentford TW8 ....131 D6
Berkeley Lo Enfield EN2 ..4 C2
New Malden KT3 ....199 C5
Berkeley Mews W1 ...237 D1
Sunbury TW16 ....194 C6
Berkeley Pl SW19 ....178 D4
Berkeley Prim Sch
TW5 ....128 D5
Berkeley Rd E12 ....78 A3
N15 ....51 B3
N8 ....49 D3
NW9 ....44 C4
Barnes SW13 ....134 A4
Hillingdon UB10 ....61 A1
Berkeley Sq
W1 ....115 B6 248 D5
Berkeley St
W1 ....115 B5 248 D4
Berkeleys The SE25 ..206 A5
Berkeley The NW11 ....47 D2
Berkeley Waye TW5 ..128 D5
Berkeley Wlk 1 N7 ....72 B6
Berkerley Ct SW15 ...156 D6
Berkhampstead Rd
DA17 ....125 C1
Berkhamsted Ave HA9 .66 C2
Berkley Cl TW2 ....152 C1
Berkley Ct 6 TW1 ....153 A4
Berkley Gr NW1 ....71 A1
Berkley Rd NW1 ....70 D1
Berkshire Ct 1 W7 ....86 D3
Berkshire Gdns
Edmonton N13 ....32 C4
Edmonton N18 ....34 B5
Berkshire Ho SE6 ....185 C6
Berkshire Rd E9 ....75 B2
Berkshire Sq CR4 ....204 A5
Berkshire Way CR4 ...204 A5
Berleley Ct NW10 ....67 C4
Bermans Way NW10 ....67 D4
Bermondsey Leather Mkt
SE1 ....253 A1
Bermondsey Mkt*
SE1 ....117 C3 263 B8
Bermondsey Sq SE1 ..263 B6
Bermondsey St
SE1 ....117 C4 253 A1
Bermondsey Sta SE16 118 A3
Bermondsey Trad Est
SE16 ....118 C1
Bermondsey Wall E
SE16 ....118 B4
Bermondsey Wall W
SE1,SE16 ....118 A4
Bermuda Ho HA1 ....64 B5
Bernal Cl SE28 ....124 D6
Bernard Angell Ho 4
SE10 ....142 B6
Bernard Ashley Dr
SE7 ....121 B1
Bernard Ave W13 ....109 B3
Bernard Cassidy St 4
E16 ....98 D2
Bernard Gdns SW19 ..179 B5
Bernard Rd N15 ....51 D4
Wallington SM5,SM6 ..219 B4
Bernard Shaw Ct 3
NW1 ....71 C1
Bernard Shaw Ho 2
NW10 ....89 B6
Bernard St WC1 94 A3 240 B5
Bernays Cl HA7 ....25 C4

Bernay's Gr SW9 .....138 B1
Bernel Dr CR0 ....223 B5
Berne Rd CR7 ....205 A4
Berners Dr W13 .....109 A6
Berners Ho N1 ......234 A4
Bernersmede SE3 ....143 A2
Berners Mews
W1 ....93 C2 239 B3
Berners Pl W1 ....239 B2
Berners Rd N1 ......234 C5
Wood Green N22 ....32 C1
Berners St W1 .93 C1 239 B2
Berner Terr 30 E1 ......96 A1
Berney Ho BR3 ....207 A4
Berney Rd CR0 ....205 B2
Bernhart Cl HA8 ....27 A3
Bernwell Rd E4 ....20 C1
Bernwood Ho 6 N4 .....51 B2
Berridge Gn HA8 ....26 C3
Berridge Mews NW6 ...69 C3
Berridge Rd SE19 .....183 C5
Berriman Rd N7 ....72 B5
Berrite Works UB7 ...104 C4
Berriton Rd HA2 ....41 B1
Berrybank Cl 4 E4 ....20 A2
Berry Cl NW10 ....67 C1
Dagenham RM10 ....81 C3
Southgate N21 ....16 D3
Berry Ct TW4 ....151 B6
Berrydale Rd UB4 ......85 A3
Berryfield Cl BR1 .....188 A1
Berry Field Cl 8 E17 ..53 D5
Berryfield Rd
SE17 ....116 D1 261 D2
Berryhill SE9 ....144 D1
Berry Hill HA7 ....25 D6
Berryhill Gdns SE9 ...144 D1
Berry Ho 25 E1 ....96 B3
10 SW11 ....136 D3
Berry La SE21 ....183 B6
Berrylands
Surbiton KT5 ....198 C3
West Barnes SW20 ...200 C5
Berrylands Ct 7 SM2 .217 D1
Berrylands Rd KT5 ....198 B3
Berrylands Sta KT5 ...198 D5
Berryman Cl RM8 ....80 C5
Berryman's La SE26 ..184 D6
Berrymead Gdns W3 .111 A4
Berrymede Inf Sch
W3 ....110 D4
Berrymede Jun Sch
W3 ....110 D4
Berrymede Rd W4 ....111 B3
Berry Pl EC1 ....234 D1
Berry St EC1 ....241 D5
Berry Way W5 ....110 A3
Bertal Rd SW17 ....180 B6
Bertha Hollamby Ct
DA14 ....190 C5
Bertha Neubergh Ho 1
SE5 ....139 A4
Berthan Gdns E17 ......54 B4
Berthon St SE8 ....141 C6
Bertie Rd NW10 ....68 A2
Penge SE26 ....184 D4
Bertram Cotts SW19 ..179 C3
Bertram Rd NW4 ....46 A3
Enfield EN1 ....6 A1
Kingston KT2 ....176 C3
Bertram St N19 ....71 B6
Bertrand Ho 11 SW16 .160 A1
Bertrand St SE13 .....141 D2
Bertrand Way SE28 ...124 C6
Bert Rd CR7 ....205 A4
Bert Reilly Ho 1 SE18 123 B1
Bertrum House Sch
SW17 ....159 A2
Bert Way EN1 ....5 D1
Berwick Ave UB4 .....106 D6
Berwick Cl HA7 ....24 D4
Berwick Cres DA15 ...167 C5
Berwick Ho 10 N2 .....30 B1
Berwick Rd DA16 .....146 B4
Newham E16 ....99 C1
Tottenham N22 ....32 D2
Berwick St W1 .93 C1 239 B1
Berwyn Ave TW3 .....129 D4
Berwyn Ho 3 N16 ......51 D1
Berwyn Rd
Mortlake SW14,TW10 ..132 D1
Streatham SE24 ....160 D3
Beryl Ave E6 ....100 A2
Beryl Harding Ho 3
SW19 ....178 D3
Beryl Ho SE18 ....123 D1
Beryl Rd W6 ....112 D1
Berystede KT2 ....176 D3
Besant Cl NW2 ....69 A5
Besant Ct N1 ....73 B3
15 SE28 ....124 B6
Besant Ho NW8 ....229 A5
Besant Rd NW2 ....69 A4
Besant Way NW10 .....67 A3
Besant Wlk N7 ....72 B6
Besford Ho 25 E2 ......96 A5
Besley St SW16 ....181 C4
Bessant Dr TW9 ......132 D4
Bessborough Gdns
SW1 ....115 D1 259 D2
Bessborough Pl
SW1 ....115 D1 259 D2
Bessborough Rd
Harrow HA1 ....42 B1
Roehampton SW15 ....156 A3
Bessborough St
SW1 ....115 D1 259 C2
Bessborough Wks
KT8 ....195 B4
Bessemer Ct 5 NW1 ...71 C1
Bessemer Grange Prim Sch
SE5 ....139 C1
Bessemer Park Ind Est 3
SE24 ....138 D1
Bessemer Rd SE5 ....139 A3
Bessie Lansbury Cl E6 100 C1
Bessingby Rd HA4 .....62 B6
Bessingham Wlk SE4 .162 D6
Besson St SE14 ......140 D4
Bessy St E2 ....96 C4
Bestwood St SE8 .....118 D2
Beswick Mews 1 NW6 69 D2
Betam Rd UB3 ....105 B4
Beta Pl 20 SW4 ....138 B1
Betchworth Cl SM1 ..218 B3
Betchworth Ho 8 N7 ..71 D3
Betchworth Rd IG3 ....79 C5
Betham Rd UB6 ....86 B4
Bethany Waye TW14 ..149 C4
Bethecar Rd HA1 ....42 C4
Bethell Ave E13,E16 ....98 D3
Ilford IG1 ....56 C2
Bethel Rd DA16 ....146 C2
Bethersden Cl BR3 ...185 B3
Bethersden Ho SE17 ..263 B2
Bethesda Ct 8 SE20 ..184 C3
Beth Jacob Gram Sch
NW4 ....46 D5
Bethlehem Ho 13 E14 .119 B6
Bethlem Royal Hospl
BR3 ....207 C2
Bethnal Green Mus of
Childhood★ E2 ....96 C4
Bethnal Green Rd
E1,E2 ....96 A4 243 D6
Bethnal Green Sta E1 ..96 B3
E2 ....96 C4
Bethnal Green Tech Coll
E2 ....95 D4
Beths Gram Sch DA5 .169 D5
Bethune Ave N11 ......30 D6
Bethune Rd N16 ....51 C2
NW10 ....89 B3
Bethwin Rd SE5 ......139 A5
Betjeman Cl HA5 ....41 C5
Betony Cl CR0 ....206 D1
Betoyne Ave E4 ....36 C6
Betsham Ho SE1 ......252 C2
Betspath Ho 6 N11 ....31 C5
Betstyle Ho 2 N10 .....31 A3
Betstyle Rd N11 ....31 B6
Betterton Dr DA14 ....169 A2
Betterton Ho WC2 ....240 B1
Betterton St
WC2 ....94 A1 240 B1
Bettons Pk E15 ....98 C6
Bettridge Rd SW6 .....135 B3
Betts Cl BR3 ....185 A1
Betts Ho E1 ....118 B6
Betts Mews E17 ....53 B3
Betts Rd E16 ....121 B6
Betts St E1 ....118 B6
Betts Way
Long Ditton KT6 ....197 B1
Penge SE20 ....184 B2
Bettswood Ct 15 SE20 184 B2
Betty Layward Prim Sch
N16 ....73 B5
Betty May Gray Ho 1
E14 ....120 A2
Beulah Ave CR7 ....183 A1
Beulah Cl HA8 ....10 D1
Beulah Cres CR7 ......183 A1
Beulah Gr CR0 ....205 A3
Beulah Hill SE19 .....183 A3
Beulah Inf Sch CR7 ..205 A6
Beulah Jun Sch CR7 ..205 A6
Beulah Rd E17 ....53 D4
Merton SW19 ....179 B3
South Norwood CR7 ...205 A6
Sutton SM1 ....217 C4
Beuleigh Ct E17 ....54 B4
Bevan Ave IG11 ....80 A1
Bevan Ct Croydon CR0 .220 C3
9 Twickenham TW1 ...153 D5
Bevan Rd SE2 ....124 B1
Cockfosters EN4 ....2 D1
Bevan St N1 ....95 A6 235 B5
Bev Callender Cl 4
SW8 ....137 B2
Bevenden St
N1 ....95 B4 235 D2
Bevercote Wlk 1
DA17 ....147 B6
Beveridge Ct 1 SE28 .124 B6
Southgate N21 ....16 A6
Beveridge Rd 1 NW10 .67 C1
Beverley Ave DA15 ...167 D4
Hounslow TW4 ....129 B1
Wimbledon SW20 .....177 D2
Beverley Cl 6 SW11 ..136 B1
Barnes SW13 ....134 A3
Chessington KT9 .....213 C4
Edmonton N21 ....17 A3
Enfield EN1 ....5 C1
Beverley Cotts SW15 .155 C1
Beverley Cres IG8 .....37 B2
Beverley Ct N14 ....15 C4
N2 ....48 D5
N5 ....72 D2
SE4 ....141 B2
5 W12 ....111 C4
9 W4 ....111 A1
Harrow HA2 ....42 B6
Hounslow TW4 ....129 B1
Northolt UB5 ....84 C5
Wimbledon SW20 .....177 D2
Beverley Dr HA8 ....44 C6
Beverley Gdns NW11 ...47 A2
Barnes SW13 ....133 D2
2 New Malden KT4 ...200 A1
Stanmore HA7 ....25 A2
Wembley HA9 ....44 C1
Beverley Ho 5 BR1 ...186 B5
Beverley Hyrst 10 CR0 221 D6
Beverley La KT2 ......177 C3
Beverley Lo 6 TW10 .154 A6
Beverley Mans TW4 ..129 B1
Beverley Path 9
SW13 ....133 D3
Beverley Rd BR2 .....226 A6
E6 ....99 D4
W4 ....111 D1
Barnes SW13 ....133 D2
Chingford E4 ....36 B4
Dagenham RM9 ....81 A4
Mitcham CR4 ....203 D5
North Cheam KT4 .....216 C6
Penge SE20 ....184 B1
Ruislip HA4 ....62 B6
Southall UB2 ....107 A3
Sunbury TW16 ....171 D2
Teddington KT1 ....175 C2
West Barnes KT3 .....200 A5
Beverley Sch KT3 .....200 A4
Beverley Trad Est
SM4 ....200 D2
Beverley Way KT3,
SW20,KT2 ....177 D2
Beverley Way (Kingston By
Pass) KT3,SW20 ......200 A6
Beverly Ct HA3 ....43 C5
Beversbrook Rd N19 ...71 D5
Beverstone Rd SW2 ..160 B6
Thornton Heath CR7 ..204 D5
Beverston Mews NW1 237 C3
Bevill Allen Cl SW17 ..180 D5
Bevill Cl SE25 ....206 A6
Bevin Cl SE16 ....119 A5
Bevin Ct WC1 ....233 D2
Bevington Prim Sch
W10 ....91 A2
Bevington Rd W10 .....91 A2
Beckenham BR3 ......185 D1
Bevington St SE16 ....118 A4
Bevin Ho 35 E2 ....96 C4
7 E3 ....97 C4
Bevin Rd UB4 ....84 B4
Bevin Sq SW17 ....158 D1
Bevin Way WC1 ....234 A2
Bevis Marks
EC3 ....95 C1 243 B2
Bewcastle Gdns EN2 ....4 A1
Bew Ct SE21 ....162 A4
Bewdley Ho N4 ....51 A2
Bewdley St N1 ....72 C1
Bewick Mews SE15 ...140 B5
Bewick St SW8 ....137 B3
Bewley Ct SW2 ....160 B5
Bewley Ho 7 E1 ......118 B6
Bewley St Stepney E1 ..118 B6
Wimbledon SW19 .....180 A4
Bewlys Rd SE27 ......182 D5
Bexhill Cl TW13 ......151 A2
Bexhill Rd N11 ....31 D5
SE4 ....163 B5
Mortlake SW14 ......133 A2
Bexhill Wlk 6 E15 .....98 C6
Bexley Coll SE2 ......146 D6
Bexley Coll (Erith Rd
Campus) DA17 ....125 D1
Bexley Gdns
Edmonton N9 ....17 B1
Ilford RM6 ....58 B4
Bexley Gram Sch
DA16 ....146 B1
Bexleyheath Sch DA6 .147 C2
Bexleyheath Sta DA7 .147 A3
Bexley High St DA5 ..169 D3
Bexley Ho SE4 ....141 A1
Bexley La DA14 ....168 C1
Bexley Rd SE9 ....167 A6
Bexley Sta DA5 ....169 C3
Beynon Rd SM5 ....218 D3
BFI London Imax Cinema
SE1 ....116 C5 251 A3
Bianca Rd SE1,SE15 ..140 A6
Bibsworth Lo N3 ....29 B1
Bibsworth Rd N3 ....29 B1
Bicester Rd TW9 .....132 D2
Bickenhall Mans W1 .237 D4
Bickenhall St
W1 ....92 D2 237 D4
Bickersteth Rd SW17 .180 D4
Bickerton Rd N19 ......71 C6
Bickley Cres BR1 .....210 A5
Bickley Ct 1 HA7 ....25 C6
Bickley Park Rd BR1,
BR7 ....210 B6
Bickley Park Sch BR1 .210 A6
Bickley Prim Sch BR1 209 C6
Bickley Rd BR1 ......187 D1
E10 ....53 D2
Bickley St SW17 .....180 D5
Bickley Sta BR1 ......210 A6
Bicknell Ho 23 E1 .....96 A1
Bicknell Rd SE5 ......139 A2
Bicknoller Rd EN1 ......5 D4
Bicknor Ho 2 E5 ....74 B3
Bicknor Rd BR6 ......211 D2
Bidborough Cl 3 BR2 208 D4
Bidborough St
N1,WC1 ......94 A4 233 A1
Biddenden Way SE9 ..188 C6
Biddenham Ho 18
SE16 ....118 D2
Bidder St E16 ....98 C2
Biddesden Ho SW3 ..257 C3
Biddestone Rd N7 ......72 B4
Biddulph Ho 23 SE18 .122 B2
Biddulph Mans W9 .....91 D4
Biddulph Rd W9 ....91 D4
Bideford Ave UB6 ....87 B5
Bideford Cl
Edgware HA8 ....26 C2
Twickenham TW13 ....151 B1
Bideford Gdns EN1 ....17 C4
Bideford Rd DA16 .....146 B5
Catford BR1 ....164 D1
Enfield EN3 ....7 B5
Ruislip HA4 ....62 B5
Bidmead Ct KT6 ......214 A5
Bidwell Gdns N11 ......31 C3
Bidwell St SE15 ......140 B4
Big Ben★ SW1 ....250 B1
Bigbury Cl N17 ....33 C3
Biggerstaff Rd E15 ....98 A6
Biggerstaff St N4 ......72 C6
Biggin Ave CR4 ....180 D2
Biggin Hill SE19 ......182 D3
Biggin Hill Cl KT2 ....175 C5
Biggin Way SE19 .....183 A3
Bigginwood Rd SW16 .182 D2
Bigg's Row SW15 ....134 D2
Big Hill E5 ....52 B1
Bigland Green Prim Sch
E1 ....96 B1
Bigland St E1 ....96 B1
Bignell Rd SE18 ......122 D1
Bignold Rd E7 ....77 A4
Bigwood Ct NW11 ......47 D4
Bigwood Rd NW11 .....47 D3
Bilberry Ho 18 E3 ......97 C2
Billet Rd E17 ....35 B2
Ilford RM6 ....58 C6
Billetts Hart Cl W7 ...108 C4
Bill Hamling Cl SE9 ..166 B2
Billingford Cl SE4 ....140 D1
Billing Ho 6 E1 ....96 D1
Billingley NW1 ....232 A5
Billing Pl
SW10 ....135 D5 265 D4
Billing Rd
SW10 ....135 D5 265 D4
Billings Cl RM9 ....80 C1
Billingsgate Mkt E14 .119 D5
Billing St
SW10 ....135 D5 265 D4
Billington Ho SW8 ...269 D1
Billington Rd SE14 ...140 D5
Billiter Sq EC3 ....243 B1
Billiter St EC3 ..95 C1 243 B1
Bill Nicholson Way N17 33 D3
Billockby Cl KT9 .....214 B2
Billsley Ct SE25 ......205 C5
Billson St E14 ....120 A2
Bilsby Gr SE9 ....187 D6
Bilton Ho SW8 ....269 C1
Bilton Rd UB6 ....87 B6
Bilton Twrs W1 ......237 D1
Bilton Way Enfield EN3 ...7 B5
Hayes UB3 ....106 B4
Bina Gdns
SW5 ....114 A2 256 A3
Binbrook Ho W10 ......90 C2
Bincote Rd EN2 ....4 B2
Binden Rd W12 ....111 D3
Bindon Gn SM4 ....201 D5
Binfield Ct SE5 ....139 A3
Binfield Rd
SW4 ....138 A4 270 B1
South Croydon CR2 ..221 D3
Bingfield St N1 .94 B6 233 C6
Bingham Cnr CR0 .....206 A1
Bingham Pl W1 93 A2 238 A4
Bingham Point 11
SE18 ....122 D2
Bingham Rd CR0 .....206 B1
Bingham St N1 ....73 B2
Bingley Rd
Ashford TW16 ....172 A3
Newham E16 ....99 C1
Southall UB6 ....86 A2
Binley Ho SW15 ......155 D5
Binney St W1 ..93 A1 238 B1
Binnie Ho SE1 ....262 A5
Binns Rd W4 ....111 C1
Binns Terr 3 W4 .....111 C1
Binsey Wlk 1 SE2 ....124 C4
Binstead Cl UB4 ....85 A2
Binstead Ho SW18 ....157 D5
Binyon Cres HA7 ....24 D5
Binyon Ho 8 N16 ......73 C4
Birbetts Rd SE9 ......166 B2
Bircham Path SE4 ....140 D1
Birchanger Rd SE25 ..206 A4
Birch Ave Edmonton N13 17 A1
Hillingdon UB7 ....82 B1
Birch Cl E16 ....98 C2
N19 ....71 C6
SE15 ....140 A3
Brentford TW8 ....131 B5
Buckhurst Hill IG9 .....21 D1
Hounslow TW3 ....130 B3
Romford RM7 ....59 D6
Teddington TW11 .....175 A5
Birch Cres UB10 ....82 B6
Birch Ct E7 ....76 D4
Chingford E4 ....35 D4
Sutton SM1 ....218 A4
9 Wallington SM6 ....219 B4
Birchdale Gdns RM6 ..58 D2
Birchdale Rd E7 ....77 C3
Birchdene Dr SE28 ..124 A5
Birchdown Ho 32 E3 ..97 D4
Birchen Cl NW9 ....67 B6
Birchend Cl CR2 .....221 B2
Birchen Gr NW9 ....67 B6
Birches Cl
Mitcham CR4 ....202 D6
Pinner HA5 ....41 A4
Birches The E12 ....78 A4
SE5 ....139 C3
2 Beckenham BR2 ...208 D5
Bushey WD23 ....8 A6
Greenwich SE7 ....143 B6
Orpington BR6 ....226 C4
Southgate N21 ....16 B5
South Norwood SE25 .183 D1
Twickenham TW4 .....151 B4
Birchfield Ho 2 E14 ..119 C6
Birchfield St E14 .....119 C6
Birch Gn NW9 ....27 C3
Birch Gr E11 ....76 C5
Acton W3 ....110 C6
Bexley DA16 ....146 A1
Lewisham SE12 ......164 D4
Upper Halliford TW17 ..171 C1
Birch Hill CR0 ....222 D3
Birch Ho SE14 ....141 B4
8 SW2 ....160 C5
Birchington Cl DA7 ..147 D4
Birchington Ct N8 .....49 D3
2 NW6 ....91 D6
Birchington Ho 1 E5 ..74 B3
Birchington Rd N8 ....49 D3
NW6 ....91 C6
Surbiton KT5 ....198 B2
Birchin La EC3 ....242 D1
Birchlands Ave SW12 .158 D4
Birch Mead BR2,BR6 ..226 C6
Birchmead Ave HA5 ...40 C5
Birchmere Lo 18 SE16 118 B1
Birchmere Row SE3 ..142 D3
Birchmore Wlk N5 .....73 A5
Birch Pk HA3 ....24 A3
Birch Rd Feltham TW13 172 D5
Romford RM7 ....59 D6
Birch Row BR2 ....210 C3
Birch Tree Ave BR4 ..224 D4
Birch Tree Ho 16 SE7 .143 C6
Birch Tree Way CR0 ..222 B6
Birch Vale Ct NW8 ...236 D6
Birchway UB3 ....106 A5
Birch Wlk CR4 ....181 B2
Birchwood Ave N10 ...49 A6
Beckenham BR3 ......207 B5
Hackbridge SM5,SM6 ..219 B5
Sidcup DA14 ....168 C1
Birchwood Cl SM4 ....201 D5
Birchwood Ct HA8 .....27 A1
Edmonton N13 ....32 D5
Birchwood Dr NW3 ....69 D5
Birchwood Gr TW12 ..173 C4
Birchwood Rd
Orpington BR5 ....211 C5
Streatham SW17 .....181 B5
Birdbrook Rd SE3,SE9 .143 C2
Birdcage Wlk
SW1 ....115 D4 249 C1
Birdham Cl BR1 ......210 A4
Birdhurst Ave CR2 ...221 B4
Birdhurst Ct SM6 .....219 C1
Birdhurst Gdns CR2 ..221 B4
Birdhurst Rd SW18 ...158 A6
Mitcham SW19 ....180 C4
South Croydon CR2 ...221 C3
Birdhurst Rise CR2 ..221 C3
Bird In Bush Rd SE15 .140 A5
Bird-in-Hand La BR1 .187 D1
Bird-In-Hand Pas
SE23 ....162 C2
Bird In Hand Yd 14
NW3 ....70 A4
Birdsall Ho 5 SE5 ....139 C2
Birdsfield La E3 ....97 B6
Bird St W1 ....238 B1
Bird Wlk TW2 ....151 B3
Birdwood Cl TW11 ...174 C6
Birkbeck Ave W3 .....111 A6
Greenford UB6 ....86 A6
Birkbeck Coll
W1 ....93 D1 239 C2
Birkbeck Ct W3 ....111 B5
Birkbeck Gdns IG8 ....21 A2
Birkbeck Gr W3 ......111 B4
Birkbeck Hill SE21 ...160 D3
Birkbeck Mews 5 E8 ..73 D3
Birkbeck Pl SE21 .....161 A2
Birkbeck Prim Sch
DA14 ....168 B1
Birkbeck Rd E8 ....73 D3
N12 ....30 A5
N8 ....50 A5
NW7 ....27 D5
W3 ....111 B5
W5 ....109 C2
Enfield EN2 ....5 B5
Ilford IG2 ....57 B4
Penge BR3 ....184 D1
Sidcup DA14 ....168 A1
Tottenham N17 ....33 D2
Wimbledon SW19 .....179 D4
Birkbeck St E2 ....96 B4
Birkbeck Sta SE20 ...206 C6
Birkbeck Way UB6 .....86 B6
Birkdale Ave HA5 ......41 C6
Birkdale Cl BR6 ......211 B2
30 SE16 ....118 B1
Erith SE28 ....102 D1
Birkdale Ct 3 UB1 .....86 A1
Birkdale Gdns CR0 ...222 D4
Birkdale Rd SE2 ......124 A2
Ealing W5 ....88 A3
Birkenhead Ave KT2 ..176 B2
Birkenhead Ho 11 N7 ..72 C3
Birkenhead St
WC1 ....94 A4 233 B2
Birkhall Rd SE6 ......164 B2
Birkwood Cl SW12 ...159 D4
Birley Lo NW8 ....229 D4
Birley Rd N20 ....14 A2
Birley St SW11 ....137 A3
Birnam Rd N4 ....72 B6
Birnbeck Ct NW11 .....47 B4
Birrell Ho 9 SW9 ....138 B3
Birse Cres NW10 ....67 C4
Birstal Gn WD19 ....22 D6
Birstall Rd N15 ....51 C4
Birtwhistle Ho 5 E3 ...97 B6
Biscay Ho 11 E1 ....96 D3
Biscay Rd W6 ....112 D1
Biscoe Cl TW5 ....129 C6
Biscoe Ho UB2 ....107 D2
Biscoe Way SE13 ....142 B2
Biscott Ho 3 E3 ....97 D3
Bisenden Rd CR0 ....221 C6
Bisham Cl CR4 ....202 D1
Bisham Gdns N6 ....49 A1
Bishop Butt Cl BR6 ..227 D5
Bishop Challoner Collegiate
Sch
E1 ....118 A6
E1 ....96 C1
Bishop Challoner Sch
BR2 ....186 B1
Bishop Ct 20 SW2 ....160 C5
Bishop Douglass RC High
Sch N2 ....48 A6
Bishop Duppa's Almshouses
7 TW10 ....154 A6
Bishop Duppas Pk
TW17 ....193 C2
Bishop Fox Way KT8 ..195 B5
Bishopgate 32 N1 .....95 C6
Bishop Gilpins Prim Sch
SW19 ....179 B5
Bishop John Robinson CE
Prim Sch SE28 ......124 C6
Bishop Ken Rd HA3 ...24 D2
Bishop King's Rd
W14 ....113 A2 254 B4
Bishop Perrin CE Prim Sch
TW2 ....151 D3
Bishop Ramsey CE Sch
HA4 ....40 A2
Bishop Ramsey CE Sch
(Annexe) HA4 ....39 D2
Bishop Rd N14 ....15 B4
Bishops Ave BR1 .....209 C6

Bishops Ave *continued*
E13 99 B6
Borehamwood WD6 10 B6
Ilford RM6 58 C3
Bishop's Ave SW6 135 A3
Bishops Ave The N2 48 B3
Bishopsbourne Ho BR1 187 B3
Bishop's Bridge Rd W2 92 A1 236 A2
Bishops Cl SE9 167 A2
W4 111 A1
Bishop's Cl E17 53 D5
N19 71 C5
Bishops Cl Barnet EN5 12 D5
Enfield EN1 6 B3
Richmond TW10 153 D1
Sutton SM1 217 C5
Bishop's Cl UB10 82 C5
Bishopscourt 8 CR0 221 D6
Bishops Ct N2 48 C5
12 W2 91 D1
Bishop's Ct EC4 241 C2
WC2 241 A2
Bishops Ct
1 Ashford TW16 171 D3
Romford RM7 59 D5
Bishopsdale Ho 8 NW6 91 C6
Bishops Dr
East Bedfont TW14 149 B5
Northolt UB5 85 A6
Bishopsford Rd SM4 202 B3
Bishopsgate EC2 95 C1 243 A2
Bishopsgate Arcade E1 243 B3
Bishopsgate Church Yd EC2 243 A2
Bishops Gn BR1 187 C2
Bishops Gr N2 48 C3
Feltham TW12 173 B6
Bishop's Hall KT1 175 D1
Bishopshalt Sch UB8 82 B4
Bishops Hill KT12 194 A2
Bishops Ho SW8 270 B3
Bishop's Mans SW6 134 D3
Bishops Mead SE5 139 A5
Bishops Park Rd SW16 182 A2
Bishop's Park Rd SW6 134 D3
Bishop's Pl SM1 218 A3
Bishops Rd N6 49 A3
Bishop's Rd W7 108 C4
Bishops Rd SW6 135 B4 264 C2
Bishop's Rd Hayes UB3 83 A1
Thornton Heath CR0 204 D2
Bishop St N1 95 A6 235 A6
Bishop's Terr SE11 116 C2 261 B4
Bishopsthorpe Rd SE26 184 D6
Bishopstone Ho 4 SW11 137 A3
Bishop Stopford's Sch EN1 6 B3
Bishop's Way E2 96 C5
Bishops Wlk
Chislehurst BR7 189 A2
South Croydon CR0,CR9 223 A3
Bishopswood Rd N6 48 D2
Bishop Thomas Grant RC Sec Sch SW16 182 B5
Bishop Wand CE Sec Sch TW16 171 D1
Bishop Way NW10 67 C1
Bishop Wilfred Wood Cl SE15 140 A3
Bishop Wilfred Wood Ct 2 E13 99 C5
Bishop Winnington-Ingram CE Sch HA4 39 B2
Bisley Cl KT4 200 C1
Bisley Ho SW19 156 D2
Bispham Rd NW10 88 B4
Bissextile Ho SE13 141 D3
Bisson Rd E15 98 A5
Bistern Ave E17 54 B6
Bittacy Bsns Ctr NW7 29 A3
Bittacy Cl NW7 28 D4
Bittacy Ct NW7 29 A3
Bittacy Hill NW7 28 D4
Bittacy Park Ave NW7 28 D5
Bittacy Rd NW7 28 D4
Bittacy Rise NW7 28 D4
Bittern Cl UB4 84 D2
Bittern Ct NW9 27 C1
8 SE8 141 C6
Chingford E4 20 B4
Bittern Ho SE1 252 A1
Bittern St SE1 252 A1
Bittoms The KT1 197 D6
Bixley Cl UB2 107 B2
Blackall St EC2 243 A6
Blackberry Cl TW17 193 C5
Blackberry Farm Cl TW5 129 A5
Blackberry Field BR5 190 A2
Blackbird Ct NW9 67 B5
Blackbird Hill NW9 67 B5
Blackborne Rd RM10 81 D2
Black Boy La N15 51 A4
Blackbrook La BR1, BR2 210 C5
Blackburn 28 NW9 27 D1
Blackburn Ct 21 SW2 160 C5
Blackburne's Mews W1 248 A5
Blackburn Rd NW6 69 D2
Blackburn Trad Est TW19 148 B5
Blackbush Ave RM6 58 D4
Blackbush Cl SM2 217 D1
Blackcap Ct NW9 27 C1
Blackdown Cl N2 30 A1
Blackdown Ho E8 74 A4
Blackenham Rd SW17 180 D6
Blackett St SW15 134 D2
Black Fan Cl EN2 5 A4
Blackfen Par DA15 168 A5
Blackfen Rd DA15 168 B5
Blackfen Sch for Girls DA15 168 B5
Blackford Rd WD19 22 D5
Blackfriars Bridge EC4 251 C5
Blackfriars Ct EC4 251 C6
Black Friars La EC4 94 D1 241 C1
Blackfriars Pas EC4 251 C6
Blackfriars Pier EC4 251 C6
Blackfriars Rd SE1 116 D4 251 C3
Blackfriars Sta EC4 116 D6 251 C6
Blackfriars Underpass EC4 116 C6 251 B6
Blackham Ho SW19 179 A4
Blackheath★ SE3 142 C4
Blackheath Ave SE3 142 C5
Blackheath Bluecoat CE Sch SE3 143 B5
Blackheath Bsns Est SE10 142 A4
Blackheath Gr SE3 142 D3
Blackheath High Sch SE3 143 A5
Blackheath High Sch (Girls) SE3 142 D3
Blackheath High Sch GPDST (Jun Dept) SE3 143 A3
Blackheath Hill SE10 142 A4
Blackheath Hospl SE3 142 C2
Blackheath Pk SE3 143 A2
Blackheath Rd SE10 141 D4
Blackheath Rise SE13 142 A3
Blackheath Sta SE3 142 D2
Blackheath Vale SE3 142 C3
Blackheath Village SE3 142 D3
Black Horse Ct SE1 262 D6
Blackhorse La E17 34 D1
Croydon CR0 206 A2
Blackhorse La Sta CR0 206 A2
Blackhorse Mews E17 52 D6
Black Horse Par HA5 40 B4
Blackhorse Rd E17 53 A5
SE8 141 A6
Black Horse Rd DA14 190 A6
Blackhorse Road E17 52 D5
Blackhorse Road Sta E17 52 D5
Blacklands Dr UB4 83 A3
Blacklands Rd SE6 186 A6
Blacklands Terr SW3 257 D3
Black Lion La W6 112 A2
Black Lion Mews 4 W6 112 A2
Blackmore Ave UB1 108 B5
Blackmore Ho N1 233 D5
2 SW18 157 D6
Forest Hill SE23 163 B3
Blackmore's Gr TW11 175 A4
Blackmore Twr 1 W3 111 A3
Blackness La BR2 225 D1
Blackpool Gdns UB4 83 C3
Blackpool Rd SE15 140 B3
Black Prince Intc DA5 169 D5
Black Prince Rd SE1,SE11 116 B2 260 D3
Black Rod Cl UB3 105 D3
Black Roof Ho 9 SE5 138 D4
Blackshaw Rd SW17 180 B5
Blacksmith Cl RM6 58 C3
Blacksmiths Ho 7 E17 53 C5
Black's Rd W6 112 C2
Blackstock Ho N5 72 D5
Blackstock Mews N4 72 D5
Blackstock Rd N4,N5 72 D6
Blackstone Ho SW1 259 A1
Dulwich SE21 161 C1
Blackstone Rd NW2 68 C4
Black Swan Yd SE1 253 A2
Blackthorn Ave UB7 104 C3
Blackthorn Ct 4 E15 76 B4
19 SE15 139 D5
Heston TW5 129 A5
6 West Norwood SW16 182 C5
Blackthorne Ave CR0 206 C1
Blackthorne Dr E4 36 B6
Blackthorn Gr DA7 147 A2
Blackthorn St E3 97 C3
Blacktree Mews 12 SW9 138 C2
Blackwall Sta E14 120 A6
Blackwall Trad Est E14 98 B2
Blackwall Tunnel E14, SE10 120 B5
Blackwall Tunnel App SE10 120 C4
Blackwall Tunnel Northern Approach E14,E3 98 A3
Blackwall Way E14 120 A6
Blackwater Cl E7 76 D4
Blackwater Ho NW8 236 D4
Blackwater St SE22 161 D6
Blackwell Cl 10 E5 74 D4
Harrow HA3 24 B3
Blackwell Gdns HA8 10 C1
Blackwell Ho 3 SW4 159 D5
Blackwood Ho 11 E1 96 B3
Blackwood St SE17 117 B1 262 C2
Blade Mews SW15 135 B1
Bladen Ho 4 E1 96 D1
Blades Ct SW15 135 B1
Blades Ho 12 SE11 138 C6
Blades Lo 16 SW2 160 C5
Bladindon Dr DA5 168 D4
Bladon Ct
Beckenham BR2 208 C6
Streatham SW16 182 A4
Bladon Gdns HA2 41 D3
Blagden's Cl N14 15 D2
Blagden's La N14 15 D2
Blagdon Ct W7 108 C6
Blagdon Rd SE13 163 D5
New Malden KT3 199 D5
Blagdon Wlk TW11 175 C4
Blagrove Rd 1 W10 91 B2
Blair Ave NW9 45 C2
Thames Ditton KT10 212 A6
Blair Cl DA15 167 C6
N1 73 A2
Hayes UB3 106 A2
Blair Ct NW8 229 C6
Beckenham BR3 185 D2
7 Catford SE6 164 D3
Blairderry Rd SW2 160 A2
Blair Ho SW9 138 B3
Blair Peach Prim Sch UB1 106 D5
Blair St E14 98 B1
Blake Ave IG11 101 D6
Blake Cl DA16 145 C4
Carshalton SM5 202 C1
Blake Ct NW6 91 C4
8 SE16 118 B1
Blakeden Dr KT10 212 D2
Blake Gdns SW6 135 D4 265 C2
Blake Hall Cres E11 55 A1
Blakehall Rd SM5 218 D2
Blake Hall Rd E11 55 A2
Blake Ho 14 N16 73 C4
1 N19 71 D3
SE1 261 A6
2 SE8 141 C6
6 Beckenham BR3 185 D4
Blake Lo N3 29 B1
Blake Mews 14 TW9 132 C4
Blakemore Rd
Streatham SW16 160 A1
Thornton Heath CR7 204 B4
Blakemore Way DA17 125 A3
Blakeney Ave BR3 185 B2
Blakeney Cl 4 E8 74 A3
N20 14 A3
5 NW1 71 D1
Blakeney Ct EN2 17 B6
Blakeney Rd BR3 185 B2
Blakenham Ct W12 112 A5
Blakenham Rd SW17 180 D6
Blaker Ct SE7 143 C5
Blake Rd E16 98 D3
N11 31 C3
Croydon CR0 221 C6
Mitcham CR4 202 C6
Blaker Rd E15 98 A6
Blakes Ave KT3 199 D3
Blakes Cl W10 90 C2
Blake's Gn BR4 208 A1
Blakes La KT3 199 D4
Blakesley Ave W5 87 C1
Blakesley Ct W5 87 C1
Blakesley Ho 4 E12 78 C5
Blake's Rd SE15 139 C5
Blakes Terr KT3 200 A4
Blakesware Gdns N9 17 B4
Blakewood Cl TW13 172 C6
Blakewood Ct SE20 184 B3
Blanca Ho 16 N1 95 C5
Blanchard Cl SE9 166 A1
Blanchard Gr EN3 7 D5
Blanchard Ho 7 TW1 153 D5
Blanchard Way E8 74 A2
Blanch Cl SE15 140 C5
Blanchedowne SE5 139 B1
Blanche Ho NW8 237 A5
Blanche Nevile Sch The N15 51 D6
Blanche St E16 98 D3
Blanchland Rd SM4 201 D4
Blandfield Rd SW12 159 A4
Blandford Ave
2 Beckenham BR3 185 A1
Twickenham TW2 151 D3
Blandford Cl N2 48 A5
Romford RM7 59 D5
Wallington CR0 220 A5
Blandford Cres E4 20 A4
Blandford Ct 6 N1 73 C1
NW6 69 A1
Blandford Ho SW8 270 C4
Blandford Rd W4 111 C3
W5 109 D4
Penge BR3 184 D1
Southall UB2 107 C2
Teddington TW11 174 C5
Blandford Sq NW1 237 B5
Blandford St W1 93 A2 238 A3
Blandford Waye UB4 84 C1
Bland Ho SE11 260 D2
Bland St SE9 143 D1
Blaney Cres E6 100 D4
Blanmerle Rd SE9 166 D3
Blann Cl SE9 165 D5
Blantyre St SW10 136 B5 266 C4
Blantyre Twr SW10 266 C4
Blantyre Wlk SW10 136 B5 266 C4
Blashford NW3 70 D1
Blashford St SE13 164 B4
Blasker Wlk E14 119 D1
Blatchford Ct KT12 194 A1
Blatchford Ho 8 RM10 81 C5
Blawith Rd HA1 42 D5
Blaxland Ho 12 W12 112 B6
Blaydon Cl HA4 39 C2
Blaydon Ct 4 UB5 63 C2
Blaydon Wlk N17 34 B3
Bleak Hill La SE18 145 D6
Blean Gr SE20 184 C3
Bleasdale Ave UB6 87 A5
Blechynden Ho 17 W10 90 D1
Blechynden St W10 112 D6
Bleddyn Cl DA15 168 C5
Bledlow Cl SE28 124 C6
Bledlow Rise UB6 86 A5
Bleeding Heart Yd EC1 241 B3
Blegborough Rd SW16 181 C4
Blemundsbury WC1 240 C4
Blendon Dr DA5 168 D5
Blendon Path 7 BR1 186 D3
Blendon Rd DA5 168 D5
Blendon Terr SE18 145 A6
Blendworth Point 4 SW15 156 B3
Blenheim 26 SW19 156 D3
Blenheim Ave IG2 56 C3
Blenheim Bsns Ctr CR4 180 D1
Blenheim Cl
Edmonton N21 17 A3
Greenford UB6 86 B5
Wallington SM6 219 C1
West Barnes SW20 200 C6
Blenheim Cres W11 113 A6 244 B6
W11 91 A1
Ruislip HA4 61 B6
South Croydon CR2 221 A1
Blenheim Ct DA15 167 B1
N19 72 A6
N7 72 A2
17 SE16 118 D5
Harrow HA3 43 A3
Richmond TW9 132 B2
South Norwood SE19 183 C2
Sutton SM2 218 A2
Blenheim Dr DA16 145 D4
Blenheim Gdns NW2 68 C3
SW2 160 B5
Kingston KT2 176 D3
Wallington SM6 219 C1
Wembley HA9 66 A5
Blenheim Gr SE15 140 A3
Blenheim Ho
6 Edmonton N9 18 A1
Hounslow TW3 129 C2
Blenheim Par 2 UB10 82 D3
Blenheim Park Rd CR2 221 A1
Blenheim Pas NW8 229 A4
Blenheim Pl TW11 174 D5
Blenheim Rd E15 76 C4
E17 53 A6
E6 99 D4
NW8 92 A5 229 B4
W4 111 C3
Bromley BR1,BR2 210 A5
Harrow HA2 41 D3
Northolt UB5 63 D2
Penge SE20 184 C3
Sidcup DA15 168 C3
Sutton SM1 217 D5
West Barnes SW20 200 C6
Blenheim Rise N15 51 D5
Blenheim St W1 238 C1
Blenheim Terr NW8 92 A5 229 A4
Blenheim Way TW7 131 A4
Blenkarne Rd SW11 158 D5
Bleriot 27 NW9 27 D1
Bleriot Rd TW5 128 C5
Blessbury Rd HA8 27 A2
Blessed Dominic RC Prim Sch NW9 27 D1
Blessed John Roche RC Sch The E14 97 C1
Blessed Sacrament RC Prim Sch N1 94 B6 233 C5
Blessington Cl SE13 142 B2
Blessington Rd SE13 142 B1
Blessing Way IG11 102 C5
Bletchingley Cl CR7 204 D5
Bletchington Ct DA17 125 C2
Bletchley Ct N1 235 C3
Bletchley St N1 95 A5 235 B3
Bletchmore Cl
Hayes UB3 105 B1
Hayes UB3 127 B6
Bletsoe Wlk N1 235 B4
Blewbury Ho 3 SE2 124 C4
Blick Ho 1 SE16 118 C3
Bligh Ho 4 SE27 183 A6
Blincoe Cl SW19 156 D2
Blind Cnr SE25 206 C5
Blissett St SE10 142 A4
Blissland Ct N12 30 A4
Bliss Mews 17 W10 91 A4
Blisworth Cl UB4 85 A3
Blisworth Ho 12 E2 96 A6
Blithbury Rd RM9 80 B2
Blithdale Rd SE2 124 A2
Blithfield St W8 255 C5
Blockley Rd HA0 65 B6
Bloemfontein Ave W12 112 B5
Bloemfontein Rd W12 112 B6
Blomfield Ct SW11 266 D2
W9 236 B6
Blomfield Mans W12 112 C5
Blomfield Rd W9 92 A2 236 A4
Blomfield St EC2 95 B2 242 D3
Blomfield Villas W2 91 D2
W9 236 A4
Blomville Rd RM8 81 A5
Blondel St SW11 137 A3
Blondin Ave W5 109 C3
Blondin St E3 97 C5
Bloomburg St SW1 259 B3
Bloomfield Cres IG2 56 D3
Bloomfield Ct N6 49 A3
Bloomfield Ho 17 E1 96 A2
Bloomfield Pl W1 248 D6
Bloomfield Rd BR2 209 D4
N6 49 A3
SE18 122 D1
Kingston KT1 198 A6
Bloomfields The IG11 79 A2
Bloomfield Terr SW1 115 A1 258 B2
Bloom Gr SE27 160 D1
Bloomhall Rd SE19 183 B5
Bloom Park Rd SW6 264 C3
Bloomsbury Cl NW7 28 A3
Ealing W5 110 B6
Bloomsbury Ct E11 54 B1
WC1 240 B3
Cranford TW5 128 B4
Pinner HA5 41 B6
Bloomsbury Ho 10 SW4 159 D5
Bloomsbury Pl SW18 158 A6
WC1 240 B3
Bloomsbury Sq WC1 94 A2 240 B3
Bloomsbury St WC1 93 D2 239 D3
Bloomsbury Way WC1 94 A2 240 B3
Blore Cl SW8 269 C1
Blore Ct W1 249 C6
Blossom Cl W5 110 A4
Dagenham RM9 103 B6
South Croydon CR2 221 D3
Blossom La EN2 5 A4
Blossom Pl E1 243 B5
Blossom St E1 95 C3 243 B5
Blossom Way
Hillingdon UB10 60 B1
Blossom Way *continued*
West Drayton UB7 104 C2
Blossom Waye TW5 129 A5
Blount St E14 97 A1
Bloxam Gdns SE9 166 A6
Bloxhall Rd E10 53 B1
Bloxham Cres TW12 173 B2
Bloxworth Cl SM6 219 C5
Blucher Rd SE5 139 A5
Blue Anchor Alley 4 TW9 132 A1
Blue Anchor La SE16 118 B2
Blue Anchor Yd E1 118 A6
Blue Ball Yd SW1 249 A3
Bluebell Ave E12 78 A3
Bluebell Cl 16 E9 96 C6
Forest Hill SE26 183 D6
Hackbridge SM6 203 B1
Orpington BR6 227 A6
Bluebell Way IG1 78 D2
Blueberry Cl IG8 37 A4
Bluebird La RM10 81 C1
Bluebird Way Cl SE28
Bluefield Cl TW12 173 C5
Blue Gate Fields Jun & Inf Schs E1 118 C6
Bluegate Mews E1 118 B6
Bluegates
Stoneleigh KT17 216 A1
Wimbledon SW19 179 A5
Bluehouse Rd E4 20 C1
Blue Lion Pl SE1 263 A6
Blue Point Ct 2 HA1 42 D4
Blue Sch The TW7 131 A2
Blundell Rd HA8 27 C3
Blundell St N7 72 A2
Blunden Cl RM8 58 C1
Blunt Rd CR0 221 B3
Blunts Ave UB7 126 C5
Blunts Rd SE9 166 C6
Blurton Rd E5 74 D4
Blydon Ct N21 16 B6
Blyth Cl 4 E14 120 B2
Twickenham TW1 152 D5
Blythe Cl SE23 163 B4
Blythe Hill BR5 190 A2
Forest Hill SE6 163 B4
Blythe Hill La SE6 163 B3
Blythe Ho 8 SE11 138 C6
Blythe Mews 2 W14 112 D3
Blythendale Ho 31 E2 96 A5
Blythe Rd W14 112 D3 254 A5
Blythe St E2 96 B4
Blythe Vale SE6 163 B3
Blyth Rd E17 53 B2
Bromley BR1 186 D2
Hayes UB3 105 C4
Woolwich SE28 124 C6
Blyth's Wharf E14 119 A6
Blythswood Rd IG3 58 A2
Blythwood Pk 10 BR1 186 D2
Blythwood Rd N4 50 A2
Pinner HA5 22 D2
Boadicea St N1 233 C5
Boadoak Ho 18 NW6 91 D6
Boardman Ave E4 19 D6
Boardman Cl EN5 13 A6
Boardwalk Pl E14 120 A5
Boarhound 25 NW9 27 D1
Boarley Ho SE17 263 A3
Boathouse Ctr The W10 90 D3
Boat Lifter Way 19 SE16 119 A2
Bob Anker Cl 1 E13 99 A4
Bobbin Cl SW4 137 C2
Bobby Moore Bridge The HA9 66 C5
Bobington Ct WC1 94 A2 240 B4
Bob Marley Way 11 SE24 138 C1
Bockhampton Rd KT2 176 B3
Bocking St E8 96 B6
Boddicott Cl SW19 157 A2
Boddington Ho SE14 140 C4
Bodeney Ho 10 SE5 139 C4
Boden Ho 4 E1 96 A2
Bodiam Cl EN1 5 C3
Bodiam Ct BR2 208 D5
Bodiam Rd SW16 181 D3
Bodicea Mews TW4 151 C5
Bodington Ct 2 W12 112 D4
Bodley Cl KT3 199 C4
Bodley Manor Way SE24 160 C4
Bodley Rd KT3 199 C4
Bodmin 28 NW9 27 D1
Bodmin Cl HA2 63 B5
Bodmin Gr SM4 201 D4
Bodmin St SW18 157 C3
Bodnant Gdns SW20 200 B6
Bodney Mans 14 E8 74 B3
Bodney Rd E5,E8 74 B3
Boeing Way UB2 106 B3
Boelyn Dr HA4 62 D6
Boevey Path
Erith DA17 125 B1
2 Erith DA17 147 B6

Bognor Gdns WD19 22 C5
Bognor Rd DA16 146 D4
Bohemia Pl 1 E8 74 B2
Bohn Rd E1 97 A2
Bohun Gr EN4 14 D5
Boileau Par W5 88 B1
Boileau Rd
Barnes SW13 134 B6
Ealing W5 88 B1
Boilerhouse SE1 253 C3
Boisseau Ho 27 E1 96 C2
Bolden St SE8 141 D3
Boldero Pl NW8 237 A5
Bolderwood Way BR4 223 D6
Boldmere Rd HA5 40 C2
Boleyn Ave EN1 6 B4
Boleyn Ct E17 53 C5
Beckenham BR3 186 A2
Buckhurst Hill IG9 21 B3
East Molesey KT8 196 B5
Boleyn Dr KT8 195 B6
Boleyn Gdns BR4 223 D6
Boleyn Ground(Upton Park) (West Ham United FC) E13,E6 99 D5
Boleyn Rd E6 99 D5
E7 77 B1
N16 73 C3
Boleyn Way EN5 2 A2
Bolina Rd SE16 118 C1
Bolingbroke Gr SW11 158 D5
Bolingbroke Ho
Beckenham BR3 207 A4
Catford BR3 185 D5
Bolingbroke Hospl The SW11 158 C6
Bolingbroke Rd W14 112 D3
Bolingbroke Way UB3, UB11 105 B5
Bolingbroke Wlk SW11 136 C4 267 A2
Bollo Bridge Rd W3 111 A4
Bollo Ct 2 W3 111 A3
Bollo La W3 110 D3
Bolney Ct KT6 197 D4
Bolney Gate SW7 247 A1
Bolney St SW8 138 B5 270 C3
Bolsover St W1 93 B3 238 D5
Bolstead Rd CR4 181 B2
Bolster Gr N22 31 D2
Bolt Ct EC4 241 B1
Boltmore Cl NW4 46 D6
Bolton Cl
Chessington KT9 214 A2
Penge SE20 184 A1
Bolton Cres SE5 138 D5
Bolton Ct SW11 268 B1
Bolton Gdns NW10 90 D5
SW5 113 D1 255 D2
Bromley BR1 186 D4
Teddington TW11 175 A4
Bolton Gdns Mews SW10 256 A2
Bolton Ho 4 SE10 120 C1
Bolton Rd E15 76 D2
NW10 89 C6
NW8 91 D6
Chessington KT9 214 A2
Chiswick W4 133 A5
Edmonton N18 33 D5
Harrow HA1 42 B5
Boltons Ct SW5 255 D2
Bolton's La TW6,UB7 127 A5
Bolton St W1 115 B5 248 D4
Boltons The
SW10 114 A1 256 A2
Wembley HA0 64 D4
Woodford IG8 37 A6
Bolton Studios SW10 256 B1
Bolton Wlk N7 72 B6
Bombay St SE16 118 B2
Bomer Cl UB7 126 C5
Bomore Rd
W11 113 A6 244 A6
Bonar Pl BR7 188 A3
Bonar Rd SE15 140 A5
Bonchester Cl BR7 188 C3
Bonchurch Cl SM2 217 D1
Bonchurch Rd W10 91 A2
Ealing W13 109 B5
Bond Cl UB7 82 B1
Bond Ct EC4 242 C1
Bondfield Ave UB4 84 A4
Bondfield Rd 4 E6 100 B2
Bond Fst Sch CR4 180 D1
Bond Gdns SM6 219 C4
Bond Ho 4 NW6 91 B5
Bonding Yard Wlk SE16 119 A3
Bond Rd Mitcham CR4 180 D1
Surbiton KT6 214 B6
Bond St E15 76 C3
Ealing W5 109 D6
Bond Street Sta W1 93 B1 238 B1
Bondway SW8 138 A6 270 B6
Boneta Rd SE18 122 B3
Bonfield Rd SE13 142 A1
Bonham Gdns RM8 80 D6
Bonham Ho W11 244 C4
Bonham Rd SW2 160 B6
Dagenham RM8 80 D5
Bonheur Rd W4 111 B4
Bonhill St EC2 95 B3 242 D5
Boniface Gdns HA3 23 D3
Boniface Rd UB10 60 D5
Boniface Wlk HA3 23 D3
Bonington Ho N1 233 C3
Enfield EN1 18 A6
Bonita Mews SE15 140 D2
Bonne Marche Terr Mews 18 SE27 183 C6
Bonner Hill Rd KT1 198 C6
Bonner Ho 3 SW15 156 A6
Bonner Prim Sch E2 96 C4
Bonner Rd E2 96 C5
Bonnersfield Cl HA1 43 A3
Bonnersfield La
Harrow HA1 42 D3
Harrow HA1,HA3 43 A3
Bonner St E2 96 C5
Bonneville Gdns SW4 159 C5
Bonneville Prim Sch SW4 159 C5
Bonnington Ct 15 UB5 84 D5
Bonnington Sq SW8 138 B6 270 C6
Bonnington Twr BR2 210 A3
Bonny St NW1 71 C1
Bonser Rd TW1 152 D2
Bonsor Ho SW8 269 B2
Bonsor St SE5 139 C5
Bonthron Ho SW15 134 C3
Bonus Pastor RC Sch BR1 186 C6
Bonville Gdns 17 NW4 46 A5
Bonville Rd BR1 186 D5
Bookbinder Cotts N20 14 D1
Booker Cl 15 E3 97 B2
Booker Rd 5 N18 34 A5
Bookham Ct CR4 202 B6
Boone Ct N9 18 C1
Boones Rd SE13 142 C1
Boone St SE13 142 C1
Boord St SE10 120 C3
Boothby Ct E4 20 A1
Boothby Ho 2 SW16 181 C5
Boothby Rd N19 71 D6
Booth Cl 10 E9 96 B6
SE28 124 B6
Booth Ho 2 SW2 160 C4
Booth La EC4 252 A6
Boothman Ho HA3 43 D6
Booth Rd NW9 27 C1
Croydon CR0 220 D6
Boothroyd Ho TW7 130 D2
Booth's Pl W1 239 B3
Boot Par HA8 26 C4
Boot St N1 95 C4
Bordars Rd W7 86 D2
Bordars Wlk W7 86 C2
Borden Ave EN1 17 B5
Border Cres SE26 184 B5
Border Gate CR4 180 D2
Border Gdns CR0 223 D4
Border Rd SE26 184 B5
Bordesley Rd SM4 201 D5
Bordeston Ct TW8 131 C2
Bordon Wlk 5 SW15 156 A4
Boreas Wlk N1 234 D3
Boreham Ave E16 99 A1
Boreham Cl E11 54 A1
Boreham Rd N22 33 A1
Boreman Ho 10 SE10 142 A6
Borgard Ho 3 SE18 144 A4
Borgard Rd SE18 122 B2
Borkwood Pk BR6 227 D4
Borkwood Way BR6 227 C4
Borland Rd SE15 140 C1
Teddington TW11 175 B3
Borneo St SW15 134 C2
Borough High St SE1 117 B5 252 C2
Borough Hill CR0 220 D5
Borough Mkt* SE1 252 C3
Borough Rd
SE1 116 D3 261 D6
Hounslow TW7 130 D4
7 Kingston KT2 176 C3
Mitcham CR4 180 C1
Borough Sq SE1 252 A1
Borough Sta The SE1 117 A4 252 B1
Borrett Cl SE17 117 A1 262 A1
Borrodaile Rd SW18 157 D5
Borrowdale NW1 232 A1
Borrowdale Ave HA3 25 A1
Borrowdale Cl IG4 56 A5
Borrowdale Ct EN2 5 A4
Borthwick Mews E15 76 C4
Borthwick Rd E15 76 C4
NW9 45 D3
Borthwick St SE8 119 C1
Borwick Ave E17 53 B6
Bosbury Rd SE6 164 A1
Boscastle Rd NW5 71 B5
Boscobel Ho 4 E8 74 B2
Boscobel Pl SW1 258 B4
Boscobel St NW8 92 B3 236 D5
Boscombe Ave E10 54 B2
Boscombe Cl E5 75 A3
Boscombe Gdns SW16 182 A4
Boscombe Ho CR0 205 B1
Boscombe Rd W12 112 A4
Merton SW19 179 D2
North Cheam KT4 200 D1
Streatham SW17 181 A4
Bose Cl N3 29 A2
Bosgrove E4 20 A2
Boss Ho SE1 253 C2
Boss St SE1 253 C2
Bostall Hill SE2 124 B1
Bostall La SE2 124 B1
Bostall Manor Way SE2 124 B2
Bostall Park Ave DA7 147 A5
Bostall Rd BR5 190 B3
Bostock Ho TW5 129 C6
Boston Bsns Pk W7 108 C3
Boston Ct
South Norwood SE25 205 D5
Sutton SM2 218 A1
Boston Gdns
Brentford TW8 109 B2
Chiswick W4 133 C6
Boston Gr HA4 39 A3
Boston Ho NW1 237 C6
23 SE5 139 A3
SW5 255 D3
Boston Manor Ho TW8 109 B1
Boston Manor Rd TW8 109 B1
Boston Manor Sta TW8 109 A2
Boston Par W7 109 A2
Boston Park Rd TW8 109 C1
Boston Pl NW1 92 D3 237 C5
Boston Rd E6 100 A4
HA8 27 A3
Ealing W7 109 A3
Thornton Heath CR0 204 C3
Bostonthorpe Rd W7 108 C4
Boston Vale W7 109 A2
Bosun Cl 8 E14 119 C4
Boswell Ct 9 W14 112 D3
WC1 240 B4
Kingston KT2 176 C2
Boswell Ho BR2 209 D4
WC1 240 B4
5 Streatham SW16 181 C5
Boswell Rd CR7 205 A5
Boswell St WC1 94 A2 240 B4
Boswood Ct TW4 129 B2
Bosworth Cl E17 35 B2
Bosworth Ho 4 W10 91 A3
Bosworth Rd N11 31 D4
W10 91 A3
Barnet EN5 1 C2
Dagenham RM10 81 C5
Botany Bay La BR7 189 A1
Botany Cl EN4 2 C1
Boteley Cl E4 20 B2
Botham Cl 6 HA8 27 A3
Botha Rd E13 99 C2
Bothwell Cl E16 98 D2
Bothwell St 4 W6 134 D6
Botolph Alley EC3 253 A6
Botolph La EC3 253 A6
Botsford Rd SW20 179 A1
Bott's Mews W2 91 C1
Botwell Common Rd UB3 105 C6
Botwell Cres UB3 83 C1
Botwell House RC Prim Sch UB3 105 D4
Botwell La UB3 105 C6
Boucher Cl TW11 174 D5
Bouchier Ho 6 N2 30 B1
Bough Beech Ct EN3 6 D6
Boughton Ave BR2 208 D2
Boughton Ho SE1 252 C2
Boughton Rd SE28 123 C3
Boulcott St E1 96 D1
Boulevard The 4 SW17 159 A2
Boullen Ct SM1 218 A4
Boulogne Ho SE1 263 C6
Boulogne Rd CR0 205 A3
Boulter Ho SE14 140 C4
Boulton Ho TW8 110 A1
Boulton Rd RM8 81 B6
Boultwood Rd E6 100 B1
Bounces La N9 18 B2
Bounces Rd N9 18 C2
Boundaries Mans 3 SW12 159 A3
Boundaries Rd
Feltham TW13 150 C3
Upper Tooting SW12 159 A3
Boundary Ave E17 53 B2
Boundary Bsns Ct CR4 202 B6
Boundary Cl Barnet EN5 1 B4
Ilford IG3 79 C4
Boundary Cl *continued*
Kingston KT1 198 D6
Penge SE20 184 A1
Southall UB2 107 C1
Boundary Ct 3 N18 33 D4
Boundary Ho 1 SE5 139 A5
Balham SW12 159 B3
Isleworth TW1 153 B6
Boundary La E13,E6 99 D3
SE17 139 A6
Boundary Pas E2 243 C6
Boundary Rd DA15 167 C6
E13 99 D4
E17 53 C3
N9 18 C5
NW8 92 A6 229 B6
Boundary Rd N2 30 B2
Boundary Rd
Mitcham SW19 180 B4
Pinner HA5 40 D2
Tottenham N22 33 A1
Wallington SM5,SM6 219 A1
Boundary Road Est NW8 92 A6 229 A5
Boundary Row SE1 251 C2
Boundary St E2 95 D3 243 C6
Boundary Way CR0 223 C3
Boundfield Rd SE6 164 C2
Bounds Green Ct N11 31 D4
Bounds Green Ind Est N11 31 C4
Bounds Green Jun & Inf Schs N11 32 A3
Bounds Green Rd N11 31 D4
Wood Green N22 32 A2
Bounds Green Sta N11 31 D3
Bourbon Ho 9 SE6 186 A6
Bourchier St W1 249 C6
Bourdillon Ct 2 SE9 166 A2
Bourdon Pl W1 248 D6
Bourdon Rd SE20 184 C1
Bourdon St W1 115 B6 248 D5
Bourke Cl NW10 67 C2
SW4 160 A5
Bourlet Cl W1 239 A3
Bourn Ave N15 51 B5
Hillingdon UB8 82 C3
New Barnet EN4 14 B6
Bournbrook Rd SE3, SE9 143 D2
Bourne Ave Hayes UB3 105 B3
Palmers Green N14 16 A2
Ruislip HA4 62 C3
Bourne Cir UB3 105 A3
Bourne Cl KT7 212 D6
Bourne Ct Chiswick W4 133 A6
Ruislip HA4 62 B3
Wanstead E11 55 A4
Woodford IG8 37 D1
Bourne Dr CR4 180 B1
Bourne Gdns E4 35 D6
Bourne Hill N13 16 B2
Bourne Ho 1 NW2 68 A5
5 SW4 137 C1
Ashford TW15 170 C5
Buckhurst Hill IG9 21 D1
Bournemead Ave UB5 84 A5
Bournemead Cl UB5 84 A4
Bournemead Way UB5 84 B5
Bourne Mews W1 238 B1
Bournemouth Cl SE15 140 A3
Bournemouth Rd SE15 140 A3
Merton SW19 179 C2
Bourne Par DA5 169 D4
Bourne Pl W4 111 B1
Bourne Prim Sch HA4 62 C2
Bourne Rd DA5 169 D5
E7,E11 76 D5
N8 50 A3
Bromley BR2 209 D5
Bournes Ho 4 N15 51 C3
Bourneside 5 N14 15 D3
Bourneside Cres 6 N14 15 D3
Bourneside Gdns SE6 186 A5
Bourne St SW1 115 A2 258 A3
Croydon CR0 220 D6
Bourne Terr W2 91 D2
Bourne The N14 16 A2
Bourne Vale BR2 208 D1
Bournevale Rd SW16 182 A6
Bourne View UB6 64 D3
Bourne Way
Cheam SM1 217 B3
Coney Hall BR2,BR4 224 D6
West Ewell KT19 215 A4
Bournewood Rd SE18, SE2 146 A5
Bournville Rd SE6 163 C4
Bournwell Cl EN4 2 D3
Bourton Cl UB3 106 A5
Bousfield Prim Sch SW10 114 A1 256 A2
Bousfield Rd SE14 140 D3
Boutcher CE Prim Sch SE1 117 D2 263 C4
Boutflower Rd SW11 136 C1
Bouverie Gdns HA3 43 D3
Bouverie Mews N16 73 C6
Bouverie Pl W2 236 D2
Bouverie Rd N16 73 C6
Harrow HA1 42 A3
Bouverie St EC4 94 C1 241 B1
Bouvier Rd EN3 6 C5
Boveney Rd SE23 162 D4
Bovill Rd SE23 162 D4
Bovingdon Ave HA9 66 C2
Bovingdon Cl 3 N19 71 C6
Bovingdon La NW9 27 C2
Bovingdon Rd SW6 135 D4 265 D1
Bovril Ho EN1 5 C2
Bowater Cl NW9 45 B4
SW2 160 A5
Bowater Gdns TW16 172 B2
Bowater Ho EC1 242 B5
Bowater Pl SE3 143 B5
Bowater Rd SE18 121 D3
Bow Brook The 20 E2 96 D5
Bow Church Sta E3 97 C4
Bow Churchyard EC2, EC4 242 B1
Bow Common La E3 97 B3
Bowden Cl TW14 149 C3
Bowden Ho 29 E3 97 D4
Bowden House Hospl (Private) HA1 64 C6
Bowden St SE11 116 C1 261 B1
Bowditch SE8 119 B1
Bowdon Rd E17 53 C2
Bowen Ct 2 N5 72 D4
Bowen Dr SE21 161 C1
Bowen Rd HA1 42 A2
Bowen St E14 97 D1
Bower Ave SE3 142 C5
Bower Cl UB5 84 C5
Bowerdean St SW6 135 D3
Bower Ho SE14 140 D4
Bowerman Ave SE14 141 A6
Bowerman Ct 1 N19 71 D6
Bowers Ho 5 IG11 78 D1
Bower St E1 96 D1
Bowers Wlk 1 E6 100 B1
Bowes Cl DA15 168 B5
Bowes Park Sta N22 32 A3
Bowes Prim Sch N11 31 D5
Bowes Rd N11 31 C5
W3 111 C6
Dagenham RM8 80 C4
Walton-on-T KT12 194 B1
Bowes Rd (North Circular Rd) N13 32 A5
Bowfell Rd W6 134 C6
Bowford Ave DA7 147 A4
Bowhill Cl SW9 138 C5
Bowie Cl SW4 159 D4
Bow Ind Pk E15 75 C1
Bow La EC2,EC4 95 A1 242 B1
N12 30 A3
Bowland Ho N4 51 A2
Bowland Rd SW4 137 D1
Woodford IG8 37 C4
Bowland Yd SW1 247 D1
Bowl Ct EC2 243 B5
Bowles Ct N12 30 C3
Bowles Rd 1 SE1 140 A6
Bowley Cl SE19 183 D4
Bowley Ho 6 SE16 118 A3
Bowley La SE19 183 D5
Bowling Cl UB10 82 B6
Bowling Green Cl SW19 156 B4
Bowling Green Ct HA9 66 B6
Bowling Green Ho SW10 266 C4
Bowling Green La EC1 94 C3 241 B6
Bowling Green Pl SE1 252 C2
Bowling Green Row 1 SE18 122 B2
Bowling Green St SE11 138 C6
Bowling Green Wlk N1 95 C4
Bowls Cl HA7 25 B5
Bowman Ave E16 120 D6
Bowman Mews E1 118 A6
Wandsworth SW18 157 B3
Bowmans Cl W13 109 B5
Bowmans Lea SE23 162 C4
Bowman's Meadow SM6 219 B5
Bowman's Mews N7 72 A5
Bowman's Pl N7 72 A5
Bowmead SE9 166 B2
Bowmore Wlk NW1 71 D1
Bowness Cl 5 E8 73 D2
Bowness Cres KT2, SW15 177 C5
Bowness Dr TW4 129 A1
Bowness Ho SE15 140 C5
Bowness Rd DA7 147 D3
Catford SE6 163 D4
Bowood Rd SW11 159 A6
Enfield EN3 6 D3
Bow Rd E3 97 C4
Bowring Gn WD19 22 C5
Bow Road Sta E3 97 C4
Bowrons Ave HA0 65 D1
Bowry Ho 14 E14 97 B2
Bow Sch E3 97 C4
Bowsley Ct TW13 150 A2
Bowsprit Point 5 E14 119 C3
Bow St E15 76 C3
WC2 94 A1 240 B1
Bowstead Ct SW11 266 D1
Bow Triangle Bsns Ctr E3 97 C3
Bowyer Cl E6 100 B2
Bowyer Ct 4 E4 20 A3
Bowyer Ho 18 N1 95 C6
Wandsworth SW18 157 D5
Bowyer Pl SE5 139 A5
Bowyer St 15 SE5 139 A5
Boxall Rd SE21 161 C5
Boxgrove Prim Sch SE2 124 C3
Boxgrove Rd SE2 124 C3
Box La IG11 102 C5
Boxley Ho 3 E5 74 B3
Boxley Rd SM4 202 A5
Boxley St E16 121 B5
Boxmoor Ho 16 E2 96 A6
9 W11 112 D5
Boxmoor Rd HA3 43 B5
Boxoll Rd RM9 81 B5
Boxshall Ho 7 SE18 144 D6
Box Tree Ho SE8 119 A1
Boxtree La HA3 24 B3
Boxtree Rd HA3 24 B3
Boxwood Cl UB7 104 B4
Boxworth Cl N12 30 B5
Boxworth Gr N1 94 B6 233 D6
Boyard Rd SE18 122 D1
Boyce Ho 1 W10 91 B4
Streatham SW16 181 C5
Boyce St SE1 251 A3
Boyce Way E13 99 A3
Boycroft Ave NW9 45 A3
Boyd Ave UB1 107 B5
Boyd Cl KT2 176 C3
Boyd Ct SW15 156 C5
Boydell Ct NW8 70 B1
Boyden Ho 8 E17 54 A6
Boyd Rd SW19 180 B4
Boyd St E1 96 A1
Boyfield St SE1 116 D4 251 D1
Boyland Rd BR1 186 D5
Boyle Ave HA7 25 A4
Boyle Cl UB10 82 B5
Boyle Farm Rd KT7 197 A3
Boyle Ho 13 DA17 125 C3
Boyle St W1 249 A6
Boyne Ave NW4 46 D5
Boyne Ct NW10 68 A1
Boyne Ho 10 E5 74 B6
Boyne Rd SE13 142 B2
Dagenham RM10 81 C5
Boyne Terr Mews W11 113 B5 244 C4
Boyson Rd 10 SE17 139 B6
Boyton Cl E1 96 D3
N8 50 A6
Boyton Ho NW8 229 D4
SE11 261 A1
Boyton Rd N8 50 A6
Brabant Rd N22 32 B1
Brabazon Ave SM6 220 A1
Brabazon Rd
Heston TW5 128 D5
Northolt UB5 85 C5
Brabazon St E14 97 D2
Brabner Ho 2 E2 96 A4
Brabourne Cl 7 SE19 183 C5
Brabourne Cres DA7 147 B6
Brabourne Hts NW7 11 C1
Brabourne Rise BR3 208 B4
Brabourn Gr SE15 140 C3
Brabrook Ct SM6 219 B3
Brabstone Ho 2 UB6 86 D5
Bracer Ho 1 N1 95 C5
Bracewell Ave UB6 65 A2
Bracewell Rd W10 90 C2
Bracewood Gdns CR0 221 D5
Bracey St N4 72 A6
Bracken Ave
Balham SW12 159 A4
Croydon CR0 223 C5
Brackenbridge Dr HA4 62 D5
Brackenbury N4 50 B1
Brackenbury Gdns W6 112 B3
Brackenbury Prim Sch W6 112 B3
Brackenbury Rd N2 48 A6
W6 112 B3
Bracken Cl E6 100 B2
Ashford TW16 171 D4
Twickenham TW4 151 C4

Brackendale
Kingston KT1 176 D1
Southgate N21 16 B2
Brackendale Cl TW5 129 D4
Brackendale Ct 2
BR3 185 C3
Bracken End TW7 152 B6
Brackenfield Cl E5 74 B5
Bracken Gdns SW13 134 A3
Brackenhill HA4 63 A4
Bracken Hill Cl 5
BR1 186 D2
Bracken Hill La BR1 186 D2
Bracken Ho 14 E3 97 C2
Bracken Mews
Chingford E4 20 A3
Romford RM7 59 D3
Brackens BR3 185 C3
Brackens The EN1 17 C4
Bracken The E4 20 A2
Brackenwood TW16 172 A2
Brackenwood Lo EN5 1 C1
Brackley Cl SM6 220 A1
Brackley Ct NW8 236 D6
Brackley Rd W4 111 C1
Beckenham BR3 185 C3
Brackley Sq IG8 37 D3
Brackley St EC1 242 B4
Brackley Terr 6 W4 111 C1
Bracklyn Ct N1 235 C4
Bracklyn St N1 235 C4
Bracknell Cl N22 32 C2
Bracknell Gate NW3 69 D3
Bracknell Gdns NW3 69 D4
Bracknell Way NW3 69 D4
Bracondale KT10 212 A3
Bracondale Rd SE2 124 A2
Bradbeer Ho 24 E2 96 C4
Bradbourne Rd DA5 169 C4
Bradbourne St SW6 135 C3
Bradbury Cl UB2 107 B2
Bradbury Ct 2 SE3 143 A5
Bradbury Ho E1 243 D2
Bradbury St 28 N16 73 C3
Bradby Ho NW8 91 D5
Braddock Cl TW7 130 D3
Braddock Ho 9 NW6 91 D6
Braddon Rd TW9 132 B2
Braddyll St SE10 120 C1
Bradenham 11 SE17 139 B6
Bradenham Ave DA16 146 A1
Bradenham Cl SE17 139 B6
Bradenham Rd
Harrow HA3 43 B5
Hayes UB4 83 C4
Braden St W9 91 D3
Bradfield Ct 14 NW1 71 B1
Bradfield Dr IG11 80 A3
Bradfield Ho 15 SW8 137 D3
Bradfield Rd E16 121 B4
Ruislip HA4 63 A3
Bradford Cl BR2 210 B1
Forest Hill SE26 184 B6
Tottenham N17 33 D4
Bradford Dr KT19 215 D2
Bradford Ho 4 W14 112 D3
Bradford Rd W3 111 C4
Ilford IG1 57 C1
Bradgate Rd SE6 163 D5
Brading Cres E11 77 B6
Brading Rd
Streatham SW2 160 B4
Thornton Heath CR0 204 B3
Brading Terr W12 112 A3
Bradiston Rd W9 91 B4
Bradley Cl N7 72 B2
Bradley Ct CR0 220 C4
Bradley Gdns W13 87 B1
Bradley Ho 4 E2 96 B5
1 E3 97 D4
SE16 118 B2
Twickenham TW1 152 D3
Bradley Mews SW12 158 D3
Bradley Rd Enfield EN3 7 A6
South Norwood SE19 183 A4
Wood Green N22 32 B1
Bradley's Cl N1 234 B4
Bradley Stone Rd E6 100 B2
Bradlord Ho SE21 161 C1
Bradman Row 7 HA8 27 A3
Bradmead
SW8 137 C5 269 A3
Bradmore Park Rd
W6 112 B2
Bradon 24 NW9 27 D1
Bradshaw Cl SW19 179 C4
Bradshawe Waye UB8 82 B2
Bradshaws Cl SE25 206 A6
Bradsole Ho 13 BR3 185 C3
Brad St SE1 116 C5 251 B3
Bradstock Ho E9 75 A1
Bradstock Rd E9 74 D2
Stoneleigh KT17 216 B3
Bradwell Ave RM10 81 C6
Bradwell Cl E18 54 D5
Bradwell Ho 9 E17 53 D6
Bradwell Ho *continued*
6 NW6 91 D6
Bradwell Mews 5 N18 34 A6
Brady Ct RM8 58 D1
Brady Ho SW4 159 D6
SW8 269 B2
Bradymead E6 100 D1
Brady St E1 96 B3
Braeburn Ct 1 EN4 2 C1
Brae Ct
2 Kingston KT2 176 C2
South Norwood SE25 183 C2
Braefoot Ct SW15 156 D6
Braemar SW15 156 D5
Braemar Ave NW10 67 B6
Thornton Heath CR7 204 D6
Wembley HA0 66 A1
Wimbledon SW18,SW19 157 C2
Wood Green N22 32 A2
Braemar Ct
4 Brentford TW8 131 D6
5 Catford SE6 164 D3
Braemar Gdns DA15 167 B1
NW9 27 B2
West Wickham BR4 208 A1
Braemar Ho W9 229 A1
Richmond TW11 175 B5
Braemar Mans W8 255 D5
Braemar Rd E13 98 D3
N15 51 C4
Brentford TW8 131 D6
North Cheam KT4 216 B5
Braemore Ct EN4 3 A1
Braemore Ho 21 SE15 140 A5
Braeside BR3 185 D5
Braeside Ave SW19 179 A2
Braeside Cl HA5 23 C3
Braeside Rd SW16 181 C3
Braeside Sch
Buckhurst Hill IG9 21 B3
Buckhurst Hill IG9 21 C2
Braes St N1 72 D1
Braesyde Cl DA17 125 B2
Brafferton Rd CR0 221 A4
Braganza St
SE17 116 D1 261 C1
Bragg Cl RM8 80 B2
Bragg Rd TW11 174 D4
Braham Ho SE11 260 D1
Braham St E1 243 D2
Brahma Kumaris World
Spiritual Univ NW10 68 A1
Braid Ave W3 89 C1
Braid Cl TW13 151 B2
Braid Ho SE10 142 A4
Braidwood Rd SE6 164 B3
Braidwood St
SE1 117 C5 253 A3
Braikenridge Ho N21 17 B5
Brailsford Cl SW19 180 C3
Brailsford Rd SW2 160 C5
Braintcroft Prim Sch
NW2 67 D5
Brainton Ave TW14 150 C4
Braintree Ave IG4 56 A5
Braintree Ho 5 E1 96 C3
Braintree Rd
Dagenham RM10 81 C5
Ruislip HA4 62 B4
Braintree St E2 96 C4
Braithwaite Ave RM7 59 C2
Braithwaite Gdns HA7 25 C2
Braithwaite Ho EC1 242 C6
14 South Bromley E14 98 B1
Braithwaite Rd EN3 7 B2
Braithwaite Twr W2 236 C4
Bramah Gn SW9 138 C4
Bramall Cl E15 76 D3
Bramall Ct N7 72 B2
Bramber WC1 233 A1
Bramber Ct TW8 110 A2
Bramber Rd N12 30 C5
W14 135 B6 264 C6
Bramble Acres Cl
SM2 217 C1
Bramblebury Rd SE18 123 A1
Bramble Cl N15 52 A5
Beckenham BR3 208 A4
Croydon CR0 223 D4
Hillingdon UB8 82 B1
Stanmore HA7 25 D3
Upper Halliford TW17 193 B6
Brambledown 4 N4 50 A2
Brambledown Cl BR2,
BR4 208 C4
Brambledown Rd
South Croydon CR2 221 C1
Wallington SM5,SM6 219 B1
Bramble Gdns W12 111 D6
Bramble Ho 12 E3 97 C2
Bramble La TW12 173 B4
Brambles Cl TW7,TW8 131 B5
Brambles Farm Dr
UB10 82 C4
Brambles The
West Drayton UB7 104 A2
8 Wimbledon SW19 179 B5
Bramblewood Cl SM5 202 C1
Brambling Ct 25 SE8 141 B6
Bramblings The E4 36 B6
Bramcote Ave CR4 202 D5
Bramcote Ct CR4 202 D5
Bramcote Gr SE16 118 C1
Bramcote Rd SW15 134 B1
Bramdean Cres SE12 165 A3
Bramdean Gdns SE12 165 A3
Bramerton NW6 68 D1
Bramerton Rd BR3 207 B6
Bramerton St
SW3 136 C6 267 A6
Bramfield Ct N4 73 A6
Bramfield Rd SW11 158 D6
Bramford Ct N14 15 D2
Bramford Rd SW18 136 A1
Bramham Gdns
SW5 113 D1 255 D2
Chessington KT9 213 D4
Bramham Ho SE22 139 C1
Bramhope La SE7 143 B6
Bramlands Cl SW11 136 C2
Bramlea Cl N6 49 A3
Bramley Ave TW17 193 C6
Bramley Cl E17 35 A1
Croydon CR2 221 A3
East Barnet N14 15 B6
Hayes UB3 106 A6
Orpington BR6 210 D1
Pinner HA5 39 D6
Twickenham TW2 152 A5
Woodford IG8 37 C3
Bramley Cres
SW8 137 D5 269 D4
Ilford IG2 56 C3
Bramley Ct DA16 146 B4
NW2 68 B5
2 Barnet EN4 2 C1
9 Chingford E4 20 A3
Feltham TW14 149 C5
Mitcham CR4 180 B1
Southall UB1 108 A6
Wallington SM6 219 C3
Bramley Gdns WD19 22 C5
Bramley Hill CR2 221 A4
Bramley Ho 19 W10 90 D1
Hounslow TW3 129 B1
Ilford IG2 56 C3
1 Kingston KT2 176 D3
5 Roehampton SW15 155 D5
Bramley House Ct EN2 5 B6
Bramleyhyrst CR2 221 A3
Bramley Lo HA0 65 D4
Bramley Rd W10 90 D1
W5 109 C3
Southgate N14 15 C6
Sutton SM1 218 B3
Bramley Way
Hounslow TW4 151 B6
West Wickham BR4 223 D6
Brampton Cl 14 E5 74 B6
Brampton Ct NW4 46 B5
Brampton Gr NW4 46 C5
Harrow HA3 43 B5
Wembley HA9 44 C1
Brampton La 4 NW4 46 C5
Brampton Manor Sch
E6 99 D3
Brampton Park Rd N22 50 C6
Brampton Prim Sch
E6 100 A4
Bexley DA16 146 D3
Brampton Rd DA7 147 A4
E6 99 D4
N15 51 A4
NW9 44 C5
Croydon CR0 205 D3
Hillingdon UB10 82 D5
Bramshaw Gdns WD19 22 D5
Bramshaw Rd E9 74 D2
Bramshaw Rise KT3 199 C3
Bramshill Gdns NW5 71 B5
Bramshill Rd NW10 89 D5
Bramshot Ave SE7 143 B6
Bramshott Ct 3 KT6 198 A3
Bramshurst NW8 91 D6
Bramston Rd NW10 90 A5
Wandsworth SW17 158 A1
Bramwell Cl TW16 172 D1
Bramwell Ho SE1 262 B5
SW1 269 A6
Bramwell Mews N1 233 D6
Brancaster Dr NW7 28 A3
Brancaster Ho 22 E1 96 D4
N5 72 D3
Brancaster Rd
Ilford E12 78 B4
Ilford IG2 57 C3
Streatham SW16 160 A1
Brancepeth Gdns IG9 21 A2
Branch Hill NW3 70 A5
Branch Pl N1 95 B6 235 D6
Branch Rd E14 119 A6
Branch St SE15 139 C5
Brancker Cl SM6 220 A1
Brancker Rd HA3 43 D6
Brancroft Way EN3 7 B4
Brand Cl N4 50 D1
Brandlehow Rd SW15 135 B1
Brandon Ho BR3 185 D5
Brandon Mews EC2 242 C4
Brandon Rd E17 54 A6
N7 72 A1
Southall UB2 107 B1
Sutton SM1 217 D4
Brandon St
SE17 117 A2 262 B3
Brandram Rd SE13 142 C1
Brandrams Wharf
SE16 118 C4
Brandreth Ct HA1 42 D3
Brandreth Rd
Newham E6 100 B1
Upper Tooting SW17 159 B2
Brandries The SM6 219 D5
Brand St SE10 142 A5
Brandville Gdns IG6 56 D5
Brandville Rd UB7 104 A4
Brandy Way SM2 217 C1
Brangbourne Rd BR1 186 A5
Brangton Rd SE11 260 D1
Brangwyn Cres SW19 180 B1
Brangwyn Ct W14 254 A5
Branham Ho 1 SE18 122 D1
Branksea St
SW6 135 A3 264 A3
Branksome Ave N18 33 D5
Branksome Cl KT12 194 D1
Branksome Ct 6 N2 48 A6
Branksome Ho SW8 270 C4
Branksome Rd SW2 160 A6
Merton SW19 179 C2
Branksome Way
Harrow HA3 44 B3
Kingston KT3 177 B2
Bransby Ct 4 N16 73 C4
Bransby Rd KT9 214 A2
Branscombe NW1 232 B5
Branscombe Ct BR2 208 C4
Branscombe Gdns N21 16 C4
Branscombe St SE13 141 D2
Bransdale Cl NW6 91 C6
Bransgrove Rd HA8 26 B3
Branston Cres BR5 211 B1
Branstone Ct 9 TW9 132 B4
Branstone Rd TW9 132 B4
Branston Ho N7 72 C3
Brants Wlk W7 86 C3
Brantwood Ave DA8 147 D5
Isleworth TW7 131 A1
Brantwood Cl E17 53 D6
Brantwood Gdns
Enfield EN2 16 A6
Redbridge IG4 56 A5
Brantwood Ho 9 SE5 139 A5
Brantwood Rd DA7 147 D2
SE24 161 A6
Tottenham N17 34 A4
Brasenose Dr SW13 134 C6
Brasher Cl UB6 64 B3
Brassett Point 3 E15 98 C6
Brassey Cl TW14 150 A3
Brassey Ho 1 E14 119 D2
Walton-on-T KT12 194 A1
Brassey Rd NW6 69 B2
Brassey Sq SW11 137 A2
Brassie Ave W3 89 C1
Brass Talley Alley 31
SE16 118 D4
Brasted Cl DA6 168 D6
Forest Hill SE26 184 C6
Brasted Lo 11 BR3 185 C3
Brathay NW1 232 B3
Brathway Rd SW18 157 C4
Bratley St 12 E1 96 A3
Bratten Ct CR0 205 B3
Braund Ave UB6 85 D3
Braundton Ave DA15 167 D3
Braunston Dr UB4 85 A3
Bravington Cl TW17 192 B4
Bravington Pl W9 91 B3
Bravington Rd W9 91 B4
Brawne Ho 12 SE17 138 D6
Braxfield Rd SE4 141 B1
Braxted Pk SW16 182 B4
Bray NW3 70 C1
Brayard's Rd SE15 140 B3
Braybourne Dr TW7 130 D5
Braybrooke Gdns
SE19 183 C3
Braybrook St W12 89 D1
Brayburne Ave SW4 137 C3
Braycourt Ave KT12 194 C2
Bray Cres SE16 118 D4
Bray Ct Chessington KT9 214 B3
Streatham SW16 182 A5
Braydon Rd N16 52 A1
Bray Dr E16 120 D6
Brayfield Terr N1 72 C1
Brayford Sq 12 E1 96 C1
Bray Pl SW3 114 D2 257 C3
Bray Rd NW7 28 D4
Brayton Gdns EN2 3 D1
Braywick Ct 9 KT2 176 C3
Braywood Rd SE9 145 B1
Brazil Cl CR0 204 A2
Breach La RM9 103 C4
Bread St EC2,EC4 242 B1
Breakspeare SE21 161 D1
Breakspear Jun & Inf Schs
UB10 60 C6
Breakspear Rd HA4,UB9 38 D3
Breakspear Rd N UB9 38 B5
Breakspear Rd S UB9,
UB10 38 C1
Breakspears Dr BR5 190 A2
Breakspears Mews
SE4 141 C3
Breakspears Rd SE4 141 C2
Breakwell Ct 16 W10 91 A3
Bream Cl N17 52 B5
Bream Gdns E6 100 C4
Breamore Cl SW15 156 A3
Breamore Ct IG3 80 A6
Breamore Rd IG3 79 D6
Bream's Bldgs
EC4 94 C1 241 A2
Bream St E3 75 C1
Breamwater Gdns
TW10 153 B1
Brearley Cl HA8 27 A3
Uxbridge UB8 60 A2
Breaside Prep Sch
BR1 187 D2
Breasley Cl SW15 134 B1
Brechin Pl
SW7 114 A2 256 B3
Brecknock Prim Sch
NW1 71 D2
Brecknock Rd N19 71 D3
Breckonmead BR1 187 C1
Breco Ho IG11 102 B4
Brecon Cl Mitcham CR4 204 A6
North Cheam KT4 216 C6
Brecon Ct N12 14 A1
7 SE9 166 C5
Brecon Gn NW9 45 C3
Brecon Ho N16 51 D1
W2 236 A2
Wandsworth SW18 157 C4
Brecon Rd W6 135 A6 264 B5
Enfield EN3 6 C1
Brede Cl E6 100 C4
Bredel Ho 1 E14 97 C2
Bredgar SE13 163 D6
Bredgar Rd N19 71 C6
Bredhurst Cl SE20 184 C4
Bredinghurst SE22 162 A4
Bredinghurst Sch
SE15 140 D1
Bredon Ct HA8 26 B6
Bredon Rd CR0 205 D2
Breer St SW6 135 D2
Breezer's Ct 15 E1 118 A6
Breezer's Hill E1 118 A6
Bremans Row SW18 158 A2
Brember Rd HA2 64 A6
Bremer Mews E17 53 D5
Bremner Rd SW7 256 B6
Brenchley Cl
Chislehurst BR7 188 C2
Hayes BR2 208 D3
Brenchley Gdns SE15,
SE22,SE23 162 D5
Brenchley Rd BR5 189 D1
Brenda Rd SW17 158 D2
Brende Gdns KT8 195 D5
Brendon Ave NW10 67 C4
Brendon Cl Esher KT10 212 A2
Harlington UB7 127 A5
Brendon Ct UB2 107 D2
Brendon Dr KT10 212 A2
Brendon Gdns
Harrow HA2 63 D4
Ilford IG2 57 C4
Brendon Gr N2 30 A1
Brendon H SM2 218 A2
Brendon Ho W1 238 A4
Brendon Rd BR7 167 B2
Dagenham RM8 59 C1
Brendon St W1 92 C1 237 B2
Brendon Villas N21 17 A3
Brendon Way EN1 17 C4
Brenley Cl CR4 203 A6
Brenley Gdns SE9 143 D1
Brenley Ho SE1 252 C2
Brent Cl DA5 169 A3
Brentcot Cl W13 87 B3
Brent Cres NW10 88 B5
Brent Cross Flyover
NW2,NW4 46 D2
Brent Cross Gdns NW4 46 D3
Brent Cross Interchange
NW2,NW4 46 D2
Brent Cross Sh Ctr
NW4 46 C2
Brent Cross Sta NW11 46 D2
Brent Ct NW11 46 D2
5 W12 111 C3
Ealing W7 108 B6
Brentfield NW10 66 D1
Brentfield Cl NW10 67 B2
Brentfield Gdns NW2 46 D2
Brentfield Ho 6 NW10 67 B1
Brentfield Prim Sch
NW10 67 B2
Brentfield Rd NW10 67 B2
Brentford Bsns Ctr
TW8 131 C5
Brentford Cl UB4 84 D3
Brentford Fountain Leisure
Centre W4 110 C1
Brentford Ho 6 TW1 153 B4
Brentford Sch for Girls
TW8 131 D6
Brentford Sta TW8 131 C6
Brent Gn NW4 46 D4
Brentham Way W5 87 D3
Brent Ho 15 E9 74 C2
3 Catford BR1 186 B5
Brenthouse Rd E9 74 C2
Brenthurst Rd NW10 67 D2
Brent Knoll Sch SE26 162 D1
Brent Lea TW8 131 C5
Brent Mans NW4 46 C4
Brentmead Cl W7 108 C6
Brentmead Gdns NW10 88 B5
Brentmead Pl NW11 46 D3
Brent New Ent Ctr
NW10 67 D2
Brenton Ct E9 75 A3
Brenton St E14 97 A1
Brent Park Ind Est
UB2 106 C3
Brent Park Rd NW4 46 B2
Brent Pl EN5 13 B6
Brent Rd E16 99 A2
Brentford TW8 131 C6
Southall UB2 106 C3
Woolwich SE18 144 D5
Brent Side TW8 131 C6
Brentside Cl W13 87 A3
Brentside Executive Ctr
TW8 131 B6
Brentside High Sch W7 86 C3
Brentside Prim Sch W7 86 C3
Brent St NW4 46 C4
Brent Trad Est NW10 67 C3
Brentvale Ave
Southall UB1 108 B5
Wembley HA0 88 B6
Brent View Rd NW9 46 A2
Brentwaters Bsns Pk
TW8 131 C5
Brent Way N3 29 C4
Brentford TW8 131 D5
Wembley HA9 66 D2
Brentwick Gdns TW8 110 A2
Brentwood Cl SE9 167 A3
Brentwood Ho 2
SE18 143 D5
Brentwood Lo NW4 46 D4
Brereton Ho 4 SW2 160 C4
Brereton Rd N17 33 D3
Bressenden Pl
SW1 115 C3 259 A6
Bressey Ave EN1 6 A4
Bressey Gr E18 36 D1
Bretherton Ct CR2 221 C2
Breton Ho EC2 242 B5
SE1 263 C6
Brett Cl N16 73 C6
15 Northolt UB5 84 D4
Brett Cres NW10 89 B6
Brett Ct N9 18 C2
Brettell St SE17 262 D1
Brettenham Ave E17 35 C2
Brettenham Prim Sch
N18 34 A6
Brettenham Rd
Chingford E17 35 C2
Edmonton N18 34 A6
Brett Gdns RM9 81 A1
Brett Ho 1 SW15 156 D4
Brett House Cl 2
SW15 156 D4
Brettinghurst 7 SE1 118 A1
Brett Manor E8 74 B3
Bretton Ho N19 50 A1
Brett Pas 28 E8 74 B3
Brett Rd E8 74 B3
Barnet EN5 12 C6
Brewers Bldgs EC1 234 C2
Brewers Ct W2 236 A2
Brewer's Gn SW1 259 C6
Brewers La 11 TW9 153 D6
Brewer St W1 115 C6 249 B6
Brewery Cl HA0 65 A4
Brewery Ind Est The
N1 235 B3
Brewery Mews Bsns Ctr 1
TW7 131 A2
Brewery Rd N7 72 A2
SE18 123 B1
Keston Mark BR2 210 A1
Brewery Sq SE1 253 C3
Brewhouse La E1 118 B5
Brewhouse Rd 3
SE18 122 B2
Brewhouse St SW15 135 A2
Brewhouse Wlk SE16 119 A5
Brewhouse Yd EC1 241 C6
Brewood Rd RM8 80 B2
Brewster Gdns W10 90 C2
Brewster Ho E14 119 B6
SE1 263 D4

Brewster Rd E10 ... 53 D1
Brian Ct N10 ... 31 B2
Brian Rd RM6 ... 58 C4
Briant Ho SE1 ... 260 D5
Briants Cl HA5 ... 23 B1
Briant St SE14 ... 140 D5
Briar Ave SW16 ... 182 B3
Briarbank Rd W13 ... 87 A1
Briar Cl N2 ... 30 A1
Buckhurst Hill IG9 ... 21 D2
Edmonton N13 ... 17 A1
Hampton TW12 ... 173 B5
Isleworth TW7 ... 152 D6
Briar Cres UB5 ... 63 D2
Briar Ct E11 ... 54 B2
E8 ... 73 D1
Cheam SM3 ... 216 C4
Hampton TW12 ... 173 D5
Briardale HA8 ... 27 B6
Wandsworth SW19 ... 157 B3
Briardale Gdns NW3 ... 69 C5
Briardale Ho N16 ... 51 C1
Briarfield Ave N3 ... 29 D1
Briar Gdns BR2 ... 208 D1
Briaris Cl 11 N17 ... 34 B3
Briar La CR0 ... 223 D4
Briar Lo E18 ... 37 C2
Briar Rd NW2 ... 68 C4
Harrow HA3 ... 43 C4
Littleton TW17 ... 192 C4
Thornton Heath SW16 ... 204 B6
Twickenham TW2 ... 152 C3
Briars The WD23 ... 8 C4
Briarswood Way BR6 ... 227 D3
Briarview Ct E4 ... 36 B4
Briar Way UB7 ... 104 C4
Briar Wlk HA8 ... 27 A3
W10 ... 91 A3
Putney SW15 ... 134 B1
Briarwood Cl NW9 ... 45 A3
Feltham TW13 ... 149 C1
Briarwood Ct 5 KT4 ... 200 A1
Briarwood Dr HA6 ... 22 A1
Briarwood Rd SW4 ... 159 D6
Stoneleigh KT17 ... 216 A2
Briary Cl NW3 ... 70 C1
Briary Ct DA14 ... 190 B5
Briary Gdns BR1 ... 187 B5
Briary Gr HA8 ... 26 D1
Briary La N9 ... 17 D1
Briary Lo BR3 ... 186 A2
Brickbarn Cl SW10 ... 266 B4
Brick Ct EC4 ... 241 A1
Brickett Cl HA4 ... 39 A4
Brick Farm Cl TW9 ... 132 D4
Brickfield Cl TW8 ... 131 C5
Brickfield Cotts SE18 ... 145 D6
Brickfield Farm Gdns
BR6 ... 227 A4
Brickfield La
Edgware EN5 ... 11 D5
Harlington UB3 ... 127 B6
Brickfield Rd
South Norwood CR7,
SW16 ... 182 D2
Wimbledon SW19 ... 179 D6
Brickfields HA2 ... 64 B6
Brickfields Way UB7 ... 104 B3
Brick La E1 ... 95 D3 243 D5
E2 ... 95 D4
Enfield EN1 ... 6 B3
Stanmore HA7 ... 25 D3
Bricklayers Arms SE1 ... 262 D5
Brick St W1 ... 115 B5 248 C3
Brickwall La HA4 ... 39 D1
Brickwood Cl SE26 ... 162 B1
Brickwood Rd CR0 ... 221 C6
Brickworth Ho 26
SW9 ... 138 C4
Bridal Mews N1 ... 234 C5
Brideale Cl SE15 ... 139 D6
Bride Ct EC4 ... 241 C1
Bride La EC4 ... 94 D1 241 C1
Bride St N7 ... 72 B2
Bridewain St SE1 ... 263 C6
Bridewell Pl 20 E1 ... 118 B5
EC4 ... 241 C1
Bridford Mews W1 ... 238 D4
Bridge App NW3 ... 71 A1
Bridge Ave W6 ... 112 C1
Ealing W7 ... 86 B2
Bridge Avenue Mans 1
W6 ... 112 C1
Bridge Cl 13 W10 ... 90 D1
Enfield EN1 ... 6 B3
Teddington TW11 ... 174 D6
Walton-on-T KT12 ... 193 D1
Bridge Ct E10 ... 53 B2
Bridge Dr N13 ... 32 B6
Bridge End E17 ... 36 A2
Bridge Field Ho 7 W2 ... 91 D1
Bridgefield Rd SM1,
SM2 ... 217 C2
Bridgefoot
SE1 ... 116 A1 260 B1
Bridge Gate N21 ... 17 A4
Bridge Gdns
East Molesey KT8 ... 196 B5
Littleton TW15 ... 171 A3
Bridge Ho E9 ... 74 D3
1 NW1 ... 71 A1
SE4 ... 141 B1
TW8 ... 109 A2
Bridge Ho S TW8 ... 109 A2
Bridge House Quay
E14 ... 120 A5
Bridge La NW11 ... 47 B4
SW11 ... 136 C4 267 B1
Bridgeland Rd E16 ... 121 A6
Bridgeman Ho 19 E9 ... 74 C1
Bridgeman Rd N1 ... 72 B1
Teddington TW11 ... 175 A4
Bridgeman St
NW8 ... 92 C5 230 A3
Bridge Meadows
SE14 ... 140 D6
Bridgend Rd SW18 ... 136 A1
Bridgenhall Rd EN1 ... 5 D4
Bridgen Ho 15 E1 ... 96 B1
Bridgen Rd DA5 ... 169 A4
Bridge Par N21 ... 17 A4
Bridge Pk 7 SW18 ... 157 C6
Wembley NW10 ... 66 D1
Bridge Pl SW1 ... 115 B2 258 D4
Croydon CR0 ... 205 B1
Bridgeport Pl 4 E1 ... 118 A5
Bridge Rd DA7 ... 147 A3
E15 ... 98 B6
E17 ... 53 B2
E6 ... 78 B1
NW10 ... 67 C2
Beckenham BR3 ... 185 B3
Chessington KT9 ... 214 A3
East Molesey KT8 ... 196 C5
Edmonton N9 ... 18 A1
Hounslow TW3 ... 130 B2
Isleworth TW3,TW7 ... 130 B2
Southall UB2 ... 107 C4
Sutton SM2 ... 217 D2
Twickenham TW1 ... 153 B5
Wallington SM6 ... 219 C3
Wembley HA9 ... 66 C5
Wood Green N22 ... 32 A2
Bridge Row CR0 ... 205 B1
Bridges Ct SW11 ... 136 B3
Bridges Ho 16 SE5 ... 139 B5
Bridges La CR0 ... 220 A4
Bridges Rd
Stanmore HA7 ... 24 D5
Wimbledon SW19 ... 179 D4
Bridges Road Mews
SW19 ... 179 D4
Bridge St SW1 ... 116 A4 250 B1
W4 ... 111 B2
Pinner HA5 ... 41 A6
Richmond TW10 ... 153 D6
Walton-on-T KT12 ... 193 D2
Bridge Terr E15 ... 76 B1
Bridge The HA3 ... 42 D5
Bridgetown Cl 5
SE19 ... 183 C5
Bridgeview 2 W6 ... 112 C1
Bridgewater Cl BR5,
BR7 ... 211 C6
Bridgewater Ct HA0 ... 65 C2
Bridgewater Gdns HA8 ... 26 B1
Bridgewater Rd E15 ... 98 A6
Ruislip HA4 ... 62 B4
Wembley HA0 ... 65 C1
Bridgewater Sq EC2 ... 242 A4
Bridgewater St EC2 ... 242 A4
Bridge Way NW11 ... 47 B4
Bridgeway Barking IG11 ... 79 D1
Wembley HA0 ... 66 B1
Bridge Way
Twickenham TW2 ... 152 A4
Uxbridge UB10 ... 60 D3
Bridgeway St
NW1 ... 93 C5 232 B3
Bridge Wharf 18 E2 ... 96 D5
Bridge Wharf Rd TW7 ... 131 B2
Bridgewood Cl SE20 ... 184 B3
Bridgewood Rd
North Cheam KT17,KT4 ... 216 A4
Streatham SW16 ... 181 D3
Bridge Yd SE1 ... 252 D4
Bridgford St SW17,
SW18 ... 158 A1
Bridgman Rd W4 ... 111 A3
Bridgnorth Ho 10
SE15 ... 140 A6
Bridgwater Ho W2 ... 236 A2
Bridle Cl Enfield EN3 ... 7 B6
Kingston KT1 ... 197 D5
Sunbury TW16 ... 194 A6
West Ewell KT19 ... 215 B3
Bridle La W1 ... 115 C6 249 B6
Twickenham TW1 ... 153 B5
Bridle Path CR0 ... 220 A5
Bridle Path The IG8 ... 36 C3
Bridlepath Way TW14 ... 149 C3
Bridle Rd
Addington CR0 ... 223 C4
Claygate KT10 ... 213 B2
Croydon CR0 ... 223 C5
Pinner HA5 ... 40 C4
Bridle Way BR6 ... 227 A4
Addington CR0 ... 223 C3
Bridle Way The SM6 ... 219 C3
Bridlington Ho SW18 ... 136 A1
Bridlington Rd N9 ... 18 B4
Bridport SE17 ... 262 B1
Bridport Ave RM7 ... 59 D3
Bridport Ho N1 ... 235 D5
6 Edmonton N18 ... 34 A5
Bridport Pl N1 ... 95 B6 235 D5
Bridport Rd
Edmonton N18 ... 33 D5
Greenford UB6 ... 85 D6
Thornton Heath CR7 ... 204 D6
Bridstow Pl W2 ... 91 C1
Brief St SE5 ... 138 D4
Brierfield NW1 ... 232 A5
Brierley CR0 ... 223 D2
Brierley Ave N9 ... 18 C3
Brierley Cl SE25 ... 206 A5
Brierley Ct W7 ... 108 C6
Brierley Rd E11 ... 76 B4
Upper Tooting SW12 ... 159 C2
Brierly Gdns E2 ... 96 C5
Brigade Cl HA2 ... 64 B6
Brigade St SE3 ... 142 D3
Brigadier Ave EN2 ... 5 A4
Brigadier Hill EN2 ... 5 A5
Briggeford Cl 5 E5 ... 74 A6
Briggs Cl CR4 ... 181 B2
Briggs Ho 20 E2 ... 95 D4
Bright Cl DA17 ... 124 D2
Bright Ct 8 SE28 ... 124 C5
Brightfield Rd SE12 ... 164 D6
Brightling Rd SE4 ... 163 B5
Brightlingsea Pl 5
E14 ... 119 B6
Brightman Rd SW18 ... 158 B3
Brighton Ave E17 ... 53 B4
Brighton Bldgs SE1 ... 263 A5
Brighton Cl UB10 ... 60 D1
Brighton Ct SW15 ... 157 B5
Brighton Dr 3 UB5 ... 63 C2
Brighton Gr SE14 ... 141 A4
Brighton Ho 7 SE5 ... 139 B4
Brighton Rd N16 ... 73 C4
N2 ... 30 A1
Belmont SM2 ... 217 D1
South Croydon CR2 ... 221 B2
Surbiton KT6 ... 197 D3
Sutton SM2 ... 218 A1
Wallend E6 ... 100 C4
Brighton Terr SW9 ... 138 B1
Brightside Rd SE13 ... 164 B5
Brightside The EN3 ... 7 A4
Bright St E14 ... 97 D2
Brightwell Cl CR0 ... 204 C1
Brightwell Cres SW17 ... 180 D5
Brightwell Ct N7 ... 72 B3
Brightwells 1 SW6 ... 135 D3
Brig Mews SE8 ... 141 C6
Brigstock Ho SE5 ... 139 A3
Brigstock Rd
Belvedere DA17 ... 125 D2
Thornton Heath CR7 ... 204 D4
Brill Ho NW10 ... 67 B5
Brill Pl NW1 ... 93 D5 232 D3
Brim Hill N2 ... 48 B5
Brimpsfield Cl SE2 ... 124 B3
Brimsdown Ave EN3 ... 7 A4
Brimsdown Ho E3 ... 98 A3
Brimsdown Jun & Inf Sch
EN3 ... 6 D2
Brimsdown Sta EN3 ... 7 A3
Brimstone Ho 8 E15 ... 76 C1
Brindishe Prim Sch
SE12 ... 164 D6
Brindle Gate DA15 ... 167 C3
Brindley Cl DA7 ... 147 C2
Wembley HA0 ... 87 D6
Brindley Ho 37 W2 ... 91 C2
22 Streatham SW12 ... 160 A4
Brindley St SE14 ... 141 B4
Brindley Way BR1 ... 187 B5
Southall UB1 ... 107 D6
Brindwood Rd E4 ... 19 C1
Brine Ct KT6 ... 197 D4
Brine Ho 10 E3 ... 97 A5
Brinkburn Cl SE2 ... 124 A2
Edgware HA8 ... 44 D6
Brinkburn Gdns HA8 ... 44 C6
Brinkley 18 KT1 ... 176 C1
Brinkley Rd KT4 ... 216 B6
Brinklow Cres SE18 ... 144 D5
Brinklow Ho W2 ... 91 D2
Brinkworth Rd IG5 ... 56 A6
Brinkworth Way E9 ... 75 B2
Brinsdale Rd NW4 ... 46 D6
Brinsley Ho 17 E1 ... 96 C1
Brinsley Rd HA3 ... 24 B1
Brinsley St 29 E1 ... 96 B1
Brinsworth Cl TW2 ... 152 B2
Brinton Wlk SE1 ... 251 C3
Brion Pl E14 ... 98 A2
Brisbane Ave SW19 ... 179 D2
Brisbane Ct N10 ... 31 B3
Brisbane Ho 3 W12 ... 112 B6
Brisbane Rd E10 ... 75 D6
Ealing W13 ... 109 A4
Ilford IG1 ... 57 A1
Brisbane St SE5 ... 139 B5
Briscoe Cl E11 ... 76 D6
Briscoe Rd SW19 ... 180 B4
Briset Rd SE9 ... 143 D1
Briset St EC1 ... 94 D3 241 C5
Briset Way N7 ... 72 B6
Bristol Cl
Stanwell TW19 ... 148 A5
Wallington SM6 ... 220 A1
Bristol Ct 11 TW19 ... 148 A5
Bristol Gdns W9 ... 91 D3
Bristol Ho SE11 ... 261 A5
1 Barking IG11 ... 80 A1
Bristol Mews W9 ... 91 D3
Bristol Park Rd 1 E17 ... 53 A5
Bristol Rd E7 ... 77 D2
Greenford UB6 ... 85 D6
Morden SM4 ... 202 A4
Briston Gr N8 ... 50 A3
Briston Mews NW7 ... 28 A3
Bristow Rd DA7 ... 147 A4
Hounslow TW3 ... 130 A2
Wallington CR0 ... 220 A4
West Norwood SE19 ... 183 C5
Britannia Cl SW4 ... 137 D1
Northolt UB5 ... 84 D4
Britannia Gate 12 E16 ... 121 A5
Britannia Junc NW1 ... 231 D6
Britannia La TW2 ... 152 A4
Britannia Rd 11 E14 ... 119 C2
N12 ... 14 A1
SW6 ... 135 D5 265 C3
Ilford IG1 ... 78 D5
Surbiton KT5 ... 198 B2
Britannia Row
N1 ... 95 A6 235 A6
Britannia St
WC1 ... 94 B4 233 C2
Britannia Way
Acton NW10 ... 88 D3
Stanwell TW19 ... 148 A4
Britannia Wlk N1 ... 235 C2
British Gr W4 ... 111 D1
British Grove Pas 2
W4 ... 111 D1
British Grove S 3 W4 ... 111 D1
British Home & Hospl for
Incurables SE27 ... 182 D5
British Legion Rd E4 ... 20 D2
British Library (Newspaper
Library) NW9 ... 45 C6
British Library The*
WC1 ... 93 D4 232 D2
British Mus*
WC1 ... 94 A2 240 A3
British St E3 ... 97 B4
British Wharf Ind Est
SE14 ... 140 D6
Britley Ho 10 E14 ... 97 B1
Brittain Ct SE9 ... 166 A3
Brittain Ho SE9 ... 166 A3
Brittain Rd RM8 ... 81 B5
Brittany Ho SW15 ... 134 C1
Brittany Point SE11 ... 261 A3
Britten Cl NW11 ... 47 D1
Elstree WD6 ... 9 D5
Brittenden Cl 1 BR6 ... 227 D2
Brittenden Par BR6 ... 227 D2
Britten Dr UB1 ... 85 C1
Britten Ho SW3 ... 257 B2
Britten St SW3 ... 114 C1 257 A2
Britton Cl SE6 ... 164 B4
Britton St EC1 ... 94 D2 241 C5
Brixham Cres HA4 ... 40 A1
Brixham Gdns IG3 ... 79 C3
Brixham Rd DA16 ... 146 D4
Brixham St E16 ... 122 C5
Brixton Day Coll SW9 ... 138 A2
Brixton Hill SW2 ... 160 B5
Brixton Hill Ct 5 SW2 ... 160 B6
Brixton Hill Pl SW2 ... 160 A4
Brixton Mkt* SW9 ... 138 C1
Brixton Oval 7 SW2 ... 138 C1
Brixton Rd SW9 ... 138 C4
Brixton Sta SW9 ... 138 C1
Brixton Station Rd
SW9 ... 138 C2
Brixton Water La SW2 ... 160 B6
Broadacre Cl UB10 ... 60 D5
Broadbent Cl N6 ... 49 B1
Broadbent St W1 ... 248 C6
Broad Berry Ct N18 ... 34 B5
Broad Bridge Cl SE3 ... 143 A5
Broad Common Est
N16 ... 52 A1
Broadcoombe CR2 ... 222 D1
Broadcroft Ave HA7 ... 25 D1
Broadcroft Rd BR5 ... 211 B2
Broad Ct WC2 ... 240 B1
Broadfield NW6 ... 69 D2
Broadfield Cl NW2 ... 68 C5
Croydon CR0 ... 220 B6
Broadfield Ct WD23 ... 8 C2
Broadfield La NW1 ... 72 A1
Broadfield Rd SE6 ... 164 C3
Broadfields Harrow HA2 ... 23 D1
Thames Ditton KT8 ... 196 C3
Broadfields Ave
Edgware HA8 ... 10 D1
Southgate N21 ... 16 C4
Broadfields Hts HA8 ... 26 D6
Broadfields Inf Sch
HA8 ... 10 C2
Broadfields Jun Sch
HA8 ... 10 D2
Broadfield Sq EN1 ... 6 B3
Broadfields Way NW10 ... 67 D3
Broadfield Way IG9 ... 21 C1
Broadford Ho 11 E1 ... 97 A3
Broadgate EC2 ... 95 C2 243 A4
Broadgate Circ
EC2 ... 95 C2 243 A3
Broadgate Rd E16 ... 99 D1
Broadgates Ave EN4 ... 1 D4
Broadgates Ct SE11 ... 261 B1
Broadgates Rd SW18 ... 158 B3
Broad Green Ave CR0 ... 204 D2
Broadhead Strand
NW9 ... 27 D2
Broadheath Dr BR7 ... 188 B5
Broadhinton Rd SW4 ... 137 C2
Broadhurst Ave
Edgware HA8 ... 26 D6
Ilford IG3 ... 79 D4
Broadhurst Cl NW6 ... 70 A2
9 Richmond TW10 ... 154 B6
Broadhurst Gdns NW6 ... 69 D2
Ruislip HA4 ... 62 C6
Broadhurst Mans NW6 ... 69 D2
Broad La EC2 ... 243 A4
N15 ... 51 D5
N15 ... 52 A5
N8 ... 50 B4
Hampton TW12 ... 173 C4
Broadlands N6 ... 49 A2
Feltham TW13 ... 151 C1
Broadlands Ave
Enfield EN3 ... 6 B2
Shepperton TW17 ... 193 A3
Streatham SW16 ... 160 A2
Broadlands Cl N6 ... 49 A2
Enfield EN3 ... 6 C2
Streatham SW16 ... 160 A2
Broadlands Ct TW9 ... 132 C5
Broadlands Lo N6 ... 48 D2
Broadlands Mans 2
SW16 ... 160 A2
Broadlands Rd BR1 ... 187 B6
N6 ... 48 D2
Broadlands Way KT3 ... 199 D3
Broad Lawn SE9 ... 166 C3
Broadlawns Ct HA3 ... 24 D2
Broadley St
NW8 ... 92 C2 237 A4
Broadley Terr
NW1 ... 92 C3 237 B5
Broadmayne SE17 ... 262 C2
Broadmead W14 ... 254 A3
Catford SE6 ... 163 C1
Broadmead Ave KT4 ... 200 A2
Broadmead Cl
Hampton TW12 ... 173 C4
Pinner HA5 ... 23 A3
Broadmead Ct 6 IG8 ... 37 A4
Broadmead Inf Sch
CR0 ... 205 B2
Broadmead Jun Sch
CR0 ... 205 B3
Broadmead Rd
Northolt UB5 ... 85 A3
Woodford IG8 ... 37 B3
Broad Oak
Ashford TW16 ... 171 D4
Woodford IG8 ... 37 B5
Broad Oak Cl BR5 ... 190 A1
Chingford E4 ... 35 C5
Broadoak Ct 8 SW9 ... 138 C2
Broadoak Ho 18 NW6 ... 91 D6
Broad Oaks KT6 ... 214 D6
Broadoaks Way BR2 ... 208 D4
Broad Sanctuary SW1 ... 250 A1
Broad St
Dagenham RM10 ... 81 C1
Teddington TW11 ... 174 D4
Broad St Ave EC2 ... 243 A3
Broadstone Ho SW8 ... 270 C3
Broadstone Pl W1 ... 238 A3
Broad St Pl EC2 ... 242 D3
Broadview NW9 ... 44 C3
Broadview Est TW19 ... 148 C4
Broadview Ho RM8 ... 58 D1
Broadview Rd SW16 ... 181 D3
Broadwalk E18 ... 54 D6
Harrow HA2 ... 41 D4
Broadwalk Ho SW7 ... 246 A1
Broadwalk La NW11 ... 47 B2
Broadwalk Sh Ctr The
HA8 ... 26 D4
Broadwall SE1 ... 116 C5 251 B4
Broadwater Farm Prim Sch
N17 ... 33 B1
Broadwater Gdns BR6 ... 227 A4
Broadwater Prim Sch
SW17 ... 180 C6
Broadwater Rd SE18 ... 123 B3
Tottenham N17 ... 33 C1
Upper Tooting SW17 ... 180 C6
Broadway DA6 ... 147 B1
E15 ... 76 B1
Broadway *continued*
SW1 ... 115 D3 259 C6
Barking IG11 ... 101 A6
Bexley DA6,DA7 ... 147 C1
Ealing W13 ... 109 A5
Ealing W7 ... 108 C5
Tolworth KT6 ... 198 D1
Broadway Arc 3 W6 ... 112 C2
Broadway Ave
Thornton Heath CR0 ... 205 B4
Twickenham TW1 ... 153 B5
Broadway Bldgs 5
W7 ... 108 C5
Broadway Cl IG8 ... 37 B4
Broadway Ct
Beckenham BR3 ... 208 A6
Wimbledon SW19 ... 179 C4
Broadway Ctr Adult Coll
SW17 ... 180 C6
Broadway Gdns
Mitcham CR4 ... 202 C5
Woodford IG8 ... 37 B4
Broadway Ho 2 E8 ... 96 B6
Broadway Mans SW6 ... 265 B3
Broadway Market E8 ... 96 B6
Broadway Market Mews 21
E8 ... 96 A6
Broadway Mews E5 ... 51 D2
Southgate N21 ... 16 D3
Bowes Park N13 ... 32 B5
Broadway Par N8 ... 50 A3
Chingford E4 ... 36 A4
Hayes UB3 ... 106 A5
West Drayton UB7 ... 104 A4
Broadway Pl SW19 ... 179 B4
Broadway Sh Ctr 5
DA6 ... 147 C1
Broadway The E13 ... 99 B5
N11 ... 31 A5
2 N14 ... 15 D3
N8 ... 50 A3
NW7 ... 27 D5
W3 ... 110 C4
Barnes SW13 ... 133 C3
Cheam SM3 ... 217 A2
Chingford E4 ... 36 B4
Dagenham RM8 ... 81 C6
Ealing W5 ... 109 D6
Edmonton N9 ... 18 A1
Greenford UB6 ... 86 A3
Harrow HA3 ... 24 D1
Merton SW19 ... 179 C3
Pinner HA5 ... 23 B3
Southall UB1 ... 107 A6
Stanmore HA7 ... 25 C5
Sutton SM1 ... 218 A4
Thames Ditton KT10 ... 196 C1
Tolworth KT6 ... 198 C1
Wallington SM6 ... 220 A4
Wembley HA9 ... 66 A5
Woodford IG8 ... 37 B4
Wood Green N22 ... 32 C1
Broadwell Ct TW5 ... 128 D4
Broadwick St
W1 ... 93 C1 239 B1
Broad Wlk NW1 ... 93 A5 231 B3
W1 ... 115 A5 248 A4
Eltham SE3,SE18 ... 144 A3
Heston TW5 ... 129 A4
Richmond TW9 ... 132 B5
Southgate N21 ... 16 B3
Broad Wlk The
W8 ... 113 D5 245 D3
Broadwood Ave HA4 ... 39 C3
Broadwood Terr W14 ... 254 D4
Broad Yd EC1 ... 241 C5
Brocas Cl NW3 ... 70 C1
Brockbridge Ho 11
SW15 ... 155 D5
Brockdene Dr BR2 ... 225 D4
Brockdish Ave IG11 ... 79 D3
Brockelbank Lo RM8 ... 80 D6
Brockenhurst KT8 ... 195 B3
Brockenhurst Ave KT4 ... 199 C1
Brockenhurst Gdns
NW7 ... 27 C5
Ilford IG1 ... 79 A3
Brockenhurst Mews 9
N18 ... 34 A6
Brockenhurst Rd CR0 ... 206 B2
Brockenhurst Way
SW16 ... 181 D1
Brocket Ho 16 SW8 ... 137 D3
Brockham Cl SW19 ... 179 B5
Brockham Cres CR0 ... 224 B1
Brockham Ct 6 SM2 ... 217 D1
Brockham Dr Ilford IG2 ... 57 A4
Streatham SW2 ... 160 B4
Brockham Ho NW1 ... 232 B5
11 Streatham SW2 ... 160 B4
Brockham St SE1 ... 262 B6
Brock Ho WC1 ... 239 C4
Brockhurst Cl HA7 ... 24 D4
Brockhurst Ho N4 ... 51 B2
Brockill Cres SE4 ... 141 A1

Brocklebank Ho 7
E16 122 C5
Brocklebank Rd SE7 121 B2
Wandsworth SW18 158 A4
Brocklebank Road Ind Est
SE7 121 A2
Brocklehurst St SE14 140 D5
Brocklesby Rd SE25 206 B5
Brockley Ave HA7 10 A1
Brockley Cl HA7 26 A6
Brockley Cross SE4 141 B2
Brockley Cross Bsns Ctr
SE4 141 A2
Brockley Gdns SE4 141 B3
Brockley Gr SE4 163 B6
Brockley Hall Rd SE4 163 A6
Brockley Hill HA7,HA8 9 D2
Brockley Hill Ho HA7 9 C3
Brockley Ho SE17 263 A2
Brockley Mews SE4 163 A6
Brockley Pk SE23 163 A4
Brockley Prim Sch
SE4 163 B6
Brockley Rd SE4 163 B6
Brockley Rise SE23 163 A4
Brockleyside HA7 26 A6
Brockley Sta SE4 141 A2
Brockley View SE23 163 A4
Brockley Way SE4 163 A6
Brockman Rise BR1 186 B6
Brockmer Ho 5 E1 118 B6
Brock Pl E3 97 D3
Brock Rd E13 99 B2
Brocks Dr SM3 217 A5
Brockshot Cl 1 TW8 131 D6
Brock St SE15 140 C2
Brockway Cl E11 76 C6
Brockweir 29 E2 96 C5
Brockwell Cl BR5 211 D4
Brockwell Ct 2 SW2 160 C6
Brockwell Ho SE11 270 D6
Brockwell Park*
SE24 160 D5
Brockwell Park Gdns
SE24 160 D4
Brockworth 8 KT2 176 D2
Broderick Ho SE21 161 C1
Brodia Rd N16 73 C5
Brodick Ho 11 E3 97 B5
Brodie Ho SE1 263 D2
7 Wallington SM6 219 B4
Brodie Rd Chingford E4 20 A2
Enfield EN2 5 A5
Brodie St SE1 117 D1 263 D2
Brodlove La E1 118 D6
Brodrick Gr SE2 124 B2
Brodrick Rd SW17 158 C2
Brograve Gdns BR3 185 D1
Broken Wharf EC4 252 A6
Brokesley St E3 97 B4
Broke Wlk E8 95 D6
1 E8 96 A6
Bromar Rd SE5 139 C2
Bromborough Gn
WD19 22 C5
Bromefield HA7 25 C2
Bromehead St 8 E1 96 C1
Brome Ho 5 SE18 144 A4
Bromell's Rd SW4 137 C1
Brome Rd SE9 144 B2
Bromfelde Rd SW4 137 D3
Bromfield Ct 20 SE16 118 A3
Bromfield St N1 234 B4
Bromhall Rd RM8 80 B3
Bromhedge SE9 166 B1
Bromholm Rd SE2 124 B3
Bromleigh Ct 1 SE21,
SE22 162 B2
Bromleigh Ho SE1 263 C6
Bromley Ave BR1 186 C3
Bromley-by-Bow Sta
E3 97 D4
Bromley Coll of F & H Ed
BR2 209 D3
Bromley Comm BR2 209 D4
Bromley Cres
Beckenham BR2 208 D6
Ruislip HA4 61 D4
Bromley Ct SE13 164 B6
Bromley BR1 186 D3
Bromley Gdns BR2 208 D6
Bromley Gr BR2 186 B1
Bromley Hall Rd E14 98 A2
Bromley High Sch for Girls
BR1 210 C5
Bromley High St E3 97 D4
Bromley Hill BR1 186 C4
Bromley Hospl BR1 209 B5
Bromley Ind Est BR1 209 D6
Bromley La BR7 189 B3
Bromley Lo 2 W3 89 A1
Bromley Manor Mans 3
BR1 209 A6
Bromley North Sta
BR1 187 A2
Bromley Pk 11 BR1 186 D2
Bromley Pl W1 239 A4
Bromley Rd BR7 188 D2
E10 53 D3
E17 53 C6
Beckenham BR2,BR3 186 B1
Beckenham BR3 185 D2
Catford SE6 163 D1
Edmonton N18 17 B1
Tottenham N17 34 A2
Bromley Rd Ret Pk
SE6 163 D2
Bromley Road Inf Sch
BR3 185 D2
Bromley South Sta
BR2 209 A6
Bromley St E1 96 D1
Brompton WC1 240 C3
Brompton Arc SW1 247 D1
Brompton Cl
Hounslow TW4 151 B6
Penge SE20 184 A1
Brompton Ct 4 HA7 25 C6
Brompton Gr N2 48 C5
Brompton Ho 3 N9 34 A6
Brompton Oratory*
SW3 114 C3 257 A5
Brompton Park Cres
SW6 135 D6 265 C5
Brompton Pl
SW3 114 C3 257 B6
Brompton Rd
SW3 114 C3 257 A5
Brompton Sq
SW3 114 C3 257 A6
Bromstone Ho 19
SW9 138 C4
Bromwich Ave N6 71 A6
Bromwich Ho 3
TW10 154 A5
Bromyard Ave W3 111 C6
Bromyard Ho 3 SE15 140 B5
Bron Ct NW6 91 C6
Brondesbury Coll for Boys
NW6 69 A1
Brondesbury Ct NW2 68 D2
Brondesbury Mews 11
NW6 69 C1
Brondesbury Park Sta
NW6 91 A6
Brondesbury Pk NW2 68 D1
Brondesbury Rd NW6 91 C5
Brondesbury Sta NW6 69 B1
Brondesbury Villas
NW6 91 C5
Bronhill Terr N17 34 A2
Bronsart Rd
SW6 135 A5 264 A3
Bronson Rd SW20 179 A1
Bronte Cl DA8 147 D5
1 E7 77 A4
Ilford IG2 56 C5
Bronte Ct 8 W14 112 D3
Bronte Ho 6 N16 73 C3
NW6 91 C4
Bronti Cl SE17 117 A1 262 B2
Bronwen Ct NW8 229 C1
Bronze Age Way DA17 125 D4
Bronze St SE8 141 C5
Brook Ave
Dagenham RM10 81 D1
Edgware HA8 26 D4
Wembley HA9 66 C5
Brook Bank EN1 6 B6
Brookbank Ave W7 86 B2
Brookbank Rd SE13 141 D2
Brook Cl Acton W3 110 C5
Finchley N12 29 A3
Ruislip HA4 39 C2
Stanwell TW19 148 B4
Upper Tooting SW17 159 A2
West Barnes SW20 200 B6
Brook Cres Chingford E4 35 D6
Edmonton N9 34 B6
Brook Ct 2 E11 76 C5
E15 76 A3
E17 53 A6
Beckenham BR3 185 B2
5 Brentford TW8 131 D6
Cheam SM3 216 C4
Edgware HA8 26 D5
Mortlake SW14 133 C2
Brookdale N11 31 C6
Brookdale Rd DA5 169 A5
E17 53 C6
SE6 163 D5
Catford SE6 163 D4
Brookdales The NW4 47 A5
Brookdene N12 29 D6
Brookdene Rd SE18,
SE2 123 D2
Brook Dr SE11 116 D2 261 C4
Harrow HA1 42 A5
Ruislip HA4 39 C2
Brooke Ave HA2 64 A5
Brooke Cl WD23 8 A4
Brooke Ct 7 KT2 175 D6
Brookehowse Rd SE6 163 D1
Brookend Rd DA15 167 C3
Brooke Rd E17 54 A5
Brooke Rd *continued*
E5,N16 74 A5
Brookes Ct EC1 241 A4
Brookes Mkt EC1 241 A4
Brooke's Mkt EC1 241 B4
Brooke St EC1 94 C2 241 A3
Brooke Way WD23 8 A4
Brookfield 1 N4 72 C6
N6 71 A5
Brookfield Ave E17 54 A5
NW7 28 B4
Carshalton SM1,SM5 218 C5
Ealing W5 87 D3
Brookfield Cl NW7 28 B4
Brookfield Cres NW7 28 B4
Harrow HA3 44 A4
Brookfield Ct 1 N12 29 D6
Greenford UB6 86 A4
Brookfield Gdns KT10 212 D2
Brookfield House Sch
IG8 36 C4
Brookfield Path IG8 36 C4
Brookfield Pk NW5 71 B5
Brookfield Prim Sch
N19 71 B6
Cheam SM3 201 A1
Brookfield Rd E9 75 A2
W4 111 B4
Edmonton N9 18 B1
Brookfields EN3 6 D1
Brookfields Ave CR4 202 C4
Brookgate N16 73 B6
Brook Gate
W1 114 D6 247 D5
Brook Gdns
Barnes SW13 133 D2
Chingford E4 35 D6
Kingston KT2 177 A2
Brook Gn W6 112 D2
Brook Green Flats 11
W14 112 D3
Brookhill Cl SE18 122 D1
East Barnet EN4 14 C6
Brookhill Ct 2 EN4 14 C5
Brookhill Rd SE18 122 D1
East Barnet EN4 14 C6
Brook Ho 3 SW4 159 C6
W3 110 C4
4 W6 112 C2
3 Edmonton N9 18 A1
3 Twickenham TW1 153 A4
Brook Hos NW1 232 B3
Brookhouse Gdns E4 36 C6
Brook House Sixth Form
Coll The E5 74 B5
Brook Ind Est UB4 106 C5
Brooking Cl RM8 80 C5
Brooking Rd E7 77 A3
Brook La BR1 187 A4
DA5 168 D5
Greenwich SE3 143 B3
Brookland Cl NW11 47 C5
Brookland Garth NW11 47 D5
Brookland Hill NW11 47 D5
Brookland Jun & Inf Schs
NW11 47 D5
Brookland Rise NW11 47 C5
Brooklands Ave DA15 167 B2
Wandsworth SW18 157 D2
Brooklands Cl TW16 171 C2
Brooklands Court
Apartments 3 NW6 69 B1
Brooklands Ct 2 NW6 69 B1
Enfield N21 17 B6
Kingston KT1 197 D5
2 Mitcham CR4 180 B1
Brooklands Dr UB6 87 D6
Brooklands Pk SE3 143 A2
Brooklands Prim Sch
SE3 143 A2
Brooklands Rd KT7 197 A1
Brooklands The TW7 130 B4
Brook Lane Bns Ctr
TW8 109 D1
Brooklea Cl NW9 27 C2
Brook Lo N8 49 D3
NW4 46 D4
Brooklyn SE20 184 A3
Brooklyn Ave SE25 206 B5
Brooklyn Cl SM5 218 C6
Brooklyn Ct W12 112 C5
Brooklyn Gr SE25 206 B5
Brooklyn Rd BR2 210 A4
Croydon SE25 206 B5
Brookmarsh Ind Est
SE10 141 D5
Brook Mdw N12 13 D1
Brook Mead KT19 215 C2
Brookmead Ave BR1,
BR2 210 B4
Brookmead Ct N20 14 A2
Brookmead Ind Est
CR4 203 C3
Brook Meadow Cl IG8 36 C4
Brookmead Rd CR0 203 C3
Brook Mews N
W2 114 B6 246 B6
Brookmill Rd SE8 141 C4
Brook Park Cl N21 16 D6
Brook Pl EN5 13 C6
Brook Rd N12 30 C3
N22 50 B6
N8 50 A5
NW2 68 A6
Buckhurst Hill IG9 21 A3
Ilford IG2 57 C3
South Norwood CR7 205 A5
Surbiton KT6 214 A6
Twickenham TW1 153 A5
Brook Rd S TW8 131 D6
Brooks Ave E6 100 B3
Brooksbank Ho 7 E9 74 C2
Brooksbank St 9 E9 74 C2
Brooksby Mews N1 72 C1
Brooksby St N1 72 C1
Brooksby's Wlk E9 74 D3
Brooks Cl SE9 166 C2
Brookscroft Rd E17 35 D2
Brooks Ct 3 SW4 138 A3
SW8 269 B4
Brookshill HA3 24 B5
Brookshill Ave HA3 24 C5
Brookshill Dr HA3 24 B5
Brooks Ho 6 SW2 160 C3
Brookside BR6 211 D2
East Barnet EN4 14 C5
Southgate N21 16 B5
Wallington SM5 219 A3
Brookside Cl Barnet EN5 13 A5
Feltham TW13 150 A1
Harrow HA3 43 D4
South Harrow HA2,HA4 63 A4
Brookside Cres 1
KT4 200 A1
Brookside Ct SW16 181 C3
Brookside Gdns EN1 6 C6
Brookside Ho N17 33 C1
Brookside Prim Sch
UB4 84 C4
Brookside Rd N19 71 C6
NW11 47 B3
Edmonton N9 34 B6
Hayes UB4 106 C6
Brookside S EN4 15 A4
Brookside Way
Croydon CR0 206 D3
Hillingdon UB10 60 B1
Brooks La W4 132 C6
Brook's Mans 5 IG3 58 B1
Brook's Mews
W1 115 B6 248 C6
Brook's Par 6 IG3 58 B1
Brooks Rd W4 110 C1
Brook's Rd E13 99 A6
Brook St DA8 147 D5
W1 115 B6 248 C6
W2 114 B6 246 D6
Kingston KT1 176 A1
5 Tottenham N17 33 D1
Brookstone Ct SE15 140 B1
Brooksville Ave NW6 91 A6
Brook Vale DA7,DA8 147 D4
Brookview Ct 11 EN1 17 C6
Brookview Rd SW16 181 C5
Brookville Rd
SW6 135 B5 264 C3
Brookway SE3 143 A2
Brook Wlk HA8 27 B4
N2 30 B2
Brookwood Ave SW13 133 D3
Brookwood Cl BR2 208 D5
Brookwood Ho SE1 251 D1
Brookwood Rd
Hounslow TW3 129 D4
Wandsworth SW18 157 C3
Broom Ave BR5 190 B1
Broom Cl BR2 210 A3
Teddington KT1,TW11 175 D3
Broomcroft Ave UB5 84 C4
Broome Ct 3 TW9 132 C4
Broome Ho 7 E5 74 B3
Broome Rd TW12 173 B2
Broome Way SE5 139 B5
Broomfield E17 53 B2
7 NW1 71 A1
Sunbury TW16 172 A2
Broomfield Ave N13 32 B5
Broomfield Cotts N13 32 A5
Broomfield Ct N13 32 A5
Broomfield Ho 4 BR5 190 B1
SE17 263 A3
Stanmore HA7 9 A1
Broomfield House Sch
TW9 132 B4
Broomfield La N13 32 B6
Broomfield Pl W13 109 B5
Broomfield Rd DA6 169 C6
Beckenham BR3 207 B6
Bowes Park N13 32 A5
Dagenham RM6 58 D2
Ealing W13 109 B5
Richmond TW9 132 B4
Surbiton KT5 198 B1
Teddington TW11 175 C4
Broomfields KT10 212 A3
Broomfield Sch N14 31 D5
Broomfield St E14 97 D2
Broom Gdns CR0 223 C5
Broomgrove Gdns HA8 26 C2
Broomgrove Rd SW9 138 B3
Broomhill Ct 2 IG8 37 A4
Broomhill Rd BR6 211 D2
SW18 157 C6
Ilford IG3 80 A6
Woodford IG8 37 A4
Broomhill Rise DA6 169 C6
Broomhill Wlk IG8 36 D3
Broomhouse La SW6 135 C2
Broomhouse Rd SW6 135 C3
Broomleigh BR1 187 A2
Broomleigh Bsns Pk
SE26 185 B5
Broomloan La SM1 217 C6
Broom Lock TW11 175 C4
Broom Mead DA6 169 C6
Broom Pk KT1 175 D3
Broom Rd Croydon CR0 223 C5
Richmond TW11 175 C5
Teddington KT1,TW11 175 C4
Broomsleigh St NW6 69 B3
Broom Water TW11 175 C5
Broom Water W TW11 175 C5
Broomwood Cl CR0 206 D4
Broomwood Hall Sch
SW12 159 A4
Broomwood Rd BR5 190 B1
SW11 159 A6
Broseley Gr SE26 185 A5
Broster Gdns SE25 205 D6
Brougham Rd E8 96 A6
W3 89 A1
Brougham St SW11 136 D3
Brough Cl SW8 270 B3
Kingston KT2 175 D5
Brough St SW8 270 B3
Broughton Ave N3 47 A6
Richmond TW10 175 C6
Broughton Ct W13 109 B6
Broughton Dr 20 SW9 138 D1
Broughton Gdns N6 49 C3
Broughton Rd SW6 135 D3
Ealing W13 109 B6
Orpington BR6 227 B6
Thornton Heath CR7 204 C3
Broughton Road App 2
SW6 135 D3
Broughton St SW8 137 B3
Broughton Street Arches
Ind Area SW11 137 A3
Brouncker Rd W3 111 A4
Browells La TW13 150 B2
Brown Bear Ct TW13 172 D6
Brown Cl SM6 220 A1
Browne Ho 13 SE8 141 C5
9 Penge SE26 184 B5
Brownfield St E14 98 A1
Brownflete Ho SE4 141 A1
Browngraves Rd UB7 127 A5
Brown Hart Gdns W1 248 B6
Brownhill Rd SE6 164 A4
Browning Ave
Carshalton SM1 218 C4
Ealing W7 86 D1
North Cheam KT4 200 B1
Browning Cl DA16 145 C4
E17 54 A5
W9 236 B5
Feltham TW12 173 B6
Browning Ct W14 264 C6
Browning Ho 10 N16 73 C4
W12 90 C1
Browning Mews W1 238 B3
Browning Rd E11 54 D2
E12 78 B2
Enfield EN2 5 B5
Browning St
SE17 117 A2 262 B3
Browning Way TW5 128 D4
Brownlea Gdns IG3 80 A6
Brownlow Cl EN4 14 B6
Brownlow Ct N2 48 A4
1 Bowes Park N11 32 A4
Brownlow Ho 7 SE16 118 A4
Brownlow Mews
WC1 94 B3 240 D5
Brownlow Rd 3 E7 77 A4
E8 96 A6
N3 29 D3
NW10 67 C1
Bowes Park N11 32 A4
6 Ealing W13 109 A5
South Croydon CR0 221 D4
Brownlow St
WC1 94 B2 240 D3
Brownrigg Rd TW15 170 C6
Brown's Bldgs EC3 243 B1
Brownspring Dr SE9 166 D1
Brown's Rd E17 53 C6
Surbiton KT5,KT6 198 B2
Brown St W1 92 D1 237 C2
Brownswell Rd N2 30 B1
Brownswood Rd N4 73 A6
Broxash Rd SW11 159 A5
Broxbourne Ave E18 55 B5
Broxbourne Ho 1 E3 97 D3
Broxbourne Rd BR6 211 D2
Wanstead E7 77 A5
Broxholme Ho SW6 265 C2
Broxholm Rd SE27,
SW16 160 C1
Broxted Rd SE6 163 B2
Broxwood Way
NW8 92 C6 230 B5
Bruce Ave TW17 193 A3
Bruce Castle Ct N17 33 C2
Bruce Castle Mus*
N17 33 C2
Bruce Castle Rd N17 33 D2
Bruce Cl DA16 146 B4
W10 90 D2
Bruce Ct DA15 189 D6
Bruce Gdns N20 14 D1
Bruce Glasier Ho 13
N19 49 D2
Bruce Gr N17 33 D1
Bruce Grove N17 33 D1
Bruce Grove Prim Sch
N17 33 D1
Bruce Grove Sta N17 33 D1
Bruce Hall Mews
SW17 181 A6
Bruce Ho 4 SW4 159 D5
W10 90 D2
5 Harrow HA1 42 D4
Harrow HA3 44 A2
Putney SW15 156 B6
Bruce Lawns SW17 181 A6
Bruce Rd E3 97 D4
NW10 67 B1
Barnet EN5 1 A2
Harrow HA3 24 C1
Mitcham CR4 181 A3
South Norwood SE25 205 B5
Bruckner St W10 91 B4
Brudenell Rd SW17 181 A6
Bruffs Meadow UB5 63 A2
Bruges Pl 13 NW1 71 C1
Brumfield Rd KT19 215 A3
Brune Ho E1 243 C3
Brunel Cl Cranford TW5 128 B5
Northolt UB5 85 B4
Penge SE19 183 D4
Brunel Ct NW10 90 A4
Brunel Est W2 91 C2
Brunel Ho E14 119 D1
4 NW5 71 B4
SW10 266 D4
Hayes UB3 105 D3
25 Streatham SW2 160 A4
Brunel Pl 8 UB1 85 D1
Brunel Rd E17 53 A3
SE16 118 C5
W3 89 C2
Brunel St E16 98 D1
Brunel Univ UB8 82 A4
Brunel Univ Coll Osterley
Campus TW7 130 D5
Brunel Univ Coll
(Twickenham Campus)
TW1 131 B1
Brunel Wlk N15 51 C5
Twickenham TW4 151 C4
Brune St E1 95 D2 243 C3
Brunlees Ho SE1 262 B5
Brunner Cl NW11 48 A4
Brunner Ho 6 SE6 186 A6
Brunner Rd E17 53 B4
Ealing W5 87 D3
Bruno Pl NW9 67 A6
Brunswick Ave N11 15 A1
Brunswick Cl DA6 146 D1
Pinner HA5 41 A3
Thames Ditton KT7 196 D1
Twickenham TW2 152 B1
Brunswick Cres N11 15 A1
Brunswick Ct EC1 234 C1
SE1 117 C4 253 B2
SW1 259 D3
Kingston KT2 175 D4
New Barnet EN4 14 B6
2 Penge SE19 184 A3
2 Wimbledon SW19 179 A3
Brunswick Gdns
W8 113 C5 245 B3
Ealing W5 88 A3
Brunswick Gr N11 15 A1
Brunswick Ho 4 E2 95 D5
N3 29 B2
NW1 237 C6
Brunswick Lo 6 E4 20 A2
Brunswick Manor
SM1 218 A4
Brunswick Mews W1 237 D2
Streatham SW16 181 D4
Brunswick Park Gdns
N11 15 A2
Brunswick Park Prim Sch
N14 15 A2
SE5 139 B5
Brunswick Park Rd
N11 15 A1
Brunswick Pk SE5 139 C4
Brunswick Pl
N1 95 B4 235 D1
Penge SE19 184 A3
Brunswick Quay SE16 118 D3

Brunswick Rd DA6 147 A1
E10 54 A1
E14 98 A1
N15 51 C5
Ealing W5 88 A4
Holdbrook EN3 7 C5
Kingston KT2 176 C2
Sutton SM1 217 D4
Brunswick Sh Ctr
WC1 94 A3 240 B6
Brunswick Sq
WC1 94 A3 240 B6
Tottenham N17 33 D4
Brunswick St E17 54 A4
Brunswick Villas 2
SE5 139 C4
Brunswick Way N11 31 B6
Brunton Pl E14 97 A1
Brushfield St
E1 95 D2 243 C4
Brushwood Ho 4 E14 97 D2
Brushwood Lo DA17 125 C2
Brussels Rd SW11 136 B1
Bruton Cl BR7 188 B3
Bruton La W1 115 B6 248 D5
Bruton Pl W1 115 B6 248 D5
Bruton Rd SM4 202 A5
Bruton St W1 115 B6 248 D5
Bruton Way W13 87 A2
Bryan Ave NW10 68 B1
Bryan Cl TW16 172 A3
Bryan Ct W1 237 C2
Bryan Ho SE16 119 B4
Bryan Rd SE16 119 B4
Bryanston Ave TW2 151 D3
Bryanston Cl UB2 107 B2
Bryanston Ct W1 237 C2
Bryanstone Ct SM1 218 A5
Bryanstone Rd N8 49 D4
Bryanston Ho 11 SE15 139 D4
Bryanston Mans W1 237 C4
Bryanston Mews E
W1 237 C3
Bryanston Mews W
W1 92 D1 237 C2
Bryanston Pl
W1 92 D2 237 C3
Bryanston Sq
W1 92 D1 237 C2
Bryanston St
W1 92 D1 237 D1
Bryant Cl EN5 13 B6
Bryant Ct E2 95 D5
Bryant Rd UB5 84 C4
Bryant St E15 76 C1
Bryantwood Rd N5,N7 72 C3
Brycedale Cres N14 15 D1
Bryce Ho 25 SE14 140 D6
Bryce Rd RM8 80 C4
Brydale Ho 2 SE16 118 D2
Bryden Cl SE26 185 A5
Brydges Pl WC2 250 A5
Brydges Rd E15 76 B3
Brydon Wlk N1 233 B6
Bryer Ct EC2 242 A4
Bryett Rd N7 72 A5
Bryher Ho W4 111 A1
Brymay Cl E3 97 C5
Brymon Ct W1 237 D3
Brynmaer Ho SW11 267 D1
Brynmaer Rd
SW11 136 D4 267 D1
Bryn-y-Mawr Rd EN1 5 D1
Bryony Cl UB8 82 B2
Bryony Rd W12 112 A6
Bryony Way TW16 172 A4
B Sky B Hq TW7 131 A6
BT Telecom Twr*
W1 93 C2 239 A4
Buccleuch Ho E5 52 A2
Buchanan Cl N21 16 B6
Buchanan Ct 16 SE16 118 D2
Buchanan Gdns NW10 90 B5
Buchanan Ho
Dulwich SE21 161 C1
Wandsworth SW18 157 C4
Buchan Ho W3 110 D4
Buchan Rd SE15 140 C2
Bucharest Rd SW18 158 A4
Buckden Cl N2 48 D5
SE12 165 A5
Buckfast Ct W13 109 A6
Buckfast Ho N14 15 C6
Buckfast Rd SM4 201 D5
Buckfast St E2 96 A4
Buck Hill Wlk
W2 114 B6 246 D5
Buckhold Rd SW18 157 C5
Buckhurst Ave CR4,
SM5 202 D1
Buckhurst Hill Ho IG9 21 B2
Buckhurst Hill Sta IG9 21 D2
Buckhurst Ho 15 N7 71 D3
Buckhurst St E1 96 B3
Buckhurst Way IG9 21 D1
Buckingham Ave
DA16 145 C1
N20 14 B4
East Molesey KT8 173 D1
Buckingham Ave *continued*
Feltham TW14 150 B5
South Norwood CR7 182 C2
Wembley UB6 87 A6
Buckingham Cl BR5 211 C2
Ealing W5 87 C2
Enfield EN1 5 C3
Hampton TW12 173 B5
Buckingham College Sch
HA1 42 C4
Buckingham Ct NW4 46 A6
2 Ealing W7 86 D3
Mitcham CR4 204 A4
Northolt UB5 85 A6
Wembley HA0 65 C2
Buckingham Dr BR7 189 A5
Buckingham Gate
SW1 115 C3 259 B6
Buckingham Gdns
East Molesey KT8 173 D1
Edgware HA8 26 B3
South Norwood CR7 182 C1
Buckingham Gr UB10 82 C5
Buckingham Ho N4 51 A1
1 Acton W3 88 C1
Richmond TW10 154 C6
Buckingham La SE23 163 A4
Buckingham Lo N10 49 C5
Buckingham Mans
NW6 69 D3
Buckingham Mews
7 N1 73 C2
NW10 89 D5
SW1 259 A6
Buckingham Palace*
SW1 115 C4 249 A1
Buckingham Palace Rd
SW1 115 B2 258 D4
Buckingham Pl SW1 259 A6
Buckingham Prim Sch
TW12 173 B5
Buckingham Rd E10 75 D5
E15 76 D3
N1 73 C2
NW10 89 D5
Edgware HA8 26 B3
Hampton TW12,TW13 173 B5
Harrow HA1 42 B4
Ilford IG1 79 B6
Kingston KT1 198 B5
Mitcham CR4 204 A4
Richmond TW10 153 D2
Wanstead E11 55 C4
Woodford E18 36 D2
Wood Green N22 32 A2
Buckingham St WC2 250 B5
Buckingham Way
SM6 219 C1
Buckingham Yd NW10 89 D5
Buck La NW9 45 B4
Buckland Cres NW3 70 B2
Buckland Ct 6 N1 95 C5
Uxbridge UB10 61 A6
Buckland Inf Sch KT9 214 B4
Buckland Rd BR6 227 C4
E10 76 A6
Chessington KT9 214 B3
Buckland Rise HA5 22 D2
Bucklands Rd TW11 175 C4
Buckland St N1 95 B5 235 D3
Buckland Way KT4 200 C1
Buckland Wlk
2 Acton W3 111 A4
Morden SM4 202 A5
Buckleigh Ave SW20 201 B6
Buckleigh Ho SW17 180 B5
Buckleigh Rd SW16 182 A3
Buckleigh Way SE19 183 D3
Buckler Gdns SE9 166 B1
Buckler's Alley SW6 264 D4
Bucklersbury EC2,EC4 242 C1
Bucklers' Way SM5 218 D5
Buckles Ct DA17 124 D2
Buckle St E1 243 D2
9 E1 96 A1
Buckley Cl SE23 162 B4
Buckley Ct 5 NW6 69 B1
Buckley Rd NW6 69 B1
Buckley St SE1 251 A3
Buckmaster Cl SE17 262 B1
1 SW9 138 C2
Buckmaster Ho 1 N7 72 B4
Buckmaster Rd SW11 136 C1
Bucknall St WC1 240 A2
Bucknall Way BR3 208 A5
Bucknell Cl SW2 138 B1
Buckner Rd SW2 138 B1
Buckrell Rd E4 20 B2
Buckridge Bldg EC1 241 A4
Buckshead Ho 19 W2 91 C2
Buck St NW1 71 B1
Buckstone Cl SE23 162 C5
Buckstone Rd N18 34 A5
Buckters Rents SE16 119 A5
Buckthorne Rd SE4 163 A6
Buckthorn Ho DA15 167 D1
Buckwheat Ct DA18 124 D3
Budd Cl N12 29 D6
Buddings Circ HA9 67 A5
Bude Cl E17 53 B4
Budge La CR4 202 D2
Budge Row EC4 242 C1
Budge's Wlk
W2 114 A5 246 B4
Budleigh Cres DA16 146 C4
Budleigh Ho 19 SE15 140 A5
Budoch Ct IG3 80 A6
Budoch Dr IG3 80 A6
Buer Rd SW6 135 A3
Bugsbys Way SE10 120 D2
Bugsby's Way SE7,
SE10 121 B2
Buick Ho 4 E3 97 C3
Bulbarrow NW8 91 D6
Bulganak Rd CR7 205 A5
Bulinca St
SW1 115 D2 259 D3
Bullace Row SE5 139 B4
Bull Alley DA16 146 B2
Bullard Rd TW11 174 D4
Bullards Pl 13 E2 96 D4
Bull Dog The (Juct)
TW15 148 A2
Bulleid Way
SW1 115 B2 258 D3
Bullen Ho 13 E1 96 B3
Bullen St SW11 136 C3
Buller Cl SE15 140 A5
Buller Rd NW10 90 D4
Barking IG11 79 C1
South Norwood CR7 205 B6
Tottenham N17 34 A1
Wood Green N22 32 C1
Bullers Cl DA14 191 A5
Bullers Wood Dr BR7 188 B3
Bullers Wood Sch
BR7 188 B2
Bullescroft Rd HA8 10 D1
Bullfinch Ct 3 SE21 161 B2
Bullingham Mans W8 245 B2
Bull Inn Ct WC2 250 B5
Bullivant St 9 E14 120 A6
Bull La BR7 189 B3
Dagenham RM10 81 D5
Edmonton N18 33 C5
Bull Rd E15 98 D5
Bullrush Cl
Carshalton SM5 218 D6
Thornton Heath CR0 205 C3
Bulls Alley SW14 133 B3
Bulls Bridge Ind Est
UB2 106 B2
Bulls Bridge Rd UB2 106 B2
Bullsbrook Rd UB4 106 C5
Bull's Cross EN1,EN2 6 A6
Bull's Gdns SW3 257 B4
Bulls Head Pas EC3 243 A1
Bull Yd SE15 140 A4
Bulmer Gdns HA3 43 D2
Bulmer Mews
W11 113 C5 245 A4
Bulow Ct 3 SW6 135 D3
Bulstrode Ave TW3 129 C2
Bulstrode Gdns TW3 129 C2
Bulstrode Pl W1 238 B3
Bulstrode Rd TW3 129 C2
Bulstrode St
W1 93 A1 238 B2
Bulwer Court Rd E11 54 B1
Bulwer Ct E11 54 B1
Bulwer Gdns EN5 2 A1
Bulwer Rd E11 54 B1
Edmonton N18 33 C6
New Barnet EN5 2 A1
Bulwer St W12 112 C5
Bunbury Ho SE15 140 A5
Bunces La IG8 36 D3
Bungalow Rd SE25 205 C5
Bungalows The E10 54 A3
Mitcham SW16 181 B3
Bunhill Row
EC1 95 B3 242 C5
Bunhouse Pl SW1 258 B2
Bunkers Hill DA14 169 B1
NW11 48 A2
Bunker's Hill DA17 125 C2
Bunning Ho N7 72 A4
Bunning Way N7 72 B1
Bunn's La NW7 27 D4
Bunsen Ho 1 E3 97 A5
Bunsen St 2 E3 97 A5
Buntingbridge Rd IG2 57 B4
Bunting Cl N9 18 D3
Mitcham CR4 202 D4
Bunting Ct NW9 27 C1
Bunton St SE18 122 C3
Bunyan Ct EC2 242 A4
Bunyan Rd E17 53 A6
Buonaparte Mews
SW1 259 C2
BUPA Bushey Hospl
WD23 8 D3
Burbage Cl
SE1 117 B3 262 C5
Hayes UB3 83 B1
Burbage Ho N1 235 D5
16 SE14 140 D6
Burbage Rd SE21,SE24 161 B4
Burbage Sch N1 95 C5
Burbank KT3 199 D6
Burberry Cl KT3 177 C1
Burbidge Rd TW17 192 C5
Burbridge Way N17 34 A1
Burcham St E14 98 A1
Burcharbro Rd SE2 146 D6
Burchell Ct WD23 8 A4
Burchell Ho SE11 260 D2
Burchell Rd E10 53 D1
SE15 140 B4
Burchetts Way TW17 192 D3
Burchett Way RM6 59 B3
Burcote Rd SW18 158 B4
Burden Cl TW8 109 C1
Burden Ho SW8 270 A3
Burdenshott Ave
TW10 132 D1
Burden Way E11 77 B6
Burder Cl N1 73 C2
Burder Rd N1 73 C2
Burdett Ave SW20 178 A2
Burdett Cl DA14 191 A5
2 Ealing W7 108 D5
Burdett Coutts &
Townshend CE Prim Sch
SW1 115 D2 259 D3
Burdett Mews 4 W2 91 D1
Burdett Rd E3 97 B2
Richmond TW9 132 B2
Thornton Heath CR0 205 B3
Burdetts Rd RM9 103 B6
Burdock Cl CR0 206 D1
Burdock Rd N17 52 A6
Burdon La SM2 217 A1
Burdon Pk SM2 217 B1
Bure Ct 10 EN5 13 D6
Burfield Cl SW17 180 B6
Burford Cl
Dagenham RM8 80 C5
Ickenham UB10 60 A4
Ilford IG6 57 A5
Burford Gdns N13 16 B1
Burford Ho 11 SW9 138 B3
1 Brentford TW8 110 A1
Burford Rd BR1 210 A5
E15 98 B6
E6 100 A4
Brentford TW8 110 A1
Forest Hill SE6 163 B2
New Malden KT4 200 A2
Sutton SM1 217 C6
Burford Way CR0 224 A2
Burford Wlk SW6 265 D3
Burgate Ct 10 SW9 138 C2
Burges Gr SW13 134 B5
Burges Rd E6 78 B1
Burgess Ave NW9 45 B3
Burgess Cl 4 TW13 173 A6
Burgess Ct
3 Southall UB1 85 D1
Wallend E12 78 C1
Burgess Hill NW2 69 C4
Burgess Ho 3 SE5 139 A5
Burgess Ind Pk SE5 139 B5
Burgess Mews SW19 179 D4
Burgess Park Mans
NW6 69 C4
Burgess Rd E15 76 C4
Sutton SM1 217 D4
Burgess St E14 97 C2
Burge St SE1 262 D5
Burghill Rd SE26 185 A6
Burghley Ave
Borehamwood WD6 11 A6
Kingston KT3 177 B2
Burghley Hall Cl
SW19 157 A3
Burghley Ho SW19 157 A1
Burghley Pl CR4 202 D5
Burghley Rd E11 54 C1
N8 50 C6
NW5 71 B4
Wimbledon SW19 179 A6
Burghley Twr W3 111 D6
Burgh St N1 94 D5 234 D4
Burgon St EC4 241 D1
Burgos Cl CR0 220 C2
Burgos Gr SE10 141 D4
Burgoyne Rd N4 50 D3
SW9 138 B2
Ashford TW16 171 D4
South Norwood SE25 205 D5
Burham Cl SE20 184 C3
Burhan Uddin Ho E1 243 C5
Burhill Gr HA5 23 A1
Buriton Ho 9 SW15 156 B3
Burke Cl SW15 133 C1
Burke Ho 1 SW11 136 B1
Burke Lo E13 99 B4
Burke St E16 98 D2
Burket Cl UB2 107 B2
Burland Rd SW11 158 D6
Burleigh Ave DA15 167 D6
Hackbridge SM6 219 B5
Burleigh Ct N17 34 A4
Burleigh Gdns N14 15 C3
Ashford TW15 171 A5
Burleigh Ho SW3 266 D5
Burleigh Ho *continued*
W10 90 D2
Enfield EN1 18 A6
Burleigh Par N14 15 D3
Burleigh Pl SW15 156 D6
Burleigh Rd
Cheam SM3 201 A1
Enfield EN1 5 C1
Hillingdon UB10 82 D6
Burleigh St WC2 250 C6
Burleigh Way EN2 5 B2
Burleigh Wlk SE6 164 A3
Burley Cl Chingford E4 35 C5
Mitcham SW16 181 D1
Burley Ho E1 96 D1
Burley Rd E16 99 C2
Burlington Arc W1 249 A5
Burlington Ave
Richmond TW9 132 C4
Romford RM7 59 D3
Burlington Cl 5 E6 100 A1
W9 91 C3
East Bedfont TW14 149 B4
Orpington BR6 226 D6
Pinner HA5 40 B6
Burlington Ct W4 133 A5
Burlington Danes Sch
W12 90 B1
Burlington Gate SW20 179 A1
Burlington Gdns
W1 115 C6 249 A5
W3 111 A5
W4 111 A1
Dagenham RM6 59 A2
Fulham SW6 135 A3
Burlington Ho NW3 70 B3
Burlington Jun Sch
KT3 199 D5
Burlington La W4 133 B5
Burlington Lo BR7 188 B3
Burlington Mews W3 111 A5
1 Putney SW15 157 B6
Burlington Pl
Fulham SW6 135 A3
Woodford IG8 21 A1
Burlington Rd N10 49 A6
W4 111 A1
Enfield EN2 5 B4
Fulham SW6 135 A3
Hounslow TW7 130 B4
New Malden KT3 199 D5
South Norwood CR7 183 B1
Tottenham N17 34 A2
Burlington Rise EN4 14 D4
Burma Rd N16 73 B4
Burmarsh 6 NW5 71 A2
Burmarsh Ct SE20 184 C2
Burma Terr 11 SE19 183 C5
Burmester Ho SW17 158 A1
Burmester Rd SW17 158 A1
Burnaby Cres W4 133 A6
Burnaby Ct 27 SE16 118 A4
Burnaby Gdns W4 132 D6
Burnaby St
SW10 136 A5 266 B3
Burnand Ho 3 W14 112 D3
Burnaston Ho 5 E5 74 A5
Burnbrae Cl N12 29 D4
Burnbury Rd SW12 159 C3
Burncroft Ave EN3 6 C3
Burndell Way UB4 84 D2
Burne Jones Ho W14 254 B3
Burnell Ave DA16 146 A3
Richmond TW10 175 C5
Burnell Gdns HA7 25 D1
Burnell Ho 10 SW2 160 C3
Burnell Rd SM1 217 D4
Burnell Wlk SE1 263 D2
Burnels Ave E6 100 C4
Burness Cl N7 72 B2
Burne St NW1 237 A4
Burnett Cl E9 74 C3
Burnett Ct SW11 267 A1
Burnett Ho 5 SE13 142 A3
Burney Ave KT5 198 B4
Burney Ho 4 SW16 181 C5
Burney St SE10 142 A5
Burnfoot Ave
SW6 135 A4 264 B1
Burnham NW3 70 C1
Burnham Ave UB10 61 A4
Burnham Cl NW7 28 A3
SE1 263 D3
Enfield EN1 5 C5
Harrow HA3 43 A5
Burnham Cres E11 55 C5
Burnham Ct NW4 46 C5
W2 245 D6
Burnham Dr KT4 216 D6
Burnham Est 8 E2 96 C4
Burnham Gdns
Cranford TW4 128 B4
Croydon CR0 205 D2
Hayes UB3 105 B3
Burnham Rd DA14 169 A2
E4 35 B5
Dagenham RM9 102 B6
Morden SM4 201 D5
Burnham St E2 96 C4
Burnham St *continued*
Kingston KT2 176 C2
Burnham Way W13 109 B3
Penge SE26 185 B5
Burnhill Ho EC1 235 A1
Burnhill Rd BR3 185 C1
Burnley Cl WD19 22 C5
Burnley Rd NW10 68 A3
SW9 138 B3
Burnsall St
SW3 114 C1 257 B2
Burns Ave DA15 168 B5
Feltham TW14 150 A5
Ilford RM6 58 C2
Southall UB1 107 C6
Burns Cl DA16 145 D4
Hayes UB4 84 A2
Mitcham SW17 180 B4
Burns Ct SM6 219 B1
Burns Ho 18 E2 96 C4
11 N16 73 C4
N7 72 B2
SE17 261 D1
Burn's Ho NW10 89 C6
Burnside RM8 58 C1
Burnside Ave E4 35 B4
Burnside Cl SE16 118 D5
Barnet EN5 1 C2
Twickenham TW1 153 A5
Burnside Cres HA0 87 D6
Burns Rd SW11 136 D3
W13 109 B4
Burn's Rd NW10 89 D6
Burns Rd HA0 88 A5
Burns Way TW5 128 D4
Burnt Ash Hill SE12 164 D5
Lewisham SE12 165 A3
Burnt Ash Hts BR1 187 B5
Burnt Ash La BR1,SE12 187 B5
Burnt Ash Prim Sch
BR1 187 A5
Burnt Ash Rd SE12 164 D6
Burnthwaite Rd
SW6 135 B5 264 D3
Burnt Oak Broadway
HA8 26 D2
Burnt Oak Fields HA8 27 A2
Burnt Oak Jun Sch
DA15 168 A3
Burnt Oak La DA15 168 B3
Burnt Oak Sta HA8 27 A2
Burntwood Cl SW18 158 C3
Burntwood Ct SW17 158 A1
Burntwood Grange Rd
SW18 158 C3
Burntwood La SW17 158 B2
Burntwood Sch SW17 158 B2
Burntwood View SE19 183 D5
Buross St E1 96 B1
Burpham Cl UB4 84 D2
Burrage Ct 17 SE16 118 D2
Burrage Gr SE18 123 A2
Burrage Pl SE18 122 D1
Burrage Rd SE18 123 A1
Burrard Ho 11 E2 96 C5
Burrard Rd NW6 69 C4
Newham E16 99 B1
Burr Cl DA7 147 B2
E1 118 A5
Burrel Ct HA1 42 B2
Burrell Cl Croydon CR0 207 A3
Edgware HA8 10 D2
Burrell Ho 4 TW1 153 B4
Burrell Row BR3 185 C1
Burrells 9 BR3 185 D1
Burrell St SE1 116 D5 251 C4
Burrell's Wharf Sq
E14 119 D1
Burrell Twrs E10 53 C2
Burrhill Ct SE16 118 D3
Burritt Rd KT1 176 C1
Burrmead Ct NW2 67 D5
Burroughs Gdns NW4 46 B5
Burroughs The NW4 46 B5
Burrow Ho 19 SW9 138 B3
Burrow Rd SE22 139 C1
Burrows Mews SE1 251 C2
Burrows Rd NW10 90 C4
Burrow Wlk SE21 161 A4
Burr Rd SW18 157 C4
Bursar St SE1 253 A3
Bursdon Cl DA15 167 D2
Bursland Rd EN3 6 D1
Burslem St E1 96 A1
Bursted Wood Prim Sch
DA7 147 D3
Burstock Rd SW15 135 A1
Burston Rd SW15 156 D6
Burstow Rd SW20 179 A2
Burtenshaw Rd KT7 197 A3
Burtley Cl N4 51 A1
Burton Bank N1 73 B1
Burton Cl
Chessington KT9 213 D1
South Norwood CR7 205 B6
Burton Ct SW3 257 D2

Burton Ct *continued*
Thames Ditton KT7 197 A3
Burton Dr EN3 7 C6
Burton Gdns TW5 129 B4
Burton Gr SE17 262 C1
Burton Ho 6 SE16 118 B4
SE5 138 D4
Penge SE26 184 B5
Burtonhole Cl NW7 28 D6
Burtonhole La NW7 28 D6
Burton Lo 5 SW15 157 B6
Burton Mews SW1 258 B3
Burton Pl WC1 232 D1
Burton Rd NW6 69 B1
SW9 138 D3
8 SW9 138 C3
Kingston KT2 176 A3
Wanstead E18 55 B6
Burtons Ct E15 76 B1
Burtons Rd TW12 174 A6
Burton St WC1 93 D3 239 D6
Burtonwood Ho N4 51 B2
Burt Rd E16 121 C5
Burtt Ho 6 N1 95 C4
Burtwell La SE21,SE27 183 B6
Burwash Ho SE1 252 D1
Burwash Rd SE18 123 B1
Burwell 2 KT1 176 C1
Burwell Ave UB6 64 C2
Burwell Cl 25 E1 96 B1
Burwell Rd E10 53 A1
Burwell Wlk 14 E3 97 C3
Burwood Ave BR2 225 B6
Pinner HA5 40 C4
Burwood Cl KT6 198 C1
Burwood Ct SE23 162 C4
Burwood Ho 11 SW9 138 D1
Burwood Pl W2 237 B2
Bury Ave Hayes UB4 83 C5
Ruislip HA4 39 A3
Bury Cl SE16 118 D5
Bury Ct EC3 243 B2
Bury Gr SM4 201 D4
Bury Hall Villas N9 17 D4
Bury Pl WC1 94 A2 240 B3
Bury Rd N22 50 C6
Chingford E4 20 C6
Dagenham RM10 81 D3
Buryside Cl IG2 57 D5
Bury St EC3 95 C1 243 B2
SW1 115 C5 249 B4
Edmonton N9 18 A3
Ruislip HA4 39 B3
Bury St W N9 17 C4
Bury Wlk SW3 114 C1 257 A2
Burywood Ct EN3 6 C3
Busbridge Ho 16 E14 97 C2
Busby Ho SW16 181 C6
Busby Pl NW5 71 D2
Busch Cl TW7 131 B4
Busch Cnr TW7 131 B4
Bushbaby Cl SE1 263 A5
Bushberry Rd E9 75 A2
Bush Cl IG2 57 B4
Bush Cotts 12 SW18 157 C6
Bush Ct N14 15 C3
7 W12 112 D4
Bushell Cl SW2 160 B2
Bushell Gn WD23 8 B2
Bushell Ho 3 SE27 183 A6
Bushell St E1 118 A5
Bushell Way BR7 188 C5
Bushey Ave BR5 211 B2
E18 54 D6
Bushey Cl Chingford E4 20 A1
Ickenham UB10 60 C6
Bushey Ct SW20 178 B1
Bushey Down SW12 159 B2
Bushey Fst Sch KT3 200 B6
Bushey Hall SE5 139 D4
Bushey Heath Prim Sch
WD23 8 B3
Bushey Hill Rd SE5 139 D4
Bushey Ho SE12 165 C1
Bushey La SM1 217 C4
Bushey Lees DA15 167 D5
Bushey Meads Sch
WD23 8 A6
Bushey Mid Sch SW20 200 B6
Bushey Rd E13 99 C5
N15 51 C3
Croydon CR0 223 C6
Hayes UB3 105 C2
Ickenham UB10 60 C6
Sutton SM1 217 C4
West Barnes SW20 178 D1
Bushey Way BR3 208 B4
Bush Fair Ct N14 15 B5
Bushfield Cl HA8 10 D2
Bushfield Cres HA8 10 D2
Bushfield Ho N5 73 A3
Bush Gr NW9 45 A2
Stanmore HA7 25 D2
Bushgrove Rd RM8 80 D5
Bush Hill N21 17 A5
Bush Hill Par EN1 17 B4
Bush Hill Park Prim Sch
EN1 18 A6
Bush Hill Park Sta EN1 17 D5
Bush Hill Rd Enfield N21 17 B5
Harrow HA3 44 B3
Bush Ind Est NW10 89 B3
Bush La EC4 117 B6 252 C6
Bushmead Cl 6 N15 51 D5
Bushmoor Cres SE18 144 D5
Bushnell Rd SW17 159 B1
Bush Rd E8 96 B6
SE8 118 D2
Littleton TW17 192 B4
Richmond TW9 132 B6
Wanstead E11 55 A2
Woodford IG9 37 D6
Bushway RM8 80 D5
Bushwood E11 55 A1
Bushwood Dr
SE1 117 D2 263 D3
Bushwood Rd TW9 132 C6
Bushy Ct KT1 175 C2
Bushy Park Gdns
TW12 174 B5
Bushy Park Rd TW11 175 B3
Bushy Rd TW11 174 D3
Business Acad The
DA18 125 A4
Business Design Ctr*
N1 94 C6 234 B5
Buspace Studios 3
W10 91 A3
Butcher Row E1 96 D1
Butchers Rd E16 99 A1
Bute Ave TW10 154 A2
Bute Ct SM6 219 C3
Bute Gdns W6 112 D2
Wallington SM6 219 C3
Bute Gdns W SM6 219 C3
Bute House Prep Sch
W6 112 D2
Bute Rd Ilford IG6 56 D4
Thornton Heath CR0 204 C1
Wallington SM6 219 C4
Bute St SW7 114 B2 256 C4
Butfield Ho 6 E9 74 C2
Butler Ave HA1 42 B2
Butler Ct Dagenham RM8 81 C6
Wembley HA0 65 A4
Butler Ho 13 E14 97 B1
32 E2 96 C4
5 SW9 138 D4
Butler Pl SW1 259 C6
Butler Rd NW10 67 D1
Dagenham RM8 80 B4
Harrow HA1 42 A2
Butler's Cotts DA7 147 C3
Butler St 33 E2 96 C4
Hillingdon UB10 82 D3
Butler's Wharf W SE1 253 C3
Butley Ct 7 E3 97 A5
Butterfield Cl 1 SE16 118 B4
Tottenham N17 33 A4
Twickenham TW1 152 D5
Butterfield Row EN2 5 A2
Butterfields E17 54 A4
Butterfield Sq 10 E6 100 B1
Butterfly La SE9 166 D5
Butterfly Wlk 2 SE5 139 B4
Butter Hill SM5,SM6 219 A4
Butteridges Cl RM9 103 B6
Buttermere NW1 231 D2
Buttermere Cl E11 76 B4
SE1 263 C3
East Bedfont TW14 149 D3
West Barnes SM4 200 D3
Buttermere Ct NW8 229 C6
Buttermere Dr SW15 157 A6
Buttermere Ho 11 E3 97 B4
N12 30 C5
Buttermere Wlk 9 E8 73 D2
Butterwick W6 112 C2
Butterworth Ct SW16 160 A1
Butterworth Gdns IG8 37 A5
Buttesland St
N1 95 B4 235 D2
Buttfield Cl RM10 81 D2
Buttmarsh Cl SE18 122 D1
Buttsbury Rd IG1 79 A3
Butts Cotts TW13 151 B1
Butts Cres TW13 151 C1
Butts Ho TW13 151 C1
Butts Piece UB5 84 B5
Butts Rd BR1 186 C5
Butts The TW8 131 D6
Buxhall Cres E9 75 B2
Buxlow Prep Sch HA9 66 A5
Buxted Rd E8 73 D1
N12 30 C5
SE22 139 C1
Buxton Cl N9 18 C2
Woodford IG8 37 D4
Buxton Cres SM3 217 A4
Buxton Ct N1 235 B2
Buxton Dr E11 54 C5
Kingston KT3 177 B1
Buxton Gdns W3 110 D6
Buxton Ho E11 54 C5
3 SW11 136 B1
Buxton Lo E11 77 B6
Buxton Rd E15 76 C3
E17 53 A5
E6 100 A4
N19 49 D1
NW2 68 B2
Chingford E4 20 B4
Ilford IG2 57 C3
Mortlake SW14 133 C2
Thornton Heath CR7 204 D4
Buxton St E1 96 A3 243 D5
Buzzard Creek Ind Est
IG11 102 A2
Byam Shaw Sch of Art
N19 71 D6
Byam St SW6 136 A3
Byards Croft SW16 181 D2
Byards Ct SE16 118 D3
Byas Ho 6 E3 97 B4
Byatt Wlk TW12 173 A4
Bychurch End 9
TW11 174 D5
Bycroft Rd UB1 85 C3
Bycroft St SE20 184 D3
Bycullah Ave EN2 4 D3
Bycullah Rd EN2 4 D3
Byefield Cl SE16 119 A4
Byelands Cl 12 SE16 118 D5
Bye The W3 89 C1
Byeways TW2 151 D1
Byeways The KT5 198 D4
Byeway The SW14 133 A2
Bye Way The HA3 24 D2
Byfeld Gdns SW13 134 A4
Byfield Ct KT3 200 A5
Byfield Rd TW7 131 A2
Byford Cl E15 76 C1
Bygrove CR0 223 D1
Bygrove Ct SW19 180 B4
Bygrove Prim Sch E14 97 D1
Bygrove Rd SW19 180 B4
Bygrove St E14 97 D1
Byland Cl N21 16 B4
Bylands Cl SE2 124 B3
Byne Rd
Carshalton SM5 218 C6
Forest Hill SE26 184 C5
Bynes Rd CR2 221 B1
Byng Pl WC1 93 D3 239 C5
Byng St E14 119 C4
Bynon Ave DA7 147 B2
Byre Rd N14 15 B5
Byrne Ho 11 SW2 160 B6
Byrne Rd SW12 159 B2
Byron Ave E12 78 A2
NW9 44 D6
Borehamwood WD6 10 C6
Cranford TW4 128 B3
Sutton SM1 218 B4
West Barnes KT3 200 A4
Woodford E18 36 D1
Byron Ave E SM1 218 B4
Byron Cl E8 96 A6
SE28 124 C5
Feltham TW12 173 B6
Forest Hill SE26 185 A6
Streatham SW16 182 A4
Walton-on-T KT12 195 A1
Byron Court Prim Sch
HA0 65 C6
Byron Ct 3 NW6 70 A1
SW3 257 B3
W7 109 A2
W9 91 C3
WC1 240 C6
Dulwich SE21 162 A3
Enfield EN2 4 D3
Harrow HA1 42 C3
1 Richmond TW10 175 D6
South Norwood CR7 183 A1
11 Wanstead E11 55 A5
Woodford E18 37 B2
Byron Dr DA8 147 D5
N2 48 B3
Byron Gdns SM1 218 C4
Byron Hill Rd HA1,HA2 64 C6
Byron Ho 5 BR3 185 D4
Byron Mews NW3 70 C4
Byron Par UB10 83 A3
Byron Rd E10 53 D1
E17 53 C6
NW2 68 B6
NW7 28 A5
Ealing W5 110 B5
Harrow HA1 42 C3
Harrow HA3 24 D1
Wembley HA0 65 C5
Byron St E14 98 A1
Byron Way Hayes UB4 83 D3
Northolt UB5 85 A4
West Drayton UB7 104 B2
Bysouth Cl N15 51 B5
Bythorn St SW9 138 B1
Byton Rd SW17 180 D4
Byward Ave TW14 150 C5
Byward St EC3 117 C6 253 B5
Bywater Ho SE18 122 A3
Bywater Pl SE16 119 A5
Bywater St
SW3 114 D1 257 C2
Byways The KT19 215 D4
Bywell Pl W1 239 A3
Bywood Ave CR0 206 D3
Bywood Terr CR0 206 C3
Byworth Wlk N19 50 A1

C

Cabbell St NW1 92 C2 237 A3
Cabinet Off SW1 250 A2
Cabinet War Rooms*
SW1 115 D4 249 D2
Cabinet Way E4 35 B4
Cable Ho WC1 234 A2
Cable Pl SE10 142 A4
Cable St E1 118 B6
Cabot Ct SE16 118 D3
Cabot Sq E14 119 C5
Cabot Way 3 E6 99 D6
Cabul Rd SW11 136 C3
Cactus Cl SE5 139 C3
Cactus Wlk W12 89 D1
Cadbury Cl
Ashford TW16 171 C3
Isleworth TW7 131 A4
Cadbury Rd TW16 171 C4
Cadbury Way 1 SE16 118 A2
Caddington Cl EN4 14 C6
Caddington Rd NW2 69 A5
Caddis Cl HA7 24 D3
Cadell Cl E2 95 D5
Cadell Ho 12 E2 95 D5
Cade Rd SE10 142 B4
Cader Rd SW18 158 A5
Cadet Dr SE1 117 D1 263 D2
Cade Tyler Ho 10
SE10 142 A4
Cadiz St SE17 117 A1 262 B1
Cadley Terr SE23 162 C2
Cadman Cl SW9 138 D5
Cadmer Cl KT3 199 C5
Cadmore Ho 4 N1 72 D1
Cadmus Cl 9 SW4 137 D2
Cadmus Ct 6 SW9 138 C4
Cadnam Lo E14 120 B3
Cadnam Point 15
SW15 156 B3
Cadogan Cl E9 75 B1
Beckenham BR3 186 B1
Harrow HA2 63 D4
Teddington TW11 174 C5
Cadogan Ct SW3 257 C3
Sutton SM2 217 D2
New Malden KT3 199 C5
Cadogan Ct Gdns
SW1 258 A4
Cadogan Gate
SW1 114 D2 257 D4
Cadogan Gdns N3 29 D2
SW3 114 D2 257 D3
Southgate N21 16 C6
Wanstead E18 55 B6
Cadogan Ho SW3 266 D5
Cadogan La
SW1 115 A3 258 A5
Cadogan Pl
SW1 114 D3 257 D5
Cadogan Rd SE18 123 A3
Kingston KT6 197 D4
Cadogan Sq
SW1 114 D3 257 D5
Cadogan St
SW3 114 D2 257 C3
Cadogan Terr E9 75 B1
Cadoxton Ave 3 N15 51 D3
Cadwallon Rd SE9 167 A2
Caedmon Rd N7 72 B4
Caerleon Cl
Claygate KT10 213 B1
Sidcup DA14 190 C5
Caerleon Terr SE2 124 B2
Caernarvon Cl CR4 204 A6
Caernarvon Ct 3 KT5 198 B4
Caernarvon Ho W2 236 A2
Caesar Ct 28 E2 96 D5
Caesar's Way TW17 193 B3
Caesars Wlk CR4 202 D4
Cahill St EC1 242 B5
Cahir St E14 119 D2
Cain Ct 2 W5 87 C2
Caine Ho W3 110 D4
Cain's La TW14 149 C6
Caird St W10 91 B4
Cairn Ave W5 109 D5
Cairndale Cl BR1 186 D3
Cairnfield Ave NW2 67 D5
Cairnfield Ct NW2 67 C5
Cairns Ho 3 N7 72 B4
Cairns Mews SE18 144 A4
Cairns Rd SW11 158 C6
Cairn Way HA7 24 D4
Cairo New Rd CR0 220 D6
Cairo Rd E17 53 C5
Caister Ho N7 72 B2
10 Balham SW12 159 B4
Caistor Ho 5 E15 98 D6
Caistor Mews SW12 159 B4
Caistor Park Rd E15 98 D6
Caistor Rd SW12 159 B4
Caithness Gdns DA15 167 D5
Caithness Ho N1 233 C6
Caithness Rd W14 112 D3
Mitcham CR4 181 B3
Calabria Rd N5 72 D3
Calais Gate SE5 138 D4
Calais St SE5 138 D4
Calbourne Rd SW12 159 A4
Calcott Wlk SE9 187 D6
Calcraft Ho 10 E2 96 C5
Caldbeck Ave KT4 200 B1
Caldecot Ct SE5 139 A3
Caldecote 3 KT1 176 C1
Caldecote Gdns WD23 8 C4
Caldecote La WD23 8 D5
Caldecot Rd SE5 139 A3
Caldecott Way E5 74 D5
Calder Ave UB6 86 D5
Calder Cl EN1 5 C2
Calder Ct SE16 119 B5
Calder Gdns HA8 44 C6
Calderon Ho NW8 230 A4
Calderon Pl W10 90 C2
Calderon Rd E11 76 B5
Calder Rd SM4 202 A4
Caldervale Rd SW4 159 D6
Calderwood St SE18 122 C2
Caldew Ct NW7 28 A3
Caldew St SE5 139 B5
Caldicote Gn NW9 45 C3
Caldwell Rd WD19 22 D6
Caldwell St
SW9 138 B5 270 D3
Caldy Rd DA17 125 D3
Caldy Wlk 15 N1 73 A2
Caleb St SE1 252 B2
Caledonia Ct IG11 102 C5
Caledonia Ho 17 E14 97 A1
Caledonian Cl 1 IG3 58 B1
Caledonian Market
SE1 117 C3 263 B6
Caledonian Rd
N1 94 B6 233 C5
N7 72 B2
Caledonian Road &
Barnsbury Sta N7 72 B1
Caledonian Road Sta
N7 72 B2
Caledonian Wharf Rd
E14 120 B2
Caledonia Rd TW19 148 A3
Caledonia St N1 233 B3
Caledon Rd E6 78 B1
Hackbridge SM5,SM6 219 A4
Cale St SW3 114 C1 257 A2
Caletock Way SE10 120 D1
Calgarth NW1 232 B3
Calgary Ct 24 SE16 118 C4
Caliban Twr 9 N1 95 C5
Calico Ho 4 SW11 136 A2
Calico Row 5 SW11 136 A2
Calidore Cl SW2 160 B5
California La WD23 8 B3
California Rd KT3 199 A6
Callaby Terr 11 N1 73 B2
Callaghan Cl SE13 142 C1
Callahan Cotts 8 E1 96 C2
Callander Rd SE6 164 A2
Callanders The WD23 8 C3
Callard Ave N13 32 D6
Callcott Ct NW6 69 B1
Callcott Rd NW6 69 B1
Callcott St W8 245 A4
Callendar Rd SW7 256 C6
Callingham Cl 17 E14 97 B2
Callingham Ho 1
SW4 138 A2
Callis Farm Cl TW19 148 A5
Callis Rd E17 53 B3
Callonfield 3 E17 53 A5
Callow St SW3 136 B6 266 C6
Calmington Rd SE5 139 C6
Calmont Rd BR1 186 C4
Calonne Rd SW19 178 D6
Calshot Ho N1 233 C4
Calshot Rd TW6 126 D3
Calshot St N1 94 B5 233 C3
Calshot Way Enfield EN2 4 D2
Harlington TW6 126 C3
Calstock NW1 232 C5
Calstock Ho SE11 261 B2
Calthorpe Gdns
Edgware HA8 26 B5
Sutton SM1 218 A5
Calthorpe St
WC1 94 B3 240 D6
Calton Ave SE21 161 C5
Calton Rd EN5 14 B5
Calver 13 NW5 71 B4
Calver Ct E17 54 B6
Calverley Cl BR3 185 D4
Calverley Cres RM10 81 C6
Calverley Gr N19 49 D1
Calverley Rd KT17 216 A2
Calvert Ave E2 95 D4
Calvert Cl
Belvedere DA17 125 D2
Sidcup DA14 191 A4
Calvert Ct 1 N19 49 C1
5 Richmond TW9 132 B1
Calvert Ho 9 W12 112 B6
Calverton SE5 139 C6
Calverton Prim Sch
E16 99 D1
Calverton Rd E6 100 C6
Calvert Rd SE10 120 D1
Calvert's Bldgs SE1 252 C3
Calvert St NW1 93 A6 231 A6
Calvin St E1 95 D3 243 C5
Calydon Rd SE7 121 B1
Calypso Cres 5 SE15 139 D5
Calypso Way SE8,SE16 119 B2
Camac Rd TW2 152 B3
Camarthen Gn NW9 45 C3
Cambalt Ho 3 SW15 156 D6
Cambalt Rd SW15 156 D6
Cambell Inf Sch RM9 80 D1
Cambell Jun Sch RM9 80 D1
Cambell Wlk N1 233 B6
Camber Ho 4 SE15 140 C6
Camberley Ave
Enfield EN1 5 C1
Wimbledon SW20 178 B1
Camberley Cl SM3 216 D5
Camberley Ct 8 SM2 217 D1
Camberley Ho NW1 231 D3
Camberley Rd TW6 126 C2
Cambert Way SE9 143 B1
Camberwell Church St
SE5 139 B4
Camberwell Coll of Arts
SE15 139 D5
SE5 139 C4
Camberwell Glebe
SE5 139 C4
Camberwell Gn SE5 139 B4
Camberwell Gr SE5 139 C3
Camberwell Green
SE5 139 A4
Camberwell New Rd
SW9 138 D5
Camberwell Rd SE5 139 A5
Camberwell Station Rd
SE5 139 A4
Camberwell Trad Est
SE5 139 A4
Cambeys Rd RM10 81 D3
Cambisgate SW19 179 A5
Camborne Ave W13 109 C4
Camborne Cl TW6 126 C2
Camborne Cres TW6 126 C2
Camborne Rd DA16 145 D3
Belmont SM2 217 D1
Croydon CR0 206 A2
Sidcup DA14 168 C1
Wandsworth SW18 157 C4
West Barnes SM4 200 D4
Harmondsworth TW6 126 C2
Camborne Way
Harlington TW6 126 C2
Heston TW5 129 C4
Cambourne Ave N9 18 D4
Cambourne Mews 6
W11 91 A1
Cambray Rd BR6 211 D2
Streatham SW12 159 C3
Cambria 6 BR3 185 D1
Cambria Cl DA15 167 C3
Hounslow TW3 129 C1
Cambria Ct TW14 150 B4
Cambria Gdns TW19 148 A4
Cambria Ho 16 E14 97 A1
Forest Hill SE26 184 A6
Cambrian Ave IG2 57 C4
Cambrian Cl SE27 160 D1
Cambrian Ct UB2 107 D2
Cambrian Gn NW9 45 C4
Cambrian Rd E10 53 C1
Richmond TW10 154 B5
Cambria Rd SE5 139 A2
Cambria St
SW6 135 D5 265 D3
Cambridge Ave DA16 145 D1
NW6 91 C5
Greenford UB6 64 D3
Kingston KT3,SW20 177 D1
Cambridge Barracks Rd 12
SE18 122 B2
Cambridge Cir
WC2 93 D1 239 D1
Cambridge Cl E17 53 B3
NW10 67 A5
Hounslow TW4 129 A1
Wimbledon SW20 178 B2
Wood Green N22 32 C2
Cambridge Cotts TW9 132 C6
Cambridge Cres 20 E2 96 B5
Teddington TW11 175 A5
Cambridge Ct 25 E2 96 B5
N16 51 C2
2 NW6 91 C5
Wimbledon SW20 178 B2
Cambridge Dr SE12 165 A6
Ruislip HA4 62 D6

Cambridge Gate NW1 238 C6
Cambridge Gate Mews NW1 238 D6
Cambridge Gdns N10 31 B2
NW6 91 C5
W10 91 A1
Enfield EN1 6 A3
Kingston KT1 176 C1
Southgate N21 17 B4
Tottenham N17 33 B3
Cambridge Gn SE9 166 D3
Cambridge Gr W6 112 B2
Penge SE20 184 B2
Cambridge Grove Rd
Kingston KT1 198 C6
13 Kingston KT1 176 C1
Cambridge Heath Rd
E1,E2 96 B4
Cambridge Heath Sta
E2 96 B5
Cambridge Ho
Ealing W13 87 A1
Fulham SW6 135 A2
2 Teddington TW11 175 A5
7 Woolwich SE18 122 B2
Cambridge Mans
SW11 267 C1
Cambridge Par EN1 6 A4
Cambridge Park Ct
TW1 153 D4
Cambridge Park Rd
E11 55 A2
Cambridge Pas 9 E9 74 C1
Cambridge Pk
Twickenham TW1 153 D5
Wanstead E11 55 A3
Cambridge Pl W8 245 D1
Cambridge Rd BR1 187 A3
E11 54 D3
NW6 91 C4
NW6 91 C5
SW11 136 D4 267 C1
W7 108 D4
Barking IG11 79 A1
Barnes SW13 133 D3
Carshalton SM5 218 C3
3 Chingford E4 20 B3
East Molesey KT8 195 B5
Hampton TW12 173 B3
Harrow HA2 41 C4
Hounslow TW4 129 A1
Ilford IG3 57 C1
Kingston KT1 176 C1
Littleton TW15 171 A3
Mitcham CR4 203 C6
New Malden KT3 199 C5
Penge SE20 206 B6
Richmond TW9 132 C5
Sidcup DA14 189 C6
Southall UB1 107 B5
Teddington TW11 175 A5
Twickenham TW1 153 D5
Walton-on-T KT12 194 B3
Wimbledon SW20 178 B2
Cambridge Rd N W4 110 D1
Cambridge Rd S 3 W4 110 D1
Cambridge Row SE18 122 D1
Cambridge Sch W6 112 B2
Cambridge Sq
W2 92 C1 237 A2
Cambridge St
SW1 115 C1 259 A2
Cambridge Terr NW1 231 C1
Edmonton N9 17 D4
Cambridge Terr Mews
NW1 231 D1
Cambstone Cl N11 15 A2
Cambus Cl UB4 85 A2
Cambus Rd E16 99 A2
Cam Ct 2 SE15 139 D6
Camdale Rd SE18 145 D5
Camden Ave
Feltham TW13 150 C3
Hayes UB4 106 D6
Camden Cl BR7 189 A2
Camden Ct 9 DA17 125 C1
Camden Gdns NW1 71 B1
Sutton SM1 217 D3
Thornton Heath CR7 204 D6
Camden Gr BR7 188 D4
Camden High St
NW1 93 C6 232 A5
Camden Hill Rd SE19 183 C4
Camden Ho 6 SE8 119 B1
Camdenhurst St E14 97 A1
Camden Jun Sch SM5 218 D4
Camden Lock Pl NW1 71 B1
Camden Mews NW1 71 D2
Camden Mkt*
NW1 93 B6 231 D6
Camden Park Rd BR7 188 C3
NW1 71 D2
Camden Pas N1 94 D6 234 C5
Camden Rd DA5 169 B4
E17 53 B3
NW1 71 D2 231 D6
Carshalton SM5 218 D4
Sutton SM1 217 D3
Camden Rd *continued*
Wanstead E11 55 B3
Camden Road Sta NW1 71 C1
Camden Row SE3 142 C3
Camden Sch for Girls The
NW5 71 C2
Camden Sq NW1 71 D2
Camden St
NW1 93 C6 232 B5
Camden Studios NW1 232 B5
Camden Town Sta
NW1 93 B6 231 D6
Camden Way BR7 188 C3
Thornton Heath CR7 204 D6
Camden Wlk N1 234 C5
Cameford Ct 20 SW12 160 A4
Camel Ct HA9 66 D6
Camelford NW1 232 B5
Camelford Ct 7 W11 91 A1
Camelford Wlk 8 W11 91 A1
Camel Gr KT2 175 D5
Camelia Ct IG8 36 C4
Camellia Ct 20 BR3 185 C3
Camellia Ho SE8 141 B5
Camellia Pl TW2 151 D4
Camellia St SW8 270 A3
Camelot Cl SE18 123 B4
Wimbledon SW19 179 C6
Camelot Ho 6 NW1 71 D2
Camelot Prim Sch
SE15 140 B6
Camel Rd E16 121 D5
Camera Pl SW10 266 C6
Cameret Ct 6 W11 112 D4
Cameron Cl N20 14 C2
Edmonton N18 34 B5
Cameron Ct 3 SW19 157 A3
Cameron Ho NW8 230 A4
SE5 139 A5
8 Bromley BR1 186 D2
Cameron House Sch
SW10 266 D5
Cameron Lo TW3 130 A1
Cameron Rd BR2 209 A4
Forest Hill SE6 163 B2
Ilford IG3 57 C1
Thornton Heath CR0 204 D3
Cameron Sq CR4 180 C2
Camerton Cl 8 E8 73 D2
Camfrey Ct N8 50 A5
Camgate Ctr The
TW19 148 B4
Camilla Cl TW16 171 D4
Camilla Ct 14 SM2 217 C1
Camilla Rd SE16 118 B2
Camille Cl SE25 206 A6
Camlan Rd BR1 186 D6
Camlet St E2 243 C6
Camlet Way EN4 1 D4
Camley St NW1 93 D5 232 D4
Camm 23 NW9 27 D1
Camm Gdns
5 Kingston KT1 176 B1
Thames Ditton KT7 196 D2
Camomile Ave CR4 180 D2
Camomile St
EC3 95 C1 243 B2
Camomile Way UB7 82 A1
Campaign Ct W9 91 B3
Campana Rd
SW6 135 C4 265 B2
Campasps Bsns Pk
TW16 193 D4
Campbell Ave IG6 57 A5
Campbell Cl SE18 144 C4
Ruislip HA4 40 A3
Streatham SW16 181 D6
Twickenham TW2 152 B3
Campbell Croft HA8 26 C5
Campbell Ct NW9 45 A3
SW7 256 A5
Dulwich SE21 162 A3
Ealing W7 108 C6
Tottenham N17 33 D2
Campbell Gordon Way
NW2 68 B4
Campbell Ho SW1 259 A1
30 W12 112 B6
W2 236 C5
6 Wallington SM6 219 B4
Campbell Rd E15 76 D4
E17 53 B5
E3 97 C4
E6 100 A6
Ealing W7 108 C6
Thornton Heath CR0 204 D3
Tottenham N17 34 A2
Twickenham TW2 152 B2
Campdale Rd N7 71 D5
Campden Cres
Dagenham RM8 80 C4
Wembley HA0 65 B5
Campden Gr
W8 113 C4 245 B2
Campden Hill
W8 113 C4 245 A2
Campden Hill Ct W8 245 B2
Campden Hill Gate
W8 245 A2
Campden Hill Gdns
W8 245 A4
Campden Hill Mans
W8 245 B4
Campden Hill Pl W14 244 D4
Campden Hill Rd
W8 113 C4 245 A2
Campden Hill Sq
W14 113 B5 244 D4
Campden Ho 4 NW6 70 B1
W8 245 B3
Campden Hos W8 245 A3
Campden House Cl
W8 245 B2
Campden Rd
Ickenham UB10 60 B4
South Croydon CR2 221 C3
Campden St
W8 113 C5 245 A3
Campe Ho 1 N10 31 A3
Campen Cl SW19 157 A2
Camperdown St E1 243 D1
Campfield Rd SE9 165 D4
Campion Cl Harrow HA3 44 B3
Hillingdon UB8 82 B2
Newham E6 122 B6
South Croydon CR2 221 C4
Campion Ct 10 HA0 88 A5
Campion Gdns IG8 37 A5
Campion Ho 15 N16 73 C3
Campion House (Seminary)
TW7 130 B4
Campion Pl SE28 124 B5
Campion Rd
Hounslow TW7 130 D4
Putney SW15 156 C6
Campion Terr NW2 68 D5
Campion Way HA8 27 A6
Camplin Rd HA3 44 A4
Camplin St SE14 140 D5
Camp Rd SW19 178 C5
Campsbourne Ho 3
N8 50 A5
Campsbourne Jun & Inf
Schs N8 50 A6
Campsbourne The N8 50 A5
Campsey Gdns RM9 80 B1
Campsey Rd RM9 80 B1
Campsfield Ho N8 50 A6
Campsfield Rd N8 50 A6
Campshill Pl SE13 164 A6
Campshill Rd SE13 164 A6
Camp Site The BR8 191 C3
Campton Hill Twrs
W8 245 A4
Campus Rd E17 53 B3
Camp View SW19 178 B5
Cam Rd E15 98 B6
Camrose Ave DA8 147 D6
Edgware HA8 26 B2
Feltham TW13 172 C6
Camrose Cl
Croydon CR0 207 A2
Morden SM4 201 C5
Camrose St SE2 124 A2
Camsey Ho 8 SW2 160 B6
Canada Ave N18 33 A4
Canada Cres W3 89 A3
Canada Gdns SE13 164 A6
Canada Rd W3 89 A2
Canada Sq E14 119 D5
Canada St SE16 118 D4
Canada Way W12 112 B6
Canadian Ave SE6 163 D3
Canal App SE8 141 A6
Canal Bldg N1 235 A4
Canal Bridge SE15 140 A6
Canal Cl E1 97 A3
W10 90 D3
Canal Gr SE15 140 B6
Canal Head Public Sq
SE15 140 A4
Canal Path 22 E2 95 D6
Canalside Studios 31
N1 95 C6
Canal St SE5 139 B6
Canal Way W10 90 D3
Canal Wlk N1 95 B6 235 D6
Croydon CR0 205 D3
Forest Hill SE26 184 C5
Canary Wharf* E14 119 D5
Canary Wharf Pier River
Bus) E14 119 B5
Canary Wharf Sta E14 119 C5
Canberra Cl NW4 46 A6
Canberra Dr UB4 84 C4
Canberra Prim Sch
W12 112 B6
Canberra Rd E6 100 B6
SE7 143 D6
Erith DA7 146 D6
Harlington TW6 126 C2
Canbury 2000 Bsns Pk 3
KT2 176 A2
Canbury Ave KT2 176 B2
Canbury Ct KT2 176 A3
Canbury Mews SE26 162 A1
Canbury Park Rd KT2 176 B2
Canbury Sch KT2 176 D4
Cancell Rd SW9 138 C4
Candahar Rd SW11 136 C3
Candida Ct 9 NW1 71 B1
Candishe Ho SE1 253 C2
Candler Mews TW1 153 A4
Candler St N15 51 B3
Candover St W1 239 A3
Candy St E3 97 B6
Caney Mews NW2 68 D6
Canfield Dr HA4 62 B3
Canfield Gdns NW6 69 D1
Canfield Ho N15 51 C3
Canfield Pl NW6 70 A2
Canford Ave UB5 85 A6
Canford Cl EN2 4 C3
Canford Gdns KT3 199 C3
Canford Pl TW11 175 C4
Canford Rd SW11 159 A6
Canham Rd W3 111 C4
South Norwood SE25 205 C6
Canmore Gdns SW16 181 C3
Cann Hall Prim Sch
E11 76 D5
Cann Hall Rd E11 76 D4
Cann Ho W14 254 B5
Canning Cres N22 32 B2
Canning Cross SE5 139 C3
Canning Ct N22 32 B2
Canning Ho 23 W12 112 B6
Canning Pas
W8 114 A3 256 A6
Canning Pl
W8 114 A3 256 A6
Canning Pl Mews W8 256 A6
Canning Rd E15 98 C5
E17 53 A6
N5 72 D5
Croydon CR0 221 D6
Harrow HA3 42 D6
Cannington 14 NW5 71 A2
Cannington Rd RM9 80 C2
Canning Town E16 98 C2
Canning Town Sta E16 98 C2
Cannizaro Rd SW19 178 D5
Cannock Ho N4 51 B2
Cannock Lo EN1 17 C5
Cannonbury Ave HA5 40 D3
Cannon Cl
Hampton TW12 173 D4
West Barnes SW20 200 C6
Cannon Dr E14 119 C6
Cannon Hill NW6 69 C3
Palmers Green N14 16 A1
Cannon Hill La SM4,
SW20 201 A5
Cannon Hill Mews N14 16 A1
Cannon Ho SE11 260 D3
Penge SE26 184 B4
Cannon La NW3 70 B5
Pinner HA5 41 A3
Cannon Pl NW3 70 B5
SE7 122 A1
Cannon Rd DA7 147 B4
Palmers Green N14 16 A1
Cannon St EC4 117 B6 252 B6
Cannon Street Rd E1 96 B1
Cannon Street Sta
EC4 117 B6 252 C6
Cannon Trad Est HA9 66 D4
Cannon Way KT8 195 D5
Cannon Wharf Bsns Ctr 12
SE8 119 A2
Canon Ave RM6 58 C4
Canon Barnett CE Prim Sch
E1 95 D1 243 D2
Canon Beck Rd SE16 118 C4
Canonbie Rd SE23 162 C4
Canonbury Cres N1 73 A1
Canonbury Ct 21 N1 72 D1
Canonbury Gr N1 73 A1
Canonbury La N1 72 D1
Canonbury Pk N N1 73 A2
Canonbury Pk S N1 73 A2
Canonbury Pl N1 72 D2
Canonbury Prim Sch
N1 72 D2
Canonbury Rd N1 72 D1
Enfield EN1 5 C4
Canonbury Sq N1 72 D1
Canonbury St N1 73 A1
Canonbury Sta N1,N5 73 A3
Canonbury Villas N1 72 D1
Canon Lane Fst & Mid Schs
HA5 40 D3
Canon Mohan Cl N14 15 B5
Canon Murnane Rd
SE1 263 C5
Canon Palmer RC Sch
IG3 57 C1
Canon Rd BR1 209 D6
Canon Row
SW1 116 A4 250 A1
Canons Cl N2 48 B2
Edgware HA8 26 B4
Canons Cnr HA8 26 A6
Canons Ct HA8 26 B4
Canons Dr HA8 26 B4
Canons High Sch HA8 26 B1
Canons L Ctr The CR4 202 D5
Canonsleigh Rd RM9 80 B1
Canons Park Cl HA8 26 A3
Canons Park Sta HA8 26 A3
Canon St N1 95 A6 235 A5
Canon's Wlk CR0 222 D5
Canopus Way
Moor Park HA6 22 A6
Stanwell TW19 148 A4
Canrobert St E2 96 B4
Cantelowes Ho EN5 12 D6
Cantelowes Rd NW1 71 D2
Canterbury SE13 164 A6
Canterbury Ave
DA14,DA15 168 C2
Redbridge IG1 56 A2
Canterbury Cl 16 SE5 139 A3
Beckenham BR3 185 D2
7 Newham E6 100 B1
Southall UB6 85 D2
Canterbury Cres SW9 138 C2
Canterbury Ct NW11 47 A3
NW6 91 C5
15 NW9 27 D1
W3 111 C5
Ashford TW15 170 B6
South Croydon CR2 221 A1
Canterbury Gr SE27,
SW16 160 C1
Canterbury Ho 6 E3 97 D4
SE1 260 D6
2 Barking IG11 80 A1
Canterbury Ind Pk 15
SE15 140 C6
Canterbury Mans NW6 69 D2
Canterbury Pl SE17 261 D3
Canterbury Rd E10 54 A3
NW6 91 C5
Feltham TW13 151 A2
Harrow HA1,HA2 42 A4
Morden SM4 202 A3
Thornton Heath CR0 204 C2
Canterbury Terr NW6 91 C5
Cantium Ret Pk SE1 140 A6
Cantley Gdns Ilford IG2 57 A3
South Norwood SE19 183 D2
Cantley Rd W7 109 A3
Canton St E14 97 C1
Cantrell Rd E3 97 C3
Cantwell Ho SE18 144 D5
Cantwell Rd SE18 144 D5
Canute Ct SW16 160 C1
Canute Gdns SE16 118 D2
Canvey St SE1 252 A4
Cape Cl IG11 78 D1
Cape Henry Ct 7 E14 120 B6
Capel KT5 198 B2
Capel Ave SM6 220 B3
Capel Cl N20 14 A1
Keston Mark BR2 210 A1
Capel Ct SE20 184 C2
Capel Gdns Ilford IG3 79 D4
Pinner HA5 41 B5
Capel Ho 17 E9 74 C1
South Oxhey WD19 22 D6
Capella Ho SE7 143 B6
Capel Lo
5 Richmond TW9 132 B4
12 Streatham SW2 160 B4
Capel Point E7 77 B4
Capel Rd E7,E12 77 C4
East Barnet EN4 14 C5
Capener's Cl SW1 248 A1
Cape Rd N17 52 A6
Capern Rd SW18 158 A3
Capital Bsns Ctr HA0 87 D5
Capital Ind Est
Belvedere DA17 125 D3
Mitcham CR4 202 D4
Capital Interchange Way
TW8 110 C1
Capital Wharf 15 E1 118 A5
Capitol Way NW9 45 A6
Capland Ho NW8 236 D6
Capland St
NW8 92 B3 236 D6
Caplan Est CR4 181 C2
Caple Ho SW10 266 B4
Caple Rd NW10 89 D5
Capper St WC1 93 C3 239 B5
Caprea Cl UB4 84 D2
Capricorn Ctr RM8 59 B2
Capri Ho E17 35 B1
Capri Rd CR0 205 D2
Capstan Cl RM6 58 B3
Capstan Ho 5 E14 120 A2
Capstan Rd SE8 119 B2
Capstan Ride EN2 4 C3
Capstan Sq E14 120 A4
Capstan Way SE16 119 A5
Capstone Rd BR1 186 D6
Capthorne Ave HA2 41 B1
Capuchin Cl HA7 25 B4
Capulet Mews 1 E16 121 A5
Capworth St E10 53 D2
Caradoc Cl W2 91 C1
Caradoc Evans Cl 1
N11 31 B5
Caradoc St SE10 120 C1
Caradon Ct E11 54 C1
Caradon Ct *continued*
7 Twickenham TW1 153 C5
Caradon Way N15 51 B5
Caranday Villas 5
W11 112 D5
Caravel Cl E14 119 C3
Caravelle Gdns 1 UB5 84 D4
Caravel Mews 14 SE8 141 C6
Caraway Cl E13 99 B2
Caraway Hts E14 120 A6
Caraway Pl SM6 219 B5
Carberry Rd 12 SE19 183 C4
Carbery Ave W3 110 B4
Carbis Cl E4 20 B3
Carbis Rd E14 97 B1
Carbroke Ho 10 E9 96 C6
Carburton St
W1 93 B3 238 D5
Cardale St 1 E14 120 A3
Cardamom Ct 7 E12 78 C4
Carden Rd SE15 140 B2
Cardiff Ho 9 SE15 140 A6
Cardiff Rd Ealing W7 109 A3
Enfield EN3 6 B1
Cardiff St SE18 145 C5
Cardigan Ct 3 W7 86 D3
Cardigan Gdns IG3 80 A6
Cardigan Rd E3 97 B5
Barnes SW13 134 A3
Richmond TW10 154 A5
Wimbledon SW19 180 A4
Cardigan St
SE11 116 C1 261 A2
Cardigan Wlk 12 N1 73 A1
Cardinal Ave
Kingston KT2 176 A4
West Barnes SM4 201 A3
Cardinal Bourne St
SE1 262 D5
Cardinal Cap Alley
SE1 252 A4
Cardinal Cl HA8 27 B3
Chislehurst BR7 189 B2
West Barnes SM4 201 A3
Worcester Park KT19,
KT4 216 A4
Cardinal Cres KT3 177 A1
Cardinal Dr KT12 194 D1
Cardinal Hinsey Cl
NW10 90 A5
Cardinal Hinsley RC High
Sch (Boys) NW10 90 A6
Cardinal Pl SW15 134 D1
Cardinal Pole RC Sch
E9 75 A3
E9 74 D1
Cardinal Rd
Feltham TW13 150 B3
Ruislip HA4 40 D1
Cardinal Road Inf Sch
TW13 150 B3
Cardinals Way N19 49 D1
Cardinal's Wlk
Ashford TW16 171 C4
Hampton TW12 174 A3
Cardinal Vaughan Memorial
Sch W14 244 A2
Cardinal Way HA3 42 C6
Cardinal Wiseman RC High
Sch UB6 86 A3
Cardinal Wiseman RC Sch
The UB6 86 A2
Cardine Mews SE15 140 B5
Cardington Sq TW4 128 D1
Cardington St
NW1 93 C4 232 B1
Cardozo Rd N7 72 A3
Cardrew Ave N12 30 B5
Cardrew Cl N12 30 B5
Cardrew Ct N12 30 B5
Cardross St W6 112 B3
Cardwell Prim Sch
SE18 122 B2
Cardwell Rd N7 72 A4
Career Ct 11 SE16 118 D4
Carew Cl N7 72 B6
Carew Ct 15 SE14 140 D6
Carew Ho 24 SE18 122 B2
West Norwood SW16 160 C1
Carew Manor Sch
SM6 219 D5
Carew Rd W13 109 C4
Ashford TW15 171 A4
Mitcham CR4 181 A1
Thornton Heath CR7 204 D5
Tottenham N17 34 A1
Wallington SM6 219 C2
Carew St SE5 139 A3
Carey Ct DA6 169 D6
20 SE5 139 A5
Carey Gdns
SW8 137 D4 269 C1
Carey Ho E5 74 B5
Carey La EC2 242 A2
Carey Pl SW1 259 C3
Carey Rd RM9 81 A4

Carey St WC2 94 B1 240 D1
Carey Way HA9 66 D4
Carfax Pl SW4 137 D1
Carfax Rd UB3 106 A2
Carfree Cl 3 N1 72 C1
Cargill Rd SW18 158 A3
Cargreen Pl SE25 205 D5
Cargreen Rd SE25 205 D5
Cargrey Ho 9 HA7 25 C5
Carholme Rd SE23 163 B3
Carillon Ct W5 109 D6
Carinthia Ct 5 SE8 119 A2
Carisbrook 2 N10 31 B1
Carisbrook Cl EN1 5 D4
Carisbrook Ct 1
SW16 160 B1
Carisbrooke Ave DA5 168 D3
Carisbrooke Cl HA7 25 D1
Carisbrooke Ct
Acton W3 111 A4
Belmont SM2 217 B1
Northolt UB5 85 B6
Carisbrooke Gdns
SE15 139 D5
Carisbrooke Ho TW10 154 C6
Carisbrooke Rd E17 53 A4
Bromley BR2 209 C5
Mitcham CR4 204 A5
Carleton Ave SM6 219 D1
Carleton Cl KT10 196 B1
Carleton Gdns N19 71 C3
Carleton Rd N7 71 D4
Carlile Cl E3 97 B5
Carlile Ho SE1 262 D5
Carlina Gdns IG8 37 B5
Carlingford Gdns CR4 181 A3
Carlingford Rd N15 50 D6
NW3 70 B4
West Barnes SM4 200 D3
Carlisle Ave EC3 243 C1
W3 89 C1
Carlisle Cl KT2 176 C2
Carlisle Gdns
Harrow HA3 43 D2
Redbridge IG1 56 A3
Carlisle Ho IG1 56 A3
Carlisle La
SE1 116 B3 260 D6
Carlisle Pl N11 31 B6
SW1 115 C3 259 A5
Carlisle Prim Sch
TW12 173 D4
Carlisle Rd E10 53 C1
N4 50 C2
NW6 91 A6
NW9 45 A6
Cheam SM1 217 B2
Hampton TW12 173 D3
Carlisle St W1 93 D1 239 C1
Carlisle Way SW17 181 A5
Carlisle Wlk 6 E8 73 D2
Carlos Pl W1 115 B6 248 C5
Carlow St NW1 232 A4
Carlton Ave
Feltham TW14 150 C5
Harrow HA3 43 B4
Hayes UB3 105 C2
South Croydon CR2 221 C1
Southgate N14 15 D6
Carlton Ave E HA9 44 A1
Carlton Ave W HA0 65 B6
Carlton Cl NW3 69 C6
Chessington KT9 213 D2
Edgware HA8 26 C5
Northolt UB5 64 A3
Carlton Cres SM3 217 A4
Carlton Ct NW2 68 C2
NW6 91 D5
SW9 138 D4
Ilford IG6 57 B6
11 Penge SE20 184 B2
South Norwood SE19 183 D2
Carlton Dr Ilford IG6 57 B6
Putney SW15 157 A6
Carlton Gdns
SW1 115 D5 249 C3
Ealing W5 109 C6
Carlton Gn DA14 189 D6
Carlton Gr SE15 140 B4
8 SE15 140 B5
Carlton Hill
NW8 92 A5 229 A4
Carlton Ho NW6 91 C5
8 NW6 91 B5
W1 237 D2
Cheam SM1 217 B2
Edmonton N21 17 A3
Hounslow TW4 151 C5
Carlton House Terr
SW1 115 D5 249 D4
Carlton Lo N4 50 C2
Carlton Mans N16 51 D1
7 NW6 69 C1
SW9 138 C1
W14 244 B2
W9 91 D4
Carlton Par HA9 44 A1
Carlton Park Ave
SW20 178 D1
Carlton Prim Sch NW5 71 A3
Carlton Rd DA14 189 D6
DA16 146 B2
DA8 147 D6
E11 54 D1
E12 77 D4
E17 35 A2
N11 31 A5
N4 50 C2
W4 111 B4
Ashford TW16 171 D3
Ealing W5 87 C1
Kingston KT3 177 C1
Mortlake SW14 133 A1
South Croydon CR2 221 B1
Walton-on-T KT12 194 B2
Carlton Sq E1 96 D3
Carlton St SW1 249 C5
Carltons The 5 SW15 157 A6
Carlton Terr E7 77 C1
Edmonton N18 33 B6
Forest Hill SE26 162 C1
Wanstead E11 55 B4
Carlton Tower Pl SW1 257 D6
Carlton Twrs SM5 218 D5
Carlton Vale NW6 91 C5
Carlton Vale Inf Sch
NW6 91 B4
Carlwell St SW17 180 C5
Carlyle Ave BR1 209 D6
Southall UB1 107 B6
Carlyle Cl N2 48 A3
NW10 89 B6
East Molesey KT8 173 D1
Carlyle Ct SW6 265 D1
Carlyle Gdns UB1 107 B6
Carlyle Ho 12 N16 73 C5
4 SE5 139 A5
SW3 266 D6
W5 109 D2
Carlyle Mans SW3 267 A5
Carlyle Mews E1 96 D3
Carlyle Pl SW15 134 D1
Carlyle Rd E12 78 A4
W5 109 C2
Croydon CR0 222 A6
Woolwich SE28 124 C6
Carlyle's Ho* SW3 267 A5
Carlyle Sq
SW3 114 B1 256 D1
Carlyon Ave HA2 63 C4
Carlyon Cl HA0 88 A6
Carlyon Ct HA0 88 B6
Carlyon Mans 1 HA0 88 A5
Carlyon Rd HA0 88 A6
Carlys Cl BR3 184 D1
Carmalt Gdns SW15 134 C1
Carmarthen Ct 4 W7 86 D3
Carmarthen Ho 8
SW15 156 C4
Carmarthen Pl SE1 253 A2
Carmel Ct W8 245 C2
Carmelite Cl HA3 24 A2
Carmelite Rd HA3 24 A1
Carmelite St
EC4 116 C6 251 B6
Carmelite Way HA3 24 A1
Carmelite Wlk HA3 24 A2
Carmen St E14 97 D1
Carmichael Cl
9 SW11 136 B2
Ruislip HA4 62 A4
Carmichael Ct 5
SW13 133 D3
Carmichael Ho 6 E14 120 A6
17 Dulwich SE21 183 C6
Carmichael Mews
SW18 158 B4
Carmichael Rd SE25 206 A5
Carminia Rd SW17 159 B2
Carnaby St*
W1 93 C1 239 A1
Carnac St SE21,SE27 161 B1
Carnanton Rd E17 36 B2
Carnarvon Ave EN1 5 D3
Carnarvon Dr UB3 105 A3
Carnarvon Rd E10 54 A4
E15 76 D2
Barnet EN5 1 A2
Woodford E18 36 D2
Carnation St SE2 124 B1
Carnbrook Rd SE3 143 D2
Carnecke Gdns SE9 166 A6
Carnegie Cl
Holdbrook EN3 7 D5
Surbiton KT6 214 B6
Carnegie Ho NW3 70 B5
Carnegie Pl SW19 156 D1
Carnegie St N1 94 B6 233 D5
Carnforth Cl KT19 214 D2
Carnforth Rd SW16 181 D3
Carnicot Ho 9 SE15 140 B4
Carnoustie Cl SE28 102 D1
Carnoustie Dr N1 72 B1
Carnwath Ho SW6 135 D2
Carnwath Rd SW6 135 D2
Caroe Ct N9 18 B3
Carole Ho 13 SE20 184 B2
Carolina Cl E15 76 C3
Carolina Rd CR7 183 A2
Caroline Cl N10 31 B1
W2 245 D5
Hounslow TW7 130 C5
South Croydon CR0 221 C4
Streatham SW16 160 B1
Caroline Ct NW11 47 A3
Ashford TW15 170 D4
Catford SE6 186 B6
Stanmore HA7 25 A4
17 Surbiton KT6 197 D2
Caroline Gdns E2 95 C4
Caroline Ho W2 245 D5
20 W6 112 C1
Caroline Martyn Ho 8
N19 49 D2
Caroline Pl SW11 137 A3
W2 245 D5
Harlington UB3 127 C5
Caroline Pl Mews W2 245 D5
Caroline Rd SW19 179 B3
Caroline St E1 96 D1
Caroline Terr
SW1 115 A2 258 A3
Caroline Wlk W6 264 A5
Carol St NW1 93 C6 232 A6
Caronia Ct 4 SE16 119 A2
Carpenter Gdns N21 16 D2
Carpenter Ho 10 E14 97 C2
6 N19 71 D4
NW11 48 A3
Carpenters Bsns Pk
E15 75 D1
Carpenters Cl EN5 13 D5
Carpenters Ct NW1 232 A6
5 Dagenham RM10 81 D2
Twickenham TW2 152 C2
Carpenter's Pl SW4 137 D1
Carpenters Prim Sch
E15 98 A6
Carpenter's Rd E15 75 D1
Carpenter St W1 248 C5
Carrara Wharf SW6 135 A2
Carrara Wlk 19 SW9 138 D1
Carr Gr SE18 122 A2
Carriage Dr E
SW11 137 A5 268 B4
Carriage Drive E
SW11 137 A5 268 B4
Carriage Drive N
SW11,SW8 137 A6 268 B5
Carriage Dr N
SW8,SW11 136 D5 267 C4
SW8,SW11 137 A6 268 B5
Carriage Dr S
SW11 137 A4 268 A2
Carriage Dr W
SW11 136 D5 267 C3
Carriage Mews IG1 79 A6
Carrick Cl TW7 131 A2
Carrick Gate KT10 212 A5
Carrick Gdns N17 33 C3
Carrick Ho N7 72 B2
SE11 261 C2
Carrick Mews SE8 141 C6
Carrill Way DA17 124 D3
Carrington Ave
Borehamwood WD6 10 D6
Hounslow TW3 151 D6
Carrington Cl
Barnet EN5 12 A6
Borehamwood WD6 11 A6
Croydon CR0 207 A2
Carrington Ct SW11 136 C1
Carrington Gdns 4 E7 77 A4
Carrington Ho W1 248 C3
Wimbledon SW19 179 C3
Carrington Lo 3
TW10 154 A6
Carrington Pl KT10 212 A4
Carrington Rd TW10 132 C1
Carrington Sq HA3 24 A3
Carrington St W1 248 C3
Carrol Cl NW5 71 B4
Carroll Cl E15 76 D3
Carroll Ho W2 246 C6
Carronade Pl SE18 123 B3
Carron Cl E14 97 D1
Carroun Rd
SW8 138 B5 270 C4
Carroway La UB6 86 B4
Carrow Rd RM9 80 B1
Carr Rd Chingford E17 35 C1
Northolt UB5 64 A1
Carrs La N21 17 B6
Carr St E14 97 A2
Carshalton, Beddington & Wallington War Memorial Hospl SM5 218 D2
Carshalton Beeches Sta
SM5 218 D2
Carshalton Coll SM5 218 D5
Carshalton Gr SM1 218 B3
Carshalton High Sch for
Boys SM5 218 C6
Carshalton High Sch for
Girls SM5 218 C5
Carshalton Park Rd
SM5 218 D3
Carshalton Pl SM5 219 A3
Carshalton Rd
Mitcham CR4 203 A4
Sutton SM1,SM5 218 B3
Carshalton Sta SM5 218 D4
Carslake Rd SW15 156 C5
Carson Rd E16 99 A2
Cockfosters EN4 2 D1
Dulwich SE21 161 B2
Carstairs Rd SE6 164 A1
Carswell Cl IG4 55 D5
Carswell Rd SE6 164 A4
Carter Cl SM6 219 D1
Carter Ct EC4 241 D1
Carteret Ho 8 W12 112 B6
Carteret St SW1 249 C1
Carteret Way SE8 119 A2
Carterhatch Jun & Inf Schs
EN1 6 B4
Carterhatch La EN1 6 A4
Carterhatch Rd EN3 6 D4
Carter Ho E1 243 C3
11 SW2 160 C6
Carter La EC4 94 D1 241 D1
Carter Pl SE17 117 A1 262 B1
Carter Rd E13 99 B6
Mitcham SW19 180 B4
Carters Cl 2 NW5 71 D2
North Cheam KT4 200 D1
Carters Hill Cl SE9 165 C3
Carters Rd N2 30 C3
Carter St SE17 117 A1 262 A1
Carter's Yd SW18 157 C6
Carthew Rd W6 112 B3
Carthew Villas W6 112 B3
Carthusian St EC1 242 A4
Cartier Circ E14 120 A5
Carting La
WC2 116 A6 250 B5
Cart La E4 20 C3
Cartmel NW1 232 A2
Cartmel Cl N17 34 B3
Cartmel Ct
Beckenham BR2 186 C1
Northolt UB5 63 A2
Cartmel Gdns SM4 202 A4
Cartmel Rd DA7 147 C4
Carton Ho 2 NW2 68 A5
4 SE16 118 A3
12 W11 112 D6
Cartwright Gdns
WC1 94 A4 233 A1
Cartwright Ho SE1 262 B5
Cartwright Rd RM9 81 B1
Cartwright St
E1 117 D6 253 D5
Cartwright Way SW13 134 B5
Carvel Ho E14 120 A1
Carver Cl 15 W4 111 A3
Carver Rd SE24 161 A5
Carville Cres TW8 110 A2
Caryl Ho 6 SW19 156 D3
Cary Rd E11 76 C5
Carysfort Rd N16 73 B4
N8 49 D4
Casby Ho 7 SE16 118 A3
Cascade Ave N10 49 C5
Cascade Cl IG9 21 D2
Cascade Rd IG9 21 D2
Casella Rd SE14 140 D5
Casewick Rd SE27 182 D6
Casey Cl NW8 92 C4 230 B1
Casimir Rd E5 74 C5
Casino Ave SE24 161 B6
Caspian Ho 7 E1 96 D2
Caspian St SE5 139 B5
Caspian Wlk E16 99 D1
Cassandra Cl UB5 64 B4
Cassanora Ct NW2 68 C2
Casselden Rd NW10 67 B1
Cassel Hospl TW10 175 D6
Cassell Ho 21 SW9 138 A3
Casserley Ho W4 111 B3
Cass Ho 23 E9 74 D2
Cassidy Rd SW6 265 A3
Cassilda Rd SE2 124 A2
Cassilis Rd TW1 153 B5
Cassinghurst SE24 161 B6
Cassiobury Ave TW14 149 D4
Cassiobury Rd E17 53 A4
Cassland Rd E9 74 D2
South Norwood CR7 205 B5
Casslee Rd SE6 163 B4
Cassocks Sq TW17 193 B2
Casson Ho 10 E1 96 A2
Casson St E1 96 A2
Castalia Sq 6 E14 120 A4
Castellain Mans W9 91 D3
Castellain Rd W9 91 D3
Castellane Cl HA7 24 D3
Castell Ho 11 SE8 141 C5
Castello Ave SW15 156 C6
Castelnau SW13 134 B5
Casterbridge NW6 91 D6
3 W11 91 C1
Casterbridge Rd SE3 143 A2
Casterton St E8 74 B2
Castile Rd SE18 122 C2
Castilion Prim Sch
SE28 102 C1
Castillon Rd SE6 164 C2
Castlands Rd SE6 163 B2
Castleacre W2 237 A1
Castle Ave Chingford E4 36 B5
Yiewsley UB7 104 B6
Castlebar Ct 5 W5 87 C2
Castlebar Hill W5 87 C2
Castlebar Mews W5 87 C2
Castle Bar Park Sta
W7 86 D2
Castlebar Pk W5 87 B2
Castlebar Rd W5 87 C1
Castlebar Sch W13 87 A2
Castle Baynard St
EC4 117 A6 252 A6
Castlebrook Cl
SE11 116 D2 261 C4
Castle Cl E9 75 A3
W3 110 D4
Ashford TW16 171 C3
Beckenham BR2 208 C6
Wimbledon SW19 156 D1
Castlecombe Dr SW19 156 D4
Castlecombe Prim Sch
SE9 188 A5
Castlecombe Rd SE9 188 A6
Castle Ct EC3 242 D1
Belmont SM2 217 C2
Forest Hill SE26 185 A6
Morden SM4 202 B4
Castleden Ho NW6 70 B1
Castledine Rd SE20 184 B3
Castle Dr IG4 56 A3
Castleford Ave SE9 166 D3
Castleford Cl N17 33 D4
Castleford Ct NW8 236 D6
Castlefrank Ho 21 N1 95 C4
Castlegate TW9 132 B2
Castlehaven Rd NW1 71 B1
Castle Hill Ave CR0 224 A1
Castle Hill Prim Sch
CR0 224 A2
Castle Ho SE1 262 A4
SW8 270 B4
10 Belmont SM2 217 C1
3 Chingford E4 36 B5
Castleigh Ct EN2 17 B6
Castle Ind Est SE17 262 A4
Castle La SW1 115 C3 259 A6
Castlemaine 8 SW11 136 D3
Castlemaine Ave CR2 221 D3
Castle Mead SE5 139 A5
Castle Mews N12 30 A5
NW1 71 B2
Castlenau Gdns SW13 134 B6
Castlenau Mans SW13 134 B6
Castlenau Row SW13 134 B6
Castle Par KT17 216 A1
Castle Pl 8 W4 111 C2
Castle Point 3 E13 99 C5
Castle Rd N12 30 B5
NW1 71 B2
Dagenham RM9 102 B6
Enfield EN3 7 A5
Isleworth TW7 130 D3
Northolt UB5 63 D1
Southall UB2 107 B3
Castlereagh St W1 237 C2
Castle St E6 99 C5
Kingston KT2 176 A1
Castleton Ave HA9 66 A4
Castleton Cl CR0 207 A3
Castleton Ct KT5 198 B4
Castleton Gdns HA9 66 A5
Castleton Ho 2 E14 120 A2
Castleton Rd SE12,SE9 187 D6
Chingford E17 36 B1
Ilford IG3 58 B1
Mitcham CR4 203 D5
Ruislip HA4 40 D1
Castletown Rd
W14 113 A1 254 B1
Castleview Cl N4 73 A6
Castle View Gdns IG1 56 B3
Castle Way
Feltham TW13 172 C6
Wimbledon SW19 156 D1
Castle Wlk TW16 194 C6
Castlewood Day Hospl
SE18 144 C4
Castlewood Dr SE9 144 B3
Castlewood Rd N16 52 A3
Barnet EN4 2 B2
Castle Yd N6 49 A2
SE1 251 D4
17 Richmond TW10 153 D6
Castor La E14 119 D6
Catalina Rd TW6 126 C2
Caterham Rd SE13 142 B2
Catesby Ho 25 E9 74 C1
Catesby St
SE17 117 B2 262 D3
Catford Br SE6 163 C4
Catford Bridge Sta
SE6 163 C4
Catford Broadway
SE6 163 D4
Catford Girls' Sch SE6 164 A1
Catford Gyratory SE6 163 D4
Catford Hill SE6 163 C3
Catford Rd SE6 163 C4
Catford Sta SE6 163 C4
Cathall Rd E11 76 B5
Cathay Ho SE16 118 B4
Cathay St 9 SE16 118 B4
Cathay Wlk UB5 85 C5
Cathcart Dr BR6 211 C1
Cathcart Hill N19 71 C5
Cathcart Rd
SW10 136 A6 266 A6
Cathcart St NW5 71 B2
Cathedral Ct EC4 241 D1
Cathedral Sch of St Saviour & St Mary Overie Prim Sch
SE1 117 A4 252 B2
Cathedral St
SE1 117 B5 252 C4
Catherall Rd N5,N16 73 A5
Catherine Baird Ct 12
SW12 159 B4
Catherine Ct
1 Ilford IG2 57 A3
2 Southgate N14 15 C6
3 Wimbledon SW19 179 B5
Catherine Dr
Ashford TW16 171 D4
Richmond TW9 132 A1
Catherine Gdns TW3 130 B1
Catherine Godfrey Ho
RM9 103 B6
Catherine Gr SE10 141 D4
Catherine Griffiths Ct
EC1 241 B6
Catherine Ho 16 N1 95 C6
Isleworth TW7 131 B4
Catherine Pl
SW1 115 C3 259 A6
Harrow HA1 42 D4
Catherine Rd Enfield EN3 7 A6
Kingston KT6 197 D4
Catherine St
WC2 116 B6 250 C6
Catherine Wheel Alley
E1 243 B3
Catherine Wheel Rd
TW8 131 D5
Catherine Wheel Yd
SW1 249 A3
Catherwood Ct N1 235 C3
Cat Hill EN4 14 D6
Cathles Rd SW12 159 B5
Cathnor Rd W12 112 B4
Catisfield Rd EN3 7 A6
Catlin Cres TW17 193 B4
Catling Cl SE23 162 D1
Catlin's La HA5 40 B5
Catlin St SE16 118 B1
Catman Ho N4 50 B1
Caton Ct BR2 186 C1
Cato Rd SW4 137 D1
Cator La BR3 185 B2
Cator Park Sch for Girls
BR3 185 A3
Cator Rd
Penge SE20,SE26 184 D5
Wallington SM5 218 D3
Cator St SE15 139 D5
SE15 139 D6
Cato St W1 92 C1 237 B2
Catsey La WD23 8 A4
Catsey Wood WD23 8 A4
Catterick Cl N11 31 A4
Cattistock Rd SE9 188 B5
Cattley Cl EN5 1 A1
Catton St WC1 240 C3
Caughley Ho SE11 261 A5
Caulfield Ct 12 NW1 71 C1
Caulfield Rd E6 78 B1
SE15 140 B3
Causeway TW14,TW4 128 B1
Causeway The N2 48 C5
SW18 157 D6
Carshalton SM5 219 A6
Chessington KT9 214 A4
Claygate KT10 212 D1
Teddington TW11 174 D4
Wimbledon SW19 178 C5
Causeyware Rd N9 18 C4
Causton Cotts 3 E14 97 A1
Causton Ho SE5 139 A5
Causton Rd N6 49 B2
Causton Sq RM10 81 C1
Causton St
SW1 115 D1 259 D2
Cautley Ave SW4 159 C6
Cavalier Cl RM6 58 D5
Cavalier Gdns UB3 83 B1
Cavalry Cres TW4 128 D1
Cavalry Gdns SW15 157 B6
Cavan Pl HA5 23 B2
Cavaye Ho SW10 266 B6
Cavaye Pl SW10 256 B1

Cavell Dr EN2 4 C3
Cavell Ho 8 N1 95 C6
Cavell Rd N17 33 B3
Cavell St E1 96 B2
Cavendish Ave DA16 145 D2
N3 29 C1
NW8 92 B5 229 D3
Ealing W13 87 A1
Harrow HA1 64 C4
Ruislip HA4 62 B3
Sidcup DA15 168 A4
West Barnes KT3 200 B5
Woodford IG8 37 B3
Cavendish Cl NW6 69 B2
NW8 92 B4 229 D2
Ashford TW16 171 D4
Edmonton N18 34 B5
Hayes UB4 83 C2
3 Putney SW15 157 A6
Cavendish Cres
Borehamwood WD6 10 C6
Borehamwood WD6 10 C6
Cavendish Ct EC2 243 B2
Ashford TW16 171 D4
5 Chingford E4 20 C4
Cavendish Dr E11 54 B1
Claygate KT10 212 C3
Edgware HA8 26 B4
Cavendish Gdns SW4 159 C5
Barking IG11 79 D3
Dagenham RM6 59 A4
Ilford IG1 56 C1
Cavendish Ho N12 30 A6
NW8 229 D3
SW8 270 A2
Twickenham TW1 153 A5
Cavendish Mans E5 74 C3
EC1 241 A5
8 NW6 69 C3
2 SW12 159 C5
Cavendish Mews N
W1 238 D4
Cavendish Mews S
W1 238 D3
Cavendish Par
Balham SW12 159 B5
Hounslow TW4 129 A3
Cavendish Pl W1 238 D2
Cavendish Prim Sch
W4 133 C5
Cavendish Rd N4 50 D3
NW6 69 B1
SW12 159 C5
Ashford TW16 171 D4
Chingford E4 36 A4
Chiswick W4 133 A4
Edmonton N18 34 B5
Mitcham SW19 180 C3
New Malden KT3 199 D5
Sutton SM2 218 A1
Thornton Heath CR0 204 D1
Cavendish Sch The
NW1 93 B6 231 D6
Cavendish Sq
W1 93 B1 238 D2
Cavendish St
N1 95 B5 235 C3
Cavendish Terr 10 E3 97 B4
Feltham TW13 150 A2
Cavendish The NW11 47 D2
Cavendish Way BR4 207 D1
Cavenham Gdns IG1 79 B5
Cave Rd E13 99 B4
Richmond TW10 175 C6
Caverleigh Way KT4 200 B2
Caverley Gdns HA3 43 D2
Caversham Ave
Cheam SM3 217 A6
Palmers Green N13 16 C1
Caversham Ct N11 15 A1
Caversham Ho N15 51 A5
7 SE15 140 A6
8 Kingston KT1 176 A1
Caversham Rd N15 51 A5
NW5 71 C2
Kingston KT1 176 B1
Caversham St
SW3 136 D6 267 C6
Caverswall St W12 90 C1
Caveside Cl BR7 188 C2
Cavour Ho SE17 261 D2
Cawdor Cres W7 109 A2
Cawnpore St SE19 183 C5
Cawston Ct 6 BR1 186 D3
Caxton Gr E3 97 C4
Caxton Hall SW1 259 C6
Caxton Rd W12 112 D4
Southall UB2 106 D3
Wimbledon SW19 180 A5
Wood Green N22 32 B1
Caxton St SW1 115 D3 259 C6
Caxton St N E16 98 D1
Caxton Trad Est UB3 105 C5
Cayford Ho 1 NW3 70 D3
Caygill Cl BR2 208 D5
Cayley Cl SM6 220 A1
Cayley Prim Sch E14 97 A1
Cayley Rd UB2 107 D3
Cayton Pl EC1 235 C1
Cayton Rd UB6 86 C5
Cayton St EC1 235 C1
Cazenove Mans 1 N16 74 A6
Cazenove Rd N16 74 A6
Chingford E17 35 C2
Cearns Ho E6 99 D6
Cecil Ave Barking IG11 79 B1
Enfield EN1 5 D1
Wembley HA9 66 B3
Cecil Cl
Chessington KT9 213 D4
Ealing W5 87 D2
Littleton TW15 171 A3
Cecil Ct NW6 69 D1
SW10 266 A6
WC2 250 A5
12 Croydon CR0 221 D6
Ealing W5 87 D2
Cecile Pk N8 50 A3
Cecil Ho 6 E5 74 C6
Chingford E17 35 C2
Cecilia Cl N2 48 A6
Cecilia Rd E8 74 A3
Cecil Lo KT9 213 D4
Cecil Mans 2 SW17 159 A2
Cecil Pk HA5 41 A5
Cecil Pl CR4 202 D4
Cecil Rd E11 76 C5
E13 99 A6
N10 31 B1
N14 15 C3
NW10 89 C6
NW9 45 C6
W3 89 A2
Ashford TW15 171 A4
Cheam SM1,SM2 217 B2
Chingford E17 35 C2
Dagenham RM6 58 D2
Enfield EN2 5 B1
Harrow HA3 42 C6
Hounslow TW3 130 A3
Ilford IG1 78 D4
Merton SW19 179 D3
Thornton Heath CR0 204 B3
Cecil Rhodes Ho NW1 232 C4
Cecil Rosen Ct HA0 65 B5
Cecil Way BR2 209 A1
Cedar Ave
Dagenham RM6 59 A4
East Barnet EN4 14 C4
Enfield EN3 6 C3
Hayes UB3 84 A1
Ruislip HA4 62 C3
Sidcup DA15 168 A4
Twickenham TW2 152 A5
Yiewsley UB7 104 B6
Cedar Cl Bow E3 97 B6
Buckhurst Hill IG9 21 D2
East Molesey KT8 196 C5
Keston Mark BR2 226 A5
Kingston KT2 177 B6
Wallington SM5 218 D2
West Norwood SE21 161 A2
Cedar Copse BR1 188 B1
Cedar Cres BR2 226 A5
Cedarcroft Rd KT9 214 B4
Cedar Ct HA8 11 A1
1 N10 31 B1
N1 73 A1
5 N11 31 C5
N20 14 B3
N3 29 C3
19 SE7 143 C6
W1 237 B2
7 Brentford TW8 131 D6
Eltham SE9 166 A5
Mortlake SW14 133 A1
Stoneleigh KT17 216 A1
3 Sutton SM2 218 A2
6 Wanstead E11 55 B4
Wimbledon SW19 156 D1
5 Woodford E18 37 A2
Cedar Dr N2 48 C5
Pinner HA5 23 C4
Cedar Gdns SM2 218 A2
Cedar Gr DA5 168 D5
W5 110 A3
Southall UB1 85 C2
Cedar Grange 10 EN1 17 C6
Cedar Ho 5 E14 120 A4
SE14 140 D4
16 SE16 118 D4
W8 255 C6
Ashford TW16 171 D3
Hayes UB4 84 C3
New Addington CR0 223 D2
Wood Green N22 32 C2
Cedar Hts NW2 69 B2
Richmond TW10 154 A3
Cedarhurst Dr SE9 165 C6
Cedar Lawn Ave EN5 13 A6
Cedar Lo SW6 134 D4
Cedarmore Ct BR7 189 A2
Cedar Mount SE9 165 D3
Cedarne Rd
SW6 135 D5 265 C3
Cedar Park Gdns RM6 58 D2
Cedar Park Rd EN2 5 A5
Cedar Pl 3 SE7 121 C1
Cedar Rd BR1 187 C1
NW2 68 C4
Cranford TW5 128 C3
Croydon CR0 221 C6
East Bedfont TW14 149 B3
East Molesey KT8 196 C5
Enfield EN2 5 A5
Sutton SM2 218 A2
Tottenham N17 33 D2
Cedar Rise N14 15 A4
Cedars Ave E17 53 C4
Mitcham CR4 203 A6
Cedars Cl NW4 46 D6
SE13 142 B2
Cedars Ct Edmonton N9 17 D2
Putney SW15 156 A5
Cedars Dr UB10 82 C5
Cedars Fst & Mid Schs
HA3 24 A2
Cedars Ho 15 E17 53 D6
21 SW2 138 B1
5 West Norwood
SW27 182 D5
Cedars Mews SW4 137 B1
Cedars Prim Sch The
TW5 128 A5
Cedars Rd E15 76 C2
SW4 137 B1
W4 111 C1
Barnes SW13 134 A3
Beckenham BR3 185 B1
Edmonton N21 16 D2
4 Edmonton N9 18 A2
Morden SM4 201 C5
Teddington KT8 175 C2
Wallington CR0 220 A4
Cedars The E9 74 D1
Buckhurst Hill IG9 21 A3
Ealing W13 87 C1
4 Kingston KT2 176 D2
Teddington TW11 174 D4
Wallington SM6 219 C4
Cedar Terr
9 Dagenham RM8 58 D2
Richmond TW9 132 A1
Cedar Tree Ct SE5 139 A4
Cedar Tree Gr SE27 182 D5
Cedarville Gdns SW16 182 B4
Cedar Way
NW1 71 D1 232 C6
Ashford TW16 171 C3
Cedar Wlk KT10 212 D2
Cedarwood BR3 185 B3
Cedarwood Ho EN2 4 D3
Cedra Ct N16 52 A1
Cedric Chambers
NW8 236 C6
Cedric Rd SE9 167 A1
Celadon Cl EN3 7 A2
Celandine Cl E3,E14 97 C2
Celandine Dr E8 73 D1
Woolwich SE28 124 B5
Celandine Way E15 98 C4
Celbridge Mews W2 91 D1
Celandine Ct E4 19 D1
Celestial Gdns SE13 142 B1
Celia Ct 7 TW9 132 B4
Celia Ho 10 N1 95 C5
Celia Rd N19 71 C4
Celtic Ave BR2 208 C6
Celtic St E14 97 D2
Cemetery La
Lower Halliford TW17 192 D2
Woolwich SE7 144 A6
Cemetery Rd E7 76 D4
Tottenham N17 33 C3
Woolwich SE2 146 B5
Cenacle Cl NW3 69 C5
Cenotaph* SW1 250 A2
Centaur Ct 3 TW8 110 A1
Centaurs Bsns Pk
TW7 131 A6
Centaur St
SE1 116 B3 260 D6
Centenary Rd EN3 7 B1
Centennial Ave WD6 9 C4
Centennial Ct WD6 9 C4
Centennial Pk HA7,WD6 9 C4
Central Ave DA16 146 A3
E11 76 B6
N2 30 B1
N2 47 D6
SW11 136 D5 267 D3
East Molesey KT8 195 B4
Edmonton N9 17 D1
Enfield EN1 6 B3
Hayes UB3 106 A6
Isleworth TW3,TW7 130 A1
Pinner HA5 41 B2
Wallington SM6 220 A3
Central Bsns Ctr NW10 67 C3
Central Cir NW4 46 B4
Central Criminal Court (Old
Bailey)* EC4 94 D1 241 D2
Central Ct 2 SE18 122 D2
Centrale Ctr CR0 221 A6
Central Foundation Lower
Sch E3 97 A4
Central Foundation Sch
EC2 95 B3 242 D6
Central Foundation Upper
Sch E3 97 B4
Central Gdns SM4 201 D4
Central Hill SE19 183 B4
Central Mans 8 NW4 46 B4
Central Middlesex Hospl
NW10 89 A4
Central Par 8 E17 53 C5
W3 110 D4
Ealing UB6 87 A4
Enfield EN3 6 C3
Feltham TW14 150 C4
Harrow HA1 42 D4
Heston TW5 129 C5
Ilford IG2 57 B3
Penge SE20 184 D3
Surbiton KT6 198 A3
Central Park Ave RM10 81 D5
Central Park Prim Sch
E6 99 D5
Central Park Rd E6 99 D5
Central Par Villas BR5 190 C1
Central Pk Est TW4 128 D1
Central Public Health
Laboratories NW9 45 C6
Central Rd
Morden SM4 201 D4
Wembley HA0 65 B3
Worcester Park KT4 216 A6
Central Sch of Speech &
Drama The NW3 70 B1
Central School of Ballet
EC1 94 C3 241 B5
Central Sq NW11 47 D3
East Molesey KT8 195 B5
4 Wembley HA9 66 A3
Central St EC1 95 A4 235 A1
Central St Martins Coll of
Art & Design (The London
Inst) WC1 94 B2 240 C3
Central St Martin's Sch of
Art & Design
W1 93 D1 239 D1
Central Terr BR3 206 D6
Central Way NW10 89 A4
SE28 124 B6
Feltham TW14 150 B6
Sutton SM5 218 C1
Centre Ave N2 30 C1
NW10 90 C4
W3 111 B5
Centre Bldg SE17 262 B4
Centre Common Rd
BR7 189 A3
Centre Ct N20 14 B2
Centre Dr E7 77 C4
Centre Hts 5 NW3 70 B1
Centre Point 3 SE1 118 A1
Centre Rd
Dagenham RM10 103 D5
Wanstead E7,E11 77 A6
Centre St E2 96 B5
Centre The
Feltham TW13 150 B2
Walton-on-T KT12 193 D1
Centre Way N9 18 D2
Centreway IG1 79 A6
Centurian Way DA18 125 C3
Centurion Cl N7 72 B1
Centurion Ct SM6 219 B6
Centurion Ho 2 RM10 81 D2
Centurion La E3 97 B5
Century Cl NW4 46 D4
Century Ho SE13 141 D3
Wembley HA9 66 B6
Century Rd E17 53 A6
Century Yd SE23 162 C2
Cephas Ave E1 96 C3
Cephas Ho 8 E1 96 C3
Cephas St E1 96 C3
Ceres Rd SE18 123 D2
Cerise Rd SE15 140 A4
Cerne Cl UB4 106 C6
Cerne Rd SM4 202 A3
Cerney Mews W2 246 C6
Cervantes Ct 11 W2 91 D1
Ceylon Rd W14 254 A5
6 W14 112 D3
Chace Com Sch EN1 5 C4
Chadacre Ave IG5 56 B6
Chadacre Ho 10 SW9 138 D1
Chadacre Rd KT17 216 B3
Chadbourn St E14 97 D2
Chadbury Ct NW7 28 A2
Chad Cres N9 18 C1
Chadd Dr BR1 210 A6
Chadd Gn E13 99 A6
Chadston Ho 17 N1 72 D1
Chadswell WC1 233 B1
Chadview Ct 2 RM6 58 D2
Chadville Gdns RM6 58 D4
Chadway RM8 58 C1
Chadwell Ave RM6 58 B2
Chadwell Heath Foundation
Sch The RM6 58 B3
Chadwell Heath Hospl
RM6 58 B4
Chadwell Heath Ind Pk
RM8 58 D1
Chadwell Heath La
RM6 58 C3
Chadwell Heath Sta
RM6 58 D2
Chadwell Prim Sch
RM6 58 C2
Chadwell St
EC1 94 C4 234 B2
Chadwick Ave
Chingford E4 36 B6
Wimbledon SW19 179 C4
Chadwick Cl
12 Ealing W7 86 D2
Roehampton SW15
Teddington TW11 175 A4
Chadwick Ct 4 SE28 124 B5
Chadwick Pl KT6 197 C3
Chadwick Rd E11 54 D3
NW10 89 D6
SE15 139 D3
Ilford IG1 78 D5
Chadwick St
SW1 115 D3 259 C5
Chadwick Way SE28 124 D6
Chadwin Rd E13 99 B2
Chadworth Ho EC1 235 A1
N4 51 A1
Chadworth Way KT10 212 B3
Chaffey Ho 6 SE7 121 C1
Chaffinch Ave CR0 206 D3
Chaffinch Cl N9 18 D3
Croydon CR0 206 D3
Tolworth KT6 214 C5
Chaffinch Rd BR3 185 A2
Chafford Way RM6 58 C5
Chagford Ct SW19 180 C3
Chagford Ho 38 E3 97 D4
NW1 237 C5
Chagford St
NW1 92 D3 237 D5
Chailey Ave EN1 5 D3
Chailey Cl TW5 128 D4
Chailey Ind Est UB3 106 A4
Chailey St E5 74 C5
Chalbury Ho 8 SW9 138 B1
Chalbury Wlk N1 234 A4
Chalcombe Rd SE2 124 B3
Chalcot Cl SM2 217 C1
Chalcot Cres
NW1 92 D6 230 D6
Chalcot Gdns NW3 70 D2
Chalcot Mews SW16 160 A1
Chalcot Rd
NW1 93 A6 231 A6
Chalcot Sch NW1 71 B1
Chalcot Sq NW1 71 A1
Chalcott Gdns KT6 197 C1
Chalcroft Rd SE13 164 C6
Chaldon Rd
SW6 135 A5 264 B4
Chale Rd SW2 160 A5
Chalet Ct CR7 204 D4
Chalfont Ave HA9 66 D2
Chalfont Ct NW1 237 D5
NW9 45 D6
3 Belvedere DA17 125 C1
12 Harrow HA1 42 D3
Chalfont Gn N9 17 C1
Chalfont Ho NW10 67 B5
2 SE16 118 B3
Chalfont Rd
Edmonton N9 17 D1
Hayes UB3 106 A4
South Norwood SE25 205 D6
Chalfont Way W13 109 B3
Chalfont Wlk 3 HA5 22 C1
Chalford 7 NW3 70 A2
Chalford Cl KT8 195 C5
Chalford Ct Ilford IG2 56 D4
15 Putney SW15 156 D5
Surbiton KT6 198 B2
Chalford Rd SE21 183 B6
Chalford Wlk IG8 37 D3
Chalgrove Ave SM4 201 C4
Chalgrove Gdns N3 47 A6
Chalgrove Prim Sch N3 47 A6
Chalgrove Rd
Sutton SM2 218 B1
Tottenham N17 34 B2
Chalice Cl SM6 219 D2
Chalice Ct N2 48 C5
Chalkenden Cl SE20 184 B3
Chalkers Cnr TW9 132 D2
Chalk Farm Rd
NW1 71 A1 231 D6
Chalk Farm Sta NW3 71 A1
Chalkhill Prim Sch HA9 66 D5
Chalk Hill Rd W6 112 D2
Chalkhill Rd HA9 67 A5
Chalk La EN4 2 D1
Chalklands HA9 67 A5
Chalkley Cl CR4 181 A1
Chalkmill Dr EN1 6 B2
Chalk Pit Ave BR5 190 C1
Chalk Pit Rd SM1 218 A3
Chalk Rd E13 99 C2
Chalkstone Cl DA16 146 A4
Chalkwell Ho 9 E1 96 D1
Chalkwell Park Ave EN1 5 C1
Challenge Cl NW10 89 C6
Challenge Rd TW15 149 B1
Challenger Ho 7 E14 119 A6
Challice Way SW2 160 B3
Challiner Ct HA1 43 A4
Challin St 1 SE20 184 C2
Challis Rd TW8 109 D1
Challoner Cl N2 30 B1
Challoner Cres W14 254 C1
Challoner Ct BR2 186 B1
Challoner Mans W14 254 C1
Challoners Cl KT8 196 B5
Challoner St
W14 113 B1 254 C1
Chalmers Ho E17 53 D4
13 SW11 136 A2
Chalmers Rd TW15 170 D5
Chalmers Rd E TW15 171 A5
Chalmers Way TW14 150 B6
Chalmer's Wlk 14
SE17 138 D6
Chalner Ho SW2 160 C3
Chaloner Ct SE1 252 C2
Chalsey Rd SE4 141 B1
Chalton Dr N2 48 B3
Chalton St NW1 93 D5 232 C3
Chamberlain Cl SE18 123 B3
Chamberlain Cotts
SE5 139 B4
Chamberlain Cres
BR4 207 D1
Chamberlain Gdns
TW3 130 A4
Chamberlain Ho 5
E1 118 C6
Chamberlain La HA5 40 A5
Chamberlain Pl E17 53 A6
Chamberlain Rd N2 30 A1
Ealing W13 109 A4
Edmonton N9 18 A2
Chamberlain St 7
NW1 70 D1
Chamberlain Way
Pinner HA5 40 B6
Surbiton KT6 198 A2
Chamberlain Wlk 5
TW13 173 A6
Chamberlayne Mans 3
NW10 90 D4
Chamberlayne Rd
NW10 90 C6
Chambers Gdns N2 30 B2
Chambers Ho 2
SW16 181 C6
Chambers La NW10 68 C1
Chambers Pl CR2 221 B1
Chambers Rd N7 72 A4
Chambers St SE16 118 A4
Chamber St
E1 117 D6 253 D6
Chambon Pl 7 W6 112 A2
Chambord Ho 24 E2 95 D4
Chambord St E2 95 D4
Chamomile Ct E17 53 C3
Champion Cres SE26 185 A6
Champion Gr SE5 139 B2
Champion Hill SE5 139 B2
Champion Pk SE5 139 B3
Champion Rd SE26 185 A6
Champlain Ho 28 W12 112 B6
Champness Cl 9
SE27 183 B6
Champness Rd IG11 79 D1
Champneys Cl SM2 217 B1
Chancel Ct W1 249 C6
Chancellor Gr SE21 161 A1
Chancellor Ho 29 E1 118 B5
SW7 256 B6
Chancellor Pas E14 119 C5
Chancellor Pl NW9 27 D1
Chancellors' Ct WC1 240 C4
Chancellor's Rd W6 112 C1
Chancellors St W6 112 C1
Chancellors Wharf 21
W6 112 C1
Chancelot Rd SE2 124 B2
Chancel St
SE1 116 D5 251 C3
Chancery Bldgs 13 E1 118 C6
Chancery La
EC4 94 C1 241 A2
Beckenham BR3 185 D1
Chancery Lane Sta
WC1 94 C2 241 A3
Chance St E2 243 C6
Chanctonbury Cl SE9 166 D1
Chanctonbury Gdns
SM2 217 D1
Chanctonbury Way N12 29 C6
Chandler Ave E16 99 A2
Chandler Cl TW12 173 C2
Chandler Ct
Feltham TW14 150 A5
2 Tolworth KT5 198 D1

Chandler Ct *continued*
8 Wallington SM6 .... 219 B2
Chandlers Ct TW14 .... 149 D4
Chandlers Field Prim Sch KT8 .... 195 C4
Chandlers Mews E14 .... 119 C4
Chandler St E1 .... 118 B5
Chandlers Way 11 SE24 .... 160 C4
Chandler Way SE15 .... 139 D5
Chandon Lo SM2 .... 218 A1
Chandos Ave N14 .... 15 C1
N20 .... 14 B3
W5 .... 109 D2
Chingford E17 .... 35 C1
Chandos Cl IG9 .... 21 B2
Chandos Cres HA8 .... 26 C3
Chandos Ct N14 .... 15 D2
Chandos Pl WC2 .... 116 A6 250 A5
Chandos Rd E15 .... 76 B3
N2 .... 30 C1
NW10 .... 89 C3
NW2 .... 68 C3
Harrow HA1 .... 42 A4
Pinner HA5 .... 40 D2
Tottenham N17 .... 33 C1
Chandos St W1 93 B2 238 D3
Chandos Way NW11 .... 47 D1
Change Alley EC3 .... 242 D1
Channel Cl TW5 .... 129 C4
Channel Ho E14 .... 97 A2
Channelsea Bsns Ctr E15 .... 98 B5
Channing Sch N6 .... 49 B1
Channon Ct 3 KT6 .... 198 A4
Chantrey Cl DA14 .... 191 A5
Chantrey Rd SW9 .... 138 B2
Chantries The HA7 .... 25 A5
Chantry Cl W9 .... 91 B3
Edgware NW7 .... 11 D4
Enfield EN2 .... 5 A5
Harrow HA3 .... 44 B4
Sunbury TW16 .... 172 A3
Chantry Cres NW10 .... 67 D2
Chantry Ct SW6 .... 135 A2
Chantry Ct Ind Est SM5 .... 218 C5
Chantry La BR2 .... 209 D4
Chantry Pl HA3 .... 23 D2
Chantry Rd
Chessington KT9 .... 214 C3
Harrow HA3 .... 23 D2
Chantry Sch UB7 .... 104 A6
Chantry Sq W8 .... 113 D3 255 C5
Chantry St N1 .... 94 D6 234 D5
Chantry The
3 Chingford E4 .... 20 A3
Hillingdon UB8 .... 82 B4
Chantry Way CR4 .... 202 B6
Chant Sq E15 .... 76 B1
Chant St E15 .... 76 B1
Chapel Cl NW10 .... 67 D2
Chapel Ct 12 EC2 .... 95 C4
N2 .... 48 C6
SE1 .... 252 C2
Hayes UB3 .... 105 D6
Chapel End Ho E17 .... 35 D2
Chapel End Inf Sch E17 35 D2
Chapel End Jun Sch E17 .... 35 D2
Chapel Farm Rd SE9 .... 166 B2
Chapel Hill N2 .... 30 C1
Chapel House St E14 .... 119 D2
Chapel La
5 Dagenham RM6 .... 58 D2
Hillingdon UB8 .... 82 C1
Pinner HA5 .... 40 D6
Chapel Market N1 .... 94 C5 234 A4
Chapel Pl 13 EC2 .... 95 C4
N1 .... 234 B4
W1 .... 238 C1
Tottenham N17 .... 33 D3
Chapel Rd DA7 .... 147 C1
Ealing W13 .... 109 B5
Hounslow TW3 .... 129 D2
Ilford IG1 .... 78 D5
Twickenham TW1 .... 153 B4
West Norwood SE27 .... 182 D6
Chapel Side W2 .... 113 D6 245 C5
Chapel St NW1 .92 C2 237 A3
SW1 .... 115 A4 248 B1
Enfield EN2 .... 5 B2
Chapel View CR2 .... 222 C1
Chapel Wlk NW4 .... 46 C5
Chapleton Ho SW2 .... 160 C6
Chaplin Cl SE1 .... 251 C2
Wembley HA0 .... 65 D2
Chaplin Cres TW16 .... 171 C4
Chaplin Ho 6 SW9 .... 138 C1
Chaplin Rd E15 .... 98 D6
2 N17 .... 51 D6
NW2 .... 68 A2

Chaplin Rd *continued*
Dagenham RM9 .... 81 A1
Wembley HA0 .... 65 D2
Chapman Cl UB7 .... 104 B3
Chapman Cres HA3 .... 44 B4
Chapman Gn N22 .... 32 C2
Chapman Ho 26 E1 .... 96 B1
2 West Norwood SE27 160 D1
Chapman Rd E9 .... 75 B2
Belvedere DA17 .... 125 D1
Thornton Heath CR0 .... 204 C1
Chapmans End BR5 .... 191 A1
Chapman's La BR5 .... 190 D1
Chapmans Park Ind Est NW10 .... 67 D2
Chapman Sq SW19 .... 156 D2
Chapman St E1 .... 118 B6
Chapone Pl W1 .... 239 C1
Chapter Cl 15 W4 .... 111 A3
Hillingdon UB10 .... 60 B1
Chapter Rd NW2 .... 68 A3
SE17 .... 116 D1 261 D1
Chapter St SW1 .... 259 C3
Chapter Way TW12 .... 173 C6
Chara Pl W4 .... 133 B6
Charcot Ho 9 SW15 .... 155 D5
Charcroft Ct 11 W14 .... 112 D4
Charcroft Gdns EN3 .... 6 D1
Chard Ho 7 N7 .... 72 B6
Chardin Ho 30 SW9 .... 138 C4
Chardin Rd 11 W4 .... 111 C2
Chardmore Rd N16 .... 52 A1
Chardwell Cl E6 .... 100 B1
Charecroft Way W12 .... 112 D4
Charfield Ct W9 .... 91 D3
Charford Rd E16 .... 99 A2
Chargeable La E13 .... 99 A3
Chargeable St E16 .... 98 D3
Chargrove Cl 24 SE16 .... 118 D4
Charing Cl BR6 .... 227 D4
Charing Cross SW1 .... 116 A5 250 A4
Charing Cross Hospl W6 .... 112 D1
Charing Cross Rd WC2 .... 93 D1 239 D1
Charing Cross Sta WC2 .... 116 A5 250 B4
Charing Ct BR2 .... 186 C1
Charing Ho SE1 .... 251 B2
Charlbert Ct NW8 .... 230 A4
Charlbert St NW8 .... 92 C5 230 A4
Charlbury Ave HA7 .... 25 D5
Charlbury Gdns IG3 .... 79 D6
Charlbury Gr W5 .... 87 C1
Charlbury Ho 1 E12 .... 78 C5
Charlbury Rd UB10 .... 60 B5
Charldane Rd SE9 .... 166 D1
Charlecote Gr SE26 .... 162 B1
Charlecote Rd RM8 .... 81 A5
Charlemont Rd E6 .... 100 C3
Charles Allen Ho EC1 .... 234 A2
Charles Auffray Ho 26 E1 .... 96 C2
Charles Babbage Cl KT9 .... 213 C1
Charles Barry Cl SW4 .... 137 C2
Charles Bradlaugh Ho 2 N17 .... 34 B3
Charles Burton Ct E5 .... 75 A4
Charles Cl DA14 .... 190 B6
Charles Cobb Gdns CR0 .... 220 C3
Charles Coveney Rd 4 SE15 .... 139 D4
Charles Cres HA1 .... 42 B2
Charles Ct N3 .... 29 D1
Charles Darwin Ho 8 E2 .... 96 B4
Bromley BR1 .... 187 B3
Charles Dickens Ct SE25 .... 206 A5
Charles Dickens Ho 1 E2 .... 96 B4
Charles Dickens Prim Sch SE1 .... 117 A4 252 A1
Charles Edward Brooke Sch SW9 .... 138 D4
Charlesfield SE12 .... 165 C1
Charles Grinling Wlk SE18 .... 122 C2
Charles Haller St 25 SW2 .... 160 C4
Charles Harrod Ct SW13 .... 134 C6
Charles Ho 1 N17 .... 33 D3
Charles Hobson Ho NW10 .... 67 C1
Charles Hocking Ho 8 W3 .... 111 A4
Charles II Pl SW3 .... 114 D1 257 C1
Charles II St SW1 .... 115 D5 249 C4
Charles La NW8 92 C5 230 A4
Charles Lamb Prim Sch N1 .... 95 A6 235 A6
Charles Lesser KT9 .... 213 D3

Charles Mackenzie Ho 7 SE16 .... 118 A2
Charles Mills Ct SW16 182 A4
Charles Pl NW1 .... 232 B1
Charles Rd E7 .... 77 C1
Dagenham RM6 .... 58 D3
Ealing W13 .... 87 A1
Merton SW19 .... 179 C2
Charles Rowan Ho WC1 .... 234 A1
Charles Sevright Dr NW7 .... 28 D5
Charles Sq N1 .95 B4 235 D1
Charles St E16 .... 121 C5
W1 .... 115 B5 248 C4
Barnes SW13 .... 133 C3
Croydon CR0 .... 221 A5
Enfield EN1 .... 17 D6
Hillingdon UB10 .... 82 D3
Hounslow TW3 .... 129 B3
Charles Staunton Ho 3 SE27 .... 183 B6
Charleston Cl TW13 .... 150 A1
Charleston St SE17 .... 262 B3
Charles Townsend Ho EC1 .... 241 C6
Charles Winchup Rd 2 E16 .... 121 B5
Charlesworth Ho 2 E14 .... 97 C1
Charleville Cir SE26 .... 184 A5
Charleville Ct SW5 .... 254 C1
Charleville Mans W14 254 B1
Charleville Rd W14 .... 113 A1 254 C1
Charlie Browns Rdbt E18 .... 37 C1
Charlmont Rd SW17 .... 180 D4
Charlotte Cl DA6 .... 169 A6
Charlotte Ct N8 .... 49 D3
Ilford IG2 .... 56 C3
5 Wembley HA0 .... 66 A2
Charlotte Ho 12 W6 .... 112 C1
Charlotte Mews W10 .... 90 D1
W1 .... 239 B4
W14 .... 254 A4
Charlotte Park Ave BR1 .... 210 A6
Charlotte Pl SW1 .... 259 A3
W1 .... 239 B3
Charlotte Rd EC2 .... 95 C3 243 A6
Barnes SW13 .... 133 D4
Dagenham RM10 .... 81 D2
Wallington SM6 .... 219 C2
Charlotte Row SW4 .... 137 C2
Charlotte Sharman Prim Sch SE11 .... 116 D3 261 C5
Charlotte Sq 5 TW10 .... 154 B5
Charlotte St W1 93 C2 239 B4
Charlotte Terr N1 .... 94 B6 233 D5
Charlow Cl SW6 .... 136 A3
Charlton Church La SE7 .... 121 C1
Charlton Cl UB10 .... 60 D6
Charlton Cres IG11 .... 101 D5
Charlton Ct 25 E2 .... 95 D6
E6 .... 100 B4
17 N7 .... 71 D3
Charlton Dene SE7 .... 143 D5
Charlton Ho NW1 .... 232 C2
5 Brentford TW8 .... 132 A6
Charlton King's Rd NW5 .... 71 D3
Charlton La SE7 .... 121 D1
Upper Halliford TW17 .... 193 B5
Upper Halliford TW17 .... 193 C5
Charlton Lo 1 NW11 .... 47 B3
Charlton Manor Prim Sch SE7 .... 143 D5
Charlton Park La SE7 .... 144 A6
Charlton Park Rd SE7 143 D6
Charlton Park Sch SE7 .... 144 A6
Charlton Pl N1 .94 D5 234 C4
Charlton Rd N9 .... 18 D4
NW10 .... 89 C6
SE3,SE7 .... 143 B6
Charlton TW17 .... 171 A1
Harrow HA3 .... 43 D5
Wembley HA9 .... 44 B1
Charlton Way SE10, SE3 .... 142 C4
Charlwood Cl HA3 .... 24 C4
Charlwood Ho SW1 .... 259 C3
1 Streatham SW2 .... 160 B3
Charlwood Pl SW1 .... 115 C2 259 B3
Charlwood Rd SW15 .... 134 D1
Charlwood Sq CR4 .... 202 B6
Charlwood St SW1 .... 115 C1 259 B2
Charlwood Terr 5 SW15 .... 134 D1
Charman Ho 18 SW2 .... 160 C5
SW8 .... 270 A4
Charmian Ave HA7 .... 25 D1
Charmian Ho 19 N1 .... 95 C5

Charminster Ave SW19 .... 179 D1
Charminster Ct 3 KT6 .... 197 D2
Charminster Rd SE12,SE9 .... 187 D6
North Cheam KT4 .... 200 D1
Charmouth Ct TW10 .... 154 B6
Charmouth Ho SW8 .... 270 C4
Charmouth Rd DA16 .... 146 C4
Charnock Ho 22 W12 .... 112 B6
Charnock Rd E5 .... 74 B5
Charnwood Ave SW19 179 D1
Charnwood Cl KT3 .... 199 C5
Charnwood Dr E18 .... 55 B5
Charnwood Gdns E14 .... 119 C2
Charnwood Ho 9 E5 .... 74 B6
Charnwood Pl N20 .... 14 A1
Charnwood Rd
Hillingdon UB10 .... 82 C5
South Norwood SE25 .... 205 B5
Charnwood St E5 .... 74 B6
Charrington Rd 2 CR0 .... 221 A6
Charrington St NW1 .... 93 D5 232 C4
Charsley Rd SE6 .... 163 D2
Chart Cl Bromley BR2 .... 186 C2
Croydon CR0 .... 206 C3
Mitcham CR4 .... 202 D5
Charter Ave IG2 .... 57 B2
Charter Cres TW4 .... 129 A1
Charter Ct N4 .... 50 C1
W1 .... 237 B3
Kingston KT3 .... 199 C6
Southall UB1 .... 107 C5
Charter Dr DA5 .... 169 A4
Charter Ho WC2 .... 240 B1
Charterhouse Ave HA0 .65 C3
Charterhouse Bldgs EC1 .... 242 A5
Charterhouse Mews EC1 .... 241 D4
Charterhouse Rd E8 .... 74 A3
Charterhouse Sq EC1 .... 94 D2 241 D4
Charterhouse Square Prim Sch The EC1 .... 94 D2 241 D3
Charterhouse St EC1 .... 241 C3
Charteris Rd N4 .... 50 C1
NW6 .... 91 B6
Woodford IG8 .... 37 B4
Charter Nightingale Hospl The NW1 .... 92 C2 237 B4
Charter Rd KT1 .... 198 D6
Charter Rd The IG8 .... 36 D4
Charter Sch The SE24 .... 161 B6
Charters Cl SE19 .... 183 C5
Charter Sq KT1 .... 176 D1
Charter Way NW3 .... 47 B5
Southgate N14 .... 15 D5
Chartes Ho SE1 .... 263 B6
Chartfield Ave SW15 .... 156 C6
Chartfield Sch SW15 .... 156 B6
Chartfield Sq SW15 .... 156 D6
Chartham Ct 13 SW9 .... 138 C2
Chartham Gr SE27 .... 160 D1
Chartham Ho SE1 .... 262 D6
Chartham Rd SE25 .... 206 B6
Chart Hills Cl SE28 .... 103 A1
Chartley Ave NW2 .... 67 C5
Harrow HA7 .... 24 D4
Charton Cl 5 DA17 .... 147 B6
Chartres Ct UB6 .... 86 B5
Chartridge SE17 .... 139 B6
Chartridge Cl
Barnet EN5 .... 12 A6
Bushey WD23 .... 8 A5
Chartridge Ct 6 HA7 .... 25 C5
Chart St N1 .... 95 B4 235 D2
Chartwell 25 SW19 .... 156 D3
Chartwell Bsns Ctr BR1 .... 209 D6
Chartwell Cl
2 Croydon CR0 .... 205 B1
Greenford UB6 .... 85 D6
Sidcup BR7,DA15 .... 167 B2
Chartwell Ct
8 Barnet EN5 .... 1 A1
2 Woodford IG8 .... 37 A3
Chartwell Dr BR6 .... 227 B3
Chartwell Gdns SM3 .... 217 A4
Chartwell Lo 5 BR3 .... 185 C3
Chartwell Pl
Cheam SM3 .... 217 B4
Harrow HA2 .... 64 B6
Chartwell Way 3 SE20 .... 184 B2
Charville Ct 8 HA1 .... 42 D3
Charville La UB4 .... 83 C5
Charville La W UB10 .... 82 D4
Charville Prim Sch UB4 83 C5
Charwood SW16 .... 182 C6
Chase Bridge Prim Sch TW2 .... 152 C5
Chase Court Gdns EN2 .... 5 A2
Chase Ct SW3 .... 257 C5
Isleworth TW7 .... 131 A3
Merton SW20 .... 179 A1

Chase Ct *continued*
Southgate N14 .... 15 C5
Wembley HA0 .... 65 D2
Chase Ctr The NW10 .... 89 B4
Chase Farm Hospl EN2 .... 4 C5
Chasefield Rd SW17 .... 180 D6
Chase Gdns
Chingford E4 .... 35 C6
Twickenham TW2 .... 152 B4
Chase Gn EN2 .... 5 A2
Chase Green Ave EN2 .... 5 A3
Chase Hill EN2 .... 5 A2
Chase La IG6 .... 57 B4
Chase Lane Inf Sch E4 35 B6
Chase Lane Jun Sch E4 35 B6
Chaseley Ct W4 .... 110 D1
Oatlands Park KT13 .... 193 C1
Chaseley St E14 .... 97 A1
Chasemore Cl CR4 .... 202 D2
Chasemore Gdns CR0 220 C3
Chasemore Ho SW6 .... 264 B4
Chase Rd NW10 .... 89 B3
Southgate N14 .... 15 D5
Chase Ridings EN2 .... 4 C3
Chase Road Trad Est NW10 .... 89 B3
Chase Side N14 .... 15 B4
Enfield EN2 .... 5 A3
Chaseside Ave SW20 .... 179 A1
Chase Side Ave EN2 .... 5 A3
Chase Side Cres EN2 .... 5 A4
Chase Side Pl EN2 .... 5 A3
Chase Side Prim Sch EN2 .... 5 A3
Chase The DA7 .... 147 D2
E12 .... 77 D4
SW4 .... 137 B2
Bromley BR1 .... 209 B6
Edgware HA8 .... 26 D2
Ickenham UB10 .... 60 C3
Loughton IG10 .... 21 D4
Pinner HA5 .... 40 C3
Pinner HA5 .... 41 B5
South Norwood SW16 .... 182 C3
Stanmore HA7 .... 25 A4
Sunbury TW16 .... 172 B2
Wallington CR0,SM6 .... 220 B3
Dagenham RM6 .... 59 A3
Chaseville Par N21 .... 16 B6
Chaseville Park Rd N21 16 B6
Chase Way N14 .... 15 C3
Chasewood Ave EN2 .... 4 D3
Chasewood Ct NW7 .... 27 B5
Chasewood Pk HA1 .... 64 C5
Chater Ho 6 E2 .... 96 D4
Chatfield Rd SW11 .... 136 A2
Thornton Heath CR0 .... 204 D1
Chatham Ave BR2 .... 209 A2
Chatham Cl NW11 .... 47 C4
Cheam SM3 .... 201 B2
Chatham Ct SW11 .... 158 D6
Chatham Ho 22 SE18 .... 122 B2
7 SE5 .... 139 C3
Chatham Pl E9 .... 74 C2
Chatham Rd E17 .... 53 A6
SW11 .... 158 D6
Kingston KT1,KT2 .... 176 C1
1 Woodford E18 .... 36 D1
Chatham St SE17 .... 117 B2 262 D4
Chatsfield Pl W5 .... 88 A1
Chatsworth Ave BR1 .... 187 B6
DA15 .... 168 A3
NW4 .... 28 C1
Merton SW20 .... 179 A1
Wembley HA9 .... 66 B3
Chatsworth Cl NW4 .... 28 C1
Coney Hall BR2,BR4 .... 224 D6
Chatsworth Cres TW3, TW7 .... 130 B2
Chatsworth Ct E5 .... 74 D4
W8 .... 255 A4
5 Stanmore HA7 .... 25 C5
Chatsworth Dr EN1 .... 18 A5
Chatsworth Est E5 .... 74 D4
Chatsworth Gdns
Acton W3 .... 110 D5
Harrow HA2 .... 41 D1
New Malden KT3 .... 199 D4
Chatsworth Ho
2 BR2 .... 209 A5
Kingston KT6 .... 197 D4
Chatsworth Inf Sch DA15 .... 168 A3
Isleworth TW3 .... 130 A1
Chatsworth Jun Sch TW3 .... 130 A1
Chatsworth Lo 1 W4 .... 111 B1
West Wickham BR4 .... 224 A6
Chatsworth Par BR5 .... 211 A4
Chatsworth Pl
Mitcham CR4 .... 202 D6
Teddington TW11 .... 175 A6
Chatsworth Rd E15 .... 76 D3
E5 .... 74 D4
NW2 .... 68 D2
Cheam SM3 .... 217 A4
Chiswick W4 .... 133 A6
Ealing W5 .... 88 B3

Chatsworth Rd *continued*
Hayes UB4 .... 84 B3
South Croydon CR0 .... 221 B5
Chatsworth Rise W5 .... 88 B3
Chatsworth Way SE27 161 A1
Chattenden Ho 8 N4 .... 51 B2
Chattern Hill TW15 .... 170 D6
Chattern Rd TW15 .... 171 A6
Chatterton Ct TW9 .... 132 B3
Chatterton Rd BR2 .... 209 D4
N4 .... 72 D5
Chatton Ct 5 NW9 .... 46 A5
Chatto Rd SW11 .... 158 D6
Chaucer Ave
Cranford TW4 .... 128 B3
Hayes UB4 .... 84 A2
Richmond TW9 .... 132 C3
Chaucer Cl N11 .... 31 D5
Chaucer Ct 17 N16 .... 73 C4
12 New Barnet EN5 .... 13 D6
Chaucer Dr SE1 .... 117 D2 263 D3
Chaucer Gdns SM1 .... 217 C5
Chaucer Gn CR0 .... 206 C2
Chaucer Ho SW1 .... 259 A1
Harrow HA2 .... 41 D4
Sutton SM1 .... 217 C5
2 West Norwood SE27 .... 183 A6
Chaucer Rd DA16 .... 145 D4
E7 .... 77 A2
SE24 .... 160 D6
W3 .... 111 A5
Ashford TW15 .... 170 B6
Chingford E17 .... 36 A1
Sidcup DA15 .... 168 C3
Sutton SM1 .... 217 C4
Wanstead E11 .... 55 A3
Chaucer Way SW17 .... 180 B5
Chaulden Ho EC1 .... 235 D1
Chauncey Cl N9 .... 18 A1
Chaundrye Cl SE9 .... 166 B5
Chauntler Cl E16 .... 121 B6
Chaville Ct N11 .... 31 A6
Cheadle Ct NW8 .... 236 D6
Cheadle Ho 11 E14 .... 97 B1
Cheam Common Inf Sch KT4 .... 216 B6
Cheam Common Jun Sch KT4 .... 216 B6
Cheam Common Rd KT4 .... 216 C5
Cheam Court Flats 1 SM3 .... 217 A2
Cheam Fields Prim Sch SM3 .... 217 A3
Cheam High Sch SM3 217 A4
Cheam Mans SM3 .... 217 A1
Cheam Park Farm Inf Sch SM3 .... 217 A5
Cheam Park Farm Jun Sch SM3 .... 217 A5
Cheam Park Way SM3 217 A2
Cheam Rd
Belmont SM2,SM3 .... 216 D1
Cheam SM1 .... 217 C2
Cheam St 4 SE15 .... 140 B2
Cheam Sta SM2 .... 217 A1
Cheam Village SM3 .... 217 A2
Cheapside EC2 .95 A1 242 B1
Edmonton N13 .... 33 A6
Chearsley SE17 .... 262 B4
Cheddar Cl N11 .... 31 A4
Cheddar Rd TW6 .... 126 C3
Cheddar Waye UB4 .... 84 B1
Cheddington Ho 9 E2 .96 A6
Cheddington Rd N18 .... 33 C6
Chedworth Cl E16 .... 98 D1
Chedworth Ho 2 E5 .... 74 A6
N15 .... 51 B5
Cheeseman Cl TW12 .... 173 A4
Cheesemans Terr W14 .... 254 C1
Chelford Rd BR1 .... 186 B5
Chelmer Cres IG11 .... 102 B5
Chelmer Rd E9 .... 74 D3
Chelmsford Cl W6 .... 134 D6
Newham E6 .... 100 B1
Chelmsford Ct N14 .... 15 D4
Chelmsford Gdns IG1 .... 56 B2
Chelmsford Ho 5 N7 .... 72 B4
Chelmsford Rd E11 .... 54 B1
E17 .... 53 C3
N14 .... 15 C4
Woodford E18 .... 36 D2
Chelmsford Sq NW10 .... 90 C6
Chelsea Barracks* SW1 .... 115 A1 258 B1
Chelsea Bridge SW1 .... 137 B6 268 C6
Chelsea Bridge Rd SW1 .... 115 A1 258 B1
Chelsea Cl NW10 .... 89 B6
Edgware HA8 .... 26 C1
Hampton TW12 .... 174 A5
New Malden KT4 .... 200 A2
Chelsea Cloisters SW3 .... 257 B3

Chelsea Coll of Art & Design SW3 114 C1 257 A1
W12 112 C4
Chelsea Cres SW10 266 B1
Chelsea Ct SW3 268 A6
[8] Chingford E4 20 A3
Chelsea Emb SW3 136 D6 267 C5
Chelsea Est SW3 267 A5
Chelsea Farm Ho SW10 266 D5
Chelsea Fields SW19 180 B2
Chelsea Gate SW1 258 B1
Chelsea Gdns SW1 258 B1
Cheam SM3 217 A4
Ealing W13 86 D2
Chelsea Harbour Design Ctr SW10 266 B2
Chelsea Harbour Dr SW10 136 A4 266 B2
Chelsea Harbour Pier SW10 266 C1
Chelsea Lo SW3 267 D6
SW6 265 C2
Chelsea Manor Ct SW3 267 B6
Chelsea Manor Gdns SW3 257 B1
Chelsea Manor St SW3 114 C1 257 B1
Chelsea Manor Studios SW3 257 B1
Chelsea Park Gdns SW3 136 B6 266 C6
Chelsea Physic Gdn* SW1 267 C6
Chelsea Reach Twr SW10 266 C4
Chelsea Sq SW3 114 B1 256 D1
Chelsea Twrs SW3 267 B6
Chelsea & Westminster Hospl SW10 136 A6 266 B5
Chelsfield Ave N9 18 D4
Chelsfield Gdns SE26 162 C1
Chelsfield Gn N9 18 D4
Chelsfield Ho SE17 263 A3
Chelsfield Point [3] E9 74 D1
Chelsham Ho [1] SW4 137 D2
Chelsham Rd SW4 137 D2
South Croydon CR2 221 B2
Chelsiter Ct DA14 189 D6
Chelston Ct [2] E11 55 B4
Chelston Rd HA4 40 A1
Chelsworth Dr SE18 145 B6
Cheltenham Ave [8] TW1 153 A4
Cheltenham Cl
Kingston KT3 199 A6
Northolt UB5 63 D2
Cheltenham Ct [8] HA7 25 C5
Cheltenham Gdns E6 100 A5
Cheltenham Ho UB3 105 A3
Cheltenham Pl [1] W3 110 D4
Harrow HA3 44 A5
Cheltenham Rd E10 54 A3
SE15 162 C6
Cheltenham Terr SW3 114 D1 257 D2
Cheltenham Villas CR7 204 C3
Chelverton Ct SW15 134 D1
Chelverton Rd SW15 134 D1
Chelwood N20 14 B2
NW5 71 A3
Chelwood Cl E4 19 D5
Chelwood Ct SW11 266 D2
Chelwood Gdns TW9 132 C3
Chelwood Ho W2 236 D1
Chenappa Cl E13 99 A4
Chenduit Way HA7 24 D5
Chene Colline Ct KT6 198 A3
Cheney Ct SE23 162 D3
Cheney Row E17 35 B2
Cheneys Rd E11 76 C5
Cheney St HA5 40 C4
Chenies Ho W2 245 C6
Chenies Mews WC1 239 C5
Chenies Pl NW1 232 D4
Chenies St WC1 93 D2 239 C4
Chenies The NW1 232 D4
Orpington BR5,BR6 211 C3
Cheniston Gdns W8 255 C6
Chennestone Cty Prim Sch TW16 172 B1
Chepstow Cl SW15 157 A6
Chepstow Cres W11 113 C6 245 A6
Ilford IG3 57 C3
Chepstow Ct W11 245 A6
Chepstow Gdns UB1 85 B1
Chepstow Pl W2 113 C6 245 B6
Chepstow Rd W2 91 C1
Croydon CR0 221 D6
Ealing W7 109 A3
Chepstow Rise CR0 221 C5
Chepstow Villas W11 113 C6 245 A6
Chequers IG9 21 B3
Chequers Cl NW9 45 C6
Orpington BR5 211 D5
Chequers Ct EC1 242 C5
[7] Croydon CR0 205 D1
Chequers Ho NW8 237 A6
Chequers La RM9 103 C5
Chequers Par
Dagenham RM9 103 C6
Edmonton N13 33 A5
Chequer St EC1 95 A3 242 B5
Chequers The HA5 40 D6
Chequers Way N13 32 D5
Cherbury Cl SE28 102 D1
Cherbury Ct N1 235 D3
Cherbury St N1 95 B5 235 D3
Cherchefells Mews HA7 25 B5
Cherimoya Gdns KT8 195 D6
Cherington Rd W7 108 D5
Cheriton Ave BR2 209 A4
Cheriton Cl
Cockfosters EN4 2 D1
[10] Ealing W5 87 C2
Cheriton Ct [4] SE12 165 A4
South Norwood SE25 205 C4
Walton-on-T KT12 194 C1
Cheriton Dr SE18 145 B6
Cheriton Ho [9] E5 74 B3
Cheriton Sq SW17 159 A2
Cherry Ave UB1 106 D5
Cherry Blossom Cl N13 32 D5
Cherry Cl E17 53 D4
W5 109 D3
Carshalton SM5 218 D6
Merton SM4 201 A5
Ruislip HA4 61 D5
[7] Streatham SW2 160 C4
Cherrycot Hill BR6 227 B4
Cherrycot Rise BR6 227 A4
Cherry Cres TW8 131 B5
Cherry Croft Gdns [2] HA5 23 B3
Cherry Ct W3 111 C5
Ilford IG6 56 D6
Pinner HA5 22 D2
Sidcup DA14 168 B1
Cherrydeal Ct E11 54 B2
Cherrydown Ave E4 19 C1
Cherrydown Cl E4 19 C1
Cherrydown Rd DA14 168 D2
Cherry Garden Ho [5] SE16 118 B4
Cherry Garden Sch SE16 118 A2
Cherry Garden St SE16 118 B4
Cherry Garth TW8 109 D1
Cherry Gdns
Dagenham RM9 81 B3
Northolt UB5 63 D1
Cherry Gr Hayes UB3 106 B5
Hillingdon UB8 83 A2
Cherry Hill
New Barnet EN5 13 D5
Stanmore HA3 24 C4
Cherry Hill Gdns CR0 220 B4
Cherry Hills WD19 23 A5
Cherry La UB7 104 C2
Cherrylands Cl NW9 67 A6
Cherry Lane Jun & Inf Schs UB7 104 B2
Cherry Laurel Wlk SW2 160 B5
Cherry Orch SE7 143 C6
West Drayton UB7 104 A4
Cherry Orchard Gdns
[7] Croydon CR0 205 B1
East Molesey KT8 195 B6
[5] South Croydon CR0 221 B6
Cherry Orchard Prim Sch SE7 143 C5
Cherry Orchard Rd BR2 226 A6
Croydon CR0 205 C1
East Molesey KT8 195 C6
Cherry Rd EN3 6 C5
Cherry Tree Ave UB7 82 B1
Cherry Tree Cl [17] E9 96 C6
Wembley HA0 65 A4
Cherrytree Ct NW9 45 A5
Cherry Tree Ct [17] SE7 143 C6
[3] Woodford E18 36 D1
Cherry Tree Dr SW16 160 A1
Cherrytree Ho [8] W10 90 D4
Cherry Tree Ho SE14 141 B3
Cherry Tree Rd E15 76 C3
N2 48 D5
Cherry Tree Rise IG9 37 D6
Cherry Trees Sch The E3 97 C4
Cherry Tree Terr SE1 253 B2
Cherry Tree Way HA7 25 B4
Cherry Tree Wlk EC1 242 B5
Beckenham BR3 207 B5
Coney Hall BR4 224 D4
Cherry Way
Upper Halliford TW17 193 C5
West Ewell KT19 215 B2
Cherry Wlk BR2 209 A1
Cherrywood Cl E3 97 A4
Kingston KT2 176 C3
Cherrywood Ct [1] TW11 175 A5
Cherrywood Dr SW15 156 D6
Cherrywood La SM4, SW20 201 A5
Cherry Wood Way W5 88 C2
Chertsey Ct SW14 132 D2
Chertsey Dr SM3 217 A6
Chertsey Ho [37] E2 95 D4
Feltham TW13 151 C1
Chertsey Rd E11 76 B6
Ashford TW15,TW16 171 B4
Feltham TW13,TW16 171 C6
Ilford IG1 79 B4
Lower Halliford TW17 192 C2
Shepperton TW17 192 A2
Twickenham TW2 152 B4
Chertsey St SW17 181 A5
Chervil Cl TW13 150 A1
Chervil Mews SE28 124 B5
Cherwell Ct
Teddington KT1 175 D3
West Ewell KT19 215 A4
Cherwell Ho NW8 236 D5
Cherwell Way HA4 39 A3
Cheryls Cl SW6 135 D4 265 D2
Cheseman St SE26 162 B1
Chesfield Rd KT2 176 A3
Chesham Ave BR2,BR5 210 D3
Chesham Cl SW1 258 A5
Chesham Cres SE20 184 C2
Chesham Ct SW18 158 B4
Chesham Flats W1 248 B6
Chesham Mews SW1 258 A6
Chesham Pl SW1 115 A3 258 A5
Chesham Rd
Kingston KT1,KT2 176 C1
Penge SE20 184 C2
Chesham St NW10 67 B5
SW1 115 A3 258 A5
Chesham Terr W13 109 B4
Cheshire Cl
Chingford, Highams Park E17 35 D2
Mitcham CR4,SW16 204 A6
Cheshire Gdns KT9 213 D2
Cheshire Ho SM4 201 D2
Cheshire Rd N22 32 B4
Cheshire St E2 95 D3 243 D6
Cheshir Ho NW4 46 C5
Chesholm Rd N16 73 C5
Cheshunt Ho [7] NW6 91 D6
Cheshunt Rd E7 77 B2
Belvedere DA17 125 C1
Chesil Ct [18] E2 96 C5
SW3 267 B6
Chesilton Rd SW6 135 B4 264 C2
Chesil Way UB4 83 D4
Chesley Gdns E6 100 A4
Chesney Cres CR0 224 A1
Chesney Ct W9 91 C3
Chesney Ho SE13 142 B1
Chesney St SW11 268 A1
Chesnut Gr N17 51 D6
Chesnut Rd N17 51 D6
Chessell Cl CR7 204 D5
Chessholme Ct TW16 171 C3
Chessholme Rd TW15 171 A4
Chessing Ct N2 48 D6
Chessington Ave DA7 147 A5
N3 47 B6
Chessington Cl KT19 215 A2
Chessington Com Coll KT9 213 D1
Chessington Ct N3 47 B6
Pinner HA5 41 B5
Chessington Hall Gdns KT9 213 D1
Chessington Hill Pk KT9 214 C3
Chessington Ho [19] SW8 137 D3
Chessington Lo N3 47 B6
Chessington Mans E10 53 C2
E11 54 C2
Chessington North Sta KT9 214 A3
Chessington Par KT9 213 D3
Chessington Park KT9 214 C4
Chessington Pk KT9 214 C4
Chessington Rd KT19 215 B1
Chessington South Sta KT9 213 D1
Chessington Way BR4 223 D6
Chesson Rd W14 135 B6 264 D6
Chesswood Way HA5 22 D1
Chestbrook Ct [12] EN1 17 C6
Chester Ave
Richmond TW10 154 B5
Chester Ave *continued*
Twickenham TW2 151 B3
Chester Cl SW1 248 C1
Ashford TW15 171 B5
Barnes SW13 134 B2
Hayes UB8 82 D1
[1] Richmond TW10 154 B5
Sutton SM1 217 C6
Chester Close N NW1 231 D2
Chester Close S NW1 231 D1
Chester Cres E8 73 D3
Chester Ct NW1 231 D1
NW5 71 A4
[4] SE5 139 B5
SE8 118 D1
[2] Acton W3 88 C1
Chester Dr HA2 41 C3
Chesterfield Ct KT6 198 A4
Chesterfield Dr KT10 213 A6
Chesterfield Flats EN5 12 D6
Chesterfield Gdns N4 50 D4
SE10 142 B5
W1 248 C4
Chesterfield Gr SE22 161 D6
Chesterfield Hill W1 115 B5 248 C4
Chesterfield Ho W1 248 B4
[6] Streatham SW16 181 C5
Chesterfield Jun & Inf Sch EN3 7 A6
Chesterfield Lo N21 16 B4
Chesterfield Mews N4 50 D4
Ashford TW15 170 A6
Chesterfield Rd E10 54 A3
N3 29 C4
Ashford TW15 170 A5
Barnet EN5 12 D6
Chiswick W4 133 A6
Enfield EN3 7 A6
West Ewell KT19 215 B1
Chesterfield St W1 248 C4
Chesterfield Way
SE15 140 C5
Hayes UB3 106 A4
Chesterford Gdns NW3 69 D4
Chesterford Ho [4] SE18 143 D5
Chesterford Rd E12 78 B3
Chester Gate NW1 231 D1
Chester Gdns
Ealing W13 87 B1
Enfield EN3 18 B5
Morden SM4 202 A3
Chester Ho N19 71 B6
[1] SE8 141 B6
Kingston KT1 176 D1
Chesterman Ct W4 133 C5
Chester Mews SW1 258 C6
Chester Pl NW1 231 C2
Chester Rd DA15 167 C6
E16 98 C3
E17 52 D4
E7 77 D1
N17 51 C6
N19 71 B6
NW1 93 B4 231 C2
Edmonton N9 18 B3
Harlington TW6 126 C2
Hounslow TW4 128 B2
Ilford IG3 57 D2
Wanstead E11 55 B3
Wimbledon SW19,SW20 178 C4
Chester Row SW1 115 A2 258 B4
Chester Sq SW1 115 B2 258 C4
Chester Sq Mews SW1 258 C5
Chester St E2 96 A3
SW1 115 A3 258 B6
Chesters The KT3 177 C2
Chester Terr NW1 93 B4 231 C2
Chesterton Cl SW18 157 C6
Greenford UB6 85 D5
Chesterton Dr TW19 148 B3
Chesterton Ho
[21] SW11 136 B2
[3] W10 91 A2
Chesterton Prim Sch SW11 137 A4 268 A1
Chesterton Rd E13 99 A4
W10 91 A2
Chesterton Sq W8 255 A3
Chesterton Terr E13 99 A4
[6] Kingston KT1 176 C1
Chester Way SE11 116 C2 261 B3
Chesthunte Rd N17 33 A2
Chestnut Alley SW6 264 D5
Chestnut Ave E7 77 B4
N8 50 A4
Brentford TW8 109 D2
Buckhurst Hill IG9 21 D1
Coney Hall BR4 224 C4
Edgware HA8 26 B4
Hampton TW12 173 C3
Chestnut Ave *continued*
Hampton, Hampton Court KT8,KT11 174 D2
[11] Mortlake SW14 133 B2
Thames Ditton KT10 196 B1
Wembley HA0 65 B3
Worcester Park KT19 215 C4
Yiewsley UB7 104 B6
Chestnut Ave N E17 54 B5
Chestnut Ave S E17 54 B4
Chestnut Cl DA15 168 A2
[1] N16 73 B6
SE14 141 B4
Ashford TW15 170 D6
Ashford TW16 171 D4
Buckhurst Hill IG9 21 D2
Carshalton SM5 202 D1
Catford SE6 186 A6
Harlington UB7 126 D5
Hayes UB3 105 C6
Southgate N14 15 D6
West Norwood SW16 182 C6
Chestnut Ct N8 49 D3
N8 50 A4
SW6 264 D6
Beckenham BR3 185 C3
[5] Croydon CR0 221 A4
Feltham TW13 172 D5
Hounslow TW3 129 C2
Kingston KT3 199 C6
Surbiton KT6 198 A2
Wembley HA0 65 B3
Chestnut Dr DA7 147 A2
Harrow HA3 24 D2
Pinner HA5 41 A3
Wanstead E11 55 A3
Chestnut Gr W5 109 D3
Cockfosters EN4 14 D6
Isleworth TW7 131 A1
Kingston KT3 199 B6
Mitcham CR4 203 D5
Penge SE20 184 C3
South Croydon CR2 222 B1
Upper Tooting SW12 159 A3
Wembley HA0 65 B3
Chestnut Grove Sch SW12 159 A3
Chestnut Ho [7] NW3 70 D2
SE4 141 B2
[1] W4 111 C2
West Norwood SE27 161 A1
Chestnut La N20 13 A3
Chestnut Pl SE19 183 D6
Chestnut Rd
Ashford TW15 170 D6
Kingston KT2 176 A3
Twickenham TW2 152 C2
West Barnes SW20 178 D1
West Norwood SE21, SE27 161 A1
Chestnut Rise SE18 123 C1
Chestnut Row N3 29 C3
Chestnuts Ct [3] E17 54 A6
Chestnuts The N2 48 D4
[1] N5 72 D4
NW9 45 C6
SE18 144 D4
[3] Erith DA17 125 B1
Penge BR3 206 D6
Uxbridge UB10 60 A1
Walton-on-T KT12 194 B1
Chestnut Way TW13 150 B1
Chestnut Wlk
Upper Halliford TW17 193 C5
Woodford IG8 37 A5
Cheston Ave CR0 207 B1
Chestwood Gr UB10 60 B1
Chettle Cl SE1 262 C6
Chettle Ct N8 50 C3
Chetwode Ho NW8 237 A6
Chetwode Rd SW17 158 D1
Chetwood Wlk [13] E6 100 A2
Chetwynd Ave EN4 14 D3
Chetwynd Dr UB10 82 B5
Chetwynd Rd NW5 71 B5
Cheval Ct SW15 134 B1
Chevalier Cl HA7 26 A6
Cheval Pl SW7 114 C3 257 B6
Cheval St E14 119 C3
Cheveney Wlk [2] BR2 209 A6
Chevening Ho BR5 190 A2
Chevening Rd NW6 91 A6
SE10 120 D1
South Norwood SE19 183 B4
Chevenings The DA14 168 C1
Cheverell Ho [24] E2 96 A5
Cheverton Rd N19 49 D1
Chevet St E9 75 A3
Chevington NW2 69 B2
Cheviot [4] N17 34 B3
Cheviot Cl Bushey WD23 8 A5
Enfield EN1 5 B3
Harlington UB3 127 B5
Cheviot Ct [16] SE14 140 C5
Enfield EN2 5 B3
Southall UB2 107 D2
Cheviot Gate NW2 69 A6
Cheviot Gdns NW2 69 A6
West Norwood SE27 182 D6
Cheviot Ho N16 51 D1
Cheviot Rd SE27 182 D5
Cheviots Hostel EN1 5 B3
Cheviot Way IG2 57 C5
Chevron Cl E16 99 A1
Chevy Rd UB2 108 A4
Chewton Rd E17 53 A5
Cheylesmore Ho SW1 258 C2
Cheyne Ave E18 54 D6
Twickenham TW2 151 B3
Cheyne Cl [6] NW4 46 B4
Keston Mark BR2 226 A5
Cheyne Ct SW3 267 C6
[1] Croydon CR0 221 D6
[4] Wallington SM6 219 B2
Cheyne Gdns SW3 136 C6 267 B5
Cheyne Hill KT5 198 B5
Cheyne Mews SW3 136 C6 267 B5
Cheyne Path W7 86 D1
Cheyne Rd TW15 171 B4
Cheyne Row SW3 136 C6 267 A5
Cheyne Wlk NW4 46 C3
SW10 136 B5 266 C4
Croydon CR0 222 A6
Southgate N21 16 D6
Cheyney Ho [2] E9 74 D2
Cheyneys Ave HA8 25 D4
Chichele Gdns CR0 221 C4
Chichele Rd NW2 68 D3
Chicheley Gdns HA3 24 A3
Chicheley Rd HA3 24 A3
Chicheley St SE1 250 D2
Chichelle Ho HA8 26 B6
Chichester Ave HA4 61 B6
Chichester Cl E6 100 A1
SE3 143 C4
Hampton TW12 173 B4
Chichester Ct
Edgware HA8 26 C4
Harrow HA2 41 B1
Northolt UB5 85 A6
[3] Sidcup DA5 169 C4
Stanmore HA7 44 A6
Stanwell TW19 148 A3
Chichester Gdns IG1 56 B2
Chichester Ho NW6 91 C5
[2] Kingston KT2 176 D2
Chichester Mews SE27 182 C6
Chichester Rd E11 76 C5
NW6 91 C5
W2 91 D2
Edmonton N9 18 A3
South Croydon CR0 221 C5
Chichester Rents WC2 241 A2
Chichester St SW1 115 C1 259 B1
Chichester Way E14 120 B2
Feltham TW14 150 C4
Chicksand Ho [13] E1 96 A2
Chicksand St E1 95 D2 243 D3
Chiddingfold N12 13 C1
Chiddingstone SE13 164 A6
Chiddingstone Ave DA7 147 B5
Chiddingstone St SW6 135 C3
Chieveley Par DA7 147 D2
Chieveley Rd DA7 147 D1
Chignell Pl [7] W13 109 A5
Chigwell Hill E1 118 B6
Chigwell Hurst Ct HA5 40 D6
Chigwell Rd
Wanstead E18 55 B6
Woodford IG8 37 D3
Chilam Ho [5] SE15 140 C6
Chilchester Ct [3] BR3 207 D6
Chilcombe Ho [6] SW15 156 A4
Chilcot Cl [13] E14 97 D1
Chilcott Cl HA0 65 C4
Child Ct E11 54 B2
Childebert Rd SW17 159 B2
Childeric Prim Sch SE14 141 A5
Childeric Rd SE14 141 A5
Childerley St SW6 135 A4 264 A2
Childerly KT1 198 C6
Childers St SE8 141 B6
Chlld La SE10 120 D3
Childs Ct UB3 106 A6
Child's Hill Prim Sch NW2 69 A5
Childs La [11] SE19 183 C4
Child's Pl SW5 255 B3
Child's St SW5 255 B3
Childs Way NW11 47 B4
Child's Wlk SW5 255 B3
Chilham Cl DA5 169 B4
Wembley UB6 87 A5
Chilham Ct [14] SW9 138 C2

Chilham Ho SE1 .... **262** D6
Chilham Rd SE8 .... 188 A6
Chillerton Rd SW17 ..... 181 B5
Chillingford Ho SW17 ..180 A6
Chillingworth Gdns
TW1 ....152 D1
Chillingworth Rd N7 ....72 C3
Chilmark Gdns KT3 ....200 A3
Chilmark Rd SW16 .....181 D2
Chiltern Ave
Bushey WD23 ....8 A5
Twickenham TW2 ....151 C3
Chiltern CI
Ickenham UB10 ....60 C6
North Cheam KT4 ....216 C6
South Croydon CR0 ....221 C5
Bushey WD23 ....8 A5
Chiltern Ct N10 ....31 A1
NW1 ....**237** C5
 SE14 ....140 C5
 SE9 ....166 C5
Harrow HA1 ....42 B4
Hillingdon UB8 ....82 D3
New Barnet EN5 ....14 A6
Chiltern Dene EN2 ......4 A1
Chiltern Dr KT5 ....198 D4
Chiltern Gdns NW2 ....68 D5
Beckenham BR3 ....208 D5
Chiltern Ho N16 .....52 C1
SE17 ....139 B6
 W10 ....91 A2
Ealing W5 ....88 A2
 Edmonton N9 ....18 A1
Chiltern Rd Bow E3 ....97 C3
Ilford IG2 ....57 C4
Pinner HA5 ....40 C6
Chiltern St W1 ..93 A2 **238** A4
Chiltern Way IG8 ......21 A1
Chilthorne CI SE6 .....163 B4
Chilton Ave W5 ....109 D2
Chilton Gr SE8 ....119 A2
Chiltonian Ind Est
SE12 ....164 D5
Chilton Rd Edgware HA8 26 C4
Richmond TW9 ....154 D4
Chilton St E2 ..95 D3 **243** D6
Chiltons The E18 ....37 A1
Chilvers CI TW2 ....152 C2
Chilver St SE10 ....120 D1
Chilwell Gdns WD19 ....22 C6
Chilworth Ct SW19 156 D3
Chilworth Gdns SM1 ..218 A5
Chilworth Mews
W2 ....92 B1 **236** C1
Chilworth St
W2 ....92 B1 **236** B1
Chimes Ave N13 ....32 C6
Chimney Ct E1 ....118 B5
Chimneys Ct SW9 178 C3
China Ct E1 ....118 C5
China Mews SW2 ..160 B4
Chinbrook Cres SE12 ..165 B1
Chinbrook Rd SE12 ...165 B1
Chinchilla Dr TW4 ....128 C3
Chindit Ho N16 .....73 A4
Chine The N10 ....49 C5
Southgate N21 ....16 D6
Wembley HA0 ....65 B3
Ching Ct E4 ....20 C1
Chingdale Rd E4 ....20 C1
Chingford Ave E4 ......19 D2
Chingford CE Inf Sch
E4 ....20 B3
Chingford CE Jun Sch
E4 ....20 B3
Chingford Foundation
Sch E4 ....19 B3
Chingford Hall Com Prim
Sch E4 ....35 B4
Chingford Hospl E4 ....20 A1
Chingford Ind Ctr E4 ..35 A5
Chingford La IG8 ....36 D5
Chingford Mount Rd
E4 ....35 A2
Chingford Rd
Chingford E17 ....35 D1
Chingford E4 ....35 C3
Chingford Sch E4 ....19 D3
Chingford Sta E4 ....20 C4
Chingley CI BR1 ....186 C4
Ching Way E4 ....35 B4
Chinnery CI EN1 ....5 D4
Chinnocks Wharf E14 119 A6
Chinnor Cres UB6 ......86 A5
Chipka St E14 ....120 A4
Chipley St SE14 ....141 A6
Chipmunk Gr UB5 ....85 A4
Chippendale Ho SW1 **258** D1
Chippendale St E5 ......74 D5
Chippenham Ave HA9 ..66 D3
Chippenham Gdns
NW6 ....91 C4
Chippenham Mews W9 91 C3

Chippenham Rd W9 ....91 C3
Chipperfield Rd BR5 ..190 A1
Chipping CI EN5 ....1 A2
Chip St SW4 ....137 D1
Chipstead Ave CR7 ...204 D5
Chipstead CI SE19 ....183 D3
Chipstead Gdns NW2 ..68 B6
Chipstead Rd SW2 160 A3
Chipstead St SW6 ....135 C3
Chirk CI UB4 ....85 A3
Chisenhale Prim Sch
E3 ....97 A5
Chisenhale Rd E3 ......97 A5
Chisholm Ct W6 ....112 A1
Chisholm Rd
Croydon CR0 ....221 C6
 Richmond TW10 ....154 B5
Chisledon Wlk E9 ....78 C6
Chislehurst Ave N12 ...30 A3
Chislehurst High St
BR7 ....188 D4
Chislehurst Rd BR6 ...211 D2
Bromley BR1,BR7 ......188 A2
Orpington,Petts Wood
BR5,BR6,BR7 ....211 A4
Richmond TW10 ....154 A6
Sidcup DA14 ....190 A5
Chislehurst & Sidcup Gram
Sch DA15 ....168 B2
Chislehurst Sta BR7 ..188 C1
Chislehurst St Nicholas CE
Prim Sch BR7 ....189 A3
Chislet NW5 ....71 A2
Chislet CI BR3 ....185 C3
Chisley Rd N15 ....51 C3
Chiswell Sq SE3 ....143 B3
Chiswell St EC1 95 B2 **242** C4
Chiswick & Bedford Park
Prep Sch W4 ....111 C2
Chiswick Ct UB10 ......220 B5
Chiswick Common Rd
W4 ....111 B2
Chiswick Com Sch
W4 ....133 B5
Chiswick Ct A5 ....41 B6
Chiswick Green Studios
W4 ....111 A2
Chiswick High Rd W4 111 C2
Chiswick Ho ★ W4 ....110 C1
Chiswick La W4 ....111 C1
Chiswick La S W4 ......133 D6
Chiswick Mall W4 .....111 D1
Chiswick Maternity Hospl
W4 ....111 C1
Chiswick Park Sta W4 111 A2
Chiswick Pier W4 ......133 C5
Chiswick Pk W4 ....110 D2
Chiswick Plaza W4 ....133 A4
Chiswick Quay W4 ....133 A4
Chiswick Rdbk W4 ....110 C1
Edmonton N9 ....18 A2
Chiswick Sq W4 ....133 C6
Chiswick Staithe W4 ..133 A3
Chiswick Terr W4 ..111 A2
Chiswick Village W4 ..132 D6
Chiswick Wharf W4 ...133 D6
Chitterfield Gate UB7 126 C5
Chitty's La RM8 ....80 D6
Chitty St W1 ...93 C2 **239** B4
Chivalry Rd SW11 .....158 C6
Chivelston SW19 ..156 D3
Chivenor Gr KT2 ......175 D5
Chivers Rd E4 ....35 C6
Choats Rd IG11 ....102 D4
Chobham Gdns SW19 156 D2
Chobham Rd E15 ....76 C3
Cholmeley Cres N6 ....49 B2
Cholmeley Lo N6 ....49 A1
Cholmeley Pk N6 ....49 B2
Cholmley Gdns NW6 ..69 C3
Cholmley Rd KT7 ......197 B3
Cholmondeley Ave
NW10 ....90 A5
Cholmondeley Wlk
TW9 ....153 C6
Chopin's Ct E1 ......118 B5
Chopwell CI E15 ....76 B1
Chorleywood Cres
BR5 ....190 A1
Choumert Gr SE15 ....140 A3
Choumert Mews SE15 140 A3
Choumert Rd SE15 ...139 D3
Choumert Sq SE15 140 A3
Chow Sq E8 ....73 D3
Chrisp Ho SE10 ....142 C6
Chrisp St E14 ....97 D1
Christabel CI TW7 ....130 D2
Christchurch Ave N12 ..30 A4
NW6 ....69 A1
Harrow HA3 ....42 D5
Harrow HA3 ....43 A5
 Teddington TW11 ...175 A5
Wembley HA0 ....66 A2

Christ Church Bentinck CE
Prim Sch NW1 92 C2 **237** B4
Christ Church CE Mid Sch
 W5 ....109 D6
Christchurch CE Prim Sch
SW3 ....136 D6 **267** C6
Christ Church CE Prim Sch
NW6 ....69 B1
SE10 ....120 C1
SE18 ....144 C4
SW11 ....136 C1
Forest Hill SE23 ....162 D2
Kingston KT3 ....199 C6
Christ Church CE
E1 ....95 D2 **243** D3
Christ Church CE Sec Sch
N12 ....30 B5
Christchurch CI N12 ...30 B3
Enfield EN2 ....5 A3
Mitcham SW19 ....180 B3
Christ Church CE NW10 89 C6
Wimbledon SW19 .....179 A5
NW6 ....69 A1
Christchurch Ct UB4 ..84 C3
Christchurch Gdns HA3 43 A5
Christchurch Ho SW2 ..66 A2
Christchurch Hill NW3 ..70 B4
Christchurch Ho
SW2 ....160 A3
Christ Church La EN5 ...1 A3
Christchurch Lo E4 .....2 D1
Christchurch Pas NW3 ..70 A5
Tottenham N15 ....51 A6
Christchurch Pk SM2 218 A1
Christ Church Prim Sch,
Hampstead NW3 ....70 B5
Christchurch Rd DA15 167 D1
Christ Church Rd N8 ...50 A3
Christchurch Rd
Harlington TW6 ....126 C2
Ilford IG1 ....79 A6
Mitcham SW19 ....180 B2
Mortlake SW14 ....155 A6
Surbiton KT5 ....198 B3
Christ Church
BR3 ....185 C1
Christ Church Sch
W4 ....93 B4 **231** D2
Christ Church Sq E9 96 C6
Christchurch St
SW3 ....136 D6 **267** C6
Christ Church Streatham CE
Prim Sch SW2 ....160 B3
Christchurch Terr
SW3 ....**267** C6
Christchurch Way
SE10 ....120 C1
Christian Ct SE16 ....119 B5
Christian Fields SW16 182 C3
Christian St E1 ....96 A1
Christie Ct N19 ......72 A6
 W14 ....110 A4
NW3 ....70 C3
Christie Dr SE25 ......206 A4
Christie Gdns RM6 .....58 B2
Christie Ho SE10 ..142 C6
 SE10 ....140 C6
West Wickham BR4 ...207 D1
Christie Rd E9 ....75 A2
Christina Sq N4 ....50 D1
Christina St EC2 ....95 B3
Christine Worsley CI
N21 ....16 D3
Christopher Ave W7 ..109 A3
Christopher Boone's
Almshouses SE13 ....142 B1
Christopher CI DA15 ..167 D6
SE16 ....118 D4
Christopher Ct
Ashford TW15 ....170 A5
Barnet EN5 ....1 A3
 Croydon CR0 ....206 A1
Christopher Gdns RM9 80 D3
Christopher Hatton Prim
Sch EC1 ......94 C3 **241** A5
Christopher N E2 ..49 D2
Christopher PI NW1 ..232 D1
Christopher Rd UB2 ..106 B2
Christopher St
EC2 ....95 B3 **242** D5
Christ's Coll NW11 .....47 D6
SE3 ....143 A4
Christ's Coll Upper Sch
N3 ....29 B1
Christ's Sch (East Side)
TW10 ....154 C6
Christ's Sch (West Side)
TW10 ....154 B6
Christ the King RC Fst Sch
N4 ....72 B6
Christ the King RC Prim Sch
N4 ....72 B6
Christ the King RC Sixth
Form Coll SE13 ....142 B2
Chryssell Rd SW9 ....138 C5
Chubworthy St SE14 ..141 A6
Chudleigh SW1 ......146 A2
Chudleigh Cres IG3 ....79 C4
Chudleigh Gdns SM1 ..218 A5
Chudleigh Rd NW6 ....68 D1
SE4 ....163 C6
Twickenham TW1,TW2 ..152 D4

Chudleigh St E1 ....96 D1
Chudleigh Way HA4 ....40 A1
Chulsa Rd SE26 ....184 B5
Chumleigh Gdns SE5 139 C6
Chumleigh St SE5 ....139 C6
Chumleigh Wlk KT5 ..198 B5
Church App DA14 .....190 B5
N2 ....30 B2
NW1 ....71 B2
Beckenham BR3 ......185 C2
Chingford E4 ....36 B4
Mortlake SW14 ....133 B2
Northolt UB5 ....63 B1
Pinner HA5 ....41 B3
Ruislip HA4 ....39 B1
Southall UB2 ....107 A3
Churchbank E17 ....53 C5
Churchbury CI EN1 ......5 C3
Churchbury La EN1 ......5 C3
Churchbury Rd SE9 ..165 D4
EN1 ....5 C3
Church CI HA8 ....27 A5
N20 ....14 C1
W8 ....113 C2
Hayes UB4 ....83 B2
Hounslow TW4 ....129 B3
West Drayton UB7 ....104 A3
Church Cres E9 ....74 D1
N10 ....49 B5
N20 ....14 C1
N3 ....29 B2
Churchcroft CI SW12 159 A4
Church Ct EC4 ....**241** B1
N9 ....18 A6
 Richmond TW10 ...153 D6
Churchdale Ct W4 ..110 D1
Churchdale Rd EN3 ...186 C6
Church Dr NW9 ....45 B1
Church Elm La RM10 ...81 C2
Church End E17 ....53 D5
Hendon NW4 ....46 B6
Church Entry EC4 .....**241** D1
Church Estate Almshouses
 TW9 ....132 B1
Church Farm House Mus★
NW4 ....46 A5
Church Farm La SM3 217 A2
Churchfield Ave N12 30 B4
Churchfield CI
Harrow HA2 ....42 A5
Hayes UB3 ....105 D6
Churchfield Ho W2 236 C5
Churchfield Mans
SW6 ....135 B3
Churchfield PI TW17 ..192 D2
Churchfield Prim Sch
N9 ....17 D3
Churchfield Rd DA16 ..146 A2
W3 ....111 A6
W7 ....108 C4
Ealing W13 ....109 C5
Walton-on-T KT12 ....194 A1
Churchfields SE10 ....142 A6
East Molesey KT8 ....195 C6
Woodford IG8 ....37 A2
Churchfields Ave
TW13 ....151 C1
Churchfields SE2 ......124 A2
Wanstead E11 ....55 A4
Church PI SW1 ....**249** B5
Upper Tooting SW17 ...181 A5
Wallington SM6 ....219 C1
Church PI E W5 ....109 D4
Uxbridge UB10 ....61 A5
Church Rd BR1,BR2 ..187 A1
DA8 ....146 B3
Feltham TW13 ....170 B6
E10 ....75 C6
E12 ....78 A3
 E1 ....35 A1
 N1 ....73 A2
N6 ....49 A3
NW10 ....67 C1
W3 ....111 A4
Ashford TW15 ....170 B6
Barnes SW13 ....134 A4
Bexley DA6,DA7 ....147 B2
Cheam SM3 ....217 A2
Claygate KT10 ....212 D1
Croydon CR0 ....221 A5
Ealing W7 ....108 C6
East Molesey KT8 ...196 B6
Enfield EN3 ....18 C6
 N17 ....73 A2
Hayes UB3 ....105 D6
NW10 ....67 C1
Acton W3 ....111 A4
Ashford TW15 ....170 B6
Barnes SW13 ....134 A4
West Barnes SW20 ...200 C6
Churchwood Gdns IG8 37 A6
Churchyard Row
SE11 ....116 D2 **261** D4
Churnfield N4 ....50 D1
Churston Ave E13 ....99 B6
Churston CI SW2 ...160 C3
Churston Dr SM4 .....201 A4
Churston Gdns N11 ....31 C4
Churston Mans WC1 ..**240** D5
Churston PI SW1 ......**259** B3
Brentford W4 ....132 D6
Churton St
SW1 ....115 C2 **259** B3
Chute Ho SW9 ......**264** D5
Chuter Ede Ho SW6 ..**264** D5
Chyngton CI DA15 ....167 D1
Chyngton Ct HA1 ....64 C6
Cibber Rd SE23 ....162 D2
Cicada Rd SW18 ......158 A6
Cicely Ho NW8 ....**229** D3
Cicely Rd SE15 ....140 A4
Cinderford Way BR1 ..186 C6
Cinema Par RM8 ....81 B6
Cinnabar Wharf Central
E1 ....118 A5
Cinnabar Wharf East
E1 ....118 A5
Cinnabar Wharf West
E1 ....118 A5
Cinnamon CI SE15 139 D5
Thornton Heath CR0 ..204 A2
Cinnamon Row
SW11 ....136 A2
Cinnamon St E1 ......118 B5
Cinnamon Wharf SE1 **253** D2
Cinque Cotts SW19 ..178 C4
Cintra Ct SE19 ....183 D4
Cintra Pk SE19 ....183 D3
Circle Ct HA0 ....65 D4

Churchill Ct continued
NW4 ....50 C2
NW2 ....68 B3
Edmonton N9 ....17 B3
Harrow HA2 ....41 D4
 Ilford IG2 ....57 C3
Northolt UB5 ....63 C3
Churchill Gardens Prim Sch
SW1 ....115 C1 **259** B1
Churchill Gdns
SW1 ....137 C6 **269** A6
Acton W3 ....88 C1
Churchill Gdns Rd
SW1 ....137 C6 **269** A6
Churchill Ho UB8 ....109 C1
Churchill Lo IG8 ....36 D4
Churchill Mews IG8 ....36 C4
Churchill PI E14 ....119 D5
Harrow HA1 ....42 C5
Churchill Rd NW2 ......68 B2
NW5 ....71 B4
Edgware HA8 ....26 C4
Newham E16 ....99 C1
South Croydon CR2 ..221 A1
Churchill Terr E4 ....19 C1
Churchill Way BR1 ..187 A1
Ashford TW16 ....172 A4
Church La E11 ....54 C1
 E17 ....53 D5
N2 ....48 B6
N8 ....50 B5
N9 ....18 A6
N17 ....33 D2
W5 ....109 D4
Chessington KT9 ......214 B2
Dagenham RM10 ......81 D2
Edmonton N9 ....17 C2
Enfield EN2 ....5 B2
Hampton TW12 ....174 A2
Isleworth TW7 ....131 B3
Kingston KT1 ....175 D1
Sunbury TW16 ....194 B6
Twickenham TW1 ....153 A3
Walton-on-T KT12 ...194 A2
Church St N 1 E15 ....98 D6
TW3 ....152 A6
Church St Sta CR0 ...221 A6
Church Terr SE13 .....142 C2
Hendon NW4 ....46 B6
 Richmond TW10 ...153 D6
Church Vale N2 ....48 D6
SE23 ....162 D2
Churchview Rd TW2 ..152 B2
Church Villa TW4 ..194 B6
Churchward Ho SE17 **261** C1
SW5 ....**254** D1
Churchway NW1 ......**232** D2
Churchway EN4 ....2 C1
Church Wlk N16 ....73 B4
N6 ....69 B1
NW9 ....67 B6
Barnes SW13 ....134 A4
Hayes UB3 ....83 D1
Mitcham SW16 ....181 C1
 Richmond TW10 ...153 D6
Thames Ditton KT7 ..196 D3
 N11 ....31 A4
West Barnes SW20 ...200 C6

Circle Gdns SW19 ....179 C1
Circle Ho E14 ....98 B1
Circle The NW2 ......67 C5
NW7 ....27 B4
SE1 ....253 D2
Circuit Rd SE28 ....124 A4
Circuits The HA5 ....40 C5
Circular Rd N17 .....51 D6
NW2 ....30 B2
Circular Way SE18 ..144 C6
Circus Lo NW8 ......229 C2
Circus Mews W1 ....237 C4
Circus Pl EC2 ....242 D3
Circus Rd NW8 .92 B5 229 C2
Circus St SE10 .....142 A5
Cirencester St W2 ...91 D2
Cirrus NW9 ....9 C5
Cissbury Ho ⑨ SE26 .162 A1
Cissbury Ring N N12 ..51 B4
Cissbury Ring N N12 ..29 C5
Cissbury Ring S N12 ..29 B5
Citizen Ho N7 ....72 C4
Citizen Rd N7 ....72 C4
Citron Terr ③ SE15 ..140 B2
Citrus Ho ④ SE8 ....119 B1
City Airport Pier E16 .120 D5
City and Islington Coll
EC1 ....94 D4 234 C1
City Banking Coll
SE1 ....117 B4 252 D2
City Bsns Ctr ⑳ SE16 118 C4
City Central Est EC1 ..235 A1
City Forum EC1 ..94 A4 235 A2
City Garden Row
N1 ....94 D5 234 D3
City Gate E1 ....96 C3
City & Guilds of London Art
Sch The SE11 ..116 C1 261 B1
City Harbour E14 ....119 D3
City & Islington Coll
N1 ....95 B6 235 C6
N4 ....72 D6
City Literature Inst The
WC2 ....94 A1 240 B2
City of London Sch
EC4 ....117 A6 252 A6
City of London Sch for Girls
EC2 ....95 A2 242 A4
City of Westminster Coll
W2 ....92 C2 237 B4
W2 ....92 B2 236 C4
City of Westminster Coll,
Maida Vale Ctr W9 ...91 D4
City of Westminster Coll,
Queens Park Ctr W9 ...91 C4
City Prospect ⑤ SE19 183 C4
City Rd EC1 .....95 A4 235 B2
City Thameslink Sta
EC4 ....94 D1 241 C1
City Wharf Ho KT17 ..197 B3
Civic Way HA7 ....62 D3
Civil Service Coll
SW1 ....115 C2 259 A3
Clabon Mews
SW1 ....114 D2 257 C4
Clack St SE16 ....118 C4
Clacton Rd E17 ....53 A3
E6 ....99 D4
Tottenham N17 ......51 D4
Claigmar Gdns N3 ....29 D2
Claire Ct N12 ....14 A1
NW2 ....69 A2
Bushey WD23 ....8 B3
Claire Gdns HA7 .....25 C5
Claire Pl E14 ....119 C3
Clairvale Rd TW5 ...129 A4
Clairview Rd SW16 ..181 B5
Clairville Gdns W7 ..108 C5
Clairville Point ⑫
SE23 ....162 D1
Clamp Hill HA7 ......24 C5
Clancarty Rd SW6 ...135 C3
Clandon Cl W3 ......110 D4
Stoneleigh KT17 ....216 A2
Clandon Ct BR1 ....187 A4
Sutton SM2 ....218 B2
Clandon Gdns N3 ....47 C6
Clandon Ho N3 ......47 C6
⑫ Kingston KT2 ....176 D4
Clandon St SE8 .....141 C3
Clanfield Ho ⑦ SW15 156 A3
Clanricarde Gdns
W2 ....113 C6 245 B5
Clapham Common*
SW4 ....137 C1
Clapham Common North
Side SW4 ....159 C6
Clapham Common South
Side SW4 ....159 C6
Clapham Common Sta
SW4 ....137 C1
Clapham Common West
Side
SW11 ....159 A6
SW4,SW11 ....136 D1
Clapham Court Terr ②
SW4 ....160 A6

Clapham Cres SW4 ..137 D1
Clapham Ct ③ SW4 ..160 A6
Clapham High St SW4 137 D1
Clapham High Street Sta
SW4 ....137 D2
Clapham Junction Est
SW11 ....136 C1
Clapham Junction Sta
SW11 ....136 C1
Clapham Manor Ct ①
SW4 ....137 D1
Clapham Manor Prim Sch
SW4 ....137 C2
Clapham Manor St
SW4 ....137 C2
Clapham Mans SW4 ..159 B5
Clapham Park Rd
SW4 ....138 A2
Clapham Park Terr ④
SW2 ....160 A6
Clapham Rd
SW9 ....138 B4 270 D2
Clapham South Sta
SW4 ....159 B5
Claps Gate La E6 ...100 D3
Clapton Comm E5 ....52 A2
Clapton Girls Tec Coll
E5 ....74 C4
Clapton Ho ⑦ E5 ....74 C6
Clapton Pas E5 ......74 C4
Clapton Sq E5 ....74 C4
Clapton Terr E5 .....52 A1
Clapton Way E5 ......74 A5
Clara Grant Prim Sch The
E3 ....97 C3
Clara Pl SE18 ......122 C2
Clare Cl N2 ....48 A6
Borehamwood WD6 ....10 B5
Clare Cnr SE9 ......166 D4
Clare Ct BR7 ....188 B2
WC1 ....233 B1
Wimbledon SW19 ....179 A4
Claredale Ct SW4 ..218 A1
Claredale Ho ③ E2 ...96 B5
Claredale St E2 ......96 B5
Clare Gdns E7 ....77 A4
Barking IG11 ....80 A1
Stratford E7 ....263 D2
Clare Grant Ho ⑨ E14 119 C3
Clare Ho E3 ....97 B6
⑧ HA8 ....27 A1
SE1 ....263 D2
Clare House Prim Sch
BR3 ....186 A1
Clare La N1 ....73 A1
Clare Lawn Ave SW14 156 C3
Clare Mkt WC2 ......240 D1
Claremont
⑥ Putney SW15 ....157 A6
Shepperton TW17 ...192 D3
Claremont Ave
Harrow HA3 ....44 A4
Sunbury TW16 ......172 B2
West Barnes KT3 ...200 B4
Claremont Cl E16 ...122 C5
⑥ Streatham SW2 ..160 B3
Orpington BR6 .....226 C4
Claremont Ct ⑧ W9 ..91 B5
Claremont Dr TW17 .192 D3
Claremont Gdns
Ilford IG3 ....79 C6
Kingston KT6 ......198 A4
Claremont Gr
Chiswick W4 ....133 C5
Woodford IG8 ....37 C4
Claremont High Sch
HA3 ....44 A4
Claremont Hts EN2 ...4 A1
Claremont La KT10 .212 A3
Claremont Pk N3 ....29 A2
Claremont Rd BR1 ..210 B5
E17 ....35 A1
E7 ....76 B5
E7 ....77 C6
W9 ....91 B5
Claygate KT10 .....212 C1
Croydon CR0 ......206 A1
Ealing W13 ....87 A2
Harrow HA3 ....24 C1
Hayes UB3 ....105 C2
Mitcham SW19 .....180 C3
Wallington SM6 ...219 C2
Wanstead E18 ....55 A6
Wood Green N22 .....32 A3
Claremont Rise SE13 142 A1
Claremont Sch ③
NW2 ....68 C6
Claremont Sq
N1 ....94 C5 234 A3
Claremont St E16 ...122 C4
SE10 ....141 D6
Edmonton N18 ......34 A4
Claremont Terr KT7 .197 B2
Claremont Way NW2 ..46 D2
Claremont Way Ind Est
NW2 ....46 C1

Clarence Ave SW4 ..159 D5
Bromley BR1,BR2 ...210 A5
Ilford IG2 ....56 C3
Kingston KT3 ......177 B1
New Barnet EN4 .....14 B6
Clarence Cl Bushey WD23 8 B4
⑤ Harrow HA3 ......44 A1
Clarence Cr NW7 ....27 C5
E16 ....112 B2
Clarence Ct NW7 ....27 C5
Clarence Gate Gdns
NW1 ....93 B4 231 D1
Clarence Gdns
NW1 ....93 B4 231 D1
Clarence Ho ⁕
SW1 ....115 C5 249 B3
Clarence La SW15 ..155 D5
Clarence Mews E5 ...74 B3
⑧ SE16 ....118 D5
Balham SW12 ......159 B4
Clarence Pl ㉕ E5 ...74 B3
Clarence Rd DA6 ...147 A1
E12 ....77 D3
E16 ....98 C3
E17 ....34 D1
E5 ....74 B4
N15 ....51 B4
NW6 ....69 B1
W4 ....110 C1
Bromley BR1,BR2 ..210 A6
Chislehurst SE9 ...166 A2
Enfield EN3 ....18 C6
Richmond TW9 ....132 C4
Sidcup DA14 ......168 B1
Sutton SM1 ....217 D3
Teddington TW11 ..175 A4
Thornton Heath CR0 ..205 B2
Wallington SM6 ...219 B3
Wimbledon SW19 ..179 D4
Wood Green N22 ...32 A3
Clarence St
Kingston KT1,KT2 ..176 A1
⑤ Richmond TW9 ..132 A1
Southall UB2 ......106 D3
Clarence Terr NW1 .237 D6
Hounslow TW3 ....129 D1
Clarence Way NW1 ..71 B1
Clarence Wlk ⑬ SW4 138 A3
Clarence CE Infants Sch
TW15 ....170 B6
Clarendon Cl ⑪ W2 247 A6
⑰ Hackney E9 .....74 C1
Clarendon Cres TW2 152 B1
Clarendon Cross ⑪ 244 B5
Clavell St ⑪ SE10 .142 A6
Clarendon Dr SW15 134 C1
Clarendon Flats W1 238 B1
Clarendon Gdns
W9 ....92 A3 236 B5
Hendon NW4 ....46 B6
Redbridge IG1 ....56 B2
Wembley HA9 ....66 A4
Clarendon Gr NW1 ..232 C2
Mitcham CR4 ......202 D6
⑨ SW19 ....179 D3
Clarendon Mews DA5 169 D3
W2 ....247 A6
Clarendon Pl
W2 ....114 C6 247 A6
Clarendon Rd E11 ...54 B1
E17 ....53 D3
N15 ....51 A5
N8 ....31 C4
N18 .....113 A6 244 B5
Ashford TW15 .....170 B6
Ealing W5 ....88 A3
Edmonton N18 ......34 A5
Harrow HA1 ....42 C3
Hayes UB3 ....105 D4
Mitcham SW19 ....180 C3
Wallington SM6 ...219 C2
Wanstead E18 ....55 A6
Wood Green N22 .....32 B1
Clarendon Rise SE13 142 A1
Clarendon St
SW1 ....115 B1 258 D2
Clarendon Terr W9 ..236 B6
Clarendon Way
BR5,BR7 ....211 D6
Chislehurst BR7 ...211 A5
Enfield N21 ....17 A5
Clarendon Wlk ⑪ W11 .91 A1
Clarens St SE6 .....163 B2
Clare Pl SW15 ......156 A4
Clare Point ⑧ NW2 ..46 D6
Clare Rd E11 ....54 B3
NW10 ....67 D1
SE14 ....141 B4
Hounslow TW4 ....129 B2
Northolt UB6 ....64 B2
Stanwell TW19 ....148 A4
Clare St E2 ....96 B5
Clareville Ct SW7 ..256 B3

Clifford Ct *continued*
W2 91 D2
Wandsworth SW18 158 B4
Clifford Dr SW9 138 D1
Clifford Gdns NW10 90 C5
Hayes UB3 105 B2
Clifford Gr TW15 170 C6
Clifford Haigh Ho
SW6 134 D5
Clifford Ho W14 254 C3
2 Beckenham BR3 185 D4
Clifford Rd E16 98 D3
N9 18 C5
Barnet EN5 1 D2
Chingford E17 36 A1
Croydon SE25 206 A5
Hounslow TW4 128 D2
Richmond TW10 153 D2
Wembley HA0 87 D6
Clifford's Inn Pas EC4 241 A1
Clifford St W1 115 C6 249 A5
Clifford Way NW10 67 D4
Cliff Rd NW1 71 D2
Cliffsend Ho 23 SW9 138 C4
Cliff Terr SE8 141 C3
Cliffview Rd SE13 141 C2
Cliff Villas NW1 71 D2
Cliff Wlk E16 98 D2
Clifton Ave E17 52 D6
N3 29 B2
Feltham TW13 150 C1
Shepherd's Bush W12 111 D5
Stanmore HA7 25 B1
Wembley HA9 66 B2
Clifton Cl 8 BR6 227 A3
Clifton Cres SE15 140 B5
Clifton Ct N4 72 C6
NW8 236 C6
SE15 140 B5
2 Beckenham BR3 185 D2
Putney SW15 156 D6
South Norwood SE25 205 C4
9 Stanwell TW19 148 A5
Surbiton KT5 198 B2
3 Woodford IG8 37 A4
Clifton Gate SW10 266 A6
Clifton Gdns N15 51 D3
2 NW11 47 B3
W4 111 B2
W9 92 A3 236 A5
Enfield EN2 16 A6
Hillingdon UB10 82 D5
Clifton Gr E8 74 A2
Clifton Hill
NW8 92 A6 229 A5
Clifton Ho E11 76 C6
E2 243 C6
Clifton Lodge (Brunel Univ
Coll Twickenham Campus)
TW1 153 B6
Clifton Mans 4 SW9 138 C1
Clifton Mews SE25 205 C5
Clifton Par TW13 172 C6
Clifton Park Ave
SW20 178 C1
Clifton Pl SE16 118 C4
W2 236 D1
Clifton Prim Sch UB2 107 A2
Clifton Rd E16 98 C2
E7 77 D2
N3 30 A2
N8 49 D3
NW10 90 A5
W9 92 A3 236 B6
Bexley DA16 146 C2
Greenford UB6 86 B3
Harlington TW6 126 D2
Harrow HA3 44 B4
Ilford IG2 57 B3
Isleworth TW7 130 C3
Kingston KT2 176 B2
Sidcup DA14 189 C6
Southall UB2 107 A2
South Norwood SE25 205 C5
Teddington TW11 174 C6
Wallington SM6 219 B3
Wimbledon SW19 178 D4
Wood Green N22 31 C2
Clifton Rise SE14 141 A5
Cliftons Roundabout
SE9,SE12 165 C5
Clifton St EC2 95 C3 243 A5
Clifton Terr N4 72 C6
Clifton The KT6 214 A6
Clifton Villas
W9 92 A2 236 A4
Cliftonville Ct SE12 165 A3
Clifton Way SE15 140 C5
Wembley HA0 88 A6
Climsland Ho SE1 251 B4
Clinch Ct 11 E16 99 A2
Cline Ho SW15 156 A6
Cline Rd N11 31 C4
Clinger Ct N1 95 C6
Clink St SE1 117 B5 252 C4
Clinton Ave
Bexley DA16 146 A1
East Molesey KT8 196 A5
Clinton Ho
New Malden KT3 199 B1
6 Surbiton KT6 197 D2
Clinton Rd E3 97 A4
E7 77 A4
N15 51 B5
Clipper Cl 3 SE16 118 D4
Clipper Ho E14 120 A1
Clipper Way SE13 142 A1
Clippesby Cl KT9 214 B2
Clipstone Ho 10 SW15 156 A6
Clipstone Mews W1 239 A4
Clipstone Rd TW3 129 C2
Clipstone St
W1 93 C2 239 A4
Clissold Cl N2 48 D6
Clissold Cres N16 73 B4
Clissold Ct N4 73 A6
Clissold Ho 4 N16 73 B6
Clissold Rd N16 73 B5
Clitheroe Ave HA2 41 C1
Clitheroe Gdns WD19 22 D6
Clitheroe Rd SW9 138 A3
Clitherow Ave W7 109 A3
Clitherow Rd TW8 109 C1
Clitterhouse Cres NW2 46 C1
Clitterhouse Jun & Inf Schs
NW2 68 D6
Clitterhouse Rd NW2 46 C1
Clive Ave N18 34 A4
Clive Ct W9 236 B6
Streatham SW16 181 D5
Tolworth KT6 214 C6
Cliveden Cl N12 30 A6
Cliveden Pl
SW1 115 A2 258 A4
Shepperton TW17 193 A3
Cliveden Rd SW19 179 B2
Clivedon Ct W13 87 B2
Clivedon Rd E4 36 C5
Clive Ho SE10 142 A6
18 SW8 137 D3
3 Croydon CR0 205 D1
Clive Lloyd Ho N15 51 A4
Clive Lo NW4 46 D3
Clive Rd
Belvedere DA17 125 C2
Enfield EN1 6 A1
Feltham TW14 150 A5
Mitcham SW19 180 C4
Teddington TW1 175 A6
West Norwood SE21,
SE27 161 B1
Clivesdale Dr UB3 106 B5
Clive Way EN1 6 A1
Cloak La EC4 117 B6 252 C6
Clochar Ct NW10 89 D6
Clock Ct E11 55 B5
Clock Ho E17 54 B5
N16 51 D2
Clock Ho The EN2 5 D6
Clockhouse Ave IG11 101 A6
Clockhouse Cl SW19 156 C2
Clock House Ct 1
BR3 185 A1
Clockhouse Junc N13 32 C5
Clockhouse La TW14,
TW15 148 D2
Clockhouse Par N13 32 C5
Clock House Par E11 55 B3
Clockhouse Pl SW15 157 A5
Clock House Rd BR3 185 A1
Clockhouse Rdbt
TW14 149 A3
Clock House Sta BR3 185 A2
Clockhouse The SW19 156 C1
Clock Tower Mews
N1 235 B5
Thamesmead SE28 124 B6
Clock Tower Pl N7 72 A2
Clock Tower Rd TW7 130 D2
Cloister Cl TW11 175 B5
Cloister Gdns HA8 27 A5
Croydon SE25 206 B3
Cloister Rd NW2 69 B6
W3 89 A2
Cloisters Ave BR1,BR2 210 B4
Cloisters Ct DA7 147 D2
N6 49 B1
Cloisters The 22 SW9 138 C4
Clonard Way HA5 23 C4
Clonbrock Rd N16 73 C4
Cloncurry St SW6 134 D3
Clone Ct 4 W12 111 C3
Clone The 5 KT2 176 D3
Clonmel Cl HA2 42 B1
Clonmell Rd N17 51 B6
Clonmel Rd TW11 174 B6
Fulham SW6 135 B4 264 D2
Clonmore St SW18 157 B3
Cloonmore Ave BR6 227 D4
Clorane Gdns NW3 69 C5
Close The BR5 211 C3
DA14 190 B5
N10 31 B1
N14 15 D2
Close The *continued*
N20 13 B2
Beckenham BR3 207 A5
Cheam SM3 201 B2
Chingford E4 36 A3
Cockfosters EN4 14 D6
Croydon SE25 206 A3
Dagenham RM6 59 A3
Hillingdon UB10 82 C6
Hounslow TW7 130 B3
Ilford IG2 57 C3
Kingston KT3 177 A1
Mitcham CR4 202 D5
Mortlake TW9 132 D2
Pinner HA5 40 C2
Pinner HA5 41 B2
1 Sidcup DA5 169 C4
Surbiton KT6 198 A3
Wembley HA0 66 A2
Wembley HA9 67 A5
Cloth Ct EC1 241 D3
Cloth Fair EC1 94 D2 241 D3
Clothier Ho SE7 122 A1
Clothier St EC3 243 B2
Cloth St EC1 95 A2 242 A4
Clothworkers Rd SE18 145 B5
Cloudesdale Rd SW17 159 B2
Cloudeslay Mans N1 234 B5
Cloudesley Pl
N1 94 C6 234 B5
Cloudesley Rd DA7 147 B4
N1 94 C6 234 A5
Cloudesley Sq
N1 94 C6 234 B6
Cloudesley St
N1 94 C6 234 B5
Clouston Cl SM6 220 A3
Clova Rd E7 77 A3
Clove Cres E14 120 B6
Clovelly Ave NW9 45 D5
Uxbridge UB10 61 A4
Clovelly Cl Pinner HA5 40 C6
Uxbridge UB10 61 A4
Clovelly Ct NW2 68 C3
Clovelly Gdns EN1 17 C4
Clovelly Ho W2 236 A2
Clovelly Rd DA7 147 A6
N8 49 D5
W4 111 B4
W5 109 C4
Hounslow TW3 129 C3
Clovelly Way BR6 211 D3
E1 96 C1
Harrow HA2 63 B6
Clover Cl E11 76 B6
Cloverdale Gdns DA15 167 D5
Clover Ho TW3 130 A4
Cloverleys IG10 21 D6
Clover Mews SW3 267 D6
Clover Way SM6 203 A1
Clove St 9 E13 99 A3
Clowders Rd SE6 163 B1
Clowes Ho 3 SW4 138 A1
Clowser Cl 4 SM1 218 A3
Cloysters Gn E1 118 A5
Cloyster Wood HA8 25 D4
Club Gardens Rd BR2 209 A2
Club Row E2 95 D3 243 C6
Clumps The TW15 171 B6
Clunbury Ave UB2 107 B1
Clunbury St N1 235 D3
Clunie Ho SW1 257 D6
Cluny Mews SW5 255 A3
Cluny Pl SE1 117 C3 263 A6
Cluse Ct N1 235 A4
Clutton St E14 97 D2
Clydach Rd EN1 5 D1
Clyde Cir N15 51 C5
Clyde Ct NW1 232 D4
Clyde Flats SW6 264 C4
Clyde Ho 9 KT2 175 D2
Clyde Pl E10 53 D2
Clyde Rd N15 51 C5
N22 31 D2
Croydon CR0 221 D6
Stanwell TW19 148 A3
Sutton SM1 217 C3
Wallington SM6 219 C2
Clydesdale EN3 6 D1
Clydesdale Ave HA7 43 D6
Clydesdale Cl
Borehamwood WD6 11 B6
Isleworth TW7 130 D2
Clydesdale Ct N20 14 B3
Clydesdale Gdns
TW10 132 D1
Clydesdale Ho DA18 125 A4
4 W11 91 B1
Clydesdale Path WD6 11 B6
Clydesdale Rd W11 91 B1
Clyde St SE8 141 B6
Clyde Terr SE23 162 C2
Clyde Vale SE23 162 C2
Clyfford Rd HA4 61 D4
Clymping Dene TW14 150 B4
Clynes Ho 3 E2 96 D4
6 Dagenham RM10 81 C5
Hayes UB4 84 A4
Clyro Ct N4 50 B1
Clyston St SW8 137 C3
Clytha Ct SE27 183 A6
Coach & Horses Yd
W1 249 A6
Coach House La N5 72 D4
Wimbledon SW19 156 D1
Coach House Mews
SE23 162 D5
Coach House Yd NW3 70 B4
Coachmaker Mews 5
SW9 138 A2
Coachman Lo N12 30 A5
Coalbrook Mans 3
SW12 159 B3
Coaldale Wlk SE21 161 A4
Coalecroft Rd SW15 156 C6
Coalport Ho SE11 261 A4
Coal Wharf Rd W12 112 D5
Coates Ave SW18 158 C5
Coates Ct NW3 70 C3
Coates Hill Rd BR1 188 C1
Coates Rd WD6 9 D4
Coate St E2 96 A5
Coates Wlk TW8 110 A1
Cobbett Rd SE9 144 A2
Twickenham TW2 151 C3
Cobbetts Ave IG4 55 D4
Cobbett St
SW8 138 B5 270 D3
Cobble La N1 72 D1
Cobble Mews N4,N5 73 A5
Cobbler's Wlk
Teddington KT1,TW11 175 A2
Teddington TW11 174 D3
Cobblestone Pl CR0 205 A1
Cobbold Ct SW1 259 C4
Cobbold Ind Est NW10 67 D2
Cobbold Mews W12 111 D4
Cobbold Rd E11 76 D5
NW10 67 D2
W12 111 D4
Cobb's Hall 1 SW6 134 D6
Cobbs Rd TW4 129 B1
Cobb St E1 243 C3
Cob Cl WD6 11 A6
Cobden Bldgs WC1 233 C2
Cobden Ct 9 SE28 124 C5
Cobden Ho 7 E2 96 A4
NW1 232 A4
Cobden Mews SE26 184 B5
Cobden Rd BR6 227 B4
E11 76 C6
Croydon SE25 206 A4
Cobham 21 NW9 27 D1
Cobham Ave KT3 200 A4
Cobham Cl 2 DA15 168 B5
SW11 158 C5
Bromley BR2 210 A2
Edgware HA8 26 D1
Enfield EN1 6 A2
Wallington SM6 220 A2
Cobham Ct CR4 180 B1
Cobham Ho IG11 101 A6
Cobham Mews 3 NW1 71 D1
Cobham Pl DA6 168 D6
Cobham Rd N22 50 D6
Chingford E17 36 A2
Heston TW5 128 C5
Ilford IG3 79 C5
Kingston KT1,KT2 176 C1
Cobland Rd SE12 187 C6
Coborn Mews 9 E3 97 B4
Coborn Rd E3 97 B4
Coborn St E3 97 B4
Cobourg Prim Sch
SE5 139 D6
Cobourg Rd SE5 139 D6
Cobourg St
NW1 93 C4 232 B1
Coburg Cl SW1 259 B4
Coburg Cres SW2 160 C3
Coburg Dwellings 10
E1 118 C6
Coburg Gdns IG5 37 D1
Coburg Rd N22 32 B1
Cochrane Cl NW8 229 D3
Cochrane Ct 3 E10 53 C1
Cochrane Mews
NW8 92 B5 229 D3
Cochrane Rd SW19 179 B3
Cochrane St
NW8 92 B5 229 D3
Coci Ho W14 254 D3
Cockburn Ho SW1 259 D1
Cockerell Rd E17 53 A3
Cockfosters Par EN4 3 A1
Cockfosters Rd EN4 2 D3
Cockfosters Sta EN4 3 A1
Cock Hill E1 243 B3
Cock La EC1 94 D2 241 D3
Cockpit Yd WC1 240 D4
Cocks Cres KT3 199 D5
Cocksett Ave BR6 227 C2
Cockspur Ct SW1 249 D4
Cockspur St
SW1 115 D5 249 D4
Cocksure La DA14 191 C6
Coda Ctr The
SW6 135 A4 264 B2
Code St E1 95 D3 243 D5
Codicote Ho 22 SE8 118 D2
Codicote Terr N4 73 A6
Codling Cl 13 E1 118 A5
Codling Way HA0 65 D4
Codrington Ct SE16 119 A5
Codrington Hill SE23 163 A4
Codrington Ho 7 E1 96 B3
Codrington Mews W11 91 A1
Cody Cl Harrow HA3 43 D6
Wallington SM6 219 D1
Cody Rd E16 98 B3
Coe Ave SE25 206 A3
Coerdale Ct EN3 7 A6
Coe's Alley EN5 1 A1
Cofers Circ HA9 66 D5
Coffey St SE8 141 C5
Cogan Ave E17 35 A2
Cohen Ho NW7 28 A6
Cohen Lo E5 75 A3
Coin St SE1 116 C5 251 A4
Coity Rd NW5 71 A2
Cokers La SE21 161 B3
Coke St E1 96 A1
Colab Ct N22 32 C2
Colas Mews 7 NW6 91 C6
Colbeck Mews
SW5 113 D2 255 D3
Colbeck Rd HA1 42 A2
Colberg Pl N16 51 D2
Colbert 1 SE5 139 D4
Colborne Ho 7 E14 119 C6
Colborne Way KT4 216 C6
Colbrook Ave UB3 105 B3
Colbrook Cl UB3 105 B3
Colburn Ave HA5 23 A4
Colburn Way SM1 218 B5
Colby Rd
Walton-on-T KT12 194 A1
West Norwood SE19 183 C5
Colchester Ave E12 78 B5
Colchester Dr HA5 40 D4
Colchester Ho 17
SW8 137 D3
Colchester Rd E10 54 A2
E17 53 C3
HA8 27 A3
Pinner HA6 22 A1
Colchester St E1 243 D2
Colchester Villas CR7 204 C3
Coldbath Sq EC1 241 A6
Coldbath St SE13 141 D3
Coldblow La SE14 140 D6
Coldershaw Rd W13 109 A4
Coldfall Ave N10 31 A1
Coldfall Prim Sch N10 30 D1
Coldham Ct N22 32 D2
Coldham Gr EN3 7 A6
Coldharbour E14 120 A5
Coldharbour Crest
SE9 166 C1
Coldharbour Ind Est
SE5 139 A3
Coldharbour La SW9 138 D2
Bushey WD23 8 A6
Hayes UB3 106 A5
Coldharbour Lane Ho
UB3 106 A5
Coldharbour Pl SE5 139 B3
Coldharbour Rd CR0 220 C3
Coldharbour Sports Ctr
SE9 166 C2
Coldharbour Way CR0 220 C3
Coldstream Gdns
SW18 157 B5
Colebeck Mews N1 72 D2
Colebert Ave E1 96 C3
Colebert Ho 20 E1 96 C3
Colebrook Cl SW19 156 D4
Colebrook Ct SW3 257 B3
Colebrooke Ave W13 87 B1
Colebrooke Ct DA14 190 B6
Colebrooke Dr E11 55 C2
Colebrooke Pl N1 234 D5
Colebrooke Row
N1 94 D5 234 C4
N1 234 C5
Colebrooke Sch
N1 94 D5 234 D4
Colebrook Ho 1 E14 97 D1
Colebrook Rd SW16 182 A2
Colebrook Rise BR2 186 C1
Colebrook Way N11 31 B5
Coleby Path 21 SE5 139 B5
Colechurch Ho 8 SE1 118 A1
Cole Cl SE28 124 B5
Cole Court Lo 7 TW1 153 A4
Coledale Dr HA7 25 C2
Coleford Rd SW18 158 A6
Cole Gdns TW5 128 A5
Colegrave Prim Sch
E15 76 B3
Colegrave Rd E15 76 B3
Colegrove Rd SE15 139 D6
Coleherne Ct
SW10 113 D1 255 D1
Coleherne Mans SW5 255 D2
Coleherne Mews
SW10 113 D1 255 C1
Coleherne Rd
SW10 113 D1 255 C1
Colehill Gdns SW6 264 A1
Colehill La
SW6 135 A4 264 B1
Cole Ho SE1 251 B1
Coleman Cl SE25 184 A1
Coleman Ct SW18 157 C4
Coleman Fields
N1 95 A6 235 B6
Coleman Mans N19 50 A2
Coleman Rd SE5 139 C5
Belvedere DA17 125 C2
Dagenham RM9 81 A2
Colemans Heath SE9 166 D1
Coleman St EC2 95 B1 242 C2
Coleman St Bldgs EC2 242 C2
Colenso Dr NW7 28 A3
Colenso Rd E5 74 C4
Ilford IG2 57 C2
Cole Park Gdns TW1 153 A5
Cole Park Rd TW1 153 A5
Cole Park View 2
TW1 153 A5
Colepits Wood Rd SE9 167 B6
Coleraine Park Prim Sch
N17 34 B2
Coleraine Rd N8,N22 50 C6
SE3 142 D6
Cole Rd TW1 153 A5
Coleridge Ave E12 78 A2
Carshalton SM1 218 C4
Coleridge Cl SW8 137 B3
Coleridge Ct W14 112 D3
11 New Barnet EN5 13 D6
2 Richmond TW10 175 D6
Coleridge Gdns NW6 70 A1
Coleridge Ho SE17 262 B2
SW1 259 B1
Coleridge Prim Sch N8 49 D2
Coleridge Rd E17 53 B5
N12 30 A5
N4,N7 72 C6
N8 49 D3
Ashford TW15 170 B6
Croydon CR0 206 C2
Coleridge Sq W13 87 A1
Coleridge Way
Hayes UB4 84 A1
West Drayton UB7 104 B2
Coleridge Wlk NW11 47 C5
Colerne Ct NW4 29 A1
Colesburg Rd BR3 185 B1
Coles Cres HA2 63 D6
Coles Ct SW11 266 D1
Coles Gn WD23 8 A3
Coles Green Ct NW2 68 A6
Coles Green Rd NW2 68 B6
Coleshill Flats SW1 258 B3
Coleshill Rd TW11 174 C4
Cole St SE1 117 A4 252 B1
Colestown St 4 SW11 136 C3
Coleswood N20 14 C3
Colesworth Ho 1 HA8 27 A1
Colet Cl N13 32 D4
Colet Gdns W14 112 D2
Colet Ho SE17 261 D1
Colette Ct 5 SE16 118 D4
Coley St WC1 94 B3 240 D5
Colfe & Hatchcliffe's Glebe
SE13 163 D6
Colfe Rd SE23 163 A3
Colfe's Prep Sch SE12 165 A5
Colfe's Sch SE12 165 B5
Colgate Ct EN5 13 A6
Colgate Ho SE13 141 D3
Colgate Pl EN3 7 C6
Colham Ave UB7 104 A5
Colham Green Rd UB8 82 C2
Colham Manor Jun & Inf
Schs UB8 82 C1
Colham Rd UB8 82 B3
Colina Mews N8,N15 50 D5
Colina Rd N8,N15 50 D4
Colin Blanchard Ho
SE4 141 C3
Colin Cl NW9 45 C5
Coney Hall BR4 224 D5
Croydon CR0 223 B5
Colin Cres NW9 45 D5
Colin Ct SW16 159 D2
Colindale Ave NW9 45 C6
Colindale Hospl NW9 45 C6
Colindale Prim Sch
NW9 45 D5
Colindale Sta NW9 45 C6
Colindeep Gdns NW4 46 A5
Colindeep La NW9,NW4 45 D5
Colin Dr NW9 45 D4
Colinette Rd SW15 134 C1
Colin Gdns NW9 45 D5
Colin Par NW9 45 C5
Colin Park Rd NW9 45 C5
Colin Rd NW10 68 A2
Colinsdale N1 234 C5
Colinton Rd IG3 80 B6
Colin Winter Ho 32 E1 96 C3
Coliston Pass SW18 157 C4
Coliston Rd SW18 157 C4

Collamore Ave SW18 158 C3
Collapit Cl HA1 41 D3
Collard Pl NW1 71 B1
College App SE10 142 A6
College Ave HA3 24 C2
College Cl E5 74 C3
Edmonton N18 33 D5
Harrow HA3 24 C3
Twickenham TW2 152 B3
College Cres NW3 70 B2
College Cross N1 72 C1
College Ct NW3 70 B2
SW3 114 D1 257 D1
3 W6 112 C1
Croydon CR0 222 A6
Ealing W5 110 A6
Enfield EN3 18 C6
College Dr Ruislip HA4 40 A2
Thames Ditton KT7 196 C2
College Fields Bsns Ctr
SW19 180 C2
College Gdns
Chingford E4 20 A3
Dulwich SE21 161 C3
Edmonton N18 34 A5
Enfield EN2 5 B4
New Malden KT3 199 D4
Redbridge IG4 56 A4
Upper Tooting SW17 158 C2
College Gn BR1 187 A2
South Norwood SE19 183 C3
College Gr NW1 232 C6
College Hill EC4 252 B6
College Hill Rd HA3 24 C3
College La NW5 71 B4
College Park Cl SE13 142 B1
College Park Rd N17 33 D4
College Park Sch W2 91 D1
College Pl E17 54 C5
NW1 93 C6 232 B5
SW10 266 A4
College Pt E15 76 D2
College Rd BR1 187 A3
E17 54 A4
NW10 90 C5
Dulwich SE19,SE21 161 C2
Ealing W13 87 B1
Enfield EN2 5 B3
Harrow HA1 42 C3
Harrow HA3 24 C2
Hounslow TW7 130 D4
Mitcham SW19 180 B4
South Croydon CR0 221 B6
Southgate N21 16 C2
Tottenham N17 33 D4
Wembley HA9 43 D1
College Rdbt 1 KT1 198 A6
College St EC4 117 A6 252 B6
College Terr E3 97 B4
N3 29 B1
College View SE9 165 D3
College Way
Ashford TW15 170 B6
Hayes UB3 106 A6
College Wlk 10 KT1 198 A6
Collent Ho 12 E9 74 C2
Collent St E9 74 C2
Collerston Ho SE10 120 D1
Colless Rd N15 51 D4
Collette Ct SE25 205 C4
Collette Ho N16 51 D1
Collett Rd SE16 118 A3
Collett Way UB2 107 D4
Colley Ho 12 N7 71 D3
Collier Cl E16 122 D6
West Ewell KT19 214 D2
Collier Dr HA8 26 C1
Collier St N1 94 B5 233 C3
Colliers Water La CR7 204 C4
Colliers Wood BR2 225 D3
Mitcham SW19 180 B3
Collier's Wood Sta
SW19 180 B3
Collindale Ave DA15 168 A3
DA8 147 D6
Collingbourne Rd
W12 112 B5
Collingham Gdns
SW5 113 D2 255 D3
Collingham Pl
SW5 113 D2 255 D4
Collingham Rd
SW5 113 D2 255 D3
Collings Cl N22 32 B4
Collington Ho SE7 143 B6
Collington St SE10 120 B1
Collingtree Rd SE26 184 C6
Collingwood Ave N10 49 A5
Tolworth KT5 199 A1
Collingwood Cl
2 Penge SE20 184 B2
Twickenham TW2,TW4 151 C4
Collingwood Ct NW4 46 C4
New Barnet EN5 13 D6
Collingwood Ho 27 E1 96 B3
Collingwood Rd N15 51 C5
Hillingdon UB8 82 D3
Mitcham CR4 202 C6
Sutton SM1 217 C4
Collingwood Sch SM6 219 B3
Collingwood St E1 96 B3
Collins Ave HA7 26 A1
Collins Ct E8 74 A2
Collins Dr HA4 62 C6
Collins Ho 4 E14 120 A6
6 SE10 120 D1
8 Barking IG11 78 D1
Collinson Ct SE1 252 A1
Edgware HA8 26 B6
Collinson Ho 13 SE15 140 A5
Collinson St SE1 252 A1
Collinson Wlk SE1 252 A1
Collins Rd N5,N16 73 A4
Collins Sq SE3 142 D3
Collins St SE3 142 C3
Collins Yd N1 234 C5
Collinwood Ave EN3 6 C2
Collinwood Gdns IG5 56 C5
Collis Prim Sch TW11 175 B4
Coll of Liberal Arts
SM1 217 D3
Coll of North East London
The
N11 31 D3
N15 51 D5
Coll of NW London
(Willesden Centre) The
NW10 67 D3
Coll Sharp Ct 42 E2 95 D4
Coll's Rd SE15 140 C4
Collyer Ave CR0 220 A4
Collyer Pl SE15 140 A4
Collyer Rd CR0 220 A4
Colman Ct N12 30 A4
Stanmore HA7 25 B4
Colman Rd E16 99 C2
Colmans Wharf 6 E14 97 D2
Colmar Cl 3 E1 96 D3
Colmer Pl HA3 24 B3
Colmer Rd SW16 182 A3
Colmore Mews SE15 140 B4
Colmore Rd EN3 6 C1
Colnbrook Ct SW17 180 B6
Colnbrook St SE1 261 C6
Colne Ct Ealing W7 86 B1
West Ewell KT19 215 A4
Colne Ho NW8 236 D5
Barking IG11 78 D2
Colne Rd E5 75 A4
Southgate N21 17 B4
Twickenham TW1,TW2 152 C3
Colne St E13 99 A4
Colney Hatch N10 31 A3
Colney Hatch La N10 31 A3
Cologne Rd SW11 136 B1
Coloma Convent Girls Sch
CR0 222 D5
Colombo Rd IG1 57 A2
Colombo St SE1 251 C3
Colomb St SE10 120 C1
Colonades The 4 SE5 139 B4
Colonels Wlk EN2 4 D2
Colonial Ave TW2 152 A5
Colonial Dr W4 111 A2
Colonial Rd TW14 149 C4
Colonnade WC1 240 B5
Colonnades The 6 E8 74 B2
Colonnade The 11 SE8 119 B2
Colosseum Ct N3 29 B1
Colroy Ct NW4 47 A4
Colson Rd CR0 221 C6
Colson Way SW16 181 C6
Colstead Ho 23 E1 96 B1
Colsterworth Rd N15 51 D5
Colston Ave SM1,SM5 218 C4
Colston Ct SM5 218 D4
Colston Rd E7 77 D2
Mortlake SW14 133 A1
Colthurst Cres N4 73 A6
Colthurst Dr N9 18 B1
Coltman Ho 1 E14 97 A1
SE10 142 A6
Colt Mews EN3 7 C6
Coltness Cres SE2 124 B1
Colton Gdns N17 51 A6
Colton Rd HA1 42 C4
Coltsfoot Dr UB7 82 A1
Columba Ho SE14 141 B4
Columbas Dr NW3 48 B1
Columbia Ave
Edgware HA8 26 D2
New Malden KT4 199 D2
Ruislip HA4 40 B1
Columbia Ct KT3 199 D2
Columbia Ho 16 E3 97 C4
Columbia Point 7
SE16 118 C3
Columbia Prim Sch E2 95 D4
Columbia Rd E13 98 D3
E2 95 D4
Columbine Ave E6 100 A2
Croydon CR2 220 D1
Columbus Gdns HA6 22 A2
Colveiw Ct SE9 165 D3
Colverson Ho 11 E1 96 C2
Colvestone Cres E8 73 D3
Colvestone Prim Sch
E8 73 D3
Colville Gdns W11 91 B1
Colville Ho 33 E2 96 C5
W11 91 B1
Colville Mews W11 91 B1
Colville Pl W1 239 B3
Colville Prim Sch W11 91 B1
Colville Rd E11 76 A5
E17 35 A1
W11 91 B1
W3 110 D3
Edmonton N9 18 B3
Colville Sq W11 91 B1
Colville Sq Mews 6
W11 91 B1
Colville Terr W11 91 B1
Colvin Cl SE26 184 C5
Colvin Gdns
Chingford E4 20 A1
Wanstead E11 55 B5
Colvin Rd E6 78 A1
Thornton Heath CR7 204 C4
Colwall Gdns IG8 37 A5
Colwall Ho 18 SW9 138 B3
Colwell Rd SE22 161 D6
Colwick Cl N6 49 D2
Colwith Rd W6 134 C6
Colwood Gdns SW19 180 B3
Colworth Gr SE17 262 B3
Colworth Rd E11 54 C2
Croydon CR0 206 A1
Colwyn Ave UB6 86 D5
Colwyn Cl SW16 181 C5
Colwyn Cres TW3 130 A4
Colwyn Gn NW9 45 C3
Colwyn Ho SE1 261 A5
Colwyn Rd NW2 68 B5
Colyer Cl SE9 166 D2
Colyer Ho SE2 124 D1
Colyton Cl DA16 146 D4
Wembley HA0 65 C2
Colyton Rd SE22 162 B6
Colyton Way N18 34 A5
Combe Ave SE3 142 D5
Combedale Rd SE10 121 A1
Combe Ho 20 W2 91 C2
Mortlake SW14 133 A3
Combe Hurst KT2 177 A5
Combe Lane Sta CR0 222 C3
Combemartin Rd
SW18 157 A3
Combe Mews 4 SE3 142 D5
Comber Cl NW2 68 B6
Comber Gr SE5 139 A5
Comber Grove Prim Sch
SE5 139 A5
Comber Ho SE5 139 A5
Combermere Rd SW9 138 B2
Morden SM4 201 D4
Comberton 10 KT1 176 C1
Comberton Rd E5 74 B6
Combeside SE18 145 D5
Combes Rd RM9 81 B1
Combe The NW1 231 D1
Combwell Cres SE2 124 A3
Comely Bank Rd E17 54 A4
Comeragh Mews W14 254 B1
Comeragh Rd
W14 113 A1 254 B1
Comer Cres UB2 108 A4
Comerford Rd SE4 141 B1
Comet Cl E12 77 D4
Comet Pl SE8 141 C5
Comet St SE8 141 C5
Comins Ho SW4 159 C6
Commerce Est E18 37 C1
Commerce Rd
Brentford TW8 131 C5
Wood Green N22 32 B2
Commerce Way CR0 220 B6
Commercial Rd E1 96 C1
Edmonton N18 33 C4
Commercial St
E1 95 D2 243 C4
Commercial Way
SE15 140 A5
Wembley NW10 88 D5
Commerell Pl SE10 120 D1
Commerell St SE10 120 C1
Commodore Ct SE8 141 C4
Commodore Ho 7
E14 120 A6
Commodore St E1 97 A3
Commondale SW15 134 C2
Common La KT10 213 A1
Common Rd
Barnes SW13 134 A2
Claygate KT10 213 A1
Stanmore HA7 8 C1
Commonside BR2 225 C4
Commonside Ct SW16 182 A4
Commonside E CR4 203 B6
Common The
Ealing W5 110 A5
Southall UB2 106 D2
Stanmore HA7 8 D2
Common View SW15 134 C2
Commonwealth Ave
21 W12 112 B6
Hayes UB3 83 B1
Commonwealth Rd
N17 34 A3
Commonwealth Way
SE2 124 C1
Community Cl
Cranford TW5 128 B4
Uxbridge UB10 61 A5
Community Coll The
E9 74 D3
E9 96 D6
Community Rd E15 76 B3
Greenford UB6 86 A6
Como Rd SE23 163 A2
Compania Bldg 12 E1 118 D6
Compass Ct SE1 253 C3
Compass Hill TW10 153 D5
Compass Ho SE8 141 D3
W2 91 D1
Compass Point 9 E14 119 C6
Compayne Gdns NW6 69 D1
Compton Ave E6 99 D5
N1 72 D2
N6 48 C2
Wembley HA0 65 C4
Compton Cl 5 HA8 27 A3
NW1 231 D1
NW11 68 D5
SE15 139 D5
Ealing W13 87 A1
Esher KT10 212 B3
Compton Cres
Chessington KT9 214 A2
Chiswick W4 133 A6
Northolt UB5 84 D6
Tottenham N17 33 A3
Compton Ct
Sutton SM1 218 A4
9 West Norwood SE19 183 C5
Compton High Sch & Sports
Coll UB5 85 A6
Compton Ho SW11 267 A2
Compton Lo N21 16 D3
Compton Pas EC1 241 D6
Compton Pl WC1 240 A6
South Oxhey WD19 23 A6
Compton Rd N1 72 D2
NW10 90 D4
Croydon CR0 206 B1
Hayes UB3 105 D6
Southgate N21 16 D3
Wimbledon SW19 179 B4
Compton Rise HA5 41 B4
Compton Sch The N12 30 C4
Compton St
EC1 94 D3 241 D6
Compton Terr N1 72 D2
Southgate N21 16 C3
Comreddy Cl EN2 4 D4
Comus Ho SE17 263 A3
Comus Pl
SE17 117 C2 263 A3
Comyn Rd SW11 136 C1
Comyns Cl E16 98 D2
Comyns Rd RM9 81 C1
Comyns The WD23 8 A3
Conal Ct SW16 181 D5
Conant Ho SE11 138 D6
Conant Mews 1 E1 118 A6
Concanon Rd SW2,
SW4 138 B1
Concert Hall App
SE1 116 B5 250 D3
Concord Bsns Ctr W3 88 D2
Concord Cl UB5 85 A4
Concord Ct KT1 198 B6
Concord Ctr W12 112 D4
Concorde Cl
Hounslow TW3 129 D3
Uxbridge UB10 82 A5
Concorde Dr E6 100 B2
Concord Ho
Kingston KT3 199 C6
5 Tottenham N17 33 D3
Concordia Wharf E14 120 A5
Concord Rd Acton W3 88 D3
Enfield EN3 18 C6
Concourse The 7 N9 18 A2
Condell Rd
SW8 137 C4 269 B1
Conder St E14 97 A1
Condor Path UB5 85 C5
Condover Cres SE18 144 D5
Condray Pl SW11 267 A3
Conduit Ct WC2 250 A6
Conduit Ho SE10 142 B4
Conduit La N18 34 C5
South Croydon CR0 222 A3
Conduit Mews
W2 92 B1 236 C1
Conduit Pas W2 236 C1
Conduit Pl W2 236 C1
Conduit Rd SE18 122 D1
Conduit St W1 115 C6 249 A6
Conduit Way NW10 67 A1
Conewood St N5 72 D5
Coney Acre SE21 161 A3
Coney Burrows E4 20 C2
Coney Gr UB8 82 C4
Coneygrove Path UB5 63 A2
Coney Hall Par BR4 224 C5
Coney Hall Rdbt BR4 224 C5
Coney Hill Rd BR4 224 D6
Coney Hill Sch BR2 224 D5
Coney Way SW8 270 D5
Conference Cl 3 E4 20 A2
Conference Ho UB8 83 A1
Conference Rd SE2 124 C2
Congers Ho SE8 141 C5
Congleton Gr SE18 123 A1
Congo Rd SE18 123 B1
Congress Rd SE2 124 C2
Congreve Ho 10 N16 73 C3
Congreve Rd SE9 144 B2
Congreve St
SE17 117 C2 263 A3
Congreve Wlk 6 E16 99 D2
Conical Cnr EN2 5 A3
Conifer Cl BR6 227 B4
Conifer Ct Ilford IG1 78 D2
23 Putney SW19 156 D3
Conifer Gdns
Enfield EN1 17 C5
Streatham SW16 160 B1
Sutton SM1 217 D6
Conifer Ho SE4 141 B1
Conifers Cl TW11 175 C3
Conifer Way
Hayes UB3 106 A6
Wembley HA0 65 C5
Coniger Rd SW6 135 C3
Coningham Ct SW10 266 B4
Coningham Mews
W12 112 A5
Coningham Rd W12 112 B4
Coningsby Cotts W5 109 D4
Coningsby Ct 4 CR4 181 A1
Coningsby Gdns E4 35 D4
Coningsby Rd N4 50 D2
W5 109 D4
Conington Rd SE13 142 A3
Conisbee Ct 3 N14 15 C6
Conisborough Cres
SE6 164 A1
Conisbrough NW1 232 A5
Coniscliffe Cl BR7 188 C2
Coniscliffe Rd N13 17 A1
Coniston NW1 232 A2
Coniston Ave DA16 145 C2
Barking IG11 79 C1
Ealing UB6 87 B4
Coniston Cl N20 14 A1
Barking IG11 79 C1
Barnes SW13 133 D5
Chiswick W4 133 A5
West Barnes SM4 200 D3
Coniston Ct 6 SE16 118 D4
W2 237 B1
Beckenham BR3 186 A2
Chessington KT9 214 A5
Edgware HA8 26 B5
Penge SE26 184 B4
3 Wallington SM6 219 B4
Conistone Way N7 72 A1
Coniston Gdns N9 18 C3
NW9 45 B4
Pinner HA5 40 A5
Redbridge IG4 56 A5
Sutton SM2 218 B2
Wembley HA9 43 C1
Coniston Ho 13 E3 97 B4
18 SE5 139 A5
Coniston Rd N10 31 B1
Catford BR1 186 C4
Croydon CR0 206 A2
Tottenham N17 34 A4
Twickenham TW2 151 D5
Coniston Way KT9 214 A5
Coniston Wlk E9 74 C3
Conlan St W10 91 A3
Conley Rd NW10 67 C2
Conley St SE10 120 C1
Connaught Ave
Ashford TW15 170 A6
Barnet, London EN4 14 D3
Chingford E4 20 B4
Enfield EN1 5 C3
Hounslow TW4 129 A1
Mortlake SW14 133 A1
Connaught Bsns Ctr
NW9 45 D4
Mitcham CR4 202 D4
Wallington CR0 220 B2
Connaught Cl E10 75 A6
W2 237 B1
Carshalton SM1 218 B6
Enfield EN1 5 C3
Hillingdon UB8 83 A3
Connaught Ct 10 E17 53 D5
1 Chingford E4 20 C4
Connaught Day Hospl
E11 54 C3
Connaught Dr NW11 47 C5
Connaught Gdns N10 49 B4
Edmonton N13 32 D6
Morden SM4 202 A5
Connaught Grange
N13 32 D6
Connaught Ho N10 49 B4
Connaught Ho *continued*
NW10 90 B4
W1 248 C5
Connaught La IG1 79 B6
Connaught Lo N4 50 C2
Connaught Mans
15 N16 73 B4
SW11 267 B1
SW6 264 A2
3 SW9 138 C1
Connaught Mews
SE18 122 C1
Ilford IG1 79 B6
Connaught Pl W2 237 C1
Connaught Rd E11 54 B1
E16 121 D5
E17 53 C4
N4 50 C2
NW10 89 C5
SE18 122 D1
Barnet EN5 12 D5
Carshalton SM1 218 B6
Chingford, Chingford Green
E4 20 C3
Ealing W13 109 B6
Harrow HA3 24 D2
Ilford IG1 79 B6
New Malden KT3 199 C5
5 Richmond TW10 154 B6
Teddington TW11,TW12 174 B5
Connaught Sch for Girls
E11 54 C1
Connaught Sch for Girls
(Annexe) E11 76 C6
Connaught Sq
W2 92 D1 237 C1
Connaught St
W2 92 C1 237 B1
Connaught Way N13 32 D6
Connell Cres W5 88 B3
Connell Ct 6 SE14 140 D6
Connell Ho 6 SM6 219 C2
Connemara Cl WD6 11 B5
Connett Ho 5 E2 96 B5
Connington 5 KT1 176 C1
Connington Cres E4 20 B1
Connoly Ct NW2 68 B5
Connop Rd EN3 6 D5
Connor Cl E11 54 C2
Connor Ct SW11 268 C1
Connor Rd RM9 81 B4
Connor St E9 96 D6
Conolly Rd W7 108 C5
Conrad Dr KT4 200 D1
Conrad Ho 12 N16 73 C3
8 SE16 119 A6
SW8 270 A4
Consfield Ave KT3 200 A4
Consolata Missionary Coll
N20 13 C1
Consort Ho NW7 27 D5
W2 245 D5
Consort Lo NW8 230 C5
Consort Mews TW7 152 B6
Consort Rd SE15 140 B3
Cons St SE1 251 B2
Constable Ave E16 121 B5
Constable Cl NW11 47 D3
Hayes UB4 83 A5
Constable Cres N15 52 A4
Constable Ct 11 SE16 118 B1
Constable Gdns
Edgware HA8 26 C1
Isleworth TW7 152 B6
Constable Ho NW3 70 D1
Enfield EN1 18 A6
14 Northolt UB5 84 D5
Constable Mews RM8 80 B4
Constable Wlk SE21 161 C1
Constance Cres BR2 208 D1
Constance Rd
Enfield EN1 17 C5
Sutton SM1 218 A4
Thornton Heath CR0 204 D2
Twickenham TW2 151 D4
Constance St E16 122 A5
Constant Ho 23 E14 119 D6
Constantine Ho SW2 160 D3
Constantine Pl UB10 82 B6
Constantine Rd NW3 70 C4
Constitution Hill
SW1,W1 115 B4 248 D2
Constitution Rise
SE18 144 C4
Consul Ho 5 E3 97 C3
Content St
SE17 117 B2 262 C3
Contessa Cl BR6 227 C3
Control Tower Rd
TW6 126 D2
Convair Wlk 11 UB5 84 D4
Convent Cl BR3 186 A3
Convent Gdns W11 91 B1
W5 109 C2
Convent Hill SE19 183 A4
Convent Lo TW15 170 D5

Convent of Jesus & Mary Language Coll NW10 .89 D6
Convent of Jesus & Mary RC Inf Sch NW2 ......68 C2
Convent Rd TW15 ....170 D5
Convent Way UB2 ....106 D2
Conway Cl HA7 ....25 A4
Conway Cres
Dagenham RM6 ....58 C3
Greenford UB6 ....86 C5
Conway Dr
Ashford TW15 ....171 A4
Hayes UB3 ....105 A3
Sutton SM2 ....217 D2
Conway Gdns Enfield EN2 5 C5
Mitcham CR4 ....204 A5
Wembley HA9 ....43 C2
Conway Gr W3 ....89 B2
Conway Ho 5 E14 ....119 D2
6 Streatham SW2 ....160 A3
Conway Mews W1 ....239 A5
Conway Prim Sch SE18 ....123 C2
Conway Rd N15 ....51 A4
NW2 ....68 C6
SE18 ....123 C2
Feltham TW13 ....172 D5
Harlington TW6 ......126 D2
Palmers Green N14 .....16 A1
Twickenham TW4 .....151 C4
Wimbledon SW20 .....178 C2
Conway St W1 .93 C3 239 A5
Conway Wlk TW12 ....173 B4
Conybeare NW3 ....70 C1
Conyers Cl IG8 ....36 C4
Conyer's Rd SW16 ....181 D5
Conyer St 10 E3 ....97 A5
Cooden Cl BR1 ....187 B3
Cookes Cl E11 ....76 D6
Cookes La SM3 ....217 A2
Cookham Cl UB2 .....107 D4
Cookham Cres SE16 ..118 D4
Cookham Dene Cl BR7 ....189 B2
Cookham Ho E2 ......243 C6
Cookham Rd BR8 .....191 C2
Cookhill Rd SE2 ......124 B3
Cooks Ferry N18 ....34 D5
Cook's Hole Rd EN2 .....5 A5
Cookson Gr DA8 ......147 D5
Cook's Rd E15 ....97 D5
SE17 ....138 D6
Coolfin Rd E16 ....99 B1
Coolgardie Ave E4 .....36 B5
Coolgardie Rd TW15 ..171 A5
Coolhurst Rd N8 ....49 D3
Cool Oak La NW9 .....45 D2
Coomassie Rd W9 .....91 B3
Coombe Ave CR0 .....221 C4
Coombe Bank KT2,KT3 177 C2
Coombe Cl Edgware HA8 26 B1
Hounslow TW3 ....129 C1
Coombe Cnr N21 ......16 D3
Coombe Cres TW12 ..173 A3
Coombe Ct
2 Beckenham BR3 ....185 B2
3 Croydon CR0 ......221 B4
Coombe Dr HA4 ......40 B1
Coombe End KT2 .....177 B3
Coombefield Cl KT3 ..199 C4
Coombe Gdns
New Malden KT3 .....199 D5
Wimbledon SW20 .....178 A2
Coombe Girls Sch KT3 177 B1
Coombe Hill Glade KT2 ....177 C3
Coombe Hill Inf Sch KT3 ....177 B2
Coombe Hill Jun Sch KT3 ....177 B2
Coombe Hill Rd KT2 ..177 C3
Coombe Ho 13 N7 .....71 D3
Coombe House Chase KT3 ....177 B2
Coombehurst Cl EN4 ....2 D3
Coombe La CR0 ......222 B3
Coombe Lane Flyover SW20 ....177 D2
Coombe La W KT2 ....177 B2
Coombe Lea BR1 .....210 A6
Coombe Lo SE7 ......143 C6
Coombe Neville KT2 ..177 B3
Coombe Pk KT2 ......177 B5
Coombe Pl KT2 ......177 A5
Coombe Rd NW10 .....67 B5
W13 ....109 B3
W4 ....111 C1
Bushey WD23 ....8 B4
Forest Hill SE26 ....184 B6
Hampton TW12 ......173 B4
Kingston KT2 ....176 C2
Kingston KT3 ....199 C6
South Croydon CR0,CR2 .221 C4
Wood Green N22 ......32 C2
Coomber Ho SW6 ....135 D2
Coombe Ridings KT2 .177 A5
Coombe Rise KT2 ....177 A2
Coombes Rd RM9 .....103 B6
Coombe Wlk SM1 ....217 D5
Coombewood Dr RM6 ..59 B3
Coombe Wood Rd KT2 ....177 A5
Coombs St N1 ....234 D3
Coomer Mews SW6 ..264 D5
Coomer Pl SW6 ....135 B6 264 D5
Cooms Wlk HA8 ....27 A2
Cooperage Cl 5 N17 ..33 D4
Cooperage The SE1 ..253 C3
Cooper Ave E17 ......35 A2
Cooper Cl SE1 ....251 B1
Cooper Cres SM5 ....218 D5
Cooper Ct E15 ....76 A3
SE18 ....144 D6
Cooper Ho NW8 .....236 C5
Hounslow TW4 ....129 B2
7 West Norwood SW27 ....182 D5
Cooper Rd NW10 ......68 A3
NW4 ....46 D3
Croydon CR0,CR9 ....220 D4
Coopersale Cl 3 IG8 ..37 C3
Coopersale Rd E9 .....74 D3
Coopers Cl E1 ....96 C3
Dagenham RM10 ....81 D2
Coopers Ct E3 ....97 B3
9 W3 ....111 A5
Isleworth TW7 ....130 D3
Coopers La NW1 .....232 D3
SE12 ....165 B2
Cooper's La E10 ......54 A1
Coopers' Lane Prim Sch SE12 ....165 B2
Coopers Lodge SE1 ..253 C2
Cooper's Rd SE1 ....117 D1 263 D2
Cooper's Row EC3 ....117 D6 253 C6
Coopers Sch BR7 ....189 A2
Cooper St 10 E16 .....98 D2
Cooper's Yd SE19 ....183 C4
Coote Gdns RM8 ......81 B5
Coote Rd DA7 ....147 B4
Dagenham RM8 ....81 B5
Cope Ho EC1 ....235 B1
Copeland Dr E14 ....119 C2
Copeland Ho SE11 ..260 D5
Upper Tooting SW17 ..180 B6
Copeland Rd E17 ......53 D3
SE15 ....140 B3
Copelands BR3 ......185 B3
Copeman Cl SE26 ....184 C5
Copenhagen Gdns W4 111 B4
Copenhagen Ho N1 ..234 A5
Copenhagen Pl E14 ....97 B1
Copenhagen Prim Sch N1 ....94 B6 233 C5
Copenhagen St N1 ....94 B6 233 C5
Cope Pl W8 ...113 C3 255 A5
Copers Cope Rd BR3 185 B3
Cope St SE16 ....118 D2
Copeswood Ct UB7 ..126 C5
Cope Yd 6 E1 ....118 A5
Copford Wlk N1 .....235 A6
Copinger Wlk HA8 ....26 D2
Copland Ave HA0 ......65 D3
Copland Cl HA0 ....65 C3
Copland Com Sch & Tech Ctr HA9 ....66 B3
Copland Mews 3 HA0 .66 A2
Copland Rd HA0 ....66 A2
Copleston Rd SE15 ..139 D2
Copley Cl 15 SE17 ...138 D6
Ealing W7 ....86 D2
Copley Dene BR1 ....187 D2
Copley Pk SW16 .....182 B4
Copley Rd HA7 ....25 C5
Coppard Gdns KT9 ..213 C2
Coppedhall 1 SE21 ..161 B2
Coppelia Rd SE3 ....142 D1
Coppen Rd RM8 ....59 B2
Copperas St SE8 ....141 D6
Copper Beech N6 .....49 A2
Copperbeech Cl NW3 ..70 B3
Copper Beech Ct N20 ..14 A1
Copper Beeches TW7 .130 B4
Copper Cl SE19 .....183 D3
Copperdale Rd UB3 ..106 A4
Copperfield Ave UB8 ..82 C3
Copperfield Dr N15 ...51 D5
Copperfield Ho 10 SE1 ....118 A4
Copperfield Mews N18 33 C5
Copperfield Rd SE28 .102 C1
Stepney E3 ....97 A2
Copperfields
5 Beckenham BR3 ....186 A2
Harrow HA1 ....42 C2
Copperfields Ct W3 ..110 C4
Copperfield St SE1 ....117 A4 252 A2
Copperfield Way BR7 .189 A4
Pinner HA5 ....41 B5
Coppergate Cl BR1 ...187 B2
Coppermead Cl NW2 ..68 C5
Copper Mill Dr TW7 ..130 D3
Coppermill La E17 .....52 D4
Copper Mill La SW17 .180 A6
Coppermill Prim Sch E17 ....52 D4
Copperwood Lo EN2 ....4 D3
Coppetts Cl N12 ......30 D3
Coppetts Ctr* N12 ....30 D3
Coppetts Rd N10 ......30 D2
Coppetts Wood Prim Sch N10 ....31 A2
Coppice Cl
Beckenham BR3 ......207 D5
Harrow HA7 ....24 D4
Ruislip HA4 ....39 B3
West Barnes SW20 ...200 C6
Coppice Dr SW15 ....156 B5
Coppice The
Ashford TW15 ....170 D4
Enfield EN2 ....4 D1
Hillingdon UB7 ....82 A1
New Barnet EN5 ....13 D5
Coppice Way E18 .....54 D6
Coppice Wlk N20 .....13 C1
Coppies Gr N11 ....31 B6
Copping Cl CR0 .....221 C4
Coppinger Ct UB7 ...104 A4
Coppin Ho SW2 .....160 D3
Coppins The
New Addington CR0 ..223 D2
Stanmore HA3 ....24 C4
2 Ilford RM6 ....58 B2
Coppock Cl SW11 ...136 C3
Coppsfield KT8 ......195 C6
Copse Ave BR4 ......223 D5
Copse Cl SE7 ....143 B6
Copse Ct SW15 ......157 A6
Copse Glade KT6 ....197 D1
Copse Hill
Belmont SM2 ....217 D1
Wimbledon SW20 ....178 B3
Copsem Dr KT10 ....212 A2
Copsem La KT10 .....212 A1
Copsem Way KT10 ..212 A2
Copse The N2 ....48 D6
Chingford E4 ....20 D3
Copse View CR2 ....223 A1
Coptefield Dr DA17 ..125 A3
Copthall Ave EC2 ....95 B1 242 D2
Copthall Bldgs EC2 ..242 D2
Copthall Cl EC2 .....242 C2
Copthall Dr NW7 ......28 A4
Copthall Gdns NW7 ...28 A3
Twickenham TW1 ....152 D3
Copthall Rd E UB10 ...60 C5
Copthall Rd W UB10 ..60 C6
Copthall Sch NW7 ....28 B3
Copthall Sports Ctr NW4 ....28 B2
Copthorne Ave BR2 ..226 B6
Streatham SW12 .....159 D4
Copthorne Chase TW15 ....170 B6
Copthorne Cl TW17 ..193 A3
Copthorne Mews UB3 105 C2
Coptic St WC1 .94 A2 240 A3
Copton Cl E3 ....97 C2
Copwood Cl N12 ......30 B6
Coral Cl RM6 ....58 C6
Coral Ho 5 E1 ....97 A3
Coraline Cl UB1 ....85 B4
Coralline Wlk 4 SE2 .124 C4
Coral Row 14 SW11 ..136 A2
Coral St SE1 ..116 C4 251 B1
Coram Ho 9 W4 .....111 C1
WC1 ....240 A6
Coram St WC1 .94 A3 240 A5
Coran Cl N9 ....18 D4
Corban Rd TW3 .....129 C2
Corbar Cl EN4 ....2 B4
Corbden Cl SE15 ....139 D4
Corbet Cl CR4,SM6 ..219 A6
Corbet Ct EC3 ....242 D1
Corbet Ho N1 ....234 A5
Corbet Pl E1 ....95 D2 243 C4
Corbett Ct SE26 .....185 B6
Corbett Gr N22 ....32 A3
Corbett Ho SW10 ...266 A6
Corbett Rd E17 ....54 A6
Wanstead E11 ....55 C3
Corbett's La SE16 ...118 C2
Corbett Villas RM8 ....58 C1
Corbicum E11 ....54 C2
Corbidge Ct SE8 ....141 D6
Corbiere Ct SW19 ...178 D4
Corbiere Ho 5 N1 .....95 C6
Corbin Ho 7 E3 ....97 D4
Corbin's La HA2 ....63 D5
Corbridge 5 N17 ......34 B3
Corbridge Cres E2 ....96 B5
Corby Cres EN2 ....4 A1
Corbyland Rd DA15 ..167 C3
Corbylands Rd DA15 .167 C4
Corbyn St N4,N19 .....50 A1
Corby Rd NW10 ....89 A5
Corby Way E3 ....97 C3
Cordelia Cl SE24 ....138 D1
Cordelia Gdns TW19 ..148 A4
Cordelia Ho 26 N1 .....95 C5
Cordelia Rd TW19 ....148 A4
Cordelia St E14 ....97 D1
Cordell Ho N15 ....51 D4
Cordingley Rd HA4 ....61 B6
Cording St E14 ....97 D2
Cordwainers Coll E8 ..74 B1
Cordwainers Ct 18 E9 ..74 C1
Cordwainers Wlk 9 E13 ....99 A5
Cordwain Ho 7 N18 ...34 A5
Cord Way 7 E14 .....119 C3
Cordwell Rd SE13 ....164 C6
Corefield Cl N11 ....15 A2
Corelli Rd SE3 ....144 A4
Corfe Ave HA2 ....63 C4
Corfe Cl UB4 ....84 C1
Corfe Ho SW8 ....270 C4
Corfe Lo SE21 ....161 B2
Corfe Twr 6 W3 .....111 A4
Corfield Rd N21 ....16 B6
Corfield St E2 ....96 B4
Corfton Lo W5 ....88 A2
Corfton Rd W5 ....88 A2
Coriander Ave E14 ....98 B1
Coriander Ct SE1 ....253 D2
Cories Cl RM8 ....80 D6
Corigan Ct 5 E11 .....76 C6
Corinium Cl HA9 ....66 B4
Corinne Rd N19 ....71 C4
Corkscrew Hill BR4 ..224 B5
Cork Sq E1 ....118 B5
Cork St W1 ...115 C6 249 A5
Cork St Mews W1 ....249 A5
Cork Tree Ho 3 SW27 ....182 D5
Cork Tree Ret Pk N18 ..35 A4
Cork Tree Way E4 ......35 A5
Corlett St NW1 ......237 A4
Cormont Rd SE5 .....138 D4
Cormorant Cl E17 .....35 A3
Cheam SM1 ....217 B3
Cormorant Ct 34 SE8 .141 B6
12 Dulwich SE21 .....161 B2
Cormorant Ho EN3 ....18 D6
Cormorant Rd E7 ......76 D3
Cornbury Ho 5 SE8 ..141 B6
Cornbury Rd HA8 ......25 D3
Cornel Ho 4 DA15 ...168 A1
Cornelia St N7 ....72 B2
Cornell Cl DA14 .....191 A4
Cornell Ho HA2 ....63 B5
Corner Fielde SW2 ..160 B3
Corner Gn SE3 ......143 A3
Corner House St WC2 250 A4
Corner Mead NW9 .....27 D2
Cornerside TW15 ....171 A3
Cornerways Harrow HA1 65 A5
Putney SW15 ....134 A1
Corney Rd W4 ....133 C6
Corney Reach Way W4 ....133 C5
Cornflower La CR0 ..206 D1
Cornflower Terr SE22 .162 B5
Cornford Cl BR2 .....209 A4
Cornford Gr SW12 ...159 B2
Cornhill EC3 ....95 B1 242 D1
Cornhill Dr EN3 ....7 A6
Cornick Ho 7 SE16 ..118 B3
Cornish Ct N9 ....18 B4
Cornish Gr SE20 .....184 B2
Cornish Ho 7 SE17 ..138 D6
Brentford TW8 ......110 B1
Cornmill La SE13 ....142 A2
Cornmow Dr NW10 ....68 A3
Cornshaw Rd RM8 .....58 D1
Cornthwaite Rd E5 ....74 C5
Cornwall Ave DA16 ..145 D2
E2 ....96 C4
N3 ....29 C3
Claygate KT10 ....212 D1
Southall UB1 ....85 C2
Wood Green N22 ......32 A2
Cornwall Cl
Barking IG11 ....79 D2
3 Pinner HA5 ....23 B3
Cornwall Cres W11 ....91 A1
Cornwall Ct 5 W7 .....86 D3
Cornwall Dr BR5 .....190 C3
Cornwall Gdns NW10 ..68 B2
SW7 ....113 D3 255 D5
Cornwall Gdns Wlk SW7 ....255 D5
Cornwall Gr W4 .....111 C1
Cornwall Ho NW1 ...237 D5
3 Putney SW15 .....156 C4
Cornwallis Ave DA15 ..167 B2
N9 ....18 C2
Cornwallis Ct SW8 ..270 A2
Cornwallis Gr N9 ......18 C2
Cornwallis Ho 24 W12 112 B6
Cornwallis Rd N19 .....72 A6
SE18 ....122 D3
Dagenham RM9 ....81 A4
Edmonton N9 ....18 B2
Walthamstow E17 .....52 D5
Cornwallis Sq N19 .....72 A6
Cornwallis Wlk SE9 ..144 B2
Cornwall Mans NW1 ..237 D5
SW10 ....266 B4
Cornwall Mews S SW7 ....256 A5
Cornwall Mews W SW7 ....255 D5
Cornwall Rd N15 ....51 B4
N4 ....50 C2
SE1 ....116 C5 251 B2
Belmont SM2 ....217 B1
Croydon CR0 ....220 D6
Edmonton N18 ....34 A5
Harrow HA1 ....42 A3
Pinner HA5 ....23 B3
Ruislip HA4 ....61 D6
Twickenham TW1 ....153 A3
Cornwall Sq SE11 ...261 D2
Cornwall St 6 E1 ....118 B6
Cornwall Terr NW1 ..237 D5
Cornwall Terr Mews NW1 ....237 D5
Corn Way E11 ....76 C5
Cornwell Ct 21 E10 ...53 D2
Cornwood Cl N2 ....48 B5
Cornwood Dr E1 ......96 C1
Cornworthy Rd RM8 ...80 C3
Corona Rd SE12 .....165 A4
Coronation Ave 1 N16 73 D4
Coronation Cl DA5 ..168 D5
Ilford IG6 ....57 A5
Coronation Ct E15 .....76 D2
W10 ....90 C2
Coronation Rd E13 ....99 C4
Acton NW10 ....88 C3
Hayes UB3 ....105 D2
Coronet Par 4 HA0 ....66 A2
Coronet St N1 ....95 C4
Corporation Ave TW4 .129 A1
Corporation Row EC1 .241 B6
Corporation St E15 ....98 D5
N7 ....72 A3
Corpus Christi RC Prim Sch SW2 ....160 B6
Kingston KT3 ....199 A6
Corrance Rd SW2,SW4 138 A1
Corri Ave N14 ....31 D6
Corrib Ct N13 ....16 B1
Corrib Dr SM1 ....218 C3
Corrib Hts N8 ....49 D3
Corrigan Cl NW4 ......46 C6
Corringham Ct NW11 ..47 C2
Corringham Ho 10 E1 ..96 D1
Corringham Rd NW11 ..47 C2
Wembley HA9 ....66 C6
Corringway NW11 .....47 D2
Ealing W5 ....88 C2
Corris Gn NW9 ....45 C3
Corry Dr SW9 ....138 D1
Corry Ho 2 E14 .....119 D6
Corsair Cl TW19 .....148 A4
Corsair Rd TW19 ....148 A4
Corscombe Cl KT2 ..177 A5
Corsehill St SW16 ...181 C4
Corseley Way E9 ......75 B2
Corsham Ho HA9 ......66 C2
Corsham St N1 .95 B4 235 D1
Corsica St N5 ....72 D2
Cortayne Rd SW6 ...135 B3
Cortis Rd SW15 .....156 B5
Cortis Terr SW15 ....156 B5
Corunna Rd SW8 ....137 C4 269 B2
Corunna Terr SW8 ..269 A2
Corvette Sq 5 SE10 ..142 B6
Corwell Gdns UB8 ....83 A1
Corwell La UB8 ....83 A1
Coryton Path W9 ......91 B3
Cosbycote Ave SE24 ..161 A6
Cosdach Ave SM6 ..219 D1
Cosedge Cres CR0,CR9 220 D3
Cosgrove Cl
Edmonton N21 ....17 A2
Hayes UB4 ....84 D3
Cosgrove Ho 11 E2 ....96 A6
Cosmo Pl WC1 ......240 B4
Cosmur Cl W12 .....111 D3
Cossall Wlk SE15 ...140 B4
Cossar Mews 10 SW2 .160 C6
Cosser St SE1 .116 C3 261 A6
Costa St SE15 ....140 A3
Coston Prim Sch UB6 ..86 A4
Costons Ave UB6 ......86 B4
Costons La UB6 ....86 B4
Coston Wlk 4 SE4 ...140 D1
Cosway Ho NW11 .....48 A3
Cosway Mans NW1 ..237 B4
Cosway St NW1 92 C2 237 B4
Cotall St E14 ....97 C2
Coteford Cl HA5 ....40 A4
Coteford Inf Sch HA5 ..40 A3
Coteford Jun Sch HA5 .39 D4
Coteford St SW17 ...181 A6
Cotelands CR0 ....221 C5
Cotesbach Rd E5 ......74 C5
Cotes Ho NW8 ....237 A5
Cotesmore Gdns RM8 ..80 C4
Cotford Rd CR7 .....205 A5
Cotham St SE17 .....262 B3
Cotherstone Rd SW2 .160 B3
Cotleigh Ave DA5 ....168 D2
Cotleigh Rd NW6 ......69 C1
Cotman Cl NW11 ......48 A3
Putney SW15 ....156 D6
Cotman Ct BR3 ....185 B2
Cotmandene Cres BR5 ....190 A1
Cotman Gdns HA8 .....26 C1
Cotman Ho NW8 .....230 A4
6 Northolt UB5 ....84 D5
Cotmans Cl UB3 .....106 A5
Coton Rd DA16 ......146 A2
Cotsford Ave KT3 ....199 B4
Cotswold Ave WD23 ....8 A5
Cotswold Cl
Hinchley Wood KT10 ..212 D6
Kingston KT2 ....177 A4
Cotswold Ct EC1 ....242 A6
N11 ....31 A6
3 Wembley UB6 ....86 D5
Cotswold Gate NW2 ...47 A1
Cotswold Gdns E6 .....99 D5
Hendon NW2 ....68 D6
Ilford IG2 ....57 B2
Cotswold Gn EN2 ....4 B1
Cotswold Ho N16 ......51 D1
Cotswold Mews SW11 266 D1
Cotswold Rd TW12 ..173 C4
Cotswold Rise BR6 ..211 D3
Cotswold St SE27 ...182 D6
Cotswold Way Enfield EN2 4 B2
North Cheam KT4 ....216 C6
Cottage Ave BR2 ....210 A1
Cottage Cl HA4 ....39 B1
Cottage Field Cl DA5, DA15 ....168 C3
Cottage Gn SE5 .....139 B5
Cottage Gr SW9 .....138 A2
Surbiton KT6 ....197 D3
Cottage Pl SW3 ....114 C3 257 A5
Cottage Rd KT19 ....215 B1
Cottage St E14 ......119 D6
Cottages The UB10 ....60 D5
Cottage Wlk 2 N16 ...73 D5
Cottenham Dr NW9 ....45 D6
Wimbledon SW20 ....178 B3
Cottenham Ho 4 N19 .72 A6
Cottenham Par SW20 .178 B1
Cottenham Park Rd SW20 ....178 C3
Cottenham Pl SW20 ..178 B3
Cottenham Rd E17 .....53 B5
Cotterill Rd KT6 .....198 B1
Cottesbrook St 9 SE14 ....141 A5
Cottesloe Ho NW8 ..237 A6
Cottesloe Mews SE1 .261 B6
Cottesmore Ct W8 ..255 D6
Cottesmore Gdns W8 ....113 D3 255 D6
Cottimore Ave KT12 ..194 B1
Cottimore Cres KT12 .194 B2
Cottimore Terr KT12 ..194 B2
Cottingham Chase HA4 62 A5
Cottingham Rd SW8 ....138 B5 270 D4
Penge SE20 ....184 D3
Cottington Rd TW13 ..172 D6
Cottington St SE11 ..261 C2
Cotton Ave W3 ....89 B1
Cotton Cl RM9 ....80 C1
Cottongrass Cl 1 CR0 206 D1
Cotton Hill BR1 ......186 B6
Cotton Ho W12 ......111 D4
18 Streatham SW12 ..160 A4
Cotton Row SW11 ....136 B2
Cotton's Gdns E2 ......95 C4
Cottons La SE1 ......252 D4
Cotton St E14 ....120 A6
Cottrell Ct SE10 .....120 D3
Cotts Cl 13 W7 ....86 D2
Couchman Ho 8 SW4 159 C5
Couchmore Ave KT10 .212 C6
Coulgate St SE4 .....141 A2
Coulsdon Ct 3 N8 .....49 D4
Coulsdon Ho 5 SW2 .160 A3
Coulson Cl RM8 ....58 C1
Coulson St SW3 ....114 D1 257 C2
Coulter Cl UB4 ....85 A3
Coulter Rd W6 ....112 B3
Coulthurst Ct SW16 ..182 A3
Coults Cres NW5 ......71 A5
Councillor St SE5 ....139 A5
Counters Ct W14 ....254 B6
Counter St SE1 ......253 A3
Countess Rd NW5 .....71 C3
Countisbury Ave EN1 ..17 D4
Countisbury Ho SE26 .162 A1
Country Way TW13, TW16 ....172 C5
County Gate BR7 ....167 A1
New Barnet EN5 ....13 D5
County Gr SE5 ......139 A4
County Ho 9 SW9 ...138 C4
County Par TW8 .....131 D5
County Rd Newham E6 .100 D2
South Norwood CR7 ..182 D1

Crescent Ho SE13 141 D3
5 Wimbledon SW20 178 D2
Crescent La SW4 159 D6
Crescent Mans N5 72 D3
W11 244 B6
Crescent Par UB10 82 C4
Crescent Pl SW3 257 B4
Crescent Rd BR1 187 A3
DA15 167 D1
E10 75 D6
E13 99 A6
E6 99 C6
N11 30 D6
N15 50 D6
N22 31 D2
N3 29 B2
N8 49 D3
SE18 122 D2
Beckenham BR3 185 D1
Chingford E4 20 C4
Dagenham RM10 81 D5
East Barnet EN4 14 C6
Edmonton N9 18 A3
Enfield EN2 4 D1
Kingston KT2 176 D3
Shepperton TW17 193 A4
Wimbledon SW20 178 D2
Woodford E18 37 C2
Crescent Rise N22 31 D2
N3 29 B2
3 N3 29 C2
East Barnet EN4 14 C6
Crescent Row EC1 242 A5
Crescent St N1 72 B1
Crescent Stables
SW15 157 A6
Crescent The DA14 189 D6
E17 53 A4
N11 31 A6
N2 47 D6
NW2 68 B5
W3 89 C1
Ashford TW15 170 B5
Barnes SW13 134 A3
Barnet EN5 1 D3
Beckenham BR3 185 C2
East Molesey KT8 195 C5
Harlington UB7 127 B5
Harrow HA2 42 A1
Ilford IG2 56 C3
Kingston KT3 177 A1
Kingston KT6 198 A4
Loughton IG10 21 D5
Lower Halliford TW17 193 D2
Sidcup DA5 168 C4
Southall UB1 107 A4
Sutton SM1 218 B3
Thornton Heath CR0 205 B3
Wembley HA0 65 B6
West Wickham BR4 208 C3
Wimbledon SW19 157 C1
Crescent View IG10 21 D6
Crescent W EN4 2 A5
Crescent Way N12 30 C4
SE4 141 C2
Orpington BR6 227 C3
South Norwood SW16 182 C3
Crescent Wood Rd
SE21,SE26 162 A1
Cresford Rd
SW6 135 D4 265 C1
Crespigny Rd NW4 46 B3
Cressage Cl UB1 85 C3
Cressage Ho 9 TW8 132 A6
Cressall Ho 8 E14 119 C3
Cresset Ho 6 E9 74 C2
Cresset Rd E9 74 C2
Cresset St SW4 137 D2
Cressfield Cl NW5 71 A3
Cressida Rd N19 49 D1
Cressingham Ct 1
DA17 125 C3
Cressingham Gr SM1 218 A4
Cressingham Rd HA8 27 B3
SE13 142 A2
Cressington Cl 4 N16 73 C3
Cress Mews BR1 186 B5
Cresswell Gdns SW5 256 A2
Cresswell Pk SE3 142 D2
Cresswell Pl
SW10 114 A1 256 B2
Cresswell Rd
Croydon SE25 206 A5
Feltham TW13 173 A6
Twickenham TW1 153 D5
Cresswell Way N21 16 C4
Cressy Ct 6 E1 96 C2
W6 112 B3
Cressy Ho SW13 134 B2
Cressy Hos 7 E1 96 C2
Cressy Pl E1 96 C2
Cressy Rd NW3 70 D4
Cresta Ct W5 88 B3
Cresta Ho NW6 70 B1
7 Bow E3 97 C3
Crestbrook Ave N13 16 D1
Crestbrook Pl N13 16 D1
Crest Ct NW4 46 C4
Crest Dr EN3 6 C5
Crestfield St N1,WC1 233 B2
Crest Gdns HA4 62 C5
Creston Way KT4 200 D1
Crest Rd NW2 68 A6
Hayes BR2 208 D2
South Croydon CR2 222 B1
Crest The NW4 46 C4
Edmonton N13 32 C6
Surbiton KT5 198 C4
10 West Norwood
SW27 182 D5
Crestview NW5 71 B5
Crest View HA5 40 D5
Crest View Dr BR5 211 A4
Crestway SW15 156 B5
Crestwood Way TW4 151 A6
Creswick Ct W3 110 D6
Creswick Rd W3 110 D6
Creswick Wlk 6 E3 97 C4
NW11 47 B5
Creton St SE18 122 C3
Crewdson Rd SW9 138 C5
Crewe Pl NW10 89 D4
Crewkerne Ct SW11 266 D2
Crews St E14 119 C2
Crewys Rd NW2 69 B6
SE15 140 B3
Crichton Ave SM6 219 D4
Crichton Rd SM5 218 D1
Crichton St SW8 137 C3
Cricketers Arms Rd EN2 5 A3
Cricketers Cl N14 15 C4
Chessington KT9 213 D4
Cricketers Mews 4
SW18 157 D6
Cricketers Wlk SE26 184 C5
Cricketfield Rd E5 74 B4
Cricket Gn CR4 202 D5
Cricket Green Sch
CR4 202 C6
Cricket Ground Rd
BR7 188 D2
Cricket La BR3 185 A4
Cricket Row N2 48 B6
Cricklade Ave SW2 160 B2
Cricklewood Broadway
NW2 68 D4
Cricklewood La NW2 69 B5
Cricklewood Sta NW2 68 D4
Cridland St E15 98 D6
Crieff Ct TW11,KT8 175 C3
Crieff Rd SW18 158 A5
Criffel Ave SW2 159 D3
Crimscott St
SE1 117 C3 263 B5
Crimsworth Rd
SW8 137 D5 269 D3
Crinan St N1 94 A5 233 B4
Cringle St
SW8 137 C5 269 A4
Cripplegate St EC1 242 B4
Cripps Gn UB4 84 B3
Crispe Ho N1 233 D5
Barking IG11 101 B5
Crispen Rd TW13 173 A6
Crispian Cl NW10 67 C4
Crispin Cl SM6 220 A6
Crispin Cres SM6 219 D6
Crispin Ct SE17 263 A3
Crispin Rd HA8 27 A4
Crispin St E1 95 D2 243 C3
Crisp Rd W6 112 C1
Cristowe Rd SW6 135 B3
Criterion Mews N19 71 D6
Crittall's Cnr DA14 190 C3
Crittenden Lo BR4 207 C1
Crockerton Rd SW17 158 D2
Crockham Way SE9 188 C6
Crocus Cl CR0 206 D1
Crocus Field EN5 13 B5
Croft Ave BR4 208 A1
Croft Cl BR7 188 B5
NW7 11 C1
Erith DA17 125 B1
Harlington UB7 127 A5
Hillingdon UB10 60 C1
Croft Ct HA4 39 D1
Croftdown Rd NW5 71 B5
Crofters Cl TW7 152 B6
Crofters Ct 9 SE8 119 A2
Crofters Way
NW1 93 D6 232 C6
Croft Gdns W7 109 A4
Ruislip HA4 39 D1
Croft Ho 12 W10 91 A4
Putney SW15 157 A5
Croft Lodge Cl IG8 37 B4
Croft Mews N12 14 A1
Crofton Ave
Chiswick W4 133 B5
Orpington BR6 227 A6
Sidcup DA5 168 D4
Crofton Gate Way SE4 163 A6
Crofton Gr E4 36 B6
Crofton Inf Sch BR5 211 B2
Crofton Jun Sch BR5 211 B2
Crofton La BR5,BR6 211 B2
Crofton L Ctr SE4 163 C5
Crofton Park Rd SE4 163 B5
Crofton Park Sta SE4 163 B6
Crofton Rd BR6 226 C5
BR6 226 D5
E13 99 B3
SE5 139 C3
Crofton Sch SE4 163 C5
Crofton Terr E5 75 A3
Richmond TW9 132 B1
Crofton Way Enfield EN2 4 C3
New Barnet EN5 13 D5
Croft Rd BR1 187 A4
Carshalton SM1 218 C3
Enfield EN3 7 A4
Merton SW19 180 A3
South Norwood SW16 182 C3
Crofts Ho 19 E2 96 A5
Croftside The SE25 206 A6
Crofts La N22 32 C3
Crofts Rd HA1 43 A4
Crofts St E1 118 A6
Croft St SE8 119 A2
Crofts The TW17 193 C5
Croft The NW10 89 D5
Barnet EN5 1 A1
Chingford E4 20 C2
Ealing W5 88 A2
Edgware HA8 26 D3
Heston TW5 129 A5
New Malden KT3 199 C4
Pinner HA5 41 B2
Ruislip HA4 62 C4
Wembley HA0 65 C3
Croft Villas HA1 43 A3
Croft Way
Richmond TW10 153 B1
Sidcup DA15 167 C1
Crogsland Rd NW1 71 A1
Croham Cl CR2 221 C1
Croham Hurst Sch
CR2 221 D3
Croham Manor Rd
CR2 221 C2
Croham Mount CR2 221 C1
Croham Park Ave CR2 221 D3
Croham Rd CR2 221 C3
Croham Valley Rd
CR2 222 B1
Croindene Rd SW16 182 A2
Crokesley Ho 2 HA8 27 A1
Cromartie Rd N19 49 D2
Cromarty Ct 5 BR1 187 C1
Cromarty Ho 8 E1 97 A2
Cromarty Rd HA8 10 D2
Cromberdale Ct N17 34 A2
Crombie Cl IG4 56 B4
Crombie Mews 5
SW11 136 C3
Crombie Rd DA15 167 B3
Cromdale Ct N16 51 D2
Crome Ho UB5 85 A5
Cromer Cl UB8 83 A1
Cromer Ct
7 Southall UB1 85 D1
Streatham SW16 160 A1
Wandsworth SW18 157 B5
Cromer Pl 5 BR6 211 B1
Cromer Rd E10 54 B2
Barnet EN5 2 A2
Croydon SE25 206 B6
Dagenham RM6 59 A3
Harlington TW6 126 C3
Streatham SW17 181 A4
Tottenham N17 34 A1
Woodford IG8 37 A6
Cromer Road Prim Sch
EN5 2 A2
Cromer St WC1 94 A4 233 B1
Cromer Terr E8 74 A3
Cromer Villas Rd
SW18 157 B5
Cromford Cl BR6 227 C5
Cromford Path 1 E5 74 D4
Cromford Rd SW18 157 C6
Cromford Way KT3 177 B2
Cromlix Cl BR7 188 D1
Crompton Ct SW3 257 A4
Crompton Ho SE1 262 B5
SW8 269 B1
W2 236 C5
Crompton Pl EN3 7 C5
Crompton St
W2 92 B3 236 C5
Cromwell Ave BR2 209 B5
N6 49 B1
W6 112 B2
New Malden KT3 199 D4
Cromwell Bsns Ctr
IG11 101 C4
Cromwell Cl N2 48 B5
W3 111 A5
2 W4 110 D1
Bromley BR2 209 B5
Walton-on-T KT12 194 B1
Cromwell Cres
SW5 113 C2 255 A4
Cromwell Ct Enfield EN3 18 D6
Cromwell Ct *continued*
15 Kingston KT2 176 C3
Wembley HA0 88 A5
Cromwell Ctr NW10 89 B4
Barking IG11 102 A4
Cromwell Ctr The RM8 59 B2
Cromwell Est E10 53 A1
Cromwell Gdns
SW7 114 B3 256 D5
Cromwell Gr W6 112 C3
Cromwell Ho SW11 268 B1
Croydon CR0 220 D5
Putney SW15 134 A1
Cromwell Hospl
SW5 113 D2 255 C4
Cromwell Lo 36 E1 96 C3
Barking IG11 79 C3
Cromwell Mans SW5 255 B4
Cromwell Mews SW7 256 D4
Cromwell Pl N6 49 B1
SW7 114 B2 256 D4
5 W3 111 A5
Mortlake SW14 133 A2
Cromwell Rd E17 54 A4
E7 77 C1
N10 31 A3
N3 30 A2
SW7 256 B4
SW9 138 D4
Beckenham BR3 207 A6
Feltham TW13 150 B3
Hayes UB3 83 B1
Hounslow TW3 129 C1
Kingston KT2 176 A2
Teddington TW11 175 A4
Thornton Heath CR0 205 B2
Walton-on-T KT12 194 B1
Wembley HA0 88 A5
Wimbledon SW19 179 D5
Worcester Park KT4 215 C5
Cromwell St TW3 129 C1
Cromwell Twr EC2 242 B4
Crondace Rd
SW6 135 C4 265 B1
Crondall Ct 7 N1 95 C5
Crondall Ho SW15 156 A3
Crondall Pl 15 N1 95 C5
Crondall St N1 95 C5
Crone Ct 5 NW6 91 B5
Cronin St SE15 139 D5
Crooked Billet E4 35 C3
Crooked Billet Yd 19
E2 95 C4
Crooked Usage N3 47 A6
Crooke Rd SE8 119 A1
Crookham Rd
SW6 135 B4 264 C1
Crook Log DA6 146 D1
Crook Log Prim Sch
DA6 146 D1
Crook Log Sports Ctr
DA16 146 D2
Crookston Rd SE9 144 C2
Croombs Rd E16 99 C2
Croom's Hill SE10 142 B5
Croom's Hill Gr SE10 142 A5
Cropley Ct N1 235 C4
Cropley St N1 95 B5 235 C4
Croppath Rd RM10 81 C4
Cropthorne Ct W9 229 B1
Crosbie 10 NW9 27 D1
Crosbie Ho 20 E17 53 D6
Crosby Cl TW13 173 A6
Crosby Ct N2 48 A5
SE1 252 C2
Crosby Rd E7 77 A2
Dagenham RM10 103 D6
Crosby Row
SE1 117 B4 252 C2
Crosby Sq EC3 243 A2
Crosby Wlk 3 E8 73 D2
Streatham SE24 160 C4
Crosfield Ct 3 W10 90 D1
Crosfield Ho W11 244 A5
Crosier Cl SE3 144 A3
Crosier Rd UB10 61 A4
Crosier Way HA4 61 C5
Crosland Pl 5 SW11 137 A2
Crossbow Ho 15 N1 95 C6
Ealing W13 109 B5
Crossbrook Rd SE3 144 A2
Cross Cl SE15 140 B3
Cross Ct 11 SE28 124 B6
SE5 139 B2
Cross Deep TW1 153 A2
Cross Deep Gdns
TW1 152 D2
Crossfield Rd N17 51 A6
NW3 70 B2
Crossfield St SE8 141 C5
Crossford St SW9 138 B3
Crossgate Edgware HA8 10 C1
Wembley UB6 65 B2
Crossharbour & London
Arena Sta E14 119 D3
Cross Keys Cl W1 238 B3
5 Edmonton N9 18 A2
Cross La DA5 169 B4
EC3 253 A5
Cross La *continued*
N8 50 B5
Cross Lances Rd TW3 129 D1
Crossland Rd CR7 204 D3
Crosslands Ave
Ealing W5 110 B5
Southall UB2 107 B1
Crosslands Rd KT19 215 B2
Crossleigh Ct 3 SE14 141 B5
Crosslet St SE17 262 D4
Crosslet Vale SE10 141 D4
Crossley St N7 72 C2
Crossman Hos 19
SW12 160 A4
Crossmead SE9 166 B3
Crossmead Ave UB6 85 C4
Crossmount Ho 13
SE5 139 A5
Crossness Rd IG11 101 D4
Cross Rd BR2 226 A6
N11 31 B5
N2 30 C1
SE5 139 C3
Chingford, Chingford Green
E4 20 C3
Croydon CR0 205 B1
Enfield EN1 5 C1
Feltham TW13 173 A6
Harrow HA1 42 B4
Harrow HA2 63 D5
Harrow HA3 25 A1
Ilford RM6 58 C2
Kingston KT2 176 B3
Merton SW19 179 C3
Romford RM7 59 C6
Sidcup DA14 190 B6
Sutton SM1 218 B3
Wood Green N22 32 C3
Cross St N1 94 D6 234 D6
2 Edmonton N18 34 A5
Hampton TW12 174 A5
Mortlake SW13 133 C2
Crossthwaite Ave SE5,
SE24 139 B1
Crosswall EC3 117 D6 253 C6
Crossway BR5 211 B4
E8,N16 73 C3
N12 30 B4
NW9 45 D5
SE28 102 D1
Dagenham RM8 80 C5
Ealing W13 87 A3
Enfield EN1 17 C4
Hayes UB3 106 A5
Pinner HA5 22 B1
Ruislip HA4 62 C4
West Barnes KT3,SW20 200 C5
Woodford IG8 37 C6
Crossway Ct SE4 141 A3
Crossway Par N22 32 D3
Crossways
Ashford TW16 171 D3
South Croydon CR2 223 B1
Sutton SM2 218 B1
Crossways Rd
Beckenham BR3 207 C5
Mitcham CR4 203 B6
Crossways The
Heston TW5 129 B5
Wembley HA9 66 C6
Crossway The
Chislehurst SE9 165 D2
Hillingdon UB10 82 B5
Tottenham N22 32 D3
Cross Way The HA3 24 C1
Croswell Cl TW17 171 A1
Croston St E8 96 A6
Crothall Cl N13 16 B1
Crouch Ave IG11 102 B5
Crouch Cl BR3 185 C4
Crouch Croft SE9 166 C1
Crouch End Hill N8 49 D2
Crouch Hall Ct N19 50 A1
Crouch Hall Rd N8 49 D3
Crouch Hill N4,N8,N19 50 A2
Crouchmans Cl SE21,
SE26 162 A1
Crouch Rd NW10 67 B1
Crowborough Ct W13 109 C6
Crowborough Path
WD19 22 D6
Crowborough Rd
SW17 181 A5
Crowden Way SE28 124 C6
Crowder St E1 118 B6
Crowfield Ho N5 73 A4
Crowfoot Cl E9 75 B3
Crowhurst SE25 206 A6
Crowhurst Cl SW9 138 C3
Crowhurst Ct N17 34 B2
Crowhurst Ho 21 SW9 138 B3
Crow La RM7,RM8 59 D2
Crowland Ave UB3 105 D2
Crowland Gdns N14 16 A4
Crowland Ho NW8 229 A5
Crowland Prim Sch
N15 52 A4
Crowland Rd N15 51 D4
South Norwood CR7 205 B5
Crowlands Ave RM7 59 D3
Crowland Terr N1 73 B1
Crowland Wlk SM4 202 A3
Crowley Cres CR0 220 C3
Crowline Wlk 1 N1 73 A2
Crowmarsh Gdns
SE23 162 C4
Crown Arc KT1 175 D1
Crown Bldgs 4 E4 20 B3
Crownbourne Ct SM1 217 D4
Crown Cl E3 97 C6
NW6 69 D2
NW7 11 D2
Hayes UB3 105 D4
Walton-on-T KT12 194 C2
Crown Close Bsns Ctr
E3 97 C6
Crown Ct EC4 242 B1
6 N10 31 A3
NW8 230 B1
SE12 165 B5
WC2 240 B1
Bromley BR1 209 D4
4 Putney SW15 134 D1
3 Twickenham TW1 153 B4
Crown Dale SE19 183 A5
Crowndale Ct NW1 232 C4
Crowndale Rd
NW1 93 C5 232 B4
Crownfield Ave IG2 57 C4
Crownfield Rd E15 76 B4
Crown Hill CR0 221 A5
Crownhill Rd NW10 89 D6
Crown Ho HA4 40 A1
Crown La BR2 209 D4
N14 15 C3
Chislehurst BR7 189 A2
Merton SM4 201 C6
South Norwood SE19,
SW16 182 C5
Crown Lane Gdns
SE27 182 C5
Crown Lane Prim Sch
SE27 182 D5
Crown Lane Spur BR2 209 D3
Crownleigh Ct SW2 160 C6
Crown Lo SW3 257 B3
Crownmead Way RM7 59 D5
Crown Mews 3 E13 99 C6
Crown Office Row
EC4 251 A6
Crown Par N14 15 C3
Morden SM4 201 D5
South Norwood SE19 182 D4
Crown Pas SW1 249 B3
Kingston KT1 175 D1
Crown Pl EC2 243 A4
NW5 71 B2
Crown Point SE19 182 D4
Crown Rd N10 31 A3
Enfield EN1 6 B2
Ilford IG6 57 B5
Kingston KT3 177 A2
Morden SM4 201 D5
Ruislip HA4 62 D3
Sutton SM1 217 D4
Twickenham TW1 153 B5
Crown Reach SW1 259 D1
Crown St SE5 139 A5
Acton W3 110 D5
Dagenham RM10 81 D2
Harrow HA2 42 C1
Crownstone Ct 1
SW2 160 C6
Crownstone Rd SW2 160 C6
Crown Terr TW9 132 B1
Crown Trad Ctr UB3 105 C4
Crowntree Cl TW7 130 D6
Crown Way UB7 104 B5
Crown Wlk HA9 66 B5
Crown Woods Sch
SE9 167 A6
Crown Woods Way
SE9 167 B6
Crown Yard TW3 130 A2
Crowshott Ave HA7 25 D2
Crows Rd E15 98 B4
Barking IG11 78 D2
Crowther Ave TW8 110 A2
Crowther Cl
SW6 135 B6 264 D5
Crowther Rd SE25 206 A5
Crowthorne Cl SW18 157 B3
Crowthorne Rd W10 90 D1
Croxall Ho KT12 194 C3
Croxden Cl HA8 44 C6
Croxden Wlk SM4 202 A3
Croxford Gdns N22 32 D3
Croxley Cl BR5 190 B1
Croxley Gn BR5 190 B2
Croxley Rd W9 91 B4
Croxted Cl SE21 161 A4
Croxted Mews SE24 161 A5
Croxted Rd SE21,SE24 161 B3
Croxteth Ho 11 SW8 137 D3
Croxton 17 KT1 176 C1
Croyde Ave
Greenford UB6 86 A4
Hayes UB3 105 C2

Croyde Cl SE9 ... 167 B4
Croydon N17 ... 33 B1
Croydon Airport Ind Est CR0 ... 220 B2
Croydon Central Sta CR0 ... 221 A6
Croydon Coll CR0 ... 221 B6
Croydon Coll Annexe CR0 ... 205 B1
Croydon Coll (Selhurst Tertiary Ctr) SE25 ... 205 B4
Croydon Flyover The CR0 ... 221 A5
Croydon Gr CR0 ... 204 D1
Croydon Ho SE1 ... 251 B2
Croydon Rd E13 ... 98 D3
Beckenham BR3 ... 207 A6
Coney Hall BR2,BR4 ... 224 D5
Harlington TW6 ... 126 D2
Keston Mark BR2,BR4, BR6 ... 225 C5
Mitcham CR0,CR4 ... 203 C4
Penge SE20 ... 184 C2
Wallington CR0 ... 220 B4
Wallington CR0,SM5, SM6 ... 219 C5
Croydon Rd Ind Est BR3 ... 206 D5
Croyland Rd N9 ... 18 A3
Croylands Dr KT6 ... 198 A2
Croysdale Ave TW16 ... 194 A6
Crozier Ho SE3 ... 143 B2
SW8 ... 270 C3
Crozier Terr E9 ... 74 D3
Crucible Cl RM6 ... 58 B3
Crucifix La SE1 ... 117 C4 253 A2
Cruden Ho 23 E3 ... 97 B5
11 SE17 ... 138 D6
Cruden St N1 ... 94 D6 234 D5
Cruickshank St WC1 ... 234 A2
Cruikshank Ho NW8 ... 230 B4
Cruikshank Rd E15 ... 76 C3
Crummock Gdns NW9 ... 45 C4
Crumpsall St SE2 ... 124 C2
Crundale Ave NW9 ... 44 C4
Crunden Rd CR2 ... 221 B1
Crusader Gdns CR0 ... 221 C5
Crusader Ind Est N4 ... 51 A3
Crusoe House Sch N1 ... 95 B4 235 C2
Crusoe Mews N16 ... 73 B6
Crusoe Rd CR4 ... 180 D3
Crutched Friars EC3 ... 117 C6 253 B6
Crutchfield La KT12 ... 194 B1
Crutchley Rd SE6 ... 164 C2
Crystal Ct SE19 ... 183 D5
Crystal Ctr The 1 HA1 ... 42 D4
Crystal Ho SE18 ... 123 D1
Crystal Palace Mus★ SE19 ... 183 D4
Crystal Palace National Sports Ctr SE20 ... 184 A4
Crystal Palace Par SE19 ... 183 D5
Crystal Palace Park Rd SE26 ... 184 B5
Crystal Palace Rd SE22 ... 162 A6
Crystal Palace Sta SE19 ... 184 A4
Crystal Palace Station Rd SE19 ... 184 A4
Crystal Terr SE19 ... 183 B4
Crystal View Ct BR1 ... 186 B6
Crystal Way
Dagenham RM8 ... 58 C1
Harrow HA1 ... 42 D4
Cuba Dr EN3 ... 6 C3
Cuba St E14 ... 119 C4
Cubitt Ho 4 SW4 ... 159 C5
Cubitt Sq UB2 ... 108 A5
Cubitt St WC1 ... 94 B4 233 D1
Cubitt Terr SW4 ... 137 C2
Cubitt Town Jun & Inf Sch E14 ... 120 A3
Cuckoo Ave W7 ... 86 C3
Cuckoo Dene W7 ... 86 B2
Cuckoo Hall La N9 ... 18 D4
Cuckoo Hall Prim Sch N9 ... 18 C4
Cuckoo Hill HA5 ... 40 C6
Cuckoo Hill Dr HA5 ... 40 C6
Cuckoo Hill Rd HA5 ... 40 D5
Cuckoo La W7 ... 108 C6
Cuda's Cl KT19 ... 215 D4
Cuddington SE17 ... 262 B4
Cuddington Ave KT19, KT4 ... 215 D5
Cuddington Com Prim Sch KT4 ... 215 D5
Cudham La N BR6 ... 227 C1
Cudham St SE6 ... 164 A4
Cudworth Ho SW8 ... 269 B1
Cudworth St E1 ... 96 B3
Cuff Cres SE9 ... 165 D5
Cuffley Ho W10 ... 90 C2
Cuff Point 12 E2 ... 95 D4
Culand Ho SE17 ... 263 A3
Culford Gdns SW3 ... 114 D2 257 D3
Culford Gr N1 ... 73 C2
Culford Mans SW3 ... 257 D3
Culford Mews N1 ... 73 C2
Culford Rd N1 ... 73 C2
N1 ... 95 C6
Culgaith Gdns EN2 ... 4 A1
Culham Ho 33 E2 ... 95 D4
21 W2 ... 91 C2
Cullen Ho W9 ... 91 B5
Cullen Way NW10 ... 89 A3
Culling Rd SE16 ... 118 C3
Cullington Cl HA3 ... 43 A5
Cullingworth Rd NW10 ... 68 B3
Culloden Cl 15 SE16 ... 118 A1
Culloden Prim Sch E14 ... 98 A1
Culloden Rd EN2 ... 4 D3
Cullum St EC3 ... 253 A6
Culmington Mans W13 ... 109 C6
Culmington Par W13 ... 109 C6
Culmington Rd
Ealing W13,W5 ... 109 C5
South Croydon CR2 ... 221 A1
Culmore Rd SE15 ... 140 C5
Culmstock Rd SW11 ... 159 A6
Culpepper Ct SE11 ... 261 A4
Culross Bldgs NW1 ... 233 A4
Culross Cl N15 ... 51 A5
Culross St W1 ... 115 A6 248 A5
Culsac Rd KT6 ... 214 A6
Culver Ct SW18 ... 157 D5
Culverden Rd SW12 ... 159 C2
Culver Gr HA7 ... 25 C1
Culverhouse WC1 ... 240 C3
Culverhouse Gdns SW16 ... 160 B1
Culverlands Cl HA7 ... 25 B6
Culverley Rd SE6 ... 164 A3
Culvers Ave SM5,CR4 ... 218 D6
Culvers House Prim Sch CR4 ... 203 A1
Culvers Retreat SM5 ... 218 D6
Culverstone Cl BR2 ... 208 D4
Culvers Way SM5 ... 218 D6
Culvert Ct SW11 ... 137 A3
Culverton Ct 5 DA14 ... 190 A6
Culvert Pl SW11 ... 137 A3
Culvert Rd N15 ... 51 C4
SW11 ... 136 D3
Culworth Ho NW8 ... 230 A4
Culworth St NW8 ... 230 A3
Cumber Ho SW18 ... 157 C3
Cumberland Ave DA16 ... 145 D1
Wembley NW10 ... 88 D4
Cumberland Bsns Pk NW10 ... 88 D4
Cumberland Cl E8 ... 73 D2
2 Twickenham TW1 ... 153 B5
8 Wimbledon SW20 ... 178 D3
Cumberland Cres W14 ... 254 B4
Cumberland Ct W1 ... 237 D1
4 Croydon CR0 ... 205 B1
Woodford IG8 ... 37 B3
Cumberland Dr DA7 ... 147 A5
Chessington KT9 ... 214 B5
Hinchley Wood KT10 ... 213 A6
Cumberland Gate W1 ... 114 D6 247 D6
Cumberland Gdns NW4 ... 29 A1
WC1 ... 234 A2
Cumberland Ho N9 ... 18 C3
Kingston KT2 ... 176 D3
1 Putney SW15 ... 156 C4
Cumberland Mans
7 NW6 ... 69 C3
W1 ... 237 C2
Cumberland Market NW1 ... 93 B4 231 D2
Cumberland Mills Sq E14 ... 120 B1
Cumberland Park Ind Est NW10 ... 90 A4
Cumberland Pk W3 ... 111 A6
Cumberland Pl NW1 ... 231 C2
Catford SE6 ... 164 D3
Sunbury TW16 ... 194 A5
Cumberland Rd E12 ... 77 D4
E13 ... 99 B3
E17 ... 35 A1
N9 ... 18 C3
W3 ... 111 A6
W7 ... 108 D4
Ashford TW15 ... 148 A1
Barnes SW13 ... 134 A4
Beckenham BR2 ... 208 D6
Croydon SE25 ... 206 B3
Harrow HA1 ... 41 D4
Richmond TW9 ... 132 C5
Stanmore HA7,HA8 ... 44 B6
Wood Green N22 ... 32 B1
Cumberland Sch E16 ... 98 D2
Cumberland St SW1 ... 115 B1 258 D2
Cumberland Terr NW1 ... 231 C3
Cumberland Terrace Mews NW1 ... 231 C3
Cumberland Villas W3 ... 111 A6
Cumberlow Ave SE25 ... 206 A6
Cumbernauld Gdns TW16 ... 171 D5
Cumberton Rd N17 ... 33 B2
Cumbrae Gdns KT6 ... 213 D6
Cumbria Ho 2 SW15 ... 157 B6
Cumbrian Gdns NW2 ... 69 A6
Cumming St N1 ... 233 D3
Cumnor Cl 23 SW9 ... 138 B3
Cumnor Gdns KT17 ... 216 A2
Cumnor Rd SM2 ... 218 A2
Cunard Cres N21 ... 17 B5
Cunard Pl EC3 ... 243 B1
Cunard Rd NW10 ... 89 B4
Cunard Wlk 3 SE16 ... 119 A2
Cundy Rd E16 ... 99 C1
Cundy St SW1 ... 115 A2 258 B3
Cunliffe Rd KT19 ... 215 D4
Cunliffe St SW16 ... 181 C4
Cunningham Cl
Dagenham RM6 ... 58 C4
West Wickham BR4 ... 223 D6
Cunningham Ct W2 ... 236 C5
Cunningham Ho 16 SE5 ... 139 B5
Cunningham Pk HA1 ... 42 B4
Cunningham Pl NW8 ... 92 B3 236 C6
Cunningham Rd N15 ... 52 A5
Cunnington St W4 ... 111 A2
Cupar Rd SW11 ... 268 B2
Cupola Cl BR1 ... 187 B5
Cureton St SW1 ... 115 D2 259 D3
Curie Gdns NW9 ... 27 C1
Curie Ho 1 HA9 ... 67 A5
Curlew Cl SE28 ... 124 D6
Curlew Ct KT6 ... 214 C5
Curlew Ho 6 SE15 ... 139 D4
SE4 ... 141 A1
Enfield EN3 ... 18 D6
Curlew St SE1 ... 117 D4 253 D2
Curlew Way UB4 ... 84 D2
Curnick's La SE27 ... 183 A6
Curran Ave DA15 ... 167 D6
Hackbridge SM6 ... 219 A5
Curran Ho SW3 ... 257 A3
Currey Rd UB6 ... 64 B2
Curricle St W3 ... 111 C5
Currie Hill Cl SW19 ... 179 B6
Currie Ho 13 SW12 ... 159 D4
Curry Rise NW7 ... 28 D4
Cursitor St EC4 ... 94 C1 241 A2
Curtain Pl EC2 ... 243 B6
Curtain Rd EC2 ... 95 C3 243 B6
Curthwaite Gdns EN2 ... 15 D6
Curtis Dr W3 ... 89 B1
Curtis Field Rd SW16 ... 182 C6
Curtis Ho 7 N11 ... 31 C5
SE17 ... 262 C2
Curtis La HA0 ... 66 A3
Curtis Rd
Twickenham TW4 ... 151 B4
West Ewell KT19 ... 215 A4
Curtis St SE1 ... 117 D2 263 C4
Curtis Way SE1 ... 263 C4
7 SE28 ... 124 B6
Curtlington Ho 3 HA8 ... 27 A1
Curve The W12 ... 112 A6
Curwen Ave E7 ... 77 B4
Curwen Rd W12 ... 112 A4
Curwen Sch E13 ... 99 A5
Curzon Ave Enfield EN3 ... 18 D6
Stanmore HA7 ... 25 A2
Curzon Cl BR6 ... 227 B4
Curzon Cres NW10 ... 67 C1
Barking IG11 ... 101 D4
Curzon Ct SE9 ... 167 A1
SW6 ... 265 D1
Curzon Gate W1 ... 248 B3
Curzon Ho W5 ... 87 B3
Curzon Pl W1 ... 248 B3
Pinner HA5 ... 40 C4
Curzon Rd N10 ... 31 B1
Ealing W5 ... 87 B3
Thornton Heath CR7 ... 204 C3
Curzon St W1 ... 115 B5 248 C4
Cusack Cl TW1 ... 174 D6
Custance Ho N1 ... 235 C3
Custance St N1 ... 235 C2
Custom House★ EC3 ... 117 C6 253 A5
Custom House for ExCeL Sta E16 ... 121 B6
Custom House Reach SE16 ... 119 B3
Cutbush Ho N7 ... 71 D3
Cutcombe Mans 22 SE5 ... 139 A3
Cutcombe Rd SE5 ... 139 A3
Cuthberga Cl IG11 ... 79 A1
Cuthbert Gdns SE25 ... 205 C6
Cuthbert Harrowing Ho EC1 ... 242 A5
Cuthbert Ho W2 ... 236 C4
Cuthbert Rd E17 ... 54 A6
Croydon CR0 ... 220 D6
8 Edmonton N18 ... 34 A6
Cuthbert St W2 ... 236 C5
Cuthill Wlk 3 SE5 ... 139 B4
Cutlers Gdns EC2 ... 243 B2
Cutlers Sq E14 ... 119 C2
Cutler St EC2 ... 243 B2
Cut The SE1 ... 116 C4 251 B2
Cutty Sark★ SE10 ... 142 A6
Cutty Sark Sta SE10 ... 142 A6
Cuxton BR5 ... 211 A4
Cuxton Cl DA6 ... 169 A6
Cuxton Ho SE17 ... 263 B2
Cyclamen Cl 4 TW12 ... 173 C4
Cyclamen Way KT19 ... 215 A3
Cyclops Mews 9 E14 ... 119 C2
Cygnet Ave TW14 ... 150 D4
Cygnet Cl NW10 ... 67 B3
Cygnet St E1 ... 243 D6
Cygnets The TW13 ... 173 A6
Cygnet Way UB4 ... 84 D2
Cygnus Bsns Ctr NW10 ... 67 D2
Cymbeline Ct 6 HA1 ... 42 D3
Cyns Ct 5 E11 ... 55 A3
Cynthia St N1 ... 233 D3
Cypress Ave N2 ... 47 D6
Twickenham TW2 ... 152 A4
Cypress Ct 5 E11 ... 76 B4
Cheam SM1 ... 217 C2
7 West Norwood SW16 ... 182 C5
Cypress Gdns SE4 ... 163 A6
Cypress Ho SE14 ... 140 D4
Cypress Inf Sch SE25 ... 183 C1
Cypress Jun Sch SE25 ... 183 C1
Cypress Lo SE25 ... 183 C1
Cypress Pl W1 ... 239 B5
Cypress Rd Harrow HA3 ... 24 B1
South Norwood SE25 ... 183 C1
Cypress Tree Cl DA15 ... 167 D3
Cyprus Ave N3 ... 29 A1
Cyprus Cl N4 ... 50 C3
Cyprus Gdns N3 ... 29 A1
Cyprus Pl 24 E2 ... 96 C5
E6 ... 122 C6
Cyprus Rd N3 ... 29 B1
Edmonton N9 ... 17 D2
Cyprus St E2 ... 96 C5
Cyprus Sta E6 ... 122 C6
Cyrena Rd SE22 ... 161 D6
Cyril Jackson Prim Sch (North Bldg) E14 ... 119 B6
Cyril Jackson Prim Sch (South Bldg) E14 ... 119 B6
Cyril Lo 2 DA14 ... 190 A6
Cyril Mans SW11 ... 267 D1
Cyril Rd DA7 ... 147 A3
Cyril Smith Ho N13 ... 32 B5
Cyril Thatcher Ho SW6 ... 265 B1
Cyrus Ho EC1 ... 241 D6
Cyrus St EC1 ... 94 D3 241 D6
Czar St SE8 ... 141 C6

D

Dabbs Hill La UB5 ... 63 C3
Dabb's La EC1 ... 241 B5
Dabin Cres SE10 ... 142 A4
Dacca St SE8 ... 141 B6
Dace Rd E3 ... 97 C6
Dacre Cl UB6 ... 85 D5
Dacre Gdns SE13 ... 142 C1
Borehamwood WD6 ... 11 B6
Dacre Ho SW3 ... 266 D5
Dacre Pk SE13 ... 142 C1
Dacre Pl SE13 ... 142 C2
Dacre Rd E11 ... 54 D1
E13 ... 99 B6
Thornton Heath CR0 ... 204 A2
Dacres Rd SE23 ... 162 D1
Dacre St SW1 ... 115 D3 259 C6
Dade Way UB2 ... 107 B1
Daerwood Cl BR2 ... 210 B1
Daffodil Cl CR0 ... 206 D1
Daffodil Gdns IG1 ... 78 D3
Daffodil Pl 7 TW12 ... 173 C4
Daffodil St W12 ... 111 D6
Dafforne Rd SW17 ... 159 A1
Dagenham Ave RM9 ... 103 A6
Dagenham Dock Sta RM9 ... 103 B5
Dagenham East Sta RM10 ... 81 D3
Dagenham Heathway Sta RM9 ... 81 B2
Dagenham Priory Comp Sch RM10 ... 103 D6
Dagenham Rd E10 ... 53 B1
Dagenham RM10 ... 81 D4
Dagger La WD23,WD6 ... 9 A6
Dagmar Ave HA9 ... 66 B4
Dagmar Ct E14 ... 120 A3
Dagmar Gdns NW10 ... 90 D5
Dagmar Mews UB2 ... 107 A3
Dagmar Pas N1 ... 234 D6
Dagmar Rd N15 ... 51 B5
N22 ... 31 D2
N4 ... 50 C2
SE5 ... 139 C4
4 Kingston KT2 ... 176 C3
Southall UB2 ... 107 A3
South Norwood SE25 ... 205 C4
Dagmar Terr N1 ... 94 D6 234 D6
Dagnall Pk SE25 ... 205 C4
Dagnall Rd SE25 ... 205 C4
Dagnall St SW11 ... 137 A4 268 A1
Dagnan Rd SW12 ... 159 C4
Dagobert Ho 25 E1 ... 96 C2
Dagonet Gdns BR1 ... 165 A1
Dagonet Rd BR1 ... 165 A1
Dahlia Gdns Ilford IG1 ... 78 D2
Mitcham CR4 ... 203 D5
Dahlia Rd SE2 ... 124 B2
Dahomey Rd SW16 ... 181 C4
Daiglen Sch The IG9 ... 21 C2
Daimler Ho 8 E3 ... 97 C3
Daimler Way SM6 ... 220 A1
Daines Cl E12 ... 78 B5
Dainford Cl BR1 ... 186 B5
Dainton Cl 2 BR1 ... 187 B2
Dainton Ho 22 W2 ... 91 C2
Daintry Cl HA3 ... 43 A5
Daintry Way E9 ... 75 B2
Dairsie Ct 2 BR1 ... 187 C1
Dairsie Rd SE9 ... 144 C2
Dairy Cl BR1 ... 187 B3
South Norwood CR7 ... 183 A1
Dairy La SE18 ... 122 B2
Dairyman Cl NW2 ... 69 A5
Dairy Meadow Prim Sch UB2 ... 107 B3
Daisy Cl CR0 ... 206 D1
Daisy Dormer Ct 11 SW9 ... 138 B1
Daisy La SW6 ... 135 C2
Daisy Rd E16 ... 98 C3
Woodford E18 ... 37 B1
Dakota Cl SM6 ...
Dakota Gdns
Newham E6 ... 100 A3
Northolt UB5 ... 85 A4
Dalberg Rd SW2 ... 160 C6
Dalberg Way SE2 ... 124 D3
Dalbury Ho 6 SW9 ... 138 B1
Dalby Rd SW18 ... 136 A1
Dalbys Cres N17 ... 33 C4
Dalby St NW5 ... 71 B2
Dalcross Rd TW4,TW5 ... 129 A3
Dale Ave Edgware HA8 ... 26 B1
Hounslow TW4 ... 129 A2
Dalebury Rd SW17 ... 158 D2
Dale Cl SE3 ... 143 A2
New Barnet EN5 ... 13 D5
Pinner HA5 ... 22 B2
Dale Croft N4 ... 73 A5
Dale Ct N8 ... 49 C5
3 Kingston KT2 ... 176 B3
Woodford E18 ... 37 A1
Dale Dr UB4 ... 83 D4
Dalefield IG9 ... 21 D3
Dale Gdns IG8 ... 37 B6
Dale Gr N12 ... 30 A5
Dale Green Rd N11 ... 15 B1
Dalehead NW1 ... 232 A3
Daleham Dr UB8 ... 82 D1
Daleham Gdns NW3 ... 70 B2
Daleham Mews NW3 ... 70 B2
Dale Ho NW8 ... 229 A6
SE4 ... 141 A1
Dale Lo N6 ... 49 C3
Dalemain Ho 5 SW8 ... 137 D3
Dalemain Mews 13 E16 ... 121 A5
Dale Park Ave SM5 ... 218 D6
Dale Park Rd SE19 ... 183 B2
Dale Rd NW5 ... 71 A3
SE17 ... 138 D6
Ashford TW16 ... 171 D3
Cheam SM1 ... 217 B4
Southall UB6 ... 85 D2
Walton-on-T KT12 ... 193 D2
Dale Row W11 ... 91 A1
Daleside Rd
Streatham SW17 ... 181 B5
West Ewell KT19 ... 215 B2
Dales Path WD6 ... 11 B6
Dales Rd WD6 ... 11 B6
Dale St W4 ... 111 C1
Dale The BR2 ... 225 D4
Dale View Ave E4 ... 20 A2
Dale View Cres E4 ... 20 A1
Dale View Gdns E4 ... 20 B1
Daleview Rd N15 ... 51 C3
Dalewood Gdns KT4 ... 216 B6
Dale Wood Rd BR6 ... 211 C1
Daley Ho W12 ... 90 B1
Daley St E9 ... 74 D2
Daley Thompson Way 7 SW8 ... 137 B2
Dalgarno Gdns W10 ... 90 C2
Dalgarno Way W10 ... 90 C3
Daling Way E3 ... 97 A5
Dalkeith Ct SW1 ... 259 D3
Dalkeith Gr HA7 ... 26 A5
Dalkeith Ho 6 SW9 ... 138 D4
Dalkeith Rd Ilford IG1 ... 79 A5
West Norwood SE21 ... 161 A4
Dallas Rd NW4 ... 46 A2
Cheam SM3 ... 217 A2
Ealing W5 ... 88 B2
Forest Hill SE26 ... 162 B1
Dallas Terr UB3 ... 105 D3
Dallega Cl UB3 ... 105 B6
Dallinger Rd SE12 ... 164 D5
Dalling Rd W6 ... 112 B2
Dallington Sch EC1 ... 94 D3 241 D6
Dallington St EC1 ... 94 D3 241 D6
Dallin Rd DA6 ... 146 D1
Woolwich SE18 ... 144 D5
Dalmain Prim Sch SE23 ... 163 A3
Dalmain Rd SE23 ... 162 D3
Dalmally Rd CR0 ... 206 A2
Dalmeny Ave N7 ... 71 D4
Thornton Heath SW16 ... 182 C1
Dalmeny Cl HA0 ... 65 C2
Dalmeny Cres TW3 ... 130 B1
Dalmeny Ct 4 SW4 ... 138 A3
Dalmeny Rd DA7,DA8 ... 147 D4
N7 ... 71 D4
New Barnet EN5 ... 14 A5
North Cheam KT4 ... 216 B5
Wallington SM5 ... 219 A1
Dalmeyer Rd NW10 ... 67 D2
Dalmore Ave KT10 ... 212 D2
Dalmore Rd SE21 ... 161 A2
Dalrymple Cl N14 ... 15 D4
Dalrymple Rd SE4 ... 141 A1
Dalston Gdns HA7 ... 26 A1
Dalston Jct E8 ... 73 D2
Dalston Kingsland Sta E8 ... 73 D3
Dalston La E8 ... 74 A3
Dalton Ave CR4 ... 180 C1
Dalton Cl BR6 ... 227 C5
Hayes UB4 ... 83 B3
Dalton Ho 9 E3 ... 97 A5
19 SE14 ... 140 D6
Dalton St SE27 ... 160 D1
Dalwood St SE5 ... 139 C4
Daly Ct E15 ... 76 A3
Dalyell Rd SW9 ... 138 B2
Damascene Wlk SE21 ... 161 A3
Damask Cres E16 ... 98 C3
Damer Ho 9 TW10 ... 154 B5
Damer Terr SW10 ... 266 B3
Dames Rd E7 ... 77 A5
Dame St N1 ... 95 A5 235 A4
Damien Ct 20 E1 ... 96 B1
Damien St E1 ... 96 B1
Damon Cl DA14 ... 168 B1
Damon Ct DA14 ... 168 B1
Damory Ho 1 SE16 ... 118 C2
Damson Dr UB3 ... 106 A6
Damsonwood Rd UB2 ... 107 C3
Danbrook Rd SW16 ... 182 A3
Dan Bryant Ho 5 SW12 ... 159 C4
Danbury Cl RM6 ... 58 D6
Danbury Mans 3 IG11 ... 78 D1
Danbury Mews SM5, SM6 ... 219 B4
Danbury St N1 ... 94 D5 234 D4
Danbury Way IG8 ... 37 C4
Danby Ct EN2 ... 5 A2
Danby Ho 23 E9 ... 74 C1
3 W10 ... 91 B4
Danby St SE15 ... 139 D2
Dancer Rd
Fulham SW6 ... 135 B4 264 C1
Richmond TW9 ... 132 C2
Dando Cres SE3 ... 143 B2
Dandridge Cl SE10 ... 120 D1
Dandridge Ho E1 ... 243 C4
Danebury W10 ... 90 C2
New Addington CR0 ... 223 D2
Danebury Ave SW15 ... 155 D5
Daneby Rd SE6 ... 164 A2
Dane Cl BR6 ... 227 B3
Sidcup DA5 ... 169 C4
Danecourt Gdns CR0 ... 221 D5
Danecroft Rd SE24 ... 161 B6
Danegrove Prim Sch EN4 ... 14 C5
Danegrove Sch EN4 ... 14 D5
Danehill Wlk DA14 ... 168 A1
Dane Ho 15 SE5 ... 139 A3
Danehurst TW8 ... 131 C5
Danehurst Gdns IG4 ... 56 B4
Danehurst St SW6 ... 135 A4 264 A2
Daneland EN4 ... 14 D5
Danemead Gr UB5 ... 63 D3
Danemere St SW15 ... 134 C2

Dane Pl E3 97 B5
Dane Rd N18 18 C1
Ashford TW15 171 B4
Ealing W13 109 C5
Ilford IG1 79 A3
Merton SW19 180 A2
Southall UB1 107 A6
Danesbury Rd TW13 150 B3
Danescombe SE12 165 A3
Danescourt Cres SM1 218 A6
Danescroft NW4 46 D4
Danescroft Ave NW4 46 D4
Danescroft Gdns NW4 46 D4
Danes Ct NW8 230 C5
Wembley HA9 66 D5
Danesdale Rd E9 75 A2
Danesfield SE5 139 C6
Danes Gate HA1 42 C6
Danes Ho W10 90 C2
Dane St WC1 240 C3
Daneswood Ave SE6 164 A1
Danethorpe Rd HA0 65 D2
Danetree Cl KT19 215 A1
Danetree Jun Sch KT19 215 A1
Danetree Rd KT19 215 A1
Danette Gdns RM8 81 B6
Daneville Rd SE5 139 B4
Danford Ho 9 N11 31 C5
Dangan Rd E11 55 A3
Daniel Bolt Cl E14 97 D2
Daniel Cl N18 34 C6
Twickenham TW4 151 B4
Upper Tooting SW17 180 C4
Daniel Ct 8 NW9 27 C2
W3 111 C6
3 Beckenham BR3 185 C3
Daniel Gdns SE15 139 D5
Daniell Ho N1 235 D4
Daniell Way CR0 204 B1
Daniel Pl NW4 46 B2
Daniel Rd W5 110 B6
Daniel's Rd SE15 140 C2
Dan Leno Wlk SW6 265 C3
Dansey Pl W1 249 C6
Dansington Rd DA16 146 A1
Danson Cres DA16 146 B2
Danson Intc DA5,DA6 168 C5
Danson La DA16 146 B1
Danson Mead DA16 146 C2
Danson Prim Sch DA16 146 A1
Danson Rd DA5,DA6, DA15 168 D6
Danson Underpass DA15 168 C5
Dante Rd SE11 116 D2 261 C4
Danube Ct 12 SE15 139 D5
Danube St SW3 114 C1 257 B2
Danvers Ho 22 E1 96 A1
Danvers Rd N8 49 D5
Danvers St SW3 136 B6 266 D5
Da Palma Ct SW6 265 A5
Daphne Ct Ealing W5 87 C1
Worcester Park KT4 215 C6
Daphne Gdns E4 20 A1
Daphne Ho N22 32 C2
Daphne St SW18 158 A5
Daplyn St 6 E1 96 A2
D'arblay St W1 93 C1 239 B1
Darby Cres TW16 172 C1
Darby Gdns TW16 172 C1
Darcy Ave SM6 219 C4
Darcy Cl N20 14 B2
D'arcy Dr HA3 43 D5
D'arcy Gdns
Dagenham RM9 103 B6
Harrow HA3 44 A5
Darcy Ho E8 96 B6
D'arcy Pl BR2 209 A5
Darcy Rd
Isleworth TW7 131 A4
Thornton Heath SW16 182 A1
D'arcy Rd SM3 216 D4
Dare Ct 2 E10 54 A2
Dare Gdns RM8 81 A5
Darell Prim Sch TW9 132 C2
Darell Rd TW9 132 C2
Daren Ct N7 72 A4
Darent Ho NW8 236 D4
4 Catford BR1 186 B5
Darenth Rd DA16 146 A4
N16 51 D1
Darfield NW1 232 A5
Darfield Rd SE4 163 B6
Darfield Way W10 90 D1
Darfur St SW15 134 D2
Dargate Cl SE19 183 D3
Darien Ho 8 E1 96 D2
17 SW11 136 B2
Darien Rd SW11 136 B2
Daring Ho 21 E3 97 A5
Darland Ct SW15 157 B5
Darlands Dr EN5 12 D6
Darlan Rd SW6 135 B5 264 D3
Darlaston Rd SW19 179 A3
Darley Cl CR0 207 A3
Darley Dr KT3 177 B1
Darley Gdns SM4 201 D3
Darley Ho SE11 260 C1
Darley Rd SW11 158 D5
Edmonton N9 17 D3
Darling Ho 5 TW1 153 D5
Darling Rd SE4 141 C2
Darling Row E1 96 B3
Darlington Ct 8 SE6 164 D3
Darlington Ho SW8 269 D3
2 Surbiton KT6 197 D2
Darlington Rd SE27 182 D5
Darmaine Cl CR2 221 A1
Darnay Ho 8 SE16 118 A3
Darndale Cl E17 35 B1
Darnell Ho 4 SE10 142 A4
9 SE10 142 A5
Darnley Ho 9 E14 97 A1
Darnley Rd E9 74 C2
Woodford IG8 37 B2
Darnley Terr 12 W11 112 D5
Darrell Ct BR2 208 C6
Darrell Rd SE22 162 A6
Darren Cl N4 50 B2
Darrick Wood Ho BR6 227 A5
Darrick Wood Inf Sch BR6 226 D5
Darrick Wood Jun Sch BR6 226 D4
Darrick Wood Rd BR6 227 B6
Darrick Wood Sec Sch BR6 226 D5
Darrick Wood Sports Ctr BR6 227 C6
Darris Cl UB4 85 A3
Darsley Dr SW8 138 A4 270 A2
Dartford Ave N9 18 D5
Dartford Gdns RM6 58 B4
Dartford Ho SE1 263 D4
Dartford St SE17 139 A6
Dartington NW1 232 B5
Dartington Ho 7 SW8 137 D3
W2 91 D2
Dartle Ct 26 SE16 118 A4
Dartmoor Wlk 17 E14 119 C2
Dartmouth Cl W11 91 C1
Dartmouth Ct SE10 142 A4
Dartmouth Gr SE10 142 A4
Dartmouth Hill SE10 142 A4
Dartmouth Ho N19 71 B6
Lewisham SE10 142 A3
Thornton Heath CR0 204 D2
Dartmouth Park Ave NW5 71 B5
Dartmouth Park Hill N19 71 B6
Dartmouth Park Rd NW5 71 B5
Dartmouth Pl
Chiswick W4 133 C6
Forest Hill SE23 162 C2
Dartmouth Rd NW2 68 D2
NW4 46 A3
Forest Hill SE23,SE26 162 C1
Hayes BR2 209 A2
Ruislip HA4 62 A5
Dartmouth Row SE10 142 A4
Dartmouth St SW1 115 D4 249 D1
Dartmouth Terr SE10 142 B4
Dartnell Rd CR0 205 D2
Darton Ct W3 111 A5
Dartrey Twr SW10 266 C4
Dartrey Wlk SW10 136 A5 266 B4
Dart St W10 91 B4
Darville Rd N16 73 D5
Darwell Cl E6 100 C5
Darwen Pl E2 96 B6
Darwin Cl BR6 227 B3
N11 15 B1
Darwin Ct E13 99 B4
NW1 231 B6
SE9 166 C5
Darwin Dr UB1 85 D1
Darwin Gdns WD19 22 C5
Darwin Ho 2 HA9 67 A5
Darwin Rd DA16 145 D2
W5 109 C2
Tottenham N22 32 D1
Darwin St SE17 117 B2 262 D4
Daryngton Dr UB6 86 C5
Daryngton Ho SW8 270 A3
Dashwood Cl DA6 169 C6
Dashwood Ct TW3 130 A1
Dashwood Ho SE21 161 D1
Dashwood Rd N8 50 B3
Dassett Rd SE27 182 D5
Data Point Bsns Ctr E16 98 B3
Datchelor Pl 14 SE5 139 B4
Datchet Ho NW1 231 D2
Datchet Rd SE6 163 B2
Datchett Ho 40 E2 95 D4
Datchwood Ct N4 73 A5
Datchworth Ct 7 EN1 17 C6
Datchworth Ho 8 N1 72 D1
Date St SE17 117 B1 262 C1
Daubeney Gdns N17 33 A3
Daubeney Pl TW12 173 D1
Daubeney Prim Sch E5 75 A4
Daubeney Rd E5 75 A4
Tottenham N17 33 A3
Daubeney Twr 2 SE8 119 B1
Dault Rd SW18 158 A5
Dauney Ho SE1 251 C1
Dave Adams Ho 7 E3 97 B5
Davenant Ho 18 E1 96 A2
Davenant Rd N19 71 D6
Croydon CR0,CR9 220 D4
Davenant St E1 96 A2
Davenport Cl TW11 175 A4
Davenport Ctr IG11 102 B5
Davenport Ho SE11 261 A5
Davenport Lo TW5 129 A5
Davenport Rd DA14 169 A2
SE6 164 A5
Daventer Dr HA7 24 D3
Daventry Ave E17 53 C3
Daventry St NW1 92 C2 237 A4
Dave Porter Hts SW19 157 A4
Daver Ct SW3 257 B1
Ealing W5 87 D3
Davern Cl SE10 120 D2
Davet Ct SW8 270 C2
Davey Cl N7 72 B2
Bowes Park N13 32 B5
Davey Lo 2 N1 72 C1
Davey Rd E9 75 C1
Davey's Ct WC2 250 A6
Davey St SE15 139 D6
David Ave UB6 86 C5
David Cl UB3 127 C5
David Coffer Ct DA17 125 D2
David Devine Ho 7 E8 74 A3
Davidge Ho SE1 251 B1
Davidge St SE1 116 D4 251 D1
David Ho 3 E14 97 D2
SW8 270 A4
8 Putney SW15 156 A6
South Norwood SE25 206 A6
David Lee Point 4 E15 98 C6
David Livingstone Prim Sch CR7 183 A2
David Mews W1 237 D4
David Rd RM8 81 A6
Davidson Gdns SW8 138 A5 270 A4
Davidson Ho 7 N19 71 C4
Davidson Inf Sch CR0 205 D2
Davidson Jun Sch CR0 205 D2
Davidson Lo CR0 205 C2
Davidson Rd CR0 205 D3
Davidson Terrs E7 77 B3
Davidson Twr BR1 187 B5
David's Rd SE23 162 C3
David St E15 76 B3
David Twigg Cl KT2 176 A2
Davies Cl CR0 206 A3
Davies La E11 76 D6
Davies Lane Jun & Inf Sch E11 76 D6
Davies Mews W1 248 C6
Davies St W1 115 B6 248 C6
Davies Walk TW7 130 B4
Da Vinci Ct 12 SE16 118 B1
Davington Gdns RM8 80 B3
Davington Rd RM8 80 B3
Davis Ho W12 112 B6
Davis Rd W3 111 D4
Chessington KT9 214 C4
Davis St E13 99 B5
Davisville Rd W12 112 A4
Davmor Ct TW8 109 C1
Davy Ho HA9 67 A6
Dawes Ave TW7 131 A1
Dawe's Cl UB10 82 A5
Dawes Ho SE17 262 C3
Dawes Rd SW6 135 B5 264 C4
Dawe's Rd UB10 82 A5
Dawes St SE17 117 B1 262 D2
Dawley Ave UB8 83 A1
Dawley Par UB3 105 A6
Dawley Rd Hayes UB3 105 B6
Hayes UB3 105 C2
Dawlish Ave
Bowes Park N13 32 A5
Wandsworth SW18 157 D2
Wembley UB6 87 A5
Dawlish Dr Ilford IG3 79 D4
Pinner HA5 41 A3
Ruislip HA4 62 B6
Dawlish Prim Sch E10 54 A1
Dawlish Rd E10 76 A6
N17 52 A6
NW2 68 D2
Dawnay Gdns SW18 158 B2
Dawnay Rd SW17, SW18 158 B2
Dawn Cl TW4 129 A2
Dawn Cres E15 98 B6
Dawn Wlk BR2 186 B1
Dawpool Rd NW2 67 D6
Daws Ho 35 W12 112 B6
Daws La NW7 28 A5
Dawson Ave BR5 190 B1
Barking IG11 79 D1
Dawson Cl SE18 123 A2
Hayes UB3 83 B2
Dawson Gdns 9 IG11 79 D1
Dawson Ho 23 E2 96 C4
5 SE5 139 C4
Dawson Pl W2 113 C6 245 B6
Dawson Rd NW2 68 C4
Kingston KT1 198 B6
Dawson St E2 95 D5
Dawson Terr N9 18 C4
Dax Ct TW16 194 C6
Daybrook Rd SW19 201 D6
Day Ho SE5 138 D5
2 SE5 139 A5
Daylesford Ave SW15 134 A1
Daymer Gdns HA5 40 C5
Daynor Ho 4 NW6 91 C6
Daysbrook Rd SW2 160 B3
Days La DA15 167 C4
Days Lane Prim Sch DA15 167 D5
Daytone Ho SW20 178 D2
Dayton Gr SE15 140 C4
Deaconess Ct 4 N15 51 D5
Deacon Ho SE11 260 D3
Deacon Mews N1 73 B1
Deacon Rd NW2 68 A2
Kingston KT2 176 B2
Deacons Cl HA5 22 B1
Deacon's Hill Rd WD6 10 C6
Deacons Hts WD6 10 C5
Deacons Leas BR6 227 B4
Deacons Rise N2 48 B4
Deacons Wlk TW12 173 C6
Deacon Way SE17 117 A2 262 B4
Deal Ct 13 NW9 27 D1
7 Southall UB1 86 A1
Deal Ho SE15 140 D6
SE17 263 B2
Deal Porters Way SE16 118 D3
Deal Rd SW17 181 A4
Deal St E1 96 A2
Dealtry Rd SW15 134 C1
Deal Wlk 3 SW9 138 C5
Dean Bradley St SW1 260 A5
Dean Cl E9 74 C3
SE16 118 D5
Hillingdon UB10 60 B1
Deancross St E1 96 C1
Dean Ct SW8 270 A3
Edgware HA8 26 D4
10 Kingston KT2 176 C3
Wembley HA0 65 B5
Dean Dr HA7 26 A1
Deane Ave HA4 62 C3
Deane Croft Rd HA5 40 C3
Deanery Cl N2 48 C5
Deanery Mews W1 248 B4
Deanery Rd E15 76 C2
Deanery St W1 115 A5 248 B4
Deane Way HA4 40 B3
Dean Farrar St SW1 259 D6
Deanfield Gdns CR0 221 B4
Dean Gdns E17 54 B5
Deanhill Ct 2 SW14 132 D1
Deanhill Rd SW14 132 D1
Dean Ho 18 E1 96 C1
N16 51 D1
N4 51 A2
SE14 141 B5
Ruislip HA4 39 B1
Dean Rd NW2 68 C2
Croydon CR0 221 B4
Hampton TW12 173 C5
Hounslow TW3 151 D6
Thamesmead SE28 124 A6
Dean Ryle St SW1 260 A4
Dean's Bldgs SE17 117 B2 262 D3
Deansbrook Cl HA8 27 A3
Deansbrook Jun & Inf Schs HA8,NW7 27 A4
Deansbrook Rd HA8 27 B4
Edgware HA8 26 D3
Deans Cl HA8 27 A4
Chiswick W4 132 D6
South Croydon CR0 221 D5
Deanscroft Ave NW9 45 A1
Dean's Ct EC4 241 D1
Dean's Dr HA8 27 B5
Deans Dr N13 32 D4
Deansfield Prim HA4 62 D4
Deansfield Prim Sch SE9 144 C2
Deans Gate Cl SE23 162 D1
Deanshanger Ho 21 SE8 118 D2
Dean's La HA8 27 A4
Dean's Mews W1 238 D2
Dean's Rd W7 108 D4
Deans Rd SM1 217 D5
Dean St E7 77 A3
W1 93 D1 239 C1
Dean Stanley St SW1 260 A5
Deansway N2 48 B5
Deans Way HA8 27 A5
Deansway N9 17 C1
Deanswood N11 31 D4
Dean's Yd SW1 259 D6
Dean Trench St SW1 260 A5
Dean Way UB2 107 D4
Dean Wlk HA8 27 B3
Dearmer Ho 6 SW2 160 C4
Dearne Cl HA7 25 A5
De'arn Gdns CR4 202 C6
Dearsley Rd EN1 6 A2
Deason St E15 98 A6
Deauville Ct 4 SE16 118 D4
14 SW4 159 C5
Deauville Mans 13 SW4 159 C5
De Barowe Mews N5 72 D3
Debdale Ho 20 E2 96 A6
Debden N17 33 B1
Debden Cl
Kingston KT2 175 D5
Woodford IG8 37 D3
De Beauvoir Cres N1 95 C6
De Beauvoir Ct N1 73 B1
De Beauvoir Pl 5 N1 73 C2
De Beauvoir Prim Sch N1 73 C2
De Beauvoir Rd N1 73 C1
De Beauvoir Sq N1 73 C1
Debenham Ct E8 96 A6
Barnet EN5 12 C6
Debham Ct NW2 68 C5
Debnams Rd SE16 118 C2
De Bohun Ave N14 15 B5
De Bohun Prim Sch N14 15 B6
Deborah Cl TW7 130 C4
Deborah Cres HA4 39 B2
Deborah Ct 7 E18 55 B6
De Broome Rd TW13 150 C3
De Burgh Ho 10 SW19 180 A3
Deburgh Rd SW19 180 A3
Debussy 9 NW9 27 D1
Decimal Ctr UB2 107 C4
Decima St SE1 117 C3 263 A6
Decimus Cl CR7 205 B5
Deck Cl SE16 118 D5
Decoy Ave NW11 47 A5
De Crespigny Pk SE5 139 B3
Dedham Ho 1 SE6 186 A6
Dee Ct W7 86 B1
Deeley Rd SW8 137 D4 269 C2
Deena Cl W3 88 B1
Deepdale N4 72 D5
Wimbledon SW19 178 D6
Deepdale Ave BR2 208 D5
Deepdale Cl N11 31 A4
Deepdale Ct 4 CR0 221 B4
Deepdene N12 30 C6
Deepdene Ave CR0 221 D5
Deepdene Cl E11 55 A5
Deepdene Ct
Beckenham BR2 208 C6
Southgate N21 16 D5
Deepdene Gdns SW2 160 B4
Deepdene Ho N16 51 B1
Deepdene Lo 5 SW2 160 B4
Deepdene Mans SW6 264 C2
Deepdene Point 9 SE26 162 D1
Deepdene Rd DA16 146 A2
SE5,SE24 139 B1
Deepwell Cl TW7 131 A4
Deepwood La UB6 86 B4
Deerbrook Rd SE24, SW2 160 D3
Dee Rd TW9 132 B1
Deerdale Rd SE24 139 A1
Deerhurst 7 KT2 176 D2
Deerhurst Cl TW13 172 B6
Deerhurst Cres TW12 174 A5
Deerhurst Ho 6 SE15 140 A6
Deerhurst Rd NW2 68 D2
Streatham SW16 182 B5
Deerings Dr HA5 40 A4
Deerleap Gr E4 19 D6
Deer Lo SW6 135 A2
Deer Park Cl KT2 176 D3
Deer Park Gdns CR4 202 B5
Deer Park Rd SW19 180 A1
Deer Park Way BR4 224 D6
Deeside Rd SW17 158 B1
Dee St E14 98 A1
Defiance Wlk SE18 122 B3
Defiant 18 NW9 27 D1
Defiant Way SM6 220 A1
Defoe Ave TW9 132 C5
Defoe Cl SW17 180 C4
Defoe Ho EC2 242 A4
5 N16 73 C5
Defoe Pl EC2 242 A4
Upper Tooting SW17 180 D6
Defoe Rd N16 73 C5
SE16 119 B4
De Frene Rd SE26 163 A1
De Gama Pl E14 119 C1
Degema Rd BR7 188 D5
Dehar Cres NW9 46 A2
Dehavilland Cl UB5 84 D4
De Havilland Rd
Edgware HA8 26 D1
Heston TW5 128 C5
De Havilland Way TW19 148 A5
Dekker Ho 19 SE5 139 B5
Dekker Rd SE21 161 C5
Delacourt Rd SE3 143 B5
Delafield Ho 18 E1 96 A1
Delafield Rd SE7 121 C1
Delaford Rd SE16 118 B1
Delaford St SW6 135 B6 264 B5
Delamare Cres CR0 206 C3
Delamere Gdns NW7 27 B4
Delamere Ho 4 N4 51 B2
Delamere Rd W5 110 A4
Hayes UB4 106 D6
Wimbledon SW20 178 D2
Delamere St W2 236 A3
Delamere Terr W2 91 D2
Delancey Pas NW1 231 D5
Delancey St NW1 93 B6 231 D5
Delancey Studios NW1 231 D5
Delany Ho SE10 142 A6
Delarch Ho SE1 251 C1
De Laune St SE17 116 D1 261 C1
Delaware Rd W9 91 D3
Delawyk Cres SE24 161 B5
Delcombe Ave KT4 200 C1
Delft Ho 8 KT2 176 B3
Delft Way 2 SE22 161 C6
Delhi Rd EN1 17 D4
Delhi St N1 94 A6 233 B5
Delia St SW18 157 D4
Delisle Rd SE28 123 C5
Delius Cl WD6 9 C5
Delius Gr E15 98 A5
Dellafield N4 72 C6
Della Path E5 74 B5
Dellbow Rd TW14 150 B6
Dell Cl E15 98 B6
Wallington SM6 219 D4
Woodford IG8 21 B1
Dellfield Cl BR3 186 A2
Dell La KT17 216 A3
Dellors Cl EN5 12 D6
Dellow Cl IG2 57 B2
Dellow Ho 6 E1 118 B6
Dellow St E1 118 B6
Dell Rd Enfield EN3 6 C5
Stoneleigh KT17 216 A2
West Drayton UB7 104 B3
Dells Cl Chingford E4 19 D4
Teddington TW11 174 D4
Dell's Mews SW1 259 B3
Dell The SE2 124 A1
Brentford TW8 131 C6
Feltham TW14 150 B4
Pinner HA5 22 D1
South Norwood SE19 183 D2
Wembley HA0 65 B3
Woodford IG8 21 B1
Dell Way W13 87 C1
Dell Wlk KT3 177 C1
Dellwood Gdns IG5 56 C6
Delme Cres SE3 143 B3
Delmey Cl CR0 221 D5
Deloraine Ho SE8 141 C4
Deloraine St SE8 141 C4
Delorme St W6 134 D6
Delphian Ct 5 SW16 182 C6
Delroy Ct N20 14 A4
Delta Bldg 4 E14 98 A1
Delta Cl KT4 215 D5
Delta Ct NW2 68 A6
Delta Gr UB5 84 D4
Delta Ho N1 235 D2
Delta Pk SW18 135 D1
Delta Rd KT4 215 C5
Delta St 3 E2 96 A4
De Lucy Prim Sch SE2 124 B4
De Lucy St SE2 124 B2
Delvan Cl SE18 144 C5
Delverton Ho SE17 261 D2
Delverton Rd SE17 261 D1
Delvino Rd SW6 135 C4 265 B1
De Mandeville Ct E4 35 A6
De Mandeville Gate EN1 6 B1
Demesne Rd SM6 219 D4
Demeta Cl HA9 67 A5
De Montfort Par 1 SW16 160 A1
De Montfort Rd SW16 160 A2

De Morgan Rd SW6 135 D2
Dempster Cl KT6 197 C1
Dempster Rd SW18 158 A6
Denberry Dr DA14 168 B1
Denbigh Cl BR7 188 B4
NW10 67 C1
W11 113 B6 244 D6
Cheam SM1 217 B3
Ruislip HA4 61 D6
Southall UB1 85 B1
Denbigh Ct E6 99 D4
1 Ealing W7 86 D2
Denbigh Dr UB3 105 A4
Denbigh Gdns TW10 154 B6
Denbigh Ho SW1 257 D6
W11 244 D6
7 W11 91 B1
Denbigh Mews SW1 259 A3
Denbigh Pl
SW1 115 C1 259 A2
Denbigh Rd E6 99 D4
W11 113 B6 244 D6
Ealing W13 87 B1
Hounslow TW3 129 D3
Southall UB1 85 B1
Denbigh St
SW1 115 C1 259 B2
Denbigh Terr
W11 113 B6 244 D6
Denbridge Rd BR1,BR7 188 B1
Denbury Ho 48 E3 97 D4
Denby Ct SE11 260 D4
Dence Ho 20 E2 96 A4
Denchworth Ho 15
SW9 138 C3
Den Cl BR2,BR3 208 B6
Dencliffe TW15 170 C5
Dendridge Cl EN1 6 B6
Dendy St SW12 159 A3
Dene Ave DA15 168 B4
Hounslow TW3 129 B2
Dene Cl SE4 141 A1
Hayes BR2 208 D1
Worcester Park KT4 215 D6
Denecroft Cres UB10 82 D6
Dene Ct W7 108 D4
Ealing W5 87 C2
Dene Gdns
Hinchley Wood KT7 213 A6
Stanmore HA7 25 C5
Dene Ho N14 15 D4
Denehurst Gdns NW4 46 C3
Acton W3 110 D5
Richmond TW10 132 C1
Twickenham TW2 152 B4
Woodford IG8 37 B6
Dene Mans 1 NW6 69 C2
Dene Rd N11 14 D2
Buckhurst Hill IG9 21 D3
Denesmead SE24 161 A6
Dene The Ealing W13 87 B2
East Molesey KT12,KT8 195 B4
South Croydon CR0 222 D4
Wembley HA9 66 A4
Denewood EN5 14 A6
Denewood Rd N6 48 D2
Dengie Wlk N1 235 A6
Denham Cl DA16 146 C2
Denham Cres CR4 202 D5
Denham Ct
Forest Hill SE26 162 B1
Southall UB1 108 A6
Denham Dr IG2 57 A3
Denham Ho 32 W12 112 B6
Denham Lo W5 88 A1
Denham Rd N20 14 D1
Feltham TW14 150 C4
Denham St SE10 121 A1
Denham Way IG11 101 D6
Denholme Rd W9 91 B4
Denise Ct HA0 65 C4
Denison Cl N2 48 A6
Denison Ho 8 E14 97 C1
Denison Rd Ealing W5 87 C3
Feltham TW13 171 D6
Mitcham SW19 180 B4
Deniston Ave DA5 169 A3
Denland Ho SW8 270 D3
Denleigh Ct N14 15 D4
Denleigh Gdns
Southgate N21 16 C4
Thames Ditton KT7 196 C3
Denman Dr NW11 47 C4
Ashford TW15 170 D4
Claygate KT10 213 A3
Denman Dr N NW11 47 C4
Denman Dr S NW11 47 C4
Denman Ho N16 73 C6
Denman Rd SE15 139 D3
Denman St W1 249 C5
Denmark Ave SW19 179 A3
Denmark Ct SM4 201 C4
Denmark Gdns SM5 218 D5
Denmark Gr N1 234 A4
Denmark Hill SE5 139 B3
Denmark Hill Dr NW9 46 A6
Denmark Hill Sta SE5 139 B3
Denmark Ho 9 SE7 122 A2
Denmark Mans 14
SE5 139 A3
Denmark Pl WC2 239 D2
Denmark Rd BR1 187 B2
N8 50 C5
NW6 91 B5
SE5 139 A3
Carshalton SM5 218 D5
Croydon SE25 206 B4
Ealing W13 109 B6
Kingston KT1 198 A6
Twickenham TW2 152 B1
Wimbledon SW19 178 D4
Denmark St 6 E11 76 C5
E13 99 B2
WC2 239 D2
Tottenham N17 34 B3
Denmark Terr NW2 48 D6
Denmead Ho 8 SW15 155 D5
Denmead Rd CR0 204 D1
Denmead Sch TW12 173 D3
Denmead Upper Sch
TW12 173 D3
Denmore Ct SM6 219 B3
Dennan Rd KT6 198 B1
Dennard Way BR6 226 C4
Denner Rd E4 19 C2
Denne Terr E8 95 D6
Dennett Rd CR0 204 C2
Dennett's Gr SE14 140 D3
Dennett's Rd SE14 140 C4
Denning Ave CR0 220 C3
Denning Cl
NW8 92 A4 229 B1
Hampton TW12 173 B5
Denning Point E1 243 D2
Denning Rd NW3 70 B4
Dennington Cl 17 E5 74 B6
Dennington Park Rd
NW6 69 C2
Denningtons The KT4 215 C6
Dennis Ave HA9 66 B3
Dennis Cl TW15 171 B3
Dennis Ct E17 36 B1
Dennis Gdns HA7 25 C5
Dennis Ho 4 E3 97 B5
Sutton SM1 217 C4
Dennis La HA7 25 B6
Dennison Point E15 76 A1
Dennis Par 1 N14 15 D3
Dennis Park Cres
SW20 179 A2
Dennis Rd KT8 196 A5
Dennis Reeve Cl CR4 180 D2
Dennis Way SW4 137 D2
Denny Cl 15 E6 100 A2
Denny Cres SE11 261 B2
Denny Gdns RM9 80 B1
Denny Rd N9 18 B3
Denny St SE11 116 C1 261 B2
Den Rd BR2 208 B6
Densham Ho NW8 229 D3
Densham Rd E15 98 C6
Densole Cl BR3 185 A2
Denstone Ho 5 SE15 140 A6
Densworth Gr N9 18 C2
Dent Ho SE17 263 A3
Denton NW1 71 A2
Denton Cl EN5 12 C6
Denton Ho N1 72 D1
Denton Rd N8 50 B3
Bexley DA16 146 C5
Edmonton N18 33 C6
Twickenham TW1 153 D5
Denton St SW18 157 D5
Denton Way E5 74 D5
Dents Rd SW11 158 D5
Denvale Trade Pk CR4 202 B5
Denver Cl BR6 211 C3
Denver Rd N16 51 C2
Denwood SE23 162 D1
Denyer Ho 1 NW5 71 B4
Denyer St
SW3 114 C2 257 B4
Denys Bldg EC1 241 A4
Denziloe Ave UB10 82 D4
Denzil Rd NW10 67 D3
Deodar Rd SW15 135 A1
Deodora Cl N20 14 D1
Depot App NW2 68 D4
Depot Rd W12 112 C6
Isleworth TW3,TW7 130 B2
Depot St SE5 139 B6
Deptford Bridge SE8 141 C4
Deptford Bridge Sta
SE8 141 C4
Deptford Broadway
SE8,SE14 141 C4
Deptford Church St
SE8 141 C5
Deptford Ferry Rd 12
E14 119 C2
Deptford Gn SE8 141 C6
Deptford Green Sch
SE14 141 B5
Deptford Green Sch
(Annexe) SE14 141 A5
Deptford High St SE8 141 C5
Deptford Park Prim Sch
SE8 119 A1
Deptford Sta SE8 141 C5
Deptford Trad Est SE8 141 A6
Deptford Wharf SE8 119 B2
Dept of Transport &
Environment SW1 259 D5
De Quincey Mews 3
E16 121 A5
De Quincey Rd N17 33 B2
Derby Ave N12 30 A5
Harrow HA3 24 B2
Romford RM7 59 D3
Derby Ct 8 E5 74 D4
Woodford E18 36 D2
Derby Gate SW1 250 A2
Derby Hill SE23 162 C2
Derby Hill Cres SE23 162 C2
Derby Ho NW4 46 C6
SE11 261 A4
Pinner HA5 22 D1
Derby Lo N3 29 B1
Derby Rd E7 77 D1
E9 96 D6
N18 34 C5
Cheam SM1,SM2 217 B2
Enfield EN3 18 C6
Greenford UB6 85 D6
Hounslow TW3 129 D1
Merton SW19 179 C3
Mortlake SW14 132 D1
Surbiton KT5,KT6 198 C1
Thornton Heath CR0 204 D1
Woodford E18 36 D2
Derby Rd Ind Est TW3 129 D1
Derbyshire St E2 96 A4
Derby St W1 248 B3
Dereham Ho 7 SE4 140 D1
Dereham Pl EC2 243 B6
Dereham Rd IG11 79 D3
Derek Ave
Chessington KT19 214 D3
Wallington SM6 219 B4
Wembley HA9 66 D1
Derek Cl KT19 214 D3
Derek Walcott Cl
SE24 160 D6
Dericote St E8 96 B6
Deri Dene Cl 2 TW19 148 A5
Derifall Cl E6 100 B2
Dering Pl CR0 221 A4
Dering Rd CR0 221 A4
Dering St W1 238 D1
Derinton Rd SW17 181 A6
Derley Rd UB2 106 D3
Dermody Gdns SE13 164 B6
Dermody Rd SE13 164 B6
Deronda Rd SE24,SW2 160 D3
Deroy Cl SM5 218 D2
Deroy Ct SM5 218 D2
Derrick Gdns SE7 121 C2
Derrick Ho 13 SW2 160 C3
Derrick Rd BR3 207 B5
Derrycombe Ho W11 91 B2
18 W2 91 C2
Derry Rd CR0,SM6 220 A5
Derry St W8 113 D4 245 C1
Dersingham Ave E12 78 C4
Dersingham Inf Sch
E12 78 C3
Dersingham Rd NW2 69 A5
Derwent NW1 232 A1
Derwent Ave NW7 27 B4
NW9 45 C4
Barnet, London EN4 14 D3
Edmonton N18 33 B5
Kingston SW15 177 C6
Pinner HA5 23 A4
Uxbridge UB10 60 C5
Derwent Cl
Claygate KT10 212 D2
East Bedfont TW14 149 D3
Derwent Cres DA7 147 C3
N20 14 A1
Stanmore HA7 25 C1
Derwent Ct N8 50 A3
8 SE16 118 D4
2 W6 112 A2
Derwent Dr BR5 211 B2
Hayes UB4 83 C2
Derwent Gdns
Redbridge IG4 56 A5
Wembley HA9 43 C2
Derwent Gr SE22 139 D1
Derwent Ho E3 97 B3
SW7 256 B4
Penge SE20 184 B1
Derwent Lo
Hounslow TW7 130 B3
North Cheam KT4 216 B6
Derwent Rd W5 109 C3
Palmers Green N13 16 B1
Penge SE20 184 B1
Southall UB1 85 B1
Twickenham TW2 151 D5
West Barnes SM4 200 D3
Derwent Rise NW9 45 C3
Derwent St SE10 120 C1
Derwentwater Mans 2
W3 111 A5
Derwentwater Prim Sch
W3 111 A5
Derwentwater Rd W3 111 A5
Derwent Wlk SM6 219 B1
Derwent Yd W5 109 C3
De Salis Rd UB10 83 A3
Desborough Cl W2 91 D2
Lower Halliford TW17 192 C2
Desborough Ct SE25 206 B5
Desborough Ho W14 264 D6
Desenfans Rd SE21 161 C5
Desford Rd E16 98 C3
Desford Way TW15 148 B2
Design Mus*
SE1 117 D4 253 D2
Desmond Ho 4 EN4 14 C5
Desmond St SE14 141 A6
Despard Ho SW2 160 C2
Despard Rd N19 49 C1
Dessouter 19 NW9 27 D1
Detherick Ct TW3 130 A1
Dethick Ct E3 97 A6
Detling Ho SE17 263 A3
Detling Rd BR1 187 A5
Detmold Rd E5 74 C6
Deutsche Schule
TW10 153 D3
Devalls Cl E6 122 C6
Devana End SM5 218 D5
Devas Rd SW20 178 C2
Devas St E3 97 D3
Devema Cl BR7 188 C2
Devenay Rd E15 76 D1
Devenish Rd SE2 124 A4
Deventer Cres 8
SE22 161 C6
De Vere Cotts W8 256 A6
De Vere Gdns
W8 114 A4 246 A1
Redbridge IG1 56 B1
Deverell St
SE1 117 B3 262 C5
De Vere Mews W8 256 A6
Devereux Ct WC2 241 A1
Devereux Ho 7 SW15 156 A6
Devereux La SW13 134 B5
Devereux Rd SW11 158 D5
Deverill Ct SE20 184 C2
Devey Cl KT2 177 B5
Devitt Ho 4 E14 119 D6
Devizes St N1 235 D5
Devon Ave TW2 152 A3
Devon Cl N17 51 D6
Chigwell IG9 21 B2
Wembley UB6 87 C6
Devoncroft Gdns TW1 153 A4
Devon Ct 3 Acton W3 88 C1
2 Ealing W7 86 D2
Devon Gdns N4 50 D3
Devon Ho E17 35 B1
Penge SE20 184 B3
5 Wanstead E11 55 A4
Devonhurst Pl 4 W4 111 B1
Devonia Gdns N18 33 A4
Devonia Rd N1 94 D5 234 D4
Devon Mans SE1 253 B2
Devon Par HA3 43 C4
Devonport W2 237 A2
Devonport Gdns IG1 56 B3
Devonport Ho 23 W2 91 C2
Devonport Rd W12 112 B4
Devonport St E1 96 D1
Devon Rd IG11 101 C6
Devon Rise N2 48 B5
Devonshire Ave SM2 218 A1
Devonshire Cl E15 76 C4
W1 238 C4
Edmonton N13 32 C6
Devonshire Cres NW7 28 D3
Devonshire Ct
Croydon CR0 207 C1
Feltham TW13 150 B2
6 Richmond TW9 132 B4
Tottenham N17 33 A4
Devonshire Dr SE10 141 D4
Long Ditton KT6 213 D6
Devonshire Gdns
Chiswick W4 133 A5
Edmonton N21 17 A4
Tottenham N17 33 A4
Devonshire Gr SE15 140 B6
Devonshire Hall 14 E9 74 C2
Devonshire Hill La N17 33 A4
Devonshire Hill Prim Sch
N17 33 B4
Devonshire Ho N12 14 A1
NW6 69 B2
SE1 262 A6
SW1 259 D2
W2 236 D4
14 Balham SW12 159 B4
Hounslow TW3 130 A2
2 Putney SW15 156 C4
10 Sutton SM2 218 A1
Devonshire Hospl
W1 93 A2 238 B4
Devonshire House Prep Sch
NW3 70 B3
Devonshire House Sch
NW3 70 A3
Devonshire Mews 2
W4 111 C1
Devonshire Mews N
W1 238 C4
Devonshire Mews S
W1 238 C4
Devonshire Mews W
W1 238 B4
Devonshire Pl NW2 69 C5
W1 93 A2 238 B4
W8 255 C5
Devonshire Place Mews
W1 238 B4
Devonshire Prim Sch
SM2 218 A1
Devonshire Rd DA6 147 A1
E17 53 C3
N9 18 C3
NW7 28 D3
W4 111 C1
W5 109 C3
Chislehurst SE9 166 A2
Edmonton N13 32 C6
Feltham TW13 173 A6
Forest Hill SE23 162 C4
Hackbridge SM5,SM6 219 A4
Harrow HA1 42 B3
Ilford IG2 57 C2
Mitcham SW17,SW19 180 C3
Newham E16 99 B1
Pinner HA5 23 B2
Pinner HA5 40 C2
Southall UB1 85 C2
Sutton SM2 218 A1
Thornton Heath CR0 205 B2
Tottenham N17 33 A4
Devonshire Row EC2 243 B3
Devonshire Row Mews
W1 238 D5
Devonshire Sq BR2 209 B5
EC2 95 C1 243 B2
Devonshire St
W1 93 B2 238 C4
W4 111 C1
Devonshire Terr
W2 92 A1 236 B1
Devonshire Way
Croydon CR0,CR9 223 B6
Hayes UB4 84 B1
Devons Rd E3 97 D3
Devons Road Sta E3 97 D3
Devon St SE15 140 B6
Devon Way
Chessington KT19 214 D3
Chessington KT9 213 C3
Hillingdon UB10 82 B5
Devon Waye TW5 129 B5
De Walden Ho NW8 230 A4
De Walden St W1 238 B3
Dewar Ho 2 SW17 180 C5
Dewar St SE15 140 A2
Dewberry Gdns E6 100 A2
Dewberry St E14 98 A2
Dewey Rd N1 94 C5 234 A4
Dagenham RM10 81 D2
Dewey St SW17 180 D5
Dewhurst Rd W14 112 D3
Dewlands Ct NW4 28 D1
Dewsbury Cl HA5 41 A3
Dewsbury Ct 5 W4 111 A2
Dewsbury Gdns KT4 216 A5
Dewsbury Rd NW10 68 A3
Dewsbury Terr NW1 231 D6
Dexter Ho 2 DA18 125 A3
Dexter Rd EN5 12 D5
Deyncourt Rd N17 33 A2
Deynecourt Gdns E11 55 C5
D'eynsford Rd SE5 139 B4
Dhonau Ho SE16 263 D4
Diadem Ct W1 239 C2
Dial Wlk The
W8 113 D4 245 D2
Diameter Rd BR5 211 A3
Diamond Cl RM8 58 C1
Diamond Est SW17 158 C1
Diamond Ho 20 E3 97 A5
Diamond Rd HA4 63 A4
Diamond St SE15 139 C5
13 NW10 67 B1
Diamond Terr SE10 142 A4
Diana Cl 45 SE8 141 B6
Woodford E18 37 B2
Diana Ct SM5 219 A1
Diana Gdns KT6 214 B6
Diana Ho 4 SW2 160 B6
Diana, Princess of Wales
Mml Wlk W2 114 A5 246 A3
Diana Rd E17 53 B6
Dianne Ct SE12 165 A3
Dianne Way EN4 2 C1
Dianthus Cl SE2 124 B1
Dibden Ho 16 SE5 139 C5
Dibden St N1 95 A6 235 A6
Dibdin Cl SM1 217 C5
Dibdin Ho W9 91 D5
Dibdin Rd SM1 217 C6
Dicey Ave NW2 68 C4
Dickens Ave N3 30 A2
Hayes UB8 82 D1
Dickens Cl DA8 147 D5
Hayes UB3 105 C2
Richmond TW10 154 A2
Dickens Ct
10 Wanstead E11 55 A5
Wembley HA0 65 C5
Dickens Dr BR7 189 A4
Dickens Ho NW6 91 C4
NW8 236 D6
SE17 261 D1
WC1 240 A6
3 Erith DA17 125 B1
Hayes UB3 105 C2
Dickens House Mus*
WC1 94 B3 240 D5
Dickens La N18 33 C5
Dickenson Cl N9 18 A3
Dickenson Ho N8 50 B3
Dickenson Rd N8 50 A2
Dickenson's La SE25 206 A3
Dickenson's Pl SE25 206 A3
Dickens Rd E6 99 D5
Dickens Sq
SE1 117 A3 262 B6
Dickens St SW8 137 B3
Dickens Wood Cl
SE19 182 D3
Dickerage Hill
Kingston KT3 199 A6
Kingston KT3 177 A1
Dickerage La KT3 199 A6
Dickerage Rd KT1,KT2,
KT3 177 A1
Dickinson Ho 21 E2 96 A4
Dickinson Rd TW13 172 D5
Dicksee Ho NW8 236 C5
Dick Shepherd Ct 17
SW2 160 C5
Dickson Fold HA5 40 D5
Dickson Ho 13 E1 96 B1
9 SE18 144 A4
Dickson Rd SE9 144 A2
Dick Turpin Way
TW14 127 D1
Didbin Ho N7 72 B6
Didsbury Cl E6 100 B6
Digby Bsns Ctr E9 74 D2
Digby Cres N4 73 A6
Digby Gdns RM10 103 C6
Digby Mans W6 112 C1
Digby Pl CR0 221 D5
Digby Rd E9 74 D2
Barking IG11 79 D1
Digby St E2 96 C4
Digby Stuart Coll
SW15 156 A6
Diggon St 16 E1 96 D2
Dighton Ct SE17 139 A6
Dighton Rd SW18 136 A1
Dignum St N1 234 A4
Digswell St N7 72 C2
Dilhorne Cl SE12 165 B1
Dilke St SW3 136 D6 267 D6
Dilloway Yd UB2 107 A4
Dillwyn Cl SE26 185 A6
Dilston Cl 1 UB5 84 C4
Dilston Gr SE16 118 C2
Dilton Gdns SW15 156 B3
Dilwyn Ct E17 35 A1
Dimes Pl 9 W6 112 B2
Dimmock Dr UB6 64 B3
Dimond Cl E7 77 A4
Dimsdale Dr NW9 45 A1
Enfield EN1 18 A5
Dimsdale Wlk 4 E13 99 A5
Dimson Cres E3 97 C4
Dinerman Ct NW8 229 B6
Dingle Cl EN5 11 D5
Dingle Gdns E14 119 C6
Dingle Rd TW15 170 D5
Dingle The UB10 82 D4
Dingley La SW16 159 D2
Dingley Pl EC1 95 A4 235 B1
Dingley Rd EC1 95 A4 235 A1
Dingwall Ave CR0 221 A6
Dingwall Gdns NW11 47 C3
Dingwall Rd
South Croydon CR0 221 B6
Wandsworth SW18 158 A4
Dinmont Ho 26 E2 96 A5
Dinmont St 1 E2 96 B5
Dinmore Ho 7 E9 96 C6
Dinnington Ho 17 E1 96 B3
Dinorben SM6 219 C1
Dinsdale Ct EN5 13 D6
Dinsdale Gdns
New Barnet EN5 13 D6
South Norwood SE25 205 C4
Dinsdale Rd SE3 142 D6
Dinsmore Rd SW12 159 B4
Dinton Ho NW8 237 A6
Dinton Rd Kingston KT2 176 B3

Dinton Rd *continued*
Mitcham SW19 180 B4
Dinwiddy Ho N1 233 C3
Diploma Ave N2 48 C5
Diploma Ct N2 48 C5
Dirleton Rd E15 98 D6
Disbrowe Rd W6 135 A6 264 B5
Discovery Bsns Pk 13 SE16 118 A3
Discovery Ho 1 E14 120 A6
Dishforth La NW9 27 C2
Disley Ct 2 UB1 85 D1
Disney Pl SE1 252 B2
Disney St SE1 252 B2
Dison Cl EN3 6 D4
Disraeli Cl SE28 124 C5
W4 111 B2
Disraeli Gdns SW15 135 B1
Disraeli Rd E7 77 A2
Acton NW10 89 B5
Ealing W5 109 D5
Putney SW15 135 A1
Diss St E2 95 D4
Distaff La EC4 252 A6
Distillery La W6 112 C1
Distillery Rd W6 112 C1
Distillery Wlk 14 TW8 132 A6
Distin St SE11 116 C2 261 A3
District Rd HA0 65 B3
Ditchburn St E14 120 A6
Ditchfield Rd UB4 85 A3
Dittisham Rd SE9 188 A6
Ditton Cl KT7 197 A2
Dittoncroft Cl CR0 221 C4
Ditton Grange Cl KT6 197 D1
Ditton Grange Dr KT6 197 D1
Ditton Hill KT6 213 D6
Ditton Hill Rd KT6 197 C1
Ditton Ho 10 E5 74 B3
Ditton Lawn KT7 197 A1
Ditton Pl 6 SE20 184 B2
Ditton Rd Bexley DA6 169 A6
Southall UB2 107 B1
Surbiton KT6 198 B1
Ditton Reach KT7 197 B3
Divis Way SW15 156 B5
Dixon Cl 4 E6 100 B1
Dixon Clark Ct N1 72 D2
Dixon Ct N4 50 C3
Dixon Ho SE2 124 C1
Dixon Pl BR4 207 D1
Dixon Rd SE14 141 A4
South Norwood SE25 205 D6
Dobbin Cl HA3 25 A1
Dobell Rd SE9 166 B6
Dobree Ave NW10 68 B1
Dobson Cl NW6 70 B1
Dobson Ho 18 SE14 140 D6
SE5 139 B5
Doby Ct EC4 252 B6
Dockers Tanner Rd 19 E14 119 C2
Dockett Eddy La KT16, TW17 192 B1
Dockett Moorings KT16 192 B1
Dockhead SE1 117 D4 253 D1
Dockhead Wharf SE1 253 D2
Dock Hill Ave SE16 118 D4
Docklands Heritage Mus* SE16 119 B5
Docklands Mus (Museum in Docklands)* E14 119 C6
Dockland St E16 122 C5
Dockley Rd SE16 118 A3
Dockley Road Ind Est 11 SE16 118 A3
Dock Offices 12 SE16 118 C3
Dock Rd E16 120 D6
Brentford TW8 131 D5
Dockside Rd E16 121 D6
Dock St E1 118 A6
Dockwell Cl TW14 128 A1
Dockwell's Ind Est TW14 150 C6
Doctors Cl SE26 184 C5
Doctor Spurstowe Almshos 9 E8 74 B2
Docura Ho N7 72 B6
Docwra's Bldgs N1 73 C2
Dodbrooke Rd SE27 160 D1
Dodd Ho 18 SE16 118 B2
Doddington Gr SE17 116 D1 261 D1
Doddington Pl 4 SE17 138 D6
Dodsley Pl N9 18 C1
Dodson St SE1 116 C4 251 B1
Dod St E14 97 C1
Doebury Wlk SE18 146 A6
Doel Cl SW19 180 A3
Doggett Rd SE6 163 C4
Doggetts Ct EN4 14 C6
Doghurst Ave UB3 126 D5
Doghurst Dr UB7 126 D5
Dog Kennel Hill SE22 139 C2
Dog Kennel Hill Sch SE22 139 C2
Dog La NW10 67 C4
Dogrose Ct 14 NW9 46 A5
Doherty Rd E13 99 A3
Dokal Ind Est UB2 107 A4
Doland Ct SW17 180 D4
Dolben Ct SE8 119 B2
Dolben St SE1 116 D5 251 D3
Dolby Rd SW6 135 B3
Dolland Ho SE11 260 D1
Dolland St SE11 260 D1
Dollar Bay E14 120 A4
Dollary Ct KT3 198 D6
Dollis Ave N3 29 B2
Dollis Brook Wlk EN5 13 A5
Dollis Cres HA4 40 C1
Dolliscroft NW7 29 A3
Dollis Ct N3 29 B2
Dollis Hill Ave NW2 68 B5
Dollis Hill Est NW2 68 A5
Dollis Hill La NW2 68 A5
Dollis Hill Sta NW2 68 A3
Dollis Hts NW2 68 B5
Dollis Jun & Inf Schs NW7 28 C3
Dollis Mews N3 29 C2
Dollis Pk N3 29 B2
Dollis Rd N3,NW7 29 B3
Dollis Valley Way EN5 13 B5
Dolman Cl N3 30 A1
Dolman Rd W4 111 B2
Dolman St SW4 138 B1
Dolphin Cl 2 SE16 118 D4
SE28 102 D1
Kingston KT6 197 D4
Dolphin Ct N7 71 D4
NW11 47 A3
Harrow HA3 24 C1
Merton SW19 179 C3
2 Wallington SM6 219 B2
Dolphin Est The TW16 171 B2
Dolphin La E14 119 D6
Dolphin Rd
Charlton TW16 171 C2
Northolt UB5 85 B5
Dolphin Rd N TW16 171 C2
Dolphin Rd S TW16 171 C2
Dolphin Rd W TW16 171 C2
Dolphin Sch SW11 158 D6
Dolphin Sq SW1 259 B1
Dolphin St KT2 176 A2
Dolphin Twr 21 SE8 141 B6
Dombey Ho 9 SE1 118 A4
4 W11 112 D5
Dombey St WC1 240 C4
Dome Hill Pk SE26 183 D6
Domelton Ho SW18 157 D5
Domett Cl SE5 139 B1
Domfe Pl E5 74 C4
Domingo St EC1 242 A5
Dominica Cl 6 E6 99 D5
Dominion Bsns Pk N9 18 D2
Dominion Ind Est UB2 107 A4
Dominion Par HA1 42 D4
Dominion Rd
Croydon CR0 205 D2
Southall UB2 107 A3
Dominion St EC2 95 B2 242 D4
Dominion Wks RM8 59 A1
Domonic Dr SE9 166 D1
Domville Cl N20 14 B2
Donaghue Cotts 13 E14 97 A2
Donald Dr RM6 58 C4
Donald Lynch Ho CR4 180 D1
Donald Rd E13 99 B6
Thornton Heath CR0 204 B2
Donaldson Rd NW6 91 B6
SE18 144 C4
Donald Woods Gdns KT5 215 A6
Doncaster Dr UB5 63 B3
Doncaster Gdns N4 51 A3
Northolt UB5 63 B3
Doncaster Gn WD19 22 C5
Doncaster Rd N9 18 B4
Doncel Ct E4 20 B4
Donegal Ho 2 E1 96 C3
Donegal St N1 94 B5 233 D3
Doneraile Ho SW1 258 C1
Doneraile St SW6 134 D4
Dongola Rd E1 97 A2
E13 99 B4
N17 51 C6
Dongola Rd W 5 E13 99 B4
Donington Ave IG6 57 A4
Donkey Alley SE22 162 A5
Donkey La EN1 6 A3
Donkin Ho 15 SE16 118 B2
Donne Ct SE24 161 A5
Donnefield Ave HA8 26 A3
Donne Ho 7 E14 97 C1
18 N16 73 B4
14 SE14 140 D6
Donnelly Ct SW6 264 B4
Donne Pl SW3 114 C2 257 B4
Mitcham CR4 203 B5
Donne Rd RM8 80 C6
Donnington Ct NW10 68 B1
11 NW1 71 B1
Donnington Ho 12 SW8 137 D3
Donnington Prim Sch NW10 90 B6
Donnington Rd NW10 90 B6
Harrow HA3 43 D3
Worcester Park KT4 216 A6
Donnybrook Rd SW16 181 D3
Donovan Ave N10 31 C1
Donovan Ct SW7 256 C1
Donovan Ho 3 E1 118 C6
Donovan Pl N21 16 B6
Don Phelan Cl SE5 139 B4
Doone Cl TW11 175 A4
Doon St SE1 116 C5 251 A4
Doradus Ct 20 SW19 156 D3
Dora Ho 1 E14 97 B1
11 W11 112 D6
Doral Way SM5 218 D3
Doran Ct E6 100 B5
Dorando Cl W12 112 B6
Doran Gr SE18 145 C5
Doran Manor N2 48 D4
Doran Wlk E15 76 A1
Dora Rd SW19 179 C6
Dora St E14 97 B1
Dorcas Ct 9 SW18 136 B1
Dorchester Ave
Edmonton N13 33 A6
Harrow HA2 42 A3
Sidcup DA5 168 D4
Dorchester Cl
Northolt UB5 63 D3
St Paul's Cray BR5 190 B3
Dorchester Ct 1 N10 49 B6
1 N1 73 C1
N14 15 B4
NW2 68 D5
SE24 161 A6
SW1 257 D5
5 Streatham SW16 160 A2
2 Woodford E18 36 D2
Dorchester Dr SE24 161 A6
Feltham TW14 149 C5
Dorchester Gdns NW11 47 C5
Chingford E4 35 C6
Dorchester Gr W4 111 D1
Dorchester Mews
New Malden KT3 199 B5
Twickenham TW1 153 C5
Dorchester Prim Sch KT4 200 C1
Dorchester Rd
Cheam SM4 202 A2
North Cheam KT4 200 C1
Northolt UB5 63 D3
Dorchester Way HA3 44 B3
Dorchester Waye
Hayes UB4 84 B1
Hayes UB4 84 C1
Dorcis Ave DA7 147 A3
Dordrecht Rd W3 111 C5
Dore Ave E12 78 C3
Doreen Ave NW9 45 B1
Doreen Capstan Ho 3 E11 76 C5
Dore Gdns SM4 201 D2
Dorell Cl UB1 85 B2
Doria Rd SW6 135 B3
Doric Ho 7 E2 96 D5
Doric Way NW1 93 D4 232 C2
Dorien Rd SW20 178 D1
Doris Emmerton Ct SW18 136 A1
Doris Rd E7 77 A1
Ashford TW15 171 B4
Dorking Cl SE8 141 B6
North Cheam KT4 216 D6
Dorking Ct N17 34 A2
Dorking Ho SE1 262 D6
Dorland Ho SE9 167 B5
Dorlcote Rd SW18 158 C4
Dorleston Ct N1 235 D6
Dorly Cl TW17 193 C4
Dorman Pl 6 N9 18 A2
Dorman Way NW8 92 B6 229 C6
Dorman Wlk NW10 67 B2
Dorma Trad Pk E10 52 D1
Dormay St SW18 157 D6
Dormer Cl E15 76 D2
Barnet EN5 12 D6
Dormer's Ave UB1 85 C1
Dormers Lo EN4 2 D3
Dormers Rise UB1 85 D1
Dormer's Wells High Sch UB1 85 C1
Dormers Wells Ho UB4 84 C2
Dormer's Wells Inf Sch UB1 107 D6
Dormer's Wells Jun Sch UB1 107 D6
Dormer's Wells La UB1 107 C5
Dormstone Ho SE17 263 A3
Dormywood HA4 39 D4
Dornan Wlk E15 98 A6
Dornberg Cl SE3 143 A5
Dornberg Rd SE3 143 B5
Dorncliffe Rd SW6 135 A3
Dorney NW3 70 C1
Dorney Ct SW6 135 A2
Dorney Rise BR5 211 D5
Dorney Way TW4 151 A6
Dornfell St NW6 69 B3
Dornoch Ho 25 E3 97 B5
Dornton Rd
South Croydon CR2 221 C3
Upper Tooting SW12, SW17 159 C2
Dorothy Ave HA0 66 A1
Dorothy Barley Inf Sch RM8 80 B3
Dorothy Barley Jun Sch RM8 80 B3
Dorothy Charrington Ho 1 SE22 162 A6
Dorothy Evans Cl DA7 147 D1
Dorothy Gdns RM8 80 B4
Dorothy Rd SW11 136 D2
Dorrien Wlk SW16 159 D2
Dorrington Ct SE25 183 C1
Dorrington Point 20 E3 97 D4
Dorrington St EC1 241 A4
Dorrit Ho 2 W11 112 D5
Dorrit Mews N18 33 C5
Dorrit St SE1 252 B2
Dorrit Way BR7 189 A4
Dorryn Ct SE26 184 D5
Dors Cl NW9 45 B1
Dorset Ave DA16 145 D1
Hayes UB4 83 C4
Southall UB2 107 C2
Dorset Bldgs EC4 241 C1
Dorset Cl NW1 237 C4
Hayes UB4 83 C4
Dorset Ct 3 N1 73 C1
3 Ealing W7 86 D2
Dorset Dr HA8 26 B4
Dorset Gdns SW16 204 B5
Dorset Ho 1 SE20 184 B2
Dorset Mans 2 W6 134 D6
Dorset Mews N3 29 C2
SW1 258 C6
Dorset Pl E15 76 B2
Dorset Rd E7 77 C1
N15 51 B5
SW8 138 B5 270 C4
W5 109 D3
Ashford TW15 148 A1
Chislehurst SE9 166 A2
Harrow HA1 42 A3
Merton SW19 179 C1
Mitcham CR4 180 C1
Penge BR3 206 D6
Wood Green N22 32 A2
Dorset Rise EC4 94 D1 241 C1
Dorset Road Inf Sch SE9 166 A2
Dorset Sq NW1 92 D3 237 C5
Dorset St W1 92 D2 237 D3
Dorset Way
Hillingdon UB10 82 B5
Twickenham TW2 152 B3
Dorset Waye TW5 129 B5
Dorton Cl 6 SE15 139 C5
Dorville Cres W6 112 B3
Dorville Rd SE12 165 A6
Dothill Rd SE18 145 A5
Douai Gr TW12 174 A2
Douay Martyrs RC Sch (Annexe) The UB10 60 D3
Doughty Ct 11 E1 118 B5
Doughty Mews WC1 94 B3 240 C5
Doughty St WC1 94 B3 240 C5
Douglas 20 NW9 27 D1
Douglas Ave
Chingford E17 35 C2
Wembley HA0 66 A1
West Barnes KT3 200 B5
Douglas Bader Ho N3 29 D4
Douglas Bldgs SE1 252 B2
Douglas Cl
Stanmore HA7 25 A5
Wallington SM6 220 A2
Douglas Cres UB4 84 D3
Douglas Ct N3 29 D1
5 NW6 69 C1
Douglas Dr CR0 223 C5
Douglas Gracey Ho SW18 157 A4
Douglas Ho
Isleworth TW1 153 B6
Putney SW15 156 A5
Douglas Johnstone Ho SW6 264 C5
Douglas Mews NW2 69 A5
Douglas Rd DA16 146 B4
5 E16 99 A2
N1 73 A1
NW6 91 B6
Chingford, Chingford Green E4 20 C3
Douglas Rd *continued*
Hounslow TW3 129 D2
Ilford IG3 58 A3
Kingston KT1 176 D1
Stanwell TW19 148 A5
Surbiton KT6 198 B1
Thames Ditton KT10 212 A6
Wood Green N22 32 C2
Douglas Rd N N1 73 A2
Douglas Rd S N1 73 A2
Douglas Robinson Ct SW16 182 A3
Douglas Sq SM4 201 C3
Douglas St SW1 115 D2 259 C3
Douglas Terr E17 35 B2
Douglas Waite Ho NW6 69 D1
Douglas Way SE8 141 B5
Doulton Ho SE11 260 D4
Doulton Mews 4 NW6 69 D2
Dounesforth Gdns SW18 157 D3
Douro Pl W8 113 D3 255 D6
Douro St E3 97 C5
Douthwaite Sq 12 E1 118 A5
Dove App E6 100 A2
Dove Cl NW7 27 D3
Northolt UB5 84 D3
Wallington SM6
Dovecot Cl HA5 40 C4
Dovecote Gdns 8 SW14 133 B2
Dove Ct Enfield EN3 18 B6
Stanwell TW19 148 A4
Dovedale Ave HA3 43 C3
Dovedale Cl DA16 146 A3
Dovedale Cotts 6 SW11 136 D3
Dovedale Ho N16 51 B2
Dovedale Rd SE22 162 B5
Dovedale Rise CR4 180 D3
Dovedon Cl N14 16 A2
Dove House Gdns E4 19 C2
Dovehouse Mead IG11 101 B5
Dovehouse St SW3 114 C1 257 A1
Dove Mews SW7 114 A2 256 B2
Dove Pk HA5 23 C3
Dover Cl NW2 68 D6
Dovercourt Ave CR7 204 C5
Dovercourt Gdns HA7 26 A5
Dovercourt La SM1 218 A5
Dovercourt Rd SE22 161 D5
Dover Ct EC1 241 C5
SE10 141 D4
Dove Rd N1 73 B2
Doverfield Rd SW2 160 A4
Dover Flats SE1 263 B3
Dover Gdns SM5 218 D5
Dover Ho 11 SE15 140 C6
SE5 138 D4
7 Beckenham BR3 185 C3
14 Penge SE20 184 B2
Dover House Rd SW15 156 B6
Doveridge Gdns N13 32 D6
Dover Mans 17 SW9 138 C2
Dove Row E2 96 A6
Dover Park Dr SW15 156 B5
Dover Patrol SE3 143 C3
Dover Rd N9 18 C2
Dagenham RM6 59 A3
South Norwood SE19 183 B4
Wanstead E12 77 C6
Woolwich SE18 145 A3
Dover St W1 115 C5 249 A4
Dover Terr TW9 132 C3
Dover Yd W1 249 A4
Doves Cl BR2 226 A6
Doves Yd N1 94 C6 234 A5
Doveton Ho 6 E1 96 C3
Doveton Rd CR2 221 B3
Doveton St 7 E1 96 C3
Dove Wlk SW1 258 A2
Dowanhill Rd SE6 164 B3
Dowdeswell Cl SW15 133 C1
Dowding Ho N6 49 A2
Dowding Pl HA7 25 A4
Dowding Rd UB10 60 B1
Dowe Ho SE3 142 C2
Dowell Ho SE21 161 D1
Dowes Ho 13 SW16 160 A1
Dowgate Hill EC4 252 C6
Dowland Ho EN1 5 D5
Dowland St W10 91 A4
Dowlas St SE5 139 C5
Dowler Ct 2 KT2 176 B2
Dowlerville Rd BR6 227 D2
Dowling Ho DA17 125 B3
Dowman Cl 2 SW19 179 D3
Downage NW4 46 C6
Downalong WD23 8 B3
Down Barns Rd HA4 62 D5
Downbarton Ho 11 SW9 138 C4
Downbury Mews 13 SW18 157 C6
Down Cl UB5 84 B5
Downderry Prim Sch BR1 186 C6
Downderry Rd BR1 186 C6
Downe Cl DA16 146 C5
Downe Ho 9 SE7 143 C6
Downe Manor Prim Sch UB5 84 B4
Downend SE18 144 D5
Downend Ct 8 SE15 139 C6
Downe Rd CR4 180 D1
Downer's Cotts SW4 137 C1
Downes Cl TW1 153 B5
Downes Ct N21 16 C3
Downey Ho 6 E1 96 D3
Downfield KT4 200 A1
Downfield Cl W9 91 D3
Downfield Ho KT3 199 B1
Down Hall Rd KT2 175 D2
Downham Ct N1 73 B1
Downham Ent Ctr SE6 164 D2
Downham La BR1 186 B5
Downham Rd N1 73 B1
Downham Way BR1 186 C6
Downhills Ave N17 51 B6
Downhills Jun & Inf Schs N15 51 B5
Downhills Park Rd N17 51 A6
Downhills Way N17 33 A1
Downhurst Ave NW7 27 B5
Downhurst Ct NW4 46 C6
Downing Cl HA2 42 A6
Downing Ct N12 29 D5
Downing Dr UB6 86 C6
Downing Ho 2 W10 90 D1
3 Merton SW19 179 C3
4 Putney SW15 156 A6
Downing Rd RM9 81 B1
Downings E6 100 C1
Downing St* SW1 116 A4 250 A2
Downland Cl N20 14 A3
Downland Ct E11 76 C6
Downleys Cl SE9 166 B2
Downman Rd SE9 144 A2
Down Pl W6 112 B1
Down Rd TW11 175 B4
Downs Ave BR7 188 B5
Pinner HA5 41 B2
Downs Bridge Rd BR3 186 B2
Downs Ct 16 E8 74 B3
12 Wimbledon SW19 178 D3
Downsell Jun & Inf Schs E15 76 B4
Downsell Rd E15 76 B4
Downsfield Rd E17 53 A3
Downshall Ave IG3 57 C3
Downshall Ct IG3 57 C3
Downs Hill BR2,BR3 186 B2
Downshire Hill NW3 70 B4
Downside
2 Putney SW15 157 A6
Sunbury TW16 172 A2
Twickenham TW1 152 D1
Downside Cl SW19 180 A4
Downside Cres NW3 70 C3
Ealing W13 87 A3
Downside Rd SM2 218 C2
Downside Wlk UB5 85 B4
Downs La 5 E5 74 B4
Downs Park Rd E5,E8 74 A3
Downs Rd E5,N16 74 A4
Beckenham BR3 185 D1
Enfield EN1 5 C1
South Norwood CR7 183 A2
Downs Side JMI Sch E5 74 A4
Down St W1 115 B5 248 C3
East Molesey KT8 195 C4
Downs The SW19, SW20 178 D3
Down St Mews W1 248 C3
Downs View TW7 131 A4
Downsview Gdns SE19 183 A3
Downs View Lo 9 KT6 198 A3
Downsview Prim Sch SE19 183 A3
Downsview Rd SE19 183 A3
Downsview Sch E5 74 B4
Downsway BR6 227 C3
Downsway The SM2 218 A1
Downton Ave SW2 160 B2
Downtown Rd SE16 119 A4
Downway N12 30 C3
Down Way UB5 84 B4
Dowrey St N1 234 A6
Dowsett Rd N17 34 A1
Dowson Cl SE5 139 B1
Dowson Ct SE13 142 B2
Dowson Ho 7 E1 96 D1
Doyce St SE1 252 A2
Doyle Gdns NW10 90 B6
Doyle Ho W3 110 D4
Doyle Rd SE25 206 A5
D'Oyley St SW1 258 A4
Doynton St N19 71 B6
Draco St SE17 139 A6
Dragonfly Cl E13 99 B4

Dragon Rd SE15 139 C6
Dragon Yd WC1 240 B2
Dragoon Rd SE8 119 B1
Dragor Rd NW10 89 A3
Drake Cl 30 SE16 118 D4
Drake Cres SE28 102 C1
Drake Croft N16 73 B6
Drake Ct 5 W12 112 B4
Dulwich SE19 183 D5
Kingston KT5 198 B5
Drakefell Rd SE4,SE14 140 D2
Drakefield Rd SW17 159 A1
Drake Ho 17 E1 96 C2
2 E14 119 A6
Drakeley Ct N5 72 D4
Drake Rd SE4 141 C2
Chessington KT9 214 C3
Harrow HA2 63 B6
Mitcham CR4 203 A3
Thornton Heath CR0 204 B2
Drakes Ct SE23 162 C3
Drakes Ctyd NW6 69 B1
Drake St WC1 240 C3
Enfield EN2 5 B4
Drakes Wlk E6 100 B6
Drakewood Rd SW16 181 D3
Draldo Ho 6 SW15 157 A6
Draper Cl DA17 125 B2
Hounslow TW7 130 B3
Draper Ct BR1 210 A5
Draper Ho SE1 261 D4
Draper Pl N1 234 D6
Drapers Almhouses 4
E3 97 C4
Draper's Cottage Homes
NW7 28 A6
Drapers Gdns EC2 242 D2
Drapers Rd E15 76 B4
N17 51 D6
Enfield EN2 4 D4
Drappers Way 8
SE16 118 A2
Draven Cl BR2 208 D2
Drawell Cl SE18 123 C1
Drax Ave SW20 178 A3
Draxmont SW19 179 A4
Draycot Rd
Tolworth KT6 198 C1
Wanstead E11 55 B2
Draycott Ave
SW3 114 C2 257 B3
Harrow HA3 43 C3
Draycott Cl NW2 68 D5
Harrow HA3 43 B3
Draycott Ct SW11 267 A2
Draycott Ho SW3 257 C3
Draycott Pl
SW3 114 D2 257 C3
Draycott Terr
SW3 114 D2 257 D3
Drayford Cl W9 91 B3
Dray Gdns SW2 160 B6
Draymans Ct 4 SW9 138 B2
Draymans Way TW7 130 D2
Drayside Mews UB2 107 B4
Drayson Mews
W8 113 C4 245 B1
Drayton Ave
Ealing W13 109 A6
Orpington BR6 210 D1
Drayton Bridge Rd
Ealing W13 87 A1
Ealing W7,W13 108 D6
Drayton Cl
Hounslow TW4 151 B6
Ilford IG1 57 B1
Drayton Ct SW10 256 B1
Tolworth KT5 214 D6
West Drayton UB7 104 B2
Drayton Gdns
SW10 114 A1 256 B1
Ealing W13 109 A6
Southgate N21 16 D4
West Drayton UB7 104 A4
Drayton Gn W13 109 A6
Drayton Gr W13 109 A6
Drayton Green Prim Sch
W13 109 A6
Drayton Green Rd
W13 109 B6
Drayton Green Sta W7 86 D1
Drayton Ho E11 54 B1
14 SE5 139 B5
Drayton Manor High Sch
W7 86 D1
Drayton Park Prim Sch
N5 72 C3
Drayton Park Sta N5 72 C3
Drayton Pk N5,N7 72 C4
Drayton Rd E11 54 B1
NW10 89 D6
Croydon CR0 220 D6
Ealing W13 109 B6
Tottenham N17 33 C1
Drayton Sch The N15 52 A3
Drayton Waye HA3 43 B3
Dreadnought St SE10 120 C3
Drenon Sq UB3 105 D6
Dresden Cl NW6 69 D2
Dresden Ho SE11 260 D4
5 SW11 137 A3
Dresden Rd N19 49 D1
Dressington Ave SE4 163 C5
Drew Ave NW7 29 A4
Drewery Ct SE3 142 C2
Drewett Ho 19 E1 96 A1
Drew Gdns UB6 64 D2
Drew Ho 12 SW16 160 A1
Drew Prim Sch E16 122 A5
Drew Rd E16 122 A5
Drewstead Rd SW16 159 D2
Driffield Ct 4 NW9 27 C2
Driffield Rd E3 97 A5
Drift The BR2 225 D5
Driftway Ho 15 E3 97 B5
Driftway The CR4 181 A2
Drinkwater Ho 11 SE5 139 B5
Drinkwater Rd HA2 63 D6
Drive Mans SW6 135 A3
Drive The BR6 227 D6
BR7 189 D2
DA8 147 D6
E17 53 D6
HA9 67 A6
N11 31 D4
N3 29 C3
N6 48 D4
N7 72 B2
NW10 89 D6
NW11 47 A2
W3 89 A1
Ashford TW15 171 B3
Barking IG11 79 D1
Barnet EN5 1 A2
Beckenham BR3 185 C2
Buckhurst Hill IG9 21 C4
Chingford E4 20 B4
Edgware HA8 26 C5
Enfield EN2 5 B4
Feltham TW14 150 C4
Harrow HA2 41 C2
Hounslow TW3,TW7 130 B3
Ickenham UB10 60 A5
Kingston KT2 177 A3
Morden SM4 202 B4
New Barnet EN5 14 A5
Redbridge IG1 56 B2
Sidcup DA14 190 B6
Sidcup DA5 168 D4
South Norwood CR7 205 B5
St Paul's Cray BR7 211 D6
Surbiton KT6 198 A2
Thames Ditton KT10 196 A1
Wanstead E18 55 A6
West Ewell KT19 215 D2
West Wickham BR4 208 B5
Wimbledon SW19,SW20 178 C3
Barking IG11 80 A2
Dr Johnson Ave SW17 159 B1
Dr Johnson's House★
EC4 241 B1
Droitwich Cl SE26 162 A1
Dromey Gdns HA3 24 D3
Dromore Rd SW15 157 A5
Dronfield Gdns RM8 80 C3
Dron Ho E1 96 C2
Droop St W10 91 A3
Drovers Ct SE13 142 A2
3 Kingston KT1 176 A1
Drovers Pl SE15 140 B5
Drovers Rd CR2 221 B3
Dr Triplett's CE Prim Sch
UB3 83 D1
Druce Rd SE21 161 C5
Druid St SE1 117 D4 253 C1
Druids Way BR2 208 B5
Drumaline Ridge KT4 215 C6
Drummer Lo N7 72 B5
Drummond Castle Ct
E7 76 D4
Drummond Cres
NW1 93 D4 232 C2
Drummond Ct N12 30 C3
Drummond Ctr CR0 221 A6
Drummond Dr HA7 24 D3
Drummond Gate SW1 259 D2
Drummond Ho 12 E2 95 D5
N2 30 A1
Drummond Rd SE16 118 B3
Croydon CR0 221 A6
Wanstead E11 55 C3
Drummonds Pl TW9 132 A1
Drummond St
NW1 93 C3 239 A6
Drummonds The IG9 21 B2
Drum St E1 243 D2
Drury Cres CR0 220 C6
Drury Ho SW8 269 A2
Drury La WC2 94 A1 240 B1
Drury Rd HA1 42 A2
Drury Way NW10 67 B3
Dryad St SW15 134 D2
Dryburgh Gdns NW9 44 C6
Dryburgh Ho SW1 258 D2
Dryburgh Mans SW15 134 C2
Dryburgh Rd SW15 134 C2
Dryden Ave W7 86 D1
Dryden Ct SE11 261 B3
Dryden Ct *continued*
11 Richmond TW10 175 D6
Dryden Ho BR2 209 D4
16 N16 73 C5
6 SE5 139 C4
Dryden Rd DA16,SE18 145 D4
Enfield EN1 17 D5
Harrow HA3 24 D2
Wimbledon SW19 180 A4
Dryden St WC2 240 B1
Dryer's Bldgs EC1 241 A3
Dryfield Cl NW10 67 A2
Dryfield Rd HA8 27 A4
Dryfield Wlk 1 SE8 141 C6
Dryhill Rd DA17 147 B6
Dryland Ave 5 BR6 227 D4
Drylands Rd N8 50 A3
Drysdale Ave E4 19 D5
Drysdale Flats 3 E8 73 D3
Drysdale Ho 20 E2 95 C4
Drysdale Pl N1 95 C4
Drysdale St N1 95 C4
Dublin Ave E8 96 A6
Du Burstow Terr W7 108 C4
Ducal St 25 E2 95 D4
Ducane Cl W12 90 C1
Du Cane Ct SW12 159 A3
Du Cane Rd W12 90 A1
Ducavel Ho SW2 160 B3
Duchess Cl N11 31 B5
Sutton SM1 218 A4
Duchess Gr IG9 21 B2
Duchess Mews W1 238 D3
Duchess of Bedford Ho
W8 245 A2
Duchess of Bedford's Wlk
W8 113 C4 245 A1
Duchess St W1 93 B2 238 D3
Duchy Rd EN4 2 B5
Duchy St SE1 116 C5 251 B4
Ducie Ho 8 SE7 143 C6
2 Putney SW15 156 C6
Ducie St SW4 138 B1
Duckett Mews N4 50 D3
Duckett Rd N4 50 D3
Duckett St E1 97 A2
Duck La W1 239 C1
Duck Lees La EN3 7 A1
Ducks Hill Rd HA4,HA6 39 A5
Duck's Wlk TW1 153 C6
Du Cros Dr HA7 25 D4
Du Cros Rd W3 111 C5
Dudden Hill La NW10 67 D3
Duddington Cl SE9 187 D6
Dudley Ave HA3,HA7 43 C6
Dudley Ct NW11 47 A4
W1 237 C1
WC2 240 A2
9 Wanstead E11 55 A4
Wembley HA0 65 D3
Dudley Dr Ruislip HA4 62 B3
West Barnes SM4 201 A2
Dudley Gdns W13 109 B4
Harrow HA2 42 B1
Dudley Ho 14 SW9 138 C3
W2 236 C3
Dudley Mews 14 SW2 160 C5
Dudley Rd N3 29 D1
NW6 91 B5
Ashford TW15 170 B6
Chingford E17 35 C1
East Bedfont TW14 149 B3
Harrow HA2 64 A6
Ilford IG1 78 D4
Kingston KT1 198 B6
Richmond TW9 132 B3
Southall UB2 106 D3
Walton-on-T KT12 194 A2
Wimbledon SW19 179 C4
Dudley St W2 236 C3
Dudlington Rd E5 74 C6
Dudmaston Mews
SW3 256 D2
Dudsbury Rd DA14 190 B4
Dudset La TW5 128 A4
Duffell Ho SE11 260 D1
Dufferin Ave EC1 242 C5
Dufferin Ct EC1 242 C5
Dufferin St EC1 95 A3 242 B5
Duffield Cl HA1 42 D4
Duffield Dr N15 51 D5
Duffield Ho N4 51 A2
Duff St E14 97 D1
Dufour's Pl W1 239 B1
Dugdale Ho 10 N7 71 D3
Duke Gdns IG6 57 B5
Duke Humphrey Rd
SE3 142 C3
Duke Of Cambridge Cl
TW2 152 B5
Duke Of Edinburgh Rd
SM1 218 B6
Duke of Wellington Pl
SW1,W1 248 B2
Duke Of York's Sq
SW3 114 D2 258 A4
Duke of York St SW1 249 B4
Duke Rd W4 111 B1
Ilford IG6 57 B5
Dukes Ave N10 49 C6
N3 29 D2
Duke's Ave W4 111 B1
Dukes Ave Edgware HA8 26 B5
Harrow HA1 42 C5
Harrow HA2,HA5 41 B3
Hounslow TW4 129 A1
Kingston KT3 199 D6
Northolt UB5 63 A1
Richmond KT2,TW10 175 D6
Dukes Cl Ashford TW15 171 A6
Hampton TW12 173 B5
Dukes Ct SE13 142 A3
SE22 162 A3
SE22 162 B6
Barking E6 100 C6
Beckenham BR3 207 A6
Ealing W13 87 B2
Dukes Gate 4 W4 111 A2
Dukes Green Ave
TW14 150 A6
Dukes Head Yd N6 49 B1
Duke's Ho SW1 259 D4
Duke Shore Wharf
E14 119 B6
Dukes La W8 113 D4 245 C2
Dukes Mews N10 49 B6
Duke's Mews W1 238 B2
Duke's Pl EC3 95 C1 243 B1
Dukes Point N6 49 B1
Duke's Rd WC1 93 D4 232 D1
Dukes Rd Acton W3 88 C3
Barking E6 100 C6
Dukes Ride UB10 60 A4
Duke St W1 93 A1 238 B1
Richmond TW10,TW9 153 D6
Sutton SM1 218 B4
Duke St Hill SE1 252 D4
Dukesthorpe Rd SE26 184 D6
Duke St Mans W1 238 B1
Duke St St James's
SW1 115 C5 249 B4
Dukes Way BR4 224 C5
Duke's Yd W1 248 B6
Dulas St N4 50 B1
Dulford St
W11 113 A6 244 A6
Dulka Rd SW11 158 D6
Dulverton NW1 232 B5
Dulverton Ct 12 KT6 198 A4
Dulverton Mans WC1 240 D5
Dulverton Prim Sch
DA15 167 B2
Dulverton Rd
DA15,DA15 167 B2
Ruislip HA4 62 A6
Dulwich Bsns Ctr
SE23 162 D3
Dulwich Coll (Endowed)
SE21 161 C2
Dulwich Coll Picture Gall★
SE21 161 C4
Dulwich Coll Prep Sch
SE21 161 C1
Dulwich Comm SE21 161 C3
Dulwich Ct SE22 162 B3
Dulwich Hamlet Jun Sch
SE21 161 B5
Dulwich High Sch for Boys
SE24 161 B6
Dulwich Hospl SE22 139 C1
Dulwich Mead SE24 161 A5
Dulwich Mews 1
SE22 139 D1
Dulwich Oaks The
SE21 161 D1
Dulwich Rd SE24 160 D5
Dulwich Village SE21 161 C5
Dulwich Village CE Inf Sch
SE21 161 C5
Dulwich Wood Ave
SE19 183 C5
Dulwich Wood Pk
SE19 183 C6
Dumain Ct SE11 261 C3
Du Maurier Ho 2 NW3 70 D3
Dumbarton Ct 16 SW2 160 A4
Dumbarton Rd SW2 160 A5
Dumbleton Cl KT2 176 D2
Dumbreck Rd SE9 144 C2
Dumont Rd N16 73 C5
Dumphreys Ho 5
SW4 159 D4
Dumpton Pl NW1 71 A1
Dunally Pk TW17 193 B2
Dunbar Ave
Beckenham BR3 207 A5
Dagenham RM10 81 C5
Thornton Heath SW16 182 C1
Dunbar Cl UB4 84 A2
Dunbar Ct 3 N12 29 D6
Sutton SM1 218 B3
Walton-on-T KT12 194 C1
Dunbar Gdns RM10 81 D3
Dunbar Rd E7 77 A2
New Malden KT3 199 A5
Tottenham N22 32 D2
Dunbar St SE27 161 A1
Dunbar Wharf 20 E14 119 B6
Dunblane Rd SE9 144 A3
Dunboe Pl TW17 193 A2
Dunboyne Rd NW3 70 D3
Dunbridge Ho 7
SW15 155 D5
Dunbridge St E2 96 B3
Duncan Cl EN5 2 A1
Duncan Ct 3 E14 98 A2
Southgate N21 16 D3
Duncan Gr W3 89 C1
Duncan Ho 3 NW3 70 D1
Duncannon Ho SW1 259 D1
Duncannon St WC2 250 A5
Duncan Rd E8 96 B6
Richmond TW9 132 A1
Duncan St N1 94 D5 234 C4
Duncan Terr
N1 94 D5 234 C4
Dunch St 30 E1 96 B1
Dunchurch Ho RM10 81 C1
Duncombe Hill SE23 163 A4
Duncombe Ho 7
SW19 156 D3
Duncombe Prim Sch
N19 50 A1
Duncombe Rd N19 49 D1
Duncrievie Rd SE13 164 B5
Duncroft SE18 145 C5
Dundalk Ho 2 E1 96 C1
Dundalk Rd SE4 141 A2
Dundas Gdns KT8 195 D6
Dundas Ho 12 E2 96 C5
Dundas Rd SE15 140 C3
Dundee Ct 36 E1 118 B5
Dundee Ho W9 229 A2
Dundee Mews EN3 7 C6
Dundee Rd E13 99 B5
Croydon SE25 206 B4
Dundee St E1 118 B5
Dundee Way EN3 7 A2
Dundee Wharf E14 119 B6
Dundela Gdns KT17,
KT4 216 B4
Dundonald Cl 6 E6 100 A1
Dundonald Prim Sch
SW19 179 B3
Dundonald Rd NW10 90 D6
Merton SW19 179 B3
Dundonald Road Sta
SW19 179 B3
Dundry Ho 8 SE26 162 A1
Duneaves HA1 64 C5
Dunedin Rd E10 75 D5
Ilford IG1 57 A1
Dunedin Way UB4 84 C3
Dunelm Gr SE27 161 A1
Dunelm St E1 96 D1
Dunfield Gdns SE6 185 D5
Dunfield Rd SE6 185 D5
Dunford Rd N7 72 B4
Dungarvan Ave SW15 134 A1
Dungeness Ho SW18 136 A1
Dunheved Cl CR7 204 C3
Dunheved Rd N CR7 204 C3
Dunheved Rd S CR7 204 C3
Dunheved Rd W CR7 204 C3
Dunhill Point 12 SW15 156 B3
Dunholme Gn N9 17 D1
Dunholme La N9 17 D1
Dunholme Rd N9 17 D1
Dunkeld Ho 13 E14 98 B1
Dunkeld Rd
Dagenham RM8 80 C6
South Norwood SE25 205 B5
Dunkery Rd SE9 166 A1
Dunkirk St 12 SE27 183 A6
Dunlace Rd E5 74 D4
Dunleary Cl TW4 151 B4
Dunley Dr CR0 224 A2
Dunlin Ct 11 SE21 161 B2
Dunlin Ho 13 SE16 118 D2
Dunloe Ave N17 51 B6
Dunloe Ct 7 E2 95 D5
Dunloe St E2 95 D5
Dunlop Pl
SE16 117 D3 263 D5
Dunlop Point 10 E16 121 B5
Dunmore Point 15 E2 95 D4
Dunmore Rd NW6 91 A6
Wimbledon SW20 178 D2
Dunmow Cl
Dagenham RM6 58 C4
3 Feltham TW13 173 A6
Dunmow Ho SE11 260 D2
Dagenham RM9 102 B6
Dunmow Rd E15 76 B4
Dunmow Wlk N1 235 A6
Dunnage Cres SE16 119 A2
Dunnet Ho 26 E3 97 B5
Dunnico Ho SE17 263 A2
Dunn Mead NW9 27 D3
Dunnock Cl N9 18 D3
Dunnock Ct 10 SE21 161 B2
Dunnock Rd E6 100 A1
Dunn's Pas WC1 240 B2
Dunn St E8 73 D3
Dunollie Pl NW5 71 C3
Dunollie Rd NW5 71 C3
Dunoon Gdns SE23 162 D4
Dunoon Ho N1 233 C5
Dunoon Rd SE23 162 C4
Dunraven Dr EN2 4 C3
Dunraven Ho 12 TW9 132 B4
Dunraven Rd W12 112 A5
Dunraven St
W1 114 D6 247 D6
Dunraven Upper Sch
SW16 160 B1
Dunrobin Ct NW3 69 D3
Dunsany Rd W14 112 D3
Dunsfold Ct 9 SM2 217 D1
Dunsfold Ho
10 Kingston KT2 176 D4
4 Streatham SW2 160 B4
Dunsfold Way CR0 223 D1
Dunsford Ct 4 HA5 23 B3
Dunsford Way SW15 156 B5
Dunsmore Cl
Bushey WD23 8 B5
Hayes UB4 85 A3
Dunsmore Rd KT12 194 B3
Dunsmore Way WD23 8 B5
Dunsmure Rd N16 51 C1
Dunstable Ct 3 SE3 143 A5
Dunstable Mews W1 238 B4
Dunstable Rd
East Molesey KT8 195 B5
Richmond TW10,TW9 132 A1
Dunstall Ho 9 SE15 140 A4
Dunstall Rd SW19,
SW20 178 C4
Dunstall Way KT8 195 D6
Dunstall Welling Est
DA16 146 B3
Dunstan Cl 2 N2 48 A6
Dunstan Glade BR5 211 B3
Dunstan Ho SE4 141 B3
Dunstan Hos 5 E1 96 C2
Dunstan Rd NW11 47 C1
Dunstan's Gr SE22 162 B5
Dunstan's Rd SE22 162 A5
Dunster Ave SM4 200 D1
Dunster Ct EC3 253 B6
Dunster Dr NW9 45 A1
Dunster Gdns NW6 69 B1
Dunster Ho SE6 163 D1
Dunsterville Way SE1 252 D1
Dunster Way
Carshalton CR4 203 A1
Harrow HA2 63 A5
Dunston Rd E8 95 D6
SW11 137 A3
Dunston St E8 95 D6
Dunton Cl KT6 198 A1
Dunton Ct 5 SE26 162 B2
Dunton Ho 14 SW16 160 A1
Dunton Rd E10 53 D2
SE1 117 D2 263 C3
Duntshill Rd SW18 157 D3
Dunvegan Cl KT8 195 D5
Dunvegan Rd SE9 144 B1
Dunwich Rd DA7 147 B4
Dunworth Mews W11 91 B1
Duplex Ride SW1 247 D1
Dupont Rd SW20 178 D1
Duppas Ave CR0 220 D4
Duppas Cl TW17 193 B4
Duppas Ct CR0 220 D5
Duppas Hill La CR0 220 D4
Duppas Hill Rd CR0 220 D4
Duppas Hill Terr CR0 220 D5
Duppas Jun Sch CR0 220 D3
Duppas Rd CR0 220 D5
Dupree Rd SE7 121 B1
Dura Den Cl BR3 185 D3
Durand Cl SM5 202 D1
Durand Gdns
SW9 138 B4 270 D1
Durand Prim Sch
SW9 138 B4 270 D1
Durand Way NW10 67 A1
Durants Lo EN3 6 D2
Durants Park Ave EN3 6 D1
Durants Rd EN3 6 D1
Durants Sch EN3 6 C4
Durant St E2 96 A4
Durban Ct E7 77 D1
Durban Ho 28 W12 112 B6
Durban Rd E15 98 C4
E17 35 B2
Beckenham BR3 185 B1
Ilford IG2 57 C1
Tottenham N17 33 D4
West Norwood SE27 183 B6
Durbin Ho 13 N9 18 A1
Durbin Rd KT9 214 B4
Durdans Ho 1 NW1 71 C1
Durdans Park Prim Sch
UB1 85 B2
Durdans Rd UB1 85 B1
Durell Gdns RM9 80 D3
Durell Rd RM9 80 D3
Durfey Ho SE5 139 B5
Durford Cres SW15 156 B3

Durham Ave
Beckenham BR2 208 D5
Hounslow TW5 107 B1
Woodford IG8 37 D5
Durham Cl SW20 178 B1
Durham Ct 3 NW6 91 C5
Teddington TW11 174 C6
Durham Hill BR1 186 D6
Durham Ho NW8 230 B1
3 Barking IG11 80 A1
Durham House St
WC2 250 B5
Durham Pl SW3 257 C1
Ilford IG1 79 A4
Durham Rd DA14 190 B5
E12 77 D4
E16 98 C3
N2 48 D6
N4,N7 72 B6
W5 109 D3
Beckenham BR2 208 D6
Edmonton N9 18 A2
Feltham TW14 150 C4
Harrow HA1 41 D4
Wimbledon SW20 178 B2
Durham Rise SE18 123 B1
Durham Row E1 97 A2
Durham St
SE11 138 B6 270 C6
Durham Terr W2 91 D1
Durley Ave HA5 41 A3
Durley Rd N16 51 C2
Durlock Ho 16 SW9 138 C4
Durlston Rd E5 74 A6
Kingston KT2 176 A4
Durnford Ho SE6 163 D1
Durnford St N15 51 C4
3 SE10 142 A6
Durning Rd SE19 183 B5
Durnsford Ave SW18,
SW19 157 C2
Durnsford Rd N11 31 D3
Wimbledon SW18,SW19 157 C1
Durrant Ct HA3 24 C2
Durrant Way BR6 227 B3
Durrell Rd SW6 264 C1
Durrell Way TW17 193 B3
Durrels Ho W14 254 D4
Durrington Ave SW20 178 C3
Durrington Park Rd
SW20 178 C2
Durrington Rd E5 75 A4
Durrington Twr 3
SW8 137 C3
Durrisdeer Ho NW2 69 B4
Dursley Cl SE3 143 C3
Dursley Gdns SE3 143 D4
Dursley Rd SE3 143 C3
Durston NW5 71 A3
Durston House Middleton's
Sch W5 87 D1
Durston House Prep Sch
W5 87 D1
Durward St E1 96 B2
Durweston Mews W1 237 D4
Durweston St W1 237 D3
Dury Rd EN5 1 B3
Dutch Gdns KT2 176 D4
Dutch Yd SW18 157 C6
Dutton Ho SW2 160 D3
Dutton St SE10 142 A4
Duxberry Cl BR2 210 A4
Duxford 21 KT1 176 C1
Duxford Ho 12 SE2 124 D4
Dwight Ct SW6 135 A3
Dycer Ho 19 E9 74 D2
Dye House La E3 97 C6
Dyer Ho TW12 173 D2
Dyers Hall Rd E11 54 C1
E11 76 B6
Dyer's La SW15 134 B1
Dykes Ct 11 SW2 160 B3
Dykes Way BR2 208 D6
Dylan Cl WD6 9 D4
Dylan Rd 2 SE24 138 D1
Belvedere DA17 125 C3
Dylan Thomas Ho N8 50 B5
Dylways SE5 139 B1
Dymchurch Cl BR6 227 C4
Ilford IG5 56 C6
Dymchurch Ho 12 E5 74 B3
Dymes Path SW19 156 D2
Dymock St SW6 135 D2
Dyneley Rd SE12 165 C1
Dyne Rd NW6 69 B1
Dynevor Rd N16 73 D5
Richmond TW10 154 A6
Dynham Rd NW6 69 C1
Dyott St WC1 239 D2
WC1,WC2 94 A1 240 A2
Dysart Ave KT2,TW10 175 C6
Dysart Sch
Kingston KT2 175 D6
Surbiton KT6 198 B2
Dysart St EC2 95 C3 243 A5
Dyson Ct NW2 46 C2
Dyson Ct *continued*
Wembley HA0 65 A4
Dyson Ho 3 SE10 120 D1
Dyson Rd E11 54 C3
E15 76 D2
Dyson's Rd N18 34 B4

E

Eade Rd N4 51 A2
Eagans Cl N2 48 B6
Eagle Ave RM6 59 A3
Eagle Cl SE16 118 C1
Enfield EN3 6 C1
Wallington SM6 220 A2
Eagle Ct EC1 241 C4
9 Dulwich SE21 161 B2
Edmonton N18 33 D4
6 Wanstead E11 55 A5
Eagle Dr NW9 27 C1
Eagle Dwellings EC1 235 B2
Eagle Hill SE19 183 B4
Eagle Ho 22 E1 96 B3
Eagle Hts 10 SW11 136 C2
Eagle La E11 55 A5
Eagle Lo E11 54 D5
NW11 47 B2
Eagle Mans N16 73 D3
Eagle Mews N1 73 C2
Eagle Pl SW1 249 B5
SW7 114 A1 256 B2
Eagle Rd Hatton TW6 127 D2
Wembley HA0 65 D1
Eaglesfield Rd SE18 144 D4
Eaglesfield Sch SE18 144 C4
Eagle St WC1 94 B2 240 C3
Eagle Terr IG8 37 B3
Eagle Trad Est CR4 202 D3
Eagle Wharf SE1 253 C3
Eagle Wharf Rd
N1 95 A5 235 B4
Ealcom Ct W5 110 B5
Ealdham Prim Sch
SE9 143 C1
Ealdham Sq SE9 143 C1
Ealing Almshouses
W5 109 D4
Ealing Broadway Ctr
W5 109 D6
Ealing Broadway Sta
W5 109 D6
Ealing Coll W13 87 B1
Ealing Common W5 110 B6
Ealing Common Sta
W5 110 B5
Ealing Gn W5 109 D5
Ealing,Hammersmith &
West London Coll
W14 113 A1 254 B1
Ealing Hospl UB1,UB2 108 B4
Ealing Park Gdns W5 109 C2
Ealing Park Mans W5 109 D3
Ealing Rd
Brentford TW8 109 D2
Northolt UB5 63 C1
Wembley HA0 66 A1
Ealing Road Trad Est
TW8 109 D1
Ealing Tertiary Coll
Acton W3 110 D5
Ealing W5 109 D5
Ealing Village W5 88 A1
Eamann Casey Ho 34
SW9 138 C4
Eamont Cl HA4 38 D2
Eamont Ct NW8 230 B4
Eamont St NW8 92 C5 230 B4
Eardley Cres
SW5 113 C1 255 B1
Eardley Point 9 SE18 122 D2
Eardley Prim Sch
SW16 181 C4
Eardley Rd
Belvedere DA17 125 C1
Streatham SW16 181 C4
Earl Cl N11 31 B5
Earldom Rd SW15 134 C1
Earle Gdns KT2 176 A3
Earlham Gr E7 77 A3
Wood Green N22 32 B3
Earlham Prim Sch E7 76 D3
Earlham Prim Schs
N22 32 C3
Earlham St
WC2 94 A1 240 A1
Earl Ho NW1 237 B5
Earlom Ho WC1 234 A1
Earl Rd SW14 133 A1
Earl Rise SE18 123 B2
Earl's Court Ex Ctr
SW5 255 A1
Earl's Court Gdns
SW5 113 D2 255 C3
Earl's Court Rd
SW5,W8 113 C2 255 B4
Earl's Court Sq
SW5 113 D1 255 C2
Earl's Court Sta
SW5 113 C2 255 B3
Earls Cres HA1 42 C5
Earlsdown Ho IG11 101 B5
Earlsferry Way N1 72 A1
Earlsfield Prim Sch
SW18 158 A2
Earlsfield Rd SW18 158 A4
Earlsfield Sta SW18 158 A3
Earlshall Rd SE9 144 C1
Earlsmead HA2 63 B4
Earlsmead Fst & Mid Sch
HA2 63 B4
Earlsmead Prim Sch
N15 51 D5
Earlsmead Rd N15 51 D4
NW10 90 C4
Earl St EC2 95 C2 243 A4
Earls Terr W8 254 D5
Earlsthorpe Mews 3
SW12 159 A5
Earlsthorpe Rd SE26 184 D6
Earlstoke St EC1 234 C2
Earlston Gr E9 96 B6
Earls Wlk W8 113 C3 255 A5
Dagenham RM8 80 B4
Earlswood Ave CR7 204 C4
Earlswood Cl 10 SE10 120 C1
Earlswood Gdns IG5 56 C6
Earlswood Ho 2 SW2 160 B3
Earlswood St SE10 120 C1
Early Mews NW1 231 D6
Earnshaw St WC1,WC2 239 D2
Earsby St W14 254 B4
Easby Cres SM4 201 D3
Easebourne Rd RM8 80 C3
Easedale Ho TW7 152 D6
Eashing Point 5
SW15 156 B3
Easleys Mews W1 238 B2
East Acton Arc W3 89 D1
East Acton Ct W3 111 C6
East Acton La W3 111 C6
East Acton Prim Sch
W3 111 C6
East Acton Sta W12 89 D1
East Arbour St E1 96 D1
East Ave E12 78 A1
E17 53 D5
NW2 48 A6
Croydon CR0 220 B3
Hayes UB3 106 A5
Southall UB1 107 B6
Wallend E6 100 C4
East Bank N16 51 C2
Eastbank Rd TW12 174 A5
East Barnet Main Sch
Barnet EN4 2 B2
East Barnet EN4 14 D5
East Barnet Rd EN4 2 B1
East Beckton District Ctr
E6 100 B2
East Block 5 E1 118 D6
Eastbourne Ave W3 89 B1
Eastbourne Gdns
SW14 133 A2
Eastbourne Mews
W2 92 A1 236 B2
Eastbourne Rd E15 98 C6
N15 51 C3
Brentford TW8 109 D1
Chiswick W4 133 A6
Feltham TW13 150 D2
Streatham SW17 181 A4
Wallend E6 100 C4
Eastbourne Terr
W2 92 A1 236 B2
Eastbournia Ave N9 18 B1
Eastbrook Ave N9 18 C4
Eastbrook Rd SE3 143 B4
Eastbury Ave
Barking IG11 101 C6
Enfield EN1 5 D4
Moor Park HA6 22 A5
Eastbury Ct
Barking IG11 101 C6
New Barnet EN5 14 A6
Eastbury Gr W4 111 C1
Eastbury Inf Sch IG11 79 D1
Eastbury Rd E6 100 C3
Kingston KT2 176 A3
Eastbury Sq IG11 101 D6
Eastbury Terr E1 96 D3
Eastcastle St
W1 93 C1 239 B2
Eastcheap EC3 117 C6 253 A6
East Churchfield Rd
W3 111 B5
Eastchurch Rd TW6 127 C2
Eastchurch Road Rdbt
TW6 127 C3
East Cl W5 88 C3
Cockfosters EN4 3 A1
Greenford UB6 86 A5
Eastcombe Ave SE7 143 B6
Eastcote BR6 211 D1
Eastcote Ave
East Molesey KT8 195 C4
Greenford UB6 65 A3
Harrow HA2 64 A6
Eastcote Ind Est HA4 40 C2
Eastcote La Harrow HA2 63 C5
Northolt UB5 63 B2
Eastcote La N UB5 63 C2
Eastcote Pl HA5 40 B3
Eastcote Prim Sch
DA16 145 B2
Eastcote Rd DA16 145 B3
Harrow HA2 64 A5
Pinner HA5 40 D4
Ruislip HA4 40 A3
Eastcote St SW9 138 B3
Eastcote Sta HA5 40 C2
Eastcote View HA5 40 C5
Eastcourt Ind Sch IG3 58 A1
East Cres N11 30 D6
Enfield EN1 17 D6
Eastcroft Rd KT19 215 C1
East Cross Ctr E15 75 C2
East Cross Route E3 97 C6
E9 75 B3
East Croydon Sta CR0 221 B6
East Ct HA0 65 C6
Eastdown Ho E8 74 A4
Eastdown Pk SE13 142 B1
East Duck Lees La EN3 7 B1
East Dulwich Gr SE22 161 C6
East Dulwich Rd SE15,
SE22 140 A1
East Dulwich Sta SE22 139 C1
East End Rd N2 48 A6
N2,N3 47 D6
N3 29 C1
East End Way HA5 41 A6
East Entrance RM10 103 D5
Eastern Ave
Ilford IG1,IG2,IG4, 56 B3
Ilford IG1,IG2,IG4 56 C3
Ilford IG2 57 B3
Pinner HA5 40 D2
Wanstead E11 55 C3
Eastern Ave W RM7 59 C5
Eastern Bsns Pk
TW16 127 D3
Eastern Perimeter Rd
TW14 127 D3
Eastern Rd E13 99 B5
E17 54 A4
N2 48 D5
SE4 141 C1
Wood Green N22 32 A2
Easternville Gdns IG2 57 A3
Eastern Way SE28 124 B4
East Ferry Rd E14 119 D2
Eastfield Gdns RM10 81 C4
Eastfield Prim Sch EN3 6 D5
Eastfield Rd E17 53 C5
N8 50 A6
Dagenham RM10 81 C4
Dagenham RM9 81 B4
Enfield EN3 6 D5
Eastfields HA5 40 C4
Eastfields Rd W3 89 A2
Mitcham CR4 181 A1
Eastfield St E14 97 A2
East Finchley Sta N2 48 C5
Eastgate Cl SE28 102 D1
East Gdns SW17 180 C4
Eastglade HA5 41 B6
Eastham Cl EN5 13 B6
East Ham Ind Est E6 100 A2
East Ham Manor Way
E6 100 C1
East Ham Meml Hospl
E7 77 D1
East Ham Sta E6 78 A1
East Harding St EC4 241 B2
East Heath Rd NW3 70 B5
East Hill SW18 158 A6
Wembley HA9 44 C1
Eastholm NW11 47 D5
Eastholme UB3 106 A5
East India Bldgs 8
E14 119 C6
East India Dock Basin
E14 120 C6
East India Dock Rd
E14 119 D6
East India Dock Road
Tunnel 17 E14 98 B1
East India Dock Wall Rd
E14 120 B6
East India Sta E14 120 B6
East La SE16 118 A4
Kingston KT1 197 D6
Wembley HA0,HA9 65 D5
Eastlake Ho NW8 236 D5
Eastlake Rd SE5 139 A3
Eastlands Cres SE21 161 D5
Eastlea Com Sch E16 98 C3
Eastlea Mews E16 98 C3
Eastleigh Ave HA2 63 D6
Eastleigh Cl NW2 67 C5
Belmont SM2 217 D1
Eastleigh Rd E17 35 B1
Eastleigh Way TW14 150 A3
Eastleigh Wlk 9
SW15 156 A4
East London Coll & Toynbee
Theatre E1 95 D2 243 D3
East London Stadium
E3 97 B2
Eastman Dental Hospl
WC1 94 B4 240 C6
Eastman Ho 7 SW4 159 C5
Eastman Rd W3 111 B4
East Mascalls 15 SE7 143 C6
Eastmead IG3 58 A2
East Mead HA4 62 D5
Eastmead Ave UB6 85 D4
Eastmead Cl BR1 188 A1
Eastmearn Rd SE21,
SE27 161 A2
East Molesey Inf sch
KT8 196 B5
Eastmont Rd KT10 212 D6
Eastmoor Pl SE7 121 D3
Eastmoor St SE7 121 D3
East Mount St E1 96 B2
Eastney Rd CR0 204 D1
Eastney St SE10 120 B1
Eastnor Rd SE9 167 A3
Easton Ho 4 SE27 160 D1
Easton St WC1 241 A6
East Park Cl RM6 59 A4
East Parkside SE10 120 D4
East Pas EC1 242 A4
East Pl SE27 183 A6
East Point 4 SE1 118 A1
Eastpole Cotts N14 3 D1
East Poultry Ave EC1 241 C3
East Putney Sta SW15 157 A6
East Ramp TW6 126 D4
East Rd DA16 146 B3
E15 99 A6
HA8 27 A2
N1 95 B4 235 D2
N2 30 C2
Dagenham RM6 59 A4
East Barnet EN4 15 A3
East Bedfont TW14 149 B4
Enfield EN3 6 C5
Kingston KT2 176 A2
West Drayton UB7 104 C2
Wimbledon SW19 180 A4
East Rochester Way
DA5,DA15,DA16,SE9 168 C5
East Row W10 91 A3
Wanstead E11 55 A3
Eastry Ave BR2 208 D3
Eastry Ho SW8 270 A3
Eastry Rd DA8 147 C5
East Sheen Ave SW14 133 B1
East Sheen Prim Sch
SW14 133 C1
Eastside Rd NW11 47 B5
East Smithfield
E1 117 D6 253 D5
East St BR1 187 A1
DA7 147 C1
SE17 117 B1 262 C2
Barking IG11 79 A1
Brentford TW8 131 C5
East Surrey Gr SE15 139 D5
East Tenter St
E1 95 D1 243 D1
East Terr DA15 167 C3
East Thamesmead Bsns Pk
DA18 125 B4
East Towers HA5 40 D3
Eastvale W3 111 D5
East View NW3 70 B6
Barnet EN5 1 B2
Chingford E4 36 A5
Eastview Ave SE18 145 C5
Eastville Ave NW11 47 B3
Eastway E3,E9 97 A6
E9,E10 75 C4
Hayes BR2 209 A2
Merton SM4,SW20 201 A5
Wallington SM6 219 C4
Wanstead E11 55 B4
East Way Croydon CR0 223 A5
Hayes UB3 106 A5
Ruislip HA4 40 A1
Eastwell Cl BR3 185 A2
Eastwell Ho SE1 262 D6
Eastwick Ct 2 SW19 156 D3
East Wickham Inf Sch
DA16 145 D4
East Wickham Jun Sch
DA16 146 A4
East Wlk East Barnet EN4 15 A3
Hayes UB3 106 A5
Eastwood Cl
7 Tottenham N17 34 B3
Woodford E18 37 A1
Eastwood Rd N10 31 A1
Ilford IG3 58 A2
West Drayton UB7 104 C4
Woodford E18 37 A1
East Woodside DA5 169 A3
Eastwood St SW16 181 C4
Eatington Rd E10 54 B4
Eaton Cl SW1 258 A3
Stanmore HA7 25 B6
Eaton Ct BR7 189 A4
Eaton Ct *continued*
Ealing W5 87 D1
Edgware HA8 26 C6
Southall UB1 107 B6
Sutton SM2 218 B2
Eaton Dr SW9 138 D1
Kingston KT2 176 C3
Eaton Gate
SW1 115 A2 258 A4
Eaton Gdns RM9 81 A1
Eaton Ho SW11 266 D1
Ealing W5 87 D1
Eaton House The Manor
Sch SW4 137 B1
Eaton La SW1 115 B3 258 D5
Eaton Mans SW1 258 A3
Eaton Mews N
SW1 115 A3 258 B5
Eaton Mews S
SW1 115 B3 258 C5
Eaton Mews W SW1 258 B4
Eaton Park Rd N13 16 D2
Eaton Pl SW1 115 A3 258 B5
Eaton Rd DA14 168 D2
NW4 46 C4
Enfield EN1 5 C1
Isleworth TW3,TW7 130 B1
Sutton SM2 218 B2
Eaton Rise Ealing W5 87 D1
Wanstead E11 55 C4
Eaton Row
SW1 115 B3 258 C5
Eatons Mead E4 19 C2
Eaton Sq SW1 115 A3 258 B5
Eaton Square Sch
SW1 115 B2 258 C4
Eaton Terr E3 97 A4
SW1 115 A2 258 B4
Eaton Terr Mews SW1 258 A4
Eatonville Rd SW17 158 D2
Eatonville Villas SW17 158 D2
Ebbisham Dr
SW8 138 B6 270 C5
Ebbisham Rd KT4 216 C6
Ebbsfleet Rd NW2 69 A4
Ebdon Way SE3 143 B2
Ebenezer Ho SE11 261 C3
Ebenezer Mussel Ho 5
E2 96 C5
Ebenezer St N1 235 C2
Ebenezer Wlk CR4 181 C2
Ebley Cl SE15 139 D6
Ebner St SW18 157 D6
Ebony Ho 10 NW3 69 D2
Ebor Cotts SW15 155 C1
Ebor St E1,E2 243 C6
Ebrington Rd HA3 43 D3
Ebsworth St SE23 162 D4
Eburne Rd N7 72 A5
Ebury Bridge Rd
SW1 115 A1 258 B1
Ebury Cl BR2 226 A5
Ebury Mews
SW1 115 B2 258 C4
Ebury Mews E SW1 258 C5
Ebury Sq SW1 258 B3
Ebury St SW1 115 B2 258 C4
Ecclesbourne Cl N13 32 C5
Ecclesbourne Gdns
N13 32 C5
Ecclesbourne Inf Sch
CR7 205 A4
Ecclesbourne Jun Sch
CR7 205 A4
Ecclesbourne Prim Sch
N1 73 B1
Ecclesbourne Rd N1 73 A1
Thornton Heath CR7 205 A4
Eccleshill 3 BR2 208 D5
Eccles Rd SW11 136 D1
Eccleston Cl BR6 211 B1
Cockfosters EN4 2 D1
Eccleston Cres RM6 58 B2
Eccleston Ct HA9 66 A3
Ecclestone Mews HA9 66 A3
Ecclestone Pl HA9 66 B3
Eccleston Ho 1 SW2 160 C5
Eccleston Mews
SW1 115 A3 258 B5
Eccleston Pl
SW1 115 B2 258 C4
Eccleston Rd W13 109 A5
Eccleston Sq
SW1 115 B2 258 D3
Eccleston Sq Mews
SW1 259 A3
Eccleston St
SW1 115 B2 258 C4
Echelford Cty Prim Sch
TW15 170 D5
Echelforde Dr TW15 170 C6
Echo Hts E4 19 D3
Eckersley St E1 243 D5
8 E2 96 A3
Eckford St N1 234 A4
Eckington Ho N15 51 B3
Eckstein Rd SW11 136 C1
Eclipse Rd E13 99 B2
Ector Rd SE6 164 C2

Edam Ct 11 DA14 168 A1
Edans Ct W12 111 D4
Edbrooke Rd W9 91 C3
Eddisbury Ho 7 SE26 162 A1
Eddiscombe Rd SW6 135 B3
Eddy Cl RM7 59 D3
Eddystone Rd SE4 163 A6
Eddystone Twr SE8 119 A1
Eddystone Wlk TW19 148 A4
Ede Cl TW4 129 B2
Edenbridge Cl 29
SE16 118 B1
Edenbridge Rd E9 74 D1
Enfield EN1 17 C5
Eden Cl NW3 69 C6
W8 255 B6
Wembley HA0 87 D6
Edencourt W5 88 B1
Edencourt Rd SW16 181 B4
Edendale W3 110 D6
Edenfield Gdns KT4 215 D5
Eden Gr E17 53 D4
N7 72 B3
Edenham High Sch
CR0 207 B2
Edenham Way W10 91 B2
Eden Ho NW8 237 A5
15 SW11 136 C2
Edenhurst Ave SW6 135 B2
Eden Lodge NW6 68 D1
Eden Mews SW17 158 A1
Eden Park Ave BR3 207 C4
Eden Park Sta BR3 207 C4
Eden Rd E17 53 D4
Croydon CR0 221 B4
Penge BR3 185 A2
West Norwood SE27 182 D5
Edensmuir Ct SE3 143 A5
Edensor Gdns W4 133 C5
Edensor Rd W4 133 C5
Eden St KT1,KT2 176 A1
Edenvale Cl CR4 181 A3
Edenvale Rd CR4 181 A3
Edenvale St SW6 136 A3
Eden Way BR3 207 C3
Eden Wlk 5 KT1 176 A1
Ederline Ave SW16 182 C1
Edgar Ct KT3 199 C6
Edgar Ho E9 75 A3
SW8 270 A4
Wanstead E11 55 A2
Edgar Kail Way SE22 139 C1
Edgarley Terr SW6 264 A1
Edgar Rd E3 97 D4
Dagenham RM6 58 D2
Twickenham TW4 151 B4
Yiewsley UB7 104 A5
Edgcott Ho W10 90 C2
Edgeborough Way
BR1 187 D2
Edge Bsns Ctr The
NW2 68 B6
Edgebury BR7,SE9 188 D6
Edgebury Prim Sch
BR7 189 A6
Edgebury Wlk BR7 167 A1
Edgecombe Cl KT2 177 B3
Edgecombe Ho
4 SE5 139 C3
Putney SW19 157 A4
Edgecoombe CR2 222 C1
Edgecote Cl 7 W3 111 A5
Edgecot Gr N15 51 C4
Edgecumbe Ct 2 CR0 206 A1
Edgefield Ave IG11 79 D1
Edgefield Ct 2 IG11 79 D1
Edge Hill SE18 144 D6
Wimbledon SW19 178 D3
Edge Hill Ave N3 47 C5
Edge Hill Ct DA14 189 D6
Edgehill Ct KT12 194 C1
Edge Hill Ct SW19 178 D3
Edgehill Gdns RM10 81 C4
Edgehill Ho 4 SW9 138 D3
Edgehill Rd BR7 189 A6
Ealing W13 87 C2
Mitcham CR4 181 B2
Edgeley La SW4 137 D2
Edgeley Rd SW4 137 D2
Edgel St SW18 135 D1
Edge Point Cl SE27 182 D5
Edge St W8 113 C5 245 B4
Edgewood Dr BR6 227 D3
Edgewood Gn CR0 206 D1
Edgeworth Ave NW4 46 A4
Edgeworth Cl NW4 46 A4
Edgeworth Cres NW4 46 A4
Edgeworth Ct 10 EN4 2 C1
Edgeworth Ho NW8 229 A6
Edgeworth Rd SE9 143 D1
Barnet EN4 2 C1
Edgington Rd SW16 181 D4
Edgington Way DA14 190 D3
Edgson Ho SW1 258 C2
Edgwarebury Ct HA8 26 C5
Edgwarebury Gdns
HA8 26 C5
Edgwarebury La HA8 10 C2
Edgware Community Hospl
HA8 26 D3
Edgware Ct HA8 26 C4
Edgware Jun & Inf Schs
HA8 26 C4
Edgware Rd NW2 68 C6
W1,W2,NW1,
NW8 92 C2 237 A3
Edgware Rd Burnt Oak
Broadway HA8 26 D3
Edgware Rd High St
HA8 26 C4
Edgware Road Sta
(Bakerloo)
NW1 92 C2 237 A3
Edgware Road Sta
(Met,Distr,Circle)
NW1 237 B3
Edgware Road The Hyde
NW9 45 C5
Edgware Road West
Hendon Broadway
NW9 46 A2
Edgware Sch The HA8 26 B6
Edgware Sta HA8 26 D4
Edgware Way (Watford
By-Pass) HA8 26 C6
Edinburgh Cl 7 E2 96 C5
Uxbridge UB10 60 D4
Edinburgh Ct E13 99 B5
10 SE16 118 D5
1 Catford SE6 164 D3
2 Kingston KT1 198 A6
West Barnes SM4 200 D4
Edinburgh Dr UB10 60 D4
Edinburgh Ho NW4 46 C6
3 W3 89 B1
W9 91 D4
Edinburgh Prim Sch
E17 53 B4
Edinburgh Rd E13 99 B5
E17 53 C4
W7 108 D4
Carshalton SM1 218 B6
Edmonton N18 34 A5
Edington 20 NW5 71 A2
Edington Rd SE2 124 B3
Enfield EN3 6 C3
Edison Bldg 11 E14 119 C4
Edison Cl E17 53 C4
Edison Ct SE10 120 D3
Edison Dr UB1 85 D1
Edison Gr SE18 145 D5
Edison Ho SE1 262 C4
10 Wembley HA9 67 A5
Edison Rd DA16 145 D4
N8 49 D3
Brimsdown EN3 7 B3
Bromley BR2 187 A1
Edis St NW1 93 A6 231 B6
Editha Mans SW10 266 A5
Edith Cavell Cl 6 N19 50 A2
Edith Cavell Way SE18 144 A4
Edith Gdns KT5 198 D2
Edith Gr SW10 136 A5 266 B4
Edith Ho 6 W6 112 C1
Edithna St SW9 138 A2
Edith Neville Prim Sch
NW1 93 D5 232 C3
Edith Pond Ct SE9 166 D2
Edith Ramsay Ho 2 E1 97 A2
Edith Rd E15 76 B3
E6 77 D1
N11 31 D3
W14 113 A2 254 B3
Dagenham RM6 58 D2
South Norwood SE25 205 B4
Wimbledon SW19 179 D4
Edith Row SW6 265 D2
Edith St E2 96 A5
Edith Summerskill Ho
SW6 264 C4
Edith Terr
SW10 136 A5 266 A4
Edith Villas
W14 113 B2 254 C2
Edith Yd SW10 266 B4
Edmansons' Cl N17 33 D2
Edmeston Cl E9 75 A2
Edmond Ct SE14 140 C4
Edmonscote W13 87 A2
Edmonton Coll of F Ed
EN3 6 C4
Edmonton Ct 5 SE16 118 C3
Edmonton Cty Lower Sch
N9 17 C3
Edmonton Cty Upper Sch
EN1 17 D4
Edmonton Green Sh Ctr
N9 18 B2
Edmonton Green Sta
N9 18 A2
Edmonton Wharf N18 34 D4
Edmund Gr TW13 151 B2
Edmund Halley Way
SE10 120 C4
Edmund Ho SE14 141 B4
SE17 261 D1
Edmund Hurst Dr E6 100 D2
Edmund Rd DA16 146 A2
Mitcham CR4 202 C6
Edmundsbury Ct Est 16
SW9 138 B1
Edmunds Cl UB4 84 C2
Edmund St SE5 139 B5
Edmunds Wlk N2 48 C5
Edmund Waller Prim Sch
SE14 140 D3
Ednam Ho SE15 140 A6
Edna Rd SW20 178 D1
Edna St SW11 136 C4 267 A1
Edred Ho E9 75 A4
Edrich Ho SW4 270 A1
Edric Ho SW1 259 D4
Edrick Rd HA8 27 A4
Edrick Wlk HA8 27 A4
Edric Rd SE14 140 D5
Edridge Cl WD23 8 A6
Edridge Ho 9 SE27 160 D1
Edridge Rd CR0 221 B5
Edward Alleyn Ho
SE21 161 C4
Edward Ave
Chingford E4 35 D4
Morden SM4 202 B4
Edward Betham CE Prim
Sch UB6 86 A5
Edward Cl Edmonton N9 17 D4
Hampton TW12 174 A5
Edward Ct 2 E16 99 A2
2 Ealing W5 87 B3
Harrow HA1 64 C6
Edward Dodd Ct N1 235 D2
Edward Edward's Ho
SE1 251 C3
Edwardes Sq
W8 113 B3 254 D5
Edward Friend Ho 6
N16 73 C5
Edward Gr EN4 14 B6
Edward Harvey Ct
DA17 125 B1
Edward Ho SE11 260 D2
W2 236 C5
Edward Kennedy Ho 18
W10 91 A3
Edward Mann Cl 12 E1 96 D1
Edward Mans 7 IG11 79 D1
Edward Mews NW1 231 D3
Edward Pauling Ho
TW14 149 D4
Edward Pauling Prim Sch
TW13 149 C2
Edward Pinner Ct 5
KT6 214 A6
Edward Pl SE8 141 B6
Edward Rd E17 52 D4
Bromley BR1 187 C3
Chislehurst BR7 188 D5
Croydon CR0 205 C2
Dagenham RM6 59 A3
Hampton TW12 174 A5
Harrow HA2 42 A6
Hatton TW14 149 C6
New Barnet EN4 14 B6
Northolt UB5 84 C5
Penge SE20 184 D4
Edward Redhead Jun & Inf
Sch E17 53 A6
Edward Robinson Ho 3
SE14 140 D5
Edward's Ave HA4 62 C2
Edwards Cl KT4 216 D6
Edward's Cotts 11 N1 72 D1
Edwards Dr N11 31 D3
Edward's La N16 73 C6
Edwards Language Sch
W5 110 A6
Edwards Mews N1 72 D1
W1 93 A1 238 A1
Edward Sq N1 233 C5
SE16 119 A5
Edwards Rd DA17 125 C2
Edward St 10 E16 99 A3
SE14 141 B5
Edward Temme Ave
E15 76 D1
Edward Tyler Rd SE12 165 C2
Edward VII Mans NW10 90 D4
Edward Way TW15 148 B2
Edward Wilson Prim Sch
W2 91 D2
Edwina Ct SM1 217 D4
Edwina Gdns IG4 56 A4
Edwin Arnold Ct DA15 189 D6
Edwin Ave E6 100 C5
Edwin Cl DA7 147 B6
Edwin Ho SE15 140 A5
Edwin Rd HA8 27 B4
Twickenham TW1,TW2 152 C3
Edwin's Mead E9 75 A4
Edwin St E1 96 C3
E16 99 A2
Edwin Stray Ho TW13 151 C1
Edwin Ware Ct 2 HA5 22 C1
Edwy Ho E9 75 B4
Edwyn Cl EN5 12 D5
Edwyn Ho SW18 157 D5
Eel Pie Island★ TW1 153 A3
Effie Pl SW6 265 B3
Effie Rd SW6 135 C5 265 B3
Effingham Cl SM2 217 D1
Effingham Ct SW19 180 C3
Effingham Ho 37 SW8 137 D3
9 Kingston KT2 176 D4
Effingham Lo 1 KT6 198 A4
Effingham Rd N8 50 C5
SE12 164 D6
Thames Ditton KT6,KT7 197 C2
Thornton Heath CR0 204 B2
Effort St SW17 180 C5
Effra Ct SW2 160 B6
South Norwood SE19 183 C3
Effra Mans SW2 160 C6
Effra Par SW2 160 C6
Effra Rd SW2 160 C6
Wimbledon SW19 179 D4
Effra Road Ret Pk
SW2 160 C6
Egan Way UB3 105 C6
Egbert Ho E9 75 A3
Egbert St NW1 93 A6 231 A6
Egbury Ho SW15 155 D5
Egerton Cl HA5 40 A5
Egerton Cres
SW3 114 C2 257 B4
Egerton Ct E11 54 B2
5 Richmond TW10 154 A6
Egerton Dr SE10 141 D4
Egerton Gdns NW4 46 B5
SW3 114 C3 257 A5
Ealing W13 87 B1
Ilford IG3 79 D5
Willesden NW10 90 C6
Egerton Gdns Mews
SW3 257 B5
Egerton Ho W4 133 A6
Egerton Pl SW3 257 B5
Egerton Rd N16 51 D2
New Malden KT3 199 D5
South Norwood SE25 205 C6
Twickenham TW2 152 C4
Wembley HA0 66 B1
Egerton Terr
SW3 114 C3 257 B5
Egerton Way UB3 126 D5
Eggardon Ct UB5 64 A2
Egham Cl Cheam SM3 217 A6
Putney SW19 157 A2
Egham Cres SM3 217 A6
Egham Ct KT6 197 D4
Egham Rd E13 99 B2
Eglantine Rd SW18 158 A6
Egleston Rd SM4 201 D3
Eglington Ct SE17 139 A6
Eglington Rd E4 20 B4
Eglinton Hill SE18 144 D5
Eglinton Prim Sch
SE18 144 C6
Eglinton Rd SE18 144 D6
Egliston Mews SW15 134 C2
Egliston Rd SW15 134 C2
Egmont Ave KT6 198 B1
Egmont Rd
New Malden KT3 199 D5
Sutton SM2 218 A1
Tolworth KT6 198 C1
Walton-on-T KT12 194 B2
Egmont St SE14 140 D5
Egremont Ho SE13 141 D3
Egremont Rd SE27 160 C1
Egret Ho 11 SE16 118 D2
Egret Way UB4 84 D2
Eider Cl E7 76 D3
Hayes UB4 84 D2
Eider Ct 39 SE8 141 B6
Eighteenth Rd CR4 204 A5
Eighth Ave Hayes UB3 106 A5
Ilford E12 78 B4
Eileen Ct BR7 188 C5
Eileen Rd SE25 205 B4
Eindhoven Cl SM5 203 A1
Einstein Ho HA9 67 A5
Eisenhower Dr E6 100 A2
Eisenhower Ho KT8 175 C2
Ekarra Ho SW8 270 B2
Elaine Ct 13 NW3 70 D2
Elaine Gr NW5 71 A3
Elaine Ho N4 50 A1
Elam Cl SE5 138 D3
Elam St SE5 138 D3
Elan Ct E1 96 B2
Eland Pl CR0 220 D5
Eland Rd SW11 136 D2
Croydon CR0 220 D5
Elba Pl SE17 117 A2 262 B4
Elberon Ave CR0 203 C3
Elbe St SW6 136 A3
Elborough Rd SE25 206 A4
Elborough St SW18 157 C3
Elbourne Trad Est
DA17 125 D3
Elbury Dr E16 99 A1
Elcho St SW11 136 C5 267 B3
Elcot Ave SE15 140 B5
Eldenwall Ind Est RM8 59 B1
Elder Ave N8 50 A4
Elderberry Gr 10 SE27 183 A6
Elderberry Rd W5 110 A4
Elder Cl DA15 167 D3
HA8 27 A5
Barnet N20 13 D3
Yiewsley UB7 104 A6
Elder Ct WD23 8 C2
Elderfield Ho 3 E14 119 C6
Elderfield Pl SW17 181 B6
Elderfield Rd E5 74 C4
Elderfield Wlk E11 55 B4
Elderflower Way E15 76 C1
Elder Gdns 9 SE27 183 A6
Elder Oak Cl SE20 184 B2
Elder Rd SE27 183 A5
Elderslie Cl BR3 207 D3
Elderslie Rd SE9 166 C6
Elder St E1 95 D3 243 C5
Elderton Rd SE26 185 A6
Eldertree Pl CR4 181 C2
Eldertree Way CR4 181 C2
Elder Wlk N1 234 D6
Elderwood Pl SE27 183 A5
Eldon Ave Croydon CR0 222 C6
Heston TW5 129 C5
Eldon Ct NW6 91 C6
Eldon Gr NW3 70 B3
Eldon Ho SW9 138 D2
Eldon Jun & Inf Schs
N9 18 C3
Eldon Pk SE25 206 B5
Eldon Rd E17 53 B5
N9 18 C3
W8 113 D3 255 D5
Tottenham N22 32 D2
Eldon St EC2 95 B2 242 D3
Eldon Way NW10 88 D5
Eldred Rd IG11 101 C6
Eldrick Ct TW14 149 B3
Eldridge Cl TW14 150 A3
Eldridge Ct SE16 118 A3
Eleanor Cl N15 51 D6
SE16 118 D4
Eleanor Cres NW7 28 D6
Eleanor Ct 13 E2 96 A6
Eleanor Gdns
Barnet EN5 12 D6
Dagenham RM8 81 B6
Eleanor Gr
Mortlake SW13 133 C2
Uxbridge UB10 60 D5
Eleanor Ho 1 NW5 71 C3
18 W6 112 C1
6 Merton SW19 179 D2
Eleanor Palmer Prim Sch
NW5 71 C4
Eleanor Rathbone Ho 1
N6 49 D2
Eleanor Rd E15 76 D2
Bowes Park N11 32 A4
Eleanor Smith Sch E13 99 B5
Eleanor St E3 97 C4
Eleanor Wlk 25 SE18 122 B2
Electra Ave TW6 127 D2
Electric Ave SW9 138 C1
Enfield EN3 7 B6
Electric Ho 12 E3 97 C4
Electric La 2 SW9 138 C1
Electric Mans 1 SW9 138 C1
Electric Par Ilford IG3 57 D1
Surbiton KT6 197 D3
Woodford E18 37 A1
Elephant & Castle
SE1 261 D4
SE1 117 A3 261 D5
Elephant & Castle Sta
SE1 116 D3 261 D5
SE17 117 A2 262 A4
Elephant La SE16 118 C4
Elephant Rd
SE17 117 A2 262 A4
Elers Rd W13 109 C4
Hayes UB3 105 B2
Eley Rd N18 34 D5
Eley's Est N18 34 D6
Elfindale Rd SE24 161 A6
Elfin Gr TW11 174 D5
Elford Cl SE9 143 C1
Elfort Rd N5 72 C4
Elfrida Cres SE6 185 C6
Elfrida Prim Sch SE6 185 C6
Elf Row E1 118 C6
Elfwine Rd W7 86 C2
Elgal Cl BR6 226 D3
Elgar N8 50 A6
Elgar Ave NW10 67 B2
W5 110 A4
Thornton Heath SW16 204 A6
Tolworth KT5,KT6 198 D2
Elgar Cl E13 99 C5
SE8 141 C5
Buckhurst Hill IG9 21 D2
Elstree WD6 9 D4
Ickenham UB10 60 C6
Elgar Ct W14 254 A5
Elgar Ho NW6 70 A1
SW1 258 D1
Hayes UB4 84 C2
Isleworth TW2 152 B5
Elgar St SE16 119 A3
Elgin Ave W12 112 B3
W9 91 D3
Ashford TW15 171 A4
Harrow HA3 25 B1
Elgin Cres
W11 113 A6 244 B6
Hatton TW6 127 C3
Elgin Ct W9 91 D3
6 Croydon CR0 221 A4
Elgin Ho 8 E14 97 D1
Northolt UB5 84 B5
Elgin Mans W9 91 D4
Elgin Mews W11 91 A1
Elgin Mews N W9 91 D4
Elgin Mews S W9 91 D4
Elgin Rd N22 31 C1
Croydon CR0 221 D6
Ilford IG3 57 C2
Sutton SM1 218 A5
Wallington SM6 219 C2
Elgood Ave HA6 22 A3
Elgood Ho NW8 229 D3
Elham Cl BR1 187 D3
Elham Ho 13 E5 74 B3
Elia Mews N1 94 D5 234 C3
Elias Pl SW8 138 C6
Elia St N1 94 D5 234 C3
Elibank Rd SE9 144 C1
Elim Est SE1 263 A6
Elim St SE1 263 A6
Elim Way E13 98 D4
Eliot Bank SE23,SE26 162 B2
Eliot Bank Prim Sch
SE23 162 B2
Eliot Ct SW18 157 D5
Eliot Dr HA2 63 D6
Eliot Gdns SW15 134 A1
Eliot Hill SE13 142 A3
Eliot Ho 10 TW10 154 B5
Eliot Mews NW8 229 A3
Eliot Pk SE13 142 A3
Eliot Pl SE3 142 C3
Eliot Rd RM9 80 D4
Eliot Vale SE3 142 B3
Elizabethan Ct N3 47 A6
Elizabeth Ave
N1 73 B1 235 B6
Enfield EN2 4 D2
Ilford IG1 79 B6
Elizabeth Barnes Ct 5
SW6 135 D3
Elizabeth Blackwell Ho
N22 32 C2
Elizabeth Cl 12 E14 97 D1
W9 236 B5
Cheam SM1 217 B6
Elizabeth Clyde Cl N15 51 C5
Elizabeth Cotts 5
TW9 132 C4
Elizabeth Ct NW8 237 B6
SE22 140 A1
SW10 266 D5
SW1 259 D5
Buckhurst Hill IG9 21 B3
Sunbury TW16 194 C6
3 Teddington TW11 174 C5
West Barnes SM4 201 A2
6 Woodford E18 37 A2
2 Woodford IG8 37 C3
Elizabeth Finn Ho
W12 112 A3
Elizabeth Fry Ho UB3 105 D2
Elizabeth Fry Pl SE18 144 A4
Elizabeth Garrett Anderson
Ho 9 DA17 125 C3
Elizabeth Garrett Anderson
Hospl NW1 93 C3 239 B6
Elizabeth Garrett Anderson
Language Coll
N1 94 B5 233 C3
Elizabeth Gdns W3 111 D5
Stanmore HA7 25 C5
Sunbury TW16 194 C6
Elizabeth Ho 46 E3 97 D4
N20 14 D1
SE11 261 B3
15 W6 112 C1
Wembley HA9 66 B3
Elizabeth Ind Est SE14 140 D6
Elizabeth Kenny Ho N1 73 A2
Elizabeth Mews NW3 70 D2
Elizabeth Pl N15 51 B5
Elizabeth Rd E6 99 D6
N15 51 C4
Elizabeth Ride N9 18 B4
Elizabeth Selby Inf Sch
E2 96 A4
Elizabeth Sq 13 SE16 119 A6
Elizabeth St
SW1 115 A2 258 B4
Elizabeth Terr SE9 166 B5
Elizabeth Way
Feltham TW13 172 C6
South Norwood SE19 183 B3
Elkanette Mews N20 14 A2

Elkington Point SE11 261 A3
Elkington Rd E13 99 B3
Elkstone Rd W10 91 B2
Ellacombe Ho 1 SW2 160 C4
Ellaline Rd W6 134 D6
Ella Mews NW3 70 D4
Ellanby Cres N18 34 B5
Elland Ho 12 E14 97 B1
Elland Rd SE15 140 C1
Ella Rd N4,N8 50 A2
Ellement Cl HA5 40 D4
Ellena Ct N14 16 A1
Ellenborough Ct N22 32 D2
Ellenborough Ho 5
W12 112 B6
Ellenborough Pl
SW15 134 A1
Ellenborough Rd
DA14 191 A5
Tottenham N22 33 A2
Ellen Cl BR1 209 D6
Ellen Ct N9 18 C2
6 Chingford E4 20 A3
Ellen Miller Ho 2 E17 54 A4
Ellen St E1 96 A1
Ellen Webb Dr HA3 42 C6
Ellen Wilkinson Ho
7 E2 96 D4
SW6 264 D5
12 Dagenham RM10 81 C5
Ellen Wilkinson Prim Sch
E6 100 A2
Ellen Wilkinson Sch for
Girls W3 88 B1
Elleray Rd TW11 174 D4
Ellerby St SW6 134 D4
Ellerdale Cl 22 NW3 70 A4
Ellerdale Rd NW3 70 A3
Ellerdale St SE13 141 D2
Ellerdine Rd TW3 130 B1
Ellerker Gdns TW10 154 A5
Ellerman Ave TW2,
TW4 151 B3
Ellerslie Ct 6 SM6 219 B2
Ellerslie Gdns NW10 90 A6
Ellerslie Ind Est SW2 160 A6
Ellerslie Rd W12 112 B5
Ellerton Ct W3 110 D4
Ellerton Gdns RM9 80 C1
Ellerton Lo N3 29 C1
Ellerton Rd
Barnes SW13 134 A4
Dagenham RM9 80 C1
Surbiton KT6 198 B1
Wandsworth SW17,
SW18 158 B3
Wimbledon SW20 178 A3
Ellery Ho SE17 262 D3
Ellery Rd SE19 183 B3
Ellery St SE15 140 B3
Ellesborough Cl WD19 22 C5
Ellesmere Ave NW7 11 B1
Beckenham BR3 185 D1
Ellesmere Cl E11 54 D4
Ruislip HA4 39 A2
Ellesmere Ct
Chiswick W4 133 B6
Lewisham SE12 165 A3
Penge SE20 184 B1
Ellesmere Gdns IG4 56 A3
Ellesmere Gr EN5 13 B6
Ellesmere Rd E3 97 A5
NW10 68 A3
Chiswick W4 133 B6
Greenford UB6 86 A3
Twickenham TW1 153 C5
Ellesmere St E14 97 D1
Ellies Mews TW15 148 A2
Ellingfort Rd E8 74 B1
Ellingham Prim Sch
KT9 213 D1
Ellingham Rd E15 76 B4
W12 112 A4
Chessington KT9 213 D2
Ellington Ct N14 15 D2
Ellington Ho SE1 262 B5
Ellington Rd N10 49 B5
Feltham TW13 171 D6
Hounslow TW3 129 D3
Ellington St N7 72 C2
Elliot Cl E15 76 C1
Wembley HA9 66 C5
Elliot Ct 5 N15 51 D5
Elliot Rd NW4 46 B3
SW9 138 D5
Elliott Ave HA4 62 B6
Elliott Gdns TW17 192 C5
Elliott Rd SW9 138 D4
W4 111 C2
Bromley BR2 209 D5
Stanmore HA7 25 A4
Thornton Heath CR7 204 D5
Elliott Sch SW15 156 C5
Elliott's Pl N1 234 D5
Elliott Sq NW3 70 C1
Elliott's Row
SE11 116 D2 261 D4
Ellis Cl HA8 27 C4
NW10 68 C2
SE9 167 A2
Elliscombe Mount 11
SE7 143 C6
Elliscombe Rd SE7 143 C6
Ellis Ct W7 86 D2
Ellisfield Dr SW15 156 A4
Ellis Franklin Ct NW8 229 A4
Ellis Ho E17 54 A4
SE17 262 C2
Ellison Gdns UB2 107 B2
Ellison Ho 1 SE13 142 A3
Ellison Rd DA15 167 B3
Barnes SW13 133 D3
Streatham SW16 182 A3
Ellis Rd Mitcham CR4 202 D3
Southall UB2 108 A5
Ellis St SW1 115 A2 258 A4
Ellistoun Ho 14 SE18 122 C2
Ellora Rd SW16 181 D5
Ellswood Ct 18 KT6 197 D2
Ellsworth St E2 96 B4
Ellwood Ct 1 W9 91 D3
Elmar Rd N15 51 B5
Elm Ave Ealing W5 110 B5
Ruislip HA4 40 B2
Elmbank N14 16 A4
Elmbank Dr BR1 187 D1
Elm Bank Gdns SW13 133 C3
Elm Bank Mans SW13 133 C3
Elmbank Way W7 86 B2
Elmbourne Dr DA17 125 D2
Elmbourne Rd SW17 159 B1
Elmbridge Ave KT5 199 A3
Elmbridge Cl HA4 40 A3
Elmbridge Dr HA4 40 A3
Elmbridge Wlk E8 74 A1
Elmbrook 2 E18 55 A6
Elmbrook Cl TW16 172 B2
Elmbrook Gdns SE9 144 A1
Elmbrook Rd SM1 217 B4
Elm Cl N19 71 C6
NW4 46 D4
Buckhurst Hill IG9 21 D2
Carshalton SM5 202 D1
Harrow HA2 41 D3
Hayes UB3 84 A1
South Croydon CR2 221 C2
Tolworth KT5 199 A2
Twickenham TW13,TW2 151 D2
Wanstead E11 55 B3
West Barnes SW20 200 C5
Elmcote HA5 22 D1
Elmcourt Rd SE21,
SE27 160 D2
Elm Court Sch SE27 161 A2
Elm Cres W5 110 A4
Kingston KT2 176 A2
Elmcroft N6 49 C2
N8 50 B4
Elmcroft Ave DA15 168 A5
NW11 47 B2
Enfield N9 18 B5
Wanstead E11 55 B5
Elmcroft Cl
Chessington KT9 214 A5
Ealing W5 87 D1
Feltham TW14 149 D5
Wanstead E11 55 B5
Elmcroft Cres NW11 47 A2
Harrow HA2 41 C6
Elmcroft Dr
Ashford TW15 170 C5
Chessington KT9 214 A5
Elmcroft Gdns NW9 44 C4
Elmcroft St E5 74 C4
Elmcroft Terr UB8 82 C1
Elm Ct EC4 251 A6
4 N3 29 C2
SE13 142 B2
SW9 138 C4
42 W2 91 C2
5 Ashford TW16 171 D3
Catford SE6 163 D3
Chingford E4 36 A4
Mitcham CR4 180 D1
Elmdale Rd N13 32 B5
Elmdene KT5 199 A1
Elmdene Cl BR3 207 B4
Elmdene Rd SE18 122 D1
Elmdon Rd
Hatton, Hatton Cross
TW6 127 D2
Hounslow TW5 129 A3
Elm Dr Harrow HA2 41 D3
Sunbury TW16 172 C1
Elmer Cl EN2 4 B2
Elmer Ct SW6 135 A3
Elmer Gdns
Edgware HA8 26 D3
Isleworth TW7 130 B2
Elmer Ho NW1 237 A4
Elmer Rd SE6 164 A4
Elmer's Dr TW11 175 B4
Elmers End Rd BR3,
SE20 206 C6
Elmers End Sta BR3 206 D5
Elmerside Rd BR3 207 A5
Elmers Rd SE25 206 A2
Elmfield Ave N8 50 A4
Mitcham CR4 181 A2
Teddington TW11 174 D5
Elmfield Cl HA1 64 C6
Elmfield Ct DA16 146 B4
Elmfield Ho 17 N2 30 B1
6 N5 73 A3
W9 91 C3
Elmfield Mans 5
SW17 159 A2
Elmfield Pk BR1 209 A6
Elmfield Rd BR1 209 A6
E17 52 D3
N2 48 B6
Chingford E4 20 B2
Southall UB2 107 A3
Upper Tooting SW17 159 B2
Elmfield Way W9 91 C2
South Croydon CR2 221 D1
Elm Friars Wlk NW1 71 D1
Elmgate Ave TW13 150 C1
Elmgate Gdns HA8 27 B6
Elm Gdns N2 48 A6
Claygate KT10 212 D2
Enfield EN2 5 B5
Mitcham CR4 203 D5
Elm Gn W3 89 C1
Elm Gr BR6 211 D1
N8 50 A3
NW2 68 D4
SE15 140 A3
Harrow HA2 41 C2
Kingston KT2 176 A2
Sutton SM1 217 D4
Wimbledon SW19 179 A3
Woodford IG8 36 D5
Yiewsley UB7 104 B6
Elmgreen Cl 8 E15 98 C6
Elmgrove Cres HA1 43 A4
Elmgrove Fst & Mid Schs
HA3 43 A5
Elmgrove Gdns HA1 43 A4
Elm Grove Par SM6 219 A5
Elm Grove Rd W5 110 A4
Elmgrove Rd
Croydon CR0 206 B2
Harrow HA1 42 D4
Elm Grove Rd SW13 134 A3
Elm Hall Gdns E11 55 B3
Elm Hatch HA5 23 B3
Elm Ho 4 E14 120 A4
2 Kingston KT2 176 B3
Elmhurst DA17 147 A6
Elmhurst Ave N2 48 B6
Mitcham CR4 181 B3
Elmhurst Ct CR0 221 B3
Elmhurst Dr E18 37 A1
Elmhurst Lo 3 SM2 218 A1
Elmhurst Mans SW4 137 D2
Elmhurst Prim Sch E7 77 B1
Elmhurst Rd E7 77 B1
Chislehurst SE9 166 A1
Enfield EN3 6 C6
Tottenham N17 33 D1
Elmhurst Sch CR2 221 B3
Elmhurst St SW4 137 D2
Elmhurst Villas SE15 140 C1
Elmington Cl DA5 169 D5
Elmington Rd SE5 139 B5
Elmira St SE13 141 D2
Elm La SE6 163 B2
Elm Lawn Cl UB8 60 A1
Elmlea Dr UB3 83 D2
Elmlee Cl BR7 188 B4
Elmley Cl 12 E6 100 A2
Elmley St SE18 123 B2
Elm Lo SW6 134 D4
Elmore Cl HA0 88 A5
Elmore Ho SW9 138 D3
Elmore Rd E11 76 B5
Enfield EN3 6 D5
Elmore St N1 73 B1
Elm Park Ave N15 52 A3
Elm Park Ct HA5 40 C6
Elm Park Gdns NW4 46 D4
SW10 114 B1 256 C1
Elm Park Ho SW10 256 C1
Elm Park La
SW3 114 B1 256 C1
Elm Park Mans SW10 266 B6
Elm Park Rd N3 29 B3
SW3 136 B6 266 C6
Edmonton N21 17 A4
Pinner HA5 40 D6
South Norwood SE25 205 D6
Walthamstow E10 53 A1
Elm Pk Stanmore HA7 25 C5
Streatham SW2 160 B4
Elm Pl SW7 114 B1 256 C2
Elm Quay SW8 269 C5
Elm Rd E11 76 B6
E17 54 A4
E7 76 D2
Barnet EN5 1 B1
Beckenham BR3 185 B1
Chessington KT9 214 A4
Elm Rd *continued*
Claygate KT10 212 D2
East Bedfont TW14 149 B4
Hackbridge SM6 203 A1
Kingston KT2 176 B2
Kingston KT3 199 B6
Mortlake SW14 133 A1
Sidcup DA14 190 A6
South Norwood CR7 205 B5
Stoneleigh KT17 215 D2
Tottenham N22 32 D2
Wembley HA9 66 A3
Elm Rd W SM4 201 B2
Elm Row NW3 70 A5
Elms Ave N10 49 B6
NW4 46 D4
Elmscott Gdns N21 17 A5
Elmscott Rd BR1 186 D5
Elms Cotts 1 CR4 180 D1
Elms Cres SW4 159 D5
Elms Ct Merton SW19 179 D3
Wembley HA0 65 A4
Elmsdale Rd E17 53 B5
Elms Gdns
Dagenham RM9 81 B4
Wembley HA0 65 A4
Elmshaw Rd SW15 156 A6
Elmshurst Cres N2 48 B5
Elmside CR0 223 D2
Elmside Rd HA9 66 C5
Elms La HA0 65 A5
Elmsleigh Ave HA3 43 C5
Elmsleigh Ct SM1 217 D5
Elmsleigh Ho TW2 152 B2
Elmsleigh Rd TW2 152 B2
Elmslie Ct SE9 166 C5
Elmslie Point 2 E3 97 B2
Elms Mews W2 246 C6
Elms Park Ave HA0 65 A4
Elms Rd SW4 159 C6
Harrow HA3 24 C3
Elm St WC1 94 B3 240 D5
Elmstead Ave BR7 188 B5
Wembley HA9 66 B6
Elmstead Cl N20 13 C2
West Ewell KT19 215 C3
Elmstead Gdns KT4 216 A5
Elmstead Glade BR7 188 B4
Elmstead La BR7 188 B5
Elmstead Rd IG3 79 D6
Elmstead Woods Sta
BR7 188 A4
Elmsted Cres DA16 146 C6
Elms The E12 78 A2
NW10 89 C5
NW9 45 A3
Ashford TW15 170 C5
Barnes SW13 133 D2
Claygate KT10 212 D1
Croydon CR0 205 A1
Elmstone Rd SW6 265 A2
Elmsway TW15 170 C5
Elmsworth Ave TW3 129 D3
Elm Terr NW2 69 C5
3 SE9 166 C5
Harrow HA3 24 B2
Elmton Ct NW8 236 C6
Elmton Way E5 74 A5
Elm Tree Ave KT10 196 C2
Elm Tree Cl
NW8 92 B4 229 C2
Ashford TW15 170 D5
Northolt UB5 85 B5
Elm Tree Ct NW8 229 C2
5 SE5 139 A4
18 SE7 143 C6
Elm Tree Rd
NW8 92 B4 229 C2
Elmtree Rd TW11 174 C5
Elm View Ct UB2 107 C2
Elm Way N11 31 A4
NW10 67 C4
North Cheam KT4 216 C5
West Ewell KT19 215 B3
Elm Wlk NW3 69 C6
Orpington BR6 226 B5
West Barnes SW20 200 D5
Elmwood Ave
Bowes Park N13 32 A5
Feltham TW13 150 B1
Harrow HA3 43 B3
Elmwood Cl
Hackbridge SM6 219 B6
Stoneleigh KT17 216 A1
Elmwood Cres NW9 45 A5
Elmwood Ct SW11 268 C2
Wembley HA0 65 A5
Elmwood Dr DA5 169 A4
Stoneleigh KT17 216 A1
Elmwood Gdns W7 86 C1
Elmwood Inf Sch CR0 204 D3
Elmwood Jun Sch
CR0 204 D2
Elm Wood Prim Sch
SE27 161 B1
Elmwood Rd SE24 161 B6
Chiswick W4 133 A6
Mitcham CR4 202 D6
Thornton Heath CR0 204 D2
Elmworth Gr SE21 161 B2
Elnathan Mews W9 91 D3
Elphinstone Ct SW16 182 A4
Elphinstone Rd E17 35 B1
Elphinstone St N5 72 D4
Elrington Rd E8 74 A2
Woodford IG8 37 A5
Elsa Ct BR3 185 B2
Elsa Rd DA16 146 C3
Elsa St E1 97 A2
Elsdale St E9 74 C2
Elsden Mews E2 96 C5
Elsden Rd N17 33 D2
Elsenham Rd E12 78 C3
Elsenham St SW18,
SW19 157 B2
Elsfield NW5 71 B3
Elsham Rd E11 76 C4
W14 113 A4 244 A1
Elsham Terr W14 244 A1
Elsiedene Rd N21 17 A4
Elsie Lane Ct W2 91 D2
Elsiemaud Rd SE4 163 B6
Elsie Rd SE22 139 D1
Elsinge Rd EN1 6 B6
Elsinore Ave TW19 148 A4
Elsinore Gdns NW2 69 A5
Elsinore Ho N1 234 A5
12 SE5 139 A3
7 SE7 122 A2
Elsinore Rd SE23 163 A3
Elsinore Way TW9 132 D2
Elsley Ct HA9 66 D2
Elsley Prim Sch HA9 66 B2
Elsley Rd SW11 137 A2
Elsley Sch SW11 137 A2
Elspeth Rd SW11 136 D1
Wembley HA0 66 A3
Elsrick Ave SM4 201 C4
Elstan Way CR0 207 A2
Elstead Ct SM4 201 A4
Elstead Ho 9 SW2 160 B4
Elsted St SE17 117 B2 262 D3
Elstow Cl SE9 166 B6
Ruislip HA4 40 D2
Elstow Gdns RM9 103 A6
Elstow Grange NW6 68 D1
Elstow Rd RM9 103 A6
Elstree Gdns DA17 125 A2
Edmonton N9 18 B3
Ilford IG1 79 A3
Elstree Hill BR1 186 C3
Elstree Hill N WD6 9 D6
Elstree Hill S WD6 9 D4
Elstree Ho 3 HA7 25 C6
Elstree Pk WD6 11 B5
Elstree Rd Bushey WD23 8 C4
Elstree WD6 9 A5
Elswick Rd SE13 141 D3
Elswick St SW6 136 A3
Elsworth Cl TW14 149 C3
Elsworthy KT7 196 C3
Elsworthy Rd
NW3 92 C6 230 A6
Elsworthy Rise NW3 70 C1
Elsworthy Terr NW3 70 C1
Elsynge Rd SW18 158 B6
Elsynge Road Mans
SW18 158 B6
Eltham CE Prim Sch
SE9 166 B6
Eltham Coll SE9 165 D2
Eltham Green Rd SE9 165 C6
Eltham Green Sch
SE9 165 D5
Eltham High St SE9 166 B5
Eltham Hill SE9 166 A6
Eltham Hill Sch SE9 166 A5
Eltham Hill Tech Coll for
Girls SE9 166 A5
Eltham Palace* SE9 166 A4
Eltham Palace Rd SE9 165 D5
Eltham Park Gdns
SE9 144 C1
Eltham Rd SE9,SE12 165 B6
Eltham Sta SE9 166 B6
Elthiron Rd
SW6 135 C4 265 B1
Elthorne Ave W7 109 A4
Elthorne Ct NW9 45 B3
Feltham TW13 150 C3
Elthorne Park High Sch
W7 108 D3
Elthorne Park Rd W7 109 A4
Elthorne Rd N19 71 D6
NW9 45 B2
Elthorne Way NW9 45 B3
Elthruda Rd SE13 164 B5
Eltisley Rd IG1 78 D4
Elton Ave Barnet EN5 13 B6
Wembley HA0 65 B3
Wembley UB6 64 D2
Elton Cl KT1 175 C3
Elton Ho 3 E3 97 B6
Elton Lo 4 W5 110 A6
Elton Pl N16 73 C3
Elton Rd KT2 176 C2
Elton St 11 N16 73 C3
Eltringham St SW18 136 A1
Elvaston Ct EN5 12 C6
Elvaston Mews SW7 256 B6
Elvaston Pl
SW7 114 A3 256 B5
Elveden Ho 13 SW9 138 D1
Elveden Pl NW10 88 C5
Elveden Rd NW10 88 C5
Elvendon Rd N13 32 A4
Elver Gdns 6 E2 96 A4
Elverson Rd SE8 141 D3
Elverson Rd Sta SE8 141 D3
Elverton St
SW1 115 D2 259 C4
Elvin Ct NW9 45 A2
Elvington Gn BR2 208 D4
Elvington La NW9 27 C2
Elvin Ho 2 E9 74 C2
Elvino Rd SE26 185 A5
Elvis Rd NW2 68 C2
Elwill Way BR3 208 B5
Elwin St E2 96 A4
Elwood Ho N5 72 D5
Elwood St N4,N5 72 D5
Elworth Ho SW8 270 D3
Elwyn Gdns SE12 165 A4
Ely Cl SW20 177 D1
Ely Cottages SW8 270 C3
Ely Court Flats SW6 264 A1
Ely Ct KT1 198 C6
Ely Gdns
Borehamwood WD6 11 B6
Redbridge IG1 56 A2
Ely Ho 22 SE15 140 A5
Barnet EN4 2 C1
Elyne Rd N4 50 C3
Ely Pl EC1 94 C2 241 B3
Ely Rd E10 54 A2
Hatton TW6 127 D3
Hounslow TW4 128 C2
Thornton Heath CR0 205 B4
Elysian Ave BR5 211 D3
Elysium Gate 7 SW6 135 B3
Elysium Pl SW6 135 B3
Elysium St SW6 135 B3
Elystan Bsns Ctr UB4 106 C6
Elystan Pl
SW3 114 D1 257 C2
Elystan St
SW3 114 C2 257 B3
Elystan Wlk N1 234 A5
Elyston Ct SW15 156 B6
Emanuel Ave W3 89 A1
Emanuel Ct W3 89 B1
Emanuel Sch SW11 158 C6
Embankment SW15 134 D3
Embankment Gdns
SW3 136 D6 267 D6
Embankment Pier
WC2 116 B4 250 B4
Embankment Pl WC2 250 B4
Embankment Sta
WC2 116 A5 250 B4
Embankment The
TW1 153 A3
Embassy Ct DA14 168 B1
Embassy Ct DA16 146 B2
N11 31 D4
NW8 229 D3
Kingston KT6 197 D4
7 Wallington SM6 219 B2
7 Wanstead E18 55 A6
Ealing W5 110 B6
Embassy Gdns BR3 185 B2
Embassy Ho 2 NW6 69 C1
Embassy Lo N3 29 B1
Emba St SE16 118 A4
Ember Cl BR5 211 A2
Embercourt Rd KT10,
KT7,KT8 196 C3
Ember Ct 14 NW9 27 D1
2 W12 111 C3
Ember Farm Ave KT8 196 B3
Ember Farm Way KT8 196 B4
Ember Gdns KT10,KT8 196 C2
Ember Ho 8 BR1 186 B5
Ember La KT10,KT8 196 B2
Emberson Ho 7 E17 54 A5
Emberton SE5 139 C6
Emberton Ct EC1 234 C1
Embleton Rd SE13 141 D1
Embleton Wlk TW12 173 B5
Embley Point 2 E5 74 B4
Embry Cl HA7 25 A6
Embry Dr HA7 25 A4
Embry Way HA7 25 A6
Emden Cl UB7 104 C4
Emden St SW6 265 D2
Emerald Cl E16 100 A1
Emerald Ct N12 30 A6
Emerald Gdns RM8 59 C1
Emerald Sq UB2 106 D3
Emerald St WC1 94 B2 240 C4
Emerson Gdns HA3 44 B3
Emerson Ho N16 73 C3
Emerson Rd IG1 56 C2
Emerson St
SE1 117 A5 252 A4
Emerton Cl DA6 147 A1
Emery Hill St SW1 259 B5

Emery St SE1 116 C3 261 B6
Emilia Cl EN3 18 B6
Emily Pl N7 72 C4
Emily St 7 E16 98 D1
Emlyn Gdns 3 W12 111 C3
Emlyn Rd W12 111 D3
Emmanuel CE Prim Sch
NW6 69 C3
Emmanuel Ct 9 E10 53 D2
Emmanuel Ho SE11 261 A3
Dulwich SE21 161 B1
Emmanuel Rd
Streatham SW12 159 D3
Northwood HA6 22 A3
Emma Rd E13 98 D5
Emma St E2 96 B5
Emmeline Ct KT12 194 C2
Emminster NW6 91 D6
Emmott Ave IG6 57 A4
Emmott Cl E1 97 A3
NW11 48 A3
Emperor's Gate
SW7 114 A2 256 A4
Empingham Ho 20
SE8 118 D2
Empire Ave N18 33 A4
Empire Ct HA9 66 D5
Empire Ho SW3 257 A5
Edmonton N18 33 B4
Empire Par
Edmonton N18 33 B4
Wembley HA9 66 C5
Empire Rd UB6 65 C1
Empire Sq N19 72 A5
Empire Way HA9 66 C4
Empire Wharf E3 97 A6
Empire Wharf Rd E14 120 B2
Empress Ave
Chingford E4 35 D3
Ilford IG1 78 C6
Wanstead E12 77 D6
Woodford IG8 36 D3
Empress Dr BR7 188 D4
Empress Mews 37 SE5 139 A3
Empress Par E4 35 C3
Empress Pl
SW5 113 C1 255 A1
Empress St SE17 139 A6
Empson St E3 97 D3
Emsworth Cl N9 18 C3
Emsworth St SW2 160 B2
Emu Rd SW8 137 B3
Ena Rd SW16 204 A6
Enard Ho 27 E3 97 B5
Enbrook St W10 91 A4
Enclave Ct EC1 241 C6
Endale Cl SM5 218 D6
Endeavour Way
Barking IG11 102 A5
Thornton Heath CR0 204 A2
Wimbledon SW19 179 D6
Endell St WC2 94 A1 240 A1
Enderby St SE10 120 C1
Enderfield Ct BR7 188 C2
Enderley Cl HA3 24 C2
Enderley Ho SE19 183 D2
Enderley Rd HA3 24 C2
Endersby Rd EN5 12 C6
Endersleigh Gdns NW4 46 A5
Endlebury Ct 3 E4 20 B2
Endlebury Rd E4 20 A2
Endlesham Ct 2
SW12 159 A4
Endlesham Rd SW12 159 A4
Endsleigh Gdns
WC1 93 D3 239 C6
Ilford IG1 56 D1
Kingston KT6 197 C3
Endsleigh Ind Est UB2 107 B2
Endsleigh Mans 4
SW16 160 A1
Endsleigh Pl WC1 239 D6
Endsleigh Rd
Ealing W13 109 A6
Southall UB2 107 A2
Endsleigh St
WC1 93 D3 239 D6
Endway KT5 198 D2
Endwell Rd SE4 141 A3
Endymion Rd N4 50 D2
SW2 160 B5
Energen Cl NW10 67 C1
NW10 67 C2
Enfield Chase Sta EN2 5 A2
Enfield Cloisters 7 N1 95 C4
Enfield Coll EN3 6 C2
Enfield Gram Sch EN2 5 B2
Enfield Gram Sch Lower
EN1 5 B3
Enfield Ho 24 SW9 138 A3
Enfield Lock Sta EN3 7 A6
Enfield Rd E8,N1 73 C1
W3 110 D4
Brentford TW8 109 D1
Enfield EN2 4 A2
Hatton TW6 127 C3
Enfield Road Rdbt
TW6 127 C3
Enfield Town Sta EN1 5 B2
Enfield Wlk TW8 109 D1
Enford St W1 92 D2 237 C4
Engadine Cl CR0 221 D5
Engadine St SW18 157 C3
Engate St SE13 142 A1
Engel Pk NW7 28 C4
Engineer Cl SE18 144 C6
Engineers Way HA9 66 C4
England's La NW3 70 D2
England Way KT3 199 A5
Englefield NW1 232 A1
Englefield Cl Enfield EN2 4 C3
Orpington BR5 211 D5
Thornton Heath CR0 205 A3
Englefield Path BR5 211 D5
Englefield Rd N1 73 C1
Engleheart Dr TW14 149 D5
Engleheart Rd SE6 164 A4
Englewood Rd SW12 159 C5
English Gardening Sch The
SW3 136 D6 267 C6
English Grounds SE1 253 A3
English Martyrs RC Prim
Sch E1 95 D1 243 D1
English St E3 97 B3
Enid St SE16 117 D3 263 D6
Enid Stacy Ho 11 N19 49 D2
Enmore Ave SE25 206 A4
Enmore Ct SW14 155 B6
Enmore Gdns SW14 155 B6
Enmore Rd
Croydon SE25 206 A4
Putney SW15 156 C6
Southall UB1 85 C3
Ennerdale Ave HA3,HA7 43 C6
Ennerdale Cl
Cheam SM1 217 B4
East Bedfont TW14 149 D3
Ennerdale Ct E11 55 A2
Ennerdale Dr NW9 45 C4
Ennerdale Gdns HA9 43 C1
Ennerdale Ho 3 N4 51 B2
Ennerdale Rd DA7 147 C4
Richmond TW9 132 B3
Ennersdale Prim Sch
SE13 164 B6
Ennersdale Rd SE13 164 B6
Ennis Ho 16 E14 97 D1
Ennismore Ave W4 111 D2
Greenford UB6 64 C3
Ennismore Gdns
SW7 114 C3 257 A6
Thames Ditton KT7 196 C3
Ennismore Gdns Mews
SW7 114 C3 257 A6
Ennismore Mews
SW7 114 C3 257 A6
Ennismore St
SW7 114 C3 257 A6
Ennis Rd N4 50 C1
SE18 145 A6
Ennor Ct KT4 216 C4
Ensbury Ho SW8 270 C4
Ensign Cl TW19 148 A3
Ensign Ct 7 E1 118 A6
Ensign Dr N13 17 A1
Ensign St E1 118 A6
Ensign Way TW19 148 A3
Enslin Rd SE9 166 C4
Ensor Mews SW7 256 C2
Enstone Rd Enfield EN3 7 A2
Ickenham UB10 60 B5
Enterprise Cl CR0 204 C1
Enterprise Ho
Barking IG11 101 D4
Chingford E4 20 A4
Walton-on-T KT12 194 B2
Enterprise Row N15 51 D4
Enterprise Way NW10 90 A4
SW18 135 C1
Teddington TW11 174 D4
Enterprize Way SE8 119 B2
Enton Pl TW3 129 D1
Epirus Mews SW6 265 A4
Epirus Rd SW6 135 B5 264 D4
Epping Cl E14 119 C2
Romford RM7 59 D6
Epping Forest* IG10 21 B6
Epping Glade E4 20 A5
Epping Ho E5 74 A6
Epping New Rd IG9 21 B5
Epping Pl N1 72 C2
Epping Way E4 19 D5
Epple Rd SW6 135 B4 264 D2
Epsom Cl DA7 147 D2
Northolt UB5 63 B3
Epsom & Ewell High Sch
KT19 215 A3
Epsom Rd E10 54 A3
Croydon CR0 220 C4
Ilford IG3 57 D3
Morden SM4 201 B2
Epsom Sq TW6 127 D3
Epstein Rd SE28 124 B5
Epworth Rd TW7,TW8 131 B5
Epworth St EC2 95 B3 242 D5
Equity Sq 29 E2 95 D4
Erasmus St
SW1 115 D2 259 D3
Erconwald St W12 89 D1
Erebus Dr SE28 123 B4
Eresby Dr BR3 207 C1
Eresby Ho SW7 247 B1
Eresby Pl NW6 69 C1
Erica Ct SW4 270 B1
Erica Gdns CR0 223 D5
Erica Ho SE4 141 B2
Wood Green N22 32 C2
Erica St W12 112 A6
Eric Cl E7 77 A4
Eric Clarke La IG11 101 A4
Ericcson Cl SW18 157 C6
Eric Fletcher Ct 7 N1 73 A1
Eric Macdonald Ho
SW6 265 B1
Eric Rd E7 77 A4
NW10 67 D2
Dagenham RM6 58 D2
Eric Shipman Terr 2
E13 99 A3
Ericson Ho N16 51 D1
SE13 142 B1
Eric St E3 97 B3
Eric Wilkins Ho 13
SE1 118 A1
Eridge Ho SE22 139 D2
Eridge Rd W4 111 B3
Erin Ct BR1 186 C3
Erindale SE18 145 B6
Erindale Ct 1 BR3 185 C2
Erindale Terr SE18 145 B6
Erith Rd DA7 147 D2
Belvedere DA17 125 D1
Erlanger Rd SE14 140 D3
Erlesmere Gdns W13 109 A3
Ermine Cl TW4 128 C3
Ermine Ho 3 N17 33 D3
Ermine Rd N15 51 D3
SE13 141 D1
Ermine Side EN1 18 A6
Ermington Rd BR7,SE9 167 A2
Ernald Ave E6 100 A5
Erncroft Way TW1 152 D5
Ernest Ave SE27 182 D6
Ernest Bevin Coll
SW17 158 C2
Ernest Cl BR3 207 C4
Ernest Cotts KT17 215 D1
Ernest Gdns W4 132 D6
Ernest Gr BR3 207 B4
Ernest Rd KT1 176 D1
Ernest Richards Twr
E17 53 B3
Ernest Simmonds Ho
SE14 140 C3
Ernest Sq KT1 176 D1
Ernest St E1 96 D3
Ernle Rd SW20 178 C3
Ernshaw Pl SW15 157 A6
Eros (Shaftesbury Meml)*
W1 115 D6 249 C5
Erpingham Rd SW15 134 C2
Erridge Rd SW19 179 C1
Errington Rd W9 91 B3
Errol Gdns Hayes UB4 84 B3
West Barnes KT3 200 A5
Errol St EC1 95 A3 242 B5
Erskine Cl SM1 218 C5
Erskine Cres N17 52 B5
Erskine Hill NW11 47 C4
Erskine Ho 7 SE7 143 C6
SW1 259 A1
Erskine Rd E17 53 B5
NW3 70 D1
Carshalton SM1,SM5 218 B5
Erwood Rd SE7 122 A1
Esam Way SW16 182 C5
Escot Rd TW16 171 C3
Escott Gdns SE9 188 A6
Escot Way EN5 12 C6
Escreet Gr SE18 122 C2
Escuan Lo N5 73 A3
Esher Ave Cheam SM3 216 D5
Walton-on-T KT12 194 A1
Esher Church Sch
KT10 212 A3
Esher Cl DA5 169 A3
Esher Coll KT7 196 C2
Esher Cres TW6 127 D3
Esher Gdns SW19 156 D2
Esher Ho 8 SW8 137 D3
Esher Mews 4 CR4 202 D6
Esher Park Ave KT10 212 A3
Esher Rd
East Molesey KT8 196 B4
Ilford IG3 79 C5
Esher Sta KT10 212 B6
Eskdale NW1 232 A3
Eskdale Ave UB5 85 B6
Eskdale Cl HA9 65 D6
Eskdale Rd DA7 147 C4
Esk Ho E3 97 B3
Eskmont Ridge SE19 183 C3
Esk Rd E13 99 B3
Esmar Cres NW9 46 A2
Esme Ho SW15 133 D1
Esmeralda Rd SE1 118 A2
Esmond Ct W8 255 D6
Esmond Gdns W4 111 B2
Esmond Rd NW6 91 B6
W4 111 B3
Esmond St SW15 135 A1
Esparto St SW18 157 D4
Essan Ho W13 87 B2
Essenden Rd
Belvedere DA17 125 C1
South Croydon CR2 221 C1
Essendine Mans W9 91 C4
Essendine Prim Sch
W9 91 C4
Essendine Rd W9 91 C4
Essex Ave TW7 130 C2
Essex Cl E17 53 A5
Romford RM7 59 D5
Ruislip HA4 40 D1
West Barnes SM4 200 D2
Essex Ct EC4 241 A1
W6 112 C3
Barnes SW13 133 D3
South Norwood SE19 183 B4
Essex Gdns N4 50 D3
Essex Gr SE19 183 B4
Essex Ho 2 E14 97 D1
4 Acton W3 88 C1
Essex Lo 5 N10 31 B1
Essex Mans E11 54 B2
Essex Park Mews W3 111 C5
Essex Pk N3 29 D4
Essex Pl W4 111 A2
Essex Place Sq W4 111 B2
Essex Prim Sch E12 78 A3
Essex Rd E10 54 A3
E12 78 A2
E17 53 A3
N1 73 A1 234 D6
NW10 67 C1
W3 111 A6
W4 111 B2
Barking IG11 79 B1
Chingford, Chingford Green
E4 20 C3
Enfield EN2 5 B1
Ilford RM6 58 C2
Romford RM7 59 D5
Woodford E18 37 B1
Essex Rd S E11 54 B2
Essex Road Sta N1 73 A1
Essex St E7 77 A3
SE18 123 A3
WC2 116 C6 251 A6
Essex Twr 4 SE20 184 B2
Essex Villas
W8 113 C4 245 A1
Essian St E1 97 A2
Essington SW15 157 A5
Essoldo Way HA8 44 B6
Estate Way E10 53 B1
Estcourt Rd
SW6 135 B5 264 C4
Croydon SE25 206 B3
Estella Ave KT3 200 B5
Estella Ho W11 112 D6
Estelle Rd NW3 70 D4
Esterbrooke St SW1 259 C3
Este Rd SW11 136 C2
Esther Cl N21 16 C4
Esther Rd E11 54 C2
Estoria Cl 22 SW2 160 C4
Estreham Rd SW16 181 D4
Estridge Cl TW3 129 C1
Estuary Cl IG11 102 B4
Eswyn Rd SW17 180 D5
Etal Ho N1 72 D1
Etchingham Ct N12 30 A3
Etchingham Park Rd
N3 29 D3
Etchingham Rd E15 76 A4
Etfield Gr DA14 190 B5
Ethelbert Cl BR1 209 A6
Ethelbert Gdns IG2 56 C4
Ethelbert Ho E9 75 A4
Ethelbert Rd
Bromley BR1,BR2 209 A6
Wimbledon SW20 178 D2
Ethelbert St SW12 159 B3
Ethel Brooks Ho SE18 144 D6
Ethelburga St
SW11 136 C4 267 B2
Ethelburga Twr SW11 267 B2
Ethel Cotts RM6 58 B6
Ethel Davis Sch RM6 58 B4
Etheldene Ave N10 49 C5
Ethelden Rd W12 112 B5
Ethel Rankin Ct 8
SW6 135 B3
Ethel Rd Ashford TW15 170 A5
Newham E16 99 B1
Ethel St SE17 262 B3
Ethelworth Ct 4 SW2 160 C3
Etheridge Rd NW2 46 C2
Etherley Rd N15 51 A4
Etherow St SE22 162 A4
Etherstone Gn SW16 182 C6
Etherstone Rd SW16 182 C6
Ethnard Rd SE15 140 B6
Ethronvi Rd DA7 147 A2
Etloe Ho E10 53 C1
Etloe Rd E10 75 C6
Eton Ave N12 30 A3
NW3 70 C1
East Barnet EN4 14 C5
Heston TW5 129 C6
New Malden KT3 199 B5
Wembley HA0 65 C4
Eton Cl SW18 157 D4
Eton College Rd NW3 70 D2
Eton Ct NW3 70 B1
Wembley HA0 65 C4
Eton Garages 11 NW3 70 C2
Eton Gr NW9 44 C5
SE13 142 C2
Eton Hall NW3 70 D2
Eton Ho N5 72 D4
Eton Manor Ct E10 75 C6
Eton Pl NW1 71 A1
Eton Rd NW3 70 D2
Harlington UB3 127 D5
Ilford IG1 79 B4
Eton Rise NW3 70 D2
Eton St TW10 154 A6
Eton Villas NW3 70 D2
Etta St SE8 141 A6
Ettrick Ho 8 E5 74 B6
Ettrick St E14 98 A1
Etwell Pl KT5 198 B3
Eugene Cotter Ho
SE17 262 D3
Eugenia Rd SE16 118 C2
Eugenie Mews BR7 188 D2
Eureka Rd 8 KT1 176 C1
Euro Bsns Ctr 3 E15 98 D6
Euro Cl NW10 68 A2
Eurolink Bsns Ctr
SW2 160 C6
Europa Pl EC1 235 A1
Europe Rd SE18 122 B3
Eusdon Cl N9 18 B1
Eustace Ho SE11 260 C4
Eustace Pl SE18 122 B2
Eustace Rd E6 100 A4
SW6 135 C5 265 A4
Dagenham RM6 58 D2
Euston Rd NW1 93 D3 239 B6
Thornton Heath CR0 204 C1
Euston Sq NW1 232 C1
Euston Square Sta
WC1 93 C3 239 B6
Euston St NW1 93 C4 232 B1
Euston Sta
NW1 93 D4 232 C1
Euston Underpass
NW1 239 A6
Evandale Rd SW9 138 C3
Evangelist Rd NW5 71 B4
Evans Cl E8 73 D2
Evans Gr TW13 151 C2
Evans Ho SW8 269 D3
34 W12 112 B6
Evans Rd SE6 164 C2
Evanston Ave E4 36 A3
Evanston Gdns IG4 56 A3
Eva Rd RM6 58 D2
Evelina Mans 8 SE5 139 B5
Evelina Rd SE15 140 C3
Penge SE20 184 D3
Eveline Ct N10 49 B4
Eveline Lowe Prim Sch
SE1 118 A1
Eveline Rd CR4 180 D2
Evelyn Ave NW9 45 B5
Ruislip HA4 39 D2
Evelyn Cl TW2 151 D4
Evelyn Cres TW16 171 D2
Evelyn Ct E8 74 A4
N1 235 C3
W1 237 C1
Croydon CR0 206 A2
Evelyn Denington Ct 2
N1 72 D1
Evelyn Denington Rd
E6 100 A3
Evelyn Dr HA5 22 D3
Evelyn Fox Ct W10 90 C2
Evelyn Gdns
SW7 114 B1 256 C1
Richmond TW9 132 A1
Evelyn Gr Ealing W5 110 B5
Southall UB1 85 B1
Evelyn Ho 3 SW2 160 B6
W12 111 D4
Evelyn Rd E16 121 B5
E17 54 A5
W4 111 B3
Cockfosters EN4 2 D1
Richmond TW10 153 C1
Richmond TW9 132 A2
Wimbledon SW19 179 D4
Evelyns Cl UB8 82 C1
Evelyns Com Sch UB7 82 B1
Evelyn St SE8 119 A1
Evelyn Terr TW9 132 A2
Evelyn Way
Sunbury TW16 171 D2
Wallington SM6 219 D4
Evelyn Wlk N1 95 B5 235 C3
Evelyn Yd W1 239 C2
Evening Hill BR3 186 A3
Evenlode Ho 5 SE2 124 C4
Evenwood Cl SW15 157 A6
Everard Ave BR2 209 A1
Everard Ct N13 16 B1
Everard Ho 24 E1 96 A1
Everard Way HA9 66 A5
Everatt Cl SW18 157 B6
Eve Rd E11 76 C4
E15 98 C5
N17 51 C6
Isleworth TW7 131 A1
Everdale Ct N2 48 C5
Everdon Rd SW13 134 A6
Everest Ct
6 Chislehurst SE9 166 A2
South Norwood SE19 183 C2
Everest Pl E14 98 A2
Everest Rd SE9 166 B6
Stanwell TW19 148 A4
Everett Cl Bushey WD23 8 C3
Pinner HA5 39 D6
Everett Ho N7 72 C4
SE17 262 C2
Everett Wlk DA17 125 B1
Everglade Ho E17 35 B1
Everglades
Beckenham BR2 208 C6
Hounslow TW3 130 A2
Everglade Strand NW9 27 D2
Evergreen Cl SE20 184 C3
Evergreen Sq 3 E8 73 D1
Evergreen Way UB3 105 D6
Everilda St N1 233 D5
Evering Rd E5,N16 74 A5
Everington Rd N10 30 D1
Everington St W6 134 D6
Everitt Rd NW10 89 B4
Everleigh St N4 50 B1
Eversfield Ct SE12 165 B2
Eversfield Gdns HA8,
NW7 27 C3
Eversfield Rd TW9 132 B3
Evershed Ho E1 243 D2
Evershed Wlk W4 111 B2
Eversholt Ct EN5 14 A6
Eversholt St
NW1 93 C4 232 B3
Evershot Rd N4 50 B1
Eversleigh Ct N3 29 C3
Eversleigh Rd E6 99 D6
N3 29 B3
SW11 137 A3
New Barnet EN5 14 A6
Eversley Ave HA9 66 C6
Eversley Cl N21 16 B5
Eversley Cres
Hounslow TW7 130 B4
Ruislip HA4 61 D6
Southgate N21 16 C5
Eversley Ho 18 E2 96 A4
Eversley Mount N21 16 B5
Eversley Park Rd N21 16 B5
Eversley Pk SW19 178 B5
Eversley Prim Sch N21 16 B5
Eversley Rd
Greenwich SE7 143 B6
Kingston KT5 198 B4
South Norwood SE19 183 B3
Eversley Way CR0 223 C5
Everthorpe Rd SE15 139 D2
Everton Bldgs NW1 232 A1
Everton Ct HA0 65 D4
Everton Dr HA7 44 A6
Everton Rd CR0 206 A1
Evesham Ave E17 35 C1
Evesham Cl
Belmont SM2 217 C1
Greenford UB6 85 D5
Evesham Ct
2 Ealing W13 109 A5
2 Richmond TW10 154 B5
Evesham Gn SM4 201 D3
Evesham Ho 1 E2 96 C5
NW8 229 A5
SW1 258 D2
Evesham Rd E15 76 D1
N11 31 D5
Morden SM4 201 D3
Evesham St W11 112 D6
Evesham Way SW11 137 A2
Ilford IG5 56 C6
Evesham Wlk SE5 139 B3
SW9 138 C3
Evry Rd DA14 190 C4
Ewald Rd SW6 135 B3
Ewanrigg Terr IG8 37 C5
Ewart Gr N22 32 C2
Ewart Pl 10 E3 97 B5
Ewart Rd SE23 162 D4
Ewe Cl N7 72 A2
Ewell By-Pass KT17 216 A1
Ewell Court Ave KT19 215 C3
Ewell Park Gdns KT17 216 A1
Ewell Park Way KT17 216 A1

Ewell Rd
Cheam SM2,SM3 216 D2
Surbiton KT5,KT6 198 B2
Thames Ditton KT6,KT7 197 B2
Tolworth KT6 198 D1
Ewelme Rd SE23 162 C3
Ewen Cres SW2 160 C4
Ewen Ho N1 233 C5
Ewer St SE1 117 A5 252 A3
Ewhurst 19 SW15 156 D5
Ewhurst Cl E1 96 C2
Ewhurst Ct CR4 202 B6
Ewhurst Rd SE4 163 B5
Exbury Ho E9 74 C2
4 SW9 138 B1
Exbury Rd SE6 163 C2
Excel Ct WC2 249 D5
Excel Ex Ctr E16 121 B6
Excelsior Cl KT1 176 C1
Excelsior Gdns SE13 142 A3
Excelsior Ind Est SE16 140 C6
Exchange Arc EC2 243 B4
Exchange Cl N11 15 A2
Exchange Ct WC2 250 B5
Exchange Mans 2 NW11 47 B2
Exchange Pl EC2 243 A4
Exchange The IG1 78 D6
Exeforde Ave TW15 170 C6
Exeter Cl E6 100 B1
Exeter Ct NW6 91 C5
Kingston KT6 198 A4
Mitcham SW19 180 C3
Exeter Gdns IG1 56 B1
Exeter Ho 11 SE15 140 A6
W2 236 A2
7 Barking IG11 80 A1
Feltham TW13 151 C2
Putney SW15 156 C5
Exeter Mans NW2 69 A2
Exeter Mews SW6 265 A4
Exeter Rd DA16 145 D3
E16 99 A2
E17 53 C4
N14 15 B4
N9 18 C2
NW2 69 A2
Croydon CR0 205 D2
Dagenham RM10 81 D2
Enfield EN3 6 D2
Harrow HA2 63 A6
Hatton TW6 127 C2
Twickenham TW13 151 B1
Exeter St WC2 116 B6 250 C6
Exeter Way 2 SE14 141 B5
Hatton TW6 127 C3
Exford Ct SW11 266 D2
Exford Gdns SE12 165 B3
Exford Rd SE12 165 B3
Exhibition Cl W12 112 C6
Exhibition Rd SW7 114 B3 256 D6
Exmoor Ho 23 E3 97 A5
Exmoor St W10 90 D2
Exmouth Ho 6 E14 119 D2
Exmouth Market EC1 94 C3 241 B6
Exmouth Mews NW1 232 B1
Exmouth Pl E8 74 B1
Exmouth Rd E17 53 B4
Bexley DA16 146 C5
Hayes UB4 83 C4
Ruislip HA4 62 C5
Exmouth St E1 96 C1
Exning Rd E16 98 D3
Exonbury NW8 91 D6
Exon St SE17 117 C2 263 A3
Explorer Ave TW19 148 A3
Express Dr IG3 58 B1
Exton Cres NW10 67 A1
Exton Gdns RM8 80 C4
Exton St SE1 116 C5 251 A3
Eyebright Cl 3 CR0 206 D1
Eyhurst Cl NW2 68 A6
Eylewood Rd SE27 183 A5
Eynella Rd SE21 161 D4
Eynham Rd W12 90 C1
Eynsford Cl BR5 211 A3
Eynsford Cres DA5, DA14 168 D3
Eynsford Ho SE1 252 C2
12 SE15 140 C6
SE17 263 A3
Eynsford Rd IG3 79 C6
Eynsford Terr UB7 82 B1
Eynsham Dr SE2 124 B3
Eynswood Dr DA14 190 C5
Eyot Gdns W6 111 D1
Eyot Gn W4 111 D1
Eyre Ct NW8 229 C4
Eyre St Hill EC1 94 C3 241 A5
Eysham Ct 8 EN5 13 D6
Eythorne Rd SW9 138 C4
Ezra St E2 95 D4

F

Faber Gdns NW4 46 A4
Fabian Rd SW6 135 B5 264 D4
Fabian St E6 100 B3
Fabyc Ho TW9 132 C5
Factory La
Croydon CR0 220 D6
Tottenham N17 33 D1
Factory Rd E16 122 A5
Factory Yd W7 108 C5
Fagg's Rd TW14 150 A6
Fairacre Hounslow TW7 130 B4
Kingston KT3 199 C6
Pinner HA5 40 A5
Fair Acres BR2 209 A4
Fairacres Putney SW15 134 A1
Ruislip HA4 39 D2
Fairbairn Gn 1 SW9 138 D4
Fairbank Ave BR6 226 D4
Fairbanks Rd N17 52 A6
Fairbourne Ho UB3 105 A3
Fairbourne Rd N17 51 C6
Fairbridge Rd N19 71 D6
Fairbrook Cl N13 32 C5
Fairbrook Rd N13 32 C4
Fairburn Ct SW15 157 A6
Fairburn Ho 9 N16 51 C1
SW5 254 D1
Fairby Ho SE1 263 D4
Fairby Rd SE12 165 B6
Faircharm Trad Est SE8 141 D5
Fairchild Cl 6 SW11 136 B3
Fairchild Ho 13 E9 74 C1
5 N1 95 C4
SW1 259 B3
Fairchild Pl EC2 243 B5
Fairchild St EC2 243 B5
Fairclough St E1 96 A1
Faircourt 14 NW3 70 D2
Faircroft N16 51 B1
Forest Hill SE26 184 C6
Faircross Ave IG11 79 A2
Faircross Par IG11 79 C3
Fairdale Gdns
Hayes UB3 106 A4
Putney SW15 134 B1
Fairdene Ct N7 72 A3
Fairey Ave UB3 105 D3
Fairfax Cl KT12 194 B1
Fairfax Gdns SE3 143 C4
Fairfax Ho 12 SW9 138 C3
5 Ealing W5 88 A4
6 Putney SW15 156 A6
Fairfax Mews E16 121 B5
N8 50 D5
Putney SW15 134 C1
Fairfax Pl NW6 70 A1
Fairfax Rd N8 50 C5
NW6 70 A1
W4 111 C3
Teddington TW11 175 B3
Fairfax Way N10 31 A3
Fairfield 4 E1 96 C2
N20 14 B4
NW1 232 A5
Pinner HA6 22 A1
Fairfield Ave NW4 46 B3
Edgware HA8 26 D3
Ruislip HA4 39 A2
Twickenham TW2 151 D3
Fairfield Cl DA15 167 D5
N12 30 A6
Enfield EN3 7 A1
Mitcham SW19 180 C3
West Ewell KT19 215 C3
Fairfield Cres HA8 26 D4
Fairfield Ct NW10 90 A6
1 SW18 157 D6
Ruislip HA4 39 B1
8 Woodford IG8 37 A4
Fairfield Dr SW18 157 D6
Harrow HA2 42 A6
Wembley UB6 87 C6
Fairfield E KT1 176 A1
Fairfield Gdns N8 50 A4
Fairfield Gr SE7 143 D6
Fairfield Ind Est KT1 198 B6
Fairfield N KT1,KT2 176 A1
Fairfield Path CR0 221 B5
Fairfield Pl KT1 198 A6
Fairfield Rd BR1 187 A3
BR5 211 B3
E17 35 A1
E3 97 C5
N8 50 A4
Beckenham BR3 185 C1
Bexley DA7 147 B3
Edmonton N18 34 A6
Ilford IG1 78 D2
Kingston KT1 176 A1
Southall UB1 85 B1
South Croydon CR0 221 C5
Woodford IG8 37 A4
Yiewsley UB7 104 A6
Fairfields SE6 163 D4
Fairfield S KT1 176 B1
Fairfields Cl NW9 45 A4
Fairfields Cres NW9 45 A4
Fairfields Rd TW3 130 A2
Fairfield St SW18 157 D6
Fairfield W KT1 176 A1
Fairfield Way
Barnet EN5 13 C6
West Ewell KT19 215 C3
Fairfoot Rd E3 97 C3
Fairford SE6 163 C3
Fairford Ave CR0 206 D4
Fairford Cl CR0 207 A4
Fairford Ct SM2 217 D1
Fairford Gdns KT4 215 D5
Fairford Ho SE11 261 B3
Fairgreen EN4 2 D2
Fairgreen Ct EN4 2 D2
Fair Green Ct 1 CR4 202 D6
Fairgreen E EN4 2 D2
Fairgreen Rd CR7 204 D4
Fairhall Ct KT6 198 B2
Fairhaven Ave CR0 206 D3
Fairhaven Ct CR2 221 A3
Fairhazel Gdns NW6 70 A1
Fairheathe SW15 156 D5
Fairholme TW14 149 C4
Fairholme Cl N3 47 A5
Fairholme Cres UB4 84 A3
Fairholme Gdns N3 47 A5
Fairholme Ho 3 KT3 199 C5
Fairholme Jun & Inf Schs TW14 149 B3
Fairholme Rd W14 113 A1 254 B1
Ashford TW15 170 B5
Cheam SM1 217 B2
Harrow HA1 42 D4
Ilford IG1 56 C2
Thornton Heath CR0 204 C2
Fairholt Cl N16 51 C1
Fairholt Rd N16 51 B1
Fairholt St SW7 257 B6
Fairhurst 4 NW6 70 A2
Fairland Ho BR2 209 B5
Fairland Rd E15 76 D1
Fairlands Ave
Sutton SM1 217 C6
Thornton Heath CR7 204 C4
Woodford IG9 21 A2
Fairlands Ct 6 SE9 166 C5
Fairlawn SE7 143 C6
Fairlawn Ave N2 48 C5
Acton W4 111 A2
Bexley DA16 146 D3
Fairlawn Cl
Claygate KT10 212 D2
Feltham TW13 173 B6
Kingston KT2 177 A4
Southgate N14 15 D5
Fairlawn Ct SE7 143 C5
3 Acton W4 111 A2
Fairlawn Dr IG8 37 A3
Fairlawnes SM6 219 B3
Fairlawn Gdns UB1 107 B6
Fairlawn Gr W4 111 A2
Fairlawn Mans SE14 140 D4
Fairlawn Pk SE26 185 A5
Fairlawn Prim Sch
Forest Hill SE23 162 C4
Forest Hill SE23 162 C3
Fairlawn Rd SW19 179 B3
Fairlawns
3 Bowes Park N11 32 A4
10 Chingford E4 20 A2
Pinner WD19 22 D1
Putney SW15 156 D6
Sunbury TW16 194 A6
Twickenham TW1 153 C5
Fairlea Pl W5 87 D3
Fair Lea Pl W5 87 C2
Fairleas 12 BR3 185 D1
Fairley House Sch SW1 259 D2
Fairlie Ct 22 E3 97 D4
1 N7 71 D4
Fairlie Gdns SE23 162 C4
Fairlight TW12 173 D5
Fairlight Ave NW10 89 C5
Chingford E4 20 B2
Woodford IG8 37 A4
Fairlight Cl Cheam KT4 216 C4
Chingford E4 20 B2
Fairlight Ct NW10 89 C5
Greenford UB6 86 B5
Fairlight Rd SW17 180 B6
Fairline Ct BR3 186 A1
Fairlop Ct E11 54 C1
Fairlop Pl NW8 229 D1
Fairlop Rd E11 54 B2
Fairmark Dr UB10 60 C2
Fairmead BR1 210 B5
Tolworth KT5,KT6 198 D1
Fairmead Cl BR1 210 B5
Heston TW5 128 D5
Kingston KT3 199 B6
Fairmead Cres HA8 11 A1
Fairmead Ct 3 E4 20 C4
Fairmead Gdns IG4 56 A4
Fairmead Ho E9 75 A4
Fairmead Rd N7,N19 72 A5
Thornton Heath CR0 204 C2
Fairmeadside IG10 21 C6
Fairmile Ave SW16 181 D5
Fairmile Ho BR5 190 A1
Teddington TW11 175 A6
Fairmont Cl DA17 125 B1
Fairmont Ho 1 E3 97 C3
Fairmount Rd SW2 160 B5
Fairoak Cl BR5 210 D2
Fairoak Dr SE9 167 B6
Fairoaks Gr EN3 6 D6
Fairseat Cl WD23 8 C2
Fair St SE1 117 D4 253 C2
Hounslow TW3 130 A2
Fairstead Lo 4 IG8 37 A4
Fairstead Wlk N1 235 A6
Fairthorn Rd SE7,SE10 121 A1
Fairview Ave HA0 65 D2
Fair View Cl E17 35 A2
Fairview Cl SE26 185 A5
Fairview Cres HA2 41 C1
Fairview Ct NW4 28 D1
Ashford TW15 170 C5
Kingston KT2 176 D2
Fairview Dr BR6 227 B4
Littleton TW17 192 B4
Fairview Gdns IG8 37 B2
Fairview Ho 14 SW2 160 B4
Fairview Pl SW2 160 B4
Fairview Rd N15 51 D3
Carshalton SM1,SM5 218 C3
Enfield EN2 4 C4
Thornton Heath SW16 182 B2
Fairview Villas E4 35 D3
Fairview Way HA8 26 C6
Fairwall Ho 9 SE5 139 C4
Fairwater Ave DA16 146 A1
Fairwater Ho TW11 175 A6
Fairway BR5 211 B4
Bexley DA6 169 A6
West Barnes SW20 200 C6
Woodford IG8 37 C5
Fairway Ave NW9 44 D6
Fairway Cl NW11 48 A2
Croydon CR0 207 A4
Hounslow TW4 150 D6
West Ewell KT19 215 A4
Fairway Ct NW7 11 B1
13 SE16 118 D4
12 SE9 166 C5
New Barnet EN5 13 D5
Fairway Dr Erith SE28 103 A1
Greenford UB6 63 D1
Fairway Est TW4 150 C6
Fairway Gdns Ilford IG1 79 A3
West Wickham BR3 208 B3
Fairway Prim Sch NW7 11 B2
Fairways E17 54 A5
Ashford TW15 170 D4
4 Hounslow TW7 130 C4
Stanmore HA7 26 A1
Teddington TW11 175 D3
Fairways Bsns Pk E10 75 A6
Fairway The BR1,BR2 210 B4
NW7 11 B1
W3 89 C1
East Molesey KT8 195 D6
Edmonton N13 17 B1
Hillingdon UB10 82 B5
Kingston KT3 177 B2
New Barnet EN5 13 D5
Northolt UB5 64 A2
Ruislip HA4 62 D5
Southgate N14 15 C5
Wembley HA0 65 B6
Fairweather Cl N15 51 C5
Fairweather Ct N13 32 B6
Fairweather Ho N7 72 A4
Fairweather Rd N16 52 A3
Fairwood Ct E11 54 B2
Fairwyn Rd SE26 185 A6
Faith Ct NW2 68 B2
Faithfull Ho N5 73 A3
Fakenham Cl NW7 28 A3
5 Northolt UB5 63 C2
Fakruddin St E1 96 A3
Falaize Ave IG1 78 D4
Falcon Ave BR1 210 A5
Falconberg Ct W1 239 D2
Falconberg Mews W1 239 D2
Falconbrook Inf Sch SW11 136 B2
Falcon Cl SE1 251 D4
Chiswick W4 133 A6
Falcon Cres EN3 18 D6
Falcon Ct EC4 241 A1
N1 234 D3
8 Dulwich SE21 161 B2
New Barnet EN5 2 A1
Ruislip HA4 61 C6
6 Wanstead E18 55 B6
Falcon Dr TW19 148 A5
Falconer Ct N17 33 A3
Falconer Wlk 12 N7 72 B6
Falcon Gr SW11 136 C2
Falcon Ho 10 SE15 139 D4
Falconhurst 4 KT6 198 A4
Falcon La SW11 136 C2
Falcon Lo NW3 69 D4
11 W9 91 C2
Falcon Pk Ind Est NW10 67 C3
Falcon Point SE1 251 D5
Falcon Rd SW11 136 C2
Enfield EN3 18 D6
Hampton TW12 173 B3
Falconry Ct KT1 198 A6
Falcon St E13 99 A3
Falcon Terr SW11 136 C2
Falcon Way E14 119 D2
NW9 27 C1
Feltham TW14 150 B6
Harrow HA3 44 A3
Sunbury TW16 171 C1
Wanstead E11 55 A5
Falconwood Ave DA16 145 C3
Falconwood Ct SE3 142 D3
Falconwood Par DA16 145 D1
Falconwood Rd CR0 223 C1
Falconwood Sta SE9 145 B1
Falcourt Cl SM1 217 D3
Falkener Ct SW11 268 B1
Falkirk Ct 11 SE16 118 D5
Falkirk Gdns WD19 22 D5
Falkirk Ho W9 91 D4
Falkirk St N1 95 C5
Falkland Ave N11 31 B6
N3 29 C3
Falkland Ho W14 254 C2
W8 255 C5
Catford SE6 186 A6
Falkland Park Ave SE25 183 C1
Falkland Pl 2 NW5 71 C3
Falkland Rd N8 50 C5
NW5 71 C3
Barnet EN5 1 A3
Falladon Ho W11 91 B2
Falling La UB7 104 A6
Falloden Way NW11 47 C5
Fallodon Ho 6 SW8 137 D3
Fallow Court Ave N12 30 A4
Fallow Ct 16 SE16 118 A1
Fallowfield N4 72 B6
Stanmore HA7 9 A1
Fallowfield Ct HA7 9 A1
Fallowfields Dr N12 30 C4
Fallows Cl N2 30 B1
Fallsbrook Rd SW16 181 C4
Falman Cl N9 18 A3
Falmer Rd E17 53 D6
N15 51 B4
Enfield EN1 5 C1
Falmouth Ave E4 36 C5
Falmouth Cl SE12 164 D6
Wood Green N22 32 B3
Falmouth Gdns IG4 55 D5
Falmouth Ho SE11 261 B2
W2 247 A6
Falmouth Rd SE1 117 A3 262 B5
Falmouth St E15 76 B3
Falmouth Way E17 53 B4
Falstaff Ct SE11 261 C3
Falstaff Ho 18 N1 95 C5
Fambridge Cl SE26 185 B6
Fambridge Rd RM8 59 C1
Fane St W14 264 D6
Fann St EC1 95 A3 242 B5
Fanshawe Ave IG11 79 A2
Fanshawe Cres RM9 81 B3
Fanshawe Rd TW10 175 C6
Fanshaw Ho 6 E17 53 D6
Fanshaw St N1 95 C4
Fantail The BR6 226 B5
Fanthorpe St SW15 134 C2
Faraday Ave DA14 168 B2
Faraday Cl N7 72 B2
Faraday Ho 6 E14 119 B6
6 NW5 71 B4
W10 91 A2
2 Balham SW12 159 B4
4 Belvedere DA17 125 C3
5 Hampton TW12 173 D4
Wembley HA9 67 A5
Faraday Lo SE10 120 D3
Faraday Rd DA16 146 A2
E15 76 D2
W10 91 A2
W3 111 A6
East Molesey KT8 195 C5
Southall UB1 107 D6
Wimbledon SW19 179 D4
Faraday Way SE18 121 D3
Thornton Heath CR0 204 B1
Fareham Ho 13 SW15 156 A3
Fareham Rd TW14 150 C4
Fareham St W1 239 C2
Farewell Pl CR4 180 C2
Faringdon Ave BR2 210 C3
Faringford Rd E15 76 C1
Farjeon Ho NW6 70 B1
Farjeon Rd SE3 143 D4
Farleigh Ave BR2 209 A2
Farleigh Ct CR2 221 A3
Farleigh Ho 7 KT2 176 D4
Farleigh Pl N16 73 D4
Farleigh Rd N16 73 D4
Farleycroft 1 CR0 206 A1
Farley Croft BR2 186 C1
Farley Ct NW1 238 A5
W14 254 C6
Farley Dr IG3 57 C1
Farley Ho SE26 162 B1
Farley Pl SE25 206 A5
Farley Rd Catford SE6 164 A4
South Croydon CR2 222 B1
Farlington Pl SW15 156 B4
Farlow Rd SW15 134 D2
Farlton Rd SW18 157 D4
Farman Terr HA3 43 D5
Farm Ave NW2 69 B5
Harrow HA2,HA5 41 C3
Streatham SW16 182 A6
Wembley HA0 65 C2
Farm Avenue Ho HA0 65 C2
Farmborough Cl HA1 42 B2
Farm Cl SW6 265 B4
Barnet EN5 12 C6
Buckhurst Hill IG9 21 C1
Coney Hall BR4 224 D5
Lower Halliford TW17 192 C2
Southall UB1 107 D6
Sutton SM2 218 B1
Uxbridge UB10 60 D6
Farmcote Rd SE12 165 A3
Farm Cotts E17 53 A3
Farm Ct NW4 46 A6
Farmdale Rd SE10 121 A1
Sutton SM5 218 C1
Farm Dr CR0 223 B6
Farm End E4 20 C6
Farmer Ho 4 SE16 118 B3
Farmer Rd E10 53 D1
Farmers Rd SE5 138 D5
Farmer St W8 245 A4
Farmfield Rd BR1 186 C5
Farm House Ct NW7 28 A3
Farmhouse Rd SW16 181 C3
Farmilo Rd E17 53 C2
Farmington Ave SM1 218 B5
Farm La SW6 135 C5 265 B4
Croydon CR0 223 B6
East Barnet N14 15 B5
Farmlands Enfield EN2 4 C4
Pinner HA5 40 A5
Farmlands The UB5 63 C2
Farmland Wlk BR7 188 D5
Farm Lane Trad Ctr SW6 135 C6 265 B5
Farmleigh N14 15 C4
Farmleigh Ho SW9 160 D6
Farm Pl W8 245 A4
Farm Rd NW10 89 B6
Edmonton N21 17 A3
Morden SM4 201 D4
Sutton SM2 218 B1
Twickenham TW4 151 A3
Thames Ditton KT10 195 C1
Farm St W1 115 B6 248 C5
Farmstead Rd
Catford SE6 185 D6
Harrow HA3 24 B1
Farm Vale DA5 169 D5
Farm View N3 47 B6
Farmway RM8 80 C5
Farm Way
Buckhurst Hill IG9 37 C6
North Cheam KT4 216 C5
Farm Wlk NW11 47 C4
Farnaby Ho 2 W10 91 B4
Farnaby Rd SE9 143 C1
Bromley BR1,BR2 186 C2
Farnan Ave E17 53 D6
Farnan Rd SW16 182 A5
Farnborough Ave E17 53 A6
South Croydon CR2 223 A1
Farnborough Cl HA9 66 D6
Farnborough Comm
Keston Mark BR2,BR6 226 B5
Orpington BR6 226 C4
Farnborough Cres
3 Hayes BR2 208 D1
South Croydon CR2 223 A1
Farnborough Ct 2 BR6 227 A3
Farnborough Hill BR6 227 C3
Farnborough Ho 1 SW15 156 A3
Farnborough Hospl BR6 226 C4
Farnborough Prim Sch BR6 227 A3
Farnborough Way BR6 227 B3
10 SE15 139 C5
Farncombe St SE16 118 A4
Farndale Ave N13 17 A1
Farndale Cres UB6 86 A4
Farndale Ho 1 NW6 91 D6
Farnell Mews SW5 255 C2
Farnell Pl W3 110 D6
Farnell Rd TW7 130 B2
Farnell's Almshouses TW7 130 D3

Farnfield Ho 12 SW2 160 B6
Farnham Cl N20 14 A4
Farnham Ct 2 N16 51 C1
2 Cheam SM3 217 A2
1 Southall UB1 86 A1
Farnham Gdns SW20 178 B1
Farnham Green Prim Sch IG3 58 A3
Farnham Ho NW1 237 B5
SE1 252 A3
Farnham Pl SE1 251 D3
Farnham Rd
Bexley DA16 146 C3
Ilford IG3 57 D2
Farnham Royal SE11 116 B1 260 D1
Farnhurst Ho 7 SW11 137 A3
Farningham Ct SW16 181 D3
Farningham Ho 9 N4 51 B2
Farningham Rd N17 34 A3
Farnley Ho 13 SW8 137 D3
Farnley Rd Chingford E4 20 C4
South Norwood SE25 205 B5
Farnsworth Ho 8 SW27 182 D5
Farnworth Ho 5 E14 120 B2
Faro Cl BR1 188 C1
Faroe Rd W14 112 D3
Farorna Wlk EN2 4 C4
Farquhar Rd
Dulwich SE19 183 D5
Wimbledon SW19 157 C1
Farquharson Rd CR0 205 A1
Farrance Rd RM6 59 A2
Farrance St E14 97 C1
Farrans Ct HA3 43 B2
Farrant Ave N22 32 D1
Farrant Cl BR6 227 D1
Farrant Ho 15 SW11 136 B2
Farr Ave IG11 102 A5
Farrell Ho E1 96 C1
Farren Rd SE23 163 A2
Farrer Ho SE8 141 C5
Farrer Mews N8 49 C5
Farrer Rd N8 49 D5
Harrow HA3 44 A5
Farrer's Pl CR0 222 D4
Farrier Cl BR1 209 D6
Hillingdon UB8 82 C1
Sunbury TW16 194 A5
Farrier Mews SE15 140 C2
Farrier Rd UB5 85 C5
Farriers Ct
Belmont SM2 217 A1
Wimbledon SW19 179 A3
Farrier St NW1 71 C1
Farriers Way WD6 11 B6
Farrier Wlk SW10 136 A6 266 A6
Farringdon La EC1 94 C3 241 B5
Farringdon Rd EC1 94 C3 241 B5
Farringdon St EC4 94 D1 241 C2
Farringdon Sta EC1 94 D2 241 C4
Farrington Pl BR7 189 B3
Farrington & Stratford House Sch BR7 189 B3
Farrins Rents SE16 119 A5
Farrow La SE14 140 C5
Farrow Pl SE16 119 A3
Farr Rd EN2 5 B4
Farthingale Wlk E15 76 B1
Farthing Alley 5 SE1 118 A4
Farthing Fields 8 E1 118 B5
Farthings Cl
Chingford E4 20 C1
Pinner HA5 40 B3
Farthing St BR6 226 B1
Farthings The 1 KT2 176 C2
Farwell Rd DA14 190 C6
Farwig La BR1 187 A2
Fashion & Design Museum The* SE1 253 A2
Fashion St E1 95 D2 243 D3
Fashoda Rd BR2 209 D5
Fassett Rd E8 74 A2
Kingston KT1 198 A5
Fassett Sq E8 74 A2
Fauconberg Ct W4 133 A6
Fauconberg Rd W4 133 A6
Faulkner Cl 6 RM8 58 D2
Faulkner Ho SW15 134 C3
Faulkner's Alley EC1 241 C4
Faulkner St SE14 140 C4
Fauna Cl RM6 58 C3
Faunce Ho 1 SE17 138 D6
Faunce St SE17 116 D1 261 C1
Favart Rd SW6 135 C4 265 B2
F Ave SE18 122 D3
Faversham Ave
Chingford E4 20 D3
Enfield EN1 17 B5
Faversham Ho NW1 232 B5
SE17 263 A1
Faversham Rd
Beckenham BR3 185 B1
Forest Hill SE6 163 B3
Morden SM4 201 D3
Fawcett Cl SW11 136 B3
West Norwood SW16 182 C6
Fawcett Est E5 52 A1
Fawcett Ho 25 SW9 138 A3
Fawcett Rd NW10 67 D1
Croydon CR0 221 A5
Fawcett St SW10 136 A6 266 A6
Fawcus Cl KT10 212 C2
Fawe Park Rd SW15 135 B1
Fawe St E14 97 D2
Fawkham Ho SE1 263 D3
Fawley Ct SE27 160 D2
Fawley Lo 2 E14 120 B2
Fawley Rd NW6 69 D3
Fawnbrake Ave SE24 161 A6
Fawn Rd E13 99 C5
Fawns Manor Cl TW14 149 A3
Fawns Manor Rd TW14 149 B3
Fawood Ave NW10 67 B1
Fayetville Ho 28 N19 49 D2
Faygate Cres DA6 169 C6
Faygate Rd SW2 160 B2
Fayland Ave SW16 181 C5
Fazal Laf IG1 79 A6
Fazerley Ct 49 W2 91 C2
Fearnley Cres TW12 173 B4
Fearnley Ho SE5 139 C3
Fearon St SE10 121 A1
Featherbed La CR0 223 B1
Feathers Pl SE10 142 B6
Featherstone Ave 4 SE23 162 C2
Featherstone Ct NW7 28 A3
Featherstone Ho UB4 84 C2
Featherstone Ind Est UB2 107 A3
Featherstone Prim Sch UB2 107 A3
Featherstone Rd NW7 28 B4
Southall UB2 107 A3
Featherstone St EC1 95 B3 242 C6
Featherstone Terr UB2 107 A3
Featley Rd SW9 138 D2
Federal Rd UB6 87 C5
Federation Rd SE2 124 C2
Fee Farm Rd KT10 212 D1
Felbridge Ave HA7 25 B2
Felbridge Cl SW16 182 C6
Felbridge Ct
Croydon CR2 221 A1
East Bedfont TW14 150 B3
Feltham TW14 150 A3
Harlington UB3 127 B6
Felbridge Ho 22 SE22 139 C2
Felbrigge Rd IG3 57 D1
Felday Rd SE13 163 D5
Felden Cl HA5 23 A3
Felden St SW6 135 B4 264 C1
Feldman Cl N16 52 A1
Felgate Mews 4 W6 112 B2
Felhampton Rd SE9 166 D1
Felhurst Cres RM10 81 D4
Feline Ct 1 EN4 14 C5
Felix Ave N8 50 A3
Felix Ct E17 53 D4
Felix La TW17 193 D3
Felix Manor BR7 189 C4
Felix Neubergh Ct EN1 5 C1
Felix Rd Ealing W13 109 A6
Walton-on-T KT12 194 A3
Felix St 19 E2 96 B5
Felixstowe Ct E16 122 D5
Felixstowe Rd N17 51 D6
NW10 90 B4
SE2 124 B3
Edmonton N9 34 A6
Fellbrigg Rd SE22 161 D6
Fellbrigg St 21 E1 96 B3
Fellbrook TW10 153 B1
Fellmongers Yd 3 CR0 221 A5
Fellowes Cl UB4 84 D3
Fellowes Ct UB3 127 B6
Fellowes Rd SM1,SM5 218 C6
Fellows Ct E2 95 D5
Fellows Rd NW3 70 C1
Fell Rd CR0 221 A5
Fells Haugh 6 W3 89 A1
Felltram Way SE7 121 A1
Fell Wlk HA8 26 D2
Felmersham Cl 2 SW4 137 D1
Felmingham Rd SE20 184 C1
Felnex Trad Est SM6 219 A6
Felsberg Rd SW2 160 A4
Fels Cl RM10 81 D5
Felsham Ho SW15 134 D2
Felsham Rd SW15 134 D2
Felspar Cl SE18 123 D1
Felstead Rd E11 55 A2
Felstead St E9 75 B2
Felstead Wharf E14 120 A1
Felsted Rd E16 99 D1
Feltham Ave KT8 196 C5
Felthambrook Ind Est TW13 150 B1
Felthambrook Way TW13 172 B6
Feltham Bsns Complex TW13 150 B2
Feltham Comm Sch TW13 150 C2
Feltham Corporate Ctr TW13 150 B1
Feltham Hill Jun Sch TW13 149 D1
Feltham Hill Rd
Ashford TW15 171 A4
Feltham TW13 172 B6
Feltham Rd
Ashford TW15 171 A6
Mitcham CR4 181 A1
Feltham Sta TW13 150 B3
Felton Cl BR5 210 D3
Felton Gdns IG11 101 C5
Felton Ho N1 235 D5
SE9 143 C1
Felton Lea DA14 189 D5
Felton Rd W13 109 C4
Barking IG11 101 C5
Felton St N1 95 B6 235 D5
Fenchurch 34 N1 95 C6
Fenchurch Ave EC3 95 C1 243 A1
Fenchurch Bldgs EC3 243 B1
Fenchurch Pl EC3 253 B6
Fenchurch St EC3 117 C6 253 B6
Fenchurch Street Sta EC3 117 C6 253 B6
Fen Ct EC3 253 A6
Fendall Rd KT19 215 A3
Fendall St SE1 117 C3 263 B5
Fender Ct 5 SW4 138 A3
Fendt Cl 8 E16 98 D1
Fendyke Rd SE2,DA17 124 D3
Fenelon Pl W14 113 B2 254 D3
Fen Gr DA15 167 D5
Fenham Rd SE15 140 B5
Fenman Ct N17 34 B2
Fenman Gdns IG3 58 B1
Fenn Cl BR1 187 A4
Fenn Ct HA1 43 A4
Fennel Cl E16 98 C3
Croydon CR0 206 D1
Fennell St SE18 144 C6
Fenner Cl SE16 118 B2
Fenner Ho 25 E1 118 B5
Fenner Sq 10 SW11 136 B2
Fenning Ct CR4 202 C5
Fenning St SE1 253 A2
Fenn St E9 74 C3
Fen St E16 120 D6
Fenstanton Ave N12 30 B5
Fenstanton Prim Sch SW2 160 C3
Fentiman Rd SW8 138 B5 270 C4
Fenton Cl BR7 188 B5
E8 73 D2
SW9 138 B3
Fenton Ho SE14 141 A5
Heston TW5 129 C6
Fenton Rd N17 33 A3
Fentons SE3 142 D5
Fenton's Ave E13 99 B5
Fenton St E1 96 B1
Fenwick Cl 16 SE18 144 C6
Fenwick Gr SE15 140 A2
Fenwick Pl SW9 138 A2
Croydon CR2 220 D1
Fenwick Rd SE15 140 A2
Ferby Ct DA15 189 D6
Ferdinand Ho 1 NW1 71 B1
Ferdinand Pl NW1 71 A1
Ferdinand St NW1 71 A1
Ferguson Ave KT5 198 B4
Ferguson Cl BR2,BR3 208 B6
Ferguson Dr W3 89 B1
Ferguson Ho SE10 142 A4
Ferguson's Cl E14 119 C2
Fergus Rd N5 72 D3
Fermain Ct E N1 95 C6
Fermain Ct N N1 95 C6
Fermain Ct W N1 95 C6
Ferme Park Rd N4,N8 50 B3
Fermor Rd SE23 163 A3
Fermoy Rd W9 91 B3
Greenford UB6 85 D3
Fern Ave CR4 203 D5
Fernbank IG9 21 B3
Fernbank Ave
Walton-on-T KT12 195 A2
Wembley HA0 64 D3
Fernbank Mews SW12 159 C5
Fernbrook Dr HA2 41 D2
Fernbrook Rd SE13 164 C5
Fern Cl 3 N1 95 C5
Ferncliff Rd E8 74 A3
Ferncroft Ave N12 30 D4
NW3 69 C4
Ruislip HA4 62 C6
Fern Ct DA7 147 C1
SE14 140 D3
Chingford E4 36 A4
Ferndale BR1 187 C1
Ferndale Ave E17 54 B4
Hounslow TW4 129 A2
Ferndale Cl DA7 147 A4
Ferndale Ct 3 SE3 142 D5
Ferndale Ho N16 51 B1
Ferndale Rd E11 76 D6
E7 77 B1
N15 51 D4
SW4,SW9 138 B1
Ashford TW15 170 A5
Croydon SE25 206 B4
Enfield EN3 7 A6
Ferndale St E6 100 D1
Ferndale Way BR6 227 B3
Ferndene NW9 45 A4
Fern Dene W13 87 B2
Ferndene Rd SE24 139 A1
Fernden Way RM7 59 D3
Ferndown
5 Kingston KT6 198 A4
Pinner HA6 22 A1
6 Wanstead E18 55 A6
Ferndown Ave BR6 211 B1
Ferndown Cl Pinner HA5 23 A3
Sutton SM2 218 B2
Ferndown Ct 6 UB1 86 A1
Ferndown Lo E14 120 A3
Ferndown Rd SE9 165 D4
South Oxhey WD19 22 C6
Ferney Meade Way TW7 131 A3
Ferney Rd EN4 15 A3
Fern Gr TW14 150 B4
Fernhall Dr IG4 55 D4
Fernham Rd CR7 205 A6
Fernhead Rd W9 91 B4
Fernhill Ct Chingford E17 36 B1
Kingston KT2 175 D5
Fernhill Gdns KT2 176 A5
Fernhill Ho E5 74 A6
Fern Hill Pl 3 BR6 227 A3
Fern Hill Prim Sch KT2 176 A4
Fernhill St E16 122 B5
Fernholme Rd SE15 162 D6
Fernhurst Gdns HA8 26 C4
Fernhurst Rd
Ashford TW15 171 A6
Croydon CR0 206 B1
Fulham SW6 135 A4 264 B2
Fernie Ho SE22 139 D2
Fern La TW5 107 B1
Fernlea Ho NW10 88 B4
Fernlea Rd
Balham SW12 159 B3
Mitcham CR4 181 A2
Fernleigh Cl W9 91 B4
Croydon CR0 220 C4
Fernleigh Ct
Harrow HA2 23 D1
Wembley HA9 44 A1
Fernleigh Rd N21 16 D2
Fernley Cl HA5 40 A5
Fern Lo 13 SW16 182 C5
Fernsbury St WC1 234 A1
Fernshaw Mans SW10 266 A5
Fernshaw Rd SW10 136 A6 266 A5
Fernside IG9 21 B3
Fernside Ave NW7 11 B1
Feltham TW13 172 B6
Fernside Ct NW4 28 D1
Fernside Rd SW12 159 A4
Ferns Rd E15 76 D2
Fern St E3 97 C3
Fernthorpe Rd SW16 181 C4
Ferntower Rd N5 73 B3
Fernways IG1 78 D4
Fern Wlk 17 SE16 118 A1
Fernwood
Wandsworth SW19 157 B3
Wood Green N22 32 A3
Fernwood Ave
Streatham SW16 181 D6
Wembley HA0 65 C2
Fernwood Cl BR1 187 C1
Fernwood Cres N20 14 D1
Ferny Hill EN4 3 A5
Ferranti Cl SE18 121 D3
Ferraro Cl TW5 129 C6
Ferrers Ave
Wallington SM6 219 D4
West Drayton UB7 104 A4
Ferrers Rd SW16 181 D5
Ferrestone Rd N8 50 B5
Ferrey Mews 20 SW9 138 C3
Ferriby Cl N1 72 C1
Ferrier Ind Est SW18 135 D1
Ferrier Point 6 E16 99 A2
Ferrier St SW18 135 D1
Ferring Cl HA2 42 A1
Ferrings SE21 161 C1
Ferris Ave CR0 223 B5
Ferris Rd SE22 140 A1
Ferron Rd E5 74 B5
Ferrour Ct N2 48 B6
Ferrybridge Ho SE11 260 D5
Ferry Ho E5 52 B1
Ferry La N17 52 B5
Barnes SW13 133 D6
Brentford TW8 132 A6
Lower Halliford TW17 192 C1
Richmond TW9 132 B6
Ferry Lane Prim Sch N17 52 B5
Ferrymead Ave UB6 85 C5
Ferrymead Dr UB6 85 C5
Ferrymead Gdns UB6 86 A5
Ferrymoor TW10 153 B1
Ferry Rd Barnes SW13 134 A4
East Molesey KT8 195 C6
Richmond TW11 175 B5
Thames Ditton KT7 197 B3
Twickenham TW1 153 B3
Ferry Sq 1 TW8 132 A6
Ferry St E14 120 A1
Ferry Wks TW17 192 C1
Festing Rd SW15 134 D2
Festival Cl DA5 168 D3
Hillingdon UB10 82 D6
Festival Pier SE1 116 B5 250 C4
Festival Pleasure Gdns SW11 136 D5 267 C3
Fetter La EC4 94 C1 241 B2
Fettes Ho NW8 229 D3
Fews Lo RM6 58 D5
Ffinch St SE8 141 C5
Field Cl BR1 187 C1
Buckhurst Hill IG9 21 C1
Chessington KT9 213 C3
Chingford E4 35 D4
Cranford TW4 128 B4
East Molesey KT8 195 D4
Harlington UB7 127 A5
Ruislip HA4 39 A1
Uxbridge UB10 60 D6
Fieldcommon La KT12 195 B1
Field Ct N7 72 A3
NW3 70 A3
WC1 240 D3
Wimbledon SW19 157 C1
Field End Ruislip HA4 62 C2
Twickenham TW11 174 D6
Field End Jun & Inf Schs HA4 62 D6
Fieldend Rd SW16 181 C2
Field End Rd HA5,HA4 40 C1
Fielders Cl 2 Enfield EN1 5 C1
Harrow HA2 42 A1
Fieldfare Rd SE28 124 C6
Fieldgate Mans 23 E1 96 A2
Fieldgate St E1 96 A2
Field Ho 4 N9 34 A6
Fieldhouse Cl E18 37 B2
Fieldhouse Rd SW12 159 C3
Fielding Ave TW2 152 A1
Fielding Ho 3 NW6 91 C4
NW8 229 A6
Chiswick W4 133 C6
Fielding Mews SW13 134 B6
Fielding Prim Sch W13 109 B3
Fielding Rd W14 112 D3
W4 111 C3
Fielding St SE17 139 A6
Fieldings The SE23 162 C3
Fielding Terr W5 110 B6
Field La Brentford TW8 131 C5
Teddington TW11 175 A5
Field Mead NW9,NW7 27 D3
Field Pl KT3 199 D3
Field Point E7 77 A4
Field Rd E7 77 A4
N17 51 C6
W6 135 A6 264 A6
Feltham TW14 150 B5
Fieldsend Rd SM3 217 A3
Fields Est E8 74 A1
Fieldside Cl BR6 227 A4
Fieldside Rd BR1 186 B5
Fields Park Cres RM6 58 D4
Field St WC1 233 C2
Fieldsway Ho N5 72 C3
Fieldview SW17,SW18 158 B3
Field View TW13 171 B6
Fieldview Ct N5 72 D3
NW9 44 C3
Fieldway BR5 211 B3
Field Way NW10 67 A1
Fieldway RM8 80 C4
Field Way
Greenford UB6 85 D6
New Addington CR0 223 D2
Ruislip HA4 39 A1
Fieldway Cres N5,N7 72 C3
Fieldway Sta CR0 223 D1
Fieldwick Ho 14 E9 74 D2
Fiennes Cl RM8 58 C1
Fife Ct 5 W3 88 C1
Fifehead Cl TW15 170 A4
Fife Rd E16 99 A2
Kingston KT2 176 A1
Mortlake SW14 155 A6
Tottenham N22 32 D3
Fife Terr N1 233 D4
Fifield Path SE23 162 D1
Fifteenpenny Fields SE9 166 C6
Fifth Ave W10 91 A4
Hayes UB3 105 D5
Ilford E12 78 B4
Fifth Cross Rd TW2 152 B2
Fifth Way HA9 66 D4
Figge's Rd CR4 181 A3
Fig Tree Cl NW10 89 C6
Filanco Ct W7 108 D5
Filby Rd KT9 214 B2
Filey Ave N16 52 A1
Filey Cl SM2 218 A1
Filey Ho SW18 136 A1
Filey Waye HA4 62 B6
Filigree Ct SE16 119 B5
Fillebrook Ave EN1 5 D3
Fillebrook Hall E11 54 C2
Fillebrook Rd E11 54 C1
Filmer Ho SW6 264 B2
Filmer Rd SW6 135 B5 264 C3
Filmer Road Studios SW6 264 B2
Filston Rd DA8 125 D1
Filton Ct 14 SE14 140 C5
Finborough Ho SW10 266 A6
Finborough Rd SW10 135 D6 265 D6
Upper Tooting SW17 180 D4
Finchale Rd SE2 124 A3
Fincham Cl UB10 61 A5
Finch Ave SE27 183 B6
Finch Cl NW10 67 B2
Barnet EN5 13 C6
Finchdean Ho SW15 155 D4
Finch Dr TW14 150 D4
Finch Gdns E4 35 C5
Finch Ho 1 SE8 141 D5
Finchingfield Ave IG8 37 C3
Finch La EC2,EC3 242 D1
Finchley Cath High Sch N12 13 D1
Finchley Central Sta N3 29 C2
Finchley Ct N3 29 D4
Finchley La NW4 46 D5
Finchley Lo N12 29 D5
Finchley Memorial Hospl N12 30 A3
Finchley Pk N12 30 B6
Finchley Pl NW8 229 C4
Finchley Rd NW11 47 B3
NW3 70 A2
NW8 229 C4
Finchley Road & Frognal Sta NW3 70 A3
Finchley Road Sta NW3 70 A2
Finchley Way N3 29 C3
Finch Lo 15 W9 91 C2
Finch Mews 3 SE15 139 D4
Finch's Ct 9 E14 119 D6
Finden Rd E7 77 C3
Findhorn Ave UB4 84 B2
Findhorn St E14 98 A1
Findon Cl SW18 157 C5
Harrow HA2 63 D5
Findon Rd W12 112 A4
Edmonton N9 18 B3
Fine Bush La HA4 38 D3
Fineran Ct 16 SW11 136 B1
Fingal St SE10 120 D1
Fingest Ho NW8 237 A6
Finians Cl UB10 60 B1
Finland Rd SE4 141 A2
Finland St SE16 119 A3
Finlays Cl KT9 214 C3
Finlay St SW6 134 D4
Finley Ct 21 SE5 139 A5
Finmere Ho 1 N4 51 A2
Finnemore Ho N1 235 A6
Finney La TW7 131 A4
Finn Ho N1 235 D2
Finnis St E2 96 B3
Finnymore Rd RM9 81 A1
Finsbury Ave EC2 242 D3
Finsbury Cir EC2 95 B2 242 D3
Finsbury Cotts N22 32 A3
Finsbury Ct EC2 242 C4
Finsbury Ho N22 32 A2
Finsbury Market EC2 243 A4
Finsbury Mkt EC2 243 A5
Finsbury Park Ave N4 51 A3
Finsbury Park Rd N4, N5 72 D6
Finsbury Park Sta N4 72 C6
Finsbury Pavement EC2 95 B2 242 D4
Finsbury Rd N22 32 B2

Finsbury Sq
EC2 ... 95 B2 242 D4
Finsbury St EC2 ... 242 C4
Finsbury Way DA5 ... 169 B5
Finsen Rd SE5 ... 139 A2
Finstock Rd W10 ... 90 D1
Finton House Sch
SW17 ... 158 D2
Finucane Ct TW9 ... 132 B2
Finucane Rise WD23 ... 8 A2
Finwhale Ho E14 ... 119 D3
Fiona Ct 9 NW6 ... 91 B5
Enfield EN2 ... 4 D2
Firbank Cl E16 ... 99 D2
Enfield EN2 ... 5 A1
Firbank Rd SE15 ... 140 B3
Fir Cl KT12 ... 194 A2
Fircroft N1 ... 94 D6 234 D6
Fircroft Gdns HA1 ... 64 C5
Fircroft Prim Sch
SW17 ... 158 D1
Fircroft Rd
Chessington KT9 ... 214 B4
Upper Tooting SW17 ... 158 D1
Fir Dene BR6 ... 226 C5
Firdene KT5 ... 199 A1
Fire Bell Alley KT6 ... 198 A3
Firebell Mews KT6 ... 198 A3
Fire Brigade Pier SE1 ... 260 B4
Firecrest Dr NW3 ... 69 D5
Firefly 7 NW9 ... 27 D1
Firefly Cl SM6 ... 220 A1
Firefly Gdns E6 ... 100 A3
Firemans Cotts N10 ... 49 A6
Fireman's Flats N22 ... 32 A2
Firepower (The Royal Artillery Mus)*
SE18 ... 122 D3
Fire Station Alley EN5 ... 1 A3
Fire Station Mews 3
BR3 ... 185 D2
Firethorn Cl HA8 ... 27 A6
Fir Gr KT3 ... 199 D3
Firhill Rd SE6 ... 163 C1
Firle Ho W10 ... 90 C2
Fir Lo SW15 ... 134 B1
Firmston Ho 9 SW14 ... 133 B2
Fir Rd Cheam SM3 ... 201 B1
Feltham TW13 ... 172 D5
Firs Ave N10 ... 49 A5
N11 ... 31 A4
Mortlake SW14 ... 133 A1
Firsby Ave CR0 ... 207 A1
Firsby Rd N16 ... 52 A1
Firs Cl N10 ... 49 A6
Claygate KT10 ... 212 C2
Forest Hill SE23 ... 163 A4
Mitcham CR4 ... 181 B2
Firscroft N13 ... 17 A1
Firs Dr TW5 ... 128 B5
Firs Farm Prim Sch
N13 ... 17 B1
Firs Ho N22 ... 32 C2
Firside Gr DA15 ... 167 D3
Firs La N21,N13 ... 17 A2
Firs Park Ave N21 ... 17 B3
Firs Park Gdns N21 ... 17 B3
First Ave E12 ... 78 A3
E13 ... 99 A4
E17 ... 53 D4
N18 ... 34 C6
NW4 ... 46 C5
W10 ... 91 B3
W3 ... 111 D5
Bexley DA7 ... 146 C5
Dagenham RM10 ... 103 D5
Dagenham RM6 ... 58 C4
East Molesey KT8 ... 195 C5
Enfield EN1 ... 17 D6
Hayes UB3 ... 105 D5
Mortlake SW14 ... 133 C2
Walton-on-T KT12 ... 194 B3
Wembley HA9 ... 65 D6
First Cl KT8 ... 196 A6
First Cross Rd TW2 ... 152 C2
First Dr NW10 ... 67 A1
Firs The DA15 ... 167 D1
E6 ... 78 A1
N20 ... 14 B3
Belmont SM2 ... 217 D1
Claygate KT10 ... 212 C2
Ealing W5 ... 87 D2
Forest Hill SE26 ... 184 C5
2 Penge SE26 ... 184 B5
Wimbledon SW20 ... 178 A3
Woodford IG8 ... 37 C3
First St SW3 ... 114 C2 257 B4
Firstway SW20 ... 178 C1
First Way HA9 ... 66 D4
Firs Wlk IG8 ... 37 A5
Firswood Ave KT19 ... 215 D3
Firth Gdns
SW6 ... 135 A4 264 A1
Firtree Ave CR4 ... 181 A1
Fir Tree Ave UB7 ... 104 C3
Fir Tree Cl Ealing W5 ... 88 A1
Fir Tree Cl *continued*
Esher KT10 ... 212 A3
5 Orpington BR6 ... 227 D3
Streatham SW16 ... 181 C5
Worcester Park KT19 ... 215 D4
Firtree Ct BR2 ... 208 D6
Fir Tree Gdns CR0 ... 223 C4
Fir Tree Gr SM5 ... 218 D1
Fir Tree Ho 11 SE14 ... 140 C5
Fir Tree Rd TW4 ... 129 A1
Fir Trees Cl SE16 ... 119 A5
Fir Tree Wlk EN1 ... 5 B2
Fir Wlk KT17,SM3 ... 216 D2
Fisher Cl Croydon CR0 ... 205 D1
Southall UB6 ... 85 C4
Holdbrook EN3 ... 7 C6
Fisher Ho 8 E1 ... 118 C6
N1 ... 234 A5
2 N19 ... 71 C5
Fisherman Cl TW10 ... 175 C6
Fishermans Dr SE16 ... 118 D4
Fishermans Wlk SE28 ... 123 C4
Fisherman's Wlk E14 ... 119 C5
Fisher Rd HA3 ... 24 D1
Fishers Cl SW16 ... 159 D1
Fishers Ct SE14 ... 140 D4
4 Teddington TW11 ... 174 D5
Fishersdene KT10 ... 213 A1
Fisher's La W4 ... 111 B2
Fisher St E16 ... 99 A2
WC1 ... 240 C3
Fisherton St
NW8 ... 92 B3 236 D6
Fisherton Street Est
NW8 ... 92 B3 236 D5
Fishguard Way E16 ... 122 D5
Fishlock Ct 6 SW4 ... 138 A3
Fishponds Rd BR2 ... 225 D3
Upper Tooting SW17 ... 180 C6
Fish St Hill EC3 ... 252 D5
Fiske Ct Barking IG11 ... 101 B5
1 Merton SW19 ... 180 A3
Sutton SM2 ... 218 A1
Tottenham N17 ... 34 A2
Fitch Ct SW2 ... 160 C6
8 Mitcham CR4 ... 181 A1
Fitzalan Rd N3 ... 47 B6
Claygate KT10 ... 212 C1
Fitzalan St
SE11 ... 116 C2 261 A4
Fitzclarence Ho W11 ... 244 A2
Fitz-George Ave W14 ... 254 A3
Fitzgeorge Ave KT2,
KT3 ... 177 B2
Fitzgerald Ave SW14 ... 133 C2
Fitzgerald Ct 1 E10 ... 53 D1
Fitzgerald Ho 14 E14 ... 97 D1
10 SW9 ... 138 C3
Hayes UB3 ... 106 B5
Fitzgerald Rd
Mortlake SW14 ... 133 B2
Thames Ditton KT7 ... 197 A3
Wanstead E11 ... 55 A4
Fitzhardinge Ho W1 ... 238 A2
Beckenham BR3 ... 185 D1
Fitzhardinge St W1 ... 238 A2
Fitzherbert Ho 11
TW10 ... 154 B5
Fitzhugh Gr SW18 ... 158 B5
Fitzjames Ave W14 ... 254 B3
Croydon CR0 ... 222 A6
Fitzjohn Ave EN5 ... 1 B1
Fitzjohn's Ave NW3 ... 70 B3
Fitzjohns Mans NW3 ... 70 A2
Fitzjohns Prim Sch
NW3 ... 70 B3
Fitzmaurice Ho 17
SE16 ... 118 B2
Fitzmaurice Pl W1 ... 248 D4
Fitzneal St W12 ... 89 D1
Fitzroy Cl N6 ... 48 D1
Fitzroy Cres W4 ... 133 B5
Fitzroy Ct N6 ... 49 C3
W1 ... 239 B5
Fitzroy Gdns SE19 ... 183 C3
Fitzroy Ho 14 E14 ... 97 B1
SE1 ... 263 D2
Fitzroy Lo N21 ... 16 D6
Fitzroy Mews W1 ... 239 A5
Fitzroy Pk N6 ... 48 D1
Fitzroy Rd NW1 ... 93 A6 231 A6
Fitzroy Sq W1 ... 239 A5
Fitzroy St W1 ... 93 C3 239 A5
Fitzroy Yd NW1 ... 231 A6
Fitzsimmons Ct 1
NW10 ... 89 B6
Fitzstephen Rd RM8 ... 80 C3
Fitzwarren Gdns N19 ... 49 C1
Fitzwilliam Ave TW9 ... 132 B3
Fitzwilliam Ho TW9 ... 131 D1
Fitzwilliam Hts 1
SE23 ... 162 C2
Fitzwilliam Mews E16 ... 121 A5
Fitzwilliam Rd SW4 ... 137 C2
Fitzwygram Cl TW12 ... 174 A5
Five Acre NW9 ... 27 D1
Fiveacre Cl CR7 ... 204 C3
Five Elms Prim Sch
RM8 ... 81 B5
Five Elms Rd BR2 ... 225 C5
Dagenham RM9 ... 81 B5
Fives Ct SE11 ... 261 C5
Fiveways SE9 ... 166 D2
Croydon CR0 ... 220 C4
Five Ways Cnr NW4 ... 28 A2
Fiveways Rd SW9 ... 138 C3
Five Ways Retail Pk
NW7 ... 27 D3
Flack Ct 14 E10 ... 53 D2
Fladbury Rd N15 ... 51 B3
Fladgate Rd E11 ... 54 C3
Flag Cl CR0 ... 206 D1
Flag Wlk HA5 ... 40 A3
Flambard Rd HA1,HA3 ... 43 A3
Flamborough Ho 11
SE15 ... 140 A4
Flamborough Rd HA4 ... 62 A5
Flamborough St E14 ... 97 A1
Flamingo Ct 2 SE8 ... 141 C5
Flamingo Gdns UB5 ... 85 A4
Flamstead Gdns RM9 ... 80 C1
Flamstead Rd RM9 ... 80 C1
Flamsted Ave HA9 ... 66 C2
Flamsteed Ho* SE10 ... 142 B5
Flamsteed Rd SE7 ... 122 A1
Flanchford Rd W12 ... 111 D3
Flanders Cres SW17 ... 180 D4
Flanders Ct E17 ... 53 A3
Flanders Mans 1 W4 ... 111 D2
Flanders Rd W4 ... 111 C2
Wallend E6 ... 100 C5
Flanders Way E9 ... 74 D2
Flank St 6 E1 ... 118 A6
Flansham Ho 2 E14 ... 97 B1
Flash La EN2 ... 5 A6
Flask Wlk NW3 ... 70 B4
Flatford Ho 2 SE6 ... 186 A6
Flavell Mews SE10 ... 120 C1
Flaxen Cl E4 ... 19 D1
Flaxen Rd E4 ... 19 D1
Flaxley Rd SM4 ... 201 D2
Flaxman Ct W1 ... 239 C1
12 Belvedere DA17 ... 125 C1
Flaxman Ho SE1 ... 261 D6
10 W4 ... 111 C1
Flaxman Rd SE5 ... 138 D3
Flaxman Terr
WC1 ... 93 D4 232 D1
Flaxman Villas N2 ... 48 A6
Flaxmore Ct DA7 ... 147 D2
South Norwood CR7 ... 183 B1
Flaxton Rd SE18 ... 145 C5
Flecker Cl HA7 ... 24 D5
Flecker Ho 6 SE5 ... 139 B5
Fleece Dr N9 ... 34 A6
Fleecefield Prim Sch
N18 ... 34 A6
Fleece Rd KT6 ... 197 C1
Fleece Wlk N7 ... 72 A2
Fleeming Cl E17 ... 35 B1
Fleeming Rd E17 ... 35 B1
Fleet Cl
East Molesey KT8 ... 195 B4
Ruislip HA4 ... 39 A3
Fleet Ct 1 W12 ... 111 C3
Fleetfield WC1 ... 233 B2
Fleet Ho 4 E14 ... 119 A6
6 SW2 ... 160 C6
Fleet Pl EC4 ... 241 C2
Fleet Prim Sch NW3 ... 70 D3
Fleet Rd NW3 ... 70 D3
Fleetside KT8 ... 195 C4
Fleet Sq WC1 ... 233 D1
Fleet St EC4 ... 94 C1 241 B1
Fleet Street Hill 11 E1 ... 96 A3
Fleet Terr SE6 ... 164 A4
Fleetway WC1 ... 233 B2
Fleetway West Bsns Pk
UB6 ... 87 B5
Fleet Wood 6 N16 ... 73 D6
Fleetwood Cl E16 ... 99 D2
Chessington KT9 ... 213 D1
South Croydon CR0 ... 221 D5
Fleetwood Ct 1 E6 ... 100 B2
Orpington BR6 ... 226 C4
8 Stanwell TW19 ... 148 A5
Fleetwood Rd NW10 ... 68 A3
Kingston KT3 ... 198 D6
Fleetwood Sq KT3 ... 198 D6
Fleetwood St N16 ... 73 C6
Fleetwood Way WD19 ... 22 C6
Fleming Cl 3 W9 ... 91 C3
Fleming Ct W2 ... 236 C4
Croydon CR0 ... 220 C3
Fleming Dr N21 ... 16 B6
Fleming Ho N4 ... 51 A1
8 SE16 ... 118 A4
8 Wembley HA9 ... 67 A5
Fleming Mead CR4 ... 180 D3
Fleming Rd SE17 ... 138 D6
Southall UB1 ... 86 A1
Fleming Way SE28 ... 124 D6
Isleworth TW7 ... 130 D1
Fleming Wlk NW9 ... 27 C1
Flemming Ave HA4 ... 62 B6
Flempton Rd E10 ... 53 A1
Fletcher Bldgs WC2 ... 240 B1
Fletcher Cl E16 ... 122 D6
Fletcher Ct 9 NW5 ... 71 B4
Fletcher Ho 22 N1 ... 95 C6
16 N16 ... 73 C4
Fletcher La E10 ... 54 A2
Fletcher Path 7 SE8 ... 141 C5
Fletcher Rd W4 ... 111 A3
Fletchers Cl BR2 ... 209 B5
Fletcher St 10 E1 ... 118 A6
Fletching Rd E5 ... 74 C5
SE7 ... 143 D6
Fletton Rd N11 ... 32 A3
Fleur Gates 7 SW19 ... 156 D4
Flexmere Rd N17 ... 33 C2
Flimwell Cl BR1 ... 186 C5
Flinders Ho 28 E1 ... 118 B5
Flint Cl 8 BR6 ... 227 D2
Flint Down Cl BR5 ... 190 A2
Flintmill Cres SE3,SE9 ... 144 A3
Flinton St
SE17 ... 117 C1 263 B2
Flint St SE17 ... 117 B2 262 D3
Flitcroft St WC2 ... 239 D1
Flitton Ho 7 N1 ... 72 D1
Floathaven Cl SE28 ... 124 A5
Flock Mill Pl SW18 ... 157 D3
Flodden Rd SE5 ... 139 A4
Flood La 4 TW1 ... 153 A3
Flood St SW3 ... 136 C6 267 B6
Flood Wlk
SW3 ... 136 C6 267 B6
Flora Cl E14 ... 97 D1
Flora Gardens Prim Sch
W6 ... 112 B2
Flora Gdns 2 W6 ... 112 B2
Dagenham RM6 ... 58 C3
Floral St WC2 ... 116 A6 250 A6
Flora St DA17 ... 125 B1
Florence Ave Enfield EN2 ... 5 A2
Morden SM4 ... 202 A4
Florence Cl KT12 ... 194 B2
Florence Ct 4 E5 ... 74 A5
W9 ... 229 B1
Wanstead E11 ... 55 C5
5 Wimbledon SW19 ... 179 A4
Florence Dr EN2 ... 5 A2
Florence Elson Cl E12 ... 78 C4
Florence Gdns
Chiswick W4 ... 133 A6
Ilford RM6 ... 58 C2
Florence Ho 20 SE16 ... 118 B1
2 SE18 ... 144 B4
7 SW18 ... 136 B1
2 SW2 ... 160 B6
10 W11 ... 112 D6
5 Kingston KT2 ... 176 B3
Florence Mans 4 NW4 ... 46 B4
SW6 ... 264 C2
Florence Nightingale Ho 11
N1 ... 73 A2
Florence Nightingale Mus*
SE1 ... 250 D1
Florence Rd BR1 ... 187 A2
E13 ... 99 A5
8 E6 ... 99 C6
N4 ... 50 C2
SE14 ... 141 B4
SE2 ... 124 C2
W4 ... 111 B3
5 Beckenham BR3 ... 185 A1
Ealing W5 ... 110 A6
Feltham TW13 ... 150 B3
6 Kingston KT2 ... 176 B3
Southall UB2 ... 106 D3
Walton-on-T KT12 ... 194 B2
Wimbledon SW19 ... 179 D4
Florence Root Ho IG4 ... 56 B4
Florence St E16 ... 98 D3
N1 ... 72 D1
NW4 ... 46 C5
Florence Terr SE14 ... 141 B4
Kingston SW15 ... 155 C1
Florence Way SW12 ... 158 D3
Florentine Ho 3 IG1 ... 78 D6
Flores Ho 10 E1 ... 96 D2
Florfield Rd E8 ... 74 B2
Florian SE5 ... 139 C4
Florian Ave SM1 ... 218 B4
Florian Rd SW15 ... 135 A1
Florida Cl WD23 ... 8 B2
Florida Ct BR2 ... 208 D5
Florida Rd CR7 ... 182 D2
Florida St E2 ... 96 A4
Florin Ct SE1 ... 253 C1
Edmonton N18 ... 33 C6
Floris Pl 7 SW4 ... 137 C2
Floriston Ave UB10 ... 61 A1
Floriston Cl HA7 ... 25 B2
Floriston Ct UB5 ... 63 D3
Floriston Gdns HA7 ... 25 B2
Florys Ct 7 SW19 ... 157 A3
Floss St SW15 ... 134 C3
Flower & Dean Wlk
E1 ... 243 D3
Flower La NW7 ... 27 D4
Flower Pot Cl N15 ... 51 D3
Flowers Cl NW2 ... 68 A5
Flowersmead SW17 ... 159 A2
Flowers Mews 1 N19 ... 71 C6
Flower Wlk The
SW7 ... 114 A4 246 B2
Floyd Rd SE7 ... 121 C1
Fludyer St SE13 ... 142 C1
Fluer De Lis St E1 ... 243 C5
Flynn Ct 12 E14 ... 119 C6
Fogerty Cl EN3 ... 7 C6
Foley Cotts KT10 ... 212 D2
Foley Ho 19 E1 ... 96 C1
Foley Mews KT10 ... 212 C2
Foley Rd KT10 ... 212 C1
Foley St W1 ... 93 C2 239 A3
Folgate St E1 ... 95 D2 243 C4
Foliot Ho N1 ... 233 C4
Foliot St W12 ... 89 D1
Folkestone Ct UB5 ... 63 D3
Folkestone Rd E17 ... 53 D5
Edmonton N18 ... 34 A6
Wallend E6 ... 100 C4
Folkingham La 6 NW9 ... 27 C2
Folkington Cnr N12 ... 29 B5
Folland 6 NW9 ... 27 D1
Follett Ho SW10 ... 266 C4
Follett St E14 ... 98 A1
Folly La E17 ... 35 A2
E4 ... 35 B3
Folly Wall E14 ... 120 A4
Fontaine Ct 3 BR3 ... 185 B2
Fontaine Rd SW16 ... 182 B3
Fontarabia Rd SW11 ... 137 A1
Fontenelle SE5 ... 139 C4
Fontenoy Ho SE11 ... 261 C3
Fontenoy Rd SW12,
SW17 ... 159 C2
Fonteyne Gdns IG8 ... 37 D1
Fonthill Cl SE20 ... 184 A1
Fonthill Ct SE23 ... 162 C4
Fonthill Ho SW1 ... 258 D2
W14 ... 254 B6
Fonthill Mews N4 ... 72 B6
Fonthill Rd N4 ... 72 C6
Font Hills N2 ... 30 A1
Fontley Way SW15 ... 156 A4
Fontmell Cl TW15 ... 170 C5
Fontmell Pk TW15 ... 170 C5
Fontwell Cl Harrow HA3 ... 24 C3
Northolt UB5 ... 63 C2
Fontwell Dr BR2 ... 210 C4
Football La HA1 ... 42 C1
Footpath The SW15 ... 156 A6
Foots Cray High St
DA14 ... 190 D4
Foots Cray La DA5,
DA14 ... 168 C3
Footscray Rd SE9 ... 166 D3
Forber Ho 25 E2 ... 96 C4
Forbes Cl NW2 ... 68 A5
Forbes Ct SE19 ... 183 C5
Forbes Ho 2 W4 ... 110 C1
Forbes St E1 ... 96 A1
Forbes Way HA4 ... 62 B6
Forburg Rd N16 ... 52 A1
Fordbridge Ct TW15 ... 170 A4
Fordbridge Rd
Ashford TW15 ... 170 B5
Lower Halliford TW16,
TW17 ... 193 D3
Sunbury TW16 ... 194 A5
Fordbridge Rdbt
TW15 ... 170 A4
Ford Cl 11 E3 ... 97 A5
Ashford TW15 ... 170 A4
Harrow HA1 ... 42 B2
Littleton TW17 ... 192 C4
Thornton Heath CR7 ... 204 D4
Fordcombe 13 NW5 ... 71 A2
Forde Ave BR1 ... 209 C6
Fordel Rd SE6 ... 164 B3
Ford End IG8 ... 37 B4
Fordham 4 KT1 ... 176 C1
Fordham Cl EN4 ... 2 C2
Fordham Rd EN4 ... 2 C2
Fordham St 7 E1 ... 96 A1
Ford Ho 2 SE18 ... 122 D1
2 New Barnet EN5 ... 13 D6
Fordhook Ave W5 ... 110 C6
Fordingley Rd W9 ... 91 B4
Fordington Ho 2
SE26 ... 162 B1
Fordington Rd N6 ... 48 D5
Fordmill Rd SE6 ... 163 C2
Ford Rd E3 ... 97 B5
Ashford TW15 ... 170 B6
Dagenham RM10 ... 81 C1
Ford's Gr N21 ... 17 A3
Fords Park Rd E16 ... 99 A1
Ford Sq E1 ... 96 B2
Ford St E16 ... 98 D1
E3 ... 97 A5
Fordwich Cl BR6 ... 211 D2
Fordwych Ct NW2 ... 69 A2
Fordwych Rd NW2 ... 69 A3
Fordyce Ho 3 SW16 ... 181 C6
Fordyce Rd SE13 ... 164 A5
Fordyke Rd RM8 ... 81 B6
Foreign, Commonwealth &
Home Offices SW1 ... 250 A2
Foreland Ct NW4 ... 29 A2
Foreland Ho W11 ... 244 A6
Foreland St SE18 ... 123 B2
Foreshore SE8 ... 119 B2
Fore St EC2 ... 95 A2 242 B3
Edmonton N18 ... 34 A6
Pinner HA5 ... 40 A4
Forest App Chingford E4 ... 20 C4
Woodford IG8 ... 37 A3
Fore St Ave EC2 ... 242 C3
Forest Ave E4 ... 20 C4
Forest Bsns Pk E17 ... 52 D2
Forest Cl
Chislehurst BR7 ... 188 C2
Wanstead E11 ... 55 A4
Woodford IG8 ... 37 B6
Forest Croft SE23 ... 162 B2
Forest Ct E11 ... 54 C5
12 N12 ... 29 D6
Chingford E4 ... 20 D3
Forestdale N14 ... 31 D6
Forestdale Ctr The
CR0 ... 223 B1
Forest Dene Ct 2
SM2 ... 218 A2
Forest Dr
Ashford TW16 ... 171 D3
Chingford IG8 ... 36 C3
Keston Mark BR2 ... 226 A4
Wanstead E12 ... 77 D5
Forest Dr E E11 ... 54 B3
Forest Dr W E11 ... 54 B2
Forest Edge IG9 ... 21 D1
Forester Rd SE15 ... 140 B2
Foresters Cl SM6 ... 219 D1
Foresters Cres DA7 ... 147 D1
Foresters Dr E17 ... 54 B5
Wallington SM6 ... 219 D1
Foresters Prim Sch
SM6 ... 219 D2
Forest Gate NW9 ... 45 C4
Forest Gate Com Sch
E7 ... 77 A3
Forest Gate Sta E7 ... 77 A3
Forest Gdns N17 ... 33 D1
Forest Glade E11 ... 54 C3
Chingford E4 ... 36 C5
Forest Gr E8 ... 73 D2
Forest Hill SE23 ... 162 C3
Forest Hill Bsns Ctr
SE23 ... 162 C2
Forest Hill Ct 6 SE26 ... 162 B1
Forest Hill Ind Est
SE23 ... 162 C2
Forest Hill Rd SE22 ... 162 B5
Forest Hill Sec Sch
SE23 ... 162 D1
Forest Hill Sta SE23 ... 162 C2
Forest Ho 9 E4 ... 20 C4
Forestholme Cl SE23 ... 162 C2
Forest Hts IG9 ... 21 A2
Forest La E7,E15 ... 76 D3
Forest Lawns BR1 ... 187 C2
Forest Lea E11 ... 54 D2
Forest Lo 1 SE23 ... 162 C1
Forest Mount Rd IG8 ... 36 B3
Forest Point E7 ... 77 B3
Forest Rd E11 ... 54 B2
E17 ... 53 C6
E7 ... 77 A4
E8 ... 73 D2
Edmonton N9 ... 18 B3
Feltham TW13 ... 150 C2
Morden SM3,SM4 ... 201 C2
Richmond TW9 ... 132 C5
Romford RM7 ... 59 D6
Woodford IG8 ... 21 A1
Forest Ridge BR2 ... 226 B4
Beckenham BR3 ... 207 C6
Forest Rise E17 ... 54 B5
Forest Sch E17 ... 54 C5
Forest Side E7 ... 77 B4
Buckhurst Hill IG9 ... 21 C3
Chingford E4 ... 20 D3
New Malden KT4 ... 199 D1
Forest St E7 ... 77 A3
Forest The E11 ... 54 C5
Forest Trad Est E17 ... 52 D6
Forest View E11 ... 54 D2
Chingford E4 ... 20 B4
Forest View Ave E10 ... 54 B4
Forest View Rd E12 ... 78 A4
Chingford E17 ... 36 A2
Forest Way BR5 ... 211 D4
6 N19 ... 71 C6
Sidcup DA15 ... 167 B4
Woodford IG8 ... 37 B6
Forfar Rd
SW11 ... 137 A4 268 B2
Tottenham N22 ... 32 D2
Forge Cl BR2 ... 209 A1
Forge Cotts W5 ... 109 D5
Forge Dr KT10 ... 213 A1
Forge La Belmont SM3 ... 217 A1
Feltham TW13 ... 173 A5
Sunbury TW16 ... 194 A6
Forge Lane Inf Sch
TW13 ... 173 A5
Forge Lane Jun Sch
TW13 ... 173 A5

Forge Mews
Addington CR0 223 C3
Sunbury TW16 194 A6
Forge Pl NW1 71 A2
Forge The UB3 127 B6
Forlong Path UB5 63 A2
Forman Ct TW1 152 D3
Forman Gr 2 UB5 84 D4
Forman Ho SE4 140 D1
Forman Pl N16 73 D4
Formby Ave HA3,HA7 43 C6
Formby Ct 9 N7 72 C3
Formosa Ho 1 E1 97 A3
Formosa St W9 91 D3
Formunt Cl E16 98 D2
Forres Gdns NW11 47 C3
Forrest Ct N7 72 C2
Forrester Path SE26 184 C6
Forresters The HA5 40 B3
Forrest Gdns SW16 204 B6
Forrest Ho SW15 134 C3
Forris Ave UB3 105 D5
Forset Ct W1 237 B2
Forset St W1 92 C1 237 B2
Forstal Cl BR2 209 A6
Forster Ho SE6 164 B1
Forster Park Prim Sch
SE6 164 C1
Forster Rd E17 53 A3
N17 51 D6
Beckenham BR3 207 A6
Streatham SW2 160 A4
Thornton Heath CR0 205 A2
Forsters Cl RM6 59 B3
Forsters Way UB4 84 B1
Forstic Wlk E1 243 D3
Forston St N1 95 A5 235 B4
Forsyte Cres SE19 183 C2
Forsyte Ct KT2 176 D2
Forsythe Ct KT3 177 C1
Forsythe Shades BR3 186 A2
Forsyth Gdns SE17 138 D6
Forsyth Ho 14 E9 74 C1
SW1 259 B3
Forsythia Cl IG1 78 D3
Forsythia Ho SE4 141 A2
Forsyth Pl EN1 17 C6
Forterie Gdns IG3 80 A4
Fortescue Ave 1 E8 74 B1
Twickenham TW2 152 A1
Fortescue Rd HA8 27 B3
Mitcham SW19 180 B3
Fortess Gr NW5 71 C3
Fortess Rd NW5 71 C4
Fortess Wlk NW5 71 B3
Forthbridge Rd SW11 137 A1
Forth Ho 28 E3 97 B5
Forties The 9 NW5 71 C3
Fortior Ct N6 49 C2
Fortis Cl E16 99 C1
Fortis Ct N10 49 A6
Fortis Gn N2,N10 48 D6
Fortis Green Ave N2 48 D5
Fortis Green Cotts N2 48 D6
Fortismere Ave N10 49 A6
Fortismere Sch N10 30 D1
Fortismere Sch (South
Wing) N10 49 A6
Fortnam Rd N19 71 D6
Fortnums Acre HA7 24 D4
Fort Rd SE1 117 D2 263 D3
Northolt UB5 63 C1
Fortrose Gdns SW12,
SW2 160 A3
Fort St E1 243 B3
E16 121 B5
Fortuna Cl N7 72 B2
Fortune Ct IG11 102 B5
Fortune Gate Rd NW10 89 C6
Fortune Green Rd NW6 69 C4
Fortune Ho EC1 242 B5
SE11 261 A3
Fortune La WD6 9 D5
Fortunes Mead UB5 63 A2
Fortune St EC1 95 A3 242 B5
Fortune Way NW10 90 A4
Fortune Wlk SE28 123 B3
Forty Acre La E16 99 A2
Forty Ave HA9 66 B6
Forty Cl HA9 66 B5
Forty Hall* EN2 5 D6
Forty Hill EN2 5 D6
Forty Hill CE Prim Sch
EN2 6 A6
Forty Hill Ho EN1 5 D5
Forty La HA9 66 D6
Forumside HA8 26 C4
Forum The KT8 195 D5
Forum Way HA8 26 C4
Forval Cl CR4 202 D4
Forward Bsns Ctr The
E16 98 B3
Forward Dr HA3 42 D5
Fosbroke Ho SW8 270 A3
Fosbury Ho 7 SW9 138 B1
Fosbury Mews W2 245 D5
Foscote Mews W9 91 C2
Foscote Rd NW4 46 B3
Foskett Ho 18 N2 30 B1
Foskett Rd SW6 135 B3
Foss Ave CR0,CR9 220 C3
Fossdene Prim Sch
SE7 121 B1
Fossdene Rd SE7 121 B1
Fossdyke Cl UB4 85 A2
Fosse Way W13 87 A2
Fossil Rd SE13 141 C2
Fossington Rd DA17 124 D2
Foss Rd SW17 180 B6
Fossway RM8 80 C6
Foster Ct E16 120 D6
4 NW1 71 C1
NW4 46 C5
Foster Ho SE14 141 B4
Foster La EC2 95 A1 242 A2
Foster Rd E13 99 A3
W3 111 C6
W4 111 B1
Fosters Cl BR7 188 B5
Woodford E18 37 B2
Fosters Old Sch DA16 146 B3
Foster's Prim Sch
DA16 146 C2
Foster St NW4 46 C5
Foster Wlk NW4 46 C5
Fothergill Cl E13 99 A5
Fothergill Dr N21 16 A6
Fotheringham Ct EN1 5 D1
Fotheringham Rd EN1 5 D1
Foubert's Pl W1 239 A1
Foulden Rd N16 73 D4
Foulden Terr N16 73 D4
Foulis Terr
SW7 114 B1 256 D2
Foulser Rd SW17 159 A1
Foulsham Rd CR7 205 B6
Foundary Ho 7 E14 97 D2
Founder Cl 2 E6 100 D1
Founders Ct EC2 242 C2
Founders Gdns SE19 183 A3
Founders Ho SW1 259 C2
Foundling Ct WC1 240 A6
Foundry Cl SE16 119 A5
Foundry Mews NW1 239 B6
Foundry Pl E1 96 C2
Fountain Cl UB8 83 A2
Fountain Ct DA15 168 B5
EC4 251 A6
SW1 258 C3
New Malden KT3 199 A5
Penge SE26 184 C4
Fountain Dr
Dulwich SE19 183 D6
Wallington SM5 218 D1
Fountain Green Sq 31
SE16 118 A4
Fountain Ho 1 NW6 69 A1
30 SE16 118 A4
W1 248 A4
Fountain Mews 1 N5 73 A4
NW3 70 D2
Fountain Pl SW9 138 C4
Fountain Rd
South Norwood CR7 183 A1
Upper Tooting SW17 180 B6
Fountains Ave TW13 151 B1
Fountains Cl TW13 151 B1
Fountains Cres N14 16 A4
Fountains The N3 29 D3
Loughton IG10 21 D4
Fountayne Bsns Ctr
N15 52 A5
Fountayne Rd N15 52 A5
N16 74 A6
Fount St SW8 137 D5 269 D3
Four Acres N12 29 D6
Fouracres EN3 7 A4
Fourland Wlk HA8 27 A4
Fournier St E1 95 D2 243 D4
Four Seasons Cl E3 97 C5
Four Seasons Cres
SM3 217 B6
Four Square Ct TW4 151 C5
Fourth Ave W10 91 A4
Hayes UB3 105 D5
Ilford E12 78 B4
Fourth Cross Rd TW2 152 B2
Fourth Way
Wembley HA9 66 D4
Wembley HA9 67 A4
Four Tubs The WD23 8 B4
Fourways 2 CR0 221 D6
Four Wents The E4 20 B2
Fovant Ct 5 SW8 137 C3
Fowey Ave IG4 55 D4
Fowey Cl E1 118 B5
Fowey Ho SE11 261 B2
Fowler Cl DA14 191 A5
SW11 136 B2
Fowler Ho N1 94 D6 234 D6
N15 51 B4
5 SE5 139 C3
SW8 269 D1
Fowler Rd E7 77 A4
N1 94 D6 234 D6
Mitcham CR4 181 A1
Fowler's Wlk W5 87 D3
Fownes St SW11 136 C2
Foxberry Ct SE4 141 B1
Foxberry Rd SE4 141 A2
Foxborough Gdns SE4 163 C6
Foxbourne Rd SW17 159 A2
Foxbury Ave BR7 189 B4
Foxbury Cl BR1 187 B4
Foxbury Rd BR1 187 B4
Fox Cl E1 96 C3
E16 99 A2
Elstree WD6 9 D5
Foxcombe CR0 223 D2
Foxcombe Cl 1 E6 99 D5
Foxcombe Rd 6
SW15 156 A3
Foxcote SE5 263 B1
Foxcroft N1 233 D3
Foxcroft Rd SE18 144 D4
Foxes Dale SE3 143 A2
Beckenham BR2 208 B6
Foxfield Prim Sch
SE18 123 A2
Foxfield Rd BR6 227 B6
Foxglove Ave BR3 185 D3
Foxglove Cl UB1 107 A6
Foxglove Ct 11 HA0 88 A5
Foxglove Gdns E11 55 C5
Foxglove La KT9 214 C4
Foxglove St W12 111 D6
Foxglove Way SM6 203 B1
Fox Gr KT12 194 B2
Foxgrove N14 16 A1
Foxgrove Path WD19 22 D5
Foxgrove Rd BR3 186 A3
Foxham Rd N19 71 D5
Fox Hill SE19 183 D3
Fox Hill Gdns SE19 183 D3
Fox Ho 2 SW11 136 B1
Foxhole Rd 2 SE9 166 A6
Fox Hollow Cl 1 SE18 123 C1
Fox Hollow Dr DA16 146 D2
Foxholt Gdns NW10 67 A1
Foxhome Cl BR7 188 C4
Fox House Rd DA17 125 D1
Fox & Knot St EC1 241 D4
Fox La BR2 225 C3
Ealing W5 88 A3
Palmers Green N13 16 B1
Foxlands Rd RM10 81 D3
Foxlees HA0 65 A4
Foxley Cl E8 74 A3
Foxley Ct SM2 218 A1
Foxley Ho 4 E3 97 D4
Foxley Rd SW9 138 D5
Thornton Heath CR7 204 D5
Foxley Sq 3 SW9 138 D4
Foxmead Cl EN2 4 B2
Foxmore St SW11 267 C1
Fox Prim Sch
W8 113 C5 245 A3
Fox Rd E16 98 D2
Foxs Path CR4 180 C1
Fox's Yd E2 243 D6
Foxtail Ho TW3 130 A4
Foxton KT1 198 C6
Foxton Gr CR4 180 B1
Foxton Ho E16 122 C4
Foxwarren KT10 212 D1
Foxwell Mews SE4 141 A2
Foxwell St SE4 141 A2
Foxwood Cl NW7 27 C6
Feltham TW13 150 B1
Foxwood Green Cl EN1 17 C5
Foxwood Rd SE3 142 D1
Foyle Rd SE3 142 D6
Tottenham N17 34 A2
Fradel Lo N16 51 B1
Framfield Cl N12 13 C1
Framfield Ct EN1 17 C5
Framfield Rd N5 72 D3
Ealing W7 86 D1
Mitcham CR4 181 A3
Framlingham Cl 2 E5 74 C6
Framlingham Cres
SE9 188 B6
Frampton NW1 71 D1
Frampton Cl SM2 217 C1
Frampton Ct 3 W3 111 A4
Frampton Ho NW8 236 D5
Frampton Park Rd E9 74 C1
Frampton Rd TW4 151 A6
Frampton St
NW8 92 B3 236 D5
Francemary Rd SE4 163 C6
Frances Ct E17 53 C3
South Norwood SE25 183 D1
Frances Grey Ho 18 E1 96 D2
Frances Rd E4 35 C4
Frances St SE18 122 B2
Franche Court Rd
SW17 158 A1
Francis Ave DA7 147 C3
Feltham TW13 150 A1
Ilford IG1 79 B6
Francis Barber Cl
SW16 182 B6
Franciscan Prim Sch
SW17 181 A5
Franciscan Rd SW17 181 A6
Francis Chichester Way
SW11 137 A4 268 B1
Francis Cl 6 E14 120 B2
Littleton TW17 192 C5
West Ewell KT19 215 B4
Francis Ct NW7 27 D5
12 SE14 140 D6
Ealing W5 110 B6
Kingston KT5 198 A5
Francis Gr SW19 179 B4
Francis Ho 11 N1 95 C6
NW10 89 D6
Francis Holland Sch
NW1 92 D3 237 D5
SW1 115 A2 258 B3
Francis Rd E10 76 A6
N2 48 D5
Harrow HA1 43 A4
Hounslow TW4 128 D3
Ilford IG1 79 B6
Pinner HA5 40 C4
Thornton Heath CR0 204 D2
Wallington SM6 219 C2
Wembley UB6 87 C6
Francis Snary Lo 11
SW18 157 C6
Francis St E15 76 C3
SW1 115 C2 259 B4
Ilford IG1 79 B6
Francis Terr N19 71 C5
Francis Wlk N1 233 C6
Francklyn Gdns HA8 10 C1
Franconia Rd SW4 159 D6
Frank Bailey Wlk E12 78 C2
Frank Barnes Prim Sch for
Deaf Children NW3 70 B1
Frank Beswick Ho
SW6 264 D5
Frank Burton Cl 4
SE7 121 B1
Frank Dixon Cl SE21 161 C3
Frank Dixon Way
SE21 161 C3
Frank Douglas Ct W6 112 A2
Frankfurt Rd SE24 161 A6
Frankham Ho 8 SE8 141 C5
Frankham St SE8 141 C5
Frank Ho SW8 270 A4
Frankland Cl SE16 118 B2
Woodford IG8 37 C5
Frankland Ho 4
SW12 159 B4
Frankland Rd
SW7 114 B3 256 C5
Chingford E4 35 C5
Franklin Bldg 6 E14 119 C4
Franklin Cl N20 14 A4
SE13 141 D4
Kingston KT1 198 C6
West Norwood SE27 160 D1
Franklin Cres CR4 203 C5
Franklin Ho 26 E1 118 B5
NW9 45 D2
Beckenham BR2 208 C6
Franklin Ind Est SE20 184 C2
Franklin Pas SE9 144 A2
Franklin Rd DA7 147 A4
Penge SE20 184 C3
Walton-on-T KT12 194 A3
Franklins Mews HA2 64 A6
Franklin Sq SW5 254 D1
Franklin's Row
SW3 114 D1 257 D2
Franklin St 43 E3 97 D4
N15 51 C3
Franklin Way CR0 204 A2
Franklyn Rd NW10 67 D2
Walton-on-T KT12 194 B3
Franks Ave KT3 199 A5
Franks Ho TW7 131 B1
Frank Slater Ho 4 IG3 58 B1
Frank Soskice Ho
SW6 264 D5
Frank St 5 E13 99 A3
Franks Wood Ave BR2,
BR5 211 A4
Frankswood Ave UB7 82 B1
Frank Towell Ct TW14 150 A3
Frank Whymark Ho 4
SE16 118 C4
Franlaw Cres N13 33 A6
Fransfield Gr SE26 162 B1
Frans Hals Ct E14 120 B3
Franshams WD23 8 C2
Frant Cl SE20 184 C3
Franthorne Way SE6 163 D1
Frant Rd CR7 204 D4
Fraserburgh Ho 28 E3 97 B5
Fraser Cl 3 E6 100 A1
Fraser Ct SW11 267 A2
Fraser Ho 3 SE18 122 C2
40 SW8 137 D3
Brentford TW8 110 B1
Fraser Rd E17 53 D3
Edmonton N9 18 B1
Wembley UB6 87 C6
Fraser Regnart Ct 12
NW5 70 D3
Fraser St W4 111 C1
Frating Cres IG8 37 B4
Frazer Ave HA4 62 C3
Frazier St SE1 116 C4 251 A1
Freame Ho N21 17 B5
Frean St SE16 118 A3
Frearson Ho WC1 233 D2
Freda Corbett Cl 9
SE15 140 A5
Frederica Rd E4 20 B4
Frederica St 4 N7 72 B1
Frederic Ho SE7 122 A3
Frederick SE16 119 B5
Frederick Charrington Ho
3 E1 96 C3
Frederick Cl
W2 114 D6 247 C6
Cheam SM1 217 B3
Frederick Cres SW9 138 D5
Enfield EN3 6 C3
Frederick Ct SW6 135 A2
Frederick Gdns
Cheam SM1 217 B3
Thornton Heath CR0 204 D3
Frederick Ho UB1 107 B6
Frederick Pl SE18 122 D1
Frederick Rd SM1 217 B3
Frederick's Pl EC2 242 C1
N12 30 A6
Frederick Sq 11 SE16 119 A6
Frederick's Row EC1 234 C2
Frederick St
WC1 94 B4 233 C1
Frederick Terr E8 73 D1
Frederic Mews SW1 248 A1
Frederic St E17 53 A4
Fredora Ave UB4 83 D3
Fred Wigg Twr E11 76 D6
Freedom Cl E17 53 A5
Freedom St SW11 136 D3
Freegrove Rd N7 72 A3
Freehold Ind Ctr TW4 150 C6
Freeland Ct W5 110 B6
Freeland Pk N3 29 A1
Freeland Rd W5 110 B6
Freelands Ave CR2 222 D1
Freelands Gr BR1 187 B2
Freelands Rd BR1 187 B2
Freeling Ho NW8 229 C6
Freeling St 7 N1 72 B1
Freeman Cl
Northolt UB5 63 A1
Upper Halliford TW17 193 C5
Freeman Dr KT8 195 B5
Freeman Ho 13 SW2 160 A4
Freeman Rd SM4 202 B4
Freemans La UB3 105 C6
Freemantle Ave EN3 18 D6
Freemantle St
SE17 117 C1 263 A2
Freemasons Rd E16 99 B1
Freemason's Rd CR0 205 C1
Freemens Hos 1 SW9 138 B1
Freesia Cl BR6 227 D3
Freethorpe Cl SE19 183 C2
Freezeland Way UB10 60 D2
Freke Rd SW11 137 A2
Fremantle Ho 14 E1 96 B3
Fremantle Rd
Belvedere DA17 125 C2
Ilford IG6 57 A6
Fremont St E9 96 C6
French Ordinary Ct
EC3 253 B6
French Pl E1 243 B6
French St TW16 172 C1
Frendsbury Rd SE4 141 A1
Frensham Cl UB1 85 B4
Frensham Ct N5 73 A3
4 NW9 46 A5
Mitcham CR4 202 B6
Frensham Dr
New Addington CR0 224 A1
Roehampton SW15 156 A2
Frensham Ho 7 KT6 198 A4
Frensham Rd DA15 167 B2
Frensham St SE15 140 A6
Frere St 6 SW11 136 C3
Fresham Ho BR2 208 D6
Freshfield Ave E8 73 D1
Freshfield Cl SE13 142 B1
Freshfield Dr N14 15 B4
Freshfields CR0 207 B1
Freshford St SW17,
SW18 158 A1
Freshwater Cl SW17 181 A4
Freshwater Ct UB1 85 C4
Freshwater Rd
Dagenham RM8 59 A1
Streatham SW17 181 A4
Freshwell Ave RM6 58 C5
Fresh Wharf Est IG11 100 D6
Fresh Wharf Rd IG11 100 D5
Freshwood Cl BR3 185 D2
Freston Gdns EN4 15 A6
Freston Pk N3 29 B1
Freston Rd W10,W11 112 D6
Freswick Ho 8 SE8 119 A2
Freta Rd DA6 169 B6
Freud Mus The* NW3 70 A2
Frewell Bldg EC1 241 A4
Frewing Cl BR7 188 C5
Frewin Rd SW18 158 B3
Friar Mews SE27 160 D1
Friar Rd UB4 84 D3
Friars Ave N20 30 C6
Roehampton SW15 155 D1
Friars Cl SE1 251 D3
Chingford E4 20 A1
Ilford IG1 57 B1
16 Northolt UB5 84 D4
Friars Ct 5 SM6 219 B4
Friars Gate Cl IG8 37 A6
Friars Gdns W3 89 B1
Friars La TW9 153 D6
Friars Mead E14 120 A3
Friars Mews SE9 166 C6
Friars Place La W3 111 B6
Friars Prim Sch
SE1 116 D4 251 D1
Friar's Rd E6 99 D6
Friars Stile Pl 9
TW10 154 A5
Friars Stile Rd TW10 154 A5
Friar St EC4 241 D1
Friars Way W3 89 B1
Friars Wlk N14 15 B4
SE2 124 D1
Friary Cl N12 30 C5
Friary La IG8 37 A6
Friary Park Ct W3 89 A1
Friary Rd N12 30 C6
SE15 140 A5
W3 89 B1
Friary Way N12 30 C6
Friday Hill E4 20 C1
Friday Hill E E4 20 C1
Friday Hill W E4 20 C2
Friday Rd CR4 180 D3
Friday St EC4 117 A6 252 A6
Frideswide Pl NW5 71 C3
Friendly Pl SE13 141 D4
Friendly St SE8 141 C4
Friendly Street Mews
SE8 141 C3
Friendship Wlk UB5 84 D4
Friends' Rd CR0 221 B5
Friend St EC1 94 D4 234 C2
Friern Barnet La N20 30 C6
Friern Barnet Rd N11 31 A5
Friern Barnet Sch N11 30 D5
Friern Bridge Ret Pk
N11 31 B4
Friern Ct N20 14 B1
Friern Mount Dr N20 14 A4
Friern Pk N12 30 B5
Friern Rd SE22 162 A5
Friern Watch Ave N12 30 B6
Frigate Ho 6 E14 120 A2
Frigate Mews SE8 141 C6
Frimley Ave SM6 220 B3
Frimley Cl
New Addington CR0 224 A1
Putney SW19 157 A2
Frimley Cres CR0 224 A1
Frimley Ct DA14 190 C5
Frimley Gdns CR4 202 C6
Frimley Ho CR4 202 C6
Frimley Rd
Chessington KT9 214 A3
Ilford IG3 79 C5
Frimley Way E1 96 D3
Frinstead Ho 1 W10 112 D6
Frinton Ct W13 87 B2
Frinton Dr IG8 36 B3
Frinton Mews IG2 56 C3
Frinton Rd DA14 169 A2
E6 99 D4
N15 51 C3
Streatham SW17 181 A4
Friston St SW6 135 D3
Friswell Pl 1 DA7 147 C1
Fritham Cl KT3 199 C3
Frith Ct NW7 29 A3
Frith Ho E2 96 A4
NW8 236 D5
Frith La NW7 29 A4
Frith Manor Sch N12 29 B5
Frith Rd E11 76 B4
Croydon CR0 221 A6
Frith St W1 93 D1 239 C1
Frithville Ct W12 112 C5
Frithville Gdns W12 112 C5
Frizlands La RM10 81 D5
Frobisher Cl HA5 40 D2
Frobisher Cres TW19 148 A4
Frobisher Ct NW9 27 C1
1 SE10 142 B6
3 W12 112 C4
Belmont SM2 217 B1
6 Forest Hill SE23 162 B2
Frobisher Gdns TW19 148 A4
Frobisher Ho 27 E1 118 B5
3 Ealing W5 88 A4
Frobisher Mews EN2 5 B1
Frobisher Pas E14 119 C5

Frobisher Pl SE14 140 C4
Frobisher Rd E6 100 B1
N8 50 C5
Frobisher St SE10 142 C6
Froebel Coll SW15 155 D5
Frogley Rd SE22 139 D1
Frogmore SW18 157 C6
Frogmore Ave UB4 83 C3
Frogmore Cl SM3 217 A5
Frogmore Ct UB2 107 B2
Frogmore Est NW10 89 A4
Frogmore Gdns
Cheam SM3 217 A4
Hayes UB4 83 C3
Frogmore Ind Est N5 73 A4
Frognal NW3 70 A3
Frognal Ave DA14 190 A4
Harrow HA1 42 D5
Frognal Cl NW3 70 A3
Frognal Cnr BR7 189 D4
Frognal Ct NW3 70 A2
Frognal Gdns NW3 70 A4
Frognal La NW3 69 D3
Frognal Par NW3 70 A2
Frognal Pl DA14 190 A5
Frognal Rise NW3 70 A4
Frognal Way NW3 70 A4
Froissart Rd SE9 166 A6
Frome Ho SE15 140 C1
Frome Rd N22 50 D6
Frome St N1 95 A5 235 A4
Fromondes Rd SM3 217 A3
Frontenac NW10 68 B1
Frontier Works N17 33 C4
Froude St SW8 137 B3
Fruen Rd TW14 149 D4
Fryatt Rd N17 33 B3
Frye Ct E3 97 B4
Fryent Cl NW9 44 C3
Fryent Cres NW9 45 C3
Fryent Ctry Park HA3, HA9 44 C2
Fryent Fields NW9 45 C3
Fryent Gr NW9 45 C3
Fryent Prim Sch NW9 45 A2
Fryent Way HA9,NW9 44 D2
Fry Ho E6 77 C1
Frying Pan Alley E1 243 C3
Fry Rd E6 77 D1
NW10 89 D6
Fryston Ave CR0 222 A6
Fuchsia St SE2 124 B1
Fulbeck Dr NW9 27 C2
Fulbeck Ho N7 72 B2
Fulbeck Way HA2 24 A1
Fulbourn 9 KT1 176 C1
Fulbourne Rd E17 36 A1
Fulbourne St E1 96 B2
Fulbrook Rd N19 71 C4
Fulcher Ho 10 N1 95 C6
13 SE8 119 B1
Fulford Mans N19 72 A5
Fulford Rd KT19 215 B1
Fulford St SE16 118 B4
Fulham Broadway SW6 135 C5 265 B3
Fulham Broadway Sta SW6 135 C5 265 B4
Fulham Cl UB10 83 A3
Fulham Cross Sec Sch SW6 135 A5 264 B2
Fulham Ct SW6 135 C4 265 A2
Fulham High St SW6 135 A3
Fulham Palace★ SW6 135 A3
Fulham Palace Rd W6 134 D6
Fulham SW6 135 A4 264 A1
Fulham Park Gdns SW6 135 B3
Fulham Park Rd SW6 135 B3
Fulham Prep Sch SW6 135 A3
Fulham Prim Sch SW6 135 C6 265 A5
Fulham Rd SW10 136 A6 266 B6
Fulham SW6 135 B4 264 D2
Fulke Ho E5 74 B5
Fullbrooks Ave KT4 199 D1
Fuller Cl 3 E2 96 A3
Orpington BR6 227 D3
Fuller Rd RM8 80 C4
Fullers Ave KT6 214 B6
Fuller's Ave IG8 36 D3
Fullers Cotts N22 32 B3
Fullers Ho 6 SW18 157 C6
Fuller's Rd E18 36 D3
Fuller St NW4 46 C5
Fullers Way N KT6 214 B5
Fullers Way S KT9 214 A5
Fuller's Wood CR0 223 C3
Fuller Terr IG1 79 B3
Fullerton Ct TW11 175 A4
Fullerton Rd SW18 158 A6
Croydon CR0 205 D2
Fuller Way UB3 105 D1
Fullwood Prim Sch IG6 57 A5
Fullwood's Mews N1 235 D2
Fulmar Ct
5 Dulwich SE21 161 B2
Surbiton KT5 198 B3
Fulmar Ho NW8 237 B5
12 SE16 118 D2
Fulmead St SW6 265 D1
Fulmer Cl TW12 173 A5
Fulmer Rd E16 99 D2
Fulmer Way W13 109 B3
Fulneck 1 E1 96 C2
Fulready Rd E10 54 B4
Fulstone Cl TW4 129 B1
Fulthorp Rd SE3 143 A3
Fulton Ct EN3 7 C5
Fulton Mews W2 246 A6
Fulton Rd HA9 66 C5
Fulwell Ct UB1 108 A6
Fulwell Park Ave TW2 152 A2
Fulwell Rd TW11,TW12 174 B6
Fulwell Sta TW11 174 B6
Fulwood Ave HA0 88 B5
Fulwood Cl UB3 83 D1
Fulwood Gdns TW1 153 A5
Fulwood Pl WC1 240 D3
Fulwood Wlk SW19 157 A3
Furber St W6 112 B3
Furham Field HA5 23 C3
Furley Ho 7 SE15 140 A5
Furley Rd SE15 140 A5
Furlong Cl SM6 203 B1
Furlong Rd N7 72 C2
Furmage St SW18 157 D4
Furneaux Ave SE27 182 D5
Furness Ho SW1 258 C2
Furness Lo 4 SW14 132 D1
Furness Rd NW10 90 A5
SW6 135 D3
Harrow HA2 41 D1
Morden SM4 201 D3
Furnival St EC4 94 C1 241 A2
Furrow La E9 74 C3
Furrows The KT12 194 C1
Fursby Ave N3 29 C4
Fursecroft W1 237 C2
Further Acre NW9 27 D1
Furtherfield Cl CR0 204 C3
Further Green Rd SE6 164 C3
Furze Cl WD19 22 C5
Furze Ct CR0 222 A6
Furzedown Dr SW17 181 B5
Furzedown Prim Sch SW17 181 A4
Furzedown Rd SW17 181 B5
Furzefield Cl BR7 188 D4
Furzefield Rd SE3 143 B5
Furzeground Way UB11 105 A5
Furzeham Rd UB7 104 A4
Furzehill Rd WD6 11 A6
Furze Inf Sch RM6 59 A3
Furzeland Ho 2 KT3 199 C2
Furze Rd CR7 205 A6
Furze St E3 97 C2
Furzewood TW16 172 A2
Fuschia Ct IG8 36 C4
Fyfe Way BR1 187 A1
Fyfield N4 72 C6
Fyfield Cl BR2,BR3 208 B5
Fyfield Ct E7 77 A2
Fyfield Ho RM9 80 B1
Fyfield Rd E17 54 B6
6 SW9 138 C2
Enfield EN1 5 C2
Woodford IG8 37 C3
Fynes St SW1 259 C4

G

Gable Cl HA5 23 C3
Gable Ct SE26 184 B6
Gable Ho 12 W4 111 C2
Gable Lo
Hadley Wood EN4 2 A5
West Wickham BR4 208 A1
Gables Ave TW15 170 B5
Gables Cl SE5 139 C4
Lewisham SE12 165 A3
Gables The BR1 187 B3
N10 49 A6
N12 29 D5
NW3 70 B6
3 SW4 137 C2
Barking IG11 79 A2
Ealing W13 87 B1
Wembley HA9 66 B5
Gabriel Cl 1 TW13 173 A6
Gabriel Ho SE11 260 C4
Gabrielle Cl HA9 66 B5
Gabrielle Ct NW3 70 B2
Gabriel St SE23 163 A4
Gabriel's Wharf★ SE1 251 A4
Gad Cl E13 99 B4
Gaddesden Ave HA9 66 B2
Gaddesden Ho EC1 235 D1
Gade Cl UB3 106 B5
Gadesden Rd KT19 215 A2
Gadsbury Cl NW9 45 D3
Gadsden Ho 6 E9 74 D2
8 W10 91 A3
Gadwall Cl E16 99 B1
Gadwall Way SE28 123 B4
Gagarin Ho SW11 136 B2
Gage Rd E16 98 C2
Gage St WC1 240 B4
Gainford Ho 18 E2 96 B4
Gainford St N1 94 C6 234 A6
Gainsboro Gdns UB6 64 C3
Gainsborough Ave E12 78 C3
Gainsborough Cl
Beckenham BR3 185 C3
Thames Ditton KT10 196 C1
Gainsborough Ct N12 29 D5
6 SE16 118 B1
W12 112 C4
Barnet EN5 1 D1
Bromley BR2 209 C5
Dulwich SE21 161 C2
Gainsborough Gdns
NW11 47 B2
NW3 70 B5
Edgware HA8 26 C1
Isleworth TW7 152 B6
Gainsborough Ho
5 E14 119 A6
N4 50 B1
3 NW3 70 A4
SW1 259 D3
Dagenham RM8 80 B4
Enfield EN1 18 A6
Gainsborough Lo HA1 42 C4
Gainsborough Mews 5
SE26 162 B1
Gainsborough Prim Sch
E15 98 C4
E9 75 C2
Gainsborough Rd E11 54 C2
E15 98 C4
N12 29 D5
W4 111 D2
Dagenham RM8 80 B5
Hayes UB4 83 B5
New Malden KT3 199 B2
Richmond TW9 132 B2
Gainsborough Sq DA7 146 D2
Gainsborough Twr 8
UB5 84 D5
Gainsford Rd E17 53 B5
Gainsford St
SE1 117 D4 253 D2
Gairloch Ho 2 NW1 71 D1
Gairloch Rd SE5 139 C3
Gaisford St NW5 71 C2
Gaitskell Ct SW11 136 C3
Gaitskell Ho 3 E17 53 D6
2 E6 99 D6
SE17 139 B6
Gaitskell Rd SE9 167 A3
Galahad Rd BR1 187 A6
Galata Rd SW13 134 A5
Galatea Sq SE15 140 B2
Galba Ct 1 TW8 131 D5
Galbraith St E14 120 A3
Galdana Ave EN5 2 A2
Galeborough Ave IG8 36 B3
Gale Cl Hampton TW12 173 A4
Mitcham CR4 202 B6
Gale Ho 10 SW2 160 B6
Galena Ho SE18 123 D1
5 W6 112 B2
Galena Rd W6 112 B2
Galen Pl WC1 240 B3
Galesbury Rd SW18 158 A5
Gales Gdns E2 96 B4
Gale St E3 97 C2
Dagenham RM9 80 D1
Galgate Cl 4 SW19 157 A3
Gallants Farm Rd EN4 14 C3
Galleon Cl SE16 118 D4
Galleon Ho 7 E14 120 A2
Galleons Dr IG11 102 A4
Gallery Ct SW10 266 A5
Gallery Gdns UB5 84 D5
Gallery Rd SE21 161 B3
Galleywall Prim Sch
SE16 118 B2
Galleywall Rd SE16 118 B2
Galleywall Road Trad Est 12
SE16 118 B2
Galleywood Ho W10 90 C2
Gallia Rd N5 72 D3
Galliard Cl N9 18 C5
Galliard Ct N9 18 A5
Galliard Rd N9 18 A5
Gallions Cl IG11 102 A4
Gallions Mount Prim Sch
SE18 123 D1
Gallions Rd
Greenwich SE7 121 A2
Newham E16 123 A6
Gallions Reach Sta
E16 122 D6
Gallions View Rd
SE28 123 C4
Gallon Cl SE7 121 C2
Gallop The
South Croydon CR2 222 B1
Sutton SM2 218 A1
Gallosson Rd SE18 123 C2
Galloway Path 5 CR0 221 B4
Galloway Rd W12 112 A5
Gallus Cl N21 16 B5
Gallus Sq SE3 143 B2
Galpin's Rd CR4,CR7 204 B5
Galsworthy Ave E14 97 A2
Ilford RM6 58 B2
Galsworthy Cl SE28 124 B5
Galsworthy Cres SE3 143 C4
Galsworthy Ho 4 W11 91 A1
Galsworthy Rd NW2 69 A4
Kingston KT2 176 D2
Galton Ho 1 SE18 144 B4
Galton St W10 91 A4
Galva Cl EN4 3 A1
Galvani Way CR0 204 B1
Galveston Ho 2 E1 97 A3
Galveston Rd SW15 157 B6
Galway Cl 28 SE16 118 B1
Galway Ho 6 E1 96 D2
EC1 235 B1
Galway St EC1 95 A4 235 B1
Galy 5 NW9 27 D1
Gambetta St 3 SW8 137 B3
Gambia St
SE1 116 D5 251 D3
Gambler Ho EC1 235 B1
Gambole Rd SW17 180 C6
Games Ho 6 SE7 143 C6
Games Rd EN4 2 D2
Gamlen Rd SW15 134 D1
Gamuel Cl E17 53 C3
Gander Green Cres
TW12 173 C2
Gander Green La KT4, SM1,SM3 217 B5
Gandhi Cl E17 53 C3
Gandolfi st 5 SE15 139 C6
Ganley Ct 19 SW11 136 B2
Gannet Ct 4 SE21 161 B2
Gannet Ho SE15 139 D4
Ganton St W1 239 B1
Ganton Wlk WD19 22 D6
Gants Hill IG2 56 C3
Gants Hill Cres IG2 56 C4
Gants Hill Sta IG2 56 C3
Gap Rd SW19 179 D5
Garage Rd W3 88 C1
Garbett Ho 2 SE17 138 D6
Garbutt Pl W1 238 B3
Garden Ave DA7 147 C2
Mitcham CR4 181 B3
Garden City HA8 26 C4
Garden Cl SE12 165 B1
Ashford TW15 171 A4
Chingford E4 35 C5
Hampton TW12 173 B5
Northolt UB5 85 A6
Roehampton SW15 156 B4
Ruislip HA4 61 D6
Wallington SM6 220 A3
Garden Cotts BR5 190 C1
Garden Ct EC4 251 A6
N12 29 D5
NW8 229 C2
10 SE9 166 C5
12 W4 111 A3
5 Belmont SM2 217 C1
4 Richmond TW9 132 B4
South Croydon CR0 221 D5
4 Stanmore HA7 25 C5
Wembley HA0 65 C5
Gardeners Rd CR0 204 D1
Garden Flats SW16 160 A1
Garden Ho 2 N2 30 B1
12 SW9 138 A3
Garden Hospl The NW4 46 C6
Gardenia Ct 1 BR3 185 C3
Gardenia Rd EN1 17 C5
Gardenia Way IG8 37 A5
Garden La Bromley BR1 187 B4
Streatham SW2 160 B3
Garden Lodge Ct N2 48 B6
Garden Mews W2 245 B5
Garden Pl 28 E2 95 D6
Garden Rd NW8 92 A4 229 B2
Bromley BR1 187 B4
Penge SE20 184 C2
Richmond TW9 132 C2
Walton-on-T KT12 194 B2
Garden Row
SE1 116 D3 261 C6
Garden Royal 16
SW15 156 D5
Garden St E1 96 D2
Gardens The N16 51 C2
SE22 140 A1
Beckenham BR3 186 A2
East Bedfont TW14 149 B5
Harrow HA1,HA2 42 A3
Pinner HA5 41 B3
Garden Suburb Jun & Inf
Schs NW11 47 B4
Garden Terr SW1 259 C2
SW7 247 B1
Garden Way NW10 67 A2
Garden Wlk
EC2 95 C3 243 A6
Beckenham BR3 185 B2
Gardiner Ave NW2 68 C3
Gardiner Cl BR5 190 C1
Dagenham RM8 80 D4
Enfield EN3 18 D5
Gardiner Ct NW10 89 B6
Gardiner Ho 3 SE18 144 A5
SW11 267 A2
Gardner Cl E11 55 B3
Gardner Ct N5 73 A4
Hounslow TW3 129 C2
Tottenham N22 32 D1
Gardner Ho
Feltham TW13 151 B2
Southall UB1 106 D6
Gardner Ind Est SE26 185 B5
Gardner Pl TW14 150 B5
Gardner Rd E13 99 B3
Gardners Cl N11 15 A2
Gardners La EC4 252 A6
Gardnor Mans 10 NW3 70 A4
Gardnor Rd NW3 70 B4
Gard St EC1 234 D2
Garendon Gdns SM4 201 D2
Garendon Rd SM4 201 D2
Garenne Ct 10 E4 20 A3
Gareth Cl KT4 216 D6
Gareth Ct SW16 159 D1
Gareth Gr BR1 187 A6
Garfield Edmonton N9 18 B3
Enfield EN2 17 B6
Garfield First Sch
SW19 180 A4
Garfield Prim Sch N11 31 C5
Garfield Rd E13 98 D3
SW11 137 A2
Chingford E4 20 B3
Enfield EN3 6 C1
2 Twickenham TW1 153 A3
Wimbledon SW19 180 A4
Garford St E14 119 C6
Garganey Ct NW10 67 B2
Gargany Wlk SE28 124 C6
Garibaldi St SE18 123 C2
Garland Dr TW3 130 A3
Garland Ho N16 73 B5
Garland Rd SE18 145 B5
Stanmore HA7 26 A2
Garlands Ct 2 CR0 221 B4
Garlands The HA1 42 D2
Garlick Hill
EC4 117 A6 252 B6
Garlies Rd SE23 163 A1
Garlinge Ho 12 SW9 138 C4
Garlinge Rd NW2 69 B2
Garman Cl N18 33 B5
Garman Rd N17 34 C3
Garnault Mews EC1 234 B1
Garnault Pl EC1 234 B1
Garnault Rd EN1 5 D5
Garner Cl RM8 58 D1
Garner Rd E17 36 A2
Garner St E2 96 A5
Garnet Ho KT4 199 B1
Garnet Rd NW10 67 C2
South Norwood CR7 205 B5
Garnet St E1 118 C6
Garnett Cl SE9 144 B2
Garnett Ho 5 NW3 70 D3
Garnett Rd NW3 70 D3
Garnett Way E17 35 A2
Garnet Wlk 8 E6 100 A2
Garnham Cl 2 N16 73 D6
Garnham St 1 N16 73 D6
Garnies Cl SE15 139 D5
Garrad's Rd SW16 159 D1
Garrard Cl DA7 147 C2
Chislehurst BR7 188 D5
Garrard Wlk NW10 67 C2
Garratt Cl CR0 220 A4
Garratt Ho 8 N16 51 C1
Garratt La
Upper Tooting SW17, SW18 180 C6
Wandsworth SW18 157 D3
Garratt Park Sch
SW18 158 A1
Garratt Rd HA8 26 C3
Garratts Rd WD23 8 A4
Garratt Terr SW17 180 C6
Garraway Ct SW13 134 C5
Garraway Ho SE21 161 D1
Garrett Cl W3 89 B2
Garrett Ho W12 90 B1
Teddington TW11 175 B4
Garrett St EC1 95 A3 242 B6
Garrick Ave NW11 47 A3
Garrick Cl SW18 136 A1
Ealing W5 88 A3
1 Richmond TW9 153 D6
Garrick Cres CR0 221 C6
Garrick Ct HA8 26 B6
Garrick Dr NW4 28 C1
SE18 123 B3
Garrick Gdns KT8 195 C6
Garrick Ho W1 248 C3
Garrick Ho *continued*
Chiswick W4 133 C6
2 Kingston KT1 198 A5
7 Streatham SW16 181 C5
Garrick Ind Est NW9 45 D4
Garrick Pk NW4 28 D1
Garrick Rd NW9 45 D3
Greenford UB6 85 D3
Richmond TW9 132 C3
Garrick's Ait KT8 174 A1
Garricks Ho KT1 175 D1
Garrick St
WC2 116 A6 250 A6
Garrick Way NW4 46 D5
Garrick Yd WC2 250 A6
Garrison Cl SE18 144 C5
Hounslow TW4 151 B6
Garrison La KT9 214 A1
Garrowsfield EN5 13 B6
Garsdale Cl N11 31 A4
Garsdale Terr SW5 254 D2
Garside Cl SE28 123 B3
Hampton TW12 173 D4
Garsington Mews SE4 141 B2
Garson Ho W2 246 C6
Garston Ho 6 N1 72 D1
Garter Way SE16 118 D4
Garth Cl Kingston KT2 176 B5
Ruislip HA4 40 D1
West Barnes SM4 200 D2
Garth Ct Chiswick W4 133 B6
Harrow HA1 42 D3
Garth Ho NW2 69 B6
Garthland Dr EN5 12 C6
Garth Mews W5 88 A3
Garthorne Rd SE23 162 D4
Garth Rd NW2 69 B6
8 W4 111 B1
Kingston KT2 176 B5
West Barnes SM4 200 D2
Garthside TW10 176 A5
Garth The N12 29 D5
Hampton TW12 173 D4
Harrow HA3 44 B3
Garthway N12 30 C4
Gartmoor Gdns SW19 157 B3
Gartmore Rd IG3 79 D6
Garton Ho 6 N6 49 D2
Garton Pl SW18 158 A5
Gartons Cl EN3 6 C1
Gartons Way SW11 136 A2
Garvary Rd E16 99 B1
Garvens SE19 183 C5
Garway Rd W2 91 D1
Gascoigne Gdns IG8 36 C3
Gascoigne Pl 17 E2 95 D4
Gascoigne Prim Sch
IG11 101 A6
Gascoigne Rd IG11 101 A5
Gascony Ave NW6 69 C1
Gascoyne Ho 2 E9 74 D1
Gascoyne Rd E9 74 D1
Gaselee St E14 120 A6
Gasholder Pl
SE11 116 B1 260 D1
Gaskarth Rd HA8 27 A1
Balham SW12 159 B5
Gaskell Rd N6 48 D3
Gaskell St SW4 138 A3
Gaskin Ho N16 73 B5
Gaskin St N1 94 D6 234 C6
Gaspar Cl SW7 255 D4
Gaspar Mews SW5 255 D4
Gassiot Rd SW17 180 D6
Gassiot Way SM1 218 B5
Gasson Ho 24 SE14 140 D6
Gastein Rd W6 134 D6
Gastigny Ho EC1 235 B1
Gaston Bell Cl TW9 132 B2
Gaston Bridge Rd
TW17 193 B3
Gaston Gate SW8 270 C2
Gaston Rd CR4 203 A6
Gaston Way TW17 193 B4
Gataker Ho 5 SE16 118 B3
Gataker St 6 SE16 118 B3
Gatcliff Cl SW1 258 B1
Gatcombe Ct BR3 185 C3
Gatcombe Ho 20 SE22 139 C2
Gatcombe Mews W5 110 B6
Gatcombe Rd 9 E16 121 A5
N19 71 D5
Gatcombe Way EN4 2 D2
Gateacre Ct DA14 190 B6
Gatebeck Ho 21 SE22 139 C2
Gate End HA6 22 A3
Gatefield Ct SE15 140 A2
Gateforth St NW8 237 A5
Gate Hill Ct W11 244 D4
Gatehill Rd HA6 22 A3
Gate Ho 4 KT6 198 A1
Gatehouse Cl KT2 177 A3
Gatehouse Sch E2 96 D5
Gatehouse Sq SE1 252 B4
Gateley Ho 6 SE4 140 D1
Gateley Rd SW9 138 B2
Gate Mews
SW7 114 C4 247 B1
Gater Dr EN2 5 B4

Gates 4 NW9 27 D1
Gatesborough St EC2 243 A6
Gates Ct SE17 262 A2
Gatesden WC1 233 B1
Gates Green Rd
BR2,BR4 225 A4
Coney Hall BR4 224 D5
Gateside Rd SW17 158 D1
Gate St WC2 94 B1 240 C2
Gatestone Ct 10 SE19 183 C4
Gatestone Rd SE19 183 C4
Gateway SE17 139 A6
Gateway Mews 4 E8 73 D3
Gateway Prim Sch
NW8 92 B3 236 D6
Gateway Rd E10 75 D5
Gateway Ret Pk E6 100 D3
Gateways KT6 198 A4
Gateways Ct SM6 219 B3
Gateways The SW3 257 B3
Richmond TW9 131 D1
Gateway Trad Est
NW10 89 D4
Gatfield Gr TW13 151 C2
Gatfield Ho TW13 151 C2
Gathorne Rd N22 32 C2
Gathorne St 19 E2 96 D5
Gatley Ave KT19 214 D3
Gatliff Rd SW1 115 B1 258 C1
Gatling Rd SE18,SE2 124 A1
Gatonby St SE15 139 D4
Gatting Cl HA8 27 A3
Gatting Way UB8 60 A2
Gatton Rd SW17 180 C6
Gattons Way DA14 191 B6
Gatward Cl N21 16 D5
Gatward Gn N9 17 D2
Gatwick Ho 3 E14 97 B1
Gatwick Rd SW18 157 B4
Gauden Cl SW4 137 D2
Gauden Rd SW4 137 D2
Gaugin Ct 13 SE16 118 B1
Gauntlet 1 NW9 27 D1
Gauntlet Cl UB5 63 A1
Gauntlett Ct HA0 65 B3
Gauntlett Rd SM1 218 B3
Gaunt St SE1 262 A6
Gautrey Rd SE15 140 C3
Gautrey Sq 5 E6 100 B1
Gavel St SE17 262 D4
Gaven Ho N17 33 C1
Gavestone Cres SE12 165 B4
Gavestone Rd SE12 165 B4
Gaviller Pl 4 E5 74 B4
Gavina Cl SM4 202 C4
Gavin Ho SE18 123 C2
Gavrelle Ho EC1 242 C5
Gawber St E2 96 C4
Gawsworth Cl E15 76 D3
Gawthorne Ave NW7 29 A5
Gawthorne Ct E3 97 C5
Gay Cl NW2 68 B3
Gaydon Ho W2 91 D2
Gaydon La NW9 27 C2
Gayfere Rd
Redbridge IG5 56 B6
Stoneleigh KT17 216 A3
Gayfere St
SW1 116 A3 260 A5
Gayford Rd W12 111 D4
Gay Ho N16 73 C3
Gayhurst SE17 139 B6
Gayhurst Ct 9 UB5 84 C4
Gayhurst Ho NW8 237 B6
Gayhurst Rd E8 74 A1
Gayhurst Sch E8 74 A1
Gaylor Rd UB5 63 B3
Gaymead NW8 91 D6
Gaynesford Rd
Forest Hill SE23 162 D2
Wallington SM5 218 D1
Gay Rd E15 98 B5
Gaysham Ave IG2 56 D4
Gaysham Hall IG5 56 D6
Gaysley Ho SE11 261 A3
Gay St SW15 134 D2
Gayton Cres NW3 70 B4
Gayton Ct
3 Harrow HA1 42 D3
New Malden KT3 199 D4
Gayton Ho E3 97 C3
Gayton Rd NW3 70 B4
SE2 124 C3
Harrow HA1 43 A3
Gayville Rd SW11 158 D5
Gaywood Cl SW2 160 C3
Gaywood Rd E17 53 C6
Gaywood St SE1 261 D5
Gaza St SE17 116 D1 261 C1
Gaze Ho 10 E14 98 B1
Gean Ct 3 E11 76 B4
Gearies Inf Sch IG2 56 D4
Gearies Jun Sch IG2 56 D4
Geariesville Gdns IG6 56 D5
Geary Ho N7 72 B3
Geary Rd NW10 68 A3
Geary St N7 72 B3
GEC Est HA9 65 D6
Geddes Pl 3 DA7 147 C1
Gedeney Rd N17 33 A2
Gedge Ct CR4 202 C5
Gedling Ho SE22 139 D2
Gedling Pl SE1 263 D6
Geere Rd E15 98 D6
Gees Ct W1 238 B1
Gee St EC1 95 A3 242 A6
Geffrey's Ct SE9 166 A1
Geffrye Ct N1 95 C5
Geffrye Mus* E2 95 D5
Geffrye St E2 95 D5
Geldart Rd SE15 140 B5
Geldeston Rd E5 74 A6
Gellatly Rd SE14 140 D3
Gell Cl UB10 60 B5
Gemini Bsns Ctr E16 98 B3
Gemini Gr UB5 85 A4
Gemini Ho SW15 134 D1
Gemma Ct BR3 185 B1
General Gordon Pl
SE18 122 D2
Generals Wlk The EN3 7 A6
General Wolfe Rd
SE10 142 B4
Genesis Cl TW19 148 B3
Genesta Rd SE18 145 A6
Geneva Cl TW17 171 C1
Geneva Ct N16 51 B1
1 Putney SW15 156 D6
Geneva Dr SW9 138 C1
Geneva Gdns RM6 59 A4
Geneva Rd
Kingston KT1 198 A5
Thornton Heath CR7 205 A4
Genever Cl E4 35 C5
Genista Rd N18 34 B5
Genoa Ave SW15 156 C6
Genoa Ho 19 E1 96 D3
Genoa Rd SE20 184 C2
Genotin Rd EN1 5 B2
Genotin Terr EN1 5 B2
Gentleman's Row EN2 5 A2
Gentry Gdns E13 99 A4
Geoffrey Chaucer Tech Coll
SE1 117 B3 262 B5
Geoffrey Cl SE5 139 A3
Geoffrey Ct SE4 141 B2
Geoffrey Gdns E6 100 A5
Geoffrey Ho SE1 262 D6
Geoffrey Jones Ct
NW10 90 A6
Geoffrey Rd SE4 141 B2
Geological Mus*
SW7 114 B3 256 D5
George Akass Ho 3
SE18 123 A1
George Beard Rd 10
SE8 119 B2
George Beare Lo 9
SW4 159 C6
George Belt Ho 8 E2 96 D4
George Comberton Wlk 3
E12 78 C3
George Cres N10 31 A3
George Ct WC2 250 B5
Buckhurst Hill IG9 21 D2
George Downing Est
N16 73 D6
George Eliot Ho SW1 259 B3
George Eliot Jun & Inf Sch
NW8 92 B6 229 C6
George Elliot Ho SE17 262 A2
George Elliston Ho 12
SE1 118 A1
George Eyre Ho NW8 229 D3
George Gange Way
HA3 42 D6
George Green's Sec Sch
E14 120 A1
George Groves Rd
SE20 184 A2
George Ho 8 SE26 184 B5
George Inn Yd SE1 252 C3
George La SE13 164 A5
Hayes BR2 209 B1
Wanstead E18 55 B6
Woodford E18 37 A1
George Lansbury Ho
7 E3 97 B4
NW10 67 C1
Wood Green N22 32 C2
George Lashwood Ct 12
SW9 138 B1
George Leybourne Ho 9
E1 118 A6
George Lindgren Ho
SW6 264 D4
George Loveless Ho 4
E2 95 D4
George Lovell Dr EN3 7 C6
George Mews NW1 232 A1
George Mitchell Com Sch
E10 53 D1
George Orwell Sch N4 50 B1
George Parr Ho N21 16 D4
George Peabody Ct
NW1 237 A4
George Rd Chingford E4 35 C4
Kingston KT2 177 A3
George Rd *continued*
New Malden KT3 199 D4
George Row SE16 118 A4
Georges Mead WD6 10 A5
George Spicer Prim Sch
EN1 5 D2
George Sq SW19 201 C6
George's Rd N7 72 B3
George's Sq SW6 264 D6
George St 6 E16 98 D1
W1 92 D1 237 D2
Barking IG11 79 A1
Ealing W7 108 C5
Hounslow TW3,TW5 129 B3
Richmond TW10 153 D6
Southall UB2 107 A2
South Croydon CR0 221 B6
George Tingle Ho SE1 263 D6
George Tomlinson Prim Sch
E11 54 C1
Georgetown Cl 4
SE19 183 C5
Georgette Pl SE10 142 A5
George Vale Ho 32 E2 96 A5
George V Ave HA2,HA5 41 C6
Georgeville Gdns IG6 56 D5
George V Way UB6 87 B6
George Walter Ho 7
SE16 118 C2
George Wyver Cl
SW18 157 A4
George Yd EC3 242 D1
W1 115 A6 248 B6
Georgiana St
NW1 93 C6 232 B6
Georgian Cl Hayes BR2 209 B1
Ickenham UB10 60 A4
Stanmore HA7 25 A3
Georgian Ct 19 E9 96 C6
3 NW4 46 B4
Croydon CR0 205 B1
Wembley HA9 66 D2
Georgian Lo HA5 40 B4
Georgian Way HA1 64 B6
Georgia Rd
New Malden KT3 199 A5
South Norwood CR7 182 D2
Georgina Ct 5 TW1 153 C5
Georgina Gdns 10 E2 95 D4
Geraint Rd BR1 187 A6
Geraldine Ct 6 NW9 46 A5
Geraldine Rd SW18 158 A6
Brentford W4 132 C6
Geraldine St SE11 261 C5
Gerald Mews SW1 258 B4
Gerald Rd E16 98 D3
SW1 115 A2 258 B4
Dagenham RM8 59 B1
Gerard Ave TW4 151 C4
Gerard Ct NW2 68 D3
Gerard Rd
Barnes SW13 133 D4
Harrow HA1 43 A3
Gerards Cl SE16 118 C1
Gerboa Ct 6 E4 36 B5
Gerda Rd SE9 167 A2
Germander Way E15 98 C4
Gernigan Ho SW18 158 B5
Gernon Rd E3 97 A5
Geron Way NW2 68 C6
Gerrard Gdns HA5 40 A4
Gerrard Ho 5 SE14 140 D5
Gerrard Pl W1 249 D6
Gerrard Rd N1 94 D5 234 D4
Gerrards Cl N14 15 C6
Gerrard's Ct W5 109 D3
Gerrard St W1 115 D6 249 D6
Gerridge Ct SE1 261 B6
Gerridge St
SE1 116 C3 261 B6
Gerry Raffles Sq E15 76 B2
Gertrude Rd DA17 125 C2
Gertrude St
SW10 136 A6 266 B5
Gervase Cl HA9 67 A5
Gervase Rd HA8 27 B2
Gervase St SE15 140 B5
Ghent St SE6 163 C2
Ghent Way E8 73 D2
Giant Arches Rd SE24 161 A5
Giant Tree Hill WD23 8 B3
Gibbards Cott 1 IG11 79 D1
Gibbfield Cl RM6 59 A6
Gibbings Ho SE1 251 D1
Gibbins Rd E15 76 A1
Gibbon Ho NW8 236 D5
Gibbon Rd SE15 140 C3
W3 111 C6
Kingston KT2 176 A3
Gibbons Rd NW10 67 C2
Gibbon's Rents SE1 253 A3
Gibbon Wlk SW15 134 A1
Gibbs Ave SE19 183 B5
Gibbs Cl SE19 183 B5
Gibbs Gn HA8 27 A6
W14 113 B1 254 D2
Gibbs Green Sch
W14 113 B1 254 D2
Gibbs Ho
6 Balham SW12 159 B4
2 Bromley BR1 186 D2
Gibbs Rd N18 34 C6
Gibbs Sq SE19 183 B5
Gibraltar Ho NW10 89 C5
Gibraltar Wlk 28 E2 95 D4
Gibson Bsns Ctr N17 33 D3
Gibson Cl E1 96 C3
Chessington KT9 213 C3
Isleworth TW7 130 B2
Southgate N21 16 C5
Gibson Ct KT10 212 D5
Gibson Gdns N16 73 D6
Gibson Ho
South Croydon CR2 221 A2
Sutton SM1 217 C4
Gibson Rd SE11 260 D3
Dagenham RM8 58 C1
Ickenham UB10 60 B4
Sutton SM1 217 D3
Gibson's Hill
South Norwood SW16 182 C3
South Norwood SW16 182 C4
Gibson Sq N1 94 C6 234 B6
Gibson St SE10 120 C1
Gideon Cl DA17 125 D2
Gideon Mews W5 109 D4
Gideon Rd SW11 137 A2
Giesbach Rd N19 71 D6
Giffard Rd N18 33 C4
Giffen Square Mkt
SE8 141 C5
Giffin St SE8 141 C5
Gifford Gdns W7 86 C2
Gifford Ho SE10 120 B1
5 SW4 137 D1
Gifford Prim Sch UB5 85 B5
Gifford St N1 72 A1
Gift La E15 98 D6
Giggs Hill BR5 190 A2
Giggs Hill Gdns KT7 197 A1
Giggs Hill Rd KT7 197 A2
Gilbert Cl SE18 144 B4
1 Merton SW19 179 D2
Gilbert Ct W5 88 B1
Gilbert Gr HA8 27 B2
Gilbert Ho 5 E17 54 A6
5 E2 96 D4
EC2 242 B3
SE8 141 C6
SW1 258 D1
SW8 270 A4
Gilbert Pl WC1 94 A2 240 A3
Gilbert Rd BR1 187 A3
SE11 116 C2 261 B4
Belvedere DA17 125 C3
Merton SW19 180 A3
Pinner HA5 40 D5
Gilbert Scott Com Inf Sch
CR2 223 A1
Gilbert Scott Com Jun Sch
CR2 223 A1
Gilbert Sheldon Ho
W2 236 D4
Gilbertson Ho 4 E14 119 C3
Gilbert St E15 76 C4
W1 93 A1 238 B1
Enfield EN3 6 C6
Hounslow TW3 130 A2
Gilbey Cl UB10 60 D4
Gilbey Rd SW17 180 C5
Gilbeys Yd NW1 71 A1
Gilbourne Rd SE18 145 D6
Gilby Ho 5 E9 74 D2
Gilda Ave EN3 19 A6
Gilda Cres N16 52 A1
Gilda Ct NW7 28 A2
Gildea Cl HA5 23 C3
Gildea St W1 238 D3
Gilden Cres NW5 71 A3
Gildersome St SE18 144 C6
Gilders Rd KT9 214 B2
Giles Coppice SE19 183 D6
Giles Ho 5 SE16 118 A3
W11 91 C1
Gilesmead SE5 139 B4
Gilfrid Cl UB8 82 D1
Gilkes Cres SE21 161 C5
Gilkes Pl SE21 161 C5
Gillam Ho 6 SE16 118 C2
Gillan Ct SE12 165 B1
Gillan Gn WD23 8 A2
Gillards Mews 6 E17 53 C5
Gillards Way E17 53 C5
Gill Ave E16 99 A1
Gill Ct SE18 123 A2
Gillender St E3 98 A3
Gillespie Prim Sch N5 72 D5
Gillespie Rd N4,N5 72 D5
Gillett Ave E6 100 A5
Gillette Cnr TW7 131 A5
Gillett Ho N8 50 A6
Gillett Pl 27 E8 73 C3
Gillett Rd CR7 205 B5
Gillett St E8,N16 73 C3
Gillfoot NW1 232 A3
Gillham Terr N17 34 A3
Gillian Ho HA3 24 C4
Gillian Park Rd SM3 201 B1
Gillian St SE13 163 D6
Gillies Ct DA14 189 C6
Gillies Ho NW6 70 B1
Gilling Ct 5 NW3 70 C2
Gillingham Mews SW1 259 A4
Gillingham Rd NW2 69 A5
Gillingham Row SW1 259 A4
Gillingham St
SW1 115 C2 259 A4
Gillings Ct EN5 1 A1
Gillison Wlk 19 SE16 118 A3
Gillman Dr E15 98 D6
Gillman Ho 23 E2 96 A5
Gillray Ho SW10 266 C5
Gill St E14 119 B6
Gillum Cl EN4 14 D3
Gilmore Cl UB10 60 C5
Gilmore Cres TW15 170 C4
Gilmore Ct N11 30 D5
Gilmore Ho SW4 136 D1
Gilmore Rd SE13 142 B1
Gilpin Ave SW14 133 B1
Gilpin Cl
Mitcham CR4 180 C1
W1 236 B3
Gilpin Cres
Edmonton N18 33 D5
Twickenham TW2 151 D4
Gilpin Ho
9 Edmonton N9 18 A1
New Malden KT3 199 C4
Gilpin Rd E5 75 A4
Gilpin Way UB3 127 B5
Gilray Ho W2 246 C6
Gilsland Rd CR7 205 B5
Gilstead Ho IG11 102 B5
Gilstead Rd SW6 135 D3
Gilston Rd
SW10 114 A1 256 B1
Gilton Rd SE6 164 C1
Giltspur St EC1 94 D1 241 D2
Gilwell Cl E4 7 D1
Gilwell Ct 8 E5 74 B4
Gippeswyck Cl HA5 22 D2
Gipsy Cnr W3 89 B2
Gipsy Hill SE19 183 C5
Gipsy Hill Sta SE19 183 C5
Gipsy La SW15 134 B2
Gipsy Moth IV* SE10 142 A6
Gipsy Rd Bexley DA16 146 D3
West Norwood SE27 183 B6
Gipsy Road Gdns SE27 183 A6
Giralda Cl E16 99 D2
Giraud St E14 97 D1
Girdlers Rd W14 112 D2
Girdlestone Wlk N19 71 C6
Girdwood Rd SW18,
SW19 157 A4
Girling Ho 9 N1 95 C6
Girling Way TW14 128 A2
Gironde Rd
SW6 135 B5 264 D3
Girtin Ho 5 UB5 84 D5
Girton Ave NW9 44 C6
Girton Cl UB5 64 A2
Girton Gdns CR0 223 C5
Girton Ho SW15 156 D5
Girton Rd
Forest Hill SE26 184 D5
Northolt UB5 64 A2
Girton Villas 6 W10 90 D1
Gisbourne Cl SM6 219 D5
Gisburn Mans N8 50 B5
Gisburn Rd N8 50 B5
Gissing Wlk N1 72 C1
Gistelwood Ho 9 TW7 131 A2
Gittens Cl BR1 186 D6
Given-Wilson Wlk E13 98 D5
Glacier Way HA0 87 D5
Gladbeck Way EN2 4 D1
Gladding Rd E12 77 D4
Glade Cl KT6 213 D6
Glade Gdns CR0 207 A2
Glade La UB2 107 D4
Gladeside Croydon CR0 206 D3
Southgate N21 16 B4
Gladeside Cl KT9 213 D1
Gladesmore Com Sch
N15 52 A4
Gladesmore Rd N15 51 D3
Glades Sh Ctr The BR1 187 A1
Gladeswood Rd DA17 125 D2
Glade The BR1 187 D1
SE7 143 C5
Croydon CR0 206 D3
Enfield EN2 4 C3
Southgate N21 16 B4
Stoneleigh KT17 216 A2
West Wickham BR4 223 D5
Woodford IG8 21 B1
Gladiator St SE23 163 A4
Glading Terr N16 73 D5
Gladioli Cl 6 TW12 173 C4
Gladsdale Dr HA5 40 B5
Gladsmuir Rd N19 49 C1
Barnet EN5 1 A3
Gladstone Ave E12 78 A1
Feltham TW14 150 B5
Gladstone Ave *continued*
Tottenham N22 32 D1
Twickenham TW2 152 B4
Gladstone Ct NW2 68 B3
SW1 259 D3
5 Merton SW19 179 C3
Gladstone Gdns TW3 130 A4
Gladstone Ho 14 E14 97 C1
Gladstone Mews
3 Penge SE20 184 C3
Wood Green N22 32 C1
Gladstone Par NW2 68 C5
Gladstone Park Gdns
NW2 68 B5
Gladstone Park Sch
NW10 68 B3
Gladstone Pl KT8 196 C4
Gladstone Rd BR6 227 A3
W4 111 B3
Buckhurst Hill IG9 21 C3
Kingston KT1 198 C6
Merton SW19 179 C3
Southall UB2 107 A4
Surbiton KT6 214 A6
Thornton Heath CR0 205 B2
Gladstone St SE1 261 C6
Gladstone Terr
SW8 137 B4 268 D2
Gladstone Way HA3 42 C6
Gladwell Rd BR1 187 A4
N8 50 B3
Gladwin Ho NW1 232 B3
Gladwyn Rd SW15 134 D2
Gladys Dimson Ho E7 76 D3
Gladys Rd NW6 69 C1
Glaisher St 2 SE10 142 A5
SE8 141 D6
Glamis Cres UB3 105 A3
Glamis Ct W3 110 D4
Glamis Est 3 E1 118 D6
Glamis Pl E1 118 C6
Glamis Rd E1 118 C6
Glamis Way UB5 64 A2
Glamorgan Cl CR4,
SW16 204 A6
Glamorgan Ct 4 W7 86 D2
Glamorgan Rd KT1 175 C3
Glanfield Rd BR3 207 B5
Glanleam Rd HA7 25 D6
Glanville Ho 4 SW12 159 C4
Glanville Rd SW2 160 A6
Bromley BR2 209 B6
Glasbrook Ave TW2 151 B3
Glasbrook Rd SE9 165 D4
Glasbury Ho 5 SW9 138 B1
Glaserton Rd N16 51 C2
Glasford St SW17 180 D4
Glasfryn Ct HA2 64 B6
Glasgow Ho W9 91 D5
Glasgow Rd E13 99 B5
Edmonton N18 34 B5
Glasgow Terr
SW1 115 C1 259 A1
Glasse Cl W13 109 A6
Glasshill St
SE1 116 D4 251 D2
Glasshouse Fields E1 118 D6
Glasshouse St
W1 115 C6 249 B5
Glasshouse Wlk
SE11 116 B1 260 C2
Glasshouse Yd EC1 242 A5
Glasslyn Rd N8 49 D4
Glassmill La BR2 186 D1
Glass St 4 E2 96 B3
Glass Yd SE18 122 C3
Glastonbury Ave IG8 37 D4
Glastonbury Ct
12 SE14 140 C5
1 Ealing W13 109 A5
Glastonbury Ho SW1 258 C2
Glastonbury Pl 25 E1 96 C1
Glastonbury Rd
Edmonton N9 18 A3
Morden SM4 201 C2
Glastonbury St NW6 69 B3
Glaston Ct W5 109 D5
Glaucus St E3 97 D2
Glazbury Rd
W14 113 A1 254 B2
Glazebrook Cl SE21 161 B2
Glazebrook Rd TW11 174 D3
Glebe Ave Enfield EN2 4 D2
Harrow HA3 44 A6
Mitcham CR4 180 C1
Ruislip HA4 62 B2
Uxbridge UB10 61 A4
Woodford IG8 37 A4
Glebe Cl 1 W4 111 C1
Uxbridge UB10 61 A4
Glebe Cotts TW13 151 C1
Glebe Cres NW4 46 C5
Harrow HA3 44 A6
Glebe Ct SE3 142 C2
Ealing W5 109 D5
Ealing W7 108 B6

Glebe Ct *continued*
Mitcham CR4 .202 D6
Palmers Green N13 .16 C1
Stanmore HA7 .25 C5
Glebe Fst & Mid Sch
HA3 .44 A5
Glebe Gdns KT3 .199 C2
Glebe Ho 8 SE16 .118 B3
7 SE18 .122 C2
Feltham TW13 .151 C1
Glebe House Dr BR2 .209 B1
Glebehyrst SE19 .183 C6
Glebe La Barnet EN5 .12 A5
Harrow HA3 .44 A5
Glebeland Gdns TW17 193 A3
Glebelands E10 .75 D6
East Molesey KT8 .195 D5
Glebelands Ave
Ilford IG2 .57 B2
Woodford E18 .37 A1
Glebelands Cl SE5 .139 C2
Glebelands Rd TW14 .150 A4
Glebe Path CR4 .202 D6
Glebe Pl SW3 .136 C6 267 A6
Glebe Prim Sch UB10 .61 B4
Glebe Rd BR1 .187 A2
E8 .73 D1
N3 .30 A2
N8 .50 B5
NW10 .68 A2
Barnes SW13 .134 A3
Belmont SM2 .217 A1
Dagenham RM10 .81 D2
Hayes UB3 .105 D5
Stanmore HA7 .25 C5
Wallington SM5 .218 D2
Glebe Sch BR4 .224 B6
Glebe Side TW1 .152 D5
Glebe Sq CR4 .202 D6
Glebe St W4 .111 C1
Glebe Terr 15 E3 .97 D4
Glebe The SE3 .142 C2
Chislehurst BR7 .189 A2
New Malden KT4 .199 D1
Streatham SW16 .181 D6
West Drayton UB7 .104 B2
Glebeway IG8 .37 C5
Glebe Way
Feltham TW13 .151 C1
West Wickham BR4 .224 B6
Gledhow Gdns SW5 .256 A3
Gledstanes Rd
W14 .113 A1 254 B1
Gledwood Ave UB4 .84 A2
Gledwood Cres UB4 .83 D2
Gledwood Ct UB4 .83 D2
Gledwood Dr UB4 .83 D2
Gledwood Gdns UB4 .84 A2
Gleed Ave WD23 .8 B2
Gleeson Dr BR6 .227 D4
Glegg Pl 3 SW15 .134 D1
Glenaffric Ave E14 .120 B2
Glen Albyn Rd SW19 .156 D2
Glenalla Rd HA4 .39 D2
Glenalmond Ho
Ashford TW15 .148 A1
2 Putney SW15 .156 D5
Glenalmond Rd HA3 .44 A5
Glenalvon Way 5 SE7 122 A2
Glena Mount SM1 .218 A4
Glenarm Coll IG1 .78 D6
Glenarm Rd E5 .74 D4
Glen Ave TW15 .170 C6
Glenavon Cl KT10 .213 A1
Glenavon Ct KT4 .216 B6
Glenavon Lo 4 E18 .55 A6
Glenavon Rd E15 .76 C1
Glenbarr Cl SE9 .144 D2
Glenbow Rd BR1 .186 C5
Glenbrook Inf Sch
SW4 .159 D5
Glenbrook Jun Sch
SW4 .159 D5
Glenbrook N EN2 .4 B1
Glenbrook Rd NW6 .69 C3
Glenbrook S EN2 .4 B1
Glenbuck Ct 6 KT6 .198 A3
Glenbuck Rd KT6 .198 A3
Glenburnie Rd SW17 .158 D1
Glencairn Dr W5 .87 C3
Glencairne Cl E16 .99 D2
Glencairn Rd SW16 .182 A3
Glen Cl TW17 .192 C5
Glencoe Ave IG2 .57 C2
Glencoe Dr RM10 .81 C4
Glencoe Mans 6 SW9 138 C5
Glencoe Rd UB4 .84 D3
Glencorse Gn WD19 .22 D6
Glen Cres IG8 .37 B4
Glen Ct 5 Bromley BR1 186 D3
9 Penge SE20 .184 B2
Sidcup DA14 .190 A6
Glendale Ave
Edgware HA8 .26 C6
Ilford RM6 .58 C2
Wood Green N22 .32 C3
Glendale Cl SE9 .144 C2
Glendale Dr SW19 .179 B5
Glendale Gdns HA9 .44 A1
Glendale Mews BR3 .185 D2
Glendale Way SE28 .124 C6
Glendall St SW9 .138 B1
Glendarvon St SW15 .134 D2
Glendevon Cl HA8 .10 D1
Glendish Rd N17 .34 B2
Glendor Gdns NW7 .27 B6
Glendower Gdns 10
SW14 .133 B2
Glendower Pl SW7 .256 C4
Glendower Prep Sch
SW7 .114 B2 256 D4
Glendower Rd
Chingford E4 .20 B3
Mortlake SW14 .133 B2
Glendown Ho 2 E8 .74 A3
Glendown Rd SE2 .124 A1
Glendun Ct W3 .111 C6
Glendun Rd W3 .111 C6
Gleneagle Lo BR3 .185 C2
Gleneagle Mews
SW16 .181 D5
Gleneagle Rd SW16 .181 D5
Gleneagles Ealing W13 .87 B2
Stanmore HA7 .25 B4
Gleneagles Cl BR6 .211 B1
21 SE16 .118 B1
South Oxhey WD19 .22 D6
Gleneagles Ct 3
TW11 .175 A5
Gleneagles Gn 1 BR6 211 B1
Gleneagles Twr 2 UB1 .86 A1
Gleneldon Mews
SW16 .182 A6
Gleneldon Rd SW16 .182 A6
Glenelg Rd SW2 .160 A6
Glenesk Rd SE9 .144 D1
Glenfarg Rd SE6 .164 B3
Glenfield Cres HA4 .39 B2
Glenfield Rd W13 .109 B4
Ashford TW15 .171 A4
Streatham SW12 .159 C3
Glenfield Terr W13 .109 B5
Glenfinlas Way SE5 .138 D5
Glenforth St SE10 .120 D1
Glengall Gr E14 .120 A3
Glengall Pass 2 NW6 .91 C6
Glengall Rd DA7 .147 A2
NW6 .91 B6
SE15 .139 D6
Edgware HA8 .10 D1
Woodford IG8 .37 B4
Glengall Terr SE15 .139 D6
Glengarnock Ave E14 .120 A2
Glengarry Rd SE22 .161 D6
Glen Gdns CR0 .220 C4
Glenham Dr IG2 .56 D4
Glenhead Cl SE9 .144 D2
Glenhill Cl N3 .29 C1
Glen Ho 6 E16 .122 C5
SW1 .259 A6
Glenhouse Rd SE9 .166 C6
Glenhurst 4 BR3 .186 A2
Glenhurst Ave DA5 .169 B3
NW5 .71 A4
Ruislip HA4 .39 A1
Glenhurst Ct SE19 .183 D5
Glenhurst Rd N12 .30 B5
Brentford TW8 .109 C1
Glenhurst Rise SE19 .183 A3
Glenilla Rd NW3 .70 C2
Glenister Ho UB3 .106 B5
Glenister Park Rd
SW16 .181 D3
Glenister Rd SE10 .120 D1
Glenister St E16 .122 C5
Glenlea Rd SE9 .166 C6
Glenloch Ct 2 NW3 .70 C2
Glenloch Rd NW3 .70 C3
Enfield EN3 .6 C3
Glenluce Rd SE3 .143 A6
Glenlyon Rd SE9 .166 C6
Glenmead IG9 .21 C3
Glenmere Ave NW7 .28 A4
Glen Mews E17 .53 B4
Glenmill TW12 .173 B5
Glenmore SW15 .156 D5
Glenmore Ho 6 TW10 154 A5
Glenmore Lawns W13 .87 A1
Glenmore Rd DA16 .145 D4
NW3 .70 C2
Glenmore Way IG11 .102 A5
Glenmount Path 1
SE18 .123 A1
Glennie Ct SE21 .162 A3
Glennie Ho SE10 .142 A4
Glennie Rd SE27,SW16 160 C1
Glenny Rd IG11 .79 A2
Glenorchy Cl UB4 .85 A2
Glenparke Rd E7 .77 B2
Glen Rd E13 .99 C3
E17 .53 B4
Chessington KT9 .214 A5
Glenridding NW1 .232 B3
Glen Rise IG8 .37 B4
Glenrosa St SW6 .136 A3
Glenrose Ct DA14 .190 B5
Glenroy St W12 .90 C1
Glensdale Rd SE4 .141 B2
Glenshaw Mans 7
SW9 .138 C5
Glenshiel Rd SE9 .166 C6
Glentanner Way SW17 158 B1
Glen Terr E14 .120 A4
Glentham Gdns SW13 .134 B6
Glentham Rd SW13 .134 B6
Glen The BR6 .226 C5
Beckenham BR2 .186 C1
Enfield EN2 .4 D1
Pinner HA5 .40 B4
Pinner HA5 .41 A2
Southall UB2 .107 B1
South Croydon CR0 .222 D5
Wembley HA9 .65 D4
Glenthorne Ave CR0 .206 C1
Glenthorne Cl SM3 .201 C1
Glenthorne Gdns
Cheam SM3 .201 C1
Ilford IG6 .56 D5
Glenthorne High Sch
SM3 .201 C1
Glenthorne Mews W6 112 B2
Glenthorne Rd E17 .53 A4
N11 .31 A5
W6 .112 B2
Kingston KT1 .198 B5
Glenthorpe SW15 .134 A1
Glenthorpe Rd SM4 .200 D4
Glenton Rd SE13 .142 C1
Glentrammon Ave
BR6 .227 D2
Glentrammon Cl BR6 .227 D3
Glentrammon Gdns
BR6 .227 D2
Glentrammon Rd BR6 227 D2
Glentworth St
NW1 .92 D3 237 D5
Glenure Rd SE9 .166 C6
Glenview SE2 .146 D6
Glen View Rd BR1 .187 D1
Glenville Ave EN2 .5 A5
Glenville Gr SE8 .141 B5
Glenville Mews SW18 .157 C4
Glenville Rd KT2 .176 C2
Glen Wlk TW7 .152 B6
Glenwood Ave NW9 .45 C1
Glenwood Cl HA1 .42 D4
Glenwood Ct
4 Sidcup DA14 .190 A6
5 Wanstead E18 .55 A6
Glenwood Gdns IG2 .56 C4
Glenwood Gr NW9 .45 A1
Glenwood Ho 3 EN5 .13 D6
Glenwood Rd N15 .50 D4
NW7 .11 C1
Forest Hill SE6 .163 C3
Hounslow TW3 .130 B2
Stoneleigh KT17 .216 A2
Glenwood Way CR0 .206 D3
Glenworth Ave E14 .120 B2
Gliddon Rd
W14 .113 A1 254 A2
Glifford Ho SW1 .259 A1
Glimpsing Gn DA18 .125 A3
Glisson Rd UB10 .82 C5
Globe Pond Rd SE16 .119 A5
Globe Prim Sch E2 .96 C4
Globe Rd E15 .76 D3
E1,E2 .96 C3
Woodford IG8 .37 C4
Globe St SE1 .117 B4 252 C1
Globe Terr 9 E2 .96 C4
Globe Theatre The★
SE1 .252 A5
Globe View EC4 .252 A6
Globe Yd W1 .238 C1
Gloster Rd KT3 .199 C5
Gloucester
W14 .113 B2 254 D3
Gloucester Ave DA16 .145 D1
NW1 .93 A6 231 B6
Sidcup DA15 .167 C2
Gloucester Cir SE10 .142 A5
Gloucester Cl NW10 .67 B1
Thames Ditton KT7 .197 A1
Gloucester Cres
NW1 .93 B6 231 C6
Staines TW18 .170 A4
Gloucester Ct EC3 .253 B5
NW11 .47 B2
SE1 .262 B6
SE22 .162 A3
6 Acton W3 .88 C1
5 Ealing W7 .86 D2
Harrow HA1 .42 C6
Redbridge IG1 .56 B2
Richmond TW9 .132 C5
8 Surbiton KT6 .197 D2
Gloucester Dr N4 .72 D6
NW11 .47 C5
Gloucester Gate NW1 231 C4
Gloucester Gate Mews
NW1 .231 C4
Gloucester Gdns NW11 47 B2
W2 .236 A2
Gloucester Gdns *continued*
Cockfosters EN4 .15 A6
Redbridge IG1 .56 A2
Sutton SM1 .217 D6
Gloucester Gr HA8 .27 B2
Gloucester Ho NW6 .91 C5
Richmond TW10 .154 C6
Gloucester Lo 9 CR0 .221 D6
Gloucester Mews W2 .236 B1
Gloucester Mews W
W2 .236 B1
Gloucester Par DA15 .168 A6
Hayes UB3 .105 A3
Gloucester Pk SW7 .256 A4
Gloucester Pl
W1 .92 D2 237 D4
Gloucester Pl Mews
W1 .92 D2 237 D3
Gloucester Prim Sch
SE15 .139 C5
Gloucester Rd E10 .53 C2
E17 .34 D1
N17 .51 B6
SW7 .114 A3 256 A4
W5 .109 C4
Acton W3 .111 A4
Croydon CR0 .205 C2
Edmonton N18 .33 D5
Enfield EN2 .5 A5
Erith DA17 .125 B1
Feltham TW13 .150 C3
Hampton TW12 .173 D3
Harrow HA1 .41 D4
Hounslow TW4 .129 A1
Ilford E12 .78 B4
Kingston KT1,KT2 .176 D1
New Barnet EN5 .14 A6
Richmond TW9 .132 C5
Teddington TW11 .174 C5
Twickenham TW2 .152 A3
Wanstead E11 .55 C4
Gloucester Road Sta
SW7 .114 A2 256 A4
Gloucester Sq 6 E2 .96 A6
W2 .92 C1 237 A1
Gloucester St
SW1 .115 C1 259 A2
Gloucester Terr
W2 .92 A1 236 B1
Gloucester Way EC1 .234 B1
Gloucester Wlk
W8 .113 C4 245 B2
Glover Cl SE2 .124 C2
Glover Dr N18 .34 C4
Glover Ho 2 NW6 .70 A1
SE15 .140 B1
Glover Rd HA5 .40 D3
Glovers Gr HA4 .38 D2
Gloxinia Wlk TW12 .173 C4
Glycena Rd SW11 .136 D2
Glyn Ave EN4 .2 B1
Glyn Cl SE25 .183 C2
Glyn Ct SE27 .160 C1
Glyndale Grange SM2 217 D2
Glyndebourne Ct 5
UB5 .84 C4
Glyndebourne Pk BR6 226 D6
Glynde Mews SW3 .257 B5
Glynde Rd DA7 .147 A2
Glynde Reach WC1 .233 B1
Glynde St SE4 .163 B5
Glyndon Rd SE18 .123 B2
Glyn Dr DA14 .190 B6
Glynfield Rd NW10 .67 C1
Glyn Mans W14 .254 B4
Glynne Rd N22 .32 C1
Glyn Rd E5 .74 D4
Enfield EN3 .6 C1
North Cheam KT4,SM3 .216 D6
Glyn St SE11 .260 C1
Glynwood Ct SE23 .162 C2
Goater's Alley SW6 .264 D3
Goat La EN1 .5 D5
Goat Rd CR4 .202 D2
Goat Wharf TW8 .132 A6
Godalming Ave SM6 .220 B3
Godalming Rd E14 .97 D2
Godbold Rd E15 .98 C4
Goddard Cl TW17 .192 B6
Goddard Ho SW19 .156 D2
Goddard Pl N19 .71 C5
Goddard Rd BR3 .207 A5
Goddards Way IG1 .57 B1
Goddarts Ho E17 .53 C6
Godfrey Ave
Northolt UB5 .85 A6
Twickenham TW2 .152 B4
Godfrey Hill SE18 .122 A2
Godfrey Ho EC1 .235 C1
Godfrey Rd SE18 .122 B2
Godfrey St E15 .98 A5
SW3 .114 C1 257 B2
Godfrey Way TW4 .151 B4
Goding St
SE11 .116 A1 260 B1
Godley Rd SW18 .158 B3
Godliman St EC4 .252 A6
Godman Rd SE15 .140 B3
Godolphin Cl N13 .32 D4
Godolphin Ho NW3 .70 C1
7 Streatham SW2 .160 C3
Godolphin & Latymer Sch
W6 .112 B2
Godolphin Pl W3 .111 B6
Godolphin Rd W12 .112 B4
Godson Rd CR0 .220 C5
Godson St N1 .234 A4
Godstone Ct 1 N16 .51 C1
Godstone Ho SE1 .262 D6
1 Kingston KT2 .176 D4
Godstone Rd
Sutton SM1 .218 A4
Twickenham TW1 .153 B5
Godstow Rd SE2 .124 C4
Godwin Cl N1 .235 B4
West Ewell KT19 .215 A2
Godwin Ct NW1 .232 B4
Godwin Ho 2 E2 .95 D5
NW6 .91 D5
6 SE18 .144 B4
Godwin Jun Sch E7 .77 B4
Godwin Prim Sch RM9 .81 A1
Godwin Rd BR1,BR2 .209 C6
E7 .77 B4
Goffers Ho SE3 .142 C3
Goffers Rd SE3,SE13 .142 C3
Goffs Rd TW15 .171 B4
Goffton Ho 14 SW9 .138 B3
Goidel Cl SM6 .219 D4
Golborne Gdns W10 .91 B3
5 W10 .91 A3
Golborne Mews 9
W10 .91 A2
Golborne Rd W10 .91 A2
Golda Cl EN5 .12 D5
Goldbeaters Gr HA8 .27 C3
Goldbeaters Prim Sch
HA8 .27 B2
Goldcliff Cl SM4 .201 C2
Goldcrest Cl E16 .99 D2
Woolwich SE28 .124 C6
Goldcrest Mews W5 .87 D2
Goldcrest Way
Bushey WD23 .8 A3
New Addington CR0 .224 B1
Golden Cres UB3 .105 D5
Golden Cross Mews 8
W11 .91 B1
Golden Ct 4 Barnet EN4 .2 C1
Ealing W7 .108 C6
10 Richmond TW9 .153 D6
Golden Hind Pl 4 SE8 119 B2
Golden La EC1 .95 A3 242 B5
Golden Manor W7 .108 C6
Golden Mews SE20 .184 C2
Golden Par 2 E17 .54 A6
Golden Plover Cl E16 .99 A1
Golden Sq W1 115 C6 249 B6
Golders Cl HA8 .26 D5
Golders Ct NW11 .47 B2
Golders Gdns NW11 .47 B2
Golders Green Coll
NW11 .47 B1
Golders Green Cres
NW11 .47 C2
Golders Green Rd
NW11 .47 A2
Golders Green Sta
NW11 .47 C1
Golders Hill Sch NW11 .47 C2
Goldersley NW11 .47 C1
Golders Manor Dr
NW11 .47 A3
Golders Park Cl NW11 .47 C1
Golders Rise NW4 .46 D4
Golders Way NW11 .47 B2
Golderton 2 NW4 .46 C5
Goldfinch Rd SE28 .123 B3
Goldhawk Ind Est The
W6 .112 B3
Goldhawk Mews 2
W12 .112 B4
Goldhawk Rd W12 .112 A3
Goldhawk Road Sta
W12 .112 C4
Goldhaze Cl IG8 .37 D3
Gold Hill HA8 .27 B4
Goldhurst Terr NW6 .70 A1
Goldie Ho N19 .49 D2
Goldie Leigh Hospl
SE2 .146 C6
Golding Cl KT9 .213 C2
Golding Ct 7 IG1 .78 C5
Golding St E1 .96 A1
Golding Terr 17 E1 .96 A1
Goldington Cres NW1 232 C4
Goldington Ct NW1 .232 C5
Goldington St
NW1 .93 D5 232 C4
Gold La HA8 .27 B4
Goldman Cl E2 .96 A3
Goldmark Ho SE3 .143 B2
Goldney Rd W9 .91 C3
Goldrill Dr N11 .15 A2
Goldsboro Rd
SW8 .137 D5 269 D3
Goldsborough Cres E4 .20 A2
Goldsborough Ho
SW8 .269 D1
Goldsdown Cl EN3 .7 A3
Goldsdown Rd EN3 .7 A3
Goldsmid St 2 SE18 .123 C1
Goldsmith Ave E12 .78 A2
NW9 .45 C3
W3 .111 B6
Dagenham RM7 .59 C2
Goldsmith Cl HA2 .41 D1
Goldsmith Ct WC1 .240 A2
Edgware HA8 .26 B6
Goldsmith Ho W3 .111 B6
Goldsmith La NW9 .45 A5
Goldsmith Rd E10 .53 D1
E17 .34 D1
N11 .30 D5
SE15 .140 A4
W3 .111 B5
Goldsmiths Bldgs W3 .111 B5
Goldsmiths Cl W3 .111 B5
Goldsmith's Coll, Univ of
London SE14 .141 A4
Goldsmith's Ct N6 .49 B3
Goldsmith's Pl 4 NW6 .91 D6
Goldsmith's Row E2 .96 A5
Goldsmith's Sq 16 E2 .96 A5
Goldsmith St EC2 .242 B2
Goldsworthy Gdns
SE16 .118 C1
Goldthorpe NW1 .232 A5
Goldwell Ho SE22 .139 C1
Goldwell Rd CR7 .204 B5
Goldwin Cl SE14 .140 C4
Goldwing Cl E16 .99 A1
Golf Cl
South Norwood SW16 .182 C2
Stanmore HA7 .25 C3
Golf Club Dr KT2 .177 B3
Golfe Rd IG1 .79 B5
Golf Rd BR1 .210 C6
Ealing W5 .88 B1
Golf Side TW2 .152 B1
Golfside Cl N20 .14 C1
Kingston KT3 .177 C1
Goliath Cl SM6 .220 A1
Gollogly Terr 9 SE7 .121 C1
Gomer Gdns TW11 .175 A4
Gomer Pl TW11 .175 A4
Gomm Rd SE16 .118 C3
Gomshall Ave SM6 .220 A3
Gondar Gdns NW6 .69 B3
Gondar Mans NW6 .69 B3
Gonson St SE8 .141 D6
Gonston Cl SW19 .157 A2
Gonville Cres UB5 .63 D2
Gonville Ho 6 SW15 .156 D5
Gonville Prim Sch
CR7 .204 B4
Gonville Rd CR7 .204 B4
Gonville St SW6 .135 A2
Gooch Ho E5 .74 B5
EC1 .241 A4
Goodall Ho 10 SE4 .140 D1
Goodall Rd E11 .76 A5
Goodbehere Ho 7
SE27 .183 A6
Gooden Ct HA1 .64 C5
Goodenough Rd SW19 179 B3
Goodey Rd IG11 .79 D1
Goodfaith Ho 16 E14 .119 D6
Goodge Pl W1 .239 B3
Goodge St W1 .93 C2 239 B3
Goodge Street Sta
W1 .93 D2 239 C4
Goodhall St NW10 .89 D4
Good Hart Pl E14 .119 A6
Goodhart Way BR4 .208 C3
Goodhew Rd CR0 .206 A3
Goodhope Ho 15 E14 .119 D6
Gooding Cl KT3 .199 A4
Goodinge Cl N7 .72 A2
Goodinge Rd N7 .72 A2
Gooding Ho 4 SE7 .121 C1
Goodison Cl WD23 .8 A6
Goodland Ho 1 KT3 .199 C2
Goodman Cres SW2 .159 D2
Goodman Rd E10 .54 A2
Goodmans Ct HA0 .65 D4
Goodman's Stile 12 E1 .96 A1
Goodman's Yd
E1,EC3 .117 D6 253 C6
Goodmayes Ave IG3 .58 A1
Goodmayes Hospl IG3 .58 A4
Goodmayes La IG3 .80 A5
Goodmayes Prim Sch
IG3 .58 B1
Goodmayes Rd IG3 .58 A1
Goodmayes Ret Pk
RM6 .58 B2
Goodmayes Sta IG3 .58 A1
Goodrich Com Sch
SE22 .162 A5
Goodrich Ct 9 W10 .90 D1
Goodrich Ho 21 E2 .96 C5
N16 .51 C2
Goodrich Rd SE22 .162 A5
Goodridge Ho E17 .36 A3

Good Shepherd RC Prim Sch
Catford BR1 186 D6
New Addington CR0 223 D1
Good Shepherd RC Prim Sch The W12 111 D4
Goodson Ho SM4 202 A2
Goodson Rd NW10 67 C1
Goodsway NW1 94 A5 233 A4
Goodway Gdns E14 98 B1
Goodwill Ho 19 E14 119 D6
Goodwin Cl
SE16 117 D3 263 D5
Mitcham CR4 202 B6
Goodwin Ct N8 50 A6
East Barnet EN4 14 C5
Goodwin Dr DA14 168 D2
Goodwin Gdns CR0, CR2 220 D2
Goodwin Ho N9 18 C3
2 SE15 140 B2
Goodwin Rd N9 18 D3
W12 112 A4
Croydon CR0 220 D3
Goodwins Ct WC2 250 A6
Goodwin St N4 72 C6
Goodwood Ave EN3 6 C6
Goodwood Cl
Morden SM4 201 C5
11 Stanmore HA7 25 C5
Goodwood Ct W1 238 D4
Goodwood Dr UB5 63 C2
Goodwood Ho 3 W4 111 A1
Penge SE26 184 B4
Goodwood Mans 4 SW9 138 C2
Goodwood Par BR3 207 A5
Goodwood Rd SE14 141 A5
Goodwyn Ave NW7 27 C5
Goodwyn Sch NW7 28 A5
Goodwyn's Vale N10 31 B2
Goodyear Ho 8 N2 30 B1
Goodyers Gdns NW4 46 D4
Goosander Ct 34 NW9 27 D1
Goosander Way SE18, SE28 123 B3
Gooseacre La HA3 43 D4
Goose Green Cl BR5 190 A1
Goose Green Trad Est SE22 140 A1
Gooseley La E6 100 C4
Goose Sq 8 E6 100 B1
Goossens Cl 1 SM1 218 A3
Gophir La EC4 252 C6
Gopsall St N1 95 B6 235 D5
Gordon Ave
Chingford E4 36 C4
Isleworth TW1 153 B6
Mortlake SW14 133 C1
Stanmore HA7 25 A4
Gordonbrock Prim Sch SE4 163 C6
Gordonbrock Rd SE4 163 C6
Gordon Cl E17 53 C3
Gordon Cres
Croydon CR0 205 D1
Hayes UB3 106 A2
Gordon Ct W12 90 C1
17 Wimbledon SW20 178 D3
Gordondale Rd SW18, SW19 157 C2
Gordon Dr TW17 193 B2
Gordon Gdns HA8 26 D1
Gordon Gr SE5 138 D3
Gordon Hill EN2 5 A4
Gordon Hill Sta EN2 4 D4
Gordon Ho 16 E1 118 C6
3 SE10 141 D5
SE12 165 A4
2 Ealing W5 88 A4
Gordon Hospl The SW1 115 D2 259 C3
Gordon House Rd NW5 71 A4
Gordon Inf Sch IG1 79 B5
Gordon Lo N16 51 B1
Gordon Pl W8 113 C4 245 B2
Gordon Prim Sch SE9 144 B1
Gordon Rd DA15 167 C6
E15 76 A4
N11 31 D3
N3 29 B3
SE15 140 B3
Ashford TW15 148 A1
Barking IG11 101 C6
Beckenham BR3 207 B6
Chingford E4 20 C4
Chiswick W4 132 D6
Claygate KT10 212 C1
Dagenham RM6 59 B3
Ealing W13 109 C6
Edmonton N9 18 B2
Enfield EN2 5 B3
Harrow HA3 42 C6
Ilford IG1 79 B5
Isleworth TW3 130 A1
Kingston KT2 176 B2
Richmond TW9 132 B3
Shepperton TW17 193 B3
Southall UB2 107 A2
Gordon Rd *continued*
Surbiton KT5 198 B2
Wallington SM5 218 D2
Wanstead E11 55 A3
Woodford E18 37 B2
Yiewsley UB7 104 A6
Gordon Sq WC1 93 D3 239 D6
Gordon St E13 99 A4
WC1 93 D3 239 C6
Gordon Way BR1 187 A2
Barnet EN5 1 B1
Gore Ct NW9 44 C4
Gorefield Ho NW6 91 C5
Gorefield Pl NW6 91 C5
Gore Rd E9 96 C6
Merton SW20 178 C1
Goresbrook Rd RM9 102 D6
Gore St SW7 114 A3 256 B6
Gorham Ho 12 SW4 159 C5
Gorham Pl W11 244 A5
Goring Gdns RM8 80 C4
Goring Rd N11 32 A4
Goring St EC3 243 B2
Goring Way UB6 86 A5
Gorleston Rd N15 51 B4
Gorleston St W14 113 A2 254 B4
Gorman Rd SE18 122 B2
Gorringe Park Ave CR4 181 A3
Gorringe Park Prim Sch CR4 181 A2
Gorse Cl E16 99 A1
Gorsefield Ho 6 E14 119 C6
Gorse Rd CR0 223 C5
Gorse Rise SW17 181 A5
Gorse Wlk UB7 82 A1
Gorst Rd NW10 89 B3
SW11 158 D5
Gorsuch Pl 1 E2 95 D4
Gorsuch St E2 95 D4
Gosberton Rd SW12 159 A3
Gosbury Hill KT9 214 A4
Gosfield Rd RM8 59 C1
Gosfield St W1 93 C2 239 A3
Gosford Gdns IG4 56 B4
Gosford Ho 21 E3 97 B5
Goshawk Gdns UB4 83 C5
Goslett Yd WC2 239 D2
Gosling Cl UB6 85 C4
Gosling Ho 1 E1 118 C6
Gosling Way SW9 138 C4
Gospatrick Rd N17 33 A2
Gospel Oak Prim Sch NW5 71 A4
Gospel Oak Sta NW5 71 A4
Gosport Ho 9 SW15 156 A3
Gosport Rd E17 53 B4
Gosport Wlk N17 52 B5
Gossage Rd SE18 123 B1
Hillingdon UB10 60 B1
Gosset St E2 96 A4
Gosshill Rd BR7 188 C1
Gossington Cl BR7 188 D6
Gosterwood St SE8 141 A6
Gostling Rd TW2 151 C3
Goston Gdns CR7 204 C6
Goswell Pl EC1 234 D1
Goswell Rd EC1 94 D4 234 D2
Gothic Ct 17 SE5 139 A5
Harlington UB3 127 B6
Gothic Rd TW2 152 B2
Gottfried Mews NW5 71 C4
Goudhurst Ho 10 SE20 184 C3
Goudhurst Rd BR1 186 D5
Gough Ho N1 234 D6
4 Kingston KT1 176 A1
Gough Rd E15 76 D4
Enfield EN1 6 B3
Gough Sq EC4 94 C1 241 B2
Gough St WC1 94 B3 240 D5
Gough Wlk 10 E14 97 C1
Gould Ct SE19 183 C5
Goulden Ho SW11 136 C3
Goulding Ct N8 50 B5
Goulding Gdns CR7 183 A1
Goulman Ho 30 E1 96 C3
Gould Rd
East Bedfont TW14 149 C4
Twickenham TW2 152 C3
Gould's Gn UB8 104 D6
Gould Terr 26 E8 74 B3
Goulston St E1 95 D1 243 C2
Goulton Rd E5 74 B4
Gourley Pl N15 51 C4
Gourley St N15 51 C4
Gourock Rd SE9 166 C6
Govan St E2 96 A6
Gover Ct 8 SW4 138 A3
Government Row EN3 7 C6
Govett Ave TW17 193 A4
Govier Cl E15 76 C1
Gowan Ave SW6 135 A4 264 A2
Gowan Ho 22 E2 95 D4
Gowan Lea 4 E18 55 A5
Gowan Rd NW10 68 B2
Gower Cl SW4 159 C5
Gower Ct WC1 239 C6
Gower Ho 12 E17 53 D6
SE17 262 B2
Barking IG11 79 A1
Hayes UB3 105 C6
Upper Tooting SW17 180 B4
Gower House Sch NW9 67 A6
Gower Mews WC1 239 D4
Gower Pl NW1, WC1 93 D3 239 C6
Gower Rd E7 77 A2
Hounslow TW7 130 D6
Gower St WC1 93 D3 239 C5
Gower's Wlk E1 96 A1
Gowland Pl BR3 185 B1
Gowlett Rd SE15 140 A2
Gowrie Rd SW11 137 A2
Graburn Way KT8 196 B6
Grace Ave DA7 147 B3
Grace Bsns Ctr CR4 202 D3
Gracechurch St EC2, EC4 252 D6
Grace Cl HA8 27 A3
SE9 165 D1
Gracedale Rd SW16 181 B5
Gracefield Gdns SW16 160 A1
Gracehill 2 E1 96 C2
Grace Ho SE11 270 D6
Penge SE26 184 B5
Grace Jones Cl E8 74 A2
Grace Path SE26 184 C6
Grace Pl E3 97 D4
Grace Rd CR0 205 A3
Graces Mews NW8 229 B3
Grace's Mews SE5 139 C3
Grace's Rd SE5 139 C3
Grace St E3 97 D4
Gradient The SE26 184 A6
Graeme Rd EN1 5 C3
Graemesdyke Ave SW14 132 D1
Grafton Cl Ealing W13 87 A1
Twickenham TW4 151 B3
Worcester Park KT4 215 C5
Grafton Cres NW1 71 B2
Grafton Ct 10 E8 74 A3
East Bedfont TW14 149 B3
Grafton Gdns N4 51 A3
Dagenham RM8 81 A6
Grafton Ho 15 E3 97 C4
12 SE8 119 B1
Grafton Inf Sch RM8 81 B6
Grafton Jun Sch RM8 81 B6
Grafton Mews W1 239 A5
Grafton Park Rd KT4 215 C6
Grafton Pl NW1 93 D4 232 D1
Grafton Prim Sch N7 72 A5
Grafton Rd NW5 71 A3
W3 111 A6
Dagenham RM8 81 A6
Enfield EN2 4 B2
Harrow HA1 42 A4
Kingston KT3 199 C6
Thornton Heath CR0 204 C1
Worcester Park KT4 215 C5
Grafton Sq SW4 137 C2
Grafton St W1 115 B6 248 D5
Grafton Terr NW5 71 A3
Grafton Way W1 239 B5
East Molesey KT8 195 B5
Grafton Yd NW5 71 B2
Graham Ave W13 109 B4
Mitcham CR4 181 A2
Graham Cl CR0 223 C6
Graham Ct BR1 187 B3
5 SE14 140 D6
Northolt UB5 63 B3
Grahame Park Way NW7,NW9 27 D2
Grahame White Ho HA3 43 D6
Graham Gdns KT6 198 A1
Graham Ho 7 N19 71 D4
N9 18 C3
5 Balham SW12 159 B4
Woolwich SE18 144 D5
Graham Lo NW4 46 B3
Graham Mans 2 E8 74 B2
11 Barking IG11 80 A1
Graham Rd DA7 147 C1
E13 99 A3
E8 74 A2
N15 50 D6
NW4 46 B3
W4 111 B3
Hampton TW12 173 C6
Harrow HA3 42 C6
Merton SW19 179 B3
Mitcham CR4 181 A2
Graham St N1 94 D5 234 D3
Graham Terr SW1 115 A2 258 B3
Grainger Cl UB5 64 A3
Grainger Ct 22 SE5 139 A5
Grainger Rd
Isleworth TW7 130 D3
Tottenham N22 33 A2
Gramer Cl E11 76 B6
Grampian Cl BR6 211 D3
Harlington UB3 127 B5
Grampian Cl *continued*
15 Sutton SM2 218 A1
Grampian Gdns NW2 47 A1
Grampians The 10 W14 112 D4
Granada St SW17 180 D5
Granard Ave SW15 156 B6
Granard Bsns Ctr NW7 27 C4
Granard Ho 20 E9 74 D2
Granard Prim Sch SW15 156 B5
Granard Rd SW11, SW12 158 D4
Granary Cl N9 18 C4
Granary Ct 3 RM6 58 D2
Granary Rd E1 96 B3
Granary St NW1 93 D6 232 C5
Granby Ho 14 SE18 122 B2
Granby Pl SE1 251 A1
Granby Rd SE18 122 D3
SE9 144 B2
Granby St E2 96 A3 243 D6
Granby Terr NW1 93 C5 232 A3
Grand Arc N12 30 A5
Grand Ave EC1 241 D4
N10 49 A5
Tolworth KT5 198 D3
Wembley HA9 66 C3
Grand Ave E HA9 66 D3
Grand Avenue Prim Sch KT5 199 A3
Grand Ct RM8 81 A5
Grand Depot Rd SE18 122 C1
Grand Dr Southall UB2 108 A4
West Barnes SM4,SW20 200 C5
Granden Rd SW16 182 A1
Grandfield Ct W4 133 B6
Grandison Rd SW11 158 D6
North Cheam KT4 216 C5
Grand Junction Wharf N1 235 A3
Grand Par N4 50 D3
Mortlake SW14 133 A1
Tolworth KT6 198 C1
Wembley HA9 66 C6
Grand Union Cl W9 91 B2
Grand Union Cres E8 96 A6
Grand Union Ind Est NW10 88 D5
Grand Union Way UB2 107 C4
Grand Vitesse Ind Est SE1 251 D3
Granfield St SW11 266 D1
Grange Ave N12 30 A5
Barnet N20 13 A4
Barnet, London EN4 14 D3
South Norwood SE25 183 C1
Stanmore HA7 25 C1
Twickenham TW2 152 C2
Woodford IG8 37 A3
Grange Cl DA15 168 A1
HA8 27 A5
East Molesey KT8 195 D5
Hayes UB3 83 C2
Heston TW5 129 B6
Woodford IG8 37 A3
Grangecliffe Gdns SE25 183 C1
Grangecourt Rd N16 51 C1
Grange Cres SE28 102 C1
Grange Ct SE15 139 D3
WC2 240 D1
Belmont SM2 217 D1
Hackbridge SM6 219 B5
Littleton TW17 192 C5
Loughton IG10 21 D6
Northolt UB5 84 C5
Pinner HA5 41 A6
Harrow HA1 64 D5
Grange Dr BR7 188 B4
Grange Farm Cl HA2 64 A6
Grange Farm Cvn Pk TW17 193 C6
Grangefield NW1 72 A1
Grange Fst & Mid Schs HA2 41 D1
Grange Gdns N14 15 D3
NW3 69 D5
Pinner HA5 41 A5
South Norwood SE25 183 C1
Grange Gr N1 73 A2
Grange Hill HA8 27 A5
South Norwood SE25 183 C1
Grangehill Pl SE9 144 B2
Grangehill Rd SE9 144 B1
Grange Ho NW10 68 B1
SE1 263 C5
6 Barking IG11 101 B6
Grange Inf Sch E13 98 D4
Grange La SE21 161 D2
Grange Lo SW19 178 D4
Grange Mans KT17 215 D1
Grangemill 11 NW5 71 B4
Grangemill Rd SE6 163 C2
Grange Mills SW12 159 C3
Grangemill Way SE6 163 C2
Grange Mus of Community History The★ NW10 67 C4
Grange Park Ave N21 17 A5
Grange Park Jun & Inf Schs UB4 83 D3
Grange Park Pl SW20 178 B3
Grange Park Prep Sch N21 16 D5
Grange Park Rd E10 53 D1
South Norwood CR7 205 B6
Grange Park Sta N21 16 D5
Grange Pk W5 110 A5
Grange Pl NW6 69 C1
Grange Prim Sch SE1 117 C3 263 A5
W5 109 D4
Grange Rd E10 53 C1
E13 98 D4
E17 53 A4
HA8 27 B4
N6 49 A3
NW10 68 B2
SE1 117 D3 263 C5
W4 110 D1
Barnes SW13 134 A4
Belmont SM2 217 C1
Borehamwood WD6 10 B6
Chessington KT9 214 A4
Ealing W5 110 A5
East Molesey KT8 195 D5
Harrow HA1 43 A4
Harrow HA2 64 B6
Hayes UB3 83 C1
Ilford IG1 79 A4
Kingston KT1 198 A6
Orpington BR6 227 A6
Southall UB1 107 A4
South Norwood SE19, SE25 183 B1
Tottenham N17 34 A4
Grange St N1 235 D5
Grange The 3 E17 53 A4
19 NW3 70 D2
SE1 117 D3 263 C5
W12 112 B3
W14 113 B2 254 C3
W3 110 D4
7 W4 110 D1
Cockfosters EN4 2 D2
Croydon CR0 223 B6
Ealing W13 87 C2
3 Wanstead E18 55 A6
Wembley HA0 66 C1
West Barnes KT3 200 A4
West Ewell KT19 215 B4
Wimbledon SW19 178 D4
Grange The(Eltham Coll Jun Sch) SE9 165 D3
Grange Vale SM2 217 D1
Grangeview Rd N20 14 A3
Grangeway N12 29 D6
NW6 69 C1
Woodford IG8 37 C6
Grangeway Gdns IG4 56 A4
Grangeway The N21 16 D5
Grange Wlk SE1 117 D3 263 C5
Grangewood DA5 169 B3
Grangewood Cl HA5 40 A4
Grangewood Ind Sch E7 77 D1
Grangewood La BR3 185 B4
Grangewood Sch HA5 39 D4
Grangewood St E6 99 D6
Grange Yd SE1 117 D3 263 C5
Granham Gdns N9 17 D2
Granite St SE18 123 D1
Granleigh Rd E11 76 C6
Gransden Ave E8 74 B1
Gransden Ho 1 SE8 119 B1
Gransden Rd W12 111 D4
Grantbridge St N1 94 D5 234 D4
Grantchester 12 KT1 176 C1
Grantchester Cl HA1 64 D5
Grant Cl N14 15 C4
Shepperton TW17 192 D3
Grant Ct 11 NW9 27 D1
2 Chingford E4 20 A3
Grantham Cl HA8 10 A1
Grantham Ct 9 SE16 118 D4
Dagenham RM6 59 B2
Grantham Gdns RM6 59 B2
Grantham Gn WD6 11 A6
Grantham Ho 12 SE15 140 A6
Ashford TW16 171 C3
Grantham Pl W1 248 C3
Grantham Rd SW9 138 A3
Chiswick W4 133 C5
Little Ilford E12 78 C4
Grant Ho 38 SW8 137 D3
Grantley Ho 2 SE14 140 D6
5 Putney SW19 156 D3
Grantley Pl KT10 212 A3
Grantley Rd TW4,TW5 128 C3
Grantley St E1 96 D3
Grantock Rd E17 36 B2
Granton Prim Sch SW16 181 C3
Granton Rd Ilford IG3 58 A1
Granton Rd *continued*
Sidcup DA14 190 C4
Streatham SW16 181 C2
Grant Pl 2 CR0 205 D1
Grant Rd SW11 136 C2
Croydon CR0 205 D1
Harrow HA3 42 D6
Grants Cl NW7 28 D3
Grants Cotts KT10 212 B6
Grant St E13 99 A4
N1 234 A4
Grantully Rd W9 91 D4
Grant Way TW7 131 A6
Granville Ave N9 18 C1
Feltham TW13 150 A2
Hounslow TW3,TW4 151 C6
Granville Cl CR0 221 C6
Granville Ct N1 235 D6
N4 50 B3
8 SE14 141 A5
Granville Gdns
Ealing W5 110 B5
South Norwood SW16 182 B3
Granville Gr SE13 142 A2
Granville Ho 18 E14 97 C1
Granville Mans
8 W12 112 C4
WC1 240 A6
Granville Mews
Sidcup DA14 190 A6
Stanmore HA7 25 A5
Granville Pk SE13 142 B2
Granville Pl N12 30 A3
SW6 265 C3
W1 93 A1 238 A1
Pinner HA5 40 D6
Granville Point NW2 69 B6
Granville Rd E17 53 D3
N12 30 A3
N4,N8 50 B3
NW2 69 B6
NW6 91 C5
Bexley DA16 146 C2
Bowes Park N13 32 B4
Hayes UB3 105 D2
Hillingdon UB10 60 D2
Ilford IG1 78 D6
Merton SW19 179 C3
Sidcup DA14 190 B6
Tottenham N22 32 D2
Wandsworth SW18 157 B4
Woodford E18 37 B1
Granville Sq 8 SE15 139 C5
WC1 94 B4 233 D1
Granville St WC1 233 D1
Granwood Ct 5 TW7 130 C4
Grape St WC2 240 A2
Grapsome Cl KT9 213 C1
Grasdene Rd SE18,SE2 146 A5
Grasmere NW1 231 D1
Grasmere Ave BR6 226 D5
W3 111 B6
Kingston SW15 177 C6
Merton SW19 201 C6
Ruislip HA4 39 A2
Twickenham TW3 151 D5
Wembley HA9 43 D1
Grasmere Cl TW14 149 D3
Grasmere Ct
Barnes SW13 134 A6
Bowes Park N22 32 B4
Forest Hill SE26 184 A5
Grasmere Gdns BR6 226 D5
Harrow HA3 25 A1
Redbridge IG4 56 B4
Grasmere Ho 19 N16 73 B4
Grasmere JMI Sch N16 73 B4
Grasmere Point 2 SE15 140 C5
Grasmere Rd BR6 226 D5
3 E13 99 A5
N10 31 B2
Bromley BR1 186 D3
Croydon SE25 206 B4
Streatham SW16 182 B5
Tottenham N17 34 A4
Grasshaven Way SE28 123 D5
Grassington Cl N11 31 A4
Grassington Rd DA14 190 A6
Grassmere Ct 6 EN1 17 C6
Grassmount SE23 162 B2
Grass Pk N3 29 B2
Grassway SM6 219 C4
Grasvenor Ave EN5 13 C5
Grasvenor Avenue Inf Sch EN5 13 C5
Grately Ho 10 SW15 156 B3
Gratton Rd W14 113 A3 254 A5
Gratton Terr NW2 68 D5
Graveley 16 KT1 176 C1
Graveley Ave WD6 11 A6
Graveley Ho 7 SE8 119 A2
Gravel Hill DA6 169 D6
N3 29 B1
South Croydon CR0,CR2 223 B1

Gravel Hill Cl DA5,DA6 169 D5
Gravel Hill Prim Sch DA6 169 D6
Gravel Hill Sta CR0 223 A2
Gravel La E1 95 D1 243 C2
Gravel Rd BR2 226 A6
Twickenham TW2 152 C3
Gravelwood Cl BR7 167 A1
Gravenel Gdns 5 SW17 180 C5
Graveney Gr SE20 184 C3
Graveney Rd SW17 180 C6
Graveney Sch SW17 181 B5
Gravesend Rd W12 112 A6
Graves Est DA16 146 B3
Gray Ave RM8 59 B1
Gray Ct 8 KT2 175 D6
Grayfriars Pas EC1 241 D2
Grayham Cres KT3 199 B5
Grayham Rd KT3 199 B5
Gray Ho SE17 262 B2
Grayland Cl BR1 187 D2
Grayland Ct WC1 233 C1
Grayling Cl E16 98 C3
Grayling Ct N17 52 B5
Ealing W5 109 D5
Grayling Rd N16 73 B6
Grayling Sq E2 96 A4
Grays Cotts UB9 38 C1
Grayscroft Rd SW16 181 D3
Grays Farm Prim Sch BR5 190 B2
Grays Farm Production Village BR5 190 B2
Grays Farm Rd BR5 190 B2
Grayshott Rd SW11 137 A2
Gray's Inn★ WC1 94 B2 240 D4
Gray's Inn Pl WC1 240 D3
Gray's Inn Rd WC1 94 B3 240 D6
Gray's Inn Sq WC1 94 C2 241 A4
Grays La TW15 170 D6
Grayson Ho EC1 235 B1
Gray's Rd UB10 60 A1
Gray St SE1 116 C4 251 B1
Grayswood Gdns SW20 178 B1
Grayswood Point 14 SW15 156 A3
Gray's Yd W1 238 B2
Graywood Ct N12 30 A3
Grazebrook Prim Sch N16 73 C6
Grazebrook Rd N16 73 B6
Grazeley Ct SE19 183 C5
Great Arthur Ho EC1 242 A5
Great Bell Alley EC2 242 C2
Great Benty UB7 104 A2
Great Brownings SE21 183 D6
Great Bushey Dr N20 13 D3
Great Cambridge Ind Est EN1 18 B6
Great Cambridge Junction N13,N18 33 B6
Great Cambridge Rd
Edmonton N9,N18 17 C3
Enfield EN1 6 A3
Great Castle St W1 239 A2
Great Central Ave HA4 62 C3
Great Central St NW1 92 D2 237 C4
Great Central Way NW10 67 B4
Great Chapel St W1 93 D1 239 C2
Great Chertsey Rd
Chiswick SW14,W4 133 B4
Feltham TW13,TW2 151 C1
Great Church La W6 112 D1
Great College St SW1 116 A3 260 A6
Great Croft WC1 233 B1
Great Cumberland Mews W1 237 C1
Great Cumberland Pl W1 92 D1 237 D1
Great Dover St SE1 117 B3 262 C6
Greatdown Rd W7 86 D2
Great Eastern Bldgs 10 E8 74 B2
Great Eastern Ent Ctr E14 119 D4
Great Eastern Pier E14 119 C1
Great Eastern Rd E15 76 B2
Great Eastern St EC2 95 C3 243 A6
Great Eastern Wharf SW11 267 B3
Great Elms Rd BR2 209 C5
Great Field 7 NW5 71 C3
NW9 27 D2
Greatfield Ave E6 100 B3
Greatfield Cl 4 N19 71 C4
SE4 141 C1
Greatfields Dr UB8 82 C2
Greatfields Rd IG11 101 B5
Great Fleete Way IG11 102 C5
Great Galley Cl IG11 102 C4
Great Gatton Cl CR0 207 A2
Great George St SW1 116 A4 250 A1
Great Guildford St SE1 117 A5 252 A3
Great Guilford Bsns Sq SE1 252 A3
Greatham Wlk 8 SW15 156 A3
Great Harry Dr SE9 166 C1
Great James St WC1 240 C4
Great Marlborough St W1 93 C1 239 A1
Great Mathers Rd SE11 261 C4
Great Maze Pond SE1 117 B4 252 D2
Great Newport St WC2 250 A6
Great New St EC4 94 C1 241 B2
Great North Rd N2 48 C5
Barnet EN5 1 A2
New Barnet EN5 13 D6
Great North Way (Barnet By-Pass) NW4 46 D6
Greatorex Ho 12 E1 96 A2
Greatorex St E1 96 A2
Great Ormond St WC1 94 B3 240 C5
Great Ormond St Hospl for Children WC1 94 B3 240 C5
Great Percy St WC1 94 C4 234 A2
Great Peter St SW1 115 D3 259 D5
Great Portland St W1 93 B2 238 D4
Great Portland Street Sta W1 93 B3 238 D5
Great Pulteney St W1 249 B6
Great Queen St WC2 94 A1 240 B2
Great Russell St WC1 94 A2 240 A3
Great Scotland Yd SW1,WC2 116 A5 250 A4
Great Smith St SW1 115 D3 259 D6
Great South West Rd TW6,TW14,TW4 126 B4
Great South-West Rd TW5 128 B2
Great Spilmans SE22 161 C6
Great St Helen's EC3 243 A2
Greatstone Ho 13 SE20 184 C3
Great Strand NW9 27 D1
Great St Thomas Apostle EC4 252 B6
Great Suffolk St SE1 116 D4 251 D3
Great Sutton St EC1 94 D3 241 D5
Great Swan Alley EC2 242 C2
Great Thrift BR5 211 A5
Great Titchfield St W1 93 C2 239 A3
Great Tower St EC3 117 C6 253 A6
Great Trinity La EC4 252 B6
Great Turnstile WC2 240 D3
Great Western Ind Pk UB2 108 A4
Great Western Rd W2, W9 91 B2
Great West Rd
Brentford TW7,TW8 131 B6
Chiswick W4,W6 133 B6
Heston TW5,TW7 129 B4
Hounslow TW5 129 B4
Hounslow TW5,TW7 130 B5
Great West Road Cedars Rd W4 133 A6
Great West Road Hogarth La W4 133 C6
Great West Trad Est TW8 131 B6
Great Winchester St EC2 95 B1 242 D2
Great Windmill St W1 115 D6 249 C6
Greatwood BR7 188 C3
Great Yd SE1 253 B2
Greaves Cl IG11 79 C1
Greaves Cotts 12 E14 97 A2
Greaves Pl SW17 180 C6
Greaves Twr SW10 266 B4
Grebe 3 NW9 27 D1
Grebe Ave UB4 84 D1
Grebe Cl E17 35 A3
Grebe Cl *continued*
E7 76 D3
Barking IG11 102 A3
Grebe Ct 11 E14 120 A4
Cheam SM1 217 B3
Grebe Terr 4 KT1 198 A6
Grecian Cres SE19 182 D4
Greek Ct W1 239 D1
Greek St W1 93 D1 239 D1
Greenacre Cl Barnet EN5 1 B5
Northolt UB5 63 B3
Greenacre Ct E8 74 A3
Greenacre Gdns E17 54 A5
Greenacre Pl SM6 219 B6
Greenacres N3 29 A1
SE9 166 C5
Green Acres DA14 189 D6
Greenacres WD23 8 B2
Green Acres CR0 221 D5
Greenacres Ave UB10 60 C5
Greenacres Cl BR6 227 A4
Greenacres Dr HA7 25 B3
Greenacres Prim Sch SE9 166 C2
Greenacre Sq 26 SE16 118 D4
Greenacre Wlk N14 15 D1
Green Arbour Ct EC1 241 C2
Green Ave NW7 27 C6
W13 109 B3
Greenaway Gdns NW3 69 D4
Greenaway Ho NW8 229 A6
WC1 234 A1
Greenaway Terr TW19 148 A3
Green Bank E1 118 B5
N12 29 D6
Greenbank Ave HA0 65 A3
Greenbank Cl E4 20 A2
Greenbank Cres NW4 47 A5
Greenbank Lo 2 BR7 188 C2
Greenbanks HA1 64 C4
Greenbay Rd SE7 143 D5
Greenberry St NW8 230 A3
Greenbrook Ave EN4 2 A4
Green CE Prim Sch The N17 51 D6
Green CE Sch Holy Trinity (Infants' Annexe) The N15 51 D5
Green Cl NW11 48 A2
NW9 45 A3
Beckenham BR2 208 C6
Carshalton SM5 218 D6
Feltham TW13 173 A5
Greencoat Ho 13 KT1 176 A1
Greencoat Pl SW1 115 C2 259 B4
Greencoat Row SW1 259 B5
Greencourt Ave HA8 26 D2
Green Court Ave CR0 222 B6
Green Court Gdns CR0 222 B6
Greencourt Ho E1 96 D3
Greencourt Rd BR5 211 C4
Greencroft HA8 27 A5
Greencroft Ave HA4 62 C6
Greencroft Cl E16 99 D2
Greencroft Gdns NW6 70 A1
Enfield EN1 5 C2
Greencroft Rd TW5 129 B4
Green Ct TW16 171 D4
Greendale NW7 27 C6
Green Dale SE22 161 C6
Greendale Cl SE22 161 C6
Greendale Ct CR2 221 A2
Green Dr UB1 107 C5
Green Dragon Ct SE1 252 C3
Green Dragon Ho WC1 240 B2
Green Dragon Jun & Inf Sch TW8 132 A6
Green Dragon La
Brentford TW8 110 B1
Southgate N21 16 D5
Green Dragon Yd 21 E1 96 A2
Greene Ct 20 SE14 140 D6
Greene Ho SE1 262 C5
Green Elms IG6 57 A6
Green End
Chessington KT9 214 A4
Edmonton N21 16 D2
Greenend Rd W4 111 C4
Greener Ho 8 SW4 137 D2
Green Farm Cl BR6 227 D3
Greenfell Mans SE8 141 D6
Greenfield Ave KT5 198 D3
Greenfield Dr BR1 187 C1
N2 48 D5
Greenfield Gdns BR5 211 B2
NW2 69 A5
Dagenham RM9 102 D6
Greenfield Ho 28 SW19 156 D3
Greenfield Rd E1 96 A1
N15 51 C4
Dagenham RM9 102 C6
Greenfields UB1 85 C1
Greenfields JMI Sch WD19 22 C5
Greenfields Sch N10 30 D2
Greenfield Way HA2 41 D6
Greenford Ave
Ealing W7 86 C1
Southall UB1 107 B6
Greenford Gdns UB6 86 A4
Greenford High Sch UB6 85 C4
Greenford Ind Est UB6 85 D6
Greenford Rd
Greenford UB6 86 A3
Greenford, Harrow HA1, UB6 64 C3
Sutton SM1 217 D4
Greenford Rdbt UB6 86 B5
Greenford Sta UB6 86 B6
Greengate UB6 65 B2
Greengate St E13 99 B4
Green Gdns BR6 227 A3
Greenhalgh Wlk N2 48 A5
Greenham Cl SE1 251 A1
Greenham Cres E4 35 B4
Greenham Ho 6 E9 96 C6
Isleworth TW7 130 B2
Greenham Rd N10 31 A1
Greenhaven Dr SE28 102 B1
Greenheath Bsns Ctr 3 E2 96 B3
Green Hedges 8 TW1 153 C5
Greenheys Dr E18 54 D6
Greenhill HA9 66 D6
NW3 70 B4
Buckhurst Hill IG9 21 C3
Sutton SM1 218 A6
Green Hill SE18 122 B1
Greenhill Cts SE7 122 B1
Greenhill Gdns UB5 85 B5
Greenhill Gr E12 78 A4
Greenhill Par EN5 13 D6
Greenhill Pk NW10 89 C6
New Barnet EN5 13 D6
Greenhill Rd NW10 89 C6
Harrow HA1 42 C3
Greenhill's Rents EC1 241 C4
Greenhills Terr 16 N1 73 B2
Greenhill Terr
Northolt UB5 85 B5
Woolwich SE18 122 B1
Greenhill Way HA9 66 D6
Harrow HA1 42 C3
Greenhithe Cl SE9 167 C4
Greenholm Rd SE9 166 D6
Green Ho The 5 SW19 157 A3
Green Hundred Rd SE15 140 A6
Greenhurst Rd SE27 182 C5
Greening St SE2 124 C2
Green La NW4 46 D4
SE9 166 D1
W7 108 C4
Ashford TW16 171 D4
Chessington KT9 214 A1
Dagenham RM8 81 B6
East Molesey KT8 195 D4
Edgware HA8 26 C5
Feltham TW13 173 A5
Hillingdon UB8 83 A2
Hounslow TW4 128 C1
Ilford IG1 79 C6
Ilford IG3 79 C6
Morden SM4 201 D3
New Malden KT3 199 A4
New Malden KT4 200 A1
Penge SE20 184 D3
Shepperton TW17 193 A4
South Norwood CR7, SW16 182 C2
Stanmore HA7 25 B5
Greenland Cres UB2 106 D3
Greenland Ho 4 E1 97 A3
SE8 118 D1
Greenland Mews SE8 118 D1
Greenland Pl NW1 231 D6
Greenland Quay SE16 118 D2
Greenland Rd
NW1 93 C6 232 A6
Barnet EN5 12 C5
Greenlands
Borehamwood WD6 11 B5
Chessington KT19 214 D3
Greenland St NW1 231 D6
Green Lane Bsns Pk SE9 166 C2
Green Lane Cotts HA7 25 B6
Green Lane Gdns CR7 183 A1
Green Lane Mews SM4 201 D3
Green Lane Prim Sch KT4 200 B2
Green Lanes N4,N8,N15 50 D2
Palmers Green N13 16 C1
West Ewell KT19 215 C1
Greenlaw Ct W5 87 D1
Greenlaw Gdns KT3 199 D2
Greenlawns N12 29 D4
Green Lawns 8 SE18 122 D2
Ruislip HA4 40 C1
Greenlaw St SE18 122 C3
Green Leaf Ave SM6 219 D4
Greenleaf Cl 8 SW2 160 C4
Greenleafe Dr IG6 56 D6
Greenleaf Prim Sch E17 53 B6
Greenleaf Rd E17 53 B6
6 E6 99 C6
Greenlea Pk SW19 180 C2
Green Leas
Ashford TW16 171 D4
Kingston KT1 198 A6
Green Leas Cl TW16 171 D4
Greenleaves Ct TW15 170 D4
Green Man Gdns W13 109 A6
Green Man Intc E11 54 D2
Green Man La
Ealing W13 109 A5
Hatton TW14 128 A1
Greenman St N1 95 A6 235 A6
Greenmead Cl SE25 206 A4
Greenmead Sch SW15 156 B6
Green Moor Link N21 16 D4
Greenmoor Rd EN3 6 C3
Greenoak Pl EN4 2 D3
Green Oaks UB2 106 D2
Greenoak Way SW19 178 D6
Greenock Rd 11 W3 111 A3
Mitcham SW16 181 D2
Greeno Cres TW17 192 C4
Green Park★ SW1,W1 115 B4 248 D2
Green Park Sta W1 115 C5 249 A4
Green Pond Cl E17 53 B6
Green Pond Rd E17 53 A6
Green Pt E15 76 C2
Green Rd N20 14 A1
East Barnet N14 15 B5
Green Ride IG10,E4 21 A6
Greenrigg Wlk HA9 66 D5
Greenroof Way SE10 120 D3
Green Sch for Girls The TW7 131 A4
Greens Ct W1 249 C6
Green's Ct W11 244 C3
Greens Ct HA9 65 D5
Greens End SE18 122 D2
Greenshank Cl E17 35 A3
Greenshields Ind Est E16 121 B5
Greenside DA5 169 A3
Dagenham RM8 58 C1
Greenside Cl N20 14 B2
Catford SE6 164 B2
Greenside Prim Sch W12 112 A4
Greenside Rd W12 112 A4
Thornton Heath CR0 204 C2
Greenslade Prim Sch SE18 145 B6
Greenslade Rd IG11 79 B1
Greensleeves Ho UB2 107 D2
Greensleeves Manor SM2 217 D2
Green St E13 99 C6
E7 77 C1
W1 115 A6 248 A6
Enfield EN3 6 D3
Sunbury TW16 172 A1
Greenstead Ave IG8 37 C4
Greenstead Cl IG8 37 C4
Greenstead Gdns
Putney SW15 156 B6
Woodford IG8 37 C4
Greenstone Mews E11 55 A3
Green Street Green Prim Sch BR6 227 D2
Greenstreet Hill SE4 140 D2
Green Terr EC1 234 B1
Green The BR1 165 A1
DA16 145 C1
DA7 147 C4
E15 76 D2
N14 15 D1
W3 89 C1
Chingford E4 20 B3
Claygate KT10 212 D2
Ealing W5 109 D6
Edmonton N9 18 A2
Feltham TW13 150 B2
Hackbridge SM6 219 A6
Hayes BR2 209 A2
Heston TW5 129 C6
Kingston KT3 177 A1
Merton SM4 201 A5
7 Richmond TW9 153 D6
Sidcup DA14 190 A5
Southall UB2 107 B4
Southgate N21 16 C4
St Paul's Cray BR5 190 B3
Sutton SM1 217 D5
Tottenham N17 33 A4
Twickenham TW2 152 C2
Uxbridge UB10 61 A6
Wallington SM5 219 A4
Wanstead E11 55 B3
Wembley HA0 65 A6
Wimbledon SW19 178 D5
Green The *continued*
Woodford IG8 37 A5
Buckhurst Hill IG9 21 B3
Green Vale DA6 168 D6
Ealing W5 88 B1
Greenvale Rd SE9 144 C1
Greenvale Specl Sch SE23 163 A1
Green Verges HA7 25 D3
Green View KT9 214 B1
Greenview Ave CR0 207 A3
Greenview Cl W3 111 C5
Greenview Ct TW15 170 B6
Greenway N20 13 C2
Green Way BR2 210 A3
Greenway
Chislehurst BR7 188 D5
Dagenham RM8 58 C1
Harrow HA3 44 A4
Hayes UB4 84 B3
Palmers Green N14 16 A2
Pinner HA5 22 B1
Wallington SM6 219 C4
West Barnes SW20 200 C5
Woodford IG8 37 C5
Green Way Eltham SE9 165 D6
Sunbury TW16 194 A5
Greenway Ave E17 54 B5
Greenway Cl N11 31 A4
1 N15 51 D5
N20 13 C2
N4 73 A6
NW9 27 B1
Greenway Ct Hayes UB4 84 B3
Ilford IG1 56 D1
Greenway Gdns NW9 27 B1
Croydon CR0 223 B5
Greenford UB6 85 D4
Green Way Gdns HA3 24 C1
Greenways
Beckenham BR3 185 C1
Forest Hill SE26 184 C6
Hinchley Wood KT10 212 C4
Greenways The 1 TW1 153 A5
Greenway The NW9 27 B1
Hounslow TW4 129 B1
Pinner HA5 41 B3
Uxbridge UB10 61 A6
Uxbridge UB8 82 A5
Green Way The HA3 24 C2
Greenwell St W1 238 D5
Greenwich Academy SE10 141 D4
Greenwich Bsns Ctr SE10 141 D5
Greenwich Bsns Pk SE10 141 D5
Greenwich Church St SE10 142 A6
Greenwich Com Coll (Charlton Ctr) SE7 121 D2
Greenwich Cres E6 100 A2
Greenwich Ct 18 E1 96 B1
Greenwich District Hospl SE10 120 D1
Greenwich High Rd SE10 141 D5
Greenwich Hts 2 SE18 144 A5
Greenwich Ind Est SE10 141 D5
SE7 121 B2
Greenwich Mkt 1 SE10 142 A6
Greenwich Park SE10 142 C5
Greenwich Park Sch SE10 142 A5
Greenwich Park St SE10 142 B6
Greenwich South St SE10 142 A4
Greenwich Sta SE10 141 D5
Greenwich View E14 119 D3
Green Wlk NW4 46 D4
SE1 263 A5
Hampton TW12 173 B4
Ruislip HA4 39 D1
Southall UB2 107 C1
Green Wlk The E4 20 B3
Green Wood NW5 71 C3
Greenwood
8 Putney SW19 156 D4
3 Woodford IG8 37 A3
Greenwood Ave
Dagenham RM10 81 D4
Enfield EN3 7 A4
Greenwood Cl DA15 168 A2
Bushey WD23 8 C3
Merton SM4 201 A5
Orpington BR5,BR6 211 C3
Thames Ditton KT7 197 A1
Greenwood Dr E4 36 B5
Greenwood Gdns N13 16 D1
Greenwood Ho
8 SE4 140 D1
WC1 234 A1
Wood Green N22 32 C2
Greenwood La TW12 173 D5

Gunpowder Sq EC4 ..241 B2
Gun St E1 ....243 C3
Gunstor Rd N16 .....73 C4
Gunter Gr HA8 .....27 B2
SW6 ......136 A5 266 A4
Gunterstone Rd
W14 ......113 A1 254 B2
Gunthorpe St
E1 ......95 D1 243 D2
Gunton Rd E5 .....74 B6
Streatham SW17 ....181 A4
Gunwhale Cl SE16 ....118 D5
Gun Wharf E1 ......118 C5
E3 ....97 A6
Gurdon Ho 3 E14 ....97 C1
Gurdon Rd SE7 .....121 A1
Gurnell Gr W13 .....86 D3
Gurney Cl E15 .....76 C3
E17 ....34 D2
Barking IG11 .....78 D2
Gurney Cres CR0 ....204 B1
Gurney Dr N2 .....48 A5
Gurney Ho 14 E2 .....96 A5
3 W2 ....91 D1
Hayes UB3 ....105 C2
Gurney Rd E15 .....76 C3
SW6 .....136 A2
Northolt UB5 .....84 C4
Wallington SM5 ....219 A4
Guru Nanak Sikh Coll
UB4 ....106 C5
Guthrie Ct SE1 ....251 B1
Guthrie St SW3 .....257 A2
Gutter La EC2 ..95 A1 242 A2
Guyatt Gdns CR4 ....181 A1
Guy Barnett Gr SE3 ...143 A2
Guy Rd CR0,SM6 ....219 D5
Guyscliff Rd SE13 ....164 A6
Guy's Hospl
SE1 .....117 B5 252 D2
Guy's Hospl Sch
SE1 ......117 B5 252 D3
Guy's Retreat IG9 .....21 C4
Guy St SE1 ...117 B4 252 D2
Gwalior Ho N14 .....15 C5
Gwalior Rd SW15 .....134 D2
Gwendolen Ave SW15 156 D6
Gwendolen Cl SW15 ..156 D6
Gwendoline Ave E13 ...99 B6
Gwendwr Rd
W14 ....113 A1 254 B2
Gwent Ct 18 SE16 ....118 D5
Gwillim Cl DA15 .....168 A6
Gwilym Maries Ho 11
E2 ......96 B4
Gwydor Rd BR3 .....206 D6
Gwydyr Rd BR2 .....208 D6
Gwyn Cl SW6 .136 A5 266 A3
Gwyn Jones Prim Sch
E11 ......54 B2
Gwynne Ave CR0 .....206 D2
Gwynne Cl W4 .....133 D6
Gwynne Ho WC1 .....234 A1
6 Streatham SW2 ....160 B3
3 Wanstead E11 .....55 A4
Gwynne Pl WC1 .....233 D1
Gwynne Rd SW11 .....136 B3
Gye Ho 2 SW4 .....138 A1
Gylcote Cl SE5 .....139 B1
Gyles Pk HA7 .....25 C2
Gyllyngdune Gdns IG3 .79 D5

H

Haarlem Rd 12 W14 ...112 D3
Haberdasher Pl 4 N1 .95 C4
Haberdasher St
N1 ......95 B4 235 D2
Habington Ho 9 SE5 .139 B5
Haccombe Rd SW19 ..180 A4
Hackbridge Park Gdns
SM5 ......218 D6
Hackbridge Prim Sch
SM5 ......203 A1
Hackbridge Rd SM5,
SM6 ......219 A6
Hackbridge Sta SM6 ..219 B6
Hackett Cl SE8 .....119 B2
Hackford Rd
SW9 ......138 C4 270 D2
Hackford Wlk SW9 ...138 C4
Hackforth Cl EN5 .....12 B6
Hackington Cres BR3 .185 C4
Hackney Central Sta
E8 ......74 B2
Hackney Cl WD6 .....11 B6
Hackney Coll (Poplar Ctr)
E3 .....97 D3
Hackney Com Coll N1 .95 C4
N4 ......51 A2
Hackney Downs Sch
E5,E8 ......74 A3
Hackney Downs Sta E8 74 B3
Hackney Free & Parochial
CE Sch (Secondary)
E9 ......74 C2
Hackney Gr E8 .....74 B2
Hackney Hospl E9 ....75 A3
Hackney Rd E2 .....96 A5
Hackney Wick E9 .....75 B2
Hackney Wick Sta E9 ..75 C2
Hackworth Point 24 E3 97 D4
Haddenham Ct SW17 .180 B6
Hadden Rd SE28 .....123 C3
Hadden Way UB6 .....64 B2
Haddington Ct 4
SE10 ......141 D5
Haddington Rd BR1 ..186 B6
Haddo Ho NW5 .....71 B4
SE10 .....141 D6
Haddon Cl Enfield EN1 ..18 A5
New Malden KT3 .....199 D4
Haddon Ct NW4 .....46 C6
W3 ......111 D6
Haddon Gr DA15 .....168 A4
Haddon Rd SM1 .....217 D4
Haddo St SE10 .....142 A6
Haden Ct N4 .....72 C6
Hadfield Cl UB1 .....85 B4
Hadfield Ho 26 E1 .....96 A1
Hadleigh Cl 16 E1 .....96 C3
Merton SW20 .....179 B1
Hadleigh Ct 8 E4 .....20 C4
Hadleigh Ho 19 E1 .....96 C3
Hadleigh Lo 5 IG8 ....37 A4
Hadleigh Rd N9 .....18 B4
Hadleigh St E2 .....96 C4
Hadleigh Wlk 1 E6 ..100 A1
Hadley Cl
Borehamwood WD6 ....10 B5
Southgate N21 .....16 C5
Hadley Ct N16 .....52 A1
Hadley Gdns W4 .....111 B1
Southall UB2 .....107 B1
Hadley Gn EN5 .....1 B3
Hadley Gn W EN5 .....1 B3
Hadley Gr EN5 .....1 A3
Hadley Green Rd EN5 ..1 B3
Hadley Hall N21 .....16 C3
Hadley Highstone EN5 ..1 B4
Hadley Ho BR5 .....189 D1
Hadley Rd DA17 .....125 B2
Barnet EN5 .....1 D2
Enfield EN2 .....4 A5
Mitcham CR4 .....203 D5
Hadley Ridge EN5 .....1 B2
Hadley St NW1 .....71 B2
Hadleyvale Ct EN5 .....1 D2
Hadley Way N21 .....16 C5
Hadley Wood Prim Sch
EN4 .....2 A5
Hadley Wood Rd
Barnet EN4 .....2 A3
Barnet EN5 .....1 C3
Hadley Wood Sta EN4 ..2 A5
Hadlow Coll (Mottingham
Ctr) SE12 .....165 C3
Hadlow Ho SE17 .....263 B2
Hadlow Pl SE19 .....184 A3
Hadlow Rd
Bexley DA16 .....146 C5
Sidcup DA14 .....190 A6
Hadrian Cl TW19 .....148 A4
Hadrian Ct SE4 .....141 C2
Barnet EN5 .....1 D1
1 Belmont SM2 .....217 D1
Hadrian Est 30 E2 .....96 A5
Hadrian's Ride EN1 .....17 D6
Hadrian St SE10 .....120 C1
Hadrian Way TW19 ...148 A4
Hadstock Ho NW1 ....232 D2
Hadyn Park Ct 13
W12 .....112 A4
Hadyn Park Rd W12 ..112 A4
Hafer Rd SW11 .....136 D1
Hafton Rd SE6 .....164 C2
Haggard Rd TW1 .....153 B4
Hagger Ct E17 .....54 B6
Haggerston Rd E8 .....95 D6
Haggerston Sch E2 .....95 D5
Hague Prim Sch E2 ....96 B3
Hague St 12 E2 .....96 A4
Ha-Ha Rd SE7,SE18 ...144 B6
Haig Ct BR7 .....188 D5
Haig Ho 4 E2 .....96 A5
Haig Pl SM4 .....201 C3
Haig Rd Hillingdon UB8 .83 A2
Stanmore HA7 .....25 C5
Haig Rd E E13 .....99 C5
Haig Rd W E13 .....99 C4
Haigville Gdns IG6 ....56 D5
Hailes Cl SW19 .....180 A4
Haileybury Ave EN1 ....17 D5
Hailey Rd DA18 .....125 C4
Hailey Rd Bsns Pk
DA18 .....125 C4
Hailsham Ave SW2 ....160 B2
Hailsham Cl KT6 .....197 D2
Hailsham Dr HA1 .....42 B6
Hailsham Ho NW8 .....237 A5
Hailsham Rd SW17 ....181 A4
Hailsham Terr N18 .....33 B5
Haimo Prim Sch SE9 .165 D6
Haimo Rd SE9 .....165 D6
Hainault Bldgs E10 ....54 A1
Hainault Bridge Par 4
IG1 .....78 D6
Hainault Ct E17 .....54 B5
Hainault Gore RM6 ....59 A4
Hainault Rd E11 .....54 B2
Dagenham RM6 .....59 B3
Ilford RM6 .....58 B6
Hainault St SE9 .....166 D3
Ilford IG1 .....78 D6
Haines Wlk SM4 .....201 D2
Hainford Cl SE4 .....140 D1
Haining Cl 3 W4 .....110 C1
Hainthorpe Rd SE27 ..182 D6
Hainton Cl E1 .....96 B1
Halberd Mews E5 .....74 B6
Halbutt Gdns RM9 ....81 B5
Halcomb St N1 .....95 C6
Halcot Ave DA6 .....169 D6
Halcrow St E1 .....96 B2
Halcyon 3 EN1 .....17 C6
Halcyon Wharf 19 E1 .118 A5
Haldane Cl N10 .....31 B3
Holdbrook EN3 .....7 D5
Haldane Pl SW18 .....157 D3
Haldane Rd E6 .....100 A4
SE28 .....124 D6
SW6 ......135 B6 264 D5
Southall UB1 .....86 A1
Haldan Rd E4 .....36 A4
Haldon Rd SW18 .....157 B5
Hale Cl BR6 .....227 A4
HA8 .....27 A5
Chingford E4 .....20 A1
Hale Ct HA8 .....27 A5
Hale Dr NW7 .....27 B4
Hale End Cl HA4 .....40 A3
Hale End Rd E17 .....36 B2
Halefield Rd N17 .....34 B2
Hale Gdns N17 .....52 A6
Acton W3 .....110 C5
Hale Grove Gdns NW7 .27 C5
Hale Ho SW1 .....259 D2
Enfield EN3 .....6 D6
Hale La NW7,HA8 .....27 B5
Hale Lo HA1 .....42 C2
Hale Rd N17 .....52 A6
Newham E6 .....100 A3
Hales Ct 5 TW11 .....175 A5
Hales Ho 3 SW12 ....159 B4
Halesowen Rd SM4 ...201 D2
Hales Prior N1 .....233 C3
Hales St SE8 .....141 C5
Hale St E14 .....119 D6
Halesworth Cl 3 E5 ...74 C6
Halesworth Rd SE13 ..141 D2
Hale The N17 .....52 A6
Chingford E4 .....36 B3
Hale Wlk W7 .....86 C2
Haley Rd NW4 .....46 C3
Half Acre TW8 .....131 D6
Half Acre Mews TW8 .131 D6
Half Acre Rd W7 .....108 C5
Half Moon Ct EC1 ....242 A3
Half Moon La SE24 ...161 A5
Halfmoon Pas E1 .....243 D1
Half Moon St
W1 ......115 B5 248 D3
Halford Cl HA8 .....26 D1
Halford Ct KT9 .....214 A1
Halford Ho 9 SW15 ..156 D6
Halford Rd E10 .....54 B4
SW6 ......135 C6 265 A5
Ickenham UB10 .....60 C3
Richmond TW10 .....154 A6
Halfway St DA15 .....167 C3
Haliburton Rd TW1,
TW7 .....131 A1
Haliday Ho N1 .....73 B2
Haliday Wlk 4 N1 .....73 B2
Halidon Cl E9 .....74 C3
Halifax 8 NW9 .....27 D1
Halifax Cl TW11 .....174 C4
Halifax Rd Enfield EN2 ...5 B3
Greenford UB6 .....85 D6
Halifax St SE26 .....162 B1
Halifield Dr DA17 .....125 A3
Haling Gr CR2 .....221 A1
Haling Manor High Sch
CR2 .....220 D1
Haling Park Gdns CR2 220 D2
Haling Park Rd CR2 ..221 A2
Haling Rd CR2 .....221 B2
Haliwell Ho 8 NW6 ...91 D6
Halkett Ho 1 E2 .....96 C6
Halkin Arc
SW1 ......114 D3 257 D6
Halkin Mews SW1 ....258 A6
Halkin Pl SW1 .....258 A6
Halkin St SW1 115 A4 248 B1
Hallam Cl BR7 .....188 B5
Hallam Ct W1 .....238 D4
Hallam Gdns HA5 .....23 A3
Hallam Ho SW1 .....259 B1
17 SW9 .....138 C4
Hallam Mews W1 .....238 D4
Hallam Rd N15 .....50 D5
Hallam Rd *continued*
Barnes SW13 .....134 B2
Hallam St W1 ..93 B2 238 D4
Hallane Ho SE27 .....183 A5
Hall Cl W5 .....88 A2
Hall Ct TW11 .....174 D5
Hall Dr Ealing W7 .....86 C1
Forest Hill SE26 .....184 C5
Halley Gdns SE13 .....142 B1
Halley Ho 15 E2 .....96 A5
8 SE10 .....120 D1
Halley Prim Sch E14 ...97 A2
Halley Rd E7,E12 .....77 D2
Halley St E14 .....97 A2
Hall Farm Cl HA7 .....25 B6
Hall Farm Dr TW2 ....152 B4
Hallfield W2 .....236 A1
Hallfield Jun & Inf Schs
W2 .....91 D1
Hallgate SE3 .....143 A2
Hall Gate NW8 .92 A4 229 B2
Hall Gdns E4 .....35 B6
Halliards The KT12 ....194 A3
Halliday Ho 29 E1 .....96 A1
Halliday Sq UB2 .....108 B5
Halliford Cl TW17 .....193 C6
Halliford Rd
Sunbury TW16 .....194 A5
Upper Halliford TW16,
TW17 .....193 D5
Halliford Sch TW17 ...193 A2
Halliford St N1 .....73 B1
Halling Ho SE1 .....252 D1
Halliwell Ct 4 SE22 ..162 A6
Halliwell Rd SW2 .....160 B5
Halliwick Court Par 2
N12 .....30 D5
Halliwick Ct 1 N12 ....30 D5
Halliwick Ho N21 .....17 B5
Halliwick Rd N10 .....31 A2
Hall La E4 .....35 B5
NW4 .....28 A1
Harlington UB3 .....127 B5
Hall Lane E4 .....35 A5
Hallmark Trad Ctr HA9 .67 A4
Hallmead Rd SM1 ....217 D5
Hall Oak Wlk NW6 .....69 B2
Hallowell Ave CR0 ....220 A4
Hallowell Cl CR4 .....203 A6
Hallowfield Way CR4 .202 C6
Hall Pl W2 .....92 B3 236 C5
Hall Rd E15 .....76 B4
E6 .....100 B6
NW8 ......92 A4 229 B2
Dagenham RM6 .....58 D3
Isleworth TW7 .....152 B6
Hall Sch SW20 .....178 D2
Hall Sch The NW3 .....70 B2
Hall Sch Wimbledon
SW15 .....156 A1
Hallside Rd EN1 .....5 D5
Hall St EC1 .....94 D4 234 D2
N12 .....30 A5
Halls Terr UB10 .....82 D3
Hallsville Prim Sch E16 99 A1
Hallsville Rd E16 .....98 D1
Hallswelle Par 1 NW11 47 B4
Hallswelle Rd NW11 ...47 B4
Hall The SE3 .....143 A2
Hall Twr W2 .....236 D4
Hall View SE9 .....165 D2
Hallywell Cres E6 ....100 B2
Halons Rd SE9 .....166 C4
Halpin Pl SE17 117 B2 262 D3
Halsbrook Rd SE3 ....143 D2
Halsbury Cl HA7 .....25 B6
Halsbury Ct HA7 .....25 B6
Halsbury Ho 4 N7 .....72 B4
Halsbury Rd W12 .....112 B5
Halsbury Rd E UB5 ....64 A4
Halsbury Rd W UB5 ....63 D3
Halsend UB3 .....106 B5
Halsey St SW3 114 D2 257 C4
Halsham Cres IG11 ....79 D3
Halsmere Rd SE5 .....138 D4
Halstead Cl 2 CR0 ...221 A5
Halstead Ct N1 .....235 D3
Halstead Gdns N21 ....17 B3
Halstead Rd
Edmonton N21 .....17 B3
Enfield EN1 .....5 C1
Wanstead E11 .....55 B4
Halston Cl SW11 .....158 D5
Halstow 12 NW5 .....71 A2
Halstow Prim Sch
SE10 .....121 A1
Halstow Rd NW10 .....90 D4
SE3,SE10 .....121 A1
Halsway UB3 .....106 A5
Halter Cl WD6 .....11 B6
Halton Cl N11 .....30 D4
Halton Cross St
N1 ......94 D6 234 D6
Haltone Ho 1 SW4 ...137 D3
Halton Ho 23 N1 .....72 D1
Halton Mans N1 .....72 D1
Halton Pl N1 .....235 A6
Halton Rd N1 ..72 D1 234 D6
Halt Robin La DA17 ...125 D2
Halt Robin Rd DA17 ..125 D2
Halyard Ho E14 .....120 A3
Hamara Ghar 5 E13 ...99 C6
Hambalt Rd SW4 .....159 C6
Hamble Cl HA4 .....61 C6
Hamble Ct KT1 .....175 D3
Hambledon SE17 .....139 B6
Hambledon Chase N4 .50 A2
Hambledon Cl UB8 ....82 D3
Hambledon Ct
5 Ealing W5 .....110 A6
9 Wallington SM6 ....219 B2
Hambledon Gdns
SE25 .....205 D6
Hambledon Ho E5 .....74 B4
2 Kingston KT2 .....176 D4
Hambledon Pl SE21 ..161 D3
Hambledon Rd SW18 .157 B4
Hambledown Rd SE9 .167 C4
Hamble St SW6 .....135 D2
Hambleton Cl KT4 ....216 C6
Hamble Wlk UB5 .....85 C5
Hambley Ho 5 SE16 ..118 B2
Hamblin Ho UB1 .....107 A6
Hamblyn Ct N16 .....51 D2
Hambridge Way SW2 .160 C4
Hambro Ave BR2 .....209 A1
Hambrook Ct 12 NW5 ..71 B4
Hambrook Rd SE25 ..206 B6
Hambro Rd SW16 ....181 D5
Hambrough Ho UB4 ...84 C2
Hambrough Prim Sch
UB1 .....107 B5
Hambrough Rd UB1 ..107 A5
Hambury Ho SW8 .....270 B5
Ham Cl TW10 .....153 C1
Ham Comm TW10 ....153 D1
Ham Ct 12 NW9 .....27 D1
Hamden Cres RM10 ....81 D5
Hamel Cl HA3 .....43 D5
Hamelton Terr RM9 ....80 C1
Hamers Ho 19 SW2 ...160 C4
Hameway E6 .....100 C3
Ham Farm Rd KT2,
TW10 .....176 A6
Hamfrith Rd E15 .....76 D2
Ham Gate Ave TW10 ..176 A6
Ham Ho★ TW10 .....153 C2
Hamilton Ave
Cheam SM3 .....217 A6
Edmonton N9 .....18 A4
Ilford IG6 .....57 A4
Tolworth KT6,SM3 ....214 C6
Hamilton Cl N17 .....51 D6
NW8 ......92 B4 229 C1
SE16 .....119 A4
Ashford TW13 .....171 D5
Cockfosters EN4 .....2 D1
Teddington TW11 .....175 B4
Hamilton Cres
Edmonton N13 .....32 C6
Harrow HA2 .....63 B5
Hounslow TW3 .....151 D6
Hamilton Ct W9 .....229 A2
9 Catford SE6 .....164 D3
Croydon CR0 .....206 A1
Ealing W5 .....110 B6
Hamilton Gdns
NW8 ......92 A4 229 B2
Hamilton Hall
NW8 ......92 A5 229 A3
Hamilton Ho 1 E14 ..119 B6
19 E3 .....97 B4
NW8 .....229 C2
W8 .....245 C2
Chiswick W4 .....133 C6
Putney SW15 .....156 A6
10 Richmond TW9 ....132 C4
Hamilton La N5 .....72 D4
Hamilton Lo 32 E1 .....96 C3
Hamilton Mews W1 ..248 C2
Hamilton Par TW13 ...172 A6
Hamilton Pk N5 .....72 D4
Hamilton Pk W N5 ....72 D4
Hamilton Pl
W1 ......115 A5 248 B3
Sunbury TW16 .....172 B3
Tottenham N17 .....33 D1
Hamilton Rd DA7 .....147 A3
E15 .....98 C4
E17 .....35 A1
N2 .....48 A6
NW10 .....68 A3
NW11 .....47 A2
W4 .....111 C4
Barnet EN4 .....2 C1
Brentford TW8 .....131 D6
Ealing W5 .....110 A6
Edmonton N9 .....18 A4
Feltham TW13 .....171 D6
Harrow HA1 .....42 C4
Hayes UB3 .....106 B6
Ilford IG1 .....78 D4
Merton SW19 .....179 D3
Sidcup DA15 .....190 A6
Southall UB1 .....107 B5
South Norwood CR7 ...205 B6
Twickenham TW2 .....152 C3
West Norwood SE27 ...183 B6
Hamilton Road Ctr E15 98 C4
Hamilton Road Ind Est
SE27 .....183 B6
Hamilton Road Mews 1
SW19 .....179 D3
Hamilton Sq N12 .....30 A4
SE1 .....252 D2
Hamilton St SE8 .....141 C6
Hamilton Terr
NW8 ......92 A4 229 B2
Hamilton Way N3 .....29 C4
Edmonton N13 .....32 D6
Hamlea Cl SE12 .....165 A6
Hamlet Cl SE13 .....142 C1
Hamlet Ct SE11 .....261 C2
1 W6 .....112 A2
14 Enfield EN1 .....17 C6
Hamlet (Day) Hospl The
TW9 .....132 A2
Hamlet Gdns W6 .....112 A2
Hamlet Ho SE9 .....166 C6
Hamlet Ind Est E9 .....75 C1
Hamlet Rd SE19 .....184 A3
Hamlet Sq NW2 .....69 A5
Hamlets Way E3 .....97 B3
Hamlet The SE5 .....139 B2
Hamlet Way SE1 .....252 D2
Hamlin Cres HA5 .....40 C4
Hamlyn Cl HA8 .....10 A1
Hamlyn Gdns SE19 ....183 C3
Hammelton Ct 4 BR1 186 D2
Hammelton Gn 2
SW9 .....138 D4
Hammelton Rd BR1 ..187 A2
Hammers La NW7 .....28 A6
Hammersley Ho 8
SE14 .....140 C5
Hammersmith Bridge Rd
W6,SW13 .....112 C1
Hammersmith Broadway 5
W6 .....112 C2
Hammersmith Flyover
W6 .....112 C1
Hammersmith Gr W6 .112 C3
Hammersmith Hospl
W12 .....90 B1
Hammersmith Rd
W14 .....254 B4
W6 .....112 D2
Hammersmith Sta W6 112 C2
Hammersmith Terr
W6 .....112 A1
Hammet Cl UB4 .....84 D2
Hammett St EC3 .....253 C6
Hammond Ave CR4 ...181 B1
Hammond Cl
Barnet EN5 .....13 B6
Greenford UB6 .....64 B3
Hampton TW12 .....173 C2
Hammond Ct 1 E10 ...75 D6
1 E17 .....53 A4
Hammond Ho E14 .....119 D3
10 SE14 .....140 C5
Hammond Lo 6 W9 .....91 C2
Hammond Rd Enfield EN1 6 B3
Southall UB2 .....107 A3
Hammonds Cl RM8 .....80 C5
Hammond St NW5 .....71 C2
Hammond Way 2
SE28 .....124 B6
Hamonde Cl HA8 .....10 D2
Hamond Sq N1 .....95 C5
Ham Park Rd E15 .....76 D1
Hampden Ave BR3 ....185 A1
Hampden Cl NW1 .....232 D4
Hampden Ct 5 N10 ....31 A3
Hampden Gurney CE Prim
Sch W1 ......92 C1 237 B2
Hampden Gurney St
W1 .....237 C1
Hampden Ho SW9 ....138 C3
Hampden La N17 .....34 A2
Hampden Rd N10 .....31 A3
N19 .....71 D6
N8 .....50 C5
Beckenham BR3 .....185 A1
Harrow HA3 .....24 A1
Kingston KT1 .....198 C6
Tottenham N17 .....34 A2
Hampden Sq N14 .....15 B3
Hampden Way N14 .....15 B2
Hampshire Cl N18 .....34 B5
Hampshire Ct 6
SW13 .....133 D3
Hampshire Hog La 11
W6 .....112 B2
Hampshire Rd N22 .....32 B3
Hampshire Sch The
SW7 ......114 C4 247 B1
Hampshire St NW5 .....71 D2
Hampson Way
SW8 ......138 B4 270 C2
Hampstead Cl SE28 ...124 B5
Hampstead Garden Suburb
Inst NW11 .....47 D4
Hampstead Gate NW3 .70 A3
Hampstead Gdns NW11 47 C3
Hampstead Gn NW3 ...70 C3
Hampstead Gr NW3 ...70 A5

Hampstead Heath★ NW3 ....70 B6
Hampstead Heath Sta NW3 ....70 C4
Hampstead High St NW3 ....70 B4
Hampstead Hill Gdns NW3 ....70 C4
Hampstead Hill Sch NW3 ....70 C3
Hampstead Hts N2 ....48 A6
Hampstead La N6 ....48 C2
Hampstead Parochial CE Prim Sch NW3 ....70 A4
Hampstead Rd NW1 ....93 C4 232 A2
Hampstead Sch NW2 ..69 A4
Hampstead Sq NW3 ...70 A5
Hampstead Sta NW3 ...70 A4
Hampstead Way NW11 .47 C3
Hampstead West 4 NW6 ....69 C2
Hampstead Wlk 1 E3 .97 B6
Hampton Cl N11 ....31 B5
NW6 ....91 C4
Wimbledon SW20 ....178 C3
Hampton Com Coll TW12 ....173 C5
Hampton Court KT8 ..196 C6
Hampton Court Ave KT8 ....196 C3
Hampton Court Cres KT8 ....196 B6
Hampton Court Landing Stage KT8 ....196 C6
Hampton Court Palace★ KT8 ....196 D6
Hampton Court Par KT8 ....196 C5
Hampton Court Rd KT1,KT8 ....197 B6
Hampton Court Sta KT8 ....196 C5
Hampton Court Way KT10,KT7,KT8 ....196 C3
Hampton Ct N1 ....72 D2
19 SE16 ....118 D5
Wood Green N22 ....31 C2
Hampton Farm Ind Est TW13 ....151 A1
Hampton Hill Bsns Pk TW12 ....174 A5
Hampton Hill Jun Mix Sch TW12 ....174 A5
Hampton Ho DA7 ....147 D3
Hampton Inf Sch TW12 ....173 C3
Hampton Jun Sch TW12 ....173 C2
Hampton La TW13 ....173 A6
Hampton Rd E11 ....54 B1
E4 ....35 B5
E7 ....77 C3
Ilford IG1 ....79 A4
North Cheam KT4 ....216 B6
Teddington TW11,TW12 ....174 C5
Thornton Heath CR0 ....205 A3
Twickenham TW2 ....152 B1
Hampton Rd E TW13 ..151 B1
Hampton Rd W TW13 .151 A1
Hampton Rise HA3 ...44 A3
Hampton Road Ind Pk CR0 ....205 A3
Hampton Sch TW12 ..173 C5
Hampton St SE1 ....116 D2 261 D3
Hampton Sta TW12 ...173 C2
Hampton Wick Inf Sch KT1 ....175 D3
Hampton Wick Sta KT1 ....175 C2
Ham Ridings TW10 ...176 B5
Ham Shades Cl 1 DA15 ....168 A1
Ham St TW10 ....153 C1
Ham The TW8 ....131 C5
Ham View CR0 ....207 A3
Ham Yd W1 ....249 C6
Hanameel St 6 E16 ...121 A5
7 E16 ....121 B5
10 E16 ....121 B5
Hana Mews E5 ....74 B4
Hanbury Cl NW4 ....46 C6
Hanbury Ct HA1 ....42 D3
Hanbury Dr N21 ....16 B6
Hanbury Ho 8 E1 ....96 A2
Hanbury Rd W3 ....110 D4
Tottenham N17 ....34 B1
Hanbury St E1 .96 A2 243 D4
Hancocke Ho 4 E17 ...53 D6
Hancock Nunn Ho 1 NW3 ....70 D1
Hancock Rd E3 ....98 A4
South Norwood SE19 ...183 B4
Handa Wlk 3 N1 ....73 A2
Handcroft Rd CR0 ....204 D1
Hand Ct WC1 ....240 D3
Handel Cl HA8 ....26 B4
Handel Ho TW2 ....152 B5
Handel Mans SW13 ...134 C5
Handel Pl NW10 ....67 B2
Handel St WC1 .94 A3 240 B6
Handel Way HA8 ....26 C3
Handen Rd SE12 ....164 D6
Handforth Rd SW9 ...138 C5
6 Ilford IG1 ....78 D5
Handley Gr NW2 ....68 D5
Handley Page Rd SM6 ....
Handley Rd E9 ....96 C6
Handowe Cl NW4 ....46 A5
Handside Cl KT4 ....200 D1
Hands Wlk E16 ....99 A1
Handsworth Ave E4 ...36 B4
Handsworth Prim Sch E4 ....36 B4
Handsworth Rd N17 ...51 B6
Handtrough Way IG11 ....100 D5
Hanford Cl SW18 ....157 C3
Hanger Ct W5 ....88 C3
Hanger Gn W5 ....88 C3
Hanger Lane Sta W5 ...88 A4
Hanger La (North Circular Rd) W5 ....88 B2
Hanger Vale La W5 ....88 B1
Hanger View Way W3 ..88 C2
Hangmans Cnr BR7 ...188 D2
Hankey Pl SE1 117 B4 252 D1
Hankins La NW7 ....11 C1
Hanley Gdns N4 ....50 B1
Hanley Pl BR3 ....185 C3
Hanley Rd N4,N19 ....50 A1
Hanmer Wlk N7 ....72 B6
Hannah Cl BR3 ....208 A6
Hannah Ct SW19 ....178 D3
Hannah Mary Way 15 SE1 ....118 A2
Hannah Mews SM6 ...219 C1
Hannan Cl NW10 ....67 A4
Hannay La N8 ....49 D2
Hannay Wlk SW16 ....159 D2
Hannell Rd SW6 ....135 A5 264 B4
Hannen Ho SE5 ....139 B2
Hannen Rd SE27 ....160 D1
Hannibal Rd E1 ....96 C2
Stanwell TW19 ....148 A4
Hannibal Way CR0 ....220 B2
Hanning Lo TW3 ....130 A1
Hannington Rd SW4 ..137 B2
Hanover Ave E16 ....121 A5
Feltham TW13 ....150 A2
Hanover Circ UB3 ....83 B1
Hanover Cl Cheam SM3 217 B4
Richmond TW9 ....132 C5
Hanover Ct N16 ....51 D2
NW9 ....45 C6
W12 ....112 A5
1 Penge SE19 ....184 A3
Hanover Dr BR7 ....189 A6
Hanover Gate Mans NW1 ....237 B6
Hanover Gdns SE11 ..138 C6
Hanover Ho NW8 ....230 A3
New Barnet EN5 ....2 A1
Tolworth KT6 ....198 C1
Hanover Mans 5 SW2 ....160 C6
Hanover Mead NW11 ..47 A3
Hanover Pk SE15 ....140 A4
Hanover Pl 12 E3 ....97 B4
WC2 ....240 B1
Hanover Prim Sch N1 235 B4
Hanover Rd N15 ....51 D5
Merton SW19 ....180 A3
Willesden NW10 ....90 C6
Hanover Sq W1 93 B1 238 D1
Hanover St W1 .93 B1 238 D1
Croydon CR0 ....220 D5
Hanover Steps W2 ...237 B1
Hanover Terr NW1 ....92 D4 230 C1
Isleworth TW7 ....131 A4
Hanover Terr Mews NW1 ....92 C4 230 B1
Hanover Way DA7 ....146 D2
Hanover West Ind Est NW10 ....89 B4
Hanover Yd N1 ....235 A4
Hansard Mews W14 ..112 D4
Hansart Way EN2 ....4 C4
Hanscomb Mews 3 SW4 ....137 C1
Hans Cres SW1 ....114 D3 257 C6
Hanselin Cl HA7 ....24 D5
Hansen Dr N21 ....16 B6
Hanshaw Dr HA8 ....27 B2
Hansler Gr KT8 ....196 B5
Hansler Rd SE22 ....161 D6
Hansol Rd DA6 ....169 A6
Hansom Terr 1 BR1 ..187 B2
Hanson Cl
Balham SW12 ....159 B4
Beckenham BR3 ....185 D4
Mortlake SW14 ....133 A2
West Drayton UB7 ....104 B3
Hanson Ct E17 ....53 D3
Hanson Gdns UB1 ....107 A4
Hanson Ho 2 E1 ....118 A6
Hanson St W1 ..93 C2 239 A4
Hans Pl SW1 ..114 D3 257 C6
Hans Rd SW3 .114 D3 257 C6
Hans St SW1 ..114 D3 257 D5
Hanway Ho 25 SW9 ...138 C4
Hanway Pl W1 ....239 C2
Hanway Rd W7 ....86 C1
Hanway St W1 ....239 C2
Hanwell Ho 24 W2 ....91 C2
Hanwell Sta W7 ....108 C6
Hanworth Ho SE5 ....138 D5
Hanworth Rd
Ashford TW16 ....172 A3
Feltham TW13 ....150 B3
Hampton TW12 ....173 C5
Hounslow TW3,TW4 ....129 D1
Twickenham TW4 ....151 B4
Hanworth Terr TW3 ...129 D1
Hanworth Trad Est TW13 ....151 A1
Hapgood Cl UB6 ....64 B3
Harben Rd NW6 ....70 A1
Harberson Rd E15 ....98 D6
Balham SW12 ....159 B3
Harberton Rd N19 ....49 C1
Harbet Rd N18 ....35 A4
W2 ....92 B2 236 D3
Harbex Cl DA5 ....169 D4
Harbinger Prim Sch E14 ....119 D2
Harbinger Rd E14 ....119 D2
Harbin Ho 5 SW2 ....160 C3
Harbledown Ho SE1 ..252 C1
Harbledown Rd SW6 .265 A2
Harbord Cl SE5 ....139 B3
Harbord Ho 5 SE16 ...118 D2
Harbord St SW6 ....134 D4
Harborne Cl WD19 ....22 C5
Harborough Ave DA15 167 D4
Harborough Rd SW16 .182 B6
Harborough Sch N19 ..71 D6
Harbour Ave SW10 ....136 A4 266 B1
Harbour Exchange Sq E14 ....119 D4
Harbour Rd SE5 ....139 A2
Harbridge Ave SW15 ..156 A4
Harbury Rd SM5 ....218 C1
Harbut Rd SW11 ....136 B1
Harcastle Cl UB4 ....85 A3
Harcombe Rd N16 ....73 C5
Harcourt Ave
DA5,DA15 ....168 C4
E12 ....78 B3
HA8 ....11 A1
Wallington SM6 ....219 B4
Harcourt Cl TW7 ....131 A2
Harcourt Field SM6 ...219 B4
Harcourt Ho 27 SW8 ..137 D3
W1 ....238 C2
5 Chingford E4 ....36 B5
Harcourt Lo 2 SM6 ...219 B4
Harcourt Rd E15 ....98 D5
N22 ....31 D2
SE4 ....141 B2
Bexley DA6,DA7 ....147 A1
Bushey WD23 ....8 A6
Merton SW19 ....179 C3
Thornton Heath CR7 ....204 C3
Wallington SM6 ....219 B4
Harcourt St W1 92 C2 237 B3
Harcourt Terr SW10 ....113 D1 255 D1
Hardcastle Cl SE25 ...206 A3
Hardcastle Ho 8 SE15 ....140 A4
Hardcourts Cl BR4 ...223 D5
Hard Ct IG8 ....37 C4
Hardel Rise SW2 ....160 D3
Hardel Wlk SE24,SW2 .160 C4
Harden Ct 1 SE7 ....122 A2
Harden Ho SE5 ....139 C3
Harders Rd SE15 ....140 B3
Hardess St SE24 ....139 A2
Hardham Ho 5 SW2 ..160 C5
Hardie Cl NW10 ....67 B3
Harding Cl SE17 ....139 A6
South Croydon CR0 ....221 D5
Harding Ct SE25 ....183 D1
Hardinge Cl UB8 ....82 D1
Hardinge Rd
Edmonton N18 ....33 C4
Willesden NW10 ....90 C6
Hardinge St E1 ....96 C1
SE18 ....122 D3
Harding Ho 16 SE18 ...122 B2
Barnes SW13 ....134 B6
Hayes UB3 ....84 B1
Harding Pl SE23 ....163 A4
Harding Rd DA7 ....147 B3
Hardings Cl KT2 ....176 B2
Hardings La SE20 ....184 D4
Hardington 2 NW1 ....71 A1
Hardman Rd SE7 ....121 B1
Kingston KT2 ....176 A1
Hardwick Cl 7 HA7 ....25 C5
Hardwick Ct 8 E11 ....55 A3
Hardwicke Ave TW5 ..129 C4
Hardwicke Ho 14 E3 ...97 D4
Hardwicke Mews WC1 ....233 D1
Hardwicke Rd W4 ....111 B2
Bowes Park N13 ....32 A4
Richmond TW10 ....175 C6
Hardwicke St IG11 ...101 A6
Hardwick Gn W13 ....87 B2
Hardwick Ho NW8 ....237 B6
14 SW8 ....137 D3
Hardwick St EC1 ....94 C4 234 B1
Hardwick's Way SW18 157 C6
Hardwidge St SE1 ....253 A2
Hardy Ave 4 E16 ....121 A5
Ruislip HA4 ....62 B3
Hardy Cl SE16 ....118 D4
Barnet EN5 ....13 A6
Pinner HA5 ....40 D2
Hardy Cotts 2 SE10 ..142 B6
Hardy Ct SE3 ....142 D6
9 Wanstead E11 ....55 A5
Hardyng Ho 4 E17 ....53 A5
Hardy Pas N22 ....32 C1
Hardy Rd E4 ....35 B4
SE3 ....142 D6
Merton SW19 ....179 D3
Hardys Cl KT8 ....196 C5
Hardy Way EN2 ....4 C4
Harebell Dr E6 ....100 C2
Hare & Billet Rd SE3 ..142 B3
Harecourt Rd N1 ....73 A2
Hare Ct EC4 ....241 A1
Haredale Ho 22 SE16 .118 A4
Haredale Rd SE24 ....139 A1
Haredon Cl SE23 ....162 D4
Harefield KT10 ....212 C5
Harefield Cl EN2 ....4 C4
Harefield Ct 6 SW19 .179 C3
Harefield Mews SE4 ..141 B2
Harefield Rd DA14 ....168 D1
N8 ....49 D4
SE4 ....141 B2
South Norwood SW16 ..182 B3
Uxbridge UB8 ....60 A3
Hare La KT10 ....212 C2
Hare Marsh E2 ....96 A3
Harenc Sch Trust DA14 ....190 C5
Hare Pl EC4 ....241 B1
Hare Row E2 ....96 B5
Haresfield Rd RM10 ....81 C2
Hare St SE18 ....122 C3
Hare Wlk N1 ....95 C5
Harewood Ave NW1 ....92 C3 237 B5
Northolt UB5 ....63 B1
Harewood Cl UB5 ....63 B1
Harewood Ct HA3 ....24 C2
Harewood Pl W1 ....238 D1
Harewood Rd
Hounslow TW7 ....130 D4
Mitcham SW19 ....180 C4
South Croydon CR2 ....221 C2
Harewood Row NW1 ..237 B4
Harewood Terr UB2 ...107 B2
Harfield Gdns 1 SE5 .139 C2
Harfield Rd TW16 ....172 D1
Harfleur Ct SE11 ....261 C3
Harford Cl E4 ....19 D4
Harford Ho SE5 ....139 A6
W11 ....91 B2
Harford Rd E4 ....19 D4
Harford St E1 ....97 A3
Harford Wlk N2 ....48 B5
Hargood Cl HA3 ....44 A3
Hargood Rd SE3 ....143 C4
Hargrave Mans 2 N19 .71 D6
Hargrave Park Prim Sch N19 ....71 C6
Hargrave Pk N19 ....71 C6
Hargrave Pl N7 ....71 D3
Hargrave Rd N19 ....71 C6
Hargraves Ho 14 W12 .112 B6
Hargwyne St SW9 ....138 B2
Haringey Pk N8 ....50 A3
Haringey Rd N8 ....50 A5
Harington Terr N18 ....17 B1
Harkett Cl HA3 ....24 D1
Harkness Ho 20 E1 ....96 A1
Harland Ave
Sidcup DA15 ....167 C2
South Croydon CR0 ....222 A5
Harland Cl SW19 ....201 D6
Harland Fst Sch CR4 ..180 B1
Harland Rd SE12 ....165 A3
Harlands Gr BR6 ....226 D4
Harlech Ct 1 SE23 ...162 C3
Harlech Gdns TW5 ...128 C5
Harlech Rd N14 ....16 A1
Harlech Twr 5 W3 ...111 A4
Harlequin Ave TW8 ...131 A6
Harlequin Cl Hayes UB4 84 D2
Isleworth TW7 ....152 C6
Harlequin Ct NW10 ....67 B2
Croydon CR2 ....221 A1
Ealing W5 ....109 C6
Harlequin Ho 1 DA18 125 A3
Harlequin Rd TW11 ...175 B3
Harlescott Rd SE15 ...140 D1
Harlesden Gdns NW10 .89 D6
Harlesden Plaza 2 NW10 ....89 D5
Harlesden Prim Sch NW10 ....89 C5
Harlesden Rd NW10 ...90 A6
Harlesden Sta NW10 ...89 B5
Harleston Cl 4 E5 ....74 C6
Harley Cl HA0 ....65 D2
Harley Cres HA1 ....42 B5
Harley Ct N20 ....14 A1
Wanstead E11 ....55 A2
Harleyford BR1 ....187 C2
Harleyford Ct SW8 ...270 C6
Harleyford Manor 8 W3 ....111 A5
Harleyford Rd SE11 ....138 B6 270 C6
Harleyford St SE11 ...138 C6
Harley Gdns BR6 ....227 C4
SW10 ....114 A1 256 B1
Harley Gr E3 ....97 B4
Harley Ho E11 ....54 B2
NW1 ....238 B5
Harley Pl W1 ...93 B2 238 C3
Harley Rd NW10 ....89 C5
NW3 ....70 B1
Harrow HA1 ....42 B5
Harley St W1 ...93 B2 238 C3
Harley Villas NW10 ....89 C5
Harling Ct 3 SW11 ...136 D3
Harlinger St SE18 ....122 A3
Harlington Bridge UB3 ....105 C1
Harlington Cl UB7 ....127 A5
Harlington Cnr UB3 ..127 B4
Harlington Com Sch UB3 ....105 B2
Harlington Rd DA7 ...147 A2
Hillingdon UB8 ....82 C3
Harlington Rd E TW13, TW14 ....150 C3
Harlington Rd W TW14 ....150 B5
Harlowe Ho 13 E8 ....95 D6
Harlow Mans 2 IG11 ..78 D1
Harlow Rd N13 ....17 B1
Harlyn Dr HA5 ....40 B6
Harlyn Prim Sch HA5 ..40 B6
Harlynwood 19 SE5 ...139 A5
Harman Ave IG8 ....36 D4
Harman Cl NW2 ....69 A5
9 SE1 ....118 A1
Chingford E4 ....36 B6
Harman Dr DA15 ....167 D5
NW2 ....69 A4
Harman Rd EN1 ....17 D6
Harmondsworth La UB7 ....126 B6
Harmondsworth Rd UB7 ....104 A2
Harmon Ho 6 SE8 ....119 B2
Harmony Cl NW11 ....47 A4
Harmony Way BR1 ....187 A1
NW4 ....46 C5
Harmood Gr NW1 ....71 B1
Harmood Ho 2 NW1 ...71 B1
Harmood St NW1 ....71 B1
Harmsworth St SE17 ....116 D1 261 C1
Harmsworth Way N20 ..13 C3
Harness Rd SE28 ....124 A4
Harold Ave Erith DA17 .125 B1
Hayes UB3 ....105 D3
Harold Ct 16 SE16 ....118 D4
Harold Est SE1 ....263 B5
Harold Gibbons Ct 12 SE7 ....143 C6
Harold Ho 16 E2 ....96 D5
Harold Laski Ho EC1 ..234 D1
Harold Maddison Ho SE17 ....261 D2
Harold Pl SE11 ....261 A1
Harold Rd E11 ....54 C1
E13 ....99 B6
N15 ....51 D4
N8 ....50 B5
NW10 ....89 B4
Chingford E4 ....20 A1
South Norwood SE19 ..183 B3
Sutton SM1 ....218 B4
Woodford IG8 ....37 A2
Haroldstone Rd E17 ...53 A4
Harold Wilson Ho SW6 ....264 D5
Harp Alley EC4 ....241 C2
Harp Bsns Ctr The NW2 ....68 A6
Harpenden Rd
Wanstead E12 ....77 C6
West Norwood SE27, SW16 ....160 D2
Harpenmead Point NW2 ....69 B6
Harper Cl N14 ....15 C6
Harper Ho 3 SW9 ....138 D2
Harper Mews SW17 ...158 A1
Harper Rd SE1 117 A3 262 B6
Newham E6 ....100 B1
Harper's Yd N17 ....33 D2
Harp Island Cl NW10 ..67 B6
Harp La EC3 ....253 A5
Harpley Sq E1 ....96 D3
Harpour Rd IG11 ....79 A2
Harp Rd W7 ....86 D3
Harpsden St SW11 ...268 A1
Harpur Mews WC1 ...240 C4
Harpur St WC1 .94 B2 240 C4
Harraden Rd SE3 ....143 C4
Harrier Ave E11 ....55 B3
Harrier Ct TW4 ....129 A3
Harrier Ho 9 SW11 ...136 C2
Harrier Mews SE28 ...123 B4
Harrier Rd NW9 ....27 C1
Harriers Cl W5 ....110 A6
Harrier Way E6 ....100 B2
Harries Rd UB4 ....84 C3
Harriet Cl E8 ....96 A6
Harriet Gdns CR0 ....222 A6
Harriet Ho SW6 ....265 D3
Harriet St SW1 ....114 D4 247 D1
Harriet Tubman Cl 21 SW2 ....160 C4
Harriet Way WD23 ....8 B4
Harriet Wlk SW1 ....114 D4 247 D1
Harringay Gdns N8 ....50 D5
Harringay Green Lanes Sta N4 ....50 D3
Harringay Rd N15 ....50 D5
Harringay Sta N4 ....50 C3
Harrington Cl NW10 ...67 B5
Wallington CR0 ....220 A6
Harrington Ct SW7 ...256 D4
9 W9 ....91 B4
6 South Croydon CR0 ..221 B6
Harrington Gdns SW7 ....114 A2 256 A3
Harrington Hill E5 ....52 B1
Harrington Hill Prim Sch E5 ....52 B1
Harrington Ho E5 ....52 C1
NW1 ....232 A2
SW1 ....259 D2
Harrington Rd E11 ....54 C1
SW7 ....114 B2 256 C4
Croydon SE25 ....206 B5
Harrington Rd Sta SE25 ....206 C6
Harrington Sq NW1 ....93 C5 232 A3
Harrington St NW1 ....93 C4 232 A2
Harrington Way SE18 .121 D3
Harriott Cl SE10 ....120 D2
Harriott Ho 11 E1 ....96 C1
Harris City Tech Coll SE19 ....183 D2
Harris Cl Enfield EN2 ....4 D4
Heston TW5 ....129 C4
Harris Cotts 1 E15 ....98 D6
Harris Ho 10 E3 ....97 C4
8 SW9 ....138 C2
Harris Lo SE6 ....164 A3
Harrison Cl N20 ....14 C3
Harrison Ho SE17 ....262 C2
Harrison Rd RM10 ....81 D2
Harrisons Ct 1 SE14 .140 D6
Harrison's Rise CR0 ..220 D5
Harrison St WC1 ....94 A4 233 B1
Harrison Way TW17 ..192 D4
Harris Rd DA7 ....147 B4
Dagenham RM9 ....81 B3
Harris St E17 ....53 B2
SE5 ....139 B5
Harris Way TW16 ....171 C2
Harrodian Sch The SW13 ....133 D5
Harrogate Ct 2 SE26 .162 A1
Harrold Ho 1 NW3 ....70 A1
Harrold Rd RM8 ....80 B3
Harrow Ave EN1 ....17 D5
Harroway Rd SW11 ...136 B3
Harrowby St W1 ....92 C1 237 B2
Harrow Cl KT9 ....213 D1
Harrow Coll HA1 ....42 C2
Harrow Coll (Harrow Weald Campus) HA3 ....24 C4
Harrowdene Cl HA0 ...65 D4
Harrowdene Ct SW19 .179 A5
Harrowdene Gdns TW11 ....175 A3
Harrowdene Rd HA0 ...65 D4
Harrow Dr N9 ....17 D3
Harrowes Meade HA8 ..10 C1
Harrow Fields Gdns HA1 ....64 C5
Harrowgate Ho 22 E9 ..74 D2
Harrowgate Rd E9 ....75 A1
Harrow Gn E11 ....76 C5

Harrow High Sch HA1 43 A3
Harrow Hospl HA2 64 C6
Harrow La E14 120 A6
Harrow Lo SM2 218 B2
Harrow Manor Way
SE2 124 C3
Harrow Mus & Her Ctr★
HA2 42 A6
Harrow-on-the-Hill Sta
HA1 42 C3
Harrow Pk HA1 64 C6
Harrow Pl E1 95 C1 243 B2
Harrow Rd E11 76 D5
2 E6 100 A6
W2 92 A2 236 B3
W2,W9 91 C3
Ashford TW15 148 C2
Barking IG11 101 C6
Carshalton SM1,SM2,
SM5 218 C2
Ilford IG1 79 A4
Wembley HA0 65 A4
Wembley HA0 65 D3
Wembley HA9 66 C2
Harrow Sch HA1 42 C1
Harrow St NW1 237 A4
Harrow View
Harrow HA1,HA2 42 B5
Hayes UB3 84 A1
Hillingdon UB10 83 A4
Harrow View Rd W5 87 B3
Harrow Way
Charlton TW17 171 A1
South Oxhey WD19 23 A6
Harrow Weald Pk HA3 24 B4
Harrow & Wealdstone Sta
HA1 42 C5
Harry Ct 15 NW9 46 A5
Harry Gosling Prim Sch
E1 96 A1
Harry Hinkins Ho
SE17 262 B1
Harry Lambourn Ho 10
SE15 140 B5
Harston 15 KT1 176 C1
Harston Dr EN3 7 C5
Hart Ct E12 78 C1
Harte Rd TW3 129 B3
Hartfield Ave
Borehamwood WD6 10 C6
Northolt UB5 84 B5
Hartfield Cl WD6 10 C6
Hartfield Cres BR4 225 A5
Merton SW19 179 B3
Hartfield Gr SE20 184 C2
Hartfield Ho UB5 84 B5
Hartfield Rd
Chessington KT9 213 D3
Hayes BR4 225 A4
Merton SW19 179 C3
Hartfield Terr E3 97 C5
Hartford Ave HA3 43 B6
Hartford Rd DA5 169 C5
West Ewell KT19 214 D2
Hart Gr Ealing W5 110 C5
Southall UB1 85 C2
Hart Grove Ct 3 W5 110 C5
Hartham Cl N7 72 A3
Isleworth TW7 131 A4
Hartham Rd N7 72 A3
Isleworth TW7 131 A4
Tottenham N17 33 D1
Hart Ho SW2 160 C3
Harting Rd SE9 166 A1
Hartington Cl BR6 227 A3
Harrow HA1 64 C4
Hartington Ct SW8 270 A2
Chiswick W4 132 D5
Hartington Rd E17 53 A3
SW8 138 A5 270 A3
Chiswick W4 133 A4
Ealing W13 109 B6
Newham E16 99 B1
Southall UB2 107 A3
Twickenham TW1 153 B5
Hartismere Rd
SW6 135 B5 264 D4
Hartlake Rd E9 75 A2
Hartland NW1 232 B5
Hartland Cl
Edgware HA8 10 C2
Enfield N21 17 A5
Hartland Ct 5 N11 30 D5
Hartland Dr
Edgware HA8 10 C2
Ruislip HA4 62 B4
Hartland Rd E15 76 D1
N11 30 D5
NW1 71 B1
NW6 91 B6
Cheam SM4 201 D2
Hampton TW12 173 D6
Isleworth TW7 131 A2
Hartlands Cl DA5 169 B5
Hartlands Cvn Pk The
TW5 128 B6
Hartland Way
Croydon CR0 223 A6
Morden SM4 201 B2
Hartlepool Ct E16 122 D5
Hartley Ave E6 100 A6
NW7 27 D5
Hartley Cl BR1 188 B1
NW7 27 D5
Hartley Ct W5 110 C5
Hartley Ho N3 29 D4
SE1 263 D4
Putney SW15 156 A6
Hartley Prim Sch E6 100 A6
Hartley Rd E11 54 D1
Bexley DA16 146 C5
Thornton Heath CR0 205 A2
Hartley St E2 96 C4
Hart Lo EN5 1 A2
Hartmann Rd E16 122 A5
Hartmoor Mews EN3 6 D6
Hartnoll Ho 4 N7 72 C3
Hartnoll St N7 72 B3
Harton Cl BR1 187 D2
Harton Lo 2 SE8 141 C4
Harton Rd N9 18 B2
Harton St SE8 141 C4
Hartopp Ct N16 73 C5
Hartopp Point SW6 264 B4
Hartsbourne Ave WD23 8 B2
Hartsbourne Cl WD23 8 B2
Hartsbourne Ct 5 UB1 86 A1
Hartsbourne Pk WD23 8 C2
Hartsbourne Prim Sch
WD23 8 B2
Hartsbourne Rd WD23 8 B2
Harts Gr IG8 37 A5
Hartshill Cl UB10 60 D2
Hartshorn Alley EC3 243 B1
Hartshorn Gdns E6 100 C3
Hart's La SE14 141 A4
Harts La IG11 78 D2
Hartslock Dr SE2 124 D4
Hartsmead Rd SE9 166 B2
Hart Sq SM4 201 C3
Hart St EC3 253 B6
Hartsway EN3 6 C1
Hartswood Gn WD23 8 B2
Hartswood Ho 10 SW2 160 A3
Hartswood Rd W12 111 D3
Hartsworth Cl E13 98 D5
Hartville Rd SE18 123 C2
Hartwell Dr E4 36 A4
Hartwell Ho 2 SE7 121 B1
Hartwell St E8 73 D2
Harvard Ct NW6 69 D3
9 SE9 166 C5
Harvard Hill W4 132 D6
Harvard Ho 3 SE17 138 D6
Putney SW15 156 D5
Harvard Mans 18
SW11 136 B1
Harvard Rd SE13 164 A6
W4 110 D1
11 W4 111 A1
Hounslow TW7 130 C4
Harvel Cres SE2 124 D1
Harvest Bank Rd BR4 225 A5
Harvest Ct
Beckenham BR3 185 C3
Littleton TW17 192 C5
Harvesters Cl TW7 152 B6
Harvest La
Loughton IG10 21 D4
Thames Ditton KT7 197 A3
Harvest Rd TW13 150 A1
Harvey Ct E17 53 C4
SW11 267 B2
Harvey Dr TW12 173 C2
Harvey Gdns E11 54 D1
SE7 121 C1
Harvey Ho 10 E1 96 B3
N1 235 D5
N8 50 A6
SW1 259 D1
Barking IG11 79 A1
Brentford TW8 110 A1
Dagenham RM6 58 D5
Twickenham TW1 153 B5
Harvey Lo 8 W9 91 C2
Harvey Mews N8 50 B4
Harvey Point 7 E16 99 A2
Harvey Rd E11 54 D1
N8 50 B4
15 SE5 139 B4
Hillingdon UB10 82 C5
Ilford IG1 78 D3
Ruislip UB5 62 C1
Twickenham TW4 151 B4
Walton-on-T KT12 194 A2
Harvey St N1 235 D5
Harvill Rd DA14 191 A5
UB9 38 A2
Harvil Rd UB9,UB10 38 A2
Harvington Sch W5 87 D1
Harvington Wlk E8 74 A1
Harvist Rd NW6 91 A5
Harwell Cl HA4 39 B1
Harwick Mans SE18 122 A3
Harwood Ave BR1 187 B1
Mitcham CR4 202 C6
Harwood Cl N12 30 C4
Wembley HA0 65 D4
Harwood Ct N1 235 D5
Putney SW15 134 C1
Harwood Dr UB10 82 B6
Harwood Point SE16 119 B4
Harwood Rd
SW6 135 D5 265 C3
Harwoods Yd N21 16 C4
Harwood Terr
SW6 135 D4 265 C2
Hascombe Ho 11
SW15 156 B3
Hascombe Terr 2
SE5 139 B3
Haselbury Rd N9 17 C1
Haseley End SE23 162 C4
Haselrigge Rd SW4 137 D1
Haseltine Prim Sch
SE26 185 B6
Haseltine Rd SE26 185 B6
Haselwood Dr EN2 4 D1
Haskard Rd RM9 80 D4
Hasker St SW3 114 C2 257 B4
Haslam Ave SM3 201 A1
Haslam Cl N1 72 C1
Uxbridge UB10 61 A6
Haslam Ct N11 31 B6
Haslam Ho 1 N1 73 A1
Haslam St SE15 139 D4
Haslemere Ave NW4 46 D3
W13 109 A3
Barnet, London EN4 14 D3
Cranford TW5 128 C3
Mitcham CR4,SW19 180 B1
Wandsworth SW18 157 D2
Haslemere Cl
Hampton TW12 173 B5
Wallington SM6 220 A3
Haslemere Ct 5 N16 51 C1
Haslemere Fst Sch
CR4 180 B1
Haslemere Gdns N3 47 B5
Haslemere & Heathrow Est
The TW4 128 B2
Haslemere Ind Est
Feltham TW14 150 A6
Wandsworth SW18 157 D2
Haslemere Rd DA7 147 C3
N8 50 A2
Ilford IG3 79 D6
Southgate N21 16 D3
Thornton Heath CR7 204 D4
Hasler Cl SE28 124 C6
Hasler Ct E12 78 A4
Haslett Rd TW17 171 C1
Hasluck Gdns EN5 14 A5
Hasmonean High Sch
(Boys) NW4 28 D1
Hasmonean High Sch
(Girls) NW7 28 A2
Hasmonean Prim Sch
NW4 46 D4
Hassard St E2 95 D5
Hassendean Rd SE3 143 B5
Hassett Rd E9 75 A2
Hassocks Cl SE23,SE26 162 B1
Hassocks Rd SW16 181 D2
Hassop Rd NW2 68 D4
Hassop Wlk SE9 188 A6
Hasted Rd SE7 121 D1
Hastings Ave IG6 57 A5
Hastings Cl 16 SE15 140 A5
New Barnet EN5 2 A1
Wembley HA0 65 C4
Hastings Dr KT6 197 C3
Hastings Ho 11 SE18 122 B2
18 W12 112 B6
Ealing W13 109 B6
Enfield EN3 6 C3
Tottenham N17 34 A2
Hastings Hos WC1 233 A1
Hastings Pl 1 CR0 205 D1
Hastings Rd BR2 226 A6
N11 31 D5
N17 51 B6
Croydon CR0 205 D1
Ealing W13 109 B6
Hastings St
WC1 94 A4 233 A1
Hastingwood Ct E17 53 D4
Hastingwood Trad Est
N18 34 D4
N18 35 A4
Hastoe Cl UB4 85 A3
Hatcham Mews Bsns Ctr
SE14 140 D4
Hatcham Park Mews
SE14 140 D4
Hatcham Park Rd
SE14 140 D4
Hatcham Rd SE15 140 C6
Hatchard Rd N19 72 A6
Hatchcroft NW4 46 B6
Hatch End High Sch
HA3 23 D2
Hatch End Sta HA5 23 C3
Hatchett Rd TW14 149 A3
Hatchfield Ho 8 N15 51 C3
Hatch Gr RM6 59 A5
Hatch La E4 20 C1
Hatch Pl TW10 176 B5
Hatch Rd SW16 182 A1
Hatch The EN3 6 D4
Hatchwoods IG8 36 D6
Hatcliffe Almshouses 8
SE10 120 C1
Hatcliffe Cl SE3 142 D2
Hatcliffe St SE10 120 D1
Hatfield Cl SE14 140 D5
Ilford IG6 56 D6
Mitcham CR4 202 B5
Hatfield Ct
Greenwich SE3 143 A5
8 Northolt UB5 84 C4
Hatfield First Sch
SM4 201 A3
Hatfield Ho E11 54 D2
EC1 242 A5
16 Kingston KT6 198 A4
Hatfield Mead SM4 201 C4
Hatfield Rd E15 76 C3
W4 111 B4
Dagenham RM9 81 A1
10 Ealing W13,W7 109 A5
Hatfields SE1 116 C5 251 B4
Hathaway Cl BR2 210 B1
Ruislip HA4 61 D4
Stanmore HA7 25 A5
Hathaway Cres E12 78 C2
Hathaway Gdns
Ealing W13 87 A2
Ilford RM6 58 D4
Hathaway Ho 3 N1 95 C4
Hathaway Prim Sch
W13 86 D2
Hathaway Rd CR0 204 D2
Hatherleigh Cl
Chessington KT9 213 D3
Morden SM4 201 C5
Hatherleigh Ho SM4 201 C5
Hatherleigh Rd HA4 62 A6
Hatherley Cres DA14 168 A2
Hatherley Ct 6 W2 91 D1
Hatherley Gdns E6 99 D4
N8 50 A3
Hatherley Gr W2 91 D1
Hatherley Ho 2 E17 53 C5
Hatherley Mews E17 53 C5
Hatherley Rd E17 53 C5
Richmond TW9 132 B4
Sidcup DA14 168 A1
Hatherley St SW1 259 B3
Hathern Gdns SE9 188 C6
Hatherop Rd TW12 173 B3
Hathersage Ct N1 73 B3
Hathersley Ho 3 SW2 160 C4
Hathorne Cl 3 SE15 140 B3
Hathway Ho 3 SE15 140 C3
Hathway St 4 SE15 140 C3
Hatley Ave IG6 57 A5
Hatley Cl N11 30 D5
Hatley Rd N4,N7 72 B6
Hat & Mitre Ct EC1 241 D5
Hatteraick St 6 SE16 118 C4
Hattersfield Cl DA17 125 B2
Hatton Cl SE18 145 B5
Hatton Cross Rdbt
TW6 127 D2
Hatton Cross Sta TW6 127 D1
Hatton Ct BR7 188 B3
Hatton Gdn EC1 94 C2 241 B4
Hatton Gdns CR4 202 D4
Hatton Gn TW14 128 A1
Hatton Ho 18 E1 118 A6
Hatton Pl EC1 241 B4
Hatton Rd
Hatton TW14,TW6 149 C6
Thornton Heath CR0 204 C1
Hatton Rd N TW6 127 B4
Hatton Row NW8 236 D5
Hatton Sch IG8 55 D6
Hatton St NW8 236 D5
Hatton Wall
EC1 94 C2 241 B4
Haughmond 4 N12 29 D6
Haunch of Venison Yd
W1 238 C1
Hauteville Court Gdns 2
W6 111 D3
Havana Rd SW18,SW19 157 C2
Havannah St E14 119 C4
Havant Rd E17 54 A6
Havelock Cl 13 W12 112 B6
Havelock Ct UB2 107 B3
Havelock Hall 8 CR0 205 D1
Havelock Ho
4 Croydon CR0 205 D1
Forest Hill SE23 162 C3
Havelock Pl HA1 42 C3
Havelock Prim Sch
UB2 107 B3
Havelock Rd DA17 125 B2
Bromley BR2 209 C5
Croydon CR0 221 D6
Harrow HA3 42 C6
Southall UB2 107 C3
Tottenham N17 34 A1
Havelock Rd *continued*
Wimbledon SW19 180 A5
Havelock St N1 94 A6 233 B6
Ilford IG1 78 D6
Havelock Terr
SW8 137 B5 268 D3
Havelock Wlk SE23 162 C2
Haven Cl SE9 166 B1
Hayes UB4 83 C3
Sidcup DA14 190 C4
Wimbledon SW19 156 D1
Haven Ct BR3 186 A1
Haven Gn W5 87 D1
Haven Green Ct W5 87 D1
Havenhurst Rise EN2 4 C3
Haven La W5 88 A1
Haven Lo NW11 47 B4
7 SE18 122 D2
15 Enfield EN1 17 C6
Haven Pl W5 109 D6
Havenpool NW8 91 D6
Haven Rd TW15 148 D1
Haven St 17 NW1 71 B1
Haven The
Ashford TW16 172 A3
East Barnet N14 15 B5
Richmond TW9 132 C2
Havenwood HA9 66 D5
Havercourt 3 NW3 70 C2
Haverfield Gdns TW9 132 C5
Haverfield Rd E3 97 A4
Haverford Way HA8 26 B2
Havergal Villas N15 50 D6
Haverhill Rd
Chingford E4 20 A3
Streatham SW12 159 C3
Havering 8 NW1 71 B1
Havering Gdns RM6 58 D4
Havering Ho N4 51 A2
Havering St E1 96 D1
Havering Way IG11 102 B4
Haverley 14 SW20 178 D3
Haversham Cl TW1 153 D5
Haversham Ct UB6 64 D2
Haversham Lo NW2 68 D3
Haversham Pl N6 70 D6
Haverstock Ct 2 BR5 190 B1
Haverstock Hill NW3 70 D2
Haverstock Rd NW5 71 A3
Haverstock Sch NW1 71 A2
Haverstock St
N1 94 D5 234 D3
Haverthwaite Rd BR6 227 B5
Havilland Ct HA8 26 B6
Havil St SE5 139 C4
Havisham Ho 23 SE16 118 A4
Havisham Pl SW16 182 D3
Hawarden Gr SE24 161 A4
Hawarden Hill NW2 68 A5
Hawarden Rd E17 52 D5
Hawberry Ho N7 72 A2
Hawbridge Rd E11 54 B1
Hawes Down Inf Sch BR4
Hawes Down Jun Sch
BR4 208 B1
Hawes La BR4 224 C6
Hawes Rd BR1 187 B2
Edmonton N18 34 B4
Hawes St N1 72 D1
Haweswater Ho TW1 152 D6
Hawfinch 29 NW9 27 D2
Hawgood St E3 97 C2
Hawkdene E4 20 A5
Hawke Ct UB4 84 C3
Hawkedale Fst Sch
TW16 193 D6
Hawke Ho 20 E1 96 D3
Hawke Park Rd N22 50 D6
Hawke Pl 25 SE16 118 D4
Hawker 28 NW9 27 D2
Hawker Ct 14 KT2 176 C3
Hawke Rd SE19 183 C4
Hawkesbury Rd SW15 156 B6
Hawkesfield Rd SE23 163 B2
Hawkesley Cl TW1 175 A6
Hawkes Rd
Feltham TW14 150 A4
Mitcham CR4 180 D2
Hawkesworth Ho 5
SW4 159 C5
Hawke Twr 4 SE14 141 A6
Hawkewood Rd TW16 194 A6
Hawkfield Ct TW7 130 C3
Hawk Ho 7 SW11 136 C2
Hawkhurst Gdns KT9 214 A4
Hawkhurst Rd SW16 181 D2
Hawkhurst Way
New Malden KT3 199 B4
West Wickham BR4 223 D6
Hawkinge N17 33 B1
Hawkins Cl NW7 27 B5
Harrow HA1 42 B2
Hawkins Ho 3 SE8 141 C6
Hawkins Rd TW11 175 B4
Hawkins Way SE6 185 C5
Hawkley Gdns SE27 160 D2
Hawkridge 19 NW5 71 A2
Hawkridge Cl RM6 58 C3
Hawksbrook La BR3 208 A3
Hawkshead NW1 232 A2
Hawkshead Cl BR1 186 C3
Hawkshead Rd NW10 67 D1
W4 111 C4
Hawkslade Rd SE15 162 D6
Hawksley Rd N16 73 C5
Hawks Mews 10 SE10 142 A5
Hawksmoor Cl 2 E6 100 A1
SE18 123 C1
Hawksmoor Mews E1 118 B6
Hawksmoor Sch SE28 124 B6
Hawksmoor St 5 W6 134 D6
Hawksmouth E4 20 A4
Hawks Rd KT1 176 B1
Hawkstone Rd SE16 118 C2
Hawkswood Sch E4 20 A6
Hawkwell Ct E4 20 A1
Hawkwell Ho RM8 81 C6
Hawkwell Wlk N1 235 B6
Hawkwood Cres E4 19 D5
Hawkwood La BR7 189 A2
Hawkwood Mount 1
E5 52 B1
Hawlands Dr HA5 41 A2
Hawley Cl TW12 173 B4
Hawley Cres NW1 71 B1
Hawley Inf Sch NW1 71 B1
Hawley Mews 4 NW1 71 B1
Hawley Rd N18 34 D5
3 NW1 71 B1
Hawley St NW1 71 B1
Hawley Way TW15 170 D5
Haworth Ct E15 76 A3
Haworth Ho 7 SW2 160 C5
Hawstead Rd SE6 163 D5
Hawsted IG9 21 B4
Hawthorn Ave Bow E3 97 B6
Bowes Park N13 32 A5
South Norwood CR7 182 D2
Hawthorn Cl BR5 211 B3
Cranford TW5 128 B5
Hampton TW12 173 C5
Hawthorn Cres SW17 181 A5
Hawthorn Ct
Putney SW15 134 B2
Richmond TW9 132 D4
8 West Norwood
SW16 182 C5
Hawthorn Ctr HA1 43 A4
Hawthorndene Cl N12 30 C4
Hawthorndene Cl BR2 225 A6
Hawthorndene Rd
BR2 225 A6
Hawthorn Dr
Coney Hall BR4 224 C4
Harrow HA2 41 C3
Hawthorne Ave
Harrow HA3 43 A3
Mitcham CR4 180 B1
Ruislip HA4 40 B2
Wallington SM5 219 A1
Hawthorne Cl BR1 210 B6
N1 73 C2
Sutton SM1 218 A6
Hawthorne Cres UB7 104 B4
Hawthorne Ct
Chingford E4 35 D4
Ealing W5 110 A5
Pinner HA6 22 A1
Hawthorne Gr NW9 45 A2
Hawthorne Ho SW1 259 B1
Hawthorne Mews UB6 86 A1
Hawthorne Rd BR1 210 B6
E17 53 C6
Edmonton N18 33 D5
Feltham TW14 150 A3
Hawthorne Way N9 17 D2
Hawthorn Farm Ave
UB5 85 A6
Hawthorn Gdns W5 109 D3
Hawthorn Gr
Edgware EN5 11 D5
Enfield EN2 5 B5
Penge SE20 184 B2
Hawthorn Hatch TW8 131 B5
Hawthorn Mews NW7 29 A2
Hawthorn Pl UB3 105 D6
Hawthorn Rd DA6 147 B1
N8 50 A6
NW10 68 A1
Brentford TW8 131 B5
Carshalton SM1,SM2,
SM5 218 C2
Wallington SM5,SM6 219 B1
Woodford IG9 37 D6
Hawthorns IG8 21 A1
Hawthorns The KT17 216 A1
Hawthorn Terr DA15 167 D6
Hawthorn Way TW17 193 B5
Hawthorn Wlk W10 91 A3
Hawtrey Ave UB5 84 D5
Hawtrey Dr HA4 40 A2
Hawtrey Rd NW3 70 C1
Haxted Rd BR1 187 B2
Haybridge Ho 1 E5 74 C6
Hay Cl E15 76 D1
Haycroft Gdns NW10 90 B6
Haycroft Mans NW10 90 A6
Haycroft Rd SW2 160 A6

Haycroft Rd *continued*
Surbiton KT6 214 A6
Hay Currie St E14 97 D1
Hayday Rd E16 99 A2
Hayden's Pl W11 91 B1
Haydock Ave UB5 63 C2
Haydock Gn UB5 63 C2
Haydock Green Flats 2 UB5 63 C2
Haydon Cl NW9 45 A5
Enfield EN1 17 C6
Haydon Ct NW9 45 A5
Haydon Dr HA5 40 A5
Haydon Ho Ealing W7 108 D5
Teddington TW11 175 C3
Haydon Park Rd SW19 179 D5
Haydon Rd RM8 80 C6
Haydon Sch HA5 39 D6
Haydon's Rd SW19 180 A4
Haydons Road Sta SW19 180 A5
Haydon St E1, EC3 117 D6 253 C6
Haydon Way SW11 136 B1
Haydon Wlk E1 243 D1
Hayes Bridge Ret Pk UB4 106 D6
Hayes Chase BR4 208 C3
Hayes Cl BR2 225 A6
Hayes Cres NW11 47 B4
Cheam SM3 216 D4
Hayes Ct 23 SE5 139 A5
Streatham SW12 160 A3
Wimbledon SW19 179 A4
Hayes End Cl UB4 83 B2
Hayes End Dr UB4 83 B3
Hayesend Ho SW17 180 A6
Hayes End Rd UB4 83 B3
Hayesford Park Dr BR2 208 D4
Hayes Garden BR2 209 A1
Hayes & Harlington Sta UB3 105 D3
Hayes Hill BR2 208 C1
Hayes Hill Rd BR2 208 D1
Hayes La BR2 209 A4
Beckenham BR2,BR3 208 B5
Hayes Manor Sch UB3 83 C1
Hayes Mead Rd BR2 208 C1
Hayes Park Sch UB4 83 D3
Hayes Pl NW1 237 B5
Hayes Prim Sch BR2 209 B1
Hayes Rd BR2 209 A5
Southall UB2 106 B2
Hayes Sch BR2 225 B6
Hayes St BR2 209 B1
Hayes Sta BR2 208 D1
Hayes Way BR3 208 B5
Hayes Wood Ave BR2 209 B1
Hayfield Pas E1 96 C3
Hayford Ct NW2 68 D5
Haygarth Pl 2 SW19 178 D5
Haygreen Cl KT2 176 D4
Hay Hill W1 115 B6 248 D5
Hay La NW9 45 B5
Hayland Cl NW9 45 B5
Hay Lane Sch NW9 45 A5
Hayles Bldgs SE11 261 D4
Hayles St SE11 116 D3 261 C4
Haylett Gdns KT1 197 D5
Hayling Ave TW13 150 A1
Hayling Cl 20 N16 73 C3
Hayling Ct SM3 216 C4
Haymaker Cl UB10 60 B1
Hayman Cres UB4 83 B5
Haymans Point SE11 260 C2
Haymarket SW1 115 D6 249 C5
Haymeads Dr KT10 212 A2
Haymer Gdns KT4 216 A5
Haymerle Ho 6 SE15 140 A5
Haymerle Rd SE15 140 A6
Haymerle Sch SE15 140 A6
Haymill Cl UB6 86 D4
Hayne Ho W11 244 A4
Hayne Rd BR3 185 B2
Haynes Cl N11 15 A1
SE3 142 C2
Tottenham N17 34 B3
Haynes Dr N9 18 B1
Haynes Ho 3 E9 74 D2
Haynes La SE19 183 C4
Haynes Rd HA0 66 A1
Hayne St EC1 94 D2 241 D4
Haynt Wlk SW20 201 A6
Hay's Galleria SE1 253 A4
Hay's La SE1 253 A4
Haysleigh Gdns SE20 184 A1
Haysleigh Ho SE20 184 B1
Hay's Mews W1 115 B6 248 C4
Hay St E2 96 A6
Haystall Cl UB4 83 C5
Haystocks E18 55 C6
Hayter Ho W12 112 A6
Hayter Rd SW2 160 B6
Haythorn Ho SW11 136 B4 266 D1
Hayton Cl 11 E8 73 D2
Hayward Cl SW19 179 D2
Hayward Ct 14 SW4 138 A3
Mitcham CR4 180 B1
Hayward Gallery* SE1 116 B5 250 D4
Hayward Gdns SW15 156 C5
Hayward Ho E5 74 B5
N1 234 A4
Hayward Rd N20 14 A2
Thames Ditton KT7 196 D1
Haywards Cl RM6 58 C4
Haywards Pl EC1 241 C6
Haywood Cl HA5 22 D1
Haywood Lo N11 31 D4
23 N7 71 D3
Haywood Rd BR2 209 D5
Haywood Rise BR6 227 C3
Hazel Ave UB7 104 C3
Hazelbank KT5 199 A1
Hazel Bank SE25 183 C1
Hazelbank Rd SE6 164 C2
Hazelbourne Rd SW12 159 B5
Hazelbury Cl SW19 179 C1
Hazelbury Gn N9 17 C1
Hazelbury Inf Sch N9 17 C1
Hazelbury Jun Sch N9 17 C1
Hazelbury La N9 17 C1
Hazel Cl N19 71 C6
NW9 27 D1
SE15 140 A3
Brentford TW8 131 B5
Croydon CR0 206 D1
Edmonton N13 17 B1
Mitcham CR4 203 D5
Twickenham TW2 152 A4
Hazelcroft HA5 23 D4
Hazelcroft Cl UB10 60 B1
Hazel Ct Ealing W5 110 A6
9 West Norwood SW16 182 C5
Hazeldean Rd NW10 67 B1
Hazeldene Dr HA5 40 C6
Hazeldene Gdns UB10 83 A6
Hazeldene Rd
Bexley DA16 146 C3
Ilford IG3 80 B6
Hazeldon Rd SE4 163 A6
Hazel Gdns HA8 26 D6
Hazel Gr Dagenham RM6 59 A6
Enfield EN1 18 A5
Feltham TW14 150 A3
Forest Hill SE26 184 D6
Orpington BR6 226 D6
Wembley HA0 88 A6
Hazelgreen Cl N21 16 D3
Hazel Ho 12 NW3 70 D2
SE4 141 B2
Hazelhurst BR3 186 B2
Hazelhurst Ct SE6 186 A5
Hazelhurst Rd SW17 180 B6
Hazellville Rd N19 49 D1
Hazel Mead EN5 12 B6
Hazelmere Cl
Feltham TW14 149 C5
Northolt UB5 85 B5
Hazelmere Ct 10 SW2 160 B3
Hazelmere Dr UB5 85 B5
Hazelmere Rd BR5 211 B5
NW6 91 B6
Northolt UB5 85 B5
Hazelmere Way BR2 209 A3
Hazelmere Wlk UB5 85 B5
Hazel Rd E15 76 C3
NW10 90 C4
Hazeltree La UB5 85 A4
Hazel Way E4 35 B4
SE1 263 C4
Hazel Wlk BR2 210 C3
Hazelwood IG10 21 D6
Hazelwood Ave SM4 201 D5
Hazelwood Cl E5 75 A5
W5 110 A4
Harrow HA2 41 D5
Hazelwood Cres N13 32 C6
Hazelwood Ct 1 NW10 67 C5
Surbiton KT6 198 A3
Hazelwood Dr HA5 22 B1
Hazelwood Ho 11 SE8 119 A2
Beckenham BR2 208 C6
Edmonton N13 32 D6
Hazelwood Jun & Inf Schs N13 32 C6
Hazelwood La N13 32 C6
Hazelwood Lo BR4 208 A2
Hazelwood Mans SW6 264 C2
Hazelwood Rd E17 53 A4
Enfield EN1 17 D5
Hazlebury Rd SW6 135 D3
Hazledean Rd CR0 221 B6
Hazledene Rd W4 133 A6
Hazlemere Bsns Ctr EN1 18 B6
Hazlemere Gdns KT4 200 A1
Hazlewell Rd SW15 156 C6
Hazlewood Cres W10 91 A3
Hazlewood Twr W10 91 B3
Hazlitt Cl TW13 173 A6
Hazlitt Ct 4 SE28 124 C5
Hazlitt Mews W14 254 A5
Hazlitt Rd W14 113 A3 254 A5
Heacham Ave UB10 61 A5
Headbourne Ho SE1 262 D6
Headcorn 10 NW5 71 A2
Headcorn Pl CR7 204 B5
Headcorn Rd BR1 187 A5
Thornton Heath CR7 204 B5
Tottenham N17 33 D3
Headfort Pl SW1 115 A4 248 B1
Headington Rd SW18 158 A2
Headlam Rd SW4 159 D4
Headlam St E1 96 B3
Headley App IG2 56 D4
Headley Ave CR0,SM6 220 B3
Headley Cl KT19 214 C2
Headley Ct SE26 184 C5
Headley Dr Ilford IG2 56 D3
New Addington CR0 224 A1
Headley Ho 5 BR5 190 B1
Heads Mews W11 91 C1
Head St E1 96 D1
Headstone Dr HA1,HA3 42 C6
Headstone Gdns HA2 42 A5
Headstone La
Harrow HA2 41 D5
Harrow HA2,HA3 23 D2
Headstone Lane Sta HA3 23 D2
Headstone Rd HA1 42 C3
Headway Cl TW10 175 C6
Heald St SE8,SE14 141 C4
Healey St NW1 71 B2
Healy Ct EN5 12 D5
Healy Dr 1 BR6 227 D4
Healy Ho 2 E3 97 C3
12 SW9 138 C5
Heanor Ct 4 E5 74 D4
Hearne Rd W4 132 C6
Hearn Rise UB5 84 D6
Hearn's Bldgs SE17 262 D3
Hearn St EC2 95 C3 243 B5
Hearnville Rd SW12 159 A3
Heart Hospl The W1 93 A2 238 B4
Heatham Pk TW2 152 D4
Heath Ave DA7 146 D6
Heathbourne Rd WD23, HA7 8 D3
Heathbrook Prim Sch SW4 137 C3
Heath Brow NW3 70 A5
Heath Bsns Ctr The TW3 130 A1
Heath Cl NW11 47 D2
Croydon CR2 220 D2
Ealing W5 88 B3
Harlington UB3 127 B5
Heathcote Gr E4 20 A2
Heathcote Rd TW1 153 B6
Heathcote Sch E4 20 C2
Heathcote St WC1 94 B4 233 C1
Heathcroft NW11 47 D1
Ealing W5 88 A3
Heathcroft Ave TW16 171 D3
Heathcroft Gdns E4 36 B2
Heath Ct E11 54 D3
N16 51 B1
2 NW3 70 A2
Uxbridge UB8 60 A1
Heathdale Ave TW4 129 A2
Heathdene N14 15 C4
Heathdene Dr DA17 125 D2
Heathdene Rd
South Norwood SW16 182 B3
Wallington SM5,SM6 219 B1
Heath Dr SW20 200 C5
Heathedge SE23,SE26 162 B2
Heatherbank BR7 188 C1
SE9 144 B3
Heather Cl E6 100 C1
SW8 137 B2
Hampton TW12 173 B2
Hillingdon UB8 82 B2
Isleworth TW7 152 B6
Heather Ct SW4 270 B1
Heatherdale Cl KT2 176 D3
Heatherdene Cl N12 30 A2
Mitcham CR4 202 C5
Heatherdene Mans 2 TW1 153 D5
Heather Dr EN2 4 D3
Heatherfold Way HA5, HA6 39 D6
Heather Gdns NW11 47 A3
Belmont SM2 217 C2
Heather Ho 7 E14 98 A1
Heather La UB7 82 A1
Heatherlands TW16 172 A4
Heatherley Ct N16 74 A5
Heatherley Dr IG5 56 B6
Heatherley Sch of Fine Art SW10 266 B3
Heather Lo N16 51 C1
Heather Park Dr HA0 66 C1
Heather Park Par HA0 66 B1
Heather Rd E4 35 B4
NW2 67 D6
Lewisham SE12 165 A3
Heatherset Cl KT10 212 A3
Heatherset Gdns SW16 182 B3
Heatherside Rd
Sidcup DA14 168 C1
West Ewell KT19 215 B1
Heathers The TW19 148 B4
Heather Way HA7 24 D4
Heather Wlk W10 91 A3
Edgware HA8 26 D5
Twickenham TW4 151 C4
Heatherwood Cl E12 77 C6
Heatherwood Dr UB4 83 B5
Heathfield BR7 189 A4
Chingford E4 20 A1
Heathfield Ave SW18 158 B4
Heathfield Cl BR2 225 C3
E16 99 D2
Heathfield Ct DA14 190 B5
5 W4 111 B1
Ashford TW15 148 A1
Penge SE20 184 C3
Wandsworth SW18 158 B4
Heathfield Dr CR4 180 C2
Heathfielde N2 48 A4
Heathfield Gdns NW11 46 D3
SW18 158 B5
W4 111 A1
Croydon CR0 221 B4
Heathfield Ho SE3 142 C3
Heathfield Inf Sch TW2 151 C3
Heathfield Jun Sch TW2 151 C3
Heathfield La BR7 189 A4
Heathfield N TW1,TW2 152 D4
Heathfield Park Dr RM6 58 B4
Heathfield Pk NW2 68 C2
Heathfield Rd BR2 225 D3
DA6 147 B1
SW18 158 B5
W3 110 D4
Bromley BR1 186 D3
Croydon CR0 221 B4
Heathfield Rise HA4 39 A2
Heathfield S TW1,TW2 152 D4
Heathfield Sch HA5 40 D2
Heathfield Sq SW18 158 B4
Heathfield Terr SE18 145 D6
W4 111 B1
Heathfield Vale CR2 223 A1
Heathgate NW11 47 D3
Heathgate Pl NW3 70 D4
Heath Gdns TW1 152 D2
Heath Gr Ashford TW16 171 D3
Penge SE20 184 C3
Heath Ho DA15 189 D6
Thornton Heath CR7 204 C4
Uxbridge UB10 60 D4
Heath Hurst Rd NW3 70 C4
Heath La SE3 142 B3
Heathland Rd N16 51 C1
Heathland Sch SW19 156 D1
Heathland Sch The TW4 151 B5
Heathlands Cl
Sunbury TW16 172 A1
Twickenham TW1 152 D3
Heathlands Ct
Hounslow TW4 151 A6
Mitcham CR4 203 A6
Heathlands Way TW4 151 A6
Heathlee Rd SE3 142 D1
Heathley End BR7 189 A4
Heath Lo WD23 8 B3
Heath Mans 4 NW3 70 A4
Putney SW15 156 D5
Heathman's Rd SW6 135 B4 264 D1
Heath Mead SW19 156 D1
Heathmere Prim Sch SW15 156 A3
Heath Park Dr BR1 210 A6
Heath Park Gdns NW3 69 D5
Heathpool Ct 8 E1 96 B3
Heath Rd SW8 137 B3
Dagenham RM6 59 A2
Harrow HA1 42 A2
Hillingdon UB10 83 A3
Isleworth TW3,TW7 130 A1
South Norwood CR7 205 A6
Twickenham TW1 152 D3
Heath Rise Hayes BR2 209 A3
Putney SW15 156 D5
Heathrow Airport London TW6 126 D3
Heathrow Bvd UB7 126 B5
Heathrow Causeway Est TW4 128 B2
Heathrow International Trad Est TW4 128 B2
Heathrow Sch UB7 126 B6
Heathrow Terminal 4 Sta TW6 149 A5
Heathrow Terminals 1,2,3 TW6 126 D2
Heath Royal SW15 156 D5
Heath's Cl EN1 5 C3
Heathshot 8 TW10 154 A5
Heathside NW3 70 B4
Heath Side BR5 211 A2
Heathside
Hinchley Wood KT10 212 C5
Twickenham TW4 151 B4
Heathside Ave DA7 147 A3
Heathside Cl
Hinchley Wood KT10 212 C5
Ilford IG2 57 B4
Heathside Prep Sch NW3 70 A4
Heath St NW3 70 A5
Heathstan Rd W12 90 A1
Heath Terr RM6 58 D2
Heath The W7 108 C5
Heath View N2 48 A5
NW5 71 A4
Heath View Cl N2 48 A5
Heathview Ct SW19 156 D2
Heath View Dr SE2 146 D6
Heathview Gdns SW15 156 C4
Heathview Rd CR7 204 C5
Heath Villas SE18 123 D1
Heathville Rd N4,N19 50 A2
Heathwall St SW11 136 D2
Heathway 6 SE3 142 D5
Croydon CR0 223 B5
Greenwich SE3 143 A5
Woodford IG8 37 C5
Heathway Ct NW3 69 C6
Heathwood Ct
1 Hounslow TW3 129 D1
Streatham SW12 159 C3
Heathwood Gdns SE7 122 A1
Heathwood Point 7 SE26 162 D1
Heaton Cl E4 20 A1
Heaton Ho 6 SE15 140 B3
SW10 266 B6
Heaton Rd SE15 140 B3
Mitcham CR4 181 A3
Heaver Rd 24 SW11 136 B2
Heavers Farm Prim Sch SE25 205 D4
Heavitree Cl SE18 123 B1
Heavitree Rd SE18 123 B1
Hebden Ct 24 E2 95 D6
Hebden Terr N17 33 C4
Hebdon Rd SW17 158 C1
Heber Prim Sch SE22 161 D5
Heber Rd NW2 68 D4
SE22 161 D5
Hebron Rd W6 112 B3
Hecham Cl E17 35 A2
Heckfield Pl SW6 135 C5 265 A3
Heckford St E1 118 D6
Hector 31 NW9 27 D2
Hector Ct 1 SW9 138 C4
Putney SW15 156 D6
Hector Ho 14 E2 96 B5
Hector St SE18 123 C2
Heddington Gr N7 72 B3
Heddon Cl TW7 131 A1
Heddon Court Ave EN4 14 D6
Heddon Court Par EN4 15 A6
Heddon Ct EN4 15 A6
Heddon Rd EN4 14 D6
Heddon St W1 249 A6
Hedge Hill EN2 4 D4
Hedge La N13 17 A1
Hedgeley IG4 56 B5
Hedgemans Rd RM9 81 A1
Hedgemans Way RM9 81 A2
Hedgemoor Ct 1 E4 36 B5
Hedgerley Gdns UB6 86 A5
Hedgerow La EN5 12 B6
Hedger's Gr E9 75 A2
Hedger St SE11 261 C4
Hedge Wlk SE6 185 D6
Hedgewood Gdns IG5 56 C4
Hedgewood Specl Sch UB4 83 C4
Hedgley Mews SE12 164 D6
Hedgley St SE12 164 D6
Hedingham Cl 6 N1 73 A1
Hedingham Rd RM8 80 B3
Hedley Ct SW15 156 D5
Hedley Ho E14 120 A3
Hedley Rd TW4 151 C4
Hedley Row N5,N16 73 B3
Hedsor Ho E2 243 C6
Heenan Cl IG11 79 A2
Heene Rd EN2 5 B4
Heidegger Cres SW13 134 B5
Heigham Rd E6 78 A1
Heighton Gdns CR0 220 D3
Heights Cl SW20 178 B3
Heights The N4 50 C3
NW3 70 A4
SE7 121 C1
Beckenham BR3 186 A3
Northolt UB5 63 C3
Heiron St SE17 138 D6
Helby Rd SW4 159 D5
Heldar Ct SE1 252 D1
Helder Gr SE12 164 D4
Helder St CR2 221 B2
Heldmann Cl TW7 130 B1
Helena Cl EN4 2 B5
Helena Ct W5 87 D2
Helena Rd E13 99 A5
E17 53 C4
NW10 68 B3
Ealing W5 87 D2
Helena Sq 12 SE16 119 A6
Helen Ave TW14 150 B4
Helen Cl N2 48 A6
East Molesey KT8 195 D5
Helen Ct N3 47 A6
Helen Gladstone Ho SE1 251 C2
Helen Ho 9 E2 96 B5
Helen Mackay Ho 9 E14 98 B1
Helen Peele Cotts 10 SE16 118 C3
Helenslea Ave NW11 47 C1
Helen's Pl E2 96 C4
Helen St SE18 122 D2
Helen Taylor Ho 5 SE16 118 A2
Helford Cl HA4 61 C6
Helgiford Gdns TW16 171 C3
Heli gan Cl BR6 227 D4
Helios Rd CR4 203 A1
Heliport Est The SW11 136 B3
Helix Gdns SW2 160 B5
Helix Ho TW7 131 B3
Helix Rd SW2 160 B5
Hellenic Coll of London SW1 114 D3 257 C5
Hellings St E1 118 A5
Helme Cl SW19 179 B5
Helmet Row EC1 242 B6
Helmore Rd IG11 79 D1
Helmsdale Cl UB4 85 A3
Helmsdale Ho NW6 91 D5
Helmsdale Rd SW16 181 D2
Helmsley 10 E18 55 A6
Helmsley Pl E8 74 B1
Helmsley St 7 E8 74 B1
Helperby Rd NW10 67 C1
Helsby Ct NW8 236 C6
Helsinki Sq SE16 119 A3
Helston NW1 232 B4
Helston Cl HA5 23 B3
Helston Ct N15 51 C4
Helston Ho SE11 261 B2
Helvetia St SE6 163 B2
Helwys Ct E4 36 A4
Hemans Est SW8 137 D5 269 D3
Hemans St SW8 137 D5 269 D3
Hemberton Rd SW9 138 A2
Hemery Rd UB6 64 B3
Hemingford Cl N12 30 B5
Hemingford Rd N1 72 B1 233 D6
Cheam SM3 216 C4
Heming Rd HA8 26 D3
Hemington Ave N11 30 D5
Hemlock Rd W12 111 D6
Hemmen La UB3 83 D1
Hemming Cl 5 TW12 173 C2
Hemmings Cl DA14 168 B2
Hemmings Ct HA8 27 A3
Hemming St E1 96 A3
Hempstead Cl IG9 21 A2
Hempstead Rd E17 36 B1
Hemp Wlk SE17 262 D4
Hemsby Rd KT9 214 B2
Hemstal Rd NW6 69 C1
Hemswell Dr NW9 27 C2
Hemsworth Ct N1 95 C5
Hemsworth St N1 95 C5
Hemus Pl SW3 257 B1
Henchman St W12 89 D1
Hendale Ave NW4 46 B6
Hendale Ho 13 E5 74 B6
Henderson Cl NW10 67 A2
Henderson Ct NW3 70 B3
8 SE14 140 D6
Henderson Dr NW8 92 B3 236 C6
Henderson Ho 7 RM10 81 C5
Henderson Rd E7 77 C2
Edmonton N9 18 B3
Hayes UB4 84 A4
Thornton Heath CR0 205 B3
Wandsworth SW18 158 C4
Hendfield Ct 5 SM6 219 B2
Hendham Rd SW17 158 D2
Hendon Ave N3 29 A2
Hendon Central NW4 46 B6
Hendon Central Sta NW4 46 B4

Hendon Coll NW9 27 D2
Hendon Coll of F Ed
NW4 46 A3
Hendon Hall Ct NW4 46 D6
Hendon Ho NW4 46 A5
Hendon La N3 29 B1
Hendon Lo NW4 46 B6
Hendon Park Mans
NW4 46 C4
Hendon Park Row
NW11 47 B3
Hendon Prep Sch NW4 46 D6
Hendon Rd N9 18 A2
Hendon Sch NW4 46 D4
Hendon Sta NW4 46 A3
Hendon Terr TW15 171 B4
Hendon Way NW2 46 C3
NW2,NW4 46 C3
Hendon Wood La NW7 12 A3
Hendre Ho SE1 263 B3
Hendren Cl UB6 64 B3
Hendre Rd
SE1 117 C2 263 B3
Hendrick Ave SW12 158 D4
Heneage La EC3 243 B1
Heneage Pl EC3 243 B1
Heneage St E1 95 D2 243 D4
Henfield Cl DA5 169 C5
N19 49 C1
Henfield Rd SW19,
SW20 179 B2
Hengelo Gdns CR4 202 B5
Hengist Rd DA8 147 D5
Eltham SE12 165 B4
Hengist Way BR2,BR3 208 C5
Hengrave Rd SE23 162 D4
Hengrove Ct DA5 169 A3
Henley Ave SM3 217 A5
Henley Cl SE16 118 C4
Greenford UB6 86 A5
Hounslow TW7 130 D4
Henley Ct N14 15 C4
NW2 68 D2
NW4 46 A6
SE15 140 A2
Mitcham CR4 203 A6
Henley Dr SE1 117 D2 263 D4
Kingston KT2 177 D3
Henley Gdns
Dagenham RM6 59 A4
Pinner HA5 40 B6
Henley Ho E2 243 D6
N12 30 B5
Henley Lo E17 53 B4
South Norwood SE25 205 D5
Henley Prior N1 233 C3
Henley Rd
Edmonton N18 33 C6
Ilford IG1 79 B4
Newham E16 122 B4
Willesden NW10 90 C6
Henleys Cnr NW11 47 B5
Henley St SW11 137 A3
Henley Way TW13 172 D5
Henlow Pl TW10 153 D2
Henlys Rdbt TW5 128 C3
Hennel Cl SE23 162 C1
Hennessy Rd N9 18 C2
Henniker Gdns E6 100 A4
Henniker Mews SW3 266 C6
Henniker Point E15 76 C3
Henniker Rd E15 76 B3
Henningham Rd N17 33 B2
Henning St
SW11 136 C4 267 A1
Henrietta Barnett Sch
NW11 47 D3
Henrietta Cl SE8 141 C6
Henrietta Ho 3 N15 51 C3
11 W6 112 C1
Henrietta Mews WC1 240 B6
Henrietta Pl W1 93 B1 238 C2
Henrietta St E15 76 A3
WC2 116 A6 250 B6
Henriques St E1 96 A1
Henry Addlington Cl
E6 100 D2
Henry Cavendish Prim Sch
SW12 159 C3
Henry Cl EN2 5 C5
Henry Compton Sec Sch
SW6 135 A4 264 A2
Henry Cooper Way
SE12 187 D6
Henry Darlot Dr NW7 29 A5
Henry Dent Cl SE5 139 B2
Henry Dickens Ct
W11 244 A4
Henry Doulton Dr
SW17 181 B6
Henry Fawcett Prim Sch
SE11 138 C6
Henry Green Prim Sch
RM8 80 D6
Henry Hatch Ct SM2 218 A1
Henry Ho NW8 230 A4
Henry Ho *continued*
SE1 251 B3
SW8 270 A4
Henry Jackson Ho
SW15 134 D2
Henry Jackson Rd
SW15 134 D2
Henry Maynard Inf Sch
E17 54 A4
Henry Maynard Jun Sch
E17 54 A4
Henry Peters Dr TW11 174 C5
Henry Rd E6 100 A5
N4 51 A1
New Barnet EN4 14 B6
Henry's Ave IG8 36 D5
Henryson Rd SE4 163 C6
Henry St BR1 187 B2
Henry Tate Mews
SW16 182 C5
Henry Wise Ho SW1 259 B3
Hensford Gdns SE26 184 B6
Henshall Point 19 E3 97 D4
Henshall St N1 73 B2
Henshawe Rd RM8 80 D5
Henshaw St
SE17 117 B2 262 C4
Henslowe Rd SE22 162 A6
Henslow Ho 11 SE15 140 A5
Henson Ave NW2 68 C3
Henson Cl BR6 226 D6
Henson Ct 3 N5 73 A4
Henson Path HA3 43 D6
Henson Pl UB5 84 C6
Henty Cl SW11 136 C4 267 B2
Henty Wlk SW15 156 B6
Henville Rd BR1 187 B2
Henwick Prim Sch
SE9 144 A2
Henwick Rd SE9 144 A2
Hepburn Gdns BR2 208 D1
Hepburn Mews SW11 158 D6
Hepple Cl TW7 131 B3
Hepplestone Cl SW15 156 B5
Hepscott Rd E9 75 C1
Hepworth Ct N1 234 D6
Barking IG11 80 A3
Cheam SM3 201 C1
Hepworth Gdns IG11 80 A3
Hepworth Ho IG8 21 A1
Hepworth Rd SW16 182 A3
Hepworth Way KT12 193 D1
Heracles 30 NW9 27 D2
Heracles Cl SM6 220 A1
Hera Ct 7 E14 119 C2
Herald Gdns SM6 219 B5
Heralds Pl SE11 261 C4
Herald St 5 E2 96 B3
Herbal Hill EC1 241 B5
Herbert Chapman Ct
N5 72 D4
Herbert Cres SW1 257 D6
Herbert Gdns NW10 90 B5
Chiswick W4 132 D6
Dagenham RM6 58 D2
Herbert Ho E1 243 C2
Herbert Mews 15 SW2 160 C5
Herbert Morrison Ho
SW6 264 C5
Herbert Morrison Prim Sch
SW8 138 A5 270 B3
Herbert Pl SE18 144 D6
Herbert Rd BR2 210 A4
DA7 147 A3
E12 78 A4
E17 53 B2
N15 51 D4
NW9 46 A3
SE18 144 D6
Ilford IG3 79 C6
Kingston KT1 198 B6
Merton SW19 179 B3
Southall UB1 107 B5
Wood Green N11 32 A3
Herbert St E13 99 A5
NW5 71 A2
Herbrand Est
WC1 94 A3 240 A6
Herbrand St
WC1 94 A3 240 A6
Hercies Rd UB10 60 C2
Hercules Pl N7 72 A5
Hercules Rd
SE1 116 B3 260 D5
Hercules St N7 72 A5
Hereford Ave EN4 14 D3
Hereford Bldgs SW3 266 D6
Hereford Ct
12 Belmont SM2 217 C1
6 Croydon CR0 205 D1
6 Ealing W7 86 D2
Harrow HA1 42 C6
Hereford Gdns SE13 164 C6
Pinner HA5 41 A4
Redbridge IG1 56 A2
Twickenham TW2 152 A3
Hereford Ho 26 SE5 139 A3
SW10 265 D4
5 SW2 138 C1
Hereford Ho *continued*
SW3 257 B6
7 Acton W3 88 C1
Hereford Mans 10 W2 91 C1
Hereford Mews 11 W2 91 C1
Hereford Pl SE14 141 B5
Hereford Rd
W2 91 C1 245 B6
W3 111 A6
W5 109 C3
Feltham TW13 150 C3
Wanstead E11 55 B4
Hereford Retreat 5
SE15 140 A5
Hereford Sq
SW7 114 A2 256 B3
Hereford St E2 96 A3
Hereford Way KT9 213 D3
Herent Dr IG5 56 B6
Hereward Gdns N13 32 C5
Hereward House Sch
NW3 70 B2
Hereward Rd SW17 180 D6
Herga Ct HA1 64 C6
Herga Rd HA3 42 D5
Heriot Ave E4 19 C2
Heriot Rd NW4 46 C4
Heriots Cl HA7 25 A6
Heritage Cl SW9 138 D2
Heritage Ct SE8 118 D1
Heritage Hill BR2 225 C3
Heritage Ho 22 SW19 156 D3
Heritage View HA1 64 D5
Herlwyn Ave HA4 61 C5
Herlwyn Gdns SW17 180 D6
Herm Cl TW7 130 A5
Hermes Cl 4 W9 91 C3
Hermes Ct 4 SW9 138 C4
Hermes Ho BR3 185 A2
Hermes St N1 234 A3
Hermes Way SM6 219 D1
Hermes Wlk UB5 85 C5
Herm Ho 10 N1 73 A2
Enfield EN3 6 D5
Hermiston Ave N8 50 A4
Hermitage Cl E18 54 D5
Claygate KT10 213 A2
Enfield EN2 4 D3
Littleton TW17 192 C5
Hermitage Ct 14 E1 118 A5
2 NW2 69 C5
3 Wanstead E18 55 A5
Hermitage Gdns NW2 69 C5
South Norwood SE19 183 A3
Hermitage La NW2 69 C5
Croydon CR0 206 A3
South Norwood SW16 182 B3
Hermitage Prim Sch
E1 118 A5
Hermitage Rd N4,N15 51 A3
South Norwood SE19 183 B4
Hermitage Row 9 E8 74 A3
Hermitage St W2 236 C3
Hermitage The
Barnes SW13 133 D4
Feltham TW13 149 D1
Forest Hill SE23 162 C3
Kingston KT1 197 D5
Richmond TW10 154 A6
Uxbridge UB8 60 A2
Hermitage Wall E1 118 A5
Hermitage Way HA7 25 A2
Hermitage Wlk E18 54 D5
Hermit Pl NW6 91 D6
Hermit Rd E16 98 D3
Hermit St EC1 234 C2
Hermon Gr UB3 106 A5
Hermon Hill E11 55 A5
Herndon Rd SW18 158 A6
Herne Cl NW10 67 B3
Herne Ct WD23 8 A4
Herne Hill SE24 139 A1
Herne Hill Ho SE24 160 D5
Herne Hill Mans SE24 161 A5
Herne Hill Rd SE24 139 A1
Herne Hill Sta SE24 160 D5
Herne Hill Stad SE24 161 B5
Herne Mews N18 34 A6
Herne Pl SE24 160 D6
Herne Rd KT6 214 A6
Heron Cl E17 35 B1
NW10 67 C2
Buckhurst Hill IG9 21 A3
Cheam SM1 217 B3
Heron Cres DA14 189 C6
Heron Ct 14 E14 120 A3
Bromley BR2 209 C5
6 Dulwich SE21 161 B2
9 Forest Hill SE23 162 C3
Ilford IG1 78 D6
5 Kingston KT1 198 A6
Ruislip HA4 61 B6
Stanwell TW19 148 A3
Herondale Ave SW18 158 C3
Heron Dr N4 73 A6
Herongate N1 235 B6
Herongate Rd E12 77 C6
Heron Hill DA17 125 B2
Heron Ho NW8 230 A3
Heron Ho *continued*
SE15 139 D4
SW11 267 B2
Ealing W13 87 A3
Teddington KT1 175 C2
Heron Ind Est E15 97 D5
Heron Mead EN3 7 C5
Heron Mews IG1 78 D6
Heron Pl SE16 119 A5
W1 238 B2
Heron Quays E14 119 C5
Heron Quays Sta E14 119 C5
Heron Rd SE24 139 A1
Croydon CR0 221 C6
Isleworth TW1 131 B1
Heronsforde W13 87 C1
Heronsgate HA8 26 C5
Heronsgate Prim Sch
SE28 123 B3
Heron's Lea N6 48 D3
Heronslea Dr HA7 26 A5
Herons Pl TW7 131 B2
Heron Sq 25 TW10 153 D6
Herons Rise EN4 2 C1
Herons The E11 54 D3
Heron Trad Est W3 88 D2
Heronway IG8 37 C6
Heron Way TW14 128 A1
Herrick Ct 4 TW10 175 D6
Herrick Ho 17 N16 73 B4
18 SE5 139 B5
Herrick Rd N5 73 A5
Herrick St
SW1 115 D2 259 D3
Herries St W10 91 A5
Herringham Rd SE7 121 C3
Herrongate Cl EN1 5 D3
Hersant Cl NW10 90 A6
Herschell Rd SE23 163 A4
Herschell's Mews SE5 139 A2
Hersham Cl SW15 156 A4
Hersham Rd KT12 194 A1
Hershell Ct 1 SW14 132 D1
Hertford Ave SW14 133 C1
Hertford Cl EN4 2 B2
Hertford Ct E6 100 B4
16 SW11 136 C2
Palmers Green N13 16 C1
Hertford Lo 10 SW19 157 A3
Hertford Pl W1 239 B5
Hertford Rd N1 95 C6
N2 48 C6
Barking IG11 78 D1
Barnet EN4 2 A2
Edmonton N9 18 B3
Enfield EN3 6 C5
Ilford IG2 57 C3
Hertford Rd High St
EN3 18 C6
Hertford Sq CR4 204 A5
Hertford St
W1 115 B5 248 C3
Hertford Way CR4 204 A5
Hertford Wlk 13 DA17 125 C1
Hertmitage The 4
SE13 142 A3
Hertslet Rd N7 72 B5
Hertsmere Rd E14 119 C6
Hertswood Ct 1 EN5 1 A1
Hervey Cl N3 29 C2
Hervey Park Rd E17 53 A5
Hervey Rd SE3 143 B4
Hesa Rd UB3 106 A6
Hesewall Cl SW4 137 C3
Hesketh Pl W11 244 A5
Hesketh Rd E7 77 A5
Heslop Ct 1 SW12 159 A3
Heslop Rd SW12 158 D3
Hesper Mews
SW5 113 D2 255 C3
Hesperus Cres E14 119 D2
Hessel Rd W13 109 B4
Hessel St E1 96 B1
Hestercombe Ave
SW6 135 B4 264 B1
Hesterman Way CR0 204 B1
Hester Rd
SW11 136 C5 267 A3
Edmonton N18 34 A5
Hester Terr TW9 132 C2
Heston Ave TW5 129 A5
Heston Com Sch TW5 129 C5
Heston Ctr The TW5 106 C1
Heston Grange TW5 129 B6
Heston Grange La
TW5 129 B6
Heston Ho 5 SE8 141 C4
W4 110 D1
Heston Ind Mall TW5 129 B5
Heston Inf Sch TW5 129 C5
Heston Jun Sch TW5 129 C5
Heston Phoenix
Distribution Pk TW5 128 C6
Heston Rd TW5 129 C5
Heston St SE14 141 C4
Hetherington Rd
SW2,SW4 138 A1
Charlton TW17 171 A1
Hetherington Way
UB10 60 A4
Hethpool Ho W2 236 C5
Hetley Gdns 1 SE19 183 D3
Hetley Rd W12 112 B4
Heton Gdns NW4 46 A5
Hevelius Cl SE10 120 D1
Hever Croft SE9 188 C6
Heverfield Ct CR4 180 D3
Hever Gdns BR1 188 C1
Heverham Rd SE18 123 C2
Hever Ho SE15 140 D6
Heversham Ho SE15 140 C6
Heversham Rd DA7 147 C4
Hewens Rd UB4 83 A3
Hewer Ho 6 SW4 159 C6
Hewer St W10 90 D2
Hewes Ho E17 52 D5
Hewett Cl HA7 25 B6
Hewett Ho 7 SE18 122 D1
Hewett Rd RM8 80 D4
Hewett St EC2 95 C3 243 B5
Hewish Rd N18 33 C6
Hewison St E3 97 B5
Hewitt Ave N22 32 D1
Hewitt Cl CR0 223 C5
Hewitt Ho 2 E4 36 B5
Hewitt Rd N8 50 D4
Hewlett Rd E3 97 A5
Hewling Ho 1 N16 73 C3
Hewtt Ho SW15 134 C3
Hexagon The N6 48 D1
Hexal Rd SE6 164 C1
Hexham Gdns TW7 131 A5
Hexham Rd Barnet EN5 1 D1
Cheam SM4 201 D1
West Norwood SE27 161 A2
Heybourne Rd N17 34 B3
Hey Bridge 9 NW1 71 B2
Heybridge Ave SW16 182 B4
Heybridge Dr IG6 57 B6
Heybridge Way E10 53 B1
Heydon Ct BR4 224 C6
Heydon Ho SE14 140 C4
Heyford Ave
SW8 138 A5 270 B4
Merton SW20 201 B6
Heyford Rd CR4 180 C1
Heygate St
SE17 117 A2 262 B4
Heylyn Sq E3 97 B4
Heynes Rd RM8 80 C4
Heysham Dr WD19 22 D5
Heysham La NW3 69 D5
Heysham Rd N15 51 B3
Heythorp St SW18 157 B2
Heythrop Dr UB10 60 B4
Heyward Ct SM2 217 C2
Heywood Ave NW9 27 C2
Heywood Ct 2 HA7 25 C5
Heywood Ho 11 SE14 140 D6
6 SW2 160 C5
Heyworth Rd E15 76 D4
E5 74 B4
Hibbert Rd E17 53 B2
Harrow HA3 24 D1
Hibbert St SW11 136 B2
Hibernia Gdns TW3 151 C6
Hibernia Point 11 SE2 124 D4
Hibernia Rd TW3 129 C1
Hibiscus Cl HA8 27 A6
Hibiscus Lo E15 76 C1
Hichisson Rd SE15 162 C6
Hickes Ho 6 NW6 70 B1
Hickey's Almshouses 7
TW9 132 B1
Hickin Cl SE7 121 D2
Hickin St 2 E14 120 A3
Hickleton NW1 232 B5
Hickling Ho 10 SE16 118 B3
Hickling Rd IG1 78 D3
Hickman Ave E4 36 A4
Hickman Cl E16 99 D2
Hickman Rd RM6 58 C2
Hickmore Wlk SW4 137 C2
Hickory Cl N9 18 A4
Hicks Ave UB6 86 C4
Hicks Cl SW11 136 C2
Hicks Ct RM10 81 D5
Hicks St SE8 119 A1
Hidaburn Ct 7 SW16 181 C6
Hidcote Gdns SW20 200 B6
Hidcote Ho 11 SM2 218 A1
Hide E6 100 C1
Hide Pl SW1 115 D2 259 C3
Hide Rd HA1 42 B5
Hide Twr SW1 259 C3
Hieover SE21 161 A2
Higgins Ho 7 N1 95 C6
Higginson Ho 2 NW3 70 D1
Higgins Wlk TW12 173 A4
Higgs Ind Est 9 SE24 138 D2
High Acre EN2 4 D2
Higham Ct 9 IG8 37 A4
Higham Hill Ho E17 34 D2
Higham Hill Rd E17 35 A1
Higham Ho E4 35 C4
Higham Pl E17 53 A6
Higham Rd N17 51 B6
Higham Rd *continued*
Woodford IG8 37 A4
Highams Lodge Bsns Ctr
E17 52 D6
Highams Park Sch E4 36 B4
Highams Park Sta E4 36 B4
Higham St E17 53 A6
Higham Station Ave E4 35 D4
Highams The E17 36 A2
High Ashton 11 KT2 176 D3
Highbanks Cl DA16 146 B5
Highbanks Rd HA5 23 D4
Highbank Way N8 50 C3
High Barnet Sta EN5 1 C1
Highbarrow Rd CR0 206 A1
High Beech
South Croydon CR2 221 C1
Southgate N21 16 B5
High Beeches DA14 191 A5
High Birch Ct 7 EN4 2 C1
Highbridge Ct 13 SE14 140 C5
Highbridge Rd IG11 100 D6
High Bridge Wharf
SE10 120 B1
Highbrook Rd SE3 143 D2
High Broom Cres BR4 207 D2
Highbury (Arsenal FC)
N5 72 D5
Highbury Ave CR7 182 D1
Highbury Cl
New Malden KT3 199 A4
West Wickham BR4 223 D6
Highbury Cnr N5 72 D2
Highbury Corner N5 72 D2
Highbury Cres N5 72 C3
Highbury Fields Sch
N5 72 D3
Highbury Gdns IG3 79 C6
Highbury Gr N5 72 D3
Highbury Grange N5 73 A4
Highbury Grove Ct N5 72 D2
Highbury Grove Sch
N5 73 A3
Highbury Hill N5 72 D4
Highbury & Islington Sta
N1 72 D2
Highbury New Pk N5 73 A4
Highbury Pk N5 72 D4
Highbury Pl N5 72 D3
Highbury Quadrant N5 73 A5
Highbury Quadrant Prim
Sch N5 73 A4
Highbury Rd SW19 179 A5
Highbury Station Rd
N1 72 C2
Highbury Terr N5 72 D3
Highbury Terrace Mews
N5 72 D3
High Cedar Dr SW20 178 B3
Highclere Rd KT3 199 B6
Highclere St SE26 185 A6
Highcliffe
Beckenham BR3 185 D2
Ealing W13 87 B2
Highcliffe Dr SW15 155 D5
Highcliffe Gdns IG4 56 A4
Highcombe SE7 143 B6
Highcombe Cl SE9 166 A3
High Coombe Pl KT2 177 B3
Highcroft N6 49 A3
NW9 45 C4
2 Kingston KT5 198 B4
Highcroft Ave HA0 88 C6
Highcroft Gdns NW11 47 B3
Highcroft Rd N19 50 A2
High Cross Ctr The
N15 52 A5
High Cross Rd N17 52 A6
Highcross Way 4
SW15 156 A3
Highdaun Dr SW16 204 B5
High Dene EN2 4 D2
Highdown KT4 215 D6
Highdown Rd SW15 156 B5
High Dr KT2,KT3 177 A1
High Elms IG8 37 A5
High Elms Rd BR6 227 A1
Highenden Ho NW8 237 A6
Highfield WD23 8 C2
Highfield Ave DA8 147 D6
NW11 47 A2
NW9 45 A4
Greenford UB6 64 D3
Orpington BR6 227 D3
Pinner HA5 41 B4
Wembley HA9 66 B5
Highfield Cl NW9 45 A4
SE13 164 B5
Long Ditton KT6 197 C1
Wood Green N22 32 C2
Highfield Ct NW11 47 A3
Mitcham CR4 202 C5
Southgate N14 15 C5
Wanstead E12 77 C6
Highfield Dr
Beckenham BR2 208 D5
Ickenham UB10 60 A5
West Ewell KT19 215 D2
West Wickham BR4 224 A5

Highfield Gdns NW11 47 A3
Highfield Gr N6 48 D1
Highfield Hill SE19 183 C3
Highfield Ho N21 16 D3
Highfield Inf Sch BR2 208 C5
Highfield Jun Sch
BR2 208 C5
Highfield Prim Sch
Edmonton N21 17 A3
Hillingdon UB10 82 D4
Highfield Rd BR1 210 B5
BR5,BR7 211 D6
DA6 169 B6
NW11 47 A3
W3 89 A2
Carshalton SM1 218 C3
Edmonton N21 16 D2
Feltham TW13 150 A2
Hounslow TW7 130 D4
Tolworth KT5 199 A2
Upper Halliford TW16 193 D4
Walton-on-T KT12 194 A1
Highfields SM1 217 C6
Highfield Sch SW18 158 C4
High Foleys KT10 213 B1
High Gables
Beckenham BR2 186 C1
Loughton IG10 21 D6
High Garth KT10 212 A2
Highgate Archway N6 49 C1
Highgate Ave N6 49 B2
Highgate Ballet Sch
NW11 47 D5
Highgate Cemetery*
N19 71 B6
Highgate Cl N6 49 A2
High Gate Edge N2 48 C4
Highgate High St N6 49 B1
Highgate Hill N19 49 C1
Highgate Ho 11 SE26 162 A1
Highgate Hts N6 49 C3
Highgate Jun Sch N6 48 D2
Highgate Prim Sch N6 48 D3
Highgate Private Hospl
N6 48 D3
Highgate Rd NW5 71 B4
Highgate Sch N6 49 A2
Highgate Spinney N8 49 D3
Highgate Sta N6 49 B3
Highgate West Hill N6 71 A6
Highgate Wlk SE23 162 C2
Highgate Wood Sch N8 49 C4
High Gr Bromley BR1 187 D2
Woolwich SE18 145 B4
Highgrove Cl BR7 188 A2
N11 31 A5
Highgrove Ct BR3 185 C3
Highgrove Ho HA4 40 A3
Highgrove Mews SM5 218 D5
Highgrove Point 2
NW3 70 A4
Highgrove Rd RM8 80 C4
Highgrove Way HA4 40 A2
High Hill Ferry 3 E5 52 B1
High Holborn
WC1 94 B2 240 C3
High La W7 86 B1
Highland Ave W7 86 C1
Highland Cotts SM6 219 C4
Highland Croft BR3 185 D4
Highland Ct E18 37 B2
Highland Dr WD23 8 A4
Highland Lo 3 SE19 183 D3
Highland Pk TW13 171 D6
Highland Rd
Bexley DA6 147 C1
Bromley BR1 186 D2
Pinner HA6 22 A1
West Norwood SE19 183 C4
Highlands N20 14 B2
Highlands Ave W3 111 A6
Southgate N21 16 B6
Highlands Cl N4 50 A2
Hounslow TW3 129 D4
Highlands Ct SE19 183 C4
Highlands Gdns IG1 56 B1
Highlands Heath
SW15 156 C4
Highlands Prim Sch
IG1 56 B1
Highlands Rd EN5 13 C6
Highlands Sch N21 6 C1
Highlands The
Barnet EN5 1 D1
Edgware HA8 26 D1
Highlawn Hall HA1 64 C5
Highlea Cl NW9 27 C2
High Level Dr SE26 184 A6
Highlever Rd W10 90 C2
High Limes 2 SE19 183 C4
High London 5 N6 49 D2
Highmead SE18 145 D5
9 Edmonton N18 34 A5
High Mead Harrow HA1 42 D4
West Wickham BR4 224 C6
Highmead Cres HA0 66 B1
High Meadow Cl HA5 40 C5
High Meadow Cres
NW9 45 B4
High Meads Rd E16 99 D1
Highmore Rd SE3 142 C5
High Mount NW4 46 A3
High Oaks EN2 4 B5
High Park Ave TW9 132 C4
High Park Rd TW9 132 C4
High Par The SW16 160 A1
High Path SW19 180 A2
High Point N6 49 A2
SE9 166 D1
Highpoint EN5 14 A6
High Range SW20 178 C3
High Rd E10 53 D3
N11 31 B5
N15,N17 51 D5
N20 14 A4
N2 48 C6
N2,N12 30 A3
NW10 68 A2
Buckhurst Hill IG9,IG10 21 C5
Bushey WD23 8 B3
Harrow HA3 24 C3
Ilford IG1 78 D6
Ilford IG1,IG3 79 C6
Ilford IG3 57 D1
Ilford RM6 58 B2
Tottenham N17 33 D2
Wembley HA0,HA9 66 A3
Woodford E18 37 A2
Wood Green N22 32 B3
High Ridge N10 31 B2
High Road Eastcote
HA5 40 B4
High Road, Ickenham
UB10 61 A6
High Road Leyton E10 75 D6
High Road Leytonstone
E11 76 C6
High Road Woodford Gn
IG8 37 A6
High Sheldon N6 48 D3
Highshore Rd SE15 139 D3
Highshore Sch SE15 139 D4
High Silver IG10 21 D6
High St BR1 187 A1
BR6 227 A3
BR6 227 D2
E13 99 A5
E15 98 A6
E17 53 B5
N14 15 D2
N8 50 B5
NW7 28 B5
Acton W3 110 D5
Barnet EN5 1 B1
Beckenham BR3 185 C1
Brentford TW8 132 A6
Cheam SM1,KT17 217 A2
Claygate KT10 212 D2
Cranford TW5 128 B5
Croydon CR0 221 A5
Croydon SE25 206 A5
Ealing W5 109 D6
East Molesey KT8 195 C5
Elstree WD6 9 D5
Feltham TW13 150 A2
Hampton TW12 174 A4
Harlington UB3 127 B6
Harrow HA1 42 C1
Harrow HA3 42 C6
Hounslow TW3 129 D2
Ilford IG6 57 A6
Kingston KT1 197 D6
New Malden KT3 199 C5
Penge SE20 184 D3
Pinner HA5 41 A6
Ruislip HA4 39 C1
Shepperton TW17 193 A3
Sidcup DA14 190 A6
Southall UB1 107 B5
South Norwood CR7 205 B5
Sutton SM1 217 D4
Sutton SM1,SM2 217 D3
Teddington KT1 175 D2
Teddington TW11 175 A5
Thames Ditton KT7 197 A3
Twickenham TW2 152 A4
Wallington SM5 219 A4
Walton-on-T KT12 194 A1
Wanstead E11 55 A4
Wembley HA9 66 B4
West Wickham BR4 207 D1
Wimbledon SW19 178 D5
Yiewsley UB7 104 A6
High St Mews SW19 179 A5
High St N E12 78 A2
E6 100 A6
Highstone Ave E11 55 A3
Highstone Ct E11 54 D3
High Street Collier's Wood
SW17,SW19 180 B4
High Street Harlesden
NW10 89 D5
High Street Harlington
TW6 127 B5
High Street Kensington Sta
W8 113 D3 245 C1
High St S E6 100 B4
High The SW16 160 A1
High Timber St EC4 252 A6
High Tor Cl BR1 187 B3
High Tor View SE28 123 C5
High Trees N20 14 A1
Croydon CR0 207 A1
East Barnet EN4 14 C6
Streatham SW2 160 C3
Uxbridge UB10 61 A6
Hightrees Ct W7 108 C6
Hightrees Ho SW12 159 A5
Highview N8 50 A2
Northolt UB5 85 A4
Woolwich SE18 144 D5
High View
6 Penge SE19 183 D3
Pinner HA5 40 C6
Highview Ave HA8 27 A6
High View Ave CR0,
SM6 220 B3
High View Cl
Loughton IG10 21 C6
South Norwood SE19 183 D1
Highview Ct 2 SW19 157 A3
High View Ct HA3 24 C3
Highview Gdns HA8 27 A6
N11 31 C5
N3 47 A6
High View Par 1 IG4 56 B4
High View Prim Sch
SW11 136 B1
Wallington SM6 220 A3
High View Rd E18 54 D6
N10 30 D2
Highview Rd Ealing W13 87 A1
Sidcup DA14 190 B6
High View Rd SE19 183 B4
Highway Bsns Pk The 7
E1 118 D6
Highway The E1 118 C6
Stanmore HA7 25 A3
Highway Trad Ctr The 6
E1 118 D6
High Wigsell TW11 175 A5
Highwood Ave N12 30 A6
Highwood Cl BR6 227 A6
Highwood Ct N12 14 A1
Barnet EN5 13 C6
Highwood Dr BR6 227 A6
Highwood Gdns IG5 56 B5
Highwood Gr NW7 27 B5
Highwood Hill NW7 11 D2
Highwood Rd N19 72 A5
High Worple HA2 41 B1
Highworth Rd N11 31 D5
Highworth St NW1 237 B4
Hilary Ave CR4 203 A6
Hilary Cl SW6 265 C4
Bexley DA7 147 D4
Hilary Ct N9 18 D3
Hilary Rd W12 111 D6
Hilbert Rd SM3 216 D5
Hilborough Cl SW19 180 A3
Hilborough Ct 1 E8 95 D6
Hilborough Rd 1 E8 73 D1
Hilborough Way BR6 227 B3
Hilda Rd E16 98 C3
E6 77 D1
Hilda Terr 2 SW9 138 C3
Hilda Vale Cl BR6 226 D4
Hilda Vale Rd BR6 226 D4
Hildenborough Gdns
BR1 186 D4
Hildenborough Ho BR3 185 B3
Hildenlea Pl BR2 186 C1
Hilditch Ho 7 TW10 154 B5
Hildred Ho SW1 258 C4
Hildreth St SW12 159 B3
Hildreth Street Mews 2
SW12 159 B3
Hildyard Rd SW6 265 B6
Hiley Rd NW10 90 C4
Hilfield La WD23 8 C6
Hilfield La S WD23 8 D5
Hilgrove Rd NW6 70 A1
Hiliary Gdns HA7 25 C1
Hillard Ct SM6 219 D2
Hillary Cres KT12 194 C1
Hillary Ct
3 Chislehurst SE9 166 A2
Stanwell TW19 148 A3
Hillary Dr TW7 152 D6
Hillary Ho E14 98 A2
Hillary Rd UB2 107 C3
Hillary Rise EN5 1 C1
Hillbeck Cl SE15 140 C5
SE15 140 C6
Hillbeck Way UB6 86 B6
Hillborne Cl UB3 106 A1
Hillboro Ct E11 54 B2
1 Woodford E18 36 D2
Hillbrook Rd SW17 181 A6
Hillbrook Sch SW17 181 A6
Hillbrow Kingston KT3 199 D6
7 Richmond TW10 154 A5
Hill Brow BR1 187 D2
Hillbrow Ct KT10 212 A4
Hillbrow Rd
Catford BR1 186 C4
Esher KT10 212 A4
Hill Bunker's DA17 125 C2
Hillbury Ave HA3 43 B4
Hillbury Rd SW17 159 B1
Hill Cl NW11 47 C3
NW2 68 B5
Barnet EN5 12 C6
Chislehurst BR7 188 D5
Harrow HA1 64 C5
Stanmore HA7 25 B6
Hillcote Ave SW16 182 C3
Hillcourt Ave N12 29 D4
Hillcourt Rd SE22 162 B5
Hill Cres N20 13 D2
Harrow HA1 43 A4
Kingston KT5 198 B4
North Cheam KT4 216 C6
Hillcrest N6 49 A2
SE24 139 B1
W11 244 C5
Hill Crest DA15 168 B4
Hillcrest N21 16 C4
Hillcrest Ave NW11 47 B4
Edgware HA8 26 D6
Pinner HA5 40 D5
Hillcrest Cl
Beckenham BR3 207 B3
Forest Hill SE26 184 A6
Hillcrest Ct NW2 69 A3
Sutton SM2 218 B2
Hillcrest Gdns N3 47 A5
NW2 68 A5
Hinchley Wood KT10 212 D5
Hillcrest Hts W5 88 A3
Hillcrest Rd BR1 187 A6
Acton W3 110 D5
Chingford E17 36 B1
Ealing W5 88 A2
Loughton IG10 21 D5
Woodford E18 37 A1
Hillcrest View BR3 207 B3
Hillcroft Ave HA5 41 B3
Hillcroft Coll KT6 198 A3
Hillcroft Cres Ealing W5 87 D1
Ruislip HA4 62 D5
Wembley HA9 66 B4
Hillcroft Rd E6 100 D2
Hillcroome Rd SM2 218 B2
Hillcross Ave SM4 201 A4
Hillcross Prim Sch
SM4 201 B5
Hill Ct NW3 70 C4
Barnet EN4 2 C1
Ealing W5 88 B3
8 Kingston KT2 176 D3
14 Kingston KT6 198 A4
Northolt UB5 63 C3
Putney SW15 156 D6
Hilldale Rd SM1 217 B4
Hilldown Ct SW16 182 A3
Hilldown Rd
Hayes BR2 208 D1
South Norwood SW16 182 B3
Hill Dr NW9 45 A1
Thornton Heath SW16 204 B6
Hilldrop Cres N7 71 D3
Hilldrop Est 4 N7 71 D4
Hilldrop La N7 71 D3
Hilldrop Rd N7 71 D3
Bromley BR1 187 B4
Hill End BR6 227 D6
SE18 144 C4
Hillersdon Ave
Barnes SW13 134 A3
Edgware HA8 26 B5
Hillersdon Ho SW1 258 C2
Hillery Cl SE17 262 D3
Hill Farm Rd W10 90 D2
Hillfield Ave N8 50 A5
NW9 45 C5
Mitcham SM4 202 C4
Wembley HA0 66 B1
Hillfield Cl HA2 42 A5
Hillfield Ct NW3 70 C3
Hillfield Ho N5 73 A3
Hillfield Mans NW3 70 C3
Hillfield Par SM4 202 B3
Hillfield Park Mews
N10 49 B5
Hillfield Pk N10 49 B5
Southgate N21 16 C2
Hillfield Rd NW6 69 C3
Hampton TW12 173 B2
Hillgate Pl W8 113 C5 245 A4
Balham SW12 159 B4
Hillgate St W8 245 A4
Hill Gr TW13 151 B2
Hill Ho E5 52 B1
Stanmore HA7 9 A1
Hill House Ave HA7 24 D3
Hill House Cl N21 16 C4
Hill House Dr TW12 173 C2
Hill House Rd SW16 182 B5
Hill House Sch
SW1 114 D3 257 D5
Hilliard Ho 15 E1 118 B5
Hilliard's Ct E1 118 C5
Hillier Cl EN5 13 D5
Hillier Gdns CR0 220 C3
Hillier Ho 1 NW1 71 D1
Hillier Lo TW12 174 B5
Hillier Pl KT9 213 D2
Hillier Rd SW11 158 D5
Hilliers Ave UB8 82 C4
Hillier's La CR0,SM6 220 A5
Hillingdon Ave TW19 148 A3
Hillingdon Circus UB10 60 D2
Hillingdon Hill UB10 82 B4
Hillingdon Hospl UB8 82 B2
Hillingdon Par 6 UB10 82 D3
Hillingdon Prim Sch
UB10 82 D4
Hillingdon Rd UB10 82 A5
Hillingdon St SE17 138 D6
Hillingdon Sta UB10 60 D3
Hillington Gdns IG8 37 D1
Hill La HA4 39 A1
Hill Lo SW11 136 B1
Hillman Cl UB8 60 A3
Hillman St E8 74 B2
Hillmarton Rd N7 72 A3
Hillmead Dr SW9 138 D1
Hill Mead Prim Sch
SW9 138 D1
Hillmont Rd KT10 212 C5
Hillmore Ct SE13 142 B2
Hillmore Gr SE26 185 A5
Hill Rd N10 30 D2
NW8 92 A5 229 B3
Carshalton SM5 218 C2
Harrow HA1 43 A4
Mitcham CR4 181 B3
Pinner HA5 41 A3
Sutton SM1 217 D3
Wembley HA0 65 B5
Hillreach SE7,SE18 122 B1
Hill Rise NW11 47 D5
Hillrise KT12 193 D2
Hill Rise Enfield N9 18 B5
Forest Hill SE23 162 B3
Greenford UB6 86 A6
Hinchley Wood KT10 213 B6
Richmond TW10 153 D6
Ruislip HA4 39 B1
Hillrise Mans N19 50 A2
Hillrise Rd N19 50 A2
Hillsboro Rd SE22 161 C6
Hillsborough Ct 11
NW6 91 D6
Hillsgrove Cl DA16 146 C5
Hillsgrove Prim Sch
DA16 146 C5
Hillside N8 49 D3
NW10 89 B6
NW9 45 B5
Barnet EN5 14 A6
Wimbledon SW19 178 D4
Hill Side EN5 14 A6
Hillside Ave N11 30 D4
Wembley HA9 66 B4
Woodford IG8 37 C5
Hillside Cl NW8 91 D5
Merton SM4 201 A5
Woodford IG8 37 C5
Hillside Cres Enfield EN2 5 B5
Harrow HA2 42 A1
Northwood HA6 22 A2
Hillside Ct NW3 69 D3
7 Kingston KT2 176 D3
Hillside Dr HA8 26 C5
Hillside Gdns E17 54 B6
N6 49 B3
Barnet EN5 1 A1
Barnet N11 31 C4
Edgware HA8 26 B6
Harrow HA3 44 A2
Northwood HA6 22 B2
Streatham SW2 160 C2
Wallington SM6 219 C1
Hillside Gr N14 15 D4
NW7 28 A3
Hillside Jun Inf Schs
HA6 22 A3
Hillside La BR2 224 D6
Hillside Mans EN5 1 B1
Hillside Rd N15 51 C3
Beckenham BR2 208 D6
Belmont SM2 217 B1
Croydon CR0 220 D4
Ealing W5 88 A2
Northwood HA6,HA5 22 B3
Southall UB1 85 C3
Streatham SW2 160 C2
Surbiton KT5 198 C4
Hillside Rise HA6 22 A3
Hillsleigh Rd
W14 113 B5 244 D4
Hills Mews 2 W5 110 A6
Hills Pl W1 239 A1
Hill's Rd IG9 21 B3
Hill St W1 115 B6 248 C4
Richmond TW10 153 D6
Hillstone Ct 5 E3 97 D3
Hillstowe St E5 74 C5
Hilltop 7 E17 53 D6
Hill Top NW11 47 D5
Cheam SM3 201 B2
Hilltop Ct NW8 70 A1
12 SW18 136 B1
Hilltop Ct continued
South Norwood SE19 183 B2
Hilltop Gdns BR6 227 C6
Hilltop Ho 7 N6 49 D2
Hilltop Rd NW6 69 C1
Hilltop Way HA7 9 A1
Hillview SW20 178 B3
Hill View CR4 204 A5
Hillview Ave HA3 44 A4
Hillview Cl Pinner HA5 23 B4
Wembley HA9 66 B6
Hillview Cres BR6 211 D1
Hill View Cres IG1 56 B3
Hillview Ct SE19 183 C6
Hill View Dr DA16 145 C3
Woolwich SE28 123 C5
Hillview Gdns NW4 46 D5
Hill View Gdns NW9 45 B4
Hillview Gdns HA2 41 C5
Hillview Rd BR7 188 D6
NW7 28 D6
Hill View Rd BR6 227 D6
Hillview Rd
Carshalton SM1 218 B5
Pinner HA5 23 B4
Hill View Rd
Claygate KT10 213 A1
Twickenham TW1 153 A5
Hillway N6 71 A6
NW9 45 C1
Hill Wood Ho NW1 232 C3
Hillworth 7 BR3 185 D1
Hillworth Rd SW2 160 C4
Hillyard Rd W7 86 C2
Hillyard St SW9 138 C4
Hillyfield E17 35 A1
Hillyfield Cl E9 75 A3
Hilly Fields Cres SE4 141 C2
Hilly Mead SW19 179 A3
Hilsea Point 7 SW15 156 B3
Hilsea St E5 74 C4
Hilton Ave N12 30 B5
Hilton Ho N7 72 A4
9 SE4 140 D1
4 Ealing W13 87 C1
Hilversum Cres 10
SE22 161 C6
Himley Rd SW17 180 D4
Hinchley Cl KT10 212 D5
Hinchley Dr KT10 212 D5
Hinchley Way KT10 213 A5
Hinchley Wood Prim Sch
KT10 213 A6
Hinchley Wood Sch
KT10 213 A6
Hinchley Wood Sta
KT10 212 D5
Hinckley Rd SE15 140 A1
Hind Ct EC4 241 B1
Hinde Mews W1 238 B2
Hindes Rd HA1 42 C4
Hinde St W1 93 A1 238 B2
Hind Gr E14 97 C1
Hindhead Cl UB8 82 D2
Hindhead Gdns UB5 85 A6
Hindhead Gn WD19 22 C5
Hindhead Point 6
SW15 156 B3
Hindhead Way SM6 220 A3
Hind Ho N7 72 C4
13 SE14 140 D6
Hindhurst Ct NW9 45 A5
Hindle Ho E8 73 D3
Hindley Ho N7 72 B5
Hindlip Ho SW8 269 C1
Hindmans Rd SE22 162 A6
Hindmans Way RM9 103 B3
Hindmarsh Cl E1 118 A6
Hindrey Rd E5 74 B3
Hindsley's Pl SE23 162 C2
Hines Ct HA1 43 A4
Hinkler Rd HA3 43 D6
Hinksey Path SE2 124 D3
Hinstock NW6 91 D6
Hinstock Rd SE18 145 A5
Hinton Ave TW4 128 D1
Hinton Cl SE9 166 A3
Hinton Ct 3 E10 75 D6
Hinton Rd SE24 138 D2
Edmonton N18 33 C6
Wallington SM6 219 C2
Hippodrome Mews
W11 244 A5
Hippodrome Pl W11 244 B5
Hiscocks Ho NW10 67 A1
Hitcham Rd E17 53 B2
Hitchcock Cl TW17 192 B6
Hitchin Sq E3 97 A5
Hitherbroom Rd UB3 106 A6
Hither Farm Rd SE3 143 C2
Hitherfield Prim Sch
SW2 160 C2
Hitherfield Rd
Dagenham RM8 81 A6
Streatham SW16,SW27 160 C1
Hither Green La SE13 164 B5

Hither Green Prim Sch
SE13 164 B5
Hither Green Sta SE13 164 C5
Hitherlands SW12 159 B2
Hitherwell Dr HA3 24 B2
Hitherwood Ct SE21 183 D6
Hitherwood Dr SE19 183 D6
Hive Cl WD23 8 B2
Hive Rd WD23 8 C2
HM Prison Wormwood
Scrubs W12 90 A1
HMS Belfast★ SE1 253 B4
Hoadly Rd SW16 159 D2
Hobart Cl N20 14 C2
Hayes UB4 84 D3
Hobart Ct Harrow HA1 42 C2
Woodford IG8 36 D6
Hobart Dr UB4 84 D3
Hobart Gdns CR7 205 B6
Hobart La UB4 84 D3
Hobart Pl SW1 115 B3 258 C6
Richmond TW10 154 B4
Hobart Rd
Dagenham RM9 80 D4
Hayes UB4 84 D3
North Cheam KT4 216 B5
Hobbayne Prim Sch
W7 86 D1
Hobbayne Rd W7 86 B1
Hobbes Wlk SW15 156 B6
Hobb's Ct SE1 253 D2
Hobbs Gn N2 48 A6
Hobbs Mews IG3 79 D6
Hobbs' Pl N1 95 C6
Hobbs Rd 5 SE27 183 A6
Hobday St E14 97 D1
Hobill Wlk KT5 198 B3
Hoblands End BR7 189 C4
Hobsons Pl 7 E1 96 A2
Hobury St
SW10 136 B6 266 C5
Hockenden La BR5,
BR8 191 D1
Hocker St 41 E2 95 D4
Hockington Ct 7 EN5 13 D6
Hockley Ave E6 100 A5
Hockley Ct 2 E18 37 A2
Hockley Ho 4 E9 74 C2
Hockley Mews IG11 101 C5
Hockliffe Ho W10 90 C2
Hockney Ct 1 SE16 118 B1
Hockworth Ho 7 N16 51 C1
Hocroft Ave NW2 69 B5
Hocroft Ct NW2 69 B5
Hocroft Rd NW2 69 B5
Hocroft Wlk NW2 69 B5
Hodder Dr UB6 86 D5
Hoddesdon Rd DA17 125 C1
Hodford Rd NW11 47 B1
Hodgkins Cl SE28 124 D6
Hodister Cl 26 SE5 139 A5
Hodnet Gr SE16 118 D2
Hodson Cl HA2 63 B5
Hodson Pl EN3 7 C5
Hoecroft Ct EN3 6 C5
Hoe La EN1 6 B5
Hoe St E17 53 C4
Hoffman Sq N1 235 D2
Hofland Rd
W14 113 A3 254 A6
Hogan Mews W2 236 C4
Hogan Way E5 74 A6
Hogarth Ave TW15 171 A4
Hogarth Bsns Pk W4 133 C6
Hogarth Cl E16 99 D2
Ealing W5 88 A2
Hogarth Cres
Mitcham SW19 180 B2
Thornton Heath CR0 205 A2
Hogarth Ct 16 E1 96 A1
EC3 253 B6
6 NW1 71 C1
Dulwich SE19 183 D6
Heston TW5 129 A5
Hogarth Gdns TW5 129 C5
Hogarth Hill NW11 47 B5
Hogarth Ho SW1 259 D3
Enfield EN1 18 A6
13 Northolt UB5 84 D5
6 West Norwood SE27 183 A6
Hogarth Ind Est NW10 90 A3
Hogarth La W4 133 C6
Hogarth Pl SW5 255 C3
Hogarth Prim Sch W4 111 C1
Hogarth Rd
SW5 113 D2 255 C3
Barking RM8 80 B3
Edgware HA8 26 C1
Hogarth Roundabout
W4 133 C6
Hogarth Way TW12 174 A2
Hogsmill Way KT19 215 A4
Holbeach Gdns DA15 167 D5
Holbeach Mews 1
SW12 159 B3
Holbeach Prim Sch
SE6 163 C4
Holbeach Rd SE6 163 D4
Holbeck Row SE15 140 A5
Holbein Ho SW1 258 A2
10 Stanmore HA7 25 C5
Holbein Mews
SW1 115 A1 258 A2
Holbein Pl
SW1 115 A2 258 A3
Holberry Ho 5 SE21 183 C6
Holberton Gdns NW10 90 B4
Holborn EC1 94 C2 241 B3
Holborn Cir EC1 94 C2 241 B3
Holborn Pl WC1 240 C3
Holborn Rd E13 99 B3
Holborn Sta
WC1 94 B2 240 C3
Holborn Way CR4 180 D1
Holbrook Cl N19 49 B1
Enfield EN1 6 A5
Holbrooke Ct N7 72 A4
Holbrooke Pl 28 TW10 153 D6
Holbrook Ho W3 89 B2
Chislehurst BR7 189 B2
5 Streatham SW2 160 B3
Holbrook La BR7 189 B3
Holbrook Rd E15 98 D5
Holbrook Way BR2 210 B4
Holburn 33 N1 95 C6
Holburne Cl SE3 143 C4
Holburne Gdns SE3 143 D4
Holburne Rd SE3 143 D4
Holburn Viaduct
EC1 94 D2 241 C3
Holcombe Hill NW7 12 A1
Holcombe Ho SW9 138 A2
Holcombe Rd N17 52 A6
1 N17 51 D6
Ilford IG1 56 C2
Holcombe St W6 112 B2
Holcote Cl DA17 125 A3
Holcroft Ct W1 239 A4
Holcroft Ho SE10 142 A4
SW11 136 B2
Holcroft Rd E9 74 C1
Holden Ave N12 29 D5
NW9 45 A1
Holdenby Rd SE4 163 A6
Holden Cl RM8 80 B5
Holden Ho N1 235 A5
12 SE8 141 C5
Holden Hts N12 13 D1
Holdenhurst Ave N12 30 A3
Holden Lo N11 31 C5
Holden Rd N12 29 D6
Holden St SW11 137 A3
Holdernesse Rd
Isleworth TW7 131 A4
6 Upper Tooting SW17 159 A2
Holderness Ho SE5 139 C2
Holderness Way SE27 182 D5
Holders Hill Ave NW4 46 D6
Holders Hill Cres NW4 28 D1
Holders Hill Dr NW4 28 D1
Holders Hill Gdns NW4 29 A1
Holders Hill Par NW7 29 A2
Holders Hill Rd NW4 28 D1
NW4,NW7 29 A2
Holdsworth Ho 5
SW2 160 C4
Holford Ho 6 SE16 118 B2
WC1 233 D2
Holford Pl WC1 233 D2
Holford Rd NW3 70 A5
Holford St WC1 234 A2
Holgate Ave SW11 136 B2
Holgate Ct HA8 26 B6
Holgate Gdns RM10 81 C2
Holgate Rd RM10 81 C3
Holgate St SE7 121 D3
Hollam Ho N8 50 B5
Holland Ave
Belmont SM2 217 C1
Wimbledon SW20 177 D2
Holland Cl
Coney Hall BR2 224 D6
New Barnet EN5 14 B4
Stanmore HA7 25 B5
Holland Ct 6 E17 54 A5
NW7 28 A4
Holland Dr SE23 163 A1
Holland Gdns W14 254 B6
Holland Gr SW9 138 C5
Holland Ho E4 36 A6
Holland House Sch
HA8 26 D6
Holland Park
W11 113 B5 244 C3
Holland Park Ave
W11 113 A5 244 B3
Ilford IG3 57 D4
Holland Park Ct W14 244 B2
Holland Park Gdns
W14 113 A4 244 A2
Holland Park Mews
W11 113 B5 244 C3
Holland Park Rd
W14 113 B3 254 D5
Holland Park Rdbt
W12 112 D4
Holland Park Sch
W8 113 B4 244 D2
Holland Park Sta
W11 113 B5 244 C3
Holland Pl W8 245 C2
Holland Rd E15 98 C4
NW10 90 B5
W14 113 A3 254 B6
Croydon SE25 206 A4
Wallend E6 78 C1
Wembley HA0 65 D2
Holland Rise Ho SW9 270 D3
Holland St
SE1 116 D5 251 D4
W8 113 C4 245 B2
Hollands The
Feltham TW13 172 D6
New Malden KT4 199 D1
Holland Villas Rd
W14 113 A4 244 A1
Holland Way BR2 224 D6
Holland Wlk N19 49 D1
W14 113 B4 244 D1
Stanmore HA7 25 A5
Hollar Rd N16 73 D5
Hollen St W1 239 C2
Holles Cl TW12 173 C5
Holles Ho 5 SW9 138 C3
Holles St W1 93 B1 238 D2
Holley Rd W3 111 C4
Hollickwood Ave N12 30 D4
Hollickwood Prim Sch
N10 31 B3
Holliday Sq 7 SW11 136 B2
Hollidge Way RM10 81 D1
Hollies Ave DA15 167 D3
Hollies Cl
South Norwood SW16 182 C4
Twickenham TW1 152 D2
Hollies End NW7 28 B5
Hollies Rd W5 109 C2
Hollies The N20 14 B3
Harrow HA3 43 A5
7 Wanstead E11 55 A4
Hollies Way 1 SW12 159 A4
Holligrave Rd BR1 187 A2
Hollingbourne Ave
DA7 147 B4
Hollingbourne Gdns
W13 87 B2
Hollingbourne Rd
SE24 161 A6
Hollingbury Ct 1 E17 53 D6
Hollingsworth Rd CR0 222 B2
Hollington Cres KT3 199 D3
Hollington Ct BR7 188 D4
Hollington Rd E6 100 B4
Tottenham N17 34 A1
Hollingworth Cl KT8 195 B5
Hollingworth Ct 7
KT6 197 D2
Hollingworth Rd BR2,
BR5 210 D2
Hollins Ho N7 72 A4
Hollisfield WC1 233 B1
Hollman Gdns SW16 182 D4
Holloway Cl UB7 104 A1
Holloway La UB7 104 B1
Holloway Rd E11 76 B5
E6 100 B4
N19 71 D6
N7 72 B4
Holloway Road Sta N7 72 B3
Holloway Sch N7 71 D3
Holloway St TW3 129 D2
Hollowfield Wlk UB5 63 A2
Hollow The IG8 36 D6
Holly Ave N2 47 D6
Stanmore HA7 26 A1
Walton-on-T KT12 194 D1
Hollybank Cl TW12 173 C5
Holly Berry La 6 NW3 70 A4
Hollybrake Cl BR7 189 B3
Hollybush Cl
Harrow HA3 24 C2
Wanstead E11 55 A4
Hollybush Gdns E2 96 B4
Hollybush Hill E11 54 D3
Holly Bush Hill 23 NW3 70 A4
Hollybush Ho 23 E2 96 B4
Holly Bush La TW12 173 C3
Hollybush Pl E2 96 B4
Hollybush Rd KT2 176 A4
Hollybush St E13 99 B4
Holly Bush Vale 9
NW3 70 A4
Holly Cl NW10 67 C1
Beckenham BR3 208 A5
Buckhurst Hill IG9 21 D1
Feltham TW13 173 A5
Holly Cott KT7 197 A1
Holly Cottage Mews
UB8 82 C2
Holly Cres
Beckenham BR3 207 B4
Chingford IG8 36 B3
Hollycroft Ave NW3 69 C5
Hollycroft Ave *continued*
Wembley HA9 66 B5
Hollycroft Cl
Harmondsworth UB7 126 C6
South Croydon CR2 221 C3
Hollycroft Gdns UB7 126 C6
Holly Ct N15 51 C5
9 Belmont SM2 217 C1
4 Sidcup DA14 190 B6
Wallington SM6 219 B1
Hollydale Cl UB5 63 D4
Hollydale Dr BR2 226 B5
Holly Dale Prim Sch
SE15 140 C3
Hollydale Rd SE15 140 C3
Hollydene SE13 164 B5
5 SE15 140 B4
Bromley BR1 186 D2
Hollydown Way E11 76 B5
Holly Dr E4 19 D4
Holly Farm Rd UB2 107 A1
Hollyfield Ave N11 30 D5
Hollyfield Rd KT5 198 B2
Hollyfield Sch KT6 198 A4
Holly Gdns UB7 104 B4
Holly Gr NW9 45 A2
SE15 140 A3
Pinner HA5 23 A2
Hollygrove WD23 8 B4
Hollygrove Cl TW3 129 B1
Holly Hedge Terr
SE13 164 B6
Holly Hill NW3 70 A4
Southgate N21 16 B5
Holly Hill Rd DA8,DA17 125 D1
Holly Ho TW8 131 C6
Holly House Hospl IG9 21 B2
Holly Lo SE13 142 B1
Harrow HA1 42 B4
Southgate N21 16 C3
4 Wimbledon SW19 179 A4
Wimbledon SW20 178 B1
Holly Lodge Gdns N6 49 A1
Holly Lodge Mans N6 71 A6
Hollymead SM5 218 D5
Holly Mews SW10 256 B1
Holly Mount NW3 70 A4
Hollymount Cl 9
SE10 142 A4
Hollymount Prim Sch
SW20 178 C2
Holly Park Est N4 50 B2
Holly Park Gdns N3 47 C6
Holly Park Prim Sch
N11 31 A5
Holly Park Rd N11 31 A5
Ealing W7 108 D5
Holly Pk N3 47 C6
N4 50 B2
Holly Pl NW3 70 A4
Holly Rd E11 54 D2
W4 111 B2
Hampton TW12 174 A4
Hounslow TW3 129 D1
Twickenham TW1 153 A3
Holly St E8 73 D1
Holly Terr N6 49 A1
Hollytree Cl SW19 156 D3
Holly Tree Ho SE4 141 B2
Holly Tree Lo EN2 4 D3
Hollyview Cl NW4 46 A3
Holly Village N6 71 B6
Holly Way CR4 203 D6
Hollywell Row
EC2 95 C3 243 A5
Holly Wlk NW3 70 A4
Enfield EN2 5 B2
Hollywood Ct W5 110 B6
Hollywood Gdns UB4 84 B1
Hollywood Mews
SW10 266 A6
Hollywood Rd E4 35 A5
SW10 136 A6 266 A6
Hollywood Way IG8 36 B4
Holman Ho 2 E2 96 D4
Holman Hunt Ho W14 254 A1
Holman Rd SW11 136 B3
West Ewell KT19 215 A3
Holmbank Dr TW17 193 C5
Holmbridge Gdns EN3 6 D1
Holmbrook NW1 232 B3
Holmbrook Dr NW4 46 D4
Holmbury Cl WD23 8 C2
Holmbury Ct
Mitcham SW19 180 C3
Upper Tooting SW17 158 D1
Holmbury Gdns UB3 105 D5
Holmbury Gr CR0 223 B1
Holmbury Ho SW9 160 D6
Holmbury Manor 6
DA14 190 A6
Holmbury Pk BR7 188 A3
Holmbury View 2 E5 52 B1
Holmbush Ct NW4 46 D4
Holmbush Rd SW15 157 A5
Holmcote Gdns N5 73 A3
Holmcroft Ho 9 E17 53 D5
Holmcroft Way BR2 210 B4
Holm Ct SE12 165 B1
Holmdale Gdns NW4 46 D4
Holmdale Rd NW6 69 C3
Chislehurst BR7 189 A5
Holmdale Terr N15 51 C3
Holmdene N12 29 D5
Holmdene Ave NW7 28 A4
SE24 161 A6
Harrow HA2 41 D6
Holmdene Cl BR3 186 A1
Holmdene Ct BR1 210 A6
Holmead Rd
SW6 135 D5 265 D3
Holmefield Ho W10 91 A3
Holme Lacey Rd SE12 164 D5
Holmeleigh Ct EN3 6 C1
Holme Rd E6 100 A6
Holmes Ave E17 53 B6
NW7 29 A5
Holmes Ct 18 SW4 138 A3
17 W4 111 A3
5 Chingford E4 20 B2
Holmesdale Ave
SW14 132 D1
Holmesdale Cl SE25 205 D6
Holmesdale Ho 12 NW6 91 C6
Holmesdale Rd N6 49 B2
Bexley DA16 146 D3
Richmond TW9 132 B4
South Norwood SE25 205 C5
Teddington TW11 175 C4
Thornton Heath CR0 205 B4
Holmesley Rd SE23 163 A5
Holmes Pl SW10 266 B6
Holmes Rd NW5 71 B3
Merton SW19 180 A3
Twickenham TW1 152 D2
Holmes Terr SE1 251 A2
Holmeswood Ct 3 N22 32 C1
Holme Way HA7 24 D4
Holmewood Gdns
SW2 160 B4
Holmewood Rd
South Norwood SE25 205 C6
Streatham SW2 160 B4
Holmfield Ave NW4 46 D4
Holmfield Ct 4 NW3 70 C2
Holmfield Ho E17 54 B5
Holm Gr UB10 60 C1
Holmhurst SE13 164 B5
Holmhurst Rd DA17 125 D1
Holmlea Ct 1 CR0 221 B4
Holmleigh Prim Sch
N16 51 C1
Holmleigh Rd N16 51 C1
Holm Oak Cl SW15 157 B5
Holmoaks Ho BR3 186 A1
Holmsbury Ho 6 N7 71 D3
Holmsdale Ho 21 E14 119 D6
6 N11 31 B6
Holmshaw Cl SE26 185 A6
Holmside Ct SW12 159 A5
Holmside Rd SW12 159 A5
Holmsley Cl KT3 199 D2
Holmsley Ho SW15 155 D4
Holmstall Ave HA8 27 A1
Holmstall Par HA8 27 A1
Holm Wlk SE3 143 A3
Holmwood 2 KT5 198 B3
Holmwood Cl
Cheam SM2 216 D1
Harrow HA2 42 A6
Northolt UB5 63 D2
Holmwood Ct DA14 189 D5
3 N16 51 D2
Kingston KT3 199 B6
Holmwood Gdns N3 29 C1
Wallington SM6 219 B2
Holmwood Gr NW7 27 B5
Holmwood Mans W3 110 C5
Holmwood Rd
Chessington KT9 214 A3
Ilford IG3 79 C6
Holne Chase N2 48 A3
Morden SM4 201 C3
Holness Rd E15 76 D2
Holocaust Meml Gdn★
W2 114 D4 247 D2
Holroyd Rd SW15 156 C6
Holsgrove Ct W3 111 C5
Holstein Way 6 DA18 125 A3
Holst Mans SW13 134 C5
Holstock Rd IG1 79 A6
Holsworth Cl HA2 42 A4
Holsworthy Ho 49 E3 97 D4
Holsworthy Way KT9 213 C3
Holt Cl N10 49 A5
Woolwich SE28 124 C6
Holt Ct E15 76 A3
Holt Ho SW2 160 C5
Holtoake Ct 1 W5 87 C3
Holtoake Ho 3 W5 87 C3
Holton St E1 96 D3
Holt Rd E16 122 A5
Wembley HA0 65 C5
Holt The Morden SM4 201 C5
Wallington SM6 219 C4
Holtwhite Ave EN2 5 A3
Holtwhite's Hill EN2 4 D4
Holwell Pl HA5 41 A5
Holwood Park Ave
BR2,BR6 226 B4
Holwood Pl 7 SW4 137 D1
Holybourne Ave SW15 156 A4
Holy Cross RC Sch
SW6 135 C4 265 A2
Holy Cross Sch The
KT3 199 C4
Holy Family RC Prim Sch
E14 119 C6
SE9 143 C1
Holy Ghost RC Prim Sch
SW12 159 A4
Holyhead Cl E3 97 C4
3 E6 100 B2
Holyhead Ct KT1 197 D5
Holy Innocents RC Prim Sch
BR6 227 D5
Holyoake Ct SE16 119 B4
Holyoake Wlk N2 48 A6
Ealing W5 87 C3
Holyoak Rd
SE11 116 D2 261 D3
Holyport Rd SW6 134 D5
Holyrood Ave HA2 63 B4
Holyrood Gdns HA8 26 D1
Holyrood Ho N4 50 D1
Holyrood Mews 11
E16 121 A5
Holyrood Rd EN5 14 B5
Holyrood St
SE1 117 C5 253 A3
Holy Trinity CE First Sch
SW19 179 D4
Holy Trinity CE Inf Sch
SW17 158 D2
Holy Trinity CE JMI Sch
E8 73 D2
Holy Trinity CE Jun Sch
Richmond TW10 132 C1
Wallington SM6 219 C4
Holy Trinity CE Prim Sch
DA15 168 A3
N2 48 B6
NW3 70 A2
SW1 114 D2 257 D4
SW1 115 A2 258 A4
Forest Hill SE23 162 C2
Streatham SW2 160 B4
Holy Trinity Coll BR1 187 C2
Holy Trinity & St Silas CE
Prim Sch NW1 71 B1
Holywell Cl 35 SE16 118 B1
2 SE3 143 A6
Stanwell TW19 148 A3
Holywell La EC2 243 B6
Holywell Way TW19 148 A3
Homan Ct N12 30 A6
Homan Ho 6 SW4 159 D4
Homebush Ho E4 19 D4
Home Cl
Carshalton SM5 218 D6
Northolt UB5 85 B4
Homecoppice Ho 1
BR1 186 D3
Homecroft Rd
Forest Hill SE26 184 C5
Tottenham N22 33 A2
Home Ct KT6 197 D4
Home Farm Cl
Thames Ditton KT7 196 D2
Upper Halliford TW17 193 C5
Home Farm Cotts BR5 190 D2
Homefarm Rd W7 86 D1
Homefield SM4 201 C5
Home Field EN5 13 B6
Homefield Ave IG2 57 C4
Homefield Cl NW10 67 A2
Hayes UB4 84 D3
Homefield Ct NW4 46 C5
Homefield Gdns N2 48 B6
Mitcham CR4,SW19 180 B1
Homefield Ho SE23 162 D1
Homefield Pk SM1,
SM2 217 D2
Homefield Pl 4 SW19 178 D5
Homefield Prep Sch
SM1 217 C3
Homefield Rd BR1 187 C2
HA8 27 B4
W4 111 D1
Walton-on-T KT12 195 A2
Wembley HA0 65 B4
Wimbledon SW19 179 A4
Homefield St 14 N1 95 C5
Homefirs Ho HA9 66 B5
Homelands Dr SE19 183 C3
Home Lea BR6 227 D3
Homeleigh Ct 8
SW16 160 A1
Homeleigh Rd SE15 162 D6
Homemead SW12 159 B2
Home Mead HA7 25 C2
Homemead Rd BR2 210 B4
Wallington CR0 203 C3
Home Office SW1 249 C1
Home Park Rd SW19 157 B1
Home Park Terr KT1 175 D1
Home Park Wlk KT1 197 D5

Home Rd SW11 136 C3
Homer Dr E14 119 C2
Homer Rd E9 75 A2
Croydon CR0 206 D3
Homer Row W1 237 B3
Homersham Rd KT1 176 D1
Homer St W1 92 C2 237 B3
Homerton Coll of Technology E9 74 C3
Homerton Gr E9 74 D3
Homerton High St E9 74 D3
Homerton Hospl E9 74 D3
Homerton Rd E9 75 B3
Homerton Row E9 74 C3
Homerton Sta E9 74 D2
Homerton Terr E9 74 C2
Homesdale Cl E11 55 A4
Homesdale Rd
BR1,BR2 209 C6
Orpington BR5,BR6 211 C2
Homesfield NW11 47 C4
Homes Of Rest (CE Temperance Society) IG1 79 B5
Homestall Rd SE22 162 C6
Homestead Ct EN5 13 C6
Homestead Gdns KT10 212 C3
Homestead Paddock N14 15 B6
Homestead Pk NW2 67 D5
Homestead Rd SW6 135 B5 264 D3
Dagenham RM8 81 B6
Homesteads The BR3 185 D4
Homestead The N11 31 B6
Homewalk Ho SE26 184 C6
Homewaters Ave TW16 171 D2
Homewillow Cl N21 16 D5
Homewood Cl TW12 173 B4
Homewood Cres BR7 189 C4
Homewood Gdns SE25 205 C4
Homewoods 2 SW12 159 C4
Homildon Ho 10 SE26 162 A1
Homington Ct KT2 176 A3
Honduras St EC1 242 A6
Honeybourne Rd NW6 69 D3
Honeybourne Way BR5 211 B1
Honeybrook Rd SW12, SW4 159 C4
Honey Cl RM10 81 D2
Honeycroft Hill UB10 60 A1
Honeyden Rd DA14 191 A4
Honeyfield N4 72 C6
Honey Hill UB10 60 B1
Honey La EC2 242 B1
Honeyman Cl NW6 68 D1
Honeypot Bsns Ctr HA7 26 A2
Honeypot Cl NW9 44 B5
Honeypot La HA3,HA7, NW9 44 B6
Honeysett Rd 1 N17 33 D1
Honeysuckle Cl UB1 107 A6
Honeysuckle Ct
2 SE12 165 A4
Ilford IG1 78 D2
Honeysuckle Gdns CR0 206 D1
Honeywell Jun & Inf Schs SW11 158 D5
Honeywell Rd SW11 158 D5
Honeywood Ho 5 SE15 140 A4
Honeywood Rd NW10 89 D5
Isleworth TW7 131 A1
Honeywood Wlk SM5 218 D4
Honister Cl HA7 25 B2
Honister Gdns HA7 25 B2
Honister Pl HA7 25 B2
Honiton Gdns 1 SE15 140 C3
Honiton Ho 30 SE5 139 A3
Honiton Rd DA16 145 D3
NW6 91 B5
Honley Rd SE6 163 D4
Honnor Gdns TW7 130 B3
Honor Oak Park Sta SE23 162 D5
Honor Oak Pk SE23 162 D5
Honor Oak Rd SE23 162 C4
Honor Oak Rise SE23 162 C5
Honwell Ho W2 91 C2
Hood Ave
East Barnet N14 15 B5
Mortlake SW14 155 A6
Hood Cl CR0 204 D1
Hoodcote Gdns N21 16 D4
Hood Ct N7 72 B5
Hood Ho 17 SE5 139 B5
Hood Lo E11 77 B6
Hood Rd SW20 177 D3
Hook KT6 214 A5
Hooke Ct SE10 142 A4
Hooke Ho 30 E3 97 A5
Hooker's Rd E17 52 D6
Hook Farm Rd BR2 209 D4
Hookham Ct SW8 269 C2
Hook Ho 9 SW27 182 D5
Hooking Gn HA2 41 D4
Hook La DA16 146 A1
Hook Lane Prim Sch DA16 146 A2
Hook Rd KT19,KT17 215 A1
Hook Rise N
Surbiton KT6 214 A5
Tolworth KT6,KT9 214 D6
Hook Rise S KT6,KT9 214 D6
Hook Rise South KT6 214 A5
Hooks Cl SE15 140 B4
Hookstone Way IG8 37 D3
Hook The EN5 14 B5
Hook Underpass KT6 214 A5
Hook Wlk HA8 27 A4
Hooper Ho 8 SW18 157 B6
Hooper Rd E16 99 A1
Hooper's Ct SW1 247 C1
Hooper's Mews 4 W3 111 A5
Hooper St E1 96 A1
Hoop La NW11 47 C2
Hoover Ho 5 SE6 186 A6
Hope Cl N1 73 A2
SE12 165 B1
2 Brentford TW8 110 A1
Dagenham RM6 58 D5
Sutton SM1 218 A3
1 Woodford IG8 37 C4
Hopedale Rd SE7 143 B6
Hopefield 3 W7 108 D5
Hopefield Ave NW6 91 A5
Hope Pk BR1 186 D3
Hopes Cl TW5 129 C6
Hope St SW11 136 B2
Hopetown St E1 243 D3
Hopewell St SE5 139 B5
Hop Gdns WC2 250 A5
Hopgood St W12 112 C5
Hopkins Cl N10 31 A3
Hopkins Ho 12 E14 97 C1
Hopkins Mews E15 98 D6
Hopkinson Ho 1 SW11 137 A3
Hopkinson's Pl NW1 231 A6
Hopkins St W1 93 D1 239 C1
Hoppers Rd N21 16 C2
Hoppett Rd E4 20 C2
Hopping La N1 72 D2
Hoppingwood Ave KT3 199 C6
Hoppner Rd UB4 83 B5
Hop St SE10 120 D3
Hopton Ct BR2 209 A1
Hopton Gdns KT3 200 A3
Hopton Ho 5 SW9 138 D3
Hopton Rd SW16 182 A5
Hopton's Gdns SE1 251 D4
Hopton St SE1 116 D5 251 D4
Hoptree Cl N12 29 D6
Hopwood Cl SW17 158 A1
Hopwood Rd SE17 139 B6
Hopwood Wlk E8 74 A1
Horace Rd E7 77 B4
Ilford IG6 57 A6
Kingston KT1 198 B6
Horatio Ho 13 E2 95 D5
Horatio Pl E14 120 A5
Horatio St 11 E2 95 D5
Horatius Way CR0 220 B2
Horbury Cres W11 113 C6 245 A5
Horbury Mews W11 113 B6 244 D5
Horder Rd SW6 135 A4 264 B1
Hordle Prom E 14 SE15 139 D5
Hordle Prom N 3 SE15 139 D5
Hordle Prom S 7 SE15 139 D5
Hordle Prom W 13 SE15 139 C5
Horizon Bldg 14 E14 119 C6
Horizon Sch N16 73 C4
Horle Wlk SE5 138 D3
Horley Cl DA6 169 C6
Horley Rd SE9 188 A6
Hormead Rd W9 91 B3
Hornbeam Cl NW7 11 D1
SE11 261 A4
Barking IG11 102 B3
Buckhurst Hill IG9 21 D1
Northolt UB5 63 B3
Hornbeam Cres TW8 131 B5
Hornbeam Gr E4 20 D1
Hornbeam Ho
6 DA15 168 A1
2 NW3 70 D2
Buckhurst Hill IG9 21 D1
Hornbeam La E4 20 C6
Hornbeam Rd
Buckhurst Hill IG9 21 D1
Hayes UB4 84 C2
Hornbeams Rise N11 31 A4
Hornbeam Terr SM5 202 C1
Hornbeam Twr E11 76 B5
Hornbeam Way BR2 210 C3
Hornblower Cl 2 SE16 119 A2
Hornbuckle Cl HA2 64 B6
Hornby Cl NW3 70 B1
Hornby Ho 6 SE11 138 C6
Horncastle Cl SE12 165 A4
Horncastle Rd SE12 165 A4
Hornchurch N17 33 B1
Hornchurch Cl KT2 175 D6
Horndean Cl 3 SW15 156 A3
Horne Ho 7 SE18 144 A4
Horner Ct E11 76 B5
Horne Rd TW17 192 C5
Horner Hos 18 N1 95 C6
Horner La 3 CR4 180 B1
Horne Way SW15 134 C3
Hornfair Rd SE7 143 D5
Horniman Dr SE23 162 C4
Horniman Grange 7 SE23 162 C3
Horniman Mus & Gdns★ SE23 162 B3
Horniman Sch SE23 162 B3
Horning Cl SE9 188 A6
Horn La SE10 121 A2
W3 89 A1
Woodford IG8 37 A3
Horn Link Way SE10 121 A2
Horn Park Cl SE12 165 B6
Horn Park La SE12 165 B5
Horn Park Prim Sch SE12 165 B4
Hornsby House Sch SW12 159 A3
Horns End Pl HA5 40 C4
Hornsey Central Hospl N8 49 D4
Hornsey La N6 49 C2
Hornsey Lane Gdns N6 49 C2
Hornsey Park Rd N8 50 B6
Hornsey Rd N7,N19 72 B6
Hornsey Rise Gdns N19 50 A2
Hornsey Sch for Girls N8 50 B4
Hornsey St N7 72 B3
Hornsey Sta N8 50 B5
Hornshay St SE15 140 C6
Horns Rd IG2,IG6 57 A4
Hornton Ct W8 245 B1
Hornton Pl W8 245 B1
Hornton St W8 113 C4 245 B2
Horrocks Ho SW15 156 B6
Horsa Rd DA8 147 D5
Eltham SE12 165 C4
Horsebridge Cl RM9 103 A6
Horsecroft Rd HA8 27 B3
Horse & Dolphin Yd W1 249 D6
Horse Fair KT1 175 D1
Horseferry Pl SE10 142 A6
Horseferry Rd E14 119 A6
SW1 115 D2 259 D4
Horseferry Rd Est SW1 259 C5
Horseguards Ave SW1 116 A5 250 A3
Horse Guards Par★ SW1 115 D5 249 D3
Horse Guards Rd SW1 115 D4 249 D2
Horse Leaze E6 100 C1
Horsell Rd BR5 190 B2
N5 72 C3
Horselydown La SE1 117 D5 253 C3
Horselydown Mans SE1 253 C2
Horsenden Ave UB6 64 D3
Horsenden Cres UB6 64 D3
Horsenden La N UB6 64 D1
Horsenden La S UB6 87 A6
Horsenden Prim Sch UB6 64 C2
Horsendon Ho 11 N7 71 D3
Horseshoe Cl E14 120 A1
NW2 68 B6
Horse Shoe Cres UB5 85 C5
Horseshoe Dr UB8 82 C1
Horse Shoe Gn SM1 217 D6
Horseshoe La
Barnet N20 12 D3
Enfield EN2 5 A2
Horse Shoe Yd W1 248 D6
Horse Yd N1 234 D6
Horsfield Gdns 1 SE9 166 A6
Horsfeld Rd SE9 165 D6
Horsfield Ho 2 N1 73 A1
Horsford Rd SW2 160 B6
Horsham Ave N12 30 C5
Horsham Ct N17 34 A2
Horsham Rd DA6 169 C6
East Bedfont TW14 149 A5
Horsley Dr
Kingston KT2 175 D5
New Addington CR0 224 A1
Horsley Ho 11 SE4 140 D1
Horsley Rd BR1 187 B2
Chingford E4 20 A2
Horsley St 3 SE17 139 B6
Horsman Ho SE5 139 A6
Horsman St SE5 139 A6
Horsmonden Cl BR6 211 D2
Horsmonden Rd SE4 163 B5
Horston Ho N4 51 A2
Hortensia Ho SW10 266 A4
Hortensia Rd SW10 136 A5 266 A4
Horticultural Pl 6 W4 111 B1
Horton Ave NW2 69 A4
Horton Bridge Rd UB7 104 B5
Horton Cl UB7 104 B5
Horton Ctry Pk KT19 214 C1
Horton Ho 13 SE15 140 C6
SW8 270 C4
W14 254 A1
Horton Ind Pk UB7 104 B5
Horton La KT19 215 A1
Horton Par UB7 104 A5
Horton Rd E8 74 B2
Yiewsley UB7 104 B5
Horton Road Ind Est UB7 104 B5
Horton St SE13 141 D2
Horton Way CR0 206 D4
Hortus Rd Chingford E4 20 A2
Southall UB2 107 B4
Horwood Ho 24 E2 96 B4
NW8 237 B6
Hosack Rd SW12,SW17 159 A2
Hoser Ave SE12 165 A2
Hosier La EC1 94 D2 241 D3
Hoskins Cl UB3 105 D1
Hoskin's Cl E16 99 C1
Hoskins St SE10 120 B1
Hospital Bridge Rd TW2 151 D3
Hospital Bridge Rdbt TW2 151 D2
Hospital of the Holy Trinity (Almshouses) 5 CR0 221 A6
Hospital Rd TW3 129 C2
Hospl for Tropical Diseases NW1 232 C5
Hospl of St John & St Elizabeth NW8 92 B5 229 C3
Hotham Cl KT8 195 C6
Hotham Prim Sch SW15 134 D1
Hotham Rd
Merton SW19 180 A3
Putney SW15 134 C2
Hotham Road Mews 12 SW19 180 A3
Hotham St E15 98 C6
Hothfield Pl SE16 118 C3
Hotspur Ind Est N17 34 B4
Hotspur Rd UB5 85 C5
Hotspur St SE11 116 C1 261 A2
Houblon Rd TW10 154 A6
Houghton Cl 10 E8 73 D2
Hampton TW12 173 A4
Houghton Rd N15 51 D5
Houghton St WC2 240 D1
Houlder Cres CR0 220 D2
Houndsden Rd N21 16 C5
Houndsditch EC3 95 C1 243 B2
Houndsfield Prim Sch N9 18 B4
Houndsfield Rd N9 18 B4
Hounslow Ave TW3 151 D6
Hounslow Bsns Pk TW3 129 D1
Hounslow Central Sta TW3 129 D2
Hounslow Ctr The TW3 129 D2
Hounslow East Sta TW3 130 A3
Hounslow Ed Ctr (Specl Sch) The TW4 129 A2
Hounslow Gdns TW3 151 D6
Hounslow Heath Jun & Inf Schs TW4 129 A2
Hounslow Heath Nature Reserve TW4 151 A5
Hounslow Manor Sch TW3 130 A2
Hounslow Rd
Feltham TW13 151 A2
Twickenham TW2,TW3 152 A5
Feltham TW14 150 B4
Hounslow Sta TW3 151 D6
Hounslow Town Prim Sch TW3 130 B2
Hounslow West Sta TW3 129 A3
Houseman Way 20 SE5 139 B5
Houses of Parliament★ SW1 116 A3 260 B6
Houston Ct 3 CR0 205 C1
Houston Rd
Forest Hill SE23 163 A1
Houston Rd *continued*
Thames Ditton KT6 197 B3
Houstoun Ct TW5 129 B5
Hove Ave E17 53 B4
Hoveden Rd NW2 69 A3
Hove Gdns SM1 201 D1
Hovenden Ho 6 SE21 183 C6
Hoveton Rd SE28 102 C1
Howard Ave DA5 168 C4
Howard Cl N11 15 A2
NW2 69 A4
Acton W3 88 D1
Ashford TW16 171 D4
Bushey WD23 8 C4
Hampton TW12 174 A4
Howard Ct SE15 140 A2
12 Barking IG11 101 B6
Beckenham BR3 186 A1
Howard Ho 8 E5 74 C6
14 SE8 141 B6
7 SW9 138 C2
W1 238 D5
Penge SE20 184 C2
Howard Mans E17 53 D6
Howard Prim Sch CR0 221 A4
Howard Rd BR1 187 A3
E11 76 C5
E17 53 D6
E6 100 B5
N15 51 C3
N16 73 B4
NW2 68 D4
Barking IG11 101 B6
Croydon SE25 206 A3
Ilford IG1 78 D4
Isleworth TW7 130 D2
New Malden KT3 199 D5
Penge SE20 184 C2
Southall UB1 85 D1
Surbiton KT5 198 B3
Howards Cl HA5 22 B1
Howards Crest Cl BR3 186 A1
Howard's La SW15 134 C1
Howard's Rd E13 99 A4
Howard St KT7 197 B3
Howard Way EN5 12 D6
Howard Wlk N2 48 B5
Howarth Rd SE2 124 A2
Howberry Cl HA8 25 D4
Howberry Rd
South Norwood CR7 183 B1
Stanmore HA7,H8 25 D4
Howbury Rd SE15 140 C2
Howcroft Cres N3 29 C3
Howcroft Ho 3 E3 97 B4
Howcroft La UB6 86 B4
Howden Cl SE28 124 D6
Howden Ct SE25 183 D1
Howden Rd SE25 183 D1
Howden St SE15 140 A2
Howell Cl RM6 58 D4
Howell Ct 2 E10 53 D2
Howell Ho 5 N7 71 D3
Howell Wlk SE1 261 D3
Howerd Way SE18 144 A4
Howes Cl N3 47 C6
Howfield Pl N17 51 D6
Howgate Rd SW14 133 B2
Howick Pl SW1 115 C3 259 B5
Howie St SW11 136 C5 267 A3
Howitt Cl 6 NW3 70 C2
Howitt Rd NW3 70 C2
Howland Ho 9 SW16 160 A1
Howland Mews E W1 239 B4
Howland St W1 93 C2 239 B4
Howland Way SE16 119 A4
Howletts La HA4 39 A3
Howletts Rd SE24 161 A5
Howley Pl W2 92 A2 236 B4
Howley Rd CR0 221 A5
Howmic Ct 1 TW1 153 C5
Howsman Rd SW13 134 A6
Howson Rd SE4 141 A1
Howson Terr TW10 154 A5
How's St E2 95 D5
Howton Pl WD23 8 B3
Hoxton Mkt 10 N1 95 C4
Hoxton Point EC1 95 C4
Hoxton Sq N1 95 C4
Hoxton St N1 95 C5
Hoylake Cres UB10 60 D6
Hoylake Gdns
Mitcham CR4 203 C6
Ruislip HA4 40 B1
South Oxhey WD19 22 D6
Hoylake Rd W3 89 C1
Hoyland Cl 4 SE15 140 B5
Hoyle Rd SW17 180 C5
Hoy St E16 98 D1
Huan Ct N20 14 C2
Hubbard Dr KT9 213 D2
Hubbard Rd SE27 183 A6
Hubbards Cl UB8 82 D1
Hubbard St E15 98 C6
Hub Buildings The 4 SW12 159 B3
Huberd Ho SE1 262 D6
Hubert Gr SW9 138 A2
Hubert Ho NW8 237 A5
Hubert Rd E6 99 D4
Hucknall Ct NW8 236 C6
Huddart St E3 97 B2
Huddleston Cl E2 96 C5
Huddlestone Rd E7 76 D4
NW2 68 B2
Huddleston Rd N7 71 C4
Hudson 27 NW9 27 D2
Hudson Cl 15 W12 112 B6
Hudson Ct
Croydon SE25 206 A5
4 Merton SW19 179 D2
3 Millwall E14 119 C1
Hudson Ho SW10 266 A4
5 W11 91 A1
Hudson Pl SE18 123 A1
Hudson Rd DA7 147 B4
Harlington UB7 127 B6
Hudsons Ho N1 235 D1
Hudson's Pl SW1 115 C2 259 A4
Hudson Way N9 18 C2
Huggin Ct EC4 252 B6
Huggin Hill EC4 252 B6
Huggins Ho 8 E3 97 C4
Huggins Pl SW2 160 B3
Hughan Rd E15 76 B3
Hugh Astor Ct SE1 261 D6
Hugh Clark Ho W13 109 A5
Hughenden Ave HA3 43 B4
Hughenden Gdns UB5 84 C4
Hughenden Rd KT4 200 A2
Hughendon EN5 1 D1
Hughendon Terr E15 76 A4
Hughes Cl N12 30 A5
Hughes Ho 28 E2 96 C4
SE17 261 D3
SE5 139 A4
15 SE8 141 C6
Hughes Mans E1 96 A3
Hughes Rd
Ashford TW15 171 A4
Hayes UB3 106 B6
Hughes Terr 6 E16 98 D2
Hughes Wlk CR0 205 A2
Hugh Gaitskell Cl SW6 264 C5
Hugh Gaitskell Ho N16 73 D6
NW10 67 D1
Hugh Herland KT1 198 A6
Hugh Mews SW1 258 D3
Hugh Morgan Ho 5 SW4 137 D2
Hugh Myddelton Prim Sch EC1 94 C4 234 B1
Hugh Platt Ho 29 E2 96 B5
Hugh St SW1 115 B2 258 D3
Hugo Ho SW1 257 D6
Hugon Rd SW6 135 D2
Hugo Rd N19 71 C4
Huguenot Pl SW18 158 A6
Huguenot Sq SE15 140 B2
Hullbridge Mews N1 235 C6
Hull Cl SE16 118 D5
Hull Ct SE5 139 B3
Hull Pl E16 123 A5
Hull St EC1 235 A1
Hulme Pl SE1 252 B1
Hulse Ave IG11 79 C2
Humber Ct W7 86 B1
Humber Dr W10 90 D3
Humber Rd NW2 68 B6
SE3 142 D6
Humberstone Rd E13 99 C4
Humberton Cl E9 75 A3
Humbolt Rd W6 135 A6 264 A5
Hume Ct N1 72 D1
Hume Ho 14 W11 112 D5
Humes Ave W7 108 D4
Hume Terr E16 99 B1
Hume Way HA4 40 A3
Humphrey Ct SW11 266 D1
Humphrey St SE1 117 D1 263 C2
Humphries Cl RM9 81 B4
Humphry Ho 10 SW15 156 D6
Hundred Acre NW9 27 D1
Hungerdown E4 20 A3
Hungerford Bridge WC2 250 C4
Hungerford Ho SW1 269 B6
Hungerford Inf Sch N7 72 A2
Hungerford Jun & Inf Schs N7 71 D2
Hungerford La WC2 250 B4
Hungerford Prim Sch N7 72 A2
Hungerford Rd N7 72 A3
4 N7 71 D2
Hungerford St 24 E1 96 B1
Hunsdon Cl RM9 81 A2
Hunsdon Ho E5 74 B5
Hunsdon Rd SE14 140 D5

Hunslett St 27 E2 ... 96 C5
Hunstanton Ho NW1 ... 237 B4
Hunston Rd SM4 ... 201 D1
Hunt Ct N14 ... 15 B4
11 Northolt UB5 ... 84 D5
Hunter Cl SE1 ... 262 D5
Borehamwood WD6 ... 11 A6
Upper Tooting SW12 ... 159 A3
Huntercrombe Gdns
WD19 ... 22 C5
Hunter Ct 8 SE5 ... 139 B1
27 Streatham SW2 ... 160 C4
Hunter Ho 1 N19 ... 71 C5
SE1 ... 251 D1
SW5 ... 255 B1
SW8 ... 269 D3
WC1 ... 240 B6
Feltham TW14 ... 150 A3
Hunter Lo 9 W9 ... 91 C2
Hunter Rd
South Norwood CR7 ... 205 B6
Wimbledon SW20 ... 178 C2
Hunters Ct 5 TW9 ... 153 D6
Hunter's Gr BR6 ... 227 A4
Hunters Gr Harrow HA3 ... 43 C5
Hayes UB3 ... 106 A4
Hunters Hall Prim Sch
RM10 ... 81 D3
Hunters Hall Rd RM10 ... 81 C3
Hunters Hill HA4 ... 62 D5
Hunters Lo 10 DA15 ... 168 A1
Hunters Mdw SE19 ... 183 C6
Hunters Rd
Chessington KT9 ... 214 A4
Ilford IG1 ... 78 D3
Hunters Sq RM10 ... 81 C4
Hunter St WC1 ... 94 A3 240 B6
Hunters The 2 BR3 ... 186 A2
Hunters Way Enfield EN2 ... 4 C4
South Croydon CR0 ... 221 C4
Hunter Wlk E13 ... 99 A5
Borehamwood WD6 ... 11 B6
Huntingdon Cl CR4,
SW16 ... 204 A5
Huntingdon Ct SW14 ... 133 A2
Huntingdon Gdns
Chiswick W4 ... 133 A5
North Cheam KT4 ... 216 C5
Huntingdon Ho SW5 ... 255 B4
Huntingdon Rd N2 ... 48 C6
N9 ... 18 C3
Huntingdon St E16 ... 98 D1
N1 ... 72 B1
Huntingfield CR0 ... 223 B1
Huntingfield Rd SW15 ... 156 A6
Huntingford Ho SW15 ... 134 C3
Hunting Gate Cl EN2 ... 4 C2
Hunting Gate Dr KT9 ... 214 A1
Hunting Gate Mews
Sutton SM1 ... 217 D5
Twickenham TW2 ... 152 C3
Huntings Farm IG1 ... 79 C6
Huntings Rd RM10 ... 81 C2
Huntley Ho 7 SE21 ... 183 C6
Huntley St WC1 ... 93 D3 239 C5
Huntley Way SW20 ... 178 A1
Huntly Dr N3 ... 29 C4
Huntly Rd SE25 ... 205 C5
Hunton St E1 ... 96 A2
Hunt Rd UB2 ... 107 C3
Hunts Cl SE3 ... 143 A3
Hunt's Ct WC2 ... 249 D5
Huntshaw Ho 37 E3 ... 97 D4
Hunt's La E15 ... 98 A5
Huntsman Cl TW13 ... 172 B6
Huntsman St SE17 ... 263 A3
Hunts Mead EN3 ... 6 D2
Hunts Mead Cl BR7 ... 188 B3
Huntsmoor Rd KT19 ... 215 B3
Huntspill St SW17 ... 158 A1
Hunts Slip Rd SE21 ... 161 C2
Huntsworth Ct SE6 ... 163 C3
Huntsworth Mews
NW1 ... 92 D3 237 C5
Hurdwick Ho NW1 ... 232 A4
Hurleston Ho 11 SE8 ... 119 B1
Hurley Cres SE16 ... 118 D4
Hurley Ct 1 W5 ... 87 C1
Hurley Ho 34 E2 ... 95 D4
SE11 ... 261 B3
Hurley Lo SE22 ... 162 C5
Hurley Rd UB6 ... 85 D2
Hurlingham Bsns Pk
SW6 ... 135 C2
Hurlingham & Chelsea Sec
Sch SW6 ... 135 C2
Hurlingham Court Mans
SW6 ... 135 C3
Hurlingham Ct SW6 ... 135 B2
Hurlingham Gdns
SW6 ... 135 B2
Hurlingham Rd DA7 ... 147 B5
Fulham SW6 ... 135 B3
Hurlingham Sq SW6 ... 135 D2
Hurlock Ho N5 ... 72 D5
Hurlock St N5 ... 72 D5
Hurlstone Rd SE25 ... 205 C4
Hurn Court Rd TW5 ... 128 D3
Hurn Ct TW5 ... 128 D3
Huron Cl 5 BR6 ... 227 D2
Huron Rd SW17 ... 159 A1
Hurren Cl SE3 ... 142 C2
Hurricane Rd SM6 ... 220 B1
Hurry Cl E15 ... 76 C1
Hursley Ct 11 KT6 ... 197 D2
Hurst Ave N6 ... 49 C3
Chingford E4 ... 19 C1
Hurstbourne KT10 ... 212 D2
Hurstbourne Cotts
DA5 ... 169 D4
Hurstbourne Gdns
IG11 ... 79 C2
Hurstbourne Ho 12
SW15 ... 155 D5
Hurstbourne Priors
CR2 ... 221 C2
Hurstbourne Rd SE23 ... 163 A3
Hurst Cl NW11 ... 47 D3
Chessington KT9 ... 214 C3
Chingford E4 ... 19 C1
Hayes BR2 ... 208 D1
Northolt UB5 ... 63 B3
Hurstcombe IG9 ... 21 A2
Hurstcourt Rd SM1 ... 217 D6
Hurst Ct
Beckenham BR3 ... 185 C3
South Norwood SE25 ... 205 D5
Woodford IG8 ... 37 B4
Hurstdene Ave BR2 ... 208 D1
Hurstdene Gdns N15 ... 51 C2
Hurstfield BR2 ... 209 A4
Hurstfield Cres UB4 ... 83 C2
Hurstfield Rd KT8 ... 195 C6
Hurst Gr KT12 ... 193 D1
Hurst Ho N1 ... 233 D3
SE2 ... 124 D1
7 Penge SE26 ... 184 B5
Hurst La SE2 ... 124 D1
East Molesey KT8 ... 196 A6
Hurst Lo N8 ... 49 D3
Hurstmead Ct HA8 ... 26 D6
Hurstmere Foundation Sch
for Boys DA15 ... 168 C3
Hurst Park Prim Sch
KT8 ... 195 C6
Hurst Pl SE2 ... 146 D6
Hurst Prim Sch DA5 ... 168 D3
Hurst Rd DA5,DA15 ... 168 C3
E17 ... 53 D6
Buckhurst Hill IG9 ... 21 D3
Croydon CR0 ... 221 B3
East Molesey KT8,KT12 ... 195 C6
Southgate N21 ... 16 C3
Walton-on-T KT8&KT12 ... 194 D5
Hurst Rise EN5 ... 1 C2
Hurst Springs DA5 ... 169 A3
Hurst St SE24 ... 160 D5
Hurstview Grange
CR2 ... 220 D1
Hurst View Rd CR2 ... 221 C1
Hurst Way CR2 ... 221 C2
Hurstway Wlk 2 W11 ... 112 D6
Hurstwood Ave DA5 ... 169 A3
Wanstead E18 ... 55 B5
Hurstwood Ct N12 ... 30 C4
NW11 ... 47 B5
Hurstwood Dr BR1 ... 210 B6
Hurstwood Rd NW11 ... 47 B5
Hurtwood Rd KT12 ... 195 B2
Husbourne Ho 8 SE8 ... 119 A2
Huson Cl NW3 ... 70 C1
Hussain Cl HA1 ... 64 D4
Hussars Cl TW4 ... 129 A2
Husseywell Cres BR2 ... 209 A1
Hutching's St E14 ... 119 C4
Hutchings Wlk NW11 ... 47 D5
Hutchins Cl E15 ... 76 A1
Hutchins Ho 8 SW4 ... 159 D4
Hutchinson Ct RM6 ... 58 D5
Hutchinson Ho 9
SE14 ... 140 C5
Hutchinson Terr HA9 ... 65 D5
Hutchins Rd SE28 ... 124 A5
Thamesmead SE28 ... 124 A6
Hutton Cl Greenford UB6 ... 64 B3
Woodford IG8 ... 37 B4
Hutton Ct 3 N4 ... 50 B1
N9 ... 18 C4
1 Ealing W5 ... 87 C2
Hutton Gdns HA3 ... 24 A3
Hutton Gr N12 ... 29 D5
Hutton Ho 22 E2 ... 96 A4
Hutton La HA3 ... 24 A3
Hutton Row 4 HA8 ... 27 A3
Hutton St EC4 ... 241 B1
Hutton Wlk HA3 ... 24 A3
Huxbear St SE4 ... 163 B6
Huxley Cl UB5 ... 85 A6
Huxley Dr RM6 ... 58 B2
Huxley Gdns NW10 ... 88 B5
Huxley Ho NW8 ... 236 D5
SE2 ... 124 D1
4 SW9 ... 138 B3
Huxley Par N18 ... 33 B5
Huxley Pl N13 ... 16 D1
Huxley Rd DA16 ... 145 D2
E10 ... 76 A6
Edmonton N18 ... 33 C6
Huxley Sayze N18 ... 33 B5
Huxley South N18 ... 33 B5
Huxley St W10 ... 91 A4
Hyacinth Cl
3 Hampton TW12 ... 173 C4
Ilford IG1 ... 78 D2
Hyacinth Dr UB10 ... 60 A1
Hyacinth Rd SW15 ... 156 A3
Hyde Cl E13 ... 99 A5
Ashford TW16 ... 171 C4
Barnet EN5 ... 1 B2
Hyde Cres NW9 ... 45 C4
Hyde Ct N20 ... 14 B1
NW9 ... 45 B2
Hounslow TW4 ... 151 B6
Hyde Estate Rd NW9 ... 45 D4
Hyde Farm Mews
SW12 ... 159 D3
Hydefield Cl N21 ... 17 B3
Hydefield Ct N9 ... 17 C2
Hyde Ho TW3 ... 130 A2
Hyde La SW11 ... 136 C4 267 A2
Hyde Park★
W2 ... 114 D5 247 C3
Hyde Park Ave N21 ... 17 B3
Hyde Park Cnr SW1 ... 248 B2
Hyde Park Corner Sta
SW1 ... 115 A4 248 B2
Hyde Park Cres
W2 ... 92 C1 237 A1
Hyde Park Gate Mews
SW7 ... 246 B1
Hyde Park Gdns
W2 ... 114 C6 246 D6
Edmonton N21 ... 17 A3
Hyde Park Gdns Mews
W2 ... 114 C6 247 A6
Hyde Park Mans NW1 ... 237 A3
Hyde Park Pl W2 ... 247 B6
Hyde Park Sq
W2 ... 92 C1 237 A1
Hyde Park Square Mews
W2 ... 237 A1
Hyde Park St
W2 ... 92 C1 237 A1
Hyde Park Twrs W2 ... 246 A5
Hyderabad Way E15 ... 76 C1
Hyde Rd N1 ... 95 C6
Bexley DA7 ... 147 B3
Richmond TW10 ... 154 B6
Hyde Sch The NW9 ... 45 D3
Hydeside Gdns N9 ... 17 D2
Hyde's Pl 12 N1 ... 72 D1
Hyde St SE8 ... 141 C6
Hyde Terr TW15,TW16 ... 171 C4
Hydethorpe Ave N9 ... 17 D2
Hydethorpe Rd SW12 ... 159 C3
Hyde Vale SE10 ... 142 A5
Hyde Way Edmonton N9 ... 17 D2
Hayes UB3 ... 105 D2
Hyde Wlk SM4 ... 201 C2
Hydon Ct N11 ... 30 D5
Hyh Ho E17 ... 35 D2
Hyland House Sch E17 ... 36 B1
Hylands Rd E17 ... 36 B1
Hylda Ct NW5 ... 71 A5
Hyleford Sch IG3 ... 79 C4
Hylton St SE18 ... 123 D2
Hyndewood 14 SE23 ... 162 D1
Hyndman Ho 5 N19 ... 71 D4
5 Dagenham RM10 ... 81 C5
Hyndman St SE15 ... 140 B6
Hynton Rd RM8 ... 80 C6
Hyperion Ho 25 E3 ... 97 A5
Streatham SW2 ... 160 B4
Hyrstdene CR0 ... 220 D4
Hyson Rd SE16 ... 118 B1
Hythe Ave DA7 ... 147 B5
Hythe Cl N18 ... 34 A6
Hythe Ho 7 SE16 ... 118 C4
Hythe Rd NW10 ... 90 A3
South Norwood CR7 ... 183 B1
Hythe Road Ind Est
NW10 ... 90 A3
Hyver Hill NW7 ... 11 B4

I

Ian Ct SE23 ... 162 C2
Ian Hamilton Ho NW1 ... 232 C2
Ian Sq EN3 ... 6 D4
Ibberton Ho SW8 ... 270 C4
W14 ... 254 B6
Ibbotson Ave E16 ... 98 D1
Ibbott St 22 E1 ... 96 C3
Iberia Ho 17 N19 ... 49 D2
Iberian Ave CR0,SM6 ... 220 A4
Ibis Ct 18 SE8 ... 141 B6
Ibis La W4 ... 133 A4
Ibis Way UB4 ... 84 D1
Ibrox Ct 3 IG9 ... 21 C2
Ibsley Gdns SW15 ... 156 A3
Ibsley Way EN4 ... 2 C1
Ibstock Place Sch
SW15 ... 155 C5
Icarus Ho 16 E3 ... 97 B4
Iceland Rd E3 ... 97 C6
Iceland Wharf SE16 ... 119 A2
Ice Wharf NW1 ... 233 B4
Ickburgh Est E5 ... 74 B6
Ickburgh Rd E5 ... 74 B5
Ickburgh Sch E5 ... 74 B5
Ickenham Cl HA4 ... 61 B6
Ickenham Rd HA4 ... 39 B1
Ickenham Sta UB10 ... 61 A4
Ickleton Rd SE9 ... 188 A6
Icknield Dr IG2 ... 56 D4
Ickworth Park Rd E17 ... 53 A5
Icough Ct SE3 ... 143 B5
Ida Rd N15 ... 51 B5
Ida St E14 ... 98 A1
Iden Cl BR2 ... 208 C6
Idlecombe Rd SW17 ... 181 A4
Idmiston Rd E15 ... 76 D3
New Malden KT4 ... 199 D2
West Norwood SE21,
SE27 ... 161 A2
Idmiston Sq KT4 ... 199 D2
Idol La EC3 ... 117 C6 253 A5
Idonia St SE8 ... 141 C5
Iffley Ho 47 E2 ... 95 D4
Iffley Rd W6 ... 112 B3
Ifield Ho SE17 ... 263 B2
Ifield Rd SW10 ... 135 D6 265 D6
Ifor Evans Pl E1 ... 96 D3
Ightham Ho SE17 ... 263 A3
Beckenham BR3 ... 185 B3
Ightham Rd DA8 ... 147 C5
Ilbert St W10 ... 91 A4
Ilchester Gdns W2 ... 245 C6
Ilchester Mans W8 ... 255 A6
Ilchester Pl
W14 ... 113 B3 254 D6
Ilchester Rd RM8 ... 80 C3
Ildersly Gr SE21 ... 161 B2
Ilderton Prim Sch
SE16 ... 118 C1
Ilderton Rd SE15,SE16 ... 140 C6
Ilex Cl TW16 ... 172 C1
Ilex Rd NW10 ... 67 D2
Ilex Way SW16 ... 182 C5
Ilford Hill IG1 ... 78 C5
Ilford Ho 14 N1 ... 73 B2
Ilford Interchange IG1 ... 78 C5
Ilford Jewish Prim Sch
IG6 ... 57 B6
Ilford La IG1 ... 78 D4
Ilford Prep Sch IG3 ... 58 A1
Ilford Ret Pk IG1 ... 79 A6
Ilford Sta IG1 ... 78 D6
Ilford Ursuline High Sch
IG1 ... 78 D6
Ilfracombe Gdns RM6 ... 58 B2
Ilfracombe Rd BR1 ... 164 D1
Iliffe St SE17 ... 116 D1 261 D2
Iliffe Yd SE17 ... 116 D1 261 D2
Ilkeston Ct 7 E5 ... 74 D4
Ilkley Cl SE19 ... 183 B4
Ilkley Ct N11 ... 31 A4
Ilkley Rd Newham E16 ... 99 C2
South Oxhey WD19 ... 22 D5
Illingworth Cl CR4 ... 202 B6
Illingworth Way EN1 ... 17 C6
Ilmington Rd HA3 ... 43 D3
Ilminster Gdns SW11 ... 136 C1
Ilsley Ct 8 SW8 ... 137 C3
Imber Cl N14 ... 15 C4
Thames Ditton KT7 ... 196 B1
Imber Court Trad Est
KT8 ... 196 B3
Imber Cross KT7 ... 196 D3
Imber Ct 4 SE9 ... 166 C5
Imber Gr KT10 ... 196 B2
Imber Park Rd KT10 ... 196 B1
Imber St N1 ... 235 C5
Immanuel Coll WD23 ... 8 C4
Immanuel & St Andrew CE
Prim Sch SW16 ... 182 A4
Impact Ct SE20 ... 184 B1
Imperial Ave 5 N16 ... 73 C4
Imperial Cl HA2 ... 41 C3
Imperial College Rd
SW7 ... 114 B3 256 C6
Imperial Coll of Science,
Technology & Medicine
SW7 ... 114 B3 256 C6
Imperial Ct N20 ... 14 A1
NW8 ... 230 B4
Wembley HA9 ... 66 C5
Harrow HA2 ... 41 C2
Imperial Dr HA2 ... 41 C3
Imperial Gdns CR4 ... 203 B6
Imperial Ho 2 E14 ... 119 B6
E3 ... 97 A4
Imperial Mews 5 E6 ... 99 D5
Imperial Pl BR7 ... 188 C2
Imperial Rd SW6 ... 265 D1
East Bedfont TW14 ... 149 C4
Wood Green N22 ... 32 A2
Imperial Sq SW6 ... 265 D2
Imperial St E3 ... 98 A4
Imperial Twrs 3 NW3 ... 70 A2
Imperial War Mus★
SE1,SE11 ... 116 C3 261 B5
Imperial Way BR7,SE9 ... 167 A1
Croydon CR0,CR9 ... 220 C2
Harrow HA3 ... 44 A3
Impington 19 KT1 ... 176 C1
Imre Cl W12 ... 112 B5
Inca Dr SE9 ... 166 D4
Inchmery Rd SE6 ... 164 A3
Inchwood BR4,CR0 ... 223 D4
Independant Jewish Day
Sch NW4 ... 46 D4
Independant Pl E8 ... 73 D3
Independents Rd SE3 ... 142 D2
Inderwick Rd N8 ... 50 B4
Indescon Ct E14 ... 119 D4
India St EC3 ... 243 C1
India Way W12 ... 112 B6
Indigo Mews N16 ... 73 B5
Indus Ct 15 SE15 ... 139 D5
Indus Rd SE7 ... 143 C5
Ingal Rd E13 ... 99 A3
Ingate Pl SW8 ... 137 B4 268 D1
Ingatestone Rd
Croydon SE25 ... 206 B5
Wanstead E12 ... 55 C1
Woodford IG8 ... 37 B3
Ingelow Ho W8 ... 245 C2
Ingelow St SW8 ... 137 B3
Ingersoll Rd W12 ... 112 B5
Enfield EN3 ... 6 C5
Ingestre Pl W1 ... 239 B1
Ingestre Rd E7 ... 77 A4
NW5 ... 71 B4
Ingham Rd NW6 ... 69 C4
Inglebert St
EC1 ... 94 C4 234 A2
Ingleborough Ct N17 ... 51 D6
Ingleborough St SW9 ... 138 C3
Ingleby Dr HA1 ... 64 B5
Ingleby Rd N7 ... 72 A5
Dagenham RM10 ... 81 D2
Ilford IG1 ... 56 D1
Ingleby Way BR7 ... 188 C5
Wallington SM6 ... 219 D1
Ingle Cl HA5 ... 41 B6
Ingledew Rd SE18 ... 123 B1
Inglefield Sq 12 E1 ... 118 B5
Ingle Ho 3 SW12 ... 159 D3
Inglehurst Gdns IG4 ... 56 B4
Inglemere Ct CR4,
SW17 ... 180 D3
Inglemere Rd
Forest Hill SE23 ... 162 D1
Mitcham CR4,SW17 ... 180 D3
Ingleshaw Wlk E9 ... 75 B2
Ingleside Cl BR3 ... 185 C3
Ingleside Gr SE3 ... 142 D6
Inglethorpe Ho 6 E5 ... 74 A6
Inglethorpe St SW6 ... 134 D4
Ingleton Ave DA16 ... 168 A6
Ingleton Rd N18 ... 34 A4
Ingleton St SW9 ... 138 C3
Ingle Way N12 ... 30 C4
Inglewood BR7 ... 189 B4
Inglewood Cl E14 ... 119 C2
Inglewood Copse BR1 ... 188 B1
Inglewood Ct 3 BR1 ... 186 D3
Inglewood Mans 11
NW6 ... 69 C3
Inglewood Rd NW6 ... 69 C3
Inglis Ct W5 ... 110 B6
Inglis Ho 1 SW15 ... 156 C6
Inglis Rd Croydon CR0 ... 205 D1
Ealing W5 ... 110 B6
Inglis St SE5 ... 138 D4
Ingram Ave NW11 ... 48 A2
Ingram Cl SE11 ... 260 D4
Stanmore HA7 ... 25 C5
Ingram Ct EN1 ... 17 D5
Ingram Ho E3 ... 97 A6
7 Harrow HA1 ... 42 D4
Teddington KT8 ... 175 C2
Ingram Lo 8 SW4 ... 159 D5
Ingram Rd N2 ... 48 C5
South Norwood CR7 ... 183 A2
Ingram Way UB6 ... 86 B6
Ingrave Ho RM9 ... 102 B6
Ingrave St SW11 ... 136 C2
Ingrebourne Ct E4 ... 19 D2
Ingrebourne Ho NW8 ... 236 D4
2 Catford BR1 ... 186 B5
Ingress St 4 W4 ... 111 C1
Inigo Jones Rd SE7 ... 144 A5
Inigo Pl WC2 ... 250 A6
Inkerman Rd NW5 ... 71 B2
Inkerman Terr W8 ... 255 B5
Inks Gn E4 ... 36 A5
Inkster Ho 8 SW11 ... 136 C2
Inkwell Cl N12 ... 14 A1
Inman Rd NW10 ... 89 C6
Wandsworth SW18 ... 158 A4
Inmans Row IG8 ... 37 A6
Inner Circ NW1 ... 93 A4 231 A2
Inner Park Rd SW19 ... 156 D2
Inner Ring E TW6 ... 126 D2
Inner Ring W TW6 ... 126 C2
Inner Temple★ EC4 ... 251 A6
Inner Temple La EC4 ... 241 A1
Innes Cl SW20 ... 179 A1
Innes Gdns SW15 ... 156 B5
Innes Lo SE23 ... 162 D1
Innes Yd CR0 ... 221 A5
Innis Ho SE17 ... 263 A2
Inniskilling Rd E13 ... 99 C5
Innovation Cl HA0 ... 88 A6
Inskip Cl E10 ... 75 D6
Inskip Rd RM8 ... 58 D1
Insley Ho 18 E3 ... 97 D4
Inst for Child Health
WC1 ... 94 B3 240 C5
Institute Pl E8 ... 74 B3
Instituto Espanol Vicente
Canada Blanch W10 ... 91 A2
Inst of Ophthalmology
EC1 ... 235 D2
Integer Gdns E11 ... 54 B2
Interchange The NW5 ... 71 B3
International Ave
TW5 ... 106 C1
International Sch of London
W3 ... 110 C2
International Trad Est
UB2 ... 106 B3
Inveagh Cl E9 ... 96 D6
Inverary Pl SE18 ... 145 B6
Inver Cl E5 ... 74 C6
Inverclyde Gdns RM6 ... 58 D5
Inver Ct W2 ... 91 D1
Inveresk Gdns KT4 ... 216 A5
Inverforth Cl NW3 ... 70 A6
Inverforth Ho NW3 ... 70 A6
Inverforth Rd N11 ... 31 B5
Invergarry Ho NW6 ... 91 D5
Inverine Rd SE7 ... 121 B1
Invermore Pl SE18 ... 123 A2
Inverness Ave EN1 ... 5 C4
Inverness Ct
8 Acton W3 ... 88 C1
10 Catford SE6 ... 164 D3
Inverness Gdns W8 ... 245 C3
Inverness Mews E16 ... 122 D5
W2 ... 245 D6
North Woolwich E16 ... 123 A5
Inverness Pl W2 ... 245 D6
Inverness Rd
Edmonton N18 ... 34 B5
Hounslow TW3 ... 129 C1
North Cheam KT4 ... 200 D1
Southall UB2 ... 107 A2
Inverness St NW1 ... 231 D6
Inverness Terr
W2 ... 113 D6 245 D6
Inverton Rd SE15 ... 140 D1
Invicta Cl BR7 ... 188 C5
18 E3 ... 97 C2
East Bedfont TW14 ... 149 D3
Invicta Ct KT9 ... 214 B3
Invicta Ctr The IG11 ... 102 A6
Invicta Gr UB5 ... 85 B4
Invicta Plaza SE1 ... 251 C4
Invicta Prim Sch SE3 ... 143 A5
Invicta Rd SE3,SE7 ... 143 A6
Inville Rd SE17 ... 117 B1 262 D1
Inwen Ct SE8 ... 119 A1
Inwood Ave TW3 ... 130 A2
Inwood Bsns Pk TW3 ... 129 D1
Inwood Cl CR0 ... 223 A6
Inwood Ct 10 NW1 ... 71 C1
Inwood Ho 19 SE22 ... 139 C2
Inwood Rd TW3 ... 130 A1
Inworth St SW11 ... 136 C3
Inworth Wlk N1 ... 235 A6
Iona Cl Catford SE6 ... 163 C4
Morden SM4 ... 201 D2
Ion Ct 8 E2 ... 96 A5
Ionian Bldg 19 E14 ... 119 A6
Ionian Ho 22 E1 ... 96 D3
Ipsden Bldgs SE1 ... 251 B2
Ipswich Ho SE4 ... 162 D6
Ipswich Rd SW17 ... 181 A4
Irby Ho SW2 ... 160 C5
Ireland Cl E6 ... 100 B2
Ireland Pl N22 ... 32 A3
Ireland Yd EC4 ... 241 D1
Irene Rd BR6 ... 211 D2
SW6 ... 135 C4 265 B1
Ireton Cl N10 ... 31 A3
Ireton Ho SW9 ... 138 C3
Ireton St 12 E3 ... 97 C3
Iris Ave DA5 ... 169 A5
Iris Cl Croydon CR0 ... 206 D1
Newham E6 ... 100 A3
Surbiton KT6 ... 198 B2
Iris Cres DA7 ... 147 B6
Iris Rd KT19 ... 214 D3
Iris Way E4 ... 35 B4
Iris Wlk 1 HA8 ... 27 A6
Irkdale Ave EN1 ... 5 D4
Iroko Ho 7 NW3 ... 69 D2
Iron Bridge Cl NW10 ... 67 C3
Southall UB2 ... 108 A5
Iron Bridge Ho NW3 ... 70 D1
Iron Bridge Rd N
UB11 ... 104 C5
Iron Bridge Rd S UB7 ... 104 C4
Iron Mill Pl SW18 ... 157 D5
Iron Mill Rd SW18 ... 157 D5
Ironmonger La
EC2 ... 95 B1 242 C1

Ironmonger Pas EC1 ..235 B1
Ironmonger Row
EC1 ..95 A4 235 B1
Ironmonger's Pl 13
E14 ..119 C2
Ironside Cl SE16 ..118 D4
Ironside Ho E9 ..75 A4
Irvine Ave HA3 ..43 B6
Irvine Cl N20 ..14 C2
Irvine Ct W1 ..239 B5
Thornton Heath CR7 ..204 C3
Irvine Ho 2 E14 ..97 D2
N7 ..72 B2
Irvine Way BR6 ..211 D2
Irving Ave UB5 ..84 D6
Irving Ct N22 ..32 D2
Irving Gr SW9 ..138 B3
Irving Ho SE17 ..261 C1
Irving Mews N1 ..73 A2
Irving Rd W14 ..112 D3
Irving St WC2 ..249 D5
Irwell Ct W7 ..86 B1
Irwell Est 25 SE16 ..118 C4
Irwin Ave SE18 ..145 C5
Irwin Cl UB10 ..60 C5
Irwin Gdns NW10 ..90 B6
Isabel Hill Cl TW12 ..173 C2
Isabella Cl N14 ..15 C4
Isabella Ct 8 TW10 ..154 B5
Isabella Dr BR6 ..227 A4
Isabella Ho SE11 ..261 C2
10 W6 ..112 C1
Isabella Rd E9 ..74 C3
Isabella St SE1 ..251 C3
Isabel St SW9 ..270 D2
Isambard Mews E14 ..120 A3
Isambard Pl SE16 ..118 C5
Iseldon Ct N7 ..72 A4
Isel Way 4 SE22 ..161 C6
Isham Rd SW16 ..182 A1
Isis Cl Putney SW15 ..134 C1
Ruislip HA4 ..39 A3
Isis Ct W4 ..132 D5
Isis Ho NW8 ..236 D5
2 Edmonton N18 ..33 D4
Isis St SW18 ..158 A2
Islamia Girls' High Sch
NW6 ..91 A6
Islamia Prim Sch NW6 ..91 A6
Islamic Coll for Advanced
Studies NW10 ..68 B2
Island Centre Way EN3 ..7 C6
Island Farm Ave KT8 ..195 B4
Island Farm Rd KT8 ..195 C4
Island Gardens Sta
E14 ..120 A1
Island Ho SW19 ..202 A5
Island Rd CR4 ..180 D3
Island Row E14 ..97 B1
Isla Rd SE18 ..145 A6
Islay Gdns TW4 ..150 D6
Isleden Ho N1 ..235 A6
Isledon Rd N4,N7 ..72 C5
Islehurst Cl BR7 ..188 C2
Isleworth Bsns Complex
TW7 ..130 D3
Isleworth Sta TW7 ..130 D3
Isleworth & Syon Sch for
Boys TW7 ..130 C5
Isleworth Town Sch
TW7 ..131 A3
Islington Est N1 95 A6 235 A6
Islington Gn N1 94 D6 234 C5
Islington Green Sch
N1 ..95 A6 235 A5
Islington High St
N1 ..94 D5 234 C4
Islington Park Mews 1
N1 ..72 D1
Islington Park St N1 ..72 D1
Islington Sixth Form Ctr
N7 ..72 C4
Islip Gdns HA8 ..27 B3
Northolt UB5 ..63 A1
Islip Manor Rd UB5 ..63 A1
Islip St NW5 ..71 C3
Ismailia Rd E7 ..77 B1
Isobel Ho
10 Ashford TW16 ..171 D3
Harrow HA1 ..42 D4
Isokon Flats 3 NW3 ..70 D3
Isom Cl E13 ..99 B4
Ivanhoe Dr HA3 ..25 B1
Ivanhoe Ho 32 E3 ..97 A5
11 Balham SW12 ..159 B4
Ivanhoe Rd SE5 ..139 D2
Hounslow TW4 ..128 D2
Ivatt Pl W14 ..113 B1 254 D1
Ivatt Way N17 ..50 D6
Iveagh Ave NW10 ..88 C5
Iveagh Cl NW10 ..88 C5
Iveagh Ct EC3 ..243 C1
4 Beckenham BR3 ..207 D6
Iveagh Ho SW10 ..266 B4
2 SW9 ..138 D3
Ivebury Ct W10 ..90 C1
Ivedon Rd DA16 ..146 C3
Ive Farm Cl E10 ..75 C6
Ive Farm La E10 ..75 C6
Iveley Rd SW4 ..137 C3
Iver Ct N1 ..73 A2
Ivere Dr EN5 ..13 D5
Iverhurst Cl DA6 ..168 D6
Iverna Ct W8 ..255 B6
Iverna Gdns
W8 ..113 C3 255 B6
Hatton TW14 ..149 B6
Iverson Rd NW6 ..69 C2
Ivers Way CR0 ..223 D1
Ives Rd E16 ..98 C2
Ives St SW3 ..114 C2 257 B4
Ivestor Terr SE23 ..162 C4
Ivimey St E2 ..96 A4
Ivinghoe Cl EN1 ..5 C4
Ivinghoe Ho 14 N7 ..71 D3
Ivinghoe Rd
Barking RM8 ..80 B3
Bushey WD23 ..8 B4
Ivor Ct N8 ..50 A3
NW1 ..237 C6
Ivor Gr SE9 ..166 D3
Ivories The N1 ..73 A1
Ivor Pl NW1 ..92 D3 237 C5
Ivor St NW1 ..71 C1
Ivory Ct TW13 ..150 A3
Ivorydown BR1 ..187 A6
Ivory Ho E1 ..253 D4
9 SW11 ..136 A2
Ivybridge Cl
2 Twickenham TW1 ..153 A4
Uxbridge UB8 ..82 A4
Ivybridge Ct 1 BR7 ..188 C2
Ivybridge Ho 18 SE22 ..139 C2
Ivybridge La WC2 ..250 B5
Ivybridge Prim Sch
TW1 ..152 D5
Ivybridge Ret Pk TW7 152 D6
Ivychurch Cl SE20 ..184 C3
Ivy Church La SE1,
SE17 ..263 C2
Ivy Cl Harrow HA2 ..63 B4
Pinner HA5 ..40 C2
Sunbury TW16 ..172 C1
Ivy Cotts UB10 ..61 A2
Ivy Cres W4 ..111 A2
Ivy Ct SE13 ..163 C6
18 SE16 ..118 A1
SE3 ..142 D1
Ivydale Prim Sch
SE15 ..140 D1
Ivydale Rd SE15 ..140 D1
Carshalton SM5 ..218 D6
Ivyday Gr SW16 ..160 B1
Ivydene KT12,KT8 ..195 B4
Ivydene Cl SM1 ..218 A4
Ivy Gdns N8 ..50 A3
Mitcham CR4 ..203 D6
Ivy Ho 6 E5 ..52 B1
Croydon CR0 ..206 D1
Ivyhouse Rd
Dagenham RM9 ..81 A2
Uxbridge UB10 ..60 D5
Ivy La TW4 ..129 B1
Ivy Lo W8 ..245 A4
Ivymount Rd SE27 ..160 C1
Ivy Rd E16 ..99 A1
E17 ..53 C3
N14 ..15 D4
NW2 ..68 C4
SE4 ..141 C1
Hounslow TW3 ..129 D1
Tolworth KT6 ..198 C1
Upper Tooting SW17 ..180 C5
Ivy St N1 ..95 C5
Ivy Terr 3 IG2 ..57 A3
Ivy Wlk RM9 ..81 A2
Ixworth Pl
SW3 ..114 C2 257 A3
Izane Rd DA6 ..147 B1

J

Jacaranda Cl KT3 ..199 C6
Jacaranda Gr E8 ..73 D1
Jack Ashley Ct 5 NW9 27 C2
Jackass La BR2 ..225 C2
Jack Barnett Way N22 ..32 B1
Jack Clow Rd E15 ..98 C5
Jack Cook Ho 9 IG11 ..78 D1
Jack Cornwell St E12 ..78 C4
Jack Goodchild Way
KT3 ..198 D6
Jacklin Gn IG8 ..37 A6
Jackman Ho 24 E1 ..118 B5
Jackman Mews NW2 ..67 C5
Jackman St E8 ..96 B6
Jackson Cl E9 ..74 D1
Uxbridge UB10 ..60 A1
Jackson Ct E7 ..77 B2
Wanstead E11 ..55 B1
Jackson Ho 16 SW11 ..136 B2
Jackson Rd BR2 ..226 B6
N7 ..72 B4
Barking IG11 ..101 B6
East Barnet EN4 ..14 C5
Uxbridge UB10 ..60 A1
Jackson's La N6 ..49 B2
Jackson's Pl CR0 ..205 C1
Jackson St SE18 ..144 C6
Jackson's Way CR0 ..223 C5
Jackson Way UB2 ..107 D4
Jack Taylor Sch
NW8 ..92 A6 229 A6
Jack Tizard Sch SW6 ..134 D4
Jack Walker Ct N5 ..72 D4
Jacob Ho 5 DA18 ..124 D4
Jacobin Lo N7 ..72 A3
Jacob Mans 1 E1 ..96 B1
Jacobs Cl RM10 ..81 D4
Jacobs Ho E13 ..99 C4
Jacobson Ct SW11 ..267 B1
Jacobson Ho E1 ..243 C2
Jacob St SE1 ..118 A4
Jacob's Well Mews
W1 ..238 B2
Jacotts Ho W10 ..90 C3
Jacqueline Cl UB5 ..85 A6
Jade Cl E16 ..99 D1
NW2 ..46 D2
Dagenham RM8 ..58 C1
Jaffe Rd IG1 ..57 B1
Jaffray Rd BR2 ..209 D5
Jaggard Way SW12 ..158 D4
Jagger Ho SW11 ..267 C2
Jago Cl SE18 ..145 A6
Jago Wlk 22 SE5 ..139 B5
Jamahiriya Sch
SW3 ..136 C6 267 A6
Jamaica Rd SE1 ..253 D1
SE16 ..118 B3
Thornton Heath CR7 ..204 D3
Jamaica St E1 ..96 C2
James Allen's Girls' Sch
SE22 ..161 C6
James Anderson Ct 29
E2 ..95 C5
James Ave NW2 ..68 C3
Dagenham RM8 ..59 B1
James Bedford Cl HA5 ..22 C1
James Boswell Cl 1
SW16 ..182 C6
James Brine Ho 6 E2 ..95 D4
James Campbell Ho 2
E2 ..96 C5
James Cl 8 E13 ..99 A5
NW11 ..47 A3
James Collins Cl W9 ..91 B3
James Ct N12 ..30 C3
NW9 ..27 C1
4 Chingford E4 ..20 B2
Northolt UB5 ..85 A5
3 Woodford E18 ..37 B1
James Dixon Prim Sch
SE20 ..184 B3
James Docherty Ho 4
E2 ..96 C5
James Dudson Ct
NW10 ..67 A1
James Est CR4 ..180 D1
James Gdns N22 ..32 D3
James Hammett Ho 9
E2 ..95 D5
James Ho E1 ..97 A3
33 SE16 ..118 D4
James Joyes Wlk 7
SE24 ..138 D1
James La E10,E11 ..54 B3
James Lee Sq EN3 ..7 C5
James Leicester Hall of
Residence N7 ..72 A2
James Lind Ho 5 SE8 119 B2
James Middleton Ho 20
E2 ..96 B4
James Newman Ct
SE9 ..166 C1
Jameson Ct 6 E2 ..96 C5
Jameson Ho SE11 ..260 C2
Jameson Lo N6 ..49 C3
Jameson Pl 11 W3 ..111 A4
Jameson St W8 ..245 B4
James Pl N17 ..33 D2
James St W1 ..93 A1 238 B1
WC2 ..116 A6 250 B6
Barking IG11 ..79 A1
Enfield EN1 ..17 D6
Hounslow TW3 ..130 B2
James Stewart Ho NW6 69 B1
James Stroud Ho
SE17 ..262 B1
Jamestown Rd
NW1 ..93 B6 231 C6
Jamestown Way E14 ..120 B6
James Wolfe Prim Sch
SE10 ..142 A5
Jamieson Ho TW4 ..151 B5
Jamuna Cl E14 ..97 A2
Jane Sabina Colard's
Almshouses 1 E17 ..54 A4
Jane St E1 ..96 B1
Janet Ct 4 DA7 ..147 C1
Janet St E14 ..119 C3
Janeway Pl 2 SE16 ..118 B4
Janeway St SE16 ..118 A4
Janice Mews 3 IG1 ..78 D5
Jansen Wlk SW11 ..136 B1
Janson Cl E15 ..76 C3
Janson Cl *continued*
NW10 ..67 C5
Janson Rd E15 ..76 C3
Jansons Rd N15 ..51 C6
Japan Cres N4 ..50 B1
Japanese Sch The
W3 ..110 C6
Japan Rd RM6 ..58 D3
Jaquets Ct DA5 ..169 C2
Jardine Rd E1 ..118 D6
Jarman Ho 13 E1 ..96 C2
SE16 ..118 D2
Jarret Ho 1 E3 ..97 C4
Jarrett Cl SW2 ..160 D3
Jarrow Cl SM4 ..201 D4
Jarrow Rd N17 ..52 B5
SE16 ..118 C1
Dagenham RM6 ..58 C3
Jarrow Way E9 ..75 A4
Jarvis Cl
1 Barking IG11 ..101 B6
Barnet EN5 ..12 D6
Jarvis Ct 2 SE10 ..142 A4
Jarvis Ho 3 SE15 ..140 A4
Jarvis Rd SE22 ..139 C1
South Croydon CR2 ..221 B2
Jashada Ho SE18 ..122 C1
Jasmin SE1 ..253 D3
Jasmine Cl Ilford IG1 ..78 D3
Orpington BR6 ..226 D6
Southall UB1 ..107 A6
Jasmine Ct SE12 ..165 A5
11 Wallington SM6 ..219 B2
Jasmine Gdns
Harrow HA2 ..63 C6
West Wickham CR0 ..223 D5
Jasmine Gr SE20 ..184 B2
Jasmine Rd KT19 ..214 D3
Jasmine Terr UB7 ..104 C4
Jasmine Way KT7 ..196 C5
Jasmin Ho SE4 ..141 B2
Jasmin Lo 17 SE16 ..118 B1
Jason Ct 2 SW9 ..138 C4
W1 ..238 B2
Jason Ho UB5 ..84 B4
Jason Wlk SE9 ..188 C6
Jasper Cl EN3 ..6 C5
Jasper Ho KT4 ..199 B1
Jasper Rd E16 ..99 D1
Penge SE19 ..183 D4
Jasper Wlk N1 ..235 C2
Java Wharf SE1 ..253 D2
Javelin Way UB5 ..84 D4
Jawahar Bagh SW16 ..182 D4
Jaycroft EN2 ..4 C4
Jay Gdns BR7 ..188 B6
Jay Ho SW15 ..134 C3
Jay Mews SW7 114 A4 246 B1
Jayson Ct 7 CR0 ..206 A1
Jean Batten Cl SM6 ..220 B1
Jean Darling Ho
SW10 ..266 C5
Jean Ho 3 SW17 ..180 C5
Jean Humbert Ho 2
SE27 ..183 B6
Jean Pardies Ho 21 E1 ..96 C2
Jebb Ave SW2 ..160 A5
Jebb St E3 ..97 C5
Jedburgh Rd E13 ..99 C4
Jedburgh St SW11 ..137 A1
Jeddo Mews W12 ..111 D4
Jeddo Rd W12 ..111 D4
Jefferies Ho 12 NW10 ..67 B1
Jefferson Bldg 3 E14 119 C4
Jefferson Cl W13 ..109 B3
Ilford IG2 ..56 D4
Jefferson Wlk 13 SE18 144 C6
Jeffrey Row SE12 ..165 B6
Jeffrey's Ct 2 SW4 ..138 A3
Jeffrey's Pl NW1 ..71 C1
Jeffrey's Rd SW4 ..138 A3
Jeffreys Rd EN3 ..7 B1
Jeffrey's St NW1 ..71 C1
Jeffs Cl TW12 ..173 D4
Jeffs Rd SM1 ..217 B4
Jefton Ct SM6 ..219 C3
Jeger Ave E2 ..95 D6
Jeken Rd SE9 ..143 C1
Jelf Rd SW2 ..160 C6
Jellicoe Ct E4 ..36 B4
Jellicoe Gdns HA7 ..25 A4
Jellicoe Ho 5 E2 ..96 A5
11 Putney SW15 ..156 D6
Jellicoe Rd 4 E13 ..99 A3
Tottenham N17 ..33 B3
Jemmett Cl KT2 ..176 D2
Jemotts Ct 9 SE14 ..140 D6
Jem Paterson Ct HA1 ..64 C4
Jengar Cl SM1 ..217 D4
Jenkins Ho SW8 ..269 C2
Jenkins La IG11 ..101 A4
Jenkinson Ho 12 E2 ..96 D4
Jenkins Rd E13 ..99 B3
Jenner Ave W3 ..89 B2
Jenner Ct N21 ..16 A6
Jenner Ho SE3 ..142 C6
5 Belvedere DA17 ..125 C3
Jenner Pl SW13 ..134 B6
Jenner Rd N16 ..73 D5
Jennett Rd CR0 ..220 C5
Jennifer Ho SE11 ..261 B3
Jennifer Rd BR1 ..164 D1
Jennings Cl KT6 ..197 C2
Jennings Ho SE10 ..120 B1
Jennings Rd SE22 ..161 D5
Jenny Hammond Cl
E11 ..76 D5
Jenny Hammond Sch
E11 ..76 C4
Jensen Ho 10 E3 ..97 C3
Jenson Way SE19 ..183 D3
Jenton Ave DA7 ..147 A3
Jephson Ct 17 SW4 ..138 A3
Jephson Ho 6 SE17 ..138 D6
Jephson Rd E7 ..77 C1
Jephson St SE5 ..139 B4
Jephtha Rd SW18 ..157 C5
Jeppo's La CR4 ..202 D5
Jerdan Pl SW6 ..265 A4
Jeremiah St 11 E14 ..97 D1
Jeremy Bentham Ho 9
E2 ..96 A4
Jeremy's Gn N18 ..34 C6
Jermyn St
SW1 ..115 C5 249 B4
Jerningham Ct SE14 ..141 A4
Jerningham Rd SE14 ..141 A4
Jerome Cres
NW8 ..92 C3 237 A6
Jerome Ct 2 N11 ..31 C5
Jerome Ho NW1 ..237 B4
Kingston KT1 ..175 D1
Jerome Pl KT1 ..175 D1
Jerome St E1 ..95 D3 243 C5
Jerome Twr 5 W3 ..110 D4
Jerrard St SE13 ..141 D2
Jerrold Lo SW15 ..134 C2
Jerrold St 24 N1 ..95 C5
Jersey Ave HA7 ..25 C1
Jersey Ct UB2 ..107 B3
Jersey Dr BR5 ..211 B3
Jersey Ho 12 N1 ..73 A2
Enfield EN3 ..6 D5
Jersey Rd E11 ..54 B1
N1 ..73 A2
W7 ..109 A4
Hounslow TW5,TW7 ..130 B5
Ilford IG1 ..78 D4
Mitcham SW17 ..181 B4
Newham E16 ..99 C1
Jersey St E2 ..96 B4
Jerusalem Pas EC1 ..241 C5
Jervis Bay Ho 8 E14 ..98 B1
Jervis Ct W1 ..238 D1
9 Dagenham RM10 ..81 D2
Jerviston Gdns SW16 ..182 C4
Jesmond Ave HA9 ..66 B2
Jesmond Cl CR4 ..203 B6
Jesmond Rd CR0 ..205 D2
Jesmond Way HA7 ..26 A5
Jessam Ave E5 ..52 B1
Jessamine Rd W7 ..108 D5
Jessel Ho SW1 ..259 D4
WC1 ..233 A1
Jesse Rd E10 ..54 A1
Jessica Rd SW18 ..158 A6
Jessie Blythe La 2
N19 ..50 A2
Jessie Duffett Ho 11
SE5 ..139 A5
Jessie's Cotts E17 ..53 A3
Jessiman Terr TW17 ..192 C4
Jesson Ho SE17 ..262 C3
Jessop Ave UB2 ..107 B2
Jessop Ct N1 ..234 D3
Jessop Prim Sch SE24 139 A1
Jessop Sq E14 ..119 C5
Jessops Way CR0 ..203 C3
Jessup Cl SE18 ..123 A2
Jeston Ho 10 SE27 ..160 D1
Jethou Ho 13 N1 ..73 A2
Jetstar Way UB5 ..85 A4
Jevington Way SE12 ..165 B3
Jevons Ho 9 NW8 ..70 B1
Jewell Ho 3 SW12 ..159 C4
Jewel Rd E17 ..53 C6
Jewish Prep Sch The
NW6 ..91 D5
Jewry St EC3 ..95 D1 243 C1
Jews Coll NW4 ..46 D5
Jews Free Sch NW1 ..71 D2
Jews Row SW18 ..136 A1
Jews Wlk SE26 ..184 B6
Jeymer Ave NW2 ..68 C3
Jeymer Dr UB6 ..86 A6
Jeypore Rd SW18 ..158 A5
JFS Sch NW9 ..44 C3
Jillian Cl TW12 ..173 C3
Jim Bradley Cl 16
SE18 ..122 C2
Jim Griffiths Ho SW6 ..264 D5
Joan Cres SE9 ..165 D4
Joan Gdns RM8 ..81 A6
Joanna Ho 7 W6 ..112 C1
Joan Player Ho EN3 ..6 D6
Joan Rd RM8 ..81 A6
Joan St SE1 ..116 D5 251 C3
Jocelin Ho N1 ..233 D5
Jocelyn Rd TW9 ..132 A2
Jocelyn St SE15 ..140 A4
Jockey's Fields
WC1 ..94 B2 240 D4
Jodane Rd SE8 ..119 B2
Jodrell Cl TW7 ..131 A4
Jodrell Rd E3 ..75 B1
Joe Hunte Ct 2 SW27 182 D5
Joel St HA5,HA6 ..40 A5
Johanna Prim Sch
SE1 ..116 C4 251 A1
Johanna St SE1 ..251 A1
John Adam St
WC2 ..116 A6 250 B5
John Aird Ct
W2 ..92 A2 236 B4
John Archer Way
SW18 ..158 B5
John Ashby Cl SW2 ..160 A5
John Austin Cl KT2 ..176 B2
John Baird Ct SE26 ..184 D6
John Baird Ho 14
SE20 ..184 C3
John Ball Prim Sch
SE3 ..142 C3
John Barker Ct NW6 ..69 A1
John Barker Ho IG1 ..79 B6
John Barnes Wlk E15 ..76 D2
John Barter Ho TW3 ..129 B3
John Betts' Ho W12 ..112 A3
John Betts Prim Sch
W6 ..112 B3
John Bond Ho 2 E3 ..97 B5
John Bradshaw Rd N14 15 D3
John Brent Ho 8 SE8 118 D2
John Buck Ho NW10 ..89 D6
John Burns Dr IG11 ..79 C1
John Burns Prim Sch
SW11 ..137 A3
John Busch Sch TW7 ..131 B4
Johnby Cl EN3 ..7 A6
John Campbell Rd 26
N16 ..73 C3
John Carpenter St
EC4 ..251 C6
John Cartwright Ho 7
E2 ..96 B4
John Chilton Sch UB5 ..63 A1
John Clifford Ho N8 ..50 A3
John Conwey Ho 23
SW2 ..160 C5
John Cornwell VC Ho 5
E12 ..78 C4
John Dee Ho 3 SW14 133 B2
John Donne Prim Sch
SE15 ..140 B4
John Drinkwater Cl
E11 ..54 D2
John Dwight Ho SW6 ..135 D2
John Felton Rd 16
SE16 ..118 A4
John Fielden Ho 10 E2 ..96 B4
John Fisher St E1 ..118 A6
John F. Kennedy Specl Sch
E15 ..98 B6
John Glynes Ct SW15 ..134 B1
John Gooch Dr EN2 ..4 D4
John Harris Ho SE15 ..140 A2
John Harrison Way
SE10 ..120 D3
John Hunt Ct 5 SE9 ..166 A2
John Islip St
SW1 ..116 A2 260 A3
John Kaye Ct TW17 ..192 C4
John Keall Ho SW15 ..134 D2
John Keats Lo EN2 ..5 B4
John Keble CE Prim Sch
NW10 ..89 D6
John Kelly Tech Colls
NW2 ..67 D5
John Kennedy Ct 1 N1 73 B2
John Kennedy Ho 1
SE16 ..118 D2
John Kennedy Lo 2
N1 ..73 B2
John King Ct 4 N19 ..71 D6
John Kirk Ho 22 SW11 136 B2
Beckenham BR3 ..207 A5
5 Streatham SW16 ..160 A1
John Knight Lo SW6 ..265 B4
John Lamb Ct HA3 ..24 C2
John Loughborough Sch
The N17 ..33 D1
John Lyon Sch The
HA2 ..42 B1
John Masefield Ho N15 51 B3
John Maurice Cl
SE17 ..117 B2 262 C4
John McDonald Ho 3
E14 ..120 A3
John McKenna Wlk 17
SE16 ..118 A3
John Milton Prim Sch
SW8 ..137 C5 269 A3
John Nettleford Ho 14
E2 ..96 B4

K

Kenilworth Rd continued
Ashford TW15,TW19 148 A1
Ealing W5 110 A5
Orpington BR5 211 A3
Penge SE20 184 D2
Stoneleigh KT17 216 A3
Kenilworth Terr 3
SM2 217 C1
Kenley N17 33 B1
Kenley Ave NW9 27 C1
Kenley Cl Barnet EN4 2 C1
Sidcup DA5 169 C4
St Paul's Cray BR7 211 C6
Kenley Gdns CR7 204 D5
Kenley Ho 6 BR5 190 B1
5 Croydon CR0 206 A1
Kenley Rd
Kingston KT1,KT3 176 D1
Merton SW19 201 C6
Twickenham TW1 153 B5
Kenley Wlk W11 244 A5
Cheam SM3 216 D4
Kenlor Rd SW17 180 B5
Kenmare Ct 5 HA7 25 C6
Kenmare Dr CR4 180 D3
Kenmare Gdns N13 33 A6
Kenmare Mans NW6 69 B3
Kenmare Rd CR7 204 C3
Kenmere Gdns HA0 88 C6
Kenmere Mans W5 87 C3
Kenmere Rd DA16 146 C3
Kenmont Gdns NW10 90 B4
Kenmont Prim Sch
NW10 90 B4
Kenmore Ave HA3 43 A6
Kenmore Cl TW9 132 C5
Kenmore Cres UB4 83 D4
Kenmore Ct NW6 69 C1
Kenmore Gdns HA8 26 D1
Kenmore Park Fst & Mid
Schs HA3 44 A6
Kenmore Rd HA3 43 D5
Kenmure Rd E8 74 B3
Kenmure Yd E8 74 B3
Kennacraig Cl 7 E16 121 A5
Kennard Ho 11 SW11 137 A3
Kennard Mans 6 N11 30 B5
Kennard Rd E15 76 B1
N11 30 D5
Kennard St 9 SW11 137 A3
Newham E16 122 B5
Kennedy Ave EN3 18 C5
Kennedy Cl BR5 211 B1
E13 99 A5
1 Mitcham CR4 181 A1
Pinner HA5 23 B4
Kennedy Cox Ho 9
E16 98 D2
Kennedy Ct TW15 171 A5
Kennedy Ho SE11 260 C2
Kennedy Path W7 86 D3
Kennedy Rd
Barking IG11 101 C6
Ealing W7 86 C2
Kennedy Wlk SE17 262 D3
Kennet Cl SW11 136 B1
Kennet Ct 4 W2 91 C2
Kennet Dr UB4 85 A2
Kenneth Ave IG1 78 D4
Kenneth Campbell Ho
NW8 236 D6
Kenneth Cres NW2 68 B3
Kenneth Ct SE11 261 B4
Kenneth Gdns HA7 25 A4
Kenneth Moor Rd 4
IG1 78 D5
Kennet Ho NW8 236 D5
Kenneth Rd RM6 59 A2
Kenneth Robbins Ho 1
N17 34 B3
Kenneth Younger Ho
SW6 264 D5
Kennet Rd W9 91 B3
Isleworth TW7 130 D2
Kennet Sq CR4 180 C2
Kennet St E1 118 A5
Kennet Wharf La EC4 252 B6
Kenninghall N18 34 C5
Kenninghall Rd E5 74 B5
N18 34 C5
Kenning Ho 6 N1 95 C6
Kenning St 12 SE16 118 C4
Kennings Way
SE11 116 C1 261 B2
Kennington Gdns KT1 197 D6
Kennington Gr SE11 270 D6
Kennington La
SE11 116 C1 260 D1
Kennington Oval
SE11 138 C6 270 D5
Kennington Palace Ct
SE11 261 A2
Kennington Park Gdns
SE17 138 D6
Kennington Park Ho
SE11 261 B1
Kennington Park Pl
SE11 138 D6
Kennington Park Rd
SE11 116 D1 261 C2
Kennington Rd
SE11 116 C2 261 A3
Kennington Sta
SE17 116 D1 261 C2
Kennoldes SE21 161 B2
Kennyland Lo NW4 46 B3
Kenny Rd NW7 29 A5
Kenrick Pl W1 238 A3
Kensal Green Cemy (All
Souls)★ NW10 90 C4
Kensal Green Sta
NW10 90 C4
Kensal Ho W10 90 D3
Kensal Rd W10 91 A3
Kensal Rise Prim Sch
NW6 90 D5
Kensal Rise Sta NW10 90 D5
Kensington Ave E12 78 B2
South Norwood CR7 182 C2
Kensington Avenue Inf Sch
CR7 182 C2
Kensington Avenue Jun Sch
CR7 182 C2
Kensington & Chelsea Coll
SW10 136 A5 266 A4
W10 91 A2
Kensington Church Ct
W8 245 C1
Kensington Church St
W8 113 C5 245 B3
Kensington Church Wlk
W8 245 C1
Kensington Cl N11 31 A4
Kensington Court Mans
W8 245 D1
Kensington Court Mews
W8 255 D6
Kensington Court Pl
W8 113 D3 255 D6
Kensington Ct 2 NW7 27 B5
W8 113 D4 245 D1
Enfield EN2 5 C5
Kensington Ct Gdns
W8 255 D6
Kensington Dr IG8 37 D1
Kensington Gardens★
W2 114 A5 246 B3
Kensington Gate
W8 114 A3 256 A6
Kensington Gdns IG1 56 B1
Kensington Gdns Sq
W2 91 D1
Kensington Gore
SW7 114 B4 246 C1
Kensington Hall Gdns
W14 254 C2
Kensington Hgts HA1 42 D3
Kensington High St
W8 113 C3 255 B6
Kensington Ho 3 NW5 71 C3
Kensington Hts W8 245 A3
Kensington Mall W8 245 B4
Kensington Mans
SW5 255 B2
Kensington Olympia Sta
W14 113 A3 254 A6
Kensington Palace★
W8 113 D5 245 D3
Kensington Palace Gdns
W8 113 D5 245 C4
Kensington Park Gdns
W11 113 B6 244 D5
Kensington Park Mews
W11 91 B1
Kensington Park Rd
W11 113 B6 244 D6
Kensington Pl
W8 113 C5 245 A4
Kensington Prep Sch
SW6 135 B4 264 D2
Kensington Prim Sch
E12 78 B2
Kensington Rd
SW7 114 C4 246 B1
Northolt UB5 85 C5
Kensington Sports Ctr
W11 244 A6
Kensington Sq
W8 113 D4 245 C1
Kensington Terr CR2 221 B1
Kensington Village
W14 113 B2 254 D3
Kensington W W14 254 A4
Kensworth Ho EC1 235 D1
Kent Ave Bexley DA16 167 D6
Dagenham RM9 103 C3
Ealing W13 87 B2
Kent Cl
Mitcham CR4,SW16 204 A5
Orpington BR6 227 C2
Kent Ct 3 E2 95 D5
NW9 27 C1
Acton W3 88 B1
Kent Dr Cockfosters EN4 15 A6
Teddington TW11 174 C5
Kentford Way UB5 85 A6
Kent Gate Way CR0 223 D3
Kent Gdns Ealing W13 87 B2
Ruislip HA4 40 B3
Kent Ho SE1 263 D1
SW1 259 C1
10 W4 111 C1
Richmond TW10 154 C6
Kent House La BR3 185 A5
Kent House Rd BR3 185 A4
Kent House Sta BR3 185 A2
Kent House Station App
BR3 184 D2
Kentish Bldgs SE1 252 C3
Kentish Rd DA17 125 C2
Kentish Town CE Prim Sch
NW5 71 C3
Kentish Town Rd NW1 71 B2
Kentish Town Sta NW5 71 C3
Kentish Town West Sta
NW5 71 B2
Kentish Way BR1,BR2 209 B6
Kentlea Rd SE28 123 C4
Kent Lo 9 SW19 156 D3
Kentmere Ho SE15 140 C6
Kentmere Rd SE18 123 C2
Kenton Ave Harrow HA1 42 D2
Southall UB1 107 C6
Sunbury TW16 173 A1
Kenton Ct W14 254 C5
2 Forest Hill SE26 185 A6
Harrow HA3 43 B3
3 Richmond TW10 153 D5
Kenton Gdns HA3 43 C4
Kenton Ho 21 E1 96 C3
N5 72 C5
Kenton La Harrow HA3 24 D3
Harrow HA3 43 C6
Kenton Park Ave HA3 43 D5
Kenton Park Cl HA3 43 C4
Kenton Park Cres HA3 43 D5
Kenton Park Par HA3 43 D4
Kenton Park Rd HA3 43 C5
Kenton Rd E9 74 D2
Harrow HA3 43 C4
Kenton St WC1 240 A6
Kenton Sta HA3 43 B3
Kenton Way UB4 83 C4
Kent Pas NW1 237 C6
Kent Rd W4 111 A3
Dagenham RM10 81 D3
East Molesey KT8 196 A5
Kingston KT1 197 D6
Richmond TW9 132 C5
Southgate N21 17 B4
West Wickham BR4 207 D1
Kent St E13 99 B4
E2 95 D5
Kent Terr NW1 92 C4 230 B1
Kent Twr SE20 184 B3
Kent View Gdns IG3 79 C6
Kent Way KT6 214 B6
Kentwell Cl SE4 141 A1
Kentwode Gn SW13 134 A5
Kent Yard SW7 247 B1
Kenver Ave N12 30 B4
Kenward Rd SE9 165 D6
Ken Way HA9 67 A5
Kenway Rd
SW5 113 D2 255 C3
Ken Wilson Ho 17 E2 96 A5
Kenwood EN1 17 C5
Kenwood Ave N14 15 D6
Kenwood Cl NW3 48 B1
Harmondsworth UB7 126 C6
Kenwood Ct NW9 45 A5
Kenwood Dr BR3 208 A6
Kenwood Gdns
Ilford IG2 56 C4
2 Wanstead E18 55 B6
Kenwood Ho★ NW3 48 C1
15 SW9 138 D1
Kenwood Rd N6 48 D3
Edmonton N9 18 A3
Kenworthy Rd E9 75 A2
Kenwrick Ho N1 233 D5
Kenwyn Dr NW2 67 D5
Kenwyn Rd SW4 137 D1
Wimbledon SW20 178 C2
Kenya Rd SE7 143 D5
Kenyngton Dr TW16 172 A5
Kenyngton Manor Prim Sch
TW16 172 A4
Kenyngton Pl HA3 43 C4
Kenyon Ho 31 SE5 139 A5
Kenyon St SW6 134 D4
Keogh Rd E15 76 D2
Kepler Ho 9 SE10 120 D1
Kepler Rd SW2,SW4 138 A1
Keppel Ho 5 SE8 119 B1
SW3 257 A3
Keppel Rd E6 100 B6
Dagenham RM9 81 A4
Keppel Row SE1 252 A3
Keppel St WC1 239 D4
Kerala Ct N17 33 D2
Kerbela St 2 E2 96 A3
Kerbey St E14 97 D1
Kerem Sch N2 48 B4
Kerfield Cres SE5 139 B4
Kerfield Pl SE5 139 B4
Kerridge Ct N1 73 C2
Kerrier Ho SW10 266 B3
Kerrington Ct 7 W12 112 C4
Kerrin Point SE11 261 A2
Kerrison Pl W5 109 D5
Kerrison Rd E15 98 B6
SW11 136 C2
Ealing W5 109 D5
Kerrison Villas W5 109 D5
Kerry N7 72 A2
Kerry Ave HA7 25 D6
Kerry Cl Newham E16 99 B1
Palmers Green N13 16 B2
Kerry Ct HA7 25 D6
Kerry Ho 5 E1 96 C1
Kerry Path SE8 141 B6
Kerry Rd SE8 141 B6
Kerscott Ho 30 E3 97 D4
Kersey Gdns SE9 188 A6
Kersfield Ho SW15 156 D5
Kersfield Rd SW15 156 D5
Kershaw Cl SW18 158 B5
Kershaw Ho 7 SE27 160 D1
Kershaw Rd RM10 81 C5
Kersley Mews SW11 267 C1
Kersley Rd N16 73 C5
Kersley St SW11 136 D3
Kerstin Cl UB3 105 D6
Kerswell Cl N15 51 C4
Kerwick Cl 1 N7 72 B1
Keslake Mans NW10 90 D5
Keslake Rd NW6 90 D5
Kessock Cl N17 52 B4
Kestlake Rd DA5 168 C5
Keston Ave BR2 225 C3
Keston CE Prim Sch
BR2 225 D3
Keston Cl Bexley DA16 146 C5
Edmonton N18 17 B1
Keston Ct DA5 169 B4
Keston Gdns BR2 225 C4
Keston Ho SE17 263 B2
Keston Mark BR2 226 A5
Keston Park Cl BR2 226 B5
Keston Rd N17 51 B5
SE15 140 A2
Thornton Heath CR7 204 C3
Kestral Ho EC1 235 A2
Kestrel Ave E6 100 A2
SE24 161 A6
Kestrel Cl NW10 67 B3
NW9 27 C1
Kingston KT2 175 D6
Kestrel Ct E17 34 D1
Ruislip HA4 61 B6
South Croydon CR2 221 A2
Kestrel Ho 4 SW11 136 C2
Enfield EN3 19 A6
Kestrel Pl SE14 141 A6
Kestrel Way UB3 105 B4
Keswick Ave
Kingston KT2,SW15 177 C5
Merton SW19 179 C1
Upper Halliford TW17 193 C6
Keswick Cl SM1 218 A4
Keswick Ct 2 SE22 162 A6
13 Catford SE6 164 D3
Keswick Dr EN3 6 C6
Keswick Gdns
Redbridge IG4 56 A5
Ruislip HA4 39 B3
Wembley HA9 66 A4
Keswick Ho 8 SE5 139 A4
Keswick Hts 9 SW15 157 A6
Keswick Lo E8 73 D2
Keswick Mews W5 110 A5
Keswick Rd BR6 211 D1
DA7 147 C4
Putney SW15 157 A6
Twickenham TW2 152 A5
West Wickham BR4 224 C6
Kettering Ct CR7 205 A5
Kettering Rd EN3 6 D6
Kettering St SW16 181 C4
Kett Gdns SW2 160 B6
Kettlebaston Rd E10 53 B1
Kettleby Ho SW9 138 D2
Kettlewell Cl N11 31 A4
Ketton Ho W10 90 C3
Kevan Ct 6 E17 53 D5
Kevan Ho SE5 139 A5
Kevelioc Rd N17 33 A2
Kevin Cl TW4 128 D3
Kevington Cl BR5 211 D5
Kevington Dr BR5,BR7 211 D5
Kew Bridge TW8 110 B1
Kew Bridge Ct 8 W4 110 C1
Kew Bridge Distribution Ctr
TW8 110 B1
Kew Bridge Rd TW8 110 B1
Kew Bridge Sta TW8 110 B1
Kew Bridge Steam Mus★
TW8 110 B1
Kew Cres SM3 217 B5
Kew Foot Rd TW9 132 A2
Kew Gardens Rd TW9 132 C4
Kew Gardens(Royal
Botanic)★ TW9 132 A4
Kew Gardens Sta TW9 132 C4
Kew Gn TW9 132 B6
Kew Green TW9 132 C6
Kew Lo 11 TW9 132 B4
Kew Obsy★ TW9 131 C2
Kew Palace★ TW9 132 A5
Kew Pier TW9 132 C6
Kew Rd N2 30 C2
Richmond TW9,W4 132 B4
Kew Ret Pk TW9 132 D4
Key Cl E1 96 B3
Keyes Ct SE22 162 A6
Keyes Rd NW2 68 D3
Keyham Ho 31 W2 91 C2
Key Ho 9 SE11 138 C6
Keymer Rd SW2 160 B2
Keynes Cl N2 48 D6
Keynes Ct 9 SE28 124 B6
Keynsham Ave IG8 36 C6
Keynsham Gdns SE9 166 A6
Keynsham Ho 2 N4 51 A2
Keynsham Rd SE9 166 A6
Cheam SM4 201 D1
Keynsham Wlk SM4 201 D1
Keyse Rd SE1 117 D3 263 C5
Keysham Ave TW5 128 A4
Keystone Cres N1 233 B3
Keywood Dr TW16 172 A4
Keyworth Cl E5 75 A4
Keyworth Pl SE1 261 D6
Keyworth Prim Sch
SE17 116 D1 261 C2
Keyworth St
SE1 116 D3 261 D6
Kezia St SE8 119 A1
Khalsa Ct N22 32 D2
Khama Rd SW17 180 C6
Khartoum Rd E13 99 B4
Ilford IG1 78 D3
Upper Tooting SW17 180 B6
Khyber Rd SW11 136 C3
Kibworth St
SW8 138 B5 270 C3
Kidbrooke Gdns SE3 143 A4
Kidbrooke Gr SE3 143 B4
Kidbrooke Interchange
SE3 143 C2
Kidbrooke La SE9 144 A1
Kidbrooke Park Cl
SE3 143 B4
Kidbrooke Park Prim Sch
SE3 143 C4
Kidbrooke Park Rd
SE12,SE3 143 B2
Kidbrooke Sch SE3 143 D3
Kidbrooke Sta SE3 143 B3
Kidbrooke Way SE3 143 B3
Kiddens BR8 191 D1
Kidderminster Pl CR0 204 D1
Kidderminster Rd CR0 205 A2
Kidderpore Ave NW3 69 C4
Kidderpore Gdns NW3 69 C4
Kidd Ho RM9 81 B4
Kidd Pl SE7 122 A1
Kidlington Way NW9 27 C2
Kierbeck Bsns Complex
E16 121 B4
Kiffen St EC2 242 D6
Kilberry Cl TW7 130 B4
Kilbrennan Ho 5 E14 98 A1
Kilburn Bridge 14 NW6 91 C6
Kilburn Gate NW6 91 D5
Kilburn High Rd NW6 91 C6
Kilburn High Road Sta
NW6 91 D6
Kilburn Ho 13 W9 91 B4
Kilburn La W10 91 A5
Kilburn Park Jun Sch
NW6 91 B5
Kilburn Park Rd NW6 91 C4
Kilburn Park Sta NW6 91 C5
Kilburn Pl NW6 91 C6
Kilburn Priory NW6 91 D6
Kilburn Sq NW6 91 C6
Kilburn Sta NW2 69 B2
Kilburn Vale NW6 91 D6
Kilburn Vale Est 13
NW6 91 C6
Kildare Cl HA4 40 C1
Kildare Ct W2 91 C1
Kildare Gdns W2 91 C1
Kildare Rd E16 99 A2
Kildare Terr W2 91 C1
Kildare Wlk E14 97 C1
Kildoran Rd SW2 160 A6
Kildowan Rd IG3 58 A1
Kilgour Rd SE23 163 A5
Kilkie St SW6 136 A3
Killarney Rd SW18 158 A5
Killburns Mill Cl SM6 219 B6
Killearn Rd SE6 164 B3
Killester Gdns KT17,
KT4 216 B4
Killick Ho SM1 217 D4
Killick St N1 94 B5 233 C3
Killieser Ave SW2 160 A2
Killigrew Ho TW16 171 C3
Killip Cl E16 98 D1
Killowen Ave UB5 64 A3
Killowen Rd E9 74 D2
Killross Rd TW14 149 B3
Killyon Rd SW8 137 C3
Kilmaine Rd
SW6 135 A5 264 B3
Kilmarnock Gdns RM8 80 C5
Kilmarnock Rd WD19 22 D6
Kilmarsh Rd W6 112 C2
Kilmartin Ave SW16 204 C6
Kilmartin Rd IG3 80 A6
Kilmington Rd SW13 134 A6
Kilmiston Ave TW17 193 A3
Kilmiston Ho TW17 193 A3
Kilmore Ho 17 E14 97 D1
Kilmorey Gdns TW1 131 B1
Kilmorey Rd TW1 131 B1
Kilmorie Prim Sch
SE23 163 A2
Kilmorie Rd SE23 163 A2
Kilmuir Ho SW1 258 B3
Kiln Cl UB3 127 B6
Kiln Ct E14 119 B6
Kilner Ho 3 SE11 138 C6
Kilner St E14 97 C2
Kiln Mews SW17 180 B5
Kiln Pl NW5 71 A3
Kilnside KT10 213 A1
Kiloh Ct 1 SW11 136 C2
Kilpatrick Ct N16 51 D1
Kilpatrick Way UB4 85 A2
Kilpeck Ho 3 N4 51 A2
Kilravock Ho SE25 205 C6
Kilravock St W10 91 A4
Kilronan 5 W3 89 B1
Kilross Rd TW14 149 C3
Kilsby Wlk RM9 80 B2
Kilsha Rd KT12 194 C3
Kilvinton Dr EN2 5 B5
Kimbell Gdns
SW6 135 A4 264 A1
Kimbell Pl SE9 143 C1
Kimber Ctr The SW18 157 C4
Kimber Ho 11 SE18 144 D6
Kimberley Ave E6 100 A5
SE15 140 C2
Ilford IG2 57 C2
Kimberley Dr DA14 168 D2
Kimberley Gate 2
BR1 186 D3
Kimberley Gdns N4 50 D4
Enfield EN1 5 D2
Kimberley Ho 7 E14 120 A3
Kimberley Ind Est E17 35 B2
Kimberley Rd E11 76 B6
E16 98 D3
E17 35 B2
NW6 91 A6
SW9 138 A2
Chingford, Chingford Green
E4 20 C3
Edmonton N18 34 B4
Penge BR3 184 D1
Thornton Heath CR0 204 D3
Tottenham N17 34 A1
Kimberley Way E4 20 C3
Kimberley Wlk KT12 194 B2
Kimber Rd SW18 157 D4
Kimble Cres WD23 8 A4
Kimble Ho 1 N7 72 A3
NW8 237 B6
Kimble Rd
Mitcham SW17 180 B4
Upper Tooting SW17 180 B5
Kimbolton Cl SE12 164 D5
Kimbolton Row SW3 257 A3
Kimmeridge Gdns 3
SE9 188 A6
Kimmeridge Rd SE9 188 A6
Kimm Ho 16 E17 53 D6
Kimpton Ct 12 SE5 139 B4
Kimpton Ho SW15 156 A4
Kimpton Link Bsns Ctr
SM3 217 B6
Kimpton Rd SE5 139 B4
Cheam SM3 217 B6
Kimpton Trade & Bsns Ctr
SM3 217 B6
Kinburn St SE16 118 D4
Kincaid Rd SE15 140 B5
Kincardine Gdns W9 91 C3
Kinch Gr HA3,HA9 44 B2
Kincraig BR7 188 C2
Kindell Ho 4 SW14 133 B2
Kinder Cl SE28 124 D6
Kinder Ho N1 235 D4
Kindersley Ho 27 E1 96 A1
Kinder St 9 E1 96 B1
Kinefold Ho N7 72 A2
Kinetic Cres EN3 7 B6
Kinfauns Rd Ilford IG3 58 B1
Streatham SW2 160 C2
King Alfred Ave SE6 185 C6
King Alfred Sch NW11 47 D1
King Arthur Cl SE15 140 C5
King Athelstan Prim Sch
KT1 198 B6
King Charles Cres KT5 198 B2

King Charles Ho SW6 265 D4
King Charles' Rd KT5, KT6 198 B3
King Charles St SW1 116 A4 250 A2
King Charles Wlk 6 SW19 157 A3
King Ct 15 E10 53 D2
Kingcup Cl CR0 206 D1
King David La E1 118 C6
Kingdon Ho 8 E14 120 A3
Kingdon Rd NW6 69 C2
King Edward Dr KT6 214 A5
King Edward Mans 12 E8 96 B6
King Edward Mews SW13 134 A4
King Edward Rd E10 54 A1
E17 53 A6
Barnet EN5 1 D1
King Edward's Gdns W3 110 C5
King Edward's Gr TW11 175 C4
King Edwards Mans SW6 265 A3
King Edward's Rd E9 96 C6
Barking IG11 101 B5
Edmonton N9 18 B4
Enfield EN3 6 D1
Ruislip HA4 39 B1
King Edward St EC1 242 A2
King Edward The Third Mews 8 SE16 118 B4
King Edward Wlk SE1 116 C3 261 B6
King Fahad Acad The W5 109 C2
King Fahed Acad W3 111 D6
Kingfield Rd W5 87 D3
Kingfield St E14 120 A2
Kingfisher Ave E11 55 B3
Kingfisher Cl
Harrow HA3 24 D3
Woolwich SE28 124 C6
Kingfisher Ct 12 E14 120 A4
11 SW11 136 C2
Cheam SM1 217 B3
East Molesey KT8 196 C5
Enfield EN2 4 B5
Hounslow TW3 151 D6
Merton SW19 179 B3
Putney SW19 157 A2
Kingfisher Dr TW10 175 B6
Kingfisher Ho SE15 139 D4
W14 254 C6
Kingfisher Lo TW11 175 A6
Kingfisher Mews SE13 163 D6
Kingfisher Sports Ctr The 12 KT1 176 A1
Kingfisher Sq 19 SE8 141 B6
Kingfisher St E6 100 A2
Kingfisher Way NW10 67 B3
Croydon CR0 206 D4
Kingfisher Wlk NW9 27 C1
King Frederick IX Ct SE16 119 B3
King Garth Mews SE23 162 C2
King Gdns CR0 220 D3
King George Ave E16 99 D1
Ilford IG2 57 B3
Walton-on-T KT12 194 D1
King George Cl TW16 171 C5
King George Hospl IG3 58 A4
King George Sq TW10 154 B5
King George St SE10 142 A5
King George's Trad Est KT9 214 C4
King George VI Ave CR4 202 D5
Kingham Cl 3 W11 112 D4
Wandsworth SW18 158 A4
King Harolds Way DA7 147 A5
King Henry Mews 7 BR6 227 D3
King Henry's Mews EN3 7 C6
King Henry's Rd NW3 70 C1
Kingston KT1,KT3 198 D6
King Henry's Reach W6 134 C6
King Henry St N16 73 C3
King Henry's Wlk N1 73 C2
King Henry's Yd 5 N16 73 C3
King Ho W12 90 B1
Kinghorn St EC1 242 A3
King James St SE1 116 D4 251 D1
King John Ct EC2 243 B6
King John St E1 96 D2
King John's Wlk SE9 166 A5
Kinglake St SE17 117 C1 263 B2
Kingly Ct W1 249 B6
Kingly St W1 115 C6 249 A6
King & Queen Cl 4 SE9 188 A6
King & Queen St SE17 117 A1 262 B2
Kingsand Rd SE12 165 A2
Kings Arbour UB2 107 A1
King's Arms Ct 22 E1 96 A2
King's Arms Yd EC2 242 C2
Kingsash Dr UB4 85 A3
Kings Ave N10 49 A6
SW4 160 A5
Bromley BR1 186 D4
Dagenham RM6 59 B3
Ealing W5 87 D1
New Malden KT3 199 D5
Wallington SM5 218 D1
King's Ave
Ashford TW16 171 D4
Buckhurst Hill IG9 21 D2
Hounslow TW3,TW5 129 D4
Southall UB1 85 D1
Southgate N21 16 D3
Woodford IG8 37 C5
Kings Avenue Sch SW4 160 A6
King's Bench St SE1 116 D4 251 D2
King's Bench Wlk EC4 241 B1
Kingsbridge N16 51 B1
Kingsbridge Ave W3 110 B4
Kingsbridge Cres UB1 85 B2
Kingsbridge Ct E14 119 C2
Edmonton N21 16 D2
Kingsbridge Ho 10 SE20 184 B2
Kingsbridge Ind Est IG11 101 C4
Kingsbridge Rd W10 90 C1
Barking IG11 101 B5
Southall UB2 107 B2
Walton-on-T KT12 194 B2
West Barnes SM4 200 D2
Kingsbridge Way UB4 83 C4
Kingsbury Green Prim Sch NW9 44 D4
Kingsbury High Sch Annexe NW9 44 D5
Kingsbury Rd N1 73 C2
NW9 44 D4
Kingsbury Sta NW9 44 C4
Kingsbury Terr N1 73 C2
Kingsbury Trad Est NW9 45 B3
Kings Chace View EN2 4 C3
Kings Chase KT8 196 A6
Kings Cl NW4 46 D5
King's Cl E10 53 D2
Kings Cl KT12 194 B1
King's Cl KT7 197 A2
Kingsclere Cl SW15 156 A4
Kingsclere Ct N12 30 C5
New Barnet EN5 14 A6
Kingsclere Pl EN2 5 A2
Kingscliffe Gdns SW19 157 B3
Kings Coll SE24 161 B5
WC2 116 B6 250 D6
Kings College Ct NW3 70 C1
King's College Hospl SE5 139 B3
King's College London NW3 69 C4
Kings College Rd NW3 70 B1
Ruislip HA4 39 D3
Kings Coll London W8 245 A2
Kings Coll London (Chelsea Campus) SW3 114 C1 257 A1
King's Coll Sch SW19 178 D4
Kingscote NW11 47 B1
Kingscote Rd W4 111 B3
Croydon CR0 206 B2
Kingston KT3 199 B6
Kingscote St EC4 251 C6
King's Court N SW3 257 A1
Kingscourt Rd SW16 160 A1
King's Court S SW3 257 A1
King's Cres N4,N5 73 A5
Kingscroft SW4 160 A5
Kingscroft Rd NW2 69 B2
King's Cross WC1 94 A4 233 B2
King's Cross Bridge WC1 233 B2
King's Cross Rd WC1 94 B4 233 D1
King's Cross Sta N1 94 A5 233 B3
King's Cross, St Pancras N1 233 A2
King's Cross (Thames Link) Sta WC1 233 B2
Kings Ct E13 99 B6
HA9 66 D6
6 N7 72 B1
NW8 230 C5
SE22 140 A1
W6 112 A2
Kings Ct *continued*
2 Buckhurst Hill IG9 21 D2
16 Kingston KT2 176 C3
10 Putney SW15 156 A4
3 Wallington SM6 219 B2
King's Ct
Beckenham BR3 207 D6
9 Ealing W5 87 C2
Wimbledon SW19 179 C4
Kingsdale Gdns W11 112 D5
Kingsdale Rd SE18 145 D6
Penge SE20 184 D3
Kingsdale Sec Sch SE21 161 C1
Kingsdown 1 SW19 178 D3
Kingsdown Ave W13 109 B4
W3 111 C6
Kingsdown Cl 28 SE16 118 B1
W10 90 D1
11 W11 91 A1
Kingsdown Ct SW11 158 C5
Kingsdowne Rd KT6 198 B2
Kingsdown Ho 1 E8 74 A3
Kingsdown Rd E11 76 C5
3 N19 72 A6
Cheam SM3 217 A3
Kingsdown Way BR2 209 A3
Kings Dr HA9 66 D6
Edgware HA8 26 B6
Surbiton KT5 198 C3
King's Dr KT7 197 B2
Kingsend HA4 39 C1
Kings Farm E17 35 D2
Kings Farm Ave TW10 132 C1
Kingsfield Ave HA1,HA2 42 A4
Kingsfield Ho 18 N16 73 C5
SE9 165 D1
Kingsfield Rd HA1 42 B2
Kingsford Com Sch E13 99 C3
Newham E6 100 B1
Kingsford St NW5 70 D3
Kingsford Way E6 100 B2
Kingsgate HA9 67 A5
Kingsgate Ave N3 47 C6
Kingsgate Bsns Ctr KT2 176 A2
Kingsgate Cl BR5 190 C1
DA7 147 A4
Kingsgate Est N1 73 C2
Kingsgate Ho 29 SW9 138 C4
Kingsgate Pl NW6 69 C1
Kingsgate Prim Sch NW6 69 C1
Kingsgate Rd NW6 69 C1
Kingston KT2 176 A2
King's Gdns 6 NW6 69 C1
Kings Gdns IG1 57 B1
King's Gr SE15 140 B4
SE15 140 B5
Kings Grange HA4 39 D1
Kingsground SE9 166 A5
Kings Hall Mews SE13 142 A2
Kings Hall Rd BR3 185 A2
Kings Head Hill E4 19 D4
King's Head Yd SE1 252 C3
King's Highway SE18, SE2 145 D6
Kingshill SE17 262 B4
Kingshill Ave
Harrow HA3 43 B5
Hayes UB4 83 D4
New Malden KT4 200 B2
Northolt UB5 84 B4
Kingshill Ct 6 EN5 1 A1
Kingshill Dr HA3 43 B6
Kings Ho 19 E14 119 B6
SW8 270 B4
Kingshold Rd E9 74 C1
Kingsholm Gdns SE9 144 A1
King's House Jun Sch TW10 154 B6
King's House Prep Sch TW10 154 B6
Kingshurst Rd SE12 165 A4
Kings Keep KT6 198 A5
King's Keep 6 SW15 156 D6
King's La SM1,SM2 218 B3
Kingsland NW8 92 C6 230 B5
Kingsland Gn 1 E8,N1 73 C2
Kingsland High St E8 73 D3
Kingsland Pas 2 E8 73 C2
Kingsland Rd E13 99 C4
E2 95 C5
Kingsland Sch E8 73 D3
Kingsland Sh Ctr E8 73 D2
Kingslawn Cl SW15 156 B6
Kingslee Ct 12 SM2 217 D1
Kingsleigh Pl CR4 202 D6
Kingsleigh Wlk BR2 208 D5
Kingsley Ave Ealing W13 87 A1
Hounslow TW3 130 A3
Southall UB1 107 C6
Sutton SM1 218 B4
Kingsley Cl N2 48 A4
Dagenham RM10 81 D4
Kingsley Ct E11 54 D3
NW2 68 B2
1 SE28 124 C5
Kingsley Ct *continued*
Bexley DA6 147 C1
Edgware HA8 10 D2
Wood Green N22 32 B3
2 Worcester Park KT4 215 D6
Kingsley Dr 1 KT4 215 D6
Kingsley Flats SE1 263 B3
Kingsley Gdns E4 35 C5
Kingsley Grange 1 E11 55 A4
Kingsley Ho NW11 48 A3
SW3 266 D5
3 SW4 137 D3
8 Kingston KT6 198 A4
Kingsley Mews BR7 188 D4
W8 255 D5
Dagenham RM9 80 D4
Kingsley Pl N6 49 A2
Kingsley Prim Sch CR9 204 C1
Kingsley Rd E7 77 A1
NW6 91 B6
Chingford E17 36 A1
Edmonton N13 32 D6
Harrow HA2 64 A5
Hounslow TW3 130 A3
Orpington BR6 227 D1
Pinner HA5 41 B5
Thornton Heath CR0 204 C1
Wimbledon SW19 179 D5
Kingsley St SW11 136 D2
Kingsley Way N2 48 A4
Kingsley Wood Dr SE9 166 B1
Kings Lo HA4 39 C1
Kingslyn Cres SE19 183 C2
Kings Mall W6 112 C2
Kingsman Par SE18 122 B3
King's Mans SW3 267 A5
Kingsman St SE18 122 B2
Kingsmead Barnet EN5 1 C1
Richmond TW10 154 B5
Kingsmead Ave NW9 45 B2
Edmonton N9 18 B3
Mitcham CR4 203 C6
North Cheam KT4 216 B5
Sunbury TW16 172 C1
Tolworth KT6 214 C6
Kingsmead Cl DA15 168 A2
Teddington TW11 175 B4
West Ewell KT19 215 B1
Kingsmead Ct N6 49 D2
Bromley BR1 186 D3
Kingsmead Dr UB5 63 B1
Kingsmead Ho E9 75 A4
Kingsmead Lo
9 Chingford E4 20 A2
Sutton SM2 218 B2
Kings Mead Pk KT10 212 C1
Kingsmead Prim Sch E9 75 A4
Kingsmead Rd SW2 160 C2
Kingsmead Sch EN1 6 A2
Kingsmead Way E5,E9 75 A4
Kingsmere BR7 188 A2
Catford SE6 163 D3
Kingsmere Cl SW15 134 D2
Kingsmere Ct NW9 44 D1
Kingsmere Pk NW9 45 A1
Kingsmere Pl N16 51 B1
Kingsmere Rd SW19 156 D2
King's Mews 1 SW4 160 A6
WC1 94 B3 240 D5
Kingsmill NW8 92 B5 229 D4
Kingsmill Bsns Pk KT1 198 B6
Kingsmill Gdns RM9 81 B3
Kingsmill Rd RM9 81 B3
Kingsmill Terr NW8 92 B5 229 D4
Kingsnorth Ho 12 W10 90 D1
Kingsnympton Pk KT2 176 D4
Kings Oak RM7 59 C6
Kings Oak Hospl (Private) The EN2 4 C5
King's Orch SE9 166 A5
King's Paddock TW12 174 A2
King's Par W12 112 A3
Willesden NW10 90 C6
Kingspark Ct E18 55 A6
King's Pas KT2 175 D2
King's Pl SE1 252 A1
Kings Pl Acton W4 111 A2
Buckhurst Hill IG9 21 D2
Loughton IG10 21 D4
King Sq EC1 95 A4 235 A1
King's Quay SW10 266 B2
Kings Rd BR6 227 D4
NW10 68 B1
King's Rd E11 54 C2
E6 99 C6
SW10 136 B6 266 C5
SW3 257 B1
Kings Rd Ealing W5 87 D2
Feltham TW13 150 C3
Harrow HA2 63 B6
Mitcham CR4 203 A6
Richmond TW10,TW9 154 B6
Walton-on-T KT12 194 B1
West Drayton UB7 104 B4
Wood Green N22 32 B2
King's Rd Barking IG11 79 A1
Chingford E4 20 B3
Edmonton N18 34 A6
Kingston KT2 176 B3
Long Ditton KT6 197 C1
Mortlake SW14 133 B2
South Norwood SE25 206 A6
Teddington TW11,TW12 174 B5
Tottenham N17 33 D2
Twickenham TW1 153 B5
Wimbledon SW19 179 C4
Kings Ride Gate TW10 132 C1
Kingsridge SW19 157 A2
Kings Road Bglws HA2 63 B5
King's Scholars' Pas SW1 259 A4
King St E13 98 D3
E13 99 A3
EC2 95 A1 242 B1
N2 48 B6
SW1 115 C5 249 B4
W3 111 A5
W6 112 A2
WC2 250 A6
Richmond TW9 153 D6
Southall UB2 107 A3
Tottenham N17 33 D2
Twickenham TW1 153 A3
King Stairs Cl SE16 118 B4
King's Terr NW1 93 C6 232 A5
8 Isleworth TW7 131 A2
Kingsthorpe Rd SE26 184 D6
Kingston Ave
Cheam SM3 217 A5
Feltham TW14 149 D5
Yiewsley UB7 104 B6
Kingston Bsns Ctr KT9 214 B5
Kingston By-Pass KT6, KT7,KT9 213 C5
Kingston By - Pass KT6 214 C5
Kingston Cl
Dagenham RM6 59 A6
Northolt UB5 85 B6
Teddington TW11 175 B4
Kingston Coll of F Ed KT1 197 D6
Kingston Coll of F Ed (M V Annex) KT2 176 A2
Kingston Cres BR3 185 B2
Kingston Gdns CR0 220 A5
Kingston Gram Sch KT2 176 B1
Kingston Hall Rd KT1 197 D6
Kingston Hill KT2 177 A5
Kingston Hill Ave RM6 59 A6
Kingston Hill Pl KT2, TW10 177 A6
Kingston Ho 2 NW6 69 A1
Kingston Ho E SW7 247 A1
Kingston Ho N SW7 247 A1
Kingston Ho S SW7 247 A1
Kingston Hospl KT2 176 D2
Kingston House Estate KT6 197 B3
Kingston La
Teddington TW11 175 B4
Uxbridge UB8 82 A4
West Drayton UB7 104 B4
Kingston Lo 2 KT3 199 C5
Kingston Mus KT1 176 A1
Kingston Pl HA3 24 D3
Kingston Rd
SW15,SW19 156 B3
Ashford TW15 170 A4
Ashford TW15,TW17 170 B4
Edmonton N9 18 A2
Ilford IG1 79 A4
Kingston KT1,KT3 199 A5
Merton SW19,SW20 179 B1
New Barnet EN4 14 B6
Southall UB2 107 B4
Teddington TW11 175 B4
Ewell KT17 215 D1
Kingston Sq SE19 183 B5
Kingston Sta KT2 176 A2
Kingston Univ
Kingston KT1 198 A6
Kingston KT2 177 B5
Kingston Univ Annex KT1 176 B1
Kingston Univ Roehampton Vale Ctr SW15 155 D1
Kingston Vale SW15 155 C1
Kingstown St NW1 93 A6 231 A6
King Street Cloisters 8 W6 112 B2
King Street Coll W12 112 C4
W6 112 C2
King Street Par 6 TW1 153 A3
Kings View Ct 1 SW20 178 D3
Kingswater Pl SW11 267 A3
Kingsway BR5 211 B4
N12 30 A4
WC2 94 B1 240 C2
Kingsway *continued*
Coney Hall BR4 224 D5
Enfield EN3 18 B6
Hayes UB3 83 A2
Mortlake SW14,TW9 132 D2
Stanwell TW19 148 A3
Wembley HA9 66 A4
West Barnes KT3 200 C4
Woodford IG8 37 C5
Kings Way Croydon CR0 220 B3
Harrow HA1 42 C5
Kingsway Bsns Pk TW12 173 B2
Kingsway Coll NW5 71 B2
Kingsway Cres HA2 42 A5
Kingsway Est N18 34 D4
Kingsway Pl EC1 241 C6
Kingsway Rd SM3 217 A1
Kingswear Ho 5 SE23 162 C2
Kingswear Rd NW5 71 B5
Ruislip HA4 62 A6
Kingswood 32 E2 96 C5
Kingswood Ave DA17 125 B2
NW6 91 A5
Beckenham BR2,BR3 208 C5
Hampton TW12 173 D4
Hounslow TW3,TW5 129 B3
Thornton Heath CR7 204 C4
Kingswood Cl BR6 211 B2
N20 14 A4
SW8 270 B3
Enfield EN1 17 D6
New Malden KT3 199 D3
Surbiton KT6 198 A2
Kings Wood Ct 4 NW6 69 C1
Kingswood Ct
Chingford E4 35 C5
7 Richmond TW10 154 B6
Kingswood Dr
Carshalton SM5 202 D1
Dulwich SE19,SE21 183 D6
Kingswood Ho 3 KT2 176 D4
Kingswood Pk N3 29 B1
Kingswood Pl SE13 142 C1
Kingswood Prim Sch SE27 183 B5
Kingswood Rd E11 54 C2
W4 111 A3
Beckenham BR2 208 C6
Ilford IG3 58 A2
Merton SW19 179 B2
Penge SE20 184 C4
Streatham SW2 160 A4
Kingswood Terr W4 111 A3
Kingswood Way SM6 220 A3
Kingsworth Cl BR3 207 A4
Kingsworthy Cl KT1 198 B6
Kings Yd E15 75 C2
Kingthorpe Rd NW10 67 B1
Kingthorpe Terr 1 NW10 67 B1
Kington Ho 16 NW6 91 D6
Kingward Ho E1 96 A2
Kingwell Rd EN4 2 B5
King William IV Gdns SE20 184 C4
King William La 3 SE10 120 C1
King William St EC4 117 B6 252 D6
King William Wlk SE10 142 A6
Kingwood Rd SW6 135 A5 264 A3
Kinlet Rd SE18 145 A4
Kinloch Dr NW9 45 C2
Kinloch St N7 72 B5
Kinloss Ct NW3 47 B5
Kinloss Gdns NW3 47 B5
Kinloss Rd SM5 202 A2
Kinnaird Ave
Bromley BR1 186 D4
Chiswick W4 133 A5
Kinnaird Cl BR1 186 D4
Kinnear Ct 2 SW20 178 D2
Kinnear Rd W12 111 D4
Kinnerton Pl N SW1 247 D1
Kinnerton Pl S SW1 247 D1
Kinnerton St SW1 115 A4 248 A1
Kinnerton Yd SW1 248 A1
Kinnoull Mans 10 E5 74 B4
Kinnoul Rd W6 135 A6 264 A6
Kinross Ave KT4 216 A6
Kinross Cl
Ashford TW16 171 D5
Harrow HA3 44 B4
Kinross Ct 1 SE6 164 D2
Kinross Dr TW16 171 D5
Kinross Ho N1 233 C6
Kinross Terr E17 35 B1
Kinsale Rd SE15 140 A2
Kinsella Gdns SW19 178 B5
Kinsey Ho SE21 183 C6
Kinsham Ho 4 E2 96 A3
Kintore Way SE1 263 C4
Kintyre Cl SW16 204 B6
Kintyre Ct 17 SW2 160 A4

Kinveachy Gdns SE7 ...122 A1
Kinver Ho N4 ...51 B2
Kinver Rd SE26 ...184 C6
Kipling Ct W7 ...108 D6
Kipling Dr SW17 ...180 B4
Kipling Ho 23 SE5 ...139 A5
Kipling Pl HA7 ...24 D4
Kipling Rd DA7 ...147 A4
Kipling St SE1 117 B4 252 D2
Kipling Terr N9 ...17 B2
Kipling Twr 3 W3 ...111 A3
Kippington Dr SE9 ...165 D3
Kirby Cl KT19 ...215 D3
Kirby Est SE16 ...118 B3
Kirby Gr SE1 ..117 C4 253 A2
Kirby St EC1 ...94 C2 241 B4
Kirby Way KT12 ...194 C3
Kirchen Rd W13 ...109 B6
Kirkby Cl N11 ...31 A4
Kirkdale SE26 ...162 B1
Kirkdale Rd E11 ...54 C2
Kirkeby Bldg EC1 ...241 A4
Kirkfield Cl W13 ...109 B5
Kirkham Rd E6 ...100 A1
Kirkham St SE18 ...145 C6
Kirk La SE18 ...145 A6
Kirkland Cl DA15 ...167 C5
Kirkland Dr EN2 ...5 A4
Kirkland Wlk 4 E8 ...73 D2
Kirkleas Rd KT6 ...198 A1
Kirklees Rd
Dagenham RM8 ...80 C3
Thornton Heath CR7 ...204 C4
Kirkley Ho N16 ...51 C1
Kirkley Rd SW19 ...179 C2
Kirkman Pl W1 ...239 C3
Kirkmichael Rd E14 ...98 A1
Kirk Rd E17 ...53 B3
Kirk Rise SM1 ...217 D5
Kirkside Rd SE3 ...143 A6
Kirk's Pl E3 ...97 B2
Kirkstall Ave N17 ...51 B5
Kirkstall Gdns SW2 ...160 A3
Kirkstall Ho SW1 ...258 C2
Kirkstall Rd SW2 ...160 A3
Kirkstead Ct E5 ...75 A4
Kirksted Rd SM4 ...201 D1
Kirkstone NW1 ...232 A2
Kirkstone Way BR1 ...186 C3
Kirkton Lo SW18 ...157 D5
Kirkton Rd N15 ...51 C5
Kirkwall Pl E2 ...96 C4
Kirkwood Rd SE15 ...140 B3
Kirn Rd W13 ...109 B6
Kirrane Cl KT3 ...199 D4
Kirtley Ho SW8 ...269 B2
Kirtley Rd SE26 ...185 A6
Kirtling St
SW8 ...137 C5 269 A4
Kirton Cl W4 ...111 B2
Kirton Rd E13 ...99 C5
Kirton Wlk HA8 ...27 A3
Kirwin Way SE5 ...138 D5
Kisharon Day Sch
NW11 ...47 B3
Kitcat Terr E3 ...97 C4
Kitchener Rd E7 ...77 B2
N17 ...51 C6
N2 ...48 C6
Chingford, Highams Park
E17 ...35 D2
Dagenham RM10 ...81 D2
South Norwood CR7 ...205 B6
Kite Ho 5 SW11 ...136 C2
Kitley Gdns SE19 ...183 D2
Kitson Rd SE5 ...139 A5
Barnes SW13 ...134 A4
Kittiwake Ct 26 SE8 ...141 B6
Kittiwake Pl SM1 ...217 B3
Kittiwake Rd UB5 ...84 D4
Kittiwake Way UB4 ...84 D2
Kitto Rd SE14 ...140 D3
Kitt's End Rd EN5 ...1 A6
Kiver Rd N19 ...72 A6
Klea Ave SW4 ...159 C5
Kleffens Ct 2 SE3 ...142 D5
Knaggs Ho 1 TW11 ...174 C5
Knapdale Cl SE23 ...162 B2
Knapmill Rd SE6 ...163 D2
Knapmill Way SE6 ...163 D2
Knapp Cl NW10 ...67 C2
Knapp Rd
Ashford TW15 ...170 B6
Bow E3 ...97 C3
Knapton Mews SW17 ...181 A4
Knaresborough Dr
SW18 ...157 D3
Knaresborough Ho 4
N4 ...51 A2
Knaresborough Pl
SW5 ...113 D2 255 C4
Knatchbull Rd NW10 ...89 B6
SE5 ...138 D4
Knebworth Ave E17 ...35 C2
Knebworth Ho 2 N16 ...73 C4
SW8 ...269 D1
Chingford E17 ...35 C2
Knebworth Rd 3 N16 ...73 C4
Knee Hill SE2 ...124 C1
Knee Hill Cres SE2 ...124 C2
Kneller Gdns TW7 ...152 B5
Kneller Ho 9 SW8 ...137 D3
4 Northolt UB5 ...84 D5
Kneller Rd SE4 ...141 A1
Isleworth TW2 ...152 B5
New Malden KT3 ...199 C2
Knight Cl RM8 ...80 C6
Knight Ct N15 ...51 C4
1 Chingford E4 ...20 A3
Knighten St E1 ...118 B5
Knighthead Point E14 119 C4
Knight Ho SE17 ...263 A3
Knightland Ho E5 ...74 B6
Knightland Rd E5 ...74 B6
Knightleas Ct NW2 ...68 C2
Knighton Cl
Croydon CR2 ...220 D1
Woodford IG8 ...37 B6
Knighton Dr IG8 ...37 B6
Knighton Gn IG9 ...21 B2
Knighton La IG9 ...21 B2
Knighton Park Rd
SE26 ...184 D5
Knighton Rd E7 ...77 A4
Knightrider Ct EC4 ...252 A6
Knightrider St EC4 ...251 D6
Knights Arc SW1 ...247 C1
Knight's Ave W5 ...110 A4
Knightsbridge
SW1,SW7 ...114 D4 247 C1
Knightsbridge Ct SW1 247 D1
Knightsbridge Gn
SW1 ...247 C1
Knightsbridge Mews
BR7 ...188 B3
Knights Cl E9 ...74 C3
Knights Ct Bushey WD23 ..8 B3
Kingston KT1 ...198 A6
Penge BR3 ...185 A2
Knightshayes Ho NW4 .28 D1
Knight's Hill SE19,SE27 182 D6
Knight's Hill Sq SE27 .182 D6
Knights Ho SE1 ...253 C2
SW5 ...254 C2
SW8 ...270 B3
Knight's Ho SW10 ...266 A4
Knight's La N9 ...18 A1
Knight's Pk KT1 ...198 A6
Knight's Pl TW2 ...152 C3
Knights Rd
Newham E16 ...121 A4
Stanmore HA7 ...25 C6
Knight's Wlk SE11 ...261 C3
Knightswood Cl HA8 ...11 A2
Knightswood Ct N6 ...49 D2
Knightswood Ho N12 ...30 A4
Knightwood Cres KT3 199 C3
Knivet Rd SW6 ...265 A5
Knobs Hill Rd E15 ...97 D6
Knockholt Rd SE9 ...165 D6
Knole Cl CR0 ...206 C3
Knole Ct UB5 ...84 C4
Knole Gate DA15 ...167 C1
Knole The SE9 ...188 C6
Knoll Ct BR6 ...227 D6
Dulwich SE19 ...183 D5
Knoll Dr N14 ...15 A4
Knoll Ho NW8 ...229 A4
Knollmead KT4,KT5 ...199 A1
Knollmead Prim Sch
KT5 ...215 A6
Knoll Rd DA5 ...169 C5
SW18 ...158 A6
Sidcup DA14 ...190 B6
Knoll Rise BR6 ...211 D1
Knolls Cl KT4 ...216 B5
Knoll The
Beckenham BR3 ...185 D2
Ealing W13 ...87 C2
Hayes BR2 ...209 A1
Knolly's Cl SE27,SW16 .160 C1
Knolly's Rd SE27,SW16 160 C1
Knot Ho SE1 ...253 C3
Knottisford St E2 ...96 C4
Knotts Green Mews
E10 ...54 A3
Knotts Green Rd E10 ...54 A3
Knowlden Ho 4 E1 ...118 C6
Knowle Ave DA7 ...147 B5
Knowle Cl SW9 ...138 C2
Knowle Lo BR7 ...188 B4
Knowle Rd BR2 ...226 A6
Twickenham TW2 ...152 C3
Knowles Cl UB7 ...104 A5
Knowles Ct 7 HA1 ...42 D3
Knowles Hill Cres
SE13 ...164 B6
Knowles Ho NW10 ...90 A6
Wandsworth SW18 ...157 D5
Knowles Wlk SW4 ...137 C2
Knowl Pk WD6 ...10 A6
Knowlton Gn 1 BR2 ...208 D4
Knowlton Ho 32 SW9 ...138 C4
Knowl Way WD6 ...10 B6
Knowsley Ave UB1 ...107 D5
Knowsley Rd SW11 ...136 D3
Knox Ct 16 SW4 ...138 A3
Knox Ho SW15 ...134 C3
Knox Rd E7 ...77 A2
Knox St W1 ...92 D2 237 C4
Knoyle Ho W14 ...254 B5
Knoyle St SE14 ...141 A6
Kobi Nazrul Prim Sch
E1 ...96 A1
Koblenz Ho N8 ...50 A6
Kohat Rd SW19 ...179 D5
Korda Cl TW17 ...192 B6
Kossuth St SE10 ...120 C1
Kotree Way 16 SE1 ...118 A2
Kramer Mews SW5 ...255 C1
Kreedman Wlk 8 E8 ...74 A3
Kreisel Wlk TW9 ...132 B6
Kuala Gdns SW16 ...182 B2
Kubrick Bsns Est E7 ...77 B4
Kuhn Way E7 ...77 A3
Kwesi Johnson Ct 4
N22 ...32 C1
Kydbrook Cl BR5 ...211 A2
Kylemore Cl 3 E6 ...99 D5
Kylemore Ct 4 W12 ...112 A4
Kylemore Rd NW6 ...69 C1
Kylestrome Ho SW1 ...258 B3
Kymberley Rd HA1 ...42 C3
Kynance Gdns HA7 ...25 C2
Kynance Mews
SW7 ...113 D3 255 D5
Kynance Pl SW7 ...256 A5
Kynaston Ave CR7 ...205 A4
Kynaston Cl HA3 ...24 B3
Kynaston Cres CR7 ...205 A4
Kynaston Ho 7 SW2 ...160 B3
Kynaston Rd BR1 ...187 A5
N16 ...73 C5
Enfield EN2 ...5 B4
Thornton Heath CR7 ...205 A4
Kynaston Wood HA3 ...24 B3
Kynersley Cl SM5 ...218 D5
Kynoch Rd N18 ...34 D6
Kyrle Rd SW11 ...159 A5
Kyverdale Rd N16 ...51 D1

L

Laburnam Ct 12 SW16 182 C5
Laburnum Cl 5 SE15 140 C5
Laburnham Ct NW2 ...69 B6
Laburnham Ho SE4 ...141 B3
Laburnham Pl SE9 ...166 C6
Laburnum Ave
Carshalton SM1 ...218 C5
Edmonton N9 ...17 D2
Tottenham N17 ...33 B3
Yiewsley UB7 ...104 B6
Laburnum Cl E4 ...35 B4
N11 ...31 A4
Laburnum Cres TW16 .172 B2
Laburnum Ct 28 E2 ...95 D6
Harrow HA1 ...41 D3
5 Mitcham CR4 ...181 A1
Stanmore HA7 ...25 C6
Laburnum Gdns
Croydon CR0 ...206 D1
Edmonton N21 ...17 A2
Laburnum Gr NW9 ...45 A2
Edmonton N21 ...17 A2
Hounslow TW3 ...129 B1
Kingston KT3 ...177 B1
Ruislip HA4 ...39 B3
Southall UB1 ...85 B3
Laburnum Ho 6 N16 ...73 B6
Dagenham RM10 ...81 C6
Laburnum JMI Sch E2 .95 D6
Laburnum Lo N3 ...29 B1
Laburnum Rd
Hayes UB3 ...105 D2
Merton SW19 ...180 A3
Mitcham CR4 ...181 A1
Laburnum St E2 ...95 D6
Laburnums The E6 ...100 A3
Laburnum Way BR2 ...210 D2
Stanwell TW19 ...148 B3
Lacebark Cl DA15 ...167 D4
Lacey Cl N9 ...18 A2
Lacey Dr Dagenham RM8 80 C5
Edgware HA8 ...26 B6
Hampton TW12 ...173 B2
Lacey Ho 6 SE13 ...142 A3
Lacey Wlk E3 ...97 C5
Lacine Ct 12 SE16 ...118 D4
Lackington St EC2 ...242 D4
Lackland Ho SE1 ...263 D2
Lacland Ho SW10 ...266 C4
Lacock Cl SW19 ...180 A4
Lacock Ct 3 W13 ...109 A5
Lacon Rd SE22 ...140 A1
Lacrosse Way SW16 ...181 D2
Lacy Rd SW15 ...134 D1
Ladas Rd SE27 ...183 A5
Ladbroke Cres W11 ...91 A1
Ladbroke Gdns
W11 ...113 B6 244 C6
Ladbroke Gr W10 ...91 A2
W11 ...113 B6 244 C6
Ladbroke Grove Ho
W11 ...244 C6
Ladbroke Grove Sta
W10 ...91 A1
Ladbroke Mews W11 .244 B3
Ladbroke Rd
W11 ...113 B5 244 C4
Enfield EN1 ...17 D5
Ladbroke Sq
W11 ...113 B6 244 D5
Ladbroke Terr
W11 ...113 B5 244 D4
Ladbroke Wlk
W11 ...113 B5 244 D4
Ladbrook Cl HA5 ...41 B4
Ladbrooke Cres DA14 .168 D1
Ladbrook Rd SE25 ...205 B5
Ladderstile Ride KT2,
TW10 ...176 D5
Ladderswood Way N11 31 C5
Ladlands SE22 ...162 A4
Lady Aylesford Ave
HA7 ...25 B5
Lady Bankes Jun & Inf Schs
HA4 ...62 A6
Lady Booth Rd 7 KT1 176 A1
Ladybower Ct 6 E5 ...74 D4
Ladycroft Gdns 6
BR6 ...227 A3
Ladycroft Rd SE13 ...141 D2
Ladycroft Way BR6 ...227 A3
Ladycroft Wlk HA7 ...25 D1
Lady Eleanor Holles Sch
The (Jun Girls)
TW12 ...173 D5
Lady Eleanor Holles Sch
The (Senior Girls)
TW12 ...173 D5
Lady Elizabeth Ho
SW14 ...133 A2
Lady Florence Ctyd 14
SE8 ...141 C5
Ladygate La HA4 ...39 A3
Lady Hay KT4 ...215 D6
Lady Margaret Prim Sch
UB1 ...85 B2
Lady Margaret Rd NW5 71 C3
Southall UB1 ...85 B2
Lady Margaret Sch
SW6 ...135 C4 265 A1
Lady Shaw Ct N13 ...16 B1
Ladysmith Ave E6 ...100 A5
Ilford IG2 ...57 C2
Ladysmith Cl NW7 ...28 A3
Ladysmith Rd E16 ...98 D4
SE9 ...166 C5
Edmonton N18 ...34 B5
Enfield EN1 ...5 D3
Harrow HA3 ...24 C1
Tottenham N17 ...34 A1
Lady Somerset Rd NW5 71 B4
Ladywell Cl SE4 ...141 C1
Ladywell Ho 7 BR5 ...190 B1
Ladywell Hts SE4 ...163 B5
Ladywell Rd SE13 ...163 D6
Ladywell St 4 E15 ...98 D6
Ladywell Sta SE13 ...163 D6
Ladywell Water Twr
SE4 ...163 C6
Ladywood Ave BR5 ...211 C4
Ladywood Rd KT6 ...214 C6
Lafitte Ho 22 N19 ...49 D2
Lafone Ave TW13 ...150 C2
Lafone Ho 11 SW2 ...160 A4
Lafone St SE1 .117 D4 253 C2
Lagado Mews SE16 ...118 D5
Lagonda Ho 11 E3 ...97 C3
Lagonier Ho EC1 ...235 B1
Laidlaw Dr N21 ...16 B6
Laindon Ho 6 N16 ...51 D1
Laing Dean UB5 ...84 C6
Laing Ho SE5 ...139 A5
Laings Ave CR4 ...180 D1
Laings Cnr CR4 ...180 D2
Lainlock Pl TW3 ...129 D4
Lainson St SW18 ...157 C4
Lairdale Cl SE21 ...161 A4
Laird Ho SE5 ...139 A5
Lairs Cl N7 ...72 A2
Laitwood Rd SW12 ...159 B3
Lakanal 14 SE5 ...139 C4
Lake Ave BR1 ...187 A4
Lake Bsns Ctr N17 ...34 A3
Lake Cl Dagenham RM8 ..80 D5
6 Wimbledon SW19 ...179 B5
Lakedale Rd SE18 ...123 C1
Lake Dr WD23 ...8 B2
Lakefield Cl SE20 ...184 B3
Lakefield Rd N22 ...32 D1
Lake Gdns
Dagenham RM10 ...81 C3
Hackbridge SM6 ...219 B5
Richmond TW10 ...153 B2
Lakehall Gdns CR7 ...204 D4
Lakehall Rd CR7 ...204 D4
Lake Ho SE1 ...252 A1
4 West Norwood
SW27 ...182 D5
Lake House Rd E11 ...77 A6
Lakehurst Rd KT19 ...215 C3
Lakeland Cl HA3 ...24 B4
Lakeman Ct CR7 ...183 A1
Lakenheath N14 ...15 D6
Laker Ct SW4 ...138 A3
Lake Rd Croydon CR0 ...223 B6
Dagenham RM6 ...58 D5
Dagenham RM9 ...103 D4
Wimbledon SW19 ...179 B5
Laker Pl SW15 ...157 A5
Lakeside
Beckenham BR3 ...207 D6
Borehamwood WD6 ...10 C6
Ealing W13 ...87 C1
Enfield EN2 ...3 D1
10 Kingston KT2 ...176 D3
Wallington SM6 ...219 B4
West Ewell KT19 ...215 C2
Lakeside Ave SE28 ...124 A5
Redbridge IG4 ...55 D5
Lakeside Cl Ruislip HA4 .39 B5
Sidcup DA15 ...168 C6
South Norwood SE25 ...184 A1
Lakeside Complex The
SE2 ...124 D5
Lakeside Cres EN4 ...14 D6
Lakeside Ct N4 ...51 A1
Lakeside Dr
Esher KT10 ...212 A2
Keston Mark BR2 ...226 A5
Lakeside Lo NW4 ...47 A5
Lakeside Rd W14 ...112 D3
Palmers Green N13 ...16 B1
Lakeside Way HA9 ...66 C4
Lakes Rd BR2 ...225 C3
Lakeswood Rd BR5 ...211 A3
Lake The WD23 ...8 B3
Lakeview 23 E3 ...96 D5
Lake View HA8 ...26 B5
Lake View Ct SW1 ...258 D6
Lakeview Ct E4 ...36 B4
Lakeview Rd DA16 ...146 B1
West Norwood SE27 ...182 D5
Lake View Terr N18 ...33 D6
Lakis Cl NW3 ...70 A4
Laleham Ave NW7 ...11 B1
Laleham Ho E2 ...243 C6
Laleham Rd
Catford SE6 ...164 A4
Littleton TW17 ...192 C4
Lambarde Ave SE9 ...188 C6
Lamb Ct 16 E14 ...119 A6
Lamberhurst Ho 14
SE15 ...140 C6
Lamberhurst Rd
Dagenham RM8 ...59 B1
West Norwood SE27 ...182 C5
Lambert Ave TW9 ...132 D2
Lambert Ho 19 N19 ...49 D2
17 SW9 ...138 C3
Lambert Lo TW8 ...109 D1
Lambert Rd N12 ...30 B5
SW2 ...160 B6
Newham E16 ...99 B1
Lambert's Pl CR0 ...205 B1
Lambert's Rd KT6 ...198 B4
Lambert St N1 ...72 C1
Lambert Way N12 ...30 A5
Lambert Wlk HA9 ...65 D5
Lambeth Coll (Brixton Ctr)
SW2 ...160 B6
Lambeth Coll (Clapham Ctr)
SW4 ...159 C6
Lambeth Coll (Tower
Bridge Ctr)
SE1 ...117 C5 253 B3
Lambeth Coll (Vauxhall Ctr)
SW8 ...137 D4 269 C2
Lambeth Ct 8 SW18 ...157 C6
Lambeth High St
SE1 ...116 B2 260 C4
Lambeth Hill EC4 ...252 A6
Lambeth Hospl SW9 ...138 B2
Lambeth Inst Strand Ctr
SW2 ...160 B4
Lambeth North Sta
SE1 ...116 C3 261 A6
Lambeth Palace*
SE1 ...116 B3 260 C5
Lambeth Palace Rd
SE1 ...116 B3 260 C6
Lambeth Pier SE1 ...260 B5
Lambeth Prospect
SE19 ...183 B4
Lambeth Rd
SE1 ...116 C3 261 B5
Thornton Heath CR0 ...204 D1
Lambeth Twrs SE11 ...261 A5
Lambeth Wlk
SE11 ...116 B2 260 D4
Lambfold Ho N7 ...72 A2
Lamb Ho SE10 ...142 A6
11 SE5 ...139 B4
28 SE5 ...139 A5
Lamb La E8 ...74 B1
Lamble St NW5 ...71 A4
Lambley Rd RM9 ...80 B2
Lambolle Pl NW3 ...70 C2
Lambolle Rd NW3 ...70 C2
Lambourn Cl 9 NW5 ...71 C4
W7 ...108 D4
Lambourne Ave SW19 179 B6
Lambourne Ct 5 IG8 ...37 C3
Lambourne Gdns
4 Barking IG11 ...79 D1
Chingford E4 ...19 C2
Enfield EN1 ...5 D3
Lambourne Gr KT1 ...176 D1
Lambourne Ho NW8 ...236 D4
SE16 ...118 D2
Lambourne Pl SE3 ...143 B4
Lambourne Rd E11 ...54 A2
Barking IG11 ...79 D1
Ilford IG3 ...79 C6
Lambourn Rd SW4 ...137 B2
Lambrook Ho 12 SE15 140 A4
Lambrook Terr
SW6 ...135 A4 264 A2
Lamb's Bldgs EC1 ...242 C5
Lamb's Cl N9 ...18 A2
Lamb's Conduit Pas
WC1 ...240 C4
Lamb's Conduit St
WC1 ...94 B3 240 C5
Lambscroft Ave SE9,
SE12 ...165 D1
Lambs Mdw IG8 ...37 D1
Lamb's Mews N1 ...234 C5
Lamb's Pas EC1 95 B3 242 C5
Lamb St E1 ...95 D2 243 C4
Lamb's Terr N9 ...17 B2
Lambs Wlk EN2 ...5 A3
Lambton Ct 2 N19 ...50 A1
Lambton Pl W11 ...244 D6
Lambton Rd N19 ...50 A1
Wimbledon SW20 ...178 C2
Lamb Wlk SE1 ...253 A1
Lamerock Rd BR1 ...186 D6
Lamerton Lo 10 TW9 ...132 B4
Lamerton St 9 SE8 ...141 C6
Lamford Cl N17 ...33 B3
Lamington St 3 W6 ...112 B2
Lamlash St SE11 ...261 C4
Lamley Ho SE10 ...141 D5
Lammas Ave CR4 ...181 A1
Lammas Gn SE26 ...162 B1
Lammas Park Gdns
W5 ...109 C5
Lammas Park Rd W5 .109 D4
Lammas Rd E9 ...74 D1
Richmond TW10 ...175 C6
Walthamstow E10 ...53 A1
Lammas Sch The E10 ...53 B1
Lammermoor Rd
SW12 ...159 B4
Lamont Rd
SW10 ...136 B6 266 C5
Lamont Rd Pas SW10 .266 C5
Lamorbey Cl DA15 ...167 D2
Lamorna Cl E17 ...36 A2
Lamorna Gr HA7 ...25 D1
Lampard Gr N16 ...51 D1
Lampern Sq 8 E2 ...96 A4
Lampeter Cl NW9 ...45 C3
Lampeter Sq W6 ...264 A5
Lamplighter Cl 31 E1 ...96 C3
Lampmead Rd SE12 ...142 D1
Lamport Cl SE18 ...122 B2
Lampson Ho 6 N19 ...71 C4
Lampton Ave TW5 ...129 D4
Lampton Ct TW5 ...129 D4
Lampton House Cl
SW19 ...178 D6
Lampton Park Rd
TW3 ...129 D3
Lampton Rd TW3,TW5 129 D3
Lampton Sch TW5 ...129 C4
Lanacre Ave NW9 ...27 C2
Lanain Ct SE12 ...164 D4
Lanark Cl W5 ...87 C2
Lanark Ct UB5 ...63 C3
Lanark Ho 11 SE1 ...118 A1
Lanark Mans 6 W12 ...112 C4
W9 ...236 B6
Lanark Pl W9 ..92 A3 236 B6
Lanark Rd W9 ..92 A4 229 A1
Lanark Sq E14 ...119 D3
Lanata Wlk UB4 ...84 D3
Lanbury Rd SE15 ...140 D1
Lancashire Ct W1 ...248 D6
Lancaster Ave
Barking IG11 ...101 C6
Hadley Wood EN4 ...2 B5
Wanstead E18 ...55 B5
West Norwood SE21,
SE27 ...161 A2
Wimbledon SW19 ...178 D5
Lancaster Cl 9 N1 ...73 C1
NW9 ...27 D3
W2 ...245 C5
Beckenham BR2 ...208 D5
Kingston KT2 ...175 D5
Stanwell TW19 ...148 A5
Tottenham N17 ...34 A3
Lancaster Cotts 1
TW10 ...154 A5
Lancaster Ct SW6 ...264 D3

Lancaster Ct continued
W2 246 B6
1 Belmont SM2 217 C1
Stanwell TW19 148 A3
Walton-on-T KT12 194 B2
West Norwood SE27 160 D2
Lancaster Dr E14 120 A5
NW3 70 C2
Lancaster Gate
W2 114 A6 246 B6
Lancaster Gate Sta
W2 114 B6 246 C6
Lancaster Gdns W13 109 B4
Kingston KT2 175 D5
Wimbledon SW19 179 A5
Lancaster Gr NW3 70 C2
Lancaster Ho Enfield EN2 5 B4
Putney SW15 134 C3
Wandsworth SW18 157 D4
Lancaster House SW1 249 A2
Lancasterian Inf Sch
N17 33 D2
Lancaster Lo 2 W11 91 A1
Lancaster Mews
3 SW18 157 D6
W2 114 A6 246 B6
2 Richmond TW10 154 A5
Lancaster Pk TW10 154 A6
Lancaster Pl
WC2 116 B6 250 C5
Hounslow TW5 128 D3
Ilford IG1 79 A4
Twickenham TW1 153 A4
1 Wimbledon SW19 178 D5
Lancaster Rd E11 76 C6
E17 34 D1
E7 77 A1
N11 31 D4
N4 50 C2
NW10 68 A3
W11 91 A1
Edmonton N18 33 D5
Enfield EN2 5 B4
Harrow HA2 41 C4
New Barnet EN4 14 B6
Northolt UB5 64 A2
Southall UB1 107 A6
South Norwood SE25 206 A6
Wimbledon SW19 178 D5
Lancaster Road Ind Est 2
EN4 14 B6
Lancaster St
SE1 116 D4 251 D1
Lancaster Stables 10
NW3 70 C2
Lancaster Terr
W2 114 B6 246 C6
Lancaster Wlk
W2 114 A5 246 B4
Hayes UB3 83 A1
Lancastrian Rd SM6 220 B1
Lancefield Ct 1 NW6 91 A5
Lancefield Ho SE15 140 B2
Lancefield St W10 91 B4
Lancell St N16 73 C6
Lancelot Ave HA0 65 D4
Lancelot Cres HA0 65 D4
Lancelot Gdns EN4 15 A4
Lancelot Par 4 HA0 65 D3
Lancelot Pl
SW7 114 D4 247 C1
Lancelot Rd DA16 146 A2
Wembley HA0 65 D3
Lance Rd HA1 42 A2
Lancer Sq W8 245 C2
Lancey Cl SE7 122 A2
Lanchester Ct W2 237 C1
Lanchester Rd N6 48 D4
Lancing Gdns N9 17 D3
Lancing Rd Ealing W13 109 B6
Feltham TW13 149 D2
Ilford IG2 57 B2
Thornton Heath CR0 204 B2
Lancing St NW1 232 C1
Lancresse Ct N1 95 C6
Landale Ho 13 SE16 118 C3
Landcroft Rd SE22 161 D5
Landells Rd SE22 162 A5
Lander Ct EN5 14 A6
Landford Rd SW15 134 C2
Landgrove Rd SW19 179 C5
Landin Ho 1 E14 97 C1
Landleys Field 21 N7 71 D3
Landmann Ho 16 SE16 118 B2
Landmann Way SE14 118 D1
Landmark Commercial Ctr
N18 33 C4
Landon Pl SW1 257 C6
Landons Cl E14 120 A5
Landon Way TW15 170 D4
Landon Wlk 14 E14 119 D6
Landor Ct N16 73 C3
Landor Ho 7 SE5 139 B5
Landor Rd SW9 138 A2
Landor Wlk 11 W12 112 A4
Landra Gdns N21 16 D5
Landrake NW1 232 B5
Landridge Dr EN1 6 B5
Landridge Rd SW6 135 B3
Landrock Rd N8 50 B3
Landscape Rd IG8 37 B3
Landseer Ave E12 78 C3
Landseer Cl
Edgware HA8 26 C1
Mitcham SW19 180 B2
Landseer Ct UB4 83 B5
Landseer Ho NW8 236 D6
SW1 259 D3
SW11 268 B1
17 Northolt UB5 84 D5
Landseer Rd N19 72 A6
Cheam SM1,SM2 217 C2
Enfield EN1 18 A6
New Malden KT3 199 B2
Lands' End WD6 9 D5
Landstead Rd SE18 145 B5
Landulph Ho SE11 261 B2
Landward Ct W1 237 B2
Lane Cl NW2 68 B5
Lane Ct SW11 158 D4
Lane End DA7 147 D2
Lane Gdns Bushey WD23 8 C4
Claygate KT10 212 D1
Lane Mews E12 78 B5
Lanercost Cl SW2 160 C2
Lanercost Gdns N14 16 A4
Lanercost Rd SW2 160 C2
Laneside HA8 27 A5
Chislehurst BR7 189 A5
Laneside Ave RM8 59 B2
Lane The NW8 92 A5 229 A3
SE3 143 A2
Laneway SW15 156 B6
Laney Bldg EC1 241 A4
Lanfranc Ct HA1 64 D5
Lanfranc Rd E3 97 A5
Lanfrey Pl W14 254 C1
Langbourne Ave N6 71 A6
Langbourne Ct E17 53 A3
Langbourne Ho 7
SW2 160 C6
Langbourne Mans N6 71 A6
Langbourne Pl E14 119 D1
Langbourne Prim Sch
SE21 161 C1
Langbourne Way
KT10 213 A2
Langbrook Rd SE3 143 D3
Langcroft Cl SM5 218 D5
Langdale NW1 232 A2
Langdale Ave CR4 202 D6
Langdale Cl BR6 226 D5
SE17 139 A6
Dagenham RM8 58 C1
Mortlake SW14 132 D1
Langdale Cres DA7 147 C4
Langdale Ct
3 Ealing W5 87 C2
9 Ilford IG1 78 D5
Langdale Dr UB4 83 C5
Langdale Gdns UB6 87 B4
Langdale Ho SW1 259 A1
Langdale Rd SE10 142 A5
Thornton Heath CR7 204 C5
Langdale St 3 E1 96 B1
Langdon Cres E6 100 C5
Langdon Ct EC1 234 D3
NW10 89 C6
Langdon Dr NW9 45 A1
Langdon Ho 1 E14 98 A1
Langdon Park Rd N6 49 C2
Langdon Park Sec Sch
E14 98 A1
Langdon Pl SW14 133 A2
Langdon Rd Barking E6 100 C6
Bromley BR2 209 B6
Morden SM4 202 A4
Langdon Sch E6 100 D6
Langdons Ct UB2 107 C3
Langdon Shaw DA14 189 D5
Langdon Way 14 SE1 118 A2
Langdon Wlk SM4 202 A4
Langford Cl E8 74 A3
7 N15 51 C3
NW8 229 B4
Langford Cres EN4 2 D1
Langford Ct NW8 229 B3
Langford Gn SE5 139 C2
Langford Ho 5 SE8 141 C6
Langford Pl
NW8 92 A5 229 B4
Sidcup DA14 168 A1
Langford Prim Sch
SW6 135 D3
Langford Rd 4 SW6 135 D3
Cockfosters EN4 2 D1
Woodford IG8 37 C4
Langfords IG9 21 D2
Langham Cl N15 50 D6
Langham Ct NW4 46 D4
Merton SW20 178 C1
4 Putney SW15 156 D6
Ruislip HA4 62 B3
12 Twickenham TW1 153 C5
Langham Dr RM6 58 B3
Langham Gdns HA8 27 A3
Ealing W13 109 B6
Richmond TW10 175 C6
Southgate N21 16 D6
Wembley HA0 65 C6
Langham Ho SW4 159 C6
Langham House Cl
TW10 175 D6
Langham Mans SW5 255 C1
Langham Park Pl BR2 208 D5
Langham Pl N15 50 D6
W1 93 B2 238 D3
Chiswick W4 133 C6
Langham Rd HA8 27 A4
N15 51 A6
Teddington TW11 175 B4
Wimbledon SW20 178 C2
Langham Sch The N15 51 A5
Langham St W1 93 B2 238 D3
Langhedge Cl N18 33 D4
Langhedge La N18 33 D4
Langhedge Lane Ind Est
N18 33 D4
Lang Ho 3 N19 71 C5
SW8 270 A3
Langholm Cl SW12 159 D4
Langholme WD23 8 A3
Langhorn Dr TW2 152 C4
Langhorne Ct 10 NW8 70 B1
Langhorne Ho 5 SE7 143 C6
Langhorne Rd RM10 81 C1
Langhurst Ho 10
SW11 137 A3
Langland Cres HA7 25 D1
Langland Dr HA5 23 A3
Langland Gdns NW3 69 D3
Croydon CR0 223 B6
Langland Ho 10 SE5 139 B5
Upper Tooting SW17 180 B5
Langler Rd NW10 90 C5
Langley Ave
North Cheam KT4,SM3 216 D6
Ruislip HA4 62 B6
Surbiton KT6 198 A1
Langley Cres HA8 11 A1
Dagenham RM9 80 D1
Harlington UB3 127 D5
Wanstead E11 55 C2
Langley Ct SW8 270 A2
WC2 250 A6
Langley Dr W3 110 D4
Wanstead E11 55 B2
Langley Gdns BR5 210 D3
Bromley BR2 209 C5
Dagenham RM9 80 D1
Langley Gr KT3 177 C1
Langley Ho BR1 187 B3
11 E5 74 B3
36 W2 91 C2
Langley La
SW8 138 A6 270 B6
Langley Manor BR3 208 A4
Langley Mans SW8 270 B6
Langley Park Rd SM1,
SM2 218 A1
Langley Park Sch for Boys
BR3 207 D3
Langley Park Sch for Girls
BR3 208 A3
Langley Pk NW7 27 C4
Langley Rd DA16 146 C6
Beckenham BR3 207 A5
Isleworth TW7 130 D3
Merton SW19 179 C2
Surbiton KT6 198 A2
Langley Row EN5 1 B4
Langley St WC2 94 A1 240 A1
Langley Way BR4 208 C2
Langmead Dr WD23 8 B3
Langmead Ho 34 E3 97 D4
Langmead St SE27 183 A6
Langmore Ct DA7 146 D2
Langmore Ho 28 E1 96 A1
Langport Ct KT12 194 C1
Langport Ho 1 SW9 138 D3
Langridge 15 NW5 71 A2
Langridge Mews
TW12 173 B4
Langroyd Rd SW17 158 D2
Langside Ave SW15 134 A1
Langside Cres N14 15 D1
Lang St E1 96 C3
Langston Hughes Cl 5
SE24 138 D1
Langthorn Ct EC2 242 D2
Langthorne Ct 4 SE6 186 A6
Langthorne Ho UB3 105 C2
Langthorne Lo 30
SW2 160 C4
Langthorne Rd E11 76 B5
Langthorne St SW6 134 D5
Langton Ave N20 14 B4
Wallend E6 100 C4
Langton Cl WC1 94 B3 240 D6
Langton Ct SW15 157 B5
Langton Ho SE11 260 D4
5 Streatham SW16 181 C6
Langton Pl SW18 157 C3
Langton Rd NW2 68 C5
Langton Rd continued
SW9 138 D5
East Molesey KT8 196 A5
Harrow HA3 24 A3
Langton Rise SE22,
SE23 162 B4
Langton St
SW10 136 A6 266 B5
Langton Way
Greenwich SE3 143 A5
South Croydon CR0 221 C4
Langtry Pl SW6 265 B6
Langtry Rd NW8 91 D6
Northolt UB5 84 D5
Langtry Wlk
NW8 92 A6 229 A6
NW8 91 D6
Langwood Chase
TW11 175 C4
Langworth Dr UB4 84 B1
Langworthy HA5 23 C4
Lanherne Ho 7 SW19 178 D3
Lanhill Rd W9 91 C3
Lanier Rd SE13 164 B5
Lanigan Dr TW3 151 D6
Lankaster Gdns N2 30 B2
Lankers Dr HA2 41 B3
Lankton Cl BR3 186 A2
Lanner Ho 2 SW11 136 C2
Lannock Rd UB3 105 D5
Lannoy Point SW6 264 B4
Lannoy Rd SE9 167 A3
Lanrick Rd E14 98 C1
Lanridge Rd SE2 124 D3
Lansbury Ave
Barking IG11 80 A1
Dagenham RM6 59 A4
Edmonton N18 33 C5
Feltham TW14 150 B5
Lansbury Cl NW10 67 A3
Lansbury Ct 4 SE28 124 B6
Lansbury Dr UB4 83 D3
Lansbury Gdns 1 E14 98 B1
Lansbury Ho 5 DA17 125 B1
Lansbury Rd EN3 6 D4
Lansbury Way N18 33 C5
Lanscombe Wlk SW8 270 A3
Lansdell Rd CR4 181 A1
Lansdown Cl KT12 194 C1
Lansdowne Ave DA7 146 D5
Orpington BR6 210 D1
Lansdowne Cl
Tolworth KT5 214 D6
Twickenham TW1 152 D3
Wimbledon SW20 178 D3
Lansdowne Copse 1
KT4 216 A6
Lansdowne Cres
W11 113 A6 244 B5
Lansdowne Ct 2 KT4 216 A6
Lansdowne Dr E8 74 A1
Lansdowne Gdns
SW8 138 A4 270 A2
Lansdowne Gr NW10 67 C4
Lansdowne Hill SE27 160 D1
Lansdowne Ho W11 244 C4
Enfield EN2 4 C3
Lansdowne La SE7 121 D1
Lansdowne Mews SE7 121 D1
W11 244 C4
Lansdowne Pl SE1 262 D6
Penge SE19 183 D3
Lansdowne Rd BR1 187 B3
E11 76 D6
E17 53 C3
E8 74 A2
N10 31 C1
N3 29 C3
W11 113 A6 244 B5
Chingford E4 19 C2
Croydon CR0 205 B1
Harrow HA1 42 C2
Hayes UB8 83 A1
Hounslow TW3 129 D2
Ilford IG3 57 D2
Stanmore HA7 25 C4
Tottenham N17 34 A2
Wanstead E18 55 A6
West Ewell KT19 215 B1
Wimbledon SW19,SW20 178 C3
Lansdowne Rise
W11 113 A6 244 B5
Lansdowne Row W1 248 D4
Lansdowne Sch SW9 138 B2
Lansdowne Terr WC1 240 B5
Lansdowne Way
SW4,SW8 138 A4 270 B1
Lansdowne Wlk
W11 113 B5 244 C4
Lansdowne Wood Cl 11
SE27 160 D1
Lansdown Ho 29 SE5 139 A3
Lansdown Rd E7 77 C1
Sidcup DA14 168 B1
Lansfield Ave N18 34 A6
Lanson Ct E11 76 D6
Lanson Ho HA8 26 C4
Lanswood Ct KT4 216 A6
Lantern Cl
Putney SW15 134 A1
Wembley HA0 65 D3
Lantern Ct 4 SW20 178 D2
Lantern Ho E14 119 C4
Lanterns Ct E14 119 C3
Lanterns The N12 29 D4
Lantern Way UB7 104 B4
Lant Ho SE1 252 A1
Lantry Ct 1 W3 110 D5
Lant St SE1 117 A4 252 B1
Lanvanor Rd SE15 140 C3
Lanyard Ho 3 SE8 119 B2
Lapford Cl W9 91 B3
Lapponum Wlk UB4 84 D2
Lapsang SE1 253 D3
Lapse Wood Wlk SE22 162 B3
Lapstone Gdns HA3 43 C3
Lapwing Ct NW9 27 C1
Tolworth KT6 214 C5
Lapwing Twr 31 SE8 141 B6
Lapwing Way UB4 84 D1
Lapworth 2 N11 31 B6
Lapworth Ct W2 91 D2
Lara Cl SE13 164 A5
Chessington KT9 214 A1
Larbert Rd SW16 181 C3
Larch Ave W3 111 C5
Larch Cl E13 99 C3
N11 31 A3
7 N19 71 C6
15 SE8 141 B6
Balham SW12 159 B2
Larch Cres Hayes UB4 84 D2
West Ewell KT19 214 D2
Larch Ct 41 W2 91 C2
Larch Dene BR6 226 C6
Larches Ave SW14 133 B1
Larches The
Edmonton N13 17 A1
Hillingdon UB10 82 D5
Larchfield Ho 2 N5 73 A3
Larch Gn NW9 27 C2
Larch Gr DA15 167 D3
Larch Ho 17 SE16 118 C4
Hayes UB4 84 C2
Larchmore Ct N19 72 A6
Larch Rd E10 75 C6
NW2 68 C4
Larch Tree Way CR0 223 C5
Larchvale Ct 4 SM2 217 D1
Larch Way BR2 210 C2
Larchwood Rd SE9 166 D2
Larcombe Cl CR0 221 D4
Larcom St
SE17 117 A2 262 B3
Larden Rd W3 111 C4
La Retraite RC Girls Sch
SW12 159 C4
Largewood Ave KT6 214 C6
Larissa St SE17 262 D3
Larix Ct NW10 90 A6
Larkbere Rd SE26 185 A6
Larken Cl WD23 8 A3
Larken Dr WD23 8 A3
Larkfield Ave HA3 43 B6
Larkfield Cl BR2 225 A6
Larkfield Rd DA14 167 D1
Richmond TW9 132 A1
Lark Hall Inf Sch SW4 137 D3
Lark Hall Jun Sch
SW4 138 A3
Larkhall La
SW4 138 A4 270 A1
Larkhall Rise SW4 137 D3
Larkham Cl TW13 149 C1
Lark Row E2 96 C6
Larksfield Gr EN1 6 B4
Larks Gr IG11 79 C1
Larkshall Bsns Ctr 2
E4 20 B2
Larkshall Cres E4 36 A6
Larkshall Ct E4 36 A5
Larkshall Rd E4 36 B6
Larkspur Cl 4 E6 100 A2
NW9 44 D4
Ruislip HA4 39 A2
Tottenham N17 33 B3
Larkspur Ct SM6 219 B1
Larkspur Gr HA8 27 A6
Larkspur Way KT19 215 A3
Larkswood Ct E4 36 B5
Larkswood Jun & Inf Sch
E4 35 D6
Larkswood Rd E4 35 D6
Larkswood Rise HA5 40 C5
Lark Way SM5 202 C2
Larkway Cl NW9 45 B5
Larmenier & Sacred Heart
RC Prim Sch W6 112 D2
Larnaca Ho SE1 263 C6
Larnach Rd W6 134 D6
Larne Rd HA4 39 D2
Larpent Ave SW15 156 C6
Larwood Cl UB6 64 B3
La Saint Union Rc Sec Sch
NW5 71 A5
Lascelles Ave HA1 42 B2
Lascelles Cl E11 76 B6
Lascelles Ho NW1 237 B5
Lascott's Rd N22 32 B4
Lashford Ho HA8 27 A4
Lassa Rd SE9 166 B6
Lassell St SE10 120 B1
Lasseter Pl SE3 142 D6
Latchett Rd E18 37 B2
Latchingdon Ct E17 52 D5
Latchmere Cl KT2,
TW10 176 A5
Latchmere Jun & Inf Schs
KT2 176 B4
Latchmere La KT2,
TW10 176 B5
Latchmere Rd SW11 136 D3
Kingston KT2 176 B4
Latchmere St 5
SW11 136 D3
Lateward Rd TW8 131 D6
Latham Cl E6 100 A1
4 Twickenham TW1 153 A4
Latham Ct
2 Bowes Park N11 32 A4
7 Northolt UB5 84 D4
Latham Ho E1 96 D1
18 E17 53 D6
Latham Rd DA6 169 C6
Twickenham TW1 152 D4
Latham's Way CR0 220 B6
Lathkill Cl EN1 18 A4
Lathkill Ct BR3 185 B2
Lathom Jun Sch E6 78 A1
Lathom Rd E6 78 B1
Lathwood Ho 6 SE26 184 B5
Latimer SE17 263 A1
Latimer Ave E6 100 B6
Latimer Cl
North Cheam KT4 216 B4
Pinner HA5 22 C2
Latimer Gdns HA5 22 C2
Latimer Ho 11 E9 74 D2
W11 244 D5
Latimer Pl W10 90 C1
Latimer Rd E7 77 B4
N15 51 C3
W10 90 C1
Barnet EN5 1 D2
Croydon CR0 220 D5
Teddington TW11 174 D5
Wimbledon SW19 179 D4
Latimer Road Sta
W10 112 D6
Latona Rd SE15 140 A6
La Tourne Gdns BR6 227 A5
Lattimer Pl W4 133 C6
Latton Cl KT12 195 A2
Latymer All Saints CE Prim
Sch N9 17 D2
Latymer Ct W6 112 D2
Latymer Rd N9 17 D3
Latymer Sch The N9 17 C2
Latymer Upper Sch
W6 112 A1
Latymer Way N9 17 C2
Lauder Cl UB5 84 D5
Lauder Ct N14 16 A4
Lauderdale Dr TW10 153 D1
Lauderdale Mans W9 91 D4
Lauderdale Rd W9 91 D4
Lauderdale Twr EC2 242 A4
Laud St SE11 116 B1 260 C2
Croydon CR0 221 A5
Laughton Ho 11 SW2 160 C5
Laughton Rd UB5 84 D6
Launcelot Prim Sch
BR1 187 A6
Launcelot Rd BR1,
SE12 187 A6
Launcelot St SE1 251 A1
Launceston Ct CR7 204 C3
Launceston Gdns UB6 65 C1
Launceston Pl
W8 114 A3 256 A5
Launceston Rd UB6 87 C6
Launch St E14 120 A3
Laundress La N16 74 A5
Laundry La 15 N1 73 A1
Laundry Mews SE23 162 D4
Laundry Rd
W6 135 A6 264 A5
Laura Cl Enfield EN1 17 C6
Wanstead E11 55 C4
Lauradale Rd N2 48 D5
Laura Pl E5 74 C4
Laurel Ave TW1 152 D3
Laurel Bank Gdns 3
SW6 135 B3
Laurel Bank Rd EN2 5 B4
Laurel Cl 5 N19 71 C6
Sidcup DA14 168 A1
Upper Tooting SW17 180 C5
Laurel Cres CR0 223 C5
Laurel Ct E8 73 D2
2 Putney SW15 156 D6
South Norwood SE25 205 C4
8 Wembley HA0 88 A5
Laurel Dr N21 16 C4
Laurel Gdns NW7 11 B1
Chingford E4 19 D4

Laurel Gdns *continued*
Ealing W7 108 C5
Hounslow TW4 129 A1
Laurel Gr
Forest Hill SE26 185 A6
Penge SE20 184 C3
Laurel Ho 5 NW3 69 D2
9 SE8 141 B6
Morden SM4 201 D4
Laurel La UB7 104 A2
Laurel Manor SM2 218 A1
Laurel Mead Ct 8 E18 37 A2
Laurel Pk HA3 24 D3
Laurel Rd Barnes SW13 134 A3
Teddington TW12 174 B5
Wimbledon SW20 178 B2
Laurel St E8 73 D2
Laurels The 8 BR1 187 B2
BR2 209 A5
N3 29 D4
Bushey WD23 8 C2
8 Belvedere DA17 125 C1
Buckhurst Hill IG9 21 C3
Laurel View N12 13 D1
Laurel Way E18 54 D5
N20 13 C1
Laurence Ct E10 53 D2
Laurence Mews 12
W12 112 A4
Laurence Pountney Hill
EC4 252 C6
Laurence Pountney La
EC4 252 D6
Laurie Gr SE14 141 A4
Laurie Ho SE1 261 D5
W8 113 C5 245 A3
Laurie Rd W7 86 C2
Laurier Rd NW5 71 B5
Croydon CR0 205 D2
Laurimel Cl HA7 25 B4
Laurino Pl WD23 8 A2
Lauriston Lo NW6 69 B2
Lauriston Rd E9 74 D1
Wimbledon SW19 178 D4
Lauriston Sch E9 96 D6
Lausanne Rd N8 50 C5
SE15 140 C4
Lavehham Ho E17 35 D2
Lavell St N16 73 B4
Lavender Ave NW9 45 A1
Mitcham CR4 180 D2
North Cheam KT4,SM3 216 C5
Lavender Cl BR2 210 A3
SW3 266 D5
Wallington SM5 219 B4
Lavender Ct SW4 270 B1
East Molesey KT8 195 D6
Lavender Gdns SW11 136 D1
Enfield EN2 4 D4
Stanmore HA3 24 C4
Lavender Gr E8 74 A1
Mitcham CR4 180 C2
Lavender Hill SW11 137 A2
Enfield EN2 4 D4
Lavender Ho 14 SE16 118 D5
Lavender Pl IG1 78 D3
Lavender Prim Sch EN2 5 C5
Lavender Rd SE16 119 A5
SW11 136 B2
Enfield EN2 5 B4
Hillingdon UB8 82 B2
Sutton SM1 218 B4
Thornton Heath CR0 204 B3
Wallington SM5 219 A4
West Ewell KT19 214 D2
Lavender Rise UB7 104 C4
Lavender St E15 76 C2
Lavender Sweep
SW11 136 D1
Lavender Terr 12
SW11 136 C2
Lavender Vale SM6 219 D2
Lavender Way CR0 206 D3
Lavender Wlk SW11 136 D1
Lavendon Ho NW8 237 B6
Lavengro Rd SE27 161 A2
Lavenham Ho E17 35 D2
Lavenham Rd SW18 157 C3
Lavernock Rd DA7 147 C3
Lavers Rd N16 73 C5
Laverstoke Gdns
SW15 156 A4
Laverton Mews SW5 255 D3
Laverton Pl SW5 255 D3
Lavidge Rd SE9 166 B2
Lavina Gr N1 233 C4
Lavington Cl E9 75 B2
Lavington Rd
Ealing W13 109 B5
Wallington CR0 220 B4
Lavington St
SE1 116 D5 251 D3
Lavinia Ct BR1 186 C3
Lavisham Ho BR1 187 B5
Lawdale Jun Sch E2 96 A4
Lawdon Gdns CR0 220 D4
Lawford Cl SM6 220 A1
Lawford Rd N1 73 C1
NW5 71 C2

Lawford Rd *continued*
Chiswick W4 133 A5
Lawfords Wharf 15
NW1 71 C1
Lawless Ho 5 E14 120 A6
Lawless St 11 E14 119 D6
Lawley Ho 10 TW1 153 D5
Lawley Rd N14 15 B4
Lawley St E5 74 C4
Lawman Ct 2 TW9 132 B4
Lawn Cl BR1 187 B3
Edmonton N9 17 D4
Kingston KT3 177 C1
Ruislip HA4 61 D5
Lawn Cres TW9 132 C3
Lawn Farm Gr RM6 59 A5
Lawnfield NW6 68 D1
Lawn Gdns W7 108 C5
Lawn House Cl E14 120 A4
Lawn La SW8 138 B6 270 C6
Lawn Rd NW3 70 D3
Beckenham BR3 185 B3
Lawns Ct HA9 66 C6
Lawnside SE3 142 D1
Lawns The N16 73 C3
SE3 142 D2
Belmont SM2 217 A1
Chingford E4 35 C5
Harrow HA5 23 D3
Sidcup DA14 190 B6
South Norwood SE19 183 B2
1 Wimbledon SW19 179 B5
Lawn Terr SE3 142 C2
Lawn The UB2 107 C1
Lawn Vale HA5 23 A1
Lawrence Ave E17 34 D2
NW7 27 D6
Edmonton N13 32 D6
Little Ilford E12 78 C4
New Malden KT3 199 C2
Lawrence Camp Ct N20 14 B1
Lawrence Cl E3 97 C5
N15 51 C5
6 W12 112 B6
Lawrence Cres
Dagenham RM10 81 D5
Edgware HA8 26 C1
Lawrence Ct N10 49 C6
N16 73 D5
NW7 27 C5
4 W3 111 A3
Lawrence Dr UB10 61 A4
Lawrence Est TW4 128 C1
Lawrence Gdns NW7 11 D1
Lawrence Hill E4 19 C2
Lawrence Ho SW1 259 D3
Bowes Park N22 32 B4
Lawrence La EC2 242 B2
Lawrence Mans SW3 267 A5
Lawrence Pl N1 233 B6
Lawrence Rd DA8 147 D5
E13 99 B6
E6 100 A6
N15 51 C5
W5 109 D2
Edmonton N18 34 B6
Hampton TW12 173 B3
Hayes BR4 225 A4
Hayes UB4 83 A5
Hounslow TW4 128 C1
Pinner HA5 40 D4
Richmond TW10 175 C6
South Norwood SE25 205 D5
Lawrence's Bldgs 1
N16 73 D5
Lawrence St E16 98 D2
NW7 27 D6
SW3 136 C6 267 A5
Lawrence Trad Est
SE10 120 C2
Lawrence Way NW10 67 B5
Lawrence Weaver Cl
SM4 201 C3
Lawrence Yd N15 51 C5
Lawrie Ct HA3 24 D3
Lawrie Park Ave SE26 184 B5
Lawrie Park Cres
SE26 184 B5
Lawrie Park Gdns
SE26 184 B5
Lawrie Park Rd SE26 184 C5
Lawson Cl Newham E16 99 C2
Wimbledon SW19 156 D1
Lawson Ct 1 N4 50 B1
13 Surbiton KT6 197 D2
Lawson Gdns HA5 40 B6
Lawson Ho 1 SE18 144 C6
17 W12 112 B6
Lawson Rd Enfield EN3 6 C4
Southall UB1 85 C3
Law St SE1 117 B3 262 D6
Lawton Rd E10 54 A1
E3 97 A4
Barnet EN4 2 B2
Laxcon Cl NW10 67 B3
Laxey Rd BR6 227 D2
Laxfield Ct E8 96 A6
Laxley Cl SE5 138 D5
Laxton Ct CR7 205 A5

Laxton Path 1 SE4 140 D1
Laxton Pl NW1 238 D6
Layard Rd SE16 118 B2
Enfield EN1 5 D4
South Norwood CR7 183 B1
Layard Sq SE16 118 B2
Laycock Prim Sch N1 72 D2
Laycock St N1 72 C2
Layer Gdns W3 110 C6
Layfield Cl NW4 46 B2
Layfield Cres NW4 46 B2
Layfield Ho 1 SE10 121 A1
Layfield Rd NW4 46 B2
Laymarsh Cl DA17 125 B3
Laymead Cl UB5 63 A2
Laystall Ct EC1 241 A5
Laystall St EC1 241 A5
Layton Cres CR0 220 D3
Layton Ct TW8 109 D1
Layton Pl TW9 132 C4
Layton Rd
Brentford TW8 109 D1
Hounslow TW3 129 D1
Layton's La TW16 171 D1
Layzell Wlk SE9 165 D3
Lazar Wlk 2 N7 72 B6
Leabank Cl HA1 64 C5
Leabank Sq E9 75 C2
Leabank View N15 52 A3
Leabourne Rd N16 52 A2
Lea Bridge Rd E10 53 C2
Lea Cl TW2 151 B4
Lea Cres HA4 61 D4
Leacroft Ave SW12 158 D4
Leacroft Cl
Southgate N21 16 D2
3 Yiewsley UB7 104 A6
Lea Ct 2 E13 99 A4
3 W12 111 C4
1 Chingford E4 20 A2
3 Hillingdon UB10 82 D3
Leadale Ave E4 19 C2
Leadale Rd N16 52 A3
Leadbeaters Cl N11 30 D5
Leadbetter Ct 10 NW10 67 B1
Leadenhall Mkt EC3 243 A1
Leadenhall Pl EC3 243 A1
Leadenhall St
EC3 95 C1 243 A1
Leadenham Ct 15 E3 97 C3
Leader Ave E12 78 C3
Leadings The HA9 67 A5
Leaf Cl KT7,KT8 196 C4
Leaf Gr SE27 182 C5
Leaf Ho 9 HA1 42 D4
Leafield Cl SW16 182 D4
Leafield La DA14 169 B1
Leafield Rd
Merton SW19,SW20 201 B6
Sutton SM1 217 C6
Leafy Gr BR2 225 C3
Leafy Oak Rd SE12 165 C1
Leafy Way CR0 221 D6
Lea Gdns HA9 66 B4
Leagrave St E5 74 C5
Lea Hall Gdns E10 53 C1
Lea Hall Rd E10 53 C1
Lea Ho E5 52 C1
NW8 237 A5
2 Edmonton N9 18 A1
Leaholme Waye HA4 39 A3
Leahurst Rd SE13 164 C6
Lea Int E9 75 C3
Leake St SE1 116 B4 250 D2
SE1 251 A1
Lealand Rd N15 51 D3
Leamington Ave BR6 227 C4
E17 53 C4
Bromley BR1 187 C5
Merton SM4 201 B5
Leamington Cl E12 78 A3
Bromley BR1 187 C5
Hounslow TW3 152 A6
Leamington Cres HA2 63 B5
Leamington Ct W3 89 B2
4 Forest Hill SE26 162 A1
Leamington Gdns IG3 79 D6
Leamington Ho 3 W11 91 B2
Edgware HA8 26 B5
Leamington Pk W3 89 B2
Leamington Pl UB4 83 D3
Leamington Rd UB2 106 D2
Leamington Rd Villas
W11 91 B2
Leamington Villas
SE13 164 C6
Leamore St W6 112 C2
Leamouth Rd E6 100 A2
South Bromley E14 98 B1
Leander Ct 27 E9 74 C1
7 NW9 27 C2
SE8 141 C4
5 Surbiton KT6 197 D2
Leander Rd SW2 160 C5
Northolt UB5 85 C5
Thornton Heath CR7 204 B5
Lea Rd
2 Beckenham BR3 185 C1
Enfield EN2 5 B4

Lea Rd *continued*
Southall UB2 107 A2
Learner Dr HA2 63 C6
Learoyd Gdns E6 122 C6
Leary Ho SE11 260 D1
Leas Cl KT9 214 B1
Leas Dale SE9 166 C1
Leas Gn BR7 189 D4
Leaside Ave N10 49 A5
Leaside Bsns Ctr EN3 7 B3
Leaside Ct UB10 82 D4
Leaside Ho 4 E5 52 B1
Leaside Mans N10 49 A6
Leaside Rd E5 52 C1
Leasowes Rd E10 53 C1
Leas The SE18 144 D4
Leatherbottle Gn
DA18 125 B3
Leather Cl CR4 181 A1
Leatherdale St 29 E1 96 C3
Leather Gdns E15 98 C6
Leatherhead Cl N16 51 D1
Leatherhead Rd KT9 213 D1
Leather La EC1 94 C2 241 B4
Leathermarket Ct SE1 253 A1
Leathermarket St
SE1 117 C4 253 A1
Leathersellers Cl EN5 1 A2
Leathsale Rd HA2 63 D5
Leathwaite Rd SW11 158 D6
Leathwell Rd SE8 141 D3
Lea Valley Prim Sch
N17 34 A3
Lea Valley Rd EN3 19 B5
Lea Valley Riding Sch
E10 52 D1
Lea Valley Technopark
N17 52 A6
Lea Valley Trad Est
N18 34 D5
Leaveland Cl BR3 207 C5
Leaver Gdns UB6 86 C5
Leavesden Rd HA7 25 A4
Leaview Ct 7 E4 20 A3
Lea View Ho E5 52 B1
Lebanon Ave TW13 172 D5
Lebanon Ct 10 TW1 153 B4
Lebanon Gdns SW18 157 C5
Lebanon Pk TW1 153 B4
Lebanon Rd SW18 157 C6
Croydon CR0 205 C1
Lebanon Road Sta
CR0 221 C6
Lebrun Sq SE3 143 B2
Lebus Ho NW8 230 A3
Le Chateau CR0 221 B5
Lechmere App IG8 37 D1
Lechmere Ave IG8 37 D1
Lechmere Rd NW2 68 B2
Leckford Rd SW18 158 A3
Leckhampton Pl 23
SW2 160 C4
Leckwith Ave DA17 147 A6
Lecky St SW7 114 B1 256 C2
Leclair Ho SE3 143 B2
L'Ecole des Petits
SW6 135 D3
Leconfield Ave SW13,
SW15 133 D2
Leconfield Ho SE5 139 C2
Leconfield Rd N5 73 B4
Leda Ave EN3 6 D5
Leda Ct 9 SW9 138 C5
Ledalle Ho NW2 68 B5
Ledam Bldg EC1 241 A4
Leda Rd SE18 122 B3
Ledbury Ho 12 SE22 139 C2
Ledbury Mews N W11 91 C1
Ledbury Mews W
W11 245 A6
Ledbury Pl 10 CR0 221 A4
Ledbury Rd W11 91 C1
Croydon CR0 221 B4
Ledbury St SE15 140 A5
Ledo Ho 1 N16 73 B4
Ledrington Rd SE19 184 A4
Ledway Dr HA9 44 B2
Lee Ave RM6 59 A3
Leechcroft Ave DA15 167 D6
Leechcroft Rd SM6 219 A5
Lee Church St SE13 142 C1
Lee Cl E17 34 D2
New Barnet EN5 2 A1
Lee Conservancy Rd E9 75 B3
Leecroft Rd EN5 1 A1
Leeds Ct EC1 241 C5
Carshalton SM5 218 D5
Catford SE6 163 D1
Leeds Rd IG1 57 B1
Leeds St N18 34 A5
Leegate SE12 164 D6
Lee Green SE12 142 D1
Lee High Rd SE12,SE13 142 C1
Lee Ho 3 N19 71 D3
Leeke St WC1 94 B4 233 C2
Leeland Mans W13 109 A5
Leeland Rd W13 109 A5
Leeland Terr W13 109 A5
Leeland Way NW10 67 D4

Lee Manor Sch SE13 164 C5
Leemount Cl NW4 46 D5
Lee Park Way N9,N18 19 A1
Lee Pk SE3 142 D2
Lee Rd NW7 28 D3
SE3 142 D1
Enfield EN1 18 A5
Merton SW19 179 D2
Wembley UB6 87 C6
Leerdam Dr E14 120 A3
Lees Ct W1 248 A6
Lees Ho SE17 262 D1
Leeside EN5 13 A5
Leeside Cres NW11 47 B4
Leeside Ind Est N17 34 B3
Leeside Rd N17 34 B4
Leeside Trad Est N17 34 C3
Leeside Works N17 34 C3
Leeson Ho 7 TW1 153 B4
Leeson Rd 12 SE24 138 C1
Leesons Hill BR5,BR7 211 D6
Leesons Way BR5 189 D1
Lees Par UB10 82 D3
Lees Pl W1 115 A6 248 A6
Lees Rd UB8 82 D3
Lee St E8 95 D6
Lee Sta SE12 165 A5
Lees The CR0 223 B6
Leet Ct N16 73 B4
Lee Terr SE3 142 C2
Lee Valley L Ctr N9 19 A3
Lee Valley Sp Ctr E15 75 D4
Leeve Ho 7 W9 91 B4
Lee View EN2 4 D4
Leeward Ct 3 E1 118 A5
Leeward Gdns SW19 179 B5
Leeway SE8 119 B1
Leeway Cl HA5 23 B3
Leewood Cl SE12 165 A5
Lefevre Wlk E3 97 B6
Leffern Rd W12 112 A4
Leff Ho 7 NW6 69 A1
Lefroy Ho SE1 252 A1
Lefroy Rd W12 111 D4
Legard Rd N5 72 D5
Legat Ct N4 51 A4
Legatt Rd SE9 165 D6
Leggatt Rd E15 98 A5
Legge St SE13 164 A6
Leghorn Rd NW10 90 A5
SE18 123 B1
Legion Cl N1 72 C1
Legion Ct SM4 201 C3
Legion Rd UB6 86 A5
Legion Terr E3 97 C6
Legion Way N12 30 C3
Legrace Ave TW4,TW5 128 D3
Leicester Ave CR4 204 A5
Leicester Cl KT4 216 C4
Leicester Ct 46 W2 91 C2
WC2 249 D6
11 Twickenham TW1 153 D5
Leicester Gdns IG3 57 C2
Leicester Ho 4 SW9 138 D2
5 Putney SW15 156 C4
2 Thames Ditton KT7 197 A2
Leicester Mews N2 48 C6
Leicester Pl WC2 249 D6
Leicester Rd N2 48 C6
NW10 67 B1
Barnet EN5 1 D1
Croydon CR0 205 C2
Wanstead E11 55 B4
Leicester Sq★
WC2 115 D6 249 D5
Leicester Square Sta
WC2 115 D6 249 D6
Leicester St WC2 249 D6
Leigham Ave SW16 160 A1
Leigham Cl SW16 182 B6
Leigham Court Rd
SW16 182 C6
Leigham Dr TW7 130 C5
Leigham Hall 3 SW16 160 A1
Leigham Hall Par 2
SW16 160 A1
Leigham Vale SE27,
SW16,SW2 160 C2
Leigh Ave IG4 55 D5
Leigh Cl KT3 199 B5
Leigh Cres CR0 223 D1
Leigh Ct 22 SW2 160 C5
Harrow HA2 42 C1
3 Woodford E18 37 A1
Leighfield Ho 5 N4 51 A2
Leigh Gdns NW10 90 C5
Leigh Ho
4 Kingston KT2 176 D4
9 Putney SW15 156 A6
Leigh Hunt Dr N14 15 D3
Leigh Orchard Cl
SW16 160 B1
Leigh Pl DA16 146 A3
EC1 241 A4
Leigh Rd E10 54 A2
N5 72 D4
Isleworth TW3 130 B1
Wallend E6 78 C2
Leigh St WC1 94 A4 233 A1

Leigh The KT2 177 C3
Leighton Ave
Little Ilford E12 78 C3
Pinner HA5 41 A6
Leighton Cl HA8 26 C1
Leighton Cres NW5 71 C3
Leighton Gdns NW10 90 C5
Thornton Heath CR0 204 D2
Leighton Gr NW5 71 C3
Leighton Ho 7 KT6 198 A3
Leighton House (Art Gall &
Mus)★ W14 254 D6
Leighton Pl NW5 71 C3
Leighton Rd NW5 71 C3
Ealing W13 109 A4
Enfield EN1 18 A6
Harrow HA3 24 B1
Leighton St CR0 204 D1
Leila Parnell Pl 14
SE7 143 C6
Leinster Ave SW14 133 A1
Leinster Ct NW6 91 C4
Leinster Gdns
W2 114 A6 246 A6
Leinster Mews W2 246 A6
Leinster Pl W2 236 A1
Leinster Rd N10 49 B5
Leinster Sq W2 91 D1
Leinster Terr W2 246 A6
Leisure Way N12 30 B3
Leitch Ho 8 NW8 70 B1
Leith Cl NW9 45 B1
Leithcote Gdns SW16 182 B6
Leithcote Path SW16 160 B1
Leith Hill BR5 190 A2
Leith Hill Gn BR5 190 A2
Leith Ho 7 N7 71 D3
13 Streatham SW2 160 B4
Leith Mans W9 91 D4
Leith Rd N22 32 D2
Leith Towers 11 SM2 217 D1
Leith Yd 3 NW6 91 C6
Lela Ave TW4,TW5 128 C3
Lelitia Cl E8 96 A6
Lelland Ho 8 SE7 122 A2
Lely Ho 3 UB5 84 D5
Leman St E1 96 A1
Lemark Cl HA7 25 C4
Le May Ave SE12 165 B1
Lemmon Rd SE10 142 C6
Lemna Ct E11 54 C2
Lemna Rd E11 54 C2
Le Moal Ho 23 E1 96 C2
Lemon Gr TW14 150 A3
Lemonwell Ct SE9 167 A6
Lemonwell Dr SE9 167 A6
Lemsford Cl N15 52 A4
Lemsford Ct N4 73 A6
Lena Cres N9 18 C2
Lena Gardens Prim Sch
W6 112 C3
Lena Gdns W6 112 C3
Lena Kennedy Cl E4 36 A4
Len Clifton Ho 13
SE18 122 B2
Lendal Terr 7 SW4 137 D2
Lenelby Rd KT6 198 C1
Len Freeman Pl SW6 264 C5
Lenham 11 NW5 71 A2
Lenham Ho SE1 252 D1
Lenham Rd DA7 147 B6
SE12 142 D1
South Norwood CR7 183 B1
Sutton SM1 218 A3
Lennard Ave BR4 224 C6
Lennard Cl BR4 224 C6
Lennard Rd BR2 210 B1
Croydon CR0 205 A1
Penge BR3 185 A4
Lennon Rd NW2 68 C2
Lennox Gdns NW10 67 D4
SW1 114 D3 257 C5
Croydon CR0 220 D4
Redbridge IG1 56 B1
Lennox Gdns Mews
SW1 257 C4
Lennox Ho 10 E9 74 C2
7 Belvedere DA17 125 C3
Lennox Rd E17 53 C3
N4,N7 72 C6
Lenor Cl DA6 147 A1
Lensbury Way SE2 124 D3
Lens Rd E7 77 C1
Lenthall Ho SW1 259 B1
Lenthall Rd E8 74 A1
Lenthorp Rd SE10 120 D2
Lentmead Rd BR1 164 D1
Lenton Rise TW9 132 A2
Lenton St SE18 123 B2
Len Williams Ct NW6 91 C5
Leo Ct 4 TW8 131 D5
Leof Cres SE6 185 D5
Leominster Rd SM4 202 A3
Leominster Wlk SM4 202 A3
Leonard Ave SM4 202 A4
Leonard Ct W8 255 A6

Lingfield Ave KT1,KT5 198 B5
Lingfield Cl EN1 17 C5
Lingfield Cres SE9,
DA16 145 B1
Lingfield Ct
Northolt UB5 85 C5
Wimbledon SW19 178 D4
Lingfield Gdns N9 18 B4
Lingfield Ho SE1 251 D1
5 W4 111 A1
Penge SE26 184 B4
Lingfield Rd
North Cheam KT4 216 C5
Wimbledon SW19 178 D4
Lingham St SW9 138 B3
Lingholm Way EN5 12 D6
Ling Rd E16 99 A2
Lingrove Gdns IG9 21 B2
Ling's Coppice SE21 161 B2
Lingwell Rd SW17 158 C1
Lingwood DA7 147 D3
Lingwood Gdns TW7 130 C5
Lingwood Rd E5 52 A2
Linhope St
NW1 92 D3 237 C5
Linkenholt Mans 3
W6 111 D2
Linkfield KT8 195 D6
Link Field BR2 209 A3
Linkfield Rd TW7 130 D3
Link La SM6 220 A2
Linklea Cl NW9 27 C3
Link Prim Sch CR0 220 A4
Link Rd N11 31 A6
Dagenham RM9 103 D5
East Bedfont TW14 149 D4
Hackbridge SM6 203 A1
Links Ave SM4 201 C5
Linkscroft Ave TW15 170 D4
Links Ct N20 14 B1
Links Dr N20 13 D3
Link Sec Sch CR0 220 B4
Links Gdns SW16 182 C3
Linkside N12 29 C4
Kingston KT3 177 C1
Linkside Cl EN2 4 C2
Linkside Gdns EN2 4 B2
Links Ind Est TW13 151 A1
Links Prim Sch SW17 181 A4
Links Rd NW2 67 D6
Acton W3 88 C1
Ashford TW15 170 A5
Mitcham SW16,SW17 181 A4
West Wickham BR4 208 A1
Woodford IG8 37 A5
Links Side EN2 4 C2
Link St E9 74 C2
Links The E17 53 A5
Linksview N2 48 D4
Links View N3 29 B3
SE18 144 D4
Links View Cl HA7 25 A4
Links View Rd
Croydon CR0 223 C5
Hampton TW12 174 A6
Linksway NW4 28 D1
Links Way
Beckenham BR3 207 C3
Streatham SW17 181 A4
Links Yd E1 243 D4
9 E1 96 A2
Link The NW2 46 A1
SE9 166 C1
Acton W3 88 D1
Enfield EN3 7 A4
Northolt UB5 63 B3
Pinner HA5 40 C2
Teddington TW11 174 D4
Wembley HA0 43 C1
Linkway N4 51 A2
Dagenham RM8 80 C4
Pinner HA5 22 D2
West Barnes SW20 200 B6
Link Way Bromley BR2 210 A2
Richmond TW10 153 B2
Linkway The EN5 13 D5
Linkwood Wlk NW1 71 D1
Linley Cres RM7 59 D6
Linley Ct
1 Dulwich SE21 183 C6
Sutton SM1 218 A4
Linley Rd N17 33 C1
Linnell Cl NW11 47 D3
Linnell Dr NW11 47 D3
Linnell Ho E1 243 C4
NW8 229 A6
Linnell Rd SE5 139 C3
Edmonton N18 34 A5
Linnet Cl N9 18 D3
Bushey WD23 8 A3
Woolwich SE28 124 C6
Linnet Mews SW12 159 A4
Linnett Cl E4 36 A6
Linom Rd SW4 138 A1
Linscott Rd E5 74 C4
Linsdell Rd IG11 101 A6
Linsey St SE16 118 A2
SE16 118 A3
Linslade Cl
Hounslow TW4 151 A6
Pinner HA5 40 B6
Linslade Ho 10 E2 96 A6
NW8 237 B6
Linstead St 1 NW6 69 C1
Linstead Way SW18,
SW19 157 A4
Linsted Ct SE9,DA15 167 C5
Linster Gr WD6 11 A6
Lintaine Cl W6 264 B5
Linthorpe Ave HA0 65 C2
Linthorpe Rd N16 51 C2
Cockfosters EN4 2 C2
Linton Cl DA16 146 B4
2 SE7 121 C1
Carshalton CR4 202 D2
Linton Gdns E6 100 A1
Linton Gr SE27 183 A5
Linton Ho 2 E3 97 C2
Linton Mead Prim Sch
SE28 124 B6
Linton Rd IG11 79 A1
Linton St N1 95 A6 235 B5
Lintons The IG11 79 A1
Linver Rd SW6 135 C3
Linwood Cl SE5 139 D3
Linwood Cres EN1 6 A4
Linzee Rd N8 50 A5
Lion Ave TW1 152 D3
Lion Cl SE4 163 C5
Littleton TW17 192 A6
Lion Ct 12 NW9 46 A5
Lion Ctr The TW13 151 A1
Lionel Gdns SE9 165 D6
Lionel Ho 5 W10 91 A2
Bowes Park N22 32 B4
Lionel Mans 14 W14 112 D3
Lionel Mews W10 91 A2
Lionel Rd SE9 165 D6
Lionel Road Jun & Inf Sch
TW8 110 A2
Lionel Road N TW8 110 A2
Lionel Road S TW8 110 B1
Lion Gate Gdns TW9 132 B2
Lion Gate Mews SW18 157 C4
Lion Mills 33 E2 96 A5
Lion Park Ave KT9 214 C4
Lion Rd DA6 147 B1
E6 100 B2
Edmonton N9 18 A2
Thornton Heath CR0 205 A4
Twickenham TW1,TW2 152 D3
Lions Cl SE12 165 D1
Lion Way TW8 131 D5
Lion Wharf Rd TW7 131 B2
Lion Yd SW4 137 D1
Liphook Cres SE23 162 C4
Liphook Rd WD19 22 D6
Lipton Cl SE28 124 C6
Lipton Rd 8 E1 96 D1
Lisa Lo 5 EN5 13 D6
Lisbon Ave TW2 152 A2
Lisbon Cl E17 35 B1
Lisburne Rd NW3 70 D4
Lisford St SE15 139 D4
Lisgar Terr
W14 113 B2 254 C4
Liskeard Cl BR7 189 A4
Liskeard Gdns SE3 143 A4
Liskeard Ho SE11 261 B2
Lisle Cl SW17 181 B6
Lisle Ct NW2 69 A5
Lisle St WC2 115 D6 249 D6
Lismirrane Ind Pk WD6 9 B5
Lismore 9 SW19 179 B5
Lismore Cl TW7 131 A3
Lismore Rd N17 51 B6
South Croydon CR2 221 C2
Lismore Wlk 4 N1 73 A2
Lissant Cl KT6 197 D2
Lisselton Ho 3 NW4 46 D5
Lissenden Gdns NW5 71 A4
Lissenden Mans NW5 71 A4
Lisson Cotts NW1 237 B4
Lisson Gr NW1,
NW8 92 C3 237 A6
Lisson Ho NW1 237 A4
Lisson St NW1 92 C2 237 A4
Lister Cl W3 89 B2
Mitcham SW19 180 C2
Lister Com Sch E13 99 B5
Lister Ct N16 73 C6
NW9 27 C1
Lister Gdns N18 33 A5
Lister Ho E1 96 A2
SE2 124 D1
SE3 142 C6
Hayes UB3 105 C2
8 Wembley HA9 67 A5
Lister Hospl
SW1 115 B1 258 C1
Lister Mews N7 72 B4
Lister Rd E11 54 D1
Lister Wlk SE28 124 D6
Liston Ho N21 16 B6
Liston Rd SW4 137 C2
Tottenham N17 34 A2
Liston Way 1 IG8 37 C3
Listowel Cl 2 SW9 138 C5
Listowel Rd RM10 81 C5
Listria Lo N16 73 D6
Listria Pk N16 73 D6
Litcham Ho 23 E1 96 D4
Litchfield Ave E15 76 C2
Morden SM4 201 B2
Litchfield Ct E17 53 C3
Litchfield Gdns NW10 68 A2
Litchfield Rd SM1 218 A4
Litchfield St WC2 249 D6
Litchfield Way NW11 48 A4
Lithgow's Rd TW14,
TW6 127 D1
Lithos Rd NW3 70 A2
Little Acre BR3 207 C6
Little Albany St NW1 238 D6
Little Argyll St W1 239 A1
Little Birches DA15 167 C2
Little Boltons The
SW10 255 D1
Little Bornes SE21 183 C6
Littlebourne 2 SE13 164 C4
Little Britain EC1 242 A3
Littlebrook Cl CR0 206 D3
Little Brownings SE23 162 B2
Littlebury Rd SW4 137 D2
Little Bury St N9 17 C4
Little Bushey La WD23 8 B5
Little Cedars N12 30 A6
Little Chelsea Ho
SW10 266 B5
Little Chester St SW1 258 C6
Little College St SW1 260 A6
Littlecombe SE7 143 B6
Little Combe Cl 13
SW15 156 D5
Little Common HA7 9 A1
Littlecote Cl SW19 157 A4
Littlecote Pl HA5 23 B2
Littlecroft SE9 144 C2
Little Ct BR4 224 C6
Littledale SE2 146 A6
Little Dimocks SW12 159 B2
Little Dorrit Ct SE1 252 B2
Little Ealing La W5 109 C2
Little Ealing Prim Sch
W5 109 C3
Little Edward St NW1 231 D2
Little Elms UB3 127 B5
Little Essex St WC2 251 A6
Little Ferry Rd TW1 153 B3
Littlefield Cl N19 71 C4
9 Kingston KT1 176 A1
Littlefield Ct UB7 126 A5
Littlefield Ho KT1 176 A1
Littlefield Rd HA8 27 A3
Little Friday Rd E4 20 C2
Little Gearies IG6 56 D5
Little George St SW1 250 A1
Little Gn TW9 131 D1
Little Grange UB6 87 A4
Little Green St NW5 71 B4
Littlegrove EN4 14 C5
Littlegrove Ct 3 EN4 14 C5
Little Halliards KT12 194 A3
Little Heath SE7 122 A1
Ilford RM6 58 B5
Little Heath Rd DA7 147 B5
Littleheath Rd CR2 222 B1
Little Heath Sch RM6 58 B5
Little Holt 8 E11 55 A4
Little Ilford La E12 78 B4
Little Ilford Sch E12 78 B3
Littlejohn Rd W7 86 D1
Little Larkins EN5 13 A5
Little Marlborough St
W1 239 A1
Littlemead KT10 212 B4
Littlemede SE9 166 B1
Littlemoor Rd IG1 79 B5
Littlemore Rd SE2 124 A4
Little Moss La HA5 23 A1
Little Newport St
WC2 249 D6
Little New St EC4 241 B2
Little Orchard Cl HA5 23 A1
Little Oxhey La WD19 23 A6
Little Park Dr TW13 151 A2
Little Park Gdns EN2 5 B2
Little Pluckett's Way
IG9 21 D3
Little Portland St W1 239 A2
Little Potters WD23 8 C4
Little Queens Rd
TW11 174 D4
Little Rd UB3 105 D4
Little Redlands BR1 188 A1
Little Road Mans SW6 264 B5
Littlers Cl SW19 180 B2
Little Russell St WC1 240 A3
Little Sanctuary SW1 250 A1
Little Smith St SW1 259 D6
Little Somerset St E1 243 C1
Little Stanmore Fst & Mid
Sch HA8 26 B2
Little St James's St
SW1 249 A3
Little St Leonards
SW14 133 A2
Littlestone Cl BR3 185 C4
Little Strand NW9 27 D1
Little Thrift BR5 211 A5
Little Titchfield St W1 239 A3
Littleton Ave E4 20 D3
Littleton CE Inf Sch
TW17 192 C6
Littleton Cres HA1 64 D6
Littleton La TW17,
TW18 192 A4
Littleton Rd Harrow HA1 64 D6
Littleton TW15,TW17 171 A3
Littleton St SW18 158 A2
Little Trinity La EC4 252 B6
Little Venice*
W9 92 A2 236 A4
Littlewood SE13 164 A5
Littlewood Cl W13 109 B3
Little Wood Cl BR5 190 A2
Littleworth Ave KT10 212 B3
Littleworth Common Rd
KT10 212 B5
Littleworth La KT10 212 B4
Littleworth Pl KT10 212 B4
Littleworth Rd KT10 212 C4
Livermere Ct 3 E8 95 D6
Livermere Rd E8 95 D6
Liverpool Gr
SE17 117 B1 262 C1
Liverpool Ho N7 72 C2
Liverpool Rd E10 54 A3
E16 98 C2
N1 234 B5
N1,N7 72 C1
W5 109 D4
Kingston KT2 176 C3
South Norwood CR7 205 A6
Liverpool St
EC2 95 C2 243 A3
Liverpool Street Sta
EC2 95 C2 243 A3
Livesey Cl KT1 198 B6
Livesey Mus* SE15 140 B6
Livesey Pl SE15 140 A6
Livingstone Ct E10 54 A3
Barnet EN5 1 A3
Stanwell TW19 148 A3
Livingstone Ho 16 SE5 139 A5
Livingstone Lo 13 W9 91 C2
Livingstone Pl E14 120 A1
Livingstone Prim Sch
EN4 2 B2
Livingstone Rd E15 98 A6
E17 53 D3
14 SW11 136 B2
Bowes Park N13 32 A5
Isleworth TW3 130 A1
Southall UB1 106 D6
South Norwood CR7 183 B1
Livity Sch The SW2 160 A6
Livonia St W1 239 B1
Lizard St EC1 95 A4 235 B1
Lizban St SE3 143 B5
Llandovery Ho 1 E14 120 A4
Llanelly Rd NW2 69 B6
Llanover Ct HA9 65 D4
Llanover Rd SE18 144 C5
Wembley HA9 65 D5
Llanthony Rd SM4 202 B4
Llanvanor Rd NW2 69 B6
Llewellyn Ct SE20 184 C2
Llewellyn St SE16 118 A4
Lloyd Ave SW16 182 A2
Lloyd Baker St
WC1 94 C4 234 A1
Lloyd Ct SE13 163 D6
Pinner HA5 40 D4
6 West Norwood SE27 160 D1
Lloyd Ho N16 73 B5
3 Beckenham BR3 185 D4
Bromley BR1 187 B5
Lloyd Mews EN3 7 C5
Lloyd Park Ave CR0 221 D4
Lloyd Park Ho E17 53 C6
Lloyd Park Sta CR0 221 D4
Lloyd Rd E6 100 B6
Dagenham RM9 81 B1
North Cheam KT4,SM3 216 D5
Walthamstow E17 52 D5
Lloyd's Ave EC3 243 B1
Lloyd's Bldg*
EC3 95 C1 243 A1
Lloyd's Pl SE3 142 C3
Lloyd Sq WC1 94 C4 234 A2
Lloyd's Row
EC1 94 D4 234 C1
Lloyd St WC1 94 C4 234 A2
Lloyds Way BR3 207 B4
Lloyd Villas SE4 141 C3
Loampit Hill SE13 141 D3
Loampit Vale SE13 142 A2
Loanda Cl 17 E8 95 D6
Loanda Ho SE15 140 C2
Loats Rd SW2 160 A5
Lobelia Cl 5 E6 100 A2
Locarno Rd 6 W3 111 A5
Greenford UB6 86 B3
Lochaber Rd SE13 142 C1
Lochaline St W6 134 C6
Lochan Cl UB4 85 A3
Lochbie 5 N4 50 A2
Lochinvar St SW12 159 B4
Lochleven Ho 9 N2 30 B1
Lochmere Cl DA8 147 D6
Lochmore Ho SW1 258 B3
Lochnagar St E14 98 A2
Lockbridge Ct 3 W9 91 C2
Lock Chase SE3 142 C2
Lock Cl UB2 108 A4
Locke Ho SW8 269 A2
Lockesfield Pl E14 119 D1
Lockesley Dr BR5 211 D3
Lockesley Sq KT6 197 D3
Locket Rd HA3 24 D1
Lockfield Ave EN3 7 B4
Lockgate Cl E9 75 B3
Lockhart Cl N7 72 B2
Enfield EN3 18 B6
Lockhart Lo 4 E4 20 C4
Lockhart St E3 97 B3
Lock Ho N16 51 D1
Lockhurst St E5 74 D4
Lockier Wlk HA9 65 D5
Lockington Rd
SW8 137 B4 268 D2
Lockmead Rd N15 52 A3
SE13 142 A2
Lock Rd TW10 175 C6
Lock's La CR4 181 A1
Locksley St E14 97 B2
Locksmeade Rd TW10 175 C6
Lock View Ct 9 E14 119 A6
Lockwood Cl SE26 184 D6
Lockwood Ct KT3 199 A5
Lockwood Ho 10 SE11 138 C6
Lockwood Ind Pk N17 52 B6
Lockwood Sq SE16 118 B3
Lockwood Way E17 34 D1
Chessington KT9 214 C3
Lockyer Est SE1 252 D1
Lockyer Ho 7 SE10 120 D1
SW8 270 A4
Putney SW15 134 D2
Lockyer St SE1 252 D1
Locomotive Dr TW14 150 A3
Locton Gn 4 E3 97 B6
Lodden Lo 13 SM2 218 A1
Loddiges Ho 5 E9 74 C1
Loddiges Rd E9 74 C1
Loddon Ho NW8 236 D5
Loder St SE15 140 C5
Lodge Ave
Borehamwood WD6 10 B6
Croydon CR0 220 C5
Dagenham RM8,RM9,IG11 80 B3
Harrow HA3 44 A5
Lodge Cl Edgware HA8 26 C4
Edmonton N18 33 A5
Hackbridge SM6 203 A1
Isleworth TW7 131 B4
Lodge Ct 3 HA0 66 A3
Lodge Dr N13 32 C6
Lodge Gdns BR3 207 B4
Lodge Hill DA16 146 B5
Redbridge IG4 56 A5
Lodgehill Park Cl HA2 63 D6
Lodge La DA5 168 D5
N12 30 A5
New Addington CR0 223 D1
Lodge Pl SM1 217 D3
Lodge Rd NW4 46 C5
NW8 92 C4 230 A1
Bromley BR1 187 C3
Sutton SM1 217 D3
Thornton Heath CR0 204 D2
Wallington SM6 219 B3
Lodge Villas IG8 36 D4
Lodge Way
Charlton TW17 171 A1
Stanwell TW15 148 A2
Lodore Gdns NW9 45 C4
Lodore Gn UB10 60 A5
Lodore St E14 98 A1
Lodsworth Ho SW11 268 A1
Lofthouse Pl KT9 213 C2
Loftie St SE16 118 A4
Lofting Rd N1 72 C1
Lofts on the Park 24 E9 74 D2
Loftus Rd W12 112 B5
Loftus Rd (Queens Park
Rangers FC) W12 112 B5
Logan Cl Enfield EN3 6 D4
Hounslow TW4 129 B2
Logan Mews W8 255 A4
Logan Pl W8 113 C2 255 A4
Logan Rd Edmonton N9 18 B2
Wembley HA9 66 A6
Loggetts SE21 161 C2
Logs Hill BR1,BR7 188 A2
Logs Hill Cl BR7 188 A2
Lohmann Ho 5 SE11 138 C6
Lois Dr TW17 192 D4
Lolesworth Cl E1 243 D3
Lollard St
SE11 116 C2 261 A3
Loman St SE1 116 D4 251 D2
Lomas Cl CR0 224 A1
Lomas St E1 96 A2
Lombard Ave Enfield EN3 6 C4
Ilford IG3 57 C1
Lombard Bsns Pk
Merton SW19 179 D1
Thornton Heath CR0 204 B2
Lombard Ct EC3 252 D6
Lombard Ho 4 SE10 142 A5
Lombard La EC4 241 B1
Lombard Rd N11 31 B5
SW11 136 B3
Merton SW19 179 D1
Lombard Rdbt CR0 204 B2
Lombard St EC3 95 B1 242 D1
Lombard Trad Est SE7 121 B2
Lombard Wall SE7 121 B2
Lombardy Pl W2 245 D5
Lombardy Ret Pk UB3 106 B6
Lomley Ho 10 SW2 160 C5
Lomond Cl N15 51 C4
Wembley HA0 66 B1
Lomond Ct HA3 42 D6
Lomond Gdns CR2 223 A1
Lomond Gr SE5 139 B5
Lomond Ho 10 SE5 139 B4
Loncroft Rd SE5 139 C6
Londale Ct SE10 142 A4
Londesborough Ho 1
N16 73 C4
Londesborough Rd
N16 73 C4
London Aquarium*
SE1 250 C1
London Bridge
EC4,SE1 117 B6 252 D5
London Bridge City Pier
SE1 117 C5 253 A4
London Bridge Hospl
SE1 117 B5 252 D4
London Bridge St
SE1 117 B5 252 D3
London Bridge Sta
SE1 117 B5 252 D3
London Business Sch
NW1 92 D3 237 C6
London Butterfly Ho*
TW8 131 B4
London Canal Mus*
N1 94 A5 233 B4
London Central Mosque*
NW8 92 C4 230 B1
London Chest Hospl E2 96 C5
London City Airport
E16 122 B5
London Clinic
NW1 93 A3 238 B5
London Coll of Fashion
EC2 95 C3 243 B6
London Coll of Fashion The
W1 238 B1
London Coll of International
Business Studies
WC1 240 B3
London Coll of Printing
SE11 116 D3 261 D5
London Ct 3 SW18 157 C6
London Docklands Visitor
Ctr E14 120 A4
London Dungeon The*
SE1 117 B5 252 D4
London Eye (Millennium
Wheel)* SE1 116 B4 250 C2
London Fields East Side
E8 74 B1
London Fields Prim Sch
E8 96 B6
London Fields Sta E8 74 B1
London Fields West Side
E8 74 A1
London Foot Hospl
W1 93 C3 239 A5
London Gas Mus The*
E3,E16 98 B3
London Group Bsns Pk
NW2 46 A1
London Ho NW8 230 B4
Edgware HA8 26 A6
London Hospital Dental Inst
E1 96 B2
London Independent Hospl
The E1 96 D2
London Ind Pk The E6 100 C2
London Inst The W1 238 C1
Streatham SW17 181 B5
London International Film
Sch WC2 94 A1 240 B1
London La E8 74 B1
Bromley BR1 186 D3
London Metropolitan Univ
E1 95 D1 243 D2
London Metropolitan Univ
(Carleton Grange Hall) 2
N7 71 D4

London Metropolitan Univ (Central Ho) E1 96 A1
London Metropolitan Univ (Coll of Tech & Design) E1 96 A1
London Metropolitan Univ (Commercial Rd) E1 96 A1
London Metropolitan Univ (Ladbrook Ho) N5 72 D3
London Metropolitan Univ (Moorgate) EC2 95 B2 242 C3
London Metropolitan Univ (North London Campus) N7 72 C3
London Metropolitan Univ (Tufnel Park Hall) N7 71 C5
London Metropolitian Univ (Spring Ho) N7 72 C2
London Mews W2 236 D2
London Nautical Sch The SE1 116 C5 251 B4
London Oratory Sch The SW6 135 C5 265 B4
London Peace Pagoda★ SW3 267 D4
London Rd E13 99 A5
SE1 116 D3 261 D6
Ashford TW15,TW18, TW19,TW14 148 B2
Brentford TW7,TW8 131 B4
Bromley BR1 186 D3
Enfield EN2 5 B1
Forest Hill SE22,SE23 162 C3
Hackbridge SM6,CR4 219 B6
Harrow HA1 64 C6
Hounslow TW3,TW7, TW1,TW8 130 B3
Kingston KT1,KT2 176 B1
Morden SM4 201 C5
Romford RM7,RM8 59 C3
Stanmore HA7 25 D6
Stoneleigh KT17 216 B3
Stoneleigh KT17,KT4, SM3 216 B3
Thornton Heath CR0, CR7,SW16 204 C3
Twickenham TW1 153 A4
Wembley HA9 66 A2
Carshalton CR4 203 A2
London Road Rdbt TW1 153 A5
London Sch of Economics & Political Science WC2 94 B1 240 D1
London St EC3 253 B6
W2 92 B1 236 C1
London Stile 5 W4 110 C1
London Terr 1 E2 96 A5
London Theological Seminary at Kensit Memorial Coll N3 29 A1
London Toy & Model Mus★ W2 114 A6 246 A6
London Transport Mus★ WC2 250 B6
London Wall EC2 95 B2 242 D3
London Wharf 4 E2 96 B6
London Zoo★ NW1 93 A5 231 A4
Lonesome Prim Sch CR4 181 B1
Lonesome Way CR4 181 C2
Long Acre WC2 94 A1 240 B1
Long Acre Ct W13 87 A2
Longacre Pl SM5 219 A2
Longacre Rd E17 36 B2
Longbeach Rd SW11 136 D2
Longberrys NW2 69 B5
Longboat Row UB1 85 B1
Longbow Ho 20 N1 95 C6
Longbridge Ho RM8 80 B4
Longbridge Rd
Barking IG11 79 C3
Dagenham RM8 80 B4
Longbridge Way SE13 164 A6
Longbury Dr BR5 190 B1
Longcliffe Ho SW18 157 D6
Longcroft SE9 166 C1
Longcrofte Rd HA8 25 D3
Longdale Sq N1 234 B6
Long Deacon Rd E4 20 C3
Long Ditton Cty Inf Sch KT6 197 C1
Longdon Wood BR2 226 A4
Longdown Rd SE6 185 C6
Long Dr W3 89 C1
Greenford UB6 85 D6
Ruislip HA4 62 D4
Long Elmes HA3 24 A2
Longfellow Rd E17 53 B3
North Cheam KT4 200 B1
Longfellow Way SE1 263 D3
Long Field NW9 27 D3
Longfield
3 Bromley BR1 186 D2
Loughton IG10 21 C6
Longfield Ave E17 53 A5
NW7 28 A3
Ealing W5 109 C6
Enfield EN3 6 C5
Hackbridge SM6 203 A1
Wembley HA9 44 A1
Longfield Cres SE23, SE26 162 C1
Longfield Ct 4 N2 48 A6
Longfield Dr
Mitcham SW19 180 C2
Mortlake SW14 154 D6
Longfield Est SE1 263 D3
Longfield Fst & Mid Schs HA2 41 C3
Longfield Ho E17 53 B4
Ealing W5 109 C6
Longfield Rd W5 87 C1
Longfield St SW18 157 C4
Longford Ave
Feltham TW14 149 D5
Southall UB1 107 D6
Stanwell TW19 148 A3
Longford Cl
Feltham TW13 151 A1
Hampton TW12 173 C6
Hayes UB4 106 D6
Longford Ct 2 E5 74 D4
6 NW4 46 C5
1 W12 111 C4
Southall UB1 107 C5
West Ewell KT19 215 A4
Longford Gdns
Hayes UB4 106 D6
Sutton SM1 218 A6
Longford Ho 7 E1 96 C1
1 Catford BR1 186 B5
Hampton TW12 173 C6
Longford Ind Est TW12 173 D4
Longford Rd TW2 151 D3
Longford Sch TW14 149 D4
Longford St NW1 93 B3 238 D6
Longford Way TW19 148 A3
Longford Wlk 9 SW2 160 C4
Longhayes Ave RM6 58 D5
Longhayes Ct RM6 58 D5
Longheath Gdns CR0 206 C4
Longhedge Ho SE26 184 A6
Longhill Rd SE6 164 B1
Longhook Gdns UB5 84 B4
Longhope Cl SE15 139 D6
Longhurst Ho 8 W9 91 B4
Longhurst Rd SE13 164 C6
Croydon CR0 206 B3
Long La DA7 147 B4
EC1 94 D2 241 D4
N2 48 B6
N3 29 D2
SE1 117 B4 252 D1
Croydon CR0 206 C3
Hillingdon UB10 60 D1
Stanwell TW15,TW19 148 B3
Longland Ct E9 75 A3
SE1 118 A1
Longland Dr N20 13 D2
Longlands Ct DA15 167 D1
E17 35 A2
W11 244 D6
Mitcham CR4 181 A2
Longlands Park Cres DA15 167 C2
Longlands Prim Sch DA15 167 C1
Longlands Rd DA15 167 D1
Longleat Ho SW1 259 C2
Longleat Rd EN1 17 C6
Longleat Villas 3 DA6 147 A1
Longleat Way TW14 149 B4
Longleigh Ho 8 SE5 139 C4
Longleigh La SE2 146 C6
Longlents Ho 3 NW10 89 B6
Longley Ave HA0 88 B6
Longley Ho 5 N19 71 C4
Longley Rd Harrow HA1 42 B5
Thornton Heath CR0 204 D2
Upper Tooting SW17 180 D4
Long Leys E4 36 A4
Longley St SE1 118 A2
Longley Way NW2 68 C5
Longman Ho 9 E2 96 B5
10 E8 95 D6
Long Mark Rd 5 E16 99 D2
Longmead BR7 188 C1
Long Mead NW9 27 D2
Longmead Dr DA14 168 D2
Longmead Ho SE27 183 A5
Long Meadow 20 N7 71 D3
Long Meadow Cl BR3, BR4 208 A2
Longmeadow Rd DA15 167 C3
Longmead Prim Sch UB7 104 A2
Longmead Rd
Hayes UB3 105 D6
Thames Ditton KT7 196 D2
Upper Tooting SW17 180 D5
Longmoor Point 14 SW15 156 B3
Longmore Ave EN4,EN5 14 B5
Longmore St SW1 115 C2 259 A3
Longnor Rd E1 96 D4
Long Pond Rd SE3 142 C4
Long Rd SW4 137 C1
Longreach Ct IG11 101 B5
Long Reach Rd IG11 101 D3
Longridge Ho SE1 262 B5
Longridge La UB1 85 D1
Longridge Rd SW5 113 C2 255 B3
Long Ridges N2 49 A6
Long's Ct W1 249 D5
Longs Ct 2 TW9 132 B1
Longshaw Prim Sch E4 20 B1
Longshaw Rd E4 20 B1
Longshore SE8 119 B2
Long St E2 95 D4
Longstaff Cres SW18 157 C4
Longstaff Rd SW18 157 C5
Longstone Ave NW10 89 D6
Longstone Rd SW17 181 B5
Longthorne Ho 20 E3 97 B4
Longthornton Rd SW16 181 D1
Longton Ave SE26 184 A6
Longton Gr SE26 184 B6
Longville Rd SE11 261 D4
Longwalk Rd UB11 104 D5
Long Wlk SE1 263 B6
SE18 144 D6
Kingston KT3 199 A6
Longwood Bsns Pk TW16 193 D4
Longwood Dr SW15 156 A5
Longwood Gdns IG2, IG6,IG5 56 C6
Longwood Par IG6 56 D6
Longworth Cl SE28 102 D1
Long Yd WC1 94 B3 240 C5
Loning The NW9 45 D5
Enfield EN3 6 C5
Lonsdale Ave
Newham E6 100 A3
Wembley HA9 66 A3
Lonsdale Cl SE12 165 D1
Edgware HA8 26 B5
Hillingdon UB8 83 A2
Newham E6 100 A3
Pinner HA5 23 A2
Lonsdale Cres IG2 56 D3
Lonsdale Dr EN2 16 A6
Lonsdale Dr N EN2 4 A1
Lonsdale Gdns CR7, SW16 204 B5
Lonsdale Ho 6 N4 51 A2
SW6 135 C2
Lonsdale Mews W11 91 B1
4 Richmond TW9 132 C4
Lonsdale Pl N1 72 C1
Lonsdale Rd E11 54 D2
NW6 91 B6
W11 91 B1
W4 111 D2
Barnes SW13 133 D5
Bexley DA7 147 B3
Croydon SE25 206 B5
Southall UB2 106 D3
Lonsdell Ho 9 SW2 160 C5
Loobert Rd N15 51 C6
Looe Gdns IG6 56 D6
Loop Rd BR7 189 A4
Lopen Rd N18 33 C6
Lopen Works N18 33 C6
Lopez Ho 4 SW9 138 A2
Lorac Ct 13 SM2 217 C1
Loraine Cl EN3 18 C6
Loraine Ct BR7 188 D5
Loraine Ho 1 SM5 219 B4
Loraine Rd N7 72 B4
Chiswick W4 132 D6
Lord Ave IG5 56 B6
Lord Chancellor Wlk KT2 177 A2
Lord David Pitt Ho 8 SE24 138 C1
Lordell Pl SW19 178 C4
Lorden Wlk 25 E2 96 A4
Lord Gdns IG5 56 B5
Lord Hills Rd W2 91 D2
Lord Holland La 5 SW9 138 C3
Lord Knyvetts Ct 3 TW19 148 A5
Lord Napier Pl W6 112 A1
Lord North St SW1 260 A5
Lord Roberts Mews SW6 265 C3
Lord Roberts Terr SE18 122 C1
Lords Cl Feltham TW13 151 A2
West Norwood SE21 161 A2
Lord's Cricket Mus★ NW8 92 B4 229 D1
Lords Ct 3 HA8 27 A3
Lordship Gr N16 73 B6
Lordship Ho 3 N16 73 B6
Lordship La SE22 161 D5
Tottenham N22 33 B2
Lordship Lane Prim Sch N22 33 A2
Lordship Park Mews N16 73 A6
Lordship Pk N16 73 B6
Lordship Pl SW3 267 A5
Lordship Rd N16 73 B6
Northolt UB5 63 A1
Lordship Terr N16 73 B6
Lord's Indoor Cricket Sch NW8 229 D2
NW8 230 A2
Lord's (MCC & Middlesex Cty Cricket Ground)★ NW8 92 B4 229 D2
Lordsmead Rd N17 33 C1
Lord St E16 122 A5
Lord's View NW8 229 D1
Lord Warwick St SE18 122 B3
Loreburn Ho 2 N7 72 B4
Lorenzo St N1,WC1 233 C2
Loretto Gdns HA3 44 A5
Lorian Cl N12 29 D6
Loring Rd N20 14 C2
Isleworth TW7 130 D3
Loris Rd W6 112 C3
Lorn Ct SW9 138 C3
Lorne Ave CR0 206 D2
Lorne Cl NW8 92 C4 230 B1
Lorne Ct SW15 156 D5
Lorne Gdns 5 W11 112 D4
Croydon CR0 206 D2
Wanstead E11 55 C5
Lorne Ho 7 E1 97 A2
3 N11 31 B5
Lorne Rd E17 53 C4
E7 77 C4
N4 50 B1
Harrow HA3 24 D1
3 Richmond TW10 154 B6
Lorn Rd SW9 138 C3
Lorraine Ct 10 NW1 71 B1
Beckenham BR3 186 A2
Lorraine Pk HA3 24 C3
Lorrimore Rd SE17 138 D6
Lorrimore Sq SE17 138 D6
Lorton Ho 9 NW6 91 C6
Loseberry Rd KT10 212 B3
Lostock Ho 10 SW8 137 D3
Lothair Rd W5 109 D4
Lothair Rd N N4 50 D3
Lothair Rd S N4 50 D2
Lothbury EC2 95 B1 242 C2
Lothian Ave UB4 84 B2
Lothian Cl HA0 65 A5
Lothian Rd SW9 138 D4
Lothrop St W10 91 A4
Lots Rd SW10 136 A5 266 B3
Loubet St SW17 180 D4
Loudoun Ave IG6 56 D4
Loudoun Rd NW8 92 A6 229 B5
Loudwater Cl TW16 194 A5
Loudwater Rd TW16 194 A5
Loughborough Ct 7 SW9 138 D2
Loughborough Junction Sta SW9 138 D2
Loughborough Pk SW9 138 D1
Loughborough Prim Sch SW9 138 D3
Loughborough Rd SE5,SW9 138 D3
Loughborough St SE11 116 B1 260 D1
Lough Rd N7 72 B2
Loughton Way IG9 21 D3
Louisa Cl E9 96 D6
Louisa Ct TW2 152 C2
Louisa Gdns E1 96 D3
Louisa Ho SW15 133 D1
Louisa St E1 96 D3
Louis Ct 3 RM10 81 D2
Louise Bennett Cl 9 SE24 138 D1
Louise Ct
4 Wanstead E11 55 B4
Wood Green N22 32 C2
Louise De Marillac Ho 18 E1 96 C2
Louise Graham Ho 5 IG11 101 B6
Louise Rd E15 76 C2
Louise White Ho 1 N19 49 D1
Louis Gdns BR7 188 B6
Louis Mews N10 31 B2
Louisville Rd SW17 159 A1
Lousada Lo N14 15 C5
Louvaine Rd SW11 136 B1
Lovage App E6 100 A2
Lovat Cl NW2 67 D5
Lovat La EC3 253 A5
Lovatt Cl HA8 26 D4
Lovatt Ct SW12 159 B3
Lovatt Dr HA4 39 D4
Lovat Wlk TW5 129 A5
Loveday Ho 2 SW2 160 C3
Loveday Rd W13 109 B5
Lovegrove St SE1 140 A6
Lovegrove Wlk E14 120 A5
Lovekyn Cl KT2 176 B1
Love La DA5 169 C5
EC2 95 A1 242 B2
SE18 122 D2
Cheam SM3 217 A2
Cheam SM4 201 D2
Croydon SE25 206 B6
Long Ditton KT6 213 D6
Mitcham CR4 202 C6
Pinner HA5 41 A6
Tottenham N17 33 D3
Lovelace Ave BR2 210 C3
Lovelace Gdns
Barking IG11 80 A4
Surbiton KT6 197 D2
Lovelace Gn SE9 144 B2
Lovelace Ho 12 E8 95 D6
Lovelace Prim Sch KT9 213 C3
Lovelace Rd
East Barnet EN4 14 C4
Surbiton KT6 197 D2
West Norwood SE21 161 A3
Loveland Mans 6 IG11 79 D1
Lovel Ave DA16 146 A3
Lovelinch Cl SE15 140 C6
Lovell Ho E8 96 A6
4 Merton SW19 180 A2
Lovell Pl SE16 119 A3
Lovell Rd
Richmond TW10 153 C1
Southall UB1 85 D1
Loveridge Mews NW6 69 B2
Loveridge Rd NW6 69 B2
Lover's Wlk W1 115 A5 248 A3
Lovett Dr SM5 202 B2
Lovette Ho 3 E3 97 C4
Lovett Way NW10 67 A3
Love Wlk SE5 139 B3
Lovibonds Ave BR6 226 D5
Hillingdon UB7 82 B1
Lowbrook Rd IG1 78 D4
Low Cross Wood La SE21 161 D1
Lowdell Cl UB7 82 A1
Lowden Rd SE24 139 A1
Edmonton N9 18 B3
Southall UB1 107 A6
Lowder Ho 6 E1 118 B5
Lowe Ave E16 99 A2
Lowell Ho 10 SE5 139 A5
Lowell St E14 97 A1
Lower Addiscombe Rd CR0 205 C1
Lower Addison Gdns W14 113 A4 244 A1
Lower Belgrave St SW1 115 B3 258 C5
Lower Boston Rd W7 108 C4
Lower Broad St RM10 103 C6
Lower Camden BR7 188 B2
Lower Church St CR0 220 D6
Lower Clapton Rd E5 74 C4
Lower Clarendon Wlk 12 W11 91 A1
Lower Comm S SW15 134 B2
Lower Coombe St CR0 221 A4
Lower Downs Rd SW20 178 D2
Lower Fosters NW4 46 C4
Lower George St 13 TW10 153 D6
Lower Gn W CR4 202 C6
Lower Gravel Rd BR2 210 B1
Lower Green Gdns KT4 200 A1
Lower Green Rd KT10 212 A6
Lower Grosvenor Pl SW1 115 B3 258 D6
Lower Grove Rd TW10 154 B6
Lower Hall La E4 35 A6
Lower Hampton Rd TW12,TW16 172 D1
Lower Ham Rd KT2 175 D4
Lower James St W1 249 B6
Lower John St W1 249 B6
Lower Kenwood Ave EN2 16 A6
Lower Lea Crossing E14,E16 120 C6
Lower Maidstone Rd N11 31 C4
Lower Mall W6 112 B1
Lower Marsh SE1 116 C4 251 A1
Lower Marsh La KT1, KT5 198 C5
Lower Merton Rise NW3 70 C1
Lower Morden La SM4 201 A3
Lower Mortlake Rd TW9 132 B2
Lower Park Rd N11 31 C5
Belvedere DA17 125 C2
Loughton IG10 21 D6
Lower Pk 5 SW15 156 D6
Lower Place Bsns Ctr NW10 89 A5
Lower Queen's Rd IG9 21 D2
Lower Rd N2 30 B2
SE16 118 C4
Belvedere DA17 125 D3
Harrow HA2 42 B1
Sutton SM1 218 A4
Lower Richmond Rd
Mortlake SW14,TW9 132 D2
Putney SW15 134 C2
Lower Robert St WC2 250 B5
Lower Sand Hills KT6 197 C2
Lower Sloane St SW1 115 A1 258 A2
Lower Strand NW9 27 D1
Lower Sunbury Rd TW12 173 C1
Lower Sydenham Sta SE26 185 B5
Lower Teddington Rd KT1 175 D2
Lower Terr NW3 70 A5
Lower Thames St EC3 117 C6 253 A5
Lower Tub WD23 8 B4
Lowerwood Ct W11 91 A1
Lower Wood Rd KT10 213 B2
Lowestoft Cl 5 E5 74 C6
Lowestoft Mews E16 122 D4
Loweswater Cl HA9 65 D6
Loweswater Ho E3 97 B3
Lowfield Rd NW6 69 C1
W3 89 A1
Low Hall Cl E4 19 D4
Low Hall La E17 53 A3
Low Ho IG11 102 A5
Lowick Rd HA1 42 C4
Lowland Gdns RM7 59 D3
Lowlands NW3 70 C2
Lowlands Rd
Harrow HA1 42 C2
Pinner HA5 40 C3
Lowman Rd N7 72 B4
Lowndes Cl SW1 258 B5
Lowndes Ct SW1 257 D6
Lowndes Lo EN5 1 D2
Lowndes Pl SW1 115 A3 258 A5
Lowndes Sq SW1 114 D4 247 D1
Lowndes St SW1 115 A3 258 A6
Lownds Ct BR1 187 A1
Lowood Ct SE19 183 D5
Lowood Ho 11 E1 118 C6
Lowood St E1 118 B6
Lowry Cres CR4 180 C1
Lowry Ct 3 SE16 118 B1
Lowry Ho N17 33 D2
Lowry Lo 2 HA0 65 D3
Lowry Rd RM8 80 B3
Lowther Cl WD6 10 B6
Lowther Dr EN2 4 A1
Lowther Hill SE23 163 A4
Lowther Ho 11 E8 95 D6
SW1 259 B1
Lowther Prim Sch SW13 134 A6
Lowther Rd E17 35 A1
N7 72 C3
Barnes SW13 133 D4
Kingston KT2 176 B2
Stanmore HA7 44 B6
Lowth Rd SE5 139 A3
Loxdon Ct RM6 58 B3
Loxford Ave E6 99 D5
Loxford Ho SW1 258 B3
Loxford La IG1 79 B3
Loxford Rd IG11 78 D2
Loxford Sch of Science & Tech IG1 79 B3
Loxham Rd E4 35 D3
Loxham St WC1 233 B1
Loxley Cl SE26 184 D5
Loxley Rd
Feltham TW12 173 B6
Wandsworth SW18 158 B3
Loxton Rd SE23 163 A3
Loxwood Cl TW14 149 C3
Loxwood Rd N17 51 C6
Loyola Prep Sch IG9 21 C3
Lubavitch House Gram Sch N2 48 A4
Lubbock Ct BR7 188 B3
Lubbock Ho 18 E14 119 D6
Lubbock Rd BR7 188 B3
Lubbock St SE14 140 C5
Lucan Ho N1 235 D5

Lucan Pl SW3 114 C2 257 B3
Lucan Rd EN5 1 A2
Lucas Ave E13 99 B6
Harrow HA2 63 C6
Lucas Ct SW11 268 B1
Forest Hill SE26 185 A5
Lucas Gdns N2 30 A1
Lucas Ho 2 SW8 137 C3
Lucas Rd SE20 184 C4
Lucas Sq NW11 47 C3
Lucas St SE4,SE8 141 C4
Lucas Vale Prim Sch
SE8 141 C4
Lucerne Cl N14 16 A1
Lucerne Ct 5 DA18 125 A3
8 Beckenham BR3 185 C3
Lucerne Gr E17 54 B5
Lucerne Mews W8 245 B4
Lucerne Rd BR6 211 D1
N5 72 D4
South Norwood CR7 205 A5
Lucey Rd SE16 118 A3
Lucey Way SE16 118 A2
Lucie Ave TW15 170 D4
Lucien Rd
Upper Tooting SW17 181 A6
Wandsworth SW18 157 D2
Lucille Ho SE26 184 B4
Lucknow St SE18 145 C5
Lucorn Cl SE12 164 D5
Lucraft Ho 12 SW2 160 A4
Luctons Ave IG9 21 C3
Lucy Ashe Ho SE17 261 D3
Lucy Brown Ho SE1 252 B3
Lucy Cres W3 89 A3
Lucy Gdns RM8 81 A5
Luddesdon Rd DA8 147 C5
Ludford Cl NW9 27 C1
Croydon CR0 220 D4
Ludgate Broadway
EC4 241 D1
Ludgate Cir
EC4 94 D1 241 C1
Ludgate Hill
EC4 94 D1 241 D1
Ludgate Sq EC4 241 D1
Ludham NW5 70 D3
Ludham Cl SE28 102 C1
Ludlow Cl BR2 209 A6
Harrow HA2 63 B4
Ludlow Ct W3 111 A4
Ludlow Rd Ealing W5 87 C3
Feltham TW13 172 A6
Ludlow St EC1 242 A6
Ludlow Way N2 48 A5
Ludovick Wlk SW15 133 C1
Ludwell Ho W14 254 B6
Ludwick Mews SE14 141 A5
Luffield Rd SE2 124 B3
Luffman Rd SE12 165 B1
Lugard Ho W12 112 B5
Lugard Rd SE15 140 B4
Lugg App E12 78 C5
Luke Ho 31 E1 96 B1
Lukes Ct N3 47 C6
Luke St EC2 95 C3 243 A6
Lukin Cres E4 20 B1
Lukin St E1 96 C1
Lullingstone Cl BR5 190 B3
Lullingstone Cres BR5 190 B3
Lullingstone Ho 20
SE15 140 C6
Lullingstone La SE13 164 B5
Lullingstone Rd 3
DA17 147 B6
Lullington Garth N12 29 B5
Borehamwood WD6 10 D6
Bromley BR1 186 C3
Lullington Rd
Dagenham RM9 81 A1
Penge SE20 184 A3
Lulot Gdns N19 71 B6
Lulworth NW1 71 D1
SE17 262 C2
Lulworth Ave
Hounslow TW5,TW7 130 A5
Wembley HA9 43 C2
Lulworth Cl HA2 63 B5
Lulworth Cres CR4 180 C1
Lulworth Ct N14 16 A1
Lulworth Dr HA5 41 A2
Lulworth Gdns HA2 63 B6
Lulworth Ho SW8 270 C3
Lulworth Rd DA16 145 D3
SE15 140 B3
Chislehurst SE9 166 A2
Lulworth Waye UB4 84 B1
Lumen Rd HA9 65 D6
Lumiere Bldg The E7 77 D3
Lumiere Ct SW17 159 A2
Lumley Cl DA17 125 C1
Lumley Ct WC2 250 B5
Lumley Flats SW1 258 A2
Lumley Gdns SM3 217 A3
Lumley Ho KT3 199 B1
Lumley Rd SM1,SM3 217 A3
Lumley St W1 238 B1
Lumsdon NW8 91 D6
Lunan Ho 12 E3 97 B5
Luna Rd CR7 205 A6
Lundin Wlk WD19 22 D6
Lund Point E15 98 A6
Lundy Dr UB3 105 C2
Lunham Rd SE19 183 C4
Lupin Cl Croydon CR0 206 D1
Streatham SW2 160 D2
Lupin Cres IG11 78 D2
Lupino Ct SE11 260 C4
Lupin Point SE1 253 D1
Lupton Cl SE12 187 B6
Lupton St NW5 71 C4
Lupus Ct SE19 183 B2
Lupus St SW1 115 C1 259 B1
Luralda Gdns E14 120 B1
Lurgan Ave W6 134 D6
Lurline Gdns
SW11 137 A4 268 B2
Luscombe Ct BR2 186 C1
Luscombe Ho SW18 157 B6
Luscombe Way
SW8 138 A5 270 A4
Lusher Ho SW15 156 D5
Lushington Ho KT12 194 C3
Lushington Rd NW10 90 B5
Catford SE6 185 D5
Lushington Terr 11 E8 74 A3
Lutea Ho SM2 218 A1
Luther Cl HA8 11 A2
Luther King Cl E17 53 A3
Luther Rd TW11 174 D5
Luton Pl SE10 142 A5
Luton Rd E13 99 A3
E17 53 B6
Sidcup DA14 168 C1
Luton St NW8 92 B3 236 D5
Luttrell Ave SW15 156 B6
Lutwyche Rd SE6 163 B2
Lutyens Ho SW1 259 A1
Luxborough Ho W1 238 A4
Luxborough St
W1 93 A2 238 A4
Luxborough Twr W1 238 A4
Luxemburg Gdns W6 112 D2
Luxfield Rd SE9 166 A3
Luxford St SE16 118 D2
Luxmore St SE4 141 B4
Luxor St SE5 139 A2
Lyall Ave SE21 183 D6
Lyall Mews
SW1 115 A3 258 A5
Lyall Mews W SW1 258 A5
Lyall St SW1 115 A3 258 A5
Lyal Rd E3 97 A5
Lyceé Francais Charles de
Gaulle (French Univ Coll)
SW7 114 B2 256 C4
Lyceé The SE11 116 C1 261 B1
Lycett Ho 10 SW2 160 A4
Lycett Pl 3 W12 112 A4
Lychgate Manor HA1 42 C2
Lych Gate Wlk UB3 105 D6
Lyconby Gdns CR0 207 A2
Lydd Cl DA15 167 C1
Lydden Ct SE9 167 C5
Lydden Gr SW18 157 D4
Lydden Rd SW18 157 D4
Lydd Rd DA7 147 B5
Lydeard Rd E6 78 B1
Lydford NW1 232 B5
Lydford Cl 22 N16 73 C3
Lydford Rd N15 51 B4
NW2 68 D2
W9 91 B3
Lydgate Ho 8 N16 73 C3
Lydhurst Ave SW2 160 B2
Lydia Lo HA1 64 C4
Lydney Cl SE15 139 C5
Putney SW19 157 A2
Lydon Rd SW4 137 C2
Lydstep Rd BR7 188 C6
Lydwell Ho 29 SW8 137 D3
Lyford Rd SW18 158 C3
Lyford St SE7 122 A2
Lygoe Ho 18 N6 49 D2
Lygoe Rd N2 30 B2
Lygon Ho 1 E2 96 A4
Lygon Pl SW1 258 C5
Lyham Cl SW2 160 A5
Lyham Rd SW2 160 A5
Lyle Cl CR4 203 A2
Lyly Ho SE1 262 D5
Lyme Farm Rd SE12 143 B1
Lyme Gr E9 74 C1
Lyme Grove Ho 2 E9 74 C1
Lymer Ave SE19 183 D5
Lyme Rd DA16 146 B4
Lymescote Gdns SM1 217 C6
Lyme St NW1 71 C1 232 A6
Lyminge Cl DA14 189 D6
Lyminge Gdns SW17,
SW18 158 C3
Lymington Ave N22 32 D1
Lymington Cl 2 E6 100 B2
Mitcham SW16 181 D1
Lymington Ct SM1 218 A5
Lymington Dr HA4 61 B6
Lymington Gdns KT19 215 D3
Lymington Mans NW6 69 D2
Lymington Rd NW6 69 D2
Dagenham RM8 58 D1
Lyminster Cl UB4 85 A2
Lympne N17 33 B1
Lympstone Gdns SE15 140 A5
Lynbridge Gdns N13 32 D6
Lynch Cl SE3 142 D3
Lynchen Cl TW5 128 B4
Lynch Wlk 2 SE8 141 B6
Lyncott Cres SW4 137 B1
Lyncourt SE3 142 B3
Lyncroft Ave HA5 41 A4
Lyncroft Gdns NW6 69 C3
Ealing W13 109 C5
Hounslow TW3 152 A6
Lyncroft Mans 4 NW6 69 C3
Lyndale NW2 69 B5
Lyndale Ave NW2 69 B5
Lyndale Cl SE3 142 D6
Lyndean Ind Est SE2 124 C3
Lynde Ho 2 SW4 137 D2
Walton-on-T KT12 194 C3
Lynden Gate SW15 156 B4
Lynden Hyrst CR0 221 D6
Lyndhurst BR7 188 D4
Lyndhurst Ave N12 30 D4
NW7 27 C4
Mitcham SW16 181 D1
Pinner HA5 22 B2
Southall UB1 107 D5
Sunbury TW16 194 A6
Tolworth KT5 198 D1
Twickenham TW2,TW4 151 C3
Lyndhurst Cl DA7 147 D2
NW10 67 B5
Orpington BR6 226 D4
South Croydon CR0 221 D5
Lyndhurst Ct
7 Belmont SM2 217 C1
11 Woodford E18 37 A2
Lyndhurst Dr E10 54 A2
New Malden KT3 199 D2
Lyndhurst Gdns N3 29 A2
NW3 70 B3
Barking IG11 79 C2
Enfield EN1 5 C1
Ilford IG2 57 B3
Pinner HA5 22 B2
Lyndhurst Gr SE5,SE15 139 D3
Lyndhurst Ho 2
SW15 156 A4
Lyndhurst House Prep Sch
NW3 70 B3
Lyndhurst Lo 3 E14 120 B2
Lyndhurst Rd DA7 147 D2
NW3 70 B3
Chingford E4 36 A3
Edmonton N18 34 A6
Greenford UB6 85 D3
Thornton Heath CR7 204 C5
Tottenham N22 32 C4
Lyndhurst Sch SE5 139 B3
Lyndhurst Sq SE15 139 D4
Lyndhurst Terr NW3 70 B3
Lyndhurst Way SE15 139 D3
Belmont SM2 217 C1
Lyndon Ave DA15 167 D6
Hackbridge SM6 219 A5
Pinner HA5 23 A4
Lyndon Rd DA17 125 C2
Lyndon Yd SW17 179 D6
Lyndum Ct N22 32 C2
Lyne Cres E17 35 B2
Lyne Ct NW9 45 B2
Lynegrove Ave TW15 171 A5
Lyneham Wlk E5 75 A3
Pinner HA5 39 D6
Lynette Ave SW4 159 C5
Lynfield Ct SE23 162 D4
Lynford Cl HA8 27 A2
Edgware EN5 11 D6
Lynford French Ho
SE17 262 A2
Lynford Gdns
Edgware HA8 10 D1
Ilford IG3 79 D6
Lynford Terr N9 17 D3
Lynhurst Cres UB10 61 B1
Lynhurst Rd UB10 61 A1
Lynmere Rd DA16 146 B3
Lynmouth Ave
Enfield EN1 17 D5
West Barnes SM4 200 D2
Lynmouth Dr HA4 62 B5
Lynmouth Gdns
Heston TW5 128 D4
Wembley UB6 65 B1
Lynmouth Rd E17 53 A4
N16 51 D1
N2 48 D5
Wembley UB6 87 B6
Lynn Cl Ashford TW15 171 B5
Harrow HA3 24 B1
Lynn Ct SW16 181 D5
Lynne Cl 7 BR6 227 D2
Lynne Ct NW6 69 D1
Forest Hill SE23 163 B4
South Croydon CR2 221 C4
Wimbledon SW20 178 B2
Lynnett Ct E9 75 A2
Lynnett Rd RM8 58 D1
Lynne Way NW10 67 C2
Northolt UB5 84 D5
Lynne Wlk KT10 212 A3
Lynn Ho SE15 140 A6
Lynn Mews E11 76 C6
Lynn Rd E11 76 C5
Balham SW12 159 B4
Ilford IG2 57 B2
Lynn St EN2 5 B4
Lynstead Cl BR1 187 C1
Lynsted Cl DA6 169 D6
Lynsted Ct 4 BR3 185 A1
Lynsted Gdns SE9 143 D2
Lynton KT7 197 A2
Lynton Ave N12 30 B6
NW9 45 D5
Ealing W13 87 A1
Lynton Cl NW10 67 D3
Chessington KT9 214 A4
Isleworth TW7 130 D1
Lynton Cres IG2 56 D3
Lynton Ct 9 W3 89 A1
Bowes Park N13 32 A5
Penge SE20 184 B2
Sutton SM2 218 A2
Lynton Est SE1 118 A2
Lynton Gdns N11 31 D4
Enfield EN1 17 C4
Lynton Grange N2 48 D6
Lynton Ho 15 W2 91 D1
Lynton Lo N5 72 D3
Lynton Mans SE1 261 A6
Lynton Mead N20 13 D2
Lynton Rd N8 50 A4
NW6 91 B5
SE1 118 D3 263
Acton W3 110 D6
Chingford E4 35 D5
Harrow HA2 63 A6
New Malden KT3 199 B4
Thornton Heath CR0 204 C3
Lynton Terr 4 W3 89 A1
Lynton Wlk UB4 83 C4
Lynwood Cl Harrow HA2 63 A5
Woodford E18 37 C2
Lynwood Dr KT4 216 A6
Lynwood Gdns
Southall UB1 85 B1
Wallington CR0 220 B4
Lynwood Gr
Orpington BR6 211 C1
Southgate N21 16 C3
Lynwood Rd Ealing W5 88 A3
Thames Ditton KT7 196 D1
Upper Tooting SW17 180 D6
Lyon Bsns Pk IG11 101 C5
Lyon Ct HA4 39 D1
Lyon Ho NW8 237 A5
Lyon Meade HA7 25 C2
Lyon Park Ave HA0 66 B2
Lyon Park Jun & Inf Schs
HA0 66 B1
Lyon Rd Harrow HA1 42 D3
Merton SW19 180 A2
Lyonsdown Ave EN5 14 A5
Lyonsdown Ct EN5 14 A6
Lyonsdown Rd EN5 14 A6
Lyonsdown Sch EN5 14 A6
Lyons Pl NW8 92 B3 236 C5
Lyon St N1 72 B1
Lyons Wlk W14 254 A4
Lyon Way UB6 86 C6
Lyoth Rd BR5 227 A6
Lyric Dr UB6 85 D3
Lyric Mews SE26 184 C6
Lyric Rd SW13 133 D4
Lysander 20 NW9 27 D2
Lysander Gdns KT5 198 B3
Lysander Gr N19 49 D1
Lysander Ho 10 E2 96 B5
Lysander Rd Ruislip HA4 61 B6
Wallington CR0 220 B2
Lysander Way BR6 227 A5
Lysia Ct SW6 134 D5
Lysias Rd SW12 159 B5
Lysia St SW6 134 D5
Lysons Wlk SW15 156 A6
Lytchet Rd BR1 187 B3
Lytchet Way EN3 6 C4
Lytchgate Cl CR2 221 C1
Lytcott Dr KT8 195 B6
Lytcott Gr SE22 161 D6
Lytham Ave WD19 22 D5
Lytham Cl SE28 103 A1
Lytham Ct 5 UB1 85 D1
Lytham Gr W5 88 B4
Lytham St
SE17 117 B1 262 C1
Lyttelton Cl NW3 70 C1
Lyttelton Ct N2 48 A4
Lyttelton Rd E10 76 A5
N2 48 A4
Lytten Ct 6 W12 112 A4
Lyttleton Ct UB4 84 C3
Lyttleton Ho 10 E9 74 C1
Lyttleton Rd N8 50 C6
Lytton Ave Enfield EN3 7 A5
Lytton Ave *continued*
Southgate N13 16 C2
Lytton Cl N2 48 B4
Northolt UB5 63 B1
Lytton Ct WC1 240 B3
Lytton Gdns SM6 219 D4
Lytton Gr SW15 157 A5
Lytton Ho 3 TW12 173 D4
Lytton Rd E11 54 C2
New Barnet EN5 2 A1
Pinner HA5 23 A3
Lytton Strachy Path 8
SE28 124 B6
Lyveden Rd SE3 143 B5
Mitcham SW17,SW19 180 D4

M

Mabbett Ho 2 SE18 144 C6
Mabel Evetts Ct UB3 106 B6
Mabel Thornton Ho 12
N16 73 B4
Maberley Cres SE19 184 A3
Maberley Ct SE19 184 A3
Maberley Rd SE19 182 C2
Mabledon Pl NW1,
WC1 232 D1
Mablethorpe Rd SW6 264 A3
Mabley St E9 75 A3
Mcadam Dr EN2 4 D3
Macallister Ho 8
SE18 144 D6
Macaret Cl N20 14 A4
Macarthur Cl E7 77 A2
MacArthur Ho 4 SW2 160 A4
Macaulay Ave KT10 212 C6
Macaulay CE Prim Sch
SW4 137 B1
Macaulay Ct SW4 137 B2
Macaulay Ho 10 N16 73 C5
2 W10 91 A2
Macaulay Rd E6 99 D5
SW4 137 B2
Macaulay Sq SW4 137 B1
Macaulay Way 2
SE28 124 B5
McAuley Cl
SE1 116 C3 261 A6
SE9 166 C6
Macbean St SE18 122 D3
Macbeth Ho 4 N1 95 C5
Macbeth St W6 112 B1
McBride Ho 5 E3 97 B5
McCall Cl SW4 138 A3
McCall Cres SE7 122 A1
McCall Ho N7 72 A4
Mccarthy Ct SW11 267 B1
McCarthy Rd TW13 172 D5
Macclesfield Rd
EC1 95 A4 235 A2
Croydon SE25 206 C4
Macclesfield St W1 249 D6
McClintock Pl EN3 7 C6
McCoid Way SE1 252 A1
Mcconnell Ho SW8 269 C1
McCormick Ho 9
SW2 160 C3
McCrone Mews 3
NW3 70 B2
McCullum Rd E3 97 B6
McDermott Cl SW11 136 C2
McDermott Rd SE15 140 A2
Macdonald Ave RM10 81 D5
Macdonald Ct TW3 130 A1
Macdonald Ho 2
SW11 137 A3
McDonald Ho 1 KT2 176 B3
Macdonald Rd E7 77 A4
N11 30 D5
N19 71 C6
Chingford E17 36 A1
McDonough Cl KT9 214 A4
McDougall Ct TW9 132 C3
McDowall Cl E16 98 D2
McDowall Rd SE5 139 A4
Macduff Rd
SW11 137 A4 268 B2
Mace Cl E1 118 B5
Mace Gateway E16 121 B6
Mace Ho 2 E17 53 D6
McEntee Ave E17 35 A2
Mace St E2 96 D5
McEwan Way E15 98 B6
Macey Ho 9 SE10 142 A6
SW11 267 A1
Macfarlane La TW7 131 A6
Macfarlane Rd W12 112 C5
Macfarren Ho 9 W10 91 A4
MacFarren Pl NW1 238 B5
McGlashon Ho 10 E1 96 A3
McGrath Rd E15 76 D2
MacGregor Ct 8 N1 95 C4
MacGregor Ho 2
SW12 159 D3
McGregor Rd W11 91 B2
Macgregor Rd E16 99 C2
Mcguffie Ct E17 53 B6
Machell Rd SE15 140 C2
McIndoe Ct N1 235 C6
McIntosh Cl SM6 220 A1
McIntosh Ho 11 SE16 118 C2
McIntyre Ct 10 SW4 138 A3
Mackay Ho 33 W12 112 B6
Mackay Rd SW4 137 B2
McKay Rd SW20 178 C4
McKellar Cl WD23 8 A2
McKenna Ho 3 E3 97 B5
Mackennal St
NW8 92 C5 230 B4
Mackenzie Cl 7 W12 112 B6
Mackenzie Ct 1 N8 50 A5
Mackenzie Ho 5 NW2 68 A5
Mackenzie Rd N7 72 B2
Penge BR3 184 D1
Mackenzie Wlk E14 119 C5
McKerrell Rd SE15 140 A4
Mackeson Rd NW3 70 D4
Mackie Ho SW2 160 C4
Mackie Rd 18 SW2 160 C4
McKiernan Ct 2
SW11 136 C3
Mc Killop Way DA14 190 C3
McKinlay Ct BR3 185 B1
McKinnon Wood Ho 23
E2 96 A4
Mackintosh La E9 74 D3
Macklin Ho SE23 162 B2
Macklin St WC2 94 A1 240 B2
Mackonochie Ho EC1 241 A4
Mackrow Wlk 11 E14 120 A6
Macks Rd SE16 118 A2
Mackworth Ho NW1 232 A2
Mackworth St NW1 232 A2
Maclean Rd SE23 163 A5
Mcleod Ct SE21 162 A3
Macleod Ho 4 SE18 144 A4
McLeod Ho 3 SE23 162 C2
McLeod Rd SE2 124 B2
Macleod Rd N21 16 A6
McLeod's Mews
SW7 113 D2 255 D4
Macleod St
SE17 117 A1 262 B1
Maclise Rd
W14 113 A3 254 A5
McManus Ho 3 SW11 136 B2
McMillan Ct 2 SE6 164 D3
Macmillan Ct HA2 41 C1
Mcmillan Ho SE4 141 A2
Macmillan Ho NW4 68 B4
NW8 230 A1
McMillan St SE8 141 C6
Macmillan Way SW17 181 B6
Mcmorran Ho N7 72 A4
McNair Rd UB2 107 D3
Macnamara Ho SW10 266 C4
Mcneil Rd SE5 139 C3
McNicol Dr NW10 89 A5
Macoma Rd SE18 145 B6
Macoma Terr SE18 145 B6
Maconochies Rd E14 119 D1
Macquarie Way E14 119 D2
McRae La CR4 202 D2
Macready Ho W1 237 B3
Macready Pl 2 N7 72 A4
Macroom Ho W9 91 B4
Macroom Rd W9 91 B4
Mac's Pl EC4 241 B2
Madame Tussaud's★
NW1 93 A3 238 A5
Mada Rd BR6 226 D5
Maddams St E3 97 D3
Maddison Cl TW11 174 D4
Maddocks Cl DA14 191 A5
Maddocks Ho 3 E1 118 B6
Maddock Way SE17 138 D6
Maddox Ct 1 E4 20 B3
Maddox St W1 248 D6
Madeira Ave BR1 186 C3
Madeira Gr IG8 37 C4
Madeira Rd E11 54 C1
Edmonton N13 16 D1
Mitcham CR4 202 D5
Streatham SW16 182 A5
Madeley Ct W5 88 A1
Madeley Rd W5 88 A1
Madeline Gr IG1 79 B3
Madeline Rd SE20 184 A3
Madge Gill Way 4 E6 100 A6
Madge Hill W7 108 C6
Madinah Rd E8 74 A3
Madingley 11 KT1 176 C1
Madingley Ct TW1 153 C6
Madison Cres DA7 146 C5
Madison Gdns
Beckenham BR2 208 D6
Bexley DA7 146 C5
Madison Ho E3 98 A4
Madras Ho IG1 78 D4
Madras Pl N7 72 C2
Madras Rd IG1 78 D4
Madrid Rd SW13 134 A5
Madron St
SE17 117 C1 263 B2

Mafeking Ave E6 100 A5
Brentford TW8 132 A6
Ilford IG2 57 B2
Mafeking Rd E16 98 D3
Enfield EN1 5 D2
Tottenham N17 34 A1
Magdala Ave N19 71 C6
Magdala Rd
Isleworth TW7 131 A2
South Croydon CR2 221 B1
Magdalen Ct SE25 206 A4
Magdalene Cl 7 SE15 140 B3
Magdalene Gdns E6 100 C3
Magdalene Ho 7
SW15 156 D5
Magdalene Rd TW17 192 B6
Magdalen Pas E1 253 D6
Magdalen Rd SW18 158 B3
Magdalen St SE1 253 A3
Magee St SE11 138 C6
Magellan Ct 9 NW10 67 B1
Magellan Ho 16 E1 96 D3
Magellan Pl 10 E14 119 C2
Magnaville Rd WD23 8 D4
Magnet Rd HA9 65 D6
Magnin Cl 5 E8 96 A6
Magnolia Cl E10 75 C6
Kingston KT2 176 D4
Magnolia Ct 2 N12 29 D6
SW11 158 D5
3 Belmont SM2 217 D1
Feltham TW14 150 A3
Forest Hill SE26 184 C5
Harrow HA3 44 B2
Hillingdon UB10 60 D2
Northolt UB5 85 A3
Richmond TW9 132 D4
Magnolia Ho 13 SE8 141 B6
Magnolia Lo E4 19 D1
Magnolia Pl SW4 160 A6
Ealing W5 87 D2
Magnolia Rd W4 132 D6
Magnolia Way KT19 215 A3
Magnolia Wharf W4 132 D6
Magpie Cl E7 76 D3
NW9 27 C1
Enfield EN1 6 A4
Magpie Hall Cl BR2 210 A3
Magpie Hall La BR2 210 B3
Magpie Hall Rd WD23 8 C2
Magpie Ho 7 E3 97 B6
Magpie Pl SE14 141 A6
Maguire Dr TW10 175 C6
Maguire St
SE1 117 D4 253 D2
Mahatma Gandhi Ind Est 11
SE24 138 D1
Mahlon Ave HA4 62 B2
Mahogany Cl SE16 119 A5
Mahon Cl EN1 5 D4
Mahoney Ho SE14 141 B4
Maida Ave W2 92 A3 236 B5
Chingford E4 19 D4
Maida Rd DA17 125 C3
Maida Vale W9 92 A4 229 A1
Maida Vale Psychiatric
Hospl W9 92 A3 236 B6
Maida Vale Sta W9 91 D4
Maida Way E4 19 D4
Maiden Erlegh Ave
DA5 169 A3
Maiden La NW1 71 D1
SE1 117 A5 252 B4
WC2 116 A6 250 B6
Maiden Rd E15 76 C1
Maidenstone Hill
SE10 142 A4
Maids of Honour Row 4
TW9 153 D6
Maidstone Bldgs SE1 252 C3
Maidstone Ho 4 E14 97 D1
Maidstone Rd N11 31 D4
Ruxley DA14 191 C3
Mail Coach Yd 24 E2 95 C4
Main Ave EN1 17 D6
Main Dr HA9 65 D5
Main Rd BR5 190 C1
Sidcup DA14,DA15 167 C1
Mainridge Rd BR7,SE9 188 C6
Main St TW13 172 D5
Mainwaring Ct 3 CR4 181 A1
Main Yd E9 75 C2
Mais Ho SE26 162 B2
Maismore St SE15 140 A6
Maison Alfort HA3 24 C2
Maisonettes The SM1 217 B3
Maitland Cl 5 SE10 141 D5
Hounslow TW4 129 B2
Maitland Ct W2 246 C6
Maitland Ho 17 E2 96 C5
SW1 269 A6
Maitland Park Rd NW3 70 D2
Maitland Park Villas
NW3 70 D2
Maitland Pl E5 74 C4
Maitland Rd E15 76 D2
Maitland Rd *continued*
Penge SE26 184 D4
Majendie Rd SE18 123 B1
Majestic Ct N4 50 D1
Majestic Way CR4 180 D1
Major Rd E15 76 B3
22 SE16 118 A3
Makepeace Ave N6 71 A6
Makepeace Mans N6 71 A6
Makepeace Rd
Northolt UB5 85 A6
Wanstead E11 55 A5
Makinen Ho IG9 21 C3
Makins St SW3 257 B3
Malabar Ct 20 W12 112 B6
Malabar St E14 119 C4
Malam Ct SE11 261 A3
Malam Gdns 3 E14 119 D6
Malatia CR2 221 A2
Malay Ho 2 E1 118 C5
Malbrook Rd SW15 134 B1
Malcolm Cl SE20 184 C3
Malcolm Cres NW4 46 A3
Malcolm Ct E7 76 D2
NW4 46 A3
Ealing W5 88 B3
Stanmore HA7 25 C5
Malcolm Dr KT6 198 A1
Malcolm Gavin Cl
SW17 158 C2
Malcolm Ho 13 N1 95 C5
Malcolm Pl E2 96 C3
Malcolm Prim Sch
SE20 184 C3
Malcolm Rd E1 96 C3
Croydon SE25 206 A3
Ickenham UB10 60 B4
Penge SE20 184 C3
Wimbledon SW19 179 A4
Malcolmson Ho SW1 259 D1
Malcolms Way N14 15 C6
Malcolm Way E11 55 A5
Malden Ave
Croydon SE25 206 B6
Northolt UB6 64 C2
Malden CE Prim Sch
KT4 199 C1
Malden Cres NW1 71 A2
Malden Ct N4 51 A3
West Barnes KT3 200 B6
Malden Green Ave
KT4 200 A1
Malden Hill KT3 199 D6
Malden Hill Gdns KT3 199 D6
Malden Junc KT3 199 D4
Malden Manor Prim Sch
KT3 199 C2
Malden Manor Sta
KT3 199 C2
Malden Pk KT3 199 D3
Malden Pl NW5 71 A3
Malden Rd NW5 71 A2
Cheam KT4,SM3 216 D4
New Malden KT3,KT4 199 D2
Malden Way KT3 200 A5
Malden Way (Kingston By
Pass) KT3,KT5 199 C4
Maldon Cl E15 76 B3
N1 235 B6
SE5 139 C2
Maldon Ct Barking E6 100 C6
Wallington SM6 219 C3
Maldon Rd W3 111 A6
Edmonton N9 17 D1
Wallington SM6 219 B3
Maldon Wlk IG8 37 C4
Malet Pl WC1 239 C5
Malet St WC1 93 D2 239 D4
Maley Ave SE27 160 D2
Malford Ct E18 37 A1
Malford Gr E18 54 D6
Malfort Rd SE5 139 C2
Malham Cl N11 31 A4
Malham Rd SE23 162 D3
Malham Road Ind Est
SE23 162 D3
Malins Cl EN5 12 C6
Mallams Mews 1
SW9 138 D2
Mallard Cl E9 75 B2
NW6 91 C6
W7 108 C4
New Barnet EN5 14 B5
Twickenham TW4 151 C4
Mallard Ct E12 78 B3
E17 54 B6
NW9 45 A2
Chingford E4 20 B4
Ilford IG1 79 A6
15 Richmond TW10 153 D5
Mallard Ho NW8 230 A3
7 SE15 139 D4
Mallard Path SE28 123 B3
Mallard Pl TW1 153 A1
Mallard Point 5 E3 97 C4
Mallards E11 55 A2
Mallards Rd
Barking IG11 102 A3
Woodford IG8 37 B3
Mallard Way NW9 45 A2
Mallard Wlk
Beckenham BR3 206 D4
Sidcup DA14 190 C4
Mall Ct W5 110 A6
Mallet Dr UB5 63 B3
Mallet Ho 11 SW15 156 A6
Mallet Rd SE13 164 B5
Malling SE13 163 D6
Malling Cl CR0 206 C3
Malling Gdns SM4 202 A3
Malling Ho 9 BR3 185 C3
Malling Way BR2 208 D2
Mallinson Ct 2 E11 76 C6
Mallinson Rd SW11 158 D6
Wallington SM6 219 D5
Mallon Gdns E1 243 D3
Mallord St
SW3 136 B6 266 D6
Mallory Bldgs EC1 241 C5
Mallory Cl SE4 141 A1
Mallory Gdns EN4 15 A4
Mallory Ho E14 98 A2
Mallory St NW8 92 C3 237 B6
Mallow Cl CR0 206 D1
Mallow Mead NW7 29 A3
Mallow St EC1 242 C6
Mallows The UB10 60 D5
Mall Rd W6 112 B1
Mall Studios 9 NW3 70 D3
Mall The 4 BR1 209 A6
SW1 115 D5 249 C3
6 Bexley DA6 147 C1
Brentford TW8 131 D6
Ealing W5 110 A6
Harrow HA3 44 B3
Kingston KT6 197 D4
Mortlake SW14 155 A6
Palmers Green N14 16 A1
Mall The (Prep Sch)
TW2 152 B1
Malmains Cl BR3 208 B5
Malmains Way BR3 208 B5
Malmesbury 31 E2 96 C5
Malmesbury Cl HA5 40 A5
Malmesbury Fst Sch
SM4 202 A2
Malmesbury Mid Sch
SM4 202 A3
Malmesbury Prim Sch
E3 97 B4
Malmesbury Rd E16 98 C2
E3 97 B5
Morden SM4 202 A3
Woodford E18 36 D2
Malmesbury Terr E16 98 D2
Malmsey Ho SE11 260 D2
Malmsmead Ho E9 75 A3
Malorees Jun & Inf Schs
NW6 68 D1
Malory Sch BR1 187 A6
Malpas Dr HA5 40 D4
Malpas Rd E8 74 B2
SE4 141 B3
Dagenham RM9 80 D2
Malta Rd E10 53 C2
Malta St EC1 241 D6
Maltby Dr EN1 6 B5
Maltby Rd KT9 214 C2
Maltby St SE1 117 D3 263 C6
Maltham Terr N18 34 B4
Malthouse Dr
Chiswick W4 133 D6
Feltham TW13 172 D5
Malthouse Pas SW13 133 C3
Malthus Path 7 SE28 124 C5
Malting Ho E14 119 B6
Maltings W4 110 C1
Maltings Cl SW13 133 C3
Maltings Lo W4 133 C5
Maltings Pl SE1 253 B2
SW6 265 D1
Maltings The BR6 211 D1
Malting Way TW7 130 D2
Malt Mill SE1 253 C3
Malton Ho SE25 205 C5
Malton Mews SE18 145 C6
1 W10 91 A1
Malton Rd W10 91 A1
Malton St SE18 145 C6
Maltravers St WC2 251 A6
Malt St SE1 140 A6
Malva Cl SW18 157 D6
Malvern Ave DA7 147 A5
Chingford E4 36 B3
Harrow HA2 63 B5
Malvern Cl W10 91 B2
Ickenham UB10 60 C6
Mitcham CR4 203 C6
Penge SE20 184 A1
Surbiton KT6 198 A1
Malvern Court SW7 256 D4
Malvern Ct
Belmont SM2 217 C1
3 Surbiton KT6 198 A1
Malvern Dr
Feltham TW13 172 D5
Ilford IG3 79 D4
Woodford IG8 37 C6
Malvern Gdns NW2 69 A6
Harrow HA3 44 A5
Malvern Ho N16 51 D1
Malvern Lo N12 30 B6
Malvern Mews NW6 91 C4
Malvern Pl NW6 91 B4
Malvern Rd E11 76 D6
E6 100 A6
E8 74 A1
N17 52 A6
N19 49 D1
N8 50 C6
NW6 91 C4
Enfield EN3 7 A6
Hampton TW12 173 C3
Harlington UB3 127 C5
Surbiton KT6 198 A1
Thornton Heath CR7 204 C5
Malvern Terr N1 234 A6
Edmonton N9 17 D3
Malvern Way W13 87 B2
Malwood Rd SW12 159 B5
Malyons Rd SE13 163 D6
Malyons Terr SE13 163 D6
Malyons The TW17 193 B3
Managers St E14 120 A5
Manatee Pl SM6 219 D5
Manaton Cl SE15 140 B2
Manaton Cres UB1 85 C1
Manbey Gr E15 76 C2
Manbey Park Rd E15 76 C2
Manbey Rd E15 76 C2
Manbey St E15 76 C2
Manbre Rd W6 134 C6
Manbrough Ave E6 100 C4
Manchester Ct E16 99 B1
Manchester Dr W10 91 A3
Manchester Gr E14 120 A1
Manchester Ho SE17 262 B2
Manchester Mans N19 49 D2
Manchester Mews
W1 238 A3
Manchester Rd E14 120 A3
N15 51 B3
South Norwood CR7 205 A6
Manchester Sq
W1 93 A1 238 B2
Manchester St
W1 93 A2 238 A3
Manchester Way RM10 81 D4
Manchuria Rd SW11 159 A5
Manciple St
SE1 117 B3 262 D6
Mandalay Ho 6 N16 73 B4
Mandalay Rd SW4 159 C6
Mandarin Ct NW10 67 B2
6 SE8 141 C6
Mandarin Way UB4 84 D1
Mandela Cl NW10 67 A1
36 W12 112 B6
Mandela Ho 18 E2 95 D4
Mandela Rd E16 99 A1
Mandela St
NW1 93 C6 232 B6
SW9 138 C5
Mandela Way
SE1 117 C2 263 B4
Manderville Ho SE1 263 D2
Mandeville Cl 5 SE3 142 D5
Merton SW19 179 A2
Mandeville Ct NW3 69 D3
Mandeville Ctyd SW11 268 A1
Mandeville Dr KT6 197 D1
Mandeville Ho 8
SW4 159 C6
Mandeville Pl W1 238 B2
Mandeville Prim Sch
E5 74 D5
Mandeville Rd N14 15 C2
Enfield EN3 7 A6
Isleworth TW7 131 A3
Littleton TW17 192 C4
Northolt UB5 63 C1
Mandeville Sch UB5 63 B2
Mandeville St E5 75 A5
Mandrake Rd SW17 158 D1
Mandrake Way 2 E15 76 C1
Mandrell Rd SW2 160 A6
Manesty Ct N14 15 D4
Manette St W1 239 D1
Manfred Ct 6 SW15 157 B6
Manfred Rd SW15 157 B6
Manger Rd N7 72 A2
Mangold Way 4 DA18 125 A3
Manilla St E14 119 C4
Manister Rd SE2 124 A3
Manitoba Ct 23 SE16 118 C4
Manitoba Gdns 6
BR6 227 D2
Manley Ct N16 73 D5
Manley Ho SE11 261 A2
Manley St NW1 231 A6
Manly Dixon Dr EN3 7 A6
Mann Cl 1 CR0 221 A5
Mannebury Prior N1 233 D3
Mannering Ho 16 SW2 160 B6
Manning Ct 3 SE28 124 B5
Manningford Cl EC1 234 C2
Manning Gdns HA3 43 D2
Manning Ho 6 E17 54 A6
3 W11 91 A1
Manning Pl TW10 154 B5
Manning Rd E17 53 A4
Dagenham RM10 81 C1
Manningtree Cl SW19 157 A3
Manningtree Rd HA4 62 B4
Manningtree St 1 E1 96 A1
Mannin Rd RM6 58 B2
Mannock Rd N22 50 D6
Mann's Cl TW7 152 D6
Manns Rd HA8 26 C4
Manny Shinwell Ho
SW6 264 D5
Manoel Rd TW2 152 A2
Manor Ave SE4 141 B3
Hounslow TW4 128 D3
Northolt UB5 63 B1
Manorbrook SE12,SE3 143 A1
Manor Circus TW9 132 C2
Manor Cl E17 35 A1
NW7 27 B5
NW9 44 D4
SE28 102 C1
Barnet EN5 1 A1
New Malden KT4 199 C1
Ruislip HA4 39 D1
Manor Cottages App
N2 30 A1
Manor Cotts N2 30 A1
Manor Court Rd W7 108 C6
Manor Cres KT5 198 C3
Manor Ct E10 53 D1
N14 15 D2
N20 14 D1
N2 48 D4
SE15 139 D4
7 SW2 160 B6
SW6 265 D1
W3 110 C2
3 Barking IG11 79 D1
Chingford, Chingford Green
E4 20 C3
Harrow HA1 42 D3
Kingston KT2 176 C2
Streatham SW16 160 A1
Surbiton KT5 198 C3
Twickenham TW2 152 A2
5 Wembley HA9 66 A3
Manordene Cl KT7 197 A1
Manordene Rd SE28 102 D1
Manor Dr N14 15 B3
N20 14 D1
NW7 27 B5
Feltham TW13 172 D5
Hinchley Wood KT10 213 A5
Sunbury TW16 172 A1
Surbiton KT5 198 C3
Wembley HA9 66 B4
West Ewell KT19 215 C2
Manor Dr N KT3,KT4 199 B2
Manor Dr The KT4 199 D1
Manor Farm Ave
TW17 192 D3
Manor Farm Cl KT4 199 C1
Manor Farm Ct E6 100 B4
Manor Farm Dr E4 20 C1
Manor Farm Rd
Thornton Heath CR7,
SW16 182 C1
Wembley HA0 87 D5
Manorfield Cl 3 N19 71 C4
Manorfield Prim Sch
E14 97 D2
Manorfields Cl BR7 211 D6
Manor Gate UB5 63 A1
Manorgate Rd KT2 176 C2
Manor Gdns N7 72 A5
SW4 137 C3
W3 110 C2
8 W4 111 C1
Hampton TW12 174 A3
Merton SW20 179 B1
Richmond TW10,TW9 132 B1
Ruislip HA4 62 C3
South Croydon CR2 221 D2
Sunbury TW16 172 A1
Manor Gr SE15 140 C6
Beckenham BR3 185 D1
Richmond TW9 132 C2
Manor Gt SW15 157 A6
Manor Hall Ave NW4 28 D1
Manor Hall Dr NW4 28 D1
Manor Hall Gdns E10 53 C1
Manor Ho E12 77 D4
N14 15 D3
NW1 237 B4
Brentford TW8 109 C1
Wallington SM6 219 B3
Manor House Ct W9 236 A5
Manor House Dr NW6 68 D1
Manor House Est HA7 25 B5
Manor House Sch W7 108 C6
Manor House Way
TW7 131 B2
Manor Inf Sch IG11 79 D2
Manor Jun Sch IG11 79 D2
Manor La SE12 164 C5
Feltham TW13 150 A2
Manor La *continued*
Harlington UB3 127 B6
Sunbury TW16 172 B1
Sutton SM1 218 A3
Manor Lane Terr SE13 164 C6
Manor Lodge NW2 68 D2
Manor Mans N7 72 A5
7 NW3 70 C2
Manor Mead Sch
TW17 192 D4
Manor Mews NW6 91 C5
SE4 141 B3
Manor Mount SE23 162 C3
Manor Oak Mans SE22 162 B5
Manor Par N16 73 D6
Harrow HA1 42 D3
Manor Park Cl BR4 207 D1
Manor Park Cres HA8 26 C4
Manor Park Dr HA2 41 D6
Manor Park Gdns HA8 26 C4
Manor Park Prim Sch
SM1 218 A3
Manor Park Rd E12 77 D4
N2 48 B6
NW10 89 D6
Chislehurst BR7 189 B2
Sutton SM1 218 A3
West Wickham BR4 207 D1
Manor Park Sta E12 77 D4
Manor Pk SE13 164 C6
Chislehurst BR7 189 B2
Richmond TW9 132 B1
Manor Pl BR7 207 D1
SE17 117 A1 262 A2
East Bedfont TW14 150 A3
Mitcham CR4 203 C6
Sutton SM1 217 D4
Walton-on-T KT12 194 A2
Manor Prim Sch E15 98 C5
Manor Rd DA15 168 A1
DA5 169 D3
E10 53 C2
E15,E16 98 C4
E17 35 A1
N16 51 C1
Ashford TW15 170 C5
Barking IG11 79 D2
Barnet EN5 1 A1
Beckenham BR3 185 D1
Belmont SM2 217 B1
Bowes Park N22 32 A4
Dagenham RM6 58 D3
Ealing W13 109 A6
East Molesey KT8 196 B5
Enfield EN2 5 B3
Harrow HA1 43 A3
Hayes UB3 84 A1
Loughton IG10 21 B5
Merton SW20 179 B1
Mitcham CR4 203 C6
Richmond TW10,TW9 132 B1
Richmond TW11 175 B5
Ruislip HA4 39 B1
South Norwood SE25 206 A6
Tottenham N17 34 B2
Twickenham TW2 152 B2
Wallington SM5,SM6 219 B3
Walton-on-T KT12 193 D2
West Wickham BR4 223 D6
Manor Rd N
Hinchley Wood KT7 213 A6
Wallington SM5,SM6 219 B4
Manor Rd S KT10 212 C4
Manor Sch NW10 90 C6
Manorside EN5 1 A1
Manorside Cl SE2 124 D2
Manorside Prim Sch
N3 30 A2
Manor Sq RM8 80 C6
Manor Street Est SW3 267 B6
Manor The W1 248 C5
Manor Vale TW8 109 C1
Manor View N3 29 D1
Manor Way BR2 210 A3
BR5 211 A5
DA5 169 C3
NW9 45 C5
W3 110 C2
Manorway Enfield EN1 17 C4
Woodford IG8 37 C5
Manor Way
Beckenham BR3 207 C6
Chingford E4 36 B6
Greenwich SE3 143 A1
Harrow HA2 41 D5
Mitcham CR4 203 C6
New Malden KT4 199 D1
Ruislip HA4 39 D1
Southall UB2 106 D2
South Croydon CR2 221 D2
Manor Waye UB8 82 A6
Manor Way The SM6 219 B4
Manpreet Ct E12 78 B3
Manresa Rd
SW3 114 C1 257 A1
Mansard Beeches
SW17 181 A5
Mansard Cl HA5 40 D6

Mansard Manor 4
SM2 .218 A1
Manse Cl UB3 .127 B6
Manse Ct DA14 .190 C5
Mansel Ct SW11 .267 B1
Mansel Gr E17 .35 C2
Mansell Ho SW8 .269 B2
Mansell Rd W3 .111 B4
Southall UB6 .85 D2
Mansell St E1 ..95 D1 243 D1
Mansel Rd SW19 .179 B4
Manse Rd N16 .73 D5
Mansergh Cl SE18 .144 A5
Mansfield Ave N15 .51 B5
East Barnet EN4 .15 A5
Ruislip HA4 .40 B1
Mansfield Cl N9 .18 A5
Mansfield Ct 27 E2 .95 D6
Mansfield Dr UB4 .83 C3
Mansfield Hill E4 .19 D3
Mansfield Ho SW15 .156 D5
Mansfield Hts N2 .48 D4
Mansfield Mews W1 .238 C3
Mansfield Pl 11 NW3 .70 A4
Mansfield Rd E17 .53 B5
NW3 .70 D4
Acton W3 .88 D3
Chessington KT9 .213 D3
Ilford IG1 .78 C6
South Croydon CR2 .221 B2
Wanstead E11 .55 B3
Mansfield St
W1 .93 B2 238 C3
Mansford St E2 .96 A5
Manship Rd CR4 .181 A2
Mansion Cl SW9 .138 C4
Mansion Gdns NW3 .69 D5
Mansion House★ EC4 242 C1
Mansion House Pl
EC3,EC4 .242 C1
Mansion House St
EC2 .242 C1
Mansion House Sta
EC4 .117 A6 252 B6
Mansions The NW6 .69 B3
Manson Mews
SW7 .114 B2 256 C3
Manson Pl
SW7 .114 B2 256 C3
Manstead Gdns RM6 .58 C2
Manston NW1 .71 C1
Tottenham N17 .33 B1
Manston Ave UB2 .107 C2
Manston Cl SE20 .184 C2
Manstone Rd NW2 .69 A3
Manston Gr KT2 .175 D5
Manston Ho W14 .254 B5
Mantell Ho SW4 .159 C6
Manthorpe Rd SE18 .123 A1
Mantilla Rd SW17 .181 A6
Mantle Rd SE4 .141 A2
Mantlet Cl SW16 .181 C3
Mantle Way E15 .76 C1
Manton Ave W7 .109 A4
Manton Cl UB3 .105 C6
Manton Ho N16 .73 B5
Manton Rd SE2 .124 A2
Holdbrook EN3 .7 C5
Mantua St 23 SW11 .136 B2
Mantus Cl E1 .96 C3
Mantus Rd E1 .96 C3
Manus Way N20 .14 A3
Manville Gdns SW17 .159 B1
Manville Rd SW17 .159 B1
Manwood Rd SE4 .163 B5
Manwood St E16 .122 B5
Manygate La TW17 .193 A3
Many Gates SW12 .159 B2
Mapesbury Ct NW2 .69 A3
Mapesbury Rd NW2 .69 A2
Mapeshill Pl NW2 .68 C2
Mapes Ho 5 NW6 .69 A1
Mape St E2 .96 B3
Maple Ave E4 .35 B4
W3 .111 C5
Harrow HA2 .63 D6
Yiewsley UB7 .104 B6
Maple Cl BR5 .211 B4
N16 .52 A3
N3 .29 C4
SW4 .159 D5
Buckhurst Hill IG9 .21 D1
Hampton TW12 .173 B4
Hayes UB4 .84 D4
Mitcham CR4 .181 B2
Ruislip HA4 .40 B3
Maple Cres DA15 .168 A5
Maplecroft Cl E6 .100 A1
Maple Ct E6 .100 C2
NW2 .68 D4
Catford SE6 .163 D3
2 Croydon CR0 .221 A4
7 Dagenham RM8 .58 D2
Kingston KT3 .199 B6
4 Pinner HA5 .22 C1
Sidcup DA14 .190 B5
11 West Norwood
SW16 .182 C5
Mapledale Ave CR0 .222 A5
Mapledene BR7 .189 A5
Mapledene Est E8 .74 A1
Mapledene Rd E8 .74 A1
Mapledown Sch NW2 .46 C2
Maple Gdns HA8 .27 C3
Stanwell TW19 .148 A2
Maple Gr NW9 .45 A2
W5 .109 D3
Brentford TW8 .131 B5
Southall UB1 .85 B2
Maple Gr Bsns Ctr
TW4 .128 C1
Maple Ho 13 E17 .53 D6
11 NW3 .70 D2
5 SE8 .141 B5
2 Kingston KT6 .198 A4
Maplehurst 2 BR2 .186 C1
Maplehurst Cl KT1 .198 A5
Maple Ind Est TW13 .150 A1
Maple Inf Sch KT6 .197 D4
Maple Leaf Dr DA15 .167 D3
Mapleleafe Gdns IG6 .56 D6
Maple Leaf Sq 27
SE16 .118 D4
Maple Lo NW9 .67 B6
Putney SW15 .157 A5
Maple Mews NW6 .91 D5
Streatham SW16 .182 B5
Maple Pl W1 .239 B5
Tottenham N17 .34 A3
Yiewsley UB7 .104 B6
Maple Rd E11 .54 C3
Hayes UB4 .84 D4
Kingston KT6 .197 D4
Penge SE20 .184 C2
Maples Pl E1 .96 B2
Maple St W1 .93 C3 239 B5
Maplestead Rd
Dagenham RM9 .102 B6
Streatham SW2 .160 B4
Maples The KT8 .175 C3
Maplethorpe Rd CR7 .204 D5
Mapleton Cl BR2 .209 A3
Mapleton Cres
Enfield EN3 .6 C5
Wandsworth SW18 .157 D5
Mapleton Rd
Chingford E4 .20 A1
Enfield EN1 .6 B3
Wandsworth SW18 .157 D5
Maple Way TW13 .150 B1
Maple Wlk W10 .90 D3
Maplin Cl N21 .16 B5
Maplin Ho 9 SE2 .124 D4
Maplin Rd E16 .99 B1
Maplin St E3 .97 B4
Mapperley Cl 3 E11 .55 A3
Mapperley Dr IG8 .36 C3
Marada Ho NW6 .69 A1
Marais W4 .133 A5
Maran Way DA18 .124 D3
Marathon Way SE28 .123 D4
Marban Rd W9 .91 B4
Marble Arch★
W1 .114 D6 247 D6
Marble Arch Sta
W1 .92 D1 237 D1
Marble Cl W3 .110 D5
Marble Dr NW2 .46 D2
Marbleford Ct 4 N6 .49 D2
Marble Hill★ TW1 .153 C4
Marble Hill Cl TW1 .153 B4
Marble Hill Gdns TW1 153 B4
Marble Ho SE18 .123 D1
W9 .91 B3
Marbrook Ct SE12 .165 C1
Marcella Rd SW9 .138 C3
Marcellina Way BR6 .227 D5
March 23 NW9 .27 D2
Marchant Ct SE1 .263 D2
Marchant Ho 13 SW2 .160 B6
Marchant Rd E11 .76 B6
Marchant St SE14 .141 A6
Marchbank Rd
W14 .135 B6 264 D6
March Ct SW15 .134 B1
Marchmont Ho 10
SW16 .181 C5
Marchmont Rd
Richmond TW10 .154 B6
Wallington SM6 .219 C1
Marchmont St
WC1 .94 A3 240 A6
March Rd 5 TW1 .153 A4
Marchside Cl TW5 .128 D4
Marchwood Cl 17 SE5 139 C5
Marchwood Cres W5 .87 D1
Marcia Rd SE1 117 C2 263 B3
Marcilly Rd SW18 .158 B6
Marcon Ct 20 E8 .74 B3
Marconi Pl N11 .31 B6
Marconi Rd E10 .53 C1
Marconi Way UB1 .85 D1
Marcon Pl E8 .74 B3
Marco Rd W6 .112 C3
Marcourt Lawns W5 .88 A3
Marcus Ct E15 .98 C6
Brentford TW8 .132 A5
Marcus Garvey Mews
SE22 .162 B6
Marcus Garvey Way 9
SE24 .138 C1
Marcus Ho 13 SE15 .139 D4
Marcus St E15 .98 D6
Wandsworth SW18 .157 D5
Marcus Terr SW18 .157 D5
Mardale Ct NW7 .28 A3
Mardale Dr NW9 .45 B4
Mardell Rd CR0 .206 D4
Marden Ave BR2 .209 A3
Marden Cres CR0 .204 B3
Marden Ho 6 E8 .74 B3
Marden Rd
Thornton Heath CR0 .204 B3
Tottenham N17 .33 C1
Marden Sq SE16 .118 B3
Marder Rd W13 .109 A4
Mardyke Ho SE17 .262 D4
Marechal Niel Ave
DA15 .167 B1
Marechal Niel Par
DA15 .167 B1
Maresby Ho E4 .19 D2
Maresfield CR0 .221 C5
Maresfield Gdns NW3 .70 A2
Mare St E8 .74 B2
E8,E2 .96 B6
Marfleet Cl SM5 .218 C6
Margaret Ave E4 .19 D5
Margaret Bondfield Ave
IG11 .80 A1
Margaret Bondfield Ho
4 E3 .97 A5
22 N7 .71 D3
Margaret Ct W1 .239 A2
Barnet EN4 .2 B1
Margaret Gardner Dr
SE9 .166 B2
Margaret Herbison Ho
SW6 .264 D5
Margaret Hill Ho N8 .50 A4
Margaret Ho 16 W6 .112 C1
Margaret Ingram Cl
SW6 .264 C5
Margaret Lockwood Cl
KT5 .198 B5
Margaret Mcmillan Ho 10
N19 .49 D2
Margaret Rd DA5 .168 D5
N16 .51 D1
Barnet EN4 .2 B1
Margaret's Ct E11 .54 B2
SE1 .252 C3
Margarets Ct HA8 .26 D5
Margaret St W1 93 C1 239 A2
Margaretta Terr
SW3 .136 C6 267 B6
Margaretting Rd E12 .55 C1
Margaret Way IG4 .56 A3
Margaret White Ho
NW1 .232 C2
Margate Rd SW2 .160 A6
Margery Fry Ct N7 .72 A5
Margery Park Rd E7 .77 A2
Margery Rd RM8 .80 D5
Margery St
WC1 .94 C4 234 A1
Margetson Ho N16 .51 D3
Margin Dr SW19 .178 D6
Margravine Gdns W14 254 A2
W6 .112 D1
Margravine Rd
W6 .112 D1 264 A6
Marham Gdns
Morden SM4 .202 A3
Wandsworth SW17,
SW18 .158 C3
Mar Ho 4 SE7 .143 C6
Maria Cl 10 SE1 .118 A2
Maria Fidelis RC Convent
Sch NW1 .93 D4 232 C2
Maria Ho 13 SW9 .138 C4
Marian Cl UB4 .84 D3
Marian Ct E9 .74 C3
Sutton SM1 .217 D3
Marian Lo 5 SW20 .178 D3
Marian Pl E2 .96 B5
Marian Rd SW16 .181 C2
Marian Sq E2 .96 B5
Marian St 2 E2 .96 B5
Marian Vian Prim Sch
BR3 .207 A4
Marian Way NW10 .67 D1
Maria Terr E1 .96 D3
Maria Theresa Cl KT3 .199 B4
Maribor 13 SE10 .142 A5
Maricas Ave HA3 .24 B2
Marie Curie SE5 .139 C4
Marie Lloyd Ct 13
SW9 .138 B1
Marie Lloyd Gdns 1
N19 .50 A2
Marie Lloyd Ho N1 .235 C3
Marien Ct E4 .36 B5
Marigold Cl UB1 .107 A6
Marigold Rd N17 .34 C3
Marigold St SE16 .118 B4
Marigold Way CR0 .206 D1
Marilea Ct W5 .109 D4
Marina App UB4 .85 A2
Marina Ave KT3 .200 B4
Marina Cl 1 BR2 .209 A6
Marina Ct 11 E3 .97 C4
Marina Dr DA16 .145 C3
Marina Gdns RM7 .59 D4
Marina Way TW11 .175 D3
Marine Dr 5 SE18 .122 B2
Barking IG11 .102 B4
Marinefield Rd SW6 .135 D3
Marinel Ho 25 SE5 .139 A5
Mariner Gdns TW10 .153 C1
Mariner Rd E12 .78 C4
Mariners Mews E14 .120 B2
Marine St SE16 .118 A3
Marine Twr 29 SE8 .141 B6
Marion Ave TW17 .192 D4
Marion Ct 4 SW17 .180 C5
Marion Gr IG8 .36 C6
Marion Rd NW7 .28 A5
Thornton Heath CR0 .205 B4
Marion Richardson Prim
Sch E1 .96 D1
Marischal Rd SE13 .142 B2
Maritime Ho 5 SW4 .137 C2
Maritime Ind Est SE7 .121 B2
Maritime Quay 6 E14 119 C1
Maritime St E3 .97 B3
Marius Mans 3 SW17 159 A2
Marius Rd SW17 .159 A2
Marjorie Gr SW11 .136 D1
Marjorie McClure Sch
BR7 .189 A2
Marjory Kinnon Sch
TW14 .149 C6
Markab Rd HA6 .22 A5
Mark Ave E4 .19 D5
Mark Cl BR2 .226 A4
DA7 .147 A4
Southall UB1 .107 D5
Markeston Gn WD19 .22 D6
Market Ct W1 .239 A2
Market Ctr The UB2 .106 B2
Market La HA8 .27 A2
Market Mews
W1 .115 B5 248 C3
Market Par E10 .53 D3
E17 .53 B6
Croydon SE25 .206 A5
1 Edmonton N9 .18 A2
Feltham TW13 .151 A2
Market Pl 2 DA7 .147 C1
N2 .48 C6
1 SE16 .118 B2
W1 .239 A2
3 W3 .111 A5
Brentford TW8 .131 C5
Enfield EN2 .5 B2
Kingston KT1 .175 D1
Market Pl The NW11 .47 D5
Market Rd N7 .72 A2
Richmond TW9 .132 C2
Market Sq BR1 .187 A1
E14 .97 D1
Market Sq The N9 .18 B2
Market St SE18 .122 C2
Wallend E6 .100 C5
Market The SM1,SM5 .202 A1
Market Way E14 .97 D1
1 Wembley HA0 .66 A3
Market Yd Mews SE1 .263 A6
Markfield Gdns E4 .19 D4
Markfield Ho N15 .52 A5
Markfield Rd N15 .52 A4
Markham Ct NW4 .46 C6
Markham Ho
1 Dagenham RM10 .81 C5
9 Dulwich SE21 .183 C6
Markham Pl SW3 .257 C2
Markham Sq
SW3 .114 D1 257 C2
Markham St
SW3 .114 C1 257 B2
Mark Ho 3 E2 .96 D5
Markhole Cl TW12 .173 B3
Markhouse Ave E17 .53 A3
Markhouse Pas E17 .53 B3
Markhouse Rd E17 .53 B3
Mark La EC3 .117 C6 253 B6
Markland Ho W10 .112 D6
Mark Lo 9 EN4 .2 C1
Markmanor Ave E17 .53 B2
Mark Mans W12 .112 A4
Mark Rd N22 .32 D1
Marksbury Ave TW9 .132 C2
Marks Gate Inf Sch
RM6 .59 A6
Marks Gate Jun Sch
RM6 .59 A6
Mark Sq EC2 .243 A6
Mark St E15 .76 C1
EC2 .243 A6
Markstone Ho SE1 .251 C1
Mark Wade Cl E12 .55 D1
Markway The TW16 .172 C1
Markwell Cl SE26 .184 B6
Markyate Ho W10 .90 C3
Markyate Rd RM8 .80 B3
Marland Ho SW1 .257 D6
Marlands Rd IG5 .56 B6
Marlang Ct BR3 .186 B2
Marlborough W9 .229 A2
11 Putney SW19 .156 D3
Marlborough Ave
3 E8 .96 A6
N14 .15 C1
Edgware HA8 .10 D1
Ruislip HA4 .39 B3
Marlborough Cl BR6 .211 D3
N20 .14 D1
SE17 .261 D3
Mitcham SW19 .180 C4
Marlborough Cres
W4 .111 C3
Harlington UB3 .127 B5
Marlborough Ct W8 .255 A4
7 Buckhurst Hill IG9 .21 C2
Harrow HA1 .42 B5
Wallington SM6 .219 C1
Marlborough Day Hospl
NW8 .92 A5 229 A4
Marlborough Dr IG5 .56 A6
Marlborough Flats
SW3 .257 B4
Marlborough Fst & Mid Sch
HA1 .42 C5
Marlborough Gdns N20 14 D1
Surbiton KT6 .197 D2
Marlborough Gr SE1 .118 A1
Marlborough Hill
NW8 .92 A6 229 B5
Harrow HA1 .42 C5
Marlborough Ho N4 .51 A1
NW8 .229 A3
Richmond TW10 .154 C6
Wimbledon SW19 .156 D1
Marlborough House
SW1 .249 B3
Marlborough La SE7 .143 C5
Marlborough Mans 5
NW6 .69 C3
Marlborough Mews
SW2 .138 B1
Marlborough Par 1
UB10 .82 D3
Marlborough Park Ave
DA15 .168 A3
Marlborough Pl
NW8 .92 A5 229 B4
Marlborough Prim Sch
SW3 .114 C2 257 B3
Marlborough Rd DA16 146 D2
E15 .76 C4
E7 .77 C1
N19 .72 A6
SE18 .123 A3
SW1 .115 C5 249 B3
W4 .111 A1
W5 .109 D4
Ashford TW15 .170 A5
Bowes Park N22 .32 B4
Brentford TW7 .131 B5
Bromley BR2 .209 C5
Chingford E4 .35 D4
Dagenham RM8 .80 C4
Edmonton N9 .18 A3
Feltham TW13 .150 D2
Hampton TW12 .173 C4
Hillingdon UB10 .82 D4
Mitcham SW19 .180 C4
Richmond TW10 .154 B5
Romford RM7 .59 D5
Southall UB2 .106 C3
South Croydon CR2 .221 A1
Sutton SM1 .217 C6
Wanstead E18 .55 A6
Marlborough Sch
Isleworth TW7 .131 A4
Sidcup DA15 .168 A4
Marlborough St
SW3 .114 C2 257 B3
Marlborough Trad Est
TW9 .132 D4
Marlborough Yd N19 .71 D6
Marlbury NW8 .91 D6
Marler Rd SE23 .163 B3
Marlesford Ct SM6 .219 C4
Marley Ave DA7 .146 D6
Marley Cl N15 .50 D5
Southall UB6 .85 C4
Marley Ho 14 W11 .112 D6
Marley Wlk NW2 .68 C3
Marlfield Cl KT4 .200 A1
Marlfield Ct KT3 .199 D2
Marlin Cl TW16 .171 C4
Marling Ct TW12 .173 B4
Marlingdene Cl TW12 173 C4
Marlings Cl BR7 .211 C5
Marlings Park Ave
BR7 .211 C6
Marlin Ho SW15 .157 A6
Marlins Cl 3 SM1 .218 A3
Marloes Cl HA0 .65 D4
Marloes Rd
W8 .113 D3 255 C5
Marlow Cl SE20 .206 B6
Marlow Cres TW1 .152 D5
Marlow Ct N14 .15 C4
NW6 .68 D1
NW9 .45 D6
1 Ealing W7 .108 C5
Marlow Dr SM3 .216 D5
Marlowe Bsns Ctr 2
SE14 .141 A5
Marlowe Cl BR7 .189 B4
Marlowe Ct SW3 .257 B3
Dulwich SE19 .183 D5
6 Kingston KT2 .175 D6
Marlowe Gdns SE9 .166 C5
Marlowe Ho 15 N16 .73 C4
SE8 .119 B1
Kingston KT1 .197 D5
Marlowe Lo CR0 .223 A6
Marlowe Rd E17 .54 A5
Marlowe Sq CR4 .203 C5
Marlowes The
NW8 .92 B6 229 C6
Marlowe Way CR0 .220 A6
Marlow Gdns UB3 .105 B3
Marlow Ho 44 E2 .95 D4
SE1 .263 C6
14 W2 .91 D1
Teddington TW11 .175 A6
Marlow Rd E6 .100 B4
Penge SE20 .184 B1
Southall UB2 .107 B3
Marlow Studio Workshops
43 E2 .95 D4
Marlow Way SE16 .118 D4
Marl Rd SW18 .136 A1
Marlston NW1 .231 D1
Marlton St SE10 .120 D1
Marlwood Cl DA15 .167 C2
Marmadon Rd SE18,
SE2 .123 D2
Marmion App E4 .35 C6
Marmion Ave E4 .35 B6
Marmion Cl E4 .35 B6
Marmion Ho 13 SW12 .159 B4
Marmion Mews 4
SW11 .137 A2
Marmion Rd SW11 .137 A1
Marmont Rd SE15 .140 A5
Marmora Ho E1 .97 A2
Marmora Rd SE22 .162 C5
Marmot Rd TW4 .128 D2
Marne Ave DA16 .146 A2
N11 .31 B6
Marnell Way TW4 .128 D2
Marner Prim Sch E3 .97 D3
Marne St W10 .91 A4
Marney Rd SW11 .137 A1
Marnfield Cres SW2 .160 B3
Marnham Ave NW2 .69 A4
Marnham Cres UB6 .85 D5
Marnham Ct HA0 .65 C3
Marnock Ho SE17 .262 C2
Marnock Rd SE4 .163 B6
Maroon St E14 .97 A2
Maroons Way SE6 .185 C5
Marqueen Twrs SW16 .182 B3
Marquess Rd N1 .73 B2
Marquess Rd N N1 .73 B2
Marquess Rd S 17 N1 .73 A2
Marquis Cl HA0 .66 B1
Marquis Ct N4 .50 B1
Barking IG11 .79 C3
1 Kingston KT1 .198 A5
Marquis Rd N4 .50 C1
NW1 .71 D2
Bowes Park N22 .32 B4
Marrabon Cl DA15 .168 A3
Marrayat Sq SW6 .264 A2
Marrick Cl SW15 .134 A1
Marrick Ho 17 NW6 .91 D6
Marrilyne Ave EN3 .7 B5
Marriner Ct UB3 .105 C6
Marriott Cl TW14 .149 B5
Marriott Ho 8 SE6 .186 A6
Marriott Rd E15 .98 C6
N10 .30 D2
N4 .50 B1
Marriotts Cl NW9 .45 D3
Marryat Ct 12 W6 .112 B2
Marryat Ho SW1 .259 A1
Marryat Pl SW19 .179 A6
Marryat Rd SW19 .179 A6
Marryatt Ct W5 .88 B1
Marsala Rd SE13 .141 D1
Marsalis Ho 2 E3 .97 C4
Marsden Rd SE15 .139 D2
Edmonton N9 .18 B2
Marsden St NW5 .71 A2
Marsden Way 2 BR6 .227 D4
Marshall Cl N11 .15 B1
SW18 .158 A5
Harrow HA1 .42 B2
Hounslow TW4 .151 B6
Marshall Ct SW4 .270 B1
Marshall Dr UB4 .83 D2
Marshall Ho N1 .235 D4
NW6 .91 B5

Marshall Ho *continued*
SE17 ... 262 C2
4 New Malden KT3 ... 199 C5
Marshall Path 10 SE28 124 B6
Marshall Rd Leyton E10 ... 75 D4
Tottenham N17 ... 33 B2
Marshalls Gr SE18 ... 122 A2
Marshall's Pl SE16 ... 263 D5
Marshall's Rd SM1 ... 217 D4
Marshall St W1 93 C1 239 B1
Marshalsea Rd
SE1 ... 117 A4 252 B2
Marsham Cl BR7 ... 188 D5
Marsham Ct SW1 ... 259 D4
19 Putney SW19 ... 156 D3
Marsham St
SW1 ... 115 D2 259 D4
Marsh Ave CR4 ... 181 A1
Marshbrook Cl SE3 ... 143 D2
Marsh Cl NW7 ... 11 D1
Marsh Ct E8 ... 74 A2
3 Merton SW19 ... 180 A2
Marsh Dr NW9 ... 45 D3
Marsh Farm Rd TW2 ... 152 D3
Marshfield St E14 ... 120 A3
Marshgate Bsns Ctr
E15 ... 98 A5
Marshgate Ctr The E15 97 D6
Marshgate La E15 ... 75 D1
Marsh Green Prim Sch
RM10 ... 103 C5
Marsh Green Rd RM10 103 C6
Marsh Hall HA9 ... 66 B5
Marsh Hill E9 ... 75 A3
Marsh Ho SW1 ... 259 D1
SW8 ... 269 B2
Marsh La E10 ... 75 C6
NW7 ... 11 C1
Stanmore HA7 ... 25 C4
Tottenham N17 ... 34 B2
Marsh Rd Pinner HA5 ... 41 A5
Wembley HA0 ... 87 D5
Marshside Cl N9 ... 18 C3
Marsh St E14 ... 119 D2
Marsh Wall E14 ... 119 D4
Marshwood Ho 10 NW6 91 C6
Marsland Cl SE17 ... 261 D1
Marsom Ho N1 ... 235 C3
Marston SE17 ... 262 B4
Marston Ave
Chessington KT9 ... 214 A2
Dagenham RM10 ... 81 C5
Marston Cl NW6 ... 70 A1
Dagenham RM10 ... 81 C5
Marston Ct DA14 ... 189 D6
Walton-on-T KT12 ... 194 C1
Marston Ho SW9 ... 138 C3
Marston Rd TW11 ... 175 B5
Marston Way SE19 ... 183 A3
Marsworth Ave HA5 ... 22 D2
Marsworth Cl UB4 ... 85 A3
Marsworth Ho 8 E2 ... 96 A6
Martaban Rd N16 ... 73 D6
Martello St E8 ... 74 B1
Martello Terr E8 ... 74 B1
Martell Rd SE21 ... 161 B1
Martel Pl E8 ... 73 D2
Marten Rd E17 ... 35 C1
Martens Ave DA7 ... 147 D1
Martham Cl SE28 ... 124 D6
Martha Rd E15 ... 76 C2
Martha's Bldgs EC1 ... 242 C6
Martha St E1 ... 96 C1
Marthorne Cres HA3 ... 24 B1
Martin Bowes Rd SE9 ... 144 B2
Martinbridge Trad Est
EN1 ... 18 B6
Martin Cl N9 ... 18 D3
Uxbridge UB10 ... 82 A5
Martin Cres CR0 ... 204 C1
Martin Ct 10 E14 ... 120 A4
Merton SW19 ... 179 C3
Southall UB2 ... 107 B4
Martindale SW14 ... 155 A6
Martindale Ave 2
E16 ... 121 A6
Martindale Ho 20 E14 119 D6
Martindale Rd
Balham SW12 ... 159 B4
Hounslow TW4 ... 129 A2
Martin Dene DA6 ... 169 B6
Martin Dr UB5 ... 63 B3
Martineau Cl KT10 ... 212 B4
Martineau Ho SW1 ... 259 A1
Martineau Mews N5 ... 72 D4
Martineau Rd N5 ... 72 D4
Martingale Cl TW16 ... 194 A5
Martingales Cl TW10 ... 153 D1
Martin Gdns RM8 ... 80 D4
Martin Gr SM4 ... 201 C6
Martin Ho SE1 ... 262 B5
SW8 ... 270 A4
6 New Malden KT3 ... 199 C5
Martini Dr EN3 ... 7 C6
Martin La EC4 ... 252 D6
Martin Prim Sch N2 ... 30 C1
Martin Rd RM8 ... 80 D4
Martin Rise DA6 ... 169 B6
Martins Cl BR4 ... 224 B6
Martins Mount EN5 ... 1 D1
Martin's Rd BR2 ... 186 D1
Martin St SE28 ... 123 C5
Martins The
Penge SE26 ... 184 B5
Wembley HA9 ... 66 B5
Martins Wlk N10 ... 31 A2
Woolwich SE28 ... 123 C5
Martin Way SW19,
SW20,SM4 ... 201 B6
Martlesham N17 ... 33 C1
Martlet Gr 5 UB5 ... 84 D4
Martlett Ct WC2 ... 240 B1
Martlett Lo NW3 ... 69 D4
Martley Dr IG2 ... 56 D4
Martley Ho SW8 ... 269 B2
Martock Cl HA3 ... 43 A5
Martock Ct 10 SE15 ... 140 B4
Martock Gdns N11 ... 31 A5
Marton Cl SE6 ... 163 C1
Marton Rd 2 N16 ... 73 C5
Martyn Ct HA8 ... 26 B6
Martyn Ho SE2 ... 146 D6
Martynside 22 NW9 ... 27 D2
Marvel Ho 5 SE5 ... 139 B5
Marvell Ave UB4 ... 84 A2
Marvels Cl SE12 ... 165 B2
Marvels La SE12 ... 165 C1
Marvels Lane Prim Sch
SE12 ... 187 D6
Marville Ho SW18 ... 158 B5
Marville Rd
SW6 ... 135 B5 264 C3
Marvin Ho 9 SE18 ... 144 D6
Marvin St 3 E8 ... 74 B2
Marwell Cl BR4 ... 224 D6
Marwick Rd UB7 ... 104 B4
Marwood Cl DA16 ... 146 B2
Mary Adelaide Cl
Kingston SW15 ... 155 C1
Kingston SW15 ... 177 C6
Mary Adelaide Ho W2 236 D4
Mary Ann Bldgs SE8 ... 141 C6
Maryatt Ave HA2 ... 63 D6
Marybank SE18 ... 122 B2
Mary Batchelor Sch (Girls)
SE5 ... 139 B4
Mary Cl HA7 ... 44 B5
Mary Datchelor Cl
SE5 ... 139 B4
Mary Dine Ct SW8 ... 270 D3
Mary Gn NW8 ... 91 D6
Marygold Ho TW3 ... 130 A4
Mary Ho 6 SW9 ... 138 B3
8 W6 ... 112 C1
Mary James Ho 29 E2 ... 96 A5
Mary Jones Ho 13 E14 119 C6
Maryland Ct KT1 ... 176 D1
Maryland Pk E15 ... 76 C3
Maryland Point E15 ... 76 C2
Maryland Prim Sch E15 76 C3
Maryland Rd E15 ... 76 B3
W9 ... 91 C3
South Norwood CR7 ... 182 D2
Tottenham N22 ... 32 C4
Marylands Ind Est E15 ... 76 C3
Maryland Sq E15 ... 76 C3
Marylands Rd W9 ... 91 D3
Maryland St E15 ... 76 C3
Maryland Sta E15 ... 76 C2
Maryland Way TW16 ... 172 A1
Maryland Wlk N1 ... 235 A6
Mary Lawrenson Pl 1
SE3 ... 143 A5
Marylebone Flyover
NW1 ... 92 C2 237 A3
Marylebone High St
W1 ... 93 A2 238 B4
Marylebone La
W1 ... 93 A1 238 B2
Marylebone Mews
W1 ... 238 C3
Marylebone Pas W1 ... 239 B2
Marylebone Rd
NW1 ... 92 D2 237 D4
Marylebone St
W1 ... 93 A2 238 B3
Marylebone Sta
NW1 ... 92 D3 237 C5
Marylee Way
SE11 ... 116 B2 260 D3
Mary Macarthur Ho
18 E2 ... 96 D4
W14 ... 264 A6
8 Belvedere DA17 ... 125 C3
11 Dagenham RM10 ... 81 C5
Mary McArthur Ho 12
N19 ... 49 D2
Marymount International
Sch KT2 ... 177 A3
Maryon Gr SE7 ... 122 A2
Maryon Mews NW3 ... 70 C4
Maryon Rd SE7 ... 122 A2
Mary Peters Dr UB6 ... 64 B3
Mary Pl W11 ... 113 A6 244 A5
Mary Rose Cl TW12 ... 173 C2
Mary Rose Mall E6 ... 100 B2
Maryrose Way N20 ... 14 B3
Mary's Ct NW8 ... 237 B6
Mary Secole Cl 21 E8 ... 95 D6
Mary St 5 E16 ... 98 D2
N1 ... 95 A6 235 B5
Mary's Terr TW1 ... 153 A4
Mary Terr NW1 ... 232 A5
Maryville DA16 ... 145 D3
Mary Wharrie Ho 4
NW3 ... 70 D1
Masbro' Rd W14 ... 112 D3
Mascalls Ct 15 SE7 ... 143 C6
Mascalls Rd SE7 ... 143 C6
Mascotte Rd 2 SW15 134 D1
Mascotts Cl NW2 ... 68 B5
Masefield Ave
Borehamwood WD6 ... 10 D6
Southall UB1 ... 107 C6
Stanmore HA7 ... 24 D5
Masefield Cres N14 ... 15 C5
Masefield Ct N5 ... 73 B3
New Barnet EN5 ... 2 A1
10 Surbiton KT6 ... 197 D2
Masefield Gdns E6 ... 100 C3
Masefield Ho 1 NW6 ... 91 C4
Masefield La UB4 ... 84 C3
Masefield Rd TW13 ... 173 B6
Masefield View BR6 ... 227 A5
Masefield Way TW19 ... 148 B3
Masham Ho 6 DA18 ... 124 D4
Mashie Rd W3 ... 89 C1
Maskall Cl SW2 ... 160 C3
Maskani Wlk SW16 ... 181 C3
Maskell Rd SW17 ... 158 A1
Maskelyne Cl
SW11 ... 136 C4 267 B2
Mason Cl DA7 ... 147 D2
E16 ... 121 A6
SE16 ... 118 A1
Hampton TW12 ... 173 B2
Wimbledon SW20 ... 178 D2
Mason Ct
4 Penge SE19 ... 183 D3
Wembley HA9 ... 66 C6
Mason Ho 16 E9 ... 74 C1
8 N11 ... 31 C5
13 SE1 ... 118 A2
Mason Rd Sutton SM1 ... 217 D3
Woodford IG8 ... 36 C6
Mason's Arms Mews
W1 ... 248 D6
Mason's Ave EC2 ... 242 C2
Masons Ave HA3 ... 42 D5
Mason's Ave CR0 ... 221 A5
Masons Hill BR2 ... 209 B5
SE18 ... 122 D2
Mason's Pl EC1 ... 235 A2
Mitcham CR4 ... 180 D2
Mason St SE17 117 B2 262 D4
Mason's Yd SW1 ... 249 B4
Wimbledon SW19 ... 178 D5
Massey Cl N11 ... 31 B5
Massey Ct 7 E6 ... 99 C6
Massie Rd E8 ... 74 A2
Massingberd Way
SW17 ... 181 B6
Massinger St SE1,SE17 263 A3
Massingham St E1 ... 96 D3
Masson Ave HA4 ... 62 C2
Mast Ct 17 SE16 ... 119 A2
Master Gunner's Pl 1
SE18 ... 144 A4
Masterman Ho 1 SE5 139 B5
Masterman Rd E6 ... 100 A4
Masters Cl SW16 ... 181 C4
Masters Ct HA4 ... 61 C6
Masters Dr SE16 ... 118 B1
Masters Lo 22 E1 ... 96 C1
Master's St 14 E1 ... 96 D2
Mast House Terr E14 ... 119 C2
Mastin Ho SW18 ... 157 C3
Mastmaker Rd E14 ... 119 C4
Maswell Park Cres
TW3 ... 152 A6
Maswell Park Rd TW3 130 A1
Matcham Rd E11 ... 76 D5
Matching Ct 13 E3 ... 97 C4
Matchless Dr SE18 ... 144 C5
Matfield Cl BR2 ... 209 A4
Matfield Rd DA17 ... 147 C6
Matham Gr SE22 ... 139 D1
Matham Rd KT8 ... 196 B4
Mathart Ct E4 ... 36 B4
Matheson Lang Ho
SE1 ... 251 A1
Matheson Rd
W14 ... 113 B2 254 C3
Mathews Ave E6 ... 100 C5
Mathews Park Ave E15 76 D2
Mathieson Ct SE1 ... 251 D1
Mathieson Ho 10 E4 ... 20 C4
Matilda Cl SE19 ... 183 B3
Matilda Ho E1 ... 118 A5
Matilda Marks-Kennedy
Jewish Prim Sch NW7 27 B5
Matilda St N1 ... 94 B6 233 D6
Matlock Cl SE24 ... 139 A1
Barnet EN5 ... 12 D6
Matlock Cres SM3 ... 217 A4
Matlock Ct NW8 ... 229 A4
7 SE5 ... 139 B1
Matlock Gdns SM1,
SM3 ... 217 A4
Matlock Pl SM1,SM3 ... 217 A4
Matlock Rd E10 ... 54 A3
Matlock St E14 ... 97 A1
Matlock Way KT3 ... 177 B2
Maton Ho SW6 ... 264 C4
Matson Ct IG8 ... 36 C3
Matson Ho 10 E9 ... 74 D2
9 SE16 ... 118 B3
Matthew Cl W10 ... 90 D3
Matthew Ct 4 E17 ... 54 A6
Mitcham CR4 ... 203 D4
Matthew Parker St
SW1 ... 249 D1
Matthews Ct N5 ... 73 A4
Matthews Ho 3 E14 ... 97 C2
Matthews Rd UB6 ... 64 B3
Matthews St SW11 ... 136 D3
Matthias Ct 12 TW10 ... 154 A5
Matthias Ho 2 N16 ... 73 C3
Matthias Rd N16 ... 73 C3
Mattingly Way 4
SE15 ... 139 D5
Mattison Rd N4 ... 50 D3
Mattock La W5,W13 ... 109 C5
Maud Cashmore Way
SE18 ... 122 B3
Maude Ho 3 E2 ... 96 A5
Maude Rd E17 ... 53 A4
SE5 ... 139 C4
Maudesville Cotts W7 108 C5
Maude Terr E17 ... 53 A5
Maud Gdns E13 ... 98 D5
Barking IG11 ... 101 D5
Maudlins Gn E1 ... 118 A5
Maud Rd E10 ... 76 A5
E13 ... 98 D5
Maudslay Rd SE9 ... 144 B2
Maudsley Ho TW8 ... 110 A1
Maudsley Hospl The
SE5 ... 139 B3
Maud St E16 ... 98 D2
Maugham Ct 5 W3 ... 111 A3
Mauleverer Rd SW2 ... 160 A6
Maundeby Wlk NW10 ... 67 C2
Maunder Rd 4 W7 ... 108 D5
Maunsel St
SW1 ... 115 D2 259 C4
Mauretania Bldg 11
E1 ... 118 D6
Maurice Ave N22 ... 32 D1
Maurice Browne Cl
NW7 ... 28 D4
Maurice Ct 3 TW8 ... 131 D5
Maurice Ho 1 SW9 ... 138 B3
Maurice St W12 ... 90 B1
Maurice Wlk NW11 ... 48 A5
Maurier Cl UB5 ... 84 C6
Mauritius Rd SE10 ... 120 C2
Maury Rd N16 ... 74 A5
Mauveine Gdns TW3 ... 129 C1
Mavelstone Cl BR1 ... 188 A2
Mavelstone Rd BR1 ... 188 A2
Maverton Rd E3 ... 97 C6
Mavery Ct 4 BR1 ... 186 D3
Mavis Ave KT19 ... 215 C3
Mavis Cl KT19 ... 215 C3
Mavis Ct 33 NW9 ... 27 D1
Mavis Wlk 9 E6 ... 100 A2
Mavor Ho N1 ... 233 D5
Mawbey Ho SE1 ... 263 D1
Mawbey Pl
SE1 ... 117 D1 263 D1
Mawbey Rd SE1 ... 263 D1
Mawbey St SW8 ... 270 A3
Mawdley Ho SE1 ... 251 B1
Mawney Cl RM7 ... 59 D6
Mawney Rd RM7 ... 59 D6
Mawson Cl SW20 ... 179 A1
Mawson Ho EC1 ... 241 A4
Mawson La W4 ... 133 D6
Maxden Ct SE15 ... 140 A2
Maxey Gdns RM9 ... 81 A4
Maxey Rd SE18 ... 123 A2
Dagenham RM9 ... 81 A4
Maxfield Cl N20 ... 14 A4
Maxim Rd N21 ... 16 C5
Maxted Pk HA1 ... 42 C2
Maxted Rd SE15 ... 139 D2
Maxwell Cl
Croydon CR0 ... 204 A1
Hayes UB3 ... 106 A6
Maxwell Ct SE21 ... 162 A3
Maxwell Gdns BR6 ... 227 D5
Maxwell Ho 12 SE18 ... 144 D6
Bowes Park N22 ... 32 B4
Chislehurst BR7 ... 188 D3
Maxwell Rd DA16 ... 146 A2
SW6 ... 135 D5 265 D3
Ashford TW15 ... 171 A4
West Drayton UB7 ... 104 B2
Maxwelton Ave NW7 ... 27 B5
Maxwelton Cl NW7 ... 27 B5
Maya Cl SE15 ... 140 B3
Mayall Cl EN3 ... 7 C5
Mayall Rd SE24 ... 160 D6
Maya Pl N11 ... 31 D3
Maya Rd N2 ... 48 A5
Maybank Ave
Wembley HA0 ... 65 A3
Woodford E18 ... 37 B1
Maybank Gdns HA5 ... 40 A4
Maybank Rd E18 ... 37 C2
May Bate Ave KT2 ... 175 D2
Maybells Commercial Est
IG11 ... 102 D5
Mayberry Pl KT5 ... 198 B2
Maybourne Cl SE26 ... 184 B5
Maybourne Grange
CR0 ... 221 C6
Maybury Cl BR5 ... 210 D4
Enfield EN1 ... 6 B5
Maybury Ct W1 ... 238 B3
Beckenham BR3 ... 185 B3
Harrow HA1 ... 42 B3
Maybury Gdns NW10 ... 68 B2
Maybury Mews N6 ... 49 C2
Maybury Rd E13 ... 99 C3
Barking IG11 ... 102 A5
Maybury St SW17 ... 180 C5
Maychurch Cl HA7 ... 25 D3
May Cl KT9 ... 214 B2
Maycroft 2 Hayes BR2 208 D1
Pinner HA5 ... 22 B1
Maycross Ave SM4 ... 201 C5
May Ct 2 SW19 ... 180 A2
Mayday Gdns SE3 ... 144 A3
Mayday Rd CR0,CR7 ... 204 D3
Mayday University Hospl
CR7 ... 204 D3
Maydeb Ct RM6 ... 59 B3
Maydew Ho SE16 ... 118 C2
Maydwell Ho 6 E14 ... 97 C2
Maye Angelou Ct E4 ... 36 A6
Mayefield Rd CR7 ... 204 B4
Mayerne Rd SE9 ... 165 D6
Mayers Ct E8 ... 74 A4
Mayesbrook Rd
Barking IG11 ... 101 D6
Dagenham RM8,IG3 ... 80 B5
Mayesford Rd RM6 ... 58 C2
Mayespark Prim Sch
IG3 ... 80 A5
Mayeswood Rd SE12 ... 187 C6
Mayfair Ave DA16 ... 146 D4
Dagenham RM6 ... 58 D3
Ilford IG1 ... 56 C1
New Malden KT4 ... 200 A1
Twickenham TW2 ... 152 A4
Mayfair Cl
Beckenham BR3 ... 185 D2
Surbiton KT6 ... 198 A1
Mayfair Ct
1 Beckenham BR3 ... 185 D2
7 Croydon CR0 ... 221 D6
1 Wimbledon SW19 ... 179 A3
Mayfair Gdns
Tottenham N17 ... 33 B4
Woodford IG8 ... 37 A3
Mayfair Pl W1 ... 248 D4
Mayfair Terr N14 ... 15 D4
Mayfield DA7 ... 147 B2
Mayfield Ave BR6 ... 211 D2
N12 ... 30 B6
N14 ... 15 D2
W13 ... 109 B4
W4 ... 111 C2
Harrow HA3 ... 43 B4
Woodford IG8 ... 37 A4
Mayfield Cl E8 ... 73 D2
SW4 ... 159 D6
Ashford TW15 ... 170 D4
Hillingdon UB10 ... 82 D4
Long Ditton KT7 ... 197 B1
Penge SE20 ... 184 B2
Mayfield Cres Enfield N9 18 B5
Thornton Heath CR7 ... 204 B4
Mayfield Ct SM2 ... 218 A1
Mayfield Dr HA5 ... 41 B5
Mayfield Gdns NW4 ... 46 D3
Ealing W7 ... 86 C2
Mayfield Ho 30 E2 ... 96 B5
N16 ... 51 C2
Mayfield Mans SW15 ... 157 B6
Mayfield Prim Sch W7 ... 86 B1
Mayfield Rd BR1 ... 210 A4
E13 ... 98 D3
E17 ... 35 A1
E8 ... 73 D1
N8 ... 50 B3
W12 ... 111 C4
Acton W3 ... 110 D6
Chingford E4 ... 20 B2
Dagenham RM8 ... 58 C1
Enfield EN3 ... 6 D3
Merton SW19 ... 179 B2
South Croydon CR2 ... 221 B1
Sutton SM2 ... 218 B2
Mayfields HA9 ... 66 C6
Mayfield Sch & Coll
RM8 ... 58 C1
Mayfields Cl HA9 ... 66 C6
Mayfield Villas DA14 ... 190 C4
Mayflower Cl SE16 ... 118 D2
Mayflower Cl *continued*
Ruislip HA4 ... 39 A3
Mayflower Ho 2 IG11 101 B6
Mayflower Lo N10 ... 31 A2
N3 ... 47 B6
Mayflower Prim Sch
E14 ... 97 D1
Mayflower Rd SW9 ... 138 A2
Mayflower St 1 SE16 ... 118 C4
Mayfly Cl HA5 ... 40 C2
Mayfly Gdns 12 UB5 ... 84 D4
Mayford NW1 ... 232 B4
Mayford Cl
Balham SW12 ... 158 D4
Penge BR3 ... 206 D6
Mayford Rd SW12 ... 159 A4
May Gdns Elstree WD6 ... 9 D5
Wembley HA0 ... 87 C4
Maygood Ho N1 ... 234 A4
Maygood St N1 94 C5 234 A4
Maygrove Rd NW6 ... 69 B2
Mayhew Cl E4 ... 19 C1
Mayhew Ct 2 SE5 ... 139 B1
Mayhill Rd Barnet EN5 ... 13 A5
Greenwich SE7 ... 143 B6
Mayland Mans 4 IG11 ... 78 D1
Maylands Dr DA14 ... 168 D1
Maylands Ho SW3 ... 257 B3
Maylands Rd WD19 ... 22 C6
Maynard Cl N15 ... 51 C4
SW6 ... 135 D5 265 D3
Maynard Ct EN3 ... 7 C5
Maynard Ho E1 ... 97 A4
SE18 ... 123 A2
Maynard Rd E17 ... 54 A4
Maynards Quay E1 ... 118 C6
Maynooth Gdns CR4 ... 202 D2
Mayo Ct W13 ... 109 B3
Mayola Rd E5 ... 74 C4
Mayo Rd NW10 ... 67 C2
Thornton Heath CR0 ... 205 B4
Walton-on-T KT12 ... 194 A2
Mayow Rd SE23,SE26 ... 184 D6
Mayplace Cl DA7 ... 147 D2
Mayplace La SE18 ... 144 D6
Mayplace Rd W DA7 ... 147 C1
Maypole Ct UB2 ... 107 B4
May Rd E13 ... 99 A5
Chingford E4 ... 35 C4
Twickenham TW2 ... 152 C3
Mayroyd Ave KT6 ... 214 C6
May's Buildings Mews
SE10 ... 142 B5
Mays Ct WC2 ... 250 A5
May's Ct SE10 ... 142 B5
May's Hill Rd BR2 ... 208 C6
Mays La EN5 ... 12 C5
Maysoule Rd SW11 ... 136 B1
Mays Rd TW11,TW12 ... 174 B5
Mayston Mews 3
SE10 ... 121 A1
May Terr IG1 ... 78 D4
Maythorne Cotts SE13 164 B5
Maytime Prep Sch IG1 ... 78 C5
Mayton St N7 ... 72 B5
Maytree Cl HA8 ... 11 A1
Maytree Ct
Mitcham CR4 ... 203 A6
Northolt UB5 ... 85 A4
May Tree Ho SE4 ... 141 B2
Maytree La HA7 ... 24 D3
Maytree Wlk SW2 ... 160 C2
Mayville Prim Sch E11 ... 76 C6
Mayville Rd E11 ... 76 C6
Ilford IG1 ... 78 D3
Mayward Ho 7 SE5 ... 139 C4
May Wlk E13 ... 99 B5
Maywood Cl BR3 ... 185 D3
May Wynne Ho E16 ... 99 B1
Maze Hill SE10,SE3 ... 142 C6
Maze Hill Lo 8 SE10 ... 142 B6
Maze Hill Specl Sch
SE10 ... 142 A5
Maze Hill Sta SE10 ... 142 C6
Mazenod Ave NW6 ... 69 C1
Maze Rd TW9 ... 132 C5
Mead Cl 3 NW1 ... 71 A1
Harrow HA3 ... 24 B2
Mead Cres
Carshalton SM1 ... 218 C4
Chingford E4 ... 36 A6
Meadcroft Ho 4 KT3 ... 199 C2
Meadcroft Rd SE17 ... 138 D6
Mead Ct NW9 ... 45 B4
Meade Cl W4 ... 132 C6
Meader Ct SE14 ... 140 D5
Meadfield HA8 ... 10 D2
Mead Field HA2 ... 63 B5
Meadfield Gn HA8 ... 10 D2
Meadfoot Rd SW16 ... 181 C2
Mead Gr RM6 ... 58 D6
Mead Ho W11 ... 244 C4
Mead House La UB4 ... 83 B3
Meadhurst Pk TW16 ... 171 C4
Mead Inf Sch The
KT19 ... 215 D4
Meadlands Dr TW10 ... 153 D2
Meadlands Prim Sch
TW10 ... 175 C6

Mead Lo W4 111 B4
Meadow Ave CR0 206 D3
Meadowbank NW3 70 D1
SE3 142 D2
Southgate N21 16 B5
Surbiton KT5 198 B3
Meadow Bank 7
SW15 157 B6
Meadowbank Cl SW6 134 C5
Meadowbank Gdns
TW5 128 B4
Meadowbank Rd NW9 45 B2
Meadowbanks EN5 12 A6
Meadowbrook Ct
TW7 130 D2
Meadow Cl DA6 169 B6
E9 75 B3
Barnet EN5 13 B5
Catford SE6 185 C5
Chingford E4 19 D3
Chislehurst BR7 188 D5
Enfield EN3 7 A5
Hinchley Wood KT10 212 D5
Northolt UB5 85 C5
Richmond TW10 154 A3
Ruislip HA4 39 D3
Sutton SM1 218 A6
West Barnes SW20 200 C5
Hounslow TW4 151 C5
Meadowcourt Rd SE3 142 D1
Meadowcroft 9 W4 110 C1
Meadow Croft BR1 210 B6
Meadowcroft Rd N13 16 C2
Meadow Dr N10 49 B6
NW4 28 C1
Meadowford Cl SE28 124 A6
Meadow Garth NW10 67 B2
Meadowgate Sch SE4 141 A2
Meadow Gdns HA8 27 A4
Meadow High Sch UB8 82 A2
Meadow Hill KT3 199 C3
Meadow La SE12 165 B1
Meadow Mews SW8 270 C5
Meadow Pl
SW8 138 A5 270 B4
Chiswick W4 133 C5
Meadow Rd
SW8 138 B5 270 C4
Ashford TW15 171 B5
Barking IG11 80 A1
Beckenham BR2 186 C1
Carshalton SM1 218 C3
Claygate KT10 212 C2
Dagenham RM9 81 B2
Feltham TW13 151 A2
Loughton IG10 21 D6
Merton SW19 180 A3
Pinner HA5 41 A5
Southall UB1 107 B6
Meadow Row SE1 262 A5
Meadows Cl E10 75 C6
Meadows Ct DA14 190 B4
Meadows End TW16 172 A2
Meadowside SE9 143 C1
Twickenham TW1 153 D4
Meadow Stile CR0 221 A5
Meadowsweet Cl
3 E16 99 D2
West Barnes KT3 200 C5
Meadow The BR7 189 A4
Meadow View DA15 168 B4
Meadowview TW17 193 A2
Meadow View HA1 42 C1
Meadowview Rd
Catford SE6 185 C5
Sidcup DA5 169 B5
West Ewell KT19 215 C1
Meadow View Rd
Hayes UB4 83 B3
Thornton Heath CR7 204 D4
Meadow Way BR6 226 C5
NW9 45 B4
Chessington KT9 214 A3
Ruislip HA4 40 B3
Wembley HA9 65 D4
Meadow Waye TW5 129 A5
Meadow Way The HA3 24 C2
Meadow Wlk
Dagenham RM9 81 B2
Ewell KT17 215 D1
Hackbridge SM6 219 B5
Wanstead E18 55 A5
West Ewell KT17,KT19 215 D1
Meadow Wood Sch
WD23 8 A6
Mead Pl E9 74 C2
Croydon CR0 205 A1
Mead Plat NW10 67 A2
Mead Rd BR7 189 A4
Edgware HA8 26 C4
Richmond TW10 153 C1
Mead Road Inf Sch
BR7 189 A4
Mead Row
SE1 116 C3 261 A6
Meads Ct E15 76 D2
Meadside Cl BR3 185 A2
Meads La IG3 57 D2
Meads Rd Enfield EN3 7 A4
Meads Rd *continued*
Tottenham N22 32 D1
Meads The HA8 27 B4
Cheam SM3 217 A5
Hillingdon UB8 82 A3
Mead The N2 30 A1
Beckenham BR3 186 A2
Ealing W13 87 B2
Ickenham UB10 60 C6
Wallington SM6 219 D2
West Wickham BR4 208 B1
Meadvale Rd
Croydon CR0 206 A3
Ealing W5 87 C3
Meadway NW11 47 D3
Ashford TW15 170 C6
Barnet EN5 1 C1
Beckenham BR3 186 A2
Enfield EN3 6 D6
Palmers Green N14 16 A2
Tolworth KT5 199 A1
Twickenham TW2 152 B3
West Barnes SW20 200 C5
Woodford IG8 37 C5
Mead Way CR0 223 A6
Meadway KT10 212 A1
Mead Way Hayes BR2 209 A3
Hayes BR2,BR4 208 D3
Ilford IG3 79 C4
Ruislip HA4 39 B3
Meadway Cl NW11 47 D3
Barnet EN5 1 C1
Pinner HA5 23 D4
Meadway Ct NW11 47 D3
Dagenham RM8 81 B6
Ealing W5 88 B2
Meadway Gate NW11 47 C3
Meadway Gdns HA4 39 B3
Meadway The SE3 142 B3
Buckhurst Hill IG9 21 D3
Meaford Way SE20 184 B3
Meakin Est SE1 263 A6
Meakin Ho N7 72 B3
Meanley Rd E12 78 A3
Meard St W1 239 C1
Meath Ho SE24 160 D5
Meath Rd E15 98 D5
Ilford IG1 79 A5
Meath St
SW11 137 B4 268 C2
Mecklenburgh Pl
WC1 240 C6
Mecklenburgh Sq
WC1 94 B3 240 C6
Medburn St NW1 232 C4
Medcalf Rd EN3 7 B6
Medcroft Gdns SW14 133 A1
Medebourne Cl SE3 143 A2
Mede Ho BR1 187 B5
Medesenge Way N13 32 D4
Medfield St SW15 156 B4
Medhurst Cl 17 E3 97 A5
Median Rd E5 74 C3
Medical Coll of St
Bartholomew's Hospl The
EC1 94 D3 241 D5
Medina Ave KT10 212 C5
Medina Ct N7 72 C5
Medina Gr N7 72 C5
Medina Ho SE15 140 C1
Medina Rd N7 72 C5
Medland Cl CR4 203 A1
Medlar Cl 1 UB5 84 D5
Medlar Ho 3 DA15 168 A1
Medlar St SE5 139 A4
Medley Rd NW6 69 C2
Medora Rd SW2 160 B4
Medresco Ho NW3 70 B3
Medusa Rd SE6,SE13 163 D5
Medway Bldgs E3 97 A5
Medway Cl
Croydon CR0 206 C3
Ilford IG1 79 A3
Medway Ct WC1 233 A1
South Norwood SE25 205 C4
Medway Dr UB6 86 D5
Medway Gdns HA0 65 A4
Medway Ho N16 73 B4
NW8 237 A4
SE1 252 D1
6 Kingston KT2 175 D2
Medway Mews 33 E3 97 A5
Medway Par 1 UB6 86 D5
Medway Rd E3 97 A5
Medway St
SW1 115 D3 259 D5
Medwin St SW4 138 B1
Meecham Ct 1 SW11 136 C3
Meerbrook Rd SE3,
SE9 143 C2
Meeson Rd E15 76 D1
Meeson St E5 75 A4
Meeting House Alley 7
E1 118 B5
Meeting House La
SE15 140 B5
Mehetabel Rd E9 74 C3
Meister Cl IG1 57 B1
Melanda Cl BR7 188 B5
Melanie Cl DA7 147 A4
Melba Ct E8 73 D1
Melbourne Ave
Bowes Park N13 32 B4
Ealing W13 109 A5
Pinner HA2,HA5 41 D6
Melbourne Cl BR6 211 C2
Ickenham UB10 60 C4
Wallington SM6 219 C3
Melbourne Ct E5 75 A4
N10 31 B3
W9 236 B6
Penge SE20 184 A3
Twickenham TW2 152 B3
Melbourne Gdns RM6 59 A4
Melbourne Gr SE22 139 D1
Melbourne Ho W8 245 A3
Hayes UB4 84 C3
Melbourne Mews
SW9 138 C4
Catford SE6 164 A4
Melbourne Pl WC2 240 D1
Melbourne Rd E10 53 D2
E17 53 A5
E6 100 B5
Ilford IG1 56 D1
Merton SW19 179 C2
Teddington TW11 175 C4
Wallington SM6 219 C3
Melbourne Sq 21 SW9 138 C4
Melbourne Way EN1 17 D5
Melbrook Ho 11 SE22 139 C2
Melbury Ave UB2 107 D3
Melbury Cl BR7 188 B4
Claygate KT10 213 B2
Melbury Ct
W8 113 B3 254 D6
Melbury Dr SE5 139 C5
Melbury Gdns SW20 178 B2
Melbury Ho SW8 270 C4
Twickenham TW2 152 B2
Melbury Rd
W14 113 B3 254 D6
Harrow HA3 44 B4
Melchester 3 W11 91 B1
Melchester Ho 1 N19 71 D5
Melcombe Ct NW1 237 C4
Melcombe Gdns HA3 44 B3
Melcombe Ho SW8 270 C3
Melcombe Pl NW1 237 C4
Melcombe Prim Sch
W6 134 D6
Melcombe St
NW1 92 D3 237 D5
Meldex Cl NW7 28 C4
Meldon Cl SW6 265 D2
Meldone KT3 199 B1
Meldone Cl KT5 198 D3
Meldrum Rd IG3 80 A6
Melfield Gdns SE6 186 A5
Melfont Ave CR7 204 D6
Melford Ave IG11 79 D2
Melford Cl KT9 214 B3
Melford Ct E5 74 B5
Dulwich SE22 162 A4
2 Sutton SM2 218 A1
Melford Rd E11 76 C6
E17 53 B5
E6 100 B4
Dulwich SE21,SE22 162 A3
Ilford IG1 79 B6
Melfort Rd CR7 204 D6
Melgund Rd N5 72 C3
Melina Cl UB3 83 B2
Melina Ct NW8 229 C1
Putney SW15 134 A2
Melina Pl NW8 92 B4 229 C1
Melina Rd W12 112 B4
Melior Ct N6 49 C3
Melior Pl SE1 253 A2
Melior St SE1 117 C4 253 A2
Meliot Rd SE6 164 B2
Melisa Ct N6 49 D2
Meller Cl SM6 220 A5
Melling Dr EN1 6 A4
Melling St SE18 145 C6
Mellington Ct 2 N16 74 A5
Mellis Ave TW9 132 D4
Mellish Cl IG11 101 D6
Mellish Ct KT6 198 A3
Mellish Flats E10 53 C2
Mellish Gdns IG8 37 A5
Mellish Ho 12 E1 96 B1
Mellish Ind Est E16 121 D3
Mellish St E14 119 C3
Mellison Rd SW17 180 C5
Mellitus St W12 89 D1
Mellor Cl KT12 195 B2
Mellor Ct 2 SW19 180 A3
Mellor Ho 2 SE21 183 C6
Mellow La E UB4 83 A3
Mellow Lane Sch UB4 83 A3
Mellow La W UB10 83 A4
Mellows Rd
Redbridge IG5 56 B6
Wallington SM6 219 D3
Mells Cres SE9 188 B6
Mell St 6 SE10 120 C1
Melody Rd SW18 158 A6
Melon Pl W8 245 B2
Melon Rd E11 76 C5
SE15 140 A4
Melrose Ave NW2 68 C3
Borehamwood WD6 10 D6
Greenford UB6 85 D5
Mitcham CR4 181 B3
Thornton Heath SW16 204 C6
Tottenham N22 32 D2
Twickenham TW2 151 D4
Wimbledon SW19 157 C1
Melrose Cl SE12 165 B3
Greenford UB6 85 D5
Hayes UB4 84 A2
Melrose Cres BR6 227 B3
Melrose Ct
5 Ealing W13 109 A5
Wandsworth SW18 157 B5
Melrose Dr UB1 107 C5
Melrose Gdns W6 112 C3
Edgware HA8 26 D1
Kingston KT3 199 B6
Melrose Ho NW6 91 C4
SW1 258 D2
Melrose Rd
1 Barnes SW13 133 D3
Merton SW19 179 C2
Pinner HA5 41 B5
Wandsworth SW18 157 B5
Melrose Sch CR4 202 C6
Melrose Terr W6 112 C3
Melrose Tudor SM6 220 A3
Melsa Rd SM4 202 A3
Melthorne Dr HA4 62 C5
Melthorpe Gdns SE3 144 A4
Melton Cl HA4 40 C1
Melton Ct SW7 256 D3
11 Croydon CR0 221 D6
Sutton SM2 218 A1
1 Twickenham TW1 153 B4
Melton Ho E5 74 A6
Melton St NW1 93 D4 232 C1
Melville Ave
Greenford UB6 64 D3
South Croydon CR2 221 D3
Wimbledon SW20 178 A3
Melville Cl UB10 61 B5
Melville Court Flats
W12 112 B4
Melville Ct SE8 119 A2
4 W4 110 C1
Melville Gdns N13 32 D5
Melville Ho SE10 142 A4
New Barnet EN5 14 B5
Melville Pl 4 N1 73 A1
Melville Rd E17 53 B6
NW10 67 B1
Barnes SW13 134 A4
Sidcup DA14 168 C2
Melville Villas Rd W3 111 B5
Melvin Ct 11 TW9 132 C4
Melvin Rd SE20 184 C2
Melwood Ho 22 E1 96 B1
Melyn Cl N7 71 C4
Memel Ct EC1 242 A5
Memel St EC1 242 A5
Memess Path 4 SE18 144 C6
Memorial Ave E15 98 C4
Memorial Cl TW5 129 B6
Memorial Hospl SE18 144 C3
Mendham Ho SE1 263 A6
Mendip Cl
Forest Hill SE26 184 C6
Harlington UB3 127 B5
North Cheam KT4 216 C6
Mendip Ct SE14 140 C6
12 SW11 136 A2
Mendip Dr NW2,NW11 69 A6
Mendip Ho 2 N4 51 B2
Mendip Hos 12 E2 96 C4
Mendip Rd SW11 136 A2
Bushey WD23 8 A5
Ilford IG2 57 C4
Mendora Rd
SW6 135 B5 264 C4
Menelik Rd NW2 69 B4
Menlo Gdns SE19 183 B3
Mennie Ho 5 SE18 144 B4
Menon Dr N9 18 B1
Menora Foundation Sch
HA8 27 A3
Menorah Gram Sch
NW11 47 A2
Menorah Prim Sch
NW11 47 A2
Menotti St 5 E2 96 A3
Menteath Ho 5 E14 97 C1
Mentmore Cl HA3 43 C3
Mentmore Terr E8 74 B1
Mentone Ct SW8 270 B2
Meon Ct TW7 130 C3
Meon Rd W3 111 A4
Meopham Rd CR4,
SW16 181 C2
Mepham Cres HA3 24 A3
Mepham Gdns HA3 24 A3
Mepham St
SE1 116 C5 251 A3
Mera Dr DA7 147 D1
Merantun Way SW19 180 A2
Merbury Cl SE13 164 B6
Merbury Rd SE28 123 C4
Merbury St SE18 122 D3
Mercator Pl E14 119 C1
Mercator Rd SE13 142 B1
Mercer Cl KT7 196 D2
Merceron Ho 3 E2 96 C4
Merceron St E1 96 B3
Mercer Pl HA5 22 C1
Mercers Cl SE10 120 D2
Mercer's Cotts 10 E3 97 A1
Mercers Pl W6 112 D2
Mercers Rd N19 71 D5
Mercer St WC2 94 A1 240 A1
Merchant Ct E1 118 C5
Merchants Cl SE25 206 A5
Merchants Lo 5 E17 53 C5
Merchant St E3 97 B4
Merchant Taylors'
Almshouses SE13 142 C1
Merchant Taylors Hall*
EC3 242 D1
Merchiston Rd SE6 164 B2
Merchland Rd SE9 167 A3
Merchon Ho N7 71 C4
Mercia Gr SE13 142 A1
Mercia Ho 9 SE5 139 A3
Mercier Rd SW15 157 A6
Mercury 25 NW9 27 D2
Mercury Ct 3 E14 119 C2
8 SW9 138 C4
Mercury Ctr TW14 150 B6
Mercury Ho TW8 109 D1
Mercury Rd TW8 109 C1
Mercury Way SE14 140 D6
Mercy Terr SE13 163 D6
Merebank La CR0,SM6 220 B3
Mere Cl Orpington BR6 226 D6
Putney SW15,SW19 156 D4
Meredith Ave NW2 68 C3
Meredith Cl HA5 22 D3
Meredith Ho 17 N16 73 C3
Meredith Mews SE4 141 B1
Meredith St E13 99 A4
EC1 234 C1
Meredyth Rd SW13 134 A3
Mere End CR0 206 D2
Mere Rd TW17 192 D3
Mereside BR6 226 C6
Meretone Cl SE4 141 A1
Meretune Ct SM4 201 B6
Merevale Cres SM4 202 A3
Mereway Industry
TW2 152 C3
Mereway Rd TW2 152 C3
Merewood Cl 1 BR1 188 C1
Mereworth Cl BR2 208 D4
Mereworth Dr SE18 145 A5
Mereworth Ho 3
SE15 140 C6
Merganser Ct 17 SE8 141 B6
Merganser Gdns SE28 123 B3
Meridan Ct SE13 142 B1
Meriden Cl BR1 187 D3
Meriden Ct SW3 257 A1
Meriden Ho 26 N1 95 C6
3 Barnet EN5 1 A1
Meridian Building
SE10 142 B5
Meridian Ct
4 Catford SE6 164 D3
Croydon CR0 220 C4
Meridian Ho SE10 120 C2
Meridian Pl E14 120 A4
Meridian Prim Sch
SE10 142 B6
Meridian Rd SE7 143 D5
Meridian Sq E15 76 B1
Meridian Trad Est SE7 121 B2
Meridian Way N9,N18 18 D1
Enfield EN3 19 A5
Meridian Wlk N17 33 C4
Merifield Rd SE9 143 C1
Merino Cl E11 55 C5
Merino Pl DA15 168 A6
Merioneth Ct 7 W7 86 D2
Merivale Rd Harrow HA1 42 A2
Putney SW15 135 A1
Merlewood Dr BR7 188 B2
Merley Ct NW9 45 A1
Merlin 26 NW9 27 D2
Merlin Cl Mitcham CR4 202 C6
4 Northolt UB5 84 C4
South Croydon CR0 221 C4
Wallington SM6 220 B2
Merlin Cres HA8 26 B2
Merlin Ct
Beckenham BR2 208 D5
6 Ealing W7 86 D3
Ruislip HA4 61 B6
Wood Green N22 32 C2
Merling Cl KT9 213 D3
Merlin Gdns BR1 165 A1
Merlin Gr BR3 207 C4
Merlin Ho NW3 69 D4
7 W4 111 B1
Enfield EN3 18 D6
Merlin Prim Sch BR1 165 A1
Merlin Rd Bexley DA16 146 A1
Wanstead E12 77 D6
Merlin Rd N DA16 146 A1
Merlins Ave HA2 63 B5
Merlins Ct WC1 234 A1
Merlin St EC1 94 C4 234 A1
Mermaid Ct N4 50 C3
SE1 117 B4 252 C2
SE16 119 B5
Mermaid Ho 8 E14 120 A6
Mermaid Twr 22 SE8 141 B6
Meroe Ct N16 73 C6
Merredene St SW2 160 B5
Merriam Ave 3 E9 75 B2
Merriam Cl E4 36 A5
Merrick Rd UB2 107 B3
Merricks Ct 5 SW14 132 D1
Merrick Sq
SE1 117 B3 262 C6
Merridale SE12 164 D6
Merridene N21 16 D5
Merrielands Cres RM9 103 B5
Merrielands Ret Pk
RM9 103 B5
Merrilands Rd KT4 200 C1
Merrilees Rd DA15 167 C4
Merrilyn Cl KT10 213 A2
Merriman Rd SE3 143 C4
Merrington Rd SW6 265 B6
Merrion Ave HA7 25 D5
Merritt Gdns KT9 213 C2
Merritt Rd SE4 163 B6
Merrivale NW1 232 B5
Southgate N14 15 D6
Merrivale Ave IG4 55 D5
Merrow Ct CR4 180 B1
Merrow St
SE17 117 B1 262 C1
Merrow Way CR0 224 A2
Merrow Wlk SE17 262 D2
Merrydown Way BR7 188 B2
Merry Fiddlers RM8 81 B6
Merryfield SE3 142 D3
Merryfield Gdns HA7 25 C5
Merryfield Ho SE12 165 C1
Merryhill Cl E4 19 D4
Merry Hill Rd WD23 8 A3
Merry Hill Sch WD23 8 A4
Merryhills Ct N14 15 C6
Merryhills Dr EN2 4 A1
Merryhills Prim Sch EN2 4 B1
Merryweather Ct 1
KT3 199 C4
Mersea Ho IG11 78 D2
Mersey Ct 10 KT2 175 D2
Mersey Ho 10 N7 72 C3
Mersey Rd E17 53 B6
Mersey Wlk UB5 85 C5
Mersham Dr NW9 44 D4
Mersham Pl
Penge SE20 184 B2
South Norwood CR7 183 B1
Mersham Rd CR7 183 B1
Merstone Ho SW18 157 D5
Merten Rd RM6 59 A2
Merthyr Terr SW13 134 B6
Merton Abbey Mills
Merton SW19 180 A2
Wandsworth SW18 157 D3
Merton Abbey Prim Sch
SW19 179 D2
Merton Ave W4 111 D2
Hillingdon UB10 60 D1
Northolt UB5 64 A3
Merton Coll SM4 201 B4
Merton Court Sch
DA14 190 C6
Merton Ct DA16 146 B3
Merton Gdns BR5 210 D4
Merton Hall Gdns
SW20 179 A2
Merton Hall Rd SW19 179 A2
Merton High St SW19 180 A3
Merton Ho SW18 157 C3
Merton Ind Pk SW19 180 A2
Merton La N6 70 D6
Merton Lo EN5 14 A6
Merton Mans SW20 178 D1
Merton Park Fst Sch
SW19 179 C1
Merton Park Par
SW19 179 B2
Merton Park Sta
SW19 179 C2
Merton Pl 9 SW19 180 A3
Merton Rd E17 54 A3
Barking IG11 79 D1
Croydon SE25 206 A4
Enfield EN2 5 B5
Harrow HA2 42 A1
Ilford IG3 57 D2
Merton SW19 179 D3
Wandsworth SW18 157 C4
Merton Rise NW3 70 C1
Merton Road Ind Est
SW18 157 C4

Merton Way
East Molesey KT8 196 A6
Hillingdon UB10 60 D1
Merttins Rd SE15 162 D6
Meru Cl NW5 71 A3
Mervan Rd SW2 138 C1
Mervyn Ave BR7,SE9 167 A2
Mervyn Rd W13 109 A3
Shepperton TW17 193 A2
Mervyn Stockwood Ho 1
SE9 167 A2
Messaline Ave W3 89 A1
Messent Rd SE9 165 D6
Messeter Pl SE9 166 C5
Messina Ave NW6 69 C1
Messiter Ho N1 233 D5
Metcalfe Ho 28 SW8 137 D3
Metcalfe Wlk 2 TW13 173 A6
Metcalf Rd TW15 170 D5
Meteor St SW11 137 A1
Meteor Way SM6 220 A1
Metford Cres EN3 7 C5
Metherell Ho N21 17 B5
Metheringham Way
NW9 27 C2
Methley Ho 8 N7 72 B6
Methley St
SE11 116 C1 261 B1
Methodist Central Hall*
SW1 115 D4 249 D1
Methuen Cl HA8 26 C3
Methuen Pk N10 49 B6
Methuen Rd DA6 147 B1
Belvedere DA17 125 D2
Edgware HA8 26 C3
Methwold Rd W10 90 D2
Metro Bsns Ctr The
SE26 185 B5
Metro Ctr Hayes UB4 106 C6
West Barnes SM4 200 D2
Metro Ind Ctr TW7 130 C3
Metropolitan Benefit
Societies Almshs 3
N1 73 C2
Metropolitan Cl 17 E14 97 C2
Metropolitan Police Cadet
Training Sch NW9 45 C6
Metro Trad Ctr HA9 66 D4
Meudon Ct KT6 197 D4
Mews Pl IG8 37 A6
Mews St E1 118 A5
Mews The N8 50 C5
Beckenham BR3 185 C2
Redbridge IG4 55 D4
Thornton Heath SW16 182 B2
Mexborough NW1 232 A5
Mexfield Rd SW15 157 B6
Meyer Gn EN1 6 A5
Meyer Ho 1 SW12 159 B4
Meymott St
SE1 116 D5 251 C3
Meynell Cres E9 74 D1
Meynell Gdns E9 74 D1
Meynell Rd E9 74 D1
Meyrick Ho 8 E14 97 C2
Meyrick Rd NW10 68 A2
SW11 136 C2
Miah Terr 10 E1 118 A5
Miall Wlk SE26 185 A6
Micawber Ave UB8 82 C3
Micawber Ct N1 235 B2
Micawber Ho 24 SE16 118 A4
Micawber St N1 95 A4 235 B2
Michael Cliffe Ho EC1 234 B1
Michael Faraday Ho
SE17 262 D1
Michael Faraday Sch
SE17 117 B1 262 D1
Michael Gaynor Cl
W7 108 D5
Michael Marshall Ho 2
SE9 167 A2
Michaelmas Cl SW20 200 C6
Michael Rd E11 54 D1
SW6 135 D4 265 D2
South Norwood SE25 205 C6
Michaels Cl SE13 142 C1
Michael Sobell Sinai Sch
HA3 44 C3
Michaelson Ho 4
SE21 183 C6
Michelangelo Ct 14
SE16 118 B1
Micheldever Rd SE12 164 D5
Michelham Gdns TW1 152 D1
Michelle Ct N12 30 A5
W3 111 B6
Michell Ho TW1 152 D3
Michels Almshouses 11
TW10 154 A6
Michelsdale Dr 3
TW9 132 A1
Michelson Ho SE11 260 D3
Michel's Row 2 TW9 132 A1
Michigan Ave E12 78 B4
Michigan Ho E14 119 C3
Michleham Down N12 29 B6
Mickledore NW1 232 B3
Mickleham Cl BR5 190 A1
Mickleham Gdns SM3 217 A2
Mickleham Rd BR5 190 A1
Mickleham Way CR0 224 B1
Micklethwaite Rd
SW6 135 C6 265 B5
Mickleton Ho 30 W2 91 C2
Midas Bsns Ctr RM10 81 D4
Midcroft HA4 39 C1
Middle Dene NW7 11 B1
Middlefield
NW8 92 B6 229 C6
Middlefielde W13 87 B2
Middlefield Gdns IG2 56 D3
Middle Green Cl 3
KT5 198 B3
Middleham Gdns N18 34 A4
Middleham Rd N18 34 A4
Middle La N8 50 A4
Teddington TW11 174 D4
Middle Lane Mews N8 50 A4
Middle Mill KT5 198 B6
Middle Park Ave SE9 165 D4
Middle Park Prim Sch
SE9 165 D4
Middle Rd 12 E13 99 A5
N10 30 C2
East Barnet EN4 14 C5
Harrow HA2 42 B1
Mitcham SW16 181 D1
Middle Row W10 91 A3
Middle Row Prim Sch
W10 91 A3
Middlesborough Rd
N18 34 A4
Middlesex Bsns Ctr
UB2 107 B4
Middlesex Coll of
Computing & Tech
HA9 66 A3
Middlesex Ct 5 W4 111 D2
Harrow HA1 42 D4
Middlesex Cty Cricket Sch
N3 29 D1
Middlesex Ho 6 SE20 184 C3
Middlesex Hospl
W1 93 C2 239 B3
Middlesex Hospl Annexe
W1 239 B4
Middlesex Pas EC1 241 D3
Middlesex Pl 13 E9 74 C2
Middlesex Rd CR4 204 A4
Middlesex St
E1 95 D2 243 C2
Middlesex Univ N17 33 D4
Middlesex Univ (Bounds
Green) N11 31 C4
Middlesex Univ (Cat Hill)
EN4 15 A6
Middlesex Univ (Enfield
Campus) EN3 18 C6
Middlesex Univ (Hendon
Campus) NW4 46 B5
Middlesex Univ Trent Park
EN4 3 C3
Middle St EC1 242 A4
Croydon CR0 221 A5
Middle Temple*
EC4 116 C6 251 A6
Middle Temple La
EC4 116 C6 251 A6
Middleton Ave E4 19 B1
Greenford UB5 86 B5
Sidcup DA14 190 C5
Middleton Bldgs W1 239 A3
Middleton Cl E4 19 B1
Middleton Ct BR1 187 B3
Middleton Dr SE16 118 D4
Pinner HA5 40 A6
Middleton Gdns IG2 56 D3
Middleton Gr N7 72 A3
Middleton Ho E8 73 D1
SE1 262 C5
Middleton Mews N7 72 A3
Middleton Rd E8 73 D1
NW11 47 C2
Carshalton CR4,SM5 202 B2
Hayes UB3 83 B2
Middleton St E2 96 B4
Middleton Way SE13 142 B1
Middleway NW11 47 D4
Middle Way Hayes UB4 84 C3
Mitcham SW16 181 D1
Middle Way The HA3 24 D1
Midfield Prim Sch
BR5 190 A3
Midfield Way BR5 190 B2
Midford Ho 1 NW4 46 D5
Midford Pl W1 239 B5
Midholm NW11 47 D5
Wembley HA9 44 C1
Midholm Cl NW11 47 D5
Midholm Rd CR0 223 A6
Midhope Ho WC1 233 B1
Midhope St WC1 233 B1
Midhurst SE26 184 C4
Midhurst Ave N10 49 A6
Midhurst Ave *continued*
Thornton Heath CR0 204 C2
Midhurst Ct N8 50 A2
Midhurst Gdns UB10 61 A1
Midhurst Hill DA6 169 C6
Midhurst Ho 6 E14 97 B1
Midhurst Par N10 49 A6
Midhurst Rd W13 109 A3
Midhurst Way E5 74 A4
Midland Pl E14 120 A1
Midland Rd E10 54 A2
NW1 94 A5 233 A3
Midland Terr NW10 89 C3
NW2 68 D5
Midleton Rd KT3 177 A1
Midlothian Rd E3 97 B3
Midmoor Rd
Merton SW19 179 A2
Streatham SW12 159 C3
Midship Cl SE16 118 D5
Midship Point E14 119 C4
Midstrath Rd NW10 67 C4
Midsummer Apmts 15
SM2 217 C1
Midsummer Ave TW4 129 B1
Midsummer Ct SE12 143 A1
Midway SM3 201 B2
Midway Ho EC1 234 D2
Midwinter Cl 3 DA16 146 A2
Midwood Cl NW2 68 B5
Mighell Ave IG4 55 D4
Milan Ct N11 31 D2
Milan Rd UB1 107 B4
Milborne Gr SW10 256 B1
Milborne Ho 11 E9 74 C2
Milborne St E9 74 C2
Milborough Cres SE12 164 C5
Milbourne La KT10 212 A3
Milbourne Lodge Jun Sch
KT10 212 B2
Milbourne Lodge Sen Sch
KT10 212 B2
Milbrook KT10 212 A2
Milburn Dr 1 UB7 104 A6
Milburn Ho SW20 178 B1
Milcote St SE1 251 D1
Milday Gr N N1 73 B3
Mildenhall Rd E5 74 C5
Mildmay Ave N1 73 B2
Mildmay Ct N1 73 B3
Mildmay Gr N N1 73 B3
Mildmay Ho 6 SW15 156 C6
Mildmay Mission Hospl
E2 95 D4
Mildmay Pk N1 73 B3
Mildmay Rd N1 73 C3
Ilford IG1 78 D5
Mildmay St N1 73 B2
Mildon Ho EN3 6 C3
Mildred Ave
Hayes UB3 105 B3
Northolt UB5 63 D3
Mildura Ct N8 50 B5
Mile End Pl E1 96 D3
Mile End Rd E1,E3 96 D3
Mile End Sta E3 97 B4
Mile End The E17 34 D2
Mile Rd
Hackbridge SM6 203 A1
Wallington CR0, CR4,
CR9 203 D1
Miles Bldgs NW1 237 A4
Miles Coverdale Prim Sch
W12 112 C4
Miles Ct E1 96 B1
Croydon CR0 220 D6
Miles Dr SE28 123 C5
Miles Ho 5 SE10 120 C1
Miles Lo E15 76 B3
Harrow HA1 42 B4
Milespit Hill NW7 28 C5
Miles Pl NW8 236 D4
Miles Rd N8 50 A6
Mitcham CR4 202 C6
Miles St SW8 138 A6 270 B5
Milestone Cl
Edmonton N9 18 A2
Sutton SM2 218 B1
Milestone Ct TW7 131 A4
Milestone Green
SW14 133 B1
Milestone Ho KT1 197 D5
Milestone Rd SE19 183 D4
Miles Way N20 14 C2
Milfoil St W12 112 A6
Milford Cl SE2 147 A6
Milford Ct 3 N16 51 C1
Southall UB1 107 C5
Milford Gdns
Croydon CR0 206 D4
Edgware HA8 26 C3
Wembley HA0 65 D3
Milford Gr SM1 218 A4
Milford La
WC2 116 C6 251 A6
Milford Mews SW16 160 B1
Milford Rd Ealing W13 109 B5
Southall UB1 107 C6
Milk St E16 122 D5
Milk St *continued*
EC2 95 A1 242 B2
Bromley BR1 187 B4
Milkwell Gdns IG8 37 B3
Milkwell Yd SE5 139 A4
Milkwood Rd SE24 138 D1
Milk Yd E1 118 C6
Millais Ave E12 78 C3
Millais Ct 10 UB5 84 D5
Millais Gdns HA8 26 C1
Millais Rd E11 76 B4
Enfield EN1 17 D6
New Malden KT3 199 C2
Millais Way KT19 215 A4
Milland Ho 11 SW15 156 A3
Millard Cl 21 N16 73 C3
Millard Ho SE8 119 B1
Millard Terr RM10 81 C2
Millbank SW1 116 A2 260 A3
Wallington SM6 219 D3
Millbank Ho KT6 198 B2
Millbank Prim Sch
SW1 115 D2 259 D3
Millbank Way SE12 165 A6
Millbourne Rd TW13 173 A6
Mill Bridge EN5 13 B5
Millbrook 1 E18 55 A6
Millbrook Ave DA16 145 B1
Millbrooke Ct 7
SW15 157 A6
Millbrook Gdns RM6 59 A3
Millbrook Ho 4 SE15 140 A6
Millbrook Rd SW9 138 D2
Edmonton N9 18 B3
Mill Cl SM5 219 A6
Mill Cnr EN5 1 B4
Millcroft Ho SE6 185 D6
Mill Ct E10 76 A5
NW7 29 A2
14 SE28 124 B6
Millender Wlk SE16 118 C2
Millennium Bsns Ctr
NW2 68 B6
Millennium Bridge*
SE1,EC4 252 A5
Millennium Dome*
SE10 120 C5
Millennium Dr E14 120 B2
Millennium Harbour
E14 119 C4
Millennium Pl 27 E2 96 B5
Millennium Prim Sch
SE10 120 D3
Millennium Sq SE1 253 D2
Millennium Way SE10 120 C3
Miller Ave EN3 7 C5
Miller Cl
Carshalton CR4 202 D2
Pinner HA5 22 C1
Miller Ct DA7 147 D2
8 NW9 46 A5
Miller Ho N15 50 D5
9 Streatham SW2 160 A4
Miller Rd
Mitcham SW19 180 B4
Thornton Heath CR0 204 C1
Miller's Ave E8,N16 73 D3
Millers Cl NW7 28 A6
Miller's Ct 1 W4 111 D1
Millers Ct 3 HA0 88 A5
Millers Green Cl EN2 4 D2
Millers Mead Ct SW19 180 B3
Miller St NW1 232 A4
Miller's Terr 1 E8 73 D3
Miller's Way W6 112 C4
Millers Wharf Ho E1 118 A5
Millers Yd N3 29 D3
Miller Wlk SE1 251 B3
Millet Rd UB6 85 D5
Mill Farm Ave TW16 171 C3
Millfarm Bsns Pk TW4 151 A4
Mill Farm Cl HA5 22 C1
Mill Farm Cres TW4 151 A3
Millfield N4 72 C6
Charlton TW16 171 B2
Kingston KT1 198 B6
Millfield Ave E17 35 B2
Millfield La N6 70 D6
Millfield Pl N6 71 A6
Millfield Rd HA8 27 A1
Twickenham TW4 151 B3
Millfields Com Sch E5 74 C4
Millfields Rd E5 74 C5
Mill Gdns SE26 162 B1
Mill Gn CR4 203 A2
Mill Green Bsns Pk
CR4 203 A2
Mill Green Rd CR4 203 A2
Millgrove St 6 SW11 137 A3
Millharbour E14 119 D4
Millhaven Cl RM6 58 B3
Mill Hill SW13 134 A2
Mill Hill Broadway Sta
NW7 27 C4
Mill Hill Circus NW7 27 D5
Mill Hill Cty High Sch
NW7 11 C2
Mill Hill East Sta NW7 29 A3
Mill Hill Gr 11 W3 110 D5
Mill Hill Ind Est NW7 27 D4
Mill Hill Rd W3 110 D4
Barnes SW13 134 A3
Mill Hill Sch NW7 28 B6
Mill Hill Terr 9 W3 110 D5
Mill Ho IG8 36 D5
Millhouse Pl SE27 182 D6
Millicent Fawcett Ct
N17 33 D2
Millicent Preston Ho 4
IG11 101 B6
Millicent Rd E10 53 B1
Milligan St E14 119 B6
Milling Rd HA8 27 B3
Millington Ho N16 73 B5
Millington Rd UB3 105 C3
Mill La NW6 69 B3
SE18 122 C1
Carshalton SM5 219 A5
Croydon CR0 220 C5
Dagenham RM6 59 A3
Sewardstone E4 7 D2
Woodford IG8 36 D5
Mill Lane Trad Est
CR0 220 B5
Millman Ct SE3 143 B5
WC1 240 C5
Millman Mews WC1 240 C5
Millman Pl WC1 240 D5
Millman St WC1 94 B3 240 C5
Millmark Gr SE14 141 A3
Millmarsh La EN3 7 B3
Millmead Bsns Ctr N17 52 B6
Millmead Ind Ctr N17 52 B6
Mill Mead Rd N17 52 B6
Millner Ct SE4 141 B3
Mill Pl BR7 188 D2
E14 97 A1
Kingston KT1 198 B6
Mill Plat TW7 131 A3
Mill Plat Ave TW7 131 A3
Mill Pond Cl
SW8 137 D5 269 D3
Millpond Est SE16 118 B4
Mill Rd E16 121 B5
Ilford IG1 78 C5
Merton SW19 180 A3
Twickenham TW2 152 A2
Mill Ridge HA8 26 C5
Mill River Trad Est EN3 7 A1
Mill Row N1 95 C6
Mills Cl UB10 82 C5
Mills Ct 7 E11 76 C5
Mills Gr 1 E14 98 A2
NW4 46 D6
Mills Ho E17 54 B6
SW8 269 B2
Millshot Cl SW6 134 C4
Millside SM5 218 D6
Millside Pl TW7 131 B3
Millson Cl N20 14 B2
Mills Row W4 111 B2
Mill St SE1 117 D4 253 D2
W1 249 A6
Kingston KT1 198 A6
Millstream Cl N13 32 C5
Millstream Rd
SE1 117 D4 253 C1
Mill Trad Est The NW10 89 A4
Mill Vale BR2 186 D1
Mill View Cl KT17 215 D1
Mill View Gdns CR0 222 D5
Millwall Dock Rd E14 119 C3
Millward Wlk 14 SE18 144 C6
Mill Way NW7 27 C5
Feltham TW14 150 B6
Millway Gdns UB5 63 B2
Millwood Rd TW3,TW7 152 A6
Millwood St 10 W10 91 A2
Mill Yd E1 118 A6
Milman Cl HA5 40 D6
Milman Rd NW6 91 A5
Milman's Ho SW10 266 C5
Milman's St
SW10 136 B6 266 C5
Milne Ct 4 E18 37 A2
Milne Field HA5 23 C3
Milne Gdns SE9 166 A6
Milne Ho 15 SE18 122 B2
Milner Dr TW2 152 B4
Milner Ho 2 SW11 136 B2
Hayes UB4 84 B4
Milner Pl N1 94 C6 234 B6
Milner Rd E15 98 C4
Dagenham RM8 80 C6
Kingston KT1 197 D6
Merton SW19 179 D2
Morden SM4 202 B4
South Norwood CR7 205 B6
Milner Sq N1 72 D1
Milner St SW3 114 D2 257 C4
Milner Wlk DA15 167 B3
Milnthorpe Rd W4 133 B6
Milo Rd SE22 161 D5
Milrood Ho 4 E1 96 D2
Milroy Wlk SE1 251 C4
Milson Rd
W14 112 D3 254 A6
Milsted Ho 23 E5 74 B3
Milton Ave E6 78 A1
N6 49 C2
NW10 89 B6
NW9 45 A6
Barnet EN5 13 B6
Carshalton SM1 218 C4
Thornton Heath CR0 205 B2
Milton Cl N2 48 A3
SE1 117 D2 263 C3
Carshalton SM1 218 B5
Hayes UB4 84 A1
Milton Court Rd SE14 141 A6
Milton Cres IG2 57 A3
Milton Ct EC2 242 C4
NW11 47 A3
SE14 141 A6
9 SW18 157 C6
Fulham SW6 135 A2
Ilford RM6 58 C2
Kingston KT2 176 A6
Twickenham TW2 152 C1
Uxbridge UB10 60 D5
Milton Dr
Borehamwood WD6 10 D6
Littleton TW17 192 A5
Milton Gdns TW19 148 B3
Milton Gr N11 31 D5
N16 73 C4
Milton Ho 19 E2 96 C4
2 SE5 139 B5
12 Beckenham BR3 185 C3
5 Kingston KT2 176 D4
Sutton SM1 217 C5
Milton House Mans E8 73 D4
Milton Lo
3 Sidcup DA14 190 A6
Southgate N21 16 D3
Twickenham TW1 152 D4
Milton Pk N6 49 C2
Milton Pl 3 N7 72 C3
Milton Rd DA16 145 D4
E17 53 C5
N15 50 D6
N6 49 C2
NW7 28 A5
1 NW9 46 A2
SE24 160 D6
W3 111 B5
Belvedere DA17 125 C2
Ealing W7 108 D6
Harrow HA1 42 C5
Mitcham CR4 181 A3
Mortlake SW14 133 B2
Sutton SM1 217 C4
Thornton Heath CR0 205 B2
Uxbridge UB10 60 D4
Wallington SM6 219 D2
Wimbledon SW19 180 A4
Hampton TW12 173 C3
Milton St EC1,
EC2 95 B2 242 C4
Milton Way UB7 104 B2
Milverton NW5 71 A3
Milverton Dr UB10 61 A4
Milverton Gdns IG3 79 D6
Milverton Ho SE23 163 A1
Milverton Rd NW6 68 C1
Milverton St
SE11 116 C1 261 B1
Milverton Way SE9 188 C6
Milward St E1 96 B2
Mimosa N15 51 B4
Mimosa Ct SW4 270 B1
Mimosa Ho UB4 84 C2
Mimosa Rd UB4 84 C2
Mimosa St
SW6 135 B4 264 D1
Mina Rd SE17 117 C1 263 B2
Merton SW19 179 C2
Minard Rd SE6 164 C3
Minchenden Cres N14 15 D1
Minchenden Ct N14 15 D2
Minchin Ho 6 E14 97 C1
Mincing La
EC3 117 C6 253 A6
Minden Rd Cheam SM3 217 B6
Penge SE20 184 B2
Minehead Ct HA2 63 C6
Minehead Rd
Harrow HA2 63 C5
Streatham SW16 182 B5
Mineral St SE18 123 C2
Minera Mews SW1 258 B4
Minerva Cl SW9 138 C5
Sidcup DA14 189 C6
Minerva Rd NW10 89 B4
Chingford E4 35 D3
Kingston KT1 176 B1
Minerva St E2 96 B5
Minerva Wlk EC1 241 D2
Minet Ave NW10 89 C5
Minet Dr UB3 106 A5
Minet Gdns NW10 89 C5
Hayes UB3 106 B5
Minet Jun & Inf Schs
UB3 106 B5
Minet Rd SE5,SW9 138 D3
Minford Gdns W14 112 D4
Mingard Wlk N7 72 B5

Ming St E14 119 C6
Minimax Cl TW14 150 A5
Ministry Way SE9 166 B2
Mink Ct TW4 128 C3
Minniedale KT5 198 B4
Minnow Wlk SE17 263 B3
Minories EC3 117 D6 253 C6
Minshaw Ct DA14 189 D6
1 Sidcup DA14 190 A6
Minshull Pl 23 BR3 185 C3
Minshull St SW8 269 C1
Minson Rd E9 96 D6
Minstead Gdns SW15 155 D4
Minstead Way KT3 199 C3
Minster Ave SM1 217 C6
Minster Dr CR0 221 C4
Minster Gdns KT8 195 B5
Minsterley Ave TW16, TW17 193 C5
Minster Rd BR1 187 B3
NW2 69 A3
Minster Wlk N8 50 A5
Minstrel Ct HA3 24 C1
Minstrel Gdns KT5 198 B5
Mint Bsns Pk 12 E16 99 A2
Mint Cl UB10 82 D4
Mintern Cl N13 16 D1
Minterne Ave UB2 107 C2
Minterne Rd HA3 44 B4
Minterne Waye UB4 84 C1
Mintern St N1 95 B5 235 D4
Minton Ho SE11 261 A4
Minton Mews 3 NW6 69 D2
Mint Rd SM5,SM6 219 B4
Mint St SE1 252 B2
Mint Wlk CR0 221 A5
Mirabel Rd SW6 135 B5 264 D4
Mirage Ctr The HA9 66 D4
Miranda Cl 16 E1 96 C2
Miranda Ct W3 88 B1
Miranda Ho 17 N1 95 C5
6 Belvedere DA17 125 C1
Miranda Rd N19 49 C1
Mirfield Ct SE20 184 A1
Mirfield St SE7 121 D3
Miriam Ct DA14 190 B6
Miriam Rd SE18 123 C1
Mirravale Trad Est RM6 59 A2
Mirren Cl HA2 63 B5
Mirror Path SE12 165 C1
Misbourne Rd UB10 82 C6
Missenden SE17 262 D1
Missenden Cl TW14 149 D3
Missenden Gdns SM4 202 A3
Missenden Ho NW8 237 A6
Mission Gr E17 53 A4
Mission Grove Prim Sch E17 53 B5
Mission Pl SE15 140 A4
Mission Sq 13 TW8 132 A6
Misterton Ct SW11 266 D2
Mistletoe Cl CR0 206 D1
Mistley Thorn IG1 56 C2
Mistral SE5 139 C4
Mistral Ct E4 19 D1
Mistys Field KT12 194 C1
Mitali Pas 13 E1 96 A1
Mitcham Garden Village CR4 203 A4
Mitcham Ho 9 SE5 139 A4
Mitcham Ind Est CR4 181 A2
Mitcham Junction Sta CR4 203 A4
Mitcham La SW16 181 C5
Mitcham Pk CR4 202 D5
Mitcham Rd E6 100 A4
Ilford IG3 57 D2
Upper Tooting SW17 180 D5
Mitcham Sta CR4 202 C5
Mitcham Vale High Sch CR4 181 B1
Mitchell 19 NW9 27 D2
Mitchell Brook Prim Sch NW10 67 C2
Mitchellbrook Way NW10 67 B2
Mitchell Cl SE2 124 C2
Belvedere DA17 125 D3
Mitchell Ct 20 E10 53 D2
Mitchell Ho 31 W12 112 B6
W4 110 D1
Mitchell Rd BR6 227 D4
Edmonton N13 33 A5
Mitchell's Pl SE21 161 C4
Mitchell St EC1 95 A3 242 B6
Mitchell Way NW10 67 A2
Bromley BR1 187 A2
Mitchell Wlk E6 100 B2
Mitchison Rd N1 73 B2
Mitchley Rd N17 52 A6
Mitford Cl KT9 213 C2
Mitford Rd N19 72 A6
Mitre Bridge Ind Pk W10 90 B3
Mitre Cl
Shepperton TW17 193 B3
Sutton SM2 218 B1
Mitre Ct EC2 242 B2
Mitre Ct *continued*
Belvedere DA17 125 C1
1 Ilford RM6 58 B2
9 Woodford E18 37 A2
Mitre Ho RM7 59 D5
Mitre Rd E15 98 C5
SE1 116 C4 251 B2
Mitre Sq EC3 243 B1
Mitre St EC3 95 C1 243 B1
Mitre The 9 E14 119 B6
Mitre Way W10 90 B2
Moatbridge Sch SE9 165 D5
Moat Cl BR6 227 D2
Moat Cres N3 47 D6
Moat Croft DA16 146 C2
Moat Ct DA15 167 D1
9 DA15 168 A1
SE9 166 B5
Moat Dr 4 E13 99 C5
Harrow HA1 42 B5
Ruislip HA4 39 C2
Moat Farm Rd UB5 63 B1
Moatfield NW6 69 A1
Moat Lo The HA1 64 C6
Moat Pl SW9 138 B2
Acton W3 88 D1
Moat Side Enfield EN3 6 D1
Feltham TW13 172 C6
Moat The KT3 177 C2
Moberly Rd SW4 159 D4
Mobey Ct SW4 270 A1
Moblin Lo IG9 21 C3
Moby Dick RM6 59 B5
Mocatta Ho 9 E1 96 B3
Modbury Gdns NW5 71 A2
Modder Pl SW15 134 D1
Model Cotts SW14 133 A2
Model Farm Cl SE9 166 A1
Modling Ho 8 E2 96 D5
Moelwyn Hughes Ct N7 71 D3
Moelyn Mews HA1 43 A4
Moffat Ct
Upper Tooting SW17 180 C6
Wimbledon SW19 179 C5
Moffat Ho 24 SE5 139 A5
Moffat Rd
Bowes Park N13 32 A4
South Norwood CR7 183 B1
Upper Tooting SW17 180 D6
Mogden La TW7 152 D6
Mohawk Ho 31 E3 97 A5
Mohmmad Khan Rd E11 54 D1
Mohr Ct N22 32 B3
Moineau 18 NW9 27 D2
Moira Cl N17 33 C1
Moira Ct SW17 159 A2
Moira Rd SE9 144 B1
Moland Mead SE16 118 D1
Molasses Ho 1 SW11 136 A2
Molasses Row 2 SW11 136 A2
Mole Abbey Gdns KT8 195 D6
Mole Ct 2 W12 111 C4
West Ewell KT19 215 A4
Mole Ho NW8 236 D5
Molember Ct KT7 196 C5
Molember Rd KT8 196 C4
Molescroft SE9 167 A1
Molesey Ave KT12,KT8 195 B4
Molesey Dr SM3 217 A5
Molesey Ho E2 243 C6
Molesey Hospl KT8 195 C4
Molesey Park Ave KT8 195 D4
Molesey Park Cl KT8 196 A4
Molesey Park Rd KT8 196 A4
Molesey Rd KT12 195 A2
Molesford Rd SW6 265 A1
Molesham Cl KT8 195 D6
Molesham Way KT8 195 D6
Molesworth Ho 9 SE17 138 D6
Molesworth St SE13 142 A2
Moliner Ct 4 BR3 185 C3
Mollie Davis Ct SE19 183 D4
Mollison Ave EN3 7 B5
Mollison Dr SM6 220 A1
Mollison Way HA8 26 C1
Molly Huggins Cl SW12 159 C4
Molton Ho N1 233 D5
Molyneux Dr SW17 181 B6
Molyneux St W1 92 C2 237 B3
Monarch Cl
Coney Hall BR4 224 D4
East Bedfont TW14 149 C4
Monarch Ct N2 48 A4
Ealing W5 87 C2
Monarch Dr E16 99 D2
Monarch Mews E17 53 D3
West Norwood SW16 182 C5
Monarch Par CR4 180 D1
Monarch Pl IG9 21 C2
Monarch Rd DA17 125 C3
Monarchs Ct 1 NW7 27 B5
Monarch's Way HA4 39 C1
Mona Rd SE15 140 C3
Mona St E16 98 D2
Monastery Gdns EN2 5 B3
Monaveen Gdns KT8 195 D6
Monck's Row SW18 157 B5
Monck St SW1 115 D3 259 D5
Monclar Rd SE5 139 B1
Moncorvo Cl SW7 114 C4 247 A1
Moncrieff Cl 4 E6 100 A1
Moncrieff St SE15 140 A3
Mondial Way UB7 127 A5
Mondragon Ho SW8 270 B2
Monega Prim Sch E12 77 D2
Monega Rd E7,E12 77 D2
Monet Ct 15 SE16 118 B1
Moneyer Ho N1 235 C2
Monica James Ho 12 DA14 168 A1
Monica Shaw Ct NW1 232 D3
Monier Rd E3 75 C1
Monivea Rd BR3 185 B3
Monk Ct W12 112 A5
Monk Dr E16 121 A6
Monken Hadley CE Prim Sch EN4 1 C4
Monkfrith Ave N14 15 B5
Monkfrith Cl N14 15 B4
Monkfrith Prim Sch N14 15 A4
Monkfrith Way N14 15 B4
Monkham's Ave IG8 37 B5
Monkham's Dr IG8 37 B5
Monkham's La IG8 37 B6
Monkleigh Rd SM4, SW20 201 A5
Monkridge 3 N8 49 D2
Monks Ave
East Molesey KT8 195 B4
New Barnet EN5 14 A5
Monks Cl SE2 124 D2
Enfield EN2 5 A3
Harrow HA2 63 D6
Ruislip HA4 62 D4
Monks Cres KT12 194 B1
Monksdene Gdns SM1 217 D5
Monks Dr W3 88 C1
Monksfield N4 72 C6
Monks Orchard Rd BR3,CR0 207 C2
Monks Orchard Sch CR0 206 D4
Monks Park Gdns HA9 66 D1
Monks Pk HA9 67 A2
Monks Rd EN2 5 A3
Monk St SE18 122 C2
Monks Way BR5 211 B1
NW11 47 B5
Beckenham BR3 207 C3
Harmondsworth UB7 126 A6
Monkswell Ct N10 31 A2
Monkswood Gdns
Borehamwood WD6 11 B6
Ilford IG5 56 C6
Monkton Ct W14 254 C6
Monkton Ho 22 E5 74 B3
32 SE16 118 D4
Monkton Rd DA16 145 D3
Monkton St SE11 116 C2 261 B4
Monkville Ave NW11 47 B5
Monkville Par 1 NW11 47 B5
Monkwell Sq EC2 242 B3
Monmouth Ave
Teddington KT1 175 C3
Wanstead E18 55 B6
Monmouth Cl W4 111 B3
Bexley DA16 146 A1
Mitcham CR4,SW16 204 A5
Monmouth Ct 9 W7 86 D2
Monmouth Gr TW8 110 A2
Monmouth Ho 5 NW5 71 B2
SW18 157 C5
Monmouth Pl W2 91 D1
Monmouth Rd E6 100 B4
N9 18 C2
W2 91 C1
Dagenham RM9 81 B3
Hayes UB3 105 D2
Monmouth St WC2 94 A1 240 A1
Monnery Rd N19 71 C5
Monnow Rd SE1 118 A2
Mono La TW13 150 B2
Monoux Almshouses E17 53 D5
Monoux Gr E17 35 C2
Monro Dr N11 31 C4
Monroe Cres EN1 6 B4
Monroe Dr SW14 154 D6
Monroe Ho 16 N19 49 D2
NW8 230 A1
Monro Gdns HA3 24 C3
Monro Ho 21 NW3 70 A4
Putney SW15 156 B6
Monro way E5 74 A4
Monsal Ct E5 75 A4
Monsell Rd N4,N5 72 D5
Monson Prim Sch SE14 140 D5
Monson Rd NW10 90 B5
SE14 140 D5
Mons Way BR2 210 A3
Montacute Rd
Bushey WD23 8 C4
Carshalton SM4 202 B3
Forest Hill SE6 163 B4
Montagu Cres N18 34 B6
Montagu Ct W1 237 D3
Montague Ave SE4 141 C1
Ealing W7 108 D5
Montague Cl SE1 252 C4
Walton-on-T KT12 194 A2
Montague Fell HA0 65 A4
Montague Gdns W3 110 C6
Montague Pl WC1 93 D2 239 D4
Montague Rd E11 76 D6
E8 74 A3
N15 52 A5
N8 50 B4
W7 108 D4
Ealing W13 87 B1
Hounslow TW3 129 D2
Merton SW19 179 D3
Richmond TW10 154 A5
Southall UB2 107 A2
Thornton Heath CR0 204 D1
Uxbridge UB8 60 A1
Montague Sq SE15 140 C5
Montague St WC1 94 A2 240 A4
Montague Street EC1 242 A3
Montague Terr 1 BR2 209 A5
Montague Way UB2 107 A3
Montagu Gdns
Edmonton N18 34 B6
Wallington SM6 219 C4
Montagu Ind Est N18 34 C6
Montagu Mans W1 92 D2 237 D3
Montagu Mews N W1 237 D3
Montagu Mews S W1 237 D2
Montagu Mews W W1 237 D2
Montagu Pl W1 92 D2 237 D3
Montagu Rd N9,N18 18 C1
NW4 46 A3
Montagu Row W1 237 D3
Montagu Sq W1 92 D1 237 D2
Montagu St W1 92 D1 237 D2
Montalt Ho IG8 36 D6
Montalt Rd IG8 36 D5
Montana Gdns
Penge SE26 185 B5
5 Sutton SM1 218 A3
Montana Rd
Upper Tooting SW17 159 A1
Wimbledon SW20 178 C2
Montbelle Prim Sch SE9 166 D1
Montbelle Rd SE9 166 D1
Montcalm Cl
Hayes BR2 209 A3
Hayes UB4 84 B4
Montcalm Ho E14 119 C3
Montcalm Rd SE7 143 D5
Montclare St E2 95 D3 243 C6
Monteagle Ave IG11 79 A2
Monteagle Ct 27 N1 95 C5
Monteagle Prim Sch RM9 102 B6
Monteagle Way E5 74 A5
SE15 140 B2
Montefiore Ct 2 N16 51 D1
Montefiore St 2 SW8 137 B3
Montem Prim Sch N7 72 B5
Montem Rd
Forest Hill SE23 163 B4
New Malden KT3 199 C5
Montem St N4 50 B1
Montenotte Rd N8 49 C4
Montesole Ct 5 HA5 22 C1
Montesquieu Terr 3 E16 98 D1
Montessori Coll SW19 179 C4
Montford Pl SE11 116 C1 261 A1
Montford Rd TW16 194 A5
Montfort Ho E14 120 A3
4 E2 96 C4
Montfort Pl SW19 156 D3
Montgo Cl 10 SW2 138 C1
Montgolfier Wlk UB5 85 A4
Montgomery Ave KT10 212 C6
Montgomery Cl DA15 167 D5
Mitcham CR4 204 A5
Montgomery Ct W4 133 A6
Montgomery Ho 5 SW14 133 B2
Montgomery Lo 34 E1 96 C3
Montgomery Rd
Acton W4 111 A2
Edgware HA8 26 B4
Montholme Rd SW11 158 D5
Monthorpe Rd 16 E1 96 A2
Montolieu Gdns SW15 156 B6
Montpelier Ave
Ealing W5 87 C2
Sidcup DA5 168 D4
Montpelier Cl UB10 82 C6
Montpelier Ct
5 Beckenham BR2 208 D5
Ealing W5 87 D2
Montpelier Gdns E6 99 D4
Ilford RM6 58 C2
Montpelier Gr NW5 71 C3
Montpelier Mews SW7 257 B6
Montpelier Pl 21 E1 96 C1
SW7 257 B6
Montpelier Prim Sch W5 87 D2
Montpelier Rd N3 30 A2
SE15 140 B4
Ealing W5 87 D2
Sutton SM1 218 A4
Montpelier Rise NW11 47 A2
Wembley HA9 43 D1
Montpelier Row SE3 142 D3
Twickenham TW1 153 C4
Montpelier Sq SW7 114 C4 247 B1
Montpelier St SW7 114 C3 257 B6
Montpelier Terr SW7 247 B1
Montpelier Vale SE3 142 D3
Montpelier Way NW11 47 A2
Montpelier Wlk SW7 114 C3 257 B6
Montrave Rd SE20 184 C3
Montreal Ho UB4 84 B4
Montreal Pl WC2 250 C6
Montreal Rd IG1 57 A2
Montrell Rd SW2 160 A3
Montrose Ave DA16 145 C2
HA8 27 B2
NW6 91 A5
Sidcup DA15 168 A4
Twickenham TW2 151 D4
Montrose Cl DA16 145 D2
Ashford TW15 171 A5
Woodford IG8 37 A6
Montrose Cres N12 30 A4
1 Wembley HA0 66 A2
Montrose Ct NW11 47 B5
NW9 27 A1
SW7 114 B4 246 D1
2 Catford SE6 164 D2
Montrose Gdns
Mitcham CR4 180 D1
Sutton SM1 217 D6
Montrose Ho E14 119 C3
SW1 248 B1
Montrose Pl SW1 115 A4 248 B1
Montrose Rd
East Bedfont TW14 149 B5
Harrow HA3 24 D1
Montrose Villas W6 112 A1
Montrose Way SE23 162 D3
Montserrat Ave IG8 36 B3
Montserrat Cl SE19 183 B5
Montserrat Rd SW15 135 A1
Montway Hts SW19 179 D3
Monument Gdns SE13 164 A6
Monument St EC3 117 B6 252 D6
Monument Sta EC3 117 B6 252 D6
Monument The★ EC3 252 D6
Monument Way N17 51 D6
Monza St E1 118 C6
Moodkee St SE16 118 C3
Moody Rd SE15 139 D4
Moody St E1 96 D4
Moon Ct SE12 143 A1
Moon La EN5 1 B2
Moon St N1 94 D6 234 C6
Moorcroft HA8 26 D2
Moorcroft Gdns BR1 210 A4
Moorcroft La UB8 82 C2
Moorcroft Rd SW16 160 A1
Moorcroft Sch UB8 82 D2
Moorcroft Way HA5 41 A4
Moordown SE18 144 D4
Moore Cl Mitcham CR4 181 B1
Mortlake SW14 133 A2
Wallington SM6 220 A1
Moore Cres RM9 102 B6
Moore Ct N1 234 C5
Moorefield Rd N17 33 D1
Moore Ho 6 E1 118 C6
10 E2 96 C4
N8 50 A5
5 SE10 120 D1
Wandsworth SW17 158 B1
1 West Norwood SE27 183 A6
Mooreland Rd BR1 187 A2
Moore Park Ct SW6 265 D4
Moore Park Rd SW6 135 D5 265 C3
Moore Rd SE19 183 A4
Moore St SW3 114 D2 257 C4
Moore Wlk E7 77 A4
Moorey Cl 2 E15 98 D6
Moorfield Ave W5 87 D3
Moorfield Rd
Chessington KT9 214 A3
Enfield EN3 6 C4
Moorfields EC2 95 B2 242 C3
Moorfields Ct 6 SW16 181 C6
Moorfields Eye Hospl EC1 95 B4 235 C1
Moorfields Highwalk EC2 242 C3
Moorfields Prim Sch EC1 95 B3 242 C6
Moorgate EC2 95 B2 242 C3
Moorgate Pl EC2 242 C2
Moorgate Sta EC2 95 B2 242 C3
Moorgreen Ho EC1 234 C2
Moorhead Way SE3 143 B2
Moorhouse 17 NW9 27 D2
Moorhouse Rd W2 91 C1
Harrow HA3 43 D6
Moorings The E16 99 C2
Moor La EC2 95 B2 242 C3
Chessington KT9 214 A3
Moorland Cl TW4 151 C4
Moorland Rd SW9 138 D1
Moorlands UB5 85 A6
Moorlands Ave NW7 28 B4
Moor Lane Jun Sch KT9 214 B3
Moormead Dr KT19 215 C3
Moor Mead Rd TW1 153 A5
Moor Park Gdns KT2 177 C3
Moor Pl EC2 242 C3
Moorside Rd BR1 186 D6
Moor St W1 239 D1
Moortown Rd WD19 22 C6
Moot Ct NW9 44 C4
Morant Ho SW9 138 B3
Morant Pl N22 32 B2
Morant St E14 119 C6
Mora Prim Sch NW2 68 C4
Mora Rd NW2 68 C4
Mora St EC1 95 A4 235 B1
Morat St SW9 138 B4 270 D2
Moravian Cl SW3 266 D5
Moravian Pl SW10 136 B6 266 D5
Moravian St 10 E2 96 C4
Moray Ave UB3 105 D5
Moray Cl HA8 10 D2
Moray Ho 8 E1 97 A3
11 Kingston KT6 198 A4
Moray Mews N4,N7 72 B6
Moray Rd N4,N7 72 B6
Mordaunt Gdns RM9 81 A1
Mordaunt Ho 4 NW10 89 B6
34 SW8 137 D3
Mordaunt Rd NW10 89 B6
Mordaunt St SW9 138 B2
Morden Court Par SM4 201 D5
Morden Ct SM4 201 D5
Morden Gdns
Greenford UB6 64 D3
Mitcham CR4 202 B5
Morden Hall SW19 201 D6
Morden Hall Rd SM4 202 A5
Morden Hill SE13 142 A3
Morden Ho 19 SW2 160 C5
Morden SM4 201 C5
Morden La SE13 142 A4
Morden Lo BR2 186 B1
Morden Mount Prim Sch SE13 141 D3
Morden Park Sch Sports Ctr SM4 201 B4
Morden Prim Sch SM4 201 C4
Morden Rd SE3 143 A3
Dagenham RM6 59 A2
Merton SW19 179 D1
Mitcham CR4,SM4 202 B5
Morden Road Mews SE3 143 A3
Morden Road Sta SW19 179 D1
Morden South Sta SM4 201 C4
Morden St SE13 141 D4
Morden Sta SW19 201 D6
Morden Way SM3 201 C2
Morden Wharf Rd SE10 120 C3
Mordern Ho NW1 237 B5
Mordon Rd IG3 57 D2
Mordred Rd SE6 164 C2
Morecambe Cl 2 E1 96 D2
Morecambe Gdns HA7 25 D6
Morecambe St SE17 117 B2 262 B2
Morecambe Terr N18 33 B6

More Cl E16 98 D1
W14 113 A2 254 A3
Morecoombe Cl KT2 176 D3
Moredown Ho 3 E8 74 A3
Moree Way N18 34 A6
More House Sch
SW1 114 D3 257 D5
Moreland Ct 3 NW2 69 C5
Moreland Prim Sch
EC1 94 D4 234 D1
Moreland St
EC1 94 D4 234 D2
Moreland Way E4 20 A1
Morella Rd SW11,
SW12 158 D4
Morell Ho 5 SW9 138 B3
Morello Ave UB8 82 D2
Morello Ct HA9 66 B5
Moremead Rd SE6 185 C6
Morena St SE6 163 D4
Moresby Ave KT5 198 D2
Moresby Rd E5 52 B1
Moresby Wlk 6 SW8 137 B3
More's Gdn SW3 266 D5
Moreton Ave TW7 130 C4
Moreton Cl E5 52 C1
N15 51 B3
NW7 28 C4
Moreton Green Fst Sch
SM4 202 B4
Moreton Ho SE16 118 B3
Upper Tooting SW17 180 B6
Moreton Pl
SW1 115 C1 259 B2
Moreton Rd N15 51 B3
Croydon CR2 221 B3
North Cheam KT4 216 B6
Moreton St
SW1 115 D1 259 C2
Moreton Terr
SW1 115 C1 259 B2
Moreton Terr Mews N
SW1 259 B2
Moreton Terr Mews S
SW1 259 B2
Moreton Twr 3 W3 110 D5
Morford Cl HA4 40 B2
Morford Way HA4 40 B2
Morgan Ave E17 54 B5
Morgan Cl RM10 81 C1
Morgan Ct 5 SW11 136 B3
Ashford TW15 170 D5
Morgan Ho SW1 259 B3
SW8 269 B2
Morgan Rd BR1 187 A3
N7 72 C3
W10 91 B2
Teddington TW11 174 C4
Morgan's La UB3 83 B2
Morgan St E16 98 D2
E3 96 D4
Morgan's Wlk SW11 267 A3
Morgan Terr RM6 58 C4
Moriah Jewish Day Sch The
HA5 41 A1
Moriatry Cl N7 72 A4
Morie St SW18 157 D6
Morieux Rd E10 53 B1
Moring Rd SW17 181 A6
Moriss Ho 5 E5 74 B6
Morkyns Wlk SE21 161 C1
Morland Ave CR0 205 C1
Morland Cl NW11 47 D1
Hampton TW12 173 B5
Mitcham CR4 202 C6
Morland Ct W12 112 B4
Morland Est E8 74 A1
Morland Gdns NW10 67 B1
Southall UB1 107 D5
Morland Ho NW1 232 B3
NW6 91 C6
SW1 260 A4
W11 91 A1
Morland Mews N1 72 C1
Morland Rd E17 52 D4
Croydon CR0 205 D2
Dagenham RM10 81 C1
Harrow HA3 44 A5
Ilford IG1 78 D6
Penge SE20 184 D4
Sutton SM1 218 A3
Morland Road Day Hospl
RM10 103 C6
Morley Ave Chingford E4 36 B3
Edmonton N18 34 A6
Tottenham N22 32 D1
Morley Cl BR6 226 D6
Morley Coll
SE1 116 C3 261 B6
Morley Cres HA8 11 A2
Ruislip HA4 62 C6
Morley Cres E HA7 43 D6
Morley Cres W HA7 43 C6
Morley Ct E4 35 B5
Beckenham BR2 208 D5
Beckenham BR3 186 B2
Morley Hill EN2 5 B5
Morley Ho N16 74 A6
Streatham SW2 160 A4
Morley Rd E10 54 A1
E15 98 D5
SE13 142 A1
Barking IG11 101 B6
Cheam SM3 201 B1
Chislehurst BR7 189 A2
Dagenham RM6 59 A4
Twickenham TW1 153 D5
Morley St SE1 116 C4 251 B1
Morna Rd SE5 139 A3
Morning La E9 74 C2
Morningside Prim Sch
E9 74 C2
Morningside Rd KT4 216 C6
Mornington Ave BR1 209 D6
W14 113 B2 254 C3
Ilford IG1 56 C2
Mornington Avenue Mans
W14 254 C3
Mornington Cl IG8 37 A6
Mornington Cres
NW1 93 C5 232 A4
Cranford TW5 128 B4
Mornington Crescent Sta
NW1 93 C5 232 A4
Mornington Ct NW1 232 A4
Mornington Gr E3 97 C4
Mornington Mews 2
SE5 139 A4
Mornington Pl NW1 232 A4
4 SE8 141 B5
Mornington Rd E11 54 D1
SE14,SE8 141 B5
Ashford TW15 171 A5
Chingford E4 20 B4
Greenford UB6 85 D3
Woodford IG8 36 D6
Mornington St
NW1 93 B5 231 D4
Mornington Terr
NW1 93 B5 231 D4
Mornington Wlk
TW10 175 C6
Morocco St
SE1 117 C4 253 A1
Morpeth Gr E9 96 D6
Morpeth Rd E9 96 D6
Morpeth Sec Sch E2 96 C4
Morpeth St E2 96 D4
Morpeth Terr
SW1 115 C3 259 A4
Morpeth Wlk N17 34 B3
Morrab Gdns IG3 79 D5
Morrel Cl EN5 2 A2
Morrel Ct 10 E2 96 A5
Morris Ave E12 78 B3
Morris Blitz Ct 2 N16 73 D4
Morris Cl BR6 227 C5
Croydon CR0 207 A4
Morris Ct 3 SE5 139 B1
Chingford E4 19 D1
Morris Gdns SW18 157 C4
Morris Ho 17 E2 96 C4
10 N19 71 C4
NW8 237 A5
1 SW4 138 A1
Morrish Rd SW2 160 A4
Morrison Ave N17 51 C6
Morrison Bldgs 3 E1 96 A1
Morrison Ct N12 30 C3
5 Barnet EN5 1 A1
Morrison Ho SW2 160 C4
Morrison Rd
Barking IG11 103 A5
Hayes UB4 84 B4
Morrison St SW11 137 A2
Morrison Yd N17 33 D1
Morris Pl N4 72 C6
Morris Rd E15 76 C4
Dagenham RM8 81 B6
Isleworth TW7 130 D2
Morriss Ho 7 SE16 118 B4
Morris St E1 96 B1
E14 97 D2
Morriston Cl WD19 22 C5
Morritt Ho 8 HA0 65 D3
Morse Cl E13 99 A4
Morshead Mans W9 91 C4
Morshead Rd W9 91 C4
Morson Rd EN3 19 A5
Morston Gdns SE9 188 B6
Mortain Ho 9 SE16 118 B2
Morten Cl SW4 159 D5
Morteyne Rd N17 33 B2
Mortgramit Sq SE18 122 C3
Mortham St E15 98 C6
Mortimer Cl 1 NW2 69 B5
Streatham SW16 159 D2
Mortimer Cres NW6 91 D6
Worcester Park KT4 215 B5
Mortimer Ct NW8 229 B3
Mortimer Dr EN1 17 C6
Mortimer Est NW6 91 D6
Mortimer Ho 6 W11 112 D5
W14 254 B3
Mortimer Lo 11 SW19 157 A3
Mortimer Market WC1 239 B5
Mortimer Pl NW6 91 D6
Mortimer Rd E6 100 B4
N1 73 C1
NW10 90 C4
Ealing W13 87 C1
Mitcham CR4 180 D2
Mortimer Sq W11 112 D6
Mortimer St W1 93 C2 239 B3
Mortimer Terr NW5 71 B4
Mortlake Cl CR0 220 A5
Mortlake Dr CR4 180 C2
Mortlake High St
SW14 133 B2
Mortlake Rd Ilford IG1 79 B4
Newham E16 99 B1
Richmond SW14,TW9 132 C4
Mortlake Sta SW14 133 A2
Mortlock Cl SE15 140 B4
Mortlock Ct E12 77 D4
Morton Cl SM6 220 B1
Morton Cres N14 31 D6
Morton Ct UB5 64 A3
Morton Gdns SM6 219 C3
Morton Ho SE17 138 D6
West Norwood SE27 183 B5
Morton Mews SW5 255 C3
Morton Pl SE1 261 A5
Morton Rd E15 76 D1
N1 73 A1
Morden SM4 202 B4
Morton Way N14 31 D6
Morvale Cl DA17 125 B2
Morval Rd SW2 160 C6
Morven Rd SW17 158 D1
Morville St E3 97 C5
Morwell St WC1 239 D3
Moscow Pl W2 245 C6
Moscow Rd
W2 113 D6 245 C6
Mosedale NW1 231 D1
Moseley Way SE10 120 D3
Moselle Ave N22 32 C1
Moselle Cl N8 50 B6
Moselle Ho 2 N17 33 D3
Moselle Pl N17 33 D3
Moselle Sch N17 51 A6
Tottenham N17 33 C1
Moselle St N17 33 D3
Mosque Terr E1 96 A2
Mosque Tower 24 E1 96 A2
Mossborough Cl N12 29 D4
Mossbury Rd SW11 136 C2
Moss Cl E1 96 A2
Pinner HA5 23 A1
Mossdown Cl DA17 125 C2
Mossford Ct IG6 56 D6
Mossford Gn IG6 57 A6
Mossford St E3 97 B3
Moss Gdns
Feltham TW13 150 A2
South Croydon CR2 222 D1
Moss Hall Cres N12 30 A4
Moss Hall Ct N12 29 D4
Moss Hall Gr N12 29 D4
Moss Hall Jun & Inf Schs
N12 29 D4
Mossington Gdns
SE16 118 C2
Moss La HA5 23 A1
Mosslea Rd BR2 209 D4
BR6 227 A5
Penge SE20 184 C4
Mossop St
SW3 114 C2 257 B4
Moss Rd RM10 81 C1
Mossville Gdns SM4 201 B5
Mosswell Ho 4 N10 31 A3
Moston Cl UB3 105 D1
Mostyn Ave HA9 66 B3
Mostyn Gdns NW10 90 D5
Mostyn Gr E3 97 C5
Mostyn Lo N5 73 A4
Mostyn Rd HA8 27 C3
SW9 138 C4
Bushey WD23 8 A6
Merton SW19 179 B1
Mosul Way BR2 210 A3
Motcomb St
SW1 115 A3 258 A6
Moth Cl SM6 220 A1
Mothers Sq The 13 E5 74 B4
Motley Ave EC2 243 A6
Motley St SW8 137 C3
Motspur Park Sta KT3 200 B4
Motspur Pk KT3 200 A3
Mottingham Ct SE9 166 B3
Mottingham Gdns
SE9 165 D3
Mottingham Prim Sch
SE9 166 B1
Mottingham Rd N9 18 D4
SE9 166 B1
Mottingham Sta SE9 166 B3
Mottisfont Rd SE2 124 B2
Moules Ct SE5 139 A5
Moulins Rd E9 74 C1
Moulsford Ho 5 N7 72 A3
32 W2 91 C2
Moulton Ave TW3,TW5 129 B3
Moundfield Rd N16 52 A3
Mound The SE9 166 C1
Mounsey Ho 10 W10 91 A4
Mountacre Cl SE26 183 D6
Mount Adon Pk SE21,
SE22 162 A4
Mountague Pl 2 E14 120 A6
Mountain Ho SE11 260 C2
Mountaire Ct NW9 45 B4
Mount Angelus Rd
SW15 155 D4
Mount Ararat Rd
TW10 154 A6
Mount Arlington 3
BR2 186 C1
Mount Ash Rd SE26 162 B1
Mount Ave Chingford E4 19 D1
Ealing W5 87 D2
Southall UB1 85 C1
Mountbatten Cl SE18 145 C6
6 West Norwood SE19 183 C5
Mountbatten Ct IG9 21 D2
Mountbatten Gdns
BR3 207 A5
Mountbatten Ho N6 49 A2
Mountbatten Mews
SW18 158 A3
Mountbel Rd HA7 25 A1
Mount Carmel RC Coll
N19 49 D1
Mount Carmel RC Sec Sch
N7 72 B3
Mount Cl BR1 188 A2
Cockfosters EN4 3 A1
Ealing W5 87 C2
Mountcombe Cl KT6 198 A2
Mountcombe Ho
SW17 180 B5
Mount Ct
6 Kingston KT2 176 D3
West Wickham BR4 224 C6
Mount Culver Ave
DA14 190 D4
Mount Dr HA9 67 A6
Bexley DA6 169 A6
Harrow HA2,HA5 41 B4
Mountearl Gdns SW16,
SW2 160 B1
Mount Eaton Ct W5 87 C2
Mount Echo Ave E4 19 D3
Mount Echo Dr E4 19 D3
Mount Ephraim La
SW16 159 D1
Mount Ephraim Rd
SW16 159 D1
Mount Felix KT12 193 D1
Mountfield NW2 69 B6
Mountfield Cl SE6 164 B4
Mountfield Ct SE13 164 B5
Mountfield Rd N3 47 C6
Ealing W5 88 A1
Wallend E6 100 C4
Mountford Ho EN2 4 D1
Mountford St 4 E1 96 A1
Mountfort Cres N1 72 C1
Mountfort Terr 1 N1 72 C1
Mount Gdns SE26 162 B1
Mount Gr HA8 27 B6
Mountgrove Rd N5 73 A5
Mount House (St Martha's
Senior Sch) The EN4 1 C4
Mounthurst Rd BR2 208 D2
Mountington Park Cl
HA3 43 D3
Mountjoy Cl SE2 124 B4
Mountjoy Ho EC2 242 A3
Mount Lo N6 49 C3
Mount Lodge SW4 137 D1
Mount Mews TW12 173 D2
Mount Mills EC1 234 D1
Mount Nod Rd SW16,
SW2 160 B1
Mount Olive Ct W7 108 C4
Mount Park Ave HA1 64 C6
Mount Park Cres W5 87 D1
Mount Park Rd
Ealing W5 87 D1
Harrow HA1 64 B5
Pinner HA5 40 A4
Mount Pk SM5 219 A1
Mount Pl 7 W3 110 D5
Mount Pleasant N14 15 D4
WC1 94 C3 241 A5
Cockfosters EN4 2 D1
Ilford IG1 79 A3
Ruislip HA4 62 D6
Wembley HA0 88 B6
West Norwood SE27 183 A6
Mount Pleasant Cres
N4 50 B2
Mount Pleasant Hill E5 74 C6
Mount Pleasant La E5 52 B1
Mount Pleasant Pl
SE18 123 B2
Mount Pleasant Rd E17 35 A1
SE13 164 A5
Ealing W5 87 C3
Kingston KT3 199 A6
Mount Pleasant Rd *continued*
Tottenham N17 33 C1
Willesden NW10 90 C6
Mount Pleasant Villas
N4 50 B2
Mount Prim Sch The
KT3 199 A6
Mount Rd NW2 68 C5
NW4 46 A3
Bexley DA6 169 A6
Chessington KT9 214 B3
Dagenham RM8 59 B1
East Barnet EN4 14 C6
Feltham TW13 151 A1
Hayes UB3 106 A4
Kingston KT3 199 B6
Mitcham CR4 180 C1
South Norwood SE19 183 B4
Wimbledon SW18,SW19 157 D2
Mount Row
W1 115 B6 248 C5
Mount Sch NW7 28 C5
Mountside HA7 25 A2
Mounts Pond Rd SE3,
SE13 142 B3
Mount Sq The NW3 70 A5
Mount St W1 115 A6 248 B5
Mount Stewart Ave
HA3 43 D2
Mount Stewart Jun & Inf
Schs HA3 43 D2
Mount Terr E1 96 B2
Mount The DA6 169 D6
E5 74 B6
HA9 67 A6
N20 14 A2
N2 30 C1
NW3 70 A5
W8 245 A3
Croydon CR2 221 A3
Kingston KT3 199 D6
North Cheam KT4 216 B4
Northolt UB5 63 D3
Mount Tyndal NW3 48 B1
Mount Vernon NW3 70 A4
Mountview NW7 11 B1
5 Streatham SW16 160 B1
Mount View Ealing W5 87 D3
Enfield EN2 4 B5
Southall UB2 106 D2
Northwood HA6 22 A4
Mountview Cl NW11 48 A1
Mountview Ct N8 50 D5
Mount View Rd N4 50 B3
NW9 45 B4
Chingford E4 20 B4
Claygate KT10 213 B1
Mountview Theatre Sch
N8 50 A3
Mount Villas SE27 160 D1
Mountwood KT8 195 D6
Mountwood Ho W5 87 D3
Mourne Ho NW3 70 A2
Movers La IG11 101 C6
Mowat Ct 3 KT4 215 D6
Mowatt Cl N19 49 D1
Mowbray Ct
South Norwood SE19 183 D2
Wood Green N22 32 C2
Mowbray Gdns UB5 85 C6
Mowbray Ho 5 N2 30 B1
Mowbray Rd NW6 69 A1
Edgware HA8 26 C6
New Barnet EN5 14 A6
Richmond TW10 153 C1
South Norwood SE19 183 D2
Mowlem Prim Sch E2 96 C5
Mowlem St E2 96 B5
Mowlem Trad Est N17 34 C3
Mowll St SW9 138 C5
Moxon Cl E13 98 D5
Moxon St W1 93 A2 238 A3
Barnet EN5 1 B2
Moye Cl 9 E2 96 A5
Moyers Rd E10 54 A2
Moylan Rd W6 135 A6 264 B5
Moyle Ho SW1 269 B6
Moyne Ho 16 SW9 138 D1
Moyne Pl NW10 88 C5
Moynihan Dr N21 16 A6
Moys Cl CR0 204 A3
Moyser Rd SW16 181 B5
Mozart St W10 91 B4
Mt Carmel RC Prim Sch
W5 109 C3
Muchelney Rd SM4 202 A3
Mudchute Sta E14 119 D2
Mudie Ho 8 SW2 160 A4
Muggeridge Cl CR2 221 B3
Muggeridge Rd RM10 81 D4
Muir Cl SW18 158 C5
Muirdown Ave SW14 133 B1
Muirfield W3 89 C1
Muirfield Cl 23 SE16 118 B1
South Oxhey WD19 22 C6
Muirfield Cres E14 119 D3
Muirfield Gn WD19 22 C6
Muirfield Rd WD19 22 C6
Muirkirk Rd SE6 164 A3
Muir Rd E5 74 A5
Muir St E16 122 A5
Mulbarton Ct BR7 189 B4
Mulberry Ave TW19 148 A3
Mulberry Bsns Ctr
SE16 118 D4
Mulberry Cl N8 50 A4
NW3 70 B4
NW4 46 C6
SE22 162 A5
SE7 143 D6
SW3 266 D5
Barnet EN4 2 B1
Chingford E4 19 C2
Northolt UB5 85 A5
Streatham SW16 181 C6
Mulberry Cres
Brentford TW8 131 C5
West Drayton UB7 104 C4
Mulberry Ct 1 E11 76 B4
EC1 234 D1
N5 72 D3
NW10 67 B2
10 W9 91 B4
Barking IG11 79 D1
4 Surbiton KT6 197 D2
Twickenham TW1 152 D1
Mulberry Ho 1 E2 96 C4
8 SE8 141 B6
Mulberry House Sch
NW2 69 A3
Mulberry La CR0 205 D1
Mulberry Mews SE14 141 B4
2 Wallington SM6 219 C2
Mulberry Par UB7 104 C4
Mulberry Pl W6 112 A1
Mulberry Rd E8 73 D1
Mulberry Sch for Girls
E1 96 B1
Stepney E1 118 B6
Mulberry St 5 E1 96 A1
Mulberry Trees TW17 193 B2
Mulberry Way Ilford IG6 57 A5
Woodford E18 37 B1
Mulberry Wlk
SW3 136 B6 266 D6
Mulgrave Chambers
SM2 217 D2
Mulgrave Hall SM2 217 D2
Mulgrave Ho 20 SE18 122 B2
Mulgrave Manor SM2 217 D2
Mulgrave Prim Sch
SE18 122 D3
Mulgrave Rd NW10 67 D4
SE18 122 C2
W14 264 C6
Belmont SM2 217 C2
Ealing W5 87 D3
Harrow HA1 65 A6
South Croydon CR0 221 B5
Mulholland Cl CR4 181 B1
Mulkern Rd N19 49 D1
Mullard Ho WC1 239 C4
Mullards Cl CR4 202 D1
Mullens Ho 7 SW15 156 C6
Mullen Twr EC1 241 A5
Muller Ho SE18 122 C1
Mullet Gdns 5 E2 96 A4
Mulletsfield WC1 233 B1
Mull Ho 13 E3 97 B5
Mullins Path SW14 133 B2
Mullion Cl HA3 23 D2
Mullion Wlk WD19 22 D6
Mulready St NW8 237 A5
Multi Way W3 111 C4
Multon Ho E9 74 C1
Multon Rd SW18 158 B4
Mulvaney Way SE1 252 D1
Mumford Rd SE24 160 D6
Muncaster Cl TW15 170 C6
Muncaster Rd SW11 159 A6
Ashford TW15 170 D5
Muncies Mews SE6 164 A2
Mundania Ct SE22 162 B5
Mundania Rd SE22 162 C5
Munday Ho SE1 262 C5
Munday Rd E16 121 A6
Munden Ho 5 E3 97 D4
Munden St
W14 113 A2 254 A4
Mundesley Cl WD19 22 C6
Mundford Rd E5 74 C6
Mundon Gdns IG1 57 B1
Mund St W14 113 B1 254 D1
Mundy Ho 8 W10 91 A4
Mundy St N1 95 C4
Mungo-Park Cl WD23 8 A2
Munnery Way BR6 226 D6
Munnings Gdns TW7 152 B6
Munro Ho SE1 251 A1
SE1 252 D1
Munro Mews W10 91 A2
Munro Rd WD23 8 A6
Munslow Gdns SM1 218 B4
Munstead Ct 12 SM2 218 A1
Munster Ave TW4 151 A6
Munster Ct
Fulham SW6 135 B3
Teddington TW11 175 C4

Munster Gdns N13 .....33 A6
Munster Rd
SW6 ....135 A4 264 B2
Teddington TW11 ......175 C4
Munster Residences
SW6 ....264 B2
Munster Sq
NW1 ....93 B3 238 D6
Munton Rd
SE1,SE17 .....117 A2 262 B4
Murchison Ave DA5 ..169 A3
Murchison Ho 1 W10 .91 A2
Murchison Rd E10 .....76 A6
Murdoch Ho 4 SE16 .118 C3
Murdock Cl E16 ....98 D1
Murdock St SE15 .....140 B6
Murfett Cl SW19 ......157 A2
Muriel Ct 17 E10 ....53 D2
Muriel St N1 ...94 B6 233 D4
Murillo Rd SE13 ......142 C1
Murley Ct N21 ....17 A4
Murphy Ho SE1 ....261 D6
Murphy St SE1 116 C4 251 A1
Murray Ave BR1 ......187 B1
Hounslow TW3 ....151 D6
Murray Cres HA5 ......22 D2
Murray Ct 5 HA1 ......42 D3
Murray Gr N1 ..95 B5 235 C3
Murray Ho 21 SE18 ...122 B2
Murray Mews NW1 ......71 D1
Murray Rd W5 ....109 C2
Richmond TW10 ....153 C2
Wimbledon SW19 .....178 D4
Murray Sq E16 ....121 B6
Murray St NW1 ....71 D1
Murray Terr NW3 ......70 B4
Musard Rd W6 135 A6 264 B6
Musbury St E1 ....96 C1
Muscal W6 ....264 A6
Muscatel Pl SE5 ......139 C4
Muschamp Inf Sch
SM5 ....218 C6
Muschamp Jun Sch
SM5 ....218 C6
Muschamp Rd SE15 ..139 D2
Carshalton SM1,SM5 ...218 C6
Muscott Ho 15 E2 ......96 A6
Muscovy Ho DA18 ....125 A4
Muscovy St EC3 ......253 B6
Museum Ho 7 E2 ......96 C4
Museum in Docklands★
E14 ....119 C6
Museum St
WC1 ....94 A1 240 A2
Musgrave Cl EN4 ....2 A4
Musgrave Cres
SW6 ....135 C4 265 B2
Musgrave Ct SW11 ....267 A2
Musgrave Rd TW7 ....130 D4
Musgrove Ho 1 E9 ....74 D2
Musgrove Rd SE14 ...141 A4
Musical Mus The★
TW8 ....132 A6
Musjid Rd 7 SW11 ...136 B3
Muslim Coll The W5 ..110 C6
Mus of Garden History★
SE1 ....260 C5
Mus of London★
EC2 ....95 A2 242 A3
Mus of Richmond★
TW10 ....153 D6
Mus of the Great Eastern
Railway★ E16 ....122 C4
Musquash Way TW4 ..128 C3
Muston Rd E5 ....74 B6
Mustow Pl 2 SW6 ....135 B3
Muswell Ave N10 ......31 B1
Muswell Hill N10 ......49 C6
Muswell Hill Bdwy N10 49 B6
Muswell Hill Jun & Inf Schs
N10 ....49 B6
Muswell Hill Pl N10 ....49 B5
Muswell Hill Rd N10 ...49 A4
Muswell Mews N10 ....49 B6
Muswell Rd N10 ....31 B1
Mutrix Rd NW6 ....91 C6
Mutton Pl NW1 ....71 A2
Muybridge Rd KT3 ....177 A1
Myatt Ct SE4 ....141 B3
Myatt Garden Prim Sch
SE4 ....141 B3
Myatt Ho SE5 ....138 D3
Myatt Rd SW9 ....138 D4
Myatts Field Ct SE5 ..139 A4
Mycenae Rd SE3 .....143 A6
Mychell Ho 8 SW19 ..180 A3
Myddelton Ave EN1 .....5 C5
Myddelton Cl EN1 ......5 D4
Myddelton Gdns N21 ..17 A4
Myddelton Ho N8 ......50 A6
Myddelton Pas
EC1 ....94 C4 234 B2
Myddelton Pk N20 .....14 B2
Myddelton Rd N8 ......50 A5
Myddelton Sq
EC1 ....94 C4 234 B2
Myddelton St
EC1 ....94 C4 234 B1
Myddleton Ave N4 .....73 A6
Myddleton Mews N22 ..32 A3
Myddleton Rd N22 .....32 B3
Myers Ho 5 SE5 .....139 A5
Myers La SE14 ....140 D6
Mylis Cl SE26 ....184 B6
Mylius Cl SE14 ....140 C4
Mylne Cl W6 ....112 A1
Mylne Ho N21 ....17 B5
Mylne St EC1 ....234 A3
Mynterne Ct 10 SW19 .156 D3
Myra St SE2 ....124 A2
Myrdle Ct 8 E1 ....96 A1
Myrdle St E1 ....96 A1
Myrna Cl SW19 ....180 C3
Myron Pl SE13 ....142 A2
Myrtle Alley SE18 ....122 C3
Myrtle Ave
Hatton TW14 ....149 C6
Ruislip HA4 ....40 B2
Myrtle Cl
Barnet, London EN4 .....14 D3
Hillingdon UB8 ....82 B2
West Drayton UB7 .....104 B3
Myrtledene Rd SE2 ...124 A1
Myrtle Gdns W7 ......108 C5
Myrtle Gr Enfield EN2 ....5 B5
Kingston KT3 ....177 A1
Myrtle Ho SE14 ....140 D4
Myrtle Rd E17 ....53 A3
E6 ....100 A6
W3 ....111 A5
Croydon CR0 ....223 C5
Edmonton N13 ....17 B1
Hampton TW12 ....174 A4
Hounslow TW3 ....130 A3
Ilford IG1 ....78 D6
Sutton SM1 ....218 A3
Myrtle Wlk 20 N1 .....95 C5
Mysore Rd SW11 .....136 D1
Myton Rd SE21 ....161 B1
Mytton Ho SW8 ......270 C3

N

N1 Shopping Ctr
N1 ....94 C5 234 B4
Nadine St SE7 ....121 C1
Nadir Ct E11 ....55 A2
Naffenton Rise IG10 ...21 D6
Nagle Cl E17 ....36 B1
Nags Head N7 ....72 B4
Nags Head Ct EC1 ....242 B5
Nag's Head La DA16 ..146 B2
Nags Head Rd EN3 ....6 D1
Nainby Ho SE11 ......261 A3
Nairn Ct
3 Wallington SM6 ....219 C2
Wimbledon SW19 ......179 D4
Nairne Gr SE5,SE24 ...139 B1
Nairn Rd HA4 ....62 C2
Nairn St E14 ....98 A2
Naish Ct N1 ....233 B6
Nallhead Rd TW13 ....172 C5
Nalton Ho 4 NW6 ......70 A1
Namba Roy Cl SW16 ..182 B6
Namton Dr CR7,SW16 .204 B5
Nan Clark's La NW7 ....11 D2
Nankin St E14 ....97 C1
Nansen Ct 1 E11 ......76 C6
Nansen Ho 7 NW10 ....67 B1
Nansen Rd SW11 .....137 A2
Nansen Village 5 N12 .29 D6
Nant Ct NW2 ....69 B6
Nantes Cl SW18 ......136 A1
Nant Rd NW2 ....69 B6
Nant St E2 ....96 B4
Naoroji St WC1 ....234 A1
Napier 15 NW9 ....27 D2
Napier Ave E14 ....119 C1
Fulham SW6 ....135 B2
Napier Cl SE14,SE8 ....141 B5
W14 ....254 C6
West Drayton UB7 .....104 B3
Napier Ct N1 ....235 C4
SE12 ....165 B1
13 Croydon CR0 ....221 D6
Fulham SW6 ....135 B2
Hayes UB4 ....84 C3
1 Surbiton KT6 ....197 D2
Napier Gr N1 ...95 A5 235 B4
Napier Lo TW15 ......171 B4
Napier Pl W14 113 B3 254 C5
Napier Rd BR2 ....209 B5
DA17 ....125 B2
E11 ....76 C5
E15 ....98 C5
N17 ....51 C6
NW10 ....90 B4
W14 ....113 B3 254 C5
Ashford TW15 ....171 B3
Croydon SE25 ....206 B5
Enfield EN3 ....18 D6
Isleworth TW7 ....131 A1
South Croydon CR2 ....221 B1
Wallend E6 ....100 C5
Wembley HA0 ....65 D2
Napier Terr N1 ....72 D1
Napier Wlk TW15 .....171 B3
Napoleon Rd E5 ....74 B5
Twickenham TW1 ......153 B4
Napton Cl UB4 ....85 A3
Narbonne Ave SW4 ...159 C6
Narborough Cl UB10 ...61 A6
Narborough St SW6 ..135 D3
Narcissus Rd NW6 .....69 C3
Nardini 12 NW9 ....27 D2
Naresby Fold HA7 .....25 C4
Narford Rd E5 ....74 A6
Narrow Boat Cl SE28 .123 B4
Narrow St E14 ....119 A6
6 Acton W3 ....110 D5
Narrow Way BR2 .....210 A3
Nascot St W12 ....90 C1
Naseby Cl NW6 ....70 A1
Hounslow TW7 ....130 C4
Naseby Ct DA14 ......189 D6
Naseby Rd
Dagenham RM10 ....81 C5
South Norwood SE19 ..183 B4
Nash Cl SM1 ....218 B5
Nash Ct HA3 ....43 B3
Nashe Ho SE1 ....262 C5
Nash Gn BR1 ....187 A4
Nash Ho 1 E17 ....53 D5
SW1 ....258 D1
Nash La BR2 ....225 A2
Nash Rd N9 ....18 C2
SE4 ....163 A6
Dagenham RM6 ....58 D5
Nash Street NW1 ....231 D2
Nash Way HA3 ....43 B3
Nasmyth St W6 ......112 B3
Nassau Path 6 SE28 .124 C5
Nassau Rd SW13 ....133 D4
Nassau St W1 ....239 A3
Nassington Rd NW3 ...70 D4
Natalie Cl TW14 .....149 B4
Natalie Mews TW2 ...152 B1
Natal Rd Bowes Park N11 32 A4
Ilford IG1 ....78 D4
South Norwood CR7 ...205 B6
Streatham SW16 .....181 D4
Nathan Ct N9 ....18 C4
Nathan Ho SE11 .....261 B3
Nathaniel Cl E1 .....243 D3
Nathaniel Ct E17 ......53 A3
Nathans Rd HA0 ....65 C6
Nathan Way SE28,SE18 123 D3
National Army Mus★
SW3 ....136 D6 267 D6
National Fan Mus★
SE10 ....142 A5
National Film Theatre★
SE1 ....250 D4
National Gallery★
W1 ....115 D6 249 D5
National Hospital for
Neurology & Neurosurgery
N2 ....48 C5
National Hospl The
WC1 ....94 A3 240 B5
National Maritime Mus★
SE10 ....142 B6
National Physical
Laboratory TW11 ....174 C4
National Portrait Gallery★
W1 ....115 D6 249 D5
National Portrait Gallery
(Annexe)★
SW1 ....115 D5 249 D4
National Postal Mus★
EC1 ....95 A1 242 A2
National Theatre
SE1 ....116 B5 250 D4
National Wks TW4 ...129 B2
Nation Way E4 ....20 A3
Natural History Mus★
SW7 ....114 B3 256 C5
Nat West Twr★ EC2 ..243 A2
Nautilus Bldg The EC1 234 B2
Naval Row E14 ......120 A6
Navarino Gr E8 ....74 A2
Navarino Mans E8 .....74 A2
Navarino Rd E8 ....74 A2
Navarre Rd E6 ....100 A5
Navarre St E2 ....243 C6
Navenby Wlk 13 E3 ....97 C3
Navestock Cl E4 ....20 A1
Navestock Ho IG11 ...102 B5
Navigator Dr UB2 ....108 A4
Navy St SW4 ....137 D2
Nayland Ho SE6 .....186 A6
Naylor Gr EN3 ....18 D6
Naylor Ho SE17 .....262 D2
33 SW8 ....137 D3
5 W10 ....91 B4
Naylor Rd N20 ....14 A2
SE15 ....140 B5
Nazareth Cl SE15 ....140 B3
Nazrul St E2 ....95 D4
Neal Ave UB1 ....85 B3
Neal Cl HA6 ....22 A2
Nealden St SW9 .....138 B2
Neale Cl N2 ....48 A6
Neale Ct N10 ....31 B3
Neal St WC2 ...94 A1 240 A1
Neal's Yd WC2 ......240 A1
Near Acre NW9 ....27 D2
Neasden Cl NW10 .....67 C3
Neasden Junc NW10 ..67 C4
Neasden La NW10 .....67 B5
NW10 ....67 C3
Neasden La N NW10 ...67 C5
Neasden Sta NW10 ....67 C3
Neasham Rd RM8 ......80 B3
Neate St SE5 ....139 C6
SE5 ....139 D6
Neath Gdns SM4 .....202 A3
Neathouse Pl SW1 ...259 A4
Neats Acre HA4 ....39 B2
Neatscourt Rd E16 ....99 D2
Nebraska St
SE1 ....117 B4 252 C1
Neckinger
SE16 ....117 D3 263 D6
Neckinger Est SE16 ..263 D6
Neckinger St SE1 ....263 D6
Nectarine Way SE13 .141 D3
Nedahall Ct 4 NW11 ...47 B2
Needham Ho SE11 ...261 A3
Needham Rd W11 ......91 C1
Needham Terr NW2 ....68 D5
Needleman St SE16 ..118 D4
Needwood Ho N4 ......51 A1
Neela Cl UB10 ....60 D4
Neeld Cres NW4 ......46 B4
Wembley HA9 ....66 C3
Neeld Ct HA9 ....66 C3
Neeld Par HA9 ....66 B3
Neil Cl TW15 ....171 A5
Neilson-Terry Ct 9
SW9 ....138 B1
Neil Wates Cres 18
SW2 ....160 C3
Nelgarde Rd SE6 .....163 C4
Nelland Ct SE6 ......163 B2
Nella Rd W6 ....134 D6
Nelldale Rd SE16 ....118 C2
Nellgrove Rd UB10 ....82 D3
Nell Gwynne Ave
TW17 ....193 B3
Nell Gwynn Ho SW3 ..257 B3
Nello James Gdns
SE27 ....183 B6
Nelson Cl 9 NW6 .....91 C4
East Bedfont TW14 ....149 D3
Hillingdon UB10 ....82 D4
Thornton Heath CR0 ...204 D1
Walton-on-T KT12 .....194 B1
Nelson Ct SE16 ......119 B5
Carshalton SM5 ....218 D5
Nelson Gdns E2 ....96 A4
Twickenham TW3,TW4 ..151 C5
Nelson Grove Rd
SW19 ....180 A2
Nelson Ho 1 W5 ......88 A4
Nelson Hospl SW20 ...179 B1
Nelson La UB10 ....82 D4
Nelson Mandela Cl N10 31 A1
Nelson Mandela Rd
SE3 ....143 C2
Nelson Pas EC1 .....235 B2
Nelson Pl N1 ....234 D3
Sidcup DA14 ....190 A6
Nelson Prim Sch
Twickenham TW2 ......151 D5
Wallend E6 ....100 C5
Nelson Rd N15 ....51 C5
N8 ....50 B3
SE10 ....142 A6
Ashford TW15 ....170 A5
Bromley BR2 ....209 C5
Chingford E4 ....35 D4
Edmonton N9 ....18 B2
Enfield EN3 ....18 D5
Erith DA17 ....125 B1
Harmondsworth TW6 ....126 B4
Harrow HA1 ....42 C1
Hillingdon UB10 ....82 D4
Merton SW19 ....180 A3
New Malden KT3 ......199 B4
Sidcup DA14 ....190 A6
Stanmore HA7 ....25 C4
Twickenham TW2,TW4 ..151 C5
Wanstead E11 ....55 B5
Nelson's Monument★
WC2 ....250 A4
Nelson Sq SE1 116 D4 251 C2
Nelsons Row SW4 ....137 D1
Nelson St E1 ....96 B1
E16 ....120 D6
E6 ....100 B5
Barking E6 ....100 C6
Nelson Terr N1 ......234 D3
Nelson Trad Est SW19 179 D2
Nemoure Rd W3 ......111 A6
Nene Gdns TW13 .....151 B2
Nene Rd TW6,UB7 ....126 D4
Nene Road Rdbt TW6 .126 D4
Nepaul Rd 17 SW11 ..136 C2
Nepean St SW15 .....156 A4
Neptune Ct 5 E14 ....119 C2
Neptune Ho 14 N16 ...73 C3
2 SE16 ....118 C3
Neptune Rd
Harlington TW6 ....127 A4
Neptune Rd *continued*
Harrow HA1 ....42 B3
Neptune St SE16 .....118 C3
Nero Ct 6 TW8 ......131 D5
Nesbit Cl SE3 ....142 C2
Nesbit Rd SE9 ....143 D1
Nesbitt Ho DA6 ......169 D6
Nesbitt Sq SE19 .....183 C3
Nesham Ho 14 N1 .....95 C6
Nesham St E1 ....118 A5
Ness St 9 SE16 ......118 A3
Nesta Rd IG8 ....36 D4
Nestle's Ave UB3 ....105 D3
Nestor Ave N21 ....16 D5
Nestor Ho 18 E2 ......96 B5
Netheravon Rd W4 ...111 D1
Ealing W7 ....108 D5
Netheravon Rd S W4 .111 D1
Netherbury Rd W5 ...109 D3
Netherby Gdns EN2 .....4 A1
Netherby Ho 23 SW8 .137 D3
Netherby Rd SE23 ....162 C4
Nether Cl N3 ....29 C3
Nethercombe Ho 1
SE3 ....143 A6
Nethercott Ho 27 E3 ...97 D4
Nethercourt Ave N3 ...29 C4
Netherfield Gdns IG11 .79 B1
Netherfield Rd N12 ....29 D5
Upper Tooting SW17 ...159 A1
Netherford Rd SW4 ..137 C3
Netherhall Gdns NW3 ..70 A3
Netherhall Way NW3 ...70 A3
Netherlands Rd EN5 ...14 B5
Netherleigh Cl N6 .....49 B1
Nether St N12 ....30 A5
N3 ....29 D4
Netherton Gr
SW10 ....136 A6 266 B5
Netherton Rd N15 .....51 B3
Isleworth TW1 ....153 B6
Netherwood 19 N2 .....30 B1
Netherwood Rd W14 .112 D4
Netherwood St NW6 ...69 C2
Nethewode Ct DA17 ..125 D3
Netley 13 SE5 ....139 C4
Netley Cl Cheam SM3 .216 D3
New Addington CR0 ...224 A1
Netley Ct IG2 ....57 B4
Netley Dr KT12 ....195 B2
Netley Gdns SM4 .....202 A2
Netley Prim Sch
NW1 ....93 C4 232 A1
Netley Rd E17 ....53 B4
Brentford TW8 ....132 A6
Cheam SM4 ....202 A2
Ilford IG2 ....57 B4
Netley Rd (W) TW6 ...127 B4
Netley St NW1 ..93 C4 232 A1
Nettlecombe NW1 .....71 D1
Nettleden Ave HA9 ....66 C2
Nettleden Ho SW3 ...257 B3
Nettlefold Pl SE27 ....160 D1
Nettlestead Cl 16 BR3 185 C3
Nettleton Rd SE14 ...140 D4
Harlington TW6 ....126 D4
Ickenham UB10 ....60 B4
Nettlewood Rd SW16 .181 D3
Neuchatel Rd SE6 ....163 B2
Nevada Cl KT3 ....199 A5
Nevada St SE10 ......142 A6
Nevena Ct 3 SW2 ....160 C6
Nevern Mans SW5 ...255 A2
Nevern Pl SW5 113 C2 255 B3
Nevern Rd SW5 .....255 A3
Nevern Sq
SW5 ....113 C2 255 B3
Nevil Ho 7 SW9 .....138 D3
Nevill Ct SW10 ......266 A4
Neville Ave KT3 .....177 B2
Neville Cl DA15 ......189 D6
E11 ....76 D5
NW1 ....232 D3
NW6 ....91 B5
SE15 ....140 A4
17 SE15 ....140 A5
Acton W3 ....111 A4
Hounslow TW3 ....129 D3
Neville Ct 10 SW12 ..159 C4
Neville Dr N2 ....48 A3
Neville Gdns RM8 .....80 D5
Neville Gill Cl SW18 ..157 D5
Neville Ho N11 ....31 A6
Neville Pl N22 ....32 B2
Neville Rd E7 ....77 B1
NW6 ....91 B5
Dagenham RM8 ....80 D5
Ealing W5 ....87 D3
Kingston KT1 ....176 C1
Richmond TW10 ......153 C2
Thornton Heath CR0 ..205 B2
Neville's Ct NW2 ......68 A5
Neville St SW7 114 B1 256 C2
Neville Terr SW7 ....256 C2
Neville Wlk SM5 .....202 C2
Nevill Rd N16 ....73 C5
Nevin Dr E4 ....19 D3
Nevin Ho UB3 ....105 A3
Nevinson Cl SW18 ...158 B5
Nevis Rd SW17 ......159 A2
Nevitt Ho N1 ....235 D3
New Acres Rd SE28 ..123 C5
Newall Ho SE1 ......262 B6
Newall Rd TW6 ......127 A4
Newark Cres NW10 ...89 B4
Newark Ct KT12 .....194 C1
Newark Ho 3 SW9 ...138 D3
Newark Knok E6 .....100 C2
Newark Par NW4 ......46 A6
Newark Rd CR2 ......221 B2
Newark St E1 ....96 B2
Newark Way NW4 .....46 A6
New Ash Cl N2 ....48 B6
New Barn Cl SM6 ....220 B2
New Barnet Sta EN5 ...14 B6
New Barns Ave CR4 ..203 D5
New Barn St E13 ......99 B3
New Beckenham Sta
BR3 ....185 B3
New Belmont Ho 4
SE23 ....162 C3
New Bentham Ct 11 N1 73 A1
Newbery Ho N1 ....73 A1
Newbiggin Path WD19 .22 C6
Newbold Cotts 4 E1 ...96 C1
Newbolt Ave SM3 ....216 D3
Newbolt Ho SE17 ....262 C2
Newbolt Rd HA7 ......24 D5
New Bond St
W1 ....115 B6 248 D6
Newborough Gn KT3 .199 B5
Newborough Ho
SW19 ....180 B3
New Brent St NW4 ....46 C4
Newbridge Ct SW17 ..180 A6
Newbridge Point 3
SE23 ....162 D1
New Bridge St
EC4 ....94 D1 241 C1
New Broad St
EC2 ....95 C2 243 A3
New Broadway
Ealing W5 ....109 D6
7 Hillingdon UB10 .....82 D3
Teddington TW12 .....174 B5
New Bsns Ctr The
NW10 ....89 D4
Newburgh Rd W3 ....111 A5
Newburgh St W1 ....239 B1
New Burlington Mews
W1 ....249 A6
New Burlington Pl
W1 ....249 A6
New Burlington St
W1 ....249 A6
Newburn Ho SE11 ....260 D2
Newburn St
SE11 ....116 B1 260 D2
Newbury Ave EN3 ......7 B6
Newbury Cl UB5 ......63 B2
Newbury Cotts 4 IG2 .57 A3
Newbury Ct DA14 ....189 D6
E5 ....75 A3
7 Wanstead E11 ....55 A5
Newbury Gdns KT19 .215 D4
Newbury Ho SW9 ....138 D3
13 W2 ....91 D1
Wood Green N22 ....32 A2
Newbury Mews NW5 ..71 A2
Newbury Park Prim Sch
IG2 ....57 B3
Newbury Park Sta IG2 .57 B3
Newbury Rd BR2 ....209 A6
Chingford E4 ....36 A4
Harmondsworth TW6 ...126 B4
Ilford IG2 ....57 C3
Newbury St EC1 .....242 A4
Newbury Way UB5 ....63 B2
New Butt La SE8 ....141 C5
Newby NW1 ....232 A2
Newby Cl EN1 ....5 C3
Newby Pl E14 ....120 A6
Newby St SW8 ......137 B2
New Caledonian Wharf
SE16 ....119 B3
New Campden Ct 7
NW3 ....70 A4
Newcastle Cl EC4 ...241 C2
Newcastle Ct EC4 ...252 B6
Newcastle Ho W1 ...238 A4
Newcastle Pl
W2 ....92 B2 236 D4
Newcastle Row EC1 ..241 B5
New Cavendish St
W1 ....93 B2 238 C3
New Change
EC4 ....95 A1 242 A1
New Chapel Sq TW13 .150 B3
New Charles St EC1 ..234 D2
New Church Ct 3
SE19 ....184 A3
New Church Rd SE5 ..139 B6
32 SE5 ....139 A5
New City Prim Sch E13 99 C4
New City Rd E13 .....99 C4

New Cl Feltham TW13 173 A5
Morden SW19 202 A6
New Colebrooke Ct SM5 219 A1
New College Ct 6 NW3 70 A2
New College Mews 4 N1 72 C1
New College Par 1 NW3 70 B1
Newcombe Ho N5 73 A3
Newcombe Pk NW7 27 C5
Wembley HA0 88 B6
Newcombe Rise UB7 82 A1
Newcombe St W8 245 B4
Newcome Gdns SW16 182 A6
Newcome Ho E5 74 B5
Newcomen Ho 5 NW5 71 B4
Newcomen Rd E11 76 D5
SW11 136 B2
Newcomen St SE1 117 B4 252 C2
New Compton St WC2 94 A1 240 A1
New Concordia Wharf SE1 253 D2
Newcourt Ho 26 E2 96 B4
Newcourt St NW8 92 C5 230 A3
New Covent Garden Flower Market SW8 138 A6 270 A5
New Covent Garden Fruit & Vegetable Mkt SW8 137 D5 269 C3
New Crescent Yd 1 NW10 89 D5
Newcroft Cl UB8 82 B2
New Cross SE14 141 B5
New Cross Gate SE14 140 D4
New Cross Gate Sta SE14 141 A5
New Cross Hospl SE14 140 C5
New Cross Rd SE14 141 A4
New Cross Sta SE14 141 B5
New Ct EC4 241 A1
N16 51 B1
13 NW3 70 A4
Northolt UB5 63 D3
Newdales Cl N9 18 A2
Newdene Ave UB5 84 D5
New Den (Millwall FC) The SE16 118 C1
Newdigate Ho 5 E14 97 B1
6 Kingston KT2 176 D4
Newell St E14 97 B1
New Eltham Sta SE9 166 D3
New End NW3 70 A5
New End Prim Sch NW3 70 A4
New End Sq NW3 70 B4
New England Est IG11 101 A5
Newent Cl SE15 139 C5
Carshalton SM5 202 D1
New Farm Ave BR2 209 A5
New Ferry App SE18 122 C3
New Fetter La EC4 94 C1 241 B2
Newfield Cl TW12 173 C2
Newfield Prim Sch NW10 67 D1
Newfield Rise NW2 68 B5
New Furness Prim Sch The NW10 90 A5
Newgale Gdns HA8 26 B2
New Garden Dr UB7 104 A4
Newgate CR0 205 A1
Newgate Cl TW13 151 A1
Newgate St EC1 94 D1 241 D2
Chingford E4 20 C1
New Globe Wlk SE1 252 A4
New Goulston St E1 243 C2
New Green Pl SE19 183 C4
Newham Acad of Music E6 100 A6
Newham Coll of FE E6 100 B5
Newham Coll of F Ed (Royal Docks Campus) E16 123 A5
Newham Ctr for Mental Health E16 99 D3
Newham General Hospl E13 99 C3
Newham Gn N22 32 C2
Newham Ho IG10 21 D5
Newham Sch of Nursing E3 97 D3
Newham Sixth Form Coll E13 99 B3
Newham's Row SE1 253 B1
Newham Way E13 99 B2
E6 100 B3
Newhaven Cl UB3 105 D2
Newhaven Cres TW15 171 B5
Newhaven Gdns SE9 143 D1
Newhaven La 3 E16 99 A2
Newhaven Rd SE25 205 B4
New Heston Rd TW5 129 B5
Newhouse 5 KT3 199 C2
Newhouse Ave RM6 58 D6
Newhouse Cl KT3 199 C2
Newhouse Wlk SM4 202 A2
Newick Cl DA5 169 D5
Newick Rd E5 74 C5
Newing Gn BR1 187 D3
Newington Barrow Way N7 72 B5
Newington Butts SE1,SE11 116 D2 261 D3
Newington Cswy SE1 117 A3 262 A6
Newington Green Mans N16 73 B3
Newington Green Prim Sch N16 73 B3
Newington Green Rd N1 73 B3
Newington Ind Est SE17 262 A3
New Inn Broadway EC2 243 B6
New Inn Pas WC2 240 D1
New Inn Sq EC2 243 B6
New Inn St EC2 243 B6
New Inn Yd EC2 95 C3 243 B6
New James Ct SE15 140 B2
New Jubilee Ct 1 IG8 37 A3
New Kelvin Ave TW11 174 C4
New Kent Rd SE1 117 A2 262 B4
New King's Prim Sch SW6 135 B3
New Kings Rd SW6 135 C3
New King's Rd SW6 135 C3 265 B1
New King St SE8 141 C6
Newland Cl HA5 23 B4
Newland Ct EC1 242 C6
Wembley HA9 66 C6
Newland Dr EN1 6 B4
Newland Gdns W13 109 A4
Newland Ho N8 50 A6
17 SE14 140 D6
Newland House Sch TW1 174 D6
Newland House Sch Annex TW1 174 D6
Newland Rd N8 50 A6
Newlands NW1 232 A2
Newlands Ave KT7 196 C1
Newlands Cl
Edgware HA8 10 A1
Southall UB2 107 A1
Wembley HA0 65 C2
Newlands Croft SE20 184 D4
Newlands Ct 8 SE9 166 C5
Streatham SW16 182 A5
Newlands Pk SE26 184 D5
Newlands Pl EN5 12 D6
Newlands Quay E1 118 C6
Newlands Rd
Thornton Heath SW16 182 A1
Woodford IG8 20 D2
Newland St E16 122 B5
Newlands The
Thames Ditton KT7 196 C1
Wallington SM6 219 D1
Newlands Way KT9 213 C3
Newling Cl E6 100 B1
New London St EC3 253 B6
New Lydenburg Commercial Est E16 121 C3
New Lydenburg St SE7 121 C3
Newlyn NW1 232 B5
Newlyn Cl Hillingdon UB8 82 C2
Orpington BR6 227 D4
Newlyn Gdns HA2 41 B2
Newlyn Rd DA16 145 D3
Barnet EN5 1 B1
Tottenham N17 33 D2
New Malden Sta KT3 199 C6
Newman Ct BR1 187 A2
Newman Pas W1 239 B3
Newman Rd BR1 187 A2
E13 99 B4
E17 52 D4
Hayes UB3 106 B6
Thornton Heath CR0 204 B1
Newman's Ct EC3 242 D1
Newman's Row WC2 240 D3
Newman St W1 93 C2 239 B3
Newman's Way EN4 2 A4
Newmarket Ave UB5 63 D3
Newmarket Gn SE9 165 D4
Newmarsh Rd SE28 123 D5
Newmill Ho E3 98 A3
New Mill Rd BR5 190 C2
Newminster Rd SM4 202 A3
Newmount NW3 70 B3
New Mount St E15 76 B1
Newnes Path SW15 134 B1
Newnham Ave HA4 40 C1
Newnham Cl
Loughton IG10 21 D5
Northolt UB5 64 A2
South Norwood CR7 183 A1
Newnham Gdns UB5 64 A2
Newnham Ho
Catford SE6 164 A1
9 Putney SW15 156 D5
Newnham Jun & Inf Schs HA4 40 C1
Newnham Lo 10 DA17 125 C1
Newnham Rd N22 32 C2
Newnhams Cl BR1 210 B6
Newnham Terr SE1 261 A6
Newnham Way HA3 44 A4
New North Pl EC2 243 A6
New North Rd N1 95 B6 235 C5
New North Road Bridge N1 235 C5
New North St WC1 94 B2 240 C4
Newnton Cl N4 51 B2
New Oak Rd N2 30 A1
New Oxford St WC1 94 A1 240 A2
New Palace Yd SW1 116 A4 250 A1
New Par Ashford TW15 170 B6
Yiewsley UB7 104 A5
New Park Ave N13 17 B1
New Park Cl UB5 63 A2
New Park Ct 26 SW2 160 A4
New Park Est N18 34 C5
New Park Ho N13 32 B6
New Park Par 14 SW2 160 A4
New Park Rd
Ashford TW15 171 A5
Streatham SW2 160 A4
New Pl CR0 223 C2
New Place Sq SE16 118 B3
New Plaistow Rd E15 98 C6
New Pond Par HA4 62 A5
Newport Ave E13 99 B3
E14 120 B6
Newport Cl EN3 7 A6
Newport Ct WC2 249 D6
Newport Ho E3 97 A4
Newport Jun & Inf Schs E10,E11 76 A6
Newport Lo 2 EN1 17 C6
Newport Mead WD19 22 D6
Newport Pl WC2 249 D6
Newport Rd E10 76 B6
E17 53 A5
Barnes SW13 134 A4
Harmondsworth TW6 126 C4
Hayes UB4 83 B2
Newport St SE11 116 B2 260 D4
New Priory Ct 9 NW6 69 C1
Newquay Cres HA2 63 A6
Newquay Ho SE11 261 A2
Newquay Rd SE6 164 A2
New Quebec St W1 237 D1
New Rd DA16 146 B3
E1 96 B2
N10 30 C2
N8 50 A4
NW7 29 A3
SE2 124 D1
Brentford TW8 109 D1
Carshalton CR4 203 A1
Chingford E4 36 A6
Dagenham RM10 103 D5
East Bedfont TW14 149 B5
East Bedfont TW14 150 B3
East Molesey KT8 195 C6
Edmonton N9 18 A2
Elstree WD6 9 D5
Esher KT10 212 A4
Feltham TW13 173 A5
Harlington TW6,UB7 127 A5
Harrow HA1 64 D4
Hillingdon UB8 83 A2
Hounslow TW3 129 D1
Ilford IG3 79 C6
Kingston KT2 176 C3
Littleton TW17 192 D6
Richmond TW10 175 C6
Tottenham N22 33 A2
New Rd Units TW3 129 D1
New River Cres N13 32 D6
New River Ct N5 73 B4
New River Sports & Recreation Ctr N22 32 D3
New River Way N4 51 B2
New Row WC2 116 A6 250 A6
Newry Rd TW1 153 A6
Newsam Ave N15 51 B4
New Scotland Yard★ SW1 115 D3 259 C6
Newsholme Dr N21 16 B6
New Southgate Ind Est 10 N11 31 C5
New Southgate Sta N11 31 B5
New Spring Gdns Wlk SE11 260 B1
New Sq WC2 94 B1 240 D2
East Bedfont TW14 149 A3
New Sq Pas WC2 241 A2
New St EC2 95 C2 243 B3
New Stanford Prim Sch SW16 181 D2
Newstead Ave BR6 227 C6
Newstead Cl N12 30 C4
Newstead Ct UB5 85 A4
Newstead Rd SE12 164 D4
Newstead Way SW19 178 D6
Newstead Wlk SM5 202 A2
Newstead Wood Sch for Girls BR6 227 B5
New Street Hill BR1 187 C5
New St Sq EC4 94 C1 241 B2
Newton Ave N10 31 B2
Acton W3 111 A4
Newton Cl E17 53 A3
Harrow HA2 63 C6
Newton Farm Fst & Mid Sch HA2 63 B6
Newton Gr W4 111 C2
Newton Ho 10 E17 54 A6
NW8 91 D6
22 SW8 137 D3
1 Stepney E1 118 B6
Newton Pl E14 119 C2
Newton Point 1 E16 98 D1
Newton Prep Sch SW8 137 B4 268 D2
Newton Rd DA16 146 A2
E15 76 B3
N15 52 A4
NW2 68 C5
W2 91 D1
Harrow HA3 24 C1
Isleworth TW7 130 D3
Wembley HA0 66 B1
Wimbledon SW19 179 A3
Newton St WC2 94 A1 240 B2
Newton's Yd 14 SW18 157 C6
Newton Terr BR2 209 D3
Newton Way N18 33 A5
Newton Wlk HA8 26 D2
New Tower Bldgs 21 E1 118 B5
Newtown Ct SW11 268 C1
SW4 159 B6
New Trinity Rd 1 N2 30 B1
New Union Cl E14 120 A3
New Union St EC2 242 C3
New Victoria Hospl KT3 177 C2
New Wanstead E11 55 A3
New Way Rd NW9 45 C5
New Wharf Rd N1 94 A5 233 B4
New Woodlands Sch BR1 186 C6
Newyears Green La UB9 38 B3
New Zealand Ave KT12 193 D1
Niagara Ave W5 109 C2
Niagara Cl N1 235 B4
Niagara Ct 6 SE16 118 C3
Niagara Ho W5 109 C2
Nibthwaite Rd HA1 42 C4
Nicholas Cl UB6 85 D5
Nicholas Ct
Chiswick W4 133 C5
Lewisham SE12 165 A3
Nicholas Gdns W5 109 D4
Nicholas Ho Ealing W13 87 C1
Penge SE26 184 B4
2 Putney SW15 156 A6
Nicholas La EC2,EC4 252 D6
Nicholas Pas EC3 252 D6
Nicholas Rd E1 96 C3
Borehamwood WD6 10 B6
Dagenham RM8 81 B5
Wallington CR0 220 A4
Nicholas Stacey Ho 3 SE7 121 B1
Nicholay Rd N19 49 D1
Nichol Cl N14 15 D3
Nicholes Rd TW3 129 C1
Nichol La BR1 187 A3
Nicholl Ho N4 51 A1
Nicholls Ave UB8 82 C3
Nicholls Point E15 99 A6
Nicholl St E2 96 A6
Nichols Cl N4 50 C1
Chessington KT9 213 C2
Nichols Ct E2 95 D5
Nichols Gn W5 88 A2
Nicholson Dr WD23 8 A2
Nicholson Ho SE17 262 C2
2 SE18 144 A4
Nicholson Rd CR0 205 D1
Nicholson St SE1 251 C3
Nickelby Cl SE28 102 C1
Nickleby Cl UB8 82 D1
Nickleby Ho 15 SE1 118 A4
7 W11 112 D5
Nicola Cl Harrow HA3 24 B1
South Croydon CR2 221 A2
Nicola Terr DA7 147 A4
Nicol Cl 6 TW1 153 B5
Nicole Ho SE25 206 A6
Nicoll Ct N10 31 B3
NW10 89 C6
Nicoll Pl NW4 46 B2
Nicoll Rd NW10 89 C6
Nicoll Way WD6 11 B6
Nicolson 14 NW9 27 D2
Nicosia Rd SW18 158 C4
Niederwald Rd SE26 185 A6
Nield Rd UB3 105 D4
Nigel Bldg EC1 241 A4
Nigel Cl UB5 85 A6
Nigel Ct N3 29 D3
Nigel Fisher Way KT9 213 D1
Nigel Mews IG1 78 D4
Nigel Playfair Ave W6 112 B1
Nigel Rd E7 77 C3
SE15 140 A2
Nigeria Rd SE7 143 D5
Nighthawk 16 NW9 27 D2
Nightingale Ave
Chingford E4 36 C5
Harrow HA1 43 B1
Nightingale Cl
Carshalton SM5 219 A6
Chingford E4 36 C6
Chiswick W4 133 A6
Pinner HA5 40 C4
Nightingale Ct 12 E14 120 A3
N4 72 B6
SW6 265 D1
1 Harrow HA1 42 D3
Penge SE19 183 D4
Sutton SM1 218 A3
1 Wanstead E11 55 B4
Nightingale Dr KT19 214 D2
Nightingale Gr SE13 164 B6
Nightingale Ho 7 E1 118 A5
21 E1 95 C6
SE18 122 C1
W12 90 C1
Hayes UB3 105 D2
Nightingale La BR1 187 D1
N8 50 A6
Balham SW11,SW12 159 A5
Richmond TW10 154 A4
Wanstead E11 55 B4
Nightingale Lo 5 W9 91 C2
Nightingale Mews SE11 261 D4
Nightingale Pl SE18 144 D6
SW10 136 A6 266 B6
Nightingale Prim Sch SE18 122 D1
Wanstead E18 55 C5
Wood Green N22 32 B2
Nightingale Rd E5 74 B5
N9 18 C4
NW10 89 D5
Carshalton SM5 219 A6
Ealing W7 108 D5
East Molesey KT8 195 D4
Hampton TW12 173 C4
Orpington BR5 211 A3
Walton-on-T KT12 194 B2
Wood Green N22 32 B3
Nightingale Sch SW17 158 C2
Nightingale Sq SW12 159 A4
Nightingales The TW19 148 B3
Nightingale Vale SE18 144 C6
Nightingale Way E6 100 A2
Nightingale Wlk SW18, SW4 159 B5
Nile Cl N16 73 D5
Nile Dr N9 18 C2
Nile Ho N1 235 C2
Nile Path 6 SE18 144 C6
Nile Rd E13 99 C5
Nile St N1 95 B4 235 C2
Nile Terr SE1, SE15 117 D1 263 D1
Nimegen Way 9 SE22 161 C6
Nimmo Dr WD23 8 B4
Nimrod 9 NW9 27 C2
Nimrod Cl UB5 84 D4
Nimrod Pas 4 N1 73 C2
Nimrod Rd SW16 181 B5
Nina Mackay Cl 10 E15 98 C6
Nine Acres Cl E12 78 A3
Nine Elms Cl TW14 149 D3
Nine Elms La SW8 137 D6 269 C5
Nineteenth Rd CR4 204 A5
Ninhams Wood BR6 226 C4
Ninth Ave UB3 106 A4
Nisbet 10 NW9 27 C2
Nisbet Ho E9 74 D3
Nita Ct SE12 165 A3
Nithdale Rd SE18 145 A5
Nithsdale Gr UB10 61 A5
Niton Cl EN5 12 D5
Niton Rd TW9 132 C2
Niton St SW6 134 D5
No 1 St SE18 122 D3
Noam Prim Sch N12 29 D6
Nobel Dr TW6 127 C5
Nobel Ho 8 SE5 139 A3
Nobel Rd N18 34 C6
Noble Cnr TW5 129 C4
Noble Ct Mitcham CR4 180 B1
Stepney E1 118 B6
Noblefield Hts N2 48 D4
Noble Ho 12 E1 118 A6
Noble St EC2 95 A1 242 A2
Noel 13 NW9 27 D2
Noel Baker Ct 4 E11 76 C6
Noel Coward Ho SW1 259 B3
Noel Ct TW4 129 B2
Noel Dene W5 109 C1
Noel Ho 3 NW3 70 B1
Noel Park Prim Schs N22 32 C1
Noel Park Rd N22 32 C1
Noel Rd N1 94 D5 234 D4
Acton W3 88 D1
Newham E6 100 A3
Noel Sq RM8 80 C4
Noel St W1 93 C1 239 B1
Noel Terr SE23 162 C2
Nolan Way E5 74 A4
Noll Ho N7 72 B6
Nolton Pl HA8 26 B2
Nonsuch Ct SM3 217 A2
Nonsuch High Sch for Girls SM3 216 D1
Nonsuch Prim Sch KT17 216 B3
Noor Ul Islam Prim Sch E10 76 A6
Nora Gdns NW4 46 D5
Norbiton Ave KT1,KT2 176 C1
Norbiton Common Rd KT1,KT3 198 D6
Norbiton Hall KT2 176 B1
Norbiton Rd E14 97 B1
Norbiton Sta KT1 176 C1
Norbreck Gdns NW10 88 B4
Norbreck Par NW10 88 B4
Norbroke St W12 111 D6
Norburn St W10 91 A2
Norbury Ave
Isleworth TW3 130 B1
Thornton Heath CR7, SW16 182 C1
Norbury Cl SW16 182 D2
Norbury Court Rd SW16 182 A1
Norbury Cres SW16 182 C1
Norbury Cross SW16 204 A6
Norbury Gdns RM6 58 D4
Norbury Gr NW7 11 C1
Norbury Hill SW16 182 D3
Norbury Manor Girls High Sch CR7 182 C2
Norbury Manor Prim Sch SW16 182 A2
Norbury Rd Chingford E4 35 C5
South Norwood CR7 205 A6
Norbury Rise SW16 204 A6
Norbury Sch HA1 42 C4
Norbury Sta SW16 182 B2
Norbury Trad Est SW16 182 B1
Norcombe Gdns HA3 43 C4
Norcombe Ho 2 N19 71 D5
Norcott Cl UB4 84 C3
Norcott Rd N16 74 A5
Norcroft Gdns SE22 162 A4
Norcutt Rd TW2 152 C3
Norden Ho 25 E2 96 B4
Norden Point NW2 46 C1
Nore Ct NW10 68 A1
Norfolk Ave N15 51 D3
Edmonton N13 32 D4
Norfolk Cl N2 48 C6
Cockfosters EN4 3 A1
Edmonton N13 32 D4
5 Twickenham TW1 153 B5
Norfolk Cres DA15 167 C4
W2 92 C1 237 B2
Norfolk Ct 4 Barnet EN5 1 A1
Surbiton KT5 198 B3
Wembley HA0 65 C2
Norfolk Gdns DA7 147 B4
Norfolk Ho E8 73 D4
EC4 252 A6
SE3 142 C6
SE8 141 C4
SW1 259 D4
13 Acton W3 88 C1
11 Merton SW19 180 A3
Penge SE20 184 C2
4 Putney SW15 156 C4
Richmond TW10 154 C6
2 South Croydon CR0 221 B6
3 Stanmore HA7 25 C5
Norfolk House Rd SW16 160 A1
Norfolk House Sch N10 31 B1
Norfolk Mans SW11 267 D1
10 SW18 157 C6
Norfolk Mews 12 W10 91 A2
Norfolk Pl DA16 146 A3
W2 92 B1 236 D2
Norfolk Rd E17 34 D1
E6 100 B6

Norfolk Rd *continued*
NW10 67 C1
NW8 92 B6 229 D5
Barking IG11 79 C1
Barnet EN5 1 C2
Claygate KT10 212 C3
Dagenham RM10 81 D3
Enfield EN3 18 B6
Feltham TW13 150 C3
Harrow HA1 41 D4
Ilford IG3 57 C2
Mitcham SW19 180 C4
South Norwood CR7 205 A6
Norfolk Row
SE1,SE11 116 B2 260 C4
Norfolk Sq W2 92 B1 236 D2
Norfolk Sq Mews W2 236 D1
Norfolk St E7 77 A3
Norgrove St SW12 159 A4
Norhyrst Ave SE25 205 D6
Norland Ho 13 W11 112 D5
Norland Pl
W11 113 A5 244 B3
Norland Place Sch
W11 113 A5 244 A3
Norland Rd W11 112 D5
Norlands Cres BR7 188 D2
Norland Sq
W11 113 A5 244 B3
Norley Vale SW15 156 A3
Norlington Rd E10,E11 54 B1
Norlington Sch for Boys
E10 54 B1
Norman Ave
Feltham TW13 151 B2
Southall UB1 107 A6
Tottenham N22 33 A2
Twickenham TW1 153 C4
Norman Butler Ho 10
W10 91 A3
Normanby Cl SW15 157 B6
Normanby Rd NW10 67 D4
Norman Cl BR6 227 A5
Tottenham N22 33 A2
Norman Cres
Heston TW5 128 D5
Pinner HA5 22 C2
Norman Ct N4 50 C2
NW10 68 A1
Dulwich SE22 162 A4
7 Hampton TW12 173 C2
Ilford IG2 57 B2
West Norwood SW16 182 C5
Woodford IG8 37 B5
Normand Mews W14 264 B6
Normand Park Prim Sch
W14 135 B6 264 D6
Normand Rd
W14 135 B6 264 C6
Normandy Ave EN5 1 B1
Normandy Cl SE26 163 A1
Normandy Dr UB3 83 A1
Normandy Ho 4 NW4 28 D1
Normandy Rd SW9 138 C4
Normandy Terr E16 99 B1
Norman Gr E3 97 A5
Norman Ho 6 E11 76 C6
SW8 270 A4
Feltham TW13 151 B2
Lower Halliford TW17 192 C2
Normanhurst TW15 170 C5
Normanhurst Ave
DA16 146 D4
Normanhurst Dr TW1 153 B6
Normanhurst Rd BR5 190 B1
Streatham SW2 160 B2
Walton-on-T KT12 194 D1
Normanhurst Sch E4 20 B4
Norman Par DA14 168 D2
Norman Rd E11 76 C6
E6 100 B3
N15 51 D4
SE10 141 D5
Ashford TW15 171 B4
Ilford IG1 78 D3
Merton SW19 180 A3
Sutton SM1 217 C3
Thornton Heath CR7 204 D4
Normans Cl NW10 67 B2
Hillingdon UB8 82 A2
Normansfield Ave KT1,
KT8 175 C3
Normanshire Dr E4 35 D6
Normans Mead NW10 67 B2
Norman St EC1 95 A4 235 B1
Normanton Ave SW18,
SW19 157 C2
Normanton Ct CR2 221 C3
Normanton Ho 6
SW4 159 C5
Normanton Pk E4 20 C2
Normanton Rd CR2 221 C2
Normanton St SE23 162 D2
Norman Way Acton W3 88 D1
Palmers Green N14 16 A2
Normington Cl SW16 182 C5
Norrice Lea N2 48 B4
Norris 11 NW9 27 D2
Norris Ho 22 E9 96 C6
Norris Ho *continued*
12 N1 95 C6
Norris St SW1 249 C5
Norroy Rd SW15 134 D1
Norrys Cl EN4 2 D1
Norrys Rd EN4 2 D1
Norse Ho 13 SE5 139 A3
Norseman Cl 3 IG3 58 B1
Norseman Way UB6 85 D6
Norstead Pl SW15 156 A2
North Access Rd E17 52 D3
North Acre NW9 27 C2
North Acton Rd NW10 89 B4
North Acton Sta W3 89 B2
Northampton Gr N1 73 B3
Northampton Pk N1 73 B2
Northampton Rd
EC1 94 C3 241 B6
Croydon CR0 222 A6
Enfield EN3 7 A1
Northampton Sq
EC1 94 D4 234 C1
Northampton St N1 73 A1
Northanger Rd SW16 182 A4
North Audley St
W1 115 A6 248 A6
North Ave Ealing W13 87 B2
Edmonton N18 34 A6
Harrow HA2 41 D3
Hayes UB3 106 A6
8 Richmond TW9 132 C4
Southall UB1 107 B6
Wallington SM5 219 A1
Northaw Ho W10 90 C3
North Bank
NW8 92 C4 230 A1
Northbank Rd E17 36 A1
North Beckton Prim Sch
E6 100 B2
North Birkbeck Rd E11 76 B5
North Block 18 E1 118 C6
Northborough Rd
SW16 182 A1
Northbourne BR2 209 A2
Northbourne Ho 21 E5 74 B3
N14 15 D4
Northbourne Rd SW4 159 D6
North Branch Ave
NW10 90 C4
Northbrook CE Sch
SE12 164 D6
Northbrook Rd SE13 164 C6
Barnet EN5 13 A5
Ilford IG1 78 C6
Thornton Heath CR0 205 B4
Wood Green N22 32 A3
Northburgh St
EC1 94 D3 241 D6
Northbury Jun & Inf Sch
IG11 79 A2
North Carriage Dr
W2 114 C6 247 B6
Northchurch SE17 262 D2
North Church Ho 19 E2 96 A6
Northchurch Rd N1 73 B1
Wembley HA9 66 C2
Northchurch Terr N1 73 C1
North Circular Rd N2 30 B2
N3,NW2,NW4 47 A4
NW10 67 C3
NW2 67 C3
Chingford, Highams Park
E17 35 D2
Edmonton N13 32 C5
Ilford IG1,E12 78 C4
Woodford E18 37 C1
North Cl DA6 146 D1
Barnet EN5 12 C6
Dagenham RM10 103 C6
East Bedfont TW14 149 B5
Merton SM4 201 A5
Northcliffe Cl KT4 215 C5
Northcliffe Dr N20 13 B3
North Colonnade E14 119 C5
North Common Rd
Ealing W5 110 A6
Uxbridge UB8 60 A3
Northcote 1 HA5 22 C1
Northcote Ave
Ealing W5 110 A6
Isleworth TW7 153 A6
Southall UB1 107 A6
Tolworth KT5 198 D2
Northcote Ho UB4 84 D2
Northcote Lodge Sch
SW11 158 D5
Northcote Rd E17 53 A5
NW10 67 C1
SW11 158 D6
Isleworth TW7 153 A6
Kingston KT3 199 B6
Sidcup DA14 189 C6
Thornton Heath CR0 205 B3
Northcott Ave N22 32 A2
North Countess Rd E17 35 B2
Northcourt W1 239 B4
North Cray Prim Sch
DA14 191 A4
North Cray Rd DA14 191 A5
North Cres E16 98 B3
N3 29 B1
WC1 239 C4
Northcroft Ct 8 W12 112 A4
Northcroft Rd W13 109 B3
West Ewell KT19 215 C1
North Crofts SE21 162 B3
North Cross Rd SE22 162 A6
Ilford IG6 57 A5
North Ct SW1 260 A5
North Dene NW7 11 B1
Hounslow TW5 129 D4
Northdene Gdns N15 51 D3
Northdown Cl HA4 61 D5
Northdown Gdns IG2 57 C4
Northdown Rd DA16 146 C3
Northdown St
N1 94 B5 233 C3
North Dr BR6 227 C4
Beckenham BR3 207 D5
Hounslow TW3,TW7 130 A3
Ruislip HA4 39 C2
Streatham SW16 181 C6
North Dulwich Sta
SE21 161 B6
North Ealing Prim Sch
W5 87 B3
North Ealing Sta W3 88 B1
North End NW3 70 A6
Buckhurst Hill IG9 21 C4
Croydon CR0 221 A6
North End Ave NW3 70 A6
North End Cres
W14 113 B2 254 C3
North End Ho
W14 113 A2 254 B3
North End La BR6 226 D1
North End Par W14 254 B3
North End Rd NW11 47 D1
W14 113 B1 254 D1
Wembley HA9 66 D5
North End Way NW3 70 A6
Northern Ave N9 17 D2
Northernhay Wlk SM4 201 A5
Northern Hts N8 49 D2
Northern Perimeter Rd
TW6 127 C4
Northern Perimeter Road
(W) TW6 126 B4
Northern Rd E13 99 B5
Northern Relief Rd
IG11 79 A2
Northesk Ho 6 E1 96 B3
North Eyot Gdns 5
W6 111 D1
Northey St E14 119 A6
North Farm IG10 21 C5
North Feltham Trad Est
TW14 128 B1
Northfield IG10 21 D6
Northfield Ave
W13,W5 109 B4
Pinner HA5 40 D5
Northfield Cl BR1 188 A2
Hayes UB3 105 D3
Northfield Cres SM3 217 A4
Northfield Gdns RM9 81 B4
Northfield Hall N6 49 A2
Northfield Ho 3 SE15 140 A6
Northfield Ind Est HA0 88 C6
Northfield Par UB3 105 D3
Northfield Path RM9 81 B4
Northfield Pk UB3 105 D3
Northfield Rd E6 78 B1
N16 51 C2
W13 109 B4
Cockfosters EN4 2 C2
Dagenham RM9 81 B4
Enfield EN3 18 B6
Heston TW5 128 D5
Northfields SW18 135 C1
Northfields Prospect
SW18 135 C1
Northfields Rd W3 89 A2
Northfields Sta W5 109 C3
Northfleet Ho SE1 252 C2
North Flower Wlk
W2 114 B6 246 C5
North Gate
NW8 92 C5 230 A3
Northgate Bsns Ctr EN1 6 B1
Northgate Ct 15 SW9 138 C2
Northgate Dr NW9 45 C3
North Gates N12 30 A2
North Gdns SW19 180 B3
North Glade DA5 169 B3
North Gn NW9 27 C3
North Gower St
NW1 93 C4 232 B1
North Gr N15 51 B4
N6 49 A2
North Greenwich Sta
SE10 120 C4
North Haringay Jun & Inf
Sch N8 50 C5
North Harrow Sta HA2 41 D4
North Hill N6 49 A3
North Hill Ave N6 48 D3
North Hill Ct N6 49 A2
North Ho 3 SE8 119 B1
North Hyde Gdns UB3 106 A2
North Hyde La UB2 107 A1
North Hyde Rd UB3 105 D3
Northiam N12 29 C6
WC1 233 B1
Northiam St E9 96 B6
Northington St
WC1 94 B3 240 D5
North La TW11 174 D4
Northlands Ave BR6 227 C4
Northlands St SE5 139 A3
Northleigh Ho 36 E3 97 D4
North Lo N22 31 D1
New Barnet EN5 14 A6
North Lodge Cl SW15 156 D6
North London Boys Sch
N16 52 A1
North London Collegiate
Sch HA7,HA8 26 A5
North London Collegiate
Sch The HA7,HA8 26 A5
North London Nuffield
Hospl EN2 4 C3
North Mall The N9 18 B2
North Mews
WC1 94 B3 240 D5
North Middlesex Hospl
N18 33 C5
Northmoor 4 SE23 162 D1
North Mount N20 14 A2
Northolm HA8 27 B6
Northolme Gdns HA8 26 C2
Northolme Rd N5 73 A4
Northolme Rise BR6 227 C6
Northolt N17 33 C1
Northolt Ave HA4 62 B3
Northolt Gdns UB6 64 D3
Northolt High Sch UB5 63 B2
Northolt Park Inf Sch
UB5 63 D3
Northolt Park Sta HA2 63 D4
Northolt Prim Sch UB5 63 A1
Northolt Rd
Harmondsworth TW6 126 A4
Harrow HA2 64 A5
Northolt Sta UB5 63 C2
Northover BR1 164 D1
North Par
Chessington KT9 214 B3
Edgware HA8 26 C1
Southall UB1 85 C1
North Pas SW18 157 C6
North Pk SE9 166 C5
North Pl Mitcham SW19 180 D3
Teddington TW11 174 D4
Northpoint BR1 187 A2
North Point UB7 104 A5
North Pole La BR2 225 A2
North Pole Rd W10 90 C2
Northport St N1 235 D5
North Prim Sch UB1 107 B6
North Rd BR1 187 B2
N2 30 C2
N6 49 A2
N7 72 A2
SE18 123 C2
W5 109 D3
Brentford TW8 132 A6
Dagenham RM6 59 A4
East Bedfont TW14 149 B5
Edgware HA8 26 D2
Edmonton N9 18 B3
Erith DA17 125 D4
Hayes UB3 83 B2
Heston TW5 128 C6
Ilford IG3 79 C6
Richmond TW9 132 C3
Southall UB1 107 C6
Surbiton KT6 197 D3
West Drayton UB7 104 B3
1 West Wickham BR4 207 D1
Wimbledon SW19 180 A4
North Residence IG3 58 B4
North Ride
W2 114 C6 247 A5
North Rise W2 237 B1
Northrop Rd TW6 127 C4
North Row W1 115 A6 248 A6
North Sheen Sta
TW10 132 C1
Northside Prim Sch
N12 30 A5
Northside Rd BR1 187 A2
North Side Wandsworth
Comm SW18 158 B6
Northspur Rd SM1 217 C5
North Sq NW11 47 C4
Edmonton N9 18 B2
North St BR1 187 A2
DA7 147 C1
E13 99 B5
NW4 46 C4
SW4 137 C2
Barking IG11 79 A1
Carshalton SM5 218 D4
Isleworth TW7 131 A2
Northstead Rd SW2 160 C2
North Tenter St E1 243 D1
North Terr SW3 257 A5
Northumberland Alley
EC3 243 B1
Northumberland Ave
DA16 145 C2
WC2 116 A5 250 A4
Enfield EN1 6 B4
Hounslow TW7 130 D4
Wanstead E12 55 C1
Northumberland Cl
TW19 148 A5
Northumberland Cres
TW14 149 C5
Northumberland Ct
3 Hounslow TW3 129 D1
South Croydon CR2 221 C3
Northumberland Gdns
BR1 210 C5
Brentford TW7 131 A5
Edmonton N9 17 D1
Mitcham CR4 203 D4
Northumberland Gr
N17 34 B3
Northumberland Heath
Prim Sch DA8 147 D5
Northumberland Ho
NW5 71 C2
Northumberland Mans
E5 74 C4
Northumberland Park Com
Sch N17 34 A3
Northumberland Park Ind
Est N17 34 B3
Northumberland Park
Sports Ctr N17 34 A3
Northumberland Park Sta
N17 34 B3
Northumberland Pk
DA8 147 D5
Tottenham N17 34 A3
Northumberland Pl W2 91 C1
26 Richmond TW10 153 D6
Northumberland Rd
E17 53 C2
E6 100 A1
Harrow HA2 41 C4
New Barnet EN5 14 A4
Northumberland St
WC2 250 A4
Northumbria St E14 97 C1
North Verbena Gdns
W6 112 A1
Northview 1 N7 72 A5
North View Ealing W5 87 C3
Pinner HA5 40 C2
Wimbledon SW19 178 C5
Northview Cres NW10 67 D4
Northview Dr IG8 37 D1
Northview Prim Sch
NW10 67 D3
North View Rd N8 49 D6
North Villas NW1 71 D2
Northway NW11 47 D4
North Way N11 31 C4
N9 18 D2
NW9 44 D6
Northway Merton SM4 201 A5
Wallington SM6 219 C4
North Way Pinner HA5 40 D5
Uxbridge UB10 60 A1
Northway Cir NW7 27 B6
Northway Cres NW7 27 C6
Northway Ct NW11 47 D4
NW7 27 B6
Northway Rd SE5 139 A2
Croydon CR0 205 D2
Northway Sch NW7 11 B1
Northways Par 2 NW3 70 B1
Northweald La KT2 175 D5
North Wembley Sta
HA0,HA9 65 D5
North Western Ave
(Watford By-Pass)
WD6 9 B5
North Westminster Com
Sch
W2 92 B2 236 D4
W9 91 C3
Northwest Pl N1 234 B4
North Wharf Rd
W2 92 B2 236 C3
Northwick Ave HA3 43 B3
Northwick Circ HA3 43 C3
Northwick Cl
NW8 92 B3 236 C6
Harrow HA1 65 B6
Northwick Ho NW8 236 B6
Northwick Park Hospl
HA1 43 A2
Northwick Park Rd
HA1 42 D3
Northwick Park Sta
HA3 43 B2
Northwick Rd
South Oxhey WD19 22 C6
Wembley HA0 87 D6
Northwick Terr
NW8 92 B3 236 C6
North Wlk W2 114 A6 246 A5
North Wlk *continued*
New Addington CR0 224 A3
Northwold Dr HA5 40 C6
Northwold Prim Sch
E5 74 A6
Northwold Rd E5,N16 74 A6
Northwood Comp Sch
HA6 22 B2
Northwood Gdns N12 30 B5
Greenford UB6 64 D3
Ilford IG5 56 C5
Northwood Hills Cir
HA6 22 A2
Northwood Hills Sta
HA6 22 A1
North Wood Lo NW3 69 D4
Northwood & Pinner Com
Hospl HA6 22 A2
Northwood Pl DA18 125 B3
Northwood Prim Sch
DA18 125 B3
Northwood Rd N6 49 B2
Forest Hill SE23 163 B3
South Norwood CR7 183 A1
Wallington SM5 219 A2
Northwood Twr 1 E17 54 A5
Northwood Way
Northwood HA6 22 A3
1 West Norwood SE19 183 C4
North Woolwich Rd
E16 121 B5
North Woolwich Rdbt
E16 121 D5
North Woolwich Sta
E16 122 C4
North Worple Way
SW14 133 B2
Norton Ave KT5 198 D2
Norton Cl Chingford E4 35 C5
Enfield EN1 6 B3
Norton Ct
Beckenham BR3 185 B2
Ilford IG2 57 B3
Norton Folgate E1 243 B4
Norton Gdns SW16 182 A1
Norton Ho 33 E1 96 B1
14 E2 96 D5
16 SW9 138 B3
5 New Malden KT3 199 C5
Norton Rd E10 53 B1
Wembley HA0 65 D2
Norval Gn 1 SW9 138 C3
Norval Rd HA0 43 B1
Norvic Ho 5 SE5 139 A3
Norway Gate SE16 119 A3
Norway Pl E14 97 B1
Norway St SE10 141 D6
Norwegian Sch SW19 178 C3
Norwich Ho 6 E14 97 D1
Norwich Mews IG3 58 A1
Norwich Pl 7 DA6 147 C1
Norwich Rd E7 77 A3
Greenford UB6 85 D6
Northwood HA6 39 D6
South Norwood CR7 205 A6
Norwich St EC4 94 C1 241 A2
Norwich Wlk HA8 27 A3
Norwood Ave HA0 88 B5
Norwood Cl
Southall UB2 107 C2
Twickenham TW2 152 B2
Norwood Dr HA2 41 C3
Norwood Gdns
Hayes UB4 84 C3
Southall UB2 107 B2
Norwood Green Inf Sch
UB2 107 B1
Norwood Green Jun Sch
UB2 107 A1
Norwood Green Rd
UB2 107 C2
Norwood Heights Sh Ctr 13
SE19 183 C4
Norwood High St
SE27 183 A6
Norwood Ho 22 E14 119 D6
Norwood Hospl SE19 183 B4
Norwood Junction Sta
SE25 206 A5
Norwood Park Rd
SE27 183 A5
Norwood Rd
Southall UB2 107 C2
West Norwood SE24,
SE27 160 D3
Norwood Terr UB2 107 D2
Notley St SE5 139 B5
Notre Dame RC Girls Sch
SE1 116 D3 261 D5
Notson Rd SE25 206 B5
Notting Barn Rd W10 90 D3
Nottingdale Sq W11 244 A4
Nottingham Ave E16 99 C1
Nottingham Ct WC2 240 A1
Nottingham Ho N4 51 A1
34 SE5 139 A3

Nottingham Pl
W1 ... 93 A2 238 A4
Nottingham Rd E10 ... 54 A3
Croydon CR2 ... 221 A3
Isleworth TW7 ... 130 D3
Upper Tooting SW17 ... 158 D3
Nottingham St W1 ... 238 A4
Nottingham Terr NW1 238 A5
Notting Hill & Ealing High Sch W13 ... 87 B2
Notting Hill Gate W11 ... 113 C5 245 A4
Notting Hill Gate Sta W11 ... 113 C5 245 A4
Nottingwood Ho W11 . 244 A6
Nova Bldg 21 E14 ... 119 C2
Nova Mews SM4 ... 201 A2
Novar Cl BR6 ... 211 D2
Nova Rd CR0 ... 205 A3
Novar Rd SE9 ... 167 A3
Novello St SW6 ... 135 C4 265 A2
Nowell Rd SW13 ... 134 A6
Nower Ct HA5 ... 41 B5
Nower Hill HA5 ... 41 B5
Nower Hill High Sch HA5 ... 41 C5
Noyna Rd SW17 ... 158 D1
Nubia Way SE6 ... 164 C1
Nuding Cl SE13 ... 141 C2
Nuffield Ct TW5 ... 129 B5
Nuffield Lo 14 W9 ... 91 C2
Nugent Ct SW16 ... 181 C6
Nugent Rd N19 ... 50 A1
South Norwood SE25 ... 205 D6
Nugents Ct HA5 ... 23 A2
Nugent's Pk HA5 ... 23 B2
Nugent Terr NW8 ... 92 A5 229 B3
Numa Ct TW8 ... 131 D5
Nun Ct EC2 ... 242 C2
Nuneaton Rd RM9 ... 81 A1
Nuneham SW16 ... 181 D6
Nunhead Cres SE15 ... 140 B2
Nunhead Gr SE15 ... 140 C2
Nunhead La SE15 ... 140 B2
Nunhead Sta SE15 ... 140 C3
Nunnington Cl SE9 ... 166 A1
Nunn's Rd EN2 ... 5 A3
Nupton Dr EN5 ... 12 C5
Nurse Cl HA8 ... 27 A2
Nursery Ave DA7 ... 147 B2
N3 ... 30 A1
Croydon CR0 ... 222 D6
Nursery Cl BR6 ... 211 D2
SE4 ... 141 B3
Croydon CR0 ... 222 D6
Dagenham RM6 ... 58 D3
Enfield EN3 ... 6 D4
Feltham TW14 ... 150 B4
Putney SW15 ... 134 D1
Woodford IG8 ... 37 B5
Nursery Ct Ealing W13 ... 87 A2
7 Tottenham N17 ... 33 D3
Nursery Gdns BR7 ... 188 D4
Enfield EN3 ... 6 D4
Hampton TW13 ... 173 B6
Hounslow TW4 ... 151 B6
Sunbury TW16 ... 171 D1
Nursery La E2 ... 95 D6
E7 ... 77 A2
W10 ... 90 C2
Nurserymans Rd N11 ... 15 A2
Nursery Rd E9 ... 74 C2
N14 ... 15 C4
N2 ... 30 B2
SW9 ... 138 B1
Loughton IG10 ... 21 C6
Merton SW19 ... 179 D1
Mitcham CR4 ... 202 C6
Pinner HA5 ... 40 C6
South Norwood CR7 ... 205 B5
Sunbury TW16 ... 171 D1
Sutton SM1 ... 218 A4
Wimbledon SW19 ... 179 A3
Nursery Row SE17 ... 262 C3
Nursery St N17 ... 33 D3
Nursery Walk Ct NW4 ... 46 B6
Nursery Wlk NW4 ... 46 C6
Nurstead Rd DA8 ... 147 C5
Nutborn Ho SW19 ... 178 D4
Nutbourne St W10 ... 91 A4
Nutbrook St SE15 ... 140 A2
Nutbrowne Rd RM9 ... 103 B6
Nutcroft Rd SE15 ... 140 B5
Nutfield Cl
Carshalton SM5 ... 218 C5
Edmonton N18 ... 34 A4
Nutfield Gdns Ilford IG3 80 A6
Northolt UB5 ... 84 C5
Nutfield Rd E15 ... 76 A4
NW2 ... 68 A5
SE22 ... 139 D1
Thornton Heath CR7 ... 204 D5
Nutfield Way BR6 ... 226 D6
Nutford Pl W1 . 92 D1 237 C2
Nuthatch Cl TW19 ... 148 B3
Nuthatch Gdns SE28 ... 123 B4
Nuthurst Ave SW2 ... 160 B2
Nutkin Wlk UB8 ... 60 A1
Nutley Terr NW3 ... 70 B2
Nutmeg Cl E16 ... 98 C3
Nutmeg La E14 ... 98 B1
Nuttall St N1 ... 95 C5
Nutter La E11 ... 55 C4
Nutt Gr HA8 ... 9 D2
Nutt St SE15 ... 139 D5
Nutty La TW17 ... 193 A6
Nutwell St SW17 ... 180 C5
Nuxley Rd DA17 ... 125 C1
NW London Jewish Day Sch NW6 ... 69 A1
Nyanza St SE18 ... 145 B6
Nye Bevan Est E5 ... 74 D5
Nye Bevan Ho SW6 ... 264 C4
Nye's Wharf SE15 ... 140 A6
Nylands Ave TW9 ... 132 C3
Nymans Gdns SW20 ... 200 B6
Nynehead St SE14 ... 141 A5
Nyon Gr SE6 ... 163 B2
Nyton Cl N19 ... 50 A1

O

Oak Apple Ct SE12 ... 165 A3
Oak Ave N10 ... 31 B3
N8 ... 50 A5
Croydon CR0 ... 223 D6
Enfield EN2 ... 4 B5
Hampton TW12,TW13 ... 173 A4
Heston TW5 ... 129 A5
Tottenham N17 ... 33 C3
Uxbridge UB10 ... 60 D6
West Drayton UB7 ... 104 C3
Oak Bank CR0 ... 224 A2
Oakbank Ave KT12 ... 195 B2
Oakbank Gr SE24 ... 139 A1
Oakbrook 3 BR3 ... 185 D1
Oakbrook Cl BR1 ... 187 B6
Oakbury Rd SW6 ... 135 D3
Oak Cl N14 ... 15 B4
Sutton SM1 ... 218 A6
Oakcombe Cl KT3 ... 177 C2
Oak Cottage Cl 11 SE6 ... 164 D3
Oak Cotts W7 ... 108 C4
Oakcourt 16 SE15 ... 139 D5
Oak Cres E16 ... 98 C2
Oakcroft SE12 ... 165 B1
Oakcroft Bsns Ctr KT9 214 B4
Oakcroft Cl HA5 ... 22 B1
Oakcroft Ho 8 KT3 ... 199 C2
Oakcroft Rd SE13 ... 142 B3
Chessington KT9 ... 214 B4
Oakcroft Villas KT9 ... 214 B4
Oak Ct BR1 ... 188 B1
Chingford E4 ... 35 D4
Oakdale N14 ... 15 B3
Beckenham BR3 ... 186 A1
Oakdale Ave
Harrow HA3 ... 44 A4
Pinner HA6 ... 22 A1
Oakdale Cl WD19 ... 22 C6
Oakdale Ct N19 ... 72 A6
Oakdale Gdns E4 ... 36 A5
Oakdale Inf Sch E18 ... 37 B1
Oakdale Jun Sch E18 ... 37 B1
Oakdale Lo NW4 ... 29 A2
Oakdale Rd E11 ... 76 B6
E7 ... 77 B1
N4 ... 51 B3
SE15 ... 140 C2
South Oxhey WD19 ... 22 C6
Streatham SW16 ... 182 A5
Woodford E18 ... 37 B1
Oakdale Way CR4 ... 203 A2
Oakdene 3 SE15 ... 140 B4
1 West Norwood SE19 . 183 C5
Oak Dene W13 ... 87 B2
Oakdene Ave BR7 ... 188 C5
Thames Ditton KT7 ... 197 A1
Oakdene Cl HA5 ... 23 B3
Oakdene Dr KT5 ... 199 A1
Oakdene Ho N16 ... 51 C1
Enfield EN2 ... 4 D2
Oakdene Lo SE20 ... 184 B3
Oakdene Mews SM3 ... 201 B1
Oakdene Pk N3 ... 29 B3
Oakdene Rd BR5 ... 211 D4
Hillingdon UB10 ... 82 D5
Oakden St SE11 ... 116 C2 261 B4
Oake Ct SW15 ... 157 A6
Oakeford Ho W14 ... 254 B5
Oakend Ho 10 N4 ... 51 B2
Oaken Dr KT10 ... 212 D2
Oakenholt Ho 1 SE2 . 124 D4
Oaken La KT10 ... 212 C3
Oakenshaw Cl KT6 ... 198 A2
Oakes Cl E6 ... 100 B1
Oakeshott Ave N6 ... 71 A6
Oakey La SE1 ... 261 A6
Oak Farm WD6 ... 11 A6
Oak Farm Jun & Inf Schs UB10 ... 82 D6
Oakfield E4 ... 35 D5
Oakfield Ave HA3 ... 43 B6
Oakfield Cl
New Malden KT3 ... 199 D4
Ruislip HA4 ... 39 D3
Oakfield Ct N3 ... 29 D2
N8 ... 50 A2
NW2 ... 46 D2
SW4 ... 160 A5
2 Ealing W5 ... 110 C5
South Croydon CR2 ... 221 A2
Oakfield Gdns
Beckenham BR3 ... 207 C4
Carshalton SM5 ... 202 D1
Edmonton N18 ... 33 C6
Greenford UB6 ... 86 B4
3 West Norwood SE19 . 183 C5
Oakfield Ho 2 IG1 ... 78 D5
Oakfield La BR2 ... 225 C4
Oakfield Lo 8 IG1 ... 78 D5
Oakfield Prep Sch SE21 ... 161 B3
Oakfield Rd E17 ... 35 A1
E6 ... 100 A6
N3 ... 29 D2
N4 ... 50 C2
Ashford TW15 ... 170 D5
Croydon CR0 ... 205 A1
Ilford IG1 ... 78 D5
Palmers Green N14 ... 16 A2
Penge SE20 ... 184 B3
Wimbledon SW19 ... 156 D1
Oakfields KT12 ... 194 A1
Oakfields Rd NW11 ... 47 A3
Oakfield St SW10 ... 136 A6 266 A6
Oakford Rd NW5 ... 71 C4
Oak Gdns HA8 ... 27 A1
Croydon CR0 ... 223 C6
Oak Gr NW2 ... 69 A4
Ruislip HA4 ... 40 B1
Sunbury TW16 ... 172 B3
West Wickham BR4 ... 208 A1
Oak Grove Rd SE20 ... 184 C1
Oakhall Ct
Ashford TW16 ... 171 D5
Wanstead E11 ... 55 B3
Oakhall Dr TW16 ... 171 D5
Oak Hall Rd E11 ... 55 B3
Oakham Cl SE6 ... 163 B2
Oakham Dr BR2 ... 208 D5
Oakham Ho W10 ... 90 C3
Oakhampton Rd NW7 ... 28 D3
Oakhill KT10 ... 213 A2
Oak Hill Chingford IG8 ... 36 C3
Surbiton KT6 ... 198 A2
Oakhill Ave NW3 ... 69 D4
Pinner HA5 ... 23 A1
Oak Hill Cl IG8 ... 36 B3
Oak Hill Coll N14 ... 15 A5
Oak Hill Cres
Chingford IG8 ... 36 C3
Surbiton KT6 ... 198 A2
Oakhill Ct SE23 ... 162 C5
Putney SW15 ... 157 B6
8 Surbiton KT6 ... 198 A3
Wimbledon SW19 ... 178 D3
Oak Hill Ct IG8 ... 36 C3
Oak Hill Gdns E4 ... 36 C2
Oak Hill Gr KT6 ... 198 A3
Oakhill Ho BR5 ... 190 A2
Oak Hill Lo NW3 ... 69 D4
Oak Hill Park Mews NW3 ... 70 A4
Oak Hill Pk NW3 ... 69 D4
Oakhill Pl SW15 ... 157 C6
Oakhill Prim Sch IG8 ... 36 C4
Oakhill Rd BR6 ... 227 D6
Beckenham BR3 ... 186 A1
Putney SW15 ... 157 B6
Sutton SM1 ... 218 A5
Thornton Heath SW16 ... 182 B2
Oak Hill Rd KT6 ... 198 A3
Oak Hill Way NW3 ... 70 A4
Oak Ho 13 DA15 ... 168 A1
8 E14 ... 120 A4
N16 ... 73 B6
11 N2 ... 30 B1
8 NW3 ... 70 D2
Penge SE20 ... 184 B1
Wood Green N22 ... 32 A3
Oakhouse Rd DA6 ... 169 C6
Oakhurst Ave DA7 ... 147 A5
East Barnet EN4 ... 14 C4
Oakhurst Cl BR7 ... 188 B2
E17 ... 54 C5
4 Teddington TW11 ... 174 C5
Oakhurst Ct E17 ... 54 C5
Oakhurst Gdns DA7 ... 147 A5
E11,E17 ... 54 C5
Chingford E4 ... 20 D3
Oakhurst Gr SE22 ... 140 A1
Oakhurst Rd KT19 ... 215 B2
Oakington 14 KT1 ... 176 C1
Oakington Ave
Harrow HA2 ... 41 C2
Hayes UB3 ... 105 B2
Oakington Ave *continued*
Wembley HA9 ... 66 B5
Oakington Dr TW16 ... 172 C1
Oakington Manor Dr HA9 ... 66 C3
Oakington Manor Prim Sch HA9 ... 66 D3
Oakington Rd W9 ... 91 C3
Oakington Way N8 ... 50 A2
Oak La E14 ... 119 B6
N11 ... 31 D4
N2 ... 30 B1
Isleworth TW7 ... 130 C1
Twickenham TW1 ... 153 A4
Woodford IG8 ... 36 D6
Oakland Pl IG9 ... 21 A2
Oakland Rd E15 ... 76 C4
Oaklands BR7 ... 189 B4
Croydon CR0 ... 220 D3
Ealing W13 ... 87 A2
Southgate N21 ... 16 B2
Oaklands Ave DA15 ... 167 D4
Enfield N9 ... 18 B5
Hounslow TW7 ... 130 D6
Thames Ditton KT10 ... 196 B1
Thornton Heath CR7 ... 204 C5
West Wickham BR4 ... 223 D5
Oaklands Cl BR5 ... 211 C3
DA6 ... 169 B6
Chessington KT9 ... 213 C4
Wembley HA0 ... 65 D3
Oaklands Ct NW10 ... 89 C6
1 Wembley HA0 ... 65 D3
Oaklands Dr TW2 ... 152 A4
Oaklands Gr W12 ... 112 A5
Oaklands Ho SE4 ... 141 B2
Oaklands Mews NW2 ... 68 D4
Oaklands Park Ave IG1 79 A6
Oaklands Pas NW2 ... 68 D4
Oaklands Pl 8 SW4 ... 137 D1
Oaklands Prim Sch W7 ... 108 D4
Oaklands Rd DA6 ... 169 B6
NW2 ... 68 D4
W7,W13 ... 109 A4
Barnet N20 ... 13 B4
Bromley BR1 ... 186 C3
Ealing W7 ... 108 D4
Mortlake SW14 ... 133 B2
Oaklands Sch
Hounslow TW3 ... 130 B2
Loughton IG10 ... 21 C6
Oaklands Sec Sch E2 ... 96 B4
Oaklands Way SM6 ... 219 D1
Oakland Way KT19 ... 215 C2
Oakleafe Gdns IG6 ... 56 D6
Oaklea Pas KT1 ... 197 D6
Oakleigh Ave N20 ... 14 C3
Edgware HA8 ... 26 D2
Tolworth KT6 ... 214 D6
Oakleigh Cl N20 ... 14 D1
Oakleigh Cres N20 ... 14 C1
Oakleigh Ct HA8 ... 27 A1
East Barnet EN4 ... 14 C5
Penge SE20 ... 184 B3
Southall UB1 ... 107 B5
Surbiton KT6 ... 214 B6
Oakleigh Gdns BR6 ... 227 C4
N20 ... 14 B3
Edgware HA8 ... 26 B5
Oakleigh Lo IG3 ... 80 A5
Oakleigh Mews N20 ... 14 A2
Oakleigh Park Ave BR7 ... 188 C2
Oakleigh Park Sta EN4 . 14 C4
Oakleigh Pk N N20 ... 14 B3
Oakleigh Pk S N20 ... 14 C3
Oakleigh Rd
Hillingdon UB10 ... 61 A1
Pinner HA5 ... 23 B4
Oakleigh Rd N N20 ... 14 C2
Oakleigh Rd S N11 ... 31 A6
Oakleigh Sch N20 ... 14 D1
Oakleigh Way
Mitcham CR4 ... 181 B2
1 Tolworth KT6 ... 198 D1
Oakley Ave Barking IG11 79 D1
Ealing W5 ... 110 C6
Wallington CR0 ... 220 A4
Oakley Cl 7 E6 ... 100 A1
Chingford E4 ... 20 A1
Ealing W7 ... 108 C6
Hounslow TW7 ... 130 B4
Oakley Cres EC1 ... 234 D3
Oakley Ct CR4 ... 203 A2
Oakley Dr DA15 ... 167 B3
SE13 ... 164 B5
Keston Mark BR2 ... 226 A5
Oakley Gdns N8 ... 50 B4
SW3 ... 136 C6 267 B6
Oakley Ho SW1 ... 257 D4
Ealing W5 ... 110 C6
Oakley Pk DA5,DA15 ... 168 C4
Oakley Pl SE1 . 117 D1 263 C1
Oakley Rd N1 ... 73 B1
Croydon SE25 ... 206 B4
Harrow HA1 ... 42 C3
Keston Mark BR2 ... 226 A6
Oakley Sq NW1 . 93 C5 232 B4
Oakley St SW3 136 C6 267 A6
Oakley Wlk W6 ... 134 D6
Oak Lo
4 Ashford TW16 ... 171 D3
Southgate N21 ... 16 B5
Wanstead E11 ... 55 A2
Oak Lodge Cl HA7 ... 25 C5
Oak Lodge Dr BR4 ... 207 D2
Oak Lodge Sch N2 ... 48 A5
Balham SW12 ... 159 A4
Oaklodge Way NW7 ... 27 D4
Oakman Ho 29 SW19 . 156 D3
Oakmead Ave BR2 ... 209 A3
Oakmead Ct HA7 ... 25 C6
Oakmeade HA5 ... 23 C4
Oakmead Gdns HA8 ... 27 B6
Oakmead Pl CR4 ... 180 C2
Oakmead Rd
Balham SW12 ... 159 B3
Wallington CR0 ... 203 D3
Oakmere Rd SE2 ... 146 A6
Oakmont Pl 6 BR6 ... 211 B1
Oak Park Gdns SW19 . 156 D3
Oak Park Mews N16 ... 73 D5
Oak Rd Ealing W5 ... 109 D6
Kingston KT3 ... 177 B1
Oakridge Dr N2 ... 48 B6
Oakridge La BR1 ... 186 B5
Oakridge Rd BR1 ... 186 C6
Oak Rise IG9 ... 21 D1
Oak Row CR4 ... 181 C1
Oaks Ave
Feltham TW13 ... 151 A2
North Cheam KT4 ... 216 B4
West Norwood SE19 ... 183 C5
Oaksford Ave SE26 ... 162 B1
Oaks Gr E4 ... 20 C2
Oakshade Rd BR1 ... 186 B6
Oakshaw Rd SW18 ... 157 D4
Oakshott Ct NW1 ... 232 C3
Oaks La Ilford IG2 ... 57 C5
South Croydon CR0 ... 222 C5
Oaks Park High Sch IG2 ... 57 C4
Oaks Rd CR0 ... 222 C4
Oaks Sh Ctr The W3 ... 111 A5
Oaks The BR2 ... 210 C3
N12 ... 29 D6
NW10 ... 68 B1
NW6 ... 68 D1
SE18 ... 123 A1
Chingford IG8 ... 36 C3
Enfield EN2 ... 4 D2
Hayes UB4 ... 83 A5
Long Ditton KT6 ... 213 C5
Ruislip HA4 ... 39 C2
Wimbledon SW19 ... 179 A4
Oaks Way Surbiton KT6 197 D1
Wallington SM5 ... 218 D1
Oakthorpe Ct N13 ... 33 A5
Oakthorpe Prim Sch N13 ... 33 A5
Oakthorpe Rd N13 ... 32 C5
Oak Tree Ave N2 ... 47 D6
Oaktree Ave N13 ... 16 D1
Oak Tree Cl Ealing W5 ... 87 C1
Stanmore HA7 ... 25 C3
Oak Tree Ct 6 SW4 ... 160 A6
Acton W3 ... 110 D6
Elstree WD6 ... 9 D5
Oak Tree Dell NW9 ... 45 B4
Oak Tree Dr N20 ... 13 D3
Oak Tree Gdns BR1 ... 187 B5
Oaktree Gr IG1 ... 79 B3
Oak Tree Ho W9 ... 91 D3
Oak Tree Rd NW8 ... 92 C4 230 A1
Oaktree Sch EN4 ... 15 A5
Oakview Gdns N2 ... 48 B5
Oakview Gr CR0 ... 207 A1
Oakview Lo NW11 ... 47 B2
Oakview Rd SE6 ... 185 D5
Oak Village NW5 ... 71 A4
Oak Way N14 ... 15 B4
W3 ... 111 C5
Oakway
Beckenham BR2 ... 186 B1
West Barnes SW20 ... 200 C5
Oak Way Croydon CR0 . 206 D3
East Bedfont TW14 ... 149 C3
Oakway Cl DA5 ... 169 A5
Oakways SE9 ... 166 D5
Oakwell Ho 24 SW8 ... 137 D3
Oak Wlk CR4 ... 203 A1
Oakwood Ave N14 ... 15 D4
Beckenham BR2,BR3 ... 186 A1
Bromley BR2 ... 209 B6
Mitcham CR4 ... 180 B1
Southall UB1 ... 107 C6
Oakwood Cl BR7 ... 188 C4
Southgate N14 ... 15 C5
Oakwood Cres
Southgate N21 ... 16 B5
Wembley UB6 ... 65 B2
Oakwood Ct 1 E6 ... 100 A6
W14 ... 113 B3 254 C6
Beckenham BR3 ... 186 A1
6 Chingford E4 ... 20 C4
Oakwood Dr HA8 ... 27 A4
Oakwood Dr *continued*
West Norwood SE19 ... 183 C4
Oakwood Gdns
Ilford IG3 ... 79 D6
Orpington BR6 ... 227 A6
Sutton SM1 ... 217 C6
Oakwood La W14 ... 113 B3 254 C6
Oakwood Park Rd N14 . 16 A5
Oakwood Pl CR0 ... 204 C3
Oakwood Rd NW11 ... 47 D4
Orpington BR6 ... 227 A6
Pinner HA5 ... 22 B1
Thornton Heath CR0 ... 204 C3
Wimbledon SW20 ... 178 A2
Oakwood Sta N14 ... 15 C6
Oakwood View N14 ... 15 D4
Oakworth Rd W10 ... 90 D2
Oarsman Pl KT8 ... 196 C5
Oasis The 4 BR1 ... 187 C1
Oast Ct 8 E14 ... 119 B6
Oast Lo W4 ... 133 C5
Oates Cl BR2 ... 208 B6
Oatfield Ho 1 N15 ... 51 C3
Oatfield Rd BR6 ... 211 D1
Oat La EC2 ... 95 A1 242 B2
Oatland Rise E17 ... 35 A1
Oatlands Ct 3 SW19 . 156 D3
Oatlands Dr KT13 ... 193 C1
Oatlands Rd EN3 ... 6 C4
Oatwell Ho SW3 ... 257 B3
Oban Cl E13 ... 99 C3
Oban Ho Barking IG11 . 101 B5
South Bromley E14 ... 98 B1
Oban Rd E13 ... 99 C4
South Norwood SE25 ... 205 B5
Oban St E14 ... 98 B1
Oberon Ho 5 N1 ... 95 C5
Oberon Way TW17 ... 192 A6
Oberstein Rd 15 SW11 136 B1
Oborne Cl SE24 ... 160 D6
O'Brian Ho 10 E1 ... 96 D4
Observatory Gdns W8 245 B2
Observatory Mews E14 ... 120 B2
Observatory Rd SW14 133 A1
Occupation La SE18 ... 144 D4
W5 ... 109 D2
Occupation Rd SE17 ... 117 A1 262 A2
W13 ... 109 B4
Ocean St E1 ... 96 D2
Ocean Wharf E14 ... 119 C4
Ockbrook 3 E1 ... 96 C2
Ockendon Rd N1 ... 73 B2
Ockham Dr BR5 ... 190 A3
Ockley Ct SM1 ... 218 A4
Ockley Ho 8 KT2 ... 176 D4
Ockley Rd
Streatham SW16 ... 160 A1
Thornton Heath CR0 ... 204 B2
Octagon Arc EC2 ... 243 A3
Octagon The NW3 ... 69 C4
Octavia Cl CR4 ... 202 C4
Octavia Ho W10 ... 91 A3
Octavia Rd TW7 ... 130 D2
Octavia St SW11 ... 136 C4 267 B1
Octavia Way 12 SE28 ... 124 B6
Octavius St SE8 ... 141 C5
October Ct BR2 ... 208 D6
October Pl NW4 ... 46 D6
Odard Rd KT8 ... 195 C5
Odell Cl IG11 ... 79 D1
Odeon Ct 1 E16 ... 99 A2
NW10 ... 89 C6
Odeon Par SE9 ... 144 A1
Wembley UB6 ... 65 B2
Odessa Inf Sch E7 ... 77 A3
Odessa Rd E7 ... 76 D4
NW10 ... 90 A5
Odessa St SE16 ... 119 B3
Odette Ct N20 ... 14 A1
Odette Duval Ho 24 E1 . 96 C2
Odette Ho 6 SE27 ... 183 B6
Odger St SW11 ... 136 D3
Odhams Wlk WC2 ... 240 B1
Odin Ho 6 SE5 ... 139 A3
O'Donnell Ct WC1 ... 240 B6
O'Driscoll Ho W12 ... 90 B1
Odyssey Bsns Pk HA4 ... 62 B3
Offa's Mead E9 ... 75 A4
Offenbach Ho 12 E2 ... 96 D5
Offenham Rd BR7,SE9 . 188 B6
Offers Ct KT1 ... 198 B6
Offerton Rd SW4 ... 137 C2
Offham Ho SE17 ... 263 A3
Offham Slope N12 ... 29 B5
Offley Ho 10 E9 ... 74 D2
Offley Pl TW7 ... 130 B3
Offley Rd SW9 ... 138 C5
Offord Cl N17 ... 34 A4
Offord Rd N1 ... 72 B1
Offord St N1 ... 72 B1
Ogden Ho TW13 ... 173 A6
Ogilby St SE18 ... 122 B2
Ogilvie Ho 11 E1 ... 96 D1
Oglander Rd SE15 ... 139 D2
Ogle St W1 ... 93 C2 239 A4

Oglethorpe Rd RM10 ... 81 C5
O'Gorman Ho SW10 ... 266 B4
O'Grady Ho 17 E17 ... 53 D6
Ohio Rd E13 ... 98 D3
Oil Mill La W6 ... 112 A1
Okeburn Rd SW17 ... 181 A5
Okehampton Cl N12 ... 30 B5
Okehampton Cres
DA16 ... 146 C4
Okehampton Rd NW10 . 90 D6
Okeover Manor SW4 .. 137 B1
Olaf Palme Ho TW13 .. 150 B1
Olaf St W11 ... 112 D6
Old Bailey EC4 . 94 D1 241 D1
Old Barn Cl SM2 ... 217 A1
Old Barrack Yd SW1 .. 248 A1
Old Bellgate Wharf
E14 ... 119 C3
Oldberry Rd HA8 ... 27 B4
Old Bethnal Green Rd
E2 ... 96 B4
Old Bexley Bsns Pk
DA5 ... 169 D4
Old Bexley CE Prim Sch
DA5 ... 169 B3
Old Bldgs WC2 ... 241 A2
Old Bond St
W1 ... 115 C6 249 A5
Oldborough Rd HA0 ... 65 C5
Old Borrowfield 7 E15 98 C6
Old Brewery Mews
NW3 ... 70 B4
Old Bridge Cl UB5 ... 85 C5
Old Bridge St KT1 ... 175 D1
Old Broad St
EC2 ... 95 B1 242 D2
Old Bromley Rd BR1 .. 186 B5
Old Brompton Rd
SW5,SW7 ... 114 A1 256 B3
Old Burlington St
W1 ... 115 C6 249 A5
Oldbury Ct E9 ... 75 A3
Oldbury Pl W1 . 93 A2 238 B4
Oldbury Rd EN1 ... 6 A3
Old Castle St
E1 ... 95 D1 243 D2
Old Cavendish St W1 . 238 C1
Old Change Ct EC4 .. 242 A1
Old Chapel Pl 2 N10 .. 49 B6
Old Charlton Rd TW17 193 A4
Old Chiswick Yd W4 .. 133 C6
Old Church Ct N11 ... 31 B5
Old Church La NW9 ... 67 B6
Ealing UB6 ... 87 A4
Stanmore HA7 ... 25 C4
Old Church Path KT10 212 A4
Old Church Rd E1 ... 96 D1
Chingford E4 ... 19 C1
Old Church St SW3 .. 256 D1
Old Claygate La KT10 . 213 A3
Old Clem Sq 12 SE18 . 144 C6
Old Compton St
W1 ... 93 D1 239 C1
Old Cote Dr TW5 ... 129 C6
Old County Hall SE1 .. 250 C2
Old Court Ho W8 ... 245 C1
Old Court (Mus & Liby)
HA0 ... 65 C3
Old Court Pl
W8 ... 113 D4 245 C1
Old Covent Garden
WC2 ... 250 B6
Old Ctyd The BR1 ... 187 B2
Old Dairy Mews
4 NW5 ... 71 B2
5 Balham SW12 ... 159 A3
Old Deer Park Gdns
TW9 ... 132 A2
Old Devonshire Rd
SW12 ... 159 B4
Old Dock Cl TW9 ... 132 C6
Old Dover Rd SE3 ... 143 B5
Oldegate Ho 1 E6 ... 99 D6
Old Farm Ave N14 ... 15 C4
Sidcup DA15 ... 167 C2
Old Farm Cl TW4 ... 129 B1
Old Farm Ct UB2 ... 107 D2
Old Farm Rd N2 ... 30 B2
Hampton TW12 ... 173 C4
Old Farm Rd E DA15 .. 168 A2
Old Farm Rd W DA15 . 167 D2
Oldfield Cl BR1 ... 210 B5
Stanmore HA7 ... 25 A5
Oldfield Farm Gdns
UB6 ... 86 B6
Oldfield Gr SE16 ... 118 D2
Oldfield Ho 14 W4 ... 111 C1
Streatham SW16 ... 181 B6
Oldfield House Sch
TW12 ... 173 B2
Oldfield Mews N6 ... 49 C2
Oldfield Prim Sch UB6 . 86 B5
Oldfield Rd BR1 ... 210 B5
DA7 ... 147 A3
N16 ... 73 C5
NW10 ... 67 D1
W3,W12 ... 111 D4
Hampton TW12 ... 173 B2
Wimbledon SW19 ... 179 A4
Oldfields Cir UB5 ... 64 A2
Oldfields Rd SM1,SM3 . 217 C6
Oldfields Trad Est
SM1 ... 217 C5
Old Fish St Hill EC4 .. 252 A6
Old Fleet La EC4 ... 241 C2
Old Fold Cl EN5 ... 1 B4
Old Fold La EN5 ... 1 B4
Old Ford Ho CR0 ... 220 A5
Old Ford Prim Sch E3 .. 97 B5
Old Ford Rd E2,E3 ... 96 D5
Old Ford Trad Ctr E3 ... 97 C6
Old Forge Cl HA7 ... 25 A6
Old Forge Cres TW17 . 192 D3
Old Forge Mews W12 . 112 B4
Old Forge Rd EN1 ... 5 D5
Old Forge Way DA14 .. 190 B6
Old Gloucester St
WC1 ... 94 A2 240 B4
Old Hall Cl HA5 ... 23 A2
Old Hall Dr HA5 ... 23 A2
Oldham Ho 10 SE21 .. 183 C6
Oldham Terr W3 ... 111 A5
Old Hatch Manor HA4 . 40 A2
Old Hill Chislehurst BR7 188 C2
Orpington BR6 ... 227 C2
Oldhill St N16 ... 52 A1
Old Homesdale Rd
BR2 ... 209 C5
Old Hospital Cl SW12,
SW17 ... 158 D3
Old House Cl SW19 .. 179 A5
Old House Gdns 9
TW1 ... 153 C5
Old Howlett's La HA4 .. 39 B3
Olding Ho 6 SW12 .. 159 C4
Old Jamaica Bsns Est 23
SE16 ... 118 A3
Old Jamaica Rd SE16 . 118 A3
Old James St SE15 ... 140 B2
Old Jewry EC2 . 95 B1 242 C1
Old Kenton La NW9 ... 44 D4
Old Kent Rd
SE1 ... 117 C1 263 B2
SE1,SE15 ... 140 B6
Old Kingston Rd KT4 . 215 A5
Old Laundry The 14
SW18 ... 136 B1
Old Lodge Pl 7 TW1 . 153 B5
Old Lodge Way HA7 ... 25 A5
Old Maidstone Rd
BR8,DA14 ... 191 B3
Old Malden La KT4 .. 215 C6
Oldman Ct SE12 ... 165 B2
Old Manor Dr TW7 ... 152 A5
Old Manor Rd UB2 ... 106 D2
Old Manor Way BR7,
SE9 ... 188 B5
Old Manor Yd SW5 ... 255 C3
Old Market Sq 11 E2 ... 95 D4
Old Marylebone Rd
NW1 ... 92 C2 237 B3
Oldmead Ho 8 RM10 ... 81 D2
Old Mill Ct E18 ... 55 C6
Old Mill Rd SE18 ... 145 B6
Old Mitre Ct EC4 ... 241 B1
Old Montague St E1 ... 96 A2
Old Nichol St
E2 ... 95 D3 243 C6
Old North St WC1 ... 240 C4
Old Nursery Pl TW15 . 170 D5
Old Oak Common La
NW10 ... 89 C3
Old Oak La NW10 ... 89 D4
Old Oak Prim Sch W12 89 D1
Old Oak Rd W3 ... 111 D6
Old Orch TW16 ... 172 C1
Old Orchard Cl
Hadley Wood EN4 ... 2 B5
Hillingdon UB8 ... 82 C1
Old Orch The NW3 ... 70 D4
Old Palace La TW9 ... 153 C6
Old Palace Prim Sch
E3 ... 97 D4
Old Palace Rd CR0 ... 221 A5
Old Palace Sch of John
Whitgift CR9 ... 220 D5
Old Palace Terr 8
TW9 ... 153 D6
Old Palace Yd 2 TW9 153 D6
Old Paradise St
SE11 ... 116 B2 260 C4
Old Park Ave SW12 .. 159 A5
Enfield EN2 ... 5 A1
Old Park Gr EN2 ... 5 A1
Old Park Ho N13 ... 32 B6
Old Park La
W1 ... 115 B5 248 C3
Old Park Mews TW5 .. 129 B5
Old Park Rd SE2 ... 124 A1
Enfield EN2 ... 4 D2
Palmers Green N13 ... 32 B6
Old Park Rd S EN2 ... 4 D1
Old Park Ridings N21 .. 17 A6
Old Park View EN2 ... 4 D2
Old Perry St BR7 ... 189 C3
Old Pound Cl TW7 ... 131 A4
Old Priory UB9 ... 38 D2
Old Pye St SW1 ... 259 C6
Old Pye Street Est
SW1 ... 259 C5
Old Quebec St W1 ... 237 D1
Old Queen St
SW1 ... 115 D4 249 D1
Old Rd SE13 ... 142 C1
Enfield EN3 ... 6 C4
Old Rectory Gdns HA8 . 26 C4
Old Redding HA3 ... 24 A6
Oldridge Rd SW12 ... 159 B4
Old Royal Free Pl N1 . 234 B5
Old Royal Free Sq
N1 ... 94 C6 234 B5
Old Royal Observatory
Greenwich (National
Maritime Mus Annexe)★
SE10 ... 142 B5
Old Ruislip Rd UB5 ... 84 C5
Old School Cl
3 Beckenham BR3 ... 185 A1
Merton SW19 ... 179 C1
Old School Cres E7 ... 77 A2
Old School Ho The EN2 . 4 D2
Old School Pl CR0 ... 220 C4
Old School Rd UB8 ... 82 B3
Old School Sq 10 E14 .. 97 C1
Thames Ditton KT7 ... 196 D3
Old School The WC1 .. 240 C4
Old Seacoal La EC4 .. 241 C1
Old South Lambeth Rd
SW8 ... 138 A5 270 B4
Old Spitalfields Mkt
E1 ... 95 D2 243 D2
Old Sq WC2 ... 241 A2
Old St E13 ... 99 B5
EC1 ... 95 B3 242 B6
Old Stable Mews N5 ... 73 A5
Old St Andrews Mans
NW9 ... 67 B6
Old Station Rd UB3 ... 105 D3
Oldstead Rd BR1 ... 186 B6
Old Street Sta
EC1 ... 95 B3 242 D6
Old Sun Wharf E14 ... 119 A6
Old Swan Wharf
SW11 ... 266 D2
Old Swan Yd SM5 ... 218 D4
Old Theatre Ct SE1 ... 252 B4
Old Town SW4 ... 137 C2
Croydon CR0 ... 220 D5
Old Tramyard SE18 ... 123 C2
Old Woolwich Rd
SE10 ... 120 B1
Old York Rd SW18 ... 157 D6
Oleander Cl BR6 ... 227 B3
O'Leary Sq E1 ... 96 C2
Olga Prim Sch E3 ... 97 A5
Olga St 13 E3 ... 97 A5
Olinda Rd N16 ... 51 D3
Oliphant St W10 ... 91 A4
Olive Blythe Ho 14 W10 91 A3
Oliver Ave SE25 ... 205 D6
Oliver Bsns Pk NW10 .. 89 A5
Oliver Cl W4 ... 132 D6
Oliver Ct SE18 ... 123 A2
Isleworth TW7 ... 130 D2
Olive Rd E13 ... 99 C4
NW2 ... 68 C4
W5 ... 109 D3
3 Merton SW19 ... 180 A3
Oliver Gdns E6 ... 100 A2
Oliver Goldsmith Prim Sch
NW9 ... 45 B4
Oliver Goldsmith Prim Schs
SE5 ... 139 D4
Oliver Gr SE25 ... 205 D5
Oliver Ho 19 SE16 ... 118 A4
SW8 ... 270 A4
W11 ... 244 B5
Oliver Mews SE15 ... 140 A3
Oliver Rd E10 ... 75 D5
E17 ... 54 A4
Kingston KT3 ... 177 A1
Sutton SM1 ... 218 B3
Oliver's Yd EC1 ... 242 D6
Olive Tree Ho N4 ... 50 C3
7 SE15 ... 140 C6
Olivette St 1 SW15 ... 134 D1
Olive Waite Ho NW6 ... 69 D1
Ollard's Gr IG10 ... 21 D6
Ollerton Gn E3 ... 97 B6
Ollerton Rd N11 ... 31 D5
Olley Cl SM6 ... 220 A2
Ollgar Cl W12 ... 111 D5
Olliffe St E14 ... 120 A3
Olmar St SE1 ... 140 A6
Olmar Wharf SE1 ... 140 A6
Olney Ho NW8 ... 237 B6
Olney Rd SE17 ... 139 A6
Olron Cres DA6 ... 169 A6
Olven Rd SE18 ... 145 A6
Olveston Wlk SM5 ... 202 B3
Olwen Mews HA5 ... 22 D1
Olyffe Ave DA16 ... 146 A3
Olyffe Dr BR3 ... 186 A2
Olympia Ex Ctr★
W14 ... 112 D3 254 A6
Olympian Ct 1 E14 ... 119 C2
Olympia Way
W14 ... 113 A3 254 B5
Olympia Yd W2 ... 245 D5
Olympic Ho W10 ... 90 C1
Olympic Ret Pk HA9 ... 66 D4
Olympic Way
Greenford UB6 ... 85 D6
Wembley HA9 ... 66 C4
Olympus Sq E5 ... 74 A5
Oman Ave NW2 ... 68 C4
Oman Ct NW4 ... 68 B4
Ombersley Ho N4 ... 51 A2
Omeara St SE1 ... 252 B3
Omega Cl E14 ... 119 D3
Omega Ho SW10 ... 266 B4
Omega Pl N1 ... 233 B3
Omega St SE14 ... 141 C4
Ommaney Rd SE14 ... 141 A4
Omnibus Way E17 ... 35 C1
Ondine Rd SE15 ... 139 D1
Onedin Point 17 E1 ... 118 A6
Onega Gate SE16 ... 119 A3
O'Neill Ho NW8 ... 229 D3
O'Neill Path 11 SE18 .. 144 C6
One Tree Cl SE23 ... 162 C5
Ongar Cl RM6 ... 58 C4
Ongar Ho 15 N1 ... 73 B2
Ongar Rd SW6 135 C6 265 B6
Onra Rd E17 ... 53 C2
Onslow Ave TW10 ... 154 A6
Onslow Avenue Mans 10
TW10 ... 154 A6
Onslow Cl Chingford E4 . 20 B2
Thames Ditton KT7 ... 196 C1
Onslow Cres BR7 ... 188 D2
Onslow Ct SW10 ... 256 B1
Onslow Dr DA14 ... 168 D2
Onslow Gdns N10 ... 49 B4
SW7 ... 114 B1 256 C2
Southgate N21 ... 16 C6
Thames Ditton KT7 ... 196 C1
Wallington SM6 ... 219 C1
Wanstead E18 ... 55 C6
Onslow Ho 1 KT2 ... 176 B2
Onslow Lo 28 SW2 ... 160 C4
Onslow Mews E SW7 . 256 C3
Onslow Mews W SW7 256 C3
Onslow Par N14 ... 15 B3
Onslow Rd
Richmond TW10 ... 154 A5
Thornton Heath CR0 ... 204 C1
West Barnes KT3 ... 200 A5
Onslow Sq
SW7 ... 114 B2 256 D3
Onslow St EC1 ... 241 B5
Onslow Way KT7 ... 196 C1
Ontario St SE1 116 D3 261 D6
Ontario Way E14 ... 119 C6
Onyx Ho KT4 ... 199 B1
Opal Cl E16 ... 99 D1
Opal Ho KT4 ... 199 B1
Opal Mews 2 IG1 ... 78 D6
Opal St SE11 .. 116 D1 261 C2
Open Air Theatre, Regent's
Park NW1 ... 231 A1
Openshaw Rd SE2 ... 124 B2
Openview SW17,SW18 . 158 B2
Operating Theatre Mus &
Herb Garret★
SE1 ... 117 B5 252 D3
Ophelia Gdns NW2 ... 69 A5
Ophir Terr SE15 ... 140 A4
Opie Ho NW8 ... 230 B4
Opossum Way TW4 ... 128 C2
Oppenheim Rd SE13 .. 142 A3
Oppidans Rd NW3 ... 70 D1
Orange Hill Rd HA8 ... 27 A3
Orange Pl SE16 ... 118 C3
Orangery La SE9 ... 166 B6
Orangery The TW10 ... 153 C2
Orange St
WC2 ... 115 D6 249 D5
Orange Yd WC2 ... 239 D1
Oratory La SW3 ... 256 D2
Oratory RC Prim Sch
SW3 ... 114 C1 257 A2
Oratory The★
SW7 ... 114 C3 257 A5
Orbain Rd
SW6 ... 135 A5 264 B3
Orbel St SW11 136 C4 267 A1
Orb St SE17 ... 117 B2 262 C3
Orchard Ave N14 ... 15 C4
N20 ... 14 B2
N3 ... 47 C6
Ashford TW15 ... 171 A4
Carshalton CR4 ... 203 A1
Croydon CR0 ... 207 A1
Erith DA17 ... 147 B6
Hatton TW14 ... 149 B6
Heston TW5 ... 129 A5
Hinchley Wood KT7 ... 213 A6
Kingston KT3 ... 199 C6
Southall UB1 ... 107 B5
Orchard Bsns Ctr
SE26 ... 185 B5
Orchard Cl DA7 ... 147 A4
N1 ... 73 A1
NW2 ... 68 A5
Orchard Cl *continued*
SE23 ... 162 C5
W10 ... 91 A2
Ashford TW15 ... 171 A4
Bushey WD23 ... 8 B3
Chingford E4 ... 35 C6
Edgware HA8 ... 26 A4
Northolt UB5 ... 64 A2
Ruislip HA4 ... 39 A2
Thames Ditton KT7 ... 197 B2
Walton-on-T KT12 ... 194 B2
Wanstead E11 ... 55 B5
Wembley HA0 ... 88 A6
West Barnes SW20 ... 200 C5
West Ewell KT19 ... 214 D2
Orchard Cotts UB3 ... 105 C4
Orchard Cres HA8 ... 27 A5
Enfield EN1 ... 5 D4
Orchard Ct E10 ... 53 D1
W1 ... 238 A2
Barnes SW13 ... 133 D2
Croydon BR3 ... 207 C1
Edgware HA8 ... 26 B5
Hounslow TW7 ... 130 B5
New Malden KT4 ... 200 A1
Southgate N14 ... 15 C5
Wallington SM6 ... 219 B3
Walton-on-T KT12 ... 193 D1
Wood Green N22 ... 32 A3
Orchard Dr SE3 ... 142 C3
Edgware HA8 ... 26 B5
Upper Halliford TW17 .. 193 C6
Orchard Gate NW9 ... 45 C5
Thames Ditton KT10 ... 196 B1
Wembley UB6 ... 65 B2
Orchard Gdns
Chessington KT9 ... 214 A4
Sutton SM1 ... 217 C3
Orchard Gn BR6 ... 227 C6
Orchard Gr BR6 ... 211 D1
BR6 ... 227 D6
Croydon CR0 ... 207 A2
Edgware HA8 ... 26 D2
Harrow HA3 ... 44 B4
Penge SE20 ... 184 A3
Orchard Hill SE13 ... 141 D4
Orchard Ho 11 SE16 ... 118 C3
SE5 ... 139 A4
W12 ... 112 A5
Orchard Jun & Inf Sch The
TW3 ... 151 C6
Orchard La
Thames Ditton KT8 ... 196 B3
Wimbledon SW20 ... 178 B2
Woodford IG8 ... 37 C6
Orchardleigh Ave EN3 ... 6 C3
Orchard Lo N12 ... 14 A1
Orchard Mead Ho
NW11 ... 69 C6
Orchardmede N21 ... 17 B5
Orchard Mews N1 ... 73 B1
Orchard Pl E14 ... 120 C6
Tottenham N17 ... 33 D3
Orchard Prim Sch E9 .. 74 C1
Orchard Rd BR1 ... 187 C2
BR6 ... 226 D3
DA16 ... 146 B2
N6 ... 49 B2
Barnet EN5 ... 1 B1
Belvedere DA17 ... 125 C2
Brentford TW8 ... 131 C6
Carshalton CR4 ... 203 A1
Chessington KT9 ... 214 A4
Dagenham RM10 ... 103 C6
Enfield EN3 ... 18 C6
Feltham TW14 ... 150 A3
Hampton TW12 ... 173 B3
Hayes UB3 ... 106 A6
Hounslow TW4 ... 151 C6
Isleworth TW1 ... 153 B6
Kingston KT1 ... 176 A1
Richmond TW9 ... 132 C2
Sidcup DA14 ... 189 C6
Sunbury TW16 ... 172 B3
Sutton SM1 ... 217 C4
Orchard Rise
Croydon CR0 ... 207 B1
Kingston KT2 ... 177 A2
Mortlake TW10 ... 132 D1
Pinner HA5 ... 39 D6
Orchard Rise E DA15 . 167 D6
Orchard Rise W DA15 . 167 C6
Orchard School Sports Ctr
SE20 ... 184 A2
Orchardson Ho NW8 . 236 D5
Orchardson St
NW8 ... 92 B3 236 D5
Orchard Sq W14 ... 254 C1
Orchard St E17 ... 53 A5
W1 ... 238 A1
Orchard Terr EN1 ... 18 A5
Orchard The N20 ... 13 D3
NW11 ... 47 C4
SE3 ... 142 B3
W4 ... 111 B2
Ealing W5 ... 87 D2
East Barnet N14 ... 15 B6
Enfield N21 ... 17 B5
Ewell KT17 ... 215 D1
Orchard The *continued*
Hounslow TW3 ... 130 A3
Orchard Way
Ashford TW15 ... 148 B2
Croydon BR3,CR0 ... 207 A3
Enfield EN1 ... 5 C2
Esher KT10 ... 212 A2
Sutton SM1 ... 218 B4
Orchard Way Prim Sch
CR0 ... 207 A2
Orchid Cl 1 E6 ... 100 A2
Chessington KT9 ... 213 C1
Southall UB1 ... 85 A1
Orchid Ct HA9 ... 66 A6
Orchid Grange N14 ... 15 C4
Orchid Lo N14 ... 15 C4
Orchid Rd N14 ... 15 C4
Orchid St W12 ... 112 A6
Orde 6 NW9 ... 27 D2
Orde Hall St
WC1 ... 94 B2 240 C4
Orde Ho 10 N16 ... 73 B4
Ordell Ct 30 E3 ... 97 B5
Ordell Rd E3 ... 97 B5
Ordnance Cl TW13 ... 150 A2
Ordnance Cres SE10 .. 120 C4
Ordnance Hill
NW8 ... 92 B6 229 D5
Ordnance Mews NW8 229 D4
Ordnance Rd E16 ... 98 D2
SE18 ... 144 C6
Enfield EN3 ... 7 B6
Oregano Cl UB7 ... 104 B6
Oregano Dr E14 ... 98 B1
Oregon Ave E12 ... 78 B4
Oregon Cl KT3 ... 199 A5
Oregon Sq BR6 ... 211 B1
Orestes Ct 8 E18 ... 55 A6
Orestes Mews 1 NW6 . 69 C3
Orford Ct Stanmore HA7 . 25 C4
Wallington SM6 ... 219 C3
West Norwood SE27 ... 160 D2
Orford Gdns TW1 ... 152 D2
Orford Rd E17 ... 53 D4
Catford SE6 ... 163 D1
Wanstead E18 ... 55 B6
Organ Crossroads
KT17 ... 216 A1
Oriana Ho 3 E14 ... 119 B6
Oriel Cl CR4 ... 203 D6
Oriel Ct NW3 ... 70 A4
6 Croydon CR0 ... 205 B1
Oriel Dr SW13 ... 134 C6
Oriel Gdns IG5 ... 56 B6
Oriel Jun & Inf Sch
TW13 ... 151 A1
Oriel Rd E9 ... 74 D2
E9 ... 75 A2
Oriel Way UB5 ... 63 D1
Oriental City NW9 ... 45 B6
Oriental Rd E16 ... 121 D5
Orient Ind Pk E10 ... 75 C6
Orient St SE11 116 D2 261 C4
Orient Way E5 ... 74 D5
Oriole Way SE28 ... 124 B6
Orion Bsns Ctr SE14 .. 118 D1
Orion Ctr The CR0 ... 220 A6
Orion Ho 20 E1 ... 96 B3
Orion Prim Sch The
NW9 ... 27 D2
Orion Rd N11 ... 31 A4
Orion Way HA6 ... 22 A6
Orissa Rd SE18 ... 123 C1
Orkney Ho N1 ... 233 C6
Orkney St SW11 ... 137 A3
Orlando Rd SW4 ... 137 C2
Orleans Cl KT10 ... 212 B6
Orleans Ct 9 TW1 ... 153 B4
Orleans Inf Sch TW1 .. 153 B4
Orleans Park Sec Sch
TW1 ... 153 B4
Orleans Rd
South Norwood SE19 .. 183 B4
Twickenham TW1 ... 153 C4
Orleston Mews N7 ... 72 C2
Orleston Rd N7 ... 72 C2
Orley Farm Rd HA1 ... 64 C5
Orley Farm Sch HA1 ... 64 B5
Orlop St SE10 ... 120 C1
Ormanton Rd SE26 ... 184 A6
Orme Ct W2 .. 113 D6 245 C5
Orme Ct Mews W2 ... 245 D5
Orme Ho 8 E8 ... 95 D6
Orme La W2 .. 113 D6 245 C5
Ormeley Rd SW12 ... 159 B3
Orme Rd
Kingston KT1,KT3 ... 176 D1
Sutton SM1 ... 217 D2
Ormerod Gdns CR4 ... 181 A2
Ormesby Cl SE28 ... 124 D6
Ormesby Way HA3 ... 44 B4
Orme Sq W2 ... 245 C5
Ormiston Gr W12 ... 112 B5
Ormiston Rd SE10 ... 121 A1
Ormond Ave
Hampton TW12 ... 173 D2

Ormond Ave *continued*
22 Richmond TW10 153 D6
Ormond Cl WC1 240 B4
Ormond Cres TW12 173 D2
Ormond Dr TW12 173 D3
Ormonde Ave BR6 227 A6
Ormonde Ct SW15 134 C1
Ormonde Gate
SW3 114 D1 257 D1
Ormonde Pl SW1 258 B3
Ormonde Rd SW14 133 A2
Ormonde Rise IG9 21 C3
Ormonde Terr
NW8 92 D6 230 C5
Ormond Ho 7 N16 73 B6
Ormond Mews WC1 240 B5
Ormond Rd N4,N19 50 A1
Richmond TW10 153 D6
Ormond Yd SW1 249 B4
Ormrod Ct W11 91 B1
Ormsby SM2 217 D1
Ormsby Gdns UB6 86 A5
Ormsby Lo 7 W4 111 C3
Ormsby Pl N16 73 D5
Ormsby Point 6 SE18 122 D2
Ormsby St E2 95 D5
Ormside St SE15 140 C6
Ormskirk Rd WD19 22 D5
Ornan Rd NW3 70 C3
Oronsay Rd 18 N1 73 A2
Orpheus Ho 25 N19 49 D2
Orpheus St SE5 139 B4
Orpington Gdns N18 17 C1
Orpington Hospl BR6 227 D4
Orpington Mans N21 16 C3
Orpington Rd
Southgate N21 16 D3
St Paul's Cray BR7 211 C6
Orpington Sta BR6 227 C6
Orpwood Cl TW12 173 B4
Orsett Mews
W2 91 D1 236 A2
Orsett St SE11 116 B1 260 D2
Orsett Terr W2 92 A1 236 A2
Woodford IG8 37 C3
Orsman Rd N1 95 C6
Orton St E1 118 A5
Orville Rd SW11 136 B3
Orwell Cl UB3 105 C6
Orwell Ct E8 96 A6
N5 73 A4
Orwell Ho W12 112 A6
Orwell Lo 2 E18 55 A5
Orwell Rd E13 99 C6
Osbaldeston Rd N16 52 A1
Osberton Rd SE12 165 A6
Osbert St SW1 259 C3
Osborn Cl E8 96 A6
Osborne Ave TW19 148 B3
Osborne Cl
Beckenham BR3 207 A5
Cockfosters EN4 2 D2
Feltham TW13 172 D5
Osborne Ct 16 E10 53 D2
Ealing W5 88 A2
10 Surbiton KT6 198 A3
Osborne Gdns CR7 183 A1
Osborne Gr E17 53 B5
Osborne Mews E17 53 B5
Osborne Pl SM1 218 B3
Osborne Rd E10 75 D6
E7 77 B3
E9 75 B2
N4 50 C1
NW2 68 B2
W3 110 D4
Buckhurst Hill IG9 21 B3
Dagenham RM9 81 B3
Enfield EN3 7 A3
Erith DA17 147 B6
Hounslow TW3,TW4 129 B2
Kingston KT2 176 A3
Palmers Green N13 16 C1
Southall UB1 86 A1
South Norwood CR7 183 A1
Walton-on-T KT12 194 A1
Osborne Sq RM9 81 B4
Osborne Way KT9 214 B3
Osborn Gdns NW7 28 D3
Osborn La SE23 163 A4
Osborn St E1 95 D2 243 D2
Osborn Terr SE3 142 D1
Osbourne Ct HA2 41 D5
Osbourne Ho TW10 154 C6
Osbourne Terr 1
SW17 181 A5
Oscar Faber Pl 8 N1 73 C1
Oscar St SE8 141 C4
Oseney Cres NW5 71 D2
Osgood Ave BR6 227 D3
Osgood Gdns 1 BR6 227 D3
O'Shea Gr E3 97 B6
Osidge JMI Sch N14 15 C3
Osidge La N14 15 B3
Osier Cres N10 30 D2
Osier Ct E1 96 D3
Osier Mews W4 133 D6
Osiers Ct 3 KT1 175 D2
Osiers Rd SW18 135 C1
Osier St E1 96 C3
Osier Way E10 75 D5
Mitcham CR4 202 D4
Oslac Rd SE6 185 D5
Oslo Ct NW8 230 A3
Mitcham SW19 180 B3
Oslo Ho 2 SE5 139 A3
Oslo Sq SE16 119 A3
Osman Cl N15 51 B3
Osmani Prim Sch E1 96 A2
Osman Rd W6 112 C3
Edmonton N9 18 A1
Osmington Ho SW8 270 D3
Osmond Cl HA2 64 A6
Osmond Gdns SM6 219 C3
Osmund St W12 89 D2
Osnaburgh St
NW1 93 B3 238 D6
Osnaburgh Terr NW1 238 D6
Osney Ho 4 SE2 124 D4
Osney Wlk SM5 202 B3
Osprey 7 NW9 27 D2
Osprey Cl E17 35 A3
E6 100 A2
Cheam SM1 217 B3
Wanstead E11 55 A5
West Drayton UB7 104 A4
Osprey Ct NW3 69 D3
7 Ealing W7 86 D3
Thornton Heath SW16 182 B1
Osprey Ho 3 E14 119 A6
E4 35 B4
SE15 139 D4
Osprey Mews EN3 18 B6
Ospringe Cl 9 SE20 184 C3
Ospringe Ct SE9 167 B5
Ospringe Ho SE1 251 B3
Ospringe Rd NW5 71 C4
Osram Ct W6 112 C3
Osram Rd HA9 65 D5
Osric Path 8 N1 95 C5
Ossian Rd N4 50 B2
Ossie Garvin Rdbt
UB4 106 C6
Ossington Bldgs W1 238 A3
Ossington Cl W2 245 B5
Ossington St
W2 113 D6 245 C5
Ossory Rd SE1 140 A6
Ossulston St
NW1 93 D4 232 D2
Ossultan Pl N2 48 A6
Ossulton Way N2 48 A5
Ostade Rd SW2 160 B4
Ostell Cres EN3 7 C5
Osten Mews
SW7 113 D3 255 D5
Osterley Ave TW7 130 B5
Osterley Cl BR5 190 A2
Osterley Cres TW7 130 D4
Osterley Ct
Hounslow TW7 130 B4
7 Northolt UB5 84 C4
Osterley Gdns UB2 108 A4
Osterley Ho 5 E14 97 D1
Osterley La
Isleworth TW7 108 C1
Southall UB2,TW7 107 D1
Osterley Lo 1 TW7 130 C4
Osterley Park* TW7 108 B1
Osterley Park Rd UB2 107 B3
Osterley Park View Rd
W7 108 C4
Osterley Rd N16 73 C4
Hounslow TW7 130 C4
Osterley Sta TW7 130 B5
Osterley Views UB2 108 B4
Osterly Gdns CR7 183 A1
Oster Terr E17 52 D4
Ostliffe Rd N13 33 A5
Oswald Rd UB1 107 A5
Oswald's Mead E9 75 A4
Oswald St E5 74 D5
Oswald Terr NW2 68 C5
Osward Pl N9 18 B2
Osward Rd SW12,
SW17 158 D2
Oswell Ho 9 E1 118 B5
Oswin St SE11 116 D2 261 D4
Oswyth Rd SE5 139 C3
Otford Cl BR1 210 C6
DA5 169 D5
Penge SE20 184 C2
Otford Cres SE4 163 B5
Otford Ho SE1 252 D1
6 SE15 140 C6
Otha Ho 13 SW9 138 A3
Othello Cl SE11 261 C2
Otho Ct 5 TW8 131 D5
Otis St E3 98 A4
Otley App IG2 56 D3
Otley Ct N11 31 A4
Otley Dr IG2 56 D3
Otley Ho N5 72 D5
Otley Rd E16 99 C1
Otley Terr E5 74 D5
Ottawa Ho 4 HA4 40 C1
Ottaway Ct E5 74 A5
Ottaway St E5 74 A5
Otterbourne Rd
Chingford E4 20 B1
1 Croydon CR0 221 A6
Otterburn Gdns TW7 131 A5
Otterburn Ho 12 SE5 139 A5
Otterburn St SW17 180 D4
Otterden Cl BR6 227 C4
Otterden St SE6 185 C6
Otterfield Rd UB7 104 A6
Otter Rd UB6 86 A3
Ottershaw Ho BR5 190 B2
Ottoman Ct W5 109 D2
Otto St SE17 138 D6
Otway Ct N4 50 B3
Otway Gdns WD23 8 C4
Oulton Cl E5 74 C6
Erith SE28 102 C1
Oulton Cres IG11 79 D3
Oulton Rd N15 51 B4
Oulton Way WD19 23 B6
Oundle Ave WD23 8 A5
Our Lady Immaculate RC
Prim Sch KT6 198 D1
Our Lady of Dolours RC
Prim Sch W2 91 D2
Our Lady of Grace RC Inf
Sch NW2 68 C6
Our Lady of Grace RC Jun
Sch NW2 68 B5
Our Lady of Grace Sch
SE7 143 B6
Our Lady of Lourdes RC
Prim Sch
N11 31 C5
N12 30 A2
SE13 142 B2
Our Lady of Lourdes RC Sch
NW10 89 A6
Our Lady of Lourds RC Prim
Sch E11 55 A3
Our Lady of Muswell Prim
Sch N10 49 A6
Our Lady of Muswell RC
Prim Sch N10 31 A1
Our Lady of the Assumption
RC Prim Sch E2 96 C5
Our Lady of the Rosary RC
Prim Sch DA15 167 C5
Our Lady of the Sacred
Heart RC Prim Sch
(Annexe) N7 72 B2
Our Lady of the Sacred
Heart RC Sch N7 72 B3
Our Lady of the Visitation
RC Prim Sch UB6 86 A3
Our Lady of Victories RC
Prim Sch
SW7 114 A2 256 B3
Putney SW15 134 D1
Our Lady Queen of Heaven
RC Sch SW19 156 D4
Our Lady RC Prim Sch
E14 97 B1
NW1 93 C6 232 B5
Our Lady's Convent High
Sch N15,N16 51 C2
Our Lady & St John's RC
Jun & Inf Sch TW8 109 C1
Our Lady & St Joseph RC
Prim Sch N1 73 C2
Our Lady & St Philip Neri
RC Prim Sch SE26 185 A6
Our Lady & St Philip Neri
RC Sch SE26 185 A6
Ouseley Rd SW12 158 D3
Outer Circ NW8 92 C4 230 B3
Outgate Rd NW10 67 D1
Outram Pl N1 94 A6 233 B6
Outram Rd E6 100 A6
N22 31 D2
Croydon CR0 221 D6
Outwich St EC3 243 B2
Outwood Ct CR2 221 A1
Outwood Ho 3 SW2 160 B4
Oval Ct HA8 27 A3
Oval Mans SE11 270 D6
Oval Pl SW8 138 B5 270 D4
Oval Prim Sch CR0 205 C1
Oval Rd NW1 93 B6 231 C6
Croydon CR0 205 C1
Oval Rd N RM10 103 D6
Oval Rd S RM10 103 D5
Oval Sta SE11 138 C6
Oval The E2 96 B5
Sidcup DA15 168 A4
Oval The (Surrey Cnty Crkt
Gd) SE11 138 C6
Oval Way SE11 116 B1 260 D1
Overbrae BR3 185 C5
Overbrook Wlk HA8 26 C3
Overbury Ave BR3 208 A6
Overbury Ct 1 BR3 208 A6
Overbury Ho 3 E5 74 D4
Overbury Rd N4,N15 51 B3
Overbury St E5 74 D4
Overcliff Rd SE13 141 C2
Overcourt Cl DA15 168 B5
Overdale Ave KT3 177 B1
Overdale Rd W5 109 C3
Overdown Rd SE6 185 D6
Overhill Rd SE21,SE22 162 A4
Overhill Way BR3 208 B4
Overlea Rd E5 52 A2
Overmead SE9 167 B4
Oversley Ho 17 W2 91 C2
Overstand Cl BR3 207 C4
Overstone Gdns CR0 207 B2
Overstone Ho 17 E14 97 C1
Overstone Rd W6 112 C2
Overstrand Mans
SW11 268 A1
Overton Cl NW10 67 A2
Hounslow TW7 130 D4
Overton Ct E11 55 A2
Overton Dr Ilford RM6 58 C2
Wanstead E11 55 B2
Overton Grange Sch
SM2 217 D1
Overton Ho SW15 155 D4
Overton Rd SE2 124 D3
SW9 138 C3
Belmont SM2 217 C1
Southgate N14 16 A6
Walthamstow E10 53 A1
Overton's Yd CR0 221 A5
Overy Ho SE1 251 C1
Ovesdon Ave HA2 41 B1
Ovett Cl SE19 183 C4
Ovex Cl E14 120 A4
Ovington Ct SW3 257 B5
Ovington Gdns SW3 257 B5
Ovington Mews SW3 257 B5
Ovington Sq
SW3 114 C3 257 B5
Ovington St
SW3 114 C2 257 B4
Owen Cl SE28 124 C5
Hayes UB4 84 B4
Thornton Heath CR0 205 B3
Owen Ct UB4 84 B4
Owen Ho 11 N19 71 C4
Feltham TW14 150 A4
5 Twickenham TW1 153 B4
Owenite St SE2 124 B2
Owen Rd Edmonton N13 33 A5
Hayes UB4 84 B4
Owen's Ct EC1 234 C2
Owen's Row EC1 234 C2
Owen St EC1 234 C3
Owens Way SE23 163 A4
Owen Way NW10 67 A3
Owen Wlk 7 SE20 184 A3
Owgan Cl SE5 139 B5
Oxberry Ave SW6 135 A3
Oxbridge Ct 4 W4 110 D1
Oxendon St
SW1,W1 115 D6 249 C5
Oxenford St SE15 139 D2
Oxenham Ho 13 SE8 141 C6
Oxenholme NW1 232 B3
Oxenpark Ave HA9 44 A2
Oxestalls Rd SE8 119 A1
Oxford Ave NW10 90 C4
Harlington TW6 127 D5
Hounslow TW5 107 C1
Merton SW20 179 A1
Oxford & Cambridge Mans
NW1 237 B3
Oxford Cir W1 93 C1 239 A1
Oxford Circus Ave W1 239 A1
Oxford Circus Sta
W1 93 C1 239 A1
Oxford Cl Edmonton N9 18 B2
Littleton TW15,TW17 171 A3
Mitcham CR4 203 C6
Oxford Cres KT3 199 B3
Oxford Ct EC4 252 C6
48 W2 91 C2
W4 110 D1
16 Acton W3 88 C1
8 Ealing W7 86 D2
17 Kingston KT6 198 A4
Oxford Dr SE1 253 B1
Ruislip HA4 62 C6
Oxford Gardens Prim Sch
W10 90 D1
Oxford Gate W6 112 D2
Oxford Gdns N20 14 B3
W10 90 D1
Brentford W4 132 C6
Edmonton N21 17 A4
Oxford Mews DA5 169 C4
Oxford Rd DA14 190 B5
E15 76 B2
N4 50 C1
NW6 91 C5
Carshalton SM2,SM5 218 C3
Ealing W5 109 D6
Edmonton N9 18 B2
Enfield EN3 18 B6
Harrow HA1 42 A3
Harrow HA3 42 D6
Ilford IG1 79 A3
Putney SW15 135 A1
South Norwood SE19 183 B4
Oxford Rd *continued*
Teddington TW11,TW12 174 B5
Wallington SM6 219 C3
Woodford IG8 37 D5
Oxford Rd N W4 110 D1
Oxford Rd S W4 110 D1
Oxford Sq W2 92 C1 237 B1
Oxford St W1 93 B1 238 D1
Oxford Way TW13 172 D6
Oxford Wlk UB1 107 B5
Oxgate Ct Par NW2 68 A6
Oxgate Ctr NW2 68 B6
Oxgate Gdns NW2 68 B6
Oxgate La NW2 68 B6
Oxhawth Cres BR2 210 D3
Oxhey Dr HA6,WD19 22 B6
Oxhey La HA5 23 C5
Oxhey Ridge Cl HA6 22 B5
Oxhey Wood JMI Schs
WD19 22 C6
Oxleas E6 100 D1
Oxleas Cl DA16 145 B3
Oxleay Rd HA2 41 C1
Oxleigh Cl KT3 199 C4
Oxley Cl SE1 118 A1
Oxleys Rd NW2 68 B5
Oxlip Cl 2 CR0 206 D1
Oxlow La RM10 81 C4
Oxonian St SE22 139 D1
Oxo Tower SE1 251 B5
Oxo Tower Wharf SE1 251 B5
Oxted Cl CR4 202 B6
Oxted Ct N16 51 C1
Oxtoby Way SW16 181 D2
Oyster Catchers Cl E16 99 B1
Oyster Catcher Terr
IG5 56 C6
Oyster Row E1 96 C1
Ozolins Way E16 99 A1

P

Pablo Neruda Cl 4
SE24 138 D1
Pace Pl E1 96 B1
Pacific Cl TW14 149 D3
Pacific Ho 15 E1 96 D3
Pacific Hts BR3 185 C3
Pacific Rd E16 99 A1
Pacific Wharf SE16 118 D5
Packenham Ho 21 E2 95 D4
24 N19 49 D2
Packham Ct KT4 216 C5
Packington Ho 22
SW9 138 A3
Packington Sq
N1 95 A6 235 A6
Packington St
N1 94 D6 234 D5
Packmores Rd SE9 167 B6
Padbury SE17 263 B1
Padbury Cl TW14 149 B3
Padbury Ct E2 95 D4
Padbury Ho NW8 237 B6
Paddenswick Ct W6 112 B3
Paddenswick Rd W6 112 A3
Paddington Cl UB4 84 D3
Paddington Com Hospl
W9 91 C2
Paddington Ct 10 W7 86 D2
Paddington Gn
W2 92 B2 236 C4
Paddington Green Prim Sch
NW8 92 B3 236 C5
Paddington St W1 238 A4
Paddington Sta
W2 92 B1 236 C2
Paddock Cl SE3 143 A3
Forest Hill SE26 184 D6
New Malden KT4 199 C1
Northolt UB5 85 C5
Orpington BR6 226 D4
Paddock Ct SW20 200 C5
Paddock Gdns SE19 183 C4
Paddock Lo 13 EN1 17 C6
Paddock Rd DA6 147 A1
NW2 68 A6
Ruislip HA4 62 D5
Paddock Sch SW15 133 D1
Paddocks Cl HA2 63 D4
Paddocks Gn NW9 44 D1
Paddocks The HA9 66 D6
Addington CR0 223 C2
Cockfosters EN4 2 D2
Paddock The UB10 60 D4
Paddock Way BR7 189 B3
Padfield Ct HA9 66 B5
Padfield Rd SE5 139 A2
Padley Cl KT9 214 B3
Padnall Ct RM6 58 D6
Padnall Rd RM6 58 D5
Padstow Cl BR6 227 D4
Padstow Ho 12 E14 119 B6
Padstow Rd EN2 4 D4
Padstow Wlk TW14 149 D3
Padua Rd SE20 184 C2
Pagden St SW8 268 D2
Pageant Ave NW9 27 C2
Pageant Cres SE16 119 B5
Pageantmaster Ct
EC4 241 C1
Pageant Wlk CR0 221 C5
Page Cl Dagenham RM9 81 A3
Hampton TW12 173 A4
Harrow HA3 44 B3
Page Cres CR0 220 D3
Page Ct NW7 28 A3
Page Green Rd N15 52 A4
Page Green Terr N15 51 D4
Page Heath La BR1 209 D6
Page Heath Villas
BR1 209 D6
Page High N22 50 C6
Page Ho SE10 142 A6
Pagehurst Rd CR0 206 B2
Page Mdw NW7 28 A3
Page Rd TW14 149 B5
Page's Ct N10 31 A1
Page's Hill N10 31 A1
Page's La N10 31 A1
Page St NW7 28 A3
SW1 115 D2 259 D4
Page's Wlk
SE1 117 C3 263 B5
Page's Yd W4 133 C6
Paget Ave SM1 218 B5
Paget Cl TW12 174 B6
Paget Ct UB7 104 A4
Paget Gdns BR7 188 D2
Paget Ho 15 E2 96 C5
Paget La TW7 130 C2
Paget Pl Kingston KT2 177 A4
Thames Ditton KT7 196 D1
Paget Rd N16 51 B1
Hillingdon UB10 83 A3
Ilford IG1 78 D4
Paget Rise SE18 144 C5
Paget St EC1 234 C2
Paget Terr SE18 144 D6
Pagham Ho W10 90 C3
Pagin Ho N15 51 C4
Pagitts Gr EN4 1 D4
Pagnell St SE14 141 B5
Pagoda Ave TW9 132 B2
Pagoda Gdns SE3 142 B3
Paignton Rd N15 51 C3
Ruislip HA4 62 A5
Paine Ct SE3 142 D6
Paines Cl HA5 41 A6
Paine's La HA5 23 A1
Pain's Cl CR4 181 B1
Painsthorpe Rd 3 N16 73 C5
Painswick Ct 1 SE15 139 D5
Painters Mews SE16 118 A2
Painters Rd IG2,RM6 58 A6
Paisley Rd
Carshalton SM5 202 B1
Tottenham N22 32 D2
Pakeman Ho SE1 251 D2
Pakeman Prim Sch N7 72 B5
Pakeman St N7 72 B5
Pakenham Cl SW12 159 A3
Pakenham St
WC1 94 B3 240 D6
Palace Ave
W8 113 D4 245 D2
Palace Court Gdns N10 49 C6
Palace Ct NW3 69 D3
SE9 166 B5
W2 113 D6 245 C5
Harrow HA3 44 A3
South Norwood CR7 205 B5
Streatham SW2 160 C2
Palace Garden Mews
W8 245 B4
Palace Gardens Terr
W8 113 D5 245 C3
Palace Gate
W8 114 A4 246 A1
Palace Gates Rd N22 31 D2
Palace Gdns
Buckhurst Hill IG9 21 D3
Enfield EN2 5 B1
Palace Gdns Mews
W8 113 D5 245 D3
Palace Gn W8 113 D5 245 C3
New Addington CR0 223 B1
Palace Gr BR1 187 B2
Penge SE19 183 D3
Palace Mans W14 254 B4
Palace Mews E17 53 B5
SW1 258 B3
SW6 264 D4
Palace of Ind HA9 66 C4
Palace Par E17 53 C5
Palace Pl SW1 259 A6
Palace Rd BR1 187 B2
N8 49 D4
East Molesey KT8 196 B6
Kingston KT1 197 D5
Penge SE19 183 D3
Ruislip HA4 63 A4
Streatham SE27,SW16,
SW2 160 C2
Wood Green N11 32 A3
Palace Sq SE19 183 D3
Palace St SW1 115 C3 259 A6

Palace View SE12 165 A2
Bromley BR1 209 B6
Croydon CR0 223 B4
Palace View Rd E4 35 D5
Palamon Ct SE1 263 D2
Palamos Rd E10 53 C1
Palatine Ave N16 73 C4
Palatine Rd N16 73 C4
Palemead Cl SW6 134 D4
Palermo Rd NW10 90 A5
Palestine Gr SW19 180 B2
Palewell Cl BR5 190 B1
Palewell Common Dr SW14 155 B6
Palewell Pk SW14 133 B1
Palfrey Pl SW8 138 B5 270 D4
Palgrave Ave UB1 107 C6
Palgrave Gdns NW1 237 A5
Palgrave Ho 4 NW3 70 D3
7 SE5 139 A5
Twickenham TW2 152 A4
Palgrave Rd W12 111 D3
Palissy St 35 E2 95 D4
Pallant Ho SE1 262 D5
Pallant Way BR6 226 C5
Pallet Way SE18 144 A4
Palliser Ct W14 254 A1
Palliser Ho 21 E1 96 D3
3 SE10 142 B6
Palliser Rd W14 113 A1 254 A1
Pallister Terr SW15 155 D2
Pall Mall SW1 115 D5 249 C3
Pall Mall E SW1 115 D5 249 D4
Pall Mall Pl SW1 249 B3
Palmar Cres DA7 147 C3
Palmar Rd DA7 147 C3
Palm Ave DA14 190 D4
Palm Cl E10 75 D5
Palm Ct N16 73 B6
17 SE15 139 D5
Beckenham BR3 207 B6
Wood Green N22 32 B3
Palmeira Rd DA16 146 D2
Palmer Ave KT4,SM3 216 C4
Palmer Cl Heston TW5 129 C4
West Wickham BR4 224 B6
Palmer Cres KT1 198 A6
Palmer Ct NW10 89 B6
Palmer Gdns EN5 12 D6
Palmer Ho 5 N19 71 C5
8 NW5 71 C4
6 SE14 140 D5
Palmer Pl N7 72 C3
Palmer Rd E13 99 B3
Dagenham RM8 58 D1
Palmer's Ct 11 N11 31 C5
Palmers Gr KT8 195 C5
Palmers Green High Sch N21 16 C2
Palmers Green Sta N13 32 B6
Palmers La EN3 6 C4
Palmers Rd E2 96 D5
Palmer's Rd N11 31 C5
Palmers Rd
Mortlake SW14 133 A2
Thornton Heath SW16 182 B1
Palmer St SW1 259 C6
Palmerston Cres SE18 145 A6
Bowes Park N13 32 B5
Palmerston Ct E17 53 B5
22 E3 96 D5
2 Buckhurst Hill IG9 21 C2
9 Surbiton KT6 197 D2
Palmerston Ctr HA3 42 D6
Palmerston Gr 4 SW19 179 C3
Palmerston Ho SW11 268 B1
W8 245 A3
Palmerston Rd BR6 227 A3
E17 53 B5
E7 77 B2
NW6 69 B1
NW6 69 C1
W3 111 A3
Bowes Park N22 32 B4
Buckhurst Hill IG9 21 C3
Harrow HA3 42 D6
Hounslow TW3 130 A4
Merton SW19 179 C3
Mortlake SW14 133 A1
Sutton SM1 218 A3
Thornton Heath CR0 205 B4
Twickenham TW2 152 C5
Wallington SM5 219 A4
Palmerston Way SW8 268 D3
Palm Gr W5 110 A3
Palm Tree Ct 3 N17 33 D1
Palm Tree Ho 2 SE14 140 D5
Pamela Ct N12 29 D4
NW10 68 A1
Pamela Gdns HA5 40 B4
Pamela Ho 14 E8 95 D6
Pamlion Ct N4 50 A2
Pams Way KT19 215 B3
Panama Ho 5 E1 96 D2
Panbro Ho 7 SE18 144 B4
Pancras La EC2 242 C1
Pancras Rd NW1 93 D5 232 D4
Pandora Ct 4 KT6 198 A3
Pandora Rd NW6 69 C2
Panfield Mews IG2 56 C3
Panfield Rd SE2 124 A3
Pangbourne NW1 232 A1
Pangbourne Ave W10 90 C2
Pangbourne Ct N20 14 A4
Upper Tooting SW17 180 A6
Pangbourne Dr HA7 26 A5
Pangbourne Ho 4 N7 72 A3
Panhard Pl UB1 107 D6
Pank Ave EN5 14 A6
Pankhurst Cl 7 SE14 140 D5
Isleworth TW7 130 D2
Pankhurst Rd KT12 194 C2
Panmuir Rd SW20 178 B2
Panmure Cl N5 72 D4
Panmure Ct 11 UB1 86 A1
Panmure Rd SE26 162 B1
Panorama Ct N6 49 C3
Pansy Gdns W12 112 A6
Panther Dr NW10 67 B3
Pantiles Cl N13 32 D5
Pantiles The BR1 210 A6
DA7 147 B5
NW11 47 B4
Bushey WD23 8 B3
Panton Cl CR0 204 D1
Panton St SW1 249 C5
Panyer Alley EC2 242 A2
Papermill Cl SM5 219 A4
Paper Mill Wharf E14 119 A6
Papillons Wlk SE3 143 A2
Papworth Gdns N7 72 B3
Papworth Way SW2 160 C4
Parade Mans 2 NW4 46 B4
19 SE5 139 A3
Parade Mews SE27, SW2 160 D2
Parade The SW11 136 D5 267 D4
Ashford TW16 171 D3
Claygate KT10 212 C2
Croydon CR0 220 B3
Greenford UB6 65 B3
2 Kingston KT2 176 A1
Paradise Pas N7 72 C3
Paradise Pl 15 SE7 122 A2
Paradise Rd SW4 138 A3
Richmond TW10 154 A6
Paradise Row E2 96 B4
Paradise St SE16 118 B4
Paradise Wlk SW3 136 D6 267 D6
Paragon Cl E16 99 A1
Paragon Ct NW4 29 A2
Paragon Gr KT5 198 B3
Paragon Mews SE1 262 D4
Paragon Pl SE3 142 D3
Surbiton KT5 198 B3
Paragon Rd E9 74 C2
Paragon The SE17 262 C4
SE3 143 A3
Paramount Bldg EC1 241 C6
Paramount Ct WC1 239 B5
Paramount Ho 8 E11 76 C5
Parayhouse Sch W12 112 B5
Parbury Rd SE23 163 A5
Parbury Rise KT9 214 A2
Parchmore Rd CR7 205 A6
Parchmore Way CR7 182 D1
Pardes House & Beis Yaakov Sch (Boys) N3 29 B1
Pardoner St SE1 117 B3 262 D6
Pardon St EC1 241 D6
Parfett St E1 96 A1
Parfew Ct 2 SE22 162 B2
Parfitt Cl NW3 48 A1
Parfrey St W6 134 C6
Pargraves Ct HA9 66 C6
Parham Dr IG2 56 D4
Paris Gdn SE1 116 D5 251 C4
Parish CE Prim Sch BR1 187 A3
Parish Church CE Inf & Jun Schs CR0 220 D5
Parish Ct KT6 198 A3
Parish Gate Dr DA15 167 C5
Parish La SE20 184 D3
Paris Ho 12 E2 96 B5
Parish Wharf 6 SE7 122 A2
Park App DA16 146 B1
Park Ave BR1 187 A4
BR6 226 C6
E15 76 C2
N3 29 D2
NW11 47 D1
NW2 68 C2
Barking IG11 79 A2
Edmonton N18 34 A6
Enfield EN1 17 C5
Ilford IG1 56 C1
Mitcham CR4 181 B3
Mortlake SW14 133 B1
Palmers Green N13 16 C1
Park Ave *continued*
Ruislip HA4 39 C3
Southall UB1 107 C5
Twickenham TW3 151 D5
Upper Halliford TW17 193 C6
Wallend E6 100 C5
Wallington SM5 219 A2
West Wickham BR4 224 A6
Woodford IG8 37 B5
Wood Green N22 32 B2
Park Ave E KT17 216 A2
Park Ave N N8 49 D5
NW10 68 B3
Park Avenue Mews CR4 181 B3
Park Avenue Rd N17 34 B3
Park Ave S N8 49 D5
Park Ave W KT17 216 A2
Park Bsns Ctr 4 NW6 91 C4
Park Chase HA9 66 B4
Park Cl 20 E9 96 C6
N12 30 B6
NW2 68 B5
SW1 247 C1
W14 113 B3 254 D6
Ealing NW10 88 B4
Hampton TW12 174 A2
Harrow HA3 24 C2
Isleworth TW3,TW7 152 A6
Kingston KT2 176 C2
Wallington SM5 218 D2
Park Cotts 10 TW1 153 B5
Park Cres N3 30 A3
W1 93 B3 238 C5
Enfield EN2 5 B1
Harrow HA3 24 C2
Twickenham TW2 152 B3
Park Cres Mews E W1 238 D5
Park Cres Mews W W1 238 C5
Park Croft HA8 27 A2
Parkcroft Rd SE12 164 D4
Park Ct E17 53 D4
N11 31 D3
N12 30 B5
SW11 268 C2
SW4 159 D6
2 Beckenham BR3 207 D6
2 Chingford E4 20 A2
Dulwich SE21 161 B1
New Barnet EN5 14 B4
New Malden KT3 199 B5
Teddington KT1 175 C2
Upper Tooting SW12 159 A3
Wallington SM6 220 A3
Wembley HA9 66 A3
Parkdale N11 31 D4
Parkdale Cres KT4 215 B5
Parkdale Rd SE18 123 C1
Park Dr NW11 47 D1
Acton W3 110 C3
Enfield N21 17 A5
Harrow HA2 41 C2
Mortlake SW14 133 B1
Stanmore HA3 24 C4
Woolwich SE7 144 A6
Park Dwellings 7 NW3 70 D3
Park End NW3 70 C4
Bromley BR1 186 D2
Parker Cl E16 122 A5
Parker Ct N1 235 B6
SW4 270 A1
Wimbledon SW19 179 A3
Parke Rd Barnes SW13 134 A4
Sunbury TW16 194 A5
Parker Ho 4 SE18 122 D1
Parker Mews WC2 240 B2
Parker Rd CR0 221 A4
Parkers Rd N10 30 C2
Parkers Row 12 SE16 118 A4
Parker's Row SE1 253 D1
Parker St E16 122 A5
WC2 94 A1 240 B2
Park Farm SE7 144 A6
Park Farm Cl N2 48 A6
Pinner HA5 40 B4
Park Farm Ct UB3 105 C6
Park Farm Rd
Bromley BR1 187 D2
Kingston KT2 176 A3
Parkfield 3 TW7 130 C4
Parkfield Ave
Feltham TW13 150 A1
Harrow HA2 24 A1
Hillingdon UB10 82 D4
Mortlake SW14 133 C1
Northolt UB5 84 D5
Parkfield Cl
Edgware HA8 26 D4
Northolt UB5 85 A5
Parkfield Cres
Feltham TW13 150 A1
Harrow HA2 24 A1
Ruislip HA4 63 A5
Parkfield Dr UB5 84 D5
Parkfield Gdns HA2 41 D6
Parkfield Ho HA2 23 D2
Parkfield Ind Est SW11 137 A3
Parkfield Par TW13 150 A1
Parkfield Prim Sch NW4 46 B2
Parkfield Rd NW10 68 B1
SE14 141 B4
Feltham TW13 150 A1
Harrow HA2 64 A5
Northolt UB5 85 A5
Uxbridge UB10 60 D6
Parkfields Croydon CR0 207 B1
Putney SW15 134 C1
Parkfields Ave NW9 45 B1
Wimbledon SW20 178 B1
Parkfields Cl SM5 219 A4
Parkfields Rd TW10 176 B5
Parkfield St N1 94 C5 234 B4
Parkfield Way BR2 210 B4
Park Flats N6 48 C2
Parkgate SE3 142 D2
Park Gate N2 48 B6
Ealing W5 87 D2
Southgate N21 16 B4
Parkgate Ave EN4 2 A4
Parkgate Cl KT2 176 D4
Parkgate Cres EN4 2 A4
Park Gate Ct TW12 174 A5
Parkgate Gdns SW14 155 B6
Parkgate House Sch SW11 137 A1
Park Gate Mans N2 48 B6
Parkgate Mews N6 49 C2
Parkgate Rd SW11 136 C5 267 B3
Wallington SM5,SM6 219 B3
Park Gates HA2 63 C4
Park Gdns NW9 44 D6
Kingston KT2 176 B5
Park Gr BR1 187 B2
E15 99 A6
N11 31 D3
Edgware HA8 26 B5
Park Grove Rd E11 76 C6
Park Hall Rd N2 48 C5
Dulwich SE21 161 B1
Park Hall Road Trad Est SE21 161 B1
Parkham Ct BR2 186 C1
Parkham St SW11 136 C4 267 A1
Parkham Way N10 31 C1
Park High Sch HA7 25 D1
Park Hill BR1 210 B5
SW4 159 D6
Ealing W5 87 D2
Forest Hill SE23 162 C3
Loughton IG10 21 D6
Richmond TW10 154 B5
Wallington SM5 218 D2
Park Hill Cl SM5 218 C3
Park Hill Ct
Croydon CR0 221 C6
Ealing W5 87 D2
Upper Tooting SW17 158 D1
Parkhill Inf Sch IG5 56 C6
Park Hill Inf Sch CR0 221 C5
Parkhill Jun Sch IG5 56 C6
Park Hill Jun Sch CR0 221 C5
Parkhill Rd DA5 169 B4
NW3 70 D3
Chingford E4 20 A4
Sidcup DA15 167 C1
Park Hill Rd
Beckenham BR2 186 C1
South Croydon CR0 221 C5
Wallington SM6 219 B1
Park Hill Rise CR0 221 D5
Park Hill Sch KT2 176 C3
Park Hill Wlk 10 NW3 70 D3
Park Ho 35 E9 74 C1
N4 72 D6
8 SE5 139 B4
Forest Hill SE26 184 A5
Sidcup DA14 190 A5
Southgate N21 16 B4
Parkholme Rd E8 74 A2
Park House Gdns TW1 153 C6
Park House Mid Sch SW19 179 B6
Parkhouse St SE5 139 B5
Parkhurst Ct N7 72 A4
Parkhurst Gdns 2 DA5 169 C4
Parkhurst Rd E17 53 A5
N11 31 A5
N7 72 A4
Bowes Park N22 32 B4
Little Ilford E12 78 C4
Sidcup DA5 169 C4
Sutton SM1 218 B4
Tottenham N17 34 A1
Parkin Ho SE20 184 D3
Parkinson Ct EC1 235 D2
N1 235 C1
Parkinson Ho 6 E9 74 C1
Park La E15 98 B6
W1 115 A6 248 A5
Park La *continued*
Cheam SM3 217 A2
Cranford TW5 128 A5
Dagenham RM6 58 D3
Edmonton N9 17 D1
Harrow HA2 63 D5
Hayes UB4 83 C3
Richmond TW9 131 D1
South Croydon CR0 221 B5
Stanmore HA7 9 A1
Teddington TW11 174 D4
Tottenham N17 34 A3
Wallington SM5,SM6 219 A3
Wembley HA9 66 A4
Parkland Ct E15 76 C3
W14 244 A2
Parkland Gdns 12 SW19 156 D3
Parkland Gr
Ashford TW15 170 C6
Hounslow TW7 130 D4
Parkland Rd
Ashford TW15 170 C6
Woodford IG8 37 B3
Wood Green N22 32 B1
Parklands N6 49 B2
SE22 162 B6
Bushey WD23 8 A5
Kingston KT5 198 B4
Parklands Cl
Hadley Wood EN4 2 B5
Ilford IG2 57 A2
Mortlake SW14 155 A6
Parklands Ct TW5 128 D3
Parklands Dr N3 47 A6
Parklands Par TW5 128 D3
Parklands Rd SW16 181 B5
Parklands Way KT4 215 C6
Parkland Wlk N4,N8 50 B2
Park Lane Cl N17 34 A3
Park Lane Prim Sch HA9 66 A3
Park Lawn CR7 183 A1
Parklea Cl NW9 27 C2
Park Lea Ct N16 51 C2
Parkleigh Ct SW19 179 D1
Parkleigh Rd SW19 179 D1
Parkleys
Richmond KT2,TW10 175 D6
Richmond, Ham Common TW10 176 A6
Park Lo 10 E1 118 B5
N12 30 A5
NW2 68 C4
11 NW8 70 B1
3 Ealing W5 87 B3
Park Lofts 7 SW4 160 A6
Park Lorne NW8 230 B1
Park Mans 5 NW4 46 B4
NW8 230 A3
SW1 247 C1
SW11 267 C1
SW6 264 B1
SW8 270 B6
W6 111 D3
Forest Hill SE26 162 C1
Park Mead DA15 168 B5
Parkmead SW15 156 B5
Park Mead HA2 63 D5
Parkmead Gdns NW7 27 D4
Park Mews BR7 188 D4
W10 91 A5
Stanwell TW19 148 B4
Parkmore Cl IG8 37 A6
Park Nook Gdns EN2 5 B6
Park Par NW10 89 D5
NW9 45 B6
Acton W3 110 C3
Hayes UB3 83 C1
Park Pl E14 119 C5
SW1 115 C5 249 A4
W3 110 C2
Ealing W5 109 D5
Hampton TW12 174 A4
Wembley HA9 66 B4
Park Place Dr W3 110 C3
Park Place Villas W2 236 B4
Park Prim Sch E15 76 D1
Park Rd BR1 187 B2
BR7 188 D4
E10 53 C1
E15 99 A6
E17 53 B4
E6 99 C6
N11 31 D3
N14 15 D4
N2 48 B6
N8 49 D4
N8,N15 50 D5
NW10 89 C6
NW1,NW8 92 C3 237 B6
NW4 46 B3
NW9 45 B2
Ashford TW15 170 D5
Barnet EN4 2 C1
Barnet EN5 1 B1
Beckenham BR3 185 C3
Cheam SM3 217 A2
Chiswick W4 133 B6
Park Rd *continued*
Ealing W7 108 D6
East Molesey KT8 196 A5
Edmonton N18 34 A6
Feltham TW13 172 D6
Hackbridge SM6 219 B6
Hampton TW12 174 A5
Hayes UB4 83 C2
Ilford IG1 79 B5
Isleworth TW3,TW7 152 A6
Isleworth TW7 131 B3
Kingston KT2,TW10 176 C3
Lower Halliford TW17 192 C1
Mitcham SW19 180 C4
New Malden KT3 199 B5
Richmond TW10 154 B5
South Norwood SE25 205 C5
Sunbury TW16 172 B3
Teddington KT1 175 C2
Teddington TW11 174 D4
Twickenham TW1 153 C5
Uxbridge UB8 60 A2
Wallington SM6 219 B3
Wanstead E12 77 B6
Wembley HA0 66 A2
Park Rd E Acton W3 111 A4
Uxbridge UB10 82 A5
Park Rd N W3 110 D4
W4 111 B1
Park Ridings N8 50 C6
Park Rise
Forest Hill SE23 163 A3
Harrow HA3 24 C2
Park Rise Rd SE23 163 A3
Park Road Ho 3 KT2 176 C3
Park Row SE10 142 B6
Park Royal NW10 88 D6
Park Royal Bsns Ctr NW10 89 A3
Park Royal Metro Ctr NW10 88 D3
Park Royal Rd NW10, W3 89 A3
Park Royal Sta W5 88 C3
Park S SW11 268 A1
Park Sch IG1 56 D1
Park Sheen 3 SW14 132 D1
Parkshot TW9 132 A1
Parkside DA14 168 B2
N3 29 D3
NW7 28 A4
SE3 142 D5
W3 111 C5
Park Side NW2 68 B4
Parkside
1 Beckenham BR3 185 D1
Cheam SM3 217 A2
Ealing W5 110 A6
Hampton TW12 174 A5
Hayes UB3 105 C6
Wimbledon SW19 178 D6
Park Side IG9 21 B2
Parkside Ave BR1 210 A5
Wimbledon SW19 178 D5
Parkside Cl SE20 184 C3
Parkside Cres N7 72 C5
Tolworth KT5 199 A3
Parkside Ct
Bowes Park N22 32 B4
2 Wanstead E11 55 A3
Parkside Dr HA8 10 C1
Parkside Est E9 96 D6
Parkside Gdns
East Barnet EN4 15 A4
Wimbledon SW19 178 D6
Parkside Lo DA17 125 D1
Parkside Rd
Belvedere DA17 125 D2
Hounslow TW3 151 D6
Parkside St SW11 268 A1
Parkside Terr N18 33 B6
Parkside Way HA2 42 A5
Park Sq E NW1 93 B3 238 D6
Park Sq Mews NW1 238 C5
Park Sq W NW1 93 B3 238 C5
Park St SE1 117 A5 252 B4
W1 115 A6 248 A5
Croydon CR0 221 A6
Teddington TW11 174 C4
Parkstead Rd SW15 156 B6
Park Steps W2 247 B6
Park St James NW8 230 C5
Parkstone Ave N18 33 D5
Parkstone Rd E17 54 A6
3 SE15 140 A3
Park Terr
Carshalton SM5 218 C5
Enfield EN3 7 A5
New Malden KT4 200 A1
Park The N6 49 A3
NW11 47 D1
Ealing W5 109 D5
Forest Hill SE23 162 C3
Sidcup DA14 190 A5
Wallington SM5 218 D3
Parkthorne Cl HA2 41 D3

Parkthorne Dr HA2 41 D3
Parkthorne Rd SW12 159 D4
Park Twrs W1 248 C3
Park View N5 73 A4
NW2 68 C4
W3 89 A2
Parkview UB6 87 A4
Park View
Kingston KT3 199 D6
Morden SM4 202 B4
Pinner HA5 23 B2
Southgate N21 16 B4
Wembley HA9 66 D3
Yiewsley UB7 104 A6
Park View Cres N11 31 B6
Park View Ct N12 30 C6
NW9 45 A5
SW18 157 C5
Parkview Ct
Fulham SW6 135 A3
Penge SE20 184 B2
Park View Dr CR4 180 B1
Park View Gdns NW4 46 D4
Redbridge IG4 56 B5
Wood Green N22 32 C2
Park View Ho SE24 160 D5
Parkview Lo BR3 207 D6
Park View Mews 24
SW9 138 B3
Park View Rd DA16 146 D2
N3 29 D2
NW10 67 D4
SE9 166 D2
Parkview Rd CR0 206 A1
Park View Rd Ealing W5 88 A2
Hillingdon UB8 82 C1
Pinner HA5 22 B3
Southall UB1 107 C5
Tottenham N17 34 A1
Park Village E
NW1 93 B5 231 D3
Park Village W
NW1 93 B5 231 C4
Park Villas RM6 58 D3
Parkville Rd
SW6 135 B5 264 C3
Park Vista SE10 142 B6
Park Walk Prim Sch
SW10 136 B6 266 C5
Parkway DA18 125 A3
NW1 93 B6 231 C5
Park Way N20 30 D6
NW11 47 A4
W3 110 C2
Parkway Hillingdon UB10 60 D1
Ilford IG3 79 D5
Palmers Green N14 16 A2
West Barnes SW20 200 D5
Woodford IG8 37 C5
Park Way
East Molesey KT8 195 D6
Edgware HA8 26 D2
Enfield EN2 4 C3
Feltham TW14 150 B4
Ruislip HA4 40 A1
Park Way Ct HA4 39 D1
Parkway Prim Sch
DA18 125 A3
Parkway The
Cranford TW5 128 B5
Hayes UB2,UB3,UB4,
TW5 106 B3
Hayes UB4 84 D2
Parkway Trad Est
TW5 128 C6
Park West W2 92 C1 237 B1
Park West Pl
W1,W2 92 C1 237 B2
Park Wlk
SW10 136 B6 266 C6
Parkwood N20 14 D2
NW8 230 C5
Beckenham BR3 185 C3
Parkwood Ave KT10 196 A1
Parkwood Gr TW16 194 A6
Parkwood Mews N6 49 B3
Parkwood Prim Sch
N4 72 D6
Parkwood Rd DA5 169 B4
Hounslow TW7 130 D4
Wimbledon SW19 179 B5
Parliament Ct NW3 70 C4
Parliament Hill NW3 70 C4
Parliament Hill Mans
NW5 71 A4
Parliament Hill Sch
NW5 71 A4
Parliament Mews
SW14 133 A3
Parliament Sq★
SW1 116 A4 250 A1
Parliament St
SW1 116 A4 250 A2
Parliament View
Apartments SE11 260 B4
Parma Cres SW11 136 D1
Parminter Ind Est 23
E2 96 B5
Parmiter St E2 96 B5
Parmoor Ct EC1 242 A6
Parnall Ho 11 SE19 183 C6
Parnell Cl HA8 27 A6
W12 112 B3
Parnell Rd E3 97 B6
Parnham St E14 97 A1
Parolles Rd N19 49 C1
Paroma Rd DA17 125 C3
Parr Cl N9 34 B6
Parr Ct N1 235 C4
Feltham TW13 172 C6
Parrington Ho 1
SW4 159 D5
Parr Pl W4 111 D2
Parr Rd E6 99 D6
Stanmore HA7 26 A2
Parr's Pl TW12 173 C3
Parr St N1 95 B5 235 C4
Parry Ave E6 100 B1
Parry Cl KT17 216 A1
Parry Ho 32 E1 118 B5
Parry Pl SE18 122 D2
Parry Rd W10 91 A4
South Norwood SE25 205 C6
Parry St SW8 138 A6 270 B6
Parsifal Coll NW3 69 C4
Parsifal Ho NW3 69 C4
Parsifal Rd NW6 69 C3
Parsley Gdns CR0 206 D1
Parsloes Ave RM9 81 A3
Parsloes Prim Sch RM9 81 B2
Parsonage Cl UB3 83 D1
Parsonage Gdns EN2 5 A3
Parsonage La DA14 191 B6
Enfield EN2 5 B3
Parsonage Manorway
DA8,DA17 147 C6
Parsonage St E14 120 A2
Parson Ct SE13 141 D2
Parsons Gn
SW6 135 C3 265 A1
Parsons Gr HA8 10 C1
Parsons Green La
SW6 135 C4 265 A2
Parsons Green Sta
SW6 135 C4 265 A1
Parsons Hill SE18 122 C3
Parsons Ho W2 236 C5
21 Streatham SW12 160 A4
Parsons Lo NW6 69 D1
Parsons Mead KT8 196 A6
Parson's Mead CR0 204 D1
Parsons Rd E13 99 C5
Edgware HA8 10 C1
Parson St NW4 46 C6
Parthenia Rd
SW6 135 C4 265 B1
Partingdale La NW7 28 D5
Partington Cl N19 49 D1
Partridge Cl 1 E16 99 D2
Barnet EN5 12 C5
Bushey WD23 8 A3
Stanmore HA7 26 A6
Partridge Ct EC1 241 C6
Partridge Dr BR6 227 A5
Partridge Gn SE9 166 C1
Partridge Ho 20 E3 97 B5
Partridge Rd
8 Hampton TW12 173 C4
Sidcup DA14 189 C6
Partridge Sq 3 E6 100 A2
Partridge Way N22 32 A2
Pasadena Cl UB3 106 B4
Pascall Ho SE17 139 A6
Pascal St SW8 137 D5 269 D4
Pascoe Rd SE13 164 B6
Pasley Cl SE17 262 A1
Pasquier Rd E17 53 A6
Passey Pl SE9 166 B5
Passfield Dr E14 97 D2
Passfield Ho SE18 123 B2
Passfield Path 13
SE28 124 B6
Passfields W14 254 C1
Catford SE6 164 A1
Passing Alley EC1 241 D5
Passingham Ho TW5 129 C6
Passmore Gdns N11 31 D4
Passmore Ho 12 N9 18 A1
Passmores Edwards Ho
N11 31 D3
Passmore St
SW1 115 A1 258 A2
Pasteur Cl NW9 27 C1
Pasteur Gdns N18 33 A5
Paston Cl SM6 219 C5
Paston Cres SE12 165 B4
Pastor Ct N6 49 C3
Pastor St SE1,
SE11 116 D2 261 D4
Pasture Cl Bushey WD23 8 A4
Wembley HA0 65 B5
Pasture Rd Catford SE6 164 D3
Dagenham RM9 81 B3
Wembley HA0 65 B5
Pastures Mead UB10 60 C2
Pastures The N20 13 B3
Patcham Terr SW8 268 D2
Patch Cl UB10 82 B6
Patching Way UB4 85 A2
Patent Ho E14 97 D2
Paternoster Row
EC2,EC4 95 A1 242 A1
Paternoster Sq
EC4 94 D1 241 D2
Pater St W8 113 C3 255 A5
Pates Manor Dr TW14 149 B4
Pathfield Rd SW16 181 D4
Path The SW19 179 D2
Patience Rd SW11 136 C3
Patio Cl SW4 159 D5
Patmore Ho 9 N16 73 C3
Patmore St
SW8 137 C4 269 B2
Paton Cl E3 97 C4
Paton Ho 3 SW9 138 B3
Paton St EC1 235 A1
Patricia Ct
Chislehurst BR7 189 B2
Woolwich SE2 146 B5
Patricia Villas N17 34 B2
Patrick Coman Ho
EC1 234 C1
Patrick Connolly Gdns 41
E3 97 D4
Patrick Rd E13 99 C4
Patriot Sq E2 96 B5
Patrol Pl SE6 163 D5
Pat Shaw Ho 2 E1 96 D3
Patshull Pl NW5 71 C2
Patshull Rd NW5 71 C2
Patson Cl E5 74 D5
Pattenden Rd SE6 163 B3
Patten Ho N4 51 A1
Patten Rd SW18 158 C4
Patterdale NW1 231 D1
Patterdale Cl BR1 186 C4
Patterdale Rd SE15 140 C5
Patterson Ct SE19 183 D4
Patterson Rd SE19 183 D4
Pattina Wlk SE16 119 A5
Pattinson Point 10 E16 99 A2
Pattison Ho 1 E1 96 D1
SE1 252 B2
Pattison Rd NW2 69 C5
Pattison Wlk SE18 123 A1
Paul Byrne Ho 3 N2 48 A6
Paul Cl E15 76 C1
Paul Ct N3 29 A1
7 Edmonton N18 34 A6
Paulet Rd SE5 138 D4
Paul Gdns CR0 221 D6
Paulhan Rd HA3 43 D5
Paul Ho 13 W10 91 A3
Paulin Dr N21 16 C4
Pauline Cres TW2 152 A3
Pauline Ho 19 E1 96 A2
Paulinus Cl BR5 190 C1
Paul Julius Cl E14 120 B6
Paul Robeson Cl E6 100 C4
Paul's Ho 5 E3 97 B2
Paulson Ho 7 IG11 78 D1
Paul St E15 98 C6
EC2 95 C3 243 A6
Paultons Ho SW3 266 D6
Paultons Sq
SW3 136 B6 266 D6
Paultons St
SW3 136 B6 266 D5
Pauntley Ho 6 N19 49 C1
Pauntley St 4 N19 49 C1
Pavan Ct 23 E2 96 C4
Paved Ct 9 TW9 153 D6
Paveley Dr
SW11 136 C5 267 A3
Paveley Ho N1 233 C3
Paveley St NW8 92 C3 237 B6
Pavement Mews 1
RM6 58 D2
Pavement Sq CR0 206 A1
Pavement The E11 54 A1
SW4 137 C1
W5 110 A3
11 West Norwood SE27 183 A6
Pavet Cl RM10 81 D2
Pavilion Ct NW3 70 B3
5 NW3 70 A4
8 NW6 91 C4
3 Wimbledon SW19 179 A3
Pavilion L Ctr The
BR1 187 A1
Pavilion Lo HA2 42 B1
Pavilion Mans 10 SW9 138 B1
Pavilion Mews N3 29 C1
Pavilion Rd
SW1 114 D3 257 D5
Redbridge IG1 56 B2
Pavilion St SW1 257 D5
Pavilion Terr W12 90 C1
Hampton KT1 197 A4
Pavilion Way HA8 27 A3
Ruislip HA4 62 C6
Pawleyne Cl SE20 184 C3
Pawsey Cl E13 99 A6
Pawson's Rd CR0 205 A4
Paxford Rd HA0 65 B6
Paxton Cl
Richmond TW9 132 B3
Walton-on-T KT12 194 C2
Paxton Ct SE9 165 C1
1 Forest Hill SE26 185 A6
Mitcham CR4 180 D1
Paxton Ho SE17 262 B2
Paxton Pl SE27 183 C6
Paxton Prim Sch SE19 183 C4
Paxton Rd BR1 187 A3
Forest Hill SE23 163 A1
Tottenham N17 34 A3
Chiswick W4 133 C6
Paxton Terr SW1 268 D6
Payens Wlk
W6 135 A6 264 A5
Paymal Ho 28 E1 96 C2
Payne Cl IG11 79 D1
Payne Ho N1 233 D5
Paynell Ct SE3 142 C2
Payne Rd E3 97 D5
Paynesfield Ave SW14 133 B2
Paynesfield Rd WD23 8 D4
Payne St SE8 141 B6
Payzes Gdns IG8 36 D5
Peabody Ave
SW1 115 B1 258 D1
Peabody Bldgs SE17 262 C3
6 SE5 139 B4
Peabody Cl SW1 268 D6
Croydon CR0 206 C1
Peabody Cotts N17 33 C2
Peabody Ct EC1 242 B5
9 SE5 139 B4
Peabody Est E1 118 A6
4 E1 118 D6
18 E2 96 B5
EC1 241 B5
EC1 242 B5
SE1 251 B3
SE1 252 A3
SW1 259 B4
SW6 135 B6 264 D6
W10 90 C2
17 W6 112 C1
WC2 240 C1
Streatham SE24 161 A4
Peabody Hill SE21 161 A3
Peabody Sq SE1 251 C1
Peabody Twr EC1 242 B5
Peabody Yd N1 235 A6
Peace Cl East Barnet N14 15 B6
Greenford UB6 86 B6
South Norwood SE25 205 C5
Peace Ct 10 NW9 46 A5
Peace Gr HA9 66 D6
Peace St SE18 144 C6
Peaches Cl SM2 217 A1
Peach Rd W10 91 A4
Feltham TW14 150 A3
Peach Tree Ave UB7 82 B1
Peachum Rd SE3 142 D6
Peach Walk Mews 23
E3 96 D5
Peacock Ave TW14 149 B3
Peacock Cl RM8 80 C6
Peacock Est N17 33 D3
Peacock St
SE17 116 D2 261 D3
Peacock Wlk E16 99 B1
Peacock Yd SE17 261 D3
Peaketon Ave IG4 55 D4
Peak Hill SE26 184 C6
Peak Hill Ave SE26 184 C6
Peak Hill Gdns SE26 184 C6
Peak Ho N4 51 A1
Peak The SE26 162 C1
Peal Gdns W13 87 A3
Peall Rd CR0 204 B3
Pear Ave TW17 193 C6
Pearce Cl 2 CR4 181 A1
Pearcefield Ave 5
SE23 162 C3
Pearce Ho N19 71 C5
7 Streatham SW2 160 A4
Pear Cl NW9 45 B5
SE14 141 A5
Pearcroft Rd E11 76 B6
Pear Ct 20 SE15 139 D5
Peardon St SW8 137 B3
Peareswood Gdns HA7 25 D2
Pearfield Ho 1 N5 73 A3
Pearfield Rd SE23 163 A1
Pearl Cl E6 100 C1
NW2 46 D2
Pearl Ct 18 NW9 46 A5
Pearl Rd E17 53 C6
Pearl St E1 118 B5
Pearlstones Ct RM10 103 C6
Pearmain Cl TW17 192 D4
Pearman St
SE1 116 C4 251 B1
Pear Pl SE1 251 A2
Pear Rd E11 76 C5
Pearscroft Ct
SW6 135 D4 265 D1
Pearscroft Rd
SW6 135 D4 265 D1
Pearse St 3 SE15 139 C6
Pearson Ct SM4 201 D4
Pearson Ho SW15 134 C3
Pearson's Ave SE8,
SE14 141 C4
Pearson St E2 95 D5
Pears Rd TW3 130 A2
Peartree Ave SW17 158 A1
Pear Tree Ave UB7 82 B1
Pear Tree Cl 23 E2 95 D6
Peartree Cl KT9 214 C3
Pear Tree Cl CR4 180 C1
Pear Tree Ct EC1 241 B5
Putney SW15 134 B1
Peartree Gdns RM8 80 B4
Pear Tree Ho SE4 141 B1
Hayes UB8 83 A1
Peartree La E1 118 C6
Peartree Rd EN1 5 C2
Pear Tree Rd TW15 171 A5
Peartree St EC1 95 A3 242 A6
Peartree Way SE10 121 A2
Peary Ho 3 NW10 67 B1
Peary Pl E2 96 C4
Peas Mead Terr E4 36 A6
Peatfield Cl DA15 167 C1
Pebworth Lo SE25 205 D5
Pebworth Rd HA1 65 A6
Peckarmans Wood
SE21,SE26 162 A1
Peckett Sq 3 N5 72 D4
Peckford Pl SW9 138 C3
Peckham Gr SE15 139 C5
Peckham High St
SE15 140 A4
Peckham Hill St SE15 140 A5
Peckham Park Prim Sch
SE15 140 A5
Peckham Park Rd
SE15 140 A5
Peckham Rd SE5 139 C4
Peckham Rye SE22 140 A1
Peckham SE15,SE22 140 B1
Peckham Rye Prim Sch
SE15 140 B2
Peckham Rye Sta
SE15 140 A3
Peckwater St NW5 71 C3
Pedlars Wlk N7 72 B3
Pedley Rd RM8 58 C1
Pedley St E1 95 D3 243 D5
Pedro St E5 74 D4
Pedworth Gdns 4
SE16 118 C2
Peebles Ct UB1 86 A1
Peek Cres SW19 178 D5
Peel Centre (Metropolitan
Police Training
Establishment) NW9 45 D6
Peel Cl Chingford E4 19 D2
Edmonton N9 18 A1
Peel Ct UB6 86 A4
Peel Dr NW9 45 D6
Redbridge IG5 56 A6
Peel Gr E2 96 C5
Peel Pass W8 245 A3
Peel Pl IG5 37 D1
Peel Prec NW6 91 C5
Peel Rd BR6 227 A3
NW6 91 B4
Harrow HA3 42 D6
Wembley HA0,HA9 65 D5
Woodford E18 36 D2
Peel St W8 113 C5 245 A3
Peel Way UB8 82 A2
Peel Yates Ho 13 SE7 122 A2
Peerglow Est EN3 18 C6
Peerless St EC1 95 B4 235 C1
Pegamoid Rd N18 18 C1
Pegasus Ct NW10 90 B4
Brentford TW8 110 B1
Kingston KT1 197 D6
Pegasus Ho 9 E1 96 D3
Pegasus Rd CR0,CR9 220 C2
Pegasus Way N11 31 B4
Peggotty Way UB8 82 D1
Pegg Rd TW5 128 D5
Peggy Quirke Ct 2
HA0 66 A2
Pegley Gdns SE12 165 A2
Pegwell Ho 19 E5 74 B3
Pegwell St SE18 145 C5
Pekin St E14 97 C1
Pekoe SE1 253 D3
Peldon Ct TW10 154 B6
Pele Ct N17 33 B3
Pelham Ave IG11 101 D6
Pelham Cl SE5 139 C2
Pelham Cotts DA5 169 D3
Pelham Cres SW7 257 A3
Pelham Ct SW3 257 A3
Pelham Ho W14 254 C3
Pelham Pl SW7 257 A3
8 Ealing W7 86 D3
Pelham Prim Sch DA7 147 C2
Pelham Rd DA7 147 C2
N15 51 D5
Ilford IG1 79 B6
Merton SW19 179 C3
Pelham Rd *continued*
Penge BR3,SE20 184 C1
Wanstead E18 55 B6
Wood Green N22 32 C1
Pelham St
SW7 114 B2 256 D4
Pelican Ho 7 SE8 119 B2
Pelier St SE17 139 A6
Pelinore Rd SE6 164 C2
Pella Ho SE11 260 D2
Pellant Rd
SW6 135 A5 264 B4
Pellatt Gr N22 32 C2
Pellatt Rd SE22 161 D6
Wembley HA9 66 A6
Pellerin Rd N16 73 C3
Pellew Ho 15 E1 96 B3
Pelling St E14 97 C1
Pellipar Cl N13 16 C1
Pellipar Gdns SE18 122 B1
Pellipar Rd SE18 122 B1
Pelly Ct 4 E17 54 A5
Pelly Rd E13 99 A5
Pelter St E2 95 D4
Pelton Ct CR2 221 A2
Pelton Rd SE10 120 C1
Pembar Ave E17 53 A6
Pemberley Chase
KT19 214 D3
Pemberley Cl KT19 214 D3
Pemberley Ho KT19 214 D3
Pember Rd NW10 90 D4
Pemberton Ct 18 E1 96 D4
Pemberton Gdns N19 71 C5
Dagenham RM6 59 A4
Pemberton Ho SE26 184 A6
Pemberton Pl 2 E8 74 B1
Esher KT10 212 A5
Pemberton Rd N4 50 D4
East Molesey KT8 196 A5
Pemberton Row EC4 241 B2
Pemberton Terr N19 71 C5
Pembridge Ave TW4 151 B3
Pembridge Cres
W11 113 C6 245 A6
Pembridge Gdns
W2 113 C6 245 A5
Pembridge Mews
W11 113 C6 245 A6
Pembridge Pl
1 SW15 157 C6
W2 113 C6 245 B6
Pembridge Rd
W11 113 C6 245 A5
Pembridge Sq
W2 113 C6 245 B5
Pembridge Villas
W11 113 C6 245 A6
Pembroke W14 254 D3
Pembroke Ave
Enfield EN1 6 B4
Harrow HA3 43 B6
Surbiton KT5 198 D4
Pembroke Bldgs NW10 90 A4
Pembroke Cl SW1 248 B1
Pembroke Ct 11 W7 86 D2
Pembroke Gdns
W8 113 C3 254 D4
Dagenham RM10 81 D5
Pembroke Gdns Cl
W8 255 A5
Pembroke Hall NW4 46 C6
Pembroke Ho 16 W2 91 D1
Acton W3 111 A4
Putney SW15 156 A6
Upper Tooting SW17 180 B5
Pembroke Mews N10 31 A2
W8 255 A5
Pembroke Pl W8 255 A5
Edgware HA8 26 C3
Isleworth TW7 130 C3
Pembroke Rd BR1 187 D1
E17 53 D4
E6 100 B2
N10 31 A3
N15 51 D4
N8 50 A5
W8 113 C2 255 A4
Edmonton N13 17 A1
Greenford UB6 85 D3
Ilford IG3 57 D2
Mitcham CR4 181 A1
Ruislip HA4 39 D1
South Norwood SE25 205 C5
Wembley HA9 65 D5
Pembroke Sq
W8 113 C3 255 A5
Pembroke St
N1 72 A1 233 B6
Pembroke Studios
W8 254 D5
Pembroke Terr NW8 229 C5
Pembroke Villas W8 255 A4
Richmond TW9 131 D1
Pembroke Way UB3 105 A3
Pembroke Wlk W8 255 A4
Pembrook Lo 2
SW16 160 B1
Pembury Ave KT4 200 A2

Pembury Cl E5 74 B3
Hayes BR2 208 D2
Pembury Cres DA14 169 A2
Pembury Ct UB3 127 B6
Pembury Ho SE5 139 C3
Pembury Pl 15 E5,E8 74 B3
Pembury Rd DA7 147 A6
E5 74 B3
Croydon SE25 206 A5
Tottenham N17 33 D1
Pemdevon Rd CR0 204 C2
Pemell Cl 27 E1 96 C3
Pemell Ho 28 E1 96 C3
Pemerich Cl UB3 105 D1
Pempath Pl HA9 65 D6
Penally Pl N1 235 D6
Penang St E1 118 B5
Penard Rd UB2 107 D3
Penarth Ct SM2 218 A1
Penarth St SE15 140 C6
Penates KT10 212 B4
Penberth Rd SE6 164 A3
Penbury Rd UB2 107 B1
Penceat Ct SE20 184 C1
Pencombe Mews W11 244 D6
Pencraig Way SE15 140 B6
Pendall Cl EN4 2 C1
Penda Rd DA8 147 D5
Pendarves Rd SW20 178 C2
Penda's Mead E9 75 A4
Pendell Ave UB3 127 D5
Pendennis Ho 15 SE8 119 A2
Pendennis Rd N17 51 B6
Streatham SW16 182 A6
Penderel Rd TW3 151 C6
Penderry Rise SE6 164 B2
Penderyn Way N7 71 D4
Pendlebury Gn 8 SE18 144 A4
Pendle Ho 13 SE26 162 A1
Pendle Rd SW16 181 B5
Pendlestone Rd E17 53 D4
Pendley Ho 18 E2 96 A6
Pendragon Rd BR1 165 A1
Pendragon Sec Sch BR1 165 A1
Pendrell Ho WC2 239 D1
Pendrell Rd SE4 141 A3
Pendrell St SE18 145 B6
Pendula Dr UB4 84 D3
Penelope Ho 20 SW9 138 C4
Penerley Rd SE6 163 D3
Penfield Lo 7 W9 91 C2
Penfields Ho N7 72 A2
Penfold Cl CR0 220 C5
Penfold Ct NW8 236 D5
7 Mitcham CR4 181 A1
Penfold Ho 14 SE18 144 D6
Penfold La DA5 168 D3
Penfold Pl NW1 92 C2 237 A4
Penfold Rd N9 18 D3
Penfold St NW8 92 B3 236 D5
Penford Gdns SE9 143 D2
Penford St SE5 138 D3
Pengarth Rd DA5 168 D5
Penge East Sta SE20 184 C4
Penge La SE20 184 D3
Penge Rd E13 99 C6
South Norwood SE25 206 A6
Penge West Sta SE20 184 B4
Penhall Rd SE7 121 D2
Penhill Rd DA5 168 C4
Penhurst Mans SW6 264 C2
Penifather La UB6 86 B4
Peninsula Ct E14 119 D3
Peninsular Cl TW14 149 C5
Peninsular Park Rd SE7 121 A2
Penistone Rd SW16 182 A3
Penketh Dr HA1 64 B5
Penmayne Ho SE11 261 B2
Penmon Rd SE2 124 A3
Pennack Rd SE15 139 D6
Penn Almshouse 1 SE10 142 A4
Pennant Mews W8 113 D2 255 C4
Pennant Terr E17 35 B1
Pennard Mans 5 W12 112 C4
Pennard Rd W12 112 C4
Pennards The TW16 194 C6
Penn Cl Greenford UB6 85 D5
Harrow HA3 43 C5
Penn Ct NW9 45 B6
Penner Cl SW19 157 A2
Penners Gdns KT6 198 A2
Pennethorne Cl E9 96 C6
Pennethorne Ho SW11 136 B2
Pennethorne Rd SE15 140 B5
Penn Gdns BR7 188 D1
Penn Ho NW8 237 A5
7 Edmonton N9 18 A1
Pennine Dr NW2 68 D6
Pennine La NW2 69 A6
Pennine Mans NW2 69 A6
Pennine Par NW2 69 A6
Pennine Way UB7 127 B5
Pennington Cl 10 SE27 183 B6
Pennington Ct 16 E1 118 A6
SE16 119 A5
Pennington Dr N21 16 A6
Pennington Lo 18 KT5 198 A4
Pennington St E1 118 B6
Pennington Way SE12 165 B2
Penniston Cl N17 33 A1
Penn La DA5 169 A5
Penn Rd N7 72 A4
Penn St N1 95 B6 235 D5
Penny Ct SW10 266 B6
Pennyfields E14 119 C6
Pennyford Ct NW8 236 C6
Penny La TW17 193 C2
Penny Mews SW12 159 B4
Pennymore Wlk W9 91 B3
Penny Rd NW10 88 D4
Penny Royal SM6 219 D2
Pennyroyal Ave E6 100 C1
Penpoll Rd E8 74 B2
Penpool La DA16 146 B2
Penrhyn Ave E17 35 C2
Penrhyn Cres
Chingford E17 35 C2
Mortlake SW14 133 A1
Penrhyn Gdns KT1 197 D5
Penrhyn Gr E17 35 C2
Penrhyn Rd KT1 198 A6
Penrith Cl
Beckenham BR3 185 D2
Putney SW15 157 A6
Penrith Pl SE27 160 D2
Penrith Rd N15 51 B4
New Malden KT3 199 B5
South Norwood CR7 183 A1
Penrith St SW16 181 C4
Penrose Gr SE17 117 A1 262 A1
Penrose Ho SE17 262 A1
Southgate N21 16 B6
Penrose St SE17 117 A1 262 A1
Penryn Ho SE11 261 C2
Penryn St NW1 93 D5 232 C4
Penry St SE1 263 B3
Pensbury Pl SW8 137 C3
Pensbury St SW8 137 C3
Pensford Ave TW9 132 C3
Penshurst 2 NW5 71 A2
Penshurst Ave DA15 168 A5
Penshurst Gdns HA8 26 D5
Penshurst Gn BR2 208 D4
Penshurst Ho 1 SE15 140 C6
Penshurst Rd DA7 147 B4
E9 74 D1
Thornton Heath CR7 204 D4
Tottenham N17 33 D3
Penshurst Way SM2 217 C1
Penshurst Wlk 4 BR2 208 D4
Pensilver Cl EN4 2 C1
Penstemon Cl N3 29 C4
Pentelow Gdns TW14 150 A5
Pentire Rd E17 36 B2
Pentland Ave
Edgware HA8 10 D2
Littleton TW17 192 C4
Pentland Cl N9 18 C2
NW11 69 A6
Pentland Ho 7 N16 51 D1
17 NW5 71 A2
Pentland Pl UB5 85 A6
Pentland Rd WD23 8 A5
Pentlands BR3 186 A2
Pentlands Cl CR4 203 B6
Pentland St SW18 158 A5
Pentland Way UB10 61 A5
Pentlow St SW15 134 C2
Pentney Rd
5 Chingford E4 20 B3
Merton SW19,SW20 179 A2
Streatham SW12 159 C3
Penton Gr N1 234 A3
Penton Ho N1 234 A3
3 SE2 124 D4
Sutton SM2 218 A1
Penton Pl SE17 116 D1 261 D2
Penton Rise WC1 94 B4 233 D2
Penton St N1 94 C5 234 A3
Pentonville Rd N1 94 B5 233 C3
Pentrich Ave EN1 6 A5
Pentridge St SE15 139 D5
Pentyre Ave N18 33 B5
Penwerris Ave TW5, TW7 130 A5
Penwerris Ct TW7 130 A5
Penwith Rd SW18 157 D2
Penwood Ho 4 SW15 155 D5
Penwortham Ct 1 N22 32 C1
Penwortham Prim Sch SW17 181 B4
Penwortham Rd SW16 181 C4
Penylan Pl HA8 26 C3
Penywern Rd SW5 113 C1 255 B2
Penzance Ho SE11 261 B2
Penzance Pl W11 113 A5 244 B4
Penzance St W11 113 A5 244 A4
Peony Ct IG8 36 C3
Peony Gdns W12 112 A6
Peperfield WC1 233 C1
Pepler Ho 17 W10 91 A3
Pepler Mews SE1 263 C1
Peploe Rd NW6 90 D5
Pepper Cl E6 100 B2
Peppermead Sq SE13 163 C6
Peppermint Cl CR0 204 A2
Peppermint Pl 5 E11 76 C5
Pepper St E14 119 D3
SE1 252 A2
Peppie Cl N16 73 C6
Pepsi Trocadero W1 249 C5
Pepys Cl UB10 60 D4
Pepys Cres 2 E16 121 A5
Barnet EN5 12 C6
Pepys Ct SW20 178 C1
Pepys Ent Ctr 12 SE8 119 B2
Pepys Ho 14 E2 96 C4
SW4 159 D6
Pepys Rd SE14 140 D3
Wimbledon SW20 178 C2
Pepys Rise BR6 211 D1
Pepys St EC3 117 C6 253 B6
Perak Ct KT5 199 A2
Perceval Ave NW3 70 C3
Perceval Ct UB5 63 C2
Percheron Cl TW7 130 D2
Percheron Ct 3 SW9 138 B2
Percheron Rd WD6 11 B5
Perch St E8 73 D4
Percival Ct N17 33 D3
Percival Gdns RM6 58 C3
Percival Rd Enfield EN1 5 D1
Feltham TW13 149 D2
Mortlake SW14 133 A1
Orpington BR6 226 D6
Percival St EC1 94 D4 234 D1
Percival Way KT19 215 B4
Percy Ave TW15 170 C5
Percy Bilton Ct TW5 129 D4
Percy Bryant Rd TW16 171 C3
Percy Bush Rd UB7 104 B3
Percy Cir WC1 94 B4 233 D2
Percy Ct 1 KT5 198 B3
Percy Gdns Enfield EN3 18 D6
Hayes UB4 83 C4
3 Isleworth TW7 131 A2
New Malden KT4 199 C1
Percy Ho 4 SW16 181 C6
Percy Mews W1 239 C3
Percy Pas W1 239 C3
Percy Rd DA7 147 A3
E11 54 C2
E16 98 C2
N12 30 A5
W12 112 A4
Carshalton CR4 203 A2
Croydon SE25 206 A4
Edmonton N21 17 A4
Hampton TW12 173 C3
Ilford IG3 58 A2
Isleworth TW7 131 A1
Penge SE20 184 D2
Romford RM7 59 D6
Twickenham TW2 152 A3
Percy St W1 93 D2 239 C3
Percy Way TW2 152 A3
Peregrine Cl NW10 67 B3
Peregrine Ct DA16 145 D4
Streatham SW16 182 B6
Peregrine Gdns CR0 223 A6
Peregrine Ho EC1 234 D2
6 SW11 136 C2
Peregrine Rd TW16 171 D1
Peregrine Way SW19, SW20 178 C3
Performing Arts & Tech Sch SE25 205 B3
Perham Rd W14 113 B1 254 B1
Peridot St E6 100 A2
Perifield SE21 161 A3
Perimeade Rd UB6 87 C5
Periton Rd SE9 143 D1
Perivale UB6 86 D5
Perivale Fst & Mid Schs UB6 87 C5
Perivale Gdns W13 87 B3
Perivale Grange UB6 87 A4
Perivale Ind Pk UB6 87 B5
Perivale La UB6 87 A4
Perivale Lo UB6 87 A4
Perivale New Bsns Ctr UB6 87 C5
Perivale Sta UB6 87 A5
Perkin Cl
Hounslow TW3 129 D1
Wembley HA0 65 B3
Perkins Ct TW15 170 B5
Perkins Ho 13 E14 97 B2
Perkins Rd IG2 57 B4
Perkins Rents SW1 259 C5
Perkins Sq SE1 252 B4
Perks Cl SE3 142 C2
Perley Ho 10 E3 97 B2
Perotti Ho SW6 135 D2
Perpins Rd SE9 167 C5
Perran Rd SE24,SW2 160 D2
Perren St NW5 71 B2
Perrers Rd W6 112 B2
Perrin Cl TW15 170 B5
Perring Est E3 97 C2
Perrin Grange HA9 66 B6
Perrin Rd HA0 65 B4
Perrin's Ct 17 NW3 70 A4
Perrin's La NW3 70 A4
Perrin's Wlk NW3 70 A4
Perronet Ho SE1 261 D5
Perry Ave W3 89 B1
Perry Cl UB8 82 D1
Perry Ct 2 N15 51 C3
5 Millwall E14 119 C1
Perryfield Way NW9 45 D3
Richmond TW10 153 B2
Perry Garth UB5 84 C6
Perry Gdns N9 17 C1
Perry Hall Prim Sch BR6 211 D3
Perry Hill SE6 163 B1
Perry Ho 24 SW2 160 A4
Perry How KT4 199 D1
Perryman Ho IG11 101 A6
Perrymans Farm Rd IG2 57 B4
Perry Mead Bushey WD23 8 A5
Enfield EN2 4 D3
Perrymead St SW6 135 D3 265 C1
Perrymount Prim Sch SE23 162 D2
Perryn Ct 1 TW1 153 A4
Perryn Ho W3 111 C6
Perryn Rd 1 SE16 118 B3
W3 111 B6
Perry Rise SE23 163 A1
Perry's Pl W1 239 C2
Perry St BR7 189 C4
Perry Street Gdns BR7 189 C4
Perry Vale SE23 162 D2
Perrywood Ho 17 E5 74 B3
Persant Rd SE6 164 C2
Perserverance Pl SW9 138 C5
Perseverance Works 18 E2 95 C4
Pershore Cl IG2 56 D4
Pershore Gr SM5 202 B3
Pert Cl N10 31 B4
Perth Ave NW9 45 B2
Hayes UB4 84 C3
Perth Cl SW20 178 A1
Perth Ct 5 SE5 139 B1
Perth Ho N1 72 B1
12 Acton W3 88 C1
Perth Rd E10 53 B1
E13 99 B5
N4 50 C1
Barking IG11 101 B6
Beckenham BR3 186 A1
Ilford IG2 56 D3
Tottenham N22 32 D2
Perth Terr IG2 57 A2
Perwell Ave HA2 41 B1
Perystreete SE23 162 C2
Petavel Rd TW11 174 C4
Peter Ave NW10 68 B1
Peter Best Ho 6 E1 96 B1
Peterboat Cl SE10 120 C2
Peterborough Ct EC4 241 B1
Peterborough Gdns IG1 56 A2
Peterborough Mews SW6 135 C3
Peterborough Prim Sch SW6 135 C3
Peterborough Rd E10 54 B3
SW6 135 C2
Carshalton SM5 202 C3
Harrow HA1 42 D2
Peterborough Villas SW6 265 C2
Peter Bradley Ct RM9 81 B1
Peter Butler Ho 6 SE1 118 A4
Peterchurch Ho SE15 140 B6
Petergate SW11 136 A1
Peterhead Ct 12 UB1 86 A1
Peter Hills Ho 6 SE16 118 A2
Peter Hills with St Mary's & St Paul's CE Prim Sch SE16 118 D5
Peter Ho SW8 270 A4
Peter James Bsns Ctr UB3 106 A4
Peter Kennedy Ct CR0 207 B3
Peterley Bsns Ctr 21 E2 96 B5
Peters Cl DA16 145 C3
Dagenham RM8 58 D1
Peters Cl *continued*
Stanmore HA7 25 D4
Peters Ct 9 W2 91 D1
Peter's Ct SW4 160 A5
Petersfield Cl N18 33 A5
Petersfield Rd W3 111 A4
Petersfield Rise SW15 156 B3
Petersham Cl
Richmond TW10 153 D2
Sutton SM1 217 C3
Petersham Dr BR5 190 A1
Petersham Gdns BR5 189 D1
Petersham Ho SW7 256 C4
Petersham La SW7 256 A6
Petersham Mews SW7 114 A3 256 B5
Petersham Pl SW7 114 A3 256 B6
Petersham Rd TW10 154 A3
Petersham Terr CR0 220 A5
Peter's La EC1 241 D4
Peter's Lo HA8 26 B4
Peter's Path SE26 184 B6
Peter St W1 115 D6 249 C6
Peterstone Rd SE2 124 B4
Peterstow Cl SW19 157 A2
Peterwood Pk CR9 220 B6
Peterwood Way CR0 220 B6
Petherton Ct NW10 90 D6
10 Harrow HA1 42 D3
Petherton Ho N4 51 A1
Petherton Rd N5 73 A3
Petiver Cl 26 E9 74 C1
Petley Rd W6 134 D5
Peto Pl NW1 238 D6
Peto St N E16 98 D1
Petrel Ct 7 SE21 161 B2
Petrie Cl NW2 69 A2
Petrie Ho 3 SE18 144 C6
Petros Gdns 1 NW3 70 A2
Petticoat Lane Mkt★ EC2 95 D2 243 C3
Petticoat Sq E1 243 C2
Petticoat Twr E1 243 C2
Pettit's Pl RM10 81 C3
Pettit's Rd RM10 81 C3
Pettiward Cl SW15 134 C1
Pettman Cres SE18, SE28 123 B3
Pettsgrove Ave HA0 65 C3
Pett's Hill UB5 63 D3
Petts La TW17 192 C5
Pett St SE7 122 A2
Petts Wood Rd BR5 211 B4
Petts Wood Sta BR5 211 A4
Petty France SW1 115 C3 259 C6
Petworth Cl UB5 63 B1
Petworth Gdns
Hillingdon UB10 83 A6
West Barnes SW20 200 B6
Petworth Ho 16 SE22 139 C2
Petworth Rd DA6 169 C6
N12 30 C5
Petworth St SW11 136 C4 267 B2
Petyt Pl SW3 136 C6 267 A5
Petyward SW3 114 C2 257 B3
Pevensey Ave N11 31 D5
Enfield EN1 5 C3
Pevensey Cl TW7 130 A5
Pevensey Ct 4 W3 110 D4
West Norwood SW16 160 C1
10 Woodford E18 37 A2
Pevensey Ho 5 E1 97 A2
Pevensey Rd E7 77 A4
Feltham TW13 151 A3
Upper Tooting SW17 180 B6
Peverel E6 100 C1
Peverel Ho RM10 81 C6
Peverett Cl N11 31 B5
Peveril Dr TW11 174 B5
Peveril Ho SE1 262 D5
Pewsey Cl E4 35 C5
Pewsham Ho N4 51 A1
Pewterers Ct N3 29 B2
Peyton Ho N11 31 A6
Peyton Pl SE10 142 A5
Pharamond NW2 68 D2
Pharaoh Cl CR4 202 D2
Pheasant Cl E16 99 B1
Phelps Ho SW15 134 D2
Phelp St SE17 139 B6
Phelps Way UB3 105 D2
Phene St SW3 136 C6 267 B6
Philadelphia Ct SW10 266 B3
Philbeach Gdns SW5 113 C1 255 A2
Phil Brown Pl 3 SW8 137 B2
Philchurch Pl 25 E1 96 A1
Phildor Ct NW11 47 A3
Philia Ho 2 NW1 71 C1
Philimore Cl SE18 123 C1
Philip Ct W2 236 C4
Enfield EN2 5 B4
Philip Gdns CR0 223 B6
Philip Ho N20 14 D2
10 NW6 91 D6
Philip La N15 51 C6
Philipot Almshouse SE9 166 B5
Philipot Path SE9 166 B5
Philippa Gdns SE9 165 D6
Philip Rd SE15 140 A2
Philips Cl CR4 203 A1
Philip St E13 99 A3
Philip Turner Est 28 E9 74 C1
Philip Wlk SE15 140 B2
Phillimore Ct W8 245 B1
Phillimore Gardens Cl W8 113 C3 255 A6
Phillimore Gdns W8 113 C4 245 A1
Willesden NW10 90 C6
Phillimore Pl W8 113 C4 245 A1
Phillimore Terr W8 255 B6
Phillimore Wlk W8 113 C3 255 B6
Phillip Ho E1 243 D3
Phillipp St N1 95 C6
Phillips Ct Edgware HA8 26 C4
Hayes UB4 84 B4
Philpot La EC3 253 A6
Philpot Sq SW6 135 D2
Philpot St E1 96 B1
Phineas Pett Rd SE9 144 A2
Phipp's Bridge Rd CR4, SW19 202 B6
Phipps Bridge Sta CR4 202 B6
Phipps Hatch La EN2 5 A5
Phipps Ho 1 SE7 121 B1
18 W12 112 B6
Phipp St EC2 95 C3 243 A6
Phoebeth Rd SE4 163 C6
Phoenix Bsns Ctr E3 97 C2
Phoenix Cl E17 35 B1
18 E8 95 D6
West Wickham BR4 224 C6
Phoenix Coll SM4 202 A4
Phoenix Ct E14 119 C2
2 SE14 141 A6
4 Brentford TW8 110 A1
Chingford E4 19 D1
Croydon SE25 206 A4
Enfield EN3 6 C5
Phoenix Dr BR2 225 D5
Phoenix High Sch W12 112 A6
Phoenix Ind Est HA1 42 D5
Phoenix Lodge Mans 1 W6 112 C2
Phoenix Pk NW2 68 A6
Phoenix Pl WC1 94 B3 240 D6
Phoenix Rd NW1 93 D4 232 C2
Penge SE20 184 C4
Phoenix Sch E3 97 B4
Phoenix Sch The NW3 70 A2
Phoenix St WC2 239 D1
Phoenix Trad Est UB6 87 D6
Phoenix Trad Pk TW8 109 D1
Phoenix Way TW5 128 D6
Phoenix Wharf Rd SE1 253 D1
Phyllis Ave KT3 200 B4
Phyllis Ho CR0 220 D4
Phyllis Hodges Ho NW1 93 D5 232 C3
Physic Pl SW3 136 D6 267 C6
Picador Ho 1 RM10 81 D2
Picardy Manorway DA17 125 D4
Picardy Rd DA17 125 C2
Picardy St DA17 125 C3
Piccadilly W1 115 C5 249 A4
Piccadilly Arc SW1 249 A4
Piccadilly Cir★ W1 115 D6 249 C5
Piccadilly Circus Sta SW1 115 D6 249 C5
Piccadilly Pl W1 249 B5
Pickard St EC1 234 D2
Pickering Ave E6 100 C4
Pickering Gdns N11 31 A4
Croydon SE25 205 D3
Pickering Ho N4 51 B2
4 SE18 122 C2
17 W2 91 D1
W5 109 C2
Pickering Mews W2 91 D1
Pickering Pl SW1 249 B3
Pickering St N1 234 D6
Pickets Cl WD23 8 C3
Pickets St SW12 159 B4
Pickett Croft HA7 25 D2
Pickett's Lock La N9 18 D2
Pickford Cl DA7 147 A3
Pickford La DA7 147 A3
Pickford Rd DA7 147 A2
Pickfords Wharf N1 235 A3
Pickhurst Gn BR2 208 D2
Pickhurst Inf Sch BR2 208 D3

Pickhurst Jun Sch BR2 208 D3
Pickhurst La BR2,BR3, BR4 208 C2
Pickhurst Mead BR2 208 D2
Pickhurst Pk BR2 208 D4
Pickhurst Rise BR4 208 B1
Pickwick Cl TW4 151 A6
Pickwick Ct SE9 166 B3
Pickwick Ho 18 SE16 118 A4
3 W11 112 D5
Pickwick Mews N18 33 C5
Pickwick Pl HA1 42 C2
Pickwick Rd SE21 161 C4
Pickwick St SE1 252 A1
Pickwick Way BR7 189 A4
Pickworth Cl SW8 270 B3
Picton Ho 1 SW4 160 A4
Picton Pl W1 238 B1
Tolworth KT6 198 C1
Picton St SE5 139 B5
Pied Bull Ct WC1 240 B3
Pied Bull Yd WC1 240 B3
Piedmont Rd SE18 123 B1
Pield Heath Ave UB8 82 C3
Pield Heath Rd UB8 82 B3
Pield Heath Sch UB8 82 A3
Pierhead Wharf 37 E1 118 B5
Pier Ho SW3 267 B5
Piermont Pl BR1 188 A1
Piermont Rd SE22 162 B6
Pier Par 3 E16 122 C5
Pierpoint Bldg 5 E14 119 C4
Pier Rd E16 122 C4
Feltham TW14 150 B6
Pierrepoint SE25 205 C6
Pierrepoint Rd W3 110 D6
Pierson Ho 12 SE19 183 C6
Pier St E14 120 A2
Pier Terr SW18 136 A1
Pier Way SE18 123 B3
Pigeon Ct E4 36 A4
Pigeon La TW12 173 C6
Piggott Ho 2 E2 96 D5
Pigott St E14 97 C1
Pike Cl BR1 187 B5
Hillingdon UB10 82 B6
Pike Rd NW7 27 B6
Pike's End HA5 40 B5
Pikestone Cl UB4 85 A3
Pikethorne SE23 162 D2
Pilgrimage St SE1 117 B4 252 C1
Pilgrim Cl SM4 201 D2
Pilgrim Hill SE27 183 A6
Pilgrim Ho SE1 262 D5
Pilgrims Cl Northolt UB5 64 A3
Palmers Green N13 32 B6
Pilgrims Cloisters 18 SE5 139 C5
Pilgrims Ct SE3 143 A4
Enfield EN1 5 B3
Pilgrim's La NW3 70 B4
Pilgrims Mews E14 120 B6
Pilgrim's Rise EN4 14 C6
Pilgrim St EC4 241 C1
Pilgrims Way 5 E6 100 A6
N19 49 D1
Wembley HA9 44 D1
Pilgrim's Way CR2 221 D3
Pilgrims Way Prim Sch SE15 140 C6
Pilkington Ct 1 NW9 46 A5
Pilkington Rd 4 SE15 140 B3
Orpington BR6 227 A6
Pillar of Fire Society Church & Bible Sch NW4 46 D4
Pillions La UB4 83 B3
Pilot Ind Ctr NW10 89 C3
Pilsden Cl SW19 156 D3
Piltdown Rd WD19 22 D6
Pilton Est The CR0 220 D6
Pilton Pl SE17 262 B2
Pimento Ct W5 109 D3
Pimilico Sta SW1 115 D1 259 C2
Pimlico Rd SW1 115 A1 258 B2
Pimlico Sch SW1 115 C1 259 B1
Pimlico Wlk 1 N1 95 C4
Pinchbeck Rd BR6 227 D2
Pinchin St E1 118 A6
Pincombe Ho SE17 262 C2
Pincott Pl SE4 140 D2
Pincott Rd
8 Bexley DA6 147 C1
Merton SW19 180 A2
Pindar St EC2 95 C2 243 A4
Pindock Mews W9 91 D3
Pine Apple Ct SW1 259 A6
Pine Ave E15 76 B3
West Wickham BR4 207 D1
Pine Cl N14 15 C4
8 N19 71 C6
Pine Cl *continued*
E10 75 D6
3 Penge SE20 184 C2
Stanmore HA7 25 B6
Pine Coombe CR0 222 D4
Pinecrest Gdns BR6 226 D4
Pinecroft DA16 146 A5
Harrow HA3 44 B4
Pinecroft Cres EN5 1 A1
Pine Ct UB5 85 A4
Pinedene 2 SE15 140 B4
Pinefield Cl E14 119 C6
Pine Gdns Ruislip HA4 62 B6
Surbiton KT5 198 C3
Pine Glade BR6 226 B4
Pine Gr N20 13 C3
N4,N19 72 B6
Wimbledon SW19 179 B5
Pine Ho 15 SE16 118 C4
Pinehurst BR7 188 D4
Pinehurst Ct 5 W11 91 B1
Pinehurst Wlk 4 BR6 211 B1
Pinelands Cl 7 SE3 142 D5
Pine Lo SW15 157 A5
Pinemartin Cl NW2 68 C5
Pine Pl UB4 83 D3
Pine Rd N11 15 A2
NW2 68 D4
Pine Ridge SM5 219 A1
Pines Ct 14 SW19 156 D3
Pines Rd BR1 188 A1
Pine St EC1 94 C3 241 A6
Pines The Southgate N14 15 C6
South Norwood SE19 182 D4
Sunbury TW16 194 A6
Woodford IG8 21 A1
Pine Tree Cl TW5 128 B4
Pine Tree Ho SE14 140 D5
Pine Tree Lo BR2 208 D5
Pine Trees Dr UB10 60 A4
Pineview Ct 5 E4 20 A3
Pine Wlk KT5 198 C3
Pinewood BR7 188 C4
Pine Wood TW16 172 A2
Pinewood Ave DA15 167 C3
Hillingdon UB8 82 B1
Pinner HA5 23 D4
Pinewood Cl BR6 211 B1
Croydon CR0 223 A5
Pinner HA5 23 D4
Pinewood Ct SW4 159 D5
Enfield EN2 4 D2
Pinewood Dr BR6 227 C3
Pinewood Gr W5 87 C1
Pinewood Pl KT19 215 B4
Pinewood Rd BR2 209 A5
SE2 146 D6
Feltham TW13 150 B1
Pinfold Rd SW16 182 A6
Pinglestone Cl UB7 126 A5
Pinkcoat Cl TW13 150 B1
Pinkerton Ct KT2 176 D1
Pinkerton Pl SW16 181 D6
Pinkham Mans W4 110 C1
Pinkham Way (North Circular Rd)
N12 30 D3
N12 31 A4
Pinkwell Ave UB3 105 B2
Pinkwell Jun & Inf Schs UB3 105 A2
Pinkwell La UB3 105 B2
Pinley Gdns RM9 102 B6
Pinnacle Hill DA7 147 D1
Pinnacle Hill N DA7 147 D1
Pinnacle Ho E14 120 A3
Pinnell Rd SE9 143 D1
Pinner Ct HA5 41 C5
Pinner Gn HA5 22 C1
Pinner Gr HA5 41 A4
Pinner Hill HA5 22 B3
Pinner Hill Rd HA5 22 C1
Pinner Ho 31 SE5 139 A3
Pinner Park Ave HA2 24 A1
Pinner Park Fst & Mid Schs HA5 41 D6
Pinner Park Gdns HA2 24 A1
Pinner Rd
Harrow HA1,HA2 42 A3
Harrow, Pinner HA2,HA5 41 C5
Pinner HA6 22 A1
Pinner Sta HA5 41 A5
Pinner View HA1,HA2 42 A4
Pinner Wood Fst & Mid Schs HA5 22 C2
Pinn Way HA4 39 C2
Pintail Cl E6 100 A2
Pintail Ct 40 SE8 141 B6
Pintail Rd IG8 37 B3
Pintail Way UB4 84 D2
Pinter Ho 30 SW9 138 A3
Pinto Cl WD6 11 B5
Pinto Way SE3 143 B1
Pioneer Cl W12 90 B1
Pioneers Ind Pk CR0 204 A1
Pioneer St SE15 140 A4
Pioneer Way W12 90 C1
Piper Cl N7 72 B2
Piper Rd KT1 198 C6
Pipers Gdns CR0 207 A2
Pipers Gn NW9 45 A4
Pipers Green La HA8 10 A1
Pipewell Rd SM5 202 C3
Pippenhall SE9 166 D5
Pippin Cl NW2 68 B5
Croydon CR0 207 B1
Pippin Ct 5 EN4 2 C1
Pippins Ct TW15 170 D4
Piquet Rd SE20 184 C1
Pirbright Cres CR0 224 A2
Pirbright Ho 11 KT2 176 D4
Pirbright Rd SW18 157 C3
Pirie St 6 E16 121 B5
Pitcairn Cl RM7 59 C5
Pitcairn Ho 1 E9 74 C1
Pitcairn Rd CR4 180 D3
Pitchford St E15 76 C1
Pitfield Cres SE28 124 A5
Pitfield Ho N5 73 A3
Pitfield St N1 95 C5
Pitfield Way NW10 67 A2
Enfield EN3 6 C4
Pitfold Cl SE12 165 B5
Pitfold Rd SE12 165 A4
Pit Ho NW10 67 B5
Pitlake CR0 220 D6
Pitman Ho 4 SE8 141 C4
Southgate N21 16 B6
Pitmans Coll HA0 65 D2
Pitman St SE5 139 A5
Pitmaston Ho 2 SE13 142 A3
Pitsea Pl E1 96 D1
Pitsea St E1 96 D1
Pitshanger Ct 2 W5 87 C3
Pitshanger La W5 87 C3
Pitshanger Manor Mus & Art Gallery* W5 109 D5
Pitt Cres SW19 179 D6
Pitt Ho 4 SW11 136 B1
Pittman Gdns IG1 79 A3
Pitt Rd BR6 227 A4
Harrow HA2 64 A6
Thornton Heath CR0, CR7 205 A4
Pitt's Head Mews W1 248 B3
Pittsmead Ave BR2 209 A2
Pitt St W8 113 C4 245 B2
Pittville Gdns SE25 206 A6
Pixfield Ct BR2 186 D1
Pixley St E14 97 B1
Pixton 11 NW9 27 C2
Pixton Way CR2 223 B1
Place Farm Ave BR5, BR6 211 B1
Plains The 7 E4 20 C4
Plaistow Gr BR1 187 B3
E15 98 D6
Plaistow Hospl E13 99 C5
Plaistow La BR1 187 C2
Plaistow Park Rd E13 99 B5
Plaistow Prim Sch E13 99 B5
Plaistow Rd E13,E15 98 D5
Plaistow Sta E13 98 D5
Plane St SE26 162 B1
Planetarium The* NW1 93 A3 238 A5
Plane Tree Cres TW13 150 B1
Planetree Ct W6 112 D2
Plane Tree Ho SE7 121 D1
SE8 141 A6
Plane Tree Wlk 4 SE19 183 C4
Plantagenet Cl KT19 215 B4
Plantagenet Gdns RM6 58 D2
Plantagenet Ho SE18 122 B3
Plantagenet Pl RM6 58 D2
Plantagenet Rd EN5 2 A1
Plantain Pl SE1 252 C2
Plantation The SE3 143 A3
Plasel Ct E13 99 B6
Plashet Gr E6 77 D1
Plashet Rd E13 77 B1
Plashet Sch E6 78 A1
Plassy Rd SE6 163 D4
Platina St EC2 242 D6
Plato Pl 1 SW6 135 B3
Plato Rd SW2 138 A1
Platt Halls (a) 35 NW9 27 D1
Platt Halls (b) 37 NW9 27 D1
Platt Halls (c) 38 NW9 27 D1
Platt's Eyot TW12 173 C1
Platt's La NW3 69 C5
Platts Rd EN3 6 C4
Platt St NW1 232 C4
Plaxdale Ho SE17 263 A3
Plaxtol Cl BR1 187 C2
Plaxtol Rd DA8 147 C5
Plaxton Ct E11 76 D5
Playfair St W6 112 C1
Playfield Cres SE22 161 D6
Playfield Rd HA8 27 A1
Playford Rd N4 72 B6
N4 72 C6
Playgreen Way SE6 185 C6
Playground Cl BR3 184 D1
Playhouse Yd EC4 241 C1
Plaza Bsns Ctr EN3 7 B3
Pleasance Rd BR5 190 B1
Pleasance Rd *continued*
Putney SW15 156 B6
Pleasance The SW15 134 B1
Pleasant Gr CR0 223 B5
Pleasant Pl N1 72 D1
Pleasant Row NW1 231 D5
Pleasant View BR6 227 A3
Pleasant View Pl BR6 227 A3
Pleasant Way HA0 87 C5
Pleasaunce Ct SE9 144 B1
Plender Ct NW1 232 B5
Plender St NW1 93 C6 232 B5
Pleshey Rd N7 71 D4
Plevna Cres N15 51 C3
Plevna Ho 1 N9 18 A1
Plevna Rd Edmonton N9 18 B1
Hampton TW12 173 D2
Plevna St E14 120 A3
Pleydell Ave W6 111 D2
Penge SE19 183 D3
Pleydell Ct EC4 241 B1
Pleydell Gdns SE19 183 D4
Pleydell St EC4 241 B1
Plimsoll Cl E14 97 D1
Plimsoll Rd N4 72 D5
Plough Ct EC3 252 D6
Plough Farm Cl HA4 39 B3
Plough La SE22 161 D5
Wallington CR0,SM6 220 A3
Wimbledon SW17,SW19 180 A6
Plough Lane Cl CR0, SM6 220 A3
Ploughmans Cl NW1 232 C6
Ploughmans End TW7 152 B6
Plough Pl EC4 241 B2
Plough Rd SW11 136 B1
West Ewell KT19 215 B1
Plough St 10 E1 96 A1
Plough Terr SW11 136 B1
Plough Way SE16 119 A2
Plough Yd EC2 243 B5
Plover Ho 4 SW9 138 C5
Plover Way SE16 119 A3
Hayes UB4 84 D2
Plowman Cl N18 33 B5
Plowman Ho SW19 156 D2
Plowman Way RM8 58 C1
Plumbers Row E1 96 A1
Plumbridge St 7 SE10 142 A4
Plum Cl TW14 150 A3
Plumcroft Prim Sch SE18 145 A6
Plume Ho SE10 141 D6
Plum Garth TW8 109 D2
Plum La SE18 145 A5
Plummer Ct SE13 163 D5
Plummer La CR4 180 D1
Plummer Rd SW4 159 D4
Plumpton Cl UB5 63 C2
Plumpton Way SM5 218 C5
Plumstead Common Rd SE18 145 A6
Plumstead High St SE18,SE2 123 C2
Plumstead Manor Sch SE18 145 B6
Plumstead Rd SE18, SE28 123 A2
Plumstead Sta SE18 123 B2
Plumtree Cl
Dagenham RM10 81 D2
Wallington SM6 219 D1
Plumtree Ct EC4 241 C2
Plymouth Ho 10 IG11 80 A1
Plymouth Rd BR1 187 B2
E16 99 A2
Plymouth Wharf E14 120 B2
Plympton Ave NW6 69 B1
Plympton Cl 8 DA17 125 B3
Plympton Pl NW1 237 A5
Plympton Rd NW6 69 B1
Plympton St NW8 237 A5
Plymstock Rd DA16 146 C5
Pocklington Cl NW9 27 C1
Pocklington Ct SW15 156 A3
Pocock Ave UB7 104 B3
Pocock St SE1 116 D4 251 D2
Podmore Rd SW18 136 A1
Poets Corner SW1 260 A6
Poet's Rd N5 73 B3
Poets Way HA1 42 C5
Pointalls Cl N3 30 A1
Point Cl SE10 142 A4
Pointer Cl SE28 102 D1
Pointer Sch The SE3 143 A5
Pointers Cl E14 119 D1
Point Hill SE10 142 A4
Point Pl HA9 66 D1
Point Pleasant SW18 135 C1
Point Terr E7 77 B3
Poland St W1 93 C1 239 B1
Polebrook Rd SE3 143 C2
Polecroft La SE6 163 B2
Polehamptons The TW12 174 A2
Pole Hill Rd
Chingford E4 20 A4
Hillingdon UB4 83 A4
Polesden Gdns SW20 178 B1
Polesworth Ho 16 W2 91 C2
Polesworth Rd RM9 80 D1
Polish Univ Abroad W6 112 A2
Polish War Meml HA4 62 C2
Pollard Cl E16 121 A6
N7 72 B4
Pollard Ho N1 233 C3
Cheam KT4 216 C4
Pollard Rd N20 14 C2
Morden SM4 202 B4
Pollard Row E2 96 A4
Pollards Cl IG10 21 C6
Pollards Cres SW16 204 A6
Pollards Hill E SW16 204 B6
Pollards Hill N SW16 204 B6
Pollards Hill S SW16 204 B6
Pollards Hill W SW16 204 B6
Pollard St E2 96 A4
Pollards Wood Rd SW16 204 A6
Pollard Wlk DA14 190 C4
Pollen St W1 238 D1
Pollitt Dr NW8 92 B3 236 D6
Pollock Ho W10 91 A3
Polperro Cl BR6 211 D3
Polperro Mans 3 NW6 69 C3
Polperro Mews SE11 261 D4
Polsted Rd SE6 163 B4
Polsten Mews EN3 7 C6
Polthorne Gr SE18 123 B2
Polworth Rd SW16 182 A5
Polygon Rd NW1 93 D5 232 C3
Polygon The NW8 229 D6
1 SW4 137 C1
Polytechnic St SE18 122 C2
Pomell Way E1 243 D2
Pomeroy Ct W11 91 A1
Pomeroy Ho 5 E2 96 D5
Pomeroy St SE14 140 C4
Pomfret Rd SE5 138 D2
Pomoja La N19 72 A6
Pomona Ho 10 SE8 119 A2
Pond Cl N12 30 C4
SE3 143 A3
Pond Cottage La BR3, BR4 207 C1
Pond Cotts SE21 161 C3
Ponders End Ind Est EN3 19 A6
Ponders End Sta EN3 19 A6
Ponder St 5 N7 72 B1
Pond Farm Est E5 74 C5
Pondfield End IG10 21 C4
Pondfield Ho 4 N5 73 A3
West Norwood SE27 183 A5
Pondfield Rd BR6 226 D5
Dagenham RM10 81 D3
West Wickham BR2 208 C1
Pond Gn HA4 61 C6
Pond Hill Gdns SM3 217 A2
Pond Ho SW3 257 A3
Pond Mead SE21 161 B5
Pond Path BR7 188 D4
Pond Pl SW3 114 C2 257 A3
Pond Rd E15 98 C5
SE3 142 D3
Pondside Cl UB3 127 B6
Pond Sq N6 49 A1
Pond St NW3 70 C3
Pond Way TW11 175 C4
Pondwood Rise BR6 211 C2
Ponler St E1 96 B1
Ponsard Rd NW10 90 B4
Ponsford St E9 74 C2
Ponsonby Pl SW1 115 D1 259 D2
Ponsonby Rd SW15 156 B4
Ponsonby Terr SW1 259 D2
Pontefract Ct UB5 63 D3
Pontefract Rd BR1 186 D5
Ponton Ho SW2 160 C3
Ponton Rd SW8 137 D6 269 D5
Pont St SW1 114 D3 257 D5
Pont St Mews SW1 257 C5
Pontypool Pl SE1 251 C2
Pool Cl Beckenham BR3 185 C5
East Molesey KT8 195 B4
Pool Ct SE6 163 C2
Poole Cl HA4 61 C6
Poole Court Rd TW5 129 A3
Poole Ct N1 73 C1
Hounslow TW5 129 A3
Poole Ho SE11 260 D5
Pool End Cl TW17 192 C4
Poole Rd E9 74 D2
West Ewell KT19 215 B2
Pooles Bldgs EC1 241 A5
Pooles Ct IG3 80 A5
Pooles La SW10 266 A3
Pooles Park Prim Sch N4 72 B6
Pooles Pk N4 72 C6
Poole St N1 95 B6 235 C5
Poole Way UB4 83 C4
Pool Ho NW8 236 D4
Poolmans St SE16 118 D4
Pool Rd
East Molesey KT12,KT8 195 B4
Harrow HA1 42 B2
Poolsford Rd NW9 45 C5
Poonah St E1 96 C1
Pope Cl
East Bedfont TW14 149 D3
Mitcham SW17,SW19 180 B4
Pope Ct 10 KT2 175 D6
Pope Ho 7 SE16 118 B2
3 SE5 139 B5
Pope John RC Prim Sch W12 112 B6
Pope Rd BR2 209 D4
Pope's Ave TW2 152 C2
Popes Dr N3 29 C2
Popes Gr CR0 223 B5
Pope's Gr TW1,TW2 152 D2
Pope's Head Alley EC3 242 D1
Pope's La W5 110 A3
Pope's Rd SW9 138 C2
Pope St SE1 253 B1
Pope Street Ct SE9 166 B3
Popham Cl TW13 151 B1
Popham Ct N16 73 C5
Popham Gdns TW9 132 D2
Popham Rd N1 95 A6 235 A6
Popham St N1 234 D6
N1 95 A6 235 A6
Poplar Ave
Mitcham CR4 180 D2
Orpington BR6 226 D6
Southall UB2 107 D3
Yiewsley UB7 104 B6
Poplar Bath St 10 E14 119 D6
Poplar Bsns Pk E14 120 A6
Poplar Cl E9 75 B3
Pinner HA5 22 D2
Poplar Cres KT19 215 A2
Poplar Ct Chingford E4 35 D4
Northolt UB5 84 C5
4 Streatham SW16 160 B1
13 Twickenham TW1 153 C5
Wimbledon SW19 179 C5
Poplar Farm Cl KT19 215 A2
Poplar Fst Sch SW19 201 C6
Poplar Gdns KT3 177 B1
Poplar Gr N11 31 A4
W6 112 C4
Kingston KT3 199 B6
Wembley HA9 67 A5
Poplar High St E14 119 D6
Poplar Ho 19 SE16 118 D4
SE4 141 B1
Poplar Mews W12 112 C5
Poplar Mount DA17 125 D2
Poplar Pl W2 113 D6 245 D6
Hayes UB3 106 A6
Woolwich SE28 124 C6
Poplar Rd SE24 139 A1
Ashford TW15 171 A5
Cheam SM3 201 B1
Merton SW19 179 C1
Poplar Rd S SW19 201 C6
Poplars Cl HA4 39 C1
Poplars Ho 14 E17 53 D6
Poplars Rd E17 53 D3
Poplar Sta E14 119 D6
Poplars The NW5 71 C3
East Barnet N14 15 B6
Poplar View HA9 65 D6
Poplar Way
Feltham TW13 150 B1
Ilford IG6 57 A5
Poplar Wlk SE24 139 A1
Croydon CR0 205 A1
Poppins Ct EC4 241 C1
Poppleton Rd E11 54 C3
Poppy Cl
Belvedere DA17 125 D4
Hackbridge SM6 203 A1
Poppy La CR0 206 C1
Porchester Ct W2 245 D6
Porchester Gate W2 246 A5
Porchester Gdn Mews W2 91 D1
Porchester Gdns W2 113 D6 245 D6
Porchester Mead BR3 185 D4
Porchester Mews W2 91 D1
Porchester Pl W2 237 B1
Porchester Rd W2 91 D1
Kingston KT1 176 D1
Porchester Sq W2 91 D1
Porchester Terr W2 114 A6 246 A6
Porchester Terr N W2 91 D1
Porch Way N20 14 D1
Porcupine Cl SE9 166 A2
Porden Rd SW2 138 B1
Porland Ct SE1 262 C6
Porlock Ave HA1,HA2 42 A1
Porlock Ho 5 SE26 162 A1
Porlock Rd EN1 17 D4
Porlock St SE1 117 B4 252 D2
Porrington Cl BR7 188 C2
Portal Cl Hillingdon UB10 60 B1

Portal Cl *continued*
Ruislip HA4 62 B4
West Norwood SE27 160 C1
Portbury Cl 16 SE15 140 A4
Portchester Cl SE24 139 B1
Portchester Ct W2 91 D1
Port Cres E13 99 B3
Portcullis Lodge Rd EN1 5 B2
Porte 10 NW9 27 D2
Portelet Ct 1 N1 95 C6
Portelet Rd E1 96 D4
Porten Hos W14 254 A5
Porten Rd W14 254 A5
Porter Rd E6 100 B1
Porters Ave RM8,RM9 80 C3
Porter Sq N19 50 A1
Porter St SE1 117 A5 252 B4
W1 237 D4
Porters & Walters Almshouses N22 32 B3
Porters Way UB7 104 B4
Porteus Rd W2 236 B4
Portgate Cl W9 91 B3
Porthcawe Rd SE26 185 B6
Porthkerry Ave DA16 146 A1
Port Ho 6 SW11 136 A2
Portia Ct 12 IG11 80 A1
Portia Way E3 97 B3
Porticos The SW3 266 C5
Portinscale Rd SW15 157 B6
Portishead Ho 29 W2 91 C2
Portland Ave DA15 168 A5
N16 51 D2
New Malden KT3 199 D2
Portland Cl RM6 59 A4
Portland Commercial Est IG11 102 C5
Portland Cotts CR0 203 D2
Portland Cres
1 Chislehurst SE9 166 A2
Feltham TW13 171 B6
Southall UB6 86 A2
Stanmore HA7 25 D1
Portland Cres W HA7 43 D6
Portland Ct 7 N1 73 C1
1 SE14 141 A6
Portland Dr EN2 5 C5
Portland Gdns N4 50 D3
Ilford RM6 58 D4
Portland Gr SW8 138 B4 270 C2
Portland Ho 20 SW2 160 C3
Portland Hospl for Women & Children The W1 238 D5
Portland Mans SE25 206 B4
Portland Mews W1 239 B1
Portland Pl W1 93 B2 238 D3
Croydon SE25 206 A5
Portland Rd N15 51 D5
W11 113 A6 244 A5
W11 113 A5 244 B4
Ashford TW15 148 A1
Bromley BR1 187 C5
Chislehurst SE9 166 A2
Croydon SE25 206 B4
Hayes UB4 83 C4
Kingston KT1 198 B6
Mitcham CR4 180 C1
Southall UB2 107 B3
Portland Rise N4 51 A1
Portland Sq 4 E1 118 B5
Portland St SE17 117 B1 262 C1
Portland Terr TW9 131 D1
Portland Village W6 112 C3
Portman Ave SW14 133 B2
Portman Cl DA7 147 A2
W1 93 A1 238 A2
Portman Dr IG8 37 D1
Portman Gate NW1 237 B5
Portman Gdns NW9 27 B1
Hillingdon UB10 60 C1
Portman Hts 1 NW3 69 C5
Portman Lo N21 16 D6
Portman Mews S W1 238 A1
Portman Pl E2 96 C4
Portman Rd KT1 176 B1
Portman Sq W1 93 A1 238 A2
Portman St W1 93 A1 238 A1
Portman The NW11 47 C2
Portman Twrs W1 237 D2
Portmeadow Wlk SE2 124 D4
Portmeers Cl E17 53 C3
Portnall Rd W9 91 B4
Portobello Ct Est W11 91 B1
Portobello Ho 6 SW27 182 D5
Portobello Mews W11 245 A5
Portobello Rd W10 91 A2
W11 113 B6 244 D6
Portobello Road Mkt★ W10 91 A2
Porton Ct KT6 197 C3
Portpool La EC1 94 C2 241 A4
Portree Cl N22 32 B3
Portree St E14 98 B1
Port Royal Pl 3 N16 73 C3
Portrush Ct 9 UB1 86 A1
Portsdown HA8 26 C5
Portsdown Ave NW11 47 B3
Portsdown Mews NW11 47 B3
Portsea Hall W2 237 B1
Portsea Ho 3 SW15 156 B3
Portsea Mews W2 237 B1
Portsea Pl W2 237 B1
Portslade Rd SW8 137 C3
Portsmouth Ave KT7 197 A2
Portsmouth Rd
Esher KT10 212 A5
Putney SW15 156 C4
Thames Ditton KT6,KT7 197 C3
Portsmouth St WC2 240 D1
Portsoken St E1,EC3 253 C6
Portswood Pl 10 SW15 155 D5
Portugal Gdns TW2 152 A2
Portugal St WC2 94 B1 240 D1
Portway E15 98 D6
Portway Gdns SE18 143 D5
Portway Sch E13 98 D6
Poseidon Ct 4 E14 119 C2
Postern Gn EN2 4 C2
Postern The EC2 242 B3
Post La TW2 152 B3
Postmill Cl CR0 222 D5
Post Office App E7 77 B3
Post Office Way SW8 137 D5 269 C4
Post Rd UB2 107 D3
Postway Mews 1 IG1 78 D5
Potier St SE1 262 D5
Potter Cl CR4 181 B1
Potterhill Ct TW11 175 B3
Potteries The EN5 13 C6
Potterne Cl 5 SW19 156 D4
Potters Cl CR0 207 A1
Pottersfield EN1 5 C1
Potters Fields SE1 117 C5 253 B3
Potters Gr KT3 199 A5
Potters Heights Cl HA5 22 B3
Potter's La Barnet EN5 1 C1
Streatham SW16 181 D4
Potters Lo E14 120 A1
Potters Mews 4 WD6 9 D5
Potters Rd SW6 136 A3
Potter's Rd EN5 1 D1
Potter St HA5 22 B2
Potter Street Hill HA5 22 B3
Pottery La W11 113 A5 244 B4
Pottery Rd TW8 132 A6
Pottery St SE16 118 B4
Pott St E2 96 B4
Poulett Gdns TW1 153 A3
Poulett Rd E6 100 B5
Poullett Ho SW2 160 D3
Poulters Wood BR2 225 D3
Poulton Ave SM1,SM5 218 B5
Poulton Cl E8 74 B2
Poultry EC2 95 B1 242 C1
Pound Cl
Long Ditton KT6 197 C1
Orpington BR6 227 B6
Pound Court Dr BR6 227 B6
Pound Green Ct 4 DA5 169 C4
Pound La NW10 68 A2
Pound Park Rd SE7 121 D2
Pound Pl SE9 166 C5
Pound St SM5 218 D3
Pountney Rd SW11 137 A2
Poverest Rd BR5 211 D4
Povey Ho SE17 263 A3
SW2 160 C5
Powder Mill La TW2, TW4 151 C3
Powell Cl
Chessington KT9 213 D3
Edgware HA8 26 B4
Wallington SM6 220 A1
Powell Ct 19 E17 53 D6
Croydon CR2 221 A4
Powell Gdns RM10 81 C4
Powell Rd E5 74 B5
Buckhurst Hill IG9 21 C4
Powell's Wlk W4 133 D6
Powergate Bsns Pk NW10 89 B4
Power Ho 12 TW9 132 C4
Power Ho The W4 111 D2
Power Rd W4 110 C2
Powerscroft Rd E5 74 C4
Sidcup DA14 190 C4
Powers Ct TW1 153 D4
Powis Ct Bushey WD23 8 B3
Edgware HA8 26 B6
Powis Gdns NW11 47 B2
W11 91 B1
Powis Ho WC2 240 B2
Powis Mews W11 91 B1
Powis Pl WC1 94 A3 240 B5
Powis Rd E3 97 D4
Powis Sq W11 91 B1
Powis St SE18 122 D2
Powis Terr W11 91 B1
Powlesland Ct 23 E14 97 A1
Powle Terr IG1 79 B3
Powlett Ho NW1 71 B2
Powlett Pl NW1 71 B1
Pownall Gdns TW3 129 D1
Pownall Rd E8 96 A6
Hounslow TW3 129 D1
Pownsett Terr IG1 79 A3
Powrie Ho 4 SW11 136 B3
Powster Rd BR1 187 B5
Powys Cl DA7 146 D6
Powys Ct N11 32 A5
Powys La
Bowes Park N13 32 A5
Palmers Green N14 32 A6
Poynder Ct 3 N7 72 A3
Poynder Lo TW7 131 A4
Poynders Ct 9 SW4 159 C5
Poynders Gdns SW12 159 C4
Poynders Rd SW12, SW4 159 D4
Poynings Rd N19 71 C5
Poynings Way N12 29 C5
Poyntell Cres BR7 189 B2
Poynter Ct 12 UB5 84 D5
Poynter Ho NW8 236 C6
10 W11 112 D5
Poynter Rd EN1 18 A6
Poynton Rd N17 34 A1
Poyntz Rd SW11 136 D3
Poyser St E2 96 B5
Praed Mews W2 236 D2
Praed St W2 92 B1 236 D2
Pragel St E13 99 C5
Pragnell Rd SE12 165 B2
Prague Pl SW2 160 A6
Prah Rd N4 72 C6
Prairie St SW8 137 B3
Pratt Mews NW1 232 A5
Pratt St NW1 93 C6 232 A6
Pratt Wlk SE1, SE11 116 B2 260 D4
Prayle Gr NW2 46 D1
Prebend Gdns W4,W6 111 D2
Prebend Mans 4 W4 111 D2
Prebend St N1 95 A6 235 A6
Precinct Rd UB3 106 A6
Precincts The SM4 201 C3
Precinct The N1 235 A5
N5 72 D3
East Molesey KT8 195 D6
Preedy Ho N1 233 D4
Premier Ct EN3 6 D5
Premier Lo N3 29 C2
Premier Park Rd NW10 88 D5
Premier Pl E14 119 C6
Prendergast Ho 7 SW4 159 D4
Prendergast Rd SE3 142 C2
Prendergast Sch SE4 141 C1
Prentice Ct 2 SW19 179 B5
Prentis Rd SW16 181 D6
Prentiss Ct SE7 121 D2
Presburg Rd KT3 199 C4
Prescelly Pl HA8 26 B2
Prescot St E1 117 D6 253 D6
Prescott Ave BR5 210 D3
Prescott Ho 18 SE17 138 D6
Prescott Pl SW4 137 D1
Presentation Mews SW2 160 B3
President Dr E1 118 B5
President Ho EC1 234 D1
President St EC1 235 A2
Prespa Cl N9 18 C2
Press Ho NW10 67 B5
Press Rd NW10 67 B5
Prestage Way E14 120 A6
Prestbury Rd E7 77 C1
Prestbury Sq SE9 188 B6
Prested Rd SW11 136 C1
Preston Ave E4 36 B4
Preston Cl SE1 263 A4
Twickenham TW2 152 C1
Preston Ct DA14 189 D6
Walton-on-T KT12 194 C1
Preston Dr DA16 146 D4
Wanstead E11 55 C4
West Ewell KT19 215 D2
Preston Gdns NW10 67 C2
Enfield EN3 7 A6
Redbridge IG1 56 A3
Preston Hill HA3 44 B3
Preston Ho SE1 263 A4
SE1 263 C6
1 SE18 122 C2
3 Dagenham RM10 81 C5
Preston Manor High Sch HA9 66 B6
Preston Park Prim Sch HA9 43 D1
Preston Pl NW2 68 A2
Richmond TW10 154 A6
Preston Rd E11 54 C3
Littleton TW17 192 C4
South Norwood SE19 182 D4
Wembley HA3,HA9 66 A6
Wimbledon SW20 177 D3
Preston Road Sta HA3 44 A1
Prestons Rd BR2 225 A6
Preston's Rd E14 120 A5
Preston Waye HA3 44 A1
Prestwich Terr SW4 159 D6
Prestwick Cl UB2 107 A1
Prestwick Ct UB1 108 A6
Prestwick Rd WD19 22 D6
Prestwood Ave HA3 43 B5
Prestwood Cl SE18 146 A6
Harrow HA3 43 B5
Prestwood Gdns CR0 205 A2
Prestwood Ho 3 SE16 118 B3
Prestwood St N1 235 B3
Pretoria Ave E17 53 A5
Pretoria Cres E4 20 A3
Pretoria Ho 3 HA4 40 C1
Pretoria Rd E11 54 B1
E16 98 D3
Chingford E4 20 B3
Ilford IG1 78 D3
Streatham SW16 181 C5
Tottenham N17 33 D4
Pretoria Rd N N18 33 D4
Pretty Cnr HA6 22 A5
Prevost Rd N11 15 A2
Priam Ho 17 E2 96 B5
Price Cl NW7 29 A4
Upper Tooting SW17 158 D1
Price Ct HA1 43 A4
Price Ho N1 235 A5
Price Rd CR0 220 D3
Prices Ct SW11 136 B2
Price's St SE1 251 D4
Price's Yd N1 233 D5
Price Way TW12 173 A4
Prichard Ct N7 72 B3
SW11 266 D1
Pricklers Hill EN5 13 D5
Prickley Wood BR2 208 D1
Priddy's Yd 4 CR0 221 A6
Prideaux Ho WC1 233 D2
Prideaux Pl W3 111 B6
WC1 94 B4 233 D2
Prideaux Rd SW9 138 A2
Pridham Rd CR7 205 B5
Priestfield Rd SE23 163 A1
Priestlands Park Rd DA15 167 D1
Priestley Cl N16 51 D2
Priestley Gdns RM6 58 B3
Priestley Ho EC1 242 B6
2 NW5 71 B2
6 Wembley HA9 67 A5
Priestley Rd CR4 181 A1
Priestley Way E17 52 D6
NW2 46 A1
Priestman Point 25 E3 97 D4
Priestmead Fst & Mid Schs HA3 43 B6
Priest Park Ave HA2 63 C6
Priests Bridge SW14 133 C2
Priest's Ct EC2 242 A2
Prima Rd SW9 138 C5
Primrose Ave Enfield EN2 5 C4
Ilford RM6 58 B2
Primrose Cl
Catford SE6 186 A5
Hackbridge SM6 203 B1
Harrow HA2 63 B5
Primrose Ct
New Malden KT4 200 A2
11 Streatham SW12 159 D4
Primrose Gdns NW3 70 C2
Ruislip HA4 62 C3
Primrose Hill EC4 241 B1
Primrose Hill★ NW1,NW3 92 D6 230 C6
Primrose Hill Ct NW3 70 D1
Primrose Hill Rd NW1,NW3 70 D1 230 C6
Primrose Hill Sch NW1 93 A6 231 B6
Primrose Hill Studios NW1 231 A6
Primrose Ho 7 SE15 140 A4
1 Richmond TW9 132 B4
Primrose La CR0 206 D1
Primrose Mans SW11 268 A2
Primrose Mews 9 NW1 70 D1
Primrose Rd E10 53 D1
Woodford E18 37 B1
Primrose Sq E9 96 C6
Primrose St EC2 95 C2 243 B4
Primrose Way HA0 87 D5
Primrose Wlk 6 SE14 141 A5
Ewell KT17 215 D1
Primula St W12 90 A1
Prince Albert Ct NW8 230 C5
Sunbury TW16 171 C3
Prince Albert Rd NW8 92 D5 230 C5
Prince Arthur Ct 19 NW3 70 A4
Prince Arthur Mews 20 NW3 70 A4
Prince Arthur Rd NW3 70 A3
Prince Charles Dr NW2 46 C2
Prince Charles Rd SE3 142 D4
Prince Charles Way SM6 219 B5
Prince Consort Dr BR7 189 B2
Prince Consort Rd SW7 114 B3 256 C6
Princedale Rd W11 113 A5 244 B4
Prince Edward Mans W2 245 B6
Prince Edward Rd E9 75 B2
Prince George Ave N14 15 D6
Prince George Rd N16 73 C4
Prince George's Ave SW20 178 C1
Prince Georges Rd SW19 180 B2
Prince Henry Rd SE7 143 D5
Prince Imperial Rd SE18 144 B4
Chislehurst BR7 188 D3
Prince John Rd SE9 166 A6
Princelet St E1 95 D2 243 D4
Prince of Orange La 3 SE10 142 A5
Prince Of Wales Cl NW4 46 B5
Prince of Wales Dr SW11 137 A4 268 A2
Prince of Wales Mans SW11 268 B2
SW4 159 B6
Prince of Wales Pas NW1 232 A1
Prince of Wales Prim Sch EN3 7 B6
Prince Of Wales Rd NW5 71 A2
SE3 142 D4
Newham E16 99 C1
Prince Of Wales' Rd SM1 218 B6
Prince Of Wales Terr W4 111 C1
W8 245 D1
Prince Rd SE25 205 C4
Prince Regent E16 99 C2
Prince Regent Ct SE16 119 A5
Prince Regent La E13 99 C3
Prince Regent Mews NW1 232 A1
Prince Regent Rd TW3 130 A2
Prince Regent Sta E16 121 C6
Prince Rupert Rd SE9 144 B1
Princes Arc SW1 249 B4
Princes Ave BR5 211 C4
N10 49 B6
N22 31 D2
N3 29 D2
NW9 44 D5
Acton W3 110 C3
Edmonton N13 32 C5
Tolworth KT6 214 C6
Wallington SM5 218 D1
Woodford IG8 37 C6
Prince's Ave UB1 85 D1
Princes Cir WC2 94 A1 240 A2
Princes Cl DA14 168 D1
N4 50 D1
NW9 44 C5
Edgware HA8 26 C5
Prince's Cl TW11,TW12 174 B6
Princes Ct NW2 69 A3
NW3 70 B4
Prince's Ct SE16 119 B3
Princes Ct
Kingston KT3 199 D6
Stepney E1 118 B6
Wembley HA9 66 A3
Princes Dr HA1 42 C6
Princes Gate SW7 114 C4 246 D1
Prince's Gate SW7 114 C4 247 A1
Princes Gate Ct SW7 246 D1
Princes Gate Mews SW7 114 B3 256 D6
Princes Gdns SW7 114 B3 256 D6
Acton W3 88 C2
Ealing W5 87 C3
Princes Ho W11 245 A5
Princes La N10 49 B6
Prince's Mews W2 113 D6 245 C6
W6 112 B1
Princes Mews TW3 129 C1
Princes Par NW11 47 A3
Princes Park Ave NW11 47 A4
Hayes UB3 105 B6
Princes Park Circ UB3 105 B6
Princes Park Cl UB3 105 B6
Princes Park La UB3 105 B6
Princes Park Par UB3 105 B6
Princes Pl SW1 249 B4
W11 113 A5 244 A4
Prince's Plain BR2 210 A1
Prince's Plain Prim Sch BR2 210 A2
Princes Rd N18 34 C6
Ashford TW15 170 B5
Buckhurst Hill IG9 21 C2
Ealing W13 109 B5
Feltham TW13 149 D1
Ilford IG6 57 B5
Kingston KT2 176 C3
Penge SE20 184 D4
Richmond TW10 154 B6
Richmond TW9 132 B4
Prince's Rd
Mortlake SW14 133 B2
Teddington TW11,TW12 174 B6
Wimbledon SW19 179 C4
Princes Rise SE13 142 A3
Princes Riverside Rd 7 SE16 118 D5
Princessa Ct EN2 17 B6
Princess Alexandra School of Nursing The E1 96 B2
Princess Alice Ho W10 90 C3
Princess Alice Way SE28 123 B4
Princess Ave HA9 66 A6
Princess Beatrice Ho SW10 255 C1
Princess Christian Coll WC1 94 A2 240 B4
Princess Cres N4 72 D6
Princess Ct NW6 69 D1
W1 237 C3
W2 245 D6
Catford BR1 186 C4
3 Croydon CR0 221 D6
11 Wimbledon SW19 178 D3
Princess Frederica CE Prim Sch NW10 90 C5
Princess Grace Hospl The W1 93 A3 238 A5
Princess La HA4 39 C1
Princess Louise Cl W2 236 D4
Princess Louise Hospl W10 90 C2
Princess Mary Ho SW1 259 D3
Princess May Prim Sch N16 73 D4
Princess May Rd N16 73 C4
Princess Mews NW3 70 B2
Kingston KT1 198 B6
Princess Par BR6 226 C5
Dagenham RM10 103 C5
Princess Park Manor N11 31 A5
Prince's Sq W2 113 D6 245 C6
Princess Rd NW1 93 A6 231 B6
NW6 91 C5
Thornton Heath CR0 205 A3
Princess St SE1 261 D5
Princes St DA7 147 B2
W1 238 D1
Prince's St EC2 95 B1 242 C1
Princes St Sutton SM1 218 B4
Tottenham N17 33 C4
Prince's St TW10,TW9 154 A6
Prince St SE8 141 B6
Prince's Terr E13 99 B6
Princes Way Acton W3 110 C3
Buckhurst Hill IG9 21 C2
Coney Hall BR4 224 D5
Croydon CR0 220 B3
Putney SW15,SW19 157 A3
Ruislip HA4 63 A4
Princes Yd W11 244 B3
Princethorpe Ho W2 91 D2
Princethorpe Rd SE26 184 D6
Princeton Ct SW15 134 D2
Princeton Mans WC1 240 C3
Princeton Mews 3 KT2 176 C2
Princeton St WC1 94 B2 240 C4
Prince William Ct TW15 170 B5
Pringle Gdns SW16 181 C6
Printers Mews E3 97 A6
Printer St EC4 241 B2
Printinghouse La UB3 105 C4
Printing House Yd 17 E2 95 C4
Printon Ho 12 E3 97 B2
Print Village Ind Est SE15 139 D3
Priolo Rd SE7 121 C1
Prior Ave SM2,SM5 218 C1
Prior Bolton St N1 72 D2

Prioress Ho 2 E3 ... 97 D4
Prioress Rd SE27 ... 160 D1
Prioress St SE1 ... 262 D5
Prior Rd IG1 ... 78 C5
Priors Croft E17 ... 35 B1
Priors Field UB5 ... 63 A2
Priors Gdns HA4 ... 62 C3
Priors Lo 4 TW10 ... 154 A5
Priors Mead EN1 ... 5 C4
Prior St SE10 ... 142 A5
Priorty Ct SE15 ... 140 C1
Prior Weston Prim Sch EC1 ... 95 A3 242 B5
Priory Ave BR5 ... 211 B3
E17 ... 53 C4
N8 ... 49 D5
W4 ... 111 C3
Cheam SM3 ... 216 D4
Chingford E4 ... 19 C1
Wembley HA0 ... 64 D4
Priory CE Prim Sch SW19 ... 179 D5
Priory Cl BR7 ... 188 B2
E4 ... 19 B1
N3 ... 29 B2
Ashford TW16 ... 172 A3
Barnet N20 ... 13 B4
Beckenham BR3 ... 207 A6
East Barnet N14 ... 15 B6
Hampton TW12 ... 173 B2
Hayes UB3 ... 106 B6
3 Merton SW19 ... 179 D2
Ruislip HA4 ... 39 D1
Stanmore HA7 ... 8 D1
Wembley HA0 ... 64 D4
Woodford E18 ... 37 A2
Priory Cres
Cheam SM3 ... 216 D4
South Norwood SE19 ... 183 A3
Wembley HA0 ... 65 A5
Priory Ct E17 ... 35 B1
E17 ... 53 B6
E6 ... 99 D6
E9 ... 74 D3
EC4 ... 241 D1
SW8 ... 137 D4 269 D2
Bushey WD23 ... 8 A3
Cheam SM1 ... 217 B3
Cheam SM3 ... 217 A4
Hounslow TW3 ... 129 D2
Ilford RM6 ... 58 B3
Putney SW15 ... 156 C5
Roehampton SW15 ... 133 D1
4 Wembley HA0 ... 88 A5
Priory Dr SE2 ... 124 D1
Stanmore HA7 ... 8 D1
Priory Field Dr HA8 ... 26 D6
Priory Gdns N6 ... 49 B3
6 W4 ... 111 C2
Ashford TW15 ... 171 B5
Barnes SW13 ... 133 D2
Ealing W5 ... 88 A4
Hampton TW12 ... 173 B2
South Norwood SE25 ... 205 D5
Wembley HA0 ... 65 A4
Priory Gn N1 ... 233 C4
Priory Gr SW8 138 A4 270 A1
Priory Grange N2 ... 48 D6
Priory Heights N1 ... 233 D4
Priory Hill HA0 ... 65 A4
Priory Ho E1 ... 243 C4
EC1 ... 241 C6
3 SE7 ... 143 C6
SW1 ... 259 C2
Priory Hospl Hayes Grove The BR2 ... 225 A6
Priory Hospl The SW15 ... 133 D1
Priory House Ct SE6 ... 163 D3
Priory La
East Molesey KT8 ... 195 D5
Roehampton SW15 ... 155 D6
Priory Leas SE9 ... 166 A3
Priory Lo 7 W4 ... 110 C1
Coney Hall BR4 ... 224 C5
Ealing W5 ... 87 C1
Priory Mans 17 NW3 ... 70 D2
SW10 ... 256 B1
Priory Park Rd NW6 ... 91 B6
Wembley HA0 ... 65 A4
Priory Pk SE3 ... 142 D2
Priory Rd E6 ... 99 D5
N8 ... 49 D5
NW6 ... 69 D1
W4 ... 111 B3
Barking IG11 ... 79 B1
Cheam SM3 ... 216 D4
Chessington KT9 ... 214 A5
Hampton TW12 ... 173 C3
Hounslow TW3 ... 152 A6
Mitcham SW19 ... 180 B3
Richmond TW9 ... 132 C5
Thornton Heath CR0 ... 204 C2
Priory Ret Pk SW19 ... 180 B3
Priory Sch SE25 ... 205 D5
Priory St 16 E3 ... 97 D4
Priory Terr NW6 ... 91 D6
Priory The N8 ... 49 D5
SE1 ... 251 C1
SE3 ... 142 D1
Croydon CR0 ... 220 C5
21 Kingston KT6 ... 198 A4
Priory View WD23 ... 8 C4
Priory Villas N11 ... 30 D5
Priory Way
Harmondsworth UB7 ... 126 A6
Harrow HA2 ... 41 D5
Southall UB2 ... 106 D3
Priory Wlk SW10 ... 114 A1 256 B1
Priscilla Ho 8 TW16 ... 171 D3
Pritchard Ho 34 E2 ... 96 A5
Pritchard's Rd E2 ... 96 A5
Pritchett Cl EN3 ... 7 C6
Priter Rd SE16 ... 118 A3
Priter Road Hostel 14 SE16 ... 118 A3
Private Rd EN1 ... 17 C6
Probert Rd SW2 ... 160 C6
Probyn Ho SW1 ... 259 D4
Probyn Rd SW2 ... 160 D2
Procter Ho 12 SE5 ... 139 B5
Procter St WC1 ... 94 B2 240 C3
Proctor Cl CR4 ... 181 A2
Proctor Ho 5 SE1 ... 118 A1
Proctors Cl TW14 ... 150 A3
Prodger 8 NW9 ... 27 D2
Progress Bsns Pk CR9 ... 220 B6
Progress Way
Croydon CR0 ... 220 B6
Enfield EN1 ... 18 A6
Wood Green N22 ... 32 C2
Prologis Pk TW4 ... 128 C1
Prome Ho 3 N16 ... 73 B4
Promenade Approach Rd W4 ... 133 C5
Promenade Mans HA8 ... 26 C5
Promenade The W4 ... 133 C4
Pronto Trad Est UB4 ... 83 C2
Prospect Cl
Belvedere DA17 ... 125 C2
Forest Hill SE26 ... 184 B6
Hounslow TW5 ... 129 B4
Ruislip HA4 ... 40 D2
Prospect Cotts SW18 ... 135 C1
Prospect Cres TW2 ... 152 A5
Prospect Hill E17 ... 53 D5
Prospect Ho 9 E17 ... 54 A6
1 E8 ... 73 D2
N1 ... 234 A3
SE1 ... 261 D5
14 W10 ... 90 D1
Prospect House Sch SW15 ... 156 D4
Prospect Pl E1 ... 118 C5
N2 ... 48 B5
4 NW2 ... 69 B5
24 NW3 ... 70 A4
6 SE8 ... 141 B6
2 W4 ... 111 B1
Bromley BR2 ... 209 B6
Tottenham N17 ... 33 C3
Wimbledon SW20 ... 178 B3
Prospect Quay SW18 ... 135 C1
Prospect Rd NW2 ... 69 C5
Barnet EN5 ... 1 D1
Kingston KT6 ... 197 C3
Woodford IG8 ... 37 C5
Prospect Ring N2 ... 48 B6
Prospect St SE16 ... 118 B4
Prospect Vale SE7, SE18 ... 122 A2
Prospect Wharf E1 ... 118 C6
Prospero Ho 7 DA17 ... 125 C1
Prospero Rd N19 ... 49 D1
Protea Cl E16 ... 98 D3
Protheroe Ho 4 N17 ... 51 D6
Prothero Gdns NW4 ... 46 B4
Prothero Ho NW10 ... 67 B1
Prothero Rd SW6 ... 135 B5 264 C4
Prout Gr NW10 ... 67 D4
Prout Rd E5 ... 74 B5
Provence St N1 ... 235 A4
Providence Ct W1 ... 248 B6
Providence Ho E9 ... 96 D6
Providence La UB3 ... 127 B5
Providence Pl N1 ... 234 C5
Providence Rd UB7 ... 104 B5
Providence Row N1 ... 233 C3
Providence Sq 4 SE1 ... 118 A4
Providence Twr 1 SE16 ... 118 A4
Provident Ind Est UB3 ... 106 A4
Provincial Terr 2 SE20 ... 184 D3
Provost Ct NW3 ... 70 D2
Provost Rd NW3 ... 70 D1
Provost St N1 ... 95 B4 235 C2
Prowse Ave WD23 ... 8 A2
Prowse Pl NW1 ... 71 C1
Pruden Cl N14 ... 15 C2
Prudent Pas EC2 ... 242 B1
Prusom's Island 8 E1 ... 118 C5
Prusom St E1 ... 118 B5
Pryors The NW3 ... 70 B5
Public Record Office EC4,WC2 ... 94 C1 241 A2
Richmond TW9 ... 132 D5
Public Record Office Mus★ EC4,WC2 ... 241 A2
Pudding La EC3 ... 252 D6
Pudding Mill La E15 ... 97 D6
Pudding Mill Lane Sta E15 ... 97 D6
Puddle Dock EC4 ... 116 D6 251 D6
Puffin Cl Barking IG11 ... 102 B4
Beckenham BR3 ... 206 D4
Puffin Terr IG5 ... 56 C6
Pugin Ct N1 ... 72 C1
Pulborough Rd SW18 ... 157 B4
Pulborough Way TW4 ... 128 C1
Pulford Rd N15 ... 51 B3
Pulham Ave N2 ... 48 B5
Pulham Ho SW8 ... 270 C3
Puller Rd EN5 ... 1 A3
Pulleyns Ave E6 ... 100 A4
Pullman Ct SW2 ... 160 B3
Pullman Gdns SW15 ... 156 C5
Pullman Mews SE12 ... 165 B1
Pullman Pl SE9 ... 166 A6
Pulross Rd SW9 ... 138 B2
Pulteney Cl 13 E3 ... 97 B6
Pulteney Gdns 9 E18 ... 55 B6
Pulteney Rd E18 ... 55 B6
Pulteney Terr N1 ... 94 B6 233 D6
Pulton Ho SE4 ... 141 A1
Pulton Pl SW6 ... 135 C5 265 A3
Puma Ct E1 ... 243 C4
Pump Alley 8 TW8 ... 131 D5
Pump Cl UB5 ... 85 C5
Pump Ct EC4 ... 241 A1
Pump House Cl SE16 ... 118 C4
Bromley BR2 ... 186 D1
Pumping Station Rd W4 ... 133 C6
Pump La SE14 ... 140 C5
Hayes UB3 ... 106 A4
Pump Pail N CR0 ... 221 A5
Pump Pail S CR0 ... 221 A5
Punchard Cres EN3 ... 7 D5
Punderson's Gdns E2 ... 96 B4
Puran Ho E13 ... 99 C5
Purbeck Ave KT3 ... 199 D3
Purbeck Dr NW2 ... 68 D6
Purbeck Ho SW8 ... 270 C3
Purbrook Est SE1 ... 253 B1
Purbrook Ho 2 SW15 ... 156 B3
Purbrook St SE1 ... 263 B6
Purcell Cres SW6 ... 135 A5 264 A4
Purcell Ho SW10 ... 266 C5
Isleworth TW2 ... 152 B5
Southall UB1 ... 85 C1
Purcell Mews NW10 ... 67 C1
Purcell Rd UB6 ... 85 D2
Purcells Ave HA8 ... 26 C5
Purcell St N1 ... 95 C5
Purchese St NW1 ... 93 D5 232 D3
Purday Ho 4 W10 ... 91 B4
Purdey Ct 3 KT4 ... 200 A1
Purdon Ho 10 SE15 ... 140 A4
Purdy St E3 ... 97 D3
Purland Cl RM8 ... 59 B1
Purland Rd SE28,SE18 ... 123 D4
Purley Ave NW2 ... 69 A6
Purley Oaks Prim Sch CR2 ... 221 B1
Purley Pl N1 ... 72 D1
Purley Rd Edmonton N9 ... 17 C1
South Croydon CR2 ... 221 B1
Purley View Terr CR2 ... 221 B1
Purley Way
Croydon CR0,CR9 ... 220 C3
Thornton Heath CR0 ... 204 B1
Purley Way Cres CR0 ... 204 B2
Purneys Rd SE9 ... 143 D1
Purrett Rd SE18 ... 123 D1
Purser Ho 3 SW2 ... 160 C5
Pursers Cross Rd SW6 ... 135 B4 264 D2
Pursewardens Cl W13 ... 109 C5
Pursley Rd NW7 ... 28 B3
Purves Rd NW10 ... 90 C5
Purvis Ho CR0 ... 205 B2
Pusey Ho 16 E14 ... 97 C1
Puteaux Ho 6 E2 ... 96 D5
Putney Bridge App SW6 ... 135 A2
Putney Bridge Rd SW15 ... 135 B1
Putney Bridge Sta SW6 ... 135 B2
Putney Comm SW15 ... 134 C2
Putney Gdns RM6 ... 58 B4
Putney Heath SW15 ... 156 C5
Putney Heath La SW15 ... 156 D5
Putney High Sch SW15 ... 156 D6
Putney High St SW15 ... 135 A1
Putney Hill SW15 ... 156 D6
Putney Hospl SW15 ... 134 C2
Putney Park Ave SW15 ... 134 A1
Putney Park La SW15 ... 156 B6
Putney Pier SW15 ... 135 A2
Putney School of Art & Design SW15 ... 135 A1
Putney Sta SW15 ... 135 A1
Putney Wharf Twr SW15 ... 135 A2
Pycombe Cnr N12 ... 29 B6
Pycroft Way N9 ... 34 A6
Pylbrook Rd SM1 ... 217 D5
Pylon Trad Est E16 ... 98 B2
Pylon Way CR0 ... 204 A1
Pym Cl EN4 ... 14 B6
Pymers Mead SE21 ... 161 A3
Pymmes Brook Ho 3 N10 ... 31 A3
Pymmes Cl
Bowes Park N13 ... 32 B5
Tottenham N17 ... 34 B2
Pymmes Gdns N N9 ... 17 D1
Pymmes Gdns S N9 ... 17 D1
Pymmes Green Rd N11 ... 15 C1
Pymmes Rd N13 ... 32 A5
Pymms Brook Dr EN4 ... 2 C1
Pynchester Cl UB10 ... 60 C6
Pyne Rd KT6 ... 198 C1
Pynfolds SE16 ... 118 B4
Pynham Cl SE2 ... 124 B3
Pynnacles Cl HA7 ... 25 B5
Pynnersmead SE24 ... 161 A6
Pyramid Ho N12 ... 30 A6
Pyrford Ho 12 SW9 ... 138 D1
Pyrland Rd N5 ... 73 B3
Richmond TW10 ... 154 B5
Pyrmont Gr SE27 ... 160 D1
Pyrmont Rd W4 ... 132 C6
Pytchley Cres SE19 ... 183 A4
Pytchley Rd SE22 ... 139 C2

Q

Quadrangle Cl SE1 ... 263 A4
Quadrangle Lo SW19 ... 179 C4
Quadrangle The E17 ... 35 B1
SE24 ... 161 A6
SW10 ... 266 B2
SW6 ... 264 A3
W12 ... 90 C1
W2 ... 237 A2
Stanmore HA7 ... 25 C3
Quadrant Arc W1 ... 249 B5
Quadrant Bsns Pk NW6 ... 91 A6
Quadrant Cl NW4 ... 46 B4
Quadrant Gr NW5 ... 70 D3
Quadrant Ho E15 ... 98 C4
Quadrant Rd
Richmond TW9 ... 131 D1
Thornton Heath CR7 ... 204 D5
Quadrant The DA7 ... 146 D5
4 W10 ... 90 D4
Richmond TW9 ... 132 A1
Sutton SM2 ... 218 A2
Wimbledon SW20 ... 179 A2
Quad Rd HA9 ... 65 D5
Quaggy Wlk SE3 ... 143 A1
Quainton Hall Sch HA1 ... 42 C4
Quainton St NW10 ... 67 B5
Quaker Ct EC1 ... 242 B6
Quaker La UB2 ... 107 C3
Quakers Course NW9 ... 27 D2
Quaker's Pl E7 ... 77 D3
Quaker St E1 ... 95 D3 243 C5
Quakers Wlk N21 ... 17 B5
Quality Ct WC2 ... 241 A2
Quantock Cl UB3 ... 127 B5
Quantock Ct UB6 ... 64 C3
Quantock Dr KT4 ... 216 C6
Quantock Gdns NW2 ... 68 D6
Quantock Ho N16 ... 51 D1
Quarrendon St SW6 ... 135 C3
Quarr Rd SM5 ... 202 C3
Quarry Park Rd SM1 ... 217 B2
Quarry Rd SW18 ... 158 A5
Quarry Rise SM1 ... 217 B2
Quarterdeck The E14 ... 119 C4
Quartermain Ho SM4 ... 202 A4
Quartermile La E10,E15 ... 75 D4
Quayside Ct 6 SE16 ... 118 D5
Quay West TW11 ... 175 B5
Quebec & Crown Wharves E14 ... 97 B1
Quebeck Ind Est SE16 ... 119 A3
Quebec Mews W1 ... 237 D1
Quebec Rd Hayes UB4 ... 84 C1
Ilford IG1 ... 56 D2
Quebec Way SE16 ... 119 A4
Quedgeley Ct 3 SE15 ... 139 D6
Queen Adelaide Ct SE20 ... 184 C4
Queen Adelaide Rd SE20 ... 184 C3
Queen Alexandra Mans WC1 ... 233 A1
Queen Alexandra's Ct 5 SW19 ... 179 B5
Queen Anne Ave BR2 ... 208 D6
Queen Anne Dr KT10 ... 212 C1
Queen Anne Gate DA7 ... 146 D2
Queen Anne Mews W1 ... 238 D3
Queen Anne Rd E9 ... 74 D2
Queen Annes Cl TW2 ... 152 B1
Queen Anne's Gate SW1 ... 115 D4 249 C1
Queen Anne's Gdns
W4 ... 111 C3
W5 ... 110 A4
Enfield EN1 ... 17 C5
Mitcham CR4 ... 202 D6
Queen Anne's Gr W4 ... 111 C3
W5 ... 110 A4
Enfield EN1 ... 17 C5
Queen Anne's Pl EN1 ... 17 C5
Queen Anne St W1 ... 93 B2 238 C3
Queen Borough Gdns BR7 ... 189 B4
Queenborough Gdns IG2 ... 56 C5
Queen Caroline St W6 ... 112 C1
Queen Charlottes & Chelsea Hospl W12 ... 90 A1
Queen Elizabeth College 15 SE10 ... 142 A5
Queen Elizabeth Ct EN5 ... 1 B1
Queen Elizabeth Gdns SM4 ... 201 C5
Queen Elizabeth Hall & Purcell Room SE1 ... 250 D4
Queen Elizabeth Hospital for Children The E2 ... 96 A5
Queen Elizabeth Hospl SE7 ... 144 A5
Queen Elizabeth II Con Ctr SW1 ... 249 D1
Queen Elizabeth II Jubilee Sch W9 ... 91 B3
Queen Elizabeth II Pier SE10 ... 120 D5
Queen Elizabeth Rd E17 ... 53 A6
Kingston KT2 ... 176 B1
Queen Elizabeth's Cl N16 ... 73 B6
Queen Elizabeth's Dr N14 ... 16 A3
Queen Elizabeth's Girls Sch EN5 ... 1 B1
Queen Elizabeth's Hunting Lodge Mus★ E4 ... 20 D4
Queen Elizabeth St SE1 ... 117 D4 253 C2
Queen Elizabeth's Wlk N16 ... 73 B6
Wallington SM6 ... 219 D4
Queen Elizabeth Wlk SW13 ... 134 B4
Queenhithe EC4 ... 252 B6
Queen Margaret Flats 22 E2 ... 96 B4
Queen Margarets Ct N1 ... 73 C3
Queen Margaret's Gr N1 ... 73 C3
Queen Mary Ave SM4 ... 200 D4
Queen Mary Cl KT9 ... 214 C5
Queen Mary Rd
Charlton TW17 ... 171 A1
South Norwood SE19 ... 182 D4
Queen Mary's Ave SM5 ... 218 D1
Queen Mary's Gdns★ NW1 ... 231 A1
Queen Mary's Hospl
DA14 ... 190 A4
NW3 ... 70 A5
Queen Mary's Univ Hospl SW15 ... 156 A5
Queen Mary, Univ of London E1 ... 97 A3
Queen of Denmark Ct SE16 ... 119 B3
Queens Acre SM3 ... 217 A1
Queens Ave N10 ... 49 B6
N20 ... 14 B2
Queen's Ave N3 ... 30 A2
Queens Ave
Feltham TW13 ... 172 C6
Stanmore HA7 ... 25 C1
Queen's Ave
Southall UB1 ... 86 A1
Southgate N21 ... 16 D3
Woodford IG8 ... 37 B5
Queensberry Ho 6 TW9 ... 153 D6
Queensberry Mews W SW7 ... 256 C4
Queensberry Pl E12 ... 78 A3
SW7 ... 114 B2 256 C4
Queensberry Way SW7 ... 256 C4
Queensborough Ct N3 ... 47 B5
Queensborough Mews W2 ... 246 A6
Queensborough Pas W2 ... 246 A6
Queensborough Terr W2 ... 113 D6 245 D6
Queensbridge Ct 1 E2 ... 95 D5
Queensbridge Inf Sch E8 ... 73 D1
Queensbridge Pk TW7 ... 152 C6
Queensbridge Rd E2,E8 ... 95 D6
E8 ... 73 D1
Queensbury IG9 ... 21 B3
Queensbury Circ Par HA3 ... 44 A6
Queensbury Ct CR7 ... 183 A1
Queensbury Rd NW9 ... 45 B2
Wembley HA0 ... 88 B5
Queensbury St N1 ... 73 A1
Queensbury Sta HA7, HA8 ... 44 B6
Queensbury Station Par HA8 ... 44 B6
Queen's CE Prim Sch The TW9 ... 132 C5
Queen's Cir SW11 ... 137 B5 268 C3
Queen's Cl Edgware HA8 ... 26 C5
Wallington SM6 ... 219 B3
Queen's Club Gdns W14 ... 135 A6 264 B6
Queen's Club The★ W14 ... 113 A1 254 B1
Queen's Coll W1 ... 93 B2 238 C3
Queenscourt HA9 ... 66 A4
Queen's Cres NW5 ... 71 A2
Queens Cres TW10 ... 154 B6
Queenscroft Rd SE9 ... 165 D5
Queens Ct E10 ... 53 C2
4 E14 ... 119 B6
E17 ... 53 C4
8 NW11 ... 47 B4
SE5 ... 139 C3
SW11 ... 268 C2
Queen's Ct E11 ... 54 C2
NW11 ... 47 C4
NW8 ... 229 C4
W2 ... 245 D5
Queens Ct
Beckenham BR3 ... 185 D3
5 Buckhurst Hill IG9 ... 21 C2
Stanmore HA7 ... 25 B1
Queen's Ct
Barnes SW13 ... 134 A2
Beckenham BR3 ... 185 C2
Croydon CR2 ... 221 A3
8 Ealing W5 ... 87 C2
1 Kingston KT2 ... 176 C3
3 Richmond TW10 ... 154 B5
Thornton Heath CR7 ... 204 C4
Queensdale Cres W11 ... 112 D5
Queensdale Pl W11 ... 244 A3
Queensdale Rd W11 ... 113 A5 244 A3
Queensdale Wlk W11 ... 244 A3
Queens Down Rd E5 ... 74 B4
Queens Dr E10 ... 53 C2
Queen's Dr N4 ... 72 D6
Queens Dr KT5 ... 198 C3
Queen's Dr Acton W3 ... 88 C1
Thames Ditton KT7 ... 197 A3
Queen's Elm Sq SW3 ... 256 D1
Queensferry Wlk N17 ... 52 B5
Queensfield Ct SM3 ... 216 C4
Queen's Gallery The★ SW1 ... 115 B4 248 D1
Queen's Gate SW7 ... 114 A3 256 B5
Queens Gate IG4 ... 56 B5
Queensgate Ct N12 ... 29 D5
Queen's Gate Gdns SW7 ... 114 A3 256 B5
Queensgate Gdns SW15 ... 134 B1
Queens Gate Gdns BR7 ... 189 B2
Queen's Gate Mews SW7 ... 114 A3 256 B6
Queensgate Pl 10 NW6 ... 69 C1
Queen's Gate Pl SW7 ... 114 A3 256 B5
Queen's Gate Pl Mews SW7 ... 114 A3 256 B5
Queen's Gate Terr SW7 ... 114 A3 256 B6
Queens Gate Villas E9 ... 75 A1
Queens Gdns NW4 ... 46 C4
Queen's Gdns W2 ... 114 A6 246 A6
Ealing W5 ... 87 C3
Heston TW5 ... 129 A4
Queen's Gr NW8 ... 92 B6 229 D5
Queen's Grove Rd E4 ... 20 B3

Queen's Head Pas
EC2 242 A2
Queen's Head St
N1 94 D6 234 D5
Queen's Head Yd SE1 252 C3
Queens Ho 1 SE17 139 B6
Queen's Ho TW11 174 D4
Queen's Hospl CR0 205 A3
Queen's House The★
SE10 142 B6
Queens Keep 10 TW1 153 C5
Queens La N10 49 B6
Queensland Ave
Edmonton N18 33 A4
Merton SW19 179 D2
Queensland Cl E17 35 B1
Queensland Ct N10 31 B3
Queensland Ho 2
E16 122 C5
Queensland Pl N7 72 C4
Queensland Rd N7 72 C4
Queens Manor Prim Sch
SW6 134 D5
Queens Mans NW4 46 B4
NW6 69 D3
Queen's Mans W6 112 D2
Queensmead
NW8 92 B6 229 D6
Queen's Mead Rd BR2 186 D1
Queensmead Sch HA4 62 D4
Queensmere Cl SW19 156 D2
Queensmere Ct SW13 134 A6
Queensmere Rd SW19 156 D2
Queen's Mews
W2 113 D6 245 C6
Queensmill Rd SW6 134 D5
Queensmill Sch SW6 135 C3
Queen's Mkt 1 E13 99 C6
Queens Par NW2 68 C2
7 NW4 46 B4
Queen's Par 3 N11 30 D5
Queens Par W5 88 B1
Queen's Par N11 32 A3
Queens Parade Cl N11 30 D5
Queens Park Com Sch
NW6 90 D6
Queens Park Ct 5
W10 90 D4
Queens Park Gdns
TW13 149 D1
Queen's Park Prim Sch
W10 91 A3
Queen's Park Sta NW6 91 B5
Queen's Pas BR7 188 D4
Queen's Pl SM4 201 C5
Queen Sq WC1 94 A2 240 B4
Queen Sq Pl WC1 240 B5
Queen's Quay EC4 252 B6
Queen's Rd BR1 187 A1
BR7 188 D4
DA16 146 B3
E11 54 C2
E13 99 C6
E17 53 C3
N3 30 A2
NW4 46 C4
SE14,SE15 140 C4
Queens Rd Hayes UB3 83 C1
Morden SM4 201 C5
Twickenham TW1 153 A3
West Drayton UB7 104 B4
Queen's Rd Barking IG11 79 A2
Beckenham BR3 185 A1
Bowes Park N11 32 A4
Buckhurst Hill IG9 21 C2
Ealing W5 88 A1
Edmonton N9 18 B2
Enfield EN1 5 C1
Feltham TW13 150 B3
Hampton TW12 173 D6
Hounslow TW3 129 D2
Kingston KT2 176 C3
Mitcham CR4 202 B6
Mortlake SW14 133 B2
New Malden KT3 199 D4
Richmond TW10 154 B5
Richmond, Richmond Park
KT2,TW10 176 C5
Southall UB2 107 A4
Teddington TW11 174 D4
Thames Ditton KT7 196 D4
Thornton Heath CR0 205 A3
Wallington SM6 219 B3
Wimbledon SW19 179 C4
Queen's Rd W E13 99 B5
Queens Reach KT8 196 C5
Queen's Ride SW13 134 B2
Queen's Rise TW10 154 B5
Queen's Road Sta
SE15 140 C4
Queen's Row SE17 139 B6
Queen St DA7 147 B2
EC4 117 A6 252 B6
W1 115 B5 248 C4
Croydon CR0 221 A4
Tottenham N17 33 C4
Queens Terr E13 99 B6
NW8 92 B5 229 C4
Queen's Terr TW7 131 A1
Queensthorpe Rd
SE26 184 D6
Queenstown Rd
SW8 137 B5 268 C4
Queenstown Road Sta
SW8 137 B4 268 D2
Queen St Pl EC4 252 B6
Queensville Rd SW12,
SW4 159 D4
Queens Walk Ho W5 87 C2
Queensway
W2 113 D6 245 D6
Queens Way NW4 46 C4
Queensway
Coney Hall BR4 224 D4
Enfield EN3 6 C1
Orpington BR5 211 A3
Sunbury TW16 172 B1
Queens Way
Croydon CR0 220 B3
Feltham TW13 172 C6
Queensway Sta
W2 113 D6 245 D5
Queens Well Ave N20 30 C6
Queenswell Jun & Inf Schs
N20 14 B2
Queens Wlk NW9 67 A6
Queen's Wlk
SW1 115 C5 249 A3
Queens Wlk
Ashford TW15 170 A6
Chingford E4 20 B3
Harrow HA1 42 C5
Ruislip HA4 62 C5
Queen's Wlk W5 87 C2
Queenswood Ave
Chingford E17 36 A2
Hampton TW12 173 D4
Hounslow TW3,TW5 129 B3
Thornton Heath CR7 204 C4
Wallington CR0,SM6 219 D4
Queenswood Ct
5 SW4 160 A6
11 West Norwood SE27 183 B6
Queenswood Gdns E11 55 B1
Queenswood Pk N3 29 A2
Queenswood Rd DA15 167 D5
Queen's Wood Rd N6 49 B3
Queenswood Rd SE23 163 A1
Queens Yd E9 75 C2
Queen's Yd W1 239 B5
Queen Terr Cotts W7 108 C4
Queen Victoria Ave
HA0 65 D1
Queen Victoria Mon★
SW1 249 A2
Queen Victoria St
EC4 117 A6 252 A6
Quelch Ho 2 N19 71 D3
Quemerford Rd N7 72 B3
Quendon Ho W10 90 C3
Quenington Ct 5
SE15 139 D6
Quennel Ho 7 SW12 159 C4
Quentington Mans
SW6 264 C2
Quentin Pl SE13 142 C2
Quentin Rd SE13 142 C2
Quernmore Cl BR1 187 A4
Quernmore Rd BR1 187 A4
N4 50 C3
Querrin St SW6 136 A3
Quested Ct 27 E8 74 B3
Quex Mews NW6 91 C6
Quex Rd NW6 91 C6
Quick Rd W4 111 C1
Quicks Rd SW19 179 D3
Quick St N1 94 D5 234 D3
Quickswood NW3 70 C1
Quiet Nook BR2 225 D5
Quill La SW15 134 D1
Quill St N4 72 C5
Ealing W5 88 A5
Quilp St SE1 252 A2
Quilter Ho 11 W9 91 B4
Quilter St E2 96 A4
SE18 123 D1
Quilting Ct 23 SE16 118 D4
Quinta Dr EN5 12 C6
Quintin Ave SW20 179 B2
Quintin Ct W4 133 A5
Quintock Ho 2 TW9 132 C4
Quinton Cl
Beckenham BR3 208 A6
Cranford TW5 128 B5
Wallington SM6 219 B4
Quinton Ho SW8 270 A4
Quinton Kynaston Sch
NW8 92 B6 229 C5
Quinton Rd KT7 197 A1
Quinton St SW18 158 A2
Quixley St E14 120 B6
Quorn Rd SE22 139 C2

R

Rabbit Row W8 245 B4
Rabbits Rd E12 78 A4
Rabbs Farm Prim Sch
UB7 104 A6
Rabournmead Dr UB5 63 A3
Raby Rd KT3 199 B5
Raby St E14 97 A1
Raccoon Way TW4 128 C3
Rachel Cl IG6 57 B6
Rachel Ct SM2 218 B1
Rachel Point E5 74 A4
Racine 15 SE5 139 C4
Rackham Cl DA16 146 B3
Rackham Mews SW16 181 C4
Racton Rd
SW6 135 C6 265 A5
Radbourne Ave W5 109 C2
Radbourne Cl E5 74 D4
Radbourne Cres E17 36 B1
Radbourne Ct HA3 43 B3
Radbourne Rd SW12 159 D3
Radcliff Bldg EC1 241 A4
Radcliffe Ave NW10 90 A5
Enfield EN2 5 A4
Radcliffe Gdns SM5 218 C1
Radcliffe Ho 10 SE16 118 B2
Radcliffe Mews TW12 174 A5
Radcliffe Path 5 SW8 137 B3
Radcliffe Rd SE1 263 B6
Harrow HA3 25 A1
South Croydon CR0 221 D5
Southgate N21 16 D3
Radcliffe Sq SW15 156 D5
Radcliffe Way UB5 84 D4
Radcot Point 2 SE23 162 D1
Radcot St SE11 261 B1
Raddington Rd W10 91 A2
Radfield Way SE9 167 B4
Radford Ho 8 E14 97 D2
N7 72 B3
Radford Rd SE13 164 A5
Radford Way IG11 101 D4
Radipole Rd
SW6 135 B4 264 C2
Radius Pk TW6 127 D1
Radland Rd E16 99 A1
Radlet Ave SE23 162 B2
Radlett Cl E7 76 D2
Radlett Pl NW8 92 C6 230 A6
Radley Ave IG3 80 A4
Radley Cl TW14 149 D3
Radley Ct 25 SE16 118 D4
3 Catford BR1 186 A6
Radley Gdns HA3 44 A5
Radley Ho NW1 237 C6
13 SE2 124 D4
Radley Lo 30 SW19 156 D3
Radley Mews W8 255 B5
Radley Rd N17 33 C1
Radley's La E18 37 A1
Radleys Mead RM10 81 D2
Radley Sq E5 74 C6
Radley Terr 1 E16 98 D2
Radlix Rd E10 53 C1
Radnor Ave DA16 168 B6
Harrow HA1 42 C4
Radnor Cl BR7 189 C4
Mitcham CR4 204 A5
Radnor Cres
Redbridge IG4 56 B4
Woolwich SE18 146 A5
Radnor Ct Ealing W7 86 D1
6 Forest Hill SE23 162 D1
Harrow HA3 24 D2
Radnor Gdns Enfield EN1 5 C4
Twickenham TW1 152 D2
Radnor Gr UB10 82 C5
Radnor Lo W2 236 D1
Radnor Mews
W2 92 B1 236 D1
Radnor Pl W2 92 C1 237 A1
Radnor Rd NW6 91 A6
SE15 140 A5
Twickenham TW1 152 D2
Radnor St EC1 95 A4 235 B1
Radnor Terr
W14 113 B2 254 C4
Radnor Way NW10 88 D3
Radnor Wlk 14 E14 119 C2
SW3 114 D1 257 C1
Croydon CR0 207 A3
Radstock Ave HA3 43 B6
Radstock Cl N11 31 A4
Radstock St SW11 267 A3
Radway Ho 38 W2 91 C2
Radwell Ho SW2 160 C6
Raebarn Ct 6 SW16 160 A1
Raebarn Gdns EN5 12 B6
Raeburn Ave
Surbiton KT3 198 D3
Tolworth KT5,KT6 198 D3
Raeburn Cl NW11 48 A3
Teddington KT1 175 D3
Raeburn Ho 7 UB5 84 D5
Raeburn Rd
Edgware HA8 26 C2
Hayes UB4 83 B5
Sidcup DA15 167 C5
Raeburn St SW2 138 A1
Raffles Ct HA8 26 B6
Raffles Ho NW4 46 B5
Rafford Way BR1 209 B6
RAF Mus★ NW9 28 A1
Ragate Ho E5 74 A5
Ragged School Mus The★
E3 97 A2
Raggleswood BR7 188 C2
Raglan Cl TW4 151 B6
Raglan Ct SE12 165 A6
SW9 138 C2
Croydon CR0,CR2 220 D3
Wembley HA9 66 C5
Raglan Jun & Inf Schs
EN1 17 C4
Raglan Prim Sch BR2 209 D5
Raglan Rd DA17 125 B2
E17 54 B4
SE18 123 A1
Bromley BR2 209 C5
Enfield EN1 17 D4
Raglan St NW5 71 B2
Raglan Terr HA2 63 D4
Raglan Way UB5 64 A2
Ragley Cl W3 111 A4
Ragwort Ct 1 SE26 184 B5
Rahere Ho EC1 235 A2
Railey Mews NW5 71 C3
Railshead Rd TW1,
TW7 131 B1
Railton Rd SE24 160 D6
Railway App N4 50 C3
SE1 252 D4
Harrow HA1,HA3 42 D5
9 Twickenham TW1 153 A4
Wallington SM6 219 B3
Railway Ave SE16 118 C4
Railway Cotts W6 112 C4
Railway Gr SE14 141 B5
Railway Pl DA17 125 C3
Railway Rd TW11 174 D6
Railway Rise SE22 139 C1
Railway Side SW13 133 C2
Railway St N1 233 B3
Ilford RM6 58 C2
Railway Terr SE13 163 D6
Chingford E17 36 A2
Feltham TW13,TW14 150 A3
Rainborough Cl NW10 67 A2
Rainbow Ave E14 119 D1
Rainbow Ct 3 SE14 141 A6
Rainbow Ind Est SW20 178 B1
Rainbow Quay SE16 119 A3
Rainbow St SE5 139 C5
Rainbow Works N15 52 A4
Raine's Foundation Sch
E2 96 B4
Raines Foundation Sec Sch
E2 96 C5
Raine St E1 118 B5
Rainford Ho 9 N7 72 B6
Rainham Cl SE9 167 C5
SW11 158 C5
Rainham Ho NW1 232 B5
Rainham Rd NW10 90 C4
Rainham Rd N RM10 81 D6
Rainham Rd S RM10 81 D4
Rainhill Way E3 97 C4
Rainsborough Ave
SE8 119 A2
Rainsford Cl HA7 25 C5
Rainsford Ct NW10 88 D5
Rainsford Ho 14 SW2 160 B6
Rainsford Rd NW10 88 D5
Rainsford St W2 237 A2
Rainstar Est N18 34 C6
Rainton Rd SE7 121 A1
Rainville Rd W6 134 C6
Raisins Hill HA5 40 C6
Raith Ave N14 15 D1
Raleigh Ave Hayes UB4 84 B2
Wallington SM6 219 D4
Raleigh Cl NW4 46 C4
Pinner HA5 40 D2
Ruislip HA4 61 D6
Raleigh Ct 2 SE16 118 D5
Beckenham BR3 185 D2
Dulwich SE19 183 D5
Ealing W13 87 B2
Wallington SM6 219 B2
Raleigh Dr N20 14 C1
Esher KT10 212 B3
Tolworth KT5 199 A1
Raleigh Gdns SW2 160 B5
Mitcham CR4 202 D6
Raleigh Ho 30 SW8 137 D3
1 Thames Ditton KT7 197 A2
Raleigh Mews N1 234 D5
6 Orpington BR6 227 D3
Raleigh Rd N10 30 C2
N8 50 C5
Enfield EN2 5 B1
Feltham TW13 149 D2
Penge SE20 184 D3
Richmond TW9 132 B2
Southall UB2 107 A1
Raleigh St N1 94 D6 234 D5
Raleigh Way
Feltham TW13 172 C5
Southgate N14 16 A3
Ralph Ct 8 W2 91 D1
Ralph Perring Ct BR3 207 C5
Ralston St SW3 257 C1
Ramac Ind Est SE7 121 B1
Rama Cl SW16 182 A3
Rama Ct HA1 64 C6
Ramac Way SE7 121 B1
Rama La SE19 183 D3
Ramar Ho 11 E1 96 A2
Rambler Cl SW16 181 C6
Rambler Ct 11 NW9 46 A5
Rame Cl SW17 181 A5
Ramilles Cl SW2 160 A5
Ramillies Pl W1 93 C1 239 A1
Ramillies Rd DA15 168 B5
NW7 11 C2
W4 111 B3
Ramillies St W1 239 A1
Ramney Dr EN3 7 A6
Rampart St E1 96 B1
Rampayne St SW1 259 C2
Rampton Cl E4 19 C1
Ramsay Ho NW8 230 A4
Ramsay Rd E7 76 D4
Acton W3 111 A4
Ramscroft Cl N9 17 C4
Ramsdale Rd SW17 181 A5
Ramsdean Ho 1
SW15 156 B3
Ramsden Rd N11 30 D5
Balham SW12 159 A4
Ramsey Cl NW9 45 D3
Greenford UB6 64 B3
Ramsey Ct N8 49 D4
Croydon CR0 220 D6
Ramsey Ho 14 SW9 138 C5
7 Merton SW19 179 D2
Ramsey Rd CR7 204 B3
Ramsey St E2 96 A3
Ramsey Way N14 15 C4
Ramsfort Ho 4 SE16 118 B2
Ramsgate Cl 8 E16 121 B5
11 E16 121 B5
Ramsgate St E8 73 D2
Ramsgill App IG2 57 D5
Ramsgill Dr IG2 57 D5
Rams Gr RM6 59 A5
Rams Pas KT1 175 D1
Ram St SW18 157 D6
Ramulis Dr UB4 84 D3
Ramus Wood Ave BR6 227 C3
Rance Ho 12 SE7 122 A2
Rancliffe Gdns SE9 144 A1
Rancliffe Rd E6 100 A5
Randal Cremer JMI Sch
E2 95 D5
Randall 9 NW9 27 D2
Randall Ave NW2 67 D5
Randall Cl
SW11 136 C4 267 A2
Randall Ct NW7 28 A3
Randall Pl SE10 142 A5
Randall Rd
SE11 116 B2 260 C3
Randall Row SE11 260 C3
Randell's Rd N1 94 A6 233 B6
Randisbourne Gdns
SE6 163 D1
Randle Rd TW10 175 C6
Randlesdown Rd SE6 163 D1
Randmore Ct 6 BR3 185 C3
Randolph App E16 99 C1
Randolph Ave
W9 92 A4 229 A1
Randolph Cl KT2 177 A5
Randolph Cres
W9 92 A3 236 A6
Randolph Ct HA5 23 C3
Randolph Gdns NW6 91 D5
Randolph Gr RM6 58 C4
Randolph Mews
W9 92 A3 236 B5
Randolph Rd BR2 210 B1
E17 53 D4
W9 92 A3 236 B5
Southall UB1 107 B4
Randolph St NW1 71 C1
Randon Cl HA2 23 D1
Ranelagh Ave
Barnes SW13 134 A3
Fulham SW6 135 B2
Ranelagh Cl HA8 26 C6
Ranelagh Dr
Edgware HA8 26 C6
Twickenham TW1 153 C6
Ranelagh Gardens Mans
SW6 135 A2
Ranelagh Gardens (site of
Chelsea Flower Show)★
SW1 115 A1 258 B1
Ranelagh Gdns 3 W6 111 D3
Chiswick W4 133 A5
Fulham SW6 135 B2
Ilford IG1 56 C1
Wanstead E11 55 C4
Ranelagh Gr
SW1 115 A1 258 B2
Ranelagh Ho SW3 257 C2
Ranelagh Mans 4
SW6 135 B3
Ranelagh Pl KT3 199 C4
Ranelagh Prim Sch E15 98 C5
Ranelagh Rd E11 76 C4
E15 98 C5
N17 51 C6
NW10 89 D5
SW1 115 C1 259 B1
W5 109 D4
Southall UB1 106 D5
Wallend E6 100 C5
Wembley HA0 65 D2
Wood Green N22 32 B2
Ranfurly Rd SM1 217 C6
Rangdon St EC3 243 C1
Rangefield Prim Sch
BR1 186 C5
Rangefield Rd BR1 186 D5
Rangemoor Rd N15 51 D4
Ranger's Rd
Buckhurst Hill IG9,IG10 21 A4
Chingford E4 20 D4
Rangers Sq SE10 142 B4
Range Villas TW17 192 A2
Range Way TW17 192 C2
Rangeworth Pl DA15 167 D1
Rangoon Ho 5 N16 73 B4
Rankin Cl NW9 45 C6
Rankine Ho SE1 262 A5
Ranleigh Gdns DA7 147 B5
Ranmere St SW12 159 B3
Ranmoor Cl HA1 42 B5
Ranmoor Gdns HA1 42 C5
Ranmore Ave CR0 221 D5
Ranmore Ct
Kingston KT6 197 D4
3 Wimbledon SW20 178 D2
Rann Ho 1 SW14 133 B2
Rannoch Cl HA8 10 D2
Rannoch Ct 9 KT6 198 A4
Rannoch Rd W6 134 D6
Rannock Ave NW9 45 C2
Ransford Ho 16 SE21 183 C6
Ransom Rd 1 SE7 121 C1
Ranston St NW1 237 A4
Ranulf Rd NW2 69 B4
Ranwell Cl 11 E3 97 B6
Ranwell Ho 10 E3 97 B6
Ranworth Rd N9 18 C2
Ranyard Cl KT9 214 B5
Raphael Ct 9 SE16 118 B1
Raphael Dr KT7 196 D2
Raphael St SW7 247 C1
Rapide 12 NW9 27 C2
Rapley Ho 19 E2 96 A4
Rashleigh Ct 8 SW8 137 B2
Rashleigh Ho WC1 233 A1
Rasper Rd N20 14 A2
Rastell Ave SW12 159 D3
Ratcliffe Cl SE12 165 A4
Ratcliffe Cross St E1 96 D1
Ratcliffe Ho 12 E14 97 A1
Ratcliffe La 18 E14 97 A1
Ratcliffe Orch 9 E1 118 D6
Ratcliff Rd E7 77 C3
Rathbone Ho 5 E16 98 D1
NW6 91 C6
10 Wimbledon SW19 178 D3
Rathbone Mkt 2 E16 98 D2
Rathbone Pl
W1 93 D1 239 C2
Rathbone Point E5 74 A4
Rathbone St E16 98 D1
W1 93 C2 239 B3
Rathcoole Ave N8 50 B4
Rathcoole Gdns N8 50 B4
Rathfern Prim Sch
SE23 163 B3
Rathfern Rd SE6 163 B3
Rathgar Ave W13 109 C5
Rathgar Cl N3 29 B1
Rathgar Rd SW9 138 D2
Rathmell Dr SW4 159 D5
Rathmore Rd SE7 121 B1
Ratier 13 NW9 27 C2
Rattray Ct 3 SE6 164 D2
Rattray Rd SW2 160 C6
Raul Rd SE15 140 A4
Raveley St NW5 71 C4
Raven Cl NW9 27 C1
Ravendale Rd TW16 171 D1
Ravenet Ct SW11 268 C1
SW4 159 B6
Ravenet St
SW11 137 B4 268 C1
Ravenfield Rd SW17 158 D1
Ravenhill Rd E13 99 C5
Raven Ho 10 SE16 118 D2
Ravenings Par IG3 58 A1
Ravenna Rd SW15 156 D6
Ravenor Ct UB6 85 D3
Ravenor Park Rd UB6 86 A4
Ravenor Prim Sch UB6 85 C4
Raven Rd E18 37 C1
Raven Row E1 96 B2
Ravensbourne 3 TW1 153 C5

Ravensbourne Ave
Bromley BR2,BR3 … 186 C2
Catford BR2 … 186 B3
Stanwell TW19 … 148 A3
Ravensbourne Coll of Design & Communication
BR7 … 188 B5
Ravensbourne Ct SE6 . 163 C4
Ravensbourne Gdns
W13 … 87 B2
Ravensbourne Ho
NW8 … 237 A4
10 Catford BR1 … 186 B5
Ravensbourne Park Cres
SE6 … 163 B4
Ravensbourne Pk SE6 163 C4
Ravensbourne Pl
SE13 … 141 D3
Ravensbourne Rd
Bromley BR1,BR2 … 209 A6
Forest Hill SE23 … 163 B3
Twickenham TW1 … 153 C5
Ravensbourne Sch The
BR2 … 209 B4
Ravensbourne Sta
BR3 … 186 B3
Ravensbury Ave SM4 . 202 A4
Ravensbury Ct CR4 .. 202 B5
Ravensbury Gr CR4 .. 202 B5
Ravensbury La CR4 .. 202 B5
Ravensbury Rd
Orpington BR5 … 211 D5
Wandsworth SW18 … 157 D2
Ravensbury Terr
SW18 … 157 D2
Ravenscar NW1 … 232 A5
Ravenscar Lo 13
SW19 … 178 D3
Ravenscar Rd
Catford BR1 … 186 C6
Surbiton KT6 … 214 B6
Ravens Cl Bromley BR2 186 D1
Enfield EN1 … 5 C3
Kingston KT6 … 197 D3
Ravenscourt 1 N16 .. 74 A5
Sunbury TW16 … 171 D2
Ravenscourt Ave W6 . 112 A2
Ravenscourt Cl HA4 .. 39 A2
Ravenscourt Gdns W6 112 A2
Ravenscourt Park Mans
W6 … 112 B3
Ravenscourt Park Prep Sch
W6 … 112 A2
Ravenscourt Park Sta
W6 … 112 B2
Ravenscourt Pk W6 .. 112 A2
Ravenscourt Pl W6 .. 112 B2
Ravenscourt Rd BR5 .. 190 B1
W6 … 112 B2
Ravenscourt Sq W6 .. 112 A3
Ravenscourt Theatre Sch
W6 … 112 B2
Ravenscraig Rd N11 .. 31 C6
Ravenscroft Ave NW11 . 47 B2
Wembley HA9 … 44 B2
Ravenscroft Cl 4 E16 .. 99 A2
Ravenscroft Cres SE9 . 166 B1
Ravenscroft Ct NW11 .. 47 B2
Ravenscroft Prim Sch
E16 … 99 A3
Ravenscroft Rd E16 … 99 A2
Acton W4 … 111 A2
Penge BR3 … 184 D1
Ravenscroft Sch N20 .. 13 B4
Ravenscroft St E2 … 95 D4
Ravensdale Ave N12 .. 30 B6
Ravensdale Com Est
N16 … 52 A3
Ravensdale Gdns
Hounslow TW4 … 129 A2
South Norwood SE19 .. 183 B3
Ravensdale Mans N8 .. 50 A3
Ravensdale Rd N16 … 51 D3
Hounslow TW4 … 129 A2
Ravensdon St
SE11 … 116 C1 261 B1
Ravensfield Cl RM9 … 80 D4
Ravensfield Gdns
KT19 … 215 C4
Ravenshaw St NW6 … 69 B3
Ravenshill BR7 … 188 D2
Ravens Ho KT1 … 175 D1
Ravenshurst Ave NW4 . 46 C5
Ravenside KT6 … 197 D4
Ravenside Cl N18 … 34 D5
Ravenslea Rd SW11,
SW12 … 158 D4
Ravensleigh Gdns
BR1 … 187 B5
Ravensmead Rd BR2 .. 186 B3
Ravensmede Way W4 111 D2
Ravensroost SE19 … 183 B2
Ravenstone
SE17 … 117 C1 263 B1
Ravenstone Prim Sch
SW12 … 159 A2
Ravenstone Rd N8 … 50 C6
NW9 … 45 D3
Ravenstone St SW12 .. 159 A3
Ravensview Ct KT6 … 197 D4
Ravens Way SE3,SE12 . 165 A6
Ravenswood DA5 … 169 A3
Ravenswood Ave
Tolworth KT6 … 214 C6
West Wickham BR4 … 208 A1
Ravenswood Cres
Harrow HA2 … 63 B6
West Wickham BR4 … 208 A1
Ravenswood Gdns
TW7 … 130 C4
Ravenswood Pk HA6 … 22 A4
Ravenswood Rd E17 … 54 A5
Balham SW12 … 159 B4
Croydon CR0 … 220 D5
Ravenswood Road Ind Est
5 E17 … 54 A5
Ravens Wood Sch
BR2 … 225 D5
Ravensworth Ct SW6 . 265 A3
Ravensworth Rd NW10 . 90 B4
SE9 … 188 B6
Raven Wharf SE1 … 253 C2
Ravey St EC2 … 95 C3 243 A6
Ravine Gr SE18 … 145 C6
Rav Pinter Cl N16 … 51 C2
Rawlings Cl 3 BR6 .. 227 D3
Rawlings Cres HA9 … 66 D5
Rawlings St
SW3 … 114 D2 257 C4
Rawlins Cl N3 … 47 A6
South Croydon CR2 … 223 B1
Rawlinson Ct NW2 … 46 C2
Rawlinson Ho SE13 .. 142 B1
Rawlinson Point 8
E16 … 98 D2
Rawnsley Ave CR4 … 202 C4
Rawreth Wlk N1 … 235 B6
Rawson Ct SW11 … 268 B1
Rawson St
SW11 … 137 B4 268 C1
Rawsthorne Cl E16 .. 122 B5
Rawstone Wlk 5 E13 .. 99 A5
Rawstorne Pl EC1 … 234 C2
Rawstorne St
EC1 … 94 D4 234 C2
Raybell Ct TW7 … 130 D3
Rayburne Ct W14 … 254 A6
Buckhurst Hill IG9 … 21 C3
Ray Cl KT9 … 213 C2
Ray Ct Ealing W13 … 109 B5
Woodford IG8 … 37 D4
Raydean Rd EN5 … 13 D6
Raydons Gdns RM9 … 81 A3
Raydons Rd RM9 … 81 A3
Raydon St N19 … 71 B6
Rayfield Cl BR2 … 210 A3
Rayford Ave SE12 … 164 D4
Ray Gdns Barking IG11 . 102 A5
Stanmore HA7 … 25 B5
Ray Ho 7 W10 … 90 D1
Rayleas Cl SE18 … 144 D4
Rayleigh Ave TW11 .. 174 C4
Rayleigh Cl N13 … 17 B1
Rayleigh Ct
2 Kingston KT1 … 176 B1
Tottenham N22 … 33 A2
Rayleigh Rd 5 E16 .. 121 B5
7 E16 … 121 B5
Edmonton N13 … 17 B1
Merton SW19 … 179 B2
Woodford IG8 … 37 C3
Rayleigh Rise CR2 … 221 C2
Ray Lodge Prim Sch
IG8 … 37 D4
Ray Lodge Rd IG8 … 37 D4
Ray Massey Way 3
E6 … 100 A6
Raymead Ave CR7 … 204 C4
Raymede Twr W10 … 90 D2
Raymere Gdns SE18 .. 145 C5
Raymond Ave W13 … 109 A3
Woodford E18 … 36 D1
Raymond Cl SE26 … 184 C5
Raymond Ct N10 … 31 A3
Raymond Postgate Ct 5
SE28 … 124 B6
Raymond Rd E13 … 99 C6
Beckenham BR3 … 207 A5
Ilford IG2 … 57 B2
Wimbledon SW19 … 179 A4
Raymond Way KT10 .. 213 A2
Raymouth Rd SE16 … 118 B2
Raynald Ho 15 SW16 .. 160 A1
Rayne Ct E18 … 54 D5
SE1 … 253 C2
Rayne Ho 1 SW12 … 159 A5
W9 … 91 D3
Rayner Ct 10 W12 … 112 C4
Rayners Cl HA0 … 65 D3
Rayners Cres UB5 … 84 B4
Rayners Gdns UB5 … 84 B4
Rayners La Harrow HA2 . 63 D6
Pinner HA5 … 41 B3
Rayners Lane Sta HA5 41 B2
Rayner's Rd SW15 … 157 A6
Rayner Twrs E10 … 53 C2
Raynes Ave E11 … 55 C2
Raynes Ct NW2 … 69 A4
Raynesfield SW20 … 200 C6
Raynes Park High Sch
KT3 … 200 B6
Raynes Park Sta
SW20 … 178 C1
Raynham W2 … 237 A2
Raynham Ave N18 … 34 A5
Raynham Ho 1 E1 … 96 D3
Raynham Prim Sch
N18 … 34 A5
Raynham Rd W6 … 112 B2
Edmonton N18 … 34 A5
Raynham Terr N18 … 34 A5
Raynor Cl UB1 … 107 B5
Raynor Pl N1 … 235 B6
Raynton Cl Harrow HA2 . 41 A2
Hayes UB4 … 83 D3
Raynton Dr Hayes UB4 .. 83 C5
Hayes UB4 … 83 D3
Raynton Rd EN3 … 6 D6
Ray Rd KT8 … 195 D4
Rays Ave N18 … 34 C6
Rays Rd N18 … 34 C6
West Wickham BR4 … 208 A2
Ray St EC1 … 241 B5
Ray Wlk N7 … 72 B6
Raywood Cl UB7 … 127 A5
Reachview Cl 14 NW1 .. 71 C1
Read Cl KT7 … 197 A2
Read Ct E17 … 53 D3
Reade Ct 6 W3 … 111 A3
Reade Ho 7 SE10 … 142 B6
Reade Wlk NW10 … 67 C1
Read Ho N11 … 30 D6
4 SE11 … 138 C6
Reading Ho SE15 … 140 A6
W2 … 236 A1
Reading La E8 … 74 B2
Reading Rd
Northolt UB5 … 64 A3
Sutton SM1 … 218 A3
Reading Way NW7 … 29 A5
Readman Ct 8 SE20 .. 184 B2
Reads Cl IG1 … 78 D5
Reapers Cl NW1 … 232 C6
Reapers Way TW7 … 152 B6
Reardon Ho 5 E1 … 118 B5
Reardon Path 31 E1 .. 118 B5
Reardon St E1 … 118 B5
Reaston St SE14 … 140 D5
Reay Prim Sch
SW9 … 138 B5 270 D3
Rebecca Ct
Beckenham BR3 … 185 C2
Sidcup DA14 … 190 B6
Rebecca Ho 10 N12 … 29 D6
Reckitt Rd W4 … 111 C1
Record St SE16 … 140 C6
Recovery St SW17 … 180 C5
Recreation Rd
Bromley BR2 … 186 D1
Forest Hill SE26 … 184 D6
Southall UB2 … 107 A2
Recreation Way CR4,
SW16 … 204 A6
Rector St N1 … 95 A6 235 A5
Rectory Bsns Ctr 5
DA14 … 190 B6
Rectory Cl N3 … 29 B2
Chingford E4 … 19 C1
Littleton TW17 … 192 C6
Long Ditton KT6 … 197 C1
Sidcup DA14 … 190 B6
Stanmore HA7 … 25 B5
West Barnes SW20 … 200 C6
Rectory Cres E11 … 55 C3
Rectory Ct E11 … 76 D5
Cranford TW5 … 128 C3
Feltham TW13 … 172 C6
Wallington SM6 … 219 C4
Woodford E18 … 36 D2
Rectory Field Cres
SE7 … 143 C5
Rectory Gdns N8 … 50 A5
SW4 … 137 C2
Beckenham BR3 … 185 C2
Northolt UB5 … 85 B6
Rectory Gn BR3 … 185 B2
Rectory Gr SW4 … 137 C2
Croydon CR0 … 220 D6
Hampton TW12,TW13 .. 173 B6
Rectory La DA14 … 190 C6
Edgware HA8 … 26 C4
Long Ditton KT6 … 197 C1
Stanmore HA7 … 25 B5
Upper Tooting SW17 .. 181 A5
Wallington SM6 … 219 C4
Rectory Orch SW19 .. 179 A6
Rectory Paddock Sch
BR5 … 190 C1
Rectory Park Ave UB5 .. 85 B4
Rectory Pl SE18 … 122 C2
Rectory Rd E12 … 78 B3
E17 … 53 D5
N16 … 73 D5
1 W3 … 111 A5
Rectory Rd *continued*
Barnes SW13 … 134 A3
Beckenham BR3 … 185 C2
Cranford TW5 … 128 C3
Dagenham RM10 … 81 D1
Hayes UB3 … 84 A1
Keston BR2 … 225 D1
Southall UB2 … 107 B3
Sutton SM1 … 217 D5
Rectory Road Sta N16 . 73 D5
Rectory Sq E1 … 96 D2
Rectory Way UB10 … 60 D5
Reculver Ho 2 SE15 .. 140 C6
Reculver Mews N18 … 34 A6
Reculver Rd SE16 … 118 D1
Red Anchor Cl SW3 .. 267 A5
Redan Pl W2 … 91 D1
Redan St W14 … 112 D3
Redan Terr SE5 … 138 D3
Red Barracks Rd 4
SE18 … 122 B2
Redberry Gr SE23,SE26 162 C1
Redbourne Ave N3 … 29 C2
Redbourne Dr SE28 .. 102 D1
Redbourne Ho 7 E14 .. 97 B1
N3 … 29 C2
Redbourn Ho W10 … 90 C3
Redbridge Coll RM6 .. 58 B4
Redbridge Ent Ctr IG1 . 79 A6
Redbridge Gdns SE5 .. 139 C5
Redbridge Inf Sch IG4 . 56 A4
Redbridge Jun Sch IG4 56 A4
Redbridge La E IG4 … 56 A4
Redbridge La W E11 … 55 C3
Redbridge Rdbt IG4 … 55 D3
Redbridge Sta IG4 … 55 D3
Redburn St
SW3 … 136 D6 267 C6
Redburn Trad Est EN3 .. 18 D5
Redcar Cl UB5 … 63 D2
Redcar Ho SE26 … 184 B4
Redcar St SE5 … 139 A5
Redcastle Cl E1 … 118 C6
Red Cedars Rd BR6 .. 211 C2
Redchurch St
E2 … 95 D3 243 C6
Redcliffe Cl SW5 … 255 C1
Redcliffe Gdns
SW10 … 135 D6 265 D6
Chiswick W4 … 132 D5
Ilford IG1 … 56 C1
Redcliffe Mews SW10 255 D1
Redcliffe Pl SW10 … 266 A5
Redcliffe Rd
SW10 … 136 A6 266 B6
Redcliffe Sch
SW10 … 136 A6 266 B6
Redcliffe Sq
SW10 … 113 D1 255 D1
Redcliffe St SW10 … 265 D6
Redcliffe Wlk HA9 … 66 D5
Redclose Ave SM4 … 201 C4
Redclyffe Rd E6 … 99 C6
Redclyffe Terr 2 SM2 217 C1
Redclyf Ho 12 E1 … 96 C3
Redcroft 5 NW6 … 69 C2
Redcroft Rd UB1 … 86 A1
Redcross Way
SE1 … 117 A5 252 B3
Redding Ho SE18 … 122 A3
Reddings Ave WD23 … 8 A6
Reddings Cl NW7 … 27 D6
Reddings The NW7 … 11 D1
Reddins Rd SE15 … 140 A6
Reddons Rd BR3 … 185 A3
Rede Ho 2 E12 … 78 C3
Rede Pl W2 … 113 C6 245 B6
Redesdale Gdns TW7 . 131 A5
Redesdale St SW3 … 267 C6
Redfern Ave TW2,TW4 151 C4
Redfern Ho 6 E13 … 98 D6
Redfern Rd NW10 … 67 C1
Catford SE6 … 164 A4
Redfield La
SW5 … 113 D2 255 C4
Redfield Mews SW5 .. 255 B4
Redriff Est SE16 … 119 B3
Redford Ave
Thornton Heath CR7 .. 204 B5
Wallington SM6 … 220 A2
Redford Cl TW13 … 149 D2
Redford Wlk N1 … 235 A6
Redgate Dr BR2 … 225 B6
Red Gates Sch CR9 .. 220 C3
Redgate Terr SW15 … 156 D5
Redgrave Cl SE25 … 205 D3
Redgrave Rd SW15 … 134 D2
Red Hill BR7 … 188 D5
Redhill Ct SW2 … 160 C2
Redhill Dr HA8 … 27 A1
Red Hill Prim Sch
BR7 … 188 D5
Redhill St NW1 .. 93 B4 231 D2
Red House La DA6 … 147 A1
Red House Rd CR0 … 203 D3
Redif Ho RM10 … 81 D4
Redington Gdns NW3 .. 69 D4
Redington Ho N1 … 233 D4
Redington Rd NW3 … 69 D4
Redknap Ho TW10 … 153 C1
Red La KT10 … 213 A2
Redland Gdns KT8 … 195 B5
Redlands N15 … 51 B5
Teddington TW11 … 175 A4
Redlands Ct BR1 … 186 D3
Redlands Prim Sch E1 . 96 C2
Redlands Rd EN3 … 7 A4
Redlands The 5 BR3 . 185 D1
Redlands Way SW2 … 160 B4
Redleaf Cl DA17 … 147 C6
Redleaves Ave TW15 . 170 D4
Redlees Cl TW7 … 131 A1
Red Leys UB8 … 60 A1
Red Lion Bsns Ctr KT6 214 B5
Red Lion Cl 9 SE17 .. 139 B6
Red Lion Ct EC4 … 241 B1
Red Lion Hill N2 … 30 B1
Red Lion La SE18 … 144 C4
Red Lion Pl SE18 … 144 C4
Red Lion Rd KT6 … 214 C6
Red Lion Row SE17 .. 139 A6
Red Lion Sq
WC1 … 94 B2 240 C3
Red Lion St
WC1 … 94 B2 240 C3
Richmond TW10 … 153 D6
Red Lion Yd W1 … 248 B4
Red Lo BR4 … 208 A2
Red Lodge Rd BR3,BR4 208 B2
Redlynch Ct
W14 … 113 A4 244 B1
Redlynch Ho 27 SW9 . 138 C4
Redman Bldg EC1 … 241 A4
Redman Cl UB5 … 84 C5
Redman Ho SE1 … 252 B1
Redman's Rd E1 … 96 C2
Redmayne Ho 15 SW9 138 B3
Redmead La E1 … 118 A5
Redmead Rd UB3 … 105 C2
Redmill Ho 24 E1 … 96 B3
Redmond Ho N1 … 233 D5
Redmore Rd W6 … 112 B2
Red Oak Cl BR6 … 226 D6
Red Pl W1 … 248 A6
Redpoll Way DA18 … 124 D3
Red Post Hill SE21,
SE24 … 161 B6
Red Post Ho E6 … 77 D1
Redriffe Rd E13 … 98 D6
Redriff Prim Sch SE16 119 A4
Redriff Rd SE16 … 119 A3
Redroofs Cl BR3 … 185 D2
Redrose Trad Ctr 1
EN4 … 14 B6
Red Rover SW13 … 134 A2
Redrup Ho 21 SE14 .. 140 D6
Redruth Cl N22 … 32 B3
Redruth Ho SM2 … 217 D1
Redruth Rd E9 … 96 C6
Red Sq The N16 … 73 B5
Redstart Cl E6 … 100 A2
SE14 … 141 A5
Redston Rd N8 … 49 D5
Redvers Rd N22 … 32 C1
Redvers St E2 … 95 C4
Redway Dr TW2 … 152 A4
Redwing Path SE28 .. 123 B4
Redwood Cl DA15 … 168 A3
N14 … 15 D4
SE16 … 119 A5
Chigwell IG9 … 21 B2
Hillingdon UB10 … 82 D5
South Oxhey WD19 … 22 D6
Redwood Ct N19 … 49 D2
NW6 … 69 A1
Northolt UB5 … 85 A4
10 Surbiton KT6 … 197 D2
Redwood Est TW5 … 128 B6
Redwood Gdns E4 … 19 D5
Redwood Mews
2 SW4 … 137 B2
Ashford TW15 … 171 B3
Redwoods SW15 … 156 A3
Redwood Twr E11 … 76 B5
Redwood Way EN5 … 12 D6
Redwood Wlk KT6 … 197 D1
Reece Mews SW7 … 256 C4
Reed Ave BR6 … 227 C5
Reed Cl E16 … 99 A2
SE12 … 165 A6
Reede Gdns RM10 … 81 D3
Reede Rd RM10 … 81 D2
Reede Way RM10 … 81 D2
Reedham Cl N17 … 52 B5
Reedham St SE15 … 140 A2
Reed Ho SW15 … 156 A5
Reedholm Villas N16 .. 73 B4
Reed Mans 6 E11 … 55 A3
Reed Pl Bsns Pk TW17 192 B1
Reed Rd N17 … 33 D1
Reedsfield Cl TW15 .. 148 D1
Reedsfield Rd TW15 . 170 D6
Reed's Pl NW1 … 71 C1
Reedworth St
SE11 … 116 C2 261 B3
Reef Ho E14 … 120 A3
Reenglass Rd HA7 … 25 D6
Rees Dr HA7 … 26 A6
Rees Gdns CR0 … 205 D3
Rees Ho 6 N17 … 33 D3
Reesland Cl E12 … 78 C2
Rees St N1 … 95 A6 235 B5
Reets Farm Cl NW9 … 45 C3
Reeves Ave NW9 … 45 B2
Reeves Cnr CR0 … 220 D6
Reeves Cnr Sta CR0 .. 220 D6
Reeves Ho SE1 … 251 A1
W1 … 248 A5
Reeves Mews
W1 … 115 A6 248 B5
Reeves Rd E3 … 97 D3
SE18 … 144 D6
Reflection The E16 .. 122 D4
Reform Row N17 … 33 D1
Reform St SW11 … 136 D3
Regal Cl E1 … 96 A2
Ealing W5 … 87 D2
Regal Cres SM6 … 219 B5
Regal Ct Edmonton N18 . 33 D5
2 Mitcham CR4 … 202 D6
Wembley HA0 … 65 D4
Regal Dr N11 … 31 B5
Regal La NW1 … 231 B5
Regal Pl 8 E3 … 97 B4
SW6 … 265 D3
Regal Way HA3 … 44 A3
Regan Ho 1 N18 … 33 D4
Regan Way N1 … 95 C5
Regatta Ho TW11 … 175 A6
Regatta Point TW8 … 132 B6
Regency Cl Ealing W5 .. 88 A1
Hampton TW12 … 173 B5
Regency Cres 3 NW4 . 28 D1
Regency Ct 21 E9 … 96 C6
Enfield EN1 … 17 B6
4 Kingston KT5 … 198 B4
4 Penge SE19 … 184 A3
Sutton SM1 … 217 D4
Wimbledon SW19 … 179 B3
Regency Dr HA4 … 39 C1
Regency Gdns KT12 .. 194 C1
Regency Ho N3 … 29 B1
Regency Lo NW3 … 70 B1
1 Buckhurst Hill IG9 .. 21 D2
Regency Mews
1 NW10 … 68 A2
Beckenham BR3 … 186 A2
Isleworth TW7 … 152 C6
Regency St
SW1 … 115 D2 259 D3
Regency Way DA7 … 147 A2
Regency Wlk
Croydon CR0 … 207 B3
8 Richmond TW10 … 154 A6
Regent Ave UB10 … 60 D1
Regent Bsns Ctr UB3 . 106 A4
Regent Cl N12 … 30 A5
Cranford TW4 … 128 B4
Harrow HA3 … 44 A3
Regent Ct 1 N16 … 51 D2
N3 … 29 D3
NW8 … 230 A1
South Norwood SE19 . 182 D4
Regent Gdns IG3 … 58 A2
Regent Ho W14 … 254 A4
Regent Lo 9 SW2 … 160 B3
Regent Pl W1 … 249 B6
Croydon CR0 … 205 D1
Wimbledon SW19 … 180 A5
Regent Rd SE24 … 160 D6
Surbiton KT5 … 198 C4
Regents Ave N13 … 32 C5
Regents Bridge Gdns
SW8 … 270 B4
Regents Canal Ho 21
E14 … 97 A1
Regents Cl Hayes UB4 .. 83 C2
South Croydon CR2 … 221 C2
Regent's Coll
NW1 … 93 A3 238 A6
Regents Ct E8 … 96 A6
22 Beckenham BR3 … 185 C3
Bromley BR1 … 186 D3
Edgware HA8 … 26 A6
1 Kingston KT2 … 176 A2
Regents Dr BR2 … 225 D3
Regents Gate Ho 20
E14 … 119 A6
Regents Mews
NW8 … 92 A5 229 B4
Regent's Park★
NW1 … 93 A4 231 A3
Regent's Park Barracks
NW1 … 231 D3
Regent's Park Rd N3 .. 47 B6
NW1 … 93 A6 231 A6
Regent's Park Sta
NW1 … 93 B3 238 C5
Regent's Park Terr
NW1 … 231 C6
Regent's Pl SE3 … 143 A3
Regents Pl IG10 … 21 D4
Regents Plaza 2 NW6 . 91 D5
Regent Sq 23 E3 … 97 D4
WC1 … 94 A4 233 B1
Belvedere DA17 … 125 D2
Regent's Row E8 … 96 A6

Regent St W1 115 C6 249 A6
W4 110 C1
Regents Wharf 3 E2 96 B6
N1 233 C4
Regina Coeli RC Prim Sch
CR2 220 D1
Reginald Ct BR3 186 A2
Reginald Pl 6 SE8 141 C5
Reginald Rd E7 77 A2
SE8 141 C5
Reginald Sorenson Ct
E11 54 B2
Reginald Sq SE8 141 C5
Regina Point SE16 118 C3
Regina Rd N4 50 B1
Ealing W13 109 A5
Southall UB2 107 A4
South Norwood SE25 206 A6
Regina Terr W13 109 B5
Regis Ct N8 50 B5
NW1 237 C4
East Bedfont TW14 149 B5
Mitcham SW19 180 C2
Regis Pl 17 SW2 138 B1
Regis Rd NW5 71 B3
Regnart Bldgs NW1 232 B1
Regnolruf Ct KT12 194 A2
Reid Cl HA5 40 A5
Reid Ct SW14 133 A3
Reidhaven Rd SE18 123 C2
Reigate Ave SM3,SM4 201 D1
Reigate Rd BR1,SE12 165 A2
Catford BR1 164 D1
Ilford IG3 79 D6
Reigate Way SM6 220 A3
Reighton Rd E5 74 A6
Reizel Cl N16 51 C1
Relay Rd W12 112 C5
Relf Rd SE15 140 A2
Reliance Sq E2 243 A6
Relko Gdns SM1 218 B3
Relton Mews SW7 257 B6
Rembrandt Cl E14 120 B3
Rembrandt Ct 10 SE16 118 B1
West Ewell KT19 215 D2
Rembrandt Rd SE13 142 C1
Edgware HA8 26 C1
Remembrance Ave N2 47 D6
Remington Rd E6 100 A1
N15 51 B3
Remington St
N1 94 D5 234 D3
Remnant St WC2 240 C2
Remsted Ho 5 NW6 91 D6
Remus Rd E3 75 C1
Renbold Ho 5 SE10 142 A4
Rendlebury Ho 17
SE18 122 B2
Rendle Cl CR0 206 A4
Rendlesham Ho 3 E5,
N16 74 A5
Rendlesham Rd E5 74 A5
Enfield EN2 4 D4
Renforth St SE16 118 C4
Renfree Way TW17 192 C2
Renfrew Cl E6 122 C6
Renfrew Ct TW5 129 A3
Renfrew Ho E17 35 B1
NW6 91 D5
Renfrew Rd
SE11 116 D2 261 C3
Hounslow TW5 129 A3
Kingston KT2 177 A3
Renmuir St SW17 180 D4
Rennell Ho 18 E9 74 D2
Rennell St SE13 142 A2
Renness Rd E17 53 A6
Rennets Cl SE9 167 C6
Rennets Wood Rd SE9 167 B6
Rennie Cotts 24 E1 96 C3
Rennie Ct SE1 251 C4
Holdbrook EN3 7 C5
Rennie Ho SE1 262 A5
Rennie St SE1 116 D5 251 C4
Renoir Ct 7 SE16 118 B1
Renovation The E16 122 D4
Renown Cl CR0 204 D1
Rensburg Rd E17 52 D3
Rensburg Villas E17 52 D4
Renshaw Cl 7 DA17 147 B6
Renshaw Ct SW19 179 A6
Renshaw Ho 11 SW27 182 D5
Renters Ave NW4 46 C3
Renton Cl SW2 160 B5
Renwick Rd IG11 102 B4
Repens Way UB4 84 D3
Rephidim St SE1 263 A5
Replingham Rd SW18 157 C3
Reporton Rd
SW6 135 A5 264 B3
Repository Rd SE7,
SE18 122 B1
Repton Ave Hayes UB3 105 B2
Wembley HA0 65 C4
Repton Cl SM1,SM5 218 C3
Repton Ct BR3 185 D2
Repton Ho 2 E14 97 A1
SW1 259 B3
Repton Rd Harrow HA3 44 B5
Repton Rd *continued*
Orpington BR6 227 D5
Repton St E14 97 A1
Re Sassoon Ho SE15 140 C4
Reservoir Cl CR7 205 B5
Reservoir Rd SE4 141 A3
Ruislip HA4 39 B5
Southgate N14 15 C6
Resolution Wlk SE18 122 B3
Restell Cl SE3 142 C6
Restmor Way SM5,
SM6 219 A6
Reston Pl SW7 246 A1
Restons Cres DA15,
SE9 167 C5
Restoration Sq SW11 266 D1
Restormel Cl TW3 151 C6
Retcar Pl N19 71 B6
Retford St E2 95 C5
Retingham Way E4 19 D2
Retreat Cl HA3 43 C4
Retreat Ho 5 E9 74 C2
Retreat Pl E9 74 C2
Retreat Rd TW9 153 D6
Retreat The NW9 45 B4
Harrow HA2 41 C2
Mortlake SW14 133 C2
North Cheam KT4 216 B6
South Norwood CR7 205 B5
Surbiton KT5 198 B3
Reunion Row E1 118 B6
Reveley Sq SE16 119 A4
Revell Rd Cheam SM1 217 B2
Kingston KT1 176 D2
Revell Rise SE18 145 D6
Revelon Rd SE4 141 A2
Revelstoke Rd SW18,
SW19 157 C2
Reventlow Rd SE9 167 A3
Reverdy Rd SE1 118 A2
Reverend Cl HA2 63 D5
Revesby Rd SM5 202 C3
Review Rd NW2 67 D6
Dagenham RM10 103 D6
Rewell St SW6 136 A5 266 A3
Rewley Rd SM4 202 B3
Rex Ave TW15 170 C5
Rex Ho TW13 151 A1
Rex Par 2 IG8 37 C4
Rex Pl W1 115 A5 248 B4
Reydon Ave E11 55 C3
Reygate Ct N4 51 A3
Reynard Cl BR1 210 C6
SE4 141 A2
Reynard Dr SE19 183 D3
Reynard Mills Trad Est
TW8 109 C1
Reynard Pl SE14 141 A6
Reynardson Rd N17 33 A3
Reynardson's Ct 3 N17 51 D6
Reynolds Ave
Chessington KT9 214 A1
Ilford RM6 58 C2
Little Ilford E12 78 C3
Reynolds Cl NW11 47 D2
Carshalton SM5 202 D1
Mitcham SW19 180 B2
Reynolds Ct E11 76 D5
Ilford RM6 58 D6
Reynolds Dr HA8 44 B6
Reynolds Ho 19 E2 96 C5
N4 50 A1
NW8 229 D3
SW1 259 D3
Enfield EN1 18 A6
Reynolds Pl SE3 143 B5
12 Richmond TW10 154 B5
Reynolds Rd SE15 140 C1
W4 111 A3
Hayes UB4 84 C3
New Malden KT3 199 B2
Reynolds Way CR0 221 C4
Rheidol Mews N1 235 A4
Rheidol Terr
N1 95 A6 235 A5
Rhein Ho N8 50 A6
Rheola Cl N17 33 D2
Rhoda St E2 95 D3 243 D6
Rhodes Ave N22 31 C2
Rhodes Avenue Prim Sch
N22 31 C2
Rhodes Ho N1 235 C2
Rhodesia Rd E11 76 B6
SW9 138 A3
Rhodes-Moorhouse Ct
SM4 201 C3
Rhodes St N7 72 B3
Rhodeswell Rd E14 97 A2
Rhodrons Ave KT9 214 A3
Rhondda Gr E3 97 B4
Rhyl Prim Sch NW5 71 A2
Rhyl Rd UB6 86 D5
Rhyl St NW5 71 A2
Rhys Ave N11 31 D3
Rialto Rd CR4 181 A1
Ribble Cl IG8 37 C4
Ribblesdale Ave N11 31 A4
Northolt UB5 63 D2
Ribblesdale Ho 11 NW6 91 C6
Ribblesdale Rd N8 50 B5
Streatham SW16 181 B5
Ribbon Dance Mews
SE5 139 B4
Ribchester Ave UB6 86 D4
Ribston Cl BR2 210 B1
Ribstone Ho 12 E9 74 D2
Ricardo Path 5 SE28 124 C5
Ricardo St E14 97 D1
Ricards Lodge High Sch
SW19 179 B5
Ricards Rd SW19 179 B5
Riccal Ct 2 NW9 27 C2
Riceyman Ho WC1 234 A1
Richard Alibon Prim Sch
RM10 81 C3
Richard Anderson Ct 1
SE14 140 D5
Richard Atkins Prim Sch
SW2 160 A4
Richard Burbidge Mans
SW13 134 C6
Richard Burton Ct 4
IG9 21 C2
Richard Challoner Sch
KT3 199 B2
Richard Cl SE18 122 A2
Richard Cloudesley Sch
EC1 95 A3 242 A5
Richard Cobden Prim Sch
NW1 93 C6 232 B5
Richard Ct EN5 1 A2
Richard Fell Ho 2 E12 78 C4
Richard Fox Ho N4 73 A5
Richard Ho 8 SE16 118 C2
Richard House Dr E16 99 D1
E6 100 A1
Richard Knight Ho
SW6 265 B2
Richard Neale Ho 2
E1 118 B6
Richards Cl Bushey WD23 8 B4
Harlington UB3 127 B6
Harrow HA1 43 A4
Hillingdon UB10 82 C6
Richards Ct BR3 184 D2
Richardson Cl 19 E8 95 D6
Richardson Ct 20 SW4 138 A3
Richardson Gdns 12
RM10 81 D2
Richardson Ho TW7 130 D2
Richardson Rd E15 98 C5
Richardson's Mews
W1 239 A5
Richards Pl E17 53 C6
Richard's Pl SW3 257 B4
Richard St 10 E1 96 B1
Richard Thornton Ho
SW19 179 C1
Richbell Pl WC1 240 C4
Richborne Terr
SW8 138 B5 270 D4
Richborough Ho 14 E5 74 B4
10 SE15 140 C6
Richborough Rd NW2 69 A4
Richens Cl TW3 130 B3
Riches Rd IG1 79 A6
Richfield Ct 4 BR3 185 B2
Richfield Rd WD23 8 A4
Richford Gate W6 112 C3
Richford Rd E15 98 D6
Richford St W6 112 C3
Richings Ho BR5 190 A2
Rich La SW5 255 C2
Richland Ho 4 SE15 140 A4
Richlands Ave KT17 216 A4
Richman Ho 10 SE8 119 B1
Richmond Adult & Com Coll
TW9 131 D1
Richmond Ave
N1 94 B6 233 D6
NW10 68 C2
Chingford E4 36 B5
Feltham TW14 149 C5
Hillingdon UB10 60 D2
Wimbledon SW20 179 A2
Richmond Bldgs W1 239 C1
Richmond Bridge
TW1 153 D5
Richmond Bridge Mans 1
TW1 153 D5
Richmond Circus TW9 132 A1
Richmond Cl E17 53 B3
Borehamwood WD6 11 B6
Richmond Coll
W8 113 D3 255 D6
Richmond TW10 154 A4
Richmond Cres
N1 94 C6 234 A6
Chingford E4 36 B5
Edmonton N9 18 A3
Richmond Ct BR1 187 B3
SW1 247 D1
12 Kingston KT2 176 C3
Mitcham CR4 202 B6
Wembley HA9 66 B6
Wimbledon SW20 178 B1
Richmond Dr TW17 193 B3
Richmond Gdns NW4 46 A4
Richmond Gdns *continued*
Harrow HA3 24 D3
Richmond Gn CR0 220 A5
Richmond Gr N1 72 D1
Surbiton KT5 198 B3
Richmond Hill TW10 154 A5
Richmond Hill Ct 5
TW10 154 A5
Richmond Ho NW1 231 D3
SE17 262 C2
12 Forest Hill SE26 162 A1
Richmond Ho(Annexe of
Rectory Sch) TW12 173 B5
Richmond International
Bsns Ctr 9 TW9 132 B1
Richmond Mans SW5 255 C2
Putney SW15 135 A2
14 Twickenham TW1 153 D5
Richmond Mews W1 239 C1
Richmond Park*
TW10 155 A3
Richmond Park Rd
Kingston KT2 176 A3
Mortlake SW14 133 B1
Richmond Pk IG10 21 D4
Richmond Pl SE18 123 A2
Richmond Rd E11 76 B6
E7 77 B3
E8 74 A1
N15 51 C3
N2 30 A1
W5 110 A4
Bowes Park N11 32 A4
Chingford E4 20 B3
Ilford IG1 79 A5
Isleworth TW7 131 A2
Kingston KT2 176 A4
New Barnet EN5 14 A6
Thornton Heath CR7 204 D5
Twickenham TW1 153 C4
Wallington CR0 220 A5
Wimbledon SW20 178 B2
Richmond St E13 99 A5
Richmond Sta TW9 132 A1
Richmond Terr
SW1 116 A4 250 A2
Richmond upon Thames
Coll TW2 152 C4
Richmond Way
W12,W14 112 D4
Wanstead E11 77 A6
Richmount Gdns SE3 143 A2
Rich St E14 119 B6
Rickard Cl NW4 46 A5
Streatham SW2 160 C3
Rickards Cl KT6 214 A6
Rickett St SW6 265 B6
Rickman Ho 26 E2 96 C3
Rickman St 25 E1 96 C3
Rickmansworth Rd
HA5 22 C1
Rick Roberts Way E15 98 B5
Rickthorne Rd 6 N19 72 A6
Rickyard Path SE9 144 A1
Riddell Ct SE1 263 C2
Ridding La UB6 64 D3
Riddons Rd SE12 187 C6
Rideout St SE18 122 B2
Rider Cl DA15 167 C5
Ride The
Brentford TW8 109 C1
Enfield EN3 6 D2
Ridgdale St E3 97 D5
Ridge Ave N21 17 B4
Ridgebrook Rd SE3,
SE9 143 D2
Ridge Cl NW4 28 D1
NW9 45 B5
SE28 123 B4
Ridge Crest EN2 4 B4
Ridge Hill NW11 47 A1
Ridge Ho 4 KT2 176 D3
Ridgemead Cl N13,N14 16 A2
Ridgemont Gdns HA8 27 A6
Ridgemount Ave CR0 222 D6
Ridgemount Cl SE20 184 B3
Ridgemount Gdns EN2 4 D3
Ridgeon Ct N22 32 B4
Ridge Rd N8 50 B3
NW2 69 B5
Cheam SM3 201 B1
Edmonton N21 17 B3
Mitcham CR4 181 B3
Ridges The E4 35 C6
Ridge Terr N21 17 A4
Ridge The DA5 169 B4
Barnet EN5 13 B6
Orpington BR6 227 B6
Surbiton KT5 198 C4
Twickenham TW2 152 B4
Ridgeview Cl EN5 12 D5
Ridgeview Rd N20 14 A1
Ridgeway BR2 225 A6
11 Richmond TW10 154 A5
Walton-on-T KT12 193 D1
Woodford IG8 37 C6
Ridge Way
Feltham TW13 151 A1
7 West Norwood SE19 183 C4
Ridgeway Ave EN4 14 D5
Ridgeway Cres BR6 227 C5
Ridgeway Crescent Gdns
BR6 227 C5
Ridgeway Ct HA5 23 C3
Ridgeway Dr BR1 187 B6
Acton W3 110 C3
Ridgeway E DA15 167 D6
Ridgeway Gdns N6 49 C2
Redbridge IG4 56 A4
Ridgeway Rd TW7 130 C4
Ridgeway Rd N TW7 130 C5
Ridgeway The N11 30 D6
N3 29 D3
NW11 47 B1
NW7 28 B6
NW9 45 B5
Acton W3 110 C3
Chingford E4 20 A3
Enfield EN2 4 B5
Harrow HA2 41 B4
Harrow HA2 41 D3
Harrow HA3 43 C3
Palmers Green N14 16 A2
Ruislip HA4 40 A2
Stanmore HA7 25 C4
Wallington CR0 220 B5
Ridgeway W DA15 167 C6
Ridgeway Wlk UB5 63 A2
Ridgewell Cl N1 235 B6
Dagenham RM10 103 D6
Forest Hill SE26 185 B6
Ridgmount Gdns
WC1 93 D2 239 C4
Ridgmount Pl WC1 239 C4
Ridgmount Rd SW18 157 D6
Ridgmount St
WC1 93 D2 239 C4
Ridgway SW19,SW20 178 D4
Ridgway Ct SW19 178 D4
Ridgway Gdns SW19 178 D3
Ridgway Pl SW19 179 A4
Ridgway Rd SW9 138 D2
Ridgway The SM2 218 B1
Ridgwell Rd E16 99 C2
Riding House St
W1 93 C2 239 A3
Ridings Ave N21 17 A6
Ridings Cl N6 49 C2
Ridings The EN4 14 B4
Ealing W5 88 B3
Sunbury TW16 172 A2
Surbiton KT5 198 C4
Riding The NW11 47 B2
Ridler Rd EN1 5 C5
Ridley Ave W13 109 B3
Ridley Cl IG11 79 D1
Ridley Ct SW16 182 A4
Ridley Ho 14 SW11 136 C2
Ridley Rd DA16 146 B4
E7 77 C4
E8 73 D3
NW10 90 A5
Beckenham BR2 208 D6
Merton SW19 179 D3
Ridley Road Mkt E8 73 D3
Ridsdale Rd SE20 184 B2
Riefield Rd SE9 167 A6
Riesco Dr CR0 222 C2
Riffel Rd NW2 68 C3
Rifle Ct SE11 138 C6
Rifle Pl W11 112 D5
Rifle Range La HA1 42 D1
Rifle St E14 97 D2
Rigault Rd SW6 135 A3
Rigby Cl CR0 220 C5
Rigby La UB3 105 A4
Rigby Mews IG1 78 C6
Rigby Pl EN3 7 C6
Rigden St E14 97 D1
Rigeley Rd NW10 90 A4
Rigg App E10 53 A1
Rigge Pl SW4 137 D1
Rigg Ho 2 SW4 160 A4
Riggindale Rd SW16 181 D6
Rignold Ho 6 SE5 139 C3
Rigo Ho 9 E1 96 D2
Riley Ho SW10 266 C5
9 Bow E3 97 C3
1 Streatham SW4 159 D4
Riley Rd SE1 117 D3 263 C6
Enfield EN3 6 C5
Riley St SW10 136 B5 266 C4
Rill Ho 24 SE5 139 C5
Rimini Ct SW12 158 D3
Rinaldo Rd SW12 159 B4
Ring Cl BR1 187 B3
Ringcroft St N7 72 C3
Ring Cross Prim Sch
N7 72 B3
Ringer's Rd BR1 209 A6
Ringford Ho SW18 157 B6
Ringford Rd SW18 157 C6
Ring Ho 14 E1 118 C6
Ringlet Cl E16 99 B2
Ringlewell Cl EN1 6 B3
Ringmer Ave
SW6 135 A4 264 B1
Ringmer Gdns 2 N19 72 A6
Ringmer Ho 15 SE22 139 C2
Ringmer Pl N21 17 B6
Ringmer Way BR1 210 B4
Ringmore Rise SE23 162 B4
Ringsfield Ho SE17 262 B1
Ringslade Rd N22 32 B1
Ringstead Ct SM1 218 B3
Ringstead Rd
Catford SE6 163 D4
Sutton SM1 218 B3
Ring Way N11 31 C4
Ringway UB2 107 A1
Ringwold Cl BR3 185 A3
Ringwood Ave N2 48 D6
Thornton Heath CR0 204 A2
Ringwood Cl HA5 40 C6
Ringwood Gdns
18 E14 119 C2
Roehampton SW15 156 A3
Ringwood Rd E17 53 B3
Ringwood Way
Hampton TW12 173 C6
Southgate N21 16 D4
Ripley Cl BR1 210 B4
New Addington CR0 224 A2
Ripley Ct 1 CR4 180 B1
Ripley Gdns
Mortlake SW14 133 B2
Sutton SM1 218 A4
Ripley Ho SW1 269 A6
13 Kingston KT2 176 D4
Mortlake SW14 133 C2
5 Penge SE26 184 B5
Ripley Mews E11 54 C3
Ripley Rd
Belvedere DA17 125 C2
Enfield EN2 5 A4
Hampton TW12 173 C3
Ilford IG3 79 D6
Newham E16 99 C1
Riplington Ct SW15 156 B4
Ripon Cl UB5 63 C2
Ripon Gdns
Chessington KT9 213 D3
Redbridge IG1 56 A2
Ripon Rd N17 51 B6
SE18 144 D6
Edmonton N9 18 B4
Ripon Way WD6 11 B6
Rippersley Rd DA16 146 A4
Ripple Ct 10 IG11 101 B6
Ripple Rd Barking IG11 101 C6
Barking RM9 102 A6
Rippleside Commercial Est
IG11 102 C5
Ripplevale Gr N1 72 B1
Rippolson Rd SE18 123 D1
Ripston Rd TW15 171 B5
Risborough SE17 262 A4
Risborough Cl 4 N10 49 B6
Risborough Dr KT4 200 A2
Risborough Ho NW8 237 B6
Risborough St SE1 251 D2
Risdon Ho 20 SE16 118 C4
Risdon St 21 SE16 118 C4
Risedale Rd DA7 147 D2
Riseholme Ho 14 SE22 139 C2
Riseldine Rd SE23 163 A5
Rise The NW10 67 B5
NW7 27 D4
Borehamwood WD6 10 B6
Buckhurst Hill IG9 21 D4
Chingford, Chingford Green
E4 20 C3
Edgware HA8 26 D5
Edmonton N13 32 C6
Greenford HA0,UB6 65 A3
Hillingdon UB10 82 B5
Sidcup DA5 168 C4
Wanstead E11 55 A4
Risinghill St N1 234 A4
Risingholme Cl HA3 24 C2
Risingholme Rd HA3 24 C1
Risings The E17 54 B5
Rising Sun Ct EC1 241 D3
Risley Ave N17 33 B2
Risley Avenue Prim Sch
N17 33 C2
Risley Ho 7 E9 74 D2
Rita Rd SW8 138 B5 270 C4
Ritches Rd N15 51 A4
Ritchie Ho N19 49 D2
8 SE16 118 C3
11 South Bromley E14 98 B1
Ritchie Rd CR0 206 B3
Ritchie St N1 94 C5 234 B4
Ritchings Ave E17 53 A5
Ritherdon Rd SW17 159 B2
Ritson Ho N1 233 C5
Ritson Rd E8 74 A2
Ritter St SE18 144 C6
Ritz Par W5 88 B3
Rivaz Pl E9 74 C2
Riven Ct 10 W2 91 D1
Rivenhall Gdns E11,E18 54 D5
Riverains The SW11 266 C1

River Ave Southgate N13 16 D2
Thames Ditton KT7 197 A2
Riverbank KT8 196 C5
River Bank
Edmonton N21 17 A4
Thames Ditton KT7 196 D4
Riverbank Rd BR1 165 A1
Riverbank Way TW8 131 C6
River Barge Cl E14 120 A4
River Brent Bsns Pk
W7 108 C3
River Cl Ruislip HA4 39 D3
Southall UB2 108 A4
Wanstead E11 55 C3
River Cotts BR5 190 C1
Rivercourt Rd W6 112 B1
River Crane Way
TW13 151 B2
River Ct SE1 251 C3
Kingston KT6 197 D4
Wanstead E11 55 C5
Riverdale Dr SW18 157 D3
Riverdale Gdns TW1 153 C6
Riverdale Rd SE18 123 D1
Erith DA8 125 D1
Feltham TW13 173 B6
Sidcup DA5 169 B5
Twickenham TW1 153 C5
Riverdene HA8 11 A1
Riverdene Rd IG1 78 D5
Riverfleet WC1 233 B2
Riverford Ho 28 W2 91 C2
River Front EN1 5 C2
River Gdns
Carshalton SM5 219 A5
Feltham TW14 150 B6
River Gdns Bsns Ctr
TW14 128 B1
River Grove Pk BR3 185 B2
Riverhead Cl E17 34 D1
River Ho Barnes SW13 133 C3
1 Forest Hill SE26 162 B1
Riverholme KT8 196 C6
Riverhope Mans SE18 122 A3
Riverine Lo HA7 25 A5
River La TW10 153 D3
Rivermead
East Molesey KT8 196 A6
Kingston KT6 197 D4
Rivermead Cl TW11 175 B5
Rivermead Ct
Ealing UB6 87 A4
Fulham SW6 135 B2
Rivermead Ho E9 75 A3
Sunbury TW16 194 C6
Rivermeads Ave TW13,
TW2 151 D1
River Mount KT12 193 D2
Rivernook Cl KT12 194 C4
River Park Gdns BR2 186 B3
River Park Rd N22 32 B1
River Pl N1 73 A1
River Rd Barking IG11 101 D3
Buckhurst Hill IG9 21 D3
River Reach TW11 175 C5
River Road Bsns Pk
IG11 101 D4
Riversdale Gdns N22 32 C2
Riversdale Prim Sch
SW18 157 C3
Riversdale Rd N5 73 A5
Thames Ditton KT7 197 A3
Riversdene N5 73 A5
Riversfield Rd EN1 5 C2
Rivers Ho 11 TW8 110 C1
Riverside NW4 46 B2
SW11 267 B4
WC1 233 B2
Forest Hill SE6 185 B6
Greenwich SE7 121 B3
Oatlands Park TW17 193 C2
Sunbury TW16 172 D1
Twickenham TW1 153 B3
Riverside Apartments
N13 32 B5
Riverside Ave KT8 196 B4
Riverside Bsns Ctr
SW18 157 D3
Riverside Bsns Pk
SW19 180 A2
Riverside Cl BR5 190 C1
E5 74 C6
Ealing W7 86 C3
Hackbridge SM6 219 B5
Kingston KT1 197 D5
Riverside Cotts IG11 101 B5
Riverside Ct SE12 142 D1
SW8 269 D6
Chingford E4 19 D5
Richmond TW11 175 C5
Riverside Dr NW11 47 A3
Chiswick W4 133 C4
Mitcham CR4 202 C4
Richmond TW10 153 B1
Riverside Est EN3 19 A5
Riverside Gdns N3 47 A6
Riverside Gdns continued
W6 112 B1
Enfield EN2 5 A3
Wembley HA0 88 A5
Riverside Ho N12 29 D6
Morden SW19 202 A5
Riverside Ind Est IG11 102 A4
Riverside Mans 4 E1 118 C5
Riverside Pl N11 15 C1
Stanwell TW19 148 A5
Riverside Prim Sch
SE16 118 A4
Riverside Rd DA14 169 A2
E15 98 A5
N15 52 A3
Stanwell TW19 148 A5
Wandsworth SW17,
SW19 158 A1
Riverside The KT8 196 B6
Riverside West SW18 135 D1
Riverside Wlk
Isleworth TW7 130 C2
3 West Wickham BR4 207 D1
Riverside Works IG11 78 D1
Riverside Workshops
SE1 252 B4
River St EC1 94 C4 234 A2
Riverstone Ct KT2 176 B2
Riverston Sch SE12 165 A6
River Terr W6 112 C1
Riverton Cl W9 91 B4
Riverview TW17 193 B2
River View EN2 5 A2
Riverview CE Sch
KT19 215 B4
Riverview Ct 14 DA17 125 C1
Riverview Gdns
Barnes SW13 134 B6
Twickenham TW1 152 D2
Riverview Gr W4 132 D6
Riverview Hts SE18 144 D5
Riverview Lo NW9 67 B6
Riverview Pk SE6 163 C2
Riverview Prim Sch
KT19 215 B4
Riverview Rd
Chiswick W4 132 D6
West Ewell KT19 215 B4
River Way SE10 120 D3
Riverway N13 32 C6
River Way
Twickenham TW13,TW2 151 D2
West Ewell KT19 215 C3
River Wlk KT12 194 A3
Riverwood La BR7 189 B2
Rivet Ho SE1 263 D2
Rivington Ave IG8 37 D1
Rivington Cres NW7 27 D3
Rivington Ct NW10 90 A6
Rivington Pl EC2 95 C4
Rivington St EC2 95 C4
Rivington Wlk 4 E8 96 A6
Rivulet Rd N17 33 A3
Rixon Ho SE18 144 D6
Rixon St N7 72 C5
Rixsen Rd E12 78 A3
Roach Rd E3 75 C1
Roach Works E3 75 C1
Roads Pl N19 72 A6
Roan Ind Est CR4 180 D2
Roan St SE10 142 A6
Robarts Cl HA5 40 B4
Robbins Hall EN3 18 D5
Robb Rd HA7 25 A4
Robert Adam St W1 238 A2
Roberta St E2 96 A4
Robert Bell Ho 2
SE16 118 A2
Robert Blair Prim Sch
N7 72 A2
Robert Browning Prim Sch
SE17 117 B1 262 C2
Robert Burns Ho N17 34 B3
Robert Cl W9 236 B5
Robert Clack Lower Sch
RM8 81 B6
Robert Clack Upper Sch
RM8 59 C1
Robert Dashwood Way
SE17 262 A3
Robert Gentry Ho
W14 254 B1
Robert Gerard Ho 7
SE27 183 B6
Robert Jones Ho 3
SE16 118 A2
Robert Keen Cl 17
SE15 140 A4
Robert Lowe Cl SE14 140 D5
Roberton Dr BR1 187 C2
Robert Owen Ho 8 E2 95 D4
Fulham SW6 134 D4
Robert Owen Lo 5 E5 74 B4
Robertsbridge Rd
SM5 202 B2
Roberts Cl SE9 167 B3
Cheam SM3 216 D1
Yiewsley UB7 104 A5
Roberts Ct N1 234 D5
Roberts Ct continued
NW10 67 C2
Chessington KT9 213 D3
Ealing W5 88 A1
Penge SE20 184 C2
Roberts Ho 2 N11 31 B5
10 SE18 144 A4
5 West Norwood SE27 160 D1
Roberts Mews SW1 258 A5
Robertson Ho 11 SE10 142 A4
4 SE18 144 B4
1 Upper Tooting SW17 180 C5
Robertson Rd E15 98 A6
Robertson St SW8 137 B3
Robert's Pl EC1 241 B6
Roberts Rd NW7 29 A4
Belvedere DA17 125 C1
Chingford, Highams Park
E17 35 D2
Robert St E16 122 D5
NW1 93 B4 231 D1
SE18 123 B2
WC2 250 B5
Croydon CR0 221 A5
Robert Sutton Ho 20
E1 96 C1
Robeson St 8 E3 97 B2
Robina Cl DA6 146 D1
Northwood HA6 22 A2
Robin Cl NW7 11 C1
Hampton TW12 173 A5
Robin Cres E6 99 D2
Robin Ct 13 E14 120 A3
Wallington SM6 219 C2
Robin Gr N6 71 A6
Brentford TW8 131 C6
Harrow HA3 44 B3
Robin Hill Dr BR7 188 A4
Robin Ho NW8 230 A3
Robin Hood SW15 155 C1
Robinhood Cl CR4 203 C6
Robin Hood Ct SM1 217 D3
Robin Hood Dr HA3 24 D3
Robin Hood Gdns 12
E14 120 A6
Robin Hood Inf Sch
SM1 217 C3
Robin Hood Jun Sch
SM1 217 D3
Robin Hood La E14 120 A6
Robinhood La CR4 203 C6
Robin Hood La
Bexley DA6 169 A6
Kingston SW15 177 C6
Sutton SM1 217 D3
Robin Hood Prim Sch
SW15 177 C5
Robin Hood Way UB6 64 D2
Robin Hood Way (Kingston
By Pass) KT2,SW15,
SW20 177 C5
Robinia Cl SE20 184 A2
Robinia Cres E10 75 D6
Robinscroft Mews
SE10 141 D4
Robins Ct SE12 165 C1
Robin's Ct SW4 160 A5
Robins Ct TW10 154 A5
Robin's Ct BR3 186 B1
Robinsfield Inf Sch
NW8 92 C5 230 A4
Robins Gr BR4 225 A5
Robinson Cres WD23 8 A3
Robinson Ct N1 234 D6
4 Richmond TW9 132 B1
Robinson Ho 11 E14 97 C2
4 W10 90 D1
Robinson Rd E2 96 C5
Dagenham RM10 81 C4
Mitcham SW19 180 C4
Robinson's Cl W13 87 A2
Robinson St SW3 267 C6
Robinwood Gr UB8 82 B3
Robinwood Pl SW15 177 B6
Robsart St SW9 138 C3
Robson Ave NW10 68 A1
Robson Cl E6 100 A1
Enfield EN2 4 D3
Robson Ct N12 30 A5
Robson Rd SE21,SE27 161 A1
Roby Ho EC1 242 A6
Roch Ave HA8 26 B1
Rochdale 8 SE19 183 C4
Rochdale Rd E10 53 C2
SE2 124 B2
Rochdale Way 4 SE8 141 C5
Roche Ho 15 E14 119 B6
Rochelle Cl SW11 136 B1
Rochelle Ct 14 E1 96 C1
Beckenham BR3 185 D3
Rochelle St 31 E2 95 D4
Rochemont Wlk 2 E8 96 A6
Roche Rd SW16 182 B2
Rochester Ave BR1 187 B1
E13 99 C6
Feltham TW13 149 D2
Rochester Cl 1 DA15 168 B5
SE3 143 C2
Enfield EN1 5 C4
Rochester Cl continued
Streatham SW16 182 A3
Rochester Ct 1 E2 96 B3
7 NW1 71 C1
NW9 45 B4
South Norwood SE25 184 A1
Rochester Dr DA5 169 C5
Pinner HA5 40 D4
Rochester Gdns
Redbridge IG1 56 B2
South Croydon CR0 221 C5
Rochester Ho SE1 252 D1
18 SE15 140 C6
Rochester Mews NW1 71 C1
Rochester Par TW13 150 A1
Rochester Pl NW1 71 C1
Rochester Rd NW1 71 C2
Carshalton SM5 218 D4
Northwood HA6 39 D6
Rochester Row
SW1 115 C2 259 B4
Rochester Sq NW1 71 C1
Rochester St SW1 259 C5
Rochester Terr NW1 71 C2
Rochester Way
SE3,SE9 143 D2
SE9 144 C2
Rochester Wlk SE1 252 C4
Roche Wlk SM5 202 B3
Rochford N17 33 C1
Rochford Ave RM6 58 C4
Rochford Cl 2 E6 99 D5
Rochford Way CR0 204 A3
Rochford Wlk 3 E8 74 A1
Rochfort Ho 4 SE8 119 B1
Rock Ave 13 SW14 133 B2
Rockbourne Rd SE23 162 D3
Rock Cl CR4 180 B1
Rockell's Pl SE22 162 B5
Rockfield Ho 2 NW4 46 D5
SE10 142 A6
Rockford Ave UB6 87 B5
Rock Gdns RM10 81 D3
Rock Grove Way SE16 118 A2
Rockhall Rd NW2 68 D4
Rockhampton Cl 4
SE27 182 C6
Rockhampton Rd
South Croydon CR2 221 C2
West Norwood SE27,
SW16 182 C6
Rock Hill SE19 183 D6
Rockingham Cl SW15 133 D1
Rockingham Ct 19
BR3 185 C3
Rockingham Gate WD23 8 A5
Rockingham St
SE1 117 A3 262 A5
Rockland Rd SW15 135 A1
Rocklands N3 29 B3
Rocklands Dr HA7 25 C1
Rockley Ct 9 W14 112 D4
Rockley Rd W14 112 D4
Rockliffe Manor Prim Sch
SE18 145 D6
Rockmount Prim Sch
SE19 183 B4
Rockmount Rd
SE18,SE2 123 D1
South Norwood SE19 183 B4
Rocks La SW13 134 A2
Rock St N4 72 C6
Rockstraw Ho 5 NW3 70 D1
Rockware Ave UB6 86 C6
Rockways EN5 11 D5
Rockwell Gdns SE19 183 C6
Rockwell Rd RM10 81 D3
Rockwood Ct N16 52 A2
Rocliffe St N1 94 D5 234 D3
Rocombe Cres SE23 162 C4
Rocque Ho SW6 264 C4
Rocque La SE3 142 D2
Rodborough Rd NW11 47 C1
Rodd Est TW17 193 B4
Roden Gdns CR0 205 C3
Rodenhurst Ct SW4 159 D6
Rodenhurst Rd SW4 159 D5
Roden St N7 72 B5
Ilford IG1 78 C5
Roderick Ho 3 SE16 118 C2
Roderick Rd NW3 70 D4
Rodgers Cl WD6 9 D5
Rodgers Ho 4 SW4 159 D4
Rodin Ct N1 234 C5
Roding Ct 6 W12 111 C4
Roding Ho N1 234 A5
Roding Hospl IG4 55 D6
Roding La IG9 21 D3
Roding La N IG8 37 D1
Roding La S IG4 55 D5
Roding Lo IG1 55 D3
Roding Mews E1 118 A5
Roding Prim Sch RM8 80 C3
Roding Rd E5 75 A3
Newham E6 100 D2
Rodings Ct E4 36 B5
Rodings The Barnet EN5 1 A1
4 Woodford IG8 37 C4
Roding Valley Sta IG9 37 D6
Roding View IG9 21 D3
Rodmarton St
W1 92 D2 237 D3
Rodmell WC1 233 B1
Rodmell Cl UB4 85 A3
Rodmell Slope N12 29 B5
Rodmere St SE10 120 C1
Rodmill La SW2 160 A4
Rodney Cl
New Malden KT3 199 C4
Pinner HA5 41 A2
Thornton Heath CR0 204 D1
Walton-on-T KT12 194 C1
Rodney Ct NW8 236 B6
Rodney Gdns
Hayes BR4 225 A4
Pinner HA5 40 C4
Rodney Ho 4 E14 119 D2
N1 233 D3
W11 245 A6
Rodney Pl E17 35 B1
SE17 117 A2 262 B4
Merton SW19 180 A2
Rodney Rd
SE17 117 B2 262 C3
Mitcham CR4 202 C6
New Malden KT3 199 C4
Twickenham TW4 151 C4
Walton-on-T KT12 194 C1
Wanstead E11 55 B5
Rodney St N1 94 B5 233 D3
Rodway Rd BR1 187 B2
Putney SW15 156 A4
Rodwell Cl 2 HA4 40 C1
Rodwell Rd SE22 161 D5
Roe 5 NW9 27 D2
Roebourne Way E16 122 C4
Roebuck Cl
Feltham TW13 172 B6
Tottenham N17 33 D4
Roebuck Ct Chingford E4 36 A3
2 New Malden KT3 199 C4
Roebuck Ho SW1 259 A6
Roebuck La IG9 21 C3
Roebuck Rd KT9 214 C3
Roedean Ave EN3 6 C5
Roedean Cl EN3 6 C4
Roedean Cres SW15 155 C6
Roe End NW9 45 A5
Roe Gn NW9 45 A4
Roe Green Jun & Inf Schs
NW9 44 D5
Roehampton CE Prim Sch
SW15 156 B4
Roehampton Cl SW15 134 A1
Roehampton Ct SW13 134 A2
Roehampton Dr BR7 189 A4
Roehampton Gate
SW15 155 C5
Roehampton High St
SW15 156 A4
Roehampton La
Putney SW15 156 A5
Roehampton SW15 156 B3
Roehampton Vale
SW15 155 D2
Roe La NW9 45 A5
Roe Way SM6 220 A2
Roffey Ct 9 NW9 46 A5
Roffey St E14 120 A4
Roger Ascham Prim Sch
E17 35 B2
Roger Dowley Ct 8 E2 96 C5
Roger's Almshouses 2
SW9 138 B1
Rogers Est 28 E2 96 C4
Rogers Gdns RM10 81 C3
Rogers Ho SW1 259 D4
9 Dagenham RM10 81 C5
Rogers Rd E16 98 D1
Dagenham RM10 81 C3
Upper Tooting SW17 180 C6
Roger St WC1 94 B3 240 D5
Roger Stone Ct NW10 67 B6
Rogers Wlk N12 13 D1
Rojack Rd SE23 162 D3
Rokeby Gdns IG8 37 A2
Rokeby Ho WC1 240 C5
9 Balham SW12 159 B4
Rokeby Pl SW20 178 B3
Rokeby Rd SE4 141 B3
Rokeby Sch E15 76 B1
Kingston KT2 177 A3
Rokeby St E15 98 C6
Rokeland Ho SE4 141 A1
Rokell Ho BR3 185 D5
Roker Park Ave UB10 60 A4
Rokesby Cl DA16 145 B3
Rokesby Pl HA0 65 D3
Rokesly Ave N8 50 A4
Rokesly Jun & Inf Schs
N8 50 A4
Roland Ct SE19 183 D2
Roland Gdns
SW7 114 A1 256 B2
Roland Mews 1 E1 96 D2
Roland Rd E17 54 B5
Roland Way SE17 262 D1
SW7 114 A1 256 B2
Roland Way continued
Worcester Park KT4 215 D6
Roles Gr RM6 59 A5
Rolfe Cl EN4 2 C1
Rolfe Ho N11 30 D6
Rolinsden Way BR2 225 D4
Rolland Ho W7 86 C2
Rollesby Rd KT19,KT9 214 C2
Rollesby Way SE28 102 C1
Rolleston Ave BR5 210 D3
Rolleston Cl BR5 210 D2
Rolleston Rd CR2 221 B1
Roll Gdns IG2 56 C4
Rollins St SE15 140 C6
Rollit Cres TW3 151 C6
Rollit Ho N7 72 C3
Rollit St N7 72 C3
Rollo Ct SW11 268 C1
Rolls Bldgs EC4 241 B2
Rollscourt Ave SE24 161 A6
Rolls Park Ave E4 35 D5
Rolls Park Rd E4 35 D5
Rolls Pas EC4 241 A2
Rolls Rd SE1 118 A1 263 D2
Rolt St SE8 141 A6
Rolvenden Gdns BR1 187 D3
Rolvenden Pl N17 34 A2
Roman Cl W3 110 D4
Feltham TW14 150 C6
Romanfield Rd SW2 160 B4
Romanhurst Ave BR2 208 C5
Romanhurst Gdns
BR2,BR3 208 C5
Roman Ind Est CR0 205 C2
Roman Rd E2,E3 96 D5
E3 97 B6
N10 31 B3
N12 30 C2
W4 111 D2
Ilford IG1 78 D2
Newham E6 100 A3
Roman Rise SE19 183 B4
Roman Road Prim Sch
E6 99 D3
Roman Sq SE28 124 A5
Roman Square Mkt 1
E3 97 B5
Roman Way N7 72 B2
4 SE15 140 C5
Croydon CR0 220 D6
Enfield EN1 17 D6
Romany Gdns E17 35 A2
Cheam SM3 201 C2
Romany Ho 8 N9 18 A1
Romany Prospect
SE19 183 B4
Romany Rise BR5 211 A1
Roma Rd E17 53 A6
Roma Read Cl SW15 156 B4
Romayne Ho SW4 137 D2
Romberg Rd SW17 159 A1
Romborough Gdns
SE13 164 A6
Romborough Way
SE13 164 A6
Romeland WD6 9 D5
Romer Ho 9 SW2 160 B6
12 W10 91 B4
Romero Cl SW9 138 B2
Romero Sq SE9 143 C1
Romey Mews W1 238 A4
Romeyn Rd SW16 160 B1
Romford Ho 17 N1 73 B2
Romford Rd E15 76 D2
E7,E12 77 C3
Romford St E1 96 B2
Romilly Dr WD19 23 A6
Romilly Rd N4 72 D6
Romilly St W1 249 D6
Romily Ct SW6 135 A3
Rommany Ct SE27 183 B6
Rommany Rd SE27 183 B6
Romney Cl NW11 48 A1
7 SE14 140 C5
Ashford TW15 171 A5
Chessington KT9 214 A4
Harrow HA2 41 C2
Tottenham N17 34 B2
Romney Ct 9 NW3 70 C2
9 W12 112 C4
16 Northolt UB5 84 D5
Romney Dr
Bromley BR1 187 D3
Harrow HA2 41 C2
Romney Gdns DA7 147 B4
Romney Ho EN1 18 A6
Romney Par UB4 83 B5
Romney Rd SE10 142 B6
Hayes UB4 83 B5
New Malden KT3 199 B3
Romney Row NW2 68 D6
Romney St
SW1 116 A3 260 A5
Romola Rd SE24,SW2 160 D3
Romsey Cl BR6 227 A4
Romsey Gdns RM9 102 D6
Romsey Ho 5 SW11 136 B1
Romsey Rd
Dagenham RM9 102 D6

Romsey Rd *continued*
Ealing W13 ....109 A6
Romulus Ct 7 TW8 ..131 D5
Ronald Ave E15 ....98 C4
Ronald Cl BR3 ....207 B4
Ronald Ho SE9 ....143 C1
Ronald Ross Prim Sch
SW19 ....157 A4
Ronaldshay N4 ....50 C1
Ronalds Rd BR1 ....187 A2
N5 ....72 C3
Ronald St E1 ....96 C1
Ronaldstone Rd DA15 167 C5
Rona Rd NW3 ....71 A4
Ronart St HA3 ....42 D6
Rona Wlk 7 N1 ....73 B2
Rondu Rd NW2 ....69 A3
Ronelean Rd KT6 ....214 B5
Ron Leighton Way E6 100 A6
Ronver Lo E4 ....20 C1
Ronver Rd SE12 ....164 D3
Rood La EC3 ..117 C6 253 A6
Rookby Ct N21 ....16 D2
Rook Cl HA9 ....66 D5
Rookeries Cl TW13 ..150 C1
Rookery Cl NW9 ....45 D4
Rookery Cotts EN4 ....3 B2
Rookery Cres RM10 ....81 D1
Rookery Dr BR7 ....188 C2
Rookery La BR2 ....209 D3
Rookery Rd SW4 ....137 C1
Rookery Way NW9 ....45 D4
Rookes Heath High Sch
HA2 ....63 C5
Rooke Way SE10 ....120 D1
Rookfield Ave N10 ....49 C5
Rookfield Cl N10 ....49 C5
Rook Lo IG1 ....55 D3
Rooksmead Rd TW16 .172 A1
Rooks Terr UB7 ....104 A4
Rookstone Rd SW17 ..180 D5
Rook Wlk E6 ....100 A1
Rookwood Ave
Wallington SM6 ....219 D4
West Barnes KT3 ....200 A5
Rookwood Gdns E4 ....20 D2
Rookwood Ho IG11 ...101 B5
Rookwood Rd N16 ....52 A2
Rootes Dr W10 ....90 D2
Ropemaker Rd SE16 ..119 A3
Ropemaker's Fields 7
E14 ....119 B6
Ropemaker St
EC2 ....95 B2 242 C4
Roper Ho 13 SE21 ....183 C6
Roper La SE1 .117 C4 253 B1
Ropers Ave E4 ....36 A5
Roper's Orchard SW3 .267 A5
Roper St 1 SE9 ....166 C5
Ropers Wlk 13 SE24 ....160 C4
Roper Way CR4 ....181 A1
Ropery Bsns Est SE7 .121 C2
Ropery St E3 ....97 B3
Rope St SE16 ....119 A3
Ropewalk Gdns 16 E1 ..96 A1
Rope Yard Rails SE18 .122 D3
Ropley St 6 E2 ....96 A5
Rosa Alba Mews N5 ....73 A4
Rosa Ave TW15 ....170 C6
Rosalind Ct 6 IG11 ....80 A1
Rosalind Ho 25 N1 ....95 C5
Rosaline Rd
SW6 ....135 A5 264 B3
Rosaline Terr SW6 ....264 B3
Rosamond St SE26 ....162 B1
Rosamund Cl CR2 ....221 B4
Rosamun St UB2 ....107 A2
Rosa Parks Ho 8
SW9 ....138 B3
Rosary Cl TW3,TW5 ..129 A3
Rosary Gdns
SW7 ....114 A2 256 B3
Ashford TW15 ....170 D6
Bushey WD23 ....8 C4
Rosary RC Inf Sch
TW5 ....129 C6
Rosary RC Jun Sch
TW5 ....129 C6
Rosary RC Prim Sch
NW3 ....70 C3
Rosaville Rd
SW6 ....135 B5 264 C3
Rosbury SW15 ....157 A5
Roscoe St EC1 ..95 A3 242 B5
Roscoff Cl HA8 ....27 A2
Roscommon Ho 2
NW3 ....70 B3
Roseacre Cl Ealing W13 .87 B2
Littleton TW17 ....192 C4
Roseacre Lo EN3 ....6 C1
Roseacre Rd DA16 ....146 B2
Rose Alley EC2 ....243 B3
SE1 ....252 B4
Rose Ave Mitcham CR4 .180 D2
Morden SM4 ....202 A4
Woodford E18 ....37 B1
Rosebank SW6 ....134 C5
2 W3 ....89 B1
Penge SE20 ....184 B3
Rosebank Ave HA0 ....64 D4
Rose Bank Cl N12 ....30 C5
Rosebank Cl TW11 ....175 A4
Rosebank Gdns E3 ....97 B5
1 W3 ....89 B1
Rosebank Gr E17 ....53 B6
Rosebank Rd E17 ....53 D3
W7 ....108 C4
Rosebank Villas E17 ....53 C5
Rosebank Way W3 ....89 B1
Rosebank Wlk NW1 ....71 D1
14 SE7 ....122 A2
Rose Bates Dr NW9 ....44 C5
Roseberry Gdns BR6 ..227 C5
N4 ....50 D3
Roseberry Pl E8 ....73 D2
Roseberry St SE16 ..118 B2
Rosebery Ave DA15 ..167 C4
E12 ....78 B2
EC1 ....94 C4 234 B1
Harrow HA2 ....63 B4
Kingston KT3 ....199 D6
South Norwood CR7 ....183 A1
Tottenham N17 ....34 A1
Rosebery Cl SM4 ....200 D3
Rosebery Ct EC1 ....241 A6
W1 ....248 C4
Chessington KT9 ....214 B3
Rosebery Gdns N8 ....50 A4
Ealing W13 ....87 A1
Sutton SM1 ....217 D4
Rosebery Ho 22 E2 ....96 C5
Rosebery Ind Pk N17 ..34 B1
Rosebery Mews N10 ....31 C1
Rosebery Rd N10 ....31 C1
SW2 ....160 A5
Cheam SM1,SM2 ....217 B2
Edmonton N9 ....18 A2
Isleworth TW3,TW7 ....152 A6
Kingston KT1 ....176 D1
Rosebery Sq EC1 ....241 A5
Kingston KT1 ....176 D1
Rosebine Ave TW2 ....152 B4
Rosebriars KT10 ....212 A3
Rose Bruford Coll SE8 141 C6
Rose Bruford Coll of
Speech & Drama
DA15 ....168 B3
Rosebury Rd SW6 ....135 D3
Rosebury Vale HA4 ....62 A6
Rose Bush Ct NW3 ....70 D3
Rose Cotts KT10 ....212 B3
Rosecourt Rd CR0 ....204 B3
Rosecroft N22 ....32 B2
Rosecroft Ave NW3 ....69 C5
Rosecroft Gdns NW2 ....68 A5
Twickenham TW2 ....152 B3
Rosecroft Rd UB1 ....85 C3
Rosecroft Wlk
Pinner HA5 ....40 D4
Wembley HA0 ....65 D3
Rose & Crown Ct EC2 .242 A2
Rose & Crown Yd
SW1 ....249 B3
Rose Ct E1 ....243 D3
N1 ....234 D6
Harrow HA2 ....64 A6
Ilford IG1 ....78 D2
7 Wembley HA0 ....88 A5
10 Wimbledon SW19 ....179 B5
Rose Dale BR6 ....226 D6
Rosedale Ave UB3 ....83 B2
Rosedale Cl SE2 ....124 B3
W7 ....108 D4
Stanmore HA7 ....25 B4
Rosedale Ct N5 ....72 D4
Rosedale Gdns RM9 ....80 B1
Rosedale Ho N16 ....51 B1
Rosedale Lo N14 ....15 B4
Rosedale Rd E7 ....77 C3
Dagenham RM9 ....80 B1
Richmond TW9 ....132 A1
Stoneleigh KT17 ....216 A3
Rosedale Terr W6 ....112 B3
Rosedene NW6 ....90 D6
Rosedene Ave
Morden SM4 ....201 C4
Southall UB6 ....85 C4
Streatham SW16 ....160 B1
Thornton Heath CR0 ....204 A2
Rosedene Gdns IG2 ....56 C5
Rosedene Terr E10 ....75 D6
Rosedew Rd W6 ....134 D6
Rose End KT4 ....200 D1
Rosefield Cl SM5 ....218 C3
Rosefield Ct EN4 ....2 D1
Rosefield Gdns E14 ....119 C6
Rose Garden Cl HA8 ....26 A4
Rose Gdns W5 ....109 D3
Feltham TW13 ....150 A2
Southall UB1 ....85 C3
Rose Glen NW9 ....45 B5
Rosehart Mews 8 W11 91 C1
Rose Hatch Ave RM6 ....58 D6
Roseheath Rd TW4 ....151 B6
Rosehill Claygate KT10 .213 A2
Hampton TW12 ....173 C2
Rose Hill
Carshalton SM4,SM5 ....202 A2
Rose Hill *continued*
Cheam SM1 ....201 D1
Rosehill Ave SM1,SM5 .202 A1
Rosehill Ct SM4 ....202 A2
Rosehill Gdns
Greenford UB6 ....64 D3
Sutton SM1 ....218 A6
Rose Hill Park W SM1 218 A6
Rosehill Rd SW18 ....158 A6
Rose La RM6 ....59 A5
Roseland Cl N17 ....33 B3
Roseland Ho SW6 ....135 A2
Rose Lawn WD23 ....8 A3
Roseleigh Ave N5 ....72 D4
Roseleigh Cl 12 TW1 .153 D5
Roselle Ct W5 ....88 A1
Rosemary Ave N3 ....29 D1
NW2 ....47 D5
East Molesey KT8 ....195 C5
Edmonton N9 ....18 B3
Enfield EN2 ....5 C4
Hounslow TW4 ....128 D3
Rosemary Branch Bridge
N1 ....235 C6
Rosemary Cl
Hillingdon UB8 ....82 C2
Thornton Heath CR0 ....204 A3
Rosemary Cotts 3
SW19 ....178 C3
Rosemary Ct 43 SE8 ..141 B6
Rosemary Dr
Redbridge IG4 ....55 D4
15 South Bromley E14 ....98 B1
Rosemary Gdns
Chessington KT9 ....214 A4
Dagenham RM8 ....59 B1
Mortlake SW14 ....133 A2
Rosemary Ho N1 ....235 D5
Rosemary La SW14 ....133 A2
Rosemary Mews N1 ....235 D6
Rosemary Rd DA16 ....145 D4
SE15 ....139 D5
Wandsworth SW17 ....158 A1
Rosemary Works Sch
N1 ....235 D5
Rosemead NW9 ....46 A2
Rosemead Ave
Feltham TW13 ....149 D2
Mitcham CR4 ....181 C1
Wembley HA9 ....66 A3
Rosemead Prep Sch
SE27 ....161 A2
Rose Mews N18 ....34 B6
Rosemont Ave N12 ....30 A4
Rosemont Mans 11
NW3 ....69 D2
Rosemont Rd NW3 ....70 A2
Acton W3 ....110 D6
Kingston KT3 ....199 A6
Richmond TW10 ....154 A5
Wembley HA0 ....88 A6
Rosemoor St
SW3 ....114 D2 257 C3
Rosemount Ct
2 Acton W3 ....110 D5
South Norwood SE25 ....205 C6
Rosemount Dr BR1 ....210 B5
Rosemount Lo W3 ....110 D6
Rosemount Point 10
SE23 ....162 D1
Rosemount Rd W13 ....87 A1
Rosemount Towers 5
SM6 ....219 C2
Rosenau Cres SW11 ....267 C1
Rosenau Rd
SW11 ....136 D4 267 C2
Rosendale Prim Sch
SE21 ....161 A4
Rosendale Rd SE21,
SE24 ....161 A3
Roseneath Ave N21 ....16 D3
Roseneath Rd SW11 ....159 A5
Roseneath Wlk EN1 ....5 C1
Rosens Wlk HA8 ....10 D1
Rosenthal Rd SE6 ....164 A5
Rosenthorpe Rd SE15 162 D6
Roserton St E14 ....120 A4
Rosery The CR0 ....206 D3
Rose Sq SW7 ....256 D2
Rose St EC4 ....241 D1
WC2 ....116 A6 250 A6
Roses The IG8 ....36 D3
Rosethorn Cl SW12 ....159 D4
Rosetta Cl SW8 ....270 B3
Rosetta Ct SE19 ....183 C3
Rosetta Prim Sch E16 ..99 B2
Rosetti Terr RM8 ....80 B4
Roseveare Rd SE12 ....187 C6
Roseville N21 ....16 C3
Roseville Ave TW3,
TW4 ....151 C6
Roseville Rd UB3 ....106 A2
Rosevine Rd SW20 ....178 C2
Roseway SE21 ....161 B5
Rose Way HA8 ....27 A6
SE12 ....165 A6
Rosewell Cl SE20 ....184 B3
Rose Wlk Surbiton KT5 .198 D4
West Wickham BR4 ....224 B6
Rosewood Ave UB6 ....65 A2
Rosewood Cl DA14 ....168 C1
Rosewood Ct 2 E11 ....76 B4
Bromley BR1 ....187 D2
Dagenham RM6 ....58 C4
Kingston KT2 ....176 C3
Rosewood Dr TW17 ..192 B4
Rosewood Gr SM1 ....218 A6
Rosewood Sq W12 ....90 A1
Rosher Cl E15 ....76 B1
Roshni Ho SW17 ....180 C4
Rosh Pinah Prim Sch
HA8 ....10 D1
Rosina Ct SW17 ....180 C5
Rosina St E9 ....74 D2
Roskeen Ct 1 SW19 ..178 C3
Roskell Rd SW15 ....134 D2
Roskild Ct HA9 ....66 B4
Roslin Ho 2 E1 ....118 D6
Roslin Rd W3 ....110 D3
Roslin Way BR1 ....187 A5
Roslyn Cl CR4 ....180 B1
Roslyn Rd N15 ....51 C4
Rosmead Rd
W11 ....113 A6 244 B6
Rosoman Pl EC1 ....241 B6
Rossal Ct SE20 ....184 B3
Rossall Cres NW10 ....88 B4
Rossanne Ho N3 ....29 D3
Ross Ave NW7 ....29 A5
Dagenham RM8 ....59 B1
Ross Cl Harrow HA3 ....24 A3
Hayes UB3 ....105 B2
Ross Ct BR7 ....188 B3
NW9 ....45 C6
Ealing W13 ....87 B2
4 Putney SW15 ....156 D4
South Croydon CR2 ....221 A2
Rossdale SM1 ....218 C3
Rossdale Dr N9 ....18 C5
NW9 ....45 A1
Rossdale Rd SW15 ....134 C1
Rosse Mews SE3 ....143 B4
Rossendale Cl EN2 ....4 D6
Rossendale Ho 7 E5 ..74 B6
Rossendale St E5 ....74 B6
Rossendale Way
NW1 ....93 C6 232 B6
Rossendon Ct 1 SM6 219 C2
Rossetti Ct WC1 ....239 C4
Rossetti Gdns Mans
SW3 ....267 C6
Rossetti Ho SW1 ....259 D3
Rossetti Mews NW8 ..229 D5
Rossetti Rd SE16 ....118 B1
Ross Ho 18 E1 ....118 B5
6 SE18 ....144 A4
Twickenham TW2 ....151 D2
Rossignol Gdns SM5 ..219 A6
Rossindel Rd TW3 ....151 C6
Rossington Cl EN1 ....6 B5
Rossington St E5 ....74 A6
Rossiter Fields EN5 ....13 B5
Rossiter Rd SW12 ....159 B3
Rossland Cl DA6 ....169 D6
Rosslyn Ave
Barnes SW13 ....133 D2
Chingford E4 ....20 D2
Dagenham RM8 ....59 C2
East Barnet EN4 ....14 C5
Feltham TW14 ....150 A5
Rosslyn Cl
Ashford TW16 ....171 C4
Coney Hall BR4 ....224 D5
Hayes UB3 ....83 B2
Rosslyn Cres
Harrow HA1 ....42 D5
Wembley HA9 ....66 A4
Rosslyn Ct NW3 ....70 C3
Rosslyn Hill NW3 ....70 B3
Rosslyn Ho 8 TW9 ....132 B4
Rosslyn Mans NW6 ....70 A2
Rosslyn Park Mews
NW3 ....70 B3
Rosslyn Rd E17 ....54 A5
Barking IG11 ....79 B1
Twickenham TW1 ....153 C5
Rossmore Ct NW1 ....237 C6
Rossmore Rd
NW1 ....92 C3 237 B6
Ross Par SM6 ....219 B2
Ross Rd
South Norwood SE25 ....205 C6
Twickenham TW2 ....152 A3
Wallington SM6 ....219 C3
Ross Way SE9 ....144 A2
Rossway Dr WD23 ....8 B6
Rosswood Gdns SM6 .219 C2
Rosswood Lo CR0 ....222 D6
Rostella Rd SW17 ....180 B6
Rostrever Gdns UB3 ..105 C5
Rostrevor Ave N15 ....51 D3
Rostrevor Gdns UB2 ..107 A1
Rostrevor Mans SW6 .264 C2
Rostrevor Rd
Fulham SW6 ...135 B4 264 C2
Wimbledon SW19 ....179 C5
Rotary St SE1 ....261 D6
Rothay NW1 ....231 D2
Rothbury Gdns TW7 ..131 A5
Rothbury Rd E9 ....75 C1
Rothbury Wlk N17 ....34 A3
Rotherfield Ct
N1 ....73 B1 235 C6
Rotherfield Prim Sch
N1 ....95 A6 235 B6
Rotherfield Rd
Enfield EN3 ....6 D6
Wallington SM5 ....219 A3
Rotherfield St
N1 ....73 A1 235 B6
Rotherham Wlk SE1 ..251 C3
Rotherhill Ave SW16 ..181 D4
Rotherhithe SE16 ....119 B5
Rotherhithe Holiday Inn
Pier SE16 ....119 B5
Rotherhithe New Rd
SE16 ....118 B1
Rotherhithe Old Rd
SE16 ....118 D2
Rotherhithe Prim Sch
SE16 ....118 D2
Rotherhithe St SE16 ..118 C4
10 SE16 ....118 B4
Rotherhithe Sta SE16 .118 C4
Rotherhithe Tunnel
SE16 ....118 D5
Rother Ho SE15 ....140 B1
Rotherwick Hill W5 ....88 B3
Rotherwick Rd NW11 ..47 C2
Rotherwood Cl SW20 .179 A2
Rotherwood Rd SW15 134 D2
Rothery St N1 ....234 D6
Rothesay Ave
Merton SW20 ....179 A1
Mortlake SW14,TW10 ..132 D1
Northolt UB6 ....64 B2
Rothesay Ct 13 SE11 ..138 C6
SE12 ....165 B1
4 Catford SE6 ....164 D2
Rothesay Rd SE25 ....205 C5
Rothley Ct NW8 ....236 C6
Rothsay Rd E7 ....77 C2
Rothsay St
SE1 ....117 C3 263 A5
Rothsay Wlk 16 E14 ..119 C2
Rothschild Rd W4 ....111 A3
Rothschild St SE27 ..182 D6
Rothwell Ct HA1 ....42 D4
Rothwell Gdns RM9 ..102 C6
Rothwell Ho TW5 ....129 C6
Rothwell Rd RM9 ....102 C6
Rothwell St NW1 ....230 D6
10 NW1 ....70 D1
Roth Wlk N7 ....72 B6
Rotten Row★
SW1 ....114 D4 247 C2
Rotterdam Dr E14 ....120 A3
Rotunda Mus★ SE18 ..122 B1
Rouel Rd SE16 ....118 A2
SE16 ....118 A3
Rougemont Ave SM4 .201 C3
Roundabout Ho HA6 ..22 A2
Roundacre SW19 ....156 D2
Roundel Cl SE4 ....141 B1
Roundell Ho 14 SE21 .183 C6
Rounders Ct 7 RM10 ..81 D2
Round Gr CR0 ....206 D2
Roundhay Cl SE23 ....162 D2
Roundhedge Way EN2 ..4 B5
Round Hill SE23 ....162 C1
Roundhill Dr EN2 ....4 B1
Roundshaw Ctr SM6 ..220 A1
Roundtable Rd BR1 ..164 D1
Roundtree Rd HA0 ....65 B3
Roundways HA4 ....61 D5
Roundway The
Claygate KT10 ....212 D2
Tottenham N17 ....33 B2
Roundwood BR7 ....188 D1
Roundwood Ave UB11 105 A5
Roundwood Cl HA4 ....39 B2
Roundwood Rd NW10 ..67 D1
Rounton Rd E3 ....97 C3
Roupell Ho 7 KT2 ....176 B3
Roupell Rd SW2 ....160 B3
Roupell St SE1 116 C5 251 B3
Rousden St NW1 ....71 C1
Rouse Gdns SE21 ....183 C6
Routemaster Cl E13 ....99 B4
Routh Ct TW14 ....149 B3
Routh Rd SW18 ....158 C4
Routh St E6 ....100 B2
Rover Ho 27 N1 ....95 C6
Rowallan Ct 3 SE6 ....164 D3
Rowallan Rd
SW6 ....135 A5 264 A3
Rowallen Par RM8 ....58 C1
Rowan N10 ....31 B1
Rowan Ave E4 ....35 B4
Rowan Cl W5 ....110 A4
Harrow HA7 ....24 D4
Kingston KT3 ....177 C1
Streatham SW16 ....181 C2
Wembley HA0 ....65 A5
Rowan Cres SW16 ....181 C2
Rowan Ct 18 SE15 ....139 D5
SW11 ....158 D5
Rowan Ct *continued*
Forest Hill SE26 ....184 C6
11 Kingston KT2 ....176 C3
Wimbledon SW20 ....178 B1
Rowan Dr NW9 ....46 A6
Rowan Gdns CR0 ....221 D5
Rowan High Sch
SW16 ....181 C1
Rowan Ho DA14 ....167 D1
NW10 ....89 C3
5 NW3 ....70 D2
East Bedfont TW14 ....149 B5
Ilford IG1 ....79 B3
Rowan Pl UB3 ....105 D6
Rowan Rd DA7 ....147 A2
W6 ....112 D2
Brentford TW8 ....131 B5
Mitcham SW16 ....181 C1
West Drayton UB7 ....104 A2
Rowans The
Ashford TW16 ....171 D5
Edmonton N13 ....17 A1
Rowan Terr W6 ....112 D2
Rowantree Cl N21 ....17 B3
Rowantree Rd
Edmonton N21 ....17 B3
Enfield EN2 ....4 D3
Rowan Way RM6 ....58 C6
Rowan Wlk BR2 ....226 B5
N19 ....71 C6
N2 ....48 A4
W10 ....91 A3
1 New Barnet EN5 ....13 D6
Rowanwood Ave
DA15 ....168 A3
Rowanwood Mews EN2 .4 D3
Rowben Cl N20 ....13 D3
Rowberry Cl SW6 ....134 C5
Rowcross St
SE1 ....117 D1 263 D2
Rowdell Rd UB5 ....85 C6
Rowden Par E4 ....35 C4
Rowden Park Gdns E4 .35 C4
Rowden Rd
Beckenham BR3 ....185 B2
Chingford E4 ....35 D4
West Ewell KT19 ....215 A4
Rowditch La SW11 ....137 A3
Rowdon Ave NW10 ....68 B1
Rowdowns Rd RM9 ....81 B1
Rowe Gdns IG11 ....102 A5
Rowe La E9 ....74 C3
Rowena Cres SW11 ....136 C3
Rowe Wlk HA2 ....63 C5
Rowfant Rd SW12,
SW17 ....159 A2
Rowhill Mans 11 E5 ....74 B4
Rowhill Rd E5 ....74 B4
Rowington Cl W2 ....91 D2
Rowland Ave HA3 ....43 C6
Rowland Ct E16 ....98 D3
Rowland Gr SE26 ....162 B1
Rowland Hill Almshouses
TW15 ....170 C5
Rowland Hill Ave N17 ..33 B4
Rowland Hill Ho SE1 ..251 C2
Rowland Hill St NW3 ..70 C3
Rowlands Ave HA5 ....23 D4
Rowlands Cl N6 ....49 A3
NW7 ....28 A3
Rowlands Rd RM8 ....81 B6
Rowland Way
Ashford TW15 ....171 B3
Merton SW19 ....179 D2
Rowley Ave DA15 ....168 B4
Rowley Cl HA0 ....66 B1
Rowley Gdns N4 ....51 A2
Rowley Green Rd EN5 ..12 A6
Rowley Ho SE8 ....141 C6
Rowley Ind Pk W3 ....110 D3
Rowley La EN5 ....11 D6
Rowley Rd N15 ....51 A4
Rowlheys Pl UB7 ....104 A3
Rowlls Rd KT1 ....198 B6
Rowney Gdns RM9 ....80 C2
Rowney Rd RM9 ....80 B2
Rowntree Cl NW6 ....69 C2
Rowntree Clifford Cl 7
E13 ....99 B4
Rowntree Path 1
SE28 ....124 B5
Rowntree Rd TW2 ....152 C3
Rowse Cl E15 ....98 A6
Rowsham Ct HA1 ....64 C5
Rowsley Ave NW4 ....46 C6
Rowstock 1 NW5 ....71 D2
Rowstock Gdns N7 ....71 D3
Rowton Rd SE18 ....145 A5
Roxborough Ave
Harrow HA1 ....42 C2
Hounslow TW7 ....130 D5
Roxborough Pk HA1 ..42 C2
Roxborough Rd HA1 ..42 B3
Roxbourne Cl UB5 ....62 D2
Roxbourne Fst & Mid Schs
HA2 ....63 A6

Roxburgh Rd SE27 182 D5
Roxburn Way HA4 61 D5
Roxby Pl SW6 135 C6 265 B6
Roxeth Ct TW15 170 C5
Roxeth Fst & Mid Sch HA2 64 B6
Roxeth Gr HA2 63 D4
Roxeth Green Ave HA2 63 D6
Roxeth Hill HA2 64 C6
Roxeth Manor Fst & Mid Schs HA2 63 C5
Roxeth Mead Sch HA2 64 B6
Roxford Cl TW17 193 C4
Roxford Ho 2 E3 97 D3
Roxley Rd SE13 163 D5
Roxton Gdns CR0 223 C3
Roxwell 10 NW1 71 B2
Roxwell Rd W12 112 A4
Barking IG11 102 A5
Roxwell Trad Pk E10 53 A2
Roxwell Way IG8 37 C3
Roxy Ave RM6 58 C2
Royal Academy of Dramatic Art★ WC1 93 D2 239 C4
Royal Acad of Arts★ W1 115 C6 249 A5
Royal Acad of Dance SW11 266 D1
Royal Acad of Music NW1 238 B5
Royal Albert Hall★ SW7 114 B4 246 C1
Royal Albert Rd E16 122 D6
Royal Albert Sta E16 122 A6
Royal Albert Way E16 122 B6
Royal Arc W1 249 A5
Royal Army Medical Coll SW1 116 A1 260 A2
Royal Ave SW3 114 D1 257 C2
Worcester Park KT4 215 C6
Royal Avenue Ho SW3 257 C2
Royal Ballet Sch The WC2 240 B1
Royal Brompton Hospl SW3 114 B1 256 C2
SW3 114 C1 257 B1
Royal Cir SE27 160 D1
Royal Cl BR6 226 D4
N16 51 C1
SE8 141 B6
Hillingdon UB7 82 B1
Ilford IG3 58 A2
Putney SW19 156 D2
Worcester Park KT4 215 C6
Royal College St NW1 93 C6 232 B6
Royal Coll of Anaesthetists WC1 94 A2 240 B4
Royal Coll of Art SW7 114 B4 246 C1
Royal Coll of Art Sculpture Sch SW11 136 C5 267 A3
Royal Coll of Midwives W1 93 B2 238 C3
Royal Coll of Music SW7 114 B3 256 C6
Royal Coll of Obstetricians & Gynaecologists NW1 92 D3 237 C6
Royal Coll of Physicians NW1 93 B3 238 D6
Royal Coll of Science SW7 114 B3 256 C6
Royal Coll of Surgeons WC2 94 B1 240 D2
Royal Connaught Apps E16 121 D5
Royal Courts of Justice WC2 94 C1 241 A1
Royal Cres W11 113 A5 244 A3
Ruislip HA4 63 A5
Royal Crescent Mews W11 112 D5
Royal Ct SE16 119 B3
SE9 166 B3
Enfield EN1 17 C5
9 Kingston KT2 176 D3
Royal Docks Rd E6 100 D2
Royal Duchess Mews SW12 159 B4
Royal Exchange★ EC3 242 D1
Royal Exchange Ave EC3 242 D1
Royal Exchange Bldgs EC3 242 D1
Royal Festival Hall★ SE1 116 B5 250 D3
Royal Free Hospl NW3 70 C3
Royal Gdns W7 109 A3
Royal Geographical Society SW7 114 B4 246 D1
Royal Hill SE10 142 A5
Royal Horticultural Society (Lawrence Hall & Conf Ctr) SW1 259 D5
Royal Horticultural Society (Lindley Hall) SW1 259 C4
Royal Hospital (Army Pensioners)★ SW1 115 A1 258 A1
Royal Hospital Rd SW3 114 D1 257 D1
Royal Hospl and Home SW15 157 A5
Royal La Hillingdon UB7 82 B1
Hillingdon UB8 82 B3
Royal Langford 3 NW6 91 D5
Royal London Est N17 34 B4
Royal London Est The NW10 89 B5
Royal London Homeopathic Hospl The WC1 94 A2 240 B4
Royal London Hospl (Mile End) The E2 96 D4
Royal London Hospl (St Clements) The E3 97 B4
Royal London Hospl (Whitechapel) The E1 96 B2
Royal Marsden Hospl SW3 114 B1 256 D2
Royal Mews KT8 196 C6
Royal Mews The★ SW1 115 B3 258 D6
Royal Military Sch of Music (Kneller Hall) TW2 152 B5
Royal Mint Pl 5 E1 118 A6
Royal Mint St E1 117 D6 253 D6
Royal National Orthopaedic Hospl W1 93 B3 238 D5
Stanmore HA7 9 C2
Royal National TNE Hospl The WC1 94 B4 233 C2
Royal Nat TN&E Hospl The W5 87 C2
Royal Naval Pl SE14 141 B5
Royal Oak Ct 9 N1 95 C4
Dagenham RM8 80 C6
Royal Oak Pl SE22 162 B5
Royal Oak Rd 5 E8 74 B2
Bexley DA6 147 C1
Royal Oak Sta W2 91 D2
Royal Opera Arc SW1 249 C4
Royal Orchard Cl SW18 157 A4
Royal Par BR7 189 A3
SE3 142 D3
SW6 264 A4
Ealing W5 88 A4
11 Dagenham RM10 81 D2
Royal Parade Mews BR7 189 A3
Royal Park Prim Sch DA14 169 A1
Royal Pl 11 SE10 142 A5
Royal Rd DA14 168 D1
E16 99 D1
SE17 138 D6
Teddington TW11 174 B5
Royal Route HA9 66 B4
Royal Russell Sch (Ballards) CR0 222 B3
Royal Sch Hampstead The NW3 70 B4
Royal St SE1 116 B3 260 D6
Royalty Mews W1 239 C1
Royalty Studios W11 91 A1
Royal United Services Mus★ SW1 250 A3
Royal Veterinary Coll NW1 93 D6 232 C5
Royal Victoria Pl E16 121 B5
Royal Victoria Sta E16 121 A6
Royal Victor Pl E3 96 D5
Royal Wlk SM6 219 B5
Roycraft Ave IG11 101 D5
Roycroft Cl
Streatham SW2 160 C3
Woodford E18 37 B2
Roydene Rd SE18 123 C1
Roydon Cl 7 SW11 136 D3
Roy Gdns IG2 57 D4
Roy Gr TW12 173 D4
Roy Ho N1 235 D5
Royle Cres W13 87 A3
Roymount Ct TW2 152 C1
Roy Ridley Ho 6 SW4 137 D2
Roy Sq E14 119 A6
Royston Ave
Carshalton SM1 218 B5
Chingford E4 35 D5
Wallington SM6 219 D4
Royston Cl
Cranford TW5 128 B4
Walton-on-T KT12 194 A1
Royston Ct 1 E13 99 A6
Hinchley Wood KT10 212 D6
Redbridge IG1 55 D3
3 Richmond TW9 132 B4
Royston Ct *continued*
Tolworth KT6 214 C6
Royston Gdns IG1 55 D3
Royston Gr HA5 23 C4
Royston Ho N11 31 A6
14 SE15 140 A6
Royston Par IG1 55 D3
Royston Park Rd HA5 23 C5
Royston Prim Sch SE20 184 D2
Royston Rd
Penge SE20 184 D2
Richmond TW10 154 A6
Royston St 25 E2 96 C5
Roystons The KT5 198 D4
Rozel Ct 3 N1 95 C6
Rozel Rd SW4 137 C2
Rubastic Rd UB2 106 C3
Rubens Rd UB5 84 D5
Rubens St SE6 163 B2
Rubin Pl EN3 7 C6
Ruby Rd E17 53 C6
Ruby St NW10 67 A1
SE15 140 B6
Ruby Triangle SE15 140 B6
Ruckholt Cl E10 75 D5
Ruckholt Rd E10 75 D5
Rucklidge Ave NW10 90 A5
Rudall Cres NW3 70 B4
Rudbeck Ho 10 SE15 140 A5
Ruddington Cl E5 75 A4
Ruddock Cl HA8 27 A3
Ruddstreet Cl SE18 123 A2
Rudge Ho 1 SE16 118 A3
Rudgwick Terr NW8 92 C6 230 B5
Rudhall Ho 4 SW2 160 C5
Rudland Rd DA7 147 D2
Rudloe Rd SW12 159 C4
Rudolf Pl SW8 270 B5
Rudolph Ct SE22 162 B4
Rudolph Rd E13 98 D5
NW6 91 C5
Rudstone Ho 10 E3 97 D4
Rudyard Ct SE1 252 D1
Rudyard Gr NW7 27 A4
Ruegg Ho 5 SE18 144 C6
Ruffetts Cl CR2 222 B1
Ruffetts The CR2 222 B1
Ruffle Cl UB7 104 B4
Rufford Cl HA3 43 A3
Rufford St N1 94 A6 233 B6
Rufford Street Mews N1 72 A1
Rufford Twr 5 W3 110 D5
Rufforth Ct 1 NW9 27 C2
Rufus Bsns Ctr SW18 157 D2
Rufus Cl HA4 63 A5
Rufus Ho SE1 263 D6
Rufus St N1 95 C4
Rugby Ave Edmonton N9 17 D3
Northolt UB6 64 B2
Wembley HA0 65 C4
Rugby Cl HA1 42 C5
Rugby Gdns RM9 80 C2
Rugby Mans W14 254 B4
Rugby Rd NW9 44 D5
W4 111 C4
Dagenham RM9 80 C2
Twickenham TW1,TW2, TW7 152 C5
Rugby St WC1 94 B3 240 C5
Rugg St E14 119 C6
Rugless Ho 2 E14 120 A4
Rugmere 4 NW1 71 A1
Ruislip Cl UB6 85 D3
Ruislip Ct HA4 61 D6
Ruislip Gardens Prim Sch HA4 61 D4
Ruislip Gardens Sta HA4 62 A4
Ruislip Lido★ HA4,HA5 39 B5
Ruislip Lido Railway★ HA4 39 B5
Ruislip Manor Sta HA4 40 A1
Ruislip Rd UB6,UB5 85 C4
Ruislip Rd E
Ealing UB6,W7 86 D3
Greenford UB6 86 B3
Ruislip St SW17 180 D6
Ruislip Sta HA4 39 D1
Rumball Ho 22 SE5 139 C5
Rumbold Rd SW6 135 D5 265 D3
Rum Cl E1 118 C6
Rumford Ho SE1 262 A5
Rumsey Cl TW12 173 B4
Rumsey Rd SW9 138 B2
Runacres Ct SE17 262 A1
Runbury Circ NW9 67 B6
Runcorn Cl N17 52 B5
Runcorn Pl W11 244 A6
Rundell Cres NW4 46 B4
Rundell Twr SW8 270 C2
Runes Cl CR4 202 C5
Runnelfield HA1 64 C5
Running Horse Yd 12 TW8 132 A6
Runnymede SW19 180 B2
Runnymede Cl TW2 151 D4
Runnymede Cres SW16 182 A2
Runnymede Ct 1 SM6 219 B2
Runnymede Gdns
Greenford UB6 86 C5
Twickenham TW2 151 D4
Runnymede Ho E9 75 A4
Richmond TW10 154 C6
Runnymede Rd TW2 151 D5
Runway The HA4 62 C3
Rupack St 3 SE16 118 C4
Rupert Ave 6 HA9 66 A3
Rupert Ct W1 249 C6
Rupert Gdns SW9 138 D3
Rupert Ho SE11 261 B3
Rupert Rd N19 71 D6
NW6 91 B5
W4 111 C3
Rupert St W1 115 D6 249 C6
Rural Way SW16 181 B3
Rusbridge Cl E8 74 A3
Ruscoe Ho 12 SW27 182 D5
Ruscoe Rd E16 98 D1
Ruscombe Way TW14 149 D4
Rusham Rd SW12 158 D4
Rushbrook Cres E17 35 B2
Rushbrook Ho 20 SW8 137 D3
Rushbrook Rd SE9 167 A2
Rushbury Ct 4 TW12 173 C2
Rushby Ct SW4 270 A1
Rush Common Mews 18 SW2 160 B4
Rushcroft Rd SW2,SW9 138 C1
Chingford E4 35 D3
Rush Croft Sch E4 35 D3
Rushcutters Ct 18 SE16 119 A2
Rushden Cl SE19 183 B3
Rushdene SE2 124 D3
Rushdene Ave EN4 14 C4
Rushdene Cl UB5 84 C5
Rushdene Cres UB5 84 C4
Rushdene Rd HA5 40 D3
Rushden Gdns NW7 28 C4
Ilford IG5 56 C6
Rushen Wlk SM5 202 B1
Rushet Rd BR5 190 A1
Rushett Cl KT7 197 B1
Rushett Rd KT7 197 B2
Rushey Cl KT3 199 B5
Rushey Gn SE6 163 D4
Rushey Green Prim Sch SE6 163 D3
Rushey Hill EN2 4 B1
Rushey Mead SE4 163 C6
Rushford Rd SE4 163 B5
Rush Green Rd RM7, RM8,RM10 59 D1
Rushgrove Ave NW9 45 D5
Rushgrove Ct NW9 45 C4
Rushgrove St SE18 122 B2
Rush Hill Mews 3 SW11 137 A2
Rush Hill Rd SW11 137 A2
Rushlake Ho 3 SW11 137 A3
Rushley Cl BR2 226 A4
Rushman Villas KT3 199 D5
Rushmead 5 E2 96 B4
Richmond TW10 153 B1
Rushmead Cl CR0 221 D4
Rushmere Ct KT4 216 A6
Rushmere Ho 2 SW15 156 A3
Rushmere Pl SW19 178 D5
Rushmon Pl SM3 217 A2
Rushmoor Cl HA5 40 B5
Rushmore Cl BR1 210 A6
Rushmore Cres 9 E5 74 D4
Rushmore Ho 9 N7 71 D3
W14 254 B5
Rushmore Prim Sch E5 74 D4
Rushmore Rd E5 74 D4
E5 75 A4
Rusholme Ave RM10 81 C5
Rusholme Gr SE19 183 C5
Rusholme Rd SW15 157 A5
Rushout Ave HA3 43 B3
Rush The SW20 179 B2
Rushton Ho 26 SW8 137 D3
Rushton St N1 95 B5 235 D4
Rushworth St SE1 116 D4 251 D1
Rushy Meadow La SM5 218 C5
Rushy Meadow Prim Sch SM5 218 C5
Ruskin Ave DA16 146 A3
E12 78 A2
Feltham TW14 149 D5
Richmond TW9 132 C5
Ruskin Cl NW11 47 D3
Ruskin Ct SE5 139 B2
SE9 166 B5
Southgate N21 16 B4
Ruskin Dr BR6 227 C5
DA16 146 A2
Ruskin Dr *continued*
North Cheam KT4 216 C6
Ruskin Gdns Ealing W5 87 D3
Harrow HA3 44 B5
Ruskin Gr DA16 146 A3
Ruskin Ho SW1 259 D3
Ruskin Par CR0 221 B3
Ruskin Park Ho SE5 139 B2
Ruskin Rd
Belvedere DA17 125 C2
Croydon CR0 220 D6
Isleworth TW7 130 D2
Southall UB1 107 A6
Tottenham N17 33 D2
Wallington SM5 219 A3
Ruskin Way SW19 180 B2
Ruskin Wlk BR2 210 B3
SE24 161 A6
Edmonton N9 18 A2
Rusland Ave BR6 227 B5
Rusland Hts HA1 42 C5
Rusland Park Rd HA1 42 C5
Rusper Cl NW2 68 C5
Stanmore HA7 25 C6
Rusper Ct SW9 138 A3
Rusper Rd N17,N22 51 A6
Dagenham RM9 80 C2
Russel Cl BR3 208 A6
Russel Ct N14 15 D6
Russell Ave N22 32 D1
Russell Cl DA7 147 C1
NW10 67 A1
SE7 143 C5
Chiswick W4 133 D6
Ruislip HA4 62 C6
Russell Ct 4 E10 53 D2
5 SE15 140 B3
SW1 249 B3
SW11 268 B1
Bromley BR1 186 D3
New Barnet EN5 2 A1
Streatham SW16 182 B5
Surbiton KT6 198 A2
Wallington SM6 219 C3
Wembley HA0 66 A1
Russell Gdns N20 14 C2
NW11 47 A3
W14 113 A3 254 A6
Ilford IG2 57 B2
Richmond TW10 153 C2
West Drayton UB7 104 C1
Russell Gdns Mews W14 113 A3 254 A6
Russell Gr NW7 27 C6
33 SW9 138 C4
Russell Ho 15 E14 97 C1
SW1 259 A2
Russell Kerr Cl W4 133 A5
Russell La N20 14 D2
Russell Lo 5 E4 20 A2
Russell Lodge SE1 262 C6
Russell Mans WC1 240 B4
Russell Par NW11 47 A3
Russell Pickering Ho 2 SW4 138 A2
Russell Pl NW3 70 C3
SE16 119 A3
Russell Prim Sch The TW10 153 D3
Russell Rd E10 53 D3
E17 53 B6
E4 35 B6
N15 51 C4
N20 14 C2
N8 49 D3
NW9 45 D3
W14 113 A3 254 B5
Bowes Park N13 32 B4
Buckhurst Hill IG9 21 C3
Enfield EN1 5 D5
Merton SW19 179 C3
Mitcham CR4 202 C6
Newham E16 99 B1
Northolt UB5 64 A3
Shepperton TW17 193 A2
Twickenham TW1,TW2 152 D5
Walton-on-T KT12 194 A3
Russell Sch The TW10 153 D2
Russell Sq WC1 94 A3 240 A5
Russell Square Mans WC1 240 B4
Russell Square Sta WC1 94 A3 240 A5
Russell St WC2 116 A6 250 B6
Russell's Wharf 2 W9 91 B3
Russell Way SM1 217 D3
Russell Wlk 4 TW10 154 B5
Russet Ave TW16, TW17 193 C6
Russet Cl UB10 83 A3
Russet Cres N7 72 B3
Russet Ct NW2 68 B5
6 Barnet EN4 2 C1
Russet Dr CR0 207 A1
Russet Ho TW3 129 B1
Russet House Sch EN1 6 B4
Russets Cl E4 36 B6
Russett Way SE13 141 D3
Russia Ct EC2 242 B2
Russia Dock Rd SE16 119 A5
Russia La E2 96 C5
Russian Submarine SE18 121 D3
Russia Row EC2 242 B1
Russington Rd TW17 193 B3
Rusthall Ave W4 111 B3
Rusthall Cl CR0 206 C3
Rusthall Mans W4 111 B2
Rustic Ave SW16 181 B3
Rustic Pl HA0 65 D4
Rustic Wlk E16 99 B1
Rustington Wlk SM4 201 B2
Ruston Ave KT5 198 D2
Ruston Gdns N14 15 A5
Ruston Mews W11 91 A1
Ruston Rd SE18 122 A3
Ruston St E3 97 B6
Rust Sq SE5 139 B5
Rutford Rd SW16 182 A5
Ruth Cl HA7 44 B5
Ruth Ct 14 E3 97 A5
Rutherford Cl
Hillingdon UB8 82 B3
Sutton SM2 218 B2
Rutherford Ho 12 E1 96 B3
Teddington TW11 174 D5
7 Wembley HA9 67 A5
Rutherford St SW1 115 D2 259 C4
Rutherford Twr 10 UB1 85 D1
Rutherford Way
Bushey WD23 8 C3
Wembley HA9 66 C4
Rutherglen Rd SE2 146 A6
Rutherwyke Cl KT17 216 A2
Ruth Ho W10 91 A3
Ruthin Cl NW9 45 C3
Ruthin Rd SE3 143 A6
Ruthven St E9 96 D6
Rutland Ave DA15 168 A4
Rutland Cl DA5 168 D3
Chessington KT9 214 B2
Mitcham SW19 180 C3
Mortlake SW14 133 A2
Rutland Ct SE5 139 B1
SW7 247 B1
15 Acton W3 88 C1
Chislehurst BR7 188 C2
Enfield EN3 18 B6
Sidcup BR7 167 A2
Rutland Dr
Morden SM4 201 C2
Richmond TW10 154 A3
Rutland Gate SW7 114 C4 247 B1
Beckenham BR2 208 D5
Belvedere DA17 125 D1
Rutland Gate Mews SW7 247 A1
Rutland Gdns N4 51 A3
SW7 114 C4 247 B1
Dagenham RM8 80 C3
Ealing W13 87 A2
South Croydon CR0 221 C4
Rutland Gdns Mews SW7 247 B1
Rutland Gr W6 112 B1
Rutland Ho 18 SE18 122 B2
W8 255 C5
6 Northolt UB5 63 C2
2 Penge SE20 184 C2
10 Putney SW15 156 C4
Tolworth KT6 198 C1
Rutland Lo SE6 163 B2
Rutland Mews E SW7 257 B6
Rutland Mews S SW7 257 A6
Rutland Mews W SW7 257 A6
Rutland Park Gdns NW2 68 C2
Rutland Park Mans NW2 68 C2
Rutland Pk NW2 68 C2
Forest Hill SE6 163 B2
Rutland Pl EC1 241 D4
Bushey WD23 8 B3
Rutland Rd E17 53 C3
E7 77 D1
E9 96 D6
Harrow HA1 42 A3
Hayes UB3 105 B2
Ilford IG1 78 D5
Mitcham SW19 180 C3
Southall UB1 85 C2
Twickenham TW2 152 B2
Wanstead E11 55 B4
Rutland St SW7 257 B6
Rutland Studios NW10 90 A4
Rutland Wlk SE6 163 B2
Rutley Cl SE11 138 D6
Rutlish Rd SW19 179 C2
Rutlish Sch (Boys) SW20 179 B1
Rutter Gdns CR4 202 B5
Rutters Cl UB7 104 C4
Rutt's Terr SE14 140 D4
Rutts The WD23 8 B3
Ruvigny Gdns SW15 134 D2

Ruvigny Mans SW15 134 D2
Ruxbury Ct TW15 148 A1
Ruxley Cl
Chessington KT19 214 D3
Sidcup DA14 191 A4
Ruxley Cnr DA14 191 A4
Ruxley Corner Ind Est DA14 190 D4
Ruxley Cres KT10 213 B1
Ruxley Ct KT19 215 A3
Ruxley Gdns TW17 193 A4
Ruxley La KT19 215 B3
Ruxley Mews KT19 214 D3
Ruxley Ridge KT10 213 A1
Ryall's Ct N20 14 D1
Ryan Cl SE9 143 C1
Ruislip HA4 40 B1
Ryan Ct SW16 182 A3
Ryan Dr TW8 131 A6
Ryan Ho 3 HA1 42 D4
Ryarsh Cres BR6 227 C4
Rycott Path SE22 162 A4
Rycroft Way N17 51 D6
Ryculff Sq SE3 142 D3
Rydal Cl NW4 29 A2
Rydal Cres UB6 87 C5
Rydal Ct Edgware HA8 26 B5
Wembley HA9 44 A2
Rydal Dr DA7 147 C4
West Wickham BR4 224 C6
Rydal Gdns NW9 45 C4
Kingston SW15 177 C5
Twickenham TW2,TW3 151 D5
Wembley HA9 43 C1
Rydal Ho 25 SW8 137 D3
Rydal Lo N17 34 A3
Rydal Rd SW16 181 D6
Rydal Water NW1 232 A1
Rydal Way Enfield EN3 18 C5
Ruislip HA4 62 C4
Ryde Ho 1 NW6 91 C6
Rydens Ho SE9 165 C1
Rydens Rd KT12 194 D1
Ryde Pl TW1 153 D5
Ryder Cl BR1 187 B5
Ryder Ct E10 75 D6
SW1 249 B4
Ryder Dr SE16 118 B1
Ryder Ho 14 E1 96 C3
5 Merton SW19 179 D2
Ryder St SW1 249 B4
Ryder's Terr
NW8 92 A5 229 A4
Ryder Yd SW1 249 B4
Ryde Vale Rd SW12 159 C2
Rydon Mews SW19 178 C3
Rydons Cl SE9 144 A2
Rydon St N1 235 B6
Rydston Cl 2 N7 72 B1
Rye Cl DA5 169 D5
Ryecotes Mead SE21 161 C3
Ryecroft Ave TW2 151 D3
Ryecroft Cres EN5 12 B6
Ryecroft Rd BR5 211 B3
SE13 164 A6
South Norwood SW16 182 C4
Ryecroft St
SW6 135 D4 265 C1
Rye Ct BR3 185 B2
Ryedale SE22 162 B5
Ryedale Ct 6 TW12 173 C2
Ryefield Ave UB10 60 D1
Ryefield Cres HA5,HA6 22 A1
Ryefield Ct HA6 22 A1
Ryefield Path 7
SW15 156 A3
Ryefield Prim Sch UB10 83 B6
Ryefield Rd SE19 183 A4
Ryegates 2 SE15 140 B3
Ryehill Ct KT3 199 D2
Rye Hill Pk SE15 140 C1
Rye La SE15 140 A3
Ryeland Cl UB7 82 A1
Ryelands Cres SE12 165 C5
Ryelands Prim Sch
SE25 206 B4
Rye Rd SE15 140 D1
Rye The N14 15 C4
Rye Way HA8 26 B4
Rye Wlk SW15 156 D6
Ryfold Rd SW19 157 C1
Ryhope Rd N11 31 B6
Ryland Cl TW13 171 D6
Ryland Ct EN2 5 B1
Rylandes Rd NW2 68 A5
Ryland Ho 11 SW16 181 C5
Ryland Rd NW5 71 B2
Rylett Cres W12 111 D3
Rylett Rd W12 111 D3
Rylston Rd
SW6 135 B6 264 C5
Edmonton N13 17 B1
Rylton Ho KT12 194 A1
Rymer Rd CR0 205 C2
Rymer St SE24 160 D5
Rymill St E16 122 C5
Rysbrack St SW1 257 C6
Rythe Cl KT9 213 C1
Rythe Ct KT7 197 A2
Rythe Ho 7 BR1 186 B5
Rythe Rd KT10 212 C3

S

Saatchi Gallery* SE1 250 C2
Sabah Ct TW15 170 C6
Sabbarton St 9 E16 98 D1
Sabella Ct E3 97 B5
Sabine Rd SW11 137 A2
Sable Cl TW4 128 C2
Sable Ct 3 KT3 199 C4
Sable St N1 72 D1
Sach Rd E5 74 B6
Sacketts Ho 24 SW9 138 C4
Sackville Ave BR2 209 A1
Sackville Cl HA2 64 B5
Sackville Gdns IG1 56 B1
Sackville Ho N8 50 A5
16 Streatham SW16 160 A1
Sackville Rd SM2 217 C1
Sackville St
W1 115 C6 249 B5
Sacred Heart High Sch
W6 112 C2
Sacred Heart Jun Sch
W6 112 D2
Sacred Heart Prim Sch,
Battersea SW11 136 C3
Sacred Heart RC High Sch
The HA3 24 C1
Sacred Heart RC Prim Sch
N20 14 C2
Putney SW15 156 A6
Ruislip HA4 61 C6
Teddington TW11 175 B3
West Barnes KT3 200 A5
Sacred Heart RC Sch The
SE5 139 A4
Saddlebrook Pk TW16 171 C3
Saddlers Cl Barnet EN5 12 B6
Borehamwood WD6 11 B5
Pinner HA5 23 C5
Saddlers Mews SW8 270 B2
Teddington KT1 175 C2
Wembley HA0 64 D4
Saddlers Path WD6 11 B6
Saddlescombe Way
N12 29 C5
Sadler Cl CR4 180 D1
Sadler Ho 17 E3 97 D4
EC1 234 C2
Sadlers Ride KT8 174 A1
Saffron Ave E14 120 B6
Saffron Cl NW11 47 B3
Thornton Heath CR0 204 A3
Saffron Ct E15 76 C3
10 N1 73 B2
Saffron Hill EC1 94 C2 241 B4
Saffron St EC1 241 B4
Saffron Way KT6 197 D1
Saffron Wharf SE1 253 D2
Sage Cl 7 E6 100 B2
Sage Mews SE22 161 D6
Sage St E1 118 C6
Sage Way WC1 233 C1
Sage Yd KT6 198 B1
Sahara Ct UB1 107 A6
Saigasso Cl E16 99 D1
Sailmakers Ct SW6 136 A2
Sail St SE11 116 C3 260 D4
Saimet 3 NW9 27 D2
Sainfoin Rd SW17 159 A2
Sainsbury Rd SE19 183 C5
St Agatha's Dr KT2 176 B4
St Agatha's Gr SM5 202 D1
St Agatha's RC Prim Sch
KT2 176 B4
St Agatha's RC Sch
KT2 176 B3
St Agnes Cl E9 96 C6
St Agnes Pl SE11 138 D6
St Agnes RC Prim Sch
E3 97 D4
St Agnes RC Sch NW2 69 A5
St Aidans Ct IG11 102 B5
St Aidan's Prim Sch N4 50 C2
St Aidan's RC Prim Sch
IG1 57 B1
St Aidan's Rd SE22 162 B6
W13 109 B4
St Albans Ave W4 111 B3
Feltham TW13 172 D5
St Alban's Ave E6 100 C4
St Alban's CE Prim Sch
EC1 94 C2 241 A4
St Alban's Cl NW11 47 C1
St Albans Cres N22 32 C2
St Alban's Cres IG8 37 A2
St Alban's Gdns TW11 175 A5
St Alban's Gr
W8 113 D3 255 D6
Carshalton SM5 202 C2
St Albans Ho 2 SW16 182 C6
St Albans La NW11 47 C1
St Albans Mans W8 255 D6
St Alban's Pl
N1 94 D6 234 C5
St Alban's RC Prim Sch
KT8 196 A4
St Alban's Rd NW10 89 C6
NW5 71 B5
St Albans Rd Barnet EN5 1 A3
Cheam SM1 217 B4
Ilford IG3 57 D2
Kingston KT2 176 A4
St Alban's Rd IG8 37 A3
St Alban's St SW1 249 C5
St Albans Studios W8 255 D6
St Albans Terr W6 264 A6
St Alban's Villas NW5 71 A5
St Alfege Pas SE10 142 A6
St Alfege Rd SE7 143 D6
St Alfege with St Peter's CE
Prim Sch SE10 142 A6
St Aloysius RC Inf Sch
NW1 232 D1
St Aloysius' RC Jun & Inf
Sch NW1 232 C2
St Aloysius RC Jun Sch
NW1 93 D5 232 D3
St Alphage Ct NW9 45 B6
St Alphage Gdn EC2 242 B3
St Alphage Highwalk
EC2 242 B3
St Alphage Wlk HA8 27 A1
St Alphege Rd N9 18 C4
St Alphonsus Rd SW4 137 D1
St Amunds Cl SE6 185 C6
St Andrews Ave HA0 65 A4
St Andrew's CE Prim Sch
N1 94 B6 233 D6
N14 15 D3
SW9 138 A3
Enfield EN1 5 C3
St Andrew's CE Sch
N20 13 B2
St Andrews Cl 25 SE16 118 B1
St Andrew's Cl N12 30 A6
NW2 68 B5
St Andrews Cl
Erith SE28 102 D1
Hinchley Wood KT7 197 B1
Ruislip HA4 62 D6
Stanmore HA7 25 C1
St Andrew's Cl
2 Hounslow TW7 130 C4
Upper Halliford TW17 193 B5
St Andrew's Ct E17 35 A1
St Andrews Ct W4 133 A4
St Andrew's Ct
Kingston KT3 199 D6
Wandsworth SW18 158 A2
St Andrews Dr HA7 25 C2
St Andrew's Gr N16 51 B1
St Andrew's Greek Sch
NW1 71 C2
St Andrew's High Sch
CR0 220 D4
St Andrew's Hill
EC4 94 D1 241 D1
St Andrews Ho 11
SE16 118 B3
St Andrew's Hospl E3 97 D3
St Andrew's Mans W1 238 A3
St Andrew's Mews N16 51 C1
St Andrews Mews
Greenwich SE3 143 A5
4 Streatham SW12 159 D3
St Andrew's Pl NW1 238 D6
St Andrews RC Prim Sch
SW16 182 A5
St Andrews Rd DA14 168 D1
E17 35 A1
N9 18 C4
NW9 45 B1
St Andrew's Rd E11 54 C3
E13 99 B4
NW11 47 B3
NW2 68 B2
W14 264 B6
W3 89 C1
W7 108 C4
St Andrews Rd SM5 218 C5
St Andrew's Rd
3 Croydon CR0 221 A4
Enfield EN1 5 B2
Hillingdon UB10 82 B6
Redbridge IG1 56 B2
Surbiton KT6 197 D3
St Andrew's Sq W11 91 A1
Surbiton KT6 197 D3
St Andrew's & St Mark's CE
Jun Sch KT6 197 D4
St Andrew St EC4 241 B3
St Andrews Terr WD19 22 C5
St Andrew & St Francis CE
Prim Sch NW2 68 A2
St Andrew's Twr UB1 108 A6
St Andrews Way E3 97 D3
St Andrew's Wharf
SE1 253 D2
St Angela's Ursuline
Convent Sch E7 77 B2
St Anna Rd EN5 12 D6
St Anne RC Prim Sch
E1 96 A3
St Annes Catholic High Sch
for Girls (Upper) N13 32 C6
St Anne's CE Prim Sch
SW18 157 D6
St Anne's Cl N6 71 A5
St Annes Cl WD19 22 C6
St Anne's Ct NW6 91 A6
W1 239 C1
St Anne's Flats NW1 232 C2
St Annes Gdns NW10 88 B4
St Anne's Pas E14 97 B1
St Anne's Prim Sch
TW19 148 A4
St Anne's RC Prim Sch
SE11 138 B6 270 C6
St Anne's Rd E11 76 B6
Wembley HA0 65 D3
St Anne's Row E14 97 B1
St Anne St E14 97 B1
St Anne's Trad Est E14 97 B1
St Ann's IG11 101 A6
St Ann's CE Prim Sch
N15 51 B4
St Ann's Cres SW18 158 A5
St Ann's Ct NW4 46 B6
St Ann's Ctr HA1 42 C3
St Ann's Gdns NW5 71 A2
St Ann's General Hospl
N4,N15 51 A4
St Ann's Hill SW18 158 A5
St Ann's Ho WC1 234 A1
St Ann's La SW1 259 D5
St Ann's Park Rd
SW18 158 A5
St Ann's Rd N15 51 B4
W11 112 D6
St Anns Rd SW13 133 D4
St Ann's Rd
2 Barking IG11 101 A6
Edmonton N9 17 D3
Harrow HA1 42 C3
St Ann's Sch Ealing W7 108 C5
Morden SM4 201 D4
St Ann's St
SW1 115 D3 259 D6
St Ann's Terr
NW8 92 B5 229 D4
St Ann's Villas
W11 112 D5 244 A3
St Ann's Way CR2 220 D2
St Anselm RC Prim Sch
UB2 107 B3
St Anselm's Ct SW16 182 A5
St Anselm's Pl W1 248 C6
St Anselm's RC Prim Sch
Harrow HA1 42 C2
Upper Tooting SW17 159 A1
St Anselms Rd UB3 105 D4
St Anthony's Ave IG8 37 C3
St Anthony's Cl 8 E1 118 A5
St Anthonys Cl SW17 158 C2
St Anthony's Ct
2 SW12 159 A5
Orpington BR6 226 D6
Upper Tooting SW17 159 A2
St Anthony's Flats
NW1 232 C3
St Anthony's Hospl
KT4 200 D1
St Anthony's RC Prim Sch
E7 77 B1
SE22 162 A5
Penge SE20 184 B2
St Anthony's Way
TW14 127 D1
St Antony's RC Prim Sch
IG8 37 A6
St Antony's Rd E7 77 B1
St Arvans Cl CR0 221 C5
St Asaph Ct SE4 140 D2
St Asaph Rd SE4 140 D2
St Aubins Ct N1 235 D6
St Aubyns E18 54 D5
St Aubyn's Ave
Hounslow TW3,TW4 151 C6
Wimbledon SW19 179 B5
St Aubyns Cl BR6 227 D5
St Aubyn's Ct SW19 179 A4
St Aubyns Gdns BR6 227 D6
St Aubyn's Prep Sch
IG8 36 D3
St Aubyn's Rd SE19 183 D4
St Aubyn's Sch IG8 36 D3
St Audrey Ave DA7 147 C3
St Augustine's Ave
BR1,BR2 210 A4
Ealing W5 88 A4
South Croydon CR2 221 A1
Wembley HA9 66 A5
St Augustine's CE High Sch
NW6 91 C5
St Augustine's CE Prim Sch
NW6 91 D5
St Augustine's Ct E11 54 D1
St Augustines Ct BR3 185 A1
St Augustine's Prim Sch
DA17 125 B2
St Augustine's RC Prim Sch
W6 135 A6 264 B5
St Augustine's RC Prim Sch
continued
Ilford IG2 56 D4
St Augustine's Rd
DA17 125 B2
NW1 71 D1
St Augustines's RC Prim
Sch SE6 186 A5
St Austell Cl HA8 26 B1
St Austell Rd SE13 142 B3
St Awdry's Rd IG11 79 B1
St Barnabas CE Prim Sch
SW1 115 A1 258 B2
St Barnabas Cl
11 SE22 161 C6
Beckenham BR3 186 A1
St Barnabas Ct HA3 24 A2
St Barnabas' Gdns
KT8 195 C4
St Barnabas Rd E17 53 C3
Mitcham CR4 181 A3
Sutton SM1 218 B3
Woodford IG8 37 C3
St Barnabas St SW1 258 B2
St Barnabas & St Philip's CE
Prim Sch W8 113 C3 255 A5
St Barnabas Terr E9 74 D3
St Barnabas Villas
SW8 138 A4 270 B2
St Bartholomews CE Prim
Sch SE26 162 C1
St Bartholomew's CE Prim
Sch SE26 184 C6
St Bartholomew's Cl
SE26 184 C6
St Bartholomew's Hospl
EC1 94 D2 241 D3
St Bartholomew's Rd
E6 100 B5
St Bede's RC Inf Sch
SW12 159 D3
St Bede's RC Prim Sch
RM6 58 C4
St Benedict's Cl SW17 181 A5
St Benedict's Jun Sch
W5 87 C2
St Benedict's Sch W5 87 D2
St Benets Cl SW17 158 C2
St Benet's Gr SM5 202 A2
St Benet's Pl EC3 252 D6
St Bernadette RC Jun Sch
SW12 159 C4
St Bernadette's RC Fst &
Mid Sch HA3 44 B5
St Bernadette's RC Prim
Sch UB10 82 D6
St Bernard Ho 6 E14 120 A3
St Bernards CR0 221 C5
St Bernards Cl 8
SE27 183 B6
St Bernards Ho 1
KT6 214 A6
St Bernard's Rd E6 99 D6
St Blaise Ave BR1 187 B1
St Bonaventure's RC Sec
Sch E7 77 A1
St Boniface Catholic Prim
Sch SW17 180 D5
St Botolph St
E1,EC3 95 D1 243 C2
St Brelades Ct N1 235 D6
St Bride's Ave EC4 241 C1
Edgware HA8 26 B2
St Brides Cl DA18 124 D4
St Bride's Pas EC4 241 C1
St Bride St EC4 94 D1 241 C2
St Catherines Cl
Chessington KT9 213 D2
Upper Tooting SW17 158 C2
St Catherine's Convent Girls
Prep & Senior Schs
TW1 153 A2
St Catherine's Ct 8
W4 111 C3
St Catherines Ct
TW13 150 A3
St Catherine's Dr
SE14 140 D3
St Catherines Farm Ct
HA4 39 A3
St Catherines Mews
SW3 257 C4
St Catherine's RC Mid Sch
SW20 200 C4
St Catherine's RC Prim Sch
EN5 1 C1
St Catherine's RC Sch for
Girls DA6 169 D6
St Catherines Rd
Chingford E4 19 C2
Ruislip HA4 39 B3
St Cecilia's Cl SM3 201 A1
St Cecilia's RC Prim Sch
SM3 216 D6
St Chads Cl KT6 197 C2
St Chad's Gdns RM6 59 A2
St Chad's Pl WC1 233 C2
St Chad's RC Prim Sch
SE25 205 C4
St Chad's Rd RM6 59 A2
St Chad's St WC1 233 B2
St Charles' Hospl W10 90 D2
St Charles Pl W10 91 A2
St Charles RC Prim Sch
W10 90 D2
St Charles RC Sixth Form
Coll W10 90 D2
St Charles Sq W10 90 D2
St Christina's Sch
NW8 92 C5 230 A3
St Christopher's Cl
TW7 130 C4
St Christophers Dr
UB3 106 B6
St Christophers Gdns
CR7 204 C6
St Christopher's Ho
NW1 232 C3
St Christopher's Hospice
SE26 184 C5
St Christopher's Mews
SM6 219 C3
St Christopher's Pl
W1 238 B2
St Christopher's Sch
NW3 70 B3
Beckenham BR3 186 A1
Wembley HA9 66 B5
St Clair Dr KT4 216 B4
St Clair Ho 18 E3 97 B4
St Clair Rd E13 99 B5
St Clair's Rd CR0 221 C6
St Clare Bsns Pk
TW12 174 A4
St Clare St EC3 243 C1
St Clement Danes CE Prim
Sch WC2 94 B1 240 C1
St Clements Ct N7 72 B2
7 SE14 140 D6
8 W11 112 D6
St Clement's Ct EC3 252 D6
St Clements Ho KT12 194 A2
St Clement's Hts SE26 184 A6
St Clement's La WC2 240 D1
St Clements Mans 3
SW6 134 D6
St Clements St N7 72 C1
St Clement & St James CE
Prim Sch
W11 112 D5 244 A3
St Cloud Rd SE27 183 B6
St Columba's Ct E15 76 C4
St Columbas Ho 2 E17 53 D5
St Columba's RC Sch for
Boys DA6 169 D6
St Columb's Ho 11 W10 91 A2
St Crispins Cl NW3 70 C4
St Crispin's Cl UB1 85 B1
St Cross St EC1 94 C2 241 B4
St Cuthberts Gdns 1
HA5 23 B3
St Cuthbert's Rd NW2 69 B2
St Cuthberts Rd N13 32 C4
St Cuthbert with St
Matthias Prim Sch
SW5 113 D1 255 C2
St Cyprian's Greek Orthodox
Prim Sch CR7 183 A2
St Cyprian's St SW17 180 D6
St Davids Cl 27 SE16 118 B1
Wembley HA9 67 A5
St David's Cl BR4 207 D2
St David's Coll BR4 207 D2
St David's Ct 1 E17 54 A6
St Davids Ct 5 E11 55 B4
St David's Ct 3 UB1 86 A1
St David's Dr HA8 26 B2
St David's Pl NW4 46 B2
St David's Sch TW15 148 B1
St David's Sq E14 119 D1
St Denis Rd SE27 183 B6
St Dionis Rd SW6 135 B3
St Domingo Ho SE18 122 B3
St Dominic RC Prim Sch
NW5 70 D3
St Dominics RC Prim Sch
E9 75 A2
St Dominic's Sixth Form
Coll (RC) HA1 64 C6
St Donatt's Rd SE14 141 B4
St Dunstans SM1 217 B2
St Dunstan's Alley
EC3 253 A5
St Dunstan's Ave W3 111 B6
St Dunstan's CE Prim Sch
SM3 217 A1
St Dunstans Cl UB3 105 D2
St Dunstan's Coll SE6 163 C3
St Dunstan's Ct EC4 241 B1
St Dunstans Gdns W3 111 B6
St Dunstan's Hill EC3 253 A5
Cheam SM1,SM3 217 A3
St Dunstan's La EC3 253 A5
Beckenham BR3 208 A4
St Dunstans Rd E7 77 C2

St Dunstan's Rd W6 ....112 D1
W7 ....108 C4
Cranford TW5 ....128 B3
Feltham TW13 ....149 D1
South Norwood SE25 ....205 D5
St Edmund RC Sch E14 ....119 C2
St Edmunds Ave HA4 ....39 B3
St Edmunds Cl DA18 ....124 D4
St Edmund's Cl NW8 ....230 C5
St Edmunds Cl SW17 ....158 C2
St Edmund's Ct NW8 ....230 C5
St Edmunds Dr HA7 ....25 A2
St Edmund's La TW2 ....151 D4
St Edmund's RC Prim Sch
Edmonton N9 ....18 B3
Twickenham TW2 ....151 D4
St Edmunds Rd N9 ....18 A4
St Edmund's Rd IG1 ....56 B3
St Edmund's Sq SW13 134 C6
St Edmund's Terr NW8 ....92 D6 230 C5
St Edward's CE Comp Sch RM7 ....59 C3
St Edward's Cl NW11 ....47 C3
St Edwards Ct 3 E10 ....54 A2
St Edward's Ct NW11 ....47 C3
St Edward's RC Prim Sch E6 ....99 C6
St Edward's RC Prim Sch NW1 ....92 C3 237 B5
St Egberts Way E4 ....20 A3
St Elizabeth Ct 8 E10 ....53 D2
N12 ....30 A6
St Elizabeth's RC Prim Sch TW10 ....154 B5
St Elmo Rd W12 ....111 D4
St Elmos Rd SE16 ....119 A4
St Elphege's RC Inf Sch SM6 ....220 A2
St Elphege's RC Jun Sch SM6 ....220 A2
St Erkenwald Mews IG11 ....101 B6
St Erkenwald Rd IG11 101 B6
St Ermin's Hill SW1 ....259 C6
St Ervan's Rd W10 ....91 B2
St Eugene de Mazenod RC Prim Sch NW6 ....91 C6
St Faith's CE Prim Sch SW18 ....158 A6
St Faith's Cl EN2 ....5 A4
St Faith's Rd SE24 ....160 D3
St Fillans Rd SE6 ....164 A4
St Francesca Cabrini Prim Sch SE23 ....162 C5
St Francis Cl BR6 ....211 C3
St Francis de Sales RC Jun Sch N17 ....33 D3
St Francis' Ho NW1 ....232 C3
St Francis Lo HA0 ....64 D5
St Francis of Assisi RC Prim Sch W11 ....112 D6
St Francis RC Prim Sch
E15 ....76 C3
SE15 ....140 A5
St Francis Rd SE22 ....139 C1
St Francis Way IG1 ....79 B4
St Francis Xavier Sixth Form Coll SW12 ....159 B5
St Gables Ct N11 ....31 D3
St Gabriel's CE Prim Sch SW1 ....115 C1 259 A1
St Gabriel's Cl E11 ....55 B1
St Gabriel's Rd NW2 ....68 D3
St George Ho SW11 ....268 B1
St George's Ave E7 ....77 B1
N7 ....71 D4
NW9 ....45 B5
W5 ....109 D4
Southall UB1 ....107 B6
St George's Battersea CE Prim Sch SW8 ....137 C5 269 B3
St George's Bickley CE Prim Sch BR1 ....187 D1
St George's Cath NW1 231 D2
St George's Cath RC Jun & Inf Sch SE1 ....116 D3 261 C6
St George's CE Prim Sch SE5 ....139 C5
St George's Circ SE1 ....116 D3 261 C6
St George's Cl NW11 ....47 B3
St Georges Cl
Erith SE28 ....102 D1
Wembley HA0 ....65 A5
St Georges Ct E17 ....54 B4
E6 ....100 B3
St George's Ct SE1 ....261 C5
SW3 ....257 A4
SW7 ....256 A5
St Georges Ct
Harrow HA3 ....43 A3
Penge SE20 ....184 B2
Putney SW15 ....135 B1
St George's Dr SW1 ....115 C1 259 A2
Ickenham UB10 ....60 B6
South Oxhey WD19 ....23 A6
St George's Field W2 ....92 C1 237 B1
St George's Gdns KT6 214 D6
St George's Gr SW17 ....158 B1
St Georges Hanover Sq Sch W1 ....115 A6 248 B5
St George's Ho NW1 ....232 B3
St George's Hospl SW17 ....180 B5
St Georges Ind Est
Kingston KT2 ....175 D5
Tottenham N22 ....32 D3
St George's La EC3 ....253 A6
St Georges Lo N10 ....49 C5
St Georges Mews 11 NW1 ....70 D1
St George's Mews SE1 261 B6
St George's RC Cath SE1 ....116 C3 261 B6
St George's RC Prim Sch
Enfield EN2 ....5 B3
Harrow HA1 ....64 D5
St George's RC Sec Sch W9 ....91 D5
St Georges Rd BR1 ....210 B6
BR5 ....211 B3
W4 ....111 B4
St George's Rd DA14 ....190 D4
E10 ....76 A5
E7 ....77 B2
NW11 ....47 B3
SE1 ....116 D3 261 C5
St Georges Rd RM9 ....81 A4
St George's Rd
Beckenham BR3 ....185 D2
Ealing W7 ....108 D5
Edmonton N9 ....18 A1
Enfield EN1 ....5 D5
Feltham TW13 ....172 D6
Isleworth TW1 ....153 B6
2 Kingston KT2 ....176 C3
Mitcham CR4 ....203 B6
Palmers Green N13 ....16 B2
Redbridge IG1 ....56 B2
Richmond TW9 ....132 B2
Wallington SM6 ....219 B3
Wimbledon SW19 ....179 B4
St Georges Rd W BR1 188 A1
St George's Residences 4 SW2 ....160 C6
St Georges's Ct EC4 ....241 C2
St Georges Sh & L Ctr HA1 ....42 C3
St Georges Sq 1 E14 ....119 A6
St George's Sq E7 ....77 B1
SE8 ....119 B2
SW1 ....115 D1 259 C1
Kingston KT3 ....199 C6
St George's Square Mews SW1 ....259 C1
St George St W1 ....115 B6 248 D6
St Georges Terr NW1 ....70 D1
St George's Way SE15 139 C6
St George's Wlk CR0 ....221 A5
St George the Martyr CE Prim Sch WC1 94 B3 240 D5
St Gerards Cl SW4 ....159 C6
St German's Pl SE3 ....143 A4
St German's Rd SE23 ....163 A3
St Gildas' RC Jun Sch N8 ....50 A3
St Giles Ave
Dagenham RM10 ....81 D1
Uxbridge UB10 ....61 A4
St Giles Cir WC1 ....93 D1 239 D2
St Giles Cl BR6 ....227 B3
Dagenham RM10 ....81 D1
St Giles Colls WC1 ....94 A2 240 B4
St Giles Ct WC2 ....240 A2
Ealing W13 ....109 C5
St Giles High St WC2 ....93 D1 239 D2
St Giles Hospl SE5 ....139 C4
St Giles Pas WC2 ....239 D1
St Giles Rd SE5 ....139 C4
St Giles' Sch CR2 ....220 D2
St Giles Twr 3 SE5 ....139 C4
St Gilles Ho 15 E2 ....96 D5
St Gothard Rd SE21, SE27 ....183 B6
St Gregory Cl HA4 ....62 C4
St Gregory RC High Sch HA3 ....43 D4
St Gregory's RC Prim Sch W5 ....87 D2
St Helena Ho WC1 ....234 A1
St Helena Pier TW9 ....153 D6
St Helena Rd SE16 ....118 D2
St Helena St WC1 ....234 A1
St Helena Terr 23 TW9 ....153 D6
St Helens KT7 ....196 D2
Saint Helens Coll UB10 60 C1
St Helen's Cres SW16 ....182 B2
St Helen's Gdns W10 ....90 D1
St Helen's Pl EC3 ....243 A2
St Helen's RC Inf Sch E17 ....54 A4
St Helen's RC Prim Sch
E13 ....99 A3
SW9 ....138 C2
St Helens Rd 7 DA18 ....124 D4
St Helen's Rd
Ealing W13 ....109 C5
Redbridge IG1 ....56 B3
Thornton Heath SW16 ....182 B2
St Helens Sch UB10 ....60 C1
St Helier Ave SM4 ....202 A3
St Helier Ct 4 N1 ....95 C6
St Helier Hospl SM5 ....202 A1
St Heliers Ave TW3, TW4 ....151 C6
St Helier's Rd E10 ....54 A3
St Helier Sta SM4 ....201 C3
St Hilda's Ave TW15 ....170 A5
St Hilda's Cl NW6 ....68 D1
St Hildas Cl SW17 ....158 C2
St Hilda's Rd SW13 ....134 B6
St Hildas Wharf E1 ....118 C5
St Hubert's Ho 1 E14 119 C3
St Hughes Cl SW17 ....158 C2
St Hugh's Rd SE20 ....184 B3
St Ignatius Coll EN1 ....6 B6
St Ignatius' RC Prim Sch N15 ....51 D3
St Ignatius RC Prim Sch TW16 ....172 A2
St Ivian Ct 3 N10 ....31 B1
St James Apartments 2 E17 ....53 A4
St James Ave N20 ....14 C1
Sutton SM1 ....217 C3
St James' Ave W13 ....109 A5
St James CE Jun Sch E7 ....77 A3
St James CE Prim Sch EN3 ....6 C3
St James Cl N20 ....14 C1
Barnet EN4 ....2 B1
St James' Cl
New Malden KT3 ....199 D4
Ruislip HA4 ....62 C6
St James Ct 11 E2 ....96 A4
SE3 ....143 B4
10 W4 ....110 C1
St James' Ct SW1 259
W4 ....111 B3
St James Ct
Thornton Heath CR0 ....204 D2
Wanstead E12 ....77 C6
St James' Ct 7 KT1 ....198 A6
St James Gate IG9 ....21 B3
St James Gdns IG6 ....58 B5
St James' Gdns HA0 ....66 A1
St James Hatcham CE Prim Sch SE14 ....141 A4
St James Independent Schs W14 ....113 A2 254 A4
St James Ind Mews SE1 ....118 A1
St James' Mans NW6 ....69 C1
St James Mews E14 ....120 A3
St James RC Prim Sch BR5 ....210 D4
St James' Rd E15 ....76 D3
St James Rd
Carshalton SM5 ....218 C5
Kingston KT1 ....175 D1
Sutton SM1,SM2 ....217 C3
St James' Rd
Edmonton N9 ....18 B2
Mitcham CR4 ....181 A3
Surbiton KT6 ....197 D3
St James's SE14 ....141 A4
St James's App EC2 ....243 A5
St James's Ave E2 ....96 C5
Beckenham BR3 ....207 A6
Hampton TW12 ....174 A5
St James's CE Prim Sch
N10 ....49 A5
SE16 ....118 A3
St James School Flats 5 N7 ....72 C3
St James's Cl NW8 ....230 C5
SE18 ....123 A1
Upper Tooting SW17 ....158 D2
St James's Cloisters 2 SE22 ....139 D1
St James's Cotts 14 TW10 ....153 D6
St James's Cres SW9 ....138 C2
St James's Ct 8 N18 ....34 A5
St James's Dr
Balham SW12,SW17 ....158 D4
Upper Tooting SW17 ....158 D3
St James's Gdns W11 ....113 A5 244 A4
St James's Gr SW11 ....136 D3
St James's La N10 ....49 B5
St James's Lo 4 CR0 ....205 C1
St James's Market SW1 ....249 C5
St James's Mews E17 ....53 A4
St James's Palace★ SW1 ....115 C5 249 B3
St James's Park★ SW1 ....249 C2
St James's Park Sta SW1 ....115 D3 259 C6
St James's Pas EC3 ....243 B1
St James's Pk CR0 ....205 A2
St James's Pl SW1 ....115 C5 249 A3
St James's RC High Sch NW9 ....27 D2
St James's RC Prim Sch TW2 ....152 C1
St James's Rd SE1,SE16 ....118 A2
Hampton TW12 ....173 D5
Thornton Heath CR0 ....205 B2
St James's Sq SW1 ....115 C5 249 B4
St James's St E17 ....53 A4
SW1 ....115 C5 249 A4
St James's & St Michael's CE Prim Sch W2 ....114 A6 246 A6
St James St W6 ....112 C1
St James's Terr NW8 ....230 C4
2 Upper Tooting SW12 ....159 A3
St James's Terrace Mews NW8 ....230 C5
St James Street Sta E17 ....53 A4
St James's Wlk EC1 ....241 C6
St James The Great RC Prim Sch SE15 ....139 D4
South Norwood CR7 ....182 D1
St James Way DA14 ....191 A5
St Jerome's Gr UB3 ....83 A1
St Joachim's RC Prim Sch E16 ....99 C1
St Joan of Arc RC Prim Sch N5 ....73 A4
St Joan's Rd N9 ....17 D2
St John Baptist CE Prim Sch BR1 ....186 A6
St John CE Prim Sch SE17 ....117 A2 262 B3
St John Cl SW6 ....265 A4
St John Evangelist RC Prim Sch N1 ....94 D5 234 C4
St John Fisher RC Fst & Mid Sch HA5 ....41 C5
St John Fisher RC Prim Sch DA18 ....125 A3
Wembley UB6 ....87 C4
West Barnes SW20 ....200 D4
St John of Jerusalem CE Prim Sch E9 ....74 C1
St John Rigby RC Coll BR4 ....224 B4
St John's Angell Town CE Prim Sch SW9 ....138 C3
St John's Ave N11 ....30 D5
NW10 ....89 D6
Putney SW15 ....156 D6
St Johns CE Fst Sch HA7 ....25 B6
St John's CE Inf Sch NW4 ....46 B4
St John's CE JMI Sch N11 ....30 D6
St Johns CE Mid Sch HA7 ....25 A6
St John's CE Prim Sch
E2 ....96 C5
N20 ....14 A2
Buckhurst Hill IG9 ....21 B3
Fulham SW6 ....135 A4 264 B1
Kingston KT1 ....198 A6
Penge SE20 ....184 C3
St John's Church Rd E9 ....74 C3
St John's Cl N20 ....14 A1
St Johns Cl N14 ....15 C5
St John's Cl HA9 ....66 A3
St Johns Concert Hall SW1 ....260 A5
St John's Cotts 2 SE20 ....184 C3
St John's Cres SW9 ....138 C2
St Johns Ct 39 E1 ....118 B5
St John's Ct E11 ....54 D1
N4 ....72 D6
N5 ....72 D4
5 NW3 ....70 A2
SE13 ....142 A3
W6 ....112 B2
Buckhurst Hill IG9 ....21 B3
2 Harrow HA1 ....42 D3
Isleworth TW7 ....130 D3
Kingston KT1 ....198 A5
St Johns Dr KT12 ....194 C1
St John's Dr SW18 ....157 D3
St John's Est SE1 ....253 C1
St John's Gdns W11 ....113 B6 244 C5
St John's Gr N19 ....71 C6
3 Barnes SW13 ....133 D3
1 Richmond TW9 ....132 A1
St John's (Highbury Vale) CE Prim Sch N5 ....72 D5
St John's Hill SW11 ....136 B1
St John's Hill Gr SW11 136 B1
St Johns Ho 5 SE17 ....139 B6
St John's La EC1 ....94 D2 241 D4
St John's Mans E5 ....74 C3
St John's Par Ealing W13 ....109 B5
3 Sidcup DA14 ....190 B6
St John's Park Mans N19 ....71 C5
St John's Path EC1 ....241 C5
St John's Pk SE3 ....143 A5
St John's Pl EC1 ....241 C5
St John's Prim Sch W13 ....109 A6
St John's RC Prim Sch SE16 ....119 A4
St John's Rd DA16 ....146 B2
E16 ....99 A1
E6 ....100 A6
N15 ....51 C3
NW11 ....47 B3
SW11 ....136 C1
St Johns Rd Ilford IG2 ....57 C2
Kingston KT3 ....199 A6
St John's Rd
Barking IG11 ....101 C6
Carshalton SM5 ....218 C5
Chingford E17 ....36 A1
Chingford E4 ....35 D6
Croydon CR0 ....220 D5
East Molesey KT8 ....196 B5
Feltham TW13 ....173 B6
Harrow HA1 ....42 D3
Isleworth TW7 ....130 D3
Orpington BR5,BR6 ....211 C3
Penge SE20 ....184 C4
Richmond TW9 ....132 A1
Sidcup DA14 ....190 B6
Southall UB2 ....107 A3
Sutton SM1 ....217 D6
Teddington KT1 ....175 C1
Wembley HA9 ....66 A3
Wimbledon SW19 ....179 A4
St John's (Shirley) CE Prim Sch CR0 ....222 D5
St John's Sq EC1 ....94 D3 241 C5
St Johns Sta SE8 ....141 C3
St John's & St Clements CE Prim Sch SE15 ....140 A2
St John St EC1 ....94 D3 241 C6
St John's Terr E7 ....77 B2
SE18 ....145 B6
W10 ....90 D3
Enfield EN2 ....5 B6
St John & St James CE Prim Sch E9 ....74 C3
Edmonton N18 ....33 D5
St Johnstone Ho 15 N12 ....29 D6
St John's (Upper Holloway) Prim Sch N19 ....71 D6
St John's Vale SE8 ....141 C3
St John's Village 4 N11 ....30 D5
St John's Villas N19 ....71 D6
W8 ....255 D5
St John's Way N19 ....49 D1
St John's Wood Ct NW8 ....229 D1
St John's Wood High St NW8 ....92 C5 230 A3
St John's Wood Park NW8 ....92 B6 229 C6
St John's Wood Prep Sch NW8 ....92 C4 230 A1
St John's Wood Rd NW8 ....92 B4 229 D1
St John's Wood Sta NW8 ....92 B5 229 C4
St John's Wood Terr NW8 ....92 C5 230 A4
St John the Baptist CE Jun Sch KT1 ....175 D3
St John the Baptist CE Prim Sch N1 ....95 C5
St John the Divine CE Jun & Inf Sch SE5 ....138 D5
St John Vianney RC Prim Sch N8 ....50 D5
St Joseph RC Prim Sch W7 ....108 C5
St Joseph's Acad SE3 ....142 C2
St Josephs Cl BR6 ....227 D4
St Joseph's Cl W10 ....91 A2
St Joseph's Coll Mill Hill Missionaries NW7 ....27 D6
St Joseph's Convent Prep Sch KT8 ....196 A4
St Joseph's Convent Prim Sch NW4 ....46 B5
St Joseph's Convent Sch E11 ....55 A3
St Josephs Ct 10 E10 ....53 D2
3 NW10 ....89 D5
St Joseph's Ct E4 ....20 B4
St Joseph's Dr UB1 ....107 B5
St Joseph's Flats NW1 232 C2
St Josephs Gr NW4 ....46 B5
St Joseph's Ho W6 ....112 D2
St Joseph's Hospice E9, E8 ....96 B6
St Joseph's RC Coll SW16 ....182 D4
St Josephs RC Fst & Mid Sch HA3 ....25 A1
St Joseph's RC Inf Sch E10 ....75 C6
South Norwood SE19 ....183 A4
St Joseph's RC Jun & Inf Sch SE1 ....117 A4 252 B2
SE16 ....118 A4
SE16 ....118 C3
St Joseph's RC Jun & Inf Schs HA9 ....66 B3
St Joseph's RC Jun Sch E10 ....53 D1
SE5 ....139 A5
South Norwood SE19 ....183 A4
St Joseph's RC Prim Sch
N19 ....49 B1
NW10 ....67 C1
SE10 ....120 C1
SE8 ....141 C5
SW18 ....157 C6
SW3 ....114 D2 257 C3
W9 ....92 A4 229 A1
WC2 ....94 A1 240 B2
Barking IG11 ....101 A6
Dagenham RM9 ....81 B4
Kingston KT1 ....176 B1
St Joseph's RC Sch BR1 ....187 B3
St Joseph's Rd N9 ....18 C3
St Joseph's St SW8 ....268 D2
St Joseph's Vale SE3 ....142 B2
St Jude's CE Prim Sch SE24 ....160 D6
St Judes Ho 6 W10 ....91 B4
St Jude's Prim Sch SE1 ....116 D3 261 C5
St Jude's Rd E2 ....96 B5
St Jude's & St Paul's Prim Sch N1 ....73 C2
St Jude St N16 ....73 C3
St Julian's Cl SW16 ....182 C6
St Julian's Farm Rd SE27,SW16 ....182 D6
St Julian's Rd NW6 ....91 C6
St Katharine Docks★ E1 ....117 D5 253 D4
St Katharine's Ho N1 ....234 A4
St Katharine's Pier E1 ....117 D5 253 D4
St Katharine's Way E1 ....117 D5 253 D4
St Katherine's Prec NW1 ....231 C4
St Katherines Rd DA18 ....124 D4
St Katherine's Row EC3 ....243 B1
St Katherine's Wlk 1 W11 ....112 D5
St Keverne Rd SE9 ....188 A6
St Kilda Rd BR6 ....211 D1
Ealing W13 ....109 A4
St Kilda's Rd N16 ....51 C1
Harrow HA1 ....42 C3
St Kitts Terr SE19 ....183 C5
St Laurence's Cl NW6 ....90 D6
St Lawrence CE Jun & Mid Sch KT8 ....196 B5
St Lawrence Cl HA8 ....26 B3
St Lawrence Ct N1 ....235 D6
St Lawrence Dr HA5 ....40 B4
St Lawrence Ho SE1 ....263 B6
St Lawrence RC Sch TW13 ....150 B2
St Lawrence St E14 ....120 A5
St Lawrence Terr W10 .91 A2
St Lawrence Way SW9 ....138 C3
St Leonards Ave HA3 ....43 C4
St Leonard's Ave E4 ....36 B4
St Leonards CE Prim Sch SW16 ....181 D5
St Leonards Cl 4 DA16 ....146 A2
St Leonard's Ct N1 ....235 D2
St Leonards Ct SW14 ....133 A2
St Leonards Gdns IG1 .79 A3
St Leonard's Gdns TW5 ....129 A4
St Leonard's Hospl N1 .95 C5
St Leonard's Rd E14 ....98 A2
NW10 ....89 B3

St Leonards Rd SW14 .133 A2
St Leonard's Rd
Claygate KT10 .212 D2
Croydon CR0 .220 D5
Ealing W13 .109 C6
Kingston KT6 .197 D4
Thames Ditton KT7 .197 A2
St Leonards Rise BR6 .227 C4
St Leonard's Sq NW5 .71 A2
Kingston KT6 .197 D4
St Leonard's St E3 .97 D4
St Leonard's Terr
SW3 .114 D1 257 D1
St Leonard's Wlk
SW16 .182 B3
St Loo Ave
SW3 .136 C6 267 B6
St Loo Ct SW3 .267 C6
St Louis Rd SE27 .183 B6
St Loy's Rd N17 .51 D6
St Lucia Dr E15 .98 D6
St Luke Ct 5 E10 .53 D2
St Luke's Ave SW4 .137 D1
Enfield EN2 .5 B5
Ilford IG1 .78 D3
St Luke's CE Prim Sch
E14 .120 B2
St Luke's CE Prim Sch
EC1 .235 A2
W9 .91 B4
Kingston KT2 .176 B2
Richmond TW9 .132 C4
West Norwood SE27 .183 A5
St Luke's Cl EC1 95 A3 242 B6
Croydon SE25 .206 B3
St Luke's Ct W11 .91 B1
St Luke's Hospl
W1 .93 C3 239 A5
St Luke's Mews W11 .91 B1
St Luke's Path 1 IG1 .78 D3
St Luke's Prim Sch
E16 .98 D1
St Luke's Rd W11 .91 B2
Uxbridge UB10 .60 A1
St Luke's Sq E16 .98 D1
St Luke's St SW3 .257 B2
St Luke's Woodside Hospl
N10 .49 A5
St Malo Ave N9 .18 C1
St Margaret Clitherow RC
Prim Sch
NW10 .67 A4
Woolwich SE28 .124 B5
St Margarets IG11 .101 B6
St Margarets Ave
DA15 .167 B1
N20 .14 A3
St Margaret's Ave N8,
N15 .50 D5
St Margarets Ave
Ashford TW15 .170 D5
Hillingdon UB8 .82 C3
St Margaret's Ave
Cheam SM3 .217 A5
Harrow HA2 .64 A5
St Margarets Bsns Ctr 11
TW1 .153 B5
St Margaret's CE Prim Sch
SE18 .123 A1
Barking IG11 .79 A1
St Margaret's Cres
SW15 .156 B6
St Margaret's Ct E15 .76 C4
Putney SW15 .134 B1
9 Twickenham TW1 .153 B5
St Margaret's Dr TW1 .153 B6
St Margaret's Gr E11 .76 D5
SE18 .145 A6
Twickenham TW1 .153 A5
St Margaret's La
W8 .113 D3 255 C5
St Margaret's Lee CE Prim
Sch SE13 .142 C1
St Margarets Lo W3 .110 D4
St Margaret's Rd N17 .51 C6
NW10 .90 C4
SE4 .141 B1
W7 .108 C4
St Margarets Rd
Edgware HA8 .26 D5
Ruislip HA4 .39 B3
St Margaret's Rd
Isleworth TW1 .153 B6
Wanstead E12 .77 C6
St Margarets Rdbt
TW1 .153 B6
St Margaret's Sch NW3 69 D4
St Margaret's Sta TW1 153 B5
St Margaret St SW1 .250 A1
St Margaret's Terr
SE18 .123 A1
St Mark's CE Prim Sch
BR2 .209 A6
SE11 .138 B6 270 D6
Croydon SE25 .206 A5
St Marks Cl 5 SE10 .142 A5
St Mark's Cl Barnet EN5 .1 D2
Harrow HA1 .43 B1
St Mark's Cres
NW1 .93 A6 231 B6
St Mark's Ct 7 E10 .53 D2
W7 .108 C4
St Mark's Fst Sch CR4 180 D1
St Marks Gate E9 .75 B1
St Mark's Gr
SW10 .135 D5 265 D4
St Mark's Hill KT6 .198 A3
St Marks Ho 6 SE17 .139 B6
St Mark's Ho 8 E17 .54 A5
St Mark's Hospl
EC1 .94 D4 234 D2
St Marks Ind Est E16 .121 D5
St Mark's Pl W11 .91 A1
Wimbledon SW19 .179 B4
St Mark's Prim Sch
N19 .72 A6
W7 .108 C4
St Mark's RC Sch TW3 129 C2
St Mark's Rd W10 .90 D2
W11 .91 A1
W7 .108 C4
Bromley BR2 .209 B6
Croydon SE25 .206 A5
Ealing W5 .110 A5
Enfield EN1 .17 D6
Mitcham CR4 .181 A1
Teddington TW11 .175 B3
St Mark's Rise E8 .73 D3
St Mark's Sq NW1 .231 A5
St Mark St E1 .95 D1 243 D1
St Martha's Convent Jun
Sch for Girls EN5 .1 A1
St Martin-in-the-Fields
High Sch for Girls
SW2 .160 C3
St Martin of Porres RC Prim
Sch N11 .31 C4
St Martin's Almshos
NW1 .232 A6
St Martin's App HA4 .39 C2
St Martin's Ave E6 .99 D5
St Martins Cl DA18 .124 D4
St Martin's Cl NW1 .232 A6
St Martins Cl WD19 .22 C6
St Martin's Cl EN1 .6 B4
St Martins Ct N1 .95 C6
St Martin's Ct WC2 .250 A6
West Norwood SE27 .160 D2
St Martin's La
WC2 .116 A6 250 A5
St Martins La BR3 .207 D4
St Martin's Le Grand
EC1 .242 A2
St Martin's Pl WC2 .250 A5
St Martin's Rd N2 .30 B2
SW9 .138 B3
Edmonton N9 .18 B2
St Martin's Sch NW7 .27 B5
St Martin's St WC2 .249 D5
St Martin's Way SW17 158 A1
St Mary Abbots CE Prim
Sch W8 .113 D4 245 C1
St Mary Abbot's Ct
W14 .254 C5
St Mary Abbot's Pl
W8 .254 D5
St Mary Abbots Terr
W14 .254 D5
St Mary at Hill
EC3 .117 C6 253 A5
St Mary Ave SM6 .219 B5
St Mary Axe
EC3 .95 C1 243 B2
St Marychurch St
SE16 .118 C4
St Mary Graces Ct E1 .253 D5
St Marylebone CE Sch The
W1 .93 A2 238 A3
St Mary le Bow Church★
EC2 .242 B1
St Mary- le-Park Ct
SW11 .267 B3
St Mary Magdalene CE Prim
Sch
N7 .72 C2
SE15 .140 B3
W2 .91 D2
St Mary Magdalens RC Prim
Sch SE4 .141 A1
St Mary Magdalen's RC
Prim Sch SW14 .133 B2
St Mary Magdelen's RC Jun
Sch NW2 .68 B2
St Mary Newington Cl
SE17 .263 B2
St Mary of the Angels RC
Prim Sch W2 .91 C1
St Mary RC Prim Sch
W10 .91 A3
St Mary Rd E17 .53 D5
St Marys IG11 .101 B6
St Mary's App E12 .78 B3
St Mary's Ave N3 .29 B1
St Marys Ave UB2 .107 D2
St Mary's Ave
Beckenham BR2 .208 C6
Teddington TW11 .174 D4
St Mary's Ave *continued*
Wanstead E11 .55 B2
St Mary's Bryanston Square
CE Sch W1 .92 D2 237 C4
St Mary's CE High Sch
(Lower & Upper) NW4 46 C6
St Mary's CE High Sch
(Middle) NW4 .46 C6
St Mary's CE Inf Sch N8 50 B5
St Mary's CE Jun Sch
N8 .50 A5
NW4 .46 B4
St Mary's CE Prim Sch
E17 .53 D5
N1 .94 D6 234 D6
N3 .29 B3
NW10 .67 C2
SE18 .122 C2
Chessington KT9 .214 B2
East Barnet EN4 .14 C5
Long Ditton KT7 .197 B1
Putney SW15 .134 D2
St Mary's CE Sch
TW19 .148 A4
St Mary's Church Sch
TW1 .153 A4
St Mary's Cl BR5 .190 B1
Chessington KT9 .214 B1
Ewell KT17 .215 D1
Sunbury TW16 .194 A5
Tottenham N17 .34 A2
St Mary's Coll TW1 .152 D1
St Mary's Cottage Hospl
TW12 .173 B2
St Mary's Cres
Hayes UB3 .105 D6
Hendon NW4 .46 B6
Hounslow TW7 .130 C5
St Marys Ct E6 .100 B3
SE7 .143 D5
St Mary's Ct E11 .54 D1
N12 .30 A3
W5 .109 D4
W6 .111 D3
Kingston KT3 .199 C6
Wallington SM6 .219 C4
St Mary's Dr TW14 .149 A4
St Mary's Est 2 SE16 .118 C4
St Mary's Flats NW1 .232 C2
St Mary's Gate W8 .255 C5
St Mary's Gdns SE11 .261 B4
St Mary's Gn 1 N2 .48 A6
St Mary's Gr N1 .72 D2
Barnes SW13 .134 B2
Chiswick W4 .132 D6
Richmond TW10,TW9 .132 B1
St Mary's Ho N1 .234 D6
W5 .109 D3
St Mary's Hospl
W2 .92 B1 236 D2
St Mary's Inf Sch E17 .53 D5
St Mary's Kilburn CE Prim
Sch NW6 .91 C6
St Mary's Lewisham CE
Prim Sch SE13 .163 D6
St Mary's Lo E11 .55 B3
St Mary's Mans NW10 .89 C6
W2 .92 B2 236 C4
St Mary's Medical Sch
W2 .92 B1 236 D2
St Mary's Mews NW6 .69 D1
St Mary's Path N1 .234 D6
St Mary's Pl SE9 .166 C5
W5 .109 D4
W8 .113 D3 255 C5
St Mary's RC High Sch
CR0 .205 A1
St Mary's RC Inf Sch
CR0 .205 B1
St Mary's RC Jun & Inf Schs
N15 .51 B4
St Mary's RC Jun Sch
E17 .54 A6
Croydon CR0 .205 B1
Wallington SM5 .218 D3
St Mary's RC Prim Sch
NW6 .91 C5
SE9 .166 C6
SW4 .159 C6
SW8 .137 B4 268 D2
W14 .112 D3
Beckenham BR3 .186 A3
Chingford E4 .20 B3
Chiswick W4 .133 C6
Enfield EN3 .6 D1
Isleworth TW7 .131 A2
Merton SW19 .179 C3
St Mary's RC Sch TW7 131 A2
St Mary's Rd E10 .76 A6
E13 .99 B5
N2 .30 B2
N8 .50 A5
N9 .18 C3
NW10 .89 C6
NW11 .47 A2
SE15 .140 C3
St Marys Rd IG1 .79 B6
St Mary's Rd Ealing W5 109 D5
East Barnet EN4 .14 D4
St Mary's Rd *continued*
East Molesey KT8 .196 B4
Hayes UB3 .105 D6
Long Ditton KT6 .197 C1
South Norwood SE25 .205 C6
Surbiton KT6 .197 D3
Wimbledon SW19 .179 B5
Worcester Park KT4 .215 C6
St Mary's Roman Catholic
Inf Sch SM5 .218 D4
St Mary's Sch Hampstead
NW3 .70 B3
St Mary's Sq W2 .236 C4
W5 .109 D4
St Mary's Stoke Newington
CE Prim Sch N16 .73 C6
St Mary's & St Peter's CE
Prim Sch TW11 .174 D5
St Mary St SE18 .122 C2
St Mary's Terr W2 .236 C4
St Mary & St Joseph's Sch
DA14 .190 A5
St Mary & St Michael Prim
Sch E1 .96 C1
St Mary & St Pancras CE
Prim Sch NW1 93 D5 232 C3
St Mary's Twr EC1 .242 B5
St Marys View HA3 .43 C4
St Mary's Wlk SE11 .261 B4
Hayes UB3 .105 D6
St Matthew's Ave KT6 .198 B1
St Matthew's CE Fst Sch
SW20 .178 A2
St Matthew's CE Prim Sch
Enfield EN3 .18 C6
Surbiton KT6 .198 A2
Yiewsley UB7 .104 A5
St Matthews Ct 6 E10 .53 D2
E15 .76 D1
N10 .31 A1
SE1 .262 A5
St Matthew's Ct TW15 170 C5
St Matthews Dr BR1 .210 B6
St Matthew's Ho 8
SE17 .139 B6
St Matthew's Lo NW1 .232 B4
St Matthew's Rd SW2 .160 B6
Ealing W5 .110 A5
St Matthew's Row E2 .96 A3
St Matthews Sch
Westminster
SW1 .115 D3 259 D6
St Matthew St SW1 .259 C5
St Matthias CE Prim Sch
E2 .95 D3 243 D6
St Matthias Cl NW9 .45 D4
St Matthias's CE Prim Sch
N16 .73 C4
St Maur Rd
SW6 .135 B4 264 D1
St Mellion Cl SE28 .102 D1
St Merryn Cl SE18 .145 B5
St Merryn Ct BR3 .185 C3
St Michael-at-Bowes CE
Jun Sch N13 .32 C4
St Michael's Alley EC3 242 D1
St Michaels Ave N9 .18 C4
St Michael's Ave HA9 .66 C2
St Michael's CE Jun & Inf
Sch N22 .32 B2
St Michael's CE Prim Sch
N6 .49 A2
NW1 .93 C6 232 A6
Enfield EN2 .5 A4
Forest Hill SE26 .185 A6
Wandsworth SW18 .157 B4
St Michaels Cl BR1 .210 A6
4 E16 .99 D2
St Michael's Cl DA18 .124 D4
N12 .30 C5
N3 .29 B1
St Michaels Cl KT4 .215 D6
St Michael's Cres HA5 .41 A3
St Michaels Ct E14 .98 A2
St Michael's Ct N11 .15 A1
NW11 .47 B2
St Michael's East Wickham
CE Sch DA16 .146 C4
St Michael's Flats
NW1 .232 C3
St Michael's Gdns W10 91 A2
St Michael's Hospl EN2 .5 B4
St Michael's RC Gram Sch
N12 .30 A5
St Michael's RC Prim Sch
E6 .100 B5
Ashford TW15 .170 C5
St Michael's RC Sch
SE16 .118 A4
St Michael's Rd DA16 .146 B2
NW2 .68 C4
SW9 .138 B3
St Michaels Rd TW15 .170 C5
St Michael's Rd
Croydon CR0 .205 A1
Wallington SM6 .219 C2
St Michael's Rise
DA16 .146 B4
St Michael's St
W2 .92 C1 237 A2
St Michael's Terr N22 .32 A2
St Michael & St Martin RC
Prim Sch TW4 .129 B2
St Michael Twr E17 .53 B4
St Mildred's Ct EC2 .242 C1
St Mildreds Rd SE12,
SE6 .164 D4
St Mirren Ct EN5 .14 A6
St Monica's RC Prim Sch
N1 .95 C4
St Nicholas CE JMI Sch
WD6 .9 D5
St Nicholas CE Prim Sch
TW17 .192 D3
St Nicholas Cl WD6 .9 D5
St Nicholas Ct SE18 .123 D1
St Nicholas Ctr SM1 .217 D3
St Nicholas Dr TW17 .192 C2
St Nicholas Elstree CE Prim
Sch WD6 .9 D5
St Nicholas' Flats
NW1 .232 C3
St Nicholas Glebe
SW17 .181 A4
St Nicholas Ho SE8 .141 C6
St Nicholas Rd SE18 .123 D2
Sutton SM1 .217 D3
Thames Ditton KT7 .196 D3
St Nicholas Sch NW9 .67 A6
St Nicholas St SE8 .141 C4
St Nicholas Way SM1 .217 D3
St Nicolas La BR7 .188 A2
St Ninian's Ct N20 .14 D1
St Norbert Gn SE4 .141 A1
St Norbert Rd SE4 .141 A1
St Olaf's Rd
SW6 .135 A5 264 B3
St Olaves Ct W2 .245 C5
St Olave's Ct EC2 .242 C1
St Olave's Est SE1 .253 B2
St Olave's Gdns SE11 .261 A4
St Olave's Mans SE11 .261 A4
St Olaves Prep Sch
SE9 .166 D2
St Olave's Rd E6 .100 C6
St Olave's Wlk SW16 .181 D1
St Olav's Sq 27 SE16 .118 C4
St Osmund's RC Prim Sch
SW13 .133 D4
St Oswald's Pl
SE11 .116 B1 260 C1
St Oswald's Rd SW16 .182 D2
St Oswulf St SW1 .259 D3
St Owen Ho SE1 .263 B6
St Pancras Almshouses 13
NW5 .70 D3
St Pancras Commercial Ctr
NW1 .232 B6
St Pancras Ct N2 .30 B1
St Pancras Hospl
NW1 .93 D6 232 C5
St Pancras Sta
WC1 .94 A4 233 A2
St Pancras Way
NW1 .93 C6 232 C6
St Patrick's RC Inf Sch
E1 .118 B5
St Patrick's RC Prim Sch
E17 .53 A5
NW5 .71 B3
SE18 .123 B2
St Paul's & All Hallows CE
Jun & Inf Sch N17 .34 A3
St Paul's Ave NW2 .68 C2
SE16 .118 D5
Harrow HA3 .44 B5
St Paul's Cath★
EC4 .95 A1 242 A1
St Paul's Catholic Coll
TW16 .172 A2
St Pauls Catholic Sch
TW16 .172 A2
St Paul's Cath Sch
EC4 .95 A1 242 A1
St Paul's CE Jun Sch
KT2 .176 C3
St Paul's CE Prim Sch
N11 .31 B5
NW3 .70 D1
NW7 .28 B6
SE17 .262 B2
W6 .112 C1
St Pauls CE Prim Sch
TW8 .131 D6
St Paul's CE Prim Sch
Chessington KT9 .214 A4
Southgate N21 .16 D4
St Paul's Church Yd
EC4 .95 A1 242 A1
St Pauls Cl W5 .110 B4
St Paul's Cl SE7 .121 D1
St Pauls Cl UB3 .105 B1
St Paul's Cl
Ashford TW15 .171 A5
Carshalton SM5 .202 C1
Chessington KT9 .213 D4
Hounslow TW3,TW4 .129 A3
St Paul's Cray Rd BR7 .189 B2
St Pauls Cres NW1 .71 D1
St Paul's Ct 5 N19 .72 A6
SW4 .137 D1
Hounslow TW4 .129 A2
St Paul's Dr E15 .76 B3
St Paul's Girls' Sch
W6 .112 D2
St Pauls Mews NW1 .71 D1
St Paul's Pl N1 .73 B2
St Paul's RC Prim Sch
Thames Ditton KT7 .196 C2
Wood Green N22 .32 B1
St Paul's RC Sec Sch
SE2 .146 A6
St Paul's Rd N1 .73 A2
St Pauls Rd
Barking IG11 .101 A6
Richmond TW9 .132 B2
St Paul's Rd
Brentford TW8 .131 D6
South Norwood CR7 .205 A6
Tottenham N17 .34 A2
St Pauls Rise N13 .32 D4
St Paul's Sch SW13 .112 A1
St Paul's Sq BR2 .187 A1
St Paul's Sta
EC2 .95 A1 242 A2
St Paul St N1 .235 B5
St Paul's Terr SE17 .138 D6
St Paul's Twr 13 E10 .53 D2
St Pauls View WC1 .234 A1
St Paul's Way E3 .97 C2
N3 .29 D3
St Paul's Way Com Sch
E3 .97 C2
St Paul's Whitechapel CE
Prim Sch E1 .118 A6
St Paul's with St Michael's
Prim Sch E8 .96 A6
St Paul's Wood Hill
BR5,BR7 .189 D1
St Paul with St Luke CE
Prim Sch E3 .97 B2
St Peter Chanel RC Prim
Sch DA14 .190 C5
St Peter in Chains RC Inf
Sch N8 .50 A3
SS Peter & Paul RC Prim
Sch BR5 .189 C1
SS Peter & Paul's RC Prim
Sch
Ilford IG1 .79 B5
Mitcham CR4 .202 D5
St Peter's Alley EC3 .242 D1
St Peters Ave N12 .30 C3
St Peter's Ave N18 .34 A6
St Petersburgh Mews
W2 .245 C6
St Petersburgh Pl
W2 .113 D6 245 C5
St Peter's CE Prim Sch
SE17 .262 D1
W9 .91 C3
St Peter's Church Ct
N1 .234 D5
St Peters Cl BR7 .189 B3
St Peter's Cl E2 .96 A5
St Peters Cl Ilford IG2 .57 D5
Upper Tooting SW17 .158 C2
St Peter's Cl Barnet EN5 .12 B6
Bushey WD23 .8 B3
Ruislip HA4 .62 D6
St Peters Ct SE12 .164 D6
SE4 .141 B3
St Peter's Ct NW4 .46 C4
St Peters Ct KT8 .195 C5
St Peter's Eaton Square CE
Sch SW1 .115 B3 258 D5
St Peter's Gdns SE27 .160 C1
St Peter's Gr W6 .112 A2
St Peters Ho N15 .52 A5
WC1 .233 B1
St Peter's Ho N16 .51 C2
4 SE17 .139 B6
St Peters La BR5 .190 A1
St Peter's London Docks CE
Prim Sch E1 .118 C5
St Peter's Path E17 .54 C5
St Peter's Pl W9 .91 D3
St Peter's Prim Sch
W6 .112 A1
South Croydon CR2 .221 C2
St Peter's RC Prim Sch
SE18 .122 D2
Dagenham RM9 .103 B6
St Peter's Rd W6 .112 A1
St Peters Rd KT1 .176 C1
St Peter's Rd
Croydon CR0 .221 B4
East Molesey KT8 .195 C5
Edmonton N9 .18 B3
Isleworth TW1 .153 B6
Southall UB1 .85 C2
St Peter's Sq E2 .96 A5
W6 .111 D1

St Peter's St N1 94 D6 234 D5
Croydon CR2 221 B3
St Peters & St Pauls RC Prim Sch EC1 94 D3 241 D6
St Peter's Street Mews N1 234 D4
St Peter's Terr SW6 264 B3
St Peter's Villas 5 W6 112 A2
St Peter's Way N1 73 C1
St Peters Way UB3 105 B1
St Peter's Way W5 87 D2
St Philip Ho WC1 234 A1
St Philip's Ave KT4 216 B6
St Philip Sq 1 SW8 137 B3
St Philip's Rd E8 74 A2
Surbiton KT6 197 D3
St Philip's Sch SW7 256 B4
Chessington KT9 213 D2
St Philip St SW8 137 B3
St Philip's Way N1 235 B5
St Philomena's Sch SM5 218 C3
St Quentin Ho SW18 158 B5
St Quentin Rd DA16 145 D2
St Quintin Ave W10 90 D2
St Quintin Gdns W10 90 C2
St Quintin Rd E13 99 B5
St Raphael's RC Prim Sch UB5 84 B5
St Raphael's Way NW10 67 A3
St Regis Cl N10 31 B1
St Regis Hts NW3 69 D5
St Richard of Chichester RC Sec Sch NW1 71 C1
St Richards Ct TW10 153 B1
St Richard's with St Andrew's CE Prim Sch TW10 153 B1
St Ronan's 2 N3 29 C2
St Ronans Cl EN4 2 B5
St Ronans Cres IG8 37 A3
St Rule St SW8 137 C3
St Savior's CE Inf Sch W5 109 D6
St Saviours SW4 137 B1
St Saviour's CE Prim Sch
E14 97 D2
E17 53 B2
SE24 139 A2
W9 91 D3
St Saviour's Coll SE27 183 B6
St Saviours Ct N22 31 D1
Harrow HA1 42 C4
St Saviours Ho 4 SE1 118 A4
St Saviour's RC Prim Sch SE13 142 A1
St Saviour's Rd SW2 160 B6
Thornton Heath CR0 205 A3
St Saviours & St Olaves CE Sch SE1 117 B3 262 D5
St Saviour's Wharf SE1 253 D2
St Scholastica's RC Prim Sch E5 74 A5
Saints Cl SE27 182 D6
Saints Dr E7 77 D3
St Silas Pl NW5 71 A2
St Simon's Ave SW15 156 C6
St Stephen's Ave E17 54 A4
W12 112 B4
Ealing W13 87 B1
St Stephen's CE Prim Sch
SE8 141 C3
SW8 138 B5 270 C4
W12 112 C4
W2 91 C2
St Stephen's Cl E17 53 D4
NW5 70 D3
NW8 230 B5
Southall UB1 85 C2
St Stephen's Cres W2 91 C1
Thornton Heath CR7 204 C6
St Stephens Ct N8 50 B3
Ealing W13 87 B1
St Stephen's Gdns W2 91 C1
3 Putney SW15 157 B6
Twickenham TW1 153 C5
St Stephen's Gr SE13 142 A2
St Stephens Ho 7 SE17 139 B6
St Stephen's Mews 34 W2 91 C2
St Stephens Par E6 77 C1
St Stephens Prim Sch E6 77 C1
St Stephen's RC Prim Sch DA16 146 A3
St Stephens Rd E6 77 C1
St Stephen's Rd E17 53 D4
E3 97 B5
St Stephens Rd EN5 12 D6
St Stephen's Rd
Ealing W13 87 C1
Enfield EN3 6 D6
Hounslow TW3,TW4 151 C6
St Stephen's Rd *continued*
Yiewsley UB7 104 A5
St Stephen's Row EC4 242 C1
St Stephen's Terr SW8 270 C3
St Swithin's La EC4 117 B6 252 C6
St Swithun's Rd SE13 164 B6
St Swithun Wells RC Prim Sch HA4 62 D5
St Teresa RC Prim Sch The RM8 80 C4
St Teresa's RC Fst & Mid Sch HA3 24 A2
St Teresa's RC Prim Sch SM4 202 B3
St Theresa Ct E4 20 B4
St Theresa's RC Sch N3 47 D6
St Theresa's Rd TW14 127 D1
St Thomas a Beckett RC Prim Sch SE2 124 A3
St Thomas Becket RC Prim Sch SE25 206 A3
St Thomas' CE Prim Sch
N16 52 A1
W10 91 A3
St Thomas' Cl KT6 198 B1
St Thomas Ct 10 E10 53 D2
Sidcup DA5 169 C4
St Thomas' Dr BR5 211 A1
Pinner HA5 23 A2
St Thomas' Gdns NW5 71 A2
St Thomas Gdns IG1 79 A2
St Thomas Ho 2 E1 96 D1
St Thomas More RC Prim Sch
SE9 144 A2
Bexley DA7 147 B3
St Thomas More RC Sch
SE9 166 C5
SW3 114 D2 257 C3
East Molesey KT8 196 A4
St Thomas More Sch N22 32 C3
St Thomas of Canterbury RC Mid Sch CR4 203 A6
St Thomas of Canterbury RC Prim Sch SW6 135 B5 264 C4
St Thomas Rd E16 99 A1
N14 15 D4
St Thomas' Rd W4 133 A6
St Thomas's Hospl SE1 116 B3 260 C6
St Thomas's Hospl Medical Sch SE1 116 B3 260 C5
St Thomas's Pl 20 E9 74 C1
St Thomas's Rd N4,N5 72 C5
NW10 89 C6
St Thomas's Sq E9 74 C1
St Thomas St SE1 117 B5 252 D3
St Thomas's Way SW6 135 B5 264 D4
St Thomas the Apostle Coll The SE15 140 C4
St Timothy's Mews 3 BR1 187 B2
St Ursula Gr HA5 41 A4
St Ursula Rd UB1 85 C1
St Ursula's Convent Sch SE10 142 B5
St Vincent Cl SE27 182 D5
St Vincent De Paul Ho 20 E1 96 C2
St Vincent De Paul RC Prim Sch SW1 115 C3 259 B6
St Vincent Ho SE1 263 C6
St Vincent Rd TW2 152 A5
St Vincent's Hospl HA5 39 D6
St Vincents RC Prim Sch SE9 188 A6
St Vincent's RC Prim Sch
W1 93 A2 238 B3
Acton W3 110 D6
Dagenham RM8 80 C6
St Vincent's RC Sch NW7 28 C5
St Vincent St W1 238 B3
St Wilfrid's Cl EN4 14 C6
St Wilfrid's Rd EN4 14 C6
St William of York RC Prim Sch SE23 163 A3
St William of York RC Sec Boys Sch (Upper) N1 72 A1
St Winefride's Ave E12 78 B3
St Winefride's RC Prim Sch E12 78 B3
St Winifred's RC Inf Sch SE12 164 C6
St Winifred's RC Jun Sch SE12 164 D4
St Winifred's Rd TW11 175 B4
Sala Ho SE3 143 B1
Salamanca Pl SE1 260 C3
Salamanca St SE1,SE11 116 B2 260 C3
Salamander Cl KT2 175 C5
Salamander Quay KT1 175 D2
Salcombe Dr
Dagenham RM6 59 B3
North Cheam SM4 200 D1
Salcombe Gdns NW7 28 C4
SW4 137 B1
Salcombe Ho 6 SE23 162 C2
Salcombe Lo NW5 71 A4
Salcombe Pk IG10 21 D6
Salcombe Prep Sch N14 15 B4
Salcombe Rd E17 53 B2
23 N16 73 C3
Ashford TW15 148 A1
Salcombe Villas 13 TW10 154 A6
Salcombe Way
Hayes UB4 83 C4
Ruislip HA4 62 A6
Salcot N4 72 B6
Salcott Rd SW11 158 D6
Wallington CR0 220 B4
Salehurst Cl HA3 44 A4
Salehurst Rd SE4 163 B5
Salem Ho 13 E9 74 D2
Salem Pl CR0 221 A5
Salem Rd W2 113 D6 245 D6
Sale Pl W2 92 C1 237 A2
Salesian Coll SW11 136 C4 267 A1
Sale St E2 96 A3
Salford Ho 4 E14 120 A2
Salford Rd SW12,SW2 159 D3
Salhouse Cl SE28 102 C1
Salisbury Ave N3 47 B6
Barking IG11 79 C1
Cheam SM1,SM2 217 B2
Salisbury Cl SE17 262 C4
Worcester Park KT4 215 D5
Salisbury Ct E9 75 A3
EC4 241 C1
N3 29 B1
15 SE16 118 A3
W4 111 C2
Edgware HA8 26 B6
Enfield EN2 5 B1
Northolt UB5 63 D3
Salisbury Gdns
Buckhurst Hill IG9 21 D2
Wimbledon SW19 179 A3
Salisbury Hall Gdns E4 35 C4
Salisbury Ho 3 E14 97 D1
N1 234 C6
SW1 259 D2
1 Ruislip HA4 40 C1
Stanmore HA7 25 A4
Wimbledon SW19 156 D1
Salisbury Lower Sch N9 18 C4
Salisbury Mans N4,N15 50 D4
Salisbury Mews BR2 210 A4
SW6 264 C3
Salisbury Pl SW9 138 D5
W1 237 C4
Salisbury Prim Sch E12 78 A3
Salisbury Rd BR2 210 A4
DA5 169 C3
E10 76 A6
E12 77 D3
E17 54 A4
E7 77 A2
N4 50 D4
W13 109 B4
Barnet EN5 1 A2
Chingford E4 19 C1
Croydon SE25 206 A3
Dagenham RM10 81 D2
East Bedfont TW6 149 A5
Edmonton N9 18 A1
Enfield EN3 7 B6
Feltham TW13 150 C3
Harrow HA1 42 B4
Hounslow TW4 128 C2
Ilford IG3 79 C6
Kingston KT3 199 B6
Pinner HA5 40 A5
Richmond TW9 132 A1
Southall UB2 107 A2
Tottenham N22 32 D1
Wallington SM5 218 D2
Wimbledon SW19 179 A3
Worcester Park KT4 215 C5
Salisbury Sq EC4 241 B1
Salisbury St NW8 237 A5
10 Acton W3 111 A4
Salisbury Terr SE15 140 C2
Salisbury Upper Sch N9 18 C4
Salisbury Wlk N19 71 C6
Salix Cl TW16 172 B3
Salix Ct N3 29 C4
Salliesfield TW2 152 B5
Sally Murray Cl E12 78 C4
Salmen Rd E13 98 D5
Salmond Cl HA7 25 A4
Salmon La E14 97 A1
Salmon Rd DA17 125 C1
Salmons Rd
Chessington KT9 214 A2
Salmons Rd *continued*
Edmonton N9 18 A3
Salmon St 6 E14 97 B1
NW9 45 A2
Salomons Rd E13 99 C2
Salop Rd E17 52 D3
Saltash Cl SM1 217 B4
Saltash Rd DA16 146 C4
Saltcoats Rd W4 111 C4
Saltcroft Cl HA9 44 D1
Saltdene N4 50 B1
Salter Cl HA2 63 B4
Salterford Rd SW17 181 A4
Salter Ho 8 SW16 181 C6
Salter Rd SE16 119 A5
Salters' Hall Ct EC4 252 C6
Salter's Hill SE19 183 B5
Salters Rd E17 54 B5
W10 90 D3
Salter St 10 E14 119 C6
NW10 90 A4
Salterton Rd N7 72 B5
Salt Hill Cl UB8 60 A3
Saltley Cl E6 100 A1
Saltoun Rd SW2,SW9 138 C1
Saltram Cl N15 51 D5
Saltram Cres W9 91 C4
Saltwell St E14 119 C6
Saltwood Gr SE17 262 C1
Salusbury Prim Sch NW6 91 B6
Salusbury Rd NW6 91 A6
Salutation Rd SE10 120 C2
Salvador SW17 180 D5
Salvatorian RC Coll HA3 24 C1
Salvia Gdns UB6 87 A5
Salvin Rd SW15 134 D2
Salway Cl IG8 37 A3
Salway Ho E10 75 D6
SW8 270 B2
Salway Pl E15 76 C2
Salway Rd E15 76 B2
Salween Ho 2 N16 73 B4
Samantha Cl E17 53 B2
Samantha Ct E11 54 C2
Samaritan Hospl for Women NW1 237 C4
Sam Bartram Cl SE7 121 C1
Sambrooke Ct EN1 17 D6
Sambrook Ho 19 E1 96 C2
Sambruck Mews SE6 163 D3
Samels Ct W6 112 A1
Samford Ho N1 234 A5
Samford St NW8 92 C3 237 A5
Samira Cl E17 53 C3
Sam Manners Ho 7 SE10 120 C1
Sam March Ho 5 E14 98 B1
Samos Rd SE20 184 B1
Sampson Ave EN5 12 D6
Sampson Cl DA17 125 A3
Sampson Ct TW17 193 A4
Sampson St E1 118 A5
Samson Ho SE18 123 A2
Samson St E13 99 C5
Samuel Cl E8 95 D6
SE14 140 D6
SE18 122 A2
Samuel Ct BR3 207 D6
Samuel Gray Gdns KT2 175 D2
Samuel Ho 15 E8 95 D6
Samuel Johnson Cl SW16 182 B6
Samuel Jones Ind Est 15 SE15 139 C5
Samuel Lewis Bldgs N1 72 C2
Samuel Lewis Trust Dwellings
6 SE5 139 A4
SW3 257 A3
SW6 135 C5 265 B4
W14 254 B4
Samuel Lewis Trust Est N15 51 C3
Samuel Rhodes Sch N1 94 C6 234 A6
Samuel Richardson Ho W14 254 C3
Samuel's Cl 2 W6 112 C2
Samuel St 6 SE15 139 D5
SE18 122 B2
Sancroft Cl NW2 68 B5
Sancroft Ct SW11 267 B2
Sancroft Rd HA3 25 A1
Sancroft St SE11 116 C1 260 D2
Sanctuary Rd TW19, TW6 148 C5
Sanctuary St SE1 252 B2
Sanctuary The DA5 168 D5
35 E1 118 B5
SW1 115 D3 259 D6
Morden SM4 201 C3
Sandale Cl N16 73 B5
Sandall Cl W5 88 A3
Sandall Ho 6 E3 97 A5
Sandall Rd NW5 71 C2
Ealing W5 88 A3
Sandal Rd Edmonton N18 34 A5
New Malden KT3 199 C5
Sandal St E15 98 C6
Sandalwood Cl 10 E1 97 A3
Sandalwood Dr HA4 39 A2
Sandalwood Ho DA15 167 D1
6 NW3 69 D2
Sandalwood Rd TW13 150 B1
Sandbach Pl SE18 123 A1
Sandbourne 12 NW8 91 D6
4 W11 91 C1
Sandbourne Ave SW19 179 D1
Sandbourne Rd SE4 141 A3
Sandbrook Cl NW7 27 B4
Sandbrook Rd N16 73 C5
Sandby Ct BR3 185 B2
Sandby Gn SE9 144 A2
Sandby Ho 6 NW6 91 C6
11 SE5 139 C4
Sandcroft Cl N13 32 D4
Sandcroft Ho SE11 260 D2
Sandells Ave
Ashford TW15 171 A6
Ashford TW15 171 A6
Sandell St SE1 251 A2
Sanderling Ct 20 SE8 141 B6
Woolwich SE28 124 C6
Sanders Cl TW12 174 A5
Sanders Ho WC1 234 A2
Streatham SW16 182 A4
Sanders La NW7 28 C3
Sanderson Cl NW5 71 B4
Sanderson Ho 7 SE8 119 B1
Sanderstead Ave NW2 69 A6
Sanderstead Cl SW12 159 C4
Sanderstead Rd
South Croydon CR2 221 B1
Walthamstow E10 53 A1
Sanders Way 3 N19 49 D1
Sandfield WC1 233 B1
Sandfield Gdns CR7 204 D6
Sandfield Pl CR7 205 A6
Sandfield Rd CR7 204 D6
Sandford Ave N22 33 A2
Sandford Cl E6 100 B3
Sandford Ct N16 51 C1
Barnet EN5 1 D2
Sandford Rd BR2 209 A5
E6 100 B4
Bexley DA6,DA7 147 A2
Sandford Row SE17 262 D2
Sandford St SW6 265 D3
Sandford Wlk 4 N16 73 D6
SE14 141 A6
Sandgate Ho 15 E5 74 B4
14 Beckenham BR3 185 C3
Ealing W5 87 C2
Sandgate La SW17, SW18 158 C3
Sandgate Rd DA16 146 C5
Sandgate St SE15 140 B6
Sandgate Trad Est SE15 140 B6
Sandham Ct SW4 270 B1
Sandham Point 10 SE18 122 D2
Sandhills CR0,SM6 219 D4
Sandhills Mdw TW17 193 A2
Sandhills The SW10 266 B6
Sandhurst Ave
Harrow HA2 41 D3
Tolworth KT5 198 D2
Sandhurst Cl NW9 44 C6
South Croydon CR2 221 C1
Sandhurst Ct SW2 138 A1
Sandhurst Dr IG3 79 D4
Sandhurst Ho 10 E1 96 C2
Sandhurst Jun & Inf Sch SE6 164 C3
Sandhurst Mkt SE6 164 A3
Sandhurst Rd DA15 168 A1
HA8,NW9 44 C6
N9 18 D5
Bexley DA5 168 D6
Catford SE6 164 B3
Sandhurst Way CR2 221 C1
Sandifer Dr NW2, NW11 68 D5
Sandiford Rd SM3 217 B6
Sandiland Cres BR2 224 D6
Sandilands CR0 222 A5
Sandilands Rd SW6 135 D4 265 C1
Sandilands Sta CR0 221 D6
Sandison St SE15 140 A2
Sandland St WC1 240 D3
Sandling Rise SE9 166 C1
Sandlings Cl SE15 140 B3
Sandlings The N22 50 D6
5 Wood Green N22 32 C1
Sandmartin Way CR4 203 A1
Sandmere Rd SW4 138 A1
Sandon Cl KT10 196 B1
Sandon Ct IG3 80 A5
Sandon Ho 5 SW2 160 A4
Sandow Cres UB3 105 D3
Sandown Ave KT10 212 A3
Sandown Cl TW5 128 A4
Sandown Gate KT10 212 B5
Sandown Ho 2 W4 111 A1
Penge SE26 184 B4
Sandown Park KT10 212 A6
Sandown Rd
Croydon SE25 206 B4
Esher KT10 212 A4
Sandown Way UB5 63 B3
Sandpiper Cl E17 34 D3
SE16 119 B4
Sandpiper Ct 11 E14 120 A3
1 SE8 141 C5
Sandpiper Rd SM1 217 B3
Sandpiper Terr IG5 56 D6
Sandpit Pl SE7 122 A1
Sandpit Rd BR1 186 C5
Sandpits Rd
Richmond TW10 153 D2
South Croydon CR0 222 D4
Sandra Cl
Hounslow TW3 151 D6
Tottenham N17 33 A2
Sandra Ho KT8 196 B4
Sandridge Cl HA1 42 C5
Sandridge Ct N4 73 A6
Sandridge St 2 N19 71 C6
Sandringham Ave SW20 179 A1
Sandringham Cl
Enfield EN1 5 C3
Ilford IG6 57 A6
1 Putney SW19 156 D3
Sandringham Cres HA2 63 D6
Sandringham Ct
18 SE16 118 D5
W1 239 B1
W9 229 B1
3 Beckenham BR3 186 A2
Edgware HA8 26 D6
Hillingdon UB10 83 A3
Putney SW15 156 D5
Sandringham Dr DA16 145 C3
Ashford TW15 170 A6
Sandringham Flats WC2 249 D6
Sandringham Gdns
N12 30 B4
N8 50 A3
Cranford TW5 128 A4
East Molesey KT8 195 C5
Ilford IG6 57 A6
Sandringham Ho W14 254 A4
Richmond TW10 154 C6
Sandringham Prim Sch E7 77 C3
Sandringham Rd BR1 187 A5
E10 54 B3
E7 77 C3
E8 73 D3
NW11 47 A2
NW2 68 B2
Barking IG11 79 D2
Northolt UB5 63 C1
Stanwell TW19,TW6 148 A6
Thornton Heath CR0 205 A4
Tottenham N22 33 A1
Worcester Park KT4 216 A5
Sandrock Pl CR0 222 D4
Sandrock Rd SE13 141 C2
Sands End La SW6 135 D4 265 D2
Sandstone TW9 132 C5
Sandstone Pl N19 71 B6
Sandstone Rd SE12 165 B2
Sandtoft Rd SE7 143 B6
Sandways 6 TW9 132 C4
Sandwell Cres 2 NW6 69 C2
Sandwell Mans 3 NW6 69 C2
Sandwich Ho 9 SE16 118 C4
WC1 233 A1
Sandwich St WC1 94 A4 233 A1
Sandwick Cl NW7 28 A3
Sandy Bury BR6 227 B5
Sandycombe Rd
East Bedfont TW14 150 A3
Richmond TW9 132 C3
Sandycoombe Rd TW1 153 C5
Sandycroft SE2 146 A6
Sandy Dr TW14 149 C3
Sandy Hill Ave SE18 122 D1
Sandy Hill La SE18 122 D2
Sandy Hill Rd SE18 122 D1
Sandyhill Rd IG1 78 D4
Sandy La BR5 190 D2
Belmont SM2 217 A1
Harrow HA3 44 C3
Mitcham CR4 181 A2
Moor Park HA6 22 A6
Richmond TW10 153 D2
Teddington KT8,TW11 175 B3
Walton-on-T KT12 194 C3
Sandy La N SM6 219 D3
Sandy La S SM6 219 C1
Sandy Lo N6 49 C2
Sandymount Ave HA7 25 D5

Sandy Rd NW3 69 D6
Sandy Ridge BR7 188 C4
Sandy's Row E1 243 B3
Sandy Way
Croydon CR0 223 B5
Walton-on-T KT12 193 D1
Sanford La 3 N16 73 D6
Sanford St SE14,SE8 141 A6
Sanford Terr N16 73 D5
Sanger Ave KT9 214 B4
Sangley Rd Catford SE6 164 A3
South Norwood SE25 205 C5
Sangora Rd 17 SW11 136 B1
Sankey Ho 23 E2 96 C5
Sansom Rd E11 76 D6
Sansom St SE5 139 B4
20 SE5 139 B5
Sans Wlk EC1 94 D3 241 C6
Santana Ho SE18 144 D5
Santley Ho SE1 251 B1
Santley St SW4 138 B1
Santos Rd SW18 157 C6
Sapcote Trad Ctr NW10 67 D2
Saperton Wlk SE11 260 D4
Saphora Cl BR6 227 B3
Sapperton Ct EC1 242 A6
Sapphire Cl E6 100 C1
Dagenham RM8 58 C1
Sapphire Ct 8 E1 118 A6
Sapphire Rd SE8 119 A2
Saracen Cl CR0 205 B3
Saracen St E14 97 C1
Sarah Bonnell Sch E15 76 C2
Sarah Ct UB5 85 B6
Sarah Ho 11 E1 96 B1
Roehampton SW15 133 D1
Sarah Swift Ho SE1 252 D2
Sara Lane Ct 31 N1 95 C5
Saratoga Rd E5 74 C4
Sara Turnbull Ho 2
SE18 122 B2
Sardeson Ho 13 SW27 182 D5
Sardinia St WC2 240 C2
Sargents Hill N2 30 C2
Sarita Cl HA3 24 B1
Sarjant Path SW19 156 D2
Sark Cl TW5 129 C5
Sark Ho 5 N1 73 A2
Enfield EN3 6 D5
Sark Wlk E16 99 B1
Sarnersfield Ho SE15 140 B6
Sarnes Ct 4 N11 31 B6
Sarnesfield Rd EN2 5 B2
Sarratt Ho W10 90 C2
Sarre Rd NW2 69 B3
Sarsden Bldgs W1 238 B1
Sarsen Ave TW3 129 C3
Sarsfeld Rd SW12,
SW17 158 D3
Sarsfield Rd UB6 87 C5
Sartor Rd SE15 140 D1
Sarum Hall Sch NW3 70 C1
Sarum Ho W11 244 D5
Sassoon 4 NW9 27 D2
Satanita Cl E16 99 D1
Satchell Mead NW9 27 D2
Satchwell Rd 24 E2 96 A4
Saul Ct 4 SE15 139 D6
Sauls Gn E11 76 C5
Saunders Cl 14 E14 119 B6
Saunders Ho 11 SW2 160 C3
Saunders Ness Rd
E14 120 B2
Saunders Rd SE18 123 D1
Hillingdon UB10 82 B6
Saunders St SE11 261 A4
Saunders Way SE28 124 B6
Saunderton Rd HA0 65 B3
Saunton Ave UB3 127 D5
Saunton Ct UB1 108 A6
Savage Gdns EC3 253 B6
Newham E6 100 B1
Savana N16 73 C6
Savannah Cl 9 SE15 139 D5
Savernake Ct HA7 25 B4
Savernake Ho N4 51 B2
Savernake Rd NW3 70 D4
Enfield N9 18 A5
Savery Dr KT6 197 C2
Savile Cl
New Malden KT3 199 C4
Thames Ditton KT7 197 A1
Savile Gdns CR0 221 D6
Saville Cres TW15 171 B4
Saville Rd E16 122 A5
W4 111 B3
Dagenham RM6 59 B2
Twickenham TW1 152 D3
Saville Row
W1 115 C6 249 A6
Enfield EN3 6 D3
Hayes BR2 208 D1
Savill Gdns SW20 200 A6
Savill Ho E16 122 D5
2 SW4 159 D5
Savill Row IG8 36 D4
Savin Lo 7 SM2 218 A1
Savona Cl 15 SW19 178 D3
Savona Ct SW20 178 D2
Savona St
SW8 137 C5 269 A3
Savoy Ave UB3 105 C1
Savoy Bldgs W12 111 D6
Savoy Circus W3 111 D6
Savoy Cl E15 98 C6
Edgware HA8 26 C5
Savoy Ct SW5 255 B4
WC2 250 B5
Savoy Hill WC2 250 C5
Savoy Par EN1 5 C2
Savoy Pier WC2 250 C5
Savoy Pl WC2 116 B6 250 C5
Savoy Row WC2 250 C6
Savoy St WC2 116 B6 250 C5
Savoy Steps WC2 250 C5
Savoy Way WC2 250 C5
Sawbill Cl UB4 84 D2
Sawkins Cl SW19 157 A2
Sawley Rd W12 112 A5
Sawmill Yd E3 97 A6
Sawtry Cl SM5 202 C2
Sawyer Cl N9 18 A2
Sawyer Ho 15 SE21 183 C6
Sawyer's Hill TW10 154 B4
Sawyers Lawn W13 87 A1
Sawyer St SE1 117 A4 252 A2
Saxby Rd SW2 160 A4
Saxham Rd IG11 101 D5
Saxlingham Rd E4 20 B1
Saxon Ave TW13 151 B2
Saxon Bsns Ctr SW19 180 A2
Saxonbury Ave TW16 172 B1
Saxonbury Cl CR4 202 B6
Saxonbury Ct 2 N7 72 A3
18 N7 71 D3
Saxonbury Gdns KT6 197 C1
Saxon Cl E17 53 C2
Hillingdon UB8 82 A2
Surbiton KT6 197 D3
Saxoncroft Ho SW16 159 D1
Saxon Cty Jun Sch
TW17 192 C4
Saxon Dr W3 88 D2
Saxonfield Cl SW2 160 B4
Saxon Gdns UB1 107 A6
Saxon Hall W2 245 C5
Saxon Ho 4 SW4 137 D1
Feltham TW13 151 B2
Saxon Rd E3 97 B5
E6 100 B3
Ashford TW15 171 B4
Bromley BR1 186 D3
Ilford IG1 78 D3
Kingston KT2 176 A2
Southall UB1 107 A6
South Norwood SE25 205 B4
Tottenham N22 32 D2
Wembley HA9 67 A5
Saxon Way N14 15 D5
Saxon Wlk DA14 190 C4
Saxony Par UB3 83 A2
Saxton Cl SE13 142 B2
Saxville Rd BR5 190 B1
Sayer Ho SE4 141 A1
Sayers Ho 4 N2 30 B1
Sayer's Wlk TW10 154 B4
Sayesbury La N18 34 A5
Sayes Court St SE8 141 B6
Sayes Ct SE8 141 B6
Scadbury Gdns BR5 190 A1
Scadbury Park Nature
Reserve* BR7 189 D4
Scads Hill Cl BR5,BR6 211 D3
Scafell NW1 232 A2
Scala St W1 239 B4
Scales Rd N17 52 A6
Scampston Mews 5
W10 90 D1
Scandrett St 38 E1 118 B5
Scarba Wlk N1 73 B2
Scarborough Rd E11 54 B1
N4 50 C1
N9 18 C4
East Bedfont TW6 149 A5
Scarborough St E1 243 D1
Scarbrook Rd CR0 221 A5
Scardale Ho 12 E5 74 B6
Scarle Rd HA0 65 D2
Scarlet Rd SE6 164 C1
Scarlette Manor Wlk 10
SE24 160 C4
Scarsbrook Ho 2
SW2 160 C5
Scarsbrook Rd SE3 143 D2
Scarsdale Pl W8 255 C6
Scarsdale Rd HA2 64 A5
Scarsdale Villas
W8 113 C3 255 B5
Scarth Rd SW13 133 D2
Scawen Cl SM5 219 A4
Scawen Rd SE8 119 A1
Scawfell St E2 95 D5
Scaynes Link N12 29 C6
Sceptre Ho 9 E1 96 C3
Sceptre Rd E2 96 C4
Schiller International Sch
BR4 224 B4
Schofield Wlk SE3 143 A5
Sch of Nursing
W1 93 C2 239 A4
Sch of Pharmacy
WC1 94 A3 240 B6
Sch of the Douay Martyrs
UB10 60 D4
Scholars Ho 6 E4 20 B3
Scholars Rd
Chingford E4 20 B3
Streatham SW12 159 C3
Scholefield Rd N19 71 D6
Scholey Ho SW11 136 C2
Schomberg Ho SW1 259 D4
Schonfeld Sq N16 51 B1
School App 22 E2 95 C4
Schoolbank Rd SE10 120 D3
School Bell Cloisters 15
E3 97 A5
Schoolbell Mews 16 E3 97 A5
School Cotts DA14 190 C5
School Flats SW8 270 A1
School Ho SE1 263 A4
Schoolhouse La E1 118 D6
School House La
TW11 175 C3
School La DA16 146 B2
Lower Halliford TW17 192 D2
Pinner HA5 41 A5
Surbiton KT6 198 B1
Teddington KT1 175 C2
School of Finance &
Management N7 72 B2
School of St David & St
Katharine The N8 50 A5
School Pas
3 Kingston KT1 176 B1
Southall UB1 107 B6
School Rd BR7 189 A3
NW10 89 B3
Ashford TW15 170 D4
Dagenham RM10 103 D6
East Molesey KT8 196 B5
Hampton TW12 174 A4
Hounslow TW3 130 A2
Ilford E12 78 B4
Littleton TW15 170 D3
Teddington KT1 175 C2
School Road Ave
TW12 174 A4
School Sq SE10 120 D3
Schoolway N12 30 B4
School Way RM8 80 C5
School Wlk TW16 193 D6
Schooner Cl E14 120 B3
1 SE16 118 D4
Barking IG11 102 B4
Schubert Rd Elstree WD6 9 D5
Putney SW15 157 B6
Science Mus*
SW7 114 B3 256 C5
Scilly Isles KT10 212 C6
Sclater St E1 243 D6
Scoles Cres SW2 160 C3
Scope Way KT1 198 A5
Scoresby St SE1 251 C3
Scoresdale SE19 183 C2
Scorton Ave UB6 87 A5
Scorton Ho 2 N1 95 C5
Scotch Comm W13 87 B2
Scotch Ho
SW1 114 D4 247 C1
Scoter Cl IG8 37 B3
Scoter Ct 23 SE8 141 B6
Scot Gr HA5 22 D3
Scotia Bldg 10 E1 118 D6
Scotia Ct 3 SE16 118 C3
Scotia Rd 24 SW2 160 C4
Scotland Gn N17 33 D1
Scotland Green Rd EN3 18 D6
Scotland Green Rd N
EN3 7 A1
Scotland Pl SW1 250 A3
Scotland Rd IG9 21 C3
Scotney Ho E9 74 C2
Scots Cl TW19 148 A3
Scotsdale Cl BR5,BR7 211 C5
Belmont SM3 217 A1
Scotsdale Rd SE12 165 B6
Scotson Ho SE11 261 A3
Scotswood St
EC1 94 C3 241 B6
Scotswood Wlk N17 34 A3
Scott Cl
Thornton Heath SW16 182 B2
West Drayton UB7 104 B2
West Ewell KT19 215 A3
Scott Ct 17 N16 73 C5
4 SW11 137 B3
W4 111 B4
Scott Ellis Gdns
NW8 92 B4 229 C1
Scottes La RM8 58 D1
Scott Farm Cl KT7 197 B1
Scott Gdns TW5 128 D5
Scott Ho 6 E13 99 A5
N1 235 C6
N7 72 B2
2 NW10 67 B1
NW8 237 A5
Scott Ho *continued*
3 Edmonton N18 34 A5
4 Erith DA17 125 B1
Richmond TW10 153 C2
Scott Lidgett Cres
SE16 118 A4
Scott's Ave
Ashford TW16 171 C3
Beckenham BR2 186 B1
Scotts Ct 6 W12 112 B4
Scotts Dr TW12 173 D3
Scotts Farm Rd KT19 215 A2
Scott's La BR2,BR3 186 B1
Scotts Park Prim Sch
BR1 187 C2
Scotts Rd BR1 187 A3
Scott's Rd E10 54 A1
W12 112 B4
Scotts Rd UB2 106 D3
Scott's Sufferance Wharf
SE1 253 D1
Scott St E1 96 B3
Scott's Way TW16 171 C3
Scott's Yd EC4 252 C6
Scott Trimmer Way
TW3 129 A3
Scottwell Dr NW9 45 D4
Scott Wilkie Prim Sch
E16 99 C1
Scoulding Ho 6 E14 119 C3
Scoulding Rd E16 99 A1
Scouler St E14 120 B6
Scout App NW10 67 C4
Scout Way NW7 27 B6
Scovell Cres SE1 252 A1
Scovell Rd SE1 252 A1
Scrattons Terr IG11 103 A5
Scriven Ct 2 E8 95 D6
Scriven St E8 95 D6
Scrooby St SE6 163 D5
Scrope Bldg EC1 241 A4
Scrubs La NW10,W10,
W12 90 B3
Scrutton Cl SW12 159 D4
Scrutton St EC2 95 C3 243 A5
Scudamore La NW9 45 A5
Scutari Rd SE22 162 C6
Scylla Cres
TW6&TW14 148 D4
Scylla Rd SE15 140 B2
East Bedfont TW14,TW6 148 D5
Seabright St 27 E2 96 B4
Seabrook Dr BR4 224 C6
Seabrook Gdns RM7 59 C2
Seabrook Rd RM8 80 D5
Seacole Cl W3 89 B2
Seacole Ct N15 51 D4
Seacole Lo N21 16 B6
Seacourt Rd SE2 124 D4
Seacroft Gdns WD19 22 D6
Seafield Rd N11 31 D6
Seaford Cl HA4 61 B6
Seaford Ho 8 SE16 118 C4
Seaford Rd E17 53 D6
N15 51 C4
Ealing W13 109 B5
Enfield EN1 5 C1
Seaford St WC1 233 B1
Seaforth Ave KT3 200 B5
Seaforth Cres N5 73 A3
Seaforth Gdns
Southgate N21 16 C3
Woodford IG8 37 C5
Worcester Park KT19 215 D3
Seaforth Lo 2 SW13 133 D3
Seaforth Pl SW1 259 B6
Seager Pl E3 97 B2
Seagrave Lo SW6 265 B6
Seagrave Rd
SW6 135 C6 265 B6
Seagrove Cl E1 96 D2
Seagry Rd E11 55 B2
Seagull Cl IG11 102 A4
Sealand Rd TW6 148 C5
Sealand Wlk UB5 85 A4
Seal Ho SE1 262 D6
Seal St E8 73 D4
Searle Ct 6 CR4 180 C2
Searle Pl N4 50 B1
Searles Cl
SW11 136 C5 267 B3
Searles Dr E6 100 D2
Searles Rd SE1 262 D4
Searson Ho SE17 261 D3
Sears St SE5 139 B5
Seasalter Ho 10 SW9 138 C4
Seasprite Cl 10 UB5 84 D4
Seath Ho 4 SE26 184 B5
Seaton Ave IG3 79 D3
Seaton Cl 6 E13 99 A3
Isleworth TW2 152 B5
Roehampton SW15 156 B4
Seaton Dr TW15 148 A2
Seaton Gdns HA4 62 A6
Seaton Point E5 74 A4
Seaton Rd Bexley DA16 146 C5
Hayes UB3 105 B3
Mitcham CR4 180 C1
Twickenham TW2 152 A5
Seaton Rd *continued*
Wembley HA0 88 A5
Seaton Sq NW7 28 D3
Seaton St N18 34 A5
Seavington Ho 3 SE5 139 C2
Sebastian Ct 10 IG11 79 D1
Sebastian Ho 22 N1 95 C5
Sebastian St
EC1 94 D4 234 D1
Sebastopol Rd N9 34 A6
Sebbon St N1 72 D1
Sebergham Gr NW7 28 A3
Sebert Rd E7 77 B4
Sebright Ho 21 E2 96 A5
Sebright Rd EN5 1 A2
Sebright Sch E2 96 A5
Secker Cres HA3 24 A2
Secker Ho SW9 138 D3
Secker St SE1 251 A3
Second Ave E12 78 A3
E13 99 A4
E17 53 C4
N18 34 C6
NW4 46 D5
W10 91 A3
W3 111 D5
Dagenham RM10 103 D5
Dagenham RM6 58 C4
Enfield EN1 17 D6
Hayes UB3 105 D5
Mortlake SW14 133 C2
Walton-on-T KT12 194 B3
Wembley HA9 65 D6
Second Cl KT8 196 A5
Second Cross Rd TW2 152 C2
Second Way HA9 66 D4
Sedan Way
SE17 117 C1 263 A2
Sedcombe Cl DA14 190 C6
Sedcote Rd EN3 18 D6
Sedding St SW1 258 A4
Seddon Ho EC2 242 A4
Seddon Rd SM4 202 B4
Seddon St WC1 94 B4 233 D1
Sedgebrook Rd SE3 143 D2
Sedgecombe Ave HA3 43 C4
Sedgefield Ct UB5 63 D3
Sedgeford Rd W12 111 D5
Sedgehill Rd SE6 185 D5
Sedgehill Sch SE6 185 D5
Sedgemere Ave N2 48 A6
Sedgemere Rd SE2 124 C3
Sedgemoor Dr RM10 81 C4
Sedge Rd N17 34 C3
Sedgeway SE6 164 D3
Sedgewick Ho SW19 156 D2
Sedgewood Cl BR2 208 D2
Sedgley Ho N4 72 B6
Sedgmoor Pl SE5 139 C5
Sedgwick Ave UB10 60 D1
Sedgwick Rd E10 76 A6
Sedgwick St E9 74 D3
Sedleigh Rd SW18 157 B5
Sedlescombe Rd
SW6 135 C6 265 A6
Sedley Cl EN1 6 B5
Sedley Ct SE26 162 B2
Sedley Ho SE11 260 D2
Sedley Pl W1 238 C1
Sedum Cl NW9 44 D4
Seeley Dr SE21 183 C6
Seelig Ave NW9 46 A2
Seely Rd SW17 181 A4
Seething La
EC3 117 C6 253 B6
Seething Wells Halls of
Residence KT6 197 C3
Seething Wells La
KT6 197 C3
Sefton Ave NW7 27 B5
Harrow HA3 24 B2
Sefton Cl BR5 211 D5
Sefton Ct TW5 129 D4
Sefton Lo 2 TW1 153 C5
Sefton Rd Croydon CR0 206 A1
Orpington BR5 211 D5
Sefton St SW15 134 C2
Segal Cl SE23 163 A4
Sekforde St
EC1 94 D3 241 C6
Sekhon Terr TW13 151 C1
Selan Gdns UB4 84 B2
Selbie Ave NW10 67 D3
Selborne 2 SW11 137 A2
Selborne Ave DA5 169 A3
E17 53 B5
Little Ilford E12 78 C4
Selborne Gdns NW4 46 A5
Wembley UB6 87 A5
Selborne Ho SE1 252 C1
Selborne Prim Sch
UB6 86 D5
Selborne Rd E17 53 C4
1 SE5 139 B3
Ilford IG1 78 C6
Kingston KT3 177 C1
Palmers Green N14 16 A1
Sidcup DA14 190 B6
South Croydon CR0 221 D5
Selborne Rd *continued*
Wood Green N22 32 B2
Selborne Wlk E17 53 B5
Selbourne Ave KT6 214 C5
Selby Chase HA4 62 B6
Selby Cl BR7 188 C4
14 E6 100 A2
Chessington KT9 214 A1
Selby Ct TW2 152 B2
Selby Gdns UB1 85 C3
Selby Gn SM5 202 C2
Selby Ho 10 SW4 159 C5
6 W10 91 A4
Selby Rd E11 76 C5
E13 99 B2
Ashford TW15 171 A4
Carshalton SM5 202 C2
Ealing W5 87 C3
Penge SE20 184 A1
Tottenham N17 33 C4
Selby St E1 96 A3
Selden Ho 2 SE15 140 C3
Selden Rd SE15 140 C3
Selden Wlk N7 72 B6
Seldon Ho SW1 259 A1
SW8 269 A3
Selena Ct N20 14 D1
Selfridges W1 238 B1
Selhurst Cl SW19 156 D3
Selhurst New Ct SE25 205 C3
Selhurst New Rd SE25 205 C3
Selhurst Park (Crystal
Palace FC) SE25 205 C5
Selhurst Pl SE25 205 C3
Selhurst Rd
Edmonton N9 17 C1
South Norwood SE25 205 C4
Selhurst Sta SE25 205 C4
Selina Ho NW8 236 D6
Selinas La RM8 59 B2
Selkirk Ct N17 33 C1
Selkirk Ho N1 233 C6
4 N16 73 C5
Selkirk Rd
Twickenham TW2 152 A3
Upper Tooting SW17 180 C6
Sellers Hall Cl N3 29 C3
Sellincourt Inf Sch
SW17 180 C4
Sellincourt Jun Sch
SW17 180 C4
Sellincourt Rd SW17 180 C4
Sellindge Cl BR3 185 B3
Sellons Ave NW10 89 D6
Sellsby Ct N11 31 B5
Sellwood Dr EN5 12 D6
Selma Ho W12 90 B1
Selman Ho 3 E9 75 A2
Selsdon Ave CR2 221 B2
Selsdon Cl KT6 198 A4
Selsdon Ct 4 UB1 85 D1
Selsdon High Sch
CR2 222 D1
Selsdon Park Rd CR0,
CR2 223 B1
Selsdon Rd E13 99 C5
NW2 67 D6
South Croydon CR2 221 B2
Wanstead E11 55 A2
West Norwood SE27 182 D6
Selsdon Road Ind Est
CR2 221 B2
Selsdon Way E14 119 D3
Selsea Pl N16 73 C3
Selsey Cres DA16 146 D4
Selsey St E14 97 C2
Selvage La NW7 27 B6
Selway Cl HA5 40 B6
Selwood Ho 1 N4 51 B2
Selwood Pl
SW7 114 B1 256 C2
Selwood Rd
Cheam SM3 201 B1
Chessington KT9 213 D4
Croydon CR0 206 B1
Selwood Terr SW7 256 C2
Selworthy Cl E11 55 A4
Selworthy Ho SW11 266 D2
Selworthy Rd SE6 163 B1
Selwyn Ave Chingford E4 36 A4
Ilford IG3 57 D3
Richmond TW9 132 B2
Selwyn Cl TW4 129 A1
Selwyn Cres DA16 146 B1
Selwyn Ct E17 53 C4
SE3 142 D2
Edgware HA8 26 D3
8 Richmond TW10 154 B6
Selwyn Ho 3 SW15 156 D5
Selwyn Inf Sch E4 36 A4
Selwyn Jun Sch E4 36 A4
Selwyn Prim Sch E13 99 A6
Selwyn Rd E13 99 B6
E3 97 B5
NW10 67 C1
New Malden KT3 199 B4

Semley Gate E9 ... 75 B2
Semley Ho SW1 ... 258 C3
Semley Pl
SW1 ... 115 B2 258 C3
Semley Rd SW16 ... 182 A1
Senate St SE15 ... 140 C3
Senators Lo 28 E3 ... 97 A5
Senator Wlk SE28 ... 123 B3
Sencler Ho SE2 ... 146 D6
Sendall Ct 13 SW11 ... 136 B2
Seneca Rd CR7 ... 205 A5
Senga Rd SM6 ... 203 A1
Senhouse Rd SM3 ... 216 D5
Senior St W2 ... 91 D2
Senlac Rd SE12 ... 165 B3
Sennen Rd EN1 ... 17 D4
Sennen Wlk SE9 ... 166 A1
Senrab St E1 ... 96 D1
Sentinel Cl UB5 ... 85 A3
Sentinel Ho NW4 ... 46 C5
Sentinel Sq NW4 ... 46 C5
September Ct UB1 ... 107 D5
September Way HA7 ... 25 B4
Sequoia Cl WD23 ... 8 B3
Sequoia Gdns BR6 ... 211 D2
Sequoia Pk HA5 ... 23 D4
Seraph Ct EC1 ... 95 A4 235 A2
Serbin Cl E10 ... 54 A2
Serenaders Rd 21
SW9 ... 138 C5
Sergeant Ind Est The
SW18 ... 157 D5
Serica Ct 14 SE10 ... 142 A5
Serjeants' Inn EC4 ... 241 B1
Serlby Ct W14 ... 254 C6
Serle St WC2 ... 94 B1 240 D2
Sermon La EC4 ... 242 A1
Serpentine Ct 10 SE16 118 D4
Serpentine Gallery★
W2 ... 114 B4 246 D2
Serpentine Rd
W2 ... 114 D5 247 C3
Serpentine The★
W2 ... 114 C5 247 B3
Service Route No 1 E15 76 B1
Service Route No 2 E15 76 B1
Service Route No 3 E15 76 B1
Serviden Dr BR1 ... 187 D2
Servite Ho SE13 ... 141 D4
Beckenham BR3 ... 185 B2
East Barnet N14 ... 15 B6
Penge SE26 ... 184 C4
Worcester Park KT4 ... 215 D6
Servite RC Prim Sch
SW10 ... 136 A6 266 A6
Servius Ct 2 TW8 ... 131 D5
Setchell Rd
SE1 ... 117 D2 263 C4
Setchell Way SE1 ... 263 C4
Seth St 18 SE16 ... 118 C4
Seton Ct 3 NW9 ... 46 A5
Seton Gdns RM9 ... 80 C1
Settle Point 11 E13 ... 99 A5
Settlers Ct 2 E14 ... 120 B6
Settles St E1 ... 96 A1
Settrington Rd SW6 ... 135 D3
Seven Acres
Carshalton SM5 ... 218 C6
Northwood HA6 ... 22 A4
Seven Dials
WC2 ... 94 A1 240 A1
Seven Kings High Sch
IG2 ... 57 B2
Seven Kings Rd IG3 ... 79 D6
Seven Kings Sta IG3 ... 57 C1
Seven Kings Way KT2 ... 176 A2
Seven Mills Prim Sch
E14 ... 119 C4
Sevenoaks Rd BR6 ... 227 D4
SE4 ... 163 B5
Sevenoaks Way BR5 ... 190 C1
Seven Sisters N15 ... 51 D4
Seven Sisters Inf Sch
N15 ... 51 B4
Seven Sisters Rd N4,N7,
N15 ... 51 A2
Seven Sisters Sta N15 ... 51 C4
Seven Stars Cnr W12 ... 112 A3
Seventh Ave
Hayes UB3 ... 106 A5
Ilford E12 ... 78 B4
Seven Ways Par IG2 ... 56 C4
Severnake Cl E14 ... 119 C2
Severn Ct 11 KT2 ... 175 D2
Severn Dr Enfield EN1 ... 6 A5
Hinchley Wood KT10 ... 213 A6
Severn Way NW10 ... 67 D3
Severus Rd SW11 ... 136 C1
Seville Ho 11 E1 ... 118 A5
Seville Mews N1 ... 73 C1
Seville St SW1 ... 247 D1
Sevington Rd NW4 ... 46 B3
Sevington St W9 ... 91 D3
Seward Rd W7 ... 109 A4
Penge BR3 ... 184 D1
Seward St EC1 ... 95 A4 235 A1
Sewardstone Gdns E4 ... 19 D6
Sewardstone Rd E2 ... 96 C5
Chingford E4 ... 19 D6
Sewdley St E5 ... 74 D5
Sewell Ho 7 N16 ... 73 C3
Sewell Rd SE28 ... 124 B4
Sewell St E13 ... 99 A4
Sextant Ave E14 ... 120 B2
Sexton's Ho 4 SE13 ... 142 A6
Seychelle Ct BR3 ... 185 D3
Seymour Ave
Tottenham N17 ... 34 A1
West Barnes SM4 ... 200 D2
Seymour Cl
East Molesey KT8 ... 196 A4
Pinner HA5 ... 23 B2
Seymour Ct N10 ... 31 A1
N16 ... 52 A1
NW2 ... 68 B6
Chingford E4 ... 20 D2
Putney SW15 ... 134 B1
Southgate N21 ... 16 B5
Seymour Dr BR2 ... 210 B1
Seymour Gdns SE4 ... 141 A2
Feltham TW13 ... 172 C6
Kingston KT5 ... 198 B4
Redbridge IG1 ... 56 B1
Ruislip HA4 ... 40 D1
Twickenham TW1 ... 153 B4
Seymour Ho NW1 ... 232 D1
1 SW8 ... 137 C3
WC1 ... 240 A6
Seymour Mews W1 ... 238 A2
Seymour Pl W1 ... 92 D1 237 C2
Croydon SE25 ... 206 B5
Seymour Rd E10 ... 53 B1
E6 ... 99 D6
N3 ... 29 D3
N8 ... 50 D4
Acton W4 ... 111 A2
Carshalton CR4 ... 203 A2
Chingford E4 ... 19 D3
East Molesey KT8 ... 196 A4
Edmonton N9 ... 18 B2
Hampton TW12 ... 174 A5
Teddington KT1 ... 175 D2
Wallington SM5 ... 219 A3
Wandsworth SW18 ... 157 B5
Wimbledon SW19 ... 156 D1
Seymour St SE18 ... 123 A3
W1 ... 92 D1 237 D1
Seymour Terr SE20 ... 184 B2
Seymour Villas SE20 ... 184 A2
Seymour Way TW16 ... 171 C3
Seymour Wlk
SW10 ... 136 A6 266 A6
Seyssel St E14 ... 120 A2
Shaa Rd W3 ... 111 B6
Shacklegate La TW11 ... 174 C6
Shackleton Cl SE23 ... 162 B2
Shackleton Ct 4 W12 ... 112 B4
2 Dulwich SE21 ... 161 B2
4 Millwall E14 ... 119 C1
7 Stanwell TW19 ... 148 A5
Shackleton Ho 5 E1 ... 118 C5
4 NW10 ... 67 B1
Shackleton Rd UB1 ... 107 B6
Shacklewell Ho 3 E8 ... 73 D4
Shacklewell La E8 ... 73 D3
Shacklewell Prim Sch
E8 ... 73 D4
Shacklewell Rd N16 ... 73 D4
Shacklewell Row E8 ... 73 D4
Shacklewell St 30 E2 ... 95 D4
Shadbolt Cl KT4 ... 215 D6
Shad Thames
SE1 ... 117 D4 253 D2
Shadwell Ct UB5 ... 85 B5
Shadwell Dr UB5 ... 85 B4
Shadwell Gdns E1 ... 118 C6
Shadwell Pierhead E1 118 C6
Shadwell Sta E1 ... 118 B6
Shady Bush Cl WD23 ... 8 A4
Shaef Way TW11 ... 175 A3
Shafter Rd RM10 ... 81 D2
Shaftesbury Ave
W1 ... 115 D6 249 D6
Enfield EN3 ... 6 D3
Feltham TW14 ... 150 A5
Harrow HA1,HA2 ... 42 A1
Harrow HA3 ... 44 A3
New Barnet EN5 ... 2 A1
Southall UB2 ... 107 C3
Shaftesbury Circ HA2 ... 42 A1
Shaftesbury Ct N1 ... 235 C3
SE1 ... 262 C6
3 SE28 ... 124 C5
1 SE5 ... 139 B1
Ilford RM6 ... 58 C2
Shaftesbury Gdns
NW10 ... 89 C3
Shaftesbury Ho 13 N16 73 C5
W2 ... 245 D6
Croydon SE25 ... 206 A3
Shaftesbury Lo 9 E14 ... 97 D1
Shaftesbury Mews
W8 ... 255 B5
Shaftesbury Park Chambers
1 SW11 ... 137 A2
Shaftesbury Prim Sch
E7 ... 77 C1
Shaftesbury Rd E10 ... 53 C1
E17 ... 53 D3
E7 ... 77 C1
N4,N19 ... 50 A1
Beckenham BR3 ... 185 B1
Carshalton SM5 ... 202 C2
Chingford E4 ... 20 B3
Edmonton N18 ... 33 D4
Richmond TW9 ... 132 A2
Shaftesbury Sch HA3 ... 23 D2
Shaftesbury St N1 ... 235 C3
Shaftesburys The
IG11 ... 101 A5
Shaftesbury Way TW2 152 B1
Shaftesbury Waye UB4 ... 84 C1
Shafteswood Ct SW17 158 D1
Shafto Mews SW1 ... 257 D5
Shafton Rd E9 ... 96 D6
Shaftsbury Ct E6 ... 100 C1
SW6 ... 265 D1
Shaftsbury Mews 2
SW4 ... 159 C6
Shaftsbury Park Prim Sch
SW11 ... 137 A3
Shafts Ct EC3 ... 243 A1
Shahjalal Ho 18 E2 ... 96 A5
Shakespeare Ave N11 ... 31 C5
NW10 ... 89 B6
Feltham TW14 ... 150 A5
Hayes UB4 ... 84 B2
Shakespeare Cl HA3 ... 44 C2
Shakespeare Cres E12 78 B2
NW10 ... 89 B6
Shakespeare Dr HA3 ... 44 B3
Shakespeare Gdns N2 ... 48 D5
Shakespeare Ho 3 E9 ... 74 C1
N14 ... 15 D2
1 Erith DA17 ... 125 B1
Shakespeare Rd DA7 ... 147 A4
E17 ... 34 D1
N3 ... 29 C2
NW7 ... 28 A6
SE24 ... 138 D1
W3 ... 111 A5
Ealing W7 ... 108 D6
Shakespeare's Globe
Theatre (site of)★
SE1 ... 252 B4
Shakespeare Twr EC2 ... 242 B4
Shakespeare Way
TW13 ... 172 C6
Shakspeare Mews 7
N16 ... 73 C4
Shakspeare Wlk N16 ... 73 C4
Shalbourne Sq E9 ... 75 B2
Shalcomb St
SW10 ... 136 A6 266 B5
Shalden Ho 6 SW15 ... 155 D5
Shaldon Dr Ruislip HA4 ... 62 C5
West Barnes SM4 ... 201 A4
Shaldon Rd HA8 ... 26 B1
Shalfleet Dr W10 ... 112 D6
Shalford NW10 ... 90 A6
3 Woodford IG8 ... 37 C4
Shalford Cl BR6 ... 227 A4
Shalford Ct N1 ... 234 C4
Shalford Ho SE1 ... 262 D6
Shalimar Gdns W3 ... 111 A6
Shalimar Lo W3 ... 111 A6
Shalimar Rd W3 ... 111 A6
Shallons Rd SE9 ... 188 D6
Shalstone Rd SW14,
TW9 ... 132 D2
Shalston Villas KT5,
KT6 ... 198 B3
Shamrock Ho SE26 ... 184 A6
Shamrock Rd CR0 ... 204 B3
Shamrock St SW4 ... 137 D2
Shamrock Way N14 ... 15 B3
Shandon Rd SW4 ... 159 C5
Shand St SE1 ... 117 C4 253 B2
Shandy St E1 ... 96 D3
Shanklin Gdns WD19 ... 22 C6
Shanklin Ho E17 ... 35 B1
Shanklin Rd N15 ... 52 A5
N8 ... 49 D4
Shannon Cl NW2 ... 68 D5
Southall UB2 ... 106 D1
Shannon Cnr KT3 ... 200 A5
Shannon Cnr Ret Pk
KT3 ... 200 A5
Shannon Commercial Ctr
KT3 ... 200 A5
Shannon Ct N16 ... 73 C5
NW10 ... 68 A2
Croydon CR0 ... 205 A1
Shannon Gr SW9 ... 138 B1
Shannon Pl
NW8 ... 92 C5 230 B4
Shannon Way BR3 ... 185 D4
Shanti Ct SW18 ... 157 C3
Shap Cres SM5 ... 202 D1
Shapland Way N13 ... 32 B5
Shapla Prim Sch E1 ... 118 A6
Shapwick Cl N11 ... 30 D5
Shardcroft Ave SE24 ... 160 D6
Shardeloes Rd SE14 ... 141 B3
Shard's Sq SE15 ... 140 A6
Sharebourne Ho SW2 160 C6
Sharland Cl CR7 ... 204 C3
Sharman Ct DA14 ... 190 A6
Sharnbrooke Cl DA16 ... 146 C2
Sharnbrook Ho W6 ... 265 A6
Sharon Cl KT6 ... 197 C1
Sharon Gdns E9 ... 96 C6
Sharon Rd W4 ... 111 B1
Enfield EN3 ... 7 A3
Sharpe Cl W7 ... 86 D2
Sharp Ho SW8 ... 137 B2
Sharples Hall St 8
NW1 ... 70 D1
Sharpness Cl UB4 ... 85 A2
Sharpness Ct 2 SE15 139 D5
Sharps La HA4 ... 39 B2
Sharratt St SE15 ... 140 C6
Sharstead St
SE17 ... 116 D1 261 C1
Sharvel La UB5 ... 84 B6
Sharwell Ho SW18 ... 157 D5
Sharwood WC1 ... 233 D3
Shaver's Pl SW1 ... 249 C5
Shaw Ave IG11 ... 103 A5
Shawbrooke Rd SE9 ... 143 D1
Shawbury Ct SE22 ... 161 D6
Shawbury Rd SE22 ... 161 D6
Shaw Cl Bushey WD23 ... 8 C2
Woolwich SE28 ... 124 B5
Shaw Ct N19 ... 72 A6
12 SW11 ... 136 B2
8 W3 ... 111 A3
Shaw Dr KT12 ... 194 C2
Shawfield Ct UB7 ... 104 A3
Shawfield Pk BR1 ... 187 D1
Shawfield St
SW3 ... 114 C1 257 B1
Shawford Ct 8 SW15 ... 156 A4
Shawford Rd KT19 ... 215 B2
Shaw Gdns IG11 ... 103 A5
Shaw Ho 5 E16 ... 122 C5
6 Erith DA17 ... 125 B1
Shaw Path BR1 ... 164 D1
Shaw Rd SE22 ... 139 C1
Catford BR1 ... 164 D1
Enfield EN3 ... 6 D4
Shaw Sq E17 ... 35 A2
Shaws Wood Cotts EN4 ... 3 C3
Shaw Way SM6 ... 220 A1
Shearing Dr SM4 ... 202 A2
Shearling Way N7 ... 72 A2
Shearman Rd SE3 ... 142 D2
Shears Ct TW16 ... 171 C3
Shearsmith Ho 14 E1 ... 118 A6
Shears The TW16 ... 171 C3
Shearwater Cl IG11 ... 102 A4
Shearwater Ct 24 SE8 141 B6
Shearwater Rd SM1 ... 217 B3
Shearwater Way UB4 ... 84 D1
Sheaveshill Ave NW9 ... 45 C5
Sheaveshill Ct NW9 ... 45 C5
Sheaveshill Par NW9 ... 45 C5
Sheen Common Dr
SW14,TW10 ... 154 C6
Sheen Court Rd TW10 132 C1
Sheen Ct TW10 ... 132 C1
Sheendale Rd TW9 ... 132 B1
Sheenewood SE26 ... 184 B6
Sheen Gate Gdns
SW14 ... 133 A1
Sheen Gr N1 ... 94 C6 234 A6
Sheen La SW14 ... 133 A1
Sheen Mount JMI Sch
SW14 ... 154 D6
Sheen Pk TW10,TW9 ... 132 A1
Sheen Rd
Orpington BR5 ... 211 D5
Richmond TW10,TW9 ... 132 B1
Sheen Way SM6 ... 220 B3
Sheen Wood SW14 ... 155 A6
Sheepcote Cl TW5 ... 128 A5
Sheepcote La SW11 ... 136 D3
Sheepcote Rd HA1 ... 42 D3
Sheepcotes Rd RM6 ... 59 A5
Sheephouse Way KT3 199 C2
Sheep La E8 ... 96 B6
Sheepwalk TW17 ... 192 B3
Sheep Walk Mews 7
SW19 ... 179 A4
Sheerness Mews E16 ... 122 D4
Sheerwater Rd E16 ... 99 D2
Sheffield Ho 14 SE15 ... 139 D4
Sheffield Rd TW14,
TW6 ... 149 A6
Sheffield Sq 2 E3 ... 97 B4
Sheffield St WC2 ... 240 C1
Sheffield Terr
W8 ... 113 C5 245 B3
Sheffield Way TW14,
TW6 ... 149 B6
Shefton Rise HA6 ... 22 A3
Shelbey Ct BR1 ... 186 D2
Shelbourne Cl HA5 ... 41 B6
Shelbourne Ho 20 N19 ... 49 D2
Shelbourne Rd N17 ... 34 B2
Shelburne Ct SW15 ... 156 D6
Shelburne Dr TW4 ... 151 C5
Shelburne Ho 9
SW16 ... 181 C5
Shelburne Rd N7 ... 72 B4
Shelbury Cl DA14 ... 168 A1
Shelbury Rd SE22 ... 162 B6
Sheldon Ave N6 ... 48 D3
Sheldon Cl SE12 ... 165 B6
Penge SE20 ... 184 B2
Sheldon Ct SW8 ... 270 A3
Barnet EN5 ... 1 D1
Sheldon Ho 9 E9 ... 74 D2
Chingford E4 ... 36 C4
Teddington TW11 ... 175 A4
Sheldon Rd DA7 ... 147 B4
NW2 ... 68 D4
Dagenham RM9 ... 81 A1
Edmonton N18 ... 33 C6
Sheldon St CR0 ... 221 A5
Sheldrake Cl E16 ... 122 B5
Sheldrake Ho 15 SE16 118 D2
Sheldrake Pl
W8 ... 113 C4 245 A2
Sheldrick Cl CR4 ... 180 B1
Shelduck Cl E15 ... 76 D3
Shelduck Ct 36 SE8 ... 141 B6
Sheldwich Terr BR2 ... 210 A3
Shelford 20 KT1 ... 176 C1
Shelford Ct 7 E5 ... 52 B1
Shelford Pl N16 ... 73 B5
Shelford Rd EN5 ... 12 C5
Shelford Rise SE19 ... 183 D3
Shelgate Rd SW11 ... 158 D6
Shell Cl BR2 ... 210 A3
Shell Ctr SE1 ... 250 D3
Shellduck Cl NW9 ... 27 C1
Shelley N8 ... 50 A6
Shelley Ave E12 ... 78 A2
Greenford UB6 ... 86 B4
Shelley Cl BR6 ... 227 C5
SE15 ... 140 B3
Edgware HA8 ... 26 C6
Greenford UB6 ... 86 B4
Hayes UB4 ... 84 A2
Shelley Cres
Heston TW5 ... 128 D4
Southall UB1 ... 85 B1
Shelley Ct 12 E10 ... 53 D2
N4 ... 50 B1
SW3 ... 267 D6
9 Kingston KT2 ... 175 D6
8 Wanstead E11 ... 55 A5
Wembley HA0 ... 65 C4
West Barnes KT3 ... 200 A4
Shelley Dr DA16 ... 145 C4
Shelley Gdns HA0 ... 65 C6
Shelley Ho 21 E2 ... 96 C4
9 N16 ... 73 C4
SE17 ... 262 B2
SW1 ... 269 A6
Shelley Rd NW10 ... 89 B6
Shelley Sch
SE11 ... 116 C2 261 B3
Shelley Way SW17 ... 180 B4
Shellgrove Rd N16 ... 73 C3
Shellness Rd E5 ... 74 B3
Shell Rd SE13 ... 141 D2
Shellwood Rd SW11 ... 136 D3
Shelly Lo EN2 ... 5 B4
Shelmerdine Cl E3 ... 97 C2
Shelson Ave TW13 ... 171 D6
Shelton Rd SW19 ... 179 C2
Shelton St WC2 94 A1 240 A1
Shene Bldg EC1 ... 241 A4
Shene Int Sch SW14 ... 133 C1
Shenfield Ho 3 SE18 ... 143 D5
Shenfield Rd IG8 ... 37 B3
Shenfield St N1 ... 95 C5
Shenley Ave HA4 ... 39 D1
Shenley Rd SE5 ... 139 C4
Heston TW5 ... 129 A4
Shenstone W13 ... 109 C5
Shenstone Gdns IG2 ... 57 D4
Shenstone Ho SW16 ... 181 C5
Shepherd Cl W1 ... 248 A6
Feltham TW13 ... 173 A6
Shepherdess Pl N1 ... 235 B2
Shepherdess Wlk
N1 ... 95 A5 235 B3
Shepherd Ho 10 E14 ... 97 D1
N7 ... 72 A2
Shepherd Mkt W1 ... 248 C3
Shepherd's Bush (Central
Line) Sta W12 ... 112 D4
Shepherd's Bush Gn
W12 ... 112 C4
Shepherd's Bush (Hamm &
City) Sta W12 ... 112 C5
Shepherd's Bush Market
W12 ... 112 C4
Shepherd's Bush Pl
W12 ... 112 D4
Shepherd's Bush Rd
W6 ... 112 C3
Shepherd's Cl N6 ... 49 B3
Shepherds Cl
Dagenham RM6 ... 58 D5
Orpington BR6 ... 227 D5
Shepperton TW17 ... 192 D3
Shepherds Ct 8 W12 112 D4
Shepherds Gn BR7 ... 189 B3
Shepherd's Hill N6 ... 49 C3
Shepherd's La E9 ... 74 D2
Shepherds Leas SE9 ... 145 B1
Shepherds Path UB5 ... 63 A2
Shepherds Pl W1 ... 248 A6
Shepherd St
W1 ... 115 B5 248 C3
Shepherds Way CR2 ... 222 D1
Shepherds Wlk NW2 ... 68 A6
Shepherd's Wlk NW3 ... 70 B4
Shepherds Wlk WD23 ... 8 B2
Shepiston La UB3 ... 105 A1
Shepley Cl SM5 ... 219 A5
Shepley Ct SW16 ... 181 C6
Shepley Mews EN3 ... 7 C6
Sheppard Cl Enfield EN1 ... 6 B5
Kingston KT6 ... 198 A5
Sheppard Dr SE16 ... 118 B1
Sheppard Ho 28 E2 ... 96 A5
18 SW11 ... 136 B2
8 Streatham SW2 ... 160 C3
Sheppard's Ct
Harrow HA1 ... 42 C2
Wembley UB6 ... 64 D2
Sheppard St E16 ... 98 D3
Shepperton Bsns Park
TW17 ... 193 A4
Shepperton Court Dr
TW17 ... 192 D4
Shepperton Ct TW17 ... 192 D3
Shepperton Rd
N1 ... 95 B6 235 C6
Littleton TW17,TW18 ... 192 A5
Orpington BR5 ... 211 A3
Shepperton Sta TW17 193 A4
Shepperton Studios
TW17 ... 192 B6
Sheppey Gdns RM9 ... 80 C1
Sheppey Ho 16 E5 ... 74 B4
Sheppey Rd RM9 ... 80 C1
Sheppey Wlk N1 ... 73 A1
Shepton Ct SW11 ... 266 D2
Shepton Hos 11 E2 ... 96 C4
Sherard Ct N19 ... 72 A5
Sherard Ho 24 E9 ... 74 C1
Sherard Rd SE9 ... 166 A6
Sheraton Bsns Ctr UB6 87 C5
Sheraton Cl WD6 ... 10 B6
Sheraton Ho SW1 ... 268 D6
Sheraton Lo HA3 ... 42 C6
Sheraton St W1 ... 239 C1
Sheraton The 22 KT6 ... 198 A4
Sherborne Ave
Enfield EN3 ... 6 C3
Southall UB2 ... 107 C2
Sherborne Cl UB4 ... 84 C1
Sherborne Cres SM5 ... 202 C2
Sherborne Ct SE20 ... 184 C1
Sherborne Gdns NW9 ... 44 C6
Ealing W13 ... 87 B2
Sherborne Ho SW1 ... 258 D2
SW8 ... 270 C3
Sherborne La EC4 ... 252 D6
Sherborne Rd BR5 ... 211 D4
Cheam SM3 ... 201 C1
Chessington KT9 ... 214 A3
East Bedfont TW14 ... 149 B3
Sherborne St
N1 ... 95 B6 235 C6
Sherboro Rd 1 N15 ... 51 D3
Sherbourne Ct 1
TW12 ... 173 C2
Sherbourne Gdns
TW17 ... 193 C2
Sherbourne Pl HA7 ... 25 A4
Sherbrooke Cl DA7 ... 147 C1
Sherbrooke Ho 9 E2 ... 96 C5
Sherbrooke Rd
SW6 ... 135 A5 264 B3
Sherbrooke Terr SW6 ... 264 B3
Sherbrook Gdns N21 ... 16 D4
Shere Cl KT9 ... 213 D3
Sheredan Rd E4 ... 36 C5
Shere Ho SE1 ... 262 C6
Shere Rd IG2 ... 56 C4
Sherfield Cl KT3 ... 198 D5
Sherfield Gdns SW15 ... 155 D5
Sheridan N8 ... 50 C5
Sheridan Bldgs WC2 ... 240 B1
Sheridan Cl UB10 ... 83 A3
Sheridan Cres BR7 ... 188 D1
Sheridan Ct NW6 ... 70 A1
SW9 ... 270 D1
Ealing W7 ... 108 D6
Harrow HA1 ... 42 B3
Hounslow TW4 ... 151 A6
Sheridan Gdns HA3 ... 43 D3
Sheridan Ho 16 E1 ... 96 C1
7 N16 ... 73 C5
SE11 ... 261 B3
Sheridan Lo EN5 ... 1 D1
Sheridan Mews E11 ... 55 B3
Sheridan Pl
Barnes SW13 ... 133 D2
Hampton TW12 ... 174 A2
Harrow HA1 ... 42 C2
Sheridan Rd DA7 ... 147 A2
E12 ... 78 B3

Sheridan Rd *continued*
E7 .76 D5
Belvedere DA17 .125 C2
Merton SW19 .179 B2
Richmond TW10 .153 C1
Sheridan St 28 E1 .96 B1
Sheridan Terr UB5 .63 D3
Sheridan Way 5 BR3 .185 B2
Sheridan Wlk NW11 .47 C3
Sheridon Ct SW5 .255 C3
Sheringdale Prim Sch
SW18 .157 B3
Sheringham NW8 .229 D6
Sheringham Ave E12 .78 B3
Southgate N14 .15 D5
Twickenham TW2 .151 C3
Sheringham Dr IG11 .80 A3
Sheringham Ho NW1 .237 B4
Sheringham Jun Sch
E12 .78 B4
Sheringham Rd N7 .72 C2
Penge SE20 .206 C6
Sheringham Twr UB1 .107 D6
Sherington Ave HA5 .23 C3
Sherington Prim Sch
SE7 .143 B6
Sherington Rd SE7 .143 B6
Sherland Rd TW1 .152 D3
Sherleys Ct HA4 .61 C6
Sherlies Ave BR6 .227 C6
Sherlock Ct NW8 .229 C6
Sherlock Holmes Mus★
NW1 .92 D3 237 D5
Sherlock Mews W1 .238 A4
Sherman Gdns RM6 .58 C3
Sherman Rd BR1 .187 A2
Shernwood Ho 1 E18 .55 A5
Sherrard Rd E7,E12 .77 D2
Sherrards Way EN5 .13 D5
Sherrick Green Rd
NW10 .68 B3
Sherriff Ct NW6 .69 C2
Sherriff Rd NW6 .69 C2
Sherringham Ave
Feltham TW13 .150 A1
Tottenham N17 .34 A1
Sherringham Ct 1 N3 .29 C2
Sherrin Rd E10 .75 D4
Sherrock Gdns NW4 .46 A5
Sherry Mews IG11 .79 B1
Sherston Ct SE1 .261 D4
WC1 .234 A1
Sherwin Ho 1 SE11 .138 C6
Sherwin Rd SE14 .140 D4
Sherwood NW6 .69 A1
Long Ditton KT6 .213 D6
Sherwood Ave
Greenford UB6 .64 C3
Hayes UB4 .84 B3
Mitcham SW16 .181 D2
Ruislip HA4 .39 C3
Wanstead E18 .55 B6
Sherwood Cl DA5 .168 C5
E17 .35 B1
Barnes SW13 .134 B2
Ealing W13 .109 B5
Sherwood Ct SE13 .141 D3
11 SW11 .136 A2
W1 .237 C3
5 West Wickham BR4 .207 D1
Sherwood Gdns E14 .119 C2
SE16 .118 B1
Barking IG11 .79 B1
Sherwood Hall 7 N2 .48 A6
Sherwood Ho N4 .51 A2
Sherwood Park Ave
DA15 .168 B5
Sherwood Park Prim Sch
DA15 .168 B5
Sherwood Park Rd
Mitcham CR4 .203 D5
Sutton SM1 .217 C3
Sherwood Park Sch
SM6 .219 D5
Sherwood Prim Sch
CR4 .203 C5
Sherwood Rd DA16 .145 C2
NW4 .46 C6
Croydon CR0 .206 B1
Hampton TW12 .174 A5
Harrow HA2 .64 A6
Ilford IG6 .57 B5
Merton SW19 .179 B3
Sherwood St N20 .14 B1
W1 .249 B6
Sherwood Terr N20 .14 B1
Sherwood Way BR4 .224 A6
Shetland Cl WD6 .11 B5
Shetland Rd E3 .97 B5
East Bedfont TW6 .149 A5
Shield Dr TW8 .131 A6
Shieldhall St SE2 .124 C2
Shield Rd TW15 .171 B6
Shifford Path SE23 .162 D1
Shillaker Ct W3 .111 D5
Shillibeer Pl W1 .237 B3
Shillingford Ho 40 E3 .97 D4
Shillingford St 22 N1 .72 D1
Shillingstone Ho W14 254 B5
Shinfield St W12 .90 C1
Shinglewell Rd DA8 .147 C5
Shinners Cl SE25 .206 A4
Shipka Rd SW12 .159 B3
Ship La SW14 .133 A3
Shiplake Ct SW17 .180 B6
Shiplake Ho 45 E2 .95 D4
Shipley Ct SE20 .184 A1
Shipley Ho 32 SW8 .137 D3
Shipman Par SE23 .163 A2
Shipman Rd
Forest Hill SE23 .162 D2
Newham E16 .99 C1
Ship & Mermaid Row
SE1 .253 A2
Ship St SE8 .141 C4
Ship Tavern Pas EC3 .253 A6
Shipton Cl RM8 .80 D5
Shipton Ho 14 E2 .95 D5
7 NW5 .71 A2
Shipton Rd UB8 .60 B4
Shipton St E2 .95 D4
Shipwright Rd SE16 .119 A4
Shipwright Yd SE1 .253 A3
Shirburn Cl SE23 .162 C4
Shirbutt St E14 .119 D6
Shirebrook Rd SE3 .143 D2
Shire Ct DA18 .124 D3
Ewell KT17 .215 D1
Shirehall Cl NW4 .46 D3
Shirehall Gdns NW4 .46 D3
Shirehall La NW4 .46 D3
Shirehall Pk NW4 .46 D3
Shire Ho E11 .76 D5
Shire Horse Way TW7 130 D2
Shire La
Farthing Street BR6,BR2 227 B2
Orpington BR6 .227 C3
Shiremeade WD6 .10 B6
Shire Pl SW18 .158 A4
Shires The TW10 .176 A6
Shirland Mews W9 .91 B4
Shirland Rd W9 .91 C3
Shirley Ave DA5 .168 D3
Carshalton SM1 .218 C4
Croydon CR0 .206 D1
Shirley Church Rd
CR0 .223 A5
Shirley Cl TW3 .152 A6
Shirley Cres BR3 .207 A5
Shirley Ct NW9 .45 B4
8 Ealing W13 .109 A5
Ilford IG2 .57 B4
Thornton Heath SW16 .204 B6
Shirley Dr TW3 .152 A6
Shirley Gdns
Barking IG11 .79 C2
Ealing W7 .108 D5
Shirley Gr N9 .18 D4
SW11 .137 A2
Shirley High Sch CR0 .222 D5
Shirley Hills Rd CR0 .222 D3
Shirley Ho 13 SE5 .139 B5
Shirley House Dr SE7 .143 C5
Shirley Lo 4 SE26 .185 A6
Shirley Oaks Hospl
CR0 .206 C2
Shirley Oaks Rd CR0 .222 D6
Shirley Park Rd CR0 .206 C1
Shirley Rd E15 .76 C1
W4 .111 B4
Croydon CR0 .206 B1
Enfield EN2 .5 A2
Sidcup DA15 .167 C1
Shirleys Cl E17 .53 D4
Shirley St E16 .98 D1
Shirley Way CR0 .223 B5
Shirlock Rd NW3 .70 D4
Shobden Rd N17 .33 B2
Shobroke Cl NW2 .68 C5
Shoebury Rd E6 .78 B1
Shoe La EC4 .94 C1 241 B2
Shoelands Ct NW9 .45 B6
Shooters Ave HA3 .43 C5
Shooters Hill SE18 .144 C4
Shooters Hill Rd
SE18,SE3,SE7 .143 D5
SE3,SE10 .142 C4
Shooters Rd EN2 .4 D4
Shoot-Up Hill NW2 .69 A2
Shore Bsns Ctr 31 E9 .74 C1
Shore Cl Feltham TW14 150 A4
Hampton TW12 .173 A5
Shorediche Cl UB10 .60 B5
Shoreditch Ct 2 E8 .73 D1
Shoreditch High St
E2 .95 C3 243 B6
Shoreditch Sta
E1 .95 D3 243 D5
Shore Gr TW13 .151 C2
Shoreham Cl DA5 .168 D3
SW18 .157 D6
Croydon CR0 .206 C3
Shoreham Rd BR5 .190 B1
Shoreham Rd (E)
TW6 .148 A6
Shoreham Rd (W)
TW6 .148 A6
Shoreham Way BR2 .209 A3
Shore Ho SW8 .137 B2
Shore Mews 30 E9 .74 C1
Shore Pl E9 .74 C1
Shore Rd E9 .74 C1
Shorncliffe Rd
SE1 .117 D1 263 C2
Shorndean St SE6 .164 A3
Shorne Cl 3 DA15 .168 B5
Shornefield Cl BR1 .210 C6
Shornells Way SE2 .124 C1
Shorrolds Rd
SW6 .135 B5 264 D4
Shortcroft Mead Ct
NW10 .68 A3
Shortcroft Rd KT17 .215 D1
Shortcrofts Rd RM9 .81 B2
Shorter St
EC3 .117 D6 253 D6
Shortgate N12 .29 B6
Short La TW15,TW19 .148 B3
Shortlands W6 .112 D2
Harlington UB3 .127 B6
Shortlands Cl DA17 .125 B3
Edmonton N18 .17 B1
Shortlands Gdns BR2 .186 C1
Shortlands Gr BR2 .208 B6
Shortlands Rd E10 .53 D2
Beckenham BR2,BR3 .208 C6
Kingston KT2 .176 B3
Shortlands Sta BR2 .186 C1
Short Path SE18 .144 D6
Short Rd E11 .76 C6
Chiswick W4 .133 C6
Stanwell TW19 .148 A5
Shorts Croft NW9 .44 D5
Shorts Gdns
WC2 .94 A1 240 A1
Shorts Rd SM5 .218 C3
Short St 7 NW4 .46 C5
SE1 .251 B2
Shortway SE9 .144 A2
Short Way N12 .30 C4
Twickenham TW2 .152 A4
Shotfield SM6 .219 B2
Shott Cl SM1 .218 A3
Shottendane Rd
SW6 .135 C4 265 A2
Shottery Cl SE9 .166 A1
Shottfield Ave SW14 .133 C1
Shottsford 1 W11 .91 C1
Shoulder of Mutton Alley 10
E14 .119 A6
Shouldham St
W1 .92 C2 237 B3
Showers Way UB3 .106 A5
Shrapnel Cl SE18 .144 A5
Shrapnel Rd SE9 .144 B2
Shreveport Ho 23 N19 .49 D2
Shrewsbury Ave
Harrow HA3 .44 A5
Mortlake SW14 .133 B1
Shrewsbury Cl KT6 .214 A6
Shrewsbury Cres NW10 89 B6
Shrewsbury Ho SE11 .270 D5
SW3 .267 A5
Shrewsbury House Sch
KT6 .214 A6
Shrewsbury La SE18 .144 D4
Shrewsbury Mews 33
W2 .91 C2
Shrewsbury Rd E7 .77 D2
N11 .31 D4
W2 .91 C1
Beckenham BR3 .207 A6
Carshalton SM5 .202 C2
Harlington TW14,TW6 .149 B5
Shrewsbury St W10 .90 C3
Shrewsbury Wlk 7
TW7 .131 A2
Shrewton Rd SW17 .180 D3
Shroffold Rd BR1 .164 D1
Shropshire Cl CR4 .204 A5
Shropshire Ct W7 .86 D1
Shropshire Pl WC1 .239 B5
Shropshire Rd N22 .32 B3
Shroton St NW1 92 C2 237 B4
Shrubberies The
Ilford IG2 .57 D4
Woodford E18 .37 A1
Shrubbery Gdns N21 .16 D4
Shrubbery Rd
Edmonton N9 .18 A1
Southall UB1 .107 C5
Streatham SW16 .182 A6
Shrubbery The
2 Surbiton KT6 .198 A1
7 Wanstead E11 .55 B4
Shrubland Gr KT4 .216 C5
Shrubland Rd E10 .53 C2
E8 .96 A6
Walthamstow E10 .53 C4
Shrublands Ave CR0 .223 C4
Shrublands Cl N20 .14 B2
Forest Hill SE26 .162 C1
Shrubsall Cl SE9 .166 A3
Shrubs Ho SW1 .259 D3
Shubbery Cl N1 .235 B5
Shurland Ave EN4 .14 B5
Shurland Gdns SE15 .139 D5
Shurlock Dr BR6 .227 A4
Shuters Sq W14 .254 C1
Shuttle Cl DA15 .167 D4
Shuttlemead DA5 .169 B4
Shuttle St E1 .96 A3
Shuttleworth Rd
SW11 .136 C3
Sibella Rd SW4 .137 D3
Sibford Ct 5 CR4 .202 D6
Sibley Cl DA6 .169 A6
Sibley Ct UB8 .83 A2
Sibley Gr E12 .78 A1
Sibthorpe Rd SE12 .165 C4
Sibthorp Rd 2 CR4 .180 D1
Sibton Rd SM5 .202 C2
Sicilian Ave WC1 .240 B3
Sidbury St
SW6 .135 A4 264 A2
Sidcup By Pass Rd
Sidcup DA14 .189 C6
St Paul's Cray BR5,BR7 .190 B3
Sidcup Hill DA14 .190 B5
Sidcup Hill Gdns
DA14 .190 C5
Sidcup Hill Prim Sch
DA14 .190 B5
Sidcup Pl DA14 .190 A5
Sidcup Rd SE9 .166 A3
Sidcup Sta DA14,DA15 .168 A2
Sidcup Tech Ctr DA14 .190 D4
Siddeley Dr TW4 .129 A3
Siddons Ct WC2 .240 C1
Siddons Ho 8 NW3 .70 D3
W2 .236 D3
Siddons La
NW1 .92 D3 237 D5
Siddons Rd
Croydon CR0 .220 D5
Forest Hill SE23 .163 A2
Tottenham N17 .34 A2
Side Rd E17 .53 B4
Sidewood Rd DA15,
SE9 .167 B3
Sidford Ho SE1 .260 D5
Sidford Pl SE1 116 B3 260 D5
Sidgwick Ho 26 SW9 .138 A3
Sidings Mews N7 .72 C4
Sidings The E11 .54 A1
Sidlaw Ho N16 .51 D1
Sidmouth Ave TW7 .130 C3
Sidmouth Dr HA4 .62 A5
Sidmouth Ho 18 SE15 .140 A5
W1 .237 B2
26 Streatham SW2 .160 C4
Sidmouth Par NW2 .68 C1
Sidmouth Rd E10 .76 A5
NW2 .68 C1
Bexley DA16 .146 C5
Sidmouth St
WC1 .94 B4 233 C1
Sidney Ave N13 .32 B5
Sidney Boyd Ct NW6 .69 C1
Sidney Elson Way E6 .100 C5
Sidney Gdns TW8 .131 D6
Sidney Godley (VC) Ho 31
E2 .96 C4
Sidney Gr EC1 .234 C3
Sidney Ho 4 E2 .96 D5
3 SE18 .144 B4
Sidney Miller Ct 8
W3 .110 D5
Sidney Rd SW9 .138 B3
Beckenham BR3 .185 A1
Croydon SE25 .206 A4
Harrow HA2 .42 A6
Twickenham TW1 .153 B5
Walton-on-T KT12 .194 B1
Wanstead E7 .77 A5
Wood Green N22 .32 B3
Sidney Sq E1 .96 C2
Sidney St E1 .96 C2
Sidworth St 6 E8 .74 B1
Siebert Rd SE3 .143 A6
Siedle Ho 9 SE18 .144 C6
Siege Ho 21 E1 .96 B1
Siemens Rd SE18 .121 D3
Sierra Dr RM9 .103 D5
Sigdon Rd E8 .74 A3
Sigers The HA5 .40 B3
Signmakers Yd NW1 .231 D5
Sigrist Sq 4 KT2 .176 A2
Silbury Ave CR4 .180 C2
Silbury Ho 9 SE26 .162 A1
Silbury St N1 .235 C2
Silchester Ct
Stanwell TW15 .148 A2
Thornton Heath CR7 .204 C5
Silchester Rd W10 .90 D1
Silecroft Rd DA7 .147 C4
Silesia Bldgs E8 .74 B1
Silex St SE1 .116 D4 251 D1
Silicone Bsns Ctr UB6 .87 C5
Silk Cl SE12 .165 A5
Silkfield Rd NW9 .45 C4
Silk Ho NW9 .45 B6
Silk Mills Path SE13 .142 A2
Silk Mills Sq E9 .75 B2
Silks Ct E11 .54 C1
Silk St EC2 .95 A2 242 B4
Silkstream Par HA8 .27 A2
Silkstream Rd HA8 .27 A2
Sillitoe Ho N1 .235 D5
Silsoe Ho NW1 .231 D3
Silsoe Rd N22 .50 B6
Silver Birch Ave E4 .35 B4
Silver Birch Cl N11 .31 A4
Forest Hill SE6 .163 B1
Ickenham UB10 .60 A4
Silver Birch Ct EN3 .18 D6
Silver Birch Gdns E6 .100 B3
Silver Birch Rd SE28 .124 A5
Silverbirch Wlk 1
NW3 .71 A2
Silverburn Ho 4 SW9 138 D4
Silver Cl SE14 .141 A5
Harrow HA3 .24 B3
Silvercliffe Gdns EN4 .2 C1
Silver Cres W4 .110 D2
Silver Ct N19 .71 C5
Silverdale NW1 .232 A2
Enfield EN2 .4 A1
Forest Hill SE26 .184 C6
Silverdale Ave IG3 .57 D4
Silverdale Cl
Cheam SM1 .217 B4
1 Ealing W7 .108 D5
Northolt UB5 .63 B3
Silverdale Ct EC1 .241 D6
Silverdale Dr
Chislehurst SE9 .166 A2
Sunbury TW16 .172 B1
Silverdale Factory Ctr
UB3 .106 A4
Silverdale Gdns UB3 .106 A4
Silverdale Par IG3 .57 D4
Silverdale Rd BR5 .211 A5
DA7 .147 D3
Chingford E4 .36 B4
Hayes UB3 .106 A4
Silverhall St TW7 .131 A2
Silverholme Cl HA3 .44 A2
Silver Ind Est N17 .33 D1
Silver Jubilee Way
TW4 .128 B3
Silver La BR4 .224 B6
Silverland St E16 .122 B5
Silverleigh Rd CR7 .204 B4
Silvermead 7 E18 .37 A2
Silvermere Rd SE6 .163 D5
Silver Pl W1 .249 B6
Silver Rd W12 .112 D6
Silvers IG9 .21 C3
Silver Spring Cl DA8 .147 D6
Silver St Edmonton N18 .33 C6
Enfield EN1 .5 B2
Silverstone Ct 6 BR1 .187 C1
Silverston Way HA7 .25 C4
Silver Street Sta N18 .33 D5
Silverthorn 15 NW6 .91 D6
Silverthorne Rd SW8 .137 B3
Silverthorn Gdns E4 .19 C2
Silverton Lo SE19 .183 C3
Silverton Rd W6 .134 D6
Silvertown Sta E16 .122 A5
Silvertown Way E16 .121 A5
Silvertree La UB6 .86 B4
Silver Way
Hillingdon UB10 .82 D5
Romford RM7 .59 D6
Silver Wlk SE16 .119 B5
Silverwood Cl BR3 .185 C3
Silvester Ho 17 E1 .96 B1
27 E2 .96 C4
2 W11 .91 B1
Pinner HA5 .40 A5
Silvester Rd SE22 .161 D6
Silvester St SE1 .252 C1
Silwood St SE16 .118 C1
Simba Ct TW1 .152 D3
Simla Ho SE1 .252 D1
Simmil Rd KT10 .212 C3
Simmons Cl N20 .14 C3
Chessington KT9 .213 C2
Simmons Gate KT10 .212 A3
Simmons Ho 16 E2 .96 A4
N7 .72 B6
Simmons La E4 .20 B2
Simmons Rd SE18 .122 D1
Simmons' Way N20 .14 C2
Simms Cl SM5 .218 C6
Simms Ct SW6 .135 A2
Simms Gdns N2 .30 A1
Simms Rd SE1 .118 A2
Simnel Rd SE12 .165 B4
Simon Cl W11 113 B6 244 D6
Simon Ct W9 .91 C4
5 Woolwich SE28 .124 B5
Simonds Rd E10 .75 C6
Simone Cl BR1 .187 D2
Simon Lo 31 SW19 .156 D3
Simon Marks (Jewish) Prim
Sch N16 .73 D6
Simon Peter Ct EN2 .4 D3
Simons Wlk E15 .76 B3
Simpson Cl N21 .16 B6
Simpson Dr W3 .89 B1
Simpson Ho NW8 .230 A1
SE11 .260 C1
Simpson Ho *continued*
Wembley HA9 .65 D6
Simpson Rd
Hounslow TW4 .151 B5
Richmond TW10 .175 C6
Simpson's Cotts BR2 .225 C5
Simpson's Rd BR2 .209 A6
E14 .119 D6
Simpson St SW11 .136 C3
Simpson Way KT6 .197 C3
Sim's Cotts KT10 .212 D2
Sims Wlk SE3 .142 D1
Sinclair Ct N5 .73 A2
21 Beckenham BR3 .185 C3
5 Croydon CR0 .221 D6
Sinclair Gdns W14 .112 D4
Sinclair Gr NW11 .46 D3
Sinclair Ho 1 SW12 .159 D3
Sinclair Mans 13 W12 112 D4
Sinclair Rd E4 .35 B5
W14 .113 A3 254 A6
Sinclairs Ho 14 E3 .97 B5
Sinclare Cl EN1 .5 D4
Singapore Rd W13 .109 A5
Singer St EC2 .235 D1
Singlegate First Sch
SW19 .180 B3
Singleton Cl
Mitcham SW17,SW19 .180 D3
Thornton Heath CR0 .205 A2
Singleton Rd RM9 .81 B3
Singleton Scarp N12 .29 C5
Sinnott Rd E17 .34 D2
Sion Ct TW1 .153 B3
Sion-Manning RC Sch for
Girls
W10 .90 D2
W10 .91 A2
Sion Rd TW1 .153 B3
Sippetts Ct IG1 .57 B1
Sipson Cl UB7 .126 C6
Sipson La UB3,UB7 .126 D6
Sipson Rd
Harmondsworth UB7 .126 C6
West Drayton UB7 .104 B2
West Drayton UB7 .104 C1
Sipson Way UB7 .126 C5
Sir Abraham Dawes Cotts
SW15 .135 A1
Sir Alexander Cl W3 .111 D5
Sir Alexander Rd W3 .111 D5
Sir Cyril Black Way 2
SW19 .179 C3
Sirdar Rd W11 113 A6 244 A5
Mitcham CR4 .181 A4
Tottenham N22 .33 A1
Sir Francis Drake Prim Sch
SE8 .119 A1
Sir George Monoux Sixth
Form Coll E17 .35 D1
Sir Henry Floyd Ct HA7 .9 B2
Sirinham Point SW8 .270 D5
Sirius Bldg 13 E1 .118 D6
Sir James Barrie Prim Sch
SW8 .137 C4 269 B1
Sir John Cass Foundation &
Redcoat CE Sec Sch
E1 .96 D2
Sir John Cass's Prim Sch
EC3 .95 C1 243 A1
Sir John Heron Prim Sch
E12 .78 B4
Sir John Kirk Cl 33
SE5 .139 A5
Sir John Lillie Prim Sch
SW6 .135 A6 264 B5
Sir Martin Bowes Ho 15
SE18 .122 C2
Sir Oswald Stoll Foundation
The SW6 .265 C4
Sir Thomas Abney Sch
N16 .51 B1
Sir Thomas More Est
SW3 .136 B6 266 D5
Sirus Rd HA6 .22 A5
Sir William Burrough Prim
Sch E14 .97 A1
Sir William Powell's
Almshos SW6 .135 A2
Sise La EC4 .242 C1
Siskin Ho 14 SE16 .118 D2
Sisley Rd IG11 .101 D6
Sispara Gdns SW18 .157 B5
Sissinghurst Cl BR1 .186 C5
Sissinghurst Ho 17
SE15 .140 C6
Sissinghurst Rd CR0 .206 A2
Sissulu Ct 9 E6 .99 C6
Sister Mabel's Way 14
SE15 .140 A5
Sisters Ave SW11 .136 D1
Sistova Rd SW12 .159 B3
Sisulu Pl SW9 .138 C2
Site of Changing of the
Guard★ SW1 .249 A1
Sittingbourne Ave EN1 .17 B5

Sitwell Gr HA7 24 D5
Siverst Cl UB5 63 D2
Sivill Ho 9 E2 95 D4
Siviter Way RM10 81 D1
Siward Rd Bromley BR2 209 C6
Tottenham N17 33 B2
Wandsworth SW17 158 A1
Six Bridges Ind Est SE1 118 A1
Sixth Ave W10 91 A4
Hayes UB3 105 D5
Ilford E12 78 B4
Sixth Cross Rd TW2 152 A1
Skardu Rd NW2 69 A3
Skeena Hill SW18, SW19 157 A4
Skeffington Rd E6 100 B6
Skeggs Ho 5 E14 120 A3
Skegness Ho 3 N7 72 B1
Skelbrook St SW18 158 A2
Skelgill Rd SW15 135 B1
Skelley Rd E15 76 D1
Skelton Cl 7 E8 73 D2
Skelton Ho N16 73 C3
Skelton Rd E7 77 A2
Skelton's La E10 53 D2
Skelwith Rd W6 134 C6
Skenfrith Ho SE15 140 B6
Skerne Rd KT2 175 D2
Sketchley Gdns SE16 118 D1
Sketty Rd EN1 5 D2
Skiers St E15 98 C6
Skiffington Cl SW2 160 C3
Skinner Ct E17 53 C4
Skinner Pl SW1 258 A3
Skinners Almshouses N13 16 C1
Skinners Company Sch (Upper) N16 51 D2
Skinner's Company's Lower Sch E5 52 B1
Skinners La EC4 252 B6
Hounslow TW5 129 D4
Skinner St EC1 94 C3 241 B6
Skipsea Ho SW18 158 B5
Skipsey Ave E6 100 B4
Skipton Cl N11 31 A4
Skipton Dr UB3 105 A3
Skipton Ho SE4 141 A1
Skipwith Bldg EC1 241 A4
Skipworth Rd E9 96 C6
Skua Ct 42 SE8 141 B6
Skyline Ct SE1 263 C5
Skylines E14 120 A4
Sky Peals Rd IG8 36 B3
Sladebrook Rd SE3 143 D2
Slade Ct NW2 69 A3
Barnet EN5 1 D2
Sladedale Rd SE18 123 C1
Slade Ho TW4 151 B5
Sladen Pl 12 E5 74 B4
Slades Cl EN2 4 C2
Slades Dr BR7 189 A6
Slades Gdns EN2 4 C2
Slades Hill EN2 4 C2
Slades Rise EN2 4 C2
Slade The SE18 145 C6
Slade Twr E10 75 C6
Slade Wlk SE17 139 A6
Slagrove Pl SE13 163 D6
Slaidburn St SW10 136 A6 266 B5
Slaithwaite Rd SE13 142 A1
Slaney Ct NW10 68 C1
Slaney Pl 1 N7 72 C3
Slater Cl 18 SE18 122 C2
Slater Ho 4 N16 51 D3
Slatter 1 NW9 27 D2
Slattery Rd TW13 150 C3
Sleaford Ho 16 E3 97 C3
Sleaford Ind Est SW8 137 C5 269 B3
Sleaford St SW8 137 C5 269 B3
Sleat Ho 9 E3 97 B5
Sledmere Ct TW14 149 C3
Slievemore Cl 8 SW4 137 D2
Sligo Ho 8 E1 96 D3
Slingsby Pl WC2 250 A6
Slippers Pl SE16 118 B3
Sloane Ave SW3 114 C2 257 B3
Sloane Avenue Mans SW3 257 C3
Sloane Ct E SW3 258 A2
Sloane Ct W SW3 258 A2
Sloane Gate Mans SW1 258 A4
Sloane Gdns BR6 227 A5
SW1 115 A2 258 A3
Sloane Ho 7 E9 74 C1
Sloane Hospl BR3 186 B2
Sloane Sq SW1 257 D3
Sloane Square Sta SW1 115 A2 258 A3
Sloane St SW1 114 D3 257 D5
Sloane Terr SW1 258 A4
Sloane Terr Mans SW1 258 A4
Sloane Wlk CR0 207 B3
Slocum Cl SE28 124 C6
Slomon Ho 2 W10 91 A4
Slough La NW9 45 A3
Sly St 7 E1 96 B1
Smaldon Cl UB7 104 C3
Smallberry Ave TW7 130 D3
Smallberry Green Prim Sch TW7 131 A4
Smallbrook Mews W2 236 C1
Smalley Cl N16 73 D5
Smallwood Prim Sch SW17 180 B6
Smallwood Rd SW17 180 B6
Smarden Cl DA17 125 C1
Smarden Gr SE9 188 B6
Smart's Pl WC1,WC2 240 B2
Edmonton N18 34 A5
Smart St E2 96 D4
Smeaton Cl KT9 213 D2
Smeaton Ct SE1 262 A5
Smeaton Rd
Holdbrook EN3 7 C6
Wandsworth SW18 157 C4
Smeaton St E1 118 B5
Smedley St SW4 137 D3
Smeed Rd E3 75 C1
Smiles Pl SE13 142 A3
Smith Cl SE16 118 D5
Smithers Ho 3 SE20 184 D3
Smithfield Mkt EC1 241 D3
Smithfield St EC1 94 D2 241 C3
Smithies Ct E15 76 A3
Smithies Rd SE2 124 B2
Smith's Ct W1 249 C6
Smithson Rd N17 33 B2
Smiths Point E13 99 A6
Smith Sq SW1 116 A3 260 A5
Smith St SW3 114 D1 257 C1
Surbiton KT5 198 B3
Smith's Yd SW18 158 A2
Smith Terr SW3 114 D1 257 C1
Smithwood Cl SW19 157 A2
Smithy St E1 96 C2
Smithy Street Sch E1 96 C2
Smock Wlk CR0 205 A3
Smoothfield TW3 129 C1
Smugglers Way SW18 135 D1
Smyrk's Rd SE17 117 C1 263 B1
Smyrna Mans 8 NW6 69 C1
Smyrna Rd NW6 69 C1
Smythe St E14 119 D6
Snakes La EN4,N14 3 C1
Snakes La E IG8 37 C4
Snakes La W IG8 37 B4
Snaresbrook Dr HA7 26 A6
Snaresbrook Hall 11 E18 55 A6
Snaresbrook Ho E18 54 D5
Snaresbrook Prim Sch E18 55 A5
Snaresbrook Rd E11 54 D5
Snaresbrook Sta E11 55 A4
Snarsgate St W10 90 C2
Sneath Ave NW11 47 B2
Snell's Pk N18 33 D4
Sneyd Rd NW2 68 C4
Snowberry Cl E11 76 B4
Snowbury Rd 6 SW6 135 D3
Snow Ct 6 HA0 65 D3
Snowden Ave UB10 82 D5
Snowden St EC2 95 C3 243 A5
Snowdon Cres UB3 105 A3
Snowdon Dr NW9 45 C3
Snowdon Rd TW6 149 A5
Snowdown Cl SE20 184 D2
Snowdrop Cl 2 TW12 173 C4
Snow Hill EC1 94 D2 241 C3
Snow Ho SE27 160 D1
Snowman Ho NW6 91 D6
Snowsfield Prim Sch SE1 117 C4 253 A2
Snowsfields SE1 117 B4 252 D2
Snowshill Rd E12 78 A3
Snowy Fielder Waye TW7 131 B3
Soames St SE15 139 D2
Soames Wlk KT3 177 C2
Soane Cl W5 109 D4
Soane Ct 8 NW1 71 C1
Soane Ho SE17 262 D1
Soane Mus* WC2 94 B1 240 C2
Soaphouse La TW8 132 A5
Soham Rd EN3 7 B6
Soho* W1 93 D1 239 C2
Soho Mills SM6 203 B1
Soho Parish CE Prim Sch W1 115 D6 249 C6
Soho Sq W1 93 D1 239 C2
Soho St W1 239 C2
Sojourner-Truth Cl 11 E8 74 B2
Solander Gdns 12 E1 118 C6
Stepney E1 118 B6
Solar Ct N3 29 D3
Soldene Ct N7 72 B2
Solebay St E1 97 A3
Solent Ct SW16 182 B1
Solent Ho 6 E1 97 A2
Solent Rd NW6 69 C3
Solent Rise E13 99 A4
Soley Mews WC1 234 A2
Solna Ave SW15 156 C6
Solna Rd N21 17 B4
Solomon Ave N9 34 A6
Solomon's Pas SE15 140 B1
Solon New Rd SW4 138 A1
Solon Rd SW2 138 A1
Solway Cl TW4 129 A2
Solway Ho 12 E1 96 D3
Solway Lo 4 IG8 37 A3
Solway Rd SE22 140 A1
Tottenham N22 32 D2
Somaford Gr EN4 14 B5
Somali Rd NW2 69 B3
Somborne Ho SW15 156 A4
Sombrook Ho SE11 261 A3
Somerby Rd IG11 79 B1
Somercoates Cl EN4 2 C2
Somer Ct SW6 265 A5
Somerfield Ho SE16 118 D1
Somerfield Rd N4 72 D6
Somerford Cl HA5 40 A5
Somerford Gr N16 73 D4
Tottenham N17 34 A3
Somerford Grove Est N16 73 D4
Somerford St E1 96 B3
Somerford Way SE16 119 A4
Somerhill Ave DA15 168 B4
Somerhill Rd DA16 146 B3
Somerleyton Rd SW9 138 C1
Somersby Est SE20 184 C3
Somersby Gdns IG4 56 B4
Somers Cl NW1 232 C4
Somers Cres W2 237 A1
Somerset Ave DA16 145 D1
Chessington KT9 213 D4
Wimbledon SW20 178 B1
Somerset Cl
New Malden KT3 199 C3
Tottenham N17 33 B1
Woodford IG8 37 A2
Somerset Ct Ealing W7 86 D1
2 Hampton TW12 173 C2
Somerset Gdns N6 49 A2
SE13 141 D3
Teddington TW11 174 C5
Thornton Heath SW16 204 B6
Tottenham N17 33 C3
Somerset Hall N17 33 C3
Somerset Ho* WC2 116 B6 250 D6
Wimbledon SW19 157 A1
Somerset Lo
9 Brentford TW8 131 D6
Putney SW15 134 B1
Somerset Rd E17 53 C3
N17 51 D6
NW4 46 C5
W4 111 B3
Brentford TW8 131 C6
Ealing W13 109 C5
Edmonton N18 33 D5
Harrow HA1 42 A4
Holdbrook EN3 7 C5
Kingston KT1 176 B1
New Barnet EN5 14 A6
Southall UB1 85 C2
Teddington TW11 174 C5
Wimbledon SW19 157 A1
Somerset Sq W14 113 B4 244 C1
Somerset Waye TW5 129 A5
Somersham Rd DA7 147 A3
Somers Pl SW2 160 B4
Somers Rd E17 53 B5
SW2 160 B5
Somers Town Est NW1 93 C5 232 B3
Somers Way WD23 8 A4
Somerton Ave TW9 132 D2
Somerton Rd NW2 69 A5
SE15 140 B1
Somertrees Ave SE12 165 B2
Somervell Rd HA2 63 C3
Somerville Ave SW13 134 C6
Somerville Ct SW16 181 D4
Somerville Ho 10 SW15 156 D5
Somerville Point SE16 119 B4
Somerville Rd
Dagenham RM6 58 C4
Penge SE20 184 D3
Sonderburg Rd 13 N7 72 B6
Sondes St SE17 139 B6
Sonia Ct N12 30 A6
Sonia Ct *continued*
Edgware HA8 26 B3
Sonia Gdns N12 30 A6
NW10 67 D4
Heston TW5 129 C5
Sonning Ct CR0 222 A6
Sonning Gdns TW12 173 A4
Sonning Ho 32 E2 95 D4
Sonning Rd CR0 206 A3
Soper Cl E4 35 B5
4 Forest Hill SE23 162 D2
Soper Mews EN3 7 C5
Sophia Cl N7 72 B2
Sophia Ho N15 51 D5
10 W6 112 C1
Sophia Rd E10 53 D1
E13 99 B2
Sophia Sq 14 SE16 119 A6
Sopwith 2 NW9 27 D2
Sopwith Ave KT9 214 A3
Sopwith Cl TW10 176 B5
Sopwith Rd TW5 128 C5
Sopwith Way SW11 268 C4
Kingston KT2 176 A2
Sorbus Ct EN2 4 D3
Sorenson Ct 2 E10 75 D6
Sorrel Cl SE28 124 A5
Sorrel Gdns E6 100 A2
Sorrel Ho TW3 130 A4
Sorrel La 18 E14 98 B1
Sorrell Cl SE14 141 A5
7 SW9 138 C3
Sorrento Rd SM1 217 D5
Sotheby Rd N5 73 A4
Sotheran Cl E8 96 A6
Sotheron Pl SW6 265 D3
Soudan Rd SW11 136 D4 267 C1
Souldern Rd 10 W14 112 D3
South Access Rd E17 53 A3
South Acre NW9 27 D1
Southacre Way HA5 22 C2
South Acton Sta W3, W4 111 A3
South Africa Rd W12 112 B6
Southall Ct UB1 107 B6
Southall Ent Ctr UB2 107 C4
Southall La TW5 106 B1
Southall Norwood Hospl UB2 107 B3
Southall Pl SE1 252 C1
Southall Sta UB1 107 B4
Southall & West London Coll UB1 107 A5
Southam Ho 9 W10 91 A3
Southampton Bldgs WC2 241 A3
Southampton Gdns CR4 204 A4
Southampton Pl WC1 240 B3
Southampton Rd NW5 70 D3
Stanwell TW19,TW6 148 B5
Southampton Row WC1 94 A2 240 B4
Southampton St WC2 250 B6
Southampton Way SE5 139 C5
Southam St W10 91 A3
South Audley St W1 115 A5 248 B4
South Ave NW11 47 D5
Chingford E4 20 A4
Richmond TW9 132 C3
Southall UB1 107 B6
Wallington SM5 219 A1
South Avenue Gdns UB1 107 B6
Southbank KT7 197 B2
South Bank KT6 198 A3
South Bank Bsns Ctr SW8 137 D6 269 D5
South Bank Lo 2 KT6 198 A3
South Bank Terr KT6 198 A3
South Bank Univ SW8 137 D4 269 D2
SE1 116 D3 261 D6
South Bermondsey Sta SE16 118 C1
South Birkbeck Rd E11 76 B5
South Black Lion La W6 112 A1
South Bldg SW1 259 B5
South Block 19 E1 118 C6
South Bolton Gdns SW10 255 D2
Southborough Cl KT6 197 D1
Southborough Ho SE17 263 B2
Southborough La BR1, BR2 210 B4
Southborough Prim Sch BR2 210 C4
Southborough Rd E9 96 D6
Bromley BR1,BR2 210 A5
Surbiton KT6 198 A1
Southborough Rd (The Lane) KT6 198 A1
Southborough Sch KT6 214 A5
Southbourne BR2 209 A2
Southbourne Ave NW9 27 B1
Southbourne Cl HA5 41 A2
Southbourne Cres NW4 47 A5
Southbourne Ct NW9 27 A1
Southbourne Gdns SE12 165 B6
Ilford IG1 79 A3
Ruislip HA4 40 B1
Southbridge Pl CR0 221 A4
Southbridge Rd CR0 221 A4
Southbridge Way UB2 107 A4
Southbrook Mews SE12 164 D5
Southbrook Rd SE12 164 D5
Thornton Heath SW16 182 A2
South Building SE10 142 B5
Southbury NW8 229 B6
Southbury Ave EN1 6 A1
Southbury Prim Sch EN3 6 C1
Southbury Rd Enfield EN1 5 D1
Enfield EN1,EN3 6 B1
Southbury Sta EN3 6 B1
South Camden Com Sch NW1 93 D5 232 C3
South Carriage Dr SW1,SW7 114 D4 247 C2
South Church Ct E6 100 B5
Southchurch Rd E6 100 B5
South Cl DA6 146 D1
N6 49 B3
Barnet EN5 1 B2
Dagenham RM10 103 C6
Morden SM4 201 C3
Pinner HA5 22 D2
Pinner HA5 41 B2
Twickenham TW2 151 C1
West Drayton UB7 104 C3
South Colonnade E14 119 C5
Southcombe St W14 254 A4
South Common Rd UB8 60 A2
Southcote Ave
Feltham TW13 150 A2
Tolworth KT5 198 D2
Southcote Rd E17 53 A4
N19 71 C4
Croydon SE25 206 B3
Southcote Rise HA4 39 B2
Southcott Ho 31 E3 97 D4
W9 236 B5
South Cres E16 98 B3
WC1 239 C3
Southcroft Ave DA16 145 C2
West Wickham BR4 224 A6
Southcroft Rd BR6 227 C5
Streatham SW17 181 A4
South Cross Rd IG6 57 A4
South Croxted Rd SE21 183 B6
South Croydon Sta CR2 221 B3
South Ct 17 SW15 156 D5
Southdean Gdns SW19 157 B2
South Dene NW7 11 B1
Southdene Ct N11 15 C1
Southdown N7 72 A2
Southdown Ave W7 109 A3
Southdown Cres
Harrow HA2 42 A1
Ilford IG2 57 C4
Southdown Dr SW20 178 D3
Southdown Rd SW20 178 D2
South Dr Orpington BR6 227 C3
Ruislip HA4 39 C1
South Ealing Cemy W5 109 D2
South Ealing Rd W5 109 D3
South Ealing Sta W5 109 D3
South Eastern Ave N9 17 D1
South Eaton Pl SW1 115 A2 258 B4
South Eden Park Rd BR3 207 D4
South Edwardes Sq W8 255 A5
South End W8 113 D3 255 D6
Croydon CR0 221 A4
Southend Cl SE9 166 D5
South End Cl NW3 70 C4
Southend Cres SE9 166 D5
South End Gn NW3 70 C4
Southend La SE6 185 C6
Southend Rd E6 78 B1
South End Rd NW3 70 C4
Southend Rd
Beckenham BR3 185 C2
Woodford IG8 37 D1
Southend Road (North Circular Rd) E17,E18 36 C2
South End Row W8 113 D3 255 D6
Southern Ave
East Bedfont TW14 150 A3
South Norwood SE25 205 D6
Southerngate Way SE14 141 A5
Southern Gr E3 97 B3
Southernhay IG10 21 D6
Southern Perimeter Rd
Harlington TW14,TW6 149 B6
Harlington TW19,TW6 148 C5
Stanwell TW6 148 C5
Southern Rd E13 99 B5
N2 48 D5
Southern Road Inf Sch E13 99 B5
Southern Road Prim Sch E13 99 B5
Southern Row W10 91 A3
Southern St N1 233 C4
Southern Way SE10 120 D3
Romford RM7 59 C3
Southerton Rd W6 112 C2
South Esk Rd E7 77 C2
Southey Ho SE17 262 B2
Southey Rd N15 51 C4
SW9 138 C4
Merton SW19 179 C3
Southey St SE20 184 D3
Southfield EN5 12 D5
Southfield Cl UB8 82 C4
Southfield Cotts W7 108 D4
Southfield Gdns TW1, TW2 174 D6
Southfield Pk HA2 41 D5
Southfield Prim Sch W4 111 C4
Southfield Rd W4 111 B4
Enfield EN3 18 C5
St Paul's Cray BR7 211 D6
Southfields Hendon NW4 46 B6
Thames Ditton KT8 196 C3
Southfields Ave TW15 170 D4
Southfields Com Coll SW18 157 C3
Southfields Ct SM3 217 C6
Southfields Rd SW18 157 C5
Southfields Sta SW18 157 B3
Southfleet Rd BR6 227 C4
South Gate Ave TW13 171 B6
Southgate Cir 3 N14 15 D3
Southgate Coll N14 15 D2
Southgate Ct N1 73 B1
Southgate Gr N1 73 B1
Southgate Ho 7 E17 54 A6
Southgate Rd N1 73 B1 235 D6
Southgate Sch EN4 15 B6
Southgate Sta N14 15 D3
Southgate Way N2 30 C2
South Gdns
Mitcham SW19 180 B3
Wembley HA9 66 C6
South Gipsy Rd DA16 146 D2
South Glade DA5 169 B3
South Gn NW9 27 C2
South Gr E17 53 B4
N15 51 B4
N6 49 A1
South Greenford Sta UB6 86 C4
South Grove Ho N6 49 A1
South Grove Prim Sch E17 53 B3
South Hampstead High Sch NW3 70 B2
South Hampstead Jun Sch NW3 70 A2
South Hampstead Sta NW8 70 A1
South Harringay Jun & Inf Schs N4 50 D4
South Harrow Sta HA2 64 A5
South Hill BR7 188 B4
South Hill Ave HA1,HA2 64 B5
South Hill Gr HA1 64 C4
South Hill Pk NW3 70 C4
South Hill Pk Gdns NW3 70 C4
South Hill Rd BR2 208 C5
Southholme Cl SE19 183 C2
Southill La HA5 40 B5
Southill Rd BR7 188 B3
Southill St E14 97 D1
South Island Pl SW9 138 C5
South Kensington Sta SW7 114 B2 256 D4
South Kenton Sta HA9 43 C1
South La Kingston KT1 197 D6
New Malden KT3 199 B3
Southlake Prim Sch SE2 124 D4
South Lambeth Pl SW8 270 B6
South Lambeth Rd SW8 138 A5 270 B4
Southland Rd SE18 145 D5
Southlands Ave BR6 227 C3
Southlands Coll SW15 156 A6
Southlands Dr SW19 156 D2
Southlands Gr BR1 210 A6
Southlands Rd BR1, BR2 209 D5
Southland Way TW7 152 B6
South La W KT3 199 B5
South Lo NW8 229 C2
6 New Barnet EN5 13 D6

South Lo *continued*
Twickenham TW2 ... 152 A5
South Lodge Ave CR4, CR7,SW16 ... 204 A5
South Lodge Cres EN2 ... 3 D1
South Lodge Dr N14 ... 15 D6
South London Montessori Sch SW11 ... 267 A1
South London Tamil Sch CR0 ... 205 A2
South Mall The N9 ... 18 A1
South Mead NW9 ... 27 D2
West Ewell KT19 ... 215 D1
Southmead Prim Sch SW19 ... 157 A3
Southmead Rd SW19 ... 157 A3
South Merton Sta SW20 ... 201 B6
South Molton La W1 ... 93 B1 238 C1
South Molton Rd E16 ... 99 A1
South Molton St W1 ... 93 B1 238 C1
Southmont Rd KT10 ... 212 C5
Southmoor Way E9 ... 75 B3
South Mount N20 ... 14 A2
South Norwood Ctry Pk★ SE25 ... 206 C5
South Norwood Hill SE19,SE25 ... 183 D1
South Norwood Prim Sch SE25 ... 206 A5
South Oak Rd SW16 ... 182 B6
Southold Rise SE9 ... 166 B1
Southolm St SW11 ... 137 B4 268 D1
South Ordnance Rd EN3 ... 7 C5
Southover BR1 ... 187 A5
N12 ... 29 C6
South Par W4 ... 111 B2
Edgware HA8 ... 26 C1
South Parade SW3 ... 114 B1 256 D2
South Park Cres
Catford SE6 ... 164 D3
Ilford IG1 ... 79 C5
South Park Ct 24 BR3 ... 185 C3
South Park Dr
Barking IG11 ... 79 C4
Ilford IG3 ... 79 C5
South Park Gr KT3 ... 199 A5
South Park Hill Rd CR2 ... 221 B4
South Park Mews SW6 ... 135 D2
South Park Prim Sch IG3 ... 79 C5
South Park Rd
Ilford IG1 ... 79 B5
Wimbledon SW19 ... 179 D4
South Park Terr IG1 ... 79 C5
South Park Villas IG3 ... 79 C4
South Park Way HA4 ... 62 C3
South Pl EC2 ... 95 B2 242 D3
Enfield EN3 ... 18 C6
Surbiton KT5 ... 198 B2
South Pl Mews EC2 ... 242 D3
Southport Rd SE18 ... 123 B2
South Quay Plaza E14 ... 119 D4
South Quay Sta E14 ... 119 D4
South Rd W5 ... 109 D2
Edgware HA8 ... 26 D2
Edmonton N9 ... 18 A3
Feltham TW13 ... 172 D5
Forest Hill SE23 ... 162 D2
Hampton TW12 ... 173 B4
Mitcham SW19 ... 180 B4
Southall UB1 ... 107 B5
Twickenham TW2 ... 152 B1
West Drayton UB7 ... 104 C3
Heston TW5 ... 128 D6
South Residence IG3 ... 58 B4
Southridge Pl SW20 ... 178 D3
South Rise W2 ... 247 B6
South Rise Prim Sch SE18 ... 123 B1
South Rise Way SE18 ... 123 B2
South Row SE3 ... 142 D3
South Ruislip Sta HA4 ... 62 C3
Southsea Rd KT1 ... 198 A5
South Sea St SE16 ... 119 B3
Southside N7 ... 71 D4
South Side W6 ... 111 D3
Southside Comm SW19 ... 178 D4
Southside Ind Est SW8 ... 269 A2
Southside Quarter 4 SW11 ... 136 D3
Southspring SE9 ... 167 B4
South Sq NW11 ... 47 D3
WC1 ... 241 A3
South St BR1 ... 187 A1
W1 ... 115 A5 248 B4
Enfield EN3 ... 18 D6
Isleworth TW7 ... 131 A2
South Tenter St E1 ... 95 D1 243 D1
South Terr N22 ... 31 D1
South Terr *continued*
SW7 ... 114 C2 257 A4
Surbiton KT6 ... 198 A3
South Thames Coll SW18 ... 157 D6
Putney SW15 ... 156 D6
South Tottenham Sta N15 ... 51 D4
South Vale Harrow HA1 ... 64 C4
West Norwood SE19 ... 183 C4
Southvale Rd SE3 ... 142 C3
South View BR1 ... 187 C1
Wimbledon SW19 ... 178 D4
Southview Ave NW10 ... 67 D3
Southview Cl SW17 ... 181 A5
South View Cl DA5 ... 169 B5
South View Cres IG2 ... 56 D3
South View Ct
8 Forest Hill SE23 ... 162 C3
South Norwood SE19 ... 183 A3
Southview Dr E18 ... 55 B6
Southview Gdns SM6 ... 219 C1
South View Rd N8 ... 50 A6
Southview Rd BR1 ... 186 B6
South View Rd HA5 ... 22 B4
South Villas NW1 ... 71 D2
Southville SW8 ... 137 D4 269 D1
Southville Cl
East Bedfont TW14 ... 149 C3
West Ewell KT19 ... 215 B1
Southville Cres TW14 ... 149 C3
Southville Jun Sch TW14 ... 149 D3
Southville Rd
East Bedfont TW14 ... 149 C4
Thames Ditton KT7 ... 197 B2
Southwark Bridge SE1,EC4 ... 117 A6 252 B5
Southwark Bridge Office Village SE1 ... 252 B3
Southwark Bridge Rd SE1 ... 117 A5 252 B3
Southwark Cath★ SE1 ... 117 B5 252 C4
Southwark Coll SE1 ... 116 D4 251 C2
SE15 ... 140 B5
Southwark Coll (Blackfriars Ctr) SE1 ... 251 C3
Southwark Coll (Camberwell Ctr) SE5 ... 139 C5
Southwark Coll (Grange Ctr) SE1 ... 263 B5
Southwark Coll (Surrey Docks Ctr) SE16 ... 118 B3
Southwark Park Est 1 SE16 ... 118 B2
Southwark Park Prim Sch SE16 ... 118 B3
Southwark Park Rd SE16 ... 118 A2 263 D4
Southwark Pl BR1 ... 210 B6
Southwark St SE1 ... 117 A5 252 A3
Southwater Cl 6 E14 ... 97 B1
Beckenham BR3 ... 185 D3
Southway N20 ... 13 C2
NW11 ... 47 D4
South Way N11 ... 31 C4
N9 ... 18 C2
Southway Hayes BR2 ... 209 A2
Wallington SM6 ... 219 C4
West Barnes SW20 ... 200 D5
South Way
Croydon CR0 ... 223 A5
Harrow HA2 ... 41 C5
Wembley HA9 ... 66 C3
Southwell Ave UB5 ... 63 C2
Southwell Gdns SW7 ... 256 A3
Southwell Grove Rd E11 ... 76 C6
Southwell Ho 13 N16 ... 73 C3
8 SE16 ... 118 B2
Southwell Rd SE5 ... 139 A2
Harrow HA3 ... 43 D3
Thornton Heath CR0 ... 204 C3
South Western Rd TW1 ... 153 B5
Southwest Rd E11 ... 54 B1
South Wharf Rd W2 ... 92 B1 236 D2
Southwick Mews W2 ... 236 D2
Southwick Pl W2 ... 237 A1
Southwick St W2 ... 92 C1 237 A2
Southwick Yd W2 ... 237 A1
South Wimbledon Sta SW19 ... 179 D3
South Wlk
Coney Hall BR4 ... 224 C5
Hayes UB3 ... 83 B2
Southwold Dr IG11 ... 80 A3
Southwold Mans W9 ... 91 C4
Southwold Prim Sch E5 ... 74 B6
Southwold Rd DA5 ... 169 D5
E5 ... 74 C6
Southwood Ave N6 ... 49 B2
Kingston KT2,KT3 ... 177 A2
Southwood Cl BR1 ... 210 B5
North Cheam KT4 ... 200 D1
Southwood Ct EC1 ... 234 C1
NW11 ... 47 D4
Southwood Dr KT5 ... 199 A1
South Woodford Sta E18 ... 37 B1
Southwood Gdns
Hinchley Wood KT10 ... 213 A5
Ilford IG2 ... 56 D5
Southwood Hall N6 ... 49 B3
Southwood Ho SE9 ... 166 D2
W11 ... 244 A6
Southwood Hospl (Geriatric) N6 ... 49 A2
Southwood Hts N6 ... 49 B2
Southwood La N6 ... 49 A2
Southwood Lawn Rd N6 ... 49 B2
Southwood Mans N6 ... 49 B3
Southwood Park N6 ... 49 A2
Southwood Prim Sch RM9 ... 81 A4
Southwood Rd SE9 ... 166 D2
Woolwich SE28 ... 124 B5
Southwood Smith Ho 4 E2 ... 96 B4
Southwood Smith St N1 ... 234 C5
South Worple Way SW14 ... 133 B2
Southwyck Ho SW9 ... 138 C1
South Yd EC1 ... 242 C4
Sovereign Bsns Ctr EN3 ... 7 B2
Sovereign Cl Ealing W5 ... 87 C2
Ruislip HA4 ... 39 C1
Stepney E1 ... 118 B6
Sovereign Cres SE16 ... 119 A6
Sovereign Ct BR2 ... 210 B3
East Molesey KT8 ... 195 B5
Harlington UB7 ... 126 D5
3 Richmond TW9 ... 132 B1
Stepney E1 ... 118 B6
Sovereign Gr HA0 ... 65 D5
Sovereign Ho 23 E1 ... 96 B3
NW7 ... 27 B6
SE18 ... 122 B3
Ashford TW15 ... 170 A6
3 Wimbledon SW19 ... 179 A4
Sovereign Mews 6 E2 ... 95 D5
Barnet EN4 ... 2 D2
Sovereign Pk NW10 ... 88 D3
Sovereign Pl HA1 ... 42 D4
Sovereign Rd IG11 ... 102 C4
Sowerby Cl SE9 ... 166 B6
Space Waye TW14 ... 150 B6
Spa Cl SE19 ... 183 C2
Spa Ct 12 SE16 ... 118 A3
Spafield St EC1 ... 241 A6
Spa Hill CR7,SE19 ... 183 B2
Spalding Cl HA8 ... 27 C3
Spalding Ct HA8 ... 26 B6
Spalding Ho SE4 ... 163 A6
Spalding Rd NW4 ... 46 C3
Streatham SW17 ... 181 B5
Spanby Rd E3 ... 97 C3
Spangate SE3 ... 142 D2
Spaniards Cl NW11 ... 48 B1
Spaniards End NW3 ... 48 B1
Spaniards Rd NW3 ... 70 A6
Spanish Pl W1 ... 238 B2
Spanish Rd SW18 ... 158 A6
Spa Rd SE16 ... 117 D3 263 D5
Sparkbridge Rd HA1 ... 42 C5
Sparke Terr 2 E16 ... 98 D1
Sparkford Gdns N11 ... 31 A5
Sparkford Ho SW11 ... 266 D2
Sparks Cl W3 ... 89 B1
Dagenham RM8 ... 80 D6
Hampton TW12 ... 173 A4
Sparrow Cl TW12 ... 173 A4
Sparrow Dr BR5 ... 211 B1
Sparrow Farm Com Jun Sch KT17 ... 216 B4
Sparrow Farm Dr TW14 ... 150 D4
Sparrow Farm Inf Sch TW14 ... 150 C4
Sparrow Farm Jun Sch TW14 ... 150 C4
Sparrow Farm Rd KT17,KT4 ... 216 B4
Sparrow Gn RM10 ... 81 D5
Sparrow's Farm L Ctr SE9 ... 167 A4
Sparrows Herne WD23 ... 8 A4
Sparrows La SE9 ... 167 A3
Sparrows Way WD23 ... 8 A4
Sparsholt Rd N19 ... 50 B1
Barking IG11 ... 101 C6
Sparta St SE10 ... 142 A4
Spa Sch SE1 ... 118 A2
Spa View 6 SW16 ... 160 B1
Speakers' Corner★ W1 ... 114 D6 247 D6
Speaker's Ct 3 CR0 ... 205 B1
Speakman Ho SE4 ... 141 A2
Spearman St 8 SE18 ... 144 C6
Spear Mews SW5 ... 113 C2 255 B3
Spearpoint Gdns IG2 ... 57 D5
Spears Rd N19 ... 50 A1
Speart La TW5 ... 129 A5
Spectrum Ho NW5 ... 71 A4
Spedan Cl NW3 ... 70 A5
Speechly Mews E8 ... 73 D3
Speed Ho EC2 ... 242 B4
Speedwell Ct 7 N12 ... 29 D6
Speedwell Ho 9 N12 ... 29 D6
Speedwell St 5 SE8 ... 141 C5
Speedy Pl WC1 ... 233 A1
Speer Rd KT7 ... 196 D3
Speirs Cl KT3 ... 199 D3
Spekehill SE9 ... 166 B1
Speke Rd CR7 ... 183 B1
Speldhurst Cl 2 BR2 ... 208 D4
Speldhurst Rd E9 ... 74 D1
W4 ... 111 B3
Spellbrook Wlk N1 ... 235 B6
Spelman Ho 14 E1 ... 96 A2
Spelman St E1 ... 96 A2
Spelthorne Coll TW15 ... 170 B6
Spelthorne Cty Inf Sch TW15 ... 171 B4
Spelthorne Gr TW16 ... 171 D3
Spelthorne La TW15, TW17 ... 171 A2
Spence Cl SE16 ... 119 B4
Spencer Ave
Bowes Park N13 ... 32 B4
Hayes UB4 ... 84 A2
Spencer Cl BR6 ... 227 D6
N3 ... 29 C1
Ealing NW10 ... 88 B4
Woodford IG8 ... 37 C5
Spencer Ct 5 BR6 ... 227 A3
Wimbledon SW20 ... 178 B2
Spencer Dr N2 ... 48 A3
Spencer Gdns SW14 ... 155 A6
Spencer Hill SW19 ... 179 A3
Spencer Hill Rd SW19 ... 179 A3
Spencer Ho NW3 ... 70 B5
NW4 ... 46 B4
31 SW8 ... 137 D3
24 Putney SW19 ... 156 D3
Wimbledon SW19 ... 156 D1
Spencer Mews W6 ... 264 A6
Spencer Park Ct SW18 ... 158 B6
Spencer Pk SW18 ... 158 B6
Spencer Pl 16 N1 ... 72 D1
SW1 ... 259 B5
Thornton Heath CR0 ... 205 B2
Spencer Rd E6 ... 99 D6
N11 ... 31 B6
N8 ... 50 B4
SW18 ... 158 B6
W3 ... 111 A5
Bromley BR1 ... 186 D3
Carshalton CR4 ... 203 A2
Chingford E17 ... 36 A1
Chiswick W4 ... 133 A5
East Molesey KT8 ... 196 A4
Harrow HA3 ... 24 C1
Hounslow TW3,TW5, TW7 ... 130 A4
Ilford IG3 ... 57 D1
Mitcham CR4 ... 203 A6
South Croydon CR2 ... 221 C3
Tottenham N17 ... 34 A2
Twickenham TW2 ... 152 C2
Wembley HA0 ... 65 C6
Wimbledon SW20 ... 178 B2
Spencer Rise NW5 ... 71 B5
Spencer St EC1 ... 94 D4 234 C1
Southall UB2 ... 106 D4
Spencer Wlk 15 NW3 ... 70 A4
Putney SW15 ... 134 D1
Spenlow Ho 2 SE16 ... 118 A3
Spenser Ct 5 TW10 ... 175 D6
Spenser Gr N16 ... 73 C4
Spenser Mews SE21 ... 161 B3
Spenser Rd SE24 ... 160 D6
Spenser St SW1 ... 259 B6
Spens Ho WC1 ... 240 C5
Spensley Wlk N16 ... 73 B5
Speranza St SE18 ... 123 D1
Sperling Rd N17 ... 33 C1
Spert St E14 ... 119 A6
Speyside N14 ... 15 C5
Spey St E14 ... 98 A2
Spezia Rd NW10 ... 90 A5
Spice Ct 2 E1 ... 118 A5
10 SW11 ... 136 A2
Spice Quay Heights SE1 ... 253 D3
Spicer Cl SE5,SW9 ... 138 D3
Walton-on-T KT12 ... 194 C3
Spicer Ct EN1 ... 5 C2
Spices Yd CR0 ... 221 A4
Spigurnell Rd N17 ... 33 B2
Spikes Bridge Rd UB1 ... 107 A6
Spilsby Cl NW9 ... 27 C1
Spindle Cl SE18 ... 122 A3
Spindle Ho 8 DA15 ... 168 A1
Spindlewood Gdns CR0 ... 221 C4
Spindrift Ave E14 ... 119 D2
Spinel Cl SE18 ... 123 D1
Spinnaker Cl IG11 ... 102 B4
Spinnaker Ct 2 KT1 ... 175 D2
Spinnaker Ho E14 ... 119 C4
Spinnells Rd HA2 ... 41 B1
Spinney Cl
Beckenham BR3 ... 207 D5
New Malden KT3 ... 199 C4
Worcester Park KT4 ... 215 D6
Yiewsley UB7 ... 104 A6
Spinney Dr TW14 ... 149 A4
Spinney Gdns
Dagenham RM9 ... 81 A3
Dulwich SE19 ... 183 D5
Spinney Oak BR1 ... 188 A1
Spinneys The BR1 ... 188 B1
Spinney The DA14 ... 191 A5
Barnes SW13 ... 134 B6
Barnet EN5 ... 1 D3
Cheam SM3 ... 216 C4
Southgate N21 ... 16 C4
Stanmore HA7 ... 26 A6
Streatham SW16 ... 159 D1
Sunbury TW16 ... 172 A2
Wembley HA0 ... 65 A5
Spire Ct 10 TW10 ... 154 A5
Spire Ho W2 ... 246 B6
Spires The EN5 ... 1 A2
Spirit Quay E1 ... 118 B5
Spital Sq E1 ... 95 C2 243 B4
Spital St E1 ... 96 A2
Spital Yd E1 ... 243 B4
Spitfire Est The TW5 ... 106 C1
Spitfire Rd SM6 ... 220 B1
Spitfire Way TW5 ... 106 C1
Splendour Wlk SE16 ... 118 C1
Spode Ho SE11 ... 261 A5
Spode Wlk NW3 ... 69 D3
Spondon Rd N15 ... 52 A5
Spoonbill Way UB4 ... 84 D2
Spooner 8 NW9 ... 27 D2
Spooner Ho TW5 ... 129 C6
Spooner Wlk SM6 ... 219 D3
Sporle Ct 6 SW11 ... 136 B2
Sportsbank St SE6 ... 164 A4
Spottons Gr N17 ... 33 A2
Spout Hill CR0 ... 223 C3
Spratt Hall Rd E11 ... 55 A3
Spray St SE18 ... 122 D2
Spreighton Rd KT8 ... 195 D5
Sprewell SW15 ... 157 A5
Spriggs Ho 14 N1 ... 72 D1
Sprimont Pl SW3 ... 114 D2 257 C2
Springall St 9 SE15 ... 140 B5
Springalls Wharf 2 SE16 ... 118 A4
Springbank N21 ... 16 B5
Springbank Rd SE13 ... 164 C5
Springbank Wlk NW1 ... 71 D1
Springbourne Ct BR3 ... 186 A2
Spring Bridge Rd W5 ... 109 D6
Spring Cl Barnet EN5 ... 12 D6
Dagenham RM8 ... 58 D1
Springclose La SM3 ... 217 A2
Spring Cnr TW13 ... 149 D1
Spring Cott 10 W12 ... 112 A4
Spring Cotts KT6 ... 197 D4
Spring Court Rd EN2 ... 4 C5
Springcroft Ave N2 ... 48 D5
Spring Ct Ealing W7 ... 108 B6
10 Wanstead E18 ... 55 B6
Springdale Rd N16 ... 73 B4
Spring Dr HA5 ... 40 A3
Springett Ho 15 SW2 ... 160 B6
Springfield E5 ... 52 B1
Bushey WD23 ... 8 B3
South Norwood SE25 ... 206 A6
Springfield Ave N10 ... 49 C6
Hampton TW12 ... 173 D4
Merton SW20 ... 201 B6
Springfield Cl N12 ... 29 D5
Stanmore HA7 ... 9 A1
Springfield Ct E5 ... 52 B1
NW3 ... 70 C1
7 W3 ... 89 A1
2 Ilford IG1 ... 78 D3
9 Kingston KT1 ... 198 A6
Wallington SM6 ... 219 B3
Springfield Dr IG2 ... 57 A3
Springfield Gdns BR1 ... 210 B5
E5 ... 52 B1
NW9 ... 45 B4
Ruislip HA4 ... 40 B1
West Wickham BR4 ... 223 D6
Woodford IG8 ... 37 C3
Springfield Gr SE7 ... 143 C6
Sunbury TW16 ... 172 A2
Springfield Ho 1 SE5 ... 139 C3
W3 ... 111 A5
Springfield Hospl SW17 ... 158 C1
Springfield La NW6 ... 91 D6
Springfield Mount NW9 ... 45 C4
Springfield Pl KT3 ... 199 A5
Springfield Rd BR1 ... 210 B5
DA16 ... 146 B2
DA7 ... 147 D1
E15 ... 98 C4
E17 ... 53 B3
E6 ... 78 B1
N11 ... 31 C5
N15 ... 52 A5
NW8 ... 92 A6 229 B5
Ashford TW15 ... 170 B5
Chingford E4 ... 20 C4
Ealing W7 ... 108 C5
Harrow HA1 ... 42 C3
Hayes UB4 ... 106 C5
Kingston KT1 ... 198 A6
Penge SE26 ... 184 B5
South Norwood CR7 ... 183 A2
6 Teddington TW11 ... 175 A5
Twickenham TW2 ... 151 C3
Wallington SM6 ... 219 B3
Wimbledon SW19 ... 179 B5
Springfield Rise SE26 ... 162 B1
Springfields 9 EN5 ... 13 D6
Springfield Wlk 3 BR6 ... 211 B1
NW6 ... 91 D6
Spring Gdns N5 ... 73 A3
SW1 ... 116 A5 250 A4
East Molesey KT8 ... 196 A5
Wallington SM6 ... 219 C3
Woodford IG8 ... 37 C3
Spring Gr Brentford W4 ... 132 C6
Hampton TW12 ... 173 D2
Loughton IG10 ... 21 D5
Mitcham CR4 ... 181 A2
Spring Grove Cres TW3,TW5 ... 130 A4
Spring Grove Prim Sch TW7 ... 130 B3
Spring Grove Rd
Hounslow TW3,TW5, TW7 ... 130 A4
Richmond TW10 ... 154 B6
Springhallow Sch W13 ... 87 A1
Spring Hill E5 ... 52 A2
Forest Hill SE26 ... 184 C6
Springhill Cl SE5 ... 139 B2
Spring Ho WC1 ... 234 A1
Merton SW19 ... 179 B2
Springhurst Cl CR0 ... 223 B4
Spring La E5 ... 52 B1
N10 ... 49 A6
Croydon SE25 ... 206 B3
Spring Lake HA7 ... 25 B6
Spring Mews W1 ... 237 D4
Spring Park Ave CR0 ... 222 D6
Springpark Dr N4 ... 51 A1
Beckenham BR3 ... 208 A6
Spring Park Prim Sch CR0 ... 223 C5
Spring Park Rd CR0 ... 222 D6
Spring Pl N3 ... 47 C6
NW5 ... 71 B3
Springpond Rd RM9 ... 81 A3
Spring Rd TW13 ... 149 D1
Springrice Rd SE13 ... 164 B5
Spring Shaw Rd BR5 ... 190 A2
Spring St W2 ... 92 B1 236 C1
Spring Terr TW10 ... 154 A6
Spring Vale DA7 ... 147 D1
Springvale Ave TW8 ... 110 A1
Springvale Ct SE12 ... 143 A1
Springvale Terr 5 W14 ... 112 D3
Spring Villa Rd HA8 ... 26 C3
Springwater WC1 ... 240 C4
Springwater Cl SE18 ... 144 C4
Springway HA1 ... 42 B2
Springwell Ave NW10 ... 89 D6
Springwell Cl SW16 ... 182 B6
Springwell Ct TW5 ... 128 D3
Springwell Jun & Inf Schs TW5 ... 129 A5
Springwell Rd
Heston TW5 ... 128 D4
West Norwood SW16 ... 182 C5
Spring Wlk E1 ... 96 A2
Springwood Cres HA8 ... 11 A2
Springwood Ct CR2 ... 221 C4
Sprowston Mews E7 ... 77 A3
Sprowston Rd E7 ... 77 A3
Spruce Ct W5 ... 110 A3
Sprucedale Gdns CR0 ... 222 D4
Spruce Hills Rd E17 ... 36 A1
Spruce Ho 15 SE16 ... 118 D4
Spruce Pk BR2 ... 208 D5
Sprules Rd SE4 ... 141 A3
Spurfield KT8 ... 195 D6
Spurgeon Ave SE19 ... 183 B2
Spurgeon Rd SE19 ... 183 B3
Spurgeon's Coll SE25 ... 183 C1
Spurgeon St SE1 ... 117 B3 262 C6
Spurling Rd SE22 ... 139 D1
Dagenham RM9 ... 81 B2
Spur Rd N15 ... 51 B5

Spur Rd *continued*
SE1 116 C4 251 A2
Brentford TW7 131 B5
Edgware HA8 26 A6
Feltham TW14 128 B1
Wallend IG11 101 A4
Spurstowe Rd E8 74 B2
Spurstowe Terr E8 74 B3
Spurway Par 2 IG2 56 B4
Square Rigger Row 7 SW11 136 A2
Square The SW6 265 A1
W6 112 C1
Hayes UB11 105 B5
Ilford IG1 56 C2
12 Richmond TW10 153 D6
Wallington SM5 219 A3
Woodford IG8 37 A5
Squarey St SW17 158 A1
Squire Ct 2 CR0 205 C1
Squire Gdns NW8 229 C1
Squire's Almshouses 7 E17 53 D5
Squires Bridge Rd KT17 192 B5
Squires Ct N3 30 A2
SW4 270 B1
Wimbledon SW19 179 C6
Squires Ho 3 SE18 144 D6
Squires La N3 30 A2
Squire's Mount NW3 70 B5
Squire's Rd TW17 192 C5
Squires The RM7 59 D3
Squires Wlk TW15 171 B3
Squires Wood Dr BR7 188 B3
Squirrel Cl TW4 128 C2
Squirrel Mews W13 109 A6
Squirrels Cl N12 30 A6
Hillingdon UB10 60 C1
Orpington BR6 211 C1
Squirrels Ct 4 KT4 215 D6
Squirrels Gn KT4 216 A6
Squirrel's La IG9 21 D1
Squirrels The SE13 142 B2
Bushey WD23 8 B5
Pinner HA5 41 B6
Squirrels Trad Est UB3 105 D3
Squirries St E2 96 A4
Stable Cl UB5 85 C5
Stable Mews SE27 183 A5
Stables End BR6 227 A5
Stables The IG9 21 C4
Stables Way SE11 116 C1 261 A2
Stable Way W10 90 C1
Stable Wlk N2 30 B2
Stable Yd Rd SW1 115 C4 249 B2
Staburn Ct HA8 27 A1
Stacey Ave N18 34 C6
Stacey Cl E10 54 B4
Stacey St N7 72 C5
WC2 93 D1 239 D1
Stack Ho SW1 258 B3
Stackhouse St SW1 257 C6
Stacy Path 21 SE5 139 C5
Staddon Ct BR3 207 A5
Stadium Bsns Ctr HA9 66 D5
Stadium Rd SE7,SE18 144 B6
Stadium Ret Pk HA9 66 C5
Stadium St SW10 136 A5 266 B3
Stadium Way HA9 66 C4
Staffa Rd E10 53 A1
Stafford Cl E17 53 B3
NW6 91 C4
Cheam SM3 217 A2
Southgate N14 15 C6
Stafford Cripps Ho 30 E2 96 C4
SW6 264 D5
Stafford Cross CR0 220 B3
Stafford Ct SW8 270 A2
W8 255 B6
Ealing W7 86 D1
Stafford Gdns CR0 220 B3
Stafford Ho SE1 263 D2
Stafford Mans SW11 267 C3
13 SW4 138 A1
13 W14 112 D3
Stafford Morris Ho 9 E15 98 C6
Stafford Pl SW1 115 C3 259 A6
Richmond TW10 154 B4
Stafford Rd E3 97 B5
E7 77 D2
NW6 91 C4
Croydon CR0 220 C4
Harrow HA3 24 A3
Kingston KT3 199 A6
Ruislip HA4 61 D4
Sidcup DA14 189 C6
Wallington CR0,SM6 220 A3
Staffordshire St SE15 140 A4

Staffordshire St *continued*
SE15 140 B4
Stafford St W1 249 A4
Stafford Terr W8 113 C3 255 A6
Stag Cl HA8 27 A1
Stagg Hill EN4 2 C6
Stag La Chigwell IG9 21 B2
Edgware HA8,NW9 45 A6
Roehampton SW15 155 D2
Stag Lane Fst & Mid Schs HA8 26 C1
Stag Pl SW1 115 C3 259 A6
Stags Ct KT7 197 A2
Stagshaw Ho 17 SE22 139 C2
Stags Way TW7 130 D6
Stainbank Rd CR4 203 B6
Stainby Cl UB7 104 A3
Stainby Rd N15 51 D5
Stainer Ho SE9 143 C1
Stainer St SE1 252 D3
Staines Ave SM3 216 D6
Staines By-Pass TW15 170 A4
Staines Rd
East Bedfont TW14 149 B4
Feltham TW14,TW3 150 C6
Ilford IG1 79 B4
Twickenham TW13,TW2 151 D1
Hounslow TW3 129 C1
Twickenham TW2 152 A1
Staines Rd E TW12, TW16 172 C2
Staines Rd W TW15 171 B3
Staines Wlk DA14 190 C4
Stainford Cl TW15 171 B5
Stainforth Rd E17 53 C5
Ilford IG2 57 B2
Staining La EC2 242 B2
Stainmore Cl BR7 189 B2
Stainsbury St 26 E2 96 C5
Stainsby Pl E14 97 C1
Stainsby Rd E14 97 C1
Stainton Rd Enfield EN3 6 C4
Lewisham SE13 164 B4
Stalbridge Ho NW1 232 A3
Stalbridge St NW1 237 B4
Stalham St SE16 118 B3
Stambourne Ho SW8 270 B2
Stambourne Way
Penge SE19 183 D3
West Wickham BR4 224 A5
Stamford Bridge Stadium (Chelsea FC) SW6 135 D5 265 C4
Stamford Brook Ave W6 111 D3
Stamford Brook Gdns 1 W6 111 D3
Stamford Brook Mans 2 W6 111 D2
Stamford Brook Rd W6 111 D3
Stamford Brook Sta W6 111 D2
Stamford Cl N15 52 A5
2 NW3 70 A5
Harrow HA3 24 C3
Southall UB1 107 C6
Stamford Ct W6 112 A2
Edgware HA8 26 B6
Stamford Dr BR2 208 D5
Stamford Gdns RM9 80 C1
Stamford Grove E 1 N16 52 A1
Stamford Grove W 4 N16 52 A1
Stamford Hill N16 51 D1
Stamford Hill Mans 1 N16 51 D1
Stamford Hill Prim Sch N15 51 B3
Stamford Hill Sta N16 51 C2
Stamford Ho N15 52 A5
Stamford Hospl W6 112 A2
Stamford Lo 2 N16 51 D2
Stamford Mans 2 N16 52 A1
Stamford Rd E6 100 A6
N1 73 C2
N15 52 A4
Dagenham RM9 80 C1
Stamford St SE1 116 C5 251 B4
Stamp Pl E2 95 D4
Stanard Cl N16 51 C2
Stanborough Cl TW12 173 B4
Stanborough Ho 4 E3 97 D3
Stanborough Pas E8 73 D2
Stanborough Rd TW3, TW7 130 B2
Stanbridge Mans SW15 134 C2
Stanbridge Pl N21 16 D2
Stanbridge Rd SW15 134 C2
Stanbrook Ct W1 249 A4
Stanbrook Rd SE2 124 B4
Stanburn Fst & Mid Schs HA7 25 C3
Stanbury Ct 16 NW3 70 D2

Stanbury Rd SE15 140 B3
SE15 140 C3
Stancroft NW9 45 C4
Standale Gr HA4 39 A4
Standard Ind Est E16 122 B4
Standard Pl 14 EC2 95 C4
Standard Rd DA6 147 A1
NW10 89 B3
Belvedere DA17 125 C1
Enfield EN3 7 A6
Hounslow TW4 129 A2
Standen Rd SW18 157 C4
Standfield Gdns RM10 81 C2
Standfield Rd RM10 81 C3
Standish Ho SE9 143 B1
6 W6 112 A2
Standish Rd W6 112 A2
Standlake Point 1 SE23 162 D1
Stane Cl SW19 179 D3
Stanedge Ct SW16 182 A5
Stanesgate Ho 20 SE15 140 A5
Stane Way SE18 144 A5
Stanetto Ct 3 RM6 58 B2
Stanfield Ho NW8 236 D6
9 Northolt UB5 84 D5
Stanfield Rd 13 E3 97 A5
Stanford Cl
Hampton TW12 173 B4
Romford RM7 59 D3
Ruislip HA4 39 A3
Stanford Ct N11 31 A5
SW6 265 D1
W8 255 D5
Stanford Ho IG11 102 B5
Stanford Pl SE1 117 C2 263 A3
Stanford Rd N11 30 D5
W8 113 D3 255 D6
Thornton Heath SW16 182 A1
Stanford St SW1 259 C3
Stanford Way SW16 181 D1
Stangate Cres WD6 11 C6
Stangate Gdns HA7 25 B6
Stangate Lo N21 16 B4
Stangate Mansi TW1 152 D1
Stanger Rd SE25 206 A5
Stanhope Ave N3 47 B6
Harrow HA3 24 B2
Hayes BR2 209 A1
Stanhope Cl 28 SE16 118 D4
Stanhope Ct N3 29 B1
Stanhope Gate W1 248 B4
Stanhope Gdns N4 51 A3
N6 49 C3
NW7 27 D5
SW7 114 A2 256 B4
Dagenham RM8 81 B5
Redbridge IG1 56 B1
Stanhope Gr BR3 207 B5
Stanhope Ho 5 N11 31 B6
N6 49 C3
SE8 141 B5
4 Putney SW15 156 C6
Stanhope Mews E SW7 114 A2 256 B4
Stanhope Mews S SW7 256 B3
Stanhope Mews W SW7 114 A2 256 B4
Stanhope Park Rd UB6 86 A3
Stanhope Pl W2 237 C1
Stanhope Prim Sch UB6 86 A3
Stanhope Rd DA7 147 A3
E17 53 D4
N12 30 A5
N6 49 C2
Barnet EN5 12 D5
Dagenham RM8 81 B5
Sidcup DA15 190 A6
Southall UB6 86 A2
South Croydon CR0 221 C5
Wallington SM5 219 A1
Stanhope Row W1 248 C3
Stanhope St NW1 93 C4 232 A1
Stanhope Terr W2 114 B6 246 D6
Stanier Cl SW5 254 D1
Stanlake Rd W12 112 C5
Stanlake Villas W12 112 C5
Stanley Ave
Barking IG11 101 D5
Beckenham BR2,BR3 208 A6
Dagenham RM8 59 B2
Greenford UB6 86 A6
Wembley HA0 66 A1
West Barnes KT3 200 A4
Stanley Bldgs NW1 233 A3
Stanley Cl SW8 270 C5
Wembley HA0 66 A1
Stanley Cres W11 113 B6 244 C6
Stanleycroft Cl TW7 130 C4
Stanley Ct
Belmont SM2 217 D1
11 Ealing W5 87 C2

Stanley Ct *continued*
Wallington SM5 219 A1
Wimbledon SW19 179 C4
Stanley Gardens Rd TW11 174 C5
Stanley Gdns NW2 68 C3
W11 244 C6
W3 111 C4
Mitcham CR4 181 A4
Wallington SM6 219 C2
Stanley Gr SW11 137 A3
Thornton Heath CR0 204 C3
Stanley Ho E11 54 C3
18 E14 97 C1
35 SW8 137 D3
Stanley Horstead Twr E10 75 D6
Stanley Inf Sch TW2 174 C6
Stanley Jun Sch TW2 174 C6
Stanley Mans SW10 266 B6
Upper Tooting SW17 158 D2
Stanley Park Dr HA0 88 B6
Stanley Park High Sch SM5 219 A2
Stanley Park Inf Sch SM5 218 D1
Stanley Park Jun Sch SM5 218 D1
Stanley Park Rd SM5, SM6 219 A1
Stanley Rd BR6 211 D1
E10 53 D3
E12 78 A3
E15 98 B6
N10 31 B3
N11 31 D5
N15 50 D5
N2 48 B6
2 NW9 46 A2
W3 111 A3
Ashford TW15 170 A5
Belmont SM2 217 D1
Bromley BR2 209 C5
Chingford E4 20 B3
Edmonton N9 17 D2
Enfield EN1 5 C2
Harrow HA2 64 A6
Ilford IG1 79 B6
Isleworth TW3 130 A1
Mitcham CR4 181 A3
Morden SM4 201 C5
Mortlake SW14 132 D1
Northwood HA6 22 A2
Sidcup DA14 168 A1
Southall UB1 107 A6
Teddington TW11,TW2 174 C5
Thornton Heath CR0 204 C3
Twickenham TW2 152 B1
Wallington SM5 219 A1
Wembley HA9 66 B2
Wimbledon SW19 179 C4
Woodford E18 36 D2
Stanley St SE14,SE8 141 B5
Stanley Studios SW10 266 B6
Stanley Tech High Sch for Boys SE25 205 D6
Stanley Terr 7 N19 72 A6
Stanmer St SW11 136 C3
Stanmore Coll HA7 25 C4
Stanmore Gdns
Richmond TW9 132 B2
Sutton SM1 218 A5
Stanmore Hill HA7 25 A6
Stanmore Ho 21 SW8 137 D3
Stanmore Lo HA7 25 B6
Stanmore Pl NW1 231 D6
Stanmore Rd E11 54 D1
N15 50 D5
Richmond TW9 132 B2
Stanmore St N1 94 B6 233 C6
Stanmore Sta HA7 25 D6
Stanmore Terr 3 BR3 185 C1
Stannard Cotts 23 E1 96 C3
Stannard Mews E8 74 A2
Stannard Rd E8 74 A2
Stannary Pl SE11 261 B1
Stannary St SE11 116 C1 261 B1
Stannet Way SM6 219 C4
Stansbury Ho 3 W10 91 A4
Stansfeld Ho SE1 263 D3
Stansfeld Rd E6 99 D1
Stansfield Rd SW9 138 B2
Cranford TW4,TW5 128 B3
Stansgate Rd RM10 81 C5
Stanstead Cl BR2 208 D3
Stanstead Gr SE23 163 B3
Stanstead Ho E3 98 A3
Stanstead Manor SM1 217 C2
Stanstead Rd
Forest Hill SE23,SE6 163 A3
Wanstead E11 55 B4
Stansted Cres DA5 168 D3
Stansted Rd TW6 148 B5
Stanswood Gdns SE5 139 C5
Stanthorpe Cl SW16 182 A5
Stanthorpe Rd SW16 182 A5
Stanton Ave TW11 174 C4

Stanton Cl
Chessington KT19 214 D3
North Cheam KT4 200 D1
Stanton Ct 5 DA15 168 A1
N16 51 B2
N3 29 C2
Stanton Ho 8 SE10 142 A6
Stanton Rd
Barnes SW13 133 D3
Thornton Heath CR0 205 A2
Wimbledon SW20 178 D2
Stanton Sq SE26 185 B6
Stanton Way SE26 185 B6
Stanway Ct 23 N1 95 C5
Stanway Gdns HA8 27 A5
Acton W3 110 C5
Stanway St N1 95 C5
Stanwell Rd
Ashford TW15 170 A6
East Bedfont TW14, TW19,TW6 148 D4
Stanwell TW15 148 A1
Ashford TW15 148 A1
Stanwick Rd W14 113 B2 254 C3
Stanworth Ct TW5 129 C5
Stanworth St SE1 253 D1
Stanyhurst SE23 163 A3
Stapelhurst Ho 18 E5 74 B3
Stapenhill Rd HA0 65 B5
Staplefield Cl
Pinner HA5 23 A3
3 Streatham SW2 160 A3
Stapleford N17 33 C1
Stapleford Ave IG2 57 C4
Stapleford Cl
Chingford E4 20 A1
Kingston KT1 198 C6
Putney SW19 157 A4
Stapleford Rd HA0 65 D1
Stapleford Way IG11 102 B4
Staplehurst Ct SW11 158 D5
Staplehurst Rd SE13 164 C6
Sutton SM5 218 C1
Staple Inn WC2 241 A3
Staple Inn Bldgs WC2 241 A3
Staples Cl SE16 119 A5
Staples Corner Bsns Pk NW2 46 B1
Staples Corner (East) NW2 46 B1
Staples Corner (West) NW2 46 B1
Staple St SE1 117 B4 252 D1
Stapleton Gdns CR0 220 C3
Stapleton Hall N4 50 B2
Stapleton Hall Rd N4 50 B2
Stapleton Ho 19 E2 96 B4
Stapleton Rd DA7 147 B6
Orpington BR6 227 D5
Upper Tooting SW17 159 A1
Stapley Rd DA17 125 C1
Staplyton Rd EN5 1 A2
Star Alley EC3 253 B6
Star and Garter Hill TW10 154 A4
Starboard Way E14 119 C3
Starcross St NW1 93 C4 232 B1
Star Ct UB10 83 A3
Starfield Rd W12 112 A4
Star & Garter Mans SW15 134 D2
Star La E16 98 C3
Starliner Ct N7 72 C2
Starling Cl
Buckhurst Hill IG9 21 A3
Pinner HA5 40 C6
Starling Ho NW8 230 A4
Starling Wlk TW12 173 A5
Starmans Cl RM9 103 A6
Star Path UB5 85 C5
Star Pl E1 118 A6
Star Prim Sch E16 98 C3
Star Rd W14 113 B1 254 C1
Hillingdon UB10 83 A3
Hounslow TW7 130 B3
Star St W2 92 C1 237 A2
Starts Cl BR6 226 C5
Starts Hill Ave BR6 226 D4
Starts Hill Rd BR6 226 D4
Starveall Cl UB7 104 B3
Star Works NW10 90 A4
Star Yd WC2 94 C1 241 A2
State Farm Ave BR6 227 A4
Staten Gdns TW1 152 D3
Statham Gr N16 73 B5
Edmonton N18 33 C5
Statham Ho SW8 269 A2
Stathard Ho 18 E1 96 C3
Station App BR6 227 D6
BR7 188 A4
BR7 188 C1
DA16 146 A3
DA7 147 A3
E17 53 C4
E7 77 B4
N11 31 B5
N12 29 D6

Station App *continued*
NW10 89 D4
SE3 143 B2
SE9 166 B3
Ashford TW15 170 B6
5 Beckenham BR3 185 C2
Belmont SM2 217 A1
Fulham SW6 135 A2
Greenford UB6 64 B1
Hampton TW12 173 C2
Hayes BR2 209 A1
Hayes UB3 105 D3
Hinchley Wood KT10 212 D5
4 Kingston KT1,KT2 176 C2
New Barnet EN5 2 A1
6 New Malden KT4 200 A1
Penge SE26 185 B5
Pinner HA5 41 A6
Richmond TW9 132 C4
Ruislip HA4 39 D1
Ruislip HA4 62 B3
Shepperton TW17 193 A4
3 South Croydon CR0 221 B6
Streatham SW16 181 D5
Sunbury TW16 172 A2
1 Surbiton KT6 198 A3
Wanstead E11 55 A4
Wembley HA0 65 B2
2 Woodford E18 37 B1
Woodford IG9 37 D6
Worcester Park KT19 216 A3
Yiewsley UB7 104 A5
Station App Rd SE1 116 C4 251 A2
Station Approach Rd W4 133 A5
Station Ave 5 SW9 138 D2
Kingston KT3 199 C6
13 Richmond TW9 132 C4
West Ewell KT19 215 D1
Station Bldgs SW20 178 C1
Station Blgs W5 110 B5
Station Cl N3 29 C2
Hampton TW12 173 D2
Station Cres N15 51 B5
SE3 121 A1
Ashford TW15 170 A6
Wembley HA0 65 B2
Station Ct 1 E10 53 D2
5 SE15 140 C3
Stationers Hall Ct EC4 241 D1
Station Est
Beckenham BR3 206 D5
1 Woodford E18 37 B1
Station Estate Rd TW14 150 B3
Station Gdns W4 133 A5
Station Hill BR2 225 A6
Station House Mews N9 34 A6
Station Par 4 N14 15 D3
NW2 68 C2
Acton W3 88 C1
Ashford TW15 170 B6
Barking IG11 79 A1
Cockfosters EN4 3 A1
Dagenham RM10 81 C2
Ealing W5 110 B5
Edgware HA8 26 A3
Feltham TW14 150 B4
Harrow HA2 63 D4
Harrow HA3 25 A1
Richmond TW9 132 C4
Ruislip HA4 61 B6
4 Upper Tooting SW12 159 A3
2 Wanstead E11 55 A4
Woodford IG9 37 D6
Station Pas SE15 140 C4
Woodford E18 37 B1
Station Pl N4 72 C6
Station Rd BR1 187 A2
BR6 227 D6
DA7 147 A2
E10 76 A5
E12 78 A4
E17 53 A4
E7 77 A4
N11 31 B5
N17 52 A6
N19 71 C5
N3 29 C1
NW10 89 D5
NW4 46 A4
NW7 27 C4
SE13 142 A2
Ashford TW15 170 B6
Ashford TW16 172 A3
Barnes SW13 133 D3
Beckenham BR2 186 C1
Belvedere DA17 125 C3
Carshalton SM5 218 D4
Chessington KT9 214 A3
Chingford E4 20 B3
Claygate KT10 212 C3
Croydon CR0 205 A1
Dagenham RM6 58 D2
Ealing W5 88 B1
Ealing W7 108 C5
Edgware HA8 26 C4

Station Rd *continued*
Esher KT10 212 B6
Hampton TW12 173 D2
Harrow HA1 42 D4
Harrow HA1,HA2 41 D4
Hayes UB3 105 C2
Hounslow TW3 129 D1
Ilford IG1 78 D5
Ilford IG6 57 B6
Kingston KT2 176 C2
Merton SW19 180 A2
New Barnet EN5 13 D6
Penge SE20 184 C4
Shepperton TW17 193 A4
Sidcup DA14,DA15 168 A1
Southgate N21 16 D3
South Norwood SE25 205 D5
Teddington KT1 175 D2
Teddington TW11 175 A4
Thames Ditton KT7 196 D2
Twickenham TW1 152 D4
West Barnes KT3 200 B4
West Drayton UB7 104 A4
West Wickham BR4 208 A1
Wood Green N22 32 B1
Station Rd N DA17 125 D3
Station Rise SE27 160 D2
Station Sq BR5 211 A4
Station St E15 76 B1
E16 122 D5
Station Terr NW10 90 D5
SE5 139 A4
Station View UB6 86 B6
Station Way
Cheam SM2,SM3 217 A1
Woodford IG9 37 D6
Station Yd TW1 153 A4
Staunton Ho SE17 263 A3
Staunton Rd KT2 176 B3
Staunton St SE8 141 B6
Staveley NW1 232 A2
Staveley Cl E9 74 C3
N7 72 A4
SE15 140 C4
8 SE15 140 B4
Staveley Ct 4 E11 55 A4
Staveley Gdns W4 133 B4
Staveley Rd
Ashford TW15 171 B4
Chiswick W4 133 B5
Staverdale Lo W14 254 D6
Stavers Ho 18 E3 97 B5
Staverton Rd NW2 68 C1
Stave Yard Rd SE16 119 A5
Stavordale Rd N5 72 D4
Carshalton SM5 202 A2
Stayner's Rd E1 96 D3
Stayton Rd SM1 217 C5
Steadfast Rd KT1 175 D2
Steadman Ct EC1 242 B6
Steadman Ho 4 RM10 81 C5
Stead St SE17 117 B2 262 C3
Steam Farm La TW14 127 D1
Stean St E8 95 D6
Stebbing Ho 8 W11 112 D5
Stebbing Way IG11 102 A5
Stebondale St E14 120 A2
Stebon Prim Sch E14 97 C2
Stedham Pl WC1 240 A2
Stedman Cl UB10 60 C5
Steedman St
SE17 117 A2 262 A3
Steeds Rd N10 30 D2
Steele App IG11 102 B5
Steele Rd E11 76 C4
N17 51 C6
NW10 89 A5
W4 111 A3
Isleworth TW7 131 A1
Steele's Mews N NW3 70 D2
Steele's Mews S NW3 70 D2
Steele's Rd NW3 70 D2
Steele Wlk DA8 147 D5
Steel's La 23 E1 96 C1
Steen Way 7 SE22 161 C6
Steep Cl BR6 227 D2
Steep Hill
South Croydon CR0 221 C4
Streatham SW16 159 D1
Steeple Cl Fulham SW6 135 A3
Wimbledon SW19 179 A6
Steeple Ct 19 E1 96 B3
Steeplestone Cl N18 33 A5
Steeple Wlk N1 235 B6
Steerforth St SW18 158 A2
Steers Mead CR4 180 D2
Steers Way SE16 119 A4
Steetley Ct 14 SM2 218 A1
Steinman Ct TW7 130 D2
Stelfax Ho WC1 233 D2
Stella Rd SW17 180 D4
Stellar Ho 4 N17 33 D4
Stellman Cl E5 74 A5
Stembridge Rd SE20 184 B1
Sten Cl EN3 7 C6
Stephan Cl E8 96 A6
Stephen Cl BR6 227 D5
Stephen Ct 18 SW19 156 D3
Stephendale Rd SW6 136 A3
Stephen Fox Ho 7
W4 111 C1
Stephen Hawking Sch
E14 97 A1
Stephen Mews W1 239 C3
Stephen Pl SW4 137 C2
Stephen Saunders Ct
SW11 158 C6
Stephens Ct E16 98 D3
SE4 141 A2
Stephens Lo N12 14 A1
Stephenson Ct SM2 217 B1
Stephenson Ho 6 NW3 70 D3
2 NW5 71 B4
SE1 262 A6
SE2 124 D1
Stephenson Rd E17 53 A4
Ealing W7 86 D1
Twickenham TW4 151 C4
Stephenson St E16 98 C2
NW10 89 D4
Stephenson Way
NW1 93 C3 239 B6
Stephen's Rd E15 98 C6
Stephen St W1 239 C3
Stepney Cswy E1 96 D1
Stepney Day Hospl E1 96 C1
Stepney Gn E1 96 D2
Stepney Greencoat CE Prim
Sch The E14 97 B1
Stepney Green Ct 3
E1 96 D2
Stepney Green Sch E1 96 D2
Stepney Green Sta E1 96 D3
Stepney High St E1 96 D2
Stepney Way E1 96 C2
Sterling Ave
Edgware HA8 26 B6
Upper Halliford TW17 193 C6
Sterling Cl NW10 68 A1
Sterling Gdns SE14 141 A6
Sterling Ho SE9 143 B1
Sterling Ind Est RM10 81 D4
Sterling Pl W5 110 A2
Sterling Rd EN2 5 B5
Sterling St SW7 257 B6
Sterling Way (North
Circular Rd) N18 33 C5
Stern Cl IG11 102 C5
Sterndale Rd W14 112 D3
Sterne St W12 112 D4
Sternhall La SE15 140 A2
Sternhold Ave SW12,
SW2 159 D2
Sterry Cres RM10 81 C3
Sterry Dr
Thames Ditton KT7 196 C3
Worcester Park KT19 215 C4
Sterry Gdns RM10 81 C2
Sterry Rd Barking IG11 101 D6
Dagenham RM10 81 C3
Sterry St SE1 252 C1
Steucers La SE23 163 A3
Stevanne Ct 1 DA17 125 C1
Steve Biko Ct W10 90 D3
Steve Biko La SE6 185 C6
Steve Biko Rd N7 72 C5
Steve Biko Way TW3 129 C2
Stevedale Rd DA16 146 C3
Stevedore St 3 E1 118 B5
Stevenage Rd
Fulham SW6 134 D4
Wallend E6 78 C2
Stevens Ave E9 74 C2
Stevens Cl
Beckenham BR3 185 C4
Hampton TW12 173 B4
Pinner HA5 40 C4
Stevens Ct BR3 185 C4
Stevens Gn WD23 8 A3
Stevens Ho KT1 175 D1
Stevens' La KT10 213 A2
Stevenson Cl EN5 14 B5
Stevenson Cres SE16 118 B1
Stevenson Ho NW8 229 A6
1 SW11 136 D3
Wembley HA9 65 D6
Stevens Rd RM8 80 C5
Stevens St SE1 263 B6
Steventon Rd W12 111 D6
Stewards Holte Wlk 3
N11 31 B6
Steward St E1 95 C2 243 B4
Stewart Ave TW17 192 C5
Stewart Cl BR7 188 D6
NW9 45 A3
Hampton TW12 173 A4
Stewart Fleming Prim Sch
SE20 206 C6
Stewart Headlam Prim Sch
E1 96 B3
Stewart Ho SE1 263 A5
Stewart Quay UB3 105 C4
Stewart Rainbird Ho 1
E12 78 C3
Stewart Rd E15 76 B4
Stewartsby Cl N18 33 A5
Stewart's Gr
SW3 114 C1 257 A2
Stewart's Rd
SW8 137 C4 269 A2
Stewart St E14 120 A4
Stew La EC4 252 A6
Steyne Rd W3 110 D5
Steyning Gr SE9 188 B6
Steynings Way N12 29 C5
Steyning Way TW4 128 C1
Steynton Ave DA5 168 D2
Stickland Rd DA17 125 C2
Stickleton Cl UB6 85 D4
Stifford Ho E1 96 C2
Stilecroft Gdns HA0 65 B5
Stile Hall Gdns W4 110 C1
Stile Hall Par 6 W4 110 C1
Stileman Ho 4 E3 97 B2
Stile Path TW16 194 A5
Stiles Cl BR2 210 B3
Erith DA8 125 D1
Stillingfleet Rd SW13 134 A6
Stillington St
SW1 115 C2 259 B4
Stillness Jun & Inf Schs
SE23 163 A5
Stillness Rd SE23 163 B5
Stilwell Dr UB8 82 B3
Stilwell Rdbt UB8 104 D6
Stipularis Dr UB4 84 D3
Stirling Ave Pinner HA5 41 A2
Wallington SM6 220 A1
Stirling Cl SW16 181 C2
Stirling Cnr EN5,WD6 11 B5
Stirling Ct EC1 241 C6
WC2 240 C1
Ealing W13 109 B6
Stirling Gr TW3 130 A3
Stirling Ho 5 SE18 122 D1
Stirling Mans NW6 70 A2
Stirling Rd E13 99 B5
E17 53 A6
SW9 138 A3
W3 110 D3
Harrow HA3 42 D6
Hayes UB3 106 B6
Stanwell TW19,TW6 148 B5
Tottenham N17 34 A2
Tottenham N22 32 D2
Twickenham TW2 151 D4
Stirling Way
Borehamwood WD6 11 B6
Thornton Heath CR0 204 A2
Stiven Cres HA2 63 B5
Stoatley Ho 10 SW15 156 A3
Stockbeck NW1 232 B3
Stockbridge Ho EN2 4 D3
Stockbury Rd CR0 206 C3
Stockdale Rd RM8 81 B6
Stockdove Way UB6 86 D4
Stocker Gdns RM9 80 C1
Stock Exchange★
EC2 242 D1
Stockfield Rd
Claygate KT10 212 C3
Streatham SW16 160 B1
Stockholm Ho E1 118 A6
Stockholm Rd SE16 118 C1
Stockholm Way 9 E1 118 A5
Stockhurst Cl SW15 134 D3
Stockingswater La EN3 7 B2
Stockleigh Hall NW8 230 B4
Stockley Cl UB7 104 D4
Stockley Ctry Pk UB7 104 C6
Stockley Farm Rd
UB7 104 D3
Stockley Park Bsns Pk
UB11 105 A5
Stockley Rd UB7,UB8,
UB11 104 D4
Stock Orchard Cres N7 72 B3
Stock Orchard St N7 72 B3
Stockport Rd SW16 181 D2
Stocks Ct 5 E1 96 D3
Stocksfield Rd E17 54 A6
Stocks Pl 16 E14 119 B6
Hillingdon UB10 82 C6
Stock St E13 99 A5
Stockton Cl EN5 2 A1
Stockton Gdns NW7 11 C1
Tottenham N17 33 A3
Stockton Ho 16 E2 96 B4
Harrow HA2 41 C1
Stockton Rd
Edmonton N18 34 B4
Tottenham N17 33 A3
Stockwell Ave SW9 138 B2
Stockwell Cl BR1 187 B1
Stockwell Gdns
SW9 138 B4 270 C1
Stockwell Gn SW9 138 B3
Stockwell La SW9 138 B3
Stockwell Park Cres
SW9 138 B3
Stockwell Park Rd
SW9 138 B4 270 D1
Stockwell Park Sch
SW9 138 B4 270 C1
Stockwell Park Wlk
SW9 138 C2
Stockwell Prim Sch
SW9 138 B2
Stockwell Rd SW9 138 B3
Stockwell St SE10 142 A6
Stockwell Sta SW4 138 A3
Stockwell Terr SW9 270 C1
Stodart Rd SE20 184 C2
Stoddart Ho SW8 270 D5
Stodmarsh Ho 28 SW9 138 C4
Stofield Gdns SE9 165 D1
Stoford Cl SW19 157 A4
Stokenchurch St
SW6 135 D4 265 C1
Stoke Newington Church St
N16 73 C6
Stoke Newington Comm
N16 73 D6
Stoke Newington High St
N16 73 D5
Stoke Newington Rd
N16 73 D4
Stoke Newington Sch
N16 73 B5
Stoke Newington Sta
N16 73 D6
Stoke Pl NW10 89 D4
Stoke Rd KT2 177 A3
Stokesby Rd KT9 214 B2
Stokes Ct N2 48 C5
Stokesley St W12 89 D1
Stokes Rd Croydon CR0 206 D3
Newham E6 100 A3
Stokley Ct N8 50 A5
Stoll Cl NW2 68 C5
Stoms Path SE6 185 C5
Stonard Rd
Dagenham RM8 80 B4
Palmers Green N13 16 C1
Stondon Pk SE23 163 A5
Stondon Wlk E6 100 A5
4 E6 99 D5
Stonebanks KT12 194 A2
Stone Bldgs
WC2 94 B2 240 D3
Stonebridge Ct 8
NW10 67 B1
Stonebridge Ctr The
N15 52 A4
Stonebridge Park HA9 66 D1
Stonebridge Park Sta
NW10 66 D1
Stonebridge Pk NW10 67 B1
Stonebridge Rd N15 51 D4
Stonebridge Sch The
NW10 89 B6
Stonebridge Sh Ctr 6
NW10 89 B6
Stonebridge Way HA9 66 D2
Stonechat Sq 6 E6 100 A2
Stone Cl SW4 137 C3
Dagenham RM8 81 B6
Yiewsley UB7 104 B5
Stonecot Cl SM3 201 A1
Stonecot Hill SM4 201 A1
Stone Cres TW14 149 D4
Stonecroft Way CR0 204 A2
Stonecutter St EC4 241 C2
Stonefield N4 72 B6
Stonefield Cl DA7 147 C2
Ruislip HA4 63 A3
Stonefield Mans N1 234 A5
Stonefield St
N1 94 C6 234 B6
Stonefield Way SE7 143 D5
Ruislip HA4 63 A3
Stone Gate 8 NW5 71 A2
Stone Gr HA8 26 B5
Stone Grove Ct HA8 26 B5
Stonegrove Gdns HA8 26 A5
Stonehall Ave IG1 56 A3
Stone Hall Rd N21 16 C4
Stoneham Rd N11 31 C5
Stonehaven BR3 185 D1
Stonehill Cl SW14 155 B6
Stonehill Ct E4 19 D4
Stonehill Rd W4 110 C1
Mortlake SW14 155 B6
Stonehills Ct SE21 161 C1
Stonehill's Mans 3
SW16 160 A2
Stonehill Woods Pk
DA14 169 D3
Stonehorse Rd EN3 18 C6
Stonehouse NW1 232 B5
Stonehouse Ct EC2 243 B2
Stonehouse Ho 27 W2 91 C2
Stone Lake Ind Pk
SE7 121 C2
Stone Lake Ret Pk
SE7 121 C2
Stoneleigh Ave
Enfield EN1 6 B4
North Cheam KT17,KT4 216 A5
Stoneleigh Broadway
KT17 216 A3
Stoneleigh Cres KT19 215 D3
Stoneleigh Ct
Redbridge IG5 56 A6
Stoneleigh Ct *continued*
4 Tottenham N17 33 D1
Stoneleigh Fst Sch
KT17 216 B4
Stoneleigh Lo 13 TW9 132 B4
Stoneleigh Park Ave
CR0 206 D3
Stoneleigh Park Rd
KT19,KT4 216 A3
Stoneleigh Pl W11 112 D6
Stoneleigh Rd
Carshalton SM5 202 C2
Redbridge IG5 56 B6
Tottenham N17 33 D1
Stoneleigh St W11 112 D6
Stoneleigh Sta KT19 216 A3
Stoneleigh Terr N19 71 B6
Stonell's Rd SW11 158 D6
Stonemasons Cl N15 51 B5
Stonenest St N4 50 B1
Stone Park Ave BR3 207 D5
Stone Pl KT4 216 A6
Stone Rd BR2 208 D4
Stones End St SE1 252 A1
Stonewall E6 100 C2
Stoneworth Ct SE25 206 A3
Stoney Alley SE18 144 C3
Stoneyard La E14 119 D6
Stoneycroft Cl SE12 164 D4
Stoney Deep TW11 175 A6
Stoneydown E17 53 A5
Stoneydown Ave E17 53 A5
Stoneydown Ho 2 E17 53 A5
Stoneydown Park Sch
E17 53 A5
Stoneyfields Gdns HA8 27 A6
Stoneyfields La HA8 27 A6
Stoney La E1 243 B2
Penge SE19 183 D4
Stoney St SE1 117 B5 252 C4
Stonhouse St SW4 137 D1
Stonor Rd
W14 113 B2 254 C3
Stonycroft Cl EN3 7 A3
Stopes St SE15 139 D5
Stopford Rd E13 99 A6
SE17 261 D1
Stopher Ho SE1 251 D1
Storace Ho 6 SW4 138 A1
Store Rd E16 122 C4
Storers Quay E14 120 B2
Store St E15 76 B3
WC1 93 D2 239 C4
Storey Ct NW8 229 C1
Storey Ho 12 E14 119 D6
Storey Prim Sch E16 122 D5
Storey Rd E17 53 B5
N6 48 D3
Storey's Gate
SW1 115 D4 249 D1
Storey St E16 122 C4
Stories Rd SE5 139 C2
Stork Rd E7 77 A2
Storksmead Rd HA8 27 C3
Storks Rd SE16 118 A3
Stormont House Sch
E5 74 B4
Stormont Rd N6 48 D2
SW11 137 A1
Stormont Way KT9 213 C3
Stormount Dr UB3 105 A4
Storrington WC1 233 B1
Storrington Rd CR0 205 D1
Story St N1 72 B1
Stothard Pl E1 243 B4
Stothard St 11 E1 96 C3
Stott Cl SW18 158 B5
Stoughton Ave SM3 217 A3
Stoughton Cl SE11 260 D3
Roehampton SW15 156 A3
Stour Ave UB2 107 C3
Stour Cl BR2 225 C4
Stourcliffe Cl W1 237 C2
Stourcliffe St W1 237 C1
Stourhead Cl 6 SW19 156 D4
Stourhead Gdns SW20 200 A6
Stour Rd E3 75 C1
Dagenham RM10 81 C6
Stourton Ave TW13 173 B6
Stowage SE8 141 D6
Stow Cres E17 35 A3
Stowe Cres HA4 39 A3
Stowe Gdns N9 17 D3
Stowe Ho 11 N16 73 C5
NW11 48 A3
Stowell Ho 2 N8 50 A5
Stowe Pl N15 51 C6
Stowe Rd W12 112 B4
Stowford Coll SM2 218 A1
Stowting Rd BR6 227 C4
Stox Mead HA3 24 B2
Stracey Rd E7 77 A4
NW10 89 B6
Strachan Pl SW19,
SW20 178 C4
Stradbroke Gr
Buckhurst Hill IG9 21 D3
Redbridge IG5 56 B6
Stradbroke Rd N5 73 A4
Stradbrook Cl HA2 63 B5
Stradella Rd SE24 161 A5
Straffan Lo 8 NW3 70 C2
Strafford Ho 9 SE8 119 B1
Strafford Rd Acton W3 111 A4
Barnet EN5 1 A2
Hounslow TW3 129 B2
Twickenham TW1 153 A4
Strafford St E14 119 C4
Strahan Rd E3 97 A4
Straightsmouth SE10 142 A5
Straight The UB2 107 A4
Strait Rd E6 122 B6
Straker's Rd SE15 140 B1
Strale Ho 17 N1 95 C6
Strand WC2 116 B6 250 C6
Strandfield Cl SE18 123 C1
Strand La WC2 250 D6
Strand-on-the-Green
W4 132 C6
Strand-on-the-Green Sch
W4 132 C6
Strand Pl N18 33 C6
Strang Ho N1 235 A5
Strangways Terr W14 254 C5
Stranraer Way N1 72 A1
1 Stanwell TW6 148 A5
Strasburg Rd
SW11 137 B4 268 C1
Stratfield Ho SE12 165 A2
Stratfield Park Cl N21 16 D4
Stratford Ave UB10 82 B5
Stratford Bus Sta E15 76 B1
Stratford Cir E15 76 B2
Stratford Cl IG11 80 A1
Stratford Ct KT3 199 B5
Stratford Ctr E15 76 B1
Stratford Gr SW15 134 D1
Stratford House Ave
BR1 210 A6
Stratford Office Village The
1 E15 76 C1
Stratford Pl W1 238 C1
Stratford Rd E13 99 A6
W8 113 C3 255 B5
Harlington TW6 149 A6
Hayes UB4 84 B3
Southall UB2 107 A2
Thornton Heath CR7 204 D6
Stratford Sta E15 76 B1
Stratford Studios W8 255 C5
Stratford Villas NW1 71 D1
Stratford Workshops
E15 98 B6
Strathan Cl SW18 157 A5
Strathaven Rd SE12 165 B5
Strathblaine Rd SW11 136 B1
Strathbrook Rd SW16 182 B3
Strathcona Rd HA9 65 D6
Strathdale SW16 182 B5
Strathdon Dr SW17 158 B1
Strathearn Ave
Harlington UB3 127 D5
Twickenham TW2 152 A3
Strathearn House W2 247 A6
Strathearn Pl
W2 114 C6 247 A6
Strathearn Rd
Sutton SM1 217 C3
Wimbledon SW19 179 C6
Stratheden Par SE3 143 A5
Stratheden Rd SE3 143 A5
Strathfield Gdns IG11 79 B2
Strathleven Rd SW2 160 A6
Strathmore Ct NW8 230 A2
Strathmore Gdns N3 29 D2
W8 245 B4
Edgware HA8 26 D1
Strathmore Rd
Teddington TW11,TW2 174 C6
Thornton Heath CR0 205 B2
Wimbledon SW19 157 C1
Strathmore Sch TW10 153 D2
Strathnairn St SE1 118 A2
Strathray Gdns NW3 70 C2
Strath Terr SW11 136 C1
Strathville Rd SW18 157 D2
Strathyre Ave SW16 204 C6
Stratton Ave EN2 5 B6
Stratton Cl DA7 147 A2
Edgware HA8 26 B4
Heston TW5 129 C4
Merton SW19 179 C1
Walton-on-T KT12 194 C1
Stratton Ct 4 N1 73 C1
10 Kingston KT6 198 A4
Strattondale St E14 120 A3
Stratton Dr IG11 79 D2
Stratton Gdns UB1 85 C1
Stratton Ho HA8 26 B6
Stratton Rd DA7 147 A2
Merton SW19 179 C1
Sunbury TW16 171 D1
Stratton St
W1 115 B5 248 D4
Strauss Rd W4 111 B4

Strawberry Hill Cl TW1 152 D1
Strawberry Hill Rd TW1 152 D1
Strawberry Hill Sta TW2 152 D1
Strawberry La SM5 219 B5
Strawberry Terr N10 30 D2
Strawberry Vale N2 30 B2
Twickenham TW1 153 A1
Strayfield Rd EN2 4 D6
Streakes Field Rd NW2 68 A6
Streamdale SE2 146 B6
Streamline Mews SE22 162 A3
Streamside Cl BR2 209 A5
Edmonton N9 17 D3
Stream Way DA17 147 C6
Streatfield Ave E6 100 B6
Streatfield Rd HA3,HA7 43 D6
Streatham Cl SW16 160 A2
Streatham & Clapham High Sch SW16 159 D1
Streatham Comm N SW16 182 B5
Streatham Common Sta SW16 181 D3
Streatham Comm S SW16 182 B4
Streatham Ct SW16 160 A1
Streatham High Rd SW16,SW2 182 A5
Streatham Hill SW2 160 A3
Streatham Hill & Clapham High Sch SW2 160 B3
Streatham Hill Sta SW2 160 A2
Streatham Pl SW2 160 A4
Streatham Rd CR4 181 A2
Streatham St WC1 240 A2
Streatham Sta SW16 181 D5
Streatham & Tooting Adult Inst SW16 160 B2
Streatham Vale SW16 181 D3
Streathbourne Rd SW17 159 A1
Streathem Wells Prim Sch SW2 160 C2
Streatleigh Par 4 SW16 160 A2
Streatley Pl NW3 70 B4
12 NW3 70 A4
Streatley Rd NW6 69 B1
Streeters La SM6 219 D5
Streetfield Mews SE3 143 A2
Streimer Rd E15 98 A5
Strelley Way W3 111 C6
Stretton Lo W13 109 B6
Stretton Mans 16 SE8 141 C6
Stretton Rd
Croydon CR0 205 C2
Richmond TW10 153 C2
Strickland Ct SE15 140 A2
Strickland Ho 26 E2 95 D4
Strickland Row SW18 158 B4
Strickland St SE8 141 C4
Strickland Way 4 BR6 227 D4
Stride Rd E13 98 D5
Strimon Cl N9 18 C2
Stringer Hos 19 N1 95 C6
Strode Cl N10 31 A3
Strode Ho 3 SW2 160 C3
Strode Rd E7 77 A4
NW10 68 A2
SW6 135 A5 264 A4
Tottenham N17 33 C1
Strome Ho NW6 91 D5
Strone Rd E7,E12 77 D2
Strone Way UB4 85 A3
Strongbow Cres SE9 166 B6
Strongbow Rd SE9 166 B6
Strongbridge Cl HA2 41 C1
Stronsa Rd W12 111 D4
Strood Ho SE1 252 D1
12 Penge SE20 184 C3
Stroud Cres SW15 156 A1
Stroudes Cl KT4 199 D2
Stroud Field UB5 63 A2
Stroud Gate HA2 63 D4
Stroud Green Gdns CR0 206 C2
Stroud Green JMI Sch N4 50 C1
Stroud Green Rd N4 50 C1
Stroud Green Way CR0 206 C3
Stroudley Ho SW8 269 B2
Stroudley Wlk E3 97 D4
Stroud Rd
Croydon SE25 206 A3
Wimbledon SW19 157 C1
Strouds Cl RM6 58 B4
Stroud Way TW15 171 A4
Strout's Pl 2 E2 95 D4
Struan Ho 11 E11 55 A4
Strudwick Ct SW4 270 B1
Strutton Ground SW1 115 D3 259 C5
Strype St E1 243 C3
Stuart Ave NW9 46 A2
W5 110 B4
Harrow HA2 63 B5
Hayes BR2 209 A1
Walton-on-T KT12 194 B1
Stuart Cl UB10 60 C2
Stuart Cres
Croydon CR0 223 B5
Hayes UB3 83 A1
Wood Green N22 32 B2
Stuart Ct Chingford E4 20 D2
2 Elstree WD6 9 D5
Stuart Evans Cl DA16 146 C2
Stuart Gr TW11 174 C5
Stuart Ho 1 E9 74 D1
5 SW4 138 A1
W14 254 A4
Stuart Lo SE25 183 C1
Stuart Mill Ho N1 233 C3
Stuart Pl CR4 180 D2
Stuart Rd DA16 146 B4
NW6 91 C4
SE15 140 C1
W3 111 A5
East Barnet EN4 14 D4
Harrow HA3 42 D6
Richmond TW10 153 B1
South Norwood CR7 205 A5
Wimbledon SW19 157 C1
Stubbs Cl NW9 45 A4
Stubbs Dr SE16 118 B1
Stubbs Ho 1 E2 96 D4
N4 50 B1
Stubbs Mews RM8 80 B4
Stubbs Point E13 99 B3
Stubbs Way SW19 180 B2
Stucley Pl 18 NW1 71 B1
Stucley Rd TW5,TW7 130 A5
Studdridge St SW6 135 C3
Studd St N1 94 D6 234 C6
Studholme Ct NW3 69 C4
Studholme St SE15 140 B5
Studio Pl SW1 247 D1
Studios Rd TW17 192 B6
Studios The 4 SW4 137 C1
SW8 269 D1
Studland SE17 262 C2
Studland Cl DA15 167 D1
Studland Ho E14 97 A1
Studland Rd Ealing W7 86 C1
Forest Hill SE26 184 D5
Kingston KT2 176 A4
Studland St W6 112 B2
Studley Ave E4 36 B3
Studley Cl E5 75 A3
Studley Ct DA14 190 B5
9 Poplar E14 120 B6
Redbridge IG4 55 D3
Studley Dr IG4 55 D3
Studley Grange Rd W7 108 D4
Studley Rd E7 77 B2
SW4 138 A3
Dagenham RM9 80 D1
Study Prep Sch The SW19 178 C5
Study Sch The KT3 199 C4
Stukeley Rd E7 77 B1
Stukeley St WC2 94 A1 240 B2
Stumps Hill La BR3 185 C4
Stunnell Ho 23 SE14 140 D6
Sturdee Ho 2 E2 96 A5
Sturdy Ho 26 E3 97 A5
Sturdy Rd SE15 140 B3
Sturge Ave E17 35 D1
Sturgeon Rd SE17 117 A1 262 A1
Sturges Field BR7 189 B4
Sturgess Ave NW4 46 B2
Sturge St SE1 117 A4 252 A2
Sturmer Way N7 72 B3
Sturminster Cl UB4 84 C1
Sturminster Ho SW8 270 D3
Sturrock Cl N15 51 B5
Sturry St E14 97 D1
Sturt St N1 235 B3
Stutfield St E1 96 A1
Stuttle Ho 9 E1 96 A3
Styles Gdns SW9 138 D2
Styles Ho SE1 251 C3
Styles Way BR3 208 A5
Sudbourne Prim Sch SW2 160 B6
Sudbourne Rd SW2 160 B6
Sudbrooke Rd SW12 159 A5
Sudbrook Gdns TW10 154 A1
Sudbrook La TW10 154 A2
Sudbury E6 100 C1
Sudbury Ave HA0 65 D4
Sudbury Court Dr HA1 65 A5
Sudbury Court Rd HA1 65 A5
Sudbury Cres BR1 187 A5
Wembley HA0 65 B3
Sudbury Croft HA0 64 D4
Sudbury Ct E5 75 A4
SW8 269 D2
Sudbury Gdns CR0 221 C4
Sudbury & Harrow Road Sta HA0 65 B3
Sudbury Heights Ave UB6 65 A3
Sudbury Hill HA1 64 C5
Sudbury Hill Cl HA0 64 D5
Sudbury Hill Harrow Sta HA1 64 C4
Sudbury Hill Sta HA1 64 C4
Sudbury Ho SW18 157 D6
Sudbury Jun & Inf Schs HA0 65 B4
Sudbury Rd IG11 79 D3
Sudbury Town Sta UB6 65 B2
Sudeley St N1 94 D5 234 D3
Sudlow Rd SW18 157 C6
Sudrey St SE1 252 A1
Suez Ave UB6 86 D5
Suez Rd EN3 7 A2
Suffield Ho SE17 261 D2
Suffield Rd 2 N15 51 D4
Chingford E4 35 D6
Penge SE20 184 C1
Suffolk Cl WD6 11 B6
Suffolk Ct Ilford IG3 57 C3
3 West Norwood SW16 182 C6
Suffolk Ho 11 Acton W3 88 C1
Penge SE20 184 C2
4 South Croydon CR0 221 B6
Suffolk La EC4 252 C6
Suffolk Park Rd E17 53 A5
Suffolk Pl SW1 249 D4
Suffolk Rd 4 E13 99 A4
N15 51 B3
NW10 67 C1
Barking IG11 79 B1
Barnes SW13 134 A5
Dagenham RM10 81 D3
Enfield EN3 18 B6
Harrow HA2 41 B4
Ilford IG3 57 C3
Sidcup DA14 190 C4
South Norwood SE25 205 D5
Worcester Park KT4 215 D6
Suffolks Prim Sch EN1 6 B3
Suffolk St E7 77 A4
SW1 115 D5 249 D4
Sugar House La E15 98 A5
Sugar Loaf Wlk 6 E2 96 C4
Sugden Rd SW11 137 A1
Long Ditton KT7 197 B1
Sugden Way IG11 101 D5
Sulby Ho SE4 141 A1
Sulgrave Gdns 11 W6 112 C4
Sulgrave Rd W6 112 C3
Sulina Rd SW2 160 A4
Sulivan Ct SW6 135 C3
Sulivan Ent Ctr SW6 135 C2
Sulivan Prim Sch SW6 135 C3
Sulivan Rd SW6 135 C2
Sulkin Ho 11 E2 96 D4
Sullivan Ave E16 99 D2
Sullivan Cl SW11 136 C2
East Molesey KT8 195 D6
Northolt UB4 84 C2
Sullivan Ct N16 51 D1
SW5 255 B4
4 Croydon CR0 206 A1
Sullivan Ho SE11 260 D3
SW1 268 D6
Isleworth TW2 152 B5
Sullivan Rd SE11 116 C2 261 B4
Sullivans Reach KT12 193 D2
Sullivan Way WD6 9 C5
Sultan Rd E11 55 B5
Sultan St SE5 139 A5
Penge BR3 184 D1
Sumal Ct E9 76 B6
Sumatra Rd NW6 69 C2
Sumburgh Rd SW12 159 A5
Summer Ave KT8 196 C4
Summercourt Rd E1 96 C1
Summerene Cl SW16 181 C3
Summerfield 6 BR1 187 B2
Summerfield Ave N12 30 C4
NW6 91 A5
Summerfield La KT6 213 D6
Summerfield Rd
Ealing W5 87 B3
Loughton IG10 21 D5
Summerfield St SE12 164 D4
Summer Gdns KT8 196 C4
Summer Gr WD6 9 D5
Summer Hill BR7 188 C1
Borehamwood WD6 10 C6
Summerhill Cl BR6 227 C5
Summerhill Gr EN1 17 C5
Summerhill Rd N15 51 B5
Summerhill Way CR4 181 A2
Summer Ho SE13 142 B1
Summerhouse Ave TW5 129 A4
Summerhouse Rd N16 73 C6
Summerland Gdns N10 49 B6
Summerland Grange N10 49 B6
Summerlands Ave W3 111 A6
Summerlands Lo BR6 226 C4
Summerlee Ave N2 48 D5
Summerlee Gdns N2 48 D5
Summerley St SW18 157 D2
Summer Rd
East Molesey KT8 196 B4
Thames Ditton KT7,KT8 196 D4
Summersby Rd N6 49 B3
Summers Cl
Belmont SM2 217 C1
Wembley HA9 44 D1
Summersell Ho SE27 183 B5
Summerside Prim Sch N12 30 B4
Summerskille Cl N9 18 B2
Summers La N12 30 B3
Summers Row N12 30 C4
Summers St EC1 241 A5
Summerstown SW17 180 A6
Summerton Way SE28 102 D1
Summer Trees TW16 172 B2
Summerville Gdns SM1 217 B2
Summerwood Rd TW1,TW7 152 D5
Summit Ave NW9 45 B4
Summit Bsns Pk The TW16 172 A3
Summit Cl N14 15 C2
NW9 45 B5
Edgware HA8 26 C3
Summit Ct NW2 69 A3
Summit Dr IG8 37 D1
Summit Est N16 52 A2
Summit Rd E17 53 D5
Northolt UB5 63 C1
Summit The TW16 172 A3
Summit Way N14 15 B2
South Norwood SE19 183 C3
Sumner Ave SE15 139 D4
Sumner Bldgs SE1 252 A4
Sumner Cl BR6 227 A4
Sumner Ct SW8 270 A2
Sumner Gdns CR0 204 C1
Sumner Ho 1 E3 97 D2
Sumner Pl SW7 114 B2 256 D3
Sumner Place Mews SW7 256 D3
Sumner Rd SE15 139 D5
Harrow HA1 42 A2
Thornton Heath CR0 204 D1
Sumner Rd S CR0 204 C1
Sumner St SE1 117 A5 252 A4
Sumpter Cl NW3 70 A2
Sun Alley 6 TW9 132 A1
Sunbeam Cres W10 90 C3
Sunbeam Rd NW10 89 B3
Sunbury Ave NW7 27 B6
Mortlake SW14 133 B1
Sunbury Cl KT12 194 A3
Sunbury Court Island TW16 194 D6
Sunbury Court Rd TW16 172 C1
Sunbury Cres TW13 171 D6
Sunbury Cross TW16 172 A3
Sunbury Cross Ctr 9 TW16 171 D3
Sunbury Ct 3 SE14 140 D6
2 Barnet EN5 1 A1
Sunbury TW16 172 D1
Sunbury Ct (Con Ctr) TW16 172 D1
Sunbury Gdns NW7 27 B5
Sunbury Ho 38 E2 95 D4
Sunbury Int Bsns Ctr TW16 171 C2
Sunbury La SW11 136 B4 266 D2
Walton-on-T KT12 194 A3
Sunbury Manor Sch TW16 171 D2
Sunbury Rd
Cheam SM3 217 A5
Feltham TW13 171 D6
Sunbury St SE18 122 B3
Sunbury Sta TW16 172 A2
Sunbury Way TW13 172 C5
Sunbury Workshops 39 E2 95 D4
Suncroft Pl SE26 162 C1
Sun Ct EC3 242 D1
Sunderland Ct
Dulwich SE22 162 A4
12 Stanwell TW19 148 A5
Sunderland Ho 26 W2 91 C2
Sunderland Mount SE23 162 D2
Sunderland Pt E16 123 A5
Sunderland Rd W5 109 D3
Forest Hill SE23 162 D2
Sunderland Terr W2 91 D1
Sunderland Way E12 77 D6
Sundew Ave W12 112 A6
Sundew Ct 6 HA0 88 A5
Sundial Ave SE25 205 D6
Sundial Ct KT5 214 D6
Sundorne Rd SE7 121 C1
Sundown Rd TW15 171 A5
Sundridge Ave DA16 145 B2
Bromley BR1,BR7 188 A3
Sundridge Ho 4 E9 74 D1
Sundridge Par BR1 187 B3
Sundridge Park Sta BR1 187 B3
Sundridge Rd CR0 206 A1
Sunfields Pl SE3 143 B5
Sun in the Sands SE3 143 B5
Sunken Rd CR0 222 C3
Sun La SE3 143 B5
Sunland Ave DA6 147 A1
Sunleigh Ct HA0 88 A6
Sunleigh Rd HA0 88 A6
Sunley Gdns UB6 87 A6
Sun Life Trad Est TW14 128 A2
Sunlight Cl SW19 180 A4
Sunlight Sq 29 E2 96 B4
Sunmead Rd TW16 194 A6
Sunna Gdns TW16 172 B1
Sunniholme Ct CR2 221 A3
Sunningdale N14 31 D5
Ealing W13 87 B2
Sunningdale Ave W3 111 C6
Barking IG11 79 B1
Feltham TW13 151 A2
Ruislip HA4 40 C1
Sunningdale Cl E6 100 B4
22 SE16 118 B1
Erith SE28 103 A1
Stanmore HA7 25 A3
3 Surbiton KT6 214 A6
Sunningdale Ct
13 Kingston KT2 176 C3
13 Southall UB1 86 A1
Sunningdale Gdns NW9 45 A4
W8 255 B5
Sunningdale Rd BR1,BR2 210 A4
Cheam SM1 217 B4
Sunningfields Cres NW4 28 B1
Sunningfields Rd NW4 46 B6
Sunninghill Ct 9 W3 111 A4
Sunninghill Gdns IG2 57 D4
Sunninghill Rd SE13 141 D3
Sunny Bank SE25 206 A6
Sunny Cres NW10 67 A1
Sunnycroft Rd
Hounslow TW3 129 D3
Southall UB1 85 C2
South Norwood SE25 206 A6
Sunnydale BR6 226 C6
Sunnydale Gdns NW7 27 C4
Sunnydale Rd SE12 165 B6
Sunnydene Ave
Chingford E4 36 B5
Ruislip HA4 62 A6
Sunnydene Gdns HA0 65 C2
Sunnydene St SE26 185 A6
Sunnyfield NW7 27 D6
Sunnyfields Prim Sch NW4 46 B6
Sunny Gardens Par NW4 28 B1
Sunny Gardens Rd NW4 46 C6
Sunny Hill NW4 46 B6
Sunnyhill Cl E5 75 A4
Sunny Hill Ct NW4 28 B1
Sunnyhill Prim Sch SW16 182 B6
Sunnyhill Rd SW16 182 A6
Sunnyhurst Cl SM1 217 C5
Sunnymead Ave CR4 203 D6
Sunnymead Ct W5 109 C6
Sunnymead Rd NW9 45 B2
Putney SW15 156 B6
Sunnymede Ave KT19 215 C1
Sunnymede Dr IG6 56 D5
Sunny Nook Gdns CR2 221 B2
Sunny Pl NW4 46 C5
Sunny Rd The EN3 6 D4
Sunnyside 3 NW2 69 B5
Walton-on-T KT12 194 C4
Wimbledon SW19 179 A4
Sunnyside Dr E4 20 A4
Sunnyside Ho 2 NW2 69 B5
Sunnyside Pl SW19 179 A4
Sunnyside Rd E10 53 C1
N19 49 D2
Ealing W5 109 D5
Ilford IG1 79 B5
Teddington TW11 174 B6
Sunnyside Rd E N9 18 A1
Sunnyside Rd N N9 18 A1
Sunnyside Rd S N9 18 A1
Sunny View NW9 45 B4
Sunny Way N12 30 C3
Sun Pas 8 SE16 118 A3
Sunray Ave BR2 210 B3
SE5,SE24 139 B1
Sunray Ave *continued*
Tolworth KT5 214 D6
Sun Rd W14 113 B1 254 C1
Sunrise Cl TW13 151 B1
Sunrise View NW7 27 D4
Sunset Ave Chingford E4 19 D3
Woodford IG8 36 D6
Sunset Ct 4 IG8 37 C3
Sunset Gdns SE25 183 D1
Sunset Rd SE28 124 A5
SE5 139 B1
Wimbledon SW19 178 B5
Sunset View EN5 1 A3
Sunshine Way CR4 180 D1
Sun St EC2 95 B2 242 D4
Sun St Pas EC2 95 C2 243 A3
Sunwell Cl SE15 140 B4
Superior Dr 4 BR6 227 D2
Surbiton Cres KT1,KT6 198 A5
Surbiton Ct KT6 197 D3
Surbiton Hall Cl KT1 198 A5
Surbiton High Sch KT1 198 A5
Surbiton High Sch Jun Sch for Girls KT1 198 A5
Surbiton Hill Pk KT5 198 C4
Surbiton Hill Rd KT6 198 A4
Surbiton Hospl KT6 198 A3
Surbiton Prep Sch KT6 198 A4
Surbiton Rd KT1 198 A5
Surbiton Sta KT6 198 A3
Surcot Ho 2 SW4 137 D3
Surlingham Cl SE28 124 D6
Surma Cl E1 96 A3
Surmans Cl RM9 102 C6
Surrendale Pl W9 91 C3
Surrey Canal Rd SE14, SE16,SE8 140 D6
Surrey Cres 1 W4 110 C1
Surrey Ct N3 47 A6
Surrey Gdns N4 51 A3
Surrey Gr SE17 263 A1
Carshalton SM1 218 B5
Surrey Ho 8 SE16 118 D5
Surrey La SW11 136 C4 267 B1
Surrey Lo SW20 178 C1
Surrey Mews SE27 183 C6
Surrey Mount SE23 162 B3
Surrey Quays Rd SE16 118 D4
Surrey Quays Sh Ctr SE16 118 D3
Surrey Quays Sta SE16 118 D2
Surrey Rd SE15 162 D6
Barking IG11 79 C1
Dagenham RM10 81 D3
Harrow HA1 42 A4
West Wickham BR4 207 D1
Surrey Row SE1 116 D4 251 D2
Surrey Sq SE17 117 C1 263 B2
Surrey Square Inf Sch SE17 117 C1 263 A2
Surrey Square Jun Sch SE17 117 C1 263 A2
Surrey St 4 E13 99 B4
WC2 116 B6 250 D6
Croydon CR0 221 A5
Surrey Terr SE17 263 B2
Surrey Water Rd SE16 118 D5
Surrey Wharf SE1 140 A6
Surridge Ct 15 SW9 138 A3
Surridge Gdns SE19 183 B4
Surr St N7 72 A3
Sury Basin KT2 176 A2
Susan Constant Ct 3 E14 120 B6
Susan Lawrence Ho 3 E12 78 C4
Susan Lawrence Prim Schs E14 97 D1
Susannah St E14 98 A1
Susan Rd SE3 143 B3
Susan Wood BR7 188 C2
Sussex Ave TW7 130 C2
Sussex Cl N19 72 A6
New Malden KT3 199 C5
Redbridge IG4 56 B4
4 Twickenham TW1 153 B5
Sussex Cres UB5 63 C2
Sussex Ct SE10 142 A6
W2 236 C1
4 Barnes SW13 133 D3
Mitcham CR4 204 A4
Sussex Gate N6 48 D4
Sussex Gdns N4 51 A4
N6 48 D4
W2 92 B1 236 D1
Chessington KT9 213 D2
Sussex Ho NW3 70 C2
Richmond TW9 132 B3
Sussex House Sch SW3 114 D2 257 C3
Sussex Lo W2 236 D1
Sussex Mans SW7 256 C3
WC2 250 B6

Sussex Mews SE6 163 C3
Sussex Mews E W2 236 D1
Sussex Mews W W2 246 D6
Sussex Pl NW1 92 D3 237 C6
W2 92 B1 236 D1
22 W6 112 C1
New Malden KT3 199 C5
Sussex Rd DA14 190 B5
DA8 147 D5
Barking E6 100 C6
Harrow HA1 42 A4
Mitcham CR4 204 A4
New Malden KT3 199 C5
Southall UB2 106 D3
South Croydon CR2 221 B2
Uxbridge UB10 61 A3
Wallington SM5 218 D2
2 West Wickham BR4 207 D1
Sussex Ring N12 29 C5
Sussex Sq W2 114 B6 246 D6
Sussex St E13 99 B4
SW1 258 D2
Sussex Way N19 49 D1
N7,N19 72 A6
Cockfosters EN4 15 B6
Sutcliffe Cl NW11 47 D4
Sutcliffe Ho UB3 84 A1
Sutcliffe Rd SE18 145 C6
Bexley DA16 146 C3
Sutherland Ave BR5 211 D4
DA16 145 C1
W9 92 A3 236 A6
Ealing W13 87 B1
Hayes UB3 106 A2
Sunbury TW16 171 D1
Sutherland Cl EN5 1 A1
Sutherland Ct N16 73 B5
NW9 44 D4
2 W9 91 C3
Sutherland Dr SW19 180 B2
Sutherland Gdns
Mortlake SW14 133 C2
North Cheam KT4 200 B1
Sunbury TW16 171 D1
Sutherland Gr
Putney SW18,SW19 157 B4
Teddington TW11 174 C5
Sutherland Ho 9 NW6 70 A2
8 SE18 144 B4
W8 255 C5
Ealing W13 109 A6
7 Putney SW15 156 C4
Richmond TW10 153 C2
Sutherland Pl W2 91 C1
Sutherland Point 1 E5 74 B4
Sutherland Rd E17 53 A6
E3 97 B5
Belvedere DA17 125 C3
Chiswick W4 133 C6
Ealing W13 87 A1
Edmonton N9 18 B3
Enfield EN3 18 D6
Southall UB1 85 B1
Thornton Heath CR0 204 C2
Tottenham N17 34 A2
Sutherland Row SW1 258 D2
Sutherland Sq
SE17 117 A1 262 A1
Sutherland St
SW1 115 B1 258 D2
Sutherland Wlk SE17 262 B1
Sutlej Rd SE7 143 C5
Sutterton St N7 72 B2
Sutton Arc SM1 217 D3
Sutton Cl
Beckenham BR3 185 D2
Pinner HA5 40 A4
Sutton Common Rd
Cheam SM3 201 C1
Sutton SM1,SM3 217 D6
Sutton Common Sta
SM1 217 D6
Sutton Courtenay Ho
SW17 180 B6
Sutton Court Rd E13 99 C4
Chiswick W4 133 A6
Hillingdon UB10 82 D6
Sutton SM1,SM2 218 A2
Sutton Cres EN5 12 D6
Sutton Ct 9 E5 74 B4
Chiswick W4 133 A6
Ealing W5 110 A5
East Molesey KT8 195 B4
Penge SE19 183 D3
Sutton SM2 218 A2
Sutton Dene TW3 129 D4
Sutton Est
SW3 114 C1 257 B2
Sutton Est The W10 90 C2
Sutton Gdns
Barking IG11 101 C5
Croydon CR0 205 D4
Sutton Gn IG11 101 C6
Sutton Gr SM1 218 B3
Sutton Gram Sch For Boys
SM1 218 A3
Sutton Hall Rd TW5 129 C5
Sutton High Sch SM1 217 D2
Sutton Ho N21 16 B6
Sutton La TW3,TW4,
TW5 129 B3
Sutton La N W4 111 A1
Sutton La S W4 133 A6
Sutton Par NW4 46 C5
Sutton Park Rd SM1,
SM2 217 D2
Sutton Pl E9 74 C3
Sutton Rd E13 98 D3
E17 34 D2
N10 31 A2
Barking IG11 101 C6
Heston TW5 129 C4
Sutton Row W1 239 D2
Sutton Sq E9 74 C3
Hounslow TW5 129 B4
Sutton St E1 96 C1
Sutton Sta SM2 218 A2
Suttons Way EC1 242 B5
Sutton Way W10 90 C2
Hounslow TW5 129 B4
Sutton Wlk
SE1 116 B5 250 D3
Swaby Rd SW17,SW18 158 A2
Swaffield Prim Sch
SW18 158 A4
Swaffield Rd SW18 158 A4
Swain Cl SW16 181 B4
Swain Rd CR7 205 A4
Swains Cl UB7 104 A4
Swain's La N6 71 B6
Swainson Ho N7 72 C4
Swainson Rd W3 111 D4
Swains Rd CR4,SW17,
SW19 180 D3
Swakeleys Dr UB10 60 C3
Swakeleys Rd UB10 60 C5
Swakeleys Rdbt UB8,
UB10 60 A4
Swakeleys Sch UB10 82 D5
Swaledale Cl N11 31 A4
Swallands Rd SE6 163 C1
Swallowbrook Bsns Ctr
UB4 106 D5
Swallow Cl SE14 140 D4
Bushey WD23 8 A3
Swallow Ct 1 SE12 165 A4
4 W9 91 C2
Chingford IG8 36 B3
Ilford IG2 56 D4
5 Ruislip HA4 40 C1
Swallow Dr NW10 67 B2
Northolt UB5 85 C5
Swallowfield NW1 231 D1
Swallowfield Rd SE7 121 B1
Swallowfield Way
UB3 105 B4
Swallow Gdns SW16 181 D5
Swallow Ho N8 50 B6
NW8 230 A4
Swallow Pk KT6 214 B5
Swallow Pl W1 238 D1
Swallows Ct 5 SE20 184 D3
Swallow St E6 100 A2
W1 115 C6 249 B5
Swaminarayan Sch The
NW10 67 B2
Swanage Ct 5 N1 73 C1
Swanage Ho SW8 270 C3
Swanage Rd SW18 158 A5
Chingford E4 36 A3
Swanage Waye UB4 84 C1
Swan App E6 100 A2
Swanbourne SE17 262 A3
Swanbourne Ho NW8 237 A6
Swanbridge Rd DA7 147 C4
Swan Cl E17 35 A3
Croydon CR0 205 C2
Feltham TW13 173 A6
Swan Ct E14 97 B1
N20 14 A2
SW3 257 B1
SW6 265 A3
Swan Ctr SW17 158 A1
Swandon Way SW18 135 D1
Swan Dr NW9 27 C1
Swanfield St E2 95 D4
Swan Ho N1 73 B1
Enfield EN3 18 C6
Swan La EC4 117 B6 252 D5
N20 14 A1
Loughton IG10 21 C4
Swan Lane Pier
EC4 117 B6 252 C5
Swanlea Sec Sch E1 96 B3
Swanley Ho SE17 263 B2
Swanley Rd DA16 146 C4
Swan Mead
SE1 117 C3 263 A5
Swan Mews SW9 138 B3
Swanmore Ct SW18 158 A5
Swann Ct 6 TW7 131 A2
Swanne Ho 12 SE10 142 A5
Swan Pas 4 E1 118 A6
Swan Pl SW13 133 D3
Swan Rd SE16 118 C4
SE18 121 D3
Feltham TW13 173 A6
Southall UB1 85 D1
Swan Rd *continued*
West Drayton UB7 104 A4
Swanscombe Ho
1 BR5 190 B1
11 W11 112 D5
Swanscombe Point 7
E16 98 D2
Swanscombe Rd W11 112 D5
5 W4 111 C1
Swansea Ct E16 122 D5
Swansea Rd Enfield EN3 6 C1
Harlington TW14,TW6 149 B5
Swansland Gdns E17 35 A2
Swansmere Sch KT12 194 C1
Swan St SE1 117 A4 252 B1
Isleworth TW7 131 B2
Swan The BR4 224 A6
Swanton Gdns SW19 156 D3
Swanton Rd DA8 147 D5
Swan Way EN3 6 D3
Swanwick Cl SW15 155 D4
Swan Wlk
SW3 136 D6 267 C6
Oatlands Park TW17 193 C2
Swan Yd N1 72 D2
Swaton Rd E3 97 C3
Swaylands Rd DA17 147 C6
Swaythling Cl N18 34 B6
Swaythling Ho 2
SW15 155 D5
Swedenborg Gdns E1 118 B6
Sweden Gate SE16 119 A2
Swedish Sch The
SW13 133 D6
Sweeney Cres SE1 253 D1
Sweet Briar Gn N9 17 D1
Sweet Briar Gr N9 17 D1
Sweet Briar Wlk N18 33 D6
Sweetcroft La UB10 60 C1
Sweetmans Ave HA5 40 D6
Sweets Way N20 14 B2
Swell Ct E17 53 D3
Swetenham Wlk SE18 123 A1
Swete St E13 99 A5
Sweyn Pl SE3 143 A3
Swift Cl E17 35 A3
Harrow HA2 63 D6
Hayes UB3 83 D1
Swift Ct SM2 217 D1
Swift Ctr CR0 220 B1
Swift Ho 24 E1 96 C1
15 N16 73 C5
1 SW9 138 C5
8 Wanstead E18 55 B6
Swift Rd Feltham TW13 173 A6
Southall UB2 107 B3
Swiftsden Way BR1 186 C4
Swift St SW6 135 B4 264 C2
Swinbrook Rd W10 91 A2
Swinburne Cres CR0 206 C3
Swinburne Ct 4 SE5 139 B1
Swinburne Ho 15 E2 96 C4
Swinburne Rd SW15 134 A1
Swinderby Rd HA0 66 A2
Swindon Cl IG3 57 C1
Swindon Rd TW6 149 A6
Swindon St W12 112 C5
Swinfield Cl TW13 173 A6
Swinford Gdns SW9 138 D2
Swingate La SE18 145 C5
Swingfield Ho 5 E9 96 C6
Swinley Ho NW1 231 D2
Swinnerton St E9 75 A3
Swinton Cl HA9 44 D1
Swinton Ho 17 E2 96 A4
Swinton Pl WC1 233 C2
Swinton St WC1 94 B4 233 C2
Swires Shaw BR2 225 D4
Swiss Cottage NW3 70 B1
Swiss Cottage Sch
NW8 92 B6 229 D6
Swiss Cottage Sta NW3 70 B1
Swiss Re Building★
EC2 243 B2
Swiss Terr 7 NW3 70 B1
Swithland Gdns SE9 188 C6
Swyncombe Ave W5 109 B2
Swynford Gdns 7 NW4 46 A5
Sybil Elgar Sch UB2 107 B3
Sybil Mews N4 50 D3
Sybil Phoenix Cl SE8 118 D1
Sybil Thorndike Casson Ho
SW5 255 B1
Sybil Thorndike Ho 7
N1 73 A2
Sybourn Inf Sch Annexe
E10 53 A1
Sybourn Jun & Inf Schs
E17 53 B2
Sybourn St E17 53 B2
Sycamore Ave DA15 167 D5
N3 47 D6
W5 109 D3
Bow E3 97 B6
Hayes UB3 105 C6
Sycamore Cl E16 98 C3
W3 111 C5
2 HA8 27 A6
Carshalton SM5 218 D4
Sycamore Cl *continued*
Chislehurst SE9 166 A2
Edmonton N9 34 A6
Feltham TW13 150 A1
New Barnet EN4 14 B5
Northolt UB5 85 A6
South Croydon CR2 221 C3
Yiewsley UB7 104 B6
Sycamore Ct E7 77 A2
N19 71 D5
NW6 91 C6
SE12 164 D5
4 SE5 139 A4
Forest Hill SE26 184 C6
Hillingdon UB8 82 C3
Hounslow TW4 129 A1
Surbiton KT6 198 A2
10 West Norwood
SW16 182 C5
Sycamore Gdns N15 51 D5
W6,W12 112 B3
Mitcham CR4 180 B1
Sycamore Gr NW9 45 A2
SE6 164 A5
Kingston KT3 199 C6
Penge SE20 184 A2
Sycamore Hill N11 31 A4
Sycamore Ho 2 N16 73 B6
18 N2 30 B1
10 NW3 70 D2
17 SE16 118 D4
3 W6 112 B4
4 Buckhurst Hill IG9 21 D2
Penge SE20 184 D4
Sycamore Lo
7 Ashford TW16 171 D3
Putney SW15 134 B2
Sycamore Mews 4
SW4 137 C2
Sycamore Rd SW19,
SW20 178 C4
Sycamore St EC1 242 A5
Sycamore Way TW11 175 C4
Sycamore Wlk 1 W10 91 A3
Ilford IG6 57 A5
Sydenham Ave
Penge SE26 184 B5
Southgate N21 16 B6
Sydenham High Sch For
Girls SE26 184 B6
Sydenham Hill SE21,
SE22,SE23,SE26,SE19 162 A1
Sydenham Hill Sta
SE21 161 D1
Sydenham Ho 16 KT6 197 D2
Sydenham Ind Est
SE26 185 B5
Sydenham Park Mans 2
SE26 162 C1
Sydenham Park Rd
SE23,SE26 162 C1
Sydenham Pk SE26 162 C1
Sydenham Rd
Forest Hill SE26 184 D5
Forest Hill SE26 185 A6
Thornton Heath CR0 205 B2
Sydenham Rise SE23 162 B2
Sydenham Sec Sch
SE26 162 B1
Sydenham Sta SE26 184 C6
Sydenham Station App
SE26 184 C6
Sydmons Ct SE23 162 C4
Sydner Mews N16 73 D4
Sydner Rd N16 73 D4
Sydney Cl SW3 256 D3
Sydney Cotts KT10 212 D2
Sydney Cres TW15 170 D4
Sydney Ct Hayes UB4 84 C3
Surbiton KT6 214 A6
Sydney Gr NW4 46 C4
Sydney Ho 4 W4 111 C2
Sydney Mews SW3 256 D3
Sydney Pl SW7 257 A3
Sydney Rd DA6 146 D1
N10 31 B3
N8 50 C5
SE2 124 D3
Ealing W13 109 A4
East Bedfont TW14 150 A3
Enfield EN2 5 B1
Richmond TW10,TW9 132 A1
Sidcup DA14 189 C6
Sutton SM1 217 C4
Teddington TW11 174 D5
Wanstead E11 55 B3
West Barnes SW20 178 D1
Woodford IG8 37 A6
Sydney Russell Sch The
RM9 80 D3
Sydney St
SW3 114 C1 257 A2
Sydney Terr KT10 212 D2
Sylva Ct 3 SW15 156 D4
Sylvana Cl UB10 82 B6
Sylvan Ave N3 29 C1
NW7 27 D4
Dagenham RM6 59 B3
Wood Green N22 32 C3
Sylvan Ct N12 29 D6
South Croydon CR2 221 A2
Sylvan Gdns KT6 197 D2
Sylvan Gr NW2 68 D4
SE15 140 B6
Sylvan Hill SE19 183 C2
Sylvan Ho N21 16 B6
Sylvan Rd E17 53 C4
E7 77 B2
Ilford IG1 79 A6
South Norwood SE19 183 D2
Wanstead E11 55 A4
Sylvan Way
Coney Hall BR4 224 C4
Dagenham RM8 80 B5
Sylvan Wlk BR1 210 B6
Sylverdale Rd CR0 220 D5
Sylvester Ave BR7 188 B4
Sylvester Ho 7 E8 74 B2
Sylvester Path 8 E8 74 B2
Sylvester Rd E17 53 B2
E8 74 B2
N2 30 B1
Wembley HA0 65 C3
Sylvestrus Cl KT1 176 C1
Sylvia Ave HA5 23 B4
Sylvia Cotts 3 SE8 141 C4
Sylvia Ct N1 235 C3
Wembley HA9 66 D1
Sylvia Gdns HA9 66 D1
Sylvia Pankhurst Ho
14 E2 96 D4
10 Dagenham RM10 81 C5
Sylvia Young Theatre Sch
NW1 237 B5
Symes Mews NW1 232 A4
Symington Ho SE1 262 C5
Symington Mews E9 74 D3
Symister Mews N1 95 C4
Symons St
SW3 114 D2 257 D3
Symphony Mews 16
W10 91 A4
Syon Gate Way
Brentford TW7,TW8 131 A5
Brentford TW8 131 B5
Syon Ho TW8 131 C2
Syon La
Brentford TW7,TW8 131 B5
Hounslow TW7 130 D6
Syon Lane Sta TW7 131 A5
Syon Lo 6 SE12 165 A4
Syon Park Cotts TW8 131 C2
Syon Park Gdns TW7 130 D5
Syringa Ho SE4 141 B2

T

Tabard Ct 3 E14 98 A1
Tabard Ho SE1 262 D6
Teddington KT1 175 C2
Tabard St SE1 117 B3 262 C6
Tabernacle Ave 7 E13 99 A3
Tabernacle St
EC2 95 B3 242 D6
Tableer Ave SW4 159 D6
Tabley Rd N7 72 A4
Tabor Ct 3 SM3 217 A2
Tabor Gdns SM2,SM3 217 B1
Tabor Gr SW19 179 B3
Tabor Rd W6 112 B3
Tachbrook Est
SW1 115 D1 259 D1
Tachbrook Mews
SW1 259 A4
Tachbrook Rd
East Bedfont TW14 149 D4
Southall UB2 106 D2
Tachbrook St
SW1 115 C2 259 B3
Tack Mews SE4 141 C2
Tadbourne Ct 1 HA8 27 A3
Tadema Ho NW8 236 D5
Tadema Rd
SW10 136 A5 266 B3
Tadlow KT1 198 C6
Tadmor Cl TW16 193 D5
Tadmor St W12 112 D5
Tadworth Ave KT3 199 D4
Tadworth Ho SE1 251 C1
Tadworth Rd NW2 68 A6
Taeping St E14 119 D2
Taffy's How CR4 202 C6
Taft Way 44 E3 97 D4
Taggs Ho KT1 175 D1
Tailworth St 15 E1 96 A2
Tait 7 NW9 27 D3
Tait Ct 9 E3 97 B6
SW8 269 D2
Tait Ho 2 N19 71 C4
SE1 251 B3
Tait Rd CR0 205 C2
Tait Rd Ind Est CR0 205 C2
Takhar Mews SW11 136 C3
Talacre Rd NW5 71 A2
Talbot Ave N2 48 B6
Talbot Cl N15 51 D5
Talbot Cres NW4 46 A4
Talbot Ct EC3 252 D6
NW9 67 B5
Talbot Gdns IG3 80 A6
Talbot Grove Ho 9
W11 91 A1
Talbot Ho E14 97 D1
N7 72 C5
Talbot Pl SE3 142 C3
Talbot Rd E7 77 A4
N15 51 D5
N6 49 A3
SE22 139 C1
W11 91 B1
W2 91 C1
Ashford TW15 170 A5
Dagenham RM9 81 B1
Ealing W13 109 A5
Harrow HA3 24 D1
Isleworth TW1,TW7 131 A1
Southall UB2 107 A2
South Norwood CR7 205 B5
Twickenham TW2 152 D3
Wallend E6 100 C5
Wallington SM5 219 A3
Wembley HA0 65 D2
Wood Green N22 31 C2
Talbot Sq W2 92 B1 236 C1
Talbot Wlk NW10 67 C2
W11 91 A1
Talbot Yd SE1 252 C3
Talcott Path 12 SW2 160 C3
Talfourd Pl SE15 139 D4
Talfourd Rd SE15 139 D4
Talgarth Rd
W14 113 A1 254 B2
W6 112 D1
Talgarth Wlk NW9 45 C4
Talia Ho E14 120 A3
Talina Ctr SW6 266 A1
Talisman Cl 2 IG3 58 B1
Talisman Sq SE26 184 A6
Talisman Way HA9 66 B5
Tallack Cl HA3 24 C3
Tallack Rd E10 53 B1
Tall Elms Cl BR2 208 D4
Talleyrand Ho SE5 139 A3
Tallis Cl E16 99 B1
Tallis Gr SE7 143 B6
Tallis St EC4 251 B6
Tallis View NW10 67 B2
Tall Trees SW16 204 B6
Talma Gdns TW2 152 C4
Talmage Cl SE23 162 C4
Talman Gr HA7 25 D4
Talma Rd SW2 138 C1
Talmudical Coll N16 51 B2
Talmud Torah Sch N16 51 D2
Talwin St E3 97 D4
Tamar Cl E3 97 B6
Tamar Ho SE11 261 B2
Tamarind Ct 8 W3 89 A1
Tamarind Ho 4 SE15 140 A5
Tamarind Yd 5 E1 118 A5
Tamarisk Sq W12 111 D6
Tamar Sq IG8 37 B4
Tamar St SE7 122 A2
Tamar Way N17 52 A6
Tamesa Ho TW17 192 C2
Tamesis Gdns KT4 215 C6
Tamian Ind Est TW4 128 C1
Tamian Way TW4 128 C1
Tamworth N7 72 A2
Tamworth Ave IG8 36 C4
Tamworth La CR4 203 B6
Tamworth Manor High Sch
CR4 203 D6
Tamworth Pk CR4 203 B6
Tamworth Pl 3 CR0 221 A6
Tamworth Rd CR0 221 A6
Tamworth St
SW6 135 C6 265 A5
Tancred Rd N4 50 D3
Tandem Ctr SW19 180 B2
Tandridge Ct SM2 217 D2
Tandridge Dr BR5,BR6 211 B1
Tandridge Pl 2 BR6 211 B1
Tanfield Ave NW2 67 D5
Tanfield Rd CR0 221 A4
Tangier Rd TW10 132 D2
Tangleberry Cl BR1 210 B5
Tangle Tree Cl N3 29 D1
Tanglewood Cl
Hillingdon UB10 82 C3
South Croydon CR0 222 C5
Stanmore HA7 8 C2
Tanglewood Way
TW13 150 B1
Tangley Gr SW15 155 D4
Tangley Park Rd
TW12 173 B4
Tanglyn Ave TW17 192 D4
Tangmere WC1 233 C1
Tottenham N17 33 B1
Tangmere Gdns UB5 84 C5
Tangmere Gr KT2 175 D5
Tangmere Way NW9 27 C1

Tanhurst Ho 27 SW2 160 A4
Tankerton Rd KT6 214 B6
Tankerton St WC1 233 B1
Tankerton Terr CR0 204 B3
Tankerville Rd SW16 182 A3
Tankridge Rd NW2 68 B6
Tanner Ho SE1 253 B1
1 Merton SW19 180 A2
Tanner Point E13 99 A6
Tanners Cl KT12 194 B3
Tanners End La N18 33 C5
Tanner's Hill SE8 141 C4
Tanners La IG6 57 A6
Tanner St SE1 117 C4 253 B1
Barking IG11 79 A2
Tanners Yd 32 E2 96 B5
Tannery Cl
Beckenham BR3,CR0 206 D4
Dagenham RM10 81 D5
Tannery Ho 20 E1 96 A2
Tannington Terr N5 72 C5
Tannsfeld Rd SE26 184 D5
Tansley Cl N7 71 D3
Tanswell St SE1 251 A1
Tansy Cl E6 100 C1
Tantallon Rd SW12 159 A3
Tant Ave E16 98 D1
Tantony Gr RM6 58 D6
Tanworth Gdns HA5 22 C1
Tan Yard La DA5 169 C4
Tanza Rd NW3 70 D4
Tapestry Cl SM2 217 D1
Tapley Ho 11 SE1 118 A4
Taplow NW3 70 B1
Taplow Ct CR4 202 C5
Taplow Ho 36 E2 95 D4
Taplow Rd N13 33 A6
Taplow St N1 95 A5 235 B3
Tappesfield Rd SE15 140 C2
Tapping Cl 5 KT2 176 C3
Tapp St E1 96 B3
Tapster St EN5 1 B2
Tara Ct
4 Beckenham BR3 185 D1
9 Buckhurst Hill IG9 21 C2
Taranto Ho 11 E1 96 D2
Tarbert Rd SE22 161 C6
Tarbert Wlk E1 118 C6
Target Cl TW14 149 C5
Target Ho W13 109 B5
Target Rdbt UB5 85 B6
Tariff Rd N17 34 A4
Tarleton Ct 2 N22 32 C1
Tarleton Gdns SE23 162 B3
Tarling Cl DA14 168 B1
Tarling Ho 27 E1 96 B1
Tarling Rd E16 98 D1
N2 30 A1
Tarling St E1 96 C1
Tarnbank EN2 16 A6
Tarnbrook Ct SW1 258 A3
Tarn St SE1 117 A3 262 A5
Tarns The NW1 232 A2
Tarnwood Pk SE9 166 B3
Tarplett Ho 22 SE14 140 D6
Tarquin Ho SE26 184 A6
Tarragon Cl SE14 141 A5
Tarragon Gr SE26 184 D4
Tarranbrae NW6 69 A1
Tarrant Ho E2 96 C4
Tarrant Pl W1 237 C3
Tarrantt Ho W14 254 B5
Tarriff Cres SE8 119 B2
Tarrington Cl SW16 159 D1
Tartan Ho 8 E14 98 A1
Tarver Rd
SE17 116 D1 261 D2
Tarves Way SE10 141 D5
Tash Pl N11 31 B5
Tasker Cl UB7 127 A5
Tasker Ho 18 E14 97 B2
Barking IG11 101 B5
Tasker Rd NW3 70 D3
Tasman Ct 9 E14 119 D2
Ashford TW16 171 C3
Tasman Ho 16 E1 118 B5
Tasmania Terr N18 33 A4
Tasman Rd SW9 138 A2
Tasman Wlk E16 99 D1
Tasso Rd W6 135 A6 264 A6
Tasso Yd W6 264 A5
Tatchbury Ho 3
SW15 155 D5
Tate Britain★
SW1 116 A2 260 A3
Tate Gdns WD23 8 C4
Tate Ho 13 E2 96 D5
Tate Modern★
EC4 116 D5 251 C3
Tate Rd Newham E16 122 B5
Sutton SM1 217 C3
Tatham Pl NW8 92 B5 229 D4
Tatnell Rd SE23 163 A5
Tattersall Cl SE9 166 A6
Tatton Cres E5,N16 51 D2
Tatum Rd NW10 67 B1
Tatum St SE17 117 C2 262 D3
Tauheed Cl N4 73 A6
Taunton Ave
Hounslow TW3 130 A3
Wimbledon SW20 178 B1
Taunton Cl SM3 201 C1
Taunton Dr N2 30 A1
Enfield EN2 4 C2
Taunton Ho W2 236 A1
Taunton Mews NW1 237 C5
Taunton Pl
NW1 92 D3 237 C6
Taunton Rd SE12 164 D6
Greenford UB6 85 D6
Taunton Way HA7 26 A1
Tavern Cl SM5 202 C2
Taverner Ho N16 73 B5
Taverners Cl W11 244 A3
Taverners Ct HA9 66 B6
Taverner Sq 4 N5 73 A4
Taverners Way E4 20 C3
Tavern La SW9 138 C3
Tavistock Ave E17 53 A6
NW7 28 D3
Wembley UB6 87 A5
Tavistock Cl N16 73 C3
Tavistock Cres W11 91 B2
Mitcham CR4 204 A5
Tavistock Ct WC1 239 D6
1 Croydon CR0 205 B1
Tavistock Gdns IG3 79 C4
Tavistock Gr CR0 205 B2
Tavistock Ho 2 W11 91 B2
Tavistock Mews 1
W11 91 B1
Tavistock Pl
WC1 94 A3 240 A6
East Barnet N14 15 B5
Tavistock Rd DA16 146 C4
E15 76 D2
E7 76 D4
N4,N15 51 B3
NW10 89 D5
W11 91 B2
4 Beckenham BR2 208 D5
Carshalton SM5 202 B1
Croydon CR0 205 B1
Edgware HA8 26 C2
Uxbridge UB10 61 A3
Wanstead E18 55 A6
Tavistock Sq
WC1 93 D3 239 D6
Tavistock St
WC2 116 A6 250 B6
Tavistock Terr N19 71 D5
Tavistock Twr SE16 119 A3
Tavistock Wlk SM5 202 B1
Taviton St WC1 93 D3 239 C6
Tavy Bridge SE2 124 C4
Tavy Cl SE11 261 B2
Tawney Rd SE28 124 B6
Tawny Cl Ealing W13 109 B5
Feltham TW13 150 A1
Tawny Way SE16 118 D2
Tayben Ave TW2 152 C5
Taybridge Rd SW11 137 A1
Tayburn Cl E14 98 A1
Tayfield Cl UB10 61 A5
Tay Ho 8 E3 97 B5
Tayler Ct NW8 229 C6
Taylor Ave TW9 132 D3
Taylor Cl 3 BR6 227 D4
Hampton TW12 174 A5
Hounslow TW3 130 A4
Tottenham N17 34 A3
Taylor Ct E15 76 A3
Ealing W13 109 C5
Penge SE20 184 C1
Taylor Ho 10 SW2 160 C3
Taylor Rd Mitcham CR4 180 C3
Wallington SM6 219 B3
Taylor's Bldgs SE18 122 D2
Taylors Cl DA14 167 D1
Taylors Ct TW13 150 A2
Taylor's Gn W3 89 C1
Taylor's La NW10 67 C1
Barnet EN5 1 B4
Forest Hill SE26 184 B6
Taylorsmead NW7 28 A5
Taymount Grange 2
SE23 162 C2
Taymount Rise SE23 162 C2
Tayport Cl N1 72 A1
Tayside Ct 6 SE5 139 B1
Tayside Dr HA8 10 D2
Taywood Rd UB5 85 B4
Teak Cl SE16 119 A5
Tealby Ct N7 72 B2
Teal Cl E16 99 D2
Teal Ct NW10 67 B2
30 SE8 141 B6
Wallington SM6 219 C3
Teale St E2 96 A5
Tealing Dr KT19 215 B4
Teal Pl SM1 217 B3
Teasel Cl CR0 206 D1
Teasel Way E15 98 C4
Teather St 20 SE5 139 C5
Tebbs Ho 14 SW2 160 C4
Tebworth Rd N17 33 D3
Teck Cl TW7 131 A3
Tedder 5 NW9 27 D3
Tedder Cl
Chessington KT9 213 C3
Hillingdon UB10 60 B1
Tedder Rd CR2 222 D1
Teddington Memorial Hospl
TW11 174 C4
Teddington Park Rd
TW11 174 D6
Teddington Pk TW11 174 D5
Teddington Sch TW11 175 C4
Teddington Sta TW11 175 A4
Ted Hennem Ho RM10 81 D5
Ted Roberts Ho 24 E2 96 B5
Tedworth Gdns SW3 257 C1
Tedworth Sq
SW3 114 D1 257 C1
Tees Ave UB6 86 D5
Tees Ct W7 86 B1
Teesdale Ave TW7 131 A4
Teesdale Cl E2 96 B5
Teesdale Gdns
Isleworth TW7 131 A4
South Norwood SE25 183 C1
Teesdale Rd E11 54 D2
Teesdale St E2 96 B5
Teesdale Yd 33 E2 96 B5
Teeswater Ct DA18 124 D3
Tee The W3 89 C1
Teevan Cl CR0 206 A2
Teevan Rd CR0 206 A2
Teignmouth Cl
6 SW4 137 D1
Edgware HA8 26 B1
Teignmouth Gdns UB6 87 A4
Teignmouth Rd NW2 68 D2
Bexley DA16 146 C3
Telcote Way HA4 40 C2
Telegraph Hill NW3 69 D5
Telegraph La KT10 212 D3
Telegraph Mews IG3 58 A1
Telegraph Pl E14 119 D2
Telegraph Rd SW15 156 C4
Telegraph St EC2 242 C2
Telemann Sq SE3 143 B2
Telfer Cl 4 W3 111 A4
Telfer Ho EC1 234 D1
8 Dulwich SE21 183 C6
Telferscot JMI Sch
SW12 159 D3
Telferscot Prim Sch
SW12 159 D3
Telferscot Rd SW12 159 D3
Telford Ave SW12,SW2 160 A3
Telford Avenue Mans 7
SW2 160 A3
Telford Cl E17 53 A2
Penge SE19 183 D4
Telford Dr KT12 194 C2
Telford Ho SE1 262 A6
8 W10 91 A2
2 Belvedere DA17 125 C3
Telford Parade Mans 8
SW2 160 A3
Telford Rd 2 NW9 46 A3
W10 91 A2
Sidcup BR7,DA15 167 B2
Southall UB1 85 D1
Twickenham TW4 151 C4
Telford Rd (North Circular
Rd) N11 31 C5
Telford Terr SW1 269 A6
Telford Way W3 89 C2
Hayes UB4 85 A2
Telham Rd E6 100 C5
Tell Gr SE22 139 D1
Tellson Ave SE18 144 A4
Telscombe Cl BR6 227 C6
Telscombe Ho SW11 268 A1
Temair Ho 1 SE10 142 A5
Temeraire St SE16 118 C4
Temperley Rd SW12 159 A4
Templar Ct RM7 59 D5
Templar Dr SE28 102 D1
Templar Ho 9 E5 74 C6
NW2 69 B2
Templar Pl TW12 173 C3
Templars Ave NW11 47 B3
Templars Cres N3 29 C1
Templars Dr HA3 24 B4
Templars Ho E15 75 D3
Templar St SE5 138 D3
Temple Ave
EC4 116 C6 251 B6
N20 14 B4
Croydon CR0 223 B5
Dagenham RM8 59 C1
Temple Cl E11 54 C2
N3 29 B1
SE18 123 A3
Templecombe Rd E9 96 C6
Templecombe Way
SM4 201 A4
Templecroft TW15 171 B4
Temple Ct SW8 270 A3
Templedene BR2 186 B1
Temple Dwellings 7
E2 96 B5
Temple Fortune Ct 9
NW11 47 B4
Temple Fortune Hill
NW11 47 C4
Temple Fortune Ho 3
NW11 47 B4
Temple Fortune La
NW11 47 C3
Temple Fortune Par 5
NW11 47 B4
Temple Gdns NW11 47 B3
Dagenham RM8 80 D5
Edmonton N21 16 D2
Temple Gr NW11 47 C3
Enfield EN2 4 D2
Temple Hall Ct 1 E4 20 B2
Temple Ho 11 E17 53 D6
4 N7 71 C5
13 SW11 136 C2
Templehof Ave NW2 46 C2
Temple La EC4 94 C1 241 B1
Temple Lo EN5 14 B4
Templeman Rd W7 86 D2
Templemead Cl W3 89 C1
Temple Mead Cl HA7 25 B4
Templemead Ho E9 75 A4
Temple Mills La E10,
E15 76 A4
Temple Mills Rd E9 75 C4
Templemore DA14 190 B5
Temple Par EN5 14 B4
Temple Pk UB8 82 C4
Temple Pl
WC2 116 B6 250 D6
Temple Rd E6 100 A6
N8 50 B5
NW2 68 C5
W4 111 A3
W5 109 D3
Croydon CR0 221 B4
Isleworth TW3 130 A1
Richmond TW9 132 B2
Temple Sheen SW14 155 A6
Temple Sheen Rd
SW14 133 A1
Temple St E2 96 B5
Temple Sta
WC2 116 C6 251 A6
Temple Terr N22 32 C1
Templeton Ave E4 35 D6
Templeton Cl 25 N16 73 C3
South Norwood SE19 183 B2
Templeton Ct E10 53 D1
Templeton Pl
SW5 113 C2 255 B3
Templeton Rd N4,N15 51 B3
Temple Way SM1 218 B5
Temple West Mews
SE11 261 C5
Templewood W13 87 B2
Templewood Ave NW3 69 D5
Templewood Gdns
NW3 69 D5
Templewood Point
NW2 69 B6
Tempsford Cl EN2 5 A2
Tempsford Ct HA1 42 D3
Temsford Cl HA2 24 A1
Tenbury Cl E7 77 D3
Tenbury Ct SW12 159 D3
Tenby Ave HA3 25 B1
Tenby Cl N15 51 D5
Dagenham RM6 59 A3
Tenby Ct E17 53 A4
Tenby Gdns UB5 63 C2
Tenby Ho N7 72 C4
W2 236 A1
Hayes UB3 105 A3
Tenby Rd DA16 146 D4
E17 53 A4
Dagenham RM6 59 A3
Edgware HA8 26 B1
Enfield EN3 6 C1
Tench St E1 118 B5
Tenda Rd SE16 118 B2
Tendring Ho SW2 160 C5
Tendring Way RM6 58 C4
Tenham Ave SW2 159 D2
Tenison Ct W1 249 A6
Tenison Way SE1 251 A3
Tenniel Cl W2 245 D6
Tennison Ave WD6 10 D6
Tennison Rd SE25 205 D4
Tennis St SE1 117 B4 252 C2
Tenniswood Rd EN1 5 C4
Tennyson Ave E12 78 A1
NW9 45 A6
Twickenham TW1 152 D3
Wanstead E11 55 A2
West Barnes KT3 200 B4
Tennyson Cl DA16 145 D4
Enfield EN3 18 D6
Feltham TW14 150 A5
Tennyson Ct SW6 265 D1
3 Richmond TW10 175 D6
Tennyson Ho SE17 262 B2
2 Erith DA17 125 B1
Tennyson Rd E10 75 D6
E15 76 C1
E17 53 B3
NW6 91 B6
NW7 28 A5
Ashford TW15 170 A5
Ealing W7 108 D6
Hounslow TW3 130 A3
Penge SE20 184 D3
Wimbledon SW19 180 A4
Tennyson St SW8 137 B3
Tensing Ct TW19 148 A3
Tensing Ho N1 72 D2
Tensing Rd UB2 107 C3
Tentelow La UB2 107 D3
Tenterden Cl NW4 46 D6
SE9 188 B6
Tenterden Dr NW4 46 D6
Tenterden Gdns NW4 46 D6
Croydon CR0 206 A2
Tenterden Gr NW4 46 D6
Tenterden Ho SE17 263 B2
Tenterden Rd
Croydon CR0 206 A2
Dagenham RM8 81 B6
Tottenham N17 33 D3
Tenterden St W1 238 D1
Tenter Ground E1 243 C3
Tent Peg La BR5 211 A4
Tent St E1 96 B3
Tenzing Ct 4 SE9 166 A2
Terborah Way 6
SE22 161 C6
Terence Ct 6 DA17 147 B6
Terence Messenger Twr
E10 75 D6
Teresa Mews E17 53 C5
Teresa Wlk N10 49 B4
Terling Cl E11 76 D5
Terling Ho W10 90 C2
Terling Rd RM8 81 C6
Terling Wlk N1 235 A6
Terminal Rdbt TW6 149 A5
Terminus Pl SW1 258 D5
Tern Ho 8 SE15 139 D4
Terrace Ave NW10 90 C4
Terrace Gdns SW13 133 D3
Terrace La TW10 154 A5
Terrace Rd E13 99 B6
E9 74 C1
Walton-on-T KT12 194 B3
Terraces The 6 SW20 178 D3
Terrace The EC4 241 B1
N2 49 A5
NW6 91 C6
9 SE8 119 B2
SW13,SW14 133 C3
Chingford E4 20 C1
1 Woodford IG8 37 A4
Terrace Wlk RM9 81 A3
Terrapin Ct SW17 159 B1
Terrapin Rd SW17 159 B1
Terrapins KT6 197 D2
Terrick Rd N22 32 A2
Terrick St W12 90 B1
Terrilands HA5 41 B6
Territorial Ho SE11 261 B3
Terront Rd N15 51 A5
Terry Ho SW2 160 C3
Tersha St TW9 132 B1
Tessa Sanderson Pl 6
SW8 137 B2
Tessa Sanderson Way
UB6 64 B3
Testerton Wlk 3 W11 112 D6
Testwood Ct W7 108 C6
Tetcott Rd
SW10 136 A5 266 A3
Tetherdown N10 49 A6
Tetherdown Prim Sch
N10 49 A5
Tetty Way BR1,BR2 187 A1
Teversham La
SW8 138 A4 270 B2
Teviot Cl DA16 146 B4
Teviot St E14 98 A2
Tewkesbury Ave
Forest Hill SE23 162 B4
Pinner HA5 41 A4
Tewkesbury Cl N15 51 B3
Tewkesbury Gdns NW9 44 D6
Tewkesbury Rd N15 51 B3
Carshalton SM5 202 B1
Ealing W13 109 A6
Tewkesbury Terr N11 31 D4
Tewson Rd SE18 123 C1
Teyham Ct SW11 158 D5
Teynham Ave EN1 17 B5
Teynham Gn BR2 209 A4
Teynham Ho SE9 167 B5
Teynton Terr N17 33 A2
Thackeray Ave N17 34 A1
Thackeray Cl
Harrow HA2 41 C1
Hayes UB8 82 D1
Isleworth TW7 131 A3
Wimbledon SW19 178 D3
Thackeray Ct SW3 257 C2
W14 254 A5
Thackeray Ct *continued*
Ealing W5 88 B1
Thackeray Dr RM6 58 B2
Thackeray Ho WC1 240 A6
Thackeray Manor
SM1 218 A3
Thackeray Mews E8 74 A2
Thackeray Rd E6 99 D5
SW8 137 B3
Thackeray St W8 255 D6
Thackery Lo TW14 149 B5
Thackran Cl N2 30 A1
Thakeham Cl SE26 184 B5
Thalia Cl SE10 142 B6
Thame Rd SE16 118 D4
Thames Ave
SW10 136 A4 266 B2
Dagenham RM9,RM13 103 D3
Wembley UB6 86 D5
Thames Bank SW14 133 A3
Thamesbank Pl SE28 102 C1
Thames Barrier Visitor
Ctr★ SE18 121 D3
Thames Circ E14 119 C2
Thames Cl TW12 173 D1
Thames Cres W4 133 C5
Thames Ct 10 SE15 139 D5
West Molesey KT8 173 D1
Thames Ditton Cty Fst Sch
KT7 196 D3
Thames Ditton Island
KT7 197 A4
Thames Ditton Jun Sch
KT7 196 D2
Thames Ditton Sta
KT7 196 D2
Thames Dr HA4 39 A3
Thames Eyot 7 TW1 153 A3
Thamesfield Ct TW17 193 A2
Thamesgate Cl TW10 175 B6
Thames Gateway Pk
RM9 103 B4
Thames Haven KT6 197 D4
Thames Hts SE1 253 C2
Thameside TW11 175 D3
Thameside Ctr TW8 132 B6
Thameside Ind Est
E16 121 D4
Thames Link Ho 7
TW9 132 A1
Thames Mead KT12 194 A2
Thames Meadow
East Molesey KT8 195 C6
Lower Halliford KT12,
TW17 193 C1
Thamesmead Sec Sch
TW17 193 B3
Thamesmead Sh Ctr
SE28 124 A6
Thamesmere Dr SE28 124 A6
Thames Pl SW15 134 D2
Thamespoint TW11 175 D3
Thames Quay E14 119 D4
SW10 266 B1
Thames Rd E16 121 D5
Barking IG11 102 A4
Chiswick W4 132 D6
Thames Reach W6 134 C6
Thames Road Ind Est
E16 121 D4
Thames Side
Teddington KT1 175 D2
Thames Ditton KT7 197 B3
Thames St SE10 141 D6
Hampton TW12 173 D1
Kingston KT1,KT2 175 D1
Sunbury TW16 194 B6
Walton-on-T KT12 193 D2
Thamesvale Cl TW3 129 C3
Thames Valley Univ
W5 109 D5
Thames View Ho
TW12 194 A3
Thames View Inf Sch
IG11 102 A5
Thames View Jun Sch
IG11 101 D5
Thames View Lodge
IG11 101 C4
Thames Village W4 133 A4
Thames Wlk
SW11 136 C5 267 A4
Thane Mans N7 72 B5
Thanescroft Gdns
CR0 221 C5
Thanet Ct 14 W3 88 C1
Thanet Dr BR2 225 D5
Thanet Ho WC1 233 A1
1 West Norwood SE27 160 D1
Thanet Lo NW2 69 A2
Thanet Pl CR0 221 A4
Thanet Rd DA5 169 C4
Thanet St WC1 94 A4 233 A1
Thane Villas N7 72 B5
Thane Works N7 72 B5
Thanington Ct DA15 167 C5
Thant Cl E10 75 D5
Tharp Rd SM6 219 D3
Thatcham Ct N20 14 A4

Thatcham Gdns N20 14 A4
Thatcher Cl UB7 104 A4
Thatchers Way TW7 152 B6
Thatches Gr RM6 59 A5
Thavie's Inn EC4 241 B2
Thaxted Ct N1 235 D3
Thaxted Ho SE16 118 C2
Dagenham RM10 81 D1
Thaxted Lo 3 E18 55 B6
Thaxted Pl 9 SW20 178 D3
Thaxted Rd SE9 167 A2
Buckhurst Hill IG9 21 D4
Thaxton Rd
W14 135 B6 264 D6
Thayers Farm Rd BR3 185 A2
Thayer St W1 93 A2 238 B2
Theatre Mus★ WC2 250 B6
Theatre Sq E15 76 B2
Theatre St SW11 136 D2
Theberton St
N1 94 D6 234 C6
Theed St SE1 116 C5 251 B3
Thelbridge Ho 28 E3 97 D4
Thelma Gdns SE3 144 A4
Thelma Gr TW11 175 A4
Theobald Cres HA3 24 A2
Theobald Rd E17 53 C2
Croydon CR0 220 D6
Theobalds Av N12 30 A6
Theobalds Ct N4 73 A6
Theobalds Park Rd EN2 4 D6
Theobald's Rd
WC1 94 B2 240 C4
Theobald St SE1 262 C5
Theodora Way HA5 39 D6
Theodore Ho 1 SW15 156 A6
Theodore Rd SE13 164 B5
Therapia La
Thornton Heath CR0 204 A2
Thornton Heath CR0 204 A3
Wallington CR0 203 D2
Therapia Lane Sta
CR0 204 A2
Therapia Rd SE22 162 C5
Theresa Rd W6 112 A2
Therfield Ct N4 73 A6
Thermopylae Gate
E14 119 D2
Theseus Ho 2 E14 98 B1
Theseus Wlk N1 234 D3
Thesiger Rd SE20 184 D3
Thessaly Ho SW8 269 A3
Thessaly Rd
SW8 137 C4 269 B2
Thesus Ho 2 E14 98 B1
Thetford Cl N13 32 D4
Thetford Ct
3 Dulwich SE21 162 B2
New Malden KT3 199 C4
Thetford Gdns RM9 103 A6
Thetford Ho SE1 263 C6
Thetford Rd
Ashford TW15 148 A1
Dagenham RM9 80 D1
New Malden KT3 199 C4
Thetis Terr TW9 132 C6
Theydon Gr IG8 37 C4
Theydon Rd E5 74 C6
Theydon St E17 53 B2
Thicket Cres SM1 218 A4
Thicket Gr
Dagenham RM9 80 C2
Penge SE20 184 A3
Thicket Rd Penge SE20 184 B3
Sutton SM1 218 A4
Thicket The UB7 82 A1
Third Ave E12 78 B3
3 E13 99 A4
E17 53 C4
W10 91 A4
W3 111 D5
Dagenham RM10 103 D5
Dagenham RM6 58 C3
Enfield EN1 17 D6
Hayes UB3 105 D5
Wembley HA9 65 D6
Third Cl KT8 196 A5
Third Cross Rd TW2 152 B2
Third Way HA9 66 D4
Thirleby Rd HA8 27 B2
SW1 115 C3 259 B5
Thirlestone Ct N10 31 A1
Thirlmere NW1 231 D2
Thirlmere Ave UB6 87 C4
Thirlmere Gdns HA9 43 D1
Thirlmere Ho 20 N16 73 B4
Isleworth TW1 152 D6
Thirlmere Rd N10 31 B2
Streatham SW16 181 D6
Thirlmere Rise BR1 186 D4
Thirsk Cl UB5 63 C2
Thirsk Rd SW11 137 A1
Mitcham CR4 181 A3
South Norwood SE25 205 B5
Thisilefield Cl DA5 168 D3
Thistlebrook SE2 124 C4
Thistlecroft Gdns HA7 25 D1
Thistle Ct N17 52 B5
Thistledene KT7 196 C3
Thistledene Ave HA2 63 A5
Thistledown Ct SE25 205 C6
Thistle Gr SW7 256 B1
Thistle Ho 6 E14 98 A1
Thistlemead BR7 188 D1
Thistlewaite Rd E5 74 B5
Thistlewood Cl 3 N7 72 B6
Thistleworth Cl TW7 130 B5
Thistley Cl N12 30 C4
Thistly Ct SE8 141 D6
Thomas a' Beckett Cl
HA0 64 D4
Thomas Arnold Prim Sch
RM9 81 B1
Thomas Baines Rd
SW11 136 B2
Thomas Burt Ho 9 E2 96 B4
Thomas Buxton Jun & Inf
Sch E1 96 A3
Thomas Cribb Mews
E6 100 B1
Thomas Ct E17 53 D4
Dagenham RM8 80 C6
Ealing W7 86 C1
Thomas Dean Rd SE26 185 B6
Thomas Dinwiddy Rd
SE12 165 B2
Thomas Doyle St SE1 261 D6
Thomas Fairchild Comm
Sch N1 95 A5 235 B4
Thomas Gamuel Prim Sch
E17 53 C3
Thomas Hardy Ho N22 32 B2
Thomas Hewlett Ho
HA1 64 C4
Thomas Ho 3 E9 74 C2
4 SW4 138 A1
Thomas Hollywood Ho 3
E2 96 C5
Thomas Jones Prim Sch
W11 91 A1
Thomas' La SE6 163 C4
Thomas More Ho EC2 242 A3
Thomas More Sq E1 118 A6
Thomas More St E1 118 A5
Thomas More Way N2 48 A6
Thomas North Terr 3
E16 98 D2
Thomas Pl W8 255 C5
Thomas Pooley Ct
KT6 198 A2
Thomas Rd E14 97 C2
Thomas Road Ind Est
E14 97 C1
Thomas's London Day Schs
SW11 136 B4 266 D2
Thomas's Prep Sch
Clapham SW11 158 D6
Thomas St SE18 122 D2
Thomas Tallis Sch
SE3 143 B2
Thomas Wall Cl SM1 217 D3
Thomas Watson Cottage
Homes The EN5 13 A6
Thompson Ave TW9 132 C2
Thompson Cl Ilford IG1 79 A6
Morden SM3 201 C1
Thompson Ho SE14 140 D6
11 W10 91 A3
Thompson Rd SE22 161 D5
Dagenham RM9 81 B5
Hounslow TW3 129 D1
Uxbridge UB10 60 A1
Thompson's Ave 6
SE5 139 A5
Thomson Cres CR0 204 C1
Thomson Ho SE17 263 A3
SW1 259 D1
Southall UB1 107 A6
Thomson Rd HA3 42 C6
Thorburn Ho SW1 248 A1
Thorburn Sq SE1 118 A2
Thorburn Way SW19 180 B2
Thoresby Ho N16 73 B5
Thoresby St N1 95 A4 235 B2
Thorkhill Gdns KT7 197 B1
Thorkhill Rd KT7 197 B2
Thornaby Gdns N18 34 B5
Thornaby Ho 15 E2 96 B4
Thorn Ave WD23 8 A3
Thornbill Ho 1 SE15 140 A5
Thornbury 3 NW4 46 C5
Thornbury Ave TW7 130 B5
Thornbury Cl N16 73 C3
Thornbury Ct W11 245 A6
Croydon CR2 221 B3
Hounslow TW7 130 C5
Thornbury Ho N6 49 C1
Thornbury Rd SW2 160 A5
Hounslow TW7 130 B4
Thornbury Sq N6 49 C1
Thornby Rd E5 74 C5
Thorn Cl BR2 210 C3
Northolt UB5 85 B4
Thorncliffe Ct SW2 160 A5
Thorncliffe Rd SW2 160 A5
Southall UB2 107 B1
Thorncombe Rd SE22 161 C6
Thorncroft Rd SM1 217 D4
Thorncroft St
SW8 138 A5 270 A3
Thorndale Ho N16 51 C1
Thorndean St SW18 158 A2
Thorndene Ave N11 15 A3
Thorndike Ave UB5 84 D6
Thorndike Cl
SW10 136 A5 266 A4
Thorndike Ho SW1 259 C2
Thorndike St
SW1 115 D2 259 C3
Thorndon Cl BR5 189 D1
Thorndon Gdns KT19 215 C4
Thorndon Rd BR5 189 D1
Thorndyke Ct HA5 23 B3
Thorne Cl DA8 147 D6
E11 76 C4
E16 99 A1
Littleton TW15 171 A3
Thorne Ho 4 E14 120 A3
34 E2 96 C4
Thorneloe Gdns CR0,
CR9 220 D3
Thorne Pas 7 SW13 133 D3
Thorne Rd
SW8 138 A5 270 B3
Thorne's Cl BR3 208 A6
Thorness Ct SW18 158 A5
Thorne St SW13,SW14 133 C2
Thornet Wood Rd
BR1 210 C6
Thornewill Ho 7 E1 118 C6
Thorney Cres
SW11 136 B5 266 D3
Thorneycroft Cl KT12 194 C3
Thorneycroft Dr EN3 7 C6
Thorneycroft Ho 11
W4 111 C1
Thorney Ct W8 246 A1
Thorney Hedge Rd
W4 110 D2
Thorney St
SW1 116 A2 260 A4
Thornfield Ave NW7 29 A2
Thornfield Ct NW7 29 A2
Thornfield Ho 4 E14 119 C6
Thornfield Par NW7 29 A3
Thornfield Rd W12 112 B4
Thornford Rd SE13 164 A6
Thorngate Rd W9 91 C3
Thorngrove Rd E13 99 B6
Thornham Gr E15 76 B3
Thorn Ham Ho SE1 262 D6
Thornham St SE10 141 D6
Thornhaugh St WC1 239 D5
Thornhill Ave SE18 145 C5
Surbiton KT6 214 A6
Thornhill Bridge Wharf
N1 233 C5
Thornhill Cres N1 72 B1
Thornhill Ct N8 49 D3
Thornhill Gdns E10 75 D6
Barking IG11 79 C1
Thornhill Gr N1 72 C1
Thornhill Ho N1 72 C1
12 W4 111 C1
Thornhill Prim Sch N1 72 C1
Thornhill Rd E10 75 D6
N1 72 C1 234 A6
Ickenham UB10 60 C4
Surbiton KT6 214 B6
Thornton Heath CR0 205 A2
Thornhill Sq N1 72 B1
Thornhill Way TW17 192 C4
Thornicroft Ho 12
SW9 138 B3
Thornlaw Rd SE27 182 D6
Thornley Cl N17 34 A3
Thornley Dr HA2 63 D6
Thornley Pl 2 SE10 120 C1
Thornsbeach Rd SE6 164 A2
Thornsett Pl SE20 184 B1
Thornsett Rd
Penge SE20 184 B1
Wandsworth SW18 157 D3
Thornsett Terr SE20 184 B1
Thornton Ave W4 111 C2
Streatham SW2 159 D3
Thornton Heath CR0 204 B3
West Drayton UB7 104 B3
Thornton Cl UB7 104 B3
Thornton Ct N7 72 A3
West Barnes SW20 200 D4
Thornton Dene BR3 185 C1
Thornton Gdns SW12 159 D3
Thornton Gr HA5 23 C4
Thornton Heath Pond
CR7 204 C4
Thornton Heath Sta
CR7 205 A5
Thornton Hill SW19 179 A3
Thornton Ho SE17 263 A3
7 Wanstead E11 55 A3
Thornton Lo CR7 205 A6
Thornton Pl W1 237 D4
Thornton Rd BR1 187 A5
E11 76 B6
N18 18 C1
Barnet EN5 1 A2
Thornton Rd *continued*
Belvedere DA17 125 D2
Carshalton SM5 202 B1
Ilford IG1 78 D4
Mortlake SW14 133 B2
Streatham SW12,SW2 159 D3
Thornton Heath CR0,CR7 204 B3
Wimbledon SW19 178 D3
Thornton Rd E SW19 178 D4
Thornton Row CR7 204 C4
Thornton St SW9 138 C3
Thornton Way NW11 47 D4
Thorntree Ct W5 88 A2
Thorntree Rd SE7 121 D1
Thorntree Sch SE7 121 B1
Thornville Gr CR4 180 B1
Thornville St SE8 141 C4
Thornwell Ct W7 108 C4
Thornwood Cl E18 37 B1
Thornwood Rd SE13 164 C6
Thornycroft Ct TW9 132 B3
Thorogood Gdns E15 76 C3
Thorold Ho SE1 252 A2
6 Streatham SW2 160 A4
Thorold Rd Ilford IG1 57 A1
Wood Green N22 32 A3
Thorparch Rd
SW8 137 D5 269 D3
Thorpebank Rd W12 112 A5
Thorpe Cl BR6 227 C6
W10 91 A1
Forest Hill SE26 184 D6
Thorpe Coombe Hospl
E17 54 A6
Thorpe Cres E17 35 B1
Thorpe Ct EN2 4 D2
Thorpedale Gdns IG6 56 D5
Thorpedale Rd N4 50 B1
Thorpe Hall W5 87 D2
Thorpe Hall Rd E17 36 A2
Thorpe Ho N1 233 D5
Thorpe Rd E6 100 B6
E7 76 D4
N15 51 C3
Barking IG11 79 B1
Chingford E17 36 A1
Kingston KT2 176 A3
Thorpewood Ave SE23,
SE26 162 B2
Thorpland Ave UB10 61 A5
Thorsden Way 2
SE19 183 C5
Thorverton Rd NW2 69 A5
Thoydon Rd E3 97 A5
Thrale Almhouses
SW16 182 A5
Thrale Rd SW16 181 C5
Thrale St SE1 252 B3
Thrasher Cl 20 E8 95 D6
Thrawl St E1 95 D2 243 D3
Thrayle Ho 2 SW9 138 B2
Threadgold Ho 8 N1 73 B2
Threadneedle St
EC2,EC3 95 B1 242 D1
Three Bridges Bsns Ctr
UB2 108 A4
Three Bridges Prim Sch
UB2 107 D3
Three Colts La E2 96 B3
Three Colt St E14 119 B6
Three Corners DA7 147 D3
Three Cups Yd WC1 240 D3
Three Kings Yd W1 248 C6
Three Meadows Mews
HA7 24 D2
Three Mill La E3 98 A4
Three Nun Ct EC2 242 B2
Three Oak La SE1 253 C2
Three Oaks Cl UB10 60 B5
Threshers Pl W11 244 A6
Thriffwood SE23,SE26 162 D1
Thrigby Rd KT9 214 B2
Thring Ho 2 SW9 138 B3
Throckmorten Rd E16 99 B1
Throgmorton Ave
EC2 95 B1 242 D2
Throgmorton St
EC2 95 B1 242 D2
Throwley Cl SE2 124 C3
Throwley Rd SM1 217 D3
Throwley Way SM1 217 D3
Thrupp Cl CR4 181 B1
Thrush Gn HA2 41 C5
Thrush St SE17 262 A2
Thunderer Rd RM9 103 B3
Thunder Rd RM9 103 B3
Thurbarn Rd SE6 185 D5
Thurland Ho 3 SE16 118 B2
Thurland Rd SE16 118 A3
Thurlby Cl HA1 43 A3
Thurlby Croft NW4 46 C6
Thurlby Rd
Wembley HA0 65 D2
West Norwood SE27 182 C6
Thurleigh Ave SW12 159 A5
Thurleigh Ct SW12 159 A5
Thurleigh Rd SW12 159 A5
Thurleston Ave SM4 201 A4
Thurlestone Ave N12 30 D4
Thurlestone Ave *continued*
Ilford IG3 79 D4
Thurlestone Cl TW17 193 A3
Thurlestone Ct 1 UB1 85 D1
Thurlestone Par
TW17 193 A3
Thurlestone Rd SE27 182 C6
Thurloe Cl SW7 257 A4
Thurloe Ct SW3 257 A3
Thurloe Pl
SW7 114 B2 256 D4
Thurloe Place Mews
SW7 256 D4
Thurloe Sq
SW7 114 C2 257 A4
Thurloe St
SW7 114 B2 256 D4
Thurlow Cl E4 35 D4
Thurlow Ct 6 E11 55 A4
Thurlow Gdns HA0 65 D3
Thurlow Hill SE21 161 A2
Thurlow Ho 17 SW16 160 A1
Thurlow Park Rd SE21,
SE24 161 A2
Thurlow Rd NW3 70 B3
W7 109 A4
Thurlow St
SE17 117 C1 263 A1
Thurlow Terr NW5 71 A3
Thurlow Twrs SE27 160 C1
Thurlston Rd HA4 62 A5
Thurnby Ct TW2 152 C1
Thurnscoe NW1 232 A5
Thursland Rd DA14 191 A5
Thursley Cres CR0 224 B1
Thursley Gdns SW19 156 D2
Thursley Ho
3 Kingston KT2 176 D3
10 Streatham SW2 160 B4
Thursley Rd SE9 166 B1
Thurso Ho NW6 91 D5
Thurso St SW17 180 B6
Thurstan Rd SW20 178 B3
Thurston Ho 4 BR3 185 D4
Thurston Ind Est SE13 141 D2
Thurston Rd SE8,SE13 141 D3
Southall UB1 85 B1
Thurtle Rd E2 95 D5
Thurza Ct TW7 130 D3
Thyer Cl BR6 227 A4
Thyra Gr N12 29 D4
Tibbatt's Rd E3 97 D3
Tibbenham Pl SE6 163 C2
Tibbenham Wlk E13 98 D5
Tibbets Cl SW19 156 D3
Tibbet's Corner SW19 156 D4
Tibbet's Ride SW19 156 D4
Tiber Gdns N1 233 B5
Ticehurst Cl BR5 190 A3
Ticehurst Rd SE23 163 A2
Tickford Cl SE2 124 C4
Tickford Ho NW8 230 A1
Tidal Basin Rd E16 120 D6
Tidbury Ct SW8 269 A3
Tidemill Prim Sch
SE8 141 C5
Tidenham Gdns CR0 221 C5
Tideside Ct SE18 122 A3
Tideswell 10 NW5 71 B4
Tideswell Rd
Croydon CR0 223 C5
Putney SW15 134 C1
Tideway Cl TW10 175 C6
Tideway Ct 9 SE16 118 D5
Tideway Ho E14 119 C4
Tideway Ind Est
SW8 137 C6 269 B5
Tideway Wharf SW13 133 C3
Tideway Yd SW13 133 C3
Tidey St E3 97 C2
Tidford Rd DA16 145 D3
Tidworth Ho 13 SE22 139 C2
Tidworth Rd E3 97 C3
Tiepigs La BR2,BR4 208 D1
Tierney Ct 4 CR0 221 D6
Tierney Rd SW2 160 A3
Tierney Terr SW2 160 A3
Tiffin Girls' Sch KT2 176 A4
Tiffin Sch KT2 176 B1
Tiger Ho WC1 232 D1
Tiger La BR2 209 B5
Tiger Way E5 74 B4
Tigris Cl N9 18 C2
Tilbrook Rd SE3,SE9 143 C2
Tilbury Cl BR5 190 B1
13 SE15 139 D5
Tilbury Ho 4 SE14 140 D6
Tilbury Rd E10 54 A2
E6 100 B5
Tildesley Rd SW15 156 C5
Tile Farm Rd BR6 227 B5
Tilehurst NW1 231 D1
Tilehurst Point 2 SE2 124 C4
Tilehurst Rd
Cheam SM3 217 A3
Wandsworth SW17,
SW18 158 B3
Tile Kiln La N6 49 C1
Edmonton N13 33 A5
Tile Kiln La *continued*
Harefield UB9 38 D2
Tileyard Rd N7 72 A1
Tilford Ave CR0 224 A1
Tilford Gdns SW19 156 D3
Tilford Ho 8 SW2 160 B4
Tilia Rd E5 74 B4
Tilia Wlk 21 SW9 138 D1
Tilleard Ho 4 W10 91 A4
Tiller Ho 30 N1 95 C6
Tiller Rd E14 119 C3
Tillet Sq SE16 119 A4
Tillett Cl NW10 67 A2
Tillet Way 4 E2 96 A4
Tilley Rd TW14 150 A3
Tillingbourne Gdns N3 47 A6
Tillingbourne Way N3 47 B5
Tillingham Way N12 29 D6
Tilling Ho 1 SE15 140 B2
Tilling Rd NW2 46 C2
Tilling Way HA9 65 D6
Tillman Ho 8 SW2 160 B3
Tillman St E1 96 B1
Tillotson Ct SW8 269 D3
Tillotson Rd
Edmonton N9 17 D2
Harrow HA3 23 D3
Ilford IG1 56 C2
Tilney Ct EC1 242 B6
Kingston KT6 197 D4
Woodford IG9 21 A2
Tilney Dr IG9 21 A2
Tilney Gdns 12 N1 73 B2
Tilney Rd Chigwell IG9 21 B2
Dagenham RM9 81 B2
Southall UB2 106 C2
Tilney St W1 248 B4
Tilson Cl 2 SE15 139 C5
Tilson Gdns SW2,SW4 160 A4
Tilson Ho SW2 160 A4
Tilson Rd N17 34 A2
Tilston Cl E11 76 D5
Tilston St SW6 264 B5
Tiltwood The W3 111 A6
Tilt Yard App SE9 166 B5
Timber Cl BR7 188 C1
Timbercroft KT19 215 C4
Timbercroft La SE18 145 C5
Timbercroft Prim Sch
SE18 145 C5
Timberdene NW4 28 D1
Timberland Cl 15
SE15 140 A5
Timberland Rd E1 96 B1
Timber Mill Way SW4 137 D2
Timber Pond Rd SE16 118 D4
Timber St EC1 242 A6
Timberwharf Rd N16 52 A3
Time Sq E8 73 D3
Times Sq SM1 217 D3
Timothy Cl 1 SW4 159 C6
Bexley DA6 169 A6
Timothy Ho DA18 125 A4
Timothy Rd E3 97 B2
Timsbury Wlk 5
SW15 156 A3
Tina Ct SW16 160 C1
Tindal St SW9 138 D4
Tinniswood Cl N5 72 C3
Tinsley Rd E1 96 C2
Tintagel Cres SE22 139 D1
Tintagel Ct EC1 241 C6
Tintagel Dr HA7 25 D6
Tintagel Ho SE20 184 A3
Tintern Ave NW9 44 D6
Tintern Cl
Putney SW15 157 A6
Wimbledon SW19 180 A4
Tintern Ct W13 109 A6
Tintern Gdns N14 16 A4
Tintern Ho NW1 231 D3
SW1 258 C3
Tintern Path NW9 45 C3
Tintern Rd
Carshalton SM5 202 B1
Tottenham N22 33 A2
Tintern St SW4 138 A1
Tintern Way HA2 41 D1
Tinto Rd E16 99 A3
Tinwell Mews WD6 11 B6
Tinworth St
SE11 116 A1 260 B2
Tippett Ct E6 100 B5
Tippetts Cl EN2 5 A4
Tipthorpe Rd SW11 137 A2
Tipton Dr CR0 221 C4
Tiptree 7 NW1 71 B1
Tiptree Cl E4 20 A1
Tiptree Cres IG5 56 C6
Tiptree Ct EN2 5 B1
Tiptree Dr EN2 5 B1
Tiptree Rd HA4 62 B4
Tirlemont Rd CR2 221 A1
Tirrell Rd CR0 205 A3
Tisbury Ct W1 249 C6
Tisbury Rd SW16 182 A1

Tisdall Pl SE17 117 B2 262 D3
Tissington Ct 4 SE16 118 D2
Titan Bsns Est 3 SE8 141 C5
Titan Ct TW8 110 B1
Titchborne Row W2 237 B1
Titchfield Rd
NW8 92 D6 230 C4
Carshalton SM5 202 B1
Enfield EN3 7 A6
Titchfield Wlk SM5 202 B2
Titchwell Rd SW18 158 B3
Tite St SW3 136 D6 267 C6
Tithe Barn Cl KT2 176 B2
Tithe Barn Way UB5 84 B5
Tithe Cl NW7 28 A2
Hayes UB4 83 D2
Walton-on-T KT12 194 B3
Tithe Ct NW4 28 A2
Tithe Farm Ave HA2 63 C5
Tithe Farm Cl HA2 63 C5
Tithe Wlk NW7 28 A2
Titian Ave WD23 8 C4
Titley Cl E4 35 C5
Titmus Cl UB8 83 A1
Titmuss Ave SE28 124 B6
Titmuss St W12 112 C4
Tivendale N8 50 A6
Tiverton Ave IG5 56 C6
Tiverton Dr SE9 167 A3
Tiverton Prim Sch N15 51 B3
Tiverton Rd N4,N15 51 B3
NW6,NW10 90 D6
Edgware HA8 26 B1
Edmonton N18 33 C5
Hounslow TW3 130 A3
Ruislip HA4 62 A5
Wembley HA0 88 A5
Tiverton St
SE1 117 A3 262 A6
Tiverton Way KT9 213 D3
Tivoli Ct SE16 119 B5
Tivoli Gdns 11 SE7 122 A2
Tivoli Rd N8 49 D4
Hounslow TW4 129 A1
West Norwood SE27 183 A5
Toad La TW4 129 B1
Tobago St E14 119 C4
Tobin Cl NW3 70 C1
Toby Ct N9 18 C4
Toby La E1 97 A3
Toby Way KT5,KT6 214 D6
Todber Ho W14 254 B5
Todd Ho 3 N2 30 B1
Todds Wlk N7 72 B6
Tokenhouse Yd EC2 242 C2
Tokyngton Ave HA9 66 C2
Toland Sq SW15 156 A6
Tolcairn Ct 2 DA17 125 C1
Tolcarne Dr HA5 40 B6
Tolchurch 2 W11 91 C1
Toley Ave HA3,HA9 44 A2
Tollbridge Cl W10 91 A3
Tollesbury Gdns IG6 57 B6
Tollet St E1 96 D3
Tollgate Dr
Dulwich SE21 161 C2
Hayes UB4 106 D6
Tollgate Ho 1 NW6 91 D5
Tollgate Prim Sch E13 99 C3
Croydon CR0 206 C3
Tollgate Rd E6 100 A2
Tollhouse Way N19 71 C6
Tollington Ct N4 72 B6
Tollington Pk N4 72 B6
Tollington Pl N4 72 B6
Tollington Rd N7 72 B4
Tollington Way N7 72 A5
Tolmers Sq
NW1 93 C3 239 B6
Tolpaide Ho SE11 261 A3
Tolpuddle Ave 2 E13 99 C6
Tolsford Rd E5 74 B3
Tolson Ho 2 TW7 131 A2
Tolson Rd TW7 131 A2
Tolverne Rd SW20 178 C2
Tolworth Cl KT6 198 D1
Tolworth Gdns RM6 58 D4
Tolworth Girls' Sch
KT6 214 B5
Tolworth Hospl KT6 214 C6
Tolworth Inf Sch KT6 198 B1
Tolworth Junc KT6 214 D6
Tolworth Jun Sch KT6 198 B1
Tolworth Par RM6 59 A4
Tolworth Park Rd KT6 214 B6
Tolworth Rd KT6 214 A6
Tolworth Rise N KT5 198 D1
Tolworth Rise S KT5 198 D1
Tolworth Sta KT5 214 D6
Tolworth Underpass
KT5,KT6 214 D6
Tomahawk Gdns 4
UB5 84 D4
Tom Coombs Cl SE9 144 A1
Tom Cribb Rd SE18,
SE28 123 B3
Tom Groves Cl E15 76 B3
Tom Hood Cl E15 76 B3
Tom Hood Sch E11 76 D5
Tom Jenkinson Rd 5
E16 121 A5
Tomkyns Ho SE11 261 A3
Tomline Ho SE1 252 A3
Tomlin's Gr E3 97 C4
Tomlinson Cl E2 95 D4
5 W4 110 D1
Tomlins Orch IG11 101 A6
Tomlin's Terr E14 97 A1
Tomlins Wlk 4 N7 72 B6
Tom Mann Cl IG11 101 C6
Tom Nolan Cl E15 98 C5
Tompion Ho EC1 241 D6
Tompion St EC1 234 D1
Tom Smith Cl SE10 142 C6
Tom Smith Ho 3 E17 54 A4
Tomson Ho SE1 263 C6
Tom Williams Ho
SW6 264 C5
Tonbridge Cres HA3 44 A5
Tonbridge Hos WC1 233 A1
Tonbridge Rd KT12,
KT8 195 B5
Tonbridge St
WC1 94 A4 233 A1
Toneborough 14 NW8 91 D6
Tonfield Rd SM3 201 B1
Tonge Cl BR3 207 C4
Tonsley Hill SW18 157 D6
Tonsley Pl SW18 157 D6
Tonsley Rd SW18 157 D6
Tonsley St SW18 157 D6
Tonstall Rd CR4 181 A1
Tooke Cl HA5 23 A2
Tookey Cl HA3 44 B2
Took's Ct EC4 241 A2
Tooley St SE1 117 C5 253 A3
Toorack Rd HA3 24 B1
Tooting Bec SW17 159 A1
Tooting Bec Gdns
SW16 181 D6
Tooting Bec Rd
Streatham SW16 181 C5
Upper Tooting, Furzedown
SW17 181 B6
Tooting Bec Sta SW17 159 A1
Tooting Broadway
SW17 180 D5
Tooting Broadway Sta
SW17 180 C5
Tooting Gr SW17 180 C5
Tooting High St SW17,
SW19 180 C5
Tooting Sta SW17 180 D4
Tootswood Rd BR2,
BR3 208 C5
Topaz Ho KT4 199 B1
Topaz Wlk NW2 46 D2
Topcliffe Dr BR6 227 B4
Topham Ho 8 SE10 142 A5
Topham Sq N17 33 A2
Topham St EC1 241 A6
Top House Rise E4 20 A4
Topiary Sq TW9 132 B2
Topley St SE9 143 D1
Topmast Point E14 119 C4
Top Pk BR3 208 C4
Topsfield Cl N8 49 D4
Topsfield Par N8 50 A3
Topsfield Rd N8 50 A4
Topsham Rd SW17 181 A6
Torbay Ct 13 NW1 71 B1
Torbay Mans NW6 91 B6
Torbay Rd NW6 69 B1
Harrow HA2 63 A6
Torbay St 15 NW1 71 B1
Torbitt Way IG2 57 D4
Torbridge Cl HA8 26 A3
Torbrook Cl DA5 169 A5
Torcross Dr SE23 162 C2
Torcross Rd HA4 62 C5
Tor Ct W8 245 B2
Torfell 5 E18 36 D1
Tor Gdns W8 113 C4 245 A2
Tor Ho N6 49 B3
Tormead Cl SM1 217 C2
Tormount Rd SE18 145 C6
Tornay Ho E9 74 C1
N1 233 C4
Toronto Ave E12 78 B4
Toronto Rd IG1 57 A1
Torquay Gdns IG4 55 D5
Torquay St W2 91 D2
Tor Rd DA16 146 C4
Torrens Ct SE5 139 B2
Torrens Rd E15 76 D2
SW2 160 B6
Torrens Sq E15 76 D2
Torrens St EC1 94 D5 234 C3
Torres Sq E14 119 C1
Torre Wlk SM5 202 C1
Torriano Ave NW5 71 D3
Torriano Cotts NW5 71 C3
Torriano Jun & Inf Schs
NW5 71 D3
Torridge Gdns SE15 140 C1
Torridge Rd CR7 204 D4
Torridon Ho NW6 91 D5
Torridon Inf Sch SE6 164 B2
Torridon Jun Sch SE6 164 B2
Torridon Rd SE13,SE6 164 B3
Torrington Ave N12 30 B5
Torrington Cl N12 30 B6
Claygate KT10 212 C2
Torrington Ct N12 30 B6
Forest Hill SE26 184 A5
Harrow HA2 63 D5
Torrington Dr HA2 63 D5
Torrington Gdns N11 31 C4
Wembley UB6 65 C1
Torrington Gr N12 30 C5
Torrington Pk N12 30 B6
Torrington Pl E1 118 A5
WC1 93 D2 239 C4
Torrington Rd
Claygate KT10 212 C2
Dagenham RM8 59 B1
Ruislip HA4 62 A5
Wanstead E18 55 A6
Wembley UB6 87 C6
Torrington Sq
WC1 93 D3 239 D5
Thornton Heath CR0 205 B2
Torrington Way SM4 201 C3
Torr Rd SE20 184 D3
Tortington Ho 1 SE15 140 B5
Torver Rd HA1 42 C5
Torver Way BR6 227 B5
Torwood Rd SW15 156 A6
Totham Lo SW20 178 B2
Tothill Ho SW1 259 D4
Tothill St SW1 115 D4 249 D1
Totland Ho SW18 157 D5
Totnes Rd DA16 146 C5
Totnes Villas N11 31 C5
Totnes Wlk N2 48 B5
Tottan Terr E1 96 D1
Tottenhall 5 NW1 71 A1
Tottenhall Inf Sch N13 32 C4
Tottenhall Rd N13 32 D4
Tottenham Court Rd
W1 93 C2 239 B4
Tottenham Court Road Sta
W1 93 D1 239 D2
Tottenham Gn E 2
N15 51 D5
Tottenham Gn E South Side
3 N15 51 D5
Tottenham Hale N15 52 A5
Tottenham Hale Ret Pk
N15 52 A5
Tottenham Hale Sta
N17 52 B6
Tottenham La N8 50 B4
Tottenham Mews W1 239 B4
Tottenham Rd N1 73 C2
Tottenham St
W1 93 C2 239 B4
Totterdown St SW17 180 D5
Totteridge Comm N20 12 C3
Totteridge Ho SW11 136 B3
Totteridge La N20 13 D3
Totteridge Rd EN3 6 D6
Totteridge Village N20 13 B3
Totteridge & Whetstone Sta
N20 14 A2
Totternhoe Cl HA3 43 C4
Totton Rd CR7 204 C6
Touchard Ho N1 235 D1
Toulmin St
SE1 117 A4 252 A1
Toulon St SE5 139 A5
Toulouse Ct 2 SE16 118 B1
Tournay Rd
SW6 135 B5 264 D4
Toussaint Wlk 18
SE16 118 A3
Tovil Cl SE20 184 B1
Tovy Ho 6 SE1 118 A1
Towcester Rd E3 98 A3
Tower 42★ EC2 243 A2
Tower Bldgs 22 E1 118 B5
Tower Br App E1,EC3 253 C5
Tower Bridge★
E1,EC3,SE1 117 D5 253 C4
Tower Bridge Bsns Complex
SE16 118 B3
Tower Bridge Bsns Sq
SE16 118 B2
Tower Bridge Piazza
SE1 253 C3
Tower Bridge Prim Sch
SE1 117 D4 253 C2
Tower Bridge Rd
SE1 117 C4 253 C3
Tower Bridge Sq SE1 253 C2
Tower Cl NW3 70 B3
Orpington BR6 227 D5
Penge SE20 184 B3
Tower Ct E5 51 D2
NW8 230 B4
WC2 240 A1
Tower Gardens Rd N17 33 B2
Towergate SE1 263 A4
Towergate Cl UB8 60 A3
Tower Gateway Sta
EC3 117 D6 253 C6
Tower Gdns KT10 213 A1
Tower Gr KT13 193 C1
Tower Hamlets Coll E1 96 C2
E1 96 D1
E14 119 D6
E14 97 D1
Tower Hamlets Rd E17 53 C6
E7 76 D3
Tower Hill
EC3 117 D6 253 C5
Tower Hill Sta
EC3 117 D6 253 C6
Tower Hill Terr EC3 253 B5
Tower La HA9 65 D5
Tower Mans SE1 263 C5
Tower Mews E17 53 C5
E5 75 A3
Tower Millennium Pier
EC3 117 C5 253 B4
Tower Mill Rd 11
SE15 139 C5
Tower Rd DA7 147 D1
NW10 68 A1
Orpington BR6 227 D5
Twickenham TW1,TW2 152 D1
Tower Rise TW9 132 A2
Tower Royal EC4 252 C6
Towers Ave UB10 83 A4
Towers Ct UB10 83 A4
Towers Pl TW10 154 A6
Towers Rd Pinner HA5 23 A2
Southall UB1 85 C3
Tower St WC2 240 A1
Towers The NW5 71 B5
1 Richmond TW9 132 B1
Tower Terr SE4 141 A1
Wood Green N22 32 B1
Tower The★
EC3 117 D6 253 C5
Tower View CR0 207 A2
Tower Wharf SE1 253 C2
Tower Wlk SE1 263 A4
Towfield Ct TW13 151 B2
Towfield Rd TW13 151 B2
Towncourt Cres BR5 211 B5
Towncourt La BR5 211 B2
Towncourt Path N4 51 A1
Townend Ct 6 BR1 186 D2
Towney Mead UB5 85 B5
Towney Mead Ct UB5 85 B5
Townfield Rd UB3 105 D5
Townfield Sq UB3 105 D6
Town Field Way TW7 131 A3
Town Hall Approach Rd
N15 51 D5
Townhall Ave 3 W4 111 B1
Town Hall Rd SW11 136 D2
Townholm Cres W7 108 D3
Town La TW19 148 A2
Townley Ct E15 76 D2
Townley Gram Sch for Girls
DA5 169 B6
Townley Rd DA6 169 B6
SE22 161 C6
Townley St
SE17 117 B1 262 C2
Townmead Bsns Ctr
SW6 136 A2
Town Meadow TW8 131 D5
Townmead Rd SW6 136 A3
Richmond TW9 132 D3
Town Quay IG11 100 D6
Town Quay Wharf
IG11 100 D6
Town Rd N9 18 B2
Townsend Ave N14 31 D6
Townsend Ho 12 SE1 118 A2
Townsend Ind Est
NW10 89 A5
Townsend La NW9 45 B3
Townsend Prim Sch
SE17 117 C2 263 A4
Townsend Rd N15 51 D4
Ashford TW15 170 A5
Southall UB1 107 A5
Townsend St
SE1,SE17 117 C2 263 A4
Townsend Way HA6 22 A3
Townsend Yd N6 49 B1
Townshend Cl DA14 190 C4
Townshend Ct NW8 230 B4
Townshend Est
NW8 92 C5 230 A4
Townshend Ho 19
SE18 122 B2
Townshend Rd
NW8 92 C6 230 A5
Chislehurst BR7 188 D5
Richmond TW9 132 B1
Townshend Terr TW9 132 B1
Towns Ho 4 SW4 137 D2
Townson Ave UB5 84 B5
Townson Way UB5 84 A5
Town The EN2 5 B2
Town Tree Rd TW15 170 C5
Towpath TW17 192 B1
Towpath Way CR0 205 D4
Towton Rd SE27 161 A2
Toxteth Ho N4 51 A2
Toynbec Cl BR7 188 D6
Toynbee Rd SW19,
SW20 179 A2
Toynbee St E1 95 D2 243 C3
Toyne Way N6 48 D3
Tracey Ave NW2 68 C3
Tracy Ct HA7 25 C3
Tracy Ho 12 E3 97 B4
Trade Cl N13 32 C6
Trader Rd E6 100 D1
Tradescant Ho 15 E9 74 C1
Tradescant Rd
SW8 138 A5 270 B3
Trade Twr 8 SW11 136 A2
Trade Winds Ct 1 E1 118 A5
Trading Estate Rd
NW10 89 A3
Traemore Ct SW16 160 C1
Trafalgar Ave SE15 139 D6
North Cheam KT4,SM3,
SM4 200 D1
Tottenham N17 33 C4
Trafalgar Bsns Ctr
IG11 101 D3
Trafalgar Cl 1 SE16 119 A2
Trafalgar Ct Barking E6 100 C6
Hounslow TW3 129 B2
West Barnes KT3 200 B6
Trafalgar Gdns E1 96 D2
W8 255 D6
Trafalgar Gr SE10 142 B6
Trafalgar Ho SE17 262 B2
Barking IG11 102 B4
Trafalgar Inf Sch TW2 152 B2
Trafalgar Jun Sch
TW2 152 B2
Trafalgar Mews E9 75 B2
Trafalgar Pl
Edmonton N18 34 A5
Wanstead E11 55 A5
Trafalgar Rd SE10 120 C1
Merton SW19 180 A3
Twickenham TW2 152 B2
Trafalgar Sq★
SW1 115 D5 249 D4
Trafalgar St
SE17 117 B1 262 D2
Trafalgar Terr HA1 42 C1
Trafalgar Trad Est EN3 7 A1
Trafalgar Way E14 120 A5
Croydon CR0 220 C6
Trafford Cl E15 75 D3
Trafford Ho N1 235 D4
Trafford Rd CR7 204 B4
Tragail SW15 157 A6
Traherne Lo 3 TW11 174 D5
Traitors Gate★
EC3 117 D5 253 C4
Tralee Ct 31 SE16 118 B1
Tramsheds The CR0,
CR4 203 D2
Tramway Ave E15 76 B1
N9 18 C4
Tramway Path CR4 202 C5
Trance Way W3 110 C3
Tranmere Ct 5 SM2 218 A1
Tranmere Ho 7 N7 72 C3
Tranmere Rd
Edmonton N9 17 D4
Twickenham TW2 151 D4
Wandsworth SW17,
SW18 158 A2
Tranquil Pass SE3 142 D3
Tranquil Vale SE3 142 C3
Transept St NW1 237 B3
Transmere Cl BR5 211 A3
Transmere Rd BR5 211 A3
Transom Cl SE16 119 A2
Transom Sq E14 119 D1
Transport Ave TW8 131 B6
Tranton Rd SE16 118 B3
Trappes Ho 2 SE16 118 B2
Traps La KT2,KT3 177 C2
Travel Clinic, Hospl for
Tropical Diseases
WC1 93 C3 239 B5
Travellers Way TW5 128 C3
Travers Cl E17 34 D2
Travers Ho 6 SE10 142 B6
Travers Rd N7 72 C5
Travis Ho SE10 142 A4
Treacy Cl WD23 8 A2
Treadgold Ho 7 W11 112 D6
Treadgold St W11 112 D6
Treadway St E2 96 B5
Treasury Buildings
SW1 250 A2
Treaty Ctr TW3 129 D2
Treaty St N1 94 B6 233 C5
Trebeck St W1 248 C3
Treborough Ho W1 238 A4
Trebovir Rd
SW5 113 C2 255 B3
Treby St E3 97 B3
Trecastle Way 3 N7 71 D4
Tredegar Rd E3 97 B5
N11 31 D3
Tredegar Sq E3 97 B4
Tredegar Terr E3 97 B4
Trederwen Rd E8 96 A6
Tredown Rd SE26 184 C5
Tredwell Cl BR2 210 A5
Tredwell Rd SE27 182 D6
Tree Cl TW10 153 D3
Treen Ave SW13 133 D2
Tree Rd E16 99 C1
Trees The N16 51 B2
Tree Tops 1 IG8 37 A6
Treetops Cl SE2 125 A1
Treetops Ct CR7 205 A4
Treetops View IG10 21 D4
Treeview Cl SE19 183 C2
Treewall Gdns BR1 187 B6
Trefgarne Rd RM10 81 C6
Trefil Wlk N7 72 A4
Trefoil Ho DA18 125 A4
Trefoil Rd SW18 158 A6
Trefusis Ct TW5 128 B4
Tregaron Ave N8 50 A3
Tregaron Gdns KT3 199 C5
Tregarvon Rd SW11 137 A1
Tregenna Ave HA2 63 C4
Tregenna Cl 1 N14 15 C6
Tregenna Ct HA2 63 C4
Tregony Rd BR6 227 D4
Trego Rd E9 75 C1
Tregothnan Rd SW9 138 A2
Tregunter Rd
SW10 114 A1 256 A1
Treherne Ct SW9 138 D4
Upper Tooting SW17 181 A6
Trehern Rd 12 SW14 133 B2
Trehurst St E5 75 A3
Trelawney Est E9 74 C2
Trelawney Ho SE1 252 A2
Trelawn Rd E10 76 A5
SW2 160 C6
Trelawny Cl E17 53 D5
Trellis Ho SW19 180 A3
Trellis Sq 1 E3 97 B4
Treloar Gdns SE19 183 B4
Tremadoc Rd SW4 137 D1
Tremaine Cl SE4 141 C3
Tremaine Rd SE20 184 B1
Trematon Ho SE11 261 B2
Trematon Pl TW11 175 C3
Tremlett Gr N19 71 C5
Tremlett Mews N19 71 C5
Trenance Gdns IG3 80 A5
Trenchard Ave HA4 62 B4
Trenchard Cl NW9 27 C2
Stanmore HA7 25 B4
Trenchard Ct SM4 201 C3
Trenchard St SE10 120 B1
Trenchold St
SW8 138 A6 270 A5
Trend Ct W13 109 B5
Trendell Ho 4 E14 97 C1
Trenholme Cl SE20 184 B3
Trenholme Rd SE20 184 B3
Trenholme Terr SE20 184 B3
Trenmar Gdns NW10 90 B4
Trenmar Lo NW10 90 B4
Trent Ave W5 109 C3
Trent CE Prim Sch EN4 2 D1
Trent Ct E11 55 A4
Trent Ctry Pk EN4 3 A3
Trent Gdns N14 15 B5
Trentham Lo 8 EN1 17 C6
Trentham St SW18 157 C3
Trent Ho SE15 140 C1
4 Kingston KT2 175 D2
Trent Rd SW2 160 B6
Buckhurst Hill IG9 21 B3
Trent Way Hayes UB4 83 C4
North Cheam KT4 216 C5
Trentwood Side EN2 4 B2
Treport St SW18 157 D4
Tresco Cl BR1 186 C4
Trescoe Gdns HA2 41 A2
Tresco Gdns IG3 80 A6
Tresco Ho SE11 261 A2
Tresco Rd SE15 140 B1
Tresham Cres
NW8 92 C3 237 A6
Tresham Rd IG11 79 D1
Tresham Wlk E9 74 C3
Tresidder Ho 10 SW4 159 D4
Tresilian Ave N21 16 B6
Tressel Cl 20 N1 72 D1
Tressillian Cres SE4 141 C2
Tressillian Rd SE4 141 C2
Trestis Cl UB4 84 D2
Treswell Rd RM9 103 A6
Tretawn Gdns NW7 11 C1
Tretawn Pk NW7 27 C6
Trevallyn Lo 1 KT2 176 D2
Trevanion Rd W14 254 B2
Treve Ave HA1 42 B2
Trevelayan Rd SW17 180 D4
Trevelyan Ave E12 78 B4
Trevelyan Cres HA3 43 D2
Trevelyan Ct KT3 199 D2
Trevelyan Gdns NW10 90 C6
Trevelyan Ho 16 E2 96 D4
SE5 138 D5

Trevelyan Ho continued
  6 Twickenham TW1 ....153 C5
Trevelyan Rd E15 ....76 D4
Trevenna Ho 12 SE23 ..162 D1
Treveris St SE1 ....251 D3
Treversh Cl 3 BR1 ....186 D2
Treverton St W10 ......90 D3
Treverton Twr W10 .....90 D2
Treves Cl N21 ....16 B6
Treves Ho 1 ....96 A3
Treville St SW15 .....156 B4
Treviso Rd SE23 ......163 A2
Trevithick Cl TW14 ...149 D3
Trevithick Ho 3 NW5 ..71 B4
  Northolt UB5 ....84 D5
  SE16 ....269 C2
Trevithick St SE8 ....141 C6
Trevone Gdns HA5 .....41 A3
Trevor Cl Harrow HA3 ..24 D3
  Hayes BR2 ....209 A2
  Isleworth TW7 .....152 D6
  New Barnet EN4 .....14 B5
  Northolt UB5 ....84 C5
Trevor Cres HA4 ......61 D4
Trevor Gdns HA8 ......27 B2
  Northolt UB5 ....84 C5
Trevor Ho 7 SW1 .....247 B1
Trevor Rd HA8 ....27 B2
  Hayes UB3 ....105 C4
  Wimbledon SW19 ...179 A3
  Woodford IG8 ....37 A3
Trevor Roberts Tutorial Coll
  NW8 ....70 B1
Trevor Sq 2 SW7 ..114 C4 247 B1
Trevor St SW7 ....114 C4 247 B1
Trevose Ho SE11 .....260 D2
Trevose Rd E17 ....36 B2
Trewenna Dr KT9 .....213 D3
Trewince Rd SW20 ...178 C2
Trewint St SW18 .....158 A2
Trewsbury Ho 2 SE24 124 D4
Trewsbury Rd SE26 ..184 D5
Triandra Way UB4 ....84 D2
Triangle Ct E16 ....99 C2
Triangle Ctr UB1 ....108 B5
Triangle Est The SE11 261 A1
Triangle Pl SW4 .....137 D1
Triangle Rd 8 E8 .....96 B6
Triangle The E8 ......96 B6
  EC1 ....241 D6
  N19 ....49 D2
  Barking IG11 ....79 A2
  Kingston KT3 ......177 A1
Tribune Ct 10 NW9 ...46 A5
Trident Gdns 6 UB5 ..84 D4
Trident Ho 10 E14 ....98 A1
Trident St SE16 .....118 D2
Trident Way UB2 ....106 B3
Trieste Ct SW12 ....158 D3
Trigon Rd
  SW8 ....138 B5 270 D4
Trilby Rd SE23 ......162 D2
Trillo Ct IG1 ....57 C2
Trimdon NW1 ....232 B5
Trimmer Ct TW7 .....152 D6
Trimmer Wlk 1 TW8 .132 A6
Trim St SE8 ....141 B6
Trinder Gdns N19 ....50 A1
Trinder Rd N4,N19 ...50 A1
  Barnet EN5 ....12 C6
Tring Ave Ealing W5 .110 B5
  Southall UB1 ....85 B1
  Wembley HA9 ....66 C2
Tring Cl IG2 ....57 B4
Tring Ct TW1 ....175 A6
Trinidad Ho 17 E14 ..119 B6
Trinidad St E14 .....119 B6
Trinity Ave N2 ....48 B6
  Enfield EN1 ....17 D5
Trinity Church Rd
  SW13 ....134 B6
Trinity Church Sq
  SE1 ....117 A3 262 B6
Trinity Cl E11 ....76 C1
  SE13 ....142 B1
  3 SW4 ....137 C1
  Hounslow TW4 ....129 A1
  Keston Mark BR2 ..210 A1
Trinity Cotts TW9 ...132 B2
Trinity Cres SW17 ..159 A2
Trinity Ct 2 N1 ....95 C6
  SE16 ....119 A4
  SE9 ....166 D5
  WC1 ....240 C6
  8 Chingford E4 .....20 A2
  Edmonton N18 .....33 D4
  Forest Hill SE23 ..162 D3
  Southgate N21 .....16 D3
  Thornton Heath SE25 205 C3
  Twickenham TW2 ..152 C2
Trinity Gdns E16 .....98 D2
  SW2,SW9 ....138 B1
  11 Wanstead E18 ...55 B6
Trinity Gn E1 ....96 C2
Trinity Ho 5 E17 .....53 D6
  SE1 ....262 C2
Trinity Homes 14 SW2 138 B1

Trinity Mews SE9 ....167 B5
  Penge SE20 ....184 B2
  Wandsworth SW18 .157 C3
Trinity Par TW3 .....129 C2
Trinity Pl DA6 ....147 B1
  EC3 ....253 C5
Trinity RC High Sch (Lower)
  IG8 ....37 A6
Trinity RC High Sch (Upper
  Sch) IG8 ....36 D6
Trinity RC High Sch (Upper)
  IG8 ....37 A6
Trinity Rd N2 ....48 B6
  Ilford IG6 ....57 A6
  Richmond TW9 ....132 B2
  Southall UB1 ......107 A5
  Wandsworth SW17,
  SW18 ....158 C4
  Wimbledon SW19 ..179 C4
  Wood Green N22 ...32 A3
  Wood Green N22 ...32 B2
Trinity Rise SE24,SW2 160 D4
Trinity Sch
  Croydon CR0 ......222 C6
  Dagenham RM10 ...81 C4
Trinity Sq EC3 ..117 C6 253 B6
Trinity St 9 E16 ......99 A2
  SE1 ....117 B3 262 C6
  Enfield EN2 ....5 A3
Trinity St Mary's CE Prim
  Sch SW12 ....159 A3
Trinity Terr IG9 ......21 B4
Trinity Way E4 ....35 B4
  W3 ....111 D6
Trio Pl SE1 ....117 A4 262 B6
Triscott Ho UB3 ....106 A5
Tristan Ct 13 SE8 ...141 B6
Tristan Ct 11 SE8 ...141 A6
Tristan S SE23 ......142 C2
Tristram Cl E17 ......54 B6
Tristram Rd BR1 ....186 D6
Triton Ct EC2 ....242 D5
Triton Ho 4 E14 .....119 D2
Triton Sq NW1 ......239 A6
Tritton Ave CR0 .....220 A4
Tritton Ho N1 ....17 B5
Tritton Rd SE21,SE27 161 A1
Triumph Cl UB7 .....127 A4
Triumph Ho 1 IG11 ..102 A4
Triumph Ho 9 IG11 ..102 A4
Triumph Trad Est N17 34 A4
Trocette Mans SE1 ..263 B6
Trojan Ct NW6 ....69 A1
  9 Ealing W7 ....109 A5
Trojan Ind Est NW10 67 D2
Trojan Way CR0 ....220 B5
Troon Cl 6 SE16 ....118 B1
  Erith SE28 ....122 C5
Troon Ho 11 E14 .....97 A1
Troon St E1 ....97 A1
Tropical Ct 2 W10 ...90 D4
Trosley Rd DA17 ....147 C6
Trossachs Rd SE22 .161 C6
Trothy Rd SE1 ....118 A2
Trotman Ho 14 SE14 140 C4
Trott Rd N10 ....31 A3
Trott St SW11 ..136 C4 267 A1
Trotwood Ho 8 SE16 118 B4
Troubridge Ct 10 W4 111 A1
Troughton Rd SE7 ..121 B1
Troutbeck NW1 ......231 D1
Troutbeck Rd SE14 .141 A4
Trouville Rd SW4 ...159 C5
Trowbridge Rd E9 ...75 B2
Trower Ho 5 E9 ......75 A2
Trowlock Ave TW11 .175 C4
Trowlock Island TW11 175 D4
Trowlock Way TW11 .175 D4
Troy Ct 8 SE18 .....122 D2
  W8 ....255 A6
Troyes Ho NW3 ......70 D3
Troy Rd SE19 ....183 B4
Troy Town SE15 ....140 A2
Troy Town Flats SE15 140 A2
Trubshaw Rd UB2 ..107 D3
Truesdale Rd E6 ...100 B1
Trulock Ct N17 ....34 A3
Trulock Rd N17 ......34 A3
Truman's Rd 22 N16 73 C3
Trumpers Way 7 W7 108 D3
Trumpeters Inn TW9 153 C6
Trumpington Rd E7 ..76 D4
Trump St EC2 ....242 B1
Trundlers Way WD23 8 C3
Trundle St SE1 .....252 A2
Trundleys Rd SE8 ..141 A6
Trundleys Rd SE8 ..118 D1
Trundleys Terr SE8 .118 D2
Truro Gdns IG1 ......56 A2
Truro Ho 2 W2 ....91 C2
Truro Rd E17 ....53 B5
  Wood Green N22 ...32 B3
Truro St NW5 ....71 A2
Truro Way UB4 ......84 C4
Truslove Rd SE27 ..182 D5
Trussley Rd W6 .....112 C3
Trust Wlk SE21 ....160 D3
Tryfan Cl IG4 ....55 A5
Tryon Cres E9 ....96 C6

Tryon St SW3 ...114 D1 257 C2
Trystings Cl KT10 ..213 A2
Tuam Rd SE18 ......145 B6
Tubbenden Cl BR6 ..227 C5
Tubbenden Dr BR6 ..227 B4
Tubbenden Jun & Inf Schs
  BR6 ....227 C5
Tubbenden La BR6 ..227 C5
Tubbenden La S BR6 227 B3
Tubbs Rd NW10 ......89 D5
Tudor Ave
  Hampton TW12 ....173 C3
  North Cheam KT4 .216 B4
Tudor Cl BR7 ....188 B2
  N6 ....49 C2
  NW3 ....70 C2
  NW7 ....28 A4
  NW9 ....67 A6
  SW2 ....160 B5
  Ashford TW15 .....170 A6
  Cheam SM3 ....217 A2
  Chessington KT9 ..214 A3
  Hampton TW12 ....174 A5
  Pinner HA5 ....40 A4
  Wallington SM6 ...219 C1
  Woodford IG8 ......52 A3
Tudor Cres EN2 ......5 A4
Tudor Ct E17 ....53 B2
  N1 ....73 C2
  6 SE16 ....118 D5
  W5 ....110 C4
  W7 ....108 C6
  Feltham TW13 .....172 C6
  Sidcup DA14 ......168 A1
  4 Stanwell TW19 ..148 A5
  Teddington TW11 ..174 D4
Tudor Ct N Wembley
  HA9 ....66 C3
Tudor Ct S Wembley
  HA9 ....66 C3
Tudor Dr Kingston KT2 176 A5
  Walton-on-T KT12 .194 D1
  West Barnes SM4 .201 A3
Tudor Ent Pk HA3 ...42 B6
Tudor Est NW10 .....88 B5
Tudor Gables NW7 ..27 D6
Tudor Gdns SW13 ..133 D6
  Harrow HA3 ....24 B1
  Kingston KT1 ......176 C3
  West Wickham BR4 224 B5
Tudor Gr E9 ....74 D4
Tudor Ho 34 E9 ......74 C1
  W14 ....112 D2
Tudor Mews 7 NW10 68 A2
Tudor Par
  Dagenham RM6 ....59 C2
Tudor Prim Sch N10 .31 A2
Tudor Rd E6 ....99 C6
  E9 ....96 B5
  N9 ....18 D3
  SE19 ....184 A1
  SE25 ....206 B4
  Ashford TW15 .....171 B4
  Barking IG11 ......101 D6
  Beckenham BR3 ...208 A6
  Hampton TW12 ....173 C1
  Harrow HA3 ....24 B1
  Hayes UB3 ....83 B1
  Kingston KT2 ......176 C3
  Pinner HA5 ....22 C1
  Southall UB1 ......107 A6
Tudor Sq UB3 ....83 B2
Tudor Stacks 6 SE24 139 D1
Tudor St EC4 ..116 C6 241 B1
Tudor Way Acton W3 110 C4
  Hillingdon UB10 ...60 C2
  Petts Wood BR5 ..211 C3
  Winchmore Hill N21 16 C4
Tudway Rd SE3 .....143 C1
Tufnell Ct 3 E3 ....97 B3
Tufnell Park Mans
  N7 ....72 C5
Tufnell Park Prim Sch
  N7 ....72 C4
Tufnell Park Rd N19,N7 71 D4
Tufnell Park Sta N19 .71 C4
Tufton Ct SW1 ......260 A5
Tufton Gdns KT8 ...177 D3
Tufton Rd E4 ....35 C6
Tufton St SW1 ..116 A3 260 A5
Tugboat St SE28 ...123 C4
Tugela Rd CR0 .....205 B3
Tugela St SE6 ......163 B2
Tugmutton Cl BR6 .226 D4
Tuke Sch SE15 .....140 B4
Tulip Cl 6 E6 ....100 B2
  Croydon CR0 .....206 D1
  Hampton TW12 ...173 B4
  Southall UB2 .....108 D2
Tulip Ct 2 IG1 ....78 C5
Tulip Gdns Chingford E4 20 B1

Tulip Gdns continued
  Ilford IG1 ....78 D2
Tullis Ho 12 E9 ......74 C1
Tull St CR4 ....202 D2
Tulse Cl BR3 ....208 A6
Tulse Hill
  Streatham SW2 ...160 C4
  Streatham SW2,SE24 160 C4
Tulse Hill Sta SE27 .160 D2
Tulse Ho SW2 ......160 C5
Tulsemere Rd SE21,
  SE27 ....161 A2
Tumbling Bay KT12 .194 A3
Tummons Gdns SE25 183 C1
Tunbridge Cl 8 BR3 208 A1
Tunbridge Ho EC1 ..234 A2
Tuncombe Rd N18 ..33 C6
Tunis Rd W12 ......112 B5
Tunley Gn 10 E14 ...97 B2
Tunley Rd NW10 ....89 A6
  Upper Tooting SW12,
  SW17 ....159 A2
Tunmarsh La E13 ...99 C4
Tunnan Leys E6 ...100 C1
Tunnel Avenue Trad Est
  SE10 ....120 B4
Tunnel Gdns N11 ...31 C2
Tunnel Link Rd TW6 148 C6
Tunnel Rd 5 SE16 ..118 D4
Tunnel Rd E TW6 ..126 D4
Tunnel Rd W TW6 .126 D4
Tunstall Cl BR6 ....227 C4
Tunstall Ct 14 TW9 132 B4
Tunstall Rd SW9 ..138 A1
  Croydon CR0 .....205 C1
Tunstall Wlk 10 TW8 132 A6
Tunstock Way DA17 125 A3
Tunworth Cl NW9 ...45 B3
Tunworth Cres SW15 155 D5
Tupelo Rd E10 ......74 B6
Tupman Ho 21 SE16 118 A4
Turberville Ho 1 SW9 138 B2
Turenne Cl SW18 ..136 A1
Turin Rd N9 ....18 D3
Turin St E2 ....96 A4
Turkey Oak Cl SE19 183 C2
Turkey St Enfield EN1 6 B6
  Enfield EN3 ....6 B6
Turkey Street Sta EN3 6 A6
Turks Cl UB8 ....82 C4
Turk's Head Yd EC1 241 D5
Turks Row
  SW3 ....114 D1 257 D2
Turle Rd N4 ....72 B6
  Thornton Heath SW16 182 A1
Turlewray Cl N4 ....50 B1
Turley Cl E15 ....98 C6
Turnagain La EC4 ..241 C2
Turnage Rd RM8 ...59 A1
Turnant Rd N17 .....33 A2
Turnberry Cl NW4 ..28 D1
  24 SE16 ....118 D1
Turnberry Way BR6 211 B1
Turnbull Ho N1 .....94 C6
Turnbury Cl SE28 ..102 D1
Turnchapel Mews 1
  SW4 ....137 B2
Turner Ave N15 .....51 C6
  Mitcham CR4 .....180 D2
  Twickenham TW2 .152 A1
Turner Cl NW11 .....47 D3
  7 SW9 ....138 D4
  Wembley HA0 .....83 A4
Turner Ct 16 SE16 .118 D4
  13 SE5 ....139 B2
Turner Ho N4 ......230 A4
  NW8 ....230 A4
Turner Lo 10 SW19 156 D3
Turner Pl SW11 ...156 D6
Turner Rd E17 ......54 A6
  Edgware HA8 .....26 B1
  New Malden KT3 .199 B2
Turners Meadow Way
  BR3 ....185 B2
Turner's Rd E3 .....97 B2
Turner St E1 ....96 B2
  E16 ....98 D1
Turners Way CR0 ..220 D6
Turneville Rd
  W14 ....135 B6 264 C6
Turney Rd SE21 ...161 B4
Turney Sch SE21 ..161 A4
Turnham Green Sta
  W4 ....111 C2
Turnham Green Terr
  W4 ....111 C2
Turnham Ho SE4 ..141 A1
Turnham Prim Sch
  SE4 ....141 A1
Turnham Rd SE4 ..141 A1
Turnmill Ho SE1 ..182 C6
Turnmill St EC1 ..94 D2 241 C4
Turnour Ho 2 E1 ...96 B1
Turnpike Cl SE8 ...141 B5

Turnpike Ct DA6 ...146 D1
Turnpike Ho EC1 ..234 D1
Turnpike La N8 .....50 C6
  Sutton SM1 ......218 A3
  Uxbridge UB10 ...82 A5
Turnpike Lane Sta N15 50 D6
Turnpike Link CR0 .221 C6
Turnpike Way TW7 .131 A4
Turnpin La 2 SE10 .142 A6
Turnstone Cl E13 ...99 A4
  NW9 ....46 A3
  Uxbridge UB10 ....60 D3
Turpentine La
  SW1 ....115 B1 258 D1
Turpin Cl EN3 ....7 C6
Turpington Cl BR2 .210 A2
Turpington La BR2 .210 A3
Turpin Ho SW11 ...268 C2
Turpin Rd TW14 ...149 D5
Turpin Way N19 ....49 D1
  Wallington SM6 ..219 B1
Turquand St SE17 .262 B3
Turret Gr SW4 .....137 C2
Turret Ho KT2 .....176 A4
Turton Ho 5 SE18 .144 D6
Turton Rd HA0 .....66 A3
Turville Ho NW8 ...237 A6
Turville St E2 ......243 C6
Tuscan Ho 30 E2 ...96 C4
Tuscan Rd SE18 ..123 B1
Tuskar St SE10 ...119 D1
Tutorial Coll of West
  London UB1 ......107 B5
Tuttlebee La IG9 ...21 A2
Tuttle Ho SW1 ....259 D1
Tweedale Ct E15 ..76 A3
Tweed Ct W7 ....86 C1
Tweeddale Gr UB10 61 A5
Tweeddale Jun & Inf Schs
  SM5 ....202 B2
Tweeddale Rd SM5 202 B1
Tweed Ho E14 .....98 A3
Tweedmouth Rd E13 99 B5
Tweedy Cl EN1 .....17 D6
Tweedy Rd BR1 ...187 A2
Tweezer's Alley WC2 251 A6
Twelve Acre Ho 5 E12 78 C5
Twelvetrees Cres 3 98 A3
Twentyman Cl IG8 ..37 A5
Twickenham Bridge
  TW1 ....153 C6
Twickenham CI CR0 220 B5
Twickenham Gdns
  Greenford UB6 ....65 A3
  Harrow HA3 ....24 C3
Twickenham Rd E11 76 B6
  Isleworth TW1,TW7 131 A2
  Richmond TW1,TW9 131 C1
  Teddington TW11 .175 A6
  Twickenham TW13 151 B1
Twickenham Rugby
  Football Union Ground ★
  TW2 ....152 C5
Twickenham Sta TW1 153 A4
Twickenham Trad Ctr
  TW1 ....152 D5
Twig Folly Cl E2 ...96 D5
Twilley St SW18 ...157 D4
Twine Cl IG11 .....102 B4
Twine Ct E1 ....96 C6
Twineham Gn N12 .29 C6
Twining Ave TW2 .152 B1
Twinn Rd NW7 .....29 A4
Twisden Rd NW5 ..71 B4
Twiss Ho 5 SE18 ..122 D1
Twybridge Way NW10 67 A5
Twyford Abbey Rd
  NW10 ....88 B4
Twyford Ave N2 ....48 D6
  Acton W3 ....110 C6
Twyford CE High Sch
  W3 ....110 C5
Twyford Cres W3 .110 C5
Twyford Ct N10 ....49 A6
  Acton W3 ....110 C5
  6 Wembley HA0 ..88 A6
Twyford Ho N5 .....51 C3
  N15 ....51 D5
Twyford Pl WC2 ..240 C2
Twyford Rd
  Carshalton SM5 .202 B1
  Harrow HA2 ....41 D2
  Ilford IG1 ....79 A3
Twyford St N1 ......94 B5
Tyas Rd E16 ....98 D3
Tyberry Rd EN3 .....6 C2
Tyburn La HA1 .....42 D2
Tyburn Tree (site of) ★
  W2 ....247 C6
Tyburn Way W1 ...247 D6
Tye La BR6 ....227 A3
Tyer's Est SE1 ....253 A2
Tyers Gate
  SE1 ....117 C4 253 A1
Tyers Ho 5 SW16 .181 C5
Tyers St SE11 .116 B1 260 C2

Tulip Gdns continued
  Ilford IG1 ....78 D2
Tullis Ho 12 E9 ......74 C1
Tull St CR4 ....202 D2
Tulse Cl BR3 ....208 A6
Tulse Hill
  Streatham SW2 ...160 C4
  Streatham SW2,SE24 160 C4
Tulse Hill Sta SE27 .160 D2
Tulse Ho SW2 ......160 C5
Tulsemere Rd SE21,
  SE27 ....161 A2
Tumbling Bay KT12 .194 A3
Tummons Gdns SE25 183 C1
Tunbridge Cl 8 BR3 208 A1
Tunbridge Ho EC1 ..234 A2
Tuncombe Rd N18 ..33 C6
Tunis Rd W12 ......112 B5
Tunley Gn 10 E14 ...97 B2
Tunley Rd NW10 ....89 A6
  Upper Tooting SW12,
  SW17 ....159 A2
Tunmarsh La E13 ...99 C4
Tunnan Leys E6 ...100 C1
Tunnel Avenue Trad Est
  SE10 ....120 B4
Tunnel Gdns N11 ...31 C2
Tunnel Link Rd TW6 148 C6
Tunnel Rd 5 SE16 ..118 D4
Tunnel Rd E TW6 ..126 D4
Tunnel Rd W TW6 .126 D4
Tunstall Cl BR6 ....227 C4
Tunstall Ct 14 TW9 132 B4
Tunstall Rd SW9 ..138 A1
  Croydon CR0 .....205 C1
Tunstall Wlk 10 TW8 132 A6
Tunstock Way DA17 125 A3
Tunworth Cl NW9 ...45 B3
Tunworth Cres SW15 155 D5
Tupelo Rd E10 ......74 B6
Tupman Ho 21 SE16 118 A4
Turberville Ho 1 SW9 138 B2
Turenne Cl SW18 ..136 A1
Turin Ho N9 ....18 D3

Turnpike Ct DA6 ...146 D1
Turnpike Ho EC1 ..234 D1

Tyers Terr
  SE11 ....116 B1 260 B1
Tyeshurst Cl SE2 ..125 A1
Tylecroft Rd SW16 182 A1
Tylehurst Gdns IG1 79 A3
Tyler Cl E2 ....95 D5
Tyler Rd UB2 ......107 D3
Tylers Ct 4 E17 ....53 C5
  5 Wembley HA0 ..88 A5
Tylers Gate HA3 ..44 A4
Tylers Path SM5 ..218 D4
Tylney Ave SE19 ..183 D5
Tylney Ho 16 E1 ...96 B1
Tylney Rd BR1 ....187 D1
  E7 ....77 C4
Tymperley Ct SW19 157 A3
Tynamara KT1 ....197 D5
Tyndale Ct 2 TW14 150 A3
Tyndale La N1 ......72 D1
Tyndale Mans N1 ..72 D1
Tyndale Terr 13 N1 72 D1
Tyndall Gdns E10 ..76 A6
Tyndall Rd DA16 ..145 D2
  E10 ....76 A6
Tyne Cl W7 ....86 C1
Tynedale Ct E14 ..119 D1
Tyneham Cl 10 SW11 137 A2
Tyne Ho 8 KT2 ....175 D2
Tynemouth Cl E6 ..101 A2
Tynemouth Dr EN1 ..6 A5
Tynemouth Rd N15 .51 D5
  SE18 ....123 C1
  Mitcham CR4 .....181 A3
Tynemouth St SW6 136 A3
Tynemouth Terr 8
  N15 ....51 D5
Tyne St E1 ....243 D2
Tynsdale Rd NW10 67 C2
Tynte Ct E9 ....75 A3
Tynwald Ho 30 SE26 162 A1
Type St E2 ....96 D5
Tyrawley Rd SW6 ..265 C2
Tyrell Cl HA1 ....64 C4
Tyrell Ct SM5 ......218 D4
Tyrols Rd SE23 ....162 D3
Tyrone Rd E6 ....100 B4
Tyron Way DA14 ..189 D5
Tyrrell Av DA16 ...168 B6
Tyrrell Ho SW1 ....269 B6
  Catford BR3 ......185 D5
Tyrrell Rd SE22 ...140 A1
Tyrrell Way NW9 ...46 A2
Tyrwhitt Rd SE4 ..141 C2
Tysoe Ave EN3 .....7 A6
Tysoe St EC1 .....234 B1
Tyson Rd SE23 ...162 C4
Tyssen Rd N16 ....73 D5
Tyssen Sch N16 ...52 A1
Tyssen St 8 ....95 C5
  N1 ....95 C6
Tytherton 10 E2 ...96 C5
Tytherton Rd N19 ..71 D5

U
Uamvar St E14 .....97 D2
Uckfield Gr CR4 ...181 A2
Uckfield Rd EN3 ....6 C6
Udall St SW1 ......259 B3
Udimore Ho W10 ..90 C2
Udney Park Rd TW11 175 A4
Uffington Rd NW10 90 B6
  West Norwood SE27 182 C6
Ufford Cl HA3 ......23 D3
Ufford Rd HA3 .....23 D3
Ufford St SE1 ..116 C4 251 B2
Ufton Ct UB5 ......84 D4
Ufton Gr N1 ....73 B1
Ufton Rd N1 ....73 B1
Uhura Sq 10 N16 ..73 C5
Ujima Ct N19 ......50 A1
  SW16 ....182 A6
Ujima Ho SW16 ...182 A6
Uk Cotts UB3 ......105 B4
Ullathorne Rd SW16 181 C6
Ulleswater Rd N14 .16 B1
Ullin St E14 ....98 A2
Ullswater SW15 ..156 D5
Ullswater Cl
  Bromley BR1 .....186 C3
  Hayes UB4 ....83 C5
  Kingston KT2,SW15 177 B6
Ullswater Cres SW15 177 B6
Ullswater Ct
  2 Woodford E18 ...37 A1
  Harrow HA2 ....41 C2
Ullswater Ho SE15 140 C6
Ullswater Rd
  Barnes SW13 .....134 A5
  West Norwood SE27,
  SW16 ....160 D2
Ulster Ct KT2 ......175 D4

Ulster Gdns N13 33 A6
Ulster Pl NW1 238 C5
Ulundi Rd SE3 142 C6
Ulva Rd SW15 134 D1
Ulverscroft Rd SE22 162 A6
Ulverstone Rd SE27 160 D2
Ulverston Rd E17 36 B1
Ulysses Rd NW6 69 B3
Umberston St E1 96 B1
Umbria St SW15 156 A5
Umfreville Rd N4 50 D3
Una Ho 7 NW5 71 B2
Under Cliff SE10 142 A4
Undercliff Rd SE13 141 D2
Underhill EN5 13 C6
Underhill Ct EN5 13 C6
Underhill Ho 7 E14 97 C2
Underhill Jun & Inf Schs EN5 13 A6
Underhill Pas NW1 231 D6
Underhill Rd SE21, SE22 162 B4
Underhill St NW1 231 D5
Underne Ave N14 15 B2
Undershaft EC3 95 C1 243 A1
Undershaw Rd BR1 164 D1
Underwood CR0 224 A3
Underwood Ct 3 E10 53 D1
Underwood Ho W6 112 B3
Underwood Rd E1 96 A3
Chingford E4 35 D5
Woodford IG8 37 D3
Underwood Row N1 235 B2
Underwood St N1 95 A4 235 B2
Underwood The SE9 166 B2
Undine Rd E14 119 D2
Undine St SW17 180 D5
Uneeda Dr UB6 86 B6
Unicorn Bldg 14 E1 118 D6
Unicorn Sch TW9 132 B4
Unicorn Works N17 34 C3
Union Cl E11 76 B4
Union Ct SW4 138 A3
45 W2 91 C2
2 Richmond TW10 154 A6
Union Dr E1 97 A3
Union Gr SW8 137 D3
Union Mews SW9 138 A3
Union Rd BR2 209 D4
N11 31 D4
SW8 137 D3
Northolt UB5 85 C5
Thornton Heath CR0 205 A2
Wembley HA0 66 A2
Union Sq N1 95 A6 235 B5
Union St E15 98 B6
SE1 117 A5 252 A3
Barnet EN5 1 A2
Kingston KT1 175 D1
Union Wlk E2 95 C4
Union Yd W1 238 D1
Unity Cl NW10 68 A2
West Norwood SE19 183 A5
Unity Mews NW1 232 C4
Unity Rd EN3 6 C6
Unity Way SE18 121 D3
Univ College Hospl (Annexe) W1 93 A2 238 B4
Univ Coll Jun Sch NW3 70 A4
Univ Coll London
W1 93 C2 239 B4
WC1 93 D3 239 C6
WC1 94 A3 240 B6
University Cl NW7 27 D3
University Coll Hospl WC1 93 C3 239 B5
University Coll Sch NW3 70 A3
University Gdns DA5 169 B4
University Mans SW15 134 D2
University of North London (Tufnel Park Hall) N7 71 C5
University Pl DA8 147 D5
University Rd SW19 180 B4
University St WC1 93 C3 239 B5
University Way E16 122 D6
Univ of East London
E15 76 C2
E15 98 B6
E6 122 C6
Barking RM8 80 A4
Univ of East London (Holbrook Ctr) E15 98 D5
Univ of Greenwich Avery Hill Campus Mansion Site SE9 167 A5
Univ of Greenwich Avery Hill Campus Southwood Site SE9 167 B4
Univ of Greenwich Rachel Mcmillan Campus SE8 141 C6
Univ of Greenwich Riverside Ho Annexe SE18 122 C3
Univ of Greenwich The SW15 156 A4
Univ of London WC1 94 A4 233 A1
Univ of London (King's Coll Hall) SE5 139 B2
Univ of London Observatory NW7 27 D4
Univ of London (Queen Mary & Westfield Coll) E1 97 A3
Univ of Westminster
NW1 93 C3 239 A6
NW8 92 C3 237 A5
W1 93 A2 238 A4
W1 93 B1 238 D2
Univ of Westminster (Harrow Campus) HA1 43 A2
Unwin Ave TW14 149 B6
Unwin Cl SE15 140 A6
Unwin Rd SW7 114 B3 256 D6
Isleworth TW7 130 C2
Upbrook Mews W2 92 A1 236 B1
Upcerne Rd SW10 136 A5 266 B3
Upchurch Cl SE20 184 B3
Upcott Ho 33 E3 97 D4
4 E9 74 C1
Upcroft Ave HA8 27 A6
Updale Rd DA14 189 D6
Upfield CR0 222 B5
Upfield Rd W7 86 D2
Upgrove Manor Way 12 SE24 160 C4
Uphall Prim Sch IG1 78 D3
Uphall Rd IG1 78 D3
Upham Park Rd W4 111 C2
Uphill Dr NW7 27 C5
NW9 45 A4
Uphill Gr NW7 27 C6
Uphill Rd NW7 27 C6
Upland Ct SE23 162 C2
Upland Inf Sch DA7 147 B2
Upland Jun Sch DA7 147 B2
Upland Rd DA7 147 B2
8 E13 99 A3
SE22 162 A5
Croydon CR2 221 B3
Sutton SM2 218 B1
Uplands BR3 185 C1
Uplands Ave E17 34 D1
Uplands Bsns Pk E17 52 D6
Uplands Cl SW14 154 D6
Uplands Ct N21 16 C4
Uplands Park Rd EN2 4 C3
Uplands Rd N8 50 B4
East Barnet EN4 15 A3
Ilford RM6 58 D6
Woodford IG8 37 D3
Uplands The HA4 40 A1
Uplands Way N21 16 C6
Upnall Ho 16 SE15 140 C6
Upney La IG11 79 D1
Upney Sta IG11 79 D1
Upnor Way SE17 263 B2
Uppark Dr IG2 57 A3
Upper Abbey Rd DA17 125 C2
Upper Addison Gdns W14 113 A4 244 A2
Upper Belgrave St SW1 115 A3 258 B6
Upper Berkeley St W1 92 D1 237 D1
Upper Beulah Hill SE19 183 C2
Upper Brighton Rd KT6 198 A2
Upper Brockley Rd SE4 141 B3
Upper Brook St W1 115 A6 248 A6
Upper Butts TW8 131 C6
Upper Caldy Wlk 14 N1 73 A2
Upper Cavendish Ave N3 47 C6
Upper Cheyne Row SW3 136 C6 267 A6
Upper Clapton Rd E5 74 B6
Upper Clarendon Wlk 13 W11 91 A1
Upper Dengie Wlk N1 235 A6
Upper Elmers End Rd BR3 207 A4
Upper Farm Rd KT8 195 B5
Upper Fosters NW4 46 C5
Upper Gn E CR4 203 A6
Upper Gn W CR4 180 D1
Upper Gr SE25 205 D5
Upper Grosvenor St W1 115 A6 248 A5
Upper Grotto Rd TW1 152 D2
Upper Ground SE1 116 C5 251 A4
Upper Grove Rd DA17 147 B6
Upper Gulland Wlk 19 N1 73 A2
Upper Halliford Rd TW17 193 C6
Upper Halliford Sta TW16 171 C1
Upper Ham Rd KT2, TW10 175 D6
Upper Harley St NW1 238 B5
Upper Hawkwell Wlk N1 235 B6
Upper Holloway Sta N19 71 D6
Upper Holly Hill Rd DA17 125 D1
Upper James St W1 249 B6
Upper John St W1 249 B6
Upper Lodge Mews TW12 174 A4
Upper Mall W6 112 B1
Upper Marsh SE1 116 B4 260 D6
Upper Montague St W1 92 D2 237 C3
Upper Mulgrave Rd SM2 217 A1
Upper North St E3,E14 97 C2
Upper Park Rd BR1 187 C2
N11 31 C5
NW3 70 D3
Belvedere DA17 125 D2
Kingston KT2 176 C4
Upper Phillimore Gdns W8 113 C4 245 A1
Upper Pk IG10 21 D6
Upper Rawreth Wlk N1 235 B6
Upper Rd E13 99 A4
N2 30 C2
Wallington SM6 219 D3
Upper Richmond Rd SW15 134 C1
Upper Richmond Rd W TW10,SW14,SW15 133 A1
Upper Selsdon Rd CR2 221 D1
Upper Sheridan Rd DA17 125 C2
Upper Shirley Rd CR0 222 D5
Upper Sq TW7 131 A2
Upper St N1 94 D6 234 C5
Upper St Martin's La WC2 250 A6
Upper Sunbury Rd TW12 173 C2
Upper Sutton La TW5 129 C4
Upper Tachbrook St SW1 259 B4
Upper Teddington Rd KT1,KT8 175 C2
Upper Terr NW3 70 A5
Upper Thames St EC4 117 A6 252 B6
Upper Tollington Pk N4 50 C1
Upperton Rd DA14 189 D5
Upperton Rd E E13 99 C4
Upperton Rd W E13 99 C4
Upper Tooting Park Mans 1 SW17 159 A2
Upper Tooting Pk SW17 158 D2
Upper Tooting Rd SW17 158 D1
Upper Town Rd UB6 85 D3
Upper Tulse Hill SW2 160 B3
Upper Vernon Rd SM1 218 B3
Upper Walthamstow Rd E17 54 B6
Upper Wickham La DA16 146 B4
Upper Wimpole St W1 93 A2 238 B4
Upper Woburn Pl NW1,WC1 93 D4 232 D1
Uppingham Ave HA7 25 C1
Upsdell Ave N13 32 C4
Upshire Ho E17 35 B1
Upstall St SE5 138 D4
Upton Ave E7 77 A1
Upton Cl NW2 69 A5
Sidcup DA5 169 B5
Upton Cross E13 99 A6
Upton Cross Prim Sch E13 99 B6
Upton Ct Penge SE20 184 C3
Southall UB1 107 D5
4 Wimbledon SW19 178 D3
Upton Day Hospl DA6 147 A1
Upton Dene SM2 217 D1
Upton Gdns HA3 43 C3
Upton La E7 77 A1
Upton Lodge Cl WD23 8 A4
Upton Park Rd E7 77 B1
Upton Park Sta E13 99 C6
Upton Prim Sch DA5 169 B6
Upton Rd SE18 145 A6
Bexley DA6 169 A6
Edmonton N18 34 A5
Upton Rd *continued*
Hounslow TW3 129 C2
South Norwood CR7 183 B1
Upton Rd S DA5 169 B5
Upton Villas 4 DA6 147 A1
Upway N12 30 C4
Upwood Rd SE12 165 A5
Thornton Heath SW16 182 A2
Urlwin St SE5 139 A6
Urlwin Wlk SW9 138 D4
Urmston Dr SW19 157 A3
Urmston Ho 3 E14 120 A2
Urquhart Ct BR3 185 B3
Ursula Lo DA14 190 B5
Ursula Mews N4 51 A1
Ursula St SW11 136 C4 267 A1
Ursuline High Sch SW20 178 D2
Urswick Gdns RM9 81 A1
Urswick Rd E5,E9 74 C3
Dagenham RM9 81 A1
Usborne Mews SW8 270 D4
Usher Rd E3 97 B5
Usk Rd SW11 136 A1
Usk St E2 96 D4
Utopia Village NW1 71 A1 231 A6
Uvedale Rd
Dagenham RM10 81 C5
Enfield EN2 17 B6
Uverdale Rd SW10 136 A5 266 B3
Uxbridge Coll
Hayes UB3 106 A6
Uxbridge UB8 60 A2
Uxbridge High Sch UB8 82 A5
Uxbridge Rd W12 112 B5
Acton W3,W5 110 C5
Ealing W13 109 C6
Feltham TW13 150 D2
Hampton TW12,TW13 173 D5
Hayes UB4 106 C6
Hillingdon UB10,UB4 83 C2
Kingston KT1,KT6 197 D4
Southall UB1,UB2,W5, W7 108 B5
Stanmore HA7 25 A5
Uxbridge Road (Harrow Weald) HA3 24 B3
Uxbridge Road (Hatch End) HA5 23 B3
Uxbridge St W8 113 C5 245 A4
Uxendon Cres HA3,HA9 44 A1
Uxendon Hill HA9 44 B2
Uxendon Manor Prim Sch HA3 44 A4

V

Vaine Ho 4 E9 75 A2
Valance Ave E4 20 D3
Valan Leas BR2 208 C6
Vale Ave WD6 10 D6
Vale Cl N2 48 D6
W9 92 A4 229 A1
Orpington BR6 226 C4
Twickenham TW1 153 A1
Vale Cres SW15 177 C6
Vale Croft
Claygate KT10 212 D1
Pinner HA5 41 A4
Vale Ct W3 111 D5
W9 92 A4 229 A1
Barnet EN5 1 D1
Wembley HA0 65 C5
Vale Dr EN5 13 C6
Vale End SE22 139 D1
Vale Est The W3 111 C5
Vale Farm Sports Ctr HA0 65 B4
Vale Gr N4 51 A2
W3 111 B5
Vale La W3 88 C2
Vale Lo SE23 162 C2
Valence Ave RM8 80 D6
Valence Cir RM8 81 A5
Valence House Mus★ RM8 81 A6
Valence Inf Sch RM8 80 D6
Valence Jun Sch RM8 80 D6
Valence Wood Rd RM8 81 A5
Valencia Rd HA7 25 C6
Valens Ho 1 SW2 160 C3
Valentia Pl SW9 138 C1
Valentine Ave DA5 169 A3
Valentine Ct SE23 162 D2
Valentine Ho 11 SW4 159 C5
Valentine Pl SE1 116 D4 251 C2
Valentine Rd E9 74 D2
Harrow HA2 64 A5
Valentine Row SE1 251 C1
Valentines High Sch IG2 56 C3
Valentines Rd IG1 56 D1
Vale of Health NW3 70 B5
Vale Rd BR1 188 C1
E7 77 B2
N4 51 A2
Claygate KT10 212 D1
Mitcham CR4 203 D5
Sutton SM1 217 D4
Worcester Park KT19, KT4 215 D5
Vale Rd N KT6 214 A6
Vale Rd S KT6 214 A6
Valerian Way E15 98 C4
Valerie Ct Belmont SM2 217 D1
Bushey WD23 8 A4
Vale Rise NW11 47 B1
Vale Row N5 72 D5
Vale Royal N7 72 A1
Valery Pl TW12 173 C3
Vale Sch The N4 51 B3
Valeswood Rd BR1 186 D5
Vale Terr N4 51 A3
Vale The N10 31 A2
NW11 69 A6
SW3 136 B6 266 D6
W3 111 C5
Ashford TW16 172 A4
Croydon CR0 222 D6
Feltham TW14 150 B5
Heston TW5 129 A6
Ruislip HA4 62 C4
Southgate N14 16 A4
Woodford IG8 37 A3
Valetta Gr E13 99 A5
Valetta Rd W3 111 D4
Valette Ct N10 49 B5
Valette Ho E9 74 C2
Valette St E8 74 B2
Valiant Cl 13 UB5 84 D4
Valiant Ho 5 SE7 121 C1
SW11 266 D1
Valiant Way E6 100 B2
Vallance Rd E1 96 A3
N22 31 C1
Vallentin Rd E17 54 A5
Valley Ave N12 30 B6
Valley (Charlton Athletic FC) The SE7 121 C1
Valley Cl HA5 22 B1
Valley Ct IG8 37 B3
Valley Dr NW9 44 D3
Valleyfield Rd SW16 182 B5
Valley Fields Cres EN2 4 C3
Valley Gdns
Mitcham SW19 180 B3
Wembley HA0 66 B1
Valley Gr SE7 121 C1
Valley Ho E5 52 C1
4 Edmonton N9 18 A1
Valley L Ctr SE9 167 A4
Valleylink Est EN3 19 A5
Valley Mews TW1 153 A2
Valley Pl KT6 198 A3
Valley Prim Sch BR2 186 D1
Valley Prospect 3 SE19 183 C4
Valley Rd BR5 190 B2
Beckenham BR2 186 C1
Streatham SW16 182 B6
Uxbridge UB10 82 A5
Valleyside SE7 121 D1
Valley Side E4 19 C3
Valley Side Par E4 19 C2
Valley View EN5 13 A5
Valley Wlk CR0 222 C6
Valliere Rd NW10 90 A4
Valliers Wood Rd DA15 167 C3
Vallis Way
Chessington KT9 213 D4
Ealing W13 87 A2
Valmar Rd SE5 139 A4
Valmar Trad Est 7 SE5 139 A4
Valnay St SW17 180 D5
Valognes Ave E17 35 A2
Valols Ho SE1 263 C6
Valonia Gdns SW18 157 B5
Vambery Rd SE18 145 A6
Vanbern Ho NW5 71 A2
Vanborough Ct 4 SM2 218 A2
Vanbrough Cres UB5 84 C6
Vanbrugh Cl 2 E16 99 D2
Vanbrugh Ct SE11 261 B3
Vanbrugh Dr KT12 194 C3
Vanbrugh Fields SE3 142 D5
Vanbrugh Hill SE10, SE3 142 D6
Vanbrugh Ho 8 E9 74 C1
Vanbrugh Mews KT12 194 C2
Vanbrugh Park Rd SE3 142 D5
Vanbrugh Park Rd W SE3 142 D5
Vanbrugh Pk SE3 142 D5
Vanbrugh Rd W4 111 B3
Vanbrugh Terr SE3 142 D4
Vanburgh Cl BR6 211 C1
Vanburgh Ho E1 243 C4
Vancouver Rd
Edgware HA8 26 D2
Forest Hill SE23 163 B2
Hayes UB4 84 B3
Richmond TW10 175 C6
Vancouver Ho 33 E1 118 B5
Vanderbilt Rd SW18 158 A3
Vanderbilt Villas 1 W12 112 D4
Vanderville Gdns N2 30 B1
Vandome Cl E16 99 B1
Vandon Ct SW1 259 B6
Vandon Pas SW1 259 B6
Vandon St SW1 259 B6
Van Dyck Ave KT3 199 B2
Vandyke Cl SW15 156 D5
Vandyke Cross SE9 166 A6
Vandy St EC2 243 A5
Vane Cl NW3 70 B4
Harrow HA3 44 B3
Vane Ho 15 N2 30 B1
Vanessa Cl DA17 125 C1
Vane St SW1 259 B4
Vanfame Ct KT3 199 D6
Vangaurd Way TW6 127 C2
Vange Ho W10 90 C2
Van Gogh Ct E14 120 B3
Vanguard Bldg 12 E14 119 C4
Vanguard Cl E16 99 B2
Thornton Heath CR0 204 D1
Vanguard Ho
7 Merton SW19 180 A3
6 Stanwell TW19 148 A5
Vanguard St SE8 141 C4
Vanguard Trad Ctr E15 98 A6
Vanguard Way SM6 220 A1
Vanneck Sq SW15 156 A6
Vanoc Gdns BR1 187 A6
Vansittart Rd E7 77 A4
Vansittart St 7 SE14 141 A5
Vanston Pl SW6 135 C5 265 B4
Vantage Mews E14 120 A5
Vant Rd SW17 180 D5
Vantrey Ho SE11 261 A3
Varcoe Rd SE16 118 C1
Vardens Rd SW11 136 B1
Varden St E1 96 B1
Vardon Cl W3 89 B1
Vardon Ho SE10 142 A4
Varey Ho E1 97 A4
Varley Ho 5 NW6 91 C6
Varley Par NW9 45 C5
Varley Rd E16 99 B1
Varley Way CR4 180 B1
Varna Rd SW6 135 B5 264 C3
Hampton TW12 173 D2
Varndell St NW1 93 C4 232 A2
Varsity Dr TW1,TW7 152 D5
Varsity Row SW14 133 A3
Vartry Rd N15 51 C3
Vassal Ho E3 97 A4
Vassall Rd SW9 138 C5
Vat Ho SW8 270 B4
Vauban Est SE16 263 D5
Vauban St SE16 117 D3 263 D5
Vaudeville Ct N4 72 C6
Vaughan Almshouses TW15 170 D5
Vaughan Ave NW4 46 A4
W6 111 D2
Vaughan Est 3 E2 95 D4
Vaughan Fst & Mid Sch HA1 42 A3
Vaughan Gdns IG1 56 B2
Vaughan Ho SE1 251 C2
Vaughan Rd DA16 145 D3
E15 76 D2
SE5 139 A2
Harrow HA1 42 B3
Thames Ditton KT7 197 B2
Vaughan St SE16 119 B4
Vaughan Way E1 118 A5
Vaughan Williams Cl SE8 141 C5
Vauxhall Bridge Rd SW1 115 C2 259 B3
Vauxhall Cross SE1,SW8 116 A1 260 B1
Vauxhall Gdns CR2 221 A2
Vauxhall Gr SW8 138 B6 270 C6
Vauxhall Prim Sch SE11 116 B1 260 D2
Vauxhall St SE11 116 B1 260 D2
Vauxhall Sta SE11 116 A1 260 B1
Vauxhall Wlk SE11 260 C2
Vawdrey Cl E1 96 C3
Vaynor Ho N7 72 A4
Veals Mead CR4 180 C2
Vectis Ct SW18 157 D5
Vectis Gdns SW17 181 B4
Vectis Rd SW17 181 B4
Veda Rd SE13 141 C1
Vega Cres HA6 22 A5

Vega Rd WD23 8 A4
Veitch Cl TW14 149 D4
Veldene Way HA2 63 B5
Velde Way 1 SE22 161 C6
Vellacott Ho W12 90 B1
Velletri Ho 17 E2 96 D5
Vellum Dr SM5 219 A5
Venables Cl RM10 81 D4
Venables St
NW8 92 B2 236 D4
Vencourt Pl W6 112 A2
Venetian Rd SE5 139 A3
Venetia Rd N4 50 D3
W5 109 D4
Venice Ct 14 SE5 139 A5
Venita Manor SE27 182 C5
Venmead Ct DA17 125 C2
Venner Rd SE26 184 C5
Venn Ho N1 233 D5
Venn St SW4 137 C1
Ventnor Ave HA7 25 B1
Ventnor Dr N20 13 D2
Ventnor Gdns IG11 79 C2
Ventnor Mans IG11 79 C2
Ventnor Rd SE14 140 D5
Belmont SM2 217 D1
Ventnor Terr N15 52 A5
Venture Cl DA5 169 A4
Venture Ct 3 SE12 165 A4
Venue St E14 98 A2
Venus Rd SE18 122 B3
Vera Ave N21 16 C6
Vera Ct 1 W2 91 D1
Vera Lynn Cl 5 E7 77 A4
Vera Rd SW6 135 A4 264 B2
Verbena Cl E16 98 D3
Verbena Gdns W6 112 A1
Verdant Ct 3 SE6 164 C4
Verdant La SE6 164 C3
Verdayne Ave CR0 222 D6
Verdi Ho 2 NW6 91 A5
Verdun Rd SE18,SE2 146 A6
Barnes SW13 134 A5
Vere Bank SW19 157 B3
Vereker Dr TW16 194 A6
Vereker Rd W14 254 B1
Vere St W1 93 B1 238 C1
Verity Cl W11 91 A1
Verity Ct N9 18 D3
Verity Ho 15 E3 97 B4
Vermeer Ct E14 120 B3
Vermont Cl EN2 4 D1
Vermont Ho E17 35 B1
Vermont Rd
Sutton SM1 217 D5
Wandsworth SW18 157 D5
West Norwood SE19 183 C4
Verne Ct 9 W3 111 A3
Verney Gdns RM9 81 A4
Verney Ho NW8 237 A6
Isleworth TW3 130 A1
Verney Rd SE16 118 B1
Dagenham RM9 81 A4
Verney St NW10 67 B5
Verney Way SE16 118 B1
Vernham Rd SE18 145 A6
Vernon Ave Ilford E12 78 B4
West Barnes SW20 178 D1
Woodford IG8 37 B3
Vernon Cl KT19 215 A2
Vernon Cres EN4 15 A5
Vernon Ct NW2 69 B5
Ealing W5 109 C6
Stanmore HA7 25 B2
Vernon Dr HA7 25 A2
Vernon Ho NW9 45 D4
SE11 260 D1
Vernon House Sch
NW10 67 B3
Vernon Mews W14 254 B3
Vernon Pl WC1 240 B3
Vernon Rd E11 54 C1
E15 76 C1
E17 53 B4
E3 97 B5
N8 50 C6
Feltham TW13 149 D2
Ilford IG3 57 D1
Mortlake SW14 133 B2
Sutton SM1 218 B3
Vernon Rise WC1 233 D2
Greenford UB6 64 B3
Vernon Sq WC1 233 D2
Vernon St
W14 113 A2 254 B3
Vernon Yd
W11 113 B6 244 C6
Veroan Rd DA7 147 A3
Verona Ct 10 SE14 140 D6
W4 111 C1
Verona Dr KT6 214 A6
Verona Rd E7 77 A1
Veronica Gdns CR4,
SW16 181 C2
Veronica Ho SE4 141 B2
Veronica Rd SW17 159 B2
Veronique Gdns IG6 57 A4
Verran Rd SW12 159 B4
Versailles Rd SE20 184 A3
Verulam Ave E17 53 B2
Verulam Ct NW9 46 A2
4 Southall UB1 86 A1
Verulam Ho 1 W6 112 C4
Verulam Rd UB6 85 C3
Verulam St EC1 94 C2 241 A4
Vervain Ho 2 SE15 140 A5
Verwood Dr EN4 2 D2
Verwood Ho SW8 270 D3
Verwood Lo 1 E14 120 B2
Verwood Rd HA2 24 A1
Veryan Ct 2 N8 49 D4
Vesage Ct EC1 241 B3
Vesey Path 15 E14 97 D1
Vespan Rd W12 112 A4
Vesta Rd SE4,SE14 141 A3
Vestris Rd SE23 162 D2
Vestry House (Mus)★
E17 53 D5
Vestry Mews 12 SE5 139 C4
Vestry Rd E17 53 D5
SE5 139 C4
Vestry St N1 95 B4 235 C2
Vevey St SE23,SE6 163 B2
Veysey Gdns RM10 81 C5
Viaduct Pl 28 E2 96 B4
Viaduct Rd N2 30 C1
Viaduct St E2 96 B4
Viaduct The Harrow HA2 64 A5
Woodford E18 37 B1
Vian St SE13 141 D2
Viant Ho 11 NW10 67 B1
Vibart Gdns SW2 160 B4
Vibart Wlk N1 233 B6
Vicarage Ave SE3 143 A5
Vicarage Cl
New Malden KT4 199 C1
Northolt UB5 63 B1
Ruislip HA4 39 B2
Vicarage Cres
SW11 136 B4 266 C1
Vicarage Ct N12 29 D5
W8 245 C2
Beckenham BR3 207 A6
East Bedfont TW14 149 A4
7 Putney SW15 156 A4
Vicarage Dr
Barking IG11 79 A1
Beckenham BR3 185 C2
Mortlake SW14 155 B6
Vicarage Farm Ct
TW5 129 B5
Vicarage Farm Rd
TW3,TW4,TW5 129 A4
Vicarage Fields KT12 194 C3
Vicarage Fields Sh Ctr The
IG11 79 A1
Vicarage Gate
W8 113 D5 245 C3
Vicarage Gdns W8 245 B3
Mitcham CR4 202 C6
Mortlake SW14 155 B6
Vicarage Gr SE5 139 B4
Vicarage Ho 1 KT1 176 B1
Vicarage La E15 76 D1
Ilford IG1 57 B1
Wallend E6 100 C4
Vicarage Pk SE18 123 A1
Vicarage Prim Sch E6 100 B4
Vicarage Rd DA5 169 D3
E10 53 D1
E15 76 D1
NW4 46 A3
SE18 123 A1
Ashford TW16 171 D4
Croydon CR0 220 C5
Dagenham RM10 81 D1
Kingston KT1,KT2 175 D1
Mortlake SW14 155 B6
Sutton SM1 217 D5
Teddington KT1,KT8 175 C2
Teddington TW11 175 A5
Tottenham N17 34 A2
Vicarage Way NW10 67 B5
Harrow HA2 41 C2
Vicarage Wlk
SW11 136 B4 266 D2
Vicars Bridge Cl HA0 88 A5
Vicar's Cl E15 99 A6
E9 96 C6
Enfield EN1 5 C3
Vicar's Green Prim Sch
HA0 87 C5
Vicars Hill SE13 141 D1
Vicar's Moor La N21 16 D4
Vicars Oak Rd SE19 183 C4
Vicar's Rd NW5 71 A3
Vicar's Wlk RM8 80 B5
Viceroy Cl N2 48 C6
Viceroy Ct NW8 230 B4
5 Croydon CR0 205 B1
Viceroy Lo 6 KT6 198 A4
Viceroy Par N2 48 C6
Viceroy Rd
SW8 138 A4 270 A2
Vic Johnson Ho 14 E3 97 B6
Vickers Cl SM6 220 B1
Vickers Ct 10 TW19 148 A5
Vickery Ct EC1 242 B6
Vickery Ho 12 SW4 138 A1
Victor Cazalet Ho N1 234 C6
Victor Gr HA0 66 A1
Victor Ho N20 14 D1
Victoria & Albert Mus★
SW7 114 B3 256 D5
Victoria Arc SW1 258 D5
Victoria Ave E6 99 D6
EC2 243 B3
N3 29 B2
Barnet EN4 2 B1
East Molesey KT8 195 D6
Hackbridge SM5,SM6 219 A5
Hillingdon UB10 60 D1
Hounslow TW3,TW4 151 C6
Surbiton KT6 197 D3
Wembley HA9 66 D2
Victoria Bglws DA14 191 B3
Victoria Bldgs 13 E8 96 B6
Victoria Bsns Ctr
DA16 146 B3
Victoria Cl Barnet EN4 2 B1
East Molesey KT8 195 C6
Harrow HA1 42 D3
Hayes UB3 83 B1
Victoria Coach Sta
SW1 115 B2 258 C3
Victoria Cotts N10 31 A1
3 E1 96 A2
Ilford IG6 57 A4
7 Richmond TW9 132 C4
Victoria Cres N15 51 C4
Merton SW19 179 B3
West Norwood SE19 183 C4
Victoria Ct 3 E1 118 A6
5 SW4 159 D5
W3 110 C4
Penge SE26 184 C4
1 Wanstead E18 55 B6
Wembley HA9 66 C2
Victoria Dock Rd E16 121 B6
Victoria Dr SW19 156 D3
Victoria Emb
WC2 116 C6 251 A5
Victoria Gdns
W11 113 C5 245 A4
Heston TW5 129 A4
Victoria Gr N12 30 B5
W8 114 A3 256 A6
Victoria Gr Mews W2 245 C5
Victoria Ho SW1 258 C2
6 SW4 159 D5
2 W12 112 A4
Edgware HA8 26 D4
Victoria Ind Est W3 89 C2
Victoria Jun Sch The
TW13 150 B3
Victoria La Barnet EN5 1 B1
Hayes UB3 105 B1
Victoria Lo 4 SW19 178 C3
Victoria Mans 8 N7 72 C3
NW10 68 B1
Victoria Mews NW6 91 C6
Wandsworth SW18 158 A3
Victorian Gr N16 73 C5
Victorian Rd N16 73 D5
Victoria Park Ct 11 E9 74 C1
Victoria Park Ind Ctr
E3 75 B1
Victoria Park Lofts E9 96 D6
Victoria Park Rd E9 74 D1
Victoria Park Sq E2 96 C4
Victoria Pas NW8 236 C6
Victoria Pl 16 TW10 153 D6
Victoria Point 10 E13 99 A5
Victoria Rd BR2 209 D4
BR7 188 C5
DA15 168 A1
E11 76 C4
E13 99 A5
N15 52 A5
N22 31 D2
N4 50 B1
NW10 89 C3
NW4 46 D5
NW6 91 B6
NW7 27 D5
W8 114 A3 256 A6
Barking IG11 78 D2
Barnet EN4 2 B1
Bexley DA6 147 C1
Buckhurst Hill IG9 21 D2
Chingford E17 36 A1
Chingford, Chingford Green
E4 20 C3
Dagenham RM10 81 D3
Ealing W5 87 B2
Edmonton N18 33 D6
Edmonton N9 17 D1
Feltham TW13 150 B3
Kingston KT1 176 B1
Mitcham CR4 180 D3
Mortlake SW14 133 B2
Ruislip HA4 62 B4
Southall UB2 107 B3
Surbiton KT6 197 D3
Sutton SM1 218 B3
Teddington TW11 175 A4
Twickenham TW1 153 B4
Victoria Rd *continued*
Wanstead E18 55 B6
Victoria Ret Pk HA4 62 D3
Victoria Rise SW4 137 B2
Victoria Sq SW1 258 D6
Victoria St E15 76 C1
SW1 115 C3 259 B5
Erith DA17 125 B1
Victoria Sta
SW1 115 B2 258 D4
Victoria Terr N4 50 C1
NW10 89 C3
Harrow HA1 42 C1
Victoria Villas TW9 132 B1
Victoria Way SE7 143 C6
Victoria Yd 31 E1 96 A1
Victor Mills Cotts BR8 191 C3
Victor Rd NW10 90 B4
Harrow HA2 42 A6
Penge SE20 184 D3
Teddington TW11 174 C6
Victors Dr TW12 173 A4
Victor Seymour Inf Sch
SM5 218 D4
Victors Way EN5 1 B2
Victor Villas N9 17 B1
Victory Ave SM4 202 A4
Victory Bsns Ctr The
TW7 130 D1
Victory Ct IG11 102 B4
Victory Day Sch
SW11 137 A4 268 A1
Victory Pl 6 E14 119 A6
SE17 117 B2 262 C4
West Norwood SE19 183 C4
Victory Prim Sch
SE17 117 A2 262 B4
Victory Rd
Merton SW19 180 A3
Wanstead E11 55 B5
Victory Road Mews 5
SW19 180 A3
Victory Way SE16 119 A4
Hounslow TW5 106 C1
Victory Wharf E14 119 A6
Victory Wlk SE8 141 C4
Video Ct N4 50 A2
Vidler Cl KT9 213 C2
Vienna Cl IG5 37 D1
View Cl N6 48 D2
Harrow HA1 42 B5
View Cres N8 49 D4
Viewfield Cl HA3 44 A2
Viewfield Rd DA5 168 C3
Wandsworth SW18 157 B5
Viewland Rd SE18 123 D1
View Point SE3 142 D2
View Rd N6 48 D3
Viewside Lo N6 49 C3
View The SE2 125 A1
Viga Rd N21 16 C5
Vigilant Cl SE26 184 A6
Vignoles Rd RM7 59 C2
Vigo St W1 115 C6 249 A5
Vi & John Rubens Ho
IG2 56 C3
Viking Cl 12 E3 97 A5
Viking Ct TW12 173 D2
Viking Fst & Mid Sch
UB5 84 D4
Viking Gdns E6 100 A3
Viking Ho 3 SE5 139 A3
3 SE7 122 A2
Viking Pl E10 53 B1
Viking Rd UB1 107 A6
Villacourt Rd SE18,SE2 146 A6
Village Arc The 2 E4 20 B3
Village Cl NW3 70 B3
Chingford E4 36 A5
Village Ct E17 53 D4
SE3 142 C2
Village Gate TW17 192 D4
Village Home The IG6 57 A6
Village Hts IG8 36 D5
Village Inf Sch RM10 81 C1
Village Mount 18 NW3 70 A4
Village Park Cl EN1 17 C5
Village Rd N3 29 A1
Enfield EN1 17 C6
Village Row SM2 217 C1
Village Sch The NW3 70 D2
Village The SE7 143 D6
SW11 136 D2
Village Way NW10 67 B4
SE21 161 B5
Ashford TW15 170 C6
Beckenham BR3 207 C6
Pinner HA5 41 B2
Village Way E HA2 41 C2
Villa Rd SW9 138 C2
Villas Rd SE18 123 A2
Villa St SE17 117 B1 262 D1
Villiers Ave
Kingston KT5 198 B5
Twickenham TW2 151 B3
Villiers Cl E10 75 C6
Kingston KT5 198 B5
Villiers Ct N20 14 A4
SW11 267 B2
Villiers High Sch UB1 107 B5
Villiers Ho W5 109 D6
Villiers Rd NW2 68 A2
Isleworth TW7 130 C3
Kingston KT1 198 B6
Penge BR3 184 D1
Southall UB1 107 B5
Villiers St WC2 250 B4
Vincam Cl TW2 151 C4
Vince Ct N1 235 D1
Vincent Ave KT5 215 A6
Vincent Cl BR2 209 B5
DA15 167 C3
Barnet EN5 1 D2
Harmondsworth UB7 126 C6
Vincent Ct N4 50 A1
NW4 46 D5
SW9 270 D1
W1 237 C2
Vincent Dr
Hillingdon UB10 82 B6
Upper Halliford TW17 193 C6
Vincent Gdns NW2 67 D5
Vincent Ho KT3 199 D5
Vincent Rd N15 51 A5
SE18 122 D2
W3 111 A3
Chingford E4 36 B4
Croydon CR0 205 C2
Dagenham RM9 81 A1
Hounslow TW4 128 D2
Hounslow TW7 130 B4
Kingston KT1 198 C6
Wembley HA0 66 B1
Wood Green N22 32 C1
Vincent Row TW12 174 A5
Vincents Cl SE16 119 A4
Vincents Path UB5 63 A2
Vincent Sq
SW1 115 D2 259 C4
Wood Green N22 32 C1
Vincent St E16 98 D2
SW1 115 D2 259 D4
Vincent Terr
N1 94 D5 234 D4
Vince St EC1 95 B4 235 D1
Vine Cl Surbiton KT5 198 B3
Sutton SM1 218 A5
West Drayton UB7 104 C2
Vine Cotts
3 Ealing W7 108 C5
Southall UB2 107 D2
Vine Ct E1 96 A2
Harrow HA3 44 A3
Vinegar St E1 118 B5
Vinegar Yd SE1 253 A2
Vine Gdns IG1 79 A3
Vine Gr UB10 60 C1
Vine Hill EC1 241 A5
Vine La SE1 117 C5 253 B3
Hillingdon UB10 82 B6
Uxbridge UB10 60 B1
Vine Lo N12 30 A4
Vine Pl Ealing W5 110 A5
Hounslow TW3 129 D1
Vine Rd BR6 227 D2
E15 76 D1
Barnes SW13 133 D2
East Molesey KT8 196 A5
Vineries Bank NW7 28 B5
Vineries Cl
Dagenham RM9 81 B2
Harmondsworth UB7 126 C6
Vineries The Enfield EN1 5 C2
Southgate N14 15 C5
Viners Cl KT12 194 C3
Vines Ave N3 29 D2
Vine Sq W14 254 D1
Vines Sch The SW11 137 A1
Vine St EC3 95 D1 243 C1
W1 249 B5
Vine St Bridge EC1 241 B5
Vinewood Ct E17 54 B4
Vineyard Ave NW7 29 A3
Vineyard Cl
Forest Hill SE6 163 C3
Kingston KT1 198 B6
Vineyard Gr N3 29 D2
Vineyard Hill Rd
SW19 179 C6
Vineyard Path SW14 133 B2
Vineyard Rd TW13 150 A1
Vineyard Row KT1,KT8 175 C2
Vineyard Sch The
TW10 154 A5
Vineyards The TW13 150 A1
Vineyard The TW10 154 A6
Vineyard Wlk EC1 241 A6
Viney Ct 9 SW4 159 D5
Vine Yd SE1 252 B2
Viney Rd SE13 141 D2
Vining St SW2,SW9 138 C1
Vinlake Ave UB10 60 C5
Vinson Ho N1 235 D3
Vinter Ct TW17 192 C4
Vintners Ct EC4 252 B6
Vintry Mews 3 E17 53 C5
Viola Ave SE2 124 B1
Feltham TW14 150 C5
Viola Ave *continued*
Stanwell TW19 148 A3
Viola Sq W12 111 D6
Violet Ave Enfield EN2 5 B5
Hillingdon UB8 82 B2
Violet Cl E16 98 C3
44 SE8 141 B6
Hackbridge SM6 203 A1
Violet Gdns CR0 220 D3
Violet Hill NW8 92 A5 229 A3
Violet Hill Ho NW8 229 A3
Violet La CR0 220 D3
Violet Rd E17 53 C3
E3 97 D3
Woodford E18 37 B1
Violet St E2 96 B3
Violet Terr UB8 82 C2
Violette Szabo Ho 4
SE27 183 B6
VIP Trad Est SE7 121 C2
Virgil Pl W1 237 C3
Virgil St SE1 116 B3 260 D6
Virginia Cl KT3 199 A5
Virginia Ct 7 SE16 118 D4
Virginia Ho 3 E14 120 A6
Teddington TW11 175 A5
Virginia Prim Sch E2 95 D4
Virginia Rd 10 E2 95 D4
South Norwood CR7 182 D2
Virginia St E1 118 A6
Virginia Wlk SW2 160 B5
Viscount Cl N11 31 B5
Viscount Ct 9 W11 91 C1
Viscount Dr E6 100 B2
Viscount Gr 3 UB5 84 D4
Viscount Point 7
SW19 179 C3
Viscount Rd TW19 148 A3
Viscount St EC1 242 A4
Viscount Way TW6 127 C1
Vista Ave EN3 6 D3
Vista Dr IG4 55 D4
Vista The SE9 165 D4
Vista Way HA3 44 A3
Vita Et Pax Sch N14 15 B6
Vittoria Ho N1 233 D5
Vittoria Prim Sch
N1 94 C5 234 A4
Viveash Cl UB3 105 D3
Vivian Ave NW4 46 B4
Wembley HA9 66 C2
Vivian Ct N12 29 D5
Vivian Gdns HA9 66 C3
Vivian Ho N4 51 B2
Vivian Mans 1 NW4 46 B4
Vivian Rd E3 97 A5
Vivian Sq SE15 140 B2
Vivian Way N2 48 B4
Vivien Cl KT9 214 A1
Vivienne Cl TW1 153 D5
Voce Rd SE18 145 B5
Voewood Cl KT3 199 D3
Vogans Mill SE1 253 D2
Vogler Ho 2 E1 118 C6
Vollasky Ho 5 E1 96 A2
Volta Cl N9 18 C1
Voltaire 2 SE5 139 D4
15 Richmond TW9 132 B4
Voltaire Ct 12 SW11 137 A3
Voltaire Rd SW4 137 D2
Voltaire Way UB3 105 C6
Volt Ave NW10 89 C4
Volta Way CR0 204 B1
Voluntary Pl E11 55 A3
Vorley Rd N19 71 C6
Voss Ct SW16 182 A4
Voss St E2 96 A4
Voyager Bsns Est 10
SE16 118 A3
Voyagers Cl IG11 102 C1
Voysey Cl N3 47 A6
Vulcan Cl E6 100 C1
Vulcan Gate EN2 4 C3
Vulcan Rd SE4 141 B3
Vulcan Sq E14 119 C2
Vulcan Terr SE4 141 B3
Vulcan Way N7 72 B2
Vyner Ct E5 74 A6
Vyner Rd W3 111 B6
Vyners Sch UB10 60 B4
Vyner St E2 96 B6
Vyners Way UB10 60 C3
Vyne The DA7 147 D2
Vyvyan Ho SE18 144 C4

W

Wadbrook St KT1 175 D1
Wadding St
SE17 117 B2 262 C3
Waddington Cl EN1 5 C1
Waddington Rd E15 76 B2
Waddington St E15 76 B2
Waddington Way
SE19 183 B2

Warner Cl E15 ....76 C3
NW9 ....46 A2
Hampton TW12 ....173 B5
Harlington UB3 ....127 B5
Warner Ct SM3 ....217 A6
Warner Ho 4 E9 ....74 D2
NW8 ....229 A2
SE13 ....141 D3
1 Beckenham BR3 ....185 D4
Warner Pl E2 ....96 A4
Warner Rd E17 ....53 A5
N8 ....49 D5
SE5 ....139 A4
Bromley BR1 ....186 D3
Warners Cl IG8 ....37 A5
Warner St EC1 .94 C3 241 A5
Warner Yd EC1 ....241 A5
Warnford Ho SW15 ....155 C5
Warnford Ind Est UB3 105 C4
Warnford Rd BR6 ....227 D3
Warnham WC1 ....233 C1
Warnham Court Rd
SM5 ....218 D1
Warnham Ho 6 SW2 .160 B4
Warnham Rd N12 ....30 C5
Warple Mews W3 ....111 C4
Warple Way W3,W12 ..111 C4
Warren Ave E11 ....76 B5
Bromley BR1 ....186 C3
Mortlake SW14,TW10 ..132 D1
Orpington BR6 ....227 D3
South Croydon CR2 ....222 D1
Warren Cl DA6 ....169 C6
N9 ....18 D4
Hayes UB4 ....84 C2
Wembley HA9 ....65 D6
West Norwood SE21 ....161 A4
Esher KT10 ....212 A4
Warren Comp Sch RM6 59 B4
Warren Cres N9 ....17 D4
Warren Ct N1 ....234 A4
N17 ....52 A6
17 Beckenham BR3 ....185 C3
6 Croydon CR0 ....205 C1
6 Ealing W5 ....87 C2
Warren Cutting KT2 ..177 B3
Warrender Prim Sch
HA4 ....39 D2
Warrender Rd N19 ....71 C4
Warrender Way HA4 ...40 A2
Warren Dr
Greenford UB6 ....86 A3
Ruislip HA4 ....40 D2
Warren Dr N KT5,KT6 .198 D1
Warren Dr S KT5 ....199 A1
Warren Dr The E11 ....55 C2
Warren Fields HA7 ....25 C6
Warren Gdns E15 ....76 B3
Warren Hill IG10 ....21 C6
Warren Ho 21 E3 ....97 D4
Warren Jun Sch RM6 ..59 B4
Warren La SE18 ....122 D3
Stanmore HA7 ....9 A2
Warren Mews W1 ....239 A5
Warren Park Rd SM1,
SM2 ....218 C2
Warren Pk KT2 ....177 A4
Warren Pond Rd E4 ...20 D4
Warren Rd BR2 ....225 A6
DA6 ....169 C6
E10 ....76 A5
NW2 ....67 D6
Ashford TW15 ....171 C3
Bushey WD23 ....8 B3
Chingford E4 ....20 A2
Croydon CR0 ....205 D1
Ickenham UB10 ....60 B4
Ilford IG6 ....57 B4
Isleworth TW2 ....152 B5
Kingston KT2 ....177 A4
Mitcham SW19 ....180 C4
Sidcup DA14 ....168 C1
Wanstead E11 ....55 C2
Warren Rise KT3 ....177 B2
Warren Road Prim Sch
BR6 ....227 D4
Warrens Shawe La HA8 10 D2
Warren St W1 ..93 C3 239 A5
Warren Street Sta
NW1 ....93 C3 239 B6
Warren Terr RM6 ....58 D5
Warren The E12 ....78 A4
Hayes UB4 ....84 A1
Heston TW5 ....129 B5
Worcester Park KT19 ...215 B5
Warren Way NW7 ....29 A4
Warren Wlk 1 SE7 ...143 C6
Warren Wood Cl BR2 .225 A6
Warriner Dr N9 ....18 A1
Warriner Gdns
SW11 ....137 A4 268 A1
Warrington Cres
W9 ....92 A3 236 A6
Warrington Gdns W9 .236 A5
Warrington Pl E14 ....120 A5
Warrington Rd
Croydon CR0 ....220 D5
Dagenham RM8 ....81 A6
Harrow HA1 ....42 C4
Warrington Rd *continued*
21 Richmond TW10 ....153 D6
Warrington Sq RM8 ....80 D6
Warrior Sq E12 ....78 C4
Warsaw Cl HA4 ....62 B2
Warspite Ho 3 E14 ..119 D2
Warspite Rd SE18 ....122 A3
Warton Rd E15 ....98 A6
Warwall E6 ....100 D1
Warwick W14 .113 B2 254 D3
Warwick Ave HA8 ....11 A1
W9 ....92 A3 236 A5
Harrow HA2 ....63 B4
Warwick Avenue Sta
W9 ....92 A3 236 A5
Warwick Chambers
W8 ....255 A6
Warwick Cl DA5 ....169 B4
Bushey WD23 ....8 C4
Hampton TW12 ....174 A3
New Barnet EN4 ....14 B6
Warwick Cres
W2 ....92 A2 236 A4
Hayes UB4 ....83 D3
Warwick Ct 3 E5 ....74 B6
N11 ....31 D4
5 N2 ....48 A6
NW2 ....69 A3
WC1 ....240 D3
1 Beckenham BR2 ....186 C1
Ealing W7 ....86 D1
Harrow HA1 ....42 C6
Merton SW19 ....179 C2
Northolt UB5 ....63 C3
Surbiton KT6 ....214 A6
Warwick Dene W5 ....110 A5
Warwick Dr SW15 ....134 B2
Warwick Gdns N4 ....51 A4
W14 ....113 B2 254 D4
Ilford IG1 ....56 D1
Thames Ditton KT7 ....196 D4
Thornton Heath CR7 ....204 C5
Warwick Gr E5 ....52 B1
Surbiton KT5 ....198 B2
Warwick Ho 10 E5 ....74 C6
N4 ....51 A1
11 SW9 ....138 C3
9 Acton W3 ....88 C1
6 Kingston KT2 ....176 A2
6 Putney SW15 ....156 C4
Warwick House St
SW1 ....249 D4
Warwick La
EC4 ....94 D1 241 D1
Warwick Lo
Cheam SM1 ....217 B4
Twickenham TW2 ....151 D1
Warwick Mans SW5 ..255 A4
Warwick Park Sch
SE15 ....139 D4
Warwick Pas EC4 ....241 D2
Warwick Pl W5 ....109 D4
W9 ....92 A2 236 A4
Warwick Pl N SW1 ...259 A3
Warwick Rd DA14 ....190 B5
E12 ....78 A3
E15 ....76 D2
E17 ....35 B1
N11 ....31 D4
W14,SW5 ....113 B2 254 D4
Ashford TW15 ....170 A5
Barnet EN5 ....1 D1
Bexley DA16 ....146 C2
Chingford E4 ....35 C5
Ealing W5 ....110 A5
Edmonton N18 ....33 D6
Enfield EN3 ....7 B6
Hounslow TW4 ....128 B2
Kingston KT3 ....199 A6
Penge SE20 ....206 B6
Southall UB2 ....107 B3
Sutton SM1 ....218 A3
Teddington KT1 ....175 C2
Thames Ditton KT7 ....196 D4
Thornton Heath CR7 ....204 C6
Twickenham TW2 ....152 C3
Wanstead E11 ....55 B4
Yiewsley UB7 ....104 A5
Warwick Row
SW1 ....115 B3 258 D6
Warwick Sch for Boys
E17 ....54 A5
Warwickshire Path
SE8 ....141 B5
Warwickshire Rd N16 ..73 C4
Warwick Sq EC4 ....241 D2
SW1 ....115 C1 259 A2
Warwick Sq Mews
SW1 ....259 A3
Warwick St
W1 ....115 C6 249 B6
Warwick Terr E17 ....54 B4
SE18 ....145 B6
Warwick Way
SW1 ....115 B2 258 D2
Warwick Yd EC1 ....242 B5
Wasdale NW1 ....231 D1
Washbrook Ho SW2 ..160 C5
Washington Ave E12 ...78 B4
Washington Cl 45 E3 ..97 D4
Washington Ct SW17 .180 D4
Washington Ho E17 ....35 B1
SW1 ....247 C1
Washington Rd E6 ....77 C1
Barnes SW13 ....134 A5
Kingston KT1 ....176 C1
North Cheam KT4 ....200 B1
2 Woodford E18 ....36 D1
Wastdale Rd SE23 ....162 D3
Watchfield Ct 7 W4 ..111 A1
Watcombe Cotts TW9 132 C6
Watcombe Rd SE25 ...206 B4
Waterbank Rd SE6 ...186 A6
Waterbeach Rd RM9 ...80 C2
Water Brook La NW4 ..46 C4
Watercress Pl N1 ....73 C1
Waterdale Rd SE2 ....146 A6
Waterden Cres E9 ....75 C3
Waterden Rd E15 ....75 C2
Waterer Ho 7 SE6 ...186 A6
Waterer Rise SM6 ....219 D2
Waterfall Cl N14 ....15 C1
Waterfall Cotts SW19 .180 B4
Waterfall Rd N11,N14 ..15 C1
Mitcham SW19 ....180 B4
Waterfall Terr SW17 ..180 C4
Waterfield Cl
Belvedere DA17 ....125 C3
Woolwich SE28 ....124 B5
Waterfield Gdns SE25 .205 C4
Waterford Rd
SW6 ....135 D5 265 C3
Watergardens The
KT2 ....177 A4
Watergate EC4 ....251 C6
Watergate Ho 5 SE18 122 C2
Watergate Sch SE13 ..141 D1
Watergate St SE8 ....141 C6
Watergate Wlk WC2 ..250 B4
Water Gdns HA7 ....25 B4
Water Gdns The
W2 ....92 C1 237 B2
Waterglade Ctr The
W5 ....109 D6
Waterhall Ave E4 ....36 C6
Waterhall Cl E17 ....34 D2
Waterhead NW1 ....232 A2
Waterhedge Mews EN1 17 D6
Waterhouse Cl E16 ....99 D2
NW3 ....70 B3
W6 ....112 D1
Waterhouse Ct 5
TW11 ....174 D5
Wateridge Cl E14 ....119 C3
Wateringbury Cl BR5 .190 B1
Water La E15 ....76 C2
SE14 ....140 C5
Edmonton N9 ....18 B4
Ilford IG3 ....79 D5
Richmond TW10,TW9 ...153 D6
Sidcup DA14 ....169 B2
Teddington KT1 ....175 D2
Twickenham TW1 ....153 A3
Water Lily Cl UB2 ....108 A4
Waterloo Bridge
SE1,WC2 ....116 B6 250 D5
Waterloo Cl E9 ....74 C3
East Bedfont TW14 ....149 D3
Waterloo East Sta
SE1 ....116 C5 251 B3
Waterloo Gdns E2 ....96 C5
Waterloo Int Sta
SE1 ....116 B4 250 D2
Waterloo Pier SE1 ....250 C2
Waterloo Pl
SW1 ....115 D5 249 C4
Waterloo Rd E10 ....53 C2
E6 ....77 C1
E7 ....76 D3
NW2 ....68 A6
SE1 ....116 C4 251 B2
Sutton SM1 ....218 B3
Waterloo Sta
SE1 ....116 C4 251 A2
Waterloo Terr N1 ....72 D1
Waterlow Ct NW11 ....47 D2
Waterlow Rd N19 ....49 C1
Waterman Bldg 4
E14 ....119 C4
Watermans Mews 1
W5 ....110 A6
Waterman St SW15 ...134 D2
Waterman Way E1 ....118 B5
Watermead TW14 ....149 C3
Watermead Ho E9 ....75 B3
Watermead La CR4 ...202 D2
Watermeadow La
SW6 ....136 A3
Watermead Rd SE6 ...186 A6
Watermeads High Sch
SM4 ....202 B3
Watermead Way N17 ..34 B1
Watermen's Sq 1
SE20 ....184 C3
Water Mews SE15 ....140 C1
Watermill Bsns Ctr EN3 .7 B3
Watermill Cl TW10 ...153 C1
Watermill La N18 ....33 C5
Watermill Way
Feltham TW13 ....151 C2
Merton SW19 ....180 A2
Watermint Quay N16 ..52 A2
Water Rd HA0 ....88 B6
Watersedge KT19 ....215 A4
Water's Edge SW6 ....134 C4
Watersfield Way HA8 ..26 A3
Waters Gdns RM10 ....81 C3
Watership Down Ho
E11 ....54 D2
Waterside E17 ....52 C3
4 Beckenham BR3 ....185 C2
Waterside Cl E3 ....97 B6
28 SE16 ....118 A4
Barking IG11 ....80 A4
Northolt UB5 ....85 B4
Surbiton KT6 ....214 A6
Waterside Ct SE13 ....142 B1
Waterside Dr KT12 ...194 B4
Waterside Pl NW1 ....231 B6
Waterside Point SW11 267 B4
Waterside Rd UB2 ....107 C3
Waterside Sch SE18 ..123 B1
Waterside Trad Ctr
W7 ....108 C3
Waterside Way SW17 .180 A5
Watersmeet Way
SE28 ....102 D1
Waterson St E2 ....95 D4
Waters Pl SW15 ....134 C3
Watersplash Cl KT1 ...198 A6
Watersplash La
Hayes UB3 ....106 A2
Southall TW5 ....106 B1
Watersplash Rd TW17 192 C5
Waters Rd Catford SE6 .164 C1
Kingston KT1 ....176 D1
Waters Sq KT1 ....198 D6
Water St WC2 ....251 A6
Water Tower Cl UB8 ...60 A3
Water Tower Hill CR0 .221 B4
Water Tower Ho W8 ..245 A3
Water Tower Pl N1 ...234 C5
Waterview Ho E14 ....97 A2
Waterworks Cnr E17 ...36 C1
Waterworks La E5 ....74 D6
Waterworks Rd SW2 ..160 B5
Watery La DA14 ....190 B4
Hayes UB3 ....105 B1
Merton SW19,SW20 ....179 B1
Northolt UB5 ....84 C5
Wates Way CR4 ....202 D3
Wateville Rd N17 ....33 A2
Watford Cl SW11 ....267 B2
Watford Rd E16 ....99 A2
Elstree WD6 ....9 C5
Harrow HA0,HA1 ....65 A5
Harrow HA1 ....43 A1
Northwood HA6 ....22 A4
Watford Way NW4 ....46 A5
Watford Way (Barnet
By-Pass) NW9 ....27 D3
Watkin Ho N16 ....51 D2
Watkin Rd HA9 ....66 D5
Watkinson Rd N7 ....72 B2
Watling Ave HA8 ....27 B2
Watling Ct EC4 ....242 B1
1 Elstree WD6 ....9 D5
Watling Gate NW9 ....45 C5
Watling Gdns NW2 ....69 A2
Watling Ho 10 SE18 ...144 C6
Watlings Cl CR0 ....207 A3
Watling St DA6,DA7 ...147 D1
EC4 ....95 A1 242 B1
4 SE15 ....139 C6
Watlington Gr SE26 ...185 A5
Watney Cotts SW14 ...133 A2
Watney Mkt E1 ....96 B1
Watney Rd SW14 ....133 A2
Watneys Rd CR4 ....203 D4
Watney St E1 ....96 B1
Watson Ave
Cheam SM3 ....217 A6
Wallend E6 ....78 C1
Watson Cl N16 ....73 B3
Mitcham SW19 ....180 C3
Watson Ho 3 SW2 ...160 A4
Watsons Lo 4 RM10 ...81 D2
Watson's Mews W1 ...237 B3
Watsons Rd N22 ....32 B2
Watson's St SE8 ....141 C5
Watson St E13 ....99 B5
Wattisfield Rd E5 ....74 C5
Watts Cl N15 ....51 C4
Watts Gr E3 ....97 D2
Watts Ho 6 W10 ....91 A2
Watt's La
Chislehurst BR7 ....189 A2
Teddington TW11 ....175 A5
Watts Point E13 ....99 A6
Watts Rd KT7 ....197 A2
Watts St E1 ....118 B5
SE15 ....139 D4
Wat Tyler Ho N8 ....50 A6
Wat Tyler Rd SE10 ....142 B4
Wauthier Cl N13 ....32 D5
Wavel Ct 7 E1 ....118 C5
7 Streatham SW16 ...160 A1
Wavell Dr DA15 ....167 C5
Wavell Ho N6 ....49 A3
Wavel Mews N8 ....49 D5
NW6 ....69 D1
Wavel Pl SE26 ....183 D6
Wavendon Ave W4 ...111 B1
Waveney Ave SE15 ....140 B1
Waveney Cl E1 ....118 A5
Waveney Ho SE15 ....140 B1
Waverley Ave E17 ....54 B6
E4 ....35 B6
Sutton SM1 ....217 D6
Tolworth KT5 ....199 A3
Twickenham TW2,TW4 ..151 C3
Wembley HA9 ....66 B3
Waverley Cl BR2 ....209 D4
East Molesey KT8 ....195 C4
Hayes UB3 ....105 B2
Woodford E18 ....37 C1
Waverley Cres SE18 ...123 B1
Waverley Ct 3 NW6 ...69 A1
W1 ....238 B4
Enfield EN2 ....5 A2
Waverley Gdns E6 ....100 A2
Barking IG11 ....101 C5
Ealing NW10 ....88 B5
Ilford IG6 ....57 B6
Northwood HA6 ....22 A2
Waverley Gr N3 ....47 A6
Waverley Ind Pk HA1 ...42 B6
Waverley Pl N4 ....50 D1
NW8 ....92 B5 229 C4
Waverley Rd E17 ....54 A6
N8 ....50 A2
SE18 ....123 B1
Croydon SE25 ....206 B6
Enfield EN2 ....4 D2
Harrow HA2 ....41 A1
Southall UB1 ....107 C6
Stoneleigh KT17,KT4 ...216 B3
Tottenham N17 ....34 B3
Woodford E18 ....37 C2
Waverley Sch EN3 ....6 C1
Waverley Sch (lower)
SE22 ....162 B6
Waverley Sch (Upper)
SE15 ....162 C6
Waverley Way SM2,
SM5 ....218 C2
Waverly Ct NW3 ....70 D2
Waverton Ho 2 E3 ....97 B6
Waverton Rd SW18 ...158 A4
Waverton St
W1 ....115 B5 248 C4
Wavertree Ct 9 SW2 .160 A3
Wavertree Rd
Streatham SW2 ....160 B3
Woodford E18 ....37 A1
Waxham NW5 ....70 D3
Waxlow Cres UB1 ....85 C1
Waxlow Ho UB4 ....84 C2
Waxlow Rd NW10 ....89 B5
Waxwell Cl HA5 ....22 D1
Waxwell La HA5 ....22 D1
Wayborne Gr HA4 ....39 A3
Waye Ave TW5 ....128 A4
Wayfarer Rd UB5 ....85 A4
Wayfield Link SE9 ....167 B5
Wayford St SW11 ....136 C3
Wayland Ave E8 ....74 A3
Wayland Ho 13 SW9 ..138 C3
Waylands UB3 ....83 B2
Waylands Ct IG1 ....79 B4
Waylands Mead BR3 ..185 D2
Waylett Ho SE11 ....261 A1
Waylett Pl Wembley HA0 65 D4
West Norwood SE27 ...160 D1
Wayman Ct E8 ....74 B2
Wayne Cl BR6 ....227 D5
Waynflete Ave CR0 ...220 D5
Waynflete Sq 16 W10 .112 D6
18 W10 ....90 D1
Waynflete St SW18 ...158 A2
Wayside NW11 ....47 A1
Mortlake SW14 ....155 A6
New Addington CR0 ....223 D2
Wayside Ave WD23 ....8 B5
Wayside Cl N14 ....15 C5
Wayside Commercial Est
IG11 ....102 A5
Wayside Ct
Isleworth TW7 ....130 C3
Twickenham TW1 ....153 C5
Wembley HA9 ....66 C5
Wayside Gdns RM10 ...81 C3
Wayside Gr BR7,SE9 ...188 B6
Wayside Mews IG2 ....56 C4
Weald Cl BR2 ....226 A6
16 SE16 ....118 B1
Weald Fst & Mid Schs
HA3 ....24 D3
Weald La HA3 ....24 B2
Weald Rd UB10 ....82 C5
Weald Rise HA3 ....24 D2
Weald Sq E5 ....74 B6
Wealdstone Rd SM3 ..217 B6
Weald The BR7 ....188 B4
Weald Way Hayes UB4 ..83 C4
Romford RM7 ....59 D3
Wealdwood Gdns HA5 .23 D4
Weale Rd E4 ....20 B1
Weall Ct HA5 ....41 A5
Weardale Ct EN5 ....12 C6
Weardale Gdns EN2 ....5 B4
Weardale Ho N4 ....51 A2
Weardale Rd SE13 ....142 B1
Wearmouth Ho 1 E3 ..97 B2
Wear Pl 13 E2 ....96 B4
Wearside Rd SE13 ....141 D1
Weatherbury 6 W2 ...91 C1
Weatherbury Ho 3
N19 ....71 D5
Weatherill Ct SE25 ....206 B3
Weatherley Cl E3 ....97 B2
Weathersfield Ct SE9 .166 B5
Weaver Cl E16 ....122 D6
South Croydon CR0 ....221 D4
Weaver Ct 2 E2 ....96 B3
Weaver Ho 13 E1 ....96 A3
Weavers Cl TW7 ....130 C1
Weavers Ho 4 E11 ....55 A3
Weaver's La
SE1 ....117 C5 253 B3
Weaver St E1 ....96 A3
Weavers Way NW1 ...232 C6
6 NW1 ....71 D1
Weaver Wlk SE27 ....182 D6
Webb Ct 6 SE28 ....124 B6
W3 ....110 D4
Webber Cl WD6 ....9 D5
Webber Ho 6 IG11 ....78 D1
Webber Row
SE1 ....116 D4 251 C1
Webber St
SE1 ....116 D4 251 C1
Webb Est E5 ....52 A2
Webb Gdns 1 E13 ....99 A3
Webb Ho SW8 ....269 D3
2 Dagenham RM10 ....81 C5
Feltham TW13 ....151 A1
Webb Pl NW10 ....89 D4
Webb Rd SE3 ....142 D6
Webbscroft Rd RM10 ..81 D4
Webb's Rd SW11 ....158 D6
Webbs Rd UB4 ....84 B4
Webb St SE1 ..117 C3 263 A5
Webheath 6 NW6 ....69 B1
Webster Gdns W5 ....109 D5
Webster Ho 16 N16 ....73 C3
Webster Rd E11 ....76 A5
SE16 ....118 A3
Weddell Ho 23 E1 ....96 D3
Wedderburn Rd NW3 ..70 B3
Barking IG11 ....101 C6
Wedgewood Ct DA5 ..169 B4
1 Beckenham BR2 ....208 D5
Wedgewood Ho SW1 .259 A1
Wedgewood Mews
W1 ....239 D1
Wedgewood Wlk NW3 .69 D3
Wedgwood Ho 17 E2 ..96 D4
SE11 ....261 A5
Wedgwood Way SE19 .183 A3
Wedlake St W10 ....91 A3
Wedmore Gdns N19 ...71 D6
Wedmore Rd UB6 ....86 B4
Wedmore St N19 ....71 D5
Weech Rd NW6 ....69 C4
Weedington Rd NW5 ...71 A3
Weedon Ho W12 ....90 A1
Weekley Sq SW11 ....136 B2
Weeks Ho TW10 ....175 C6
Weigall Rd SE12,SE3 ..143 A1
Weighhouse St W1 ...238 B1
Weighton Rd
Harrow HA3 ....24 B2
Penge SE20 ....184 B1
Weihurst Ct SM1 ....218 C3
Weihurst Gdns SM1 ...218 B3
Weimar St SW15 ....135 A2
Weirdale Ave N20 ....14 D2
Weir Hall Ave N18 ....33 B4
Weir Hall Gdns N18 ....33 B5
Weir Hall Rd N18 ....33 B4
Weir Ho 8 SW12 ....159 C4
Weir Rd Sidcup DA5 ...169 D4
Streatham SW12 ....159 C4
Walton-on-T KT12 ....194 A3
Wimbledon SW18,SW19 157 D1
Weir's Pas NW1 ....232 D2
Weiss Rd SW15 ....134 D2
Welbeck Ave BR1 ....187 B6
DA15 ....168 A3
Hayes UB4 ....84 B3
Welbeck Cl N12 ....30 B5
New Malden KT3 ....199 D4
Stoneleigh KT17 ....216 A1
Welbeck Ct W14 ....254 C4
Hayes UB4 ....84 B3
Welbeck Mans 10 NW6 .69 C3
Welbeck Rd E6 ....99 D4
Carshalton SM1,SM5 ...218 B6
East Barnet EN4 ....14 C5
Harrow HA2 ....41 D1
Carshalton SM5 ....202 C1

Welbeck St W1 .93 B1 238 C2
Welbeck Villas N21 ...17 A3
Welbeck Way W1 ...238 C2
Welbeck Wlk SM5 ...202 B1
Welbourne Prim Sch
N17 ...52 A6
Welby Ho N19 ...49 D2
Welby St SE5 ...138 D4
Welch Pl HA5 ...22 C2
Welcome Ct E17 ...53 C2
Weldon Cl HA4 ...62 B2
Weldon Ct
Southgate N21 ...16 B6
Thornton Heath CR7 ..204 D4
Weldon Dr KT8 ...195 B5
Weld Pl N11 ...31 B5
Welfare Rd E15 ...76 C1
Welford Cl E5 ...74 D5
Welford Ct 12 NW1 ...71 B1
7 SW8 ...137 C3
Welford Pl SW19 ...179 A6
Welham Rd SW16,
SW17 ...181 B4
Welhouse Rd SM5 ...202 C1
Wellacre Rd HA3 ...43 B3
Wellan Cl DA15,DA16 ..168 B6
Welland Gdns UB6 ...86 D5
Welland Ho SE15 ...140 C1
Welland Mews E1 ...118 A5
Wellands Cl BR1 ...188 B1
Welland St SE10 ...142 A6
Well App EN5 ...12 C6
Wellbrook Rd BR6 ...226 C4
Wellby Ct 1 E13 ...99 C5
Well Cl Ruislip HA4 ...63 A5
Streatham SW16 ...182 B6
Wellclose Sq E1 ...118 A6
Wellclose St 11 E1 ...118 A6
Well Cottage Cl E11 ...55 C2
Well Ct EC4 ...242 B1
Wellday Ho 2 E9 ...75 A2
Welldon Cres HA1 ...42 C3
Welldon Park Fst Sch
HA2 ...64 A4
Welldon Park Mid Sch
HA2 ...64 A4
Weller Ho 20 SE16 ...118 A4
Weller St SE1 ...252 A2
Wellesley Ave W6 ...112 B3
Wellesley Cl 8 SE7 ...121 C1
Wellesley Court Rd 1
CR0 ...221 B6
Wellesley Cres TW2 ...152 C1
Wellesley Ct
W9 ...92 A4 229 A2
Cheam SM3 ...201 A1
Twickenham TW2 ...152 C1
Wellesley Gr CR0 ...221 B6
Wellesley Ho NW1 ...232 C1
Wellesley Park Mews
EN2 ...4 D3
Wellesley Pl NW1 ...232 C1
Wellesley Rd E17 ...53 C3
NW5 ...71 A3
W4 ...110 D1
Croydon CR0 ...205 A1
Harrow HA1 ...42 C4
Ilford IG1 ...57 A1
Sutton SM2 ...218 A2
Twickenham TW2 ...152 C1
Wanstead E11 ...55 A4
Wood Green N22 ...32 C1
Wellesley Road Sta
CR0 ...221 B6
Wellesley St E1 ...96 D2
Wellesley Terr
N1 ...95 A4 235 B2
Wellfield Ave N10 ...49 B6
Wellfield Rd SW16 ...182 B6
Wellfit St 6 SE24 ...138 D2
Wellgarth UB6 ...65 B2
Wellgarth Rd NW11 ...47 D1
Well Gr N20 ...14 B3
Well Hall Par SE9 ...144 B1
Well Hall Pleasaunce★
SE9 ...144 A1
Well Hall Rd SE9 ...144 B1
Well Ho 11 N9 ...18 A1
Wellhouse Rd BR3 ...207 C5
Wellingfield Ct 1
DA16 ...146 A2
Welling High St DA16 .146 B2
Welling Sch DA16 ...146 B4
Wellings Ho UB3 ...106 B5
Welling Sta DA16 ...146 A3
Wellington N8 ...50 A5
1 NW9 ...27 D3
Wellington Arch★
SW1 ...248 B2
Wellington Ave DA15 .168 A5
N15 ...52 A3
SE18 ...123 A3
Chingford E4 ...19 D2
Edmonton N9 ...18 B1
Hounslow TW3,TW4 ...151 C6
North Cheam KT4 ...216 C5
Wellington Ave *continued*
Pinner HA5 ...23 B2
Wellington Bldgs 14 E3 97 C4
SW1 ...258 B1
Wellington Cl SE14 ..140 D4
W11 ...91 C1
Walton-on-T KT12 ...193 D1
Wellington Cres KT3 ..199 A6
Wellington Ct NW8 ..229 D3
SW1 ...247 C1
SW18 ...158 C6
SW6 ...265 D1
WC2 ...250 A6
Ashford TW15 ...170 A6
Stanwell TW19 ...148 A4
5 Surbiton KT6 ...198 A3
Teddington TW12 ...174 B5
Wellington Gdns SE7 .121 C1
Teddington TW12,TW2 ..174 B6
Wellington Gr SE10 ..142 B5
Wellington Ho 18 NW3 .70 D2
4 Ealing W5 ...88 A4
Northolt UB5 ...63 C1
Stanmore HA7 ...9 A1
Wellington Hospl (North)
NW8 ...92 B5 229 D3
Wellington Hospl (South)
NW8 ...92 B5 229 D3
Wellington Mans
1 E10 ...53 C1
N16 ...73 D4
Wellington Mews
SE22 ...140 A1
Streatham SW16 ...159 D1
Wellington Mus (Apsley
Ho)★ SW1 ...115 A4 248 B2
Wellington Par DA15 .168 A6
Wellington Park Est
NW2 ...68 A6
Wellington Pl N2 ...48 C4
NW8 ...92 B4 229 D2
Wellington Prim Sch
E3 ...97 C4
Chingford E4 ...19 D2
Hounslow TW3 ...129 B3
Wellington Rd E17 ...53 A5
E6 ...100 B5
E7 ...76 D4
NW10 ...90 D4
NW8 ...92 B5 229 D3
W5 ...109 C3
Ashford TW15 ...170 A5
Bexley DA5 ...168 D6
Bromley BR2 ...209 C5
Enfield EN1 ...17 C5
Erith DA17 ...125 B1
Harrow HA3 ...42 C6
Hatton TW14 ...149 C6
Pinner HA5 ...23 B2
Teddington TW12,TW2 ..174 B6
Thornton Heath CR0 ..204 D2
Walthamstow E10 ...53 A1
Wanstead E11 ...55 A4
Wimbledon SW19 ...157 C2
Wellington Rd N TW4 .129 B2
Wellington Rd S TW4 .151 B6
Wellington Row E2 ...96 A4
Wellington Sq
SW3 ...114 D1 257 C2
Wellington St SE18 ...122 C2
WC2 ...116 B6 250 C6
1 Barking IG11 ...101 A6
Wellington Terr 2 E1 .118 B5
Harrow HA1 ...42 B1
Wellington Way E3 ...97 C4
Welling Way DA16 ...145 B2
Well La SW14 ...155 A6
Wellmead IG3 ...58 A2
Wellmeadow Rd W7 ..109 A2
Catford SE13,SE6 ...164 C3
Wellow Wlk SM5 ...202 B1
Well Rd NW3 ...70 B5
Barnet EN5 ...12 C6
Wells Cl 2 Northolt UB5 84 C4
South Croydon CR2 ...221 C3
Wells Ct N1 ...73 C3
16 NW3 ...70 A4
1 NW6 ...91 C5
Wells Dr NW9 ...45 B1
Wells Gdns
Dagenham RM10 ...81 D3
Redbridge IG1 ...56 A2
Wells Ho BR1 ...187 B5
EC1 ...234 C2
9 SE16 ...118 C3
12 W10 ...91 A3
4 Barking IG11 ...80 A1
Ealing W5 ...109 D6
Wells Ho The NW3 ...70 B4
Wells House Rd NW10 .89 C2
Wellside Gdns SW14 ..155 A6
Wells Mews W1 ...239 B2
Wellsmoor Gdns BR1 .210 C6
Wells Park Ct SE26 ...184 B6
Wells Park Rd SE26 ...184 B6
Wells Pl SW18 ...158 A4
Wells Prim Sch IG8 ...37 A6
Wells Rd BR1 ...188 B1
W12 ...112 C4
Wells Rise NW8 92 D6 230 C5
Wells Sq WC1 ...233 D1
Wells St W1 ...93 C1 239 B2
Well St E15 ...76 C2
E9 ...74 C1
Wellstead Ave N9 ...18 D4
Wellstead Rd E6 ...100 C5
Wells Terr N4 ...72 C6
Wells The N14 ...15 D4
Wells Way SE5 ...139 C6
SW7 ...114 B3 256 C6
Wells Yd 2 N7 ...72 C3
Well Wlk NW3 ...70 B5
Wellwood Ct SW15 ...134 C1
Wellwood Rd IG3 ...58 A2
Welsby Ct W5 ...87 C2
Welsford St SE1 ...118 A2
Welsh Cl E13 ...99 A4
Welsh Harp Field Centre
NW9 ...45 B1
Welsh Ho 14 E1 ...118 B5
Welshpool Ho 22 E8 ...96 A6
Welshpool St 1 E8 ...96 B6
Welshside NW9 ...45 C3
Welshside Wlk NW9 ...45 C3
Welstead Ho 5 E1 ...96 B1
Welstead Way W4 ...111 D2
Weltje Rd W6 ...112 A1
Welton Ho E1 ...96 D2
SE5 ...139 C4
Welton Rd SE18 ...145 C5
Welwyn Ave TW14 ...149 D5
Welwyn St E2 ...96 C4
Welwyn Way UB4 ...83 C3
Wembley HA0 ...65 D2
Wembley Arena HA9 ...66 C4
Wembley Bsns Ctr HA9 66 D5
Wembley Central Sta
HA9 ...66 A3
Wembley Commercial Ctr
HA9 ...65 D6
Wembley Conference Ctr
HA9 ...66 C4
Wembley Exhibition Halls
HA9 ...66 C4
Wembley High Sch
HA0 ...65 C5
Wembley Hill Rd HA9 ...66 B4
Wembley Hospl HA0 ...65 D2
Wembley Manor Jun & Inf
Schs HA9 ...66 A5
Wembley Park Dr HA9 ...66 B5
Wembley Park Sta HA9 66 C5
Wembley Rd TW12 ...173 C2
Wembley Stadium HA9 66 C3
Wembley Stadium Ind Est
Wembley HA9 ...66 C5
Wembley HA9 ...66 D4
Wembley Stadium Sta
HA9 ...66 B3
Wembley Way HA9 ...66 D2
Wemborough Rd HA7 ..25 C3
Wembury Rd N6 ...49 B2
Wemyss Rd SE3 ...142 D3
Wendela Ct HA1 ...64 C6
Wendell Park Prim Sch
W12 ...111 D4
Wendell Rd W12 ...111 D4
Wenderholme CR2 ...221 B3
Wendle Ct SW8 ...270 A5
Wendling NW5 ...70 D3
Wendling Rd SM1,SM5 218 B6
Wendon St E3 ...97 B6
Wendover NW9 ...45 D3
SE17 ...117 C1 263 A1
Wendover Cl UB4 ...85 A3
Wendover Ct 4 NW2 ...69 C5
W1 ...238 A3
W3 ...89 A3
Bromley BR2 ...209 B6
Wendover Dr KT3 ...199 D3
Wendover Ho W1 ...238 A3
Wendover Rd BR1,BR2 209 B6
NW10 ...89 D5
SE9 ...143 D2
Wendover Way
Bexley DA16 ...146 A1
Bushey WD23 ...8 A5
Wendy Cl EN1 ...17 D5
Wendy Ho N12 ...30 B5
Wendy Way HA0 ...88 A6
Wengham Ho W12 ...112 A6
Wenham Ho SW8 ...269 A3
Wenlake Ho EC1 ...242 A6
Wenlock Ct N1 ...235 D3
Wenlock Gdns 13 NW4 .46 A5
Wenlock Rd HA8 ...27 A4
N1 ...95 A5 235 B3
Wenlock St N1 .95 B5 235 C3
Wennington Rd E3 ...96 D5
Wensdale Ho E5 ...74 A6
Wensley Ave IG8 ...37 A3
Wensley Cl SE9 ...166 B5
Barnet N11 ...31 A4
Wensleydale Gdns
TW12 ...173 D3
Wensleydale Ho 8 N4 .51 A2
Wensleydale Rd TW12 173 D3
Wensley Rd N18 ...34 B4
Wentland Cl SE6 ...164 B2
Wentland Rd SE6 ...164 B2
Wentway Ct W13 ...87 A3
Wentwood Ho 1 E5 ...74 B6
Wentworth Ave N3 ...29 C3
Borehamwood WD6 ...10 B6
Wentworth Cl BR2 ...225 A6
N3 ...29 D3
SE28 ...102 D1
Ashford TW15 ...170 D6
Long Ditton KT6 ...213 D6
Morden SM4 ...201 C2
Orpington BR6 ...227 C3
Wentworth Cres SE15 .140 A5
Hayes UB3 ...105 B3
Wentworth Ct W6 ...264 A5
Barnet EN5 ...1 A2
20 Kingston KT6 ...198 A4
Southall UB2 ...106 C2
2 Surbiton KT6 ...214 A6
Twickenham TW2 ...152 C1
Wandsworth SW18 ...157 D5
Wentworth Dr HA5 ...40 A4
Wentworth Dwellings
E1 ...243 C2
Wentworth Gdns N13 ..16 D1
Wentworth Hall NW7 ..28 C5
Wentworth Hill HA9 ...44 B1
Wentworth Lo N3 ...29 D3
Wentworth Mews E3 ...97 B4
Wentworth Pk N3 ...29 D3
Wentworth Pl HA7 ...25 B4
Wentworth Rd E12 ...77 D4
NW11 ...47 B3
Southall UB2 ...106 D2
Thornton Heath CR0 ...204 C2
Wentworth St
E1 ...95 D2 243 D3
Wentworth Way HA5 ...41 A5
Wenvoe Ave DA7 ...147 D3
Wepham Cl UB4 ...84 D2
Wernbrook St SE18 ...145 A6
Werndee Rd SE25 ...206 A5
Werneth Hall Rd IG5 ...56 C6
Werrington St
NW1 ...93 C5 232 B3
Werter Rd SW15 ...135 A1
Wesleyan Pl NW5 ...71 B4
Wesley Ave E16 ...121 B5
NW10 ...89 B4
Hounslow TW3 ...129 B3
Wesley Cl N7 ...72 B6
SE17 ...261 D3
Harrow HA2 ...64 A6
Wesley Ho SE24 ...161 B5
Wesley Rd E10 ...54 A2
N10 ...30 C2
NW10 ...89 A6
Hayes UB3 ...84 A1
Wesley Sq W11 ...91 A1
Wesley St W1 ...238 B3
Wessex Ave SW19 ...201 C6
Wessex Cl
Hinchley Wood KT10,
KT7 ...212 D6
Ilford IG3 ...57 C3
Kingston KT1,KT2 ...176 D2
Wessex Ct
Putney SW15 ...156 D6
5 Stanwell TW19 ...148 A5
Wessex Dr HA5 ...23 A3
Wessex Gardens Prim Sch
NW11 ...47 A1
Wessex Gdns NW11 ...47 A1
Wessex Ho 4 N19 ...71 D5
SE1 ...263 D1
Wessex La UB6 ...86 B5
Wessex Rd TW6 ...126 A2
Wessex St E2 ...96 C4
Wessex Way NW11 ...47 A1
Wesson Ho 3 CR0 ...206 A1
Westacott UB4 ...83 C2
Westacott Cl N19 ...49 D1
West Acton Prim Sch
W3 ...88 D1
West Acton Sta W3 ...88 C1
West App BR5 ...211 A4
West Arbour St E1 ...96 D1
West Ave E17 ...53 D4
N2 ...47 D6
N3 ...29 C4
NW4 ...46 D4
Hayes UB3 ...105 D6
Pinner HA5 ...41 B2
Southall UB1 ...107 B6
Wallington SM6 ...220 A3
West Avenue Rd E17 ...53 D5
West Bank N16 ...51 C2
Barking IG11 ...100 D6
Enfield EN2 ...5 A3
Westbank Rd TW12 ...174 A4
West Barnes La KT3,
SW20 ...200 B5
Westbeech Rd N22 ...50 C6
Westbere Dr HA7 ...25 D5
Westbere Rd NW2 ...69 A3
West Block 17 E1 ...118 C6
Westbourne Ave W3 ...89 B3
Cheam SM3 ...217 A6
Westbourne Cl UB4 ...84 C3
Westbourne Cres W2 .246 C6
Westbourne Ct W2 ...236 A2
Westbourne Dr SE23 .162 D2
Westbourne Gdns W2 .91 D1
Westbourne Gr
W11 ...113 B6 244 D6
W2,W11 ...91 C1
Westbourne Gr Mews 7
W11 ...91 C1
Westbourne Gr Terr
W2 ...91 D1
Westbourne Ho SW1 .258 C2
Heston TW5 ...129 C6
8 Twickenham TW1 ...153 B4
Westbourne Par 4
UB10 ...82 D3
Westbourne Park Rd
W11 ...91 B1
W2 ...91 C1
Westbourne Park Sta
W11 ...91 B2
Westbourne Park Villas
W2 ...91 C2
Westbourne Pl N9 ...18 B1
Westbourne Prim Sch
SM1 ...217 C5
Westbourne Rd DA7 ..147 A5
N7 ...72 B2
Croydon CR0 ...205 D3
Feltham TW13 ...149 D1
Hillingdon UB8 ...82 D3
Penge SE26 ...184 D4
Westbourne St
W2 ...114 B6 246 C6
Westbourne Terr
W2 ...92 A1 236 B2
Westbourne Terr Mews
W2 ...236 A2
Westbourne Terr Rd
W2 ...92 A2 236 A3
Westbridge Cl W12 ...112 A5
Westbridge Prim Sch
SW11 ...267 B2
Westbridge Rd
SW11 ...136 C4 267 A2
West Brompton Sta
SW5 ...113 C1 255 B1
Westbrook Ave TW12 .173 B3
Westbrook Cl EN4 ...2 B2
Westbrook Cres EN4 ...2 B2
Westbrook Ct SE3 ...143 B4
Westbrooke Cres
DA16 ...146 C2
Westbrooke Rd DA15 .167 B2
Bexley DA16 ...146 C2
Westbrooke Sch DA16 146 D2
Westbrook Ho 5 E2 ...96 C4
5 SW4 ...159 C6
Westbrook Rd SE3 ...143 B4
Heston TW5 ...129 B5
South Norwood CR7 ...183 B1
Westbrook Sq EN4 ...2 B2
West Brow BR7 ...188 D5
Westbury Ave
Claygate KT10 ...212 D2
Southall UB1 ...85 C3
Tottenham N22 ...32 D1
Wembley HA0 ...66 A1
Westbury Cl Ruislip HA4 .40 A2
Shepperton TW17 ...192 D3
Westbury Ct SW4 ...159 B5
3 Barking IG11 ...101 B6
Beckenham BR3 ...185 D2
1 Buckhurst Hill IG9 ...21 C2
Tottenham N22 ...33 A1
Westbury Gr N12 ...29 C4
Westbury Ho 1 E17 ...53 C5
Westbury House Sch The
KT3 ...199 B4
Westbury La IG9 ...21 C2
Westbury Lodge Cl
HA5 ...40 D6
Westbury Pl 2 TW8 ...131 D6
Westbury Rd E17 ...53 C5
E7 ...77 B2
N12 ...29 D5
Barking IG11 ...101 B6
Beckenham BR3 ...207 A6
Bowes Park N11 ...32 A4
Bromley BR1 ...187 D2
Buckhurst Hill IG9 ...21 C3
Ealing W5 ...88 A1
Feltham TW13 ...150 D3
Ilford IG1 ...78 C6
New Malden KT3 ...199 B4
Penge SE20 ...184 D2
Thornton Heath CR0 ...205 B3
Wembley HA0 ...66 A1
Westbury Terr E7 ...77 B2
Westbush Ct 1 W12 ...112 B4
West Carriage Dr
W2 ...114 C5 247 A4
West Central Ave NW10 90 B4
West Central St WC1 .240 A2
West Chantry HA3 ...23 D2
Westchester Ct NW4 ...46 D6
Westchester Dr NW4 ...46 D6
Westchester Ho W2 ..237 C1
West Cl Ashford TW15 ..170 A6
Barnet EN5 ...12 B6
Cockfosters EN4 ...3 A1
Edmonton N9 ...17 D1
Greenford UB6 ...86 A5
Wembley HA9 ...44 B1
Westcliff Ho 13 N1 ...73 B2
Westcombe Ave CR0 ..204 B2
Westcombe Ct 1 SE3 142 D5
Westcombe Dr EN5 ...13 C6
Westcombe Hill SE3,
SE10 ...143 A6
Westcombe Park Lo
UB4 ...83 B2
Westcombe Park Rd
SE3 ...142 D5
Westcombe Park Sta
SE3 ...121 A1
West Common Rd
BR2 ...225 B5
Westcoombe Ave
SW20 ...177 D2
Westcote Rd SW16 ...181 C5
Westcote Rise HA4 ...39 A2
Westcott Cl BR1 ...210 A4
2 N15 ...51 D3
Westcott Cres W7 ...86 C2
Westcott Ho 1 E14 ...119 D6
Westcott Rd SE17 ...138 D6
West Cotts NW6 ...69 C3
Westcroft Cl NW2 ...69 A4
Enfield EN3 ...6 C5
Westcroft Ct NW9 ...44 D4
3 W6 ...112 A2
Westcroft Gdns SM4 ..201 B5
Westcroft Rd SM5,SM6 219 A4
Westcroft Sq W6 ...112 A2
Westcroft Way NW2 ...69 A4
West Cromwell Rd
W14 ...113 B1 254 D2
West Cross Ctr TW8 ..131 B6
West Cross Route
W10,W11 ...112 D6
West Cross Way TW8 .131 B6
West Croydon Sta
CR9 ...205 A1
West Ct E17 ...53 D5
Hounslow TW7 ...130 A5
Wembley HA0 ...65 C6
Westdale Rd SE18 ...144 D6
Westdean Ave SE12 ...165 C3
Westdean Cl SW18 ...157 D5
Westdown Rd E15 ...76 A4
Catford SE6 ...163 C4
West Dr Stanmore HA3 ..24 B4
Streatham SW16 ...181 C6
West Drayton Park Ave
UB7 ...104 A3
West Drayton Prim Sch
UB7 ...104 A4
West Drayton Rd UB8 ..82 D1
West Drayton Sta UB7 104 A5
West Drive Gdns HA3 ..24 B4
West Dulwich Sta
SE21 ...161 B3
West Ealing Bsns Ctr
W13 ...109 A6
West Ealing Sta W13 .109 B6
West Eaton Pl SW1 ..258 A4
West Eaton Pl Mews
SW1 ...258 A4
West Ella Rd NW10 ...67 C1
West End Ave E10 ...54 B4
Pinner HA5 ...40 D5
West End Cl NW10 ...67 A1
West End Ct NW6 ...69 D1
Pinner HA5 ...40 D5
West End Gdns UB5 ...84 C5
West End La NW6 ...69 D2
Harlington UB7 ...127 A5
Pinner HA5 ...40 D5
West End Rd
Ruislip HA4,UB5 ...62 A4
Ruislip UB5 ...62 C1
Southall UB1 ...107 A5
Westerdale Ct N5 ...72 D4
Westerdale Rd 2
SE10 ...121 A1
Westerfield Rd 1 N15 .51 D4
Westergate W5 ...88 A2
Westergate Rd SE2 ...147 A6
Westerham NW1 ...232 A5
13 Kingston KT6 ...198 A4
Westerham Ave N9 ...17 C1
Westerham Dr DA15 ..168 B5
Westerham Ho SE1 ..262 D6
Westerham Lo 10 BR3 185 C3
Westerham Rd E10 ...53 D2
Keston BR2 ...225 D2
Westerland BR7 ...189 A4
Westerley Cres SE26 ..185 B5
Western Ave NW11 ...46 D3
W3 ...89 B1
Hillingdon HA4,UB4,UB5,
UB10 ...61 C1
Northolt UB5 ...85 C6
Northolt UB5,UB6 ...85 B6
Ruislip UB8,UB9,UB10 ...60 B3
Wembley UB6 ...87 C4

Western Avenue Bsns Pk W3 ... 88 D3
Western Ct N3 ... 29 C4
4 W3 ... 89 B1
3 W9 ... 91 B5
Southall UB2 ... 107 A3
Western Dr TW17 ... 193 B3
Western Eye Hospl The NW1 ... 92 D2 237 C4
Western Gdns W5 ... 110 C6
Western Ho 1 W9 ... 91 B3
Western International Market UB2 ... 106 B2
Western La SW12 ... 159 A4
Western Mews W9 ... 91 B3
Western Par EN5 ... 13 D6
Western Pl 13 SE16 ... 118 C4
Western Rd E13 ... 99 C5
E17 ... 54 A4
N2 ... 48 D5
NW10 ... 89 A3
SW9 ... 138 C2
Ealing W5 ... 109 D6
Mitcham CR4,SW19 ... 180 C1
Southall UB2 ... 106 D2
Sutton SM1 ... 217 C3
Wood Green N22 ... 32 B1
Western Terr W6 ... 112 A1
Western View UB3 ... 105 D4
Westernville Gdns IG2 ... 57 A2
Western Way SE28 ... 123 C4
New Barnet EN5 ... 13 D5
Western Wharf 2 SE15 ... 140 A6
West Ewell Inf Sch KT19 ... 215 B3
Westferry Cir E14 ... 119 C5
Westferry Rd E14 ... 119 C3
Westferry Sta E14 ... 119 C6
Westfield 1 BR6 ... 227 A3
NW3 ... 69 C4
Loughton IG10 ... 21 C6
Westfield Cl NW9 ... 45 A6
SW10 ... 266 A3
Cheam SM1 ... 217 B4
Enfield EN3 ... 7 A2
Westfield Ct 1 W10 ... 90 D4
Kingston KT6 ... 197 D4
Westfield Dr HA3 ... 43 D5
Westfield Gdns HA3 ... 43 D5
Westfield Ho 6 SE16 ... 118 D2
Westfield La HA3 ... 43 D5
Westfield Pk HA5 ... 23 B3
Westfield Rd NW7 ... 11 C1
Beckenham BR3 ... 185 B1
Cheam SM1 ... 217 B4
Croydon CR0 ... 220 D6
Dagenham RM9 ... 81 B4
Ealing W13 ... 109 A5
Kingston KT6 ... 197 D4
Mitcham CR4 ... 180 D1
Walton-on-T KT12 ... 195 A2
Westfields SW13 ... 133 D2
Westfields Ave SW13 ... 133 C2
Westfields Gdns RM6 ... 58 C3
Westfields Rd W3 ... 88 D2
Westfields Sch SW13 ... 133 D2
Westfield St SE18 ... 121 D3
Westfield Way E1 ... 97 A3
Ruislip HA4 ... 61 D5
West Finchley Sta N3 ... 29 D4
West Garden Pl W2 ... 237 B1
West Gate W5 ... 88 A4
Westgate Bsns Ctr W10 ... 90 D3
2 W10 ... 91 A3
Westgate Ct 16 SW9 ... 138 C2
6 Beckenham BR3 ... 186 A2
Lewisham SE12 ... 165 A3
Westgate Est TW14 ... 148 D3
Westgate Rd Beckenham BR3 ... 186 A2
Croydon SE25 ... 206 B5
Westgate St E8 ... 96 B6
Westgate Terr SW10 ... 135 D6 265 D6
West Gdns Mitcham SW19 ... 180 C4
Stepney E1 ... 118 B6
Westglade Ct HA3 ... 43 D4
West Gr SE10 ... 142 B4
Woodford IG8 ... 37 C5
West Green Pl UB6 ... 86 B6
West Green Prim Sch N15 ... 51 A5
West Green Rd N15 ... 51 B5
Westgrove La SE10 ... 142 A4
West Grove Prim Sch N14 ... 15 D4
West Halkin St SW1 ... 115 A3 258 A6
West Hallowes SE9 ... 166 A3
West Hall Rd TW9 ... 132 D4
West Ham Church Prim Sch E15 ... 98 D6
West Ham La E15 ... 76 C1
West Hampstead Mews NW6 ... 69 D2
West Hampstead Sta NW6 ... 69 C2
West Hampstead Thameslink Sta NW6 ... 69 C2
West Ham Sta E15 ... 98 C4
West Harding St EC4 ... 241 B2
West Harrow Sta HA1 ... 42 A3
West Hatch Manor HA4 ... 39 D2
Westhay Gdns SW14 ... 154 D6
West Heath Ave NW11 ... 47 C1
West Heath Cl NW3 ... 69 C5
West Heath Ct NW11 ... 47 C1
West Heath Dr NW11 ... 47 C1
West Heath Gdns NW3 ... 69 C5
West Heath Rd NW3 ... 69 D5
SE2 ... 146 D6
West Hill N6 ... 49 A1
Harrow HA2 ... 64 C6
Putney SW15 ... 157 A5
South Croydon CR2 ... 221 C1
Wembley HA9 ... 44 B1
Westhill Ct W11 ... 244 D6
West Hill Ct N6 ... 71 A5
West Hill Hall HA2 ... 64 C6
Westhill Pk N6 ... 70 D6
N6 ... 71 A6
West Hill Prim Sch SW18 ... 157 C6
West Hill Rd SW18 ... 157 B5
West Hill Way N20 ... 13 D3
West Ho Barking IG11 ... 78 D2
4 Penge SE20 ... 184 D3
9 Streatham SW12 ... 159 C4
Westholm NW11 ... 47 D5
Westholme BR6 ... 211 D2
Westholme Gdns HA4 ... 40 A1
Westhope Ho 18 E2 ... 96 A4
Westhorne Ave SE9, SE12 ... 165 C5
Westhorpe Gdns NW4 ... 46 C6
Westhorpe Rd SW15 ... 134 C2
West House Cl SW19 ... 157 A3
Westhurst Dr BR7 ... 188 D5
West India Ave E14 ... 119 C5
West India Dock Rd E14 ... 119 C6
West India Ho 1 E14 ... 119 C6
West India Quay Sta E14 ... 119 C6
West Kensington Ct W14 ... 254 C2
West Kensington Mans W14 ... 254 C1
West Kensington Sta W14 ... 113 B1 254 C2
West La SE16 ... 118 B4
Westlake 10 SE16 ... 118 C2
Westlake Cl Hayes UB4 ... 85 A3
Palmers Green N13 ... 16 C1
Westlake Rd HA9 ... 65 D6
Westland Cl TW19 ... 148 A5
Westland Ct 9 UB5 ... 84 D4
Westland Dr BR2,BR4 ... 224 D6
Westland Ho 1 E16 ... 122 C5
Westland Lo 1 BR1 ... 187 C1
Westland Pl N1 ... 235 C2
Westlands Cl UB3 ... 106 A2
Westlands Ct KT8 ... 196 C5
Westlands Terr 3 SW12 ... 159 C5
Westlea Rd W7 ... 109 A3
West Lea Sch N9 ... 17 C1
Westleigh Ave SW15 ... 156 C6
Westleigh Ct N12 ... 29 D4
12 Wanstead E11 ... 55 A4
Westleigh Dr BR1 ... 188 A2
Westleigh Gdns HA8 ... 26 C1
West Links HA0 ... 87 D4
Westlinton Cl NW7 ... 29 A4
West Lodge Ave W3 ... 110 C5
West Lodge Ct W3 ... 110 C5
West Lodge Fst & Mid Schs HA5 ... 40 D5
West Lodge Sch DA15 ... 168 A1
West London Shooting Grounds UB5 ... 84 B5
West London Stad The W12 ... 90 B2
Westly Ct NW2 ... 68 D2
Westmacott Dr TW14 ... 149 D3
Westmacott Ho NW8 ... 236 D5
West Mall W11 ... 245 B4
Westmark Point 13 SW15 ... 156 B3
Westmead SW15 ... 156 B5
West Mead Ruislip HA4 ... 62 C4
West Ewell KT19 ... 215 C2
Westmead Cnr SM5 ... 218 C4
Westmead Rd SM1 ... 218 B4
Westmeath Ho NW2 ... 68 A5
Westmere Dr NW7 ... 11 B1
West Mersea Cl 9 E16 ... 121 B5
West Mews SW1 ... 259 A3
West Middlesex Univ Hosp TW7 ... 131 A3
Westmill Ct N4 ... 73 A6
Westminster Abbey★ SW1 ... 116 A3 260 A6
Westminster Abbey Choir Sch SW1 ... 115 D3 259 D6
Westminster Ave CR7 ... 182 D1
Westminster Boating Base SW1 ... 269 C6
Westminster Bridge SE1,SW1 ... 116 A4 250 B1
Westminster Bridge Rd SE1 ... 116 B4 250 C1
Westminster Cath★ SW1 ... 115 C3 259 A5
Westminster Cath Choir Sch SW1 ... 115 C2 259 B4
Westminster Cath RC Prim Sch SW1 ... 115 D1 259 D2
Westminster City Hall SW1 ... 259 B6
Westminster City Sch SW1 ... 259 B6
Westminster Cl East Bedfont TW14 ... 150 A3
Teddington TW11 ... 175 A5
Westminster Coll of Bsns & Computing HA9 ... 66 A3
Westminster Ct 22 SE16 ... 118 D5
5 SW18 ... 157 C6
South Norwood CR7 ... 183 A1
Wanstead E11 ... 55 B3
Westminster Dr N13 ... 32 A5
Westminster Gdns SW1 ... 260 A4
Barking IG11 ... 101 C5
Chingford, Chingford Green E4 ... 20 C3
Westminster Ind Est E16 ... 121 D3
Westminster Kingsway Coll SW11 ... 137 A4 268 B2
WC1 ... 94 B4 233 C1
Westminster Pier SW1 ... 250 B1
Westminster Rd Carshalton SM1,SM5 ... 218 B6
Ealing W7 ... 108 C5
Edmonton N9 ... 18 B3
Westminster Sch SW1 ... 116 A3 260 A6
Westminster Sta SW1 ... 116 A4 250 B1
Westmoat Cl BR3 ... 186 A3
Westmont Rd KT10 ... 212 C6
Westmoor Gdns EN3 ... 6 D3
Westmoor Rd EN3 ... 6 D3
Westmoor St SE7 ... 121 D3
Westmore Ct SW15 ... 157 A6
Westmoreland Ave DA16 ... 145 C1
Westmoreland Ho NW10 ... 90 A4
Westmoreland Pl 5 BR1 ... 209 A6
SW1 ... 258 D1
Ealing W5 ... 87 D2
Westmoreland Rd BR2 ... 209 A5
HA3,NW9 ... 44 B5
SE17 ... 139 B6
Barnes SW13 ... 134 A4
Beckenham BR2,BR3 ... 208 D5
Westmoreland St W1 ... 238 B3
Westmoreland Terr SW1 ... 115 B1 258 D1
Penge SE20 ... 184 B3
Westmorland Cl 3 Twickenham TW1 ... 153 B5
Wanstead E12 ... 77 D6
Westmorland Ct 12 KT6 ... 197 D2
Westmorland Dr SM2 ... 217 D1
Westmorland Rd BR2 ... 209 A5
E17 ... 53 C3
Harrow HA1 ... 41 D4
Westmorland Sq CR4 ... 204 A4
Westmorland Way CR4 ... 203 D4
Westmount Ct W5 ... 88 B2
Westmount Rd SE9 ... 144 C1
West Norwood Sta SE27 ... 160 D1
West Oak BR3 ... 186 B2
Westoe Rd N9 ... 18 B2
Weston Ave East Molesey KT8 ... 195 B5
Thames Ditton KT10,KT7 ... 196 C2
Westonbirt Ct 6 SE15 ... 139 D6
Weston Ct N20 ... 14 A4
N4 ... 73 A5
3 Kingston KT1 ... 198 A6
Weston Dr HA7 ... 25 B2
Weston Ed Ctr The SE5 ... 139 A3
West One Ho W1 ... 239 A3
Westone Mans 5 IG11 ... 79 D1
Weston Gdns TW7 ... 130 C4
Weston Gn Dagenham RM9 ... 81 B4
Thames Ditton KT7 ... 196 C1
Weston Gr 1 BR1 ... 186 D2
Weston Green Prep Sch KT7 ... 196 C1
Weston Green Rd KT7 ... 196 C2
Weston Ho 9 E9 ... 96 C6
4 NW6 ... 69 A1
Weston Park Cl KT7 ... 196 C1
Weston Park Prim Sch N8 ... 50 B4
Weston Pk N8 ... 50 B3
Kingston KT1 ... 176 A1
Thames Ditton KT10,KT7 ... 196 C1
Weston Rd W4 ... 111 A3
Bromley BR1 ... 186 D3
Dagenham RM9 ... 81 A4
Enfield EN2 ... 5 B3
Ruislip HA4 ... 61 D1
Thames Ditton KT7 ... 196 C1
Weston Rise N1, WC1 ... 94 B4 233 D2
Weston St SE1 ... 117 B4 252 D2
Weston Wlk 3 E8,E9 ... 74 B1
Westover Hill NW3 ... 69 C6
Westover Rd SW18 ... 158 A5
Westow Hill SE19 ... 183 D4
Westow St SE19 ... 183 C4
Westpark W5 ... 87 D1
West Park Ave TW9 ... 132 D4
West Park Cl Heston TW5 ... 129 B6
Ilford RM6 ... 58 D4
West Park Rd Richmond TW9 ... 132 C4
Southall UB2 ... 108 B5
West Parkside SE10 ... 121 A2
Greenwich SE10 ... 120 D3
West Pk SE9 ... 166 A3
West Pl SW19 ... 178 C5
West Point 2 SE1 ... 118 A1
Westpoint Beckenham BR2 ... 208 B6
Putney SW15 ... 156 D5
Westpoint Trad Est W3 ... 88 D2
Westpole Ave EN4 ... 3 B1
Westport Ct UB4 ... 84 C3
Westport Rd E13 ... 99 B3
Westport St E1 ... 96 D1
West Poultry Ave EC1 ... 241 C3
West Quarters W12 ... 90 A1
West Quay Dr UB4 ... 85 A2
West Ramp TW6 ... 126 C4
West Rd E15 ... 98 D6
N2 ... 30 B2
SW3 ... 136 D6 267 D6
SW4 ... 159 D6
Dagenham RM6 ... 59 A3
Ealing W5 ... 88 A2
East Barnet EN4 ... 15 A3
East Bedfont TW14 ... 149 B4
Kingston KT2,KT3 ... 177 A2
Tottenham N17 ... 34 B4
West Drayton UB7 ... 104 B3
West Ridge Gdns UB6 ... 86 A5
West Row W10 ... 91 A3
Westrow SW15 ... 156 C5
Westrow Dr IG11 ... 80 A2
Westrow Gdns IG3 ... 79 D5
West Ruislip Elementary Sch UB10 ... 61 A5
West Ruislip Sta HA4 ... 61 A6
West Sheen Vale TW9 ... 132 B1
Westside N2 ... 48 D6
NW4 ... 28 B1
West Side Comm SW19 ... 178 C5
Westside Ct 1 W9 ... 91 C3
West Smithfield EC1 ... 94 D2 241 D3
West Sq SE11 ... 116 D3 261 C5
West St BR1 ... 187 A1
DA7 ... 147 B2
E11 ... 76 C5
E17 ... 53 D4
26 E2 ... 96 B5
WC2 ... 93 D1 239 D1
Carshalton SM5 ... 218 D4
Croydon CR0 ... 221 A4
Harrow HA1 ... 42 C1
Sutton SM1 ... 217 D3
West Street La SM5 ... 218 D4
West Street Pl 1 CR0 ... 221 A4
West Surrey Ests TW15 ... 171 A2
West Sutton Sta SM1 ... 217 C4
West Temple Sheen SW14 ... 154 D6
West Tenter St E1 ... 95 D1 243 D1
West Terr DA15 ... 167 C3
West Thames Coll TW7 ... 130 C4
West Thamesmead Bsns Pk SE28 ... 123 D3
West Thornton Prim Sch CR0 ... 204 B3
West Towers HA5 ... 40 D3
West Twyford Prim Sch NW10 ... 88 C5
Westvale Mews W3 ... 111 C4
Westview W7 ... 86 C1
West View Dagenham RM6 ... 58 C4
East Bedfont TW14 ... 149 A4
Westview Cl NW10 ... 67 D3
W10 ... 90 C1
Westview Cres N9 ... 17 C4
Westview Ct 3 WD6 ... 9 D5
Westview Dr IG8 ... 37 D1
West View Gdns WD6 ... 9 D5
Westville Rd W12 ... 112 A4
Thames Ditton KT7 ... 197 A2
Westward Rd E4 ... 35 B5
Westward Way HA3 ... 44 A3
West Warwick Pl SW1 ... 259 A3
Westway W10,W12 ... 112 A6
West Way BR5 ... 211 B4
HA8 ... 27 A4
NW10 ... 67 B5
Westway SW20 ... 200 C5
West Way Croydon CR0 ... 223 A5
Edmonton N18 ... 33 B6
Hounslow TW5 ... 129 B4
Pinner HA5 ... 40 D5
Ruislip HA4 ... 39 D1
Shepperton TW17 ... 193 B3
West Wickham BR4 ... 208 C3
Westway Cl SW20 ... 200 B6
Westway Cross Sh Pk UB6 ... 86 C6
Westway Ct UB5 ... 85 C6
Westway (Elevated Rd) W10 ... 91 B2
West Way Gdns CR0 ... 222 D6
Westway Lo 35 W2 ... 91 C2
Westways KT19 ... 215 D4
West Ways HA6 ... 22 A1
Westwell 4 NW5 ... 71 A2
Westwell Rd SW16 ... 182 A4
Westwell Road App SW16 ... 182 A4
Westwick 7 KT1 ... 176 C1
Westwick Gdns W14 ... 112 D4
Cranford TW4,TW5 ... 128 B3
West Wickham Sta BR3 ... 208 A2
West Wlk East Barnet EN4 ... 15 A3
Hayes UB3 ... 106 A5
Westwood Ave Harrow HA2 ... 63 D4
South Norwood SE19 ... 183 A2
Westwood Cl BR1 ... 209 D6
Esher KT10 ... 212 A5
Ruislip HA4 ... 38 D3
Westwood Ct Enfield EN1 ... 17 C5
3 Forest Hill SE23 ... 162 C3
7 Wimbledon SW19 ... 179 B5
Westwood Gdns SW13 ... 133 D2
Westwood Hill SE26 ... 184 B6
Westwood Ho 5 N4 ... 51 B2
W12 ... 112 C5
Westwood La DA16 ... 145 D1
Westwood Language College for Girls SE19 ... 183 B3
Westwood Pk SE23 ... 162 B4
Westwood Pl SE26 ... 184 A6
Westwood Prim Sch DA16 ... 145 C1
Westwood Rd 12 E16 ... 121 B5
Barnes SW13 ... 133 D2
Ilford IG3 ... 58 A2
Westwood Sch WD23 ... 8 B2
West Woodside DA5 ... 169 A3
Westwood Tech Coll DA16 ... 145 C1
Wetheral Ct SW17 ... 180 B6
Wetheral Dr HA7 ... 25 C1
Wetherby Cl UB5 ... 63 D2
Wetherby Ct SE25 ... 183 C1
Wetherby Gdns SW5 ... 114 A2 256 A3
Wetherby Mans SW5 ... 255 C2
Wetherby Mews SW5 ... 255 D2
Wetherby Pl SW7 ... 114 A2 256 B3
Wetherby Rd EN2 ... 5 A4
Wetherby Way KT9 ... 214 A1
Wetherden St E17 ... 53 B2
Wetherell Rd E9 ... 96 D6
Wetherill Rd N10 ... 31 A2
Wetland Centre The★ SW13 ... 134 B5
Wevco Wharf SE15 ... 140 B6
Wexford Ho 9 E1 ... 96 C2
Wexford Rd SW12 ... 158 D4
Weybourne St SW18 ... 158 A2
Weybridge Ct 19 SE16 ... 118 B1
Weybridge Ho N4 ... 51 A2
Weybridge Point 11 SW11 ... 136 D3
Weybridge Rd CR7 ... 204 C5
Wey Ct KT19 ... 215 A4
Weydown Cl SW19 ... 157 A3
Weyhill Ho 27 SE5 ... 139 A3
Weyhill Rd 6 E1 ... 96 A1
Wey Ho NW8 ... 236 D5
Weylands Cl KT12 ... 195 B1
Weylond Rd RM8 ... 81 B5
Weyman Rd SE3 ... 143 C4
Weymarks The N17 ... 33 B4
Weymouth Ave NW7 ... 27 C5
W5 ... 109 C3
Weymouth Cl 1 E6 ... 100 D1
Weymouth Ct 5 E2 ... 95 D5
Belmont SM2 ... 217 C1
15 Streatham SW2 ... 160 B4
Weymouth Ho SW8 ... 270 C3
Bromley BR2 ... 186 D1
Weymouth Mews W1 ... 93 B2 238 C4
Weymouth Rd UB4 ... 83 C4
Weymouth St W1 ... 93 B2 238 C4
Weymouth Terr E2 ... 95 D5
Weymouth Wlk HA7 ... 25 A4
Whadcoat St N4 ... 72 C6
Whadden Ho 10 SE5 ... 139 C2
Whaddon Ho SW1 ... 247 D1
Whalebone Ave RM6 ... 59 B3
Whalebone Gr RM6 ... 59 B3
Whalebone La E15 ... 76 C1
Whalebone La N RM6 ... 59 A6
Whalebone La S RM6, RM8 ... 59 B2
Whales Yd E15 ... 76 C1
Wharfdale Cl N11 ... 31 A4
Wharfdale Rd N1 ... 94 A5 233 B4
Wharfedale Ct 5 E5 ... 74 D4
Wharfedale Gdns CR7, SW16 ... 204 B6
Wharfedale St SW10 ... 255 C1
Wharf La TW1 ... 153 A3
Wharf Pl E2 ... 96 B6
Wharf Rd E15 ... 98 B6
N1 ... 95 A5 235 A3
NW1 ... 93 D6 232 D5
Enfield EN3 ... 19 A5
Wharfside HA0 ... 88 A6
Wharfside Rd E16 ... 98 C2
Wharf St E16 ... 98 C2
Wharncliffe Dr UB1 ... 108 B5
Wharncliffe Gdns SE25 ... 183 C1
Wharncliffe Rd SE25 ... 183 C1
Wharton Cl NW10 ... 67 C2
Wharton Ho SE1 ... 263 C6
Wharton Rd BR1 ... 187 B2
Wharton St WC1 ... 94 B4 233 D1
Whateley Rd SE22 ... 161 D6
Penge SE20 ... 184 D3
Whatley Ave SW20 ... 201 A6
Whatman Rd SE23 ... 162 D4
Wheatfields E6 ... 100 D1
Enfield EN3 ... 7 A3
Wheatfield Way KT1 ... 176 A1
Wheathill Ho SE20 ... 184 B1
Wheathill Rd SE20 ... 206 B6
Wheatland Ho 7 SE22 ... 139 C2
Wheatlands TW5 ... 129 C6
Wheatlands Rd SW17 ... 159 A1
Wheatley Cl NW4 ... 28 A1
Wheatley Gdns N9 ... 17 C2
Wheatley Ho NW5 ... 71 B4
3 Putney SW15 ... 156 A4
Wheatley Mans 8 IG11 ... 80 A1
Wheatley Rd TW7 ... 130 D2
Wheatley's Ait TW16 ... 194 A4
Wheatley St W1 ... 238 B3
Wheatly Cres UB3 ... 106 A6
Wheat Sheaf Cl E14 ... 119 D2
Wheatsheaf Cl UB5 ... 63 A3
Wheatsheaf La SW6 ... 134 C5
SW8 ... 270 B4
Wheatsheaf Par 6 BR4 ... 207 D1
Wheatsheaf Terr SW6 ... 264 D3
Wheatstone Cl SW19 ... 180 C2
Wheatstone Ho 7 W10 ... 91 A2
Wheatstone Rd W10 ... 91 A2
Wheeler 2 NW9 ... 27 D3
Wheeler Ct 5 SW11 ... 136 B2
Wheeler Gdns N1 ... 233 B6
Wheelers Cross IG11 ... 101 B5
Wheelers Dr HA4 ... 39 A3
Wheeler's St SM1 ... 217 C5
Wheelock Cl DA8 ... 147 D5
Wheelwright St N7 ... 72 B1
Whelan Way SM6 ... 219 D5
Wheldon Ct SE1 ... 253 C2
Wheler Ho E1 ... 243 C5
Wheler St E1 ... 95 D3 243 C5
Whellock Rd W4 ... 111 C3
Whernside Cl SE28 ... 124 C6
Whetstone Cl N20 ... 14 B2
Whetstone Park WC2 ... 94 B1 240 C2
Whetstone Rd SE3 ... 143 D4
Whewell Rd N19 ... 72 A6
Whichcote St SE1 ... 251 A3

Whidborne Bldgs WC1 233 A1
Whidborne Cl SE8 141 C3
Whidborne St WC1 233 B1
Whimbrel Cl SE28 124 C6
Whimbrel Way UB4 84 D2
Whinchat Rd SE18, SE28 123 B3
Whinfell Cl SW16 181 D5
Whinyates Rd SE9 144 A2
Whippendell Cl BR5 190 B2
Whippendell Way BR5 190 B1
Whippingham Ho 17 E3 97 B4
Whipps Cross E17 54 B4
Whipps Cross Ho E17 54 B4
Whipps Cross Hospl E10,E11 54 B3
Whipps Cross Rd E11 54 C3
Whiskin St EC1 94 D4 234 C1
Whisperwood Cl HA3 24 C3
Whistler Gdns HA8 26 B1
Whistler Mews 2 SE15 139 D5
Dagenham RM8 80 B3
Whistlers Ave SW11 136 B5 266 D3
Whistler St N5 72 D3
Whistler Twr SW10 266 A3
Whistler Wlk SW10 266 B4
Whiston Ho 18 N1 72 D1
Whiston Rd E2 96 A6
Whitakers Lo EN2 5 B4
Whitbread Cl N17 34 A2
Whitbread Ctr EC1 242 C5
Whitbread Rd SE4 141 B1
Whitburn Rd SE13 142 A1
Whitby Ave NW10 88 D4
Whitby Ct N7 72 A4
Whitby Gdns NW9 44 C6
Carshalton SM1,SM5 218 B6
Whitby Ho NW8 229 A5
Whitby Rd SE18 122 B2
Carshalton SM1,SM5 218 B6
Harrow HA2 64 A5
Ruislip HA4 62 C6
Whitby St E1 243 C6
Whitcher Cl SE14 141 A6
Whitcher Pl NW1 71 C2
Whitchurch Ave HA8 26 B3
Whitchurch Cl HA8 26 B4
Whitchurch Ct SW17 180 B6
Whitchurch Fst & Mid Schs HA7 25 D3
Whitchurch Gdns HA8 26 B4
Whitchurch Ho 16 W10 90 D1
Catford SE6 164 A1
Whitchurch La HA8 26 B3
Whitchurch Rd W11 112 D6
Whitcomb Ct W1 249 D5
Whitcombe Mews TW9 132 D4
Whitcomb St WC2 115 D6 249 D5
Whiteadder Way E14 119 D2
Whitear Wlk E15 76 B2
Whitebarn La RM10 103 C6
Whitebeam Ave BR2 210 C3
Whitebeam Cl SW9 270 D3
Whitebeam Ho 3 NW3 70 D2
White Bear Pl NW3 70 B4
White Bear Yd EC1 241 A5
White Bridge Ave CR4 202 B6
White Bridge Cl TW14 149 D5
White Butts Rd HA4 62 D5
Whitechapel High St E1 95 D1 243 D2
Whitechapel Rd E1 96 B2
Whitechapel Sta E1 96 B2
Whitechurch La 2 E1 96 A1
White City W10 90 C1
White City Cl W12 112 C6
White City Est 21 W12 112 B6
White City Rd W12 112 C6
White City Sta W12 112 C6
Whitecliff Ho SW18 157 D5
White Conduit St N1 234 B4
Whitecote Rd UB1 86 A1
White Craig Cl HA5 23 C5
Whitecroft Cl BR3 208 B5
Whitecroft Way BR3 208 B5
Whitecross Pl EC2 242 D4
Whitecross St EC1 95 A3 242 B5
White Cube art gallery* N1 95 C4
Whitefield Ave NW2 46 C1
Whitefield Cl SW15 157 A5
Whitefield Sch NW11 46 D2
Chingford E17 36 A1
Whitefoot La BR1 164 B1
Whitefoot Terr BR1 164 D1
Whitefriars Ave HA3 24 C1
Whitefriars Centre Coll HA3 42 C6
Whitefriars Ct N12 30 B5
Whitefriars Dr HA3 24 C1
Whitefriars Fst & Mid Sch HA3 24 C1
Whitefriars St EC4 94 C1 241 B1
Whitefriars Trad Est HA3 24 B1
White Gate Gdns HA3 24 D3
Whitegates 4 EN5 13 D6
White Gdns RM10 81 C2
Whitehall SW1 250 A2
Whitehall Cres KT9 213 D3
Whitehall Ct SW1 116 A5 250 B3
Whitehall Gdns SW1 250 A3
Acton W3 110 C5
Chingford, Chingford Green E4 20 C3
Chiswick W4 132 D6
Whitehall La IG9 21 A2
Whitehall Lo N10 49 A6
Woodford IG8 21 A1
Whitehall Mans 3 N19 49 C1
Whitehall Park Rd W4 132 D6
Whitehall Pk N19 49 C1
Whitehall Pl WC2,SW1 116 A5 250 A3
Wallington SM5 219 B4
Whitehall Prim Sch E4 20 C2
Whitehall Rd W7 109 A4
Bromley BR2 209 D5
Chingford E4 20 C2
Harrow HA1 42 C2
Thornton Heath CR7 204 C4
Woodford IG8 21 A1
Whitehall St N17 33 D3
White Hart Ct EC2 243 A3
White Hart La NW10 67 D2
Mortlake SW13 133 C2
White Hart Lane Sch N22 32 D3
White Hart Lane Sta N17 33 D3
White Hart Lane (Tottenham Hotspur FC) N17 34 A3
White Hart Rd SE18 123 C2
White Hart Rdbt UB5 84 D5
White Hart St EC4 241 D2
SE11 116 C1 261 B2
White Hart Terr N17 33 D3
White Hart Yd SE1 252 C3
Whitehaven Cl BR2 209 A5
Whitehaven St NW8 237 A5
Whitehead Cl Edmonton N18 33 B5
Wandsworth SW18 158 A4
Whitehead Ct N10 31 A2
Whitehead Ho 8 SW15 156 D6
Whitehead's Gr SW3 114 C2 257 B3
White Heart Ave UB8 83 A2
Whiteheath Ave HA4 39 A2
Whiteheath Inf Sch HA4 39 A3
Whiteheath Jun Sch HA4 39 A2
White Heron Mews TW11 174 D4
White Ho N9 18 C2
2 SW11 136 B3
3 Streatham SW4 159 D4
Whitehorn Ho 6 E1 118 C5
White Horse Hill BR7, SE9 188 C6
White Horse La E1 96 D2
Whitehorse La SE25 205 C5
Whitehorse Manor Inf Sch CR7 205 B5
Whitehorse Manor Jun Sch CR7 205 B5
Whitehorse Mews SE1 261 C6
Whitehorse Rd E1 97 A2
White Horse Rd E1 97 A1
E6 100 B4
Whitehorse Rd CR0, CR7 205 B3
White Horse St W1 115 B5 248 D3
White Horse Yd EC2 242 C2
White Ho The N17 51 C6
NW1 238 D6
White House Ct N14 15 D2
1 Beckenham BR3 186 A2
White House Dr HA7 25 C6
Whitehouse Est E10 54 A3
White House La EN2 5 A4
Whitehouse Way N14 15 B1
White Kennett St E1 243 B2
Whitelands Coll, Roehampton, Univ of Surrey SW18 157 A4
Whitelands Ho SW3 257 D2
Whiteledges W13 87 C1
Whitelegg Rd E13 98 D5
Whiteley Ho 9 SW4 159 D4
Whiteley Rd SE19 183 B5
Whiteleys Ctr W2 91 D1
Whiteleys Ho TW13 151 C1
Whiteleys Par 5 UB10 82 D3
Whiteleys Way TW13 151 C1
White Lion Ct EC3 243 A1
White Lion Hill EC4 116 D6 251 D6
White Lion St N1 94 C5 234 B3
White Lion Yd W1 248 C6
White Lo 7 Ealing W5 87 C2
South Norwood SE19 182 D3
Whitelock Ho 21 E9 74 D2
White Lodge Cl N2 48 B3
Sutton SM2 218 A1
White Lodge The Royal Ballet Sch TW10 155 B3
Whitely Ct TW13 151 B1
Whiteness Ho 18 SW9 138 C4
White Oak Dr BR3 186 A1
White Oak Gdns DA15 167 D4
Whiteoak Ho SE19 183 A3
Whiteoaks La UB6 86 B5
White Orchards Barnet N20 13 B3
Stanmore HA7 25 A5
White Post La E9 75 C2
White Post St SE14, SE15 140 C5
White Rd E15 76 C1
Whites Ave IG2 57 C3
Whites Dr BR2 208 D2
White's Grounds SE1 117 C4 253 B2
White's Grounds Est SE1 253 B2
White's Mdw BR1 210 C5
White's Row E1 95 D2 243 C3
White's Sq SW4 137 D1
White St UB2 106 D4
Whitestile Rd TW8 109 D1
Whitestone La NW3 70 A5
Whitestone Wlk NW3 70 A5
Whitethorn Ave UB7 104 B6
Whitethorn Gdns Croydon CR0 222 B6
Enfield EN2 17 B6
Whitethorn Pl UB7 104 B5
Whitethorn St E3 97 C2
Whiteways NW4 46 D5
Whitewebbs Way BR5 189 D2
Whitfield Ct SW4 270 A1
3 Dulwich SE21 183 C6
Redbridge IG1 56 B2
Whitfield Gdns W1 239 B4
Whitfield Ho NW8 237 A5
Whitfield Pl W1 239 B5
Whitfield Rd DA7 147 B5
E6 77 C1
SE10,SE13 142 B4
Whitfield St W1 93 C2 239 B4
Whitford Gdns CR4 202 D6
Whitgift Ave CR2 221 A3
Whitgift Ct CR2 221 A3
Whitgift Ctr CR0 221 A6
Whitgift Ho SE11 260 C4
SW11 267 A2
Croydon CR2 221 A3
Whitgift Sch CR2 221 A3
Whitgift St SE11 116 B2 260 C4
Croydon CR0 221 A5
Whiting Ave IG11 78 D1
Whitings Hill Prim Sch EN5 12 C6
Whitings Rd EN5 12 C6
Whitings The IG2 57 C4
Whitings Way E6 100 C2
Whitington Ave EC3 243 A1
Whitland Rd SM5 202 B1
Whitley Cl TW19 148 A5
Whitley Ho SW1 269 B6
Whitley Rd N17 33 C1
Whitlock Dr SW19 157 A3
Whitman Ho 20 E2 96 C4
Whitman Rd E3 97 A3
Whitmead Cl CR2 221 C2
Whitmore Cl N11 31 B5
Whitmore Comm Sch N1 235 C6
Whitmore Gdns NW10 90 C5
Whitmore High Sch HA1,HA2 42 A1
Whitmore Ho 20 E1 95 C6
N11 30 D6
Whitmore Rd N1 95 C6
Beckenham BR3 207 B6
Harrow HA1 42 A2
Whitnell Ct 7 SW15 156 D6
Whitnell Way SW15 156 D6
Whitney Ave IG4 55 D5
Whitney Ho 6 SE22 139 C2
Whitney Rd E10 53 D2
Whitney Wlk DA14 191 A4
Whitstable Cl Beckenham BR3 185 B2
Ruislip HA4 61 C6
Whitstable Ho 11 W10 90 D1
Whitstable Pl 9 CR0 221 A4
Whitsters Ho SE1 253 C2
Whittaker 3 NW9 27 D3
Whittaker Ave TW10, TW9 153 D6
Whittaker Ct SW4 270 B1
Whittaker Pl 24 TW10 153 D6
Whittaker Rd E6 77 D1
Cheam SM3 217 B5
Whittaker St SW1 258 A3
Whittaker Way 17 SE1 118 A2
Whittam Ho SE27 183 A5
Whitta Rd E12 77 D4
Whittell Gdns SE26 162 C1
Whitten Lo N12 30 C6
Whittingham 6 N17 34 B3
Whittingham Ct W4 133 C5
Whittingstall Mans SW6 264 D1
Whittingstall Rd SW6 135 B4 264 D1
Whittington Ave UB4 83 D2
Whittington Ct N2 48 D4
Penge SE20 184 B1
Whittington Hospl The N19 71 C6
Whittington Mews N12 30 A6
Whittington Rd N22 32 A3
Whittington Way HA5 41 A4
Whittle 4 NW9 27 D3
Whittlebury Cl SM5 218 D1
Whittlebury Ho N4 51 A2
Whittle Cl E17 53 A2
Southall UB1 85 D1
Whittle Rd Heston TW5 128 C5
Southall UB2 107 D4
Whittlesea Cl HA3 24 A3
Whittlesea Path HA3 24 A2
Whittlesea Rd HA3 24 A2
Whittlesea Sch HA3 24 A3
Whittlesey St SE1 116 C5 251 B3
Whitton NW3 70 D1
Whitton Ave E UB6 65 A2
Whitton Ave W UB5,UB6 64 B3
Whitton Cl UB6 65 B2
Whitton Dene Isleworth TW3,TW7 152 B5
Isleworth TW3,TW7 152 B6
Whitton Dr UB6 65 A2
Whitton Manor Rd TW7 152 A5
Whitton Rd Hounslow TW3 151 D6
Twickenham TW1 153 A4
Whitton Road Rdbt TW1 152 D5
Whitton Sch TW2 151 D2
Whitton Sta TW2 152 A4
Whitton Waye TW2, TW3 151 C5
Whitton Wlk E3 97 C4
Whitwell Ho 11 E5 74 B6
Whitwell Rd E13 99 A4
Whitworth Cres EN3 7 C6
Whitworth Ho SE1 262 B5
Whitworth Rd SE18 144 C5
South Norwood SE25 205 D5
Whitworth St SE10 120 C1
Whorlton Rd SE15 140 B2
Whychcote Point NW2 46 C2
Whymark Ave N22 50 D6
Whytecroft TW5 128 D5
Whyteville Ho E7 77 B2
Whyteville Rd E7 77 B2
Whytlaw Ho 11 E3 97 B2
Wickers Oake SE19 183 D6
Wicker St 2 E1 96 B1
Wicket Rd UB6 87 A4
Wickets The TW15 170 A6
Wicket The CR0 223 C3
Wickfield Ho 29 SE16 118 A4
Wickford Ho 4 E1 96 C3
Wickford St E1 96 C3
Wickford Way E17 52 D5
Wickham Ave Cheam KT4,SM3 216 C3
Croydon CR0 207 A1
Wickham Chase BR4 208 C2
Wickham Cl E1 96 C2
Enfield EN3 6 C2
New Malden KT3 199 D4
Wickham Common Prim Sch BR4 225 A4
Wickham Court Rd BR4 224 A6
Wickham Cres BR4 224 A6
Wickham Ct DA16 145 C3
Wickham Gdns SE4 141 B2
Wickham Ho SW15 156 D5
Wickham La SE2,SE18 146 A6
Wickham Mews SE4 141 B3
Wickham Rd SE4 141 B2
Beckenham BR3 207 D6
Chingford E4 36 A3
Croydon CR0 207 B1
Harrow HA3 24 B1
Wickham St DA16 146 A4
SE11 116 B1 260 C2
Bexley DA16 145 C3
Wickham Way BR3 208 A4
Wick Ho 1 KT1 175 D2
Wick La E3 75 B1
E3 97 C6
Wickliffe Ave N3 29 A1
Wickliffe Gdns HA9 66 D6
Wicklow Ct SE26 184 C5
Wicklow Ho N16 51 D1
Wicklow St WC1 94 B4 233 C2
Wick Mews 1 E9 75 A2
Wick Rd E9 75 A2
Hackney E9 74 D2
Teddington TW11 175 C3
Wicks Cl SE12 187 D6
Wick Sq E9 75 B2
Wickstead Ho TW8 110 B1
Wicksteed Ho SE1 262 B5
Wickway Ct 7 SE15 139 D6
Wickwood St SE5 138 D3
Widdenham Rd N7 72 B4
Widdicombe Ave HA2 63 A6
Widdin St E15 76 C1
Widecombe Ct N2 48 B4
Widecombe Gdns IG4 56 A5
Widecombe Ho 33 SE5 139 A3
Widecombe Rd SE9 166 A1
Widecombe Way N2 48 B5
Widegate St E1 243 B3
Widenham Cl HA5 40 C4
Wide Way CR4 203 D6
Widewing Cl TW11 175 B3
Widford 8 NW1 71 B2
Widford Ho N1 234 C3
Widgeon Cl E16 99 B1
Widgeon Path SE28 123 B3
Widley Rd W9 91 C3
Widmer Ct TW5 129 A3
Widmore Lodge Rd BR1 187 D1
Widmore Rd BR1 187 C1
Hillingdon UB8 82 D3
Widnes Ho 6 N7 72 C3
Wieland Rd HA6 22 A3
Wigan Ho E5 52 B1
Wigeon Way UB4 84 D1
Wiggins La TW10 153 C2
Wiggins Mead NW9 27 D3
Wigginton Ave HA9 66 D2
Wightman Rd N4,N8 50 C4
Wighton Mews TW7 130 C3
Wigley Rd TW13 150 D3
Wigmore Ct 4 W13 109 A5
Wigmore Hall W1 238 C2
Wigmore Pl W1 93 B1 238 C2
Wigmore Rd SM5 202 C1
Wigmore St W1 93 A1 238 B2
Wigmore Wlk SM5 218 B6
Wigram Ct SW11 267 A2
Wigram Ho 6 E14 119 D6
Wigram Rd E11 55 C3
Wigram Sq E17 54 A6
Wigston Cl N18 33 C5
Wigston Rd E13 99 B3
Wigton Gdns HA7 26 A2
Wigton Pl SE11 261 B1
Wigton Rd E17 35 B2
Wilberforce Ct 2 SE28 124 C5
Edgware HA8 26 B6
Wilberforce Ho 4 SW11 136 B2
Wilberforce Prim Sch W10 91 A4
Wilberforce Rd N4 72 D6
N4,N5 73 A5
NW9 46 A3
Wilberforce Way SW19 178 D4
Wilbraham Ho SW8 270 A3
Wilbraham Pl SW1 258 A4
Wilbury Prim Sch N18 33 B5
Wilbury Way N18 33 B5
Wilby Mews W11 113 B5 244 D4
Wilcox Cl SW8 270 B4
Wilcox Gdns TW17 192 B6
Wilcox Ho 6 E3 97 B2
Wilcox Pl SW1 259 B5
Wilcox Rd SW8 138 A5 270 A4
Sutton SM1 217 D4
Teddington TW11 174 B6
Wildcroft Gdns HA8 25 D4
Wildcroft Manor SW15 156 C4
Wildcroft Rd SW15 156 C4
Wild Ct WC2 94 B1 240 C2
Wilde Cl E8 96 A6
Wilde Pl Edmonton N13 32 D4
Wandsworth SW18 158 B4
Wilder Cl HA4 40 B1
Wilde Rd DA8 147 D5
Wilderness Mews SW4 137 B1
Wilderness Rd BR7 188 D3
Wilderness The East Molesey KT8 196 A4
Wilderness The *continued* Hampton TW12 173 D6
Wilderton Rd N16 51 C2
Wildfell Rd SE6 163 D4
Wild Goose Dr SE14 140 C4
Wild Hatch NW11 47 C3
Wilding Ho 17 E9 74 D2
Wild March Ct EN3 7 A6
Wild's Rents SE1 117 C3 263 A6
Wild St WC2 94 B1 240 C1
Wildwood Cl SE12 164 D4
Wildwood Gr NW3 48 A1
Wildwood Rd NW11 48 A2
Wildwood Rise NW11 48 A1
Wildwood Terr NW3 48 A1
Wilford Cl EN2 5 B2
Wilford Ho 3 SE18 122 D1
Wilford Rd CR0 205 A2
Wilfred Fienburgh Ho N7 71 D4
Wilfred Owen Cl SW19 180 A4
Wilfred St SW1 115 C3 259 A6
Wilfrid Gdns W3 89 A2
Wilkes Rd 3 TW8 132 A6
Wilkes St E1 95 D2 243 D4
Wilkie Ho SW1 259 D2
Wilkins Cl Hayes UB3 105 D1
Mitcham CR4 180 C2
Wilkins Ho SW1 269 A6
Wilkinson Cl UB10 83 A6
Wilkinson Ct SW17 180 B6
Wilkinson Ho N1 235 D3
Isleworth TW7 130 D2
Wilkinson Rd E16 99 C1
Wilkinson St SW8 138 B5 270 C3
Wilkinson Way W4 111 B4
Wilkin St NW5 71 B2
Wilks Gdns CR0 207 A1
Wilks Pl N1 95 C5
Willan Rd N17 33 C1
Willan Wall E16 120 D6
Willard St SW8 137 B2
Willbury Ho 4 N7 71 D3
Willcocks Cl KT9 214 A5
Willcott Rd W3 110 D5
Will Crooks Gdns SE9 143 D1
Willenfield Rd NW10 89 A5
Willenhall Ave EN5 14 A5
Willenhall Ct EN5 14 A5
Willenhall Dr UB3 105 C6
Willenhall Rd SE18 122 D1
Willersley Ave BR6 227 B5
DA15 167 D4
Willersley Cl DA15 167 D3
Willesden Community Hospl The NW10 68 A1
Willesden Green Sta NW2 68 C2
Willesden High Sch NW10 90 B6
Willesden Junction Sta NW10 89 D4
Willesden La NW2,NW6 68 D2
Willes Rd NW5 71 B2
Willet Cl 3 UB5 84 C4
Willett Cl BR5 211 C3
Willett Ho 7 E13 99 A5
SW9 138 A2
Willett Pl CR7 204 C4
Willett Rd CR7 204 C4
Willett Way BR5,BR6 211 C3
William Allen Ho HA8 26 B3
William Atkinson Ho N17 33 C3
William Banfield Ho 10 SW6 135 B3
William Barefoot Dr SE9 166 C1
William Bellamy Inf Sch RM10 81 C6
William Bellamy Jun Sch RM10 81 C6
William Booth Meml Training Coll SE5 139 B3
William Booth Rd SE20 184 A2
William Brown Ct SE27 160 D2
William Byrd Sch UB3 127 A6
William Carey Way HA1 42 C3
William Caslon Ho 28 E2 96 B5
William Channing Ho 6 E2 96 B4
William C Harvey Sch N17 33 B1
William Cl SE13 142 A2
Finchley N2 30 B1
Southall UB2 108 A4
William Covell Cl EN2 4 B5
William Ct 4 Ealing W5 87 C2
Ilford IG6 57 B5
William Davies Prim Sch E7 77 D2

William Davis Prim Sch E2 .96 A3
William Dromey Ct NW6 .69 B1
William Dunbar Ho NW6 .91 B5
William Dyce Mews 1 SW16 .181 D6
William Ellis Sch NW5 .71 A5
William Ellis Way 16 SE16 .118 A3
William Evans Ho 9 SE8 .118 D2
William Ford CE Jun Sch RM10 .81 C1
William Gdns SW15 .156 B6
William Guy Gdns 47 E3 .97 D4
William Harvey Ho 1 SW19 .157 A3
William Ho NW2 .68 C5
Edmonton N13 .32 D4
William Hunt Mans SW13 .134 C6
William IV St WC2 .116 A6 250 A5
William Margrie Cl 1 SE15 .140 A3
William Mews SW1 .114 D4 247 D1
William Morley Cl E6 .99 D6
William Morris Acad W6 .112 D1
William Morris Cl E17 .53 B6
William Morris Ho W6 .134 D6
William Morris Mid Sch CR4 .203 D6
William Morris Sch E17 .35 A2
William Morris Way SW6 .136 A3
William Patten Prim Sch N16 .73 D6
William Pl 31 E3 .97 B5
William Rainbird Ho 8 N17 .33 D3
William Rathbone Ho 3 E2 .96 B4
William Rd NW1 .93 C4 232 A1
Sutton SM1 .218 A3
Wimbledon SW19 .179 A3
William Rushbrooke Ho 4 SE16 .118 A2
Williams Ave E17 .35 B2
William Saville Ho 2 NW6 .91 B5
William's Bldgs 1 E2 .96 C3
Williams Cl SW6
Williams Dr TW3 .129 C1
Williams Gr
Kingston KT6 .197 C3
Wood Green N22 .32 C2
Williams Ho 9 E3 .97 C4
9 E9 .96 B6
14 Streatham SW2 .160 C3
Williams La
Morden SM4 .202 A4
Mortlake SW14 .133 A3
William Smith Ho 10 DA17 .125 C3
Williamson Cl SE10 .120 D1
Williamson Ct SE17 .262 A1
Williamson Rd N4 .50 D3
Williamson St N7 .72 A4
Williamson Way NW7 .29 A4
William Sq 15 SE16 .119 A6
Williams Rd UB2 .107 A2
William's Rd W13 .109 A5
William St E10 .53 D3
SW1 .114 D4 247 D1
Barking IG11 .79 A1
Carshalton SM5 .218 D5
Tottenham N17 .33 D3
Williams Terr CR0 .220 C2
William Torbitt Prim Sch IG2 .57 D4
William Tyndale Prim Sch N1 .72 D1
William Winter Ct 29 SW2 .160 C4
William Wood Ho 3 SE26 .162 C1
Willifield Way NW11 .47 C4
Willingale Cl IG8 .37 C4
Willingdon Rd N22 .32 D1
Willingham Cl 4 NW5 .71 C3
Willingham Terr NW5 .71 C3
Willingham Way KT1 .176 C1
Willington Ct E5 .75 A5
Willington Prep Sch SW19 .179 B5
Willington Rd SW9 .138 A2
Willis Ave SM2 .218 C2
Willis Ho 7 E14 .119 D6
2 Ilford E12 .78 C5
Willis Rd E15 .98 D5
Thornton Heath CR0 .205 A2
Willis St E14 .97 D1
Willows The CR0 .223 A6
Will Miles Ct 6 SW19 180 A3
Willmore End SW19 .179 D1
Willoughby Ave CR0 .220 B4
Willoughby Gr N17 .34 B3
Willoughby Hall Dyslexia Ctr NW3 .70 B4
Willoughby Ho 34 E1 .118 B5
EC2 .242 C3
Willoughby La N17 .34 B3
Willoughby Mews N17 .34 B3
Willoughby Park Rd N17 .34 B3
Willoughby Rd N8 .50 C5
NW3 .70 B4
Kingston KT2 .176 B2
Twickenham TW1 .153 D6
Willoughby St WC1 .240 A3
Willoughbys The SW14 .133 C1
Willoughby Way SE7 .121 B2
Willow Ave DA15 .168 A5
Barnes SW13 .133 D3
Yiewsley UB7 .104 B6
Willowbank SW6 .135 A2
Willow Bank TW10 .153 B1
Willowbank Rd SE15 .139 D6
Willow Bridge Rd N1 .73 A2
Willowbrook Rd
Southall UB2 .107 C3
Stanwell TW19 .148 A2
Willow Bsns Pk SE26 .162 C1
Willow Cl BR2 .210 B4
Brentford TW8 .131 C6
Buckhurst Hill IG9 .21 D1
12 Catford SE6 .164 D3
Sidcup DA5 .169 B5
Willow Cotts
Carshalton CR4 .202 D2
Feltham TW13 .151 A1
Richmond TW9 .132 C6
Willowcourt Ave HA3 .43 B4
Willow Ct EC2 .243 A6
N7 .72 B3
SW9 .138 C4
40 W2 .91 C2
7 E11 .76 C6
Ashford TW16 .171 C3
Beckenham BR3 .185 C2
Chiswick W4 .133 C5
8 Dagenham RM8 .58 D2
Edgware HA8 .26 A6
Harrow HA3 .24 D2
Ilford IG1 .79 A3
Kingston KT3 .198 D6
3 Streatham SW16 .160 B1
Thornton Heath CR7 .205 B4
Willow Ctr The CR4 .202 D3
Willow Dean HA5 .22 D1
Willowdene N6 .48 D2
1 SE15 .140 B4
5 SE15 .140 B5
Willow Dene WD23 .8 C4
Willowdene Cl TW2 .152 A4
Willowdene Ct N20 .14 A4
Willow Dene Sch SE18 .145 C4
Willow Dr EN5 .1 A1
Willow End N20 .13 C2
Northwood HA6 .22 A4
Surbiton KT6 .198 A1
Willow Farm La SW15 134 B2
Willowfields Cl SE18 .123 C1
Willowfield Sec Sch E17 .52 D6
Willow Gdns
Heston TW5 .129 C4
Ruislip HA4 .61 D6
Willow Gn NW9 .27 C2
Borehamwood WD6 .11 B6
Willow Gr BR7 .188 D4
E13 .99 A5
Ruislip HA4 .39 D1
Willow Hall NW3 .70 B4
Willowhayne Dr KT12 .194 B2
Willowhayne Gdns KT4 .216 C4
Willow Ho 14 N2 .30 B1
9 NW3 .70 D2
W10 .90 D3
Feltham TW14 .150 B6
Willow La SE18 .122 C2
Mitcham CR4 .202 D3
Willow Lo
6 Ashford TW16 .171 D3
Fulham SW6 .134 D4
New Barnet EN5 .14 A6
Putney SW15 .134 B2
Willow Lodge 10 SW8 .137 B2
Willow Manor SM1 .217 B4
Willowmead Cl W5 .87 D2
Willowmere KT10 .212 A4
Willow Mount CR0 .221 C5
Willow Pl SW1 115 C2 259 B4
Willow Rd NW3 .70 B4
W5 .110 A4
Dagenham RM6 .59 A3
Enfield EN1 .5 C3
Willow Rd *continued*
New Malden KT3 .199 A5
Wallington SM6 .219 B1
Willows Ave SM4 .201 D4
Willows Cl HA5 .22 C1
Willows Sch The UB4 .84 D3
Willow St EC2 .95 C3 243 A6
Chingford E4 .20 B4
Willows Terr NW10 .89 D5
Willows The N20 .14 A1
Beckenham BR3 .185 C2
Claygate KT10 .212 C2
Wallend E12 .78 C1
Loughton IG10 .21 D6
Willow Tree Cl E3 .97 B6
Willowtree Cl UB10 .61 A5
Willow Tree Cl
Hayes UB4 .84 C3
Wandsworth SW18 .157 D3
Willow Tree Ct DA14 .189 D5
5 Wembley HA0 .65 D3
Willow Tree La UB4 .84 C3
Willow Tree Prim Sch UB5 .63 A2
Willowtree Way SW16 182 C2
Willow Tree Wlk BR1 .187 B2
Willow Vale BR7 .188 D4
W12 .112 A5
Willow View SW19 .180 B2
Willow Way N3 .29 D3
9 W11 .112 D6
Forest Hill SE26 .162 C1
Sunbury TW16 .194 A5
Twickenham TW2 .151 D2
Wembley HA0 .65 A5
West Ewell KT19 .215 B2
Willow Wlk BR6 .226 D5
E17 .53 B4
N15 .50 D5
12 N2 .30 B1
SE1 .117 D2 263 C4
Cheam SM1,SM3 .217 B5
Southgate N21 .16 B5
Willow Wood Cres SE25 .205 C3
Willrose Cres SE2 .124 B1
Willsbridge Ct 1 SE15 .139 D6
Wills Cres TW3 .151 D5
Wills Gr NW7 .28 B5
Willshaw St SE14 .141 C4
Will Thorne Pav The E16 .100 A1
Wilman Gr E8 .74 A1
Wilmar Cl UB4 .83 B3
Wilmar Gdns BR4 .207 D1
Wilmcote Ho W2 .91 D2
Wilmer Cl TW10 .176 B5
Wilmer Cres KT2,TW10 176 B5
Wilmer Gdns N1 .95 C6
Wilmer Ho 5 E3 .97 A5
Wilmer Lea Cl E15 .76 B1
Wilmer Pl N16 .73 D6
Wilmers Ct 5 NW10 .89 B6
Wilmer Way N14 .31 D5
Wilmington Ave W4 .133 B5
Wilmington Ct SW16 .182 A3
Wilmington Gdns IG11 .79 C1
Wilmington Sq WC1 .94 C4 234 A1
Wilmington St WC1 .234 A1
Wilmot Cl N2 .30 A1
SE15 .140 A5
Wilmot Pl NW1 .71 C1
Ealing W7 .108 C5
Wilmot Rd E10 .75 D6
N17 .51 B6
Wallington SM5 .218 D3
Wilmot St E2 .96 B3
Wilmount St SE18 .122 D2
Wilna Rd SW18 .158 A4
Wilnett Ct 4 RM6 .58 B2
Wilnett Villas 5 RM6 .58 B2
Wilsham St W11 .113 A5 244 A4
Wilshaw Ho 10 SE8 .141 C5
Wilsmere Dr HA3 .24 C3
Wilson Ave CR4 .180 C2
Wilson Cl Croydon CR2 .221 B3
Wembley HA9 .44 B2
Wilson Dr HA9 .44 B2
Wilson Gdns HA1 .42 A2
Wilson Gr SE16 .118 B4
Wilson Ho NW6 .70 A1
2 SE7 .143 C6
39 SW8 .137 D3
Wilson Rd E6 .99 D4
SE5 .139 C4
Chessington KT9 .214 B2
Redbridge IG1 .56 B2
Wilson's Ave 2 N17 .33 D1
Wilson's Pl E14 .97 B1
Wilson's Rd W6 .112 D1
Wilson's Sch SM6 .220 A2
Wilson St E17 .54 A4
EC2 .95 B2 242 D4
Southgate N21 .16 C4
Wilstone Cl UB4 .85 A3
Wiltern Ct NW2 .69 A2
Wilthorne Gdns RM10 .81 D1
Wilton Ave W4 .111 C1
Wilton Cres
SW1 .115 A4 248 A1
Merton SW19 .179 B2
Wilton Ct 16 E1 .96 B1
N10 .31 A1
4 Richmond TW10 .154 A6
7 Woodford IG8 .37 A4
Wilton Est E8 .74 A2
Wilton Gdns
East Molesey KT8 .195 C6
Walton-on-T KT12 .194 D1
Wilton Gr Merton SW19 179 B2
New Malden KT3 .199 D3
Wilton Ho 8 SE22 .139 C2
Wilton Mews
SW1 .115 B3 258 B6
Wilton Par TW13 .150 B2
Wilton Pl SW1 115 A4 248 A1
2 Beckenham BR3 .208 A6
4 Harrow HA1 .42 D3
Wilton Rd N10 .31 A1
SE2 .124 C2
SW1 .115 C2 259 A4
Cockfosters EN4 .2 D1
Hounslow TW4 .128 D2
Mitcham SW19 .180 C3
Wilton Row SW1 .248 A1
Wilton Sq N1 .95 B6 235 C6
Wilton St SW1 115 B3 258 C6
Wilton Terr SW1 .258 A6
Wilton Villas N1 .235 C5
Wilton Way E8 .74 A2
Wilton Wlk TW13 .150 B3
Wiltshire Cl NW7 .27 D5
SW3 .257 C3
Wiltshire Ct 2 N4 .50 B1
Barking IG11 .79 A2
Wiltshire Gdns N4 .51 A3
Twickenham TW2 .152 A3
Wiltshire La HA5 .40 A5
Wiltshire Rd SW9 .138 C2
Thornton Heath CR7 .204 C6
Wiltshire Row
N1 .95 B6 235 D5
Wilverley Cres KT3 .199 C3
Wimbart Rd SW2 .160 B4
Wimbledon Bridge SW19 .179 B4
Wimbledon Central SW19 .179 B4
Wimbledon Chase Prim Sch SW20 .179 A2
Wimbledon Chase Sta SW20 .179 A1
Wimbledon Cl 2 SW20 .178 D3
Wimbledon Coll SW19 .178 D3
Wimbledon Common★ SW19 .178 B6
Wimbledon Common Prep Sch SW19 .178 D3
Wimbledon High Sch SW19 .179 A4
Wimbledon Hill Rd SW19 .179 B4
Wimbledon House Sch SW19 .179 C2
Wimbledon Lawn Tennis Mus★ SW19 .157 A1
Wimbledon Park Ct SW19 .157 B3
Wimbledon Park First Sch SW19 .157 D2
Wimbledon Park Rd SW18,SW19 .157 B3
Wimbledon Park Side SW19 .156 D3
Wimbledon Park Sta SW19 .157 C1
Wimbledon Rd SW17 .180 A6
Wimbledon Sch of Art SW19 .179 A2
Wimbledon Sch of Art Annexe SW19 .179 C3
Wimbledon Sta SW19 .179 B4
Wimbledon Stadium SW17 .180 A6
Wimbledon Stadium Bsns Ctr SW17 .157 D1
Wimbledon Windmill Mus★ SW19 .156 C1
Wimbolt St E2 .96 A4
Wimborne 2 DA14 .190 B6
Wimborne Ave
Hayes UB4 .84 B1
Southall UB2 .107 C2
Wimborne Cl SE12 .164 D6
Buckhurst Hill IG9 .21 C2
North Cheam KT4 .200 C1
Wimborne Ct 1 UB5 .63 C2
Wimborne Dr HA8,NW9 .44 C6
Pinner HA5 .41 A2
Wimborne Gdns W13 .87 B2
Wimborne Ho E16 .120 D6
NW1 .237 B5
SW8 .270 D3
Wimborne Ho *continued*
Croydon CR0 .206 C4
Upper Tooting SW12 .159 C1
Wimborne Rd
Edmonton N9 .18 A2
Tottenham N17 .33 C1
Wimborne Way BR3 .207 A5
Wimbourne Ct N1 .235 C4
Mitcham SW19 .180 B3
South Croydon CR2 .221 C2
Wimbourne St
N1 .95 B5 235 C4
Wimpole Cl
Bromley BR2 .209 C5
1 Kingston KT1 .176 C1
Wimpole Mews
W1 .93 B2 238 C3
Wimpole St W1 93 B1 238 C2
Wimshurst Cl CR0 .204 A1
Winans Wlk SW9 .138 C3
Winant Ho 17 E14 .119 D6
Wincanton Cres UB5 .63 C3
Wincanton Gdns IG6 .56 D6
Wincanton Rd SW18 .157 B4
Winchcombe Rd SM5 .202 C1
Winchcomb Gdns SE9 143 D2
Winchelsea Ave DA7 .147 B5
Winchelsea Cl SW15 .156 D6
Winchelsea Ho 11 SE16 .118 C4
Winchelsea Rd E7 .77 A4
N17 .51 C6
NW10 .89 B6
Winchelsey Rise CR2 .221 D2
Winchendon Rd
Fulham SW6 .135 B4 264 D2
Teddington TW11,TW12 .174 B6
Winchester Ave NW6 .69 A1
NW9 .44 C6
Heston TW5 .129 B6
Winchester Cl SE17 .261 D3
Beckenham BR2 .208 D6
Enfield EN1 .17 C6
Kingston KT2 .176 D3
11 Newham E6 .100 B1
Winchester Ct W8 .245 C2
Belvedere DA17 .125 C1
Winchester Dr HA5 .40 D4
Winchester Ho 18 E3 .97 B4
1 SE18 .143 D5
SW3 .266 D5
W2 .236 A1
5 Barking IG11 .80 A1
Winchester Pk BR2 .208 D6
Winchester Pl 6 E8 .73 D3
N6 .49 B1
Winchester Rd N6 .49 B1
NW3 .70 B1
Beckenham BR2 .208 D6
Bexley DA16 .146 D3
Chingford E4 .36 A3
Edmonton N9 .18 A3
Harlington UB3 .127 C5
Harrow HA3 .44 A5
Ilford IG1 .79 B5
Northwood HA6 .40 A6
Twickenham TW1 .153 B5
Twickenham TW13 .151 B1
Walton-on-T KT12 .194 A1
Winchester Sq SE1 .252 C4
Winchester St
SW1 .115 B1 258 D2
Acton W3 .111 A4
Winchester Wlk SE1 .252 C4
Winchet Wlk CR0 .206 C3
Winchfield Cl HA3 .43 C3
Winchfield Ho SW15 .155 D5
Winchfield Rd SE26 .185 A5
Winch Ho SW10 .266 B4
Winchilsea Cres KT8 .174 A1
Winchilsea Ho NW8 .229 D1
Winchmore Hill Rd N14,N21 .16 A4
Winchmore Hill Sta N21 .16 D4
Winchmore Sch N21 .17 A2
Winchmore Villas N21 .16 B4
Winchstone Cl TW17 .192 B5
Winckley Cl HA3 .44 B4
Wincott St SE11 .116 C2 261 B3
Wincrofts Dr SE9 .145 B1
Windall Cl SE20 .184 A2
Windborough Rd SM5 219 A1
Windcott Ct HA3 .43 C2
Windermere NW1 .231 D2
12 Putney SW15 .156 D5
Windermere Ave N3 .47 C6
NW6 .91 A6
Merton SW19 .201 D6
Ruislip HA4 .40 D2
Wembley HA9 .43 C1
Windermere Cl BR6 .226 D5
East Bedfont TW14 .149 D3
Stanwell TW19 .148 A2
Windermere Ct
Barnes SW13 .133 D6
Barnet EN5 .1 D1
Carshalton SM5 .219 A5
Windermere Ct *continued*
Wembley HA9 .43 C2
Windermere Gdns IG4 .56 A4
Windermere Gr HA9 .43 C1
Windermere Hall HA8 .26 B5
Windermere Ho E3 .97 B3
Isleworth TW1 .152 D6
Windermere Point 3 SE15 .140 C5
Windermere Rd N10 .31 B2
N19 .71 C6
W5 .109 C3
Croydon CR0 .205 D1
Kingston SW15 .177 C5
Mitcham SW16 .181 D1
Southall UB1 .85 B2
West Wickham BR4 .224 C6
Windermere Way UB7 104 B5
Winders Rd SW11 .136 C3
Windfield Cl SE26 .184 D6
Windham Rd TW9 .132 B2
Winding Way RM8 .80 C5
Windlass Pl SE8 .119 A2
Windlesham Gr SW19 156 D3
Windley Cl SE23 .162 C2
Windmill WC1 .240 C4
Windmill Alley 7 W4 .111 C2
Windmill Ave UB2 .108 A4
Windmill Bridge Ho 1 CR0 .205 C1
Windmill Bsns Ctr UB2 .108 A5
Windmill Bsns Village TW16 .171 C2
Windmill Cl NW2 .69 A5
11 SE1 .118 A2
3 SE13 .142 A3
Ashford TW16 .171 C3
Kingston KT6 .197 C2
Windmill Ct NW2 .69 A2
W5 .109 C2
Windmill Dr BR2 .225 C4
SW4 .159 B6
Windmill Gdns EN2 .4 C2
Windmill Gr CR0 .205 A3
Windmill Hill NW3 .70 A5
1 NW3 .70 A4
Enfield EN2 .5 A2
Ruislip HA4 .39 D1
Windmill Ho SE1 .251 B3
Windmill La E15 .76 B2
Bushey WD23 .8 C3
Edgware EN5 .11 D5
Isleworth TW7,UB2,W7 .108 C2
Southall UB2 .108 A4
Southall UB6 .86 A2
Thames Ditton KT7 .197 B2
Windmill Lo TW16 .171 C2
Windmill Pas 10 W4 .111 C2
Windmill Rd SW18 .158 B5
W4 .111 C2
Brentford TW8,W5 .109 C1
Charlton TW16 .171 C2
Edmonton N18 .33 B6
Hampton TW12 .174 A5
Mitcham CR4 .203 C5
Roehampton SW19 .156 B1
Thornton Heath CR0 .205 A2
Windmill Rd W TW16 .171 C1
Windmill Rise KT2 .176 D3
Windmill Row SE11 .261 A1
Windmill St W1 93 D2 239 C3
Bushey WD23 .8 C3
Windmill Terr TW17 .193 C2
Windmill Trad Est TW16 .171 C2
Windmill Way HA4 .39 D1
Windmill Wlk SE1 .251 B2
Windmore Cl HA0 .65 A3
Windrose Cl SE16 .118 D4
Windrush KT3 .199 A5
Windrush Cl SW11 .136 B1
Chiswick W4 .133 A5
Ickenham UB10 .60 B4
Windrush Ho NW8 .236 D4
Windrush La SE23 .162 D1
Windrush Prim Sch SE28 .124 B5
Windrush Rd NW10 .89 B6
Windsock Cl 1 SE16 .119 B2
Windsor Ave E17 .35 A1
Cheam SM3 .217 A5
East Molesey KT8 .195 C6
Edgware HA8 .10 D1
Hillingdon UB10 .60 D1
Merton SW19 .180 A2
New Malden KT3 .199 A4
Windsor Cl N3 .29 A1
Brentford TW8 .131 B6
Chislehurst BR7 .188 D5
Harrow HA2 .63 C5
Pinner HA6 .22 A1
West Norwood SE27 .183 A6
Windsor Cres
Harrow HA2 .63 C5
Wembley HA9 .66 D5

Windsor Ct BR1 210 A6
E17 53 B6
N11 30 D5
N14 15 C4
NW11 47 A3
NW3 69 C4
20 SE16 118 D5
SW11 136 B3
4 SW18 157 C6
SW3 257 B2
2 SW4 137 C1
W2 245 C6
Bushey WD23 8 A4
Fulham SW6 135 A2
South Norwood SE19 183 C2
Sunbury TW16 172 A3
Windsor Ctr The SE27 183 A6
Windsor Dr EN4 14 D5
Windsor Gdns W9 91 C3
Hayes UB3 105 B3
Wallington CR0 220 A5
Windsor Gr SE27 183 A6
Windsor Ho 4 E2 96 D4
N1 235 B4
N4 51 A1
NW1 231 D2
NW2 69 A2
2 NW4 28 D1
4 W4 111 A1
7 Northolt UB5 63 C2
Windsor Mews
Catford SE6 164 A3
Forest Hill SE23 163 A3
Windsor Park Rd UB3 127 D5
Windsor Pk SW19 180 A2
Windsor Pl SW1 259 B4
Windsor Rd DA6 147 A1
E10 75 D6
E7 77 C3
N3 29 A1
N7 72 A5
NW2 68 B2
Ashford TW16 172 A4
Barnet EN5 12 D5
Chingford E4 35 D6
Cranford TW4,TW5 128 C3
Dagenham RM8 81 A5
Ealing W5 110 A6
Harrow HA3 24 B2
Ilford IG1 79 A4
Kingston KT2 176 A3
Palmers Green N13 16 C1
Richmond TW9 132 B3
Southall UB2 107 B3
South Norwood CR7 182 D1
Teddington TW11 174 B5
Tottenham N17 34 A1
Wanstead E11 77 A6
Worcester Park KT4 216 A6
Windsor St N1 94 D6 234 D6
Windsor Terr
N1 95 A4 235 B2
Windsor Way
W14 113 A2 254 A4
Windsor Wharf E9 75 B3
Windsor Wlk SE5 139 B3
Walton-on-T KT12 194 D1
Windspoint Dr SE15 140 B6
Windus Rd N16 51 D1
Windus Wlk N16 51 D1
Windy Ridge BR1 188 A2
Windy Ridge Cl SW19 178 D5
Wine Cl E1 118 C6
Wine Office Ct EC4 241 B2
Winery La KT1 198 B6
Winey Cl KT9 213 C1
Winfield Ho SW11 136 B3
Winford Ct 15 SE15 140 A4
Winford Ho E3 75 B1
Winford Par 9 UB1 85 D1
Winforton St SE10 142 A4
Winfrith Rd SW18 158 A3
Wingate Cres CR0 204 A3
Wingate Ho 26 E3 97 D4
8 N16 73 B4
Wingate Rd W6 112 B3
Ilford IG1 78 D3
Sidcup DA14 190 C4
Wingate Trad Est N17 33 D3
Wingfield Ct 10 E14 120 B6
Wingfield Ho 16 E2 95 D4
NW6 91 D5
Wingfield Mews SE15 140 A2
Wingfield Prim Sch
SE3 143 B2
Wingfield Rd E15 76 C4
E17 53 D4
Kingston KT2 176 C4
Wingfield St SE15 140 A2
Wingfield Way HA4 62 B2
Wingford Rd SW2 160 A5
Wingham 3 NW5 71 A2
Wingham Ho 3 SE26 184 B5
Wingmore Rd SE24 139 A2
Wingrad Ho 14 E1 96 C2
Wingrave SE17 262 C3
Wingrave Rd W6 134 C6
Wingreen 13 NW8 91 D6
Wingrove Rd SE6 164 C2
Wings Cl SM1 217 C4
Winicotte Ho W2 236 D4
Winifred Cl EN5 11 D5
Winifrede Paul Ho 7
NW5 71 B4
Winifred Pl N12 30 A5
Winifred Rd
Dagenham RM8 59 A1
Hampton TW12 173 C6
Merton SW19 179 C2
Winifred St E16 122 B5
Winifred Terr EN1 17 D4
Winkfield Rd E13 99 B5
Wood Green N22 32 C2
Winkley Ct N10 49 B5
Harrow HA2 63 C5
Winkley St 6 E2 96 B5
Winkworth Cotts 13 E1 96 C3
Winlaton Rd BR1 186 B6
Winmill Rd RM8 81 B5
Winn Common Rd
SE18 145 C6
Winnett St W1 249 C6
Winningales Ct IG5 56 A6
Winnings Wlk UB5 63 A2
Winnington Cl N2 48 B3
Winnington Ho
8 SE5 139 A5
19 W10 91 A3
Winnington Rd N2 48 B3
Enfield EN3 6 C6
Winnipeg Dr 3 BR6 227 D2
Winnipeg Ho UB4 84 B3
Winn Rd SE12 165 B3
Winns Ave E17 53 B6
Winns Mews N15 51 C5
Winns Prim Sch E17 35 B1
Winns Terr E17 53 C6
Winsbeach E17 36 B1
Winscombe Cres W5 87 D3
Winscombe Ct W5 87 D3
Winscombe St N19 71 B6
Winscombe Way HA7 25 A5
Winsford Rd SE6 163 B1
Winsford Terr N18 33 B5
Winsham Gr SW11 159 A6
Winsham Ho NW1 232 D2
Winslade Ho 4 E5 74 B6
Winslade Rd SW2 160 A6
Winslade Way SE6 163 D4
Winsland Mews W2 236 C2
Winsland St W2 92 B1 236 C2
Winsley St W1 239 B2
Winslow SE17 263 A1
Winslow Cl 2 NW10 67 C5
Pinner HA5 40 B3
Winslow Gr E4 20 C2
Winslow Rd W6 134 C6
Winslow Way TW13 151 A1
Winsmoor Ct EN2 4 D2
Winsor Prim Sch E6 100 C1
Winsor Terr E6 100 C2
Winstanley Rd SW11 136 B2
Winston Ave NW9 45 C2
Winston Cl Harrow HA3 24 D4
Romford RM7 59 D5
Winston Ct 7 BR1 187 B2
Harrow HA3 23 D3
Winston Ho WC1 239 D6
Winston Rd N16 73 B4
Winston Way IG1 79 A5
Winston Wlk W4 111 B2
Winter Ave E6 100 A6
Winterborne Ave BR6 227 B5
Winterbourne Ho
W11 244 A5
Winterbourne Jun & Inf
Schs CR7 204 C5
Winterbourne Rd
Dagenham RM8 80 C6
Forest Hill SE6 163 B3
Thornton Heath CR7 204 C5
Winter Box Wlk TW10 154 B6
Winterbrook Rd SE24 161 A5
Winterburn Cl N11 31 A4
Winterfold Cl SW19 157 A2
Wintergreen Cl 7 E6 100 A2
Winterleys 7 NW6 91 B5
Winter Lo 10 SE16 118 A1
Winter's Ct E4 19 D1
Winterslow Ho 20 SE5 139 A3
Winters Rd KT7 197 B2
Winterstoke Gdns NW7 28 A5
Winterstoke Rd SE6 163 B3
Winterton Ct KT1 175 D2
Winterton Ho 15 E1 96 C1
Winterton Pl SW10 266 B6
Winterwell Rd SW2 160 A6
Winthorpe Rd SW15 135 A1
Winthrop Ho 10 W12 112 B6
Winthrop St E1 96 B2
Winthrop Wlk HA9 66 A5
Winton Ave N11 31 C3
Winton Cl N9 18 D4
Winton Ct 15 KT6 197 D2
Winton Gdns HA8 26 B3
Winton Prim Sch
N1 94 B5 233 C3
Winton Rd BR6 226 D4
Winton Way SW16 182 C5
Wintour Ho HA9 65 D6
Wirrall Ho 15 SE26 162 A1
Wirral Wood Cl BR7 188 C4
Wisbeach Rd CR0 205 B4
Wisden Ho SW8 270 D5
Wisdom Ct 5 TW7 131 A2
Wisdons Cl RM7,RM9 59 D1
Wise La NW7 28 A4
Wiseman Ct 12 SE19 183 C5
Wiseman Rd E10 75 C6
Wise Rd E15 98 B6
Wiseton Rd SW17 158 D3
Wishart Rd SE3 143 D3
Wishaw Wlk N13 32 A4
Wisley Ho SW1 259 C2
Wisley Rd SW11 159 A6
St Paul's Cray BR5 190 B3
Wistaria Cl BR6 226 D6
Wisteria Cl NW7 27 D4
Ilford IG1 78 D3
Wisteria Rd SE13 142 B1
Wistow Ho 14 E2 96 A6
Witanhurst La N6 49 A1
Witan St E2 96 B4
Witchwood Ho 11
SW9 138 C2
Witcombe Point 13
SE15 140 A4
Witham Ct E10 75 D5
Upper Tooting SW17 158 D1
Witham Ho 35 SE5 139 A3
Witham Rd
Dagenham RM10 81 C3
Ealing W13 109 B5
Hounslow TW7 130 B4
Penge SE20 206 C6
Witherby Cl CR0 221 C4
Witherington Rd N5 72 C3
Withers Cl KT9 213 C2
Withers Mead NW9 27 D2
Withers Pl EC1 242 B6
Witherston Way SE9 166 C1
Withington Rd N2 30 C2
Withycombe Rd SW19 156 D4
Withy Ho 4 E1 96 D3
Withy La HA4 39 A4
Withy Mead E4 20 B1
Witley Cres CR0 224 A2
Witley Ct UB2 107 B2
Witley Gdns UB2 107 B2
Witley Ho 2 SW2 160 B4
Witley Ind Est UB2 107 B2
Witley Point 8 SW15 156 B3
Witley Rd N19 71 C6
Witney Cl
Ickenham UB10 60 B4
Pinner HA5 23 B4
Witney Path SE23 162 D1
Wittenham Way E4 20 B1
Witten Ho KT3 199 B1
Wittering Cl KT2 175 D5
Wittering Ho 9 SW11 136 D3
Wittersham Rd BR1 186 D5
Wittingham Com Prim Sch
E17 35 A2
Witts Ho KT2 198 B6
Wivenhoe Cl SE15 140 B2
Wivenhoe Ct TW4 129 B1
Wivenhoe Rd IG11 102 B5
Wiverton Rd SE26 184 C5
Wixom Ho SE9 143 C1
Wix Prim Sch SW4 137 B1
Wix Rd RM9 102 D6
Wix's La SW4 137 B1
Woburn W13 87 B2
Woburn Cl SE28 102 D1
Bushey WD23 8 A5
Wimbledon SW19 180 A4
Woburn Ct 32 SE16 118 B1
1 DA6 147 A1
Croydon CR0 205 A1
Richmond TW9 132 B2
4 Woodford E18 37 A1
Woburn Pl WC1 94 A3 240 A5
Woburn Rd
Carshalton SM5 202 C1
Croydon CR0 205 A1
Woburn Sq
WC1 93 D3 239 D5
Woburn Twr 14 UB5 84 D4
Woburn Wlk WC1 232 D1
Wodehouse Ave SE15 139 D4
Wodehouse Ct 10 W3 111 A3
Woffington Cl KT1,KT8 175 C2
Woking Cl SW15 133 D1
Wolcot Ho NW1 232 B3
Woldham Pl BR2 209 C5
Woldham Rd BR2 209 C5
Wolds Dr BR6 226 C4
Wolfe Cl Hayes BR2 209 A3
Hayes UB4 84 B4
Wolfe Cres 34 SE16 118 D4
SE7 121 D1
Wolfe Ho 19 W12 112 B6
Wolferton Rd E12 78 B4
Wolf Fields Prim Sch
UB2 107 B2
Wolfington Rd SE27 182 D6
Wolfram Cl SE13 164 C6
Wolfson Ct NW11 47 A2
SE1 253 D2
Wolfson Hillel Prim Sch
N14 15 D5
Wolftencroft Cl SW11 136 B2
Wollaston Cl SE1 262 A4
Wolmer Cl HA8 26 D6
Wolmer Gdns HA8 10 C1
Wolmer Rd HA8 26 D6
Wolseley Ave SW18,
SW19 157 C2
Wolseley Gdns W4 132 D6
Wolseley Rd E7 77 B1
N8 49 D4
Acton W4 111 A2
Carshalton CR4 203 A2
Harrow HA3 42 C6
Wood Green N22 32 B2
Wolseley St
SE1 117 D4 253 D1
Wolsey Ave E17 53 B6
Wallend E6 100 C4
Wolsey Cl
Isleworth TW3 130 A1
Kingston KT2 176 D2
Southall UB2 108 A3
Wimbledon SW20 178 B3
Worcester Park KT19,
KT4 216 A4
Wolsey Cres SM4 201 B2
Wolsey Ct NW6 70 A1
SE9 166 B5
Bromley BR1 186 D3
Wolsey Dr
Kingston KT2 176 A4
Walton-on-T KT12 194 D1
Wolsey Gr HA8 27 B3
Wolsey Ho 2 TW12 173 D4
Wolsey Inf Sch CR0 224 A1
Wolsey Jun Sch CR0 224 A1
Wolsey Mews NW5 71 C2
Orpington BR6 227 D3
Wolsey Rd N1 73 B3
Ashford TW15 170 B6
Ashford TW16 171 D4
East Molesey KT8 196 B5
Enfield EN1 6 B3
Hampton TW12 174 A4
Wolsey St E1 96 C2
Wolsey Way KT9 214 C3
Wolstenholme HA7 25 B5
Wolstonbury N12 29 C5
Wolvercote Rd SE2 124 D4
Wolverley St E2 96 B4
Wolverton SE17 263 A2
Wolverton Ave KT2 176 C2
Wolverton Gdns W6 112 D2
Ealing W5 110 B6
Wolverton Mans W5 110 B5
Wolverton Rd HA7 25 B3
Wolverton Way N14 15 C6
Wolves La N22 32 C4
Womersley Rd N4,N8 50 B3
Wonford Cl KT2,KT3 177 C2
Wontner Cl 5 N1 73 A1
Wontner Rd SW12,
SW17 158 D2
Wooburn Cl UB8 82 D3
Woodall Cl 24 E14 119 D6
Chessington KT9 213 D2
Woodall Ho TW7 130 D2
Woodall Rd EN3 18 D5
Woodbank Rd BR1 164 D1
Woodbastwick Rd
SE26 185 A5
Woodberry Ave
Edmonton N21 16 D2
Harrow HA2 42 A5
Woodberry Cl NW7 28 D3
Ashford TW16 172 A4
Woodberry Cres N10 49 B6
Woodberry Down N4 51 A2
Woodberry Down Com Prim
Sch N4 51 A2
Woodberry Gdns N12 30 A4
Woodberry Gr N12 30 A4
N4 51 A2
Woodberry Way N12 30 A4
Chingford E4 20 A4
Woodbine Cl TW2 152 B2
Woodbine Gr Enfield EN2 5 B5
Penge SE20 184 B3
Woodbine La KT4 216 C5
Woodbine Pl E11 55 A3
Woodbine Rd DA15 167 C3
Woodbines Ave KT1 197 D6
Woodbine Terr E9 74 C2
Woodborough Rd
SW15 134 B1
Woodbourne Ave
SW16 159 D1
Woodbourne Cl SW16 160 A1
Woodbourne Dr KT10 212 D2
Woodbourne Gdns
SM6 219 B1
Woodbridge Cl 10 N7 72 B6
4 NW2 68 A5
Woodbridge Ct N16 73 B5
Woodbridge High Sch
IG8 37 B3
Woodbridge Ho E11 54 D1
Woodbridge Rd IG11 79 D3
Woodbridge St
EC1 94 D3 241 C6
Woodbrook Rd SE2 146 B6
Woodbrook Sch BR3 185 B2
Woodburn Cl NW4 46 D4
Woodbury Cl
Croydon CR0 221 D6
Wanstead E11 55 B5
Woodbury Ct 1 W13 87 B3
Woodbury Ho 4 SE26 162 B1
Woodbury Park Rd
W13 87 B3
Woodbury Rd E17 53 D5
Woodbury St SW17 180 C5
Woodchester Sq W2 91 D2
Woodchurch Cl DA14 167 B1
Woodchurch Dr BR1 187 D3
Woodchurch Ho 15
SW9 138 C4
Woodchurch Rd NW6 69 D1
Wood Cl E2 96 A3
NW9 45 B2
Harrow HA1 42 B2
Woodclyffe Dr BR7 188 C1
Woodcock Ct HA3 44 A2
Woodcock Dell Ave
HA3 43 D2
Woodcock Hill HA3 43 C3
Woodcock Ho 4 E14 97 C2
Woodcocks E16 99 D2
Woodcombe Cres
SE23 162 C3
Woodcote Ave NW7 28 C4
Thornton Heath CR7 204 D5
Wallington SM6 219 B1
Woodcote Cl Enfield N9 18 C5
Kingston KT2 176 B5
Woodcote Dr BR6 211 B2
Woodcote Ho 4 SE8 141 B6
Woodcote Mews
Loughton IG10 21 D4
Wallington SM6 219 B2
Woodcote Pl 1 SE27 182 D5
Woodcote Rd
Wallington SM6 219 C1
Wanstead E11 55 A2
Woodcott Ho 1 SW15 156 A4
Woodcroft SE9 166 B1
South Croydon CR0 221 C5
Southgate N21 16 C3
Wembley UB6 65 A2
Woodcroft Ave NW7 27 C4
Stanmore HA7 25 A2
Woodcroft Cres UB10 82 D6
Woodcroft Jun & Inf Schs
HA8 27 C3
Woodcroft Mews SE8 119 A2
Woodcroft Rd CR7 204 D3
Wood Dene 6 SE15 140 B4
Wood Dr BR7 188 A4
Woodedge Cl E4 20 D3
Woodend
South Norwood SE19 183 A4
Sutton SM1 218 A6
Thames Ditton KT10 212 A6
Wood End UB3 83 C1
Wood End Ave HA2 64 A4
Wood End Cl UB5 64 B3
Woodend Gdns EN2 4 A1
Wood End Gdns UB5 64 A3
Wood End Green Rd
UB3 83 C1
Wood End Inf Sch UB5 64 B3
Wood End Jun Sch
UB6 64 B3
Wood End La UB5 63 D3
Wood End Park Jun & Inf
Sch UB3 105 A6
Woodend Rd E17 36 A1
Wood End Rd HA1,UB5 64 B4
Wood End Way UB5 64 A3
Wooder Gdns E7 77 A4
Wooderson Cl SE25 205 C5
Woodfall Ave EN5 13 B6
Woodfall Rd N4 72 C6
Woodfall St SW3 257 C1
Woodfarrs SE5 139 B1
Wood Field NW3 70 D3
Woodfield Ave NW9 45 C5
Ealing W5 87 C3
Streatham SW16 159 D1
Wallington SM5 219 A1
Wembley HA0 65 C5
Woodfield Cl
1 Enfield EN1 5 C1
South Norwood SE19 183 A3
Woodfield Cres W5 87 D3
Woodfield Ct SW16 159 D1
Woodfield Ctr The
SW16 159 D2
Woodfield Dr EN4 15 A3
Woodfield Gdns KT3 199 D4
Woodfield Gr SW16 159 D1
Woodfield Ho 6 E5 74 B6
11 Forest Hill SE23 162 D1
New Malden KT3 199 D4
Woodfield Pl W9 91 B3
Woodfield Rd W9 91 B2
Cranford TW4,TW5 128 B3
Ealing W5 87 C3
Hinchley Wood KT10,
KT7 212 D6
Woodfield Rise WD23 8 B4
Woodfield Sch NW9 45 C1
Woodfields Ct SM1 218 A5
Woodfield Way N11 31 D3
Woodford Ave IG2,IG4,
IG5,IG8 56 B5
Woodford Bridge Rd
IG4 56 A5
Woodford Cres HA5 22 B1
Woodford Cty High Sch
IG8 36 D4
Woodforde Ct UB3 105 B1
Woodford Green Prep Sch
IG8 37 A4
Woodford Ho 13 SE18 144 D6
5 Wanstead E18 55 A5
Woodford New Rd E17 54 C6
Woodford E18 36 D3
Woodford Pl HA9 44 A1
Woodford Rd E7 77 B4
Wanstead E18 55 A6
Woodford Sta IG8 37 B4
Woodford Trad Est IG8 37 D1
Woodgate Ave KT9 213 D3
Woodgate Cres HA6 22 A4
Woodgate Dr SW16 181 D3
Woodger Rd W12 112 C4
Woodget Cl E6 100 A1
Woodgrange Ave N12 30 B4
Ealing W5 110 C5
Enfield EN1 18 A5
Harrow HA3 43 D4
Woodgrange Cl HA3 43 D4
Woodgrange Ct 1
BR2 208 D1
Woodgrange Gdns EN1 18 A5
Woodgrange Inf Sch
E7 77 B4
Woodgrange Mans
HA3 43 C4
Woodgrange Park Sta
E12 77 D3
Woodgrange Rd E7 77 A3
Woodgrange Terr EN1 18 A5
Wood Green Sta N22 32 C1
Woodhall NW1 232 A1
Woodhall Ave
Dulwich SE21 161 D1
Pinner HA5 23 A2
Woodhall Dr
Dulwich SE21 161 D1
Pinner HA5 23 A2
Woodhall Gate HA5 22 D3
Woodhall Ho SW18 158 B5
Woodhall La WD19 23 A6
Woodhall Sch WD19 23 A6
Woodham Ct E11 54 D5
Woodham Rd SE6 164 A1
Woodhatch Cl 16 E6 100 A2
Woodhaven Gdns IG6 57 A5
Woodhayes BR7 188 D4
Woodhayes Rd SW19,
SW20 178 C4
Woodhead Dr BR6 227 C6
Woodheyes Rd NW10 67 C3
Woodhill SE7,SE18 122 A2
Woodhill Cres HA3 43 D3
Woodhill Prim Sch
SE18 122 A2
Wood Ho 6 NW6 91 B5
4 SW4 137 D3
Woodhouse Ave UB6 86 D5
Woodhouse Cl
Hayes UB3 105 C3
Wembley UB6 86 D5
Woodhouse Eaves HA6 22 A5
Woodhouse Gr E12 78 A2
Woodhouse Rd E11 76 D5
N12 30 C4
Woodhouse Sixth Form Coll
N12 30 B4
Woodhurst Ave BR5 211 A3
Woodhurst Rd SE2 124 A2
W3 111 A6
Woodington Cl SE9 166 C5
Woodison St E3 97 A3
Woodknoll Dr BR7 188 B2
Wood La N6 49 B3
NW9 45 B2
W12 112 C6
Dagenham RM10 81 A5
Hounslow TW7 130 D5
Ruislip HA4 61 C6
Stanmore HA7 9 B2
Woodford IG8 36 D5
Woodland App UB6 65 A2
Woodland Cl NW9 45 A3
Uxbridge UB10 60 D6
West Ewell KT19 215 C2

Woodland Cl *continued*
West Norwood SE19 183 C4
Woodford IG8 21 B1
Woodland Cres SE10 142 C6
18 SE16 118 D4
Woodland Ct NW4 47 A4
Cheam SM1 217 C2
10 Wanstead E11 55 A4
Woodland Gdns E17 54 C5
N10 49 B4
Isleworth TW7 130 C2
Woodland Gr SE10 120 C1
Woodland Hill SE19 183 C4
Woodland Rd N11 31 B5
Chingford E4 20 A3
Penge SE19 183 D4
Thornton Heath CR7 204 C5
Woodland Rise N10 49 B5
Wembley UB6 65 A2
Woodlands N12 30 A4
NW11 47 A4
SW4 137 B1
Beckenham BR3 185 D3
Harrow HA2 41 C5
West Barnes SW20 200 D5
Woodlands Ave DA15 167 C3
N3 30 A2
Acton W3 110 D5
Dagenham RM6 59 A2
Kingston KT3 177 B2
Ruislip HA4 40 D2
Wanstead E11 55 B1
Worcester Park KT4 216 A6
Woodlands Cl BR1 188 B1
NW11 47 A4
Claygate KT10 212 D1
Woodlands Ct NW10 90 D6
9 Bromley BR1 186 D2
Dulwich SE22 162 B4
Southall UB1 107 C6
Woodlands Dr
Harrow HA7 24 D4
Sunbury TW16 172 C1
Woodlands Gr TW7 130 C3
Woodlands Gt SW15 157 B6
Woodlands Inf Sch IG1 79 B3
Woodlands Jun Sch
IG1 79 B3
Woodlands Par TW15 171 A4
Woodlands Park Jun & Inf
Schs N15 51 A4
Woodlands Park Rd
N15 51 A4
SE10 142 C6
Woodlands Rd BR1 188 B1
DA7 147 A2
E11 76 C6
E17 54 A6
N9 18 C3
Barnes SW13 133 D2
Enfield EN2 5 B4
Harrow HA1 42 D4
Ilford IG1 79 A5
Isleworth TW7 130 C3
Southall UB1 106 D5
Surbiton KT6 197 D2
Woodlands St SE13 164 B4
Woodland St 2 E8 73 D2
Woodlands The N14 15 B3
N5 73 A4
Isleworth TW7 130 D3
Lewisham SE13 164 B4
Mitcham CR4 203 A6
South Norwood SE19 183 A3
Stanmore HA7 25 B5
Thames Ditton KT10 212 A6
Woodlands Way SW15 157 B6
Woodland Terr SE7 122 A2
Woodland Way BR5 211 A4
NW7 27 D4
SE2 124 D2
Croydon CR0 207 A1
Merton SM4 201 B5
Mitcham CR4 181 A3
Southgate N21 16 C2
Tolworth KT5 214 D6
West Wickham BR4 224 A5
Woodford IG8 21 B1
Woodland Wlk NW3 70 C3
9 SE10 120 C1
Chessington KT19 214 C2
Woodlane High Sch
W12 90 B1
Woodlawn Cl SW15 157 B6
Woodlawn Cres TW2 151 D2
Woodlawn Dr TW13 150 D2
Woodlawn Rd SW6 134 D4
Woodlea Dr BR2 208 C4
Woodlea Lo EN1 17 C5
Woodlea Rd N16 73 C5
Woodleigh
1 Kingston KT5 198 B4
3 Woodford E18 37 A2
Woodleigh Ave N12 30 C4
Woodleigh Ct N22 32 B2
Woodleigh Gdns
SW16 160 A1
Woodley Cl SW17 180 D3
Woodley La SM1,SM5 218 C5
Woodlodge 4 SW19 179 B5
Wood Lodge Gdns
BR1 188 A3
Wood Lodge La BR4 224 A5
Woodman La E4 20 C6
Woodman Par 4 E16 122 C5
Woodmans Gr NW10 67 D3
Woodmans Mews W12 90 B2
Woodman St E16 122 C5
E16 122 D5
Woodmansterne Prim Sch
SW16 181 D2
Woodmansterne Rd
Mitcham SW16 181 D2
Sutton SM5 218 C1
Wood Mead N17 34 A4
Woodmere SE9 166 B3
Woodmere Ave CR0 206 D2
Woodmere Cl
10 SW11 137 A2
Croydon CR0 206 D2
Woodmere Ct N14 15 B4
Woodmere Gdns CR0 206 D2
Woodmere Way BR3 208 B4
Woodnook Rd SW16 181 B5
Woodpecker Cl
Bushey WD23 8 A3
Enfield N9 18 B5
Harrow HA3 24 D2
Woodpecker Mews
SE13 142 B1
Woodpecker Rd
6 SE14 141 A6
Woolwich SE28 124 C6
Wood Point 8 E16 99 A2
Woodquest Ave SE24 161 A6
Wood Rd TW17 192 C5
Wood Ride Barnet EN4 2 B4
Orpington BR5 211 C5
Woodridge Cl EN2 4 C4
Woodridge Prim Sch
N12 13 C1
Woodridings Ave HA5 23 B2
Woodridings Cl HA5 23 B3
Woodridings Ct N22 31 D2
Woodriffe Rd E11 54 B2
Wood Rise HA5 40 A4
Woodrow SE18 122 B2
Woodrow Ave UB4 83 D3
Woodrow Cl UB6 65 B1
Woodrow Ct 3 N17 34 B3
Woodruff Ho SW2 160 C5
Woodrush Cl 4 SE14 141 A5
Woodrush Way RM6 58 D5
Woodseer St
E1 95 D2 243 D4
Woodsford SE17 262 C1
Woodsford Sq
W14 113 A4 244 B2
Woodshire Rd RM10 81 D5
Woods Ho SW8 269 A2
Woodside N10 49 A6
NW11 47 C4
Buckhurst Hill IG9 21 C2
Palmers Green N13 16 C1
Walton-on-T KT12 194 A1
Wimbledon SW19 179 B5
Woodside Ave N12 30 A6
N6 48 D5
Chislehurst BR7 189 A5
Croydon SE25 206 B4
Thames Ditton KT10 196 C2
Wembley HA0 88 A6
Woodside Cl Ruislip HA4 39 B3
Stanmore HA7 25 B5
Tolworth KT5 199 A2
Wembley HA0 88 A6
Woodside Court Rd
CR0 206 A2
Woodside Cres DA15 167 C1
Woodside Ct 8 N12 29 D6
Ealing W5 110 A5
Enfield EN2 4 D4
Woodside End HA0 88 A6
Woodside Gdns
Chingford E4 35 D4
Tottenham N17 33 D1
Woodside Gn SE25 206 A3
Woodside Gr N12 14 A1
Woodside Grange Rd
N12 29 D6
Woodside Ho SW19 179 B4
Woodside Jun & Inf Sch
CR0 206 A2
Woodside Jun & Inf Schs
E17 54 A6
Woodside La DA5 168 D5
N12 14 A1
Woodside Park Ave
E17 54 B5
Woodside Park Rd N12 30 A6
Woodside Pk SE25 206 B3
Woodside Pl HA0 88 A6
Woodside Rd BR1 210 A4
E13 99 C3
Croydon SE25 206 B3
Kingston KT2 176 A3
Kingston KT3 177 C1
Northwood HA6 22 A3
Woodside Rd *continued*
Sidcup DA15 167 C1
Sutton SM1 218 A5
Woodford IG8 37 A6
Wood Green N22 32 C3
Woodside Sch DA17 125 D2
Woodside Sta SE25 206 B3
Woodside Way
Croydon CR0 206 C3
Streatham CR4 181 C2
Wood's Mews
W1 115 A6 248 A6
Woodsome Rd NW5 71 B5
Wood's Pl SE1 263 B5
Woodspring Rd SW19 157 A2
Wood's Rd SE15 140 B4
Wood St E16 121 B6
E17 54 B5
EC2 95 A1 242 B2
W4 111 C1
Barnet EN5 1 A1
Carshalton CR4 203 A2
Kingston KT1 175 D1
Kingston KT2 176 A2
Woodstar Ho 3 SE15 140 A5
Woodstead Gr HA8 26 A4
Woods The
Moor Park HA6 22 A5
Uxbridge UB10 60 D4
Woodstock Ave NW11 47 A2
W13 109 A3
Cheam SM3 201 B2
Isleworth TW7 153 A6
Southall UB1 85 B4
Woodstock Cl DA5 169 B3
Stanmore HA7 26 A1
Woodstock Cres N9 18 B5
Woodstock Ct SE11 260 D2
SE12 165 A5
Kingston KT2 176 D1
Woodstock Dr UB10 60 B4
Woodstock Gdns
Beckenham BR3 185 D3
Hayes UB4 83 D2
Ilford IG3 80 A6
Woodstock Gr W12 112 D4
Woodstock Ho 2 N5 73 A4
Hayes UB3 83 B2
Woodstock La N KT6 213 C6
Woodstock La S KT10,
KT6 213 C4
Woodstock Mews W1 238 B3
Woodstock Rd E7 77 C1
N4 50 C1
NW11 47 B1
W4 111 C3
Bushey WD23 8 D4
Chingford E17 36 B1
South Croydon CR0 221 B5
Wallington SM5,SM6 219 A3
Wembley HA0 66 B1
Woodstock Rise SM3 201 B2
Woodstock St W1 238 C1
Woodstock Terr E14 119 D6
Woodstock The SM3 201 B2
Woodstock Way CR4 181 C1
Woodstone Ave KT17,
KT4 216 A3
Wood Street Sta E17 54 B5
Woodsyre SE26 183 D6
Woodthorpe Rd
Ashford TW15 170 A6
Putney SW15 134 B1
Woodtree Cl NW4 28 C1
Wood Vale N10 49 C4
Dulwich SE22 162 B4
Woodvale Ave SE25 183 D1
Woodvale Ct BR1 187 B1
South Norwood SE25 205 D6
Woodvale Way NW11 68 D5
Woodvale Wlk SE27 183 A5
Woodview Ave E4 36 A6
Woodview Cl N4 50 D2
Kingston SW15 177 B6
Orpington BR6 227 A6
Woodville SE3 143 B4
Woodville Cl SE12 165 A6
Teddington TW11 175 A6
Woodville Ct 3 SE10 142 A4
Woodville Gdns NW11 46 D2
Ealing W5 88 A1
Ilford IG6 56 D5
Ruislip HA4 39 A2
Surbiton KT6 197 D2
Woodville Gr 2 DA16 146 A2
Woodville Ho SE1 263 C6
Woodville Rd E11 54 D1
E17 53 B5
N16 73 C3
NW11 47 A2
NW6 91 B5
Barnet EN5 1 D2
Ealing W5 87 D1
Morden SM4 201 C5
Richmond TW10 153 C1
South Norwood CR7 205 B6
Woodford E18 37 B1
Woodville St 16 SE7 122 A2
Woodville The W5 87 D1
Woodward Ave NW4 46 A4
Woodward Cl KT10 212 D2
Woodwarde Rd SE22 161 C5
Woodward Gdns
Dagenham RM9 80 C1
Harrow HA7 24 D3
Woodward Rd RM9 80 C1
Wood Way BR6 226 C6
Woodway Cres HA1 43 A3
Woodwell St SW18 158 A6
Wood Wharf SE10 142 A6
Woodyard Cl NW5 71 A3
Woodyard La SE21 161 C4
Woodyates Rd SE12 165 B4
Woolacombe Rd SE3 143 C3
Woolacombe Way
UB3 105 C2
Woolcombes Ct 4
SE16 118 D5
Woolden Ho 2 E4 20 C4
Wooler St
SE17 117 B1 262 D2
Woolf Cl SE28 124 B5
Woolf Ct 7 W3 111 A3
Woolf Mews WC1 240 A6
Woollaston Rd N4 50 D3
Woolley Ho SW9 138 D2
Woollon Ho 1 E1 96 C1
Woolmead Ave NW9 46 A2
Woolmer Gdns N18 34 A5
Woolmer Ho 2 E5 74 B6
Woolmer Rd N18 34 A5
Woolmore Prim Sch
E14 120 A6
Woolmore St E14 120 A6
Woolneigh St SW6 135 D3
Woolpack Ho 1 E9 74 C2
Wool Rd SW20 178 B4
Woolridge Way E9 74 C1
Woolstaplers Way
SE16 118 A2
Woolston Cl E17 34 D1
Woolstone Ho 7 E2 96 A6
Woolstone Rd SE23 163 A2
Woolven Ho SE3 142 D6
Woolwich Arsenal Sta
SE18 122 D2
Woolwich Church St
SE7,SE18 122 A3
Woolwich SE18 122 C3
Woolwich Comm
SE18 144 C6
Woolwich Dockyard Ind Est
SE18 122 A3
Woolwich Dockyard Sta
SE18 122 B2
Woolwich & Greenwich
Com Coll SE18 123 A2
Woolwich High St
SE18 122 C3
Woolwich Manorway
E16 122 D4
Woolwich Manor Way
E16 122 D5
E6 100 C1
Woolwich New Rd
SE18 122 D2
Woolwich Poly Sch for Boys
SE28 124 A5
Woolwich Rd DA7 147 C2
Belvedere DA17 125 C1
Erith SE2 125 B1
Greenwich SE7,SE10 121 C2
Wooster Gdns E14 98 B1
Wootton KT10 212 A4
Wootton Gr N3 29 C2
Wootton Ho SE9 167 B5
Wootton St
SE1 116 C5 251 B3
Worbeck Rd SE20 184 C1
Worcester Ave N17 34 A3
Worcester Cl NW2 68 B5
Croydon CR0 223 C6
Mitcham CR4 181 A1
Worcester Cres NW7 11 C1
Woodford IG8 37 C6
Worcester Ct N12 29 D5
44 W2 91 C2
Ashford TW15 170 D5
Ealing W7 86 D1
Harrow HA1 42 C6
Walton-on-T KT12 194 C1
Worcester Park KT4 215 C5
Worcester Dr W4 111 C4
Ashford TW15 170 D5
Worcester Gdns
SW11 158 D6
Northolt UB6 64 B2
Redbridge IG1 56 A2
Worcester Park KT4 215 C5
Worcester Ho SE11 261 A5
W2 236 A1
9 Putney SW15 156 C4
Worcester Mews 2
NW6 69 D2
Worcester Park Rd
KT4 215 B5
Worcester Park Sta
KT4 200 A1
Worcester Rd E17 34 D1
Belmont SM2 217 C1
Ilford E12 78 B4
11 Wimbledon SW19 179 B5
Worcesters Ave EN1 6 A5
Worcesters Prim Sch
EN1 5 D5
Wordsworth N8 50 C5
Wordsworth Ave E12 78 A1
E18 54 D6
Greenford UB6 86 B5
Wordsworth Ct HA1 42 B2
Wordsworth Dr KT4,
SM3 216 C4
Wordsworth Ho NW6 91 C4
15 SE18 144 C6
Wordsworth Par 1
N15 50 D5
Wordsworth Pl 11 NW5 70 D3
Wordsworth Rd DA16 145 C4
N16 73 C4
SE1 263 D3
Hampton TW12,TW13 173 B6
Penge SE20 184 D3
Wallington SM6 219 D2
Wordsworth Way UB7 104 B2
Wordsworth Wlk NW11 47 C5
Worfield St
SW11 136 C5 267 B3
Worgan St
SE11 116 B1 260 C2
SE16 118 D2
Working Men's Coll The
NW1 93 C5 232 A4
Worland Rd E15 76 C1
World Bsns Ctr TW6 127 A4
Worlds End La BR6 227 D1
World's End La EN2 4 B1
World's End Pas
SW10 266 C4
World's End Pl SW10 266 B4
Worley Ct NW2 68 D5
Worlidge St W6 112 C1
Worlingham Rd SE22 139 D1
Wormholt Park Prim Sch
W12 112 A6
Wormholt Rd W12 112 A5
Wormwood St EC2 243 A2
Wornington Rd W10 91 A2
Wornum Ho 3 NW6 91 A5
Woronzow Rd
NW8 92 C6 230 A5
Worple Ave
Isleworth TW7 153 A6
Wimbledon SW19 178 D3
Worple Cl HA2 41 B1
Worple Ct SW19 179 A4
Worple Prim Sch TW7 131 A1
Worple Rd
Isleworth TW7 131 A1
Wimbledon SW19,SW20 178 D2
Worple Road Mews
SW19 179 B4
Worple St SW14 133 B2
Worple Way Harrow HA2 41 B1
Richmond TW10 132 A1
Worship St EC2 95 C3 243 A5
Worslade Rd SW17 180 B6
Worsley Bridge Jun Sch
BR3 185 C3
Worsley Bridge Rd
BR3,SE6 185 C5
Worsley Ct N3 29 D4
Worsley Gr E5 74 A4
Worsley Ho 9 SE23 162 B2
Worsley Rd E11 76 C4
Worsopp Dr SW4 159 C6
Worth Cl BR6 227 C4
Worthfield Cl KT19 215 B1
Worth Gr SE17 262 C1
Worthing Cl 5 E15 98 C6
Worthing Rd TW5 129 B6
Worthington Cl CR4 203 B6
Worthington Ho EC1 234 B2
16 Streatham SW2 160 C4
Worthington Rd KT6 198 B1
Wortley Rd E6 77 D1
Thornton Heath CR0 204 C2
Worton Ct TW7 130 C1
Worton Gdns TW7 130 B3
Worton Hall Ind Est
TW7 130 C1
Worton Rd TW7 130 C2
Worton Way TW3,TW7 130 B3
Wotton Ct 8 E14 120 B6
Wotton Rd NW2 68 C5
18 SE8 141 B6
Wouldham Rd E16 98 D1
Wragby Rd E11 76 C5
Wrampling Pl N9 18 A3
Wrangthorne Wlk
CR0 220 C4
Wray Ave IG5 56 C6
Wrayburn Ho 25 SE16 118 A4
Wray Cres N4 72 B6
Wray Ct N4 72 B6
Wrayfield Rd SM3 216 D5
Wray Ho 11 SW2 160 A3
Wraysbury Cl TW4 151 A6
Wrays Way UB4 83 C3
Wrekin Rd SE18 145 A5
Wren Ave NW2 68 C4
Southall UB2 107 B2
Wren Cl E16 98 D1
N9 18 D3
Wren Cres WD23 8 A3
Wren Ct CR0 221 B4
Wren Gdns RM9 80 D3
Wren Ho 27 E3 97 A5
SW1 259 C1
4 Hampton TW12 173 D4
Wren Landing E14 119 C5
Wrenn Ho SW13 134 C6
Wren Path SE28 123 B4
Wren Rd SE5 139 B4
Dagenham RM9 80 D3
Sidcup DA14 168 C1
Wrens Ave TW15 171 A6
Wren's Park Ho E5 74 B6
Wren St WC1 94 B3 240 D6
Wrentham Ave NW10 90 D5
Wrenthorpe Rd BR1 186 C6
Wren View N6 49 C1
Wrenwood Way HA5 40 B5
Wrestlers Ct EC3 243 A2
Wrexham Rd E3 97 C5
Wricklemarsh Rd SE3 143 D4
Wrigglesworth St
SE14 140 D5
Wright Cl SE13 142 B1
Wright Gdns TW17 192 C4
Wright Ho SW15 156 B6
Wrighton Ct SM1 217 B2
Wright Rd TW5 128 C5
Wrights Cl RM10 81 D4
Wright's Gn SW4 137 D1
Wright's La
W8 113 D3 255 C6
Wrights Pl NW10 67 A2
Wright's Rd E3 97 B5
Wrights Rd SE25 205 C6
Wright's Row SM5 219 B4
Wrights Wlk SW14 133 B2
Writtle Ho 35 NW9 27 D1
Wrotham Ho SE1 262 D6
Beckenham BR3 185 B3
Wrotham Rd DA16 146 C4
11 NW1 71 C1
Barnet EN5 1 A3
Ealing W13 109 C5
Wrottesley Rd NW10 90 A5
SE18 145 A6
Wroughton Rd SW11 158 D5
Wroughton Terr NW4 46 B5
Wroxall Rd RM9 80 C2
Wroxham Gdns N11 31 D3
Wroxham Rd SE28 124 D6
Wroxton Rd SE15 140 C3
Wrythe Gn SM5 218 D5
Wrythe Green Rd SM5 218 D5
Wrythe La SM1,SM5,
SM4 218 C5
Wulfstan St W12 89 D1
Wyatt Cl SE16 119 B4
Bushey WD23 8 C4
Feltham TW13 150 D3
Hayes UB4 84 A2
Wyatt Ct HA0 66 A1
Wyatt Dr SW13 134 B5
Wyatt Ho NW8 236 D5
SE3 142 D3
Wyatt Park Mans 1
SW2 160 A2
Wyatt Park Rd SW2 160 B2
Wyatt Rd E7 77 A2
N5 73 A5
Wyatt's La E17 54 A6
Wybert St NW1 239 A6
Wyborne Ho NW10 67 A1
Wyborne Prim Sch
SE9 166 D3
Wyborne Way NW10 67 A1
Wyburn Ave EN5 1 B2
Wyche Gr CR2 221 A1
Wycherley Cl SE3 142 D5
Wycherley Cres EN5 13 D5
Wychwood Ave
Edgware HA8 25 D4
South Norwood CR7 205 A6
Wychwood Cl
Ashford TW16 172 A4
Edgware HA8 25 D4
Wychwood End N6 49 C2
Wychwood Gdns IG5 56 C5
Wychwood Ho N4 51 A2
Wychwood Way SE19 183 B4
Wyclif Ct EC1 234 C1
Wycliffe Cl DA16 145 D4
Wycliffe Ho 18 N16 73 C4
Wycliffe Rd SW19 179 D4
Wyclif St EC1 234 C1
Wycombe Ct SE3 143 A5
Wycombe Gdns NW11 69 C6
Wycombe Ho NW8 237 A6
Wycombe Pl SW18 158 A5

Wycombe Rd
Redbridge IG2 .... 56 B4
Tottenham N17 .... 34 A2
Wembley HA0 .... 88 C6
Wydell Cl SM4 .... 200 D3
Wydenhurst Rd CR0 .. 206 B2
Wydeville Manor Rd
SE12 .... 187 B6
Wye Cl BR6 .... 211 D2
Ashford TW15 .... 170 D6
Ruislip HA4 .... 39 A3
Wye Ct W13 .... 87 B2
Wyemead Cres E4 .... 20 C2
Wyersdale Ho N4 ...... 51 A2
Wye St SW11 .... 136 B3
Wyevale Cl HA5 .... 40 A6
Wyfold Ho 10 SE2 .... 124 D4
Wyfold Rd
SW6 .... 135 A5 264 A3
Wyke Cl TW7 .... 130 D6
Wyke Gdns W7 .... 109 A3
Wykeham Ave RM9 .... 80 C2
Wykeham Cl UB7 .... 126 C6
Wykeham Ct NW4 ...... 46 C4
Wykeham Gn RM9 ...... 80 C2
Wykeham Hill HA9 ...... 44 B1
Wykeham Ho SW19 .. 179 C2
Wykeham Prim Sch
NW9 .... 67 C5
Wykeham Rd NW4 ...... 46 C4
Harrow HA3 .... 43 B5
Wykeham Rise N20 .... 13 A3
Wykehurst Ho SW17 .. 180 B5
Wyke Rd E3 .... 75 C1
Merton SW20 .... 178 C1
Wylchin Cl HA5 .... 39 D6
Wyldes Cl NW11 .... 48 A1
Wyldfield Gdns N9 .... 17 D2
Wyld Way HA9 .... 66 D2
Wyleu St SE23 .... 163 A4
Wylie Rd UB2 .... 107 C3
Wyllen Cl E1 .... 96 C3
Wylo Dr EN5 .... 12 A5
Wymering Mans 6 W9 91 C4
Wymering Rd W9 ...... 91 C4
Wymondham Ct NW8 229 D6
Wymond St SW15 .... 134 C2
Wynan Rd E14 .... 119 D1
Wynard Terr SE11 .... 260 D2
Wynash Gdns SM5 .... 218 C3
Wynaud Ct N22 .... 32 B4
Wynbourne Ct SE20 .. 184 B1
Wyncham Ave DA15 .. 167 C3
Wynchgate Harrow HA3 24 C3
Southgate N14 .... 16 A4
Wyncroft Cl BR1 ...... 210 B6
Wyndale Ave NW9 ...... 44 C3
Wyndcliff Rd SE7 ...... 143 B6
Wyndcroft Cl EN2 .... 4 D2
Wyndham Cl
Belmont SM2 .... 217 C1
Orpington BR6 .... 211 A1
Wyndham Cres N19 .... 71 C5
Hounslow TW4 .... 151 C5
Wyndham Ct W7 ...... 109 A2
Wyndham Deedes Ho 27
E2 .... 96 A5
Wyndham Ho SW1 .. 258 A3
Wyndham Mews W1 .. 237 C3
Wyndham Pl W1 .... 237 C3
Wyndham Rd E6 ...... 77 D1
SE5 .... 139 A5
W13 .... 109 B3
Barnet, London EN4 ...... 14 D3
Kingston KT2 .... 176 B3
Wyndham St
W1 .... 92 D2 237 C4
Wyndham Yd W1 .... 237 C3
Wyneham Rd SE24 .... 161 B6
Wynell Rd SE23 ...... 162 D1
Wynford Pl DA17 ...... 147 C6
Wynford Rd N1 .94 B5 233 D4
Wynford Way SE9 .... 166 B1
Wynlie Gdns HA5 ...... 22 B1
Wynn Bridge Cl IG8 .. 37 D2
Wynndale Rd E18 ...... 37 B2
Wynne Ct 4 TW7 .... 131 A2
Wynne Ho SE14 ...... 140 D4
Wynne Rd SW9 ...... 138 C3
Wynn's Ave DA15 ...... 168 A6
Wynnstay Gdns
W8 .... 113 C3 255 B6
Wynter Ho 20 SW9 .... 138 B3
Wynter St SW11 ...... 136 A1
Wynton Gdns SE25 .. 205 D4
Wynton Pl W3 .... 88 D1
Wynyard Ho SE11 .... 260 D2
Wynyatt St EC1 .94 D4 234 C2
Wyre Gr Edgware HA8 .. 10 D1
Hayes UB3 .... 106 A2
Wyresdale Cres UB6 .. 86 D4
Wyteleaf Cl HA4 ...... 39 A3
Wytham Ho NW8 .... 236 D5
Wythburn Ct W1 .... 237 C2
Wythburn Pl W1 .... 237 C2
Wythenshawe Rd RM10 81 C5
Wythens Wlk SE9 .... 166 D5
Wythes Cl BR1 ...... 188 B1
Wythes Rd E16 ...... 122 A5
Wythfield Rd SE9 .... 166 B5
Wyvenhoe Rd HA2 ...... 64 A5
Wyvern Est The KT3 .. 200 A5
Wyvil Prim Sch
SW8 .... 138 A5 270 B4
Wyvil Rd SW8 .138 A5 270 A4
Wyvis St E14 .... 97 D2

X

Xavier Ho E17 .... 35 B1

Y

Yabsley St E14 .... 120 A5
Yaldam Ho SE1 .... 263 A3
Yalding Ho 20 E5 ...... 74 B3
Yalding Rd SE16 ...... 118 A2
Yale Cl TW4 .... 151 B6
Yale Ct NW6 .... 69 D3
Yarborough Rd SW19 .180 B2
Yardley Cl E4 .... 19 D6
Yardley Ct SM3 ...... 216 D4
Yardley La E4 .... 19 D6
Yardley Prim Sch E4 .. 20 A5
Yardley St WC1 ...... 234 A1
Yarmouth Cres N17 .... 52 B4
Yarmouth Pl W1 ...... 248 C3
Yarnfield Sq 14 SE15 .. 140 A4
Yarnton Way DA17,
DA18 .... 125 B3
Yarrow Cres E6 ...... 100 A2
Yarrow Ho 10 E14 .... 120 A3
W10 .... 90 C2
Yateley St SE18 ...... 121 D3
Yatesbury Ct E5 ...... 75 A3
Yates Ct NW2 .... 68 D2
Yates Ho 15 E2 .... 96 A4
Yatton Ho W10 .... 90 C2
Yeading Ave HA2 ...... 41 A1
Yeading Ct UB4 .... 84 C3
Yeading Fork UB4 ...... 84 C3
Yeading Gdns UB4 ...... 84 B2
Yeading Ho UB4 ...... 84 D2
Yeading Jun & Inf Schs
UB4 .... 84 C2
Yeading La Hayes UB4 .. 84 B2
Hayes, Northolt UB4,UB5 .84 C4
Yeadon Ho W10 ...... 90 C2
Yeames Cl W13 .... 87 A1
Yearby Ho W10 .... 90 C3
Yeate St N1 .... 73 B1
Yeatman Rd N6 .... 48 D3
Yeats Cl NW10 .... 67 C2
Yeend Cl KT8 .... 195 C5
Yeldham Ho W6 ...... 112 D1
Yeldham Rd W6 ...... 112 D1
Yellowhammer Ct NW9 27 C1
Yelverton Lo TW1 .... 153 C4
Yelverton Rd SW11 .. 136 B3
Ye Market CR0 ...... 221 B3
Yenston Cl SM4 ...... 201 C3
Yeoman Cl E16 ...... 122 D6
West Norwood SE27 .. 160 D1
Yeoman Ct TW5 ...... 129 B5
Yeoman Ho SE1 ...... 263 D2
Yeoman Rd UB5 ...... 63 A1
Yeomans Acre HA4 .... 40 A3
Yeomans Mews TW7 .. 152 B6
Yeoman's Row
SW3 .... 114 C3 257 B5
Yeoman St SE8 ...... 119 A2
Yeomans Way EN3 ...... 6 C3
Yeoman's Yd E1 ...... 253 D6
Yeo St E3 .... 97 D2
Yeovil Cl BR6 .... 227 C6
Yeovil Ho N7 .... 72 B6
W10 .... 90 C3
Yeovilton Pl KT2 ...... 175 C5
Yerbury Prim Sch N19 .71 D5
Yerbury Rd N19 ...... 71 D5
Yesodey Hatorah Sch
N16 .... 51 D2
Yester Dr BR7 .... 188 A3
Yester Pk BR7 .... 188 B4
Yester Rd BR7 .... 188 B3
Yew Ave UB7 .... 104 A6
Yew Cl IG9 .... 21 D2
Yewdale Cl BR1 ...... 186 C4
Yewfield Rd NW10 .... 67 D2
Yew Gr NW2 .... 68 D4
Yew Ho SE14 .... 141 B3
Yews The TW15 ...... 170 D6
Yew Tree Ave N2 ...... 47 D6
Yew Tree Cl DA16 .... 146 A4
Yewtree Cl Harrow HA2 .41 D5
Wood Green N22 ...... 31 C2
Yew Tree Cl
New Malden KT4 ...... 199 C1
Southgate N21 .... 16 C4
Yew Tree Cotts KT10 . 212 B6
Yew Tree Ct 4 NW11 .. 47 B4
Elstree WD6 .... 9 D5
8 Sutton SM2 ...... 218 A1
Yew Tree Gdns RM6 .... 59 A4
Yew Tree Grange 2
W5 .... 109 C6
Yew Tree Ho KT4 .... 199 C1
Yew Tree Rd W12 .... 111 D6
Yewtree Rd BR3 ...... 207 B6
Yew Tree Rd UB10 ...... 82 B6
Yew Trees TW17 ...... 192 B5
Yew Tree Wlk TW4 .... 151 B6
Yew Wlk HA1 .... 42 C1
Yiewsley Ct UB7 ...... 104 A5
Yoakley Rd N16 .... 73 C6
Yoke Cl N7 .... 72 A2
Yolande Gdns SE9 .... 166 A6
Yonge Pk N4,N7 ...... 72 C5
York Ave DA15 ...... 167 D2
SE17 .... 262 B2
Ealing W7 .... 108 C5
Hayes UB3 .... 83 A1
Mortlake SW14 ...... 155 A6
Stanmore HA7 .... 25 B1
York Bldgs
WC2 .... 116 A6 250 B5
York Bridge
NW1 .... 93 A3 238 A6
York Cl 17 SE5 ...... 139 A3
Ealing W7 .... 108 C5
Morden SM4 .... 201 D5
Newham E6 .... 100 B1
York Ct Beckenham BR3 186 B2
Kingston KT2 .... 175 D4
Wallington SM6 ...... 219 C3
York Gate NW1 ...... 238 B5
Southgate N14 .... 16 A4
York Gr SE15 .... 140 C4
York Hill SE27,SW16 .. 160 D1
York Ho N1 .... 233 C3
N5 .... 72 C3
3 N7 .... 71 D2
1 NW4 .... 28 D1
SE1 .... 116 B3 260 D5
SW3 .... 257 D2
York Ho *continued*
W1 .... 237 C4
W3 .... 111 A6
W8 .... 245 C2
10 Acton W3 .... 88 C1
Chingford E4 .... 35 C6
Enfield EN2 .... 5 B4
Forest Hill SE26 ...... 184 C5
1 Ilford IG1 .... 78 D6
4 Kingston KT2 ...... 176 B3
Richmond TW10 ...... 154 C6
Richmond TW9 ...... 132 C4
South Norwood SE25 .. 205 C5
York House Pl
W8 .... 113 D4 245 C2
Yorkland Ave DA16 .. 145 D1
Yorkley Ho W10 ...... 90 C3
York Mans 1 NW9 .... 46 A3
SW11 .... 268 B2
W1 .... 238 A4
York Mews NW5 ...... 71 B3
Ilford IG1 .... 78 C5
York Par NW9 .... 46 A3
Brentford TW8 ...... 109 D1
York Pl SW11 .... 136 B2
WC2 .... 250 B5
Ilford IG1 .... 78 C6
York Place Mans
NW1 .... 237 D4
York Rd E10 .... 76 A5
E17 .... 52 D4
E7 .... 77 A2
N11 .... 31 D4
SE1 .... 116 B4 250 D2
SW11,SW18 .... 136 B2
W3 .... 89 B1
W5 .... 109 C3
Belmont SM1,SM2 .... 217 C1
Brentford TW8 ...... 109 D1
Chingford E4 .... 35 C5
Edmonton N18 .... 34 B5
Hounslow TW3 ...... 129 D2
Ilford IG1 .... 78 C6
Kingston KT2 .... 176 B3
New Barnet EN5 ...... 14 B6
Pinner HA6 .... 22 A1
4 Richmond TW10 .... 154 B6
Southgate N21 .... 17 B4
Teddington TW11 ...... 174 C6
Thornton Heath CR0 .. 204 C2
Wimbledon SW19 .... 180 A4
York Rise BR6 ...... 227 C6
NW5 .... 71 B5
York Road Bsns Ctr
SW11 .... 136 B3
Yorkshire Cl N16 ...... 73 C5
Yorkshire Gdns N18 .... 34 B5
Yorkshire Grey SE9 .. 165 D6
Yorkshire Grey Yd
WC1 .... 240 C3
Yorkshire Rd E14 ...... 97 A1
Mitcham CR4 .... 204 A5
York Sq 14 E14 .... 97 A1
York St W1 .... 92 D2 237 D4
Barking IG11 .... 101 A6
York St *continued*
Carshalton CR4 ...... 203 A2
Twickenham TW1 .... 153 A3
York St Chambers W1 237 C4
York Terr EN2 .... 5 A5
York Terr E
NW1 .... 93 A3 238 B5
York Terr W
NW1 .... 93 A3 238 A5
Yorkton St E2 .... 96 A5
York Way N1 .... 233 B5
N1,N7,NW1 .... 72 A1
N20 .... 14 D1
Chessington KT9 .... 214 A1
Twickenham TW13 .... 151 B1
York Way Ct N1 ...... 233 B5
Youngmans Cl EN2 ...... 5 A4
Young Rd E16 .... 99 C1
Young's Bldgs EC1 .... 242 B6
Youngs Ct SW11 .... 268 B1
Youngs Rd IG2 .... 57 B4
Young St W8 .113 D4 245 C1
Yoxall Ho W10 .... 90 C3
Yoxley App IG2 .... 57 A3
Yoxley Dr IG2 .... 57 A3
Yukon Rd SW12 ...... 159 B4
Yuletide Cl NW10 ...... 67 C2
Yunus Khan Cl E17 .... 53 C4

Z

Zampa Rd SE16 ...... 118 C1
Zander Ct E2 .... 96 A4
Zangwill Ho NW6 ...... 91 B5
Zangwill Rd SE18,SE3 .143 D4
Zealand Ave UB7 .... 126 A5
Zealand Ho 11 SE5 .. 139 A3
4 SE7 .... 122 A2
Zealand Rd E3 .... 97 A5
Zennor Rd SW12 .... 159 C3
Zenoria St SE22 ...... 139 D1
Zermatt Rd CR7 ...... 205 A5
Zetland Ho W8 ...... 255 C6
Zetland St E14 .... 98 A2
Zion Ho 6 E1 .... 96 C1
Zion Pl CR7 .... 205 B5
Zion Rd CR7 .... 205 B5
Zoar St SE1 .. 117 A5 252 A4
Zodiac Ct CR0 ...... 204 D1
Zodiac Ho 3 E3 ...... 97 C3
Zoffany St N19 ...... 71 D6

List of numbered locations

This atlas shows thousands more place names than any other London street atlas. In some busy areas it is impossible to fit the name of every place.

Where not all names will fit, some smaller places are shown by a number. If you wish to find out the name associated with a number, use this listing.

The places in this list are also listed normally in the Index.

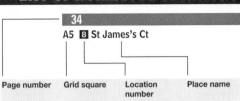

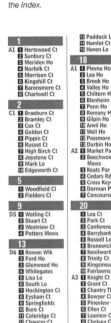

1
A1 1 Hertswood Ct
2 Sunbury Ct
3 Meriden Ho
4 Norfolk Ct
5 Morrison Ct
6 Kingshill Ct
7 Baronsmere Ct
8 Chartwell Ct

2
C1 1 Braeburn Ct
2 Bramley Ct
3 Cox Ct
4 Golden Ct
5 Pippin Ct
6 Russet Ct
7 High Birch Ct
8 Joystone Ct
9 Mark Lo
10 Edgeworth Ct

5
1 Woodfield Cl
2 Fielders Cl

9
D5 1 Watling Ct
2 Stuart Ct
3 Westview Ct
4 Potters Mews

13
D6 1 Rowan Wlk
2 Ford Ho
3 Glenwood Ho
4 Whitegates
5 Lisa Lo
6 South Lo
7 Hockington Ct
8 Eysham Ct
9 Springfields
10 Bure Ct
11 Coleridge Ct
12 Chaucer Ct

14
B6 1 Redrose Trad Ctr
2 Lancaster Road Ind Est
C5 1 Feline Ct
2 Brookhill Ct
3 Littlegrove Ct
4 Desmond Ho

15
C6 1 Tregenna Cl
2 Catherine Ct
3 Conisbee Ct
4 Ashmead
D3 1 Dennis Par
2 Broadway The
3 Southgate Cir
4 Station Par
5 Bourneside
6 Bourneside Cres

17
C6 1 Wade Ho
2 Newport Lo
3 Halcyon
4 Lerwick Ct
5 Anchor Ct
6 Grassmere Ct
7 Datchworth Ct
8 Trentham Lo
9 Austin Ct
10 Cedar Grange
11 Brookview Ct
12 Chestbrook Ct
13 Paddock Lo
14 Hamlet Ct
15 Haven Lo

18
A1 1 Plevna Ho
2 Lea Ho
3 Brook Ho
4 Valley Ho
5 Chiltern Ho
6 Blenheim Ho
7 Penn Ho
8 Romany Ho
9 Gilpin Ho
10 Anvil Ho
11 Well Ho
12 Passmore Ho
13 Durbin Ho
A2 1 Market Par
2 Beechwood Mews
3 Keats Par
4 Cedars Rd
5 Cross Keys Cl
6 Dorman Pl
7 Concourse The

20
1 Lea Ct
2 Park Ct
3 Conference Cl
4 Berrybank Cl
5 Russell Lo
6 Brunswick Lo
7 Kenilworth Ct
8 Trinity Ct
9 Kingsmead Lo
10 Fairlawns
A3 1 Knight Ct
2 Grant Ct
3 Chantry The
4 Bowyer Ct
5 Pineview Ct
6 Ellen Ct
7 Leaview Ct
8 Chelsea Ct
9 Bramley Ct
10 Garenne Ct
11 Kendal Ct
B2 1 Temple Hall Ct
2 Larkshall Bsns Ctr
3 Endlebury Ct
4 James Ct
5 Holmes Ct
B3 1 Maddox Ct
2 Village Arc The
3 Cambridge Rd
4 Crown Bldgs
5 Pentney Rd
6 Scholars Ho
7 Cranworth Cres
C4 1 Connaught Ct
2 Woolden Ho
3 Fairmead Ct
4 Lockhart Lo
5 Cavendish Ct
6 Oakwood Ct
7 Plains The
8 Hadleigh Ct
9 Forest Ho
10 Mathieson Ho

21
C2 1 Westbury Ct
2 Palmerston Ct
3 Ibrox Ct
4 Richard Burton Ct
5 Queens Ct
6 Gunnels Ct & Hastingwood Ct
7 Marlborough Ct
8 Avenue The
9 Tara Ct
D2 1 Regency Lo
2 Kings Ct
3 Beech Ct
4 Sycamore Ho

22
C1 1 Northcote
2 Edwin Ware Ct
3 Chalfont Wlk
4 Maple Ct
5 Montesole Ct

23
B3 1 St Cuthberts Gdns
2 Cherry Croft Gdns
3 Cornwall Cl
4 Dunsford Ct

25
C5 1 Belgrave Gdns
2 Heywood Ct
3 Norfolk Ho
4 Garden Ct
5 Chatsworth Ct
6 Chartridge Ct
7 Hardwick Cl
8 Cheltenham Ct
9 Cargrey Ho
10 Holbein Ho
11 Goodwood Cl
C6 1 Bickley Ct
2 Kelmscott Ct
3 Elstree Ho
4 Brompton Ct
5 Kenmare Ct

27
A1 1 Colesworth Ho
2 Crokesley Ho
3 Curtlington Ho
4 Clare Ho
5 Kedyngton Ho
A3 1 Tadbourne Ct
2 Truman Cl
3 Lords Ct
4 Hutton Row
5 Compton Cl
6 Botham Cl
7 Bradman Row
A6 1 Iris Wlk
2 Sycamore Cl
B5 1 Monarchs Ct
2 Kensington Ct
C2 1 Rufforth Ct
2 Riccal Ct
3 Lindholme Ct
4 Driffield Ct
5 Jack Ashley Ct
6 Folkingham La
7 Leander Ct
8 Daniel Ct
9 Nimrod
10 Nisbet
11 Pixton
12 Rapide
13 Ratier
D1 1 Gauntlet
2 Guilfoyle
3 Grebe
4 Gates
5 Galy
6 Folland
7 Firefly
8 Halifax
9 Debussy
10 Crosbie
11 Grant Ct
12 Ham Ct
13 Deal Ct
14 Ember Ct
15 Canterbury Ct
16 Beaumont Ct
17 Cirrus
18 Defiant
19 Dessouter
20 Douglas
21 Cobham
22 Clayton
23 Camm
24 Bradon
25 Boarhound
26 Bodmin
27 Bleriot
28 Blackburn
29 Audax
30 Anson
31 Albatross
32 Arran Ct
33 Mavis Ct
34 Goosander Ct
35 Platt Halls (a)
36 Writtle Ho
37 Platt Halls (b)
38 Platt Halls (c)
D2 1 Slatter
2 Sopwith
3 Saimet
4 Sassoon
5 Roe
6 Orde
7 Osprey
8 Prodger
9 Randall
10 Porte
11 Norris
12 Nardini
13 Noel
14 Nicolson
15 Napier
16 Nighthawk
17 Moorhouse
18 Moineau
19 Mitchell
20 Lysander
21 Lillywhite
22 Martynside
23 March
24 Kemp
25 Mercury
26 Merlin
27 Hudson
28 Hawker
29 Hawfinch
30 Heracles
31 Hector
D3 1 Wellington
2 Wheeler
3 Whittaker
4 Whittle
5 Tedder
6 Cranwell Ct
7 Tait
8 Spooner

28
D1 1 York Ho
2 Windsor Ho
3 Regency Cres
4 Normandy Ho
5 Allerton Ct

29
C2 1 Sherringham Ct
2 St Ronan's
3 Crescent Rise
4 Elm Ct
D6 1 Brookfield Ct
2 Magnolia Ct
3 Dunbar Ct
4 Haughmond
5 Nansen Village
6 Beechcroft Ct
7 Speedwell Ct
8 Woodside Ct
9 Speedwell Ho
10 Rebecca Ho
11 Ashbourne Ct
12 Forest Ct
13 Beecholme
14 Greville Lo
15 St Johnstone Ho

30
B1 1 New Trinity Rd
2 Garden Ho
3 Todd Ho
4 Sayers Ho
5 Mowbray Ho
6 Bouchier Ho
7 Cleveland Ho
8 Goodyear Ho
9 Lochleven Ho
10 Berwick Ho
11 Oak Ho
12 Willow Wlk
13 Craven Ho
14 Willow Ho
15 Vane Ho
16 Foskett Ho
17 Elmfield Ho
18 Sycamore Ho
19 Netherwood
D5 1 Halliwick Ct
2 Halliwick Court Par
3 Queen's Par
4 St John's Village
5 Hartland Ct
6 Kennard Mans
7 Bensley Cl

31
A3 1 Campe Ho
2 Betstyle Ho
3 Pymmes Brook Ho
4 Mosswell Ho
5 Hampden Ct
6 Crown Ct
B1 1 Cedar Ct
2 Carisbrook
3 St Ivian Ct
4 Barrington Ct
5 Essex Lo
B5 1 Caradoc Evans Cl
2 Roberts Ho
3 Lorne Ho
B6 1 Grovefield
2 Lapworth
3 Stewards Holte Wlk
4 Sarnes Ct
5 Stanhope Ho
6 Holmsdale Ho
C5 1 Barbara Martin Ho
2 Jerome Ct
3 Limes Cl
4 Arnos Grove Ct
5 Cedar Ct
6 Betspath Ho
7 Curtis Ho
8 Mason Ho
9 Danford Ho
10 New Southgate Ind Est
11 Palmer's Ct

32
A4 1 Brownlow Ct
2 Latham Ct
3 Fairlawns
4 Beaumaris
C1 1 Penwortham Ct
2 Tarleton Ct
3 Holmeswood Ct
4 Kwesi Johnson Ct
5 Sandlings The

33
D1 1 Honeysett Rd
2 Wilson's Ave
3 Palm Tree Ct
4 Stoneleigh Ct
5 Brook St
D3 1 Charles Ho
2 Moselle Ho
3 Ermine Ho
4 Kathleen Ferrier Ct
5 Concord Ho
6 Rees Ho
7 Nursery Ct
8 William Rainbird Ho
D4 1 Regan Ho
2 Isis Ho
3 Boundary Ct
4 Stellar Ho
5 Cooperage Cl

34
A5 1 Angel Pl
2 Cross St
3 Scott Ho
4 Beck Ho
5 Booker Rd
6 Bridport Ho
7 Cordwain Ho
8 St James's Ct
9 Highmead
A6 1 Walton Ho
2 Alma Ho
3 Brompton Ho
4 Field Ho
5 Bradwell Mews
6 Angel Corner Par
7 Paul Ct
8 Cuthbert Rd
9 Brockenhurst Mews
B3 1 Kenneth Robbins Ho
2 Charles Bradlaugh Ho
3 Woodrow Ct
4 Cheviot
5 Corbridge
6 Whittingham
7 Eastwood Cl
8 Alnwick
9 Bamburgh
10 Bellingham
11 Briaris Cl

36
B5 1 Hedgemoor Ct
2 Hewitt Ho
3 Castle Ho
4 Bailey Ct
5 Harcourt Ho
6 Gerboa Ct
D1 1 Chatham Rd
2 Washington Rd
3 Cherry Tree Ct
4 Grosvenor Lo
5 Torfell
D2 1 Hillboro Ct
2 Dorchester Ct

37
A1 1 Chiltons The
2 Ullswater Ct
3 Leigh Ct
4 Woburn Ct
A2 1 Lindal Ct
2 Hockley Ct
3 Woodleigh
4 Milne Ct
5 Cedar Ct
6 Elizabeth Ct
7 Silvermead
8 Laurel Mead Ct
9 Mitre Ct
10 Pevensey Ct
11 Lyndhurst Ct
A3 1 New Jubilee Ct
2 Chartwell Ct
3 Greenwood
4 Solway Lo
A4 1 Terrace The
2 Broomhill Ct
3 Clifton Ct
4 Fairstead Lo
5 Hadleigh Lo
6 Broadmead Ct
7 Wilton Ct
8 Fairfield Ct
9 Higham Ct
A6 1 Tree Tops
2 Cranfield Ct
B1 1 Station Est
2 Station App
3 James Ct
C3 1 Liston Way
2 Elizabeth Ct
3 Coopersale Cl
4 Sunset Ct
5 Lambourne Ct
C4 1 Hope Cl
2 Rex Par
3 Shalford
4 Rodings The

40
C1 1 Salisbury Ho
2 Rodwell Cl
3 Pretoria Ho
4 Ottawa Ho
5 Swallow Ct

42
D3 1 Nightingale Ct
2 St John's Ct
3 Gayton Ct
4 Wilton Pl
5 Murray Ct
6 Cymbeline Ct
7 Knowles Ct
8 Charville Ct
9 Lime Ct
10 Petherton Ct
12 Chalfont Ct
D4 1 Crystal Ctr The
2 Blue Point Ct
3 Ryan Ho
5 Bruce Ho
7 Ingram Ho
8 Arless Ho
9 Leaf Ho

46
A2 1 Milton Rd
2 Stanley Rd
A3 1 York Mans
2 Telford Rd
A5 1 Pilkington Ct
2 Cousins Ct
3 Seton Ct
4 Frensham Ct
5 Chatton Ct
6 Geraldine Ct
7 Swynford Gdns
8 Miller Ct
9 Roffey Ct
10 Peace Ct

11 Rambler Ct
12 Lion Ct
12 Wenlock Gdns
13 Dogrose Ct
14 Harry Ct
16 Tribune Ct
17 Bonville Gdns
18 Pearl Ct
B4
1 Vivian Mans
2 Parade Mans
3 Georgian Ct
4 Florence Mans
5 Park Mans
6 Cheyne Cl
7 Queens Par
8 Central Mans
C5
1 Courtney Ho
2 Golderton
3 Thornbury
4 Brampton La
5 Ashwood Ho
6 Longford Ct
7 Short St
D5
1 Midford Ho
2 Rockfield Ho
3 Lisselton Ho
4 Acrefield Ho

47
B2
1 Berkeley Ct
2 Exchange Mans
3 Beechcroft Ct
4 Nedahall Ct
B3
1 Charlton Lo
2 Clifton Gdns
B4
1 Hallswelle Par
2 Belmont Par
3 Temple Fortune Ho
4 New Tree Ct
5 Temple Fortune Par
6 Courtleigh
7 Arcade Ho
8 Queens Ct
9 Temple Fortune Ct
B5
1 Monkville Par
2 Ashbourne Par

48
A6
1 St Mary's Gn
2 Dunstan Cl
3 Paul Byrne Ho
4 Longfield Ct
5 Warwick Ct
6 Branksome Ct
7 Sherwood Hall

49
B6
1 Dorchester Ct
2 Old Chapel Pl
3 Athenaeum Pl
4 Risborough Ct
C1
1 Calvert Ct
2 Academy The
3 Whitehall Mans
4 Pauntley St
5 Archway Hts
6 Pauntley Ho
D1
1 Louise White Ho
2 Levison Way
3 Sanders Way
D2
1 Eleanor Rathbone Ho
2 Christopher Lo
3 Monkridge
4 Marbleford Ct
5 High London
6 Garton Ho
7 Hilltop Ho
8 Caroline Martyn Ho
9 Arthur Henderson Ho
10 Margaret Mcmillan Ho
11 Enid Stacy Ho
12 Mary McArthur Ho
13 Bruce Glasier Ho
14 John Wheatley Ho
15 Keir Hardie Ho
16 Monroe Ho
17 Iberia Ho
18 Lygoe Ho
19 Lambert Ho
20 Shelbourne Ho
21 Arkansas Ho
22 Lafitte Ho
23 Shreveport Ho
24 Packenham Ho
25 Orpheus Ho

26 Fayetville Ho
27 Bayon Ho
D4
1 Kelland Ct
2 Veryan Ct
3 Coulsdon Ct

50
A1
1 Beeches The
2 Lambton Ct
A2
1 Marie Lloyd Gdns
2 Jessie Blythe La
3 Leyden Mans
4 Brambledown
5 Lochbie
6 Edith Cavell Cl
A5
1 Mackenzie Ct
2 Stowell Ho
3 Campsbourne Ho
B1
1 Lawson Ct
2 Wiltshire Ct
3 Hutton Ct
D5
1 Wordsworth Par

51
A2
1 Finmere Ho
2 Keynsham Ho
3 Kilpeck Ho
4 Knaresborough Ho
5 Leighfield Ho
6 Lonsdale Ho
7 Groveley Ho
8 Wensleydale Ho
9 Badminton Ct
B2
1 Selwood Ho
2 Mendip Ho
3 Ennerdale Ho
4 Delamere Ho
5 Westwood Ho
6 Bernwood Ho
7 Allerdale Ho
8 Chattenden Ho
9 Farningham Ho
10 Oakend Ho
C1
1 Godstone Ct
2 Farnham Ct
3 Milford Ct
4 Cranleigh Ct
5 Haslemere Ct
6 Belmont Ct
7 Hockworth Ho
8 Garratt Ho
9 Fairburn Ho
C3
1 Oatfield Ho
2 Perry Ct
3 Henrietta Ho
4 Bournes Ho
5 Chisley Rd
6 Twyford Ho
7 Langford Cl
D1
1 Stamford Hill Mans
2 Montefiore Ct
3 Berwyn Ho
4 Clent Ho
5 Chiltern Ho
6 Laindon Ho
7 Pentland Ho
D2
1 Regent Ct
2 Stamford Lo
3 Holmwood Ct
D3
1 Sherboro Rd
2 Westcott Cl
3 Cadoxton Ave
4 Slater Ho
D4
1 Westerfield Rd
D5
1 Greenway Cl
2 Tottenham Gn E
3 Tottenham Gn E South Side
4 Deaconess Ct
5 Elliot Ct
6 Bushmead Cl
7 Beaufort Ho
8 Tynemouth Terr
D6
1 Holcombe Rd
2 Chaplin Rd
3 Reynardson's Ct
4 Protheroe Ho

52
A1
1 Stamford Grove E
2 Stamford Mans
3 Grove Mans
4 Stamford Grove W
B1
1 Hawkwood Mount
2 Holmbury View
3 High Hill Ferry
4 Leaside Ho
5 Courtlands

6 Ivy Ho
7 Shelford Ct

53
A4
1 Hammond Ct
2 St James Apartments
A5
1 Bristol Park Rd
2 Stoneydown Ho
3 Callonfield
4 Hardyng Ho
C1
1 Wellington Mans
2 Clewer Ct
3 Cochrane Ct
C5
1 Westbury Ho
2 Hatherley Ho
3 Vintry Mews
4 Tylers Ct
5 Merchants Lo
6 Gillards Mews
7 Blacksmiths Ho
8 Central Par
D1
1 Fitzgerald Ct
2 Bechervaise Ct
3 Underwood Ct
D2
1 Station Ct
2 Howell Ct
3 Atkinson Ct
4 Russell Ct
5 St Luke Ct
6 St Matthews Ct
7 St Mark's Ct
8 St Elizabeth Ct
9 Emmanuel Ct
10 St Thomas Ct
11 Beaumont Ho
12 Shelley Ct
13 St Paul's Twr
14 Flack Ct
15 King Ct
16 Osborne Ct
17 Muriel Ct
18 All Saints Twr
19 St Josephs Ct
20 Mitchell Ct
21 Cornwell Ct
D5
1 Nash Ho
2 St Columbas Ho
3 Attlee Terr
4 Astins Ho
5 Lindens The
6 Kevan Ct
7 Squire's Almshouses
8 Berry Field Cl
9 Holmcroft Ho
10 Connaught Ct
D6
1 Hollingbury Ct
2 Mace Ho
3 Gaitskell Ho
4 Hancocke Ho
5 Trinity Ho
6 Fanshaw Ho
7 Hilltop
8 Batten Ho
9 Bradwell Ho
10 Walton Ho
11 Temple Ho
12 Gower Ho
13 Maple Ho
14 Poplars Ho
15 Cedars Ho
16 Kimm Ho
17 O'Grady Ho
18 Latham Ho
19 Powell Ct
20 Crosbie Ho

54
A2
1 Ayerst Ct
2 Dare Ct
3 St Edwards Ct
A4
1 Jane Sabina Colard's Almshouses
2 Ellen Miller Ho
3 Tom Smith Ho
A5
1 Northwold Twr
2 Walnut Ct
3 Albert Whicher Ho
4 Pelly Ct
5 Ravenswood Road Ind Est
6 Holland Ct
7 Emberson Ho
8 St Mark's Ho
9 Alfred Villas
A6
1 St David's Ct
2 Golden Par
3 Chestnuts Ct
4 Matthew Ct
5 Gilbert Ho
6 Manning Ho
7 Southgate Ho
8 Boyden Ho

9 Prospect Ho
10 Newton Ho

55
A3
1 Aldham Hall
2 Parkside Ct
3 Mapperley Cl
4 Weavers Ho
5 Cyns Ct
6 Reed Mans
7 Thornton Ho
8 Hardwick Ct
A4
1 Kingsley Grange
2 Station Par
3 Gwynne Ho
4 Staveley Ct
5 Devon Ho
6 Thurlow Ct
7 Hollies The
8 Little Holt
9 Dudley Ct
10 Woodland Ct
11 Struan Ho
12 Westleigh Ct
A5
1 Sherwood Ho
2 Orwell Ct
3 Hermitage Ct
4 Gowan Lea
5 Woodford Ho
6 Eagle Ct
7 Newbury Ct
8 Shelley Ct
9 Hardy Ct
10 Dickens Ct
11 Byron Ct
A6
1 Millbrook
2 Elmbrook
3 Grange The
4 Glenavon Lo
5 Glenwood Ct
6 Ferndown
7 Embassy Ct
8 Orestes Ct
9 Walbrook
10 Helmsley
11 Snaresbrook Hall
B4
1 Nightingale Ct
2 Chelston Ct
3 Grosvenor Ct
4 Louise Ct
5 St Davids Ct
6 Cedar Ct
7 Shrubbery The
B6
1 Victoria Ct
2 Kenwood Gdns
3 Thaxted Lo
4 Albert Rd
5 Albert Ho
6 Falcon Ct
7 Deborah Ct
8 Swift Ho
9 Pulteney Gdns
10 Spring Ct
11 Trinity Gdns

56
B4
1 High View Par
2 Spurway Par

57
A3
1 Catherine Ct
2 Lincoln Ct
3 Ivy Terr
4 Newbury Cotts

58
B1
1 Caledonian Cl
2 Talisman Ct
3 Norseman Ct
4 Frank Slater Ho
5 Brook's Mans
6 Brook's Par
B2
1 Mitre Ct
2 Coppins The
3 Stanetto Ct
4 Wilnett Ct
5 Wilnett Villas
D2
1 Pavement Mews
2 Chadview Ct
3 Granary Ct
4 Bedwell Ct
5 Chapel La
6 Faulkner Ct
7 Maple Ct
8 Willow Ct
9 Cedar Terr

63
C2
1 Wimborne Ct
2 Haydock Green Flats
3 Brighton Dr
4 Blaydon Ct
5 Fakenham Ct
6 Rutland Ho
7 Windsor Ho

65
D3
1 Oaklands Ct
2 Lowry Lo
3 Morritt Ho
4 Lancelot Par
5 Willow Tree Ct
6 Snow Ct

66
A2
1 Montrose Cres
2 Peggy Quirke Ct
3 Copland Mews
4 Coronet Par
5 Charlotte Ct
A3
1 Market Way
2 Lodge Ct
3 Central Sq
4 Manor Ct
5 Rupert Ave

67
A5
1 Curie Ho
2 Darwin Ho
3 Priestley Ho
4 Rutherford Ho
5 Fleming Ho
6 Lister Ho
7 Edison Ho
B1
1 Kingthorpe Terr
2 Scott Ho
3 Peary Ho
4 Shackleton Ho
5 Amundsen Ho
6 Brentfield Ho
7 Nansen Ho
8 Stonebridge Ct
9 Magellan Ct
10 Leadbetter Ct
11 Viant Ho
12 Jefferies Ho
13 Diamond St
C1
1 Beveridge Rd
C5
1 Hazelwood Ct
2 Winslow Cl

68
A2
1 Regency Mews
2 Tudor Mews
A5
1 Bourne Ho
2 Carton Ho
3 Woodbridge Cl
4 Mackenzie Ho
5 Banting Ho

69
A1
1 Fountain Ho
2 Kingston Ho
3 Waverley Ct
4 Weston Ho
5 Mapes Ho
6 Athelstan Gdns
7 Left Ho
B1
1 Alma Birk Ho
2 Brooklands Ct
3 Brooklands Court Apartments
4 Cleveland Mans
5 Buckley Ct
6 Webheath
B5
1 Mortimer Cl
2 Sunnyside Ho
3 Sunnyside
4 Prospect Pl
C1
1 Linstead St
2 Embassy Ho
3 Acol Ct
4 Kings Wood Ct
5 Douglas Ct
6 King's Gdns
7 Carlton Mans
8 Smyrna Mans
9 New Priory Ct
10 Queensgate Pl
11 Brondesbury Mews
C2
1 Dene Mans
2 Sandwell Cres
3 Sandwell Mans
4 Hampstead West
5 Redcroft
C3
1 Orestes Mews
2 Walter Northcott Ho
3 Polperro Mans
4 Lyncroft Mans
5 Marlborough Mans
6 Alexandra Mans
7 Cumberland Mans
8 Cavendish Mans
9 Ambassador Ho
10 Welbeck Mans
D2
1 Alder Ho

11 Inglewood Mans
C5
1 Portman Hts
2 Hermitage Ct
3 Moreland Ct
4 Wendover Ct
D2
1 Beswick Mews
2 Worcester Mews
3 Minton Mews
4 Doulton Mews
5 Laurel Ho
6 Sandalwood Ho
7 Iroko Ho
8 Banyan Ho
9 Ebony Ho
10 Rosemont Mans

70
A1
1 Harrold Ho
2 Glover Ho
3 Byron Ct
4 Nalton Ho
A2
1 Petros Gdns
2 Heath Ct
3 Imperial Twrs
4 Fairhurst
5 St John's Ct
6 New College Ct
7 Chalford
8 Sutherland Ho
A4
1 Windmill Hill
2 Highgrove Point
3 Gainsborough Ho
4 Heath Mans
5 Pavilion Ct
6 Holly Berry La
7 New Campden Ct
8 Benham's Pl
9 Holly Bush Vale
10 Gardnor Mans
11 Mansfield Pl
12 Streatley Pl
13 New Ct
14 Bird In Hand Yd
15 Spencer Wlk
16 Wells Ct
17 Perrin's Ct
18 Village Mount
19 Prince Arthur Ct
20 Prince Arthur Mews
21 Monro Ho
22 Ellerdale Cl
23 Holly Bush Hill
24 Prospect Pl
B1
1 New College Par
2 Northways Par
3 Noel Ho
4 Campden Ho
5 Centre Hts
6 Hickes Ho
7 Swiss Terr
8 Leitch Ho
9 Jevons Ho
10 Langhorne Ct
11 Park Lo
12 Avenue Lo
B2
1 Belsize Park Mews
2 Baynes Mews
3 McCrone Mews
B3
1 Belsize Court Garages
2 Roscommon Ho
3 Akenside Ct
C2
1 Banff Ho
2 Glenloch Ct
3 Havercourt
4 Holmfield Ct
5 Gilling Ct
6 Howitt Cl
7 Manor Mans
8 Straffan Lo
9 Romney Ct
10 Lancaster Stables
C3
1 Eton Garages
D1
1 Hancock Nunn Ho
2 Higginson Ho
3 Duncan Ho
4 Mary Wharrie Ho
5 Rockstraw Ho
6 Cleaver Ho
7 Chamberlain St
8 Sharples Hall St
9 Primrose Mews
10 Rothwell St
11 St Georges Mews

2 Hornbeam Ho
3 Whitebeam Ho
4 Aspen Ho
5 Rowan Ho
6 Beech Ho
7 Chestnut Ho
8 Oak Ho
9 Willow Ho
10 Sycamore Ho
11 Maple Ho
12 Hazel Ho
13 Elaine Ct
14 Faircourt
15 Walham Ct
16 Stanbury Ct
17 Priory Mans
18 Wellington Ho
19 Grange The
D3
1 Cayford Ho
2 Du Maurier Ho
3 Isokon Flats
4 Palgrave Ho
5 Garnett Ho
6 Stephenson Ho
7 Park Dwellings
8 Siddons Ho
9 Mall Studios
10 Park Hill Wlk
11 Wordsworth Pl
12 Fraser Regnart Ct
13 St Pancras Almshouses

71
A1
1 Bridge Ho
2 Hardington
3 Mead Cl
4 Rugmere
5 Tottenhall
6 Beauvale
7 Broomfield
A2
1 Silverbirch Wlk
2 Penshurst
3 Wingham
4 Westwell
5 Chislet
6 Burmarsh
7 Shipton Ho
8 Stone Gate
9 Leysdown
10 Headcorn
11 Lenham
12 Halstow
13 Fordcombe
14 Cannington
15 Langridge
16 Athlone Ho
17 Pentland Ho
18 Beckington
19 Hawkridge
20 Edington
B1
1 Ferdinand Ho
2 Harmood Ho
3 Hawley Rd
4 Hawley Mews
5 Leybourne St
6 Barling
7 Tiptree
8 Havering
9 Candida Ct
10 Lorraine Ct
11 Donnington Ct
12 Welford Ct
13 Torbay Ct
14 Bradfield Ct
15 Torbay St
16 Leybourne Rd
17 Haven St
18 Stucley Pl
B2
1 Ashington
2 Priestley Ho
3 Leonard Day Ho
4 Old Dairy Mews
5 Monmouth Ho
6 Alpha Ct
7 Una Ho
8 Widford
9 Hey Bridge
10 Roxwell
B4
1 Denyer Ho
2 Stephenson Ho
3 Trevithick Ho
4 Brunel Ho
5 Newcomen Ho
6 Faraday Ho
7 Winifrede Paul Ho
8 Wardlow
9 Fletcher Ct
10 Tideswell
11 Grangemill
12 Hambrook Ct
13 Calver
C1
1 Durdans Ho
2 Philia Ho
3 Bernard Shaw Ct
4 Foster Ct

80 A1
10 Plymouth Ho
11 Graham Mans
12 Portia Ct

81
C5 1 Markham Ho
2 Webb Ho
3 Preston Ho
4 Steadman Ho
5 Hyndman Ho
6 Clynes Ho
7 Henderson Ho
8 Blatchford Ho
9 Rogers Ho
10 Sylvia Pankhurst Ho
12 Ellen Wilkinson Ho
D2 1 Picador Ho
2 Centurion Ho
3 Louis Ct
4 Watsons Lo
5 Carpenters Ct
6 Bell Ho
7 Rounders Ct
8 Oldmead Ho
9 Jervis Ct
10 Bartletts Ho
11 Royal Par
12 Richardson Gdns

82
D3 1 Marlborough Par
2 Blenheim Par
3 Lea Ct
4 Westbourne Par
5 Whiteleys Par
6 Hillingdon Par
7 New Broadway

84
C4 1 Dilston Cl
2 Wells Cl
3 Willet Cl
4 Merlin Cl
5 Glyndebourne Ct
6 Albury Ct
7 Osterley Ct
8 Hatfield Ct
9 Gayhurst Ct
D4 1 Caravelle Gdns
2 Forman Ho
3 Viscount Gr
4 Tomahawk Gdns
5 Martlet Gr
6 Trident Gdns
7 Latham Ct
8 Jupiter Ct
9 Westland Ct
10 Seasprite Cl
11 Convair Wlk
12 Mayfly Gdns
13 Valiant Cl
14 Woburn Twr
15 Brett Cl
16 Friars Ct
D5 1 Medlar Cl
2 Cranberry Cl
3 Lely Ho
4 Kneller Ho
5 Girtin Ho
6 Cotman Ho
7 Raeburn Ho
8 Gainsborough Twr
9 Stanfield Ho
10 Millais Ct
11 Hunt Ct
12 Poynter Ct
13 Hogarth Ho
14 Constable Ho
15 Bonnington Ct
16 Romney Ct
17 Landseer Ho

85
D1 1 Thurlestone Ct
2 Disley Ct
3 Burgess Ct
4 Selsdon Ct
5 Lytham Ct
6 Abbeydale Ct
7 Cromer Ct
8 Brunel Pl
9 Winford Par
10 Rutherford Twr

86
A1 1 Farnham Ct
2 Gleneagles Twr
3 Birkdale Ct
4 Verulam Ct
5 Hartsbourne Ct
6 Ferndown Ct
7 Deal Ct
8 St David's Ct
9 Portrush Ct
10 Alnmouth Ct
11 Panmure Ct
12 Peterhead Ct
13 Sunningdale Ct
D2 1 Denbigh Ct
2 Devon Ct
3 Dorset Ct
4 Glamorgan Ct
5 Gloucester Ct
6 Hereford Ct
7 Merioneth Ct
8 Oxford Ct
9 Monmouth Ct
10 Paddington Ct
11 Pembroke Ct
12 Chadwick Cl
13 Cotts Cl
D3 1 Berkshire Ct
2 Buckingham Ct
3 Cardigan Ct
4 Carmarthen Ct
5 Cornwall Ct
6 Merlin Ct
7 Osprey Ct
8 Pelham Pl
D5 1 Medway Par
2 Brabstone Ho
3 Cotswold Ct

87
B3 1 Woodbury Ct
2 Edward Ct
3 Park Lo
C1 1 Hurley Ct
2 Amherst Gdns
3 Tudor Ct
4 Hilton Ho
C2 1 Hutton Ct
2 Cain Ct
3 Langdale Ct
4 Castlebar Ct
5 Warren Ct
6 White Lo
7 Queen's Ct
8 King's Ct
9 Cheriton Ct
10 Stanley Ct
11 Juniper Ct
C3 1 Holtoake Ct
2 Pitshanger Ct
3 Holtoake Ho

88
A4 1 Nelson Ho
2 Gordon Ho
3 Frobisher Ho
4 Wellington Ho
5 Fairfax Ho
A5 1 Carlyon Mans
2 Ainslie Ct
3 Millers Ct
4 Priory Ct
5 Tylers Ct
6 Twyford Ct
7 Rose Ct
8 Laurel Ct
9 Sundew Ct
10 Campion Ct
11 Foxglove Ct
C1 1 Buckingham Ho
2 Chester Ct
3 Devon Ct
4 Essex Ho
5 Fife Ct
6 Gloucester Ct
7 Hereford Ho
8 Inverness Ct
9 Warwick Ho
10 York Ho
11 Suffolk Ho
12 Perth Ho
13 Norfolk Ho
14 Thanet Ct
15 Rutland Ct
16 Oxford Ct

89
A1 1 Avon Ct
2 Bromley Ho
3 Walter Ct
4 Lynton Terr
5 Acton Ho
6 Fells Haugh
7 Springfield Ct
8 Tamarind Ct
9 Lynton Ct
B1 1 Rosebank Gdns
2 Rosebank
3 Edinburgh Ho
4 Western Ct
5 Kilronan
B6 1 Fitzsimmons Ct
2 Bernard Shaw Ho
3 Longlents Ho
4 Mordaunt Ho
5 Wilmers Ct
6 Stonebridge Sh Ctr
D5 1 New Crescent Yd
2 Harlesden Plaza
3 St Josephs Ct

90
D1 1 Kelfield Ct
2 Downing Ho
3 Crosfield Ct
4 Robinson Ho
5 Scampston Mews
6 Girton Villas
7 Ray Ho
8 Walmer Ho
9 Goodrich Ct
10 Kingsnorth Ho
11 Whitstable Ho
12 Kingsnorth Ho
13 Bridge Cl
14 Prospect Ho
15 Whitchurch Ho
16 Blechynden Ho
18 Waynflete Sq
19 Bramley Ho
D4 1 Westfield Ct
2 Tropical Ct
3 Chamberlayne Mans
4 Quadrant The
5 Queens Park Ct
6 Warfield Yd
7 Cherrytree Ho

91
A1 1 Malton Mews
2 Lancaster Lo
3 Manning Ho
4 Galsworthy Ho
5 Hudson Ho
6 Cambourne Mews
7 Camelford Ct
8 Camelford Wlk
9 Talbot Grove Ho
10 Clarendon Wlk
11 Kingsdown Cl
12 Lower Clarendon Wlk
13 Upper Clarendon Wlk
A2 1 Murchison Ho
2 Macaulay Ho
3 Chesterton Ho
4 Chiltern Ho
5 Lionel Ho
6 Watts Ho
7 Wheatstone Ho
8 Telford Ho
9 Golborne Mews
10 Millwood St
11 St Columb's Ho
12 Norfolk Mews
A3 1 Sycamore Wlk
2 Westgate Bsns Ctr
3 Buspace Studios
4 Bosworth Ho
5 Golborne Gdns
6 Appleford Ho
7 Adair Twr
8 Gadsden Ho
9 Southam Ho
10 Norman Butler Ho
11 Thompson Ho
12 Wells Ho
13 Paul Ho
14 Olive Blythe Ho
15 Katherine Ho
16 Breakwell Ct
17 Pepler Ho
18 Edward Kennedy Ho
A4 1 Winnington Ho
2 Slomon Ho
3 Stansbury Ho
4 Tilleard Ho
5 Selby Ho
6 Mundy Ho
7 Macfarren Ho
8 Mounsey Ho
9 Courtville Ho
10 Croft Ho
11 Batten Ho
12 Bantock Ho
13 Banister Ho
14 Symphony Mews
17 Bliss Mews
A5 1 Lancefield Ct
2 Verdi Ho
3 Wornum Ho
B1 1 Tavistock Mews
2 Silvester Ho
3 Melchester
4 Clydesdale Ho
5 Pinehurst Ct
6 Colville Sq Mews
7 Denbigh Ho
8 Golden Cross Mews
B2 1 Blagrove Rd
2 Tavistock Ho
3 Leamington Ho
B3 1 Western Ho
2 Russell's Wharf
B4 1 Boyce Ho
2 Farnaby Ho
3 Danby Ho
4 Purday Ho
5 Naylor Ho
6 St Judes Ho
7 Leeve Ho
8 Longhurst Ho
9 Harrington Ct
10 Mulberry Ct
11 Quilter Ho
12 Romer Ho
13 Kilburn Ho
B5 1 Claremont Ct
2 William Saville Ho
3 Western Ct
4 Bond Ho
5 Crone Ct
6 Wood Ho
7 Winterleys
8 Carlton Ho
9 Fiona Ct
C1 1 Shottsford
2 Tolchurch
3 Casterbridge
4 Sandbourne
5 Anglebury
6 Weatherbury
7 Westbourne Gr Mews
8 Rosehart Mews
9 Viscount Ct
10 Hereford Mans
11 Hereford Mews
C2 1 Ascot Ho
2 Ashgrove Ct
3 Lockbridge Ct
4 Swallow Ct
5 Nightingale Lo
6 Hammond Lo
7 Penfield Lo
8 Harvey Lo
9 Hunter Lo
10 Barnard Lo
11 Falcon Lo
12 Johnson Lo
13 Livingstone Lo
14 Nuffield Lo
15 Finch Lo
16 Polesworth Ho
17 Oversley Ho
18 Derrycombe Ho
19 Buckshead Ho
20 Combe Ho
21 Culham Ho
22 Dainton Ho
23 Devonport Ho
24 Hanwell Ho
25 Truro Ho
26 Sunderland Ho
27 Stonehouse Ho
28 Riverford Ho
29 Portishead Ho
30 Mickleton Ho
31 Keyham Ho
32 Moulsford Ho
33 Shrewsbury Mews
34 St Stephen's Mews
35 Westway Lo
36 Langley Ho
37 Brindley Ho
38 Radway Ho
39 Astley Ho
40 Willow Ct
41 Larch Ct
42 Elm Ct
C4 1 Masefield Ho
2 Austen Ho
3 Fielding Ho
4 Park Mews
5 John Ratcliffe Ho
6 Wymering Mans
7 Pavilion Ct
8 Nelson Cl
C5 1 Wells Ct
2 Cambridge Ct
3 Durham Ct
C6 1 Ryde Ho
2 Glengall Pass
3 Leith Yd
4 Daynor Ho
5 Varley Ho
6 Sandby Ho
7 Colas Mews
8 Bishopsdale Ho
9 Lorton Ho
10 Marshwood Ho
11 Ribblesdale Ho
12 Holmesdale Ho
13 Kilburn Vale Est
14 Kilburn Bridge
D1 1 Vera Ct
2 Alexander Mews
3 Gurney Ho
4 Burdett Mews
5 Greville Lo
6 Hatherley Ct
7 Bridge Field Ho
8 Ralph Ct
9 Peters Ct
10 Riven Ct
11 Cervantes Ct
12 Bishops Ct
13 Newbury Ho
14 Marlow Ho
15 Lynton Ho
16 Pembroke Ho
17 Pickering Ho
D3 1 Ellwood Ct
D5 1 Tollgate Ho
2 Regents Plaza
3 Royal Langford
D6 1 Farndale Ho
2 Birchington Ct
3 Greville Mews
4 Goldsmith's Pl
5 Remsted Ho
6 Bradwell Ho
7 Cheshunt Ho
8 Haliwell Ho
9 Braddock Ho
10 Philip Ho
11 Hillsborough Ct
12 Sandbourne
13 Wingreen
14 Toneborough
15 Silverthorn
16 Kington Ho
17 Marrick Ho
18 Broadoak Ho
19 Boadoak Ho

95
C4 1 Pimlico Wlk
2 Aske Ho
3 Hathaway Ho
4 Haberdasher Pl
5 Fairchild Ho
6 Burtt Ho
7 Enfield Cloisters
8 McGregor Ct
9 Royal Oak Ct
10 Hoxton Mkt
11 Bath Pl
12 Chapel Ct
13 Chapel Pl
14 Standard Pl
15 Cleeve Ho
16 Printing House Yd
17 Perseverance Works
18 Crooked Billet Yd
19 Drysdale Ho
20 Castlefrank Ho
21 School App
22 Basing House Yd
23 Mail Coach Yd
12 Bacchus Wlk
13 Malcolm Ho
14 Homefield St
15 Crondall Pl
16 Blanca Ho
17 Miranda Ho
18 Falstaff Ho
19 Charmian Ho
20 Myrtle Wlk
21 Arden Ho
22 Sebastian Ho
23 Stanway Ct
24 Jerrold St
25 Rosalind Ho
26 Cordelia Ho
27 Monteagle Ct
28 John Parry Ct
29 James Anderson Ct
30 Ben Jonson Ct
31 Sara Lane Ct
32 Walbrook Ct
C6 1 Portelet Ct
2 Trinity Ct
3 Rozel Ct
4 St Helier Ct
5 Corbiere Ho
6 Kenning Ho
7 Higgins Ho
8 Cavell Ho
9 Girling Ho
10 Fulcher Ho
11 Francis Ho
12 Norris Ho
13 Kempton Ho
14 Nesham Ho
15 Crossbow Ho
16 Catherine Ho
17 Strale Ho
18 Horner Hos
19 Stringer Hos
20 Whitmore Ho
21 Nightingale Ho
22 Fletcher Ho
23 Arrow Ho
24 Archer Ho
25 Meriden Ho
26 Rover Ho
27 Bowyer Ho
28 Longbow Ho
29 Tiller Ho
30 Canalside Studios
31 Bishopgate
32 Holborn
33 Fenchurch
D4 1 Gorsuch Pl
2 Strout's Pl
3 Vaughan Est
4 George Loveless Ho
5 Baroness Rd
6 James Brine Ho
7 Arthur Wade Ho
8 Robert Owen Ho
9 Sivill Ho
10 Georgina Gdns
11 Old Market Sq
12 Cuff Point
13 Bakers Rents
14 Leopold Bldgs
15 Dunmore Point
16 Wingfield Ho
17 Gascoigne Pl
18 Mandela Ho
19 Virginia Rd
20 Briggs Ho
21 Packenham Ho
22 Gowan Ho
23 Chambord Ho
24 Ducal St
25 Strickland Ho
26 Alliston Ho
27 Gibraltar Wlk
28 Equity Sq
29 Shacklewell St
30 Rochelle St
31 Sonning Ho
32 Culham Ho
33 Hurley Ho
34 Palissy St
35 Chertsey Ho
36 Sunbury Ho
37 Sunbury Workshops
40 Datchett Ho
41 Hocker St
42 Coll Sharp Ct
43 Marlow Studio Workshops
44 Marlow Ho
45 Shiplake Ho
46 Wargrave Ho
47 Iffley Ho
D5 1 Queensbridge Ct
2 Godwin Ho
3 Kent Ct
4 Brunswick Ho
5 Weymouth Ct
6 Sovereign Mews
7 Dunloe Ct
8 Cremer Bsns Ctr
9 James Hammett Ho
10 Allgood St
11 Horatio St
12 Cadell Ho
13 Horatio Ho
14 Shipton Ho
D6 1 Hilborough Ct
2 Scriven Ct
3 Livermere Ct
4 Angrave Ct
5 Angrave Pas
6 Benfleet Ct
7 Belford Ho
8 Orme Ho
9 Clemson Ho
10 Longman Ho
11 Lowther Ho
12 Lovelace Ho
13 Harlowe Ho
14 Pamela Ho
15 Samuel Ho
16 Acton Ho
17 Loanda Cl
18 Phoenix Cl
19 Richardson Cl
20 Thrasher Cl
21 Mary Secole Cl
22 Canal Path
23 Pear Tree Cl
24 Hebden Ct
25 Charlton Ct
26 Laburnum Ct
27 Mansfield Ct
28 Garden Pl
29 Amber Wharf

96
A1 1 Manningtree St
2 Whitechurch La
3 Morrison Bldgs
4 Mountford St
5 Mulberry St
6 Weyhill Rd
7 Fordham St
8 Myrtle St
9 Buckle St
10 Plough St
11 Goodman's Stile
12 Mitali Pas
13 Basil Ho
14 Hogarth Ct
15 Ropewalk Gdns
16 Golding Terr
17 Delafield Ho
18 Drewett Ho
19 Harkness Ho
20 Batson Ho
21 Danvers Ho
22 Bicknell Ho
23 Everard Ho
24 Philchurch Pl
25 Hadfield Ho
26 Kindersley Ho
27 Langmore Ho
28 Halliday Ho
29 Berner Terr
30 Victoria Yd
A2 1 Arthur Deakin Ho
2 Albert Cotts
3 Victoria Cotts
4 Boden Ho
5 Vollasky Ho
6 Daplyn St
7 Hobsons Pl
8 Hanbury Ho
9 Links Yd
10 Casson Ho
11 Ramar Ho
12 Greatorex Ho
13 Chicksand Ho
14 Spelman Ho
15 Tailworth St
16 Monthorpe Rd
17 Bloomfield Ho
18 Davenant Ho
19 Pauline Ho
20 Tannery Ho
21 Green Dragon Yd
22 King's Arms Ct
23 Fieldgate Mans
24 Mosque Tower
A3 1 Bentworth Ct
2 Kerbela St
3 Fuller Cl
4 Kinsham Ho
5 Menotti St
6 Barwell Ho

7 Grimsby St
8 Eckersley St
9 Stuttle Ho
10 McGlashon Ho
11 Fleet Street Hill
12 Bratley St
13 Weaver Ho
14 John Pritchard Ho
A4 1 Lygon Ho
2 Brabner Ho
3 Delta St
4 Tillet Way
5 Mullet Gdns
6 Elver Gdns
7 Cobden Ho
8 Lampern Sq
9 Jeremy Bentham Ho
10 Waring Ho
11 St James Ct
12 Hague St
13 Westhope Ho
14 Johnson Ho
15 Yates Ho
16 Simmons Ho
17 Swinton Ho
18 Eversley Ho
19 Rapley Ho
20 Dence Ho
21 Dickinson Ho
22 Hutton Ho
23 McKinnon Wood Ho
24 Satchwell Rd
25 Lorden Wlk
A5 1 London Terr
2 Sturdee Ho
3 Maude Ho
4 Haig Ho
5 Jellicoe Ho
6 Ropley St
7 Guinness Trust Bldgs
8 Ion Ct
9 Moye Ct
10 Morrel Ct
11 Courtauld Ho
12 Drummond Ho
13 Atkinson Ho
14 Gurney Ho
15 Halley Ho
16 Goldsmith's Sq
17 Ken Wilson Ho
18 Shahjalal Ho
19 Crofts Ho
20 April Ct
21 Sebright Ho
22 Beechwood Ho
23 Gillman Ho
24 Cheverell Ho
25 Besford Ho
26 Dinmont Ho
27 Wyndham Deedes Ho
28 Sheppard Ho
29 Mary James Ho
30 Hadrian Est
31 Blythendale Ho
32 George Vale Ho
33 Lion Mills
34 Pritchard Ho
A6 1 Broke Wlk
2 Rochemont Wlk
3 Marlborough Ave
4 Rivington Wlk
5 Magnin Cl
6 Gloucester Sq
7 Woolstone Ho
8 Marsworth Ho
9 Cheddington Ho
10 Linslade Ho
11 Cosgrove Ho
12 Blisworth Ho
13 Eleanor Ct
14 Wistow Ho
15 Muscott Ho
16 Boxmoor Ho
17 Linford Ho
18 Pendley Ho
19 North Church Ho
20 Debdale Ho
21 Broadway Market Mews
22 Welshpool Ho
23 Ada Ho
B1 1 Jacob Mans
2 Wicker St
3 Langdale St
4 Walford Ho
5 Welstead Ho
6 Peter Best Ho
7 Sly St
8 Barnett St
9 Kinder St
10 Richard St

11 Sarah Ho
12 Mellish Ho
13 Dickson Ho
14 Joscoyne Ho
15 Bridgen Ho
16 Wilton Ct
17 Silvester Ho
18 Greenwich Ct
19 Tylney Ho
20 Damien Ct
21 Siege Ho
22 Melwood Ho
23 Colstead Ho
24 Hungerford St
25 Burwell Cl
26 Chapman Ho
27 Tarling Ho
28 Sheridan St
29 Brinsley St
30 Dunch St
31 Luke Ho
32 Turnour Ho
33 Norton Ho
B3 1 Rochester St
2 Weaver Ct
3 Greenheath Bsns Ctr
4 Glass St
5 Herald St
6 Northesk Ho
7 Codrington Ho
8 Heathpool Ct
9 Mocatta Ho
10 Harvey Ho
11 Blackwood Ho
12 Rutherford Ho
13 Bullen Ho
14 Fremantle Ho
15 Pellew Ho
16 Ashington Ho
17 Dinnington Ho
18 Bartholomew Sq
19 Steeple Ct
20 Orion Ho
21 Fellbrigg St
22 Eagle Ho
23 Sovereign Ho
24 Redmill Ho
25 Berry Ho
26 Grindall Ho
27 Collingwood Ho
B4 1 Charles Dickens Ho
2 Adrian Bolt Ho
3 William Rathbone Ho
4 Southwood Smith Ho
5 Rushmead
6 William Channing Ho
7 John Cartwright Ho
8 Charles Darwin Ho
9 Thomas Burt Ho
10 John Fielden Ho
11 Gwilym Maries Ho
12 Joseph Priestley Ho
13 Wear Ho
14 John Nettleford Ho
15 Thornaby Ho
16 Stockton Ho
17 Barnard Ho
18 Gainford Ho
19 Stapleton Ho
20 James Middleton Ho
21 Kedleston Wlk
22 Queen Margaret Flats
23 Hollybush Ho
24 Horwood Ho
25 Norden Ho
26 Newcourt Ho
27 Seabright St
28 Viaduct Pl
29 Sunlight Sq
B5 1 Dinmont St
2 Marian St
3 Claredale St
4 Bradley Ho
5 Connett Ho
6 Winkley St
7 Temple Dwellings
8 Argos Ho
9 Helen Ho
10 Lysander Ho
11 Antenor Ho
12 Paris Ho
13 Nestor Ho
14 Hector Ho

15 Ajax Ho
16 Achilles Ho
17 Priam Ho
18 Peabody Est
19 Felix St
20 Cambridge Cres
21 Peterley Bsns Ctr
22 Beckwith Ho
23 Parminter Ind Est
24 Ted Roberts Ho
25 Cambridge Ct
26 West St
27 Millennium Pl
28 William Caslon Ho
29 Hugh Platt Ho
30 Mayfield Ho
31 Apollo Ho
32 Tanners Yd
33 Teesdale Yd
B6 1 Welshpool St
2 Broadway Ho
3 Regents Wharf
4 London Wharf
5 Warburton Ho
6 Triangle Rd
7 Warburton Rd
8 Williams Ho
9 Booth Cl
10 Albert Cl
11 King Edward Mans
12 Victoria Bldgs
13 Woollon Ho
C1 1 Dundalk Ho
2 Anne Goodman Ho
3 Newbold Cotts
4 Kerry Ho
5 Zion Ho
6 Longford Ho
7 Bromehead St
8 Athlone Ho
9 Jubilee Mans
10 Harriott Ho
11 Brayford Sq
12 Clearbrook Way
13 Rochelle Ct
14 Winterton Ho
15 Sheridan Ho
16 Brinsley Ho
17 Dean Ho
18 Foley Ho
19 Robert Sutton Ho
20 Montpelier Pl
21 Masters Lo
22 Steel's La
23 Swift Ho
24 Glastonbury Pl
C2 1 Fulneck
2 Gracehill
3 Ockbrook
4 Fairfield
5 Cressy Ct
6 Cressy Hos
7 Callahan Cotts
8 Wexford Ho
9 Sandhurst Ho
10 Colverson Ho
11 Beckett Ho
12 Jarman Ho
13 Wingrad Ho
14 Armsby Ho
15 Miranda Cl
16 Drake Ho
17 Louise De Marillac Ho
18 Sambrook Ho
19 St Vincent De Paul Ho
20 Jean Pardies Ho
21 Clichy Ho
22 Le Moal Ho
23 Odette Duval Ho
24 Dagobert Ho
25 Charles Auffray Ho
26 Boisseau Ho
27 Paymal Ho
C3 1 William's Bldgs
2 Donegal Ho
3 Frederick Charrington Ho
4 Wickford Ho
5 Braintree Ho
6 Doveton Ho
7 Doveton St
8 Cephas Ho
9 Sceptre Ho
10 Bancroft Ho
11 Stothard Ho
12 Redclyf Ho

13 Winkworth Cotts
14 Ryder Ho
15 Hadleigh Ho
16 Hadleigh Cl
17 Amiel St
18 Stathard Ho
19 Barbanel Ho
20 Colebert Ho
21 Kenton Ho
22 Ibbott St
23 Stannard Cotts
24 Rennie Cotts
25 Rickman St
26 Rickman Ho
27 Pemell Cl
28 Pemell Ho
29 Leatherdale St
30 Gouldman Ho
31 Lamplighter Cl
32 Hamilton Lo
33 Cleveland Gr
34 Montgomery Lo
35 Bardsey Pl
36 Cromwell Lo
37 Colin Winter Ho
C4 1 Allport Mews
2 Mulberry Ho
3 Gretton Ho
4 Merceron Ho
5 Montfort Ho
6 Westbrook Ho
7 Sugar Loaf Wlk
8 Museum Ho
9 Globe Terr
10 Moravian St
11 Shepton Hos
12 Mendip Hos
13 Academy Ct
14 Pepys Ho
15 Swinburne Ho
16 Moore Ho
17 Morris Ho
18 Burns Ho
19 Milton Ho
20 Whitman Ho
21 Shelley Ho
22 Keats Ho
23 Dawson Ho
24 Bradbeer Ho
25 Forber Ho
26 Hughes Ho
27 Silvester Ho
28 Rogers Est
29 Pavan Ct
30 Stafford Cripps Ho
31 Sidney Godley (VC) Ho
32 Butler Ho
33 Butler St
34 Thorne Ho
35 Bevin Ho
36 Tuscan Ho
C5 1 Evesham Ho
2 James Campbell Ho
3 Thomas Hollywood Ho
4 James Docherty Ho
5 Ebenezer Mussel Ho
6 Jameson Ct
7 Edinburgh Cl
8 Roger Dowley Ct
9 Sherbrooke Ho
10 Calcraft Ho
11 Burrard Ho
12 Dundas Ho
13 Barnes Ho
14 Paget Ho
15 Maitland Ho
16 Chesil Ct
17 Reynolds Ho
18 Cleland Ho
19 Goodrich Ho
20 Rosebery Ho
21 Sankey Ho
22 Cyprus Pl
23 Royston St
24 Stainsbury St
25 Hunslett St
26 Baildon
27 Brockweir
28 Tytherton
29 Kingswood
C6 1 Halkett Ho
2 Christ Church Sq
3 Swingfield Ho
4 Greenham Ho
5 Dinmore Ho
6 Anstey Ho
7 Weston Ho

10 Carbroke Ho
11 Bluebell Cl
16 Cherry Tree Cl
18 Georgian Ct
19 Park Cl
21 Regency Ct
22 Norris Ho
D1 1 Pattison Ho
2 St Thomas Ho
3 Arbour Ho
4 Bladen Ho
5 Antill Terr
6 Billing Ho
7 Dowson Ho
8 Lipton Rd
9 Chalkwell Ho
10 Corringham Ho
11 Ogilvie Ho
12 Edward Mann Cl
13 Lighterman Mews
D2 1 Roland Mews
2 Morecambe Cl
3 Stepney Green Ct
4 Milrood Ho
5 Panama Ho
6 Galway Ho
7 Caspian Ho
8 Darien Ho
9 Rigo Ho
10 Flores Ho
11 Taranto Ho
12 Aden Ho
13 Frances Grey Ho
14 Master's St
15 Diggon St
D3 1 Raynham Ho
2 Pat Shaw Ho
3 Colmar Cl
4 Withy Ho
5 Stocks Ct
6 Downey Ho
7 Bay Ct
8 Sligo Ho
9 Pegasus Ho
10 Barents Ho
11 Biscay Ho
12 Solway Ho
13 Bantry Ho
14 Aral Ho
15 Pacific Ho
16 Magellan Ho
17 Levant Ho
18 Adriatic Ho
19 Genoa Ho
20 Hawke Ho
21 Palliser Ho
22 Ionian Ho
23 Weddell Ho
D4 1 Stubbs Ho
2 Holman Ho
3 Clynes Ho
4 Windsor Ho
5 Gilbert Ho
6 Chater Ho
7 Ellen Wilkinson Ho
8 George Belt Ho
9 Ayrton Gould Ho
10 O'Brian Ho
11 Sulkin Ho
12 Jenkinson Ho
13 Bullards Pl
14 Sylvia Pankhurst Ho
15 Mary Macarthur Ho
16 Trevelyan Ho
17 Wedgwood Ho
18 Pemberton Ct
19 Walter Besant Ho
20 Barber Beaumont Ho
21 Brancaster Ho
22 Litcham Ho
D5 1 Kemp Ho
2 Piggott Ho
3 Mark Ho
4 Sidney Ho
5 Pomeroy Ho
6 Puteaux Ho
7 Doric Ho
8 Modling Ho
9 Longman Ho
10 Ames Ho
11 Alzette Ho
12 Offenbach Ho
13 Tate Ho
14 Norton Ho
15 St Gilles Ho
16 Harold Ho
17 Velletri Ho
18 Bridge Wharf
19 Gathorne St

20 Bow Brook The
22 Palmerston Ct
23 Peach Walk Mews
24 Lakeview
25 Caesar Ct
97
A1 1 Coltman Ho
2 Repton Ho
3 Causton Cotts
4 Darnley Ho
5 Mercer's Cotts
6 Troon Ho
7 Ratcliffe Ho
8 Wakeling St
9 York Sq
10 Cambria Ho
11 Caledonia Ho
12 Ratcliffe La
13 Bekesbourne St
14 John Scurr Ho
15 Regents Canal Ho
16 Basin App
17 Powlesland Ct
A2 1 Waley St
2 Edith Ramsay Ho
3 Andaman Ho
4 Atlantic Ho
5 Pevensey Ho
6 Solent Ho
7 Lorne Ho
8 Cromarty Ho
9 Greaves Cotts
10 Donaghue Cotts
11 Ames Cotts
A3 1 Formosa Ho
2 Galveston Ho
3 Arabian Ho
4 Greenland Ho
5 Coral Ho
6 Anson Ho
7 Lindop Ho
8 Moray Ho
9 Azov Ho
10 Sandalwood Cl
11 Broadford Ho
A5 1 Bunsen Ho
2 Bunsen St
3 Beatrice Webb Ho
4 Margaret Bondfield Ho
5 Wilmer Ho
6 Sandall Ho
7 Butley Ct
8 Josseline Ct
9 Dalton Ho
10 Brine Ho
11 Ford Cl
12 Viking Cl
13 Stanfield Rd
14 Ruth Ct
15 School Bell Cloisters
16 Schoolbell Mews
17 Medhurst Cl
18 Olga St
19 Conyer St
20 Diamond Ho
21 Daring Ho
22 Crane Ho
23 Exmoor Ho
24 Grenville Ho
25 Hyperion Ho
26 Sturdy Ho
27 Wren Ho
28 Ardent Ho
29 Senators Lo
30 Hooke Ho
31 Mohawk Ho
32 Ivanhoe Ho
B1 1 Dora Ho
2 Flansham Ho
3 Gatwick Ho
4 Ashpark Ho
5 Newdigate Ho
6 Salmon St
7 Midhurst Ho
8 Redbourne Ho
9 Southwater Cl
10 Aithan Ho
11 Britley Ho
12 Cheadle Ho
13 Elland Ho
14 Butler Ho
15 Fitzroy Ho
16 Leybourne Ho
B2 1 Wearmouth Ho
2 Elmslie Point
3 Grindley Ho
4 Stileman Ho
5 Baythorne St
6 Wilcox Ho

8 Robeson St
9 Couzens Ho
10 Perley Ho
11 Whytlaw Ho
12 Printon Ho
13 Perkins Ho
14 Bowry Ho
15 Booker Cl
16 Tunley Gn
17 Callingham Cl
18 Tasker Ho
B4 1 Trellis Sq
2 Sheffield Sq
3 Howcroft Ho
4 Astra Ho
5 Byas Ho
6 George Lansbury Ho
7 Regal Pl
8 Coborn Mews
9 Cavendish Terr
10 Buttermere Ho
11 Tracy Ho
12 Hanover Pl
13 Coniston Ho
14 St Clair Ho
15 Verity Ho
16 Icarus Ho
17 Whippingham Ho
18 Winchester Ho
19 Hamilton Ho
20 Longthorne Ho
B5 1 Roman Square Mkt
2 John Bond Ho
3 McKenna Ho
4 Dennis Ho
5 McBride Ho
6 Libra Rd
7 Dave Adams Ho
8 Tay Ho
9 Sleat Ho
10 Ewart Pl
11 Brodick Ho
12 Lunan Ho
13 Mull Ho
14 Sinclairs Ho
15 Driftway Ho
16 Clayhall Ct
17 Berebinder Ho
18 Stavers Ho
19 Barford Ho
20 Partridge Ho
21 Gosford Ho
22 Gullane Ho
23 Cruden Ho
24 Anglo Rd
25 Dornoch Ho
26 Dunnet Ho
27 Enard Ho
28 Fraserburgh Ho
29 Forth Ho
30 Ordell Ct
31 William Pl
B6 1 Hampstead Wlk
2 Waverton Ho
3 Elton Ho
4 Locton Gn
5 Birtwhistle Ho
6 Clare Ho
7 Magpie Ho
8 Atkins Ct
9 Tait Ct
10 Ranwell Ho
11 Ranwell Cl
12 Tufnell Ct
13 Pulteney Ct
14 Vic Johnson Ho
C1 1 Landin Ho
2 Charlesworth Ho
3 Gurdon Ho
4 Trendell Ho
5 Menteath Ho
6 Minchin Ho
7 Donne Ho
8 Denison Ho
9 Anglesey Ho
10 Gough Wlk
11 Baring Ho
12 Hopkins Ho
13 Granville Ho
14 Gladstone Ho
15 Russell Ho
16 Pusey Ho
17 Overstone Ho
18 Stanley Ho
19 Old School Sq
C2 1 Bredel Ho
2 Linton Ho
3 Matthews Ho
4 Woodcock Ho
5 Limborough Ho
6 Maydwell Ho
7 Underhill Ho

8 Meyrick Ho
9 Ambrose Ho
10 Carpenter Ho
11 Robinson Ho
12 Bramble Ho
13 Bilberry Ho
14 Bracken Ho
15 Berberis Ho
16 Busbridge Ho
17 Metropolitan Cl
18 Invicta Cl
19 Bellmaker Ct
C3 1 Fairmont Ho
2 Healy Ho
3 Zodiac Ho
4 Buick Ho
5 Consul Ho
6 Bentley Ho
7 Cresta Ho
8 Daimler Ho
9 Riley Ho
10 Jensen Ho
11 Lagonda Ho
12 Ireton St
13 Navenby Wlk
14 Burwell Wlk
15 Leadenham Ct
16 Sleaford Ho
C4 1 Jarret Ho
2 Marsalis Ho
3 Lovette Ho
4 Drapers Almhouses
5 Mallard Point
6 Creswick Wlk
7 Bevin Ho
8 Huggins Ho
9 Williams Ho
10 Harris Ho
11 Marina Ct
12 Electric Ho
13 Matching Ct
14 Wellington Bldgs
15 Grafton Ho
16 Columbia Ho
17 Berkeley Ho
D1 1 Colebrook Ho
2 Essex Ho
3 Salisbury Ho
4 Maidstone Ho
5 Osterley Ho
6 Norwich Ho
7 Clarissa Ho
8 Elgin Ho
9 Shaftesbury Lo
10 Shepherd Ho
11 Jeremiah St
12 Elizabeth Cl
13 Chilcot Cl
14 Fitzgerald Ho
15 Vesey Path
16 Ennis Ho
17 Kilmore Ho
D2 1 Sumner Ho
2 Irvine Ho
3 David Ho
4 Brushwood Ho
5 Limehouse Cut
6 Colmans Wharf
7 Foundary Ho
8 Radford Ho
D3 1 Broxbourne Ho
2 Roxford Ho
3 Biscott Ho
4 Stanborough Ho
5 Hillstone Ct
D4 1 Bradley Ho
2 Prioress Ho
3 Alton Ho
4 Foxley Ho
5 Munden Ho
6 Canterbury Ho
7 Corbin Ho
8 Barton Ho
9 Jolles Ho
10 Rudstone Ho
11 Baxter Ho
12 Baker Ho
13 Insley Ho
14 Hardwicke Ho
15 Glebe Terr
16 Priory St
17 Sadler Ho
18 Ballinger Point
19 Henshall Point
20 Dorrington Point
21 Warren Ho
22 Fairlie Ct
23 Regent Sq
24 Hackworth Point
25 Priestman Point

26 Wingate Ho
27 Nethercott Ho
28 Thelbridge Ho
29 Bowden Ho
30 Kerscott Ho
31 Southcott Ho
32 Birchdown Ho
33 Upcott Ho
34 Langmead Ho
35 Limscott Ho
36 Northleigh Ho
37 Huntshaw Ho
38 Chagford Ho
39 Ashcombe Ho
40 Shillingford Ho
41 Patrick Connolly Gdns
42 Lester Ct
43 Franklin St
44 Taft Way
45 Washington Cl
46 Elizabeth Ho
47 William Guy Gdns
48 Denbury Ho
49 Holsworthy Ho

98
A1 1 Langdon Ho
2 Balfron Twr
3 Tabard Ct
4 Delta Bldg
5 Kilbrennan Ho
6 Thistle Ho
7 Heather Ho
8 Tartan Ho
9 Trident Ho
A2 1 Mills Gr
B1 1 Lansbury Gdns
2 Duncan Ho
3 Theseus Ho
4 Adams Ho
5 Jones Ho
6 Sam March Ho
7 Arapiles Ho
8 Athenia Ho
9 Jervis Bay Ho
10 Gaze Ho
11 Ritchie Ho
12 Circle Ho
13 Dunkeld Ho
14 Braithwaite Ho
15 Rosemary Dr
16 Sorrel La
17 East India Dock Road Tunnel
C6 1 Barnby Sq
2 Barnby St
3 Brassett Point
4 David Lee Point
5 Worthing Cl
6 Bexhill Wlk
7 Old Borrowfield
8 Elmgreen Cl
9 Stafford Morris Ho
10 Nina Mackay Cl
D1 1 Newton Point
2 Sparke Terr
3 Montesquieu Terr
4 Crawford Point
5 Rathbone Ho
6 George St
7 Emily St
8 Sabbarton St
D2 1 Radley Terr
2 Rathbone Mkt
3 Thomas North Terr
4 Bernard Cassidy St
5 Mary St
6 Hughes Terr
7 Swanscombe Point
8 Rawlinson Point
9 Kennedy Cox Ho
10 Cooper St
D6 1 Harris Cotts
2 Moorey Cl
3 Euro Bsns Ctr
4 Ladywell St
5 Caistor Ho
6 Redfern Ho

99
A2 1 Odeon Ct
2 Edward St
3 Newhaven La
4 Ravenscroft St
5 Douglas Rd

6 Ferrier Point
7 Harvey Point
8 Wood Point
9 Trinity St
10 Pattinson Point
11 Clinch Ct
12 Mint Bsns Pk
A3 1 Webb Gdns
2 Eric Shipman Terr
3 Warmington St
4 Jellicoe Rd
5 Frank St
6 Seaton Cl
7 Tabernacle Ave
8 Upland Rd
9 Clove St
10 Edward St
A4 1 Bob Anker Cl
2 Third Ave
3 Suffolk Rd
A5 1 Lettsom Wlk
2 Ashburton Terr
3 Grasmere Rd
4 Dimsdale Wlk
5 Rawstone Wlk
6 Scott Ho
7 Willett Ho
8 James Cl
9 Cordwainers Wlk
10 Victoria Point
11 Settle Point
12 Middle Rd
A6 1 Royston Ct
B4 1 Barbers Alley
2 Grengate La
3 Augurs La
4 Surrey St
5 Dongola Rd W
6 Bernersyde Point
7 Rowntree Clifford Ct
C5 1 Wellby Ct
2 Bishop Wilfred Wood Cl
3 Castle Point
4 Moat Dr
C6 1 Queen's Mkt
2 Tolpuddle Ave
3 Crown Mews
4 Lilac Ct
5 Hamara Ghar
6 Greenleaf Rd
7 Massey Ct
8 Florence Rd
9 Sissulu Ct
10 Austin Ct
D2 1 Partridge Cl
2 Vanbrugh Cl
3 Meadowsweet Cl
4 St Michaels Cl
5 Long Mark Rd
6 Congreve Wlk
D5 1 Foxcombe Cl
2 Rochford Cl
3 Stondon Wlk
4 Imperial Mews
5 Dominica Cl
D6 1 Oldegate Ho
2 Gaitskell Ho
3 Cabot Way

100
A1 1 Hadleigh Wlk
2 Hawksmoor Ct
3 Fraser Cl
4 Moncrieff Cl
5 Burlington Cl
6 Dundonald Cl
7 Oakley Cl
8 Ashwell Cl
A2 1 Orchid Cl
2 Bellflower Cl
3 Partridge Cl
4 Larkspur Cl
5 Lobelia Cl
6 Stonechat Sq
7 Wintergreen Cl
8 Garnet Wlk
9 Mavis Wlk
10 Beacons Cl
11 Abbess Cl
12 Elmley Cl
13 Chetwood Wlk
14 Selby Cl
15 Denny Cl
16 Woodhatch Cl
A6 1 Oakwood Ct
2 Harrow Rd
3 Ray Massey Way
4 Madge Gill Way
5 Pilgrims Way
B1 1 Bowers Wlk

2 Barton Cl
3 Clayton Cl
4 Dixon Cl
5 Gautrey Sq
6 Wakerly Cl
7 Canterbury Cl
8 Goose Sq
9 Coventry Cl
10 Butterfield Sq
11 Winchester Cl
B2 1 Fleetwood Cl
2 Lymington Cl
3 Holyhead Cl
4 Bondfield Rd
5 Tulip Cl
6 Ambrose Cl
7 Sage Cl
8 Lindwood Cl
D1 1 Weymouth Cl
2 Founder Cl
3 Admirals Ct

101
A1 1 Arlington Park Mans
2 Sandown Ho
3 Goodwood Ho
4 Windsor Ho
5 Lingfield Ho
6 Ascot Ho
7 Watchfield Ct
8 Belgrave Ct
9 Beverley Ct
10 Beaumont Ct
11 Harvard Rd
12 Troubridge Ct
A2 1 Chiswick Green Studios
2 Bell Ind Est
3 Fairlawn Ct
4 Dukes Gate
5 Dewsbury Ct
6 Chiswick Terr
A3 1 Blackmore Twr
2 Bollo Ct
3 Kipling Twr
4 Lawrence Ct
5 Maugham Ct
6 Reade Ct
7 Woolf Ct
8 Shaw Ct
9 Verne Ct
10 Wodehouse Ct
11 Greenock Rd
12 Garden Ct
13 Barons Gate
14 Cleveland Rd
15 Chapter Ct
16 Carver Cl
17 Beauchamp Ct
18 Holmes Ct
A4 1 Belgrave Cl
2 Buckland Wlk
3 Frampton Ct
4 Telfer Cl
5 Harlech Twr
6 Corfe Twr
7 Barwick Ho
8 Charles Hocking Ho
9 Sunninghill Ct
10 Salisbury St
11 Jameson Pl
A5 1 Rectory Rd
2 Derwentwater Mans
3 Market Pl
4 Hooper's Mews
5 Cromwell Rd
6 Locarno Rd
7 Edgecote Cl
8 Harleyford Manor
9 Coopers Ct
B1 1 Chatsworth Ct
2 Prospect Pl
3 Townhall Ave
4 Devonhurst Pl
5 Heathfield Ct
6 Horticultural Pl
7 Merlin Ho
8 Garth Rd
C1 1 Glebe Cl
2 Devonshire Mews
3 Binns Terr
4 Ingress St
5 Swanscombe Rd
6 Brackley Terr
7 Stephen Fox Ho
8 Manor Gdns
9 Coram Ho
10 Flaxman Ho
11 Thorneycroft Ho
12 Thornhill Ho
13 Kent Ho
14 Oldfield Ho
C2 1 Chestnut Ho
2 Bedford Ho

D4 1 Cheltenham Pl
2 Beaumaris Twr
3 Arundel Ho
4 Pevensey Ct
5 Jerome Twr
6 Anstey Ct
7 Bennett Ct
8 Gunnersbury Ct
D5 1 Lantry Ct
2 Rosemount Ct
3 Moreton Twr
4 Acton Central Ind Est
5 Rufford Twr
6 Narrow St
7 Mount Pl
8 Sidney Miller Ct
9 Mill Hill Terr
10 Mill Hill Gr

111
A1 1 Wellington St
2 St Ann's Rd
3 Bamber Ho
B6 1 Jarvis Cl
2 Mayflower Ho
3 Westbury Ct
4 Millicent Preston Ho
5 Louise Graham Ho
6 Grange Ho
7 Basing Ho
8 Barnes Ho
9 Lexham Ho
10 Ripple Ct
11 Waldegrave Ct
12 Howard Ct

104
A6 1 Milburn Dr
2 Cousins Cl
3 Leacroft Cl

108
C5 1 Marlow Ct
2 Andrews Ct
3 Vine Cotts
4 Benjamin Ct
5 Broadway Bldgs
D5 1 Silverdale Ct
2 Burdett Cl
3 Hopefield
4 Maunder Rd

109
A5 1 Glastonbury Ct
2 Evesham Ct
3 Lacock Ct
4 Wigmore Ct
5 Melrose Ct
6 Brownlow Rd
7 Chignell Pl
8 Shirley Ct
9 Trojan Ct
10 Hatfield Rd
C6 1 Abbey Lo
2 Yew Tree Grange
3 Abinger Ct

110
A1 1 Burford Ho
2 Hope Ct
3 Centaur Ct
4 Phoenix Ct
A6 1 Watermans Mews
2 Hills Mews
3 Grosvenor Ct
4 Elton Cl
5 Hambledon Ct
C1 1 Surrey Cres
2 Forbes Ho
3 Haining Cl
4 Melville Ct
5 London Stile
6 Stile Hall Par
7 Priory Lo
8 Kew Bridge Ct
9 Meadowcroft
10 St James Ct
C5 1 Grosvenor Par
2 Oakfield Ct
3 Hart Grove Ct
4 Grosvenor Ct
D1 1 Churchdale Ct
2 Cromwell Cl
3 Cambridge Rd S
4 Oxbridge Ct
5 Tomlinson Cl
6 Gunnersbury Mews
7 Grange The
8 Gunnersbury Cl

3 Bedford Cnr
4 Sydney Ho
5 Bedford Park Cnr
6 Priory Gdns
7 Windmill Alley
8 Castle Pl
9 Jonathan Ct
10 Windmill Pas
11 Chardin Rd
12 Gable Ho
C3 1 Fleet Ct
2 Ember Ct
3 Emlyn Gdns
4 Clone Ct
5 Brent Ct
6 Abbey Ct
7 Ormsby Lo
8 St Catherine's Ct
C4 1 Longford Ct
2 Mole Ct
3 Lea Ct
4 Wandle Ct
5 Beverley Ct
6 Roding Ct
7 Crane Ct
D1 1 Miller's Ct
2 British Grove Pas
3 British Grove S
4 Beresforde Rd
5 North Eyot Gdns
D2 1 Flanders Mans
2 Stamford Brook Mans
3 Linkenholt Mans
4 Prebend Mans
5 Middlesex Ct
D3 1 Stamford Brook Gdns
2 Hauteville Court Gdns
3 Ranelagh Gdns

112
A2 1 Hamlet Ct
2 Derwent Ct
3 Westcroft Ct
4 Black Lion Mews
5 St Peter's Villas
6 Standish Ho
7 Chambon Pl
8 Court Mans
A4 1 Victoria Ho
2 Lycett Pl
3 Kylemore Ct
4 Alexandra Ct
5 Lytten Ct
6 Becklow Mews
7 Northcroft Ct
8 Bailey Ct
9 Spring Cott
10 Landor Wlk
11 Laurence Mews
12 Hadyn Park Ct
13 Askew Mans
B2 1 Albion Gdns
2 Flora Gdns
3 Lamington St
4 Felgate Mews
5 Galena Ho
6 Albion Mews
7 Albion Ct
8 King Street Cloisters
9 Dimes Pl
10 Clarence Ct
11 Hampshire Hog La
B4 1 Westbush Ct
2 Goldhawk Mews
3 Sycamore Ho
4 Shackleton Ct
5 Drake Ct
6 Scotts Ct
B6 1 Abercrombie Ho
2 Bathurst Ho
3 Brisbane Ho
4 Bentinck Ho
5 Ellenborough Ho
6 Lawrence Cl
7 Mackenzie Ho
8 Carteret Ho
9 Calvert Ho
10 Winthrop Ho
11 Auckland Ho
12 Blaxland Ho
13 Havelock Cl
14 Hargraves Ho
15 Hudson Cl
16 Phipps Ho

17 Lawson Ho
18 Hastings Ho
19 Wolfe Ho
20 Malabar Ct
21 White City Est
22 Commonwealth Ave
23 Charnock Ho
24 Canning Ho
25 Cornwallis Ho
26 Champlain Ho
27 Grey Ho
28 Durban Ho
29 Baird Ho
30 Campbell Ho
31 Mitchell Ho
32 Denham Ho
33 Mackay Ho
34 Evans Ho
35 Daws Ho
36 Mandela Cl
C1 1 Bridge Avenue Mans
2 Bridgeview
3 College Ct
4 Beatrice Ho
5 Amelia Ho
6 Edith Ho
7 Joanna Ho
8 Mary Ho
9 Adela Ho
10 Sophia Ho
11 Henrietta Ho
12 Charlotte Ho
13 Alexandra Ho
14 Bath Pl
15 Elizabeth Ho
16 Margaret Ho
17 Peabody Est
18 Eleanor Ho
19 Isabella Ho
20 Caroline Ho
21 Chancellors Wharf
22 Sussex Pl
C2 1 Phoenix Lodge Mans
2 Samuel's Cl
3 Broadway Arc
4 Brook Ho
5 Hammersmith Broadway
C4 1 Verulam Ho
2 Grove Mans
3 Frobisher Ct
4 Library Mans
5 Pennard Mans
6 Lanark Mans
7 Kerrington Ct
8 Granville Mans
9 Romney Ct
10 Rayner Ct
11 Sulgrave Gdns
12 Bamborough Gdns
D3 1 Grosvenor Residences
2 Blythe Mews
3 Burnand Ho
4 Bradford Ho
5 Springvale Terr
6 Ceylon Rd
7 Walpole Ct
8 Bronte Ct
9 Boswell Ct
10 Souldern Rd
11 Brook Green Flats
12 Haarlem Rd
13 Stafford Mans
14 Lionel Mans
D4 1 Vanderbilt Villas
2 Bodington Ct
3 Kingham Cl
4 Clearwater Terr
5 Lorne Gdns
6 Cameret Ct
7 Bush Ct
8 Shepherds Ct
9 Rockley Ct
10 Grampians The
11 Charcroft Ct
12 Addison Park Mans
13 Sinclair Mans
D5 1 St Katherine's Wlk
2 Dorrit Ho
3 Pickwick Ho
4 Dombey Ho
5 Caranday Villas
6 Mortimer Ho
7 Nickleby Ho
8 Stebbing Ho
9 Boxmoor Ho
10 Poynter Ho
11 Swanscombe Ho
12 Darnley Terr

13 Norland Ho
14 Hume Ho
D6 14 Frinstead Ho
7 Hurstway Wlk
8 Testerton Wlk
4 Grenfell Wlk
5 Grenfell Twr
6 Barandon Wlk
8 Treadgold Ho
9 St Clements Ct
9 Willow Way
10 Florence Ho
11 Dora Ho
12 Carton Ho
13 Agnes Ho
14 Marley Ho
15 Waynflete Sq

118

A1 1 Alison Ct
2 West Point
3 Centre Point
4 East Point
5 Proctor Ho
6 Tovy Ho
7 Brettinghurst
8 Colechurch Ho
9 Harman Cl
10 Avondale Ho
11 Lanark Ho
12 George Elliston Ho
13 Eric Wilkins Ho
14 Archers Lo
15 Culloden Cl
16 Fallow Ct
17 Fern Wlk
18 Ivy Ct
19 Winter Lo
A2 1 Cadbury Way
2 Robert Bell Ho
3 Robert Jones Ho
4 William Rushbrooke Ho
5 Helen Taylor Ho
6 Peter Hills Ho
7 Charles Mackenzie Ho
8 Drappers Way
9 Abbey Gdns
10 Maria Cl
11 Windmill Cl
12 Townsend Ho
13 Mason Ho
14 Langdon Way
15 Hannah Mary Way
16 Kotree Way
17 Whittaker Way
A3 1 Rudge Ho
2 Spenlow Ho
3 Darnay Ho
4 Carton Ho
5 Giles Ho
6 Bowley Ho
7 Casby Ho
8 Sun Pas
9 Ness St
10 Voyager Bsns Est
11 Dockley Road Ind Est
12 Spa Ct
13 Discovery Bsns Pk
14 Priter Road Hostel
15 Salisbury Ct
16 William Ellis Way
17 John McKenna Wlk
18 Toussaint Wlk
19 Gillison Wlk
20 Bromfield Ct
21 Ben Smith Way
22 Major Rd
23 Old Jamaica Bsns Est
A4 1 Providence Twr
2 Springalls Wharf
4 St Saviours Ho
5 Providence Sq
6 Farthing Alley
7 Peter Butler Ho
7 Brownlow Ho
8 Fleming Ho
9 Dombey Ho
10 Copperfield Ho
11 Tapley Ho
12 Parkers Row
13 Wade Ho
14 Bardell Ho
15 Nickleby Ho
16 John Felton Rd
17 Pickwick Ho
18 Oliver Ho

20 Weller Ho
21 Tupman Ho
22 Haredale Ho
23 Havisham Ho
24 Micawber Ho
25 Wrayburn Ho
26 Dartle Ct
27 Burnaby Ct
28 Waterside Ho
29 Wickfield Ho
30 Fountain Ho
31 Fountain Green Sq
A5 1 Trade Winds Ct
2 Spice Ct
3 Leeward Ct
4 Bridgeport Pl
5 Tamarind Yd
6 Cope Yd
7 Nightingale Ho
8 St Anthony's Ct
9 Stockholm Way
10 Miah Terr
11 Seville Ho
12 Douthwaite Sq
13 Codling Cl
14 Hermitage Ct
15 Capital Wharf
16 Cinnabar Wharf East
17 Cinnabar Wharf Central
18 Cinnabar Wharf West
19 Halcyon Wharf
A6 1 Conant Mews
2 Hanson Ho
3 Victoria Ct
4 Swan Pas
5 Royal Mint Pl
6 Flank St
7 Ensign St
8 Sapphire Ct
9 George Leybourne Ho
10 Fletcher St
11 Wellclose St
12 Hatton Ho
13 Shearsmith Ho
14 Breezer's Ct
15 Pennington Ct
16 Onedin Point
17 Liberty Pl
B1 1 Hockney Ho
2 Toulouse Ct
3 Lowry Ct
4 Barry Ho
5 Lewis Ct
6 Gainsborough Ct
7 Renoir Ct
8 Blake Ct
9 Raphael Ct
10 Rembrandt Ct
11 Constable Ct
12 Da Vinci Ct
13 Gaugin Ct
14 Michelangelo Ct
15 Monet Ct
16 Weald Cl
17 Jasmin Lo
18 Birchmere Lo
19 Weybridge Ct
20 Florence Ho
21 Gleneagles Cl
22 Sunningdale Cl
23 Muirfield Cl
24 Turnberry Cl
25 St Andrews Cl
26 Kingsdown Cl
27 St Davids Cl
28 Galway Cl
29 Edenbridge Cl
30 Birkdale Cl
31 Tralee Ct
32 Woburn Ct
33 Belfry Cl
34 Troon Cl
35 Holywell Cl
B2 1 Market Pl
2 Trappes Ho
3 Thurland Ho
4 Ramsfort Ho
5 Hambley Ho
6 Holford Ho
7 Pope Ho
8 Southwell Ho
9 Mortain Ho
10 Radcliffe Ho
11 Southwark Park Est
12 Galleywall Road Trad Est
13 Trevithick Ho
14 Barlow Ho
15 Donkin Ho
16 Landmann Ho

17 Fitzmaurice Ho
18 Dodd Ho
B3 1 Perryn Rd
2 Chalfont Ho
3 Prestwood Ho
4 Farmer Ho
5 Gataker Ho
6 Gataker St
7 Cornick Ho
8 Glebe Ho
9 Matson Ho
10 Hickling Ho
11 St Andrews Ho
B4 1 Butterfield Cl
2 Janeway Pl
3 Trotwood Ho
4 Cranbourn Ho
5 Cherry Garden Ho
6 Burton Ho
7 Morriss Ho
8 King Edward The Third Mews
9 Cathay St
10 Rotherhithe St
B5 1 China Ct
2 Wellington Terr
3 Stevedore St
4 Portland Sq
5 Reardon Ho
6 Lowder Ho
7 Meeting House Alley
8 Farthing Fields
9 Oswell Ho
10 Park Lo
11 Doughty Ct
12 Inglefield Sq
13 Chopin's Ct
14 Welsh Ho
15 Hilliard Ho
16 Clegg St
17 Tasman Ho
18 Ross Ho
19 Wapping Dock St
20 Bridewell Pl
21 New Tower Bldgs
22 Tower Bldgs
23 Chimney Ct
24 Jackman Ho
25 Franklin Ho
26 Frobisher Ho
27 Flinders Ho
28 Chancellor Ho
29 Beechey Ho
30 Reardon Path
31 Parry Ho
32 Vancover Ho
33 Willoughby Ho
34 Sanctuary The
35 Dundee Ct
36 Pierhead Wharf
37 Scandrett St
38 St Johns Ct
B6 1 Newton Ho
2 Richard Neale Ho
3 Maddocks Ho
4 Cornwall St
5 Brockmer Ho
6 Dellow Ho
7 Bewley Ho
8 Artichoke Hill
C2 1 Damory Ho
2 Antony Ho
3 Roderick Ho
4 Pedworth Gdns
5 Beamish Ho
6 Gillam Ho
7 George Walter Ho
8 Richard Ho
9 Adron Ho
10 Westlake
11 McIntosh Ho
C3 1 Blick Ho
2 Neptune Ho
3 Scotia Ct
4 Murdoch Ho
5 Edmonton Ct
6 Niagara Ct
7 Columbia Point
8 Ritchie Ho
9 Wells Ho
10 Helen Peele Cotts
11 Orchard Ho
12 Dock Offices
13 Landale Ho
14 Courthope Ho
C4 1 Mayflower St
2 St Marys Est
3 Ropack St
4 Frank Whymark Ho

5 Adams Gardens Est
6 Hatteraick St
7 Hythe Ho
8 Seaford Ho
9 Sandwich Ho
10 Winchelsea Ho
11 Kenning St
12 Western Pl
13 Ainsty St
14 Pine Ho
15 Beech Ho
16 Larch Ho
17 Seth St
18 Turner Ct
19 Risdon Ct
20 Risdon St
21 Aylton Est
22 Manitoba Ct
23 Calgary Ct
24 Irwell Est
25 City Bsns Ctr
26 St Olav's Sq
C5 1 John Rennie Wlk
2 Malay Ho
3 Wainwright Ho
4 Riverside Mans
5 Shackleton Ho
6 Whitehorn Ho
7 Wavel Ct
8 Prusom's Island
C6 1 Gosling Ho
2 Vogler Ho
3 Donovan Ho
4 Knowlden Ho
5 Chamberlain Ho
6 Moore Ho
7 Thornewill Ho
8 Fisher Ho
9 All Saints Ct
10 Coburg Dwellings
11 Lowood Ho
12 Solander Gdns
13 Chancery Bldgs
14 Ring Ho
15 Juniper St
16 Gordon Ho
17 West Block
18 North Block
19 South Block
D2 1 John Kennedy Ho
2 Brydale Ho
3 Balman Ho
4 Tissington Ct
5 Harbord Ho
6 Westfield Ho
7 Albert Starr Ho
8 John Brent Ho
9 William Evans Ho
10 Raven Ho
11 Egret Ho
12 Fulmar Ho
13 Dunlin Ho
14 Siskin Ho
15 Sheldrake Ho
16 Buchanan Ct
17 Burrage Ct
18 Biddenham Ho
19 Ayston Ho
20 Empingham Ho
21 Deanshanger Ho
22 Codicote Ho
D4 1 Schooner Cl
2 Dolphin Cl
3 Clipper Cl
4 Deauville Ct
5 Colette Ct
6 Coniston Ct
7 Virginia Ct
8 Derwent Ct
9 Grantham Ct
10 Serpentine Ct
11 Career Ct
12 Lacine Ct
13 Fairway Ct
14 Harold Ct
15 Spruce Ho
16 Cedar Ho
17 Sycamore Ho
18 Woodland Cres
19 Poplar Ho
20 Adelphi Ct
21 Basque Ct
22 Aberdale Ct
23 Quilting Ct
24 Chargrove Cl
25 Radley Ct
26 Greenacre Sq
27 Maple Leaf Sq
28 Stanhope Cl
29 Hawke Pl
30 Drake Cl

31 Brass Talley Alley
32 Monkton Ho
33 James Ho
34 Wolfe Cres
D5 1 Clarence Mews
2 Raleigh Ct
3 Katherine Cl
4 Woolcombes Ct
5 Tudor Ct
6 Quayside Cl
7 Princes Riverside Rd
8 Surrey Ho
9 Tideway Ct
10 Edinburgh Ct
11 Falkirk St
12 Byelands Cl
13 Gwent Ct
14 Lavender Ho
15 Abbotshade Rd
16 Bellamy's Ct
17 Blenheim Ct
18 Sandringham Ct
19 Hampton Ct
20 Windsor Ct
21 Balmoral Ct
22 Westminster Ct
D6 1 Barnardo Gdns
2 Roslin Ho
3 Glamis Est
4 Peabody Est
5 East Block
6 Highway Trad Ctr The
7 Highway Bsns Pk The
8 Cranford Cotts
9 Ratcliffe Orch
10 Scotia Bldg
11 Mauretania Bldg
12 Compania Bldg
13 Sirius Bldg
14 Unicorn Bldg
15 Keeper Wharf

119

A2 1 Trafalgar Cl
2 Hornblower Cl
3 Cunard Wlk
4 Caronia Ct
5 Carinthia Ct
6 Freswick Ho
7 Graveley Ho
8 Husbourne Ho
9 Crofters Ct
10 Pomona Ho
11 Hazelwood Ho
12 Cannon Wharf Bsns Ctr
13 Bence Ho
14 Clement Ho
15 Pendennis Ho
16 Lighter Cl
17 Mast Ct
18 Rushcutters Ct
19 Boat Lifter Way
A6 1 St Georges Sq
2 Drake Ho
3 Osprey Ho
4 Fleet Ho
5 Gainsborough Ct
6 Victory Pl
7 Challenger Ho
8 Conrad Ho
9 Lock View Ct
10 Shoulder of Mutton Alley
11 Frederick Sq
12 Helena Sq
13 Elizabeth Sq
14 Sophia Sq
15 William Sq
16 Lamb Ct
17 Lockside
18 Ionian Bldg
19 Regents Gate
B1 1 Gransden Ho
2 Daubeney Twr
3 North Ho
4 Rochfort Ho
5 Keppel Ho
6 Camden Ho
7 Sanderson Ho
8 Berkeley Ho
9 Strafford Ho
10 Richman Ho
11 Hurleston Ho
12 Grafton Ho
13 Fulcher Ho
14 Citrus Ho
B2 1 Windsock Cl
2 Linberry Wlk
3 Lanyard Ho
4 Golden Hind Pl

5 James Lind Ho
6 Harmon Ho
7 Pelican Ho
8 Bembridge Ho
9 Terrace The
10 George Beard Rd
11 Colonnade The
12 Pepys Ent Ctr
B6 1 Hamilton Ho
2 Imperial Ho
3 Oriana Ho
4 Queens Ct
5 Brightlingsea Pl
6 Faraday Ho
7 Ropemaker's Fields
8 Oast Ct
9 Mitre The
10 Bate St
11 Joseph Irwin Ho
12 Padstow Ho
13 Bethlehem Ho
14 Saunders Ct
15 Roche Ho
16 Stocks Pl
17 Trinidad Ho
18 Grenada Ho
19 Kings Ho
20 Dunbar Wharf
21 Limekiln Wharf
C1 1 Hudson Ct
2 Shackleton Cl
3 Perry Ct
4 Maritime Quay
C2 1 Olympian Ct
2 Aphrodite Ct
3 Mercury Ct
4 Poseidon Ct
5 Neptune Ct
6 Artemis Ct
7 Hera Ct
8 Ares Ct
9 Cyclops Mews
10 Magellan Pl
11 Britannia Rd
12 Deptford Ferry Rd
13 Ironmonger's Pl
14 Radnor Wlk
15 Ashdown Wlk
16 Rothsay Wlk
17 Dartmoor Wlk
18 Ringwood Gdns
19 Dockers Tanner Rd
20 Apollo Bldg
21 Nova Bldg
C3 1 St Hubert's Ho
2 John Tucker Ho
3 Clare Grant Ho
4 Gilbertson Ho
5 Bowsprit Point
6 Scoulding Ho
7 Cord Way
8 Cressall Ho
9 Alexander Ho
10 Kedge Ho
C4 1 Jefferson Bldg
2 Waterman Bldg
3 Pierpoint Bldg
4 Franklin Bldg
5 Bellamy Cl
6 Bosun Ct
7 Edison Bldg
8 Vanguard Bldg
C6 1 West India Ho
2 Birchfield Ho
3 Elderfield Ho
4 Thornfield Ho
5 Gorsefield Ho
6 Arborfield Ho
7 Colborne Ho
8 East India Bldgs
9 Compass Point
10 Salter St
11 Kelly Ct
12 Flynn Ct
13 Mary Jones Ho
14 Horizon Bldg
15 Berber Pl
D2 1 Brassey Ho
2 Triton Ho
3 Warspite Ho
4 Rodney Ho
5 Conway Ho
6 Exmouth Ho
7 Akbar Ho
8 Arethusa Ho
9 Tasman Ct
D6 1 Westcott Ho
2 Corry Ho
3 Malam Gdns
4 Devitt Ho
5 Leyland Ho
6 Wigram Ho
7 Willis Ho
8 Balsam Ho

9 Finch's Ct
10 Poplar Bath St
11 Lawless St
12 Storey Ho
13 Abbot Ho
14 Landon Wlk
15 Goodhope Ho
16 Goodfaith Ho
17 Winant Ho
18 Lubbock Ho
19 Goodwill Ho
20 Martindale Ho
21 Holmsdale Ho
22 Norwood Ho
23 Constant Ho
24 Woodall Cl

120

A2 1 Betty May Gray Ho
2 Castleton Ho
3 Urmston Ho
4 Salford Ho
5 Capstan Ho
6 Frigate Ho
7 Galleon Ho
8 Barons Lo
A3 1 Cardale St
2 Hickin St
3 John McDonald Ho
4 Thorne Ho
5 Skeggs Ho
6 St Bernard Ho
7 Kimberley Ho
8 Kingdon Ho
9 Lingard Ho
10 Yarrow Ho
11 Sandpiper Ct
12 Nightingale Ct
13 Robin Ct
14 Heron Ct
A4 1 Llandovery Ho
2 Rugless Ho
3 Ash Ho
4 Elm Ho
5 Cedar Ho
6 Castalia Sq
7 Walkers Lo
8 Antilles Bay
9 Alice Shepherd Ho
10 Oak Ho
11 Ballin Ct
12 Grebe Ct
13 Kingfisher Ct
A6 1 Discovery Ho
2 Mountague Pl
3 Virginia Ho
4 Collins Ho
5 Lawless Ho
6 Carmichael Ho
7 Commodore Ho
8 Mermaid Ho
9 Bullivant St
10 Anderson Ho
11 Mackrow Wlk
12 Robin Hood Gdns
B2 1 Verwood Lo
2 Fawley Lo
3 Lyndhurst Lo
4 Blyth Cl
5 Farnworth Ho
6 Francis Cl
B6 1 Settlers Ct
2 Susan Constant Ct
3 Adventurers Ct
4 Bartholomew Ct
5 Atlantic Ct
6 Cape Henry Ct
7 Wotton Ct
8 Studley Ct
9 Wingfield Ct
C1 1 Bellot Gdns
2 Thornley Pl
3 King William La
4 Bolton Ho
5 Miles Ho
6 Mell St
7 Sam Manners Ho
8 Hatcliffe Almshouses
9 Woodland Wlk
10 Earlswood Ct
D1 1 Baldrey Ho
2 Christie Ho
3 Dyson Ho
4 Cliffe Ho
5 Moore Ho
6 Collins Ho
7 Lockyer Ho

8 Halley Ho
9 Kepler Ho

121
A1 **1** Layfield Ho
2 Westerdale Rd
3 Mayston Mews
A5 **1** Capulet Mews
2 Pepys Cres
3 De Quincey Mews
4 Hardy Ave
5 Tom Jenkinson Rd
6 Hanameel St
7 Kennacraig Cl
8 Gatcombe Rd
9 Badminton Mews
10 Holyrood Mews
11 Britannia Gate
12 Dalemain Mews
A6 **1** Clements Ave
2 Martindale Ave
B1 **1** Phipps Ho
2 Hartwell Ho
3 Nicholas Stacey Ho
4 Frank Burton Cl
B5 **1** Beaulieu Ave
2 Charles Winchup Rd
3 Audley Dr
4 Julie Garfield Mews
5 Julia Garfield Mews
6 Rayleigh Rd
7 Pirie St
8 Hanameel St
9 Ramsgate Cl
10 West Mersea Cl
11 Hanameel St
12 Dunlop Point
13 Ramsgate Cl
14 Westwood Rd
C1 **1** Ransom Rd
2 Linton Cl
3 Cedar Pl
4 Gooding Ho
5 Valiant Ho
6 Chaffey Ho
7 Benn Ho
8 Wellesley Ho
9 Gollogly Terr

122
A2 **1** Harden Cl
2 Albion Cl
3 Viking Ho
4 Zealand Ho
5 Glenalvon Way
6 Parish Wharf
7 Elsinore Ho
8 Lelland Ho
9 Denmark Ho
10 Jutland Ho
11 Tivoli Gdns
12 Rance Ho
13 Peel Yates Ho
14 Rosebank Wlk
15 Paradise Pl
16 Woodville St
B2 **1** Bowling Green Row
2 Sara Turnball Ho
3 Brewhouse Rd
4 Red Barracks Rd
5 Marine Dr
6 Cambridge Ho
7 Hastings Ho
8 Cambridge Barracks Rd
9 Len Clifton Ho
10 Granby Ho
11 Milne Ho
12 Harding Ho
13 Rendlebury Ho
14 Rutland Ho
15 Townshend Ho
16 Mulgrave Ho
17 Murray Ho
18 Chatham Ho
19 Biddulph Ho
20 Carew Ho
21 Eleanor Wlk
C2 **1** Preston Ho
2 Lindsay Ho
3 Fraser Ho
4 Pickering Ho
5 Watergate Ho
6 Grinling Ho
7 Glebe Ho

12 Slater Cl
13 Elliston Ho
15 Sir Martin Bowes Ho
16 Jim Bradley Cl
17 Bathway
18 Limavady Ho
C5 **1** Westland Ho
2 Queensland Ho
3 Pier Par
4 Woodman Par
5 Shaw Ho
6 Glen Ho
7 Brocklebank Ho
D1 **1** Branham Ho
2 Ford Ho
3 Wilford Ho
4 Parker Ho
5 Stirling Ho
6 Twiss Ho
7 Hewett Ho
D2 **1** Beresford Sq
2 Central Ct
3 Walpole Pl
4 Anglesea Ave
5 Troy Ct
6 Ormsby Point
7 Haven Lo
8 Green Lawns
9 Eardley Point
10 Sandham Point
11 Bingham Point

123
A1 **1** Glenmount Path
2 Claymill Ho
3 George Akass Ho
B1 **1** Bert Reilly Ho
C1 **1** Fox Hollow Cl
2 Goldsmid St

124
B5 **1** Rowntree Path
2 Macaulay Way
3 Manning Ct
4 Chadwick Ct
5 Simon Ct
B6 **1** Beveridge Ct
2 Hammond Way
3 Leonard Robbins Path
4 Lansbury Ct
5 Raymond Postgate Ct
6 Webb Ct
7 Curtis Way
8 Lytton Strachy Path
9 Keynes Ct
10 Marshall Path
11 Cross Ct
12 Octavia Way
13 Passfield Ct
14 Mill Ct
15 Besant Ct
C4 **1** Binsey Wlk
2 Tilehurst Point
3 Blewbury Ho
4 Coralline Wlk
5 Evenlode Ho
C5 **1** Kingsley Ct
2 Wilberforce Ct
3 Shaftesbury Ct
4 Hazlitt Ct
5 Ricardo Path
6 Nassau Path
7 Malthus Path
8 Bright Ct
9 Cobden Ct
D4 **1** Oakenholt Ho
2 Trewsbury Ho
3 Penton Ho
4 Osney Ho
5 Jacob Ho
6 Masham Ho
7 St Helens Rd
8 Clewer Ho
9 Maplin Ho
10 Wyfold Ho
11 Hibernia Point
12 Duxford Ho
13 Radley Ho

125
A3 **1** Harlequin Ho
2 Dexter Ho
3 Argall Ho
4 Mangold Way
5 Lucerne Ct
6 Holstein Way
7 Abbotswood Cl
8 Plympton Cl
9 Benedict Cl
B1 **1** Shakespeare Ho
2 Tennyson Ho
3 Dickens Ho
4 Chestnuts The

3 Scott Ho
5 Lansbury Ho
6 Shaw Ho
C1 **1** Stevanne Ct
2 Tolcairn Ct
3 Chalfont Ct
4 Alonso Ct
5 Ariel Ct
6 Miranda Ho
7 Prospero Ho
8 Laurels The
9 Camden Ct
10 Newnham Lo
11 Court Lo
12 Flaxman Ct
13 Hertford Wlk
14 Riverview Ct
C3 **1** Cressingham Ct
2 Telford Ho
3 Kelvin Ho
4 Faraday Ho
5 Jenner Ho
6 Keir Hardy Ho
7 Lennox Ho
8 Mary Macarthur Ho
9 Elizabeth Garrett Anderson Ho
10 William Smith Ho
11 Baden Powell Ho
12 Baird Ho
13 Boyle Ho

129
D1 **1** Heathwood Ct
2 Aldermead
3 Northumberland Ct

130
C4 **1** Osterley Lo
2 St Andrew's Cl
3 Parkfield
4 Fairways
5 Granwood Ct
6 Grovewood Ct

131
A2 **1** Brewery Mews Bsns Ctr
2 Tolson Ho
3 Percy Gdns
4 Wynne Ct
5 Wisdom Ct
6 Swann Ct
7 Shrewsbury Wlk
8 King's Terr
9 Gistelword Ho
D5 **1** Galba Ct
2 Servius Ct
3 Maurice Ct
4 Leo Ct
5 Otho Ct
6 Nero Ct
7 Romulus Ct
D6 **1** Brockshot Cl
2 Westbury Pl
3 Braemar Ct
4 Brook Ct
5 Clifden Ho
6 Cedar Ct
7 Cranbrook Ct
8 Somerset Lo
9 Alexandra Rd
10 Berkeley Ho

132
A1 **1** St John's Gr
2 Michel's Row
3 Michelsdale Dr
4 Blue Anchor Alley
5 Clarence St
6 Sun Alley
7 Thames Link Ho
8 Benns Wlk
A6 **1** Ferry Sq
2 Wilkes Rd
3 Albany Par
4 Charlton Ho
5 Albany Ho
6 Alma Ho
7 Griffin Ct
8 Cressage Ho
9 Tunstall Wlk
10 Trimmer Wlk
11 Running Horse Yd
12 Mission Sq
13 Distillery Wlk
B1 **1** Towers The
2 Longs Ct
3 Sovereign Ct
4 Robinson Ct

5 Calvert Ct
6 Bedford Ct
7 Hickey's Almshouses
8 Church Estate Almshouses
9 Richmond International Bsns Ctr
B4 **1** Abercorn Mews
2 Primrose Ho
3 Lawman Ct
4 Royston Ct
5 Garden Ct
6 Capel Lo
7 Devonshire Ct
8 Celia Ct
9 Rosslyn Ho
10 Branstone Ct
11 Lamerton Lo
12 Kew Lo
13 Dunraven Ho
14 Stoneleigh Lo
15 Tunstall Ct
16 Voltaire
C4 **1** Clarendon Ct
2 Quintock Ho
3 Broome Ct
4 Lonsdale Mews
5 Sandways
6 Victoria Cotts
7 North Ave
8 Grovewood
9 Hamilton Ho
10 Melvin Ct
11 Power Ho
12 Station Ave
13 Blake Mews
D1 **1** Hershell Ct
2 Deanhill Ct
3 Park Sheen
4 Furness Lo
5 Merricks Ct

133
B2 **1** Rann Ho
2 Craven Ho
3 John Dee Ho
4 Kindell Ho
5 Montgomery Ho
6 Avondale Ho
7 Addington Ct
8 Dovecote Gdns
9 Firmston Ho
10 Glendower Gdns
11 Chestnut Ave
12 Trehern Rd
B3 **1** Archer Ho
2 White Ho
3 Powrie Ho
4 Seaforth Lo
5 St John's Gr
6 Sussex Ct
7 Carmichael Ct
8 Hampshire Ct
9 Thorne Pas
10 Beverley Path

134
D1 **1** Olivette St
2 Mascotte Rd
3 Glegg Pl
4 Crown Ct
5 Charlwood Terr
D6 **1** Cobb's Hall
2 Dorset Mans
3 St Clements Mans
4 Bothwell St
5 Hawksmoor St

135
B3 **1** Plato Pl
2 Mustow Pl
3 Laurel Bank Gdns
4 Ranelagh Mans
5 Churchfield Mans
6 Bear Croft Ho
7 Elysium Gate
8 Ethel Rankin Ct
9 Arthur Henderson Ho
10 William Banfield Ho
D3 **1** Brightwells
2 Broughton Road App
3 Bulow Ct
4 Langford Ct
5 Elizabeth Barnes Ct
6 Snowbury Rd

136
A2 **1** Molasses Ho

2 Molasses Row
3 Cinnamon Row
4 Calico Ho
5 Calico Row
6 Port Ho
7 Square Rigger Row
8 Trade Twr
9 Ivory Ho
10 Spice Ct
11 Sherwood Ct
12 Mendip Ct
13 Chalmers Ho
14 Coral Row
B1 **1** Burke Ho
2 Fox Ho
3 Buxton Ho
4 Pitt Ho
5 Romsey Ho
6 Beverley Cl
7 Florence Ho
8 Linden Ct
9 Dorcas Ct
10 Johnson Ct
11 Agnes Ct
12 Hilltop Ct
13 Courtyard The
14 Old Laundry The
15 Oberstein Rd
16 Fineran Ct
17 Sangora Rd
18 Harvard Mans
B2 **1** Benham Cl
2 Milner Ho
3 McManus Ho
4 Wilberforce Ho
5 Wheeler Ct
6 Sporle Ct
7 Holliday Sq
8 John Parker Sq
9 Carmichael Cl
10 Fenner Sq
11 Clark Lawrence Ct
12 Shaw Ct
13 Sendall Ct
14 Livingstone Rd
15 Farrant Ho
16 Jackson Ho
17 Darien Ho
18 Sheppard Ho
19 Ganley Ct
20 Arthur Newton Ho
21 Chesterton Ho
22 John Kirk Ho
23 Mantua St
24 Heaver Rd
B3 **1** Archer Ho
2 White Ho
3 Powrie Ho
4 Morgan Ct
5 Fairchild Ct
6 Musjid Rd
C2 **1** Kiloh Ct
2 Lanner Ho
3 Grifton Ho
4 Kestrel Ho
5 Kite Ho
6 Peregrine Ho
7 Hawk Ho
8 Inkster Ho
9 Harrier Ho
10 Eagle Hts
11 Kingfisher Ct
12 Lavender Terr
13 Temple Ho
14 Ridley Ho
15 Eden Ho
16 Hertford Ct
17 Nepaul Rd
C3 **1** Meecham Ct
2 McKiernan Ct
3 Banbury St
4 Colestown St
5 Crombie Mews
6 Frere St
D3 **1** Stevenson Ho
2 Ambrose Mews
3 Harling Ct
4 Southside Quarter
5 Latchmere St
6 Dovedale Cotts
7 Royden Ct
8 Castlemaine
9 Wittering Ho
10 Berry Ho
11 Weybridge Point

137
A2 **1** Shaftesbury Park Chambers
2 Selborne
3 Rush Hill Mews
4 Marmion Mews
5 Crosland Pl

6 Craven Mews
5 Basnett Rd
6 Woodmere Cl
7 Tyneham Cl
A3 **1** Hopkinson Ho
2 Macdonald Ho
3 Rushlake Ho
4 Bishopstone Ho
5 Dresden Ho
6 Millgrove St
7 Farnhurst Ho
8 Walden Ho
9 Kennard St
10 Langhurst Ho
11 Kennard Ho
12 Voltaire Ct
13 Barloch Ho
B2 **1** Turnchapel Mews
2 Redwood Mews
3 Phil Brown Pl
4 Bev Callender Cl
5 Keith Connor Cl
6 Tessa Sanderson Pl
7 Daley Thompson Way
8 Rashleigh Ct
9 Abberley Mews
10 Willow Lodge
11 Beaufoy Rd
B3 **1** St Philip Sq
2 Montefiore St
3 Gambetta St
4 Scott Ct
5 Radcliffe Path
6 Moresby Wlk
C1 **1** Polygon The
2 Windsor Ct
3 Trinity Cl
4 Hanscomb
5 Studios The
6 Bourne Ho
C2 **1** Clapham Manor Ct
2 Clarke Ho
3 Gables The
4 Sycamore Mews
5 Maritime Ho
6 Floris Pl
C3 **1** Seymour Ho
2 Lucas Ho
3 Durrington Twr
4 Amesbury Twr
5 Fovant Ct
6 Allington Ct
7 Welford Ct
8 Ilsley Ct
D1 **1** Kendoa Rd
2 Felmersham Cl
3 Abbeville Mews
4 Saxon Ho
5 Gifford Ho
6 Teignmouth Cl
7 Holwood Pl
8 Oaklands Pl
D2 **1** Chelsham Ho
2 Lynde Ho
3 Greener Ho
4 Towns Ho
5 Hugh Morgan Cl
6 Roy Ridley Ho
7 Lendal Terr
8 Slievemore Cl
9 Cadmus Cl
D3 **1** Haltone Ho
2 Surcot Ho
3 Kingsley Ho
4 Wood Ho
5 Dalemain Ho
6 Fallodon Ho
7 Dartington Ho
8 Esher Ho
9 Kneller Ho
10 Lostock Ho
11 Croxteth Ho
12 Donnington Ho
13 Farnley Ho
14 Hardwick Ho
15 Bradfield Ho
16 Brocket Ho
17 Colchester Ho
18 Clive Ho
19 Chessington Ho
20 Rushbrook Ho
21 Stanmore Ho
22 Newton Ho
23 Netherby Ho
24 Oakwell Ho
25 Rydal Ho
26 Rushton Ho
27 Metcalfe Ho
28 Lydwell Ho
29 Raleigh Ho

31 Spencer Ho
32 Shipley Ho
33 Naylor Ho
34 Mordaunt Ho
35 Stanley Ho
36 Alderley Ho
37 Effingham Ho
38 Grant Ho
39 Wilson Ho
40 Fraser Ho

138
A1 **1** Morris Ho
2 Gye Ho
3 Clowes Ho
4 Thomas Ho
5 Stuart Ho
6 Storace Ho
7 Bedford Ho
8 Ascot Ct
9 Ascot Par
10 Ashmere Ho
11 Ashmere Gr
12 Vickery Ho
13 Stafford Mans
14 Beresford Ho
A2 **1** Callingham Ho
2 Russell Pickering Ho
3 Lopez Ho
4 Coachmaker Mews
A3 **1** Barling Ct
2 Jeffrey's Ct
3 Brooks Ct
4 Dalmeny Ct
5 Fender Ct
6 Fishlock Ct
7 Bedser Ct
8 Gover Ct
9 Clarence Wlk
10 Barton Ct
11 Allom Ct
12 Garden Ho
13 Otha Ho
14 Hayward Ct
15 Surridge Ct
16 Knox Ct
17 Jephson Ct
18 Holmes Ct
19 McIntyre Ct
20 Richardson Ct
21 Cassell Ho
22 Packington Ho
23 Bain Ho
24 Enfield Ho
25 Fawcett Ho
26 Sidgwick Ho
27 Jowett Ho
28 Beckett Ho
29 Arden Ho
30 Pinter Ho
31 Barrington Ct
B1 **1** Freemens Hos
2 Roger's Almshouses
3 Gresham Almshouses
4 Exbury Ho
5 Glasbury Ho
6 Dalbury Ho
7 Fosbury Ho
8 Chalbury Ho
9 Neilson-Terry Ct
10 Pavilion Mans
11 Daisy Dormer Ct
12 George Lashwood Ct
13 Marie Lloyd Ct
14 Trinity Homes
15 Lethaby Ho
16 Edmundsbury Ct Est
17 Regis Pl
18 Belvedere Pl
19 Alpha Ho
20 Beta Pl
21 Cedars Ho
B2 **1** Turberville Ho
2 Thrayle Ho
3 Percheron Ct
4 Draymans Ct
B3 **1** Maurice Ho
2 Thring Ho
3 Paton Ho
4 Huxley Ho
5 Morell Ho
6 Mary Ho
7 Beale Ho
8 Rosa Parks Ho
9 Birrell Ho
10 Waltham Ho
11 Burford Ho
12 Thornicroft Ho
13 Addington Ho
14 Goffton Ho
15 Redmayne Ho

16 Norton Ho
17 Aytoun Ct
18 Colwall Ho
19 Burrow Ho
20 Wynter Ho
21 Crowhurst Ho
22 Lidcote Gdns
23 Cumnor Cl
24 Park View Mews
C1 1 Electric Mans
2 Electric La
3 Connaught Mans
4 Clifton Mans
5 Hereford Ho
6 Chaplin Ho
7 Brixton Oval
8 Lord David Pitt Ho
9 Marcus Garvey Way
10 Montgo Cl
11 Bob Marley Way
12 Leeson Rd
C2 1 Buckmaster Cl
3 Albermarle Ho
4 Goodwood Mans
5 Angell Park Gdns
6 Fyfield Rd
7 Howard Ho
8 Harris Ho
9 Broadoak Ct
10 Burgate Ct
11 Witchwood Ho
12 Blacktree Mews
13 Chartham Ct
14 Chilham Ct
15 Northgate Ct
16 Westgate Ct
17 Dover Mans
C3 1 Norval Gn
2 Hilda Terr
4 Church Gn
5 Lord Holland La
7 Sorrell Cl
8 Burton Rd
9 Holles Ho
10 Leys Ct
11 Warwick Ho
12 Fairfax Ho
13 Wayland Ho
14 Dudley Ho
15 Denchworth Ho
16 Fitzgerald Ho
17 Lambert Ho
18 Chute Ho
19 Bedwell Ho
20 Ferrey Mews
21 Serenaders Rd
C4 1 Hector Ct
2 Jason Ct
3 Creon Ct
4 Hermes Ct
5 Argos Ct
6 Cadmus Ct
7 Appollo Ct
8 Mercury Ct
9 County Ho
10 Seasalter Ho
11 Downbarton Ho
12 Garlinge Ho
13 Maria Ho
14 Alvanley Ho
15 Woodchurch Ho
16 Durlock Ho
17 Hallam Ho
18 Whiteness Ho
19 Bromstone Ho
20 Penelope Ho
21 Melbourne Sq
22 Cloisters The
23 Cliffsend Ho
24 Sacketts Ho
25 Hanway Ho
26 Brickworth Ho
27 Redlynch Ho
28 Stodmarsh Ho
29 Kingsgate Ho
30 Chardin Ho
31 Annesley Ho
32 Knowlton Ho
33 Russell Gr
34 Eamann Casey Ho
C5 1 Swift Ho
2 Listowel Cl
3 Deal Wlk
4 Plover Ho
5 Aigburth Mans
6 Glencoe Mans
7 Glenshaw Mans
8 Cleveland Mans
9 Leda Ct
10 Jupiter Ct
11 Juno Ct
12 Healy Ho
13 Ashton Ho
14 Ramsey Ho
15 Annesley Ho
16 Cowley Rd
C6 1 Sherwin Ho
3 Kilner Ho
4 Read Ho
5 Lohmann Ho
6 Hornby Ho
7 Abel Ho
8 Blythe Ho
9 Key Ho
10 Lockwood Ho
11 Alverstone Ho
12 Blades Ho
13 Rothesay Ct
D1 1 Mahatma Ganhi Ind Est
2 Dylan Rd
3 Bessemer Park Ind Est
4 Pablo Neruda Cl
5 Langston Hughes Cl
6 Walt Whitman Cl
7 James Joyes Wlk
8 Alice Walker Cl
9 Louise Bennett Cl
10 Chadacre Ho
11 Burwood Ho
12 Pyrford Ho
13 Wangford Ho
14 Ashford Ho
15 Kenwood Ho
16 Moyne Ho
17 Elveden Ho
19 Carrara Wlk
20 Broughton Dr
21 Tilia Wlk
21 Angela Davis Ind Est
D2 1 Mallams Mews
2 Amberley Ct
3 Harper Ho
4 Leicester Ho
5 Station Ave
6 Wellfit St
7 Loughborough Ct
8 Belinda Rd
9 Higgs Ind Est
D3 1 Langport Ho
2 Iveagh Ho
3 Newark Ho
4 Edgehill Ho
5 Hopton Ho
6 Ashby Ho
7 Nevil Ho
D4 1 Fairbairn Gn
2 Hammelton Gn
3 Foxley Sq
4 Silverburn Ho
5 Butler Ho
6 Dalkeith Ho
7 Turner Cl
8 Bathgate Ho
9 Black Roof Ho
D6 1 Faunce Ho
2 Garbett Ho
3 Harvard Ho
4 Doddington Pl
5 Kean Ho
6 Jephson Ho
7 Cornish Ho
8 Bateman Ho
9 Molesworth Ho
10 Walters Ho
11 Cruden Ho
12 Brawne Ho
13 Prescott Ho
14 Chalmer's Wlk
15 Copley Cl

139

A3 1 Bergen Ho
2 Oslo Ho
3 Viking Ho
4 Jutland Ho
5 Norvic Ho
6 Odin Ho
7 Baltic Ho
8 Nobel Ho
9 Mercia Ho
10 Kenbury Gdns
11 Zealand Ho
12 Elsinore Ho
13 Norse Ho
14 Denmark Mans
15 Dane Ho
16 Canterbury Cl
17 York Cl
18 Kenbury Mans
19 Parade Mans
20 Winterslow Ho
21 Lilford Ho
22 Cutcombe Mans
23 Bartholomew Ho
24 Guildford Ho
25 Boston Ho
26 Hereford Ho
27 Weyhill Ho
28 Lichfield Ho
29 Lansdown Ho
30 Honiton Ho
31 Pinner Ho
32 Baldock Ho
33 Widecombe Ho
34 Nottingham Ho
35 Witham Ho
36 Barnet Ho
37 Empress Mews
A4 1 Bertha Neubergh Ho
2 Mornington Mews
3 Badsworth Rd
4 Sycamore Ct
5 Elm Tree Ct
6 Samuel Lewis Trust Dwellings
7 Valmar Trad Est
8 Keswick Ho
9 Mitcham Ho
A5 1 Boundary Ho
2 Day Ho
3 Burgess Ho
4 Carlyle Ho
5 Myers Ho
6 Thompson's Ave
7 Palgrave Ho
8 Winnington Ho
9 Brantwood Ho
10 Lowell Ho
11 Jessie Duffett Ho
12 Otterburn Ho
13 Crossmount Ho
14 Venice Ct
15 Bowyer St
16 Livingstone Ho
17 Gothic Ct
18 Coniston Ho
19 Harlynwood
20 Carey Ct
21 Finley Ct
22 Grainger Ct
23 Hayes Ct
24 Moffat Ho
25 Marinel Ho
26 Hodister Cl
27 Arnot Ho
28 Lamb Ho
29 Kipling Ho
30 Keats Ho
31 Kenyon Ho
32 New Church Rd
33 Sir John Kirk Cl
B1 1 Shaftesbury Ct
2 Mayhew Ct
3 Morris Ct
4 Swinburne Ct
5 Perth Ct
6 Tayside Ct
7 Matlock Ct
8 Hunter Ct
9 Turner Ct
B3 1 Selborne Rd
2 Hascombe Terr
B4 1 Joiners Arms Yd
2 Butterfly Wlk
3 Cuthill Wlk
4 Colonades The
5 Artichoke Mews
6 Peabody Bldgs
7 Brighton Ho
8 Park Ho
9 Peabody Ct
10 Lomond Ho
11 Lamb Ho
12 Kimpton Ct
13 Belham Wlk
14 Datchelor Pl
15 Harvey Rd
B5 1 Masterman Ho
2 Milton Ho
3 Pope Ho
4 Chester Ct
5 Marvel Ho
6 Flecker Ho
7 Landor Ho
8 Evelina Mans
9 Habington Ho
10 Langland Ho
11 Drinkwater Ho
12 Procter Ho
13 Shirley Ho
14 Drayton Ho
15 Bridges Ho
16 Cunningham Ho
17 Hood Ho
18 Herrick Ho
19 Dekker Ho
20 Sansom St
20 Houseman Way
21 Coleby Path
22 Jago Wlk
B6 1 Queens Ho
2 Arnside Ho
3 Horsley St
4 St Peter's Ho
5 St Johns Ho
6 St Marks Ho
7 St Stephens Ho
8 St Matthew's Ho
9 Red Lion Cl
10 Boyson Rd
11 Bradenham
C2 1 Harfield Gdns
2 Karen Ct
3 Seavington Ho
4 Appleshaw Ho
5 Birdsall Ho
6 Whitney Ho
7 Wheatland Ho
8 Wilton Ho
9 Walcot Ho
10 Whadden Ho
11 Melbrook Ho
12 Ledbury Ho
13 Tidworth Ho
14 Riseholme Ho
15 Ringmer Ho
16 Petworth Ho
17 Stagshaw Ho
18 Ivybridge Ho
19 Inwood Ho
20 Gatcombe Ho
21 Gatebeck Ho
22 Felbridge Ho
23 Cowdray Ho
C3 1 Springfield Ho
2 Craston Ho
3 Walters Ho
4 Edgecombe Ho
5 Fowler Ho
6 Rignold Ho
7 Chatham Ho
C4 1 Barnwell Ho
2 Brunswick Villas
3 St Giles Twr
4 Bentley Ho
5 Dawson Ho
6 Dryden Ho
7 Mayward Ho
8 Longleigh Ho
9 Fairwall Ho
10 Bodeney Ho
11 Sandby Ho
12 Vestry Mews
13 Netley
14 Lakanal
15 Racine
C5 1 Tower Mill Rd
2 Tilson Cl
6 Dorton Cl
8 Granville Sq
10 Farnborough Way
13 Hordle Prom W
15 Samuel Jones Ind Est
16 Dibden Ho
17 Marchwood Cl
18 Pilgrims Cloisters
19 Beacon Ho
20 Teather St
21 Stacy Path
22 Rumball Ho
23 Ballow Cl
24 Rill Ho
C6 3 Pearse St
4 Watling St
5 Gandolfi st
7 Andoversford Ct
8 Downend Ct
D1 1 Dulwich Mews
2 St James's Cloisters
D4 1 Colbert
2 Voltaire
3 Finch Mews
4 Charles Coveney Rd
5 Crane St
6 Curlew Ho
7 Mallard Ho
8 Tern Ho
9 Crane Ho
10 Falcon Ho
11 Bryanston Ho
12 Basing Ct
13 Marcus Ho
14 Sheffield Ho
D5 2 Whistler Mews
1 Painswick Ct
2 Sharpness Ct
3 Hordle Prom N
4 Mattingly Way
5 Calypso Cres
6 Samuel St
7 Hordle Prom S
8 Cinnamon Cl
9 Savannah Cl
10 Thames Ct
11 Amstel Ct
12 Danube Ct
13 Tilbury Cl
14 Hordle Prom E
15 Indus Ct
16 Oakcourt
17 Palm Ct
18 Rowan Ct
19 Blackthorn Ct
20 Pear Ct
21 Lidgate Rd
D6 1 Willsbridge Ct
2 Cam Ct
3 Quedgeley Ct
4 Saul Ct
5 Quenington Ct
6 Westonbirt Ct
7 Wickway Ct

140

A3 1 William Margrie Cl
2 Choumert Sq
3 Parkstone Rd
4 Atwell Rd
A4 2 Angelina Ho
3 Jarvis Ho
4 Richland Ho
5 Honeywood Ho
6 Wakefield Ho
7 Primrose Ho
8 Hardcastle Ho
9 Dunstall Ho
10 Purdon Ho
11 Flamborough Ho
12 Lambrook Ho
13 Witcombe Point
14 Yarnfield Sq
15 Winford Ct
16 Portbury Cl
17 Robert Keen Cl
A5 1 Thornbill Ho
2 Vervain Ho
3 Woodstar Ho
4 Tamarind Ho
5 Hereford Retreat
6 Haymerle Ho
7 Furley Ho
8 Applegarth Ho
9 Freda Corbett Cl
10 Rudbeck Ho
11 Henslow Ho
12 Lindley Ho
13 Collinson Ho
14 Sister Mabel's Way
15 Timberland Cl
16 Hastings Cl
17 Neville Cl
18 Sidmouth Ho
19 Budleigh Ho
20 Stanesgate Ho
21 Braemore Ho
22 Ely Ho
A6 1 Bowles Rd
2 Western Wharf
3 Northfield Ho
4 Millbrook Ho
5 Denstone Ho
6 Deerhurst Ho
7 Caversham Ho
8 Battle Ho
9 Cardiff Ho
10 Bridgnorth Ho
11 Exeter Ho
12 Grantham Ho
13 Aylesbury Ho
14 Royston Ho
B2 1 Tilling Ho
2 Goodwin Ho
3 Citron Terr
4 Cheam St
B3 1 Walkynscroft
2 Ryegates
3 Hathorne Cl
4 Pilkington Rd
5 Russell Ct
6 Heaton Ho
7 Magdalene Cl
B4 1 Willowdene
2 Pinedene
3 Oakdene
4 Beechdene
5 Hollydene
6 Wood Dene
8 Staveley Cl
9 Carnicot Ho
10 Martock Ct
11 Kendrick Ct
B5 1 Tortington Ho
2 Credenhill Ho
3 Bromyard Ho
4 Hoyland Cl
5 Willowdene
6 Ashdene
7 Acorn Par
8 Carlton Gr
9 Springall St
10 Harry Lambourn Ho
C3 1 Honiton Gdns
2 Selden Ho
3 Hathway Ho
4 Hathway St
5 Station Ct
C5 1 Ambleside Point
2 Grasmere Point
3 Windermere Point
4 Roman Way
5 Laburnham Cl
7 Romney Cl
8 Hammersley Ho
9 Hutchinson Ho
10 Hammond Ho
11 Fir Tree Ho
12 Glastonbury Ct
13 Highbridge Ct
14 Filton Ct
15 Chiltern Ct
16 Cheviot Ct
C6 1 Penshurst Ho
2 Reculver Ho
3 Mereworth Ho
4 Camber Ho
5 Chilam Ho
6 Otford Ho
7 Olive Tree Ho
8 Aspen Ho
9 Lewis Silkin Ho
10 Richborough Ho
11 Dover Ho
12 Eynsford Ho
13 Horton Ho
14 Lamberhurst Ho
15 Canterbury Ind Pk
16 Upnall Ho
17 Sissinghurst Ho
18 Rochester Ho
19 Leybourne Ho
20 Lullingstone Ho
D1 1 Laxton Path
2 Barlings Ho
3 Bayfield Ho
4 Coston Wlk
5 Coverham Ho
6 Gateley Ho
7 Dereham Ho
8 Greenwood Ho
9 Hilton Ho
10 Goodall Ho
11 Horsley Ho
12 Jordan Ho
D5 1 Richard Anderson Ct
2 Palm Tree Ho
3 Edward Robinson Ho
4 Antony Ho
5 Gerrard Ho
6 Palmer Ho
7 Pankhurst Cl
D6 1 Harrisons Ct
2 Grantley Ho
3 Sunbury Ct
4 Tilbury Ho
5 Graham Ct
6 Connell Ct
7 St Clements Ct
8 Henderson Ct
9 Jemotts Ct
10 Verona Ct
11 Heywood Ho
12 Francis Ct
13 Hind Ho
14 Donne Ho
15 Carew Ct
16 Burbage Ho
17 Newland Ho
18 Dobson Ho
19 Dalton Ho
20 Greene Ct
21 Redrup Ho
22 Tarplett Ho
23 Stunnell Ho
24 Gasson Ho
25 Bryce Ho
26 Barnes Ho
27 Barkwith Ho
28 Bannister Ho
29 Apollo Ind Bsns Ctr

141

A5 1 Batavia Ho
2 Marlowe Bsns Ctr
3 Batavia Mews
4 Woodrush Cl
5 Alexandra St
6 Primrose Wlk
7 Vansittart St
8 Casella Ct
9 Cottesbrook St
A6 1 Portland Ct
2 Phoenix Ct
3 Rainbow Ct
4 Hawke Twr
6 Woodpecker Rd
B5 1 Austin Ho
2 Exeter Way
3 Crossleigh Ct
4 Mornington Pl
5 Maple Ho
B6 1 Chester Ho
2 Lynch Wlk
3 Arlington Ho
4 Woodcote Ho
5 Cornbury Ho
6 Prospect Pl
7 Akintaro Ho
8 Mulberry Ho
9 Laurel Ho
10 Linden Ho
11 Ashford Ho
12 Wardalls Ho
13 Magnolia Ho
14 Howard Ho
15 Larch Cl
16 Ibis Ct
17 Merganser Ct
18 Wotton Rd
19 Kingfisher Sq
20 Sanderling Ct
21 Dolphin Twr
22 Mermaid Twr
23 Scoter Ct
24 Shearwater Ct
25 Brambling Ct
26 Kittiwake Ct
28 Guillemot Ct
29 Marine Twr
30 Teal Ct
31 Lapwing Twr
34 Cormorant Ct
36 Shelduck Ct
39 Eider Ct
40 Pintail Ct
41 Tristan Ct
42 Skua Ct
43 Rosemary Ct
44 Violet Cl
45 Diana Cl
C4 1 Admiralty Cl
2 Harton Lo
3 Sylvia Cotts
4 Pitman Ho
5 Heston Ho
C5 1 Sandpiper Ct
2 Flamingo Ct
3 Titan Bsns Est
4 Rochdale Way
5 Speedwell St
6 Reginald Pl
7 Fletcher Path
8 Frankham Ho
9 Cremer Ho
10 Wilshaw Ho
11 Castell Ho
12 Holden Ho
13 Browne Ho
14 Lady Florence Ctyd
15 Covell Ct
C6 1 Dryfield Wlk
2 Blake Ho
3 Hawkins Ho
4 Grenville Ho
5 Langford Ho
6 Mandarin Ct
8 Bittern Ct
9 Lamerton St
10 Armada St
11 Armada Ct
12 Benbow Ho
13 Oxenham Ho
14 Caravel Mews
15 Hughes Ho
16 Stretton Mans
D5 1 Finch Ho
2 Jubilee The
3 Gordon Ho
4 Haddington Ct
5 Maitland Cl
6 Ashburnham Retreat

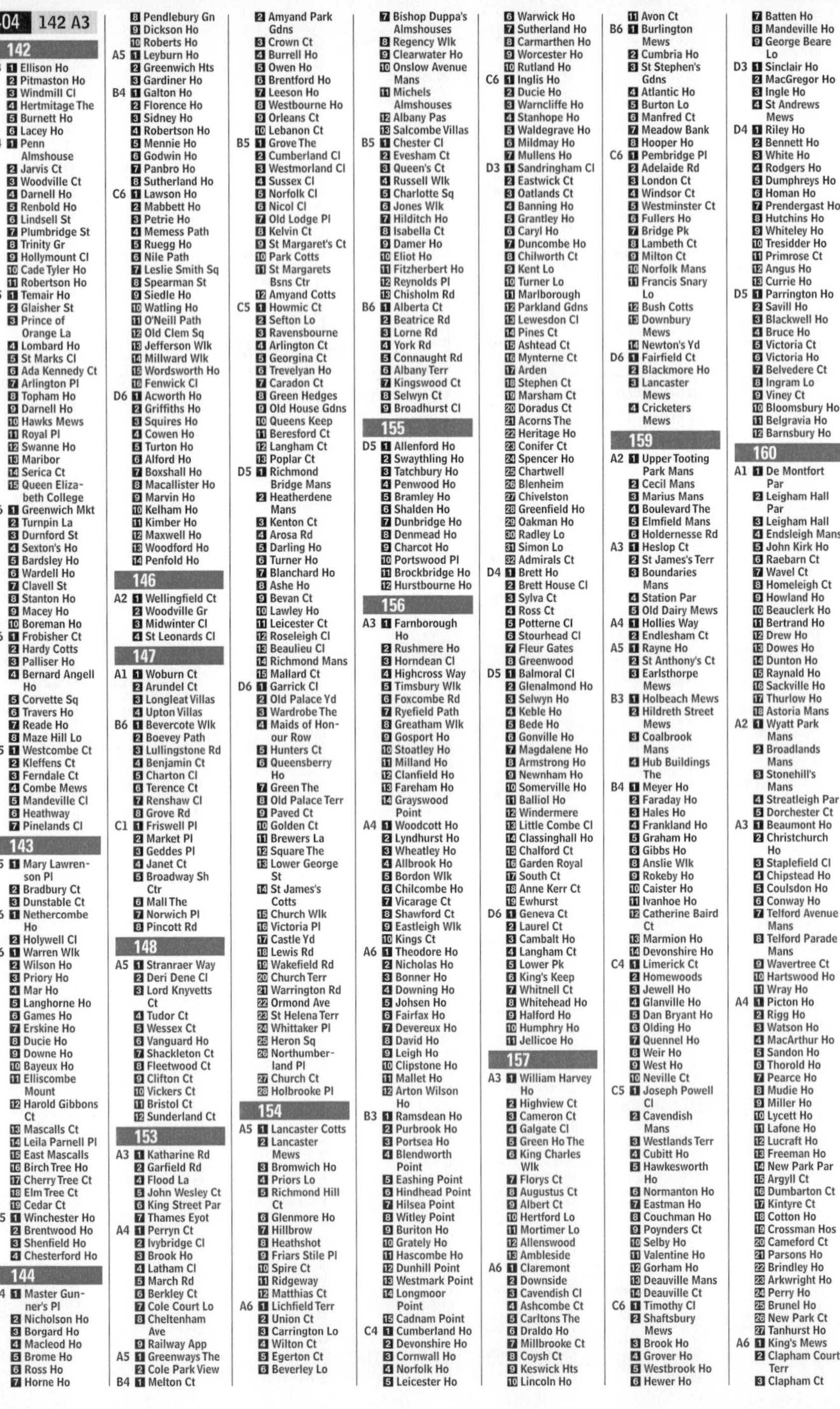

4 Clapham Park Terr
5 Queenswood Ct
6 Oak Tree Ct
7 Park Lofts
B1 1 Carisbrook Ct
2 Pembrook Lo
3 Willow Ct
4 Poplar Ct
5 Mountview
6 Spa View
B3 1 Charlwood Ho
2 Earlswood Ho
3 Balcombe Ho
4 Claremont Cl
5 Holbrook Ho
6 Gwynne Ho
7 Kynaston Ho
8 Tillman Ho
9 Regent Lo
10 Hazelmere Ct
11 Dykes Ct
B4 1 Archbishop's Pl
2 Witley Ho
3 Outwood Ho
4 Dunsfold Ho
5 Deepdene Lo
6 Warnham Ho
7 Albury Lo
8 Tilford Ho
9 Elstead Ho
10 Thursley Ho
11 Brockham Ho
12 Capel Lo
13 Leith Ho
14 Fairview Ho
15 Weymouth Ct
16 Ascalon Ct
17 China Mews
18 Rush Common Mews
B6 1 Beatrice Ho
2 Florence Ho
3 Evelyn Ho
4 Diana Ho
5 Brixton Hill Ct
6 Austin Ho
7 Manor Ct
8 Camsey Ho
9 Romer Ho
10 Gale Ho
11 Byrne Ho
12 Farnfield Ho
13 Marcham Ho
14 Rainsford Ho
15 Springett Ho
16 Mannering Ho
17 Waldron Ho
C3 1 Valens Ho
2 Loveday Ho
3 Strode Ho
4 Ethelworth Ct
5 Harbin Ho
6 Brooks Ho
7 Godolphin Ho
8 Sheppard Ho
9 McCormick Ho
10 Taylor Ho
11 Saunders Ho
12 Talcott Path
13 Derrick Ho
14 Williams Ho
15 Baldwin Ho
16 Churston Cl
17 Neil Wates Cres
18 Burnell Ho
19 Portland Ho
C4 1 Ellacombe Ho
2 Booth Ho
3 Hathersley Ho
4 Brereton Ho
5 Holdsworth Ho
6 Dearmer Ho
7 Cherry Cl
8 Greenleaf Cl
9 Longford Wlk
10 Scarlette Manor Wlk
11 Chandlers Way
12 Upgrove Manor Way
13 Ropers Wlk
14 Tebbs Ho
15 Bell Ho
16 Worthington Ho
17 Courier Ho
18 Mackie Rd
19 Hamers Ho
20 Kelyway Ho
21 Harriet Tubman Cl
22 Estoria Cl
23 Leckhampton Pl
24 Scotia Rd
25 Charles Haller St
26 Sidmouth Ho

27 Hunter Ct
28 Onslow Lo
29 William Winter Ct
30 Langthorne Lo
C5 1 Eccleston Ho
2 Scarsbrook Ho
3 Purser Ho
4 Rudhall Ho
5 Hardham Ho
6 Heywood Ho
7 Haworth Ho
8 Birch Ho
9 Lonsdell Ho
10 Lomley Ho
11 Laughton Ho
12 Bascome St
13 Dudley Mews
14 Herbert Mews
15 Blades Lo
16 Dick Shepherd Ct
17 Charman Ho
18 Morden Ho
19 Bishop Ct
20 Blackburn Ct
21 Leigh Ct
22 John Conwey Ho
C6 1 Crownstone Ct
2 Brockwell Ct
3 Nevena Ct
4 St George's Residences
5 Hanover Mans
6 Fleet Ho
7 Langbourne Ho
8 Turnmill Ho
9 Cossar Mews
10 Carter Ho
D1 1 Thanet Ho
2 Chapman Ho
3 Beaufoy Ho
4 Easton Ho
5 Roberts Ho
6 Lloyd Ct
7 Kershaw Ho
8 Wakeling Ho
9 Edridge Ho
10 Jeston Ho
11 Lansdowne Wood Cl

161
B2 1 Coppedhall
2 Shackleton Ct
3 Bullfinch Ct
4 Gannet Ct
5 Fulmar Ct
6 Heron Ct
7 Petrel Ct
8 Falcon Ct
9 Eagle Ct
10 Dunnock Ct
11 Dunlin Ct
12 Cormorant Ct
C6 1 Velde Way
2 Delft Way
3 Arnhem Way
4 Isel Way
5 Kempis Way
6 Terborah Way
7 Steen Way
8 Deventer Cres
9 Nimegen Way
10 Hilversum Way
11 St Barnabas Ct

162
A1 1 Tunbridge Ct
2 Harrogate Ct
3 Bath Ct
4 Leamington Ct
5 Porlock Ho
6 Cissbury Ho
7 Eddisbury Ho
8 Dundry Ho
9 Silbury Ho
10 Homildon Ho
11 Highgate Ho
12 Richmond Ho
13 Pendle Ho
14 Tynwald Ho
15 Wirrall Ho
A6 1 Greyfriars
2 Dorothy Charrington Ho
3 Keswick Ct
4 Kendall Ct
5 Halliwell Ct
B1 1 River Ho
2 Fordington Ho
3 Woodbury Ho
4 Gainsborough Mews
5 Forest Hill Ct
B2 1 Bromleigh Ct
2 Parfew Ct

3 Thetford Ct
4 Attleborough Ct
5 Dunton Ct
6 Frobisher Ct
7 Julian Court Path
8 Grizedale Terr
9 Worsley Ho
C1 1 Forest Lo
2 Sydenham Park Mans
3 William Wood Ho
C2 1 Fitzwilliam Hts
2 Taymount Grange
3 McLeod Ho
4 Featherstone Ave
5 Kingswear Ho
6 Salcombe Ho
C3 1 Hartech Ct
2 Angela Ct
3 Westwood Ct
4 New Belmont Ho
5 Pearcefield Ave
6 Waldram Pl
7 Horniman Grange
8 South View Ct
9 Heron Ct
10 Katherine Ct
D1 1 Standlake Point
2 Radcot Point
3 Newbridge Point
4 Northmoor Point
5 Kelmscott Point
6 Radnor Ct
7 Heathwood Point
8 Ashleigh Point
9 Deepdene Point
10 Rosemount Point
11 Woodfield Ho
12 Clairville Point
13 Trevenna Ho
14 Hyndewood
D2 4 Soper Cl

164
C4 1 Beaumont Terr
2 Littlebourne
3 Verdant Ct
D2 1 Kinross Ct
2 Montrose Ct
3 Rattray Ct
D3 1 Edinburgh Ct
2 McMillan Ct
3 Rowallan Ct
4 Meridian Ct
5 Braemar Ct
6 Barrow Ct
7 Blair Ct
8 Darlington Ct
9 Hamilton Ct
10 Inverness Ct
11 Oak Cottage Cl
12 Willow Ct
13 Keswick Ct

165
A4 1 Swallow Ct
2 Honeysuckle Ct
3 Venture Ct
4 Cheriton Ct
5 Askham Ct
6 Syon Lo

166
A2 1 Portland Cres
2 Bourdillon Ct
3 Hillary Ct
4 Tenzing Ct
5 John Hunt Ct
6 Everest Ct
A6 1 Horsfield Gdns
2 Foxhole Rd
C5 1 Roper St
2 Arcade The
3 Elm Terr
4 Imber Ct
5 Ashcroft Ct
6 Fairlands Ct
7 Brecon Ct
8 Newlands Ct
9 Harvard Ct
10 Garden Ct
11 Chiltern Ct
12 Fairway Ct

167
A2 1 Mervyn Stockwood Ho
2 Michael Marshall Ho

3 Keith Sutton Ho

168
A1 1 Ham Shades Cl
2 Aspen Ho
3 Medlar Ho
4 Cornel Ho
5 Stanton Ct
6 Hornbeam Ho
7 Beech Ho
8 Spindle Ho
9 Moat Ct
10 Hunters Lo
11 Edam Ct
12 Monica James Ho
13 Oak Ho
14 Crescent Ct
B5 1 Rochester Ct
2 Cobham Cl
3 Shorne Cl
4 Warne Pl

169
C4 1 Close The
2 Parkhurst Gdns
3 Chichester Ct
4 Pound Green Ct

171
D3 1 Bishops Ct
2 Ash Lo
3 Lime Lo
4 Oak Lo
5 Elm Ct
6 Willow Lo
7 Sycamore Lo
8 Priscilla Ho
9 Sunbury Cross Ctr
10 Isobel Ho

173
A6 1 Gabriel Ct
2 Metcalfe Wlk
3 Dunmow Ct
4 Burgess Cl
5 Chamberlain Wlk
C2 1 Sherbourne Ct
2 Somerset Ct
3 Jubilee Ho
4 Rushbury Ct
5 Hemming Ct
6 Ryedale Ct
7 Norman Ct
C4 1 Begonia Ct
2 Snowdrop Cl
3 Hyacinth Ct
4 Cyclamen Ct
5 Jonquil Gdns
6 Gladioli Ct
7 Daffodil Pl
8 Partridge Rd
D4 1 Acorn Cl
2 Wolsey Ho
3 Lytton Ho
4 Wren Ho
5 Faraday Ho

174
C5 1 Knaggs Ho
2 Keeling Ho
3 Elizabeth Ct
4 Oakhurst Ct
D5 1 Waldegrave Ct
2 Gresham Ho
3 Traherne Lo
4 Fishers Ct
5 Waterhouse Ho
6 Walpole Pl
7 Walpole Cres
8 Alice Mews
9 Bychurch End

175
A5 1 Cherrywood Ct
2 Cambridge Ho
3 Gleneagles Ct
4 Christchurch Ave
5 Hales Ct
6 Springfield Rd
D2 1 Wick Ho
2 Spinnaker Ct
3 Osiers Ct
4 Trent Ho
5 Arun Ho
6 Medway Ho
7 Avon Ho
8 Tyne Ho
9 Clyde Ho
10 Mersey Ho
11 Severn Ct
12 John Williams Cl
D6 1 Byron Ct
2 Coleridge Ct
3 Tennyson Ct

4 Herrick Ct
5 Spenser Ct
6 Marlowe Ct
7 Brooke Ct
8 Gray Ct
9 Shelley Ct
10 Pope Ct
11 Dryden Ct

176
A1 1 Cleave's Almshos
2 Parade The
3 Drovers Ct
4 Gough Ho
5 Eden Wlk
6 Alderman Judge Mall
7 Lady Booth Rd
8 Caversham Ho
9 Littlefield Ct
10 Bentall Sh Ctr The
11 Adams Wlk
12 Kingfisher Sports Ctr The
13 Greencoat Ho
A2 1 Regents Ct
2 Walter St
3 Canbury 2000 Bsns Pk
4 Sigrist Sq
5 Ashway Ctr
6 Warwick Ho
B1 1 Vicarage Ho
2 Rayleigh Ct
3 School Pas
4 Chippenham
5 Camm Gdns
6 Onslow Ho
7 Dowler Ct
B3 1 McDonald Ho
2 Elm Ho
3 Dale Ct
4 York Ho
5 Florence Ho
6 Florence Rd
7 Roupell Ho
8 Delft Ho
C1 1 Wimpole Ct
2 Burwell
3 Caldecote
4 Fordham
5 Connington
6 Chesterton Terr
7 Westwick
8 Eureka Rd
9 Fulborn
10 Comberton
11 Madingley
12 Grantchester
13 Cambridge
14 Grove Rd
15 Harston
16 Graveley
17 Croxton
18 Brinkley
19 Impington
20 Shelford
21 Duxford
C2 1 Farthings The
2 Brae Ct
3 Princeton Court
4 Station App
C3 1 Queen's Ct
2 St George's Rd
3 Park Road Ho
4 Dagmar Rd
5 Tapping Ct
6 Arthur Rd
7 Borough Rd
8 Belvedere Ct
9 Braywick Ct
10 Dean Ct
11 Rowan Ct
12 Richmond Ct
13 Sunningdale Ct
14 Hawker Ct
15 Cromwell Ct
16 Kings Ct
D2 1 Trevallyn Lo
2 Chichester Ho
3 Beechcroft
4 Cedars The
5 Liddlesdale Ho W
6 Liddlesdale Ho E
7 Deerhurst
8 Brockworth
9 Alderton
D3 1 Bramley Ho
2 Abinger Ho
3 Thursley Ho
4 Ridge Ho
5 Clone The
6 Mount Ct

7 Hillside Ct
8 Hill Ct
9 Royal Ct
10 Lakeside
11 High Ashton
D4 1 Godstone Ho
2 Hambledon Ho
3 Kingswood Ho
4 Leigh Ho
5 Milton Ho
6 Newdigate Ho
7 Farleigh Ho
8 Ockley Ho
9 Effingham Ho
10 Dunsfold Ho
11 Pirbright Ho
12 Clandon Ho
13 Ripley Ho

178
D2 1 Roskeen Ct
2 Chimneys Ct
3 Rosemary Cotts
4 Victoria Lo
5 Beaufort Ho
6 Kinnear Ct
7 Ranmore Ct
8 Lantern Ct
9 Crescent Ho
D3 1 Kings View Ct
2 Wimbledon Ct
3 Beryl Harding Ho
4 Upton Ct
5 Marian Lo
6 Terraces The
7 Lanherne Ho
8 Cumberland Cl
9 Thaxted Pl
10 Rathbone Ho
11 Princess Ct
12 Downs Ct
13 Ravenscar Lo
14 Haverley
15 Savona Cl
16 Beaumont Ct
17 Gordon Ct
D5 1 Lancaster Pl
2 Haygarth Pl
3 Allington Cl
4 Homefield Pl

179
A3 1 Mayfair Ct
2 Brunswick Ct
3 Pavilion Ct
A4 1 Walham Rise
2 Grosvenor Ct
3 Sovereign Ho
4 Holly Lo
5 Florence Ct
6 Linden Cotts
7 Sheep Walk Mews
B5 1 Lawns The
2 Prentice Ct
3 Catherine Ct
4 Woodlodge
5 Queen Alexandra's Ct
6 Lake Cl
7 Westwood Ct
8 Brambles The
9 Lismore
10 Rose Ct
C3 1 Ashbourne Terr
2 Sir Cyril Black Way
3 Downing Ho
4 Palmerston Gr
5 Gladstone Ct
6 Harefield Ct
7 Viscount Point
D2 1 Gilbert Cl
2 Becket Ct
3 Priory Cl
4 Hudson Ct
5 Ryder Ho
6 Eleanor Ho
7 Ramsey Ho
D3 1 Hamilton Road Mews
2 Dowman Cl

180
A2 1 Tanner Ho
2 May Ct
3 Marsh Ct
4 Lovell Ho
A3 1 Fiske Ct
2 Mellor Ct
3 Olive Rd
4 Allerton Ho
5 Victory Road Mews
6 Will Miles Ct
7 Vanguard Ho

8 Mychell Ho
9 Merton Pl
10 De Burgh Ho
11 Norfolk Ho
12 Hotham Road Mews
B1 1 Ripley Ct
2 Brooklands Ct
3 Horner La
C2 1 Linford Ct
2 Searle Ct
3 Gunnell Ct
C5 1 Robertson Ho
2 Dewar Ho
3 Jean Ho
4 Marion Ct
5 Gravenel Gdns
D1 1 Elms Cotts
2 Sibthorp Rd
3 Armfield Cotts

181
A1 1 Kennedy Cl
2 Pearce Cl
3 Mainwaring Ct
4 Coningsby Ct
5 Laburnum Ct
6 Beaumont Ct
7 Penfold Ct
8 Fitch Ct
A5 1 Osbourne Terr
2 Limetree Wlk
C5 1 Tyers Ho
2 Boothby Ho
3 Adams Ho
4 Burney Ho
5 Boswell Ho
6 Chesterfield Ho
7 Garrick Ho
8 Levett Ho
9 Shelburne Ho
10 Marchmont Ho
11 Ryland Ho
C6 1 Walmsley Ho
2 Chambers Ho
3 Fordyce Ho
4 Percy Ho
5 Langton Ho
6 Moorfields Ct
7 Hildaburn Ct
8 Salter Ho
D6 1 William Dyce Mews

182
C5 1 Belltrees Gr
2 Ash Ct
3 Alder Ct
4 Beech Ct
5 Acacia Ct
6 Blackthorn Ct
7 Cypress Ct
8 Hawthorn Ct
9 Hazel Ct
10 Sycamore Ct
11 Maple Ct
12 Laburnam Ct
13 Fern Lo
C6 1 James Boswell Ct
2 St Albans Ct
3 Suffolk Ct
4 Rockhampton Cl
5 Delphian Ct
D5 1 Woodcote Pl
2 Joe Hunte Ct
3 Cork Tree Ho
4 Lake Ho
5 Cedars Ho
6 Portobello Ho
7 Cooper Ho
8 Farnsworth Ho
9 Hook Ho
10 Crest The
11 Renshaw Ho
12 Ruscoe Ho
13 Sardeson Ho

183
A6 1 Moore Ho
2 Chaucer Ho
3 Bushell Ho
4 Bligh Ho
5 Hobbs Rd
6 Hogarth Ho
7 Goodbehere Ho
8 Astley Ho
9 Elder Gdns
10 Elderberry Gr
11 Pavement The
12 Dunkirk St
B6 1 Josef Perrin Ho
2 Jean Humbert Ho

3 Charles Staunton Ho
4 Violette Szabo Ho
5 Lilian Rolfe Ho
6 Odette Ho
7 Robert Gerard Ho
8 St Bernards Cl
9 Champness Cl
10 Pennington Cl
11 Queenswood Ct
C4 **1** Northwood Way
2 High Limes
3 Valley Prospect
4 Plane Tree Wlk
5 City Prospect
6 Bankside Way
7 Ridge Way
8 Rochdale
9 Barrington Wlk
10 Gatestone Ct
11 Childs La
12 Carberry Rd
13 Norwood Heights Sh Ctr
C5 **1** Oakdene
2 Thorsden Way
3 Oakfield Gdns
4 Georgetown Cl
5 Bridgetown Cl
6 Mountbatten Cl
7 Brabourne Cl
8 Alexandra Wlk
9 Compton Ct
10 Battenberg Wlk
11 Burma Terr
12 Wiseman Ct
C6 **1** Linley Ct
2 Mellor Ho
3 Whitfield Ct
4 Michaelson Ho
5 Holberry Ho
6 Hovenden Ho
7 Huntley Ho
8 Telfer Ho
9 Markham Ho
10 Oldham Ho
11 Parnall Ho
12 Pierson Ho
13 Roper Ho
14 Roundell Ho
15 Sawyer Ho
16 Ransford Ho
17 Carmichael Ho
18 Bonne Marche Terr Mews
D3 **1** Hetley Gdns
2 Claybourne Mews
3 Highland Lo
4 Mason Ct
5 Kendall Ct
6 High View

184
A3 **1** Hanover Ct
2 Brunswick Ct
3 New Church Ct
4 Regency Ct
5 Owen Wlk
6 Bargrove Cl
7 Beaver Ct
B2 **1** Dorset Ho
2 Collingwood Cl
3 Chartwell Way
4 Essex Twr
5 Appletree Cl
6 Ditton Pl
7 Kelvin Ct
8 Readman Ct
9 Glen Ct
10 Kingsbridge Ho
11 Carlton Ct
12 Benhurst Ct
13 Carole Ho
14 Dover Ho
15 Bettswood Ct
B5 **1** Ragwort Ct
2 Firs The
3 Wingham Ho
4 Seath Ho
5 Ripley Ho
6 Lathwood Ho
7 Hurst Ho
8 George Ho
9 Browne Ho
10 Beacon Ho
11 Bailey Ho

12 Agate Ho
C2 **1** Challin St
2 Rutland Ho
3 Pine Cl
C3 **1** Watermen's Sq
2 St John's Cotts
3 Gladstone Mews
4 Middlesex Ho
5 Bethesda Ct
6 Ospringe Ct
7 Goudhurst Ho
8 Walmer Ho
9 Strood Ho
10 Greatstone Ho
11 John Baird Ho
D3 **1** Groombridge Ho
2 Provincial Terr
3 Smithers Ho
4 West Ho
5 Swallows Ct

185
A1 **1** Clock House Ct
2 Blandford Ave
3 Old School Ct
4 Lynsted Ct
5 Florence Rd
A6 **1** Paxton Ct
2 Kenton Ct
3 Grove Ct
4 Shirley Lo
B2 **1** Ashton Ct
2 Coombe Ct
3 Fontaine Ct
4 Richfield Ct
5 Sheridan Way
C1 **1** Christ Church Rd
2 Lea Rd
3 Stanmore Terr
C2 **1** Erindale Ct
2 Bearsted Terr
3 Beck River Pk
4 Waterside
5 Station App
C3 **1** Gardenia Ct
2 Brackendale Ct
3 Daniel Ct
4 Moliner Ct
5 Chartwell Lo
6 Randmore Ct
7 Dover Ho
8 Lucerne Ct
9 Malling Ho
10 Westerham Lo
11 Brasted Lo
12 Milton Ho
13 Bradsole Ho
14 Sandgate Ho
15 Adelaide Ct
16 Nettlestead Ct
17 Warren Ct
18 Alton Ct
19 Rockingham Ct
20 Camellia Ct
21 Sinclair Ct
22 Regents Ct
23 Minshull Pl
24 South Park Ct
D1 **1** Parkside
2 Tudors The
3 Oakbrook
4 Tara Ct
5 Redlands The
6 Cambria
7 Hillworth
8 Kelsey Gate
9 Burrells
10 Lincoln Lo
11 Courtlands
12 Fairleas
13 Ashdown Cl
D2 **1** Mayfair Ct
2 Clifton Ct
3 Fire Station Mews
D4 **1** Warner Ho
2 Clifford Ho
3 Lloyd Ho
4 Thurston Ho
5 Byron Ho
6 Blake Ho
7 Keats Ho

186
A2 **1** White House Ct
2 Hunters The
3 Sandringham Ct
4 Glenhurst
5 Copperfields
6 Westgate Ct
A6 **1** Dedham Ho
2 Flatford Ho
3 Radley Ct
4 Langthorne Ct
5 Hoover Ho
6 Brunner Ho
7 Waterer Ho
8 Marriott Ho
9 Bourbon Ho
B5 **1** Longford Ho
2 Ingrebourne Ho
3 Brent Ho
4 Darent Ho
5 Beverley Ho
6 Wandle Ho
7 Rythe Ho
8 Ember Ho
9 Crane Ho
10 Ravensbourne Ho
C1 **1** Warwick Ct
2 Maplehurst
3 Mount Arlington
4 Arundel Ct
D2 **1** Weston Gr
2 Gibbs Ho
3 Longfield
4 Hammelton Ct
5 Bracken Hill Cl
6 Townend Ct
7 Treversh Ct
8 Cameron Ho
9 Woodlands Ct
10 Blythwood Pk
11 Bromley Pk
D3 **1** Homecoppice Ho
2 Kimberley Gate
3 Inglewood Ct
4 Mavery Ct
5 Glen Ct
6 Cawston Ct
7 Blendon Path

187
B2 **1** Hansom Terr
2 Dainton Ct
3 St Timothy's Mews
4 Andringham Lo
5 Kendall Lo
6 Summerfield
7 Winston Ct
8 Laurels The
C1 **1** Westland Lo
2 Dairsie Ct
3 Beechfield Cotts
4 Oasis The
5 Cromarty Ct
6 Silverstone Ct

188
A6 **1** Beaconsfield Par
2 Cranley Par
3 Kimmeridge Gdns
4 King & Queen Cl
5 Merewood Cl
C2 **1** Alpine Copse
2 Ivybridge Ct
3 Greenbank Lo

190
A6 **1** Minshaw Ho
2 Cyril Lo
3 Milton Lo
4 Glenwood Ct
5 Culverton Ct
6 Holmbury Manor
B1 **1** Swanscombe Ho
2 Haverstock Ct
3 Arrandene Ho
4 Broomfield Ho
5 Headley Ho
6 Ladywell Ho
B6 **1** Chudleigh
2 Wimborne
3 St John's Par
4 Holly Ct
5 Rectory Bsns Ctr

197
A2 **1** Raleigh Ho
2 Leicester Ho
3 Gresham Ho
D2 **1** Napier Ct
2 Darlington Ho
3 Charminster Ct
4 Mulberry Ct
5 Leander Ct
6 Clinton Ho
7 Hollingworth Ct
8 Gloucester Ct
9 Palmerston Ct
10 Redwood Ct
11 Hursley Ct
12 Westmorland Ct
13 Lawson Ct
14 Alexander Ct
15 Winton Ct
16 Sydenham Ho
17 Caroline Ct
18 Ellswood Ct
19 Masefield Ct

198
A1 **1** Ash Tree Cl
2 Shrubbery The
3 Malvern Ct
4 Gate Ho
A3 **1** Station App
2 South Bank Lo
3 Bramshott Ct
4 Pandora Ct
5 Wellington Ct
6 Glenbuck Ct
7 Leighton Ho
8 Oakhill Ct
9 Downs View Ct
10 Osborne Ct
A4 **1** Effingham Lo
2 Maple Ho
3 Channon Ct
4 Falconhurst
5 Ferndown
6 Viceroy Lo
7 Frensham Ho
8 Kingsley Ho
9 Rannoch Ct
10 Stratton Ct
11 Moray Ho
12 Dulverton Ct
13 Westerham
14 Hill Ct
15 Assheton-Bennett Ho
16 Hatfield Ho
17 Oxford Ct
18 Pennington Lo
19 Austin Ho
20 Wentworth Ct
21 Priory The
22 Sheraton The
A5 **1** Marquis Ct
2 Garrick Ho
A6 **1** College Rdbt
2 Edinburgh Ct
3 Weston Ct
4 Grebe Terr
5 Heron Ct
6 Agar Ho
7 St James' Ct
8 Grove Ct
9 Springfield Ct
10 College Wlk
B3 **1** Percy Ct
2 Holmwood
3 Middle Green Cl
B4 **1** Woodleigh
2 Highcroft
3 Caernarvon Ct
4 Regency Ct
D1 **1** Oakleigh Way
2 Chandler Ct

199
C2 **1** Goodland Ho
2 Furzeland Ho
3 Oakcroft Ho
4 Meadcroft Ho
5 Newhouse
C4 **1** Merryweather Ct
2 Roebuck Ct
3 Sable Ct
C5 **1** Acacia Ho
2 Kingston Lo
3 Fairholme Ho
4 Marshall Ho
5 Norton Ho
6 Martin Ho

200
A1 **1** Brookside Cres
2 Beverley Gdns
3 Purdey Ct
4 Avenue The
5 Station App

202
D6 **1** Fair Green Ct
2 Regal Ct
3 Lewes Ct
4 Esher Mews
5 Sibford Ct

205
B1 **1** Tavistock Ct
2 Chartwell Ct
3 Speaker's Ct
4 Cumberland Ct
5 Viceroy Ct
6 Oriel Ct
7 Cherry Orchard Gdns
C1 **1** Windmill Bridge Ho
2 Squire Ct
3 Houston Ct
4 St James's Lo
5 Kendal Ho
6 Warren Ct
7 Kendal Ct
D1 **1** Hastings Pl
2 Grant Pl
3 Clive Ho
4 Havelock Ho
5 Bellmore Ct
6 Hereford Ct
7 Chequers Ct
8 Havelock Hall

206
A1 **1** Farleycroft
2 Edgecumbe Ct
3 Wesson Ho
4 Sullivan Ct
5 Kenley Ho
6 Christopher Ct
7 Jayson Ct
D1 **1** Cottongrass Cl
2 Oxlip Cl
3 Eyebright Cl

207
1 North Rd
2 Sussex Rd
3 Riverside Wlk
4 Christie Ho
5 Sherwood Ct
6 Wheatsheaf Par
D6 **1** Park Ct
2 Chichester Ct
3 Iveagh Ct

208
A6 **1** Overbury Ct
2 Wilton Pl
D1 **1** Woodgrange Ct
2 Maycroft
3 Farnborough Cres
D4 **1** Knowlton Gn
2 Speldhurst Cl
3 Bidborough Cl
4 Penshurst Wlk
D5 **1** Wedgewood Ct
2 Birches The
3 Eccleshill
4 Tavistock Rd
5 Montpelier Ct

209
A5 **1** Montague Terr
2 Chatsworth Ho
A6 **1** Marina Ct
2 Cheveney Wlk
3 Bromley Manor Mans
4 Mall The
5 Westmoreland Pl

211
B1 **1** Gleneagles Gn
2 Tandridge Pl
3 Springfield Wlk
4 Pinehurst Wlk
5 Cromer Pl
6 Oakmont Pl

214
A6 **1** St Bernards Ho
2 Wentworth Ct
3 Sunningdale Cl
4 Arklow Mews
5 Edward Pinner Ct

215
D6 **1** Kingsley Dr
2 Kingsley Ct
3 Mowat Ct
4 Squirrels Ct

216
A6 **1** Lansdowne Copse
2 Lansdowne Ct

217
A2 **1** Crown Court Flats
2 Tabor Ct
C1 **1** Lancaster Ct
2 Redclyffe Terr
3 Kenilworth Terr
4 Lincoln Terr
5 Garden Ct
6 Ashwood Pk
7 Lyndhurst Ct
8 Banbury Ct
9 Holly Ct
10 Castle Ho
11 Balmoral Ct
12 Hereford Ct
13 Lorac Ct
14 Camilla Ct
15 Midsummer Apmts
D1 **1** Hadrian Ct
2 Magnolia Ct
3 Larchvale Ct
4 Alford Ct
5 Brockham Ct
6 Berrylands Ct
7 Camberley Ct
8 Dunsfold Ct
9 Courtlands
10 Leith Towers
11 Kingslee Ct

218
A1 **1** Beauclere Ho
2 Melford Ct
3 Elmhurst Lo
4 Mansard Manor
5 Tranmere Ct
6 Beechcroft Lo
7 Savin Lo
8 Yew Tree Ct
9 Avondale Ct
10 Devonshire Ho
11 Hidcote Ho
12 Munstead Ct
13 Lodden Lo
14 Steetley Ct
15 Grampian Ct
A2 **1** Grosvenor Ct
2 Forest Dene Ct
3 Cedar Ct
A3 **1** Goossens Ct
2 Cliffe Wlk
3 Marlins Ct
4 Clowser Ct
5 Montana Gdns

219
B2 **1** Runnymede Ct
2 Dolphin Ct
3 Kings Ct
4 Cheyne Ct
5 Hendfield Ct
6 Ellerslie Ct
7 Embassy Ct
8 Chandler Ct
9 Hambledon Ct
10 Wallington Ct
11 Jasmine Ct
B4 **1** Loraine Ho
2 Harcourt Lo
3 Coniston Ct
4 Alcester Ct
5 Friars Ct
6 Campbell Ho
7 Brodie Ho
8 Lesley Ct
9 Birch Ct
10 Airborne Ho
C2 **1** Rossendon Ct
2 Mulberry Mews
3 Nairn Ct
4 Wallington Sq
5 Rosemount Towers
6 Connell Ho
7 Ashby Grange

221
A4 **1** West Street Pl
2 Maple Ct
3 St Andrew's Rd
4 Albury Ct
5 Chestnut Ct
6 Elgin Ct
7 Beechfield Ct
8 Barham Ct
9 Whitstable Pl
10 Ledbury Pl
A5 **1** Mann Cl
2 Halstead Ct
A6 **1** Otterbourne Rd
2 Charrington Rd
3 Tamworth Pl
4 Priddy's Yd
5 Hospital of the Holy Trinity (Almshouses)
6 Bellhill
B4 **1** Holmlea Ct
2 Garlands Ct
3 Coombe Ct
4 Deepdale Ct
5 Galloway Path
B6 **1** Wellesley Court Rd
2 Norfolk Ho
3 Station App
4 Suffolk Ho
5 Cherry Orchard Gdns
D6 **1** Cheyne Ct
2 Fourways
3 Princess Ct
4 Tierney Ct
5 Sinclair Ct
6 Guinness Ct
7 Mayfair Ct
8 Bishopscourt
9 Gloucester Lo
10 Beverley Hyrst
11 Melton Ct
12 Cecil Ct
13 Napier Ct

227
A3 **1** Westfield
2 Farnborough Ct
3 Fern Hill Pl
4 Churchill Ct
5 Spencer Ct
6 Ladycroft Gdns
7 Crabbs Croft Cl
8 Clifton Ct
D2 **1** Brittenden Cl
2 Wardens Field Cl
3 Winnipeg Dr
4 Superior Dr
5 Huron Cl
6 Manitoba Gdns
A3 **1** Lynne Cl
2 Flint Cl
D3 **1** Bakers Mews
1 Osgood Gdns
2 Amberley Ct
3 Rawlings Cl
4 Beblets Cl
5 Fir Tree Cl
6 Raleigh Mews
7 King Henry Mews
B4 **1** Healy Dr
2 Marsden Way
3 Taylor Cl
4 Strickland Way
5 Dryland Ave
6 Adcot Wlk
7 Lichlade Cl

➕ Hospitals with accident and emergency departments are highlighted in green

A

Acton Hospital W3 ...110 C4

➕ Ashford Hospital,
Stanmore Road, Ashford,
Middlesex TW15 3AA .148 A2
📞 01784 884488

Athlone House (The Middlesex Hospital)
N6 ....48 D1

Atkinson Morley Hospital SW20 ....178 B3

B

Barking Hospital
IG11 ....79 D1

Barnes Hospital
SW14 ....133 C4

Beckenham Hospital BR3 ...185 B1

Bethlem Royal Hospital The BR3 .207 C2

Blackheath Hospital SE3 ......142 C2

Bolingbroke Hospital The SW11 ....158 C4

Bowden House Hospital (Private) HA1 ....64 C6

British Home and Hospital for Incurables
SW16 ....182 D5

➕ Bromley Hospital
Cromwell Avenue, Bromley,
Kent BR2 9AJ 209 B5
📞 020 8289 7000

Brompton Hospital
SW3 ......114 B1 256 C2

BUPA Bushey Hospital WD2 ....8 D3

C

Carshalton, War Memorial Hospital
SM5 ....218 D2

Cassel Hospital
TW10 ....175 C6

Castlewood Day Hospital SE18 ....144 C4

➕ Central Middlesex Hospital
Acton Lane, Park Royal,
London, NW10 7NS ..89 A4
📞 020 8965 5733

Central Public Health Laboratory NW9 ....45 C6

Chadwell Heath Hospital
RM6 ....58 B4

➕ Charing Cross Hospital
Fulham Palace Road, London
W6 8RF (A&E entrance off
St Dunstan's Road) .112 D1
📞 020 8846 1234

Charter Nightingale Hospital The
NW1 ....92 C2 237 B4

➕ Chase Farm Hospital
The Ridgeway, Enfield,
Middlesex, EN2 8JL ...4 C5
📞 020 8366 6600

Chelsea Hospital for Women
SW3 ......114 C1 257 A4

➕ Chelsea and Westminster Hospital
369 Fulham Road, London
SW10 9NH ..136 A6 266 B5
📞 020 8746 8000

Chingford Hospital
E4 ....20 A1

Chiswick Maternity Hospital W4 ....111 D1

Clayponds Hospital and Day Treatment
Ctr TW8 ....110 A2

Clementine Churchill Hospital The HA1 ...64 D5

Colindale Hospital
NW9 ....45 C6

Connaught Day Hospital E11 ......54 C3

Coppetts Wood Hospital
N10 ....30 D2

Cromwell Hospital
SW5 ......113 D2 255 C4

D

Devonshire Hospital
W1 ....93 A2 238 B4

Dulwich Hospital
SE22 ....139 C1

E

➕ Ealing Hospital
Uxbridge Road, Southall,
Middlesex UB1 3HW .108 B4
📞 020 8574 2444

East Ham Memorial Hospital E7 ......77 D1

Eastman Dental Hospital
WC1 ......94 B4 240 C6

Edgware General Hospital HA8 ......26 D3

Elizabeth Garrett Anderson and Obstetric Hospital
WC1 ....93 C3 235 B5

F

Farnborough Hospital
BR6 ....226 C4

Finchley Memorial Hospital N12 ....30 A3

Fitzroy Nuffield Hospital
W1 ....92 D1 237 C2

G

Garden Hospital The
NW4 ....46 C6

Goldie Leigh Hospital
SE2 ....146 C6

Goodmayes Hospital
IG3 ....58 A4

Gordon Hospital The
SW1 ......115 D2 259 C3

Great Ormond St Hospital for Children
WC1 ......94 B3 240 C5

➕ Greenwich District Hospital
Vanbrugh Hill, Greenwich,
London, SE10 9HE ..120 D1
📞 020 8858 8141

Grovelands Priory
N14 ....16 A3

Guy's Hospital
SE1 ......117 B5 252 D2

H

Hackney Hospital E9 75 A3

Hamlet (Day) Hospital The TW9 ....132 A2

➕ Hammersmith Hospital
Du Cane Road, London
W12 0HS 90 B1
📞 020 8383 1111

Harrow Hospital HA2 64 C6

➕ The Heart Hospital
W1 ....93 B2 238 C3

➕ Hillingdon Hospital
Pield Heath Road, Uxbridge,
Middlesex UB8 3NN ..82 B2
📞 01895 238282

➕ Homerton University Hospital
Homerton Rd, E9 6SR 74 D3

Hornsey Central Hospital
N8 ....49 D4

Hospital for Tropical Diseases WC1 ...232 C5

Hospital of St John and St Elizabeth
NW8 ....92 B5 229 C3

I

Inverforth House Hospital
NW3 ....70 A6

J

Jewish Home and Hospital at Tottenham The N15 ....51 D5

K

➕ King George Hospital
Barley Lane, Goodmayes,
Ilford, Essex IG3 8YB .58 A4
📞 020 8983 8000

➕ King's College Hospital
Denmark Hill, (A&E in Ruskin Wing) SE5 6JH 139 B3
📞 020 7737 4000

Kings Oak Hospital (Private) The EN2 ...4 C5

Kingsbury Hospital
NW9 ....44 C5

➕ Kingston Hospital
Galsworthy Road, Kingston-
upon-Thames, Surrey
KT2 7QB 176 D2
📞 020 8546 7711

L

Langthorne Hospital
E11 ....76 B5

➕ Lewisham Hospital
High Street, Lewisham,
London SE13 6JH ..163 D6
📞 020 8333 3000

Lister Hospital
SW1 ......115 B1 258 C1

London Bridge Hospital
SE1 ......117 B5 252 D4

London Chest Hospital
E2 ....96 C5

London Clinic
NW1 ....93 A3 238 B5

London Foot Hospital
W1 ....93 C3 239 A5

London Hospital (Mile End) The E2 .96 D4

London Hospital (St Clements) The E3 ....97 B4

London Independent Hospital The E1 ....96 D2

M

Maida Vale Psychiatric Hospital W9 92 A3 236 B6

Manor House Hospital
N11 ....47 D1

Marlborough Day Hospital
NW8 ......92 A5 229 A4

Maudsley Hospital The
SE5 ....139 B3

➕ Mayday University Hospital
Mayday Road, Thornton
Heath CR7 7YE 204 D3
📞 020 8401 3000

Memorial Hospital
SE18 ....144 C3

Middlesex Hospital
W1 ....93 C2 239 B3

Mildmay Mission Hospital E2 ......95 C4

Molesey Hospital
KT8 ....195 C4

Moorfields Eye Hospital
EC1 ......95 B4 235 C1

Morland Road Day Hospital RM10 ...103 C6

N

National Hospital for Neurology and Neurosurgery N2 ..48 C5

National Hospital The
WC1 ......94 A3 240 B5

National Physical Laboratory TW11 .174 C4

Nelson Hospital
SW20 ....179 B1

New Cross Hospital
SE14 ....140 C5

New Victoria Hospital
KT3 ....177 C2

➕ Newham General Hospital
Glen Road, Plaistow,
London E13 8SL 99 C3
📞 020 7476 4000

Normansfield Hospital
KT8 ....175 C3

North London Nuffield Hospital EN2 ......4 C5

➕ North Middlesex Hospital
Sterling Way, Edmonton,
N18 1QX 33 C5
📞 020 8887 2000

➕ Northwick Park Hospital
Watford Road, Harrow,
Middlesex HA1 3UJ .43 A2
📞 020 8864 3232

Northwood Pinner and District Cottage Hospital
HA6 ....22 A2

Norwood Hospital
SE19 ....183 B4

O

Orpington Hospital
BR6 ....227 D4

P

Paddington Com Hospital
W9 ....91 C2

Penny Sangam Day Hospital UB2 ....107 B3

Plaistow Hospital
E13 ....99 C5

Portland Hospital for Women and Children
The W1 ....93 B3 238 D5

Princess Grace Hospital
The W1 ...93 A3 238 A5

Princess Louise Hospital
W10 ....90 C2

Priory Hospital The
SW15 ....133 D1

Putney Hospital
SW15 ....134 C2

Q

Queen Charlotte's Hospital W12 ....90 B1

Queen Elizabeth Hospital for Children The E2 96 A5

Queen Elizabeth Hospital
SE18 ....144 A5

➕ Queen Mary's Hospital
Frognal Avenue, Sidcup,
Kent DA14 6LT 190 A4
📞 020 8302 2678

Queen Mary's Hospital
NW3 ....70 A5

Queen Mary's University Hospital SW15 ...156 A5

Queen's Hospital
CR0 ....205 A3

R

Roding Hospital IG4 55 D6

Royal Brompton and Nat Heart Hospital The
SW3 ......114 C1 257 A2

Royal Ear Hospital
WC1 ......93 C3 239 B5

➕ Royal Free Hospital
Pond Street, London
NW3 2QG 70 C3
📞 020 7794 0500

Royal Hospital
SW15 ....157 A5

Royal London Homeopathic Hospital The
WC1 ......94 A2 240 B4

➕ Royal London Hospital (Whitechapel)
Whitechapel Road, London
E1 1BB 96 B2
📞 020 7377 7000

Royal Marsden Hospital
SW3 ......114 B1 256 D2

Royal Masonic Hospital
W6 ....112 A2

Royal National Orthopaedic Hospital
HA7 ....9 C2
W1 ....93 B3 238 D5

Royal Nat TN&E Hospital The W5 ......87 C2
WC1 ......94 B4 233 C2

S

St Andrew's Hospital
E3 ....97 D3

St Ann's General Hospital
N4,N15 ....51 A4

St Anthony's Hospital
KT4 ....200 D1

St Bartholomew's Hospital
EC1 ......94 D2 241 A3

St Charles' Hospital
W10 ....90 D2

St Christopher's Hospice
SE26 ....184 C5

➕ St George's Hospital
Blackshaw Road, London
SW17 ....180 B5
📞 020 8672 1255

St Giles Hospital
SE5 ....139 C4

➕ St Helier Hospital
Wrythe Lane, Carshalton,
Surrey SM5 1AA 202 A1
📞 020 8296 2000

St Joseph's Hospice
E9,E8 ....96 B6

St Leonard's Hospital
N1 ....95 C5

St Luke's Hospital
W1 ....93 C3 239 A5

St Luke's Woodside Hospital
N10 ....49 A5

St Mark's Hospital
EC1 ......95 D4 234 D2

St Mary's Hospital
HA1 ....43 A2

St Mary's Cottage Hospital TW12 ...173 B2

➕ St Mary's Hospital
Praed Street, London
W2 1NY ...92 B1 236 D2
📞 020 7886 6666

St Michael's Hospital
EN2 ....5 B4

St Pancras Hospital
NW1 ......93 D6 232 C5

➕ St Thomas's Hospital
Lambeth Palace Road,
London
SE1 7EH ..116 B3 260 C6
📞 020 7928 9292

St Vincent's Hospital
HA5 ....39 C1

Samaritan Hospital for Women NW1 .....237 C4

Shirley Oaks Hospital
CR0 ....206 C2

Sloane Hospital
BR3 ....186 B2

South Western Hospital
SW9 ....138 B2

Southwood Hospital (Geriatric) N6 ....49 A2

Springfield Hospital
SW17 ....158 C1

Stepney Day Hospital
E1 ....96 C1

Surbiton Hospital
KT6 ....198 A3

T

Teddington Memorial Hospital TW11 ...174 C4

Thorpe Coombe Hospital
E17 ....54 A6

Tolworth Hospital
KT6 ....214 C6

Travel Clinic, Hospital for Tropical Diseases
WC1 ......93 C3 239 B5

U

➕ University College Hospital
A&E at Cecil Fleming House,
Grafton Way, London
WC1E 3BG ...93 C3 239 B5
📞 020 7387 9300

Upton Day Hospital
DA6 ....147 A1

W

Wanstead Hospital
E11 ....55 B5

Wellington Hospital (North)
NW8 ......92 B5 229 D3

Wellington Hospital (South)
NW8 ......92 B5 229 D3

Wembley Hospital
HA0 ....65 D2

➕ West Middlesex University Hospital
Twickenham Road,
Isleworth, Middlesex
TW7 6AF 131 A3
📞 020 8560 2121

Western Hospital
The NW1 ..92 D2 237 C4

➕ Whipps Cross Hospital
Whipps Cross Road,
Leytonstone
London E11 1NR 54 B3
📞 020 8539 5522

➕ Whittington Hospital
Highgate Hill, London,
N19 5NF 71 C6
📞 020 7272 3070

Willesden Community Hospital The NW10 .68 A1

Winifred House Hospital
EN5 ....11 D5

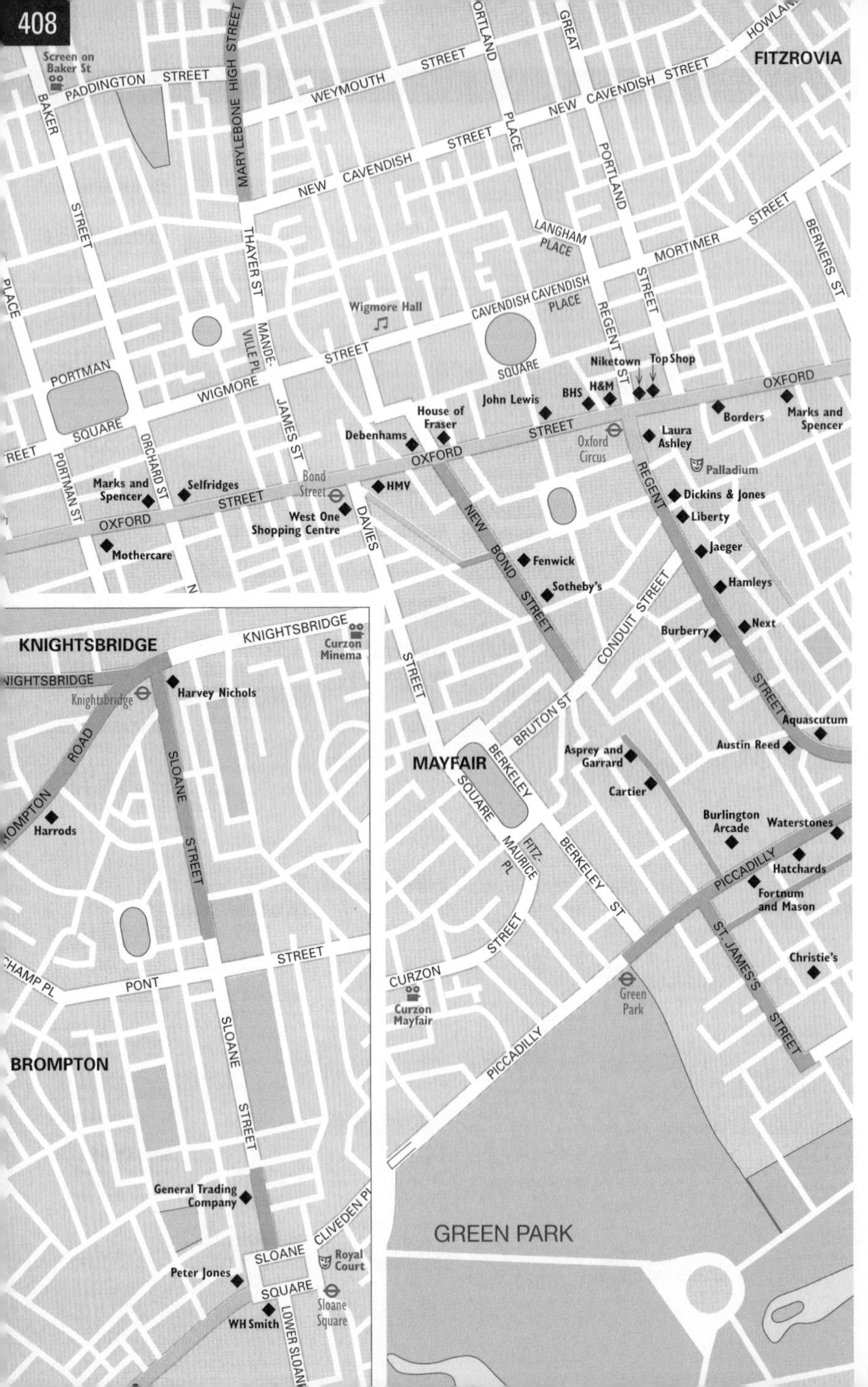

FITZROVIA

Screen on Baker St

Wigmore Hall

House of Fraser

Niketown
Top Shop
H&M
BHS
John Lewis

Debenhams

Oxford Circus

Borders

Marks and Spencer

Laura Ashley

Palladium

Marks and Spencer

Selfridges

HMV

Dickins & Jones

Liberty

West One Shopping Centre

Mothercare

Jaeger

Fenwick

Hamleys

Sotheby's

Burberry

Next

KNIGHTSBRIDGE

Curzon Minema

Aquascutum

Harvey Nichols

Austin Reed

MAYFAIR

Asprey and Garrard

Cartier

Burlington Arcade

Waterstones

Harrods

Hatchards

Fortnum and Mason

Christie's

General Trading Company

Curzon Mayfair

Green Park

BROMPTON

Peter Jones

GREEN PARK

WH Smith

Sloane Square

Royal Court

Cinemas, theatres shopping streets

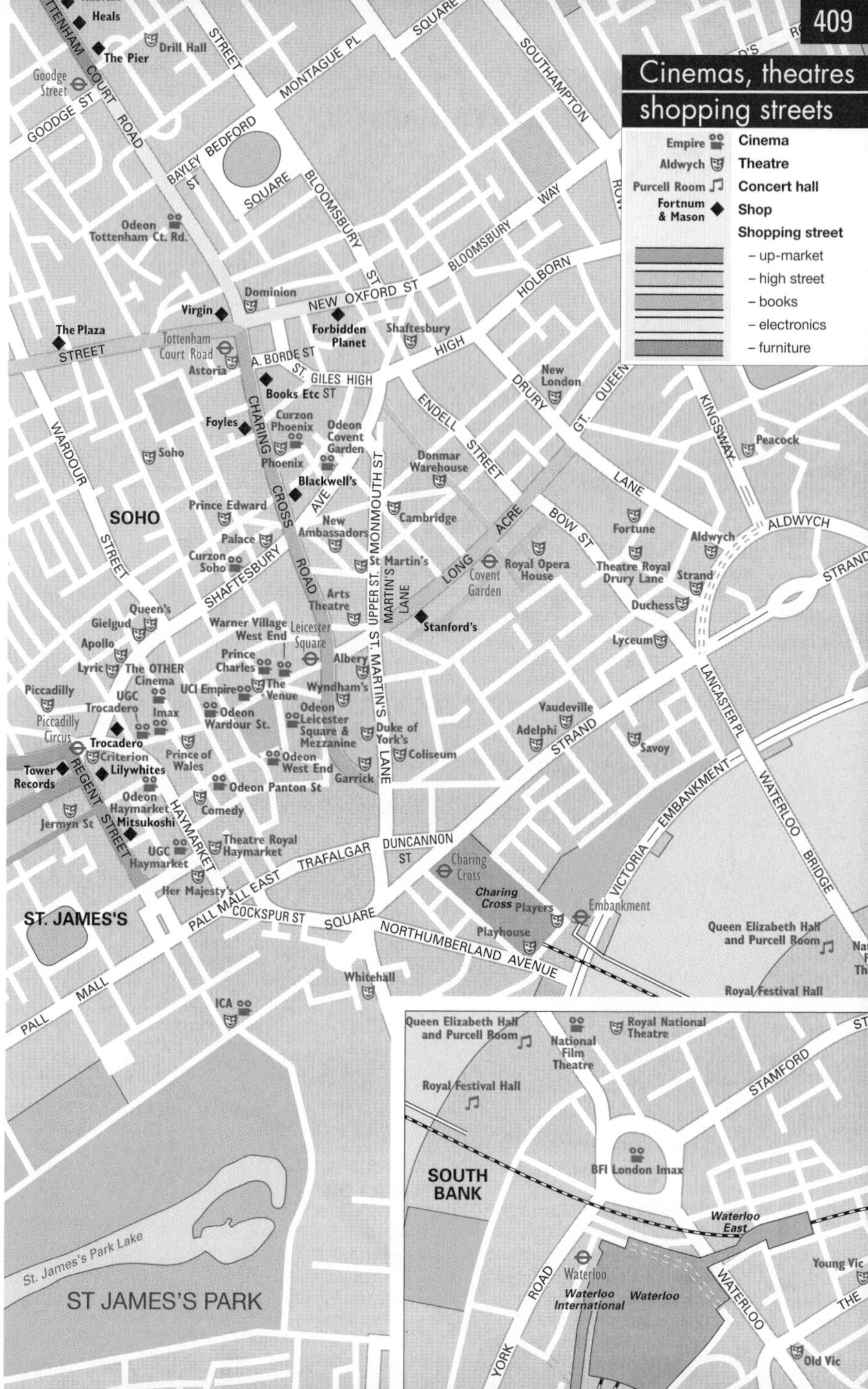

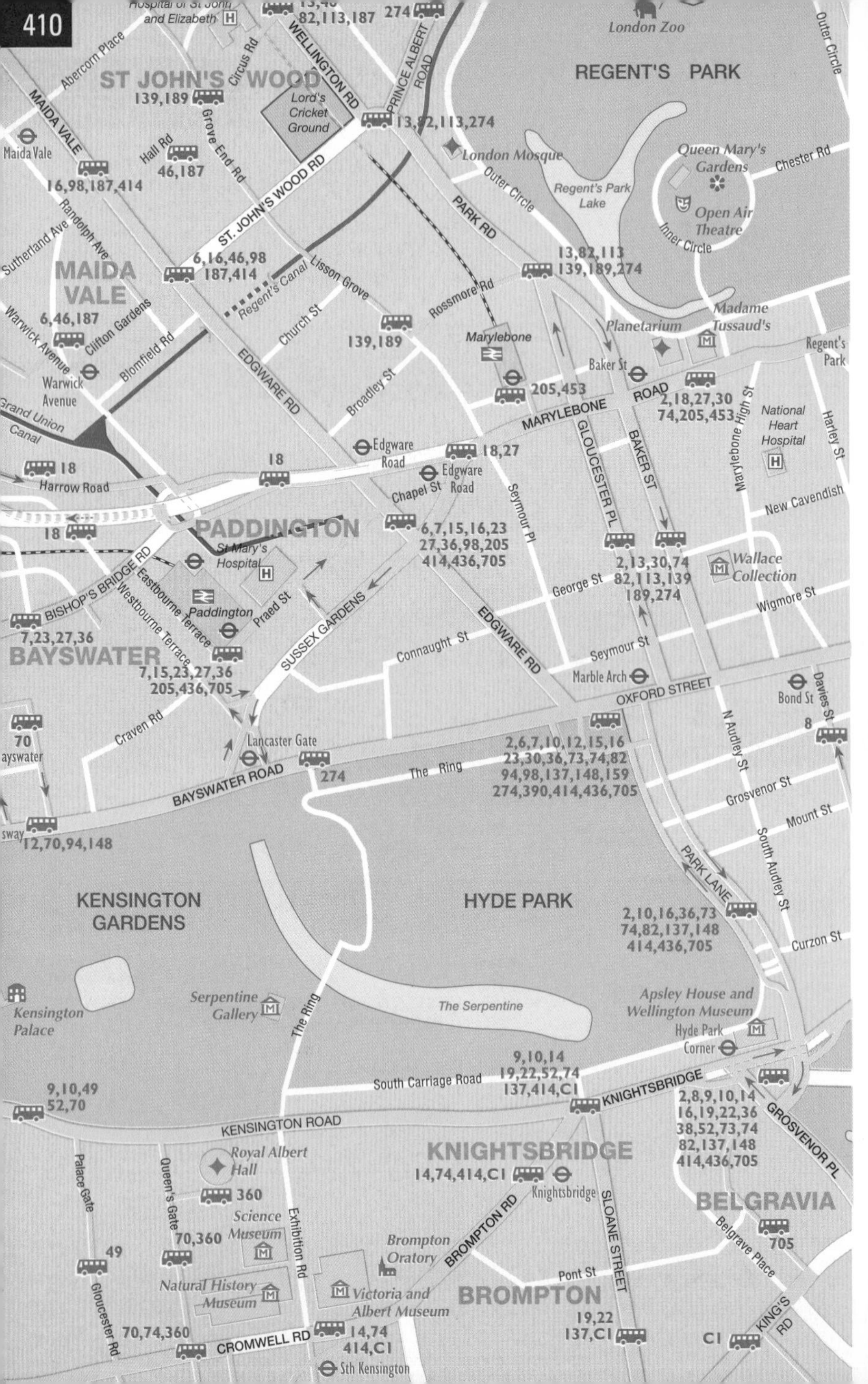

London Zoo
REGENT'S PARK
Outer Circle
ST JOHN'S WOOD
Hospital of St John and Elizabeth
82,113,187
274
WELLINGTON RD
PRINCE ALBERT ROAD
Abercorn Place
Circus Rd
139,189
Lord's Cricket Ground
13,82,113,274
London Mosque
Queen Mary's Gardens
Chester Rd
MAIDA VALE
Maida Vale
Hall Rd
46,187
Grove End Rd
ST. JOHN'S WOOD RD
16,98,187,414
Outer Circle
Regent's Park Lake
Open Air Theatre
Inner Circle
PARK RD
Randolph Ave
Sutherland Ave
6,16,46,98
187,414
13,82,113
139,189,274
Regent's Canal
Lisson Grove
Rossmore Rd
6,46,187
Clifton Gardens
Warwick Avenue
Blomfield Rd
Church St
139,189
Marylebone
Planetarium
Madame Tussaud's
Regent's Park
Warwick Avenue
Grand Union Canal
EDGWARE RD
Broadley St
Baker St
205,453
MARYLEBONE ROAD
2,18,27,30
74,205,453
Marylebone High St
National Heart Hospital
Harley St
18
Harrow Road
18
Edgware Road
18,27
Edgware Road
Chapel St
Seymour Pl
GLOUCESTER PL
BAKER ST
New Cavendish
18
PADDINGTON
St Mary's Hospital
6,7,15,16,23
27,36,98,205
414,436,705
2,13,30,74
82,113,139
189,274
Wallace Collection
BISHOP'S BRIDGE RD
Eastbourne Terrace
Westbourne Terrace
Paddington
Praed St
SUSSEX GARDENS
EDGWARE RD
George St
Wigmore St
7,23,27,36
BAYSWATER
7,15,23,27,36
205,436,705
Connaught St
Seymour St
Marble Arch
OXFORD STREET
Bond St
Davies St
8
70
Bayswater
Craven Rd
Lancaster Gate
274
BAYSWATER ROAD
The Ring
2,6,7,10,12,15,16
23,30,36,73,74,82
94,98,137,148,159
274,390,414,436,705
N Audley St
Grosvenor St
Mount St
12,70,94,148
KENSINGTON GARDENS
HYDE PARK
PARK LANE
South Audley St
2,10,16,36,73
74,82,137,148
414,436,705
Curzon St
Kensington Palace
Serpentine Gallery
The Ring
The Serpentine
Apsley House and Wellington Museum
Hyde Park Corner
9,10,14
19,22,52,74
137,414,C1
South Carriage Road
9,10,49
52,70
KNIGHTSBRIDGE
KENSINGTON ROAD
2,8,9,10,14
16,19,22,36
38,52,73,74
82,137,148
414,436,705
GROSVENOR PL
Palace Gate
Queen's Gate
Royal Albert Hall
360
KNIGHTSBRIDGE
14,74,414,C1
Knightsbridge
SLOANE STREET
BELGRAVIA
Exhibition Rd
Science Museum
70,360
49
Gloucester Rd
Brompton Oratory
BROMPTON RD
705
Belgrave Place
Natural History Museum
Victoria and Albert Museum
Pont St
BROMPTON
70,74,360
CROMWELL RD
14,74
414,C1
19,22
137,C1
C1
KING'S RD
Sth Kensington